organizational behavior

third edition

organizational behavior

MICHAEL A. HITT
Texas A&M University

C. CHET MILLER
University of Houston

ADRIENNE COLELLA
Tulane University

WILEY

John Wiley & Sons, Inc.

Vice President & Publisher	George Hoffmann
Executive Editor	Lise Johnson
Assistant Editor	Sarah Vernon
Marketing Manager	Karolina Zarychta
Assistant Marketing Manager	Laura Finely
Production Manager	Dorothy Sinclair
Production Editor	Sandra Dumas
Creative Director	Harry Nolan
Interior Designer	Lucia Tirondola
Cover Design	Howard Grossman
Executive Media Editor	Allison Morris
Associate Media Editor	Elena Santa Maria
Photo Department Manager	Hilary Newman
Photo Editor	Jennifer MacMillan
Photo Researcher	Lisa Passmore
Production Management Services	MPS Limited, a Macmillan Company

This book was typeset in 10/12 Sabon Regular at MPS and printed and bound by Quad/Graphics Versailles. The cover was printed by Quad/Graphics Versailles.

The paper in this book was manufactured by a mill whose forest management programs include sustained yield-harvesting of its timberlands. Sustained yield harvesting principles ensure that the number of trees cut each year does not exceed the amount of new growth.

This book is printed on acid-free paper.

Founded in 1807, John Wiley & Sons, Inc. has been a valued source of knowledge and understanding for more than 200 years, helping people around the world meet their needs and fulfill their aspirations. Our company is built on a foundation of principles that include responsibility to the communities we serve and where we live and work. In 2008, we launched a Corporate Citizenship Initiative, a global effort to address the environmental, social, economic, and ethical challenges we face in our business. Among the issues we are addressing are carbon impact, paper specifications and procurement, ethical conduct within our business and among our vendors, and community and charitable support. For more information, please visit our website: www.wiley.com/go/citizenship.

ISBN 13	978-0470-52853-2
ISBN 13	978-0470-92090-9

Printed in the United States of America.
10 9 8 7 6 5 4 3 2

To Aunt Jinny
for all of the love and support
you have given us over the years.
We are blessed to have you
in our lives

—MIKE

To Laura Cardinal,
who keeps the smiles
and joy coming.
I am indeed looking forward
to our next chapter together.

—CHET

To Jessica and Rebecca.
You make me proud
and you make me smile.

—ADRIENNE

about the authors

Michael A. Hitt

Texas A & M University

Michael Hitt is currently a Distinguished Professor of Management at Texas A&M University and holds the Joe B. Foster Chair in Business Leadership. He received his Ph.D. from the University of Colorado. Dr. Hitt has coauthored or co-edited 26 books and authored or coauthored many journal articles. A recent article listed him as one of the ten most cited authors in management over a 25-year period. The *Times Higher Education* listed him among the top scholars in economics, finance and management and tied for first among management scholars with the highest number of highly cited articles. He has served on the editorial review boards of multiple journals and is a former editor of the *Academy of Management Journal*. He is the current co-editor of the *Strategic Entrepreneurship Journal*. He received the 1996 Award for Outstanding Academic Contributions to Competitiveness and the 1999 Award for Outstanding Intellectual Contributions to Competitiveness Research from the American Society for Competitiveness. He is a Fellow in the Academy of Management and in the Strategic Management Society, a Research Fellow in the National Entrepreneurship Consortium and received an honorary doctorate from the Universidad Carlos III de Madrid for his contributions to the field. He is a former President of the Academy of Management, a Past President of the Strategic Management Society and a member of the Academy of Management Journals' Hall of Fame. He received awards for the best article published in the *Academy of Management Executive* (1999), *Academy of Management Journal* (2000), and the *Journal of Management* (2006). In 2001, he received the Irwin Outstanding Educator Award and the Distinguished Service Award from the Academy of Management. In 2004, Dr. Hitt was awarded the Best Paper Prize by the Strategic Management Society. In 2006, he received the Falcone Distinguished Entrepreneurship Scholar Award from Syracuse University.

C. Chet Miller

University of Houston

Dr. C. Chet Miller is the Bauer Professor of Organizational Studies at the Bauer School of Business, University of Houston. He received his Ph.D. from the University of Texas at Austin. He also received his B.A. from the University of Texas, where he was a member of Phi Beta Kappa and a Summa Cum Laude graduate.

Since working as a shift manager and subsequently completing his graduate studies, Dr. Miller has served on the faculties of Baylor University, Wake Forest University, and the University of Houston. He also has been a visiting faculty member at Cornell University and a guest instructor at Duke University. He is an active member of the Academy of

Management and the Strategic Management Society. He currently serves on the editorial boards of *Organization Science* and *Academy of Management Journal,* and is a past associate editor of *Academy of Management Journal.* Awards and honors include an outstanding young researcher award, nominations of several papers for honors, and teaching awards from multiple schools,

Dr. Miller has worked with a number of managers and executives. Through management-development programs, he has contributed to the development of individuals from such organizations as ABB, Bank of America, Krispy Kreme, La Farge, Red Hat, State Farm Insurance, and the U.S. Postal Service. His focus has been change management, strategic visioning, and high-involvement approaches to managing people.

Dr. Miller's published research focuses on the functioning of executive teams, the design of organizational structures and management systems, and the design of strategic decision processes. His publications have appeared in *Organization Science, Academy of Management Journal, Academy of Management Executive, Strategic Management Journal, Journal of Organizational Behavior,* and *Journal of Behavioral Decision Making.*

Dr. Miller teaches courses in the areas of organizational behavior, organization theory, and strategic management.

Adrienne Colella

Tulane University

Dr. Adrienne Colella is the A.B. Freeman Professor of Doctoral Studies and Research at the A.B. Freeman School of Business at Tulane University. She has also been a faculty member at the Mays Business School, Texas A&M University and at Rutgers University.

She received her Ph.D. and Masters degree from the Ohio State University in Industrial/ Organizational Psychology and her B.S. degree from Miami University. Dr. Colella is a fellow of the American Psychological Association and the Society for Industrial and Organizational Psychology, Division 14 of the APA. She will be the President of the Society of Industrial and Organizational Psychology in 2011.

Dr. Colella's main research focuses on treatment issues regarding persons with disabilities in the workplace and workplace accommodation. She has also published on a variety of other organizational behavior and human resources topics such as discrimination, pay secrecy, performance appraisal, motivation, socialization, and employee selection. Her research appears in the *Journal of Applied Psychology, Personnel Psychology, Academy of Management Journal, Academy of Management Review, Research in Personnel and Human Resource Management, Human Resource Management Review, Journal of Applied Social Psychology,* and the *Journal of Occupational Rehabilitation,* among other places. She is the editor of a Society of Industrial and Organizational Psychology Frontiers Series book on the psychology of workplace discrimination. Dr. Colella serves (or has served) on the editorial boards of *Personnel Psychology, Journal of Applied Psychology, Academy of Management Journal, Journal of Organizational Behavior, Human Resource Management Review, Human Performance, SIOP Frontier's Series, Human Resource Management,* and *Journal of Management.* She is an ad hoc reviewer for most other journals in the management field and federal funding agencies. Her research has been funded by a variety of national, state, and university sources.

Dr. Colella teaches undergraduate, masters-level, and Ph.D. level courses in Human Resource Management and Organizational Behavior.

brief contents

contents

preface

A few years ago, the following statement appeared on the cover of *Fast Company*, "The best leaders know where all of the great companies start. It's the people. ..." Despite all of the major technological advances made and the substantial increases in the power of computers (both hardware and software) that allow us to perform many functions more easily than in the past and to accomplish some tasks that we could not do in the past, all of this activity is driven by people. People developed Apple's iPod and iPad. People developed and implemented Twitter and Facebook. We communicate on cell phones and small laptop computers developed by people. Our automobiles are serviced by people; at restaurants we eat food prepared by people; we enjoy college and professional sports played by people. People are the drivers of organizations and make or break their success. Ed Breen, CEO of Tyco suggests that ideas provided by people are the basis of winning competitive battles because companies compete with their brains as well as their brawn. In support of this argument, Anne Mulcahy, former chairman of the board and former CEO of Xerox argues that people were the primary reason for Xerox's turnaround in performance. They attracted highly talented employees, motivated them and they were highly productive.[1]

Purpose

We wrote this book for several reasons. First, we wanted to communicate in an effective way the knowledge of managing people in organizations. The book presents up-to-date concepts of organizational behavior (OB) in a lively and easy-to-read manner. The book is based on classic and cutting-edge research on the primary topic of each chapter. Second, we wanted to emphasize the importance of people to the success of organizations. We do so by communicating how managing people is critical to implementing an organization's strategy, gaining an advantage over competitors, and ensuring positive organizational performance. This approach helps students to better understand the relevance of managing people, allowing the student to integrate these concepts with knowledge gained in other core business courses. To emphasize the importance of people, we use the term *human capital*. People are important assets to organizations; application of their knowledge and skills is necessary for organizations to accomplish their goals.

New to the Third Edition

A number of changes have been made to enrich the content of the book and to ensure that it is up-to-date with current organizational behavior research and managerial practice. For example, we have changed or updated all chapter opening cases (Exploring Behavior in Action), and all major case examples in the content of the chapters (e.g., Experiencing Organizational Behavior, Managerial Advice). The few that were not changed represent classic examples (such as on the U.S. Civil War). Several of the major changes to the content are described below:

- New materials were added on the topic of firms gaining value from the knowledge learned by expatriates (Chapter 3).
- New materials were added on ethics and corruption (Chapter 3).
- Critical information was added on attractiveness and weight bias in our discussion of perception (Chapter 4).
- A new section focused on social dominance orientation as an individual difference was incorporated (Chapter 5).
- A new section was added on subconscious goals, an area of leading-edge research on goal setting (Chapter 6).
- Additional information was included on overload and job loss as important stressors (Chapter 7).
- Our discussion of communication networks was substantially modified and updated (Chapter 9).
- Building on our discussion of moods and emotions in Chapter 5, an explanation of how these characteristics of human functioning affect decision making was added to Chapter 10.
- New material was added in the crucial areas of workplace aggression and violence (Chapter 12).
- A new section was added on ambidextrous organizations, a topic of growing importance in OB (Chapter 13).
- A new section on top management changes was incorporated, along with new material on institutional changes and training (Chapter 14).

In addition to the above, a new section on Human Resource Management Applications was added at the end of each chapter. These sections explain how individuals in the human resource management function can use major OB concepts to more effectively manage human capital in the organization (e.g., management development programs, compensation programs, selection processes).

By popular demand, we have brought back part-ending cases, an approach used in the first edition. We also have a case on ethics at the end of the book that can be used with the content in several chapters throughout the book. The cases are completely new and engaging.

We have added approximately 300 new references from the research literature and many more from popular press articles on managerial practice. Although we have made important revisions and updated materials to reflect current managerial practice, we have maintained all of the basic OB content that instructors found to be valuable and all of the pedagogical approaches that supported students' efforts to learn. Therefore, this third edition represents continued improvement of a high-quality teaching and learning tool. It continues to be written in an easy style and is user friendly, as were the first two editions of the book.

Value Provided by this Book

Managing OB involves acquiring, developing, managing, and applying the knowledge, skills, and abilities of people. A strategic approach to OB rests on the premise that people are the foundation for any firm's competitive advantage. Providing exceptionally high quality products and services, excellent customer service, best-in-class cost structure, and other advantages are based on the capabilities of the firm's people, its human capital. If organized and managed effectively, the knowledge and skills of the people in the firm are the basis for gaining an advantage over competitors and achieving long-term financial success.

Individual, interpersonal, and organizational characteristics determine the behavior and ultimately the value of an organization's people. Factors such as individuals' technical skills, personality characteristics, personal values, abilities to learn, and abilities to be self-managing are important bases for the development of organizational capabilities. At the interpersonal level, factors such as quality of leadership, communication within and between groups, and conflict within and between groups are noteworthy in the organization's ability to build important capabilities and apply them to achieve its goals. Finally, at the organizational level, the culture and policies of the firm are also among the most important factors, as they influence whether the talents and positive predispositions of individuals are effectively used. Thus, managing human capital is critical for an organization to beat its competition and to perform effectively.

This book explains how to effectively manage behavior in organizations. In addition, we emphasize how effective behavioral management relates to organizational performance. We link the specific behavioral topic(s) emphasized in each chapter to organizational strategy and performance through explicit but concise discussions. We also provide short cases and examples to highlight the relationships.

Therefore, we emphasize the importance of managing OB and its effect on the outcomes of the organization. This is highly significant because a number of organizations routinely mismanage their workforce. For example, some organizations routinely implement major reductions in the workforce (layoffs, downsizing) whenever they experience performance problems. How does an organization increase its effectiveness by laying off thousands of its employees? The answer is that it rarely does so.[2] Layoffs reduce costs but they also result in losses of significant human capital and valuable knowledge. These firms then suffer from diminished capabilities and their performance decreases further. Research shows that firms increasing their workforce during economic downturns enjoy much stronger performance when the economy improves.[3] These firms have the capabilities to take advantage of the improving economy, whereas firms that downsized must rebuild their capabilities and are less able to compete effectively. The firms listed annually in *Fortune's* "100 Best Companies to Work for" are consistently among the highest performers in their industries (e.g., Starbucks, Whole Foods Market, Marriott, American Express).

Concluding Remarks

The knowledge learned from a course in organizational behavior is important for managers at all levels: top executives, middle managers, and lower-level managers. While top executives may understand the strategic importance of managing human capital, middle and lower-level managers must also understand the linkage between managing behavior effectively and the organization's ability to formulate and implement its strategy. Managers do not focus solely on individual behavior. They also manage interpersonal, team, intergroup, and interorganizational relationships. Some refer to these relationships as "social capital." The essence of managing organizational behavior is the development and use of human capital and social capital.

Jack Welch, former CEO of GE, suggested that he and his management team used management concepts that energized armies of people allowing them to dream, dare, reach, and stretch their talents in order to do things they never thought possible. This book presents concepts that will help students to gain the knowledge needed to effectively manage behavior in organizations. This, in turn, helps in the implementation of the organization's strategy, affects the organization's productivity, allows the organization to gain advantages over its competitors, and therefore contributes to the organization's overall performance.

MAH
CCM
AJC

1 Hitt, M.A., Haynes, K.T., & Serpa, R. 2010. Strategic leadership for the twenty-first century. *Business Horizons*, in press.

2 Krishnan, H., Hitt, M.A., & Park, D. 2007. Acquisition premiums, subsequent workplace reductions and post-acquisition performance. *Journal of Management Studies*, 44: 709–732; Nixon, R.D., Hitt, M.A., Lee, H. & Jeong, E. 2004. Market reactions to announcements of corporate downsizing actions and implementation strategies. *Strategic Management Journal*, 25: 1121–1129.

3 Greer, C.R., & Ireland, T.C. 1992. Organizational and financial correlates of a 'contrarian' human resource investment strategy. *Academy of Management Journal*, 35: 956–984.

FOCUS AND PEDAGOGY

The book explains and covers all organizational behavior topics, based on the most current research available. Unlike other OB texts, it uses the lens of an organization's strategy as a guide. Elements of the book through which we apply this lens include:

Exploring Behavior in Action

Each chapter opens with a case, grounding the chapter in a real-world context. Some of the companies featured include Men's Wearhouse, McDonalds, W. L. Gore & Associates, Starbucks, and FedEx.

---

exploring behavior in action

Diversity in the Los Angeles Fire Department

Melissa Kelley had a rich background in firefighting. Early in life, she learned from her grandfather, who worked as a firefighter. In college, she learned through coursework as a fire-science major. After college, she spent five years learning and honing her skills as a firefighter with the California Department of Forestry.

Armed with her experiences and passion for the work, she joined the Los Angeles Fire Department in 2001. Although aware of possible discrimination and harassment against women in the department, she did not hesitate to join when presented with the opportunity. In her words, "I was willing to overlook … the dirty jokes, the porn, the … mentality. … I just wanted to be part of the team." To her, only two simple rules applied: "Do not touch me. Do not hurt me on purpose."

The Strategic Importance of …

Links the issues in the opening case to the organizational behavior topic of the chapter. The issues are discussed in light of their importance to organization strategy and ultimately how they affect the organization's performance.

> *"The Strategic Importance of … and The Strategic Lens are appropriate 'bookends' for the chapter; they set up how decision making is strategic and reinforce that at the end of the chapter."*
>
> (PAM ROFFOL-DOBIES,
> UNIVERSITY OF MISSOURI KANSAS CITY)

the strategic importance of Organizational Diversity

As the LAFD case shows, negative reactions to diversity can have harmful effects on an organization. These reactions, including discrimination and harassment of various forms, often lead to lawsuits, turnover, reduced satisfaction, and performance issues. In the most effective organizations, associates and managers understand the value of diversity and capitalize on it to improve performance. Moreover, associates and managers cannot escape diverse workgroups and organizations. Differences in gender, race, functional background, and so on are all around us. The United States is a particularly diverse country with respect to race and ethnicity, and current demographic trends indicate that its population will become even more diverse.

LAFD's legal troubles, financial settlement costs, and public embarrassment have led to renewed efforts to change the culture. The changing nature of the firefighter's job, where 80 percent of fire calls no longer involve structural or brush fires, probably has helped in this process.[1] Many organizations, however, have not needed public embarrassment or changing jobs to motivate diversity efforts. Many organizations, particularly large ones, have voluntarily adopted diversity manage-

ment with fewer than 100 workers. Over 79 percent of human resource managers at Fortune 1000 companies said they believed that successfully managing diversity improves their organizations.[3]

Diversity, if properly managed, can help a business build competitive advantage. For example, hiring and retaining managers and associates from various ethnicities can help an organization better understand and serve an existing diverse customer base. Diversity among associates also might help the organization attract additional customers from various ethnic groups. Diverse backgrounds and experiences incorporated into a work team or task force can help the organization more effectively handle an array of complex and challenging problems. Kevin Johnson, Co-President of Platforms and Services at Microsoft, puts it this way: "[W]e must recognize, respect, and leverage the different perspectives our employees bring to the marketplace as strengths. Doing so will ensure that we will be more competitive in the global marketplace, will be seen as an employer of choice, and will be more creative and innovative …."[4]

In the case of nonprofit organizations or governmental units such as the Los Angeles Fire Department, diversity

withheld from donation. In the case of the Los Angeles Fire Department, diverse captains, firefighters, and paramedics could better communicate with and predict the behavior of the diverse citizenry of Los Angeles. This would enable the department to better serve the city. It also would position it to receive more resources from the city and state and would increase its likelihood of being chosen over other organizations for additional duties in the Los Angeles area.

Many individuals feel most comfortable interacting and working with people who are similar to them on a variety of dimensions (such as age, race, ethnic background, education, functional area, values, and personality).[5] They must, however, learn to work with all others in an organization to achieve common goals. In a truly inclusive workplace, everyone feels valued and all associates are motivated and committed to the mission of the organization. Such outcomes are consistent with a high-involvement work environment and can help organizations achieve competitive advantage.

We begin this chapter by defining organizational diversity and distinguishing it from other concepts, such as affirmative action. Next, we describe

Experiencing Organizational Behavior

These two Exploring Organizational Behavior sections in each chapter apply the key concepts of the chapter. Real-world case situations are used including such topics as women, work, and stereotypes; Google and high-quality associates; Coca-Cola's new fizz; extreme jobs; and communication at J. Crew. Each discussion highlights the connection between an OB concept and the organization's strategy and performance.

> *"The Experiencing OB section is also useful since it provides a conceptual view of the changing approach to OB. I like the idea that it walks the students through a situation and then summarizes the prospects for acting successfully."*
>
> (MARIAN SCHULTZ, UNIVERSITY OF WEST FLORIDA)

> *"After reading the Experiencing OB section on the football league, I also found that the example was an excellent choice. My classroom includes both traditional and nontraditional students, ranging in age from 20–72 and I think it is important to provide a variety of examples that everyone can relate to in the course."*
>
> (MARILYN WESNER,
> GEORGE WASHINGTON UNIVERSITY)

EXPERIENCING ORGANIZATIONAL BEHAVIOR

Diversity at the Top

©MANDEL NGAN/Getty Images, Inc.

On November 4, 2008, the United States elected Barack Obama as president. President Obama personifies the concept of diversity in terms of race, ethnicity, and geography. His black father was from a small town in Kenya and his white mother was from Kansas. His parents met in Hawaii, where he was born. President Obama's parents were divorced when he was 2 years old. When he was six years old, his mother remarried a man from Indonesia, and the family moved there. At the age of ten, Barack Obama returned to Hawaii to live with his maternal grandparents. He has a half-sister who is part Indonesian and is married to a man who is Chinese Canadian. President Obama's wife, Michelle Obama, is African American. In an interview with Oprah Winfrey, President Obama described his family get-togethers as "mini United Nations meetings." He said he had some relatives that looked like Bernie Mac and some that looked like Margaret Thatcher. The Obama family clearly exemplifies the diversity inherent in the United States.

President Obama's intrapersonal diversity and strong beliefs that diversity in governance is necessary is reflected in the diversity of his cabinet. Thirty-four percent of his officials are female, 11 percent are black, 8 percent are Hispanic, and 4 percent are Asian. While these do not seem like large numbers, they reflect more diversity than was present in past administrations' cabinets. This diversity is expected to increase as President

Obama's tenure in office lengthens and he brings in new officials.

The presidency of Barack Obama brings up the question of whether the United States has overcome problems with racial, ethnic, and gender discrimination. Is the leadership in this country finally reflective of the population? Unfortunately, this is still not the case, as evidenced by the demography of corporate leaders. At the end of 2008, there were 5 black, 7 Latino, 7 Asian, and 13 female (2 of whom are Asian) CEOs of Fortune 500 companies. This means that 94 percent of Fortune 500 CEOs were white, non-Hispanic males. Examining the composition of boards of directors reveals the same lack of diversity. A Catalyst 2009 study of Fortune 500 companies revealed that women held 15.2 percent of board seats and women of color held 3.1 percent of all board director positions. Women held only 2 percent of board chair positions. These numbers have remained relatively consistent over the past five years. A study on African American representation on corporate boards found that representation had decreased from 8.1 percent in 2004 to 7.4 percent in 2008. In a recent study of Fortune 100 boards, the Alliance for Board Diversity (a

joint effort among organizations concerned with board diversity) concluded that:

- There is a severe underrepresentation of women and minorities on corporate boards when compared to general U.S. population demographics for race and gender.
- Particular areas of concern include the lack of representation of minority women and of Asian Americans and Hispanics.
- There is a recycling of the same minority individuals—especially African American men—as board members. Minority and female board members hold more seats per person than do white males.
- Very few boards have representation from all groups. Only four boards had representation by all four groups (women, African Americans, Asian Americans, and Hispanics).

Will the diversity evident in the Obama administration filter down to

Managerial Advice

These sections provide advice for future managers and make a connection to the organization's strategy and performance. Examples of Managerial Advice include multinational corporations and "glocalization", Phil Jackson's leadership success, surfing for applicants on MySpace and Facebook, managing virtual teams, finding a fit at Home Depot, and "green" policies and practices.

Promoting a Positive Diversity Environment

Robin Ely, Debra Meyerson, and Martin Davidson are professors at Harvard University, Stanford University, and the University of Virginia, respectively. In conjunction with the human development and organizational learning professionals at Learning as Leadership, they have developed several principles designed to ensure that members of various social identity groups do not become trapped in low-quality workplace relationships. These principles are designed to encourage engagement and learning. The principles are perhaps best applied in the context of individuals experiencing uncomfortable events that are open to interpretation, such as when the member of a minority group is told by someone from the majority that she is being too aggressive, or when a man is told by a woman that he is acting as his grandfather might have acted. The principles are listed below:

a. *Pause to short circuit the emotion and reflect.* Individuals who have experienced an uncomfortable event should take a few moments to identify their feelings and consider a range of responses.

b. *Connect with others in ways that affirm the importance of relationships.* Individuals who have experienced an uncomfortable event should reach out to those who have caused the difficulty, thereby valuing relationships.

c. *Question interpretations and explore blind spots.* Individuals who have experienced an uncomfortable event should engage in self-questioning as well as the questioning of others. They should be open to the interpretations that others have of the situation, while realizing that their own interpretations might be correct.

d. *Obtain genuine support that doesn't necessarily validate initial points of view but, rather, helps in gaining broader perspective.* Individuals who have experienced an uncomfortable event should seek input from those who will challenge their initial points of view on the situation.

e. *Shift the mindset.* Individuals who have experienced an uncomfortable event should be open to the idea that both parties might need to change to some degree.

©Tom Grill/Corbis

Sources: R.J. Ely, D.E. Meyerson, and M.N. Davidson. 2006. "Rethinking Political Correctness," *Harvard Business Review*, 84 (September); Learning as Leadership, "Research," 2007, at http://www.learnaslead.com/index.php.

Organizational diversity, when managed effectively, has many benefits for organizations. In general, effectively managed diversity programs contribute to an organization's ability to achieve and maintain a competitive advantage. Diversity in teams at all levels can be helpful in solving complex problems because heterogeneous teams integrate multiple perspectives. This benefit applies to the upper-echelon management team as well as to project teams, such as new-product-development teams, much lower in the organization. Not only can the diversity help resolve complex problems, but it also better mirrors U.S. society. Thus, it signals to potential associates and potential customers that the organization understands and effectively uses diversity. As a result, the organization has a larger pool of candidates for potential associates from which it can select the best. In addition, the organization is likely to have a larger potential market because of its understanding of the products and services desired by a diverse marketplace. Having a diverse organization that reflects the demographic composition of U.S. society is smart business.[106]

Critical Thinking Questions

1. How does organizational diversity contribute to an organization's competitive advantage?

2. What actions are required to create diversity in an organization, particularly in one that has homogeneous membership at present?

3. How does diversity in an organization affect its strategy?

The Strategic Lens

The Strategic Lens section concludes each chapter. The section explains the topic of the chapter through the lens of organizational strategy. Highlighted is the critical contribution of the chapter's concepts to the organization's achievement of its goals. The Strategic Lens concludes with *Critical Thinking Questions* that are designed to emphasize the student's knowledge of the OB topic, its effects on the organization's strategy, and its effects on organizational functioning.

Thinking about Ethics

1. Suppose that an organization has discriminated in the past. Should it now simply stop its discriminatory practices, or should it also take specific actions to increase its diversity by targeting, hiring, and promoting minorities ahead of nonminorities? Discuss.

2. Should all managers and associates in an organization be required to undergo diversity training regardless of their desire to do so? Why or why not?

3. Are there any circumstances in which it is appropriate to discriminate against a particular class of people (such as women)? If so, explain the circumstances. If not, explain why.

4. Women are not a minority in the population but represent a minority in the U.S. workforce, particularly in some occupations. Why has this occurred in U.S. society (or your home country, if applicable)?

5. Should all cultures and modes of conduct be tolerated, even if they conflict with the values of the organization? Why or why not?

6. What percentage of the organization's budget should be invested in building and maintaining an effective diversity management program? How should this percentage compare with other major budget items?

Thinking about Ethics

Given the growing importance of ethics, the "Thinking about Ethics" feature at the end of every chapter provides an opportunity to analyze various ethical dilemmas that confront today's managers. Students are asked to apply OB concepts to realistic ethical issues to determine the most ethical course of action.

Human Resource Management Applications

This new feature at the end of each chapter highlights the importance of OB concepts to human resource management and how managers can use these concepts to more effectively manage human capital in the organization. Students will learn various ways in which managers can use management-development programs, compensation programs, and selection processes.

Human Resource Management Applications

The Human Resource Management (HRM) function plays a key role in a firm's capability to manage diversity. Often diversity officers and initiatives are housed within HRM departments. The following are several activities that an HRM department can use to manage diversity.

A major function of HRM departments is developing, conducting, and evaluating *training* programs. Diversity training programs are integral to any diversity management effort. HRM departments are also likely to evaluate the effectiveness of these programs.

In many organizations, *employee recruitment* is centralized through the HRM department. Thus, they are concerned with advertising to, locating, and attracting potential associates from groups traditionally underrepresented in the organization.

Employee selection may also be centralized through the HRM department. In order to facilitate an organization's diversity goals, the HRM department must make certain that methods used to hire associates (e.g., interviews, job knowledge test, personality tests) are not biased against certain group members.

An important aspect of many diversity programs is an organizational *diversity climate audit*, which surveys associates to determine their feeling of inclusion and satisfaction with diversity initiatives. This audit is often the responsibility of the HRM department.

Building Your Human Capital

To help students better know themselves and develop needed skills in organizational behavior, a personal assessment instrument is included in each chapter. This includes information on scoring and interpreting the results. Assessments, for example, are focused on approaches to difficult learning situations, the propensity to be creative, skill at managing with power, and the ability to tolerate change.

> *"The Building Your Human Capital segment is unique. Students need to recognize the importance of the topics for developing their personal skills. This section does a good job in forwarding that idea."*
>
> (CEASAR DOUGLAS, FLORIDA STATE UNIVERSITY)

---

building your human capital
What's Your DQ (Diversity Quotient)?

How well do you handle diversity? Your ability to be flexible, work with many different types of people, and deal with ambiguous situations will be crucial to a successful career in the twenty-first century. The following assessment will allow you to determine whether you have had the experience necessary to help in successfully navigating a diverse work environment.

Use the following scale to answer the questions below:

1 point = never	3 points = three or four times
2 points = once or twice	4 points = four or more times

In the last month, how often did you ...?

1. See a foreign movie.
2. Speak a language other than your first language.
3. Visit an art or history museum.
4. Have a conversation with someone who was of a different race.
5. Have a conversation with someone who was from a different country.
6. Attend a social event where at least half of the people differed from you in race or ethnic background.
7. Visit a church that was of a religion different from yours.

An Organizational Behavior Moment

The applied, hypothetical case at the end of each chapter gives students an opportunity to apply the knowledge they have gained throughout the chapter. Each case concludes with questions. Teaching suggestions are included in the instructor's resources.

> *"The case was a good illustration of what life as a manger is like and it lends itself to a discussion of what might keep a manager from being highly involved."*
>
> (DEBORAH BUTLER, GEORGIA STATE UNIVERSITY)

---

an organizational behavior moment
Project "Blow Up"

Big State University (BSU) is proud of the success of its international executive MBA (EMBA) program. The program is designed to bring together promising middle- and higher-level managers from around the globe for an exceptional learning experience. BSU's EMBA program has been ranked very highly by the business press. Alumni praise the program for its excellent faculty, networking opportunities, and exposure to colleagues from around the world. Students in the program can either attend weekend classes on BSU's campus or participate through distance-learning technology from campuses around the world.

One of the defining features of the program is the first-year team project. Students are randomly assigned to five-member teams. Each team has a faculty advisor, and each must develop a business plan for a startup company. A major part of the business plan involves developing a marketing strategy. The teams begin the project during orientation week and finish at the end of the next summer. Each team must turn in a written report and a business plan and make an hour-long presentation to the other students and faculty as well as several executives from well-respected multinational companies. Students must earn a passing grade on

Team Exercise

These experiential exercises expand the student's learning through activities and engage students in team building skills. Teaching suggestions are included in the instructor's resources.

> *"The Exercise at the end of the chapter seemed like a great way to get students involved and to help them understand the material."*
>
> (Sharon Purkiss,
> California State University at Fullerton)

---

team exercise
What Is It Like to Be Different?

One reason people have a difficult time dealing with diversity in others or understanding why it is important to value and respect diversity is that most people spend most of their lives in environments where everyone is similar to them on important dimensions. Many people have seldom been in a situation in which they felt they didn't belong or didn't know the "rules." The purpose of this exercise is to have you experience such a situation and open up a dialogue with others about what it feels like to be different and what you can personally learn from this experience to become better at managing diversity in the future.

STEP 1: Choose an event that you would not normally attend and at which you will likely be in the minority on some important dimension. Attend the event.

- You can go with a friend who would normally attend the event, but not one who will also be in a minority.
- Make sure you pick a place where you will be safe and where you are sure you will be welcomed, or at least tolerated. You may want to check with your instructor about your choice.
- Do not call particular attention to yourself. Just observe what is going on and how you feel.

Some of you may find it easy to have a minority experience, since you are a minority group member in your everyday life. Others may have a more difficult time. Here are some examples of events to consider attending:

- A religious service for a religion totally different from your own.
- A sorority or fraternity party where the race of members is mostly different from your own.
- A political rally where the politics are different from your own.

SUPPLEMENTS

Instructor's Resource Guide

The Instructor's Resource Guide includes an Introduction with sample syllabi, Chapter Outlines, Chapter Objectives, Teaching Notes on how to integrate and assign special features within the text, and suggested answers for all quiz and test questions found in the text. The Instructor's Resource Guide also includes additional discussion questions and assignments that relate specifically to the cases, as well as case notes, self-assessments, and team exercises. The Instructor's Resource Guide can be accessed on the Instructor portion of the Hitt website at http://www.wiley.com/college/hitt.

Test Bank

This robust Test Bank consists of true/false (approximately 60 per chapter), multiple choice (approximately 60 per chapter), short-answer (approximately 25 per chapter), and essay questions (approximately 5 per chapter). Further, it is specifically designed so that questions will vary in degree of difficulty, ranging from straightforward recall to more challenging application questions to ensure student mastery of all key concepts and topics. The organization of test questions also offers instructors the most flexibility when designing their exams. A **Computerized Test Bank** provides even more flexibility and customization options to instructors. The Computerized Test Bank requires a PC running Windows. This electronic version of the Test Bank includes all the questions from the Test Bank within a test-generating program that allows instructors to customize their exams and also to add their own test questions in addition to what is already available. Both the Test Bank and Computerized Test Bank are available for viewing and download on the Instructor portion of the Hitt Website at http://www.wiley.com/college/hitt.

Power Point Presentations

These PowerPoint Presentations provide another visual enhancement and learning aid for students, as well as additional talking points for instructors. Each chapter's set of interactive PowerPoint slides includes lecture notes to accompany each slide. Each presentation includes roughly 30 slides with illustrations, animations, and related web links interspersed appropriately. The PowerPoint Presentations can be accessed on the Instructor portion of the Hitt website at http://www.wiley.com/college/hitt

Lecture Notes

Lecture Notes provide an outline of the chapter and knowledge objectives, highlighting the key topics/concepts presented within each chapter. Power-Point slides have been integrated, where relevant, and the lecture notes suggest to instructors when it's best to show the class each slide within a particular chapter's PowerPoint Presentation.

Web Quizzes

Online quizzes with questions varying in level of difficulty have been designed to help students evaluate their individual comprehension of the key concepts and topics presented within each chapter. These web quizzes are available at http://www. wiley.com/college/hitt. Each chapter's quiz includes 10 questions, including true/false and multiple choice questions. These review questions, developed by the Test Bank author, Melinda Blackman, have been created to provide the most effective and efficient testing system for students as they prepare for more formal quizzes and exams. Within this system, students have the opportunity to "practice" responding to the types of questions they'll be expected to address on a quiz or exam.

Prelecture and Postlecture Quizzes

The Prelecture and Postlecture Quizzes can be found exclusively in *WileyPLUS*. These quizzes consist of multiple-choice and true/false questions which vary in level of detail and difficulty while focusing on a particular chapter's key terms and concepts. This resource allows instructors to quickly and easily evaluate their students' progress by monitoring their comprehension of the material both before and after each lecture.

The prelecture quiz questions enable instructors to gauge their students' comprehension of a particular chapter's content so they can best determine what to focus on in their lecture.

The postlecture quiz questions are intended to be homework or review questions that instructors can assign to students after covering a particular chapter. The questions typically provide hints, solutions or explanations to the students, as well as page references.

Personal Response System (PRS)

Personal Response System or "Clicker" questions have been designed for each chapter to spark additional in-class discussion and debate. These questions are drawn from the Test Bank and the web quizzes. For more information on PRS content, please contact your local Wiley sales representative.

Organizational Behavior Lecture Launcher Video

Video clips from the BBC and CBS News, ranging from 2 to 10 minutes in length tied to the current news topics in organizational behavior are available on DVD. These video clips provide an excellent starting point for lectures. An instructor's manual for using the lecture launcher is available on the Instructor's portion of the Hitt website. For more information on the OB Lecture Launcher, please contact your local Wiley sales representative.

Business Extra Select Online Courseware system

This program (available at http://www.wiley.com/college/bxs) provides instructors with millions of content resources from an extensive database of cases, journals, periodicals, newspapers, and supplemental readings. This courseware system lends itself extremely well to the integration of real-world content within organizational behavior to enable instructors to convey the relevance of the course content to their students.

Companion Website

The text's website at www.wiley.com/college/hitt contains myriad resources and links to aid both teaching and learning, including the web quizzes described above.

ACKNOWLEDGMENTS

We thank the many people who helped us develop this book. We owe a debt of gratitude to the following people who reviewed this book through its development and revision, providing us with helpful feedback. Thanks to those professors who provided valuable feedback for the third edition: Lon Doty, San Jose State University; Don Gibson, Fairfield University; Richard J. Gibson, Embry-Riddle Aeronautical University; Aden Heuser, Ohio State University; Arlene Kreinik, Western Connecticut State University; Lorianne D. Mitchell, East Tennessee State University; Wendy Smith, University of Delaware; and Hamid Yeganeh, Winona State University. Also, thanks to those professors who reviewed the book in its prior editions and helped us hone its approach and focus: Syed Ahmed, Florida International University; Johnny Austin, Chapman University; Rick Bartlet, Columbus State Community College; Melinda Blackman, California State University–Fullerton; Fred Blass, Florida State University; H. Michael Boyd, Bentley College; Regina Bento, University of Baltimore; Ralph Brathwaite, University of Hartford; David Bush, Villanova University; Mark Butler, San Diego State University; Steve Buuck, Concordia University; Jay Caulfield, Marquette University; William Clark, Leeward Community College; Marie Dasborough, University of Miami; Michelle Duffy, University of Kentucky; Michael Ensby, Clarkson University; Cassandra Fenyk, Centenary College; Meltem Ferendeci-Ozgodek, Bilkent University; Dean Frear, Wilkes University; Sharon Gardner, College of New Jersey; James Gelatt, University of Maryland–University College; John George, Liberty University; Lucy Gilson, University of Connecticut-Storrs; Mary Giovannini, Truman State University; Yezdi Godiwalla, University of Wisconsin–Whitewater; Elaine Guertler, Lees-McRae College; Carol Harvey, Assumption College; David Hennessy, Mt. Mercy College; Kenny Holt, Union University; Janice Jackson, Western New England College; Paul Jacques, Western Carolina University; William Judge, University of Tennessee–Knoxville; Barbara Kelley, St. Joseph's University; Molly Kern, Baruch College; Robert Ledman, Morehouse College; James Maddox, Friends University; Bill Mellan, Florida Sothern College; Lorianne Mitchell, East Tennessee State University; Edward Miles, Georgia State University; Atul Mitra, University of Northern Iowa; Christine O'Connor, University of Ballarad; Regina O'Neill, Suffolk University; Laura Paglis, University of Evansville; Ron Piccolo, University of Central Florida; Chris Poulson, California State Polytechinal University–Pomana; Sharon Purkiss, California State University-Fullerton; David Radosevich, Montclair State University; William Reisel, St. John's University; Joe Rode, Miami University of Ohio; Pam Roffol-Dobies, University of Missouri–Kansas City; Sammie Robinson, Illinoise Wesleyan University; Bob Roller, Letourneau University; Sophie Romack, John Carroll University; William Rudd, Boise State College; Joel Rudin, Rowan University; Jane Schmidt-Wilk, Maharishi University of Management; Mel Schnake, Valdosta State University; Holly Schroth, University of California–Berkeley; Daniel Sherman, University of Alabama–Huntsville; Randy Sleeth, Virginia Commonwealth University; Shane Spiller, Morehead State University; John Stark, California State University–Bakersfield; Robert Steel, University of Michigan–Dearborn; David Tansik, University of Arizona; Tom Thompson, University of Maryland–University; Edward Tomlinson, John Carroll University; Tony Urban, Rutgers University–Camden; Fred Ware, Valdosta State University College; and Joseph Wright, Portland Community College. We also greatly appreciate the guidance and support we received from the excellent Wiley team consisting of George Hoffman, Lise Johnson, Karolina Zarychta, Sarah Vernon, and Sandra Dumas. We also acknowledge and thank former members of the editorial team who made contributions to this edition: Jayme Heffler, Kim Mortimer, and Jennifer Conklin. Our colleagues at Texas A&M University, University of Houston, and Tulane University have also provided valuable support by providing intellectual input through discussions and debates. There are many people over the years that have contributed to our own intellectual growth and development and led us to write this book. For all of your help and support, we thank you. Finally, we owe a debt of gratitude to our many students from whom we have learned and to the students who have used this text and provided feedback directly to us and through their instructors. Thank you.

MAH
CCM
AC

WHOLE FOODS,
whole people

Whole Foods Market is the largest natural food retailer in the world. With operations located primarily in the United States and also in Canada and the United Kingdom, Whole Foods sells natural and organic food products that include produce, meat, poultry, seafood, grocery products, baked and prepared goods, many drinks such as beer and wine, cheese, floral products, and pet products. The origin of the company dates to 1978 when John Mackey and his girlfriend used $45,000 in borrowed funds to start a small natural food store then named SaferWay. The store was located in Austin, Texas. John and his girlfriend lived in the space over the store (without a shower) because they were "kicked out" of their apartment for storing food products in it.

and its equipment was damaged. The total losses were approximately $400,000, and the company had no insurance. Interestingly, customers and neighbors helped the staff of the store to repair and clean up the damage. Creditors, vendors, and investors all partnered to help the store reopen only 28 days after the flood. With their assistance, Whole Foods survived this devastating natural disaster.

Whole Foods started to expand in 1984 when it opened its first store outside of Austin. The new store was located in Houston, followed by another store in Dallas and one in New Orleans. It also began acquiring other companies that sold natural foods, which helped to increase its expansion into new areas of the United States. In 2007, it expanded into international markets by opening its first Whole Foods branded store

In 1980, Mackey developed a partnership with Craig Weller and Mark Skiles, merging SaferWay with Weller's and Skiles's Clarksville Natural Grocer to create the Whole Foods Market. Its first store opened in 1980 with 12,500 square feet and 19 employees. This was a very large health food store relative to others at that time. There was a devastating flood in Austin within a year of its opening and the store was heavily damaged. Much of its inventory was ruined

in London, England. (In 2004, it acquired a small natural foods company in the United Kingdom, Fresh & Wild, but did not use the Whole Foods brand until opening its new store in London.) It also acquired one of its major U.S. competitors, Wild Oats, in 2007. It now has more than 54,000 employees in about 280 stores with annual sales of $7.95 billion. Thus, Whole Foods has become a major business enterprise and the most successful natural and organic food retailer in the world.

MANAGING HUMAN CAPITAL

Whole Foods Market has done a number of things right, thereby achieving considerable success. Yet, many people believe that one of the best things it has done is to implement an effective people-management system. Each Whole Foods store employs approximately 40 to as many as 650 associates. All of the associates are organized into self-directed teams; associates are referred to as team members. Each of the teams is responsible for a specific product or service area (e.g., prepared foods, meats and poultry, customer service). Team members report to a team leader, who then works with store management, referred to as store team leaders. The team members are a critically important part of the Whole Foods operation. Individuals are carefully selected and trained to be highly knowledgeable in their product areas, to offer friendly service, and to make critical decisions related to the types and quality of products offered to the public. Thus, they operate much differently than most "employees" in retail grocery

outlets. These team members work together with their team leader to make a number of decisions with regard to their specific areas, and they contribute to store level decisions as well. Some observers have referred to this approach as "workplace democracy." In fact, many of the team members are attracted to Whole Foods because of the discretion they have in making decisions regarding product lines and so on. Of course, there are other attractions such as the compensation. For example, the company's stock option program involves employees at all levels. In fact, 94 percent of the stock options offered by the company have been presented to nonexecutive members, including front-line team members. The company pays competitive wages and pays 100 percent of the health insurance premium for all associates working at least 30 hours per week, which includes 89 percent of its workforce. Although the annual deductible is high ($2,500), each associate receives a grant of up to $1,800 annually in a Personal Wellness Account to be used for health care out-of-pocket costs. All of the benefit options are voted on by the associates in the company. Current programs include options for dental, vision, disability, and life insurance in addition to the full medical coverage for full-time associates.

Whole Foods follows a democratic model in the selection of new associates. For example, potential new team members can apply for any one of the 13 teams that operate in most Whole Foods Markets. Current team members participate in the interview process and actually

vote on whether to offer a job to prospective colleagues. A candidate is generally given a four-week trial period to determine whether he or she has potential. At the end of that trial period, team members vote on whether to offer a permanent job to the candidate. The candidate must receive a two-thirds majority positive vote from the unit team members in order to be hired.

Teams also receive bonuses if they perform exceptionally well. They set goals relative to prior performance and must achieve those goals to attain a bonus. Exceptionally high-performing teams may earn up to $2 an hour more than their current wage base.

The top management of Whole Foods believes that the best philosophy is to build a shared identity with all team members. They do so by involving them in decisions and encouraging their participation at all levels in the business. They empower employees to make decisions and even allow them to participate in the decision regarding the benefit options, as noted above. All team members have access to full information on the company. It is referred to as Whole Foods' open-book policy. In this open-book policy, team members have access to the firm's financial records, which include compensation information for all associates and even the top management team and the CEO. Therefore, the firm operates with full transparency regarding its associates. This approach emphasizes the company's core values of collaboration and decentralization. The company attracts people who share those core values and tries to reward a highly engaged and productive workforce.

The company also limits the pay of top executives to no more than 19 times the lowest paid associate in the firm. While this amount has been increased over time in order to maintain competitive compensation for managers, it is still well below industry averages for top management team members. And, in recent times, John Mackey, the CEO, announced that he no longer will accept a salary above $1 annually or the stock options provided to him. Thus, his salary was reduced from $1 million to $1 per year. The money saved from his salary is donated to a fund to help needy associates.

The outcomes of this unique system for managing human capital have been impressive. For example, Whole Foods' voluntary turnover is much lower than the industry average. The industry average is almost 90 percent annually, but Whole Foods' data show that it has a voluntary turnover rate of approximately 26 percent. In addition, Whole Foods was ranked number 22 in the top 100 best companies to work for by *Fortune* magazine in 2009. It has been on the top 100 best companies to work for list for the past 12 years, and its ranking has been as high as number 5 (in 2007) but has always been among the best in the top 100.

In addition to its flat organization structure (few layers of management between associates and top managers) and decentralized decision making (e.g., selection of new associates), the company believes that each employee should feel a stake in the success of the company. In fact, this

---

TABLE 1   Whole Foods' Declaration of Interdependence (Five Core Values)

1. Selling the highest-quality natural and organic food products available.
2. Satisfying and delighting customers.
3. Supporting team member excellence and happiness.
4. Creating wealth through profits and growth.
5. Caring about communities and the environment.

---

is communicated in its "Declaration of Interdependence." The Declaration of Interdependence suggests that the company has five core values. They are listed in Table 1.

The company attempts to support team member excellence and happiness through its empowering work environment in which team members work together to create the results. In such an environment, they try to create a motivated work team that achieves the highest possible productivity. There is an emphasis on individuals taking responsibility for their success and failure and seeing both as opportunities for personal and organizational growth.

The company develops self-directed work teams and gives them significant decision-making authority to resolve problems and build a department and product line to satisfy and delight the customers. The company believes in providing open and timely information and in being highly transparent in all of its operations. It also focuses on achieving progress by continuously allowing associates to apply their collective creativity and intellectual capabilities to build a highly competitive and successful organization. Finally, the company emphasizes a shared fate

among all stakeholders. This is why there are no special privileges given to anyone, not even to top managers. It is assumed that everybody works together to achieve success.

SOCIAL AND COMMUNITY RESPONSIBILITIES

Whole Foods Market takes pride in being a responsible member of its community and of society. For example, it emphasizes the importance of sustainable agriculture. In particular, the firm tries to support organic farmers, growers, and the environment by a commitment to using sustainable agriculture and expanding the market for organic products. In this regard, the Whole Foods Market launched a program to loan approximately $10 million annually to help independent local producers around the country to expand. It holds seminars and teaches producers how to move their products onto grocery shelves and how to command and receive premium prices for their products. These seminars and related activities have been quite popular. As an example, its first seminar held in Colorado a few years ago attracted 130 growers, which was almost twice as many as expected. Overall, the Whole Foods Market does business with more than 2,400 independent growers.

Whole Foods Market also supports its local communities in other ways. For example, the company promotes active involvement in local communities by giving a minimum of 5 percent of its profits each year to a variety of community and nonprofit organizations. These actions encourage philanthropy and outreach in the communities that Whole Foods serves.

Whole Foods Market also tries to promote positive environmental practices. The company emphasizes the importance of recycling and reusing products and reducing waste wherever possible. Furthermore, Whole Foods was the first retailer to build a supermarket that met environmental standards of the Leadership in Energy and Environmental Design Green Building Rating System (LEED). It was the largest corporate purchaser of wind credits in the history of the United States when it purchased enough to offset 100 percent of its total electricity use in 2006. Finally, Whole Foods announced a new initiative a few years ago to create an animal compassion standard that emphasizes the firm's belief in the needs of animals. The company developed standards for each of the species that are used for foods and sold through their supermarkets.

Whole Foods launched a program to encourage higher wages and prices paid to farmers in poor countries, while simultaneously promoting environmentally safe practices. In fact, the company donates a portion of its proceeds to its Whole Planet Foundation, which in turn provides microloans to entrepreneurs in developing countries.

Very few, if any, major corporations, including competing supermarket chains, have established programs that rival those of the Whole Foods Market to meet social and community responsibilities.

SOME BUMPS IN THE ROAD

While the Whole Foods Market has been a highly successful company, it still has experienced some problems along the way. Obviously, it has produced a concept that has been imitated by other natural foods companies and a number of competing supermarkets as well. Yet, in general, Whole Foods has been able to maintain its competitive advantage and market leadership, partly by being the first to the market and partly because of its practices, which continue to generate a strong reputation and a positive company image. Yet, a number of firms have developed competing products and are making headway in selling organic foods, including some regular large supermarket chains. Even Wal-Mart has begun to offer organic foods in its grocery operations. In order to maintain its leadership and to continue to command a premium price, Whole Foods Market must continuously differentiate its products and its image so that people will buy from it rather than from competitors.

The top management of the Whole Foods Market has been strongly opposed to unionization. The belief is that the company pays workers well and treats them with dignity and respect and that a union is likely to interfere in its relationships with associates. Mackey, the CEO of the company, suggests that it is a campaign to "love the worker, not a union." Yet, the first union for Whole Foods was voted in at its Madison, Wisconsin, store. The vote by the Madison associates was 65 to 54 in favor of organizing a union. When this vote was announced, Mackey referred to it as a sad day in the history of the company. He suggested that the associates had made a mistake and believed that they would eventually realize the error of their ways. However, the Whole Foods Market executives have been able to fend off union efforts at other stores, including a campaign launched in 2009 that the company referred to as "union awareness training."

Another problem became evident in 2007, when it was announced that Mackey had, for a few years, posted on a Yahoo! financial message board anonymous online critiques of competitors and self-congratulating statements about the Whole Foods Market. These comments were made using a pseudonym so no one knew that he was the CEO of Whole Foods. This action was strongly criticized by analysts and others, and several questioned the ethics of his actions. Given that Whole Foods has emphasized its ethical approach to business and suggested that it conducts fair and open operations, such actions could be potentially harmful to the Whole Foods Market image and reputation. In fact, the company launched an investigation of his actions. In addition, the Securities and Exchange Commission (SEC) investigated some of the postings to Internet chat rooms by Mackey in which he used a pseudonym. The concern was that he may have released information that should not have been provided to the market. The Whole Foods' Board completed its investigation and reaffirmed its support for Mackey. In addition, the SEC investigated the incident but concluded that no enforcement action would be taken against the company or the CEO.

FIRM PERFORMANCE AND THE FUTURE

Whole Foods Market has performed well over the past several years, sustaining significant growth in sales and profits. Its stock price has also generally performed well. However, during the period 2005–2008, some analysts argued that the stock was overvalued, partly because they did not believe that Whole Foods' growth rate and returns could be sustained.

Undoubtedly, being able to maintain the growth rate will be difficult as the competition in its natural and organic foods grows and as the number of markets and opportunities narrows, particularly in the United States. This is especially of concern given the changed behaviors caused by the recent economic recession. Yet, some analysts are bullish on Whole Foods' stock. The price of its stock doubled early in 2009; according to some analysts, these outcomes portend the future because Whole Foods' business model seems to be strong in the face of a challenging economic environment. The company is highly profitable and continues to outperform its direct competitors.

Mackey has stated on several occasions that he does not make decisions on the basis of Wall Street's reactions. He argues that investors should not invest in his stock for the short term. Rather, they should look

for long-term value increases because he will make decisions in the best interest of the shareholders for the long term. Perhaps this approach will provide better returns over time, but only time will tell. Clearly, Whole Foods Market has been a very positive force in dealing with its associates through its highly unique means of managing human capital. It also has built a strong positive reputation and differentiated its products in the eyes of consumers. Yet, there are some challenges with which the firm must deal, such as growing competition and potential unionization. While the future likely remains bright, further evaluation will be needed to determine whether there will be continued growth and positive returns for all stakeholders of the Whole Foods Market.

Source: Whole Foods Market logo used with permission.

REFERENCES

1. 100 best companies to work for: Whole Foods Market 2009. *Fortune*, at http://money.cnn.com. accessed on June 15.
2. S. Cendrowski. 2009. What about Whole Foods? *Fortune*, July 20: 26.
3. Declaration of interdependence. 2007. Whole Foods Market website, at http://www.wholefoodsmarket.com, April 29.
4. C. Dillow. Innovating toward health care reform, the Whole Foods way. 2009. *Fast Company.com*, at http://fastcompany.com, August 12.
5. P.J. Erickson & L. Gratton. 2007. What it means to work here. *Harvard Business Review*, March: 85 (3): 104–112.
6. J.P. Fried. 2007. At Whole Foods, a welcome sign for immigrants seeking jobs. *New York Times*, at http://www.nytimes.com, April 29.
7. S. Hammer & T. McNicol. 2007. Low-cow compensation. *Business 2.0*, May: 62.
8. M. Hogan. 2007. Whole Foods: A little too rich? *BusinessWeek*, at http://www.businessweek.com, July 21.
9. P. Huetlin. 2007. Flagship Whole Foods opens in London. *BusinessWeek*, at http://www.businessweek.com, July 5.
10. L. Hunt. 2005. Whole Foods Market, Inc. At http://www.marketbusting.comlcasestudies, March 30.

11. D. Kesmodel & J. Eig. 2007. Unraveling rahodeb: A grocer's brash style takes unhealthy turn. *Wall Street Journal Online*, at http://oniine.wsj.com, July 30.
12. N.S. Koehn & K. Miller. 2007. John Mackey and Whole Foods Market. *Harvard Business School Case #9-807-111*, May 14.
13. J. Mackey. 2007. I no longer want to work for money. *Fast Company*, at http://www.fastcompany.com, February.
14. A. Nathans. 2003. Love the worker, not the union, a store says as some organize. *New York Times*, at http://www.nytimes.com, May 24.
15. Our core values. 2009. Whole Foods Market website, at http://www.wholefoodsmarket.com, April 29.
16. K. Richardson & D. Kesmodel. 2007. Why Whole Foods investors may want to shop around. *Wall Street Journal Online*, at http://online.wsj.com, November 23.
17. C. Rohwedder. 2007. Whole Foods opens new front. *Wall Street Journal Online*, at http://online.wsj.com, June 6.
18. S. Smith. 2009. Something stinks at Whole Foods. *Counterpunch*, at http://www.counterpunch.org, May 8–10.
19. J. Sonnenfeld. 2007. What's rotten at Whole Foods. *Business Week*, at http://www.businessweek.com, July 17.

20. B. Steverman. 2009. Wal-Mart vs. Whole foods. *Business-Week*, at http://www.businessweek.com, May 14.
21. S. Taub. 2008. Whole Foods "blogging" probe dropped by SEC. *CFO*, at http://www.cfo.com, April 28.
22. S. Thurm. 2007. Whole Foods CEO serves up heated word for FTC. *Wall Street Journal Online*, at http://online.swj.com, June 27.
23. Welcome to Whole Foods Market. 2009. Whole Foods Market website, http://www.wholefoodsmarket.com, August 30.
24. J.E. Wells & T. Haglock. 2005. Whole Foods Market, Inc. *Harvard Business School Case #9-705-476*, June 9.
25. Whole Foods closes buyout of Wild Oats. 2007. *New York Times*, at http://www.nytimes.com, August 29.
26. Whole Foods Market soars to #5 spot on *Fortune's "100 Best Companies to Work For"* list. Whole Foods Market website, at http://www.wholefoodsmarket.com, January 9.
27. Whole Foods Market. 2007. Wikipedia, at http://www.wikipedia.com, September 2.
28. Whole Foods promotes local buying. 2007. *New York Times*, at http://www.nytimes.com, April 29.

WHOLE FOODS CASE DISCUSSION QUESTIONS

Chapter 1
1. Describe how Whole Foods uses human capital as a source of competitive advantage.
2. Identify the aspects of high-involvement management contained in Whole Foods' approach to managing its associates.

Chapter 2
1. Compared to other companies in the service sector, is Whole Foods more or less likely to experience discrimination problems? Explain your answer.
2. How could Whole Foods' democratic model of selection interfere with the development or continuance of a diverse workforce? What should it do to prevent difficulties?

Chapter 3
1. How do you think that globalization will affect Whole Foods over time? Please explain several ways it could affect the company operations.
2. In what ways can national culture affect the management of human capital? Will Whole Foods have to adapt its democratic approach to selecting new team members or the benefits it provides to its associates as it expands further into international markets?

Chapter 4
1. To what extent do you think that training and associate learning would be more important for Whole Foods than for other grocery stores?
2. What type of perceptual problems on the part of associates and the public may have resulted from the scandal regarding John Mackey's blog activities?

Chapter 5
1. Given the nature of Whole Foods' jobs and the way in which associates are selected, what type of personality traits are important for Whole Foods' associates to possess?

2. Compared to the industry average, Whole Foods has a low turnover rate and is consistently ranked as a great place to work. Why do you think Whole Foods' associates are so satisfied and committed to the organization?

Chapter 6
1. Are Whole Foods' team members likely to experience problems with procedural and/or distributive justice? Explain.
2. Which of the major motivational practices are emphasized by Whole Foods in its management system? For example, do they include meaningful rewards, tying rewards to performance, designing enriched jobs, providing feedback, or clarifying expectations and goals?

Chapter 7
1. Based on the demand–control and effort–reward models of stress, are Whole Foods' team members likely to experience a great deal of stress? What about its executives?
2. Does Whole Foods need a wellness program? Why or why not?

Chapter 8
1. Is John Mackey a transformational leader? Why or why not?
2. Based on contingency theories of leadership, what approach to leadership should be used by Whole Foods' team leaders?

Chapter 9
1. Whole Foods' open-book policy allows all associates to have full access to all information about the company and its executives. Would this degree of open communication work as well in other companies? Why or why not? What impact do you think this degree of transparency has on the attitudes and behavior of Whole Foods' associates?

2. What ethical issues arise from John Mackey's use of a pseudonym to post opinions, information, and critiques on blog sites?

Chapter 10

1. What decision styles does John Mackey appear to use? Do these fit his situation?
2. Which group decision-making pitfalls appear most likely within Whole Foods' teams, and which decision-making techniques would you recommend to counter those pitfalls?

Chapter 11

1. What policies and procedures does Whole Foods enact that allow it to develop successful associate teams?
2. What impact do you think that the process of allowing team members to vote on hiring new members has on the dynamics and performance of the Whole Foods teams?

Chapter 12

1. Whole Foods' "Declaration of Interdependence" states that two of the company's core values are "creating wealth through profits and growth" and "caring about our communities and the environment." Often, these two values are in conflict for many companies. How does Whole Foods resolve this conflict?

2. Whole Foods has been opposed to the unionization of its associates. However, associates in a Madison, Wisconsin, store voted to become unionized. What type of conflicts or power struggles may have caused this to occur?

Chapter 13

1. Analyze the effects of the democratic approach to store operations and hiring new associates on store performance.
2. What does the transparency about company financial data and associate and managers' compensation communicate about Whole Foods' culture? How does the Declaration of Interdependence reflect aspects of Whole Foods' culture?

Chapter 14

1. Analyze how Whole Foods has managed change over the years since it started.
2. Whole Foods now faces a significant amount of competition. How should it respond to the changes in the competitive landscape of its industry? What future challenges do you envision for Whole Foods' market?

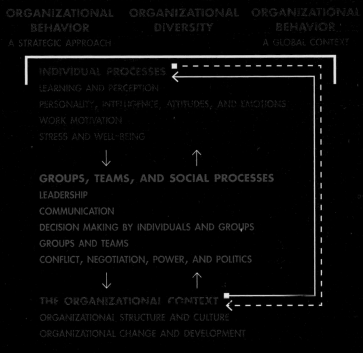

ORGANIZATIONAL
BEHAVIOR
A STRATEGIC APPROACH

ORGANIZATIONAL
DIVERSITY

ORGANIZATIONAL
BEHAVIOR
A GLOBAL CONTEXT

INDIVIDUAL PROCESSES
LEARNING AND PERCEPTION
PERSONALITY, INTELLIGENCE, ATTITUDES, AND EMOTIONS
WORK MOTIVATION
STRESS AND WELL-BEING

GROUPS, TEAMS, AND SOCIAL PROCESSES
LEADERSHIP
COMMUNICATION
DECISION MAKING BY INDIVIDUALS AND GROUPS
GROUPS AND TEAMS
CONFLICT, NEGOTIATION, POWER, AND POLITICS

THE ORGANIZATIONAL CONTEXT
ORGANIZATIONAL STRUCTURE AND CULTURE
ORGANIZATIONAL CHANGE AND DEVELOPMENT

PART 1

the strategic lens

This book describes the rich and important concepts that make up the field of organizational behavior. We have based the book on cutting-edge research as well as current practices in organizations. Beyond this, the book is unique in presenting these concepts through a strategic lens. That is, in each chapter, we explain the strategic importance of the primary concepts presented in the chapter. Our discussions emphasize how managers can use knowledge of these concepts to improve organizational performance.

In Part I, we develop and explain the strategic lens for organizational behavior. To begin, we describe in **Chapter 1** the concept of competitive advantage and how behavior in an organization affects the organization's ability to gain and maintain an advantage over its competitors. Gaining and maintaining a competitive advantage is critical for organizations to perform at high levels and provide returns to their stakeholders (including owners). We emphasize the importance and management of human capital for high performance and describe the high-involvement organization and how to manage associates to achieve it.

Chapter 2 examines the critical topic of organizational diversity. Given the demographic diversity in the United States, all organizations' workforces are likely to become increasingly diverse. Thus, it is important to understand diversity and how to manage it effectively in order to gain a competitive advantage. This chapter explains how these outcomes can be achieved.

Chapter 3 discusses managing organizations in a global environment. International markets offer more opportunities but also are likely to present greater challenges than domestic markets. Understanding the complexities of managing in international markets is a necessity. It is especially important to understand how to manage diverse cultures and operations in varying types of institutional environments.

The three chapters of Part I provide the setting for exploring the topics covered in the chapters that follow.

a strategic approach to organizational behavior

exploring behavior in action

Strategic Use of Human Capital: A Key Element of Organizational Success

In their book, *The New American Workplace,* James O'Toole and Edward Lawler described the existence of high-involvement, high-performance companies that spanned many industries. Examples of such companies are Nucor, W.L. Gore & Associates, Proctor & Gamble, and the Men's Wearhouse, among others. For example, Proctor & Gamble adopted high-involvement work practices at some of its manufacturing facilities, including empowerment of work teams to allocate the tasks among their members, establish their own work schedules, recruit new members to their team and even to select the methods used to accomplish their tasks. In addition, P&G invests in building human capital, and much of the training is done by P&G managers instead of human resource management or training specialists. In fact, P&G views work life as a career-long learning and development process. P&G has a different "college" for educating its workforce in the knowledge and skills needed for their current and future jobs. The company also carefully screens all candidates in the hiring process. The company received approximately 400,000 applications in 2009 for entry-level management positions and hired fewer than 2,000 (less than one-half of one percent).

The Men's Wearhouse is another company benefiting from high-involvement work practices. George Zimmer, founder and chief executive officer (CEO) of the Men's Wearhouse, described his company's approach in managing the people who carry out day-to-day work:

> We give people the space they need to be creative, set goals, define strategies, and implement a game plan. We call it "painting our own canvas." Our people like that freedom and the underlying trust behind it.

❓ knowledge objectives

After reading this chapter, you should be able to:

1. Define organizational behavior and explain the strategic approach to OB.
2. Provide a formal definition of *organization*.
3. Describe the nature of human capital.
4. Discuss the conditions under which human capital is a source of competitive advantage for an organization.
5. Describe positive organizational behavior and explain how it can contribute to associates' productivity.
6. Explain the five characteristics of high-involvement management and the importance of this approach to management.

Under this philosophy, individuals are given substantial discretion in choosing work methods and goals. Training is both quantitatively and qualitatively greater at the Men's Wearhouse than at the vast majority of retailers. Such training provides the base for effective use of discretion by individuals. Reward systems that value individual and team productivity help to encourage the type of behavior that is desired. Responsibility and accountability complement the system.

The base for the system of discretion and accountability is a core set of workplace beliefs, including the following:

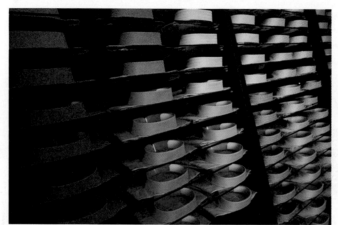
©iStockphoto

1. Work should be fulfilling.

2. Workplaces should be fearless and energized.

3. Work and family life should be balanced.

4. Leaders should serve followers.

5. Employees should be treated like customers.

6. People should not be afraid to make mistakes.

The success of the Men's Wearhouse should promote frequent attempts to imitate its practices, but this has not been the case. Instead, confronted with difficult industry conditions, managers in many retailing firms have attempted to minimize costs through low compensation and little training. They have implemented supervision and surveillance systems designed to tightly control employees. Many companies make assumptions about their workforce, but their actions do not allow the human potential existing in their workforce.

Yet, some of the highest-performing companies treat their associates in a different way. The leadership of these companies believe that valuing people is crucial for business success. They believe they get more out of their employees by providing them power and autonomy, and the results support this belief. These companies continue to grow, have low labor costs and achieve high profits while paying high compensation because of the productivity of their workforce. For ex-

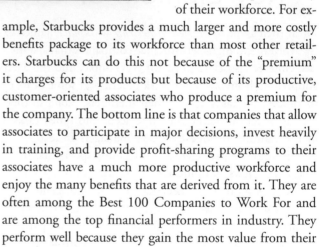

ample, Starbucks provides a much larger and more costly benefits package to its workforce than most other retailers. Starbucks can do this not because of the "premium" it charges for its products but because of its productive, customer-oriented associates who produce a premium for the company. The bottom line is that companies that allow associates to participate in major decisions, invest heavily in training, and provide profit-sharing programs to their associates have a much more productive workforce and enjoy the many benefits that are derived from it. They are often among the Best 100 Companies to Work For and are among the top financial performers in industry. They perform well because they gain the most value from their human capital.

Sources: "Fulfillment at Work," *Men's Wearhouse,* September 27, 2009, at http://www.menswearhouse.com; R. Crockett. 2009. "How P&G Finds and Keeps a Prized Workforce," *BusinessWeek,* Apr. 9, at http://www.businessweek.com; "Fortune 100 Best Companies to Work For 2009," *CNNMoney,* Feb. 2, 2009, at http://www.money.cnn.com; J. O'Toole and E. E. Lawler, III. 2007. "A Piece of Work," *Fast Company,* Dec. 19, at http://www.fastcompany.com; M. Cianciolo. 2007. "Tailoring Growth at Men's Wearhouse: Fool by the Numbers," *The Motley Fool,* May 23 at http://www.fool.com; C.A. O'Reilly and J. Pfeffer. 2000. *Hidden Value: How Great Companies Achieve Extraordinary Results with Ordinary People* (Boston: Harvard Business School Press); G. Zimmer. 2005. "Building Community through Shared Values, Goals, and Experiences," at http://www.menswearhouse.com/home_page/common_threads; G. Zimmer. 2005. "Our Philosophy," at http://www.menswearhouse.com/home_page/common_threads.

the strategic importance of Organizational Behavior

The examples of Men's Wearhouse, Proctor & Gamble, and Starbucks show the powerful difference that a firm's human capital can make. Faced with less-than-favorable industry characteristics and a labor pool that many find unattractive in the retail field, Men's Wearhouse and Starbucks have succeeded in part by paying careful attention to human behavior. Any firm can sell men's clothing and coffee, but it requires special management to effectively embrace and use to advantage the complexities and subtleties of human behavior. From the motivational and leadership practices of managers to the internal dynamics of employee-based teams to the values that provide the base for the organization's culture, successful firms develop approaches that unleash the potential of their people (human capital).

In the current highly competitive landscape, the ability to understand, appreciate, and effectively leverage human capital is critical in all industries. A strategic approach to organizational behavior is focused on these issues. In this chapter, we introduce the concept of organizational behavior and explain how to view it through a strategic lens in order to enhance organizational performance.

To introduce the strategic approach to organizational behavior, or OB, we address several issues. First, we define organizational behavior and discuss its strategic importance for organizational performance. Next, we explore the concept of human capital and its role in organizations. We then discuss how human capital most likely contributes to a competitive advantage for an organization. An explanation of high-involvement management follows. This form of management is helpful in developing and using human capital and is becoming increasingly important as firms search for ways to maximize the potential of all of their people (managers and nonmanagers). In the final section of the chapter, we describe the model and plan for the concepts explained in this book.

Basic Elements of Organizational Behavior

Important resources for businesses and other types of organizations include technologies, distribution systems, financial assets, patents, and the knowledge and skills of people. **Organizational behavior** involves the actions of individuals and groups in an organizational context. **Managing organizational behavior** focuses on acquiring, developing, and applying the knowledge and skills of people. The **strategic OB approach** rests on the premise that people are the foundation of an organization's competitive advantages.[1] An organization might have exceptionally high-quality products and services, excellent customer service, best-in-class cost structure, or some other advantage, but all of these are outcomes of the capabilities of the organization's people—its human capital. If organized and managed effectively, the knowledge and skills of the people in the organization drive sustainable competitive advantage and long-term financial performance.[2] Thus, the strategic approach to OB involves organizing and managing the people's knowledge and skills effectively to implement the organization's strategy and gain a competitive advantage.

Individual, interpersonal, and organizational factors determine the behavior and the ultimate value of people in an organization; these factors are shown in Exhibit 1-1. For individuals, factors such as the ability to learn, the ability to be self-managing, technical skills, personality characteristics, and personal values are important. These elements represent or are related to important capabilities. At the interpersonal level, factors such

organizational behavior
The actions of individuals and groups in an organizational context.

managing organizational behavior
Actions focused on acquiring, developing, and applying the knowledge and skills of people.

strategic OB approach
An approach that involves organizing and managing people's knowledge and skills effectively to implement the organization's strategy and gain a competitive advantage.

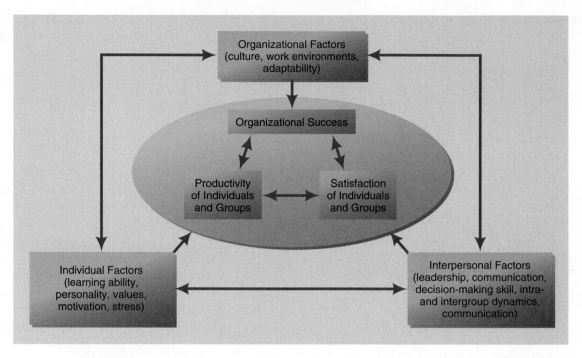

Exhibit 1-1 Factors and Outcomes of a Strategic Approach to Organizational Behavior

as quality of leadership, communication within and between groups, and conflict within and between groups are noteworthy. These elements influence the degree to which the capabilities of individuals are unleashed and fully utilized within an organization. Finally, at the organizational level, the culture and policies of the organization are among the most important factors, as they influence whether the talents and positive attitudes of individuals are effectively leveraged to create positive outcomes.

The factors discussed above interact to produce the outcomes of productivity, satisfaction, and organizational success. *Productivity* refers to the output of individuals and groups, whereas *satisfaction* relates to the feelings that individuals and groups have about their work and the workplace. *Organizational success* is defined in terms of competitive advantage and ultimately financial performance. In essence, then, a strategic approach to organizational behavior requires understanding how individual, interpersonal, and organizational factors influence the behavior and value of the people in an organization, where value is reflected in productivity, satisfaction, and ultimately the organization's competitive advantages and financial success.

The Importance of Using a Strategic Lens

Studying organizational behavior with a strategic lens is valuable for managers and aspiring managers at all levels of the organization, as well as for the workers who complete the basic tasks. For example, effective senior managers spend much of their time talking with insiders and outsiders about vision, strategy, and other major issues crucial to the direction of the organization.[3] Senior leaders make the strategic decisions for the firm.[4] Skills in conceptualizing, communicating, and understanding the perspectives of others are critical for these discussions, and these skills are addressed by strategic OB. Senior managers also spend time helping middle managers to define and redefine their roles and to manage conflict, because middle managers are often central to the organization's communication networks.[5] Skills in listening, conflict management, negotiating, and motivating are crucial for these activities. Finally, senior managers invest effort in shaping the internal norms and informal practices of the organization (that is, creating and maintaining the culture). Skill in interpersonal influence is an important part of this work. The strategic approach to OB addresses each of these issues.

In recent times, senior managers have commonly been referred to as *strategic leaders*.[6] However, exercising strategic leadership is not a function of one's level in the organization; rather, it is a matter of focus and behavior. Strategic leaders think and act strategically, and they use the skills noted above to motivate people and build trusting relationships to help implement the organization's strategy. Although their primary tasks differ from senior managers, middle and lower-level managers also can act as strategic leaders in the accomplishment of their tasks.[7]

Effective middle managers spend much of their time championing strategic ideas with senior managers and helping the firm to remain adaptive.[8] They also play an important role in implementing the organization's strategy. They serve as champions of the strategy and work with other middle managers and lower-level managers to build the processes and set them in motion to implement the strategy. Skills in networking, communicating, and influencing are important for these aspects of their work. Middle managers also spend time processing data and information for use by individuals at all levels of the firm, requiring skills in analysis and communication. When delivering the strategic initiatives to lower-level managers, skills in communicating, motivating, understanding values, and managing stress are among the most important. A strategic approach to OB addresses each of these aspects of managerial work.

Effective lower-level managers spend a great deal of their time coaching the firm's **associates**—our term for the workers who carry out the basic tasks.[9] Skills in teaching, listening, understanding personalities, and managing stress are among the most important for performing these activities. Lower-level managers also remove obstacles for associates and deal with personal problems that affect their work. Skills in negotiating and influencing others are critical for removing obstacles, whereas skills in counseling and understanding personalities are important for dealing with personal problems. Finally, lower-level managers expend effort to design jobs, team structures, and reward systems. Skills in analysis, negotiating, and group dynamics are among the most important for these activities. The strategic approach to OB addresses each of these aspects of managerial work.

Lower-level managers will be more effective when they understand the organization's strategy and how their work and that of their associates fit into the strategy. Much of what they do is required to implement the strategy. It is also helpful for these managers to take a longer-term view. If they do not take a strategic approach, many of these managers are likely to focus on short-term problems. In fact, they may emphasize resolving problems without examining how they can prevent them in the future. Taking a strategic approach enables them to use their skills to prevent problems, implement the strategy effectively, and complete their current tasks efficiently while remaining focused on the future.

associates
The workers who carry out the basic tasks.

Despite the relevance of formal study in OB, some people believe that managers can be successful solely on the basis of common sense. If this were true, fewer organizations would have difficulty unleashing the potential of people, and there would be less dissatisfaction and unhappiness with jobs. Also, if this were true, absenteeism and turnover rates would be lower. The truth is that fully leveraging the capabilities of people involves subtleties that are complex and difficult to manage. Common sense cannot be the only basis of action for managers. Effective managers deeply understand that knowledge about people and organizations is the true source of their success.

Without meaningful working knowledge of OB, managers' efforts to be successful resemble those of the drunkard and his keys. According to this classic story, the drunkard dropped his keys by the car but could not find them because it was very dark there. So, instead of bringing light to the appropriate area, he looked under a nearby streetlight where he could see better![10]

Managers in today's fast-paced organizations cannot afford to adopt the drunkard's approach when working with associates and each other, especially not in a challenging economic environment with significant competition. They must avoid looking for answers where it is easiest to see. Managers are often unsuccessful when they fail to develop the insights and skills necessary for working with others effectively.

In closing our discussion regarding the importance of understanding organizational behavior, we focus on the findings of two research studies. In both studies, the investigators examined the impact of formal business education on skills in information gathering, quantitative analysis, and dealing with people.[11] Significantly, they found that business education had positive effects on these important skills, including the interpersonal skills of leadership and helping others to grow. These findings suggest that understanding a strategic approach to OB can add value to our managerial knowledge and skills. There is no substitute for experience, but formal study can be very helpful in providing important insights and guidance.

Foundations of a Strategic Approach to Organizational Behavior

Insights from several disciplines inform our understanding of OB. The field builds on behavioral science disciplines, including psychology, social psychology, sociology, economics, and cultural anthropology. A strategic approach to OB, however, differs from these disciplines in two important ways. First, it integrates knowledge from all of these areas to understand behavior in organizations. It does not address organizational phenomena from the limited perspective of any one discipline. Second, it focuses on behaviors and processes that help to create competitive advantages and financial success. Unlike basic social science disciplines, where the goal is often to understand human and group behavior, the goal of the strategic OB approach is to improve the performance of organizations.

One might ask the following questions: Can taking courses in psychology, social psychology, sociology, economics, and cultural anthropology provide the knowledge needed to be an effective manager or to successfully accept the responsibility of working as a key member of an organization? Is it necessary to take a course in organizational behavior?

Acquiring knowledge directly from other disciplines can inform the study of organizational behavior. Knowledge from other disciplines, however, is not a substitute for the unique understanding and insights that can be gained from studying OB from a strategic perspective. As noted earlier, a strategic approach to OB integrates useful concepts from other disciplines while emphasizing their application in organizations.

Gaining an effective working knowledge of organizational behavior helps those who want to become successful managers. The following points summarize this important field of study:

1. There are complexities and subtleties involved in fully leveraging the capabilities of people. Common sense alone does not equip the manager with sufficient understanding of how to leverage human capabilities.

2. Managers must avoid the allure of seeking simple answers to resolve organizational issues. A working knowledge of OB helps managers gain the confidence required to empower associates and work with them to find creative solutions to problems that arise. The complexity of organizational life requires that managers and associates perform at high levels to contribute to organizational success and to achieve personal growth.

3. The strategic approach to OB integrates important behavioral science knowledge within an organizational setting and emphasizes application. This knowledge cannot be obtained from information derived independently from other specialized fields (psychology, economics, and the like).

Definition of an Organization

As we have already emphasized, OB is focused on organizations and what happens inside them. This is important, because organizations play an important role in modern society. Several commentators from Harvard University expressed it this way: "Modern societies are not market economies; they are organizational economies in which companies are the chief actors in creating value and advancing economic progress."[12] But what is an organization? Below we provide a formal definition of this term.

Although it is sometimes difficult to define the term *organization* precisely, most people agree that an organization is characterized by these features:[13]

- Network of individuals
- System
- Coordinated activities
- Division of labor
- Goal orientation
- Continuity over time, regardless of change in individual membership

Thus, we define an **organization** as a collection of individuals, whose members may change over time, forming a coordinated system of specialized activities for the purpose of achieving specific goals over an extended period of time.

A prominent type of organization is the business organization, such as Intel, Microsoft, or Procter & Gamble. There are other important types of organizations as well. Public-sector organizations (e.g., government organizations), for example, have a major

organization
A collection of individuals forming a coordinated system of specialized activities for the purpose of achieving certain goals over an extended period of time.

Creating Innovation: Leading and Managing the Human Capital at Apple

BusinessWeek has ranked Apple as the most innovative company for the past several years (2007–2009). And, largely because of Apple's successful innovations, Steve Jobs has been chosen by *Fortune* as the CEO of the decade (2000–2009). How has Apple achieved this lofty status? The following statement by Apple CEO, Steve Jobs explains, "Innovation has nothing to do with how many R&D dollars you have. When Apple came up with the Mac, IBM was spending at least 100 times more on R&D. It's not about money. It's about the people you have, how they're led, and how much you get it." In the early 1990s, Apple redesigned its workplace for the R&D associates, providing them both with private offices and also common areas where they could gather and share ideas, engage in teamwork, and generally discuss their research. A former manager at Apple notes that Apple's success is based on empowering its associates, delegating authority and responsibility down in the organization, and allowing the people a lot of freedom.

The results are obvious. *BusinessWeek* describes Apple as the creative king. For example, to launch the iPod, Apple's immensely successful portable music player, it integrated seven different innovations. It was able to create these innovations because of the innovation culture created at Apple and the high-quality scientists and engineers it has attracted to the company. Apple managers encourage and nurture a sense of community in which a passion for creative designs and innovation exists. Apple's designs have been described as more elegant, functional for customers, and effective than those developed by competitors. In short, Apple sets the standard in design. Apple and other innovative companies are the stars today and in the future. For example, Apple's iPhone has changed the standard in the wireless communications industry.

Apple is very careful in the hiring process by recruiting people who share its values and are passionate about what they do. In addition, they provide substantial training to build their skills and to emphasize the importance of working as a team. Yet, associates are valued as individuals; for example, staff associates in the Apple retail stores have personal business cards. This approach also suggests caring and quality to customers, not typical of most retail organizations.

Steve Jobs is a critical component of Apple's success, as suggested by his selection as the CEO of the decade. His vision and ability to see opportunities in future markets where others see only challenges has helped Apple rise above competitors and perform better than most other businesses in the world. Yet, his vision is only as good as the creativity and productivity of Apple's managers and associates. Warren Bennis states it this way, "The real test of exemplary leadership ... [is in] developing a deep, talented bench who ... can unite a company and unleash creativity in their own way." Michael Hawley, professional pianist and computer scientist, says that he thinks "of Apple as a great jazz orchestra." Hawley suggested that Apple has a talented staff and that the conductor's job is largely nominal at this stage.

© Justin Sullivan/Getty Images, Inc.

© Justin Sullivan/Getty Images, Inc.

It involves continuing to attract highly talented members and adding energy in places where they are needed.

Apple's performance in the first decade of the 21st century has been exceptional. Sales of each of its major products have increased dramatically (several of those products were developed and introduced to the market in this decade). And the market value of the company increased by over $250 billion during the decade. Thus, Apple's passion for innovation and the power of its human capital portends a very bright future for the company.

Sources: A. Lashinsky. 2009. "The Decade of Steve: How Apple's Imperious, Brilliant CEO Transformed American Business," *Fortune*, Nov. 23, pp. 93–100; "The 50 Most Innovative Companies," *BusinessWeek*, at http://bwnt.businessweek.com/interactive_reports/innovative_50_2009, Nov. 16, 2009; S. Lohr. 2009. "One Day You're Indispensible, the Next Day ...," *New York Times*, at http://www.nytimes.com, Jan. 18; A. Frankel. 2007. "Magic Shop," *Fast Company*, at http://www.fastcompany.com, Dec. 19; J. Scanton. 2007. "Apple Sets the Design Standard," *BusinessWeek.com*, at http://www.businessweek.com, Jan. 8; B. Helm. 2005. "Apple's Other Legacy: Top Designers," BusinessWeek.com, www.businessweek.com, Sept. 6; R. Enderle. 2004. "Apple's Competitive Advantage," *TechNewsWorld*, at http://www.technewsworld.com/story, Mar. 8.

presence in most countries. Although we focus primarily on business firms in this book, the strategic approach to OB applies to the public sector as well as the not-for-profit sector. For example, we can discuss motivating associates in the context of business firms, but motivating people is important in all types of organizations. Some organizations may have more motivational problems than others, but the knowledge of how to motivate workers is critical for managers in all types of situations.

As explained in the *Experiencing Organizational Behavior* feature, Apple has achieved significant success because of its innovations. In turn, Apple's innovations are due to the quality associates working in design, its innovation culture, and the way managers lead by empowering the associates to be creative and develop innovations. Apple's strategic leaders (exemplified by its CEO, Steve Jobs) are willing to take risks, and they nurture the innovation culture. But it also requires strategic leadership to implement Apple's innovation strategy throughout the company. As noted in the quote by Apple CEO Steve Jobs, the basic component of Apple's innovation is its human capital. Thus, Apple invests significant resources and energy into attracting, holding, and leading effectively high-quality human capital.

The Role of Human Capital in Creating Competitive Advantage

We have already noted the importance of human capital and competitive advantage to strategic OB. We now examine these concepts more closely.

The Nature of Human Capital

An organization's resource base includes both tangible and intangible resources. Property, factories, equipment, and inventory are examples of tangible resources. Historically, these types of resources have been the primary means of production and competition.[14] This is less true today because intangible resources have become critically important for organizations to successfully compete in the global economy. Intangible resources, including the reputation of the organization, trust between managers and associates, knowledge and skills of associates, organizational culture, brand name, and relationships with customers and suppliers, are the organization's nonphysical economic assets that provide value.[15] Such assets are often deeply rooted in a company's history and experiences, for they tend to develop through day-to-day actions and accumulate over time.[16] On a comparative basis, it is more difficult to quantify the value of intangible resources than that of tangible resources, but the importance of intangible resources continues to increase nonetheless.

human capital
The sum of the skills, knowledge, and general attributes of the people in an organization.

Human capital is a critical intangible resource. As a successful business executive recently stated, "Burn down my buildings and give me my people, and we will rebuild the company in a year. But leave my buildings and take away my people . . . and I'll have a real problem."[17] As we highlighted in the opening case, **human capital** is the sum of the skills, knowledge, and general attributes of the people in an organization.[18] It represents capacity for today's work and the potential to exploit tomorrow's opportunities. Human capital encompasses not only easily observed skills, such as those associated with operating machinery or selling products, but also the skills, knowledge, and capabilities of managers and associates for learning, communicating, motivating, building trust, and effectively working on teams. It also includes basic values, beliefs, and attitudes.

Human capital does not depreciate in value as it is used, but rather, it is commonly enhanced through use. Contrast this with tangible resources—for example, manufacturing equipment—whose productive capacity or value declines with use. In economic terms, we can say that human capital does not suffer from the law of diminishing returns. In fact, increasing returns are associated with applications of knowledge because knowledge tends to expand with use.[19] In other words, we learn more as we apply knowledge. Knowledge, then, is "infinitely expansible" and grows more valuable as it is shared and used over time.[20]

Knowledge has become a critical resource for many firms.[21] Knowledge plays a key role in gaining and sustaining an advantage over competitors. Firms that have greater knowledge about their customers, markets, technologies, competitors, and themselves can use this knowledge to gain a competitive advantage. Because most knowledge in organizations is held by the managers and associates, it is important to acquire and hold a highly knowledgeable workforce to perform well.[22] Because of the importance of knowledge and human capital, firms need to invest in continuous development of their human capital. The goal is to enhance organizational learning and build the knowledge and skills in the firm. In short, firms try to acquire and enrich their human capital.[23]

The importance of human capital and knowledge is explained in the *Experiencing Organizational Behavior* on innovation. Apple is able to be a leader in innovation largely because of its high-quality human capital and the manner in which it empowers its associates working in design. These associates developed and designed the highly successful iPod and iPhone, for which major sales have been achieved.

competitive advantage
An advantage enjoyed by an organization that can perform some aspect of its work better than competitors can or in a way that competitors cannot duplicate, such that it offers products/services that are more valuable to customers.

The Concept of Competitive Advantage

A **competitive advantage** results when an organization can perform some aspect of its work better than competitors can or when it can perform the work in a way that competitors cannot duplicate.[24] By performing the work differently from and better than competitors, the organization offers products/services that are more valuable for the customers.[25] For example, Apple developed and marketed the iPod, which took significant market share from Sony's previously highly successful Walkman MP3 players. Its iPhone did the same in the wireless communications market. As noted by the statement by Steve Jobs, Apple's CEO, the primary difference in Apple's ability to create innovation is its people and how they are led.

Human Capital as a Source of Competitive Advantage

Although human capital is crucial for competitive advantage, not all organizations have the human resources needed for success. The degree to which human capital is useful for creating true competitive advantage is determined by its value, rareness, and difficulty to imitate.[26]

Value

In a general sense, the value of human capital can be defined as the extent to which individuals are capable of handling the basic work of an organization. Lawyers with poor legal training do not add value to a law firm because they cannot provide high-quality legal services. Similarly, individuals with poor skills in painting and caulking do not add value to a house-painting company.

More directly, **human capital value** can be defined as the extent to which individuals are capable of producing work that supports an organization's strategy for competing in the marketplace.[27] In general, business firms emphasize one of two basic strategies. The first involves creating low-cost products or services for the customer while maintaining acceptable or good quality.[28] Buyers at the Closeout Division of Consolidated Stores, Inc., for example, scour the country to purchase low-cost goods. Their ability to find such goods through manufacturers' overruns and discontinued styles is crucial to the success of Closeout, the largest U.S. retailer of closeout merchandise. The buyers' skills allow the division to sell goods at below-discount prices.[29] The second strategy involves differentiating products or services from those of competitors on the basis of special features or superior quality and charging higher prices for the higher-value goods.[30] Ralph Lauren designers, for example, create special features for which customers are willing to pay a premium.[31]

Human capital plays an important role in the development and implementation of these strategies. For example, top managers are generally highly valuable resources for the firm. Their human capital as perceived by investors coupled with the strategic decisions that they make affect the investors' decisions about whether to invest in the firm.[32] Yet, most senior managers' knowledge and skills become obsolete very quickly because of the rapidly changing competitive landscape. Thus, these managers must invest time and effort to continuously enrich their capabilities in order to maintain their value to the firm.[33] Overall, managers must expend considerable effort to acquire quality human capital and demonstrate to the firm's external constituencies its value.[34]

Rareness

Human capital rareness is the extent to which the skills and talents of an organization's people are unique in the industry.[35] In some cases, individuals with rare skills are

human capital value
The extent to which individuals are capable of producing work that supports an organization's strategy for competing in the marketplace.

human capital rareness
The extent to which the skills and talents of an organization's people are unique in the industry.

hired into the organization. Corporate lawyers with relatively rare abilities to reduce the tensions of disgruntled consumers, programmers with the unusual ability to produce thousands of lines of code per day with few errors, and house painters who are exceptionally gifted can be hired from the outside. In other cases, individuals develop rare skills inside the organization.[36] Training and mentoring programs assist in these efforts.

Sales associates at Nordstrom, an upscale retailer, have several qualities that are relatively rare in the retailing industry. First, they tend to be highly educated. Nordstrom explicitly targets college graduates for its entry-level positions. College graduates are willing to accept these positions because of their interest in retailing as a career, because managers are commonly drawn from the ranks of successful salespeople, and because Nordstrom's strong incentive-based compensation system provides financial rewards that are much higher than the industry average. Second, sales associates at Nordstrom have both the willingness and the ability to provide "heroic service." This type of service at times extends to delivering merchandise to the homes of customers, changing customers' flat tires, and paying for customers' parking. Nordstrom's culture, which is based on shared values that support exceptional customer service, is an important driver of heroic service. Some believe that Nordstrom's culture is more important to the company's performance than are its strategy and structure and even its compensation system.[37]

Imitability

human capital imitability
The extent to which the skills and talents of an organization's people can be copied by other organizations.

Human capital imitability is the extent to which the skills and talents of an organization's people can be copied by other organizations.[38] A competing retailer, for example, could target college graduates and use a promotion and compensation system similar to Nordstrom's. If many retailers followed this approach, some of the skills and talents at Nordstrom would be attracted to its competitors in the industry.

The skills and talents most difficult to imitate are usually those that are complex and learned inside a particular organization. Typically, these skills involve *tacit knowledge*,[39] a type of knowledge that people have but cannot articulate. Automobile designers at BMW, the German car manufacturer, cannot tell us exactly how they develop and decide on effective body designs. They can describe the basic process of styling with clay models and with CAS (computer-aided styling), but they cannot fully explain why some curves added to the auto body are positive while others are not. They just know. They have a feel for what is right.[40] As a result, those firms that manage their knowledge effectively can make their skills and capabilities difficult to imitate by competitors.[41]

The culture of an organization represents shared values, which in turn partially determine the skills and behaviors that associates and managers are expected to have.[42] In some cases, organizational culture promotes the development and use of difficult-to-imitate skills and behavior. Southwest Airlines, for example, is thought to have a culture that encourages people to display spirit and positive attitudes that are valuable, rare, and difficult to duplicate at other airlines. Spirit and attitude result from complex interactions among people that are challenging to observe and virtually impossible to precisely describe. Associates and managers know the spirit and attitude are there. They cannot, however, fully explain how they work to create value for customers.[43]

Overall Potential for Competitive Advantage

For human capital to be the basis for sustainable competitive advantage, it must satisfy all three conditions discussed earlier: it must be valuable for executing an organization's strategy, it must be rare in the industry, and it must be difficult to imitate. An organization that hires individuals with valuable but common skills does not have a basis for competitive advantage, because any organization can easily acquire those same skills. As shown in Exhibit 1-2, the human capital in such an organization can contribute only to competitive parity; that is, it can make the organization only as good as other organizations but not better. An organization that hires individuals with valuable and rare skills, or an organization that hires individuals with valuable skills and then helps them to develop additional rare skills, has the foundation for competitive advantage, but perhaps only in the short run. The organization may not have the foundation for long-term competitive advantage because other organizations may be able to copy what the organization has done. For long-term advantage through people, an organization needs human capital that is valuable, rare, and difficult to imitate.[44]

Although the value, rareness, and low imitability of skills and talents are crucial for competitive advantage, alone they are not enough. These three factors determine the potential of human capital. To translate that potential into actual advantage, an organization must leverage its human capital effectively.[45] An organization may have highly talented, uniquely skilled associates and managers, but if these individuals are not motivated or are not given proper support resources, they will not make a positive contribution. Thus, sustainable competitive advantage through people depends not only on the skills and talents of those people, but also on how they are treated and deployed.[46] In the next section, we discuss a general approach for effectively developing and leveraging

Are human resources in the firm . . .

Valuable?	Rare?	Difficult to Imitate?	Supported by Effective Management?	Competitive Implications	Performance
No	—	—		Competitive Disadvantage	Below normal
Yes	No	—		Competitive Parity	Normal
Yes	Yes	No		Temporary Competitive Advantage	Above normal
Yes	Yes	Yes		Sustained Competitive Advantage	Above normal

Exhibit 1-2   Human Capital and Competitive Advantage

Source: Adapted from J. Barney and P. Wright. 1999. "On Becoming a Strategic Partner," *Human Resource Management,* 37: 31–46.

Leveraging Human Capital with Twitter and Other Social Networking Tools: Managing the Tweets

Originally, businesses were concerned with the explosion in social networking tools used by people inside their organization (and externally as well). The concerns focused on staff members spending time on personal networking to the exclusion of completing tasks on their jobs. Thus, managers feared the loss of productivity. Yet, they began to realize the potential for the social networking tools such as Twitter and others. Some of the social networking tools are more personalized (i.e., Facebook is better suited to individualized interests, perhaps). But,

©AP/Wide World Photos

Twitter holds special promise to further business-related goals.

Twitter has been promoted to build brand names, enhance internal relationships among those who need to coordinate their tasks, and in building a broad sense of community within the organization. Twitter can help managers to obtain broad inputs for making decisions and to gain associates' commitment to decisions made. It can also be used to support or even change the organization's culture. Twitter (and other social networking tools) is also useful to build and maintain relationships with customers/clients. It may even be useful in attracting new customers for the organizations' products and services. Managers and associates can use Twitter to serve as brand ambassadors. Companies such as Dell, Whole Foods, JetBlue, Starbucks, Popeyes, and Home Depot use Twitter to further business goals. For example, JetBlue offers Twitter-based customer service. Whole Foods uses Twitter to communicate with customers, learning more about their tastes and interests, posting news about new food podcasts and inviting them to upcoming company events. Many of

these companies monitor what is said about them on Twitter. It is a way of monitoring their brand equity with the public and especially with customers.

The social networking sites are popular means of accessing the Internet. For example, more than 150 million people use Facebook and about 50 percent of them use it daily. Facebook achieved more than 1 billion visits monthly in 2009. Facebook is used in more than 170 countries, suggesting that social networking is cross cultural and is a global phenomenon. Recent research by Nielsen shows that Facebook is more popular than e-mail as a communications tool. Social networking now accounts for approximately 10 percent of all time spent on the Internet. Twitter use in 2009 was more than 1,000 percent higher than in 2008. The top three social networking tools are Facebook, MySpace, and Twitter.

Thus, companies are trying to harness the power of social networking to facilitate the productivity of managers and associates and to promote their business brands and goods and services in the marketplace. Social networking tools can help to enhance the capabilities of their human capital.

Sources: L. Safko. 2009. "The twitter about twitter." *Fast Company*, June 13, at http://www.fastcompany.com; M. Colin & D. MacMillan. 2009. "Managing the tweets," *BusinessWeek*, June 1, pp 20–21; A. Yee. 2009. "Social network rankings—Who's hot and who's not," *Ebizq*, April 13, at http://www.ebizq.net; C.D. Marcan. 2009. "10 Twitter tips for the workplace," *PCWorld*, April 12, at http://www.pcworld.com; L. King. 2009. "Put twitter to work," *PCWorld*, March 29, at http://www.pcworld.com; M. Gotta. 2009. "Twitter in the workplace," March 6, at http://mikeg.typepad.com; J.F. Rayport. 2009. "Social networks are the new web portals," *BusinessWeek*, January 21, at http://www.businessweek.com; J. Owyang. 2009. "A collection of social network stats for 2009," January 11, at http://www.web-strategist.com; L. Watrous. 2008. "The role of twitter in business," November 19, at http://www.brighthub.com; A. Smarty. 2008. "16 Examples of huge brands using twitter for business," October 7, at http://www.searchenginejournal.com; R. King. 2008. "How companies use twitter to bolster their brands," *BusinessWeek*, September 6, at http://www.businessweek.com.

human capital. As a prelude, we explore a unique new tool that can be used for leveraging human capital in the workplace, microblogging as a social networking tool in the *Managerial Advice* feature.

As suggested in the *Managerial Advice,* companies are trying to harness the potential power of social networking tools to facilitate the human capital in the organization and to increase its productivity. Because of the critical nature of human capital to gaining and maintaining competitive advantages, the countries and companies operating in them must invest heavily in attracting the best available talent and in developing managers' and associates' capabilities. It is also critical that their capabilities be fully used. Thus, social networking tools can help to use the skills and capabilities of the organization's human capital.

The previous arguments and research underscore the strategic value of human capital.[47] Because of the potential value of human capital to an organization, the way it is managed is critical. We next discuss *positive organizational behavior.*

Positive Organizational Behavior

Positive organizational behavior grew out of positive organizational psychology, which developed to avoid focusing on trying to "fix" what was wrong with people. Rather, **positive organizational behavior** focuses on nurturing individuals' greatest strengths and helping people use them to their and the organization's advantage.[48] Positive OB suggests that people will likely perform best when they have self-confidence, are optimistic (hope), and are resilient.[49]

People are healthier and more productive if they have a strong self-efficacy with regard to the work that they are doing. Thus, managers should try to build associates' self-efficacy for the tasks assigned to them. Yet, we know from research that the effects of self-efficacy are perhaps more important on average in the United States than in many other countries.[50] In addition to the self-efficacy of individual associates, recent research suggests the importance of the efficacy of teams' performance. To the extent that a team believes that it can accomplish its assigned tasks, the team's performance is likely to be higher.[51]

Leaders who practice positive organizational behavior build stronger ties with their associates and peers.[52] Research suggests that more than 25 percent of associates express distrust in their leaders.[53] Rebuilding trust after it has dissolved represents a significant challenge.[54] Alternatively, leaders are able to rebuild trust by developing positive psychological capital among their associates. And when positive psychological capital exists within units and organizations, individuals tend to be more highly motivated and persist longer in trying to achieve goals. Therefore, such units perform at higher levels.[55]

Individuals who are managed in a positive manner and who take a personally positive approach to outperform the other candidates often are healthier mentally and physically. These people are likely to have a positive self-concept, lead life with a purpose, and have quality relationships with other people. Such people tend to be healthier, happier, and more productive and thus usually experience less stress on the job.[56] As such, managers should help their associates to develop positive emotions in themselves and others. It helps them to develop the means and implement them so as to achieve success within the organization.[57]

positive organizational behavior
An approach to managing people that nurtures each individual's greatest strengths and helps people use them to their and the organization's advantage.

Providing leadership that encourages and nurtures positive emotions often requires the application of *emotional intelligence (EI)*. Persons with strong EI have self-awareness, possess good social skills, display empathy, have strong motivation, and regulate their own behavior without the oversight of others (discussed in more depth in Chapter 5).[58] Leaders using EI build trusting relationships with their associates, exhibit optimism, and build associates' efficacy by providing the training needed and empowering them to complete the task without direct oversight.[59] The leadership approach using positive OB resembles *high-involvement management,* which we discuss next.

High-Involvement Management

high-involvement management

Involves carefully selecting and training associates and giving them significant decision-making power, information, and incentive compensation.

High-involvement management requires that senior, middle, and lower-level managers all recognize human capital as the organization's most important resource. Sometimes referred to as "high-performance management" or "high-commitment management," the **high-involvement management** approach involves carefully selecting and training associates and giving them significant decision-making power, information, and incentive compensation.[60] Combining decision power with important tactical and strategic information provides associates with the ability to make or influence decisions about how to complete tasks in ways that create value for the organization. Associates are closer to the day-to-day activities than are others in the organization, and empowering them through high-involvement management allows them to use their unique knowledge and skills.[61] In general, empowerment can increase the likelihood that associates will provide maximum effort in their work, including a willingness to: (1) work hard to serve the organization's best interests, (2) take on different tasks and gain skills needed to work in multiple capacities, and (3) work using their intellect as well as their hands.[62]

Key Characteristics of High-Involvement Management

Five key characteristics of high-involvement management have been identified. We summarize these characteristics in Exhibit 1-3 and examine them further in the following discussion.

Selective Hiring

Sound selection systems are the first crucial characteristic of the high-involvement approach. An organization must select the right people if managers are to delegate authority and information to associates. Efforts to generate a large pool of applicants and to assess applicants through rigorous evaluations, including multiple rounds of interviews with managers and peers, are important in the selection process.[63] These efforts help to identify the most promising candidates while promoting the development of commitment on the part of the individuals chosen. Individuals selected in the course of thorough processes often respect the integrity of the organization.

Another important part of the selection process involves examining applicants' fit with the organization's culture and mission; selecting new hires solely on the basis of technical skills is a mistake. In situations where most or all of the required technical skills can be taught by the organization, it is quite acceptable to pay less attention to existing skills and more attention to cultural fit (along with the person's ability to learn the needed

EXHIBIT 1-3 Dimensions of High-Involvement Management

Aspect	Description
Selective Hiring	Large pools of applicants are built through advertising, word of mouth, and internal recommendations. Applicants are evaluated rigorously using multiple interviews, tests, and other selection tools. Applicants are selected on the basis not only of skills but also of fit with culture and mission.
Extensive Training	New associates and managers are thoroughly trained for job skills through dedicated training exercises as well as on-the-job training. They also participate in structured discussions of culture and mission. Existing associates and managers are expected or required to enhance their skills each year through in-house or outside training and development. Often, existing associates and managers are rotated into different jobs for the purpose of acquiring additional skills.
Decision Power	Associates are given authority to make decisions affecting their work and performance. Associates handle only those issues about which they have proper knowledge. Lower-level managers shift from closely supervising work to coaching associates. In addition to having authority to make certain decisions, associates participate in decisions made by lower-level and even middle managers.
Information Sharing	Associates are given information concerning a broad variety of operational and strategic issues. Information is provided through bulletin boards, company intranets, meetings, posted performance displays, and newsletters.
Incentive Compensation	Associates are compensated partly on the basis of performance. Individual performance, team performance, and business performance all may be considered.

skills).[64] This is the approach taken by the Men's Wearhouse. A number of studies show the impact of cultural fit on satisfaction, intent to leave the organization, and job performance.[65] For example, a study of newly hired auditors in the largest accounting firms in the United States found that lack of fit with the organizational culture caused dissatisfaction and lower commitment among these auditors.[66] Furthermore, work context can affect the creative output of individuals so that individuals wishing to use their creative capabilities are attracted to organizations with cultures that promote the expression of creativity in work.[67] Finally, research suggests that careful selection of new associates leads to the provision of better customer service that in turn produces higher financial performance for the firm.[68]

Extensive Training

Training is the second vital component of high-involvement management. Without proper education and training, new hires cannot be expected to perform adequately.[69] And even when new hires are well trained for a position, it is important to help them build skills and capabilities beyond those needed in their present position. Furthermore, socialization into the norms of the organization is an important part of initial training. For existing associates, ongoing training in the latest tools and techniques is crucial.

Although valid calculations of return on investment for training are difficult to make, several studies reinforce the value of training. One study involving 143 *Fortune* 1000 companies reported that training significantly affected productivity, competitiveness, and employee satisfaction. (Training included job skills, social skills, quality/statistical analysis, and cross-training in different jobs.)[70]

Decision Power

The third key dimension of high-involvement management is decision-making power—providing associates with the authority to make some important decisions while inviting them to influence other decisions. For example, in a mass-production firm, such as Dell Computer, a single associate might have the authority to stop an entire production line to diagnose and address a quality problem. The associate might also have the authority, in conjunction with co-workers, to contact a supplier about quality problems, to schedule vacation time, and to discipline co-workers behaving in inappropriate ways. Beyond this decision-making authority, an associate might have significant input to capital expenditure decisions, such as a decision to replace an aging piece of equipment.

In many cases, decision power is given to teams of associates. In fact, self-managed or self-directed teams are a central part of most high-involvement systems.[71] With regard to our mass-production example, such a team might include the individuals working on a particular production line, or it might include individuals who complete similar tasks in one part of a production line. The tellers in a particular branch bank can operate as a team, the nurses in a particular hospital unit on a particular shift could be a team, and junior brokers in an investment banking firm might act as a formal team in a particular area. Teams working in high-involvement contexts often achieve the outcomes desired by the organization.[72]

Many studies of decision-making power have been conducted over the years. In general, these studies support giving associates bounded authority and influence. The study of *Fortune* 1000 firms discussed earlier assessed the impact of associates' holding significant decision power. As with training, the executives in the 143 firms reported a positive effect on productivity, competitiveness, and employee satisfaction.[73] Another recent study of empowering associates found that it enhanced knowledge sharing within and the efficacy of teams that in turn increased performance.[74]

Information Sharing

The fourth characteristic of high-involvement management is information sharing. In order for associates to make effective decisions and provide useful inputs to decisions made by managers, they must be properly informed. Furthermore, sharing information among team members promotes collaboration, coordination and high team performance.[75] Examples of information that could be shared include the firm's operating results and business plan, costs of materials, costs of turnover and absenteeism, potential technologies for implementation, competitors' initiatives, and results and roadblocks in supplier negotiations. At AES, a Virginia-based power company, so much information had been shared with associates that the Securities and Exchange Commission (SEC) identified every employee of the firm as an insider for stock-trading purposes. This was unusual; typically, only those at the top of a firm have enough information to be considered insiders by the SEC.

Incentive Compensation

The fifth and final dimension of high-involvement management is incentive compensation. This type of compensation can take many forms, including the following:

- Individual piece-rate systems, where associates are compensated based on the amount produced or sold
- Individual incentive systems, where associates receive bonuses based on short- or long-term performance
- Knowledge or skill-based pay, where associates are paid based on the amount of knowledge or number of skills they acquire
- Profit sharing, where associates earn bonuses based on company profits
- Gain sharing, where associates share in a portion of savings generated from employee suggestions for improvement

In the study of *Fortune* 1000 firms mentioned earlier, executives indicated that incentive pay positively affected productivity and competitiveness.[76]

Evidence for the Effectiveness of High-Involvement Management

Considering the five aspects of high-involvement management as a coherent system, research evidence supports the effectiveness of the approach. One study, for example, found this approach to have a positive effect on the performance of steel mini-mills.[77] In this study, 30 U.S. mini-mills were classified as having a control orientation or a commitment orientation. Under the control orientation, employees were forced to comply with detailed rules, had little decision-making authority or influence, received limited training and information, and had no incentive compensation. Under the commitment orientation, which closely resembled the high-involvement approach described above, employees had strong training; information on quality, costs, productivity, and usage rates of materials; incentive pay; the authority to make decisions regarding workflow scheduling and new equipment; and input into strategic decisions. The mills with commitment systems had lower rates of unused materials, higher productivity, and lower associate turnover.

In another study, 62 automobile plants around the world were classified as using traditional mass production or flexible production.[78] Under the traditional mass-production system, employees did not participate in empowered teams, whereas employees under the flexible approach participated in such teams. Companies that used the flexible system also offered employees more cross-training in different jobs and opportunities for incentive compensation. Furthermore, these companies displayed fewer symbols of higher status for managers (no reserved parking, no separate eating areas, and so on). The plants with flexible production had 47.4 percent fewer defects and 42.9 percent greater productivity than those with traditional production systems.

In a third study, firms were drawn from many different industries, ranging from biotechnology to business services.[79] Firms placing strong value on their people had a 79 percent probability of surviving for five years after the initial public offering (IPO), whereas firms placing low value on their people had a 60 percent probability of surviving five years.

©iStockphoto

Other studies have shown that high-involvement systems promote stronger relationships in the workplace and provide environments where associates and managers feel empowered. As such, they have higher job satisfaction and productivity. In turn, they service the organization's customers effectively to promote high customer satisfaction.[80]

Demands on Managers

When a high-involvement approach has all of the characteristics identified above, associates are fully and properly empowered. High-involvement managers place significant value on empowerment because empowered associates have the tools and support required to create value for the organization. But managers implementing high-involvement approaches must take specific and calculated actions to promote empowerment. We turn now to a discussion of the demands a high-involvement approach places on managers.

Because they believe strongly in empowering associates, high-involvement managers constantly seek to identify situations in which responsibility can be delegated. The intent is to move decision making to the lowest organization level at which associates have the information and knowledge required to make an effective decision. Managing through encouragement and commitment rather than fear and threats, high-involvement managers respect and value each associate's skills and knowledge. In addition, effective managers understand that cultural differences in a diverse workforce challenge them to empower people in ways that are consistent with their uniqueness as individuals.[81] Listening carefully to associates and asking questions of them in a genuine attempt to understand their perspectives demonstrates managerial respect and facilitates attempts to be culturally sensitive. People who feel respected for their values as well as for their skills and knowledge are motivated to act in a prudent and forthright manner in completing their assigned work. Over time, empowered, respected associates increase their confidence in their ability to help create value for the organization.

Trust between managers and associates is critical in a high-involvement organization. Managers must trust associates not to abuse their decision power. For their part, associates must trust managers not to punish them for mistakes when they are trying to do the right thing for the organization. Furthermore, research has shown that trust between associates and those formally responsible for their behavior has a positive effect on the organization's financial performance. Thus, effective managers invest effort in building and maintaining trust. In so doing, they dramatically increase their credibility with associates.[82] Confident in their abilities as well as their associates' abilities, high-involvement managers recognize that they don't have all the knowledge necessary for the organization to be successful. As a result, they work with their peers and associates to find solutions when problems arise.[83] Managers employing a high-involvement approach to management of their associates exhibit many of the characteristics of a transformational leader (this leadership approach is discussed in more depth in Chapter 8).[84]

High-involvement managers think continuously about how human capital can be used as the foundation for competitive advantage. Is there another way to use our people's skills and knowledge to further reduce costs or to more crisply differentiate the products we produce? How can the creativity of our empowered associates be used to create more value for the organization? How can we use information our associates gather through their work with people outside our organization (such as customers and suppliers) to make certain we are currently doing things that will allow us to shape the competitive advantages needed to be successful tomorrow? Finding answers to these questions and others that are unique to a particular organization can lead to long-term success.

As suggested in the *Experiencing Organizational Behavior* feature, firms use their core strengths to provide value to customers. And core strengths are commonly based on human capital, which is clearly the case with Pixar. Pixar's managers and associates have been critical to the production of ten major animated film successes. Pixar largely exhibits the characteristics of a high-involvement organization. It empowers its associates with considerable authority to determine their work projects, schedule, and how they will complete most of their work. Pixar hires top talent and gains the most from their capabilities. The freedom it provides its associates, the development of their skills and the culture promoting a happy, trusting and collaborative atmosphere retain their services for Pixar over the long term. It has been described as the "corporation of the future."[85] Pixar's success suggests why there is now global competition for the best human capital.[86] The Pixar experience suggests the importance of human capital for all organizations in order to compete effectively in the highly complex and challenging global economy they face in the current environment.

Organization of the Book

Our objective in this book is to provide managers, aspiring managers, and even individual contributors with the knowledge they need to perform effectively in organizations, especially in today's high-involvement organizations. Essentially, the book offers readers a working knowledge of OB and its strategic importance. The book has 14 chapters divided into four parts. The titles of the parts and the topics of the chapters are presented in Exhibit 1-4, which graphically depicts the model for the book.

As suggested in the exhibit, the strategic approach to OB emphasizes how to manage behavior in organizations to achieve a competitive advantage. The book unfolds in a logical sequence. In Part I, The Strategic Lens, we explain the strategic approach to OB (Chapter 1) and then discuss the importance of managing diversity in organizations (Chapter 2) and describe how organizations must operate in a global context (Chapter 3). In Part II, Individual Processes, we focus on the individual as the foundation of an organization's human capital, emphasizing the development of a sound understanding of individuals and how they affect each other and the organization's success. Topics considered include learning and perception (Chapter 4), personality (Chapter 5), motivation (Chapter 6), and stress (Chapter 7). In Part III, Groups, Teams, and Social Processes, we examine the effects of interpersonal processes on individual and organizational outcomes. Specific interpersonal processes include leadership (Chapter 8), communication (Chapter 9), decision making (Chapter 10), group dynamics (Chapter 11), and conflict (Chapter 12). Finally, in Part IV, The Organizational Context, we examine several organization-level processes and phenomena. Using insights from the book's first three parts, we study organizational design and culture (Chapter 13) and organizational change (Chapter 14). Overall, the book takes you on an exciting journey through managerial opportunities and problems related to behavior in organizations.

Pixar: An Organization of Happy, Innovative People

Pixar is one of the most successful and unique organizations in its industry and perhaps anywhere. It has produced ten major movie hits, and they are all highly creative and computer animated. The highly acclaimed movies include *Toy Story, A Bug's Life, Monsters Inc, Finding Nemo, The Incredibles, Cars,* and *Wall·E,* among others. In fact, all of Pixar's movies have been successful, which is an incredible feat. And they developed these movies in a highly unique way, not in the tradition of Hollywood. A typical movie involves a number of free agents in key positions brought together for a single, albeit major, movie project. Yet, all of Pixar's movies are developed and produced totally by its in-house staff.

Pixar's success is due to the incredible talent of its managers and associates and how it manages its human capital. It begins with a thorough recruiting and careful selection process. The firm searches for people who are innovative with good communication skills. In fact, the people in charge of hiring like to find people who have failed but overcame the failure. Randy Nelson, the person in charge of recruiting, explains the reason why these people are attractive to Pixar, "the core skill of innovators is error recovery not failure avoidance." But identifying and hiring top human capital is only the first step on the road to success. Managing this talent in ways that allow the people to reach their potential and to be highly productive in their tasks is highly critical to Pixar's success.

Pixar leaders build teams of people and expect them to work together to produce their end product. Everyone is expected to participate. When they have problems to solve, they do it as a team. In fact, all 200 to 250 members of a production group are encouraged and expected to offer their ideas. Essentially, the company produces team innovations. Pixar University was created, and all members of the organization (artists, software programmers, accountants, security guards) are encouraged to take courses up to four hours per week. PU offers 110 different courses, essentially a complete curriculum on making films. In these courses, they also learn to collaborate and to trust each other. In addition, they build new capabilities and sometimes discover new passions.

The culture of Pixar emphasizes teamwork, honesty, communication, collaboration in an environment where people can have fun and pursue their passions. Interdisciplinary learning is encouraged, creativity is rewarded, and intensity is prized. Taking risks is valued. One analyst claimed that Pixar's culture "out-Googled Google." The end results of the top human capital and effective management of it has been a string of hit movies. And the success has been aided by the ability of Pixar not only to attract and develop highly talented staff but also to keep it. Turnover at Pixar is less than five percent annually.

George Lucas, the legendary filmmaker (creator of *Star Wars*) founded Pixar in the 1970s. He sold it to Steve Jobs in the late 1980s for $10 million. Jobs sold Pixar to Walt Disney in 2006 for $7.4 billion. When one considers that the major assets of this company are a building, some computer equipment, and about 400 people, one can understand the potential value of excellent human capital and managing that talent to gain the most from it.

© CARS (2006) Directed byJohn Lasseter, Photo provided by Buena VistaPictures/Photofest

Sources: G. Adams. 2009. "Pixar: The real toon army," *The Independent,* September 23, at http://license.icopyright.net; C. Kuang. 2009. "Pixar's approach to HR," *Fast Company,* February 8, at http://www.fastcompany.com; E. Catmull. 2008. "How Pixar fosters collective creativity," *Harvard Business Review,* September, at http://hbr.harvardbusiness.org; W.C. Taylor. 2008 "Bill Taylor: Pixar's blockbuster secrets," *BusinessWeek,* July 8, at http://www.businessweek.com; C. Hawn. 2008. "Pixar's Brad Bird on fostering innovation," *The GigaOM Network,* April 17, at http://www.gigaom. com; T. Balf. 2007. "Out of juice? Recharge!" *Fast Company,* December 18, at http://www.fastcompany.com; M. Greer. 2006. "Pixar U and whistling while you work," *The Motley Fool,* November 16, at http://www.fool.com.

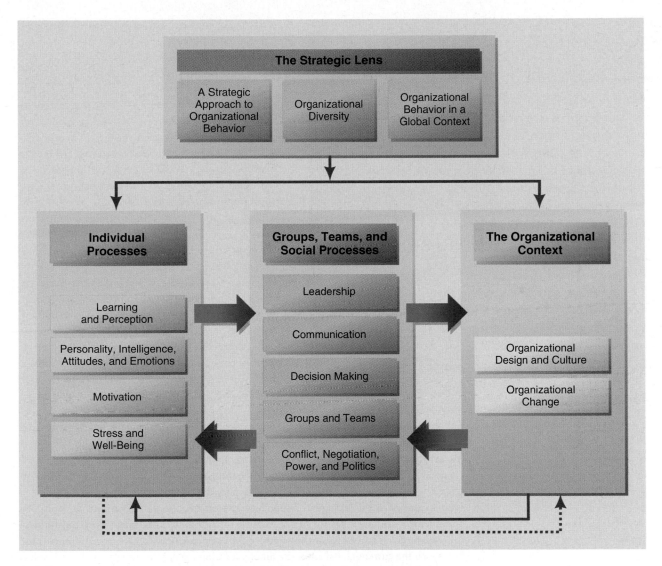

Exhibit 1-4 Managing Organizational Behavior for Competitive Advantage

What This Chapter Adds to Your Knowledge Portfolio

In this chapter, we have examined the strategic importance of organizational behavior to the success of individuals and organizations. In addition, we have discussed the nature of human capital and the circumstances under which it can be the source of competitive advantage for an organization. Finally, we have explored the high-involvement approach to management. To summarize, we have covered the following points:

- The strategic approach to organizational behavior involves knowledge and application of how individual, interpersonal, and organizational factors influence the behavior and value of an organization's people, where value is represented by productivity, satisfaction, and ultimately the organization's competitive advantages and financial success.

?back to the knowledge objectives

1. What is organizational behavior? Why is it important for managers and aspiring managers to study OB using a strategic approach? Can the study of a field such as psychology substitute for a strategic approach to organizational behavior? Why or why not?
2. What is an organization? What are the defining characteristics of an organization?
3. What is human capital? Be specific.
4. How does human capital provide the basis for competitive advantage?
5. What is positive organizational behavior and how can it contribute to associates' productivity?
6. What are the five characteristics of high-involvement management? What evidence exists to support the effectiveness of this approach?

- A strategic approach to organizational behavior is important because it addresses key issues for managers at all levels of the organization. For senior managers, the strategic approach to OB provides guidance for activities such as shaping the internal norms and practices of the organization. For middle managers, it provides guidance on matters such as implementing the strategic initiatives designed by senior managers. For lower-level managers, taking a strategic approach to OB helps with coaching and negotiating, among other important activities necessary to effectively implement the organization's strategy. Managers who lack an appreciation for the subject matter of organizational behavior are likely to experience less-successful careers.

- A strategic approach to organizational behavior builds on knowledge from the behavioral sciences. It differs from these fields, however, in two important ways. First, it integrates knowledge from these fields, rather than taking the narrow view of any one of them. Second, it focuses on behaviors and processes that help to create competitive advantages and financial success for the organization. Other fields often adopt the goal of understanding individual and group behavior without also understanding how such knowledge can contribute to enhancing the performance of organizations.

- An organization is formally defined as a collection of individuals, whose members may change over time, formed into a coordinated system of specialized activities for the purpose of achieving certain goals over some extended period of time.

- Human capital is an intangible resource of the organization. It represents capacity for current work and potential for future work. It includes the skills, knowledge, capabilities, values, beliefs, and attitudes of the people in the organization. Human capital is important because in the current global economy, an organization's ability to create something of value for customers comes largely from the know-how and intellect embodied in its people rather than from machinery and other tangible assets.

- Human capital can be a source of competitive advantage for an organization when it has *value* (it is relevant for the organization's strategy), is *rare* (skills and knowledge are possessed by relatively few outside the organization), and has *low imitability* (other organizations cannot easily duplicate the skills and knowledge). These three characteristics set the stage for gaining an advantage. For human capital to be a source of competitive advantage, it must be managed effectively.

- Positive organizational behavior focuses on nurturing individuals' greatest strengths and helping people use them to their and the organization's advantage. Positive OB suggests that people will likely perform best when they have self-confidence, are optimistic (hope), and are resilient. People are healthier and more productive if they have a strong self-efficacy with regard to the work that they are doing. Individuals who are managed in a positive manner and who take a personally positive approach to outperform the other candidates often are healthier mentally and physically.

- High-involvement management is an important method for developing and leveraging human capital. This approach has five key components: (1) selective hiring, (2) extensive training, (3) decision power, (4) information sharing, and (5) incentive compensation. Collectively, these five aspects of high-involvement management yield empowered workers.

- The effectiveness of high-involvement management is supported by strong evidence. In studies of many industries, high-involvement management has been found to lead to high productivity, satisfaction, financial success, and competitiveness.

Key Terms

organizational behavior, p. 13

managing organizational behavior, p. 13

strategic OB approach, p. 13

associates, p. 15

organization, p. 17

human capital, p. 20

competitive advantage, p. 20

human capital value, p. 21

human capital rareness, p. 21

human capital imitability, p. 22

positive organizational behavior, p. 25

high-involvement management, p. 26

Human Resource Management Applications

Recruitment and *selection* are critical Human Resource Management (HRM) functions because they provide the human capital necessary to accomplish the work in the organization. The examples of Apple and Pixar show the importance of human capital to an organization's success. Organizations employing high-involvement management use selective hiring practices.

Training is an HRM function designed to help managers and associates increase their knowledge and to develop new skills and abilities. Pixar University provides a good example of how extensive training contributes to organization performance. Training may be especially critical to help managers build the capabilities to understand and apply the techniques of high-involvement management (e.g., empowering associates).

Compensation is an HRM function that is important to the high-involvement management approach. In high-involvement management, often some of the managers' and associates' compensation is based on their performance and that of the organization. They may also be paid to acquire additional knowledge and skills (incentive compensation).

---

building your human capital

Career Style Inventory

Different people approach their careers in different ways. Some, for example, attempt to obtain as much power as possible in order to control personal and organizational outcomes. Others emphasize hard work and cooperative attitudes. The questionnaire that follows is designed to assess your tendencies, as well as your beliefs about the approaches of most managers. Following the questionnaire, we describe four distinct approaches to careers, some of which are more useful in high-involvement organizations than others.

Instructions

A number of descriptive paragraphs appear below. They describe sets of beliefs or perceptions that vary among individuals. The paragraphs are divided into four sections: Life Goals, Motivation, Self-Image, and Relations with Others. Please evaluate each paragraph as follows:

1. Read the paragraph. Taking the paragraph as a whole (using all of the information in the paragraph, not just one or two sentences), rate the paragraph on a scale from "not characteristic of me" (1) to "highly characteristic of me" (7). If you are currently a full-time

student, rate each paragraph on the basis of how you believe you would feel if you were working full-time in an organization. If you are a part-time student with a career, rate each paragraph on the basis of how you actually feel.

1	2	3	4	5	6	7
Not characteristic of me		Somewhat characteristic of me		Generally characteristic of me		Highly characteristic of me

2. In addition, rate each paragraph in terms of the way you would *like* to be, regardless of how you are now. Rate each on a scale from "would not like to be like this" (1) to "would very strongly like to be like this" (7).

1	2	3	4	5	6	7
I would not like to be like this		I would somewhat like to be like this		I would generally like to be like this		I would very strongly like to be like this

3. Finally, rate each paragraph in terms of how descriptive it is of most managers, from "not at all characteristic of most managers" (1) to "very characteristic of most managers" (7). In providing this assessment, think about managers with whom you have worked, managers you have read about or heard about, and managers you have seen in videos.

1	2	3	4	5	6	7
Not at all characteristic of most managers		Somewhat characteristic of most managers		Generally characteristic of most managers		Very characteristic of most managers

Questionnaire

Please be as honest, realistic, and candid as possible in your self-evaluations. Try to accurately describe yourself, not represent what you think others might want you to say or believe. In general, individuals do not have high scores on every question.

A. Life Goals

1. I equate my personal success in life with the development and success of the organization for which I work. I enjoy a sense of belonging, responsibility, and loyalty to an organization. If it were best for my organization, I would be satisfied with my career if I progressed no higher than a junior- or middle-management level.

    How characteristic is this of you (1–7)?_____

    How much would you like to be like this (1–7)?_____

    How characteristic is this of most managers (1–7)?_____

2. I have two major goals in life: to do my job well and to be committed to my family. I believe strongly in the work ethic and want to succeed by skillfully and creatively accomplishing goals and tasks. I also want to be a good family person. Work and family are equally important.

How characteristic is this of you (1–7)?_____
How much would you like to be like this (1–7)?_____
How characteristic is this of most managers (1–7)?_____

3. My goal in life is to acquire power and prestige; success for me means being involved in a number of successful, diverse enterprises. I generally experience life and work as a jungle; like it or not, it's a dog-eat-dog world, and there will always be winners and losers. I want to be one of the winners.

How characteristic is this of you (1–7)?_____
How much would you like to be like this (1–7)?_____
How characteristic is this of most managers (1–7)?_____

4. I tend to view life and work as an important game. I see my work, my relations with others, and my career in terms of options and possibilities as if they were part of a strategic game that I am playing. My main goal in life is to be a winner at this game while helping others to succeed as well.

How characteristic is this of you (1–7)?_____
How much would you like to be like this (1–7)?_____
How characteristic is this of most managers (1–7)?_____

B. Motivation

1. My interest in work is in the process of building something. I am motivated by problems that need to be solved; the challenge of work itself or the creation of a quality product gets me excited. I would prefer to miss a deadline rather than do something halfway—quality is more important to me than quantity.

How characteristic is this of you (1–7)?_____
How much would you like to be like this (1–7)?_____
How characteristic is this of most managers (1–7)?_____

2. I like to take risks and am fascinated by new methods, techniques, and approaches. I want to motivate myself and others by pushing everyone to the limit. My interest is in challenge, or competitive activity, where I can prove myself to be a winner. The greatest sense of exhilaration for me comes from managing a team of people and gaining victories. When work is no longer challenging, I feel bored and slightly depressed.

How characteristic is this of you (1–7)?_____
How much would you like to be like this (1–7)?_____
How characteristic is this of most managers (1–7)?_____

3. I like to control things and to acquire power. I want to succeed by climbing the corporate ladder, acquiring positions of greater power and responsibility. I want to use this power to gain prestige, visibility, and financial success and to be able to make decisions that affect many other people. Being good at "politics" is essential to this success.

How characteristic is this of you (1–7)?_____
How much would you like to be like this (1–7)?_____
How characteristic is this of most managers (1–7)?_____

4. My interest in work is to derive a sense of belonging from organizational membership and to have good relations with others. I am concerned about the feelings of people with whom I work, and I am committed to maintaining the integrity of my organization. As long as the organization rewards my efforts, I am willing to let my commitment to my organization take precedence over my own narrow self-interest.

How characteristic is this of you (1–7)?_____
How much would you like to be like this (1–7)?_____
How characteristic is this of most managers (1–7)?_____

C. Self-Image

1. I am competitive and innovative. My speech and my thinking are dynamic and come in quick flashes. I like to emphasize my strengths and don't like to feel out of control. I have trouble realizing and living within my limitations. I pride myself on being fair with others; I have very few prejudices. I like to have limitless options to succeed; my biggest fears are being trapped or being labeled as a loser.

   How characteristic is this of you (1–7)?_____
   How much would you like to be like this (1–7)?_____
   How characteristic is this of most managers (1–7)?_____

2. My identity depends on being part of a stable, noteworthy organization. I see myself as a trustworthy, responsible, and reasonable person who can get along with almost anyone. I'm concerned about making a good impression on others and representing the organization well. I may not have as much toughness, aggressiveness, and risk-taking skills as some, but I make substantial contributions to my organization.

   How characteristic is this of you (1–7)?_____
   How much would you like to be like this (1–7)?_____
   How characteristic is this of most managers (1–7)?_____

3. My sense of self-worth is based on my assessment of my skills, abilities, self-discipline, and self-reliance. I tend to be quiet, sincere, and practical. I like to stay with a project from conception to completion.

   How characteristic is this of you (1–7)?_____
   How much would you like to be like this (1–7)?_____
   How characteristic is this of most managers (1–7)?_____

4. I tend to be brighter, more courageous, and stronger than most of the people with whom I work. I see myself as bold, innovative, and entrepreneurial. I can be exceptionally creative at times, particularly in seeing entrepreneurial possibilities and opportunities. I am willing to take major risks in order to succeed and willing to be secretive if it will further my own goals.

   How characteristic is this of you (1–7)?_____
   How much would you like to be like this (1–7)?_____
   How characteristic is this of most managers (1–7)?_____

D. Relations with Others

1. I tend to dominate other people because my ideas are better. I generally don't like to work closely and cooperate with others, I would rather have other people working for me, following my directions. I don't think anyone has ever really helped me freely; either I controlled and directed them, or they were expecting me to do something for them in return.

   How characteristic is this of you (1–7)?_____
   How much would you like to be like this (1–7)?_____
   How characteristic is this of most managers (1–7)?_____

2. My relations with others are generally good. I value highly those people who are trustworthy, who are committed to this organization, and who act with integrity in the things that they do. In my part of the organization, I attempt to sustain an atmosphere of cooperation, mild excitement, and mutuality. I get "turned off" by others in the organization who are out for themselves, who show no respect for others, or who get so involved with their own little problems that they lose sight of the "big picture."

   How characteristic is this of you (1–7)?_____
   How much would you like to be like this (1–7)?_____
   How characteristic is this of most managers (1–7)?_____

3. At times, I am tough and dominating, but I don't think I am destructive. I tend to classify other people as winners and losers. I evaluate almost everyone in terms of what they can do for the team. I encourage people to share their knowledge with others, trying to get a work atmosphere that is both exciting and productive. I am impatient with those who are slower and more cautious, and I don't like to see weakness in others.

> How characteristic is this of you (1–7)?_____
>
> How much would you like to be like this (1–7)?_____
>
> How characteristic is this of most managers (1–7)?_____

4. My relations with others are generally determined by the work that we do. I feel more comfortable working in a small group or on a project with a defined and understandable structure. I tend to evaluate others (both peers and managers) in terms of whether they help or hinder me in doing a craftsman-like job. I do not compete against other people as I do against my own standards of quality.

> How characteristic is this of you (1–7)?_____
>
> How much would you like to be like this (1–7)?_____
>
> How characteristic is this of most managers (1–7)?_____

When you have evaluated each paragraph, follow the instructions below and "score" the questionnaire.

Scoring Key for Career Style Inventory

To calculate scores for each of the four primary career orientations, add up your scores for individual paragraphs as shown below. For example, to obtain your "characteristic of me" score for the orientation known as "craftsperson," add your "characteristic of me" scores for paragraph 2 under Life Goals, paragraph 1 under Motivation, paragraph 3 under Self-Image, and paragraph 4 under Relations with Others.

Scores can range from 4 to 28. A score of 23 or higher can be considered high. A score of 9 or lower can be considered low.

	Characteristic of me	Would like to be like this	Characteristic of most managers
Craftsperson Orientation			
Life Goals—Paragraph 2	_____	_____	_____
Motivation—Paragraph 1	_____	_____	_____
Self-Image—Paragraph 3	_____	_____	_____
Relations with Others—Paragraph 4	_____	_____	_____
TOTAL scores for Craftsperson	_____	_____	_____
Company Orientation			
Life Goals—Paragraph 1	_____	_____	_____
Motivation—Paragraph 4	_____	_____	_____
Self-Image—Paragraph 2	_____	_____	_____
Relations with Others—Paragraph 2	_____	_____	_____
TOTAL scores for Company Man/Woman	_____	_____	_____
Jungle Fighter Orientation			
Life Goals—Paragraph 3	_____	_____	_____
Motivation—Paragraph 3	_____	_____	_____
Self-Image—Paragraph 4	_____	_____	_____
Relations with Others—Paragraph 1	_____	_____	_____
TOTAL scores for Jungle Fighter	_____	_____	_____

Strategic Game Orientation

Life Goals—Paragraph 4   _____   _____   _____

Motivation—Paragraph 2   _____   _____   _____

Self-Image—Paragraph 1   _____   _____   _____

Relations with Others—Paragraph 3   _____   _____   _____

TOTAL scores for Gamesman/
  Gameswoman   _____   _____   _____

Descriptions of the Four Primary Career Orientations

- The *Craftsperson,* as the name implies, holds traditional values, including a strong work ethic, respect for people, concern for quality, and thrift. When talking about work, such a person tends to show an interest in specific projects that have a defined structure. He or she sees others, peers as well as managers, in terms of whether they help or hinder the completion of work in a craftsman-like way.

  The virtues of craftspersons are admired by almost everyone. In high-involvement organizations, craftspersons are valuable because they respect people and work hard and smart. On the downside, they can become overly absorbed in perfecting their projects, which can slow them down and harm their leadership on a broader stage.

- *The Jungle Fighter* lusts for power. He or she experiences life and work as a jungle where "eat or be eaten" is the rule and the winners destroy the losers. A major part of his or her psychic resources is budgeted for a personal department of defense. Jungle fighters tend to see their peers as either accomplices or enemies and their associates as objects to be used.

  There are two types of jungle fighters: lions and foxes. The lions are the conquerors who, when successful, may build an empire. The foxes make their nests in the corporate hierarchy and move ahead by stealth and politicking. The most gifted foxes rise rapidly by making use of their entrepreneurial skills. In high-involvement organizations, jungle fighters can cause many problems. They tend not to value people. Leveraging human capital may take place, but only in limited ways for the purpose of self-gain.

- *The Company Man or Woman* bases personal identity on being part of a protective organization. He or she can be fearful and submissive, seeking security even more than success. These are not positive attributes for high-involvement organizations. On the other hand, the company man or woman is concerned with the human side of the company, interested in the feelings of people, and committed to maintaining corporate integrity. The most creative company men and women sustain an atmosphere of cooperation and stimulation, but they tend to lack the daring to lead in competitive and innovative organizations.

- The *Strategic Gamesman or Gameswoman* sees business life in general, and his or her career in particular, in terms of options and possibilities, as if he or she were playing a game. Such a person likes to take calculated risks and is drawn to new techniques and methods. The contest is invigorating, and he or she communicates enthusiasm, energizing peers and associates like the quarterback on a football team. Unlike the jungle fighter, the gamesman or gameswoman competes not to build an empire or to pile up riches, but to gain the exhilaration of victory. The main goal is to be known as a winner, along with the rest of the team.

  The character of a strategic gamesman or gameswoman, which might seem to be a collection of near paradoxes, is very useful in a high-involvement organization. Such a person is cooperative but competitive, detached and playful but compulsively driven to succeed, a team player but a would-be superstar, a team leader but often a rebel against bureaucratic hierarchy, fair and unprejudiced but contemptuous of weakness, tough and dominating but not destructive. Balancing these issues is important in a team-oriented organization, where associates and managers at all levels are expected to work together for personal and organizational success.

Source: Adapted from *Experiences in Management and Organizational Behavior*, 4th ed. (New York: John Wiley & Sons, 1996). Original instrument developed by Roy J. Lewicki.

---

an organizational behavior moment

All in a Day's Work

After earning a business degree with a major in marketing, Ann Wood went to work for Norwich Enterprises as a research analyst in the Consumer Products Division. While working, she also attended graduate school at night, receiving her MBA in three years. Within a year of reaching that milestone, Ann was promoted to manager of market research. Ann became assistant director of marketing after another three years. After a stay of slightly less than 24 months in that position, Ann was appointed director of marketing for the Consumer Products Division. In this new role, she leads many more people than in her previous roles—85 in total across three different groups: market research, marketing strategy and administration, and advertising and public relations.

Ann felt good this morning, ready to continue working on several important projects that Anil Mathur, Norwich's executive vice president for marketing, had assigned to her. Ann felt that she was on a fast track to further career success and wanted to continue performing well. With continuing success, she expected an appointment in Norwich's international business operations in the near future. Ann was pleased about this prospect, as international experience was becoming a prerequisite at Norwich for senior-level managerial positions—her ultimate goal. Several problems, however, were brought to her attention on what she thought was going to be a good day at the office.

As Ann was entering the building, Joe Jackson, the current manager of the market research group, stopped her in the hall and complained that the company's intranet had been down about half of the night. This technical problem had prevented timely access to data from a central server, resulting in a delay in the completion of an important market analysis. Ann thought that immediately jumping in to help with the analysis would be useful in dealing with this matter. She had promised Anil that the analysis would be available to him and other upper-level managers this morning. Now it would have to be finished on a special priority basis, delaying work on other important projects.

Joe also told Ann that two of his analysts had submitted their resignations over the last 24 hours. Ann asked, "Why are we having so much trouble with turnover?" The manager responded, "The market is tight for smart analysts who understand our product lines. We've been having problems hiring anyone with the skills we need, much less people who have any loyalty. Maybe we should offer higher starting salaries and more attractive stock options if we expect to have much hope of keeping the people we need." Ann asked Joe to develop a concrete proposal about what could be done to reduce turnover, promising to work with him to resolve the issue.

Just as she reached her office, Ann's phone rang. It was Brooke Carpenter, the manager of market strategy and administration. "I'm glad you're here, Ann. I need to talk to you now. I'm on my way." As Brooke came through the door, Ann could tell that he was quite upset. He explained that two of his people had discovered through searches on the Internet that the average pay for their type of work was 7 percent higher than what they were currently earning. Sharing this information with co-workers had created an unpleasant environment in which people were concentrating on pay instead of focusing on tasks to be completed. Ann had a conference call coming in a few minutes, stopping her from dealing with the matter further, but she asked Brooke to set up a time when the two of them could meet with his people to talk about their concerns.

After her conference call, Ann spent the rest of her morning dealing with e-mails that were primarily related to dissatisfaction with her department's work. Most of these concerned the delays that other Norwich units were experiencing in receiving outputs from her department. The problem was complicated by the inability to retain workers.

Ann had just returned from lunch when her phone rang. "Ann, it's Brooke. Can you meet with us at 2:30 this afternoon? I know that this is short notice, but we really do need to talk with my people." Although the time was inconvenient, given that Anil expected his analysis today, Ann knew that dealing with issues concerning Brooke's associates was also important. Plus, she believed that Anil's report was about to be finished by the research group, taking that immediate problem off her plate.

The meeting with Brooke and his people lasted almost an hour. Not surprisingly, other concerns surfaced during the conversation. Ann thought to herself that this was to be expected. Her managerial experience indicated that complaints about pay often masked concerns about other issues. She learned that people weren't satisfied with the technology made available to them to do their work or Norwich's commitment to training and development. Young and eager to advance, Brooke's associates wanted assurances from Ann that Norwich would spend more money and time to develop their skills. Ann agreed to the importance of skill development—both for associates and for Norwich. She said that she would examine the matter and provide feedback to them. "It may take some time, but my commitment to you is that I'll work hard to make this happen. While I can't promise much about the pay structure overnight, I'll also investigate this matter to become more informed. Brooke and I will work on this together so you can have direct access to what is going on." Ann wanted to deal with these issues, knowing that their resolution had the potential to help both associates and the company reach their goals.

Ann then spent a couple of hours dealing with still more e-mail messages, a few phone calls, and other requests that reached her desk

during the day. Anil received the report he needed and seemed to be satisfied. Although she had been busy, Ann felt good as she left for home around 8:30 that night. Nothing came easily, she thought.

Discussion Questions

1. Describe the people-related problems or issues Ann Wood faced during the day. Did she handle these effectively? If not, what do you believe she should have done?

2. Is Ann Wood a high-involvement manager? If so, provide evidence. If not, how well do you think she'll perform in her new job as head of marketing?

3. Assume that Ann Wood wants her managers and associates to be the foundation for her department's competitive advantages. Use the framework summarized in Exhibit 1-2 (in the chapter text) to assess the degree to which Ann's people are a source of competitive advantage at this point in time.

---

team exercise

McDonald's: A High-Involvement Organization?

One experience most people in North America and Europe have shared is that of dining in the hamburger establishment known as McDonald's. In fact, someone has claimed that thirtieth-century archeologists may dig into the ruins of our present civilization and conclude that twenty-first-century religion was devoted to the worship of golden arches.

Your group, Fastalk Consultants, is known as the shrewdest, most insightful, and most overpaid management consulting firm in the country. You have been hired by the president of McDonald's to make recommendations for improving the motivation and performance of personnel in their franchise operations. Some of the key activities in franchise operations are food preparation, order-taking and dealing with customers, and routine clean-up operations.

The president of McDonald's must always be concerned that his company's competitors, such as Burger King, Wendy's, Jack in the Box, Dunkin' Donuts, various pizza establishments, and others, have the potential to make heavy inroads into McDonald's market. Thus, he hired a separate market research firm to investigate and compare the relative merits of the sandwiches, french fries, and drinks served by McDonald's and the competitors and asked the market research firm to assess the advertising campaigns of the competitors. Hence, you will not be concerned with marketing issues, except as they may affect employee behavior. The president wants you to evaluate the organization's franchises to determine their strengths and weaknesses of how they manage their associates hoping their work will be productive. He is very interested in how the restaurants' management approach compares to high-involvement management and the impact on their approach on McDonald's.

The president has established an unusual contract with you. He wants you and your colleagues in the firm to make recommendations based on your observations as customers. He does not want you to do a complete analysis with interviews, surveys, or behind-the-scenes observations.

STEPS

1. Assemble into groups of four to five. Each group will act as a separate Fastalk consulting team.

2. Think about your past visits to McDonald's. What did you see and experience? How was the food prepared and served? What was the process? Did the employees seem to be happy with

their work? Did they seem to be well trained and well suited for the work? Did the supervisor act as a coach or a superior? Your instructor may ask you to visit a McDonald's in preparation for this exercise and/or to research the organization via the Internet or school library.

3. Assess McDonald's on each dimension of high-involvement management.
4. Develop recommendations for the president of McDonald's.
5. Reassemble as a class. Discuss your group's assessments and recommendations with the rest of the class, and listen to other groups' assessments. Do you still assess McDonald's in the same way after hearing from your colleagues in the class?
6. The instructor will present additional points for consideration.

Source: Adapted from *Experiences in Management and Organizational Behavior,* 4th ed. (New York: John Wiley & Sons, 1996). Original version developed by D.T. Hall and F.S. Hall.

Endnotes

1. Wang, H.C., He, J. & Mahoney, J.T. 2009. Firm-specific knowledge resources and competitive advantage: The roles of economic- and relationship-based employee governance mechanisms. *Strategic Management Journal,* 30: 1265–1285.
2. Holcomb, T.R., Holmes, R.M. & Connelly, B.L., 2009. Making the most of what you have: Managerial ability as a source of resource value creation. *Strategic Management Journal,* 30: 457–485; Athey, R. 2008. It's 2008: Do you know where your talent is? Connecting people to what matters. *Journal of Business Strategy,* 29 (4): 4–14; ; Barney, J.B. 1991. Firm resources and sustained competitive advantage. *Journal of Management,* 17: 99–120; Hitt, M.A., & Ireland, R.D. 2002. The essence of strategic leadership: Managing human and social capital. *Journal of Leadership and Organizational Studies,* 9: 3–14.
3. Ling, Y., Simsek, Z., Lubatkin, M.H. & Veiga. J.F. 2008. Transformational leadership's role in promoting corporate entrepreneurship: Examining the CEO=TMT interface, *Academy of Management Journal,* 51: 557–576; Kor, Y.Y. 2006. Direct and interaction effects of top management team and board compositions on R&D investment strategy. *Strategic Management Journal,* 27: 1081–1099; Heifetz, R.A., & Laurie, D.L. 1997. The work of the leader. *Harvard Business Review,* 75(1): 124–134; Ireland, R.D., & Hitt, M.A. 1999. Achieving and maintaining strategic competitiveness in the 21st century: The role of strategic leadership. *Academy of Management Executives,* 13(1): 43–57.
4. Adegbesan, J.A. 2009. On the origins of competitive advantage: Strategic factor markets and heterogeneous resource complementarity. *Academy of Management Review,* 34: 463–475; Elbanna, S., & Child, J. 2007. Influences on strategic decision effectiveness: Development and test of an integrative model. *Strategic Management Journal,* 28: 431–453.
5. Cocks, G. 2009. High performers down under: Lessons from Australia's winning companies. *Journal of Business Strategy,* 30 (4): 17–22; Pappas, J.M., & Woolridge, B. 2007. Middle managers divergent strategic activity: An investigation of multiple measures of network centrality. *Journal of Management Studies,* 44: 323–341.
6. Finklestein, S., Hambrick, D.C., & Cannella, A.A. 2008. *Strategic leadership: Top executives and their effects on organizations.* New York: Oxford University Press.
7. Hitt, M.A., Black, S., & Porter, L. 2008. *Management.* Upper Saddle River, NJ: Prentice Hall.
8. Pappas & Woolridge. Middle managers divergent strategic activity; Huy, Q.N. 2001. In praise of middle managers. *Harvard Business Review,* 76(8): 73–79; Sethi, D. 1999. Leading from the middle. *Human Resource Planning,* 22(3): 9–10.
9. Manz, C., & Neck, C.P. 2007. *Mastering self leadership.* Upper Saddle River, NJ: Prentice Hall.
10. Faris, G.F. 1969. The drunkard's search in behavioral science. *Personnel Administration,* 32(1): 11–18.
11. Boyatzis, R.E., Baker, A., Leonard, L., Rhee, K., & Thompson, L. 1995. Will it make a difference? Assessing a value-added, outcome-oriented, competency-based professional program. In R.E. Boyatzis, S.S. Cowan, & D.A. Kolb (Eds.), *Innovation in professional education: Steps on a journey from teaching to learning.* San Francisco: Jossey-Bass; Kretovics, M.A. 1999. Assessing the MBA: What do our students learn? *The Journal of Management Development,* 18: 125–136.
12. Ghoshal, S., Bartlett, C.A., & Moran, P. 1999. A new manifesto for management. *Sloan Management Review,* 40(3): 9–20.
13. Etzioni, A. 1964. *Modern organizations.* Englewood Cliffs, NJ: Prentice Hall.
14. Dess, G.G., & Picken, J.C. 1999. *Beyond productivity: How leading companies achieve superior performance by leveraging their human capital.* New York: AMACOM.
15. Sirmon, D.G., & Hitt, M.A. 2009. Contingencies within dynamic managerial capabilities: Interdependent effects of resource investment and deployment on firm performance. *Strategic Management Journal,* 30: 1375–1394; Six, F., & Sorge, A. 2008. Creating a high-trust organization: An exploration into organizational policies that stimulate interpersonal trust building. *Journal of Management Studies,* 45: 857–884; Dickson, G.W., & DeSanctis, G. 2001. *Information technology and the future enterprise.* Upper Saddle River, NJ: Prentice Hall.

16. Hitt, M.A., Ireland, R.D., & Hoskisson, R.E. 2011. *Strategic management: Competitiveness and globalization.* Mason, OH: South-Western Cengage Learning.

17. Nelson, M.C. 2000. Facing the future: Intellectual capital of our workforce. *Vital Speeches of the Day*, December 15: 138–143.

18. Dess & Picken, *Beyond productivity*; Hitt, Ireland, & Hoskisson, *Strategic management.*

19. Day, J.D., & Wendler, J.C. 1998. The new economics of the organization. *The McKinsey Quarterly*, 1998 (1): 4–17.

20. Dess & Picken, *Beyond productivity.*

21. McGee, J., & Thomas, H. 2007, Knowledge as a lens on the jigsaw puzzle of strategy. *Management Decision*, 45: 539–563.

22. Dragoni. L., Tesluk, P.E., Russell, J.A. & Oh, I.-S. 2009. Understanding managerial development: Integrating developmental assignments, learning orientation, and access to developmental opportunities in predicting managerial competencies, *Academy of Management Journal*, 52: 731–743; McGee, J., & Thomas, H. 2007, Knowledge as a lens on the jigsaw puzzle of strategy. *Management Decision*, 45: 539–563.

23. Salk, J., & Lyles, M.A. 2007. Gratitude, nostalgia and what now? Knowledge acquisition and learning a decade later. *Journal of International Business Studies*, 38: 19–26; Gupta, A.K., Smith, K.G., & Shalley, C.E. 2006. The interplay between exploration and exploitation. *Academy of Management Journal*, 49: 693–706.

24. Porter, M.E. 1980. *Competitive strategy.* New York: Free Press; Porter, M.E. 1985. *Competitive advantage.* New York: Free Press.

25. Sirmon, D.G., Hitt, M.A., & Ireland, R.D. 2007. Managing firm resources in dynamic environments to create value: Looking inside the black box. *Academy of Management Review*, 32: 273–292.

26. Our discussion of the value, rare, and nonimitable terms draws significantly from: Barney, J.B., & Wright, P.M. 1998. On becoming a strategic partner: The role of human resources in gaining competitive advantage. *Human Resource Management*, 37: 31–46.

27. Barney, J.B., & Clark, D.N. 2007. *Resource-based theory: Creating and sustaining competitive advantage.* New York: Oxford University Press; Barney, Firm resources and sustained competitive advantage; Barney & Wright, On becoming a strategic partner; Lepak, D.P., & Snell, S.A. 1999. The human resource architecture: Toward a theory of human capital allocation and development. *Academy of Management Review*, 24: 31–48.

28. Porter, *Competitive strategy.*

29. Hitt, Ireland, & Hoskisson, *Strategic management.*

30. Porter, *Competitive strategy.*

31. Hitt, Ireland, & Hoskisson, *Strategic management.*

32. Smith, W.S. 2009. Vitality in business: Executing a new strategy at Unilever. *Journal of Business Strategy*, 30 (4): 31–41; Higgins, M.C., & Gulati, R. 2006. Stacking the deck: The effects of top management backgrounds on investor decisions. *Strategic Management Journal*, 27: 1–25.

33. Henderson, A.D., Miller, D., & Hambrick, D.C. 2006. How quickly do CEOs become obsolete? Industry dynamism, CEO tenure, and company performance. *Strategic Management Journal*, 27: 447–460.

34. Ployhart, R.E. 2006. Staffing in the 21st century: New challenges and strategic opportunities. *Journal of Management*, 32: 868–897.

35. Newbert, S.L. 2007. Empirical assessments of the resource-based view of the firm: An assessment and suggestions for future research. *Strategic Management Journal*, 28: 121–146; Barney & Wright, On becoming a strategic partner; Lepak & Snell, The human resource architecture.

36. Laamanen, T. & Wallin, J. 2009. Cognitive dynamics of capability development paths. *Journal of Management Studies*, 46: 950–981.

37. Pfeffer, J. 1994. *Competitive advantage through people: Unleashing the power of the work force.* Boston: Harvard Business School Press.

38. Barney & Wright, On becoming a strategic partner.

39. Ibid.

40. Bangle, C. 2001. The ultimate creativity machine: How BMW turns art into profit. *Harvard Business Review*, 79(1): 47–55.

41. Bogner, W.C., & Bansal, P. 2007. Knowledge management as the basis of sustained high performance. *Journal of Management Studies*, 44: 165–188.

42. Tsui, A.S., Wang, H., & Xin, K.R. 2006. Organizational culture in China: An analysis of culture dimensions and culture types. *Management and Organization Review*, 2: 345–376.

43. Pfeffer, *Competitive advantage.*

44. Barney & Wright, On becoming a strategic partner.

45. Sirmon, D.G., Gove, S. & Hitt, M.A. 2008. Resource management in dyadic competitive rivalry: The effects of resource bundling and deployment. *Academy of Management Journal*, 51: 918–935; Sirmon, Hitt, & Ireland, Managing firm resources in dynamic environments to create value.

46. Sirmon & Hitt, Contingencies within dynamic managerial capabilities; Bowman, C., & Swart, J. 2007. Whose human capital? The challenge of value capture when capital is embedded. *Journal of Management Studies*, 44: 488–505.

47. Collins, C.J., & Smith, K.G. 2006. Knowledge exchange and combination: The role of human resource practices in the performance of high-technology firms. *Academy of Management Journal*, 49: 544–560; Reed, K.K., Lubatkin, M., & Srinivasan, N. 2006. Proposing and testing an intellectual capital-based view of the firm. *Journal of Management Studies*, 43: 867–893.

48. West, B.J., Patera, J.L. & Carsten, M.K. 2009. Team-level positivity: Investigating positive psychological capacities and team level outcomes. *Journal of Organizational Behavior*, 30: 249–267; Luthans, F. 2002. The need for and meaning of positive organizational behavior. *Journal of Organizational Behavior*, 23: 695–706.

49. Avey, J.B. Luthans, F. & Smith, R.M. 2010. Impact of psychological capital on employee well-being over time. *Journal of Occupational Health Psychology,*15: 17–28.

50. Luthans, F. 2006. The impact of efficacy on work attitudes across cultures. *Journal of World Business*, 41: 121–132.

51. Gibson, C.B., & Earley, P.C. 2007. Collective cognition in action: Accumulation, interaction, examination, and accommodation in the development and operation of group efficacy beliefs in the workplaces. *Academy of Management Review*, 32: 438–458.

52. Walumbwa, F.O., Luthans, F, Avey, J.B. & Oke, A. 2009. Authentically leading groups: The mediating role of collective psychological capital and trust. *Journal of Organizational Behavior*, 30: 1–21.

53. Keyton, J. & Smith, F.L. 2009. Distrust in leaders: Dimensions, patterns and emotional intensity. *Journal of Leadership and Organizational Studies*, 16: 6–18; Luthans, F. & Avolio, B.J. 2009. The point of positive organizational behavior. *Journal of Organizational Behavior*, 30: 291–307.

54. Gillespie, N., & Dietz, G. 2009. Trust repair after an organization-level failure. *Academy of Management Review*, 34: 127–145.

55. Gooty, J., Gavin, M. Johnson, P.D., Frazier, M.L., & Snow, D.B. 2009. In the eyes of the beholder: Transformational leadership, positive psychological capital and performance. *Journal of Leadership and Organizational Studies*, 15: 353–367.

56. Cooper, C.L., Quick, J.C. & Schabracq, M.J. 2010. Epilogue. In C.L. Cooper, J.C. Quick & M.J. Schabracq (Eds.), *Work and health psychology: The handbook*. Hoboken, NJ: John Wiley & Sons; Quick, J.C., Macik-Frey, M., & Cooper, C.L. 2007. Managerial dimensions of organizational slack. *Journal of Management Studies*, 44: 189–205.

57. Fineman, S. 2006. On being positive: Concerns and counterpoints. *Academy of Management Review*, 31: 270–291.

58. Goleman, D. 2004. What makes a leader? *Harvard Business Review*, 82 (January): 82–91.

59. McKee, A., & Massimillian, D. 2006. Resonant leadership: A new kind of leadership for the digital age. *Journal of Business Strategy*, 27(5): 45–49.

60. The five aspects of high-commitment management that are used in this book are the most commonly mentioned aspects. See, for example, the following: Arthur, J.B. 1994. Effects of human resource systems on manufacturing performance and turnover. *Academy of Management Journal*, 37: 670–687; Becker, B., & Gerhart, B. 1996. The impact of human resource management on organizational performance: Progress and prospects. *Academy of Management Journal*, 39: 779–801; Guthrie, J.P. 2001. High-involvement work practices, turnover, and productivity: Evidence from New Zealand. *Academy of Management Journal*, 44: 180–190; MacDuffie, J.P. 1995. Human resource bundles and manufacturing performance: Organizational logic and flexible production systems in the world auto industry. *Industrial and Labor Relations Review*, 48: 197–221; Pfeffer, The human equation; Pfeffer, J., & Veiga, J.F. 1999. Putting people first for organizational success. *Academy of Management Executive*, 13(2): 37–48.

61. Zatzick, C.D., & Iverson, R.D. 2006. High-involvement management and workforce reduction: Competitive advantage or disadvantage. *Academy of Management Journal*, 49: 999–1015.

62. Takeuchi, R, Chen, G. & Lepak, D.P., 2009. Through the looking glass of a social system: Cross-level effects of high-performance work systems on employees' attitudes. *Personnel Psychology*, 62: 1–29; Baron, J.N., & Kreps, D.M. 1999. *Strategic human resources: Frameworks for general managers*. New York: John Wiley & Sons.

63. Ployhart, Staffing in the 21st century; Pfeffer, *The human equation*; Pfeffer & Veiga, Putting people first for organizational success.

64. Ibid.

65. For example, see Erdogan, B., Liden, R.C., & Kraimer, M.L. 2006. Justice and leader-member exchange: The moderating role of organizational culture, *Academy of Management Journal*, 49: 395–406.

66. O'Reilly, C.A., Chatman, J., & Caldwell, D.F. 1991. People and organizational culture: A profile comparison approach to assessing person-organization fit. *Academy of Management Journal*, 34: 487–516.

67. Perry-Smith, J.E. 2006. Social yet creative: The role of social relationships in facilitating individual creativity. *Academy of Management Journal*, 49: 85–101.

68. Van Iddekinge, C.H., Ferris, G., Perrewe, P., Perryman, A., Blass, F.R. & Thomas, D. 2009. Effects of selection and training on unit-level performance over time: A latent growth modelling approach. *Journal of Applied Psychology*, 94: 829–843.

69. Ng, T.W.H., & Feldman, D.C. 2009. How broadly does education contribute to job performance? *Personnel Psychology*, 62: 89–134.

70. Lawler, E.E., Mohrman, S.A., & Benson, G. 2001. *Organizing for high performance: Employee involvement, TQM, reengineering, and knowledge management in the Fortune 1000*. San Francisco: Jossey-Bass.

71. Manz & Neck, *Mastering self leadership*; Pfeffer, *The human equation*; Pfeffer & Veiga, Putting people first for organizational success.

72. Hulsheger, U.R., Anderson, N. & Salgado, J.F. 2009. Team-level predictors of innovation at work: A comprehensive meta-analysis spanning three decades of research. *Journal of Applied Psychology*, 94: 1126–1145.

73. Lawler, Mohrman, & Benson, *Organizing for high performance*.

74. Srivastava, A., Bartol, K.M., & Locke, E.A., 2006. Empowering leadership in management teams: Effects on knowledge sharing, efficacy and performance. *Academy of Management Journal*, 49: 1239–1251.

75. Mesmer-Mangus, J.R. & DeChurch, L.A. 2009. Information sharing and team performance: A meta-analysis, *Journal of Applied Psychology*, 94: 535–546.

76. Lawler, Mohrman, & Benson, *Organizing for high performance*.

77. Arthur, Effects of human resource systems on manufacturing performance and turnover.

78. MacDuffie, Human resource bundles and manufacturing performance.

79. Welbourne, T.M., & Andrews, A.O. 1996. Predicting the performance of initial public offerings: Should human resource management be in the equation? *Academy of Management Journal*, 39: 891–919.

80. Gittell, J.H., Seidner, R., & Wimbush, J. 2010. A relational model of how high-performance work systems work. *Organization Science*, 21: 490–506; Liao, H., Toya, K., Lepak, D.P. & Hong, Y. 2009. Do they see eye to eye? Management and employee perspectives of high-performance work systems and

influence processes on service quality. *Journal of Applied Psychology*, 94: 371–391.

81. Kirkman, B.L., Chen, G., Farh, J.-L., Chen, Z.X., & Lowe, K.B. 2009. Individual power distance orientation and follower reactions to transformational leaders: A cross-level, cross-cultural examination. *Academy of Management Journal*, 52: 744–764.

82. Davis, J.H., Schoorman, F.D., Mayer, R.C., & Tan, H.H. 2000. The trusted general manager and business unit performance: Empirical evidence of a competitive advantage. *Strategic Management Journal*, 21: 563–576; Mayer, R.C., Davis, J.H., & Schoorman, F.D. 1995. An integrative model of organizational trust. *Academy of Management Review*, 20: 709–734.

83. Guaspari, J. 2001. How to? Who cares! *Across the Board*, May/June: 75–76.

84. Gong, Y., Huang, J.-C. & Farh, J.-L. 2009. Employee learning orientation, transformational leadership, and employee creativity: The mediating role of employee creative self-efficacy. *Academy of Management Journal*, 52: 765–778.

85 Taylor, W.C., 2008. Bill Taylor: Pixar's blockbuster secrets. *BusinessWeek*, at http://www.businessweek.com, July 10.

86 Lewin, A.Y., Massini, S. & Peeters, C. 2009. Why are companies offshoring innovation? The emerging global race for talent. *Journal of International Business Studies*, 40: 901–925.

organizational diversity

exploring behavior in action

Diversity in the Los Angeles Fire Department

Melissa Kelley had a rich background in firefighting. Early in life, she learned from her grandfather, who worked as a firefighter. In college, she learned through coursework as a fire-science major. After college, she spent five years learning and honing her skills as a firefighter with the California Department of Forestry.

Armed with her experiences and passion for the work, she joined the Los Angeles Fire Department in 2001. Although aware of possible discrimination and harassment against women in the department, she did not hesitate to join when presented with the opportunity. In her words, "I was willing to overlook … the dirty jokes, the porn, the … mentality. … I just wanted to be part of the team." To her, only two simple rules applied: "Do not touch me. Do not hurt me on purpose."

According to media accounts, the first of her rules was violated early in her career with the LAFD. Soon after joining the department, a male colleague entered her bed at the firehouse. He then attempted to kiss and touch her. She resisted and the colleague left, but for several weeks following the incident he clucked like a chicken whenever she was present.

During a routine training exercise later in her career, the second rule came into sharp focus. While the rule probably was not violated explicitly, it is relevant nonetheless to the events that occurred. Following a fire call, Ms. Kelley engaged in the "Humiliator" drill, a drill that involves lifting and positioning a heavy ladder, climbing the ladder with a large saw, and using the saw to cut through metal bars in a window. Although she had previously demonstrated the abilities needed for the drill, on that particular day she dropped the ladder onto her head,

knowledge objectives

After reading this chapter, you should be able to:

1. Define organizational diversity and distinguish between affirmative action and diversity management.

2. Distinguish among multicultural, plural, and monolithic organizations.

3. Describe the demographic characteristics of the U.S. population and explain their implications for the composition of the workplace.

4. Discuss general changes occurring in the United States that are increasing the importance of managing diversity effectively.

5. Understand why successfully managing diversity is extremely important for high-involvement work organizations.

6. Discuss the various roadblocks to effectively managing a diverse workforce.

7. Describe how organizations can successfully manage diversity.

resulting in her helmet becoming stuck between two of its rungs. She immediately felt pain and could not lift her arm to free herself, saying in a later interview: "In my head I'm thinking, I'm dying. My arm is messed up. My back is hurting. My legs are going to give out if I don't get this ladder off me." She continued to struggle with the ladder while showing obvious signs of pain. One colleague apparently tried to help but was stopped. Others reportedly cursed at the struggling firefighter. In the end, Ms. Kelley was taken to a local hospital where multiple injuries were discovered. She subsequently had to be reassigned as a dispatcher. In reflecting on the events of that day, she summed up the situation this way: "Those were my teammates. They would help a dog pinned under a ladder. But they wouldn't help me."

©iStockphoto

Ms. Kelley's experiences are not unique. Alicia Mathis, a captain who joined the LAFD in 1989, also reports being approached in bed at a firehouse. She filed a complaint with the California Department of Fair Employment and Housing. Ruthie Bernal settled a lawsuit related to sexual advances that were followed by harsh treatment when the advances were rejected. Interestingly, Ms. Bernal reports that such advances and subsequent harsh treatment occurred in three different situations involving three different firefighters. Beyond sexual advances, other inappropriate acts have been reported, including mouthwash bottles being filled with inappropriate substances, unflattering female training experiences being captured on video and circulated among male colleagues, sexual materials being delivered, and disproportionately difficult training/testing being applied. In a survey released by the City Controller, 80 percent of women reported discrimination as an issue.

Beyond gender-based problems, race also has played a role in the Los Angeles Fire Department. In a racially charged incident that took place a few years ago, an African American firefighter ate dog food that had been put into his spaghetti at a firehouse. The nature of this incident remains a matter of controversy, as some claim it was harmless horseplay. Even so, because of a history of racial discrimination and harassment, it sparked outrage and a lawsuit. In the survey just mentioned, 87 percent of African Americans reported discrimination as an issue. Hispanics have also reported problems.

The overall effects of these gender and racial issues have been significant. Beyond the loss of talented individuals and the reduced opportunity to attract talented women and minorities, the LAFD has had to pay millions of dollars to settle lawsuits. For example, Brenda Lee was recently awarded more than $6.2 million in a discrimination, harassment, and retaliation case against the LAFD and her former supervisor for being harassed because she is African American, female, and gay.

Job satisfaction also has been affected for some individuals of both genders and all races. In addition, turmoil at the top of the organization has been significant, as multiple fire chiefs have been fired because of the discrimination and harassment. Has the ultimate mission of the organization been compromised? The mission is to "preserve life and property, promote public safety and foster economic growth. ..." Given the loss of talent, reduced satisfaction for some, and turmoil at the top, the effective pursuit of the mission has not been helped.

The news is not all bad, however. City and fire department officials have taken steps to remedy the situation. Surveys designed to stay abreast of the problems have been conducted, as noted earlier. Events such as "Black History Month Recruitment Exposition and Family Carnival" have been held. A new fire chief committed to a positive culture has been hired. The first female African American fire captain has been installed.

Sources: S. Banks. 2006. "Firehouse Culture an Ordeal for Women," *Los Angeles Times*, Dec. 3, p. A.1; S. Glover. 2007. "Rising Star Caught in Turmoil at the LAFD," *Los Angeles Times*, Feb. 12, B.1; D. Hernandez. 2006. "Bringing Diversity to the Force," *Los Angeles Times*, Feb. 6, B.4; J. Kandel. 2006. "Hostile Acts," *The IRE Journal* 29, no. 4: 22; LAFD, "Core Values," 2007, at http://www.joinlafd.org/CoreValues.htm; L. Richardson. 2006. "Audit Faults Fire Dept.," *Los Angeles Times*, Jan. 27, p. B.4; L. Richardson. 2006. "L.A. Fire Captain Alleges Gender Bias," *Los Angeles Times*, Sept. 28, p. B.4. "Lesbian firefighter in L.A. wins $6.2 mil. in discrimination case." *Jet*, July 30, 2007, at FindArticles.com. http://findarticles.com/p/articles/mi_m1355/is_4_112/ai_n27328045.

the strategic importance of Organizational Diversity

As the LAFD case shows, negative reactions to diversity can have harmful effects on an organization. These reactions, including discrimination and harassment of various forms, often lead to lawsuits, turnover, reduced satisfaction, and performance issues. In the most effective organizations, associates and managers understand the value of diversity and capitalize on it to improve performance. Moreover, associates and managers cannot escape diverse workgroups and organizations. Differences in gender, race, functional background, and so on are all around us. The United States is a particularly diverse country with respect to race and ethnicity, and current demographic trends indicate that its population will become even more diverse.

LAFD's legal troubles, financial settlement costs, and public embarrassment have led to renewed efforts to change the culture. The changing nature of the firefighter's job, where 80 percent of fire calls no longer involve structural or brush fires, probably has helped in this process.[1] Many organizations, however, have not needed public embarrassment or changing jobs to motivate diversity efforts. Many organizations, particularly large ones, have voluntarily adopted diversity management programs aimed at recruiting, retaining, and motivating high-quality associates from all demographic backgrounds. Most *Fortune* 500 companies, for example, have diversity management programs.[2] A full 78 percent of organizations with 10,000 or more employees report having a diversity strategy, as compared with 44 percent of companies with 100 to 999 employees and 31 percent in companies

with fewer than 100 workers. Over 79 percent of human resource managers at *Fortune* 1000 companies said they believed that successfully managing diversity improves their organizations.[3]

Diversity, if properly managed, can help a business build competitive advantage. For example, hiring and retaining managers and associates from various ethnicities can help an organization better understand and serve an existing diverse customer base. Diversity among associates also might help the organization attract additional customers from various ethnic groups. Diverse backgrounds and experiences incorporated into a work team or task force can help the organization more effectively handle an array of complex and challenging problems. Kevin Johnson, Co-President of Platforms and Services at Microsoft, puts it this way: "[W]e must recognize, respect, and leverage the different perspectives our employees bring to the marketplace as strengths. Doing so will ensure that we will be more competitive in the global marketplace, will be seen as an employer of choice, and will be more creative and innovative ...."[4]

In the case of nonprofit organizations or governmental units such as the Los Angeles Fire Department, diversity can help build a form of competitive advantage. For instance, hiring and retaining managers and associates from both genders and multiple ethnic groups could help a nonprofit organization better understand its actual and potential client base as well as its actual and potential donors. Thus, the organization might be able to attract resources that would have gone to another nonprofit organization or that would have been

withheld from donation. In the case of the Los Angeles Fire Department, diverse captains, firefighters, and paramedics could better communicate with and predict the behavior of the diverse citizenry of Los Angeles. This would enable the department to better serve the city. It also would position it to receive more resources from the city and state and would increase its likelihood of being chosen over other organizations for additional duties in the Los Angeles area.

Many individuals feel most comfortable interacting and working with people who are similar to them on a variety of dimensions (such as age, race, ethnic background, education, functional area, values, and personality).[5] They must, however, learn to work with all others in an organization to achieve common goals. In a truly inclusive workplace, everyone feels valued and all associates are motivated and committed to the mission of the organization. Such outcomes are consistent with a high-involvement work environment and can help organizations achieve competitive advantage.

We begin this chapter by defining organizational diversity and distinguishing it from other concepts, such as affirmative action. Next, we describe the forces in a changing world that have made diversity such a crucial concern. We then discuss possible benefits of effective diversity management, followed by roadblocks to such management and to the development of an inclusive workplace. We conclude the chapter with a discussion of what can be done to successfully manage a diverse organization.

Diversity Defined

diversity
A characteristic of a group of people where differences exist on one or more relevant dimensions such as gender.

Diversity can be defined as a characteristic of a group of people where differences exist on one or more relevant dimensions such as gender.[6] Notice that diversity is a *group* characteristic, not an individual characteristic. Thus, it is inappropriate to refer to an individual as "diverse." If the group is predominantly male, the presence of a woman will make the group more diverse. However, if the group is predominantly female, the presence of a particular woman will make the group more homogeneous and less diverse.

In practice, diversity is often defined in terms of particular dimensions, most commonly gender, race, and ethnicity. Other important dimensions also exist.[7] These include age, religion, social class, sexual orientation, personality, functional experience (e.g., finance, marketing, accounting), and geographical background (e.g., background in the Canadian province of Ontario versus the province of Saskatchewan).[8] Any characteristic that would influence a person's identity or the way he or she approaches problems and views the world can be important to consider when defining diversity.[9] Two diversity scholars put it this way: "the effects of diversity can result from any attribute that people use to tell themselves that another person is different."[10] Visible attributes (e.g., race, gender, ethnicity),[11] attributes directly related to job performance (e.g., education and functional experience),[12] and rare attributes[13] are the most likely to be seen as important. Examples of how some large organizations define diversity appear below:

> **Texas Instruments:** "Diversity refers to the ways in which people differ. This includes obvious differences such as race and gender, and more subtle differences in religion and culture, as well as variations in work styles, thoughts and ideas."[14]
>
> **Microsoft:** "[Diversity] means not only having a workforce balanced by race, ethnic origin, gender, sexual orientation, and gender identity and expression, but also having a workforce that embraces differences in approaches, insights, ability, and experience."[15]
>
> **Bank of America:** "Our commitment to diversity is ... about creating an environment in which all associates can fulfill their potential without artificial barriers, and in which the team is made stronger by the diverse backgrounds, experiences and perspectives of individuals."[16]

Affirmative action programs (AAPs) differ from diversity management programs. This important distinction should be noted before proceeding. AAPs are specific measures an organization takes to remedy and/or prevent discrimination. The key idea is to ensure fair representation of women and racial and ethnic minorities in the workplace. In the United States, federal contractors (with 50 or more employees or government contracts over $50,000) are required to have AAPs. Other organizations may voluntarily adopt an AAP or may be court-ordered to adopt a program to remedy discriminatory practices. Central features of AAPs include a utilization analysis, which indicates the proportion of women and minorities hired and occupying various positions; goals and timetables for remedying underutilization of women and minorities; specific recruiting practices aimed at recruiting women and minorities (for example, recruiting at traditionally African American universities); and provision of developmental opportunities.[17] AAPs do not require that specific hiring quotas be implemented (which may be illegal) or that standards for selection and promotion be lowered. Also, AAPs usually provide temporary action; once women and minorities are appropriately represented in an organization, the AAP (with the exception of monitoring) is no longer necessary.

EXHIBIT 2-1 Differences between Affirmative Action Programs and Diversity Management Programs

	Affirmative Action	Diversity Management
Purpose	To prevent and/or remedy discrimination	To create an inclusive work environment where all associates are empowered to perform their best
Assimilation	Assumes individuals will individually assimilate into the organization; individuals will adapt	Assumes that managers and the organizations will change (i.e., culture policies, and systems foster an all-inclusive work environment)
Focus	Recruitment, mobility, and retention	Creating an environment that allows all associates to reach their full potential
Cause of Diversity Problems	Does not address the cause of problems	Attempts to uncover the root causes of diversity problems
Target	Individuals identified as disadvantaged (usually racial and ethnic minorities, women, people with disabilities)	All associates
Time Frame	Temporary, until there is appropriate representation of disadvantaged groups	Ongoing, permanent changes

Sources: Adapted from R.R. Thomas, Jr. 1992. "Managing Diversity: A Conceptual Framework," in S.E. Jackson et al. (Eds.), *Diversity in the Workplace* (New York: Guilford Press), pp. 306–317. Society for Human Resource Management, "How Is a Diversity Initiative Different from My Affirmative Action Plan?," 2004, at http://www.shrm.org/diversity.

In contrast, diversity management programs are put in place to improve organizational performance. Because of their different goals, these programs differ from AAPs in several ways,[18] as summarized in Exhibit 2-1. Diversity management programs address diversity on many dimensions. They are often meant to change the organizational culture to be more inclusive and to enable and empower all associates. In addition, they focus on developing people's ability to work together.

When diversity is managed successfully, a multicultural organization is the result.[19] A **multicultural organization** is one in which the organizational culture fosters and values differences. As Google, a company often praised for their diversity initiatives, states on their website "At Google, we don't just accept difference—we thrive on it. We celebrate it. And we support it, for the benefit of our employees, our products and our community." People of any gender, ethnic, racial, and cultural backgrounds are integrated and represented at all levels and positions in the organization. Because of the effective management of diversity, there is little intergroup conflict. Very few organizations in the United States or elsewhere are truly multicultural organizations; most organizations are either plural or monolithic.

Plural organizations have diverse workforces and take steps to be inclusive and respectful of people from different backgrounds. However, diversity is tolerated rather than valued and fostered. Whereas multicultural organizations take special actions to make the environment inclusive and to ensure that all members feel valued, plural organizations focus on the law and on avoiding blatant discrimination.[20] Furthermore, people of various backgrounds may not be integrated throughout the levels and jobs of the organization, as they are in multicultural organizations. For example, even though a company may

multicultural organization
An organization in which the organizational culture values differences.

plural organization
An organization that has a diverse workforce and takes steps to be inclusive and respectful of differences, but where diversity is tolerated rather than truly valued.

employ a large number of women, most of them may be in secretarial jobs. Plural organizations may also have human resource management policies and business practices that exclude minority members, often unintentionally. For example, many companies reward people for being self-promoters; that is, people who brag about themselves and make their achievements known are noticed and promoted, even though their achievements may not be as strong as those who do not self-promote. However, self-promoting behavior may be quite unnatural for people from cultural backgrounds where modesty and concern for the group are dominant values, such as the Japanese and Chinese cultures.[21] Finally, we would expect more intergroup conflict in plural organizations than in multicultural organizations because diversity is not proactively managed.

monolithic organization
An organization that is homogeneous.

Finally, **monolithic organizations** are homogeneous. These organizations tend to have extreme occupational segregation, with minority group members holding low-status jobs. Monolithic organizations actively discourage diversity; thus, anyone who is different from the majority receives heavy pressure to conform. Most U.S. organizations have moved away from a monolithic model because changes in the external environment and the workforce have required them to do so.[22] In the next section, we describe what these changes have been.

Forces of Change

Over the past 20 years, several important changes in the United States and in many other countries have focused more attention on diversity, and these trends are expected to continue. The most important changes are: (1) shifts in population demographics, (2) increasing importance of the service economy, (3) the globalization of business, and (4) new management methods that require teamwork.

Changing Population Demographics

Over the past ten years, more than one-third of people entering the U.S. workforce have been members of racial or ethnic minority groups.[23] Moreover, the proportion of racial and ethnic minorities in the workforce is expected to increase indefinitely. The situation is similar in some European countries.[24]

Exhibit 2-2 provides data on trends that affect the workforce in the United States. It shows, for example, that non-Hispanic white people are expected to decrease as a percentage of the overall population, moving from almost 65 percent to less than 50 percent by 2050 (note that most Hispanics are racially white). The percentage of the population from Hispanic origins (any race) is expected to almost double, from just under 16 percent to almost 30 percent. The Asian American population is also expected to grow, from approximately 5 percent to 9 percent of the overall population. The expansion of the Hispanic American and Asian American populations is due in part to immigration. The percentage of black Americans (some of whom are of Hispanic origin) is expected to remain stable at around 13 percent.

Exhibit 2-2 also shows a trend related to the continued aging of the U.S. population. The decade between 2000 and 2010 saw a growth spurt in the group made up of people aged 45 through 64. This spurt reflects the aging of the post–World War II baby boom generation—people born between 1946 and 1964. A major U.S. labor shortage is expected between 2015 and 2025 as members of the baby boom generation retire.[25] Thus,

EXHIBIT 2-2 Projected U.S. Population Demographics

Percentage by Race or Hispanic Origin	2010	2030	2050
White, alone	79.5	76.6	74.0
Black, alone	12.9	13.1	13.0
Asian, alone	5.3	7.3	9.2
More than one	1.8	2.6	3.7
Hispanic origin (all races)	15.8	22.6	29.6
White (not Hispanic origin)	64.7	55.5	46.3

Percentage by Age	2010	2030	2050
0–4	6.8	6.5	6.4
5–17	17.4	17.0	16.7
18–24	9.9	9.1	9.0
25–44	26.8	25.5	25.2
45–64	26.1	22.6	22.4
65+	12.5	19.3	20.2

Percentage by Sex	2010	2030	2050
Male	49.1	49.1	49.2
Female	50.9	50.9	50.8

Source: U.S. Census Bureau, "U.S. Population Projections," 2009. At http://www.census.gov/population/www/projections/summarytables.html.

it will be even more important for organizations to be able to attract and retain talented associates. Another aspect of the aging population also will likely influence the composition of the labor force. As can be seen in the exhibit, the population over 65 years old will continue to grow. In 2050, it is expected that one in five Americans will be 65 years old or older. If people work beyond the traditional retirement age of 65 due to improved health and the Age Discrimination Act (which protects people 40 and older from discrimination such as being forced to retire), the workforce will continue to age.

Finally, Exhibit 2-2 indicates that the proportion of men and women in the population is likely to remain stable. While women make up 50.9 percent of the population, approximately 48 percent of the labor force is female.[26] This number has grown from 40 percent in 1975 and is expected to increase slightly over the next decade,[27] indicating that proportionally more women than men will be entering the workforce. About 73 percent of mothers work, and about 60 percent of mothers who work have children under the age of three.[28] In contrast, less than 50 percent of mothers worked in 1975. The number of combined hours per week that married couples with children work increased from 55 in 1969 to 66 in 2000.[29] These trends create a need for policies that take family issues into consideration and that deal with the differing issues of workers who have children versus those who do not have children.

Increase in the Service Economy

The U.S. Bureau of Labor Statistics has predicted that the number of service-producing jobs (including those in transportation, utility, communications, wholesale and retail

©AP/Wide World Photos

trade, finance, insurance, real estate, and government) will grow by approximately 17 percent between 2004 and 2014.[30] Service jobs are projected to make up more than 78 percent of all jobs in the United States by 2014.[31] Importantly, a service-based economy depends on high-quality interactions between people, whether between beauticians and their clients, home health-care workers and their patients, or human resource managers and their corporate associates. Because diversity within these and other customer groups is increasing, the service economy demands greater understanding and appreciation of diversity.[32]

The Global Economy

Globalization of the business world is an accelerating trend, gaining momentum from the increasing ease of communication, the opening of new markets, and growth in the number of multinational firms. In 2006, the United States exported $1,437 billion in goods and services and imported $2,202 billion in goods and services.[33] Since 2003, the export figure has increased by more than 40 percent in nominal dollars, while the import figure has increased by 45 percent.[34] Most of the largest companies in the world (for example, GE, Exxon, and Toyota) are the largest owners, worldwide, of foreign assets.[35] These same companies employ millions of workers outside of their home countries. Also, many of these companies require workers in their home countries to work with people from other parts of the world. Finally, many companies now conduct worldwide searches for managers and executives, so that the world serves as the labor market.

The continuing growth of globalization indicates that people will be working with others from different countries and cultures at an ever-increasing rate. Furthermore, many U.S. associates will work outside the United States with people who speak different languages, are accustomed to different business practices, and have different worldviews. As globalization increases, the need for successful diversity management also increases. You will read more about global issues in Chapter 3.

Requirements for Teamwork

Organizations that wish to succeed must respond to increasing globalization, rapidly changing technology and knowledge, and increasing demands for meaningfulness of associates' work. Teamwork is one way to provide better-quality goods and services, because people are more likely to become engaged and committed to the goals of the organization when they are members of strong teams. Whole Foods Market provides an example. At this very successful U.S.-based international provider of organic foods, everyone is assigned to a small, self-directed team.[36]

Teamwork requires that individuals work well together. Having diverse teams may allow for synergistic effects, where the variety of team experiences, attitudes, and viewpoints leads to better team performance.[37] However, to realize these positive effects, diversity must be managed effectively. Teams are discussed in more detail in Chapter 11.

Diversity Management and High-Involvement Organizations

High-involvement organizations expect their associates to respect, learn from, and help one another. They also recognize that associates must be committed to the organization in order to use training, information, and decision power in appropriate ways. Managing diversity effectively is important in the achievement of these aims. Individuals, groups, organizations, and even society as a whole can benefit.

Individual Outcomes

Associates' perceptions of the extent to which they are valued and supported by their organization have a strong effect on their commitment to the organization and their job involvement and satisfaction.[38] In the case of associates who are different from those around them, a positive, inclusive climate for diversity is necessary for full engagement in the work.[39] Research has found that women, racial and ethnic minority group members, and people with disabilities have less positive attitudes toward their organizations, jobs, and careers when they feel that their organizations have poor climates for diversity.[40] In addition, when an organization encourages and supports diversity, individuals are less likely to feel discriminated against and to be treated unfairly. When people feel they have been treated unfairly, they react negatively by withdrawing, performing poorly, retaliating, or filing lawsuits.[41]

Consider the case of a person whose religion forbids alcohol use, requires prayer at certain times of the day, and considers sexual jokes and materials offensive. This person, though, works in an environment where many deals are made over drinks in the local bar, where co-workers tease him because of his daily prayers, and where office walls are covered with risqué pictures. It is likely that this person feels uncomfortable in the office and devalued by his co-workers, leading to dissatisfaction and low commitment to his associates and the organization. Furthermore, he may avoid uncomfortable social activities where important information is exchanged and work accomplished, thus hurting his job performance. A work environment and culture that are sensitive, respectful, and accepting of this person's beliefs would likely result in a more committed, satisfied, and higher-performing associate.

With respect to individuals who are in the majority, diversity management programs must be sensitive to their needs as well. Otherwise, the ideals of diversity management will not be met and outcomes for some individuals will be less positive than they should be. In the United States, white men are often in the majority in a given organizational situation. For them, diversity management can be threatening. One study showed that white men placed less value on efforts to promote diversity.[42] Another study showed that white men perceived injustice when laid off in disproportionate numbers in the face of active diversity management, but did not perceive injustice in the face of disproportionate layoffs in situations without active diversity management.[43] To ensure commitment, satisfaction, and strong performance among those in a majority group, organizational leaders must: (1) carefully build and communicate the case for diversity by citing the forces of change discussed earlier and (2) ensure fair decision processes and fair outcomes for all.

Organizations that create, encourage, and support diversity make all associates feel valued and provide them with opportunities to reach their full potential and be truly engaged in their work. This is a necessary condition of high-involvement work environments.

To put it another way, creating and successfully managing diversity is a necessary condition for achieving a high-involvement work environment.

Group Outcomes

Diversity should have positive effects on the outcomes of organizational groups, particularly on decision-making, creative, or complex tasks.[44] This is because individual group members have different ideas, viewpoints, and knowledge to contribute, resulting in a wider variety of ideas and alternatives being considered.[45] Individuals who are different in terms of age, gender, race, ethnicity, functional background, and education often think about issues differently.[46]

For example, have you ever wondered why phones have rounded edges instead of sharp corners and why there is often a raised dot on the "5" key? One reason is that design groups at AT&T include people who have disabilities, including visual impairments. Rounded corners are less dangerous for people who cannot see the phone, and a raised dot on the "5" key allows people who cannot see to orient their fingers on the keypad. Ohmny Romero, who has worked as a manager in AT&T's technical division and is visually impaired, stated that AT&T associates with disabilities become involved in developing new technologies because they want to "give back" to their community.[47] As a result, everyone has less dangerous phones and keypads that can be used when it is difficult to see. These innovations might never have come about if AT&T design teams had not included members with disabilities and respected their inputs.

In spite of its potential benefits, diversity has been described as a "mixed blessing" in terms of outcomes for organizational groups.[48] Indeed, research has produced mixed results, with some studies showing positive effects but other studies failing to show such effects.[49] There are two issues to consider in interpreting these research outcomes. First, fault lines can be present in situations characterized by diversity. *Fault lines* occur when two or more dimensions of diversity are correlated. For example, if all/most of the young people on a cross-functional task force represent marketing while all/most of the older individuals represent product engineering, then a fault line is said to exist. Fault lines merge multiple identities (e.g., young and marketing focused) to produce barriers to effective collaboration within a group. Research on this phenomenon is relatively new, but has produced findings suggesting poor group outcomes.[50]

Second, problems can develop in all situations characterized by some level of diversity. People often label group members who are different from themselves as "out-group members" and like them less,[51] leading to difficulties in group problem solving and decision making. Diverse organizational groups are more likely to experience personal conflict, problems in communication, and conflict among subgroups.[52]

In light of the above issues, the goal becomes one of facilitating the positive effects of diversity while eradicating the potentially negative effects. One way of harnessing the positive potential of group diversity, while avoiding the negative, is to establish a common identity for the group and to focus on common goals.[53] Richard Hackman, a leading researcher and consultant in the area of teams, has pointed out the importance of common goals for a team, as well as the importance of coaching for team problems.[54] Furthermore, when a company has a positive diversity culture, the problems associated with group diversity are much less likely to occur.[55] An organization that implements effective diversity programs, philosophies, and practices tends to avoid the problems associated with diversity, allowing it to yield the benefits that can be so important.[56] We develop these ideas later in this chapter.

Organizational Outcomes

As discussed above, diversity can lead to more satisfied, motivated, and committed associates who perform more effectively at their individual tasks. Properly managed, diversity can also lead to better-performing and more innovative groups. Therefore, diversity, through its effects on individual and group outcomes, is likely to affect the bottom-line performance of the organization.[57]

Despite the importance of the issue, little systematic research has been conducted that explicitly examines whether the diversity of an organization's workforce is tied to bottom-line performance. One exception is a study that examined the effect of racial and ethnic diversity in the banking industry. Diversity was positively related to the productivity, return on equity, and market performance of banks, but only when the bank had a corporate strategy that reflected growth. The positive relationship between diversity and firm performance was not found in banks that were pursuing a downsizing strategy. In these banks, greater diversity tended to result in poorer performance.[58] Another exception is a large-scale study commissioned by business executives and conducted by researchers at MIT's Sloan School of Management, Harvard Business School, the Wharton School, Rutgers University, the University of Illinois, and the University of California at Berkeley.[59] This research examined the impact of demographic diversity on various aspects of firm performance in several *Fortune* 500 companies. Diversity was found to have no straightforward effects on performance. The researchers concluded that organizations need to manage diversity more effectively, especially because of the potential benefits that diversity offers. That is, diversity alone does not guarantee good corporate performance. It's what the company does with diversity that matters!

In addition to diversity in the workforce, diversity among those leading an organization might have effects. During the past decade or so, the business press has called for an increase in the demographic diversity of boards of directors and upper-echelon management teams.[60] Indeed, the number of women and racial/ethnic minority group members on corporate boards and in top executive positions has been consistently increasing.[61]

This trend appears to make good sense. A recent study of *Fortune* 500 firms found that the companies with the highest representation of women in top positions strongly outperformed those with the poorest representation of women in terms of return on equity and return to shareholders.[62] Other studies have found that the demographic diversity of boards of directors (in terms of race, gender, and age) is positively related to firm performance.[63] Thus, demographic diversity on boards can have a direct positive impact on the organization. One reason for this effect is that women and minorities who actually make it to the top may be better performers and better connected than typical board members.[64] Thus, including them on boards of directors usually increases the quality and talent of the board; the same is usually true for the upper-echelon management team. Another reason for positive outcomes is that by having demographically diverse boards and management teams, companies are sending positive social signals that attract both associates and potential shareholders.[65]

Other types of diversity on boards of directors and upper-echelon management teams also might be beneficial to the firm's bottom-line performance. Research suggests that diversity in functional areas, educational background, social/professional networks, and length of service can have positive effects on firm performance through better decision making.[66] Again, the diversity must be managed properly for benefits to appear.

Societal and Moral Outcomes

In order to have a society based on fairness and justice, U.S. federal laws prohibit employers from discriminating against applicants or employees on the basis of age, gender, race, color, national origin, religion, or disability. Discrimination is an expensive proposition for companies. Some recent awards to plaintiffs resulting from either out-of-court settlements or court cases include the following:

- Ford Motor Company paid out $10.5 million for age discrimination and $8 million for sex discrimination.
- Coca-Cola paid out $192.5 million for race discrimination.
- Texaco paid out $176 million for race discrimination.
- CalPERS paid out $250 million for age discrimination.
- Shoneys paid out $132.5 million for race discrimination.
- Rent-A-Center paid out $47 million for sex discrimination.
- Information Agency and Voice of America paid out $508 million for sex discrimination.
- Wal-Mart recently paid $17.5 million to settle a class action lawsuit regarding discrimination against African Americans in recruitment and hiring of truck drivers for its private fleet. The company is currently dealing with the largest discrimination lawsuit in history. There is an unresolved class action suit filed by two million current and former female employees for sex discrimination.

Apart from these direct costs, firms suffer other losses when suits are filed against them, including legal costs, bad publicity, possible boycotts, and a reduction in the number of job applicants. One study found that stock prices increased for companies that won awards for affirmative action and diversity initiatives, whereas they fell for companies that experienced negative publicity because of discrimination cases.[67] Exhibit 2-3 summarizes applicable federal laws. Individual states may also have laws that protect people from discrimination based on additional characteristics, such as sexual orientation and marital status.

EXHIBIT 2-3   Federal Laws Preventing Employment Discrimination

Law	Employers Covered	Who Is Protected
Title VII of the 1964 Civil Rights Act, Civil Rights Act of 1991	Private employers, state and local governments, education institutions, employment agencies, and labor unions with 15 or more individuals	Everyone based on race, color religion, sex, or national origin
Equal Pay Act of 1963	Virtually all employers	Men and women who perform substantially equal work
Age Discrimination in Employment Act of 1967	Private employers, state and local governments, education institutions, employment agencies, and labor unions with 20 or more individuals	Individuals who are 40 years old or older
Title I of the Americans with Disabilities Act of 1990	Private employers, state and local governments, education institutions, employment agencies, and labor unions with 15 or more individuals	Individuals who are qualified and have a disability

Source: U.S. Equal Employment Opportunity Commission, 2002, http://www.eeoc.gov/facts/qanda.html.

Diversity at the Top

On November 4, 2008, the United States elected Barack Obama as president. President Obama personifies the concept of diversity in terms of race, ethnicity, and geography. His black father was from a small town in Kenya and his white mother was from Kansas. His parents met in Hawaii, where he was born. President Obama's parents were divorced when he was 2 years old. When he was six years old, his mother remarried a man from Indonesia, and the family moved there. At the age of ten, Barack Obama returned to Hawaii to live with his maternal grandparents. He has a half-sister who is part Indonesian and is married to a man who is Chinese Canadian. President Obama's wife, Michelle Obama, is African American. In an interview with Oprah Winfrey, President Obama described his family get-togethers as "mini United Nations meetings." He said he had some relatives that looked like Bernie Mac and some that looked like Margaret Thatcher. The Obama family clearly exemplifies the diversity inherent in the United States.

President Obama's intrapersonal diversity and strong beliefs that diversity in governance is necessary is reflected in the diversity of his cabinet. Thirty-four percent of his officials are female, 11 percent are black, 8 percent are Hispanic, and 4 percent are Asian. While these do not seem like large numbers, they reflect more diversity than was present in past administrations' cabinets. This diversity is expected to increase as President Obama's tenure in office lengthens and he brings in new officials.

The presidency of Barack Obama brings up the question of whether the United States has overcome problems with racial, ethnic, and gender discrimination. Is the leadership in this country finally reflective of the population? Unfortunately, this is still not the case, as evidenced by the demography of corporate leaders. At the end of 2008, there were 5 black, 7 Latino, 7 Asian, and 13 female (2 of whom are Asian) CEOs of *Fortune* 500 companies. This means that 94 percent of *Fortune* 500 CEOs were white, non-Hispanic males. Examining the composition of boards of directors reveals the same lack of diversity. A Catalyst 2009 study of *Fortune* 500 companies revealed that women held 15.2 percent of board seats and women of color held 3.1 percent of all board director positions. Women held only 2 percent of board chair positions. These numbers have remained relatively consistent over the past five years. A study on African American representation on corporate boards found that representation had decreased from 8.1 percent in 2004 to 7.4 percent in 2008. In a recent study of *Fortune* 100 boards, the Alliance for Board Diversity (a

©MANDEL NGAN/Getty Images, Inc.

joint effort among organizations concerned with board diversity) concluded that:

- There is a severe underrepresentation of women and minorities on corporate boards when compared to general U.S. population demographics for race and gender.

- Particular areas of concern include the lack of representation of minority women and of Asian Americans and Hispanics.

- There is a recycling of the same minority individuals—especially African American men—as board members. Minority and female board members hold more seats per person than do white males.

- Very few boards have representation from all groups. Only four boards had representation by all four groups (women, African Americans, Asian Americans, and Hispanics).

Will the diversity evident in the Obama administration filter down to corporate America? Gloria Castillo, president of Chicago United (an organization that advocates for diversity in business) suggests that the Obama administration will help change things. She states "The Obama lesson for corporate directors and C.E.O.'s is that they must accept accountability for proactively seeking out executives of difference to unleash even greater innovation in their enterprises. ... [O]nce they institute true diversity and inclusion in their businesses, other leaders throughout the organizations must follow that lead and actively create an environment that fully engages the best qualified stakeholders ... regardless of ethnicity." In the next Experiencing Organizational Behavioral section "Women, Work, and Stereotypes" we indicate that women are advancing into management positions. Will women and minorities continue their integration into the very top positions, as evidenced in the White House? Only time will tell.

Sources: E.J. Cepeda. November 11, 2008. At "More Diversity in Workplace? Black Man in White House No Silver Bullet, But a Start". At http://www.huffingtonpost.com/esther-j-cepeda/more-diversity-in-workpla_b_142938.html; Oprah Winfrey Interview with Barack Obama, January 11, 2009. At http://www.oprah.com/media/20090112_inaug_diversity.; " Meet Barack." At http://www.barackobama.com/about/; J.A Barnes. June 20, 2009. Obama's Team: The Face Of Diversity. National *Journal Magazine*. At http://www.nationaljournal.com/njmagazine/nj_20090620_3869. php; "Fortune 500 Black, Latino, and Asian CEOs." July 22, 2009. Diversity Inc. At http://www.diversityinc.com/content/1757/article/3895/?Fortune_500_Black_Latino_Asian_CEOs; D. Jones. January 2, 2009. "Women CEOs slowly gain on Corporate America". At http://www.usatoday.com/money/companies/management/2009-01-01-women-ceos-increase_N.htm.; "2009 Catalyst Census of the Fortune 500 Reveals Women Missing From Critical Business Leadership' December 9, 2009. At http://www.catalyst.org/press-release/161/2009-catalyst-census-of-the-fortune-500-reveals-women-missing-from-critical-business-leadership; "African Americans Lost Ground on Fortune 500 Boards" July 21, 2009. At http://urbanmecca.net/news/?p=7649; "Alliance for Board Diversity: Fact Sheet" December 2009. Catalyst. At http://www.catalyst.org/press-release/117/alliance-for-board-diversity-fact-sheet.

Companies that manage diversity well do not discriminate, and their associates are less likely to sue for discrimination. Managing diversity means more than just avoiding discrimination, however. In addition to legal reasons for diversity, there are also moral reasons.

The goal of most diversity programs is to foster a sense of inclusiveness and provide all individuals with equal opportunity—an important cultural value in the United States and in many other countries. Although many countries pride themselves on equality and inclusiveness, they take very different approaches to encourage these ideals. For example, in the United States, differences across groups are highlighted and even celebrated, and laws are used to help in the advancement of minority and disadvantaged groups. In France, differences are downplayed as unimportant and there is limited affirmative action to promote the advancement of minority groups. Britain takes the middle road by recognizing differences but with limited affirmative action to promote fair outcomes in society.[68]

Roadblocks to Diversity

In the preceding section, we focused on the potential benefits of creating and managing diversity in organizations. Organizations working to institute effective diversity management programs face a number of obstacles, however. In this section, we consider the roadblocks to creating an inclusive workplace.

Prejudice and Discrimination

Prejudice refers to unfair negative attitudes we hold about people who belong to social or cultural groups other than our own. Racism, sexism, and homophobia are all examples of prejudice. Prejudice influences how we evaluate other groups ("Arabs are bad," "People with disabilities are to be pitied") and can also lead to emotional reactions, such as hate, fear, disgust, contempt, and anxiety. Unfair **discrimination** is behavior that results in unequal treatment of individuals based on group membership. Examples of discrimination include paying a woman less than a man to do the same work, assigning people with disabilities easier jobs than others, and not promoting Asian Americans to leadership positions.

Prejudice and discrimination do not have to be overt or obvious. Consider racism as an example. Overt prejudice and discrimination toward racial minorities have been on the decline in the United States since passage of the 1964 Civil Rights Act.[69] Whites have become more accepting of residential integration and interracial marriage over the past several decades, for example. However, prejudice and discrimination still exist in more subtle forms, a phenomenon often referred to as "modern racism."[70] In general, **modern racism** occurs when people know that it is wrong to be prejudiced against other racial groups and believe themselves not to be racists. However, deep-seated, perhaps unconscious, prejudice still exists in these people, conflicting with their belief that racism is wrong.

People who are modern racists do not make racial slurs or openly treat someone of another race poorly. However, they may discriminate when they have an opportunity to do so, and then attribute their discriminatory behavior to another cause (such as poor performance) or hide their discriminatory behavior. In some cases, the discrimination is unintentional.

A recent study demonstrates modern racism in action.[71] Participants were asked to evaluate candidates for a university peer counseling position. White participants evaluated either a black or a white candidate. The qualifications of the candidates were varied, so that sometimes the candidates had very good qualifications, sometimes they had very bad qualifications, and sometimes qualifications were ambiguous and less obviously good or bad. The white evaluators showed no discriminatory behavior toward black candidates who had either very good or very bad qualifications. These candidates were chosen (or rejected) as frequently as white candidates with similar credentials. However, when qualifications were ambiguous and it was not obvious what hiring decision was appropriate, the evaluators discriminated a great deal against black candidates. When qualifications were ambiguous, black candidates were chosen only 45 percent of the time, whereas white candidates with ambiguous qualifications were chosen 76 percent of the time.

Most research and discussion concerning modern racism has focused on whites' attitudes toward and treatment of blacks. However, evidence reveals that the same dynamics occur with non-Hispanic white behavior toward Hispanics, men's behavior toward women, nondisabled individuals' behavior toward people with disabilities, and heterosexuals' behavior toward homosexuals.[72] Further, minority group members may hold negative attitudes toward majority group members, and one minority group may hold

prejudice
Unfair negative attitudes we hold about people who belong to social or cultural groups other than our own.

discrimination
Behavior that results in unequal treatment of individuals based on group membership.

modern racism
Subtle forms of discrimination that occur despite people knowing it is wrong to be prejudiced against other racial groups and despite believing they are not racist.

©Tyler Edwards/Photodisc/Getty Images, Inc.

negative attitudes toward another. Regardless of the source, prejudice and discrimination can prevent people from working effectively, getting along with one another, and reaping the benefits that can be derived from a diverse workforce.

Prejudice and discrimination can serve as barriers to effectively managing diversity, leading to stress, poor performance, feelings of injustice, and poor organizational commitment on the part of its victims.[73] In addition to preventing an organization from becoming a high-involvement workplace, prejudice and discrimination, as discussed above, can also be costly in terms of lawsuits and poor public relations. The Los Angeles Fire Department has experienced this firsthand. Thus, diversity management programs must eliminate prejudice and discrimination before they can be effective and foster a high-involvement work environment.

Stereotyping

stereotype

A generalized set of beliefs about the characteristics of a group of individuals.

A **stereotype** is a generalized set of beliefs about the characteristics of a group of individuals. Stereotypes are unrealistically rigid, often negative, and frequently based on factual errors.[74] When individuals engage in stereotyping, they believe that all or most members of a group have certain characteristics or traits. Thus, when we meet a member of that group, we assume that the person possesses those traits.

The problem with stereotypes is, of course, that they ignore the fact that the individuals within any group vary significantly. We can always find examples of someone who fits our stereotype; alternatively, we can just as easily find examples of people who do not fit the stereotype. For example, a common stereotype is that black people are poor.[75] However, the overwhelming majority of black people are middle class (just as are the majority of white people). It is statistically easier to find a middle-class black person than a poor one—and yet the stereotype persists.

Stereotyping is particularly difficult to stop for several reasons. First, stereotypes are very difficult to dispel. When we meet someone who has characteristics that are incongruent with our stereotypes (a smart athlete, a rich black person, a socially skilled accountant, or a sensitive white male), we ignore the discrepancy, distort the disconfirming information, see the individual as an exception to the rule, or simply forget the disconfirming information.[76] Thus, disconfirming information is not as likely as it should be to change stereotypes.

Second, stereotypes guide what information we look for, process, and remember.[77] For example, suppose I believe that all accountants are socially inept. When I meet an accountant, I will look for information that confirms my stereotype. If the accountant is alone at a party, I will assume he or she is antisocial. I will remember instances of when the accountant was quiet and nervous around people. I may also actually "remember" seeing the accountant acting like a nerd, even if I actually did not. Thus, my stereotype is guiding how I process all information about this person based on his or her membership in the accountant group.

Third, stereotypes seem to be an enduring human quality; we all hold stereotypes. Stereotyping is so prevalent in part because it allows us to simplify the information that we deal with on a day-to-day basis.[78] Another reason is that it allows us to have a sense of predictability. That is, if we know a person's group membership (such as race, occupation, or gender), we also believe we have additional information about that person based on our stereotype for that group. Thus, the stereotype provides us with information about other people that enables us to predict their behavior and know how to respond to them. The comedian Dave Chappelle provides an amusing example of this in a skit in which he plays a fortuneteller. Instead of relying on mystic powers, he relies on his stereotypes. Given the race and gender of a phone-in caller, fortuneteller Chappelle can identify all sorts of information about the person's life (like whether the person is calling from prison or is on drugs).

Because stereotypes can drive behavior and lead to unrealistic or false assumptions about members of other groups, they can have very detrimental effects on interpersonal relations. Stereotypes can also have direct effects on individuals' careers by causing unfair treatment. In essence, when we rely on stereotypes to make judgments about an individual, rather than obtaining factual information, we are engaging in faulty decision making that causes harm. Exhibit 2-4 lists some common stereotypes for select groups.

The *Experiencing Organizational Behavior* feature shows that many individuals continue to stereotype women, and to harm their outcomes. Over time, changes in how women are viewed might be aided by examples of success and ambition among women

EXHIBIT 2-4 Common Stereotypes Applied to Various Groups of People

Women	People with Disabilities	White Men
Dependent	Quiet	Responsible for society's problems
Passive	Helpless	Competitive
Uncompetitive	Hypersensitive	Intelligent
Unconfident	Bitter	Aggressive
Unambitious	Benevolent	Ignorant
Warm	Inferior	Racist
Expressive	Depressed	Arrogant

Black People	Japanese Men	Jewish People
Athletes	Meticulous	Rich
Underqualified	Studious	Miserly
Poor	Workaholics	Well-educated
Good dancers	Racist	Family-oriented
Unmotivated	Unemotional	Cliquish
Violent	Defer to authority	Status conscious
Funny	Unaggressive	Good at business

Athletes	Accountants	Arab People
Dumb	Smart	Terrorists
Strong	Nerdy	Extremely religious
Sexist	Unsociable	Extremely sexist
Macho	Good at math	Rich
Male	Bad dressers	Hate Americans
Uneducated	Quiet	Jealous of Americans
Greedy	Dishonest	Don't value human life

Sources: M.E. Heilman. 1983. "Sex Bias in Work Settings: The Lack of Fit Model," in B.M. Staw and L.L. Cummings (Eds.), *Research in Organizational Behavior, Vol. 5* (Greenwich, CT: JAI Press), pp. 269–298; C.S. Fichten and R. Amsel. 1986. "Trait Attributions about College Students with a Physical Disability: Circumplex Analysis and Methodological Issues," *Journal of Applied Social Psychology*, 16: 410–427; Reprinted with permission of the publisher. From *Cultural Diversity in Organizations: Theory, Research and Practice*, © 1993 by T.H. Cox, Jr., Berrett-Koehler Publishers, Inc., San Francisco, CA. All rights reserved. www.bkconnection.com.

Women, Work, and Stereotypes

Over the past three decades, women in Western, industrialized nations have achieved a great deal in workplace acceptance, respect, and advancement. In fields as diverse as accounting, risk management, general management, and police work, women have made substantial progress. For example, chief financial officers, polled a few years ago by America's Community Bankers, reported substantial increases in the number of women managers in their banks. *Women in Business* recently reported that the percentage of women holding supervisory roles had increased from 20 percent to almost 50 percent in a recent 30-year period. *Fortune* 500 firms reported a few years ago that women in officer positions had increased from 2 percent to more than 10 percent.

With this advancement, it would seem that stereotypes characterizing women as submissive, frivolous, indecisive, and uncommitted to the workplace have been eliminated. Even though one study found that stereotypes of women were becoming more compatible with beliefs about what it takes to be a good manager, problems still exist. Consider the language used in major media outlets to describe some businesswomen.

Carly Fiorina, former chief executive officer of Hewlett-Packard, has been characterized as being "as comfortable with power as any woman could be." A former chief executive at Mattel, Jill Barad—who admittedly had some problems—was slighted with the following dismissive statement: "She should have stuck to marketing, rather than worrying her pretty little head about running the company." Darla Moore, who contributed $25 million to the University of South Carolina School of Business, was characterized as a "babe in business." This type of language may help to keep gender stereotypes alive. Stereotypical language and images routinely found in such places as television commercials, radio ads, and travel brochures may also contribute.

Further evidence that gender stereotypes are not dead comes from the financial sector. According to Sheila McFinney, an organizational psychologist familiar with Wall Street, "Stereotypes about women's abilities run rampant in the financial industry. A lot of men in management feel that women don't have the stomach for selling on Wall Street." In support of this statement, a number of Wall

Street firms have been forced to settle major harassment and discrimination claims with thousands of current and former women associates. Interestingly, women are more prevalent in finance than in many other functional areas.

Finally, evidence that suggests ongoing stereotypes comes from a 2007 survey conducted by *Elle* magazine in conjunction with MSNBC .com. Sixty-thousand respondents from a variety of occupations and industries answered questions about women and men as leaders. Approximately half of them indicated that women and men have differing abilities, with women being less able than men. Women, however, were given high marks for supportive environments.

© Steve Hix/Somos Images/Corbis

Sources: "Women Accountants Advance in Management Ranks," *Community Banker,* 10, no. 4 (2001): 52; J. Anderson. 2006. "Six Women at Dresdner File Bias Suit," *New York Times,* Jan. 10, C.1; C. Daily and D.R. Dalton. 2000. "Coverage of Women at the Top: The Press Has a Long Way to Go," *Columbia Journalism Review,* 39, no. 2: 58–59; M.K. Haben. 2001. "Shattering the Glass Ceiling," *Executive Speeches,* 15, no. 5: 4–10; M.-L. Kamberg. 2005. "A Woman's Touch," *Women in Business,* 57, no. 4: 14–17; M. Ligos. 2000. "Nightmare on Wall Street," *Sales and Marketing Management,* 152, no. 2: 66–76; E. Tahmincioglu. 2007. "Men Rule—At Least in Workplace Attitudes," at http://www.msnbc.msn.com/id/17345308; E. E. Duehr, & J.E. Bono. 2006. Men, women, and managers: Are stereotypes finally changing? *Personnel Psychology,* 59: 815–846.

leaders. Anne Mulcahy, CEO of Xerox, and Meg Whitman, former CEO of eBay, are examples. Mulcahy has been instrumental in turning around a company that was near death only a few years ago.[79] Whitman helped to build eBay from a very small company to one in which millions of people do more than $50 billion in business annually. Her vision for eBay was ambitious and included changing consumers' current emphasis on buying at retail stores. Although competition and market dynamics have cooled the company's growth to some degree, eBay continues to be strong.[80]

Differences in Social Identity

Everyone's personal self-identity is based in part on his or her membership in various social groups.[81] This aspect of self-identity is referred to as "social identity." **Social identity** is defined as a person's knowledge that he or she belongs to certain social groups, where belonging to those groups has emotional significance.[82] In describing yourself, you might respond with a statement such as "I am a Catholic," "I am Jewish," "I am a member of my sorority," "I am of Puerto Rican descent," "I am an African American," or "I am a Republican." Such a statement describes an aspect of your social identity structure. Exhibit 2-5 provides examples of overall structures.

social identity
A person's knowledge that he or she belongs to certain social groups, where belonging to those groups has emotional significance.

Having a social identity different from that of the majority can be very difficult, for several reasons. First, a person's social identity becomes more salient, or noticeable, when the person is in the minority on an important dimension. Accordingly, racial and ethnic minorities are much more likely to state that their membership in a racial or ethnic group is an important part of their self-concept.[83] For example, in one study, researchers said to people, "Tell me about yourself."[84] Only one out of every 100 white people mentioned

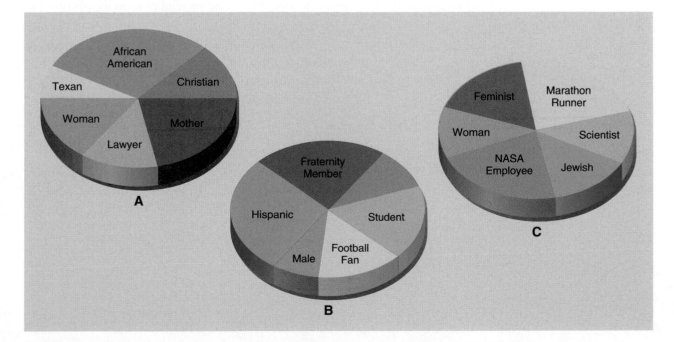

Exhibit 2-5 Sample Social-Identity Structures

that she was white. However, one in six black respondents mentioned his race, and one in seven Hispanic respondents mentioned ethnicity. Also, many women remark that they are more conscious of being female when they are in a work environment that is all male than when they are in a mixed-gender group. When a person's minority social identity becomes salient, the person is made more aware that he or she is different from the majority of people in the situation.

Second, having a social identity different from that of the majority may make people feel they have to behave in ways that are unnatural for them in certain contexts. Feeling that they are acting out a false role will in turn lead to stress and dissatisfaction.[85] For example, women operating in an all-male environment may try to act more like men in order to fit in and meet others' expectations.[86] In discussing being an African American in a predominantly white business world, Kenneth I. Chenault, CEO of American Express, says that he had to learn how to become comfortable dealing with multiple cultures with different expectations. He states, "I learned very early on how to move between both worlds and develop a level of comfort and confidence no matter what world I'm operating in."[87] Clearly, if you belong to the majority group, you do not have to learn how to act in different worlds.

A third issue resulting from differences in social identities is that often minority group members fear losing this social identity.[88] Social identity is often a source of pride and honor.[89] Thus, being forced to "check their identity at the gate" creates a sense of loss and discomfort for many people.

A final issue related to differences in social identities concerns the fact that people often evaluate others based on their membership in social groups. People tend to favor members of their own groups because their group membership is often tied to feelings of high self-esteem.[90] We think people who belong to our own group must somehow be better than those who do not belong. In other words, we tend to categorize people according to in-group and out-group membership,[91] and we tend to favor members of our own group—the in-group—and disfavor those whom we have categorized as belonging to an out-group. We often exaggerate the positive attributes of our own group and the negative aspects of the out-group. Furthermore, we are more likely to have stereotypes regarding out-group members and to ignore differences among out-group members.[92] So, for example, members of the legal department, who have strong identities as lawyers, may view other associates who are not lawyers as being similar, less savvy, and peripheral to the success of the company. In contrast, the lawyers are more likely to see other lawyers as individuals, and think they are smarter and are central to the company's success. In conclusion, social identity dynamics can be a roadblock to successful diversity management because they foster forming in-groups and out-groups and can lead to stress and dissatisfaction among those with minority identities.

Power Differentials

Power is not equally distributed among the individuals and groups in an organization. Individuals gain power in many ways—by having expert knowledge or a powerful formal position, by controlling valuable rewards or important resources, or by being irreplaceable, for example.[93] In some organizations that rely on selling, the individuals in the sales and marketing departments have most of the power, whereas the individuals in the human resources and accounting departments have less power. An executive secretary controlling those who are allowed to meet with and speak to the CEO also has power. In essence, this secretary controls everyone's communication with top management.

On the other hand, people are also awarded or deprived of power and status for reasons that have nothing to do with work life. On a societal level, groups of people have what is called *ascribed* status and power. **Ascribed status** is status and power that is assigned by cultural norms and depends on group membership.[94] In other words, societal culture defines who has power and who does not. In North America, women, racial and ethnic minorities, and people with disabilities, among other groups, are traditionally perceived to be of lower status than white men.[95] Thus, members of these groups have traditionally had less power in the workplace than white men. When such power differentials exist, they can prevent an organization from developing an inclusive workplace for at least two reasons.

First, research has shown that high-status individuals speak more and use stronger influence tactics than members of low-status groups.[96] Thus, low-status individuals may not have a chance to contribute as much to group problem-solving tasks. When people do not feel free to speak up, a major benefit of diversity is lost because different ideas and viewpoints are not presented. This phenomenon also causes problems because it perpetuates status differentials and may lead to frustration and dissatisfaction among people who do not feel free to speak up.

Second, people belonging to groups with different amounts of power and status may avoid interacting with one another and may form cliques with members of their own groups.[97] High-status groups may downgrade, ignore, or harass members of low-status groups. Associates in low-status groups may stay away from high-status associates in order to avoid rejection or humiliation. This tendency to form cliques undermines diversity efforts by setting the stage for increased conflict among groups.

ascribed status
Status and power that is assigned by cultural norms and depends on group membership.

Poor Structural Integration

You may have heard phrases such as "pink-collar ghetto" and "glass ceiling." These phrases refer to the tendency for women and members of racial and ethnic minority groups to be "stuck" in certain occupations or at certain levels in an organization. Recall from the earlier part of this chapter that one criterion for having a truly multicultural organization is that people from traditionally underrepresented groups appear at all levels and in all occupations. Exhibit 2-6 illustrates a well-integrated organization and a poorly integrated organization.

Note in the figure that 35 percent of the employees in both Company A and Company B are either female and/or a member of a racial minority group. So if we look only at the total number of employees, then we might conclude that both companies are equally well integrated. Such a conclusion would be erroneous, however.

In Company A, on average across functional areas, only .5 percent of top management jobs are held by women or minorities. At the same time, on average across functional areas, 70 percent of the lowest-level jobs are held by women and minorities. These figures indicate that women and minorities are extremely underrepresented in high-level positions and overrepresented in low-level (low-status, low-power, and low-pay) positions. Furthermore, in Company A, women and racial minorities are severely underrepresented in the areas of finance, marketing, and sales. Coca-Cola was sued by African Americans because it resembled Company A (to some degree) despite having talented people in the minority group. The company settled in 2000 for $192.5 million.[98]

Company A
Poorly Integrated

Functional Area

Level	Finance	Marketing	HR	Sales	Average across functions
Top Management	0%	0%	2%	0%	.5%
Mid Management	0%	1%	10%	2%	3.25%
Supervisor	0%	5%	15%	5%	6.25%
Staff	25%	25%	40%	26%	29%
Line Worker	60%	65%	80%	75%	70%

Company B
Well Integrated

Functional Area

Level	Finance	Marketing	HR	Sales	Average across functions
Top Management	35%	35%	35%	35%	35%
Mid Management	35%	35%	35%	35%	35%
Supervisor	35%	35%	35%	35%	35%
Staff	35%	35%	35%	35%	35%
Line Worker	35%	35%	35%	35%	35%

The numbers in each cell represent the percentage of people in each job level and functional area who are female and/or racial and ethnic minority group members.

The total percentage of employees for both companies who are female and/or a racial ethnic minority is 35%.

Exhibit 2-6 Examples of Poorly Integrated and Well-Integrated Organizations

Contrast these patterns with those in Company B. In that company, women and minorities are represented in all areas in proportion to their total representation in the company. Company B illustrates the ideal distribution for an inclusive organization—which occurs infrequently.

Data compiled in 2003 by the Equal Employment Opportunity Commission suggest that U.S. companies look more like Company A than Company B.[99] White males made up about 37 percent of the workforce in private industry but held about 56 percent of the executive and managerial jobs. In contrast, they only held about 13 percent of lower-level clerical jobs and 21 percent of service jobs. White women, who made up almost 33 percent of the workforce, held almost 55 percent of clerical jobs. Black people (both men and women) made up almost 14 percent of the workforce but held less than 7 percent of executive and managerial jobs. Black women were overrepresented in clerical and service jobs, and black men were overrepresented in operations and laborer jobs. This pattern held true for most other minority groups as well.

Why are social groups so unequally distributed across occupations and job levels? Many explanations have been offered, with discrimination being a common one. Lack of skills on the part of groups holding lower-level positions is also cited frequently. Whatever the reason, poor integration of women and minorities in organizations can present several roadblocks to creating a multicultural environment.

- Poor integration creates power and status differentials, which then become associated with gender or race.
- Poor integration fosters negative stereotypes.

- Where integration is poor overall, women and minorities who do reach higher levels may have token status. That is, since they may be the only persons of their race or gender in that type of job, they will be considered an exception.[100]
- Where integration is poor, most women and minorities may feel that it is impossible for them to rise to the top.

Communication Problems

Communication can be a roadblock to establishing an effective diversity environment. One potential communication problem arises when not everyone speaks the same language fluently. Associates who are less fluent in the dominant language may refrain from contributing to conversations. Furthermore, groups may form among those who speak the same language, excluding those who do not speak that language. Finally, many misunderstandings may occur because of language differences. For example, U.S. college students often complain that having teachers who are not fluent in English makes it difficult for them to understand class lectures.

Another communication problem arises because different cultures have different norms about what is appropriate. For example, African Americans, Hispanics, and Asians are less likely than Anglo Americans to feel they can speak freely during meetings.[101] Common areas of communication disagreement among cultures include the following:

- Willingness to openly disagree
- The importance of maintaining "face," or dignity
- The way agreement is defined
- The amount of time devoted to establishing personal relationships
- Willingness to speak assertively
- Mode of communication (written, verbal)
- Personal space and nonverbal communication

While communication differences exist for people from different backgrounds, it is important not to stereotype. Some individuals from a particular background will not share the communication preferences often associated with that background.

Effectively Creating and Managing Diversity

Organizations face many roadblocks to creating multicultural environments, but these roadblocks are not insurmountable. In this section, we discuss some strategies for effectively creating and managing diversity.

Most large companies and many small companies have in recent years instituted some type of diversity management plan. These plans have varied in effectiveness, from being very successful at creating a diverse, inclusive, and productive workplace to having no effect or to actually having negative effects. Because so many diversity programs have been instituted, there is substantial knowledge about what works and what does not work. The U.S. Department of Commerce studied 600 firms that had been cited for having excellent diversity climates.[102] The study revealed several criteria for success, including commitment by the organization's leaders, integration of the program with the organization's strategic plan, and involvement of all associates.

Commitment of the Organization's Leaders

The first criterion for having an effective diversity program is genuine commitment from the organization's upper-level leadership. Insincere support of diversity is damaging. Leaders must take ownership of diversity initiatives and effectively communicate the vision that inclusiveness is important. Actions that corporate leaders have initiated to ensure that the message comes across include the following:

- High-ranking leaders send relevant communications through multiple channels, such as intranet postings, policy statements, formal newsletters, meetings, speeches, and training programs.
- One high-ranking leader personally leads all diversity efforts. He holds town meetings and eats lunch in the cafeteria to talk about diversity.
- Multiple high-ranking executives sponsor employee councils devoted to fostering cross-cultural communication. The councils are all-inclusive—anyone who wants to join can do so. Therefore, anyone can "have the ears" of executives on diversity issues.
- Managers at all levels are held accountable for advancing diversity initiatives.

The *Managerial Advice* feature focuses on ideas that managers can use to promote positive work environments. The actions recommended are valuable for associates but are most important for managers because they have the strongest effects on the organization's culture.

Integration with the Strategic Plan

The second criterion for effective diversity management requires that diversity be linked to the organization's strategic plan. That is, it is necessary to be clear about the ways in which diversity can contribute to the strategic goals, directions, and plans of the organization. The organization must develop ways of defining and measuring diversity effectiveness and then use these measures in the strategic planning process. Common measures of diversity effectiveness focus on:

- Increased market share and new customer bases
- External awards for diversity efforts
- Associates' attrition rate
- Associates' work satisfaction
- Associates' and managers' satisfaction with the workplace climate

Another tactic for elevating diversity to the strategic level involves making it a core value and part of the formal mission statement of the organization. Many organizations that truly value diversity express this as a core value and include their beliefs in a mission statement. These statements go beyond the common catchphrase that "We are an affirmative action employer." For example, one of six principles in Starbucks' mission statement is: "Embrace diversity as an essential component in the way we do business." Another is: "Provide a great work environment and treat each other with respect and dignity."[103]

Associate Involvement

The third criterion for effective diversity management calls for the involvement of all associates. Diversity programs can produce suspicion or feelings of unfairness in some associates, particularly if they misinterpret the program's purpose. Some individuals may feel they are excluded from the program, whereas others may feel that it infringes on benefits

Promoting a Positive Diversity Environment

©Tom Grill/Corbis

obin Ely, Debra Meyerson, and Martin Davidson are professors at Harvard University, Stanford University, and the University of Virginia, respectively. In conjunction with the human development and organizational learning professionals at Learning as Leadership, they have developed several principles designed to ensure that members of various social identity groups do not become trapped in low-quality workplace relationships. These principles are designed to encourage engagement and learning. The principles are perhaps best applied in the context of individuals experiencing uncomfortable events that are open to interpretation, such as when the member of a minority group is told by someone from the majority that she is being too aggressive, or when a man is told by a woman that he is acting as his grandfather might have acted. The principles are listed below:

a. *Pause to short circuit the emotion and reflect.* Individuals who have experienced an uncomfortable event should take a few moments to identify their feelings and consider a range of responses.

b. *Connect with others in ways that affirm the importance of relationships.* Individuals who have experienced an uncomfortable event should reach out to those who have caused the difficulty, thereby valuing relationships.

c. *Question interpretations and explore blind spots.* Individuals who have experienced an uncomfortable event should engage in self-questioning as well as the questioning of others. They should be open to the interpretations that others have of the situation, while realizing that their own interpretations might be correct.

d. *Obtain genuine support that doesn't necessarily validate initial points of view but, rather, helps in gaining broader perspective.* Individuals who have experienced an uncomfortable event should seek input from those who will challenge their initial points of view on the situation.

e. *Shift the mindset.* Individuals who have experienced an uncomfortable event should be open to the idea that both parties might need to change to some degree.

Sources: R.J. Ely, D.E. Meyerson, and M.N. Davidson. 2006. "Rethinking Political Correctness," *Harvard Business Review*, 84 (September); Learning as Leadership, "Research," 2007, at http://www.learnaslead.com/index.php.

they are currently enjoying. It is important for diversity programs to address the needs of both majority group members and minority group members. Organizations can use many methods to obtain input from associates. Some of these include:

- Discussion groups made up of all types of associates who help in developing, implementing, and evaluating the program
- Employee satisfaction surveys
- Cultural diversity audits, which help the company studying the diversity culture and environment of the organization
- Informal employee feedback hotlines where associates can provide unsolicited feedback

Another common way of involving associates in diversity programs is to develop and support *affinity groups*—groups that share common interests and serve as a mechanism for the ideas and concerns of associates to be heard by managers. Affinity groups are also good sources of feedback about the effectiveness of diversity initiatives. Finally, these groups can provide networking opportunities, career support, and emotional support to their members. Ford Motor Company has the following affinity groups: Ford-Employee African American Ancestry Network; Ford Asian Indian Association; Ford Chinese Association; Ford Finance Network; Ford Gay, Lesbian, or Bisexual Employees; Ford Hispanic Network Group; Professional Women's Network; Ford's Parenting Network; Women in Finance; Ford Interfaith Network; Middle Eastern Community @ Ford Motor Company; and Ford Employees Dealing with Disabilities.[104]

Finally, another way of involving all associates is through training. Training programs often include an explanation of the business necessity for effectively managing diversity, along with empathy training, cross-cultural knowledge instruction, and exercises to help associates avoid stereotyping and engaging in offensive or prejudicial treatment of others. To create a truly inclusive environment, diversity programs also need to teach people how to value and respect diversity rather than just tolerate it.

Denny's, the U.S. restaurant chain, is an example of a company that has implemented the three aspects of diversity management discussed here. Following lawsuits and settlements in the 1990s, Jim Anderson became the CEO in 1996 and drove true commitment to diversity. Anderson himself was committed to building what Roosevelt Thomas, an expert on corporate diversity, terms a *diversity-mature* organization, in which the mission and vision of the company includes a diversity management component.

To fully integrate the management of diversity into its mission, Denny's requires all managers and associates to participate in diversity training sessions. In addition, they are held accountable for their behavior. Associates who engage in inappropriate behavior are

THE STRATEGIC LENS

Organizational diversity, when managed effectively, has many benefits for organizations. In general, effectively managed diversity programs contribute to an organization's ability to achieve and maintain a competitive advantage. Diversity in teams at all levels can be helpful in solving complex problems because heterogeneous teams integrate multiple perspectives. This benefit applies to the upper-echelon management team as well as to project teams, such as new-product-development teams, much lower in the organization. Not only can the diversity help resolve complex problems, but it also better mirrors U.S. society. Thus, it signals to potential associates and potential customers that the organization understands and effectively uses diversity. As a result, the organization has a larger pool of candidates for potential associates from which it can select the best. In addition, the organization is likely to have a larger potential market because of its understanding of the products and services desired by a diverse marketplace. Having a diverse organization that reflects the demographic composition of U.S. society is smart business.[106]

Critical Thinking Questions

1. How does organizational diversity contribute to an organization's competitive advantage?

2. What actions are required to create diversity in an organization, particularly in one that has homogeneous membership at present?

3. How does diversity in an organization affect its strategy?

put on notice and must indicate how they will change their behavior in the future. Those who do not change their behavior are terminated. More blatant transgressions, such as racial slurs, result in immediate termination.

Overall, companies such as Denny's use diversity initiatives in at least seven different areas:[105]

1. Recruiting (e.g., diverse recruiting teams, minority job fairs)
2. Retention (e.g., affinity groups, on-site child care)
3. Development (e.g., mentoring programs, leadership development programs)
4. External partnerships (e.g., minority supplier programs, community outreach)
5. Communication (e.g., addresses by high-ranking leaders, newsletters)
6. Training (e.g., awareness training, team building)
7. Staffing and infrastructure (e.g., dedicated diversity staffs, executive diversity councils).

What This Chapter Adds to Your Knowledge Portfolio

In this chapter we discussed the importance of diversity to organizations and the need to effectively manage diversity. We also discussed the forces of change that have made diversity a primary concern of many organizations, and we described some of the more common roadblocks to successfully managing diversity. Finally, we discussed the essential components of an effective diversity program. To summarize, we made the following points:

- *Organizational diversity* refers to differences among the individuals in an organization. Important differences are those that are personally important to people and affect the way in which they perceive the world. Common dimensions of diversity include race, ethnicity, gender, disability, functional area, sexual orientation, and parenthood.
- Diversity programs are aimed at developing inclusive work cultures, which are important in high-involvement work environments. Affirmative action programs are aimed at making sure there is fair representation or numbers of various groups within jobs and organizations. Affirmative action programs can be legally mandated or voluntarily adopted.

back to the knowledge objectives

1. What is organizational diversity, and how does diversity management differ from affirmative action? Do these kinds of programs have anything in common?
2. Distinguish between multicultural, plural, and monolithic organizations. How might these organizations differ in the types of policies they use? For example, how would they differ in terms of staffing practices?
3. What trends can be seen in the demographic characteristics of the U.S. population? What are the implications of these trends for organizational diversity?
4. What other changes are occurring in the environment that contribute to the importance of managing diversity effectively? Why do these changes have this effect?
5. Why is successfully managing diversity important to high-involvement work organizations? Give specific examples.
6. What problems do discrimination, prejudice, and stereotyping create in an organization attempting to manage a diverse workforce?
7. How do social identities, power differentials, and poor structural integration affect the successful management of diversity?
8. What does a diversity program need in order to be effective? How would you determine whether your diversity program was effective?

- Multicultural organizations have diverse associates and are inclusive of all associates. Plural organizations have reasonably diverse associates and tolerate diversity. Monolithic organizations are homogeneous and do not tolerate diversity.

- The U.S. population is getting older and more diverse in terms of race and ethnicity. Other changes that are occurring in the environment include an increasing service economy, increasing globalization, and increasing need for teamwork. These changes make management of diversity more important today than ever.

- Successfully managing diversity is important because it can lead to more committed, better satisfied, better-performing employees, attraction of the best talent, better group decision making, and potentially better financial performance for the organization. Effectively managing diversity also ensures that the moral principle that everyone be treated fairly will be upheld. Furthermore, effective diversity management can result in fewer lawsuits for discrimination.

- Discrimination, prejudice, stereotyping, differing social identities, power differentials, poor structural integration, and communication concerns have a negative impact on managing a diverse workforce.

- Organizations that successfully manage diversity have senior managers who fully support diversity initiatives, tie their diversity plans to the overall strategic goals of the organization, and ensure involvement from all associates through a variety of mechanisms.

Thinking about Ethics

1. Suppose that an organization has discriminated in the past. Should it now simply stop its discriminatory practices, or should it also take specific actions to increase its diversity by targeting, hiring, and promoting minorities ahead of nonminorities? Discuss.

2. Should all managers and associates in an organization be required to undergo diversity training regardless of their desire to do so? Why or why not?

3. Are there any circumstances in which it is appropriate to discriminate against a particular class of people (such as women)? If so, explain the circumstances. If not, explain why.

4. Women are not a minority in the population but represent a minority in the U.S. workforce, particularly in some occupations. Why has this occurred in U.S. society (or your home country, if applicable)?

5. Should all cultures and modes of conduct be tolerated, even if they conflict with the values of the organization? Why or why not?

6. What percentage of the organization's budget should be invested in building and maintaining an effective diversity management program? How should this percentage compare with other major budget items?

Key Terms

diversity, p. 50

multicultural
   organization, p. 51

plural organization, p. 51

monolithic
   organization, p. 52

prejudice, p. 61

discrimination, p. 61

modern racism, p. 61

stereotype, p. 62

social identity, p. 65

ascribed status, p. 67

Human Resource Management Applications

The Human Resource Management (HRM) function plays a key role in a firm's capability to manage diversity. Often diversity officers and initiatives are housed within HRM departments. The following are several activities that an HRM department can use to manage diversity.

A major function of HRM departments is developing, conducting, and evaluating *training* programs. Diversity training programs are integral to any diversity management effort. HRM departments are also likely to evaluate the effectiveness of these programs.

In many organizations, *employee recruitment* is centralized through the HRM department. Thus, they are concerned with advertising to, locating, and attracting potential associates from groups traditionally underrepresented in the organization.

Employee selection may also be centralized through the HRM department. In order to facilitate an organization's diversity goals, the HRM department must make certain that methods used to hire associates (e.g., interviews, job knowledge test, personality tests) are not biased against certain group members.

An important aspect of many diversity programs is an organizational *diversity climate audit,* which surveys associates to determine their feeling of inclusion and satisfaction with diversity initiatives. This audit is often the responsibility of the HRM department.

---

building your human capital

What's Your DQ (Diversity Quotient)?

How well do you handle diversity? Your ability to be flexible, work with many different types of people, and deal with ambiguous situations will be crucial to a successful career in the twenty-first century. The following assessment will allow you to determine whether you have had the experience necessary to help in successfully navigating a diverse work environment.

Use the following scale to answer the questions below:

1 point = never	3 points = three or four times
2 points = once or twice	4 points = four or more times

In the last month, how often did you …?

1. See a foreign movie.
2. Speak a language other than your first language.
3. Visit an art or history museum.
4. Have a conversation with someone who was of a different race.
5. Have a conversation with someone who was from a different country.
6. Attend a social event where at least half of the people differed from you in race or ethnic background.
7. Visit a church that was of a religion different from yours.
8. Visit a place where people spoke a language different from your first language.
9. Do something you've never done before.
10. Attend a cultural event (art show, concert).
11. Eat ethnic food.
12. Visit a foreign country.
13. Watch a program about world (non-U.S.) history.
14. Read a book about another culture.

15. Watch a movie or TV show about another culture.
16. Attend a social event where you didn't know anyone.
17. Read a book written by a foreign author.
18. Listen to music from a different culture.
19. Attend an event where you were in a minority based on any demographic characteristic (age, gender, race, ethnicity, religion, sexual orientation).
20. Learn something new about a country or culture other than your own.
21. Study a different language.
22. Attend an event about a different culture (an ethnic festival, a concert by musicians from a different culture, a student meeting of an ethnic group).
23. Have a conversation with someone from a different social class.
24. Develop a friendship with someone from a different background.
25. Discuss world affairs with someone who disagreed with you.

Scoring: Add up your total points for the 25 questions.
Scoring can range from 25 to 100

25–39: Your current environment is rather homogeneous. You can increase your DQ by making a concerted effort to reach out to people who are different from you, attend events that expose you to different cultures, and learn about people and cultures that differ from yours. Your score may be low because you live in an area where there is little diversity in people or cultural events. You will need to go out of your way to gain exposure to different cultures.

40–59: Your current environment could be more diverse than it currently is. You can increase your DQ by making a concerted effort to reach out to people who are different from you, attend events that expose you to different cultures, and learn about people and cultures that differ from yours.

60–79: Your environment is fairly culturally diverse. Look more closely at your scores for each question and determine whether there are any areas in which you can broaden your horizons even further. Perhaps, for example, you read and watch materials that expose you to different cultures but do not personally interact frequently with people who are different from you. If that is the case, join a club where you are likely to meet people different from yourself.

80–100: Your environment is quite culturally diverse. You experience a great deal of cultural variety, which should help prepare you for working in a culturally diverse work environment.

---

an organizational behavior moment

Project "Blow Up"

Big State University (BSU) is proud of the success of its international executive MBA (EMBA) program. The program is designed to bring together promising middle- and higher-level managers from around the globe for an exceptional learning experience. BSU's EMBA program has been ranked very highly by the business press. Alumni praise the program for its excellent faculty, networking opportunities, and exposure to colleagues from around the world. Students in the program can either attend weekend classes on BSU's campus or participate through distance-learning technology from campuses around the world.

One of the defining features of the program is the first-year team project. Students are randomly assigned to five-member teams. Each team has a faculty advisor, and each must develop a business plan for a startup company. A major part of the business plan involves developing a marketing strategy. The teams begin the project during orientation week and finish at the end of the next summer. Each team must turn in a written report and a business plan and make an hour-long presentation to the other students and faculty as well as several executives from well-respected multinational companies. Students must earn a passing grade on the project to graduate from the program. The project is also a good way of meeting and impressing important executives in the business community.

The A-Team consists of five people, who did not know each other before the project began. They are:

- **Rebecca**—A 27-year-old marketing manager for a large, high-end Italian fashion company. Rebecca is a white female of Italian descent who was born and raised in New York City. Rebecca earned her bachelor's degree in business at the University of Virginia's McIntire Business School when she was 22. She speaks English, Italian, and Spanish fluently. She speaks a little German and Japanese as well. Rebecca is single. Her job involves analyzing worldwide markets and traveling to the 136 stores around the world that carry her company's clothes. She hopes the EMBA from BSU will help her to be promoted to an executive position.

- **Aran**—The 52-year-old founder and CEO of an Egyptian management consulting firm. His firm employs 12 people who consult with local companies on issues involving information systems. Aran is an Egyptian male who is a fairly devout Muslim. He earned his business degree 25 years ago at the American University in Cairo. He speaks English and Arabic fluently. Aran is married with two adult children. He is attending BSU's program because he wants to retire from his consulting firm and become an in-house information systems consultant to a large multinational firm.

- **Katie**—A 30-year-old financial analyst at a large Wall Street firm. At present, Katie's job requires little travel, but she works long hours as a financial analyst. Katie is an American female who does not consider herself to have any strong ethnic roots. She earned her business degree two years ago from New York University. Before going to college, she worked as a bank teller on Long Island. She was concerned about her lack of progress and went back to college to get a degree. She now wants to further her education to open up even more opportunities. Katie speaks only English. She is married but has no children. However, she cares for her elderly mother, who lives nearby in New Jersey.

- **Cameron**—A 23-year-old Internet entrepreneur who heads his own small but successful company. He is the youngest student BSU has ever accepted. He was something of a child prodigy, graduating from Georgia Tech at the age of 19 with a degree in computer science. Cameron is a single, African American male who has lived all over the United States. His company is based in Austin, Texas. He speaks only English. He is attending BSU's program because, though confident of his technical expertise, he

would like to learn more about business, since he is planning to expand his company.

- **Pranarisha**—A 31-year-old manager for a nongovernmental organization (NGO) that provides support to poverty-stricken areas of Thailand. Pranarisha's job is to coordinate efforts from a variety of worldwide charitable organizations. She speaks four languages fluently; however, she is not fluent in English. She graduated from the most prestigious university in Thailand. She is married with a four-year-old son and is a devout Buddhist. She is attending BSU's program at the request of her organization, so she can help to make the organization more efficient.

The A-Team was doomed almost as soon as the project began. The team's first task was to decide how roles would be allocated to individuals on the team.

Aran: Before we begin, we need to decide what everyone will be doing on this project, how we will divide and coordinate the work. Since I have the most experience, I should serve in the executive function. I'll assign and oversee everyone's work. I will also give the presentation at the end of the project, since I know how to talk to important people. Cameron will be in charge of analyzing the financial feasibility of our project, developing the marketing plan, and evaluating the technical operations. The girls will assist him in …

Rebecca (Interrupting): Hold on a minute! First, we are not girls! Second, Cameron, Katie, and I decided last night over beers at happy hour that I should handle the marketing plan, Cameron the technical aspects, and Katie the financial aspects. You can serve as the coordinator, since you're not going to be attending class on campus—you can keep track of everything when we submit electronic reports.

Cameron: Yeah—your role would be to just make sure everyone is on the same page, but we'd individually decide how to conduct our own projects.

Aran: This team needs a leader and I …

Cameron and Katie (in unison): Who says?

Rebecca: We're all responsible adults, and since the three of us are most accustomed to the Western way of doing business—which as we all know focuses on *individual empowerment*—then we'll get the most out of the project doing it our way.

Aran: You are all young and inexperienced. What do you know about the business world?

Katie: I know a lot more about finance than you.

Rebecca: Get with the twenty-first century. Just because we're women doesn't mean …

Cameron: He isn't just ragging on women. He's ragging on me, too.

Katie: Yeah, but at least he gave you a real job. You're a guy—"Boy Wonder."

Cameron: What kind of crack was that? After all, you two didn't start your own company. You're a number cruncher, and Rebecca sells dresses, and …

Rebecca: I think we need to stop this right now, and the four of us need to decide once and for all who is doing what!

Katie: Four of us? Wasn't our team supposed to have five people? Where's that other woman? The one from Vietnam? Parisa? Prana? Whatever her name is?

At this point, Professor Bowell, the group's advisor, walks in and tells them that the team is to be disbanded. Pranarisha had walked out of the group meeting (without anyone noticing) and informed Dr. Bowell that she just couldn't take it any longer. She had come here to learn how to run an organization more efficiently and how to work with businesspeople. However, she was so disheartened by the way the group was acting, she was going to quit the program. This was the first time in over 10 years that Dr. Bowell had heard of anyone quitting the program in the first week because of the behavior of the members of her team. The advisor just didn't see any way that this group of individuals could get their act together to become a functioning team.

Discussion Questions

1. What happened with the A-Team? Why did the group process break down? What dimensions of diversity were responsible for the conflict?
2. Describe which barriers to effectively managing diversity were present in this situation.
3. What could have been done to manage the group process better?

---

team exercise

What Is It Like to Be Different?

One reason people have a difficult time dealing with diversity in others or understanding why it is important to value and respect diversity is that most people spend most of their lives in environments where everyone is similar to them on important dimensions. Many people have seldom been in a situation in which they felt they didn't belong or didn't know the "rules." The purpose of this exercise is to have you experience such a situation and open up a dialogue with others about what it feels like to be different and what you can personally learn from this experience to become better at managing diversity in the future.

STEP 1: Choose an event that you would not normally attend and at which you will likely be in the minority on some important dimension. Attend the event.

- You can go with a friend who would normally attend the event, but not one who will also be in a minority.
- Make sure you pick a place where you will be safe and where you are sure you will be welcomed, or at least tolerated. You may want to check with your instructor about your choice.
- Do not call particular attention to yourself. Just observe what is going on and how you feel.

Some of you may find it easy to have a minority experience, since you are a minority group member in your everyday life. Others may have a more difficult time. Here are some examples of events to consider attending:

- A religious service for a religion totally different from your own.
- A sorority or fraternity party where the race of members is mostly different from your own.
- A political rally where the politics are different from your own.

STEP 2: After attending the event, write down your answers to the following questions:

1. How did you feel being in a minority situation? Did different aspects of your self-identity become salient? Do you think others who are in minority situations feel as you did?
2. What did you learn about the group you visited? Do you feel differently about this group now?
3. What did people do that made you feel welcome? What did people do that made you feel self-conscious?

4. Could you be an effective team member in this group? How would your differences with group members impact on your ability to function in this group?
5. What did you learn about managing diversity from this exercise?

STEP 3: Discuss the results of the exercise in a group as assigned by the instructor.

Endnotes

1. Bamattre, W. (former LAFD Fire Chief), as reported in Richardson, L. 2006. Audit faults fire department. *Los Angeles Times*, January 27, B.4.
2. See, for example, Ball, P., Monaco, G., Schmeling, J., Schartz, H., Blanck, P. 2005. Disability as diversity in *Fortune* 100 companies. *Behavioral Sciences and Law*, 23: 97–121; Jolna, K.A. 2003. Beyond race and gender? Doctoral Dissertation. Atlanta, GA: Emory University; Society of Human Resources Management. 1997. *SHRM survey of diversity of programs*. Alexandria, VA: Society for Human Resources Management.
3. Samdahl, E. November 6, 2009. "Most Companies Don't Measure the Bottom-Line Impact of Diversity Programs," at http://hrmtoday.com.; Campbell, T. 2003. Diversity in depth. *HRMagazine*, 48(3): 152.
4. Johnson, K. 2007. Kevin Johnson, Diversity Executive Workgroup Sponsor, on executive commitment. At http://www.microsoft.com/about/diversity/exec.mspx.
5. Schneider, B., Goldstein, H.W., & Smith, D.B. 1995. The ASA framework: An update. *Personnel Psychology*, 48: 747–773.
6. Ely, R.J., & Thomas, D.A. 2001. Cultural diversity at work: The effects of diversity perspectives on work group processes and outcomes. *Administrative Science Quarterly*, 46: 229–274.
7. See, for example, Kochan, T., Bezrukova, K., Ely, R., Jackson, S., Joshi, S., Jehn, K., Leonard, J., Levine, D., & Thomas, D. 2003. The effects of diversity on business performance: Report of the diversity research network. *Human Resource Management*, 42: 3–21.
8. For additional commentary on the various dimensions, see the following: Ball, C., & Haque, A. 2003. Diversity in religious practice: Implications of Islamic values in the public workplace. *Public Personnel Management*, 32: 315–328; Bantel, K.A., & Jackson, S.E. 1989. Top management and innovations in banking: Does the composition of the top team make a difference? *Strategic Management Journal*, 10: 107–124; Barsade, S.G., Ward, A.J., Turner, J.D.F., & Sonnenfeld, J.A. 2000. To your heart's content: A model of affective diversity in top management teams. *Administrative Science Quarterly*, 45: 802–837; Cummings, J.N. 2004. Work groups, structural diversity, and knowledge sharing in a global organization. *Management Science*, 50: 352–365; Ely, R.J., & Thomas, D.A. 2001. Cultural diversity at work: The effects of diversity perspectives on work group processes and outcomes. *Administrative Science Quarterly*, 46: 229–274; Kochan et al., The effects of diversity on business performance; Richard, O.C., Ford, D., & Ismail, K. 2006. Exploring the performance effects of visible attribute diversity: The moderating role of span of control and organizational life cycle. *International Journal of Human Resource Management*, 17: 2091–2109.
9. Konrad, A.M. 2003. Special issue introduction: Defining the domain of workplace diversity scholarship. *Group and Organization Management*, 28: 4–18.
10. Williams, K.Y., & O'Reilly, C.A. 1998. Demography and diversity in organizations: A review of 40 years of research. In L.L. Cummings & B.M. Staw (Eds.), *Research in Organizational Behavior*, 20: 77–140. Greenwich, CT: JAI Press, p. 81.
11. Ibid.
12. See, for example, Jehn, K.A., Northcraft, G.B., & Neale, M.A. 1999. Why differences make a difference: A field study of diversity, conflict, and performance in groups. *Administrative Science Quarterly*, 44: 741–763.
13. Kanter, R.M. 1977. *Men and women of the corporation*. New York: Basic Books.
14. Texas Instruments. 2009. Diversity and inclusion. At http://www.ti.com/corp/docs/csr/empwellbeing/diversity.
15. Microsoft. 2007. Message from Claudette Whiting. At http://www.microsoft.com/about/diversity/fromoffice.mspx?pf=true.
16. Bank of America. 2007. Fact sheets. At http://careers.bankofamerica.com/learnmore/factsheets.asp.
17. U.S. Department of Labor. 2002. Facts on Executive Order 11246—Affirmative Action. At www.dol.gov/esa/regs/compliance/ofccp/aa.htm.
18. Thomas, R.R., Jr. 1992. Managing diversity: A conceptual framework. In S.E. Jackson & Associates (Eds.), *Diversity in the workplace*. New York: Guilford Press, pp. 306–317.
19. Cox, T.H., Jr. 1993. *Cultural diversity in organizations: Theory, research, and practice*. San Francisco, CA: Berrett-Koehler Publishers.
20. Gilbert, J.A., & Ivancevich, J.M. 2000. Valuing diversity: A tale of two organizations. *Academy of Management Review*, 14: 93–106.
21. Farh, J.L., Dobbins, G.H., & Cheng, B. 1991. Cultural relativity in action: A comparison of self-ratings made by Chinese and U.S. workers. *Personnel Psychology*, 44: 129–147.
22. Cox, *Cultural diversity in organizations*.
23. See, for example, Campbell, T. 2003. Diversity in depth. *HRMagazine*, 48(3): 152.
24. Farouky, J. 2007. The many faces of Europe. *Time International*, 169 (9): 16–20.
25. U.S. Department of Labor. 2000. Working in the 21st century. At http://www.bls.gov/opub/home.htm.
26. U.S. Equal Employment Opportunity Commission. 2003. Occupational employment in private industry by race/ethnic group/sex, and by industry. At http://www.eeoc.gov/stats/jobpat/2003/national.html.
27. U.S. Department of Labor, Working in the 21st century.
28. Ibid.

29. Ibid.

30. Bureau of Labor Statistics. 2005. Economic and employment projections. At http://www.bls.gov/news.release/ecopro.toc.htm.

31. Ibid.

32. See, for example, Jackson, S.E., & Alvarez, E.B. 1992. Working through diversity as a strategic imperative. In S.E. Jackson & Associates (Eds.), *Diversity in the workplace,* pp. 13–29.

33. U.S. Department of Commerce. 2007. FT900: U.S. International trade in goods and services. At http://www.census. gov/foreign-trade/Press-Release/current_press_release/press.html#current.

34. Ibid.

35. Hitt, M.A., Ireland, D.I., & Hoskisson. 2007. *Strategic management: Competitiveness and globalization* (7th ed.). Stamford, CT: Thompson Learning.

36. Whole Foods Market. 2007. Our core values. At http://www. wholefoodsmarket.com/company/corevalues.html.

37. Cox, T.H., & Blake, S. 1991. Managing cultural diversity: Implications for organizational competitiveness. *Academy of Management Executive,* 5(3) 45–56; Jackson & Alvarez, Working through diversity as a strategic imperative.

38. Eisenberger, R., Huntington, R., Hutchison, S., & Sowa, D. 1986. Perceived organizational support. *Journal of Applied Psychology,* 71: 500–507; Eisenberger, R., Fasolo, P., & Davis-LaMastro, V. 1990. Perceived organizational support and employee diligence, commitment, and innovation. *Journal of Applied Psychology,* 75: 51–59.

39. Cox, *Cultural diversity in organizations;* McKay, P.F., Avery, D.R., & Morris, M.A. 2008. Mean racial differences in employee sales performance: The moderating role of diversity climate. *Personnel Psychology,* 61:349–374.

40. Hicks-Clarke, D., & Iles, P. 2000. Climate for diversity and its effects on career and organizational perceptions. *Personnel Review,* 29: 324–347.

41. For research on these outcomes, see: Colquitt, J.A., Conlon, D.E., Wesson, M.J., Porter, C.O.L.H., & Ng, K.Y. 2001. Justice at the millennium: A meta-analytic review of 25 years of organizational justice research. *Journal of Applied Psychology,* 86: 425–445; Goldman, B.M. 2001. Toward an understanding of employment discrimination claiming by terminated workers: Integration of organizational justice and social information processing theories. *Personnel Psychology,* 54: 361–386; Goldman, B.M. 2003. The application of referent cognitions theory to legal-claiming by terminated workers: The role of organizational justice and anger. *Journal of Management,* 29: 705–728; Skarlicki, D.P., & Folger, R. 2003. Broadening our understanding of organizational retaliatory behavior. In R.W. Griffin & A.M. O'Leary-Kelly (Eds.), The *darkside of organizational behavior.* San Francisco, CA: Jossey-Bass, pp. 373–402.

42. Kossek, E.E., & Zonia, S.C. 1993. Assessing diversity climate: A field-study of reactions to employer efforts to promote diversity. *Journal of Organizational Behavior,* 14: 61–81.

43. Mollica, K.A. 2003. The influence of diversity context on white men's and racial minorities' reactions to disproportionate group harm. *Journal of Social Psychology,* 143: 415–431. Jehn, Northcraft, & Neale, Why differences make a difference.

44. Bantel, K.A., & Jackson, S.E. 1989. Top management and innovations in banking: Does the composition of the top team make a difference? *Strategic Management Journal,* 10: 107–124; Jackson, S.E. 1992. Consequences of group composition for the interpersonal dynamics of strategic issue processing. *Advances in Strategic Management,* 8: 345–382.

45. For research related to these dimensions, see: Hambrick, D.C., Cho, S.T., & Chen, M.J. 1996. The influence of top management team heterogeneity on firm's competitive moves. *Administrative Science Quarterly,* 41: 659–684; Jackson, S.E., May, K., & Whitney, K. 1995. Diversity in decision making teams. In R.A. Guzzo & E. Salas (Eds.), *Team effectiveness and decision making in organizations.* San Francisco, CA: Jossey-Bass, pp. 204–261; Jehn, Northcraft, & Neale, Why differences make a difference; Wood, W. 1987. Meta-analysis of sex differences in group performance. *Psychological Bulletin,* 102: 53–71; Zajac, E.J., Golden, B.R., & Shortell, S.M. 1991. New organizational forms for enhancing innovation: The case of internal corporate joint ventures. *Management Science,* 37: 170–184.

46. Grensing-Phophal, L. 2002. Reaching for diversity: What minority workers hope to get from diversity programs is what all employees want in the workplace. *HRMagazine,* 47 (5): 52–56.

47. Williams & O'Reilly, Demography and diversity in organizations.

48. Van Knippenberg, D., & Schippers, M.C. 2007. Work group diversity. *Annual Review of Psychology,* 58: 515–541.

49. See, for example, Li, J.T., & Hambrick, D.C. 2005. Factional groups: A new vantage on demographic faultlines, conflict, and disintegration in work teams. *Academy of Management Journal,* 48: 794–813; Molleman, E. 2005. Diversity in demographic characteristics, abilities and personality traits: Do faultlines affect team functioning? *Group Decision and Negotiation,* 14: 173–193; Rico, R., Molleman, E., Sanchez-Manzanares, M., & Van der Vegt, G.S. 2007. The effects of diversity faultlines and team task autonomy on decision quality and social integration. *Journal of Management,* 33: 111–132; Sawyer, J.E., Houlette, M.A., & Yeagley, E.L. 2006. Decision performance and diversity structure: Comparing faultlines in convergent, crosscut, and racially homogeneous groups. *Organizational Behavior and Human Decision Processes,* 99: 1–15.

50. Williams & O'Reilly, Demography and diversity in organizations.

51. See, for example, Richard, O.C., Kochan, T.A., & McMillan-Capehart. 2002. The impact of visible diversity on organizational effectiveness: Disclosing the contents in Pandora's black box. *Journal of Business and Management,* 8: 265–291; Pelled, L.H. 1996. Demographic diversity, conflict, and work group outcomes: An intervening process theory. *Organization Science,* 7: 615–631.

52. Williams & O'Reilly, Demography and diversity in organizations.

53. Hackman, J.R. 2002. *Leading teams: Setting the stage for great performances.* Boston, MA: Harvard Business School Press.

54. Richard, Kochan, & McMillan-Capehart, The impact of visible diversity on organizational effectiveness.

55. Ibid.

56. Cox, *Cultural diversity in organizations;* Cox & Blake, Managing cultural diversity.

57. Richard, O.C. 2000. Racial diversity, business strategy, and firm performance: A resource based view. *Academy of Management Journal,* 43: 164–177.

58. Kochan, T., Bezrukova, K., Ely, R., Jackson, S., Joshi, A., Jehn, K. Leonard, J., Levine, D., & Thomas, D. 2003. The effects

of diversity on business performance: Report of the Diversity Research Network. *Human Resource Management,* 42: 3–21.

59. See, for example, Fletcher, A.A. 2000. Business and race: Only halfway there. *Fortune,* 141 (5): 76–77.

60. See, for example, Westphal, J., & Zajac, E. 1997. Defections from the inner circle: Social exchange, reciprocity and the diffusion of board independence in U.S. corporations. *Administrative Science Quarterly,* 42: 161–183.

61. Sellers, P. 2004. By the numbers: Women and profits. *Fortune,* at http://www.fortune.com/fortune/subs/article/0,15114,582783, 00.html.

62. Siciliano, J.I. 1996. The relationship of board member diversity to organizational performance. *Journal of Business Ethics,* 15: 1313–1320.

63. Hillman, A.J., Cannella, A.A., Jr., & Harris, I.C. 2002. Women and racial minorities in the boardroom: How do directors differ? *Journal of Management,* 28: 747–763.

64. Ibid.

65. Bantel, & Jackson, Top management and innovations in banking; Hambrick, Cho, & Chen, The influence of top management team heterogeneity on firm's competitive moves.

66. Wright, P., Ferris, S.P., & Kroll, M. 1995. Competitiveness through management of diversity: Effects on stock price evaluation. *Academy of Management Journal,* 38: 272–287.

67. Cowell, A. 2005. What Britain can tell France about rioters. *The New York Times,* November 20, 4.4.

68. Dovidio, J.F., Gaertner, S.L., Kawakami, K., & Hodson, G. 2002. Why can't we just get along? Interpersonal biases and interracial distrust. *Cultural Diversity and Ethnic Minority Psychology,* 8: 88–102.

69. Bobo, L.D. 2001. Racial attitudes and relations at the close of the twentieth century. In N.J. Smelser, W.J. Wilson, & F. Mitchell (Eds.), *Racial trends and their consequences (Vol. 1).* Washington, DC: National Academic Press, pp. 264–301.

70. McConahay, J.B. 1986. Modern racism, ambivalence, and the modern racism scale. In J.F. Dovidio & S.L. Gaertner (Eds.), *Prejudice, discrimination, and racism.* Orlando, FL: Academic Press, pp. 91–125.

71. Dovidio, J.F., & Gaertner, S.L. 2000. Aversive racism and selection decisions: 1989 and 1999. *Psychological Science,* 11: 319–323.

72. For example research, see: Cleveland, J.N., Vescio, T.K., & Barnes-Farrell, J.L. 2005. Gender discrimination in organizations. In R.L. Dipboye, & A. Colella (Eds.), *Discrimination at work: The psychological and organizational bases.* Mahwah, NJ: Lawrence Erlbaum; Colella, A., & Varma, A. 2001. The impact of subordinate disability on leader-member exchange dynamics. *Academy of Management Journal,* 44: 304–315; Dovidio, J.F., Gaertner, S.L., Anastasio, P.A., & Sanitaso, R. 1992. Cognitive and motivational bases of bias: The implications of aversive racism for attitudes towards Hispanics. In S. Knouse, P. Rosenfeld, & A. Culbertson (Eds.). *Hispanics in the workplace.* Newbury Park, CA: Sage, pp. 75–106; Hebl, M.R., Bigazzi Foster, J., & Dovidio, J.F. 2002. Formal and interpersonal discrimination: A field study of bias toward homosexual applicants. *Personality and Social Psychology Bulletin,* 28: 815–825.

73. Dipboye, R.L. & Colella, A. 2005. The dilemmas of workplace discrimination. In R.L. Dipboye & A. Colella (Eds.), *Discrimination*

74. Cox, *Cultural diversity in organizations.*

75. Crocker, J., Fiske, S.T., & Taylor, S.E. 1984. Schematic bases of belief change. In J.R. Eiser (Ed.), *Attitudinal judgment.* New York: Springer-Verlag, pp. 197–226; Weber, R., & Crocker, J. 1983. Cognitive processes in the revision of stereotypic beliefs. *Journal of Personality and Social Psychology,* 45: 961–977.

76. von Heppel, W., Sekaquaptewa, D., & Vargas, P. 1995. On the role of encoding processes in stereotype maintenance. In M.P. Zanna (Ed.), *Advances in experimental social psychology, Vol. 27.* San Diego, CA: Academic Press, pp. 177–254.

77. Fiske, S.T. 1998. Stereotyping, prejudice, and discrimination. In D.T. Gilbert, S.T. Fiske, & G. Lindzey (Eds.), *The handbook of social psychology, Vol. 2* (4th ed.). New York: McGraw-Hill, pp. 357–411.

78. Cox, *Cultural diversity in organizations.*

79. Helft, M. 2007. Xerox's strategy pays off with a new search venture. *The New York Times,* February 9, C.3; Maney, K. 2006. Mulcahy traces steps of Xerox's comeback. *USA Today,* September 21, 4B.

80. Ireland, R.D., Hoskisson, R.E., & Hitt, M.A. 2006. *Understanding business strategy.* Mason, OH: South-western Publishing; Stone, B. 2007. eBay beats the estimates for 4th-quarter earnings. *New York Times,* January 25, C.3; Vara, V. 2007. eBay's strong earnings, outlook help to quiet critics, for now. *Wall Street Journal,* January 25, A.3.

81. Brewer, M.B., & Miller, N. 1984. Beyond the contact hypothesis: Theoretical perspectives on desegregation. In N. Miller & M.B. Brewer (Eds.), *Groups in contact.* San Diego, CA: Academic Press, pp. 281–302; Tajfel, H. 1978. *Differentiation between social groups: Studies in the social psychology of intergroup relations.* San Diego, CA: Academic Press; Ashforth, B., & Mael, F. 1989. Social identity theory and the organization. *Academy of Management Review,* 14: 20–39.

82. Abrams, D., & Hogg, M.A. 1990. An introduction to the social identity approach. In D. Abrams & M.A. Hogg (Eds.), *Social identity theory: Constructive and critical advances.* New York: Springer-Verlag, pp. 1–9.

83. Cox, *Cultural diversity in organizations.*

84. McGuire, W.J., McGuire, C.V., Child, P., & Fujioka, T. 1978. Salience of ethnicity in the spontaneous self-concept as a function of one's ethnic distinctiveness in the social environment. *Journal of Personality and Social Psychology,* 36: 511–520.

85. Cox, *Cultural diversity in organizations.*

86. Ely, R.J. 1994. The effects of organizational demographics and social identity on relationships among professional women. *Administrative Science Quarterly,* 39: 203–239.

87. Cited in Slay, H.S. 2003. Spanning two worlds: Social identity and emergent African American leaders. *Journal of Leadership and Organizational Studies,* 9: 56–66.

88. Cox, *Cultural diversity in organizations.*

89. Abrams & Hogg, An introduction to the social identity approach.

90. Turner, J.C. 1975. Social comparison and social identity: Some prospects for intergroup behavior. *European Journal of Social Psychology,* 5: 5–34.

91. Hogg, M.A., & Terry, D.J. 2000. Social identity and self-categorization processes in organizational contexts. *Academy of Management Review,* 25: 121–140.

92. Ibid.

93. French, J.R.P., & Raven, B. 1959. The bases of social power. In D. Cartwright (Ed.), *Social power.* Ann Arbor: University of Michigan, Institute for Social Research, pp. 150–167; Pfeffer, J., & Salancik, G.R. 1978. *The external control of organizations: A resource dependence view.* New York: Harper and Row.

94. Sidananius, J., & Pratto, F. 1999. *Social dominance.* Cambridge, UK: Cambridge University Press.

95. Ibid.

96. Kalkhoff, W., & Barnum, C. 2000. The effects of status-organizing and social identity processes on patterns of social influence. *Social Psychology Quarterly,* 63: 95–115.

97. Konard, A.M. 2003. Special issue introduction: Defining the domain of workplace diversity scholarship. *Group and Organizational Management,* 28: 4–18.

98. For additional details, see Deogun, N. Coke was told in '95 of need for diversity. *Wall Street Journal,* May 20, A.3; McKay, B. 2000. Coke settles bias suit for $192.5 million. *Wall Street Journal,* November 17, A.3.

99. U.S. Equal Employment Opportunity Commission. 2005. Occupational employment in private industry by race/ethnic group/sex, and by industry. At http://archive.eeoc.gov/stats/jobpat/2005/national.html.

100. Kanter, *Men and women of the corporation.*

101. Winters, M.F. 2003. Globalization presents both opportunities and challenges for diversity. At http://search.shrm.org/search?q=cache:8b6YiQjDjFoJ:www.shrm.org/diversity/library_published/nonIC/CMS_012382.asp+++globalization1challenges1diversity&access=p&output=xml_no_dtd&ie=UTF-8&lr=&client=shrm_frontend&num=10&site=&proxystylesheet=shrm_frontend&oe=ISO-8859-1.

102. U.S. Department of Commerce and Vice President Al Gore's National Partnership for Reinventing Government Benchmarking Study. 1998. Best practices in achieving workplace diversity. Washington, DC: U.S. Department of Commerce.

103. Starbucks. 2007. Starbucks mission statement. At http://www.starbucks.com/aboutus/environment.asp.

104. Ford Motor Company. 2007. Valuing diversity. At http://www.mycareer.ford.com/ONTHETEAM.ASP?CID=15.

105. Jayne, M.E.A., & Dipboye, R.L. 2004. Leveraging diversity to improve business performance: Research findings and recommendations for organizations. *Human Resource Management,* 43: 409–424.

106. Cox, T.H. 2001. *Creating the multicultural organization: A strategy for capturing the power of diversity.* San Francisco: Jossey-Bass.

organizational behavior in a global context

exploring behavior in action

McDonald's Thinks Globally and Acts Locally

In 1948, brothers Richard and Maurice McDonald opened the first McDonald's restaurant in San Bernardino, California. Over the next decade, hundreds of McDonald's restaurants were built alongside the new interstate highway systems in the United States. McDonald's was one of the first restaurants to make fast food available to the newly mobile American population. In 1967, McDonald's decided to go international and opened its first restaurant outside the United States in Richmond, British Columbia. Today there are over 32,000 McDonald's restaurants in 122 countries. And, its international operations have become highly important to McDonald's financial performance. For example, its restaurants in Europe now produce more revenues than its restaurants in the United States, despite the fact that McDonald's has more units in the United States. McDonald's success in international operations is partially because it has adapted to the cultural differences in the various foreign locations of its restaurants.

Trying to maintain a global brand is difficult because of the different cultural expectations experienced across different countries. It is important to ensure a positive reputation for the company and also maintain the quality of its products. So, McDonald's had to build and sustain a reputation for quality products and efficient service globally while simultaneously meeting consumer expectations across different cultures. McDonald's developed a competitive advantage because the company has taken steps to know, understand, and service customers' needs without compromising its core strengths (fast, easy, clean meals for families to enjoy). An example of McDonald's adaptation to cultural differences is exhibited in how McDonald's dispenses its food products in order to respect and serve its Israeli customers. All meat served in McDonald's restaurants located in Israel is 100 percent kosher. McDonald's operates both kosher and nonkosher restaurants in Israel. The kosher restaurants are closed on Saturday and on religious holidays, while the nonkosher restaurants remain open for those customers who do not

knowledge objectives

After reading this chapter, you should be able to:

1. Define *globalization* and discuss the forces that influence this phenomenon.
2. Discuss three types of international involvement by associates and managers and describe problems that can arise with each.
3. Explain how international involvement by associates and managers varies across firms.
4. Describe high-involvement management in the international arena, emphasizing the adaptation of this management approach to different cultures.
5. Identify and explain the key ethical issues in international business.

strictly adhere to kosher law. In the kosher restaurant, the menu includes no dairy products and food is prepared in accordance with kosher law. In addition, McDonald's supports the local communities by obtaining many of its food products (e.g., beef, potatoes, lettuce, etc.) from local suppliers. In Israel, it obtains 80 percent of its food supplies within the country.

To display the efficiency and cleanliness of its restaurants in Egypt, McDonald's operates an open-door policy, in which customers are invited to visit their kitchens to view the preparation of the food. In this way, consumers can view how McDonald's restaurants prepare their food efficiently, maintaining quality and in ways that meet high health and safety standards. For example, employees must wash their hands with disinfectant soap every 30 minutes and continuously wash and disinfect utensils. The tours provided to customers fulfill a process of transparency and have elicited highly positive customer responses and expressions of appreciation.

©ZAHID HUSSEIN/Reuters/Landov LLC

Other examples of how McDonald's adapts to local culture and ways of life include vegetarian meals in India, with local creations such as the McPuff and the McVeggie. Today, 70 percent of the menu in India has been altered to meet the customers' needs and desires. In Europe, McDonald's introduced a menu featuring salads, fruit, and the option of substituting carrots in Happy Meals for French fries, a menu modification made to appeal to health-conscious consumers. These same menu items have been offered in the United States as well. So, while the menu may be different in some ways, the McDonald's experience around the world is consistent by offering quality, great service, cleanliness, and value. It is equally important to develop a culturally appropriate strategy for a new international location. Innovation is successful when it is culturally appropriate. In Brazil, McDonald's promotes an afternoon meal rather than a lunch meal. This change was made because Brazilians prefer their main meal at midday, often eating at a leisurely pace with business associates.

There are many abroad who are concerned about having companies like McDonald's expand their restaurants globally, such as the concerns expressed about a McDonald's restaurant opening in the food court adjoining France's famous Louvre museum. Countering some of these concerns is McDonald's commitment to important local social concerns. For example, McDonald's supports Conservation International's efforts to protect wild pandas, a threatened species. Taking this further, McDonald's announced a local treasures program in China to encourage children to learn about their country's special environment and rare animals. Another example is McDonald's major donation to the Dubai Autism Center as a part of McDonald's World Children's Day campaign.

McDonald's is regularly adapting its restaurants and marketing tactics to reflect cultural, architectural, and regional differences within each country. Even in the United States, McDonald's adapts to local communities. In Maine, McDonald's offers lobster rolls. And in Michigan, customers can purchase Halal McNuggets, chicken that is processed under strict religious supervision in order to cater to the 150,000 Muslims who live in the Detroit area. Thus, McDonald's is a prime example of a company that thinks globally and acts locally.

Sources: "Welcome to McDonald's Israel", McDonald's, Nov. 22, 2009, www.mcdonalds.com; E. Ganley. 2009. "McDonald's to Become Mona Lisa's New Neighbor," *Business Week*, Oct. 5, www.businessweek.com; S.E.D. Aloui & Y. Genena. 2009. "McDonald's Egypt continues the 'Open Door' program," AMEinfo, June 28, at http://www.ameinfo.com; N. El Ajou. 2008. "McDonald's UAE Concludes its 7th World Children's Day Campaign," AMEinfo, Dec. 24, 2008; K. Capell. 2008. "A Golden Recipe for McDonald's Europe," *Business Week*, July 17; "McDonalds's and Conservation International Team Up to Protect China's Panda Habitats", McDonalds, June 10, 2008, at http://www.crmcdonalds.com; Nini Bhan and Brad Nemer. 2006. "Brand Magic in India," *Business Week*, May 8, at http://www.businessweek.com; Beth Carney. 2005. "In Europe, the Fat Is in the Fire," *Business Week*, Feb. 8, at http://www.businessweek.com; Conrad P. Kottak. 2003. McDonald's in Brazil: Culturally Appropriate Marketing, *Ethnographic Solutions*, at http://www.ethnographic-solutions.com.

the strategic importance of Organizational Behavior in a Global Context

The *Exploring Behavior in Action* discussion of McDonald's shows how one firm operates on the world stage and emphasizes the importance of cross-cultural knowledge and skills. Because of substantial competition and differing cultural expectations across the many countries in which McDonald's has restaurants, the company has strong needs for flexibility and for efficiency in resource use. McDonald's has developed a global reputation for providing clean restaurants and fast and easy meals for value-conscious families. From strategic locations, the firm develops, produces, sells, and supports its products for the world marketplace. To be successful, however, this firm must be especially attentive to local cultural values and desired foods. McDonald's always provides some consistent products on its menu regardless of location (e.g., the Big Mac) but it also provides menu items adapted to the local cultural tastes (such as vegetable meals in India and kosher foods in Israel). Obviously, McDonald's has trained its managers to be sensitive to local culture and yet to take advantage of global efficiencies. Actions such as those used by McDonald's to take advantage of the different international markets opened due to globalization have led to higher overall firm performance.[1]

To create cost advantages, to pursue growth, or to spread risk across different markets, many firms have adopted strategies that call for investment in foreign countries. Such involvement can take many forms, including the creation of company-owned manufacturing or back-office facilities, company-owned marketing and sales units, and/or alliances with companies based in a particular foreign country. In all cases, effectively handling cross-country cultural differences is crucial. Executing competitive strategies would be impossible without an understanding of how these differences affect day-to-day relationships among associates and managers, as well as relationships with external parties (such as suppliers and customers).[2]

One of the most famous examples of a corporate failure that emphasizes the importance of cultural differences is Walt Disney Company's attempt to execute a strategy involving efficient operations and exceptional customer service in its theme park located close to Paris.[3] American leaders of the Euro Disney project failed to understand some European workplace norms that produced a less friendly approach to guests in the park. Disney leaders also failed to anticipate the uproar over grooming and dress requirements for associates, including "appropriate undergarments," and they did not recognize the potential for conflict between individuals of different nationalities. One of the 1,000 associates and lower-level managers who departed in the first nine weeks of Euro Disney's operation commented, "I don't think [non-European supervisors] realized what Europeans were like." Concerning the park, a critic expressed the feelings of the French elite: "A horror made of cardboard, plastic, and appalling colors; a construction of hardened chewing gum and idiotic folklore taken straight out of comic books written for obese Americans."[4] Failure to fully appreciate and respond to cultural differences contributed to a disastrous early period for Euro Disney. Its performance suffered, but having learned several hard lessons, the company improved its practices in the park and increased its performance as well.

Because of the importance of globalization and the related diversity and ethical issues it poses, we present examples and applications involving firms operating in multiple countries throughout the book. In this chapter, we discuss these issues in depth. We open the chapter with a discussion of globalization, addressing the opportunities and challenges that globalization presents for nations and firms. Next, we discuss the ways in which associates and managers can deal with international problems and the pitfalls to avoid in their activities. A discussion of high-involvement management follows, with a focus on how this management approach can be tailored to different countries and regions of the world. Finally, we describe ethical issues frequently confronted by firms with substantial international involvement.

Forces of Globalization

In a global economy, products, services, people, technologies, and financial capital move relatively freely across national borders.[5] Tariffs, currency laws, travel restrictions, immigration restrictions, and other barriers to these international flows become less difficult to manage. Essentially, a global economy provides firms with a unified world market in which to sell products and services, as well as a unified world market for acquiring the resources needed to create those products and services.

globalization

The trend toward a unified global economy where national borders mean relatively little.

Globalization, the trend toward a more global economy, has increased substantially since 1980. Direct foreign investment by firms based in developed countries has increased. While several developed countries suffered a recession early in the twenty-first century, there were healthy increases in direct foreign investments made by them through 2007. In fact, such investments reached an all-time high in 2007. In this year, the total stock of direct foreign investments achieved $15 trillion in value.[6] However, the global economic recession led to a reduction in the total amount of direct foreign investments in 2008 and 2009. Yet, with the recovery, projections call for increases in direct foreign investment in 2010 and several years beyond.[7] These investments represent increased interest in producing goods and services in foreign countries. Exporting goods and services into other countries increased over the same time period. Exports have grown at a high rate in recent years except during the major global recession.[8] Interestingly, in recent years, significant amounts of foreign investment has been focused on emerging-economy countries such as China and India. Furthermore, these emerging economies have been making major foreign investments in other countries. Their growing economic power is evident in the projections that within the next few decades China and India are expected to have the largest and third largest economies, respectively, in the world.[9] The results of globalization are evident in the fact that major multinational firms obtain almost 55 percent of their sales from outside their home country and almost 50 percent of their assets and associates reside outside of their home country.[10] Clearly, goods and services flowed across borders in record amounts at the end of the twentieth century and early in the twenty-first century, with firms such as Toyota leading the way.

Many national leaders promote globalization as a means for economic growth inside their countries as well as in the world as a whole. Most economists agree that a highly global economy would be beneficial for most countries. Goods, services, and the resources needed to produce them freely flowing across borders likely reduce the costs of doing business, resulting in economic stimulation.[11] It has been estimated that genuine free trade (i.e., trade with no tariffs) in manufactured goods among the United States, Europe, and Japan would result in a 5 to 10 percent annual increase in the economic output of these three areas. Genuine free trade in services would increase economic output by an additional 15 to 20 percent.[12]

culture

Shared values and taken-for-granted assumptions that govern acceptable behavior and thought patterns in a country and give a country much of its uniqueness.

Despite the potential economic benefits, officials in a number of nations have expressed concerns about globalization's long-term effects on societal culture.[13] **Culture** involves shared values and taken-for-granted assumptions about how to act and think.[14] Many fear that unique cultures around the world will disappear over time if the world becomes one unified market for goods and services. They argue that cultural distinctiveness—indeed what makes a country special—will disappear as similar products and services are sold worldwide.[15] Individuals with these concerns took notice when a Taiwanese Little League baseball team playing in the United States was comforted by a McDonald's restaurant because it reminded them of home.[16] In developing nations, there are also concerns over labor exploitation and natural resource depletion. In wealthy nations, there are concerns over the export of jobs to low-wage countries and the possibility that wealthy nations ultimately will need to lower their wage structures in order to compete in a truly global economy.[17]

From the perspective of an individual company, there are many reasons to consider substantial international involvement (see Exhibit 3-1). First, a firm may want to expand sales efforts across borders in order to sustain growth. Opportunities for growth may have been exhausted in the home country (e.g., if the market is saturated), but owners, business analysts, and the media often demand continuing sales and profit growth.[18] Second, a firm may be able to reduce its business risk by selling its products and services in a number of different countries. By diversifying its sales across a number of regions of the world, a company may be able to offset bad economic times when they occur in one part of the world with good economic times in other parts of the world. Third, a firm may enjoy greater economies of scale by expanding its markets internationally. This applies most often to manufacturing firms. Hyundai, for example, could not develop operations with efficient scale by serving only the domestic South Korean automobile market.[19] To achieve a reasonable cost structure, the firm needed to build and sell more automobiles than the South Korean market could handle. The larger volume of automobiles manufactured and sold allows them to obtain quantity discounts on raw materials purchased and to spread their fixed costs across more autos, thereby reducing their cost per unit (increasing their profit margins). Fourth, when locating units internationally, a firm may enjoy location advantages such as low labor costs, specialized expertise, or other valuable resources.[20]

Clearly, globalization and the value to be gained from participating in international markets is changing the competitive landscape for many firms, regardless of their home base.[21] Even many smaller and younger firms are now participating in international markets. The openness of markets and advancing technology (and lower costs of this technology) provide opportunities for young and small firms as well as for older, larger, and established firms.[22] These opportunities in international markets have been prompted by changes in many countries' institutional environments. For example, several emerging-economy countries have reduced regulations to allow more foreign firms to enter their markets (e.g., China and India). In this way, their economies have grown larger and their firms have learned new capabilities, allowing them to compete more effectively in their home markets and abroad. Thus, the countries' institutional environments affect home and foreign country firms' strategies.[23] Institutional environments contribute to the opportunities and challenges depicted in Exhibit 3-1.

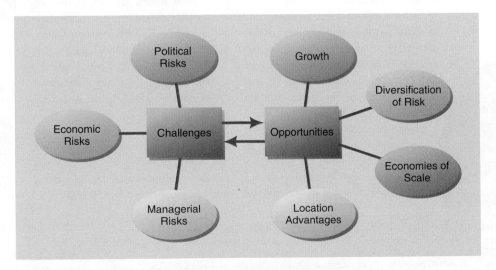

Exhibit 3-1   Opportunities and Challenges for Firms with International Involvement

MANAGERIAL ADVICE

Multinational Corporations Achieving Glocalization

Globalization has greatly increased the interactions among countries and cultures. The vast improvements in communication technologies (and transportation as well) have affected much of what we do across the world. The world's financial markets have become tightly integrated, as shown by the world recession in 2008–2009. The political actions of opening country markets and the entry into those markets by multinational corporations (MNCs) have jointly increased the amount and speed of globalization. MNCs sell more than $11 trillion in goods globally on an annual basis. And, although MNCs have been blamed for a number of ills (e.g., violation of workers' rights, harm to the natural environment, etc.), they have also enriched the fortunes of people in less-developed countries. MNCs have played a major role in the economic development in important regions of the world such as China, India, and even Latin America.

However, MNCs now face a number of challenges, including significant competition from major companies in emerging markets such as Tata, Cemex, and Lenova, among others. These companies are not only competing effectively in their home markets, but they are also developing capabilities (ability to successfully enter new foreign markets, building global resource bases) to become major forces in global markets. Thus, MNCs must not only develop major global capabilities but also must learn the local markets well and acquire knowledge from these countries/markets that can be diffused throughout the company to enhance their ability to compete in global markets. This is sometimes called glocalization.

The CEO of GE's business unit in India suggests that serving customers in 10 countries having significant cultural diversity in the managerial and professional associate ranks is a tremendous asset. He argues that the knowledge held by this group, especially the local insight, allows the company to be well positioned to exploit opportunities as they arise in local markets. In addition, using the insight afforded by the cultural diversity allows the management team to "see around the corner" regarding expectations for the future and thereby to stay ahead of the competition.

Procter & Gamble (P&G) has also learned to gain greater value from its international operations. Specifically, they design units and programs to help them acquire new knowledge available in certain countries and regions. They then use this knowledge to enrich their products, services, and processes in other regions of the world. In this way, they stay ahead of their global and local competitors. For example, in China, they have encouraged reluctant research and development (R&D) researchers to speak up and share their ideas with others. In so doing, they have enhanced their R&D output there and also added unique knowledge to their global R&D efforts.

These efforts are especially important because it is predicted that the Asian region, led by a strong China, will be the most influential geographic region for the global economy by 2020. And this means that Asian MNCs are also likely to be even more highly influential by this time. Thus, Western MNCs will experience increasing competitive challenges from this region of the world. They can only remain competitive by taking actions such as those noted by GE and P&G.

©Courtesy of Proctor & Gamble

Sources: "Earning staff's respect was pivotal for GE capital man," *Wall Street Journal*, Nov. 16, 2009, at http://www.wsj.com; V. Govindarajan. 2009. "The case for 'reverse innovation' now," *BusinessWeek*, Oct. 26, at http://www.businessweek.com; R.O. Crockett. 2009. "P&G gets reticent researchers to speak up," *BusinessWeek*, Oct. 2, at http://www.businessweek.com; "Asian multinational corporations poised for global success and Asian region may be world's most influential economy by 2020," *Fleishman-Hillard Point of View*, Sept. 10, 2009, at http://pov.fleishman.com; D. Patel. 2009. "Multinational corporations in an increasingly globalized world," *Prospect*, Feb. 3, at http://www.prospectjournal.ucsd.edu.

These powerful forces encourage many firms to expand into international markets, but there are substantial risks. These risks can be classified as political, economic, and managerial.[24]

- *Political risks* relate to instability in national governments, the threat of civil or international war, and the threat of state-sponsored terrorism. These risks create uncertainty, and they can result in the destruction of assets and disruption of resource flows.[25] One of the most difficult situations occurs when a government nationalizes an industry, meaning that it takes over the assets of private companies, often with little or no compensation provided to the firms.
- *Economic risks* relate to fluctuations in the value of foreign currencies and the possibility of sudden economic contraction in some countries.[26] When a foreign country's currency declines in value relative to the home country's currency, assets and earnings in that foreign country are worth less, and exporting to that country becomes more difficult, as exported goods cost more there.
- *Managerial risks* relate to the difficulties inherent in managing the complex resource flows required by most international firms.[27] Tariffs, logistics, and language issues can become a significant challenge as a firm does business in an increasing number of countries. Radically new marketing programs and distribution networks may be needed as firms enter new countries. Some executives and managers are better at managing these complexities than are others.

The *Managerial Advice* segment explains how managers develop their firm's capabilities to compete effectively in global markets. They must develop a global mindset but also understand local market requirements. The most effective firms such as GE and P&G enter markets with the intent to learn. Firms can gain valuable ideas in foreign markets that they can then use in business units competing in other regions of the world.[28] Multinational firms based in Western (developed) countries have a number of advantages. However, companies from Asia, particularly China and India, are building their resources and capabilities. They will be formidable competitors in the coming decade.

The Globalization Experience for Associates and Managers

For individual associates and managers, international exposure or experience can occur in several ways, which we discuss below. In each case, opportunities for personal learning, growth, and advancement are substantial. Several pitfalls, however, must be avoided.

Internationally Focused Jobs

An individual may work directly on international issues as part of her day-to-day job. Although dealing with finance issues, accounting concerns, information technology tasks, and so on can be challenging in a purely domestic context, adding an international dimension usually creates situations with significant complexity. Individuals who thrive on challenge are well suited to these environments. At Dow Chemical, for example, international finance activities are often demanding because of the firm's exposure to fluctuations in the value of many different countries' currencies. With manufacturing facilities in dozens of countries and sales in well over 100 countries, Dow faces substantial currency risk.

Associates and managers who hold internationally focused jobs are often members of geographically dispersed teams. Many of these teams complete work related to new marketing programs, new-product-development projects, and other nonroutine initiatives. Other teams focus on routine issues, such as product flow from central manufacturing facilities. In many cases, associates and managers working on geographically dispersed teams have different working and decision styles because of cultural differences. Some prefer starting meetings with social rather than business topics, others prefer an autocratic rather than an egalitarian team leader, and still others prefer indirect to direct confrontations. To facilitate their work, team members use a complex set of tools to communicate, including electronic mail, Internet chat rooms, company intranets, teleconferencing, videoconferencing, and perhaps occasional face-to-face meetings.[29] Individuals complete team-related tasks around the clock as they live and work in different time zones, creating additional coordination challenges.

Because international teams largely rely on electronically mediated communication to coordinate and accomplish their work, they are often referred to as **virtual electronic teams**.[30] Although virtual teams are efficient, a virtual world with little face-to-face communication combined with substantial cross-cultural differences sets the stage for misperceptions and misunderstandings. Small disagreements can escalate quickly, and trust can be strained. One study showed that virtual teams with substantial cross-cultural differences often exhibit lower trust than virtual teams with more cross-cultural similarities.[31] Low trust, suggesting little confidence that others will maintain their promises, be honest, and not engage in negative politics, is harmful to the team's efforts.[32] Researchers have discovered several potential negative outcomes for virtual teams with low trust, including unwillingness to cooperate, poor conflict resolution, few or no goals established, poor risk mitigation, and lack of adjustment to the virtual format for work.[33] Although trust is important for any group, it is particularly important for virtual teams because of the propensity for misunderstanding as well as the absence of traditional direct supervision.[34]

The initial communications of a virtual cross-cultural team may be particularly important in the development of trust. When early communication is task-focused, positive, and reciprocated (i.e., questions and inputs do not go unanswered), a phenomenon known as **swift trust** can occur.[35] Swift trust occurs when individuals who have little or no history of working together, but who have a clear task to accomplish, quickly develop trust in one another based on interpersonal communication. Although social communication (i.e., friendly, non-task-related) can help to maintain this trust, task-related exchanges that facilitate the team's progress are critical.[36]

In the face of possible trust issues, it is important for managers to help team members identify with the team. According to identity theory, when an individual identifies with a team, he feels connected to it, and he takes very seriously his role as a team member. Failure to identify with the team often results in withholding of effort on team projects, a common problem.[37] Steps can be taken to increase the chances that an individual will identify with the international team. First, it is important to provide training in international negotiating and conflict resolution.[38] Techniques that are sensitive to cultural differences and focused on collaborative outcomes work best. Exhibit 3-2 provides specific ideas on how managers can be sensitive to cultural differences. Second, it is important to have team members jointly develop a unified vision.[39] The shared experience of discussing the future of the team, its goals and aspirations, can draw people together. Finally, it is helpful for team members to spend some time in face-to-face meetings, especially early in a team's life.[40] Face-to-face meetings increase the chances that team members will identify personal

virtual electronic teams
Teams that rely heavily on electronically mediated communication rather than face-to-face meetings as the means to coordinate work.

swift trust
A phenomenon where trust develops rapidly based on positive, reciprocated task-related communications.

> **EXHIBIT 3-2**   **Learning about a Counterpart's Culture**
>
> - Don't attempt to identify another's culture too quickly. Common cues (name, physical appearance, language, accent, and location) may be unreliable. In a global economy and multicultural societies, some people are shaped by more than one culture.
>
> - Beware of the Western bias toward taking actions. In some cultures, thinking and talking affect relationships more than actions do.
>
> - Try to avoid the tendency to formulate simple perceptions of others' cultural values. Most cultures are highly complex, involving many dimensions.
>
> - Don't assume that your values are the best for the organization. For example, U.S. culture is individualistic, and this is often assumed to be productive. While individual competition and pride can be positive to some degree, cultural values in India and China emphasize the importance of family, friends, and social relationships, making associates in these countries highly loyal to the organizations for which they work, and this is positive as well. Loyalty to the organization is less common among U.S. associates.
>
> - Recognize that norms for interactions involving outsiders may differ from those for interactions between compatriots. Trust is especially important in some cultures and greatly affects interactions with others.
>
> - Be careful about making assumptions regarding cultural values and expected behaviors based on the published dimensions of a person's national culture. Different ages, genders, and even geographic regions may cause differences within a country.
>
> Source: Based on work in M. Javidan & R.J. House. 2001. Cultural acumen for the global manager. *Organizational Dynamics*, 29(4): 289–305; C.J. Robertson, J.A. Al-Khatib, M. Al-Habib, & D. Lanoue. 2001. Beliefs about work in the Middle East and the convergence versus divergence of values. *Journal of World Business*, 36(3): 223–244; S.E. Weiss. 1994. Negotiating with "Romans"—Part 2. *MIT Sloan Management Review*, 35 (3): 85–99.

similarities, and these similarities contribute to understanding and cooperation.[41] Absent face-to-face interactions, videoconferencing provides richer communication than Internet chat rooms and teleconferencing because of the value of seeing each other. In one study, members of international teams reported that it was even helpful to have photographs of teammates posted in the workplace.[42]

Although research on the role of personal characteristics is not conclusive, several characteristics appear to play important roles in the success of cross-cultural virtual teams.[43] Individuals who value diversity, flexibility, and autonomy may offer more positive contributions to both the task and social aspects of the team. A general disposition to trust, a significant degree of trustworthiness, relational skills (involving the ability to work with others who possess different knowledge), and skills for communicating through electronic means are also important to success in virtual teams.

Foreign Job Assignments

Individuals may accept foreign job assignments that entail dealing directly with the complexities of operating in a foreign culture. These people are referred to as **expatriates**, or "expats" for short.[44] Foreign experience can be exciting because of the new and different work situations that are encountered. The opportunity outside of work to learn about and

expatriate
An individual who leaves his or her home country to live and work in a foreign land.

live in a different culture can also be valuable. Many companies indicate that international experience results in faster promotions and makes associates more attractive to other companies because of the enhanced knowledge and capabilities they develop. In addition to the knowledge gained by expatriates, they also provide a means of transferring knowledge from the home company to foreign subsidiaries. In other words, expatriates carry with them the knowledge of the industry, technology, and firm.[45] Using expatriate managers also can facilitate coordination between the home office and foreign subsidiaries.[46]

Petroleum engineers, management consultants, operations managers, sales managers, and information technology project managers are among the common candidates for international assignments. According to recent relocation trends, international assignments are commonly made to fill skill gaps in foreign units, to launch new units, to facilitate technology transfer to another country, and to help build management expertise in a foreign unit.[47]

International assignments, however, should be treated with caution. Many things can go wrong, resulting in poor job performance and an early return to the home country.[48] **Culture shock** is a key factor in failure. This stress reaction can affect an individual who faces changes in and uncertainty over what is acceptable behavior.[49] Some behaviors that are acceptable in the home country may not be acceptable in the new country, and vice versa. For example, in many cultures, one of the hands (either the left or the right, depending on the culture) is considered dirty and should not be used in certain situations. This

culture shock
A stress reaction involving difficulties coping with the requirements of life in a new country.

can be difficult for an American or European to remember. In addition, simple limitations such as an inability to acquire favorite foods, read road signs, and communicate easily often cause stress.

Beyond the associate's or manager's experience of culture shock, a spouse may also experience stress. Research suggests that spousal inability to adjust to the new setting is a significant cause of premature departure from a foreign assignment.[50] One study suggested that spousal adjustment occurs on three dimensions: (1) effectiveness in building relationships with individuals from the host country, (2) effectiveness in adjusting to local culture in general, and (3) effectiveness in developing a feeling of being at home in the foreign country.[51] This same study showed that spouses who spoke the language of the host country adjusted much more effectively. Spouses with very young children also fared better because that spouse will likely spend a great deal of time engaged in the same activities as before the move—child care in the home. Familiar activities make the adjustment easier. In short, the family plays an important role in the ability of the associate or manager to adjust to and be effective in foreign assignments.[52]

©Hans Neleman/Photonica/Getty Images, Inc.

ethnocentrism
The belief that one's culture is better than others.

Individuals exposed to **ethnocentrism** in foreign assignments can also experience stress. Ethnocentrism is the belief that one's culture is superior to others, and it can lead to discrimination and even hostility.[53] In some cases, discrimination is subtle and even unintentional. It nonetheless can harm an expatriate's ability to adjust.

A number of remedies have been proposed to reduce or eliminate expatriate stress. In most cases, these remedies include screening and training before departure, training and social support after arrival in the country, and support for the individual returning to the home country.

Predeparture activities set the stage for success. Such activities include favoring for selection those individuals who have personal characteristics associated with success in foreign assignments. Although there are no simple relationships between personal characteristics and success in foreign posts, associates and managers who possess strong interpersonal skills, are flexible, and are emotionally stable often adapt effectively as expatriates.[54] Even so, predeparture training often plays a more important role than do personal characteristics.

Training can take many forms; a firm may provide books and CDs or arrange for role playing and language training, for example.[55] An expert on training for expatriates has offered the following advice.[56]

- *Train the entire family, if there is one.* If the spouse or children are unhappy, the expatriate assignment is more likely to be unsuccessful.
- *Conduct the predeparture orientation one to two months prior to departure.* The associate or manager and the family can forget information provided earlier than that, and if the orientation occurs too close to departure, the individuals may be too preoccupied to retain training information. Activities such as packing and closing up a home must be handled and will occupy family members in the days immediately prior to moving.
- *Include in the training key cultural information.* The Aperian Global consulting firm provides training for associates selected for expatriate assignments. The firm recommends providing side-by-side cultural comparisons of the home and host cultures, an explanation of the challenges that will likely be faced and when, lifestyle information related to areas such as tipping and gift-giving, and personal job plans for the jobholder, with an emphasis on cultural issues that help the expatriate to thrive in the new environment.[57]
- *Concentrate on conversational language training.* The ability to converse with individuals is more important than the ability to fully understand grammar or to write the foreign language.
- *Be prepared to convince busy families of the need for training.* Families with little foreign experience may not recognize the value of predeparture training.

After arrival, additional training may be useful, especially if little training was provided before departure. Language training may continue, and initial cultural exposure may bring new questions and issues. Host-country social support is also important, particularly in the early months. Individuals familiar with the country may assist in showing newcomers the area, running errands, identifying appropriate schools, and establishing local bank accounts.[58]

Finally, reintegration into the home country should be carefully managed following an international assignment. And companies should be especially mindful to take advantage of the knowledge these individuals have gained through the expatriate assignment. In fact, if managed effectively, the learning by associates and managers can provide them with additional capabilities and thereby increase their motivation and job performance after they return.[59] Such actions by the firm are even more important because research suggests that many associates and managers returning from foreign assignments leave their companies in the first year or two.[60] Old social and political networks may not be intact; information technology may have changed; and key leaders with whom important relationships existed may have departed. Each of these factors can influence the decision to leave. Career planning and sponsors inside the company can help in understanding the new landscape.

The Glass Ceiling, the Glass Floor, and the Glass Border: The Global Business Environment for Women

There are many women who experience barriers preventing them from reaching career aspirations. For international women, these barriers may be even stronger. For example, women in Asian and Middle Eastern countries often experience these barriers because of cultural values and traditions. For many women, marriage and male chauvinism are primary reasons they are unable to reach their career potential. All countries should be concerned about this problem because of the need for more human capital, which is especially troubling when they are not fully utilizing the human capital available.

With the population rapidly aging and most able-bodied men already employed in many economies (especially in strong economies such as China), companies throughout the world need more women associates. They will need to develop and effectively utilize all of the organization's human capital. The current situation has led Korean companies to adopt global business practices that include rewarding performance regardless of seniority or gender.

Interestingly, this is a global phenomenon. While there are some high-profile women executives in the United States, such as Indra Nooyi (CEO of Pepsico), Ursula Burns (CEO of Xerox) and Irene Rosenfeld (CEO of Kraft), the percentage of women in top executive positions has not

increased in recent years. For example, one survey showed that only about 10 percent of the executives and board members were women

©Image Source/Getty Images, Inc.

at the 400 largest publicly traded companies in California. In addition, a study of the top 100 companies based in Massachusetts showed that only 8.6 of their executives were women. A global study by Grant Thornton International found that only 24 percent of senior executive positions in privately held companies were held by women. In fact, 34 percent of the companies had no women executives. There were a few bright spots, however. In the Philippines, 47

percent of the senior management positions were held by women and 42 percent were held by women in Russia. In total, these data suggest that the glass ceiling continues to exist in most countries.

One prominent analyst of the general treatment of women, Shere Hite, argues that they also experience a glass floor. The glass floor hinders even lateral movement into other positions at the basic level. The glass floor barriers include short-term job contracts, child-care tasks, labor markets divided along gender lines, caring for elderly family members, etc. Many of these are the result of culture- and gender-based biases.

The third concern is the glass border. For example, it remains problematic in many Asian cultures to have a woman in charge. Even though women have been a part of the workforce for a long time, for the most part their roles have been limited to staff entry-level positions and lower-level positions in manufacturing; rarely are they found in managerial or executive positions. A glass border (which is an unseen and strong discriminatory barrier) exists, blocking women from accessing many managerial and executive-level positions. It is important to note that many Asian companies are still family-owned, with the men in the family in higher-level positions than the women. In addition, Asian companies often are unwilling to support having the female as the expatriate while her husband remains at his job in the home country. In addition, in some Asian cultures, men rarely help to care for the children, thereby requiring women who work outside the home to rely on female relatives for babysitting. Finally, patriarchal attitudes are difficult to change, especially at the office. Many clients still ask to replace women consultants with men and some bankers continue to require female CEOs to obtain loan guarantees from their husbands.

There is some light beginning to shine in some parts of the world. For example, in 2009 the first two female Islamic judges were appointed in the Palestinian territories. In the Arab countries, these are the first women judges outside of Sudan. In addition, the Saudi king appointed the first women to his council of ministers. While these represent a minor crack in the glass ceiling, these are positive steps for women.

Even though there is an increase in the number of female nonexecutives and a few positive appointments of women to leadership positions, the change in the number becoming executives and directors has been small. To overcome this problem, companies must promote on the basis of merit and ignore gender in the workplace. Women must continue to work hard to break these barriers and overcome the glass ceilings, floors, and borders. Given the demographics around the world, the most successful companies will have a healthy number of women leaders. They will be successful because they are taking advantage of the total human capital available.

Sources: "Women still hold less than a quarter of senior management positions in privately held businesses," *Grant Thornton International,* Nov. 21, 2009, at http://www.internationalbusinessreport.com; Amy Laskowsky. 2009. "The Glass Ceiling Remains Strong," Nov. 20, www.bu.edu; Don Thompson. 2009. "Study finds women still face difficult time breaking through glass ceiling at Calf. Companies," Nov. 19, at http://www.baltimoresun.com; Steve Tobak. 2009. "Is there still a glass ceiling for women in business?" Aug. 24, at http://www.blogs.bnet.com; Diane Tucker. 2009. "Arab women beginning to crack the glass ceiling," March 18, at http://www.huffingtonpost.com; Nasser Shiyoukhi. 2009. "2 Palestinian women crack the glass ceiling in court," Feb. 24, at http://www.abcnews.go.com; Hiroko Tashiro & Ian Rowley. 2005. "Japan: The Glass Ceiling Stays Put," *BusinessWeek,* May 2, at http://www.businessweek.com.

Although participation by women appears to be increasing,[61] women historically have not had as many opportunities for expatriate assignments as men. Managers must be sensitive to this deficit because they need to develop and effectively utilize all of the organization's human capital. As explained in the *Experiencing Organizational Behavior* feature, there are several reasons for the development of this **glass border**. By not providing women with international assignments, they are failing to develop women's knowledge and capabilities for higher-level jobs. As a result, these organizations may not be able to exploit strategic opportunities in international markets because of a shortage of human capital. And interestingly, some research suggests that women are often more effective in expatriate roles because they tend to be flexible and develop a more empowering identity in order to be effective in a variety of situations.[62] The plight of women executives is largely a global phenomenon, as the segment suggests. Women professionals in many countries must contend with glass ceilings, glass borders, and even glass floors. The human capital represented by these women presents a significant opportunity for businesses. Companies that utilize all of their human capital effectively are more likely to gain a competitive advantage.

glass border
The unseen but strong discriminatory barrier that blocks many women from opportunities for international assignments.

Foreign Nationals as Colleagues

Beyond gaining international exposure and experience through a job focused on international work or through a foreign assignment, an associate or manager can gain international experience in other ways. For example, associates and managers may work in a domestic unit with people from other countries or may report to a manager/executive who has relocated from another country. In the United States, H-1B visas allow skilled foreign professionals to live and work in the country for up to six years. L1 visas allow workers in foreign-based multinational companies to be transferred to the United States. Finally, J1 visas allow foreign students to fill seasonal jobs in U.S. resort areas, including jobs as waiters, lifeguards, fast-food cooks, and supermarket clerks. In fact, in recent years the demand for foreign skilled workers has been growing in many countries, including the United States.[63]

With hundreds of thousands of visas approved each year, an individual born in the United States and working in a domestic company may therefore work alongside a foreign national. U.S.-based associates and managers at Microsoft, for example, often work with foreign nationals. An associate there observed, "I am surrounded every day by people from many diverse cultural and ethnic backgrounds, each contributing their unique ideas and talents so that people around the world can realize their full potential."[64] True to its multicultural profile, Microsoft supports a number of international worker groups, including Brazilian, Chinese, Filipino, Hellenic, Indian, Korean, Malaysian, Pakistani, Singaporean, and Taiwanese groups.[65]

Working side by side with individuals from other countries can indeed be a rich and rewarding experience, but problems sometimes develop. As already noted, individuals from different countries often have different values and different ways of thinking—and even different norms for behavior in business meetings.[66] Although differences in values and thought patterns can be a source of creativity and insight, they also can create friction. Preferences for different working styles and decision styles can be particularly troublesome.[67]

A key aspect of the cultural effects on international working relationships is high versus low context cultural values.[68] In **high-context cultures**, such as Japan and South Korea, individuals value personal relationships, prefer to develop agreements on the basis of trust, and prefer slow, ritualistic negotiations.[69] Understanding others and understanding particular messages depend in large part on contextual cues, such as the other person's job, schooling, and nationality. Being familiar with a person's background and current station in life is crucial, and likely important in establishing trust-based relationships in international exchange relationships.[70] In **low-context cultures**, such as the United States and Germany, individuals value performance and expertise, prefer to develop agreements that are formal and perhaps legalistic, and engage in efficient negotiations.[71] Understanding others in general and understanding particular messages depend on targeted questioning. Written and spoken words are crucial; contextual cues tend to carry less meaning.

A related aspect of culture is monochronic versus polychronic time.[72] Individuals with a **monochronic time orientation** prefer to do one task or activity in a given time period. They dislike multitasking; they prefer not to divert attention from a planned task because of an interruption; and they usually are prompt, schedule-driven, and time-focused.[73] North Americans and Northern Europeans are usually viewed as relatively monochronic. In contrast, individuals with a **polychronic time orientation** are comfortable engaging in more than one task at a time and are not troubled by interruptions.[74] For these individuals, time is less of a guiding force, and plans are flexible. Latin Americans and Southern Europeans are often polychronic. Individuals from the Southern region of Asia are also largely polychronic, but many Japanese do not fit this pattern.

Understandably, individuals from high-context cultures can have difficulty working with people from low-context cultures. A high-context individual may not understand or appreciate the direct questioning and task orientation of a low-context individual. As a result, the high-context individual can experience hurt feelings, causing him or her discomfort in a low-context culture. In the same way, a low-context person can be frustrated

high-context cultures
A type of culture where individuals use contextual cues to understand people and their communications and where individuals value trust and personal relationships.

low-context cultures
A type of culture where individuals rely on direct questioning to understand people and their communications and where individuals value efficiency and performance.

monochronic time orientation
A preference for focusing on one task per unit of time and completing that task in a timely fashion.

polychronic time orientation
A willingness to juggle multiple tasks per unit of time and to have interruptions, and an unwillingness to be driven by time.

with the pace and focus of a high-context culture. In addition, monochronic individuals may experience conflict with people who are more polychronic. People who are driven by schedules and who do not appreciate interruptions often are frustrated by the more relaxed view of time held by polychronic people. To alleviate these cross-cultural difficulties, training in cultural differences is crucial in order to build managers' cultural intelligence. **Cultural intelligence** helps people understand others' behavior, with the ability to separate those aspects that are universally human from those that are unique to the person and those that are based in culture. It allows managers to understand and respond effectively to people from different cultures.[75] Cultural intelligence is important for managers, as they need to be sensitive to these differences when they evaluate the performance of associates and assign rewards based on these evaluations.[76]

cultural intelligence
The ability to separate the aspects of behavior that are based in culture from those unique to the individual or all humans in general.

Opportunities for International Participation

Associates' and managers' opportunities for international experiences differ across firms. Purely domestic firms offer few opportunities beyond perhaps working with foreign nationals who have been hired or trying to compete with foreign firms operating in the local markets where they sell their goods. Firms that export their goods into foreign markets offer more opportunities, because some individuals are needed for internationally focused work, such as international accounting, and a few are needed to staff foreign sales offices. Firms that have more substantial commitments to foreign operations usually provide even greater opportunities for international work, but the amount and type of opportunities vary with the type of strategy. Furthermore, the different approaches to markets in separate countries used by firms affect associates' and managers' behavior and job satisfaction.[77] As shown in Exhibit 3-3, we can classify firms with substantial commitments to foreign operations as multidomestic, global, or transnational.

EXHIBIT 3-3 International Approaches and Related Organizational Characteristics

	Multidomestic	Global	Transnational
Local responsiveness			
Local production	High	Low	Medium
Local R&D	High	Low	Medium
Local product modification	High	Low	Medium/High
Local adaptation of marketing	High	Low/Medium	Medium/High
Organizational design			
Delegation of power to local units	High	Low	Medium/Low
Interunit resource flows between and among local units	Low	Low/Medium	High
International resource flows from and/or controlled by corporate headquarters	Low	High	Low/Medium
International participation			
Opportunities for associates and managers	Low	High	High

Source: Information in this exhibit is based on A.-W. Harzing. 2000. "An Empirical Analysis and Extension of the Bartlett and Ghoshal Typology of Multinational Companies," *Journal of International Business Studies*, 31: 101–120.

Multidomestic Firms

multidomestic strategy
A strategy by which a firm tailors its products and services to the needs of each country or region in which it operates and gives a great deal of power to the managers and associates in those countries or regions.

Firms that use a **multidomestic strategy** tailor their products and services for various countries or regions of the world.[78] When customer tastes and requirements vary substantially across countries, a firm must be responsive to these differences. Tastes often vary, for example, in consumer packaged goods. Unilever, the British/Dutch provider of detergents, soaps, shampoos, and other consumer products, is a prime example by offering different versions of its products in various parts of the world.[79] It produces, for example, approximately 20 brands of black tea in order to meet the unique tastes of individuals in different countries.

Firms such as Unilever often transfer power from the corporate headquarters to units based in various countries or homogeneous regions of the world (i.e., local units).[80] These units typically are self-contained—they conduct their own research and development, produce their own products and services, and individually market and distribute their goods. This approach is expensive because geographically based units do not share resources or help one another as much as in firms using other international strategies. Yet, it may be important to allow autonomy when the subsidiary is a long distance from the home office, especially when that distance entails major differences in culture and institutional environments. In these cases, the subsidiary needs to develop a strategy that fits its competitive environment, and the home office is less likely to be of help in doing so.[81]

Among firms with substantial foreign commitments, multidomestic firms provide fewer opportunities for associates, lower-level managers, and midlevel managers to participate in international activities. Individuals tend to work within their home countries and have little interaction with people located in other geographical locations. Individuals in each unit are focused on their unit's country or homogeneous set of countries (region). Interunit learning, interunit transfers of people, and interunit coordination are rare in firms using a multidomestic strategy.

Global Firms

global strategy
A strategy by which a firm provides standard products and services to all parts of the world while maintaining a strong degree of central control in the home country.

Firms following a **global strategy** offer standardized products and services in the countries in which they are active.[82] When cost pressures demand efficient use of resources and when tailoring to local tastes is not necessary, a firm must do all it can to manage its resources efficiently. It is costly to develop, produce, and market substantially different versions of the same basic product or service across different countries. For example, Microsoft does not significantly tailor the functionality of Windows for different countries. Nor does Cemex, the world's third largest cement company, tailor its cement for different countries. While the firm sells almost 240 million metric tons of cement annually across four major regions of the world, the firm provides the same product in all countries where it operates.

Cemex exhibits many features typical of global firms.[83] First, key decisions related to: (1) products and services, (2) research and development, and (3) methods for serving each country are often made at corporate headquarters in Monterrey, Mexico. (In contrast, firms using the multidomestic strategy make key decisions locally.) Second, country- and region-based units do not have a full complement of resources covering all of the major functions (production, marketing, sales, finance, research and development, human resources). For example, Cemex has operations in more than 50 countries but only has manufacturing operations in select parts of the world. A great deal of manufacturing also takes place in the home country of Mexico, and the product is then exported to other countries. By not having manufacturing plants located in and dedicated to each country or even each region, and by having large-scale manufacturing facilities in select locations, Cemex efficiently uses its resources. Cemex also focuses significant attention on global coordination. With units depending on decisions and resources controlled by the home country as well as resources from other countries, coordinating a global flow of information and resources is crucial. One means of growth for Cemex has been by acquisition. Fortunately, the strong global coordination used by the firm helps to rapidly integrate major acquisitions.

Compared with firms following a multidomestic strategy, firms using the global strategy provide more opportunities for associates and managers to participate in international activities. For example, many individuals in the home country and in foreign units must coordinate effectively to ensure a smooth flow of worldwide resources. Thus, many jobs are internationally oriented. In addition, there are often a large number of expatriate assignments. Global firms treat the world as a unified market and frequently transfer people across borders. Thus, in any given unit, there may be a significant number of foreign nationals. As noted earlier, expatriates learn and transfer knowledge across borders. Yet, to achieve the most learning at the team level requires the firm to consciously manage the flow of knowledge across the organization.[84]

Transnational Firms

Firms using a **transnational strategy** attempt to achieve both local responsiveness and global efficiency.[85] In industries where both of these criteria are important for success, a careful integration of multidomestic and global approaches is necessary. Thus, a transnational strategy calls for more tailoring to individual countries than is typically found in global firms but generally less tailoring than in multidomestic firms.

Such an approach also requires the deployment of more resources in a given country than is typical in the global firm but fewer resources in each country than is typical in the multidomestic firm. Finally, the approach calls for less central direction from the corporate headquarters than the global strategy but more central coordination than the multidomestic strategy. In a transnational firm, interdependent geographical units must work closely together to facilitate interunit resource flows and learning. In the multidomestic firm, these flows are trivial. In the global firm, they are largely controlled by corporate headquarters.

Ogilvy & Mather Worldwide, a U.S.-based advertising subsidiary of WPP, a worldwide marketing communications group, uses a transnational strategy.[86] At one time, the firm used a strategy that most closely resembled a multidomestic approach. Ogilvy & Mather tailored the advertising it produced to different areas of the world based on local customs, expressions, sensibilities, and norms for humor. To support this strategy, it had strong, self-contained local units. Clients, however, began to object to costs, and because many of these clients were becoming global firms, they wanted a more unified message spread around the world through advertising. Ogilvy & Mather began to pursue global efficiency and local responsiveness simultaneously. It refers to itself as "the most local of internationals and the most international of the locals." It has more than 450 offices in 120 countries across the globe.[87]

transnational strategy
A strategy by which a firm tailors its products and services to some degree to meet the needs of different countries or regions of the world but also seeks some degree of standardization in order to keep costs reasonably low.

To prevent local units from reinventing largely the same advertising campaign (in other words, unnecessarily tailoring campaigns to the local market), Ogilvy & Mather implemented international teams that were assigned to service major accounts.[88] These teams create ad campaigns and send them to local units for implementation. One team is called Ogilvy*Action*, designed to provide a full range of brand activation services to customers on a global basis.[89] Local units pursue local accounts and have complete control over them but are constrained in their ability to pursue and oversee international work.

Overall, individual associates and managers have many opportunities for international exposure and experiences in firms using a transnational approach. Geographically based units are highly interdependent because they must exchange resources, and they often must coordinate these resource exchanges for their benefit as well. Rich personal networks and formal coordination mechanisms such as international work teams are developed to handle the interdependence. International meetings and travel are very important, and foreign assignments are common. Interestingly, the location of the headquarters for these firms is less important and some move their headquarters unit from their traditional home country when they adopt the transnational strategy. Normally, these moves are designed to respond to external stakeholders such as shareholders and financial markets.[90]

High-Involvement Management in the International Context

High-involvement management provides associates with decision power and the information they need to use that power effectively. As discussed in Chapter 1, firms that adopt this approach often perform better than other firms. Although most evidence supporting the effectiveness of the high-involvement approach has been collected from domestic units of North American firms,[91] sound evidence has come from other countries as well. Studies, for example, have been conducted in automobile plants worldwide,[92] in a variety of firms in New Zealand,[93] and in firms in 11 different countries.[94] A study in China suggested that such practices enhanced short-term associates' feelings of competence and increased their commitment to the organization.[95]

Although available evidence is supportive of high-involvement management, care must be taken when implementing this approach in different cultures. Modifying the approach to fit local circumstances is crucial.[96] In this section, we discuss several dimensions of national culture that should be considered. The dimensions are drawn from the GLOBE (Global Leadership and Organizational Behavior Effectiveness) research program, in which a number of researchers studied issues regarding organizational behavior in 61 countries.[97]

Dimensions of National Culture

As shown in Exhibit 3-4, the GLOBE project uses nine dimensions of national culture. Four of these dimensions have been used by many other researchers over the years. These four dimensions were originally developed by the Dutch social scientist Geert Hofstede[98] and they are listed first.

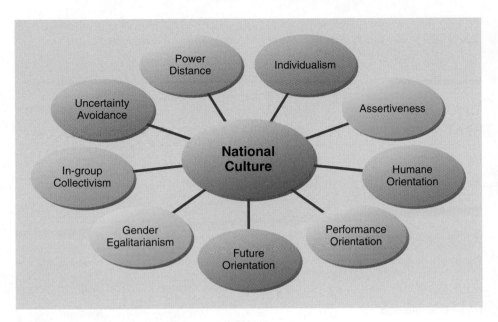

Exhibit 3-4 Dimensions of National Culture

1. *Uncertainty avoidance* is the degree to which members of a society wish to avoid unpredictable lives. It is focused on a society's desire for orderliness through formal procedures and rules as well as through strong norms that govern behavior. Countries with high scores do not value free spirits. Such countries include Austria and Germany. Countries with lower scores include Russia and Hungary. The United States has a midrange score.

2. *Power distance* is the degree to which members of a society expect power to be unequally distributed. This dimension corresponds to expectations for strong autocratic leadership rather than more egalitarian leadership. Strong central governments and centralized decision structures in work organizations are frequently found in countries with high scores. For example, Russia scores high on this dimension. Alternatively, Denmark and the Netherlands have low scores on power distance.

3. *Individualism* is the degree to which members of society are comfortable focusing on personal goals and being rewarded for personal efforts and outcomes. In individualistic cultures, personal outcomes are valued. Countries scoring high on individualism include Italy and Germany. Countries scoring low on this dimension include Japan, Singapore, and South Korea.[99]

4. *Assertiveness* is the degree to which members of society are aggressive and confrontational. In his original work, Hofstede labeled this aspect of culture "masculinity." Examples of countries with high scores on this dimension are the United States, Austria, and Germany. Examples of countries with low scores are Sweden and Kuwait.

5. *In-group collectivism* indicates how much members of society take pride in the groups and organizations to which they belong, including the family. China and India have high scores on this dimension in the GLOBE research.

EXHIBIT 3-5 National Culture in India, Germany, and the United States

Culture Dimension	India	Germany	United States
Uncertainty avoidance	Medium	High	Medium
Power distance	Medium/High	Medium	Medium/Low
Individualism	Medium	High	Medium
Assertiveness	Low/Medium	High	High
In-group collectivism	High	Low/Medium	Medium/Low
Gender egalitarianism	Low	Medium/Low	Medium
Future orientation	Medium	Medium	Medium
Performance orientation	Medium	Medium	High
Humane orientation	High/Medium	Low	Medium

Source: Based on the GLOBE Project.

6. *Gender egalitarianism* refers to equal opportunities for women and men. Sweden and Denmark score high on this dimension.

7. *Future orientation* is the degree to which members of the society value long-term planning and investing in the future. Denmark and the Netherlands are among those scoring high on this dimension.

8. *Performance orientation* is the degree to which members of society appreciate and reward improvement and excellence in schoolwork, athletics, and work life. The United States, Taiwan, Hong Kong, and Singapore have high performance orientations.

9. *Humane orientation* is the degree to which members of society value generous, caring, altruistic behavior. Countries scoring high on this dimension include the Philippines and Malaysia.

Exhibit 3-5 compares India, Germany, and the United States on all nine culture dimensions.

Research has shown that national culture affects major business practices.[100] For example, decisions to enter particular international markets are affected by the cultural dimensions of the targeted country.[101] In particular, the cultural distance between a firm's home country and the country targeted for entry has a major impact. *Cultural distance* refers to the extent of the differences in culture between countries.[102] Therefore, managers must pay careful attention to culture in designing and implementing management practices in each country.

In the *Experiencing Organizational Behavior* feature, we learn of the pioneering work of Geert Hofstede to identify the universal dimensions of national culture. He also discovered that national culture had a stronger effect on the behavior of managers and associates than did organizational culture. Hofstede's work suggested the need to understand and manage diverse cultures. This need is highlighted in the problems experienced in

Managing Diverse Cultures

Geert Hofstede pioneered the study of culture in the workplace and conducted research to examine global variations in the psychology of work and of organizations, which affected international human resource management. While working at IBM in 1968, he noticed that although the company had a strong company culture, there were variations in cultural values among the employees of IBM subsidiaries around the world. Between 1968 and 1972, he surveyed over 116,000 employees. His survey responses from over 40 countries showed general similarities within cultural groups, even when their social and economic histories were profoundly different. For example, Hong Kong and mainland China have more in common with each other but are quite different from Sweden and the United States. Hofstede found that values we observe in the workplace reflect much deeper cultural attributes, suggesting that the impact of national culture on the workplace is much greater than that of the organization's culture. His work has profound meaning for managers employed by multinational organizations.

Managers and top executives of companies seeking to expand globally need to recognize the complexities of cross-border collaboration. Difficulty in managing people is magnified when even small differences in perceptions and expectations occur, making collaboration difficult, as reflected in the cross-cultural problems that occurred in the merger between Daimler and Chrysler. Some experts believed that the merger had substantial potential because of the different but complementary capabilities possessed by the two firms. However, that potential was not realized partly because of national cultural differences between Germans and Americans. The Germans in Daimler disliked Chrysler managers' unstructured approach, while American Chrysler managers found the German Daimler managers too rigid and formal. The culture clash disallowed effective integration of the two firms and their respective associates. Many Chrysler managers left the organization, and the potential synergy between the two firms was never realized. Daimler eventually sold the Chrysler business at a tremendous loss over what it paid to acquire it.

Managers may need to utilize different concepts and methods for different times and places. Managers need to be aware of the local cultures' values, social ideals, and their workplace behavior and attitudes. Multinational companies engaging in cross-border mergers can be successful when they have managers who possess "cultural intelligence," the ability to understand and effectively manage different values and expectations existing in different parts of the world. Several firms have promoted diversity in their workforce as a means of managing and taking advantage of many cultures in the world. For example, Siemens believes that a diverse workforce can be a competitive advantage because it helps the company to understand and better serve its customers across the world. Siemens currently employs more than 430,000 managers and associates representing 140 different nationalities in its top 10 markets. To encourage collaboration and communication among its workforce members, it has launched several networks such as the Global Leadership Organization of Women (GLOW Network) and the diversity ambassadors program. The diversity ambassadors are 100 specially selected managers and associates who are profiled and share their success stories while serving as role models and mentors for others in the company.

©Siemens AG

Other companies are also promoting diversity as a way to take advantage of culturally diverse knowledge and ways of thinking. For example, ABB has a highly diverse board of directors with members from Belgium, Finland, France, Germany, India, Scotland, Sweden, Switzerland, and the United States. Procter & Gamble (P&G) also promotes a diverse workforce. The firm does so to understand and maintain a good relationship with its customers around the world and its global suppliers as well. P&G's CEO stated that "Diverse organizations will out-think, out-innovate and out-perform a homogeneous organization. ..."

Sources: "Siemens AG—Diversity," Siemens, Nov. 22, 2009, at http://www.siemens.com; G. Schoech. 2009. "Diversity to strengthen Siemens leadership—catching up or taking the lead?" Gehson Lehrman Group, March 17, at http://www.glgroup.com; H. Brown. 2009. "Diversity does matter," Forbes, July 21, at http://www.forbes.com; "No. 14: Procter & Gamble," Diversity Inc., May, 2007, at http://www.diversityinc.com; Morgan Witzel. 2003. "Geert Hofstede: The Quantifier of Culture," Financial Times, Aug. 25, at http://www.ft.com; M.A. Hitt, R.S. Harrison, & R.D. Ireland. 2001. Mergers and Acquisitions: A Guide to Creating Value for Stakeholders, New York: Oxford University Press.

the merger between Daimler Benz and Chrysler, in which the managers of the respective firms were not understanding and tolerant of the cultural attributes that differed from their own. Yet, other companies recognize the value of diversity and have promoted it in various ways. For example, Siemens does so through its global networks to encourage collaboration across cultures and its diversity ambassadors program. ABB has a highly diverse board of directors, and P&G promotes diversity because it will provide the company with a competitive advantage. With increasing globalization, understanding and managing diverse cultures has become a critical managerial attribute for competitive success in international markets.

National Culture and High-Involvement Management

High-involvement management must be implemented in accordance with a country's cultural characteristics. Although not every individual from a country will possess all of the cultural characteristics associated with that country, many people will share these traits. In the next section, we discuss how information sharing and decision power can be adapted to different levels of power distance, uncertainty avoidance, individualism, and assertiveness.[103]

Information Sharing

A firm's leaders must share tactical and strategic information if empowered individuals and teams are to make high-quality decisions. In cultures high in uncertainty avoidance, associates must have information to clarify issues and provide basic direction. If they lack such information, anxiety and poor performance can result. Where uncertainty avoidance is low, associates need less information of this kind. Rather, increasing information that encourages new ideas and ways of thinking can be useful. In cultures where assertiveness is high, associates want information that clearly and directly informs them what is needed for effective performance. In addition, they desire continuous information on how well they are performing. In cultures with low assertiveness, associates do not want information that is exclusively focused on performance and bottom-line business goals. Instead, they desire information on improving soft processes such as teamwork. Similarly, associates in individualistic cultures desire information regarding their individual jobs and responsibilities; they are less interested in information on team, department, and company issues. Associates in collectivistic cultures tend to have the opposite needs. Finally, associates in high-power-distance cultures do not expect to receive a great deal of information and may not pay much attention to it if they receive it. For these individuals, careful training in information use is often required. In low-power-distance cultures, associates expect information and put it to use when it is received. Thus, cultural attributes affect the type and amount of information shared and the knowledge learned in organizations.[104]

Decision Power and Individual Autonomy

Some high-involvement systems give a great deal of decision power to individual associates rather than to teams. In cultures characterized by high uncertainty avoidance, such autonomy can cause stress because it is associated with less direction from above as well as less support from peers. To avoid stress, clear boundaries must be set for how the autonomy is used, and managers must be readily available to provide direction. In cultures with low uncertainty avoidance, associates do not need direction and are generally able to tolerate uncertainty regarding the boundaries to their authority. In high-assertiveness cultures, associates are likely to use autonomy creatively to achieve task success. In low-assertiveness cultures, associates may channel too much of their autonomy into work on soft issues such as relationships and social networks. Managers must guard against any such excesses. In countries characterized by an individualistic culture, associates appreciate autonomy provided to individuals rather than to teams, and emphasize individual goals. Because of this focus, managers may need to explicitly channel associates' attention to any required group or team tasks. In countries characterized by a collectivistic culture, associates are unlikely to be motivated by individual autonomy. Managers may wish to emphasize autonomy at the team level in such cultures. Finally, in cultures characterized by high power distance, autonomy may be difficult to implement. Associates expect a great deal of direction from managers. In this situation, managers may want to provide small increases in autonomy over time, allowing associates to become accustomed to having discretion. Managers may want to maintain a fairly strong role even in the long run. In cultures characterized by low power distance, associates welcome autonomy from managers and can channel their efforts to be more innovative.[105]

Decision Power and Self-Managing Teams

In cultures with high uncertainty avoidance, associates need clear boundaries for self-managing teams, and managers must be readily available for mentoring and coaching.[106] In cultures with low uncertainty avoidance, teams can define their own roles. In countries characterized by high assertiveness, teams often are task-focused. For low-assertiveness cultures, associates frequently devote a great deal of time to soft issues, such as team dynamics, requiring managers to monitor the time focused on such issues. In cultures characterized by individualism, managers must pay particular attention to team training for associates and to the design of team-based reward systems. Alternatively, in cultures characterized by collectivism, managers have a more favorable situation because associates prefer teamwork. Finally, in cultures characterized by high power distance, associates may have difficulties using their decision power if their manager is too visible. Managers must be less visible and resist the temptation to offer a great deal of assistance to the team. Where power distance is low, associates work comfortably with the manager as an equal or as a coach rather than a supervisor.

AES, a U.S.-based power-generation company, is known for its high-involvement management system. Associates enjoy tremendous freedom to make decisions individually and in teams. Firing vendors for safety violations, expending funds from capital budgets, and making key decisions about important day-to-day work are common for associates. With careful selection and training, and with access to key information, AES associates typically use their freedom wisely.

As AES began to grow and establish operations in several countries, many analysts and reporters questioned whether its high-involvement system and underlying values could be applied in an international context. Although AES leaders remained committed to the system, they realized that some modifications might be needed for a particular country. Therefore, while the core of the approach was preserved, some aspects were altered to fit each local culture.

When entering Nigeria, for example, AES responded appropriately to the prevailing culture. Norman Bell, the lead on the Nigerian project, and his AES colleagues encountered high power distance and high individualism among the associates in Nigeria. These prominent cultural values initially forced Bell to adopt a more autocratic management system. Bell needed time to delegate decision power to associates, and teams required training and team-based reward systems.

AES used the same basic approach in its operations across 29 countries and 25,000 managers and associates: high-involvement management built on the company's core values with sensitivity to local cultural differences.[107] Thus, executives and managers at AES effectively used the high-involvement approach on a global basis while modifying the approach to fit local cultures. The high-involvement approach facilitated the global strategy used by AES. Therefore, it helped top managers to implement the firm's strategy.

Ethics in the International Context

A critically important issue in globalization and international business is ethics. The *American Heritage Dictionary* defines ethics as "principle[s] of right or good conduct; a system of moral principles and values." Implicit in this definition is the idea that ethical conduct can be different in different cultures. What one society deems "appropriate conduct" may be unacceptable to another. For example, nepotism that is unacceptable in many Western cultures is often more acceptable in relationship-oriented cultures. Alternatively, the use of formal contracts and lawsuits are highly acceptable in many Western cultures but are perceived negatively in other cultures.[108] Thus, **international ethics** are complex.

international ethics
Principles of proper conduct focused on issues such as corruption, exploitation of labor, and environmental impact.

Corruption is often considered to be the misuse of power for private gain.[109] Three issues are prominent in discussions of proper conduct in developed nations: (1) corruption, (2) exploitation of labor, and (3) environmental impact.[110] For corruption, the chief issue involves bribing foreign public officials in order to win business. Asking for payment of bribes is based partially on culture and partly on economic needs and institutional weaknesses in a country.[111] Many developed nations have taken steps to fight corruption because it creates uncertainty and results in a reduction of merit-based decision making. The United States, for example, passed the Foreign Corrupt Practices Act in 1977 to prevent U.S. managers from bribing foreign officials. (See Exhibit 3-6 for a recent ranking of countries based on corruption.) Exploitation of labor involves the employment of children, the forced use of prison labor, unreasonably low wages, and poor working conditions. In one well-known example involving a line of clothing produced for Wal-Mart, Chinese women were working 84 hours per week in dangerous conditions while living in monitored dormitories with 12 persons to a room.[112] Americans and others expressed their strong unhappiness with this practice, and Wal-Mart discontinued it. Finally, environmental impact relates to pollution and overuse of scarce resources. From global warming to clear cutting of forests, the concerns are many. In the United States and globally, many people have become more sensitive to the environment because of the obvious effects of global warming.

The economic development of countries with higher levels of corruption tends to suffer. For example, countries with high corruption index scores as shown in Exhibit 3-6 often receive less direct investment from foreign firms. In addition, the foreign investment in these countries more commonly comes from firms based in other countries with greater corruption.[113] Thus, corruption harms the country and its citizens.

EXHIBIT 3-6   Absence of Corruption in Select Countries

Rank	Country	Rank	Country
1	New Zealand	158	Tajikistan
2	Denmark	162	Angola
3	Singapore	162	Congo Brazzaville
3	Sweden	162	Democratic Republic of Congo
5	Switzerland	162	Guinea-Bissau
6	Finland	162	Kyrgyzstan
6	Netherlands	162	Venezuela
8	Australia	168	Burundi
8	Canada	168	Equatorial Guinea
8	Iceland	168	Guinea
11	Norway	168	Haiti
12	Hong Kong	168	Iran
12	Luxembourg	168	Turkmenistan
14	Germany	174	Uzbekistan
14	Ireland	175	Chad
16	Austria	176	Iraq
17	Japan	176	Sudan
17	United Kingdom	178	Myanmar
19	United States	179	Afghanistan
20	Barbados	180	Somalia

Source: Rankings are drawn from Transparency International's Corruption Perception's Index 2009 for 180 countries (http://www.transparency.org). Scores are based on the perceptions of the degree of corruption as seen by businesspeople and country analysts. The score ranges from 10 (highly clean) to 0 (highly corrupt).

The United Nations, the World Bank, the International Labor Organization, the World Trade Organization, and the Organization for Economic Co-operation and Development are among many organizations that advocate a unified set of global ethical standards to govern labor practices and general issues related to international business. As shown in the Exhibit 3-7, business leaders from Japan, Europe, and North America in the Caux Round Table have developed a list of expectations for companies engaging in international business. These ethical standards are intended to govern what strategies managers select and how they implement those strategies in dealings with others, both within and outside their organizations.

EXHIBIT 3-7 Caux Round Table Principles for Business

Business leaders from Japan, Europe, and North America formed the Caux Round Table in 1986 to promote moral values in business. The principles they developed are based on two ideals: *kyosei* and human dignity. *Kyosei*, a Japanese concept, means "living and working together for the common good, enabling cooperation and mutual prosperity to exist with healthy and fair competition." The seven specific principles the executives promote are listed below:

1. *The Responsibilities of Business.* The value of a business to society is the wealth and employment it creates and the marketable products and services it provides to consumers at a reasonable price commensurate with quality. To create such value, a business must maintain its economic health and viability, but survival is not a sufficient goal. Businesses have a role to play in improving the lives of all of their customers, associates, and shareholders by sharing with them the wealth they have created. Suppliers and competitors as well should expect businesses to honor their obligations in a spirit of honesty and fairness. As responsible citizens of the local, national, regional, and global communities in which they operate, businesses have a part in shaping the future of those communities.

2. *The Economic and Social Impact of Business.* Businesses established in foreign countries to develop, produce, or sell should also contribute to the social advancement of those countries by creating productive employment and helping to raise the purchasing power of their citizens. Businesses also should contribute to human rights, education, welfare, and vitalization of the countries in which they operate.

   Businesses should contribute to economic and social development not only in the countries in which they operate, but also in the world community at large, through effective and prudent use of resources, free and fair competition, and emphasis upon innovation in technology, production methods, marketing, and communications.

3. *Business Behavior.* While accepting the legitimacy of trade secrets, businesses should recognize that sincerity, candor, truthfulness, the keeping of promises, and transparency contribute not only to their own credibility and stability but also to the smoothness and efficiency of business transactions, particularly on the international level.

4. *Respect for Rules.* To avoid trade frictions and to promote freer trade, equal conditions for competition, and fair and equitable treatment for all participants, businesses should respect international and domestic rules. In addition, they should recognize that some behavior, although legal, can still have adverse consequences.

5. *Support for Multilateral Trade.* Businesses should support the multilateral trade systems of the General Agreement in Tariffs and Trade (GATT) World Trade Organization (WTO), and similar international agreements. They should cooperate in efforts to promote the progressive and judicious liberalization of trade and to relax those domestic measures that unreasonably hinder global commerce, while giving respect to national policy objectives.

6. *Respect for the Environment.* A business should protect and, where possible, improve the environment, promote sustainable development, and prevent the wasteful use of natural resources.

7. *Avoidance of Illicit Operations.* A business should not participate in or condone bribery, money laundering, or other corrupt practices: indeed, it should seek cooperation with others to eliminate these practices. It should not trade in arms or other materials used for terrorist activities, drug traffic, or other organized crime.

Sources: Caux Round Table, "Principles for Business," 2007, at http://www.cauxroundtable.org; P. Carlson and M.S. Blodgett. 1997. "International Ethics Standards for Business: NAFTA, CAUX Principles and Corporate Code of Ethics," *Review of Business*, 18, no. 3: 20–23.

THE STRATEGIC LENS

Organizations large and small must develop strategies to compete in the global economy. For some organizations, strategies leading to direct investment in foreign operations are valuable for growth, lower costs, and better management of the organization's risk. For other organizations, only exporting goods and services for selling in other countries is sufficient to meet their goals. For still other firms, particularly small ones, participation in international markets may be limited, but competition from foreign firms in their local domestic markets may require that they respond with competitive actions. In all cases, understanding other cultures and effectively managing cross-cultural activities and contexts are crucial. Without insight and sensitivity to other cultures, senior managers are unlikely to formulate effective strategies. Without appreciation for other cultures, associates and midlevel and lower-level managers can also fail in their efforts to implement carefully developed strategic plans. Furthermore, managers must prepare associates to work in international environments. This preparation often requires training and international assignments. Managers must also develop all of the organization's human capital—including women, who often have not had as many opportunities for expatriate assignments as men—and must ensure that the organization has the capabilities to take advantage of and exploit opportunities in international markets when they are identified. Cultural diversity among the firm's human capital can be an advantage if managers use it effectively. Many organizations operate or sell their products in foreign markets. Thus, managers and associates must understand cultural diversity and use this knowledge to their advantage in managing it.

Critical Thinking Questions

1. Given the complexity and challenges in operating in foreign countries, why do organizations enter international markets?

2. How can understanding and managing cultural diversity among associates contribute positively to an organization's performance?

3. How can being knowledgeable of diverse cultures enhance an individual's professional career?

What This Chapter Adds to Your Knowledge Portfolio

In this chapter, we have defined globalization and discussed the forces that influence it. We have also discussed three types of international involvement on the part of associates and managers: internationally focused jobs, foreign job assignments, and working with foreign nationals in the home country. After describing differing opportunities for international involvement, we explored dimensions of culture from the GLOBE project and examined the implications of cultural differences for high-involvement management. Finally, we examined issues regarding ethics in international settings. More specifically, we covered the following points:

- Globalization is the trend toward a global economy whereby products, services, people, technologies, and financial capital move relatively freely across national borders. Globalization increased dramatically in the last 20 years of the twentieth century and in the first decade of the twenty-first century.

- Globalization presents opportunities and challenges for nations. The principal opportunity is for economic growth. Challenges include the possible loss of a nation's cultural uniqueness as uniform goods and services become commonplace throughout the world. For developing nations, additional challenges include the

back to the knowledge objectives

1. What is globalization?
2. What are the three types of international involvement available to associates and managers? What problems can be encountered with each type?
3. How do opportunities for international involvement differ in firms emphasizing multidomestic, global, and transnational strategies? Which type of firm would you prefer to join and why?
4. What are the key dimensions of national culture that influence the success of high-involvement management? How should high-involvement management be adapted to differences in culture?
5. What are several international standards for ethical behavior by businesses (refer to the Caux Round Table Principles)? Briefly discuss each one.

protection of labor from exploitation and natural resources from depletion. For wealthy nations, additional challenges include prevention of job loss to lower-wage countries and preservation of high-level wage structures at home.

- Globalization presents opportunities and challenges for organizations. Opportunities include growth, risk reduction through diversification, greater economies of scale, and location advantages (e.g., moving into an area with a particularly talented labor pool). Challenges include political risk (instability of national governments, threat of war, and threat of state-sponsored terrorism), economic risk (fluctuation in the value of foreign currencies and the possibility of sudden economic contraction in some countries), and managerial risk (difficulties inherent in managing the complex resource flows required in a global or transnational firm).

- Individuals can be involved in the international domain through internationally focused jobs. Such individuals work from their home countries but focus on international issues as part of their day-to-day work. Membership in one or more virtual teams is often part of the job. Members of a virtual team coordinate their activities mainly through videoconferencing, teleconferencing, chat rooms, and e-mail. Having some face-to-face meetings and taking steps to ensure that individuals identify with the team facilitate team success.

- Individuals can also be involved in the international domain through foreign job assignments. These individuals are known as expatriates, and they often are on a fast track for advancement. In their new countries, expatriates may experience culture shock, a stress reaction caused by the foreign context. Failure of a spouse to adjust and strong ethnocentrism in the host country are two additional factors leading to stress for expats. Careful screening of candidates for foreign assignments and rich cultural training can reduce stress and improve chances for success.

- Individuals can be involved in the international domain by working alongside foreign nationals. This is often exciting and rewarding, but cultural differences must be appreciated and accommodated, particularly those differences related to low- versus high-context values and monochronic versus polychronic time values.

- Some executives and managers choose a multidomestic strategy for their firm's international activities. This strategy, involving tailoring products and services for different countries or regions, tends to be used when preferences vary substantially across local markets where the firm has subsidiary operations. Because country-based or regionally based units are focused on their own local domains, associates and managers have limited opportunities for international exposure and experience.

- Some executives and managers choose a global strategy for their firm's international activities. This strategy, involving standardized products and services for world markets, tends to be emphasized when needs for global efficiency are strong.

Country- or region-based units are not self-contained, independent, or exclusively focused on local markets. Instead, at a minimum, each unit interacts frequently and intensively with the home country, and probably with some units located in other countries. Global firms offer associates and managers many more opportunities for international involvement than do multidomestic firms.

- Some executives and managers choose a transnational strategy for their firm's international activities. This strategy balances needs for local responsiveness and global efficiency through a complex network of highly interdependent local units. Associates and managers enjoy many opportunities for international involvement in transnational firms.

- National cultures differ in many ways. Four dimensions have proven to be particularly useful in understanding these differences: uncertainty avoidance, power distance, individualism, and assertiveness. Organizational behavior researchers have proposed five other dimensions: in-group collectivism, gender egalitarianism, future orientation, performance orientation, and humane orientation.

- High-involvement management must be adapted to differences in national culture. Two aspects of this management approach, information sharing and decision power, are particularly important for adaptation.

- Many groups, including the World Trade Organization and the Caux Round Table, have developed guidelines for ethics in the international context. Key issues for developed countries include: (1) corruption, (2) exploitation of children, and (3) environmental impact.

Thinking about Ethics

1. Some have argued that globalization is a negative process because it can destroy national cultures. Do senior managers in global firms have a responsibility to prevent such damage? Or is their primary responsibility to maximize profits for their shareholders?

2. The members of cross-cultural virtual teams are prone to misperceptions and misunderstandings due to the lack of rich face-to-face communication. Under these circumstances, should a manager terminate an individual who has been a source of interpersonal problems in the context of such a team? Explain your answer.

3. A hard-working and generally effective associate has shown little appreciation for the cultural diversity in his unit. In fact, he has expressed some minor hostility toward several foreign nationals in the workplace. Also, he has not taken cross-cultural training seriously. How should the manager respond?

4. An experienced expatriate has hired underage labor at a cheap rate in order to save money. How should her firm respond to this situation?

Key Terms

globalization, p. 86
culture, p. 86
virtual electronic teams, p. 90
swift trust, p. 90
expatriate, p. 91
culture shock, p. 92
ethnocentrism, p. 92

glass border, p. 95
high-context cultures, p. 96
low-context cultures, p. 96
monochronic time
    orientation, p. 96
polychronic time
    orientation, p. 96

cultural intelligence, p. 97
multidomestic
    strategy, p. 98
global strategy, p. 98
transnational
    strategy, p. 99
international ethics, p. 106

Human Resource Management Applications

The Human Resource Management (HRM) function plays a key role in a firm's capability to manage international operations and to compete effectively in global markets. Following are several activities in which they facilitate management in the firm.

The HRM unit is often responsible for establishing the policies related to expatriate assignments. For example, there are often important *compensation* issues that must be handled for expatriates. Questions must be answered, such as: (1) Should they receive extra pay while on assignment away from home (Commonly, they retain their current home and must have living quarters in the foreign location as well)? (2) How are the tax differences in the different countries to be handled? (3) Do they need additional or different benefits (e.g., health care) in the foreign location?

Training (an HRM responsibility) plays a key role in expatriate assignments and in building managerial capabilities. For example, associates and managers undertaking expatriate assignments often receive cultural training to prepare them to live and work in the new cultural environment. Training may also be used to help managers learn how to more effectively manage in a global market environment. Frequently, such training will emphasize the value of cultural diversity and effectively using all of the organization's available human capital. *Career planning* (an HRM responsibility) is important for identifying when to give associates and managers expatriate assignments based on the knowledge and skills needed for the future positions in positions projected for their careers in the organization.

---

building your human capital

Assessment of Openness for International Work

In this age of globalization, it is important to clearly understand your own feelings about international teams and assignments. In the following installment of *Building Your Human Capital,* we present an assessment of openness for international work. The assessment measures specific attitudes and behaviors thought to be associated with this type of openness.

Instructions

In the following assessment, you will read 24 statements. After carefully reading each statement, use the accompanying rating scale to indicate how the statement applies to you. Rate yourself as honestly as possible.

	Never				Often
1. I eat at a variety of ethnic restaurants.	1	2	3	4	5
2. I attend foreign films.	1	2	3	4	5
3. I read magazines that address world events.	1	2	3	4	5
4. I follow world news on television or the Internet.	1	2	3	4	5
5. I attend ethnic festivals.	1	2	3	4	5
6. I visit art galleries and/or museums.	1	2	3	4	5
7. I attend the theater, concerts, ballet, etc.	1	2	3	4	5
8. I travel widely within my own country.	1	2	3	4	5

	Strongly Disagree				Strongly Agree
9. I would host a foreign exchange student.	1	2	3	4	5
10. I have extensively studied a foreign language.	1	2	3	4	5

11.	I am fluent in another language.	1	2	3	4	5
12.	I have spent substantial time in another part of the world.					
13.	I visited another part of the world by the age of 18.	1	2	3	4	5
14.	My friends' career goals, interests, and education are diverse.	1	2	3	4	5
15.	My friends' ethnic backgrounds are diverse.	1	2	3	4	5
16.	My friends' religious affiliations are diverse.					
17.	My friends' first languages are diverse.	1	2	3	4	5
18.	I have moved or been relocated substantial distances.	1	2	3	4	5
19.	I hope the company I work for (or will work for) will send me on an assignment to another part of the world.	1	2	3	4	5
20.	Foreign-language skills should be taught in elementary school.	1	2	3	4	5
21.	Traveling the world is a priority in my life.	1	2	3	4	5
22.	A year-long assignment in another part of the world would be a fantastic opportunity for me and/or my family.	1	2	3	4	5
23.	Other cultures fascinate me.	1	2	3	4	5
24.	If I took a vacation in another part of the world, I would prefer to stay in a small, locally owned hotel rather than a global chain.	1	2	3	4	5

Scoring Key for Openness to International Work

Four aspects of openness to international work have been assessed. To create scores for each of the four, combine your responses as follows:

Extent of participation in cross-cultural activities: Item 1 + Item 2 + Item 3 + Item 4 + Item 5 + Item 6 + Item 7 + Item 8

Participation scores can range from 8 to 40. Scores of 32 and above may be considered high, while scores of 16 and below may be considered low.

Extent to which international attitudes are held: Item 9 + Item 19 + Item 20 + Item 21 + Item 22 + Item 23 + Item 24

Attitude scores can range from 7 to 35. Scores of 28 and above may be considered high, while scores of 14 and below may be considered low.

Extent of international activities: Item 10 + Item 11 + Item 12 + Item 13 + Item 18

Activity scores can range from 5 to 25. Scores of 20 and above may be considered high, while scores of 10 and below may be considered low.

Degree of comfort with cross-cultural diversity: Item 14 + Item 15 + Item 16 + Item 17

Diversity scores can range from 4 to 20. Scores of 16 and above may be considered high, while scores of 8 and below may be considered low.

High scores on two or more aspects of openness, with no low scores on any aspects, suggest strong interest in and aptitude for international work.

Source: Based on P.M. Caligiuri, R.R. Jacobs, & J.L. Farr. 2000. "The Attitudinal and Behavioral Openness Scale: Scale Development and Construct Validation," *International Journal of Intercultural Relations*, 24: 27–46.

an organizational behavior moment
Managing in a Foreign Land

Spumonti, Inc., is a small manufacturer of furniture. The company was founded in 1987 by Joe Spumonti, who had been employed as a cabinetmaker in a large firm before he decided to open his own shop in the town of Colorado Springs. He soon found that some of his customers were interested in special furniture that could be built to complement their cabinets. Joe found their requests easy to accommodate. In fact, it wasn't long before their requests for custom furniture increased to the point that Joe no longer had time to build cabinets.

Joe visited a banker, obtained a loan, and opened a larger shop. He hired several craftspeople, purchased more equipment, and obtained exclusive rights to manufacture a special line of furniture. By 1997, the business had grown considerably. He then expanded the shop by purchasing adjoining buildings and converting them into production facilities. Because of the high noise level, he also opened a sales and administrative office several blocks away, in the more exclusive downtown business district.

Morale was very good among all associates. The workers often commented on Joe Spumonti's dynamic enthusiasm, as he shared his dreams and aspirations with them and made them feel like members of a big but close-knit family. Associates viewed the future with optimism and anticipated the growth of the company along with associated growth in their own responsibilities. Although their pay was competitive with that provided by other local businesses, it was not exceptional. Still, associates and others in the community viewed jobs with Spumonti as prestigious and desirable. The training, open sharing of information, and individual autonomy were noteworthy.

By 2009, business volume had grown to the extent that Joe found it necessary to hire a chief operating officer (COO) and to incorporate the business. Although incorporation posed no problem, the COO did. Joe wanted someone well acquainted with modern management techniques who could monitor internal operations and help computerize many of the procedures. Although he preferred to promote one of his loyal associates, none of them seemed interested in management at that time. Ultimately, he hired Wolfgang Schmidt, a visa holder from Germany who had recently completed his MBA at a German university. Joe thought Wolfgang was the most qualified among the applicants, especially with his experience in his family's furniture company in Germany.

Almost immediately after Wolfgang was hired, Joe began to spend most of his time on strategic planning and building external relationships with key constituents. Joe had neglected these functions for a long time and felt they demanded his immediate attention. Wolfgang did not object to being left on his own because he was enthusiastic about his duties. It was his first leadership opportunity.

Wolfgang was more conservative in his approach than Joe had been. He did not like to leave things to chance or to the gut feel of the associates, so he tried to intervene in many decisions the associates previously had been making for themselves. It wasn't that Wolfgang didn't trust the associates; rather, he simply felt the need to be in control. Nonetheless, his approach was not popular.

Dissatisfaction soon spread to most associates in the shop, who began to complain about lack of opportunity, noise, and low pay. Morale was now poor, and productivity was low among all associates. Absenteeism increased, and several longtime associates expressed their intention to find other jobs. Wolfgang's approach had not been successful, but he attributed its failure to the lack of employee openness to new management methods. He suggested to Joe that they give a pay raise to all associates "across the board" to improve their morale and reestablish their commitment. The pay raise would cost the company $120,000 annually, but Joe approved it as a necessary expense.

Morale and satisfaction did not improve, however. Shortly after the pay raise was announced, two of Spumonti's senior associates accepted jobs at other companies and announced their resignations. Wolfgang was bewildered and was considering recommending a second pay increase.

Discussion Questions

1. What weaknesses do you see in Joe's handling of Wolfgang?
2. Could Joe have anticipated Wolfgang's approach?
3. Can Wolfgang's career at Spumonti be saved?

team exercise
International Etiquette

A business traveler or expatriate must be aware of local customs governing punctuality, greetings, introductions, gift-giving, dining behavior, and gestures. Customs vary dramatically around the world, and what is accepted or even valued in one culture may be highly insulting in another. Many business deals and relationships have been harmed by a lack of awareness. In the exercise that follows, your team will compete with other teams in a test of international etiquette.

STEP 1: As an individual, complete the following quiz by selecting T (True) or F (False) for each item.

a. In Japan, slurping soup is considered bad manners.	T	F
b. In Italy, giving chrysanthemums is appropriate for a festive event.	T	F
c. In Ecuador, it is generally acceptable to be a few minutes late for a business meeting.	T	F
d. In England, the "V" sign formed with two fingers means victory when the palm faces outward but is an ugly gesture if the palm is facing inward.	T	F
e. In China, a person's surname is often given or written first with the given name appearing after.	T	F
f. In Japan, shoes are generally not worn past the doorway of a home.	T	F
g. In Brazil, hugs among business associates are considered inappropriate.	T	F
h. In Germany, use of formal titles when addressing another person is very common.	T	F
i. In Saudi Arabia, crossing one's legs in the typical style of U.S. men may cause problems.	T	F
j. In China, green hats are a symbol of achievement for men.	T	F
k. In China, a gift wrapped in red paper or enclosed in a red box is appropriate for celebrating a successful negotiation.	T	F
l. In Kuwait, an invitation to a pig roast would be warmly received.	T	F
m. In India, a leather organizer would be warmly received as a gift.	T	F
n. In Japan, it is most appropriate to give a gift with two hands.	T	F
o. In Iraq, passing a bowl or plate with the left hand is appropriate.	T	F
p. In Saudi Arabia, ignoring a woman encountered in a public place is insulting to the woman's family.	T	F

STEP 2: Assemble into groups of four to five, using the assignments or guidelines provided by the instructor.

STEP 3: Discuss the quiz as a group, and develop a set of answers for the group as a whole.

STEP 4: Complete the scoring form that follows using the answer key provided by your instructor.

Number of answers that I had correct: _____
Average number of answers that individuals in the group had correct: _____
Number of answers that the group had correct following its discussion: _____

International mastery:	13–15 correct
International competence:	9–12 correct
International deficiency:	5–8 correct
International danger:	1–4 correct

STEP 5: Designate a spokesperson to report your group's overall score and to explain the logic or information used by the group in arriving at wrong answers.

Endnotes

1. Dastidar, P. 2009. International corporate diversification and performance: Does firm self-selection matter? *Journal of International Business Studies*, 40: 71–85; Gande, A., Schenzler, C. & Senbet, L.W. 2009. Valuation of global diversification. *Journal of International Business Studies*, 40: 1515–1532; Makino, S., Isobe, T., & Chan, C.M. 2005. Does country matter? *Strategic Management Journal*, 25: 1027–1043.

2. Bouquet, C, Morrison, A., & Birkinshaw, J. 2009. International attention and multinational enterprise performance. *Journal of International Business Studies*, 40: 108–131.

3. Loveman, G., Schlesinger, L., & Anthony, R. 1993. *Euro Disney: The first 100 days*. Boston: Harvard Business School Publishing.

4. Ibid.

5. Hitt, M.A., Ireland, R.D., & Hoskisson, R.E. 2011. *Strategic management: Competitiveness and globalization* (9th ed.). Mason, OH: South-Western Cengage Learning.

6. United Nations Conference on Trade and Development. 2008. *World Investment Report*, New York, U.S.A.; United Nations Conference on Trade and Development. 2009. *World Investment Report*, New York, U.S.A.

7. United Nations Conference on Trade and Development. 2010. *World Investment Report*, New York, U.S.A.

8. World Trade Organization. 2009. *World Trade Report* 2009. Geneva, Switzerland.

9. Hitt, M.A. & He, X. 2008. Firm strategies in a changing global competitive landscape. *Business Horizons*, 51: 363–369.

10. *World Investment Report*, 2005. Transnational corporations and the internationalization of R&D. Geneva, Switzerland: United Nations Conference on Trade and Development (UNTAD).

11. Wiersema, M.E. & Bowen, H.P. Corporate diversification: The impact of foreign competition, industry globalization and product diversification. *Strategic Management Journal*, 29: 115–132; Malik, O.R. & Kotabe, M. 2009. Dynamic capabilities, government policies and performance in firms from emerging economies: Evidence from India and Pakistan. *Journal of Management Studies*, 46:421–450.

12. Hitt, Ireland, & Hoskisson, *Strategic management.*

13. For a discussion of this issue, see Asgary, N., & Walle, A.H. 2002. The cultural impact of globalization: Economic activity and social change. *Cross Cultural Management*, 9(3): 58–75; Holton, R. 2000. Globalization's cultural consequences. *The Annals of the American Academy of Political and Social Science*, 570: 140–152; Zhelezniak, O. 2003. Japanese culture and globalization. *Far Eastern Affairs*, 31(2): 114–120.

14. Hall, P.A. & Soskice, D. 2001. An introduction to the varieties of capitalism. In P. A. Hall & D. Soskice (Eds.), *Varieties of capitalism: The institutional foundations of comparative advantage*. Oxford, UK: Oxford University Press, 1–68; Hall, E.T. 1976. *Beyond culture*. New York: Anchor Books–Doubleday.

15. Sheth, J.N. 2006. Clash of cultures or fusion of cultures? Implications for international business. *Journal of International Management*, 12: 218–221; Gong, W. 2009. National culture and global diffusion of business-to-consumer e-commerce. *Cross Cultural Management*, 16: 83–101.

16. Asgary & Walle, The cultural impact of globalization.

17. Friedman, T.L. 2005. *The world is flat*. New York: Farrar, Straus and Giroux.

18. Towsend, J.D., Yeniyurt, S., & Talay, M.B. 2009. Getting to global: An evolutionary perspective of brand expansion in international markets. *Journal of International Business Studies*, 40: 539–558.

19. Hitt, Ireland & Hoskisson, *Strategic management.*

20. Ibid.; Hitt, M.A., Tihanyi, L., Miller, T., & Connelly, B. 2006. International diversification: Antecedents, outcomes and moderators. *Journal of Management*, 32: 831–867; Bruton, G.D., Ahlstrom, D., & Puky, T. 2009. Institutional differences and the development of entrepreneurial ventures: A comparison of the venture capital industries in Latin America and Asia. *Journal of International Business Studies*, 40:762–778.

21. Meyer, K. 2006. Global focusing: From domestic conglomerates to global specialists. *Journal of Management Studies*, 43: 1109–1144.

22. Sapienza, H.J., Autio, E., George, G., & Zahra, S. 2006. A capabilities perspective on the effects of early internationalization on firm survival and growth. *Academy of Management Review*, 31: 914–933; Madhaven, R. & Iriyama, A. 2009. Understanding global flows of venture capital: Human networks as the carrier wave of globalization. *Journal of International Business Studies*, 40: 1241–1259.

23. Hitt, M.A., Franklin, V., & Zhu, H. 2006. Culture, institutions and international strategy. *Journal of International Management*, 12: 222–234

24. Hitt, Ireland, & Hoskisson, *Strategic management*

25. Xia, J., Boal, K., Delios, A. 2009. When experience meets national institutional environmental change: Foreign entry attempts of U.S. firms in the central and Eastern European region. *Strategic Management Journal*, 30: 1286–1309.

26. Lin, Z, Peng, M.W., Yang, H. & Sun, S.L. 2009. How do networks and learning drive M&As? An institutional comparison between China and the United States. *Strategic Management Journal*, 30: 1113–1132.

27. Estrin, S., Baghdasaryan, D. & Meyer, K.E. 2009. The impact of institutional and human resource distance on international entry strategies. *Journal of Management Studies*, 461171–1196.

28. Chung, W. & Yeaple, S. 2008. International knowledge sourcing: Evidence from U.S. firms expanding abroad. *Strategic Management Journal*, 29: 1207–1224.

29. Shapiro, D.L., Furst, S.A., Spreitzer, G.M., & Von Glinow, M.A. 2002. Transnational teams in the electronic age: Are team identity and high performance at risk? *Journal of Organizational Behavior*, 23: 455–467.

30. Cohen, S.G., & Gibson, C.B. 2003. In the beginning: Introduction and framework. In C.B. Gibson & S.G. Cohen (Eds.), *Virtual teams that work: Creating conditions for virtual team effectiveness*. San Francisco: Jossey-Bass.

31. Gibson, C.B., & Manuel, J.A. 2003. Building trust: Effective multicultural communication processes in virtual teams. In Gibson & Cohen (Eds.), *Virtual teams that work.*

32. Kim, P.H., Dirks, K.T., & Cooper, C.D. 2009. The repair of trust: A dynamic bilateral perspective and multilevel conceptualization. *Academy of Management Review*, 34: 401–422.

33. Shin, Y. 2004. A person–environment fit model for virtual organizations. *Journal of Management*, 30: 725–743. Also see: Grabowski, M., & Roberts, K.H. 1999. Risk mitigation in virtual organizations. *Organization Science*, 10: 704–721; Jarvenpaa, S.L., & Leidner, D.E. 1999. Communication and trust in global virtual teams. *Organization Science*, 10: 791–815; Kasper-Fuehrer, E.C., & Ashkanasy, N.M. 2001. Communicating trustworthiness and building trust in interorganizational virtual organizations. *Journal of Management*, 27: 235–254; Raghuram, S., Garud, R., Wiesenfeld, B., & Gupta, V. 2001. Factors contributing to virtual work adjustment. *Journal of Management*, 27: 383–405.

34. Shin, A person–environment fit model for virtual organizations.

35. Jarvenpaa & Leidner, Communication and trust in global virtual teams.

36. Chua, R.Y.J., Morris, M.W., & Ingram, P. 2009. Guanxi vs networking: Distinctive configurations of affect- and cognition-based trust in the networks of Chinese vs American managers. *Journal of international Business Studies*, 40: 490–508.

37. Blackburn, R.S., Furst, S.A., & Rosen, B. 2003. Building a winning virtual team: KSAs, selection, training, and evaluation. In Gibson & Cohen (Eds.), *Virtual teams that work*; Shapiro, Furst, Spreitzer, & Von Glinow, Transnational teams in the electronic age.

38. Weiss, S.E. 1994. Negotiating with "Romans"—Part 2. *Sloan Management Review*, 35(3): 85–99.

39. Blackburn, Furst, & Rosen, Building a winning virtual team.

40. Shapiro, Furst, Spreitzer, & Von Glinow, Transnational teams in the electronic age.

41. Cramton, C.D., & Webber, S.S. 2002. *The impact of virtual design on the processes and effectiveness of information technology work teams*. Fairfax, VA: George Washington University.

42. Blackburn, Furst, & Rosen, Building a winning virtual team.

43. Shin, A person–environment fit model for virtual organizations.

44. Brock, D.M., Shenkar, O., Shoham, A., & Siscovick, I.C. National culture and expatriate deployment, *Journal of International Business Studies*, 39: 1293–1309.

45. Li, S. & Scullion, H. 2006. Bridging the distance: Managing cross-border knowledge holders. *Asia Pacific Journal of Management*, 23: 71–92; Nielsen, B.B. and Nelson, S. 2009. Learning and innovation in international strategic alliances: An empirical test of the role of trust and tacitness. *Journal of Management Studies*, 46: 1031–1056.

46. Reiche, B.S., Harzing, A.-W. & Kraimer, M.L. 2009. The role of international assignees' social capital in creating inter-unit intellectual capital: A cross-level model. *Journal of International Business Studies*, 40: 509–526.

47. Tan, D., & Mahoney, J. T. 2006. Why a multinational firm chooses expatriates: Integrating resource-based, agency and transaction costs perspectives. *Journal of Management Studies*, 43: 457–484; Brannen, M.Y., & Peterson, M.F. 2009. Merging without alienating: Interventions promoting cross-cultural organizational integration and their limitations. *Journal of International Business Studies*, 40: 468–489.

48. Andreason, A.W. 2003. Direct and indirect forms of in-country support for expatriates and their families as a means of reducing premature returns and improving job performance. *International Journal of Management*, 20: 548–555; McCall, M.W., & Hollenbeck, G.P. 2002. Global fatalities: When international executives derail. *Ivey Business Journal*, 66(5): 74–78.

49. Black, J.S., & Gregersen, H.B. 1991. The other half of the picture: Antecedents of spouse cross-cultural adjustment. *Journal of International Business Studies*, 3: 461–478; Sims, R.H., & Schraeder, M. 2004. An examination of salient factors affecting expatriate culture shock. *Journal of Business and Management*, 10: 73–87

50. See, for example: Andreason, Direct and indirect forms of in-country support for expatriates and their families as a means of reducing premature returns and improving job performance; Tung, R. 1982. Selection and training procedures of U.S., European, and Japanese multinationals. *California Management Review*, 25(1): 57–71.

51. Shaffer, M.A., & Harrison, D.A. 2001. Forgotten partners of international assignments: Development and test of a model of spouse adjustment. *Journal of Applied Psychology*, 86: 238–254.

52. Rothausen, T.J. 2009. Management work-family research and work-family fit. *Family Business Review*, 22: 220–234.

53. Gouttefarde, C. 1992. Host national culture shock: What management can do. *European Management Review*, 92(4): 1–3.

54. Andreason, Direct and indirect forms of in-country support for expatriates and their families as a means of reducing premature returns and improving job performance; Caligiuri, P.M. 2002. The big five personality characteristics as predictors of expatriate's desire to terminate the assignment and supervisor-rated performance. *Personnel Psychology*, 53: 67–98; McCall & Hollenbeck, Global fatalities; Sims & Schraeder, An examination of salient factors affecting expatriate culture shock.

55. For a recent information company training in cross-cultural environments see: Beck, N., Labst, R., & Walgenbach, P. 2009. The cultural dependence of vocational training. *Journal of International Business Studies*, 40: 1374–1395.

56. Frazee, V. 1999. Culture and language training: Send your expats prepared for success. *Workforce*, 4(2): 6–11.

57. Aperian Global, 2007. Global assignment services. At http://www.aperianglobal.com/practice_areas_global_assignment_services. asp.

58. Sims & Schraeder, An examination of salient factors affecting expatriate culture shock.

59. Furuya, N., Stevens, M.J., Bird, A., Oddou, G., & Mendenhall, M. 2009. Managing the learning and transfer of global management competence: Antecedents and outcomes of Japanese repatriation effectiveness. *Journal of International Business Studies*, 40: 200–215.

60. Oddou, G., Osland, J.S. & Blakeney, R.N. 2009. Repatriating knowledge: Variables influencing the "transfer" process. *Journal of International Business Studies*, 40: 181–199. Black, J.S., & Gregersen, H. 1999. The right way to manage expatriates. *Harvard Business Review*, 77(2): 52–63; Paik, Y., Segaud, B., & Malinowski, C. 2002. How to improve repatriation management: Are motivations and expectations congruent between the company and expatriates? *International Journal of Manpower*, 23: 635–648; Stroh, L., Gregersen, H., & Black, S. 1998. Closing the gap: Expectations versus reality among repatriates. *Journal of World Business*, 33: 111–124.

61. Fisher, C.M. 2002. Increase in female expatriates raises dual-career concerns. *Benefits & Compensation International*, 32(1): 73.

62. Janssens, M., Cappellen, T., & Zanoni, P. 2006. Successful female expatriates as agents: Positioning oneself through gender, hierarchy and culture. *Journal of World Business*, 41: 133–148.

63. Manning, S., Massini, S., & Lewin, A.Y. 2008. A dynamic perspective on next-generation offshoring: The global sourcing of science and engineering talent. *Academy of Management Perspectives*, 22(3): 35–54; Farrell, D., Laboissiere, M.A., & Rosenfeld, J. 2006. Sizing the emerging global labor market: Rational behavior from both companies and countries can help it work. *Academy of Management Perspectives*, 20 (4): 23–34.

64. Anonymous. 2003. College careers: Pride in diversity. At http://www.microsoft.com/college/diversity/jose.asp.

65. Microsoft Corporations. 2007. Pride in diversity: Diversity & employee groups. At http://members.microsoft.com/careers/mslife/diversepride/employeegroups.mspx.

66. Rothhausen, T.J., Gonzales, J.A., & Griffin, A.E.C. 2009. Are all the parts there everywhere? Facet job satisfaction in the United States and the Philippines. *Asia Pacific Journal of Management*, 26: 681–700.

67. Tomlinson, F., & Egan, S. 2002. Organizational sensemaking in a culturally diverse setting: Limits to the "valuing diversity" discourse. *Management Learning*, 33: 79–98.

68. Hall, *Beyond culture*.

69. Fitzgerald, M. 2007. Can you ace this test? A new exam forces managers to prove their mettle. *Fast Company*, February: 27.

70. Katsikeas, C.S., Skarmeas, D., & Bello, D.C. 2009. Developing successful trust-based international exchange relationships. *Journal of International Business Studies*, 40: 132–155.

71. Munter, M. 1993. Cross-cultural communication for managers. *Business Horizons*, 36(3): 69–78.

72. Hall, E.T. 1983. *The dance of life: The other dimension of time.* New York: Anchor Books.

73. Bluedorn, A.C., Felker, C., & Lane, P.M. 1992. How many things do you like to do at once? An introduction to monochronic and polychronic time. *Academy of Management Executive*, 6(4): 17–26; Wessel, R. 2003. Is there time to slow down? As the world speeds up, how cultures define the elastic nature of time may affect our environmental health. *Christian Science Monitor*, January 9: 13.

74. Bluedorn, Felker, & Lane. 1992. How many things do you like to do at once? Wessel, Is there time to slow down?

75. Earley, P.C., & Ang, S. 2003. *Cultural intelligence: Individual interactions across cultures.* Stanford, CA: Stanford University Press.

76. Williamson, I.O., Burnett, M.F. & Bartol, K.M. 2009. The interactive effect of collectivism and organizational rewards on affective organizational commitment. *Cross Cultural Management*, 16: 28–43.

77. Zhou, K.Z., Li, J.J., Zhou, N., & Su, C. 2008. Market orientation, job satisfaction, product quality and firm performance: Evidence from China. *Strategic Management Journal*, 29: 985–1000.

78. Bartlett, C.A., & Ghoshal, S. 1998. *Managing across borders: The transnational solution* (2nd ed.). Boston: Harvard Business School Press; Harzing, A.-W. 2000. An empirical analysis and extension of the Bartlett and Ghoshal typology of multinational companies. *Journal of International Business Studies*, 31: 101–120; Hitt, Ireland, & Hoskisson, *Strategic management*.

79. Unilever N.V./Unilever PLC. 2007. About Unilever. At http://www.unilever.com/ourcompany/aboutunilever/introducingunilever/asp.

80. Li, L. 2005. Is regional strategy more effective than global strategy in the U.S. service industries? *Management International Review*, 45: 37–57; Harzing, An empirical analysis and extension of the Bartlett and Ghoshal typology of multinational companies.

81. Harzing, A.-W., & Nooderhaven, N. 2006. Geographical distance and the role and management of subsidiaries: The case of subsidiaries down-under. *Asia Pacific Journal of Management*, 23: 167–185; Capron, L., & Guillen, M. 2009. National corporate governance institutions and post-acquisition target reorganization. *Strategic Management Journal*, 30: 803–833.

82. Bartlett & Ghoshal, Managing across borders: The transnational solution; Harzing, An empirical analysis and extension of the Bartlett and Ghoshal typology of multinational companies; Hitt, Ireland, & Hoskisson, *Strategic management*.

83. This is Cemex. 2009. Cemex web site. At http://www.cemex.com/tc/tc_lp.asp, December.

84. Zellmer-Bruhn, M., & Gibson, C. 2006. Multinational organization context: Implications for team learning and performance. *Academy of Management Journal*, 49: 501–518; Zhang, Y., Dolan, S., Lingham, T., & Altman, Y. 2009. International strategic human resource management: A comparative case analysis of Spanish firms in China. *Management and Organization Review*, 5: 195–222.

85. Bartlett & Ghoshal, Managing across borders: The transnational solution; Harzing, An empirical analysis and extension of the Bartlett and Ghoshal typology of multinational companies; Hitt, Ireland, & Hoskisson, *Strategic management*.

86. Ibarra, H., & Sackley, N. 1995. *Charlotte Beers at Ogilvy & Mather Worldwide.* Boston: Harvard Business School Publishing.

87. Ogilvy & Mather. 2009. Company information. At http://www.ogilvy.com/company.

88. Bentley, S. 1997. Big agencies profit from global tactics. *Marketing Week*, 19(43): 25–26.

89. Ogilvy & Mather. 2009. About OgilvyAction. At http://www.ogilvy.com/#/About/Network/OgilvyAction.aspx, December.

90. Birkinshaw, J., Braunerhjelm, P., & Holm, U. 2006. Why some multinational corporations relocate their headquarters overseas. *Strategic Management Journal*, 27: 681–700.

91. See, for example, Zatzick, C.D., & Iverson, R.D. 2006. High-involvement and workforce reduction: Competitive advantage or disadvantage? *Academy of Management Journal*, 49: 999–1015.

92. MacDuffie, J.P. 1995. Human resource bundles and manufacturing performance: Organizational logic and flexible production systems. *Industrial and Labor Relations Review*, 48: 197–221.

93. Guthrie, J.P. 2001. High-involvement work practices, turnover, and productivity: Evidence from New Zealand. *Academy of Management Journal*, 44: 180–190.

94. Black, B. 1999. National culture and high commitment management. *Employee Management*, 21: 389–404.

95. Huang, X., Shi, K., Zhang, Z., & Cheung, Y.L. 2006. The impact of participative leadership behavior on psychological empowerment and organizational commitment in Chinese state-owned enterprises: The moderating role of organizational tenure. *Asia Pacific Journal of Management*, 23: 345–367.

96. Benito, G.R.G., Petersen, B., & Welch, L.S. 2009. Towards more realistic conceptualizations of foreign operation modes. *Journal of International Business Studies*, 40: 1455–1470.

97. House, R., Javidan, M., Hanges, P., & Dorfman, P. 2002. Understanding cultures and implicit leadership theories across the globe: An introduction to project GLOBE. *Journal of World Business*, 37: 3–10; Javidan, M., & House, R.J. 2001. Cultural acumen for the global manager: Lessons from Project GLOBE. *Organizational Dynamics*, 29: 289–305.

98. Hofstede, G. 1984. *Culture's consequences: International differences in work-related values (abridged edition).* Beverly Hills, CA: Sage Publications.

99. Witt, M.A., & Redding, G. 2009. Culture, meaning and institutions: Executive rationale in Germany and Japan. *Journal of International Business Studies*, 40: 859–885.

100. Leung. K., Bhagat, R.S., Buchan, N.R., Erez, M., & Gibson, C.B. 2005. Culture and international business: Recent advances and their implications for future research. *Journal of International Business Studies*, 36: 357–378.

101. Rothaermel, F.T., Kotha, S., & Steensma, H.K. 2006. International market entry by U.S. Internet firms: An empirical analysis of country risk, national culture and market size. *Journal of Management*, 32: 56–82; Bhaskaran, S., & Gligorovska, E. 2009. Influence of national culture on transnational alliance relationships. *Cross Cultural Management*, 16: 44–61.

102. Zaheer, S., & Zaheer, A. 2006. Trust across borders. *Journal of International Business Studies*, 37: 21–29.

103. Randolph, W.A., & Sashkin, M. 2002. Can organizational empowerment work in multinational settings? *Academy of Management Executive*, 16: 112–115.

104. Michailova, S., & Hutchings, K. 2006. National cultural influences on knowledge sharing: A comparison of China and Russia. *Journal of Management Studies*, 43: 383–405; Wong, A., & Tjosvold, D. 2006. Collectivist values for learning in organizational relationships in China: The role of trust and vertical coordination. *Asia Pacific Journal of Management*, 23: 299–317.

105. van der Vegt, G.S., van de Vliert, E., & Huang, X. 2005. Location-level links between diversity and innovative climate depend on national power distance. *Academy of Management Journal*, 48: 1171–1182.

106. Newburry, W., & Yakova, N. 2006. Standardization preferences: A function of national culture, work interdependence and local embeddedness. *Journal of International Business Studies*, 37: 44–60.

107. AES Company home page, 2009, at http://www.aes.com/aes/index?page=home, December; Hamilton, M.M. 2003. AES's new power structure: Struggling utility overhauls corporate (lack of) structure. *The Washington Post*, June 2, E1; McMillan, J., & Dosunmu, A. 2002. Nigeria. Palo Alto, CA: Stanford Graduate School of Business; O'Reilly, C.A., & Pfeffer, J. 2000. *Hidden value: How great companies achieve extraordinary results with ordinary people.* Boston: Harvard Business School Press.

108. Hooker, J. 2009. Corruption from a cross-cultural perspective. *Cross Cultural Management*, 16: 251–267.

109. Rodriguez, P., Siegel, D.S., Hillman, A., & Eden, L. 2006. Three lenses on the multinational enterprise: Politics, corruption, and corporate social responsibility. *Journal of International Business Studies*, 37: 733–746; Meschi, P.-X. 2009. Government corruption and foreign stakes in international joint ventures in emerging economies. *Asia Pacific Journal of Management*, 26: 241–261.

110. Davids, M. 1999. Global standards, local problems. *The Journal of Business Strategy*, 20: 38–43.

111. Sanyal, R. 2009. The propensity to bribe in international business: The relevance of cultural variables. *Cross Cultural Management*, 16: 287–300.

112. Davids, Global standards, local problems.

113. Cuervo-Cazurra, A. 2006. Who cares about corruption? *Journal of International Business Studies*, 37: 807–822; Ralston, D.A., Egri, C.P., Garcia Carranza, M.T., Ramburuth, P., et al., 2009. Ethical preferences for influencing superiors: A 41-society study. *Journal of International Business Studies*, 40: 1022–1045.

COOPERATING AND communicating across cultures

Americans and Germans Working in a Project Team

Markus Pudelko
University of Edinburgh Management School

This case was written by Dr Markus Pudelko, The University of Edinburgh Management School. It is intended to be used as the basis for class discussion rather than to illustrate either effective or ineffective handling of a management situation. The case was compiled from generalized experience and on relevant literature, in particular Schroll-Machl, S. (1996) 'Kulturbedingte Unterschiede im Problemlösungsprozeß bei deutsch-amerikanischen Arbeitsgruppen', in Thomas, A. (ed) *Psychologie interkulturellen Handelns*, Göttingen et al: Hogrefe, 383–409).

Reference no 406-034-1.

1. SITUATION: THE PROJECT IS DOMINATED BY GERMANS

The American perspective

Introduction

Two months ago I was sent by my company from our Philadelphia headquarters to Stuttgart in order to prepare the launch of a new product on the European market. The product, a laser for eye surgery, was developed by a joint venture between us and our German partner. Even though the joint venture belongs in equal shares to both companies it was agreed that our German partner would take the lead in introducing the product on the European market and that we would have the say for launching the product in North America. For all other regions both partners agreed to work in tandem.

So I was selected to represent our company on what was otherwise a German team. Even though I had never worked in Germany before, I was considered to be the natural candidate for the assignment: I speak fluent German as my wife is German. In addition, I thought I was also culturally quite well prepared for the job. Next to speaking the language and having gotten used to putting up with my wife's tick for over-punctuality, I also regularly travel to Germany to visit my wife's family. Also, I have had frequent e-mail exchanges and telephone conversations with our German partners. But now, after two months working around the clock with my German team colleagues, I realize how difficult it has been for me to cooperate and communicate effectively with them. Our project of preparing the launch of our new laser is finished now and in the end we did a good job, but it was very tough and certainly not without frictions. Now I am happy and relieved to be returning to the States.

Planning phase

The problems already started with our first meeting. We were supposed to define our key objectives, our main challenges and our overall strategy. I was expecting something like a brainstorming session, in order to develop some general ideas and solutions, select the best ones, develop a plan and delegate specific tasks to the project team members. I anticipated this meeting to last for one morning or so. Instead, we sat there for three full days. All details were discussed at great length, but no concrete decisions were taken, no real plan was developed and no clear-cut objectives were formulated. The Germans love to see themselves as "Volk der Dichter und Denker" (people of poets and thinkers), but we don't have to endlessly dispute everything and act like a bunch of little Immanuel Kants in order to get a laser on the market! In the beginning, I patiently sat there, joined the discussion and thought it best to just go with the flow. On the second day, however, I became increasingly impatient and suggested several times to focus on what we should do now and then start working. But I was only looked at with amazement and was told that this was still much too early for any specific plan and so our philosophy seminar continued. Much of the third day of the debate I hardly bothered to pay attention anymore.

At the end of day three we finally came up with a decision of where to go from there, but I still was not content. We had wasted a lot of time to achieve so little. This was all very inefficient. How would we ever get the project finished if we continued like this? And moreover, I still did not have a precise idea of what I was supposed to do now. My German team members had discussed all issues at great length and from every possible perspective and developed a fantastic picture of the overall problem, but spent little time on spelling out our next activities. Many details which were relevant to our tasks were mentioned in our lengthy discussions but were never systematically summarized on a chart. How could I remember everything which was said during a three day long discussion? Furthermore, we came up with overall objectives to achieve, but never specified any broken down targets. How can we effectively work without having specific targets by which we can measure our progress and our performance along the way? An overall objective is just not providing enough guidance. To summarize, the Germans are obsessed with their focus on the problem, whereas we Americans focus more on solutions.

Working under the team leader

I would have expected my German team leader to be much more decisive. He was the boss, so he should have called the shots. But no, in particular during the planning phase he consistently asked his team members what they were thinking, was patiently listening to everyone and acted more like just another team member. For a while I would have listened to everyone's opinion, but then I would just have made my mind up, announced my decision, delegated the tasks and controlled the outcome.

I also got particularly annoyed that the team leader frequently interfered in my work. He kept insisting that I had to double-check every little detail before I pass it on to other team members. I don't like to be controlled all the time, I know what I am doing. At the end of the assignment I am happy to get evaluated on my performance, but until then I prefer to be left alone, so that I can do my job. My team leader also constantly reminded me to observe certain procedural rules of which the company seemed to have an endless amount. It seemed to me that they followed their internal procedural rules for the sake of it. It is like the red traffic lights. No German pedestrian crosses the street on red, even if no car is in sight for miles.

Another thing, I thought our team leader was a poor motivator. Instead of pushing people, making them excited about the job and provide them with encouraging feedback, our team leader was always very reserved, formal and fact oriented. No emotions ever came across. Sometimes a pat on the shoulder wouldn't do any harm.

Working with the team members

Not only had I no clear understanding of what I was supposed to do when we started our assignments, I also didn't have a good understanding of what my German colleagues were working on. And there was little exchange of information among us. I am used to working sequentially on a clear set of well broken down targets and at every step of the way getting the information I need from my colleagues. However, whenever I went over to my team members and asked them a specific question, they did answer me politely, but I had the impression they felt disturbed by me asking them questions. Everyone just worked on his or her own.

Furthermore, I was deliberately brought in to share my specific know-how with the Germans. But when we started working on our assignments no one came to see me and asked me for advice. They probably thought they knew everything better and didn't need my expertise. But then why did they want an expert from the States on their team?

I was also puzzled by how badly my German counterparts reacted when I suggested some changes in our strategy. Whenever we hit a problem, it seemed natural for me to adapt our strategy, after all one cannot foresee everything at first and one needs to keep an open mind and remain flexible. It is through trial and error that objectives are reached. But no, we had to stick to our grand master-plan, because so much time was invested in reaching it in the first place.

The German perspective
Introduction

For two months we had Jim, a marketing expert from our joint venture partner in the States, here in Stuttgart. His job was to help us in preparing the launch of our new laser on the European market. He was certainly well qualified for the job and also a really nice guy. He even spoke fluent German. That facilitated our job greatly. Otherwise it would have been quite odd, on a team with 16 Germans and one American, to speak English all the time. It's not so much of a problem during a formal meeting, when everyone listens to what the one speaking has to say. But what about a more informal setting, over lunch for example? If the American is listening, it's fine to talk in English, but if he directs his attention to someone else, should I then continue talking in English with my other German colleagues, as he might want to enter our conversation again? It is completely awkward to talk among Germans in English, searching for words for what you could otherwise express so easily in your own language. Also, to adapt to the Anglo-Saxon style and not look overly formal, we use first names when speaking in English. But it is very embarrassing to call my boss "Hans" when talking in English and then switch right away to "Herr Doktor Fischer" when speaking German again. In the end, with English entering our company communication more and more, we even tend to avoid addressing by name colleagues we have known for years, out of pure confusion over what to say. Therefore, we were really relieved when we heard that our American colleague was speaking German, it saved us from a lot of potentially embarrassing situations. But, as we found out, mastering the language is one thing, being able to truly communicate is a completely different story. I think Jim had no clue of how we do things here and he was little willing to adapt, always thinking that the American way is the only one which makes sense.

Planning phase

First, all members of a newly established team gather all relevant information and discuss them intensively. The objective is to reach a holistic understanding of the problems to be solved. During this phase team leader and team members cooperate on quite equal terms. The team leader is more the moderator of this thought process. Our deliberations are rather complex and abstract, with the intention to establish an overall conceptual foundation that covers all possible eventualities, assumptions and ramifications which lead to a set of logical conclusions. In this process we focus on the underlying principles but already include all potentially relevant details to get to the bottom of our problem. From the multitude of information and ideas we subsequently generate the solution to our problem. By doing so, we frequently recur to theories and scholarly methods. Subsequently, the group decides which tasks need to be tackled in order to reach the overall objective. It is expected that every team member brings his or her expertise and thoughts into this discussion process. The decisions to be reached should be based on a general consensus, be supported by everyone and be regarded as final. The decisions taken at this meeting will direct all ensuing activities. This process might take some time in the beginning, but in the end it might well save us time as we don't need to go back to the drawing board anymore. Unfortunately, Jim didn't understand this concept at all. We tried to encourage him to share with us his perspective on our project. In fact, we specifically asked for an American expert who could share with us the experiences won on the American market, but he just didn't come forward with his knowledge. We found this particularly unhelpful. Instead, he always tried to push us prematurely to break up the work into individual assignments, but at this initial phase we barely started to grasp the problem we were facing. How are we supposed to break our work down into assignments if we collectively still don't fully understand what we are trying to achieve? After some time he even stopped paying full attention to our deliberations. But once we fully understood the problem, developed our strategy and subsequently started working we noticed that Jim just had not grasped the concept which was the basis of our work. Typical American: no willingness to invest time in the beginning to thoroughly understand a problem, just focusing on setting some superficial targets and then seeing later on how one gets along and muddling your way through. We prefer to do things a lot more methodically.

Working under the team leader

Once we reached an agreement about what to do, all the team members started working on their assignments. They had a good understanding of our overall objective and how we wanted to achieve this. We had discussed all eventualities during the planning phase, so everyone had all the information which was needed and was now ready to focus fully on working individually on his or her job. That is everyone except Jim. As he hadn't paid attention when we had discussed our overall strategy, he was subsequently unable to understand what was expected from him. Instead, he felt confused by not having targets nicely broken down for him, so that he didn't have to think about the overall picture but could sequentially tick off one job after the other. This is what I call intellectual laziness. I also thought Jim had completely different expectations from me as his team leader. He expected me to show more authority and be less participatory while we planned our project. I tried to explain to him my more "democratic" understanding of my role as team leader, that I perceived myself more as a "primus inter pares". As team leader I have probably the best technical know-how about our project and all its details, and this is also what my team members expect from me. However, this does not mean that I tell my team what they have to do, I moderate more the decision making process, keep the group together, promote consensus and control the outcome. It is only in the case of conflict that I will enforce a decision. But I think he considered this leadership concept just as a weakness. Also, during the implementation phase he wanted more guidance from me, as he continuously asked me what exactly he should be doing and the exact target against which his performance would be measured. I think our German team members are much more independent in the way they do their job.

Jim also seemed quite annoyed when I tried to align his work to our way of operating and insisted he knew best how to do his job. I should judge his results, not his methods, he said. However, we have certain procedures here and everyone is expected to follow them. I understand that while we have all worked here for at least 10 years and know our company procedures very well, all this was unknown to Jim. But he should have at least shown some respect for our methods and should have tried to follow them, instead of insisting on doing things in his own way. Furthermore, it only makes sense to check on someone regularly and not just evaluate the final result, because by then it can be already too late to adjust things.

Working with the team members

While all team members were concentrating on their jobs, Jim bothered them all the time with specific questions. If he had paid more attention in the first place, this would have been completely unnecessary. During the implementation phase we prefer to work individually in a focused way on our own and don't need much communication with other members of the team. At that stage group meetings only take place if another exchange of information is considered necessary. The incentive to such meetings can come from anybody in the group. And if we come together, we tend to have again a holistic discussion of the entire project, but this time based on a more advanced degree of understanding. What we certainly don't like is to make some little changes here and there, because it might be momentarily more convenient. We try to come up with fundamental solutions to fundamental problems and some quick fixes will only endanger the overall applicability of these solutions. We therefore expect that everybody sticks to what was initially agreed upon and solves their tasks in a way they will be in harmony to our overall plan. If we have to correct any mistakes then we will do this in a very systematic and thorough way and try to understand all possible effects a change in plan will have. Consequently, we were not too pleased that whenever a problem occurred Jim was willing to throw overboard everything we had carefully elaborated on and just try out something different. Changing direction without prior intensive reflection is a sign of sloppiness. Good solutions should last a long time and we try to work here for the long-term.

When we had the final meeting in which he presented us the results of his work, we noticed that he had actually done quite a good job. However, a little more modesty about his work would have been appropriate. He was also somewhat playing out too much his certainly well established presentation skills. I would have preferred a little more substance in his presentation and less of a show. For example, instead of just telling us his conclusions of what we should be doing and elaborating on that, he should first have explained more about the way he developed his proposals.

To sum up, I had thought the Americans were such great managers. But now, having had the experience of working with Jim, I honestly believe that our way of doing business makes more sense.

2. SITUATION: THE PROJECT IS DOMINATED BY AMERICANS

The German perspective

Introduction

While our company was responsible for the launch of the new laser in Europe, our American partners called the shots for the North American market. Still, I was sent over from our headquarters in Stuttgart to share with our American partners the experiences we gained in Germany and to make sure that our interests were also sufficiently considered on the American turf. In principle, the task wasn't that difficult, as we hardly had any genuine conflicts of interest. It was just a matter of getting it right. But, as it turned out, working with the Americans was not so easy. I always thought they were so professional, however I wasn't overly impressed by how the project was managed. But in the end we did alright and I am glad to return home now.

Planning phase

Problems had already started in the planning phase. I am an expert in my field and could have contributed more thoroughly to the definition of our overall strategy. Instead, I was given right away specific targets and was expected to reach them in a very short period of time. But were these really the best targets I could have been given? I would have preferred to give more of my input during the all important planning phase. I was actually not overly convinced about the underlying assumptions on which our strategy was based. But for the sake of speed a thorough collection of information and discussion did not take place. How should one do quality work on this basis?

Working under the team leader

Right from the word go, I was put under so much time pressure that there was no way that I could deliver something with real substance. And yet to my surprise what I did was good enough for my American team leader. Well, it wasn't for me. And indeed later on I had to substantially modify my original suggestions once more information became available. All these subsequent improvements here and there annoyed me greatly. These are indications of sloppy work and in the end cost more time and energy than if we had invested a little more thought in the first place. Moreover, these "quick and dirty" solutions and quick fixes are not exactly testament to the upholding of high quality standards. There was no sense of perfection.

I was always astonished to see how quickly my American team leader reached a decision. He briefly thought about a problem, announced his decision and that was it. Never any doubts about possibly being wrong. Also the other team members just accepted his decisions without ever questioning them. They were even expecting our team leader to make specific decisions all the time, so that they knew exactly what to do. Despite the casual tone in the company, my American colleagues were much more hierarchy oriented compared to what I am used to in Germany. Even though we are much more formal in Germany, I thought in the American company the atmosphere was in the end more authoritarian. This actually came as quite a surprise to me, as I wasn't expecting this.

The head of the department insisted that everybody addressed him by first name, but at the same time he wouldn't have the slightest problem firing someone as soon as he detected some underperformance. By contrast, in Germany we would never call our boss by first name (and neither would he address us by first name) even though we have known each other for more than ten years. But he would also never fire someone who works loyally for the company, after all we are a team, care for each other and the company has a social responsibility.

I was also put off by the speeches our team leader gave us all the time. I guess they were supposed to motivate us, but for me that was just cheap pep talk, probably copied from these motivation seminars the Americans are so fond of. However, what I really appreciated was the feed-back our team leader gave us, particularly as it always focused on the positive. I think that is something I'd also like to see in Germany.

Working with the team members

While working on our assignments, frequent adaptations had to be made. If we all had followed more precise procedures this could have been entirely avoided. Moreover, as long as we met our individual targets my American team colleagues didn't even care if the overall result made any sense or not. No team member except the leader has any holistic concern for the entire project and feels responsible for the greater picture. I found it somewhat of a paradox that the Americans, the archetype of capitalists, were almost as obsessed with reaching specific targets as the communists were under the centrally planned economy.

At one instance, I was criticized, because my work didn't fit with what the others were doing. But this was exactly my point. If we don't bother to make a detailed picture for ourselves in the first place, how should I know what to do? But I was only told I should have checked with my team members.

I always had problems with these informalities. I don't mind enjoying a drink after work, but during work we should refrain from joking around. As we say in German: "Work is work and schnaps are schnaps." I also noticed that women in the company don't like to be treated with special courtesy. Whenever I held a door open for a woman or, after a working lunch, helped a woman with her coat, I was looked at as if I was doing something bad.

And when we discussed our final results, I felt my American colleagues were all highlighting their individual inputs by far too much. We are all team members and there is no reason to brag about one's own achievements. All my American team members at first appeared to be so collegial but in the end everyone was fighting for his or her own. Everyone pretends to be good buddy with the others, but at the same time I have never seen so much open and almost aggressive competition among team members. In this company they always talk about their team spirit, but I think that is all corporate propaganda.

The American perspective
Introduction

For two months we had Klaus working with us in order to prepare the presentation of our new laser system on the North American market. Klaus had been sent over by our German joint venture partner. He was certainly very competent and in addition a really nice guy, once one got to know him a little better. Nevertheless, working with him proved to be quite difficult, he just drove us nuts with his complete inflexibility. What can you say, a real German.

Planning phase

Klaus just couldn't focus on specific targets and solutions. When we had our first meeting in order to decide who does what, Klaus wanted to drag us into a long discussion about fundamental issues which we just perceived as either irrelevant or something to think about at a later stage. He wanted to plan everything down to the last detail. But you just can't foresee everything and therefore you have to adapt and be flexible along the way. But Klaus just misunderstood our flexibility and open-mindedness for superficiality which of course is nonsense. A first planning meeting should be solution driven. What exactly do we want to achieve? Once we understand this, we identify the specific steps we need to take in order to get there. The main task of the team leader in the planning phase is to assign specific team members to clearly defined tasks and develop a time plan, specifying what and when tasks should be achieved. With the delegation of responsibilities the planning process is finished and off you go.

Working under the team leader

Klaus was always quite nervous about the fact that as team leader I expected him to be fully responsible for his assignment. When I told him his evaluation would be primarily based on his results he got quite anxious about it, always saying that the final result could depend on many things some of which could well be beyond his control. But as a manager you have to stand up for your own performance. No excuses.

In our company it is the team leader who defines the overall objective and specific targets, who structures the assignments, and delegates responsibilities. Subsequently, during the implementation phase, the team leader is always available for questions, provides constant feed-back, supports the information exchange, keeps the morale of the team up, controls whether the various tasks are achieved on time and evaluates the team members according to their individual performance. Overall, the team leader has a strong position, he pushes the project forward.

In the end, Klaus came up with some good results, but in the final presentation he was completely underselling himself. How should people see whether you are a high performer if you can't even show how good you

are? Also, instead of telling us his proposal right away he started out explaining at great lengths the specific assumptions on which his proposal was based, the various alternative solutions he formulated, what his selection criteria were etc. etc. When we all thought he would never come to the point, he finally told us what his proposal was. That was quite a clumsy way of doing a presentation.

Working with the team members

Once Klaus got his assignment he complained that he didn't have enough information to do his job. But that is what a manager is about: to make decisions under uncertainty. And if you don't have the information you need, well, then get it. First he complained that we hadn't discussed the problem enough, but then he just never really communicated with his team members or participated in the ongoing exchange of information. While we continuously popped into each others' offices to clarify things, Klaus just sat in his office and worked by himself.

When we get our tasks from our team leader we are expected to clearly structure our working schedule and solve each single task, one after the other. The trial-and-error principle is an important and often used mechanism. In this phase we use our own knowledge but also frequently ask our colleagues for advice. This implementation phase is usually characterized by an intense information exchange. We see constant feed-back from both team leader and team members as essential to achieving our individual tasks. This information exchange takes place in a very informal way, through e-mails, telephone calls, dropping by at others' offices or just a quick chat on the corridor. Everyone is available

at every point in time for a short discussion. We frequently circulate written documentation to update each other on the various working steps. If we feel that we can improve the final solution by modifying our plan we do so at every stage in the process. If one solution doesn't work we try the next one. To quickly come up with a solution is important, but to be prepared to quickly drop a decision if a better one is found is equally important. This way we constantly improve the final outcome. For all this, good time management is important so that we can stick to the initial time plan. But I think Klaus had little understanding for all that.

Overall, I think Klaus should loosen up a bit. He can actually be quite a humorous guy and when we went to a bar after work we often had a good laugh. But the next day at work he was dead serious again, never made a joke and came across as rather unfriendly and cold. In particular, the secretaries didn't like him much, as he never spoke a private word with them, only focused on the job. Also female colleagues felt at times rather uncomfortable with his manners. They thought of the special attention and courtesy he paid them as rather sexist. I don't think he meant it in that way, but female managers in this country prefer to be treated as fully equal to men and that includes no preferential treatment.

Anyway, Klaus will be going back to Germany now. It was interesting to see how differently people from other countries act and behave. And I am relieved to say that our way of doing things clearly appears to me to make most sense.

ORGANIZATIONAL   ORGANIZATIONAL   ORGANIZATIONAL
      BEHAVIOR   DIVERSITY   BEHAVIOR
  A STRATEGIC APPROACH   A GLOBAL CONTEXT

INDIVIDUAL PROCESSES
LEARNING AND PERCEPTION
PERSONALITY, INTELLIGENCE, ATTITUDES, AND EMOTIONS
WORK MOTIVATION
STRESS AND WELL-BEING

$\downarrow$ $\uparrow$

GROUPS, TEAMS, AND SOCIAL PROCESSES
LEADERSHIP
COMMUNICATION
DECISION MAKING BY INDIVIDUALS AND GROUPS
GROUPS AND TEAMS
CONFLICT, NEGOTIATION, POWER, AND POLITICS

$\downarrow$ $\uparrow$

THE ORGANIZATIONAL CONTEXT
ORGANIZATIONAL STRUCTURE AND CULTURE
ORGANIZATIONAL CHANGE AND DEVELOPMENT

PART 2

individual processes

The chapters in Part I provided the strategic lens that is central to discussions throughout the book, and they explained how organizational diversity and the global environment affect all organizations. In Part II, we explore important concepts related to individual-level processes in organizations.

Chapter 4 explains the concepts of learning and perception. Through individual learning, associates gain the knowledge and skills they need to perform their jobs in organizations. Individual learning contributes to the value of an organization's human capital and provides the base for organizational learning, both of which are critical for organizations to capture a competitive advantage.

Chapter 5 focuses on personality, intelligence, attitudes, and emotions. Managers in organizations need to understand how each of these human characteristics affects individual behavior. Personality and intelligence are an important determinant of a person's behavior and performance and cannot be easily changed. Thus, organizations must learn how to select associates with desirable personalities and intelligence levels to maximize the value of their human capital. However, attitudes and emotions can and do vary. Attitudes and emotions affect behavior, and managers can have a significant effect on individuals' behavior by taking actions that affect their attitudes and emotions.

Chapter 6 examines a fundamental concept in organizational behavior: motivation. Individuals can be motivated in various ways and by various factors. Because individual motivation is highly critical to individual and organizational productivity, understanding how to motivate is vital to effective management.

Chapter 7 deals with stress and well-being, critical issues in today's workplace. While some stress can be functional, much of the stress individuals experience can have negative effects on their productivity and health. When managers understand the causes and consequences of stress, they can attempt to manage it to reduce dysfunctional outcomes.

learning and perception

The Strategic Importance of Learning and Perception

VF Corporation, headquartered in Greensboro, North Carolina, is the world's largest apparel manufacturer, with revenues of $7 billion plus annually. Chances are that you have several items of their clothing in your closet. Their more than thirty brands include: Wrangler, Lee, Vans, The North Face, 7 for all mankind, and Jansport. In 2004, the VF Corporation launched a new growth plan, that has been incredibly successful. The goal of this plan was to transform the VF Corporation in a global lifestyle apparel company. At the center of the plan are six Growth Drivers, one of which is building new growth enablers. The company describes this goal as: "Taking our company to new heights requires new capabilities and skills, and we've invested in areas that are specifically designed to support our growth. ... [W]e know that providing our leaders and associates with new tools and training that stretches their capabilities is crucial to our continued success." Thus, associate learning, development, and knowledge sharing has become one of the crucial drivers of the VF Corporation's new strategy. Tom Nelson, VF Corporation's manager of global sourcing states, "Learning and development makes a significant contribution to the company's ongoing success."

VF Asia Ltd., a subsidiary of VF Corporation located in Hong Kong, took this directive very seriously. This subsidiary totally reorganized its learning unit, which had previously been somewhat piecemeal, with a program here, a learning opportunity there. Tommy

knowledge objectives

After reading this chapter, you should be able to:

1. Describe the effects on learning of positive reinforcement, negative reinforcement, punishment, and extinction.
2. Discuss continuous and intermittent schedules of reinforcement.
3. Explain how principles of learning can be used to train newcomers as well as to modify the behavior of existing associates.
4. Describe the conditions under which adults learn, in addition to rewards and punishments.
5. Describe some specific methods that organizations use to train associates.
6. Discuss learning from failure.
7. Identify typical problems in accurately perceiving others and solutions to these problems.
8. Explain the complexities of causal attributions and task perception.

Lo, learning and development manager, guided the two-person regional training team by first creating a strategy. The company's 780 employees were grouped into one of four learning categories, determined by their level in the organization and the content that needed to be learned and skills developed. These categories are personal competencies, functional leadership, managerial leadership, and strategic leadership. Furthermore, all functions associated with training, performance review and development, feedback, and reward were grouped together in the same program. Thus, training and development is tied to on-the-job performance. A further part of the firm's learning and development strategy was to keep as many programs

©Martin Gerten/epa/Corbis

and initiatives as possible in-house rather than outsourcing them to vendors and contractors. Not only is this cost-effective, but it makes the most use out of in-house knowledge and talent. Finally, although VF Asia is across the world from its parent company, learning and development at the subsidiary is well integrated with that which takes place at headquarters. Tommy Lo belongs to the VF Global Learning Community, which shares new ideas and best practices through conference calls, and certain employees attend corporate learning programs such as the VF Leadership Institute.

There are many specific initiatives in place, all of which are tied to company core competencies. One concern was leadership development. To that end, Lo and his team developed a senior executive curriculum and middle-manager-level curriculum. Another concern was turnover.

Thus, they developed a program to improve managers' interviewing skills, so that they would be better at judging job candidates. Turnover decreased from 26.8 percent in 2007 to 19.3 percent in 2008. In order to improve associates' ability to deal with customers from diverse cultures, the SELF (Self Enhancement Learning Fundamentals) program was initiated. This is an online training program covering topics such as etiquette and negotiations. Associates can use this program at their own leisure. Overall, the 780 associates at VF Asia Ltd. underwent 14,200 hours of training in 2008.

The vast majority of organizations do not assess the effectiveness of their training programs beyond getting participants' reactions to the programs. Things are different at VF Asia Ltd. Learning goals are tied into individual performance evaluations and to the strategic goals of the organization. Monthly learning and development summaries are sent to executives. VF Asia Ltd. makes sure its training and development dollars are well spent. In 2009, this focus on learning was recognized with a BEST award by the American Society for Training and Development (ASTD). The criteria for this award are:

- learning has an enterprise-wide role
- learning has value in the organization's culture
- learning links to individual and organizational performance
- investment is made in learning and performance initiatives

Sources: ASTD BEST Awards. At http://www.astd.org/ASTD/aboutus/AwardsandBestPractices/bestAwards/; ASTD Learning Circuits, Nov. 17, 2009. At http://www.astd.org/LC/news.htm. J.J. Salopek, P. Harris, P. Ketter, M. Laff, & J. Llorens. 2009. "Success is in the details." *T + D*, Oct. 63, 10 ; pp. 36–38. VF Corporation. Dec. 2009. At http://www.vfc.com/about/our-strategy/growth-drivers.

The redevelopment of VF Asia Ltd.'s learning and development strategy illustrates the importance of learning to the overall strategic goals of the organization. The learning processes in this organization serve to develop current associates so that they have the knowledge, skills, and abilities to allow the organization to grow. Associates simply do not go through one-time training programs—what they learn in training is later assessed as part of their job performance and is thus tied to individual rewards. As we will soon discuss, rewards play an important role in the learning process.

At a second level, learning processes help VF Asia tie individual training, development, performance evaluation, and rewards to the overall strategic vision of the organization. The corporate strategy and goals determine what is to be learned, and the success of training and development initiatives are evaluated at the executive level by the degree to which they achieve the firm's strategic goals. Learning is fully integrated into the culture at VF Asia Ltd. and is therefore viewed as an important part of the organization's success by associates and leaders at all levels in the firm.

To be competitive in the dynamic twenty-first century, an organization must have associates and managers who can effectively learn and grow. Continuous learning based on trying new things plays a critical role in an organization's capability to gain and sustain a competitive advantage. Organizations can improve only when their human capital is enriched through learning. Their human capital must be better and produce more value for customers than their competitors to gain an advantage in the marketplace and to maintain that advantage.[1] Furthermore, providing developmental opportunities to associates helps organizations attract and retain the people most interested in personal growth and becoming better at their work. Thus, managers need to develop the means for associates and all managers to continuously improve their knowledge and skills.

To open this chapter, we explore the fundamentals of learning, including contingencies of reinforcement and various schedules of reinforcement. From there, we apply learning principles to the training of newcomers and the purposeful modification of existing associates' behavior. We focus on specific conditions helpful to learning, the use of behavior modification, simulations, and how people can learn from failure. Next, we move to a discussion of perception. Accurately perceiving characteristics of people, attributes of tasks, and the nature of cause-and-effect relationships is critical to properly assessing and learning from experiences. Several mental biases, however, can interfere with accurate perceptions.

Fundamental Learning Principles

When individuals first enter an organization, they bring with them their own unique experiences, perceptions, and ways of behaving. These patterns of behavior have developed because they have helped these individuals cope with the world around them. However, associates introduced to a new organization or to new tasks may need to learn new behaviors that will make them effective in the new situation. Associates and managers must therefore be acquainted with the principles and processes that govern learning.

In the field of organizational behavior, **learning** refers to relatively permanent changes in human capabilities that occur as a result of experience rather than a natural growth process.[2] These capabilities are related to specific learning outcomes, such as new behaviors, verbal information, intellectual skills, motor skills, attitudes, and cognitive strategies. Both parts of this definition are important. First, learning takes place only when changes in capabilities occur. Ultimately, these changes should result in changed behavior, since true learning represents adaptation to circumstances, and this must be reflected in behavior. Furthermore, this change should be relatively permanent until a new response is learned

learning
A process through which individuals change their relatively permanent behavior based on positive or negative experiences in a situation.

to the given situation. Second, learning is driven by experience with a particular situation. An associate may gain insights into a situation by thoughtfully trying different approaches to see what happens, by randomly trying different actions in a trial-and-error process, or by carefully observing others' actions. In all cases, however, the associate has gained experience in the situation—experience that affects behavior when the situation occurs again. Change in one's capabilities due to a natural growth process (e.g., gaining muscle strength) is not learning.

Operant Conditioning and Social Learning Theory

Most behavior exhibited by associates and managers is intentional in the sense that a given behavior is designed to bring about a positive consequence or avoid a negative consequence. Some associates shake hands when they see each other in the morning because it feels good and expresses respect or affection. Other associates apply the brakes on a forklift to avoid an accident. Managers may not develop close social relationships with their organization's associates in order to avoid the complications that can result. All of these behaviors have been learned.

operant conditioning theory

An explanation for consequence-based learning that assumes learning results from simple conditioning and that higher mental functioning is irrelevant.

Operant conditioning theory and social learning theory both can be used to explain learning. Both are reinforcement theories based on the idea that behavior is a function of its consequences.[3] **Operant conditioning theory** traces its roots at least back to a famous set of experiments involving cats, dogs, and other animals in the late 1800s.[4] The goal of the experiments was to show that animals learn from the consequences of their behavior in a very straightforward way—that presentation of a reward, such as food, conditions an animal to repeat the rewarded behavior in the same or similar situations. In later years, researchers such as B.F. Skinner emphasized this same conditioning in people.[5] These researchers, known as *behaviorists,* adopted the position that higher mental processes typically ascribed to human beings are irrelevant for behavior because all human learning is the result of simple conditioning, just as in cats, rats, dogs, and monkeys. In other words, people do not need to think to learn.

social learning theory

An explanation for consequence-based learning that acknowledges the higher mental functioning of human beings and the role such functioning can play in learning.

While operant conditioning explains a great deal of human learning, later scientists argued that people can learn in other ways. The most prominent of these theories is social learning theory. **Social learning theory**, developed by psychologist Albert Bandura, rejects the idea that higher mental processes are nonexistent or irrelevant in humans.[6] This theory emphasizes that humans can observe others in a situation and learn from what they see. Thus, humans do not need to directly experience a particular situation to develop some understanding of the behaviors that are rewarded in that situation.

Contingencies of Reinforcement

The basic elements of learning include:

- The situation (sometimes referred to as "the stimulus situation")
- The behavioral response of the associate or manager to the situation
- The consequence(s) of the response for the associate or manager

These elements interact to form contingencies of reinforcement. These contingencies, explained below, describe different types of consequences that can follow behavioral responses.

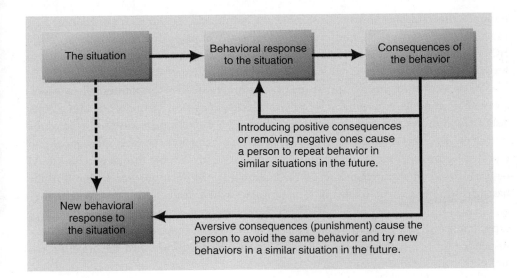

The situation

Behavioral response
to the situation

Consequences of
the behavior

Introducing positive consequences
or removing negative ones cause
a person to repeat behavior in
similar situations in the future.

New behavioral
response to
the situation

Aversive consequences (punishment) cause the
person to avoid the same behavior and try new
behaviors in a similar situation in the future.

Exhibit 4-1   Effects of Reinforcing Consequences on Learning New Behaviors

Positive and Negative Reinforcement

As shown in Exhibit 4-1, when the consequences of a behavior are positive in a particular situation, individuals are likely to repeat that behavior when the situation occurs again. The introduction of positive consequences, such as peer approval for an associate's correction of quality problems, increases the likelihood of that behavior being repeated in similar settings. This is called **positive reinforcement**. Similarly, when a particular behavior in a given situation results in the removal of previous negative consequences, the likelihood of repeating the behavior in similar settings will probably increase. Thus, the removal of negative consequences is called **negative reinforcement**. If working harder and smarter removes the frown from a manager's face, an associate may attempt to work harder and smarter.

Punishment

When behavior results in the introduction of a negative consequence, individuals are less likely to repeat the behavior. This is called **punishment**. Punishment differs from negative reinforcement in that an undesirable consequence is introduced rather than removed. Punishment reduces the likelihood of a behavior, whereas negative reinforcement increases the likelihood. An associate who is reprimanded by peers for returning a few minutes late from lunch experiences punishment, as does an associate whose manager assigns him less preferred work hours in response to tardiness.

Punishment must be used judiciously in organizations because it can create a backlash both among those punished and among those who witness the punishment.[7] It is imperative when punishment is doled out that it be made contingent upon associates engaging in negative behavior.[8] Several examples illustrate this problem. At the *Providence Journal,* a newspaper organization in the northeastern United States, senior management reprimanded two individuals and suspended a third for an editorial cartoon that seemed to poke fun at the publisher. Union officials and many union members believed the punishments were too harsh, resulting in ill will at a time when relations were already strained.[9] At Fireman's Fund, the leadership of a Tampa office terminated an associate who had "dangerous and violent propensities." Although termination was probably a reasonable

positive reinforcement
A reinforcement contingency in which a behavior is followed by a positive consequence, thereby increasing the likelihood that the behavior will be repeated in the same or similar situations.

negative reinforcement
A reinforcement contingency in which a behavior is followed by the withdrawal of a previously encountered negative consequence, thereby increasing the likelihood that the behavior will be repeated in the same or similar situations.

punishment
A reinforcement contingency in which a behavior is followed by a negative consequence, thereby reducing the likelihood that the behavior will be repeated in the same or similar situations.

response, the result was far from reasonable; the terminated individual returned intending to harm former co-workers, illustrating the complexity of managing punishment.[10] At the IRS, some managers failed to discipline associates for tardiness, extended lunches, and so forth in a consistent manner, resulting in numerous problems.[11]

What constitutes an appropriate use of punishment in an organization? When associates exhibit minor counterproductive behaviors, such as rudeness to a peer or a lunch that lasts a few minutes too long, punishment involving a verbal reprimand can be delivered informally by peers or a manager. For more serious behaviors, such as intentional and repeated loafing or consistently leaving the workplace early, a more formal process should be used. Based on requirements set by the National Labor Relations Act, Union Carbide has successfully used the following formal process when dealing with problems as they unfold over time: (1) the problem is discussed informally, and the associate is reminded of expectations; (2) the associate receives one or more written reminders; (3) the associate is suspended for one day, with pay, and asked to consider his future with the organization; and (4) the associate is terminated.[12]

Whether they are imposing minor informal punishment or major formal punishment, associates and managers should follow several guidelines:

- Deliver the punishment as quickly as possible following the undesirable behavior.
- Direct the punishment at specific behaviors that have been made clear to the recipient.
- Deliver the punishment in an objective, impersonal fashion.
- Listen to the offending party's explanation before taking action.

The problems at Korean Air discussed in the *Managerial Advice* feature were caused at least in part by the overuse of punishment. Clearly, as the case illustrates, the use of punishment at this airline played a role in the crash. Being struck by a person above you in the organization is a particularly difficult situation, even for those in an authoritarian culture. Such an approach is inappropriate in a high-involvement organization. In complex situations, associates and managers need the input of others to avoid making possibly serious errors such as those leading to the Korean Air crash. The changes implemented by the new president of the airline and the director of flight operations have helped to resolve the problem. Because Korean culture respects traditional authority, changing the culture at this airline was difficult.[13] Yet the changes were important for the airline to compete in a global marketplace.

Extinction

extinction
A reinforcement contingency in which a behavior is followed by the absence of a previously encountered positive consequence, thereby reducing the likelihood that the behavior will be repeated in the same or similar situations.

Because punishment can be a difficult process to manage, organizations may instead desire to extinguish dysfunctional behavior by removing its reinforcing consequences. This procedure is called **extinction**. It is difficult to use extinction, however, unless a manager has full control over all reinforcing consequences. For instance, an associate may be consistently late to work because he prefers to avoid morning rush-hour traffic or likes to sleep late. Missing the rush hour and sleeping late are both activities that offer rewarding consequences for being late to work. Associates and managers desiring to extinguish this behavior are unlikely to be able to remove these reinforcing consequences.

The reinforcing consequences of some dysfunctional work behaviors, however, may be completely removable. For example, an associate may have developed a habit of regularly

Punishment Taken Too Far

At 1:00 A.M. on August 6, 1997, the pilots of a Korean Air 747 prepared to land at the Guam airport. Because the airport's glide slope guidance system had been turned off for maintenance and because the airport's radio beacon was located in a nonstandard position, the landing was more difficult than usual. A rainstorm further complicated the situation. Under these conditions, the captain needed frank and timely advice from a fully informed and empowered co-pilot and flight engineer. Sadly, no such advice was given by the intimidated subordinates. The resulting crash claimed 228 lives.

The suboptimal cockpit climate on board the aircraft that morning seems to have been caused in part by Korean Air's authoritarian culture, which included heavy-handed punishment delivered by captains for unwanted subordinate input and mistakes. Park Jae Hyun, a former captain with the airline and then a flight inspector with the Ministry of Transportation, believed that teamwork in the cockpit was nearly impossible in the existing "obey or else" environment, where co-pilots "couldn't express themselves if they found something wrong with the captain's piloting skills." This

©Charles Polidano/Touch the Skies/Alamy

environment was perhaps most clearly evident during training. An American working as a pilot for the airline reported, "I've seen a captain punch a co-pilot ... for a mistake and the co-pilot just said, 'Oh, sorry, sorry.'" Another American reports being hit as well, but as an outsider he did not accept the abuse and said to the captain, "Do it again and I'll break your arm."

Korean officials, American officials, and many others believed change was necessary to prevent additional accidents and to generally improve the organization. Following another crash and the forced resignations of key leaders in the late 1990s, new leaders inside Korean Air took actions to change the authoritarian, punishment-oriented culture. Yi Taek Shim, the new president, vowed that cultural and technological problems would be addressed whatever the cost. Koh Myung Joon, who became the new director of flight operations, sought captains for training duty who had "the right temperament," meaning they would not use inappropriate, heavy-handed

punishment but rather would focus on positive reinforcement for desired behavior. These leaders clearly had useful insights. Korean Air has had an excellent safety record in the twenty-first century, and crucial relationships with partner airlines have been strengthened.

Consistent with actions and outcomes at Korean Air, Francis Friedman of Time & Place Strategies in New York has said that individuals in positions of authority should not "get into a kick-the-dog mentality." Even Simon Kukes, a Russian who achieved notoriety as CEO of Tyumen Oil, has suggested that managers should not "yell, scream, and try to find someone to punish." This is interesting advice, given the general authoritarian culture in Russia.

Sources: "Korean Air Is Restructuring Its Flight Operations Division," *Aviation Week & Space Technology,* 152, no. 21 (2000): 21; "Cargo Airline of the Year: Korean Air Cargo," *Air Transport World,* 40, no. 2 (2000): 30–31; W.M. Carley and A. Pasztor. 1999. "Pilot Error: Korean Air Confronts Dismal Safety Record Rooted in Its Culture," *Wall Street Journal,* July 7; Z. Coleman and M. Song. 2001. "Inquiry Blames Cockpit Crew for KAL Crash," *Wall Street Journal,* June 6, P.M. Perry. 2001. "Cage the Rage," *Warehousing Management,* 8, no. 2: 37–40; P. Starobin. 2001. "The Oilman as Teacher," *BusinessWeek,* June 25, G. Thomas. 2000. "Korean Air CEO Vows 'No More Excuses,'" *Aviation Week & Space Technology,* 153, no. 1: 48; G. Thomas. 2002. "The Yin and Yang of Korean Air," *Air Transport World,* 39, no. 10: 26–29.

visiting the manager's office to complain about her co-workers. Most of the complaints are trivial, and the manager wishes to extinguish this practice. However, the fact that the manager has appeared to be attentive and understanding is a positive, reinforcing consequence. The manager may therefore extinguish the behavior by refusing to listen whenever this associate complains about her co-workers. (During a useful conversation with the associate, the manager would, of course, be attentive; only the dysfunctional behavior should be extinguished.) To use extinction, then, managers must recognize the reinforcing consequences of a behavior, and these consequences must be controllable.

Extinction is supposedly used to eliminate dysfunctional behavior. However, this phenomenon can also result in unintended consequences by extinguishing desirable behavior. In a study of hospital employees, some researchers found that when managers failed to provide feedback for good performance (a reward), employees performed more poorly and became unsatisfied with their jobs.[14]

Schedules of Reinforcement

Positive and negative reinforcement are powerful tools in many situations. To fully leverage these two tools, it is important to understand schedules of reinforcement.[15] These schedules determine how often reinforcement is given for desired behavior. Reinforcement does not necessarily need to follow every instance of a positive behavior.

continuous reinforcement

A reinforcement schedule in which a reward occurs after each instance of a behavior or set of behaviors.

The simplest schedule is **continuous reinforcement**, whereby reward occurs after each instance of a particular behavior or set of behaviors. This schedule tends to produce reasonably high rates of the rewarded behavior because it is relatively easy for an individual to understand the connection between a behavior and its positive consequences.[16] Behavior in organizations, however, often is not reinforced on a continuous schedule, for several reasons. First, once initial learning has occurred through training and/or coaching, continuous reinforcement is not required to maintain learned behavior. Second, in today's organizations, both managers and associates are presumed to be self-managing, at least to some degree. Thus, they do not need continuous reinforcement of positive actions.

intermittent reinforcement

A reinforcement schedule in which a reward does not occur after each instance of a behavior or set of behaviors.

Intermittent reinforcement, then, is often used to maintain learned behavior. Schedules can vary by rewarding responses only after a specified number of correct behaviors have occurred or after a specified amount of time has passed. The four most common intermittent schedules found in organizations are as follows:

1. *Fixed interval.* With this schedule, a reinforcement becomes available only after a fixed period of time has passed since the previous reinforcement. For example, an associate at an airport car rental counter might receive a dollar and praise for saying "May I help you?" rather than using the grammatically incorrect "Can I help you?" Because the manager delivering the reinforcement has a limited amount of money and time to devote to this bonus plan, he might listen from his back office for the proper greeting only after two hours have passed since his last delivery of reinforcement. Upon hearing the greeting after the two-hour interval, the manager would provide the next reinforcement. A fixed-interval schedule like this one can make the desired behavior more resistant to extinction than the continuous schedule because the associate is not accustomed to being reinforced for every instance of the desired behavior. However, it can also yield lower probabilities of the desired behavior immediately after reinforcement has

occurred because the person may realize that no additional reinforcement is possible for a period of time. Moreover, it can yield generally low probabilities of the desired behavior if the fixed interval is too long for the situation.[17] Overall, this schedule of reinforcement tends to be the least effective.

2. *Variable interval*. With this second schedule, a reinforcement becomes available after a variable period of time has passed since the previous reinforcement. In our car rental example, the manager might listen for and reward the desired greeting one hour after the previous reinforcement and then again after one half hour, and then again after three hours. This schedule can produce a consistently high rate of the desired behavior because the associate does not know when reinforcement might be given next. If, however, the average time between reinforcements becomes too great, the variable-interval schedule can lose its effectiveness.[18]

3. *Fixed ratio*. With this third reinforcement schedule, a reinforcer is introduced after the desired behavior has occurred a fixed number of times. In our car rental example, the manager might listen closely to all of the greetings used by a given associate and reward the desired greeting every third time it is used. In industrial settings, managers may create piece-rate incentive systems whereby individual production workers are paid, for example, $5.00 after producing every fifth piece. Although the fixed-ratio schedule can produce a reasonably high rate of desired behavior, it can also result in a short period immediately following reinforcement when the desired behavior does not occur.[19] Such outcomes occur because associates and managers relax following reinforcement, knowing they are starting over.

4. *Variable ratio*. With our final schedule, a reinforcement is introduced after the desired behavior has occurred a variable number of times. The manager of our car rental counter may listen closely all day to the greetings but, because of money and time constraints, reward only the first desired greeting, the fifth, the eight, the fifteenth, the seventeenth, and so on. This schedule of reinforcement tends to produce consistently high rates of desired behavior and tends to make extinction less likely than under the other schedules.[20] The variable-ratio schedule is very common in many areas of life, including sports: baseball and softball players are reinforced on this schedule in their hitting, basketball players in their shot making, anglers in their fishing, and gamblers in their slot machine activities. In business organizations, salespersons are perhaps more subject to this schedule than others, with a variable number of sales contacts occurring between actual sales.

Exhibit 4-2 summarizes various schedules of reinforcement.

Social Learning Theory

Although the principles of operant conditioning explain a great deal of learning that takes place, people also learn in other ways. *Social learning theory*—and later, *social cognitive theory*—argues that in addition to learning through direct reinforcement, people can also learn by anticipating consequences of their behavior and by modeling others.[21] In other words, learning occurs through the mental processing of information.[22]

According to these approaches to learning, one way that associates can learn is through symbolization and forethought.[23] People have the ability to symbolize events and

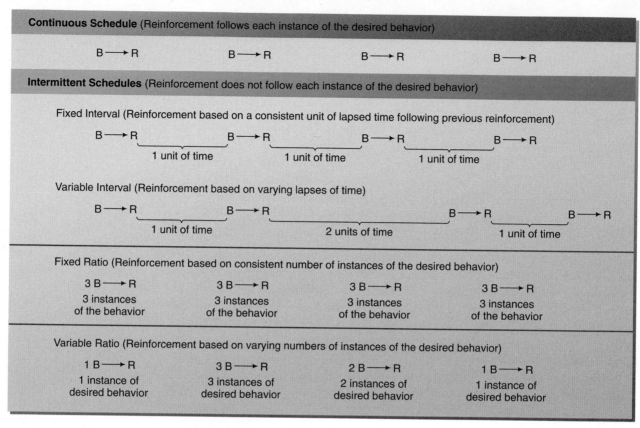

Exhibit 4-2   Schedules of Reinforcement

to anticipate consequences. This means that rather than having to directly experience possible consequences of one's behavior, a person can try out various scenarios in his or her mind to determine what potential consequences may result from a particular behavior. For example, if a manager has to make a decision about whether to open a new branch office, she can rely on past experience to come up with symbolic representation of the problem and then anticipate what outcomes may occur if she decides to open the new office.

According to social learning theory, people also learn by observing others. Rather than having to experience consequences first-hand, associates can observe the behavior of others and the results of that behavior.[24] When results are positive, then associates will model the behavior demonstrated by the other person. For example, if an associate is trying to learn how to give presentations, rather than try out many different presentation styles, he may observe his supervisor, who is a wonderful presenter, and then model the supervisor's presentation style. Associates are most likely to model the behavior of people they perceive to be competent, powerful, friendly, and of high status within the organization.[25]

Social learning theory also states that an individual's belief that he will be able to perform a specific task in a given situation is important to learning. This belief is referred to as one's **self-efficacy**.[26] When associates have high self-efficacy toward a particular task, they believe that they can perform that task well. People will not engage in behaviors or will perform poorly when they do not believe that they are able to accomplish the task at a satisfactory level. Athletes are often trained to visualize themselves performing extremely well

self-efficacy
An individual's belief that he or she will be able to perform a specific task in a given situation.

in order to increase their self-efficacy, and consequently their performance. A great deal of research has shown that self-efficacy increases performance and learning, beyond ability.[27] If there are two people with the same ability, the person with the higher self-efficacy will tend to perform better and learn more.

Other Conditions for Learning

In addition to learning through consequences and observing others, more recent research has noted that the following conditions help facilitate adult learning:[28]

- *Associates need to know why they are learning what they are learning.* People become more motivated to learn when they understand why what they are learning is important.[29] For example, in order for associates to successfully train to engage in safe behaviors, they must first understand what constitutes safe behavior and then understand the consequences of not engaging in these behaviors.[30] In order for associates to know why they are learning what they are learning, they must be provided with specific learning objectives.[31] Also, allowing associates to either directly or vicariously experience the negative effects of *not* learning may help them understand why learning the material is important.[32] We discuss learning from failure in more detail later in this chapter.
- *Associates need to use their own experiences as the basis for learning.* Many teaching and learning experts believe that people learn best when they can tie newly learned material to their past experiences, take an active role in their own learning, and are able to reflect on their learning experiences.[33] According to the experiential learning perspective, it is imperative for learning to include active experimentation and reflective observation.[34] This is why many MBA programs include team exercises to teach teamwork skills. Rather than just reading about the importance of teamwork and how to achieve it, students actually experience their lessons and later are asked to reflect upon what they have learned.
- *Associates need to practice what they have learned.* Practicing means repetitively demonstrating performance stated in the learning objectives. Overlearning due to constant practice improves the likelihood that associates will engage in newly learned behaviors once they leave the learning situation.[35] Overlearning means that performing the new behavior takes little conscious thought, so that the performance becomes automatic.
- *Associates need feedback.* A great deal of research has been conducted on the effects of feedback on learning.[36] Feedback can facilitate learning by providing associates with information about what they should be learning and it can also act as a reward. Feedback is most conducive to learning when associates are comfortably familiar with the material to be learned or when the material is relatively simple.[37]

Training and Enhancing the Performance of Associates

The learning concepts discussed thus far have been successfully used over the years to train newcomers as well as to improve the performance of existing associates. To achieve positive results when training a newcomer, managers often reinforce individuals as they move closer to the desired set of behaviors. The following steps capture the most important elements in the process:

1. Determine the new behaviors to be learned.
2. For more complex behavior, break the new behavior down into smaller, logically arranged segments.
3. Demonstrate desired behaviors to the trainee. Research indicates that modeling appropriate behaviors is very useful.[38] Research also indicates that unless the key behaviors are distinctive and meaningful, the trainee is not likely to remember them on the job.[39]
4. Have the trainee practice the new behaviors in the presence of the trainer.
5. Make reinforcement contingent on approximations of desired behavior. At the outset, mild reinforcement can be given for a good start. As the training continues, reinforcement should be given only as progress is made. Reinforcement should be immediate, and over time behavior should be reinforced only if it comes closer to the ultimate desired behavior.[40]

In newcomer training, managers in many organizations use this approach. Trilogy, a software firm based in Austin, Texas, uses positive reinforcement as new hires work through successively more difficult assignments in a boot camp that lasts several months.[41] E.L. Harvey & Sons, a refuse collector based in Westborough, Massachusetts, has used positive reinforcement as well as mild punishment in its training and orientation program for new drivers.[42] Dallas-based Greyhound Bus Company has used positive reinforcement and mild punishment as drivers master proper city, rural, and mountain driving techniques. As one recent trainee stated, "You're not going to be perfect the first time. Some things you'll get used to doing. I'll get better."[43]

Organizations use numerous methods to train employees.[44] On-the-job training methods include orientation programs, organizational socialization experiences, apprenticeship training, coaching, formal mentoring, job rotation, career development activities, and technology-based training. Off-site training methods include instructor-led classrooms, videoconferencing, corporate universities and institutes, and virtual-reality simulators. Learning can also take place informally through trial-and-error, informal mentoring relationships, interactions with co-workers, and from learning from one's mistakes. We highlight three learning methods below: OB Mod, simulation learning, and learning from failure.

OB Mod

OB Mod
A formal procedure focused on improving task performance through positive reinforcement of desired behaviors and extinction of undesired behaviors.

To improve the performance of existing associates on ongoing tasks, organizations must be concerned not only with developing good habits but also with breaking bad ones. As an aid in this process, a formal procedure known as *organizational behavior modification,* or **OB Mod**, is often used.[45] The basic goal of OB Mod, which some refer to as *performance management,* is to improve task performance through positive reinforcement of desirable behaviors and elimination of reinforcements that support undesirable behaviors.[46] Its value lies in the specific, detailed steps that it offers.

As shown in Exhibit 4-3, the OB Mod framework can be represented as a simple flowchart. In the initial steps, managers determine desirable and undesirable behaviors and assess the extent to which individuals are currently exhibiting those behaviors. Desirable

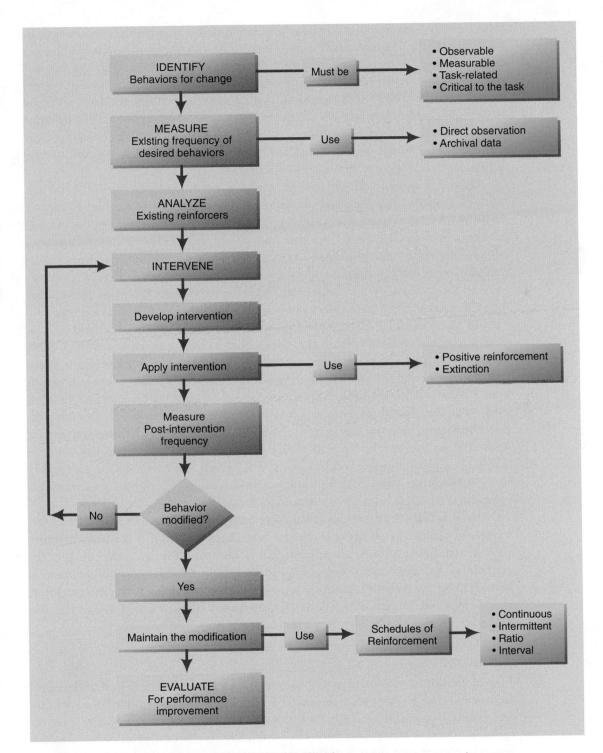

Exhibit 4-3   Shaping Behavior through OB Modification

Source: Adapted from Luthans, F., & Stajkovic, A.D. 1999. "Reinforce for Performance: The Need to Go Beyond Pay and Even Rewards," *Academy of Management Executive,* 13 (2): 49–57.

behaviors may be as simple as using a production machine or answering the telephone in a different way. In the next step, the functional analysis, managers determine reinforcers that can be used to increase the frequency of desired behavior (e.g., praise, preferential work arrangements, time off) and reinforcers that must be eliminated to extinguish undesirable behaviors (e.g., social approval from co-workers for loafing). Next, managers apply the knowledge they have gained concerning reinforcers in an effort to alter behavior in a fruitful way. If successful in this step, they can develop an appropriate reinforcement schedule for the future. Finally, the impact of modified behaviors on job performance indicators, such as units produced per day, is assessed.

Research has been generally supportive of OB Mod. One study found that PIGS (positive, immediate, graphic, and specific) feedback, coupled with social reinforcement for desired behavior (e.g., praise, attention, compliments), improved the delivery of quality service by tellers in a bank.[47] Another study found that feedback coupled with social reinforcement and time off helped overcome significant performance problems among municipal workers.[48] In Russia, a study determined that feedback and social reinforcement improved the quality of fabric produced by textile workers.[49] Overall, research has found an average performance gain of 17 percent when OB Mod was explicitly used.[50]

OB Mod research reveals that performance improvements tend to be greater in manufacturing organizations (33 percent on average) than in service organizations (13 percent on average).[51] This difference across types of organizations highlights a weakness of the OB Mod approach. For jobs that are complex and nonroutine, such as those found in some service organizations (e.g., accounting firms, law firms, and hospitals), OB Mod tends to be less effective. In complex jobs, where excellent performance in core job areas (successful audits, effective surgical procedures) is based on deep, rich knowledge and on skills that can take months or years to develop, short-term interventions based on the simple principles of operant conditioning and social learning may not yield particularly strong performance gains.[52] For organizations seeking to develop their human capital for competitive advantage, this limitation must be considered.

OB Mod research also reveals another important fact: performance feedback coupled with social reinforcements can be as effective as feedback coupled with monetary reinforcers.[53] In the studies of bank tellers, municipal workers, and Russian textile workers, for example, no monetary reinforcement was involved. For managers and organizations, this is very important. Although managers, as part of high-involvement management, should provide fair financial compensation overall, they do not necessarily need to spend significant amounts of money to improve performance.

Simulations

In some situations, an associate or manager may take a particular action with unclear consequences.[54] This happens when the effects of an action combine with the effects of other factors in unpredictable ways. Suppose, for example, that a team leader brings pizza to celebrate a week of high productivity. The team members express appreciation and appear generally pleased with the gesture, but the appreciation is not overwhelming. The team leader may conclude that having a pizza party is not worth the trouble. She may be correct, or she may be incorrect because other factors may have contributed to the situation. At the time of the pizza party, a key member of the team was out caring for a sick parent. In addition, rumors circulated among the team members that the new plant controller did

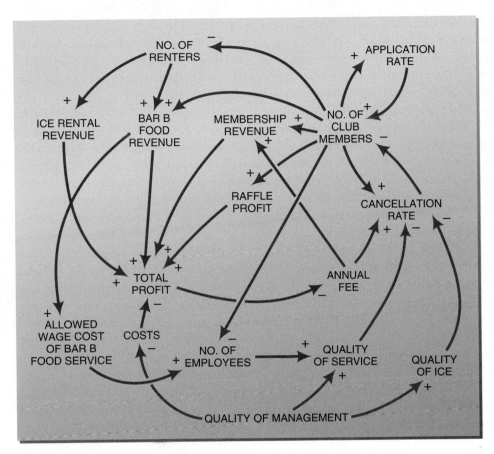

Exhibit 4-4 Causal Relationships at a Sports Club

Note: A "+" between two variables indicates a direct, noninverse relationship. When the variable at the start of an arrow exhibits an increase, there is upward pressure on the variable at the end of that arrow. When the variable at the start exhibits a decrease, there is downward pressure on the variable at the end. A "−" between two variables indicates an inverse relationship. When the variable at the start of an arrow exhibits an increase, there is downward pressure on the variable at the end of that arrow. When the variable at the start exhibits a decrease, there is upward pressure on the variable at the end.

Source: Reprinted by permission, R.D. Hall. 1983. "A Corporate System Model of a Sports Club: Using Simulation as an Aid to Policy Making in a Crisis," *Management Science*, 29 (1): 52–64, the Institute for Operations Research and the Management Sciences (INFORMS), 901 Elkridge Landing Road, Suite 400, Linthicum, Maryland 21090-2909 USA.

not embrace high-involvement management. Did these two factors affect the team's reaction to the pizza?

In this example, the team leader could discuss the situation with team members in order to better understand their reactions. Other situations may be so complex that discussions with team members may not be adequate. Consider the complex situation facing the general manager at a Canadian curling club. He plans to increase the annual membership fee to enhance profits. As shown in Exhibit 4-4, the annual fee does influence profits, but the effects are not clear. On the one hand, increasing the annual fee has a positive effect on revenue from membership fees because members who stay are paying more, and this in turn has a positive effect on profits. On the other hand, increasing the annual fee puts upward pressure on the cancellation rate among members and therefore downward pressure on the total number of club members. As the number of club members declines, revenue is lost, which reduces profits. What actual effect, then, will an increase in the membership fee have? Is the overall effect positive or negative? Perhaps an increase up to a point results in more revenue from the members who stay than is lost from the members who leave. But where is the point at which total revenue begins to decline? A further complication is that factors other than the membership fee influence revenues and costs and profits.

simulation
A representation of a real system that allows associates and managers to try various actions and receive feedback on the consequences of those actions.

In situations where a complex system of variables exists and we have some understanding of how the variables affect one another, a **simulation** may be a useful tool for understanding the effects of a potential action. A simulation mimics the real system but allows us to take one action at a time to understand its effects. In our curling club example, the relationships among the variables shown in Exhibit 4-4 could be developed into a simulation. If the manager of the club wanted to change the annual fee to affect profits, he could implement various increases in this fee within the simulation to observe the effects.

Although simulations are important and useful, they typically represent simplified models of reality. For this reason, and because some situations are too complex to be accurately represented in simulations, some organizations prefer to substitute or augment simulations with formal experimentation in the real world.[55] The idea is to have associates and managers try different approaches, even though some will no doubt fail to discover which approach seems to work best under particular conditions. Such experimentation has often been used in the development of technology for new products,[56] and it has also been used in areas such as setting the strategic direction of the organization.[57] Bank of America is one of many organizations that regularly conducts experiments.[58] It has a number of branches specifically designated for testing new ideas in décor, kiosks, service procedures, and so on.

Learning from Failure

High-involvement firms often attempt to leverage their human capital in ways that will enhance innovation.[59] Accordingly, they often empower associates and managers to experiment. In addition to the formal experimentation discussed earlier, these organizations often promote informal and smaller-scale experimentation in almost all areas of organizational life, ranging from a manager trying a new leadership style to an associate on the assembly line trying a new method of machine setup. Such experimentation yields learning that otherwise would not occur. A manager's leadership style may have been working well, but trying a new style will provide him with information on the effectiveness of the new style.

Experimentation, however, does not always result in success; by its nature, it often produces failure. New approaches sometimes are less effective than old ways of doing things. New product ideas sometimes are not attractive in the marketplace. Gerber Singles (adult foods produced by the baby food company), Life-Savers Soda (carbonated beverages produced by the candy maker), and Ben-Gay Aspirin (pain relievers produced by the heating-rub company) are reasonable ideas that failed in the marketplace.[60]

The key is to learn from failure.[61] A failure that does not result in learning is a mistake; a failure that results in learning is an intelligent failure. Intelligent failures are the result of certain kinds of actions:[62]

- Actions are thoughtfully planned.
- Actions have a reasonable chance of producing a successful outcome.

"We Are Ladies and Gentlemen Serving Ladies and Gentlemen"

©Keith Bedford/The New York Times/Redux Pictures

This credo of the Ritz-Carlton Hotel Associates may seem simple. However, in order to enact it, associates must go through constant training of a quality that led *Training* magazine to name the Ritz-Carlton the number-one company for employee training and development in 2007. The Ritz-Carlton is known for its exemplary service, which has been recognized by two Malcolm Baldrige National Quality Awards and consistently high rankings in travel periodicals of the world's greatest hotels. The Ritz-Carlton has 78 hotels worldwide, with at least 14 other projects underway; 38,000 associates work for the company.

All Ritz-Carlton associates are expected to go for what the company calls the "wow" factor by not only meeting guests' needs but also anticipating them. If you order your favorite drink at a Ritz-Carlton in Hong Kong, the bartender at the Ritz-Carlton in New Orleans will know what you want when you sit down at his bar. Special room requests, such as M&Ms in the minibar, will be met each time someone visits a Ritz-Carlton without the guest ever having to ask for the favor. Special software makes such anticipatory service doable. However, this type of service could never be carried out without exceptional associate service performance.

In order to reach this performance level, all associates go through constant training throughout their careers with the Ritz-Carlton. It all begins with a two-day orientation session taught by master trainers. However, training does not stop there. New associates go through at least 310 hours of training in their first year, where they are personally paired with a departmental trainer. They receive a training certification, much like mastercraftsmen, when they can demonstrate mastery of their job. Reviews take place on days 21 and 365.

New employees are not the only associates who receive constant training. All Ritz-Carlton associates are trained continuously. Methods of training include:

- Daily meetings, where all employees give and receive feedback on what has been done right and what has been done wrong. Time is also spent discussing one of the Ritz-Carlton's 12 service values.

- On-the-job training by mentors and training directors.

- Classroom training delivery.

- Good performance is clearly rewarded either monetarily or by verbal praise. Ritz-Carlton Associates are almost twice as likely as other hotel associates to report

that they receive constructive feedback and are clearly rewarded.

Unlike many other companies, the Ritz-Carlton also devotes a great deal of time to evaluating their training programs, using knowledge tests, performance appraisals, associate and guest surveys, and quantitative service-quality measures. Their training programs are responsible for the fact that the Ritz-Carlton sets industry standards for the total revenue per hours worked, employee satisfaction, low turnover rates, and customer satisfaction. In fact, the Ritz-Carlton training methods are so successful that the company began the Leadership Center, which provides training to associates, mostly senior managers, from other companies.

Sources: http://corporate.ritzcarlton.com. Anonymous, "Ritz-Carlton: Redefining Elegance (No. 1 of the Training Top 125),"*Training*, Mar. 1, 2007, at http://www.trainingmag.com; Lampton, B. 2003. "My Pleasure,"*ExpertMagazine. com*, Dec. 1, at http://www.expertmagazine.com; The Ritz-Carlton Hotel Company, L.L.C., "Application Summary for the Malcolm Baldrige National Quality Award," 2000, at http://corporate.ritzcarlton.com.; Ritz-Carlton Press Release facts sheet. December, 2009, at http://corporate.ritzcarlton.com/en/Press/FactSheet.htm.

- Actions are typically modest in scale, to avoid putting the entire firm or substantial parts of it at risk.
- Actions are executed and evaluated in a speedy fashion, since delayed feedback makes learning more difficult.
- Actions are limited to domains that are familiar enough to allow proper understanding of the effects of the actions.

Firms serious about experimentation and intelligent failure create cultures that protect and nurture associates and managers willing to take calculated risks and to try new things.[63] Such cultures have visible examples of individuals who have been promoted even after having failed in trying a new approach. Such cultures also have stories of associates who have been rewarded for trying something new even though it did not work out. At IDEO, a product design firm based in Palo Alto, California, the culture is built on the idea that designers should "fail often to succeed sooner."[64] At 3-M, the global giant based in St. Paul, Minnesota, the culture is built on the idea that thoughtful failure should not be a source of shame.[65]

Learning from failure, OB Mod, and simulations are just three ways in which organizations can train associates. Many organizations, such as the Ritz-Carlton Hotel Company, use multiple methods as evidenced in the *Experiencing Organizational Behavior* feature. The Ritz-Carlton provides an excellent example of the strategic importance of training and continuous employee learning. Although the Ritz-Carlton Hotel Company spends much more on associate training than its competitors, the company sees payoff from its training on all important indicators. Customer satisfaction is higher and associates work harder and turn over less frequently at the Ritz-Carlton than they do at other hotels. This superb performance has led the Ritz-Carlton to win almost every prestigious business and training award, while making it an exceptionally successful company.

Perception

perception
A process that involves sensing various aspects of a person, task, or event and forming impressions based on selected inputs.

As we have shown in the preceding sections, associates and managers who can effectively learn from experience, and help others to do so, contribute positively to an organization's human capital and therefore contribute positively to its capacity to develop sustainable competitive advantage. To further develop the story of learning, we now turn to issues of **perception**. If an associate or manager does not perceive people, tasks, and events accurately, learning from experience is difficult. If an associate or manager does not perceive the world accurately, he will base his behavior on inaccurate perceptions of the world rather than on reality.

Associates and managers are constantly exposed to a variety of sensory inputs that influence their perceptions. Sensory inputs refer to things that are heard, seen, smelled, tasted, and touched. These inputs are processed in the mind and organized to form concepts pertaining to what has been sensed or experienced. For instance, an associate in a catering firm may sense a common item such as a loaf of bread. He touches it, squeezes it, smells it, looks at its shape and color, and tastes it. His mind processes all of the sensory inputs, and he forms ideas and attitudes about that loaf of bread and the bakery that produced it. He may determine that the bread is fresh or stale, good or bad, worth the price or not, and may subsequently decide whether products of this particular bakery are to be used. These are his perceptions of the bread and of the producer.

Perception comprises three basic stages:[66]

1. *Sensing various characteristics of a person, task, or event.* This stage consists of using the senses (touch, sight, smell, and so on) to obtain data. Some data in the environment, however, cannot be detected by the sensory organs. For example, operators of the Three Mile Island nuclear facility, which almost melted down in the 1970s, could not sense that a relief valve was stuck open in the nuclear core because they could not see it and the instrument panel indicated that it was closed.[67] Some data, though accessible, are not sensed. Engineers and managers with NASA and Morton Thiokol failed to sense certain features of their booster rockets when considering whether to launch the ill-fated *Challenger* shuttle in the 1980s.[68]

2. *Selecting from the data those facts that will be used to form the perception.* An individual does not necessarily use all of the data that she senses. At times, a person may be overloaded by information and unable to use all of it. For example, U.S. Defense Department officials dealt with overwhelming amounts of data from various sources with regard to the events of September 11 and the conflict in Iraq. At other times, a person may purposely exclude information that is inconsistent with her other existing perceptions. A manager who firmly believes an associate is a weak performer, for example, may discount and ultimately exclude information suggesting otherwise.[69] Accurate perception, however, requires the use of all relevant information.

3. *Organizing the selected data into useful concepts pertaining to the object or person.* An individual must order and sort data in a way that is useful in establishing approaches to dealing with the world. We now explore this aspect of perception in discussing perceptions of people.

©Ron Galella/WireImage/Getty Images, Inc.

©E.Neitzel/WireImage/Getty Images, Inc.

Perceptions of People

Shortcomings in the ability to sense the full range of data, to select appropriate data for further processing, and to organize the data into useful information can lead to inaccurate perceptions about people.[70] These erroneous perceptions in turn can interfere with learning how to best interact with a person and can lead to poor decisions about and actions toward the person. Effective associates and managers are able to develop complete and accurate perceptions of the various people with whom they interact—customers, sales representatives, peers, and so on. An effective manager, for example, knows when a sales representative is sincere, when an associate has truly achieved superior performance, and when another manager is dependable. These accurate perceptions are crucial to a firm's human capital that contributes to competitive advantage. Next, we discuss several factors that influence the process of perceiving other people. These factors are shown in Exhibit 4-5.

The Nature of the Perceiver

The perception process is influenced by several factors related to the nature of the perceiver. Impaired hearing or sight and temporary conditions such as those induced by alcohol or prescribed medications can, of course, affect perception. Beyond those challenges, the most important factors are the perceiver's familiarity with the other person, the perceiver's existing feelings about the other person, and the emotional state of the perceiver.

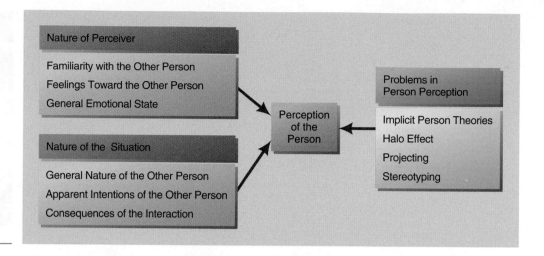

Exhibit 4-5   Person Perception

Familiarity with the person is important. On the one hand, an individual may have more accurate perceptions of people with whom she has had a substantial history. Over time, the individual has had many opportunities to observe those people. On the other hand, an individual may pay more attention to newcomers, making extra efforts to notice and process data about them.

If an individual has put a great deal of effort over time into properly understanding certain people, she probably has developed accurate perceptions of their characteristics and abilities. If, however, those characteristics and abilities change, or if the people act in ways that are not consistent with their longstanding characteristics and abilities, the perceiving individual may not accurately interpret the new characteristics or behaviors. In this case, the perceiver may be too focused on existing beliefs about the friends and associates to accurately interpret new characteristics or behaviors. A manager who has had an excellent, trusting relationship with an associate over many years may thus disregard evidence of lying or poor performance because it does not fit preexisting conceptions of the person.[71]

An individual's feelings about another person also may affect the perception process. If the individual generally has positive feelings toward a particular person, he may view the person's actions through a favorable lens and thus may interpret those actions more positively than is warranted. In contrast, if the individual generally has negative feelings toward a particular person, he may view the person's actions through an unfavorable lens and thus interpret those actions more negatively than is warranted.

Research conducted at a large multinational firm provides evidence for these commonsense effects. In this research, 344 middle managers were rated by 272 superiors, 470 peers, and 608 associates. The feelings of the 1,350 raters were assessed through measures of admiration, respect, and liking. Raters who had positive feelings toward a particular ratee consistently rated his or her performance more leniently than they should have. Raters who had negative feelings rated performance too severely.[72]

An individual's emotional state may also affect perceptions of others. If the individual is happy and excited, she may perceive others as more exuberant and cheerful than they really are. If the individual is sad and depressed, she may perceive others as more unhappy than they really are or even as more sinister than they really are. For example, in one study, several women judged photographs of faces after they had played a frightening game called "Murder." Those women perceived the faces to be more menacing than did women who had not played the game.[73]

The Nature of the Situation

Factors present in a situation can affect whether an associate or manager senses important information, and these factors can influence whether this information is used in perceptions. Relevant factors are numerous and varied. Three of them are discussed here: obvious characteristics of the other person, the other person's apparent intentions, and the consequences of interactions with the person.

As previously discussed, an individual's perceptions of another person can be influenced by his own internal states and emotions. In addition, the individual's perceptions of another person are affected by that person's most obvious characteristics (those that stand out). For instance, the perceiver is likely to notice things that are intense, bright, noisy, or in motion. He is also likely to notice highly attractive and highly unattractive people, people dressed in expensive clothes and those dressed in clothes reflecting poor taste, and bright, intelligent people or extremely dull-witted ones. He is less likely to notice normal or average people. This effect on perceptions has been demonstrated in research.[74]

In organizations, extremely good and bad performers may be noticed more than average associates. Managers must be aware of this tendency because most associates are average. Large numbers of associates may go unnoticed, unrewarded, and passed over for promotions, even though they have the potential to contribute to a firm's goals and to the achievement of competitive advantage.

An individual's perceptions may also be affected by the assumed intentions behind another person's actions. If, for example, assumed intentions are undesirable from the perceiver's point of view, the other person may be seen as threatening or hostile.[75]

Finally, an individual may be affected by the consequences of a single interaction with another person. If the consequences are basically positive, the individual is likely to perceive the other person favorably. If, however, the results of the interaction are negative, the individual is more likely to view the other person unfavorably.

©Tobi Corney/Getty Images, Inc.

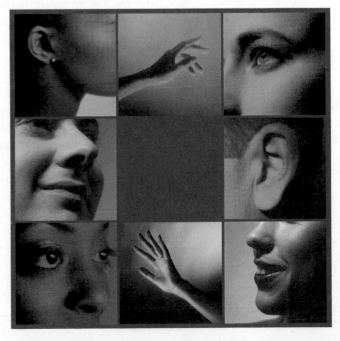

In one study, a researcher's accomplice was the only member of a work group to fail on the assigned task. The study included two conditions. In one condition, the accomplice's failure prevented the other members from receiving payment for the task. This accomplice was perceived unfavorably (as less competent, less dependable, and less likable). In a second condition, the other members received payment despite the accomplice's failure. This accomplice was seen as being more competent, dependable, and likable, even though the actual level of performance was the same as the first accomplice's.[76]

Problems in Person Perception

The preceding discussion shows that perceiving others accurately can be challenging. In fact, some of the most noteworthy conflicts in organizations have been the result of misperceiving others. In a well-known example involving Apple Computer, a midlevel manager in charge of distribution misperceived the character and motives of a manager in charge of one of the manufacturing operations, resulting in a battle that was unnecessarily protracted.[77] The distribution manager almost resigned her job with the organization before realizing the other manager was not committed to dismantling the existing distribution function. Because perceptions influence how associates and managers behave toward one another, it is important to strengthen our understanding of the perceptual process so that our perceptions of others reflect reality.

The perceptual process is influenced by factors associated with both the perceiver and the general situation. The problems that prevent the formation of accurate perceptions arise from factors that can be ordered into four general problem groups: implicit personality theories, halo effect, projecting, and stereotyping.

implicit person theories
Personal theories about what personality traits and abilities occur together and how these attributes are manifested in behavior.

People hold **implicit person theories**,[78] which are personal theories about what personality traits and abilities occur together and how these attributes are manifested in behavior. For example, if an associate notices that her colleague's office is brightly decorated and messy, she may infer that this associate will be very talkative and outgoing because her implicit personality theory states that messiness and extraversion go together.[79] One type of implicit personality theory that individuals hold concerns whether people believe that personality traits and abilities are fixed and unchangeable in people.[80] Those who believe that people cannot change are called *entity theorists,* while those who believe that people's attributes such as skills and abilities can change and develop are called *incremental theorists.* Research has shown that managers who hold an entity theorist perspective are less likely to help and coach their subordinates because they believe that their behavior is unchangeable.[81]

halo effect
A perception problem in which an individual assesses a person positively or negatively in all situations based on an existing general assessment of the person.

The **halo effect** occurs when a person makes a general assessment of another person (such as "good" or "bad"), and then uses this general impression to interpret everything that the person does, regardless of whether the general impression accurately portrays the behavior.[82] With regard to the halo effect, if a person is perceived as generally "good," a manager or associate will tend to view the person in a positive way in any circumstance or on any evaluative measure. Thus, if Marianne is perceived as being a generally "good" person, she may be seen as an active, positive force in the organization's culture even if she is actually neutral in promoting a positive culture. If Ted is perceived as being a "bad" person, he may be considered insolent and cunning even if he does not truly exhibit those particular negative traits. In the many studies of this phenomenon, halo error has been found in ratings given to job candidates, teachers, ice skaters, and others.[83]

projecting
A perception problem in which an individual assumes that others share his or her values and beliefs.

Assuming that most other people have the same values and beliefs as we do is known as **projecting**. For example, a production manager may think that lathe operators should always check with her on important decisions. The production manager may also believe that the lathe operators prefer this checking to making their own decisions. This may be an inaccurate perception, however, and the lathe operators may complain about the need to check with the manager. Obviously, falsely believing that other persons share our beliefs can lead to ineffective behavior. Specific problems include overestimating consensus, undervaluing objective assessments, and undervaluing those with opposing views.[84]

stereotyping
A perception problem in which an individual bases perceptions about members of a group on a generalized set of beliefs about the characteristics of a group of individuals.

As already noted in Chapter 2, when an individual has preconceived ideas or perceptions about a certain group of people, **stereotyping** can occur. When the individual meets someone who is obviously a member of a particular group, he may perceive that person as having the general characteristics attributed to the group rather than perceiving the person as an individual with a unique set of characteristics.[85] For example, a manager may perceive union members (a group) to be strong, assertive troublemakers. When she meets John, a union member, she perceives him to be a troublemaker simply because he is a union member. This type of perceptual problem is commonly found among managers who deal ineffectively with union leaders, associates who deal ineffectively with members of the other gender, and associates who deal ineffectively with members of other ethnic groups.

To fully leverage its human assets, an organization must have associates and managers who respect one other and appreciate the unique characteristics of each person. Stereotyping can interfere with these outcomes. Effective, productive interactions require accurate perceptions of people, and stereotypes are frequently incorrect, for two reasons. First, the stereotyped characteristics of a group may simply be wrong. Erroneous stereotypes may result from a number of factors, such as fear of a group and contact with only a select subset of a group. Obviously, when the stereotype itself is inaccurate, applying the stereotype to an individual can only result in error. Second, even if stereotyped characteristics of a group are generally correct, any given individual within the group is unlikely to have all, or even most, of the characteristics attributed to the group.

One basis for stereotyping individuals is their physical attractiveness. Elysa Yanowitz was fired by L'Oreal USA, Inc. for not firing a Macy's saleswoman who was "not good looking enough."[86] A company executive said, "Get me somebody hot" for the job. Annette McConnell, a sales company employee who weighed 300 pounds, was told by a manager that "they were going to lay me off because people don't like buying from fat people."[87] It is well documented that people associate those who are physically attractive with positive qualities and those who are unattractive with negative qualities.[88] Thus, perceptions of a person's attractiveness and/or weight can influence how they are evaluated on the job and even how much they get paid.[89] For example, overweight women were found to earn 7 to 30 percent less than normal-weight women performing at the same level in the same jobs.[90] Such bias, while usually not illegal, is strategically unsound for organizations. Bias of this type means that organizations are making less-than-optimal decisions about how to use their human capital.[91] Furthermore, such unfair treatment can be demoralizing and stressful and may lead associates to perform at less-than-optimal levels.[92] In some cases, such as the L'Oreal case, such treatment can lead to charges of sex discrimination when men and women are held to different attractiveness standards.[93] As discussed in Chapter 2, such cases are extremely costly for organizations, not to mention the individuals involved.

Self-Perception

It is widely recognized that perceptions of others have important consequences, but an individual's perception of self may have important consequences as well. Individuals who perceive themselves as highly competent are likely to try new approaches to tasks and perhaps be more productive than their peers. Self-confidence is a powerful force. In an examination of lower-level managers, self-perceptions of competence were found to play a significant role in task performance.[94]

Attributions of Causality

As individuals consider the behavior of others, they will perceive that actions have various causes. Different people, however, may see the same behavior as being caused by different

Great Bear Wilderness Crash

Flight SEA04GA192 took off from Glacier National Park airport on September 20, 2004. On board were five people, including pilot Jim Long, 60; Chief of Party, Ken Good, 58; and forestry scientists Davita Bryant, 32; Matthew Ramige, 29; and Jodee Hogg, 23. They were heading for Schafer Meadows, an airstrip in 1.5 million acres of Montana wilderness. They were heading out to collect forestry data for the U.S. Forest Service. The weather that day was horrible, with low clouds obscuring mountain peaks. Flight SEA04GA192 never reached her destination. Two days later, only two of the crew members barely survived, Matthew Ramige and Jodee Hogg. The rest of the crew lay dead at the site of the plane crash in the Great Bear Wilderness.

The weather, which had hampered visibility, led pilot Long to abandon the planned flight course. The plane flew into a boxed canyon with mountain walls on three sides and no way out. At the last minute, Long attempted to turn out of the canyon and crashed into the side of the mountain. Pilot Long and forestry scientist Bryant were killed at the time of the crash. Ken Good died at the crash site the following morning. The next day, Ramige and Hogg walked out of the canyon by themselves, without being rescued. They were found two days later when they reached civilization. Thus, apart from the disaster of the crash, there was also the failure of the search team to find the survivors.

While weather seems the most obvious cause of this problem, closer examination reveals that human error, based on a lack of learning and misguided perceptions, played a role in this disaster. Based on recollections of survivors Hogg and Ramige, there was confusion between pilot Long and Chief of Party Good when the plane ran into trouble. When trying

©AP/Wide World Photos

to call in the plane's location, Good was unable to do so.

"Ken tried to radio in and Jim—I think Jim ended up actually making the radio because Ken didn't know the code word. ... [H]e looked at Jim and said, What's your number? ... He's like, Okay, How do you do it? And Jim's like, Here. Just let me do it. And Ken is like, I really want to do it, blah, blah, blah. ..."

Furthermore, while Good had superior knowledge of the area, Long failed to take his advice, possibly because he did not know how to

factors. For example, suppose two people observe someone busily working at a task. Both may conclude that he is being positively reinforced for the task, but they may disagree about the nature of the reinforcement. One of the observers may believe that the person is making diligent efforts "because the boss is looking and smiling," whereas the other observer may believe the efforts are caused by the satisfaction inherent in doing the task. As evidenced in the *Experiencing Organizational Behavior* section, Pilot Long inaccurately concluded that Ken Good's lack of knowledge about how to radio was due to a general lack of knowledge, and thus, later ignored his expert advice about their location. He could have concluded that Ken Good's lack of knowledge about the radio was simply due to his not knowing the correct password. The process of deciding what caused the behavior is known as *attribution*.[95]

Internal–External Attribution

A person's behavior is often interpreted as having been caused by either internal factors (such as personality, attitudes, and abilities) or external factors (such as organizational

call in their location. Thus, he attributed Long's inability to use the radio as being due to his general lack of knowledge, and may have assumed he didn't know about anything. Indeed, right before the crash, pilot Long had radioed in a wrong position, after arguing with Good about it. Clearly, if these two men had been able to learn from each other, this disaster may have been avoided. Furthermore, Long was a retired chemist, who had very little experience flying in this type of terrain and certainly under these weather conditions. He just did not have the experience to handle the crisis situation.

A second tragic aspect of this disaster is that the search party arrived at the site of the accident the next day, September 21, after searching the wrong location. They surveyed the crash site and declared that there were no survivors, when in fact Hogg and Ramige had left the site after realizing that the search plane flying overhead had not seen them. Rather than looking for the survivors, it was just assumed that they were dead and that their bodies had been burned in the plane crash. Search efforts were canceled and the families were notified that their loved ones had perished. When asked to explain how they had made this mistake, the searchers blamed the survivors, rather than their own misreading of the scene. They stated, "There were no footprints leaving the site, no piled rocks, no written message—nothing indicating anyone had survived or left the area." Clearly, they had failed to learn from their error and engaged in making self-serving bias attributions for their failure to rescue the survivors.

In the end, learning, or lack of it, played a big role in this disaster. If Long and Good had been willing or able to learn from each other, the crash may have been avoided. If the search team were more accurate in their perceptions, Ken Good's life may have been saved and Jodee Hogg and Matthew Ramige would not have had to suffer for two days in the bitter cold wilderness while severely wounded.

Sources: W.S. Becker, & M.J. Burke. 2008. "Shared decision making in a wilderness aviation accident." In M. Burke (Chair), Shared Decision Making in Singular Events. Symposium at the 2008 Annual Meeting of the Academy of Management, Anaheim, California; W.S. Becker. 2007. "Missed Opportunities: The Great Bear Wilderness Disaster," Organizational Dynamics, 36; 363–376.; National Transportation Safety Board (NTSB. (2005). Aircraft Accident Report: SEA04GA192, Essex, MT, September 20, 2004. Washington, D.C. Probable Cause and Narrative Report; U.S. Department of Agriculture Forest Service (USFS) (2005). Accident Investigation Factual Report. Press Release FS-025A USDA Forest Service, 9/23/2004.

resources, luck, and uncontrollable influences). When making these internal–external attributions, we depend to a great extent on our perceptions of the consistency, consensus, and distinctiveness associated with the behavior.

- *Consistency* is the extent to which the same person behaves in the same manner in the same situation over time (he returns from lunch late every day).
- *Consensus* is the degree to which other people in the same situation behave in the same manner (everyone returns from lunch late).
- *Distinctiveness* is the degree to which the same person tends to behave differently in other situations (he returns from lunch late every day but does not come to work late in the morning or leave work early at night).[96]

As shown in Exhibit 4-6, when we see a person's behavior as high in consistency, low in consensus, and low in distinctiveness, we tend to attribute that behavior to internal factors. If the behavior is low in consistency, high in consensus, and high in distinctiveness, we tend to attribute the behavior to external factors. If the behavior is perceived as having

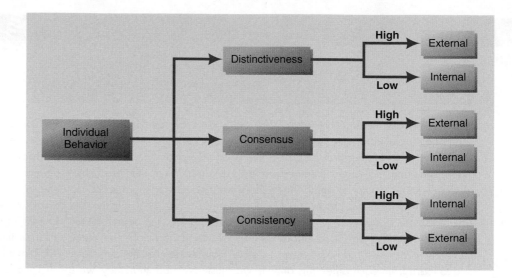

Exhibit 4-6
Attribution Theory

a mixed profile (such as high in consistency and high in distinctiveness with consensus being neutral), we often are biased toward internal attributions.

Studies have highlighted many situations in which internal and external attributions play major roles in attitudes and behavior. For example, one study suggests that unemployment counselors and their clients are influenced by these attributions in contrasting ways. On the one hand, unemployed persons are at the greatest risk for mental depression when they believe their situation is caused by uncontrollable external factors. The less control we perceive ourselves to have over events, the more likely we are to become despondent. On the other hand, a counselor is more likely to help an unemployed person if she sees that the unemployment is caused by uncontrollable external factors. If the counselor has attributed the cause of a client's unemployment to an internal factor (such as poor attitude or low motivation), she is less likely to be helpful.[97] Interestingly, researchers suggest that, in general, observers tend to overestimate the impact of internal causes on other people's behavior and underestimate the effect of external causes. This general tendency is called the **fundamental attribution error**.[98]

fundamental attribution error

A perception problem in which an individual is too likely to attribute the behavior of others to internal rather than external causes.

Attributions of Success and Failure

Monitoring and responding to poor performance are important tasks for managers and, in high-involvement organizations, for associates as well. To respond appropriately, managers must accurately assess the cause of any poor performance they observe. If they are unable to accurately identify the cause, individuals could suffer or benefit unjustly. Unfortunately, several troublesome attributional tendencies play a role.

First, the fundamental attribution error has an effect, although it may be minor. This error causes managers to attribute the behavior of others to internal factors. Thus, an individual's poor performance may have an external cause, but a manager may attribute it to an internal cause. For example, equity fund managers who perform poorly are often subjected to unfair criticism from those above them in the firm. Although skill is involved, fund-manager performance is often determined by uncontrollable factors.

Second, the **self-serving bias** plays a role, and it often has a significant effect on attributions. This bias works as follows. We have a strong tendency to attribute our own successes to internal factors (a high level of skill or hard work) and our own failures to

self-serving bias

A perception problem in which an individual is too likely to attribute the failure of others to internal causes and the successes of others to external causes, whereas the same individual will be too likely to attribute his own failure to external causes and his own successes to internal causes.

external causes (a difficult task or bad luck). Conversely, we tend to attribute someone else's success to external factors and someone else's failures to internal factors. We saw this bias at work when the rescue team in the Great Bear Wilderness case blamed the survivors for the team's failure to recognize that there had been survivors.

The fundamental attribution error and the self-serving bias work together to produce a significant bias toward assessments of internal causation for poor performance.[99] This bias means that managers and others make evaluation errors more often than they should. Was the Three Mile Island nuclear disaster in the late 1970s a function of several unforeseeable events coming together unexpectedly or a function of simple operator error? Operators received much of the blame, but it is not clear that they deserved it.[100] Are failures of new ventures typically a function of uncontrollable market developments or the missteps of entrepreneurs? Entrepreneurs receive much of the blame from venture capitalists,[101] but they may not deserve as much blame as they receive.

Task Perception

As we have described, perceptions of people and their behavior are created in subjective ways. Similarly, perceptions of tasks develop through subjective and sometimes idiosyncratic processes. Factors such as intelligence, age, and gender have been found to influence perceptions of tasks. One study, for example, found that individuals with higher levels of intelligence perceive more complexity in various tasks than individuals with lower levels of intelligence.[102] In addition, many studies have found that individuals with higher levels of satisfaction in the workplace perceive more autonomy and variety in their tasks than individuals with lower levels of satisfaction. In a study focused on

THE STRATEGIC LENS

Organizations compete on the basis of their resources. The strongest organizations usually win the competitive battles if their managers develop effective strategies and implement them well. To be competitive, managers use the organization's resources to create capabilities to act.[107] A critical component of these capabilities is knowledge. In fact, Bill Breen of *Fast Company* suggests that "Companies compete with their brains as well as their brawn. Organizations today must not only outgun and outhustle competitors, they must also outthink them. Companies win with ideas."[108]

Given the importance of knowledge in gaining a competitive advantage, learning is critical to organizational success. Managers and associates must continuously learn if they are to stay ahead of the competition. Perception is a key component of learning. It is particularly important to top executives, as they must carefully and thoroughly analyze their organization's external environment, with special emphasis on competitors. If they do not perceive their environment correctly, these executives may formulate ineffective strategies and cause the organization to lose its competitive advantage. Understanding the concepts of learning and perception, then, is absolutely essential to the effective operation of an organization.

Critical Thinking Questions

1. How does the knowledge held by managers and associates affect the performance of an organization?

2. What are some important ways in which associates can learn and thereby enhance their stock of knowledge? What role does perception play in the learning process?

3. What are the connections between learning, perception, and organizational strategies?

past graduates of a Hong Kong university, satisfaction and job perceptions were assessed multiple times over a two-year period. Satisfaction was found to influence job perceptions to a greater extent than job perceptions were found to influence satisfaction.[103]

How managers and associates perceive their jobs has important implications for behavior and outcomes. Task perceptions have been linked to intrinsic motivation as well as job performance.[104] They have even been linked to mood.[105] One group of researchers proposed that employees first perceive their jobs at an information level, then perceive the tasks at an evaluative level, and thereafter react to their jobs behaviorally and emotionally.[106] The process of task perception and the resulting effects on behavior have important consequences for organizations. We explore these issues in greater depth in Chapter 6.

What This Chapter Adds to Your Knowledge Portfolio

In this chapter, we have discussed basic learning principles and described how they can be used in effectively training and developing associates and managers. We have discussed problems that can occur in complex learning situations and how these problems can be avoided. Finally, we have seen many problems associated with perception processes. For individuals to function as effectively as possible, these perception issues must be understood and managed. At a more detailed level, we have covered the following points:

- Learning is the process by which we acquire new, relatively permanent, behaviors from experience. Operant conditioning theory and social learning theory are important explanations for how learning from experience works in practice. Learning new behaviors involves three basic elements: the situation, the behavioral response to the situation, and the consequences of that response for the person.

- Positive reinforcement involves the presentation of positive consequences for a behavior, such as praise for working hard, which increases the probability of an individual repeating the behavior in similar settings. Negative reinforcement is the removal of a negative consequence following a behavior, such as taking an employee off probation, which also increases the probability of an individual repeating the behavior. Punishment involves the presentation of negative consequences, such as a reduction in pay, which reduces the probability of repeating a behavior. Extinction refers to the removal of all reinforcing consequences, which can be effective in eliminating undesired behaviors.

- Various schedules of reinforcement exist for learning, including continuous reinforcement and several types of intermittent schedules. Although continuous schedules are rare in organizational settings, several applications of intermittent schedules can be found. Strategic use of reinforcement schedules helps in effectively shaping the behavior of newcomers and modifying the behavior of current associates and managers.

- In addition to direct reinforcement or punishment, individuals also learn by anticipating potential outcomes associated with certain behaviors and by modeling similar or important others.

- Self-efficacy is an important condition for learning to occur. Other important conditions are that people know why they are learning what they are learning, that they can tie the material to be learned to their own previous experiences, that they have the opportunity to practice, and that they receive feedback.

- People learn through many formal and informal mechanisms in organizations. Three examples are OB Mod programs, simulations, and learning from failure.

- Perception refers to the way people view the world around them. It is the process of receiving sensory inputs and organizing these inputs into useful ideas and concepts. The process consists of three stages: sensing, selecting, and organizing.

- Person perception is influenced by several factors associated with the nature of the perceiver, including the perceiver's familiarity with the person, feelings toward the person, and general emotional state. Situational factors influencing person perception include the general nature of the other person, that person's apparent intentions, and the anticipated or actual consequences of the interaction between perceiver and perceived.

back to the knowledge objectives

1. Explain the difference between negative reinforcement and punishment. Give examples of how each process might be used by managers with their associates.
2. What are four intermittent schedules of reinforcement? Give an example of how each schedule might be used by managers with their associates.
3. Explain how an instructor might effectively apply OB Mod in the classroom.
4. What can an organization do to promote learning from failure?
5. What can organizations do to train people to deal with complex and novel problems?
6. What are implicit person theories and the halo effect? How can an individual overcome a tendency to make these mistakes?
7. Give an example of a situation in which you attributed someone's behavior to internal or external factors. What influenced the attribution?

- Four general perceptual problems are implicit person theories, halo effect, projecting, and stereotyping. Implicit person theories are individuals' beliefs about the nature of human personality and attributes that can influence how they perceive other people. Halo effect is similar but involves having a general impression of a person and allowing it to affect perceptions of all other aspects of the person. Projecting is the tendency to believe that other people have characteristics like our own. Stereotyping occurs when we have generalized perceptions about a group that we apply to an individual who belongs to that group.

- Attribution refers to the process by which individuals interpret the causes of behavior. Whether behavior is seen as resulting from internal or external forces is influenced by three factors: distinctiveness, consistency, and consensus. Beyond these factors, there is a general tendency to attribute someone else's failures to internal causes.

Thinking about Ethics

1. Should associates be punished for making mistakes? If so, for what types of mistakes should they be punished? Are there mistakes for which they should not be punished? If so, what are they?

2. Should all associates be given the opportunity to learn new skills? If not, explain. Should some associates have greater learning opportunities than others? If so, when should this occur?

3. Are there circumstances when it is acceptable to use perceptual stereotypes of others? Explain why or why not.

4. Are accurate perceptions always necessary? In what situations (if any) is it less important to ensure that perceptions are accurate?

5. You are a manager of a unit with 15 associates. These associates have varying levels of education (high school to college-educated) and varying levels of skills and motivation. In your organization, associates receive higher pay for acquiring new and valuable skills. How would you decide to whom you would give learning opportunities and to whom you would not provide such opportunities?

Key Terms

learning, p. 133

operant conditioning
theory, p. 134

social learning theory, p. 134

positive reinforcement, p. 135

negative reinforcement, p. 135

punishment, p. 135

extinction, p. 136

continuous reinforcement,
p. 138

intermittent reinforcement,
p. 138

self-efficacy, p. 140

OB Mod, p. 142

simulation, p. 146

perception, p. 148

implicit person theories,
p. 152

halo effect, p. 152

projecting, p. 152

stereotyping, p. 152

fundamental attribution
error, p. 156

self-serving bias, p. 156

Human Resource Management Applications

Training is usually carried out with the human resource management (HRM) function. In addition to conducting the actual training, the HRM department may also conduct a needs analysis to determine what type of training is needed and by whom and follow through with an evaluation of the training. It may be the HRM department's responsibility to make sure that the organization realizes a financial and/or performance return on their investment of training dollars.

Many companies also offer outside learning opportunities for their associates. For example, some companies may pay for college tuition or reimburse expenses for adult learning classes. This type of learning opportunity is often viewed as a benefit of employment, and the HRM function involves developing such benefit plans.

---

building your human capital

Assessment of Approaches Used to Handle Difficult Learning Situations

Associates and managers often face difficulties in learning from experience. When there is little opportunity to learn from experience and when experience is unclear, individuals at all levels in an organization may draw the wrong conclusions. Interestingly, individuals vary in how they handle these situations. Some are prone to contemplate major issues alone. Others tend to discuss major issues with others. Both approaches can be useful, but extremes in either direction may be risky. In this installment of *Building Your Human Capital,* we present an assessment tool focused on approaches to handling difficult learning situations.

Instructions

In this assessment, you will read 12 phrases that describe people. Use the rating scale below to indicate how accurately each phrase describes *you.* Rate yourself as you generally are now, not as you wish to be in the future, and rate yourself as you honestly see yourself. Keep in mind that very few people have extreme scores on all or even most of the items (a "1" or a "5" is an extreme score); most people have midrange scores for many of the items. Read each item carefully, and then circle the number that corresponds to your choice from the rating scale.

1 Not at all like me	2 Somewhat unlike me	3 Neither like nor unlike me	4 Somewhat like me	5 Very much like me

1. Spend time reflecting on things.	1	2	3	4	5
2. Enjoy spending time by myself.	1	2	3	4	5
3. Live in a world of my own.	1	2	3	4	5
4. Enjoy my privacy.	1	2	3	4	5
5. Don't mind eating alone.	1	2	3	4	5
6. Can't stand being alone.	1	2	3	4	5
7. Do things at my own pace.	1	2	3	4	5
8. Enjoy contemplation.	1	2	3	4	5
9. Prefer to be alone.	1	2	3	4	5
10. Have point of view all my own.	1	2	3	4	5
11. Don't like to ponder over things.	1	2	3	4	5
12. Want to be left alone.	1	2	3	4	5

Scoring Key for Approaches to Handling Difficult Learning Situations

To create your score, combine your responses to the items as follows:

Private reflection = (Item 1 + Item 2 + Item 3 + Item 4 + Item 5 + Item 7 + Item 8 + Item 9 + Item 10 + Item 12) + (12 − (Item 6 + Item 11))

Scores can range from 12 to 60. Scores of 50 and above may be considered high, while scores of 22 and below may be considered low. Other scores are moderate. High scores suggest that a person prefers to spend time alone considering major issues (high private reflection). Such a person spends quality quiet time considering the possibilities. Low scores suggest that a person prefers to talk through problems with others (low private reflection). This type of person spends time exchanging information and viewpoints with others.

Additional Task

Think of a time when you faced a major problem with no clear answer. Did you handle the situation mostly by thinking alone, mostly by consulting with others, or with a mix of these two approaches? How effective was your approach? Explain.

Source of the Assessment Tool: International Personality Item Pool (2001). A Scientific Collaboration for the Development of Advanced Measures of Personality Traits and Other Individual Differences, at http://ipip.ori.org.

---

an organizational behavior moment
It's Just a Matter of Timing

Teresa Alvarez ate dinner slowly and without enthusiasm. Mike, her husband of only a few months, had learned that Teresa's "blue funks" were usually caused by her job. He knew that it was best to let her work out the problem alone. He excused himself and went to watch TV. Teresa poked at her dinner, but the large knot in her stomach kept her from eating much.

She had been very excited when Vegas Brown had approached her about managing his small interior decorating firm.

At the time, she was a loan officer for a local bank and knew Vegas through his financial dealings with the bank. As Vegas explained to her, his biggest problem was in managing the firm's financial assets, mostly because the firm was undercapitalized. It was not a severe problem, he assured her. "Mostly," he had said, "it's a cash flow problem. We have to be sure that the customers pay their accounts in time to pay our creditors. With your experience, you should be able to ensure a timely cash flow."

Teresa thought this was a good opportunity to build her managerial skills, since she had never had full responsibility for a company. It also meant a substantial raise in salary. After exploring the opportunity with Mike, she accepted the job.

During her first week with Vegas, she discovered that the financial problems were much more severe than he had led her to believe. The firm's checking account was overdrawn by about $40,000. There was a substantial list of creditors, mostly companies that sold furniture and carpeting to the firm on short-term credit. She was astonished that this financial position did not seem to bother Vegas.

"All you have to do, Teresa, is collect enough money each day to cover the checks we have written to our creditors. As you'll see, I'm the best sales rep in the business, so we have lots of money coming in. It's just a matter of timing. With you here, we should turn this problem around in short order."

Teresa, despite her misgivings, put substantial effort into the new job. She worked late almost every day and began to realize that it was more than simple cash-flow timing. For example, if the carpet layers made an error or if the furniture came in damaged, the customer would refuse to pay. This would mean that the customer's complaint must be serviced. However, the carpet layers disliked correcting service complaints, and furniture reorders might take several weeks.

Thus, Teresa personally began to examine all customer orders at crucial points in the process. Eventually, this minimized problems with new orders, but there remained a large number of old orders still awaiting corrections.

Teresa also arranged a priority system for paying creditors that eased some financial pressures in the short run and that would allow old, noncritical debts to be repaid when old customer accounts were repaid. After six months, the day arrived when the checking account had a zero balance, which was substantial progress. A few weeks later, it actually had a $9,000 positive balance. During all this time Teresa had made a point of concealing the financial status from Vegas. But with the $9,000 positive balance, she felt elated and told Vegas.

Vegas was ecstatic, said she had done a remarkable job, and gave her an immediate raise. Then it was Teresa's turn to be ecstatic. She had turned a pressure-packed job into one of promise. The future looked exciting, and the financial pressures had developed into financial opportunities. But that was last week.

This morning Vegas came into Teresa's office and asked her to write him a check for $30,000. Vegas said everything was looking so good that he was buying a new home for his family ($30,000 was the down payment). Teresa objected violently. "But this will overdraw our account by $21,000 again. I just got us out of one hole, and you want to put us back in. Either you delay the home purchase or I quit. I'm not going to go through all the late nights and all the pressure again because of some stupid personal decision you make. Can't you see what it means for the business to have money in the bank?"

"No, I can't!" Vegas said sternly. "I don't want to have money in the bank. It doesn't do me any good there. I'll just go out and keep selling our services, and the money will come in like always. You've proved to me that it's just a matter of timing. Quit if you want, but I'm going to buy the house. It's still my company, and I'll do what I want."

Discussion Questions

1. What did Teresa learn?
2. Other than quitting, what can Teresa do to resolve the problem? What learning and perception factors should she consider as she analyzes the situation?
3. If you were an outside consultant to the firm, could you recommend solutions that might not occur to Teresa or Vegas? What would they be?

---

team exercise

Best Bet for Training

Management-development programs are expensive. When organizations are determining which of several managers to send to these programs, they must evaluate each person. Some of the criteria considered might be whether the manager has the ability to learn, whether the manager and the organization will benefit, and whether a manager is moving into or has recently moved into a new position. The purpose of this exercise is to evaluate three potential candidates for developmental training, thus gaining insight into the process.

The exercise should take about 20 minutes to complete and an additional 15 to 20 minutes to discuss. The steps are as follows.

1. Read the following case about *High Tech International*.
2. Assemble into groups of four.
3. List the criteria you should consider for determining which of the three managers to send to the training program.
4. Choose the manager to send using the criteria developed in step 3.
5. Reassemble. Discuss your group's choice with the rest of the class, and listen to other groups' choices and criteria. Do you still prefer your group's choice? Why or why not?
6. The instructor will present additional points for consideration.

High Tech International

High Tech International has reserved one training slot every other year in an off-site leadership-development program. The program emphasizes personal and professional assessment and requires six days of residency to complete. High Tech's vice president for human resources must choose the manager to attend the next available program, which is to be run in three months. The cost of the program is high, including a tuition fee of $7,500, round-trip airfare, and lodging. The challenge is to choose the individual who has the greatest capacity to learn from the assessment and apply that learning back in the organization. Because of prior commitments and ongoing projects, the list of nominees has been narrowed to three:

- Gerry is slated for a major promotion in four months from regional sales manager to vice president for marketing. Her division has run smoothly during the past three years. Anticipating the move upward, she has asked for training to increase her managerial skills. Gerry is to be married in two months.

- John was a supervisor over a portion of a production process for two years before being promoted one year ago to manager of the entire process. His unit has been under stress for the past eight months due to the implementation of new technology and a consequent decline in productivity and morale. No new technological changes are planned in John's unit for at least another year.

- Bill has been considered a "fast-tracker" by his colleagues in the organization. He came to the company four years ago, at the age of 37, as a vice president for foreign operations. Historically, this position has been the stepping stone for division president. In the past year, Bill has displayed less energy and enthusiasm for the work. Eight months ago Bill and his wife separated, and two months ago he was hospitalized temporarily with a mild heart problem. For one month twice a year Bill has to travel abroad. His next trip will be in four months.

Endnotes

1. Hitt, M.A., Bierman, L., Shimizu, K., & Kochhar, R. 2001. Direct and moderating effects of human capital on strategy and performance in professional service firms: A resource-based perspective. *Academy of Management Journal*, 44: 13–28; Sirmon, D.G., Hitt, M.A., & Ireland, R.D. 2007. Managing resources in dynamic environments to create value: Looking inside the black box. *Academy of Management Review*, 32, 273–292.

2. Gange, R.M., & Medsker, K.L. 1996. *The conditions of learning*. Fort Worth, TX: Harcourt-Brace.

3. Luthans, F., & Stajkovic, A.D. 1999. Reinforce for performance: The need to go beyond pay and even performance. *Academy of Management Executive*, 13(2): 49–57.

4. Thorndike, E.L. 1898. Animal intelligence. *Psychological Review*, 2: all of issue 8; Thorndike, E.L. 1911. *Animal intelligence: Experimental studies*. New York: Macmillan.

5. Hull, C.L. 1943. *Principles of behavior*. New York: D. Appleton Century; Skinner, B.F. 1969. *Contingencies of reinforcement: A theoretical analysis*. Englewood Cliffs, NJ: Prentice Hall.

6. Bandura, A. 1996. *Social foundations of thought and action: A social cognitive theory*. Englewood Cliffs, NJ: Prentice Hall; Kreitner, R., & Luthans, F. 1984. A social learning theory approach to behavioral management: Radical behaviorists "mellowing out." *Organizational Dynamics*, 13 (2): 47–65.

7. Podsakoff, P.M., Bommer, W.H., Podsakoff, N.P., & MacKenzie, S.B. 2006. Relationships between leader reward behavior and punishment behavior and subordinate attitudes, perceptions, and behaviors: A meta-analytic review of existing and new research. *Organizational Behavior and Human Decision Processes,* 99: 113–142.

8. Trevino, L.K., 1992. The social effects of punishment in organizations: A justice perspective. *Academy of Management Review,* 17: 647–676.

9. Strupp, J. 2000. No providence in Rhode Island. *Editor and Publisher,* 133 (11): 6–8.

10. Friedman, S. 1994. Allstate faces suit over Fireman's Fund Shooting. *National Underwriter,* 98 (39): 3.

11. Guffey, C.J., & Helms, M.M. 2001. Effective employee discipline: A case of the Internal Revenue Service. *Public Personnel Management,* 30: 111–127.

12. Ibid.

13. Hitt, M.A., Lee, H., & Yucel, E. 2002. The importance of social capital to the management of multinational enterprises: Relational networks among Asian and western firms. *Asia Pacific Journal of Management,* 19: 353–372.

14. Hinkin, T.R., & Schreisheim, C.A. 2004. "If you don't hear from me you know you are doing fine": The effects of management nonresponse to employee performance. *Cornell Hotel and Restaurant Administration Quarterly,* 45: 362–373.

15. Latham, G.P., & Huber, V. 1992. Schedules of reinforcement: Lessons from the past and issues for the future. *Journal of Organizational Behavior Management,* 12(1): 125–149.

16. Scott, W.E., & Podsakoff, P.M. 1985. *Behavioral principles in the practice of management.* New York: John Wiley & Sons.

17. Ibid.

18. Ibid.

19. Ibid.

20. Ibid.

21. Bandura, A. 1986. *Social foundations of thought and action.* Englewood Cliffs, NJ: Prentice Hall; Bandura, A. 2001. Social cognitive theory: An agentic perspective. *Annual Review of Psychology,* 52: 1–26.

22. Stajkovic, A.D., Luthans, F., & Slocum, J.W., Jr. 1998. Social cognitive theory and self-efficacy: Going beyond traditional motivational and behavioral approaches. *Organizational Dynamics,* 26: 62–74.

23. Ibid.

24. Bandura, *Social foundations of thought and action.*

25. Wexley, K.N, & Latham, G.P. 2002. *Developing and training human resources in organizations* (3rd ed.). Upper Saddle River, NJ: Prentice Hall.

26. Bandura, A. 1997. *Self-efficacy: The exercise of self-control.* New York: W.H. Freeman.

27. Judge, T.A., & Bono, J.E. 2001. Relationship of core self-evaluations traits, self-esteem, generalized self-efficacy, locus of control and emotional stability with job satisfaction and job performance: A meta-analysis. *Journal of Applied Psychology,* 86: 80–93; Judge, T.A., Jackson, C.L., Shaw, J.C., Scott, B.A., & Rich, B.L. 2007. Self-efficacy and work-related performance: The integral role of individual differences. *Journal of Applied Psychology,* 92: 107–127; Stajkovic, A.D., & Luthans, F. 1998. Social cognitive theory and

work-related performance: A meta-analysis. *Psychological Bulletin,* 124: 240–261.

28. Noe, R.A. 1999. *Employee training and development.* Boston: Irwin McGraw-Hill.

29. Colquitt, J., Lepine, J., & Noe, R.A. 2000. Toward an integrative theory of training motivation: A meta-analytic pat analysis of 20 years of research. *Journal of Applied Psychology,* 85: 678–707.

30. Burke, M.J., Bradley, J., & Bowers, H.N. 2003. Health and safety programs. In J.E. Edwards, J. Scott, & N.S. Raju (Eds.), *The human resources-evaluation handbook.* Thousand Oaks, CA: Sage, pp. 429–446.

31. Noe, *Employee training and development.*

32. Burke, M.J., Holman, D., & Birdi, K. 2006. A walk on the safe side: The implications of learning theory for developing effective safety and health training. In G.P. Hodgkinson, & J.K. Ford (Eds.), *International review of industrial and organizational psychology, vol. 21.* Hoboken, NJ: John Wiley & Sons, pp. 1–44.

33. Weill, S., & McGill, I. 1989. *Making sense of experiential learning.* Buckingham, UK: SRHE/OU Press.

34. Kolb, D.A. 1984. *Experiential learning: Experience as the source of learning and development.* Englewood Cliffs, NJ: Prentice Hall.

35. Ford, J.K., Smith, E.M., Weissbein, D.A., Gully, S.M., & Salas, E. 1998. Relationships of goal orientation, metacognitive memory, and practice strategies with learning outcomes and transfer. *Journal of Applied Psychology,* 83: 218–233.

36. Kluger, A.N., & DeNisi, A.S. 1996. The effects of feedback interventions on performance: Historical review, a meta-analysis and a preliminary feedback intervention theory. *Psychological Bulletin,* 119:254–284.

37. Ibid.

38. Bandura, A. 1977. *Social learning theory.* Englewood Cliffs, NJ: Prentice Hall.

39. Mann, R.B., & Decker, P.J. 1984. The effect of key behavior distinctiveness on generalization and recall in behavior modeling training. *Academy of Management Journal,* 27: 900–910.

40. Sidman, M. 1962. Operant techniques. In A.J. Bachrach (Ed.), *Experimental foundations of clinical psychology.* New York: Basic Books.

41. Tichy, N.M. 2001. No ordinary boot camp. *Harvard Business Review,* 79(4): 63–70.

42. Fickes, M. 2000. Taking driver training to new levels. *Waste Age,* 31 (4): 238–248.

43. Robertson, G. 2001. Steering true: Greyhound's training is weeding-out process. *Richmond Times-Dispatch,* May 14: B1, B3.

44. Wexley & Latham, *Developing and training human resources in organizations.*

45. Luthans, F., & Kreitner, R. 1975. *Organizational behavior modification.* Glenview, IL: Scott & Foresman; Luthans, F., & Kreitner, R. 1985. *Organizational behavior modification and beyond.* Glenview, IL: Scott & Foresman.

46. Frederiksen, L.W. 1982. *Handbook of organizational behavior management.* New York: John Wiley & Sons.

47. Luthans, F., & Davis, E. 1991. Improving the delivery of quality service: Behavioral management techniques. *Leadership and Organization Development Journal,* 12(2): 3–6.

48. Nordstrom, R., Hall, R.V., Lorenzi, P., & Delquadri, J. 1988. Organizational behavior modification in the public sector. *Journal of Organizational Behavior Management,* 9 (2): 91–112.

49. Welsh, D.H.B., Luthans, F., & Sommer, S.M. 1993. Managing Russian factory workers: The impact of U.S.-based behavioral and participatory techniques. *Academy of Management Journal,* 36: 58–79; Welsh, D.H.B., Luthans, F., & Sommer, S.M. 1993. Organizational behavior modification goes to Russia: Replicating an experimental analysis across cultures and tasks. *Journal of Organizational Behavior Management,* 13 (2): 15–35.

50. Stajkovic, A.D., & Luthans, F. 1997. A meta-analysis of the effects of organizational behavior modification on task performance, 1975–95. *Academy of Management Journal,* 5: 1122–1149.

51. Ibid.

52. Schneier, C.J. 1974. Behavior modification in management. *Academy of Management Journal,* 17: 528–548.

53. Stajkovic & Luthans, A meta-analysis of the effects of organizational behavior modification on task performance, 1975–95.

54. Levitt, B., & March, J.G. 1988. Organizational learning. *Annual Review of Sociology,* 14: 319–340.

55. Thomke, S. 2001. Enlightened experimentation: The new imperative for innovation. *Harvard Business Review,* 79 (2): 66–75.

56. Thomke, S.H. 1998. Managing experimentation in the design of new products. *Management Science,* 44: 743–762.

57. Nicholls-Nixon, C.L., Cooper, A.C., & Woo, C.Y. 2000. Strategic experimentation: Understanding change and performance in new ventures. *Journal of Business Venturing,* 15: 493–521.

58. Thomke, S. 2003. R&D comes to service: Bank of America's pathbreaking experiments. *Harvard Business Review,* 81(4): 70–79.

59. Pfeffer, J. 1998. *The human equation.* Boston: Harvard Business School Press.

60. Master, M. 2001. Spectacular failures. *Across the Board,* 38 (2): 20–26.

61. McGrath, G. 1999. Falling forward: Real options reasoning and entrepreneurial failure. *Academy of Management,* 24: 13–30; Sitkin, S.B. 1992. Learning through failure: The strategy of small losses. *Research in Organizational Behavior,* 14: 231–266.

62. Sitkin, Learning through failure.

63. Shimizu, K., & Hitt, M.A. 2004. Strategic flexibility: Managerial capability to reverse poor strategic decisions. *Academy of Management Executive,* 18, 44–59.

64. Thomke, Enlightened experimentation.

65. Ibid.

66. Robinson, H. 1994. *Perception.* New York: Routledge.

67. Perrow, C. 1984. *Normal accidents: Living with high-risk technologies.* New York: Basic Books.

68. Tufte, E.R. 1997. *Visual and statistical thinking: Displays of evidence for making decisions.* Cheshire, CT: Graphics Press.

69. Einhorn, H.J., & Hogarth, R.M. 1978. Confidence in judgment: Persistence in the illusion of validity. *Psychological Review,* 85: 395–416; Wason, P.C. 1960. On the failure to eliminate hypotheses in a conceptual task. *Quarterly Journal of Experimental Psychology,* 20: 273–283.

70. Bierhoff, H.-W. 1989. *Person perception.* New York: Springer-Verlag; Heil, J. 1983. *Perception and cognition.* Berkeley: University of California Press.

71. Jacobs, R., & Kozlowski, S.W.J. 1985. A closer look at halo error in performance ratings. *Academy of Management Journal,* 28: 201–212.

72. Tsui, A.S., & Barry, B. 1986. Interpersonal affect and rating errors. *Academy of Management Journal,* 29: 586–599.

73. Murray, H.A. 1933. The effects of fear upon estimates of the maliciousness of other personalities. *Journal of Social Psychology,* 4: 310–329.

74. See, for example, Assor, A., Aronoff, J., & Messe, L.A. 1986. An experimental test of defensive processes in impression formation. *Journal of Personality and Social Psychology,* 50: 644–650.

75. Berkowitz, L. 1960. Repeated frustrations and expectations in hostility arousal. *Journal of Abnormal and Social Psychology,* 60: 422–429.

76. Jones, E.E., & deCharms, R. 1957. Changes in social perception as a function of the personal relevance of behavior. *Sociometry,* 20: 75–85.

77. Jick, T., & Gentile, M. 1995. Donna Dubinsky and Apple Computer, Inc. (Part A). Boston: Harvard Business School Publishing.

78. Mehl, M.R., Gosling, S.D., & Pennebaker, J.W. 2006. Personality in its natural habitat: Manifestations and implicit folk theories of personality in daily life. *Journal of Personality and Social Psychology,* 90: 862–877.

79. Gosling, S.D., Ko, S.J., Mannarelli, T., & Morris, M.E. 2002. A room with a cue: Personality judgments based on offices and bedrooms. *Journal of Personality and Social Psychology,* 82: 379–398.

80. Dweck, C.S. 1999. *Self-theories: Their role in motivation, personality, and development.* Philadelphia, PA: Psychology Press.

81. Heslin, P.A., Vandewalle, D., & Latham, G.P. 2006. Keen to help: Managers' implicit person theories and their subsequent employee coaching. *Personnel Psychology,* 59: 871–902.

82. Guilford, J.P. 1954. *Psychometric methods.* New York: McGraw-Hill.

83. Becker, B.E., & Cardy, R.L. 1986. Influence of halo error on appraisal effectiveness: A conceptual and empirical reconsideration. *Journal of Applied Psychology,* 71: 662–671; Jacobs, R., & Kozlowski, S.W.J. 1985. A closer look at halo error in performance ratings. *Academy of Management Journal,* 28: 201–212; Nisbett, R.D., & Wilson, T.D. 1977. The halo effect: Evidence for unconscious alteration of judgments. *Journal of Personality and Social Psychology,* 35: 250–256; Solomon, A.L., & Lance, C.E. 1997. Examination of the relationship between true halo and halo error in performance ratings. *Journal of Applied Psychology,* 82: 665–674.

84. Gross, R.L., & Brodt, S.E. 2001. How assumptions of consensus undermine decision making. *Sloan Management Review,* 42(2): 86–94.

85. See, for example, Finkelstein, L.M., & Burke, M.J. 1998. Age stereotyping at work: The role of rater and contextual factors on evaluation of job applicants. *Journal of General Psychology,* 125: 317–345.

86. "L'Oreal to Ask S.C. to Review Ruling on the Firing of Unattractive Worker," *Metropolitan New Enterprise,* Apr. 14, 2003, at http://www.metnews.com.

87. Tahmincioglu, E. (Jan. 26, 2007) It's Not Easy for Obese Workers, MSNBC.com, at http://www.msnbc.msn.com.

88. Dion K., Berscheid, E., & Walster, E. (1972). What is beautiful is good. *Journal of Personality and Social Psychology,* 24: 285–290.

89. Hosoda, M., Stone-Romero, E.F., & G. Coats. 2003. The effects of physical attractiveness on job-related outcomes: A meta-analysis of experimental studies. *Personnel Psychology,* 26: 431–462; Rudolph, C.W., Wells, C.L., Weller, M.D., Baltes, B. 2009. A meta-analysis of empirical studies of weight-based bias in the workplace. *Journal of Vocational Behavior,* 74: 1–10.

90. Fikkan, J., & Rothblum, E. 2005. Weight bias in employment. In K.D. Brownell, R.M. Puhl, M.B. Schwartz, & L. Rudd (Eds.), *Weight bias: Nature, consequences, and remedies* (pp. 15-28). New York: The Guilford Press.

91. Dipboye, R.L., & Colella, A. 2005. *Discrimination at work: The psychological and organizational bases.* Mahwah, NJ: Lawrence Erlbaum Associates.

92. Ibid.

93. Corbett, W.R. 2007. The ugly truth about appearance discrimination and the beauty of our employment discrimination law. *Duke Journal of Gender Law and Policy,* 14: 153–175.

94. McEnrue, M.P. 1984. Perceived competence as a moderator of the relationship between role clarity and job performance: A test of two hypotheses. *Organizational Behavior and Human Performance,* 34: 379–386.

95. Heider, F. 1958. *The psychology of interpersonal relations.* New York: John Wiley & Sons.

96. Kelley, H.H., & Michela, J. 1981. Attribution theory and research. *Annual Review of Psychology,* 31: 457–501.

97. Young, R.A. 1986. Counseling the unemployed: Attributional issues. *Journal of Counseling and Development,* 64: 374–377.

98. Harvey, J.H., & Weary, G. 1984. Current issues in attribution theory and research. *Annual Review of Psychology,* 35: 428–432.

99. Mitchell, T.R., & Green, S.G. 1983. Leadership and poor performance: An attributional analysis. In J.R. Hackman, E.E. Lawler, & L.W. Porter (Eds.), *Perspectives on behavior in organizations.* New York: McGraw-Hill.

100. Perrow, *Normal accidents: Living with high risk technologies.*

101. Ruhnka, J.C., & Feldman, H.D. 1992. The "Living Dead" phenomenon in venture capital investments. *Journal of Business Venturing,* 7: 137–155.

102. Ganzach, Y., & Pazy, A. 2001. Within-occupation sources of variance in incumbent perception of complexity. *Journal of Occupational and Organizational Psychology,* 74: 95–108.

103. Wong, C., Hui, C., & Law, K.S. 1998. A longitudinal study of the perception–job satisfaction relationship: A test of the three alternative specifications. *Journal of Occupational and Organizational Psychology,* 71: 127–146.

104. Hackman, J.R., Oldham, G., Janson, R., & Purdy, K. 1975. A new strategy of job enrichment. *California Management Review,* 17(4): 57–71.

105. Saavedra, R., & Kwun, S.K. 2000. Affective states in job characteristic theory. *Journal of Organizational Behavior,* 21 (Special Issue): 131–146.

106. Slusher, E.A., & Griffin, R.W. 1985. Comparison processes in task perceptions, evaluations, and reactions. *Journal of Business Research,* 13: 287–299.

107. Simon, D., Hitt, M.A., & Ireland, D. 2007. Managing resources in dynamic environments to create value. *Academy of Management Review,* 32:273–292.

108. Breen, B. 2004. Hidden asset. *Fast Company,* March: 93.

personality, intelligence, attitudes, and emotions

exploring behavior in action

I Know She's Smart and Accomplished ... But Does She Have "Personality"?

Answer "true" or "false" to the following questions:

It's maddening when the court lets guilty criminals go free.
Slow people irritate me.
I can easily cheer up and forget my problems.
I am tidy.
I am not polite when I don't want to be.
I would like the job of a race car driver.
My teachers were unfair to me in school.
I like to meet new people.

The way you answer these questions, or similar items, could determine whether you get the job or not. These questions are examples of the types found on personality tests commonly used to hire people for jobs. One survey found that over 30 percent of employers use some form of personality test when hiring employees. Another survey found that 29 percent of adults aged 18 to 24 took a personality test in the past two years in order to be considered for a job. One of the largest testing companies, Unicru (now a part of Kronos), tested over 11 million candidates in one year for companies such as Universal Studios. Personality testing has taken the employment field by storm. Employers are no longer relying only on stellar resumes and amazing experience, they also care about whether an applicant has the right temperament to carry out the job and fit in with the organization. "Although personality-based testing has been around for years, it's now in the spotlight," said Bill Byham, CEO of

knowledge objectives

After reading this chapter, you should be able to:

1. Define *personality* and explain the basic nature of personality traits.
2. Describe the Big Five personality traits, with particular emphasis on the relationship with job performance, success on teams, and job satisfaction.
3. Discuss specific cognitive and motivational concepts of personality, including locus of control and achievement motivation.
4. Define *intelligence* and describe its role in the workplace.
5. Define an *attitude* and describe how attitudes are formed and how they can be changed.
6. Discuss the role of emotions in organizational behavior.

Development Dimensions International, a consulting firm that is a leader in the personality testing field.

So, what are the right answers? That depends on what the employer is looking for. Common things that employers look for are conscientiousness, ability to handle stress, ability to get along with others, potential leadership, problem-solving style, and service orientation. Different employers look for different personality profiles, and often it depends on the job being sought.

For example, Karen Schoch, who hires employees for Women & Infants Hospital of Rhode Island, states, "A person must be qualified to do the job, but they also require the right personality. We're a hospital that puts a premium on patient care, and we want people who can deliver the concept." Thus, she looks for people who have a blend of compassion, diplomacy, energy, and self-confidence.

©iStockphoto

Harbor Group LLC, a Houston financial advisory firm, examines dominance, influence, steadiness, and conscientiousness to predict how its associates will handle stress. David Hanson, a founding principal at First Harbor, states "Stress can result in lower productivity, increased absenteeism, tardiness, and high employee turnover." Thus, it is important for his company to identify how people deal with stress so that they can develop ways to counteract the effects of stress.

Southwest Airlines, a company well known for its relaxed, fun culture, takes creating a relaxed, warm environment on its flights seriously. To accomplish this goal, Southwest Airlines carefully screens job applicants to ensure that only individuals with personalities and attitudes consistent with the desired culture are hired. Libby Sartain, former vice president of the People Department at Southwest, put it this way: "If we hire people who don't have the right attitude, disposition, and behavioral characteristics to fit into our culture, we will start to change that culture." Herb Kelleher, former CEO, has said, "We look for attitudes; people with a sense of humor who don't take themselves too seriously. We'll train you on whatever it is you have to do, but the one thing Southwest cannot change in people is inherent attitudes." Thus, Southwest tests people for kindness and creativity.

These four organizations all have different cultures and work environments. Therefore, they all look for different personality traits in new employees. The extent to which the personality of associates fits with an organization's culture has been found to have a positive impact on both associates and the organization, and personality testing is one way to make sure that employees have the right disposition to mesh with the organization's culture. This emphasis on cultural fit is found in many high-involvement organizations, where identifying and selecting individuals who complement a carefully developed and maintained culture is a highly important task.

One example of a company that has used personality testing to directly impact its bottom line is Outback Steakhouse. Personality testing helped Outback to identify applicants who would fit the firm's needs. Better hiring decisions resulted in growth in revenues and higher profits over time. As a result, associate turnover was reduced by 50 percent, decreasing the company's recruitment and training costs by millions of dollars. A popular and valid personality test is the Hogan Personality Inventory (HPI). Using this test in employee selection led to 50 percent reduced turnover in a retail company, 48 percent improved productivity in an insurance company, decreased accidents resulting in lost time among hospital workers, and an increase of $308,000.00 per year in sales in a bank.

Sources: "Why is Personality Testing Important to Recruitment," January 12, 2010, at http://www.hoganassessments.com/_hoganweb/documents/Why%20Personality%20Testing%20is%20Important%20to%20Recruitment.pdf; A.E. Cha. 2005. "Employers Relying on Personality Tests to Screen Applicants," *Washington Post*, Mar. 27, p. A01; A. Overholt. 2002. "True or False: You're Hiring the Right People," *Fast Company*, Issue 55, Jan. p. 110; S.B. Fink. 2006. "Getting Personal: 10 Reasons to Test Personality Before Hiring," *Training*, Issue 43, Nov. p. 16; V. Knight. 2006. "Personality Tests as Hiring Tools," *Wall Street Journal (Eastern Edition)*, Mar. 15,

Sources: *(continued from page 168)* p. B3A; B. Dattner. 2004. "Snake Oil or Science? That's the Raging Debate on Personality Testing," *Workforce Management*, Issue 83 (10), Oct., p. 90, accessed at www.workforce3.com, Mar. 2007; E. Frauenheim. 2006. "The (Would Be) King of HR Software," *Workforce Management*, Issue 85 (15), Aug. 14, pp. 34–39, accessed at www.workforce3.com, Mar. 2007; www.kronos.com, accessed Mar. 2007; K. Brooker. 2001. "The Chairman of the Board Looks Back," *Fortune* 143, no. 11: 62–76; R. Chang. 2001. "Turning into Organizational Performance," *Training and Development* 55, no. 5: 104–111; K. Ellis. 2001. "Libby Sartain," *Training* 38, no. 1: 46–50; L. Ellis. 2001. "Customer Loyalty," *Executive Excellence* 18, no. 7: 13–14; K. Freiberg & J. Freiberg. 1996. *Nuts!: Southwest Airlines' Crazy Recipe for Business and Personal Success* (Austin, TX: Bard Press); K. Freiberg & J. Freiberg. 2001. "Southwest Can Find Another Pilot," *Wall Street Journal (Eastern Edition)*, Mar. 26, p. A22; H. Lancaster. 1999. "Herb Kelleher Has One Main Strategy: Treat Employees Well," *Wall Street Journal (Eastern Edition)*, Aug. 31, p. B1; S.F. Gale. 2002. "Three Companies Cut Turnover with Tests," *Workforce* 81, no. 4: 66–69.

the strategic importance of Personality, Intelligence, Attitudes, and Emotions

The discussion of personality testing in *Exploring Organizational Behavior in Action* illustrates how important it is for organizations to select the right individuals. Everyone has individual differences that cannot be easily changed. As Herb Kelleher mentioned above, organizations can train people to do only so much; there are individual differences in people that are not easily influenced. In this chapter we explore three such differences: personality, intelligence, and emotions. We also explore another individual difference: attitudes that can be more easily affected by one's organizational experience. All of these human attributes influence organizational effectiveness by influencing associates' performance, work attitudes, motivation, willingness to stay in the organization, and ability to work together in a high-involvement environment.

In Chapter 1, we stated that an important part of high-involvement work systems was that organizations engage in selective hiring, illustrating the importance of hiring people with the right set of attributes. A great deal of research has been done that has shown that certain traits, such as conscientiousness[1] and intelligence,[2] are related to associates' performance. Associates' traits have also

been linked to how likely they will be to engage in counterproductive work behavior, such as being frequently absent or stealing.[3] In addition to traits directly affecting performance, the degree to which associates' traits fit the work environment and culture is also linked with how satisfied and committed associates are to their organization[4] and how likely they will be to remain in the organization.[5] Furthermore, the attributes of top leaders in the organization have a direct impact on organizational functioning by relating to the group dynamics among top decision makers[6] and the strategic decisions they make.[7] Thus, the individual traits and attitudes of everyone in the organization can have an important impact on the functioning of that organization.

Because personalities have such important effects on behavior in organizations, care must be taken in adding new people. For a manufacturing firm emphasizing stable, efficient operations because it competes on the basis of low cost, hiring newcomers who are serious, conscientious, and emotionally stable is logical. For a manufacturing firm competing on the basis of frequent process and product innovations, hiring newcomers who embrace change and are inquisitive is important. Furthermore, as

you will learn in this chapter, it is critical to hire associates who fit the characteristics of the particular jobs they will hold. Inside the same firm, personalities suitable for the tasks required in sales may be less suitable for the tasks involved in research and development. Although personality, intelligence, attitudes, and emotions are not perfect predictors of job performance and should never be used alone in selection decisions, they are important.

In this chapter, we open with a discussion of fundamentals of personality, including its origins and the degree to which it changes over time. Building on this foundation, we examine a major personality framework, the Big Five, that has emerged as the most useful for understanding workplace behaviors. Next, we discuss several cognitive and motive-based characteristics of personality not explicitly included in the major framework. Next, we examine intelligence, another individual difference that has become a controversial topic in employee selection. We then move on to an exploration of attitudes, including attitude development and change as well as several important types of workplace attitudes. Finally, we address emotions and their role in organizations.

Fundamentals of Personality

The term *personality* may be used in several ways. One common use—or, rather, misuse—of the word is in describing the popularity of our classmates or colleagues. We may think that Hank has a pleasant personality or that Susan is highly personable. In your high-school yearbook, someone was probably listed with the title of Mr. or Ms. Personality. When *personality* is used in this way, it means that person is popular or well liked. This meaning has little value, however, in understanding or predicting behavior. To know that some people are popular does not enable us to have a rich understanding of them, nor does it improve our ability to interact with them.

For our purposes, personality describes a person's most striking or dominant characteristics—jolly, shy, domineering, assertive, and so on. This meaning of personality is more useful because a set of rich characteristics tells us much about the behavior we can expect a person to exhibit and can serve as a guide in our interactions with her.

personality
A stable set of characteristics representing internal properties of an individual, which are reflected in behavioral tendencies across a variety of situations.

More formally, **personality** is a stable set of characteristics representing the internal properties of an individual, which are reflected in behavioral tendencies across a variety of situations.[8] These characteristics are often referred to as "traits" and have names such as dominance, assertiveness, and neuroticism. More important than the names of personality traits, however, is the meaning given to them by psychologists. The traditional meaning of personality traits rests on three basic beliefs:

1. Personality traits are individual psychological characteristics that are relatively enduring—for example, if a person is introverted or shy, he or she will likely remain so for a long period of time.

2. Personality traits are major determinants of one's behavior—for example, an introverted person will be withdrawn and exhibit nonassertive behavior.

3. Personality traits influence one's behavior across a wide variety of situations—an introverted person will be withdrawn and nonassertive at a party, in class, in sports activities, and at work.

Some researchers and managers have criticized these traditional beliefs about personality traits, believing instead that personality can undergo basic changes. They believe, for example, that shy people can become more assertive and outgoing. Furthermore, by examining our own behaviors, we may learn that sometimes we behave differently from situation to situation. Our behavior at a party, for example, may be different from our behavior at work.

Still, we often can observe consistencies in a person's behavior across situations. For example, many people at various levels of Scott Paper saw Al Dunlap act in hard-hearted ways and exhibit outbursts of temper when he served this company as CEO. Many individuals at Sunbeam, where he next filled the CEO role, observed the same behaviors. Apparently, family members also experienced similar treatment. When Dunlap was fired by the board of directors at Sunbeam, his only child said, "I laughed like hell. I'm glad he fell on his ...."[9] His sister said, "He got exactly what he deserved."[10]

Determinants of Personality Development

To properly understand personality, it is important to examine how it develops. Both heredity and environment play important roles in the development of personality.

Heredity

From basic biology, we know that parents provide genes to their children. Genes in turn determine height, hair color, eye color, size of hands, and other basic physical characteristics. Similarly, genes seem to influence personality, as demonstrated in three different types of studies.

The first type of study involves examinations of identical twins. Identical twins have identical genes and should therefore have similar personalities if genes play an important role. Moreover, if genes influence personality, identical twins separated at birth should have more similar adult personalities than regular siblings or fraternal twins who have been raised apart. This is precisely the case, as has been found in a number of studies.[11] Consider identical twins Oskar and Jack, who were parented by different people. Oskar was raised in Germany by his Roman Catholic maternal grandmother, whereas Jack was raised outside Germany by his Jewish father. As adults, however, both of the brothers were domineering, prone to anger, and absentminded.[12]

The second type of study involves assessments of newborns. Because newborns have had little exposure to the world, the temperaments they exhibit—including their

©Siri Stafford/Getty Images, Inc.

activity levels, adaptability, sensitivity to stimulation, and general disposition—are probably determined to a large degree by genetics. If newborn temperament in turn predicts personality later in life, a link between genes and personality is suggested. Several studies have provided evidence for this relationship. In one such study, newborns ranging in age from 8 to 12 weeks were tracked into adult life. Temperament in the early weeks of life was found to predict personality later in life.[13]

The third type of study supporting genetic effects focuses directly on genes. In several studies, researchers have identified distinct genes thought to influence personality. Gene D_4DR serves as a useful example. This gene carries the recipe for a protein known as *dopamine receptor,* which controls the amount of dopamine in the brain. Dopamine is crucial because it seems to affect initiative and adventure-seeking. Individuals with a long version of the gene, where a key sequence of DNA repeats itself six or more times, are more likely to be adventure-seeking than individuals with a short version of the gene.[14]

Although genes clearly play an important role in personality, we must be careful not to overemphasize their effects. Researchers typically believe that 50 percent of adult personality is genetically determined. Furthermore, we should not conclude that a single magical gene controls a particular aspect of personality. The best information currently available suggests that combinations of genes influence individual personality traits.[15] For example, gene D_4DR plays an important role in how much adventure a person desires, but other genes also affect this trait.

Environment

Beyond genes, the environment a person experiences as a child plays an important role in personality. In other words, what a child is exposed to and how she is treated influence the type of person she becomes. Warm, nurturing, and supportive households are more likely to produce well-adjusted, outgoing individuals.[16] Socioeconomic circumstances of the household may also play a role, with favorable circumstances being associated with value systems that promote hard work, ambition, and self-control.[17] Events and experiences outside the home can also affect personality. Schools, churches, and athletic teams are important places for lessons that shape personality.

Although research suggests that personality is reasonably stable in the adult years,[18] events and experiences later in life can affect personality. Reports have described, for example, how a heart attack survivor reaches deep inside to change himself. In addition, some psychological theories suggest that change may occur over time. One theory proposes a model of personality that includes possible transitions at various points in life, including infancy, early childhood, late childhood, the teenage years, early adulthood, middle adulthood, and late adulthood, for instance.[19] The specific changes that might occur are less important than the fact that change is possible.

The Big Five Personality Traits

For managers and associates to effectively use personality traits in predicting behavior, they must work with a concise set of traits. But thousands of traits can be used to describe a person. Which traits are most useful? Which correspond to the most meaningful behavioral tendencies in the workplace? These questions have puzzled researchers for many years. Fortunately, a consensus among personality experts has emerged to focus on five traits. These traits, collectively known as the Big Five, include extraversion, conscientiousness, agreeableness, emotional stability, and openness to experience, as shown in Exhibit 5-1.

Extraversion

extraversion
The degree to which an individual is outgoing and derives energy from being around other people.

The **extraversion** trait was an important area of study for many well-known psychologists in the early-to-middle portion of the twentieth century, including Carl Jung, Hans

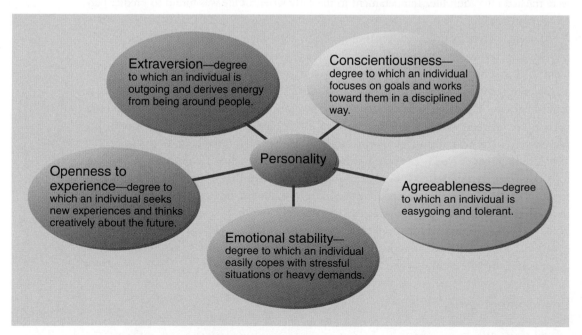

Exhibit 5-1 The Big Five Personality Traits

Eysenck, and Raymond Cattell. For Jung and many of his contemporaries, this aspect of personality was considered the most important driver of behavior. Extraversion is the degree to which a person is outgoing and derives energy from being around other people. In more specific terms, it is the degree to which a person: (1) enjoys being around other people, (2) is warm to others, (3) speaks up in group settings, (4) maintains a vigorous pace, (5) likes excitement, and (6) is cheerful.[20] Herb Kelleher of Southwest Airlines clearly fits this mold, as does Carol Bartz, current CEO of Yahoo![21]

Research has shown that people scoring high on this dimension, known as *extraverts,* tend to have a modest but measurable performance advantage over introverts in occupations requiring a high level of interaction with other people.[22] Specific occupations where extraverts have been found to perform particularly well include sales and management. In contrast, *introverts,* who do not score high on extraversion, tend to do particularly well in occupations such as accounting, engineering, and information technology, where more solitary work is frequently required. For any occupation where teams are central, or in a high-involvement organization where teams are emphasized, extraverts may also have a slight edge, as teams involve face-to-face interaction, group decision making, and navigation of interpersonal dynamics.[23] A team with a very high percentage of extraverts as members, however, may function poorly, for too many team members may be more interested in talking than in listening. Finally, research suggests that extraversion is related to job satisfaction, with extraverts exhibiting slightly more satisfaction regardless of the specific conditions of the job situation.[24]

Conscientiousness

The **conscientiousness** trait has played a central role in personality research in recent years. Many current personality researchers believe this dimension of personality has the greatest effect of all personality dimensions on a host of outcomes in the workplace. *Conscientiousness* is the degree to which a person focuses on goals and works toward them in a disciplined way. In specific terms, it is the degree to which a person: (1) feels capable, (2) is organized, (3) is reliable, (4) possesses a drive for success, (5) focuses on completing tasks, and (6) thinks before acting.[25]

conscientiousness
The degree to which an individual focuses on goals and works toward them in a disciplined way.

Research has shown that individuals scoring high on conscientiousness have a performance edge in most occupations and tend to perform well on teams.[26] This is to be expected, because irresponsible, impulsive, low-achievement-striving individuals generally are at a disadvantage in activities both inside and outside the workplace. In an important study, hundreds of individuals were tracked from early childhood through late adulthood.[27] Their success was assessed in terms of job satisfaction in midlife, occupational status in midlife, and annual income in late adulthood. Conscientiousness, which was fairly stable over the participants' lifetimes, positively affected each of these success measures. This is the reason companies such as Microsoft, Bain & Company, and Goldman Sachs emphasize conscientiousness when searching for new associates.[28] Interestingly, research shows that conscientiousness has a stronger positive effect on job performance when the person also scores high on agreeableness, the trait considered next.[29]

Agreeableness

The **agreeableness** trait has also received a great deal of attention in recent years. *Agreeableness* is the degree to which a person is easygoing and tolerant—the degree to which a person: (1) believes in the honesty of others, (2) is straightforward, (3) is willing to help

agreeableness
The degree to which an individual is easygoing and tolerant.

others, (4) tends to yield under conflict, (5) exhibits humility, and (6) is sensitive to the feelings of others.[30]

Research has not shown a consistent pattern of job outcomes for individuals scoring high or low on agreeableness. After all, being agreeable and disagreeable can be valuable at different times in the same job. A manager, for example, may need to discipline an associate in the morning but behave very agreeably toward union officials in the afternoon. A salesperson may need to be tough in negotiations on one day but treat a long-standing customer with gracious deference on the next day.

Agreeable individuals do, however, seem to be consistently effective in teamwork.[31] They are positive for interpersonal dynamics, as they are sensitive to the feelings of others and often try to ensure the participation and success of all team members. Teams with many members who are agreeable have been found to perform well.[32] Having an extremely high percentage of very agreeable team members, however, may be associated with too little debate on important issues. When teams must make important decisions and solve non-routine problems, having some individuals with lower scores on agreeableness may be an advantage.

Emotional Stability

emotional stability
The degree to which an individual easily handles stressful situations and heavy demands.

The trait of **emotional stability** relates to how a person copes with stressful situations or heavy demands. Specific features of this trait include the degree to which a person: (1) is relaxed, (2) is slow to feel anger, (3) rarely becomes discouraged, (4) rarely becomes embarrassed, (5) resists unhealthy urges associated with addictions, and (6) handles crises well.[33] Research has shown that emotionally stable individuals tend to have an edge in task performance across a large number of occupations.[34] This is reasonable, for stable individuals are less likely to exhibit characteristics that may interfere with performance, such as being anxious, hostile, and insecure. Similarly, emotionally stable individuals seem to have modest but measurable advantages as team members.[35] Several studies reveal that teams perform more effectively when composed of members scoring high on this trait.[36] Furthermore, when individuals are high on emotional stability, in combination with high extraversion and high conscientiousness, they are more likely to have team leadership potential, than those who do not have this personality profile.[37] Finally, research shows that emotional stability is positively linked to job satisfaction, independent of the specific conditions of the job situation.[38]

Openness to Experience

openness to experience
The degree to which an individual seeks new experiences and thinks creatively about the future.

The **openness** trait is the degree to which a person seeks new experiences and thinks creatively about the future. More specifically, openness is the degree to which a person: (1) has a vivid imagination, (2) has an appreciation for art and beauty, (3) values and respects emotions in himself and others, (4) prefers variety to routine, (5) has broad intellectual curiosity, and (6) is open to reexamining closely held values.[39] Research suggests that both individuals scoring high and individuals scoring low on openness can perform well in a variety of occupations and can function well on teams.[40] Those who score high on this dimension of personality, however, are probably more effective at particular tasks calling for vision and creativity, such as the creative aspects of advertising, the creative aspects of marketing, and many aspects of working in the arts. At W.L. Gore and Associates, maker of world-renowned Gore-Tex products (such as sealants and fabrics), strong openness is valued for many aspects of engineering, sales, and marketing because the company has been successful through innovation and wants to keep its culture of creativity, discovery, and initiative.[41] Individuals with lower openness scores may be more effective in jobs calling for strong adherence to rules, such as piloting airplanes and accounting.

The Big Five as a Tool for Selecting New Associates and Managers

Given the links between important competencies and specific personality traits, it is not surprising that personality assessment can play a role in hiring decisions. Although no single tool should be used as the basis for hiring new associates and managers, personality assessment can be a useful part of a portfolio of tools that includes structured interviews and skills evaluations. In some reviews of available tools, Big Five assessments have been shown to provide useful predictions of future job performance.[42] It is important, however, to develop a detailed understanding of how personality traits predict performance in a specific situation. Such understanding requires that the general information just discussed be supplemented by: (1) an in-depth analysis of the requirements of a particular job in a particular organization and (2) an in-depth determination of which traits support performance in that particular job. In some cases, only certain aspects of a trait may be important in a specific situation. For example, being slow to anger and not prone to frustration may be crucial aspects of emotional stability for particular jobs, whereas being relaxed may be much less important for these jobs. Call center operator positions call for this particular combination of characteristics. They have to respond positively to customers, even when customers are rude or hostile.[43]

The Big Five and High-Involvement Management

We now turn to competencies that are important for high-involvement management. Combinations of several Big Five traits likely provide a foundation for important competencies. Although research connecting the Big Five to these competencies has not been extensive, the evidence to date suggests important linkages.

Recall that high-involvement management focuses on developing associates so that substantial authority can be delegated to them. Available research suggests that managers' competencies in developing, delegating, and motivating are enhanced by high extraversion, high conscientiousness, and high emotional stability.[44] This research is summarized in Exhibit 5-2 and is consistent with our earlier discussion, which pointed out that conscientious, emotionally stable individuals have advantages in many situations and that extraverts have a slight advantage in situations requiring a high level of interaction with people.

As might be expected, available research also indicates that these same characteristics provide advantages to associates in high-involvement organizations. For associates, competencies in self-development, decision making, self-management, and teamwork are crucial. Conscientious, emotionally stable individuals are likely to work at these competencies, and being an extravert may present a slight advantage.[45] Agreeableness and openness do not appear to have consistent effects on the competencies discussed here.

EXHIBIT 5-2 The Big Five and High-Involvement Management

Competencies	Description	Big Five Traits*
For Managers		
Delegating to others	Patience in providing information and support when empowering others, but also the ability to confront individuals when there is a problem	E+ C+ A− ES+ O+
Developing others	Interest in sharing information, ability to coach and train, and interest in helping others plan careers	E+ (C+) A++ ES+ (O+)
Motivating others	Ability to bring out the best in other people, desire to recognize contributions of others, and in general an interest in others	E++ C+ (A+) ES+
For Associates		
Decision-making skills	Careful consideration of important inputs, little putting off of decisions, and no tendency to change mind repeatedly	E+ C++ A− ES+ O+
Self-development	Use of all available resources for improvement, interest in feedback, and lack of defensiveness	E+ C++ A+ ES+ (O−)
Self-management	Little procrastination, effective time management, and a focus on targets	E+ C+ (A−)
Teamwork	Willingness to subordinate personal interests for the team, ability to follow or lead depending on the needs of the team, and commitment to building team spirit	E+ C+ A++ ES+ O+

* Entries in the exhibit are defined as follows: E = extraversion, C = conscientiousness, A = agreeableness, ES = emotional stability (many researchers define this using a reverse scale and use the label "need for stability" or "neuroticism"), and O = openness to experience. A"+" indicates that higher scores on the trait appear to promote the listed competency. A "++" indicates that higher scores on a trait appear to have very significant effects on the listed competency. Similarly, a "−" indicates that low levels of a trait appear to promote the listed competency. Parentheses are used in cases where some aspects of a trait are associated with the listed competency but the overall trait is not. For example, only the first and fourth aspects of conscientiousness (feels capable and possesses a drive for success) have been found to be associated with the competency for developing others.

Source: Adapted from P.J. Howard and J.M. Howard. 2001. *The Owner's Manual for Personality at Work* (Austin, TX: Bard Press).

Cognitive and Motivational Properties of Personality

We turn next to several cognitive and motivational concepts that have received attention as separate and important properties related to personality. They are defined as follows (see Exhibit 5-3):

- *Cognitive properties*—properties of individuals' perceptual and thought processes that affect how they typically process information
- *Motivational properties*—stable differences in individuals that energize and maintain overt behaviors

Cognitive Concepts

Differences in how people use their intellectual capabilities may result in vastly different perceptions and judgments. Personality concepts that focus on cognitive processes help us

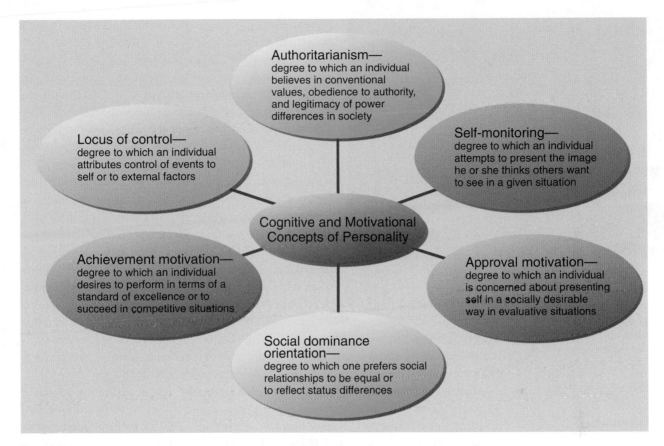

Exhibit 5-3   Cognitive and Motivational Concepts of Personality

to understand these differences. Three such concepts are locus of control, authoritarianism, and self-monitoring.

The personality concept of **locus of control** refers to a person's tendency to attribute the cause or control of events either to herself or to factors in the external environment. People who tend to believe that they have control over events are said to have an "internal" locus of control. Those who consistently believe that events are controlled by outside forces in the environment have an "external" locus of control.[46]

Internals believe they can control what happens to them. This often leads them to engage in work and leisure activities requiring greater skill[47] and to conform less to group influences.[48] Internals, then, tend to think they can be successful if they simply work hard enough, and this belief may be reflected in their work habits, especially on difficult tasks. They also tend to exhibit a greater sense of well-being, a finding that holds worldwide.[49] *Externals* believe that what happens to them is more a matter of luck or fate, and they see little connection between their own behavior and success or failure. They are more conforming and may therefore be less argumentative and easier to supervise. Structured tasks and plenty of supervision suit them well. Overall, associates with an internal locus of control experience more positive work outcomes than people with an external locus of control, including higher motivation and less job stress.[50]

The original research on **authoritarianism** began as an effort to identify people who might be susceptible to anti-Semitic ideologies. Over time, the concept evolved into its

locus of control
The degree to which an individual attributes control of events to self or external factors.

authoritarianism
The degree to which an individual believes in conventional values, obedience to authority, and legitimacy of power differences in society.

©Janie Barrett/Fairfax photos/Redux Pictures

social dominance orientation
A general attitudinal orientation concerning whether one prefers social relationships to be equal or to reflect status differences.

self-monitoring
The degree to which an individual attempts to present the image he or she thinks others want to see in a given situation.

achievement motivation
The degree to which an individual desires to perform in terms of a standard of excellence or to succeed in competitive situations.

present meaning—the extent to which a person believes in conventional values, obedience to authority, and the legitimacy of power and status differences in society.[51] Authoritarianism has been extensively researched. Individuals who score high on this concept tend to believe that status and the use of power in organizations are proper. They are submissive to people in power and aggressive toward those who break rules.[52] Furthermore, they may be more willing to accept unethical behavior in others when those others are in powerful or high-status positions.[53] Such people tend to adjust readily to rules and regulations and emerge as leaders in situations requiring a great deal of control by the manager.

Related to authoritarianism, is **social dominance orientation (SDO)**.[54] SDO refers to a general attitudinal orientation concerning whether one prefers social relationships to be equal or to reflect status differences. Furthermore, people with a high SDO view their own groups as superior and dominant over other "outgroups."[55] SDO is negatively related to the Big Five personality traits agreeableness and openness to experience.[56] People high in SDO have also been found to be more likely to discriminate against job applicants from different demographic groups[57] and prefer to work in nondiverse organizations[58] as compared with people low in SDO.

Self-monitoring is an important personality concept that describes the degree to which people are guided by their true selves in decisions and actions. It determines whether people are fully consistent in behavior across different situations. Low self-monitors follow the advice given by Polonius to Laertes in Shakespeare's *Hamlet*[59]: "To thine own self be true." Low self-monitors ask, "Who am I, and how can I be me in this situation?"[60] In contrast, high self-monitors present somewhat different faces in different situations. They have been referred to as "chameleon-like," as they try to present the appropriate image to each separate audience.[61] High self-monitors ask, "Who does this situation want me to be, and how can I be that person?"[62]

High self-monitors can be quite effective in the workplace, with a tendency to outperform low self-monitors in several areas.[63] Because they are highly attentive to social cues and the thoughts of others, they are sometimes more effective at conflict resolution. Because they are attentive to social dynamics and the expectations of others, they frequently emerge as leaders. Because they are more likely to use interpersonal strategies that fit the desires of other people, they tend to perform well in jobs requiring cooperation and interaction. Management is one such job, and research indicates that high self-monitors are more effective managers. In one study, MBA graduates were tracked for five years after graduation. MBAs who were high self-monitors received more managerial promotions.[64]

Motivational Concepts

Motivational concepts of personality are reflected more in a person's basic needs than in his or her thought processes. Two important concepts in this category are achievement motivation and approval motivation.

Achievement motivation is commonly referred to as the need for achievement (or *n-Ach*). It is an important determinant of aspiration, effort, and persistence in situations where performance will be evaluated according to some standard of excellence.[65]

Thus, need for achievement is the strength of a person's desire to perform in terms of a standard of excellence or to succeed in competitive situations. Unlike most conceptualizations of personality traits, need for achievement has been related to particular situations. That is, it is activated only in situations of expected excellence or competition. The interaction of personality and the immediate environment is obvious in this theory, and it affects the strength of motivation.

Persons with a high need for achievement set their goals and tend to accept responsibility for both success and failure. They dislike goals that are either extremely difficult or easy, tending to prefer goals of moderate difficulty. They also need feedback regarding their performance. People with a high need for achievement are also less likely to procrastinate than people with a low need for achievement.[66]

This personality characteristic is often misinterpreted. For example, some may think that need for achievement is related to desire for power and control. High need achievers, however, tend to focus on task excellence rather than on power.

Approval motivation is another important motive-based personality concept. Researchers have noted the tendency for some people to present themselves in socially desirable ways when they are in evaluative situations. Such people are highly concerned about the approval of others. Approval motivation is also related to conformity and "going along to get along."[67]

approval motivation
The degree to which an individual is concerned about presenting himself or herself in a socially desirable way in evaluative situations.

Ironically, the assessment of one's own personality is an evaluative situation, and persons high in approval motivation tend to respond to personality tests in socially desirable ways. In other words, such people will try to convey positive impressions of themselves. Such tendencies lead individuals to "fake" their answers to personality questionnaires according to the perceived desirability of the responses. Many questionnaires contain "lie" scales and sets of items to detect this social approval bias. Such precautions are especially important when personality tests are used to select, promote, or identify persons for important organizational purposes.

Some Cautionary and Concluding Remarks

Personality characteristics may change to some degree, and situational forces may at times overwhelm the forces of personality. People can adjust to their situations, particularly those who are high self-monitors. An introverted person may be somewhat sociable in a sales meeting, and a person with an external locus of control may on occasion accept personal responsibility for his failure. Furthermore, some people can be trained or developed in jobs that seem to conflict with their personalities. Fit between an individual's personality and the job does, however, convey some advantages. Overall, the purpose of measuring personality is to know that some people may fit a given job situation better than others. For those who fit less well, we may want to provide extra help, training, or counseling before making the decision to steer them toward another position or type of work. We also note that personality testing in organizations should focus only on "normal" personality characteristics. According to the Americans with Disabilities Act (1990), it is illegal to screen out potential employees based on the results of personality tests designed to measure psychological disabilities (e.g., depression or extreme anxiety).

The information on personality and performance presented in this chapter has been developed largely from research in the United States and Canada. Research in Europe is reasonably consistent,[68] but other parts of the world have been studied less. Great care must be taken in applying the results of U.S.- and Canadian-based research to other regions of the world.

"I Have Ketchup in My Veins"

Patricia Harris uses the above phrase to describe her commitment and fit with the McDonald's Corporation. Ms. Harris, currently a Vice President of McDonald's Corporation, USA. and the Global Chief Diversity Officer, began her career with the company over 30 years ago. She started at McDonald's in 1976 in a secretarial position and soon began rising through the ranks, while attending college part-time and raising a family. Many of Ms. Harris's positions have been in human resource management, and she is often attributed in making McDonald's a current leader and early forerunner in promoting employee diversity, leading the company to win the coveted Equal Employment Opportunity Commission's "Freedom to Compete Award" in 2006 and the national Restaurant Association's Diversity Award in 2009, among many other honors concerning diversity.

Several attributes of Patricia Harris have led to her phenomenal career. First of all, she is high on conscientiousness. Ms. Harris's colleagues describe her as "driven," and she has often "stepped out of her comfort zone" to take on new job challenges. She is also goal-driven to develop diversity processes and programs to help build McDonald's business all over the world. While being extremely performance-focused, Ms. Harris also displays agreeableness by serving as a mentor to many other McDonald's associates

©Nathan Mandell Photography

and crediting her own mentors and team members when asked about her success. Her high need for achievement came through when, early in her career, she told her boss and mentor: "I want your job!" Ms. Harris also has a strong internal locus of control because she focuses on making her environment and the company's a better place to work. Finally, she demonstrates a great deal of intelligence in dealing with her job. In addition to a temperament that makes her very well suited for her career, she also possesses the knowledge and intelligence that have helped make McDonald's a leader in diversity. Rich Floersch, Executive Vice President in Charge of Human Relations, states: "She's very well informed, a true student of diversity. She is good at analyzing U.S. diversity principles and applying them in an international market. She's also a good listener who understands the business and culture very well."

Patricia Harris would probably be a success anywhere she worked—yet her true passion for McDonald's and its diversity initiatives seems to set her apart from most other executives. In 1985, when Ms. Harris was first asked to become an affirmative action manager, she was apprehensive about taking the job because affirmative action was not a popular issue at the time. She overcame her apprehension and started on her path to dealing with diversity issues. She states that "this job truly became my passion. It's who I am, both personally and professionally." By working on diversity issues, Ms. Harris was able to realize not only her professional goals, but also her personal goals of helping women and minorities. Ray Kroc, the founder of McDonald's, stated that "None of us is as good as all of us," focusing on the importance of inclusion and ownership by all employees. This value permeates McDonald's corporate vision and also coincides with the personal vision of Patricia Harris. Harris says that her company's mission "is to create an environment in which everyone within McDonald's global system is able to contribute fully regardless of role." Thus, not only is she extremely competent at her job, she is also passionate about her job and her organization. Patricia Harris exemplifies what happens when an individual's traits, abilities, and passion line up with the vision of the organization.

Sources: K. Whitney. Jan. 18, 2009. Diversity is everybody's business at McDonald's. *Diversity Executive.* At http://www.diversity-executive.com/article.php?article=480; McDonald's, May 14, "National Restaurant Association Honors McDonald's With Diversity Award" at http://www.aboutmcdonalds.com/mcd/csr/news/national_restaurant.5.html?DCSext.destination=http://www.aboutmcdonalds.com/mcd/csr/news/national_restaurant.5.html; A. Pomeroy. Dec. 2006. "She's Still Lovin' It," *HRMagazine,* Dec., pp. 58–61; anonymous staff writer. 2007. "An Interview with Pat Harris, Vice President Diversity Initiatives with McDonald's Corporation" at http://www.employmentguide.com/careeradvice/Leading_the_Way-in_Diversity. html, accessed Apr. 18, 2007; J. Lawn. 2006. "Shattered Glass and Personal Journeys," *FoodManagement,* July, at http://www.food-management.com/article/13670; anonymous. 2005. "Ray Kroc: Founder's Philosophies Remain at the Heart of McDonald's Success," *Nation's Restaurant News,* Apr. 11, at http://findarticles.com/p/articles/mi_m3190/is_15_39/ai_n13649039.

In conclusion, determining the personality and behavioral attributes of higher performers in an organization can help a firm to improve its performance over time, as suggested in the *Experiencing Organizational Behavior* feature. Patricia Harris, Vice President of McDonald's Corporation, USA, and Global Chief Diversity Officer, exemplifies such a high performer whose personality fits the organization's strategies and goals.

Intelligence

In the preceding section, we saw how important personality is to organizational behavior and achieving a high-involvement workplace. There is another stable individual difference that can greatly affect organizational behavior, particularly job performance. This trait is *cognitive ability*, more commonly referred to as **intelligence**. *Intelligence* refers to the ability to develop and understand concepts, particularly more complex and abstract concepts.[69] Despite its importance, intelligence as an aspect of human ability has been somewhat controversial. Some psychologists and organizational behavior researchers do not believe that a meaningful general intelligence factor exists. Instead, they believe that many different types of intelligence exist and that most of us have strong intelligence in one or more areas. These areas might include the following:[70]

intelligence
General mental ability used in complex information processing.

- *Number aptitude*—the ability to handle mathematics
- *Verbal comprehension*—the ability to understand written and spoken words
- *Perceptual speed*—the ability to process visual data quickly
- *Spatial visualization*—the ability to imagine a different physical configuration— for example, to imagine how a room would look with the furniture rearranged
- *Deductive reasoning*—the ability to draw a conclusion or make a choice that logically follows from existing assumptions and data
- *Inductive reasoning*—the ability to identify, after observing specific cases or instances, the general rules that govern a process or that explain an outcome—for example, to identify the general factors that play a role in a successful product launch after observing one product launch at a single company
- *Memory*—the ability to store and recall previous experiences

Most psychologists and organizational behavior researchers who have extensively studied intelligence believe, however, that a single unifying intelligence factor exists, a factor that blends together all of the areas from above. They also believe that general intelligence has meaningful effects on success in the workplace. Existing evidence points to the fact that general intelligence is an important determinant of workplace performance and career success.[71] This is particularly true for jobs and career paths that require complex information processing, as opposed to simple manual labor. Exhibit 5-4 illustrates the strong connection between intelligence and success for complex jobs.

Although the use of intelligence tests is intended to help organizations select the best human capital, as explained in the *Experiencing Organizational Behavior* feature on page 183, their use is controversial. It is controversial because some question the ability of these tests to accurately capture a person's true level of intelligence. Also, there can be legal problems with intelligence tests if they result in an adverse impact. However, if a test accurately reflects individual intelligence, it can help managers select higher-quality associates. The superior human capital in the organization will then lead to higher productivity and the ability to gain an advantage over competitors. A competitive advantage, in turn, usually produces higher profits for the organization.[72]

EXHIBIT 5-4 Intelligence and Success

Job	Effects of Intelligence
Military Jobs*	**Percentage of Success in Training Attributable to General Intelligence**
Nuclear weapons specialist	77%
Air crew operations specialist	70%
Weather specialist	69%
Intelligence specialist	67%
Fireman	60%
Dental assistant	55%
Security police	54%
Vehicle maintenance	49%
General maintenance	28%
Civilian Jobs**	**Degree to which General Intelligence Predicts Job Performance (0 to 1 scale)**
Sales	.61
Technical assistant	.54
Manager	.53
Skilled trades and craft workers	.46
Protective professions workers	.42
Industrial workers	.37
Vehicle operator	.28
Sales clerk	.27

* *Source:* M.J. Ree and J.A. Earles. 1990. *Differential Validity* of a Differential Aptitude Test, AFHRL-TR-89–59 (San Antonio, TX: Brooks Air Force Base).
** *Source:* J.E. Hunter and R.F. Hunter. 1984. "Validity and Utility of Alternative Predictors of Job Performance," *Psychological Bulletin* 96: 72–98.

Attitudes

It is sometimes difficult to distinguish between an individual's personality and attitudes. The behavior of Southwest associates and managers described in the opening case, for example, might be interpreted by some as based primarily on attitudes rather than personality, whereas others might believe that personality plays a larger role. Regardless, managers are concerned about the attitudes of associates because they can be major causes of work behaviors. Positive attitudes frequently lead to productive efforts, whereas negative attitudes often produce poor work habits.

An **attitude** is defined as a persistent mental state of readiness to feel and behave in a favorable or unfavorable way toward a specific person, object, or idea. Close examination of this definition reveals three important conclusions. First, attitudes are reasonably stable.

attitude
A persistent tendency to feel and behave in a favorable or unfavorable way toward a specific person, object, or idea.

Intelligence and Intelligence Testing in the National Football League

Each spring, representatives of National Football League teams join a large group of college football players in Indianapolis, Indiana. They are in town to participate in the so-called draft combine, where the players are given the opportunity to demonstrate their football skills. After showing their speed, strength, and agility, the players hope to be selected by a team early in the draft process and to command a large salary. For some, success at the combine is critical to being chosen by a team. For others, success is important because the combine plays a role in determining the amount of signing bonuses and other financial incentives.

Talented football players work to achieve the best physical condition they can in anticipation of the important evaluations. They focus on the upcoming medical examinations, weightlifting assessments, 40-yard dashes, vertical- and broad-jump tests, and tackling-dummy tests. They may be less focused on another key feature of the draft combine—the intelligence test. The practice of testing general intelligence has been a fixture of the NFL since the early 1970s. The test that is used by all teams, the Wonderlic Personnel Test, has 50 questions and a time limit of 12 minutes in its basic version.

©PCN/Corbis Images

Teams place different levels of importance on the intelligence test. The Green Bay Packers, for example, historically have not put a great deal of emphasis on it. "The Wonderlic has never been a big part of what we do here," said former Green Bay general manager and current consultant Ron Wolf. "To me, it's [just] a signal. If it's low, you better find out why it's low, and if the guy is a good football player, you better satisfy your curiosity." The Cincinnati Bengals, in contrast, have generally taken the test very seriously, in part "because it is the only test of its kind given to college players." In Atlanta, former head coach Dan Reeves showed his faith in the intelligence-testing process by choosing a linebacker who was equal in every way to another linebacker, except for higher intelligence scores. In New York, intelligence and personality testing has been taken to an extreme for the NFL. The Giants organization has used a test with nearly 400 questions. The late Giants manager, George Young, stated, "Going into a draft without some form of psychological testing on the prospects is like going into a gunfight with a knife."

Can a player be too smart? According to some, the answer is yes. "I've been around some players who are too smart to be good football players," said Ralph Cindrich, a linebacker in the NFL many years ago. Many others have the opinion that high intelligence scores are indicative of a player who will not play within the system but will want to improvise too much on the field and argue with coaches too much off the field. There isn't much evidence, however, to support this argument. Many successful quarterbacks, for example, have had high scores. Super Bowl winner Tom Brady of the New England Patriots scored well above average, as did the New York Giants' Eli Manning.

Quarterbacks score higher on the test than players in several other positions but do not score the highest. Average scores for various positions are shown below, along with scores from the business world for comparison. A score of 20 correct out of 50 is considered average and equates to approximately 100 on a standard IQ test. Any score of 15 (the lowest score shown below) or above represents reasonable intelligence.

Offensive tackles—26

Centers—25

Quarterbacks—24

Fullbacks—17

Safeties—19

Wide receivers—17

Chemists—31

Programmers—29

News reporters—26

Halfbacks—16

Salespersons—24

Bank tellers—17

Security guards—17

Warehouse workers—15

Many players become tense over the NFL intelligence test. What types of questions are causing the anxiety? A sample of the easier questions follows (to learn more, go to www. wonderlic.com):

1. The 11th month of the year is: (a) October, (b) May, (c) November, (d) February.

2. Severe is opposite of: (a) harsh, (b) stern, (c) tender, (d) rigid, (e) unyielding.

3. In the following set of words, which word is different from the others? (a) sing, (b) call, (c) chatter, (d) hear, (e) speak.

4. A dealer bought some televisions for $3,500. He sold them for $5,500, making $50 on each television. How many televisions were involved?

5. Lemon candies sell at 3 for 15 cents. How much will $1\frac{1}{2}$ dozen cost?

6. Which number in the following group of numbers represents the smallest amount? (a) 6, (b) .7, (c) 9, (d) 36, (e) .31, (f) 5.

7. Look at the following row of numbers. What number should come next? 73 66 59 52 45 38.

8. A plane travels 75 feet in $\frac{1}{4}$ second. At this speed, how many feet will it travel in 5 seconds?

9. A skirt requires $2\frac{1}{3}$ yards of material. How many skirts can be cut from 42 yards?

10. ENLARGE, AGGRANDIZE. Do these words: (a) have similar meanings, (b) have contradictory meanings, (c) mean neither the same nor the opposite?

11. Three individuals form a partnership and agree to divide the profits equally. X invests $4,500, Y invests $3,500, Z invests $2,000. If the profits are $2,400, how much less does X receive than if profits were divided in proportion to the amount invested?

Sources: D. Dillon. 2001. "Testing, Testing: Taking the Wonderlic," *Sporting News.com*, Feb. 23, at www.sportingnews. com/voices/dennis_dillon/20010223.html; K. Kragthorpe. 2003. "Is Curtis Too Smart for NFL?" Utah Online, Apr. 23, at www.sltrib.com/2003/Apr/04232003/Sports/50504.asp; J. Litke. 2003. "Smarter Is Better in the NFL, Usually: But Not Too Smart to Be Good Football Players," *National Post (Canada)*, May 1, p. S2; J. Magee. 2003. "NFL Employs the Wonderlic Test to Probe the Minds of Draft Prospects," SignOnSanDiego.com, Apr. 20, at www.signonsandiego. com/sports/nfl/magee/200304209999–ls20nflcol.html; J. Merron. 2002. "Taking Your Wonderlics," ESPN Page 2, Feb. 2, at www.espn.go.com/page2/s/closer/020228.html; T. Silverstein. 2001. "What's His Wonderlic? NFL Uses Time-Honored IQ Test as Measuring Stick for Rookies," *Milwaukee Journal Sentinel*, Apr. 18, p. C1 ; A. Barra. 2006. "Do These NFL Scores Count for Anything?" *Wall Street Journal (Eastern Edition)*, Apr. 25, p. D.6

Unless people have strong reasons to change their attitudes, they will persist or remain the same. People who like jazz music today will probably like it tomorrow, unless important reasons occur to change their musical preferences.

Second, attitudes are directed toward some object, person, or idea; that is, we may have an attitude toward our job, our supervisor, or an idea the college instructor presented. If the attitude concerns the job (for example, if a person dislikes monotonous work), then the attitude is specifically directed toward that job. We cannot extend that negative job attitude to an attitude toward jazz music.

Third, an attitude toward an object or person relates to an individual's behavior toward that object or person. In this sense, attitudes may influence our actions. For example, if an individual likes jazz music (an attitude), he may go to a jazz club (a behavior) or buy a jazz CD (a behavior). If an associate dislikes her work (an attitude), she may avoid coming to work (absenteeism behavior) or exert very little effort on the job (poor productivity behavior). People tend to behave in ways that are consistent with their feelings. Therefore, to change an unproductive worker into a productive one, it may be necessary to deal with that worker's attitudes.

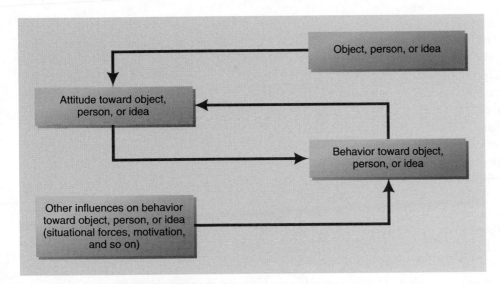

Exhibit 5-5 Influence of Attitudes on Behavior

As illustrated in Exhibit 5-5, our behavior toward an object, person, or idea is influenced by our attitudes. In turn, our attitudes are constantly developing and changing as a result of our behaviors. It is important to recognize that our behaviors are also influenced by other factors, such as motivational forces and situational factors. We therefore can understand why behaviors are not always predictable from attitudes. For example, we may have a strong positive attitude about a close friend. But we might reject an opportunity to go to a movie with that friend if we are preparing for a difficult exam to be given tomorrow. Thus, attitudes include behavioral tendencies and intentions, but our actual behaviors are also influenced by other factors.

Attitude Formation

Understanding how attitudes are formed is the first step in learning how to apply attitude concepts to organizational problems. This understanding can be developed by examining the three essential elements of an attitude: (1) cognitive, (2) affective, and (3) behavioral.[73]

- The *cognitive* element of an attitude consists of the facts we have gathered and considered about the object, person, or idea. Before we can have feelings about something, we must first be aware of it and think about its complexities.
- The *affective* element of an attitude refers to the feelings one has about the object or person. Such feelings are frequently expressed as like or dislike of the object or person and the degree to which one holds these feelings. For example, an employee may love the job, like it, dislike it, or hate it.
- Finally, most attitudes contain a *behavioral* element, which is the individual's intention to act in certain ways toward the object of the attitude. As previously explained, how we behave toward people may depend largely on whether we like or dislike them based on what we know about them.

The formation of attitudes may be quite complex. In the following discussion, we examine some ways in which attitudes are formed.

Learning

Attitudes can be formed through the learning process.[74] As explained in Chapter 4, when people interact with others or behave in particular ways toward an object, they often experience rewards or punishments. For example, if you touch a cactus plant, you may experience pain. As you experience the outcomes of such behavior, you begin to develop feelings about the objects of that behavior. Thus, if someone were to ask you how you felt about cactus plants, you might reply, "I don't like them—they can hurt." Of course, attitudes can also develop from watching others experience rewards and punishments. A person may not touch the cactus herself, but a negative attitude toward cacti could develop after she watches a friend experience pain.

Self-Perception

People may form attitudes based on simple observations of their own behaviors.[75] This is called the *self-perception effect*, and it works as follows. An individual engages in a particular behavior without thinking much about that behavior. Furthermore, no significant positive rewards are involved. Having engaged in the behavior, the person then diagnoses his actions, asking himself what the behavior suggests about his attitudes. In many instances, this person will conclude that he must have had a positive attitude toward the behavior. Why else would he have done what he did? For example, an individual may join co-workers in requesting an on-site cafeteria at work, doing so without much thought. Up to that point, the person may have had a relatively neutral attitude about a cafeteria. After having joined in the request, however, he may conclude that he has a positive attitude toward on-site cafeterias.

Influencing people through the foot-in-the-door technique is based on the self-perception effect. This technique involves asking a person for a small favor (foot-in-the-door) and later asking for a larger favor that is consistent with the initial request. After completing the small favor with little thought, the target often concludes that she has a positive view toward whatever was done, and therefore she is more likely to perform the larger favor. In one study of the foot-in-the-door technique, researchers went door-to-door asking individuals to sign a petition for safer driving.[76] The request was small and noncontroversial; thus, most people signed the petition without much thought. Weeks later, colleagues of the researchers visited these same people and asked them to put a large, unattractive sign in their yards that read "Drive Carefully." These same colleagues also approached other homeowners who had not been asked for the initial small favor. Fifty-five percent of the individuals who had signed the petition agreed to put an ugly sign in their yards, whereas only 17 percent of those who had not been asked to sign the petition agreed to the yard sign.

Need for Consistency

A major concept associated with attitude formation is consistency.[77] Two well-known theories in social psychology, *balance theory* and *congruity theory*, are important to an understanding of attitude consistency. The basic notion is that people prefer that their attitudes be consistent with one another (in balance or congruent). If we have a specific attitude toward an object or person, we tend to form other consistent attitudes toward related objects or persons.

A simple example of attitude formation based on consistency appears in Exhibit 5-6. Dan is a young accounting graduate. He is impressed with accounting theory and thinks that accountants should work with data to arrive at important conclusions for management. Obviously, he has a positive attitude toward accounting, as illustrated by the plus sign between Dan and accounting in the exhibit. Now suppose that Dan's new job requires him to work with someone who dislikes accounting (represented by the minus sign between

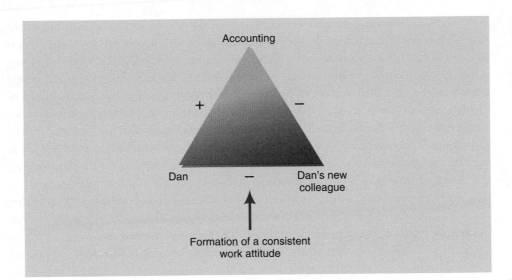

Exhibit 5-6 Formation of Consistent Attitudes

the new colleague and accounting). In this case, Dan may form a negative attitude toward the person in order to have a consistent set of attitudes. Dan likes accounting and may have a negative attitude toward those who do not.

Two Important Attitudes in the Workplace

The two most thoroughly examined attitudes in organizational behavior are job satisfaction and organizational commitment. Job satisfaction is a broad attitude related to the job. A high level of satisfaction represents a positive attitude toward the job, while a low level of satisfaction represents a negative attitude. Organizational commitment, as defined here, is a broad attitude toward the organization as a whole. It represents how strongly an individual identifies with and values being associated with the organization. Strong commitment is a positive attitude toward the organization, whereas weak commitment is a less positive attitude. As we discuss below, these two attitudes can impact behavior that is important to the functioning of an organization; thus, it is important to consider job satisfaction and organizational commitment as desirable aspects of human capital.[78]

Job Satisfaction and Outcomes

Organizations need to be concerned with the satisfaction of their associates, because job satisfaction is linked to many important behaviors that can have an impact on the bottom line of an organization's performance. Satisfaction has a highly positive effect on intentions to stay in the job and a modest effect on actually staying in the job.[79] Factors such as attractive job openings during a booming economy and reaching retirement age can cause satisfied people to leave, but in general satisfaction is associated with low turnover. With the costs of replacing a departed worker generally quite high, maintaining higher levels of satisfaction is important. High satisfaction also has a modestly positive effect on regular attendance at work.[80] Factors such as a very liberal sick-leave policy can, however, cause even highly satisfied associates and managers to miss work time. Satisfaction also has a moderately strong relationship with motivation.[81]

Job satisfaction has a reasonably straightforward relationship with intention to stay, actually staying, absenteeism, and motivation. In contrast, the specific form of the relationship between satisfaction and job performance has been the subject of a great deal of contro-versy. Many managers and researchers believe that high satisfaction produces strong per-formance. This idea seems reasonable, for a positive attitude should indeed result in strong effort and accountability. Other managers and researchers, however, believe that it is strong performance that causes workers to be satisfied with their jobs. For this second group of investigators, a positive attitude does not cause strong performance but strong performance does cause a positive attitude. Still others believe that satisfaction and performance are not related or are only weakly related. For this last group, factors other than attitudes, such as skills and incentive systems, are believed to have much stronger effects on job performance.

A recent study has helped to put these differences of opinion into perspective.[82] In this study, all previously published research on satisfaction and performance was synthe-sized using modern quantitative and qualitative techniques. The study concluded with an integrative model suggesting that all three of the groups mentioned above are correct to some degree. High satisfaction causes strong performance, strong performance also causes high satisfaction, and the relationship between the two is weaker in some situations. On this last point, low conscientiousness and the existence of simple work are examples of fac-tors that may cause the relationship to be weaker. Individuals who have positive attitudes toward the job but who are lower in conscientiousness may not necessarily work hard, which weakens the effects of job satisfaction on performance. In addition, strong perform-ance at simple work does not necessarily result in strong satisfaction, which weakens the effects of performance on satisfaction. For engineers, managers, and others with complex jobs, performance and satisfaction have a reasonably strong connection.

Organizational Commitment and Outcomes in the Workplace

Similar to satisfaction, commitment has important effects on intentions to stay in the job and modest effects on actually staying in the job and attending work regularly.[83] Com-mitment also is significantly related to motivation. Interestingly, length of employment plays a role in the relationship between commitment and staying in the job. A high level of organizational commitment tends to be more important in decisions to stay for associates and managers who have worked in their jobs for less time.[84] For longer-term employees, simple inertia and habit may prevent departures independent of the level of commitment to the organization. Commitment also has positive effects on job performance, but the effects are somewhat small.[85] This link to performance appears to be stronger for manag-ers and professionals. Although the relationship between commitment and regular job performance is not extremely strong, organizational commitment does have a very strong relationship with discretionary organizational citizenship behaviors, such as helping others and taking on voluntary assignments.[86]

Causes of Job Satisfaction and Organizational Commitment

Given that job satisfaction and organizational commitment can impact on many impor-tant organizational behaviors, it is imperative that organizations understand what makes their associates satisfied and committed. Many of the same factors that lead to job satisfac-tion also lead to organizational commitment. These factors include:

- Role ambiguity[87]
- Supervision/leadership[88]
- Pay and benefits[89]

- Nature of the job[90]
- Organizational climate[91]
- Stress[92]
- Perceptions of fair treatment[93]

Although these factors have all been linked to satisfaction and commitment, the relationships are not always so simple. For example, in order to best understand whether someone will be satisfied with a given dimension of her work, you need to consider her comparison standard. People compare desirable facets of their work with what they expect to receive or what they think they should receive.[94] So, while one person may be very satisfied with earning $100,000 per year, another person may find this amount unsatisfactory because she was expecting to earn more.

Another complication arises when we consider that associates may be committed to their organization for different reasons. There are three general reasons why people are committed to their organizations.[95] **Affective commitment** is usually what we think of when we talk about organizational commitment because it means someone has strong positive attitudes toward the organization. **Normative commitment** means that someone is committed to the organization because he feels he should be. Someone who stays with their organization because he does not want to let his co-workers down is normatively committed. Finally, associates may experience **continuance commitment**, which means that they are committed to the organization because they do not have any better opportunities. Different factors affect different types of commitment.[96] For example, benefits may affect continuance commitment, for example, when a person is committed to an organization only because her retirement plan will not transfer to another organization. On the other hand, benefits may not influence how positive one feels about the organization, so that benefits would be unrelated to affective commitment.

One other thing to note about the factors affecting satisfaction and commitment is that the presence of high-involvement management is particularly important. Individuals usually have positive experiences working with this management approach, and thus strong satisfaction and commitment is likely to develop through the learning mechanism of attitude formation. As part of high-involvement management, individuals are selected for organizations in which their values fit, they are well trained, they are encouraged to think for themselves, and they are treated fairly (e.g., receive equitable compensation).

Finally, satisfaction and commitment are not totally dependent on situational factors; personality also can play a role. Some individuals have a propensity to be satisfied and committed, whereas others are less likely to exhibit positive attitudes, no matter the actual situation in which they work.[97] In addition to one's personality disposition, emotions can also affect job attitudes. Thus, we discuss emotions in the workplace later in this chapter.

affective commitment
Organizational commitment due to one's strong positive attitudes toward the organization.

normative commitment
Organizational commitment due to feelings of obligation.

continuance commitment
Organizational commitment due to lack of better opportunities.

Attitude Change

Personality characteristics are believed to be rather stable, as we have seen, but attitudes are more susceptible to change. Social forces, such as peer pressure or changes in society, act on existing attitudes, so that over time attitudes may change, often in unpredictable ways. In addition, in many organizations, managers find they need to be active in changing employee attitudes. Although it is preferable for associates to have positive attitudes toward the job, the manager, and the organization, many do not. When the object of the attitude cannot be changed (for example, when a job cannot be redesigned), managers must work directly on attitudes. In such cases, it is necessary to develop a systematic approach to change attitudes in favorable directions. We discuss two relevant techniques next.

Persuasive Communication

Most of us experience daily attempts by others to persuade us to change our attitudes. Television, radio, and Internet advertisements are common forms of such persuasive communication. Political campaigns are another form. Occasionally, a person who is virtually unknown at the beginning of a political campaign (such as Bill Clinton) can win an election by virtue of extensive advertising and face-to-face communication.

The persuasive communication approach to attitude change consists of four elements:[98]

1. *Communicator*—the person who holds a particular attitude and wants to convince others to share that attitude

2. *Message*—the content designed to induce the change in others' attitudes

3. *Situation*—the surroundings in which the message is presented

4. *Target*—the person whose attitude the communicator wants to change

Several qualities of the communicator affect attitude change in the target. First, the communicator's overall credibility has an important effect on the target's response to the persuasion attempt. Research shows that people give more weight to persuasive messages from people they respect.[99] It is more difficult to reject messages that disagree with our attitudes when the communicator has high credibility.

Second, people are more likely to change their attitudes when they trust the intentions of the communicator. If we perceive that the communicator has something to gain from the attitude change, we are likely to distrust his or her intentions. But if we believe the communicator is more objective and less self-serving, we will trust his or her intentions and be more likely to change our attitudes. Individuals who argue against their own self-interests are effective at persuasion.[100]

Third, if people like the communicator or perceive that person to be similar to them in interests or goals, they are more likely to be persuaded.[101] This is one reason that movie stars, athletes, and other famous people are used for television ads. These people are widely liked and have characteristics that we perceive ourselves to have (correctly or incorrectly) or that we would like to have.

Finally, if the communicator is attractive, people have a stronger tendency to be persuaded. The effects of attractiveness have been discussed in studies of job seeking and political elections. The most notable example is the U.S. presidential election of 1960. By many accounts, Richard Nixon had equal, if not superior, command of the issues in the presidential debates that year, but the more handsome John Kennedy received higher ratings from the viewing public and won the election.[102]

The message involved in the communication can also influence attitude change. One of the most important dimensions of message content is fear arousal. Messages that arouse fear often produce more attitude change.[103] For example, a smoker who is told that smoking is linked to heart disease may change his attitude toward smoking. The actual amount of fear produced by the message also seems to play a role. If the smoker is told that smoking makes teeth turn yellow, rather than being told of a link to heart disease, the fear is weaker, and the resulting attitude change also is likely to be weaker.

Greater fear usually induces larger changes in attitudes, but not always. Three factors beyond amount of fear play a role:[104] (1) the probability that negative consequences will actually occur if no change in behavior is made, (2) the perceived effect of changing behavior, and (3) the perceived ability to change behavior. Returning to our smoker, even if the message regarding smoking risk arouses a great deal of fear, he still may not alter his attitude if he does not believe that he is likely to develop heart disease, if he has been smoking for so many years that he does not believe that quitting now will help the situation, or if he does not believe he can stop smoking.

So far, we have discussed how the communicator and the message affect attitude change. In general, each affects the degree to which the target believes the attitude should be changed. Frequently, however, people are motivated by factors outside the actual persuasion attempt. Such factors may be found in the situation in which persuasion is attempted. We can see a good example of this when a person is publicly reprimanded. If you have ever been present when a peer has been publicly chastised by an instructor, you may have been offended by the action. Instead of changing your attitude about the student or the student's skills, you may have changed your attitude about the instructor. Other situational factors include the reactions of those around you. Do they smile or nod their heads in approval when the communicator presents her message? Such behaviors encourage attitude change, whereas disapproving behavior may influence you to not change your attitudes.

Finally, characteristics of the target also influence the success of persuasion. For example, people differ in their personalities, their perceptions, and the way they learn. Some are more rigid and less willing to change their attitudes—even when most others believe that they are wrong. Locus of control and other characteristics also influence attitudes. People with high self-esteem are more likely to believe that their attitudes are correct, and they are less likely to change them. Therefore, it is difficult to predict precisely how different people will respond, even to the same persuasive communication. The effective manager is prepared for this uncertainty.

Cognitive Dissonance

Another way in which attitudes can change involves **cognitive dissonance.** Like balance and congruity theories, discussed earlier in this chapter, dissonance theory deals with consistency.[105] In this case, the focus is usually on consistency between attitudes and behaviors—or, more accurately, inconsistency between attitudes and behaviors. For example, a manager may have a strong positive attitude toward incentive compensation, which involves paying people on the basis of their performance. This manager, however, may refuse workers' requests for such a compensation scheme. By refusing, she has created an inconsistency between an attitude and a behavior. If certain conditions are met, as explained below, this inconsistency will create an uneasy feeling (dissonance) that causes the manager to change her positive attitude.

What are the key conditions that lead to dissonance and the changing of an attitude? There are three.[106] First, the behavior must be substantially inconsistent with the attitude rather than just mildly inconsistent. Second, the inconsistent behavior must cause harm or have negative consequences for others. If no harmful or negative consequences are involved, the individual exhibiting the inconsistent behavior can more easily move on without giving much consideration to the inconsistency. Third, the inconsistent behavior must be voluntary and not forced, or at least the person must perceive it that way.

In our example, the manager's behavior satisfies the first two conditions. It was substantially inconsistent with her attitude, and it had negative consequences for the workers

cognitive dissonance
An uneasy feeling produced when a person behaves in a manner inconsistent with an existing attitude.

MANAGERIAL ADVICE

Job Satisfaction Takes a Dive!

©iStockphoto

In 1987, a majority, 61.1 percent, of Americans responded that they were satisfied with their jobs. This was the first year that the Conference Board, a global independent membership organization that collects and disseminates information for senior executives around the world, surveyed workers about their job satisfaction. At the end of 2009, following a steady decrease over the years, that figure had plummeted to 45.3 percent. A less-scientific MSNBC poll of almost 45,000 people found that less than 34 percent of respondents were satisfied or somewhat satisfied with their jobs and 11.5 percent hated every part of their jobs.

The Conference Board survey found that while satisfaction has decreased for all age groups, it is particularly bad for younger workers. Less than 36 percent of those under 25 years old are satisfied with their jobs, as compared with a satisfaction rate of 47 percent for those 45 to 54 years old. These results also held across all income brackets. Furthermore, satisfaction decreased for all specific aspects of one's job, including: job design, organizational health, managerial quality, and extrinsic rewards.

Why are Americans so unhappy with their jobs? One could argue it is because of the economic downturn experienced during 2008 and 2009. Associates are required to do more, are afraid of losing their jobs, and are likely to receive fewer extrinsic rewards ("no raises this year!"). However, this is not the entire story. "It says something troubling about work in America. It is not about the business cycle or one grumpy generation," says Linda Barrington, managing director of human capital at the Conference Board. On of the major reasons that respondents were dissatisfied with their jobs was because the jobs were uninteresting. Ratings of interest in one's work dropped almost 19 percentage points between 1987 and 2009, with only about half of respondents currently finding their jobs interesting. Americans are finding their jobs increasingly boring and unengaging. Other reasons given for job dissatisfaction included salaries that were not keeping up with inflation, job insecurity, and health care costs.

These findings should be a wake-up call for employers. John Gibbons, program director of employee engagement research and services at the Conference Board, says "Widespread job dissatisfaction negatively affects employee behavior and retention, which can impact enterprise-level success." Lynn Franco, director of the Conference Board's Consumer Research Center, concurs, "What's really disturbing about growing job dissatisfaction is the way it can play into the competitive nature of the U.S. work force down the road and on the growth of the U.S. economy—all in a negative way." John Hollon warns, "my counsel for managers and executives is simple: If you ignore these numbers, you do so at your own peril." It is imperative that managers pay attention to these findings, given the effects that low satisfaction and commitment can have on the climate, functioning, and bottom-line success of an organization.

Sources: http://www.conference-board.org/aboutus/about.cfm; The Conference Board. Jan. 5, 2010, "U.S. Job Satisfaction at Lowest Level in Two Decades," at http://www.conference-board.org/utilities/pressDetail. cfm?press_ID=3820. MSNBC, Jan. 5, 2010. "Are you satisfied with your job?" at http://business.newsvine.com/_question/2010/01/05/3716711-are-you-satisfied-with-your-job?threadId=759420&pc=25&sp=25#short%20comment; MSNBC, Jan. 5, 2010. "Job satisfaction falls to a record low: Economists warn discontent could stifle innovation, hurt U.S. productivity," at C:\Documents and Settings\Administrator\My Documents\Americans' job satisfaction falls to record low - Careers- msnbc_com.mht; J. Hollon. Jan. 5, 2010. "A Ticking Time Bomb: Job Satisfaction Hits Record-Low Levels," *Workforce Management*, at C:\Documents and Settings\Administrator\My Documents\Workforce Blogs - The Business of Management.mht.

who wanted incentive pay. We have no way of knowing whether the third condition was met because we do not know whether someone higher in the organization ordered the manager to refuse the requests for incentive compensation or whether a union agreement prohibited such a compensation scheme. If the manager's behavior was not forced by a higher-level manager or an agreement, dissonance is more likely to occur, leading to a change of the manager's attitude toward incentive pay from positive to negative.

If an executive had wanted to change this manager's attitude toward incentive pay, he could have gently suggested that such pay not be used. If the manager acted on this suggestion, she may have experienced dissonance and changed the attitude because her behavior was at least partly voluntary. She was not required to act in a manner inconsistent with her attitude, but she did so anyway. To eliminate the uneasy feeling associated with the inconsistent behavior, she may convince herself that she does not like incentive pay as much as she previously thought.

Emotions

During a sales force team meeting, Chad became frustrated with team leader Bob's presentation. He felt that Bob was ignoring the needs of his unit. In a pique of anger, Chad yelled out that Bob was hiding something from everyone and being dishonest. Bob's reaction to Chad's outburst was to slam his fist on the table and tell him to be quiet or leave. Next door, in the same company, Susan had just learned that her team had won a coveted account. She jumped with joy and was all smiles when she ran down the hall to tell her teammates. Everyone she passed grinned and felt better when they saw Susan running past their desks.

Chad, Bob, and Susan are all displaying their emotions at work. Despite the common norms that associates should hide their emotions when they are at work,[107] people are emotional beings, and emotions play a big role in everyday organizational behavior. Indeed, organizational scholars have recently begun studying the role emotions play at work,[108] and organizations have become more concerned with the emotions of their employees. For example, Douglas Conant, CEO of Campbell Soup, says that in his company care is taken to make sure that employees focus their emotions on their jobs, so that employees "fall in love with (the) company's agenda."[109]

Emotions are complex reactions that have both a physical and a mental component. These reactions include anger, happiness, anxiety, pride, contentment, and guilt. Emotional reactions include a subjective feeling accompanied by changes in bodily functioning such as increased heart rate or blood pressure.[110] Emotions can play a part in organizational functioning in several ways. First, associates' emotions can directly affect their behavior. For example, angry associates may engage in workplace violence[111] or happy employees may be more likely to help other people on the job.[112] Another way in which emotions come into play at work is when the nature of the job calls for associates to display emotions that they might not actually be feeling. For example, on a rocky airplane ride, flight attendants have to appear calm, cool, and collected, while reassuring passengers that everything is okay. However, these flight attendants may have to do this while hiding their own fear and panic. This dynamic is called *emotional labor*. Finally, both business scholars and organizations have become concerned with what has been termed *emotional intelligence*. We turn now to discussions of these three roles that emotions play in organizational behavior.

emotions
Complex subjective reactions that have both a physical and mental component.

Direct Effects of Emotions on Behavior

Emotions can have several direct causal effects on behavior. The relationship between emotions and other important behaviors, such as job performance, is less clear. While it would seem most likely that positive emotions would always lead to high performance, this is not always the case. In some instances, negative emotions, such as anger, can serve as a motivator. Research on creativity demonstrates this point. Some researchers have found that positive emotions increase creativity,[113] while others have found that negative emotions lead to greater creativity.[114] Positive emotions should lead to greater creativity because when people feel good they are more likely to be active and inquisitive. On the other hand, negative emotions, such as fear, can serve as a signal that something is amiss, leading people to search for creative solutions to solve the problem. Indeed, a recent study found that people were most creative when they were experiencing emotional ambivalence, that is, both positive and negative emotions at the same time.[115]

The direct effects of emotions can be either beneficial or harmful to organizational effectiveness. The impact of these emotions, whether negative or positive, is even greater when one considers the phenomenon of **emotional contagion**. Emotional contagion occurs when emotions experienced by one or a few members of a work group spread to other members.[116] One study found that leaders' emotions were particularly important in influencing the emotions of followers.[117] This study indicated that charismatic leaders have a positive influence on organizational effectiveness because they are able to induce positive emotions in their followers. Thus, angry and anxious leaders are likely to develop followers who are angry and anxious, whereas leaders who are happy and passionate about their work are likely to develop followers who experience the same emotions. Exhibit 5-7 summarizes the direct effects of emotions.

emotional contagion
Phenomenon where emotions experienced by one or a few members of a work group spread to other members.

EXHIBIT 5-7 The Direct Effects of Emotion

Positive Emotions Influence:
Social activity
Altruism and helping behavior
Effective conflict resolution
Job satisfaction
Motivation
Organizational citizenship behavior

Negative Emotions Influence:
Aggression against co-workers
Aggression toward the organization
Workplace deviance
Job dissatisfaction
Decision making
Negotiation outcomes

Sources: S. Lyubomirsky, L. King, & E. Deiner. 2005. The benefits of frequent positive affect: Does happiness lead to success? *Psychological Bulletin*, 131: 803–855; T.A. Judge, B.A. Scott, & R. Ilies. 2006. Hostility, job attitudes, and workplace deviance: Test of a multilevel model. *Journal of Applied Psychology*, 91: 126–138; M.S. Hershcovis, N. Turner, J. Barling, K.A. Arnols, K.E. Dupre, M. Inness, M.M. LeBlanc, & N. Sivanathan. 2007. Predicting workplace aggression: A meta-analysis. *Journal of Applied Psychology*, 92; 228–238; A.P. Brief, H.M. Weiss. 2002. Organizational behavior: Affect in the workplace. In S.T. Fiske (Ed.), *Annual Review of Psychology*, 53: 279–307. Palo Alto, CA: Annual Reviews.

Emotional Labor

Many service and sales jobs require that individuals display certain emotions, regardless of what they are really experiencing. For example, flight attendants are expected to be warm and cordial, call center employees are expected to keep their cool when customers are hostile toward them, and sales associates are expected to be enthusiastic about the product they are selling, no matter what they actually feel. The process whereby associates must display emotions that are contrary to what they are feeling is termed **emotional labor**.[118] Organizations often indicate to employees what emotions they must express and under what circumstances. When these required emotions, or display rules, are contrary to what associates are actually feeling, they can experience stress, emotional exhaustion, and burnout.[119] Emotional labor does not always lead to overstressed employees. When associates actually come to feel the emotions they are required to display, they can experience positive outcomes such as greater job satisfaction.[120]

Even when associates may not feel the emotions they are required to express, several factors can influence whether this acting will have a negative outcome on associates' well-being. First, the manner in which supervisors enforce display rules can influence whether emotional labor is harmful to associates.[121] When supervisors are quite demanding, associates will become more exhausted. Another factor that influences the effects of emotional labor is the self-identities of associates.[122] When associates have a strong self-identity as a service worker or a caregiver then they will be less likely to experience negative effects from emotional labor. For example, a hospice care worker may feel tired and frustrated, but behave in a caring and nurturing manner with her patients. If the care worker has a strong self-identity as a caregiver, she will experience less exhaustion from her emotional labor. Finally, when associates have networks of supportive people and caring mentors, the negative effects of emotional labor will be mitigated.[123]

emotional labor
The process whereby associates must display emotions that are contrary to what they are feeling.

Emotional Intelligence

Are some people just better dealing with emotions, theirs and others, than are other people? The past decade or so has seen an explosion in what has been termed the concept of **emotional intelligence** in both the study and practice of management. The best-accepted definition of emotional intelligence (EI) is that it is the ability to

- Accurately appraise one's own and others' emotions.
- Effectively regulate one's own and others' emotions.
- Use emotion to motivate, plan, and achieve.[124]

A person displaying high emotional intelligence can accurately determine his or her own emotions and the effect those emotions will have on others, then go on to regulate the emotions to achieve his or her goals.

Emotional intelligence has been linked to career success, leadership effectiveness, managerial performance, and performance in sales jobs.[125] It also is the subject of many management development programs, popular books,[126] and articles that may at times inflate the value of emotional intelligence relative to cognitive intelligence.[127] The specific abilities generally associated with emotional intelligence include:[128]

- **Self-awareness.** Associates with high self-awareness understand how their feelings, beliefs, and behaviors affect themselves and others. For example, a supervisor knows that her reaction to a valuable (and otherwise high-performing)

emotional intelligence
The ability to accurately appraise one's own and others' emotions, effectively regulate one's own and others' emotions, and use emotion to motivate, plan, and achieve.

associate's chronic lateness and excuses is one of anger, but she realizes that if she displays this anger, it will cause the associate to withdraw even further.

- **Self-regulation.** Self-regulation is the ability to control one's emotions. The supervisor may feel like yelling at the associate or being punitive in making work assignments; however, if she is high in self-regulation, she will choose her words and actions carefully. She will behave in a manner that will more likely encourage the associate to come to work on time rather than make the associate withdraw even more.

- **Motivation or drive.** This characteristic is the same as achievement motivation, discussed previously in this chapter, and drive, discussed above under trait theories. Associates with high EI want to achieve for achievement's sake alone. They always want to do things better and seek out feedback about their progress. They are passionate about their work.

- **Empathy.** Effective empathy means thoughtfully considering others' feelings when making decisions and weighting those feelings appropriately, along with other factors. Consider again our example of the supervisor dealing with the tardy associate. Suppose she knows that the associate is frequently late because he is treated poorly by the work group. The supervisor can display empathy by acknowledging this situation and can act on it by attempting to change work arrangements rather than punishing the associate for being late. Thus, she can remove an obstacle for the associate and perhaps retain an associate who performs well and comes to work on time.

- **Social skill.** Social skill refers to the ability to build effective relationships with the goal of moving people toward a desired outcome. Socially skilled associates know how to build bonds between people. Often, leaders who appear to be

THE STRATEGIC LENS

Understanding personality, intelligence, attitudes, and emotions enables managers to more effectively manage the behavior of their associates. Selecting new associates based on personality and intelligence can have an impact on organizational performance, as demonstrated by Outback Steakhouse and the National Football League. Hiring associates who fit its culture in turn enables an organization to better implement its strategy, as illustrated by the success of Patricia Harris at McDonald's. Organizations can further increase existing associates' organizational fit, performance, and tenure by creating work environments that lead to positive attitudes and emotionally healthy environments. Furthermore, from the examples presented throughout the chapter and summarized above, we can see how knowledge of personality, intelligence, attitudes, and emotions allows executives to more effectively implement their strategies through management of behavior in their organizations.

Critical Thinking Questions

1. Specifically, how can you use knowledge of personality, attitudes, intelligence, and emotions to make better hiring decisions?

2. If top executives wanted to implement a strategy that emphasized innovation and new products, how could they use knowledge of personality, attitudes, and emotions to affect the organization's culture in ways to enhance innovation?

3. How could a manager use knowledge about personality and attitudes to form a high-performance work team?

socializing with co-workers are actually working to build relationships and exercise their influence in a positive manner.

While emotional intelligence is quite a popular concept right now, it is not without its critics.[129] One major criticism is that emotional intelligence is not intelligence at all, but rather a conglomeration of specific social skills and personality traits. Another criticism is that sometimes emotional intelligence is so broadly defined that it is meaningless. Nonetheless, the basic abilities that make up emotional intelligence are important influences on organizational behavior, whether they form one construct called *emotional intelligence* or are simply considered alone.

What This Chapter Adds to Your Knowledge Portfolio

In this chapter, we have discussed personality in some detail. We have seen how personality develops and how important it is in the workplace. We have also discussed intelligence. If an organization is to be successful, its associates and managers must understand the effects of personality and intelligence and be prepared to act on this knowledge. Moving beyond enduring traits and mental ability, we have examined attitude formation and change. Without insights into attitudes, associates and managers alike would miss important clues about how a person will act in the workplace. Finally, we have briefly examined emotions and their various roles in behavior and organizational life. More specifically, we have made the following points:

- Personality is a stable set of characteristics representing the internal properties of an individual. These characteristics, or traits, are relatively enduring, are major determinants of behavior, and influence behavior across a wide variety of situations.
- Determinants of personality include heredity and environment. Three types of studies have demonstrated the effects of heredity: (1) investigations of identical twins, (2) assessments of newborns and their behavior later in life, and (3) direct examinations of genes. Studies of environmental effects have emphasized childhood experiences as important forces in personality development.
- There are many aspects of personality. Five traits, however, have emerged as particularly important in the workplace. These traits, collectively known as the Big Five, are extraversion, conscientiousness, agreeableness, emotional stability, and openness to experience.
- Extraversion (the degree to which a person is outgoing and derives energy from being around people) tends to affect overall job performance, success in team interactions, and job satisfaction. For performance, fit with the job is important, as extraverts have at least modest advantages in occupations calling for a high level of interaction with other people, whereas introverts appear to have advantages in occupations calling for more solitary work.
- Conscientiousness (the degree to which a person focuses on goals and works toward them in a disciplined way) also affects job performance, success as a team member, and job satisfaction. Higher levels of conscientiousness tend to be positive for these outcomes.
- Agreeableness (the degree to which a person is easygoing and tolerant) does not have simple, easily specified effects on individual job performance but does appear to contribute positively to successful interactions on a team.
- Emotional stability (the degree to which a person handles stressful, high-demand situations with ease) affects job performance, success as a team member, and job satisfaction. Higher levels of emotional stability tend to be positive.
- Openness to experience (the degree to which a person seeks new experiences and thinks creatively about the future) does not have simple links to overall job performance, success

back to the knowledge objectives

1. What is meant by the term *personality*? What key beliefs do psychologists traditionally hold about personality traits?

2. What are the Big Five traits, and how do they influence behavior and performance in the workplace? Give an example of someone you know whose personality did not fit the job he or she had. This could be a person in an organization in which you worked, or it could be a person from a school club or civic organization. What was the outcome? If you had been the individual's manager, how would you have attempted to improve the situation?

3. Describe a situation in which a manager's or a friend's locus of control, authoritarianism, social dominance orientation, self-monitoring, need for achievement, or approval motivation had an impact on your life.

4. What is intelligence, and what is its effect in the workplace?

5. How are attitudes similar to and different from personality? How do attitudes form? How can managers change attitudes in the workplace? Assume that the target of the attitude cannot be changed (that is, the job, boss, technology, and so on cannot be changed). Be sure to address both persuasive communication and dissonance.

6. What is the relationship between emotions and attitudes? Describe the emotions displayed by a past or current boss and explain how those emotions affected your job.

at teamwork, or job satisfaction, but individuals scoring higher on this aspect of personality do appear to have an edge in specific tasks calling for vision and creativity.

- The Big Five personality traits may play a role in high-involvement management. Certain combinations of these traits seem to provide a foundation for the competencies needed by managers and associates. Absent these trait combinations, individuals may still be effective in high-involvement systems, but they may need to work a little harder.

- A Big Five assessment can be useful in selecting new associates and managers but must be combined with other tools, such as structured interviews and evaluations of the specific skills needed for a particular job.

- Beyond the Big Five, several cognitive and motivational personality concepts are important in the workplace. Cognitive concepts correspond to perceptual and thought processes and include locus of control, authoritarianism, social dominance orientation, and self-monitoring. Motivational concepts correspond to needs in individuals and are directly involved in energizing and maintaining overt behaviors. They include achievement motivation and approval motivation.

- There are many areas of intelligence, including number aptitude, verbal comprehension, and perceptual speed. Most psychologists who have extensively studied intelligence believe these various areas combine to form a single meaningful intelligence factor. This general intelligence factor has been found to predict workplace outcomes.

- An attitude is a persistent mental state of readiness to feel and behave in favorable or unfavorable ways toward a specific person, object, or idea. Attitudes consist of a cognitive element, an affective element, and a behavioral element.

- Attitudes may be learned as a result of direct experience with an object, person, or idea. Unfavorable experiences are likely to lead to unfavorable attitudes, and favorable experiences to favorable attitudes. Attitudes may also form as the result of self-perception, where an individual behaves in a certain way and then concludes he has an attitude that matches the behavior. Finally, attitudes may form on the basis of a need for consistency. We tend to form attitudes that are consistent with our existing attitudes.

- Job satisfaction and organizational commitment are two of the most important workplace attitudes. Job satisfaction is a favorable or unfavorable view of the job, whereas organizational commitment corresponds to how strongly an individual identifies with and values being associated with the organization. Both of these attitudes affect intentions to stay in the job, actual decisions to stay, and absenteeism. They are also related to job performance, though not as strongly as some other factors. Attitudes may change through exposure to persuasive communications or cognitive dissonance. Persuasive communication consists of four important elements: the communicator, message, situation, and target. Dissonance refers to inconsistencies between attitude and behavior. Under certain conditions, a behavior that is inconsistent with an existing attitude causes the attitude to change. Key conditions include: (1) the behavior being substantially inconsistent with the attitude, (2) the behavior causing harm or being negative for someone, and (3) the behavior being voluntary.

- Emotions are the subjective reactions associates experience that contain both a psychological and physiological component. Emotions can influence organizational behavior directly, as the basis of emotional labor, or through associates' emotional intelligence.

Thinking about Ethics

1. Is it appropriate for an organization to use personality tests to screen applicants for jobs? Should organizations reject applicants whose personalities do not fit a particular profile, ignoring the applicants' performance on previous jobs, their capabilities, and their motivation?

2. Should organizations use intelligence tests to screen applicants even though the accuracy of such tests is questioned by some? Why or why not?

3. Are there right and wrong values? How should values be used to manage the behavior of associates in organizations?

4. Can knowledge of personality, attitudes, and values be used inappropriately? If so, how?

5. Is it appropriate to change people's attitudes? If so, how can a person's attitudes be changed without altering that person's values?

Key Terms

personality, p. 170
extraversion, p. 172
conscientiousness, p. 173
agreeableness, p. 173
emotional stability, p. 174
openness to experience, p. 174
locus of control, p. 177
authoritarianism, p. 177

social dominance orientation, p. 178
self-monitoring, p. 178
achievement motivation, p. 178
approval motivation, p. 179
intelligence, p. 181
attitude, p. 182
affective commitment, p. 189

normative commitment, p. 189
continuance commitment, p. 189
cognitive dissonance, p. 191
emotions, p. 193
emotional contagion, p. 194
emotional labor, p. 195
emotional intelligence, p. 195

Human Resource Management Applications

Personality traits and intelligence are often used in employee selection. Human Resource Management (HRM) departments are often charged with developing selection procedures or choosing vendors of selection tests. Furthermore, HRM departments are often responsible for conducting job analyses to determine what traits and abilities are necessary to perform various jobs.

HRM departments conduct employee surveys and climate audits to assess the satisfaction and commitment of current employees. Exit interviews may also be conducted to determine why people leave the organization.

Finally, Employee Assistance Programs (EAPs) are part of the HRM function. These programs help employees cope with problems resulting from emotional strain on the job.

building your human capital

Big Five Personality Assessment

Different people have different personalities, and these personalities can affect outcomes in the workplace. Understanding your own personality can help you to understand how and why you behave as you do. In this installment of *Building Your Human Capital,* we present an assessment tool for the Big Five.

Instructions

In this assessment, you will read 50 phrases that describe people. Use the rating scale below to indicate how accurately each phrase describes you. Rate yourself as you generally are now, not as you wish to be in the future; and rate yourself as you honestly see yourself. Keep in mind that very few people have extreme scores on all or even most of the items (a "1" or a "5" is an extreme score); most people have midrange scores for many of the items. Read each item carefully, and then circle the number that corresponds to your choice from the rating scale.

1	2	3	4	5
Not at all like me	Somewhat unlike me	Neither like nor unlike me	Somewhat like me	Very much like me

1.	Am the life of the party.	1	2	3	4	5
2.	Feel little concern for others.	1	2	3	4	5
3.	Am always prepared.	1	2	3	4	5
4.	Get stressed out easily.	1	2	3	4	5
5.	Have a rich vocabulary.	1	2	3	4	5
6.	Don't talk a lot.	1	2	3	4	5
7.	Am interested in people.	1	2	3	4	5
8.	Leave my belongings around.	1	2	3	4	5
9.	Am relaxed most of the time.	1	2	3	4	5
10.	Have difficulty understanding abstract ideas.	1	2	3	4	5
11.	Feel comfortable around people.	1	2	3	4	5
12.	Insult people.	1	2	3	4	5
13.	Pay attention to details.	1	2	3	4	5
14.	Worry about things.	1	2	3	4	5
15.	Have a vivid imagination.	1	2	3	4	5
16.	Keep in the background.	1	2	3	4	5
17.	Sympathize with others' feelings.	1	2	3	4	5
18.	Make a mess of things.	1	2	3	4	5
19.	Seldom feel blue.	1	2	3	4	5
20.	Am not interested in abstract ideas.	1	2	3	4	5
21.	Start conversations.	1	2	3	4	5
22.	Am not interested in other people's problems.	1	2	3	4	5
23.	Get chores done right away.	1	2	3	4	5

24.	Am easily disturbed.	1	2	3	4	5
25.	Have excellent ideas.	1	2	3	4	5
26.	Have little to say.	1	2	3	4	5
27.	Have a soft heart.	1	2	3	4	5
28.	Often forget to put things back in their proper place.	1	2	3	4	5
29.	Get easily upset.	1	2	3	4	5
30.	Do not have a good imagination.	1	2	3	4	5
31.	Talk to a lot of different people at parties.	1	2	3	4	5
32.	Am not really interested in others.	1	2	3	4	5
33.	Like order.	1	2	3	4	5
34.	Change my mood a lot.	1	2	3	4	5
35.	Am quick to understand things.	1	2	3	4	5
36.	Don't like to draw attention to myself.	1	2	3	4	5
37.	Take time out for others.	1	2	3	4	5
38.	Shirk my duties.	1	2	3	4	5
39.	Have frequent mood swings.	1	2	3	4	5
40.	Use difficult words.	1	2	3	4	5
41.	Don't mind being the center of attention.	1	2	3	4	5
42.	Feel others' emotions.	1	2	3	4	5
43.	Follow a schedule.	1	2	3	4	5
44.	Get irritated easily.	1	2	3	4	5
45.	Spend time reflecting on things.	1	2	3	4	5
46.	Am quiet around strangers.	1	2	3	4	5
47.	Make people feel at ease.	1	2	3	4	5
48.	Am exact in my work.	1	2	3	4	5
49.	Often feel blue.	1	2	3	4	5
50.	Am full of ideas.	1	2	3	4	5

Scoring Key

To determine your scores, combine your responses to the items above as follows:

Extraversion = (Item 1 + Item 11 + Item 21 + Item 31 + Item 41) + (30 − (Item 6 + Item 16 + Item 26 + Item 36 + Item 46))

Conscientiousness = (Item 3 + Item 13 + Item 23 + Item 33 + Item 43 + Item 48) + (24 − (Item 8 + Item 18 + Item 28 + Item 38))

Agreeableness = (Item 7 + Item 17 + Item 27 + Item 37 + Item 42 + Item 47) + (24 − (Item 2 + Item 12 + Item 22 + Item 32))

Emotional stability = (Item 9 + Item 19) + (48 − (Item 4 + Item 14 + Item 24 + Item 29 + Item 34 + Item 39 + Item 44 + Item 49))

Openness to experience = (Item 5 + Item 15 + Item 25 + Item 35 + Item 40 + Item 45 + Item 50) + (18 − (Item 10 + Item 20 + Item 30))

Scores for each trait can range from 10 to 50. Scores of 40 and above may be considered high, while scores of 20 and below may be considered low.

Source: International Personality Item Pool. 2001. A Scientific Collaboration for the Development of Advanced Measures of Personality Traits and Other Individual Differences (http://ipip.ori.org).

an organizational behavior moment

Whatever Is Necessary!

Marian could feel the rage surge from deep within her. Even though she was usually in control of her behavior, it was not easy to control her internal emotions. She could sense her rapid pulse and knew that her face was flushed. But she knew that her emotional reaction to the report would soon subside in the solitary confines of her executive office. She would be free to think about the problem and make a decision about solving it.

Marian had joined the bank eight months ago as manager in charge of the consumer loan sections. There were eight loan sections in all, and her duties were both interesting and challenging. But for some reason there had been a trend in the past six months of decreasing loan volume and increasing payment delinquency. The month-end report to which she reacted showed that the past month was the worst in both categories in several years.

Vince Stoddard, the president, had been impressed by her credentials and aggressiveness when he hired her. Marian had been in the business for 10 years and was the head loan officer for one of the bank's competitors. Her reputation for aggressive pursuit of business goals was almost legendary among local bankers. She was active in the credit association and worked long, hard hours. Vince believed that she was the ideal person for the position.

When he hired her, he had said, "Marian, you're right for the job, but I know it won't be easy for you. Dave Kattar, who heads one of the loan sections, also wanted the job. In fact, had you turned down our offer, it would have been Dave's. He is well liked around here, and I also respect him. I don't think you'll have any problems working with him, but don't push him too hard at first. Let him get used to you, and I think you'll find him to be quite an asset."

But Dave was nothing but a "pain in the neck" for Marian. She sensed his resentment from the first day she came to work. Although he never said anything negative, his aggravating way of ending most conversations with her was, "Okay, Boss Lady. Whatever you want is what we'll do."

When loan volume turned down shortly after her arrival, she called a staff meeting with all of the section heads. As she began to explain that volume was off, she thought she noticed several of the section heads look over to Dave. Because she saw Dave only out of the corner of her eye, she couldn't be certain, but she thought he winked at the other heads. That action immediately angered her—and she felt her face flush. The meeting accomplished little, but each section head promised that the next month would be better.

In fact, the next month was worse, and each subsequent month followed that pattern. Staff meetings were now more frequent, and Marian was more prone to explode angrily with threats of what would happen if they didn't improve. So far she had not followed through on any threats, but she thought that "now" might be the time.

To consolidate her position, she had talked the situation over with Vince, and he had said rather coolly, "Whatever you think is necessary." He hadn't been very friendly toward her for several weeks, and she was worried about that also.

"So," Marian thought to herself, "I wonder what will happen if I fire Dave. If I get him out of here, will the others shape up? On the other hand, Vince might not support me. But maybe he's just waiting for me to take charge. It might even get me back in good graces with him."

Discussion Questions

1. What role did personality play in the situation at the bank? Which of the Big Five personality traits most clearly influenced Marian and Dave? Which of the cognitive and motivational aspects of personality played a role?
2. Working within the bounds of her personality, what should Marian have done when trouble first seemed to be brewing? How could she have maintained Dave's job satisfaction and commitment?
3. How should Marian proceed now that the situation has become very difficult?

team exercise

Experiencing Emotional Labor

Have you ever been forced to smile at someone who was annoying you? Have you ever had to be calm when you felt very afraid? If so, you have probably engaged in emotional labor. The purpose of this exercise is to examine how emotional labor can affect us in different ways and the factors that impact the toll that emotional labor can take on us.

STEPS

1. At the beginning of class, assemble into teams of six to eight people.
2. During the next 30 minutes of class, each individual will be required to follow emotional display rules for one of the following emotions:
   a. Happiness
   b. Anger
   c. Compassion and caring
   d. Fear

   Assign the display rules so that at least one person is displaying each emotion.
3. Each person is to display his or her assigned emotion during the next 30 minutes of class lecture or activity—*no matter what he or she actually feels!*
4. At the end of the 30 minutes (or when instructed by your teacher), re-form into groups and address the following questions:
   a. How difficult was it for you to display your assigned emotion? Was your assigned emotion different from how you actually felt? Did your felt emotions begin to change to coincide with your displayed emotion?
   b. To what extent did the type of emotion required (e.g., happiness versus anger) influence your reaction to this exercise?
   c. How much longer could you have continued displaying your assigned emotion? Why?
5. Appoint a spokesperson to present the group's conclusions to the entire class.

Source: Adapted from *Experiences in Management and Organizational Behavior*, 4th ed. New York: John Wiley & Sons, 1997.

Endnotes

1. Barrick, M.R., & Mount, M.K. 1991. The Big Five personality dimensions and performance: A meta-analysis. *Personnel Psychology*, 44: 1–26.
2. Hough, L.M., Oswald, F.L., & Ployhart, R.E. 2001. Determinants, detection, and amelioration of adverse impact in personnel selection procedures: Issues, evidence and lessons learned. *International Journal of Selection and Assessment*, 9: 152–194; Schmidt, F.L., & Hunter, J.E. 1998. The validity and utility of selection methods in personnel psychology: Practical and theoretical implications of 85 years of research findings. *Psychological Bulletin*, 124: 262–274.
3. Marcus, B., Lee, K., & Ashton, M.C. 2007. Personality dimensions explaining relationships between integrity tests and counterproductive behavior: Big Five, or one in addition? *Personnel Psychology*, 60: 1–35.
4. Kristof-Brown, A.L., Zimmerman, R.D., & Johnson, E.C. 2005. Consequences of individuals' fit at work: A meta-analysis of person-job, person-organization, person-group, and person-supervisor fit. *Personnel Psychology*, 58: 281–342; Arthur, W., Bell, S.T., Villado, A.J., & Doverspike, D. 2006. The use of person-organization fit in employment decision making: An assessment of its criterion related validity. *Journal of Applied Psychology*, 91: 786–801.
5. McCulloch, M.C., & Turban, D.B. 2007. Using person-organization fit to select employees for high turnover jobs. *International Journal of Selection and Assessment*, 15: 63.
6. Peterson, R.S., Smith, D.B., & Martorana, P.V. 2003. The impact of chief executive officer personality on top management team dynamics: One mechanism by which leadership affects organizational performance. *Journal of Applied Psychology*, 88: 795–808.
7. Miller, D., & Toulouse, J-M. 1986. Chief executive personality and corporate strategy and structure in small firms. *Organizational Science*, 32: 1389–1410.
8. Eysenck, H.J., Arnold, W.J., & Meili, R. 1975. *Encyclopedia of psychology (Vol. 2)*. London: Fontana/Collins; Fontana, D. 2000. *Personality in the workplace*. London: Macmillan Press; Howard, P.J., & Howard, J.M. 2001. *The owner's manual for personality at work*. Austin, TX: Bard Press.
9. Byrne, J.A. 1998. How Al Dunlap self-destructed. *Business Week*, July 6, 58–64.
10. Ibid.
11. See, for example, Bouchard, T.J., Lykken, D.T., McGue, M., Segal, N.L., & Tellegen, A. 1990. Sources of human psychological differences: The Minnesota study of twins reared apart. *Science*, 250: 223–228; Shields, J. 1962. *Monozygotic twins*. London: Oxford University Press.
12. Ibid.
13. Chess, S., & Thomas, A. 1987. *Know your child: An authoritative guide for today's parents*. New York: Basic Books.
14. Hamer, D., & Copeland, P. 1998. *Living with your genes*. New York: Doubleday; Ridely, M. 1999. *Genome: The autobiography of a species in 23 chapters*. New York: HarperCollins.
15. Ridely, M. 1999. *Genome: The autobiography of a species in 23 chapters*. New York: HarperCollins.

16. Friedman, H.S., & Schustack, M.W. 1999. *Personality: Classic theories and modern research.* Boston: Allyn and Bacon.

17. McCandless, B. 1969. *Children: Behavior and development.* London: Holt, Rinehart, & Winston.

18. Costa, P.T., & McCrae, R.B. 1993. Set like plaster: Evidence for the stability of adult personality. In T. Heatherton and J. Weimberger (Eds.), *Can personality change?* Washington, DC: American Psychology Association.

19. Erikson, E. 1987. *A way of looking at things: Selected papers from 1930 to 1980.* New York: W.W. Norton.

20. Costa, P.T., & McCrae, R.R. 1992. *NEO PI-R: Professional manual.* Odessa, FL: Psychological Assessment Resources.

21. Reuters. January 13, 2009. Yahoo names software exec Bartz as new CEO. At http://www.reuters.com/article/idUSN1340746920090113.

22. Barrick, M.R., & Mount, M.K. 1991. The Big Five personality dimensions and performance: A meta-analysis. *Personnel Psychology,* 44: 1–26; Barrick, M.R., Mount, M.K., & Judge, T.A. 2001. Personality and performance at the beginning of the new millennium: What do we know and where do we go next? *International Journal of Selection and Assessment,* 9: 9–30; Hurtz, G.M., & Donovan, J.J. 2000. Personality and job performance: The Big Five revisited. *Journal of Applied Psychology,* 85: 869–879; Mount, M.K., Barrick, M.R., & Strauss, G.L. 1998. Five-factor model of personality and performance in jobs involving interpersonal interactions. *Human Performance,* 11: 145–165.

23. de Jong, R.D., Bouhuys, S.A., & Barnhoorn, J.C. 1999. Personality, self-efficacy, and functioning in management teams: A contribution to validation. *International Journal of Selection and Assessment,* 7: 46–49.

24. Judge, T.A., Heller, D., & Mount, M.K. 2002. Five-factor model of personality and job satisfaction: A meta-analysis. *Journal of Applied Psychology,* 87: 530–541.

25. Costa, P.T., & McCrae, R.R. 1992. *NEO P-R: Professional manual.* Odessa, FL: Psychological Assessment Resources.

26. Barrick, M.R., & Mount, M.K. 1991. The Big Five personality dimensions and performance: A meta-analysis. *Personnel Psychology,* 44: 1–26; Barrick, M.R., Mount, M.K., & Judge, T.A. 2001. Personality and performance at the beginning of the new millennium: What do we know and where do we go next? *International Journal of Selection and Assessment,* 9: 9–30.

27. Judge, T.A., Higgins, C.A., Thoresen, C., & Barrick, M.R. 1999. The Big Five personality traits, general mental ability, and career success across the life span. *Personnel Psychology,* 52: 621–652.

28. Bain & Company, 2007. Springboard: People. www.bain.com/bainweb/Join_Bain/people_places.asp; Goldman Sachs Group, Inc. 2007. Our people. www2.goldmansachs.com/careers/inside_goldman_sachs/our_people/index.html; Microsoft. 2007. Meet Our People. http://members.microsoft.com/careers/mslife/meetpeople/default.aspx.

29. Witt, L.A., Burke, L.A., Barrick, M. R., & Mount, M.K. 2002. The interactive effects of conscientiousness and agreeableness on job performance. *Journal of Applied Psychology,* 87: 164–169.

30. Costa, P.T., & McCrae, R.R. 1992. *NEO P-R: Professional manual.* Odessa, FL: Psychological Assessment Resources.

31. Barrick, M.R., Mount, M.K., & Judge, T.A. 2001. Personality and performance at the beginning of the new millennium: What do we know and where do we go next? *International Journal of Selection and Assessment,* 9: 9–30.

32. Kichuk, S.L., & Weisner, W.H. 1997. The Big Five personality factors and team performance: Implications for selecting successful product design teams, *Journal of Engineering and Technology Management,* 14: 195–221; Neuman, G.A., Wagner, S.H., & Christiansen, N.D. 1999. The relationship between work-team personality composition and the job performance of teams. *Group and Organization Management,* 24: 28–45; Neuman, G.A., & Wright, J. 1999. Team effectiveness: beyond skills and cognitive ability. *Journal of Applied Psychology,* 84: 376–389.

33. Costa, P.T., & McCrae, R.R. 1992. *NEO P-R: Professional manual.* Odessa, FL: Psychological Assessment Resources.

34. Barrick, M.R., & Mount, M.K. 1991. The Big Five personality dimensions and performance: A meta-analysis. *Personnel Psychology,* 44: 1–26.

35. Barrick, M.R., Mount, M.K., & Judge, T.A. 2001. Personality and performance at the beginning of the new millennium: What do we know and where do we go next? *International Journal of Selection and Assessment,* 9: 9–30.

36. Kichuk, S.L., & Weisner, W.H. 1997. The Big Five personality factors and team performance: Implications for selecting successful product design teams. *Journal of Engineering and Technology Management,* 14: 195–221; Thomas, P., Moore, K.S., & Scott, K.S. 1996. The relationship between self-efficacy for participating in self-managed work groups and the Big Five personality dimensions. *Journal of Organizational Behavior,* 17: 349–363.

37. Hirschfeld, R.R., Jordan, M.H., Thomas, C.H., & Field, H.S. 2008. Observed leadership potential of personnel in a team setting: Big Five traits and proximal factors as predictors. *International Journal of Selection and Assessment,* 16: 385-402.

38. Judge, T.A., Heller, D., & Mount, M.K. 2002. Five-factor model of personality and job satisfaction: A meta-analysis. *Journal of Applied Psychology,* 87: 530–541.

39. Costa, P.T., & McCrae, R.R. 1992. NEO P-R: *Professional manual.* Odessa, FL: Psychological Assessment Resources.

40. Barrick, M.R., Mount, M.K., & Judge, T.A. 2001. Personality and performance at the beginning of the new millennium: What do we know and where do we go next? *International Journal of Selection and Assessment,* 9: 9–30.

41. W.L. Gore & Associates. 2007. Careers: North America. www.gore.com/careers/north_america_careers.html.

42. Hough, L.M., Oswald, F.L., & Ployhart, R.E. 2001. Determinants, detection, and amelioration of adverse impact in personnel selection procedures: Issues, evidence and lessons learned. International *Journal of Selection and Assessment,* 9: 152–194; Schmidt, F.L., & Hunter, J.E. 1998. The validity and utility of selection methods in personnel psychology: Practical and theoretical implications of 85 years of research findings. *Psychological Bulletin,* 124: 262–274; Tett, R.P., Jackson, D.N., & Rothstein, M. 1991. Personality measures as predictors of job performance. Personnel Psychology, 44: 703–742.

43. Wilk, S.L. & Moynihan, L.M. 2005. Display rule regulators: The relationship between supervisors and worker emotional exhaustion. *Journal of Applied Psychology*, 90: 917–927.

44. Howard, P.J., & Howard, J.M. 2001. *The owner's manual for personality at work*. Austin, TX: Bard Press.

45. Ibid.

46. Spector, P.E. 1982. Behavior in organizations as a function of employee's locus of control. *Psychological Bulletin*, 91: 482–497.

47. Kabanoff, B., & O'Brien, G.E. 1980. Work and leisure: A task-attributes analysis. *Journal of Applied Psychology*, 65: 596–609.

48. Spector, P.E. 1982. Behavior in organizations as a function of employee's locus of control. *Psychological Bulletin*, 91: 482–497.

49. Spector, P.E., Cooper, C.L., Sanchez, J.I., O'Driscoll, M., Sparks, K., Bernin, P., Bussing, A., Dewe, P., Hart, P., Lu, L., Miller, K., De Moraes, L.R., Ostrognay, G.M., Pagon, M., Pitariu, H.D., Poelmans, S.A.Y., Radhakrishnan, P., Russinova, V., Salamatov, V., Salgado, J.F., Shima, S., Siu, O., Stora, J.B., Teichmann, M., Theorell, T., Vlerick, P., Westman, M., Widerszal-Bazyl, M., Wong, P.T., & Yu, S. 2002. Locus of control and well-being at work: How generalizable are western findings? *Academy of Management Journal*, 45: 453–466.

50. Ng, T.W.H., Sorensen, K.L., & Eby, L.T. 2006. Locus of control at work: A meta-analysis. *Journal of Organizational Behavior*, 27: 1057–1087.

51. Blass, T. 1977. *Personality variables in behavior*. Hillsdale, NJ: Lawrence Erlbaum Associates.

52. Altmeyer, B. 1998. The other "authoritarian personality." In M.P. Zanna (Ed.), *Advances in experimental social psychology (Vol. 30)*. San Diego: Academic Press, pp. 47–92.

53. Son Hing, L.S., Bobocel, D.R., Zanna, M.P., and McBride, M.V. 2007. Authoritarian dynamics and unethical decision making: High social dominance orientation leaders and high right-wing authoritarian followers. *Journal of Personality and Social Psychology*, 92: 67–81.

54. Sidanius, J., & Pratto, F. 1999. *Social dominance: An intergroup theory of social hierarchy and oppression*. New York: Cambridge University Press.

55. Pratto, F., Sidanius, J., Stallworth, L.M., & Malle, B.F. 1994. Social dominance orientation: A personality variable predicting social and political attitudes. *Journal of Personality and Social Psychology*, 67: 741–763.

56. Sibley, C.G., & Duckitt, J. 2008. Personality and prejudice: A meta-analysis and theoretical review. *Personality and Social Psychology Review*, 12: 248–279.

57. Umphress, E.E., Simmons, A.L., Boswell, W.R., & Triana, M.d.C. 2008. Managing discrimination in selection: The influence of directives from an authority and social dominance orientation. *Journal of Applied Psychology*, 93: 982–993; Petersen, L.E., & Dietz, J. 2000. Social discrimination in a personnel selection context: The effects of an authority's instruction to discriminate and followers' authoritarianism. *Journal of Applied Social Psychology*, 30: 206–220.

58. Umphress, E.E., Smith-Crowe, K., Brief, A.P., Dietz, J., & Watkins, M.B. 2007. When birds of a feather flock together and when they do not: Status composition, social dominance orientation and organizational attractiveness. *Journal of Applied Psychology*, 92: 396–409; McKay, P.F., & Avery, D.R. 2006. What has race got to do with it? Unraveling the role of racioethnicity in job seekers' reactions to site visits. *Personnel Psychology*, 59: 395–429.

59. Mehra, A., Kilduff, M., & Brass, D.J. 2001. The social networks of high and low self-monitors: Implications for workplace performance. *Administrative Science Quarterly*, 46: 121–146.

60. Snyder, M. 1979. Self-monitoring processes. *Advances in Experimental Social Psychology*, 12: 85–128.

61. Mehra, A., Kilduff, M., & Brass, D.J. 2001. The social networks of high and low self-monitors: Implications for workplace performance. *Administrative Science Quarterly*, 46: 121–146.

62. Snyder, M. 1979. Self-monitoring processes. *Advances in Experimental Social Psychology*, 12: 85–128.

63. Day, D.V., Schleicher, D.J., Unckless, A.L., & Hiller, N.J. 2002. Self-monitoring personality at work: A meta-analytic investigation of construct validity. *Journal of Applied Psychology*, 87: 390–401.

64. Kilduff, M., & Day, D.V. 1994. Do chameleons get ahead? The effects of self monitoring on managerial careers. *Academy of Management Journal*, 37: 1047–1060.

65. Blass, T. 1977. *Personality variables in behavior*. Hillsdale, NJ: Lawrence Erlbaum Associates.

66. Steel, P. 2007. The nature of procrastination: A meta-analytic and theoretical review of quintessential self-regulatory failure. *Psychological Bulletin*, 133: 65–94.

67. Blass, T. 1977. *Personality variables in behavior*. Hillsdale, NJ: Lawrence Erlbaum Associates.

68. See, for example, Salgado, J.F. 1997. The five factor model of personality and job performance in the European Community. *Journal of Applied Psychology*, 82: 30–43.

69. Locke, E.A. 2005. Why emotional intelligence is an invalid concept. *Journal of Organizational Behavior*, 26: 425–431.

70. Dunnette, M.D. 1976. Aptitudes, abilities, and skills. In M.D. Dunnette (Ed.), *Handbook of industrial and organizational psychology*. Chicago: Rand McNally.

71. Hunter, J.E., & Hunter, R.F. 1984. Validity and utility of alternative predictors of job performance. *Psychological Bulletin*, 96: 72–98; Hunter, J.E., & Schmidt, F.L. 1996. Intelligence and job performance: Economic and social implications. *Psychology, Public Policy, and Law*, 2: 447–472; Salgado, J.F., & Anderson, N. 2002. Cognitive and GMA testing in the European Community: Issues and evidence. *Human Performance*, 15: 75–96; Schmidt, F.L. 2002. The role of general cognitive ability and job performance: Why there cannot be a debate. *Human Performance*, 15: 187–210; Schmidt, F.L., & Hunter, J.E. 1998. The validity and utility of selection methods in personnel psychology: Practical and theoretical implications of 85 years of research findings. *Psychological Bulletin*, 124: 262–274.

72. Simon, D.G., Hitt, M.A., & Ireland, R.D. 2007. Managing firm resources in dynamic environments to create value: Looking inside the black box. *Academy of Management Review*, 32: 273–292.

73. Katz, D., & Stotland, E. 1959. Preliminary statement to a theory of attitude structure and change. In S. Kock (Ed.), *Psychology: A study of science* (3rd ed.). New York: McGraw-Hill.

74. Petty, R.E., & Cacioppo, J.T. 1981. *Attitudes and persuasion: Classic and contemporary approaches*. Dubuque, IA: Wm. C. Brown.

75. Bem, D.J. 1972. Self-perception theory. In L. Berkowitz (Ed.), *Advances in experimental social psychology (Vol. 6)*. New York: Academic Press.

76. Freedman, J.L., & Fraser, S.C. 1966. Compliance without pressure: The foot-in-the-door technique. *Journal of Personality and Social Psychology*, 4: 195–202.

77. Heider, F. 1958. *The psychology of interpersonal relations*. New York: John Wiley & Sons; Osgood, C.E., & Tannenbaum, P.H. 1955. The principle of congruity in the prediction of attitude change. *Psychological Review*, 62: 42–55.

78. Holtom, B.C., Mitchell, T.R., & Lee, T.W. 2006. Increasing human and social capital by applying embeddedness theory. *Organizational Dynamics*, 35: 316–331.

79. Mitchell, T.R., Holtom, B.C., Lee, T.W., Sablynski, C.J., & Erez, M. 2001. Why people stay: Using job embeddedness to predict voluntary turnover. *Academy of Management Journal*, 44: 1102–1121; Tett, R.P., & Meyer, J.P. 1993. Job satisfaction, organizational commitment, turnover intention, and turnover: Path analyses based on meta-analytic findings. *Personnel Psychology*, 46: 259–293.

80. Scott, K.D., & Taylor, G.S. 1985. An examination of conflicting findings on the relationship between job satisfaction and absenteeism: A meta-analysis. *Academy of Management Journal*, 28: 599–612.

81. Kinicki, A.J., McKee-Ryan, F.M., Schriesheim, C.A., & Carson, K.P. 2002. Assessing the construct validity of the Job Descriptive Index: A review and meta-analysis. *Journal of Applied Psychology*, 87: 14–32.

82. Judge, T.A., Thoresen, C.J., Bono, J.E., & Patton, G.K. 2001. The job satisfaction-job performance relationship: A qualitative and quantitative review. *Psychological Bulletin*, 127: 376–407.

83. Gellatly, I.R., Meyer, J.P., & Luchak, A.A. 2006. Combined effects of the three commitment components on focal and discretionary behaviors: A test of Meyer and Herscovitch's propositions. *Journal of Vocational Behavior*, 69: 331–345; Meyer, J.P., Stanley, D.J., Herscovitch, L., & Topolnytsky, L. 2002. Affective, continuance, and normative commitment to the organization: A meta-analysis of antecedents, correlates and consequences. *Journal of Vocational Behavior*, 61: 20–52.

84. Wright, T.A., & Bonett, D.G. 2002. The moderating effect of employee tenure on the relation between organizational commitment and job performance: A meta-analysis. *Journal of Applied Psychology*, 87: 1183–1190.

85. Riketta, M. 2002. Attitudinal organizational commitment and job performance. *Journal of Organizational Behavior*, 23: 257–266.

86. Gellatly, I.R., Meyer, J.P., & Luchak, A.A. 2006. Combined effects of the three commitment components on focal and discretionary behaviors: A test of Meyer and Herscovitch's propositions. *Journal of Vocational Behavior*, 69: 331–345.

87. Meyer, J.P., Stanley, D.J., Herscovitch, L., & Topolnytsky, L. 2002. Affective, continuance, and normative commitment to the organization: A meta-analysis of antecedents, correlates and consequences. *Journal of Vocational Behavior*, 61: 20–52; Kalbers, L.P., & Cenker, W.J. 2007. Organizational commitment and auditors in public accounting. *Managerial Auditing Journal*, 22: 354–375.

88. Vandenberghe, C., Bentein, K., & Stinglhamber, F. 2004. Affective commitment to the organization, supervisor, and work group: Antecedents and outcomes. *Journal of Vocational Behavior*, 64: 47–71.

89. Ford, M.T., Heinen, B.A., & Langkamer, K.L. 2007. Work and family satisfaction and conflict: A meta-analysis of cross-domain relations. *Journal of Applied Psychology*, 92: 57–106.

90. Meyer, J.P., Stanley, D.J., Herscovitch, L., & Topolnytsky, L. 2002. Affective, continuance, and normative commitment to the organization: A meta-analysis of antecedents, correlates and consequences. *Journal of Vocational Behavior*, 61: 20–52.

91. Schulte, M., Ostroff, C., & Kinicki, A.J. 2006. Organizational climate and psychological climate perceptions: A cross-level study of climate-satisfaction relationships. *Journal of Occupational and Organizational Psychology*, 79: 645–671.

92. Podsakoff, N.P., LePine, J.A., & LePine, M.A. 2007. Differential challenge stressor-hindrance relationships with job attitudes, turnover intentions, and withdrawal behavior: A meta-analysis. *Journal of Applied Psychology*, 92: 438–454.

93. Colquitt, J.A., Conlon, D.E., Wesson, M.J., Porter, C.O.L.H., & Ng, K.Y. 2001. Justice at the millennium: A meta-analytic review of 25 years of organizational justice research. *Journal of Applied Psychology*, 86: 425–445.

94. Locke, E. A. 1976. The nature and causes of job satisfaction. In M. D. Dunnette (Ed.), *Handbook of industrial and organizational psychology*. Chicago: Rand McNally, pp. 1297–1343.

95. Meyer, J.P., & Allen, N.J. 1997. *Commitment in the workplace: Theory, research, and application*. Thousand Oaks, CA: Sage.

96. Meyer, J.P., Stanley, D.J., Herscovitch, L., & Topolnytsky, L. 2002. Affective, continuance, and normative commitment to the organization: A meta-analysis of antecedents, correlates and consequences. *Journal of Vocational Behavior*, 61: 20–52.

97. Ilies, R., Arvey, R.D., & Bouchard, T.J. 2006. Darwinism, behavioral genetics, and organizational behavior: A review and agenda for future research. *Journal of Organizational Behavior*, 27: 121–141.

98. Deaux, K., Dane, F.C., Wrightsman, L.S., & Sigelman, C.K. 1993. *Social psychology in the 90s*. Pacific Grove, CA: Brooks/Cole.

99. Aronson, E., Turner, J., & Carlsmith, J. 1963. Communicator credibility and communication discrepancy. *Journal of Abnormal and Social Psychology*, 67: 31–36; Hovland, C., Janis, I., & Kelley, H.H. 1953. *Communication and persuasion*. New Haven, CT: Yale University Press.

100. Eagly, A.H., Chaiken, S., & Wood, W. 1981. An attributional analysis of persuasion. In J. Harvey, W.J. Ickes, & R.F. Kidd (Eds.), *New directions in attribution research (Vol. 3)*. Hillsdale, NJ: Lawrence Erlbaum Associates; Walster, E., Aronson, E., & Abrahams, D. 1966. On increasing the persuasiveness of a low prestige communicator. *Journal of Experimental Social Psychology*, 2: 325–342.

101. Berscheid, E. 1966. Opinion change and communicator–communicatee similarity and dissimilarity. *Journal of Personality and Social Psychology*, 4: 670–680.

102. McGinniss, J. 1969. *The selling of the president*, 1968. New York: Trident Press.

103. Leventhal, H. 1970. Findings and theory in the study of fear communications. In L. Berkowitz (Ed.), *Advances in experimental social psychology (Vol. 5)*. New York: Academic Press.

104. Rogers, R.W. 1983. Cognitive and physiological processes in fear appeals and attitude change: A revised theory of protection

motivation. In J. Cacioppo, & R. Petty (Eds.), *Social psychophysiology*. New York: Guilford Press; Maddux, J.E., & Rogers, R.W. 1983. Protection motivation and self-efficacy: A revised theory of fear appeals and attitude change. *Journal of Experimental Social Psychology*, 19: 469–479.

105. Festinger, L.A. 1957. *A theory of cognitive dissonance*. Stanford, CA: Stanford University Press.

106. Deaux, K., Dane, F.C., Wrightsman, L.S., & Sigelman, C.K. 1993. *Social psychology in the 90s*. Pacific Grove, CA: Brooks/Cole.

107. Johnson, P.R., & Indvik, J. 1999. Organizational benefits of having emotionally intelligent managers and employees. *Journal of Workplace Learning*, 11: 84–90.

108. Fisher, C.D., & Ashkanasy, N.M. 2000. The emerging role of emotions in work life: An introduction. *Journal of Organizational Behavior*, 21: 123–129.

109. Hymowitz, C. 2006. Business is personal, so managers need to harness emotions. *Wall Street Journal (Eastern Edition)*, November 13, p. B.1.

110. Lazarus, R.S., & Lazarus, A.D. 1994. *Passion and reason: Making sense of emotions*. New York: Oxford University Press.

111. Hershcovis, M.S., Turner, N., Barling, J., Arnols, K.A., Dupre, K.E., Inness, M., LeBlanc, M.M., & Sivanathan, N. 2007. Predicting workplace aggression: A meta-analysis. *Journal of Applied Psychology*, 92: 228–238.

112. George, J.M. & Brief, A.P. 1992. Feeling good—doing good: A conceptual analysis of mood at work—organizational spontaneity. *Psychological Bulletin*, 112: 310–329.

113. Isen, A.M., Daubman, K.A., & Nowicki, G.P. 1987. Positive affect facilitates creative problem solving. *Journal of Personality and Social Psychology*, 52: 1122–1131.

114. George, J.M., & Zhou, J. 2002. Understanding when bad moods foster creativity and good ones don't: The role of context and clarity of feelings. *Journal of Applied Psychology*, 87: 687–697.

115. Ting Fong, C. 2006. The effects of emotional ambivalence on creativity. *Academy of Management Journal*, 49: 1016–1030.

116. Barsade, S. 2002. The ripple effect: Emotional contagion and its influence on group behavior. *Administrative Science Quarterly*, 47: 644–675; Hatfield, E., Cacioppo, J.T., & Rapson, R.L. 1994. *Emotional contagion*. Cambridge, England: Cambridge University Press.

117. Bono, J.E., & Ilies, R. 2006. Charisma, positive emotions and mood contagion. *The Leadership Quarterly*, 17(4): 317–334.

118. Hochschild, A.R. 1983. *The managed heart: Commercialization of human feeling*. Berkeley, CA: University of California Press; Ashforth, B.E., & Humphrey, R.H. 1993. Emotional labor in service roles: The influence of identity. *Academy of Management Review*, 18: 88–115.

119. Cropanzano, R., Weiss, H. M., & Elias, S. M. 2004. The impact of display rules and emotional labor on psychological well-being at work. In P.L. Perrewé, & D.C. Ganster (Eds.), *Research in occupational stress and well-being (Vol. 3)*. Amsterdam: Elsevier, pp. 45–89; Schaubroeck, J., & Jones, J.R. 2000. Antecedents of workplace emotional labor dimensions and moderators of their effects on physical symptoms. *Journal of Organizational Behavior*, 21: 163–183.

120. Zapf, D., & Holz, M. 2006. On the positive effect and negative effects of emotion work in organizations. *European Journal of Work and Organizational Psychology*, 15: 1–26.

121. Wilk, S.L., & Moynihan, L.M. 2005. Display rule "regulators": The relationship between supervisors and worker emotional exhaustion. *Journal of Applied Psychology*, 90: 915–927.

122. Wilk & Moynihan Display rule "regulators"; Ashforth, B.E., & Humphrey, R.H. 1993. Emotional labor in service roles: The influence of identity. *Academy of Management Review*, 18: 88–115.

123. Bozionelos, N. 2006. Mentoring and expressive network resources: Their relationship with career success and emotional exhaustion among Hellenes employees involved in emotion work. *Journal of Human Resource Management*, 17: 362–378.

124. Salovey, P., & Mayer, J. 1990. Emotional intelligence. *Imagination, Cognition, and Personality*, 9: 185–211.

125. Kerr, R., Garvin, J., Heaton, N., & Boyle, E. 2006. Emotional intelligence and leadership effectiveness. *Leadership and Organizational Development Journal*, 27: 265–279; Cote, S., & Miners, C.T.H. 2006. Emotional intelligence, cognitive intelligence, and job performance. *Administrative Science Quarterly*, 51: 1–28; Semadar, A., Robins, G., & Ferris, G.R. 2006. Comparing the validity of multiple social effectiveness constructs in the prediction of managerial job performance. *Journal of Organizational Behavior*, 27: 443–461. Rozell, E.J., Pettijohn, C.E., & Parker, R.S. 2006. *Journal of Marketing Theory and Practice*, 14: 113–125; Rooy, D.L., & Viswasvaran, C. 2004. Emotional intelligence: A meta-analytic investigation of predictive validity and nomonological net. *Journal of Vocational Behavior*, 65: 71–95.

126. Goleman, D. 1995. *Emotional intelligence*. New York: Bantam.

127. Locke, E.A. 2005. Why emotional intelligence is an invalid concept. *Journal of Organizational Behavior*, 26: 425–443.

128. Goleman, D. 2004. What makes a leader? *Harvard Business Review*, Jan. 2004: 82–91; Goleman, D. 1995, *Emotional intelligence*, New York: Bantam; Fineman, S. 2005. Appreciating emotion at work: Paradigm tensions. *International Journal of Work Organisation and Emotion*, 1: 4–19.

129. Locke, E.A. 2005. Why emotional intelligence is an invalid concept. *Journal of Organizational Behavior*, 26: 425–431; Murphy, K.R. (Ed.) 2006. *A critique of emotional intelligence: What are the problems and how can they be fixed?* Mahwah, NJ: Lawrence Erlbaum Associates; Fineman, S. 2005. Appreciating emotion at work: Paradigm tensions. *International Journal of Work Organisation and Emotion*, 1: 4–19.

work motivation

exploring behavior in action

exploring behavior in action
Work Motivation at W.L. Gore & Associates

knowledge objectives

After reading this chapter, you should be able to:

1. Define work motivation and explain why it is important to organizational success.

2. Discuss how managers can use Maslow's need hierarchy and ERG theory to motivate associates.

3. Describe how need for achievement, need for affiliation, and need for power relate to work motivation and performance.

4. Explain how Herzberg's two-factor theory of motivation has influenced current management practice.

5. Discuss the application of expectancy theory to motivation.

6. Understand equity theory and procedural justice, and discuss how fairness judgments influence work motivation.

7. Explain how goal-setting theory can be used to motivate associates.

8. Describe how jobs can be enriched and how job enrichment can enhance motivation.

9. Based on all major theories of work motivation, describe specific actions that can be taken to increase and sustain employee motivation.

On January 1, 1958, Wilbert and Genevieve Gore founded a small company to develop applications of polytetrafluoroethylene (PTFE). Wilbert, a chemist and research scientist, tended to the technical work while Genevieve handled accounting and other business matters.

Wilbert Gore initially focused on applications in the emerging computer industry, where PTFE's insulation characteristics were potentially useful in cables and circuit boards. After solving a number of technical issues, he and his company succeeded with cable and wire products. Some of these products eventually landed on the moon as part of the technology used in the Apollo space program. More recently, they have been incorporated into the U.S. space shuttle program. Moving beyond cables and wires, Gore has created a number of leading products for a number of industries. Best known among consumers for waterproof Gore-Tex fabrics, the company also places products in industries such as aerospace, automotive, chemical processing, computing, telecommunications, environmental protection, medical/health care, pharmaceutical, biotechnology, and textiles. Gore-Tex fabrics were used in the uniforms of the 2010 U.S. Olympic snowboarding team.

Having previously experienced bureaucratic roadblocks in highly structured organizations, Wilbert Gore designed a different kind of company to support the work with PTFE. Using the term *lattice structure* to signify an emphasis on informal communication and fluid work networks, he set up a company that focused on equality among people as well as freedom for those people to pursue their own ideas and projects. To a significant degree, individuals were and still are expected to define their own jobs within areas that interest them. Assigned sponsors help both new and existing Gore personnel with job definition.

Formal leadership assignments are less common at Gore than in more structured companies. Instead of formal assignments, Gore looks for individuals who have attracted "followers" for their ideas and projects. Thomas Malone, a professor at Massachusetts Institute of Technology, has studied the company and summarizes the approach as follows: "The way you become a [leader] is by finding people who want to work for you. … In a certain sense, you're elected rather than appointed. It's a democratic structure inside a business organization."

©Tyler Stableford/Stone/Getty Images

Culturally, four principles govern the behavior of individuals within W.L. Gore & Associates:

- The ability to make one's own commitments and keep them
- Freedom to encourage, help, and allow other associates to grow in knowledge, skill, and scope of responsibility
- Consultation with others before undertaking actions that could impact the reputation of the company
- Fairness to each other and everyone with whom contact is made

These structural and cultural features of the company set the stage for personal fulfillment and growth. The official Gore website puts it this way: "Everyone can quickly earn the credibility to define and drive projects. Sponsors help associates chart a course in the organization that will offer personal fulfillment while maximizing their contribution to the enterprise." Current CEO Terri Kelly said this: "We work hard at maximizing individual

potential … and cultivating an environment where creativity can flourish." He later stated that "Thanks largely to the pioneering corporate culture established by our founders … Gore is a place where innovation thrives and where every individual has the ability to contribute to the success of the enterprise … our culture is our biggest competitive advantage."

Of course, Gore is not for everyone. Individuals who work at the company must tolerate a certain amount of ambiguity and must thrive in autonomous settings. Moreover, they must value personal growth in the workplace. While many or even most individuals desire personal growth, some do not. Through rigorous selection procedures, Gore tends to find the right people. The result is a highly motivated and effective workforce.

The emphasis on fairness also affects motivation and effectiveness. In many companies, pay systems promote dysfunctional internal competition and jealousy. At W.L. Gore & Associates, the pay system tends to promote a sense of equity and justice. A key aspect of the system is the sponsor. Each individual at Gore has a sponsor, either a peer or a leader, who is responsible for ensuring fair pay. The sponsor collects information on contributions and achievements from an individual's peers and leaders and then shares this information with a compensation committee. Overall, Gore's approach can be summarized as follows: "Unlike companies which base an employee's pay on the evaluations of one or two people—or supervisors' opinions alone—Gore involves many [people] in the process. Our goal: internal fairness and external competitiveness."

Recognition and success have resulted from Gore's practices. For example, W.L. Gore & Associates has been listed for 12 consecutive years on the Fortune list of the "Best 100 Companies to Work For." It has also been listed as a top company for which to work in German, Italian, and British rankings, and indeed in rankings for the entire European Union. It has received awards for many technological breakthroughs. Financially, the privately held company has enjoyed consistently strong performance.

Going forward, the company seems poised for continued success. Today Gore has approximately 9,000 associates located in 30 countries worldwide, with manufacturing facilities in the United States, Germany, Scotland, Japan, and China and sales offices around the world. Their annual revenues are $2.5 billion. As it continues to grow, the company seems intent on maintaining its current structure and culture.

Sources: D. Anfuso. 1999. "Core Values Shape W.L. Gore's Innovative Culture," *Workforce,* 78 no. 3: 48–53; A. Deutschman. 2004. "The Fabric of Creativity," *Fast Company*, no. 89: 54–59; Gore & Associates, "Compensation," 2007, at http://www.gore.com/en_xx/careers/benefits/compensation.html; Gore & Associates, "Corporate Culture," 2007, at http://www.gore.com/en_xx/aboutus/culture/index.html; Gore & Associates, "Fast Facts," 2010, at http://www.gore.com/en_xx/aboutus/fastfacts/index.html; P. Kriger. 2006. "Power of the Individual," *Workforce Management,* 85, no. 4: 1–7; F. Shipper and C.C. Manz. 1993 "W.L. Gore & Associates, Inc.," Pinnacle Management Strategy Case Base; M. Weinreb. 2003. "Power to the People," *Sales and Marketing Management,* 155, no. 4: 30–35; W.L. Gore and Associates Press Release (Jan. 22, 2009), "W.L. Gore and Associates Marks 12th Year as One of Nation's Best," at http://www.gore.com/en_xx/news/FORTUNE2009.html; Gore and Associates, "About Us." at http://www.gore.com/en_xx/aboutus/index.html.

the strategic importance of Work Motivation

Formulating strategies that can deliver competitive advantage is not easy. Senior managers working with other individuals engage in countless conversations, meetings, experiments, and analyses in order to create or modify company strategies. Implementing strategies and engaging in the day-to-day behaviors that help to create competitive advantage also are not easy tasks. Hard work is involved. Managers and associates must be willing to deliver strong efforts if a firm is to succeed.[1]

With strong efforts being so important, work motivation is a crucial topic in any discussion of organizational behavior. People must be motivated if they are to effectively engage in the behaviors and practices that bring advantage and success to a firm.

It is important to note that different strategies require different types of people and behavior, and therefore different approaches to motivation. W.L. Gore has adopted a general strategy of differentiation based on innovation and creativity. Differentiating in this way requires people who can think differently, experiment in smart ways, accept responsibility, and appreciate the learning that accompanies failed efforts. The strategy also requires people who want to be challenged and grow in the workplace. To fully motivate such people, resources for trying new ideas must be made available, including time. Opportunities to develop new skills and polish old ones are important. Recognition for successes and pats on the back for strong efforts that unexpectedly did not bear fruit also might be useful. Pay, while important, often takes a backseat.

There are many ways to motivate people. Hence, there is no simple answer to the question of what managers should do to increase and sustain their associates' motivation. A great deal is known, however, about how people are motivated. In this chapter, we describe the major theories of work motivation and the practices that are most likely to increase and sustain strong efforts. We begin by formally defining what is meant by *motivation*. Next, we describe fundamental theories of work motivation, including both content and process theories. To synthesize these theories, we close the main body of the chapter by distilling useful management practices.

What Is Motivation?

Man and machine ... work in close harmony to achieve more than either could alone. Machines bring precision and capacity. They make our lives easier, perfect our processes, and in many ways, enrich our quality of life. But people possess something that machines don't—human spirit and inspiration. Our people work continuously at setting goals and tracking results for ongoing improvement as an overall business. They are an inspiration and their goals and accomplishments have won Branch-Smith Printing recognition on the highest of levels.[2]

This quotation from Branch-Smith Printing, a 2002 recipient of the Malcolm Baldrige National Quality Award, gets at the heart of motivation: it is the spirit and inspiration that leads people to apply their human capital to meet the goals of the organization. In Chapter 1, we discussed the strategic importance of human capital to the success of a firm. However, human capital alone is not enough to ensure behaviors that support organizational performance. Associates must translate their human capital into actions that result in performance important to the achievement of organizational goals. Motivation is the process through which this translation takes place.

Consider the following example. A manager has three assistants reporting to her. They have similar levels of experience and education. However, they have different levels of ability for the tasks at hand, and they perform at different levels. It is interesting that the person with the least ability has outperformed his counterparts. How can a person with less ability outperform individuals who have greater abilities? The answer may be that he is more motivated to apply his abilities than the others. The two other assistants are approximately equal to one another in their motivation to perform, judging by the fact that they work equally hard, and yet one of these assistants outperforms the other. How can this be when they are equally motivated? The answer may lie in their different ability levels. Thus, we can see that a person's level of performance is a function (f) of both ability and motivation:

$$\text{Performance} = f(\text{Ability} \times \text{Motivation})$$

Now consider another scenario. Two salespersons are equally motivated and have the same ability, yet one of them outperforms the other. How can we explain this, if performance is a function of ability and motivation? In this case, the better performer has a more lucrative sales territory than the other salesperson. Thus, environmental factors can also play a role in performance.

This brings us to our definition of work motivation. We know from the preceding discussion that ability and certain environmental factors exert influences on performance that are separate from the effects of motivation. **Motivation**, then, refers to forces coming from within a person that account for the willful direction, intensity, and persistence of the person's efforts toward achieving specific goals, where achievement is not due solely to ability or to environmental factors.[3] Several prominent theories offer explanations of motivation. Most of the theories can be separated into two groups: those concerned largely with content and those concerned largely with process. In the next two sections, we consider theories in each of these two groups.

motivation
Forces coming from within a person that account for the willful direction, intensity, and persistence of the person's efforts toward achieving specific goals, where achievement is not due solely to ability or to environmental factors.

Content Theories of Motivation

Content theories of motivation generally focus on identifying the specific factors that motivate people. These theories are, for the most part, straightforward. Four important content theories of motivation are Maslow's need hierarchy, Alderfer's ERG theory, McClelland's need theory, and Herzberg's two-factor theory.

Hierarchy of Needs Theory

One of the most popular motivation theories, frequently referred to as the **hierarchy of needs theory**, was proposed in the 1940s by Abraham Maslow.[4] According to Maslow, people are motivated by their desire to satisfy specific needs. Maslow arranged these needs in

hierarchy of needs theory
Maslow's theory that suggests people are motivated by their desire to satisfy specific needs, and that needs are arranged in a hierarchy with physiological needs at the bottom and self-actualization needs at the top. People must satisfy needs at lower levels before being motivated by needs at higher levels.

hierarchical order, with physiological needs at the bottom, followed by safety needs, social and belongingness needs, esteem needs, and, at the top, self-actualization needs. In general, lower-level needs must be substantially met before higher-level needs become important. Below, we look at each level and its theoretical implications in organizational settings.

1. *Physiological needs.* Physiological needs include basic survival needs—for water, food, air, and shelter. Most people must largely satisfy these needs before they become concerned with other, higher-order needs. Money is one organizational award that is potentially related to these needs, to the extent that it provides for food and shelter.

2. *Safety needs.* The second level of Maslow's hierarchy concerns individuals' needs to be safe and secure in their environment. These needs include the need for protection from physical or psychological harm. People at this level might consider their jobs as security factors and as a way to keep what they have acquired. These managers and associates might be expected to engage in low-risk job behaviors, such as following rules, preserving the status quo, and making career decisions based on security concerns.

3. *Social and belongingness needs.* Social needs involve interaction with and acceptance by other people. These needs include the desire for affection, affiliation, friendship, and love. Theoretically, people who reach this level have primarily satisfied physiological and safety needs and are now concerned with establishing satisfying relationships with other people. Although a great deal of satisfaction may come from family relationships, a job usually offers an additional source of relationships. Managers and associates at this level may thus seek supportive co-worker and peer-group relationships.

4. *Esteem needs.* Esteem needs relate to feelings of self-respect and self-worth, along with respect and esteem from peers. The desire for recognition, achievement, status, and power fits in this category. People at this level may be responsive to organizational recognition and awards programs and derive pleasure from having articles about them published in the company newsletter. Money and financial rewards may also help satisfy esteem needs, because they provide signals of people's "worth" to the organization.

©Ryan McVay/Getty Images, Inc.

5. *Self-actualization needs.* A person's need for self-actualization represents her desire to fulfill her potential, maximizing the use of her skills and abilities. People at the self-actualization level are less likely to respond to the types of rewards described for the first four levels. They accept their own achievements and seek new opportunities to use their unique skills and talents. They often are highly motivated by work assignments that challenge these skills, and they might even reject common rewards (salary increase, promotion) that could distract them from using their primary skills. Only a few people are assumed to reach this level.

As mentioned, these needs are arranged in hierarchical order, with physiological needs the lowest and self-actualization the highest. According to Maslow's theory, each need is prepotent over all higher-level needs until it has been satisfied. A prepotent need is one that predominates over other needs. For example, a person at the social and belongingness level will be most concerned with rewards provided by meaningful relationships and will not be so concerned with esteem-related rewards, such as public recognition or large bonuses. It follows that a satisfied need is no longer a motivator. For example, after a person's social needs are met, she will no longer be concerned with developing and maintaining relationships but will instead be motivated to seek esteem-related rewards. The need hierarchy theory is supposed to apply to all normal, healthy people in a similar way.

The need hierarchy theory has not been well supported by empirical research.[5] Research has indicated that a two-level hierarchy of lower-order and higher-order needs may exist, but it has not found much support for the five specific need categories proposed by Maslow. One reason for this finding may be the context of the studies. Most people in the United States, where the studies typically have been done, have satisfied their basic needs and are faced with a complex system of means to satisfy their higher-order ones. It may be difficult for researchers to separate the needs these people experience into the five specific categories proposed by Maslow.

In addition, the idea of prepotency has been questioned.[6] Some researchers have noted that several needs may be important at the same time. For example, a person can simultaneously have strong social, esteem, and self-actualization needs. Even Maslow's clinical studies showed that the idea of prepotency is not relevant for all individuals.[7]

A final problem with the need hierarchy theory involves a practical concern. It is difficult to determine the present need level for each associate and the exact rewards that would help satisfy that associate's specific needs. For example, a person's concern with being popular with co-workers may be related to either social and belongingness needs or esteem needs (or both). Being popular can mean that one is liked, but it can also mean that one has high status in the group. If a manager is attempting to diagnose the meaning behind a person's desire to be popular, she could make an erroneous judgment. As another example, money can be used to meet both physiological and esteem needs, but it may not have the desired effect in all cases where esteem is the key issue. In general, it is challenging for managers to apply the need hierarchy to motivate associates.

Although the need hierarchy theory has many weaknesses, it is historically important because it focused attention on people's esteem and self-actualization needs. Previously, behaviorism had been the dominant approach to understanding human motivation. As you may recall, behaviorism proposes that people's behaviors are motivated solely by extrinsic rewards. The need hierarchy, in contrast, suggests that the behavior of many people is motivated by needs reflecting a human desire to be recognized and to grow as an individual. Beyond its historical significance, the need hierarchy also continues to guide some research in fields such as humanistic psychology.[8]

ERG Theory

ERG theory, developed by Clayton Alderfer, is similar to Maslow's need hierarchy theory in that it also proposes need categories.[9] However, it includes only three categories: existence needs (E), relatedness needs (R), and growth needs (G). The relationship of these categories to those of Maslow's need hierarchy theory is shown in Exhibit 6-1. As you can see in the exhibit, existence needs are similar to Maslow's physiological and safety needs,

ERG theory
Alderfer's theory that suggests people are motivated by three hierarchically ordered types of needs: existence needs (E), relatedness needs (R), and growth needs (G). A person may work on all three needs at the same time, although satisfying lower-order needs often takes place before a person is strongly motivated by higher-level needs.

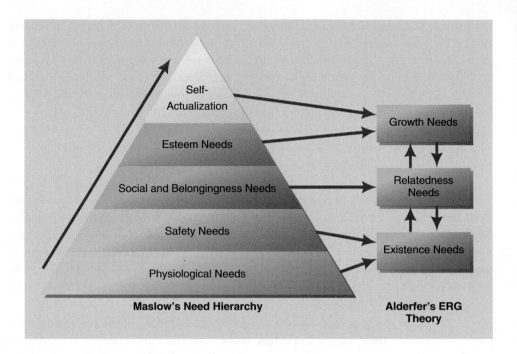

Exhibit 6-1 Maslow's Need Hierarchy and Alderfer's ERG Theory Compared

relatedness needs are similar to Maslow's social and belongingness needs, and growth needs are similar to Maslow's needs for esteem and self-actualization. Growth needs are particularly important in an organization such as W.L. Gore & Associates.

ERG theory differs from Maslow's theory in two important ways. First, the notion of prepotency is not fixed in ERG theory. A person's existence needs do not necessarily have to be satisfied before she can become concerned about her relationships with others or about using her personal capabilities. Her desire to meet the existence needs may be stronger than her desire to meet the two other types of needs, but the other needs may still be important. The need hierarchy theory proposes that the hierarchy is fixed and that physiological needs must be largely satisfied before other needs become important.

Second, even when a need is satisfied, it may remain the dominant motivator if the next need in the hierarchy cannot be satisfied. For instance, if a person has satisfied his relatedness needs but is frustrated in trying to satisfy his growth needs, his desire for relatedness needs again becomes strong (recall that a satisfied need is no longer a motivator in the need hierarchy theory). Alderfer called this the frustration-regression process.[10] Thus, it is possible that a need may never cease to be a motivator. An associate who has many friends and is very well liked may continue to seek friends and social approval if frustrated in satisfying growth needs. Understanding this is important for managers because it may provide them with the reasons for a person's behavior.

ERG theory has more research support than Maslow's hierarchy of needs. For example, some research has found evidence for the meaningfulness of the three categories of needs.[11] Support has also been found for several of Alderfer's basic propositions, such as the concept that a satisfied need may remain a motivator.[12] Indeed, relatedness and growth needs have been found to increase as they are satisfied. In other words, the more they are satisfied, the more they are desired. However, more research on ERG theory is necessary to test its usefulness under different conditions. In general, ERG theory may be viewed as a refinement of the need hierarchy theory.[13]

Theory of Achievement, Affiliation, and Power

A third theory, largely developed by David McClelland, also uses need classifications and focuses on the needs for achievement, affiliation, and power. Some have referred to these as learned needs because they are influenced by cultural background and can be acquired over time.[14] The three needs are also viewed as independent, meaning a person can be high or low on any one or all three needs. Although all three needs are important, the need for achievement has received the most attention from researchers because of its prominent organizational effects.[15]

Need for Achievement

Need for achievement, first discussed in Chapter 5, was originally defined by McClelland and his colleagues as a "desire to perform well against a standard of excellence."[16] People with a high need for achievement feel good about themselves when surpassing a standard that is meaningful to them. Further, people with a high need for achievement prefer to set their own goals rather than to have no goals or to accept the goals set for them by others. Specifically:

need for achievement
The need to perform well against a standard of excellence.

- They tend to set goals of moderate difficulty that are achievable.
- They like to solve problems rather than leave the results to chance. They are more interested in achieving the goal than in the formal rewards they may receive, although they recognize the value of their inputs and tend to earn good incomes.
- They prefer situations in which they receive regular, concrete feedback on their performance.[17]
- They are positive thinkers who find workable solutions to life's hurdles and challenges.[18]
- They assume strong personal responsibility for their work.

Some consider the achievement motive to be a component of self-actualization.[19] Consistent with this belief, people high on need for achievement tend to do well in challenging jobs but do less well in boring or routine jobs. In a study of sales and sales support personnel, individuals with high achievement needs had positive outcomes only when occupying more demanding, technically oriented roles.[20] Related to this finding, people who aspire to be entrepreneurs frequently have a high need for achievement.[21] Also, managers who have high achievement needs tend to manage differently relative to those who have lower achievement needs because of a more pronounced goal orientation.[22]

Although need for achievement is thought to be a relatively stable characteristic in adults, it is possible to train adults to increase their need for achievement. This training includes the following steps:[23]

1. Teach people how to think like persons with a high need for achievement. This includes teaching people how to imagine the achievement of desired goals and mentally rehearse the steps necessary to reach those goals.

2. Teach and encourage people to set challenging but realistic work-related goals.

3. Give people concrete feedback about themselves and their performance. Ensure that people are knowledgeable about their behavior and its outcomes.

4. Create *esprit de corps*.

In organizations such as W.L. Gore & Associates, people with high achievement needs are generally positive. Such people, however, can react negatively to the ambiguity found in these organizations. Without reasonably clear pathways to success, high achievement needs can go unmet in any given time period.

Need for Affiliation

need for affiliation
The need to be liked and to stay on good terms with most other people.

People with a high **need for affiliation** have a strong desire to be liked and to stay on good terms with most other people. Affiliative people tend not to make good managers. They are more concerned with initiating and maintaining personal relationships than with focusing on the task at hand. In one study, managers of product development units were assessed. Those with high needs for affiliation were seen as less influential and as having less-influential units. They also had units with weaker innovation profiles.[24]

Need for affiliation is a particularly important consideration in today's world, where working from home as virtual contributors is common. About 17 percent of the U.S. workforce works from home at least two days per week. At IBM, 42 percent of the workforce works from home, on the road, or at a client location. Significant percentages of people work virtually at Sun Microsystems, Convergys, and many other companies.

Without daily contact with other associates or managers, individuals with strong affiliation needs might have difficulty developing strong relations and assessing how well they are liked. They may be particularly prone to feelings of isolation and dissatisfaction. To combat these and other issues, companies that rely heavily on virtual contributors have introduced a host of technologies and practices. To ensure satisfied and productive workers, they generally have provided key technologies that help people stay connected, such as laptops, Internet access, and a personal digital assistant. Many companies also support instant messaging and provide sophisticated collaboration software. Companies such as Sun Microsystems, Ernst & Young, and Deloitte & Touche designate office and conference space for associates who occasionally stop in. Also, some managers insist on face-to-face team meetings every now and then.[25]

Need for Power

need for power
The desire to influence people and events.

The **need for power** can be defined as the desire to influence people and events. According to McClelland, there are two types of need for power: one that is directed toward the good of the organization (*institutional power*) and one that is directed toward the self (*personal power*).[26] People high in the need for institutional power want to influence others for altruistic reasons—they are concerned about the functioning of the organization and have a desire to serve others. They are also more controlled in their exercise of power. In contrast, those high in the need for personal power desire to influence others for their own personal gain. They are more impulsive in exercising power, show little concern for other people, and are focused on obtaining symbols of prestige and status (such as big offices).

Research has shown that a high need for institutional power is critical for high-performing managers. People with a high need for institutional power are particularly good at increasing morale, creating clear expectations, and influencing others to work for the good of the organization. Need for institutional power seems to be more important than need for achievement in creating managerial success,[27] although blending both is perhaps better than having one or the other.

As discussed in the *Managerial Advice* feature, the Hay Group has conducted a great deal of research on managers' needs. Its consultants apply this work in the firm's well-regarded global consulting practice. Importantly, Hay research shows that a strong need for achievement can create problems. Such problems, however, are less likely to occur when a

Managers over the Edge

The Hay Group, an internationally renowned consulting firm, studies managers' needs for achievement, affiliation, and power. Through its McClelland Center, it continues the work that David McClelland began many years ago.

In a recent report, the organization identified changes in the needs of tens of thousands of managers, most of them from the United States. In terms of average strength, need for achievement exhibited a substantial increase from the mid-1980s, with most of the increase occurring after 1995. Moreover, it became by far the strongest need. Need for affiliation exhibited little change during the key time period, but slipped from the strongest to the second strongest need. Need for power weakened and then strengthened over the time period. Overall, the average strength of this need exhibited little net change, ending the time period close to where it began. In terms of rank, it settled into a distant third place.

While increased need for achievement among managers implies many positive behaviors and outcomes, very high levels of this need can create problems for two reasons. First, a strong achievement need in a manager can set the stage for coercive tendencies, particularly when this need is paired with relatively weak needs for affiliation and institutional power. These coercive tendencies result from the manager wanting to achieve at

any cost while having limited needs to be liked and to build engaged associates. Hay research on IBM managers showed these tendencies in action. High-need-for-achievement managers with lower needs for affiliation and institutional power produced inferior work climates through less delegation, less effort in connecting associates' work to the overall strategy and mission of the organization, more command-and-control behaviors, and more instances of taking over work that should be done by others.

Second, a strong achievement need can set the stage for shortcuts and illicit actions, all in the name of achievement. Again, this is of most concern when high need for achievement is paired with relatively weak needs for affiliation and institutional power. Hay researchers cite Jeffery Skilling as a relevant example. Skilling was sentenced to prison for his role in the fall of Enron.

Scott Spreier, a senior consultant with The Hay Group; Mary Fontaine, a vice president at Hay; and Ruth Malloy, director of research at Hay's McClelland Center recently provided a set of guidelines designed to help high-achievement managers avoid problems.

- **Understand needs**. Without explicitly understanding their own personal needs in the workplace, managers cannot manage those needs. Understanding needs can

©Stockbyte/Getty Images, Inc.

be accomplished by simply thinking about valued activities and outcomes or by using available assessment tools (one popular tool will be presented in this chapter's installment of *Building Your Human Capital*).

- **Manage needs**. Having gained awareness of their needs, managers can take actions to handle them effectively. A manager with quite a strong achievement need might ask a trusted colleague to monitor his behavior for coercion. Such a manager might also seek training focused on the benefits of delegation and an empowered workforce. Finally, she might channel some of the need for achievement into nonwork pursuits (e.g., competitive golf).

Sources: Hay Group, "About Hay Group," 2007, at http://www.haygroup.com/ww/About/Index.asp?id=495; Hay Group, "A Recent Rise in Achievement Drive among Today's Executives," 2006, at http://www.haygroup.com/ww/Media/index.asp; Hay Group, "The McClelland Center Fact Sheet," 2002, at http://www.haygroup.com/wwResearch/Detail.asp?PageID=703; S.W. Spreier, M.H. Fontaine, & R.L. Malloy. 2006. "Leadership Run Amok: The Destructive Potential of Overachievers," *Harvard Business Review*, 84, no. 6: 72–82.

strong achievement need is blended and balanced with a significant need for institutional power and perhaps also with some level of need for affiliation.

Two-Factor Theory

two-factor theory
Herzberg's motivation theory that suggests that job satisfaction and dissatisfaction are not opposite ends of the same continuum but are independent states and that different factors affect satisfaction and dissatisfaction.

The **two-factor theory** (sometimes called the *dual-factor theory*) is based on the work of Frederick Herzberg.[28] It has some similarities to the other need theories, but it focuses more on the rewards or outcomes of performance that satisfy individuals' needs. The two-factor theory emphasizes two sets of rewards or outcomes—those related to job satisfaction and those related to job dissatisfaction. This theory of motivation suggests that satisfaction and dissatisfaction are not opposite ends of the same continuum but are independent states. In other words, the opposite of high job satisfaction is not high job dissatisfaction; rather, it is low job satisfaction. Likewise, the opposite of high dissatisfaction is low dissatisfaction. It follows that the job factors leading to satisfaction are different from those leading to dissatisfaction, and vice versa. Furthermore, receiving excess quantities of a factor thought to decrease dissatisfaction will not produce satisfaction, nor will increasing satisfaction factors overcome dissatisfaction.

motivators
Job factors that can influence job satisfaction but not dissatisfaction.

The factors related to job satisfaction have been called *satisfiers,* or **motivators**. These are factors that, when increased, will lead to greater levels of satisfaction. They include:

- Achievement
- Recognition
- Responsibility
- Opportunity for advancement or promotion
- Challenging work
- Potential for personal growth

hygienes
Job factors that can influence job dissatisfaction but not satisfaction.

The factors related to dissatisfaction have been called dissatisfies, or **hygienes**. When these factors are deficient, dissatisfaction will increase. However, providing greater amounts of these factors will not lead to satisfaction—only to less dissatisfaction. Hygiene factors include:

- Pay
- Technical supervision
- Working conditions
- Company policies, administration, and procedures
- Interpersonal relationships with peers, supervisors, and subordinates
- Status
- Security

Research has not generally supported Herzberg's two-factor theory.[29] One criticism is that the theory is method-bound—meaning that support can be found for the theory only when Herzberg's particular methodology is used. Researchers using different methodologies to test the theory have not found support. A second criticism is that the theory confuses job satisfaction and motivation. As discussed in Chapter 5, job satisfaction does not always lead to increased motivation. Happy associates are not always motivated associates. The causal path can also go the other way—with motivation, and consequently performance, influencing satisfaction—or there may be no relationship at all. A third criticism is that motivators and hygienes may not be uniquely different. For example, some factors, such as pay, can affect both satisfaction and dissatisfaction. Pay can help satisfy basic food and shelter needs (hygiene), but it can also provide recognition (motivator).

Despite the criticisms of two-factor theory, managers tend to find it appealing. Indeed, Herzberg's 1965 *Harvard Business Review* article on this theory was reprinted in a more recent *Harvard Business Review* volume (January 2003), indicating that these ideas continue to be popular with managers. At a practical level, the theory is easy to understand and apply. To motivate associates, managers should provide jobs that include potential for achievement and responsibility. They should also try to maintain the hygiene factors at an appropriate level to prevent dissatisfaction. Thus, managers can motivate associates by manipulating job-content factors and can prevent associate dissatisfaction by manipulating the job context or environment.

Perhaps the most important managerial conclusion is that organizations should not expect high productivity in jobs that are weak in motivators, no matter how much they invest in hygienes. Simply providing good working conditions and pay may not result in consistently high performance. Thus, managers now give much more attention to how jobs are designed. Indeed, Herzberg's work helped launch the current focus on enriched jobs that emphasize responsibility, variety, and autonomy. This focus is consistent with high-involvement management, a key theme of our book.

Conclusions Regarding Content Theories

The four content theories we have just discussed address the factors that affect motivation. These factors include associates' needs and the various job and contextual attributes that might help them meet these needs. All four theories are popular among managers because each has an intuitive logic and is easy to understand. Although research support for the theories has not been strong overall, the theories have been useful in developing specific managerial practices that increase motivation and performance. Further, these theories can be integrated with process theories, discussed next.

Process Theories of Motivation

Whereas content theories emphasize the *factors* that motivate, process theories are concerned with the *process* by which such factors interact to produce motivation. One of the weaknesses of content theories is the assumption that motivation can be explained by only one or two factors, such as a given need or the content of a job. As we have seen, human motivation is much more complex than that. In most cases, several conditions interact to produce motivated behavior. Process theories take this complexity into account. Process theories generally focus on the cognitive processes in which people engage to influence the direction, intensity, and persistence of their behavior. Three important process theories of motivation are expectancy theory, equity theory, and goal-setting theory.

Expectancy Theory

The first process theory to recognize the effects of multiple, complex sources of motivation was Victor Vroom's **expectancy theory**.[30] Expectancy theory suggests that managers and associates consider three factors in deciding whether to exert effort.

expectancy theory
Vroom's theory that suggests that motivation is a function of an individual's expectancy that a given amount of effort will lead to a particular level of performance, instrumentality judgments that indicate performance will lead to certain outcomes, and the valences of outcomes.

expectancy
The subjective probability that a given amount of effort will lead to a particular level of performance.

First, they consider the probability that a given amount of effort will lead to a particular level of performance. For example, an associate might consider the probability that working on a report for an extra four hours will lead to a significant improvement in that report. This probability is referred to as an **expectancy**.

The second factor individuals consider is the perceived connection between a particular level of performance and important outcomes. For example, the associate cited above would consider the potential outcomes of a better report. She may believe there is a strong positive connection between a better report and (1) praise from her supervisor and (2) interesting future assignments. In other words, she may perceive that good performance makes these outcomes very likely. She may also believe that there is a weak positive connection between a better report and an increase in pay, meaning she believes that good performance makes this outcome only slightly more likely to occur. Overall, she is interested in the effects of good performance on three outcomes. Each perceived connection between performance and an outcome is referred to as an **instrumentality**.

instrumentality
Perceived connections between performance and outcomes.

The third factor is the importance of each anticipated outcome. In our example, the associate may believe that more praise from her boss, better assignments, and an increase in pay would bring her a great deal of satisfaction. As a result, these outcomes have high valence. **Valence** is defined as the value placed on an outcome.

valence
Value associated with an outcome.

In essence, expectancy theory suggests that people are rational when deciding whether to expend a given level of effort. The following equation formally states how people implement expectancy theory:

$$MF = E \times \Sigma (I \times V)$$

where:

MF = Motivational force.

E = Expectancy, or the subjective probability that a given level of effort will lead to a particular level of performance. It can range from 0 to +1. Further, the expectancy of interest usually corresponds to the probability that strong effort will result in good performance.[31] Thus, an expectancy of zero means that an individual thinks there is no chance that strong effort will lead to good performance. An expectancy of one means that an individual thinks it is certain that strong effort will lead to good performance. For a given person in a given situation, self-esteem, previous experience with the task, and availability of help from a manager can influence this subjective probability.[32]

I = Instrumentality, or the perceived connection between a particular level of performance and an outcome. Instrumentality can range from −1 to +1, because it is possible for a performance level to make an outcome less likely as well as make an outcome more likely. For example, an instrumentality of −.8 indicates that an individual expects that performing at a particular level would make an outcome very unlikely (e.g., praise from co-workers might be unlikely because of jealousy).

V = Valence, or the value associated with an outcome. Valence can be negative or positive, because some outcomes may be undesirable while others are desirable.

Exhibit 6-2 illustrates the expectancy theory process.

As an example, consider a car salesman who is considering the possibility of selling 15 automobiles next month. Would he attempt to sell that many cars? Assume that our salesman believes there is a .7 probability that strong effort would result in the desired performance. Also, assume that he perceives the following connections between performance

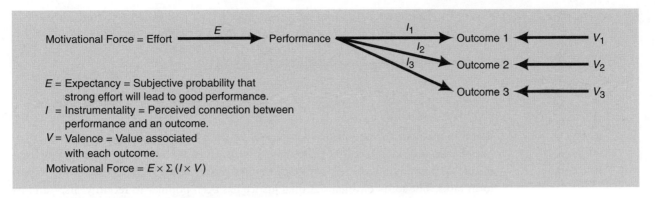

Exhibit 6-2 Expectancy Theory

and four key outcomes: +.9 for a $1,000 bonus, +.8 for strong praise from his managers, +.9 for high intrinsic satisfaction, and −.7 for meaningful praise from co-workers.[33] Finally, assume valences for these outcomes of 5, 3, 4, and 1 (on a scale from 1 to 5, where 1 means not valued at all and 5 means highly valued). Based on these beliefs and perceptions, our salesman probably would be motivated to attempt to sell the automobiles. He believes there is a good chance that his strong effort would result in success (expectancy of .7), and he perceives strong positive connections between performance and three valued outcomes (instrumentalities of .9, .8, and .9) while perceiving a strong negative connection to a nonvalued outcome (−.7) (he perceives that success probably would yield no praise, and perhaps even scorn, from co-workers, but he does not care).

Another example of expectancy theory in action is a study of over 400 police officers' productivity in terms of drug arrests.[34] This study found that officers who made the most arrests were more likely to have: (1) received specialized training in drug interdiction, and perceived that they had sufficient time in their shift to properly investigate suspected drug offenses (high expectancies); (2) perceived that drug arrests were rewarded by their agency (high instrumentality); and (3) perceived that management saw drug enforcement as a priority (high valence).

Research has generally been supportive of expectancy theory.[35] Criticisms, however, have been expressed concerning how the components of expectancy theory are measured, how they should be combined, and the impact of individual differences. For example, it has been shown that all three components of expectancy theory predict motivation better when they are considered together than when any one component is examined alone. However, the three components do not appear to have equal strength in affecting motivation. That is, the desirability of outcomes may be the most important element in the equation. Not surprisingly, valence seems to be most important.[36] Another issue results from consideration of individual differences. For example, people who have high consideration of others are less likely to engage in the rational, outcome-maximizing decision-making processes underlying expectancy theory.[37] Although subsequent research has led to revised versions of Vroom's original model, the basic components remain the same.[38]

Expectancy theory has clear implications for managers. In order to increase motivation, managers can do one or more of the following:

• Heighten expectancy by increasing associates' beliefs that strong effort will lead to higher levels of performance.

- Increase instrumentalities by clearly linking high performance to outcomes.
- Increase valence by providing outcomes that are highly valued.

We discuss specific procedures later in this chapter.

Equity Theory

The notion of fairness and justice has been of concern to human beings throughout written history and undoubtedly before that as well. Thus, it should not be surprising that people's perception of how fairly they are being treated influences their motivation to perform tasks. The study of organizational justice has been popular in recent years,[39] and its popularity is likely to continue with the increasing incidence of corporate scandals (such as those involving Enron and Arthur Andersen) and discrimination lawsuits.[40] Further, the concept of equity has taken on added importance with the demands by minority groups and women for equitable treatment on the job.[41]

equity theory
A theory that suggests motivation is based on a person's assessment of the ratio of outcomes she receives (e.g., pay, status) for inputs on the job (e.g., effort, ability) compared to the same ratio for a comparison other.

The basic model for using the fairness concept to explain human motivation comes from J. Stacey Adams's **equity theory**.[42] According to this theory, motivation is based on a person's assessment of the ratio of outcomes she receives (e.g., pay, status) for inputs on the job (e.g., effort, ability) compared with the same ratio for a comparison other, frequently a co-worker. Thus, in assessing equity, the person makes the following comparison:

$$\frac{\text{My Outcomes}}{\text{My Inputs}} \text{ vs. } \frac{\text{Other's Outcomes}}{\text{Other's Inputs}}$$

After making the comparison, the person forms equity perceptions. Based on the perceptions of equity or the lack of it, people make *choices* about the action to take (e.g., how much effort to exert to perform the task). Equity exists when the person's ratio of outcomes to inputs is equal to that of the other person, and inequity exists when the ratios are not equal. Inequity may result, for example, when one person is paid more than the other for the same inputs or when one person provides less input for the same pay. Note that an individual may compare his outcome/input ratio to the average ratio of several other people, but often the comparison is to one other person.

When individuals perceive inequity, they can reduce it in several ways. Consider the following tactics (pay is the focus here, but other inputs can affect perceptions of inequity):

- *Increasing or decreasing inputs.* Underpaid associates could decrease their effort, whereas overpaid associates could increase their effort to resolve inequity. This reaction to inequity demonstrates how equity perceptions can influence motivation.
- *Changing their outcomes.* If underpaid associates convince their supervisor to increase their pay, inequity is resolved. It is less likely, but possible, that overpaid workers would seek a salary reduction. However, they may seek to reduce or give up other outcomes, such as not taking interesting assignments or taking a less desirable office.
- *Distorting perceptions of their inputs and outcomes.* If it is not possible to actually change inputs or outcomes, inequitably paid associates may distort their perceptions of the situation. One common erroneous perception by underpaid workers is that their jobs offer many psychological benefits. Overpaid workers often believe they are working much harder than they actually are.

- *Distorting perceptions of the inputs or outcomes of the referent other.* This is similar to distorting perceptions of one's own inputs and outcomes to resolve inequity. For example, if an associate feels she is underpaid compared to her co-worker, she can reason that the co-worker really does stay late more often or has a degree from a better school and thereby the co-worker has higher inputs.
- *Changing the referent other.* If an associate perceives inequity in comparison to one co-worker, it may be easiest to find a co-worker who compares more favorably.
- *Leaving the organization.* In cases where inequity is resistant to other forms of resolution, associates may be motivated to resign from the organization and seek a more equitable situation elsewhere.

Research generally suggests that inequity is an important concept.[43] For example, some individuals have been found to respond to overpayment by increasing their effort and performance.[44] When these individuals believe they are being paid more than they deserve, they increase their inputs to bring them into balance with outcomes. In general, different individuals have been found to react differently to inequity. *Sensitives* are individuals who pay a great deal of attention to outcome/input ratios and are motivated to resolve any inequity, whether the inequity is favorable or unfavorable to them. *Benevolents* are tolerant of inequity that is unfavorable but are not comfortable with inequity that favors them. *Entitleds* do not tolerate unfavorable inequity but are comfortable with inequity that favors them.[45] In the overall population, many people exhibit behavior that seems consistent with the entitleds.

Professional athletes provide interesting case studies for the inequity concept, as indicated by frequent headlines telling us that some "star" is upset about his compensation. These highly paid athletes evidently feel that their outcome/input ratios—their salaries compared with their contributions to their teams—do not measure up to those of similar athletes in the same sport. In 2001, Alex Rodriguez, a young and talented professional baseball player, agreed to a 10-year, $252 million contract to play for the Texas Rangers. Even in the era of exceptional salaries for professional sports figures, this amount seemed almost outrageous. The contract provided Rodriguez, known as A-Rod to his fans, $25.2 million annually. However, that is not all. If by chance anyone in professional baseball negotiated a higher salary in the 10 years of his contract, A-Rod would be given that figure plus $1. In other words, his contract guaranteed that he would be the highest-paid professional baseball player for a decade.[46] Yet, partly because of this very high compensation level, he was traded to the New York Yankees, where he has had both good times and bad.[47]

Perceptions of inequity have several important effects in the workplace.[48] For example, research has found that feelings of inequity can lead to negative employee behaviors such as theft and revenge.[49] On the positive side, feelings of equity frequently lead to outcome satisfaction and job satisfaction,[50] organizational commitment,[51] and organizational citizenship behaviors.[52] *Organizational citizenship behavior* refers to an associate's willingness to engage in organizationally important behaviors that go beyond prescribed job duties, such as helping co-workers with their work or expending extra effort to bring positive publicity to the organization.[53]

Perceptions of inequity often are defined in terms of **distributive justice**, a form of justice that relates to perceptions of fairness in outcomes. Another type of justice is also important, however. **Procedural justice** is the degree to which procedures used to determine outcomes seem fair.[54] Research shows that when outcomes are unfavorable, people

distributive justice
The degree to which people think outcomes are fair.

procedural justice
The degree to which people think the procedures used to determine outcomes are fair.

are likely to be concerned with the fairness used in determining those outcomes.[55] People will be less likely to have negative reactions to unfavorable or questionable outcomes when they perceive that procedures used to arrive at the outcomes are fair. Procedures based on the following rules are more likely to be perceived as fair:[56]

- People should feel that they have a voice in the decision process. For example, good performance-appraisal systems allow associates to provide input into the evaluation process.
- Procedures should be applied consistently. For example, the same criteria should be used to decide on everyone's pay increase.
- Procedures should be free from bias.
- Procedures should be based on accurate information.
- A mechanism should be in place for correcting faulty outcome decisions. Such mechanisms sometimes involve formal grievance procedures.
- Procedures should conform to the prevailing ethical code.
- People should be treated with respect.
- People should be given reasons for the decisions. For example, survivors of a layoff are much more likely to remain motivated if the reasons for the layoff are explained.[57] Overall, equity and procedural-justice concepts can help managers understand associates' reactions to decisions about rewards. As discussed earlier, individuals at W.L. Gore & Associates have already mastered the use of equity and procedural justice.

Goal-Setting Theory

goal-setting theory
A theory that suggests challenging and specific goals increase human performance because they affect attention, effort, and persistence.

Goal-setting theory, developed by Edwin Locke, posits that goals enhance human performance because they direct attention and affect effort and persistence.[58] Given the nature of human beings, individuals are likely to be committed to the achievement of goals after they have been set and to exert effort toward goal attainment.[59] Indeed, goals serve as reference points that energize behavior.[60] The positive effects of goals on work motivation is one of the strongest findings in research on organizational behavior. Goal setting has been found to increase the motivation of associates in a multitude of jobs, such as air traffic controllers, truck drivers, faculty researchers, marine recruits, managers, social workers, nurses, research and development workers, truck maintenance workers, and weightlifters.[61] To effectively set goals for associates, managers should address several factors, including goal difficulty, goal specificity, goal commitment, participation in goal setting, and feedback:

- *Goal difficulty.* How difficult should the performance goal be? Should the goal be easy, moderately difficult, or very difficult to achieve?
- *Goal specificity.* How specific should the expected outcome be (e.g., number of parts assembled), or can goals be more loosely defined (do your best)?
- *Goal commitment.* What will make associates commit to goals?
- *Participation in setting goals.* How important is it for associates to have input in selecting the goals and levels of performance to be achieved? If important, how should they be involved?
- *Feedback.* To what extent should associates be informed of their progress as they work toward the performance goals?

Goal Difficulty

From the perspective of expectancy theory and achievement motivation theory, we might expect that associates exert the maximum effort at work when their performance goals are set at moderate levels of difficulty (i.e., somewhat difficult but achievable). Goals that are too difficult may be rejected by associates because the expectancy is low (strong effort would not lead to goal attainment). A number of researchers, however, have found that associates exert more effort when they have goals that are difficult to a significant degree. This has been found to be true of engineers and scientists, loggers, and many experimental subjects working on a variety of tasks in laboratory settings.[62] Thus, it seems that goals should be as difficult as possible, but not unreasonable. Stretch goals that are extremely difficult can be quite demotivating.

Goal Specificity

Performance goals can be explicitly stated, clear in meaning, and specific in terms of quantity or quality of performance. For example, a goal might be to "generate twenty-seven pages of edited copy with an error rate of less than one error per ten pages in each work period" or "make twelve new customer contacts each month." The nature of some tasks, however, makes it difficult to clearly determine and state the exact performance levels that should be achieved. In such cases, a performance goal can be stated only in vague terms, such as "do your best" or "increase sales during the month."

Many studies have shown that specific goals lead to better performance than do vague goals, such as "do your very best."[63] If a goal is to act as a motivator, it must establish a specific target toward which people can direct their effort. Managers are likely to find this aspect of setting goals to be challenging because many jobs involve activities that are difficult to specify. For example, it may be difficult for a manager to be specific about an engineer's goals; yet the manager must make the attempt, or the engineer's motivation could be adversely affected.

Goal Commitment

In general, associates must accept and be committed to reaching externally set goals for these goals to be motivating. A great deal of research has been conducted on the factors that influence people's commitment to externally set goals. Expectancy theory provides a useful framework for organizing these factors; people will be committed to goals that: (1) carry a reasonable expectation of being attained and (2) are viewed as desirable to attain.[64] A summary of the factors that can affect goal commitment is presented in Exhibit 6-3.

Participation in Setting Goals

A practical question for a manager, especially during performance-counseling sessions with associates, is, "Should I set performance goals for the associate on the basis of my own knowledge and judgment of her abilities, or should I allow the associate to provide input and have some degree of control over them?" Importantly, associates who participate in setting a goal rather than having it dictated to them might be more satisfied with the goal and be more committed to it, resulting in stronger performance.[65] While some researchers have failed to find a relationship between participation in goal setting and performance,[66] others have found that performance is better when associates participate in setting goals.[67] Also, as discussed earlier, individuals with high achievement needs tend to dislike assigned goals.

EXHIBIT 6-3 Factors Affecting Goal Commitment

Factors Increasing the Desirability of Attaining a Given Goal

1. The goal is set by or in conjunction with an appropriate authority figure.
2. The goal fosters a sense of self-achievement and potential for development.
3. The goal is set by or in conjunction with someone who is trustworthy.
4. The goal is set by or in conjunction with someone who is supportive and promotes self-efficacy.
5. Peers are committed to the goal.
6. The goal assigner, if there is one, provides a rationale for the goal.
7. The goal provides a challenge to prove oneself and meets ego needs.
8. The goal is public.

Factors Increasing the Perceived Ability of Attaining a Given Goal

1. There is high self-efficacy on the task.
2. There are successful role models.
3. The task is not impossibly difficult.
4. Expectancy for success is high.
5. There is competition with others.

Source: Based on E.A. Locke, & G.P. Latham. 1990. *A Theory of Goal Setting and Task Motivation* (Englewood Cliffs, NJ: Prentice Hall).

Subconscious Goals

Some management research has demonstrated that goals do not have to be consciously assigned to influence motivation and performance.[68] That is, people do not need to be consciously aware that they have been given a goal in order for the goal to influence their behavior. Studies examining this phenomenon usually use supraliminal priming to assign goals. Supraliminal priming involves consciously providing people with achievement information, but in a manner that appears to be unrelated to the task that they are about to perform.[69] For example, people may be asked to circle words in a large matrix of letters or they may be asked to unscramble words to make sentences. Those who are being assigned goals are given words or sentences having to do with motivation and achievement ("win" or "the man will succeed"), along with other neutral words or sentences. Later they are asked to perform some task. Research has found that those who are primed with achievement goals outperform those who are not primed with goals[70] and that this effect can last quite awhile.[71] It appears that subconsciously primed goals lead people to set higher self-set goals than do non-goal-oriented primes.[72] This line of research is still very new and most of it has been conducted in the laboratory, so it remains to be seen to what extent subconscious goals can be primed in actual workplace settings and to what extent these subconscious goals will affect behavior.[73] However, one preliminary study found that subconscious goals can be primed (in this case there was a picture of a woman winning a race to show achievement) and do increase motivation and performance in the workplace.[74]

Feedback

The motivational effect of providing feedback to associates about their progress toward performance goals is well established. In fact, feedback on performance, even in the absence of established goals, is likely to have a positive effect on motivation.[75] However,

Making Visible Changes

Imagine a grand ballroom filled with people in black ties and ball gowns. The crowd hushes as the award ceremony begins. A young woman in a red dress steps up on stage to receive her award: a $40,000 bonus. The woman is 25-year-old Lara Hadad, whose total pay package, including her bonus, will be almost a quarter of a million dollars. Lara is joining other colleagues who together are receiving 11 cars, a trip to Greece, and part of $8.7 million in bonuses.

Interestingly, Lara doesn't work for a large multinational firm. She is a hair stylist with Visible Changes hair salons. Visible Changes is an innovator in the hair salon industry. The company was started in 1977 in Houston, Texas. At the time, hairdressing was considered a risky business, and the McCormacks—the entrepreneurs who started the firm—had a difficult time convincing mall owners and bankers to support their project. However, the McCormacks implemented a management philosophy that has made them leaders in their field. Visible Changes has been recognized in *Inc.* magazine's list of the fastest-growing companies in the United States and won Salon Entrepreneur of the Year at the Global Salon Business Awards in Barcelona, Spain. Furthermore, in an industry plagued by high turnover and employment problems, Visible Changes associates have a low turnover rate and high satisfaction. The firm currently has 17 locations in major Texas malls with a total of over 800 associates. And each salon averages over $2 million in annual sales—well above the industry average.

How did the McCormacks build such a high-performance climate? Most of their success has been due to the way they motivate their employees:

©Digital Vision

- They provide well-defined career paths, and the performance standards required to move from one level to another are well known by stylists. For example, to move from a senior cutter to a master cutter (with an associated increase in pay and potential bonuses), a stylist must increase the total number of haircuts given from 7,000 to 14,000, be requested by 65 percent of his clients, and complete additional education. Training and encouragement help to establish positive expectancies for these performance levels.

- They provide valued rewards and benefits, showing employees that they are a part of the company "family" and that the company cares about them. For example, they have a profit-sharing plan whereby the company makes yearly contributions to associates' accounts. Associates are fully vested after 7 years, and the average person has about $100,000 in her account after 10 years. Such a plan is highly unusual in the hair salon industry. Furthermore, in addition to bonuses, employees are rewarded with cars, public-recognition ceremonies, and travel to interesting locations. The "manager of the year" receives a one-carat diamond and the use of the company Mercedes. If she wins three times consecutively, she gets to keep the car! All these perks are based on meeting and exceeding clear performance standards. John McCormack promised his employees that should any of their children want to go to medical school, the company would pay for it. Several employees have taken him up on this offer.

- They set specific, challenging goals for each time period and reward people for achieving them. The stylists at Visible Changes make three times the industry average, with some earning six-figure incomes. The industry average is below $18,500. Beginning stylists are guaranteed $7 per hour; however, they are free to make as much as they can in commissions and bonuses.

- In order to encourage customer service performance, commissions and bonuses are based on the number of requests by customers, amount of products sold, and general performance of the stylist. When requested by name, the stylist receives an extra 10% commission. When that happens 50% of the time the bonus increases an additional 10%, and then again by another 10% when a stylist is requested by name 75% of the time. When a stylist is among the top 50 requested in the entire chain, he or she earns another super bonus.

- They provide support for their stylists to help them build their client base. For example, they provide brochures, business cards, and coupons.
- They avoid layoffs of associates.
- They engage associates in a variety of organizational decisions.

The McCormacks have been industry pioneers in the ways they motivate and provide support to their associates. Thus, their company is an industry leader. Other salons are copying their methods by introducing such things as better benefits packages and profit-sharing plans. We might say that the McCormacks have made significant Visible Changes.

Sources: D. Lauk. 2003. "Up Close: Local Company Puts Employees First," 11 News (Houston, Texas), Apr. 14, at http://www.khou.com; I. MacMillan & R.G. McGrath. 2000. *The Entrepreneurial Mindset: Strategies for Continuously Creating Opportunity in an Age of Uncertainty* (Cambridge, MA: Harvard Business School Press); Visible Changes, "Careers," 2010, at http://www.visiblechanges.com/Careers.aspx; Visible Changes, "Stylist," 2010, at http://www.visiblechanges.com/Stylist.aspx; Leadership-and-Motivation Training. Jan. 29, 2010. "Managing Change in the Workplace," at http://www.leadership-and-motivation-training.com/managing-change-in-the-workplace.html; A. Ragsdale. May 30, 2007. "Texas CEO makes big promise to employees". Houstonist.com at http://houstonist.com/2007/05/30/texas_ceo_makes.php.

feedback is especially important when performance goals exist and when they are relatively difficult to achieve. In this case, feedback permits an associate to gauge his actual progress toward the goal and make corresponding adjustments in his efforts. Such adjustments are unlikely in the absence of feedback. Thus, the presence of both goals and feedback exerts a positive influence on employee motivation.

Conclusions Regarding Process Theories

Expectancy theory, equity theory, and goal-setting theory emphasize the processes that occur in motivation. Expectancy theory focuses on people as rational decision makers: "If I exert a given amount of effort, how likely is it that my performance will result in outcomes I value?" The manager's job in this case is to develop situations in which associates have high expectancies and strong performance is rewarded. Equity theory focuses more on people's general feelings about how fairly they are being treated. This theory suggests that managers must take into account how associates are comparing themselves with others in the organization; a manager's treatment of one individual can influence the motivation of others. Finally, goal-setting theory suggests that managers can motivate associates by setting or helping to set goals.

In the *Experiencing Organizational Behavior* feature, the importance of associates' motivation is emphasized. The owners of Visible Changes, the McCormacks, ensure challenging goals for their associates and then pay them handsome bonuses for meeting those goals. They also focus on expectancies held by associates and use a variety of meaningful rewards. Finally, they support associates' growth needs through an education program, and they allow associates to participate in decisions. As a result, associates earn well above the industry average, and turnover is exceptionally low. The associates' high motivation and strong performance have made Visible Changes a top performer in its industry. Thus, Visible Changes is an industry leader both in methods of motivating associates and in company performance.

EXHIBIT 6.4   Motivation Practices Resulting from Motivation Theories

Motivation Theories	Motivation Practices				
	Find Meaningful Individual Rewards	**Tie Rewards to Performance**	**Redesign Jobs**	**Provide Feedback**	**Clarify Expectations and Goals**
Need Hierarchies Maslow ERG	X		X	X	
McClelland's Needs	X	X	X	X	X
Herzberg's Two-Factor Theory			X		
Expectancy Theory	X	X		X	X
Equity Theory	X	X		X	X
Goal-Setting Theory		X		X	X

Note: The fact that there is no X in a particular cell indicates that the theory has nothing specific to say about the practice, not that the theory says the practice is ineffective.

Motivating Associates: An Integration of Motivation Theories

Viewed as a set, the various motivation theories may suggest that motivation is highly complex and even confusing. That is not actually the case, however. Motivating associates and junior managers can be undertaken in a reasonably straightforward and meaningful way. While there are no foolproof approaches, there are sound tactics to use. Exhibit 6-4 identifies connections between the various motivation theories and five categories of motivation practices that managers can use. As shown in the exhibit, multiple theories have similar implications for managers. We discuss these implications in the remainder of the chapter.

Find Meaningful Individual Rewards

All of the content theories suggest that individuals vary in what they find motivating. Furthermore, expectancy theory implies that individuals assign different valences to outcomes. This means that by tailoring individual rewards to individual needs and desires, companies can create a competitive advantage in attracting and motivating associates. One area in which this is obvious is the provision of benefits. An unmarried 28-year-old associate with no children likely places different values on various retirement and insurance plans relative to a 50-year-old associate with three children in college, for example.

One mistake that managers often make when trying to determine what motivates individual associates involves placing too much emphasis on extrinsic rewards (e.g., pay increases, bonuses, pay level, job security, job titles) while underemphasizing intrinsic rewards (e.g., satisfaction based on exciting and challenging work, feelings of accomplishment).[76] Indeed, one survey of a random sample of U.S. adults indicated that they ranked "important work" as the most important aspect of their jobs. Pay was ranked third. When, however, these same people were asked what motivates "other people," 75 percent responded that pay was the primary motivator of others.[77] Apparently, most people feel that they are motivated by outcomes that meet higher-order growth or achievement needs, but they think others are primarily motivated by money as a way to meet physiological and security needs.

Some research has shown that if a person receives extrinsic rewards for performing an intrinsically satisfying task, he may attribute the performance to external forces, with a resulting reduction in his intrinsic interest in the job.[78] This suggests that relying too heavily on extrinsic rewards can cause people to lose any natural interest they have in performing their jobs. However, this position has been challenged by some researchers, who argue that in work situations, extrinsic rewards are necessary for motivation on any kind of task. Despite the mixed research,[79] it is clear that managers must be concerned with both extrinsic and intrinsic rewards and not overemphasize either, striving instead for an appropriate balance between the two (keeping in mind that the appropriate balance differs across different people or types of people).

Individuals may vary in what they find motivating based on their position in the organization. People in different jobs and at different levels may have different concerns. Indeed, when *Harvard Business Review* asked a dozen top leaders to state their most important thoughts on motivating people, Liu Chuanzhi, chairman of the Legend Group of Beijing, noted that a leader must establish different incentives for people at different levels in the organization.[80] He divided his organization into three groups and provided appropriate incentives for each group:

- The company's executives wanted a sense of ownership in the company, so the company gave all of its executives stock, an unusual practice in Chinese state-owned organizations. They also wanted recognition, so they were given opportunities to speak to the media.
- Midlevel managers wanted to become senior-level managers. The major incentives applied to this group involved opportunities to display and develop their knowledge, skills, and abilities, so they would be in a better position to achieve promotions within the company.
- Associates wanted outcomes that would provide a sense of stability and security. Thus, based on their performance, they received predictable bonuses. Furthermore, they were allowed to participate in decisions regarding how bonuses were allotted.

Tie Rewards to Performance

A basic characteristic of high-involvement management involves tying rewards to performance. The importance of this tactic is supported by many theories concerning human motivation and learning. One of the basic principles of operant conditioning (Chapter 4) is that rewards should be tied directly to performance to encourage the desired behavior. This basic proposition is reflected in the process theories of motivation as well. Expectancy theory proposes that motivation is a function of the perceived connections between performance and outcomes. To the extent that people have experience with performance leading to rewards, they will develop stronger instrumentalities.

Equity theory suggests that performance in the recent past (an input) should play a role in rewards (outcomes). In addition, justice research indicates that linking performance and rewards should result in greater motivation because the reward decisions will be viewed as more ethical and unbiased as people are rewarded based on their achievement and contribution. Finally, goal-setting theory suggests that providing rewards for the achievement of goals can help associates accept and become committed to those goals, although external rewards are not necessarily required for goals to affect motivation.[81]

Although tying rewards to performance may seem obvious and simple, managers often find it to be challenging. One reason for this problem is that performance is sometimes difficult to measure.[82] How does one evaluate the work of an R&D professional whose job entails developing and testing many new ideas, most of which will not result in usable products? What if an individual is highly interdependent with others? Can his individual contributions be clearly assessed? Further, some managers may supervise too many employees to closely observe and easily evaluate the contributions of all of them. If one cannot measure or evaluate performance accurately, then one cannot link performance to rewards. To partially address these issues, managers can have their direct reports undertake self-assessments and generate peer assessments. These tactics coupled with managers' knowledge of performance are often very helpful.

Another problem with tying rewards to performance is that managers may have little flexibility with rewards, particularly financial rewards. For example, a manager may be able to give an average raise of only 3 percent to her employees. If the bottom third of performers are given 2 percent increases, to adjust for the cost of living, this means the best performers can receive only 4 percent increases. Associates are not likely to see this small differential as being commensurate with performance differences. Such a small differential can produce low instrumentalities or perceptions of inequity.

Such problems with flexibility underscore the importance of nonfinancial rewards. Although managers may be restricted in how they can distribute financial rewards, they often can be more creative in assigning other types of rewards based on performance. For example, high-performing associates can be given job assignments that allow them to develop new skills, or they can be given credits toward payment of tuition at a local university. The Society for Human Resource Management surveyed its members and developed a list of over 150 creative rewards that companies offer their associates. These included the services of an ergonomics consultant, sophisticated office chairs, textbook money, funding to attend conferences in exotic locations, allowing pets at work, concierge services, free dinners, and flexible work hours.

To think more deeply about tying financial rewards to performance, consider the case of Susan. Susan supervises 10 customer call-center representatives. One of her associates, Angelo, clearly outperforms the others. Angelo's customer satisfaction ratings are much higher than those of the others, he handles the most calls, and there have been no complaints against him. Susan is highly pleased with Angelo's performance, especially because he has been on the job for only one month. Susan's worst performer is Jessica, who has the lowest customer service rating, handles an average number of calls, and has been the target of several customer complaints about rudeness. Jessica has worked in the unit for the past three years, which is a long tenure for a customer service representative. It's time to assign pay increases, and Susan's boss told her that her budget for salaries would be only 4 percent. This means that her employees can receive, on average, only a 4 percent raise. Susan is considering an 8 percent increase for Angelo and no increase for Jessica. However, when she begins to assign pay increases, she has a change of heart. She realizes that if she gives Angelo an 8 percent increase and gives no pay increase to Jessica, Angelo will receive more overall pay than Jessica, who has been on the job much longer. Susan doesn't want to alienate Jessica, because it is difficult to retain people on the job (and Jessica has a tendency to react quite negatively to bad news). In the end, Susan gives Angelo a 5 percent pay increase and Jessica a 3 percent pay increase. Three months later, Susan notices that Angelo's customer service rating has decreased and that he is handling fewer calls. Jessica's performance hasn't improved either. In fact, the number of complaints against her has increased.[83]

Susan's dilemma illustrates several common pitfalls in tying financial rewards to performance.

One problem is that Susan didn't differentiate more between Angelo's and Jessica's pay increases because of her fear that Jessica would become angry. This is a common reaction of managers when distributing financial rewards. Too often, managers are overly focused on superficial harmony, and they mistakenly distribute rewards equally or nearly equally rather than equitably based on performance. Monica Barron, a management consultant from AMR research, has stated, "You should make your best performers role models and say to others 'Here's what you can do to get one of these checks.'"[84]

A second problem was that Susan really wanted to reward performance, but instead she ended up rewarding tenure. Jessica received a larger pay increase because she had remained with the organization and in the job for a relatively long time. If Susan was asked whether mediocre, or even poor, performers should be rewarded for remaining on the job, she would probably answer "No." This might not have happened if Susan had clearly established what performance she expected from associates and how that performance would be rewarded.

A third problem was Susan's dilemma of having a budget of only 4 percent for pay increases. Her situation reflects the current state for many companies. Indeed, Robert Heneman, a compensation expert from Ohio State University, has said that managers "need a 7 percent or 8 percent [compensation increase] just to catch anybody's attention."[85] Thus, the amount of money Susan had for rewards limited her flexibility.

Beyond the simple amount of money available, how the money is used also can make a difference. A frequent issue is too much emphasis placed on merit pay increases (i.e., year-to-year pay increases). With such a focus, rewards provided for good performance in any given year are maintained in an associate's pay regardless of future performance. In addition, such an approach is often inflexible in dealing with economic downturns (because higher levels of pay are locked in for some individuals who are no longer performing among the best). Finally, the approach constrains managers from being able to provide a wide distribution of rewards. There are more creative ways to provide merit-based pay, including profit sharing and bonuses.

Redesign Jobs

Job redesign is viewed as a way to make jobs more intrinsically meaningful to people and thus more likely to satisfy higher-order needs. Job redesign generally takes one of two forms: job enlargement or job enrichment.

Job Enlargement

job enlargement
The process of making a job more motivating by adding tasks that are similar in complexity relative to the current tasks.

Job enlargement involves adding tasks with similar complexity to the current tasks. The added tasks offer more variety and often require the use of different skills. However, the additional tasks are not of greater complexity and therefore offer little opportunity for personal growth. Some refer to this practice as *horizontal job loading*.

An example of job enlargement involves giving a data entry specialist the additional task of filing correspondence. In this case, a different skill is utilized, but filing is no more complex than routine data entry. Even so, by providing variety, job enlargement may prevent boredom in simple tasks. However, the effects may be only temporary because the tasks do not offer more challenges or opportunities for personal growth. Overall, research has shown that the effects of job enlargement are mixed. Some studies have found that job enlargement produces positive results, whereas others have not.[86] Individuals with lower growth needs may benefit the most.

Job Enrichment

For our purposes, **job enrichment** can be differentiated from job enlargement by the complexity of tasks added to the job. Job enrichment is frequently referred to as *vertical job loading*. In enriched jobs, workers have greater responsibility for accomplishing assigned tasks; it may be said that they become "managers" of their own jobs. The concept of job enrichment was popularized by Herzberg's two-factor concept of motivation, which emphasizes responsibility, achievement, and the work itself as motivators. The concept of job enrichment also is consistent with McClelland's notion of developing a strong need for achievement and with Maslow's and Alderfer's ideas about meeting higher-order needs.

job enrichment
The process of making a job more motivating by increasing responsibility.

Many organizations, including AT&T, Corning, IBM, and Procter & Gamble, have implemented job enrichment programs. Usually, job enrichment involves adding tasks formerly handled at levels higher in the hierarchy. Boeing, for example, has implemented job enrichment by using work teams, empowering employees to work on their own ideas, and providing continuous learning opportunities. Because job enrichment involves giving associates greater control over their work, expanded job duties, and greater decision power, job enrichment is an integral part of high-involvement management.

Numerous studies have found positive results from job enrichment using outcome variables such as job satisfaction, commitment to the organization, and performance.[87] However, job enrichment programs are not always successful. To be effective, such programs must be carefully planned, implemented, and communicated to associates and must also take into account individual differences.[88]

Interestingly, many individuals who are currently entering the workforce may embrace enriched jobs to a greater degree than some others have. These individuals are members of Generation Y, those born between 1981 and 1993. According to Deloitte Consulting, members of Generation Y love challenges in the workplace, appreciate the opportunity to be flexible and explore new ideas, and want to make a difference.[89]

©Adrian Bradshaw/epa/Corbis

The work of two researchers, Richard Hackman and Greg Oldham, has been very influential in specifying how to enrich jobs so that the motivating potential of the jobs is increased. They identified five job characteristics important in the design of jobs—skill variety, task identity, task significance, autonomy, and feedback:[90]

- *Skill variety* refers to the degree to which associates utilize a broad array of skills in doing their jobs.
- *Task identity* is the extent to which job performance results in an identifiable piece of work. Contrast the situation in which an

assembly line worker's entire job is screwing bolts into one piece of metal versus the situation in which that associate is responsible for turning out an entire dashboard assembly.

- *Task significance* is the extent to which a job has an impact on the organization. It is important because people need to see how the work they do contributes to the functioning of the organization.
- *Autonomy* means that the associate has the independence to schedule his or her own work and influence the procedures with which it is carried out.
- *Feedback* involves obtaining accurate information about performance.

Hackman and Oldham propose that these five characteristics affect three psychological states: feeling of the work's meaningfulness, feeling of responsibility for the work done, and knowledge of results of personal performance on the job. Skill variety, task identity, and task significance affect the feeling of meaningfulness. Feeling of responsibility is affected by autonomy, and knowledge of results is affected by feedback. The following formula combines these factors to compute a motivating potential score (MPS) for a given job:[91]

$$MPS = \frac{(\text{Skill variety} + \text{Task identity} + \text{Task Significance}) \times \text{Autonomy} \times \text{Feedback}}{3}$$

Research has been generally supportive of the Hackman and Oldham model, finding that associates' perceptions of task characteristics relate to intrinsic motivation and performance.[92] However, several factors have been found to influence whether employees are motivated by enriched jobs. The most heavily researched factor is growth need strength.[93] People with high growth need strength tend to be more motivated by enriched jobs than those with low growth need strength. Perceptions of job characteristics have also been found to relate to job satisfaction and growth satisfaction.[94] Indeed, in one poll, one of the major reasons given for the decline in the job satisfaction of U.S. associates, is that they perceive their jobs to be boring and unengaging.[95] On the negative side, however, enriched jobs, which require more skill variety, responsibility, and control, can also be more stressful to certain associates.[96]

As discussed in the *Experiencing Organizational Behavior* feature, there are steps managers can take to ensure that the demands of enriched jobs are successfully handled. When managers provide a proper setting and resources, associates interested in growth and challenge usually rise to the occasion.

Provide Feedback

Feedback is critical to motivation from a variety of perspectives. Those high in need for achievement seek it, it is necessary for the development of expectancies and instrumentalities, it can influence perceptions of fairness by providing explanations for decisions, and it enhances the goal-setting process. A great deal of research has been conducted on the effects of performance feedback. A review of this research resulted in the following implications for making feedback effective:[97]

- Feedback is most effective when provided in conjunction with goals.
- Feedback should be repeated and provided at regular intervals. Robert Eckert, chairman and CEO of Mattel, states this succinctly: "People can't and won't do much for you if no one in the organization knows what's going on, what you expect of them. ... And talking to them once a quarter is not enough."[98]

Connecting People in the Workplace

Enriched jobs have the potential to be highly motivating and rewarding. Such jobs, however, place significant demands on jobholders. To ensure success in dealing with these demands, individuals must rely on one another. In a recent report, Deloitte Research, an arm of Deloitte & Touche, put it this way: "Work has always been done through relationships. But as jobs become more complex, people increasingly depend on one another, whether it's to design software, lead a call center, or sell a service."

To facilitate connections among people, Deloitte recommends a number of tactics:

- *Design physical space that fosters connections.* Proximity and layout matter. Being located far away from others who have relevant knowledge and insight can be particularly harmful to those with complex jobs. A lack of face-to-face interactions, the richest type, can be harmful to those who have such jobs. Also, an absence of dedicated areas for collaborative discussions as well as areas for quiet contemplation can be detrimental.

- *Build an organizational cushion of time and space.* Overly busy associates and managers often do not have the time to consult with others. With today's leaner organizations and stretched people, connecting to other people in rich ways can be difficult. Yet, those connections can improve productivity and quality in the long run, particularly for those who have complex jobs.

- *Cultivate communities.* Without a sense of community, associates and managers may not seek out those who have relevant knowledge and insight. Communities revolve around shared interests and goals, and they foster a sense of shared identity and belonging.

- *Stimulate rich networks of high-quality relationships.* Many associates and managers have limited informal networks of colleagues. Without a rich network that stretches across departments, divisions, and hierarchical levels, individuals are blocked from key sources of information and problem solving. In some organizations, explicit mapping of informal networks is carried out and those with deficient networks are counseled on how to improve.

- *Provide collaboration tools.* A lack of interactive, real-time collaborative technologies can be a roadblock for some types of jobs. Tools such as shared whiteboards and interactive decision-support systems can be quite useful. Wikis are also becoming useful (these involve open-access information sites whose core content can be edited by anyone at any time).

©Beau Lark/Corbis

Sources: R. Athey. 2004. "It's 2008: Do You Know Where Your Talent Is?—Part 1" (New York: Deloitte & Touche USA); R. Athey. 2007. "It's 2008: Do You Know Where Your Talent Is?—Part 2" (New York: Deloitte & Touche USA); C. Mamberto. 2007. "Instant Messaging Invades the Office," *Wall Street Journal*, July 24, B.1; D. Fichter. 2005. "The Many Forms of E-Collaboration," *Online*, July-Aug., pp. 48–50.

- Feedback should contain information about how associates can improve their performance. It is not enough to tell people whether they did well or poorly; performance strategies and plans must also be part of the message.
- Feedback should come from a credible source. The person giving the feedback should have the authority to do so and should also have sufficient knowledge of the recipient's performance.

- Feedback should focus on the performance, not on the person. In other words, feedback should always refer specifically to a performance measure, as in "Your performance is poor because you missed your quota by 10 percent," not "Your performance is poor because you are not a very good salesperson."

Clarify Expectations and Goals

The importance of goal setting to associates' motivation is made explicit in goal-setting theory. However, goal setting is also important from other motivational perspectives. Goal setting can be used to strengthen the relationships important in expectancy theory. For example, because goals help people analyze and plan performance, their effort-performance expectancies may be enhanced. Also, higher goals may be associated with higher outcome valences. Furthermore, goal setting is an important part of need for achievement because people high in this characteristic tend to set moderately difficult and reachable goals for themselves.

Many organizations have adopted goal setting, for two reasons. One is the motivating potential of goals; the other is that goals often can serve to align individual motives with organizational goals. One formal management program that aims to align motives and goals is referred to as management by objectives (MBO). Throughout the organization, individuals meet with their managers to agree on expectations for the upcoming time period.

THE STRATEGIC LENS

Associates' motivation is very important in all types of organizations. In general, associates who have greater motivation perform at higher levels, and this helps to implement the organization's strategy. When the associates achieve their goals, the strategy is implemented. When the strategy is implemented effectively, the organization achieves higher performance. This result was evident in the case of W.L. Gore and later in the example of Visible Changes. The goals of associates at Visible Changes related to the strategic goal of the organization to provide high-quality service to its customers.

As part of motivation and performance, individuals must work with others to achieve success on interdependent tasks. Karl Malone, a former professional basketball player, experienced firsthand the disappointment that can occur when colleagues are unwilling to work together. He moved from the Utah Jazz to the Los Angeles Lakers in order to have a better chance to be on a championship team. He gave up a great deal of money as well as status as the sole star on a team in order to move, and he was highly motivated to perform well for the Lakers.[99] The Lakers, however, failed to play effectively as a team, and as a result they failed to win the championship. For organizations to achieve their goals and enjoy strong performance, associates and managers must be motivated not only to perform their individual tasks well but also to coordinate their activities with others in the organization to ensure that the organization's strategy is well implemented and success is ensured.

Critical Thinking Questions

1. Assume that you are managing a talented but unmotivated associate. Also assume that organizational resources needed for the job are generally sufficient. What factors would you consider first in attempting to motivate the associate? Why those factors?

2. A number of theories of motivation suggest that different rewards might be important to different people. How difficult is it to reward people differently for performing the same or similar work?

3. How will your individual motivation affect your career opportunities?

What This Chapter Adds to Your Knowledge Portfolio

In this chapter, we have discussed work motivation in some detail. We have defined motivation, discussed both content and process theories of motivation, and described how these theories can be integrated and translated into managerial practice. More specifically, we have made the following points:

- Motivation refers to forces coming from within a person that account for the willful direction, intensity, and persistence of the person's efforts toward achieving specific goals, where achievement is not due solely to ability or to environmental demands.

- Content theories of motivation generally are concerned with identifying the specific factors (such as needs, hygienes, or motivators) that motivate people. They tend to be somewhat simplistic and are easily understood by managers. The basic implications of these theories suggest that managers must take individual needs into account when trying to decipher what motivates associates.

- Maslow's need hierarchy includes five levels of needs: physiological, safety, social and belongingness, esteem, and self-actualization. These needs are arranged in prepotent hierarchical order. Prepotency refers to the concept that a lower-order need, until satisfied, is dominant in motivating a person's behavior. Once a need is satisfied, the next higher need becomes the active source of motivation. Research has not been very supportive of Maslow's theory; however, this theory has served as the basis for other theories and practices that have received empirical support.

- ERG theory is similar to Maslow's hierarchy but does not consider prepotency to be relevant. The three needs in ERG theory are existence, relatedness, and growth. A person may work on all three needs at the same time, although satisfying lower-order needs often takes place before a person is strongly motivated by higher-level needs.

- Achievement, affiliation, and power needs are the focus of McClelland's theory. Practitioners have given the most attention to the need for achievement. People with a high need for achievement like to establish their own goals and prefer

back to the knowledge objectives

1. What do we mean by work motivation, and how does it relate to performance? Why is individual work motivation important to organizational success?

2. What assumptions do Maslow's need hierarchy and ERG theory make about human motivation? How can managers use these theories to motivate associates? How do need for achievement, need for affiliation, and need for power differ? How do these needs relate to work performance and motivation? How would you distinguish McClelland's notion of needs from those of other content theorists?

3. What does Herzberg's two-factor theory of motivation say about human motivation? How has it influenced current management practice?

4. What does expectancy theory suggest about people and motivation at work? When does expectancy theory best explain motivation? What implications does this theory have for managers?

5. What do equity theory and ideas from procedural justice suggest about motivation? How do fairness judgments influence work motivation, and how can managers ensure that associates perceive judgments as having been made fairly?

6. What are the basic tenets of goal-setting theory? What should a manager keep in mind when engaging in goal setting with his associates?

7. How does job enrichment affect associates' motivation to perform? To make sure job enrichment has the desired effects, what should the organization consider?

8. Considering the various theories of motivation, what can managers do to increase motivation?

moderately difficult ones. They seek feedback on their achievements and tend to be positive thinkers. However, the need that most distinguishes effective managers from nonmanagers is the need for institutionalized power.

- Herzberg's two-factor theory identifies two types of organizational rewards: those related to satisfaction (motivators) and those related to dissatisfaction (hygienes). It also raises the issue of intrinsic and extrinsic rewards. One important application of this theory, job enrichment, is widely practiced today.

- Whereas content theories emphasize the factors that motivate, process theories are concerned with the process by which such factors interact to produce motivation. They generally are more complex than content theories and offer substantial insights and understanding. Their application frequently results in highly motivated behaviors.

- Expectancy theory suggests that motivation is affected by several factors acting together. This theory emphasizes associates' perceptions of the relationship between effort and performance (expectancy), the linkage between performance and rewards (instrumentalities), and anticipated satisfaction with rewards (valence). Managers can influence employee motivation by affecting one of these areas but can have greater impact by affecting more than one.

- Equity theory considers the human reaction to fairness. According to this theory, a person compares her outcome/input ratio with that of another person, often a co-worker, to determine whether the relationship is equitable. An inequitable situation causes an individual to alter inputs or outcomes, distort his or her perception of inputs or outcomes, change the source of comparison, or leave the organization. Associates' perceptions of procedural justice can also influence how they react to perceived inequities.

- Goal-setting theory is concerned with several issues that arise in the process of setting performance goals for employees, including goal difficulty, goal specificity, goal commitment, associates' participation, and feedback. In general, goals should be difficult but realistic and specific. Participation and feedback are also useful for increasing the effectiveness of goals in influencing motivation.

- Motivation theories support the use of several managerial practices to increase associates' motivation: (1) find meaningful individual rewards; (2) tie rewards to performance; (3) redesign jobs through enlargement or enrichment; (4) provide feedback; and (5) clarify expectations and goals.

Thinking about Ethics

1. Is there anything wrong with providing no pay increase to a person whose performance is average or below average? What are the implications of this action?

2. If the rewards provided are equitable, must the process used in providing them be fair? Why or why not?

3. Suppose a manager has provided what she believes is an equitable reward to an associate but he does not believe it is fair. What are the manager's responsibilities to the associate?

4. Is it appropriate for managers to set higher goals for some associates and lower goals for others performing the same job? Why or why not?

5. Is it acceptable to terminate an associate for being openly critical of managers? What effect will such actions probably have on other associates?

6. Can senior managers terminate whistle-blowers who report what they believe to be wrongdoing by managers? Would the termination be acceptable if the whistle-blowers truly believed that the managers were in the wrong but, in fact, the managers' actions had been judged as appropriate by independent external observers?

Key Terms

motivation, p. 211

hierarchy of needs theory, p. 211

ERG theory, p. 213

need for achievement, p. 215

need for affiliation, p. 216

need for power, p. 216

two-factor theory, p. 218

motivators, p. 218

hygienes, p. 218

expectancy theory, p. 219

expectancy, p. 220

instrumentality, p. 220

valence, p. 220

equity theory, p. 222

distributive justice, p. 223

procedural justice, p. 223

goal-setting theory, p. 224

job enlargement, p. 232

job enrichment, p. 233

Human Resource Management Applications

Human Resource Management (HRM) practices play a large role in fostering associates' motivation. Most obvious is HRM's role in determining and administering compensation and benefits packages. Often, the HRM department must determine what to compensate the people in various positions. This requires research of external markets and analyses of the jobs in question. Furthermore, strategic decisions must be made on how to compensate people. What should the salary/bonus ratio be? What should the average pay increase be, and how should individual raises be determined?

Performance appraisal and feedback are an important part of managing associates' motivation. HRM departments train managers in the performance-appraisal system, and frequently in how to conduct appraisals and give feedback. HRM departments may also develop the performance-appraisal procedures and policies used in an organization, as well as monitor the process. HRM departments may also develop goal-setting programs, train employees in the use of these programs, and then assess the results in terms of increased productivity.

HRM departments can also conduct associate surveys to assess whether they are engaged with their work, what they find rewarding, and whether they feel that their efforts are being rewarded. This information can be then used to design performance-management programs, evaluation programs, and compensation policies. Also, should there be a need for job design, HRM departments could be responsible for introducing and implementing these changes.

---

building your human capital

Assessing Your Needs

Look at the picture to the right for 60 seconds. *Turn the picture over or close your book* and take 15 to 20 minutes to write a story about what you see happening in the picture. Your story should be at least one to two pages in length and it should address the following issues:

1. Who are the people in the picture? What is their relationship?
2. What is currently taking place in the picture? What are the people doing?
3. What took place in the hour preceding the taking of the picture?
4. What will take place in the hour following the taking of the picture?

©John-Francis Bourke/Corbis

This exercise is based on a tool, the Thematic Apperception Test, used by McClelland and associates to assess people's needs for achievement, affiliation, and power. The Hay Group and other leading consulting and development firms continue to use this type of tool. To determine where you fall on the three needs, do the following:

1. Give yourself one point for need for achievement every time one of the following themes appears in your story:
   - Your story involves a work or competitive situation.
   - Feedback is being given or received.
   - Goals or standards are being discussed.
   - Someone is taking responsibility for his or her work.
   - Someone is expressing pride over his or her own accomplishments or those of another person.

2. Give yourself one point for need for affiliation every time one of the following themes appears in your story:
   - The relationship between the characters is personal.
   - Help is being given or received.
   - Encouragement, comfort, empathy, or affection is being given or received.
   - Someone is expressing a desire to be close to the other person.
   - The characters are engaged in or talking about social activities

3. Give yourself one point for need for power every time one of the following themes appears in your story:
   - The relationship between the characters is hierarchical. Someone has higher status than the others.
   - Someone is trying to get someone else to do something.
   - Someone is attempting to get others to work together.
   - Someone is concerned about reaching organizational goals.
   - Someone is evoking rules, policies, or regulations.

Add up your points for each of the needs, and answer the following questions.

1. What is your dominant need? That is, in which category did you have the most points? What does this suggest about you?
2. Does this assessment seem valid to you? Why or why not?
3. If you are not as high on need for achievement as you thought you would be, what can you do to increase it?

Sources: D.C. McClelland et al. 1958. "A Scoring Manual for the Achievement Motive," in J.W. Atkinson (Ed.), Motives in Fantasy, Action and Society (New York: Van Nostrand); C.D. Morgan & H.A. Murray. 1935. "A Method for Investigating Fantasies: The Thematic Apperception Test," Archives of Neurology and Psychiatry, 34: 289–306.

an organizational behavior moment
The Motivation of a Rhodes Scholar

Frances Mead, compensation director for Puma Corporation, was pleased because she had just hired an individual whom she considered to be highly qualified to fill the position of benefits administrator. Dan Coggin was an extremely bright fellow. He had graduated summa cum laude with a B.S. degree in finance from the University of Chicago. He had then traveled to England for a year of study as a Rhodes Scholar. After returning from England, he had worked for a large bank in the investments area for a year. He had then accepted the position of benefits administrator in the corporate personnel department at Puma, headquartered in Salt Lake City, Utah.

Dan felt good about his new job. He would be well paid and have a position of some status. Most importantly, the job was located in Utah. Dan had always enjoyed the outdoors, and he liked to backpack, camp, and do some mountain climbing. Salt Lake City was the perfect location for him.

He arrived on the job happy and ready to tackle his new responsibilities. Dan's financial background aided him greatly in his new job, where he was responsible for the development and administration of the pension plan, life and health insurance packages, employee stock purchase plan, and other employee benefit programs. Within a month, Dan had learned all of the program provisions and had things working smoothly. Frances was satisfied with her selection for benefits administrator. In fact, she expected Dan to move up in the department ranks rapidly. Dan was enjoying himself, particularly his opportunities to get into the mountains. His only concern was that he did not seem to have enough time to enjoy his outdoor activities. After six months, he had his job mastered. He was quite talented, and the job did not present a strong challenge to him.

Frances recognized Dan's talents and wanted him to evaluate Puma's complete benefits package for the purpose of making needed changes. Frances believed that Puma's benefits package was outdated and needed to be revised. With Dan's abilities, Frances thought new programs could be designed without the help of costly outside consultants.

She held several discussions with Dan, encouraging him to evaluate the total benefits package. However, at the end of a year on the job, Dan had accomplished little in the way of evaluation. He seemed to be constantly thinking of and discussing his outdoor activities. Frances became concerned about his seeming lack of commitment to the job.

In the ensuing months, Dan's performance began to slack off. He had had the current programs running smoothly shortly after his arrival, but complaints from employees regarding errors and time delays in insurance claims and stock purchases began to increase. Also, he was making no progress in the evaluation of the benefit package and thus no progress in the design of new benefit programs. In addition, he began to call in sick occasionally. Interestingly, he seemed to be sick on Friday or Monday, allowing for a three-day weekend.

It was obvious that Dan had the ability to perform the job and even more challenging tasks. However, Frances was becoming concerned and thought that she would have to take some action.

Discussion Questions

1. Using ERG theory, explain the reasons for the situation described in the case.
2. Using expectancy theory, explain the reasons for the situation.
3. Using the integration framework found in the last major section of the chapter, describe what actions Frances should and should not take.

---

team exercise

Workplace Needs and Gender

Do women and men have similar needs in the workplace? Do they exhibit similar levels of need for achievement, need for affiliation, and need for power? In this exercise, you will have the opportunity to address these questions.

STEPS

1. As an individual, think about women's and men's achievement, affiliation, and power needs. On average, do women and men exhibit similar levels of these needs? Spend five minutes on this step.
2. Assemble into groups of four or five. Each group should consist of both women and men (two or three of each). Spend 15 minutes completing the next steps.
3. Decide as a group whether:
   a. Women and men exhibit similar levels of the need for achievement.
   b. Women and men exhibit similar levels of the need for affiliation.
   c. Women and men exhibit similar levels of the need for institutional power.
   d. Women and men exhibit similar levels of the need for personal power.
4. Identify the reasons for your group's beliefs.
5. Appoint a spokesperson to present the group's ideas to the class.

Endnotes

1. Hitt, M.A., Ireland, R.D., & Hoskisson, R.E. 2007. *Strategic management: Competitiveness and globalization* (7th ed.). Cincinnati, OH: South-Western.

2. Branch-Smith Printing. 2007. Accomplishments & Quality Awards. At http://www.branchsmith.com/bsaawards.html.

3. Kanfer, R. 1995. Motivation. In N. Nicholson (Ed.), *Encyclopedic dictionary of organizational behavior.* Cambridge, MA: Blackwell Publishing, pp. 330–336.

4. Maslow, A.H. 1943. A theory of human motivation. *Psychological Review,* 50: 370–396; Maslow, A.H. 1954. *Motivation and personality.* New York: Harper.

5. Wahba, M.A., & Bridwell, L.G. 1976. Maslow reconsidered: A review of the research on the need hierarchy theory. *Organizational Behavior and Human Performance,* 15: 212–225; Kanfer, R. 1990. Motivation theory and industrial and organizational psychology. In M.D. Dunnette & L. Hough (Eds.), *Handbook of industrial and organizational psychology (Vol. 1).* Palo Alto, CA: Consulting Psychologists Press, pp. 75–170.

6. Ibid.

7. Ibid.

8. See, for example, Laas, I. 2006. Self-actualization and society: A new application for an old theory. *Journal of Humanistic Psychology,* 46: 77–91; Zalenski, R.J., & Raspa, R. 2006. Maslow's hierarchy of needs: A framework for achieving human potential in hospice. *Journal of Palliative Medicine,* 9: 1120–1127.

9. Alderfer, C.P. 1972. *Existence, relatedness and growth human needs in organizational settings.* New York: The Free Press.

10. Ibid.

11. See, for example, Wanous, J.P., & Zwany, A. 1977. A cross sectional test of need hierarchy theory. *Organizational Behavior and Human Performance,* 16: 78–97.

12. See, for example, Alderfer, C.P., Kaplan, R.E., & Smith, K.K. 1974. The effect of variations in relatedness need satisfaction on relatedness desires. *Administrative Science Quarterly,* 19: 507–532.

13. Arnolds, C.A., & Boshoff, C. 2002. Compensation, esteem valence and job performance: An empirical assessment of Alderfer's ERG theory. *International Journal of Human Resource Management,* 13: 697–719.

14. McClelland, D.C. 1966. That urge to achieve. *Think,* 32: 19–23.

15. McClelland, D.C. 1961. *The achieving society.* Princeton, NJ: Van-Nostrand.

16. McClelland, D.C., Atkinson, J.W., Clark, R.A., & Lowell, E.L. 1953. *The achievement motive.* New York: Appleton-Century-Crofts.

17. McClelland, That urge to achieve.

18. Korn, E.R., & Pratt, G.J. 1986. Reaching for success in new ways. *Management World,* 15 (7): 6–10.

19. Hershey, P., & Blanchard, K.H. 1972. *Management and organizational behavior.* New York, NY: Prentice-Hall.

20. Eisenberger, R., Jones, J.R., Stinglhamber, F., Shanock, L., & Randall, A.T. 2005. Flow experiences at work: For high achievers alone? *Journal of Organizational Behavior,* 26: 755–775.

21. See Shaver, K.G. 1995. The entrepreneurial personality myth. *Business and Economic Review,* 41 (3): 20–23.

22. Hall, J. 1976. To achieve or not: The manager's choice. *California Management Review,* 18: 5–18.

23. McClelland, D.C. 1965. Toward a theory of motivation acquisition. *American Psychologist,* 20: 321–333; Steers, R.M. 1981. *An introduction to organizational behavior.* Glenview, IL: Scott, Foresman, & Co.

24. Frischer, J. 1993. Empowering management in new product development units. *Journal of Product Innovation Management,* 10: 393–401.

25. Material related to virtual workers was drawn from: King, R. 2007. Working from home: It's in the details. *Business Week,* special report at http://www.businessweek.com/technology/content/feb2007/tc20070212_457307.htm.

26. McClelland, D.C. 1975. *Power: The inner experiences.* New York: Irvington; McClelland, D.C., & Burnham, D.H. 1976. Power is the great motivator. *Harvard Business Review,* 54 (2): 100–110 (reprinted in 1995 and in 2003).

27. McClelland & Burnham, Power is the great motivator.

28. Herzberg, F., Mausner, B., & Synderman, B. 1959. *The motivation to work.* New York: John Wiley & Sons; Herzberg, F. 1966. *Work and the nature of man.* Cleveland, OH: World Publishing.

29. House, R., & Wigdor, L. 1967. Herzberg's dual-factor theory of job satisfaction and motivation: A review of the empirical evidence and a criticism. *Personnel Psychology,* 20: 369–380; Dunnette, M.D., Campbell, J., & Hakel, M. 1967. Factors contributing to job dissatisfaction in six occupational groups. *Organizational Behavior and Human Performance,* 2: 143–174.

30. Vroom, V.H. 1964. *Work and motivation.* New York: John Wiley & Sons.

31. See, for example, Ferris, K.R. 1977. A test of the expectancy theory of motivation in an accounting environment. *The Accounting Review,* 52: 605–615; Reinharth, L., & Wahba, M.A. 1975. Expectancy theory as a predictor of work motivation, effort expenditure, and job performance. *Academy of Management Journal,* 18: 520–537.

32. See Pinder, C.C. 1984. *Work motivation.* Glenview, IL: Scott & Foresman.

33. In Vroom's original theory, extrinsic rewards were the focus. In some later work, intrinsic rewards were also a point of emphasis.

34. Johnson, R.R. 2009. Explaining patrol officer drug arrest activity through expectancy theory. *Policing: An International Journal of Police Strategies & Management,* 32: 6–20.

35. Durocher, S., Fortin, A., & Cote, L. 2007. Users' participation in the accounting standard-setting process: A theory-building study. *Accounting, Organizations, and Society,* 32: 29–59; House, R.J., Shapiro, H.J., & Wahba, M.A. 1974. Expectancy theory as a predictor of work behavior and attitudes: A reevaluation of empirical evidence. *Decision Sciences,* 5: 481–506; Kanfer, R. 1990. Motivation theory and industrial and organizational psychology. In Dunnette & Hough (Eds.), *Handbook of industrial and organizational psychology (Vol. 1);* Landy, F.J., & Trumbo, D.A. 1980. *Psychology of work behavior* (2nd ed.). Homewood, IL: Dorsey Press, pp. 343–351; Wahba, M.A., & House, R.J., 1972. Expectancy

theory in work and motivation: Some logical and methodological issues. *Human Relations,* 27: 121–147; Watson, S. 2006. "A multi-theoretical model of knowledge transfer in organizations: Determinants of knowledge contribution and knowledge reuse." *Journal of Management Studies,* 43: 141–173.

36. Landy & Trumbo, *Psychology of work behavior.*

37. Korsgaard, M.A., Meglino, B.M., & Lester, S.W. 1997. Beyond helping: Do other-oriented values have broader implications in organizations? *Journal of Applied Psychology,* 82: 160–177.

38. For one revised model, see: Porter, L.W., & Lawler, E.E. 1968. *Managerial attitudes and performance.* Homewood, IL: Irwin-Dorsey.

39. See, for example, Camerman, J. 2007. The benefits of justice for temporary workers. *Group & Organization Management,* 32: 176–207; Cropanzano, R., Rupp, D.E., Mohler, C.J., & Schmincke, M. 2001. Three roads to organizational justice. In G. Ferris (Ed.), *Research in personnel and human resources management.* Oxford, UK: Elsevier Science, pp. 1–113; Greenberg, J., Ashton-James, C.E., & Ashkanasy, N.M. 2007. Social comparison processes in organizations. *Organizational Behavior and Human Decision Processes,* 102: 22–41; Wong, Y.-T., Ngo, H.-Y., & Wong, C.-S. 2006. Perceived organizational justice, trust, and OCB: A study of Chinese workers in joint ventures and state-owned enterprises. *Journal of World Business,* 41: 344–355.

40. Pasturis, P. 2002. The corporate scandal sheet. At http://www.Forbes.com.

41. See Cox, T. 2001. *Creating the multicultural organization: A strategy for capturing the power of diversity.* San Francisco: Jossey-Bass.

42. Adams, J.S. 1965. Inequity in social exchange. In L. Berkowitz (Ed.), *Advances in experimental social psychology (Vol. 2).* New York: Academic Press, pp. 267–299.

43. Colquitt, J.A., Conlon, D.E., Wesson, M.J., Porter, C.O.L.H., & Ng, K.Y. 2001. Justice at the millennium: A meta-analytic review of 25 years of organizational justice research. *Journal of Applied Psychology,* 86: 425–445; Greenberg, Ashton-James, & Ashkanasy, Social comparison processes in organizations.

44. Greenberg, J., & Leventhal, G. 1976. Equity and the use of over-reward to motivate performance. *Journal of Personality and Social Psychology,* 34: 179–190.

45. See, for example, Bing, M.N., & Burroughs, S.M. 2001. The predictive and interactive effects of equity sensitivity in teamwork-oriented organizations. *Journal of Organizational Behavior,* 22: 271–290; Huseman, R.C., Hatfield, J.D., & Miles, E.W. 1987. A new perspective on equity theory: The equity sensitivity construct. *Academy of Management Review,* 12: 222–234.

46. For details of this story, see: Boswell, T. 2000. A Texas-sized mistake involving no lone star. *The Washington Post,* December 12, p. D.01; Simmons, M. 2003. A-Rod hits the jackpot, super Mario returns. At www.askmen.com.

47. White, P. 2007. How A-Rod learned to relax and enjoy N.Y.: In a turnabout he's on a roll but Yankees aren't. *USA Today,* May 4, p. 1A.

48. Colquitt, Conlon, Wesson, Porter, & Ng, Justice at the millennium.

49. Greenberg, J. 1993. Stealing in the name of justice: Informational and interpersonal moderators of theft reactions to underpayment inequity. *Organizational Behavior and Human Decisions Processes,*

54: 81–103; Umphress, E.E., Ren, L.R., Bingham, J.B., & Gogus, C.I. 2009. The influence of distributive justice on lying and stealing from a supervisor. *Journal of Business Ethics,* 86: 507–518; Hershcovis, M.S. et al. 2007. Predicting workplace aggression: A meta-analysis. *Journal of Applied Psychology,* 92: 228–238; Jones, D.A. 2009. Getting even with one's supervisor and one's organization: Relationships among types of injustice, desires for revenge, and counterproductive work behaviors. *Journal of Organizational Behavior,* 30, 525–542.

50. Loi, R., Yan, J., & Diefendorff, J.M. 2009. Four-factor justice and daily job satisfaction: A multilevel investigation. *Journal of Applied Psychology,* 94, 770–781; Colquitt, Conlon, Wesson, Porter, & Ng, Justice at the millennium.

51. Colquitt, Conlon, Wesson, Porter, & Ng, Justice at the millennium.

52. Colquitt, Conlon, Wesson, Porter, & Ng, Justice at the millennium.

53. Borman, W. C., & Motowidlo, S. J. 1993. Expanding the criterion domain to include elements of contextual performance. In N. Schmitt & W. C. Borman (Eds.), *Personnel selection in organizations.* San Francisco: Jossey-Bass, pp. 71–98. Organ, D. W. 1988. *Organizational citizenship behavior: The good soldier syndrome.* Lexington, MA: Lexington Books.; Organ, D.W. 1997. Organizational citizenship behavior: It's construct clean-up time. *Human Performance,* 10: 85–97.

54. Distributive and procedural justice are the two most studied types of justice. A third type, however, has been distilled and has received some attention. This third type, interactional justice, relates to quality of interpersonal treatment, typically from the supervisor. In our chapter, we focus on the main two anchors of justice phenomena. For additional discussion, see, for example, Olkkonen, M.-E., & Lipponen, J. 2006. Relationships between organizational justice, identification with the organization and work unit, and group related outcomes. *Organizational Behavior and Human Decision Processes,* 100: 202–215; Roch, S.G., & Shanock, L.R. 2006. Organizational justice in an exchange framework: Clarifying organizational justice distinctions. *Journal of Management,* 32: 299–322.

55. Brockner, J., & Wiesenfeld, B.M. 1996. An integrative framework for explaining reactions to decisions: Interactive effects of outcomes and procedures. *Psychological Bulletin,* 120: 189–208; Thibaut, J., & Walker, L. 1975. *Procedural justice: A psychological analysis.* Hillsdale, NJ: Lawrence Erlbaum.

56. Bies, R.J., & Moag, J.F. 1986. Interactional justice: Communication criteria of fairness. In R.J. Lewicki, B.H. Sheppard, & M.H. Bazerman (Eds.), *Research on negotiations in organizations (Vol. 1).* Greenwich, CT: JAI Press, pp. 43–55; Leventhal, G.S. 1980. What should be done with equity theory: New approaches to the study of fairness in social relationships. In K. Gergen, M. Greenberg, & R. Willis (Eds.), *Social exchange: Advances in theory and research.* New York: Plenum, pp. 27–55; Thibaut & Walker, *Procedural justice.*

57. Brockner, J., DeWitt, R.L., Grover, S., & Reed, T. 1990. When it is especially important to explain why: Factors affecting the relationship between managers' explanations of a layoff and survivors' reactions to the layoff. *Journal of Experimental Social Psychology,* 26: 389–407.

58. Locke, E.A., & Latham, G.P. 1990. *A theory of goal setting and task performance.* Englewood Cliffs, NJ: Prentice Hall.

59. Locke, E.A. 1968. Toward a theory of task motivation and incentives. *Organizational Behavior and Human Performance,* 3: 157–189.

60. Heath, C., Larrick, R.P., & Wu, G. 1999. Goals as reference points. *Cognitive Psychology,* 38: 79–109.

61. Locke & Latham, *A theory of goal setting and task performance.*

62. Locke, E.A., & Latham, G.P. 1979. Goal setting: A motivational technique that works. *Organizational Dynamics,* 8 (2): 68–80.

63. See, for example: Motowidlo, S.J., Loehr, U., & Dunnette, M.D. 1978. A laboratory study of the effects of goal specificity on the relationship between probability of success and performance. *Journal of Applied Psychology,* 63: 172–179.

64. Locke & Latham, *A theory of goal setting and task performance.*

65. Locke, Toward a theory of task motivation and incentives; Renn, R.W. 1998. Participation's effects on task performance: Mediating roles of goal acceptance and procedural justice. *Journal of Business Research,* 41: 115–125.

66. Latham, G.P., & Marshall, H.A. 1982. The effects of self-set, participatively set and assigned goals on the performance of government employees. *Personnel Psychology,* 35: 399–404; Latham, G.P., Steele, T.P., & Saari, L.M. 1982. The effects of participation and goal difficulty on performance. *Personnel Psychology,* 35: 677–686.

67. Renn, Participation's effect on task performance.

68. Latham, G.P., Stajkovic, A.D., & Locke, E.A. 2010. The relevance and viability of subconscious goals in the workplace. *Journal of Management,* 36: 234–255.

69. Chartrand, T. L, & Bargh, J. A. 2002. Nonconscious motivations: Their activation, operation, and consequences. In D. Tesser, A. Stapel, & J. V. Wood (Eds.), *Self and motivation: Emerging psychological perspectives.* Washington, DC: American Psychological Association, pp. 13–41.

70. Stajkovic, A. D., Locke, E. A., Bandura, A., & Greenwald, J. 2009a. *Effects of subconscious self efficacy on performance.* Paper presented at the Academy of Management, Philadelphia; Stajkovic, A.D., Locke, E.A., Bandura, A., & Greenwald, J. 2009b. The effects of subconscious self-efficacy on performance and mediation of conscious self-efficacy and conscious self-set goals. In A.D. Stajkovic (Chair), *Subconscious goals, self efficacy, need for achievement: The latest priming research.* Symposium at the annual meeting of the Society of Industrial-Organizational Psychology, New Orleans; Stajkovic, A. D., Locke, E. A., & Blair, E. S. 2006. A first examination of the relationships between primed subconscious goals, assigned conscious goals, and task performance. *Journal of Applied Psychology,* 91: 1172–1180.

71. Shantz, A., & Latham, G. P. 2009. An exploratory field experiment on the effect of subconscious and conscious goals on employee performance. *Organizational Behavior and Human Decision Making Processes,* 109: 9–17.

72. Stajkovic, Locke, Bandura, & Greenwald, The effects of subconscious self-efficacy on performance and mediation of conscious self-efficacy and conscious self-set goals.

73. Latham, Stajkovic, & Locke, The relevance and viability of subconscious goals in the workplace.

74. Shantz, A., & Latham, G.P. 2009. An exploratory field experiment on the effect of subconscious and conscious goals on employee performance.

75. Becker, L.J. 1978. Joint effect of feedback and goal setting on performance: A field study of residential energy conservation. *Journal of Applied Psychology,* 63: 428–433.

76. Morse, G. 2003. Why we misread motives. *Harvard Business Review,* 81 (1): 18.

77. Ibid.

78. Deci, E.L. 1972. Effects of noncontingent rewards and controls on intrinsic motivation. *Organizational Behavior and Human Performance,* 8: 217–229.

79. See, for example: Pate, L.E. 1978. Cognitive versus reinforcement views of intrinsic motivation. *Academy of Management Review,* 3: 505–514.

80. Chuanzhi, L. Set different incentive levels. *Harvard Business Review,* 81 (1): 47.

81. Locke & Latham, *A theory of goal setting and task performance.*

82. Kerr, S. 1975. On the folly of rewarding A, while hoping for B. *Academy of Management Journal,* 18: 769–783.

83. This story is based on the following materials: Bates, S. 2003. Top pay for best performers. *HR Magazine,* 48 (1): 31–38; Leventhal, G.S. 1976. The distribution of rewards and resources in groups and organizations. In L. Berkowitz & E. Walster (Eds.), *Advances in Experimental Social Psychology (Vol. 9).* New York: Academic Press, pp. 91–131; Mizra, P., & Fox, A. 2003. Reward the best, prod the rest. *HR Magazine,* 48 (1): 34–35.

84. Bates, Top pay for best performers

85. Ibid.

86. Aldag, R.J., & Brief, A.P. 1979. *Task design and employee motivation.* Glenview, IL: Scott, Foresman, pp. 42–43.

87. See, for example, Ford, R. 1969. *Motivation through the work itself.* New York: American Management Association; Fried, Y., & Ferris, G.R. 1987. The validity of the job characteristics model: A review and meta-analysis. *Personnel Psychology,* 40: 287–322; Walton, R.E. 1972. How to counter alienation in the plant. *Harvard Business Review,* 50 (6): 70–81; Whittington, J.L., Goodwin, V.L., & Murray, B. 2004. Transformational leadership, goal difficulty, and job design: Independent and interactive effects on employee outcomes. *The Leadership Quarterly,* 15: 593–606.

88. Hulin, C.L. 1971. Individual differences and job enrichment: The case against general treatments. In J. Maher (Ed.), *New perspectives in job enrichment.* Berkeley, CA: Van Nostrand Reinhold; Aldag & Brief, *Task design and employee motivation.*

89. Deloitte Consulting. 2005. *Who are the millennials (aka Generation Y)?* New York: Deloitte & Touche USA.

90. Hackman, J.R., & Oldham, G.R. 1974. *The job diagnostic survey: An instrument for the diagnosis of jobs and the evaluation of job design projects,* Technical Report No. 4. New Haven, CT: Yale University, Department of Administrative Sciences.

91. Hackman, J.R., & Oldham, G.R. 1976. Motivation through the design of work: Test of a theory. *Organizational Behavior and Human Decision Performance,* 16: 250–279.

92. See, for example, Abbott, J.B., Boyd, N.G., & Miles, G. 2006. Does type of team matter? An investigation of the relationships between job characteristics and outcomes within a team-based environment. *The Journal of Social Psychology,* 146: 485–507; Fried & Ferris, The validity of the job characteristics model.

93. Kanfer, Motivation; Fried & Ferris, The validity of the job characteristics model.

94. Fried & Ferris, The validity of the job characteristics model.

95. The Conference Board, January 5, 2010, "U.S. Job Satisfaction at Lowest Level in Two Decades" at http://www.conference-board.org/utilities/pressDetail.cfm?press_ID=3820; Hollon, J. January 5, 2010. "A Ticking Time Bomb: Job Satisfaction Hits Record-Low Levels," Workforce Management at http://www.workforce.com/wpmu/bizmgmt/category/recession/.

96. Schaubroeck, J., Ganster, D.C., & Kemmerer, B.E. 1994. Job complexity, "type A" behavior, and cardiovascular disorder: A prospective study. *Academy of Management Journal*, 37: 426–439;

Dwyer, D.H., & Fox, M.L. 2000. The moderating role of hostility in the relationship between enriched jobs and health. *Academy of Management Journal*, 43: 1086–1096.

97. Kluger, A.N., & DeNisi, A.S. 1996. The effects of feedback interventions on performance: A historical review, a meta-analysis, and a preliminary feedback intervention theory. *Psychological Bulletin*, 119: 254–284.

98. Eckert, R.A. 2003. Be a broken record. *Harvard Business Review*, 81 (1): 44.

99. Miller, P. 2003. Signed, delivered: Malone cannot hide his excitement about playing for a title in L.A. *Salt Lake Tribune*, July 18, at http://www.sltrib.com.

stress and well-being

Striking for Stress at Verizon

The pay is good, and sales bonuses can be generous. So why did Verizon call-center service representatives go on strike for 18 days several years ago? The answer in part is excessive stress.

Verizon, a *Fortune* 100 telecommunications company with revenues of more than $107 billion, depends on call-center representatives to provide positive customer service. These representatives provide the service link between the company and its customers. They answer many calls each day, covering a wide range of service issues. In addition, they sell products to the customers who call (such as caller ID services and DSL high-speed Internet access). The representatives are monitored electronically and in person on such factors as courtesy, length of calls, and sales of products.

knowledge objectives

After reading this chapter, you should be able to:

1. Define *stress* and distinguish among different types of stress.
2. Understand how the human body reacts to stress and be able to identify the signs of suffering from too much stress.
3. Describe two important models of workplace stress and discuss the most common work-related stressors.
4. Recognize how different people experience stress.
5. Explain the individual and organizational consequences of stress.
6. Discuss methods that associates, managers, and organizations can use to manage stress and promote well-being.

They are also closely monitored for tardiness, break times, and attendance. Failure to meet strict performance standards can lead to severe penalties, such as probation, suspension, or "separation from the payroll." Finally, service representatives are required to work overtime.

Call-center representatives are well paid and can earn commissions on sales. Over the years, they have voiced few complaints about the pay associated with the job. They have, however, voiced complaints about other issues. Associates said the following a few years ago:

> You are constantly monitored on everything that you do. Every call is timed …, If you go to the bathroom too long they say something about it.
>
> It is very stressful because we don't have enough people. … People aren't treated as people anymore. The company only sees us as numbers and dollar signs. …
>
> You're worried that before you let the customer go, you have to offer [sell] him something, no matter how upset he is, because the person sitting next to you or in that observation room is going to mark you off.

In addition to the above issues, one associate complained of being forced to sell a product to a person who was calling to have phone service shut off for a dead relative.

Several associates complained that managers monitored employees for personal reasons rather than to evaluate performance.

The Communication Workers of America (CWA), representing the call-center associates, and Verizon settled the strike that partially resulted from these workplace conditions. The settlement attempted to alleviate some of the more stressful conditions. Some of the changes included:

©AP/Wide World Photos

- Advance notification of monitoring and limits on the number of calls that can be monitored based on associates' performance.
- Monitoring only during regular working hours—not during overtime hours.
- Face-to-face feedback on monitoring within 24 hours of observation.
- Permission to be away from phones for 30 minutes per day to do paperwork.
- The formation of a CWA–Verizon committee to examine stressful conditions.
- Funding for work and family support programs.
- At some locations, recording of performance at the team level rather than the individual level.

- Split shifts, job sharing, and limited flextime at various locations.
- Limits on overtime at some locations—for example, 24-hour advance notice of overtime, 7.5 hours per week limit on mandatory overtime, and 15-minute breaks for every three hours of overtime worked.

Although the new contract addressed many of the call-center associates' complaints, some still argue that not enough has been done. To that end, some call-center associates and other employees have threatened to strike again over the last few years.

Overall, though, Verizon seems to have addressed these issues. Verizon has received awards and recognition recently from *Working Mother, LATINAStyle, CEO, Training*, and several other periodicals. Yet contention still remains. Verizon call-center employees still express frustration with the stress experienced on their jobs. For example, Abbey Bailey-Parrish recently stated that her call center job in Roanoke Virginia was a source of "constant pressure" due to an atmosphere of fear about being fired and the push to get callers to buy new products that they could not afford. She said "If you check your values at the door, this is a great job for you because the pay is great."

Sources: Anonymous, "Union Rejects Contract Offer—Verizon Communication Workers Speak on Issues in Strike," Aug. 2000, at http://www.wsws.org/articles/2000/aug2000/cwa-a15.shtml; Communication Workers of America, "Protections against Abusive Monitoring, Adherence, and Sales Quotas in CWA Contracts," 2003, at http://www.cwa-union.org/workers/customers/protections.asp; Communication Workers of America, "Contract Improvements for CWA Customer Service Professionals: 1999–Spring 2001," 2003, at http://www.cwa-union.org/workers/customers/improv_99-01.asp; K. Maher. 2001. "Stressed Out: Can Worker Stress Get Worse?" *Wall Street Journal,* Jan. 16: B1; L. Caliri. 2003. "'The Call Center Is a Gold-Plated Sweatshop': A Retired Employee of Roanoke Center Says Verizon Strike Likely as Workers Complain about Work Stress," *roanoke.com*, August, at www.roanoke.com/roatimes/news/story152897.html; Verizon Communications, "Executive Center: Awards and Honors," 2007, at http://www22.verizon.com/about/executivecenter/besttoflists/bestoflists_index.html; Verizon Communications, "Verizon Careers," 2007, at http://www22.verizon.com/jobs/. A. Sharma. 2008. "Verizon-Union Deal Averts Strike Three-Year Pact Will Create Jobs; Ratification Awaits," *Wall Street Journal,* Aug. 11, at http://online.wsj.com/article/SB121840111215927955.html. Verizon News Release. Verizon named to working mother magazine's List of 100 Best Companies." Sept. 23, 2009, at http://newscenter.verizon.com/press-releases/verizon/2009/verizon-named-to-working.html. D. Adams. "Views differ on call-center experience" July 19, 2009, Roanoke.com at http://www.roanoke.com/news/roanoke/wb/212332.Verizon Website. "Investor Relations" February 9, 2010 at http://investor.verizon.com/profile/overview.aspx

the strategic importance of Workplace Stress

By most standards, call-center service representatives have stressful jobs. Of course, individuals in other jobs also can experience stress, and such stress can lead to poor performance, workplace violence, sabotage, substance abuse, and other types of maladaptive behaviors; depression; and increased health-care costs.[1] It has been estimated that 75 percent of all medical problems are directly attributable to stress.[2] Time away from work is also an issue. According to the U.S. Bureau of Labor Statistics, individuals with substantial occupational stress missed 23 days of work per person (the median number), with 44 percent of absences lasting more than 31 days—much longer than absences resulting from injuries and illnesses.[3]

As suggested by the Verizon call-center case, many jobs and organizational policies can cause stress. Rapid technological changes, long work hours, repetitive computer work, work–family issues, and a growing service economy can also lead to stress. Given the many sources of stress, it is not surprising that a National Institute for Occupational Safety and Health (NIOSH) report on stress at work indicates that 26 to 40 percent of Americans find their work to be very or extremely stressful.[4] A survey by Northwestern National Life found that 25 percent of people believe their jobs to be the most stressful aspect of their lives.[5] A 2009 Gallup survey indicated that 31 percent of respondents were somewhat or completely dissatisfied with the stress produced in their jobs.[6] Finally, a Marlin Company survey of attitudes in the American workplace found that 43 percent of respondents believed managers at their companies did not help associates deal with stress.[7]

Although not all stress is bad (some of it can have positive outcomes, as explained later in this chapter), much of it is dysfunctional and, as we have seen, costly to organizations in terms of lost human capital and lower productivity. As a result, managers at all levels are increasingly aware of the effects of their decisions and actions on the stress of others. Indeed, it is imperative that managers effectively deal with the stress of those around them if they are to develop/maintain a high-involvement, high-performance workforce.

Given the prevalence of stress in the workplace and the high direct and indirect costs of stress at work, it should be a priority item on the agenda of top executives. In fact, many top executives also experience significant stress. The CEO makes decisions that affect many people. The strategy adopted by the organization affects the jobs performed by managers and associates. Poor decisions concerning strategy may mean that some people lose their jobs because of decreased demand for the organization's products or services, for example.

Top executives also make decisions to acquire or merge with other firms, and they must decide how many people will be laid off as a result of an acquisition or merger. Sometimes, too, they make decisions to lay off employees simply to cut costs. Layoffs create stress for the associates and managers who lose their jobs and for the survivors as well. Survivors experience stress because of job insecurity. In addition, research shows that they often feel guilty because their friends and co-workers were chosen to lose their jobs and they were not.[8] For stress to be as low as possible, those chosen to be laid off as well as survivors must view the actions of the senior leaders to be fair and humane. Research has shown that communicating effectively about the layoffs, implementing layoffs by careful selection of the units (those less valuable to the organization), and helping those laid off (e.g., providing severance pay, providing services to help them find new jobs) produces better outcomes.[9] For example, these actions result in investors seeing managers as more effective and more likely to produce higher performance, and thus stock price is positively affected.[10]

In the first section of this chapter, we define stress and related concepts. In the two sections that follow, we (1) present two important models of workplace stress that explain why and when people experience stress, and (2) discuss common workplace stressors. Next, we discuss individual characteristics that can cause people to experience more stress or help them cope with stressors. We then describe individual and organizational outcomes resulting from stress reactions. Finally, we present methods that associates, managers, and organizations can use to combat the effects of stress.

Workplace Stress Defined

Unfortunately, we all know what it feels like to be stressed. For some people, stress manifests itself as an upset stomach. For others, heart palpitations and sweaty palms signal stress. The list of stress reactions is almost endless and differs from individual to individual. Even though we know what stress feels like, we may not know just how to define it. In fact, stress is a difficult concept to define, and researchers have argued over its definition and measurement for many years.[11]

For our purposes, **stress** can be defined as a feeling of tension that occurs when a person perceives that a given situation is about to exceed her ability to cope and consequently could endanger her well-being.[12] In such situations, people first ask themselves: "Am I in trouble or danger?" and then ask, "Can I successfully cope with this situation?" If people respond with "yes" to the first question and "no" to the second, they are likely to experience stress. Extending this definition, we can define **job stress** as the feeling that one's capabilities, resources, or needs do not match the demands or requirements of the job.[13]

Consider a call-center representative who has a child in day care who must be picked up at 5:30 P.M. The representative has sole responsibility for picking up his child because his wife is out of town. At 4:58 P.M., as the representative is beginning to close down his station, his supervisor walks over and tells him that he must stay and work for another two hours. If the representative refuses to stay, he can be put on probation or even be fired, but he cannot think of anyone to call to pick up his child for him. Clearly, the demands of this situation are taxing his ability to cope, and therefore stress results. It is easy to see why being notified about overtime at least 24 hours in advance was such an important issue for Verizon's call-center representatives.

There are several important issues regarding the definition of stress. First, the level of stress experienced depends on *individual* reactions to a situation. Therefore, an event experienced by one person as stressful may not be as stressful to another person. For example, some people find stopping at a traffic light while driving to be stressful, whereas others do not. A second issue is that the source of stress, or *stressor,* can be either real or imagined. People do not actually need to be in danger to experience stress—they have only to *perceive* danger.

Stress can be defined as acute or chronic.[14] **Acute stress** is a short-term reaction to an immediate threat. For example, an associate might experience acute stress when being reprimanded by a supervisor or when not able to meet a deadline. **Chronic stress** results from ongoing situations. For example, it can result from living in fear of future layoffs or from having continuing problems with a supervisor. The constant monitoring in the call centers also is an example of a stressor likely to result in chronic stress.

Reactions involving chronic stress are potentially more severe than those involving acute stress because of the way the body responds. Stress makes demands that create an imbalance in the body's energy supply that is difficult to restore. The body reacts with a special physiological response commonly referred to as the **stress response**. A stress response is an unconscious mobilization of the body's energy resources that occurs when the

stress
A feeling of tension that occurs when a person perceives that a situation is about to exceed her ability to cope and consequently could endanger her well-being.

job stress
The feeling that one's capabilities, resources, or needs do not match the demands or requirements of the job.

acute stress
A short-term stress reaction to an immediate threat.

chronic stress
A long-term stress reaction resulting from ongoing situations.

stress response
An unconscious mobilization of energy resources that occurs when the body encounters a stressor.

©Somos/Veer/Getty Images, Inc.

> **EXHIBIT 7-1**   Some Stress-Related Conditions
>
> **Conditions That Can Result from Acute Stress**
>
> Alertness and excitement
> Increase in energy
> Feelings of uneasiness and worry
> Feelings of sadness
> Loss of appetite
> Short-term suppression of the immune system
> Increased metabolism and burning of body fat
>
> **Conditions That Can Result from Chronic Stress**
>
> Anxiety and panic attacks
> Depression
> Long-term disturbances in eating (anorexia or overeating)
> Irritability
> Lowered resistance to infection and disease
> Diabetes
> High blood pressure
> Loss of sex drive
>
> Source: Adapted from: Mayo Clinic, "Managing Work Place Stress: Plan Your Approach." 2003, at http://www.mayoclinic.com/invoke.cfm?id=HQ01442.

body encounters a stressor.[15] The body gears up to deal with impending danger by releasing hormones and increasing the heartbeat, pulse rate, blood pressure, breathing rate, and output of blood sugar from the liver.[16] If stress is short-lived, or acute, then stress responses tend to be short term. If, on the other hand, stress lasts over a period of time, with little relief, stress responses begin to wear down the body and result in more serious problems. Exhibit 7-1 displays some of the conditions that can be caused by acute and by chronic stress.

Not all demands that associates and managers encounter on the job lead to negative stress responses. Sometimes people become energized when faced with difficulties. Hans Seyle, one of the most influential stress researchers, distinguished between eustress and dystress.[17] **Eustress** is positive stress that results from facing challenges and difficulties with the expectation of achievement. Eustress is energizing and motivating.[18] Stressors do not necessarily have to be perceived in a negative manner, since they are often the result of a positive experience or result in positive outcomes.[19] For example, a promotion may result in more stressful responsibility but is viewed in a very favorable light, or completing a stressful assignment may lead to a feeling of achievement. Indeed, some research suggests that a certain level of stress is necessary for maximum performance.[20] Too little stress can produce boredom and even apathy, whereas reasonable levels of stress increase alertness and concentration. However, as stress increases, it reaches a point at which the effects become negative. If a high level of stress continues for prolonged periods, **dystress**, or bad stress, results. Note that we use the general term *stress* to refer to dystress throughout the book. This type of stress overload can lead to the physiological and psychological problems discussed here.

eustress
Positive stress that results from facing challenges and difficulties with the expectation of achievement.

dystress
Negative stress; often referred to simply as stress.

How can you tell when stress is reaching a negative level? Dr. Edward Creagan, an oncologist at the Mayo Clinic, identifies five basic signs in everyday life that indicate you are under too much stress:[21]

1. You feel irritable.
2. You have sleeping difficulties. Either you are sleepy all the time, or you have problems falling asleep and/or staying asleep.
3. You do not get any joy out of life.
4. Your appetite is disturbed. Either you lose your appetite, or you cannot stop eating.
5. You have relationship problems and difficulties getting along with people who are close to you.

Two Models of Workplace Stress

We have seen that workplace stress, or job stress, can occur when individuals perceive the demands of the workplace to outweigh their resources for coping with those demands. We turn now to two popular and important models of workplace stress—the **demand–control** model[22] and the **effort–reward imbalance model**.[23]

Demand–Control Model

The demand–control model is focused on two factors that can create situations of job strain and ultimately the experience of stress. Job strain is a function of the following two factors:

1. The workplace demands faced by an associate or manager
2. The control that an individual has in meeting those demands

Workplace demands are aspects of the work environment that job holders must handle. Examples of workplace demands abound in the call-center example at the beginning of this chapter and include long hours, pressure to handle calls quickly, and being subjected to monitoring. *Control* refers to the extent to which individuals are able to (or perceive themselves as able to) affect the state of job demands and to the amount of control they have in making decisions about their work. In the call-center example, one issue of the greatest concern to associates was their lack of control over how many hours they worked.

The demand–control model suggests that job strain is highest when job demands are high and control is low. In this condition, individuals face stressors but have little control over their situation. Call-center associates who must try to sell a product to every caller—with no authority to decide whether a particular caller needs or can afford the product—operate in a state of high strain and consequently experience stress. Compare this with a situation in which a call-center associate has a sales quota but also has the power to decide what products to try to sell and to whom to sell them. In this situation, the associate could exercise a great deal of creativity in determining how to classify customers so that their needs are met and still meet her sales goals. This situation exemplifies the "Active" condition in which both demands and control are high. The result is similar to the notion of eustress discussed earlier. Individuals are most likely to be energized, motivated, and creative in this condition.[24] Less research has been done on the other two conditions, labeled

demand–control model
A model that suggests that experienced stress is a function of both job demands and job control. Stress is highest when demands are high but individuals have little control over the situation.

effort–reward imbalance model
A model that suggests that experienced stress is a function of both required effort and rewards obtained. Stress is highest when required effort is high but rewards are low.

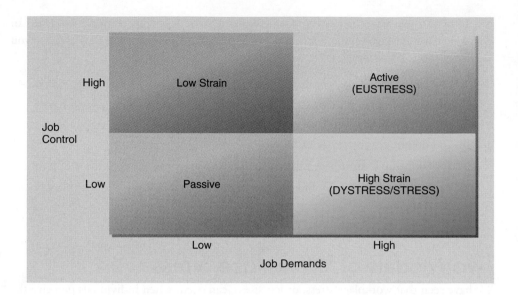

Exhibit 7-2 The Demand–Control Model of Workplace Stress

Source: R. Karasek. 1989. Control in Workplace and its Health-Related Aspects. In S.L. Sauter, J.J. Hurrell, Jr., & C.L. Cooper (Eds.), *Job Control and Worker Health*. New York: John Wiley & Sons, pp. 129–159.

"Low Strain" and "Passive," which are characterized by low demands. In any event, people facing these conditions are unlikely to experience stress. The demand–control model is depicted in Exhibit 7-2.

Research on the demand–control model has yielded somewhat mixed results. Some research has found that people in the high-strain condition are more likely to experience stress-related health problems, such as coronary heart disease and high blood pressure.[25] Other research has found less support for the model.[26] On balance, most researchers agree that both demands and control are important factors in explaining stress. However, how they work together, what constitutes job control, and the role of other variables (such as social support) must be considered in refining the demand–control model of workplace stress.[27] Furthermore, control may have only a buffering effect if it serves to reduce a person's perception of job demands.[28]

Effort–Reward Imbalance Model

The effort–reward imbalance model is focused on two factors, as depicted in Exhibit 7-3:

1. The effort required by an associate or manager
2. The rewards an individual receives as a result of the effort

Exhibit 7-3 The Effort–Reward Imbalance Model of Stress

Source: Adapted from: J. Siegrist. 1999. Occupational Health and Public Health in Germany, In P.M. Le Blanc, M.C.W. Peeters, A. Bussing, & W.B. Schaufeli (Eds.), *Organizational Psychology and Healthcare: European Contributions*. Munchen: Rainer Hampp Verlag.

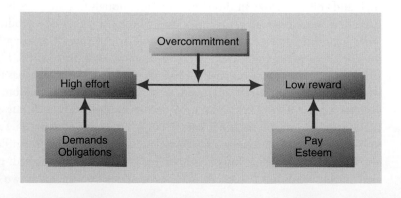

Effort required relates to the performance demands and obligations of the job. It is very similar to the demand dimension in the demand–control model, but it is somewhat more narrowly focused on the job itself rather than on broader aspects of the overall work environment. Rewards include extrinsic (e.g., pay) and intrinsic (e.g., esteem) outcomes of the work.

The effort–reward imbalance model highlights the fact that a combination of strong required efforts and low rewards violates the principle of reciprocity. Ongoing violation of this principle results in strong negative emotions and harmful changes in the autonomic nervous system. Although an individual facing such a situation could simply exit, many stay because of: (1) limited opportunities in the labor market, (2) hope for changes in the situation, and (3) excessive work-related overcommitment.[29] Overcommitment, the factor that most researchers have focused on, is driven by achievement motivation and approval motivation.

Research has yielded generally supportive results for the effort–reward imbalance model. For example, in a study of hospital workers, effort–reward imbalance predicted musculoskeletal injury.[30] In a synthesis of 45 studies, effort–reward imbalance predicted a variety of negative outcomes.[31] The relevance of overcommitment has been questioned (it may not play an important role), but other aspects of the model appear to be valid.

Organizational and Work-Related Stressors

A great deal of research has focused on identifying the specific aspects of the work environment likely to cause associates and managers to experience stress—that is, the factors that act as **stressors**. Organizational and work-related causes of stress include role conflict, role ambiguity, work overload, occupation, resource inadequacy, working conditions, management style, monitoring, job insecurity, and incivility.[32] We examine these factors next.

stressors
Environmental conditions that cause individuals to experience stress.

Role Conflict

All of us have many roles (student, fraternity/sorority member, athlete, spouse, associate). Many times, these roles are reasonably compatible. Sometimes, however, they are not compatible and create conflicting demands and requirements. This situation, known as **role conflict**, has been demonstrated to be a significant work stressor and is often associated with dissatisfaction, tardiness, absenteeism, and turnover.[33] It has been labeled a hindrance stressor in recent stress research.[34]

A specific example of role conflict and its connection to stress is provided by the case of flight attendants after the September 11 terrorist attacks.[35] Prior to the attacks, the flight attendants' role focused on providing service to passengers—"service with a smile." However, since September 11, flight attendants, under federal rulings, have been required to perform extraordinary security procedures and to scrutinize passengers. It is difficult to provide friendly service (customer service role) while taking extreme security precautions (security role). Pat Friend, president of the Association of Flight Attendants, noted that before the attacks, flight attendants could ignore or "grin and bear" unruly passenger behavior. Now, however, they are required to treat the mildest infraction as a "level-one" threat. This approach has produced an increase in passenger complaints,

role conflict
A situation in which different roles lead to conflicting expectations.

stress-management programs for flight attendants, and a study of job stress sponsored by a major flight attendants' union.

Apart from conflict among work roles, it is not uncommon for a person's work and nonwork roles to conflict. For example, a person's job demands may conflict with a role as a spouse and mother or father. Such conflict was seen in the Verizon case, and it can be quite serious. One study, for example, connected work–family conflict to mental issues. Individuals with high levels of such conflict exhibited mood problems, anxiety, and substance use. This was true for women and men, with single mothers and married fathers having the highest levels of work–family tension.[36] Overall, men and women seem to exhibit similar levels of work–family issues.[37]

The discussion in the *Managerial Advice* feature highlights a number of useful ideas for managing work–life conflict. Ensuring an appropriate balance between work and personal lives is crucial to the well-being and productivity of associates and managers. Because high-involvement organizations expect a great deal from associates, these organizations must pay particular attention to work–life balance among those individuals.

Role Ambiguity

role ambiguity
A situation in which goals, expectations, and/or basic job requirements are unclear.

Role ambiguity refers to the situation in which jobholders are unclear about the goals, expectations, or requirements of their jobs. Under ambiguous job demands, people are unsure of what is expected of them and how they will be evaluated. A number of management jobs have high role ambiguity; thus, ambiguity is another contributor to the high stress often experienced in managerial jobs.

Ambiguity on the job creates tension and anxiety.[38] Reactions to this stress are likely to be emotional. Moreover, role ambiguity has been shown to have strong negative effects on job motivation and performance, even stronger than role conflict in many instances. Further, it often has stronger effects on tardiness, absenteeism, and turnover than does role conflict.[39] Finally, role ambiguity seems to be most problematic when the job demands are perceived as quite challenging.[40]

Work Overload

Another common cause of stress in organizations is work overload. Overload can be quantitative (too much work) or qualitative (work is too complex). Research suggests that qualitative overload creates more stress than quantitative overload. For example, qualitative work overload has been found to create greater depression, less enjoyment of work, and greater hostility.[41] In a study of nurses, those with an overload of complex cases were sick more frequently.[42] Therefore, managers should be very sensitive to overloading associates with work that is too complex for them.

Evidence suggests that workload has been increasing over the past few decades.[43] In one study of high earners, 62 percent reported working more than 50 hours per week, 35 percent reported working more than 60 hours per week, and 10 percent reported working more than 80 hours per week.[44] The majority of these respondents also reported qualitative overload such as unpredictability, a fast pace with tight deadlines, and 24/7 client demands. U.S. workers are not the only ones experiencing overload, it appears to be a global phenomenon. The problem of work overload and its ensuing

Restoring and Maintaining Work–Life Balance

©Photodisc/Getty Images, Inc.

Work–life conflict is a serious source of stress in many parts of the world. Work demands have increased for many people because of longer working hours, heightened speed and complexity of the work world, and advances in communication technology that tie together workplaces and workers 24 hours per day. At the same time, personal lives have become more complex, particularly for those with families. Families have become complicated by increases in dual-career couples, increases in the number of long-distance relationships, greater needs for taking care of parents and other older family members, and more time-consuming non–school activities for children. Work–family conflict leads to role conflict, interpersonal conflict, dissatisfaction, exhaustion, time pressures, and guilt, all of which can lead to increased stress.

To help individuals cope in today's world, organizations such as the Mayo Clinic, the National Mental Health Association, and WebMD have developed useful ideas. Their advice is particularly important for managers, professionals, and other white-collar workers who have high-demand jobs. Here is our adaptation of their advice:

- *Focus on what is truly important.* Track and record all activities for one week, those that are work-related and those that are not. Prioritize the items on the list. At work, delegate tasks that are less important or personally less enjoyable. At home, outsource less enjoyable tasks. If mowing the lawn is not an enjoyable task, outsource it if possible. At both work and home, delete nonessential tasks. Less important, non-enjoyed, and nonessential tasks clutter the days of a surprising number of people.
- *Take advantage of work-related options.* If commuting is time-consuming and stressful, consider telecommuting some days, or request longer working hours on some days to avoid going to the office on other days. If onsite day-care is offered, consider using it to simplify drop-off and pickup routines. If financial services are offered onsite or nearby through a credit union, consider using those services to avoid traveling to a financial institution for face-to-face transactions.
- *Protect nonwork time.* Do not allow work-related matters to creep into nonwork time. Rejuvenation is crucial. Attempt to complete less desirable personal tasks (e.g., laundry, changing the bed linen) on work days so that days off can be spent on more enjoyable activities.

- *Manage your personal time.* Rather than going out multiple times to handle different errands, use multipurpose outings. Cook multiple meals for the week during a single evening. Complete multiple chores simultaneously whenever possible and comfortable (such as washing clothes and preparing dinner).
- *Set aside specific time each week for recreation.* Stay away from cell phones and work-related computing while enjoying activities with family and friends.

If stress becomes unmanageable, employee-assistance programs might be helpful. Given the complexity of today's world, some companies now offer programs designed specifically to help managers and associates strengthen relationships with spouses and significant others. For a suite of helpful tools, techniques, and resources, see the Mayo Clinic Stress Center at http://www.mayoclinic.com/health/stress/SR99999.

Sources: Mayo Clinic. 2006, "Work-life balance: Ways to Restore Harmony and Reduce Stress," at http://www.mayoclinic.com/health/work-life-balance/WL00056; National Mental Health Association, 2007, "Finding Your Balance: At Work and at Home," at http://www.nmha.org/go/finding-your-balance-at-work-and-home; R. Silverman. 2007. "Working on Your Marriage—At Work," *Wall Street Journal*, May 31, p. D.1; E. White. 2006. "How to Balance Home-Life Issues with Work Duties," *Wall Street Journal*, Aug. 22, p. B.8; WebMD. 2006, "5 Tips for Better Work-Life Balance," at http://www.webmd.com/balance/guide/5-strategies-for-life-balance?page=1; Livingston, B.A., & Judge, T. 2008. Emotional responses to work-family conflict: An examination of gender role orientation among working men and women. *Journal of Applied Psychology*, 93: 207–216; Cooper, C, Lu, L., Kao, S., Chang, T. & Wu, H. 2008. Work-family demands, work flexibility, work/family conflict and their consequences for work. *International Journal of Stress Management*, 15: 1–21; Eby, L.T., Maher, C.P., & Butts, M.M. 2010. The intersection of work and family life: The role of affect. *Annual Review of Psychology*, 61: 599–622.

stress-related health consequences has become so prevalent in Japan that they have special terms to describe the phenomenon: "karoshi," which means "work to death" and "karo-jisatsu," which means "suicide by overwork."[45] Causes for the growth in overload are far ranging, from economic downturns leading to more work for fewer employees, more competitive work environments, and the increasing ease with which employees are available because of technology. "BlackBerry Thumb" has become an actual medical condition.

Occupation

In accordance with the models of stress discussed above, occupations characterized by high demands and strong required efforts can generate stress. Statistics from the U.S. Department of Labor indicate that white-collar occupations are associated with a higher proportion of stress cases than the blue-collar and service occupations combined.[46] Technical, sales, and administrative support personnel contribute most of these cases, but managerial and professional occupations also contribute a substantial number of them. Although the white-collar occupations may allow greater control and offer substantial rewards, demands and requirements for people holding these jobs are typically much greater than in other occupations. On the other hand, the effects of control and rewards are demonstrated in research findings that suggest senior managers (upper-level executives, such as CEOs) experience less stress than middle managers. Even though demands on the senior managers may be greater, these managers are also likely to have more control,[47] and they frequently have generous reward packages.

Resource Inadequacy

People may also experience job stress when they lack needed resources.[48] Having inadequate resources makes it difficult to accomplish tasks effectively and efficiently and can therefore increase job demands or lessen control. There may be too few people, too little support, or inadequate material to accomplish a task, placing pressure on the person who has responsibility for the task. Severe resource shortages caused by situations such as loss of sales may lead to other stressful events, such as layoffs. As mentioned earlier, layoff decisions are stressful for the managers who make them, for those who lose their jobs, and even for those who stay. Those who remain on the job experienced stress before the layoff decision (because of uncertainty about who would be laid off), experienced the loss of friends and co-workers who were laid off, and then must endure added pressures to accomplish tasks with fewer workers.

Working Conditions

The job environment can have major effects on job attitudes and reactions. The job environment includes both physical surroundings (lighting, temperature, noise, office arrangements, and so on) and psychological aspects (such as peer relationships, warmth, and perceived rewards). If the working conditions are unpleasant, they can be stressful. For example, working with inadequate lighting, loud noise, or uncomfortable temperatures or working in isolation from others creates pressure and stress.[49]

Management Style

Management style significantly affects the psychological climate of the workplace, and certain styles of dealing with subordinates create more stress than others. For example, one study found that high scores on Machiavellianism (managing through fear) were negatively related to job satisfaction and positively related to job tension.[50] Certain types of jobs and associate personalities may interact with managerial style to produce stress. For example, directive managerial styles may produce less stress on routine jobs and with associates who prefer a more structured environment. However, for people in professional jobs and for those who prefer more personal involvement and self-determination in their jobs, a less directive managerial style produces less stress.

Monitoring

Relatively recent developments in technology have led to an explosion of stricter monitoring of associates' behavior—both work-related and non-work-related. Organizations are able to read associates' e-mail, detect websites they visit, listen to phone conversations, and keep track of any work they do electronically. As illustrated in our opening feature, Verizon's call-center associates frequently mentioned phone monitoring as a source of stress. Monitoring can cause associates to experience increased demands and loss of control at the same time, making monitoring extremely stressful.[51] Demands are increased because associates feel that they must always be "on" and that any mistake will be noticed. Control is lessened because associates who are being monitored may feel that they have little discretion in how they do their jobs. Call-center associates, for example, complained about having to follow strict scripts when they felt that it was inappropriate and would even hinder performance.

Job Insecurity

In the early part of the twenty-first century, the U.S. unemployment rate increased somewhat, and more organizations became involved in mergers and acquisitions, downsizing, and moving work offshore. The economic downturn beginning in 2008 has led to record numbers of jobs lost and unemployment rates over 9 percent. As a result, U.S. associates today are more likely to experience insecurity about keeping their jobs. Job insecurity can be an enormous stressor.[52]

Incivility in the Workplace

Have you ever been annoyed by someone taking a cell phone call while you were in a meeting, or by someone sending rude jokes over the Internet, or by someone purposefully failing to include you in a conference call? If so, then you have experienced **incivility** at work. *Incivility* is defined as slightly deviant behavior with ambiguous intent to harm another person.[53] Slightly deviant behavior means that the behavior is not overtly aggressive, physical, or violent. Ambiguous intent means that the perpetrator behaves in a way so that he or she can deny the intent to harm someone else. Incivility at work has been found to be related to job stress, mental health, and physical health of employees,[54] as well as other outcomes that impact an organization's bottom line.[55] Incivility in the workplace is discussed in more detail in the *Experiencing Organizational Behavior* feature.

incivility
Slightly deviant behavior with ambiguous intent to harm another person.

EXPERIENCING ORGANIZATIONAL BEHAVIOR

Incivility on the Job: The Cost of Being Nasty

On September 9, 2009, President Barack Obama was giving a speech to a joint session of congress about health care issues. In the middle of the President's speech, Republican Representative Joe Wilson from South Carolina very loudly and angrily said "You lie!" President Obama paused and said "That's not true." and then continued on.

Wilson's behavior went against all the norms and mores for decorum and respect in this type of event, where proper behavior is somewhat ritualized. After receiving pressure from his colleagues, Wilson came back an hour later with the following apology: "This evening I let my emotions get the best of me. While I disagree with the President's statement, my comments were inappropriate and regrettable. I extend sincere apologies to the President for this lack of civility." Several days later, when Wilson refused to apologize to his colleagues in Congress about his outburst, House Democrats, and some Republicans, reprimanded him. *New York Times* columnist, Maureen Dowd, wrote of the incident "It was a rare triumph for civility in a country that seems to have lost all sense of it."

Have we become an uncivil society, and does this behavior generalize to the workplace (outside of congressional meetings with the President)? A 10-year-long study by Christine Pearson and Christine Porath suggests that we have. In their survey of thousands of employees, 96 percent reported experiencing incivility at work, and nearly half reported that were treated rudely once or more a week. Ninety-nine percent reported that they had witnessed incivility being inflicted on other people. Another study by Lilia Cortina and her colleagues found that 71 percent of employees reported being the targets of incivility in the past five years. Examples of incivility include:

- passing blame for our own mistakes
- taking credit for other's efforts
- checking e-mail or texting during meetings
- talking down to others
- belittling others
- withholding information
- paying little attention to others' opinions
- making demeaning remarks about someone
- avoiding someone

Clearly, workplace incivility is a common occurrence, and according to Porath and Pearson's study, an expensive one for organizations. They found that associates who were

©Radius Images/Alamy

victims of uncivil treatment reacted by generally withdrawing from work. About half of the respondents said they decreased effort, time at work, or the quality of their work, so not surprisingly, 66 percent reported that their performance declined. Almost 80 percent said they became less committed to their organizations and 12 percent said they quit their jobs as a direct result of being the victim of incivility. Lilia Cortina and Vicki Magley's studies of thousands of other people in several professions found further costs of incivility in that it was a major stressor and was related to negative mental and physical health outcomes.

Sources: C. Pearson & C. Porath. 2009. *The cost of bad behavior: How incivility is costing your business and what you can do about it.* New York: Penguin Group; C.L. Porath, & C.M. Pearson. 2010. The cost of bad behavior. *Organizational Dynamics*, 39: 64–71; M. Dowd. Sept. 15, 2009. "Rapping Joe's Knuckles." *The New York Times*, at http://www.nytimes.com/2009/09/16/opinion/16dowd.html; A. Graves. Sept. 16, 2009. "Joe Wilson." *The New York Times*, at http://topics.nytimes.com/top/reference/timestopics/people/w/addison_graves_wilson/index.html; L. M. Cortina, V. J. Magley, J. H. Williams, & R. D. Langhout. 2001. Incivility at the workplace: Incidence and impact. *Journal of Occupational Health Psychology*, 6 (1): 64–80; S. Lim, L. M Cortina, & V. J Magley. 2008. Personal and workgroup incivility: Impact on work and health outcomes. *Journal of Applied Psychology*, 93: 95–107; L. M. Cortina, & V. J. Magley. 2009. Patterns and profiles of response to incivility in the workplace. *Journal of Occupational Health Psychology*, 14: 272–288.

Individual Influences on Experiencing Stress

Earlier, in defining *stress,* we noted that individuals vary in how they respond to external stressors. For example, some individuals may be energized by quite demanding workloads, whereas others respond with negative stress reactions. A great deal of research has examined characteristics that are likely to influence how an individual reacts to stress. These characteristics include Type A versus Type B personality, self-esteem, hardiness, and gender.

Type A versus Type B Personality

Many researchers have studied people with Type A and Type B personalities and how they respond to stress. People with **Type A personalities** are competitive, aggressive, and impatient. Type A's may push themselves to achieve higher and higher goals until they become frustrated, irritated, anxious, and hostile. Type A behavior is exemplified by the driver who blasts the car horn when the car in front of him is a second too slow in moving through an intersection after the light has turned green. In the words of the two physicians who focused attention on this phenomenon:

> The Type A pattern is an action–emotion complex that can be observed in any person who is aggressively involved in a chronic, incessant struggle to achieve more and more in less and less time, and if required to do so, against the opposing efforts of other things or other persons. It is not psychosis or a complex of worries or fears or phobias or obsessions, but a socially acceptable—indeed often praised—form of conflict.[56]

People with Type B personalities are quite different. They tend to be less competitive, less aggressive, and more patient.

People with Type A personalities are more susceptible to stress-induced illness.[57] Type A individuals may experience more stress for two reasons. First, given their competitive and aggressive tendencies, they may actually create more stressors in their environments. For example, Type A people have been known to increase work overload on their own, whereas Type B people are more reasonable.[58] Second, Type A people are more likely to appraise any given event as a stressor than are Type B people.[59]

Self-Esteem

Research has found that people with high self-esteem suffer fewer negative effects from stress than people with low self-esteem.[60] People with high self-esteem, in general, experience greater well-being and may be more resistant to the effects of stressors. Furthermore, people with high self-esteem are more likely to engage in active coping behaviors when they experience stressful demands relative to those with low self-esteem. For example, when faced with a heavy workload, people with high self-esteem may break tasks down into manageable units and prioritize their work so that they can begin to tackle excessive work demands. In contrast, someone with low self-esteem may withdraw from the work or procrastinate, making the work overload even worse. Consequently, people with high self-esteem are more likely to gain control over stressful situations and decrease the amount of stress they experience.

Hardiness

Individuals who are high in **hardiness** tend to have a strong internal commitment to their activities, have an internal locus of control, and seek challenge in everyday life. Research

Type A personality
A personality type characterized by competitiveness, aggressiveness, and impatience.

hardiness
A personality dimension corresponding to a strong internal commitment to activities, an internal locus of control, and challenge seeking.

has shown that people who are high in hardiness experience less severe negative stress reactions than those who are low in hardiness.[61] For example, one study showed that managers in a public utility who had scored high on hardiness had fewer illnesses following exposure to significant stress.[62]

Perhaps the most important aspect of hardiness is locus of control. Recall from Chapter 5 that people with an internal locus of control are likely to view themselves as responsible for the outcomes they experience. Those with an external locus of control are more likely to view themselves as victims of fate or luck. It is not surprising that people with an internal locus of control are more likely to develop active coping strategies and to perceive that they have control when experiencing stressful work demands. However, research has shown that the relationship between stress and locus of control may be more complex because people who have an extreme internal locus of control are likely to blame themselves for negative events and thus experience more responsibility, a stressor.[63]

Gender

Although the evidence is not entirely conclusive, women and men do not seem to differ in how stressful they perceive a given stressor to be.[64] They do, however, seem to cope differently. More specifically, women seek more emotional social support (comfort and a shoulder to lean on), seek more instrumental social support (specific support to solve a problem), engage in more positive self-talk, and exhibit rumination (thinking over the situation).[65] Social support tends to be an effective coping strategy.[66]

Beyond the above issues, women might be exposed to more stressors in the workplace. In some cases, women are paid less than men are for similar work. They are more likely than men to experience discrimination and stereotyping and to work in service industries that are stressful (such as nursing). Research suggests that women experience a greater variety of stressors in the workplace than men.[67] Some studies directly comparing the stress experienced by men and women at work also suggest that women experience more stress overall.[68] The U.S. Bureau of Labor Statistics reported that for every case of stress leading to work absence for men, there were 1.6 cases for women.[69]

Individual and Organizational Consequences of Stress

It should be clear by now that stress can be detrimental to developing a high-involvement, high-performance work organization. High-involvement organizations require that associates be engaged and motivated to perform at high levels and that their individual capabilities be used in the most productive and efficient manner. However, the consequences of work stress can sabotage managerial attempts to develop such an environment. The following discussion focuses on the individual and organizational consequences of stress.

Individual Consequences

Individual consequences of stress can be classified as psychological, behavioral, or physiological.

Psychological Consequences

Psychological responses to stress include anxiety, depression, low self-esteem, sleeplessness, frustration, family problems, and burnout.[70] Some of these psychological reactions are more severe than others. Their importance and overall effect on individual behavior and physical condition depend on their degree or level. Extreme frustration or anxiety can lead to other, more severe behavioral and physiological problems.

One important psychological problem is **burnout**. Associates and managers experiencing burnout show little or no enthusiasm for their jobs and generally experience constant fatigue. These individuals often complain bitterly about their work, blame others for mistakes, are absent from work more and more often, are uncooperative with co-workers, and become increasingly isolated.[71] Burnout often occurs in jobs that require individuals to work closely and intensely with others under emotionally charged conditions (nursing is an example). Burnout is a major concern in American industry and governmental organizations.

burnout
A condition of physical or emotional exhaustion generally brought about by stress; associates and managers experiencing burnout show various symptoms, such as constant fatigue, or lack of enthusiasm for work, and increasing isolation from others.

Behavioral Consequences

Behavioral consequences of stress include excessive smoking, substance abuse (alcohol, drugs), accident proneness, appetite disorders, and even violence.[72] Probably the most severe behavioral consequences are substance abuse and violence.

Substance abuse, unfortunately, has become much more common in the United States in recent years. The Department of Health and Human Services has reported that alcohol, tobacco, and other drug-related problems cost U.S. businesses over $100 billion every year.[73] Studies have shown that alcoholics and other drug users in the workforce exhibit the following characteristics:[74]

- They are much less productive than other associates.
- They use three times as many sick days as other associates.
- They are more likely to expose themselves and co-workers to serious safety hazards because of poor judgment and coordination. Up to 40 percent of industrial fatalities are linked to alcohol and drug consumption.
- They are five times more likely to file worker's compensation claims. In general, they are subject to higher rates of absenteeism, accidents, and sickness.
- They report missing work frequently because of hangovers.
  Each year, 500 million workdays are lost because of alcoholism.

©John Sleeman/Photodisc/Getty Images, Inc.

Although there are many reasons for alcoholism and drug abuse, many people use alcohol and drugs as a means of handling stress. Alcohol and some drugs are depressants that can substantially reduce emotional reactions. Studies have shown that in small doses, alcohol has little effect. However, with moderate-to-heavy consumption, alcohol can substantially reduce tension, anxiety, fear, and other emotional reactions to disturbing situations.[75] Drugs can have the same effects. Alcohol and drugs, then, give people a means of blocking stress reactions when they cannot control the situation. Of course, emotions are suppressed only as long as the individual continues to consume large quantities of alcohol or drugs. Because the disturbing situation still exists, emotional reactions return when the effects of drugs or alcohol wear off, leading to continued usage of these substances.

Another serious behavioral consequence of stress is workplace violence. The Occupational Safety and Health Administration (OSHA) reports that approximately two million workers are victims of workplace violence every year. Homicide is the third leading cause of workplace fatalities. Workplace violence can be either physical or mental, as in the case of excessive taunting or harassment. Many cases of tragic outbursts at work are related to stressful working conditions. The case of Mark O. Barton offers an example.

On July 31, 1999, Barton shot and killed 9 people and injured 13 more at two Atlanta day-trading organizations. In the previous days, he had killed his wife and two children by hammering them to death. After being spotted by the police at a gas station a few hours after the shootings, Barton shot and killed himself. What caused Barton to commit these unspeakable acts of violence? While the causes of such behavior are highly complex, one contributing factor was the extreme stress involved in day trading.[76]

Day trading involves the buying and selling of stocks on a very-short-term basis. Traders often use their own money, and they can experience heavy gains and losses daily. In the month before the killings, Mark Barton had lost $105,000. Day traders have no security and no regular paycheck. Some have said that day traders must have a casino mentality.[77] Christopher Farrell, author of *Day Trading Online,* states: "A day trader makes a living at the game; you live or die by your profit and loss. You never get away from it. It's on your mind twenty-four hours a day. You don't have a steady paycheck."[78] Although day trading is not as popular as it once was, it continues to be a widespread phenomenon.[79]

Stress probably was not the only factor that led to Barton's deadly outburst; he most likely suffered from personality disorders. However, the stress of trading may have been one factor that set him off. And while Barton's behavior may have been extreme, workplace violence is so prevalent that we have nicknames for it, such as "going postal," "desk rage," and "air rage" to describe it.

Physiological Consequences

Physiological reactions to stress include high blood pressure, muscle tension, headaches, ulcers, skin diseases, impaired immune systems, musculoskeletal disorders (such as back problems), and even more serious ailments, such as heart disease and cancer.[80] Stress has also been linked to obesity, a rising health epidemic worldwide.[81] Stress can be directly related to physiological problems, or it can make existing conditions worse. As we mentioned earlier, it has been estimated that 75 percent of all medical problems are directly attributable to stress.[82] The physical ailments noted above may lower productivity while on the job and increase absences from work (thereby reducing overall productivity even more).

Rick Speckmann exemplifies the debilitating physiological effects that can result from stress.[83] Speckmann was a hard-driving entrepreneur, burned out from the stress of running his executive search company in Minneapolis. One day, at age 40, Speckmann experienced an intense tightness in his chest after exercising. He was promptly sent to the hospital in an ambulance, where he received a battery of tests. The final diagnosis: acute overstress. Luckily, Speckmann paid attention to this lesson and changed his lifestyle to a less stressful one. It is important to note that physiological stress begins with normal biological mechanisms. Recall from our earlier discussion that the stress response prepares the body to deal with impending danger by releasing hormones and increasing the heartbeat, pulse rate, blood pressure, breathing rate, and output of blood sugar from the liver. These physiological changes helped primitive human beings respond to danger.[84] Such a physiological response to stress is often referred to as the *fight-or-flight response*. However, the stress response is best adapted for dealing with acute stress. As noted earlier, it is chronic stress, and the physiological responses to it, that can lead to physical ailments. The human body has not yet adapted well to an environment of continuous stress. Therefore, individual responses to stress can be severe and costly.

Organizational Consequences

Stress has consequences for organizations as well as for individuals. These consequences follow from the effects on individuals that include lower motivation, dissatisfaction, lower job performance, increased absenteeism, increased turnover, and lower quality of relationships at work. Research has shown strong connections between stress, job dissatisfaction, turnover, and health-care costs.[85] Stress-related illnesses cost companies millions of dollars in insurance and worker's compensation claims. Employees who report high levels of stress have health-care expenditures that are 50 percent higher than those reporting lower levels of stress.[86] Exhibit 7-4 gives some perspective to these costs.

Furthermore, individual consequences of stress may interact to cause organizational problems. For example, behavioral problems, such as violence, and psychological consequences, such as anxiety, can lower the quality of the relationships between co-workers, resulting in distrust, animosity, and a breakdown in communications. When individuals frequently miss work because of stress-related illness, their colleagues may become resentful at having to take over their work while they are absent.[87] We have already discussed the increased safety risks for everyone that result from one person's alcohol or drug use. Thus, the organizational consequences of stress can be dangerous as well as costly. Fortunately, many organizations and professionals, including companies, government agencies (NIOSH, OSHA), medical doctors, and psychologists, have recognized the importance of addressing stress in the workplace, and a variety of techniques have been developed to combat stress-induced problems. We now turn to a discussion of actions that can be taken to alleviate the debilitating effects of stress on individuals and organizations.

EXHIBIT 7-4 Managerial Costs of Job Stress

The cost of job stress to American industry can be estimated at $200 billion per year due to:

Absenteeism
Diminished productivity
Compensation claims
Health insurance
Direct medical expenses

To put this figure into perspective, consider the following:

Total U.S. corporate profits were $897.6 billion in 2006 (after taxes, with inventory valuation and capital accounted for).

The entire U.S. gross domestic product (the market value of the nation's goods and services) was approximately $13,246 billion in 2006.

Sources: 2007, at http://www.bca.gov/national/txt/dpga.txt; Bureau of Economic Analysis, 2007, at http://www.bea.gov/national/xls/gdplev.xls; J. Cahill, P.A. Landsbergis & P.L. Schnall. 1995. "Reducing Occupational Stress," at http://workhealth.org/prevention/prred.html.

Managing Workplace Stress

Individual associates and managers can implement a number of tactics to more effectively deal with stress. Similarly, organizations can be helpful in alleviating stress. They also can be mindful of stressful working conditions that cause stress in the first place.

Individual Stress Management

Based on the models of stress discussed earlier in this chapter, associates and managers can avoid workplace stress by finding jobs that provide a personally acceptable balance between demands and control, and between effort required and rewards. They can also propose that a dysfunctional job be redesigned. Further, they can avoid or reduce some stress by following the tactics for work–life balance presented in the earlier *Managerial Advice* feature. Beyond these tactics, individuals can adopt several positive tactics for coping with existing stress. The goal is to develop healthy ways of coping. Because individuals experience multiple sources of stress, using multiple tactics for coping is beneficial.

One of the most important tactics is regular exercise. Three areas are important: endurance, strength, and flexibility.[88] Endurance activities maintain or increase aerobic capacity. Key activities include regular walking, treadmill walking, jogging, running, cycling, and swimming. Extreme amounts of endurance exercise are not required. Moderate amounts improve fitness and reduce mortality.[89] Moderate exercise has been defined as 30 minutes of sustained activity three to four times per week, at a heart rate that is above the normal rate but below the maximum rate. An individual's target heart rate can be calculated by subtracting his age from 220, and then taking 65 to 80 percent of that number.[90]

Strength activities maintain or improve muscle mass and can prevent loss of bone mass as well. Key activities include weight training and aqua-aerobics. Twenty minutes of these types of exercises three times per week can provide important benefits.[91] Flexibility activities maintain or improve range of motion and energy. Stretching is the key activity. Stretching various muscle groups three times per week provides important and sustainable benefits.[92]

A second tactic for coping with stress is proper diet. Diet affects energy, alertness, and overall well-being. According to research conducted at the Cooper Institute, four key areas should be considered.[93] First, it is important to monitor fat intake. Adults over 30 should obtain no more than 20 to 25 percent of calories from fat per day. Younger adults also should be careful with fat consumption. Fifty to 70 percent of calories should come from complex carbohydrates (drawn from fruits, vegetables, and whole grain foods, not from candy and cakes). Ten to 15 percent of calories should come from protein (drawn from fish, poultry, and meats). Second, it is important to consume a reasonable amount of fiber, both insoluble and soluble. Third, consumption of calcium is important. Fourth, consumption of foods rich in antioxidants can be helpful. Antioxidants seem to be helpful in preventing damage caused by normal bodily operations involving oxygen.

In today's world, implementing a proper diet can be difficult. Time for grocery shopping and cooking is often limited. Many companies (not to mention school cafeterias) make the situation worse by providing or facilitating the consumption of junk food. In a poll conducted by Harris Interactive for the Marlin Company (a workplace communications company), 63 percent of respondents reported that vending machines on the job mostly contain junk food, such as potato chips, candy bars, and cookies. In a second poll, 74 percent of respondents reported that it is common for special occasions to be celebrated with candy, cookies, or cake. Even on routine workdays, accessible candy bowls are in many cubicles and offices.

A third tactic for coping with stress involves the development and use of social-support networks.[94] Social support is very important. Research has shown that such support is positively related to cardiovascular functioning and negatively related to perceived stress, anxiety, and depression.[95] Having friends and family to talk with about problems can be quite useful (emotional social support). Having friends and family who can offer specific suggestions, provide resources, and break down barriers can also be quite useful (instrumental social support).

A fourth tactic involves the use of relaxation techniques. For some, meditation, yoga, and visualization of serene settings work very well. For others, a simple walk in the park is more useful.

Other tactics include developing and using planning skills, being realistic about what can be accomplished, and avoiding unnecessary competition.

Organizational Stress Management

Organizations can help to reduce stress or help managers and associates deal more effectively with stress. To reduce stress, the following actions can be taken. These actions are consistent with high-involvement management:

- Increase individuals' autonomy and control. According to the demand–control model, increased control should help to keep experienced stress to manageable levels.
- Ensure that individuals are compensated properly. According to the effort–rewards imbalance model, proper compensation should help to keep experienced stress to manageable levels.
- Maintain job demands/requirements at healthy levels.
- Ensure that associates have adequate skills to keep up-to-date with technical changes in the workplace.
- Increase associate involvement in important decision making.
- Improve physical working conditions. For example, use ergonomically sound equipment and tools.
- Provide for job security and career development. Provide educational opportunities so that associates can continue to improve their skill sets. Use job redesign and job rotation to expand associates' skill sets.
- Provide healthy work schedules. Avoid constant shifting of schedules. Allow for flextime or other alternative work schedules.
- Improve communication to help avoid uncertainty and ambiguity.

In addition to actions taken to reduce stress, organizations can help associates and managers cope with stress and its effects. Specifically, they can encourage some managers to be "toxin handlers" and they can implement wellness programs. These are discussed next.

Toxin handlers, a term coined by renowned educator and consultant Peter Frost, are people who take it upon themselves to handle the pain and stressors that are part of everyday life in organizations.[96] Frost argues that toxin handlers are necessary for organizations to be successful, even though their contributions are often overlooked. Without the efforts of these organizational heroes, both individual and organizational well-being and productivity would suffer.

Managers can become more efficient, compassionate toxin handlers. Frost lists the following behaviors as necessary for handling the pain, strain, and stress of others:

- Read your own and others' emotional cues and understand the impact that emotional cues have on others. For example, be aware that when you show signs of anger, the most common response will be defensiveness or hostility. This can begin a cycle of negative emotions and nonproductive behavior that could have been avoided. The ability to avoid negative behaviors is one of the major components of emotional intelligence.
- Keep people connected. Devise ways in which people at work can react to each other as human beings. This can be accomplished by encouraging intimacy and fun.
- Empathize with those who are in pain. Actively listen with compassion.
- Act to alleviate the suffering of others. Providing a shoulder to cry on might be appropriate. Arranging for discreet financial aid to an associate in need might be useful.
- Mobilize people to deal with their pain and get their lives back on track. Actively acknowledge problems, encourage helping behavior, and celebrate achievements.
- Create an environment where compassionate behavior toward others is encouraged and rewarded.

Wellness programs are very popular and important tools that organizations use to manage stress and its effects.[97] These programs include health screenings, health advice, risk-management programs, smoking cessation, weight control, and exercise. The main goal is to develop/maintain a healthy and productive workforce. In some organizations, health coaches are used to proactively monitor participating associates and managers. These coaches, often nurses, offer advice based on health-screening information as well as ongoing medical events and drug prescriptions.[98]

The wellness program at Johnson & Johnson (J&J) is one of the oldest and most recognized. Originally called "Live for Life," the program has helped thousands of people lead healthier lives. In terms of company benefits, assessments have shown positive returns to the bottom line through enhanced productivity and lower health-care costs. In 2002, one estimate suggested that savings just from reduced medical expenditures have been approximately $224 per person per year, which translates into a total of $22.4 million per year based on J&J's employment base of 100,000.[99] In 2008, J&J estimates that it avoided $15.9 million in health care costs for its U.S. employees alone. J&J has exceeded its program goals given that:

- 96 percent of employees are tobacco-free.
- 94 percent of employees have blood pressures of 140/90 or better.
- 93 percent of employees have total cholesterol levels below 240.
- 68 percent of employees are physically active, defined as 30 minutes of activity three or more times each week.[100]

Evidence suggests that wellness programs provide benefits to both individuals and organizations. As such, organizations want as many people as possible to participate. Participation, though, is voluntary. As discussed in the next *Experiencing Organizational Behavior* feature, incentives have been used to raise participation levels. These incentives, however, have a dark side, and legal issues have arisen.

Incentives for Participating in Wellness Programs

Evidence supporting the bottom-line impact of wellness programs has begun to accumulate. Overall, research suggests a return of three dollars for every one dollar spent, with some recent estimates suggesting a return of six dollars per dollar spent on a wellness program. In one recent evaluation of programs at organizations such as LL Bean, Duke University, and General Motors, returns on investment were very positive.

With substantial benefits available, incentives designed to increase participation are now offered by many companies. Indeed, according to a 2008 Harris Interactive poll, 91 percent of employers "believed they could reduce their health care costs by influencing employees to adopt healthier lifestyles." Because participation by associates and managers is voluntary, these incentives are very important. At Baptist Health Florida, individuals who complete the wellness program's health assessment receive an additional $10,000 in life insurance survivor benefits. At IBM, individuals who complete a health risk assessment at the start of the year are given up to two $150 payments. At Scotts Miracle-Gro, associates receive a $10 monthly fitness center membership fee, which is reimbursable after 120 uses of the center, free health coaching,

free medical services for employees and covered dependents, and free prescriptions for generic drugs.

At some companies, however, incentives have become heavy-handed, and this is a source of growing concern. Employees at Weyco who failed to have mandated medical tests and evaluations in 2006 paid an additional $65 per month for insurance premiums. After 2006, additional increases have come into play for those who continue to resist the program. Employees at Scotts Miracle-Gro Company who failed to have "requested" evaluations saw $40 per month added to their insurance premiums. Moreover, all employees were subjected to investigation by an outside health-management company. This company used data-mining techniques and available databases to uncover any health problems or risks. Those who had issues/risks were assigned a health coach and an action plan was developed. Individuals who failed to comply with the action plan saw $67 per month added to their insurance premiums.

Although it makes sense to have people with higher risks pay more for insurance, there are some problems to consider. First, health assessments are becoming less and less voluntary and seek very personal information (e.g., information on depression, the quality

of a relationship with a spouse/partner, parents' causes of death). Is it appropriate to provide, directly or indirectly, this information to an employer? Second, the use of financial incentives tied to health plan costs and the pushing of action plans based on health status may bring legal issues. Certainly, charging people in certain categories (i.e., smokers) more for health insurance can be a complex undertaking. In the United States, the Health Insurance Portability and Accountability Act (HIPAA), the Americans with Disabilities Act (ADA), and Bona Fide Wellness Program Exceptions (BFWP) must be considered, along with applicable state laws.

Overall, the use of heavy-handed incentives (and indeed punishments) is becoming more common as companies strive for a smarter, fitter workforce. Only time will tell how accepted these practices become.

©Ryan McVay/Stone/Getty Images, Inc.

Sources: L. Chapman. 2006. "Wellness Programs Hitting Their Stride," *Benefits & Compensation Digest*, 43, no. 2: 15–17; M. Conlin. 2007. "Get Healthy or Else: One Company's All-out Attack on Medical Costs," *BusinessWeek*, Feb. 26, pp. 58–69; R. Dotinga. 2006. "Can Boss Insist on Healthy Habits?" *Christian Science Monitor*, Jan. 11, p. 15; D. Koffman, R. Goetzel, V. Anwuri, K. Shore, D. Orenstein, & T. Lapier. 2005. "Heart Healthy and Stroke Free," *American Journal of Preventive Medicine*, 29: 113–121; L. McGinley. 2006. "Health Costs: The Big Push for Wellness," *Wall Street Journal*, July 16, p. 2A; M. McQueen. 2006. "The Road to Wellness Is Starting at the Office: Employers' Efforts to Push Preventative Care Begin to Show Both Health and Cost Benefits," *Wall Street Journal*, Dec. 5, p. D1; T.M. Simon, F. Bruno, N. Grossman, & C. Stamm. 2006. "Designing Compliant Wellness Programs: HIPAA, ADA, and State Insurance Laws," *Benefits Law Journal*, 19, no. 4: 46–59; T. Walker. 2007. "Businesses Justify Worker Incentives," *Managed Healthcare Executive*, 17, no. 5: 18; L. Hand. Winter, 2009. Employer health incentives: Employee wellness programs prod workers to adopt healthy lifestyles. *Harvard Public Health Review*. At http://www.hsph.harvard.edu/news/hphr/winter-2009/winter09healthincentives.html.

Stress is an important component of organizational life. Although some stress has positive effects on people's behavior, much stress is dysfunctional. Stress affects everyone in the organization—top executives, middle and lower-level managers, and associates at all levels. All of these individuals represent human capital to an organization. We know that human capital is important because it represents much of the knowledge and skill in an organization and affects task performance. Effective task performance and problem solving are necessary for an organization to gain and hold a competitive advantage, which in turn results in positive outcomes for the organization and its external stakeholders. However, dysfunctional stress prevents associates and managers from fully utilizing their knowledge and applying it in their jobs. When this occurs, their productivity suffers, and organizational performance is harmed. If many associates and managers are overstressed, the organization may suffer millions of dollars in extra costs and lower profits. In short, top executives who want the strategies they develop to be successfully implemented must manage the stress in their organizations. Overall, managers' ability to prevent stress and help associates cope with the stress they experience will have a major impact on the performance of individuals and the organization as a whole.

Critical Thinking Questions

1. How can good stress be distinguished from bad stress? How much stress is too much stress?

2. How can managing stress in an organization contribute to improved strategy implementation and organizational performance?

3. How much stress do you currently experience? How can reducing your stress increase your performance in school and enhance your life in general?

What This Chapter Adds to Your Knowledge Portfolio

In this chapter, we have discussed workplace stress, focusing on its causes and consequences and what can be done to help manage it. A high-involvement, high-performance workplace requires that associates perform at their best; however, stress can prevent them from doing so. If an organization is to compete successfully, it is important both to manage the stress experienced by associates and to eliminate some of the sources of stress. In summary, we have made the following points.

- Stress is a feeling of tension experienced by an individual who feels that the demands of a situation are about to exceed her ability to cope. It can also be acute (short-term) or chronic (long-term). Not all stress has negative effects; eustress is positive stress that results from facing challenges with an expectation of achievement.
- The demand–control model of stress suggests that experienced stress is a function of both job demands and job control. Stress is highest when demands are high but control is low. The effort–reward imbalance model suggests that stress comes about when effort required is high but rewards are low.
- Organizational and work-related stressors include role conflict, role ambiguity, work overload, occupation, resource inadequacy, working conditions, management style, monitoring, job insecurity, and incivility.
- Individual differences can influence how people experience stress, react to stress, and cope with stress. These individual differences include Type A versus

Type B personalities, self-esteem, hardiness, and gender.

- The consequences of stress are serious for both individuals and organizations. For the individual, stress can lead to psychological consequences, such as burnout; behavioral consequences, such as substance abuse and violence; and physiological consequences, such as high blood pressure, impaired immune systems, and heart disease. Many medical problems are attributed to stress.

- Organizational consequences of stress include lower job performance across a number of people, higher absenteeism and turnover rates, lower quality of work relationships, increased safety risks, and increased health-care and insurance costs.

- Associates and managers can do many things to help manage their own stress. Coping tactics include exercise, healthy diets, social support, and relaxation techniques.

- Organizations can reduce the stress experienced by associates and managers by reducing stressors. They also can encourage toxin handlers and implement wellness programs.

back to the knowledge objectives

1. What do we mean by *stress*? What are the distinguishing features of acute and chronic stress, and eustress and dystress? Does all stress result in negative consequences?
2. How does the human body react to stress? What are the outcomes of this reaction? How can you tell if you or someone you know may be suffering from too much stress?
3. What are the general causes of workplace stress according to the demand–control model? What are the general causes of stress according to the effort–reward imbalance model? What implications do these models have for creating a high-involvement workplace? What are the most common workplace stressors?
4. What types of people are likely to experience the most stress at work? If you are experiencing too much stress, what can you do to help manage it?
5. What specific effects does workplace stress have on individuals and organizations?
6. What can organizations do to prevent and manage workplace stress? What specific changes can they make?

Thinking about Ethics

1. What responsibility do senior managers have to understand how their decisions affect the stress experienced by other managers and by associates?

2. Do managers have any responsibility to help associates manage stress caused by life events outside of work? Explain.

3. What actions should a manager take if she has an associate experiencing burnout?

4. Do organizations have a responsibility to offer programs or benefits that can help associates manage stress, such as more vacations, flexible work arrangements, and wellness programs? Why or why not?

5. Is it appropriate for employers to seek detailed personal information in order to make recommendations for wellness action plans?

Key Terms

stress, p. 249
job stress, p. 249
acute stress, p. 249
chronic stress, p. 249
stress response, p. 249
eustress, p. 250

dystress, p. 250
demand–control
   model, p. 251
effort–reward imbalance
   model, p. 251
stressors, p. 253

role conflict, p. 253
role ambiguity, p. 254
incivility, p. 257
Type A personality, p. 259
hardiness, p. 259
burnout, p. 261

Human Resource Management Applications

Human Resource Management (HRM) departments play a big role in helping organizations and their associates assess and manage stress. Employee Assistance Programs (EAPs), which are designed to help associates deal with personal, mental health, and physical health concerns are a part of the HRM function. EAPs also involve developing programs that serve to prevent or buffer stress.

Employers often use incentives and sanctions to motivate associates to engage in healthy behaviors and learn how to cope with stress. This often involves modifications to benefits programs, which are handled by HRM departments.

Finally, the HRM department may conduct surveys to assess stressors in the work environment and associates' perceptions of stress.

---

building your human capital

How Well Do You Handle Stress?

One of the most famous stress studies was published in 1960 and illustrated that it was possible to predict the likelihood that a person would succumb to stress-related illnesses within two years. The study resulted in the following list of life events with assigned points that can be used to predict a person's chances of becoming ill. The list is slightly modified to reflect modern life. Even though this research is almost 40 years old, the questionnaire still predicts stress-related illness.

To find out how likely you are to experience health problems due to stress, mark each life event that you have experienced in the last 12 months.

RANK	LIFE EVENT	POINT VALUE
1	Death of a spouse or life partner	100
2	Divorce or breakup with life partner	73
3	Marital separation or separation from life partner	65
4	Jail term	63
5	Death of close family member	63
6	Personal injury or illness	53
7	Marriage	50
8	Fired from job or laid off	47
9	Relationship reconciliation	45
10	Retirement	45
11	Change in health of family member	44
12	Pregnancy	40
13	Sex difficulties	39
14	Gain of new family member	39
15	Major business readjustment	39
16	Change in financial state	38
17	Death of close friend	37
18	Change in one's line of work	36
19	Change in number of arguments with spouse or partner	35
20	Taking on large mortgage or debt	31
21	Foreclosure of mortgage or loan	30
22	Change in work responsibilities	29
23	Child leaving home	29
24	Trouble with in-laws	29
25	Outstanding personal achievement	28

RANK	LIFE EVENT	POINT VALUE
26	Spouse or partner's work begins or stops	26
27	Beginning or ending schooling	26
28	Change in living conditions	25
29	Revision of personal habits (e.g., diet, quit smoking)	24
30	Trouble with boss	23
31	Change in work hours or conditions	20
32	Change in residence	20
33	Change in schools	20
34	Change in recreation	19
35	Change in church activities	19
36	Change in social activities	18
37	Taking on a small mortgage or debt	17
38	Change in sleep habits	16
39	Change in number of family get-togethers	15
40	Change in eating habits	15
41	Vacation	13
42	Christmas (or other major holiday)	12
43	Minor violations of the law	11

Scoring

Total the point values of the life events that you marked. Use the total to assess your risk of health problems, as follows:

Up to 150 points	You are unlikely to experience health problems due to stress.
151–300 points	You have a 50 percent chance of experiencing health problems due to stress.
301 or more points	You have an 80 percent chance of experiencing health problems due to stress.

Source: Adapted from T. Holmes & R. Rahe. 1967. "Holmes-Rahe Social Readjustment Rating Scale," *Journal of Psychosomatic Research*, 11: 213–218.

---

an organizational behavior moment
Friend or Associate?

Walt strode angrily to the kitchen to see Tony. Tony had begun showing up late for work and had missed several shifts altogether. In fact, Walt had had to cover his shift last night. The problem was that Walt really liked Tony despite the drinking problem. "I even named my kid after him," Walt thought to himself.

He had first met Tony when they both worked at the old Frontier Hotel. Tony was the chef, and Walt was headwaiter. Perhaps because they were both in their late thirties and headed nowhere, they really hit it off. Even in those days, Tony had a taste for the booze. Tony's marriage was breaking up, and he seemed to be lost. Walt often traveled the bars looking for Tony when he had missed a few days of work. He would get Tony sobered up and help him straighten it out with the boss. Tony would be okay for two or three months, and then it would happen all over again. Throughout all this time, Walt remained a faithful friend, believing that some day Tony would straighten himself out.

It was during one of Tony's good periods that the idea of starting a restaurant came up. Tony encouraged Walt to start a place of his own. Walt thought the idea was crazy, but Tony insisted on having Walt meet another friend, Bill, who might be interested in backing the idea. After several meetings and a lot of planning, they opened a small place, converting an old two-story home into a quaint Italian restaurant.

Walt and Bill were full partners, and Tony was to be the chef. They had both tried to convince Tony to join them in partnership, but he had refused. It had something to do with losing his freedom, but Walt was never sure what Tony had meant by that.

The restaurant had been an almost-instant success. Within a year, they had to move to a larger location. Walt couldn't believe how much money he was making. He took care of his associates, sharing his revenues generously with them and frequently acknowledging their efforts. Tony was earning nearly twice what he had made at the Frontier and seemed to be happy.

Then, about a week ago, Tony didn't come in to work. He hadn't called in sick; he just didn't show up. Walt was a little worried about him, but he covered the shift and went over to Tony's the next morning. Tony answered the door still half asleep, and Walt demanded an explanation.

Groggily, Tony explained, "I met the nicest woman you ever saw. Things were going so well, I just couldn't leave her. You understand, don't you?"

Walt laughed. It was all right with him if his friend had met someone and was happy. After all, Tony was a friend first and an associate second. "Sure, Tony. Just meet her a little earlier next time, okay? Can't do without a chef every day, you know."

Tony came to work late the next couple of nights, showed up the third night on time, but missed the last two. Although Walt was a patient man, he found it irritating to have to work Tony's shifts. After all, he was the boss. And then it happened. While complaining about Tony's "love life" to one of the other cooks, Walt nearly dropped a pizza platter when the cook said, "What love life, Walt? Tony's drinking again. I saw him last night over at Freddie's place on my way home. He was so drunk he didn't even recognize me."

Walt was worried. It had been almost two years since Tony had "gone on the wagon." He was concerned and irritable when a waitress, Irene, came up to the front and said, "Walt, Tony's in the back—drunk. He says he wants his money. He looks awful."

Discussion Questions

1. Could Tony's problem with alcohol be stress-related? Explain why or why not.
2. What should Walt do in this circumstance to help Tony cope?
3. Is Tony savable? Do the benefits outweigh the costs of trying to save him?

---

team exercise

Dealing with Stress

1. If you have not done so already, complete the assessment presented in *Building Your Human Capital*. In addition to the periodic stressors identified in that assessment, identify and list any ongoing stressors (demanding classes, a teacher who is not treating you appropriately, etc.).
2. Write down what you currently do to cope with stress. Be specific in commenting on each element found in the section entitled "Individual Stress Management" (e.g., endurance exercise, instrumental social support, meditation).
3. Give your results from Steps 1 and 2 to two classmates, as identified by your instructor (if you have privacy concerns, consult with your instructor).
4. Receive results from the same two classmates, and evaluate the effectiveness of their coping strategies in light of their stressors.
5. Team up with the other two people and discuss your evaluations.

   Steps 1–4 should take about 30 minutes to complete, and step 5 should take about 20–30 minutes.

Endnotes

1. Manning, M.R., Jackson, C.N., & Fusilier, M.R. 1996. Occupational stress, social support, and the costs of health care. *Academy of Management Journal, 39*: 738–751; Webster, J.R., Beehr, T.A., & Christianson, N.D. 2009. Toward a better understanding of the effects of hindrance and challenge stressors on work behavior. *Journal of Vocational Behavior, 76*: 68–77. Netterstrøm, B., Conrad, N., Bech, P., Fink, P., Olsen, O., Rugulies, R., & Stansfeld, S. 2008. The relation between work-related psychosocial factors and the development of depression. *Epidemiologic Reviews, 30*:118–132.

2. Hughes, G.H., Person, M.A., & Reinhart, G.R. 1984. Stress: Sources, effects, and management. *Family and Community Health, 7*: 47–58.

3. U.S. Bureau of Labor Statistics. 2006. Occupational stress and time away from work. At http://www.bls.gov/opub/ted/1999/oct/wk3/art03.htm (originally published in 1999).

4. Sauter, S, Murphy, L., Colligan, M., Swanson, N., Hurrell, J., Scharf, F., Sinclair, R., Grubb, P., Goldenhar, L., Alterman, T., Johnston, J., Hamilton, A., & Tisdale, J. 1999. *Stress … At Work.*

Publication No. 99–101. Washington, D.C.: National Institute for Occupational Safety and Health.

5. Ibid.

6. The Gallup Poll. 2009. Work and Work Place. At http://www.gallup.com/poll/1720/Work-Work-Place.aspx.

7. The Marlin Company. 2003. Workplace behavior: Gossip, stress, rudeness. At http://www.themarlincompany.com/Media Room/PollResults.aspx.

8. Brockner, J., Grover, S., Reed, T.F., & DeWitt, R.L. 1992. Layoffs, job insecurity and survivors' work effort: Evidence of an inverted-U relationship. *Academy of Management Journal,* 35: 413–425.

9. See, for example, Hopkins, S.M., & Weathington, B.L. 2006. The relationship between justice perceptions, trust, and employee attitudes in a downsized organization. *The Journal of Psychology,* 140: 477–498; Mishra, K.E., Spreitzer, G.M., & Mishra, A.K. 1998. Preserving employee morale during downsizing. *Sloan Management Review,* 39(2): 83–95.

10. Nixon, R.D., Hitt, M.A., Lee, H., & Jeong, E. 2004. Market reactions to announcements of corporate downsizing actions and implementation strategies. *Strategic Management Journal,* 25: 1121–1129.

11. Dewe, P. 1991. Primary appraisal, secondary appraisal and coping: Their role in stressful work encounters. *Journal of Occupational and Organizational Psychology,* 64: 331–351.

12. See, for example, Lazarus, R.S., & Folkman, S. 1984. *Stress, appraisal and coping.* New York: Springer; Medline Plus Medical Encyclopedia. 2007. Stress and Anxiety. At http://www.nlm.nih.gov/medlineplus/ency/article/003211.htm.

13. Sauter et al., *Stress … At Work.*

14. Mayo Clinic. 2003. Managing work place stress: Plan your approach. At http://www.mayoclinic.com/invoke.cfm?id=HQ01442; Mayo Clinic. 2006. Understand your sources of stress. At http://www.mayoclinic.com/health/stress-management/SR00031.

15. Quick, J.C., & Quick, J.D. 1984. *Organizational stress and preventive management.* New York: McGraw-Hill.

16. Mayo Clinic, Managing work place stress.

17. Seyle, H. 1982. History and present status of the stress concept. In L. Goldberger and S. Breiznitz (Eds.), *Handbook of stress.* New York: Free Press, pp. 7–17.

18. Simmons, B.L., & Nelson, D.L. 2007. Eustress at work: Extending the holistic stress model. In D.L. Nelson & C.L. Cooper (eds.), *Positive organizational behavior.* London: Sage, pp. 40–54.

19. Beehr, T.A. & Grebner, S.I. 2009. When stress is less (harmful). In A.-S.G. Antiniou, C.L. Cooper, G.P. Chrousos, C.D. Speilberger, & M.W. Eysenck (Eds.) Handbook of managerial behavior and occupational health. Northhampton, MA: Edward Elgar Publishing, Inc., pp. 20–34.

20. McGrath, J.E. 1976. Stress and behavior in organizations. In M.D. Dunnette (Ed.), *Handbook of industrial and organizational psychology.* Chicago: Rand McNally, pp. 1351–1395.

21. From Mayo Clinic, Managing work place stress.

22. Karasek, R. 1979. Job demands, job decision latitude, and mental strain: Implications for job redesign. *Administrative Science Quarterly,* 24: 285–306; Karasek, R. 1989. Control in the workplace and its health related aspects. In S.L. Sauter, J.J. Hurrell, & C.L. Cooper (Eds.), *Job control and worker health.* New York: John Wiley & Sons, pp. 129–159; Karasek, R., Theorell, T., 1990. Healthy Work: Stress, Productivity, and the Reconstruction of Working Life. Oxford, United Kingdom: Basic Books.

23. Siegrist, J. 1996. Adverse health effects of high-effort/low-reward conditions. *Journal of Occupational Health Psychology,* 1: 27–41; Siegrist, J. 1999. Occupational health and public health in Germany. In P.M. Le Blanc, M.C.W. Peeters, A. Büssing, & W.B. Schaufeli (Eds.), *Organizational psychology and healthcare: European contributions.* München: Rainer Hampp Verlag, pp. 35–44; Siegrist, J., Siegrist, K., & Weber, I. 1986. Sociological concepts in the etiology of chronic disease: The case of ischemic heart disease. *Social Science & Medicine,* 22: 247–253.

24. Ibid.

25. See, for example, Karasek, Control in the workplace and health related aspects; Stansfeld, S., & Candy, B. 2006. Psychosocial work environment and mental-health: A meta-analytic review. *Scandinavian Journal of Work Environment & Health,* 32: 443–462.

26. Daniels, K., & Guppy, A. 1994. Occupational stress, social support, job control, and psychological well-being. *Human Relations,* 47: 1523–1544; Ganster, D.C., & Schaubroeck, J. 1991. Work stress and employee health. *Journal of Management,* 17: 235–271; Perrewe, P.L., & Ganster, D.C. 1989. The impact of job demands and behavioral control on experienced job stress. *Journal of Organizational Behavior,* 10: 213–229.

27. Daniels & Guppy, Occupational stress, social support, job control, and psychological well-being.

28. Flynn, N, James, J.E. 2009. Relative effects of demand and control on task-related cardiovascular reactivity, task perceptions, performance accuracy, and mood. *International Journal of Psychophysiology, 72,* 217–227.

29. Siegrist, Adverse health effects of high-effort/low-reward conditions; van Vegchel, N., de Jonge, J., Bosma, H., & Schaufeli, W. 2005. Reviewing the effort-reward imbalance model: Drawing up the balance of 45 empirical studies. *Social Science & Medicine,* 60: 1117–1131.

30. Gillen, M., Yen, I.H., Trupin, L., Swig, L., Rugulies, R., Mullen, K., Font, A., Burian, D., Ryan, G., Janowitz, I., Quinlan, P.A., Frank, J., & Blanc, P. 2007. The association of status and psychosocial and physical workplace factors with musculoskeletal injury in hospital workers. *American Journal of Industrial Medicine,* 50: 245–260.

31. van Vegchel, de Jonge, Bosma, & Schaufeli, Reviewing the effort-reward imbalance model.

32. Kahn, R.L., & Byosiere, P. 1992. Stress in organizations. In M.D. Dunnette & L.M. Hough (Eds.), *Handbook of industrial and organizational psychology (Vol. 3).* Palo Alto, CA: Consulting Psychologists Press, pp. 571–650.

33. Jackson, S.E., & Schuler, R. 1985. A meta-analysis and occupational critique of research on role ambiguity and role conflict in work settings. *Organizational Behavior and Human Decision Processes,* 36: 16–78; Jamal, M. 1984. Job stress and job performance controversy: An empirical assessment. *Organizational Behavior and Human Performance,* 33: 1–21; Kalliath, T., & Morris, R. 2002. Job satisfaction among nurses: A predictor of burnout levels. *Journal of Nursing Administration,* 32: 648–654; O'Driscoll, M.P., & Beehr, T.A. 1994. Supervisor behaviors, role stressors and uncertainty as predictors of personal outcomes for

subordinates. *Journal of Organizational Behavior,* 15: 141–155; Piko, B.F. 2006. Burnout, role conflict, job satisfaction and psychosocial health among Hungarian health care staff. *International Journal of Nursing Studies,* 43: 311–318.

34. Podsakoff, N.P., LePine, J.A., & LePine, M.A. 2007. Differential challenge stressor-hindrance stressor relationships with job attitudes, turnover intentions, turnover, and withdrawal behavior: A meta-analysis. *Journal of Applied Psychology,* 92: 438–454.

35. Barnes, B. 2003. The new face of air rage. *Wall Street Journal (Eastern Edition),* Jan. 10: W1.

36. Wang, J.L., Afifi, T.O., Cox, B., & Sareen, J. 2007. Work-family conflict and mental disorders in the United States: Cross-sectional findings from the National Comorbidity Survey. *American Journal of Industrial Medicine,* 50: 143–149.

37. Byron, K. 2005. A meta-analytic review of work-family conflict and its antecedents. *Journal of Vocational Behavior,* 67: 169–198.

38. Glazer, S., & Beehr, T.A. 2005. Consistency of implications of three role stressors across four countries. *Journal of Organizational Behavior,* 26: 467–487; Jackson & Schuler, A meta-analysis and occupational critique of research on role ambiguity and role conflict in work settings.

39. Jamal, Job stress and job performance controversy.

40. Lang, J., Thomas, J.L., Bliese, P.D., & Adler, A.B. 2007. Job demands and job performance: The mediating effect of psychological and physical strain and the moderating effect of role clarity. *Journal of Occupational Health Psychology,* 12: 116–124.

41. Shaw, J.B., & Weekley, J.A. 1985. The effects of objective workload variations of psychological strain and post-work-load performance. *Journal of Management,* 11: 87–98; Ganter & Schaubroeck, Work stress and employee health.

42. Rauhala, A., Kivimäki, M., Fagerström, L., Elovainio, M., Virtanen, M., Vahtera, J., Rainio, A., Ojaniemi, K., & Kinnunen, J. 2007. What degree of work overload is likely to cause increased sickness absenteeism among nurses? Evidence from the RAFAELA patient classification system. *Journal of Advanced Nursing,* 57: 286–295.

43. Hewlett, S.A. & Luce, C.B. December 2006. Extreme jobs: The dangerous allure of the 70-hour workweek. *Harvard Business Review,* 43: 49–59.

44. Ibid.

45. Kanai, A. 2009. "Karoshi (Work to Death)" in Japan. *Journal of Business Ethics,* 84:209–216.

46. U.S. Bureau of Labor Statistics. 1999. Issues in labor statistics: Summary 99-10. At http://www.bls.gov/opub/ils/pdf/opbils35.pdf.

47. Ivancevich, J.M., Matteson, M.T., & Preston, C. 1982. Occupational stress, Type A behavior, and physical well-being. *Academy of Management Journal,* 25: 373–391.

48. Jamal, Job stress and job performance controversy.

49. Kahn & Byosiere, Stress in organizations.

50. Holton, C.J., 1983. Machiavellianism and managerial work attitudes and perceptions. *Psychological Reports,* 52: 432–434.

51. Aiello, J.R., & Kolb, K.J. 1995. Electronic performance monitoring and social context: Impact on productivity and stress. *Journal of Applied Psychology,* 80: 339–353.

52. Reisel, W., & Banai, M. 2002. Job insecurity revisited: Reformulating with affect. *Journal of Behavioral and Applied Management,* 4: 87–96.

53. Andersson, L. M., & Pearson, C. M. 1999. Tit for tat? The spiraling effect of incivility in the workplace. *Academy of Management Review,* 24: 452–471.

54. Lim, S., Cortina, L.M., & Magley, V.J. 2008. Personal and work-group incivility: Impact on work and health outcomes. *Journal of Applied Psychology,* 93: 95–107.

55. C. Pearson & C. Porath. 2009. *The cost of bad behavior: How incivility is costing your business and what you can do about it.* New York: Penguin Group.

56. Friedman, M., & Rosenman, R.H. 1974. *Type A behavior and your heart.* New York: Knopf, p. 47.

57. Kahn & Byosiere, Stress in organizations; Ganster & Schaubroeck, Work stress and employee health; Sanz, J., Garcia-Vera, M.P., Magan, I., Espinosa, R., & Fortun, M. 2007. Differences in personality between sustained hypertension, isolated clinic hypertension and normotension. *European Journal of Personality,* 21: 209–224.

58. Froggatt, K.L., & Cotton, J.L. 1987. The impact of Type A behavior pattern on role overload-induced stress and performance attributions. *Journal of Management,* 13: 87–90.

59. Ganster & Schaubroeck, Work stress and employee health.

60. Ibid.

61. Jimenez, B.M., Natera, N.I.M., Munoz, A.R., & Benadero, M.E.M. 2006. Hardy personality as moderator variable of burnout syndrome in firefighters. *Psicothema,* 18: 413–418; Kobasa, S.C.O., & Puccetti, M.C. 1983. Personality and social resources in stress resistance. *Journal of Personality and Social Psychology,* 45: 839–850; McCalister, K.T., Dolbier, C.L., Webster, J.A., Mallon, M.W., & Steinhardt, M.A. 2006. Hardiness and support at work as predictors of work stress and job satisfaction. *American Journal of Health Promotion,* 20: 183–191.

62. Kobasa, S.C., Maddi, S.R., & Kahn, S. 1982. Hardiness and health: A prospective study. *Journal of Personality and Social Psychology,* 42: 168–177.

63. Ganster & Schaubroeck, Work stress and employee health.

64. See, for example, Martocchio, J.J., & O'Leary, A.M. 1989. Sex differences in occupational stress: A meta-analytic review. *Journal of Applied Psychology,* 74: 495–501; Tamres, L.K., Janicki, D., & Helgeson, V.S. 2002. Sex differences in coping behavior: A meta-analytic review and an examination of relative coping. *Personality and Social Psychology Review,* 6: 2–30; Vagg, P.R., Speilberger, C.D., & Wasala, C.F. 2002. Effects of organizational level and gender on stress in the workplace. *International Journal of Stress Management,* 9: 243–261.

65. Tamres, Janicki, & Helgeson, Sex differences in coping behavior; Torkelson, E., & Muhonen, T. 2004. The role of gender and job level in coping with occupational stress. *Work and Stress,* 18: 267–274.

66. Daniels & Guppy, Occupational stress, social support, job control, and psychological well-being.

67. McDonald, K.M., & Korabik, K. 1991. Sources of stress and ways of coping among male and female managers. In R.L. Perrewe (Ed.), *Handbook on job stress.* New York: Select Press, pp. 185–199; Lim, V.K.G., & Thompson, S.H.T. 1996. Gender differences in occupational stress and coping strategies among IT personnel. *Women in Management Review,* 11: 20–29.

68. Nelson, D.L., & Quick, J.C. 1985. Professional women: Are distress and disease inevitable? *Academy of Management Review,* 10: 206–213.

69. Webster, Y., & Bergman, B. 1999. Occupational stress: Counts and rates. *Compensation and Working Conditions,* Fall: 38–41.

70. Nelson & Quick, Professional women.

71. For a more extensive list, see: Mayo Clinic. 2006. Job burnout: Know the signs and symptoms. At http://www.mayoclinic.com/health/burnout/WL00062.

72. Quick, J.C., & Quick, J.D. 1985. *Organizational stress and preventive management.* New York: McGraw-Hill.

73. U.S. Department of Health and Human Services. 1995. Alcohol, tobacco and other drugs in the workforce. At http://www.health.org/govpubs/m1006; U.S. Department of Health and Human Services. 2010. Division of Workplace Programs: Drugs in the workplace. At http://workplace.samhsa.gov/DrugTesting/Files_Drug_Testing/FactSheet/factsheet041906.aspx

74. Ibid

75. Bandura, A. 1969. *Principles of behavior modification.* New York: Holt, Rinehart & Winston; Cook, R., Walizer, D., & Mace, D. 1976. Illicit drug use in the Army: A social-organizational analysis. *Journal of Applied Psychology,* 61: 262–272.

76. Colarusso, D. 1999. Over the edge: Amateur traders stressed beyond capacity to cope. *ABC News.com,* at http://abcnews.go.com/sections/business?TheStreet/daytraders_990729.html; Immelman, A. 1999. The possible motives of Atlanta day-trading mass murderer Mark O. Barton. *Unit for the Study of Personality in Politics,* at http://www.csbsju.edu/uspp/Research/Barton.html.

77. Harmon, A. 1999. "Casino mentality" linked to day trading stresses. *New York Times,* Aug. 1, p. 1.16.

78. Colarusso, Over the edge: Amateur traders stressed beyond capacity to cope.

79. For additional information on day trading, go to http://www.daytraders.com.

80. Quick & Quick, *Organizational stress and preventive management*; Sauter et al., *Stress ... At Work.*

81. Chrousos, G.P., & Gold, P.W. 1992. The concepts of stress and stress system disorders: Overview of physical and behavioral homeostasis. *Journal of the American Medical Association,* 267: 1244–1252. Peeke, P. 2000. *Fight fat after forty.* New York: Penguin.

82. Hughes, G.H., Pearson, M.A., & Reinhart, G.R. 1984. Stress: Sources, effects, and management. *Family and Community Health,* 6: 47–58.

83. Margoshes, P. 2001. Take the edge off. *Fortune Small Business,* June 23, at http://www.fortune.com/smallbusiness/articles/0,15114,358931,00.html.

84. Quick & Quick, *Organizational stress and preventive management.*

85. Kemery, E.R., Bedeian, A.G., Mossholder, K.W., & Touliatos, J. 1985. Outcomes of role stress: A multisample constructive replication. *Academy of Management Journal,* 28: 363–375; Manning & Jackson, Occupational stress, social support, and the costs of health care; Parasuraman, S., & Alluto, J.A. 1984. Sources and outcomes of stress in organizational settings: Toward the development of a structural model. *Academy of Management Journal,* 27: 330–350.

86. Sauter et al., *Stress ... At work.*

87. Colella, A. 2001. Coworker distributive fairness judgments of the workplace accommodation of employees with disabilities. *Academy of Management Review,* 26: 100–116.

88. Neck, C.P., & Cooper, K.H. 2000. The fit executive: Exercise and diet guidelines for enhancing performance. *Academy of Management Executive,* 14 (2): 72–83.

89. Blair, S.N., Kohl, H.W., Paffenbarger, R.S., Clark, D.G., Cooper, K.H., & Gibbons, L.W. 1989. Physical fitness and all-cause mortality: A prospective study of healthy men and women. *Journal of the American Medical Association,* 262: 2395–2401.

90. Neck & Cooper, The fit executive: Exercise and diet guidelines for enhancing performance.

91. For additional details, see Cooper, K.H. 1995. *It's better to believe.* Nashville: Thomas Nelson, Inc.

92. For additional details, see Neck & Cooper, The fit executive. For important safety tips, see Blake, R. 1998. Don't take muscle flexibility for granted. *Executive Health's Good Health Report,* 34 (12): 7–8. In general, individuals with any health concerns should consult a physician prior to beginning a new exercise program.

93. For details, see: Cooper, K.H. 1996. *Advanced nutritional therapies.* Nashville: Thomas Nelson, Inc.; Neck & Cooper, The fit executive.

94. R. Cieslak. 2009. Social support in the work stress context. In A.-S.G. Antiniou, C.L. Cooper, G.P. Chrousos, C.D. Speilberger, & M.W. Eysenck (Eds.) *Handbook of managerial behavior and occupational health.* Northhampton, MA: Edward Elgar Publishing, Inc., pp. 427-436.

95. Clay, R.A. 2001. Research to the heart of the matter. *Monitor on Psychology,* 32: 42–45; Schirmer, L.L., & Lopez, F.G. 2001. Probing the social support and work strain relationship among adult workers: Contributions of adult attachment orientations. *Journal of Vocational Behavior,* 59: 17–33.

96. Frost, P.J. 2003. *Toxic emotions at work.* Boston: Harvard Business School Press.

97. For general information, see: Wellness Councils of America, 2007, WELCOA Overview. At http://www.welcoa.org/presskit/index.php. Note that we are using the term "wellness" broadly to include a number of health and general well-being initiatives.

98. See, for example: Schoeff, M. 2006. UPS employees get advice from health coaches. *Workforce Management,* 85 (16): 14.

99. Ozminkowski, R.J., Ling, D., Goetzel, R.Z., Bruno, J.A., Rutter, K.R, Isaac, F., & Wang, S. 2002. Long-term impact of Johnson & Johnson's Health and Wellness Program on health care utilization and expenditures. *Journal of Occupational and Environmental Medicine,* 44: 21–29.; Edwards, J.R., & Greenwood, P. Johnson & Johnson: The Live for Life Program (a). Darden Case No. UVA-OB-0412. At http://www.jnj.com/connect/caring/employee-health/?flash=true; Johnson & Johnson webpage. 2010. Protecting our people. At http://ssrn.com/abstract=1421087. Note that some controversy exists over the exact benefits received by J&J, but most analysts agree that the impact has been substantially positive.

100. Johnson & Johnson. 2010. Protecting our people. At http://ssrn.com/abstract=1421087. Note that some controversy exists over the exact benefits received by J&J, but most analysts agree that the impact has been substantially positive.

BRUSSELS AND
bradshaw

Shannon Thomson wrote this case under the supervision of Professor Alison Konrad solely to provide material for class discussion. The authors do not intend to illustrate either effective or ineffective handling of a managerial situation. The authors may have disguised certain names and other identifying information to protect confidentiality.

Ivey Management Services prohibits any form of reproduction, storage or transmittal without its written permission. Reproduction of this material is not covered under authorization by any reproduction rights organization. To order copies or request permission to reproduce materials, contact Ivey Publishing, Ivey Management Services, c/o Richard Ivey School of Business, The University of Western Ontario, London, Ontario, Canada, N6A 3K7; phone (519) 661-3208; fax (519) 661-3882; e-mail cases@ivey.uwo.ca.

In all my years as the acting Business Development Manager, I have never seen a more talented individual who repeatedly received such poor reviews from her peers. She seemed like a great hire at the time. I can't understand what happened to make her so bitter and frustrated.

— Kelly Richards

INTRODUCTION

It was August 26, 2008, and Audrey Locke, summer intern at Brussels and Bradshaw Investment Bank (B&B), had come to the end of another frustrating day. With reluctance, she made her way to Kelly Richards's office. There she would receive her final review, which would end with Richards's decision whether to offer Locke full-time employment in September. Locke was uneasy. Despite working tirelessly to appear eager, intelligent and organized to her superiors, she had received almost entirely bad reviews from the members of her project teams. To make matters worse, Locke often found herself to be the subject of rumors and pranks, all of which had caused her to grow increasingly disheartened and less productive.

As Locke collected herself outside Richards's door, she reflected on the last four months of her employment. Would this review bear more positive results, given her continued effort to reconcile personal conflict with her co-workers? Should she raise the unresolved issues that had overshadowed her internship with mistrust and frustration? Most importantly, would her hard work be rewarded with a full-time offer of employment at the end of the meeting? As Locke raised her hand to knock on Richards's office door, she couldn't help but wonder what, if any, issues she should raise with Richards and whether, if given the opportunity, she should accept B&B's offer of employment for September.

BRIEF HISTORY OF INVESTMENT BANKING

Despite its title, investment banking was historically neither investing nor banking. Instead, it was the business of raising or supplying capital for clients during growth or expansion, when the required cash was not available within the organization. Throughout the world, governments and companies financed much of their operational development and monetary needs through investment bank lending. This arrangement created a global need for such services to facilitate corporate and economic activity. As investment banking evolved, these institutions grew both in size and importance, resulting in many of the largest players operating in multiple countries. Currently, most investment banks offered commercial and investment banking services, which diversified their risk and product offerings in an increasingly complex and competitive global banking environment.

Rivalry between investment banks has continued to this day, particularly concerning retention of clients, investor support and capital,

and the recruitment of top undergraduate and MBA students. The competitiveness of an investment banking firm derived primarily from its staff because innovation, expertise and maintenance of customer relations all played vital roles in the quantity and quality of deals "closed" in any given year. This approach carried important implications for investment banks because the loss of key personnel also included the loss of current or potential clients connected with each employee.

A firm's credibility and reputation depended largely on the exposure and magnitude of the deals "closed" by its staff. Therefore, losing clients and key employees to a competitor was a devastating occurrence that firms aimed to keep to an absolute minimum. Despite the competitive compensation and prestige of an investment banking position, in recent years investment banks found it increasingly difficult to retain experienced employees. For example, an entry-level analyst, typically hired directly after completing a relevant undergraduate degree, worked between 80 and 120 hours a week for two to three years. The training and experience gained in these initial years, as well as the generous compensation, were increasingly viewed by analysts as a platform from which to apply to graduate school or to pursue another facet of the financial industry, such as private equity. The growing popularity of hedge funds also provided another exit from investment banking. This trend of using a brief stint in investment banking as a jump-off point for other career pursuits had grown substantially

in recent years, making it difficult for investment banks to retain their home-grown talent for more senior positions.

Investment banking was never known for its work–life balance or for its progressive human resources policies; however, the lucrative bonuses were often enough to initially attract and keep employees within the firm for at least the first few years. Throughout an investment banker's career, a substantial portion of compensation was derived from performance-based bonuses. A defection of personnel from one firm to another was often seen as a loss of confidence in the ability of the abandoned firm to produce products and opportunities that were more lucrative than those of the competitor firm that gained the new employee. Given the relatively small social and professional circles within the financial industry, this view could be devastating for a firm's recruiting prospects and its business reputation going forward.

Since the beginning in 2007, the economic downturn connected to the credit crises in the United States had sparked an industry-wide slow down in both the dollar value and frequency of deals. This effect, in turn, intensified firms' competition for business and their need to retain personnel.

INVESTMENT BANKING

An investment bank's primary function was to raise capital and provide advisory services during corporate mergers and acquisitions (M&As). As a result, numerous products and divisions of expertise were necessary within a firm to meet the unique challenges of a diverse client base. Often, the opportunities within the market outweighed the capital available to finance them. Thus, investment bankers needed to remain aware of economic conditions, business trends and market performance to maintain an acute ability to assess the risk, demand and appetite in the market for particular financial offerings. In addition, a keen understanding of monetary and international policy was critical because firms were becoming increasingly global and, therefore, faced more risk and opportunities when dealing with foreign clients.

Organizational Structure

Investment banks were characterized by five basic levels of authority: junior analyst, senior analyst, associate, vice president and managing director (see Exhibit 1). Each of these levels existed within assigned product and

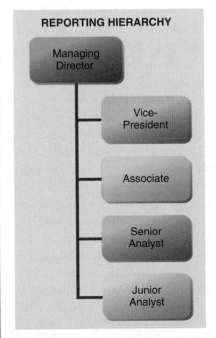

REPORTING HIERARCHY

- Managing Director
  - Vice-President
  - Associate
  - Senior Analyst
  - Junior Analyst

Exhibit 1 Reporting Hierarchy

EXHIBIT 2   Product and Industry Groups

	Product Groups		
Industry Groups	Debt Capital Markets	Equity Capital Markets	Merger and Acquisition Expertise
Natural Resources			
Consumer Retail			
Financial Institutions			
Real Estate			
Technology			
Media			
Industrial			

---

industry groups. Product groups included debt capital markets, equity capital markets and M&A expertise; whereas industry groups included natural resources, consumer retail, financial institutions, real estate, technology, media and industrial (see Exhibit 2). The purpose of these groups was to hone expertise in multiple areas of business industry, allowing employees within each group to develop expertise in their assigned area. As a result, many project teams were cross-staffed. For example, if a real estate company needed to raise equity to fulfill its intention to acquire another company, the deal could be staffed by analysts from the M&A, equity capital markets and real estate groups. This cross-staffing allowed investment banks to harness proficiencies from multiple areas to benefit one transaction, thus allowing for more innovative and tailored strategic advising.

Project Teams

Project teams were typically staffed by at least one employee from each

organizational level, depending on the timeline and magnitude of the potential deal. Junior and senior analysts, being the entry-level employees, were assigned most of the technical grunt work on pitch books and in deal teams. They built most of the valuation models and performed the majority of financial-based analysis, overseen by the associate. The vice president and managing director set the strategic direction of the pitch books and actively managed the client relationships. Project teams were typically coordinated by an independent individual within the company. Selection of the project teams was based primarily on availability and the technical skills of the employee.

Profit Generation

Investment banking analysts spent the majority of their time working on pitch books, which were essentially business plans based on a financial product, idea or valuation technique. The purpose of the pitch book was to educate the client about the opportunity and entice them to buy in.

These books required anywhere from a few days to a week to put together and acted as a means to market the bank's advisory services and to drum up new business for the bank. Once a pitch was approved, the deal went "live," taking anywhere from a few weeks to a month to complete.

Profit was derived from "closing" these live deals by collecting a fee for providing transaction advice on corporate M&As and by gaining a margin on the issuance and sale of securities. This activity was conducted in both the debt and equity capital markets. Advisory revenue and the value of transaction margins varied depending on the market focus of the investment bank. Some banks focused on the high-end market, targeting large companies and major deals, whereas others focused on the middle to low-end markets. These markets dealt with smaller companies and consequently smaller transactions. Lastly, investment banks earned profit by insuring bonds through the use of credit default swaps.

Compensation

The compensation of investment bankers was notoriously competitive, bonus-driven and known to escalate greatly with seniority. For example, an entry-level Canadian investment banking analyst could expect a beginning annual base salary of at least $65,000, with bonus potential of $20,000[1] per year, depending on personal and company-wide financial results. As seniority increased, compensation levels throughout the industry were largely based on the

---

[1]All funds in Canadian dollars unless specified otherwise.

---

performance of the individual, with vice presidents generally compensated at approximately $1,000,000 per year, including their bonus. Bonuses were paid once, at the end of the year, and were calculated by evaluating the number of deals an employee was involved with, the employee's ability to work with others, the bank's general performance and other benchmarks outlined in a firm's review structure.

BRUSSELS AND BRADSHAW

Founded in 1915, Brussels and Bradshaw (B&B) had become a well-respected and established financial institution, with net revenues of $42 billion and net profit of $15 billion in 2007. By 2008, B&B was operating globally in more than 25 countries, with a particular focus in the United States, England, Canada and Hong Kong. B&B prided itself on its innovative ability to adapt to market trends and close some of the largest deals in North America. B&B was a leader in the creation of block trading, the privatization movement, and one of the first financial institutions to hire MBAs on Wall Street. B&B's mission statement had always been "To offer our clients competitive, innovative and feasible solutions for the betterment of their organization and community environments." As a result, B&B management regarded the client as king and often worked its employees to the bone to meet tight project deadlines for clients. Even employees at the associate and VP levels had come to expect working through weekends and holidays (including Christmas Eve and New Year's Day) when closing a large deal.

Throughout its history, B&B's strategic activities had focused on growing the investment banking arm of the company, with substantial resources used to recruit newly graduated young talent and to groom analysts for more senior roles within the company. As was standard throughout the industry, B&B offered services in investment banking, sales and trading, asset management, commercial banking and various other financial services. Within the last 30 years of its history, B&B had offered these services worldwide to a diversified client base to gain more global market share.

The Summer Internship Position

Since 1985, B&B had recruited and hired undergraduates in their final year of business school to work from May to August in B&B's regional offices across the continent. The internship experience was largely meant as a screening process for potential full-time candidates. The experience also allowed undergraduates to experience the firm's culture — thereby recommending the firm as an employer to their well-educated colleagues. For the last five years, B&B's internships always began in Chicago, where summer interns from all offices throughout North America attended two weeks of initial training to learn basic valuation techniques and sophisticated methods of financial statement analysis. The training was entirely quantitative and very intense. After completing their training, interns were expected to spend their first few weeks in their respective regional office, acting as a "helper" to existing deal teams. Interns spent these first few weeks getting acquainted with the jargon, models and expectations surrounding the junior analyst role.

The 2008 summer internship position (see Exhibit 3) paid approximately $20,000 for the contracted term of 14 weeks. The difficulty of the work depended largely on how capable the analysts proved themselves to be and the projects available during their employment. As the summer progressed, interns became responsible for the full array of junior analyst activities and in return saw an increase in the hours

---

EXHIBIT 3 Brussels and Bradshaw Summer Internship Job Posting

Description of the Company:
Since its inception 93 years ago, Brussels and Bradshaw, Canada's largest investment banking institution, has operated globally in over 25 countries with a particular focus on contributing to the economies of North America through investor capital and sound financial advisory.

Brussels and Bradshaw has built a solid reputation based on consistently stellar financial performance and employee development. Our values of leadership, intelligence and innovation have shaped our past success and the employees which make our firm one of the best in the industry. At Brussels and Bradshaw, you will experience accelerated learning in a fast-paced environment full of bright and driven individuals. Our summer internship program is an ideal way to launch your career in investment banking, by joining a winning firm that wants to help you achieve your greatest potential.

The Summer Internship Position:
We are looking for driven, highly intelligent individuals who seek an environment of constant learning and change. You will work alongside other motivated individuals throughout the 14 week summer internship program. As an intern at Brussels and Bradshaw you will be provided with two initial weeks of investment banking training in Chicago, Illinois, a diverse array of assignments in multiple project teams, and assigned the work and daily responsibilities of a full time junior analyst.

Qualifications:
Candidates must be currently working towards a B.A., B.S., or B.B.A. in accounting, finance, business or applied economics. A minimum of one statistics, and two finance courses, must be successfully completed in order to apply.

Skill and Competency Requirements:
- Solid understanding of various equity and debt instruments
- Proficient problem-solving, quantitative and analysis skills
- Fundamental understanding of valuation theory, methodologies and their application
- Excellent verbal and written communication skills
- Team player with high energy and demonstrated initiative
- Self-starter with the ability to balance multiple tasks in the face of competing priorities
- Self-motivated with strong independent work ethic
- Highly skilled in Microsoft Excel and Office applications
- 1–2 years of work experience in a financial analyst position or related role

The position will entail the following responsibilities:
1) Building, using, and expanding on financial models.
2) Performing discounted cash flow, financial valuation, and multiples-based analyses.
3) Participation in collecting, synthesizing and applying product and industry research

Qualified applicants who are interested in this position should submit their cover letter, resume and unofficial university transcript via email to Kelly Richards, at KRichards@BrusselsandBradshaw.com

they were expected to be in the office. The first two weeks of work ranged between 70 and 80 hours per week, steadily increasing over the term and typically peaking at 120 hours per week in mid-June. This pace lasted until the conclusion of the internship at the end of August. At B&B, similar to other investment banks, the expected office hours were unspoken, as was the rule that summer interns were expected to be both the first employees in at 9:00 a.m. and the last to leave, at approximately 3 a.m.

B&B had always invested substantial resources into recruiting and interviewing top candidates to ensure the interns they hired were well suited for both the work and the corporate environment. To remain competitive, B&B always strived to communicate to undergraduates the importance of employee satisfaction to the firm strategy. B&B typically hired two to three summer interns for each major regional office throughout North America; however, given the state of the economy, Audrey Locke was the only intern of more than 300 applicants who was hired for the Toronto office in 2008. Locke was chosen after four rounds of intense interviews with multiple managing directors from Toronto.

The Toronto Office

B&B's Toronto office was small in relation to its other North American offices. With three managing directors, four vice presidents, four associates and three full-time analysts, B&B was a top-heavy organization. Teams had always been staffed by the business department manager (BDM), Kelly Richards, on two of

the most common types of projects: pitches and live transactions. Given the small size of the office, analysts such as Locke were often assigned to work with the same people, or alternatively were paired with employee members from other regional offices. Locke, for example, spent a quarter of her summer working for Don Spenser, a managing director in New York, whom she had never met. Despite the lack of direct communication, Locke had quite enjoyed the tasks and feedback she received from Spenser. In addition, Spenser had been thrilled with her work and gave her glowing reviews.

Corporate Culture

B&B attributed much of its growth and success to its corporate culture, and it prided itself on a "work hard, play hard" mentality whereby employees were expected to work toward hard-fast deadlines until the work was finished. Often a typical day for a junior or intermediate analyst would average 12 hours, with little supervision besides check-ins to have their work proofed and to ensure the project was on track. Associates and vice presidents sometimes assumed a fraternity mentality toward analysts, initiating them with the same aggressive treatment they had received. Creating false deadlines, assigning projects with no real purpose and applying unnecessary pressure to multiple projects were not uncommon. Often these pranks were not for humor's sake, but to see how well analysts fared under such constant treatment. Senior employees of all ranks often turned a blind eye if an analyst was struggling as a result, despite the rising turnover rate of

summer interns and junior analysts. The company had come to view the summer internships as a "weeding out" process whereby only the strong would remain until the end of the summer. At B&B, an analyst who left the internship early was viewed as having been too weak to commit to the industry and therefore was better off in another field or firm. Junior analysts were particularly susceptible to this treatment.

Without a formal human resources representative, analysts had no one to speak to about such treatment; thus, interpersonal conflict between employees was either dealt with by those involved or completely ignored. Associates, VPs and managing directors also deliberately ignored employee issues and complaints about the work environment or interpersonal conflict. In the words of Blake Cooper, one of the managing partners of the Toronto office:

> We cannot afford to get soft on our people by listening to analysts whine and complain about each other. Once you start, where does it stop? They'll figure out how to get along on their own if you let them. These are professionals. We are all here to make money and the only way to make money in this business is to work together. Those that want to get ahead will recognize that — and those are the people we want at B&B.

In addition, requests for any time off, regardless of how brief, had to be submitted and approved by one of the managing partners. Despite the expectation of long hours during the workweek, the taking of sick days and requests for time off for medical appointments were met with great resistance and gossip among the superiors. Although such requests were never formally held against an employee, the prestige of an employee's future projects and the timeline for promotion were often altered as punishment without any formal communication to the targeted employee.

KELLY RICHARDS

Kelly Richards had been the BDM at B&B for the last 10 years and was the only employee in the office without a finance background. Her duties were strictly administrative, including printing pitch books, scheduling project teams and submitting qualified resumes to the managing directors of the Toronto office. Although Richards assumed some of the tasks of a human resources employee, her position held no real authority over hiring, firing, promotion or professional discipline for poor reviews or misconduct. These functions were handled by the manager partners as a means to hire those whom the partners felt would work best within the established culture at B&B.

Richards did not have her CHRP (Certified Human Resources Professional) certification and was therefore not trained in conflict resolution, benefits and compensation, or any of the other human resource functions typically taught during the certification process. Even if employees spoke to Richards about such issues, as often was the case, Richards had no authority to enforce behavioral change or punishment for poor treatment of subordinates. Because Richards conducted all performance reviews and scheduled the project teams, she often received requests from one employee not to be staffed with another. However, given the expertise and product/industry functions of the organization, these requests could rarely be honored. As a result of Richards's limited authority, she was given little respect by any of the company's associates, VPs and managing directors. Richards was compensated at a competitive salary for her title and duties. It was well known at B&B that Richards had three children and a husband who had recently been fired from his position as a high school teacher.

AUDREY LOCKE

Audrey Locke had enjoyed the recruitment process of finding a summer internship position. Because of her grade point average (GPA) of 3.9 and a solid resume of related financial experience (see Exhibit 4), Locke finished the recruitment process with five competitive summer internship offers at some of the largest investment banks in the country. Despite the stellar reputation of each of the banks, Locke had been intent on B&B since attending their information session. With its prestigious reputation, competitive recruitment process and global presence, Locke viewed B&B as a strong career move to start her finance career. Despite being warned by some of her friends about the intensity of the position, Locke was excited to begin work at B&B's regional office in Toronto on May 5, 2008.

In mid-April, Locke received an information package that outlined what she could expect during her summer work term. A letter from Richards was also enclosed, detailing two important points of contact for Locke. An assigned mentor, Jake Frescott, a senior analyst who had been at B&B for only one year after transferring from a competitor would be available to Locke once a week to help her with the technical aspects of her position. In addition, a "buddy" would be assigned to Locke as someone to interact with on a more informal level. Christine Page, a first-year analyst in the Toronto office, was Locke's assigned buddy. Richards had paired Locke with Page because they had both attended the Richard Ivey School of Business at the University of Western Ontario. Page and Locke were the only two females in the Toronto office. The letter concluded by saying that Richards was looking forward to meeting Locke and would provide formal introductions to both Page and Frescott during Locke's first week.

CHRISTINE PAGE

Christine Page had been employed with B&B since her summer internship placement at the New York City office in 2006. Page had worked on many large deals that summer and had been offered a full-time position at the Toronto office, which included a staggering signing bonus due to her proven work ethic and quantitative abilities. Page had been given no notice of her buddy assignment and therefore made little effort to get to know Locke in her first few weeks because they were both incredibly busy on different projects. It was not until Locke's fourth week that Richards provided the formal

EXHIBIT 4   Audrey Locke's Resume

EDUCATION

Richard Ivey School of Business, London, Ontario   2009
Candidate for Bachelor of Arts, Honours Business Administration, Dean's Honour List

University of Toronto, Toronto, Ontario   2005–2007
Honours Applied Math, Dean's Honour List, Faculty of Mathematics, 2005–2007
Recipient of Continuing Scholarship for Academic Excellence

EMPLOYMENT

The Richard Ivey School of Business, London, Ontario   2006–2007
Research Assistant
- Assisted finance professor with intensive research project by providing executive compensation data through the use of proxy statements for over 300 companies.
- Investigated and rectified 25 anomalies between the information stored in archives and the information listed on the annual corporate proxy statements.
- Compiled, analyzed and drew conclusions from compiled data, writing a comprehensive report of findings and data trends.

Ernst & Young, Toronto, Ontario   Summer 2007
Audit & Assurance Summer Analyst
- Verified corporate accounting systems through the use of cash receipts, journal vouchers, weighted-average cost purchase cut-offs, currency triangulation and unrecorded liability tests to guarantee they were recorded properly.
- Performed stock counts and inventory ageing tests, ensuring that Ernst & Young's values were consistent with company records.
- Corrected two major accounting errors amounting to $60,000 during first audit engagement.

Kraft Foods Inc., Toronto, Ontario   Summer 2005–2007
Summer Financial Planning Analyst, Customer Finance
- Led a project to recover invalid charges from a distributor by collecting sufficient evidence to reverse incorrect deductions of $1.2 million.
- Evaluated sales promotion and incentive programs, providing recommendations to improve effectiveness and eliminate $500,000 of unnecessary costs from the current budget, and ensuring synchronization among the category team, the sales force and the finance department.
- Developed an inventory projection model to estimate inventory levels in the customer's warehouse and prevent unanticipated fluctuations in sales from month to month.

TRAINING, TEAMWORK AND LEADERSHIP

Wall Street Prep Course—Completed intensive financial valuation and modeling course   2008

VP Finance—Finance Club—Managed club budget, bank account, and club audits   2007–2008

Royal Conservatory of Music—Completed grade 9 certification in violin and piano   1995–Present

introduction between Locke and Page and discussed the importance of the "buddy" role in Locke's anticipated development. Following this introduction, Page took the liberty of taking Locke for lunch to give her some advice about the expectations and projects of the firm. Locke was taken aback by Page's invested interest to see her succeed, but warmed to her company. Page made a concentrated effort throughout Locke's remaining work term to check in and speak with her at least three times a week. As the only two female analysts in the Toronto office, Locke and Page were coined the "sorority girls" by two of the associates. Despite twice mentioning to Richards the promised introduction to her assigned mentor, by the end of the summer Locke had not been introduced to Frescott, who had passed Locke multiple times in the office without saying hello.

TROUBLE BREWING

In Chicago, Locke had enjoyed her training, which she found to be relatively easy. During Locke's first day in the Toronto office, Richards showed her to her designated work station and promptly left, saying she would follow up with her later that day. Locke was soon approached by Sean Petterson, a long-time associate at B&B who had experienced difficulty moving above his current position. Petterson promptly plopped a pile of papers on Locke's desk and mumbled something about compiling the data before noon. After skimming through the pages to get a feel for the work, Locke went to find Petterson, only to learn that he had left for a meeting and would not be back

until 3 p.m. Upon Petterson's return, Locke had completed what she thought he would have expected. He looked over the first two pages and frowned. "Summer interns ... every year you all seem to become more incompetent." Petterson gave it back to Locke. "Don't worry about it, I'll do it myself."

Locke did not see Richards again until the following week when, at Locke's request, they met briefly in Richards's office. Locke said:

I'm just not feeling like I know what my responsibilities are here. When I've done my work, I'm not sure who I should report to for more. Also, when I have questions there doesn't seem to be anyone to ask. What do you suggest I do?

Richards smiled and replied:

The work will come when it needs to be done, your job is to sit and wait for it. You are here to help make deals happen so sit tight and work when you're told to. Also, I've been hearing complaints that you've been listening to music while you've been working — don't let me find out about that again. Now if you'll excuse me, I've got a conference call to attend in about five minutes.

Locke left Richards's office discouraged and upset. Locke had never listened to music while at the office. Who would have lied to Richards about something she had never done? As Locke returned to her desk, Petterson was waiting for her, angrily tapping his fingers on her chair. "Where have you been? This was supposed to be done two hours ago!

Do you have any idea how important this deadline is?" This outburst was only the beginning of the type of behavior that Locke would come to expect from Petterson on a daily basis. Often around 10 p.m. when he began to get increasingly tired, he would call Locke into his office, close the door and raise his voice while complaining about her formatting and assumption decisions. Locke often stood by her assumptions and explained her judgments to learn why they needed adjusting; however, Petterson always cut her off saying, "I don't have time to teach you things you should already know."

As the weeks progressed, Richards staffed Locke with Petterson on every project despite Locke's request to be staffed with another project manager. Locke's first formal review from Petterson comprised scathing remarks about Locke's personality and work performance, remarking that she was arrogant, slow to meet deadlines and too friendly with Page. Petterson had never liked Page, who had experienced similar run-ins with Petterson when she had been a junior analyst. Although never proven or formally addressed, Petterson had a tendency to be harder on female analysts than male analysts. Although Richards was aware of this tendency, she made no effort to change Petterson's approach.

Many of the weeks following held similar experiences. Locke continued to work longer hours than anyone else in the office without complaint. Although she remained unsure about the expectations and communication lines of her position, Locke worked quietly and diligently, making sure she completed all projects by their deadlines. Locke found it frustrating that Petterson would play games with her, often giving her a deadline of Wednesday at 2 a.m. without really needing the work until Friday at noon. When Locke raised this issue with Richards, Richards looked at Locke sourly: "Audrey, are you questioning the competency of your project manager because of your interpersonal issues? You need to learn to deal with these things yourself." Following that brief discussion, Locke decided not to call Petterson on his false deadlines because she didn't want to feed him more ammunition for her next performance review. Locke remained irritated, however, by the lack of feedback and recognition regarding her sound technical abilities.

Unknown to Locke, her work was being routinely reviewed by Richards. Although much of her work was submitted directly to Petterson, Locke had one assignment that was submitted directly to Page. When Page submitted it to Richards for review, Page was immediately called into Richards's office only to be met with accusations:

No summer intern has ever been capable of building this type of model with such precision. I know you and Locke are friends, Page, but you're not doing her any favors by increasing the quality of her work before submitting it to me.

Despite her expected confidentiality about the issue, Page thought Locke should be aware of the accusation and told her what had been said during the meeting. Locke was distraught and offended. When she asked Page for advice, Page responded:

I know you're working hard. You just have to keep your head down, do your work and get through the first few years. I had similar treatment. There's just nothing you can do about it.

THE FINAL REVIEW

Locke cleared her throat and focused on her objectives for the coming meeting. After the negative treatment and feedback she had received, Locke desperately wanted Richards to understand and appreciate her concentrated effort to be a valuable employee. Despite her negative experience, Locke was still keen on a career in finance, and, at the very least, she wanted to end her internship with B&B on a high note. Locke was two minutes early for her meeting with Richards and knocked confidently on the door. The next 10 minutes would decide her future at B&B. Locke wondered what, if anything, she could say so that Richards could see her summer experience from her perspective and whether, in the larger scheme of things, it would even make a difference.

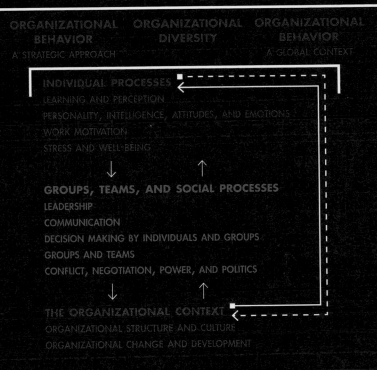

PART 3

groups, teams, and social processes

In Part II, we examined individual-level processes that affect organizational behavior. In Part III, we explore group, team, and social processes, which can directly or indirectly affect behavior in organizations. Knowledge of each of these types of processes helps managers achieve and maintain a competitive advantage. Therefore, each has important strategic implications for the organization.

Chapter 8, the first chapter in Part III, discusses various concepts related to leadership and explains what makes a leader effective. In the chapter, we pay special attention to the effects of leadership on motivation and productivity. **Chapter 9** explores communication in organizations. Communication is critical for achieving objectives because it provides the information on which people in organizations act. In addition, leaders communicate in order to motivate individuals and teams and to obtain the behavior desired.

Chapter 10 describes individual and group decision making. Decision making is a critical dimension of leadership and has substantial effects on organizational behavior. In **Chapter 11**, we turn to an examination of group dynamics and teams. Because organizations make frequent use of teams (groups of associates integrated to accomplish specified goals), understanding and managing teams can be essential to organizational success. Finally, in **Chapter 12**, we explore power, conflict, politics, and negotiations within organizations. Both the exercise of power and occurrences of conflict can have either functional or dysfunctional consequences. Chapter 12 provides an understanding of how managers can achieve functional outcomes.

leadership

Maria Yee and the Green Furniture Revolution

A number of issues confront the global furniture industry. Perhaps the most important of these is the loss of hardwood forests in many parts of the world. This loss threatens the supply of raw materials for furniture makers, and it also affects the air-cleansing capacity of the earth's tree stock and the potential for rainfall downwind of lost timberland. In addition, toxic lacquers and adhesives are commonplace in furniture manufacturing. Ethylene oxide is one example. Problematic fabric-embedded chemicals are ubiquitous as well, including perfluorooctanoic acid for stain and water resistance as well as decabromodiphenyl ether for flame retardation.

To combat these problems, a number of forward-thinking entrepreneurs have worked on green (i.e., sustainable) technologies for high-quality furniture materials and manufacturing. Their work, however, has been an uphill struggle. Hardwoods from sustainable sources are not always easy to find. Alternatives to traditional hardwoods, such as bamboo, can be difficult to transform into attractive, durable tables, chairs, and dressers. Alternatives to traditional adhesives can be challenging to develop. Safe and easy-to-produce compounds offering important flame-retardant qualities are not readily available. Perhaps most difficult, the costs of green technologies are typically greater than traditional methods, and consumers are not necessarily ready to pay higher prices. In a survey conducted by the market-research firm NPD Group, 64 percent of respondents supported green products but only 38 percent were willing to pay for them.

Against this difficult backdrop, Maria Yee has attempted to successfully implement green technologies in the furniture industry. Born in mainland China, Ms. Yee immigrated to the United States, where she founded

knowledge objectives

After reading this chapter, you should be able to:

1. Define *leadership* and distinguish between formal and informal leaders.
2. Demonstrate mastery of the trait concept of leadership.
3. Compare and contrast major behavioral theories of leadership.
4. Explain contingency theories of leadership, emphasizing how they relate leadership effectiveness to situational factors.
5. Describe transformational leaders.
6. Integrate concepts and ideas from behavioral, contingency, and transformational leadership.
7. Discuss several additional topics of current relevance, including leader–member exchange, servant leadership, gender effects on leadership, and global differences in leadership.

her company, Maria Yee Inc., in 1988. With manufacturing located in China, the company initially relied on wood reclaimed from destroyed Chinese buildings. Later, it used hardwoods grown by reasonably managed Chinese growing companies. From there, the company moved toward hardwoods sourced only from growers using principles of true sustainable production, including preservation of biological diversity, limited harvesting, and respect for forest workers and local communities. Along with the pursuit of sustainably produced hardwoods, the company began in 2002 to experiment with bamboo boards. By 2009, approximately 50 percent of its products were based on innovative materials called BambooTimbre and

©iStockphoto

RidgeBamboo. Because bamboo is a grass rather than a tree, a stand of bamboo can be harvested and replanted in five-year cycles, which makes it a rapidly renewable resource under prevailing standards. Beyond its approach to wood and boards, Maria Yee Inc. also has taken seriously the challenge of developing or encouraging others to develop nontoxic or less toxic lacquers, adhesives, sealers, water guards, stain guards, and flame retardants. Finally, the company has used a number of recycled raw materials for fuel and other inputs in the manufacturing process.

In 2009, Maria Yee Inc. had grown from a one-person hobby to a 30-million-dollar business with two manufacturing sites and hundreds of employees. A number of successful patent applications had been filed for a variety of materials and processes. Key customers included Crate & Barrel, Room & Board, and Magnolia Home Theatre. How has this success been achieved, given the tremendous competition in the furniture industry and the difficulties associated with green strategies in that industry?

The key to Ms. Yee's success seems to lie at least partially in her passion for a sustainable world and her ability to inspire others to share in her pursuit of such a world

through the activities of the company. Her vision demands a company that follows a moral path of protecting the environment while delighting end users with safe and elegantly designed furniture, and to produce that furniture in a way that ensures that associates in the manufacturing plants are healthy and happy. Commenting on the vision, Ms. Yee said this, "Being green is not just for marketing. … Because I'm a human, I want to take a very small step to protect the environment. We actually did so much more on green than we told people. We did it because of our beliefs."

Beyond the compelling vision and the ability to enlist others in pursuit of that vision, Ms. Yee is known for her coaching and development of others. She has, for example, helped to develop local Chinese management talent for her manufacturing facilities. She has also insisted on well-trained associates, and has paid them wages above average for the area while offering a full range of benefits.

Ms. Yee, however, is not just a people-oriented person. She can also be a tough taskmaster when necessary. During a recent visit to one of the manufacturing sites, an observer noted that she was "both encouraging and tough, insisting they sweat the details and strive for perfection." After discovering a table that had not been sanded properly, she asked, "Which one of you is going to be responsible for this?"

Overall, Ms. Yee is a smart, confident, high-energy person with insight into both people and technical issues. One observer had this to say, "I have not met a lot of people like Maria. … She clearly is someone who is very focused, very hard-working, gives incredible attention to detail, very customer-focused, respectful of the environment, and a strong leader. Clearly a very strong leader with impeccable standards." Another put it this way: "We love her intense level of working. … She's always available to us directly. … That's something that makes the relationship special." Indeed, Ms. Yee is a special person on a mission.

Sources: S. Fornoff. 2007. "What's in Furniture? It's Enough to Make You Sick," *San Francisco Chronicle*, Oct. 24, p. G.1; Maria Yee Inc., "Maria's Story," 2010, at http://www.mariayee.com/about/maria/index.php; Maria Yee Inc., "Who We Are," 2010, at http://www.mariayee.com/about/index.php; M. Shao. 2009. "A Fine Green Niche," *Stanford Social Innovation Review*, Fall, pp. 68–71; M. Shao & G. Carroll. 2009. *Maria Yee Inc.: Making 'Green' Furniture in China* (Stanford, CA: Stanford Graduate School of Business).

the strategic importance of Leadership

Maria Yee has displayed remarkable leadership for a number of years. As a visionary who can inspire others, she has provided important direction and energy. Although not operating at the same level or with the same scope, she is similar in many ways to Mohandas Gandhi and Margaret Thatcher in the political domain and Bill Hewlett and Dave Packard in the business world. Beyond vision, Ms. Yee also demonstrates a crucial balance between people and technical issues. As discussed in this chapter, strong leadership involves attention to both.

Ms. Yee's leadership has had a profound impact on her company. Research has not always revealed such a strong link between the leadership of senior executives and organizational performance,[1] but the overall body of evidence does provide a number of supportive studies. One study focused on the leadership of chief executives and showed positive effects for performance among *Fortune* 500 firms. These effects were especially strong for firms operating in uncertain environments.[2] In another study, chief executives of major league baseball clubs were examined in the United States. Again, leadership had positive effects, in this case on team winning percentage and fan attendance.[3] In both of these studies, the leaders who exhibited a transformation, which includes vision creation, had the strongest positive effect on performance. We discuss

transformational leadership in this chapter.

Consistent with these studies, a survey of chief executive officers (CEOs) conducted by the Center for Creative Leadership showed that almost 80 percent of respondents believe leadership development throughout the organization is the most important factor or one of the top five factors in achieving a competitive advantage in the market.[4] The survey respondents also reported that leadership quality is linked to a firm's financial performance. CEOs of firms with superior performance were more likely to indicate that their companies support the development of leadership skills through human resource systems, that there is a shared understanding of the nature of effective leadership, and that their leadership development practices are tailored to meet individual needs.

Actions taken by senior managers correspond to the original definition of *strategic leadership*.[5] Certainly, the CEO and those working directly with him are very important given the substantial influence they have in designing the organization's strategy and overseeing its implementation. Effective implementation, however, involves all leaders in the organization. Thus, the concept of strategic leadership has been extended in recent years to include leaders from all levels.

In this context, strategic leadership covers a spectrum of behaviors for those below the rank of senior

management. For example, this type of leadership might entail developing a vision for the unit or group being led, a vision that is consistent with the overall strategy of the firm.[6] Furthermore, recent work has focused on the importance of strategic leaders' managing the resources under their direction, to include financial capital but especially human capital and valuable interpersonal relationships (social capital). Particular emphasis has been placed on the importance of providing effective leadership that enhances associates' productivity (i.e., managing human capital well) and building and maintaining important relationships both within the organization (with associates and other leaders) and externally (e.g., with alliance partners). Those who manage this human and social capital well are effective leaders.[7] Based on this work, we assert that leadership is necessary in building and maintaining a high-involvement, high-performance workforce.

In this chapter, we examine the concept of leadership. We begin by describing its fundamental nature. Next, we address three types of theories that have historically been used to explain leadership effectiveness: trait theories, behavioral theories, and contingency approaches. We then focus on more recent developments in leadership theory: the transformational and charismatic approaches. We close with a discussion of several additional topics of current relevance and importance.

The Nature of Leadership

We usually attribute the success or failure of an organization to its leaders. When a company or an athletic team is successful, for example, it is the president or coach who receives much of the credit. These individuals are also subject to criticism if the company does not meet its goals or the team has a losing season.

Leadership has been defined in many ways, but most definitions emphasize the concept of influence. Here, we define **leadership** as the process of providing general direction and influencing individuals or groups to achieve goals.[8] A leader can be formally designated by the organization (formal leader) or can provide leadership without such formal designation (informal leader).

Leaders can do many things to provide direction and to influence people. These activities include providing information, resolving conflicts, motivating followers, anticipating problems, developing mutual respect among group members, and coordinating group activities and efforts.[9] Warren Bennis, who has studied leadership for a number of years, suggests that effective leaders are concerned with "doing the right things" rather than "doing things right."[10] The right things, according to Bennis, include the following:

- Creating and communicating a vision of what the organization should be
- Communicating with and gaining the support of multiple constituencies
- Persisting in the desired direction even under bad conditions
- Creating the appropriate culture and obtaining the desired results

From this definition of leadership, company presidents and many managers can be identified as leaders. Coaches, basketball captains, and football quarterbacks are leaders. Army drill sergeants are leaders. The person who organizes a social gathering is also a leader. In other words, many people serve as either formal or informal leaders, and almost anyone can act as a leader. However, some positions provide more opportunities to display leadership behavior than others. And not all people in positions that call for leader behavior (e.g., managerial positions) act as leaders. For example, a manager who merely follows rules and fails to provide direction to and support for his associates is not acting as a leader.

Trait Theory of Leadership

At one time, it was thought that some people were born with certain traits that made them effective leaders, whereas others were born without leadership traits.[11] The list of traits generated by this early research was substantial (in the thousands) and included physical characteristics (such as height and appearance), personality characteristics (such as self-esteem and dominance), and abilities (such as intelligence and verbal fluency). Additional traits that were thought to characterize leaders are presented in Exhibit 8-1.

Early trait research has been criticized for several reasons. For example, the methodology used to identify the traits was poor. Investigators simply generated lists of traits by loosely comparing people who were labeled as leaders with those who were not—without actually measuring traits or systematically testing for meaningful differences. A second criticism is that the list of traits associated with leadership grew so large it became meaningless. A third criticism is that the results of this research were inconsistent—different leaders possessed different traits. Finally, no leadership trait was found to relate consistently to unit or organizational performance, and different situations seemed to require different

leadership
The process of providing general direction and influencing individuals or groups to achieve goals.

> **EXHIBIT 8-1**   Traits Associated with Leadership
>
> | | | | |
> |---|---|---|---|
> | Energy | Achievement drive | Initiative | Sense of humor |
> | Appearance | Adaptability | Insightfulness | Tolerance for stress |
> | Intelligence | Aggressiveness | Integrity | Interpersonal skill |
> | Judgment | Enthusiasm | Persistence | Prestige |
> | Verbal fluency | Extraversion | Self-confidence | Tact |
>
> Source: Based on A.C. Jago. 1982. "Leadership: Perspectives in Theory and Research," *Management Science*, 28: 315–336.

traits.[12] Although famous leaders (e.g., Abraham Lincoln, Gandhi, Martin Luther King, Jr.) had "special" traits, a close examination reveals differences among them. Numerous studies conducted to determine the traits that relate to effective leadership found that not all leaders possess the same traits.

Nevertheless, the notion of leadership traits has been revived in recent years.[13] Research has demonstrated that leaders usually are different from other people. It is now believed, however, that many of the traits (or characteristics) that are possessed by leaders can be learned or developed (i.e., leaders are not born but are made). Moreover, possessing leadership traits is not enough to make a person a successful leader; he must also take specific actions necessary for strong leadership.[14] The measurement and understanding of personal characteristics have improved since the early twentieth century, and modern researchers have proposed that important leadership traits can be categorized as follows:[15]

- *Drive*. Drive refers to the amount of ambition, persistence, tenacity, and initiative that people possess. Leaders must have the energy and will to continue to act during turbulent and stressful times. Drive and ambition are also important to a leader's ability to create a vision and engage in behavior to achieve the vision.
- *Leadership motivation*. Leadership motivation refers to a person's desire to lead, influence others, assume responsibility, and gain power. We must distinguish here between two types of motives. Leaders can have a *socialized power motive*, whereby they use power to achieve goals that are in the organization's best interests or in the best interests of followers. In contrast, a leader with a *personalized power motive* desires power solely for the sake of having power over others.
- *Integrity*. Leaders with honesty are truthful and maintain consistency between what they say and what they do. Followers and others in the organization are not likely to trust a leader who does not have these characteristics.
- *Self-confidence*. Leaders must be confident in their actions and show that confidence to others. People who are high in self-confidence are also able to learn from their mistakes, react positively to stress, and remain even-tempered and display appropriate emotions.
- *Cognitive ability*. Leaders who possess a high degree of intelligence are better able to process complex information, solve problems, and deal with changing environments.
- *Knowledge of the domain*. Knowledge of the domain in which they are engaged allows leaders to make better decisions, anticipate future problems, and understand the implications of their actions.

Reforming a Rotten Apple and an Evil City

©Brian Harkin/Getty Images, Inc.

William Bratton was appointed police commissioner of New York City in 1994 at perhaps one of the worst times in the history of the huge New York City Police Department (NYPD). New York City had experienced three decades of increasing crime rates, and some critics claimed that there was nothing the police department could do about it. Bratton, who had previously worked his way up through the Boston Police Department, faced a challenge that had been unresolved by his predecessors, and he had to handle the problem without an increase in resources.

Mr. Bratton became the head of the Los Angeles Police Department in 2002 at one of the worse times in its history. Los Angeles had just become the murder capital of the United States. The city was operating under federal supervision because of a number of corruption scandals and civil rights violations. Relations between the police and citizens were strained. As in New York, many questioned whether Bratton could handle the situation.

To say that William Bratton exhibited successful leadership would be an understatement. Within two years, his leadership of the NYPD made New York City one of the safest large cities in the world. Felony crimes fell 39 percent, theft decreased 35 percent, and murders dropped 50 percent. Public confidence in the police department, reported in Gallup polls, soared from 37 percent to 73 percent. Not only was the NYPD effective in fighting crime, but police

officers were also happier with their jobs, reporting record levels of job satisfaction. In Los Angeles, violent crimes declined by nearly 50 percent during Bratton's leadership from 2002 to 2009. The federal supervision ended. Approval ratings from the public soared to 83%.

Does William Bratton exhibit the leadership traits suggested by modern research? Yes, he does:

Drive. Bratton has been called a "cannonball," which provides an idea of his drive and ambition. Bratton shows passion for his vision that police should be held accountable for reducing crime and that success should be measured by how much crime, disorder, and fear are reduced.

Leadership motivation. From his early years in the Boston Police Department, Bratton expressed the desire to lead it some day. When he was leaving the New York City police commissioner's job, he entertained the idea of running for mayor. Today, he is considering various leadership posts. He has been mentioned as a possible candidate for the U.S. senate, governor of New York, and director of the FBI.

Integrity. Bratton's actions have always supported his words. Even in the face of opposition from political contingencies and civil liberties groups, he has remained committed to police accountability and zero-tolerance policies. Bratton has not tailored his messages

to his audiences. For example, he has said, "One of the things people like about me is that when I'm talking to a black audience I'm not talking any different than when I'm talking to a white audience." Furthermore, he has been tough on corruption, firing officers who are dishonest.

Self-confidence. Bratton has always displayed self-confidence, particularly in the face of adversity. His self-confidence has sometimes been interpreted as arrogance; however, over his career he has learned the difference between the two.

Cognitive ability. One of the most telling indications of Bratton's strong cognitive ability is the strategic manner in which he has approached managing the country's largest police departments.

Knowledge of the domain. Bratton worked his way through the ranks of the Boston Police Department, gaining knowledge about how policing works from the bottom up. As the NYPD police commissioner, he would ride the subway to work so that he had a better understanding of what was going on in the street. In Los Angeles, he would regularly visit barbershops, parks, and other gathering places to better understand the community.

Openness to new experiences. Bratton has been open to new ideas and change. He has frequently adopted the new ideas of others during his career. In Los Angeles, he changed his approach to minority relations, as the situation was quite different relative to what he had experienced in New York.

Extraversion. One of the key attributes that Bratton has brought to the policing is his hands-on approach and vigorous pace. From informal chats with community leaders to Sunday dinners with his inner circle in New York, he has embraced people and the energy they create for him.

Beyond the traits listed above, Bratton undertook a number of specific actions that led to success and to his being named "Police Executive of the 20th Century" (and having his photo on the cover of Time). His success has been attributed to four major actions:

1. He endorsed decentralization, giving strong authority and autonomy to precinct/division commanders. Instead of having to deal with bureaucratic policies that prevented them from combating crime, commanders were able to deal more aggressively and decisively with it and do so with more understanding, involvement, and commitment from the communities in which they served.

2. He engaged in systematic strategic planning to analyze crime patterns and use of resources. The end result was more efficient use of resources. More police officers were assigned to higher-crime areas, and more focus was placed on common and serious crimes.

3. He adopted the *Compstat process.* This process uses computerized crime statistics, electronic maps, and management meetings where precinct/division heads are held accountable (and rewarded or reprimanded) for the crime activity in their precincts.

4. He instigated a controversial policy known as zero-tolerance crime fighting. Police officers were required to arrest people for seemingly petty crimes such as graffiti writing, panhandling, and minor vandalism. The philosophy behind this policy is that if a neighborhood is plagued by petty crime, it appears to be out of control—reducing the felt presence of the police and making criminals feel freer to commit more serious crimes.

Although there are critics of Bratton's zero-tolerance style of policing and questions about some of his other tactics, the fact remains that crime was substantially reduced in both New York and Los Angeles, and police relations with their communities were strengthened. Few doubt that Bratton is an effective leader.

Sources: W.J. Bratton, & P. Knobler. 1998. *The Turnaround: How America's Top Cop Reversed the Crime Epidemic* New York: Random House; G. Kahn. 2009. "Bratton Joins Private Sector after 7 Years as L.A.'s Top Cop," *Wall Street Journal*, Aug. 6, p. A.2; W.C. Kim, & R. Mauborgne. 2003. "Tipping Point Leadership," *Harvard Business Review*, 81, no. 4: 60–69; J. Newfield & M. Jacobson. 2000. "An Interview with William Bratton," at http://www.tikkun.org/magazine/index.cfm/action/tikkun/issues/tik0007/article/000727.html; J. Zengerie. 2009. "Repeat Defender: After Taming Crime in Los Angeles Bill Bratton Has Won Over Skeptics Who Doubted His Success in New York," *New York*, Nov. 30, pp. 12–16.

- *Openness to new experiences.* Being open to new ideas and approaches is associated with flexibility, which can be very important in today's dynamic world.
- *Extraversion.* Leaders who enjoy being around people, prefer to maintain a vigorous pace, and seek excitement are more likely to be proactive in engaging both problems and opportunities.

William Bratton, former chief of police for New York City and now retired head of the Los Angeles Police Department, exhibits these traits. As discussed in the *Experiencing Organizational Behavior* feature, he has leveraged them to create positive outcomes in the areas of enhanced public safety and reduced crime. He also has exhibited the characteristics of strategic leaders that were explained earlier. For example, he engaged in strategic planning in both New York and Los Angeles and effectively implemented the resulting strategies. To implement these strategies, he decentralized authority to leverage the talents of various leaders and used effective communication processes to enhance coordination. He used his knowledge of policing to have a strong positive effect on police-department performance.

Most studies of leaders have concluded that the traits focused on here are important. As noted, however, although specific traits may be necessary for a person to be an effective leader, ultimately she must take action to be successful.

Before ending this discussion of trait theory, it is important to mention charisma. Think of famous (or infamous) leaders such as John F. Kennedy, Adolf Hitler, Winston Churchill, Eleanor Roosevelt, Martin Luther King, Jr., Ronald Reagan, and Barbara Jordan. Many people believe that all of these individuals possessed charisma. *Charisma* is usually defined by the effect it has on followers. Charismatic leaders inspire their followers to change their needs and values, follow visionary quests, and sacrifice their own personal interests for the good of the cause. Traditionally, charisma was thought of as a personality trait. However, conceptualizing charisma as a simple personality trait has been subject to criticism. In addition, charisma has been difficult to define precisely, and different leaders have displayed charisma in different ways.

The notion of charisma has become popular again in modern theories. Charismatic leadership, though possibly based in personality to some degree, can be learned over time (at least partially) and is ultimately reflected in a leader's behavior. Thus, it is best described by the leader's behavior and her relationship to followers.[16] We discuss charisma in more detail later in this chapter in the section on transformational leadership.

Behavioral Theories of Leadership

In response to the heavy reliance in the earlier part of the twentieth century on trait theory and the notion that leaders are born and not developed, large research projects were conducted at the University of Michigan and the Ohio State University to examine what leaders actually did to be effective. This research concentrated largely on leadership style. Although both managerial thought and scholarly investigation have progressed beyond these two lines of research, this work provided the foundation for more contemporary theories of leadership, such as the transformational leadership approach discussed later in the chapter.

University of Michigan Studies

The leadership studies at the Institute for Social Research of the University of Michigan were conducted by such scholars as Rensis Likert, Daniel Katz, and Robert Kahn. The studies involved both private and public organizations, including businesses from numerous industry groups. These studies examined two distinct styles of leader behavior: **the job-centered** and **employee-centered styles.**[17]

The job-centered leader emphasizes employee tasks and the methods used to accomplish them. A job-centered leader supervises individuals closely (provides instructions, checks frequently on performance) and sometimes behaves in a punitive manner toward them. Alternatively, an employee-centered leader emphasizes employees' personal needs and the development of interpersonal relationships. An employee-centered leader

job-centered leadership style
A behavioral leadership style that emphasizes employee tasks and the methods used to accomplish them.

employee-centered leadership style
A behavioral leadership style that emphasizes employees' personal needs and the development of interpersonal relationships.

frequently delegates decision-making authority and responsibility to others and provides a supportive environment, encouraging interpersonal communication.

To measure these styles, leaders completed a questionnaire consisting of a number of items. Based on their responses, they were classified as either job-centered or employee-centered. The effectiveness of these leaders was then examined by measuring factors such as the productivity, job satisfaction, absenteeism, and turnover rates of those being led.

The results of these studies were inconsistent. In some cases, units whose leaders used a job-centered style were more productive, whereas in other cases units with employee-centered leaders were more productive. The job-centered style, however, resulted in less-productive units more often than did the employee-centered style. In addition, even when productivity was high, employees with job-centered leaders had lower levels of job satisfaction than those who worked with employee-centered leaders. Therefore, many of the researchers involved in the studies concluded that the employee-centered style was more effective.

The situations in which job-centered leaders were effective could not be explained well. In addition to style, then, other factors seemed to affect a leader's effectiveness. In addition, the leadership style examined in these studies was unidimensional. A leader was classified as either job-centered or employee-centered but could not possess characteristics of both styles. This oversimplification no doubt affected the results of the research.

If we consider the case of Police Commissioner William Bratton, discussed in the earlier *Experiencing Organizational Behavior* feature, it is clear why the unidimensional view of leadership behavior is problematic. Although Bratton displayed a job-centered style by carefully monitoring police officers' performance and providing rewards or punishment based on that performance, he also demonstrated an employee-centered style by decentralizing authority and opening communication channels within the department. Similarly, Maria Yee from the opening case displayed both the job-centered and employee-centered styles.

Ohio State University Studies

At around the same time that the University of Michigan studies were being conducted, leadership studies were underway at Ohio State University led by such scholars as Ralph Stogdill and Edwin Fleishman. These studies emphasized a two-dimensional view of leaders' behavior. The two independent dimensions of leadership behavior were initiating structure and consideration.

Initiating structure indicates behavior that establishes well-defined patterns of organization and communication, defines procedures, and delineates the leader's relationships with those being led. Leaders who initiate structure emphasize goals and deadlines and ensure that employees are assigned tasks and know what performance is expected from them.

Consideration refers to behavior that expresses friendship, develops mutual trust and respect, and builds strong interpersonal relationships with those being led. Leaders who exhibit consideration offer support to their employees, use employees' ideas, and frequently allow them to participate in decisions.[18]

These two concepts are similar to the ones used in the Michigan studies—initiating structure is similar to job-centered leadership, while consideration is similar to employee-centered leadership. The important difference is that leaders can exhibit characteristics of both. Thus, an individual could be classified in any of the four cells shown in Exhibit 8-2,

initiating structure
A behavioral leadership style demonstrated by leaders who establish well-defined patterns of organization and communication, define procedures, and delineate their relationships with those being led.

consideration
A behavioral leadership style demonstrated by leaders who express friendship, develop mutual trust and respect, and have strong interpersonal relationships with those being led.

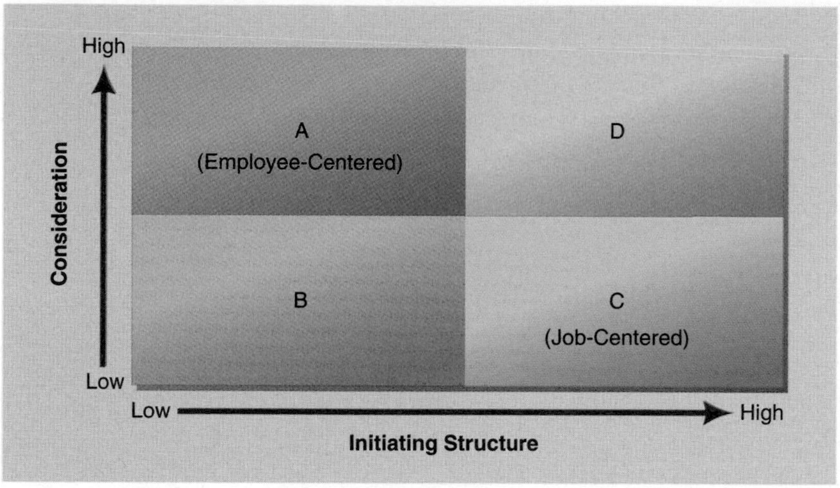

Exhibit 8-2 Comparison of Initiating Structure and Consideration with Job-Centered and Employee-Centered Concepts

whereas the Michigan approach artificially forced a person to be classified in either Cell A or Cell C.

Various studies have examined the linkage between these two dimensions of leader behavior and effectiveness. Results of early research suggested that leaders high in both initiating structure and consideration were more effective than other leaders. However, further studies showed that the relationship between leaders' behavior and their effectiveness, as measured by factors such as employee productivity, satisfaction, and turnover, was more complicated. In addition, each of the leader-behavior dimensions might affect various outcomes in different ways (structuring might have stronger effects on productivity, whereas consideration seems to have stronger effects on satisfaction, for example). A 2004 review of studies on initiating structure and consideration showed that the basic ideas of the Ohio State studies still applied.[19] Newer theories of leadership, however, present a more complex and complete view.

Contingency Theories of Leadership

Studies of trait and behavioral leadership concepts hinted at the importance of situational factors in leader effectiveness. Those studies led other researchers to conclude that effective leadership practices are "contingent" on the situation. Contingency leadership concepts were then developed. The two best known are the aptly named *contingency theory of leadership effectiveness* and the *path–goal theory of leadership*.

Fiedler's Contingency Theory of Leadership Effectiveness

contingency theory of leadership effectiveness
A theory of leadership that suggests that the effectiveness of a leader depends on the interaction of his style of behavior with certain characteristics of the situation.

The **contingency theory of leadership effectiveness** was developed by Fred Fiedler.[20] According to this theory, the effectiveness of a leader depends on the interaction of the leader's behavioral style with certain characteristics of the situation.

Leader Style

Different leaders may, of course, exhibit different styles of behavior. Fiedler explains that leaders' behavior is based on their motivational needs. The most important needs of leaders, according to Fiedler, are interpersonal-relationship needs and task-achievement needs. As you can see, these are similar to the concepts used in the Michigan and Ohio State studies.

The relative importance of these needs to a leader determines the leader's style. In determining which need is strongest, the esteem for the least-preferred co-worker (LPC) must be assessed.[21] If leaders describe their least-preferred co-worker mainly in negative terms (uncooperative, unfriendly), they obtain a low LPC score, which indicates a task-oriented leader whose task-achievement needs have first priority. Leaders who describe their least-preferred co-worker in positive terms (cooperative, friendly) receive a high LPC score. A high score indicates that the leader has a relationship-oriented style where interpersonal relationship needs have first priority.

Perhaps you have had a supervisor who focused mainly on the work to be done and did not engage in much personal interaction with those being led. This supervisor would probably have a low LPC score and be considered task-oriented. Contrast this person with another leader you have known who really cared about others and put a great deal of effort into maintaining positive relationships with everyone. This leader would have a high LPC score and be considered relationship-oriented. Which of these styles is most effective? That depends on situational characteristics.

Situational Characteristics

In some situations, leaders have more control over the work environment. In the context of Fiedler's contingency theory, this means that leaders can influence events in a straightforward way and work systematically toward desired outcomes. Important situational characteristics that determine a leader's level of control include leader–member relations, task structure, and position power.

- **Leader–member relations** correspond to the degree to which a leader is respected, is accepted as a leader, and has friendly interpersonal relations. When a leader has the respect and admiration of those who are led, he tends to have more control over the situation. He can more easily influence events and outcomes. This is the most important of the three situational variables.
- **Task structure** is the degree to which tasks can be broken down into easily understood steps or parts. When a leader deals with structured tasks, she has more control over the situation. She can more easily influence events and drive for goal achievement.
- **Position power** is the degree to which a leader can reward, punish, promote, or demote individuals in the unit or organization. When a leader can reward and punish, he has greater control and influence over the situation.[22]

leader–member relations
The degree to which a leader is respected, is accepted as a leader, and has friendly interpersonal relations.

task structure
The degree to which tasks can be broken down into easily understood steps or parts.

position power
The degree to which a leader can reward, punish, promote, or demote individuals in the unit or organization.

Situational Favorableness

The amount of control a leader has determines the favorableness of the situation. In the most favorable situations, leader–member relations are good, the tasks are highly structured, and the leader has strong position power. In the least favorable situations, leader–member relations are poor, tasks are unstructured, and leader position power is weak. Situations may, of course, vary between these two extremes.

Consider leading a project team for this course. Suppose that you have the respect of the team members, you are engaged in a set of tasks that can be easily managed, and you

Effective Leader	Task-Oriented (Low LPC)			Relationship-Oriented (High LPC)			Task-Oriented (Low LPC)	
Situational Favorableness	Favorable			Intermediate Favorableness			Unfavorable	
Leader–Member Relations	Good	Good	Good	Good	Poor	Poor	Poor	Poor
Task Structure	Structured	Structured	Un-structured	Un-structured	Structured	Structured	Un-structured	Un-structured
Leader Position Power	Strong	Weak	Strong	Weak	Strong	Weak	Strong	Weak
Situation	I	II	III	IV	V	VI	VII	VIII

Exhibit 8-3 Fiedler's Contingency Model of Leadership Effectiveness

are able to assign participation grades. This represents a favorable situation in which you, as leader, could easily influence events and outcomes. Now suppose instead that you do not get along with the members of the team, you are engaged in a set of tasks that are difficult to manage, and you have no power to reward or punish team members. This would be a very unfavorable situation, in which you would have much less influence over events and probably would have more difficulty working toward goal achievement.

Leadership Effectiveness

The leader's effectiveness is determined by the interaction of the leader's style of behavior and the favorableness of the situational characteristics. The leader's effectiveness is judged by the performance of the group being led. The linkages involving the leader's effectiveness, her style of behavior, and situational favorableness are shown in Exhibit 8-3.

Fiedler's research on the contingency model has shown that task-oriented leaders are more effective in highly favorable (I, II, III) and highly unfavorable (VII, VIII) situations, whereas relationship-oriented leaders are more effective in situations of intermediate favorableness (IV, V, VI). More specifically, the correlations between LPC scores and group performance in favorable and unfavorable situations is negative (performance was higher when LPC was lower). The correlation between LPC and group performance in situations of intermediate favorableness is positive (performance was higher when LPC was higher).[23]

Fiedler has also found that leaders may act differently in different situations. Relationship-oriented (high-LPC) leaders often display task-oriented behaviors under highly favorable conditions and display relationship-oriented behaviors in situations that are unfavorable or intermediate in favorableness. Conversely, task-oriented (low-LPC) leaders often display task-oriented behaviors in situations that are unfavorable or intermediate in favorableness but display relationship-oriented behaviors in favorable situations.[24] These findings help to explain why various leadership styles are effective in different situations, as discussed below.

Favorable situations do not require leaders to provide strong oversight or frequent task-focused inputs. Tasks can be accomplished with less direction from the leader.

task-oriented (low-LPC) leader's interpersonal needs are activated in favorable situations; however, the relationship-oriented (high-LPC) leader's needs for task achievement are activated in favorable situations. The low-LPC leader is thus more effective in favorable situations because they require leaders to provide encouragement, support, and interpersonal trust (relationship-oriented behavior).

Unfavorable situations require stronger oversight and more task-focused inputs. In such situations, the high-LPC leader's natural needs for interpersonal relations are activated, which creates difficulties. On the other hand, the low-LPC leader's natural needs for task achievement are activated. This matches the requirements of the situation.

Situations of intermediate favorableness provide neither of these extremes. Where the task is unstructured, a naturally relationship-oriented leader may be necessary to get the group to use its creativity to solve problems. Where leader-member relations are poor, a naturally relationship-oriented leader may be better able to overcome the negative relations with the group and build trust.

According to the contingency model, then, a leader cannot be effective in all situations by exhibiting only one leadership style. Fiedler believes that individuals should be matched with situations in which their leadership styles are likely to be most effective. Lacking the ability to reassign leaders, the characteristics of the situation should be changed to provide an effective match between the leader's style and the favorableness of the situation.

Fiedler conducted extensive research on the contingency model, and most of his research provided support for it.[25] Furthermore, the general observation that previously successful leaders do not always perform well after moving to a new job provides some support for a central idea in Fiedler's theory—leaders have a certain style and cannot easily adjust to a new context. In a study of senior managers who had departed from GE, lack of fit with a new job situation was cited as a cause of difficulties.[26] Still, the overall pool of research has provided only mixed support for Fiedler's ideas.[27] One issue is the simplicity of the model. It incorporates only two narrow behavioral styles (task and relationship). Moreover, it does not explain outcomes for the middle-LPC leader. Interestingly, some research suggests that the middle-LPC leader may be more effective than either the high- or low-LPC leader. Because the middle-LPC leader is more flexible and is not constrained by one orientation, she may better adapt to multiple situations.[28] Another concern has been the validity of the LPC measure. Critics believe that other measures of leader behavior are more reliable and valid.[29] A final concern has been the model's failure to explicitly address followers' satisfaction with leaders. Some research, however, has found the model to predict follower satisfaction.[30]

These criticisms do not reduce the importance of Fiedler's model. It represents one of the first comprehensive attempts to explain a complex subject. In addition, a significant amount of research supports the model, and researchers continue to investigate and attempt to extend it.

The Path–Goal Leadership Theory

The **path–goal leadership theory** was originally developed by Martin Evans[31] and Robert House.[32] The theory, which is based on expectancy concepts from the study of motivation, emphasizes a leader's effects on subordinates' goals and the paths used to achieve those goals. It provides a bridge to the modern study of leadership.

path–goal leadership theory
A theory of leadership based on expectancy concepts from the study of motivation, which suggests that leader effectiveness depends on the degree to which a leader enhances the performance expectancies and valences of her subordinates.

Recall from Chapter 6 that *expectancies* relate to the perceived probability of goal attainment and *valences* correspond to the value or attractiveness of goal attainment. Leadership can affect employees' expectancies and valences in several ways:

- Facilitating employees' efforts to achieve task goals (effort → performance expectancy). Effective leaders help employees (through encouragement, training, and technical direction, for example) believe that their efforts on a task will lead to goal attainment. As part of this, leaders address any barriers perceived by a given employee.
- Tying extrinsic rewards (pay raise, recognition, promotion) to accomplishment of task goals (performance → reward instrumentality).
- Linking individuals to tasks for which goal attainment is personally valuable (valence). In other words, leaders can assign individuals to tasks that they will find rewarding.

These tactics used by leaders increase effectiveness; employees achieve higher performance because of their increased motivation on the job. Specific behaviors through which these tactics are implemented must be tailored, however, to the situation. More so than Fielder's theory, the path–goal theory highlights the ability of managers to tailor their behaviors.[33]

Leader Behavior and Situational Factors

The path–goal leadership theory focuses on several types of leader behavior and situational factors. The main types of leader behavior are as follows:[34]

directive leadership
Leadership behavior characterized by implementing guidelines, providing information on what is expected, setting definite performance standards, and ensuring that individuals follow rules.

supportive leadership
Leadership behavior characterized by friendliness and concern for individuals' well-being, welfare, and needs.

achievement-oriented leadership
Leadership behavior characterized by setting challenging goals and seeking to improve performance.

participative leadership
Leadership behavior characterized by sharing information, consulting with those who are led, and emphasizing group decision making.

- **Directive leadership** behavior is characterized by implementing guidelines, providing information on what is expected, setting definite performance standards, and ensuring that individuals follow the rules.
- **Supportive leadership** behavior is characterized by being friendly and showing concern for well-being, welfare, and needs.
- **Achievement-oriented leadership** behavior is characterized by setting challenging goals and seeking to improve performance.
- **Participative leadership** behavior is characterized by sharing information, consulting with those who are led, and emphasizing group decision making.

Directive leadership and achievement-oriented leadership are related to the earlier concepts of job-centered style (Michigan studies), initiating structure (Ohio State studies), and task orientation (Fiedler's contingency theory of leadership effectiveness). Supportive leadership and participative leadership are related to the concepts of employee-centered style (Michigan studies), consideration (Ohio State studies), and interpersonal orientation (Fiedler's contingency theory of leadership effectiveness).

There are two sets of situational factors: subordinates' characteristics (such as needs, locus of control, experience, and ability) and characteristics of the work environment (such as task structure, interpersonal relations in the group, role conflict, and role clarity). The effectiveness of various leader behaviors depends on these situational factors.

Interaction of Leader Behavior and Situational Factors

Path–goal theory specifies a number of interactions between leader behavior and situational factors, with these interactions influencing outcomes. Researchers, however, have provided only mixed support for the theory,[35] with some studies supporting it and others failing to support it.[36] Relationships that appear to be valid are listed below:

- Associates with an internal locus of control (who believe outcomes are a function of their own behavior) are likely to be more satisfied with a participative leader. Individuals with an external locus of control (who believe outcomes are a function of chance or luck) are more likely to be effective with directive leaders.
- Associates who have a high need for affiliation are likely to be more satisfied with a supportive leader. Supportive leaders fulfill their needs for close personal relationships.
- Associates with a high need for security probably will be more satisfied with a directive leader who reduces uncertainty by providing clear rules and procedures.
- Supportive and participative leaders are more likely to increase satisfaction on highly structured tasks. Because the tasks are routine, little direction is necessary. Directive leaders are more likely to increase satisfaction on unstructured tasks, where individuals (particularly those with less experience and ability) often need help in clarifying an ambiguous task situation.
- Directive leadership is often more effective on unstructured tasks because it can increase an employee's expectation that effort will lead to task-goal accomplishment (particularly when employees have less experience and/or ability). Supportive leadership is often more effective on structured tasks because it can increase a person's expectation that accomplishing goals will lead to extrinsic rewards.[37]
- Associates with a high need for growth who are working on a complex task probably perform better with a participative or achievement-oriented leader. Because they are intrinsically motivated, they appreciate information and difficult goals that help in achievement. Individuals with a low growth need strength working on a complex task perform better with directive leaders.[38]

A summary of these interactions involving leader behavior and situational factors is presented in Exhibit 8-4. Although any number of situational factors could play roles in leader effectiveness,[39] those discussed here have been shown to be important.

Situational Factors		
Subordinate Characteristics	Characteristics of the Work Environment	Effective Leader Behaviors
Internal Locus of Control		Participative
External Locus of Control		Directive
High Need for Affiliation		Supportive
High Need for Security		Directive
	Structured Task	Supportive
	Unstructured Task	Directive
High Growth Need Strength	Complex Task	Participative Achievement Oriented
Low Growth Need Strength	Complex Task	Directive
High Growth Need Strength	Simple Task	Supportive
Low Growth Need Strength	Simple Task	Supportive

Exhibit 8-4 Interaction of Leader Behavior and Situational Factors

MANAGERIAL ADVICE

Phil Jackson and Leadership Success

Phil Jackson's success as a coach in the National Basketball Association (NBA) is legendary. He has won eleven championships, six with the Chicago Bulls and five with the Los Angeles Lakers. He has more playoff victories than anyone else in the history of the league and has the best winning percentage in playoff games among coaches with significant playoff experience. He also sports the best winning percentage in regular season games.

Some have suggested that Jackson's success is due only to having great players, such as Michael Jordan, Shaquille O'Neal, and Kobe Bryant. But the facts do not support this. In both Chicago and Los Angeles, the great players did not win championships until Jackson arrived.

So what makes him special? One answer to this question is his philosophy of leadership. His philosophy, which has been influenced by Zen Buddhism, embraces humility, respect for others, and a belief in the interconnected nature of humankind. Jackson said this:

In terms of leadership, this means treating everyone with the same care and respect you give yourself—and trying to understand their reality without judgment. When we can do that, we begin to see that we all share human struggles, desires, and dreams.

In essence, Jackson applies a philosophy that suggests less directive leadership, which fits the situation he faces in the NBA. His players typically have strong ability, a great deal of experience, and strong growth needs in terms of wanting to achieve on the basketball court. In addition, the relevant tasks are relatively structured. Under these conditions, directive leadership behaviors would be less desirable, and Jackson is known to be one of the least-directive coaches during basketball games.

In Los Angeles, Jackson helped his star player, Kobe Bryant, rebuild respect with his fellow players after a tumultuous period. Although tensions continue to arise from time to time, Jackson helped to make the situation better. He did so by advising Bryant to exhibit fewer directive behaviors in his own leadership. In Bryant's words:

Sometimes it's best if you just step back and kind of guide

©AP/Wide World Photos

them a little bit and allow them to learn on their own. Very subtle. That's … one of the things he taught me. …

Within his overall approach, Jackson tailors his leadership to circumstances. If players are less experienced or have growth needs that are dormant, he is more directive. His goal is to be "invisible," but he would not advise such invisibility in all situations.

Sources: Basketball-Reference.com, "Phil Jackson," 2009, at http://www.basketball-reference.com/coaches/jacksph01c.html; M. Bresnahan. 2007. "Leader Counsel," *Los Angeles Times*, Feb. 20, p. D.1; D. Dupree. 2002. "Phil Jackson: Zen and Now," *USA Today.com*, June 6, at http://www.usatoday.com/sports/nba/02playoffs/2002-06-05-cover-jackson.htm; P. Jackson, & H. Delehanty. 1995. "Sacred Hoops" New York: Hyperion; NBA Encyclopedia, "All-Time Regular Season Victories-Coaches," 2009, at http://www.nba.com/history/records/victories_coaches.html; J.P. Pfeffer, & R.I. Sutton. 2006. "*Hard Facts, Dangerous Half-truths, & Total Nonsense*" Boston: Harvard Business School Press.

Conclusions Regarding Contingency Theories

Contingency leadership concepts are more difficult to apply than the trait or behavioral concepts because they are more complex. But when appropriately used, they are more practical and should therefore lead to higher levels of effectiveness. In essence, they require that leaders correctly diagnose a situation and identify the behaviors that are most appropriate (those that best fit the characteristics of the situation). Also, contingency theories imply that a leader might need to change her approach over time. Among those being led, abilities and experience levels change, as do other features of the situation, suggesting that leaders must change their approaches.[40] Finally, path–goal theory implies that leaders might need to treat individuals differently within the same unit or organization.[41] If individuals in a unit are different, then leaders can benefit from approaching them in different ways, at least to some degree.

In order to be successful, leaders must act in ways that fit the situation in which they find themselves. Phil Jackson, one of basketball's great coaches, leads in a way that fits his situation. His story is presented in the *Managerial Advice* feature.

Although important and useful, contingency theories of leadership have received less attention in recent years. The dynamic business environment and rapid technological advancements of the past two decades have combined to create the need for a new approach to leadership.[42] We next turn to one of the most significant contemporary paradigms for leadership.

Transformational Leadership

The need for organizations to change and adapt rapidly while creating a high-performance workforce has become increasingly apparent in recent years. To stay competitive, business leaders must be able to inspire organizational members to go beyond their ordinary task requirements and exert extraordinary levels of effort and adaptability. As a result, new approaches to leadership have emerged.

Transactional leadership[43] provides a useful starting point in this discussion. This type of leadership focuses primarily on leaders' extrinsic exchange relationships with followers—that is, the degree to which leaders provide what followers want in response to good performance. Followers comply with leaders' wishes to gain desired rewards. Transactional leaders have the following four specific characteristics:[44]

1. They understand what followers want from their work, and they attempt to deliver these rewards if deserved.

2. They clarify the links between performance and rewards.

3. They exchange rewards and promises of rewards for specified performance.

4. They respond to interests of followers only if performance is satisfactory.

Transactional leaders are characterized by contingent reward behavior and active management-by-exception behavior.[45] *Contingent reward behavior* involves clarifying performance expectations and rewarding followers when those expectations are met. *Active management-by-exception* behavior is demonstrated when a leader clarifies minimal performance standards and punishes those who do not perform up to the standards. Transactional leaders consistently monitor the performance of their followers.

In contrast to this extrinsic exchange-based approach, **transformational leadership** involves motivating followers to do more than expected, to continuously develop and

transactional leadership
A leadership approach that is based on the exchange relationship between followers and leaders. Transactional leadership is characterized by contingent reward behavior and active management-by-exception behavior.

transformational leadership
A leadership approach that involves motivating followers to do more than expected, to continuously develop and grow, to increase self-confidence, and to place the interests of the unit or organization before their own. Transformational leadership involves charisma, intellectual stimulation, and individual consideration.

grow, to increase their level of self-confidence, and to place the interests of the unit or organization before their own.[46] Transformational leaders do the following three things:

1. They increase followers' awareness of the importance of pursuing a vision or mission and the strategy required.

2. They encourage followers to place the interests of the unit, organization, or larger collective before their own personal interests.

3. They raise followers' aspirations so that they continuously try to develop and improve themselves while striving for higher levels of accomplishment.

Transformational leadership results from both personal characteristics and specific actions. Three characteristics have been identified with transformational leaders: charisma, intellectual stimulation, and individual consideration.[47] **Charisma** refers specifically to the leader's ability to inspire emotion and passion in his followers and to cause them to identify with the leader.[48] A charismatic leader displays confidence, goes beyond self-interest, communicates and lives up to organizational values, draws attention to the purpose of the organization or mission, and speaks optimistically and enthusiastically. The second characteristic, *intellectual stimulation,* is the leader's ability to increase the followers' focus on problems and to develop new ways of addressing them. Leaders who provide intellectual stimulation reexamine assumptions, seek out different views, and try to be innovative. Finally, individual consideration involves supporting and developing followers so that they become self-confident and desire to improve their performance. Leaders showing *individual consideration* provide individualized attention to followers, focus on followers' strengths, and act as teachers and coaches.

A great deal of research has focused on how transformational leaders behave—that is, what they do to become transformational leaders. The list of common behaviors includes the following:[49]

- Transformational leaders articulate a clear and appealing vision, which is beneficial to the followers.
- They communicate the vision through personal action, emotional appeals, and symbolic forms of communication (such as metaphors and dramatic staged events).
- They delegate significant authority and responsibility.
- They eliminate unnecessary bureaucratic constraints.
- They provide coaching, training, and other developmental experiences to followers.
- They encourage open sharing of ideas and concerns.
- They encourage participative decision making.
- They promote cooperation and teamwork.
- They modify organization structure (such as resource allocation systems) and policies (such as selection and promotion criteria) to promote key values and objectives.

The proactive and energetic nature of transformational leadership hints at an opposite approach, called *laissez-faire* or *passive-avoidant* leadership.[50] Leaders displaying a laissez-faire style are not proactive, react only to failures or chronic problems, avoid making decisions, and are often absent or uninvolved in followers' activities. Such leaders typically do not have positive outcomes.[51] Leaders who strongly display transformational leadership do not display laissez-faire behaviors.

charisma
A leader's ability to inspire emotion and passion in his followers and to cause them to identify with the leader.

Commander D. Michael Abrashoff exemplified transformational leadership during his days on the USS *Benfold*.[52] First, Abrashoff's charisma was evident in several different ways. He demonstrated confidence with his informal but passionate manner. Consistent with this, he said the following: "I divide the world into believers and infidels. What the infidels don't understand … is that innovative practices combined with true empowerment produce phenomenal results." He focused on the vision of extreme readiness in order to protect the United States, and he communicated that vision clearly to all crew members, often meeting with them individually. He tried to link each crew member's tasks to the vision. He also went beyond self-interest, saying, "Anyone on my ship will tell you that I'm a low maintenance CO. It's not about me; it's about my crew."

©Reuters/Corbis

Abrashoff demonstrated his ability to create intellectual stimulation by continuously reexamining the way things were done on the ship and changing procedures when a better way was found. He stated, "There is always a better way to do things." During his first few months on the *Benfold*, he thoroughly analyzed all operations. He questioned everyone involved in each operation to find out whether they had suggestions for how to do things better. They almost always did.

Finally, Abrashoff displayed individual consideration by meeting individually with all new recruits on the ship and asking three questions: "Why did he/she join the Navy? What's his/her family situation like? What are his/her goals while in the Navy—and beyond?" He said that getting to know the sailors as individuals and linking that knowledge to the vision for the ship was critical. He always treated the sailors with respect and dignity. For example, he had the ship's cooks train at culinary schools so that the food would be the best of any ship in the Navy. Furthermore, he created learning opportunities for the crew. He wanted the crew to take the time to thoroughly learn their jobs and develop the skills necessary for job success and promotion.

The *Benfold* achieved notable performance, both in terms of reduced maintenance and repair budgets and in terms of combat-readiness indicators such as gunnery scores. At one point, the ship was considered the best in the U.S. Navy's Pacific Fleet, and it was awarded the prestigious Spokane Trophy. Furthermore, the commitment and satisfaction of the crew was quite high. One hundred percent of the crew signed up for a second tour of duty (the average for the Navy at the time was 54 percent).

Systematic research on transformational leadership is still being conducted. However, several conclusions have become apparent. First, leaders can be trained to exhibit transformational leadership behaviors.[53] Second, leaders can display both transformational and transactional leadership styles.[54] William Bratton provides a clear example of this. While exhibiting many charismatic qualities and decentralizing authority (transformational leadership), he also closely monitored officers' performance and rewarded or punished that performance accordingly (transactional leadership). Likewise, Maria Yee provides a clear example. While inspiring a shared vision and empowering individuals to make decisions (transformational leadership), she has also rewarded key performers and generally held people accountable (transactional leadership).

Third, both transformational and transactional leadership can be positive.[55] Transactional leadership has been associated with follower satisfaction, commitment, performance, and in some cases organizational citizenship (contingent reward behavior appears to be more positive than active management by exception).[56] Transformational leadership has also been linked to follower satisfaction and commitment, unit performance, organizational performance, and individual performance.[57] There are some differences. For example, the effects of transformational leadership seem to be stronger at the unit level than at the individual level (collective unit outcomes versus the outcomes of individuals). Furthermore, transformational leaders are viewed as better leaders by their followers and are more likely to enhance the self-concepts of followers.[58] This can pay important dividends in terms of confidence and sustained efforts. Finally, transformational leaders seem to be more effective in bringing about significant change in a unit or organization,[59] which explains why this form of leadership receives so much attention in today's fast-paced world. By focusing on shared visions of the future and collective interests, transformational leaders promote change.[60]

A unique study used historical data to assess U.S. presidents' charismatic leadership (part of transformational leadership). The study found that presidential charisma was positively related to presidential performance (measured by the impact of the president's decisions and various ratings by historians).[61] Another particularly interesting study found that the market value (stock price) of companies led by charismatic leaders was higher than the market value of other companies. This study also found that external stakeholders were more likely to make larger investments in a firm led by a charismatic leader than in firms whose leaders did not display charismatic qualities.[62] In another study, transformational leaders positively affected the outcomes of a strategic acquisition.[63] Because diversification and growth strategies often involve acquisitions of other firms, this is an important finding. As mentioned, however, it appears that both types of leadership can be effective; the organizational context may determine which one should be emphasized.[64] Transactional leadership perhaps should be a greater part of the leadership mix in stable situations, where significant change is not required. Transformational leadership perhaps should be a greater part of the mix in more dynamic situations, where associates must perform outside of explicit expectations, in terms of either providing extraordinary effort or being innovative. Overall, though, an integration of transformational and transactional leadership approaches seems to provide the most effective leadership strategy.[65] The basic relationships are shown in Exhibit 8-5.

Very recently, transformational leadership theory has been put to use in the pursuit of more ethical behavior in organizations. We describe this work in the *Experiencing Organizational Behavior* feature.

The scandals described in the *Experiencing Organizational Behavior* feature dramatically illustrate the effects of leaders on the performance of an organization. Unfortunately, they show the negative effects of leadership. The leaders at Enron, for example, destroyed all value in a multibillion-dollar corporation, and many people lost their jobs and all retirement savings because of the unethical leadership.

Additional Topics of Current Relevance

In closing our discussion of leadership, we cover several additional topics relevant to leading in today's workplaces. We discuss leader–member exchange, servant leadership, gender effects on leadership, and global differences in leadership.

Ethical Leadership? Authentic Leadership!

The twenty-first century seems to have brought an all-time low in ethical behavior by corporate leaders. A record number of top executives have been caught in outrageous scandals, leading to a large drop in public confidence in business leadership. Here are some examples:

- In one of the most widely reported scandals, numerous Enron executives—including former CEO Kenneth Lay; former COO, president, and CEO Jeffrey Skilling; and former CFO Andrew Fastow—were indicted on various charges, including conspiracy, fraud, and money laundering. Fastow alone was indicted on 788 charges and was sentenced to a 10-year prison term in return for pleading guilty to conspiracy and agreeing to help prosecutors with the rest of the cases. Enron declared bankruptcy in December 2001—the scandal involved, among other things, outrageous attempts to cover up the company's poor performance. Arthur Andersen LLP, the accounting firm that served as Enron's auditor, was convicted in June 2002 of obstruction of justice for destroying Enron documents. The Enron fiasco had a terrible financial impact on thousands of employees, who had most of their retirement in Enron stock, as well as on shareholders and on the company's creditors, who have received little of what they are owed.

- Samuel D. Waksal, founder of ImClone Systems, pleaded guilty in October 2002 to charges of securities fraud, perjury, and obstruction of justice. He played a major role in the flurry of stock sales that occurred after he learned that the Food and Drug Administration was not going to approve one of ImClone's new cancer drugs.

- The Waksal case led to the even-more-publicized trial of Martha Stewart, the popular lifestyle guru, who stood trial on charges related to her sale of ImClone stock. As part of the trial, many personally embarrassing details about Stewart's behavior were revealed (e.g., her tendency to treat employees badly). She was convicted and sent to prison.

- Bernard Madoff was jailed in 2009 for running a giant Ponzi scheme that cost investors billions of dollars. Paying earlier investors with the money of later investors rather than generating actual investment returns has been a popular crime over the years, but the scale of Madoff's fraud was epic. Charities that had entrusted funds to Madoff were among the hardest hit. Several had to close their doors. Retirees were also hard hit.

- In an alleged Ponzi scheme, financier R. Allen Stanford of the Stanford Financial Group was indicted in 2009. Laura Pendergest-Holt, the firm's chief investment officer, was also indicted not only for possible involvement in the Ponzi scheme but also for obstruction of justice. Billions of investor dollars have been lost.

©Stan Honda/AFP/Getty Images, Inc.

The large number of scandals (and there were many more than reported here) has led to a public outcry demanding that the management community, including business schools, place more emphasis on the ethical behavior of leaders. In response to this demand, new conceptualizations of leadership have been advanced. One such conceptualization is authentic leadership, proposed by Fred Luthans and Bruce Avolio.

Building on the research regarding transformational leadership, which partially addresses the quality of moral behavior, Luthans and Avolio posit the need to focus attention on developing leaders who are not only transformational but also authentic. An authentic leader is someone who is genuine, trustworthy, and truthful. Authentic leaders "own" their thoughts, emotions, and beliefs and act according to their true selves. These leaders have the following qualities:

- They are guided by values that focus on doing what's right for their constituencies.

- They try to act in accordance with their values.
- They remain transparent. That is, they are aware of their own shortcomings and discuss these shortcomings with others. Others are free to question them.
- They "walk the talk." That is, they model confidence, hope, optimism, and resiliency.

- They place equal weight on getting the task accomplished and developing associates.
- They continuously develop themselves.
- They have developed the values and personal strength they need to deal with ambiguous ethical issues.

The concept of authentic leadership is important in today's complex business environment. Future

leadership development and training should encompass authentic qualities so that leaders will be less likely to succumb to greed and dishonesty. Perhaps with this new stage in leadership development, images of executives from major companies being led away in handcuffs and innocent people being emotionally and financially devastated by corporate corruption will be a less common sight!

Sources: Associated Press, "Timeline of Events in Enron Scandal," press release, Feb. 19, 2004; A. Efrati, T. Lauricella, & D. Searcey. 2008. "Top Broker Accused of $50 Billion Fraud," *Wall Street Journal*, Dec. 12, p. A.1; B. George, P. Sims, A. McLean, & D. Mayer. 2007, "Discovering Your Authentic Leadership," *Harvard Business Review*, 85, pp. 129–138; F. Luthans & B.J. Avolio. 2003 "Authentic Leadership," in K.S. Cameron, J.E. Dutton, & R.E. Quinn (Eds.), *Positive Organizational Scholarship* San Francisco: Berrett-Koehler; E. Perez, & S. Stecklow. 2009. "Stanford is Indicted in Fraud, Surrenders," *Wall Street Journal*, June 19, p. C.1; "The Perp Walk," *BusinessWeek Online*, Jan. 13, 2003, at http://www.businessweek.com/print/magazine/content/03_02/bb3815660.htm.

Leader–Member Exchange

leader–member exchange
A model of leadership focused on leaders developing more positive relationships with some individuals and having more positive exchanges with these individuals.

The **leader–member exchange** (LMX) model builds on a simple idea: leaders develop different relationships with different followers.[66] A leader develops positive relationships with some followers but develops less positive relationships with others. An individual's ability to contribute at a high level is one factor that determines the relationship with the leader. An individual's similarity to the leader, in terms of personality and interests, is another factor.[67]

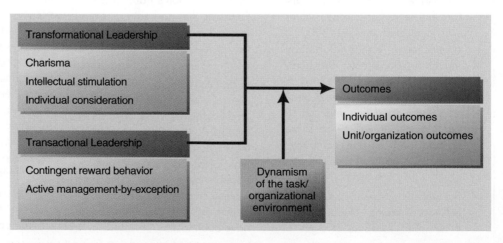

Exhibit 8-5 The Effects of Transformational and Transactional Leadership

Individuals who have positive relationships with the leader are members of an in-group. They experience leader–member exchange characterized by mutual trust, mutual support, and the provision of substantial resources. Individuals who have less positive relationships with the leader are members of an out-group. They experience out-group leader–member exchange characterized by more formality, less respect, lack of mutual support, and fewer opportunities for growth. Research on the LMX model indicates that members of an out-group tend to have lower levels of satisfaction, commitment, and performance.[68]

The existence of an out-group is inconsistent with high-involvement management. The high-involvement approach requires selection and retention of qualified individuals, proper training and coaching for each of them, and meaningful work for each of them. This is not simply a moral imperative. As explained in Chapter 1, organizational performance is at stake. Leaders should provide opportunities for all employees, or at least for as many as possible.

Servant Leadership

Similar to authentic leadership, **servant leadership** overlaps with the transformational tradition.[69] It includes elements such as valuing individuals, developing people, building community, conceptualizing, exhibiting foresight, and displaying wisdom.[70] Its distinctive focus, however, lies with an emphasis on serving others, both inside and outside the organization. Servant leaders want to serve others. They want to serve those who follow them. Their self-concepts are those of servants rather than leaders. And they often do not seek out leadership roles. Rather, such roles are thrust upon them.

servant leadership
An approach to leadership focused on serving others.

Max De Pree, former CEO of Herman Miller, often told a story that illustrates the key idea. In his words:

> I arrived at the local tennis club just after high school students had vacated the locker room. Like chickens, they had not bothered to pick up after themselves. Without thinking too much about it, I gathered up all their towels and put them in a hamper. A friend of mine quietly watched me do this and then asked me a question that I've pondered many times over the years. "Do you pick up towels because you're the president of the company? Or are you the president because you pick up towels?"[71]

The premise of the first question is more consistent with servant leadership. It suggests a mentality of "I am the leader, therefore I serve," rather than "I am the leader, therefore I lead."[72]

Systematic research into the effects of servant leadership is very limited. Even so, the research that is available suggests positive effects on associates' job satisfaction and commitment to the organization.[73] James Blanchard, former CEO of Synovus Financial Corporation, put it this way:

> The heart of the servant-leader brings order, brings meaning to employees. When employees feel order and meaning and that they are part of a team that stands for something good, that there is a higher calling than just working to get a paycheck, that they are improving mankind, there is an energy level that explodes and great things happen.[74]

Gender Effects on Leadership

Do women lead differently relative to men? Given the increase in the number of women in the U.S. workforce since the 1970s and the concern over the glass ceiling facing women who wish to advance in U.S. corporations,[75] it is not surprising that a great deal of attention has been focused on this question. For over three decades, researchers have investigated the issue of gender and leadership, and this research has been characterized by a great deal of debate.[76] There are reasons to believe that women often lead differently (for better or worse) than men, and there are also reasons to expect no differences in how men and women lead, particularly in U.S. work organizations.

One argument suggesting that women and men behave differently as leaders is referred to as the **structural–cultural model** of leader behavior.[77] This model suggests that because women often experience lack of power, lack of respect, and certain stereotypical expectations that result from cultural norms and stereotypes, they must behave differently from men to be effective leaders.[78] For example, followers are likely to expect different behaviors from women than from men. Thus, a female leader who acts aggressively might be viewed as mean-spirited or overly emotional, whereas a man behaving in the same way might be thought of as strong, confident, or passionate. Women may also be pressured to conform to certain gender-role stereotypes, such as being more interpersonally oriented and nurturing.[79] In essence, they are required to find a way to lead while making associates comfortable by exhibiting behavior consistent with gender-role stereotypes. Women who do this will not necessarily be less effective leaders because, as we discussed above, the effectiveness of specific leader behaviors depends on situational factors. Therefore, when the situation calls for a leader who emphasizes concern and caring for followers, women exhibiting nurturing behavior and strong interpersonal skills are likely to be effective and perhaps will be better at leading than men.[80]

In contrast, the **socialization model** suggests that there should be no differences in the way male and female leaders behave.[81] According to this argument, when all newcomers enter an organization, they are socialized into the organization's norms and accepted ways of behaving. Regardless of gender, all who advance to leadership positions have experienced the same organizational socialization and therefore are likely to display similar leader behaviors.[82] Therefore, women and men who have advanced into leadership positions will behave in the same way in a given organization. Across all organizations, both women and men will display a variety of behaviors.

Research evidence exists for both points of view. On the one hand, some studies have found that women display more interpersonal and social behaviors in small groups assembled as part of formal experiments, whereas men display more task-oriented behaviors.[83] Other studies have found women to be more democratic and participative than men in both experimental situations and in real organizations.[84] On the other hand, some research examining female leaders in organizational work settings has found no differences in the way male and female leaders behave.[85] Interestingly, in one study of almost 700 middle-level and executive managers, female managers and executives engaged more frequently in both stereotypical female behaviors (interpersonal behaviors) and stereotypical male behaviors (task-oriented behaviors).[86] In this case, the organization highly valued both types of behaviors—and it appeared that female leaders had to demonstrate those behaviors to a greater degree than did men. In conclusion, answering the question of whether women and men lead differently is not simple.[87] Overall, a number of studies support the idea that some stereotypical differences exist among managers, but the evidence is not quite as clear as we would like it to be. Moreover, studies that are supportive of this idea tend to reveal differences that are quite small in magnitude (i.e., women and men might differ but only to a small degree).

structural–cultural model
A model holding that because women often experience lack of power, lack of respect, and certain stereotypical expectations, they develop leadership styles different from those of the men.

socialization model
A model proposing that all leaders in a particular organization will display similar leadership styles, because all have been selected and socialized by the same organization.

The arguments concerning the differences or lack thereof between male and female leaders could be extended to differences between racial/ethnic minority leaders and white majority leaders. However, less research has been done on this issue than on gender differences. Results tend to show weak differences or no differences.[88] However, to address this issue more fully we need to better understand glass-ceiling issues that also affect racial/ethnic minority group members.

Global Differences in Leadership

As discussed in greater detail in Chapters 2 and 3, the U.S. workforce has become more diverse. In particular, globalization has produced situations in which U.S. managers lead associates socialized in different cultures, international managers lead U.S. associates, and work groups are made up of people from different cultures who must work together. Most of the theories and findings discussed so far in this chapter have focused primarily on the North American workforce, which values participation in decision making, narrow power distance (power should be equally shared), a high-performance orientation (people should be rewarded for good performance), significant individualism, and reasonably strong orientation toward the future (planning, investing, delaying gratification).[89] We can easily understand why leaders who are charismatic, engender participation, and provide relevant rewards for high performance are effective with this workforce.

©AP/Wide World Photos

But what happens in a culture that values collectivism (i.e., the group is viewed as more important than individuals) or has a high power distance (where people believe that power should be hierarchically distributed)? Such views are common in Arabic cultures such as Egypt and Morocco.[90] Would effective leadership take a different form? Or are there universal truths about what makes a good leader? As Michael Marks, CEO of Flextronics, a multinational manufacturing company, points out, "I have learned that in every place we operate, in every country, the people want to do a good job [and] there is no place where people can't do a world class job. ... This isn't to say we approach every region with cookie-cutter uniformity."[91]

The U.S. National Science Foundation funded a worldwide project, headed by Robert House, to examine whether leadership differs across different cultures and whether the effectiveness of different types of leadership varies by culture. This study is referred to as the *GLOBE* project (Global Leadership and Organizational Behavior Effectiveness).[92] It was first introduced in Chapter 3. Findings from the GLOBE project, based on surveys of thousands of people, cluster countries into groups with shared histories and values. Below is a description of the ideal leader for four cultural clusters:

1. *Anglo cluster*[93] (Australia, Canada, England, Ireland, New Zealand, South Africa [white sample], and United States): The ideal leader demonstrates charismatic influence and inspiration while encouraging participation. Ideal leaders are viewed as being diplomatic, delegating authority, and allowing everyone to have their say.

2. *Arabic Cluster*[94] (Egypt, Morocco, Kuwait, and Qatar, with Turkey also being included with these Arabic countries): Ideal leaders need to balance a paradoxical set of expectations. On one hand, they are expected to be charismatic and powerful, but on the other, they are expected not to differentiate themselves from others and to have modest styles. Leaders are also expected to have a great deal of power and to direct most decisions and actions.

3. *Germanic cluster*[95] (Austria, Germany, the Netherlands, and Switzerland): The ideal leader is one who is charismatic and participative, and who conceptualizes her relationships in a team-like fashion.

THE STRATEGIC LENS

Leadership is a critically important concept in organizational behavior and equally important for the performance of organizations. As demonstrated in this chapter, leaders have direct and strong effects on the performance of the individuals and teams they lead. At all levels in the organization, leaders often have major goals for performance, and they provide the context and take actions that affect and support efforts to achieve those goals. Leaders at the top of organizations, with input from lower-level leaders and associates, establish the strategies designed to achieve the organization's overall goals. Furthermore, the actual achievement of those goals is based strongly on the quality of the leadership they and other leaders throughout the organization provide in the implementation of strategies. In such implementations, leaders may need to be directive while simultaneously exhibiting compassion for their associates.

For strategies to be effective, they need to be formulated and implemented within a context of appropriate organizational values and with a working knowledge of the global environment. In addition, organizational strategies can be more effectively implemented when the value of diversity is understood and used to advantage. Research has shown that entering international markets with current products helps the firm achieve economies of scale (reduces the cost for each product sold), but selling goods in international markets has additional benefits that are even greater. For example, organizations operating in international markets often gain access to new knowledge. People from different cultures develop different ways of thinking and operating. As a result, leaders can obtain new ideas from employees, customers, and suppliers in international markets and incorporate them into their domestic operations and other foreign operations as well.[99]

International operations provide an excellent opportunity to gain benefits from diversity, as discussed in Chapters 2 and 3. For example, some firms develop teams composed of people from multiple ethnic and cultural backgrounds. With effective leadership, these heterogeneous teams often produce more creative ideas and solutions to problems. Also, they can better understand diverse customers and satisfy their needs.[100] Although the global context is complex, effective leadership adjusts to it and uses the multicultural environments to benefit the organization. Thus, leaders who espouse and exhibit ethical values, understand and use a diverse workforce to benefit the organization, and adapt to and extract knowledge from different environments in international markets contribute to an organization's capability to achieve and sustain a competitive advantage. These leadership characteristics contribute to the formulation of better strategies and to more effective implementation of those strategies.[101]

Critical Thinking Questions

1. How should leaders approach individuals, units, and organizations suffering from poor performance?

2. Why is ethical leadership often of utmost importance to various stakeholders?

3. Should women and men lead in different ways?

4. *Southern Asia cluster*[96] (India, Indonesia, Iran, Malaysia, Philippines, and Thailand): The ideal leader is humane, participative, and charismatic. Leaders are expected to be benevolent while maintaining a strong position of authority.

The findings from the GLOBE project suggest that charismatic leadership is viewed as effective and desirable across all cultures. Other dimensions of leadership, such as participation, humaneness, and team orientation, vary in importance across cultures. As numerous CEOs of multinational firms have indicated,[97] today's managers need to develop the cultural sensitivity required to understand differences in leadership requirements across national boundaries and cultures in order to develop highly productive multinational workforces.[98]

What This Chapter Adds to Your Knowledge Portfolio

In this chapter, we have discussed ideas about what makes a leader effective. We have covered trait theories, behavioral theories, contingency theories, and transformational leadership theory. All of these theories are related and build on one another. In specific terms, the following points were made:

- Leadership is the process of providing general direction and influencing individuals or groups to achieve goals.
- Trait theories of leadership propose that a person must possess certain characteristics to become a leader. Older trait theories held that leaders were born, not made. More modern trait theories state that certain characteristics are necessary but not sufficient for a person to be an effective leader and that many leadership characteristics can be developed or learned. Eight core traits of leaders are drive, leadership motivation, integrity, self-confidence, cognitive ability, knowledge of the relevant domain, openness to new experiences, and extraversion. Charisma may also be important.
- The Michigan studies focused on two distinct behavioral leadership styles—job-centered and employee-centered. The job-centered leader emphasizes tasks and the methods used to accomplish them. The employee-centered leader emphasizes employees and their needs and the development of interpersonal relationships. Research on which style is more effective has been inconclusive.
- The Ohio State studies focused on two dimensions of leader behavior: initiating structure and consideration. Leaders exhibiting initiating structure establish well-defined patterns of structure and communication, defining both the work activities and the relationship between leaders and subordinates. A leader showing consideration expresses friendship and develops mutual trust and strong interpersonal relationships with subordinates. Leaders may possess any combination of these two dimensions. Early research indicated that leaders exhibiting high levels of both initiating structure and consideration were most effective. However, later research showed that leadership effectiveness is more complex than this simple idea suggests.
- Fiedler's contingency model of leadership suggests that effectiveness depends on the match between a leader's style and the degree of favorableness of the situation. The important situational characteristics in this model are leader–member relations, task structure, and the leader's position power. Situational favorableness is determined by the amount of control a leader has. Fiedler's research indicates

? back to the knowledge objectives

1. What is leadership, and why is it important for organizations?

2. Are leaders born or made? Explain your answer. What are the core traits possessed by effective leaders?

3. Considering the findings from the Michigan and Ohio State studies, what do you think is the most effective leadership style? Give reasons to support your choice.

4. What key situational variables are related to leadership effectiveness in Fiedler's model of leadership effectiveness and in the path–goal model of leadership? In what ways do contingency models fall short in specifying a complete picture of effective leadership?

5. How do transformational and transactional leaders differ? What kind of results can be expected from each type of leader?

6. How do the leader–member exchange and servant–leadership models differ?

7. Explain why male and female leaders might engage in different leadership behaviors. What does the evidence show with respect to differences in leadership?

8. Describe the characteristics of an effective leader in each of the following clusters of countries: Anglo, Arabic, Germanic, and Southern Asia.

that task-oriented leaders are more effective in highly favorable or highly unfavorable situations, whereas relationship-oriented leaders are more effective in situations of intermediate favorableness. Fiedler's model has been criticized, but it is one of the first contingency concepts proposed and is supported by some research.

- The path–goal leadership model proposed by Robert House is based on the expectancy concept of motivation. Leaders positively influence individuals by enhancing their beliefs about the attainability of goals, giving consistent rewards for task-goal achievement, and assigning tasks that have valuable rewards for people being managed. Research has provided support for many of the specific predictions of the theory.

- Transformational leadership has been the subject of recent attention. Transactional leaders, who provide a useful contrast to transformational leaders, provide clear expectations and reward or punish followers based on their performance. Followers comply with leaders' wishes to gain desired rewards. Transformational leaders motivate followers to do more than expected, to continuously develop and grow, to build up their own confidence, and to put the interests of the team or organization before their own. They display charisma, intellectual stimulation, and individual consideration of followers. Research shows that both types of leadership can be positive and even necessary, with the appropriate degree of emphasis on each varying with the context (stable versus dynamic situations).

- Leader–member exchange is focused on the nature of the relationship between a leader and an individual in his unit/organization. When a positive relationship exists, the individual is a member of an in-group and experiences positive interactions. When a less positive relationship exists, the individual is a member of an out-group and experiences less positive interactions. Research shows that out-group members have lower satisfaction, commitment, and performance.

- Servant leadership means serving others. Research has been scant, but a number of individuals report success with the approach.

- Whereas the structural–cultural model suggests that there are significant differences in the leadership styles used by men and women, the socialization model holds that men and women experience the same organizational socialization and therefore exhibit the same leadership behaviors in U.S. work organizations. Research is mixed.

- The globalization of business has helped us understand that leaders must exhibit different styles to be effective in different regions of the world. For example, in the Anglo region, the ideal leader demonstrates charismatic influence and inspiration while encouraging participation, whereas in the Arabic region leaders are expected to have a great deal of power and to direct most decisions and actions.

Thinking about Ethics

1. What ethical responsibilities do leaders have in the organizations in which they work? What are the primary ethical issues involved in the leader's relationship to the organization?

2. What is more important, associates' productivity or leaders' exhibiting ethical behaviors? Is ethical behavior more important even if the result is poor performance? Why or why not?

3. Are ethical leaders more effective than leaders who exhibit unethical behaviors? Explain why or why not.

4. Assume that you are the leader of a marketing group and have been trying for some time to acquire a large new customer in a foreign country. One of your sales representatives reports that a competitor has offered a bribe to a key official of the company to obtain the contract. If you do not respond, your organization will likely lose this major new contract and your group will probably not meet its sales goal for the year. What should you do? Explain the reasons for your recommendation.

Key Terms

leadership, p. 292
job-centered leadership
   style, p. 296
employee-centered leadership
   style, p. 296
initiating structure, p. 297
consideration, p. 297
contingency theory of leadership effectiveness, p. 298
leader–member
   relations, p. 299

task structure, p. 299
position power, p. 299
path–goal leadership
   theory, p. 301
directive leadership, p. 302
supportive leadership,
   p. 302
achievement-oriented
   leadership, p. 302
participative leadership,
   p. 302

transactional leadership,
   p. 305
transformational leadership,
   p. 305
charisma, p. 306
leader–member exchange,
   p. 310
servant leadership, p. 311
structural–cultural
   model, p. 312
socialization model, p. 312

Human Resource Management Applications

The Human Resource Management (HRM) function plays a key role in a firm's ability to develop leaders at all levels of the firm. Several specific activities managed by the HRM department are particularly important.

In many organizations, the development of a comprehensive leadership model is partly the responsibility of the HRM unit. These models specify the precise behaviors and values that are expected in the organization. In many ways, these models define the culture of the organization. Culture is crucial for effective execution of strategies and attainment of organizational goals, as discussed in Chapter 13.

The administration of internal leadership development programs is also an important responsibility for many HRM units. These face-to-face programs are designed to raise the skill levels of new and experienced managers. Frequently, internal instructors are augmented with university-based faculty to facilitate the introduction of leading-edge knowledge.

The development and administration of intranet- and Internet-based programs are also tasks for HRM units. These programs can encompass many tactical and strategic topics, ranging from time management and motivating through goals to vision creation and articulation.

---

building your human capital

Are You a Transformational Leader?

Individuals lead in different ways. Understanding your own leadership behavior is very useful in assessing its appropriateness. In this chapter's *Building Your Human Capital,* we provide an assessment tool for transformational, transactional, and laissez-faire leadership.

Instructions

If you currently hold or have recently held a leadership position, ask several individuals who have experienced your leadership to respond to the questions that appear below. Your leadership position could involve managing a formal work unit in a company, leading a temporary team in an organization, being captain of an intramural basketball team, being pledge chairwoman for a sorority, and so on. If you do not have recent leadership experience, then complete a self-assessment, being very honest with yourself about the behaviors that you probably would exhibit in a future leadership role. Alternatively, you could complete the assessment with another leader in mind (i.e., rate someone who has been a leader for a unit or organization in which you have been a member).

For each item, tell your respondents to rate the frequency with which you engage in the behavior described. Also tell them that few people have extreme scores (low or high) on all or even most items (a "1" or a "4" is an extreme score). Have each respondent circle the appropriate number beside the item, using the following scale (note that "L" stands for Leader):

1 Never	2 Infrequently	3 Frequently	4 Always

1. L goes beyond self-interest.	1	2	3	4
2. L has my respect.	1	2	3	4
3. L displays power and confidence.	1	2	3	4
4. L talks of values.	1	2	3	4
5. L models integrity.	1	2	3	4
6. L considers the integrity dimension of situations.	1	2	3	4
7. L emphasizes the collective mission.	1	2	3	4
8. L talks optimistically.	1	2	3	4
9. L expresses confidence.	1	2	3	4
10. L talks enthusiastically.	1	2	3	4
11. L arouses awareness about important issues.	1	2	3	4
12. L reexamines assumptions.	1	2	3	4
13. L seeks different views.	1	2	3	4
14. L suggests new ways.	1	2	3	4
15. L suggests different angles.	1	2	3	4
16. L individualizes attention.	1	2	3	4
17. L focuses on your strengths.	1	2	3	4

18.	L teaches and coaches.	1	2	3	4
19.	L differentiates among us.	1	2	3	4
20.	L clarifies rewards.	1	2	3	4
21.	L assists based on effort.	1	2	3	4
22.	L rewards your achievements.	1	2	3	4
23.	L recognizes your achievements.	1	2	3	4
24.	L focuses on your mistakes.	1	2	3	4
25.	L puts out fires.	1	2	3	4
26.	L tracks your mistakes.	1	2	3	4
27.	L concentrates on failures.	1	2	3	4
28.	L reacts to problems but only when very serious.	1	2	3	4
29.	L reacts to only the biggest failures.	1	2	3	4
30.	L displays a philosophy of "If it's not broke, don't fix it."	1	2	3	4
31.	L reacts to problems, if chronic.	1	2	3	4
32.	L avoids involvement.	1	2	3	4
33.	L is absent when he or she is needed.	1	2	3	4
34.	L avoids deciding.	1	2	3	4
35.	L delays responding.	1	2	3	4

Scoring

Items 1–11: These items measure **charisma**. To calculate your score, sum the points given to you by each respondent and then divide by the number of respondents (i.e., calculate the average total score given by the respondents). If your score is above 29, then you display significant charisma. If the score is greater than 41, then you score very high on charisma.

Items 12–15: These items measure **intellectual stimulation**. If the total score for these items (averaged across respondents) is greater than 10, then you display significant intellectual stimulation. If the score is greater than 14, you score very high on intellectual stimulation.

Items 16–19: These items measure **individualized consideration**. If you scored higher than 11 (averaged across respondents), you display individual consideration to a significant degree. If the score is greater than 15, then you score very high on individual consideration.

Items 20–23: These items measure **contingent reward behavior**. If you scored higher than 10 (averaged across respondents), you display contingent reward behavior to a significant degree. If the score is greater than 14, then you score very high on contingent reward behavior.

Items 24–27: These items measure **management-by-exception behavior**. If you scored higher than 7 (averaged across respondents), you demonstrate management-by-exception behavior to a significant degree. If the score is greater than 11, then you score very high on management-by-exception behaviors.

Items 28–35: These items measure tendencies toward **laissez-faire** leadership. If you scored more than 8 (averaged across respondents), you display passive behavior to some degree. If the score is greater than 16, then you score very high on passive leadership.

Transformational leaders are characterized by charisma, intellectual stimulation, and individualized consideration. If you scored high on these three scales, then you are a good example of a transformational leader.

Transactional leaders provide contingent rewards and exhibit management-by-exception behaviors. If you scored high on these two scales, then you engage in transactional leadership. It is possible for a leader to be high on both transformational and transactional leadership.

Laissez-faire managers score high on avoidant/passive behaviors. If you scored high on the last set of items, then you are most likely a passive leader.

Source: Based on B.J. Avolio, B.M. Bass, and D.I. Jung. 1999. "Re-examining the Component of the Transformational and Transactional Leadership Using the Multifactor Leadership Questionnaire," *Journal of Occupational and Organizational Psychology*, 72: 441–462.

an organizational behavior moment
The Two Presidents

Frances Workman had been president of Willard University for less than two years, but during that time she had become very popular throughout the state. Frances was an excellent speaker and used every opportunity to speak to citizen groups statewide. She also worked hard to build good relationships with the major politicians and business leaders in the state. This was not easy, but she managed to maintain favorable relationships with most.

She also had worked on the internal structure of the organization, streamlining the administrative component. She started a new alumni club to help finance academic needs, such as new library facilities and higher salaries for faculty and staff. In addition, she lobbied the state legislature and the state university co-ordinating board for a larger share of the state's higher education budget dollars. Her favorable image in the state and her lobbying efforts resulted in large increases in state funding for Willard. Interestingly, Frances was so busy with external matters that she had little time to bother with the daily operations of the university. However, she did make the major operational decisions. She delegated the responsibility for daily operations to her three major vice presidents.

Before Frances's arrival, Willard University had several presidents, none of whom had been popular with the state's citizens or particularly effective in managing the university's internal affairs. The lack of leadership resulted in low faculty morale, which affected student enrollment. Willard had a poor public image. Frances worked hard to build a positive image, and she seemed to be succeeding.

Another state university, Eastern State, had Alvin Thomas as president. Al had been president about three years. He was not as popular externally as Frances. He was not a particularly effective speaker and did not spend much time dealing with the external affairs of the university. Al delegated much of that responsibility to a vice president. He did work with external groups but in a quieter and less conspicuous way than Frances did.

Al spent much of his time working on the internal operation of the university. When he arrived, he was not pleased to find that Eastern was under censure by the American Association of University Professors (AAUP) and that the university had a large number of students without adequate faculty. In addition,

Eastern was not involved in externally funded research. Al was committed to developing a quality university. Although he did not change the fundamental administrative structure of Eastern, he did extend considerable responsibilities to each of his vice presidents. He had high performance expectations for those on his staff, set ambitious goals, and reviewed every significant decision made in the university, relying heavily on his vice presidents and deans to implement them effectively. He developed a thorough planning system, the first of its kind at Eastern. He maintained good relations with the board of regents, but faculty viewed him as somewhat "stilted" and indifferent.

Frances projected a positive image to people in the state and along with that had built a positive image of Willard. The results of her efforts included an increase in enrollment of more than a thousand students in the past year. This occurred when enrollments were declining for most other colleges and universities in the state. Willard received the largest budget increase ever from the state university coordinating board and the state legislature. Finally, the outside funds from her special alumni club totaled almost $2 million in its first year. Faculty morale was higher, but faculty members viewed Frances warily because of her external focus.

In contrast, Eastern received an average budget increase similar to those it had received in the past. Although Eastern still had more students than Willard, its student enrollment declined slightly (by almost 300 students). However, the university was removed from AAUP censure. Externally funded research had increased by approximately $2 million during the previous year. Faculty morale was declining, and most faculty members did not believe they had an important voice in the administration of the university.

Discussion Questions

1. Based on the information provided, describe Frances's and Al's leadership styles.
2. What are the important factors that the leaders of Willard and Eastern must consider in order to be effective?
3. Compare and contrast Frances's and Al's effectiveness as leaders of their respective universities. What did each do well? What could each have done to be more effective?

team exercise
Coping with People Problems

The purpose of this exercise is to develop a better understanding of leadership through participation in a role-play in which a leader must cope with an employee problem.

Procedure

1. Assemble into three-person teams.
2. Within each team, one person should be selected as Don Martinez, the manager; one person selected as John Williams, the subordinate; and one person as the observer.
3. Each person should read his or her role and prepare to role-play the situation (allow 10 minutes for reading and preparing for roles). Each person, except the observer, should read only the role assigned. The observer should read all role materials.
4. After preparation, each team will engage in the role-play for approximately 20 minutes.
5. Following the role-play, each observer will answer the relevant questions and prepare to discuss how the leader (Don Martinez) handled the subordinate's (John Williams') problem.
6. Reassemble as a class. Each observer will describe the leadership situation in his or her team.
7. The instructor will present additional points for consideration.

Role for Don Martinez

You are manager of material control for Xenex Corp. You have had the job for five years and have almost 15 years of managerial experience. You enjoy working at Xenex, although advancement opportunities have become somewhat limited in the firm and budget constraints have been nontrivial in recent months. Four supervisors report to you, and John Williams is one of them. John is supervisor of inventory control. He has 22 people under his direction and has held the position for nine years. He is a good supervisor, and his unit performance has never been a problem.

However, in recent weeks you've noticed that John seems to be in a bad mood. He doesn't smile and has snapped back at you a couple of times when you've made comments to him. Also, one of his lead persons in the warehouse quit last week and claimed John had been "riding" him for no apparent reason. You think there must be some problem (maybe at home) for John to act this way. It is uncharacteristic.

John made an appointment to see you today and you hope that you can discuss this problem with him. You certainly want to deal with the problem because John has been one of your best supervisors.

Role for John Williams

You have been supervisor for inventory control for Xenex Corp. for almost nine years. You've had this job since about six months after graduating from college. When you took the job, Xenex was much smaller, but the job was a real challenge for a young, inexperienced person. The job has grown in complexity and number of people supervised (now 22).

Don Martinez, your boss, is manager of material control. He has held the job for about five years. When he was selected for the position, you were a little disappointed that you were not promoted to it, because you had done a good job. However, you were young and needed more experience, as the director of manufacturing told you.

Overall, Don has been a fairly good manager, but he seems to have neglected you during the past couple of years. You have received good pay increases, but your job is boring now. It doesn't present any new challenges. You just turned 31 and have decided that it's time to move up or go elsewhere. In past performance-appraisal sessions, you tried to talk about personal development and your desire for a promotion, but Don seemed unresponsive.

You've decided that you must be aggressive. You have done a good job and don't want to stay in your present job forever. You believe that you have been overlooked and ignored and don't intend to allow that to continue.

The purpose of your meeting today is to inform Don that you want a promotion. If the company is unable or unwilling to meet your needs, you are prepared to leave. You intend to be aggressive.

Role for Observer

You are to observe the role-play with Don Martinez and John Williams without participating. Please respond to the following based on this role-play:

1. Briefly describe how the situation evolved between Don and John.

_____

_____

_____

_____

_____

2. What leadership style did Don use in trying to deal with John?

_____

_____

_____

_____

3. How was the problem resolved?

_____

_____

_____

_____

4. How could Don have handled the situation more effectively?

_____

_____

_____

Endnotes

1. Pfeffer, J., & Sutton, R.I. 2006. _Hard facts, dangerous half-truths, & total nonsense: Profiting from evidence based management._ Boston: Harvard Business School Press, pp. 187–214.

2. Waldman, D.A., Ramirez, G.C., House, R.J., & Puranam, P. 2001. Does leadership matter? CEO leadership attributes and probability under conditions of perceived environmental uncertainty. _Academy of Management Journal,_ 44: 134–143.

3. Resick, C.J., Whitman, D.S., Weingarden, S.A., & Hiller, N.J. 2009. The bright-side and the dark-side of CEO personality: Examining core self-evaluations, narcissism, transformational leadership, and strategic influence. _Journal of Applied Psychology,_ 94: 1365–1381.

4. Haapniemi, P. 2003. Leading indicators: The development of executive leadership. At http//www.ccl.org.

5. Finkelstein, S., & Hambrick, D. 1996. _Strategic leadership._ St Paul, MN: West Publishing Co.

6. For additional insights related to vision creation as an aspect of strategic leadership, see Ireland, R.D., & Hitt, M.A. 1999. Achieving and maintaining strategic competitiveness in the 21st century: The role of strategic leadership. _Academy of Management Executive,_ 13(1): 43–57.

7. Hitt, M.A., & Ireland, R.D. 2002. The essence of strategic leadership: Managing human and social capital. _Journal of Leadership and Organizational Studies,_ 9(1): 3–14.

8. Wesley, K.N., & Yukl, G.A. 1975. _Organizational behavior and industrial psychology._ New York: Oxford University Press, pp. 109–110.

9. Kouzes, J.M., & Posner, B.Z. 2002. _The leadership challenge._ San Francisco: Jossey-Bass.

10. Bennis, W. 1982. The artform of leadership. _Training and Development Journal,_ 36(4): 44–46.

11. Kirkpatrick, S.A., & Locke, E.A. 1991. Leadership: Do traits matter? _Academy of Management Executive,_ 5: 48–60.

12. Stogdill, R.M. 1974. _Handbook of leadership: A survey of theory and research._ New York: Free Press.

13. Judge, T.A., Piccolo, R.F., & Kosalka, T. 2009. The bright and dark sides of leader traits: A review and theoretical extension of the leader trait paradigm. *Leadership Quarterly*, 20: 855–875; Zaccaro, S.J. 2007. Trait-based perspectives of leadership. *American Psychologist*, 62: 6–16.

14. Kirkpatrick & Locke, Leadership: Do traits matter?

15. Our list of important traits is based heavily on the work of Kirkpatrick & Locke, Leadership: Do traits matter? It also reflects the following: Judge, T.A., Hono, J.E., Ilies, R., & Gerhardt, M.W. 2002. Personality and leadership: A qualitative and quantitative review. *Journal of Applied Psychology*, 87: 765–780; Judge, Piccolo, & Kosalka, The bright and dark sides of leader traits: A review and theoretical extension of the leader trait paradigm; Peterson, S.J., Walumbwa, F.O., Byron, K., & Myrowitz, J. 2009. CEO Positive psychological traits, transformational leadership, and firm performance in high-technology start-up and established firms. *Journal of Management*, 35: 348–368.

16. Bass, B.M., & Avolio, B.J. 1990. The implications of transactional and transformational leadership for individual, team, and organizational development. In W.A. Pasmore, & R.W. Woodman (Eds.), *Research in organizational change and development, Vol. 4*. Greenwich, CT: JAI Press, pp. 231–272; House, R.J., Spangler, W.D., & Woycke, J. 1991. Personality and charisma in the U.S. presidency: A psychological theory of leader effectiveness. *Administrative Science Quarterly*, 36: 364–396.

17. Likert, R. 1961. *New patterns of management*. New York: McGraw-Hill.

18. Stogdill, *Handbook of leadership*.

19. Judge, T.A., Piccolo, R.F., & Ilies, R. 2004. The forgotten ones? The validity of consideration and initiating structure in leadership research. *Journal of Applied Psychology*, 89: 36–51.

20. Fiedler, F.E. 1967. *A theory of leadership effectiveness*. New York, NY: McGraw-Hill.

21. Ibid.

22. For additional information on situational factors, see Fiedler, F.E. 1993. The leadership situation and the black box in contingency theories. In M.M. Chemers, & R.Y. Ayman (Eds.), *Leadership theory and research: Perspectives and directions*. New York, NY: Academic Press, pp. 2–28.

23. Fiedler, F.E. 1971. Validation and extension of the contingency model of leadership effectiveness: A review of empirical findings. *Psychological Bulletin*, 76: 128–148.

24. Fiedler, F.E. 1972. Personality, motivational systems, and behavior of high and low LPC persons. *Human Relations*, 25: 391–412.

25. Chemers, M.M., & Skrzypek, C.J. 1972. Experimental test of the contingency model of leadership effectiveness. *Journal of Personality and Social Psychology*, 24: 173–177; Fiedler, F.E., & Chemers, M.M. 1972. *Leadership and effective management*. Glenview, IL: Scott, Foresman.

26. Groysberg, B., McLean, N., & Nohria, N. 2006. Are leaders portable? *Harvard Business Review*, 84 (5): 92–100.

27. For meta-analyses of LPC research, see Peters, L.H., Hartke, D.D., & Pohlmann, J.T. 1985. Fiedler's contingency theory of leadership: An application of the meta-analysis procedures of Schmidt and Hunter. *Psychological Bulletin*, 97: 274–285; Schriesheim, C.A., Tepper, B.J., & Tetrault, L.A. 1994. Least-preferred co-worker score, situational control, and leadership effectiveness: A meta-analysis of contingency model performance predictions. *Journal of Applied Psychology*, 79: 561–573.

28. Kennedy, J.K. 1982. Middle LPC leaders and the contingency model of leadership effectiveness. *Organizational Behavior and Human Performance*, 30: 1–14.

29. Green, S.C., & Nebeker, D.M. 1977. The effects of situational factors and leadership style on leader behavior. *Organizational Behavior and Human Performance*, 20: 368–377; Hare, A.P., Hare, S.E., & Blumberg, H.H. 1998. Wishful thinking: Who has the least preferred co-worker? *Small Group Research*, 29: 419–435; Shiflett, S. 1981. Is there a problem with the LPC score in leader match? *Personnel Psychology*, 34: 765–769; Singh, B. 1983. Leadership style and reward allocation: Does Least Preferred Co-Worker scale measure task and relation orientation? *Organizational Behavior and Human Performance*, 32: 178–197.

30. Rice, R.W. 1981. Leader LPC and follower satisfaction: A review. *Organizational Behavior and Human Performance*, 28: 1–25.

31. Evans, M.C. 1970. The effects of supervisory behavior on the path-goal relationship. *Organizational Behavior and Human Performance*, 7: 277–298.

32. House, R.J. 1971. A path-goal theory of leadership effectiveness. *Administrative Science Quarterly*, 16: 321–338.

33. Liden, R.C., & Antonakis, J. 2009. Considering context in psychological leadership research. *Human Relations*, 62: 1587–1605.

34. For work that followed the original specification of the theory, see: Fulk, J., & Wendler, E.R. 1982. Dimensionality of leader-subordinate interactions: A path-goal investigation. *Organizational Behavior and Human Performance*, 30: 241–264; House, R.J., & Mitchell, T.R. 1974. Path-goal theory of leadership. *Journal of Contemporary Business*, 3: 81–99; Podsakoff, P.M., Todor, W.D., Grover, R.A., & Huber, V.L. 1984. Situational moderators of leader reward and punishment behaviors: Fact or fiction? *Organizational Behavior and Human Performance*, 34: 21–63.

35. For a quantitative synthesis of research, see: Woffard, J.C., & Liska, L.Z. 1993. Path-goal theories of leadership: A meta-analysis. *Journal of Management*, 19: 857–876. For a supportive study in Taiwan, see: Silverthorne, C. 2001. A test of path-goal leadership theory in Taiwan. *Leadership and Organizational Development Journal*, 22: 151–158.

36. For additional insight on the mixed results, see: House, R.J. 1996. Path-goal theory of leadership effectiveness: Lessons, legacy, and a reformulated theory. *Leadership Quarterly*, 7: 305–309.

37. For additional insight, see: House, R.J., & Dessler, G.A. 1974. Path-goal theory of leadership: Some post hoc and a priori tests. In J.G. Hunt & L.L. Larsen (Eds.), *Contingency approaches to leadership*. Carbondale: Southern Illinois University Press, pp. 29–59.

38. For additional insight, see: Griffin, R.W. 1979. Task design determinants of effective leader behavior. *Academy of Management Review*, 4: 215–224; and Johnsen, A.L., Luthans, F., & Hennessey, H.W. 1984. The role of locus of control in leader influence behavior. *Personnel Psychology*, 37: 61–75.

39. Podsakoff, P.M., MacKenzie, S.B., Ahearne, M., & Bommer, W.H. 1995. Searching for a needle in a haystack: Trying to identify illusive moderators of leadership behaviors. *Journal of Management*, 21: 422–470.

40. For details of one framework emphasizing this point, see: Hersey, P., & Blanchard, K.H. 1988. *Management of organizational behavior: Utilizing human resources* (5th ed.). Englewood Cliffs, NJ: Prentice Hall.

41. See, for example: Schriesheim, C.A., Castro, S.L., Zhou, X., & DeChurch, L.A. 2006. An investigation of path-goal and transformational leadership theory at the individual level of analysis. *Leadership Quarterly,* 17: 21–38.

42. For related commentary from the key figure in path-goal theory, see: House, R.J. 1999. Weber and the neocharismatic paradigm. *Leadership Quarterly,* 10: 563–574.

43. Bass & Avolio, The implications of transactional and transformational leadership for individual, team, and organizational development; Whittington, J.L., Coker, R.H., Goodwin, V.L., Ickes, W. 2009. Transactional leadership revisited: Self-other agreement and its consequences. *Journal of Applied Social Psychology,* 39: 1860–1886.

44. Bass, B.M. 1985. *Leadership and performance beyond expectations.* New York: Free Press.

45. Bass & Avolio, The implications of transactional and transformational leadership for individual, team, and organizational development.

46. Bass, *Leadership and performance beyond expectations*; Bass & Avolio, The implications of transactional and transformational leadership for individual, team, and organizational development.

47. Others have specified four or more characteristics, but our three are grounded in the original work and have proven useful. For additional details, see: Judge, T.A., & Piccolo, R.F. 2004. Transformational and transactional leadership: A meta-analytic test of their relative validity. *Journal of Applied Psychology,* 89: 755–768; Rafferty, A.E., & Griffin, M.A. 2004. Dimensions of transformational leadership: Conceptual and empirical extensions. *Leadership Quarterly,* 15: 329–354.

48. Charisma has been studied as a standalone concept by a number of researchers and has spawned its own research tradition. It is, however, an integral part of the broader concept of transformational leadership. For details of the origins of charismatic leadership research, see House, R.J. 1977. A 1976 theory of charismatic leadership. In J.G. Hunt, & L.L. Larsen (Eds.), *Leadership: The cutting edge.* Carbondale, IL: South Illinois University Press, pp. 189–207. For example research studies, see: Howell, J.M., & Hall-Merenda, K.E. 1989. A laboratory study of charismatic leadership. *Organizational Behavior and Human Decision Process,* 43: 243–269; Shamir, B., Zakay, E., Breinin, E., & Popper, M. 1998. Correlates of charismatic leader behavior in military units: Subordinates' attitudes, unit characteristics, and superiors' appraisals of leader performance. *Academy of Management Journal,* 41: 387–409.

49. Yukl, G., & Van Fleet, D.D. 1992. Theory and research on leadership in organizations. In M.D. Dunnette & L.M. Hough (Eds.), *Handbook of industrial and organizational psychology* (2nd Ed.), Vol. 3. Palo Alto, CA: Consulting Psychologists Press, pp. 147–197.

50. Avolio, B.J., Bass, B.M., & Jung, D.I. 1999. Re-examining the components of transformational and transactional leadership using the Multifactor Leadership Questionnaire. *Journal of Occupational and Organizational Psychology,* 72: 441–462.

51. Hinkin, T.R., & Schriesheim, C.A. 2008. An examination of "nonleadership": From laissez-faire leadership to leader reward omission and punishment omission." *Journal of Applied Psychology,* 93: 1234–1248; Judge & Piccolo, Transformational and transactional research; Skogstad, A., Einarsen, S., Torsheim, T., Assland, M.S., & Hetland, H. 2007. The destructiveness of laissez-faire leadership behavior. *Journal of Occupational Health Psychology,* 12: 80–92.

52. LaBarre, P. 1999. The agenda–Grass roots leadership. *Fast Company,* 23 (April): 114–120.

53. Bass & Avolio, The implications of transactional and transformational leadership for individual, team, and organizational development.

54. Bass, B.M., Avolio, B.J., Jung, D.I., & Berson, Y. 2003. Predicting unit performance by assessing transformational and transactional leadership. *Journal of Applied Psychology,* 88: 207–218.

55. Bass, Avolio, Jung, & Berson, Predicting unit performance by assessing transformational and transactional leadership; DeGroot, T., Kiker, D.S., & Cross, T.C. 2000. A meta-analysis to review organizational outcomes related to charismatic leadership. *Canadian Journal of Administrative Sciences,* 17: 356–371; Judge & Piccolo, Transformational and transactional research; Lowe, K.B., Kroeck, K.G., & Sivasubramaniam, N. 1996. Effectiveness correlates of transformational and transactional leadership: A meta-analytic review. *Leadership Quarterly,* 7: 385–425.

56. Lowe, Kroeck, & Sivasubramaniam, Effectiveness correlates of transformational and transactional leadership; Podsakoff, P.M., Bommer, W.H., Podsakoff, N.P., & MacKenzie, S.B. 2006. Relationships between leader reward and punishment behaviour and subordinate attitudes, perceptions, and behaviors: A meta-analytic review of existing and new research. *Organizational Behavior and Human Decision Processes,* 99: 113–142.

57. Bass & Avolio, The implications of transactional and transformational leadership for individual, team, and organizational development; Lowe, Kroeck, & Sivasubramaniam, Effectiveness correlates of transformational and transactional leadership; Peterson, Walumbwa, Byron, & Myrowitz. CEO positive psychological traits, transformational leadership, and firm performance in high-technology start-up and established firms; Rowold, J., & Laukamp, L. 2009. Charismatic leadership and objective performance indicators. *Applied Psychology—An International Review,* 58: 602–621; Shamir, B., House, R.J., & Arthur, M.B. 1993. The motivational effects of charismatic leadership: A self-concept based theory. *Organizational Science,* 4: 577–594.

58. Ruggieri, S. 2009. Leadership in virtual teams: A comparison of transformational and transactional leaders. *Social Behavior and Personality,* 37: 1017–1021; Shamir, House, & Arthur, The motivational effects of charismatic leadership.

59. See, for example: Nemanich, L.A., & Keller, R.T. 2007. Transformational leadership in an acquisition: A field study of employees. *Leadership Quarterly,* 18: 49–68.

60. Bass & Avolio, The implications of transactional and transformational leadership for individual, team, and organizational development.

61. House, R.J., Spangler, W.D., & Woycke, J. 1991. Personality and charisma in the U.S. presidency: A psychological theory of leader effectiveness. *Administrative Science Quarterly,* 36: 364–396.

62. Flynn, F.J., & Staw, B.M. 2004. Lend me your wallets: The effect of charismatic leadership on external support for an organization. *Strategic Management Journal,* 25: 309–330.

63. Nemanich & Keller, Transformational leadership in an acquisition.

64. Ibid.

65. Bass, Avolio, Jung, & Berson, Predicting unit performance by assessing transformational and transactional leadership.

66. Graen, G.B. 1976. Role-making processes within complex organizations. In M.D. Dunnette (Ed.), *Handbook of industrial and organizational psychology.* Chicago: Rand McNally, pp. 1201–1245; Graen, G., Novak, M., & Sommerkamp, P. 1982. The effects of leader-member exchange and job design on productivity and satisfaction: Testing a dual attachment model. *Organizational Behavior and Human Performance,* 30: 109–131.

67. For research related to factors that influence leader-member relationships, see Sparrowe, R.T., & Liden, R.C. 1997. Process and structure in leader-member exchange. *Academy of Management Review,* 22: 522–552.

68. Chen, Z., Lam, W., & Zhong, J.A. 2007. Leader-member exchange and member performance: A new look at individual-level negative feedback-seeking behavior and team-level empowerment climate. *Journal of Applied Psychology,* 92: 202–212; DeConinck, J.B. 2009. The effect of leader-member exchange on turnover among retail buyers. *Journal of Business Research,* 62: 1081–1086; Gerstner, C.R., & Day, D.V. 1997. Meta-analytic review of leader-member exchange theory: Correlates and construct issues. *Journal of Applied Psychology,* 82: 827–844; Ilies, R., Nahrgang, J.D., & Morgeson, F.P. 2007. Leader-member exchange and citizenship behaviors: A meta-analysis. *Journal of Applied Psychology,* 269–277.

69. Barbuto, J.E., & Wheeler, D.W. 2006, Scale development and construct clarification of servant leadership. *Group & Organization Management,* 31: 300–326.

70. Ibid.; Smith, B.N., Montagno, R.V., & Kuzmenko, T.N. 2004. Transformational and servant leadership: Content and contextual comparisons. *Journal of Leadership & Organizational Studies,* 10 (4): 8091; Spears, L. 1995. Servant leadership and the Greenleaf legacy. In L.C. Spears (Ed.), *Reflections on leadership.* New York: John Wiley & Sons.

71. Max De Pree, quoted in: Sendjaya, S., & Sarros, J.C. 2002. Servant leadership: Its origin, development, and application in organizations. *Journal of Leadership & Organizational Studies,* 9 (2): 57–64.

72. Ibid.

73. Avolio, B.J., Walumbwa, F.O., & Weber, T.J. 2009. Leadership: Current theories, research, and future directions. *Annual Review of Psychology,* 60: 421–449.

74. James Blanchard, quoted in: Sendjaya & Sarros, Servant leadership.

75. Cleveland, J.N., Stockdale, M., & Murphy, K.R. 2000. *Men and women in organizations: Sex and gender issues at work.* Mahwah, NJ: Lawrence Erlbaum.

76. Ibid.

77. Dobbins, G.H., & Platz, S.J. 1986. Sex differences in leadership: How real are they? *Academy of Management Review,* 11: 118–127; Powell, G.N. 1990. One more time: Do female and male managers differ? *Academy of Management Executive,* 4: 68–75.

78. Kanter, R.M. 1977. *Men and women of the corporation.* New York: Basic Books.

79. Heilman, M.E. 1995. Sex stereotypes and their effects in the workplace: What we know and what we don't know. *Journal of Social Behavior and Personality,* 10: 3–26; Eagly, A.H., & Karau, S.J. 2002. Role congruity theory of prejudice toward female leaders. *Psychological Review,* 109: 573–598.

80. Bass, B.M., & Avolio, B.J. 1997. Shatter the glass ceiling: Women may make better managers. In K. Grint (Ed.), *Leadership: Classical, contemporary, and critical approaches.* Oxford, United Kingdom: Oxford University Press, pp. 199–210.

81. Bartol, K.M., Martin, D.C., & Kromkowski, J.A. 2003. Leadership and the glass ceiling: Gender and ethnic group influences on leader behaviors at middle and executive managerial levels. *Journal of Leadership and Organizational Studies,* 9: 8–16.

82. Eagly, A.H., & Johnson, B.T. 1990. Gender and leadership style: A meta-analysis. *Psychological Bulletin,* 108: 233–256; Ragins, B.R., & Sundstrom, E. 1989. Gender and power in organizations: A longitudinal perspective. *Psychological Bulletin,* 105: 51–88.

83. Wheelan, S.A., & Verdi, A.F. 1992. Differences in male and female patterns of communication in groups: A methodological artifact? *Sex Roles,* 27: 1–15.

84. Eagly & Johnson, Gender and leadership style.

85. Dobbins & Platz, Sex differences in leadership; Powell, One more time. Also, see van Engen, M.L., & Willemsem, T.M. 2004. Sex and leadership styles: A meta-analysis of research published in the 1990s. *Psychological Reports,* 94: 3–18.

86. Bartol, Martin, & Kromkowski, Leadership and the glass ceiling.

87. For an additional point of view see: Eagly, A.H. 2007. Female leadership advantage and disadvantage: Resolving the contradictions. *Psychology of Women Quarterly,* 31: 1–12.

88. Bartol, Martin, & Kromkowski, Leadership and the glass ceiling.

89. Hofstede, G. 1980. *Culture's consequences: International differences in work related values.* London: Sage; Ashkanasy, N.M., Trevor-Roberts, E., & Earnshaw, L. 2002. The Anglo cluster: Legacy of the British Empire. *Journal of World Business,* 37: 28–39.

90. Kabasakal, H., & Bodur, M. 2002. Arabic cluster: A bridge between East and West. *Journal of World Business,* 37: 40–54.

91. Marks, M. In search of global leaders. *Harvard Business Review,* 81 (8): 43–44.

92. House, R.J., Hanges, P.J., Javidan, M., Dorfman, P.W., Gupta, V., & GLOBE Associates. 2004. *Cultures, leadership, and organizations: GLOBE—a 62 nation study (Vol. 1).* Thousand Oaks, CA: Sage Publishing; House, R.J., Javidan, M., Dorfman, P.W., & de

Luque, M.S. 2006. A failure of scholarship: Response to George Graen's critique of GLOBE. *Academy of Management Perspectives,* 20 (4): 102–114; Javidan, M., House, R.J., Dorfman, P.W., Hanges, P.J., & de Luque, M.S. 2006. Conceptualizing and measuring cultures and their consequences: A comparative review of Globe's and Hofstede's approaches. *Journal of International Business Studies,* 37: 897–914.

93. Ashkanasy, Trevor-Roberts, & Earnshaw, The Anglo cluster.

94. Kabasakal & Bodur, Arabic cluster.

95. Szabo, E., Brodbeck, Den Hartog, D.N., Reber, G., Weibler, J., & Wunderer, R. 2002. The Germanic Europe cluster: Where employees have a voice. *Journal of World Business,* 37: 55–68.

96. Gupta, V., Surie, G., Javidan, M., & Chhokar, J. 2002. Southern Asia Cluster: Where the old meets the new? *Journal of World Business,* 37: 16–27.

97. Marks, In search of global leaders.

98. For additional information related to the GLOBE project, go to http://www.thunderbird.edu/wwwfiles/ms/globe. Also see: Chhokar, J.S., Brodbeck, F.C., & House, R.J. 2007. *Culture and leadership across the world.* Mahwah, NJ: Lawrence Erlbaum Associates.

99. Hitt, M.A., Hoskisson, R.E., & Kim, H. 1997. International diversification: Effects on innovation and firm performance in product diversified firms. *Academy of Management Journal,* 40: 767–798.

100. Hitt, M.A., Keats, B.W., & DeMarie, S. 1998. Navigating in the new competitive landscape: Building strategic flexibility and competitive advantage in the 21st century. *Academy of Management Executive,* 12 (4): 22–42.

101. Hitt, M.A., Ireland, R.D., & Hoskisson, R.E. 2007. *Strategic management: Competitiveness and globalization* (7th ed.). Cincinnati, OH: South-Western.

communication

exploring behavior in action
IBM and Virtual Social Worlds

For a recent IBM conference, participants arrived at a wonderful facility featuring a plush reception area, well-equipped meeting rooms, a support library, informal mingling spaces, picnic grounds, and relaxing gardens. Greeters offered directions to meeting rooms as well as other assistance. Kiosks also offered important information on conference activities. Once underway, the conference itself included three keynote speakers and 37 breakout sessions.

The individuals attending the conference were not physically present. Instead, they participated remotely in a virtual social world. Unlike social media such as YouTube (a simple content community), Facebook (a social networking site), or Wikipedia (an asynchronous knowledge-building endeavor), virtual worlds offer real-time interactions where people exist in a three-dimensional setting as self-generated representations of themselves (i.e., avatars). Participants can communicate using voice rather than text, utilize virtual equipment of all kinds, walk around in cleverly constructed settings, and sit down with others in venues such as cafés. Providers of virtual social worlds such as Second Life have created sophisticated systems (http://secondlife.com).

Although most often thought of as places that individuals go to socialize or live secret alternative lives, virtual social worlds can be used for collaborative meetings, training, and a number of other organizational purposes. In fact, virtual worlds are becoming viable alternatives to face-to-face meetings and training sessions even in cases where complex and important information must be exchanged. The ability for back-and-forth conversations and the ability to read body language is very helpful in this regard. Participants can offer ideas, ask questions, and even show a limited range of emotions within the virtual world.

Was IBM's conference successful? Yes it was! IBM estimates that it saved several hundred thousand U.S. dollars in comparison to what the conference would have

knowledge objectives
After reading this chapter, you should be able to:

1. Explain why communication is strategically important to organizations.
2. Describe the fundamental communication process.
3. Discuss important aspects of communication that affect the organization or its units, including networks and the direction of communication flow.
4. Define interpersonal communication and discuss the roles of formal versus informal communication, communication media, communication technology, and nonverbal communication.
5. Describe organizational and individual barriers to effective communication.
6. Understand how organizations and individuals can overcome communication barriers.

cost had it been done on a face-to-face basis. Moreover, the presentations were well received, with many sessions running long as participants continued to chat. Also, participants met on their own at the end of each day for conversations over virtual cocktails. This meant that people were informally networking, which is one reason to have a conference. Overall, the learning, information development, and social outcomes were much greater than they would have been with less rich substitutes for face-to-face interactions such as web chats, teleconferences, and videoconferences.

Based on its success, IBM is now actively using virtual social worlds for a number of purposes, including:

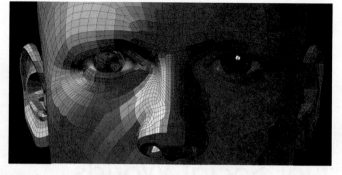

©Carol & Mike Werner/Visuals Unlimited, Inc./Getty Images, Inc.

- Events (e.g., Human Capital Management University)
- White-board Brainstorming (e.g., metaverse-brainshare application integration)
- Mentoring (e.g., mentoring from the corporate learning group)
- New employee orientation (e.g., Fresh Blue Program in China)
- Simulations and rehearsals (e.g., energy-efficient data center)
- Software development (e.g., Bluegrass-Rational Jazz Team)

In a different type of virtual social world, participants engage in games known as massively multiplayer online role playing games (MMORPG). World of Warcraft and Star Wars Galaxies are examples. World of Warcraft describes itself this way: "Players assume the roles of Warcraft heroes as they explore, adventure, and quest across a vast world. … Whether adventuring together or fighting against each other in epic battles, players will form friendships, forge alliances, and compete with enemies for power and glory."

IBM has partnered with Seriosity, a software company that develops organizational tools, to study leadership in MMORPGs. Opportunities to lead abound in these online games, where it is crucial to craft a vision for the future, create ways to attain that future through raids and other techniques, motivate others to join and sustain the fight, and make sense of events and outcomes in a complex and fluid setting. Individuals who are successful and move up the game-world hierarchies may have leadership skills that can generalize to the real world, particularly to situations that are dynamic and uncertain.

Although this work is in its early stages, the research carried out by IBM suggests that successful gamers can be effective corporate leaders. One participant said this,

> I've grown more accustomed now to directing various aspects of running the [on-line battle coalition] and providing a vision and leadership to members, Follow-up and assertiveness now feel more natural to me, even in real life. It has been an amazing opportunity to push myself beyond my boundaries.

Another participant had this to say,

> Finally, I … rallied the troops to revive one another and try again, mostly because I didn't know what else to do. It was me, this girl, talking to a room of 39 guys. And to my shock and surprise, everyone complied. … That was a defining moment for me.

Surveys also provide useful evidence. A survey of IBM managers and associates active in online games revealed that 50 percent of respondents believed game-playing had improved their real-world leadership. Forty percent indicated that they had applied specific techniques from the gaming world to improve leadership outcomes at IBM.

IBM clearly has benefited from the interactions that occur in virtual social worlds. What does the future hold? With developments occurring so rapidly, it is difficult to say.

Sources: L. Cherbakov, R. Brunner, R. Smart, & C. Lu. 2009. "Virtual Spaces: Enabling Immersive Collaborative Enterprise, Part 1," at http://www.ibm.com/developerworks/webservices/library/ws-vitualspaces; IBM Global Innovation Outlook, "Virtual Worlds, Real Leaders: Online Games Put the Future of Business Leadership on Display," 2007, at http://www.ibm.com/ibm/ideasfromibm/us/giogaming/073007/index.shtml; A.M. Kaplan, & M. Haenlein. 2009. "The Fairyland of Second Life: Virtual Social Worlds and How to Use Them," *Business Horizons*, 52, no. 6, pp. 563–572; Linden Lab, "Case Study: How Meeting in Second Life Transformed IBM's Technology Elite into Virtual World Believers," 2009, at http://secondlifegrid.net/casestudies/IBM; S. Morrison. 2009. "A Second Chance for Second Life: Northrop, IBM Use Virtual World as Setting for Training, Employee Meetings," *Wall Street Journal*, Aug. 19, p. B.5; World of Warcraft, "Intro to WOW," 2010, at http://www.worldofwarcraft.com/info/beginners/index.html.

the strategic importance of Communication

Good communication is vital to better organizational performance. Effective communication is important because few things are accomplished in organizations without it.[1] Managers must communicate with their subordinates in order for jobs to be performed effectively. Top management must communicate organizational goals to the associates who are expected to achieve them. Many jobs require coordination with others in the organization, and coordination requires communication. In fact, communication is such an important part of a manager's job that managers spend between 50 and 90 percent of their time at work communicating.[2] Top managers must digest information, shape ideas, coordinate tasks, listen to others, and give instructions. Decisions and policies are of little value unless they are fully understood by those who must implement them.[3] Good communication is also the basis for effective leadership, the motivation of subordinates, and the exercise of power and influence. It is also necessary for establishing effective relations with important external entities, such as suppliers, consumers, and government agencies.

Communication systems in organizations affect numerous outcomes that are central to an organization's functioning and competitive advantage. These include productivity,[4] quality services and products,[5] reduced costs, creativity, job satisfaction, absenteeism, and turnover.[6] In other words, organizational communication is interrelated with organizational effectiveness.[7] Indeed, surveys asking managers to give the reasons for project failures cite communication problems as an important, if not the most important, explanation.[8]

Given the importance of organizational communication, it is troubling that a number of managers find communication a challenging task. One study found that many managers underestimate the complexity and importance of superior–subordinate communications.[9] In addition, although research confirms that communication is an integral part of corporate strategy,[10] an important survey showed that only 22 percent of line associates and 41 percent of their supervisors understand the organization's strategy and that 54 percent of organizations do a poor job of communicating their strategy.[11] Thus, it appears that organizations and managers at middle and high levels have much to learn about effective communication. Also, it is not surprising that a recent survey of corporate trainers found that 44 percent of their organizations planned to greatly increase their budgets for communication training for managers and senior leaders.[12]

Communication can take many forms, such as face-to-face discussions, phone calls, e-mails, letters, memos, notes posted on electronic bulletin boards, and presentations to people who are physically in the same room. As seen in the case of IBM, communication can also occur inside virtual social worlds. These worlds offer a number of advantages that can address some of the problems plaguing communication. For example, the use of virtual social worlds might help managers and associates express themselves more freely when facing contentious issues. The use of this new creative medium could unlock previously frozen interactions, and it could facilitate the inputs of shy or conflict-avoidant people. For discussing or conveying the organization's strategy, the use of virtual social worlds might help senior managers to more effectively and less expensively reach various groups of geographically dispersed managers and associates. The fundamental purposes of communication are to provide information and instructions, to influence others, and to integrate activities.[13] Virtual social worlds have a great deal to offer in accomplishing these tasks.

In this chapter, we examine a variety of issues related to communication in organizations. In the first section, we discuss the fundamental communication process. Next, we describe aspects of communication that affect the organization or major units within it. We then discuss interpersonal communication—that is, communication between and among individual associates. Finally, after describing various barriers to effective communication, we present ways in which these barriers can be overcome to build a successful communication process.

The Communication Process

communication
The sharing of information between two or more people to achieve a common understanding about an object or situation.

encoding
The process whereby a sender translates the information he or she wishes to send in a message.

communication medium or communication channel
The manner in which a message is conveyed.

decoding
The process whereby a receiver perceives a sent message and interprets its meaning.

feedback
The process whereby a receiver encodes the message received and sends it or a response to it back to the original sender.

Communication involves the sharing of information between two or more people to achieve a common understanding about an object or situation. Successful communication occurs when the person receiving the message understands it in the way that the sender intended. Thus, communication does not end with the message sent. We also need to consider the message that is received. Think of a time when you meant to compliment someone, but the person understood your remark as an insult. This was not successful communication—the message received was not the same as the one sent.

Communication can be viewed as a process, as shown in Exhibit 9-1. The starting point in the communication process is the sender—the person who wishes to communicate a message. To convey information, the sender must first encode it. **Encoding** involves translating information into a message or a signal.[14] The encoded message is then sent through a **communication medium**, or **communication channel**, to the intended receiver. Communication media are numerous and include writing, texting, face-to-face verbal exchanges, verbal exchanges without face-to-face contact (e.g., phone conversations), and e-mail.

Once the message has been received, the receiver must decode it. In **decoding**, the receiver perceives the message and interprets its meaning.[15] To ensure that the meaning the receiver attaches to the message is the same as the one intended by the sender, feedback is necessary. **Feedback** is the process through which the receiver encodes the message received and sends it or a response to it back to the original sender. Communication that includes feedback is referred to as *two-way* communication. If feedback is not present (resulting in *one-way* communication), the receiver may walk away with an entirely different interpretation from that intended by the sender.

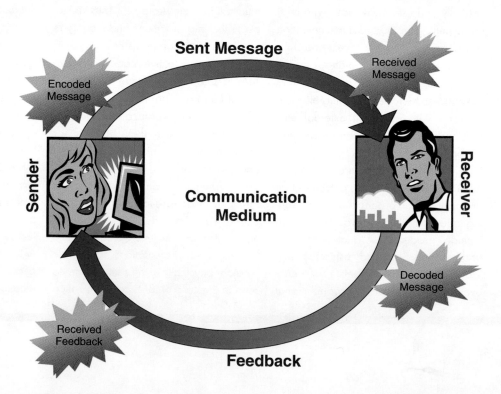

Exhibit 9-1 Sent Message

All parts of the communication process are important. A communication breakdown can occur in any part of the process. For example, information must be encoded into a message that can be understood as the sender intended. In addition, some forms of media may not be as effective as others in communicating the meaning of a particular message. Some communication media are richer than others—that is, they provide more information.[16] Consider e-mail as an example. People often use symbols such as ":)" to indicate intent (in this case, humor) because the medium is not very rich. If the message had been spoken, the humorous intent could have been indicated by the sender's tone of voice or facial expression. We describe more barriers to effective communication, as well as more details about media richness, later in the chapter.

Organizational Communication

Communication occurs at several different levels. On one level is the communication that occurs between and among individuals. This is referred to as *interpersonal communication,* and we discuss it in the next section. Here, we focus on *organizational communication*— that is, the patterns and types of communication that occur at the organizational and unit levels. The purpose of organizational communication is to facilitate the achievement of the organization's goals. As we have already seen, communication is a necessary part of almost any action taken in an organization, ranging from transmitting the organization's strategy from top executives to integrating operations among different functional areas or units. Organizational communication involves the use of communication networks, policies, and structures.[17]

Communication Networks

Communication networks represent patterns of communication (who communicates with whom). Thus, they correspond to the structure of communication flows in the organization and they affect coordination, innovation, and performance.[18] There are a variety of possible patterns, and a few of the more common ones are presented in Exhibit 9-2.

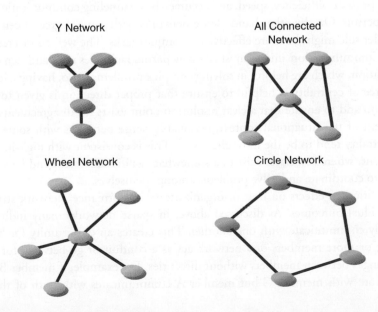

Y Network

All Connected Network

Wheel Network

Circle Network

Exhibit 9-2 Communication Networks

sparse networks
A communication network in which most or all network members communicate with only a few other members.

dense networks
A communication network in which most or all network members communicate with many other members.

centralized networks
A communication network in which one or a few network members dominate communications.

decentralized networks
A communication network in which no single network member dominates communications.

Each line shown in the exhibit represents two-way communication and, as such, counts as two network connections for the purposes of this chapter.

Networks can be characterized in terms of their density.[19] In **sparse networks**, there are few connections among members. In **dense networks**, there are many connections. The wheel, Y, and circle networks depicted in Exhibit 9-2 are sparse. In the wheel, for example, most members communicate regularly with only one other person, resulting in a density score of only .33 (10 connections among 6 people divided by 30 possible connections). In contrast, the well-connected network is dense, with a density score of .80 (16 connections among 5 people divided by 20 possible connections.

Networks can also be characterized in terms of their centralization.[20] In **centralized networks**, all communications pass through a central point or points, so that one or a few members of the network control most of the information exchanges. The wheel and the Y networks depicted in Exhibit 9-2 are examples of centralized networks. In the wheel, one member of the network communicates with every other member while the other members do not communicate with one another. In the Y network, one network member communicates with three other members while most of the others communicate with only one other member. Traditional organizational hierarchies, where subordinates communicate mostly or only with their bosses, who in turn communicate with their bosses, represent centralized networks. Companies in which units do not communicate with one other but only with a central headquarters, which then simultaneously coordinates all the units, are also centralized.

In **decentralized networks**, no single member of the network dominates information exchanges. The circle and the well-connected networks are examples. In the circle, each member of the network talks with two others. In the well-connected network pictured here, one member of the network communicates with each of the other four, but those other four members also communicate with almost everyone else. Centralization is somewhat higher in the well-connected network relative to the circle, but it is not excessively high.

To some degree, the effectiveness of networks depends on situational factors such as type of work and goals of the unit or organization.[21] For example, sparse highly centralized networks such as the wheel and the Y can be effective in accomplishing simple tasks. These structures promote efficiency, speed, and accuracy by channeling communication through a central person. On the other hand, dense networks with some degree of centralization in the leader role might be more effective for complex tasks. The well-connected network fits here. Communication among most or many parties facilitates trust and rich exchanges of information, which are helpful in solving complex problems. Also, having a leader with some degree of centrality is helpful to ensure that proper direction is given to the unit/organization and to ensure that a clear resolution point exists for disagreements. Overall, independent of the situational context, reasonably dense networks with some degree of leader centrality tend to be the most effective.[22] This is consistent with high-involvement management, where associates exist in a somewhat egalitarian system and have bounded authority to coordinate and solve problems among themselves.

In addition to effects on unit or organizational performance, network structure affects individual outcomes. As discussed above, in sparse networks many individuals do not directly communicate with one another. This creates an opportunity for brokerage, where one or more members of a network act as a conduit or go-between for information exchanges between members without direct ties. For example, if member B does not communicate with member C but member A communicates with both of them, then member A is said to be a broker of the B–C relationship. Individuals who broker a number of relationships tend to have more positive outcomes in terms of power, job performance, and financial compensation, even after controlling for factors such as hierarchical level and education.[23] Importantly, brokers in networks are not necessarily in formal leadership positions.

The networks depicted in Exhibit 9-2 involve five or six individuals; however, networks are often considerably larger. For example, the manufacturing department in a mid-sized company might have hundreds of people in it. Social scientists have been developing theories that can be used to explain and predict outcomes in these large organizational networks. In recent years, scientists and mathematicians also have been developing sophisticated network models and analytical techniques to study diverse phenomena such as stock market crashes, the relationships among CEOs, the spread of disease, and the spread of computer viruses.[24]

For example, in the late 1990s, Toyota had a brief brush with disaster that has been attributed to its heavy reliance on affiliated companies. Interestingly, the situation was resolved quickly through the network structure that connected the affiliates.[25]

To accomplish its goals, Toyota depends on a large number of affiliated companies. Those companies provide Toyota with the parts it needs to manufacture vehicles. They are independent, and each one focuses on making a unique part (such as electrical components or seat covers). At the same time, the companies are integrated because all of them must endorse Toyota's strict production system guidelines and protocols.

One of the companies in the Toyota network is Aisin Seiki, which produces a number of products including P-valves—brake devices that help prevent cars from skidding. The production of P-valves requires high precision, and the P-valves are a necessary component of every vehicle. If production of P-valves stops, Toyota cannot complete the manufacture of any vehicles. Aisin Seiki was the sole provider of P-valves for Toyota, and all the valves were made in one plant. In 1997, this plant burned down, and it was predicted that production would stop for at least a month—which would have severely harmed Toyota. However, because of the close coordination and effective communication among the various parts of the network, other plants were able to pick up the production of the precision P-valves with only about three days' preparation! Within a week, Toyota was once more manufacturing cars. Toyota's amazingly quick recovery can be attributed to the integration of all the members of its network.

Direction of Organizational Communication

Communication within organizations can occur in any of three directions: downward, upward, or horizontally.

Downward Communication

Downward communication, which refers to communication from senior managers to junior managers and from junior managers to associates, is necessary to provide job instructions, information on organization policies, and performance feedback. Downward communication can also be used to inform those at lower levels about the organization's goals and about changes faced by the organization. Downward communication, however, is

downward communication
Communication that flows from superior to subordinate.

©Michael Hitoshi/Digital Vision/ Getty Images, Inc.

frequently deficient in this regard. Lower-level managers and associates often complain about the lack of information on goals and changes being made in the organization, as mentioned in the earlier discussion of potential uses of communication through virtual social worlds.

An example of the importance of downward communication can be seen in the acquisition of a large consumer-goods manufacturing company. The company was acquired by a large conglomerate, but no downward communication had taken place informing associates of the effects they would experience. A rumor began to circulate among the acquired company's highly professional finance department staff suggesting that the department was to be reduced to a record-keeping function. All major financial responsibilities were supposed to be transferred to the financial staff at the conglomerate's headquarters. Because of this rumor, many of the finance department's professional staff members sought and obtained jobs with other organizations. When top management realized the problem, it immediately announced that the rumor was false and assured associates that the financial responsibilities would remain in their organization. Even so, the acquired company had lost almost 50 percent of its financial staff before this downward communication occurred. With a large number of acquisitions and mergers occurring in the current time period, particularly in the financial area with such combinations as Wachovia and Wells Fargo, downward communication regarding merger details must be proactively managed.[26]

Upward Communication

upward communication
Communication that flows from subordinate to superior.

Upward communication, which flows from associates to junior managers and from junior managers to senior managers, is necessary to provide feedback on downward communication and to provide ideas and information. It can, however, be difficult to achieve in an effective way. Thus, it is one of the less frequently used forms of communication in organizations. Common channels for upward communication include departmental meetings, "open-door" policies, suggestion boxes, attitude surveys, participation in decisions, grievance procedures, and exit interviews. Upward communication may be necessary for hierarchical superiors to monitor the effectiveness of decisions, gather information on problems and opportunities, ensure that jobs are being done properly, and maintain morale among those lower in the organization. However, it will not occur in organizations where superiors give the impression that they do not want to hear negative feedback or where subordinates do not trust superiors and fear reprisals. Upward communication can also be costly to organizations because policies and procedures must be developed to carry it out and also because it requires managers' time.[27]

Upward communication seems to be particularly difficult in larger organizations, probably because relationships in large organizations are more complex and formalized.[28] Certainly, larger size may inhibit the quantity of interactions between superiors and subordinates; however, the quality of the interaction is the most critical element.[29] Meg Whitman, the CEO of eBay until recently, fostered upward communication through her practice of enabling those at lower levels in the organization to be totally honest with her. So successful was this approach that a newly minted MBA associate at eBay once felt free to proclaim that almost anyone could manage the company—implying that Whitman's job as CEO was easy. Because Whitman enabled associates to communicate upward, this brash young MBA is still an associate with the company.[30] Another organization, Connecticut Bank, encouraged upward communication through employee attitude surveys. When survey results revealed that associates were dissatisfied with written communications in the

Communication at J. Crew: Mickey Drexler

Zena Olijnyk became extremely frustrated when responding to a promotional e-mail from J. Crew advertising the "retro-dot" mini skirt. She immediately tried to order the skirt online, but her size was not available. In a pique, she fired off an e-mail to J. Crew's customer service department complaining about sending promotional e-mail ads for items that were sold out. She received a response immediately from a customer service representative who told her that the demand was much larger than expected and then apologized. She was still annoyed, so she asked that her complaint be forwarded to someone higher up—maybe even the CEO. The next day, Zena received the following e-mail from someone named Millard Drexler:

> Thx much for taking time to send email-have copied our team-it has been somewhat difficult for us to forecast demand on our fashion merchandise as have not expected the reaction we have been getting-your points about how we handle are right on-have been trying to communicate more effectively than doing right now, and obviously not doing a great job. If one of [our] team members not already searching your size, please let know if still interested.

Millard "Mickey" Drexler is the chairman and CEO of J. Crew. He took over the company after being forced out of the GAP in 2002, where he had been for 19 years. Drexler left the GAP because of a 29-month decline in profits. However, Drexler is the person credited with putting the GAP on the map, turning the company into a $14.5 billion business, and revolutionizing the way the world dresses (some say he invented "casual chic"). He has done the same for J. Crew, taking the company from a failing business that lost $40 million in 2002 to one of the most profitable retail clothing companies in 2010. Even Michelle Obama has endorsed the company by wearing and discussing a J. Crew outfit on NBC's *Tonight Show*. Drexler turned J. Crew around by bringing in his own team, raising prices while raising quality, applying his uncanny talent for spotting clothing trends, cutting operating costs, and engaging in a communication style that is somewhat unique among CEOs.

Not only does Drexler e-mail and call unhappy customers, he habitually drops by J. Crew stores around the country to get a feel for what's selling, what's not, and what is happening in individual stores and to get input from sales associates in those stores. He walks into stores and quizzes customers about what they think and what they want. He also keeps in close contact with individual store managers. Once a week Drexler holds a conference call with store managers across the country. He asks them specific questions about what's going on in their stores, such as how customers reacted to a window display featuring suits (they liked it; sales rose dramatically). While Drexler is in his office at J. Crew

©Ben Baker/Redux Pictures

headquarters, he spends most of his time running around, sticking his head into cubicles to personally talk with all associates. A recent survey found that most associates complain about a lack of face-to-face contact with the "higher-ups" and about not being asked their opinion. It seems unlikely that J. Crew team members would ever feel this way.

Drexler's communication style is also unique. He's loud, boisterous, infectiously passionate about the business, and incredibly honest when he voices his frequent opinions. A colleague from his GAP days described him as letting it all hang out—he does victory dances when pleased and yells when frustrated. In response to a pair of shorts shown to him by the design team, Drexler responded, "This is a monster! No one is doing these!" Another colleague stated "Mickey's fun, but he was making so much noise we had to close the doors. He yells and screams. ..."

In the end, it is not surprising that Mickey Drexler has taken what was known as a failing, staid, preppy clothing company and turned it into an exciting, profitable, and much-talked-about success story. Through his direct and passionate communication with all stakeholders in the business, he seems to have channeled his energy and excitement.

Sources: B. Ebenkamp. 2009. "Marketer of the Year: Mickey Drexler," *Mediaweek*, 19, no. 32: pp. 26–27; M. Gordon. 2004. "Mickey Drexler's Redemption," *New York*, Nov. 29, pp. 40–41; L. Lee. 2006. "J. Crew's Smart-Looking IPO," *BusinessWeek*, June 28, at http://www.businessweek.com/print/investor/content/jun2006/pi20060628_109690. htm; A. Maitland. 2006. "Employees Want to Hear It Straight from The Boss's Mouth," *Financial Times*, Dec. 1, p. 12; Z. Olijnyk. 2007. "Now That's Service," *Canadian Business Online*, Feb. 20, at http://candianbusiness.com/shared/print.jsp?content= 20070220_130900_5412; T. Rozhon. 2004. "A Leaner J. Crew Is Showing Signs of a Turnaround," *New York Times*, June 24, at http://query.nytimes.com/gst/fullpage.html?res=9D02EFD6123F937A35755C0A96 29C8; S.M. Sears. 2009. "The Queen of J. Crew," *Barron's*, 89, no. 14: M9.

organization, the bank focused on reducing the quantity and improving the quality of written information transfers. Communication quality improved, and so did employee satisfaction and productivity. Finally, as illustrated in the *Experiencing Organizational Behavior* feature, J. Crew CEO Mickey Drexler makes it quite easy for his subordinates to communicate directly with him by frequently dropping by J. Crew stores.

Horizontal Communication

horizontal communication

Communication that takes place between and among people at the same level.

Horizontal communication, which takes place between and among people at the same level, is also important but is frequently overlooked in the design of organizations. Co-ordination among organizational units is facilitated by horizontal communication. For example, the manufacturing and marketing departments must coordinate and integrate their activities so that goods will be available for sales orders. This frequently is achieved through face-to-face conversations, phone conversations, and e-mail. Formal integrating positions may also be used to facilitate horizontal communications between units. These positions are often referred to as "boundary-spanning positions" because the position holders cross the boundaries that separate different units.[31] For example, some human resource departments have representatives or liaison members in each functional unit of the organization to coordinate and communicate staffing, compensation, and performance-management activities.[32]

Some time ago, organizations began to use communication from all three directions in the area of performance appraisal. Almost all *Fortune* 500 companies use 360-degree multi-rater feedback to evaluate senior managers.[33] Such feedback includes performance appraisals from peers (horizontal communication), subordinates (upward communication), and superiors (downward communication).[34] Evaluations from customers/clients, and suppliers are also sought in some cases.

There are, however, some problems with 360-degree feedback. One problem with subordinates evaluating superiors is that retaliation for negative performance evaluations can occur. Another problem is that peers may be politically motivated to either overrate or underrate their co-workers. Thus, it is usually recommended that upward and horizontal appraisals be used only for training and development purposes and that the superiors' evaluation be given more weight when appraisals are used to make personnel decisions (such as those involving promotions and pay raises).[35] However, if superiors do take their own 360-degree feedback seriously, and change their behavior as a result of feedback from subordinates and peers, the loyalty of subordinates will also increase.[36]

Interpersonal Communication

We now move from the organizational level to the interpersonal level of communication. **Interpersonal communication** involves a direct verbal or nonverbal interaction between two or more active participants.[37] Interpersonal communication can take many forms, both formal and informal, and be channeled through numerous media and technologies. Furthermore, people can communicate without even intending to do so, through nonverbal communication. In this section, we discuss each of these issues: formal versus informal communication, communication media, technology, and nonverbal communication.

interpersonal communication
Direct verbal or nonverbal interaction between two or more active participants.

Formal versus Informal Communication

Interpersonal communication can be formal or informal. **Formal communication** follows the formal structure of the organization (e.g., superior to subordinate) and entails organizationally sanctioned information. A major drawback of formal communication is that it can be slow. In contrast, **informal communication** involves spontaneous interaction between two or more people outside the formal organization structure. For example, communication between peers on their coffee break may be considered informal communication.

formal communication
Communication that follows the formal structure of the organization (e.g., superior to subordinate) and entails organizationally sanctioned information.

The informal system frequently emerges as an important source of communication for organization members.[38] Managers must recognize it and be sensitive to communication that travels through informal channels (such as the grapevine). In addition, managers may find that the informal system enables them to reach more members than the formal one. Another benefit of informal communication is that it can help build solidarity and friendship among associates.[39]

informal communication
Communication that involves spontaneous interaction between two or more people outside the formal organization structure.

Effective communication is crucial in implementing the organization's strategy. However, there is a downside to informal interpersonal communication—rumors and gossip. **Rumors** entail unsubstantiated information of universal interest. People often create and communicate rumors to deal with uncertainty.[40] This is why rumors are so prevalent during times of organizational upheaval, particularly during mergers and acquisitions. For example, in 2000, the Coca-Cola Company undertook a major restructuring to overcome its lagging financial performance.[41] During this period, persistent (and untrue) rumors flourished—such as "Coke is leaving Atlanta," "They're removing the flagpoles so that the American flag doesn't fly over the company," and "The CEO is leaving." These rumors resulted in dissatisfaction, loss of morale, and turnover, and senior management had to spend a great deal of time overcoming and eliminating them.

rumors
Unsubstantiated information of universal interest.

Gossip is information that is presumed to be factual and is communicated in private or intimate settings.[42] Often, gossip is not specifically work-related and focuses on things such as others' personal lives. Furthermore, gossip usually reflects information that is third-hand, fourth-hand, and even farther removed from the person passing it along. Gossip can cause problems for organizations because it reduces associates' focus on work, ruins reputations, creates stress, and can lead to legal problems. People are thought to engage in gossip in order to gain power or friendships or to enhance their own egos. For

gossip
Information that is presumed to be factual and is communicated in private or intimate settings.

example, groups of low-status office workers may try to keep their supervisor in check by continuously gossiping about him and thus threatening his reputation. Interestingly, good performers might also use gossip as an indirect weapon against poor performance. Even this use of gossip does not help unit performance and in fact can harm it.[43]

To avoid rumors in the workplace, managers are advised to provide honest, open, and clear information in times of uncertainty. Rumors should be addressed by those in a position to know the truth. To combat gossip, managers can include questions in 360-degree evaluations to identify individuals who habitually traffic in irrelevant, unsubstantiated information. Offenders can then be asked to end their dysfunctional behavior. Some organizations have dealt with rumors by placing restrictions on idle chatter.

Communication Media

Interpersonal communication, as already mentioned, can be based on many different media, and different media vary in degree of richness. Recall that *richness* describes the amount of information a medium can convey. Richness depends on: (1) the availability of feedback, (2) the use of multiple cues, (3) the use of effective language, and (4) the extent to which the communication has a personal focus.[44] Face-to-face verbal communication is the richest medium.[45] Think about all that happens during a face-to-face interaction. Suppose that you (the sender) are talking to a friend. If your friend does not understand the message or interprets it inaccurately, she can let you know either verbally or nonverbally (e.g., with a puzzled expression). In the interaction, you use multiple cues, including tone of voice, semantics (the words that are used), facial expressions, and body language. You use natural language and thus communicate more precise meaning. Finally, because you and your friend are face-to-face, it is easy to create a personal focus in the message.

Research has ordered common communication media in terms of richness.[46] In order of richest to least rich, they are:

1. Face-to-face communication
2. Telephone communication
3. Electronic messaging (such as e-mail and instant messaging)
4. Personal written text (such as letters, notes, and memos)
5. Formal written text (such as reports, documents, bulletins, and notices)
6. Formal numerical text (such as statistical reports, graphs, and computer printouts)

Virtual social worlds have not been included in the research discussed above because communication through this medium is too new. The experiences of IBM discussed in the opening case suggest, however, that this medium scores well in terms of richness. Immediate feedback is possible, multiple cues are available, including some emotional reactions, effective language can be used, and the communication can be personalized.[47]

For a particular communication task, choosing from among available media involves a trade-off between the richness of a medium and the cost (especially in time) of using it. For example, it is much easier and quicker to send someone a brief e-mail rather than to find his phone number, call him, and have a phone conversation, yet the phone conversation would likely yield richer information exchange. Research on media richness has not produced consistent results, but much of it suggests that effective managers will use richer media as the message becomes more equivocal.[48] Equivocal messages are those that can be interpreted in multiple ways. "We're having a meeting in the boardroom at 2 P.M. on Thursday" is an unequivocal message. "Your performance is not what I expected" is an equivocal message. Research has also shown that managers will use richer media when the message is important and when they feel the need to present a positive self-image.[49]

Another factor that influences the choice of media corresponds to organizational norms that indicate which types of communication media are desirable.[50] Some organizations have strong norms that employees communicate in a face-to-face manner, resulting in many meetings and chatting in the office. Other organizations have strong norms for using electronic communications and the Internet. One study found that associates' use of e-mail and instant messaging was highly dependent on their organization's norms for the use of these approaches.[51]

Communication Technology

Modern technology allows organizations and their members to communicate quickly, across any distance, and to collaborate more effectively than ever before.[52] Indeed, in order for organizations to remain competitive, they need to constantly keep up-to-date on modern communication technologies.[53] For example, after the great blackout of 2003 struck the eastern United States and Canada, IBM employees were able to fall back on instant messaging to continue working, while many other organizations, which did not use wireless technology, were crippled.

Communication technology will continue to rapidly advance. The world wide web, private intranets, virtual private networks (VPNs), web-based conferencing technologies, cell phones, and multifeatured mobile communication devices (e.g., iPhones) did not exist or were not commonly used 15 years ago.[54] Today, these technologies and the new forms of communication they support are all around us. For example, billions of e-mail messages are sent via the Internet each day from company accounts. Instant messaging is now used by the vast majority of companies worldwide. Even blogging has become more popular within the business world:

- As of December 2009, approximately 16 percent of *Fortune* 500 companies had created blogs (informal electronic communication sites that reach a wide audience) and made them available to the public. Many more had blogs that were available only internally for use by the company's managers and associates.[55] Examples of publicly available blogs are:
  - Coca Cola Conversations (Coca Cola)
  - Fast Lane Blog (General Motors)
  - Nuts about Southwest (Southwest Airlines)
- Hundreds if not thousands of CEOs and top executives worldwide now have personal blogs to communicate with associates, clients/customers, and the general public.[56] Individuals with blogs available to the public include:
  - John Mackey, CEO, Whole Foods Market
  - Tom Glocer, CEO, Reuters
  - Marc Cuban, Chairman, HDNet, and Owner, Dallas Mavericks Basketball Club

Organizations have been creating blogs to provide information related to advertising and corporate decisions and to seek information related to consumer thinking in the

EXHIBIT 9-3 Communicating with Customers

22-February-2007
Dear JetBlue Customers,

We are sorry and embarrassed. But most of all, we are deeply sorry.

Last week was the worst operational week in JetBlue's seven year history. Following the severe winter ice storm in the Northeast, we subjected our customers to unacceptable delays, flight cancellations, lost baggage, and other major inconveniences. The storm disrupted the movement of aircraft, and, more importantly, disrupted the movement of JetBlue's pilots and in-flight crewmembers who were depending on those planes to get them to the airports where they were scheduled to serve you. With the busy President's Day weekend upon us, rebooking opportunities were scarce and hold times at 1-800-JETBLUE were unacceptably long or not even available, further hindering our recovery efforts.

Words cannot express how truly sorry we are for the anxiety, frustration and inconvenience that we caused. This is especially saddening because JetBlue was founded on the promise of bringing humanity back to air travel and making the experience of flying happier and easier for everyone who chooses to fly with us. We know we failed to deliver on this promise last week.

We are committed to you, our valued customers, and are taking immediate corrective steps to regain your confidence in us. We have begun putting a comprehensive plan in place to provide better and more timely information to you, more tools and resources for our crewmembers and improved procedures for handling operational difficulties in the future. We are confident, as a result of these actions, that JetBlue will emerge as a more reliable and even more customer responsive airline than ever before.

Most importantly, we have published the **JetBlue Airways Customer Bill of Rights**—our official commitment to you of how we will handle operational interruptions going forward—including details of compensation. I have a video message to share with you about this industry leading action.

You deserved better—a lot better—from us last week. Nothing is more important than regaining your trust and all of us here hope you will give us the opportunity to welcome you onboard again soon and provide you the positive JetBlue Experience you have come to expect from us.

Sincerely,

David

Source: http://www.jetblue.com/aboutourcompany/flightlog/archive_February2007/.html.

general marketplace.[57] For example, Stonyfield Farm, the largest organic yogurt company in the world, uses blogs to interact with its customers on health-related topics relevant to the yogurt business.[58] When JetBlue Airways canceled half of its flights and kept passengers waiting in planes on the runway for up to 11 hours, they had a great deal of apologizing to do—especially for a company known for its customer service.[59] One way in which the company regained its service reputation was through Chairman David Neeleman's blog message to the passengers and the general public. This message is presented in Exhibit 9-3.

Although the adoption of communication technologies and the new forms of communication they support can be beneficial, new communication technologies can also create issues for organizations and individuals. One common problem is *information overload,* which is discussed later in this chapter. Another problem is that the new technology makes it easier to leak private or secret information to an unintended audience, often with unintended consequences. For example, Mark Jen, a programmer at Google, blogged about the company's unfavorable health plan.[60] This blog caused Jen to be fired and served as a warning to other bloggers at Google. Finally, as illustrated in the *Managerial Advice* feature, personal privacy concerns that did not exist 10 years ago are now very apparent.

Surfing for Applicants

Eva Montibello, a marketing manager with a Boston-based firm, was sorting through job applications, when a member of her staff came up and told her to check out a particular applicant's MySpace page. Eva did, and was quite shocked to find many compromising photos of the applicant, including one involving Jell-O wrestling. When this applicant was asked about the photos in her interview, she laughed it off and was quite silly about them. In the end, the unprofessional photos and unprofessional response to the photos were a factor in why this applicant was not hired by Eva's firm.

In recent years, the way in which companies recruit associates has gone through a revolution because of the availability of technology that allows employers to connect with and get information about potential job applicants. It used to be that when an individual applied for a job, the hiring organization had access only to information provided by past employers, schools, and/or the applicant. Now, for many people, there exists an abundance of information in cyberspace, and organizations are using this information to evaluate job candidates. Employers have access to information about candidates that they would never dream of asking about in an interview, such as social activities, religious activities, friends, and what people really think about their old bosses.

In a 2006 survey by executive search firm ExecuNet, 77 percent of recruiters said they use search engines to check out job candidates. In a 2009 Career-Builder.com survey of 2,600 hiring managers, 45 percent reported using search engines to gather information on applicants, with many specifically checking social networking sites such as Facebook and MySpace. According to the CareerBuilder survey, recruiters found these searches quite informative. Thirty-five percent indicated that candidates had been rejected based on information found in social networking sites. Among those recruiters screening out candidates, the following issues were cited:

©AP/Wide World Photos

- Candidate posted provocative/inappropriate photos or information (53 percent).
- Candidate posted content about drinking or drug use (44 percent).
- Candidate bad-mouthed one or more previous employers, co-workers, or clients (35 percent).
- Candidate demonstrated poor communication skills (29 percent).
- Candidate made discriminatory remarks (26 percent).
- Candidate posted information on qualifications that conflicted with information provided directly to the company (24 percent).
- Candidate shared confidential information from one or more previous employers (20 percent).

To avoid problems and to present a positive image, job seekers must be proactive. Rosemary Haefner (Vice President of Human Resources at CareerBuilder), Dave Willmer (Executive Director of a talent management company), and a number of other experts in recruiting and job searches have offered helpful advice. Collectively, they suggest the following:

- Conduct a comprehensive search of your name using major search engines (for common names, the search can be narrowed by adding employer names and/or relevant cities).
- For any web-based content that can be directly controlled, delete entries that could cast a negative light on your candidacy (see list of items presented above).
- For content that cannot be directly controlled (e.g., information someone else has posted about you), contact the relevant parties and request that the information be deleted or modified. If some negative content cannot be deleted, be prepared to discuss it in an interview.
- Reconsider your friends. Searches of social networking sites will turn up information not only on you but also on your friends and their comments to you.

- Consider creating your own professional group on sites such as Facebook or BrightFuse.com. Such a group would cast a positive light on your candidacy and might lead to important contacts.
- Present yourself in a positive way by: (1) communicating effectively when blogging and posting to social networking sites; (2) providing evidence of creativity and initiative in your web-based content; and (3) mentioning awards, accolades, and positive references in your web-based content.

Overall, the message is quite clear: people must be aware of the electronic image that they project. Not only do recruiters screen people out based on negative information found in cyberspace, they also look for positive information there.

Sources: D. Aucoin. 2007. "MySpace vs. Workplace," *Boston Globe,* May 29, at http://www.boston.com/news/globe/living/articles/2007/05/29/myspace_vs_workplace; M. Brandel. 2007. "How to 'Get Found' On the Web," *Computerworld,* March 26, vol. 41, no. 13, p. 30; W.M. Bulkeley. 2006. "Technology (A Special Report)—The Inside View: Employee Blogs Can Put a Human Face on Companies, But That's Not Always a Good Thing," *Wall Street Journal (Eastern Edition),* New York: April 3, p. R.7;.R. Haefner. 2009. "More Employers Screening Candidates via Social Networking Sites," at http://www.careerbuilder.com/Article/CB-1337-Getting-Hired-More-Employers-Screening-Candidates-via-Social-Networking-Sites/; D. Willmer. 2009. "Managing Your Digital Footprint," *T + D,* 63 no. 6: pp. 84–85.

Nonverbal Communication

nonverbal communication

Communication that takes place without using spoken or written language, such as communication through facial expressions and body language.

We can easily understand the concept of verbal communication, which involves written or spoken language; however, **nonverbal communication** is frequently as important or even more important. Forms of nonverbal communication include facial expressions, tone of voice, personal appearance (such as dress), contact or touch, and various mannerisms. In general, nonverbal communications fall into three categories: body language, paralanguage, and gestures. *Body language* (sometimes referred to as "kinesics") includes facial expressions; the use of hands, arms, and legs; and posture. *Paralanguage* refers to how something is said, such as how tone of voice, pitch of voice, and silence are used. *Gestures* are signs used to convey specific meanings (such as making a circle with your fingers to indicate "okay" or shrugging your shoulders to indicate "I don't know").

All of us have had a great deal of experience with nonverbal communication. In fact, between 60 and 90 percent of all interpersonal communication is nonverbal.[61] You have probably heard the adage "actions speak louder than words" or heard someone say they received "good vibes" from someone else. These phrases refer to nonverbal communication. One of the reasons that we place so much weight on nonverbal behavior is that it is "leaky behavior." Leaky behaviors are those that we cannot control. Therefore, people may be more likely to express their true feelings through nonverbal means rather than through verbal means, which are easy to control.

Nonverbal communication is important because, along with the sender's verbal expressions, it provides information about the person's attitudes and emotional or mental state. For example, a person's tone of voice, facial expression, and body movements can give us information about the person's feelings (timidity, enthusiasm, anger), which may either support or conflict with the words used. Nonverbal communication can also provide a useful form of feedback. Facial expressions can show whether the receiver understands the sender's message and how he or she feels about it. For this reason, face-to-face communication is frequently more effective than written communication, as we have already seen. In general, therefore, a manager should try to provide job directions and discuss performance through face-to-face communication with associates.

Because nonverbal behavior is more difficult to control than verbal behavior, it can reveal whether a person is lying. This issue has been given a great deal of attention, especially in light of its practical implications. For example, U.S. Customs officials were able to increase their hit rate in spotting drug carriers from 4.2 percent to 22.5 percent after they had been trained to read body language.[62] In the area of business negotiations, it is particularly important that people be able to read body language to identify when others are being deceptive. It is also important for negotiators to be aware of their own nonverbal cues.[63] For example, experienced negotiators often are able to determine whether the other party is lying through nonverbal cues such as the following:

- Subtle shifts in the pitch or tone of a person's voice[64]
- Long pauses before answering a question[65]
- Certain mannerisms, such as shifting limbs, licking one's lips repeatedly, scratching, or grooming[66]
- Fleeting smiles[67]

Another issue involves cultural differences in nonverbal communication. Given the increase in diversity within U.S. organizations and the globalization of the business world, it has become very important for people to understand these differences. Members of different cultures vary a great deal in how they present themselves and in their norms for nonverbal communication. Some of these differences are discussed later in the chapter. However, one aspect of nonverbal communication appears to be the same for all human beings. People of all cultures seem to discern and label facial expressions showing certain basic emotions in the same way.[68] These basic emotions include fear, disgust, surprise, happiness, and anger. Therefore, people in a variety of countries such as the United States, Spain, Argentina, New Guinea, and Japan are all likely to recognize a smile as a sign of happiness and a scowl as a sign of disgust.

Barriers to Effective Communication

At the beginning of this chapter, we emphasized how important timely, accurate, and informative communication is to an organization's overall performance and to the individuals who work within the firm. We also pointed out that organizations experience many communication problems. Here, we address the barriers to effective communication. These barriers can be categorized into organizational and individual sources.[69]

Organizational Barriers

Organizational barriers to effective communication include information overload, information distortion, jargon, time pressures, cross-cultural barriers, and breakdowns in the communication network.

Information Overload

In our present-day organizations, managers and associates are frequently burdened with more information than they can process. This overload occurs for several reasons. First, organizations face higher levels of uncertainty because of escalating change and turbulence in the external environment, so they obtain more information to reduce the uncertainty. Second, the increasing complexity of tasks and organizational structures creates a need for more information. Again, organizations employ more specialists to provide the needed information, placing greater information-processing burdens on organizational members. Third, ongoing developments in technology increase the amount of information available to associates and managers.

As mentioned, when associates or managers are overloaded with information, they cannot process all of it. Instead, they may try to escape the situation, or they may prioritize information so that some is attended to and the rest is ignored. Consider what happens when you are at a party and there are several conversations going on around you, music is playing, and someone is watching the game on TV. It is impossible to focus on everything. In order to focus on a specific conversation, you need to tune out everything else. Selecting only a portion of the available information for use, however, can result in inaccurate or incomplete communication in the organizational context.[70]

In recent years, the development and widespread use of cell phones, e-mail, and instant messaging has further increased the information overload problem—anyone can contact anyone anywhere. People in most organizations send and receive e-mail messages at work on a regular basis. Therefore, even associates at lower levels can quickly and easily send messages to higher-level managers, although this is frowned upon in many organizations. Similarly, top executives can communicate messages almost instantaneously to all associates regardless of their location. Obviously, this technology contributes to information overload, particularly for managers at higher levels. With these advances in technology, we are facing two overload problems that were not so common only a few years ago: forwarding frenzies and spamming.

Forwarding frenzies occur because electronic communication makes it very easy to pass on information to everyone. One common behavior is to forward messages to anyone who might have even the remotest interest. Thus, we receive many messages that we need to process but in which we do not have any real interest.

As you are no doubt aware, spam is unsolicited electronic junk mail. Despite anti-spam legislation in many states and increasingly sophisticated filtering systems that guard against offensive spam, the amount of spam with which people must cope at work is increasing at an alarming rate. Indeed, *InformationWeek* reported that almost 80 percent of all e-mail sent in a recent month was spam mail.[71] A study conducted by researchers at the University of Maryland estimated that spam mail cost U.S. businesses almost $22 billion due to time lost by associates reading and deleting junk mail.[72]

One way in which organizations are trying to deal with the overload caused by electronic messaging and e-mail is by adopting newer, web-based interactive technologies for internal communications. These include blogs, wiki sites, and social networking sites. With this technology, messages are all posted in one place, avoiding redundancy.

Information Distortion

It is common for information to be distorted, either intentionally or unintentionally. Unintentional distortion can occur because of honest mistakes or time pressure. On the other hand, intentional distortion often occurs because of competition between work units in an organization. Departments frequently have to compete for scarce resources in their operating budgets. Research has suggested that some units may believe that they can compete more effectively by distorting or suppressing information, thus placing their competitors at a disadvantage by keeping accurate information from them.[73] This is not a healthy situation, but it can occur if managers are not careful.

Suppression or distortion of information can (and does) also occur when a subordinate has more information than his manager. One study found that some subordinates suppress or misrepresent information about budgets when they have private information unknown to the manager.[74] For example, associates may suppress information about the amount of travel expenses, leaving the supervisor to discover the problem at audit time.

Specialty Area Jargon

One problem in large, complex organizations concerns the proliferation of specialists. Specialists are highly knowledgeable within their own fields but often have limited understanding of other fields. In addition, they often have their own "language," or jargon. It may be difficult for two specialists in different fields to communicate effectively with one another because they use different terminology. For example, a financial specialist may use terms such as *EBITA*, *accelerated depreciation*, and *P and L statement*. An information-systems specialist may use terms such as *firmware*, *hexadecimal*, *bytes*, and *PLII*. Each must understand the other's terminology if the two are to communicate.

Time Pressures

In most organizations, work needs to be done under deadlines, which create time pressures and constrain an individual's ability to communicate. When people are under time pressure, they sometimes do not carefully develop a message before sending it.[75] In addition, the pressure of a deadline often does not allow time to receive feedback, so the sender may not know whether the receiver accurately perceived the message.

Cross-Cultural Barriers

As discussed in Chapter 3, the business world is becoming more global, increasing the amount of regular cross-cultural communication. Effective cross-cultural communication is necessary for the financial success of international ventures.[76] Communication problems cause many expatriate managers to fail in their international assignments, leading to the removal of the manager or the failure of the international venture. These failures cost multinational corporations billions of dollars.[77] Many U.S. firms compete in foreign markets, and increasing numbers of foreign firms have moved into the U.S. market in recent years. Also, millions of U.S. workers are foreign-born. Thus, North American workers must deal with cross-cultural communication issues even in domestic locations. Exhibit 9-4 lists common differences in communication patterns in the United States and other cultures.

Cross-cultural barriers involve lack of language fluency or a broader lack of cultural fluency.[78] Even though English is frequently used for business around the world,[79] the potential for language barriers continues to exist in cross-cultural communications. Independently of whether English is used, one or more parties to a conversation might not speak the chosen language as well as others. Also, research has shown that many messages coming into a foreign unit of a firm arrive in the local language.[80] If knowledge of that language is weak, then trouble can ensue. Those who learn the local language often earn more respect within the culture.

Because many products are sold internationally, language is a very important consideration in product names and slogans. Major companies have experienced poor results by trying to use North American English names for products sold in foreign countries, especially when they have ignored how the name translated into other languages. For example, Enco (the former name of Exxon petroleum company) means "stalled car" in Japanese. Direct translation of advertising slogans presents similar problems. The slogan "Come alive with Pepsi," for instance, translated into "Come out of the grave" in German.

EXHIBIT 9-4 Examples of Cultural Differences between the United States and Other Cultures

Communication	In the United States	Elsewhere
Eye contact	Direct	In many Asian countries, extended eye contact is unacceptable.
Time orientation	Punctual—"Time is money"	Asian and Latin American cultures have longer time horizons; resolving issues is more important than being on time.
Answering questions	Direct and factual	Many Asian cultures view being direct as rude and aggressive.
Self-presentation	Self-promotion rewarded	Many other cultures (e.g., Asian, Russian) find this rude.
Posture	Open body posture preferred (e.g., arms relaxed)	In Japan, a closed body posture is preferred (e.g., crossed arms and legs).
Indicating "no"	Shaking one's head from side to side	In Bulgaria, the "no" signal means "I'm listening," rather than "I disagree."

cultural fluency
The ability to identify, understand, and apply cultural differences that influence communication.

Language fluency is one dimension of what is known as **cultural fluency**—the ability to identify, understand, and apply cultural differences that influence communication.[81] Language fluency is necessary for cultural fluency but is not enough by itself. Take, for example, the situation faced by Sue, an expatriate manager. When she was in Singapore, she asked a hotel clerk, who spoke English fluently, for the location of the health spa. She had seen several signs indicating that the hotel had opened a new spa, but none of the signs gave the location. The clerk responded that the hotel had no spa, although Sue kept arguing, "But I saw the signs!" After asking others and finally finding the spa, Sue concluded that the first clerk either had lied to her or was totally incompetent. Had she understood that many Asian cultures uphold the value of "face," or unwillingness to experience the embarrassment of saying "I don't know," she might have interpreted the situation differently.

Network Breakdowns

Breakdowns in the communication network frequently occur in large organizations because so much information flows through those networks. Many things can interfere with the flow—mail can be misplaced, messages may not be received by those targeted, and people can forget to relay pieces of information. Larger organizations have more problems because messages must flow through more people, increasing the probability that a message will be transmitted inaccurately at some point.

Breakdowns can also involve technology. The aftermath of Hurricane Katrina provides a vivid example. The *Experiencing Organizational Behavior* feature illustrates the strategic importance of managing communications technology and the information exchanges they support. When companies lose servers due to power outages or when malware infects intranets or when BlackBerrys will not function because of systemwide failure, the results might not be death and mayhem on the scale of Hurricane Katrina, but the chaos and financial losses can be substantial.

Communication Casualties

©AP/Wide World Photos

On August 29, 2005, Hurricane Katrina ripped through the Gulf Coast, devastating hundreds of thousands of homes, leveling entire towns, and resulting in over 1,800 deaths. After the storm, several levees surrounding Lake Pontchartrain failed, causing 80 percent of the city of New Orleans to be covered in water. For blocks and blocks, all that was visible from aerial views were rooftops, often with desperate people on top trying to flag down rescue helicopters. Cars and refrigerators floated down main streets. In many areas, the only way to get around was by boat. Swimming in the toxic, sludgy floodwater was extremely dangerous, even though it was the only way many people were able to save their lives. Some weren't so lucky, as dead bodies were often found floating down the streets of once-active and charming neighborhoods.

As if the disaster weren't enough, the attempt by authorities to respond to the disaster was shockingly inept, with a few exceptions, such as the efforts of the U.S. Coast Guard. Thousands of people waited on rooftops or overpasses for days to be rescued from the flood, without adequate food or water in insufferable heat. Looting was rampant in the city, with reports that even some New Orleans police officers were taking part in the activities. About 30,000 people were trapped in the Superdome without basic necessities, under a leaking roof, and in filthy conditions. It took five days to rescue these

people. Another 15,000 to 20,000 people were stranded at the Ernest N. Morial Convention Center, right outside the famed French Quarter, suffering from the same heat, filth, and lack of food and water as those in the Superdome. People who needed medicine for diseases such as diabetes, hypertension, and asthma became critically ill because of the lack of medical care. Rumors of rape and murder terrified the crowds. Approximately 15 percent of the police force deserted. The rest of the nation looked on in horror while watching TV reports of scenes that one would never imagine taking place in a major U.S. city.

Since that late-summer week in 2005, a great deal of examination of what went wrong has taken place. Why weren't agencies, such as the Federal Emergency Management Association (FEMA), the Red Cross, or the New Orleans Police Department able to come to the aid of New Orleanians sooner and more effectively? Blame can be, and has been, placed on many. One factor, however, that everyone agrees thwarted rescue attempts and fostered the chaos following Katrina was a major failure of communications.

In order to deal effectively with such a crisis, rescue agencies and first responders, such as FEMA, the New Orleans Police Department, the Red Cross, the Louisiana National Guard, and local rescue organizations, must be able to work together, which means they must be able to communicate among themselves. There is a need for strong communication related to the extent and form of damage, what type of problems are emerging, where the damage has occurred, and what type of aid is needed and where. Also, in order to prevent panic, people affected by the crisis must be provided with communications about what has happened, safety procedures, potential dangers, and instructions for further action. In the case of Katrina, the communication system needed to accomplish these tasks was broken:

- Millions of telephone lines were knocked down.
- Thirty-eight 911 call centers went down.
- Local wireless networks had considerable damage, making most cell phones in the area useless.
- Thirty-seven of 41 radio stations in New Orleans were unable to broadcast.
- The NOPD's communications system was inoperable for three days.

Six out of eight police headquarters were flooded, making it impossible to establish command centers. There was a severe shortage of satellite phones that allowed for communication.

- Hundreds of first responders were able to communicate through only two radio channels, jamming the system and causing great delays in the communication of vital information.
- Verizon Wireless did have generators for its cell towers; however, a number of these were stolen and a fuel truck bringing fuel to the generators was stopped at gunpoint and its fuel taken.
- FEMA did not provide New Orleans with a mobile multimedia communications unit (used in emergencies) until four days after the storm.

In the case of Katrina, the breakdown of communication technology proved to be disastrous. What could have prevented this situation? Clearly, technology could have been more up-to-date and in better condition. More redundancies in communication systems also would have been helpful. Beyond these technology issues, better planning before the storm hit would have been beneficial.

Were lessons learned? Perhaps. The City of New Orleans and the entire Gulf Coast seemed better prepared for Gustav, which struck as a Category 2 hurricane just southwest of New Orleans in 2008. Houston and most of the surrounding areas of Texas seemed to be reasonably well prepared for Ike, which also struck as a Category 2 hurricane in 2008.

Sources: Select Bipartisan Committee to Investigate the Preparation for and Response to Hurricane Katrina, "A Failure of Initiative," U.S. Government Printing Office, Feb. 15, 2006, at http://www.gpoaccess.gov/congress/index.html; D. Brinkley. 2006. *The Great Deluge* New York: Harper Collins; W. Haygood, & A.S. Tyson. 2005. "It Was as If All of Us Were Already Pronounced Dead," *Washington Post*, Sept. 15, p. A01; M. Hunter. 2006. "Deaths of Evacuees Push Death Toll to 1,577," *Times Picayune*, May 19, at http://www.nola.com; C. Landry. 2008. "After the Storms," *Oil & Gas Journal*, 106 no. 48: A7–A9; M. Williams. 2008. "Thousands Flee from New Orleans: Hurricane Gustav Described as 'The Storm of the Century,'" *The Glasgow Herald*, Sept. 1, p. A2.

Individual Barriers

We have examined several organizational factors that can make effective communication difficult. Individual factors, however, are the most commonly cited barriers to effective communication. These factors include differing perceptual bases, semantic differences, status differences, consideration of self-interest, issues related to personal space, and poor listening skills.

Differing Perceptions

One of the most common communication problems occurs when the sender has one perception of a message and the receiver has another. Differing perceptions are caused by differing frames of reference. Our expectations or frames of reference can influence how we recall and interpret information.[82]

This communication problem is vividly displayed in an exchange that occurred between a coach and a quarterback in a hotly contested U.S. football game. There were 16 seconds left in the game. The team was behind by one point and had the ball on its opponent's 20-yard line with no timeouts remaining. A field goal would win the game. The safest thing to do would be to call a running play and then kick a field goal. The coach decided, however, that it was necessary to risk a pass play because no timeouts were left. (If the pass was dropped, the clock would stop. If it was caught in the end zone, the game would be won.)

The coach told the quarterback to call the play that they had discussed in practice for just such a situation. But they had discussed two plays (one a pass into the end zone and the other a running play). The quarterback assumed the coach wanted to take the safest course and called the running play. He handed off to the fullback, who carried the ball into the middle of the line. A big pileup ensued, and the clock continued to run. Before the quarterback could get off another play, time had run out, and the team lost the game. The coach and the quarterback had two different perceptions of the meaning of one message.

Semantic Differences

Semantics refers to the meaning people attach to symbols, such as words and gestures. Because the same words may have different meanings to different people, semantic differences can create communication problems. For example, the word *profit* has a positive connotation to most professionals in business, but for others it has a negative connotation as they interpret it to mean "rip-off" or "exploitation." Such differences are evident in the problems U.S. oil, pharmaceutical, and insurance companies have had in explaining their profits to the general public in the face of political attacks from Washington.

One reason for semantic differences inside organizations relates to the proliferation of specialists, as we mentioned earlier. Specialists tend to develop their own jargon; such terminology may have little meaning or a different set of meanings to a person outside the specialist's field. A second reason for semantic differences relates to variance in cultural background. This issue was also discussed earlier.

Status Differences

Status differences can result from both organizational and individual factors. Organizations create status differences through titles, offices, and support resources, but individuals attribute meaning to these differences. Status differences can lead to problems of source credibility and can create problems that block upward communication.[83] Sometimes, for example, subordinates are reluctant to express an opinion that is different from their managers', and managers—because of either time pressures or arrogance—may strengthen status barriers by not being open to feedback or other forms of upward communication. To be effective communicators, managers must overcome status differences with those who report to them.

Consideration of Self-Interest

Often, information provided by a person is used to assess her performance. For example, it is not uncommon for firms to request information from managers about their units' performance. Data such as forecasts of future activity, performance standards, and recommendations on capital budgets are often used in determining the managers' compensation. Research shows that where data accuracy cannot be independently verified, managers sometimes provide information that is in their own self-interest.[84] Although they might not intentionally distort the information that is sent, they might provide incomplete data, selecting only information that is in their own best interests.

Personal Space

All of us have a *personal space* surrounding our bodies. When someone enters that space, we feel uncomfortable. The size of the personal space differs somewhat among individuals; it also differs by gender and across cultures.[85] Women seem to have smaller personal spaces than men. Similarly, the typical personal space in some cultures (such as some European and South American cultures) is smaller than that in other cultures (such as the United States). Personal space affects, for example, how close together people stand when conversing. Suppose someone from a culture where the norm is to stand close together is talking with someone from a culture where the norm is to stand farther apart. The first person will tend to move forward as the second backs away, with each trying to adjust the space according to a different cultural norm. Each may consider the other discourteous, and it will be difficult for either to pay attention to what the other is saying. In this case, the difference in personal space can be a barrier to communication.

Poor Listening Skills

A frequent problem in communication rests not with the sender but with the receiver. The receiver must listen in order to hear and understand the sender's message, just as the sender must listen to feedback from the receiver. Managers spend more than 50 percent of their time in verbal communication, and some researchers estimate that they spend as much as 85 percent of this time talking. This does not leave much time for listening and receiving feedback. Perhaps more importantly, it has been estimated that managers listen with only about 25 percent efficiency.[86] Therefore, they hear and understand only 25 percent of what is communicated to them verbally. This can lead the speaker to become annoyed and discouraged, thus creating a bad impression of the listener.[87] Poor listening is not conducive to high-involvement management, because it breaks down the communication process and limits information sharing. Later we discuss ways in which listening can be improved.

Overcoming Communication Barriers

Several actions can be taken to address the problems identified in this chapter. We discuss those actions next.

Conduct Communication Audits

Analyzing the organization's communication needs and practices through periodic communication audits[88] is an important step in establishing effective communication. A **communication audit** examines an organization's internal and external communication to assess communication practices and capabilities and to determine needs. Communication audits can be conducted in-house (for example, by the Human Resource Management department) or by external consulting firms. Communication audits often are used to ascertain the quality of communication and to pinpoint any deficiencies in the organization. Audits can be conducted for the entire organization or for a single unit within the organization.

communication audit
An analysis of an organization's internal and external communication to assess communication practices and capabilities and to determine needs.

Communication audits usually examine the organization's communication philosophy and objectives, existing communication programs, communication media, quantity and quality of personal communications, and employee attitudes toward existing communications. The following is a recommended method for conducting a communication audit:

- Hold a planning meeting with all major parties to determine a specific approach and gain commitment to it.

- Conduct interviews with top management.
- Collect, inventory, and analyze communication material.
- Conduct associate interviews.
- Prepare and administer a questionnaire to measure attitudes toward communication.
- Communicate survey results.[89]

Improve Communication Climates

An organization's **communication climate** corresponds to associates' perceptions of the quality of communication within the organization.[90] The communication climate is important because it influences the extent to which associates identify with their organization.[91] Organizations can overcome communication barriers by establishing a communication climate where mutual trust exists between senders and receivers, communication credibility is present, and feedback is encouraged. Managers also should encourage a free flow of downward, upward, and horizontal communication.[92] People must be comfortable in communicating their ideas openly and in asking questions when they do not understand or they want to know more. Information should be available and understandable. People in organizational units should be allowed to develop their own communication systems independently for an effective communication climate.[93]

communication climate
Associates' perceptions regarding the quality of communication within the organization.

Encourage Individual Actions

Managers and associates can also act as individuals to help overcome communication barriers. Experts recommend the following ways to improve interpersonal communication.

Know Your Audience

People often engage in what communication expert Virgil Scudder refers to as "me to me to me" communication.[94] With this phrase, Scudder is describing communicating with others as if you were communicating with yourself. Such communication assumes that others share your frame of reference and, in the absence of feedback, that people interpret the message as you intend it. Take, for example, an information technology expert trying to explain to his technologically unsophisticated colleagues how to use new computer software. He may use jargon that they do not understand, not fully explain the steps, and mistake their dumbfounded silence for understanding. In the end, the IT professional believes he has done his job and taught others how to use the new program. However, because of poor communication, his colleagues learned little and are frustrated. To communicate effectively, people must know their audience, including the audience's experience, frames of references, and motivations.

Select an Appropriate Communication Medium

Earlier, we discussed how various communication media differ in richness. When messages are complex and/or important, use of rich media, such as face-to-face communication, should be considered.[95] Also, when dealing with complex/important information, it can be beneficial to use several media—for example, by following a face-to-face communication with an e-mail message summarizing the discussion.

Regulate Information Flow and Timing

Regulating the flow of information can help to alleviate communication problems. Regulating flow involves discarding information of marginal importance and conveying only significant information. That is, do not pass on irrelevant information, or else important messages may be buried by information overload or noise.

The proper timing of messages is also important. Sometimes people are more likely to be receptive to a message and to perceive it accurately than at other times. Thus, if you have an important message to send, you should not send it when recipients are about to leave work, are fully engaged in some other task, or are receiving other communication.

Encourage Feedback Related to Understanding

Communication should be a two-way process. To ensure that the received message is interpreted as intended, feedback from the recipient is necessary. Some guidelines that individuals can use to obtain feedback are as follows:

- Ask recipients to repeat what they have heard.
- Promote and cultivate feedback, but don't try to force it.
- Reward those who provide feedback and use the feedback received. For example, thank people for providing feedback.
- Respond to feedback, indicating whether it is correct.[96] In other words, obtain feedback, use it, and then feed it back to recipients.

Listen Actively

As mentioned earlier, poor listening skills are a common barrier to effective communication. Listening is not a passive, naturally occurring activity. People must actively and consciously listen to others in order to be effective communicators. Exhibit 9-5 outlines the steps in being an active listener.

EXHIBIT 9-5 **Steps to Effective Listening**

1. **Stop talking.** Often, we talk more than we should without giving the other person a chance to respond. If we are thinking about what we will say when we talk, we cannot focus attention on the person to whom we wish to listen. Do not interrupt.

2. **Pay attention.** Do not allow yourself to be distracted by thinking about something else. Often, we need to make an active effort to pay attention when others are speaking.

3. **Listen empathetically.** Try to take the speaker's perspective. Mirror the speaker's body language and give him or her nonjudgmental encouragement to speak.

4. **Hear before evaluating.** Do not draw premature conclusions or look for points of disagreement. Listen to what the person has to say before jumping to conclusions or judgment.

5. **Listen to the whole message.** Look for consistency between the verbal and the nonverbal messages. Try to assess the person's feelings or intentions, as well as just facts.

6. **Send feedback.** In order to make sure that you have heard correctly, paraphrase what was heard and repeat it to the person you were listening to.

Organizations cannot accomplish their goals without using effective communication practices. Managers and leaders must communicate with associates to ensure that they understand the tasks to be done. In doing so, they need to use a two-way communication process to make certain that communication is understood as intended. Without effective communication, human capital in the organization will be underutilized and will not be leveraged successfully. Organizations that do not use their human capital well usually implement their strategies ineffectively, and so their performance suffers. In this circumstance, a firm might unnecessarily change its strategy because senior managers do not realize that strategy implementation—not the actual strategy—was the problem. Of course, with continued poor performance, CEOs are likely to lose their jobs.[97]

Information serves as a base for developing organizational strategies. Usually, the organization gathers significant amounts of information on its markets, customers, and competitors to use in the development of the best strategy. Interestingly, some organizations use blogging to gather intelligence on their competitors. In addition, before selecting a strategy, managers frequently obtain information on the organization's strengths and weaknesses. To get all of this information requires substantial communication with internal and external parties. If managers do not communicate well, they are unlikely to obtain the information needed to develop the correct strategy. Therefore, top executives must ensure that they communicate effectively and that all managers (and hopefully associates) do so as well. Good communication is the base on which most of what happens in the organization depends.

Critical Thinking Questions

1. For which tasks in a manager's job is effective communication critical? Explain.
2. Which contributes more to an organization's performance—oral communication or written communication? Justify your answer.
3. What are the strengths and weaknesses in your personal communication abilities? How can you best take advantage of your strengths and overcome your weaknesses to have a successful career?
4. What impact is rapidly developing communication technology likely to have on communication in organizations?

What This Chapter Adds to Your Knowledge Portfolio

In this chapter, we have discussed the communication process and have examined both organizational and interpersonal communication issues. We have also described organizational and individual barriers to communication, along with ways of overcoming these barriers. To summarize, we have covered the following points:

- The communication process is a two-way process in which a sender encodes a message, the message travels through a communication medium to the receiver, and the receiver decodes the message and returns feedback to the sender. Effective communication occurs when the received message has the same meaning as the sent message.
- Two important aspects of organizational communication are communication networks and the direction of communication flow. Networks can be sparse or dense and centralized or decentralized. Communication can occur in a downward, upward, or horizontal direction; in the case of 360-degree feedback, it occurs in all three directions.

?back to the knowledge objectives

1. Why is communication strategically important to organizations?
2. How would you describe an effective communication process?
3. What are the advantages and disadvantages of the various types of communication networks?
4. How are upward, downward, and horizontal communication accomplished?
5. Define *interpersonal communication*. How do formal and informal communication processes differ?
6. What is media richness, and how do different communication media vary in richness?
7. How can technology affect the communication process?
8. How does nonverbal communication contribute to the communication process?
9. What are six organizational barriers to effective communication?
10. What are six individual barriers to effective communication?
11. What are communication audits, and how are they conducted?
12. What specific actions can individuals take to overcome communication barriers?

- Important aspects of interpersonal communication include its formal or informal nature, media choices, communication technology, and nonverbal dynamics.
- Common barriers to effective communication that occur at the organizational level are information overload, information distortion, jargon, time pressures, cross-cultural barriers, and breakdowns in the communication network.
- Common individual barriers to effective communication include differing perceptions, semantic differences, status differences, self-interest, issues related to personal space, and poor listening skills.
- Organizations can improve communication effectiveness by conducting communication audits and creating positive communication climates.
- Individuals can improve their interpersonal communication by knowing their audience, selecting appropriate communication media, regulating information flow and timing, encouraging feedback, and engaging in active listening.

Thinking about Ethics

1. Do managers have a compelling reason to tell the truth to everyone (associates, customers, suppliers, and so forth)? Are there any circumstances in which it is ethically acceptable not to tell the truth? Explain.

2. Do people who are central to communication networks within organizations have a responsibility to pass on important information they receive? Explain.

3. What ethical issues are related to the use of "the grapevine"?

4. In the *Managerial Advice* feature, we discussed how organizations are using the Internet to check up on job applicants. Are there potential legal and ethical concerns with this practice?

Key Terms

communication, p. 330
encoding, p. 330
communication medium or communication channel, p. 330
decoding, p. 330
feedback, p. 330

sparse networks, p. 332
dense networks, p. 332
centralized networks, p. 332
decentralized networks. p. 332
downward communication, p. 333

upward communication, p. 334
horizontal communication, p. 336
interpersonal communication, p. 337
formal communication, p. 337

Human Resource Management Applications

The Human Resource Management (HRM) function is charged with helping to make managers and associates better communicators. Specific activities that are often managed by the HRM department are briefly discussed below.

Many HRM units offer training to aid in the development of interview skills. Managers in various units of the organization interview potential job candidates. In high-involvement organizations, associates often interview candidates as well. In these interviews, managers and associates must effectively convey questions and actively listen to answers, paying close attention not only to the verbal answers but also to the body language and gestures that might provide additional insights.

HRM units also develop performance-appraisal forms and systems, including those used for 360-degree assessments. In developing the relevant materials and instructions, representatives of the HRM function emphasize the sensitivity and importance of the communication that occurs in appraisal sessions.

Beyond the traditional tasks discussed above, some leading-edge HRM units are using web-based technology to: (1) develop procedures for recruiting through blogs, (2) establish standardized procedures for checking on candidates through social networking sites, and (3) create permanent information and application centers within virtual social worlds.

---

building your human capital

Presentation Dos and Don'ts

Making presentations can be one of the most challenging communication exercises faced by anyone, especially those who are not accustomed to presenting. Below is a quiz to help you determine how you fare in giving public presentations. The first 16 questions are presentation "dos" while the second 16 questions are presentation "don'ts."

Answer the questions based on your own recollections of presentations you have given. Perhaps an even better assessment of your presentation effectiveness would involve having a friend in the audience fill out this questionnaire for you when you are giving a presentation. In answering the questions, use the following scale:

1	2	3	4	5
Rarely	Seldom	Sometimes	Frequently	Almost Always

Presentation "Dos"

When you are making a presentation to a group of people, how often do you:

1. Think about the audience's collective point of view?
2. Acknowledge that the audience may be different from you?
3. Do research on who constitutes your audience?

4. Tailor your message to suit the audience?
5. Provide a clear outline of what you are going to discuss?
6. Provide illustrative visual information?
7. Summarize your main points?
8. Make between three and six major points?
9. Gauge the audience's reaction as you proceed?
10. Ask the audience for feedback?
11. Stop and provide clarification when the audience seems confused?
12. Solicit questions?
13. Use body language to get your points across?
14. Maintain eye contact with the audience?
15. Modulate your tone of voice to keep people interested?
16. Show enthusiasm for your topic?

Presentation "dos" scoring:

Add together your scores on the items for each section below. If you scored less than 16 in a particular section, you need to work on that aspect of your presentation style.

Questions 1–4: Knowing your audience. Total score on questions 1–4: _____

Questions 5–8: Structure. Total score on questions 5–8: _____

Questions 9–12: Feedback. Total score on questions 9–12: _____

Questions 13–16: Animation. Total score on questions 13–16: _____

Presentation "Don'ts"

When you are making a presentation to a group of people, how often do you:
1. Present information at the most difficult level possible, because it will make you appear knowledgeable?
2. Assume everyone in the audience agrees with you?
3. Make the presentation as simple as possible so even the least-educated person will understand?
4. Believe that if a presentation works with one crowd, it will work with another?
5. Present very detailed visual information to make sure the audience picks up on all the details?
6. Avoid a summary because it should be obvious what you have already said?
7. Get distracted by random questions?
8. Attempt to be extremely thorough in getting all of your points across, even if it means you don't have time to explain all of them?
9. Look out over the heads of the people in the audience?
10. Refuse questions in order to get your message across?
11. Ignore signs of confusion or lack of interest in the audience because it will just get you off your point?
12. Focus all your attention on a friendly face in the audience?
13. Read from your notes?
14. Make nervous gestures (fidget with your hair, tap your foot, rattle your change, or the like)?
15. Speak in monotone because it is more authoritative?
16. Speak as quickly as possible?

Presentation "don'ts" scoring:

Add together your scores on the items for each section below. If you scored more than 8 in a particular section, you need to work on that aspect of your presentation style.

Questions 1–4: Knowing your audience. Total score on questions 1–4: _____

Questions 5–8: Structure. Total score on questions 5–8: _____

Questions 9–12: Feedback. Total score on questions 9–12: _____

Questions 13–16: Animation. Total score on questions 13–16: _____

Explanation of Section Topics

Knowing your audience: In order to reach audience members and engage their interest, you must understand their point of view, their motivation for hearing your presentation, their attitudes about what you are saying, and their level of knowledge about your topic.

Structure: To get your message across, it is usually best to keep it organized and fairly simple—stick to a few major, important points. If some members of the audience want more details, offer to speak to them later, provide handouts, or give them a source of further information. If your visual presentation is too complicated, the audience will be reading your slides rather than listening to you.

Feedback: Remember that feedback is an essential part of the communication process. You need to be aware of how your audience is responding so that you can further tailor your presentation to ensure that audience members understand or are engaged with what you are telling them. Do not ignore their reactions.

Animation: Everyone has experienced both "good speakers" and "boring speakers." Don't be one of the latter. Be lively, animated, and show enthusiasm for your subject. If you don't, your audience won't either.

---

an organizational behavior moment

Going North

"Roll 'em!"

"Take number 64. Lights. Camera. Action!"

"Jane, I've missed you so much these past few weeks."

"I know, my darling. I've missed you, too."

"We must make up for lost time."

"Cut, cut, cut! Tom, you're playing this scene like a frozen polar bear. This is a tender love scene!" Helen screamed in her loudest, shrillest voice. "You're supposed to play it with feeling and tenderness. You want to make people think you love Jane."

"Helen, I could play the part better if you'd just get off my back. I knew more about romance when I was a teenager than you do now. Who are you to tell me how to play a love scene?" Tom shot back.

Helen called out, "That's all for today, everybody. We can let our mechanical lover calm down and maybe get in a better mood for this scene tomorrow."

With that Tom stomped off the set, and everyone began to disperse.

Helen Reardon is the producer and director of the film *Going North*, based on a novel that had stayed on the bestseller list for 16 months. Helen is considered to be one of the best directors in Hollywood. She already has two Academy Awards to her credit and many hit motion pictures.

Tom Nesson is a promising young actor. His most recent film, *The Western Express*, was well received at the box office and

thrust him into the limelight. In fact, one of the reasons he was chosen to play the leading male part in *Going North* was his current popularity. He is considered by industry insiders as a potential superstar.

All went well on the set for the first few weeks. But then problems began to arise. First came arguments between the set-design and wardrobe staff. There were feelings that the sets and the costumes didn't match. Some thought that the colors even clashed at times. The question was, "Whose fault is it?" Of course, each group blamed the other.

Later, the makeup staff walked off the job, claiming that they were being asked to work unreasonable hours. Helen did have a penchant for shooting movies at odd hours, particularly if the scene called for it. The makeup staff claimed that they had an informal agreement with studio management about the hours they would work and that this agreement had been violated. Although studio executives convinced them to return to work, the "peace" was an uneasy one. Now there was this blowup between Helen and Tom. Everyone hoped that the problems between the two were temporary.

The next day, everybody was back on the set on time except Tom. He came in about 10 minutes late. He explained that the makeup people were slow in getting his makeup on. No one questioned this, and they began where they had left off the previous day.

"Take number one. Lights. Camera. Action! … Take number 9. … Take number 19. … Take number 31. … " Finally, Helen yelled "Cut! Tom, we've got to find a way to get this right. We can't go on like this forever. What do you suggest?"

"I suggest you shoot it like it is. The scene was good. I've done it well several times, but you seem to keep finding small things wrong."

"Tom, do you really know what love is? Your acting doesn't show it."

With that Tom exploded. "Yes, I know what love is, but you obviously don't." He then left the set, shouting, "I'm not coming back on the set until you're gone!"

Helen left the set immediately, going straight to the studio executive offices. She barged into the president's office and stated, "Either you get rid of Tom Nesson on this movie, or I go!"

The studio executives were in a quandary. They did not want to lose either Helen or Tom. Neither had a history of being difficult to work with. They were not sure what was causing the problem. This movie seemed to be causing all kinds of problems, with the wildcat strike by makeup staff and the disagreements between wardrobe and set design. They obviously needed to examine all of the circumstances involved in the making of this film.

Discussion Questions

1. What do you suppose is really causing the problem between Helen and Tom? Explain.
2. Discuss the problems between the set design and wardrobe staff and those with the makeup department.
3. Could any of the problems in this case have been prevented? If so, how? How can the problems now be solved?

---

team exercise

Communication Barriers

This exercise demonstrates the importance of communication in organizations and shows how barriers affect communications.

Procedure

1. With the aid of the instructor, the class will be divided into teams of three to five persons.
2. The teams will perform the following tasks:

   - Identify all of the major ways in which your institution communicates with students (catalog, registration, advising, etc.). Be as specific as possible. Write each of these down.

   - Determine instances in which communication problems arise between the institution and students (for example, where students need more or better information). Write these down.

   - Identify specific barriers that make effective communication between students and the institution difficult. Write these down.

   - Development recommendations to overcome the barriers and solve the communication problems previously noted.

   The instructor will allow 30 minutes for the teams to complete their analyses.

3. The teams will present their lists of means of communication, communication problems, and recommendations, in that order. First, each team will present one item from the means-of-communication list, then the next team will present one, and so on, until all communication means have been presented. This same procedure will be followed for communication problems and recommendations, respectively. The instructor will compile a list of all the teams' responses.

4. The instructor will guide a discussion of this exercise, noting the similarity of communication problems in all types of organizations.

   The presentation and discussion should require about 30 minutes.

Endnotes

1. Monge, P.R., Farace, R.V., Eisenberg, E.M., Miller, K.I., & White, L.L. 1984. The process of studying process in organizational communication. *Journal of Communication,* 34: 234–243.

2. Whitely, W. 1984. An exploratory study of managers' reactions to properties of verbal communication. *Personnel Psychology,* 37: 41–59.

3. Shapiro, I.S. 1984. Managerial communication: The view from inside. *California Management Review,* 27: 157–172.

4. Clampitt, P.G., & Downs, C.W. 1993. Employee perceptions of the relationship between communication and productivity: A field study. *Journal of Business Communications,* 30: 5–28.

5. Pinto, M.B., & Pinto, J.K. 1991. Determinants of cross-functional cooperation in the project implementation process. *Project Management Journal,* 22: 13–20.

6. Ammeter, A.P., & Dukerich, J.M. 2002. Leadership, team building, and team member characteristics in high performance project teams. *Engineering Management Journal,* 14: 3–10; Henderson, L.S. 2004. Encoding and decoding communication competencies in project management—an exploratory study. *International Journal of Project Management,* 22: 469–476.

7. Snyder, R.A., & Morris, J.H. 1984. Organizational communication and performance. *Journal of Applied Psychology,* 69: 461–465.

8. Thomas, D. 2005. Poor communication makes UK workers less productive. April 6, 2005, at www.PersonnelToday.com; Computing Technology Industry Association Press Release. March 6, 2007. "Poor communications is the most frequent cause of project failure, CompTIA web poll reveals." At http://www.comptia.org/pressroom/get_pr.aspx?prid=1227.

9. Whitely, W. 1984. An exploratory study of managers' reactions to properties of verbal communication. *Personnel Psychology,* 37: 41–59.

10. Hinske, G. 1985. The uneven record of the corporate communicators. *International Management,* 40: 2.

11. Collison, J., & Frangos, C. 2002. Aligning HR with organization strategy survey. Society for Human Resource Management Research Report. Alexandria, VA: Society for Human Resource Management.

12. Dewhurst, S. 2007. Key findings from the pulse survey. *Strategic Communication Management,* 11 (1): 6–7.

13. Humphreys, M.A. 1983. Uncertainty and communication strategy formation. *Journal of Business Research,* 11: 187–199.

14. Clevenger, T., Jr., & Matthews, J. 1971. *The speech communication process.* Glenview, IL: Scott Foresman.

15. Ibid.

16. Daft, R.L., & Lengel, R.H. 1986. Organizational information requirements: Media richness and structural design. *Management Science,* 32: 554–571.

17. Greenbaum, H.H. 1974. The audit of organizational communication. *Academy of Management Journal,* 17: 739–754.

18. Cross, R., Ehrlich, K., Dawson, R., & Helferich, J. 2008. Managing collaboration: Improving team effectiveness through a network perspective., *California Management Review,* 50 (4): 74-98; Shaw, M.E. 1964. Communication networks. In L. Berkowitz (Ed.), Advances in experimental social psychology. New York: Academic Press, pp. 111–147.

19. Gargiulo, M., Ertug, G., & Galunic, C. 2009. The two faces of control: Network closure and individual performance among knowledge workers. *Administrative Science Quarterly,* 54: 299-333; Wong, S.-S. 2008. Task knowledge overlap and knowledge variety: The role of advice network structures and impact on group effectiveness. *Journal of Organizational Behavior,* 29: 591–614.

20. Friedrich, T.L., Vessey, W.B., Schuelke, M.J., Ruark, G.A., & Mumford, M.D. 2009. A framework for understanding collective leadership: The selective utilization of leader and team expertise within networks. *The Leadership Quarterly,* 20: 933–958; Wong, Task knowledge overlap and knowledge variety.

21. Leavitt, H.J. 1951. Some effects of certain communication patterns on group performance. *Journal of Abnormal and Social Psychology,* 46: 38–50.

22. Balkundi, P. & Harrison, D.A. 2006. Ties, leaders, and time in teams: Strong inference about network structure's effects on team viability and performance. *Academy of Management Journal,* 49: 49–68; Friedrich, Vessey, Schuelke, Ruark, & Mumford, A framework for understanding collective leadership. Also see: Balkundi, P., Barsness, Z., & Michael, J.H. 2009. Unlocking the Influence of leadership network structures on team conflict and viability. *Small Group Research,* 40: 301–322.

23. Burt, R.S. 2007. Secondhand brokerage: Evidence on the importance of local structure for managers, bankers, and analysts. *Academy of Management Journal,* 50: 119–148; Burt, R.S. 2006. *Brokerage and closure.* New York: Oxford University Press; Pfeffer, J. 2008. A note on social networks and network structure. Stanford, CA: Stanford Graduate School of Business.

24. Watts, D. 2003. *Six degrees: The science of a connected age.* New York: W.W. Norton.

25. Ibid.

26. Sidel, R. 2009. Next crisis for U.S. Banks? Integration: Merger waves poses test to system. *Wall Street Journal,* Jan. 9: C.1; Whittaker, K.D. 2009. Wachovia fades to black. *Atlanta Tribune: The Magazine,* 22 (10): 46–47.

27. Bolton, P., & Dewatripont, M. 1994. The firm as a communication network. *Quarterly Journal of Economics,* 109: 809–839.

28. Freibel, G., & Raith, M. 2004. Abuse of authority and hierarchical communications. *Rand Journal of Economics,* 35: 224–244.

29. Jablin, F.M. 1982. Formal structural characteristics of organizations and superior–subordinate communication. *Human Communication Research,* 8: 338–347.

30. Sellers, P. 2004. Most powerful women in business. *Fortune,* October 4, at http://www.fortune.com.

31. Katz, D., & Kahn, R.L. 1978. *The social psychology of organizations* (2nd ed.). New York: John Wiley & Sons.

32. Collison & Frangos, Aligning HR with organization strategy survey.

33. Ghorpade, J. 2000. Managing five paradoxes of 360-degree feedback. *Academy of Management Executive,* 14: 140–150.

34. Lussier, R.N., & Achua, C.F. 2004. *Leadership: Theory, application, skill development* (2nd ed.). Eagan, MN: Thomson Southwestern.

35. Bettenhausen, K.L., & Fedor, D.B. 1997. Peer and upward appraisals: A comparison of their benefits and problems. *Group and*

Organization Management, 22: 236–263; Freibel & Raith, Abuse of authority and hierarchical communications.

36. Atwater, L.E., & Brett, J.F. 2006. 360-degree feedback: Does it relate to changes in employee attitudes? *Group and Organization Management,* 31: 578–600.

37. Huseman, R.C., Lahiff, J.M., & Hatfield, J.D. 1976. *Interpersonal communication in organizations.* Boston, MA: Holbrook Press, p. 5.

38. Kurland, N.B., & Pelled, L.H. 2000. Passing the word: Toward a model of gossip and power in the workplace. *Academy of Management Review,* 25: 428–439.

39. Michelson, G., & Mouly, V.S. 2004. Do loose lips sink ships? The meaning, antecedents, and consequences of rumor and gossip in organizations. *Corporate Communications: An International Journal,* 9: 189–201.

40. Ibid.

41. McKay, B. 2000. At Coke layoffs inspire all manner of peculiar rumors, *Wall Street Journal (Eastern Edition),* October 17: p. A1.

42. Kurland, N.B., & Pelled, L.H. 2000. Passing the word.

43. Loughry, M.L., & Tosi, H.L. 2008. Performance implications of peer monitoring. *Organization Science,* 19: 876–890.

44. Sheer, V.C., & Chen, L. 2004. Improving media richness theory: A study of interaction goals, message valence, and task complexity in manager–subordinate communication. *Management Communication Quarterly,* 18: 76–93.

45. Daft, R.L., & Lengel, R.H. 1986. Organizational information requirements: Media richness and structural design. *Management Science,* 32: 554–571.

46. Trevino, L.K., Lengel, R.H., Bodensteiner, W., Gerloff, E., & Muir, N. 1990. The richness imperative and cognitive style: The role of individual differences in media choice behavior. *Management Communication Quarterly,* 4: 176–197.

47. Davis, A., Khazanchi, D., Murphy, J., Zigurs, I., & Owens, D. 2009. Avatars, people, and virtual worlds: Foundations for research in metaverses. *Journal of the Association for Information Systems,* 10: 90–117.

48. Daft, R.L., & Lengel, R.H. 1986. Organizational information requirements: Media richness and structural design. *Management Science,* 32: 554–571.

49. Sheer, V.C., & Chen, L. 2004. Improving media richness theory: A study of interaction goals, message valence, and task complexity in manager–subordinate communication. *Management Communication Quarterly,* 18: 76–93.

50. Fulk, J. 1993. Social construction of communication technology. *Academy of Management Journal,* 36: 921–950.

51. Turner, J.W., Grube, J.A., Tinsley, C.H., Lee, C., & O'Pell, C. 2006. Exploring the dominant media: How does media use reflect organizational norms and affect performance? *Journal of Business Communication,* 43: 220–250.

52. Fontaine, M.A., Parise, S., & Miller, D. 2004. Collaborative environments: An effective tool for transforming business processes. *Ivey Business Journal Online,* May–June: 1–7.

53. Desanctis, G., & Fulk, J. (Eds.). 1999. *Shaping organizational form: Communication, connection, and community.* Thousand Oaks, CA: Sage Publications.

54. Fontaine, M.A., Parise, S., & Miller, D. 2004. Collaborative environments: An effective tool for transforming business processes. *Ivey Business Journal Online,* May–June: 1–7.

55. Fortune 500 Business Blogging Wiki. At http://www.socialtext.net/bizblogs/index.cgi.

56. For more information, see CEO Blogwatch, at http://www.ceoblogwatch.com.

57. Baker, S., & Green, H. 2005. Blogs will change your business. *BusinessWeek online.* May 2. At www.businessweek.com/print/magazine/content/05_18/b3931001_mz001.htm.

58. Gard, L. 2005. Online extra: Stonyfield Farm's blog culture. May 2. At www.businessweek.com/print/magazine/content/05_18/b3931005_mz001.htm.

59. CBS/AP. 2007. JetBlue Attempts to calm passenger furor. CBS News. February 15. At http://www.cbsnews.com.stories/2007/02/15/national/printable2480665.shtml.

60. Baker, S., & Green, H. 2005. Blogs will change your business. *BusinessWeek online.* May 2. At www.businessweek.com/print/magazine/content/05_18/b3931001_mz001.htm.

61. Mehrabian, A. 1968. Communication without words. *Psychology Today,* 2: 53–55.

62. Davis, A., Pereira, J., & Buckley, W.M. 2002. Silent signals: Security concerns bring new focus on body language. *Wall Street Journal,* Aug. 15, p. A.1.

63. Schweitzer, M.E., Brodt, S.E., & Croson, R.T.A. 2002. Seeing and believing: Visual access and strategic use of deception. *International Journal of Conflict Management,* 13: 258–275.

64. Streeter, L.A., Krauss, R.M.N., & Geller, V. 1977. Pitch changes during attempted deception. *Journal of Personality and Social Psychology,* 35: 345–350.

65. Kraut, R.E. 1978. Verbal and nonverbal cues in the perception of lying. *Journal of Personality and Social Psychology,* 36: 380–391.

66. Ibid.

67. Davis, Pereira, & Buckley, Silent signals.

68. Ekman, P., & Oster, H. 1979. Facial expressions of emotion. *Annual Review of Psychology,* 30: 527–554.

69. Brown, D.S. 1975. Barriers to successful communication: Part 1. *Management Review,* 64: 24–29; Brown, D.S. 1976. Barriers to successful communication: Part 2. *Management Review,* 65: 15–21.

70. Marcus, H., & Zajonc, R.B. 1985. The cognitive perspective in social psychology. In G. Lindzey & E. Aronson (Eds.), *The handbook of social psychology* (3rd ed). New York: Random House, pp. 137–230.

71. Gaudin, S. 2007. Report: Spam levels rise for fifth month in a row. *InformationWeek,* March 1. At http://www.informationweek.com/story/showArticle.jhtml?articleID=197700567.

72. Claburn, T. 2005. Spam costs billions. *InformationWeek.* February 3. At http://www.informationweek.com/story/showArticle.jhtml?articleID=59300834.

73. Morgan, C.P., & Hitt, M.A. 1977. Validity and factor structure of House and Rizzo's effectiveness scales. *Academy of Management Journal,* 20: 165–169.

74. Bairman, S., & Evans, J.H., III. 1983. Pre-decision information and participative management control systems. *Journal of Accounting Research,* 21: 371–395.

75. Graham, J.R. 2002. Who do we thank (and curse) for e-mail? *Agency Sales,* November, 32: 23–26.

76. Harvey, M.G., & Griffith, D.A. 2002. Developing effective intercultural relationships: The importance of communication strategies. *Thunderbird International Business Review,* 44: 455–476.

77. Fisher, G.B., & Hartel, C.E.J. 2003. Cross-cultural effectiveness of Western expatriate–Thai client interactions: Lessons learned from IHRM research and theory. *Cross Cultural Management,* 10: 4–29.

78. Beamer, L. 1992. Learning intercultural communication competence. *Journal of Business Communication,* 29: 285–303.

79. Kranhold, K. 2004. Lost in translation?: Managers at multinationals may miss the job's nuances if they speak only English. *Wall Street Journal (Eastern Edition),* May 18, p. B.1.

80. Kilpatrick, R.H. 1984. International business communication practices. *Journal of Business Communication,* 21: 33–44.

81. Scott, J.C. 1999. Developing cultural fluency: The goal of international business communication instruction in the 21st century. *Journal of Education for Business,* 74: 140–144.

82. Marcus, H., & Zajonc, R. 1985. The cognitive perspective in social psychology. In G. Lindzey & E. Aronson (Eds.), *The handbook of social psychology* (3rd ed.), Vol. 1. New York: Random House, pp. 127–230.

83. Athanassiades, J.C. 1973. The distortion of upward communication in hierarchical organization. *Academy of Management Journal,* 16: 207–226.

84. Dye, R.A. 1983. Communication and post-decision information. *Journal of Accounting Research,* 21: 514–533.

85. Cohen, L.R. 1982. Minimizing communication breakdowns between male and female managers. *Personnel Administrator,* 27: 57–58.

86. Inman, T.H., & Hook, B.V. 1981. Barriers to organizational communication. *Management World,* 10: 34–35.

87. McKechnie, D.S., Grant, J., & Bagaria, V. 2007. Observation of listening behaviors in retail service encounters. *Managing Service Quality,* 17 (2): 116–113.

88. Kopec, J.A. 1982. The communication audit. *Public Relations Journal,* 38: 24–27; Quinn, D., & Hargie, O. 2004. Internal communication audits: A case study. *Corporate Communications: An International Journal,* 9: 146–158.

89. Ibid.

90. Goldhaber, G.M. 1993. *Organizational communication.* Dubuque, IA: Brown and Benchmark.

91. Bartels, J., Pruyn, A., De Jong, M., & Joustra, I. 2007. Multiple organizational identification levels and the impact of perceived external prestige and communication climate. *Journal of Organizational Behavior,* 28: 173–190.

92. Monge, Farace, Eisenberg, Miller, & White, The process of studying process in organizational communication.

93. Poole, M.S. 1978. An information-task approach to organizational communication. *Academy of Management Review,* 3: 493–504.

94. Scudder, V. 2004. The importance of communication in a global world. *Vital Speeches of the Day,* 70: 559–562.

95. Trevino, Lengel, Bodensteiner, Gerloff, & Muir, The richness imperative and cognitive style.

96. Gelb, B.D., & Gelb, G.M. 1974. Strategies to overcome phony feedback. *MSU Business Topics,* 22: 5–7.

97. Colvin, G. 2005. CEO knockdown. *Fortune,* April 4: 19–20.

decision making by individuals and groups

Dawn Ostroff's Decision Making at the CW Television Network

As president of the new CW Television Network, Dawn Ostroff faced many challenges in the spring of 2006. Chief among these was programming the lineup of shows for the network's first season. One issue making this a difficult task was the newness of the operation. Recently created through a combination of the WB network and UPN, the combined entity had no viewer base. What mix of existing shows versus exciting new shows would draw former WB and UPN viewers? What mix of shows would motivate former WB and UPN viewers to find and watch the new network? In some markets, WB viewers would need to find the old UPN station. In other markets, UPN viewers would need to find the old WB station. In still other markets, both WB and UPN viewers would need to find a completely new station carrying CW.

A second issue was the reduction in primetime hours available. The combination of WB and UPN had resulted in a shift from 23 centrally scheduled primetime hours to 13 centrally scheduled hours. Which existing shows should be cut? With a lineup of shows such as *America's Next Top Model* (UPN), *WWE Smackdown* (UPN), *Veronica Mars* (UPN), *Gilmore Girls* (WB), *Reba* (WB), *Smallville* (WB), and *One Tree Hill* (WB), this issue was noteworthy.

Ostroff attacked the programming task with her usual zeal. As an individual, she considered a number of factors, such as the importance of retaining current WB and UPN viewers, the passion that WB and UPN viewers displayed in lobbying for particular shows, the overall popularity of existing shows as assessed by Nielsen ratings,

knowledge objectives

After reading this chapter, you should be able to:

1. Describe the fundamentals of decision making, including the basic steps and the need to balance ideal and satisfactory decisions.
2. Discuss four important decision-making styles, emphasizing the effectiveness of each one.
3. Explain the role of risk-taking propensity and reference points.
4. Define cognitive bias and explain the effects of common types of cognitive bias on decision making.
5. Explain the role of moods and emotions in decision making.
6. Discuss common pitfalls of group decision making.
7. Describe key group decision-making techniques.
8. Explain the factors managers should consider in determining the level of associate involvement in managerial decisions.

and the current and future preferences of the new network's demographic target group (18-to-34-year-olds). As a leader, she considered the views of others as well. Two dozen individuals were involved in the decision making, with a group of six providing strong inputs for the final lineup of shows. Given the nonroutine and complex nature of the situation, incorporating information and opinions from other people was crucial.

Although Ostroff had a great deal of information at her disposal, she did not become mired in evaluating detailed information. Instead, she tended to keep the big picture in mind and used her judgment in evaluating alternatives. In her words,

> Ultimately the people who are successful in this business have a tacit ability to make right decisions based on a wide variety of inputs; they are able to integrate those inputs into what seems to be a gut decision. Deciding on programming is not formulaic.

In the end, Ostroff and her group decided to use mostly existing shows, emphasizing the more popular ones. Although some of these shows had begun to fade and none were top performers in the overall Nielsen ratings, they believed their strategy to be the best one for developing an audience quickly. Exciting new shows would have to wait.

The new CW network performed as well as could be expected in its first season of operation. Although the network had no established track record, no direct ownership of stations in large markets, and limited resources, it attracted a small but meaningful audience. Some were disappointed with the performance, believing that the network had used too many fading shows and had not established a consistent identity, but most saw a foundation for the future. CW executives and affiliate stations remained optimistic.

©CW Network, Timothy White/The Kobal Collection, Ltd.

To aggressively pursue success over the long run, Ostroff has maintained her focus on the big picture and has continued to draw from her group of advisors, particularly John Maatta, the chief operating officer of the network. Taking into account factors such as Nielsen ratings, web-based use of their shows, affiliate interests, and repositioning of the CW brand toward young women, they have made a number of changes to the lineup since the early days. Some of the shows from the first season have been dropped, particularly those such as *WWE Smackdown* that did not fit the new focus on young women. A few shows have been retained, such as *Smallville* and *One Tree Hill*. New shows have been added, including *Gossip Girl, Vampire Diaries,* and remakes of *90210* and *Melrose Place.* For the 2008–2009 season, these changes produced some success, with the CW network having the largest percentage increase in DVR use among broadcast networks, an 18 percent increase in ratings within its target demographic of 18-to-34-year-old women, more than 200 million Internet streams from CW.com, and strong download traffic from Apple's iTunes for shows such as *Gossip Girls* and *Vampire Diaries* (within iTunes, these two shows are among the most popular purchases on a per-episode basis). For the 2009–2010 season, CW scheduled as much prime-time scripted programming as NBC. This is an indicator of maturity and growth at the network.

Has success been ensured for the long run? This is a difficult question. The situation remains challenging at the small network, but as of mid-2010 Ostroff has made and continues to make decisions that have the potential to pay off. Given her history of accomplishments and awards, she may have created a viable network for many years to come.

Sources: J. Benson. 2007. "Is This the CW's New Reality?" *Broadcasting & Cable,* March 26, p. 12; A. Elberse and S.M. Young. 2008. The CW: *Launching a Television Network* (Boston: Harvard Business School Press); M. Fernandez. 2007. "Youth Must Be Served: The Revitalized CW Seeks to Regain the 18 to 34 Crowd," *Los Angeles Times,* July 11, p. E.1; M. Guthrie. 2009. "The CW: New Year, New Focus," *Broadcasting & Cable,* May 25, p. 16; C. Littleton. 2006. "Dialogue with Dawn Ostroff and John Maata," *Hollywood Reporter,* Feb. 28, pp. 1–2; M. Miller. 2007. "CW Forms a Plan of Action: 'Online Nation' and 'Gossip Girls,' with Web Components, Are Meant to Woo the 18–34 Group," *Los Angeles Times,* July 21, p. E.17; S. Schechner, & Y.I. Kane. 2009. "Apple TV Proposal Gets Some Nibbles, "*Wall Street Journal,* Dec. 22, p. B.1; M. Schneider. 2007. "Young CW Makes Brand Stand," *Variety,* Jan. 8, p. 22.

the strategic importance of # Decision Making

Individuals in charge of businesses make very important decisions. When we think about these decisions, we tend to think of decisions that are strategic in nature, such as adding or deleting products and services. However, these individuals also make other important decisions that have strategic implications. For example, deciding to outsource a function can have implications for effectively implementing a strategy. As another example, deciding to hire a particular person as a senior manager can affect strategy implementation.

The decisions made by individuals at the top of an organization are important because they often have the greatest effects on the organization's performance. However, the decisions of other managers also affect performance; frequently, even decisions by lower-level managers have significant effects on the success of the organization.[1] In particular, managers throughout the organization make decisions about the actions needed to implement strategic decisions. The quality and speed of those decisions affect the success of strategy-implementation efforts.

The example of Dawn Ostroff at the CW Network provides important insights into decision making, and not only for those at the top. Ostroff made many important decisions related to programming, advertising formats, organizational structure, personnel, logos, and trademarks. Other managers in the firm made decisions that supported her efforts. Managers in charge of web-based offerings made some of the decisions related to the availability and timing of online links to episodes of television shows. Managers courting and working with advertisers made decisions related to commercials. Beyond the many managerial decisions, associates made choices in areas ranging from broadcast standards to development resources of new shows. And in many instances, joint decisions were made by groups of people.

Faced with numerous challenges in her job, Ostroff gathered information, discussed issues with managers and associates, and made choices based on the big picture and even intuition. This approach can be effective. As you will learn in this chapter, however, not all decision makers follow this approach. Indeed, personal styles vary, and different situations call for different approaches. Furthermore, cognitive biases affect decision makers, causing them to collect less information or poor information in some cases. The cognitive models used by managers to make decisions are affected by the amount and type of their education and experience. For example, a manager with an engineering degree and several years of experience in an engineering unit and a manager with a degree in marketing and several years of experience in a marketing unit are likely to approach the same problem in very different ways.[2]

In this chapter, we open with a discussion of the fundamentals of decision making, including the basic steps and the need for balance between ideal and satisfactory decisions. Following this, we cover individual decision making, focusing on individual decision styles, risk taking, cognitive biases, and moods and emotions. Next, we examine the important area of group decision making. Key topics include techniques for improving group decisions and tools for evaluating how well groups have done. Finally, we address a crucial question: To what extent should a manager involve associates in a particular decision? While high-involvement management, an important concept presented in this book, requires managers to delegate many decisions to associates and to involve them in many others, under some circumstances a manager should make a decision alone or with limited input from associates. A framework is offered to guide managers in addressing this issue.

Fundamentals of Decision Making

decisions
Choices of actions from among multiple feasible alternatives.

Decisions are choices. We make decisions every day. We decide when we want to get up in the morning, what clothes we will wear, what we will eat for breakfast, and what our schedule of activities will be. We also make more important decisions. We decide what college or university to attend, what our major will be, what job to accept, what career path to follow, and how to manage our finances. Each time we make a purchase, a decision is involved. Clearly, decision-making activities are important to each of us.

They are also important to organizations. Making decisions is one of the primary activities for senior managers. Senior managers make decisions related to things such as entering new businesses, divesting existing business, and coordinating the units of the firm. Other managers in the firm make decisions regarding how a unit should be organized, who should lead various work groups, and how job performance should be evaluated. In a high-involvement organization, associates also make many important decisions. They may decide on scheduling of work, job-rotation schedules, vacation time, approaches to various tasks, and ways to discipline an individual for problem behavior. Overall, decision-making skills are critical to organizational effectiveness.

Basic Steps in Decision Making

As a process, decision making involves multiple steps, as shown in Exhibit 10-1. First, effective decision making begins with a determination of the problem to be solved. Problems are typically gaps between where we are today and where we would like to be tomorrow. We need a new associate in the work group but do not have one. We have excess cash in the firm but do not know where to invest it. We are experiencing quality problems and must correct them.

Two individuals examining the same situation may see the problem differently. Consider the following example. A manufacturing unit has a broken machine. One person might define the problem in terms of the need to repair the machine or perhaps buy a new

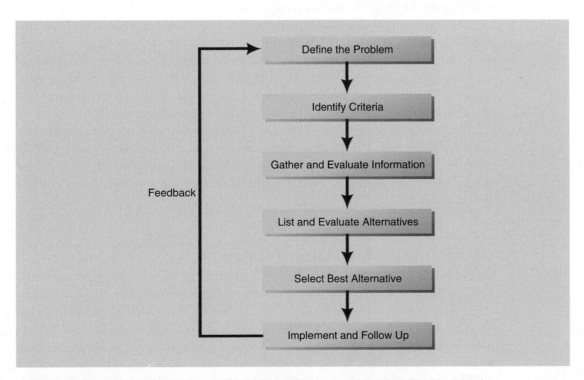

Exhibit 10-1   The Decision-Making Process

one. When developing possible solutions later in the process, she would focus either on a set of possible companies to do the repair work or a set of possible new machines. Another person might define the problem very broadly in terms of a need to return the manufacturing unit to an operational status. By broadening the problem, this person would gain access to a larger range of alternative solutions. Alternatives might include buying a new machine, repairing the existing machine, outsourcing the work, using a different type of machine already on hand to do the work, redesigning the workflow so that the machine is no longer needed, and so on. Overly narrow problem definitions are a chief concern in decision making, as they restrict options.[3]

The next step in decision making, identification of decision criteria, requires the decision maker to determine exactly what is important in solving the problem. In the case of purchasing a new machine to replace a broken one, she might consider price, maintenance costs, tolerance levels that can be achieved, size, delivery speed, and so on. Decision criteria determine what information the decision maker needs to collect in order to evaluate alternatives, and they help her explain the choice that she ultimately makes.[4] Failure to thoroughly identify important criteria results in faulty decision making.

After the decision criteria have been identified, the decision maker must gather and process information to better understand the decision context and to discover specific alternatives that might solve the problem. In discovering or identifying possible alternatives, she should be careful not to constrain or evaluate the alternatives to any significant degree, because in so doing she may prematurely eliminate more creative or novel approaches. In this context, two truisms should be understood.[5] First, a decision maker cannot choose an alternative that has not been considered. Second, a decision maker cannot choose an alternative that is better than the best alternative on the list. Therefore, careful attention to developing the list of alternatives is important.

The next step in the decision-making process involves evaluating all relevant alternatives. To complete this step, the decision maker assesses each alternative using each criterion. When purchasing a new machine, she would rate each machine on the criteria of price, projected maintenance costs, tolerance levels, size, delivery speed, and so on. After evaluating each alternative, the decision maker chooses the alternative that seems to best satisfy the criteria, thereby solving the problem in the best manner possible.

The decision-making process does not end when the decision is made. The decision must be implemented, and the decision maker must follow up and monitor the results to ensure that the adopted alternative solved the problem. By monitoring the outcomes, the decision maker may determine that the chosen alternative did not work. A new problem then must be solved.

Optimal versus Satisfactory Decisions

A decision maker typically wants to make an effective decision. For the purposes of this book, we define an effective decision as one that is timely, acceptable to those affected by it, and satisfactory in terms of the key decision criteria.[6] Although the systematic, logical process outlined in Exhibit 10-1 may not be ideal in all situations, such as when a decision must be made very quickly, it does serve as a useful framework for producing effective decisions.

The process of making decisions is not as simple, however, as it may seem from reviewing standard decision-making steps like those shown in the exhibit. Each step is more complex than it appears on the surface. Furthermore, individuals and groups cannot always make decisions that maximize their objectives, because to make such decisions we must have complete knowledge about all possible alternatives and their potential results. Complete knowledge would allow us to choose the best possible alternative, but it is unlikely that we actually would have complete knowledge for any real-world decisions. Thus, we tend to make **satisficing decisions**, or what many psychologists and economists refer to as boundedly rational decisions.[7]

satisficing decisions
Satisfactory rather than optimal decisions.

There are two important reasons that people often make satisfactory decisions rather than optimal, maximizing ones. First, as already suggested, we do not have the capability to collect and process all of the information relevant for a particular decision. In theory, the number of alternatives that could be considered for most decisions is very large, as are the number of people who could be consulted and the number of analyses that could be completed. However, most of us, and certainly managers, lack the time and other resources required to complete these activities for most decisions. Consider the simple situation of hiring an individual to head a new public relations unit. Literally millions of people could possibly fill that role. Would the company consider millions of people so that the absolute best person could be found? No! Most likely, a convenient group of perhaps two dozen people would be considered.

Second, we often display a tendency to choose the first satisfactory alternative discovered. Because we are busy and typically want to conserve the resources used in making any one decision, we often stop searching when we find the first workable alternative. Research has indicated, however, that some individuals are more likely than others to choose the first satisfactory option.[8] Some continue to search for additional alternatives after encountering the first satisfactory one, thereby increasing their odds of finding a better solution. This is an important individual difference that is of interest to managers and those interested in organizational behavior.

Individual Decision Making

Decision making is a cognitive activity that relies on both perception and judgment. If two people use different approaches to the processes of perception and judgment, they are likely to make quite different decisions, even if the facts and objectives are identical. Although many individual characteristics can affect an individual's decision process, the four psychological predispositions isolated by noted psychologist Carl Jung are of special importance for decision making in organizations. We consider these next and then turn to other factors that influence an individual's decision making, including degree of acceptable risk and cognitive biases.

Decision-Making Styles

According to Jung's theory, an individual's predispositions can affect the decision process at two critical stages: (1) the perceiving of information and (2) the judging of alternatives. Decisions, then, reflect the person's preference for one of two perceptual styles and one of two judgment styles. How these styles relate to the decision process is illustrated in Exhibit 10-2. Although some have questioned the usefulness of Jung's ideas, research has offered reasonable support for those ideas,[9] and assessment tools based on his work are very popular in the corporate world.

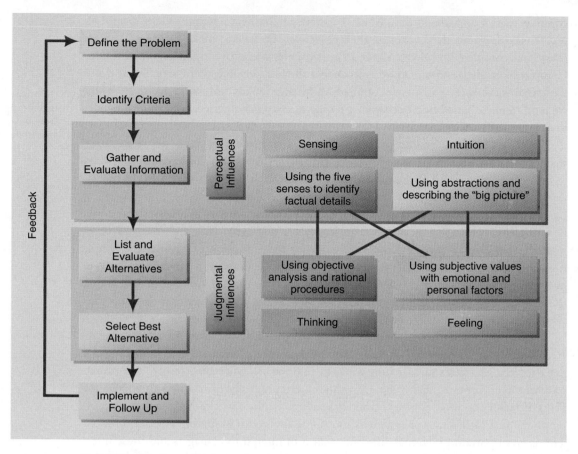

Exhibit 10-2 Influence of Decision Styles

Gathering Information

Individuals may differ in how they gather information to use in making decisions. As described in Chapter 4, gathering information involves perceptual processes. Some individuals prefer information that is concretely grounded and readily accessible through the five basic senses, whereas others prefer abstractions and figurative examples as sources.

An associate or manager who relies on facts gathered directly by the five senses is said to use a **sensing** style.[10] Such a person believes in experience and typically wants to focus on rules and regulations, step-by-step explanations, and fact checking. Decision makers who use a sensing style are concerned primarily with developing a factual database that will support any resulting decision.

People who prefer this style of gathering information see themselves as practical and realistic. They work steadily in the early stages of the decision process and enjoy the information-gathering stage. Such persons observe the actual situation very carefully: specific details, concrete examples, real experiences, practicalities, and literal statements. They are down-to-earth people who believe that creativity involves much effort. Steve Ballmer, CEO of Microsoft, seems to fit this profile. He is attracted to facts and hard data and sees things as "black or white, on or off."[11]

Decision makers who use the **intuition** style dislike details and the time required to sort and interpret them.[12] These people become impatient with routine details and often

sensing
A decision style focused on gathering concrete information directly through the senses, with an emphasis on practical and realistic ideas.

intuition
A decision style focused on developing abstractions and figurative examples for use in decision making, with an emphasis on imagination and possibilities.

perceive information in large chunks—for example, as holistic, integrated abstractions. A decision made using this style is often based on imagination. Intuitive people believe that creativity comes from inspiration rather than concentrated effort.

Although this second style may appear to be illogical and risky, many consultants and senior managers believe that it can be an effective approach. Managers with good intuition may be better able to cope with rapid change and crisis situations. They frequently have a vision for the future and can react quickly to urgent needs. Former U.S. president Bill Clinton has been classified as having the intuition style,[13] as has former British prime minister Margaret Thatcher.[14] Dawn Ostroff of the CW network also seems to fit the profile.

Overall, both the sensing and intuition styles of perception can be effective, but their effectiveness may vary depending on the context. The sensing style may be most appropriate for jobs where routine decisions are typical.[15] In one relevant study, researchers examined how loan officers handled a number of lending decisions.[16] Individuals with a sensing style used more information and made better choices. The intuition style may be most appropriate for jobs where novel decisions and a need for creativity are common. Research on innovation illustrates this point. In one important study, individuals responsible for new business ideas in a *Fortune* 500 company were divided into two groups of equal size, with one group representing the sensing style and the other representing the intuition style.[17] In the sensing group, individuals displayed less creativity and identified ideas that resulted in only $15.2 million of profit during the period of the study. Individuals in the intuition group displayed more creativity and delivered $197.5 million in profit.

Specific situations in which the intuition style may prove valuable include the following:

- When a high level of ambiguity exists
- When few or no precedents exist
- When facts are limited
- When facts don't clearly indicate which way to go
- When time is limited and there is pressure to make the right decision
- When several plausible alternative solutions exist with good arguments for each

Evaluating Alternatives

Jung proposed that once information has been gathered, decision makers again diverge in their approaches, tending to adopt either a thinking style or a feeling style to make judgments. As seen in Exhibit 10-2, there is no fixed relationship between a person's information-gathering style and his judgment style. A person using a sensing style of gathering information may use either a thinking or a feeling style in evaluating and judging the alternatives. Similarly, an intuitive information gatherer may use either of the judgment styles.

Managers and associates who use an impersonal, rational approach to arrive at their judgments are said to prefer a **thinking** style.[18] Decision makers who use the thinking style to derive conclusions from their perceptions are objective, analytical, logical, and firm.

thinking
A decision style focused on objective evaluation and systematic analysis.

People who use this style are concerned with principles, laws, and objective criteria. They find it easy to critique the work and behavior of others but are often uncomfortable dealing with people's feelings. Thinkers prefer objective analysis and fair decisions based on standards and policies. They are able to discipline and reprimand people, even fire them, if necessary. They are firm and may seem detached and impersonal to subordinates. Their apparently detached nature is likely due to the organized and structured approach they prefer. They would seldom leap to a conclusion without fully evaluating a substantial number of alternatives. They are often conservative in their decisions.

At the other extreme, people who prefer to rely on their emotions and personal, subjective judgments are said to use a **feeling** style.[19] People concerned with feelings emphasize the maintenance of harmony in the workplace. Their judgments are influenced by their own or others' personal likes and dislikes. Such persons are subjective, sympathetic, and appreciative in their decisions. They also dislike decision problems that would require them to say unpleasant things to people. Managers who use a feeling approach frequently give more weight to maintaining a friendly climate in the work group than to effective task achievement. These managers often interpret problems as having been caused by interpersonal factors rather than by other issues.

Both the thinking and feeling styles are important in organizations. The thinking style is consistent with careful decision making, and a number of studies have shown this style to be effective. In one study, for example, real estate agents were asked to provide information on decision style as well as performance in selling properties.[20] Those who used the thinking style tailored their approach to selling based on circumstances and reported stronger performance. The feeling style, however, also can have positive effects. Concern for the feelings and morale of those around us is important.

To take advantage of the positive outcomes of each style and to balance the factors considered in a decision, a decision maker who emphasizes the feeling style should consult with one or more others who emphasize the thinking style. Similarly, decision makers who emphasize the thinking style should consult with those who use the feeling style. Because most managers at all levels in an organization tend to emphasize the thinking style,[21] they are likely to benefit from seeking out a feeling type. In addition, when a manager creates a team to address a problem and make a decision, she is likely to benefit from including both styles on the team.

Using Decision Styles

Although it may seem that decision-making styles are fixed, there is some flexibility in the styles used by managers and associates. As stated by Jung and later researchers, a decision style is simply a preference.[22] Many experienced decision makers are able to adjust their styles as need dictates, at least to some degree. Microsoft's Steve Ballmer, for example, clearly emphasizes the thinking style but at times seems capable of adopting the feeling style. As a thinker, he tends to be objective, logical, and analytical, and perhaps a bit impersonal as well, but he can also take into account the feelings of others. He has been known to scream, yell, and even be sarcastic and then feel badly about the behavior and attempt to make amends.[23] Dawn Ostroff appears to emphasize the thinking style, but not as strongly as Ballmer. She, therefore, probably moves more easily between thinking and feeling.

The accounting and marketing examples discussed in the *Managerial Advice* feature represent a larger problem involving many functional areas. Associates and managers in many areas can have personal styles that work well most of the time but interfere with effectiveness on occasion. Although not all individuals working in a given functional area think in the same way, they often share some general tendencies. The mind-stretching techniques briefly discussed in the advice segment can be quite helpful in addressing the problem of limited styles by extending ways of thinking about situations and broadening the decision styles used. Using the Six Thinking Hats technique, for example, enabled MDS SCIEX to save $1 million on a single project. Similarly, Hermann International's

feeling
A decision style focused on subjective evaluation and the emotional reactions of others.

Nurturing Alternative Decision Styles

©Digital Vision

Many accounting students and practicing accountants combine the sensing and thinking styles. In fact, many accountants are attracted to the accounting field because it allows them to emphasize rules, procedures, facts, and analysis. The structure in professional accounting activities appeals to them. They must, for example, follow generally accepted accounting principles in creating and analyzing financial data for their companies or clients. In contrast, many marketing students and practicing marketers combine the intuition and feeling styles. Marketers are often drawn to the marketing field because it allows them to engage in creative problem solving and requires an understanding of the feelings of others.

Although accountants and marketers may need to emphasize the decision styles that fit the type of work they generally do, they must be careful not to overemphasize those styles. Accountants, for example, can be too narrowly focused on standard data and analysis, thereby failing to take a strategic view of financial information in the firm. In one case, a controller was asked by the CEO to provide a summary of the firm's financial position. She proceeded to tell him about debits and credits that had been recorded on certain dates. The firm's chief financial officer, who was also present at the meeting, described the CEO's reaction this way:

As she continued, you could literally see the CEO's eyes cross.

He turned in frustration and said, "No, what I mean is, where are we ... ? What do we need to work on?"

In reflecting on this experience, the chief financial officer concluded that: (1) many accountants are biased toward a belief that having more data is better and (2) many accountants hide behind "a mass of data." He recommended that accountants focus on the strategic objectives of the firm and provide written or oral communications that interpret analyses in light of those objectives.

Some marketers also have "blind spots." For those marketers who work in the more strategic, creative areas of marketing, detailed study of a statistical market analysis is often not appealing, but such work may provide key insights. Even in areas of marketing that are more quantitative, such as marketing research, individuals may not be evaluating the data carefully enough. In the words of a successful consultant:

[M]any, both within and outside the profession, don't think marketing research has fulfilled its mandate. ... Researchers have become too long on observation, description and problem identification, and too short on rigorous hypothesis testing, analysis-based conclusions and accurate predictions.

In reflecting on the state of marketing research, this consultant suggested additional training in rigorous methods, among other tactics.

To maximize effectiveness, accountants and marketers must be comfortable with alternative decision styles. They must use their "whole brains," in the words of a *Harvard Business Review* article. To support such efforts, several companies offer training programs and materials. The de Bono Group, for example, offers training called Six Thinking Hats. The purpose is to promote the use of different ways of thinking (go to http://debonogroup.com). Numerous companies have used de Bono resources, including 3-M, AT&T, Federal Express, Intel, Microsoft, PPG, The New York Times, and Procter & Gamble. Herrmann International offers a brain dominance assessment and creative ideas for working with decision styles (go to http://www.hbdi.com). Many companies have also utilized Herrmann resources, including American Express, Citibank, Coca-Cola, DuPont, General Electric, IBM, MTV, Starbucks, and Weyerhaeuser. Overall, 70 percent of *Fortune* 500 companies have used Herrmann resources.

Sources: K.A. Brown, & N.L. Hyer. 2002. "Whole-Brain Thinking for Project Management," *Business Horizons*, 45, no. 3: 47–57; de Bono Group, "What We Do," 2010, at http://debonogroup.com/what_we_do.php; B. Hamilton. 2003. "How to Be a Top Strategic Advisor," *Strategic Finance*, 84, no. 12: 41–43; Herrmann International, "Why Herrmann International," 2010, at http://www.hbdi.com/WhyUs/index.cfm; D. Leonard & S. Straus. 1997. "Putting Your Company's Whole Brain to Work," *Harvard Business Review*, 75, no. 4: 112–121; W.D. Neal. 2002. "Shortcomings Plague the Industry," *Marketing News*, 36, no. 19: 37–39; P.D. Tieger, & B. Barron-Tieger. 2001. *Do What You Are: Discover the Perfect Career for You Through the Secrets of Personality Type*, 3rd ed. New York: Little, Brown; P. Wheeler. 2001. "The Myers-Briggs Type Indicator and Applications to Accounting Education and Research," *Issues in Accounting Education*, 16: 125–150.

brain dominance technique has been credited with helping DuPont-Mexico gain new clients, worth millions of dollars in total additional revenue. Overall, the use of these techniques can enhance organizational performance.

Degree of Acceptable Risk

Risk exists when the outcome of a chosen course of action is not certain.[24] Most decisions in business carry some degree of risk. For example, a manager may be considering two candidates for a new position. One of them has a great deal of experience with the type of work to be performed and has been very steady, though not outstanding, in her prior jobs, whereas the other has limited experience but seems to have great potential. If the manager chooses the first candidate, the likelihood of poor work performance is relatively low but not zero. If he chooses the second candidate, the likelihood of poor work performance is higher, but there is also a chance of excellent performance, performance that would be out of reach for the first candidate. Who should be chosen?

risk-taking propensity
Willingness to take chances.

In choosing between less and more risky options, an individual's **risk-taking propensity**, or willingness to take chances, often plays a role.[25] Two persons with different propensities to take risks may make vastly different decisions when confronted with identical decision situations and information. One who is willing to face the possibility of loss, for example, may select a riskier alternative, whereas another person will choose a more conservative alternative. U.S. businessman Donald Trump is known for taking risks. Over the years, he has made and lost and made again significant amounts of money in buying and selling real estate.[26]

In making decisions, individuals with lower risk-taking propensities may collect and evaluate more information. They may even collect more information than they need to make the decision. In one study, managers made hiring decisions in a practice exercise.[27] Managers with low risk-taking propensity used more information and made decisions more slowly. Although information is important, managers and associates with low risk-taking propensities must avoid becoming paralyzed by trying to obtain and consider too much detailed information. Conversely, those with high risk-taking propensities must avoid making decisions with too little information.

reference point
A possible level of performance used to evaluate one's current standing.

Beyond general risk-taking propensity, reference points play an important role in many decisions.[28] A **reference point** can be a goal, a minimum acceptable level of performance, or perhaps the average performance level of others, and it is used to judge one's current standing. If a particular individual's current position in an ongoing activity is below his reference point, he is more likely to take a risk in an attempt to move above the reference point. If his current position is above the reference point, he is less likely to take risks. For example, a manager of a division in a consumer products firm who is below the goal she has set for profitability may undertake a risky project in order to meet her goal. A manager who is above a reference point she has adopted is less likely to take on such a project. In an extreme case, a student in a finance course who is performing below the level he considers minimally acceptable may decide to take drugs to help him stay awake all night studying for the next exam, or he may even decide to cheat. A student who is above his reference point is less likely to engage in these types of risky behavior. A poker player who has just lost a big hand, and is therefore below his performance goals, may adopt a riskier approach to the game, while a player who has just won a big hand is less likely to exhibit such a shift, even though he is better positioned to take on more risk.[29]

Each individual chooses, consciously or unconsciously, his own reference point in a given situation. Two different students are likely to have different minimally acceptable performance levels for a class, and these different levels can serve as their respective reference points. In a recent study, senior managers from small firms subjectively rated disappointment with their firms' business performance.[30] In some cases, managers were disappointed with a level of performance that other leaders endorsed as very positive. Clearly, reference points differed. Moreover, managers expressing dissatisfaction based on their individual reference points were more likely to undertake particularly risky projects.

Cognitive Biases

Individuals often make mistakes in decision making. Although carelessness, sloppiness, fatigue, and task overload can be contributing factors, some mistakes are caused by simple **cognitive biases.** Such biases represent mental shortcuts.[31] Although these shortcuts can be harmless and save time, they often cause problems. Being aware of their existence is an important step in avoiding them.

The **confirmation bias** is particularly important, because it often has strong effects on the type of information gathered. This bias leads decision makers to seek information that confirms beliefs and ideas formed early in the decision process.[32] Rather than also search for information that might disconfirm early beliefs, as a thorough decision process requires, individuals subconsciously seek only information that supports their early thinking. Failing to look for disconfirming information is particularly likely if a decision maker is revisiting a decision that has already been made and partially or fully implemented.

The following story illustrates the problem. An equities broker is concerned about a company in which many of his clients have invested. Because of some recent R&D failures, the company's long-term growth prospects are not as strong as originally expected. The broker's initial position, however, is to recommend that his clients retain the stock; he believes in the company's management and does not want to recommend divesting based only on one sign of possible trouble. Before making a decision, he calls two other brokers who are acquaintances and who also remain supporters of the company. He wants to understand why they continue to be positive about the firm. In the end, he decides to stay the course without seeking the opinions of other brokers who have recommended divesting the company's stock. In other words, he makes his decision having contacted only those who were likely to agree with his initial thinking. Research suggests that this is a common occurrence.[33]

In addition to business domains, research also reveals the presence of confirmation bias in medicine, where doctors may have some tendency to seek only confirming data after forming initial diagnostic impressions.[34] Similarly, research reveals the confirmation bias in the legal system, where police investigators and prosecutors may have some tendency to seek only confirming data after forming initial opinions.[35] Clearly, the potential for problems caused by confirmation tendencies is quite significant.

The **ease-of-recall bias** is also important because it affects the amount and type of information that is gathered and evaluated. In the context of this bias, a decision maker gathers information from his own memory and relies on information that he can easily recall.[36] Unfortunately, easily recalled information may be misleading or incomplete. Vivid and recent information tends to be easily recalled but may not be indicative of the overall situation. In performance appraisals, for example, a supervisor may recall a vivid incident

cognitive biases
Mental shortcuts involving simplified ways of thinking.

confirmation bias
A cognitive bias in which information confirming early beliefs and ideas is sought while potentially disconfirming information is not sought.

ease-of-recall bias
A cognitive bias in which information that is easy to recall from memory is relied upon too much in making a decision.

such as an angry disagreement between two associates while forgetting many common instances of good performance. When selecting a new supplier for a key raw material, a manager may find one or two informal stories of poor performance easier to remember than the comprehensive numbers in an evaluative report on the various alternative suppliers. As the brutal despot Joseph Stalin once said, "A single death is a tragedy, a million deaths is a statistic."[37]

anchoring bias
A cognitive bias in which the first piece of information that is encountered about a situation is emphasized too much in making a decision.

Another bias is the **anchoring bias**. Here, decision makers place too much emphasis on the first piece of information they encounter about a situation.[38] This initial information then has undue influence on ideas, evaluations, and conclusions. Even when decision makers acquire a wide range of additional information (thereby avoiding the confirmation bias), initial information can still have too much influence.

In one study of this phenomenon, auditors from the largest accounting firms in the United States were asked about management fraud.[39] Some of the auditors were asked if executive-level fraud occurred in more than 10 out of every 1,000 client organizations. Then they were asked to estimate the actual incidence rate. Others in the study were asked if executive-level fraud occurred in more than 200 out of every 1,000 client organizations. Auditors in this latter group also were asked to estimate the actual incidence rate. Interestingly, auditors in the first group estimated the actual fraud rate to be 16.52 per 1,000 client organizations whereas auditors in the second group estimated the fraud rate to be 43.11. Despite answering the same question about actual fraud, trained auditors in the most prestigious accounting firms appear to have anchored on arbitrary and irrelevant numbers (10 in the first group and 200 in the second).

sunk-cost bias
A cognitive bias in which past investments of time, effort, and/or money are heavily weighted in deciding on continued investment.

Finally, the **sunk-cost bias** causes decision makers to emphasize past investments of time and money when deciding whether to continue with a chosen course of action.[40] Decision makers are reluctant to walk away from past investments, preferring to build on them and make them successful. Decision makers should, however, treat a past investment as a *sunk cost*—a cost that is unrecoverable and irrelevant—and focus on the future costs and benefits of continued investment. For example, when the CEO of a small business returns to a loan officer at the local bank saying that he needs another $250,000 to succeed, the loan officer should not consider the first $250,000 that was loaned. She should consider the likelihood that a new $250,000 will truly help the small firm succeed. What is the probability of success going forward? What has occurred in the past is not directly relevant to the new decision.

The power of the sunk-cost bias is illustrated by its role in the deaths of a number of Mt. Everest climbers. Rob Hall's ill-fated 1996 expedition provides one of the best known examples.[41] Hall was co-founder of Adventure Consultants, a company specializing in guiding individuals to the highest peaks in the world. By the mid-1990s, he had guided 39 clients to the summit of Everest. To avoid problems, Hall used a prespecified turnaround time for the final leg of the journey. If the summit could not be reached by a particular time in the afternoon, the party returned to the intermediate camp used during the previous night. Although the technology of climbing—clothing, supplemental oxygen, tents, and so on—has improved dramatically since the early days of Everest climbs, it still is crucial to avoid being anywhere near the uninhabitable summit as darkness approaches.

Even with the prespecified turnaround time, Rob Hall lost his life and the lives of several in his party in May 1996. In part, these deaths happened because Hall ignored his turnaround rule. In this fateful ascent, he and his party encountered delays and slow progress on the final leg. Despite the delays and the slipping schedule, Hall pressed on and failed to send back clients who were obviously struggling. These clients had invested a great deal in the effort to climb Mount Everest and did not want to be sent down after coming so far. Several members of the party did, however, decide to turn around without being forced down by Hall, prompting the following observation:

> In order to succeed you must be exceedingly driven, but if you're too driven you're likely to die. Above 26,000 feet, moreover, the line between appropriate zeal and reckless summit fever becomes grievously thin. Thus, the slopes of Everest are littered with corpses. Taske, Huthchison, Kasischke, and Fischbeck [party members who turned back] had each spent as much as $70,000 and endured weeks of agony to be granted this one shot at the summit ... and yet, faced with a tough decision, they were among the few who made the right choice that day.[42]

Moods and Emotions

Moods and emotions are two aspects of affective phenomena in organizations.[43] **Moods** are affective states that correspond to general feelings disconnected from any particular event or stimulus in the workplace. Moods typically are described in generic terms, such as positive or negative, good or bad. **Emotions** correspond to more specific feelings that are often tied to particular events, people, or other stimuli. Also, emotions typically are described in terms of discrete forms, such as fear and anger. Research in the field of organizational behavior has increasingly emphasized moods and emotions in the workplace.

Mood appears to have important effects on decision making, but those effects are complex and not fully understood at this point.[44] On the one hand, individuals in positive moods seem to neglect the details of decision situations. This can lead to poor outcomes when such details are crucial. On the other hand, individuals in positive moods seem to exhibit more breadth in ideas considered, which can create more exploration, less conservatism, more creativity, and perhaps more risk taking. These decision attributes are positive in situations calling for fresh ideas or bold steps. In one study of the mood phenomenon, foreign exchange traders with positive moods were found to exhibit more confidence and risk taking, but their overall performance was lower than those in bad moods presumably because details mattered in the trading context.[45] In another study, auditors with positive moods were found to be less conservative than auditors in bad moods.[46]

Emotion also appears to have important effects on decision making. In recent years, one of the most studied emotions has been regret. Regret is an aversive emotion involving self-blame that comes from unwanted outcomes.[47] One possible reaction to this aversive emotion involves avoiding in the future a choice that has led to a poor outcome (i.e., not repeating a choice associated with failure when faced with a similar decision situation in the future). Although this reaction often is appropriate, it can be dysfunctional. For example, bad luck can create an unwanted outcome even though a good choice has been made. In that situation, a viable choice might be ruled out of future consideration when it should not be.[48] In contrast to the above circumstances, decision makers sometimes avoid full feedback so as to limit their knowledge of bad outcomes, which makes avoiding a truly poor choice difficult in the future.[49]

Another reaction to regret involves self-management. This reaction can protect the ego of the decision maker. When engaged in self management, decision makers may:[50]

1. Attempt to reverse the decision

2. Run from the decision by denying responsibility for it

moods
Affective states corresponding to general positive or negative feelings disconnected from any particular event or stimulus.

emotions
Affective states corresponding to specific feelings, such as anger, that tend to be associated with particular events, people, or other stimuli.

Anger and Fear in Recent U.S. Elections

Barack Obama earned an impressive victory in the U.S. presidential election of 2008. In part, his success was based on personal qualities such as charisma and strong oratorical skills. His success also was driven by a strong team of strategic advisors, including David Axelrod and David Plouffe. These advisors helped to develop important strategies, such as the very strong emphasis on being consistent with the political message even when setbacks and unexpected problems occurred. Energized grassroots organizations also played a role in the election outcome, as did unprecedented use of web-based media and a focus on young people.

Despite all of those positives, the victory was improbable in many ways. Obama had little leadership experience. He also had somewhat limited political experience, having served for only a few years in the U.S. Senate and roughly eight years in the Illinois state legislature. Obama also

had a number of friends and political connections that made many mainstream Americans more than a little uneasy. Reverend Jeremiah Wright is the most famous example. Wright had a long history of controversial remarks on a wide range of issues.

Scott Brown also recently earned an impressive political victory. In Brown's case, the election focused on one of Massachusetts's two seats in the U.S. Senate. Although perhaps not as gifted a campaigner as Obama, Brown worked hard to generate a win in the January 2010 special election to replace the deceased Edward Kennedy. Brown traveled widely in the state and talked with potential voters in a down-to-earth style that won high praise. He successfully applied lessons from a number of effective previous campaigns for local and state offices. He also drew on his lengthy and dedicated service in the National Guard, where he had achieved the rank of lieutenant colonel.

©Joe Raedle/Getty Images, Inc.

Scott Brown's victory was even more improbable than Obama's. He ran as a Republican in a heavily Democratic state. Moreover, he sought the Senate seat formerly held by the popular Democrat Kennedy, which meant many voters for sentimental reasons thought a Democratic candidate should have the seat. Also, his legislative record was somewhat undistinguished, and his opponent had Obama campaigning for her, albeit late in the game.

3. Argue that other alternative choices would not have led to a better outcome

4. Attempt to suppress self-knowledge of the unwanted outcome

5. Engage in after-the-fact justifications of the decision by using, for example, a self-affirmation such as "I did the best that I could".

A second often-studied emotion is anger. This emotion is widely believed to have important, potentially problematic effects on decision making. First, anger may cause decision makers to be less effective gatherers and evaluators of information.[51] Second, anger may lead to lower perceived risk unwanted decision consequences, particularly in comparison to the effects that other negative emotions have on perceived risk (e.g., fear).[52] A study of public attitudes and beliefs concerning terrorism illustrates the connection to risk.[53] Individuals who were angry about terrorism estimated the probability of future attacks as relatively small.

Obama and Brown overcame strong odds to earn their victories. Personal styles and abilities as well as strong campaign teams certainly played important roles, but the reinforcement of existing anger or the creation of new anger among voters also played a role, and a very strong one. For Obama, a key element of his overall strategy entailed positioning his opponent as an extension of then president George Bush, which leveraged the anger many American's felt toward Bush over the Iraq war, perceived corporate favoritism, and enormous government spending. Beyond simply linking the opponent to Bush to leverage existing anger, the Obama team also actively sought to create more anger related to the state of the country.

In the case of Brown, a key element of his overall strategy entailed leveraging existing anger over tactics being used in the U.S. Congress and also leveraging existing anger and creating more of it over economic conditions. He positioned himself as a Washington outsider while criticizing those working in the nation's capital. His success prompted one reporter to say this, "People are so angry out here in the real world, they can't see straight."

The strategic use of anger by Obama and Brown was no doubt critical to their success. Both candidates had a substantial number of potentially damaging attributes, as well as potentially formidable opponents. Anger among voters, though, can result in relatively low perceived risks for bold actions that address the anger, which means such voters may be willing to take a chance on a newcomer with substantial negatives. Obama and Brown could have reduced their focus on anger, while putting greater emphasis on people's fears over where the country was heading, but that approach may not have worked as well. Further, these candidates could have deemphasized anger to some degree while focusing even more on inspiring visions for the future (both candidates did put a great deal of energy into visions for the future). While inspiring visions are very powerful, this approach also may not have worked as well in their political situations.

Sources: M. Creamer. 2008. "Barack Obama and Audacity of Marketing," *Advertising Age*, Nov. 10, pp. 1–2; R. W. Forsyth. 2010. "The New Dismal," *Barron's*, Jan. 25, pp. 7–8; E. Hornick. 2010. "Independents' Anger in Massachusetts: A sign of Things to Come?," *CNN.com*, Jan. 21, at http://www.cnn.com/2010/POLITICS/01/21/mass.independent. vote/index.html; R. Lizza. 2008. "Battle Plans: How Obama Won," *The New Yorker*, Nov. 17, pp. 46–55; D. Weigel. 2010. "Conservative Grassroots Strategy Propels Brown to the Senate," *Washington Independent*, Jan. 20, at http:// washingtonindependent.com/74251/conservative-grassroots-strategy-propels-brown-to-senate.

Nonetheless, they preferred relatively bold, risky preventive measures and had relatively little concern for the consequences. Those who were fearful of terrorism estimated the probability of attacks as relatively large. Even so, they preferred less direct, less risky preventive measures as they were concerned about the consequences of bolder actions. These dynamics are explored further in the *Experiencing Organizational Behavior* feature.

Group Decision Making

We often view decision making as an individual activity, with thoughtful individuals making good or bad organizational decisions. For example, it is easy to credit the success of Intel in the 1990s microchip industry to the effective decision making of

©Karen Moskowitz/Getty
Images, Inc.

Andy Grove, the CEO for many years. But it is common for a number of people to participate in important organizational decisions, working together as a group to solve organizational problems. This is particularly true in high-involvement organizations, where associates participate in many decisions with lower-level and middle-level managers and where lower-level and middle-level managers participate in decisions with senior-level managers. In high-involvement organizations, teams of associates also make some decisions without managerial input. In this way, human capital throughout the organization is utilized effectively.

Group decision making is similar in some ways to the individual decision making we described earlier. Because the purpose of group decision making is to arrive at a preferred solution to a problem, the group must use the same basic decision-making process—define the problem, identify criteria, gather and evaluate information, list and evaluate alternatives, and choose the best alternative and implement it.

On the other hand, groups are made up of multiple individuals, resulting in dynamics and interpersonal processes that make group decision making different from decision making by an individual.[54] For instance, some members of the decision group will arrive with their own expectations, problem definitions, and predetermined solutions. These characteristics are likely to cause some interpersonal problems among group members. Also, some members will have given more thought to the decision situation than others, members' expectations about what is to be accomplished may differ, and so on. Thus, a group leader may be more concerned with turning a collection of individuals into a collaborative decision-making team than with the development of individual decision-making skills. In this section, we consider these and other issues in group decision making.

Group Decision-Making Pitfalls

Although group decision making can produce positive outcomes, the social nature of group decisions sometimes leads to undesired results. In fact, group processes that occur during decision making often prevent full discussion of facts and alternatives. Group norms, member roles, dysfunctional communication patterns, and too much cohesiveness may deter the group, thereby producing ineffective decisions. Researchers have identified several critical pitfalls in decision-making groups. These include groupthink, common information bias, diversity-based infighting, and the risky shift (see upper half of Exhibit 10-3).

Groupthink

groupthink
A situation in which group members maintain or seek consensus at the expense of identifying and debating honest disagreements.

When group members maintain or seek consensus at the expense of identifying and earnestly debating honest disagreements, **groupthink** is said to occur.[55] Focusing too much attention on consensus, especially early in a decision process, can result in a faulty decision. Many important ideas and alternative courses of action may not be seriously considered.

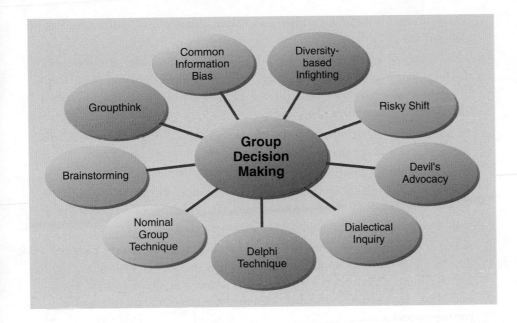

Exhibit 10-3 Group Decision-Making Phenomena—Pitfalls and Techniques

This type of group phenomenon can occur under a number of different conditions, including the following:

- Group members like one another and therefore do not want to criticize each other's ideas.[56]
- Group members have high regard for the group's collective wisdom and therefore yield to early ideas or the ideas of a leader.[57]
- Group members derive satisfaction from membership in a group that has a positive self-image and therefore try to prevent the group from having any serious divisions.[58]

In essence, then, a variety of factors can cause group members to avoid surfacing divergent opinions and ideas within the group.

Groupthink may be most likely when a group that has a positive image is under threat, such as when a management team faces a tough competitor or when a presidential administration faces possible military engagement.[59] At Enron, the failed energy company, managers valued being part of the leadership of a company perceived as progressive, innovative, and sophisticated. Being employed by Enron, and especially being a part of the favored group in the company, was powerfully reinforcing. This seems to have contributed to managers' tendency to agree with increasingly risky investments and accounting tricks.[60]

At least eight specific symptoms are associated with groupthink:

1. *Self-censorship.* Group members who recognize flaws or errors in the group position tend to remain quiet during group discussions and avoid issues that might upset the group.

2. *Pressure.* Group members apply pressure to any member who expresses opinions that threaten group consensus and harmony.

3. *Unanimity.* Censorship and pressure lead to the illusion of unanimous support for the final group decision. Members who have been quiet are assumed to be in

complete agreement, which further discourages consideration of other decision alternatives.

4. *Rationalization.* Many group members build complex rationales that effectively discount warnings or information that conflict with their thinking. Thus, sources of negative information are discredited in group discussions. Such actions often narrow the decision alternatives considered.

5. *Invulnerability.* Group members may develop an illusion of invulnerability, which causes them to ignore any dangers. As a result, they become overly optimistic and take unwarranted risks; the group seriously overestimates its collective wisdom.

6. *Mindguards.* Certain group members take on the social role of "mindguard." They attempt to shield the group from any facts, criticisms, or evaluations that may alter the illusion of unanimity and invulnerability.

7. *Morality.* Most group members believe in the morality of the group's position. The members may even speak about the inherent morality of what they are doing and the immorality of opposing views. This can result in decisions that ignore ethical and legal issues as viewed by the broader society and lead to negative consequences for others.

8. *Stereotypes.* Group members may develop negative stereotypes of other people and groups. These stereotypes can protect their own position and block the possibility of reasonable negotiations with outsiders.

As the most discussed group decision-making phenomenon, groupthink has been linked to a number of actual decisions.[61] Many of these have been U.S. government or military decisions, in part because a great deal of groupthink research has been conducted in the United States and access to important materials for assessing U.S. decision making is reasonably good. Examples include the decision of Admiral Kimmel and his advisors to focus on training instead of defense of Pearl Harbor prior to its being attacked in 1941, the decision of President John F. Kennedy and his cabinet to authorize an invasion of Cuba at the Bay of Pigs in 1960, and the decision of President Lyndon Johnson and his inner circle to escalate the war in Vietnam in the mid-1960s.[62] At NASA, examples in which groupthink may have played a role include the decision to launch the *Challenger* Shuttle in 1986[63] and the handling of the Hubble telescope.[64] For business firms, examples abound, with many of them involving boards of directors.[65] Groupthink has also been found in self-managing work teams.[66] This has implications for high-involvement organizations.

Groupthink does not guarantee a poor decision but simply increases the likelihood of such a result. When good judgment and discussion are suppressed, the group can still be lucky. However, because the purpose of group decision making is to increase the likelihood of a good decision, managers must take steps to reduce groupthink. Such steps are discussed later in this chapter.

common information bias

A bias in which group members overemphasize information held by a majority or the entire group while failing to be mindful of information held by one group member or a few members.

Common Information Bias

Some information a group might consider in making a decision may be held by one or a few group members. Other pieces of information are held by most or all group members. The **common information bias** leads groups to unconsciously neglect information held by one group member or a few members while focusing on more commonly held information in the group, thereby neglecting potentially important issues and ideas.[67]

The common information bias defeats one of the presumed advantages of group decision making—the availability of unique information, ideas, and perspectives brought to the process by individual group members.

The following study illustrates this phenomenon.[68] First, managers were asked to evaluate PeopleSoft as an alternative to the firm's existing accounting and enterprise management software. Next, these managers assembled to discuss whether adopting People-Soft would be positive for the firm. Concerns and ideas held by one or a few members received less attention than concerns and ideas held by most or all group members, resulting in a very limited group discussion.

Diversity-based Infighting

When groupthink is an issue, one or more members of the group typically act to suppress diverse ideas, and many members censor themselves. With the common information bias, individuals subconsciously focus on common information and ideas. Thus, in many groups, diverse ideas are not discussed. In other groups, however, diverse ideas are emphasized. Although this is generally positive for group decision making, it can become extreme.

Instead of creating rich discussions and insight, diverse ideas can create ill will and fractured groups.[69] Such **diversity-based infighting** is likely to occur when individuals feel very strongly about their ideas and no mechanisms to channel disagreement in productive ways have been instituted. As discussed in the next section, mechanisms that can help channel diversity include formal brainstorming procedures and the formal use of devil's advocacy.

diversity-based infighting
A situation in which group members engage in unproductive, negative conflict over differing views.

Risky Shift

As discussed earlier, most decisions involve some degree of risk. Because decision-making groups are composed of individuals, it would seem that risk taken by a group should be the same as the average risk that would have been taken by the individual group members acting alone. But the social forces involved in group decisions make this assumption incorrect.

Research on the risk taken by groups in making decisions began in the 1960s, when investigators compared individual and group decisions on the same problems.[70] Possible solutions to the problems ranged from relatively safe alternatives with moderate payoffs to relatively risky options with higher potential payoffs. Contrary to expectations, groups consistently made riskier decisions than individuals. This finding has since been called the **risky shift** phenomenon.

Subsequent analysis of these findings and additional research have determined that decisions made by groups are not always riskier. In fact, they are sometimes more cautious. However, group decisions seem to shift toward increased risk more often than toward increased cautiousness.[71] Several explanations for such shifts have been offered, but the most common and most powerful explanation involves diffusion of responsibility. Because individual group members believe that no single person can be blamed if the decision turns out poorly, they can shift the blame entirely to others (the group). This diffusion of individual responsibility may lead members to accept higher levels of risk in making a group decision.[72]

risky shift
A process by which group members collectively make a more risky choice than most or all of the individuals would have made working alone.

Group Decision-Making Techniques

As the preceding discussion makes clear, groups may flounder when given a problem to solve. It is important, therefore, to understand the techniques that can be used to encourage full and effective input and discussion before the group reaches a decision. Several

©Andreas Pollok/Getty Images, Inc.

brainstorming
A process in which a large number of ideas are generated while evaluation of the ideas is suspended.

techniques have been developed, including brainstorming, the nominal group technique, the Delphi technique, dialectical inquiry, and devil's advocacy (see Exhibit 10-3).

Brainstorming

For major decisions, it is usually important to generate a wide variety of new ideas during the data-gathering and alternative-generation phases of decision making. Increasing the number of ideas during these phases helps ensure that important facts or considerations are not overlooked. Unfortunately, if the group evaluates or critiques each new idea as it is introduced in a group meeting, individual members may withhold other creative ideas because they fear critical comments. In contrast, if ideas are not evaluated immediately, members may offer a number of inputs, even if they are uncertain of the value of their ideas. This is the essence of **brainstorming**.[73]

Brainstorming within groups has the following basic features:

- Imagination is encouraged. No idea is too unique or different, and the more ideas offered the better.
- Using or building on the ideas of others is encouraged.
- There is no criticism of any idea, no matter how bad it may seem at the time.
- Evaluation is postponed until the group can no longer think of any new ideas.

Many companies—such as IDEO, a Silicon Valley product design firm—use this basic approach.[74] Research supports the approach, as it suggests that groups using brainstorming often generate more ideas than groups that do not use brainstorming.[75] However, research also suggests that groups following this approach do not do as well as individuals brainstorming alone.[76] In one study, for example, a brainstorming group developed 28 ideas, and 8.9 percent of them were later judged as good ideas by independent experts.[77] The same number of people engaging in solitary brainstorming developed a total of 74.5 ideas, with 12.7 percent judged as good ideas.

Why is group brainstorming often less effective than individual brainstorming? One problem may be that group members believe criticism will not be entirely eliminated but will simply remain unspoken.[78] In other words, if a member contributes a unique idea, she may believe that others are silently ridiculing it. Another problem may be that some group members are simply distracted by the significant amount of discussion in a group brainstorming session.[79]

Two techniques may be helpful in overcoming the problems of standard group brainstorming. First, *brain-writing* can be used. In a common version of brain-writing, group members stop at various points in a group meeting and write down all of their ideas.[80] Then the written ideas are placed on a flipchart or whiteboard by an individual assigned the task of pooling the written remarks. By moving from an oral to a written approach, and by introducing anonymity, this method makes many individuals feel less inhibited. Furthermore, less talking takes place in the room, so distractions are reduced. Second, *electronic brainstorming (EBS)* can be used. In a common version of EBS, group members sit around a table with computer stations in front of them.[81] Each individual attempts to develop as many ideas as possible and enter them into a database. As an idea is entered, it is projected onto a large screen that everyone can see. Because there is anonymity, individuals feel less inhibited, and because there is less talking in the room, they are not distracted. Individuals can, however, build on the ideas of others as they appear on the screen.

Nominal Group Technique

Another technique used to overcome some of the inhibiting forces in group decision making is called the **nominal group technique**. This technique shares some features of brainwriting and electronic brainstorming. In its basic form, it calls for a decision meeting that follows four procedural rules:[82]

1. At the outset, individuals seated around a table write down their ideas silently and without discussion.

2. Each member presents one idea to the group. After the initial round has been completed, each member presents a second idea. The process is repeated until all ideas have been presented. No group discussion is permitted during this period.

3. After the ideas have been recorded on a blackboard or a large flipchart or in a computer database for projection, the members discuss them. The major purpose here is to clarify and evaluate.

4. The meeting concludes with a silent and independent vote or ranking of the alternative choices. The group decision is determined by summing or pooling these independent votes.

The nominal group technique eliminates a great deal of interaction among group members. Discussion and interaction occur only once during the entire process. Even the final choice of an alternative occurs in silence and depends on an impersonal summing process. Proponents of this technique believe that inhibitions are overcome at crucial stages, whereas group discussion occurs at the time it is needed for evaluation. Research has suggested that the technique yields better results than a standard group brainstorming session.[83]

Delphi Technique

Brainstorming and the nominal group technique generally require group members to be in close physical proximity (seated around a table, for example). However, groups using the **Delphi technique** do not meet face-to-face. Instead, members are solicited for their judgments at their various homes or places of business.[84] In the most common approach, group members respond to a questionnaire about the issue of interest. Their responses are summarized and the results are fed back to the group. After receiving the feedback, individuals are given a second opportunity to respond and may or may not change their judgments.

Some Delphi approaches use only two sets of responses, whereas others repeat the question–summary–feedback process several times before a decision or conclusion is reached. The final decision is derived by averaging or otherwise combining the members' responses to the last questionnaire; often, the members' responses become more similar over time. Although some research has been supportive of this technique,[85] it is a highly structured approach that can inhibit some types of input, especially if some individuals feel constrained by the particular set of questions posed. Even so, the Delphi technique is an option to consider, especially when members of the group are geographically dispersed.

nominal group technique
A process for group decision making in which discussion is structured and the final solution is decided by silent vote.

Delphi technique
A highly structured decision-making process in which participants are surveyed regarding their opinions or best judgments.

Dialectical Inquiry and Devil's Advocacy

The techniques for group decision making explained above are more concerned with increasing the number of ideas generated than with directly improving the quality of the final solution. Although having a greater number of ideas enhances the possibility that a superior alternative will be identified, other techniques can help the group find the best choice.

Two key approaches are dialectical inquiry and devil's advocacy. These approaches counter the tendency of groups to avoid conflict when evaluating alternative courses of action and to prematurely smooth over differences within the group when they occur.[86] In its basic form, **dialectical inquiry** calls for two different subgroups to develop very different assumptions and recommendations in order to encourage full discussion of ideas. The two subgroups debate their respective positions. **Devil's advocacy** calls for an individual or subgroup to argue against a recommended action put forth by other members of the group. Thus, both dialectical inquiry and devil's advocacy use "constructive" conflict. Proponents assert that both are learning-oriented approaches because the active debates can help the group to discover new alternatives and to develop a more complete understanding of the issues involved in the decision problems.[87] In spite of these similarities, however, there are important differences between the two approaches.

The dialectical inquiry technique requires group members to develop two distinct points of view. More specifically, one subgroup develops a recommendation based on a set of assumptions, and a second subgroup develops a significantly different recommendation based on different assumptions. Debate of the two opposing sets of recommendations and assumptions maximizes constructive conflict, and the resulting evaluation of the two points of view helps ensure a thorough review and also helps to promote the development of new recommendations as differences are bridged. Devil's advocacy, however, requires the group to generate only one set of assumptions and a single recommendation, which are then critiqued by the devil's advocate (or advocates) (this devil's advocacy process can be repeated over time with additional recommendations).

Research on these techniques suggests that both are effective in developing high-quality solutions to problems.[88] At the same time, however, they can result in somewhat lower levels of group satisfaction than approaches such as brainstorming.[89] This outcome is probably due to the intragroup conflict that can arise when these methods are used. Still, both approaches are apt to be effective in controlling undesirable group phenomena that suppress the full exploration of issues. Because both approaches aim to create constructive conflict through assigned roles, they are not likely to cause major dissatisfaction among group members.

dialectical inquiry
A group decision-making technique that relies on debate between two subgroups that have developed different recommendations based on different assumptions.

devil's advocacy
A group decision-making technique that relies on a critique of a recommended action and its underlying assumptions.

Who Should Decide? Individual versus Group Decision Making

In this closing section, we first provide guidance on how a manager should approach a decision that he must make. Should he make the decision alone, should he invite limited participation by associates, or should he use a group decision-making approach with associates? Following the discussion of associate involvement in managerial decisions, we summarize the general advantages and disadvantages of having an individual versus a group make a decision.

Associate Involvement in Managerial Decisions

Although associates in high-involvement firms make many important decisions, other decisions remain for managers to address, perhaps with the assistance of associates. For these latter decisions, managers must determine the correct level of associate involvement in the decision-making process. Two researchers, Victor Vroom and Philip Yetton, point out that the correct level of involvement depends on the nature of the decision problem itself.[90] If the manager can diagnose the nature of the problem, he can determine the degree to which a group of associates should participate.

The Vroom–Yetton method requires the manager first to diagnose the problem situation and then to determine the extent to which associates will be involved in the decision-making process. The optimal extent of involvement depends on the probable effect participation will have on: (1) the quality of the decision, (2) the acceptance or commitment subordinates exhibit when implementing the decision, and (3) the amount of time needed to make the decision.[91]

As you can see in Exhibit 10-4, there are several levels of involvement, ranging from the manager's making the decision alone to a fully participative group approach. Vroom and Yetton suggest that managers can determine the best strategy for associate participation by asking seven diagnostic questions. This procedure yields a decision tree that indicates the most effective level of participation, as shown in Exhibit 10-5. It is not always necessary, however, to ask all seven questions to determine the level of involvement because some branches of the decision tree end after a few questions are asked.

Research has supported the Vroom–Yetton method. The method predicts the technical quality, subordinate acceptance, and overall effectiveness of final solutions.[92]

EXHIBIT 10-4 *Managerial Approaches to Associate Involvement in Decision Making*

Approach

Low ↑ Level of Associate Involvement in Decision ↓ High	**AI**—Manager solves the problem or makes the decision alone, using the information to which she has current access.
	AII—Manager requests information but may not explain the problem to associates. The associates' role in the process is to provide specific information; associates do not generate or evaluate alternatives.
	CI—Manager explains the problem to the relevant associates one by one, requesting their input without discussing the problem as a group. After discussing it with each of the relevant associates, the manager makes the decision alone. It is unclear whether the decision reflects the associates' input.
	CII—Manager explains the problem to associates as a group. The manager obtains group members' ideas and suggestions. Afterward, the manager makes the decision alone. The associates' input may or may not be reflected in the manager's decision.
	GII—Manager explains the problem to the associates in a group setting. They work together to generate and evaluate alternatives and agree on a solution. The manager acts as a facilitator, guiding the discussion, focusing on the problem, and ensuring that the important issues are examined. The manager does not force the group to accept her solution and will accept and implement a solution supported by the group.

Source: Adapted from V.H. Vroom, & A.G. Jago. 1978. "On the validity of the Vroom–Yetton Model," *Journal of Applied Psychology*, 69: 151–162; V.H. Vroom, & P.W. Yetton. 1973. *Leadership and Decision Making*. Pittsburgh, PA: University of Pittsburgh Press.

A: Is there a quality requirement such that one solution is likely to be more rational than another (is it worth working hard to find the best possible solution, or will any number of solutions work reasonably well)?

B: Do I have sufficient information to make a high-quality decision?

C: Is the problem structured (do I know the questions to ask and where to look for relevant information)?

D: Is acceptance of the decision by associates critical to effective implementation (if implementation would be relatively easy, then full acceptance is less important; if implementation would be pursued out of loyalty, then full acceptance is less important)?

E: If I were to make the decision by myself, is it reasonably certain that it would be accepted by my associates?

F: Do the associates share the organization's goals to be attained in solving this problem?

G: Is conflict among associates likely in preferred solutions?

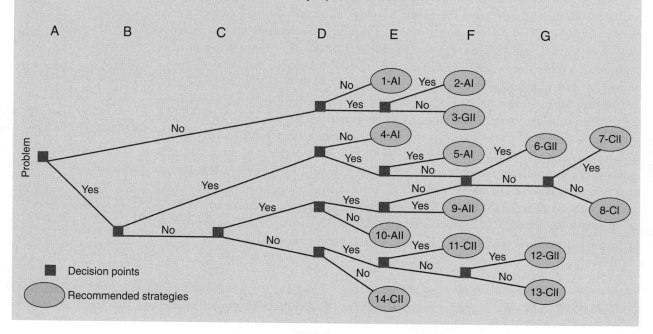

Exhibit 10-5 Decision Tree Method for Diagnosing the Appropriate Level of Subordinate Involvement in Decisions

Source: V.H. Vroom & P.W. Yetton, 1973. *Leadership and Decision Making.* Pittsburgh, PA: University of Pittsburgh Press.

As shown in the *Experiencing Organizational Behavior* feature, the success of many U.S. Civil War generals was at least partially determined by a proper level of subordinate involvement in decisions. Like a top general during the Civil War, a CEO must decide on the proper level of involvement for the other senior managers. When, for example, the CEO needs to address a complex strategic decision (such as whether to enter a new market), she probably should fully involve other managers in the decision, given the need for a variety of inputs. The input from other top-level managers can be especially valuable when the team members are heterogeneous in their backgrounds and knowledge.[93] As you can see, the Vroom–Yetton model is useful not only for lower-level managers deciding on the appropriate level of involvement for associates but also for generals deciding on the level of involvement for subordinate officers and for senior managers deciding on the level of involvement for those who report directly to them.

One final point is important. When a group decision approach is to be used (Type GII), the manager must determine how much agreement should exist within the group.

Must all the members agree on the decision, or will the manager accept the decision even though some members disagree? Typically, managers seek either a majority or a unanimous decision from the decision-making group.[94] Seeking agreement from a majority has several advantages over seeking unanimous agreement, including increased speed and reduced risk of impasse.[95] Trying to obtain unanimity, however, generally creates more discussion and often causes group members to explore the assumptions that underlie the positions and preferences held within the group.[96] Managers must balance these factors when deciding which approach to use for group decision making.

Value of Individual versus Group Decision Making

Under the proper conditions, group decision making should increase the number of ideas generated and improve the evaluation of alternatives. Such outcomes are desirable because they generally produce better decisions. However, our earlier discussion of group decision

The Vroom–Yetton Model and Military Decisions during the U.S. Civil War

©Mark Wilson/Getty Images

The U.S. Civil War remains one of the bloodiest conflicts in human history. Both the North and the South sustained heavy losses in this fight over the abolition of slavery, economic issues, and states' rights. Eventually, the North won the conflict, preserving the national union that had been established only decades earlier.

In deciding how and when to conduct battles, Northern and Southern generals needed information on the opposing side's troop locations, troop strength, and logistical weaknesses. They also needed information on the condition of their own forces, the nature of terrain where a battle might be fought, and so on. After considering the available information and after collecting as much new information as desired, the generals made decisions related to battle strategy.

As in business-related decision making, these generals could have involved others in making decisions or could have made decisions alone. General McClellan of the North, for example, orchestrated the Battle of Antietam without much input from others, using information he had available (in terms of Exhibit 10-4, the AI approach). General Robert E. Lee of the South followed this same approach at the Battle of Antietam (AI approach) but used a different approach at the Battle of Chancellorsville. At Chancellorsville, he collected substantial information from his subordinate commanders before making the decision on his own (AII approach).

Interestingly, the Vroom–Yetton framework seems to predict the success of generals in Civil War battles. For example, at the Battle of Shiloh,

General Grant of the North faced a situation in which: (1) the quality of the decision was important, (2) the decision maker (Grant himself) did not have enough information to make a quality decision, (3) the problem was not well structured, and (4) acceptance by subordinate officers was not crucial for implementation (Situation 14 in Exhibit 10-5). Grant sought information but not ideas from his officers and made the battle-strategy decision alone (AII approach). Group discussion and idea generation would have been beneficial, however, because the problem was unstructured. Grant did not meet his objectives at Shiloh.

At the Battle of Gettysburg, General Meade of the North faced a situation in which: (1) the quality of the decision was important, (2) the decision maker (Meade himself) had the crucial information, and (3) acceptance by subordinate officers was not crucial for implementation (Situation 4 in Exhibit 10-5). Meade alone made the key decision related to strategy, without collecting substantial new information from others (AI approach, perhaps close to an AII approach). As predicted by the Vroom–Yetton model, he met his objectives.

In the following table, a number of battles are profiled. As shown, the model correctly predicts outcomes in 10 of 12 cases.

Battle/Commanders	Problem Type	Recommended Decision Approach	Style Used	Outcome (Relative to Original Objective)
Battle of Shiloh				
General Grant	14	CII	AII	Not Achieved
General Johnston	12	GII	AII	Not Achieved
Battle of Antietam				
General McClellan	5	AI	AI	Achieved
General Lee	9	AII	AI	Not Achieved
Battle of Chancellorsville				
General Hooker	14	CII	AI	Not Achieved
General Lee	5	AI	AII	Achieved
Battle of Gettysburg				
General Meade	4	AI	AI	Achieved
General Lee	11	CII	AI	Not Achieved
Battle of Chickamauga				
General Rosecrans	11	CII	AII	Not Achieved
General Bragg	11	CII	AI	Not Achieved
Battle of Nashville				
General Thomas	11	CII	AII	Achieved
General Hood	13	CII	AI	Not Achieved

Sources: Adapted from W.J. Duncan, K.G. LaFrance, & P.M. Ginter. 2003. "Leadership and Decision Making: A Retrospective Application and Assessment," *Journal of Leadership and Organizational Studies*, 9: 1–20 (principal source); B.J. Murphy. 2004. "Grant versus Lee," *Civil War Times Illustrated*, 43, no. 1: 42–52; United States War Department, *The War of the Rebellion: A Compilation of the Official Records of the Union and Confederate Armies*, multiple series and volumes within series (Washington, DC: Government Printing Office, 1880–1891).

making suggested that these results are not guaranteed. Furthermore, the generation of ideas and their evaluation are not the only outcomes from group decision making. Commitment and satisfaction of participants must also be considered.

Important considerations for judging the overall value of group decision making as opposed to individual decision making include the time needed to reach the decision, the costs of making it, the nature of the problem, the satisfaction and commitment of employees affected by the decision, and opportunities for personal growth (see Exhibit 10-6).

Time

Not surprisingly, groups typically take more time to reach decisions than do individuals. There are several reasons for this difference:

- Many social needs are met by the group (exchanging greetings, talking about the weekend, and so forth). The time required to meet these needs increases the time needed to reach a decision.
- More ideas and opinions are held by the group, and discussing these increases the time required. The use of techniques such as brainstorming and dialectical inquiry also adds to the time required.

ADVANTAGES	DISADVANTAGES
Groups can accumulate more knowledge and facts and thus generate more and better alternatives.	Groups take more time to reach decisions than do individuals.
Groups often display superior judgement when evaluating alternatives, especially for complex problems.	Group social interactions may lead to premature compromise and failure to consider all alternatives fully.
Group involvement in decisions leads to a higher level of acceptance of the decisions and greater satisfaction.	Groups are sometimes dominated by one or two "decision leaders," which may reduce acceptance, satisfaction, and quality.
Group decision making can result in growth for members of the group.	Managers may rely too much on group decisions, leading to loss of their own decision and implementation skills.

Exhibit 10-6 Advantages and Disadvantages of Group Decision Making

- Arrangements for the group meeting place, format, and assembly must be made, taking more time.

Managers must consider the importance of time in their decisions, as well as the potential quality of the decisions. Some decisions must be made immediately. In other situations, time may be available for decision making. When time is an important consideration, the manager may elect to do one of the following:

- Make the decision alone.
- Use the group for advice only.
- Use an already-existing group to minimize the arrangement time.
- Use a majority-decision rule rather than requiring unanimity.
- Use the nominal group technique to reduce lengthy discussion time.

Cost

It is also inevitable that group decision making costs more than individual decision making. Time costs money, especially when expensive managers and associates are involved. The additional time must be multiplied by the number of members in the group and their respective financial compensation levels to arrive at the total cost. The additional cost of group decision making can be substantial. Therefore, managers must determine whether the decision is important enough to warrant the extra cost.

Nature of the Problem

Members of a group typically have more information and ideas than does a single individual.[97] If the information and ideas are discussed and integrated, group decisions will often be better informed than individual decisions. Many groups, however, have difficulty managing their collective knowledge. Groupthink and common information bias can prevent information from coming to the surface. Diversity-based infighting and the risky shift can prevent sound integration of information. However, the decision-making techniques discussed in this chapter, such as devil's advocacy, can help the group to overcome these negative social forces and create high-quality decisions.

The nature of the problem being examined should be considered in choosing the approach to use. Complex problems that require many different types of input tend to be solved more effectively by groups than by individuals. Deciding whether to develop a new product, for example, may require specialized knowledge of production facilities, engineering and design capabilities, market forces, government legislation, labor markets, and financial considerations. Thus, a group should be better at making this decision. In one study focused on new-product decision making, groups were in fact more effective than individuals.[98]

Satisfaction and Commitment

Even though quality is not consistently improved by group decision making, individual satisfaction and commitment to the final solution are often enhanced.[99] These outcomes may result from several factors. First, group members may change their attitudes toward the various alternatives as a result of the group's discussions. In addition, "team spirit" may develop as group members discover similarities among themselves.

Finally, it simply may be that people who share in an important activity such as decision making feel more "ownership" of the decision than when they are excluded from it. Commitment as a result of sharing in decision making has been consistently demonstrated by research, as seen in the classic work of Kurt Lewin. During World War II in the United States, there was a scarcity of good cuts of meat but an abundance of organ meats (liver, kidneys, and so forth). Lewin thought that households could be persuaded to buy organ meats if they participated in the decision to do so. He arranged to meet with two groups to test his belief.[100] One group was given an informative lecture on the value of using organ meats. The other group was given the same information, but members then were asked to discuss it among themselves and arrive at a group decision on whether to use such meat. It was found that the group decision resulted in a much higher rate of consumption (32 percent versus 3 percent). The implementation of the decision was more effective because the group had arrived at the decision. Members of the group were satisfied and committed to it because it was their decision, not someone else's.

Personal Growth

The opportunity for personal growth provided by participation in group decision making is a benefit that is often overlooked. Advancement in a career depends on the ability to learn new skills. One of the most important skills to be learned is how to make decisions, and participation in group decision making may be an ideal opportunity for individuals to acquire this skill.

What This Chapter Adds to Your Knowledge Portfolio

In this chapter, we have discussed individual and group decision making. We have covered the major steps in decision making, taking note of decision makers' tendencies to make satisficing rather than optimal decisions. In discussing individuals, we have emphasized decision styles, approaches to risk, cognitive biases, and moods and emotions. To be successful, an organization's associates and managers must understand these elements

THE STRATEGIC LENS

ecision making is the essence of management. The primary task of managers is to make decisions. Top-level managers decide what products and services to provide and what markets to enter. Middle managers decide where to locate facilities and how many products to manufacture. Lower-level managers decide what tasks should be assigned to particular associates and when certain associates should be laid off. Therefore, the quality of managers' decisions at all levels has a major effect on the success of an organization. If managers decide to enter the wrong markets or to hire less than the best applicants, the organization's performance is likely to suffer. If, however, they decide on excellent products for the market and hire outstanding associates and motivate them to achieve, the organization is likely to flourish. Thus, understanding how to make effective decisions is necessary to be a successful manager; and organizations must have managers who are effective decision makers if they are to achieve their goals.[101] All strategic decisions—down to decisions regarding what holidays to allow for associates—affect the organization's performance.

Critical Thinking Questions

1. You are a manager of a unit with 25 associates. You have just been informed that you must lay off 20 percent of the associates in your unit. What process will you follow to make the decision and to implement it?

2. If you made a decision that your manager told you was important for the organization and later you learned that you made an error in that decision, what actions would you take? Assume that others will not notice the error for some time.

3. You make decisions on a daily basis. Do you find it difficult to make decisions, especially those of importance? What can you do to improve your decision-making abilities?

---

of individual decision making. In discussing groups, we have focused on a set of problems that can affect group decision making and have described techniques for avoiding or overcoming these problems. Finally, we have discussed a model for assessing the extent to which associates should be involved in managerial decisions. In summary, we have made the following points:

- Decisions are choices. Decision making is a process involving several steps: defining the problem, identifying criteria for a solution, gathering information, evaluating alternatives, selecting the best alternative, and implementing the decision.
- Satisfactory rather than optimal decisions are common. Satisficing occurs because: (1) individuals cannot gather and process all information that might be relevant for a particular decision and (2) individuals have a tendency to stop searching after the first acceptable solution has been found.
- Decision styles represent preferred ways of gathering information and evaluating alternatives. For gathering information, associates and managers can have either a sensing style or an intuition style. With the sensing style, individuals focus on concrete information that is directly available through the five senses. They also tend to focus on rules and facts and are usually practical and realistic. They often are effective in jobs requiring routine decision making. With the intuition style, individuals dislike details and tend to focus on abstractions and figurative examples. They are often effective in jobs that require nonroutine decisions and creativity. For evaluating alternatives, associates and managers can have either a thinking or

❓ back to the knowledge objectives

1. What are the basic steps in decision making? How should a decision maker approach the problem-definition step? Why do decision makers usually fail to achieve optimal decisions?

2. What are the four Jungian decision styles, and how do they influence decisions and effectiveness in the workplace? Give an example of a person you know who had a decision style that did not seem to fit his or her role in an organization. This could be a person in an organization in which you have worked, or it could be a person from a school club or civic organization. What were the outcomes for this person in terms of satisfaction and performance? If you had been the individual's manager, how would you have managed the situation?

3. Describe a personal situation involving a reference point. Were you above or below your reference point? What was the effect on your behavior?

4. Which cognitive bias worries you the most, and why?

5. Compare the four primary pitfalls of group decision making. If you had to choose one, which would you prefer to deal with as a manager, and why?

6. What are the major group decision-making techniques? If you were dealing with diversity-based infighting, which of these techniques would you try first, and why?

7. What factors should a manager consider when deciding on the level of associate involvement in a decision? What shortcomings do you see in the Vroom–Yetton model?

a feeling style. With the thinking style, individuals focus on objective criteria and systematic analysis. With the feeling style, individuals use subjective approaches and are concerned with the emotional reactions of others. Although the thinking style is consistent with careful decision making, organizations need both thinkers and feelers to achieve a balance.

- Risk-taking propensity and reference points affect an individual's overall approach to risk. Risk-taking propensity relates to a person's willingness to take chances, whereas a reference point refers to a possible level of performance that a person uses to evaluate current standing. When a person has a strong propensity for risk and is below his reference point, risk taking is likely.

- Cognitive biases represent mental shortcuts that often cause problems. Four important biases are: confirmation bias (information confirming early beliefs and ideas is sought, but potentially disconfirming information is not sought), ease-of-recall bias (information that is easy to recall from memory is relied on too much), anchoring bias (the first piece of information encountered about a situation is emphasized too much), and the sunk-cost bias (past investments are weighted much too heavily).

- Moods and emotions are both part of the affective make-up of an individual. Moods correspond to general positive or negative feelings, while emotions correspond to more specific, discrete feelings such as anger and fear. Both moods and emotions can affect decision making.

- Several pitfalls are associated with group decision making. First, groupthink occurs when group members are too focused on consensus, particularly early in a decision process. This problem may occur because: (1) group members like one another and do not want to criticize each other's ideas, (2) group members have high regard for the group's collective wisdom and therefore yield to early ideas or the ideas of a leader, and (3) group members derive satisfaction from membership in a group that possesses a positive self-image and therefore they try to prevent the group from having any serious divisions. Second, the common information bias leads group members to unconsciously focus on information that is held by many members of the group while ignoring information held by only one or a few group members. Third, diversity-based infighting relates to disagreements being channeled in unproductive ways. Finally, the risky shift occurs when a group makes a more risky choice than individuals would have made (on average) when working separately.

- Several techniques exist to address the problems that may arise in group decision making. Brainstorming is a heavily used technique, but in its traditional form it fails in comparisons with individual brainstorming. Brain-writing and electronic brainstorming are useful alternatives. Nominal group technique, Delphi technique, dialectical inquiry, and devil's advocacy also can be very useful.

- Associates make many decisions in high-involvement firms. Managers address many other decisions but may involve associates in those decisions. The Vroom–Yetton model offers advice for assessing the proper level of involvement. To diagnose the situation, seven key questions are asked, and then a suggested approach is found through a decision tree.

- Groups have both advantages and disadvantages in decision making. One advantage is better quality, or at least a significant chance of better quality, particularly when complex decisions are being made. This advantage is based on the fact that groups bring more knowledge and facts to the decision and engage in a richer assessment of alternatives. Other advantages include better acceptance of decisions, greater satisfaction in the organization, and personal growth for group members. Time is one of several disadvantages associated with using a group to make a decision.

Thinking about Ethics

1. You are a senior vice president with responsibility for a major business division in a large company. The CEO has decided that the firm has to cut costs and that a large layoff of associates is necessary. He has asked you to decide how many associates should be laid off in your division. You know that the CEO wants a significant reduction in costs, which points to the large layoff. Of course, a layoff has a substantial effect on associates' lives. Should you recommend a large layoff to please the CEO or a smaller one, justifying a smaller layoff with plans to save money in other areas and increase sales? Explain your reasoning.

2. Suppose your manager continues to invest more money in a failing project in which he has already made a significant investment. Does this decision present ethical concerns? If so, describe these concerns. If not, explain. Would you report any concerns to his boss?

3. You are charged with the responsibility of deciding the location for the new manufacturing plant in your division. The current facility is old. In addition, the new facility will use advanced technology, but the workforce in the community does not have the skill levels needed to staff it. Thus, you will likely decide on a location in another state. You also must make decisions on when and how to close the current plant. This will mean laying off 300 associates currently working at the plant. How will you tell them that they will lose their jobs soon? Should you provide severance pay or other help? How will you make these decisions?

4. If an individual observes a group decision in which groupthink has occurred, does she have an obligation to report it to her superiors in order to prevent a serious error in the decision for the organization? Does she take any risks in taking such an action?

5. The risky shift occurs when a group makes a choice riskier than the choice group members would have made individually. Is it unethical for an individual group member to assume more risk when he is part of a group? What issues should be considered with regard to the level of risk involved in a group decision?

Key Terms

Human Resource Management Applications

The Human Resource Management (HRM) function is usually involved in strengthening decision making in the organization. More specifically, the HRM unit may offer training in the fundamentals of decision making, including tactics for problem definition, strategies for information search, and techniques for alternative generation and evaluation. The HRM unit also may offer training in and critiques of group decision making. Creating synergy in group decision making can be difficult, and HRM specialists tend to spend quite some time on these issues. Beyond hands-on training and interventions, they might develop survey items for merit reviews focused on how individuals behave and perform in a group decision situation.

---

building your human capital

Decision Style Assessment

Different people use different decision styles. Understanding how you approach the gathering of information and the evaluation of alternatives can help make you a better decision maker. Such an understanding clarifies your strengths and weaknesses, which better positions you to deal effectively with them. Below, we present an assessment tool for decision styles.

Instructions

In this assessment, you will read 24 phrases that describe people. Please use the rating scale below to indicate how accurately each phrase describes *you*. Rate yourself as you generally are now, not as you wish to be in the future. Rate yourself as you honestly see yourself. Please read each item carefully, and then circle the number that corresponds to your choice from the rating scale.

1	2	3	4	5
Not at all like me	Somewhat unlike me	Neither like nor unlike me	Somewhat like me	Very much like me

	1	2	3	4	5
1. Do things in a logical order	1	2	3	4	5
2. Do things that others find strange.	1	2	3	4	5
3. Come straight to the point.	1	2	3	4	5
4. Like to get lost in thought.	1	2	3	4	5
5. Sympathize with the homeless.	1	2	3	4	5
6. Do things by the book.	1	2	3	4	5

7. Believe in a logical answer for everything.	1	2	3	4	5
8. Enjoy wild flights of fantasy.	1	2	3	4	5
9. Am not as strict as I could be.	1	2	3	4	5
10. Seldom daydream.	1	2	3	4	5
11. Get a head start on others.	1	2	3	4	5
12. Love to daydream.	1	2	3	4	5
13. Let people pull my leg.	1	2	3	4	5
14. Seldom get lost in thought.	1	2	3	4	5
15. Dislike imperfect work.	1	2	3	4	5
16. Swim against the current.	1	2	3	4	5
17. Do things in a halfway manner.	1	2	3	4	5
18. Take deviant positions.	1	2	3	4	5
19. Let my attention wander off.	1	2	3	4	5
20. Do unexpected things.	1	2	3	4	5
21. Believe in an eye for an eye.	1	2	3	4	5
22. Have no sympathy for criminals.	1	2	3	4	5
23. Reason logically.	1	2	3	4	5
24. Believe that criminals should receive help rather than punishment.	1	2	3	4	5

Scoring Key for Decision Style Assessment

To create scores, combine your responses to the items as follows:

Sensing vs. intuition = (Item 2 + Item 4 + Item 8 + Item 12 + Item 16 + Item 18 + Item 20) + (18 − (Item 6 + Item 10 + Item 14))

Thinking vs. feeling = (Item 1 + Item 3 + Item 7 + Item 11 + Item 15 + Item 21 + Item 22 + Item 23) + (36 − (Item 5 + Item 9 + Item 13 + Item 17 + Item 19 + Item 24))

Scores for sensing versus intuition can range from 10 to 50. Scores below 30 suggest a sensing style, while scores of 30 and above suggest an intuition style. More extreme scores (very low or very high) indicate a stronger preference for one style over another. Scores from 26 to 34 suggest weaker preferences for a particular style.

Scores for thinking versus feeling can range from 14 to 70. Scores of 42 and above suggest a thinking style, while scores below 42 suggest a feeling style. More extreme scores (very low or very high) indicate a stronger preference for one style over another. Scores from 37 to 47 suggest weaker preferences for a particular style.

Source: International Personality Item Pool (2001). A Scientific Collaboration for the Development of Advanced Measures of Personality Traits and Other Individual Differences (http://ipip.ori.org).

an organizational behavior moment
Decision Making at a Nuclear Power Facility

Part A. Harry, the Reluctant Maintenance Man

Harry opened his lunch bucket and was disappointed to find two tuna fish sandwiches again. "Damn," he muttered to himself, "four days in a row." He would have to get on his daughter,

Susan, again. She graciously prepared his lunch most days but did not always provide the variety he liked. Of course, Susan would explain that she had other things to do besides providing him with a full lunch menu.

Across the cafeteria, Dan Thompson was eating with one of the design engineers, Marty Harris. Dan didn't like to talk shop while eating, but today had decided to continue a previous discussion over lunch. Dan was the supervisor of technical maintenance and had noticed that several of his people were reluctant to follow maintenance procedures. He had been told that the specifications were too complex to understand, that the procedures were often unnecessary, and that the plant engineers did not really appreciate maintenance problems. On the one hand, Dan realized that most of their complaints were just excuses for "doing things their own way." On the other hand, he didn't really know which procedures were important and which were not. That's why he had asked Marty to meet with him.

"Look, Dan," Marty was saying, "I know these procedures are complex. But damn it, nuclear power plants are complex—and potentially risky. Every specification, every procedure has a reason for being there. If your maintenance people ignore one procedure, they might get by with it and nothing happens. But one of them just might do it at the wrong time, and something could go haywire. You might explain that we have safety and cost to consider. If we lost expensive equipment, how'd they like to pay for it? Not much, I bet. If they lose a finger or get exposed to too much radiation, they wouldn't like that either. Now, just tell your people that the specifications and procedures, if followed, are the guarantee that things won't go wrong. They can count on it. If they take shortcuts, I won't guarantee a thing."

Dan nodded. This really wasn't what his maintenance staff wanted. They had hoped for a little flexibility, but he was going to have to tell them to follow the procedures. They wouldn't like it, but they would have to do it.

Later that afternoon, Dan met with his unit and relayed the instructions. He reminded them of the rules and disciplinary actions for not following procedures. At the end of the meeting, he couldn't decide whether it had done any good.

On Thursday, Harry noticed that he had been assigned the routinely scheduled maintenance on the three auxiliary feedwater (AFW) pumps. These pumps were normally used only for startup and shutdown and as emergency backup. When the main feedwater system malfunctioned, these pumps would activate to keep the system from "drying out." The procedure also specified that the pumps should be serviced and tested one at a time and that, at most, one pump should be out of service at a time.

"That's horse manure," Harry thought. "Takes three hours to service the pumps that way. I can do it in two if I shut 'em down together. Two's better than three. Those stupid design people have probably never tried to service one of these things."

Harry didn't bother to open the manual for pump servicing. He had serviced these pumps several times in the past and felt no need to do it from the book any longer. He reached over and shut off three discharge valves, set out his equipment, and got to work. Two hours later he was done. He packed up his tools and hurried to get home.

Part B. System Breakdown

Marv Bradbury was working the graveyard shift. Most technicians didn't like this shift, but Marv didn't mind it at all. In fact, he thrived on it. Over the past few months, he had discovered that he enjoyed the solitude. He also liked to sleep in the mornings. Many of his co-workers thought he was nuts, but he didn't mind. He especially liked the extra responsibility that the graveyard shift put on the technician position.

Marv's job in the nuclear generating plant was particularly important. His primary job was to monitor a series of dials and readouts in the control room. Most of the time, the job was a little monotonous because the system was so automatic. However, if the readings indicated some variance in the system, Marv's responsibilities were great. He would have to interpret the readings, diagnose the problem, and—if the automatic correcting system failed—initiate corrective actions. For two reasons, Marv never worried about the enormous responsibilities of his job. First, the system was fault-free and self-correcting. It was a good system with no weaknesses. Second, Marv was exceptionally qualified and had a great deal of understanding about the system. He always knew what he had to do in the event of a problem and was capable of doing it. Several years of training had not been wasted on him.

It was about 4 A.M. when he noticed the feedwater dial reading begin to move rapidly. Temperature in the system was increasing quickly. The readings alerted Marv that the main system was malfunctioning, and he knew just what to do. He glanced over to the AFW indicator lights to be sure they were activated. The lights switched on, and he knew everything was in order. Obviously, he would have to find the malfunction in the main system, but for the time being everything was okay. The temperature in the cooling system should drop back down to normal as the AFW pumps took over.

Suddenly, the indicator light for the pressurizer relief valve showed that it had opened. In rapid succession the high reactor tripped, and the hot leg temperature in the primary loop increased to about 607 degrees Fahrenheit.

Marv knew the system was in severe trouble and got on the phone to get help. Before he could get back, the high-pressure injection pump had started, and he could feel an unusual and threatening vibration that shouldn't be there. Indicators showed that the steam generators were drying out, but that didn't make sense—the auxiliaries were running. He knew that if they dried out, the temperature was really going to go up and that the core was going to be damaged. "Why the hell isn't that secondary loop running?" he yelled to himself.

It took eight minutes to get someone down to the auxiliary pump room and discover that the three valves were still closed. They opened the valves, but it was too late. Now no one seemed to know what to do.

Discussion Questions

1. Analyze the critical problem in Part A of the case. Did Dan handle it in the best way? What decision styles did he use?
2. In what important ways is Harry's behavior different from Marv's?
3. How might group decision making be applied at the end of Part B?
4. What alternatives do you see for reducing the possibility of a similar problem in the future?

---

team exercise

Group Decision Making in Practice

In this chapter, we discussed several techniques for group decision making. The purpose of this exercise is to demonstrate two of the techniques and to show how they facilitate group decision activities. The exercise should take about 40 minutes to complete.

Procedure

1. The instructor will assign you to either a group that will use brain-writing and dialectical inquiry (BD group) or a group that will engage in general discussion (GD group).
2. All groups will list as many ideas as possible concerning the general problem, "How can the college of business enhance its reputation among the business leaders in the regional business community?" This should take no more than 20 minutes. Each BD group will follow the rules of brain-writing to generate the list of ideas. Each GD group will discuss the issue in a group setting.
3. All groups will develop a final recommendation. Each BD group will follow the dialectical inquiry method. Each GD group will again engage in general discussion.
4. The instructor will lead a discussion about your experiences.

Endnotes

1. Hitt, M.A., Ireland, R.D., & Hoskisson, R.E. 2009. *Strategic management: Competitiveness and globalization* (8th ed.). Cincinnati, OH: South-Western.
2. Hitt, M.A., & Tyler, B.B. 1991. Strategic decision models: Integrating different perspectives. *Strategic Management Journal*, 12: 327–351.
3. Bazerman, M.H., & Moore, D.A. 2009. *Judgment in managerial decision making* (7th ed.). New York: John Wiley & Sons.
4. Hammond, J.S., Keeney, R.L., & Raiffa, H. 1999. *Smart choices: A practical guide to making better decisions*. Boston: Harvard Business School Press.
5. Ibid.
6. Based on Huber, G.P. 1980. *Managerial decision making*. Glenview, IL: Scott, Foresman.
7. Simon, H. 1957. *Administrative behavior*. New York: Macmillan.
8. Cecil, E.A., & Lundgren, E.F. 1975. An analysis of individual decision making behavior using a laboratory setting. *Academy of Management Journal*, 18: 600–604; Schwartz, B., Ward, A., Monterosso, J., Lyubomirsky, S., White, K., & Lehman, D.R. 2002. Maximizing versus satisficing: Happiness is a matter of choice. *Journal of Personality and Social Psychology*, 83: 1178–1197.
9. Most research based on Jung's ideas has used the Myers–Briggs Type Indicator (MBTI). For a review of relevant research in organizational behavior, see Gardner, W.L., & Martinko, M.J. 1996. Using the Myers-Briggs Type Indicator to study managers: A literature review and research agenda. *Journal of Management*, 22: 45–83. For a recent study based on the MBTI, see Davies, J., & Thomas H., 2009. What do business school deans do? Insights from a UK study. *Management Decision*, 47: 1396–1419; For supportive research on the internal consistency and test–retest reliability associated with the MBTI, see Capraro, R.M., & Capraro, M.M. 2002. Myers-Briggs Type Indicator score reliability across studies: A meta-analytic reliability generalization study. *Educational and Psychological Measurement*, 62: 590–602; and see Myers, I.B., & McCaulley, M.H. 1989. *Manual: A guide to the development and use of the Myers-Briggs Type Indicator*. Palo Alto, CA: Consulting Psychologists Press. For research on the construct validity associated with the MBTI, see Carlyn, M. 1977. An assessment of the Myers-Briggs Type Indicator. *Journal of Personality Assessment*, 41: 461–473; and see Thompson, B., & Borrello, G.M. 1986. Construct validity of the Myers-Briggs Type Indicator. *Educational and Psychological Measurement*, 60: 745–752. For

research on temporal stability, see Salter, D.W., Evans, N.J., & Forney, D.S. 2006. A longitudinal study of learning style preferences on the Myers-Briggs type indicator and learning style inventory. *Journal of College Student Development,* 47: 173–184; For criticism of the MBTI, see, for example, Pittenger, D.J. 1993. The utility of the Myers-Briggs Type Indicator. *Review of Educational Research,* 63: 467–488.

10. Gardner & Martinko, Using the Myers-Briggs Type Indicator to study managers; Jaffe, J. 1985. Of different minds. *Association Management,* 37 (October): 120–124.

11. Leibovich, M. 2000. Alter egos: Two sides of high-tech brain trust make up a powerful partnership. *The Washington Post,* December 31, p. A.01.

12. Gardner & Martinko, Using the Myers-Briggs Type Indicator to study managers; Jaffe, Of different minds.

13. Lyons, M. 1997. Presidential character revisited. *Political Psychology,* 18: 791–811.

14. Kiersey.com. 2007. The rationals. At http://keirsey.com/personality/nt.html.

15. Gardner & Martinko, Using the Myers-Briggs Type Indicator to study managers.

16. Rodgers, W. 1991. How do loan officers make their decisions about credit risks? A study of parallel distributed processing. *Journal of Economic Psychology,* 12: 243–365.

17. Stevens, G.A., & Burley, J. 2003. Piloting the rocket of radical innovation. *Research Technology Management,* 46: 16–25.

18. Gardner & Martinko, Using the Myers-Briggs Type Indicator to study managers; Jaffe, Of different minds.

19. Ibid.

20. McIntyre, R.P. 2000. Cognitive style as an antecedent to adaptiveness, customer orientation, and self-perceived selling performance. *Journal of Business and Psychology,* 15: 179–196.

21. Gardner & Martinko, Using the Myers-Briggs Type Indicator to study managers; Jaffe, Of different minds.

22. Jaffe, Of different minds.

23. See the following: Leibovich, Alter egos; Lohr, S. 2007. Preaching from the Ballmer pulpit. *The New York Times,* January 28, p. 3.1; Schlender, B. 2004. Ballmer unbound. *Fortune,* 149 (2): 117–124; Schlender, B. 2007. The wrath of Ballzilla. *Fortune,* 155 (8): 70.

24. Bazerman & Moore, *Judgment in managerial decision making;* Hammond, Keeney, & Raiffa, *Smart choices.*

25. Dahlback, O. 1990. Personality and risk taking. *Personality and Individual Differences,* 11: 1235–1242; Dahlback, O. 2003. A conflict theory of group risk taking. *Small Group Research,* 34: 251–289; March, J.G. 1994. *A primer on decision making.* New York: The Free Press.

26. Lashinsky, A. 2004. For Trump, fame is easier than fortune. *Fortune,* 149 (4): 38; Shawn, T. 1996. Donald Trump: An ex-loser is back in the money. *Fortune,* 134 (2): 86–88.

27. Taylor, R.N., & Dunnette, M.D. 1974. Influence of dogmatism, risk-taking propensity, and intelligence on decision-making strategies for a sample of industrial managers. *Journal of Applied Psychology,* 59: 420–423.

28. Jegers, M. 1991. Prospect theory and the risk-return relation. *Academy of Management Journal,* 34: 215–225; Kahneman, D., & Tversky, A. 1979. Prospect theory: An analysis of decision under risk. *Econometrica,* 47: 263–291; Larrick, R.P., Heath, C., Wu, G. 2009. Goal induced risk taking in negotiation and decision making. *Social Cognition,* 27: 342–364; Tversky, A., & Kahneman, D. 1986. Rational choice and the framing of decisions. *Journal of Business,* 59: 251–278; Wakker, P.P. 2003. The data of Levy and Levy (2002) "Prospect theory: Much ado about nothing?" actually support prospect theory. *Management Science,* 49: 979–981.

29. Smith, G., Levere, M., & Kurtzman, R. 2009. Poker player behavior after big wins and big loses. *Management Science,* 55: 1547–1555.

30. Simon, M., Houghton, S.M., & Savelli, S. 2003. Out of the frying pan...? Why small business managers introduce high-risk products. *Journal of Business Venturing,* 18: 419–440.

31. Tversky, A., & Kahneman, D. 1974. Judgment under uncertainty: Heuristics and biases. *Science,* 185: 1124–1131.

32. Bazerman & Moore, *Judgment in managerial decision making;* Hammond, Keeney, & Raiffa, *Smart choices;* Hogarth, R. 1980. *Judgment and choice.* New York: John Wiley & Sons.

33. Einhorn, H.J., & Hogarth, R.M. 1978. Confidence in judgment: Persistence in the illusion of validity. *Psychological Review,* 85: 395–416; Jones, M., & Sugden, R. 2001. Positive confirmation bias in the acquisition of information. *Theory and Decision,* 50: 59–99; Wason, P.C. 1960. On the failure to eliminate hypotheses in a conceptual task. *Quarterly Journal of Experimental Psychology,* 12: 129–140.

34. Pines, J.M. 2006. Profiles in patient safety: Confirmation bias in emergency medicine. *Academic Emergency Medicine,* 13: 90–94; Tschan, F, Semmer, N.K., Gurtner, A., Bizzari, L., Spychiger, M., Breuer, M., & Marsch, S.U. 2009. Explicit reasoning, confirmation bias, and illusory transactive memory. *Small Group Research,* 40: 271–300; Schawb, A.P. 2008. Putting cognitive psychology to work: Improving decision making in the medical encounter. *Social Science and Medicine,* 67: 1861–1869.

35. Ask, K., & Granhag, P.A. 2007. Motivational bias in criminal investigators' judgments of witness reliability. *Journal of Applied Social Psychology,* 37: 561–591; Ask, K., Rebelius, A., Granhag, P.A. 2008. The 'elasticity' of criminal evidence: A moderator of investigator bias. *Applied Cognitive Psychology,* 22: 1245–1259; O'Brien, B. 2009. Prime suspect: An examination of factors that aggravate and counteract confirmation bias in criminal investigations. *Psychology, Public Policy, and Law,* 15: 315–334.

36. Bazerman & Moore, *Judgment in managerial decision making.*

37. Time.com. 2004. Person of the year: Notorious leaders—Joseph Stalin. http://www.time.com/time/personoftheyear/archive/photohistory/stalin.html.

38. Bazerman & Moore, *Judgment in managerial decision making.*

39. Joyce, E.J., & Biddle, G.C. 1981. Anchoring and adjustment in probabilistic inference in auditing. *Journal of Accounting Research,* 19: 120–145.

40. Hammond, Keeney, & Raiffa, *Smart choices;* Roberto, M.A. 2002. Lessons from Everest: The interaction of cognitive bias, psychological safety, and system complexity. *California Management Review,* 45 (1): 136–158.

41. Coffey, M. 2006. The ones left behind. *Outside,* 31 (9): 80–82; Roberto, M.A. 2002. Lessons from Everest: The interaction of cognitive bias, psychological safety, and system complexity.

California Management Review, 45 (1): 136–158; Roberto, M.A., & Carioggia, G.M. 2003. *Mount Everest—1996.* Boston: Harvard Business School Publishing; Turner, P.S. 2003. Going up: Life in the death zone. *Odyssey,* 12 (8): 19.

42. Krakauer, J. 1997. *Into thin air: A personal account of the Mount Everest disaster.* New York: Villard Books.

43. Andrade, E.B., Ariely, D. 2009. The enduring impact of transient emotions on decision making. *Organizational Behavior and Human Decision Process,* 109: 1–8; Brief, A.P., & Weiss, H.M. 2002. Organizational behavior: Affect in the workplace. *Annual Review of Psychology,* 53: 279–307.

44. Bramesfeld, K.D., & Casper, K. 2008. Happily putting the pieces together: A test of two explanations for the effects of mood on group-level information processing. *British Journal of Social Psychology,* 47: 285–309; Cianci, A.M., & Bierstaker, J.L. 2009. The impact of positive and negative mood on the hypothesis generation and ethical judgments of auditors. *Auditing—A Journal of Practice & Theory,* 28 (2): 119–144; Englich, B., & Sodor, K. 2009. Moody experts—How mood and expertise influence judgmental anchoring. *Judgment and Decision Making,* 4: 41-50; Forgas, J.P. 2006. Affect in social thinking and behavior. New York: Psychology Press; Martin, L.L., & Clore, G.L. 2001. Theories of mood and cognition: A user's guidebook. Mahwah, NJ: Erlbaum.

45. Au K., Chan F., Wang D., & Vertinsky I. 2003. Mood in foreign exchange trading: Cognitive processes and performance. *Organizational Behavior and Human Decision Processes,* 91:322–338.

46. Chung, J.O.Y., Cohen, J.R., & Monroe, G.S. 2008. The effects of moods on auditors inventory valuation decisions. *Auditing—A Journal of Practice and Theory,* 27 (2): 137–159.

47. Zeelenberg, M. & Pieters, R. 2007. A theory of regret regulation 1.0. *Journal of Consumer Psychology,* 17: 3–18.

48. Ratner, R.K., & Herbst, K.C. 2005. When good decisions have bad outcomes: The impact of affect on switching behavior. *Organizational Behavior and Human Decision Processes,* 96: 23–37.

49. Reb, J., & Connolly, T. 2009. Myopic regret avoidance: Feedback avoidance and learning in repeated decision making. *Organizational Behavior and Human Decision Processes,* 109: 182–189;

50. Zeelenberg, & Pieters, A theory of regret regulation 1.0.

51. Lerner, J.S., & Tiedens, L.Z. 2006. Portrait of the angry decision maker: How appraisal tendencies shape anger's influence on cognition. *Journal of Behavioral Decision Making,* 19: 115–137.

52. Lerner, & Tiedens, Portrait of the angry decision maker: How appraisal tendencies shape anger's influence on cognition; Weber, E.U., & Johnson, E. J. 2009. Mindful judgment and decision making. *Annual Review of Psychology,* 60: 53–85.

53. Lerner, J.S., Gonzalez, R.M., Small, D.A, & Fischoff, B. 2003. Affects of fear and anger on perceived risks of terrorism: A natural field experiment. *Psychological Science,* 14: 144–150.

54. For an excellent example of social interactions in decision making, see Anderson, P.A. 1983. Decision making by objection and the Cuban missile crisis. *Administrative Science Quarterly,* 28: 201–222.

55. For the original formulation of groupthink, see the following: Janis, I.L. 1972. *Victims of groupthink: A psychological study of foreign-policy decisions and fiascos.* Boston: Houghton Mifflin; Janis, I.L. 1982. *Groupthink: Psychological studies of policy decisions and fiascos* (revised version of *Victims of groupthink).* Boston:

Houghton Mifflin. For later variants of the groupthink model, see the following examples: Hart, P.T. 1990. *Groupthink in government: A study of small groups and policy failure.* Amsterdam: Swets & Zeitlinger; Turner, P.E., & Pratkanis, A.R. 1998. A social identity maintenance model of groupthink. *Organizational Behavior and Human Decision Processes,* 73: 210–235; Whyte, G. 1998. Recasting Janis's groupthink model: The key role of collective efficacy in decision fiascos. *Organizational Behavior and Human Decision Processes,* 73: 163–184. For an interesting critique of some past groupthink research, see Henningsen, D.D., Henningsen, M.L.M., Eden, J., & Cruz, M.G. 2006. Examining the symptoms of groupthink and retrospective sensemaking. *Small Group Research,* 37: 36–64. Also see: Haslam, S.A., Ryan, M.K., Postmes, T., Spears, R., Jetten, J., & Webley, P. Sticking to our guns: Social identity as a basis for the maintenance of commitment to faltering organizational projects. *Journal of Organizational Behavior,* 27: 607–628.

56. See, for example: Callaway, M.R., & Esser, J.K. 1984. Groupthink: Effects of cohesiveness and problem-solving procedures on group decision making. *Social Behavior and Personality,* 12: 157–164; Courtright, J.A. 1978. A laboratory investigation of groupthink. *Communication Monographs,* 45: 229–246; Janis, *Victims of groupthink.*

57. Whyte, Recasting Janis's groupthink model.

58. See, for example, Turner & Pratkanis, A social identity maintenance model of groupthink; Turner, M.E., & Pratkanis, A.R. 1997. Mitigating groupthink by stimulating constructive conflict. In C. De Dreu, & E. Van de Vliert (Eds.), *Using Conflict in Organizations.* London: Sage.

59. Turner & Pratkanis, A social identity maintenance model of groupthink; Turner & Pratkanis, Mitigating groupthink by stimulating constructive conflict.

60. Stephens, J., & Behr, P. 2002. Enron's culture fed its demise: Groupthink promoted foolhardy risks. *The Washington Post,* January 27, p. A.01.

61. For summaries of published case research, see: Esser, J.K. 1998. Alive and well after 25 years: A review of groupthink research. *Organizational Behavior and Human Decision Processes,* 73: 116–141; Park, W. 2000. A comprehensive empirical investigation of the relationships among variables of the groupthink model. *Journal of Organizational Behavior,* 21: 873–887.

62. Janis, *Victims of groupthink;* Tetlock, P.E., Peterson, R.S., McGuire, C., Chang, S., & Field, P. 1992. Assessing political group dynamics: A test of the groupthink model. *Journal of Personality and Social Psychology,* 63: 403–425.

63. Moorehead, G., Ference, R., & Neck, C.P. 1991. Group decision fiascos continue: Space Shuttle *Challenger* and revised groupthink framework. *Human Relations,* 44: 539–550.

64. Chisson, E.J. 1994. *The Hubble wars.* New York: Harper-Perennial.

65. Horton, T.R. 2002. Groupthink in the boardroom. *Directors and Boards,* 26(2): 9; Hymowitz, C. 2003. Corporate governance: What's your solution? *Wall Street Journal,* February 24: R8.

66. Manz, C.C., & Sims, H.P. 1982. The potential for "groupthink" in autonomous work groups. *Human Relations,* 35: 773–784.

67. Kim, P.H. 1997. When what you know can hurt you: A study of experiential effects on group discussion and performance.

Organizational Behavior and Human Decision Processes, 69: 165–177; Stasser, G., & Titus, W. 1985. Pooling of unshared information in group decision making: Biased information sampling during discussion. *Journal of Personality and Social Psychology,* 48: 1467–1478.

68. Hunton, J.E. 2001. Mitigating the common information sampling bias inherent in small-group discussion. *Behavioral Research in Accounting,* 13: 171–194.

69. De Dreu, C.K.W., & Weingart, L.R. 2003. Task versus relationship conflict, team performance, and team member satisfaction: A meta-analysis. *Journal of Applied Psychology,* 88: 741–749; Miller, C.C., Burke, L.M., & Glick, W.H. 1998. Cognitive diversity among upper-echelon executives: Implications for strategic decision processes. *Strategic Management Journal,* 19: 39–58.

70. Stoner, J. 1968. Risky and cautious shifts in group decisions: The influence of widely held values. *Journal of Experimental Social Psychology,* 4: 442–459.

71. See, for example: Dahlback, A conflict theory of group risk taking.

72. Dahlback, A conflict theory of group risk taking; Mynatt, C., & Sherman, S.J. 1975. Responsibility attribution in groups and individuals: A direct test of the diffusion of responsibility hypothesis. *Journal of Personality and Social Psychology,* 32: 1111–1118; Wallach, M.A., Kogan, N., & Bem, D.J. 1964. Diffusion of responsibility and level of risk taking in groups. *Journal of Abnormal and Social Psychology,* 68: 263–274.

73. Osborn, A.F. 1957. *Applied imagination* (revised edition). New York: Scribner.

74. Thompson, L. 2003. Improving the creativity of organizational work groups. *Academy of Management Executive,* 17 (1): 96–109.

75. Bouchard, T. 1971. Whatever happened to brainstorming? *Journal of Creative Behavior,* 5: 182–189.

76. Mullen, B., Johnson, C., & Salas, E. 1991. Productivity loss in brainstorming groups: A meta-analytic integration. *Basic and Applied Social Psychology,* 12: 3–23; Stroebe, W., & Nijstad, B.A. 2004. Why brainstorming in groups impairs creativity: A cognitive theory of productivity losses in brainstorming groups. *Psychologische Rundschau,* 55: 2–10; Taylor, D.W., Berry, P.C., & Block, C.H. 1958. Does group participation when using brainstorming facilitate or inhibit creative thinking? *Administrative Science Quarterly,* 3: 23–47.

77. Diehl, M., & Stroebe, W. 1987. Productivity loss in brainstorming groups: Toward a solution of a riddle. *Journal of Personality and Social Psychology,* 53: 497–509.

78. Camacho, L.M., & Paulus, P.B. 1995. The role of social anxiousness in group brainstorming. *Journal of Personality and Social Psychology,* 68: 1071–1080; Thompson, Improving the creativity of organizational workgroups.

79. Thompson, Improving the creativity of organizational workgroups.

80. Ibid. Also see: Heslin, P.A. 2009. Better than brainstorming? Potential contextual boundary conditions to brainwriting for idea generation in organizations. *Journal of Occupational and Organizational Psychology,* 82: 129–145.

81. Ibid. Also see: DeRosa, D.M., Smith, C.L., & Hantula, D.A. 2007. The medium matters: Mining the long-promised merit of group interaction in creative idea generation tasks in a meta-analysis of the electronic group brainstorming literature. *Computers in Human Behavior,* 23: 1549–1581; Lynch, A.L., Murthy, U.S., & Engle, T.J. 2009. Fraud brainstorming using computer-mediated communication: The effects of brainstorming technique and facilitation. *The Accounting Review,* 84: 1209–1232.

82. Van de Ven, A., & Delbecq, A. 1974. The effectiveness of nominal, Delphi, and interacting group decision processes. *Academy of Management Journal,* 17: 605–621.

83. For supporting evidence, see: Gustafson, D.H., Shukla, R., Delbecq, A., & Walster, W. 1973. A comparative study in subjective likelihood estimates made by individuals, interacting groups, Delphi groups, and nominal groups. *Organizational Behavior and Human Performance,* 9: 280–291. Also see: Asmus, C.L., & James, K. 2005. Nominal group technique, social loafing, and group creative project quality. *Creativity Research Journal,* 17: 349–354.

84. Van de Ven & Delbecq, The effectiveness of nominal, Delphi, and interacting group decision processes.

85. See, for example, Landeta, J. 2006. Current validity of the Delphi method in social sciences. *Technology Forecasting & Social Change,* 73: 467–482; Van de Ven & Delbecq, The effectiveness of nominal, Delphi, and interacting group decision processes.

86. For early research on these two techniques, see the following: Mason, R. 1969. A dialectical approach to strategic planning. *Management Science,* 15: B403–B411; Mason, R.O., & Mitroff, I.I. 1981. *Challenging strategic planning assumptions,* New York: Wiley; Schweiger, D.M., Sandberg, W.R., & Ragan, J.W. 1986. Group approaches for improving strategic decision making: A comparative analysis of dialectical inquiry, devil's advocacy, and consensus. *Academy of Management Journal,* 29: 51–71.

87. Cosier, R.A. 1983. Methods for improving the strategic decision: Dialectic versus the devil's advocate. *Strategic Management Journal,* 4: 79–84; Mitroff, I.I. 1982. Dialectic squared: A fundamental difference in perception of the meanings of some key concepts in social science. *Decision Sciences,* 13: 222–224.

88. Schwenk, C. 1989. A meta-analysis on the comparative effectiveness of devil's advocacy and dialectical inquiry. *Strategic Management Journal,* 10: 303–306; Valacich, J.S., & Schwenk, C. 1995. Structuring conflict in individual, face-to-face, and computer-mediated group decision making: Carping versus objective devil's advocacy. *Decision Sciences,* 26: 369–393.

89. Schweiger, Sandberg, & Ragan, Group approaches for improving strategic decision making.

90. Vroom, V.H., & Yetton, P.W. 1973. *Leadership and decision making.* Pittsburgh, PA: University of Pittsburgh Press.

91. Ibid.

92. Field, R.H.G. 1982. A test of the Vroom-Yetton normative model of leadership. *Journal of Applied Psychology,* 67: 523–532; Field, R.H.G., & House, R.J. 1990. A test of the Vroom-Yetton model using manager and subordinate reports. *Journal of Applied Psychology,* 75: 362–366; Tjosvold, D., Wedley, W.C., & Field, R.H.G. 1986. Constructive controversy, the Vroom–Yetton model, and managerial decision-making. *Journal of Occupational Behaviour,* 7: 125–138; Vroom, V.H., & Jago, A.G. 1978. On the validity of the Vroom-Yetton Model. *Journal of Applied Psychology,* 69: 151–162; Vroom, V.H., & Jago, A.G. 2007. The role of the situation in leadership. *American Psychologist,* 62: 17-24.

93. Hitt, Ireland, & Hoskisson, *Strategic management.*

94. For discussions of consensus vs. majority rule, see: Hare, A.P. 1976. *Handbook of small group research* (2nd ed.). New York: Free Press; Miller, C.E. 1989. The social psychological effects of group decision rules. In P.B. Paulus (Ed.), *Psychology of Group Influence.* Hillsdale, NJ: Erlbaum; Mohammed, S., & Ringseis, E. 2001. Cognitive diversity and consensus in group decision making: The role of inputs, processes, and outcomes. *Organizational Behavior and Human Decision Processes,* 85: 310–335.

95. Mohammed & Ringseis, Cognitive diversity and consensus in group decision making.

96. Ibid.

97. Maier, N.R.F. 1967. Assets and liabilities in group problem solving: The need for an integrative function. *Psychological Review,* 74: 239–249.

98. Schmidt, J.B., Montoya-Weiss, M.M., & Massey, A.P. 2001. New product development decision-making effectiveness: Comparing individuals, face-to-face teams, and virtual teams. *Decision Sciences,* 32: 575–600.

99. Maier, Assets and liabilities in group problem solving.

100. Weiner, B. 1977. *Discovering psychology.* Chicago: Science Research Associates.

101. For an interesting history of the study of decision making, see: Buchanan, L., & O'Connell, A. 2006. A brief history of decision making. *Harvard Business Review,* 84 (1): 32-41.

groups and teams

exploring behavior in action

Teamwork at Starbucks

Although a few setbacks have occurred in recent years, Starbucks remains one of the most successful business stories in history. The company's growth and financial success have been nothing short of phenomenal. As of early 2010, Starbucks has more than 16,000 retail outlets in more than 45 countries. For the 2009 fiscal year, sales were $9.7 billion. In the most recent quarter for which data are available, the company's profits soared as the global recession eased. In addition to its retail coffee shops and kiosks, with which you are probably familiar, the company has entered several successful joint ventures and partnerships. For example, a partnership with PepsiCo produces the bottled coffee drink Frappuccino, and a joint venture with Unilever produces Starbucks coffee-flavored ice cream, which is sold in grocery stores. A partnership with Capitol Records resulted in a series of Starbucks jazz CDs. Furthermore, Starbucks has partnered with other companies, including United Airlines and Barnes & Noble Bookstores—all of which exclusively serve or sell Starbucks coffee. The list of industry awards is also impressive, including national and international awards for best management, humanitarian efforts, brand quality, and workplace experiences.

Much has been written about the sources of success at Starbucks. Several factors have been singled out for attention—effective branding, superior product quality, product innovation, superior customer service, innovative human resource practices, effective real estate strategies, and exceptional corporate social responsibility, for example. However, to anyone who has ever visited a Starbucks, another factor for its success is apparent—the teamwork of Starbucks "baristas" (the associates who take orders and who make and serve coffee and food).

knowledge objectives

After reading this chapter, you should be able to:

1. Describe the nature of groups and teams and distinguish among different types of teams.
2. Explain the criteria used to evaluate team effectiveness.
3. Discuss how various aspects of team composition influence team effectiveness.
4. Understand how structural components of teams can influence performance.
5. Explain how various team processes influence team performance.
6. Describe how teams develop over time.
7. Know what organizations can do to encourage and support effective teamwork.
8. Understand the roles of a team leader.

Watching the baristas at work in a busy Starbucks can be like watching a well-choreographed ballet. Baristas are making elaborate coffee drinks, serving up dessert, taking orders at record speed, answering customer questions, helping each other out when needed, and seemingly enjoying their work. Starbucks is legendary for its customer service, and teamwork is an important part of how this service is delivered. The extent to which baristas work together as a team, then, is an important aspect of Starbucks' success. And baristas are not only part of their shop's team—they are also part of the corporate Starbucks team.

Starbucks fosters a teamwork-based culture in many ways. It begins by hiring baristas who have the desires and skills to be successful team players. For potential job applicants, Starbucks puts it this way:

©Kevin P. Casey/©AP/Wide World Photos

> What's it like to work at Starbucks? We call each other "partners." We understand, respect, appreciate and include different people. We hear each partner's voice. And we learn from each other.

Training is an important element in this culture as well. Within their first month, all baristas receive many hours of training (most other coffee shops barely train their counter staff). New baristas are trained in the exact methods for making Starbucks drinks, care and maintenance of machinery, and customer service practices. In addition, they receive training in how to interact with each other. One of the guiding principles in Starbucks' mission statement involves providing a great work environment where people treat each other with respect and dignity. Historically, all baristas have been trained in the "Star Skills": (1) maintain and enhance (others') self-esteem; (2) listen and acknowledge; and (3) ask questions.

Another factor leading to increased teamwork and commitment to the company is Starbucks' generous benefits package. Baristas receive higher pay, better health benefits, and more vacation time than the industry norm. Even part-time employees receive benefits. Furthermore, Starbucks has a stock option plan (the Bean Stock plan) in which baristas can participate if they wish to.

Yet another way in which Starbucks fosters teamwork is by providing numerous communication channels so that every barista can communicate directly with headquarters. These communication channels include e-mail, suggestion cards, and regular forums with executives.

These are some of the most telling signs of Starbucks' desire to create a teamwork culture.

Sources: M. Gunther. 2006. "How UPS, Starbucks, Disney Do Good," *Fortune,* Feb. 25, at http://money.cnn.com/2006/02/23/news/companies/mostadmired_fortune_responsible/index.htm; D. Kesmodel. 2009. "Earnings: Starbucks Says Demand Perking Up: Coffee Retailer Reports Surge in Earnings as Cost Cuts Pay Off, Raises Outlook for 2010," *Wall Street Journal,* Nov. 6, p. B.5; Starbucks, "Our Starbucks Mission," 2010, at http://www.starbucks.com/mission/default.asp; Starbucks, "Starbucks Posts Strong Fourth Quarter and Fiscal 2009 Results," 2009, at http://investor.starbucks.com; Starbucks, "The Partner Experience," 2010, at http://www.starbucks.com/aboutus/jobcenter_partner_experience.asp; A.A. Thompson, J.E. Gamble, & A.J. Strickland. 2006. *Strategy: Winning in the Marketplace* (Chicago: McGraw-Hill); G. Weber. 2005. "Preserving Starbucks Counter Culture," *Workforce Management,* Feb., pp. 28–34

the strategic importance of Groups and Teams

U.S. organizations, following popular practice in other countries such as Japan, have adopted teamwork as a common way of doing work. The focus on teams in U.S. organizations developed during the 1980s. By 1993, 91 percent of *Fortune* 1000 companies used work teams, and 68 percent used self-managed work teams.[1] The presence of teamwork in business has only become greater since then. Indeed, after complaints from recruiters and advice from executives concerning the lack of interpersonal skills and teamwork skills of new graduates, many elite MBA programs have added teamwork training to the MBA curricula.[2]

Effective work teams have a synergistic effect on performance. **Synergy** means that the total output of a team is greater than the output that would result from adding together the outputs of the individual members working alone. Working in a team can produce synergy for several reasons. Team members are given more responsibility and autonomy; thus, they are empowered to do their jobs. Greater empowerment can produce higher motivation and identification with the organization.[3] Work teams also allow employees to develop new skills that can increase their motivation and satisfaction.[4] In addition,

work teams can provide a means for employees to be integrated with higher levels in the organization, thereby aligning individual goals with the organization's strategy.[5] Finally, work teams can promote creativity, flexibility, and quick responses to customer needs.[6] These outcomes can be seen in the teams of baristas that work in Starbucks' stores.

Organizations have reported a great deal of success with work teams. Studies have documented tenfold reductions in error rates and quality problems, product-to-market cycles cut in half, and 90 percent reductions in response times to problems.[7] Extremely effective teams, often known as *high-performance work teams*, are able to achieve extraordinary results. A team of this kind seems to act as a whole rather than as a collection of individuals.[8]

In many companies, the organization's strategy is developed by a team of senior managers. Research has shown that heterogeneous teams that work together effectively develop strategies that lead to higher organizational performance.[9] Heterogeneity of backgrounds and experiences among team members has been shown to produce more and diverse ideas, helping to resolve complex problems more effectively. The

quality of strategic decisions made by the management team affects the organization's ability to innovate and to create strategic change. Teams of top executives are used to make strategic decisions because of the complexity and importance of such decisions.[10] The senior management team at Starbucks, for example, made the strategic decisions to develop new products (such as Cinnamon Dolce Latte) and to enter new international markets (such as Russia and India). To make such important decisions, the team must work together effectively.

For the reasons noted above, the development and management of teams is highly critical to organizational performance. However, simply having people work together as a team does not guarantee positive outcomes. Teams must be effectively composed, structured, developed, managed, and supported in order to become high-performance work teams. In this chapter, we begin by exploring the nature of teams and their effectiveness. We then examine the factors that affect team performance. Next, we describe how teams develop and change overtime. Finally, we explain how to develop an effective team and how to manage teams.

The Nature of Groups and Teams

synergy
An effect wherein the total output of a team is greater than the combined outputs of individual members working alone.

For over 100 years, social science research has focused on studying collections of people interacting together. It is often said that human beings are social animals and that we seek out interactions with others. Organizations provide many opportunities for such interactions. Business transactions such as planning and coordinating require that individuals interact. Also, because associates are assigned to work units on the basis of their work skills and backgrounds, they are likely to find others with whom they share common interests.

Furthermore, organizations frequently structure work so that jobs are done by associates working together. Two terms are used to define these clusters of associates: *groups* and *teams*.

Groups and Teams Defined

There are many definitions for both *group and team,* with most researchers using the terms interchangeably.[11] For our purposes, the term **group** can be defined in very general terms as "two or more interdependent individuals who influence one another through social interaction."[12] In this chapter, however, our focus is more specific: we are mainly interested in teams—groups of individuals working toward specific goals or outcomes.[13] The common elements in the definition of a **team** are as follows:[14]

1. Two or more people,
2. with work roles that require them to be interdependent,
3. who operate within a larger social system (the organization),
4. performing tasks relevant to the organization's mission,
5. with consequences that affect others inside and outside the organization,
6. and who have membership that is identifiable to those who are in the team and to those who are not in the team.

This definition helps us understand what a team is and is not. For example, mere assemblies of people are not teams. A crowd watching a parade is not a team because the people have little, if any, interaction, nor are they recognized as a team. A collection of people who interact with and influence each other, such as a sorority or a book club, can be thought of as a general group. When the goals of a group become more specific, such as winning a game, we refer to the group as a team (baseball team, project team, senior management team, and so forth). The baristas at Starbucks work as a team because they work interdependently toward the goal of serving customers, are recognized by others as a team, and most likely perceive themselves as a team.

Several types of groups and teams exist within organizations that differ in important ways. These differences may affect how the group or team is formed, what values and attitudes are developed, and what behaviors result. In the discussion that follows, we describe various types of groups and teams.

Formal and Informal Groups

Both formal and informal groups exist within organizations. People become members of **formal groups** because they are assigned to them. Thus, in our terminology, teams are formal groups. To complete their tasks, members of these teams must interact. They often share similar task activities, have complementary skills, and work toward the same assigned goals. They recognize that they are part of the team, and the team exists as long as the task goals remain.[15] Examples of such teams are a faculty department, a highway crew, a small unit of production workers in an aircraft plant, and an assigned project team for class.

Many groups that are not formally created by management arise spontaneously as individuals find others in the organization with whom they wish to interact. These **informal groups** form because their members share interests, values, or identities. Membership in an informal group depends on voluntary commitment. Members are not assigned, and they may or may not share common tasks or task goals. They do,

group
Two or more interdependent individuals who influence one another through social interaction.

team
Two or more people with work roles that require them to be interdependent, who operate within a larger social system (the organization), performing tasks relevant to the organization's mission, with consequences that affect others inside and outside the organization, and who have membership that is identifiable to those on the team and those not on the team.

formal groups
Groups to which members are formally assigned.

informal groups
Groups formed spontaneously by people who share interests, values, or identities.

however, share other social values and attitudes, and their group goals are often related to individual social needs. For example, groups of employees may gather to go to Happy Hour on Friday afternoons or to play in a fantasy football league. The informal group may exist regardless of any formal purpose, and it endures as long as social satisfaction is achieved. Because of their various characteristics, informal groups are not considered teams.

Identity Groups

identity groups
Groups based on the social identities of members.

In Chapter 2, we discussed the importance of social identity. Associates often form groups based on their social identities, such as gender identity, racial identity, or religious identity. These groups are referred to as **identity groups**.[16] Individuals belong to many identity groups that are not based on membership in the work organization (e.g., Hispanic, female, Catholic). Thus, any member of a team is also a member of several identity groups. Effective team performance can be more difficult to achieve when team members belong to different identity groups or when their identification with these groups conflicts with the goals and objectives of the team.[17] For example, suppose most of the members of a team are white North Americans who prefer a decision-making process in which all arguments are open and group members are encouraged to debate and question each other publicly. Some of the team members, however, identify with the Japanese culture, in which publicly contradicting someone is viewed as impolite. These team members will likely find the team's decision-making process to be uncomfortable and disrespectful, and they may not participate. Thus, team functioning will be impaired.

Virtual Teams

virtual teams
Teams in which members work together but are separated by time, distance, or organizational structure.

First discussed in Chapter 3, a **virtual team** is made up of associates who work together as a team but are separated by time, distance, or organizational structure.[18] Exhibit 11-1 displays common tools through which virtual teams operate. The benefits of virtual

---

EXHIBIT 11-1 Tools Commonly Used by Virtual Teams

Audio conferencing (traditional or Internet-based)
Videoconferencing (room to room from two or three locations or via dispersed micro-electronic equipment)
Online chat rooms
E-mail and online bulletin boards
Keypad voting systems
Project-management software
Instant messaging
Messaging boards
Web conferencing
Blogs and wiki sites

Sources: D. Mittleman, & R.O. Briggs. 1999. "Communicating Technologies for Traditional and Virtual Teams." In E. Sundstrom, & Associates (Eds.), *Supporting Work Team Effectiveness*, pp. 246–270; W. Combs, & S. Peacocke. 2007. "Leading Virtual Teams," *T&D*, 61, no. 2, pp. 27–28; B. Williamson. 2009. "Managing at a Distance," *BusinessWeek*, July 27, p. 64.

teams are obvious—they allow people who are physically separated to work together. Virtual teams, however, have been shown to be less effective than face-to-face teams in many instances.[19]

There are several reasons for this outcome. First, because fewer opportunities exist for informal discussions, trust can be slower to develop among virtual team members. Second, virtual team members rely on communication channels that are less rich than face-to-face interactions. (Chapter 9 discussed communication richness.) Consequently, misunderstandings are more likely to occur among team members. Third, it is more difficult for virtual teams to develop behavioral norms. Finally, it is easier for some members to be free riders (those who do not contribute effectively to the team's work), thereby causing frustration among other team members. Thus, it is very important that virtual teams be managed well, because they have a tendency to fall apart if care is not taken to maintain the team.

Research has shown that the effectiveness of virtual teams increases as a function of the number of face-to-face meetings members actually have.[20] Also, virtual teams in which members have a great deal of empowerment (authority to make their own decisions and act without supervision) are more effective than virtual teams with little empowerment. The impact of empowerment becomes even more important when virtual teams have little face-to-face interaction.[21] Finally, virtual teams are more effective when led by transformational leaders.[22] In fact, transformational leadership (involving vision, attention to collective interests, and lofty aspirations) seems to be more important for the success of virtual teams than for the success of face-to-face teams.[23] This type of leadership facilitates the development of trust, positive team norms, and commitment to the team and team task, each of which is particularly difficult in virtual situations.

When implemented properly, virtual teams can increase productivity and save companies millions of dollars.[24] For example, IBM has shortened its project completion times and reduced person-hours with virtual teams. Marriott Corporation has saved millions of dollars by reducing the number of person-hours required for certain tasks. By using same-time, different-place technology, Hewlett-Packard has connected research and development teams in California, Colorado, Japan, Germany, and France so that all teams can participate in the same presentation.

Functional Teams

Teams can be distinguished by the type of work they do and the purpose they serve. Types of functional teams include the following:[25]

- *Production teams*—groups of associates who produce tangible products (e.g., automotive assemblers or a team of restaurant chefs)
- *Service teams*—groups of associates who engage in repeated transactions with customers (e.g., sales teams or Starbucks baristas)
- *Management teams*—groups of managers who coordinate the activities of their respective units (e.g., senior management teams)
- *Project teams*—groups of associates (often from different functional areas or organizational units) who temporarily serve as teams to complete a specific project (e.g., new-product development teams)
- *Advisory teams*—groups of associates formed to advise the organization on certain issues (e.g., disability groups who advise on the technical aspects of various products)

Self-Managing Teams

Self-managing teams have a great deal of autonomy and control over the work they do.[26] Usually self-managing teams are responsible for completing a whole piece of work, an entire project, or a significant portion of a product or service delivery process. For example, rather than working only on one part of an automobile, a self-managing auto-assembly team might build the whole automobile or a significant portion of it. Although a self-managing team typically has formal supervision from above, the supervisor's role is to facilitate team performance and member involvement rather than to direct the team. The members of the team make important decisions that in other types of teams are made by the supervisor, such as assigning members to specific tasks, setting team performance goals, and even deciding the team's pay structure. Team members are also held more accountable for team performance.

Self-managed work teams can lead to many benefits, including more satisfaction for workers, lower turnover and absenteeism, increased productivity, and higher-quality work.[27] These benefits result because members of self-managed work teams are more engaged in their work and more committed to the team. However, the effectiveness of self-managed teams can be thwarted by several factors, including leaders who are too autocratic.[28]

A well-known example of a self-managed work team is the Orpheus Chamber Orchestra, the orchestra without a conductor. Orpheus musicians collaborate to take on leadership roles usually reserved for the conductor. The orchestra is incredibly flexible, with members moving into and out of roles as the need arises. As a result of this collaboration and flexibility, orchestra members always give their best performance, rather than acting passively as they might when working under the direction of a conductor. The Orpheus Chamber Orchestra is more successful (sells more tickets, takes in more money, and receives more positive reviews) and has lower turnover and greater member loyalty than many other orchestras.[29]

In this chapter's first *Experiencing Organizational Behavior* feature, teams at McKinsey & Company are highlighted. Unlike the barista teams at Starbucks, the consulting teams at McKinsey are temporary project teams. While both the barista and consulting teams operate predominantly in a face-to-face mode, there is a substantial amount of virtual work for McKinsey teams as they access supporting resources from offices dispersed globally (and some virtual work is also carried out between/among team members). Further, both sets of teams experience empowerment, although in McKinsey's case the teams are more clearly in the self-managing category. For McKinsey, there is also a great deal of complexity. This is often the case with project teams inside and outside consulting. Project teams typically have diverse members who must bridge differences against the backdrop of a temporary existence. A well-developed, time-tested and globally deployed approach to project work helps McKinsey address the inherent difficulties.

Team Effectiveness

How do we know when a team is effective? When a team reaches its performance goals, does this alone mean it was effective? Consider a class project in which a team turns in one report and everyone on the team receives the same grade. If the project earns an A, can we say the team was effective? What if only one person on the team did all the work and

Teams at McKinsey & Company

©JEON HEON-KYUN/epa/Corbis

cKinsey & Company is one of the most revered consulting firms in the world. Through 90 offices in more than 50 countries, it offers a broad array of services in areas such as competitive strategy, organizational behavior and change, risk management, and corporate finance. Its mission is simple:

To help leaders make distinctive, lasting, and substantial improvements in performance, and constantly build a great firm that attracts, develops, excites, and retains exceptional people.

Similar to other major firms in the consulting industry, McKinsey & Company relies on project teams to accomplish its objectives. These teams are small, usually comprising fewer than 10 members. They are also temporary. Once a project has been completed, the team disbands and its members join new teams working with different clients. Each team generally has a mix of tenures represented, including a partner, an associate partner, an engagement manager, several associates, and one or more business analysts. Members of the team are drawn from more than 7,000 individuals positioned globally.

In addition to these core elements, McKinsey emphasizes dissent within its teams. If anyone on a team believes that inappropriate choices are being made, that individual has a responsibility to speak up. The firm says this to candidates for positions:

All McKinsey consultants are obligated to dissent if they believe something is incorrect or not in the best interests of the client. Everyone's opinion counts. While you might be hesitant to disagree with the team's most senior member or the client, you're expected to share your point of view.

In a typical work week, team members fly on Monday morning or Sunday evening to the client's site. During the week, individuals complete technical tasks working alone; create presentation materials alone or with others; join face-to-face team meetings; and participate in face-to-face meetings with representatives of the client. They use teleconferences, video conferences, and e-mail exchanges to access supporting resources at various McKinsey offices. Late nights are common. Lunches and dinners often involve substantive tasks or socializing with the client. On Friday afternoon or evening, team members fly home.

Clearly, the life of a consultant is complex and dynamic. Consultants must work effectively with teammates who are diverse in many ways, including their areas of expertise, national origins, levels in the firm, religions, races, and genders. They must travel constantly and work long hours. They must move to a newly forming team every two to six months. And they must live up to very high performance expectations. To ensure that consultants and their teams perform well and avoid undue stress, McKinsey & Company emphasizes the fundamentals that we would expect: sophisticated selection systems for new hires, proper training, sound information technology, and effective leadership. Perhaps more important than these tactics, McKinsey emphasizes consistent consulting methodologies at each of the more than 90 offices worldwide. This is difficult but crucial, as it allows each consultant who joins a new project team to know what to expect from others and to provide what others expect from him (recall that team members for a project are drawn from various locations around the world). The familiarity and predictability created by this approach adds structure to an otherwise complex and dynamic situation.

Also, McKinsey has addressed a history of stress and voluntary turnover by reducing travel to some degree and by generally being more attentive to work–life balance. These efforts have paid off, but stress and turnover remain issues in the consulting industry.

To further experience the complex McKinsey team environment, take the company's leadership test at http://www.mckinsey.com/locations/swiss/career/team_leader/index.asp.

Sources: H. Coster. 2007. "Baby Please Don't Go," *Forbes*, Oct. 15, p. 86; McKinsey & Company, "About Us: What We Believe," 2010, at http://www.mckinsey.com/aboutus/whatwebelieve/index.asp; McKinsey & Company, "McKinsey Careers: Teams," 2010, at http://www.mckinsey.com/careers/what_will_it_be_like_if_i_join/the_day_to_day/teams.aspx; McKinsey & Company, "McKinsey Careers: The Day-to-Day," 2010, at http://www.mckinsey.com/careers/what_will_it_be_like_if_i_join/the_day_to_day.aspx; A. Taylor. 1998. "Consultants Have a Big People Problem," *Fortune*, April 13, pp. 162–166.

everyone else loafed? The person who did all the work is likely to be angry and dissatisfied, while the others have learned nothing and walk away with the idea that it pays to loaf, especially when they have a conscientious teammate. In this case, it would have been better to have individuals work separately, even though the final product was successful. Because outcome by itself is not enough, team effectiveness is measured on several dimensions: knowledge criteria, affective criteria, and outcome criteria. A final consideration in team effectiveness is whether a team is even needed to perform the work, or whether the work is best performed by individuals.

Knowledge Criteria

Knowledge criteria reflect the degree to which the team continually increases its performance capabilities.[30] Teams are more effective when team members share their knowledge with one another and develop a collective understanding of the team's task, tools and equipment, and processes, as well as members' characteristics.[31] This shared knowledge is referred to as the team's *mental model*.[32] Shared mental models allow team members to have common expectations and agreed-upon courses of action, improve information processing and decision making, and facilitate problem solving.[33] Another knowledge-based criterion for team effectiveness is team learning—the ability of the team as a whole to learn new skills and abilities over time.[34] Clearly, in the class project example discussed above, this criterion was not met.

Affective Criteria

Affective criteria address the question of whether team members have a fulfilling and satisfying team experience.[35] One important affective criterion is the team's affective tone, or the general emotional state of the team.[36] It is important that the team, as a whole, have a positive, happy outlook on their work. Unfortunately, it is easy for even one member to contaminate the mood of a team.[37] The team's affect influences the way they communicate and their cohesion, as discussed later.

Outcome Criteria

Outcome criteria refer to the quantity and quality of the team's output[38] or the extent to which the team's output is acceptable to clients.[39] The outcome should reflect synergy, as described earlier in the chapter. Another important outcome criterion is team viability—that is, the ability of the team to remain functioning as long as needed.[40] Research has shown that teams have a tendency to "burn out" over time. One study, for example, found that the performance of research-and-development teams peaks at around years 2 to 3 and shows significant declines after year 5.[41] This decline in performance can be due to teams becoming overly cohesive (which can lead to groupthink, as discussed in Chapter 10) or to breakdowns in communication between team members. Often teams are created to deal with changing environments and uncertainty. Consider, for example, a military special operations team that must operate secretly in a foreign and hostile environment. In this case, a team's ability to adapt to the environment becomes an extremely important outcome.[42]

Is the Team Needed?

As stated earlier, teamwork has become very popular in business, as well as other types of organizations. However, is teamwork always the best way to accomplish a job? According to

Jon Katzenbach, a popular team consultant to companies such as Citicorp, General Electric, and ExxonMobil, some situations do not call for teamwork and are better handled by individuals working alone.[43] He argues that because teams are popular, managers often "jump on the team bandwagon" without giving a thought to whether a team is needed in the first place. He offers the following diagnostic checklist to determine whether a team should be created:

- Does the project really require collective work? If the work can be done by individuals working alone without any need for integration, teamwork is not necessary and merely adds to the burden by creating additional coordination tasks.
- Do team members need to focus on collective work a significant portion of the time? Can they instead focus on different aspects of the project most of the time? If the latter, then it might be more efficient to assign specific duties to individuals, rather than make the team responsible for all duties.
- Do people on the team hold one another accountable? Mutual accountability signals greater commitment to the team.

If there is a situation where these criteria are not met, then perhaps it is better to not use a team to accomplish the job.

Factors Affecting Team Effectiveness

As discussed in the opening section on the strategic importance of teams, when used properly, teams can yield great performance benefits to organizations. Teams can create synergy for several reasons, including greater goal commitment, a greater variety of skills and abilities applied to task achievement, and a greater sharing of knowledge. However, teamwork can also lead to poorer performance than individuals working alone, as suggested earlier. In addition to performing their regular work-related tasks and achieving organizational goals, team members must also deal with any interpersonal problems that arise, overcome the propensity to be lazy that some individuals might exhibit, coordinate tasks between/among individuals, and implement effective communication within the team. This extra "teamwork" can be quite substantial and can produce a significant **process loss**,[44] which is the difference between actual and potential team performance. If teams are not able to achieve synergy, less positive outcomes will result.

To ensure that the benefits of teamwork outweigh the process loss that occurs from it, teams must be structured and managed properly. Literally thousands of studies in almost every type of organizational context have examined factors that influence team effectiveness. We focus on three factors: team composition, team structure, and team processes.

Team Composition

Team composition is important because it addresses who members of the team are and what human resources (skills, abilities, and knowledge) they bring to the team. When managers assign associates to teams, they often make three questionable assumptions, which can lead to mistakes:[45]

1. They assume that people who are demographically similar and share beliefs will work better together, and so they attempt to compose teams that are somewhat homogeneous in these areas.

process loss
The difference between actual and potential team performance that is caused by diverting time and energy into maintaining the team as opposed to working on substantive tasks.

2. They assume that everyone knows how or is suited to work in a team.

3. They assume that a larger team size is always better.

In this section, we address these issues.

Diversity

In Chapter 2, we explored in depth the impact of demographic diversity on group performance. Some studies have found negative effects for demographic diversity,[46] others have found positive effects,[47] and still others have found no effect.[48] Another type of diversity that can impact team performance corresponds to differences in important beliefs among team members. Much of the research on belief diversity has taken place in the context of senior management teams, exploring how differences in beliefs regarding the attractiveness of various strategies/goals impact management-team performance and consequently firm performance. Consistent with research on demographic diversity, the impact of belief diversity on performance has been mixed.[49] Overall, the effects of demographic and belief diversity on team performance seem to depend on several factors:[50]

- *Type of task.* Diversity seems to have more positive effects when the team's tasks require complex problem solving such as that demanded by the pursuit of innovation and creativity.[51] Experiences with diverse teams at McKinsey are consistent with this idea.
- *Outcome.* Diversity may have a positive effect on performance but a negative effect on members' reactions to the team and subsequent behaviors, such as turnover.[52]
- *Time.* Diversity can have negative effects in the short run but positive effects in the long run.[53]
- *Type of diversity.* If team members are diverse on factors that lead them to have different performance goals or levels of commitment to the team the relationship between diversity and performance can be negative.[54]
- *Fault lines.* If team members exhibit diversity along two or more dimensions and those dimensions converge, then diversity can be negative.[55] For example, team members on a product development team might fall into the following two camps: (1) older male engineers and (2) younger female marketers. In this case, age, gender, and functional background converge such that two quite different subgroups exist.

Personality

The relationship between members' personalities and team performance can be quite strong, but the exact relationship depends on the type of task that the team is trying to accomplish. Researchers have several ways of determining the personality of the team; however, all methods are based on aggregating individuals' scores. The personality traits that have important effects on team performance include agreeableness (the ability to get along with others and cooperate) and emotional stability (the tendency to experience positive rather than negative emotions).[56] Also, the greater the degree of conscientiousness among team members, the higher the team's performance tends to be.[57] This is particularly true when the team's task involves planning and performance rather than creativity. It appears that agreeable team members contribute to team performance by fulfilling team maintenance roles, whereas conscientious team members perform critical task roles.[58] Finally, team-level extraversion and openness to experience can be positively related to

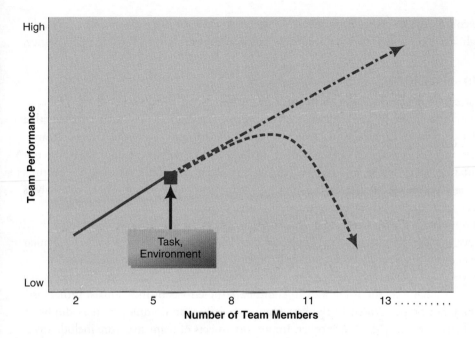

High

Low

Team Performance

Task,
Environment

2   5   8   11   13 . . . .

Number of Team Members

Exhibit 11-2 The Relationship between Team Size and Team Performance

performance in situations requiring nonroutine decision making and creative tasks.[59] (All of these personality traits are discussed in Chapter 5.)

Team Orientation

Some individuals are better at working on teams than others because they like working on teams and have the requisite skills. **Team orientation** refers to the extent to which an individual works well with others, wants to contribute to team performance, and enjoys being on a team.[60] When a team comprises many members who have a positive team orientation, that team will adapt and perform better than a team whose members do not have such an orientation.[61] Notice that both Starbucks and McKinsey & Company hire associates based on their teamwork orientation, among other things.

team orientation
The extent to which an individual works well with others, wants to contribute to team performance, and enjoys being on a team.

Size

There is no one ideal number of team members for all situations. Many studies have examined the relationship of team size and team performance, and two lines of thought have emerged. These two ideas are depicted in Exhibit 11-2.

The first suggests that the relationship between team size and team performance is shaped like an inverted U.[62] As teams become larger, the diversity of skills, talents, ideas, and individual associate inputs into the task is greater, leading to improved performance. However, as the number of team members continues to increase, the need for cooperation and coordination also increases. At some point, the effort that goes into managing the team will outweigh the benefits of having more members, and team performance will begin to decline.

Other researchers, however, have found that performance increases linearly with team size without ever showing a downturn.[63] This linear relationship most likely results when a team avoids the problems associated with too many members, such as social loafing (to be discussed later in the chapter), poor coordination, and worsening communication. Thus, the relationship between team size and performance probably depends on team skill at process management, and it also no doubt depends on factors such as the scope of the task or the complexity of the environment.[64] When task scope and environmental complexity are high, more team members are needed for task accomplishment and strong performance.

Team Structure

Team structure refers to the ongoing means of coordinating formal team efforts. The contribution of structure to team achievement is evident. For example, consider a bank with a loan department and a collection department (each department can be considered a team). One department is assigned tasks related to making loans, such as credit analysis, interest computation, loan closing, and filing. These are somewhat dissimilar tasks but they form a sequential chain related to the lending process—loans cannot be closed until credit analysis has been performed and interest computed. Thus, grouping the tasks in one department under one leader makes sense. The other department is assigned phone collections, field collections, and repossessing tasks. These tasks are less sequential but they are very similar to one another. Task similarity is another basis for grouping tasks under one leader.

Beyond grouping together tasks and the individuals assigned to them, it is necessary to use additional structural methods to coordinate the efforts of individuals. Otherwise, tasks may not be performed in the best manner possible, and employees may duplicate their efforts or work against each other. Important aspects of team structure include roles, norms and task structure.

Team Member Roles

roles
Expectations shared by group members about who is to perform what types of tasks and under what conditions.

Team **roles** are expectations shared by team members about who will perform what types of tasks and under what conditions.[65] Roles can be formally assigned, or they can be informally adopted by team members. Some members primarily serve in leadership roles, and others take the roles of followers. The leadership role does not need to be formally assigned or to be a function of formal authority. Leaders can emerge informally in groups.

task roles
Roles that require behaviors aimed at achieving the team's performance goals and tasks.

Apart from leadership roles, all teams need to have members fulfilling both task roles and socioemotional, or expressive, roles.[66] **Task roles** involve behaviors aimed at achieving the team's performance goals and tasks. **Socioemotional roles** require behaviors that support the social aspects of the team. A team member may also emphasize **destructive individual roles**, which involve behaviors that place that individual's needs and goals above those of the team.[67] As we would expect, these roles impede team performance rather than facilitate it. Exhibit 11-3 depicts examples of specific task, socioemotional, and individual roles.

socioemotional roles
Roles that require behaviors that support the social aspects of the organization.

destructive individual roles
Roles involving self-centered behaviors that put individual needs and goals ahead of the team.

As a team becomes more stable and structured, the roles of individual members often become resistant to change.[68] Group social pressures tend to keep members "in their place," and the team resists outside forces that would change members' roles, even if these roles were not the ones assigned by the formal organization.

Norms

norms
Informal rules or standards that regulate the team's behavior.

Norms are informal rules or standards that regulate the team's behavior. Norms tend to emerge naturally in a team and are part of the team's mental model, although occasionally they are systematically recorded. Norms serve the purpose of regulating team members' behavior and providing direction. When individual team members violate team norms, some type of punishment or sanction is usually applied. For example, Hudson Houck, the offensive line coach for the 1996 Dallas Cowboys, stated that anyone on the team who didn't work hard all the time (a team norm) was shunned.[69]

EXHIBIT 11-3 Team Member Roles

Role	Function
Task Roles	
Initiator/Contributor	Suggests new ideas, solutions, or ways to approach the problem
Information Seeker	Focuses on getting facts
Information Giver	Provides data for decision making
Elaborator	Gives additional information, such as rephrasing, examples
Opinion Giver	Provides opinions, values, and feelings
Coordinator	Shows the relevance of various specific ideas to the overall problem to be solved
Orienter	Refocuses discussion when the team gets off topic
Evaluator/Critic	Appraises the quality of the team's work
Energizer	Motivates the team when energy falters
Procedural Technician	Takes care of operational details, such as technology
Recorder	Takes notes and keeps records
Socioemotional Roles	
Encourager	Provides others with praise, agreement, warmth
Harmonizer	Settles conflicts among other members
Compromiser	Changes his or her position to maintain team harmony
Gatekeeper	Controls communication process so that everyone gets a chance to participate
Standard Setter	Discusses the quality of the team process
Observer	Comments on the positive or negative aspects of the team process and calls for changes
Follower	Accepts others' ideas and acts as a listener
Destructive Individual Roles	
Aggressor	Attacks others
Blocker	Unnecessarily opposes the team
Dominator	Manipulatively asserts authority
Evader	Focuses on expressing own feelings and thoughts that are unrelated to the team goals
Help Seeker	Unnecessarily expresses insecurities
Recognition Seeker	Calls unnecessary attention to himself or herself

Sources: K.D. Benne and P. Sheets. 1948. "Functional Roles of Group Members," *Journal of Social Issues*, 4: 41–49. D.R. Forsyth. 1999. *Group Dynamics* (Belmont, CA: Wadsworth Publishing Company).

Team norms can become very powerful and resistant to change. Witness a situation such as a regular team meeting, or even a college class, where everyone sits in the same seat at every meeting. Any change in seating can cause unease on the part of group or team members. In these situations, seating norms develop to curb the social unease that could result from choosing a different seat at every meeting. No one has to wonder why someone is or is not sitting next to her. Nor does anyone have to worry about how others will interpret his motives for a seating choice.

Although norms allow teams to function smoothly, they can sometimes be harmful to team members. Research on the causes of eating disorders in young women illustrates this fact.[70] Certain groups, such as cheerleading squads, sororities, and dance troupes, have particularly high rates of bulimia among their members. Examination of these groups has indicated that they often develop group norms of binging and purging. Instead of considering this behavior to be abnormal and unhealthy, team members come to view it as a normal way of controlling weight. Because norms are not always positive, it is important that teams develop norms that foster team productivity and performance and promote the welfare of individual members.

Task Structure

Task structure has been shown to be an important determinant of how teams function and perform.[71] Several typologies have been proposed for categorizing tasks. One of the most popular typologies emphasizes the following: (1) whether tasks can be separated into subcomponents, (2) whether tasks have quantity or quality goals, and (3) how individual inputs are combined to achieve the team's product.[72]

First, then, we consider whether a task can be broken down into parts. Tasks such as playing baseball, preparing a class project, and cooking a meal in a restaurant are **divisible tasks** because they can be separated into subcomponents. Thus, different individual associates can perform different parts of the task. **Unitary tasks** cannot be divided and must be performed by a single individual. Examples of unitary tasks are reading a book, completing an account sheet, and talking to a customer on the phone. If a particular goal or mission requires the completion of unitary tasks, it may not be advantageous for a team to complete the mission.

Second, we consider the goals of the task. Tasks with a quantity goal are called maximization tasks. Examples of **maximization tasks** include producing the most cars possible, running the fastest, and selling the most insurance policies. Tasks with a quality goal are referred to as optimization tasks. **Optimization tasks** often require innovation and creativity. Examples of optimization tasks include developing a new product and developing a new marketing strategy. As mentioned earlier, diverse teams tend to perform better on optimization tasks.

Finally, we consider how individual inputs are combined to achieve the team's product. The manner in which this is done places a limit on how well the team can perform. We can classify how inputs are combined by determining whether a task is additive or compensatory and whether it is disjunctive or conjunctive.

Additive tasks are those in which individual inputs are simply added together—for example, pulling a rope or inputting data. When members' inputs are additively combined, team performance will often be *better than the best individual's performance* because of social facilitation processes (discussed later in the chapter).[73] *Compensatory tasks* are those in which members' individual performances are averaged together to arrive at the team's overall performance. For example, members of a human resource management team may individually estimate future labor demands in the organization, and the total projection may then be based on the average of the managers' estimates. The potential team performance on this type of task is likely to be *better than the performance of most of the individual members*.

Disjunctive tasks are those in which teams must work together to develop a single, agreed-upon product or solution. A jury decision is an example of a disjunctive task. Usually, disjunctive tasks result in team performance that is *better than that of most of the individual members but not as good as the best member's performance*.[74] *Conjunctive tasks* are those in which all members must perform their individual tasks to arrive at the team's overall performance. Examples of conjunctive tasks are assembly lines and trucks moving in a convoy. Teams working on conjunctive tasks *cannot perform any better than their worst*

---

divisible tasks
Tasks that can be separated into subcomponents.

unitary tasks
Tasks that cannot be divided and must be performed by an individual.

maximization tasks
Tasks with a quantity goal.

optimization tasks
Tasks with a quality goal.

individual performers. For example, an assembly line cannot produce goods at a rate faster than the rate at which its slowest member performs.

Team Processes

Team processes are the behaviors and activities that influence the effectiveness of teams. Team processes have strong effects on outcomes. Team processes include cohesion, conflict, social facilitation, social loafing, and communication.

Cohesion

Team cohesion refers to members' attraction to the team.[75] **Interpersonal cohesion** is the team members' liking or attraction to other team members. **Task cohesion** is team members' attraction and commitment to the tasks and goals of the team.[76] Team cohesion is an important criterion because research indicates that cohesion affects team performance outcomes and viability.[77] Furthermore, members of cohesive teams are more likely to be satisfied with their teams than are members of noncohesive teams.[78]

Cohesive teams are likely to have strong performance when there is task cohesion.[79] When there is only interpersonal cohesion, performance is likely to be low. In fact, if team members really like each other and enjoy spending time together but are not committed to their organizational tasks and goals, they will perform worse than if they were not interpersonally cohesive. A classic study of factory workers illustrates these effects.[80] Interpersonally cohesive teams committed to organizationally sanctioned performance goals performed the best, whereas interpersonally cohesive teams without commitment to such goals performed the worst—even worse than non–interpersonally cohesive teams lacking commitment to the performance goals. Finally, it is worth noting that cohesion also has stronger effects on performance when there is a great deal of interdependence among team members.[81]

In the *Experiencing Organizational Behavior* feature, we discuss a form of behavior that is consistent with both task and interpersonal cohesion—*backing-up behavior*. As in many jobs, performers in the Cirque du Soleil must be ready to take over for their team members at a moment's notice and do more than their fair share.

The support that team members provide to each other can be quite important in the performance of the team and the unit in which it operates. The *Experiencing Organizational Behavior* feature describes the necessity of backing-up behavior by Cirque du Soleil performers. However, this behavior is necessary in almost all teams. Think of the need for backup among police officers. Backing-up behavior may be one of the strongest indicators of team effectiveness, because not only is everyone on the team doing his or her share, but each member is willing to take on others' work when assistance is needed or to fill in any gaps. Teams that engage in backing-up behavior are displaying the spirit of high-involvement management by going beyond what is merely necessary to get the job done.

Conflict

When the behaviors or beliefs of a team member are unacceptable to other team members, conflict occurs. Several types of intragroup (within-team) conflict exist; they include personal conflict (sometimes referred to as "relationship conflict"), substantive conflict (sometimes referred to as "task conflict"), and procedural conflict (sometimes referred to as "process conflict").

interpersonal cohesion
Team members' liking or attraction to other team members.

task cohesion
Team members' attraction and commitment to the tasks and goals of the team.

Backup at Cirque Du Soleil

Chances are that you have seen a performance by Cirque du Soleil (approximately 15 million people saw their performances in 2009). What started out as a band of street performers in 1984 in Quebec, Canada, has grown into a business with over 5,000 employees (1,200 are performing artists), a number of touring companies that perform all over the world, and resident shows in Las Vegas, Orlando, New York, Tokyo, and Macau. Cirque du Soleil has come to redefine what we mean by the term *circus*. There are no animals, the shows are aimed at adult audiences, and performances provide visuals not seen before, such as the shows conducted under water ("O") and the amazing costumes. The company builds its brand on creativity and teamwork.

Cirque du Soleil hires people from all over the world, searching for people with various talents, ranging from being an acrobat and scuba-certified, to doing gymnastics on rollerblades. It does not just look for run-of-the mill acrobats, jugglers, and trapeze artists. Everyone must meet certain artistic qualifications and be predisposed to teamwork. Indeed, because about 20 percent of the artists turn over (due to injury or retirement) every year, Cirque has resorted to creating its own training camps, such as a camp for contortionists in Mongolia, to make sure it has a constant supply of talent.

Once artists are cast, they go through an eight-week boot camp where they learn how to operate as a team. One important aspect of this teamwork is the ability to be flexible, creative, and work off of other performers. Their coach, Boris Verkhovsky, states that this is not always easy, because many are trained athletes who are accustomed to performing on their own using strict protocols rather than engaging in artistic performances. An important part of a Cirque performer's job is to be able to back up other performers. As with many jobs, such as police officers or retail sales clerks, it is important that these performers be able to monitor the performance of all of their team members and be able to step in when there is trouble, a team member is overtaxed, or the artistic role requires it. Thus, providing backup to other performers is an essential component of all Cirque du Soleil artists' jobs. Consider the job of an aerialist who relies on her team members for safety support should she make a mistake during her routine.

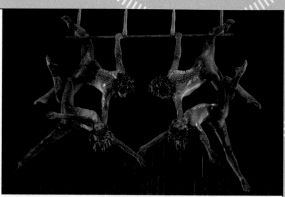

©ALFREDO ALDA/epa/Corbis

Research has addressed the issue of who is likely to provide backup, who is likely to receive it, and under what conditions backing-up behaviors are likely to occur. When team members are highly conscientious and emotionally stable, they are more likely to provide backup to team members in need. Team members must also be knowledgeable about others' job responsibilities, as well as their own, in order to provide backup. When the team member who needs help is highly conscientious and extraverted, he or she will more likely receive backup from other team members. Finally, when team members perceive that the person who needs backing up has a larger workload or fewer resources to accomplish his or her work, they are more likely to provide the support needed.

Sources: Cirque du Soleil, "Cirque Du Soleil at a Glance," 2009, at http://www.cirquedusoleil.com/cirquedusoleil/pdf/pressroom/en/cds_en_bref_en.pdf; R.M. McIntyre, & E. Salas. 1995. "Measuring and Managing for Team Performance: Emerging Principles from Complex Environments," in R.A. Guzzo et al. (Eds.), *Team Effectiveness and Decision Making in Organizations* (San Francisco: Jossey-Bass, pp. 9–45); C.O.L.H. Porter et al. 2003. "Backing Up Behaviors in Teams: The Role of Personality and Legitimacy of Need," *Journal of Applied Psychology*, 88: 391–403; L. Tischler. 2005. "Join the Circus," *Fast Company*, July 5, at http://www.fastcompany.com/magazine/96/cirque-du-soleil.

Personal conflicts result when team members simply do not like each other. As we might expect, people assigned to a team are more likely to experience this sort of conflict than are people who choose to belong to the same informal group. Personal conflict may be based on personality clashes, differences in values, and differences in likes and dislikes. No disagreement over a specific issue is necessary for personal conflict to occur. One study of business executives found that 40 percent of their conflicts resulted from personal dislike rather than disagreement over a specific issue.[82]

Substantive conflicts occur when a team member disagrees with another's task-related ideas or analysis of the team's problem or plans. For example, a design team whose task is developing a better product may disagree about whether they should focus on making the product more attractive or making it easier to use. Substantive conflicts can often lead to greater creativity and innovation, if they do not become personal conflicts.[83]

Finally, *procedural conflicts* occur when team members disagree about policies and procedures. That is, they disagree on how to work together. For example, a member of a virtual team may believe that the correct way to work as a team is to check in by e-mail with other members at least twice a day. Furthermore, he may believe that team members should respond immediately to such e-mails. Other team members, however, may believe that checking in so frequently is a waste of time and may want to contact others only when necessary. Group norms develop as a way to avoid procedural conflicts. Teams may also develop specific policies or rules to avoid conflicts of this kind. Robert's Rules of Order are one such device because they specifically define how group meetings should be conducted.

Depending on the specific type, conflict can have negative or positive consequences for team effectiveness.[84] Personal conflict tends to be negative because it interferes with cooperation and a healthy task focus. On the other hand, substantive conflict can be positive, particularly for tasks involving creativity and innovation. This type of conflict generates multiple ideas and sets the stage for the best ones to be emphasized. Openly confronting and discussing the different task ideas is important, however. Ignoring differences of opinion is less helpful. Overall, substantive conflict can be beneficial when teams cooperatively problem solve, develop positive norms, and create a consistent team mental model.[85] Procedural conflict has not been studied often enough for firm conclusions to be drawn, but it certainly would have negative effects if not addressed to some degree.

Social Facilitation

In the late 1890s, Norman Triplett, a bicyclist and early social scientist, noticed that cyclists performed better racing against others than when they were timed cycling alone.[86] This effect—that is, when the presence of others improves individual performance—has been termed the **social facilitation effect**. Social facilitation suggests that teamwork can lead to increased performance because others are present.

Several reasons for the social facilitation effect have been suggested. One is that the presence of human beings creates general arousal in other human beings.[87] This general arousal then leads to better performance. Another explanation is that the presence of others arouses evaluation apprehension, so that people perform better because they think they are being evaluated.[88] Whatever the reason, social facilitation seems to occur only when people are performing well-learned, simple, or familiar tasks.[89] The presence of others can actually decrease performance on tasks that are complex or unfamiliar. For example, someone who is not accustomed to giving speeches is likely to perform more poorly when speaking in front of others relative to practicing alone.

social facilitation effect
Improvement in individual performance when others are present.

Social Loafing

social loafing

A phenomenon wherein people put forth less effort when they work in teams than when they work alone.

Research suggests that the simple act of grouping individuals together does not necessarily increase their total output; in fact, people working together on a common task may actually perform at a lower level than they would if they were working alone. This phenomenon is called **social loafing**[90] or shirking,[91] and it can obviously result in serious losses. There are three primary explanations for the social loafing effect. First, if individual outputs are not identifiable, associates may shirk because they can get away with poor performance. Second, if associates, when working in teams, expect their teammates to loaf then they may reduce their own efforts to establish an equitable division of labor.[92] In this case, individual team members do not have a team identity and place their own good (working less) over the good of the team. Finally, when many individuals are working on a task, some individuals may feel dispensable and believe that their own contributions will not matter.[93] This is likely to happen when individuals think that they have low ability and cannot perform as well as other team members.[94]

Research on shirking supports these explanations. In one study, individuals were asked to pull alone as hard as possible on a rope attached to a strain gauge. They averaged 138.6 pounds of pressure while tugging on the rope. When the same individuals pulled on the rope in groups of three, however, they exerted only 352 pounds of pressure, an average of 117.3 pounds each. In groups of eight, the individual average dropped even lower, to an astonishing 68.2 pounds of pressure. This supports the first explanation of social loafing—that the less identifiable the individual's output is, the more the individual loafs.[95] Also, if the people with the least physical strength decrease their pressure the most, then there would also be support for the dispensability explanation.

In a second study, participants expected to work on a group task. Some of the subjects were told by a co-worker (a confederate of the researchers) that the co-worker expected to work as hard on the group task as she had on an individual task. Other participants were told that the co-worker expected to work less hard on the group task than on the individual task. In a third condition, nothing was said about the co-worker's intention. In the group task, the participants who had been told to expect lower performance from their co-worker reduced their efforts. However, the participants who had been told to expect no slacking of effort from the co-worker maintained their effort during the group task.[96] This supports the second explanation of social loafing—that individuals reduce their efforts to establish an equitable division of labor when they expect their co-workers to slack off in their efforts.

Students often experience social loafing. It occurs frequently when students are assigned to team projects in one of their courses. Inevitably, when student teams work on a class project, one or two members coast along, not "pulling their own weight." These "loafers" frequently miss the project team's meetings, fail to perform their assigned tasks, and so on. They rely on the fact that the more motivated members will complete the project without their help. The loafers still expect to share the credit and obtain the same grade, because the professor may not be concerned about determining who worked and who did not. One study examining social loafing in student groups found that the most common reasons for loafing were perceptions of unfairness (i.e., others were loafing) and perceived dispensability because one was not as talented as others.[97]

Social loafing is always a possibility in work teams, especially in teams that have limited task cohesion. For example, in a study of almost 500 work team members, 25 percent expressed concern that members of their teams engaged in social loafing. This can be extremely costly to organizations, because creating and supporting work teams requires investments in such things as new technology to aid teamwork, coordination efforts, more complicated pay systems, and restructuring of work. Thus, when teams perform worse than individuals, not only are performance and productivity lower, but costs are also higher.

Social loafing can occur in any team at any level in an organization. And because social loafing clearly results in lower productivity, it is a serious problem. At the least, when social loafing occurs, the organization's human capital is underutilized. Fortunately, managers can use several methods to address this problem.[98] First they can make individual contributions visible. This can be accomplished by using smaller rather than larger teams, using an evaluation system where everyone's contributions are noted, and/or appointing someone to monitor and oversee everyone's contributions. The second thing that can be done is to foster team cohesiveness by providing team-level rewards, training members in teamwork, and selecting "team players" to be on the team.

Communication

Team members must communicate to effectively coordinate their productive efforts. Task instructions must be delivered, results must be reported, and problem-solving discussions must take place. Because communication is crucial, teams create many formal communication processes, which may include formal reports (such as profit-and-loss statements), work schedules, interoffice memoranda, and formal meetings.

But informal communication also is necessary. Associates need and want to discuss personal and job-related problems with each other. Informal communication is a natural consequence of group processes. The effectiveness and frequency of communication are affected by many of the same factors that lead to group formation and group structure. For example, frequency of communication is partially the result of the opportunity to *interact*. People who share the same office, whose jobs are interconnected, and who have the same working hours are likely to communicate more frequently. Thus, the opportunity to interact leads to both group formation and frequent communication. This is why virtual teams are more likely to be effective when they have more face-to-face interaction.[99]

In addition to affecting task performance, communication frequency and effectiveness are related to team member satisfaction, particularly in cohesive teams. Increased communication enhances team members' satisfaction with their membership on the team. Also, communication becomes more rewarding as team membership increases in importance and satisfaction to associates.[100] Thus, communication is both a cause and a consequence of satisfaction with the team.

Team Development

The nature of interactions among team members changes over time. Teams behave differently when they meet for the first time relative to when they have been together long enough to be accustomed to working together. At the beginning of a team's life cycle, members may spend more time getting to know each other than they do on the task. As time progresses, however, the team often becomes more focused on performance. According to Bruce Tuckman's group development model, teams typically go through four stages over their life cycle: forming, storming, norming, and performing.[101]

During the *forming* stage, associates come to teams without established relationships but with some expectations about what they want in and from the team. The new team members focus on learning about each other, defining what they want to accomplish, and determining how they are going to accomplish it. Sometimes personality conflicts or disagreements arise about what needs to be done or how the team should go about doing it. At this point, the team has entered the *storming* stage, marked by conflict among team members. If the team is to be successful, team members need to resolve or manage personal conflicts and work through substantive and procedural conflicts in order to reach sufficient agreement on desired performance outcomes and processes. In working through substantive and procedural conflicts, the team will come to some understanding concerning desired outcomes, rules, procedures, and norms for team behavior. This is the *norming* stage, in which team members cooperate with each other and become more cohesive. Once the team has established norms and is working as a cohesive whole, it enters the *performing* stage. In this stage, team members are more committed to the team, focus on task performance, and are generally more satisfied with the team experience.[102]

Most teams experience some sort of end. Individual members may leave, or the team may be formally disbanded when its mission has been accomplished. Thus, teams ultimately go through a fifth stage, *adjourning,* when individuals begin to leave the team and terminate their regular contact with other team members. Adjourning can result from voluntary actions on the part of team members, as when a team member takes a job with another organization or retires. It can also result from actions over which team members have little control, such as reassignment by the parent organization or the end of a project. When individual members of a cohesive team leave, the remaining members often experience feelings of loss, and the team becomes less cohesive and less structured, until it no longer exists, unless new members replace the members who have left. In this instance, the team is similar to a new team, and the process of team development is likely to begin again.

Teams may not go through all of the stages described above in all situations. For example, the members of a newly formed team belong to the same organization and may already know each other. They are also likely to be familiar with performance expectations and may even share similar work-related values. Thus, the forming and storming stages are not needed. Furthermore, the nature of the team's work can influence the formation of the team. Most research on Tuckman's stage theory has focused on simple teams that worked on a single project and whose members were relative strangers.[103] Thus, the theory may not apply to teams that work on complex projects or that have members who have had a long history together.

punctuated equilibrium model (PEM)
A model of team development that suggests that teams do not go through linear stages but that team formation depends on the task at hand and the deadlines for that task.

The **punctuated equilibrium model (PEM)** of team development provides an alternative view of development over time.[104] This model suggests that teams do not go through linear stages but that team formation depends on the deadlines for the task at hand. The PEM is essentially a two-stage model representing two periods of equilibrium "punctuated" by a shift in focus. In the first stage, team members get to know one another and engage in norming activities. The focus at this stage is the development of socioemotional roles. When the deadline for the team's work approaches, the team undergoes a dramatic change in functioning. This is the point at which the "punctuation" occurs. After this point is reached, the team refocuses its activities on performing the task. Thus, the focus shifts to task roles. This model contrasts with Tuckman's stage model because it suggests that team life-cycle stages are determined by temporal aspects of the task, not by social dynamics within the team. Exhibit 11-4 compares the two models. Overall, research suggests that the PEM model best describes the development of teams working on a very specific, clearly time-bounded task.[105]

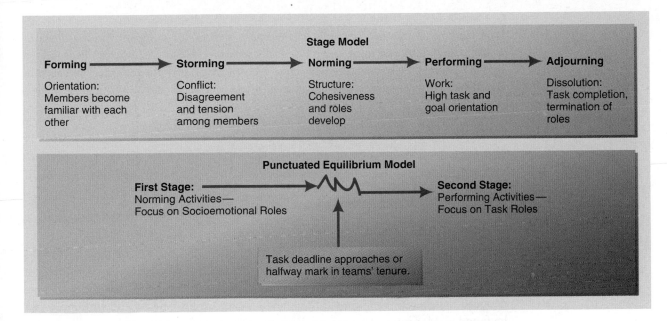

Exhibit 11-4 Models of Team Development

Sources: B.W. Tuckman. 1965. "Developmental Sequences in Small Groups," *Psychological Bulletin*, 6: 384–399; B.W. Tuckman, & M.A.C. Jensen. 1977. "Stages of Small Group Development," *Group and Organizational Studies*, 2: 419–427; C.J.G. Gersick. 1988. "Time and Transition in Work Teams: Toward a New Model of Group Development," *Academy of Management Journal*, 31: 9–41; C.J.G. Gersick. 1989. "Marking Time: Predictable Transitions in Task Groups," *Academy of Management Journal*, 32: 274–309; D.R. Forsyth. 1999. *Group Dynamics* (Belmont, CA: Wadsworth Publishing Company).

Managing for Effective Teams

To experience the potential gains of teamwork, organizations must provide support for teams to work effectively. An organization cannot simply declare that it will increase the level of teamwork without planning, training, selecting, and rewarding people for teamwork. Following are several "best practices" for managing effective teams.

Top Management Support

Effective teamwork requires support from the top of the organization.[106] All organizations that are known for their teamwork, such as Xerox, Harley-Davidson, FedEx, and Boeing, have senior management teams that actively promote teamwork. Several management practices can help senior management to support team effectiveness:[107]

- Have an explicit vision and strategic plan that serves as the basis for determining desirable team outcomes.
- Use results-oriented measurement of team outcomes and expect all leaders in the organization to do the same.
- Actively include associates and managers at all levels in the decision-making process related to the use of teams.
- Make an explicit decision about using teams and tie the decision to business objectives.
- Actively manage and review support systems for teams.

Senior management at Starbucks, described in the chapter-opening case, clearly follows these recommended practices. For example, two of the company's stated missions are to make profits and to be environmentally sensitive. These missions are incorporated into the baristas' performance assessments. The company also provides mechanisms that enable baristas to regularly communicate and share their ideas with senior management.

Support Systems

Support systems are aspects of organizational life that allow a team to function well. Support systems include technology, information systems, selection of team members, training, rewards, and leadership.

Technology

It is important that teams have access to the technology they need to do their work. This includes the technology necessary to carry out tasks (such as tools and computer software) and also technology to help team members coordinate their work. Many technologies are designed to help teams communicate and interact more fully and efficiently. Examples can be found at McKinsey & Company. Each team member has access to personal computing technology as well as mobile communication devices. Each member has access to the Internet for web-conferencing and other tasks. Also important for success, team members should have input into the adoption or development of communication technologies.[108]

Information Systems

Teams must have the necessary information to act, but they frequently need more information than they possess. An example is provided by the now-defunct People Express Airlines, which used customer service teams to conduct much of the airline's business.[109] The customer service teams needed important information, such as future bookings, to do their work; however, executives were reluctant to allow them access to this information because they were afraid that it might leak out to their competitors.

Teams can also suffer from receiving too much information.[110] Often, information technology can provide people with a flood of information; but as discussed in Chapter 9, too much information creates overload. In such situations, associates may not know to what information they should attend. They may become overwhelmed and attend to only a portion of the information, or perhaps attend to none of it, or they may even shut the system down entirely. A related problem is information unavailable in the form most useful to the team. To address this problem, it is important that teams have "user-friendly" information systems.

Selection of Team Members

Traditionally, it is recommended that organizations select team members with the knowledge, skills, and abilities to perform their individual jobs and with values that fit well with the organizational culture.[111] However, team members also have other roles to fulfill. For example, they may perform teamwork roles, such as energizing the team or soliciting and elaborating on the ideas of others. Furthermore, because teamwork often involves a variety of activities, a broader set of skills may be necessary for team-based jobs. Thus, teamwork selection needs to consider more factors than selection for a traditional job. Following are some suggestions for selecting team members:[112]

- Tailor the staffing process to the type of team. For example, paper-and-pencil personality tests may be appropriate for service teams but not for senior management teams.
- Conduct a teamwork analysis to identify the knowledge, skills, and abilities needed to perform both individual task work and teamwork.
- Consider political issues. It may be important to have members representing different constituencies on a team. For example, a university's internal review board that evaluates whether faculty research is ethical in its treatment of human subjects includes a community member who does not have ties to the university community and does not do research.
- Carefully consider who is to do the assessment of potential team members' knowledge, skills, and abilities and who will decide whom to select. It is often useful to have members of the team itself involved in the selection process.

Rewards

If people are to work together effectively as a team, they must be rewarded as a team. Team members have little motivation to engage with and support each other if they are rewarded only for their individual performance. Thus, it is important that the reward system for teams have multiple components, some of which reflect team performance. One such reward system is a profit-sharing plan in which associates receive bonuses based on the profits generated by their team. Furthermore, if the teamwork requires cross-functional work and knowledge, team members may receive skill-based or knowledge-based pay. Such pay is determined by what skills and knowledge associates acquire rather than by how they perform on specific tasks. Finally, team-based pay should be provided for only those aspects of performance under the team's control.[113]

Leadership

A team's leadership is crucial to the effectiveness of the team.[114] Team leaders can naturally emerge, or they can be assigned based on special skills or authority. Successful team leaders must fulfill three roles.[115]

The first role, team liaison, requires the leader to network with information sources both inside and outside the team, creating a bridge between the two. Outside sources include suppliers, clients, customers, other teams, and higher levels of management. In the liaison role, a team leader also acts as a representative of the team and watches out for the team's interests. In essence, the team leader connects the team to the outside world.

Another leader role involves direction setting. The leader must ensure the development of a direction for team action. This means that the leader must develop or help to develop short-term action strategies based on the long-term organizational strategies developed by the senior management team. Overall, the leader must help to translate those long-term strategies into directions, goals, and action plans for team members.

Finally, the team leader must serve as the team's operational coordinator. This role represents the management of the team's work and processes. The major responsibilities of this role are to recognize each member's contributions and decide how to best integrate the various team members' contributions; to monitor team performance and functioning

The Pros and Cons of Experiential Teambuilding

©Michael Pole/Corbis

Experiential teambuilding is used by many organizations around the world. The general idea is to move a team outside of its day-to-day routines and place it in a situation where fun and challenging activities are offered. The goal is to create stronger camaraderie and commitment among team members. Strengthening skills in the areas of problem solving and goal setting are also a part of the plan in many cases. Example activities include:

- Murder mysteries—Participants attempt to solve a murder staged by actors.
- Improv sessions—Participants engage in comedic improvisation exercises.
- Ropes courses—Participants help one another to navigate a series of challenges involving ropes that range from ground level to 10 to 12 feet above the ground.
- Scavenger hunts—Participants compete in subteams to decipher clues that lead to valuable items.
- Family feuds—Participants engage in a version of the storied game show.
- Boats—Participants form subteams to build and race boats made from barrels, boards, and ropes.

These types of activities are very popular in the business world. Despite their popularity, critics have questioned their effectiveness. Judith Mair, a German entrepreneur in the communication and advertising field,

famously complained that corporate fun and games blurred the distinction between business and personal lives, eroded the German work ethic, and imperiled the German economy. Other critics have not been quite this harsh, but have questioned the ability of experiential teambuilding to create real behavioral change in the workplace. The key concern is that teambuilding activities often are not tied to specific workplace problems.

Merrick Rosenberg, Chief Learning Officer at Team Builders Plus, understands the issues but believes they are not insurmountable. In his view, the first step is to score teams in terms of the degree to which they have deep problems with conflict, lack of trust, and lack of cooperation. For teams with few problems, simple participation in a teambuilding activity can provide a valued break from routine and a boost to morale. For teams with many problems, the basic experience is not enough. Instead, preactivity personality tests and surveys to determine specific problems must be emphasized so that teambuilding can be tailored to specific needs. Based on these assessments, particular activities can be chosen, particular individuals can be selected for certain subteams or leadership roles, and particular points can be made when instructors debrief the activities. Also, follow-up contacts, either virtually or through face-to-face meetings, become quite important for reinforcing lessons from the teambuilding experience.

Studies suggest that well-executed experiential teambuilding does in fact provide reasonable benefits. A recent participant put it this way:

We had a wonderful time! Facing a set of challenges that were very different than what we do 50–60 hours a week, we all learned different and surprising things about each other. … I think we will be a closer, better team for it.

David Goldstein, founder of a very successful company called Teambonding, certainly agrees with this assessment. He points out that well-designed team-based play delivers results because it: (1) is involving, (2) is low risk, (3) explores team dynamics, (4) promotes self-awareness, (5) builds trust, (6) shows the value of the team, (7) promotes pleasure, and (8) provides specific problem-solving and communication lessons. Based on scientific analysis and real-world applications, the power of experiential teambuilding for creating better attitudes and performance seems to be reasonably strong.

Sources: D. Goldstein. 2009. "The Power of Play," at http://www.teambonding.com/blog; H.L. Gillis, & E. Speelman. 2008. "Are Challenge (Ropes) Courses an Effective Tool? A Meta-Analysis," *The Journal of Experiential Education,* 31: pp. 111–135; J. Harkin. 2003. "Executives Go Out To Play," *New Statesmen,* Feb. 10, p. 18; C. Klein, D. DiazGranados, E. Salas, H. Le, C.S. Burke, R. Lyons, & G.F. Goodwin. 2009. "Does Team Building Work?" *Small Group Research,* 40: pp. 181–222; M. Rosenberg. 2007. "Beyond the Basics of Experiential Learning," *T&D,* 61, no. 12: pp. 26–28; Teambonding, "Programs," 2010, at http://www.teambonding.com/programs.

and make necessary changes if feedback indicates problems; and to ensure that the team is operating in a psychological climate that will enable it to function effectively.

Training

The thousands of team training programs and methods that exist speak to the criticality of adequate team training. Recall from an earlier section that one of the assumptions often held by managers is that people know how and are suited to work on teams. This is questionable in many cases. Team-building training generally focuses on four different types of skills:[116] (1) interpersonal skills, especially communication, supportiveness, and trust; (2) problem-solving skills, which allow team members to identify problems, generate solutions, and evaluate solutions; (3) goal-setting skills, and (4) role-clarification skills, which allow members to articulate role requirements and responsibilities.

A great deal of research has been done on the effectiveness of team training in improving team performance. This research shows that training has positive but somewhat weak effects on performance outcomes while having stronger positive effects on team members' evaluations of their team.[117] We should note that most of this research has been conducted on intact teams whose members had considerable experience working together. As a result, these teams had existing structures, roles, and norms, which probably made them more difficult to change. Training is likely to have a greater impact on the performance of newly formed teams.

In the *Managerial Advice* feature, a specific and important type of team training is profiled.

THE STRATEGIC LENS

In recent times much of the organization's work has been accomplished by teams. Some teams correspond to formal units of the firm (e.g., a department), some teams exist within formal units, and some teams cut across formal units. The work begins with the senior management team, which develops the organization's vision and the strategies intended to help realize the vision. These strategies are implemented by teams throughout the organization. For example, when the organization's goal is innovation, cross-functional teams are often assigned to develop new products. Members of these teams commonly represent research and development, marketing, and manufacturing units. Sometimes additional team members are drawn from customers and also external suppliers, who will provide materials for the new products.

Because of the pervasive use and importance of teams, an organization's performance ultimately depends on its teams' effectiveness. The effectiveness of the baristas in Starbucks stores, for example, has been largely responsible for the success of the overall organization. The design of teams, the selection of team members, and team leadership and management are all critical for organizational success. As a result, strategic leaders should invest significant effort in developing and managing teams.

Critical Thinking Questions

1. Think of some teams of which you have been a member. How successful were they? To what do you attribute your teams' success or lack thereof?

2. Why do organizations use teams to accomplish the work that needs to be done? What value do teams provide?

3. Someday you will be a leader of a team. What processes will you use to select team members? What specific actions will you take to manage the team to ensure high team productivity?

? back to the knowledge objectives

1. What makes a collection of people a team? How does a team differ from a group? What are some different types of teams?
2. To determine whether a team is effective, what should be measured?
3. What composition factors should a manager consider in designing an effective team? Would these factors differ depending on the type of team being formed?
4. What are the important aspects of team structure? How does each affect team performance?
5. What types of team processes can have a positive influence on team performance? What processes can have negative effects?
6. How do the stage model and the punctuated equilibrium model of team development differ?
7. What can organizations do to encourage and support effective teamwork?
8. What are some important team leader roles? Describe an example from your own experience of a team leader who filled one or more of these roles.

What This Chapter Adds to Your Knowledge Portfolio

This chapter discussed the importance of teams and teamwork in organizations. We began by discussing the nature of groups and teams and their different forms. Then, we addressed the criteria that should be used to determine whether a team is effective and the factors that influence team effectiveness. Next, we examined how teams develop over time. Finally, we described ways in which organizations and leaders can promote team effectiveness. To summarize, we focused on the following points:

- A group can be defined in very general terms as "two or more interdependent individuals who influence one another through social interaction." A team is a group that consists of two or more people who work interdependently within an organization, with tasks that are relevant and consequential for the organization's mission, and who are identified as a team by people within and outside the team.

- Groups and teams can be classified in a number of ways. Both formal and informal groups arise in organizations. People in organizations often belong to identity groups based on their social identities, such as gender identity, racial identity, or religious identity. Types of teams include virtual teams, functional teams, and self-managing teams. The type and purpose of the team can affect how the team develops and functions.

- Team effectiveness is measured in terms of the team's learning and cognition, team members' feelings about the team, and team outputs and viability.

- The composition of the team influences the team's effectiveness. The diversity of members, their personality, and the size of the team all influence team effectiveness.

- The structure of a team, including the roles held by members, the norms, and the task structure, can all influence a team's effectiveness.

- The processes used and experienced by the team also influence team performance. Team processes include team cohesion, conflict among team members, social facilitation, social loafing, and communication.

- Teams change and develop over time. The stage model of development proposes that teams experience four developmental stages: forming, storming, norming, and performing. A fifth stage, in which the team disbands, is adjourning. The punctuated equilibrium model of team development holds that teams undergo a shift from interpersonally focused to task-focused when the deadline for the team project moves closer.

- Organizations can promote effective teamwork through senior management support, technical and informational support, selecting appropriate people for teamwork, training people in teamwork skills, and rewarding team performance.
- Effective team leaders are also important for teamwork. They act as liaisons, ensure proper direction, and operationally coordinate team activities.

Thinking about Ethics

1. Should associates be required to work in teams if they prefer not to do so—that is, if they prefer to be evaluated based only on their individual efforts? What are the implications of allowing people such choices (positive or otherwise)?

2. Is it appropriate to exclude some members from teams when status and long-term rewards (such as promotions) in an organization are based largely on team performance?

3. What types of sanctions (if any) should be imposed on team members identified as engaging in social loafing? Who should apply those sanctions (if any)?

4. What are team leaders' responsibilities with regard to political processes within the organization? That is, when other individuals outside the team promote their own self-interests at the expense of the organization, especially when these actions have negative effects on the team's productivity, what should team leaders do? How can they best fulfill these responsibilities to the team and to the organization?

Key Terms

synergy, p. 404
group, p. 405
team, p. 405
formal groups, p. 405
informal groups, p. 405
identity groups, p. 406
virtual teams, p. 406
process loss, p. 411
team orientation, p. 413
roles, p. 414

task roles, p. 414
socioemotional roles, p. 414
destructive individual roles, p. 414
norms, p. 414
divisible tasks, p. 416
unitary tasks, p. 416
maximization tasks, p. 416
optimization tasks, p. 416

interpersonal cohesion, p. 417
task cohesion, p. 417
social facilitation effect, p. 419
social loafing, p. 420
punctuated equilibrium model (PEM), p. 422

Human Resource Management Applications

The Human Resource Management (HRM) function often plays a very large role in creating effective teams for an organization. Specific activities executed by the HRM department are as follows:

HRM units offer selection tools that can help to find team-oriented individuals. HRM professionals often develop specific interview questions designed to highlight team orientation. They also may develop case experiences that can reveal a person's predispositions. Finally, they may obtain personality tests that can provide information on team skills and interests. Tests of the Big Five personality traits are useful for this purpose (see Chapter 5).

HRM units also develop or otherwise make available team training. This training may involve webinars, lunch-and-learn lectures, and testing. It may involve the assignment of a mentor to difficult team members. It may also involve outsourced experiential teambuilding.

HRM units often help to design reward structures to promote team spirit and performance. For teams with disjunctive tasks, the reward structure should emphasize team outcomes to a substantial degree, with an individual's rewards being a function of those outcomes. For teams with conjunctive tasks, the reward system should put significant emphasis on individual accomplishments.

---

building your human capital
Do You Have a Team?

The benefits of teamwork are clearly outlined in this chapter. Not only can teams increase organization-related performance and contribute to the competitive advantage of the organization, they can also increase individual well-being. This has led the business world to adopt teamwork whenever possible. However, sometimes what we call a team does not really function as a team. Think of a team that you belong to, whether it is a sports team, a class project team, or a work team. Answer the following questions below to determine whether your team is really operating as a team:

1. To what extent is your team working interdependently?
   - Do team members work well together?
   - Are there problems in coordinating the team's activities?
   - Do people work together, or do they mostly do their work independently of one another?
   - What happens when a team member does not perform up to standards?
2. Is your team structured as a team?
   - Is the team organized?
   - Is it clear who is supposed to be doing what?
   - Are there conflicts over who is in charge?
3. Is your team interpersonally cohesive?
   - Is your team close or tight-knit?
   - Do team members like each other?
   - Do team members frequently quit the team?
4. Does your team have an identity?
   - Does your team have a name (either formal or informal)?
   - Are team members proud to tell others that they are a part of this team?
   - Do the team members have a sense of shared identity with each other?
   - Do team members put the team goals above their own personal goals?
   - Do team members work hard to reach the team's goals?
   - Does the team have a specific mission that everyone is clear about?

Source: Information adapted from and based on D.R. Forsyth. 1999. *Group Dynamics* (Belmont, CA: Wadsworth).

---

an organizational behavior moment
The New Quota

"One club." Jack closed his hand and, almost imperceptibly, leaned forward a little. To most people, such a movement would have gone unnoticed. But all three of the others knew that Jack's opening bid was a little weak.

"Pass."

"Three no trump." Bill was gleeful. He had 16 points, and this would be the first hand he had played this lunch hour. He watched as Jack spread his hand and noted that the play would be uneventful.

"Bid three, making four," Dennis said as he penciled down the score. "Got time for another?"

"Not really. Gotta get back to the grind," Steve grimaced as he spoke. "Listen, what do you guys think about the new quota?"

"It's ridiculous!" Bill was anxious to find out how his co-workers felt, and he also wanted to express his own opinion. "When I came here five years ago, we were supposed to wire three assemblies an hour. Now we're supposed to do eight. They aren't paying me that much more. I think it stinks."

"I do, too." Dennis was usually pretty low key. But as he spoke, his eye began to twitch, revealing his anxiety. "I'm not sure that I could meet it even if I tried, and I'm sure as hell not going to try. They can have my stinking job if they want. Only reason I stick around here, anyway, is because you guys are such lousy bridge players."

They all laughed. Then Jack, seeing that Steve was waiting, said, "Eight's possible, but I think some of us are going to be laid off if we all do it. I was talking to this guy over in engineering the other day, and he explained how to make a jig that lets you just lay those wires in real easy. I tried it and it really works. It saved me about six minutes on the first assembly. Of course, I went back and told him it didn't work. I just don't want to do eight—won't help any of us if we do."

Steve looked curiously at Jack. "So that's what you were up to! I saw you really pushing a couple of days ago and thought you'd lost your screws. Anyway, I'm glad you guys feel the same as me. It makes me feel a lot better. Don't figure the boss will do much to us if he thinks an old pro like Jack can't do eight."

It was several days later when Dave, the shop supervisor, was called to the manager's office. Dave knew that it was going to be about the quota, and he didn't know exactly what he was going to say. Mr. Martin was on the phone but motioned for him to sit down.

When he hung up, he faced Dave and said, "That was Pacific Electronics. They want to know if we can meet the shipping schedule or not. What do I tell them when I call back?"

"I don't know, honestly. The guys have picked their speed up some, but I don't think we're going to do better than six-and-a-half, maybe seven."

"That won't cut it, Dave. This new business is important. If we can't handle it, we'll have to cut back some workers. We have too many budget problems without it. Are you sure they're really trying?"

"Yes!" Dave responded. "Jack even tried a new jig that engineering thought up, but it didn't seem to help. Maybe if we added some more incentive bonus it would help. I don't know."

"We can't do that. Costs are already too high. We're being hurt on scrap rate, too. You just go back there and really push them. I'm going to tell Pacific that we can meet the schedule. Now you get that crew of yours to do it!"

Discussion Questions

1. What factors seem to be influencing team performance here?
2. Identify the team norms and goals. Are they compatible with organizational objectives?
3. How does the team function to meet individual needs? If you were Dave, what team concepts would you apply? Why?

---

team exercise

Virtual versus Real Teams

As discussed in this chapter, the use of virtual teams is common in the business world. Although virtual teams can save an organization time and money, they can also have their disadvantages. The purpose of this exercise is to explore the different dynamics that occur between face-to-face teams and virtual teams.

Procedure

DAY 1

1. The instructor will randomly divide the class into teams of five to seven people. The instructor will designate half of the teams as face-to-face teams and the other half as virtual teams.
2. Each team is responsible for developing a new school logo and branding slogan. They will have approximately one week to do this.

INTERIM PERIOD (APPROXIMATELY ONE WEEK)

1. Each team is responsible for completing its task outside class. Face-to-face teams can meet any time they desire and can also use electronic means of communication. Virtual teams may not meet face-to-face but can use any form of electronic communication to complete their task. Virtual teams also should not discuss the task in class. In addition, it is not necessary for all team meetings to include everyone on the team but several members should be present and all members should participate in some of the meetings.

2. The task is to develop a new school logo and branding slogan. Each team must also develop a three- to five-minute presentation of its product to present in class on Day 2 of the exercise.
3. Before class, each team should prepare answers to the following questions:
   a. How many meetings between team members took place? To what extent were these meetings productive?
   b. What were the most frustrating aspects of working on this project?
   c. To what extent did everyone contribute to the project?
   d. What type of communication problems arose in your team?
   e. To what extent was your team congenial? Were there misunderstandings? How well do team members now understand each other?
   f. How difficult was it to coordinate your work?

DAY 2 (APPROXIMATELY ONE WEEK AFTER DAY 1)
1. Each team presents its logo and slogan to the class.
2. The class votes on which team has the best logo and slogan.
3. The instructor leads the class in a discussion of their answers to the above questions and the different dynamics between face-to-face and virtual teams.

Endnotes

1. Lawler, E.E., III, Mohrman, S.A., & Ledford, G.E. 1995. *Creating high performance organizations: Practices and results in Fortune 1000 companies.* San Francisco: Jossey-Bass.
2. Fisher, A. 2007. The trouble with MBAs. *Fortune,* April 23, at http://cnnmoney.printhis.clikckability.com/pt/cpt?action=cpt&title+The trouble+with+MBAs.
3. Kirkman, B.L., Rosen, B., Tesluk, P.E., & Gibson, C.B. 2004. The impact of team empowerment on virtual team performance: The moderating role of face-to-face interaction. *Academy of Management Journal,* 47: 175–192.
4. Hackman, J.R., & Oldham, G.R. 1980. *Work redesign.* Reading, MA: Addison-Wesley.
5. Cohen, S.G., Ledford, G.E., & Spreitzer, G.M. 1996. A predictive model of self-managed work team effectiveness. *Human Relations,* 49: 643–679.
6. Sundstrom, E. 1999. The challenges of supporting work team effectiveness. In E. Sundstrom, & Associates (Eds.), *Supporting work team effectiveness: Best management practices for fostering high performance.* San Francisco: Jossey-Bass, pp. 3–23.
7. Ibid.
8. Labich, K. 1996. Elite teams get the job done. *Fortune,* February 19: 90–99.
9. Finkelstein, S., & Hambrick, D.C. 1996. *Strategic leadership: Top executives and their effects on organizations.* St. Paul, MN: West Publishing Company.
10. Ireland, R.D. Hoskisson, R.E., & Hitt, M.A. 2005. *Understanding business strategy.* Mason, OH: South-Western Thomson Publishing.
11. Koslowski, S.W.J., & Bell, B.S. 2004. Work groups and teams in organizations. In W.C. Borman, D.R. Ilgen, & R.J. Klimoski, (Eds.), *Handbook of psychology, Vol. 12: Industrial and organizational psychology.* Hoboken, NJ: Wiley, pp. 333–374; West, M.A. 1996. Preface: Introducing work group psychology. In M.A. West (Ed.), *Handbook of work group psychology.* Chichester, United Kingdom: John Wiley & Sons, pp. xxvi–xxxiii; Guzzo,

R.A. 1995. Introduction: At the intersection of team effectiveness and decision making. In R.A. Guzzo, E. Salas, & Associates (Eds.), *Team effectiveness and decision making in organizations.* San Francisco: Jossey-Bass, pp. 1–8.
12. Forsyth, D.R. 1999. *Group dynamics.* Belmont, CA: Wadsworth, p. 5.
13. Guzzo, Introduction.
14. Ibid.
15. Mitchell, T. 1978. *People in organizations: Understanding their behavior.* New York: McGraw-Hill, p. 176.
16. Alderfer, C.P. 1987. An intergroup perspective on group dynamics. In J. Lorsch (Ed.), *Handbook of organizational behavior.* Upper Saddle River, NJ: Prentice Hall, pp. 190–210.
17. Chao, G.T. 2000. Levels issues in cultural psychology research. In K.J. Klein & S.W.J. Koslowski (Eds.), *Multilevel theory, research, and methods in organizations.* San Francisco: Jossey-Bass, pp. 308–346.
18. See, for example, Furumo, K. 2009. The impact of conflict and conflict management style on deadbeats and deserters in virtual teams. *Journal of Computer Information Systems,* 49 (4): 66–73; Mittleman, D., & Briggs, R.O. 1999. Communicating technologies for traditional and virtual teams. In E. Sundstrom & Associates (Eds.), *Supporting work team effectiveness.* San Francisco: Jossey-Bass, pp. 246–270.
19. Furst, S.A., Reeves, M., Rosen, B., & Blackburn, R.S. 2004. Managing the life cycle of virtual teams. *Academy of Management Executive,* 18: 6–20.
20. Kirkman, Rosen, Tesluk, & Gibson, The impact of team empowerment on virtual team performance. Also, see Hill, N.S., Bartol, K.M., Tesluk, P.E., & Langa, G.A. 2009. Organizational context and face-to-face interaction: Influences on the development of trust and collaborative behaviors in computer-mediated groups. *Organizational Behavior and Human Decision Processes,* 108: 187–201.
21. Kirkman, Rosen, Tesluk, & Gibson, The impact of team empowerment on virtual team performance.

22. Joshi, A., Lazarova, M.B., & Liao, H. 2009. Getting everyone on board: The role of inspirational leadership in geographically dispersed teams. *Organization Science*, 20: 240–252; Ruggieri, S. 2009. Leadership in virtual teams: A comparison of transformational and transactional leaders. *Social Behavior and Personality*, 37: 1017–1021.

23. Purvanova, R.K., & Bono, J.E. 2009. Transformational leadership in context: Face-to-face and virtual teams. *The Leadership Quarterly*, 20: 343–357.

24. Mittleman, & Briggs, Communicating technologies for traditional and virtual teams.

25. Sundstrom, E., McIntyre, M., Halfhill, T., & Richards, H. 2000. Work groups: From the Hawthorne studies to work teams of the 1990s and beyond. *Group Dynamics: Theory, Research, and Practice*, 4: 44–67.

26. Hackman, J.R. 1986. The psychology of self-management in organizations. In M.S. Pollack, & R.O. Perlogg (Eds.), *Psychology and work: Productivity change and employment*. Washington, DC: American Psychological Association, pp. 85–136; Manz, C.C. 1992. Self-leading work teams: Moving beyond self-management myths. *Human Relations*, 45: 1119–1140.

27. Cohen, S.G., & Ledford, G.E., Jr., 1994. The effectiveness of self-managing teams: A quasi-experiment. *Human Relations*, 47: 13–43; Manz, C.C., & Sims, H.P., Jr. 1987. Leading workers to lead themselves: The external leadership of self-managing work teams. *Administrative Science Quarterly*, 32: 106–128.

28. Druskat, V.U., & Wheeler, J.V. 2003. Managing from the boundary: The effectiveness leadership of self-managing work teams. *Academy of Management Journal*, 46: 435–457; Stewart, G.L., & Manz, C.C. 1995. Leadership for self-managing work teams: A typology and integrative model. *Human Relations*, 48: 347–370.

29. Orpheus Chamber Orchestra. 2010. History. http://www.orpheusnyc.com/history.html; Pfeffer, J. 2007. *What were they thinking?: Unconventional wisdom about management*. Boston: Harvard Business School Press; Seifert, H. 2001. The conductor-less orchestra. *Leader to leader*, No. 21, http://www.pfdf.org/leaderbooks/121/summer2002/seifter.html.

30. Hackman, J.R. 2002. *Leading teams: Setting the stage for great performances*. Boston; Harvard Business School Press.

31. Canon-Bowers, J.A., Salas, E., & Converse, S.A. 1993. Shared mental models in expert team decision making. In N.J. Castellan (Ed.), *Individual and group decision making*. Hillsdale, NJ: Erlbaum, pp. 221–246.

32. Klimoski, R.J., & Mohammed, S. 1994. Team mental model: Construct or metaphor? *Journal of Management*, 20: 403–437.

33. Edwards, B.D., Day, E.A., Arthur, W., Jr., & Bell S.T. 2006. Relationships among team ability composition, team mental models, and team performance. *Journal of Applied Psychology*, 91: 727–736.

34. Koslowski & Bell, Work groups and teams in organizations.

35. Hackman, *Leading teams*.

36. George, J.M. 1990. Personality, affect, and behavior in groups. *Journal of Applied Psychology*, 75: 107–116.

37. Barsade, S.G., Ward, A., Turner, J., & Sonnenfeld, J. 2000. To your heart's content: A model of affective diversity in top management teams. *Administrative Science Quarterly*, 45: 802–836.

38. Shea, G.P., & Guzzo, R.A. 1987. Groups as human resources. In K.M. Rowland, & G.R. Ferris (Eds.), *Research in personnel and human resource management (Vol. 5)*. Greenwich, CT: JAI Press, pp. 323–356.

39. Hackman, *Leading teams*.

40. Hackman, J.R. 1987. The design of work teams. In J. Lorsch (Ed.), *Handbook of organizational behavior*. New York: Prentice Hall, pp. 315–342.

41. Katz, R., & Allen, T.J. 1988. Investigating the not invented here (NIH) syndrome: A look at performance, tenure, and communication patterns of 50 R&D project groups. In M.L. Tushman, & W.L. Moore (Eds.), *Readings in the management of innovation*. New York: Ballinger, pp. 293–309.

42. Burke, C.S., Stagl, K.C., Salas, E., Pierce, L., & Kendall, D. 2006. Understanding team adaptation: A conceptual analysis and model. *Journal of Applied Psychology*, 91: 1189–1207.

43. Katzenbach, J., 1997. *Teams at the top*. Boston, MA: Harvard Business Press.

44. Steiner, I.D. 1972. *Group processes and productivity*. New York: Academic Press.

45. Hackman, *Leading teams*.

46. Kochan, T., et al. 2003. The effects of diversity on business performance: Report of the diversity research network. *Human Resource Management*, 42: 3–21.

47. Ely, R.J., & Thomas, D.A. 2001. Cultural diversity at work: The effects of diversity perspectives on work group processes and outcomes. *Administrative Science Quarterly*, 46: 229–274; Bantel, K.A., & Jackson, S.E. 1989. Top management and innovations in banking: Does the composition of the top team make a difference? *Strategic Management Journal*, 10: 107–124; Jackson, S.E., Brett, J.F., Sessa, V.I., Cooper, D.M., Julin, J.A., & Peyroonnin, K. 1991. Some differences make a difference: Individual dissimilarity and group heterogeneity as correlates of recruitment, promotions, and turnover. *Journal of Applied Psychology*, 76: 675–689; Pelled, L.H., Eisenhardt, K.M., & Xin, K.R. 1999. Exploring the black box: An analysis of work group diversity, conflict, and performance. *Administrative Science Quarterly*, 44: 1–28.

48. Campion, M.A., Medsker, G.J., & Higgs, A.C. 1993. Relations between work group characteristics and effectiveness: Implications for designing effective work groups. *Personnel Psychology*, 46: 823–850.

49. Barkema, H.G., & Shvyrkov, O. 2007. Does top management team diversity promote or hamper foreign expansion? *Strategic Management Journal*, 28: 663–680; Miller, C.C., Burke, L.M., & Glick, W.H. 1998. Cognitive diversity among upper-echelon executives: Implications for strategic decision processes. *Strategic Management Journal*, 19: 39–58; Perretti, F., & Giacomo, N. 2007. Mixing genres and matching people: A study in innovation and team composition in Hollywood. *Journal of Organizational Behavior*, 28: 563–586; Simons, T., Pelled, L.H., & Smith, K.A. 1999. Making use of difference: Diversity, debate, and decision comprehensiveness in top management teams. *Academy of Management Journal*, 42: 662–673; Ward, A.J., Lankau, M.J., Amason, A.C., Sonnenfeld, J.A., & Agle, B.R. 2007. Improving the performance of top management teams. *MIT Sloan Management Review*, Spring: 84–90.

50. Argote, L., & McGrath, J.E. 1993. Group processes in organizations: Continuity and change. In C.L. Cooper, & I.T. Robertson (Eds.), *International review of industrial and organizational psychology (Vol. 8)*. New York: John Wiley & Sons, pp. 333–389.

51. Jackson, S.E., May, K.E., & Whitney, K. 1995. Understanding the dynamics of diversity in decision making teams. In R.A. Guzzo, E. Salas, & Associates (Eds.), *Team effectiveness and decision making in organizations*. San Francisco: Jossey-Bass, pp. 204–261.

52. Koslowski & Bell, Work groups and teams in organizations.

53. Watson, W.E., Kumar, K., & Michaelson, L.K. 1993. Cultural diversity's impact on interaction process and performance: Comparing homogeneous and diverse task groups. *Academy of Management Journal*, 36: 590–602.

54. Barkema, H.G., & Shvyrkov, O. 2007. Does top management team diversity promote or hamper foreign expansion?

55. Bezrukova, K., Jehn, K.A., Zanutto, E.L., & Thatcher, S.M.B. 2009. Do workgroup faultlines help or hurt? A moderated model of faultlines, team identification, and group performance; Lau, D.C., & Murnighan, J.K. 1998. Demographical diversity and faultlines: The compositional dynamics of organizational groups. *Academy of Management Review*, 23: 325–340.

56. Mount, M.K., Barrick, M.R., & Stewart, G.L. 1998. Five-Factor model of personality and performance in jobs involving interpersonal interactions. *Human Performance*, 11: 145–165.

57. Barrick, M.R., Stewart, G.L., Neubert, M.J., & Mount, M.K. 1998. Relating member ability and personality to work-team processes and team effectiveness. *Journal of Applied Psychology*, 83: 377–391; Bell, S.T. 2007. Deep-level composition variables as predictors of team performance: A meta-analysis. *Journal of Applied Psychology*, 92: 595.

58. Stewart, G.L. 2003. Toward an understanding of the multilevel role of personality in teams. In M.R. Barrick, & A.M. Ryan (Eds.), *Personality and work: Reconsidering the role of personality in organizations*. San Francisco: Jossey-Bass, pp. 183–204.

59. Neuman, G.A., & Wright, J. 1999. Team effectiveness: Beyond skills and cognitive ability. *Journal of Applied Psychology*, 84: 376–389.

60. Burke, Stagl, Salas, Pierce, & Kendall, Understanding team adaptation.

61. Ibid.

62. Nieva, V.F., Fleishman, E.A., & Reick, A. 1985. *Team dimensions: Their identity, their measurement, and their relationships. (Research Note #12)*. Washington, DC: U.S. Army Research Institute for the Behavioral and Social Sciences.

63. Campion, M.A., Medsker, G.J., & Higgs, A.C. 1993. Relations between work group characteristics and effectiveness: Implications for designing effective work groups. *Personnel Psychology*, 46: 823–850.

64. Koslowski & Bell, Work groups and teams in organizations.

65. Porter, L., Lawler, E., III, and Hackman, J. 1975. *Behavior in organizations*. New York: McGraw-Hill, p. 373.

66. Forsyth, D.R. 1999. *Group dynamics*. Belmont, CA: Wadsworth, p. 5.

67. Benne, K.D., & Sheets, P. 1948. Functional roles of group members. *Journal of Social Issues*, 4: 41–49.

68. Hackman, *Leading teams*.

69. Labich, K. 1996. Elite teams get the job done. *Fortune*, February 19: 90–99.

70. Crandall, C.S. 1988. Social contagion of binge eating. *Journal of Personality and Social Psychology*, 55: 588–598.

71. Hackman, The design of work teams.

72. Steiner, *Group processes and productivity*.

73. Forsyth, D.R. 1999. *Group dynamics. Belmont*, CA: Wadsworth.

74. Ibid.

75. Evans, C.R., & Jarvis, P.A. 1980. Group cohesion: A review and re-evaluation. *Small Group Behavior*, 11: 359–370.

76. Ibid.

77. Barrick, Stewart, Neubert, & Mount, Relating member ability and personality to work-team processes and team effectiveness; Hambrick, D.C. 1995. Fragmentation and other problems CEOs have with their top management teams. *California Management Review*, 37: 110–127; Mullen, B., & Copper, C. 1994. The relationship between group cohesiveness and performance: An integration. *Psychological Bulletin*, 115: 210–227.

78. Hackman, J.R. 1992. Group influences on individuals in organizations. In M.D. Dunnette & L.M. Hough (Eds.), *Handbook of industrial and organizational psychology (Vol. 3)*. Palo Alto, CA: Consulting Psychologists Press, pp. 199–267.

79. Mullen, & Copper, The relationship between group cohesiveness and performance.

80. Seashore, S.E. 1954. *Group cohesiveness in the industrial work group*. Ann Arbor: University of Michigan, Institute for Social Research.

81. Gully, S.M., Devine, D.J., & Whitney, D.J. 1995. A meta-analysis of cohesion and performance: Effects of levels of analysis and task interdependence. *Small Group Research*, 26: 497–520.

82. Morrill, C. 1995. *The executive way*. Chicago: University of Chicago Press.

83. Forsyth, *Group dynamics.*.

84. Amason, A.C., & Schweiger, D.M. 1994. Resolving the paradox of conflict, strategic decision making and organizational performance. *International Journal of Conflict Management*, 5: 239–253; Jehn, K.A. 1995. A multimethod examination of the benefits and detriments of intragroup conflict. *Administrative Science Quarterly*, 40: 256-282; Jehn, K.A., Greer, L., Levine, S., & Szulanski, G. 2008. The effects of conflict types, dimensions, and emergent states on group dynamics. *Group Decision and Negotiation*, 17: 465–495; Tekleab, A.G., Quigley, N.R., Tesluk, P.E. 2009. A longitudinal study of team conflict, conflict management, cohesion, and team effectiveness. *Group & Organizational Management*, 34: 170–205.

85. Forsyth, *Group dynamics*.

86. Ibid.

87. Zajonc, R.B. 1980. Compresence. In P.B. Paulus (Ed.), *Psychology of group influence*. Hillsdale, NJ: Erlbaum, pp. 35–60.

88. Cottrell, N.B. 1972. Social facilitation. In C.G. McClintock (Ed.), *Experimental social psychology*. New York: Holt, Rinehart, & Winston, pp. 185–236.

89. Bond, M.H., & Titus, L.J. 1983. Social facilitation: A meta-analysis of 241 studies. *Psychological Bulletin*, 94: 265–292.

90. Latane, B., Williams, K., & Harkins, S. 1979. Many hands make light the work: The causes and consequences of social loafing. *Journal of Personality and Social Psychology*, 47: 822–832.

91. Alcian, A.A., & Demsetz, H. 1972. Production information costs, and economic organization. *American Economic Review*, 62: 777–795.

92. Price, K.H., Harrison, D.A., & Gavin, J.A. 2006. Withholding inputs in team contexts: Member composition, interaction processes, evaluation structure, and social loafing. *Journal of Applied Psychology,* 91: 1375–1384; Jackson, J.M., & Harkins, S.G. 1985. Equity in effort: An explanation of the social loafing effect. *Journal of Personality and Social Psychology,* 49: 1199–1206.

93. Karau, S.J., & Williams, K.D. 1993. Social loafing: A meta-analytic review and theoretical integration. *Journal of Personality and Social Psychology,* 65: 681–706.

94. Kerr, N., & Bruun, S. 1983. Dispensability of effort and group motivational losses: Free rider effects. *Journal of Personality and Social Psychology,* 44: 78–94.

95. Latane, Williams, & Harkins, Many hands make light the work.

96. Jackson, J.M., & Harkins, S.G. 1985. Equity in effort: An explanation of the social loafing effect. *Journal of Personality and Social Psychology,* 49: 1199–1206.

97. Price, Harrison,, & Gavin, Withholding inputs in team contexts.

98. Vermeulen, P., and Benders, J. 2003. A reverse side of the team medal. *Team Performance Management: An International Journal,* 9: 107–114.

99. Kirkman, Rosen, Tesluk, & Gibson, The impact of team empowerment on virtual team performance.

100. Reitz, J. 1977. *Behavior in organizations.* Homewood, IL: Richard D. Irwin, p. 301.

101. Tuckman, B.W. 1965. Developmental sequences in small groups. *Psychological Bulletin,* 63: 384–399; Tuckman, B.W., & Jensen, M.A.C. 1977. Stages of small group development. *Group and Organizational Studies,* 2: 419–427.

102. Koslowski, & Bell, Work groups and teams in organizations.

103. Ibid.

104. Gersick, C.J.G. 1988. Time and transition in work teams: Toward a new model of group development. *Academy of Management Journal,* 31: 9–41; Gersick, C.J.G. 1989. Marking time: Predictable transitions in task groups. *Academy of Management Journal,* 32: 274–309.

105. Chang, A., Bordia P., & Duck, J. 2003. Punctuated equilibrium and linear progression: Toward a new understanding of group development. *Academy of Management Journal,* 46: 106–117.

106. Hitt, M.A., Nixon, R.D., Hoskisson, R.E., & Kochhar, R. 1999. Corporate entrepreneurship and cross-functional fertilization: Activation, process and disintegration of a new product design team. *Entrepreneurship, Theory & Practice,* 23: 145–167.

107. Sundstrom, E. 1999. Supporting work team effectiveness: Best practices. In E. Sundstrom, & Associates (Eds.), *Supporting work team effectiveness: Best management practices for fostering high performance.* San Francisco: Jossey-Bass, pp. 301–342.

108. Sundstrom, Supporting work team effectiveness.

109. Hackman, Group influences on individuals in organizations.

110. Ibid.

111. Heneman, H.G. III, & Judge, T.A. 2003. *Staffing organizations.* Middleton, WI: Mendota House.

112. Klimoski, R.J., & Zukin, L.B. 1999. Selection and staffing for team effectiveness. In E. Sundstrom, & Associates (Eds.), *Supporting work team effectiveness: Best management practices for fostering high performance.* San Francisco: Jossey-Bass, pp. 63–91.

113. Sundstrom, Supporting work team effectiveness.

114. McIntyre, R.M., & Salas, E. 1995. Measuring and managing for team performance: Emerging principles from complex environments. In R.A. Guzzo, E. Salas, & Associates (Eds.), *Team effectiveness and decision making in organizations.* San Francisco: Jossey-Bass, pp. 9–45.

115. Chen, G., Kirkman, B.L., Kanfer, R., Allen, D., & Rosen, B. 2007. A multilevel study of leadership, empowerment, and performance in teams. *Journal of Applied Psychology,* 92: 331–346; Zaccaro, S.J., & Marks, M.A. 1999. The roles of leaders in high-performance teams. In E. Sundstrom, & Associates (Eds.), *Supporting work team effectiveness: Best management practices for fostering high performance.* San Francisco: Jossey-Bass, pp. 95–125.

116. Salas, E., Rozell, D., Driskell, J.D., & Mullen, B. 1999. The effect of team building on performance: An integration. *Small Group Research,* 30: 309–329.

117. Ibid; Klein, C., DiazGranados, D., Salas, E., Le, H., Burke, C.S., Lyons, R., & Goodwin, G.F. 2009. Does Team Building Work? *Small Group Research,* 40. 181–222

conflict, negotiation, power, and politics

Green Conflict

In November 2007, Thomas Falk, the CEO of Kimberly-Clark Corporation, arrived at the University of Wisconsin where he would deliver an address on corporate governance as part of the annual Director's Summit (a meeting designed for the continuing education of board members from various companies). As he began to work through his PowerPoint presentation, the audience noticed some peculiar slides, slides that pointedly protested Kimberly-Clark's use of old-growth forests for its tissue paper products (Kleenex, Cottonelle, Scott, and other brands). After terminating the presentation and adjourning early for lunch, the directors and others in attendance found interesting menus at their tables. Those menus included entries such as "Songbird Stir-fry" and "Caribou Clearcut Cake." The appetizer was "Social Conflict Scramble." Clearly, Greenpeace activists had been active that day!

After speaking at the Consumer Electronics show in Las Vegas in 2003, Michael Dell was confronted by a group of angry environmental activists from the Silicon Valley Toxics Coalition. They were dressed as prisoners and shackled to PCs. The protest was against Dell's then-practice of using prison labor and unsafe practices to recycle old computers while competitors such as Hewlett-Packard were using much safer and more effective means. In 2005, Greenpeace activists dumped hundreds of used PCs outside of Wipro headquarters in Bangalore, India, to protest the computer assembler's lack of a "take-back" recycling practice. Greenpeace mounted a different type of campaign to motivate Apple to become more environmentally

knowledge objectives

After reading this chapter, you should be able to:

1. Explain how conflict can be either functional or dysfunctional and distinguish among various types of conflict.
2. Discuss common causes of conflict.
3. Describe conflict escalation and the various outcomes of conflict.
4. Explain how people respond to conflict and under what circumstances each type of response is best.
5. Understand how organizations can manage conflict.
6. Describe the basic negotiation process as well as effective strategies and tactics for negotiating.
7. Explain why organizations must have power to function, and discuss how people gain power in organizations.
8. Define organizational politics and the tactics used to carry out political behavior.

responsive by creating the "Green My Apple" website in 2006. In 2007, the Center for Health, Environment, and Justice staged a huge protest against Target stores for using PVC vinyl. The protest included newspaper ads against Target, a petition to the CEO, letters to store managers, and picketing at individual stores. In 2009, the World Wildlife Federation presented a petition with 50,000 signatures to ExxonMobil protesting activities that endanger the Western gray whale.

©DIETER NAGL/AFP/Getty Images, Inc.

These are just six out of thousands of examples where conflict between environmental groups and business corporations has surfaced. Traditionally, the goals of the environmental groups have included reducing carbon emissions, protecting wildlife and natural habitats, avoiding the use of poisonous substances, recycling, and the development and use of sustainable products and energy sources. Corporate goals have usually centered on providing value to shareholders—meaning companies typically benefit from using the least expensive products, processes, energy sources, and labor practices to produce their goods and services. Typically, environmentally sound business practices have not been the most cost (or profit) effective. Thus, it is no surprise that there is a long history of conflict between environmental groups and business firms.

However, things are beginning to change, with environmentalist organizations working together with business corporations to obtain mutual benefit. In fact, in order for many organizations to survive now, they must work with environmental groups. For example, when William K. Reilly was contemplating a private equity takeover of TXU corporation, a Texas utilities firm, a major drawback was that TXU did not have support from environmentalist organizations. In order for the deal to go through, TXU had to win support from those organizations. TXU had been doing battle with Environmental Defense, a major environmentalist organization, over the opening of 11

coal-fired power plants. As part of the deal negotiation, Environmental Defense was brought in. After harrowing negotiations, the new owners of TXU agreed to Environmental Defense's terms and dropped 8 of the original 11 proposed plants. When asked why environmentalists' support was so important for the TXU deal, Reilly responded, "We all swim in the same culture—and the culture is going green."

TXU is not the only company forming partnerships with environmentalist organizations. Shortly after the 2003 protest against their recycling policies, Dell joined together with Silicon Valley Toxics Coalition to develop a state-of-the-art recycling plan. DuPont, which is known as a green leader in its industry, employs Paul Gilding, the former head of Greenpeace, to work on its environmental policies and practices. In a much-publicized campaign, Walmart is working with Conservation International and the consulting firm BlueSkye to become a leader in environmentally sound retail practices. Walmart's former CEO, Lee Scott, stated that what started out as a defensive strategy in response to public protests over Walmart's environmental practices has turned out to be exactly the opposite.

Kimberly-Clark also has been working with environmental groups. In 2009, it agreed to alter its procurement policy by: (1) avoiding the use of fiber from the world's most sensitive forests, (2) giving preference to FSC (Forest Stewardship Council) certified fiber over other virgin wood, and (3) using postconsumer recycled fiber (e.g., from office paper) in some products rather than virgin fiber or preconsumer recycled fiber (e.g., wood chips from furniture manufacturing). For Kimberly-Clark, these changes will reduce the protests and pressure from activists while not substantially affecting the bottom line. For activists, the agreement is not perfect but the changes do mean more protection for ancient forests and their wildlife. For example, the National Resource Defense Council estimates that 425,000 trees would be saved annually if each U.S. household replaced once per year a 500-sheet roll of non-recycled bathroom tissue with a roll made from 100 percent recycled material. In 2009, an iPhone app was introduced to help consumers determine which tissue and bath tissue products are the most positive for the environment.

Sources: Anonymous. 2008. "Gotcha: CEO's Presentation Foiled," *Greenpeace Update*, Spring, p. 7; Associated Press. 2003. "Environmentalists at Vegas Trade Show Protest Dell's Recycling," press release, Jan. 9; J. Carey & M. Arndt. 2007. "Hugging the Tree-Huggers: Why So Many Companies Are Suddenly Linking Up with Eco Groups—Hint: Smart Business," *BusinessWeek,* Mar. 12, pp. 66–67; Center for Health, Environment, and Justice. 2007. "Target Faces Mounting Pressure to Phase Out Toxic Products & Packaging on Day of Annual Shareholder Meeting," news release, May 24, at http://www.besafenet.com/pvs/ newsreleases/target_may_24_doa_ release. htm; Greenpeace, "About Kimberly-Clark's Campaign, Aug. 5, 2009, at http://www.greenpeace.org/canada/en/recent/kimberly-clark-and-greenpeace/about-kimberly-clark-s-campain; Greenpeace. 2007. "Green My Apple Bears Fruit," June 1, at http://www.greenpeace.org/ use/news/green-my-apple-bears-fruit; M. Gunther. 2006. "The Green Machine," *Fortune,* July 31, pp. 42–45; J. Ribeiro. 2005. "Greenpeace Protests Recycling Policies," *PCWorld,* Sept. 6, at http://www.pcworld.com/printable/article/ id.122419/printable.html; B. Walsh. 2009. "A Delicate Undertaking," *Time,* June 22, p. 97; World Wildlife Fund. 2009. "Exxon Ignores Pleas from 50,000 People to Stop Threatening Rare Whales," Aug. 9, at http://worldwildlife.org/who/media/press/2009/WWFPresitem13143b.html.

the strategic importance of Conflict, Negotiation, Power, and Politics

The *Exploring Behavior in Action* feature illustrates a fundamental conflict between environmental organizations and businesses that was once believed to be a zero-sum game, where one side had to win and the other had to lose. It was thought that businesses could either act responsibly toward the environment and thus decrease profits (environmentalists win) or they could operate to increase profits at the expense of the environment (business wins). However, today many environmental organizations and businesses are handling this conflict in a different manner so that effective compromises or even win–win outcomes are achieved. Environmentalists have learned to work with businesses to develop more environmentally friendly practices rather than to protest and embarrass them. At the same time, many businesses have come to view being environmentally responsible as a profitable business strategy.[1]

For those businesses that have been able to solve this conflict, the payoff has been immense. First, many practices that are environmentally sound have also served to save businesses money. For example, DuPont has saved over $2 billion from reductions in energy use since 1990.[2] Another way in which companies benefit is by improving sustainability of the environment. This is a long-term perspective whereby companies operate so as not to deplete their resources thereby ensuring that they can operate in the future. For example, Walmart, one of the largest purveyors of seafood, has developed a program of sustainable fishing practices to maintain commercial stocks of fish, which can become depleted.[3] Finally, companies' reputations are bolstered by acting in an environmentally responsible manner.[4] There are many very public "report cards" (e.g., the Dow Jones Sustainability Index and the FTSE4Good Index) that evaluate how well companies perform in terms of environmental responsibility as well as other types of social responsibility.[5] Company reputation has been linked to profits,[6] associates' morale,[7] and the ability to recruit top talent.[8] In this case, effectively dealing with and resolving conflict has been shown to have a very important strategic impact on firm performance.

In this chapter, we examine the nature of conflict, the process of negotiation, the exercise of power, and the political behavior that is common in organizations. We begin by defining conflict and differentiating among different types of conflict. We then turn to the causes of conflict, its outcomes, and various responses to it. After discussing conflict-resolution techniques in organizations, we conclude with a discussion of power and politics.

The Nature of Conflict

Conflict is a "process in which one party perceives that its interests are being opposed or negatively affected by another party."[9] In this chapter, we focus on conflict between individuals and between organizational units, with some attention given to interorganizational conflict as well. As we noted in the opening discussion, some conflicts are dysfunctional and some are not. In this section, we look more closely at the difference between functional and dysfunctional conflict and then describe three major types of conflict.

conflict
A process in which one party perceives that its interests are being opposed or negatively affected by another party.

Dysfunctional and Functional Conflict

Dysfunctional conflict is conflict that interferes with performance. Conflict can be dysfunctional for several reasons. First, conflict with important constituencies can create doubt about the organization's future performance in the minds of shareholders, causing stock prices to drop.[10] For example, this happened when Greenpeace protested Shell Oil's sinking of the oil rig, Brent Spar, in the North Sea.[11] Second, conflict can cause people to exercise their own individual power and engage in political behavior directed toward achieving their own goals at the expense of attaining organizational goals. Third, conflict can have negative effects on interpersonal relationships, as shown in Exhibit 12-1. Finally, it takes time, resources, and emotional energy to deal with conflict, both on an interpersonal and an organizational level. Thus, resources that could be invested in achieving the organization's mission are used in the effort to address the conflict. One survey showed that managers spend approximately 25 percent of their time dealing with conflict. In some fields (such as hospital administration and management of municipal organizations), managers can spend as much as 50 percent of their time managing conflict. Managers have rated conflict management as equal to or higher in importance than planning, communicating, motivating, and decision making.[12]

dysfunctional conflict
Conflict that is detrimental to organizational goals and objectives.

As mentioned, however, conflict need not be dysfunctional. Conflict that has beneficial results for both the organization and the individual is considered **functional conflict**.[13] An organization without functional conflict frequently lacks the energy and ideas to create effective innovation. Indeed, to encourage functional conflict in groups, some managers have implemented a formal dialectical-inquiry or devil's advocacy approach (described in

functional conflict
Conflict that is beneficial to organizational goals and objectives.

EXHIBIT 12-1   Effects of Conflict

Effects on Individuals	Effects on Behavior	Effects on Interpersonal Relationships
• Anger	• Reduced motivation and productivity	• Distrust
• Hostility	• Avoidance of other party	• Misunderstandings
• Frustration	• Emotional venting	• Inability to see other's perspective
• Stress	• Threats	• Questioning of other's intentions
• Guilt	• Aggression (psychological or physical)	• More negative attitudes toward others
• Low job satisfaction	• Quitting	• Changes in the amount of power
• Embarrassment	• Absenteeism	• Changes in the quality of communication
	• Biased perceptions	• Changes in the amount of communication
	• Stereotyped thinking	
	• Increased commitment to one's perspective	
	• Demonizing others	

Chapter 10). For example, the person serving as devil's advocate has the responsibility of questioning decisions to ensure that as many alternatives as possible are considered.[14]

By stimulating energy and debate, conflict can have a number of functional consequences for organizations, including the following:

- Facilitation of change
- Improved problem solving or decision making
- Enhanced morale and cohesion within a group (based on conflict with other groups)
- More spontaneity in communication
- Stimulation of creativity and, therefore, productivity[15]

Types of Conflict

Three types of conflict occur in the workplace: personal conflict, substantive conflict, and procedural conflict.[16] As shown in Exhibit 12-2, unresolved personal conflict and procedural conflict tend to be dysfunctional, but ongoing or periodic substantive conflict can prove constructive.

personal conflict
Conflict that arises out of personal differences between people, such as differing values, personal goals, and personalities.

As mentioned in Chapter 11, **personal conflict** refers to conflict that arises out of personal and relationship differences between people—differing values, personal goals, personalities, and the like. Individuals involved in personal conflict often report disliking one another, making fun of one another, being angry with or jealous of one another, having problems with each other's personalities, or perceiving each other as enemies.[17] Personal conflict is likely to result in poor performance.[18] This form of conflict creates distrust, misunderstanding, and suspicion and reduces goodwill.[19] As a result, associates have trouble focusing their attention fully on their job responsibilities and find it difficult to work together toward organizationally relevant goals.

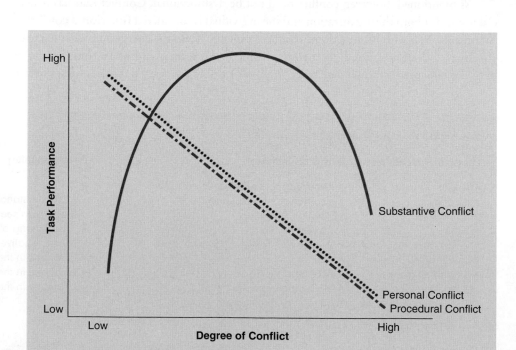

Exhibit 12-2 The Effects of Different Types of Conflict on Task Performance

The second type of conflict, **substantive conflict**, occurs over work content, tasks, and task goals.[20] In essence, differing opinions exist for task-related issues. One example of substantive conflict relates to an event described as the "Great Petunia War."[21] Two types of military retailers sell goods to military personnel: commissaries and post exchanges. In 1997, these retailers entered into a turf war over who had the right to sell garden plants and flowers. The battle soon escalated to include cooking oil, fruits and vegetables, and other types of food. These retailers were in conflict over their work goals. The conflict became so heated that two generals had to get involved because the conflict was threatening a proposal to reduce costs by integrating the operations of both retailers in the same facility on some bases. Substantive conflicts do not have to result in poor performance, if managed correctly.[22] Moderate levels of substantive conflict can actually increase performance. Even somewhat higher levels might lead to creative, positive outcomes if collaborative problem solving is emphasized. We discuss these issues later in this chapter.

©Libby Welch/Alamy

substantive conflict
Conflict that involves work content, tasks, and task goals.

procedural conflict
Conflict that arises over how work should be completed.

The third type of conflict, **procedural conflict**, concerns how work should be completed.[23] Procedural conflict occurs, for example, when students working together on a project disagree about who will work on which parts of the project or whether they should meet face to face or communicate by e-mail. Unresolved procedural conflict has been found to negatively affect performance. If individuals cannot decide who should be responsible for completing a task or how it should be done, there is little chance that they will accomplish their goals or even complete the project.[24]

Causes of Conflict

Conflict within organizations can be caused by many factors, which are frequently interrelated. To manage conflict effectively, managers should understand the causes of conflict and be able to diagnose them. Some of the more common causes are structural factors, communication factors, cognitive factors, individual characteristics, and the history of relations between the parties.

Structural Factors

Among the structural factors that can lead to conflict are increased specialization, interdependency among parties, centralization versus decentralization, and physical layout.

Increased Specialization

As organizations become larger and more diverse, they require more specialization for effective operation. For example, smaller organizations may have general human resource managers who perform most or all of the Human Resource Management functions, but larger organizations frequently have specialists for employment, labor relations, training, compensation, and affirmative action. This situation represents specialization within one function. Organizations also add new functional areas as they serve a more diverse public. Dividing up the work in this manner is referred to as *differentiation*. Effective organizations become more differentiated as they grow larger or as their external environment becomes more complex.[25]

Increasing specialization has many positive benefits, but it also creates a greater potential for conflict. Specialists frequently view issues from different perspectives. They also often differ with regard to time perspectives and goals. For example, within a human resource unit the training specialists may have different perspectives relative to the compensation specialists. Also, a research and development department often operates within a long-term time frame because developing a product and preparing it for manufacture often require several years. However, a production department operates within a much shorter time frame, perhaps a few weeks (the time required to produce the products for a given order). Conflict can result when the research and development department is late in developing and testing product prototypes, thereby creating scheduling delays for the production department.

Interdependency

In most organizations, work must be coordinated between/among units and between/among individuals inside those units. The more interdependent units or individuals are, the more the potential for conflict exists. A good example of interdependence can be found within state governments. Many state employees work under what is referred to as a *merit system*. This system is designed to alleviate political patronage; employment is based on a person's merit. A Human Resource Management agency based on the merit system is used to screen applicants for state employment and to maintain lists of those who are eligible for certain jobs within state government. When a state agency has a job opening, it must request a list of eligible applicants from the merit system. The state agency, then, depends on the merit system, and the merit system exists to serve state agencies. If the merit system is slow in responding to a request, conflict can occur.

Interdependency can result from limited resources or from required coordination in the timing and sequencing of activities. All organizations have limited resources and attempt to find the most efficient way to divide the resources and accomplish tasks. For example, an organization orders new computers for many of its associates. However, before the associates can use the computers, the company computer technician must hook them up. If there is only one technician and each job takes an hour, competition will arise among associates for the technician's time. One study found that competition for limited resources often leads to dysfunctional conflict. In this case, such competition caused units to distort and suppress information needed by other units.[26]

Centralization Versus Decentralization

Both centralization and decentralization of authority can cause conflict, but each causes a different form of conflict. At the level of the overall organization, centralized authority means that one individual makes decisions for all units or that one higher unit makes decisions for all other units. Centralization can lessen conflict between units because all units are more likely to share the same goals and perspectives in a centralized system. However, conflict between individuals and their supervisors within units or between individual units and the decision-making unit can arise because individuals and units have less control over their own work situations.

For example, many organizations have centralized recruiting; that is, the human resource department recruits associates for jobs in all departments. Centralized recruiting has many advantages for the organization. It ensures that Equal Employment Opportunity Commission rules are followed, and it can save the organization money by avoiding duplication of effort.[27] However, many units may resent the human resource department's control over whom they hire (after all, the people in the unit have to work with the new hires). The hiring goals of the human resource department may be different from those of the individual units. Thus, conflict can arise between individual units and the human resource department.

Decentralized authority means that each unit manager can make important decisions. Although decentralized authority can reduce conflict between superiors and subordinates within a unit, because subordinates have more control over their work situations, it also creates the potential for more conflict between units because decisions made by one unit may conflict with decisions made by another. Furthermore, these decisions may reflect biased perceptions associated with the separate units.

Physical Layout

The physical layout of work environments can produce conflict through several mechanisms. In Chapter 11, we discussed how virtual work teams, whose members are physically separated from one another, are more likely to suffer from poor communication that can lead to conflict. Conflict can also arise when associates must work too closely together.[28] Associates commonly work in small, crowded cubicles that do not allow for privacy or personal space—a phenomenon sometimes termed the "Dilbertization effect" (after the comic-strip character).[29] Associates in such environments experience a stressful type of interdependency. Because everyone is continuously in view and can be easily overheard when talking, even in private conversations, conflict can arise. Conflict is especially likely if associates are unaware of the effect their behavior is having on others around them. For example, someone with a loud phone voice can be particularly irritating to co-workers. Furthermore, such environments do not allow associates to handle sensitive matters in private, a situation that can further increase conflict.[30] In the *Experiencing Organizational Behavior* feature, Herman Miller's approach to physical layout for teamwork is discussed. Their ideas offer substantial benefits.

Communication

As discussed in Chapter 9, a common cause of conflict is poor communication, which can lead to misunderstandings and allow barriers to be erected.[31] Probably the easiest way to prevent conflict is to ensure good communication. One of the authors observed conflict caused by poor communication a few years ago in a consulting case. The situation involved two company vice presidents who did not communicate well with one another. They would *talk* to each other, but neither of them would *listen* to the other. As a result, misunderstandings occurred and were never resolved. There were frequent heated arguments in meetings. This hostility extended to their respective departments, and problems of coordination became evident. The conflict became so bad that the chief executive officer asked one of the vice presidents to resign.

Both too little and too much communication can lead to conflict.[32] On the one hand, when there is too little communication, associates do not know enough about each other's intentions, goals, or plans. Coordination becomes difficult, and misunderstandings are more likely to occur, which can result in conflict. On the other hand, too much

Herman Miller, Designing for Teamwork

©Michael L. Abramson/
Time & Life Pictures/Getty Images, Inc.

Herman Miller, Inc. was voted onto *Fortune* magazine's list of most admired companies in 2009, for the 21st time in the past 23 years. The company, which designs furniture, primarily for the workplace, and provides consulting and research services for office design, consistently wins awards for being a great place to work. Herman Miller, founded in 1923 by D.J. DePree, is one of the largest office furniture companies in the world and had sales of $1.63 billion in its most recent fiscal year. Thus, the company itself serves as its own best advertisement for the products and services it sells. Overall, its purpose is quite simple: "To Design and Build a Better World."

Part of its foundation for providing great work environments involves fostering teamwork through the physical design of the company's offices. The company has made the following suggestions for arranging an area that is conducive to teamwork:

First it is important to delineate boundaries, so that everyone has their own private space over which they feel ownership. At the same time, associates should always be able to see each other, which makes for easier collaboration. Next, a collaborative workspace should be created in a quiet secluded space. Holding team meetings in more public, central spaces, allows "outsiders" to intrude on the team's meeting. It is also important that team members be provided with furniture they can arrange themselves. This allows the team to reconfigure itself to suit the task. For example, when one person on the team is presenting information to the others, that would require a different furniture arrangement than if everyone were working collectively on the same document. Finally, it is important for team members to create ways to signal each other that they are unavailable and should not be disturbed.

Herman Miller follows these suggestions in the design of its own workspaces, particularly those in which creative teams are working. However, the design team is quick to point out that simply arranging the physical layout of the office space is not enough to support teamwork, although it greatly facilitates it. Rather, the company must also have a culture, management system, and reward system that fosters positive personal and task relationships. Herman Miller incorporates these types of elements in several ways. For example, the company has an employee-participation and profit-sharing plan. To complement this plan, all employees are taught during orientation about how to link their team's performance to the profits of the company.

Looking to the future, the company believes that balancing more effectively the needs for interaction and solitude will depend on advances in cognitive science. New developments connecting cognitive processing and the design of the work environment are likely to better identify factors that contribute to distraction. These developments are also likely to yield more sophisticated aids and tactics for cognitive processing in the work place. Clearly, Herman Miller is thinking ahead.

Sources: Herman Miller. 2010. "About Us: Overview," at http://www.hermanmiller.com/About-Us/Overview; Herman Miller. 2010. "About Us: For Our Investors," http://www.hermanmiller.com/About-Us/For-Our-Investors; Herman Miller. 2008. "Making Room for Collaboration," at http://www.hermanmiller.com/MarketFacingTech/hmc/research_summaries/pdfs/wp_Collaboration.pdf; Herman Miller. 2007. "Making Teamwork Work," at http://www.hermanmiller.com; J.C. Sarros, B.K. Cooper, & J.C. Santora. 2007, May–June. "The Character of Leadership," *Ivey Business Journal,* at http://www.iveybusinessjournal.com/article.asp?intArticle_ID=689.

communication can also result in information overload and misunderstandings that cause conflict. Other factors leading to poor communication are discussed in Chapter 9.

Cognitive Factors

Certain beliefs and attitudes can lead to conflict. Two such cognitive factors involve differing expectations and one party's perceptions of the other party.

Differing Expectations

People sometimes differ in their expectations about jobs, careers, and managerial actions. A common example of such differences involves professional associates (such as research scientists, accountants, or attorneys) and managers. Professional associates often perceive themselves as being loyal to their professions and define their careers as extending beyond a particular organization. In so doing, they focus on those activities valued by the profession, which the management of the organization does not necessarily value. This can lead to lower organizational loyalty and potentially to conflict between these associates and management. If the differences in expectations are great and conflict ensues, the associates may even leave the organization.[33] Thus, managers must be aware of this potential problem and work to reduce differences in expectations.

Perceptions of the Other Party

The perceptions that one party holds about another can set the stage for conflict. One person may perceive that another has extremely high goals and that these goals will interfere with his own goal attainment.[34] For example, if Smith perceives that a co-worker, Johnson, desires to be promoted at any cost, Smith might fear that Johnson will try to steal his work or sabotage his performance to "beat the competition." In general, perceptions that result in conflict include the perception that the other party's intentions are harmful, violate justice norms, are dishonest, or are counter to one's own intentions.[35]

Individual Characteristics

Individual characteristics that may lead to conflict include personality factors, differences in the value placed on conflict, and differences in goals.

Personality

The Type A personality trait has been linked to increased conflict. Recall from Chapter 7 that people with Type A personalities are competitive, aggressive, and impatient.[36] One study found that managers with Type A personalities reported more conflict with subordinates.[37] Because people with Type A personalities are more competitive, they are more likely to perceive others as having competing goals, even when this is not the case.

Another type of personality characteristic likely to influence how people experience and react to conflict is *dispositional trust*. People who are low in trust are less likely to cooperate with others[38] and less likely to try to find mutually beneficial solutions when conflict arises.[39] When people are high in trust, they are more likely to concede to another party during conflicts, especially when it appears that the other party is upset or disappointed.[40] High-trust individuals are more likely than others to become vulnerable because they have positive expectations about the motives of others.[41]

Differences in personality across people can also facilitate conflict. People high in conscientiousness plan ahead, are organized, and desire feedback. While working on a project, a person high in conscientiousness wants to plan the project out, start early, set clear goals, and consistently seek feedback. Someone who is low in conscientiousness may see these actions as unnecessary, creating the potential for procedural conflict. Note that it is not the degree of conscientiousness per se that leads to conflict here; it is the difference in this trait between two people who must work together.

Differences Across People in the Perceived Value of Conflict

People vary in the degree to which they value conflict. Some people think conflict is necessary and helpful, whereas others avoid it at all costs. There are important cultural differences as well in the way people view conflict.[42] People in Western cultures tend to view conflict as an inevitable and sometimes beneficial aspect of life. Those in some Asian cultures (such as Chinese) believe that conflict is bad and should be avoided.[43] These value differences make it more difficult to resolve conflicts when the parties are from different cultures. Value differences are most likely to get in the way of conflict resolution when the parties have a high need for closure.[44] That is, when people desire for there to be closure to a situation, they will resort to their strongest cultural norms to guide their decision making. So an American with a high need for closure might seek out solutions that put her at the best advantage for prevailing, whereas a Chinese associate with a high need for closure would focus on avoiding the conflict and maintaining harmony.

Goals

By definition, when individuals have competing or contrary goals, they often engage in conflict. In addition, certain aspects of individual goals make conflict more likely.[45] Associates with lofty goals, rigid goals, or competitive goals are more likely to experience conflict, especially when they are strongly committed to the goals.

Differences in goals can result from structural characteristics of the organization, such as increased specialization and interdependency. Recall our earlier example of the merit system for state-government employees. The merit system has the goal of ensuring that only qualified candidates are on the eligible-for-hire list and that all applicants are given a fair chance. A state agency wants qualified applicants for a job opening, but it also needs the position filled quickly so that the required work is done. It takes time to be fair to all and to be cautious about who is on the eligible list, which can delay getting the list to the state agency. Meanwhile, the agency may have a vacant job and a work backlog during the delay. In this case, differences in goals generate conflict. As the difference between the goals of two units becomes greater, the likelihood that conflict will occur increases. Organizations with structures that align individual and subgroup goals with those of the organization experience less conflict.[46]

History

Previous relationships between two parties can influence the likelihood of conflict in the future. Past performance and previous interactions are two such relationship factors.

Past Performance

When individuals or groups receive negative feedback because of poor past performance, they often perceive it as a threat.[47] When a threat is perceived, individuals frequently attempt to deal with it by becoming more rigid, exerting more control over deviant group members and ideas, and restricting the flow of communication.[48] When people become more rigid and communicate less, personal, substantive, and procedural issues can become heated. Thus, when past performance is poor, the chances for conflict are greater.[49]

Previous Interactions

Individuals who have experienced conflict in the past are more likely to experience it in the future.[50] Previous conflict can influence the probability of future conflict in several ways. First, the parties often engage in the same conflict-inducing behaviors. Second, the parties likely distrust one another. Third, they may expect conflict, and this expectation may become a self-fulfilling prophecy. Think of the old story of the warring Hatfield and McCoy families. These two families had been fighting so long that younger members of each family did not know what had caused the initial conflict. All they had learned was to engage in conflict with the other family.

Later in the chapter we discuss the negotiation process, which is an illustration of how associates and managers attempt to resolve conflict. Negotiation situations are influenced by the negotiators' previous interactions. Research has shown that negotiators' history of negotiation in terms of the quality of deals they arranged influences how they negotiate in other situations—even if they are negotiating with a different person.[51] Negotiators who have a history of not being able to reach a satisfactory conclusion during previous negotiations are much more likely to reach unfavorable solutions in future negotiations than those who have had a successful negotiation history.

Conflict Escalation and Outcomes

As we have just seen, conflict has many causes, and they are often interrelated. For example, structural factors such as specialization are related to differences in goals and perceptions. The physical environment can cause conflict because it can interfere with communication. However a conflict begins, though, there are only a certain number of ways in which it can end.

Fortunately, most cases of conflict are resolved, although not necessarily in a manner satisfactory to both parties or to the organization (as in the earlier example, where two vice presidents were in conflict and one was fired by the CEO). In this section, we discuss conflict escalation and then focus on conflict outcomes.

Conflict Escalation

Conflict escalation is the process whereby a conflict intensifies over time. Escalation is characterized by several features. Tactics become increasingly severe on both sides, and the number of issues grows. In addition, the parties become more and more deeply involved in the conflict. Eventually, as their goals shift from caring about their own welfare and outcomes to trying to harm the other party, they lose sight of their own self-interests.[52]

Many reasons have been proposed for conflict escalation. Some experts feel that escalation is inevitable unless direct measures are taken to resolve the conflict.[53] Others believe

conflict escalation
The process whereby a conflict grows increasingly worse over time.

that conflicts do not have to escalate. Rather, there are certain general conditions that make escalation more likely. These include the following:

- Cultural differences exist between the parties.[54]
- The parties have a history of antagonism.[55]
- The parties have insecure self-images.[56]
- Status differences between the parties are uncertain.[57]
- The parties have informal workplace ties to one another.[58]
- The parties do not identify with one another.[59]
- One or both parties have the goal of escalating the conflict in order to beat the other party.[60]

Conflict escalation might involve overt expressions of workplace aggression. This aspect of escalation may be one-sided, where one party becomes more hostile than the other(s). These issues are taken up in the next *Experiencing Organizational Behavior* feature.

Conflict Outcomes

There are five ways in which conflict can end in terms of how the outcome satisfies each party's concerns, interests, or wishes: lose–lose, win–lose, lose–win, compromise, and win–win.

Lose–Lose

In this conflict outcome, neither party gets what was initially desired. In aggression situations, lose–lose outcomes are often seen. The aggressor often fails to obtain an initially desired goal such as a promotion or continued employment, and he also frequently fails to obtain true satisfaction through the aggressive behavior. The aggrieved sometimes fails to achieve desired peace in the workplace, and can suffer many negative consequences beyond that.

Win–Lose or Lose–Win

In either of these outcome scenarios, one party's concerns are satisfied, whereas the other party's concerns are not. This type of outcome is obviously not advantageous for the losing party, and it often is not particularly advantageous for the organization. Such outcomes can be difficult to avoid, however. When conflicts involve "zero-sum," or distributive, issues, one party can gain only at the expense of the other. This can cause each party to attempt to fully satisfy its concerns at the expense of the other party. For example, consider a situation in which two opposing parties are competing for a limited number of resources. The more of the resources one party obtains, the less of the resources the other party obtains. When United Airlines fought its unions following the 9/11 attacks on New York, distributive issues were at the heart of the conflict.[61] Each dollar obtained by the unions for salaries and pension benefits represented a dollar out of the pocket of the airline.

Compromise

Compromise occurs when both parties give in to some degree on an issue or set of issues. Had management at United Airlines been willing to agree to somewhat less drastic pay cuts, then the unions in exchange could have moderated their demands in other strongly contested areas, such as pensions. Indeed, compromise was actually achieved several times

Workplace Aggression

On January 12, 2010, a disgruntled ex-employee of an Atlanta-area Penske truck rental facility visited his former employer. He arrived at the start-time of his former shift wearing camouflage clothing. According to police reports, the ex-employee then entered the work site and began shooting. Two individuals were killed and several others were critically injured, including the former supervisor of the alleged assailant.

On January 7, 2010, an employee of ABB's St. Louis–area transformer plant arrived at work with more than his lunch pail. He also had an assault rifle, two shotguns, and two handguns. He proceeded to kill three co-workers, seriously wound five others, and kill himself. The individual had been a party to a lawsuit related to the retirement plan.

In an office situation, a disagreement erupted. Soon, one party had the other pinned against a wall with punch after punch being delivered to the individual's face. Blood was everywhere. In another situation, an unhappy subordinate led his supervisor to a vault under false pretenses. He then locked the supervisor in the vault and turned the lights off. In another instance, a disagreement arose between two supervisors over who would deliver layoff notices. One supervisor threw a large, filled envelope at the other.

The events discussed above represent workplace aggression. This type of aggression involves behavior by one or more individuals that is designed to physically or psychologically harm a worker or multiple workers in a workplace setting. Including murders involving co-workers (or former co-workers) as well as murders committed by customers, clients, and the general public, several hundred to over one thousand workplace murders occur in any given year in the United States. Other physical forms of aggression such as fights or shoving affect millions each year. Milder acts of aggression, such as psychological bullying, affect even more. In one survey, the U.S. Bureau of Labor Statistics reported that about 50 percent of establishments with more than 1,000 employees had experienced some form of noteworthy workplace aggression in the previous 12-month period, with roughly 34 percent of the establishments having experienced co-worker–on–co-worker aggression.

The stereotypical portrait of workplace aggressors involves young white males who have poor self-esteem and/or aggressive personalities, perhaps coupled with substance abuse issues. This stereotype seems to be both right and wrong. Males with self-esteem issues and/or aggressive personalities (or anger as a general trait) do seem to be somewhat more likely to commit acts of workplace aggression. Abusers of alcohol also are more likely to commit such acts. On the other hand, individuals who are young and/or white do not appear to carry a higher likelihood of aggression in the workplace. Beyond demographic and personality factors, lack of justice in the organization and constraints on task performance are predictive of aggression.

In addition to the human suffering, the financial costs of workplace aggression are staggering (billions of dollars each year). To reduce these costs, many tactics have been suggested. The president of PCM Consultants, Chuck Mannila, suggests the following actions, with a particular emphasis on reducing or avoiding the most severe forms of aggression:

- Adopt a zero-tolerance policy
- Implement a formal workplace prevention program
- Train managers and associates to address the issues
- Take every threat seriously
- Immediately investigate all threats
- Implement tighter security
- Provide access to employee assistance programs

Sources: J. Barling, K.E. Dupre, & E.K. Kelloway. 2009. "Predicting Workplace Aggression and Violence," *Annual Review of Psychology*, 60:671–692; Bureau of Labor Statistics. 2005. "Survey of Workplace Prevention, 2005," at http://www.bls.gov/iif/oshwc/osnr0026.pdf; A. Gomstyn. 2009. "Workplace Horror Stories: Yale and Beyond," *ABC News.com*, Sept. 21, at http://abcnews.go.com/Business/workplace-horror-stories-yale/story?id=8615343; C. Mannila. 2008. "How to Avoid Becoming a Workplace Violence Statistic," *T + D*, 62(7): 60–66; K. Nolan, V. Dagher. 2010. "Workplace Shooting in St. Louis Leaves Four Dead, *Wall Street Journal*, Jan. 8, p. A.5; K. Rowson. 2010. "Police Sources: Penske Gunman Was Fired," *11Alive.com*, Jan. 13, at http://www.11alive.com/rss/rss_story.aspx?storyid=139675; D. Yusko. 2010. "Official Drops Claim Over Tossed Envelope," Timesunion.com, Jan. 16, at http://www.timesunion.com/ASPStories/Story.asp?StoryID=889607.

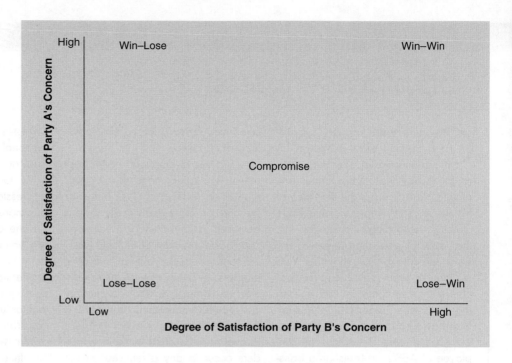

Exhibit 12-3 Possible Conflict Outcomes

Source: Adapted from K.W. Thomas. 1992. "Conflict and Negotiation Processes." In M.D. Dunnette, & L.M. Hough (Eds.), *Handbook of Industrial and Organizational Psychology, Vol. 3* Palo Alto, CA: Consulting Psychologists Press, pp. 651–717.

during the travails at United. For example, a compromise resulted in employees' accepting more substantial pay cuts than they wanted while management agreed to more employee stock ownership than it wanted. Compromise can be a desirable solution to conflict.

Win–Win

A win–win situation occurs when both parties get what they want. Consider a situation in which a union bargains for increased pay, but management does not have the resources to increase pay. A win–win situation would occur if the union decided to accept specific productivity incentives. Increases in productivity would be accompanied by cash bonuses, thus increasing union members' pay to the levels they desired in the first place. Management would win because productivity (and consequently profit) would be expected to increase, in turn covering the higher pay. Exhibit 12-3 depicts the five conflict outcomes.

Responses to Conflict

People respond to conflict in different ways. One person may try to win at all costs, whereas another person may try to ensure that both her own concerns and those of the other party are met. There are five potential responses to conflict, as well as situations in which each response is appropriate.[62] Each response is described in terms of assertiveness and cooperativeness.[63] Here, *assertiveness* refers to the extent to which a party tries to satisfy his, her, or its own concerns. *Cooperativeness* refers to the extent to which a party attempts to satisfy the other party's concerns.

1. *Competing.* A party with a competing response attempts to win at the expense of the other party. Other names for this response include *forcing* and *dominating.* This style is useful when quick, decisive action is required, when an unpopular course of action must be taken, or when the other party will take advantage

of noncompetitive behavior. For example, some countries have more lenient copyright laws than the United States, leading to a proliferation of imitative (knockoff) goods (such as fake Gucci purses, Adidas sneakers, and Rolex watches). The Calvin Klein Company used a competing conflict response in dealing with counterfeiters by establishing a worldwide network to investigate and take legal action against any organization counterfeiting its goods.[64]

2. *Accommodating.* An accommodating response is the opposite of a competitive style. A person using an accommodating response will forgo his own concerns so that the concerns of the other party can be met. For example, when someone has to work on a holiday, an associate may agree to work on the holiday so that a co-worker can have the holiday off, in order to avoid conflict. An accommodating style may be used by a party who believes that he cannot win. It may also be useful when the issue is less important to one party than to the other. An individual or unit can adopt an accommodating style in return for a favor at a future time.

3. *Avoiding.* A party who exhibits an avoiding response neglects both her own concerns and those of the other party. An avoiding style may be necessary to allow emotions to cool down or as a means of delaying decisions until effective solutions can be found. IBM has avoided conflict by refusing to do business in countries that allow bribery of public officials.[65]

4. *Compromising.* Compromising responses are those in which a party tries to partially meet both his own concerns and those of the other party. A compromising response is best used when the parties are of relatively equal power, when temporary settlements to complex problems are required, when there is time pressure, and as a backup when collaboration (described next) is unsuccessful.

5. *Collaborating.* Collaborating responses are attempts to fully meet the concerns of both parties. To use a collaborating response, the parties must work together to identify solutions in which both parties can win.[66] This type of response is most likely to result in the win–win outcome described earlier. A collaborating response is best used when both parties' concerns are too important to ignore and when the objective is to learn and to gain commitment.

Negotiation

The resolution of conflict usually requires negotiations between the conflicting parties. **Negotiation** is a process through which two or more parties with different preferences and interests attempt to agree on a solution through back-and-forth communication. Furthermore, the parties are committed to achieving a peaceful means of dispute resolution.[67]

In the resolution of conflict, the parties often engage in bargaining that requires them to engage in several reactions to conflict such as compromise, collaboration, accommodation, or competition. Although each party usually approaches negotiations with the intent to gain the most benefits for its side, for negotiations to be successful, all parties must bargain in good faith. Managers should build their skills in negotiation because they will be called on to negotiate in many situations. The political skills explained later can be useful to managers in negotiations if they use them for the benefit of the organization to achieve a negotiated agreement whereby both or all parties gain benefit and agree to abide

negotiation
A process through which parties with different preferences and interests attempt to agree on a solution.

by the decision. Depending on the circumstances, a manager can serve as a mediator or an arbitrator in negotiations. A mediator acts as a neutral third party who facilitates a positive solution to the negotiations, whereas an arbitrator acts as a third party with the authority to require an agreement. In reality, managers often serve in both roles simultaneously, and require tact and strong interpersonal skills to achieve negotiated agreement in a conflict situation. The skills and means of negotiation depend on the negotiator's bargaining strategy.

Negotiation Strategies

distributive bargaining
A strategy that: (1) involves a competing, win–lose approach and (2) tends to be used when one party's goals are in direct conflict with the goals of another party.

integrative bargaining
A strategy that: (1) involves a collaborative, win–win approach and (2) tends to be used when the nature of the problem permits a solution that is attractive to both parties.

Negotiators typically emphasize one of two strategies.[68] The **distributive bargaining** strategy involves a competing, win–lose approach. It tends to be used when one party's goals are in direct conflict with the goals of another party. For example, if a buyer and a supplier are negotiating over the price of a product, the higher the agreed-upon price, the bigger the win for the supplier and the bigger the loss for the buyer. On the other hand, the **integrative bargaining** strategy involves a collaborative, win–win approach. This strategy tends to be used when the nature of the problem permits a solution that is attractive to both parties. Sometimes what appears to be a distributive situation at the beginning can be turned into an integrative strategy by broadening the issues under consideration. For example, if the above buyer were to also offer the supplier bigger orders and offer to buy additional products in return for a lower price on the product under negotiation, then an integrative solution could be reached. The buyer would get a lower price; the supplier would get increased volume, an issue that it feels much more strongly about. Depending on what type of strategy a negotiator is using, different types of tactics are appropriate and likely to be effective. These tactics are listed in Exhibit 12-4.

Apart from the issues directly under negotiation, there is often the long-term relationship between parties to consider. Most often during negotiations, the parties desire to remain friendly, trustful, and respectful of each other. For example, if a company was negotiating with an environmental group and the negotiations turned hostile, future relationships between the two groups would remain antagonistic. The company might do only what is absolutely required to meet the terms of negotiations and fail to develop new ways in which to protect the environment. The environmental group might then give only a weak endorsement to the company or refuse to work with it on environmental practices. The activities aimed at influencing the attitudes and relationships of the negotiating parties are referred to as **attitudinal structuring**.[69] Examples of tactics to use for attitudinal structuring are also presented in Exhibit 12-4.

attitudinal structuring
Activities aimed at influencing the attitudes and relationships of the negotiating parties.

The Negotiation Process

There are generally four stages that a negotiation process should follow:[70]

1. *Preparation.* Prior to any negotiation, each party outlines the specific goals he or she hopes to achieve. At this point, negotiators must determine their best alternative to a negotiated agreement (BATNA). This is the least that the negotiator is willing to accept. Also, during the preparation stage, negotiators should engage in self-analysis and opponent analysis. It is important for negotiators to understand their own tendencies and behavior during negotiations as well as those of the other party. At this stage the following questions should be asked about the other party:
   a. What is the other party's position and power? Must the other party confer with other people to make concessions?

EXHIBIT 12-4 Negotiation Tactics

Distributive Tactics
- Convince the other that breaking off negotiations would be costly for him/her/it.
- Convince the other that you feel very committed to reaching your target outcome.
- Prevent the other from making a firm commitment to an outcome close to her target.
- Allow the other to abandon his position without loss of face or other cost.
- Convince the other that your own target outcome is fair.
- Convince the other that her target outcome is unfair.
- Convince the other that important third parties favor your own target outcome.
- Use nonhostile humor to build positive affect.
- Distract the other to impair his ability to concentrate.

Integrative Tactics
- Show the other that his/her/its concerns are important to you.
- Show the other that your target outcome is too important to compromise.
- Show the other that a win–win outcome is a possibility.
- Demonstrate that you are flexible with respect to various solutions.
- Insist on fair criteria for deciding among possible solutions.
- Make collaborative norms salient.
- Minimize use of behaviors or tactics that would cause negative emotions.
- Provide an emotionally supportive climate.
- Shield the other from emotional distractions.

Attitudinal Structuring Tactics
- Use language similar to the other party's.
- Dissociate oneself from others not liked by the opponent.
- Associate oneself with others the opponent likes.
- Reward opponent's behavior.
- Express appreciation.
- Remind opponent of role obligations.
- Assist opponent in working through negative attitudes.
- Return favors.
- Fight the antagonism, not the antagonist.

Sources: K.W. Thomas. 1992. "Conflict and Negotiation Processes," in M.D. Dunnette & L.M. Hough (Eds.), *Handbook of industrial and organizational psychology, Vol. 3* Palo Alto, CA: Consulting Psychologists Press, pp. 651–717; R.E. Walton, & R.B. McKersie. 1965. *A Behavioral Theory of Labor Negotiations* New York: McGraw-Hill.

---

   b. What does the other party consider a "win"?

   c. What is the history of the other party's negotiating style? Does she tend to focus on the distributive strategy or rely on the integrative strategy?

2. *Determining the negotiation process.* Determine the timeline, place, and structure of the negotiations. Also, agreements should be made about confidentiality, the sharing of information, and how agreements will be approved. At this point, who will be present during the negotiation process should be clarified.

3. *Negotiating the agreement.* During this stage the actual negotiation takes place and negotiation strategies and tactics are used.

4. *Closing the deal.* At this stage, both parties should be quite clear about the conclusion of the negotiations and the particulars of the final agreement. Final

agreements should be formalized and it should be made clear what each party's responsibility is in implementing the agreement.

The process outlined above appears to be quite formal. However, it should be followed in any form of negotiation, ranging from negotiating one's pay increase to negotiating major merger and acquisition deals. In the *Managerial Advice* feature, we explore a common type of negotiation scenario—that of negotiating one's salary when taking a new job.

MANAGERIAL ADVICE

A Costly Conflict Resolution: The Importance of Negotiation

Jane and Rob are very happy today. Both were offered jobs at ABSCO in the management trainee program. Because Jane and Rob had the same qualifications, ABSCO offered them the same salary of $40,000 per year. This was Rob's dream job, so he accepted right away. This was also Jane's dream job; however, she realized that she would be working in an area where the cost of living was high, and when this was taken into consideration, she would be making less than many of her colleagues in similar positions. So Jane negotiated her salary up to $42,500.

At ABSCO, pay increases are calculated as a percentage of salary. As can be seen in the chart, given the pay-raise schedule, Jane's initial increase over Rob of $2,500 will grow to nearly $3,500 at the end of a five-year period. Over that time, Jane will make almost $14,700 more than Rob. Should they both stay at ABSCO, Jane's salary will continue to grow faster than Rob's, even if they receive the same percentage increases. Thus, Rob's failure to negotiate a higher salary will mean that he is likely to receive less compensation than Jane for the rest of his career at ABSCO.

Salary negotiations are a classic case of conflict. The hiring organization wants to minimize its costs (lower compensation), whereas the applicant wants to earn as much as possible. This involves a distributive issue, as described earlier, in which two parties are contesting a limited resource. The conflict must be resolved. When you negotiate your salary, how can you participate effectively in this resolution? Advice abounds for how to negotiate your salary, but most experts agree on the fundamentals. Below are some commonly prescribed steps that you can take:

1. Do your homework. Know what you are worth on the job market and what the industry standards are for the position you are being offered. Numerous sources of information exist to help you with this task, including:

   • Salary survey information at your university's career services center.
   • Job listings that indicate salaries for similar positions.

	Raise	Rob's Salary	Jane's Salary
Year 1	—	$40,000.00	$42,500.00
Year 2	5%	42,000.00	44,625.00
Year 3	10%	46,200.00	49,087.50
Year 4	10%	50,820.00	53,996.25
Year 5	10%	55,902.00	59,395.88

©Royalty-Free/Corbis

As suggested in the *Managerial Advice* feature, the natural conflict over salary and its resolution are important to both the organization and the individual involved. Jane negotiated a higher salary before accepting the job offer, but Rob did not do so. Therefore, even though Rob and Jane had equal qualifications, they were compensated differently. Furthermore, assuming that they perform at equal levels over time and thus receive the same percentage pay increases, the gap between Jane's salary and Rob's will grow. Furthermore,

- Online salary surveys such as those found at JobStar.
- Friends, other students, and networking contacts.
- Websites that allow you to calculate the cost of living for various parts of the country; $40,000 goes a lot further in Houston than it does in New York City.

2. Determine your best alternative to a negotiated agreement (BATNA). This is the lowest offer you will consider; you will reject any offer lower than your BATNA. Your BATNA is a dynamic cutoff. You should always strive to increase it. One way to do this during salary negotiations is to have alternative job offers. The best current offer becomes your BATNA.

3. Know what salary you want— your target salary. Your BATNA is your least acceptable outcome. Your target salary is your preferred outcome.

4. Never make vague counteroffers, such as "I need more money." Be prepared to offer a specific salary range and a justification for the salary range. This is where your homework will come in handy. Ensure that the range you specify to the company does not limit your possibilities for negotiation. For example, if you specify your BATNA (say, $30,000) as the low end of your range, you may not be able to get more than your minimal acceptable amount. This does not mean you should communicate an unrealistically high figure, however. Suggesting unrealistically high figures leaves a bad impression with the organization.

5. Although you should not be vague, neither should you say, "I need X amount of dollars." This indicates that you are unwilling to negotiate. On the one hand, the organization can say no and withdraw the offer. On the other hand, if the

organization accepts immediately, you may experience "winner's remorse," whereby you feel that your suggested amount was too low.

6. Be realistic. Often, when organizations offer salaries for entry-level positions, they leave little room for negotiation. The higher you go in the organization, the more room there usually is for negotiation.

7. Be polite and direct during negotiations.

8. Never inflate your past salary or experience. Be honest in all aspects of the negotiation.

9. Remember to calculate benefits as part of the offer package. One offer may have a lower salary figure but a much more generous retirement plan. Again, do your homework.

10. Do not play "hard to get" when you have little bargaining power.

Sources: D. Gordon. 2004. "Suggested Salary Negotiation Guidelines for Recent College Graduates," at http://www.adguide.com/pages/articles/article257.htm; C. Krannich & R.L. Krannich. 2004. "30 Salary Negotiation Mistakes to Avoid," at http://www.washingtonpost.com/wl/jobs/Content?Content=/Career_Advic.../impactadvice8.html; L.L. Thompson. 2008. *The Mind and Heart of the Negotiator*, 4th ed. Upper Saddle River, NJ: Prentice Hall.

although the organization may save almost $14,700 over a five-year period, it may also lose a productive associate. Rob is likely to be unhappy about the difference in pay if he discovers it (which is likely). As we explained in Chapter 6, in the discussion of equity theory, Rob will feel that he is not being treated equitably. Consequently, he might search for a job with another organization. Unfortunately, if it leads to conflict between Rob and the organization, he is likely to depart for a job elsewhere. In this case, the organization loses valuable human capital.

Before closing this section on negotiation, it is important to point out that associates negotiate all the time in everyday work life. When we think of negotiations, we tend to think of formalized negotiations such as labor–management bargaining or merger-and-acquisition talks. However, negotiations take place whenever there are two or more parties who need to come to an agreement about a proposed course of action. Negotiation is just a means of trying to influence others to obtain outcomes that one desires. Thus, a major issue that underlies all negotiations as well as conflict situations is power.[71] When two parties try to influence each other to attempt to maximize their own outcomes or attain a target outcome, the issue of power can be critical to resolving the conflict.

Power

power
The ability to achieve desired outcomes.

The concept of power is one of the most pervasive in the study of organizational behavior.[72] **Power** is generally defined as the ability to achieve desired outcomes.[73] Power can also be thought of as the ability of one person to get another person to do something.[74] Thus, any time someone persuades another person to do something, he or she is exercising power. For example, a coach who requires players to do pushups is exercising power. A secretary who has the boss change her schedule to accommodate an associate is also exercising power.

Often, power is thought to be negative. However, little would be accomplished if power were not exercised on a regular basis.[75] Whether or not the exercise of power is harmful depends on the intent of the person holding the power. A manager who exercises power to meet organizational goals is using power in a positive, productive way. In contrast, a manager who exercises power to promote his personal interests, at the expense of others, is misusing power.

Power exists on different levels. Individuals and organizational units can have power. For example, a student body president can have power to influence university policy. Powerful units such as academic departments that bring in a great deal of external money can also influence university policy, as can the alumni association. It is generally easy to identify people in an organization or social unit who have power.[76] Think of an organization to which you belong, for example, and identify who has the power in that organization.

Bases of Individual Power

Power in organizations can come from many sources. John French and Bertram Raven developed one of the most commonly used typologies for describing the bases of power.[77] It includes five categories: legitimate power (formal authority), reward power, coercive power, expert power, and referent power.

Legitimate Power

People derive **legitimate power** (or formal authority) from the positions they hold in the organization. Legitimate power is narrow in scope because it can be applied only to acts that are defined as legitimate by everyone involved. For example, after being elected to a second term in 2004, President George W. Bush replaced many of the cabinet members from his first term. This was an exercise in legitimate power because the president has the formal authority to choose his cabinet members. However, when Attorney General Alberto Gonzales fired many U.S. attorneys, he came under fire because he was viewed as not having the legitimate authority to do so and his motives were questioned.[78]

legitimate power
Power derived from position; also known as formal authority.

Reward Power

Reward power results when one person has the ability or perceived ability to provide another with desired outcomes (i.e., the person controls or is believed to control desired resources). In the long run, reward power is limited by the person's actual ability to supply desired outcomes. For example, a supervisor may have power because she can assign pay raises to associates. However, if the company has a bad year, and the supervisor is not permitted to give pay raises, then she loses this source of power. Reward power is not limited to formal sources, such as the supervisor's power to give raises; it can also come from informal sources. For example, a secretary who often controls his boss's schedule may then reward associates with access to the boss.

reward power
Power resulting from the ability to provide others with desired outcomes.

Coercive Power

Coercive power exists when one person believes that another person has the ability or perceived ability to punish people. Coercive power is usually considered a negative form of power; thus, its use should be limited. Overuse or inappropriate application of this type of power can produce unintended results. For example, associates might respond with negative or undesired behaviors. Like reward power, coercive power can be derived from informal as well as formal sources. For example, an associate who spreads negative gossip about others may have coercive power because others fear that he will spread negative gossip about them.[79] Coercive power is limited by the fact that those being influenced must be highly dependent on the person wielding the power.[80]

coercive power
Power resulting from the ability to punish others.

Expert Power

Expert power arises from special expertise or technical knowledge that is valuable to others or the organization. Expert power is limited by the degree to which this expertise is irreplaceable. For example, an associate can gain power by becoming the only person in the unit who knows how to use certain software. However, if others learn to use the software, this person's power will be diminished.

expert power
Power resulting from special expertise or technical knowledge

Referent Power

People are said to have **referent power** when others are attracted to them or desire to be associated with them. For example, it has been found that executives who have prestigious reputations among their colleagues and shareholders have greater influence on strategic decision-making processes in their firms.[81] Referent power is the most resilient type of power because it is difficult to lose once it has been achieved. In addition, referent power can be used to influence a wide range of behaviors.[82]

referent power
Power resulting from others' desire to identify with the referent.

An Example of Power

The use of different power bases is not mutually exclusive. Associates and managers can use multiple bases at one time. The past CEO of Disney, Michael Eisner, is an example of someone who drew power from a variety of sources.[83] During the years of Eisner's reign at Disney (1984–2006), the entertainment giant went through a number of ups and downs. Owing to Eisner's efforts in his early years, the company's performance improved dramatically. In later years, Disney experienced a number of complex issues: hostile takeover threats; the acquisition of Miramax Studios and Capital Cities/ABC; conflict with Bob and Harvey Weinstein of Miramax; a successful alliance with Pixar Animation studios; the dissolution of the alliance with Pixar; the very public and contentious resignation of Jeffrey Katzenberg as president of Disney; constant battles with Disney family member Roy Disney; and the expensive hiring and resignation of Eisner's friend, Michael Ovitz.

For a long time, Eisner was incredibly successful in maintaining power over Disney, despite opposition from shareholders, other Disney companies, the Disney family, and even his own executives. How did he do it? Numerous reports exist about Eisner's strategies for increasing and holding his power.

First, Eisner had a great deal of legitimate power. He was both the chairman of the board of directors and the CEO. These positions allowed him to make managerial decisions while at the same time having the authority to evaluate those decisions. He also had the power to hire and fire executives and board members, almost guaranteeing that he was surrounded by people who supported him. This led to complaints by Eisner's detractors that he dominated the board by filling it with his own people, who often did not work in the best interests of other shareholders.

A second way in which Eisner obtained power was by lavishing attention on board members, important investors (like Warren Buffett and Sid Bass), members of the Disney family, and even the widows of former executives. In this way, he was able to curry favor with important Disney stakeholders.

Eisner was also a genius at using information. He wooed board members to support him by constantly supplying them with information. He stated "If I filled them in, made them my partner, if things didn't go so well, the likelihood of, 'I told you so' and those kind of reactions would not exist." At the same time, he controlled communication between executives and board members so that any disagreements, important discussions, or decisions had to go through him. When Eisner wanted to fire Michael Ovitz only months after hiring him, he went through elaborate procedures, talking to board members without Ovitz's knowledge and spreading the word that Ovitz wasn't working out.

Another way that Eisner maintained power was to divide those who might oppose him and to make himself indispensable. He encouraged and allowed rivalries between executives and board members to develop so that other important decision makers were unable to form a cohesive unit. He also refused to train or plan for who would succeed him in the chairman and CEO roles, thus making his departure a problem for Disney.

Finally, Eisner maintained power by restricting the power of others. One of the reasons that the Weinstein brothers wanted to separate Miramax from Disney was that Eisner tried to stop them from releasing the movie *Fahrenheit 911,* which was critical of the Bush administration. Ovitz's experiences seem to be parallel. According to Michael Ovitz, Eisner implied in the hiring process that the chief financial officer and the corporate operations chief would report to Ovitz. However, Ovitz soon learned at a dinner party that both of these men would report to Eisner.

By March 2004, Disney shareholders had become highly dissatisfied. Led by Roy Disney, among others, they participated in a 43 percent no-confidence vote to oust Eisner as the chairman of the Disney board. One of the major factors leading to this vote was the $140 million severance pay package that Eisner gave to Ovitz after Ovitz had been at Disney for only 15 months. Shareholders argued that they had not been given enough information about this deal and that the cost was detrimental to the company. They believed that Disney board members had buckled under Eisner's pressure at shareholders' expense. By December 2005, Eisner had stepped down as chairman; however, he stated that he planned to remain as CEO of Disney until his retirement in 2006.

It appears that Michael Eisner's use of power was sometimes inappropriate. This was a special concern because Eisner was both chairman and CEO of Disney. Thus, he already had significant legitimate power. Furthermore, his position also gave him reward power throughout the entire company. Because of his efforts in turning around Disney after he became CEO, many perceived him to have expert power. In addition, his prominent position afforded him referent power. His actions regarding Michael Ovitz suggest that he used coercive power as well. He fired Ovitz but only after conducting a negative campaign with members of the board of directors. He then gave Ovitz an exceptionally large severance pay package. It seems that Eisner may often have acted in his own best interests and not in the best interests of the company or its shareholders. This story perhaps suggests why Disney's performance suffered during the last years of Eisner's reign.

Strategic Contingencies Model of Power

Individuals and organizational units can also obtain power by being able to address the strategic problems that an organization faces. This is referred to as the **strategic contingencies model of power**.[84] For example, when an organization is in a highly innovative industry, where success depends on being able to develop new products, the research and development (R&D) department and its key people have a great deal of power. The R&D unit has the knowledge (human capital) critical for the success of the firm's strategy to produce innovations and compete effectively in its industry. Consider the pharmaceutical industry. Pharmaceutical firms must introduce valuable new drugs regularly, especially as their patents on their current drugs expire. Without new drugs, their revenues will decrease, and the firms will eventually die. The knowledge and expertise needed to develop new drugs is very important to the company strategy. Thus, the R&D units in pharmaceutical firms often have significant power. Essentially, these units control resources that are valuable to the organization.[85]

Units or individuals may obtain power, then, by identifying the strategic contingencies faced by an organization and gaining control over them. For example, in the United Airlines situation discussed earlier in this chapter, management (which controls the financial resources) gained more power by arguing that financial difficulties were critical and could be solved only by the unions' agreement to salary and pension concessions. However, the unions (which control the human capital in some ways) gained power by highlighting the importance and sensitivity of operations. They did this through disruptive work slow-downs. The most immediate problem for the organization, then, was to get its flights running on schedule again. The strategy of operating flights on time and satisfying customers was negatively affected by the union's exercise of its power. Thus, the unions controlled the most important resources for the strategy and had more power at that point.

If units or people are able to identify the contingencies important to the organization's strategy and performance and control them, they should be able to maintain their bases of

strategic contingencies model of power
A model holding that organizational units and people gain power by being able to address the major problems and issues faced by the organization.

power. They can then use that power to require the organization to act in ways that benefit them. Take, for example, an athletic department that brings a great deal of alumni money to its university. Because of its ability to provide the university with financial resources, the athletic department has power. The department then uses that power to demand that the university provide more resources to the athletic department. In so doing, the athletic department gains even more power.

Strategic contingency power is related to dependency.[86] Dependency occurs when a unit or person controls something that another unit/person wants or needs. For example, in the popular TV show *The Sopranos,* all the gangsters were dependent on Tony Soprano, the mob boss. Because Tony controlled all of the mob's "businesses" (such as phone-card fraud rings and truck-hijacking operations), the gangsters were able to make a living only if Tony allowed them to operate one of these businesses.

Beyond dependency, a key source of power in the structural contingencies model is the ability to cope with uncertainty.[87] Uncertainty creates threats for the organization. Anyone who can help reduce this uncertainty by addressing key issues will gain power. In the opening case, it was implied that environmental organizations have achieved greater power and influence with businesses. There are several reasons for this, including the uncertainties of tougher environmental regulations and the growing public concern with environmental issues. Environmental organizations gain power because they can help businesses deal with these uncertainties.

Another source of power involves being irreplaceable.[88] One of the power moves made by Michael Eisner at Disney was to avoid developing a succession plan. After all, if no one was prepared to replace him, the board would be unlikely to ask him to resign.[89] In contrast, Jack Welch, the former CEO of General Electric, announced 10 years before stepping down that finding a successor was the most important job he had to do.[90]

Finally, strategic contingency power can result from controlling the decision process, either by setting parameters on the types of solutions that are acceptable or by controlling the range of alternatives to be considered.[91] For example, consider a class project in which student project teams must choose a company to analyze. If a team member states that he knows what types of projects the professor prefers and what types of projects have received good grades in the past, he can gain a great deal of control over the group's decision making regarding the type of project on which they will work.

Organizational Politics

organizational politics
Behavior that is directed toward furthering one's own self-interests without concern for the interests or well-being of others.

When conflict is present in organizations, associates are likely to engage in political behavior. Indeed, politics are a fact of life in most organizations.[92] **Organizational politics** corresponds to behavior that is directed toward furthering one's own self-interests without concern for the interests or well-being of others.[93] The goal of political behavior is to exert influence on others. One survey of top-level executives and human resource managers indicated that organizational politics are on the rise.[94] Seventy percent of survey respondents said that they had been harmed by the political behavior of others and 45 percent said they had gained power and influence by acting politically. We now discuss the conditions under which political behavior is more likely to occur.[95]

Political behavior can occur at several levels. At the individual level, it involves an associate or manager who uses politics to suit his best interests, such as an individual who attempts to take sole credit for a project that was jointly completed. Political behavior at the group level often takes place in the form of coalitions. **Coalitions** are groups whose members act in an integrated manner to actively pursue a common interest. For example, when a new CEO must be chosen for an organization, groups of shareholders may act together to influence the board of directors' choice of a particular successor. Politics can also occur at the organizational level, such as when particular organizations hire lobbyists who try to influence congresspersons' votes on issues important to that organization.

Political tactics can also be aimed at any target. *Upward political influence* refers to individual or group influence on those in a superior position, such as their manager. *Lateral politics* refers to attempts to influence targets at the same hierarchical level. Finally, *downward influence* refers to attempts to influence those lower down in the hierarchy.

What do politics look like in organizations? In other words, what do people do to engage in political behavior? A great deal of research has examined the political tactics used within or by organizations.[96] These tactics include the following:

- *Rational persuasion.* A rational persuasion tactic involves using logical arguments or factual information to persuade targets that the persuader's request will result in beneficial outcomes. For example, a sales associate who is the number-one seller may tell her boss all the benefits of switching to a purely commission-based compensation system while ignoring the potential disadvantages.
- *Consultation.* A consultation tactic requires getting the target to participate in the planning or execution of whatever the politician wants accomplished. For example, a CEO who wants to implement a specific strategy would consult associates and managers at every relevant organizational level to gain their support for her plan. These consultations, though, may be quite cynical because the CEO is not really interested in anyone's input.
- *Personal appeal.* A personal appeal tactic often focuses on the target's loyalty or affection. For example, an associate may remind targets about how he has always supported their ideas and causes before asking them to support his idea.
- *Ingratiation.* An ingratiation tactic makes the target feel good by flattering or helping him. For example, a person may tell a colleague how valuable he is before asking for his support.
- *Inspirational appeal.* An inspirational appeal tactic is used to generate the enthusiasm and support of targets by appealing to their important values and ideals. For example, to obtain a target's support for her new web-based advertising plan, a person may appeal to an ecology-conscious target by explaining how electronic advertising saves trees as opposed to advertising in newspapers and magazines.
- *Exchange.* Using an exchange tactic, a person volunteers a favor in order to gain a favor in return. This is exemplified by the old axiom, "I'll scratch your back if you'll scratch mine."
- *Coalition.* As discussed above, a coalition tactic is used when people with common interests join together to pursue their interests. For example, a coalition is represented by ethnic and minority group members who band together to promote organizational diversity.
- *Legitimizing.* A legitimizing tactic involves making a request seem legitimate or official. For example, an associate who wants to complete a project in a certain manner will try to convince targets that this is "how management wants it done."

coalition
A group whose members act together to actively pursue a common interest.

- *Pressure.* A pressure tactic involves threats, nagging, or demands as a means of influencing targets. For example, an associate who threatens to expose a target's secret if the target does not comply with her wishes is using pressure tactics.

Events from a few years ago at Morgan Stanley, the large financial services firm, illustrate the use of some of these political tactics.[97] Over the five-year period ending in April 2005, Morgan Stanley stock lost one-third of its value, and the company was performing worse than its major competitors. In March 2005, a group of eight disgruntled Morgan Stanley ex-executives initiated a process intended to oust the CEO, Philip Purcell. Because they collectively owned only 1.1 percent of Morgan Stanley shares, they needed to convince other shareholders that Purcell should go.[98] One action they took involved sending a letter to other shareholders blaming the company's poor performance solely on Purcell's leadership. Because there are likely to be many causes for an organization's poor performance, this statement can be seen as a legitimizing tactic because they state the cause of the problem with assumed expertise (substantial experience in Morgan Stanley and the industry). The ex-executives also personally courted shareholders, displaying ingratiation. Another tactic involved speaking passionately about the future of Morgan Stanley. This was done by Robert Scott, who was the ex-president and would-be-CEO of the company. Unfortunately for Scott, many investors were concerned only with short-term profit, so his inspirational appeal held little sway over investors. As one independent analyst noted, "People who hold those shares are going to want something concrete before they give up their votes"[99]; he suggested that the ex-executives use an exchange tactic instead. As of late April 2005, Purcell continued as CEO, but the walls were beginning to crumble. Many important Morgan Stanley executives and senior analysts were deserting for competitors, and a large shareholder publicly expressed support for the disgruntled former ex-executives. In June of 2005, Purcell resigned.[100]

Research has examined the issue of who is better or more successful in behaving politically. One line of research has found that personality is related to the types of political tactics people are likely to use.[101] For example, extraverts are likely to use inspirational appeals and ingratiation, whereas people high on conscientiousness are most likely to use rational appeals. Also, people have varying abilities to engage in political behavior. Some people are quite good at it, but others are more transparent in their actions, thus alerting the target to their intentions. Research has identified an individual difference known as political skill that affects the successful use of political tactics. **Political skill** is the ability to effectively understand others at work and to use this knowledge to enhance one's own objectives.[102] People with strong political skills have the following qualities:[103]

political skill
The ability to effectively understand others at work and to use this knowledge to enhance one's own objectives.

- They find it easy to imagine themselves in others' positions or take another's point of view.
- They can understand situations and determine the best response. They can adjust their behavior to fit the situation.
- They develop large networks and are known by a great many people.
- They can easily gain the cooperation of others.
- They make others feel at ease.

Individuals with strong political skills can use them to the advantage of the organization (e.g., gaining the cooperation of diverse groups). Using political skills for one's own political gain, however, can harm the organization. Therefore, political skills can be positive, but only if used to achieve the appropriate goals.

Managing conflict and power are important to the success organizations enjoy. As we learned in the chapter opener, companies such as Kimberly-Clark, Dell, and DuPont have learned to develop useful solutions with environmental organizations, which not only has had a positive impact on the companies' performance but will also benefit society. Most strategic leaders must deal with conflict while making decisions. Some of this conflict is functional; it produces better decisions because it forces consideration of a broader range of ideas and alternatives. Much of the conflict that occurs in organizations is dysfunctional, however. If the organization's strategy is to be effectively implemented, this conflict must be resolved, or at least managed. Negotiation is one way to resolve conflict.

Some conflict can be resolved through the exercise of power. In addition, people and units that have power because they control critical contingencies or resources can add a great deal of value to the organization. Most strategic leaders have considerable power, especially legitimate power, and their use of power is necessary for the achievement of their organizations' goals. Yet, they must exercise their power appropriately, or it could produce undesired consequences. Michael Eisner exercised his power primarily for his own benefit rather than for the best interests of the organization. By exercising power in this way, he created considerable internal politics (e.g., others vying for influence and working in their own best interests) throughout the organization. As a result, Disney's performance suffered. Similarly, the exercise of political behavior at Morgan Stanley cost the organization valuable human capital. The use of political tactics often has negative consequences for the organization. However, the attributes of people with political skills are not negative. These skills, such as easily gaining cooperation from others, can be especially helpful to managers. The skills are negative only if they are used for personal gain at the expense of others and the organization. They are especially bad when exercised in a negative way by the CEO or other top managers (e.g., at Morgan Stanley) because they tend to have significant effects on the organization.

Critical Thinking Questions

1. Can you describe a situation in which conflict was functional (i.e., it had positive outcomes)? If so, in what ways was the conflict functional?

2. A strategic leader must use power in many actions that she takes. In what ways can she exercise this power to achieve positive outcomes?

3. How can knowledge of conflict, negotiations, power, and politics in organizations help you be more successful in your career? Please be specific.

What This Chapter Adds to Your Knowledge Portfolio

This chapter has explored conflict, negotiation, power, and politics in organizations. It has covered the nature and types of conflict, causes of conflict, outcomes of conflict, responses to conflict, and how organizations can manage conflict. The chapter has also discussed various sources of power. In summary, we have made the following points:

- Conflict is a process in which one party perceives that its interests are being opposed or negatively affected by another party. Conflict can be either functional or dysfunctional for organizational effectiveness. Functional conflict leads to creativity and positive change. Dysfunctional conflict detracts from the achievement of organizational goals.
- Conflict can be classified as personal, substantive, or procedural. Personal conflict corresponds to relationship issues; substantive conflict concerns the work that is to be done; and procedural conflict concerns how work is to be accomplished.

back to the knowledge objectives

1. Under what circumstances can conflict be functional? When is conflict dysfunctional? Which of the basic types of conflict are likely to be dysfunctional, and why?
2. Why does conflict often develop?
3. What is conflict escalation, and what conditions make it likely? What are other possible outcomes of conflict?
4. How do people respond to conflict, and under what circumstances is each type of response most effective?
5. What can organizations do to manage conflict?
6. Describe basic negotiating strategies and the tactics most likely to accomplish those strategies.
7. Why is the exercise of power necessary for organizations to operate effectively? What are some of the ways in which people gain power in organizations?
8. Why is political behavior common in organizations? How do people go about carrying out political behavior, and what makes them successful at it?

- Causes of conflict include structural arrangements (e.g., specialization), communication problems, cognitive factors (e.g., differing expectations), individual characteristics (e.g., personality), and the history of the parties (e.g., their previous interactions).
- Conflict escalation occurs when the conflict is not resolved and becomes worse. Possible resolution outcomes of conflict include lose–lose, win–lose/lose–win, compromise, and win–win.
- Parties to a conflict can adopt one of several responses to the conflict: competing, accommodating, avoiding, compromising, or collaborating. These responses vary in the degree to which they reflect assertiveness and cooperativeness on the part of conflicting parties.
- Often negotiations are required to resolve conflict. In some cases, managers act as a third party, using both mediator and, if necessary, arbitrator roles to achieve a negotiated settlement.
- Distributive and integrative negotiation strategies focus on either winning or reaching a mutually beneficial outcome. Attitudinal restructuring focuses on developing positive feelings and relationships between negotiating parties.
- Power is the ability of those who hold it to achieve the outcomes they desire. Nothing would be accomplished in organizations if individuals did not exercise power.
- Individuals can obtain power through several means. The bases of power include legitimate power, reward power, coercive power, expert power, and referent power. Referent power can influence a wider range of behaviors than the other four types of power.
- The strategic contingencies model of power suggests that units or individuals can obtain power by being able to address the important problems or issues facing the organization. Power can be obtained by identifying the critical contingencies facing an organization, creating dependency, being able to cope with uncertainty, being irreplaceable, and controlling the decision-making process.
- Organizational politics is a fact of life in most organizations. Political behavior can be carried out through a wide range of tactics. The extent to which a politician is successful in achieving his or her own goals depends on political skill.

Thinking about Ethics

1. Under what circumstances is it ethically appropriate to use coercive power? When should managers not use coercive power to deal with problems in organizations?
2. How can a manager know when conflict is functional? How can conflict be managed to ensure that it remains functional? Do managers have a responsibility to ensure that conflict is functional or to eliminate dysfunctional conflict?

3. You are chairman of the board and CEO of a major corporation. Is it appropriate for you to select the other board members? Why or why not?

4. If you control resources that are critical to an organization, you have power. Are there circumstances in which it would be acceptable to use that power to garner more resources for your unit (and thus more power)?

5. You have recently hired five new associates in your unit, all of whom have excellent knowledge and skills. Each was offered a beginning annual salary of $100,000. Four of them accepted the salary offered, but one negotiated for $5,000 more. Should you give each of the other associates $5,000 more as well? Over time, such an action would cost your unit and the organization considerable money. If you take no action, what do you expect the long-term consequences to be?

Key Terms

conflict, p. 439
dysfunctional conflict, p. 439
functional conflict, p. 439
personal conflict, p. 440
substantive conflict, p. 441
procedural conflict, p. 441
conflict escalation, p. 447
negotiation, p. 451

distributive bargaining,
   p. 452
integrative bargaining, p. 452
attitudinal structuring, p. 452
power, p. 456
legitimate power, p. 457
reward power, p. 457
coercive power, p. 457

expert power, p. 457
referent power, p. 457
strategic contingencies model
   of power, p. 459
organizational politics,
   p. 460
coalition, p. 461
political skill, p. 462

Human Resource Management Applications

The Human Resource Management (HRM) function plays an important role in managing conflict and power in an organization. First, HRM units can develop or obtain selection tools that assist in the identification of individuals who are prone to destructive conflict and self-interested politics. Such individuals can then be screened out of the selection process, or if hired they can be monitored for dysfunctional behavior.

Second, HRM units can develop or identify external training programs that deliver crucial negotiation skills. External training programs are available from management development firms and also from major universities. Northwestern University and Harvard University are two of the leading U.S. providers of negotiation programs.

Third, HRM units can provide mediation and counseling services for severe situations involving dysfunctional personal conflict. This type of mediation and counseling is difficult to enact in an effective way, requiring formally trained individuals to maximize the chances of success.

Related to the above, HRM units must stand ready to assist managers and associates in dealing with anyone who exhibits workplace aggression. Sophisticated actions are required.

building your human capital
Are You Ready to Manage with Power?

All types of managerial tasks require the exercise of power. After all, power is the ability to get others to do something you want them to do. Thus, any time you find yourself in a situation in which you need to get others to do something, you need to exercise power. However, many people are uncomfortable thinking about power and its use. The next time you find yourself in a situation in which you need to influence others, consider the following questions before acting:

1. What are your goals? What are you trying to accomplish?
2. Who will be influential in allowing you to achieve your goal? Who is dependent on you for certain outcomes?
3. How do you think others will feel about what you are trying to do? Do you think there will be resistance?
4. What are the power bases of those you wish to influence? For example, do they have reward power? Referent power?
5. What are your bases of power and influence? What rewards or valued outcomes can you control? What type of power can you exert to gain more control over the situation?

---

an organizational behavior moment

The Making of the Brooklyn Bluebirds

The Brooklyn Bluebirds is a professional baseball team. Years ago, it was the best team in professional baseball. Then it hit a period of almost 10 years without a pennant. Recently, though, things have been looking up. A new owner, Trudy Mills, acquired the Bluebirds and proclaimed that she intended to make them world champions again.

Trudy quickly began to use her wealth to rebuild the team by acquiring big-name players in the free-agent draft. She also signed a manager well known for his winning ways, Marty Bellman. Marty was also known for his "fighting ways" on and off the field. However, Trudy was more concerned with his winning record.

The first year of Trudy's and Marty's tenure, the Bluebirds came in second in the division, showing it was a team to be reckoned with. Trudy acquired even more big-name players in the free-agent draft. Everyone was predicting a pennant for the Bluebirds in the coming year.

The year began with great expectations. During the first month, the Bluebirds looked unstoppable. At the end of the month, the team was in first place with a record of 20 wins and 7 losses. But then problems began. Rumors of conflict between players were reported in the sports columns. Russ Thompson, a five-year veteran and starting first baseman, publicly stated that he wanted to renegotiate his contract. (He was unhappy that Trudy had brought in so many players at much higher salaries than his.) He and his lawyer met with Trudy and the Bluebirds' general manager, but the meeting ended in disagreement. Both Russ and Trudy were angry.

The team's record began to deteriorate, and by the All-Star Game at midseason, the Bluebirds had lost as many games as they had won and were back in fourth place. Right after the All-Star break, Marty decided he had to make a move. He benched both Russ Thompson and Mickey Ponds, a well-known player with a multimillion-dollar contract. Marty called them to his office and said, "You guys are not playing baseball up to your abilities. I think you've been loafing. When you decide to start playing baseball and quit counting your money or worrying how pretty you look on television, I'll put you back in the starting lineup. Until then, you can sit on the bench and cheer for your teammates."

Russ responded hotly, "The owner won't pay me what I'm worth, and now you won't play me. I don't want to play for the Bluebirds anymore. I'm going to ask to be traded." Mickey was no happier than Russ. "I'm going to Trudy. You can't bench me. You're the biggest jerk I've ever played for!"

At that, both players left his office, got dressed, and left the ballpark. Later, a few minutes before game time, Marty received a phone call in his office. It was Trudy, and she was upset. "Why did you bench Russ and Mickey? I hired you to manage the team, not create more problems. They're two of our best players, and the customers pay to see them play. I want you to apologize to them and put them back in the starting lineup."

Marty was not known for his diplomacy. "You hired me to manage, and that's just what I'm doing. Keep your nose out of my business. You may own the team, but I manage it. Russ and Mickey will stay benched until I say otherwise!" With that, Marty slammed the receiver down and headed for the field to get the game under way.

Discussion Questions

1. Describe the types of conflict that seem to exist within the Bluebirds organization. What are the causes?
2. Is the conflict functional, dysfunctional, or both? Explain.
3. Assume that Trudy has hired you as a consultant to help her resolve the conflict. Describe the steps that you would take.

team exercise
Managing Conflict

The purpose of this exercise is to develop a better understanding of the conflict-management process by examining three different conflict situations.

Procedure

1. With the aid of the instructor, the class will be divided into four- or five-person teams.
2. The teams should read each case and determine:
   a. Which conflict response should be used to manage the conflict (this may require starting with one style and moving to others as the situation changes).
   b. Which negotiation tactics should be used to resolve the conflict.
3. Each team should appoint a leader to explain its results to the class.
4. The instructor should call on the teams to explain the conflict response and negotiation tactics recommended. The information should be recorded on a board or flipchart for comparisons. The situations should be discussed one at a time.
5. The instructor will lead a general discussion regarding the application of conflict responses and negotiation tactics.

This exercise usually requires about 25 minutes for case analyses and another 20 to 30 minutes (depending on the number of teams) for class discussion.

Case Incident 1

You are James Whittington, manager of internal auditing. The nature of your position and of your unit's work often put you in conflict with managers of other units. Most of your audits are supportive of the actions taken in the audited units, although some are not. Nonetheless, the managers seem to resent what they consider an intrusion on their authority when the audits are conducted. You have come to accept this resentment as a part of your job, although you would prefer that it didn't occur. One case has been a particular problem. Bill Wilson, manager of compensation in the human resource department, has created problems every time your auditors have worked in his department. He has continually tried to hold back information necessary for the audit. Unfortunately, during the last year and a half, you have had to audit activities in his department several times.

Your department now has been assigned to audit the incentive bonus calculations for executives made by Bill's department. Bill was irate when he discovered that you were again going to audit his employees' work. When he found out about it, he called your office and left a message for you not to send your employees down, because he was not going to allow them access to the information. You are now trying to decide how to respond.

Case Incident 2

Irene Wilson is manager of corporate engineering and has a staff of 17 professional engineers. The group is project-oriented and thus must be flexible in structure and operation. Irene likes to hire only experienced engineers, preferably with division experience in the firm. However, during the past several years, the market for engineers has been highly competitive. Owing to shortages of experienced personnel, Irene has had to hire a few young engineers right after college graduation.

Robert Miller was one of those young engineers. Robert was considered a good recruit, but his lack of experience and arrogance have created some problems.

Irene has tried to work with him to help him gain the needed experience but has not yet discussed his arrogant attitude with him.

Last week, Robert got into an argument with several engineers from the International Division with whom he was working on a project. One of them called Irene, and she met with Robert and discussed it with him. Irene thought Robert would do better after their discussion. However, a few minutes ago, Irene received a call from the project manager, who was very angry. He and Robert had just had a shouting match, and he demanded that Robert be taken off the project. Irene did not commit to anything but said she would call him back. When Irene confronted Robert about the phone call that she had just received, he turned his anger on her. They also had an argument. Irene believes Robert has potential and does not want to lose him, but he has to overcome his problems.

Case Incident 3

Steve Bassett, a supervisor in the marketing research department, is scheduled to attend a meeting of the budget committee this afternoon at 1:30. Sarah McDonald, supervisor of budget analysis, is also a member of the committee. It has been a bad day for Steve; he and his wife argued about money as he left the house, one of his key employees called in sick, and the company's intranet went down at 9:00 this morning. Steve is not fond of being a member of this committee and really does not care to waste his valuable time listening to Sarah today. (He thinks that Sarah talks too much.)

Steve arrives at Sarah's office at 1:38 P.M. After glancing at her watch and offering a few harmless pleasantries, Sarah begins her assessment of the budget committee's agenda. Although not exciting, everything seems to be all right until she mentions how poorly Steve's unit has been responding to the budgeting department's requests for information. Steve becomes visibly irritated and tells Sarah that nothing good has ever come out of these committee meetings and that she places entirely too much emphasis on them. Sarah responds by noting that Steve has not followed company policy about preparing budget information. These failures, she reasons, are the causes of his inability to achieve positive results. Having heard this comment, Steve states, in a loud voice, that whoever designed the company's policy did not know a thing about the budgeting process.

Sarah realizes that she and Steve are in disagreement and that she should try to deal with it. How, she wonders, should she deal with Steve?

Endnotes

1. Dechant, K., & Altman, B. 1994. Environmental leadership: From compliance to competitive advantage. *Academy of Management Executive*, 8: 7–27; Porter, M.E., & Kramer, M.R., 2006. The link between competitive advantage and corporate social responsibility. *Harvard Business Review*, 84 (12): 78–92.
2. Porter & Kramer, The link between competitive advantage and corporate social responsibility.
3. Shatwell, J. 2007. The net loss of overfishing. At http:www .conservation.org/xp/frontlines/partners/06060601.xml.
4. Grayson, D., & Hodges, A. 2004. *Corporate social opportunity*. Sheffield, United Kingdom: Greenleaf.
5. Chatterji, A., & Levine, D. 2006. Breaking down the wall of codes: Evaluating non-financial performance measurement. *California Management Review*, 48(2): 29–51.
6. Orlitzky, F., Schmidt, F., & Rynes, S. 2003. Corporate social and financial performance: A meta-analysis. *Organizational Studies*, 24: 403–411.
7. Collier, J., & Esteban, R. 2007. Corporate social responsibility and employee commitment. *Business Ethics*, 16 (1): 12–31.
8. Turban, D.B., & Greening, D.W. 1997. Corporate social performance and organizational attractiveness to perspective employees. *Academy of Management Journal*, 40: 848–868.
9. Wall, J.A., Jr., & Callister, R.R. 1995. Conflict and its management. *Journal of Management*, 21: 515–558.
10. Bromiley, P. 1990. On the use of finance theory in strategic management. In P. Shrivastava and R. Lamb (Eds.), *Advances in strategic management (Vol. 6)*. Greenwich, CT: JAI Press, pp. 71–98; Nixon, R.D., Hitt, M.A., Lee, H., & Jeong, E. 2004. Market reactions to announcements of corporate downsizing actions and implementation strategies. *Strategic Management Journal*, 25: 1121–1129; Orlitzky, Schmidt, & Rynes, Corporate social and financial performance.
11. Porter, & Kramer, The link between competitive advantage and corporate social responsibility.
12. Lippitt, G.L. 1982. Managing conflict in today's organizations. *Training and Development Journal*, 36: 66–72, 74.
13. Pelled, L.H. 1996. Demographic diversity, conflict, and work group outcomes: An intervening process theory. *Organizational*

Science, 6: 615–631; Tjosvold, D. 1991. Rights and responsibilities of dissent: Cooperative conflict. *Employee Responsibilities and Rights Journal,* 4: 13–23.

14. Herbert, T.T. 1977. Improving executive decisions by formalizing dissent: The corporate devil's advocate. *Academy of Management Review,* 2: 662–667.

15. Eisenhardt, K., & Schoonhoven, C. 1990. Organizational growth: Linking founding team, strategy, environment, and growth among U.S. semiconductor ventures: 1978–1988. *Administrative Science Quarterly,* 35: 504–529.

16. Jehn, K.A. 1997. A qualitative analysis of conflict types and dimensions in organizational groups. *Administrative Science Quarterly,* 42: 530–557; Jehn, K.A., Greer, L., Levine, S., & Szulanski, G. 2008. The effects of conflict types, dimensions, and emergent states on group dynamics. *Group Decision and Negotiation,* 17: 465–495.

17. Ibid.

18. Jehn, K.A., & Mannix, E.A. 2001. The dynamic nature of conflict: A longitudinal study of intragroup conflict and group performance. *Academy of Management Journal,* 44: 238–251; Tekleab, A.G., Quigley, N.R., Tesluk, P.E. 2009. A longitudinal study of team conflict, conflict management, cohesion, and team effectiveness. *Group & Organizational Management,* 34: 170-205.

19. Deutsch, M. 1969. Conflicts: Productive and destructive. *Journal of Social Issues,* 25: 7–41.

20. Jehn, A qualitative analysis of conflict types and dimensions in organizational groups; Jehn, Greer, Levine, & Szulanski, The effects of conflict types, dimensions, and emergent states on group dynamics.

21. Smolowitz, I. 1998. Organizational fratricide: The roadblock to maximum performance. *Business Forum,* 23: 45–46.

22. Amason, A.C. 1996. Distinguishing the effects of functional and dysfunctional conflict on strategic decision making: Resolving a paradox for top management teams. *Academy of Management Journal,* 39: 123–148; Eisenhardt, & Schoonhoven, Organizational growth; Jehn, K.A. 1995. A multimethod examination of the benefits and detriments of intragroup conflict. *Administrative Science Quarterly,* 40: 256–282; Schweiger, D., Sandberg, W., & Rechner, P. 1989. Experiential effects of dialectical inquiry, devil's advocacy, and consensus approaches to strategic decision making. *Academy of Management Journal,* 29: 745–772; Tjosvold, D. 1991. Rights and responsibilities of dissent: Cooperative conflict. *Employee Responsibilities and Rights Journal,* 4: 13–23. For a different but contested view, see De Dreu, C.K.W., & Weingart, L.R. 2003. Task versus relationship conflict, team performance, and team member satisfaction. *Journal of Applied Psychology,* 88: 741–749.

23. Jehn, A qualitative analysis of conflict types and dimensions in organizational groups; Jehn, Greer, Levine, & Szulanski, The effects of conflict types, dimensions, and emergent states on group dynamics.

24. Jehn, K.A., Northcraft, G., & Neale, M. 1999. Why differences make a difference: A field study of diversity, conflict, and performance in workgroups. *Administrative Science Quarterly,* 44: 741–763.

25. Jones, G.R. 2009. *Organizational theory, design, and change.* Upper Saddle River, NJ: Prentice Hall; Lawrence, P.R., & Lorsch, J.W. 1967. *Organization and environment: Managing differentiation and integration.* Boston: Harvard University Press.

26. Morgan, C.P., & Hitt, M.A. 1977. Validity and factor structure of House—Rizzo's effectiveness scales. *Academy of Management,* 20: 165–169; Hitt, M.A., & Morgan, C.P. 1977. Organizational climate as a predictor of organizational practices. *Psychological Reports,* 40: 1191–1199.

27. Heneman, H.G. III, & Judge, T.A. 2003. *Staffing organizations.* Boston: McGraw-Hill/Irwin.

28. Wall & Callister, Conflict and its management.

29. Moline, A. 2001. Conflict in the work place. *Plants, Sites, and Parks,* 28: 50–52.

30. Ibid.

31. Filley, A.C. 1975. Interpersonal *conflict resolution.* Glenview, IL: Scott Foresman, p. 10.

32. Putnam, L.L., & Poole, M.S. 1987. Conflict and negotiation. In F.M. Jablin, L.L. Putnam, K.H. Roberts, & L.W. Porter (Eds.), *Handbook of organizational communication: An interdisciplinary perspective.* Newbury Park, CA: Sage, pp. 549–599.

33. Shafer, W.E., Park, L.J., & Liao, W.M. 2002. Professionalism, organizational-professional conflict, and work outcomes: A study of certified accountants. *Accounting, Auditing, and Accountability Journal,* 15: 46–68.

34. Kaplowitz, N. 1990. National self-images, perception of enemies, and conflict strategies: Psychopolitical dimensions of international relations. *Political Psychology,* 11: 39–81.

35. Wall, & Callister, Conflict and its management.

36. Kahn, R.L., & Byosiere, P. 1992. Stress in organizations. In M.D. Dunnette, & L.M. Hough (Eds.), *Handbook of industrial and organizational psychology (Vol. 3).* Palo Alto, CA: Consulting Psychologists Press, pp. 571–650.

37. Baron, R.A. 1990. Countering the effects of destructive criticism: The relative efficacy of four interventions. *Journal of Applied Psychology,* 75: 235–245.

38. Yamagishi, T. 1986. The provision of a sanctioning system as a public good. *Journal of Personality and Social Psychology,* 50: 110–116.

39. De Dreu, C.K.W., Geibels, E., & Van de Vliert, E. 1998. Social motives and trust in integrative negotiation: The disruptive effects of punitive capability. *Journal of Applied Psychology,* 83: 408–422.

40. Van Kleef, G.A., & De Dreu, C.K.W. 2006. Supplication and appeasement in conflict and negotiation: The interpersonal effects of disappointment, worry, guilt, and regret. *Journal of Personality and Social Psychology,* 91: 124–142.

41. Rousseau, D.M., Sitkin, S.B., Burt, R.S., & Camerer, C. 1998. Not so different after all: A cross-discipline view of trust. *Academy of Management Review,* 23: 393–404.

42. Augsberger, D.W. 1992. Conflict *mediation across cultures: Pathways and patterns.* Louisville, KY: Westminster/John Knox.

43. Leung, K. 1995. Negotiation and reward allocations across cultures. In P.C. Earley, & M. Erez (Eds.), *New perspectives on industrial/organizational psychology.* San Francisco: Jossey-Bass, pp. 640–675.

44. Fu, J.H., Morris, M.W., Lee, S., Chao, M., Chiu, C., & Hong, Y. 2007. Epistemic motives and cultural conformity: Need for closure, culture, and context as determinants of conflict judgments. *Journal of Personality and Social Psychology,* 92: 191–207.

45. Wall, & Callister, Conflict and its management.

46. Ibid.

47. Staw, B., Sandelands, L., & Dutton, J. 1981. Threat-rigidity effects in organizational behavior: A multi-level analysis. *Administrative Science Quarterly,* 26: 501–524.

48. Ibid.

49. Peterson, R.S., & Behfar, K.J. 2003. The dynamic relationship between performance feedback, trust and conflict in groups: A longitudinal study. *Organizational Behavior and Human Decision Processes,* 92: 102–112.

50. Wall, & Callister, Conflict and its management.

51. O'Connor, K.M., Arnold, J.A., & Burris, E.R. 2005. Negotiators' bargaining histories and their effects on future negotiation performance. *Journal of Applied Psychology,* 90: 350–362.

52. Pruitt, D.G., & Rubin, J.Z. 1986. *Social conflict: Escalation, stalemate, and settlement.* New York: McGraw-Hill.

53. Deutsch, M. 1990. Sixty years of conflict. *International Journal of Conflict Management,* 1: 237–263.

54. Fisher, R.J. 1990. *The social psychology of intergroup and international conflict resolution.* New York: Springer-Verlag.

55. Ember, C.R., & Ember, M. 1994. War, socialization, and interpersonal violence: A cross-cultural study. *Journal of Conflict Resolution,* 38: 620–646.

56. Pruitt, D.G., & Carnevale, P.J. 1993. *Negotiation in social conflict.* Pacific Grove, CA: Brooks/Cole.

57. Ibid.

58. Morrill, C., & Thomas, C.K. 1992. Organizational conflict management as disputing process. *Human Communication Research,* 18: 400–428.

59. Retzinger, S.M. 1991. Shame, anger, and conflict: Case study of emotional violence. *Journal of Family Violence,* 6: 37–59.

60. Brockner, J., Nathanson, S., Friend, A., Harbeck, J., Samuelson, C., Houser, R., Bazerman, M.H., & Rubin, J.Z. 1984. The role of modeling processes in the "knee deep in the big muddy" phenomenon. *Organizational Behavior and Human Performance,* 33: 77–99.

61. Helyar, J. 2002. United We Fall. *Fortune,* 145 (4): 90–96; Skertic, M. 2004. United Asks Cuts in Pay of Up to 18%. *Chicago Tribune,* Nov. 6, at http://www.chicagotribune.com/classified/jobs/promo/chi-0411060211nov06,0,973948,print.stor.

62. Thomas, K.W. 1976. Conflict and conflict management. In M. Dunnette (Ed.), *Handbook of industrial and organizational psychology.* Chicago: Rand McNally, pp. 889–935.

63. Thomas, K.W. 1992. Conflict and negotiation processes. In M.D. Dunnette, & L.M. Hough (Eds.), *Handbook of industrial and organizational psychology (Vol. 3).* Palo Alto, CA: Consulting Psychologists Press, pp. 651–717.

64. Buller, P.F., Kohls, J.J., & Anderson, K.S. 2000. When ethics collide: Managing conflict across cultures. *Organizational Dynamics,* 28: 52–66.

65. Ibid.

66. Lippitt, G.L. 1982. Managing conflict in today's organizations. *Training and Development Journal,* 36: 66–72, 74.

67. Lewicki, R.J., Saunders, D.M., & Barry, B. 2009. *Negotiation* (6th ed.). Boston: McGraw-Hill/Irwin.

68. Walton, R.E., & McKersie, R.B. 1965. *A behavioral theory of labor negotiations.* New York: McGraw-Hill.

69. Ibid.

70. Cormack, G.W. 2005. *Negotiation skills for board professionals.* Mill Creek, WA: CSE Group; Dietmeyer, B. *Negotiation: A breakthrough four-step process for effective business negotiation.* Chicago: Dearborn Trade; Sperber, P. 1983. *Fail-safe business negotiating.* Englewood Cliffs, NJ: Prentice Hall; Thompson, L.L. 2008. *The mind and heart of the negotiator* (4th ed.). Upper Saddle River, NJ: Prentice Hall.

71. Somech, A., & Drach-Zahavy, A. 2002. Relative power and influence strategy: The effects of agent-target organizational power on superiors' choices of influence strategies. *Journal of Organizational Behavior,* 23: 167–181.

72. Dahl, R.A. 1957. The concept of power. *Behavioral Science,* 2: 201–215.

73. Salancik, G.R., & Pfeffer, J. 1977. Who gets power and how they hold on to it: A strategic contingency model of power. *Organizational Dynamics,* 5: 3–21.

74. Dahl, The concept of power.

75. Pfeffer, J. 1992. Understanding power in organizations. *California Management Review,* 34: 29–50.

76. Salancik & Pfeffer, Who gets power and how they hold on to it.

77. French, J.R.P., & Raven, B. 1959. The bases of social power. In D. Cartwright (Ed.), *Studies in social power.* Ann Arbor: University of Michigan Institute for Social Research, pp. 160–167.

78. Eggen, D. 2007. Deputy attorney general defends prosecutor firings. *Washington Post,* February 7, at http://washintonpost.com/wp-dyn/content/article/2007/02/06/AR2007020600732.htm.

79. Kurland, N.B., & Pelled, L.H. 2000. Passing the word: Toward a model of gossip and power in the workplace. *Academy of Management Review,* 25: 428–438.

80. Bacharach, S.B., & Lawler, E.J. 1980. *Power and politics in organizations.* San Francisco: Jossey-Bass.

81. Finkelstein, S. 1992. Power in top management teams: Dimensions, measurement, and validation. *Academy of Management Journal,* 35: 505–539.

82. French & Raven, The bases of social power.

83. Crawford, K. 2004. Eisner vs. Ovitz: This time in court, *CNN Money,* Oct 15, at http://money.cnn.com/2004/10/15/news/fortune500/ovitz; Levine, G. 2004. Eisner: Disney, Miramax talks staggered, *Forbes,* May 12, at http://www.forbes.com/2004/05/12/0512autofacescan03.html; McCarthy, M. 2004. Eisner foes keep up the pressure, *USA Today,* March 16, at usatoday.com/money/media/2004-03-16-eisner_x.htm; McCarthy, M. 2004. Disney strips chairmanship from Eisner, *USA Today,* March 3, at http://www.usatoday.com/money/media/2004-03-03disney-shareholder-meeting_x.htm; Orwall, B. 2004. Behind the scenes at Eisner's Disney: Beleaguered CEO, Ovitz, we're headed in opposite directions from the start, *Los Angeles Daily News,* November 23, at http://www.dailynews.com/cda/article/print/0,1674,200%257E20950%257E2554402,00.html; Smith, E., & Miller, S. 2009. Remembrances: A Namesake Who Reanimated Disney. *Wall Street Journal,* Dec. 17: A.22; Surowiecki, J. 2004. Good grooming, *The New Yorker,* October 4, at http://www.newyorker.com/talk/content/?011004ta_talk_surowiecki.

84. Salancik & Pfeffer. Who gets power and how they hold on to it.

85. Hillman, A.J., & Dalziel, T. 2003. Boards of directors and firm performance: Integrating agency and resource dependence perspectives. *Academy of Management Review,* 28: 383–396.

86. Pfeffer, J. 1981. *Power in organizations.* Marshfield, MA: Pitman Publishing.

87. Ibid.

88. Ibid.

89. Surowiecki, J. 2004. Good grooming. *The New Yorker,* October 4, at http://www.newyorker.com/talk/content/?011004ta_ talk_surowiecki.

90. Ibid.

91. Pfeffer, *Power in organizations.*

92. Mintzberg, H. 1985. The organization as political arena. *Journal of Management Studies,* 22: 133–154.

93. Kacmar, K.M., & Baron, R.A. 1999. Organizational politics: The state of the field, links to related processes, and an agenda for future research. In G.R. Ferris (Ed.), *Research in personnel and human resource management (Vol. 17).* Stamford, CT: JAI Press, pp. 1–39; Zivnuska, S., Kacmar, K.M., Witt, L.A., Carlson, D.S., & Bratton, V.K. 2004. Interactive effects of impression management and organizational politics on job performance. *Journal of Organizational Behavior,* 25: 627–640.

94. Anonymous. 2002. Politics at work: Backstabbing, stolen ideas, scapegoats. *Director,* 56: 74–80.

95. Poon, J.M.L. 2003. Situational antecedents and outcomes of organizational politics perceptions. *Journal of Managerial Psychology,* 18: 138–155.

96. Yukl, G., Kim, H., & Falbe, C.M. 1996. Antecedents of influence outcomes. *Journal of Applied Psychology,* 81: 309–317.

97. Popper, M. 2004. Morgan Stanley's board must end inaction, investor Matrix says. *Bloomberg.com,* April 21, at www. bloomberg.com/apps/news?pid=10000103&sid=aluJZFE02LOA &refer=us.

98. Martinez, M.J. 2005. Uphill fight for Morgan Stanley dissidents. *Associated Press,* April 8, at www.biz.yahoo.com/ap/0504080morgan_stanley.html.

99. Ibid.

100. Davis, A. 2005. Mack Takes Step to Clean House: Morgan Stanley CEO Bids Adieu to Crawford, but Move Will Cost Firm's Shareholders $32 Million. *Wall Street Journal,* July 12: C.1

101. Cable, D.M., & Judge, T.A. 2003. Managers' upward influence tactic strategies: The role of manager personality and supervisor leadership style. *Journal of Organizational Behavior,* 24: 197–214.

102. Ahearn, K.K., Ferris, G.R., Hochwater, W.A., Douglas, C., & Ammeter, A.P. 2004. Leader political skill and team performance. *Journal of Management,* 30: 309–327.

103. Ferris, G.R., Treadway, D.C., Kolodinsky, R.W., Hochwater, W.A., Kacmar, C.J., Douglas, C., & Frink, D.D. 2005. Development and validation of the political skill inventory. *Journal of Management,* 31: 126–152.

BRIGHT AND DEDICATED:
what more do you want?

H. Richard Eisenbeis, Colorado State University—Pueblo
Sue Hanks, Colorado State University—Pueblo
Linda Shaw, Colorado State University—Pueblo

Susan Reynolds carefully studied her first annual performance review at Marco Pictures, a highly successful motion picture company headquartered in Los Angeles. Although in many respects the review was favorable, she was disturbed by the following comments made by Anita Lockwood, her immediate supervisor (Appendix I and Appendix II):

My only concern is Susan's tendency to stay in her office and avoid contact with others in the company. As the controller, she should be involved with the production, postproduction, licensing, royalties, and other departments. She should be aware of the activity going on in each and should "touch base" with the department heads periodically to determine the future requirements of the accounting department.

She should also become more involved in the personnel matters of the department. She should be aware at all times of the status of work in the department and should be the first 'manager' to tackle personnel problems as they arise.

As Susan reflected on these comments, the following thoughts went through her mind:*

Perhaps I should have listened to Bill, my assistant, confidant, and

---

*These are direct quotes from one of the principal characters. The names of the firm and people involved in the case have been disguised.

This case was presented to the North American Case Research Association at its annual meeting October 27–29, 2005, North Falmouth, MA. We want to thank the editor of the *Case Research Journal and* the anonymous reviewers for their time and valuable suggestions.

colleague (at Marco), who advised me to find a job where I didn't have to supervise people, and where my considerable auditing skills would be more valued. He also suggested that perhaps instead of worrying, I should have spent more time looking for another position. Maybe, he was right.

But, my job with Marco is consistent with those where audit managers with my skills and experience end up and perform very effectively. I like this job. I like these responsibilities. Why isn't this working? Maybe I had better be moving on.

But, Anita has been good to me. I don't want to take advantage of Marco by not telling her that I am in the process of looking for another position. It would be just plain unfair for me to remain on the payroll knowing I may soon be leaving.

MARCO PICTURES, INC.

Marco Pictures was founded by two individuals, who became highly successful in distributing motion pictures in international markets. In the 1970s and 1980s, these two men decided to make a relatively inexpensive movie that became a monumental box office hit. Because of the success of this movie, the partners decided to make more motion pictures, capitalizing upon their international distribution experience to finance these movies by "pre-selling" the rights in worldwide markets. By September 1986, the movie and its sequel had generated worldwide box office revenues of more than $390 million.

In 1986, Marco became a publicly traded company. By 1990, Marco had consolidated assets of $632 million. Consolidated net income for the year ending December 31, 1990, was $61 million on revenues of $269 million.

In the high risk motion picture industry companies must make a large investment in the production of each motion picture while gambling that the movie will be well received in theaters and other venues. Often a picture's success in future markets depends largely on its success in theaters. Even movies that are highly acclaimed by critics are not guaranteed a profitable outcome.

Marco operated under three basic principles that were established to minimize shareholder risk:

1. to produce and distribute a limited number of "event" motion pictures (movies with casts and themes having major box office appeal),
2. to finance those productions through "pre-sales" of exhibition rights in the various media around the world, and
3. to maximize return on investment from "ancillary" markets such as video, television, and merchandizing.

The financial group at Marco was headed by Anita Lockwood (vice president of finance) and included the accounting, payroll, royalty, and cash management departments. Although Susan Reynolds, in her position as controller, was nominally in charge of the twelve-person accounting department and reported to Anita Lockwood, there was no formal organizational chart. Those accounting personnel who had been with the company since its inception, as well as those who had worked directly with Anita before her career move from controller to vice president, continued to report directly to Anita after her promotion. Moreover, Anita directly assigned projects to personnel in all departments regardless of position. This lack of formal reporting lines was somewhat consistent for the entertainment industry, and especially for a company that was still young and entrepreneurial.

Anita Lockwood

Anita Lockwood, 37, grew up in an affluent Los Angeles suburb. She was the younger of two sisters and was quite vivacious. She had initially planned to become an elementary school teacher, but eventually attained a master's degree in accounting. She began her accounting career with the audit division of a big-six accounting firm. After two years, Anita left public accounting to work in the accounting department of a large entertainment company where, in her capacity as manager of general ledger reporting, she supervised several accounting clerks and worked closely with other accounting supervisors. A year after Anita's former supervisor had departed the company to accept the controller position at Marco Pictures, he was promoted to the position of vice president of finance. Faced with filling the controller position, he remembered Anita's professional competencies and managerial ability and offered her the position. Recognizing the future opportunities she might have, she eagerly accepted. Later, when he was promoted to chief financial officer, he once more chose Anita to be his successor.

After her promotion to vice president, one of Anita's first responsibilities was to find a new controller. During the search and interview process she learned that Susan, who had worked in the same big-six accounting firm with Anita, was looking for new employment challenges and opportunities. Anita had been impressed by Susan's auditing and accounting skills and believed that Susan would be a valuable addition for Marco. Following interviews by Anita and Marco's CEO, Anita offered Susan the job. Anticipating that this would be a smart career move, Susan accepted.

Susan Reynolds

Susan Reynolds was born and raised in rural America. Growing up, her activities were restricted to public school, household chores, and church activities. Religion was very important to Susan's family and her parents were strict disciplinarians. Spending her formative years in this environment, Susan developed a strong work ethic and a respect for authority. She was also quite reserved and shared little about her personal life with anyone other than her few close friends. Her parents were strong supporters of higher education, even though both had managed only to earn a high school education. Graduating as valedictorian of her high school class, Susan went on to complete an undergraduate degree in accounting maintaining a 3.88 GPA.

Upon graduation, she was recruited by several of the leading accounting firms and eventually accepted a position with a big-six accounting firm in Los Angeles.

Within two years Susan was promoted to audit senior and three years later to audit manager, a position she held for four years prior to her move to Marco. Susan's responsibilities included being in charge of the audit of a large entertainment client. The assignment included coordinating the activities of two other audit seniors and supervising two to three staff members. She was most comfortable and motivated in her position as audit manager when she was designated as the second manager on a project. The primary manager would be in charge of the more ambiguous aspects of the task, such as developing and maintaining interpersonal relationships, while Susan worked behind the scenes making sure that all the details of the assignment were carried out as required. In situations where responsibilities were not well defined, such as following through on client billings and maintaining client contacts, Susan was often uncomfortable.

THE CURRENT SITUATION AT MARCO

"What a fantastic office! What a fantastic job!" Susan often marveled at her large corner office overlooking Sunset Boulevard. Tower Records was located right across the street and she recalled that not long ago she watched in awe the throng of people standing in line hoping for a chance to get the autograph of a famous recording artist. In the evening

she was able to see the sun setting over Hollywood. Nevertheless, even before receiving her annual performance review, she began to feel apprehensive that something was not quite right.

Susan's earliest projects with Marco had gone smoothly. Her schedules had been concise and reasonable and the external auditors had been able to finish in less time than the previous year, resulting in substantial savings for Marco. Susan worked closely with the auditors and welcomed the interaction with them and the opportunity to learn more about Marco's corporate structure and its international ventures. But, as she was assigned other projects, her enthusiasm waned. Her first concerns surfaced after seven months, when Anita's office was moved to the opposite corner of the building. Before the move, Susan could catch Anita in the mornings for a short chat about what was going on within the departments before she had settled into her schedule for the day. Gone were the days when Anita would spend an hour here and there with her, telling her about the company's ongoing operations, its key players, and the company's financial strategies. She was also concerned that the participations/royalties and payroll clerks offices—two departments with which she had to work very closely—were now located closer to Anita's office than hers.

However, these morning meetings were no longer feasible. Anita commuted 60 miles to work and her time in traffic was often unpredictable. By the time Susan was certain that she had arrived, Anita was often busy with others or engrossed in her current spreadsheet project. Susan felt that just "touching base" was not a valid reason for interrupting Anita's train of thought. Consequently, Susan felt they talked all too briefly and then only about specific questions regarding Susan's current projects. Although Susan knew that Anita was busy, she often wished that Anita would hold weekly staff meetings so she would know more about what was going on in the department and the company. As a result of Anita's move, Susan suddenly felt out of the loop.

Susan's Reflections

One of Susan's first assignments had been to complete the annual U.S. Department of Commerce survey. Anita's instructions had been:

This survey needs to be completed as soon as possible. We've already extended the due date once. This project will be a good way for you to learn where specific financial information can be found in the general ledger and files. It will also be a good way for you to learn about Marco's operations. Feel free to ask me any questions you may have as you compile the data and write the final report.

After successfully completing the project, Anita had Susan undertake some of the department's more routine activities, giving Susan the following instructions:

Until we hire an assistant controller, I want you to review the invoice packages before the checks are taken to Joe (the chief

financial officer) for signature. We're just now finishing the financial package for May. Joe wants us to reduce the time it's taking to close the general ledger at the end of the month and prepare the financial package for his review. Beginning the last week of June, I also want you to start working with the participation/royalty and pay clerks to make sure they get their journal entries prepared and posted as quickly as possible. Once we have the final copy of May's package, we can go through it together so you can see how each department contributes to the final product.

Susan had been performing as expected for three months when Anita was finally successful in hiring an assistant controller to support Susan.

Bill Mayer

Bill Mayer (30) was a recent graduate of UCLA with a master's degree in accounting. Prior to returning to school to pursue his graduate degree, he had completed two years active duty with the Army reserves and been employed by a small accounting firm in Los Angeles. Upon completing his MS in accounting, Bill passed the CPA exam on his first attempt and immediately began searching for a more challenging position than was possible with his current employer. He was brought to Anita's attention by a member of UCLA's accounting faculty, an acquaintance of Anita's, who had heard through the grapevine that Marco was searching for an assistant controller. An interview followed during which Anita became convinced

that Bill would be a perfect fit. She found him to be outgoing and personable and was impressed with his academic performance and his recommendations from his previous employer. Susan had also expressed to Anita that she believed Bill would be a welcome addition to the team. Susan and Bill began an enduring cordial relationship.

Once Bill was on board, Anita gave the following instructions to Susan and her new assistant:

Now that Bill is on board, I want him to review all of accounts payables work. I also want him to orchestrate the month-end closing process, as well as the preparation of the financial package. I want you (Susan) to review the financial package before I do. Then, I'll review it before we give it to Joe. Deloitte and Touche will be here in two weeks to audit Marco International's financial statements. Here's a list of the schedules you need to prepare and have ready for them when they arrive. I also want you to provide access to all the documents they may need and answer any questions that may arise.

THREE MONTHS LATER

Although Bill was a welcome addition to the accounting department, as time passed Bill assumed more and more responsibility, and Susan began to feel that her talents were not being utilized to the extent that they should be. In addition Anita seemed to be becoming more distant. For example, one night as Susan was leaving the office, she noticed that

Anita was working late. On her way out, Susan stopped by Anita's office and asked:

"Is it going to be another late one?"

"Looks like it," Anita replied.

"Anything I can do to help?"

"No, Charles (Marco's CFO) wants me to run some new numbers through this pro forma for his meetings tomorrow," Anita answered.

"Sure you couldn't use some help?"

"No, but thanks for asking"

"Okay, see you in the morning."

"Have a good evening"

It bothered Susan that Anita would not let her help and seemed to be so determined to do the work herself. "But, she's the boss and in reality this appears to be how she prefers to do things," she thought. Another concern was that although Anita had instructed her to review the month-end financial package before passing it to her for review, over the next few months Susan's review came to be concurrent with Anita's or was skipped altogether. Having these responsibilities taken from her further increased her anxieties.

Susan would have preferred to have more interaction with others in the department but felt left out when it came to administrative and personnel matters. She believed that if more information was shared with her, she would have been able to help the department run more smoothly. She knew she had more to offer than she had the opportunity to give. For example, Susan recalled

the time when Bill had told her that he and Anita were getting ready to dismiss the cash management clerk in her department. She knew nothing of the decision until right before Bill and Anita had asked him to clean out his desk! Susan believed that Bill informed her only so that she would be ready for any commotion should it arise.

Moreover, Susan was not enjoying her current assignment. It involved a lengthy analysis of all the transactions posted to the "intercompany" accounts between Marco and Marco International over the last two years. This long, complex and tedious project required that Susan spend countless hours doing the work herself. Although she wished that she could have delegated some of the work, in the past Anita had indicated that she had taken sole responsibility for this undertaking. Susan believed that Anita also expected her to do the entire project without assistance.

As the task of analyzing the intercompany accounts began to drag on, Susan began to think more and more about her current situation. It bothered her that she was receiving inadequate feedback from Anita. And, although Susan continued to view Bill as a close friend, she began to have concerns about her willingness to share supervisory responsibilities with him—especially those tasks she found to be distasteful—and how this would affect her overall performance review. Several questions went through her mind: Shouldn't Anita be giving me more direction? Why doesn't Anita tell me directly if she is dissatisfied with my

performance and what she expects me to do differently? What exactly are my supervisory duties? What does it really mean to "manage" this department? What should I do at this point?

It had been very different in public accounting where each assignment had an overall plan from which it was easy to identify each person's specific duties. And, although she had had supervisory responsibilities, the staff members under her direction were all self-motivated high achievers who required little or no direct supervision.

Because of Susan's doubt, her belief that asking for more direction would reflect negatively on her performance, and her increasing concerns about her overall value to Marco, her self-confidence and self-esteem began to suffer. She was troubled that working diligently and producing accurate reports and schedules was simply not enough.

ANITA'S REFLECTIONS AND THE ANNUAL PERFORMANCE REVIEW

In preparing for Susan's upcoming year-end performance evaluation, Anita thought about Susan's initial orientation into the accounting department. When Susan began her employment at Marco, Anita recalled that she had spent quite a bit of time with Susan talking about the company, how its projects were going, and its financial status. In addition to expecting that Susan complete the special projects assigned, Anita anticipated that Susan would easily be able to assume the day-to-day supervisory responsibilities in the department. However, as projects were assigned to Susan, it appeared that she tended to become so engrossed in each project that important departmental personnel matters were neglected. One example was a situation that occurred earlier in the year when it became necessary to discharge the cash management clerk. In her position as controller, Anita had expected Susan to be more involved in overseeing the clerk's performance and noting or correcting any improprieties. She believed that Susan had failed to appropriately monitor and manage the situation. This aspect of Susan's management style concerned Anita.

Anita wanted to make sure that her upcoming evaluation of Susan's performance included her appreciation for the significant and substantial contributions that she had made to the accounting department over the last year. She also, however, had to include her concerns in the evaluation. Specifically, she needed to convey to Susan the need to develop her interpersonal skills and to take the appropriate disciplinary action on her own when necessary. Anita considered how she could best approach Susan without causing bad feelings that might lead to the loss of one of Marco's most valuable employees.

Anita had expected Susan to be more of a "take-charge" person and to be more outgoing and assertive. She had had excellent references and had been highly spoken of by those with whom she had previously worked. Although Susan produced excellent reports and analyses that required minimal input from Anita, she had not made any obvious effort to assume responsibility for directing and supervising the department personnel. No one could deny that Susan was highly motivated and an outstanding performer on the tasks she was assigned. But, Anita wondered why Susan was so reluctant to perform these duties at Marco. She performed them in her previous position; why isn't she doing it here?

The following week, Anita met with Susan to discuss Susan's annual performance evaluation. Anita began the discussion by saying:

You've been at Marco for over a year now and it's time we evaluated your performance. Let me begin by telling you that you're doing a great job and we're giving you a nine percent salary increase. I am pleased with your overall contribution to the accounting department over the past year. You did an excellent job with the Touche Ross audit of Marco International and with the Ernst and Young audit of the company's financial statements.

However, I am concerned that you appear to feel uncomfortable working with other managers within the company. I want you to begin attending the monthly production meetings. These meetings should give you a feeling of where the company's projects are in the production process and the problems encountered, some of which may have accounting implications. You'll also have the opportunity to get to know more of the people within various departments. And, we'll figure out some other ways in which you can interact more with the other managers.

Take a couple of minutes to read through your Employee Evaluation Report (Appendix I and Appendix II) and let's go over any concerns you might have.

Susan's Reaction

As Susan read the evaluation, she failed to notice the many positive comments. Never in her 32 years had she felt more of a failure. "What should I do now?" she thought. "I know I have terrific technical and administrative skills. How can I become a better manager? Or, should I even try?" Intellectually, she knew how important it was to her career that she display strong interpersonal skills and she knew that she should have been more involved in personnel matters and politics within the department. She disliked dealing with conflict and being even marginally involved in internal politics. And, quite truthfully, she didn't know what steps to take to become more aware and involved. She believed that Anita's recommendations would undoubtedly help, but she was afraid that it would take more energy and time than was possible on both their parts. But, once again, as was typical of Susan, she chose not to share her feelings with Anita and signed the evaluation. With copy in hand, she returned to her office overlooking Sunset Boulevard to further consider her options.

APPENDIX I: SUSAN REYNOLDS' EMPLOYEE EVALUATION REPORT

EMPLOYEE EVALUATION REPORT

Date of this evaluation ____1/22____   Date of previous evaluation _____

Reason for evaluation.   ☒ General Performance.   ☒ Salary Increase.   ☐ Promotion.

Name ____Susan Reynolds____   Soc. Sec. No. ____444-55-2222____

Job Title ____Controller____   Dept. ____Accounting____   Clock No. _____

Date Hired ____9/15____   Time Employed ____one____ ☒ Years ☐ Months

Education: ☐ Elementary   ☐ Junior H.S.   ☐ Senior H.S.   ☐ College 1 2 3 **4**

Current Salary $ ____85,000____ per ____year____ Time employed at this rate ____one____ ☒ Years ☐ Months

Date of last previous increase _____   Previous rate of pay $ _____ per _____

Time employed at present job _____ ☐ Years ☐ Months   Date of last promotion _____

ATTENDANCE RECORD   ☒ Excellent   ☐ Good   ☐ Poor

Number of days absent this year _____ Approved days _____ Unauthorized days _____

Number of days absent last year _____ Approved days _____ Unauthorized days _____

Number of days late this year _____ Number of days late last year _____

WORK PERFORMANCE

Ability to do job assigned: ☐ Superior   ☐ Meets Standard   ☐ Below Standard

Comments on job ability: _____

____See attached____

Comparison to previous evaluation: ☐ Improved   ☐ No Change   ☐ Negative

Productivity: ☐ Superior   ☐ Meets Standard   ☐ Below Standard

Comments on productivity: ____Susan's ability to complete projects in a timely manner is excellent. She is an extremely hard worker and always puts in whatever time is necessary to complete projects on time.____

Comparison to previous evaluation: ☐ Improved   ☐ No Change   ☐ Negative

Ability to follow instructions: ☒ Excellent   ☐ Good   ☐ Poor

Comments on ability to follow instructions: _____

_____

_____

Comparison to previous evaluation: ☐ Improved   ☐ No Change   ☐ Negative

				—Comparison to previous evaluation—		
Cooperation	☒ Excellent	☐ Good	☐ Poor	☐ Improved	☐ No Change	☐ Negative
Attitude	☒ Excellent	☐ Good	☐ Poor	☐ Improved	☐ No Change	☐ Negative
Initiative	☐ Excellent	☒ Good	☐ Poor	☐ Improved	☐ No Change	☐ Negative
Work Habits	☒ Excellent	☐ Good	☐ Poor	☐ Improved	☐ No Change	☐ Negative

Comments on cooperation, attitude, initiative and work habits: _____

_____

_____

_____

_____

PERSONAL

Relationship with fellow employees: ☐ Well liked   ☐ Accepted   ☐ Other (explain below)

_____

_____ See attached _____

_____

Relationship with customers: ☐ Excellent   ☐ Good   ☐ Unsatisfactory (explain below)

_____

_____ n/a _____

_____

Comparison to previous evaluation   ☐ Improved   ☐ No Change   ☐ Negative

Personality (check those which apply):

☐ Friendly   ☐ Out-going   ☒ Courteous   ☐ Aloof   ☒ Neat in appearance   ☐ Untidy

☐ Enjoys work   ☒ Dependable   ☒ Conscientious   ☐ Calm under pressure   ☐ Nervous

Complains excessively   ☐ Negative influence on others   ☐ Positive influence on others

Desire for achievement: ☐ High   ☒ Average   ☐ Low

SUMMARY OF EVALUATION

Overall evaluation: ☒ Positive   ☐ Negative

Overall comparison to previous evaluation: ☐ Improved   ☐ No Change   ☐ Poorer

Continued employment: ☒ Recommended   ☐ Not recommended

Salary increase: ☒ Recommended   ☐ Not recommended

Recommended salary increase: $ ___8,000 – 9%___ per __year__ Effective __1/22__

Promotion: ☐ Recommended   ☐ Not recommended.   Job Change: ☐ Recommended   ☐ Not recommended

Recommended promotion: _____ Effective _____

Recommended job change: _____ Effective _____

COMMENTS

   The overall performance of Susan's work is excellent, except for the area discussed in the attachment. This, however, is not such a problem that she cannot perform her work satisfactorily.

Date _____ Evaluated by ___Anita Lockwood_____

Date _____ Recommendations approved by _____

APPENDIX II: ATTACHMENT TO SUSAN REYNOLDS' ANNUAL EVALUATION OF 1/22

Susan has been a valuable addition to the accounting department. In the past year she has assumed responsibility for:

1. Accounting related to our foreign tax structure
2. Overseeing the audit of Marco and its subsidiaries by Deloitte and Touche
3. Mentoring the reporting requirements to US Commerce Dept. re: foreign ownership of US corporations
4. Coordinating and completing audit schedules for year end and quarterly reviews by Ernst & Young
5. Coordinating the gathering of information and documents for completion of the tax return

Susan is very reliable and her strong technical skills have been instrumental in accomplishing many special projects. For example:

1. Analysis of the foreign/domestic inter company balances and activity.
2. Foreign vs. domestic cash flow statements.

Susan has been very helpful in completing these and other day-to-day projects. Her work is always accurate and she is always willing to do whatever is necessary to complete the task at hand, even if it means working through the night!

My only concern is Susan's tendency to stay in her office and avoid contact with others in the company. As the controller, she should be involved with the production, postproduction, licensing, royalties, and other departments. She should be aware of the activity going on in each and should "touch base" with the department heads periodically to determine what requirements of the accounting department will be made in the future.

She should also become more involved in the personnel matters of the department. She should be aware at all times of the status of work in the department and should be the first "manager" to tackle personnel problems as they arise.

I'll work with Susan in the near future to provide opportunities for her to develop these interpersonal skills and I feel that with little effort she should be able to improve in this area.

ORGANIZATIONAL
BEHAVIOR
A STRATEGIC APPROACH

ORGANIZATIONAL
DIVERSITY

ORGANIZATIONAL
BEHAVIOR
A GLOBAL CONTEXT

INDIVIDUAL PROCESSES
LEARNING AND PERCEPTION
PERSONALITY, INTELLIGENCE, ATTITUDES, AND EMOTIONS
WORK MOTIVATION
STRESS AND WELL-BEING

GROUPS, TEAMS, AND SOCIAL PROCESSES
LEADERSHIP
COMMUNICATION
DECISION MAKING BY INDIVIDUALS AND GROUPS
GROUPS AND TEAMS
CONFLICT, NEGOTIATION, POWER, AND POLITICS

THE ORGANIZATIONAL CONTEXT
ORGANIZATIONAL STRUCTURE AND CULTURE
ORGANIZATIONAL CHANGE AND DEVELOPMENT

PART 4

the organizational context

In the final part of the book, we examine the organizational context for the individual and group processes discussed in Parts II and III. Thus, we began the book with a chapter that presented the strategic lens for managing behavior in organizations, and we end with two chapters that explain the organizational processes and context for that behavior.

In **Chapter 13**, we discuss structure and organizational culture. The organization's structure can have a significant effect on behavior. Organizational culture is based on shared values in the organization. Therefore, the fit between individual values and organizational values is important. Organizational culture can significantly influence associates' and managers' behavior. It can affect individuals' motivation and attitudes as well as team processes such as leadership and conflict.

Chapter 14, the last chapter in the book, focuses on organizational change and development. Most organizations exist in dynamic environments requiring them to change regularly in order to adapt to environmental changes. Shifting environments also require that organizations develop flexibility in their strategies. Being flexible, however, necessitates taking an approach to change that associates and managers in the organization will accept. Most people dislike and resist change because of the uncertainty involved. This chapter explains how managers can develop a change process that unfreezes associates' attitudes and allows them to accept change. The chapter also discusses organization development, a form of internal consulting aimed at improving communication, problem solving, and learning in the organization. The problem-solving process involves diagnosing the problem, prescribing interventions, and monitoring progress. The change processes and problem-resolution processes discussed in this chapter draw on many of the concepts explored in the previous chapters of this book.

organizational structure and culture

Growth and Structure Provide an Integrated Portfolio of Services at FedEx

Many companies have goals designed to achieve growth and diversification of the markets they serve, both product and geographical. These long-term goals are often maintained even during economic recessions such as that experienced at the end of the first decade of the twenty-first century. Growth can be achieved by developing new products and services internally or by acquiring other organizations. Growth by external acquisition has been popular because it is often a faster and less risky means of achieving the desired growth. FedEx's corporate strategy involved both of these approaches.

In 1971, Federal Express Corporation was founded in Little Rock, Arkansas. Early in its history, FedEx used internal development to achieve rapid growth. In 1983, Federal Express achieved $1 billion in revenue; it made its first acquisition in 1984, Gelco Express International, launching its operations in the Asia Pacific region. Five years later, Federal Express purchased Flying Tigers to expand its international presence. That same year, Roberts Express (now FedEx Custom Critical) began providing services to Europe. In 1995, FedEx acquired air routes from Evergreen International with authority to serve China and opened an Asia Pacific Hub in Subic Bay, Philippines, launching the FedEx AsiaOne Network. By 1996, FedEx Ground achieved 100 percent coverage in North America. In 1998, FedEx acquired Caliber Systems, Inc. and created FDX Corporation. This series of acquisitions made FedEx a $16 billion transportation powerhouse. But the acquisitions and growth continued. In 1999, Federal Express Corporation acquired Caribbean Transportation Services. In January 2000, FDX Corporation was renamed

knowledge objectives

After reading this chapter, you should be able to:

1. Define key elements of organizational structure, including both structural and structuring dimensions.
2. Explain how corporate and business strategies relate to structure.
3. Explain how environment, technology, and size relate to structure.
4. Define organizational culture, and discuss the competing values cultural framework.
5. Discuss socialization.
6. Describe cultural audits and subcultures.
7. Explain the importance of a fit between individual values and organizational culture.

FedEx Corporation. Also in 2000, FedEx Trade Networks was created with the acquisitions of Tower Group International and WorldTariff.

In 2001, FedEx acquired American Freightways; in 2004, it acquired Kinko's for $2.4 billion and also Parcel Direct; and it completed its acquisitions in 2007, with its purchase of Chinese shipping partner DTW Group in order to obtain more control over and access to services in secondary Chinese cities.

As suggested by the large list of acquisitions, FedEx's strategy to achieve growth was realized. It also diversified the company's portfolio of services. For example, it acquired Kinko's to expand the company's retail services through the 1,200-plus Kinko's stores.

©AP/Wide World Photos

In addition, by acquiring Parcel Direct, FedEx was able to expand services for customers in the e-tail and catalog segments. All of the companies acquired by FedEx Corp were carefully selected to ensure a corporate culture with a positive service-oriented spirit, thereby providing a good fit with FedEx. For example, in 2009, FedEx continued to be listed among *Fortune*'s 100 Best Companies to Work For and in the top ten of *Fortune*'s World's Most Admired Companies.

Because of the growth and additional services, FedEx adopted a multidivisional structure. FedEx Corporation provides strategic direction and consolidated financial reporting for the operating companies that are collectively under the FedEx name worldwide (FedEx Express, FedEx Ground, FedEx Freight, FedEx Kinko's Office and Print Services, FedEx Custom Critical, FedEx Trade Networks, and FedEx Services). Because of the growth in the size and scope of the company, FedEx delegated significant authority to the divisions. Together, the various divisions are FedEx, but independently, each division offers flexible, specialized services that represent an array of supply chain, transportation, and business and related information services. Operating independently, each FedEx company manages its own specialized network of services. The FedEx Corporation acts as the hub, allowing its decentralized divisions to work together worldwide. FedEx

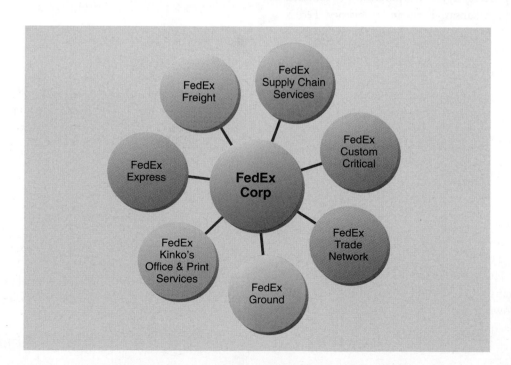

coordinates the activities of operating divisions in ways that integrate them to provide customers a unique and powerful portfolio of services globally.

Along with its competitive array of services, FedEx remains innovative and sensitive to its environment. For example, in 2010, it implemented a new service, Sense-aware, a sensor-enabled device that provides real-time data on the location and other important information (e.g., temperature) of a package. The device allows FedEx and customers to monitor the condition and travel of highly important and sensitive packages. In addition, FedEx also has initiatives to promote a sustainable environment. In 2009, for example, it announced plans to install the largest rooftop solar power system in the United States at its major distribution facility in New Jersey. Therefore, despite an exceptionally difficult global economy in 2009, two analysts predicted that FedEx would "soar like an eagle" in 2010.

Sources: Associated Press. 2009. "FedEx Meets Estimates but Gives Cautious Forecast," *New York Times,* Dec. 17, www.nytimes.com; Paul Rubillo & Tom Reese. 2009. "FedEx Flies Like an Eagle," *Forbes,* Dec. 8, www.forbes.com; Cliff Kuang. 2009. "If the Delivery Guy Drops Your Package, Senseaware Updates You Online," *Fast Company,* Nov. 24, at http://www.fastcompany.com; Stephanie N. Metha. 2009. "Smart Phones. Smart networks. Smart Packages?" *Fortune,* Nov.17, at http://www.fortune.com; Ariel Schwartz. 2009. "FedEx to Build Largest Rooftop Solar Array in U.S.," *Fast Company,* July 30, at http://www.fastcompany.com; Mitch Jackson. 2009. "Is the Overnight Envelope Anti-green?" *Money,* May 1, at http://www.cnnmoney.com; "Best Big Companies to Work for," *Money,* April 27, 2009, www.cnnmoney.com; Associated Press. 2007. "FedEx Completes Acquisition of DTW Group," *BusinessWeek,* Feb. 28, at http://www.businessweek.com; Sarah Murray. 2006. "Putting the House in Order," *Financial Times,* Nov. 8, at http://www.ft.com; Dean Foust. 2006. "Taking Off Like 'a Rocket Ship,'" *BusinessWeek*, Apr. 3, at http://www.businessweek.com; 2007. "About FedEx," *FedEx Homepage,* at http://www.fedex.com.

organizational structure
Work roles and authority relationships that influence behavior in an organization.

organizational culture
The values shared by associates and managers in an organization.

the strategic importance of Organizational Structure and Culture

When considering the implementation of organizational strategies, we often focus on the roles of strong leaders, talented managers and associates, and effective processes such as communication and conflict management. Although all these factors are important, as emphasized in prior chapters, they provide only part of the support to implement an organization's strategy. The organization's structure and culture also play crucial roles in strategy implementation.

Organizational structure refers to the formal system of work roles and authority relationships that govern how associates and managers interact with one another.[1] To properly implement a strategy, an organization must build a structure ensuring that formal and informal activities and initiatives support strategic goals. Structure influences communication patterns among individuals and groups and the degree to which they have the discretion to be innovative. If, for example, a strategy calls for rapid responses in several dynamic and different markets, it is important to create divisions around those markets and delegate authority to managers in those divisions so that they can act when necessary, similar to the decentralized divisions created by FedEx as described in the *Exploring Behavior in Action.* Firms that fail to design and maintain effective structures experience problems. FedEx also coordinates activities across its divisions in order to achieve synergies among its various services and geographical markets. Doing this enhances FedEx's performance.

An appropriate culture is also required to implement strategy effectively and achieve strong overall performance. **Organizational culture** involves shared values and norms that influence behavior.[2] It is a powerful force in organizations. For example, Google's organizational culture has been touted as one reason for its phenomenal success. We examine the specific characteristics of Google's culture later in this chapter.

As one of the top companies to work for and one of the most admired companies in the world, FedEx is known to have a special culture as well. FedEx grew rapidly early in its existence by internally expanding its services and especially by reaching new geographical markets. It then began to expand into international markets, partly by acquisition (e.g., its acquisition of Flying Tigers). It also used acquisitions to diversify the services that it offered. An example of this expansion was the acquisition of Kinko's with its 1,200 retail outlets across the United States to support the diversification strategy and divisional structure. Over time, FedEx had to adopt a new structure in order to manage its diversified portfolio of services and geographical markets. The new divisional structure granted significant autonomy to each operating business (division) with corporate coordination across the divisions to achieve synergy in offering customers integrated services. FedEx was careful in its acquisitions to ensure that the acquired firms fit well with its positive customer-oriented culture. Both organizational structure and culture influence the behavior of managers and associates and therefore play a critical role in the success of an organization's strategy and its overall organizational performance.

In this chapter, we explore issues related to structure and culture. We open with a discussion of the fundamental elements of structure, emphasizing how they influence the behavior and attitudes of managers and associates. Next, we discuss the link between strategy and structure as well as the structural implications of environmental characteristics, internal technology, and organizational size. In the second part of the chapter, we focus on culture. Cultural topics include the competing values model of culture, socialization, cultural audits, and subcultures. We close with a discussion of person–organization fit.

Fundamental Elements of Organizational Structure

The structure of an organization can be described in two different but related ways. First, **structural characteristics** refer to the tangible, physical properties that determine the basic shape and appearance of an organization's hierarchy,[3] where **hierarchy** is defined in terms of the reporting relationships depicted in an organization chart. Essentially, an organization's structure is a blueprint of the reporting relationships, distribution of authority, and decision making in the organization.[4] These characteristics influence behavior, but their effects are sometimes subtle. Second, **structuring characteristics** refer to policies and approaches used to directly prescribe the behavior of managers and associates.[5]

Structural Characteristics

Structural characteristics, as mentioned, relate to the basic shape and appearance of an organization's hierarchy. The shape of a hierarchy is determined by its height, spans of control, and type of departmentalization.

Height refers to the number of levels in the organization, from the CEO to the lower-level associates. Tall hierarchies often create communication problems, as information moving up and down the hierarchy can be slowed and distorted as it passes through many different levels.[6] Managers and associates can be unclear on appropriate actions and behaviors as decisions are delayed and faulty information is disseminated, causing lower satisfaction and commitment. Tall hierarchies also are more expensive, as they have more levels of managers.[7]

A manager's **span of control** is to the number of individuals who report directly to her. A broad span of control is possible when a manager can effectively handle many individuals, as is the case when associates have the skills and motivation they need to complete their tasks autonomously.

Broad spans have advantages for an organization. First, they result in shorter hierarchies (see Exhibit 13-1), thereby avoiding communication and expense problems.[8] Second, they promote high-involvement management because managers have difficulty micromanaging people when there are larger numbers of them. Broad spans allow for

structural characteristics
The tangible, physical properties that determine the basic shape and appearance of an organization's hierarchy.

hierarchy
The reporting relationships depicted in an organization chart.

structuring characteristics
The policies and approaches used to directly prescribe the behavior of managers and associates.

height
The number of hierarchical levels in an organization, from the CEO to the lower-level associates.

span of control
The number of individuals a manager directly oversees.

more initiative by associates.[9] In making employment decisions, many individuals take these realities into consideration.

Spans of control can be too broad, however. When a manager has too many direct reports, she cannot engage in important coaching and development activities. When tasks are more complex and the direct reports more interdependent, a manager often requires a relatively narrow span of control to be effective. It has been argued that a CEO's span of control should not exceed six people because of the complexity and interdependency of work done by direct reports at this level.[10]

Many older companies have removed layers of management and increased spans of control in recent years, whereas younger companies, such as AES, avoided unnecessary layers and overly narrow spans from the beginning.[11] Because of their profound effects on behavior and attitudes among associates and managers, spans of control are of concern to many organizations such as PricewaterhouseCoopers (PwC).[12] Through their Saratoga Institute, managers and consultants at PwC track spans of control in various industries and use the resulting insights in various reports and consulting engagements. They reported a few years ago that the median span for all managers in all industries was seven. An earlier *Wall Street Journal* report indicated an average span of nine. Yet, the Saratoga Institute reports that managerial spans of control have been increasing in recent years due to reductions in the number of managers in the recent global economic recession.[13]

Departmentalization describes the approach used in grouping resources within an organization. As highlighted in the opening case, one of the two basic options is the functional form of departmentalization, in which resources related to a particular functional area are grouped together (see Exhibit 13-2). The functional form provides several potential advantages, including deep specialized knowledge in each functional area (because functions are the focus of the firm) and economies of scale within functional areas (resources can be shared by all individuals working within each functional area).[14] This form, however, also has a potential major weakness: managers and associates in each functional department can become isolated from those who work in other departments, which harms coordinated action and causes slow responses to major industry changes that require two or more functional areas to work together.[15] Lateral relation mechanisms, discussed in a later section, can help to overcome this weakness.

If an organization has multiple products or services or operates in multiple geographical areas, it can group its resources into divisions (see Exhibit 13-3). The divisional form offers several benefits, such as better coordination among individuals in functional areas. Functional resources have been divided among the divisions, and associates and managers in the smaller functional departments within each division tend to coordinate with one another relatively easily. With smaller departments, people tend to be closer to one another, and there are fewer barriers (formal or informal) to direct communication. A second, related benefit is rapid response to changes in the industry that call for a cross-functional response. Because associates and managers in the various functional areas coordinate more effectively, response times are often faster. A third benefit is tailoring to the

©Gerard Fritz/Getty Images, Inc.

departmentalization
The grouping of human and other resources into units, typically based on functional areas or markets.

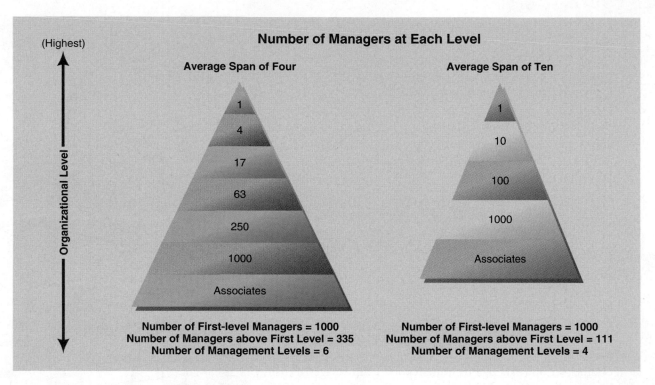

Exhibit 13-1 Average Span of Control: Effects of Height of the Hierarchy

different product/service or geographical markets. This occurs because the people in each division are dedicated to their own markets.[16]

The divisional form is not without its drawbacks, however. Two of the most important are (1) lack of collaboration across the product/service or geographic markets (individuals in one division can become isolated from those in other divisions) and (2) diseconomies of scale within functional areas (individuals in a given functional area but working on different markets cannot share resources as they can in the functional structure).[17] As described in the *Exploring Behavior in Action* feature, FedEx developed a diverse set of businesses offering a portfolio of services. To manage these businesses efficiently and to offer customers the most effective services, FedEx implemented a divisional structure.

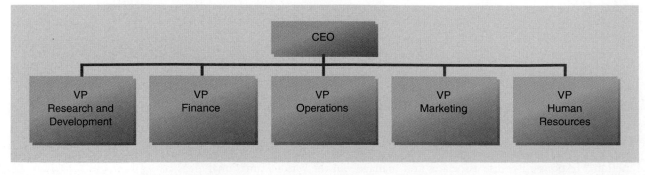

Exhibit 13-2 Simplified Functional Organization

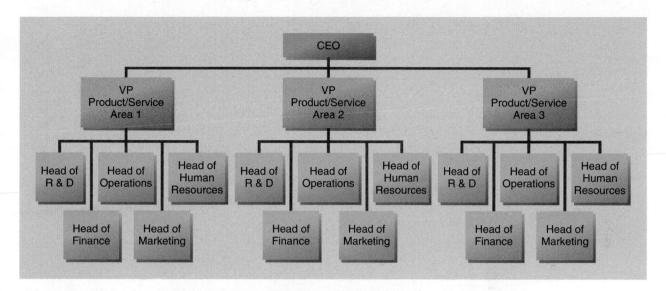

Exhibit 13-3   Simplified Divisional Organization

Hybrid forms also exist, with some functional areas divided across divisions, while others remain intact at the corporate level, often for cost reasons. *Network* organizations are another option, where many or most functional areas are outsourced to other organizations.[18] Home builders are usually network organizations, as they often do not complete their own architectural work and typically outsource to subcontractors much of the actual construction work. Nike is generally considered to be a network organization because it outsources manufacturing and other types of work.

The network approach has been emphasized by a number of firms in recent years, at least to some degree. Its chief benefit lies in allowing a firm to focus on what it does best while outsourcing the rest.[19] Quality control, however, is sometimes an issue, and coordination of internal and external efforts is often a substantial problem. Effective information technology that facilitates coordination across organizational boundaries is crucial.

Structuring Characteristics

Whereas structural characteristics indirectly affect behavior, *structuring* characteristics relate to policies and approaches used to directly prescribe the behavior of managers and associates. This second category of structure includes centralization, standardization, formalization, and specialization.

Centralization refers to the amount of decision-making authority that is held at the top of the organization.[20] In centralized organizations, top-level managers retain most authority, leaving less for mid- and lower-level managers and very little for associates. This is not consistent with high-involvement management, and research suggests that centralized organizations generally perform less well.[21] There are several conditions, however, that call for a significant degree of centralization. We discuss this issue in a later section.

Standardization refers to the existence of rules and standard operating procedures. When standardization is high, managers and associates are expected to follow prearranged approaches to their work. Under these circumstances, their behavior is very predictable. Although standardization is sometimes necessary for efficiency and safety, it reduces

centralization
The degree to which authority for meaningful decisions is retained at the top of an organization.

standardization
The degree to which rules and standard operating procedures govern behavior in an organization.

formalization
The degree to which rules and operating procedures are documented on paper or in company intranets.

specialization
The degree to which associates and managers have jobs with narrow scopes and limited variety.

opportunities for individual initiative, creativity, and self-directed collaboration with others inside and outside the organization. Thus, it can negatively affect motivation and satisfaction for many. **Formalization** is a closely related phenomenon; it is the degree to which rules and procedures are documented. **Specialization** is the degree to which managers and associates have narrow jobs that use focused skills; usually these jobs offer little variety. As discussed in Chapter 6, narrow jobs can negatively affect motivation, satisfaction, and performance for individuals who want to be challenged and to grow in the workplace. Yet, in some self-managed teams with associates having higher levels of specialization, some degree of formalization can produce positive results.[22]

The Modern Organization

Structural and structuring characteristics combine to create very different types of organizations. Some in the field of organizational behavior label the two fundamental types *organic* versus *mechanistic*.[23] Others label these types *learning* versus *nonlearning*.[24] Still others use the labels *boundaryless* versus *traditional* to make the same basic distinction.[25] In all cases, the more flexible empowering type of structure (i.e., organic, learning, or boundaryless) is associated with fewer management levels; broader spans of control; and lesser amounts of centralization, standardization, formalization, and specialization. Departmentalization at the top of the firm can be either functional or divisional. The flexible approach provides freedom for lower-level managers and associates to think for themselves, to communicate with anyone who could be helpful, and to try new ideas.

Although substantial freedom may exist, it is not unlimited, nor should it exist without alternative mechanisms designed to ensure that managers and associates are working for the common good of the organization. First, even in relatively organic firms there is some standardization, and some decisions are made by middle and senior-level managers. At Southwest Airlines, pilots and flight attendants have more freedom than at other airlines, but they still must follow applicable laws and safety rules.[26] Interestingly, research shows that new-venture firms need structure and thus often are more successful if their organization structure is less organic.[27] In addition, new-venture firms often are "boundaryless" in that they must operate in networks to gain access to needed resources. While these alliances may be critical to their survival, it can be difficult for them to break into an existing network of relationships. Working across these organizational boundaries requires that they not be too standardized or formalized. They need flexibility.[28]

Second, alternative mechanisms are used to ensure that individuals are working for the good of the organization. These mechanisms include selection systems, socialization schemes, and leadership processes. Selection systems should be designed to identify individuals who share the values of the organization. Socialization schemes, discussed later in this chapter, should be designed to further shape values and to promote a shared vision of the organization's future. Similarly, strong leadership at the top of the firm instills shared purpose among managers and associates. Shared values and vision act as guides to behavior, and reduce the chances of lower-level managers and associates acting in ways that are counterproductive. Reward systems also are used to promote appropriate behavior. Although lower-level managers and associates may not realize it, powerful forces guide their behavior in organizations characterized by relative freedom of thought and action.

Through the 1960s and into the 1970s, freedom in most organizations was severely limited. Over time, however, the value of unleashing human capital throughout an organization became widely recognized. Today, senior leaders in modern organizations tend to favor organic structures. Although this is positive, given that organic structures are closely aligned with high-involvement management, there are situations in which some aspects of this approach are not appropriate.

Factors Affecting Organizational Structure

Senior managers must choose the structures to use for their firms. Middle and lower-level managers often are involved in these choices and play a key role in the implementation of the choices. Factors that should be considered in designing the structure of the firm include strategy, external environment, internal technology, and organizational size.

The Role of Strategy

An organization's task environment is composed of customers, suppliers, competitors, government regulatory agencies, and perhaps unions. These are external components with which the organization frequently interacts and that have an effect on the organization.[29] Organizations adapt to their environments through formal strategies. In turn, these strategies affect the organization's structure.

Corporate Strategy

Corporate strategy is the overall, predominant strategy of the organization. It determines the direction for the total organization. Senior managers formulating corporate strategies focus on the organization's stockholders and other critical external constituents. Their strategies can be oriented toward growth, diversification, or both.[30]

Almost all types of organizations use **growth** as a measure of success. Awards are given for growth, such as the Growth Strategy Leadership Award given by the consulting firm Frost and Sullivan.[31] Under some circumstances, senior leaders are even willing to trade profits for increasing sales. Growth can be achieved through internal development or by external acquisition. Although the internal growth strategy is an attractive option, growth by external acquisition is popular with many companies.[32] Cisco Systems, a maker of telecommunication equipment, is known for its frequent acquisitions.[33] Acquisition is often a faster method of achieving growth, but it does carry some risk, in part because cultural differences between firms often cause difficulties in the post-acquisition integration of operations.[34] Some firms that have diversified through multiple acquisitions later retrenched and sold off prior acquisitions because of poor performance.[35]

Each of these two growth strategies has implications for structure. For example, firms using an internal-growth strategy are likely to have larger marketing and research and development (R&D) departments. It is also probable that authority for decisions is decentralized to the heads of these departments. In contrast, firms following an external acquisition strategy are likely to have the more well-developed financial and legal functions required to analyze and negotiate acquisitions. These firms may even have a separate specialized planning and acquisitions department. For example, given the number of acquisitions completed by FedEx over time, the company likely has enriched these functions.

Diversification has also been a common and popular corporate strategy. Diversification involves adding products or services different from those currently in the firm. Firms may diversify for several reasons, but the primary one is to reduce overall risk by decreasing dependency on one or a few product markets.[36] Thus, if demand for one of the firm's products falls, the other products may continue to sell.[37] Firms may also diversify the geographic markets they serve by entering new foreign markets.[38] Most companies start out

corporate strategy
The overall approach an organization uses in interacting with its environment. The emphasis is placed on growth and diversification.

growth
Relates to increases in sales as well as associates and managers.

diversification
Related to the number of different product lines or service areas in the organization.

EXHIBIT 13-4   Matches between Diversification Strategy and Structure

Diversification	Structure
Single product	Functional
Dominant product (few products)	Functional
Dominant product (several products)	Divisional
Related product	Divisional
Unrelated product	Divisional
Unrelated product	Holding company

as *single-product firms*, which are firms where more than 95 percent of annual sales come from one product. *Dominant-product firms* obtain 70 to 94 percent of their sales from one product. Most companies following a diversification strategy move on to become *related-product firms*, where less than 70 percent of annual sales come from one product and the various products are related to one another. The most diversified firms are classified as *unrelated-product firms*. In these firms, less than 70 percent of annual sales come from any one product, and the firm's various products are unrelated to the primary core business.[39]

As firms become more diversified, research suggests that they should adopt the divisional form.[40] In other words, they should develop divisions for each of their end-product businesses. Also, as firms become more diversified and divisionalized, authority should be delegated to the divisions.[41]

Matches between diversification and structure are shown in Exhibit 13-4. Single-product and most dominant-product firms should use a functional structure, where the major units of the organization are based on the functions performed (marketing, production, finance) rather than on products. Related-product and most unrelated-product firms should use a divisionalized structure. Large, highly diversified unrelated-product firms may use a *holding company* structure, in which the operating divisions are extremely autonomous.[42] Firms with functional structures are sometimes referred to as *U-form* (unitary) *organizations* and firms with divisionalized structures as *M-form* (multidivisional) *organizations*. Over time, FedEx changed from a single-product firm to a related-product firm. As such, it implemented the divisional structure and decentralized primary authority to make decisions to the heads of each division. Because the businesses are all related, the corporate office coordinated activities across the divisions to offer customers the full portfolio of FedEx's services (as described in the *Exploring Behavior in Action* feature).

Business Strategy

business strategy
How a firm competes for success against other organizations in a particular market.

Firms must formulate business strategies in addition to corporate strategies. A **business strategy** is developed for a particular product/service market and is a plan of action describing how the firm will operate in a particular market.[43]

Business strategies are necessary to ensure effective competitive actions in the different markets in which a firm intends to operate. One popular competitive strategy involves maintaining low internal costs as a basis for low prices offered to customers. Consumers interested in buying the least expensive goods in a particular market are targeted. To effectively implement this strategy, efficiency and control are important inside the firm or division utilizing this approach, and a somewhat more mechanistic structure is useful, if not taken to an extreme.[44] The structure used to implement a low-cost strategy often emphasizes functions, and the decisions are also centralized to maintain economies of scale in operations.[45] A second popular competitive strategy involves product/service differentiation. Consumers are targeted who are willing to pay more for a product/service that is different in some meaningful way (higher quality, superior technology, faster availability). To effectively implement this strategy, flexibility and initiative are useful for staying ahead of the competition, and a more organic structure can be helpful in supporting these needs.[46] To be effective, each strategy requires a unique set of internal resources (e.g., human capital as illustrated in the IDEO example) that can be used to effectively implement the strategy.[47]

In the *Experiencing Organizational Behavior* segment, IDEO illustrates four key points. First, this firm shows how a differentiation strategy can be used in the business of designing products and services. IDEO has distinguished itself through its unique approach to working with clients, and it promotes the innovation and initiative required to maintain its edge by using an organic structure. Second, the firm highlights the fact that companies occasionally supplement their internal human capital as they work to create a competitive advantage in the marketplace. All or most of IDEO's clients have talented associates and managers. Yet, on occasion they still need outside assistance. Third, IDEO promotes design thinking throughout their and their clients' organizations. In so doing, innovation is integrated into the organization's culture and DNA. Finally, the IDEO case again illustrates the value of teams with diverse members, as explained in Chapters 2 and 11. Teams provided invaluable help for IDEO and its client firms to implement a strategy of innovation designed to create or maintain a competitive advantage.

A more advanced form of the divisional structure, strategic business units (SBUs) are sometimes used for more complex firms. Large firms with multiple diversified businesses sometimes group their businesses into SBUs. At General Electric, for example, businesses are grouped into SBUs that include GE Advanced Materials, GE Commercial Finance, GE Consumer Finance, GE Consumer and Industrial Products, GE Energy, GE Healthcare, GE Infrastructure, GE Insurance Solutions, GE Transportation, and NBC Universal.[48] A business strategy is then formulated for each separate SBU, thus allowing the complex organization to be more effectively managed. The key to developing effective strategies for each SBU is the appropriate grouping of businesses. Each group must have commonalities among its businesses for a coherent strategy to be developed. These commonalities may correspond to market relatedness, shared technology, or common distinctive competencies.[49]

The Role of the Environment

Environmental forces account for many differences between organizations, and they have a marked effect on the way organizations conduct business.[50] Because organizations must obtain their inputs from the external environment, their relationships with suppliers and customers are critical. They also must satisfy governmental regulations, adapt to changes in the national and world economies, and react to competitors' actions.

Environment and Basic Structure

Managers must closely monitor their organization's external environment. However, some environments are more difficult to monitor than others because they are more uncertain (complex and changing). A number of researchers have found that the degree of

IDEO and the Differentiation Strategy

The computer mouse, stand-up toothpaste containers, Palm V, i-Zone cameras, patient-friendly waiting rooms, and shopper-friendly intimate apparel displays. Differentiation is not easy, but these products and services helped to differentiate Apple Computer, Procter & Gamble, Palm Inc., Kaiser Permanente, and Warnaco. In cooperation with IDEO, Shimano, a global company headquartered in Japan, developed an innovative new bicycle introduced in 2007. Ford is working closely with IDEO to design its new hybrid electric vehicle that will closely meet the needs of its customers. Ford refers to its project as SmartGauge with Eco-Guide to design a more-connected, fuel-efficient driving experience. IDEO is now the design firm that many organizations use to help design their new products and services. What is the secret of IDEO's success? It may have something to do with the associates and managers at IDEO, a design firm based in Palo Alto, California.

The people of IDEO have a long history of helping firms design award-winning products and services. More recently, IDEO has begun offering consulting and training in innovation and culture change. To make a difference, IDEO's associates and managers rely on a simple concept—empathy. Although this concept may not be conventional, IDEO's record of success is difficult to question. The purpose of this training and IDEO's approach more generally is to inculcate "design thinking" even into the top leaders of the organization.

Empathy for the customer is created in clients through a set of time-tested, systematic research methods. First, IDEO forms a diverse team composed of client and IDEO members. Team members from IDEO may represent the disciplines of cognitive psychology, environmental psychology, anthropology, industrial design, interaction design, mechanical engineering, and business strategy. Team members from the client firm are key decision makers. With the team in place, observations in the real world are orchestrated. Team members observe how people use relevant products and services. For a project focused on intimate apparel, team members followed women as they shopped for lingerie, encouraging the shoppers to verbalize everything they were thinking. Team members may even act as customers themselves. For a health-care project, team members received care at various hospitals and documented their experiences by video and other media.

Second, team members engage in brainstorming. After some preliminary work, the designers, engineers, social scientists, and individuals from the client company engage in intense interactions to develop a rich understanding of an existing product/service design or of the needs in a novel product category. Unlike some group sessions, IDEO's brainstorming sessions have been compared to managed chaos.

Third, team members engage in rapid prototyping. This is one of the characteristics that have made IDEO famous. IDEO associates and managers believe in the power of trying many different ideas rather than just talking about them. Rudimentary versions of products and services are quickly constructed and examined.

Finally, team members implement the fruits of their labor. Detailed design and engineering work is completed, and the team works closely with clients to ensure a successful launch. In many other design firms, team members simply turn over their work with little follow-up.

The critical component in this according to the president and one of the founders, Tim Brown, is design thinking. He suggests that all of these actions will not work effectively without this component. Innovation must be a part of the organization's DNA, Brown suggests. This thinking requires work across functions and combines creative confidence with analytic ability. This type of thinking is now used by Steelcase and Procter & Gamble, both of which have used it to become highly innovative companies.

IDEO has become so popular that many firms send their managers to the firm to observe the organic structure and to be trained in innovative thinking and action. These managers use what they have learned to enhance the operations and structures of their own firms. IDEO's approach continues to be highly successful. In 2009, it tied with Samsung for the most IDEA awards (eight) given for the top designs of the year.

Sources: IDEO. 2009. "Hybrid Electric Vehicle Dashboard Interaction for Ford Motor Company," at http://www. ideo.com, Dec. 29; V. Wong. 2009. "How to Nurture Future Leaders," *BusinessWeek*, at http://www.businessweek. com, Sept. 30; T. Brown. 2009. "Change by Design," *BusinessWeek*, at http://www.businessweek.com, Sept. 24; C. Kuang. 2009. "Big Awards for the Year's Best industrial Designs," *FastCompany*, at http://www.fastcompany. com, July 30; 2007. "Coasting Bicycle Design Strategy for Shimano," at http://www.ideo.com/ideo.asp, Apr. 16; B. Moggridge. 2006. *Designing Interactions*, Boston: MIT Press; IDEO. 2004. "About Us: Methods," at http://www. ideo.com/about/index.asp?x=3&y=3.

environmental uncertainty experienced by managers is related to the type of structure an organization utilizes. And, this is especially important today because of the high uncertainty of environments in which many organizations must operate.[51] Classic research indicated that effective organizations exhibit a match between environmental characteristics and organizational structures.[52] Although the evidence is not entirely consistent, a number of other researchers have found similar results, using mostly small organizations or units of larger ones.[53]

The classic study reported the following important findings:

- Effective organizations experiencing high environmental uncertainty tend to be more organic because lower-level managers and associates must be able to think for themselves. They must be able to respond to events quickly.
- Effective organizations experiencing low environmental uncertainty tend to be less organic. Mid and senior-level managers in conjunction with operations specialists can create efficient and effective rules and operating procedures. They can gain sufficient insight to understand and anticipate most situations that will arise and carefully create procedures to handle those situations.

It is important to understand the reasons for differences in functional departments within an organization. Because separate departments focus on different areas of the external environment, they often exhibit different types of structure. R&D, for example, is focused on technological advances and the changing pool of knowledge in the world. The relatively high level of uncertainty involved often requires a more organic structure with longer time horizons for decision making and planning and a greater emphasis on interpersonal relationships to promote important discussions and information sharing. In contrast, the accounting function is focused on more slowly evolving developments in accounting standards. The relatively low level of uncertainty generally supports use of a less organic structure, with shorter time horizons and lower emphasis on interpersonal relationships. In effective organizations, then, differences in the level of uncertainty in subenvironments create differences in functional departments.

Recent work suggests that environmental uncertainty also affects the way resources should be managed in organizations. For example, organizations operating in uncertain environments need to constantly enrich their current capabilities and even create new ones. Thus, they continuously train their managers and associates to upgrade their skills and are on the lookout for new associates with "cutting-edge" knowledge that can add to the organization's stock of knowledge. They also need to search for opportunities in the environment and to engage in entrepreneurial behavior to maximize the use of their capabilities to provide products and services that create value for their customers.[54] IDEO, as explained in the *Experiencing Organizational Behavior* feature, is helping firms to be more entrepreneurial and create products that are valued by their customers. All of the research then suggests that managers must continuously scan their firm's external environment to identify factors that may affect how the firm should act. Their scanning behavior is even more important in dynamic environments.[55]

Environment and Integration

Functional departments within a single-product firm or a division of a larger firm must be integrated. They must share information and understand one another in order to coordinate their work.[56] Thus, organizations must be structured to provide the necessary

environmental uncertainty
The degree to which an environment is complex and changing; uncertain environments are difficult to monitor and understand.

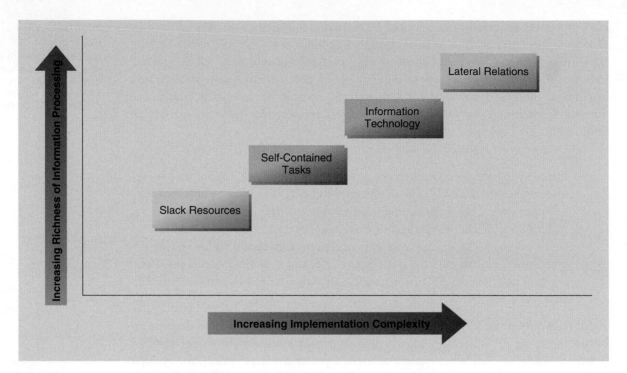

Exhibit 13-5 Integration in Organizations

information, or perhaps to reduce the need for it. Structural arrangements that address information needs are particularly important when the environment is uncertain. Useful arrangements include: (1) creation of slack resources, (2) creation of self-contained tasks, (3) investment in information technology, and (4) creation of traditional lateral relations.[57] Exhibit 13-5 shows the relationship of these elements of organizational structure and information processing needs.

The creation of **slack resources** reduces the need for interdepartmental information processing. Departments can operate more independently. Examples of slack resources include having extra time to complete tasks that other departments need as inputs and maintaining large inventories of raw materials provided by others. Although these extra resources reduce information exchange needs, they are costly.

The creation of **self-contained tasks** reduces the need for interdepartmental processing of information. This approach provides departments with more of the resources they need to do the job. For example, a department's tasks may require the help of a design engineer and a process engineer on a part-time basis. Instead of having a group of design engineers to which various departments would come when they need help, a design engineer is specifically assigned to each department, with nonengineering work used to fill any unused time. This method reduces the need for coordination between groups (e.g., the engineering group and other groups needing engineering services) and thereby reduces information-processing requirements.

Unlike the two elements of structure discussed above, **information technology** facilitates the processing of information rather than reducing the need to process it. This technology can help to transfer information up and down the hierarchy as well as horizontally from department to department. E-mail, web-based discussion boards, chat rooms, and Twitter

slack resources
An integration technique whereby a department keeps more resources on hand than absolutely required in order to reduce the need for tight communication and coordination with other departments.

self-contained tasks
An integration technique whereby a department is given resources from other functional areas in order to reduce the need to coordinate with those areas.

information technology
An overall set of tools, based on microelectronic technology, designed to provide data, documents, and commentary as well as analysis support to individuals in an organization.

are examples of simple tools that facilitate communication and coordination. An information repository is a more complex tool for integration. Such a repository requires individuals in various departments to deposit documents, data, and commentary in an open-access central database. An enterprise resource planning (ERP) system is an even more complex tool. ERP systems provide a common set of planning and analysis capabilities across departments, as well as a platform for electronically sharing evolving plans and analyses. This type of system has provided important benefits in the integration of departments,[58] particularly when the system has been explicitly designed to support the organization's strategy. An ERP system has even been used to coordinate the cross-functional curriculum of a business school.[59]

In addition to facilitating integration across existing departments in an organization, information technology has helped to flatten organizations and has promoted project-based structures.[60] Shorter hierarchies are consistent with high-involvement management because they push decision authority to the lowest levels of the organization and increase the speed and quality of decisions as a result. Such hierarchies would not be possible, however, without information technology to ensure that associates and lower-level managers have the information they need to make sound decisions. Project-based structures utilize individuals from various departments to work on complex projects requiring intense and integrated efforts. In some cases, these individuals are temporarily assigned to a project on a full-time basis. In other instances, individuals participate part-time as project members and part-time as members of their functional departments. In both cases, information technology ensures that project participants working on different aspects of the overall project understand the goals and activities of those working in other areas. Without sophisticated information technology, individuals could not integrate the various aspects of the project as effectively or as rapidly, resulting in some complex projects not being undertaken and others being handled more slowly through the traditional hierarchy.

Relations among departments are based on the need for coordinating their various tasks. Because **lateral relations** increase information flow at lower levels, decisions requiring interdepartmental coordination need not be referred up the hierarchy. Lateral relations are traditional elements of structure used to help organizations process more information. These relations may be facilitated by information technology but often are based on face-to-face communication. A number of alternative lateral processes can be used. Listed in order of least complex to most complex, they are as follows:

lateral relations
Elements of structure designed to draw individuals together for interchanges related to work issues and problems.

- *Direct contact* involves two individuals who share a problem and work directly with one another to solve it.
- *Liaison roles* are temporary coordination positions established to link two departments that need to have a large amount of contact.
- *Task forces* are temporary groups composed of members from several departments who solve problems affecting those departments.
- *Teams* are *permanent* problem-solving groups for continuous interdepartmental problems.
- *Integrating roles* are permanent positions designed to help with the coordination of various tasks.
- *Managerial linking roles* are integrative positions with more influence and decision-making authority.
- *Matrix designs* establish dual authority between functional managers (marketing manager, engineering manager) and project or product managers (leisure furniture manager, office furniture manager).

The Role of Technology

Within an organization, *technology* refers to the knowledge and processes required to accomplish tasks. It corresponds to the techniques used in transforming inputs into outputs. The relationship of technology and structure has been described in several ways, as discussed below.

Technology and Structure: A Manufacturing Framework

Early work on the relationship between technology and organization structure focused on manufacturing technology: small-batch production, mass production, and continuous-process production.[61]

This research found that technological complexity influenced structure and that effective organizations exhibited matches between technology and structure.[62]

Today, new types of technology are being used in smaller and larger manufacturing operations alike. Technology can equalize the competition between smaller and larger organizations. The use of advanced manufacturing technology (AMT), computer-aided design (CAD), and computer-aided manufacturing (CAM) helps firms of all sizes to customize their strategies by manufacturing products of high variety at lower costs and to commercialize new products in a shorter amount of time.[63] These technologies have been integrated to create forms of "mass customization." **Mass customization** is a process that integrates sophisticated information technology and management methods in a flexible manufacturing system with the ability to customize products in a short time.[64] Organizations using mass customization need a more flexible and organic structure.[65]

mass customization
A manufacturing technology that involves integrating sophisticated information technology and management methods to produce a flexible manufacturing system with the ability to customize products for many customers in a short time.

Technology and Structure: A Broader Framework

The link between technology and structure using a broader view of technology is useful in both manufacturing and service organizations. In this view, technology is defined as the number of different problem types that are encountered over time (*task variability*) and the degree to which problems can be solved using known steps and procedures (*task analyzability*).[66] Based on these two dimensions, he delineated four types of technology:

1. *Routine:* There is little variation in the fundamental nature of problems encountered over time, but any new problems can be solved using readily available methods.

2. *Craft:* There is little variation in the fundamental nature of problems encountered over time, but any new problems often require a novel search for unique solutions.

3. *Engineering:* There is significant variation in the fundamental nature of problems encountered over time, and new problems can be solved using readily available methods.

4. *Nonroutine:* There is significant variation in the fundamental nature of problems encountered over time, and new problems often require new methods to find unique solutions.

Exhibit 13-6 provides examples of organizations with these types of technologies. To be most effective, firms should match their structure to the technology used. Nonroutine organizations should adopt an organic structure; craft and engineering organizations should adopt a moderately organic structure; and routine organizations should adopt the least organic structure.[67] Essentially, as routineness increases, organic structures become somewhat less useful.

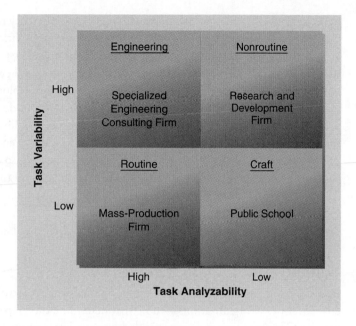

Exhibit 13-6 Organizations and Technology

These technology concepts can be applied to an organization as a whole or to units within the organization. For example, the technology of W. L. Gore, the maker of Gore-Tex fabric, can be described as a mixture of routine and craft technology at the firm level, but its R&D area can be described as nonroutine. Any unit can be assessed with respect to task variability and task analyzability and placed into one of the four technology categories. A number of studies have shown that technology influences structure at the unit level and that effective units exhibit a significant match between technology and structure.[68]

The Role of Organizational Size

It is not surprising that size has implications for organizational structure.[69] As an organization grows, it generally becomes taller; otherwise, the average span of control for managers becomes too large. As organizations increase in size, formalization also tends to increase to help maintain order. However, centralization tends to decrease, as senior managers cannot comprehend all of the organization's work and make all decisions.

The most important measure of size is the number of associates and managers. Research shows that managerial decisions regarding structure are based on the factors that are most salient to managers. Because people are highly important to most managers, managerial decisions on structure are often influenced by the number of people for whom the managers have responsibility.[70]

A common outcome of larger organizations and the heightened formalization and standardization that accompanies growing size is inertia.[71] Large formal organizations often have more standardized policies and routines for managers and associates to follow. These attributes often produce a resistance to change and thus lower innovation. Yet, innovation is a critical component of competitiveness for most organizations in our current global economic environment. The potential for inertia in large organizations and the need for innovation have led to the development of ambidextrous structures and practices.

Ambidextrous organizations balance the formalization and standardization that help to achieve efficiency and the flexibility required to explore new ideas and opportunities

ambidextrous organization
An organization structure that balances formalization and standardization to help to achieve efficiency and flexibility.

necessary to be innovative.[72] The intent is to achieve efficiency to exploit the firm's current capabilities and simultaneously explore to learn new capabilities, discover new technologies, and develop new products and services.[73] To do so first requires top management to have a shared vision of an ambidextrous organization and to develop an incentive system to reward the achievement of both exploitation and exploration. This often requires transformational leadership (as discussed in Chapter 8) and design thinking, such as that promoted by IDEO.[74] Another dimension involved in building an ambidextrous organization is the structure. Often, firms trying to achieve the needed balance maintain some parts of the organization with formalized routines but then also develop semi-autonomous units that have significant freedom to explore new ideas and unique approaches to problems.[75] These approaches allow the organization to unbundle operations and processes to manage the costs of operations but also pursue the development of technological innovations. This type of organization, structure, and leadership is becoming more common.[76]

Summary Comments on Structure

In summary, corporate strategy and organizational size have strong effects on the structural characteristics of organizations—those that determine the shape and appearance of the hierarchy. Corporate strategy is a particularly strong determinant of departmentalization, and size is an especially strong determinant of height and spans of control. Business strategy, environmental uncertainty, and technological nonroutineness have strong effects on unit structuring within organizations, as well as the overall structure of the organization.

An important study has shown how business strategy, environmental uncertainty, technological nonroutineness, and structure work together to influence performance in organizational units as well as in small organizations.[77] In this study, strong performance was associated with consistency among these factors:

- Uncertain environments led to strategies based on differentiation and innovation, which in turn led to nonroutine work, all of which were matched by organic structure.
- More certain environments led to strategies based on low costs and efficiency, which in turn led to routine work, all of which were matched by a less organic structure.

Other studies have provided similar results,[78] suggesting that managers in effective firms create consistency across strategy, environment, technology, and structure.

Organizational Culture

Culture is closely related to most other concepts in the field of organizational behavior, including structure, leadership, communication, groups, motivation, and decision making.[79] Culture is affected by and can also affect these other areas of organizational functioning and it is related to social, historic, and economic issues as well.[80] Thus, it is an important and encompassing concept.

Google's organizational culture is described in the *Experiencing Organizational Behavior* feature. Google's culture is highly informal, with a decentralized structure designed to enhance associates' creativity. Google must be doing something right because it is a highly successful company. Its culture and structure, along with its interrelated management model, have attracted significant human capital, which is one of the reasons for its success. Google's approach is highly similar to a high-involvement organization.

Google Culture Attracts High-Quality Associates

*L*arry Page and Sergy Brin graduated from Stanford University in 1995 with computer science degrees. They wanted to build a search engine that would retrieve selective information from the vast amount of data available on the Internet. In 1997, they named their search engine "Backrub," and in 1998 they renamed it "Google" (*Google* is a play on googol, the mathematical term for a + followed by 100 zeros—a reference to organizing the seemingly infinite Web). By 2003, it was the most preferred search engine in the world because of its precision and speed in delivering the desired data in searches. But their success can also be attributed to Google's organizational culture.

In organizing the firm, Page and Brin avoided unnecessary managerial hierarchies, creating a decentralized structure, and giving their engineers significant autonomy to encourage creative thinking. Google has a small management hierarchy and most engineers work in teams of three, with project leadership rotating among them. These teams had complete autonomy and freedom to create, reporting directly to the vice president. Open communication is encouraged and employees are free to approach top management as desired. They are allowed to communicate with anyone in any department. Employees were also asked to eat in the cafeteria so they could meet others in the company and create opportunities for them to share and discuss technical ideas or issues. In addition,

©Kate Lacey/The New York Times/Redux Pictures

every Friday afternoon all employees are provided information about new products and the company's financial performance. Google's emphasis on innovation and commitment to cost containment requires each employee to be a contributor. The decentralized model of management and open lines of communication are essential parts of Google's organizational culture. And the organizational structure and culture have helped the firm attract and retain the most talented individuals in the field. Although still a young firm, Google's work culture has become legendary in Silicon Valley.

Larry and Sergy wanted to create a fun place to work and use incentives that could attract top talent. Google headquarters, known as the *Googleplex*, was decorated with lava lamps, giant plastic balls, and bright colors. Employees are also allowed to bring their pets to work and are provided free snacks, lunch, and dinner, prepared by an award-winning former chef to the Grateful Dead. The founders said that the free, healthy meals came about after calculating the time saved from driving off-site and reduced health-care costs. They have even provided a Webcam that monitors the cafeteria lunch line, so employees can avoid a long wait. Employees are also provided recreational activities, which include workout gyms, assorted video games, pool tables, ping-pong tables, and roller-skater hockey. Additional benefits include flexible work hours, company-paid, midweek ski trips to Squaw Valley, and maternity/paternity leave with 75 percent pay. A benefit addition in 2008 was free afternoon tea service. The company reportedly has the best package of benefits available, even after some minor benefit cuts in 2009 due to the major economic recession.

A few people have criticized Google's organizational culture and management model. Some believe that Google has outgrown the informal culture and that it will not be able to sustain the growth and still maintain the informal lines of communication. Critics argue that even though engineers are free to pursue individual projects, the informality makes it difficult to coordinate and plan activities. Alternatively, as Google has grown much larger (from 1,000 to almost 15,000 managers and associates), sustaining its culture has been more challenging. A few associates have complained that they now feel a distance between them and management. They express concerns that the firm has become more bureaucratic. And, Google has begun losing some of its top talent, especially those who have increased their wealth with Google stock ownership and have departed to establish their own business. Yet, Google continues to be highly innovative. It was ranked as the second most innovative company in *BusinessWeek*'s 2009 rankings of the top 25 most innovative companies. In addition, Google continues to be ranked at the top of *Fortune*'s 100 best companies to work for.

But Google continues to engage its associates, involving them in addressing major issues, maintaining a flat organization, and striving to keep the entrepreneurial spirit alive. Thus, although it is losing some of the talent recruited in past years, it continues to attract some of the top talent in the industry. For example, in 2008, it received almost 1 million applications for the 3,000 positions it was trying to fill.

Google's culture and its talented associates have allowed it to continue to enhance its Internet search capabilities, maintaining its competitive advantage over formidable rivals such as Microsoft and Yahoo!. The culture and structure encourages and facilitates the development of innovative new services by associates, helping Google to remain one of the most successful companies in the world.

Sources: Staff of the Corporate Executive Board. 2009. "Involve Your Employees," Says Google, CEB, *Business Week*, Dec. 11, at http://www.businessweek.com; Andrzej Zwaniechi. 2009. "Google Aims to Retain Entrepreneurial Spirit as It Grows," America.gov, Oct. 28, at http://www.america.gov; "Google Hits Reset on Company Culture," Glassdoor, Oct. 8, 2009, at http:// www.glassdoor.com; Elizabeth Montailbano. 2009. "At 10-year mark, Google's glossy façade shows cracks," Macworld, Sept. 8, at http://www.macworld.com; "The 25 Most Innovative Companies," *Business-Week*, Apr. 20, 2009, at http://www.businessweek.com; Adam Lashinsky. 2008. "Can Google three-peat?" *Money*, Jan. 31, at http://www.cnnmoney.com; B-School News. 2006. "They Love it Here, and Here, and Here," *Business-Week*, June 4, at http://www.businessweek.com; Jade Chang. 2006. "Behind the Glass Curtain," *BusinessWeek*, July 18, at http://www.businessweek.com.

Organizational cultures are based on shared values, as described earlier.[81] As noted, culture begins with shared values, which then produce norms that govern behavior. Behavior produces outcomes that are reinforced or punished, thereby bolstering the culture. Thus, any culture, positive or negative, becomes self-reinforcing and difficult to change. The process of culture development and reinforcement is shown in Exhibit 13-7.

The strength of an organization's culture is based to some degree on the homogeneity of associates and managers and the length and intensity of shared experiences in the organization.[82] The longer a culture is perpetuated, the stronger it becomes because of its self-reinforcing nature. An organization's culture not only reinforces critical values but also important behaviors. For example, Google's culture could be described as a learning culture in which new knowledge is created, acquired externally, diffused internally,[83] and applied to create innovative services for Google's markets and customers. Organizational culture also affects an organization's ability to resolve problems and to create change. For example, in an open culture in which managers and associates are engaged (i.e., a high-involvement organization), more alternatives are likely to be generated and considered to resolve problems. Also, the open communication can help to resolve conflicts if they exist.[84] In addition, the openness of communications between managers and associates (exemplified by Google) and transparency because of the high involvement makes all participants more open to change. And, by participating in creating the change, managers and associates are more likely to be committed to it.[85]

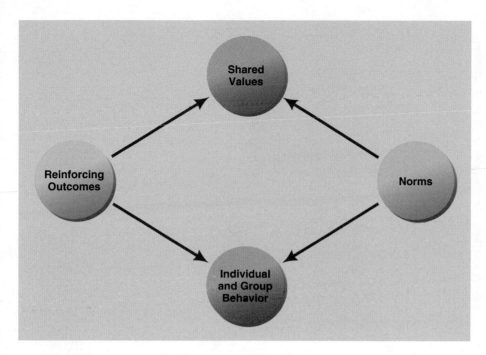

Exhibit 13-7   Process of Developing Organizational Culture

Competing Values Model of Culture

One of the most popular models of culture in business firms is the competing values model, in which two value dimensions are central.[86] The first dimension relates to the value placed on *flexibility and discretion* versus *stability and control*. In some organizations, managers and associates believe in the power and usefulness of flexibility and discretion, while in other organizations individuals believe in the power of a stable work situation where control is strongly maintained. Ambidextrous organizations, described earlier, achieve a balance in these values through the culture and structure. The second dimension relates to the value placed on an *internal focus* coupled with *integration* versus an *external focus* coupled with *differentiation* in the marketplace. In some organizations, associates and managers prefer to focus internally; in other organizations, individuals have an external orientation.

Four types of culture result from different combinations of these dimensions (see Exhibit 13-8):

1. *Clan*—strong value placed on flexibility and discretion with a focus inside the organization. Leaders tend to be mentors and coaches. Effectiveness is evaluated in terms of the cohesion and morale of individuals inside the firm and tacit knowledge held. Overall, the organization tends to be a friendly place to work, with a great deal of commitment and loyalty.

2. *Hierarchy*—strong value placed on control and stability with a focus inside the organization. Leaders tend to be monitors and organizers. Effectiveness is measured in terms of efficiency and orderly coordination. The organization tends to be a formal and standardized place to work, with emphasis on explicit knowledge.[87]

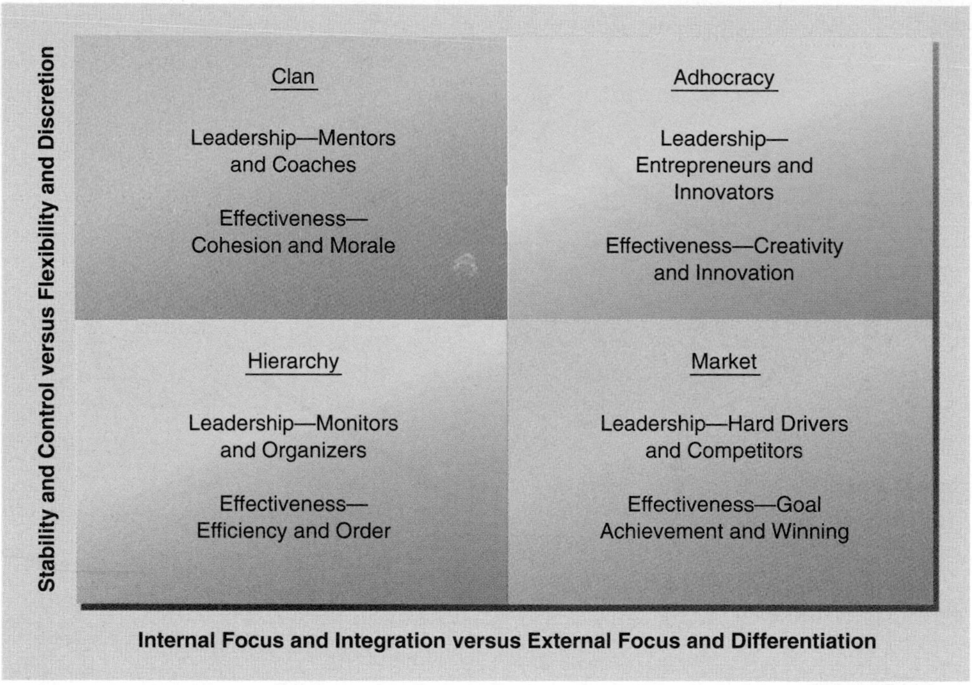

Exhibit 13-8 Competing Values Model of Organizational Culture

3. *Market*—strong value placed on control and stability with a focus outside the organization. Leaders tend be driven and competitive. Effectiveness is measured in terms of goal achievement and beating the competition in the marketplace. The organization can be a difficult place to work because there is a constant focus on results and doing better than colleagues.

4. *Adhocracy*—strong value placed on flexibility and discretion with a focus outside the organization. Leaders tend to be entrepreneurial and innovative, perhaps even visionary. Effectiveness is evaluated in terms of creativity and leading-edge innovation in the marketplace. The organization tends to be a vibrant place to work, with significant risk taking.

Organizations usually possess elements of all four cultural types. In fact, organizations need all four because morale, innovation, success relative to competitors in the marketplace, and efficiency are all important for long-term performance and survival.[88] In most cases, however, an organization emphasizes one cultural type over another. Each culture can be useful as a point of emphasis, depending on circumstances. Hierarchy, for example, might be emphasized in an organization pursuing a low-cost business strategy in all of its product lines. In such an organization, however, managers must be careful not to allow the emphasis on hierarchy to become too great. If hierarchy is overemphasized, it will be difficult to incorporate the decision- and team-related aspects of high-involvement management.[89] Furthermore, research suggests that the hierarchy culture can reduce commitment and satisfaction. Market culture could be useful in industries that are highly competitive. Clan culture is often more useful for organizations operating in regulated industries or in small new-venture firms where working with good colleagues and positive working relationships are emphasized more than financial compensation. Google has used such a culture since its beginning. However, even as a large, more established organization, Google continues to use this culture successfully. Adhocracy might be emphasized in an organization pursuing the differentiation strategy in its product lines.

Clearly, organizational cultures affect managers' and associates' behaviors and thus organizational performance. The core values of an organization serve to attract new associates who share similar values or at least are comfortable with the organization's values.[90] For example, research has shown that organizational culture affects the extent to which associates are willing to accept changes in an organization. Specifically, associates who perceive an organizational culture that positively values human relations are more willing to participate in and accept changes made by the organization.[91] In addition, other studies have shown that when the organizational culture promotes respect for people, associates are more likely to view relationships with leaders more positively, to trust others, and to perceive that the organization treats associates fairly.[92] Therefore, such cultures are likely to support an organization's competitive advantage because of a motivated workforce and low turnover among associates.[93]

Cultural Socialization

Newcomers are taught an organization's culture through **socialization**—the imparting of the organization's values. Socialization can take several forms. Based on groundbreaking work by noted culture researchers John Van Maanen and Ed Schein, researchers have focused on three sets of issues: context, content, and social dynamics.[94]

Context refers to whether newcomers are exposed to key values through a collective or an individual process, and whether they experience a formal or an informal approach. In a collective process, all newcomers experience the same socialization events (videos, senior leadership greetings, exercises, receptions, stories, and so on). In an individual process, the experiences are unique. With a formal approach, newcomers learn about the organization away from the jobs they will be taking (off-the-job learning and training), whereas an informal approach puts them in their jobs immediately (on-the-job learning and training). To maximize absorption of an organization's values, a collective, formal approach may be best. This approach ensures that newcomers are exposed to a standard set of tactics in a focused manner away from the pressures of the new job. Bain and Company, a management consulting firm, illustrates this approach. It uses a formal standard induction program to provide specific training and to build cohesiveness and a sense of identity with the firm. This is supported by excellent materials on the Bain website that explain the company's culture and provide consultants' journals with valuable information on the jobs the new recruits will likely hold. In the program and on the website, information is provided to reinforce the idea that senior colleagues serve as mentors and coaches.[95]

Content refers to whether newcomers are provided information on the probable sequence of development activities and job rotations for the first year or two in the organization, and whether they are given specific information on the likely duration of each activity.

socialization
A process through which an organization imparts its values to newcomers.

©Goodshoot/Corbis

With detailed information on upcoming development activities, newcomers experience less uncertainty. They have a better sense of where they are going in the organization. When information provided to newcomers conveys a variable and random situation (no set sequence of development activities and no estimates of duration times), newcomers are less able to discern a clear path to success and advancement. This latter situation can create satisfaction and commitment issues.

Social dynamics refer to whether newcomers experience serial or disjunctive processes and whether they are exposed to an investiture or a divestiture approach. Newcomers experiencing a serial approach have experienced organizational members as role models. The disjunctive process does not formally establish contact with experienced associates and managers, forcing newcomers to make sense of the situation on their own. With the investiture approach, positive social support is provided from the beginning rather than negative information through a hazing process. The combination of serial and investiture techniques yields better socialization experiences.

In a high-involvement organization, socialization is usually an easier task, as the process begins before employment, during the selection process. Most applicants are rigorously screened with the purpose of discouraging those who may not fit the culture. For example, at Southwest Airlines, the socialization process begins well before the applicant is hired. Applicants are exhaustively screened by a number of interviewers. The interview team does not oversell Southwest but describes both the advantages and disadvantages of working for the firm. The purpose is to make sure that the applicant's values and objectives mesh with those of the airline.[96] The process has been highly effective, as Southwest's culture is often given credit for the company's success. In 2009, Southwest Airlines was ranked number 7 in *Fortune* magazine's list of the most admired corporations in the United States.[97]

Integrating new associates into the organization's culture is important, especially for maintaining the culture. Research has shown that organizations with highly integrative cultures, whether they are focused on associate development and harmony or customer orientation and innovation often perform better than organizations that pay less attention to their cultures.[98]

Cultural Audits

cultural audit
A tool for assessing and understanding the culture of an organization.

Managers must understand and monitor their organization's current culture to develop and effectively manage it.[99] Thus, a **cultural audit** should be conducted periodically. This type of audit is an analysis designed to uncover shared values and beliefs in an organization. It should identify the strengths and weaknesses of the current culture with respect to the support it provides for the achievement of the organization's goals.[100]

The following five steps may be used in conducting a cultural audit:[101]

1. Analyze the process and content of the socialization of new associates and managers (interview those directly involved in socialization).

2. Analyze responses to critical incidents in the organization's history (construct an organizational biography from documents and interviews of past and present associates and managers).

3. Analyze the values and beliefs of culture creators (founders) and carriers (current leaders) (observe and/or interview the founders and current leaders).

4. Explore anomalies or puzzling features discovered in other analyses (initiate joint problem-solving sessions with current leaders in the organization).

5. Examine the linkage of the current organizational culture to its goals.

A cultural audit is a complex and sometimes lengthy process that should be conducted only after careful planning and preparation. The results of an audit might indicate a culture that is not well developed or might disclose the presence of subcultures. An underdeveloped culture poses less of a problem than one that is dysfunctional, fully developed, and self-reinforcing, because the less-developed culture can be more easily influenced and its path altered if necessary.

Subcultures

It is possible for **subcultures** to develop in an organization, particularly when no dominant organizational culture exists or when the organization is diverse and geographically dispersed.[102] Subcultures are based on values shared by a group rather than by an organization as a whole. Some of the values of the subculture are similar to and others are dissimilar from the organization's values and the values of other groups. The existence of subcultures complicates the development and management of an organizational culture.

In large, diverse organizations, some researchers advocate viewing organizational culture as a system of integrated subcultures rather than a unified set of values.[103] In such cases, senior managers need to understand each subculture, ensure that it is appropriate for its market segment, and decide whether it fits with critical organizational values. Thus, a manager's purpose is to encourage the integration of critical organizational values in each subculture.

It is possible for a subculture to include values that are counter to those of the overall organization. Such a counterculture may be difficult to manage. Although a counterculture often creates problems, it can also produce positive outcomes. For example, a counterculture can induce a revolution, forcing change in a staid, outmoded culture. It also may encourage the development of new and creative ideas not allowed by existing norms of the organizational culture.[104]

It is also possible that some subcultures are related to national culture. This may be even more likely in large countries where there are several regional cultures that differ in some values (e.g., China, United States). Research has shown that attributes of national culture (e.g., extent of collectivism) interact with managerial actions such as rewards provided to affect how associates react to the organization (e.g., their commitment to the organization).[105] However, some research has found that national culture has only a small influence on organizational culture.[106]

The *Managerial Advice* segment provides an example of a misfit between a key manager and the company's culture. Bob Nardelli was hired as CEO of Home Depot to make some changes. He did so, but went further than desired by the board. His changes strongly revised the culture of the firm, making it control-oriented, thereby losing the entrepreneurial spirit among store managers and associates. While Home Depot likely needed better control systems, Nardelli's changes went too far. Although Home Depot has made several positive changes since Nardelli's departure, the effects of his tenure as CEO have been long lasting. This example shows the importance of a person–organization fit, discussed next.

subcultures
In the organizational context, groups that share values that differ from the main values of the organization.

Finding a Fit at Home Depot

Research indicates that similarity in values and goals attracts individuals to specific organizations. When an individual's management style and values are not congruent with the organization's culture, problems can develop. This is the reason why problems developed after Home Depot hired Bob Nardelli as CEO in 2000. Home Depot wanted to remain adaptive and make some necessary changes to increase stock prices by bringing in a key individual that the board of directors felt could accomplish these goals. In addition, the board believed that Nardelli's ideas might prompt reflection and help Home Depot make needed changes to impress investors and "pump up" its stock price.

In the early years, Home Depot founders Bernie Marcus and Arthur Blank took it personally if a customer left without buying something. Home Depot's culture was similar to a clan, as the founders placed strong value on flexibility, leaders tended to be mentors and coaches, and they worked to achieve group cohesion and high morale among the associates. The organization was known to be a friendly place to work, and they established a decentralized, entrepreneurial business model. Home Depot

©Scott Olson/Getty Images

was famous for its freewheeling, entrepreneurial spirit, with individual stores operated in a highly autonomous manner. All aspects of the store operations were the responsibility of local management. Using that model, it became the fastest-growing retailer in U.S. history, expanding from a three-store startup in 1979 to a $45 billion chain in 2000. The substantial growth caused the company to struggle with its internal systems and controls, and change was necessary in order to accommodate and manage additional growth.

However, Nardelli's changes were too significant and conflicted with the Home Depot culture. After five years with Nardelli as CEO, the company felt more like a military organization. He embarked on an aggressive plan to centralize control, and to support this change Home Depot invested more than $1 billion in new technology. To help generate the desired data, the company purchased self-checkout aisles and inventory management systems. Nardelli felt it was important to measure everything that occurred in the company and hold executives accountable for meeting "their numbers." He implemented a management model that imported ideas, people, and platitudes from the military, which was a key part of the move to reshape Home Depot into a more centralized organization. The culture he was trying to create was similar to a hierarchy culture, emphasizing control, and stability with leaders monitoring and organizing in an efficient manner. In making these changes, Nardelli failed to keep the entrepreneurial spirit alive in the company.

Some former executives said that Nardelli had created a "culture of fear" and a demoralized staff, which in turn caused customer service to wane. While some praised Nardelli for bringing greater discipline and structure, others blamed him for eroding the entrepreneurial culture at Home Depot. Many on Wall Street felt that Nardelli never understood the value of the previous organizational culture. Associates did not embrace the new culture and some feel this was the reason Home Depot struggled with customer satisfaction and performance in the stock market. Thus, the fit between an individual and the organization was unsuccessful and had debilitating effects on the company's performance.

In early 2007, it was announced that Nardelli departed the company in a disagreement with the board of directors. Home Depot has not fully recovered since, although it has made a number of positive changes. Because of its lost sales to rivals and poor stock market performance, it also sold its entire supply business in 2007. It also closed 15 underperforming stores in 2008 and closed 34 EXPO design stores in 2009. Along with these actions, 7,000 people were laid off, including 10 percent of the corporate officers. One of the first actions taken by the new CEO, Frank Blake, after assuming the position was to abolish the daily catered lunch for top executives. He encouraged his colleagues to eat in the cafeteria with the company's other home office managers and associates. In addition, in 2009, he promoted Marvin Ellison to executive vice president of U.S. stores because of his emphasis on customer service. Home Depot lost many customers to rivals such as Lowe's because of the poor customer service during Nardelli's tenure as CEO. But, the customers who have come back to Home Depot in recent times have had a positive experience.

Home Depot remains a large company, ranked 25th on *Fortune's* list of the largest 500 corporations. But it continues to struggle because of the poor fit between Nardelli and the company and perhaps the industry as well.

Sources: Jean Niemi. 2009. "The Home Depot to Launch Exclusive Martha Stewart Living Brand," Home Depot, Sept. 14, at http://www.phx.corporate-ir.net; Jena McGregor. 2009. "Smart Cost-Cutting: How Home Depot Built It in," *BusinessWeek*, Aug. 4, at http://www.businessweek.com; Jena McGregor. 2009. "Marvin Ellison: Home Depot's Mr. Fixit?" *BusinessWeek*, May 7, at http://www.businessweek.com; "25. Home Depot," *Fortune*, May 4, 2009, at http://www.cnnmoney.com; Michael Barbaro. 2007. "Home Depot Gets a Fresh Coat of Less-Glossy Paint," *The New York Times*, Feb. 8, at http://www.nytimes.com; Theresa Forsman. 2000. "The Maverick's Manual for Entrepreneurial Success," *BusinessWeek*, Dec. 5, at http://www.businessweek.com; Brian Grow. 2006. "Renovating Home Depot," *BusinessWeek*, Mar. 6, at http://www.businessweek.com; Julie Creswell & Michael Barbaro. 2007. "Home Depot Ousts Chief," *International Herald Tribune*, Jan. 4, at http://www.iht.com.

Person–Organization Fit

As suggested throughout this discussion of structure and culture, the fit between an individual and the organization has important implications for satisfaction, commitment, intent to turnover, and job performance.[107] **Values** are abstract ideals related to proper life goals and methods for reaching those goals. As such, individual values often underlie groups of attitudes. Although people may have thousands of attitudes, most likely they have only a few-dozen values.[108] Thus, values are more general than attitudes and form the basis for how we should behave. For example, we could have the underlying value that family time is highly important and a corresponding negative attitude toward a colleague who works most nights and many weekends.

Values emerge as individuals mature and as they develop the ability to form general concepts from their accumulated experiences. Also, during value formation, the value judgments of people we respect influence the nature of our values. Finally, as discussed in Chapter 2, national and ethnic culture affects the development of values.

Once formed, values serve as frames of reference that help guide people's behavior in many different contexts. Values can be modified or refined as a result of new experiences but are much more resistant to change than are attitudes. Thus, individuals will not change their values to join a particular organization. Rather, they make choices based on the agreement between their personal values and those of the organization. Many organizations try to select new associates who share the values consistent with their organizational culture. For example, the individuals who work at Southwest Airlines are likely to share values concerning equality, hard work and having fun at work, partly because of the

values
Abstract ideals that relate to proper life goals and methods for reaching those goals.

recruitment practices of Southwest and partly due to the choices made by individuals on where they prefer to work.

Values develop along two dimensions: (1) the types of personal goals that one ought to have and (2) the types of behaviors that one ought to use in reaching those goals.[109] These two dimensions are sometimes referred to as the end–means dimensions of values. Thus, individuals may develop an end value that they should seek a life of prosperity and a means value that they should be ambitious and hardworking to achieve that goal. These values complement each other by specifying a general goal in life and identifying acceptable behaviors for reaching it. A list of "end" values and "means" values is shown in Exhibit 13-9.

Research has shown that basic personal values affect individual reactions to job situations.[110] Our satisfaction with the type of work we do, the rules imposed by the organization, career advancement opportunities, and other organizational factors are evaluated in terms of our values. Workers' reactions to jobs in different cultures may vary because of differing basic value systems. For example, the basic value systems in the United States emphasize

EXHIBIT 13-9   Types of Personal Values

End (Goal) Values	Means (Behavior) Values
Prosperity	Ambition and hard work
Stimulating, active life	Open-mindedness
Achievement	Competence
World peace	Cheerfulness
Harmony in nature and art	Cleanliness
Equality	Courageousness
Personal and family security	Forgiving nature
Freedom	Helpfulness
Happiness	Honesty
Inner peace	Imagination
Mature love	Independence and self-reliance
National security	Intelligence
Pleasure and enjoyment	Rationality
Religion and salvation	Affection and love
Self-respect	Obedience and respect
Social respect	Courtesy
Friendship	Responsibility
Wisdom	Self-discipline

Source: Adapted from M. Rokeach. 1973. *The Nature of Human Values* (New York: The Free Press).

self-reliance and initiative, whereas in Japan basic value systems emphasize self-sacrifice, obedience, and cooperation. As explained in Chapter 3, this difference has implications for how high-involvement management systems should be developed in different cultures.

When an individual's values and preferences do not fit prevailing structural arrangements, she may be a less-satisfied and a less-positive contributor to the organization. Similarly, and perhaps more importantly, when an individual's values are not congruent with the

THE STRATEGIC LENS

We have emphasized that an organization's structure and culture play important roles in the implementation of its strategy. For example, if an organization's business strategy is to be a "first mover" in the market, it must be innovative in order to develop and introduce new products before competitors do so. To be entrepreneurial and innovative, the organization needs an organic structure, one that is flexible and decentralized. A centralized mechanistic structure would not allow managers and associates the freedom to be creative and take the risks necessary to identify market opportunities and develop innovative products. Similarly, the culture of the organization must allow for the use of intuition and risk-taking behaviors because associates and managers should not be afraid of making errors or failing. To be successful over time, most organizations must be ambidextrous.

In the chapter, we mentioned that Southwest Airlines has been highly successful because of its culture and its ability to hire new associates and managers who fit well with the culture. Southwest has followed an integrated low-cost/differentiation business strategy since its founding. Many airlines have tried to imitate this strategy but have been unable to reproduce Southwest's success. These competitors have

failed to realize that Southwest uses not only low cost but also a differentiated high-quality service provided through its associates. Southwest's associates have fun at work and work together as a team. These attributes come through in the service provided and also help the airline to hold down its costs. Thus, Southwest Airlines' unique strategy, which integrates low cost and differentiation, is implemented effectively because of its culture and human resource management system.[116] Other airlines could not reproduce and effectively implement this integrated strategy because they could not imitate Southwest's culture.

A strategy will be only as effective as its implementation. If the strategy is well formulated, and the structure and the culture fit the strategy well, the organization will achieve higher performance. Congruence among strategy, structure, and culture is necessary to achieve the highest possible organization performance.

Culture's effects on strategy are also often evident in mergers and acquisitions. Many mergers between companies fail. Often these failures occur not because of financial or technical problems but because the companies involved have vastly different organizational cultures.[117] One company may be entrepreneurial and flexible, for example, whereas the other may be traditional and rigid. Merging

these two cultures is problematic, at the least.

Therefore, senior managers who expect their firm to acquire another firm should understand the target firm's culture and what must be done to integrate it. They must also act immediately after the completion of the acquisition to merge the cultures. Doing so will require developing shared values between the two firms. Cisco Systems is well known for its ability to integrate acquisitions.[118] This firm assigns key people to preacquisition integration teams and carefully includes individuals from the firm being acquired.

Critical Thinking Questions

1. Consider an organization of which you are a member or an associate. What is the structure in this organization? Is it centralized or decentralized? Is it organic and flexible? How would you change the structure in this organization to make it more effective?

2. How would you describe the culture in the organization identified in your answer to question 1? How does the culture affect members' behavior in the organization?

3. When you become a manager, what type of culture will you establish in your unit? What values do you want to emphasize? Why?

organization's culture, problems are likely to develop. In fact, when the lack of fit is between the CEO and the organization's culture, the problems are likely to be more severe, as in the case of Home Depot and Bob Nardelli. The outcomes are consistent with a great deal of research suggesting that similarity in values and goals attracts individuals to one another and to organizations.[111] Job applicants as well as associates and managers in an organization should assess applicant fit with structure and culture prior to making final employment decisions. Selection for fit is a key aspect of high-involvement management, as discussed in Chapter 1.

Interestingly, socialization can bridge some differences between newcomer preferences and organizational structure and between newcomer values and organizational culture. Socialization achieves this function by highlighting how a person's preferences and values may fit in unseen or partial ways. To some small degree, socialization also may alter a newcomer's preferences. In one study based on the socialization framework presented earlier, individuals exposed to strong socialization efforts exhibited more congruence between their personal attributes and the organization's structure and culture. (This was true even after taking into account the initial level of congruence.)[112]

Although personal fit with structure and culture is important, two issues must be addressed. First, an organization that hires only those who fit existing organizational characteristics may find it difficult to make major changes when they become necessary.[113] With individuals throughout the organization sharing preferences and values, the organization may be resistant to change. To remain adaptive, an organization may want to hire a few key individuals who do not fit. Their ideas may prompt reflection and thereby help the organization to change if necessary. These issues are addressed more fully in Chapter 14. Second, an organization that hires only those who fit may inadvertently discriminate against minorities or foreign nationals.[114] Such an organization fails to experience the benefits from having a multicultural workforce, as discussed in Chapter 2. Perhaps the best advice is to hire for fit, but with a relatively broad definition of fit allowing exceptions and a specific plan for nurturing the exceptions, no matter what their differences.[115]

What This Chapter Adds to Your Knowledge Portfolio

In this chapter, we described several aspects of structure and explained how strategy, environment, technology, and firm size influence structure. We also discussed the competing values culture framework, as well as socialization, subcultures, and cultural audits. Person–organization fit has also been addressed. In summary, we have made the following points:

- Organizational structure is the formal system of work roles and authority relationships that govern how associates and managers interact with one another. Structure can be described using structural characteristics, which determine the shape and appearance of an organization's hierarchy. These characteristics include height, spans of control, and departmentalization (functional versus divisional grouping of resources). Structure can also be described using structuring characteristics, which directly prescribe behavior. These include centralization (the amount of decision authority held at the top of the organization), standardization (the existence of rules and standard operating procedures), formalization (the degree to which rules and procedures exist in written form), and specialization (the degree to which associates and managers have narrow jobs). Modern organizations tend to emphasize configurations of structural and structuring characteristics that yield a substantial amount of freedom for lower-level managers and associates.

- Strategy plays an important role in organizational structure. Corporate strategy corresponds to the emphasis placed on growth and diversification in a firm. An emphasis on growth through internal development suggests the need for substantial research and development and marketing departments. An emphasis on growth though acquisition suggests the need for well-developed financial and legal functions. Diversification must be matched by type of departmentalization, with a single business strategy and a dominant-product strategy calling for a functional structure and higher levels of diversification calling for a divisional structure. Business-level strategies represent the method of competing in a particular product or service market. Low-cost and differentiation are two popular strategies, with the low-cost strategy calling for a less organic structure and differentiation requiring a more organic structure.

? back to the knowledge objectives

1. Compare and contrast the structural and structuring aspects of organizational structure.
2. Assume you manage a firm with three substantially different product lines. A differentiation strategy is used for each product line. What structure choices would you make, and why?
3. Assume you manage a small R&D department. When making choices concerning structure, would you be more concerned about the external environment, more concerned about technology, or equally concerned about the external environment and technology? Explain your answer.
4. What are the four types of culture in the competing values model? In which would you prefer to work, and why?
5. What is socialization? Describe a situation in which you were socialized into an organization (a club, a business firm, a church, or a volunteer organization).
6. What is a cultural audit? Why should organizations conduct cultural audits?
7. How does an organization ensure a fit between its associates' values and its organizational culture?

- The external environment also plays a role in structure. Uncertain environments (those that are complex and changing) create a need for organic structure. They also increase the need for integration among functional departments focused on the same market. Elements of structure that address integration include slack resources, self-contained tasks, information technology, and lateral relations. Furthermore, different levels of uncertainty may be experienced by different functional departments, resulting in a need to differentiate the departments, with some being more organic than others.
- Technology, too, plays a role in structure. An early framework suggests that technological complexity determines the structure required in small manufacturing firms. More recent work demonstrates that mass customization can be used in manufacturing firms of all sizes and that organic structure facilitates this approach. Recent work has also focused on technological nonroutineness in manufacturing and service organizations, suggesting that high levels of nonroutineness in small organizations and units of larger ones should be matched with more organic structures.
- Finally, organizational size plays a role in structure. Large organizations must be taller and more formalized in order to ensure smooth functioning. Centralization tends to decrease, however, because senior managers cannot make all decisions. However, as organizations grow in size, the potential increases that they will suffer from inertia. To avoid or overcome inertia, organizations must try to develop

ambidextrous attributes. Ambidextrous organizations balance formalization and flexibility and thereby are able to maintain efficiency while also being innovative.

- Organizational culture represents shared values that influence behavior. The competing values culture model is an important and popular framework for analyzing cultural phenomena in organizations. The model is based on two value dimensions: (1) flexibility and discretion versus stability and control and (2) internal focus coupled with integration versus an external focus coupled with differentiation in the marketplace. Based on these two dimensions, four culture types emerge: clan, hierarchy, market, and adhocracy.

- Socialization involves imparting an organization's values to newcomers. Socialization is accomplished by exposing individuals to experiences that highlight the organization's values. In designing socialization activities, managers and associates should consider context (collective and formal versus individual and informal), content (sequential and fixed versus variable and random), and social dynamics (serial and investiture versus disjunctive and divestiture).

- Culture audits are formal analyses designed to uncover shared values in an organization. They involve: (1) analyzing the process and content of socialization, (2) analyzing how the organization has responded to critical incidents in its history, (3) analyzing the values and beliefs of founders and current leaders, and (4) exploring any puzzling findings from the earlier analyses.

- Subcultures can develop in an organization. In large, diverse organizations, the organizational culture can be seen as a system of integrated subcultures rather than a unified set of values. Although subcultures can sometimes cause problems when they are substantially inconsistent with the overall culture of the organization, they can also help to produce fresh insights and ideas.

- Individuals bring values to the organization. The fit between individual values and organization values can be important. If there is a misfit, individuals are likely to be unproductive or become dissatisfied and leave.

Thinking about Ethics

1. Organizations can have some units with organic structures and others with mechanistic structures. Is it equitable to allow some associates a great deal of freedom and flexibility and to tightly control the behaviors of the others? Why or why not?

2. Intuit's CEO, Steve Bennett, is fond of saying, "If you don't involve me in the takeoff, don't involve me in the crash." When a firm performs poorly, do the managers who design and implement a mechanistic structure have responsibilities to protect the jobs of associates who have relatively little involvement and opportunity to affect the firm's results?

3. An organization, such as Southwest Airlines, might not hire a person who is fully qualified for the job but who is thought to be a poor fit with the firm's organizational culture. What are the ethical implications, if any? Explain your answer.

4. In a market organizational culture, associates may be encouraged to compete against one another, with the emphasis on winning. What are the ethical implications, if any? Explain your answer.

5. An organization with an adhocracy culture encourages risk taking and allows associates to make errors. How do managers operating in such a culture decide when an associate is doing a poor job and should be laid off? Should the organization specify a maximum acceptable number of errors? Explain your answer.

Key Terms

Human Resource Management Applications

The Human Resource Management (HRM) function is often responsible for several applications of the concepts explained in this chapter. For example, *managerial training* programs help managers learn how to develop the most effective structures for their context (e.g., when to use an organic structure). They may also be responsible for the *organization development* function that helps managers to identify when and how to make needed changes such as structure changes.

The HRM department often has responsibility for designing, implementing and interpreting *culture surveys* (to assess the current culture and identify changes needed if any). In addition, they frequently conduct *culture audits*.

Finally, the HRM function has the responsibility for *recruitment* and *selection* of new human capital. Therefore, HRM professionals play a major role in maintaining the person–organization fit.

---

building your human capital

An Assessment of Creativity

Many organizations use a differentiation strategy that calls for initiative and creativity. Many of these same organizations have an adhocracy culture, where innovation and risk taking are valued. Not all individuals, however, are equally suited for these organizations. This assessment focuses on creativity. Although an individual's propensity to be creative can vary from situation to situation, his or her general tendencies provide useful insight.

Instructions

In this assessment, you will read 50 statements that describe people. Use the rating scale below to indicate how accurately each statement describes you. Rate yourself as you generally are now, not as you wish to be in the future; and rate yourself as you honestly see yourself. Read each item carefully, and then circle the number that corresponds to your choice from the rating scale.

1	2	3	4	5
Strongly Disagree	Disagree	In Between or Don't Know	Agree	Strongly Agree

1. I always work with a great deal of certainty that   1   2   3   4   5
I am following the correct procedures for solving
a particular problem.

2. It would be a waste of time for me to ask questions if I had no hope of obtaining answers.	1	2	3	4	5
3. I feel that a logical step-by-step method is best for solving problems.	1	2	3	4	5
4. I occasionally voice opinions in groups that seem to turn some people off.	1	2	3	4	5
5. I spend a great deal of time thinking about what others think of me.	1	2	3	4	5
6. I feel that I may have a special contribution to give to the world.	1	2	3	4	5
7. It is more important for me to do what I believe to be right than to try to win the approval of others.	1	2	3	4	5
8. People who seem unsure and uncertain about things lose my respect.	1	2	3	4	5
9. I am able to stick with difficult problems over extended periods of time.	1	2	3	4	5
10. On occasion I get overly enthusiastic about things.	1	2	3	4	5
11. I often get my best ideas when doing nothing in particular.	1	2	3	4	5
12. I rely on intuitive hunches and the feeling of "rightness" or "wrongness" when moving toward the solution of a problem.	1	2	3	4	5
13. When problem solving, I work faster analyzing the problem and slower when synthesizing the information I've gathered.	1	2	3	4	5
14. I like hobbies that involve collecting things.	1	2	3	4	5
15. Daydreaming has provided the impetus for many of my more important projects.	1	2	3	4	5
16. If I had to choose from two occupations other than the one I now have or am now training for, I would rather be a physician than an explorer.	1	2	3	4	5
17. I can get along more easily with people if they belong to about the same social and business class as myself.	1	2	3	4	5
18. I have a high degree of aesthetic sensitivity.	1	2	3	4	5
19. Intuitive hunches are unreliable guides in problem solving.	1	2	3	4	5
20. I am much more interested in coming up with new ideas than in trying to sell them to others.	1	2	3	4	5
21. I tend to avoid situations in which I might feel inferior.	1	2	3	4	5
22. In evaluating information, the source of it is more important to me than the content.	1	2	3	4	5
23. I like people who follow the rule "business before pleasure."	1	2	3	4	5
24. One's own self-respect is much more important than the respect of others.	1	2	3	4	5
25. I feel that people who strive for perfection are unwise.	1	2	3	4	5
26. I like work in which I must influence others.	1	2	3	4	5
27. It is important for me to have a place for everything and everything in its place.	1	2	3	4	5

28. People who are willing to entertain "crackpot" ideas are impractical.   1 2 3 4 5

29. I rather enjoy fooling around with new ideas, even if there is no practical payoff.   1 2 3 4 5

30. When a certain approach to a problem doesn't work, I can quickly reorient my thinking.   1 2 3 4 5

31. I don't like to ask questions that show my ignorance.   1 2 3 4 5

32. I can more easily change my interests to pursue a job or career than I can change a job to pursue my interests.   1 2 3 4 5

33. Inability to solve a problem is frequently due to asking the wrong questions.   1 2 3 4 5

34. I can frequently anticipate the solution to my problems.   1 2 3 4 5

35. It is a waste of time to analyze one's failures.   1 2 3 4 5

36. Only fuzzy thinkers resort to metaphors and analogies.   1 2 3 4 5

37. At times I have so enjoyed the ingenuity of a crook that I hoped he or she would go scot-free.   1 2 3 4 5

38. I frequently begin work on a problem that I can only dimly sense and cannot yet express.   1 2 3 4 5

39. I frequently tend to forget things, such as names of people, streets, highways, and small towns.   1 2 3 4 5

40. I feel that hard work is the basic factor in success.   1 2 3 4 5

41. To be regarded as a good team member is important to me.   1 2 3 4 5

42. I know how to keep my inner impulses in check.   1 2 3 4 5

43. I am a thoroughly dependable and responsible person.   1 2 3 4 5

44. I resent things being uncertain and unpredictable.   1 2 3 4 5

45. I prefer to work with others in a team effort rather than solo.   1 2 3 4 5

46. The trouble with many people is that they take things too seriously.   1 2 3 4 5

47. I am frequently haunted by my problems and cannot let go of them.   1 2 3 4 5

48. I can easily give up immediate gain or comfort to reach the goals I have set.   1 2 3 4 5

49. If I were a college professor, I would rather teach factual courses than those involving theory.   1 2 3 4 5

50. I'm attracted to the mystery of life.   1 2 3 4 5

Scoring Key

Combine the numbers you have circled, as follows:

Item 4 + Item 6 + Item 7 + Item 9 + Item 10 + Item 11 + Item 12 + Item 15 + Item 18 + Item 20 + Item 24 + Item 29 + Item 30 + Item 33 + Item 34 + Item 37 + Item 38 + Item 39 + Item 40 + Item 46 + Item 47 + Item 48 + Item 50 + [162 − (Item 1 + Item 2 + Item 3 + Item 5 + Item 8 + Item 13 + Item 14 + Item 16 + Item 17 + Item 19 + Item 21 + Item 22 + Item 23 + Item 25 + Item 26 + Item 27 + Item 28 + Item 31 + Item 32 + Item 35 + Item 36 + Item 41 + Item 42 + Item 43 + Item 44 + Item 45 + Item 49)]

Total scores can be interpreted as follows:

210–250	Very creative
170–209	Somewhat creative
130–169	Neither creative nor noncreative
90–129	Not very creative
50–89	Noncreative

Source: Adapted from D.D. Bowen, R.J. Lewicki, D.T. Hall, & F.S. Hall. 1997. *Experiences in Management and Organizational Behavior* (New York: John Wiley & Sons).

---

an organizational behavior moment

How Effective Is Hillwood Medical Center?

Sharon Lawson is the administrator of Hillwood Medical Center, a large hospital located in Boston, Massachusetts. She has been its administrator for almost five years. Although it has been a rewarding position, it has not been without its frustrations. One of Sharon's primary frustrations has been her inability to determine how she should measure the effectiveness of the hospital.

The chief medical officer, Dr. Ben Peters, thinks that the only way to measure the effectiveness of a hospital is the number of human lives saved, compared with the number saved in other, similar hospitals. But the board to which Sharon reports is highly concerned about the costs of running the hospital. Hillwood is non-profit but has no outside sponsors, and so it must remain financially solvent without contributions from another major institution.

In order to be reimbursed for Medicare and Medicaid patients, the hospital must meet the licensing requirements of the state health department, as well as the requirements of the U.S. Department of Health and Human Services. Sharon finds that some of these requirements reflect minimum standards, whereas others are more rigid. She also finds that the demands of the administrative board and those of doctors on the staff frequently conflict. She must mediate these demands and make decisions to maximize the effectiveness of the hospital.

Sharon's day begins when she arises at 6:00 A.M., exercises, showers, has a quick breakfast, and heads for the office. She usually arrives at the office around 7:15 A.M. She likes to get there before others so that she can review and plan her day's activities without interruption. Today she sees that she has an appointment at 8:30 A.M. with a member of the state health department concerning its recent inspection. At 10:00 A.M., she has an administrative staff meeting. At 2:00 P.M., she has scheduled a meeting with the medical staff, and at 4:00 P.M. she has an appointment with the hospital's attorney. (She also has a luncheon appointment with an old college friend who is in town for a few days.) It looks as if her day is well planned.

At 8:15, Sharon receives a call from Dr. Ramon Garcia, chief of surgery.

"Sharon, I must see you. Do you have time now so that we could talk about an important matter?"

"Ramon, I have an appointment in fifteen minutes and probably won't be free until about eleven this morning. Would that be okay?"

"I guess so. I don't have much choice, do I?" With that, he hangs up.

At 8:30, Sharon ushers in Holly Wedman from the state health department. She learns that Hillwood has passed the general inspection but that some areas need to be improved. The kitchen meets only minimum standards for cleanliness, and some other areas are questionable. The inspectors also questioned hospital procedures that allow many people access to the drug supplies. (Sharon recalls that she tried to tighten up those procedures only two months ago, but the medical staff complained so strongly that she relented and made no change.) The state health department representative requests that appropriate changes be made and notes that these areas will be given especially rigorous scrutiny at the next inspection in six months. As the meeting ends, Sharon looks at her watch. It is 9:55—just enough time to make it to the conference room for her next meeting.

The administrative staff meeting begins normally, but after about 30 minutes, Helen Mathis, controller, asks to speak.

"Sharon, when are we going to get the new computer software we requested six months ago?"

"I don't know, Helen. I've discussed it with the board, but they've been noncommittal. We'll have to try to build it into next year's budget."

"But we need it now. We can't process our billing efficiently. Our accounts receivable are too large. We're going to run into a cash-flow problem soon if we don't find other ways to increase our billing efficiency."

Sharon thought, "Cash-flow problems. I wonder how those fit into Dr. Peters's definition of effectiveness."

It is finally decided that Sharon will make a new and stronger request to the board for the computer software.

At 11:00 sharp, Dr. Garcia comes stomping into Sharon's office, exhibiting his usual crusty demeanor. "Sharon, we have a serious problem on our hands. I've heard through the grapevine that a malpractice suit will be filed against one of our surgeons, Dr. Chambers."

"That's nothing new; we get several of those a year."

"Yes, but I think this one may have some merit, and the hospital is jointly named in the suit."

"What do you mean?"

"Well, I've suspected for several months that Dr. Chambers has been drinking a lot. He may have performed an operation while under the influence. I've talked to several people who were in the operating room at the time, and they believe that he was drunk."

"Oh, no! If you suspected this why didn't you do something?"

"What was I supposed to do? Accuse one of the oldest and most respected members of our surgical staff? You just don't accuse a person like that without proof. We've got to meet with Chambers now and confront him."

"Well, set up a meeting."

"I already have. His only free time was at lunch, so I took the liberty of scheduling a meeting with him for you and me at that time."

"I already have an engagement. I can't do it today. Try to set one up tomorrow."

Dr. Garcia, obviously feeling a great deal of stress, explodes, "You administrators are never available when we need you. Your only concern is holding down costs. We're talking about human lives here. Chambers may do it again before tomorrow."

Sharon seethes at his insinuation. "If that mattered to you, why did you wait until you heard of the malpractice suit to do something about it?"

Garcia leaves, slamming the door.

Sharon goes to lunch with her friend, but she can't enjoy it. Her mind is on problems at the hospital. She can hardly wait for the 2:00 P.M. medical staff meeting.

The meeting begins with only about half of the doctors in attendance, which is not unusual. Most of them will show up before the meeting is over. Much of the time is taken up discussing why the hospital has not purchased an upgraded piece of standard diagnostic equipment used in body scanning. Of course, it "only" costs $1

million. The meeting ends without resolving the problem. Sharon agrees to buy the equipment next year but does not have the money for it in this year's budget. The doctors do not fully understand why it cannot be purchased now if it can be purchased next year.

As soon as Sharon gets back to her office, her secretary gives her a message to call Terry Wilson, one of the third-floor pediatric nurses. Terry had said it was urgent.

"Terry, this is Sharon Lawson. What can I do for you?"

"Ms. Lawson, I thought you should know. The nurses in pediatrics are planning a walkout tomorrow."

"What? A walkout? Why?" Sharon is beginning to get a headache.

"Yes, a walkout. The nurses feel that Supervisor Tyson is a tyrant, and they want her replaced."

"Terry, can you get a group of those nurses together and meet me in my office in fifteen minutes? Be sure to leave several to cover the floor while you're gone."

"Okay. See you in a few minutes."

Sharon and the nurses meet and discuss the situation. The nurses are quite adamant but finally agree to give Sharon a week to investigate the situation and attempt to resolve it. A meeting is scheduled for next week to review the situation.

The hospital's attorney has to wait for almost 20 minutes because Sharon's meeting with the nurses runs past 4:00 P.M. Finally they meet, and as Sharon feared, he brings news of the malpractice suit filed against Dr. Chambers and Hillwood. They discuss the steps that should be taken and how the situation with Dr. Chambers should be handled from a legal viewpoint. Obviously, some hard decisions will have to be made.

The attorney leaves at 5:30, and Sharon sits in her office pondering the day's problems. She also thinks of her original problem: how to measure Hillwood's effectiveness.

Discussion Questions

1. Describe the culture or cultures at Hillwood. Are there subcultures?
2. How would you recommend that Sharon measure effectiveness at Hillwood? What do you think some of the effectiveness criteria might be?

team exercise
Words-in-Sentences Company

In this exercise, you will form a "mini-organization" with several other people. You will also compete with other companies in your industry. The success of your company will depend on your planning and organizational structure. It is important, therefore, that you spend some time thinking about the best design for your organization.

Step 1: 5 Minutes

Form companies and assign workplaces. The total class should be divided into small groups of four or five individuals. Each group should consider itself a company.

Step 2: 10 Minutes

Read the directions below and ask the instructor about any points that need clarification. Everyone should be familiar with the task before beginning Step 3.

You are members of a small company that manufactures words and then packages them in meaningful (English-language) sentences. Market research has established that sentences of at least three words but not more than six words are in demand.

The "words-in-sentences" (WIS) industry is highly competitive in terms of price, and several new firms have recently entered the market. Your ability to compete depends on efficiency and quality control.

GROUP TASK

Your group must design and participate in running a WIS company. You should design your organization to be as efficient as possible during each 10-minute production run. After the first production run, you will have an opportunity to reorganize your company if you want to.

RAW MATERIALS

For each production run, you will be given a "raw material word or phrase." The letters found in the word or phrase serve as the raw materials available to produce new words in sentences. For example, if the raw material word is *organization,* you can produce the following words and sentence: "Nat ran to a zoo."

PRODUCTION RULES

Several rules must be followed in producing "words-in-sentences." If these rules are not followed, your output will not meet production specifications and will not pass quality-control inspection.

1. A letter may appear only as often in a manufactured word as it appears in the raw-material word or phrase; for example, *organization* has two o's. Thus, *zoo* is legitimate, but *zoology* is not—it has too many o's.
2. Raw-material letters can be used over again in new, different manufactured words.
3. A manufactured word may be used only once in a sentence and in only one sentence during a production run; if a word—for example, *zoo*—is used once in a sentence, it is out of stock.
4. A new word may not be made by adding s to form the plural of an already used manufactured word.
5. A word is defined by its spelling, not its meaning.
6. Nonsense words or nonsense sentences are unacceptable. All words must be in the English language.
7. Names and places are acceptable.
8. Slang is not acceptable.

MEASURING PERFORMANCE

The output of your WIS company is measured by the total number of acceptable words that are packaged in sentences in the available time. The sentences must be legible, listed on no more than two sheets of paper, and handed to the quality-control review board at the completion of each production run.

DELIVERY

Delivery must be made to the quality-control review board 30 seconds after the end of each production run.

QUALITY CONTROL

If any word in a sentence does not meet the standards set forth above, all of the words in the sentence will be rejected. The quality-control review board (composed of one member from each company) is the final arbiter of acceptability. In the event of a tie vote on the review board, a coin toss will determine the outcome.

Step 3: 15 Minutes

Design your organization's structure using as many group members as you see fit to produce your words-in-sentences. There are many potential ways of organizing. Since some are more efficient than others, you may want to consider the following:

1. What is your company's objective?
2. How will you achieve your objective? How should you plan your work, given the time allowed?
3. What degree of specialization and centralization is appropriate?
4. Which group members are more qualified to perform certain tasks?

   Assign one member of your group to serve on the quality-control review board. This person may also participate in production runs.

Step 4: 10 Minutes—Production Run 1

1. The instructor will hand each WIS company a sheet with a raw material word or phrase.
2. When the instructor announces "Begin production," you are to manufacture as many words as possible and package them in sentences for delivery to the quality-control review board. You will have 10 minutes.
3. When the instructor announces "Stop production," you will have 30 seconds to deliver your output to the quality-control review board. Output received after 30 seconds does not meet the delivery schedule and will not be counted.

Step 5: 10 Minutes

1. The designated members of the quality-control review board will review output from each company. The total output should be recorded (after quality-control approval) on the board.
2. While the review board is completing its task, each WIS company should discuss what happened during Production Run 1.

Step 6: 5 Minutes

Each company should evaluate its performance and organization. Companies may reorganize for Run 2.

Step 7: 10 Minutes—Production Run 2

1. The instructor will hand each WIS company a sheet with a raw-material word or phrase.
2. Proceed as in Step 4 (Production Run 1). You will have 10 minutes for production.

Step 8: 10 Minutes

1. The quality-control review board will review each company's output and record it on the board. The totals for Runs 1 and 2 should be tallied.
2. While the board is completing its task, each WIS company should prepare an organization chart depicting its structural characteristics for both production runs and should prepare a description of its structuring characteristics.

Step 9: 10 Minutes

Discuss this exercise as a class. The instructor will provide discussion questions. Each company should share the structure information it prepared in Step 8.

Source: Adapted from D.D. Bowen, R.J. Lewicki, D.T. Hall, & F.S. Hall. 1997. *Experiences in Management and Organizational Behavior* (New York: John Wiley & Sons).

Endnotes

1. Etzioni, A. 1964. *Modern organization.* Englewood Cliffs, NJ: Prentice Hall; Jones, G.R. 2010. *Organizational theory, design and change* (6th ed.). Englewood Cliffs, NJ: Pearson-Prentice Hall.

2. Ravashi, D. & Schultz, M. 2006. Responding to organizational identity threats: Exploring the role of organizational culture. *Academy of Management Journal,* 49: 433–458; Gerhart, B. 2009. How much does national culture constrain organizational culture? *Management and Organization Review,* 5: 241–259.

3. Campbell, J.P., Bownas, D.A., Peterson, N.G., & Dunnette, M.D. 1974. The measurement of organizational effectiveness: A review of the relevant research and opinion. Report Tr-71-1, San Diego, Navy Personnel Research and Development Center; Dalton, D.R., Todor, W.D., Spendolini, M.J., Fielding, G.J., & Porter, L.W. 1980. Organization structure and performance: A critical review. *Academy of Management Review,* 5: 49–64.

4. Keats, B. W. & O'Neill, H. 2001. Organizational structure: Looking through a strategy lens, in M.A. Hitt, R.E. Freeman, and J.S. Harrison (eds.), *Handbook of strategic management,* Oxford, United Kingdom: Blackwell Publishers, pp. 520–542.

5. Campbell, Bownas, Peterson, & Dunnette, The measurement of organizational effectiveness; Dalton, Todor, Spendolini, Fielding & Porter, Organization structure and performance.

6. Child, J. 1984. *Organization: A guide to problems and practices* (2nd ed.). London: Harper & Row; Larson, E.W., & King, J.B. 1996. The systematic distortion of information: An ongoing challenge to management. *Organizational Dynamics,* 24 (3): 49–61; Nahm, A.Y., Vonderembse, M.A., & Koufteros, X.A. 2003. The impact of organizational structure on time-based manufacturing and plant performance. *Journal of Operations Management,* 21: 281–306.

7. Child, *Organization: A guide to problems and practices.*

8. Ibid.

9. Bohte, J., & Meier, K.J. 2001. Structure and the performance of public organizations: Task difficulty and span of control. *Public Organization Review,* 1: 341–354; Worthy, J.C. 1950. Organizational structure and employee morale. *American Sociological Review,* 15: 169–179.

10. Jones, *Organizational theory, design and change.*

11. Paine, L.S., & Mavrinac, S.C. 1995. *AES Honeycomb.* Boston: Harvard Business School Publishing; AES Corporation 2005 Annual Report, at http://www.aes.com, March 3, 2007.

12. Davison, B. 2003. Management span of control: How wide is too wide? *The Journal of Business Strategy,* 24 (4): 22–29.

13. *The Saratoga Review,* 2009. Talent strategies for tough times: Reductions in force. PricewaterhouseCoopers, July 4–5.

14. Duncan, R. 1979. What is the right organization structure? Decision tree analysis provides the answer. *Organizational Dynamics,* 7 (3): 59–80.

15. Ibid.

16. Ibid.

17. Ibid.

18. Rank, O.N., Robins, G.L. & Pattison, P.E. 2010. Structural logic of intraorganizational networks. *Organization Science,* in press; Maria, J., & Marti, V. 2004. Social capital benchmarking system: Profiting from social capital when building network organizations. *Journal of Intellectual Capital,* 5: 426–442; Miles, R.E., Snow, C.C., Mathews, J.A., Miles, G., & Coleman, H.J. 1997. Organizing in the knowledge age: Anticipating the cellular form. *Academy of Management Executive,* 11 (4): 7–20.

19. Zhiang, L., Peng, M.W., Yang, H. & Sun, S.L. 2009. How do networks and learning drive an institutional comparison between China and the United States? *Strategic Management Journal,* 30: 1113–1132; Zhiang, L., Yang, H. & Arya, B. 2009. Alliance partners and firm performance: Resource complementarity and status association, *Strategic Management Journal,* 30: 921–940; Hitt, M.A., Ireland, R.D., & Hoskisson, R.E., 2011. *Strategic management: Competitiveness and globalization.* Cincinnati, OH: Cengage South-Western Publishing .

20. Mintzberg, H. 1993. *Structuring in fives: Designing effective organizations.* Englewood Cliffs, NJ: Prentice Hall; Zabojnik, J. 2002. Centralized and decentralized decision making in organizations. *Journal of Labor Economics,* 20: 1–21.

21. Huber, G.P., Miller, C.C., & Glick, W.H. 1990. Developing more encompassing theories about organizations: The centralization-effectiveness relationship as an example. *Organization Science,* 1: 11–40; Tata, J., & Prasad, S. 2004. *Journal of Managerial Issues,* 16: 248–265.

22. Bunderson, J.S., & Boumgarden, P. 2010. Structure and learning in self-managed teams: Why "bureaucratic" teams can be better learners, *Organization Science,* in press.

23. Burns, T., & Stalker, G.M. 1966. *The management of innovation.* London: Tavistock Institute; Jones, *Organization theory, design and change.*

24. The term "learning organization" has been defined in many different ways. As it stands, there is considerable confusion and disagreement concerning its proper definition. Many *users* of the term, however, focus on aspects of structure just as we do here. See, for example, Dodgson, M. 1993. Organizational learning: A review of some literatures. *Organization Studies,* 1: 375–394. Also see Goh, S.C. Toward a learning organization: The strategic building

blocks. *S.A.M. Advanced Management Journal*, 63 (2): 15–22; For general insights, see Garvin, D.A. 1993. Building a learning organization. *Harvard Business Review*, 71 (4): 78–91.

25. The term "boundaryless organization" has been defined in various ways. Users of the term, however, generally refer to individuals having freedom and incentives to work across internal and external organizational boundaries. For a broad discussion, see Ashkenas, R., Ulrich, D., Jick, T., & Kerr, S. 1995. *The boundaryless organization*. San Francisco, CA: Jossey-Bass.

26. Freiberg, K., & Freiberg, J. 1996. *Nuts!: Southwest Airlines' crazy recipe for business and personal success*. Austin, TX: Bard Press.

27. Sine, W.D., Mitsuhashi, H., & Kirsch, D.A., 2006. Revisiting Burns and Stalker: Formal structure and new venture performance in emerging economic sectors, *Academy of Management Journal*, 49: 121–132.

28. Ahuja, G., Polidoro, F. & Mitchell, W. 2009. Structural homophily or social asymmetry? The formation of alliances by poorly embedded firms, *Strategic Management Journal*, 30: 941–956.

29. Thompson, J.P. 1967, *Organizations in action*. New York: McGraw-Hill; Hitt, M.A., Ireland, R.D., & Hoskisson, R.E. 2011. *Strategic management: Competitiveness and globalization*. Mason, OH: Cengage South-Western.

30. Hitt, M.A., Ireland, R.D., & Palia, K.A. 1982. Industrial firm's grand strategy and functional importance: Moderating effects of technology and uncertainty. *Academy of Management Journal*, 3: 265–298.

31. Anonymous. 2004, Dec. 19. Growth Strategy Leadership Award Given to Technology Company. *Medical Devices & Surgical Technology Week*, Atlanta, p. 25.

32. Hitt, M.A., Harrison, J.S., & Ireland, R.D. 2001. *Mergers and acquisitions: A guide to creating value for stakeholders*. New York: Oxford University Press; Hitt, M.A., King, D., Krishnan, H., Makri, M. Schijven, M. Shimizu, K. & Zhu, H. 2009. Mergers and acquisitions: Overcoming pitfalls, building synergy, and creating value. *Business Horizons*, 52: 523–529.

33. Holloway, C.A., Wheelwright, S.C., & Tempest, N. 1999. *Cisco Systems, Inc.: Acquisition integration for manufacturing*. Palo Alto, CA: Stanford Graduate School of Business.

34. Weber, Y., & Menipaz, E. 2003. Measuring cultural fit in mergers and acquisitions. *International Journal of Business Performance Management*, 5: 54–72.

35. Shimizu, K., & Hitt, M.A. 2005. What constrains or facilitates the divestiture of formerly acquired firms? The effects of organizational inertia. *Journal of Management*, 31: 50–72.

36. Palich, L.E., Cardinal, L.B., & Miller, C.C. 2000. Curvilinearity in the diversification-performance linkage: An examination of over three decades of research. *Strategic Management Journal*, 21: 155–174; David, P., O'Brien, J.P., Yoshikawa, T. & Delios, A. 2010. Do shareholders or stakeholders appropriate the rents from corporate diversification? The influence of ownership structure. *Academy of Management Journal*, in press.

37. Lim., E.N., Das, S.S. & Das, A. 2009. Diversification strategy, capital structure, and the Asian financial crisis (1997-1998): Evidence from Singapore firms. *Strategic Management Journal*, 30: 577–594.

38. Wiersema, M.F. & Bowen, H.P. 2008. Corporate diversification: The impact of competition, industry globalization and product diversification. *Strategic Management Journal*, 29: 115–132; Dastidar, P. 2009. International corporate diversification and performance: does firm self-selection matter? *Journal of International Business Studies*, 40: 71–85.

39. Hitt, Ireland & Hoskisson, *Strategic management*.

40. Galan, J.I. & Sanchez-Bueno, M.J. 2009. The continuing validity of the strategy-structure nexus: New findings, 1993-2003. *Strategic Management Journal*, 30: 1234–1243.

41. Hitt, Ireland, & Hoskisson, *Strategic management*.

42. Grinyer, P.H., Yasai-Ardekani, M. , & Al-Bazzaz, S. 1980. Strategy, structure, environment, and financial performance in 48 United Kingdom companies. *Academy of Management Journal*, 23:193–220; Hitt, & Ireland. Relationships among corporate level distinctive competence, diversification strategy, corporate structure and performance.

43. Porter, M.E. 1980. *Competitive strategy: Techniques for analyzing industries and competitors*. New York: The Free Press.

44. See, for example: Govindarajan, V. 1988. A contingency approach to strategy implementation at the business unit level: Integrating administrative mechanisms with strategy. *Academy of Management Journal*, 31: 828–853; Jones. *Organizational theory, design and change*.

45. Hoskisson, R.E., Hitt, M.A., Ireland, R.D., & Harrison, J.S. 2008. *Competing for advantage*, Cincinnati, OH: Thomson South-Western.

46. See, for example: Govindarajan, A contingency approach to strategy implementation at the business unit level: Integrating administrative mechanisms with strategy; Jones. *Organizational theory, design and change*; Vorhies, D.W., & Morgan, N.A. 2003. A configuration theory assessment of marketing organization fit with business strategy and its relationship with marketing performance. *Journal of Marketing*, 67: 100–115.

47. Holcomb, T.R., Holmes, Jr., R.M, & Connelley, B.L. 2009. Making the most of what you have: Managerial ability as a source of resource value creation. *Strategic Management Journal*, 30: 457–485.

48. General Electric. 2004. Our company: Business directory. At http://www.ge.com/en/company/ businesses/index.htm.

49. Bourgeois, L.J. 1980. Strategy and environment: A conceptual integration. *Academy of Management Review*, 5: 25–29.

50. Delmas, M.A. & Toffel, M.W. 2008. Organizational responses to environmental demands: Opening the black box, *Strategic Management Journal*, 29: 1027–1055.

51. Marren, P. 2009. Uncertainty cubed, *Journal of Business Strategy*, 30 (4): 52–54; Oriani, R. & Sobrero, M. 2008. Uncertainty and the market valuation of R&D within a real options logic, *Strategic Management Journal*, 29: 343–361.

52. Lawrence, P.R., & Lorsch, J.W. 1967. *Organization and environment*. Boston: Harvard Business School Press.

53. Naman, J.L., & Slevin, D.P. 1993. Entrepreneurship and the concept of fit: A model and empirical tests. *Strategic Management Journal*, 14: 137–153; Negandhi, A., & Reimann, C. 1973. Task environment, decentralization and organizational effectiveness. *Human Relations*, 26: 203–214; Priem, R.L. 1994. Executive judgement, organizational congruence, and firm performance. *Organization Science*, 421–437; Nadkarni, S. & Barr, P.S. 2008, Environmental context, managerial cognition, and strategic

action: An integrated view, *Strategic Management Journal*, 29: 1395–1427.

54. Sirmon, D.G., Hitt, M.A., & Ireland, R.D. 2007. Managing firm resources in dynamic environments to create value: Looking inside the black box. *Academy of Management Review*, 32: 273–292.

55. Garg, V.K., Walters, B.A., & Priem, R.L. 2003. Chief executive scanning emphases, environmental dynamism, and manufacturing firm performance. *Strategic Management Journal*, 24: 725–744.

56. Jarzabkowski, P., & Balogun, J. 2009. The practice and process of delivering integration through strategic planning, *Journal of Management Studies*, 46: 1255–1288.

57. Galbraith, J. 1973. *Designing complex organizations*. Reading, MA: Addison-Wesley.

58. Al-Mudimigh, Z.M., & Al-Mashari, M. 2001. ERP software implementation: An integrative framework. *European Journal of Information Systems*, 10: 216–226; Davenport, T. 2000. *Mission critical: Realizing the promise of enterprise systems*. Boston: Harvard Business School Press.

59. Johnson, T., Lorents, A.C., Morgan, J., & Ozmun, J. 2004. A customized ERP/SAP model for business curriculum integration. *Journal of Information Systems Education*, 15: 245–253.

60. Huber, G.P. 2004. *The necessary nature of future firms: Attributes of survivors in a changing world*. Thousand Oaks, CA: Sage Publications.

61. Woodward, J. 1965. *Industrial organization: Theory and practice*. London: Oxford University Press.

62. Harvey, E., 1968. Technology and the structure of organizations. *American Sociological Review*, 33: 241–259; Zwerman, W.L. 1970. *New perspectives on organizational effectiveness*. Westwood, CT: Greenwood.

63. Hitt, M.A., Keats, B.W., & Demarie, S.M. 1998. Navigating in the new competitive landscape: Building strategic flexibility and competitive advantage in the 21st century. *Academy of Management Executive*, 12(4):22–42.

64. Kotha, S. 1995. Mass customization: Implementing the emerging paradigm for competitive advantage. *Strategic Management Journal*, 16: 21–42; Pine, B. 1993. *Mass customization*. Boston, MA: Harvard Business School Press.

65. Hitt, M.A. 2000. The new frontier: Transformation of management for the new millennium. *Organizational Dynamics*, 28 (3): 7–17.

66. Ibid.

67. Ibid.

68. See, for example: Argote, L. 1982. Input uncertainty and organizational coordination in hospital emergency units. *Administrative Science Quarterly*, 27: 420–434; Drazin, R., & Van de Ven, A.H. 1985. Alternative forms of fit in contingency theory. *Administrative Science Quarterly*, 30: 514–539; Schoonhoven, C.B. 1981. Problems with contingency theory: Testing assumptions hidden within the language of contingency theory. *Administrative Science Quarterly*, 26: 349–377.

69. Child, *Organization: A guide to problems and practices*.

70. Ford, J.D., & Hegarty, W.H. 1984. Decision makers' beliefs about the causes and effects of structure: An exploratory study. *Academy of Management Journal*, 27: 271–291.

71. Peli, G. 2009, Fit by founding, fit by adaptation: Reconciling conflicting organization theories with logical formalization, *Academy of Management Review*, 34: 343–360.

72. Luo, Y., & Rui, H. 2009. An ambidexterity perspective toward multinational enterprises from emerging economies. *Academy of Management Perspectives*, 23 (4): 49–70; Simsek, Z. 2009. Organizational ambidexterity: Towards a multilevel understanding, *Journal of Management Studies*, 46: 597–624.

73. Simsek, Z., Heavey, C., Veiga, J.F., & Souder, D. 2009. A typology for aligning organizational ambidexterity's conceptualizations, antecedents and outcomes. *Journal of Management Studies*, 46: 864–894.

74. Jansen, J.J.P., George, G., Van den Bosch, F.A.J., & Volberda, H.W. 2008. Senior team attributes and organizational ambidexterity: The moderating role of transformational leadership. *Journal of Management Studies*, 45: 982–1007.

75. Fang, C., Lee, J., & Schilling, M.A. 2009. Balancing exploration and exploitation through structural design: The isolation of subgroups and organizational learning. *Organization Science*, in press.

76. Taylor, A. 2010. The next generation: Technology adoption and integration through internal competition in new product development. *Organization Science*, 21: 23–41; Leiblein, M.J. & Madsen, T.L. 2009. Unbundling competitive heterogeneity: Incentive structures and capability influences on technological innovation. *Strategic Management Journal*, 30: 711–735.

77. Doty, D.H., Glick, W.H., & Huber, G.P. 1993. Fit, equifinality, and organizational performance: A test of two configurational theories. *Academy of Management Journal*, 36: 1196–1250.

78. See, for example: Burton, R.M., Lauridsen, J., & Obel, B. 2002. Return on assets loss from situational and contingency misfits. *Management Science*, 48: 1461–1485.

79. See, for example: Burton, R.M., Lauridsen, J., & Obel, B. 2002. Return on assets loss from situational and contingency misfits. *Management Science*, 48: 1461–1485.

80. Deetz, S. 1985. Critical-cultural research: New sensibilities and old realities. *Journal of Management*, 11: 121–136.

81. Chatman, J.A., & Cha, S.E. 2003. Leading by leveraging culture. *California Management Review*, 45 (4): 20–34; Keeley, M. 1983. Values in organizational theory and management education. *Academy of Management Review*, 8: 376–386.

82. Tetrick, L.E., & Da Silva, N. 2003. Assessing culture and climate for organizational learning. In S.E. Jackson, M.A. Hitt, & A. DeNisi (Eds.), *Managing knowledge for sustained competitive advantage*. San Francisco, CA: Jossey-Bass, pp. 333–359; Schein, E.H. 1984. Coming to a new awareness of organizational culture. *Sloan Management Review*, 25 (2): 3–16.

83. Joo, B.-K. & Lim, T. 2009. The effects of organizational learning culture, perceived job complexity, and proactive personality on organizational commitment and intrinsic motivation. *Journal of Leadership and Organizational Studies*, 16: 48–60.

84. Ren, H. & Gray, B. 2009. Repairing relationship conflict: How violation types and culture influence the effectiveness of restoration rituals. *Academy of Management Review*, 34: 105–126.

85. Latta, G.F. 2009. A process model of organizational change in cultural context (OC3 Model), *Journal of Leadership and Organizational Studies*, 16: 19–37.

86. Cameron, K.S., & Quinn, R.E. 1999. *Diagnosing and changing organizational culture: Based on the competing values framework.* Reading, MA: Addison-Wesley.

87. Turner, K.L., & Makhija, M.V. 2006. The role of organizational controls in managing knowledge. *Academy of Management Review,* 31: 197–217.

88. Bernard, C. 2009. Cultural innovation in software design: The new impact of innovation planning methods. *Journal of Business Strategy,* 30(2/3): 57–69; Quinn, R.E. 1988. *Beyond rational management.* San Francisco, CA: Jossey-Bass.

89. Goodman, E.A., Zammuto, R.F., & Gifford, B.D. 2001. The competing values framework: Understanding the impact of organizational culture on the quality of work life. *Organization Development Journal,* 19 (3): 59–68.

90. van Rekom, J., van Riel, C.B.M., & Wierenga, B. 2006. A methodology for assessing organizational core values. *Journal of Management Studies,* 43: 175–201.

91. Jones, R.A., Jimmieson, N.L., & Griffiths, A. 2005. The impact of organizational culture and reshaping capabilities on change implementation success: The mediating role of readiness for change. *Journal of Management Studies,* 42: 361–386.

92. Pech, R.J. 2009. Delegating and devolving power: A case study of engaged employees. *Journal of Business Strategy,* 30(1): 27–32.

93. Erdogan, B., Liden, R.C., & Kraimer, M.L. 2006. Justice and leader-member exchange: The moderating role of organizational culture. *Academy of Management Journal,* 49: 395–406.

94. Cable, D.M., & Parsons, C.K. 2001. Socialization tactics and person-organization fit. *Personnel Psychology,* 54: 1–23; Jones, G.R, 1986. Socialization tactics, self-efficacy, and newcomers' adjustments to organizations. *Academy of Management Journal,* 29: 262–279. Also see Van Maanen, J., & Schein, E.H. 1979. Toward a theory of organizational socialization. *Research in Organizational Behavior,* 1: 209–264.

95. Bain & Company. 2007. At http://www.bain.com, April 17.

96. Freiberg & Freiberg, *Nuts*!

97. Most admired companies. 2009. CNNMoney.com, at http://money.cnn.com/magazines/fortune/mostadmired/2009/full_list/index.html, Jan. 21, 2010.

98. Zander, U., & Zander, L. 2010. Opening the grey box: Social communities, knowledge and culture in acquisitions. *Journal of International Business Studies,* 41: 27–37; Tsui, A.S., Wang, H., & Xin, K.R. 2006. Organizational culture in China: An analysis of culture dimensions and culture types. *Management and Organization Review,* 2: 345–376.

99. Wilkins, A.L. 1983. The culture audit: A tool for understanding organizations. *Organizational Dynamics,* 12: 24–38.

100. Culture Audit. 2007. Smith Weaver Smith Accelerated Cultural Transformation, at http://www.smithweaversmith.com.

101. Schein, Coming to a new awareness.

102. Wilkins, A.L. 1983. Efficient cultures: Exploring the relationship between culture and organizational performance. *Administrative Science Quarterly,* 28: 468–481.

103. Riley, P. 1983. A structurationist account of political culture. *Administrative Science Quarterly,* 28: 414–437.

104. Martin, J., & Siehl, C. 1983. Organizational culture and counterculture: An uneasy symbiosis. *Organizational Dynamics,* 12: 52–64.

105. Williamson, I.O., Burnett, M.F. & Bartol, KM. 2009. The interactive effect of collectivism and organizational rewards on affective organizational commitment, *Cross Cultural Management,* 16: 28–43.

106. Gerhard, B. 2008. How much does national culture constrain organizational culture? *Management and Organization Review,* 5: 241–259.

107. Chatman & Cha, Leading by leveraging culture; Kristof, A.L. 1996. Person-organization fit: An integrative review of its conceptualizations, measurement, and implications. *Personnel Psychology,* 49: 1–48; O'Reilly, C.A., Chatman, J.A., & Caldwell, D.F. 1991. People and organizational culture: A profile comparison approach to assessing person-organization fit. *Academy of Management Journal,* 14: 487–516; Tziner, A. 1987. Congruency issue retested using Fineman's achievement climate notion. *Journal of Social Behavior and Personality,* 2: 63–78; Vandenberghe, C. 1999. Organizational culture, person-culture fit, and turnover: A replication in the health care industry. *Journal of Organizational Behavior,* 20: 175–184.

108. Ronen, S. 1978. Personal values: A basis for work motivation set and work attitude. *Organizational Behavior and Human Performance,* 21: 80–107.

109. Rokeach, M. 1973. *The nature of human values.* New York: The Free Press.

110. Ronen, Personal values.

111. Schneider, B. 1987. The people make the place. *Personnel Psychology,* 40: 437–453.

112. Cable & Parsons, Socialization tactics and person-organization fit.

113. See, for example, Bowen, D.E., Ledford, G.E., & Nathan, B.R. 1991. Hiring for the organization, not the job. *Academy of Management Executive,* 5 (4): 35–51.

114. See, for example, Lovelace, K., & Rosen, B. 1996. Differences in achieving person-organization fit among diverse groups of managers. *Journal of Management,* 22: 703–722.

115. For additional insights, see Powell, G. 1998. Reinforcing and extending today's organizations: The simultaneous pursuit of person-organization fit and diversity. *Organizational Dynamics,* 26 (3): 50–61.

116. Hitt, Ireland, & Hoskisson, *Strategic management: Competitiveness and globalization.*

117. Hitt, Harrison, & Ireland. 2001. *Mergers and acquisitions*; Cartwright, S., & Cooper, C.L. 1993. The role of culture compatibility in successful organizational marriage. *Academy of Management Executive,* 7 (2): 57–70.

118. Holloway, Wheelwright, & Tempest, Cisco Systems, Inc.

organizational change and development

Reinventing the Dream at Starbucks

Howard Schultz, the entrepreneurial force behind the organization, provided the guiding vision and a golden touch in building Starbucks into a huge company with 16,700+ stores at the beginning of 2010. Although Starbucks has achieved amazing success, it has experienced some "bumps in the road" along the way. In 2008, Starbucks began experiencing a reduction in its average sales per store for the first time in its history. The decline continued for 2008 and 2009. There are several reasons for the weakness in Starbucks's performance. Among them are increased competition (from national and local coffee wholesalers and retailers such as Green Mountain Coffee roasters and others introducing gourmet coffees, such as McDonald's) and the global recession's causing potential customers to reduce their discretionary purchases (Starbucks coffee is viewed by most as a luxury item). As a result there was a stock-price decline that became serious for Starbucks shareholders because it made its shares less attractive to potential investors.

In January 2010, Starbucks announced its first quarterly increases since 2008 in average sales per store open at least one year; and its quarterly profit tripled. The 4 percent increase was achieved through a series of major changes in Starbucks' operations. Prior to these changes, Howard Schultz stepped back in as the chief executive officer (CEO). One of his first actions as CEO was to announce the closing of several unprofitable stores. Eventually, Starbucks closed almost 800 stores and reduced the number of managers and associates by approximately 18,000 across its U.S. and international operations. Although, these actions were designed to stem the performance declines, Schultz felt that much more was needed to rejuvenate Starbucks and its performance.

A second action taken by Schultz was to conduct a thorough organizational analysis to identify the

knowledge objectives

After reading this chapter, you should be able to:

1. Describe three major internal pressures for change.
2. Identify and explain six major external pressures for change.
3. Describe the three-phase model of planned change.
4. Discuss important tactical choices involving the speed and style of a change effort.
5. Explain the four general causes of resistance to change and the tactics that can be used to address each cause.
6. Discuss the role of the DADA syndrome in organizational change.
7. Describe the basic organization development (OD) model and discuss OD interventions, including relationship techniques and structural techniques.

problems that precipitated the weak performance over recent years. This analysis identified several problems, chief among them was the lost focus on customers' desires. In becoming a large company with standardized products and store designs, customers thought Starbucks had also become sterile. Customers preferred coffee that was unique and customized to their tastes. Based on these findings, Schultz initiated other actions.

As described in Chapter 11, Starbucks has a strong team-based culture. Schultz engaged managers and associates to help redesign their local stores in ways that best fit with the local community and its interests. The structure was changed to include more geographic regional groups, allowing them to focus on the drinks desired most in their

©Scott Olson/Getty Images Inc.

areas (e.g., cold drinks in the southern U.S. region and espresso in the Pacific Northwest region). Starbucks has also increased its innovation of new products such as the new instant coffee, Via. The company is refocusing its attention on customer needs and service. Schultz asked the managers and associates (Starbucks refers to them as "partners") to invest energy in attentiveness to customers, providing them excellent service, and to be innovative in adapting their operations to local community values.

Howard Schultz recently expressed concerns that in the drive to increase its size and gain the economies of scale, the company may have compromised the "soul" of its original stores. He is now in the process of reinventing Starbucks to recapture that soul.

Sources: C.C. Miller. 2010. "Now at Starbucks: A Rebound," *The New York Times*, Jan. 21, at http://www.nytimes.com; M. Montandon. 2010. "Bean Counters No More: Starbucks Finding Success by Thinking Local," *Fast Company*, Jan. 21, at http://www.fastcompany.com; A.M. Heher. 2010. "Starbucks Rallies, Sets Sights Overseas," *The Seattle Times*, Jan. 21, at http://www.seattletimes.nwsource.com; M. Allison. 2010. "Starbucks Reports Strong First-Quarter Results as Via, International Sales Take Off," *The Seattle Times*, Jan. 21, at http://www.seattletimes.nwsource.com; J. Jargon. 2010. "Starbucks Growth Revives, Perked by Via," *The Wall Street Journal*, Jan. 21, at http://www.wsj.com; B.J. Barr. 2010. "Now Brewing Starbucks Gets a Makeover," *The New York Times Style Magazine*, Jan. 11, at http://www.tmagazine.blogs.nytimes.com; M. Bartiromo. 2008. "Howard Schultz on Reinventing Starbucks," *BusinessWeek*, Apr. 9, at http://www.businessweek.com; 2008. "Starbucks Makes Organizational Changes," Restaurant News Resource, Feb. 25, at http://www.restaurantnewsresource.com.

the strategic importance of Organizational Change and Development

Few, if any, organizations can remain the same for very long and survive. A classic case is Polaroid Corporation, which shows the outcome of being too slow to change. Polaroid introduced instant photography to the market and at one time was among the top 50 corporations in the United States.

However, in 2001, it declared bankruptcy, and in 2002, what was left of the company was sold to Bank One's OEP Imaging Unit and then sold again in 2005 to the Petters Group. Polaroid's problem was its failure to adapt in a timely way to technological change. The company lost its market because it was too slow to recognize the importance of digital imaging technology and then too slow to change after competitors developed digital cameras.[1]

The development of a new technology created the need for change at Polaroid. Although top managers are responsible for instituting such changes, managers and associates lower in the organization must help because of their knowledge of the environment (markets, customers, competitors, technology, government regulations, and so forth). All managers should actively scan the environment for changes and help to identify external opportunities and threats. Unfortunately, Polaroid's managers did not perceive the threat to their existing business quickly enough to transform the firm. After learning of the need for a change, these managers began the difficult process of designing and implementing a new approach, but they were unable to do so in time to avoid failure. Competitors developed and introduced new cameras using digital technology before Polaroid could do so, causing Polaroid to lose a substantial share of its market.

In contrast, Starbucks has achieved considerable success since its founding. The company has been recognized for its high-involvement management practices (the manner in which it has valued and managed its human capital), environmentally conscious policies, accessibility to those with disabilities, and high-quality coffees. Yet, although Starbucks did change significantly over time, it had become rather predictable in store format and standardized coffee-product offerings. And it encountered significant competition from such unlikely sources as McDonald's and Dunkin Donuts, a recessionary economy, and disgruntled customers. Its sales per store began

declining, and its profits followed a similar path. Thus, Howard Schultz stepped back into the CEO position and instituted a number of changes. After downsizing the number of stores and the workforce, the firm made several other very important changes. The company reinstituted its strong focus on customer service and satisfaction. It began to remodel its stores, tailoring the décor to local community preferences. And it reinvigorated its focus on innovation, exemplified by its introduction of the new instant coffee, Via. Many of these changes were implemented by engaging managers and associates to gain their recommendations. Thus, Starbucks continued its commitment to high-involvement practices—effectively using the talents of associates and enhancing their motivation—which helped to reduce resistance to change by lower-level managers and associates. Some experts believe that effective management of human capital and developing effective ways of dealing with change have contributed significantly to Starbucks's ability to build and maintain a competitive advantage. Starbucks's leaders showed their concern by recapturing the soul that had made Starbucks successful. After experiencing two years of decline,

these changes began to pay dividends as the company's sales and profits began to increase again.

Change often involves an entire firm, as in the Starbucks case. In other instances, a single division or work group must change. To be prepared for either situation, managers must understand and appreciate change and possess the skills and tools necessary for implementing it. In high-involvement organizations, associates also play key roles in planning and implementing change, and they, too, must possess appropriate skills and tools.

In this chapter, we discuss organizational change and renewal. First, we examine internal and external pressures for change. Such pressures must be properly understood for effective change to occur. Next, we describe the basic process of planned change and consider important tactical decisions involved in a change effort. Building on this foundation, we then address the important topic of resistance to change. Individuals and groups often resist change, and the ability to diagnose causes of resistance and deal with them effectively is crucial. Finally, we discuss a set of assessment techniques and change tactics, collectively known as *organizational development*.

Pressures for Organizational Change

Organizations constantly face pressure for change; in order to cope, they must be agile and react quickly.[2] Organizations that understand and manage change well tend to be the most effective.[3] As suggested by Exhibit 14-1, pressures for change can be categorized as internal or external.

Internal Pressures for Change

Although many pressures for change exist in the external environments of organizations, some pressures are more closely identified with internal dynamics. Aspiration–performance

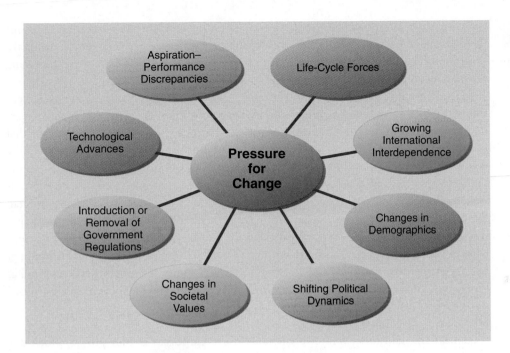

Exhibit 14-1 Internal and External Pressures for Organizational Change

discrepancies, natural life-cycle forces, and changes in the CEO or top management team are three of the most important pressures.

Aspiration–Performance Discrepancies

Perhaps the most fundamental pressure for change involves **aspiration–performance discrepancies,** or differences between aspirations and current performance.[4] When an individual, work group, division, or organization is not meeting its expectations (often expressed in goals), changes in tactics, strategies, and processes often follow. Failing to live up to expectations is an uncomfortable state that often motivates change. Some changes motivated by failing to satisfy aspirations include divesting poorly performing units[5] or acquiring other businesses to access resources that will hopefully allow the firm to achieve its aspirations.[6]

To fully appreciate the role of aspirations, it is important to understand how they develop. Research has identified three factors.[7] First, past aspirations play a role in current aspirations. Thus, if an associate had high expectations of herself yesterday, she is likely to have high expectations today as well. This point underscores an important phenomenon: stickiness in aspirations. Stickiness exists when individuals, units, and organizations are slow to revise their aspirations even when those aspirations appear to be too high or too low. One study, for example, found that units of a company adjusted performance aspirations less than might be expected in the face of information suggesting that greater change, either up or down, was warranted.

Second, past performance plays an important role. If performance in the recent past was below target levels, aspirations are likely to be reduced, although stickiness places limits on the degree of adjustment in the short run. Conversely, if performance has been above target levels, it is common for aspiration levels to be increased to some degree. For example, in the early days, Starbucks executives learned that it was relatively easy to perform well in a high-growth environment, and thus they increased the firm's aspiration levels. Although such changes in aspiration levels may seem benign, they can be harmful.

aspiration–performance discrepancies
Gaps between what an individual, unit, or organization wants to achieve and what it is actually achieving.

Poorly performing individuals, units, and organizations may reduce aspiration levels instead of making changes sufficient to increase performance. Alternatively, individuals, units, and organizations that are performing well may increase aspiration levels, causing satisfaction with current performance to be fleeting.

Third, comparisons with others play a role in determining aspirations. A management trainee may compare himself with other management trainees. A firm often compares itself with other firms in the same industry. When comparisons with similar others suggest that better performance is possible (especially when the firm's performance is perceived to be below par), aspirations will likely increase and strategies will be formulated to achieve the higher aspirations.[8] Similarly, when comparisons suggest that others are performing less well, aspirations are likely to decrease. For example, one study found that leaders of retail financial-service units that were performing poorly in comparison with other financial-service units increased their aspirations, whereas leaders of units performing well in comparison with others lowered their aspirations.[9] This latter finding is particularly intriguing, because it suggests that many individuals and business units are content to be as good as others but not necessarily better. This obviously did not apply to the founders of Starbucks.

Life-Cycle Forces

life-cycle forces
Natural and predictable pressures that build as an organization grows and that must be addressed if the organization is to continue growing.

Organizations tend to encounter predictable **life-cycle forces** as they grow.[10] Not every organization experiences the same forces in the same way as others, but most organizations face similar pressures. Although several models of the organizational life cycle have been proposed, an integrative model best highlights the key pressures that organizations experience. This model has four stages: entrepreneurial, collectivity, formalization and control, and elaboration (see Exhibit 14-2).

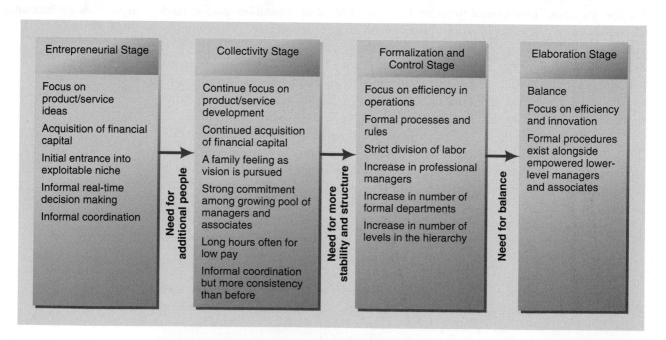

Exhibit 14-2 Integrative Life-Cycle Model

Source: Based on R.E. Quinn, & K. Cameron. 1983. "Organizational Life Cycles and Shifting Criteria of Effectiveness." *Management Science*, 24: 33–51.

In the *entrepreneurial stage,* founders and perhaps initially a few managers and associates develop ideas for products or services, acquire financial capital, and take actions to enter a niche in the marketplace. This is an exciting time, but after the market has been entered and success achieved, growth requires founders to add managers and associates. Processes must be introduced for selecting, training, and coordinating these individuals. In the *collectivity stage,* founders, managers, and associates continue to emphasize product or service development and fund-raising. Individuals in the young organization tend to feel like a family as they pursue the vision that attracted them to the firm. Individuals often work long hours for relatively low pay, and they tend to be highly committed. Informal communication and coordination are important, but founders often begin to handle more managerial responsibilities and fewer entrepreneurial responsibilities than they would like. As the firm continues to grow, professional managers and formal processes must be incorporated to resolve or prevent coordination and control problems.

In the *formalization and control stage,* managers and associates are guided by formal processes and rules, a strict division of labor, and a stable organizational structure. And they emphasize efficiency more than innovation. Functional disciplines such as accounting and operations management are elevated in status. As the firm continues to grow, more rules and procedures are often added, along with a greater number of management levels. Eventually, managers and associates can become alienated from the firm, partly because they lose discretion in decision making. Furthermore, in larger organizations, newer associates and managers do not have a connection to the original vision, and overall commitment may be lower. To prevent or overcome these problems, a renewed effort to empower both managers and associates should be considered. At Starbucks, Schultz and other leaders maintained their commitment to a high-involvement workplace, which helped the company postpone some of the negative side effects of the formalization stage. Starbucks grew rapidly and thus reached this stage more quickly than many firms. The firm continued to grow and eventually was unable to prevent the negative effects of this stage and thereby suffered performance declines. However, Schultz responded quickly with changes that now appear to be working, as evidenced in the *Exploring Behavior in Action* segment.

Unilever, a large multinational firm, began to experience declines in market share and profits largely due to more aggressive competitors such as Procter & Gamble and more innovative competitors such as Reckitt Benckiser. When the performance problems surfaced in 2005, top managers decided a change was in order. Its growth strategy appeared to have been unsuccessful. However, a thorough analysis showed that the strategy was correct but that Unilever had failed in its execution (implementation) of the strategy. To improve execution, the company streamlined its structure and developed a process referred to as "strategy in action," which involved mobilizing teams to implement the planned actions based on the strategies, and then a review process to monitor the results and make adjustments where needed to ensure success. This process was communicated to all 180,000 managers and associates. One of the outcomes was a significant increase in the amount of collaboration across teams and units. Unilever achieved its strategic vision in 2010 partly because of the changes implemented.[11]

In the *elaboration stage,* managers and associates experience a more balanced, mature organization. Formal rules and processes exist alongside empowered lower-level managers and associates. Efficiency concerns coexist with concerns for innovation and renewal. As discussed in Chapter 13, balancing these concerns is challenging but possible. Starbucks currently exemplifies this stage, especially with the changes it has implemented.

Overall, some firms handle life-cycle forces reasonably well; Starbucks and Unilever are examples of such firms. Other firms handle these issues less well. In these cases, there is often a change in the leadership of the organization that can trickle down through the organization. If effective leaders are chosen to replace the previous ones and the transition is handled in an orderly manner, the organization can experience positive outcomes from the change.[12]

Changes in Top Management

changes in top management
Involve the replacement of top management team members who retire or depart the company for other reasons.

Changes in top management involve the replacement of top management team members who retire or depart the company for other reasons (e.g., resign). The changes often begin with the selection of a new CEO. When CEOs and other members of the top management team have been in their positions for some time, the organization can experience inertia. In these cases, it is more difficult to identify, develop, and implement changes. The reason for the inertia is an overly strong commitment to the current strategy and courses of action. Such commitment may be because of high performance in the past or because the managers feel personally invested in the approach they chose and implemented (e.g., feel their reputation is at stake).[13] To overcome the inertia caused by the unwillingness of top managers to make needed changes, a change in the CEO and perhaps other members of the top management team may be necessary.[14]

A new CEO and new members of the top management team, bring unique ideas on how to deal with problems the organization is experiencing. They also have no special commitment to the previous strategies and actions, unless they represent an inside succession. However, to make major changes, it is common for the new top managers to be chosen from outside the organization.[15] New top managers often select and implement new strategies that can turn around the organization's performance.[16]

Of course, not all new managers will be successful. Some may not make changes and others may make changes that do not adequately meet the challenges faced. As a result, some new managers may be replaced after a short tenure.[17] In particular, when an organization needs changes, perhaps they should search for specific types of individuals to undertake the top leadership roles. For example, managers with a strong belief in their capabilities have been found to be more entrepreneurial.[18] Thus, firms that require more innovation to be competitive may need such individuals in their top management team. Careful selection of a new leader can help an organization create the type of change needed.

External Pressures for Change

Along with internal pressures, organizations face external pressures for change. Organizations must be sensitive to these external pressures, or they may not survive. For example, if an organization does not react to changes in the market for its product, the demand for its product probably will decline. Such was the case for Polaroid, as discussed earlier. The new digital cameras introduced to the market by Polaroid's competitors greatly reduced the demand for Polaroid's products. When Polaroid was unable to respond quickly, it filed for bankruptcy and ceased to exist as an independent business.

External pressure for change comes from several sources, including technological advances, the introduction or removal of government regulations, changes in societal values, shifting political dynamics, changing demographics, and growing international interdependency (see Exhibit 14-1).

Technological Advances

Scientific knowledge, produced by both companies and universities, has been developing rapidly over the past 50 years.[19] For example, in 2007, there were 23,750 scientific journals that published 1.35 million pages.[20] With advances in research methods and a continuing need for answers to many important research questions, the rapid development of knowledge is expected to continue.

Technological advances are based on advances in scientific knowledge. Such advances can lead to incremental or radical changes in how services and products are designed, produced, and delivered. Two facts illustrate the point that scientific knowledge drives technology. First, scientific knowledge is routinely cited in patent

©Photodisc/Getty Images

applications, with the number of scientific articles cited per patent on the increase in the United States, Germany, France, Britain, and other countries.[21] Second, the number of patents granted by the U.S. Patent Office is increasing at a growing rate, which matches the growth in science. In the first half of the twentieth century, patents granted increased by 50 percent.[22] In the second half of the twentieth century, they quadrupled.[23] These rapid changes can be seen in technologies of recent origin, such as advancements in wireless communications technologies, advanced manufacturing technologies, and nanotechnologies.[24] New technologies are being developed faster than they can be implemented. A prime example is provided by new developments in microelectronic technology, which occur before previous developments can be fully implemented.

Firms must adapt to technological advances or risk becoming outdated and ineffective.[25] Manufacturing firms, for example, must adopt new manufacturing technologies or suffer disadvantages in cost, quality, or speed relative to their competition in the marketplace.[26] Firms that failed, or were slow, to take advantage of computer-aided manufacturing, computer-aided design, and modern manufacturing resource planning experienced competitive disadvantages.

Changes in Government Regulations and Other Institutions

The U.S. government has the responsibility to regulate commerce for the common good. Much of the regulation is initiated because of societal pressures. Major regulation has been implemented over the years in areas such as civil rights and equal opportunity, environmental protection, and worker safety and health.

In recent times, regulations have been implemented that establish fuel-efficiency standards for automobile manufacturers, requirements for regional telephone companies to provide competitors access to their hardwired networks, and rules limiting telemarketers' ability to call people's homes.[27] The Drug-Free Workplace Act was passed to encourage employers to test associates for drugs and to implement employee assistance programs for substance abuse. Additional rules and regulations have been enacted since the original legislation to enhance effects. However, these regulations have been only partially effective in achieving the goals. For one thing, it covers only employers with federal contracts. In addition, the programs implemented by employers vary in their effectiveness.[28] Without question, however, organizations must adapt to regulatory changes.

Institutional changes such as in the rule of law can have a major effect on economic activity and especially on the willingness of foreign firms to enter markets.[29] Often firms are especially interested in the rule of law such as in relation to intellectual property rights (i.e., protection of copyrights and patents) and to corrupt practices (e.g., bribery).[30] Clearly, uncertainty related to regulations and the potential for changes may cause firms to postpone investments or to change their strategies.[31] Clearly, regulations can influence firm changes. For example, the U.S. government recently implemented new regulations on banks, and particularly those receiving funds from the government, to remain solvent. The banks are required to maintain ceilings on executive pay until they pay back all of the monies provided to them.[32]

The U.S. government also occasionally removes regulations created in earlier times. The airline, trucking, and communication industries, for example, have been largely deregulated. Such deregulation also requires changes. For example, firms in deregulated industries typically must adapt to a more competitive environment, which many firms in these industries have found difficult to do. Many airlines that prospered in the regulated era, such as Pan Am and Braniff, failed under deregulation.

Changes in Societal Values

Changes in societal values are normally seen in four ways. First, changing values influence consumer purchases, affecting the market for an organization's products or services. Second, society's values are evidenced in employee attitudes, behaviors, and expectations. Third, they affect potential investors in the company. Finally, society's values are represented in government regulations. The changing social values regarding environmental consciousness have had a major influence on organizational strategies and practices, as shown in the *Managerial Advice* segment.

Because of the increasing concerns about global warming, many people throughout the world have become sensitive to environmental issues. The importance of green issues is reflected by consumers' buying behaviors, by investors' purchases of stock in companies, and in other ways as well. The interest in green issues has encouraged Boeing, ExxonMobil, and Coca-Cola Enterprises to develop environmentally sensitive policies and practices as explained in the *Managerial Advice* segment. For example, ExxonMobil is developing a biofuel from algae that consumes carbon dioxide and thus helps to reduce emission of greenhouse gases.

The influence of societal values on consumer purchases can have a major effect on organizations. For example, Americans have become increasingly hostile to products manufactured by companies using questionable practices in foreign countries. Such practices include child labor, periods of intense overtime work, and very low wages. In past decades, individuals thought less about these issues, and firms could neglect them as well. Today, firms must be very careful.

Other influences of societal values are more indirect. They affect politicians who enact laws such as the Drug-Free Workplace Act. With over $200 billion in costs to organizations because of associates' substance abuse, the employee-assistance programs promoted by the Act are important to save lives and reduce costs to organizations from substance abuse.[33] Thus, societal values also influence government regulation, which in turn places external pressures on the organization.

Shifting Political Dynamics

Political pressures, both national and international, can influence organizational operations. The political philosophy of those elected to office affects legislation and the interpretation of existing legislation and government policies. For example, President Ronald

Social Pressures for "Green" Policies and Practices: The War against Carbon Emissions

©AP/Wide World Photos

While in times past, financing or regulatory approval were the most critical concerns for many major investments, in current times many investors are focused on the company's environmental sustainability policies and actions. Many companies have realized that changing their environmental policies—making them more green—will actually contribute to their bottom line, improve their public image, and make them more attractive to many investors. *Sustainability* in simple terms means meeting our current human needs without harming future generations. It is a major cause among environmentalists, human rights activists, and economic-development experts. And it has become important to many in the global society, such that companies are expected to be environmentally conscious. In the past, sustainability often meant higher costs for companies, but in current times, better environmental and social practices can yield strategic advantages. Customers are shifting their loyalties to companies that embrace the concept of sustainability.

The Boeing Company found that air used to cool its computers at its four-acre information technology processing site in Seattle was seeping out through openings in the floor. Those openings were plugged with insulation, thereby saving approximately 685,000 kilowatt-hours of electricity and $55,000 annually. Although the cost reduction is meaningful, this action also reduced Boeing's carbon emissions. Boeing voluntarily reports its carbon emissions to the Carbon Disclosure Project. This project provides companies with information about ways to measure their emissions and compare them with their rivals (industry data). Scientists suggest that companies and energy providers produce 45 percent of the carbon emissions that contribute to global warming. Many companies are reporting these data and sharing information on their reductions in carbon emissions with the public to convince potential customers and investors that they are green.

Companies are beginning to make major investments in green projects. For example, ExxonMobil announced in 2009 that it will invest in a $600 million project to develop a new biofuel from algae. If the project is successful it could represent a major advancement in the sustainability war because algae can be grown using land and water unsuitable for other uses (e.g., food production) and algae consumes carbon dioxide, the major contributor to greenhouse gases. Likewise, GE announced a $1.4 billion contract to produce and provide maintenance service for 338 large wind turbines. The turbines are to be located in Oregon and produce renewable energy for Southern California Edison. This is the largest order for wind turbines that GE has ever had.

Other companies are also investing in energy-saving projects. For example, Clorox is expanding its line of eco-friendly cleaners (Green Works), which have been highly successful in the market. In fact, sales have exceeded expectations by 600 percent. In addition, Coca-Cola Enterprises, the largest bottler of Coke drinks, announced plans to double the size of its fleet of hybrid trucks to 327 vehicles. McKinsey & Co. projected that the many efforts to reduce energy consumption will lead to a 17 percent decline in energy use in 2020 as compared with 2008. Although U.S. regulators do not require companies to quantify the effects of their environmental practices, these practices have become a powerful indicator of future market performance. Thus, responding positively to environmental pressures may help companies achieve long-term survival.

Sources: L. Kaufman. 2009. "NYT: Emissions Disclosure as Business Virtue," MSNBC, Dec. 29, at http://www.msnbc. msn.com; 2009. "GE Inks Largest Wind Turbine Contract Ever," MSNBC, Dec. 10, at http://www.msnbc.msn.com; A. Stone. 2009. "Honeywell: Green and Clean," *Forbes*, Nov. 2, at http://www.forbes.com; 2009. "Exxon Makes First Big Biofuel Investment," MSNBC, July 14, at http://www.msnbc.msn.com; J. Makower. 2009. "In Recession, Business Keeps Going Green," *BusinessWeek*, Feb. 2, at http://www.businessweek.com; J. Carey. 2007. "Hugging the Tree-Huggers," *BusinessWeek*, Mar. 12, at http://www. businessweek.com; Speeches. 2007. At http://www. thecoca-colacompany.com/presscenter; P. Engardio. 2007. "Beyond the Green Corporation," *BusinessWeek*, Jan. 29, at http://www.businessweek.com.

Reagan's views on U.S. defense spending created massive shifts in government expenditures that affected firms in several industries. These firms had to gear up to meet the government demand. International politics also influence organizational change. For example, the major changes in the former Soviet Union exemplified by the destruction of the wall separating East and West Germany led to a decline in the Cold War and thereby a reduction in U.S. defense spending (in turn leading to a downsizing of several industries). In addition, disagreements over proper tariffs between the European Union and the United States, for example, can cause uncertainty and perhaps higher costs for a firm if tariffs increase. Faced with increased tariffs in an important export market, a firm may need to enhance its efficiency to avoid being forced to raise prices to noncompetitive levels. Alternatively, it may need to shift exports to other markets.

Changes in Demographics

As discussed in Chapter 2, the average age of U.S. citizens has been increasing, along with the proportion of U.S. residents who belong to groups other than non-Hispanic whites. To deal with these changes, many organizations have altered internal practices to ensure fair treatment for people of all races and ages. Diversity programs designed to increase understanding across different groups have become common. Further changes in the demographic profile of the nation may require additional organizational changes.

Firms also have introduced products and marketing tactics designed to appeal to a broader mix of individuals or to a particular targeted niche that has grown in importance. In North Carolina, where the Hispanic population is growing rapidly as compared with most other states, auto dealers and service businesses have added Spanish-speaking associates; and Time-Warner Cable has created a special TV package targeting Hispanic viewers in the state.[34]

Age and income distribution are additional demographic characteristics of importance for workforce composition and marketplace opportunities. For example, Florida now has the largest percentage of citizens aged 65 or over (17.6 percent). This demographic has significant implications for the type of products and services likely to be in demand in that state. Incomes enjoyed by families are also important for the types of products and services likely important for particular geographic markets. The extent to which the income is produced by dual-career couples also has workforce implications. For example, dual-career couples are often less willing to accept international assignments because of the inability of the spouse to move with them.[35]

Growing International Interdependence

You have probably heard someone say that "the world is getting smaller." Or, in recent times a common statement is "the world is becoming flatter." Clichés such as this are frequently used to describe the growing interdependency among countries in the world today. The United States is no longer as self-sufficient as it once was. Growing interdependencies are created by many factors. At the national level, countries may have mutual national defense goals, which are implemented through organizations such as the North Atlantic Treaty Organization (NATO). At the organizational level, a company may need natural resources that it cannot obtain in its own country, or a firm from one country may establish operations in another.[36] One result of interdependency is that organizations must be concerned about what happens throughout the world, even if they have no operations outside the United States. As such, managers need to develop a global mindset whereby they are attentive to changes around the world, analyzing their potential influences on their organization.[37] For example, events in the Middle East have an effect on most major organizations in the United States in some way. International interdependencies provide both opportunities and constraints.[38] Many firms have found that international markets present more opportunities for sales growth than U.S. markets, as discussed in Chapter 3. Likewise, organizations have to remain flexible in their international activities, adapting to major events (e.g., acts of terror; major political changes in a country that likely will lead to changes in important policies) when they occur.[39]

Planned Change

How does an organization respond to pressures for change? One possibility is **planned change,** which involves deliberate efforts to transform an organization or a subunit from its current state to a new state. Planned change may be evolutionary over time, or can be more revolutionary, involving major changes in a shorter period of time.[40] To effectively move the organization from one state to another, those managing the change must consider a number of issues in three distinct parts of the change process.[41] Resistance to change may develop along the way, however.

planned change
A process involving deliberate efforts to move an organization or a unit from its current undesirable state to a new, more desirable state.

Process of Planned Change

Change is typically thought of as a three-phase process that transforms an organization from an undesirable state through a difficult transition period to a desirable new state. Although researchers tend to agree on the nature of these three phases,[42] different names for the phases have been used by different people.

Kurt Lewin, a noted social psychologist, provided the most commonly used labels: *unfreezing, transforming,* and *refreezing*.[43] That is, the change process involves unfreezing an organization from its current state, moving (changing) it to a new state, and refreezing it in the new state (see Exhibit 14-3).

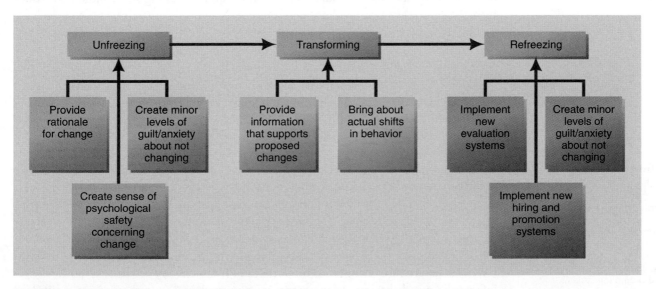

Exhibit 14-3 Process of Planned Change

Unfreezing

unfreezing
A phase in the change process in which leaders help managers and associates move beyond the past by providing a rationale for change, by creating guilt and/or anxiety about not changing, and by creating a sense of psychological safety concerning the change.

Unfreezing involves three activities.[44] First, change leaders provide a rationale—a reason why individuals in the organization should de-commit from the status quo. In particular, they need to motivate managers and associates to break out of the path dependence that currently exists;[45] instead of going down the same path, they need to select and start on a new path.[46] The leaders may accomplish this by providing information on poor financial performance, an impending regulatory change, or a new technological development. Second, leaders create at least minor levels of guilt or anxiety about not changing. Although causing undue negative emotion is not the intent, creation of psychological discomfort can be motivating. Leaders may create such a feeling by discussing the negative outcomes that the organization and its managers and associates will suffer if changes are not made. Third, leaders create a sense of psychological safety concerning the change. Managers and associates must believe they can successfully change.[47] Tactics that change leaders might use include the following:

- Reminding individuals that they have successfully changed in the past
- Communicating to individuals that managers and associates in other organizations in similar circumstances have successfully changed
- Explaining to individuals that support and training will be available for the specific changes to be made

Transforming

transforming
A phase in the change process in which leaders help to implement new approaches by providing information that supports proposed changes and by providing resources and training to bring about actual shifts in behavior.

Transforming involves three key activities.[48] First, change leaders must provide information and evidence that supports the proposed changes. Without supporting information, managers and associates may not have faith in what they are being asked to do, and they will not be committed. Pilot tests, outside experts, and data on how others have benefited from similar changes can be effective tactics. Furthermore, as noted in our discussion of transformational leaders in Chapter 8, a compelling vision of the future also can be useful in building commitment to proposed changes. Indeed, such a vision is likely to be crucial for creating change. Second, any potential constraints to making the change must be removed by the change leaders. This might require investing more money to reduce financial constraints or providing more training to remove constraints due to associates' capability limitations.[49] Third, change leaders must be able to shift behavior and implement the change.[50] They must arrange for the resources required for change, such as new equipment or budgets, and they must ensure that education and training are available. With resources and training in place, actual change can begin.[51] Feedback on progress can be used to make any necessary adjustments along the way. Small wins, or quick and highly visible successes, can be helpful in supporting this stage of the change process.

Refreezing

refreezing
A phase in the change process in which leaders lock in new approaches by implementing evaluation systems that track expected behaviors, by creating reward systems that reinforce expected behaviors, and by ensuring that hiring and promotion systems support the new demands.

Refreezing involves three interrelated activities.[52] First, change leaders implement evaluation systems that track expected behaviors after the change, and they implement permanent training systems to continuously upgrade relevant knowledge and skills. If, for example, working in teams is part of a new approach to production work in a particular organization, an individual's willingness to contribute to a team must be measured and must also be enhanced when necessary. Second, change leaders arrange for permanent reward structures, involving both monetary and nonmonetary rewards, to positively reinforce the new behaviors. Many managers suggest that, "You get what you reward."[53] Third, change leaders ensure that new hiring and promotion systems and other forms of support are designed to satisfy the altered demands.[54]

The Radical Transformation of Novartis

Several years after the pharmaceutical firm Novartis emerged from a merger, Dan Vasella, CEO, decided to make radical changes. Part of the reason for these changes was the lack of new "blockbuster" drugs in Novartis's pipeline. These new drugs were needed to replace major revenue-producing drugs in the firm's current portfolio that were scheduled to go off of patents and thus faced competition from makers of generic drugs (which would be marketed at a much lower price). In fact, the whole drug industry faces this problem, as few have new blockbuster drugs in their pipelines. Vasella decided that a major problem for Novartis and, indeed, all drug makers was that their research was not based strongly enough in science. Rather, the research targeted big diseases because of the opportunity to earn major returns. Vasella decided to include in the long and costly testing process required for the approval of new drugs only drugs that were backed by proven science. Often this means that the drugs are more targeted for very specific diseases, some of which may not affect large numbers of people. Thus, unless the drugs can help control multiple diseases, they promise only small returns. This approach changes the whole business model for drugs.

Vasella met resistance to this change from his marketing managers and others. He moved forward anyway. He hired a new person to head the R&D operations who was a strong academic scientist/researcher but did not have industry experience. He also moved the major research laboratories from Switzerland to Cambridge, Massachusetts, to be near Harvard and MIT. The research scientists were quite unhappy about the change in location, change in policy, and change in leadership. Thus, the changes were radical and also created uncertainty and concern among many of the managers and associates in the company.

His changes were praised by some management experts. For example, well-known management consultant, Ram Charan, said that Vasella was trying to change the existing paradigm in the industry rather than being a prisoner to it. Another management expert suggested that he had "the mind of a long-term strategist."

Vasella continued to make changes in the top executive ranks and finally in building a new and expensive corporate headquarters and research facilities. The new facilities were designed to be more open and to facilitate more communication among managers and associates, especially across units and functions. It is designed to promote cross-disciplinary perspectives and problem solving. A Harvard psychologist was consulted to help with the design and explain its value to people in the company. Yet, the change bothered people because it was dramatically different from what they had previously.

While many of the changes were based in logic and appeared to have the support of specialists who understood their value, Vasella

experienced significant resistance in the company. And, shareholders and analysts wanted better business performance to enhance the value of the firm's stock. Thus, in January 2010, it was announced that Vasella would depart the CEO position while remaining as chairman of the board. Joe Jimenez was promoted to be the new CEO. Jimenez had done a good job as head of the firm's dominant drug unit. Prior to his position with Novartis, Jimenez's experience was primarily in sales and marketing. He takes over the firm after a strong financial performance by Novartis in 2009. However, analysts are concerned about their lack of major drugs approved for the market and a recent and costly acquisition of the U.S. eye-care group, Alcon. Novartis paid $50 billion to acquire Alcon.

Thus, Jimenez has a full and challenging agenda in a highly competitive market and tough economic environment.

Sources: 2010. "New Novartis CEO: Cafepharma Reader, Former Heinz Exec," *The Wall Street Journal*, Jan. 26, at http://www.wsj.com; 2010. "Novartis Taps Joe Jimenez as CEO," *The New York Times*, Jan. 26, at http://www.nytimes. com; A. Jack & H. Simonian. 2010. "Novartis in Stealthy Pursuit of Change," *Financial Times*, Jan. 26, at http://www. ft.com; H. Plumridge. 2010. "New Novartis Chief Needs Surgery Skills," *The Wall Street Journal*, Jan. 26, at http:// www. wsj.com; N. Ouroussoff. 2009. "Many Hands, One Vision," *The New York Times*, Dec. 27, at http://www.nytimes.com; K. Capell. 2009. "Novartis: Radically Remaking its Drug Business," *BusinessWeek*, June 11, at http://www.businessweek. com; K. Capell. 2008. "Novartis Moves to the Next Stage," *BusinessWeek*, Oct. 20, at http://www.businessweek.com.

The *Experiencing Organizational Behavior* feature illustrates major changes implemented by Novartis. The changes described are substantial and represent a major departure from the way that research to identify major new drugs is commonly conducted in the industry. Overall, the changes implemented appear to be positive for the company and to hold value for future performance. They received praise from several management experts. However, the process used by the CEO to develop and implement the changes does not follow the process outlined herein. For example, rather than unfreezing the managers and associates in the organization, the CEO decided on the changes and announced them with little input from key managers. As a result, he encountered resistance from managers in the marketing unit (a very important function in the pharmaceutical industry) and from research scientists who not only had to change the focus of their research but also had to move from Switzerland to the United States, the new location of Novartis's research laboratories. The resistance likely produced less-effective changes or at least delayed the firm's ability to most effectively implement the changes. The end results were that the shareholders were unhappy with the financial performance of the firm and a new CEO was put in place to improve it. We conclude that Vasella appeared to have identified many positive changes for the company but followed a poor process to implement the changes in the company. Thus, they have not been as effective as they might have been.

The Novartis example emphasizes that the time and attention change leaders spend on the unfreezing phase can have a significant effect on the success of the change. When change leaders fail to treat unfreezing as a distinct and crucial phase, they often encounter problems, as Vasella obviously did. Without explicit attention to unfreezing, resistance to change is likely to be strong. Failure to focus attention on this phase, however, is common and is a source of failure in many change efforts. Two additional points are important. First, managers and associates should not expect all change activities to occur sequentially. Thus, activities important in one phase of the process may overlap activities necessary in the next phase.[55] For example, change leaders may engage in various activities in the moving phase while continuing to convince people of the need to change, an activity associated with the unfreezing phase. Although it is very useful to think in terms of three distinct phases, a measure of flexibility is required in actually creating change.

Second, a team of change leaders, rather than a single individual, should guide an organization through a major change effort. Relying on a single leader is risky because there is too much work required for one person to handle.[56] Deciding how best to unfreeze people, developing a vision, communicating a vision, generating small wins, and overseeing numerous change projects require more than one key change leader.[57]

In constructing the team, several factors should be considered. According to a well-known researcher and business consultant, John Kotter, four factors are crucial:[58]

1. *Position power* plays a role. Individuals with power based on their formal positions can block change or at least slow it down. Including some of these individuals on the team will leave fewer potential resisters who have the power to slow or resist the change.
2. *Informal credibility* is important. Individuals who have credibility are admired and respected and can be effective in selling change. Associates often are selected as change leaders based on this criterion.

3. *Expertise* is a relevant factor. Individuals on the team should possess knowledge related to the problems requiring the change effort and should have diverse points of view on potential solutions.
4. *Proven leadership* is crucial. The team needs individuals who can lead other managers and associates through the transition.

The size of the team is also a concern. There is little agreement on how large or small the team of change leaders should be, but the size of the organization that will be changed plays a role.[59] Six may be sufficient in a smaller organization or in a division of a larger organization. Fifteen or more may be required in a larger organization. However, as the team grows, it will be more difficult to coordinate and manage.

Important Tactical Choices

Change leaders must make many decisions. Among these are two important tactical decisions, the first involving speed and the second involving style.[60] Although these issues have no right or wrong answers, certain criteria must be considered when making informed choices.

Speed of Change

A fundamental decision in any change effort involves speed. A fast process, where unfreezing, moving, and refreezing occur quickly, can be useful if an ongoing problem will cause substantial damage in the near term.[61] Senior managers, for example, often initiate rapid change when they realize that organizational strategies or structure no longer provide value to customers. When Charlotte Beers became CEO of Ogilvy and Mather, a global advertising firm, the firm was out of step with the needs of the advertising industry, was losing important customers, and was suffering from declining overall performance. To save the firm, she and her circle of senior advisors created a vision, designed transformational change, and orchestrated its implementation in a matter of months.[62]

Overall, criteria that can be usefully considered when deciding on speed include:[63]

- *Urgency:* If the change is urgent, a faster pace is warranted.
- *Degree of support:* If the change is supported by a wide variety of people at the outset, a faster pace can be used.
- *Amount and complexity of change:* If the change is small and simple, a faster pace often can be used; but if the change is large, more time may be required.[64]
- *Competitive environment:* If competitors are poised to take advantage of existing weaknesses, a faster pace should be considered.
- *Knowledge and skills available:* If the knowledge and skills required by the new approach exist in the firm or can be easily acquired, a faster pace can be used.
- *Financial and other resources:* If the resources required by the change are on hand or easily acquired, a faster pace can be considered.

Style of Change

A second fundamental decision involves style. When using a top-down style, change leaders design the change and plan its implementation with little participation from those below them in the hierarchy. In contrast, when using a participatory style, change leaders seek the ideas and advice of those below them and then use many of those ideas.

Unfortunately, the Novartis CEO did not use a participatory style, and his top-down approach likely dulled the effectiveness of the changes he desired to implement. A transformational leadership style would have been more successful in this case.[65]

In a high-involvement organization, leaders use a participatory style whenever possible. Participation can be useful in generating ideas and developing commitment among those who will be affected by a change.[66] Participation, however, can be time-consuming and expensive, as meetings, debates, and synthesis of multiple sets of ideas take significant time. Overall, the following criteria are useful in evaluating the degree to which a participatory approach should be used:[67]

- *Urgency:* If the change is urgent, a participatory approach should not be used, as it tends to be time-consuming.
- *Degree of support:* If the idea of changing is supported initially by a wide variety of people, a participatory approach is less necessary.
- *Referent and expert power of change leaders:* When change leaders are admired and are known to be knowledgeable about pertinent issues, a participatory approach is less necessary.

Resistance to Change

Although organizations experience both internal and external pressures to change, they frequently encounter strong resistance to needed changes. **Resistance to change** involves efforts to block the introduction of new ways of doing things. Dealing with resistance is one of the most important aspects of a manager's job. In a high-involvement organization, associates also must take responsibility for helping to motivate change among their peers.

Resistance may be active or passive.[68] Individuals may actively argue and use political connections in the firm to stop a change. In extreme cases of active resistance, resisters may sabotage change efforts through illegal means. In other cases, individuals passively resist change, which is more difficult to detect. Resisters may act as though they are trying to make the change a success, but in reality they are not. This often occurs in organizations that have attempted to change too frequently in the recent past, because individuals in these organizations have become tired of change.[69]

Resistance to change can usually be traced to one or more of the following four causal factors: lack of understanding, different assessments, self-interest, and low tolerance for change.[70]

resistance to change
Efforts to block the introduction of new approaches. Some of these efforts are passive in nature, involving tactics such as verbally supporting the change while continuing to work in the old ways; other efforts are active in nature, involving tactics such as organized protests and sabotage.

Lack of Understanding

The first possible cause is lack of understanding. In some cases, individuals are unsure of what a change would entail. They resist because they do not understand the change.[71] For example, change leaders may decide to redesign jobs in a manufacturing facility using job enrichment. Such a redesign can result in substantial benefits to associates in the affected jobs, as discussed in Chapter 6. If, however, change leaders fail to explain the expected changes, some associates may begin to make false assumptions. They may, for example, believe that if job enrichment is implemented, their pay status will change from hourly wages to established salaries (with no overtime or incentive pay provided). Thus, they resist the change.

The key to avoiding or handling resistance to change based on lack of understanding is to communicate clearly what the change entails.[72] Many organizational researchers have emphasized the importance of rich communication for successful change. Meetings, articles in newsletters, and articles on company intranets are examples of possible communication tools.

Different Assessments

A second possible cause of resistance involves differing assessments of the change. Associates and managers who resist on this basis believe that the change would have more costs and fewer benefits than claimed by those who desire the change.[73] In this case, it is often not that the resisters have inaccurate or insufficient information, but rather that they understand the change but disagree with change leaders about the likely outcome. For example, a midlevel manager may resist an increase in product diversification because she sees more costs from the loss of focus than do those who are encouraging the change. Furthermore, she may see less potential for synergy across product lines than others do. Increased diversification may or may not be beneficial to a firm. Many factors are involved, and the situation is usually quite complex. Thus, honest disagreements are common when a firm is considering product-line expansion. Obviously, this is true for many other changes as well.

To prevent or deal with resistance based on different assessments, change leaders should consider including potential or actual resisters in the decision-making process.[74] This focus on participation serves two purposes. First, change leaders can ensure that they have all of the information they need to make good decisions.[75] Individuals resisting on the basis of different assessments may have more and better information than change leaders, making their resistance to change positive for the organization. Change leaders must explore why resisters feel the way they do.

Second, by emphasizing participation, change leaders can help to ensure procedural justice for actual or potential resisters.[76] In the context of organizational change, **procedural justice** is defined as perceived fairness in the decision process. Individuals are more likely to believe the process is fair and are more likely to trust the organization and change leaders if they are included in the decision process. One study showed the potential power of procedural justice. Associates in two U.S. power plants who believed they had input into change-related decisions felt more obligated to treat the organization well, trusted management to a greater degree, and expressed an intention to remain with the organization.[77]

procedural justice
In the context of organizational change, the perceived fairness of the change process.

Self-Interest

Individuals who resist change because of self-interest believe that they will lose something of value if the change is implemented.[78] Power, control over certain resources, and a valued job assignment are examples of things that could be lost. For example, the head of marketing in a small, rapidly growing firm might resist the establishment of a unit devoted to new-product development. If such a unit were established, he would lose his control over product development. Another example of self-interest is when individuals oppose an appointment to a higher-level position on the basis of gender or ethnicity.[79] Finally, managers and associates may resist change when they have no incentives to support it and could actually lose resources if changes are made such as in the current U.S. health care system (i.e., government payments are tied to specific actions and may not be made if innovations changing the treatments are made).[80]

To combat this type of resistance, change leaders can try to reason with resisters, explaining that the health of the organization is at stake. Leaders can also transfer resisters or, in extreme cases, ask them to leave the organization. Another option is to adopt a more coercive style and insist on compliance. In rare cases, when the resisters are extremely valuable to the organization and other tactics have failed or are unavailable, change leaders can negotiate in an effort to overcome the resistance.[81] Valuable resisters who are managers can be offered larger budgets or a valued new assignment for favored subordinates, for example. In the case of associates, additional vacation time might be offered. These actions, however, should be undertaken only under exceptional circumstances because they may create expectations on the part of other managers or associates.

Low Tolerance for Change

Associates and managers who resist on the basis of low tolerance for change fear the unknown. They have difficulty dealing with the uncertainty inherent in significant change. Such resistance leads to higher commitment to the current activities and thus organizational inertia (very slow or no change).[82] A manager, for example, may resist a change that seems good for the organization but that will disrupt established patterns. He may not be able to cope emotionally with the uncertainty and be concerned about having the capability to perform in the new situation.[83] Change leaders should offer support to these resisters.[84] Kind words, emotional support, and attention to training and education that properly prepare the individuals for the planned changes are appropriate tactics.

Research has shown that certain individual characteristics are associated with low tolerance for change. Lack of self-efficacy is perhaps the most important of these characteristics.[85] An associate or manager low in self-efficacy does not believe that he or she possesses or can mobilize the effort and ability needed to control events in his or her life. In the workplace, this translates into uncertainty about the capacity to perform at reasonable levels.[86] Another factor is low risk tolerance.[87] Individuals who do not tolerate risk very well often dislike major change. In a study of 514 managers from companies headquartered in Asia, Australia, Europe, and North America, poor views of self and low risk tolerance were found to harm the ability to deal with change.[88] In particular, openness to change is critical for organizations to be innovative.[89]

The DADA Syndrome

DADA syndrome
A sequence of stages—
denial, anger, depression,
and acceptance—through
which individuals can
move or in which they can
become trapped when faced
with unwanted change.

Beyond the resistance to change discussed above, change leaders must realize that associates and managers can become trapped in the so-called **DADA syndrome**—the syndrome of denial, anger, depression, and acceptance.[90] This syndrome highlights what can occur when individuals face unwanted change. In the denial stage, individuals ignore possible or current change; in the anger stage, individuals facing unwanted change become angry about the change; and in the depression stage, they experience emotional lows. Finally, in the acceptance stage, they embrace the reality of the situation and try to make the best of it. Not all individuals who experience this syndrome move through all of the stages sequentially, but many do. Some, however, remain in the anger or depression stage, resulting in negative consequences for them and the organization.

In a well-known incident, Donna Dubinsky at Apple Computer experienced the DADA syndrome.[91] Dubinsky headed the distribution function at Apple in the mid-1980s. She had performed well in her time at Apple and was considered to be a valuable part of the organization. Even so, Steve Jobs, chairman of the board at the time, began to criticize distribution and called for wholesale changes in the way this unit functioned. Dubinsky, incredulous that her unit was being questioned, decided the issue would go away on its own (denial stage). But the issue did not go away. Instead, Jobs asked the head of manufacturing in one of the operating divisions to develop a proposal for a new approach to distribution. Dubinsky still could not believe her unit would be changed, particularly without her input. Over time, however, she became defensive and challenged the criticisms (anger stage).

Transforming Cisco into a Recession-Proof Growth Machine

Cisco experienced its share of problems during the first decade of the twenty-first century. The two recessions during this time were especially unkind to technology-based firms. Yet, John Chambers, CEO of Cisco, has designed and implemented substantial changes in the organization. In his view, he is positioning the firm to be a growth machine for many years to come. To do so has required that he take several aggressive actions to transform the firm and to take these actions during a significant recession. However, because the firm has been well managed over the years, Chambers has $40 billion in cash that can be invested in aggressive actions.

First, Cisco has made a number of acquisitions and formed strategic alliances, both of which have the purpose of broadening Cisco's reach in attractive markets. For example, Cisco recently acquired companies with products and capabilities in the Internet videoconferencing, web security, and large-data-management markets. It also recently formed a joint venture, partnering with EMC, which expands Cisco's networking capabilities. These actions have special significance for Cisco's future. For example, Cisco predicts that 80 percent of the Internet data traffic will be in video form within four years.

©Steve Marcus/Reuters/Corbis

This could be especially important because Cisco is currently the largest seller of networking equipment in the world.

Cisco managers believe that collaboration will play a major role in business operations in the future, particularly to take advantage of human capital in the organization. As such organizations are likely to be decentralized networks of managers and associates working to accomplish the broad goals of the organization. The expectation is that the collaboration fostered by this environment will lead to more innovation and enhanced operational effectiveness. Some refer to this approach as collaborative social networking. And these networks will require tools that facilitate the communication and collaboration. The tools focus on video, collaboration, and virtualization.

In addition, Cisco has made substantial changes in its structure and mode of operation. The reorganization has produced a much flatter structure, with people and managers organized in teams. The teams are empowered to make decisions that commit resources and act without central management approval. Managers and teams have compensatory incentives to work with other teams (i.e., collaborate) to develop new products and take advantage of new market opportunities. The structure then represents a distributed network with the hope of making fast decisions to move into new markets shortly after the market opportunity is identified. The bold promise is, "Power to the people and profits to the company."

Chambers suggests that with these changes, his company should be able to achieve annual sales growth of 12 to 15 percent. For a company with annual sales of $36 billion, this amount of increase per year is not trivial. Given Cisco's positive record and the changes made to resemble more of a high-involvement organization, many believe that this level of growth is achievable.

Cisco made major changes in its organization largely by acquiring products and capabilities to enter markets new to the firm and by dramatically changing the organizational structure and approach to management. The decentralized and distributed social networks of managers and associates help to produce greater innovation and to act quickly to exploit opportunities after they are identified. Chambers has been more successful in making changes and in producing positive results than the

CEO of Novartis. As noted previously, although the changes made by the Novartis CEO appeared to be good ones, the process used to create the change and implement it was ineffective. The CEO at Cisco encountered

less resistance than the changes in Novartis, because Cisco empowered managers and associates who in turn helped implement the change. As a result one could predict greater future success for Cisco than for Novartis.

Sources: A. Greenberg. 2010. "Cisco Aims Telepresence at Consumers' TVs," *Forbes,* Jan. 6, at http://www.forbes.com; D. Clark. 2009. "Tech Firms Jockey Ahead of Recovery," *The Wall Street Journal,* Dec. 31, at http://www.wsj.com; J. Fortt. 2009. "Cisco: We're a Growth Machine," *Fortune,* Dec. 9, at http://www.cnnmoney.com; A. Dugdale. 2009. "Cisco's Collaboration Platform: Facebook for Business?" *Fast Company,* Nov. 9, at http://www.fastcompany.com; A.S. Cohen. 2009. "The Latest Tech Tool? People Power," *Fortune,* Nov. 9, at http://www.cnnmoney.com; A. Greenberg. 2009. "Cisco Preps for Recovery," *Forbes,* Nov. 2, at http://www.forbes.com; E. McGirt. 2008. "How Cisco's CEO John Chambers Is Turning the Tech Giant Socialist," *Fast Company,* Nov. 25, at http://www.fastcompany.com.

Concerned with the process through which Jobs was attempting to change distribution, senior management in the company protested, which led to the creation of a task force to examine distribution issues. Dubinsky continued to be defensive as a member of this task force. As it became clear that the task force would endorse Jobs's proposed changes, however, Dubinsky reached an emotional low (depression stage). She was eventually revived by conversations at a retreat for executives. There, Dubinsky realized she had not invested her considerable talents in effectively handling the criticisms and plans for change in the distribution function. She went on the offensive and asked that she be allowed to develop her own proposal for change (acceptance). She was allowed to do so, and after examining the concerns and alternatives, she recommended major changes—changes that were different from Jobs's original ideas. Dubinsky's ideas were incorporated in the final plan.

Change leaders should be sensitive to the potential for the DADA syndrome. To prevent associates and managers from entering the DADA stages or to ensure they do not become mired in the anger or depression stage, leaders must monitor their organizations for actual or potential resistance to change. If resistance is discovered, its cause must be diagnosed and addressed.

Organization Development

Leaders must recognize internal and external pressures for change and introduce initiatives designed to cope with them. In addition, leaders can proactively position their organizations to better recognize the need for change and to more easily implement change when necessary. In other words, leaders can develop their organizations so that communication, problem solving, and learning are more effective.

To achieve these goals, **organization development (OD)** is useful. Although researchers have not always agreed on the specific features of organization development, they agree that its purpose is to improve processes and outcomes in organizations.[92] OD has had its share of critics in recent years but it has produced some worthwhile results.[93]

organization development (OD)
A planned organization-wide continuous process designed to improve communication, problem solving, and learning through the application of behavioral science knowledge.

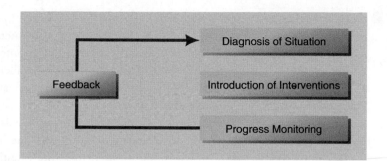

Exhibit 14-4 Basic Organization Development Model

OD can be defined as a planned, organization-wide, continuous process designed to improve communication, problem solving, and learning through the application of behavioral science knowledge.[94] With its roots in humanistic psychology, OD is grounded in values of individual empowerment and interpersonal cooperation.[95] Thus, it is consistent with the high-involvement management approach.

The Basic OD Model

The basic OD model uses a medical approach, in which organizations are treated when they suffer ill health. OD researchers and practitioners diagnose the illness, prescribe interventions, and monitor progress.[96] Exhibit 14-4 provides an overview.

Diagnosis

Diagnosis is an important step in organization development. Without effective diagnosis, managers will not understand what their organization really needs, and the chosen course of action will likely be ineffective.

Although the diagnostic approaches used by physicians and managers are similar, the tools they use vary. Over the years, physicians' diagnostic tools have become quite sophisticated (laboratory tests, CT scans, MRIs, electrocardiograms, and so on). Those of the manager, though useful, are less precise. Even so, our knowledge of diagnostic tools has increased rapidly in recent years.

Diagnostic devices for managers include interviews, surveys, group sociometric devices, process-oriented diagnosis, and accurate records (e.g., performance records). Of these tools, the most frequently used are surveys and individual and group interviews.[97] Managers can conduct many different surveys, including job-satisfaction surveys (such as the Job Description Index), organization climate or culture surveys (such as the Organizational Practices Questionnaire), job design measures (such as the Job Diagnostic Survey), and assessments of leaders (such as the Leadership Practices Inventory). In many cases, standard survey forms can be used; in other cases, surveys may need to be custom-designed for the situation. These diagnostic tools can be useful in determining needed interventions. Some organizations administer surveys to employees on a regular basis, such as annually, to identify problems.

Interventions

After the situation has been diagnosed, interventions can be prescribed. Organization development interventions include different forms of group training, team building, and job redesign.[98] The most appropriate technique will vary with the situational factors involved.

Unfortunately, there are no ready-made answers that can be used for all situations. Several of the more important techniques are described later in this chapter.

Proper implementation is crucial in organization development. For example, job enrichment may be useful when individuals desire more challenging jobs and more responsibility. Providing such jobs can enhance intrinsic motivation and satisfaction, yielding empowered individuals who are better positioned for effective problem solving and learning. OD leaders must properly prepare the individuals for job enrichment, however, even though they may have requested it. Overall, the interventions must be well planned. Increased job responsibilities often raise the question, "Don't I deserve more pay if I'm performing a more responsible job?" OD leaders must be prepared to answer such questions.

A well-trained OD specialist should play an important role in any intervention.[99] Often, managers who understand only one or two specific OD techniques attempt to use these approaches to solve whatever problem exists. But the techniques must match the situation, or the likelihood of failure is high. Furthermore, people who are not fully knowledgeable about organization development frequently have problems implementing a successful program. For example, only experts in group training, team building, or conflict resolution should implement those particular OD change techniques.

Progress Monitoring

The effects of the interventions must be evaluated after an appropriate interval.[100] The evaluation is important to ensure that the objectives have been met.[101] A common evaluation technique is the survey, which may be used to diagnose a problem and then reused after an OD technique has been implemented to determine what progress has been made toward resolving the problem. Other evaluation tools may be used as well. In any case, the main criterion for evaluation is to determine whether the original objectives have been accomplished. Some OD tools such as process consultation have evaluation processes built into them.[102]

If the evaluation shows that objectives have not been accomplished, further efforts may be necessary. A new or modified approach may be designed and implemented. The type and degree of these actions depend on why the objectives were not reached and by how far they were missed. Questions such as "Was the original process correct?" and "Was it correctly implemented?" must be answered.

Frequently, some modifications are needed to increase the positive benefits of OD work, but if care has been taken in the OD process, wholesale changes are unnecessary at this stage. Because a comprehensive OD program is continuous, the process of sensing the organization's need for development is continuous. In this way, an organization is in a constant state of renewal and regularly checks its health.

Organization Development Interventions

The interventions used to create organizational change are at the heart of organization development. Here, we describe several of the more important OD intervention techniques. Research suggests that using more than one technique is generally superior to using a single technique.[103] For convenience of discussion, we have placed the interventions into two groups: techniques directly focused on how individuals relate to one another[104] and techniques focused on structure and systems[105] (see Exhibit 14-5).

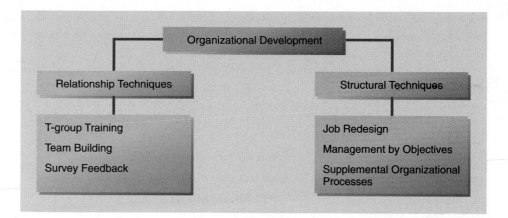

Exhibit 14-5
Organization Development Interventions

Relationship Techniques

Relationship techniques focus on how individuals perceive and respond to one another. T-group training, team building, survey feedback, and more general training are among the most important techniques in this category.

In **t-group training,** individuals participate in various interpersonal and group situations to better understand how they act, how others perceive their actions, and how others react to them.[106] In many cases, individuals involved in this type of training do not know one another before the group experience. Participating with strangers rather than work colleagues helps to promote honest behavior. T-group training is aimed at helping individual associates and managers learn about themselves in a group setting and then transfer that learning to the workplace. An individual often is able to learn about unintended negative effects created by certain types of behavior, for example, and then change that behavior, resulting in a positive effect on the workplace environment.

T-group training must be used carefully and only with a trained, qualified facilitator. The facilitator plays an important role in increasing the chances of success. The use of this technique is declining because it can produce negative outcomes for some people (e.g., those who are insecure). Thus, group participants must be chosen with great care. Neglecting to take such care is one reason that OD efforts fail.

Team building, a cornerstone of organization development, is a technique that requires members of a team to work together to understand their problems and implement solutions.[107] A team is any group of associates and/or managers who work together to accomplish a task (see Chapter 11 for additional details). The problems faced by teams usually involve substantive team tasks (e.g., technical design problems for a new-product-development team), the processes of the team (e.g., weaknesses in problem solving), and interpersonal relationships among team members (e.g., difficulties based on differences in personality).

In successful applications of team building, team members focus mostly on substantive tasks rather than on process and interpersonal issues.[108] While team members concentrate on substantive problem solving, a skilled leader can introduce interpersonal and other process guidance as needed.[109]

Overall, the team-building process can help to positively reinforce relations among team members and may be particularly useful for teams experiencing conflict, lack of cohesiveness, or ambiguous goals. Team building can be important for self-managed teams and teams that have new leaders.[110] New leaders taking over the responsibility for a team

t-group training
Group exercises in which individuals focus on their actions, how others perceive their actions, and how others generally react to them; participants often learn about unintended negative consequences of certain types of behavior.

team building
A process in which members of a team work together and with a facilitator to diagnose task, process, and interpersonal problems within the team and create solutions.

often find that team building reduces suspicion, increases trust, and promotes a healthy working relationship. At times, the use of a third-party consultant may be necessary to guide the process, particularly when conflict is present.

In summarizing their experiences, two OD researchers have offered a useful list of team-building tips:[111]

1. Get the *right people together* for
2. a large *block of uninterrupted time*
3. to work on *high-priority problems or opportunities* that
4. *they have identified* and have them work
5. in *structured ways* to enhance the likelihood of
6. *realistic solutions and action plans,* which are then
7. *implemented* enthusiastically and
8. *followed up to assess* actual versus expected results.

survey feedback
Data obtained from questionnaires; managers receive the data for their units and are expected to hold unit meetings to discuss problems.

The **survey feedback** technique emphasizes the collection and use of data from questionnaires.[112] Although all OD efforts involve collecting data through surveys and interviews as part of diagnosing the organization's situation, surveys can also be used as an intervention following diagnosis. If, for example, the diagnosis suggests that poor motivation among associates is driven partly by a feeling of lack of input, using surveys more frequently may be helpful in changing this feeling.

The first step in the survey feedback technique involves collecting data on how individuals feel about various aspects of leadership and interpersonal relations within the unit, as well as broader organizational issues. Each manager in the organization receives a summary of the survey results for her unit. An internal or external OD consultant meets with the manager to discuss the results. A second meeting is then arranged for the manager to present the findings to associates and lower-level managers. The OD consultant often attends this unit meeting to explain any technical aspects of the data. The unit members then work together to interpret the findings, understand problems, and find solutions.

It is important that all information from a survey be discussed. Positive information is crucial in helping to build and maintain a positive climate. Negative information is critical for understanding problems.

training
A process used in OD to help managers and associates to gain skills and capabilities needed to accomplish tasks in their jobs.

Training is a process used in OD to help managers and associates to gain skills and capabilities needed to accomplish tasks in their jobs.[113] It is common, for example, to provide managers leadership training to help them become more effective leaders. Training can also enrich managers' and associates' capabilities that help prepare them for future positions in the organization. Such training provides the organization with more flexibility, allowing it take advantage of new opportunities that are identified.[114] Training is a common tool used universally by all types of organizations. In addition, training is a global phenomenon. For example, most multinational enterprises have their managers and associates participate in training in their subsidiaries throughout the world. However, they do have to adjust their processes and content to adapt to local cultural values.[115]

Structural Techniques

Structural OD techniques, as the name implies, involve adjustments in the organization's structure. In the field of organization development, some structural interventions are focused on changing tasks; others are focused on changing the method of setting task objectives; and still others are broadly focused on communication, problem solving, and learning. Commonly used techniques include job redesign, management by objectives (MBO), and supplemental organizational elements.

The **job redesign** technique may include job enlargement, job enrichment, or both.[116] As discussed in Chapter 6, job enlargement involves adding tasks that offer more variety and that may require the use of different skills. The additional tasks, however, are not of greater complexity. Some refer to this as horizontal loading. Job enrichment involves adding more complex tasks, generally by incorporating tasks formerly handled by managers (e.g., scheduling of maintenance on a production machine) and staff specialists (e.g., making quality-control decisions). Thus, associates whose jobs are enriched have greater responsibility because they begin to manage their own jobs individually or as members of self-managing teams.

Much of the emphasis on the redesign of jobs in organization development grew out of controversy surrounding boring, repetitive tasks often seen in mass-production systems. Many observers, believing that repetitive tasks led to an alienated workforce, proposed to enrich jobs by providing more challenging tasks. Through enrichment, associates become more engaged problem solvers. Because managers no longer need to closely supervise the routine activities of associates, they can focus more of their attention on helping to solve key organizational problems and helping to establish a learning orientation in their units. In current organizations, jobs are often enriched by assigning coordination responsibilities related to interdependent tasks. And, these tasks frequently require collaboration with people and units based in other countries.[117]

When an organization uses **management by objectives (MBO)**, individuals negotiate task objectives with their managers at each level in the organization. (See Chapter 6 for a more detailed discussion of participation in setting goals and the motivational properties of goals.) This technique changes the objective-setting structure from one determined by the supervisor to one in which both supervisor and subordinates participate. Once set, objectives are used in performance assessments.

As an OD technique, MBO involves several specific steps.[118] First, information collected from organization members, senior managers, and perhaps others is used to diagnose organizational problems. This diagnosis provides a focus for MBO efforts. After diagnosis, senior managers and others can define major organizational objectives. Next, workshops about the MBO process generally are conducted for all managers to help them understand and use the technique correctly.

Objectives for middle managers are then defined by teams of middle and senior managers. Objectives for lower-level managers are set by teams of lower-level and middle managers, with senior managers also possibly involved. Finally, objectives for associates are established by teams of associates and managers. The participatory approach embedded in MBO often yields associates and managers who are more satisfied with and committed to the organization. As a result, they are more likely to be enthusiastic problem solvers who are open to learning.

Management by objectives can be a useful technique, but it does carry risks.[119] First, objectives can be rather static and inflexible, while the environment is constantly changing. People may have to change their focus and what they do in order to meet changing environmental demands. Second, an associate's accomplishments are often influenced by factors outside of his control. Thus, performance assessments tied to meeting objectives can be unfair. Third, a strong focus on objective attainment may mean that intangible aspects of the job for which objectives have not been set are ignored.

Finally, senior managers can create **supplemental organizational** processes to enhance communication, problem solving, and learning. Examples of such processes include

job redesign
Enlargement or enrichment of jobs; enrichment is the better method to enhance motivation for effective problem solving, communication, and learning.

management by objectives (MBO)
A management process in which individuals negotiate task objectives with their managers and then are held accountable for attainment of those objectives.

supplemental organizational processes
Processes in which associates and/or managers have ongoing meetings for the purpose of understanding and addressing important problems.

quality circles, safety councils, regular union-management meetings, and periodically scheduled management retreats. At the core, these supplemental processes involve ongoing meetings of associates and/or managers for the purpose of understanding and addressing important problems. Team building, with its attention to process and interpersonal issues, sometimes is involved.

Senior managers at General Electric used a number of OD interventions to improve honest communication, problem solving, and learning. Their efforts had remarkable results.[120] The management–union meetings implemented in the transportation division constituted a supplemental organizational process. Work-out was also a supplemental process, and it involved aspects of team building as well. The boundaryless organization involved job redesign, as individuals were expected to search across unit lines for ideas—an activity formerly outside their domain. Many analysts believe that the work-out and boundaryless organization concepts contributed to GE's phenomenal performance during the 20 years of Jack Welch's tenure as CEO. During this time, GE created more value for shareholders than any other company in the world.[121]

Beginning with the efforts of Thomas Edison, over the years GE has provided significant advances in many useful products, including the incandescent light bulb, x-ray equipment, the electric fan, radios, TVs, and turbines. But despite GE's history of innovation in product development and its overall success, the company had become stale and out of step with its environment by the time Welch took over as CEO in 1981. Many associates and managers were unhappy and unproductive, and financial performance was beginning to decline. Internal processes and structures were hindering rather than helping. But, OD interventions helped to create a healthier company. Through these interventions, associates and lower-level managers became more motivated to help identify needed changes, middle and senior managers had better forums for information exchange, and everyone had greater incentives to develop, borrow, and share ideas. The outcome was highly positive for GE's shareholders, managers, and associates.

Organizational Learning

Most organizational development and change require learning. The changes may be based on learning new capabilities, new processes, or adding new knowledge that helps the organization more effectively use its current capabilities and processes. Thus, managing organizational change entails managing knowledge transfers and development.[122] Learning how to more effectively use current knowledge is referred to as **exploitative learning**. Alternatively, **exploratory learning** involves creating new knowledge and being innovative.[123]

exploitative learning
Learning how to more effectively use current knowledge.

exploratory learning
Creating new knowledge and being innovative.

As explained earlier, some of the OD techniques also involve learning about relationships and building relationship skills.[124] Some of this learning can eventually be integrated into and enrich current organizational routines (e.g., regular processes and approaches for problem solving) or create new ones.[125] But, it is critical to emphasize that organizational change is successful in the long term only if learning occurs. For example, the changes that enhanced GE's phenomenal performance during Jack Welch's tenure as CEO were based on managers learning how to make effective decisions that created value for the organization. And, in turn, managers must help the associates who work with her to learn as well.[126] Individual learning is important to solicit creative ideas from associates and to build their capabilities to participate in problem-solving activities important in high-involvement organizations.[127]

Organization Development across Cultures

The growth of multinational corporations and the global marketplace requires that the cultural implications of OD programs be considered. Behavioral science techniques may not work the same way in different cultures, and methods of managing successful organizations can vary across cultures. Managers hoping to implement an OD program in a culture different from their own must avoid an ethnocentric attitude (assuming that everyone is similar to those back home) as well as stereotyping.

To implement OD successfully in different cultures, those involved should demonstrate the following qualities:

- *Flexibility*—openness to new approaches, ideas, and beliefs and willingness to change one's own behavior
- *Knowledge of specific cultures*—understanding of the beliefs and behavior patterns of different cultures (see Chapter 3 for a discussion of cultural differences)
- *Interpersonal sensitivity*—the ability to listen to and resolve problems with people from different cultures[128]

THE STRATEGIC LENS

Organizations must adapt to their external environments in order to survive, grow, and achieve financial success. Organizations design their strategies to engage in actions that give them an advantage over their competitors. Because most organizations exist in dynamic environments, they have to adjust their strategies regularly. Implementing strategies and adjustments to them requires the involvement and support of all managers and associates in the organization. Therefore, identifying the need for major changes and implementing those changes are critical determinants of organizational success. Managers must overcome resistance to change and effectively use the human capital in the organization to achieve and sustain a competitive advantage. Yet, the largest challenge in creating organizational change is in changing the behavior of people. This conclusion is supported by research showing that 90 percent of people who have serious heart disease find it highly difficult to change their lifestyle even though they understand the importance of doing so for their personal health.[129] One can easily surmise that if people cannot change their lifestyle when it affects their health, changing their behavior for the good of the organization is likely to be even more difficult. Research also shows that events creating a need for substantial change (often referred to as "discontinuous change") rarely trigger a response until they are perceived as a threat to survival.[130]

The examples of major changes implemented at Starbucks, Cisco, and GE show the importance of managing organizational change, as well as the potential importance of OD interventions. The major organizational changes implemented at GE are reportedly the primary reason that Jack Welch enjoyed so much success as CEO during his 20-plus years in that role. Alternatively, the major changes recently implemented at Starbucks and Cisco are positioning them to be successful in the future. Developing and implementing effective organizational strategies and managing organizational change are interdependent.

Critical Thinking Questions

1. Why do organizations need to make changes on a regular basis? What are the major causes of these changes?

2. Why is it so difficult for people to change their behavior, even when they know it is important to do so?

3. If you were in a managerial position and believed that a major change in your unit's structure was needed, what actions would you take to ensure that the change was made effectively?

What This Chapter Adds to Your Knowledge Portfolio

In our final chapter, we have discussed change in organizations. More specifically, we have discussed pressures for change, a three-phase change model, two critical tactical decisions, and resistance to change. We have also examined organization development, offering a definition and basic model, along with a set of techniques. In summary, we have made the following points:

- Organizations experience pressures for change, some of which are internal. Aspiration–performance discrepancies constitute one internal source of pressure. These discrepancies are simply differences between desired and actual performance. Past aspirations, past performance, and comparisons with others affect today's aspirations. Life-cycle forces constitute a second internal source of pressure. When organizations grow, pressure tends to build at certain predictable points, forcing organizations to respond. If an organization responds effectively, it tends to move through several stages: entrepreneurial, collectivity, formalization, and elaboration. Changes in the persons occupying top management positions often produce broader organizational changes. First, new managers are not committed to previous strategies and decisions made. Second, new managers bring unique ideas and perhaps a different vision for the organization. In turn, these reduce resistance to change and provide directions for change.

- Organizations experience a host of external pressures for change. Such pressures originate with technological advances, the introduction or removal of government regulations, changes in societal values, shifting political dynamics, changes in demographics, and growing international interdependencies.

- Planned change entails deliberate efforts to move an organization or a subunit from its current state to a new state. Such change is typically thought of as a three-phase process comprising unfreezing, transforming, and refreezing. Unfreezing involves providing a rationale for change, producing minor levels of guilt or anxiety about not changing, and creating a psychological sense of safety concerning the change. Transforming involves providing information that supports the proposed change and creating actual change. Refreezing focuses on implementing evaluation systems to track expected new behaviors and training systems to ensure continuous upgrading of relevant knowledge and skills. It also involves creating permanent reward structures to reinforce the new behaviors, as well as hiring and promotion systems that support the new approaches.

- Decisions related to speed and style must be made in all planned change projects. Whether movement toward change should be fast or slow depends on the urgency of the change, the degree of support for changing, the amount or complexity of the change, the competitive environment, the knowledge and skills available to support the change, and the availability of financial and other resources necessary to implement the change. Style involves using a top-down or participatory approach. Key criteria for this decision are the urgency of the change, the degree of support for changing, the referent and expert power of change leaders, and organizational norms.

- Resistance to change can be traced to a general set of causes: lack of understanding, different assessments, self-interest, and/or low tolerance for change. To address lack of understanding, change leaders should ensure proper communication about proposed changes. To address different assessments, leaders should include actual or potential change resisters in the decision-making process in order to learn as much as possible about their thinking and to create a sense that all voices are being heard. To address self-interest, leaders must consider a host of tactics, including transferring resisters or even terminating their employment, using a coercive style to ensure compliance, and in rare situations, negotiating compliance. Finally, to address low tolerance for change, change leaders should offer emotional support and ensure proper education and training to break the inertia.

- Individuals facing unwanted change may move through a series of stages known as denial, anger, depression, and acceptance. Change leaders must understand this so-called DADA syndrome. To prevent associates and others from experiencing it, they must monitor their organizations for potential and actual resistance to change and deal effectively with resistance when it is identified.

- Organization development is an applied field of study focused on improving processes and outcomes in organizations. It can be formally defined as a planned, organization-wide, continuous process designed to improve communication, problem solving, and learning. Because it has roots in humanistic psychology, it is grounded in values of individual empowerment and interpersonal cooperation. The basic OD model has three steps: diagnosis, intervention, and progress monitoring.

? back to the knowledge objectives

1. What are the three major sources of internal pressure for organizational change? In your opinion, which of these three is most difficult to handle? Why?
2. What are the six major sources of external pressure for organizational change? In your opinion, which of these is most difficult to handle? Why?
3. What is involved in each phase of the unfreezing–transforming–refreezing model of planned change?
4. What are the factors to consider in deciding whether a fast or slow approach to change is best? What are the factors to consider in deciding whether a top-down or participatory approach to change is best? Describe a situation in which you were either a change recipient or a change leader and a poor choice was made for at least one of these two decisions (use an example from an organization in which you currently work or formerly worked, or use a voluntary organization, a church, a sports team, or a fraternity/sorority).
5. Compare the four basic causes of resistance to change. If you had to choose one, which would you prefer to deal with as a manager, and why?
6. What is the DADA syndrome?
7. What is organization development? Provide a definition as well as a basic model. A number of interventions can be used in organization development. As a manager, which of these interventions would you prefer to use, and why?

- The various interventions used in organization development can be classified as either relationship techniques or structural techniques. Relationship techniques, which focus on how individuals perceive and respond to one another, include t-group training, team building, survey feedback, and more general skills training. Structural techniques, which involve adjustments to the structural aspects of an organization, include job redesign, management by objectives, and supplemental structural elements. OD techniques involve organizational learning in order to create the desired change.

- Cultural differences must be considered when organization development techniques are being used. Techniques must be chosen in light of the prevailing culture. To implement OD successfully in different cultures, those involved should be flexible, understand the various cultures, and possess interpersonal sensitivity.

Thinking about Ethics

1. The entrepreneurial stage of an organization's life cycle is an exciting time. But while the founders are deciding how they will enter new markets and what products they will offer, do they have any obligation to consider the general public's interests in these decisions? In this chapter, we suggested that managers can adopt a coercive style to overcome resistance to change when it is based on self-interest. Do managers have any responsibility to people whose resistance is based on self-interest? Explain.

2. When implementing OD interventions, how should managers deal with people who have low self-efficacy?

3. What ethical issues are involved in implementing major organizational changes in which a large number of associates are laid off? How should these issues be handled?

4. Suppose you identify a person going through the DADA process in response to an organizational change. Should you intervene or leave the person alone to move through the stages on his or her own? Explain your answer. If the person is in the anger stage, how can you intervene successfully?

Key Terms

aspiration–performance
    discrepancies, p. 531
life-cycle forces, p. 532
changes in top management,
    p. 534
planned change, p. 539
unfreezing, p. 540
transforming, p. 540
refreezing, p. 540

resistance to change, p. 544
procedural justice, p. 545
DADA syndrome, p. 546
organization development
    (OD), p. 548
t-group training, p. 551
team building, p. 551
survey feedback, p. 552
training, p. 552

job redesign, p. 553
management by objectives
    (MBO), p. 553
supplemental organizational
    processes, p. 553
exploitative learning, p. 554
exploratory learning, p. 554

Human Resource Management Applications

The Human Resource Management (HRM) function likely plays an important role in helping the organization to change as it desires and to achieve the objectives of that change. For example, they should have a small group of people who carefully diagnose the pressures for changes and to develop recommendations as to what changes should be made. This activity may be a part of an *organization development* unit within the HRM function.

In addition, the HRM function is commonly in charge of the organization development techniques used in the organization. They either have an internal team to design and implement them or they hire an external consultant to do so. These include *t-group training, team building, survey feedback,* and more general *skills training.*

HRM also commonly guides *job redesign* programs and helps implement *management-by-objectives* programs along with any other techniques designed to help managers and associates learn new capabilities and improve the job performance.

---

building your human capital

An Assessment of Low Tolerance for Change

People differ in their tolerance for change. Low self-efficacy and low risk tolerance are two important factors that affect tolerance for change. Although an individual's self-efficacy and risk tolerance may vary from situation to situation, overall scores on these factors provide insight into general tendencies. Understanding these tendencies can help you to understand how and why you behave as you do. In this installment of Building Your Human Capital, we present an assessment tool for efficacy and risk.

Instructions

In this assessment, you will read 19 phrases that describe people. Use the rating scale below to indicate how accurately each phrase describes you. Rate yourself as you generally are now, not as you wish to be in the future, and rate yourself as you honestly see yourself. Keep in mind that very few people have extreme scores on all or even most of the items (a "1" or a "5" is an extreme score); most people have midrange scores for many of the items. Read each item carefully, and then circle the number that corresponds to your choice from the rating scale that follows.

1	2	3	4	5
Not at all like me	Somewhat unlike me	Neither like nor unlike me	Somewhat like me	Very much like me

1. Enjoy being reckless	1	2	3	4	5
2. Become overwhelmed by events	1	2	3	4	5
3. Would never go hang-gliding or bungee-jumping	1	2	3	4	5
4. Readily overcome setbacks	1	2	3	4	5
5. Take risks	1	2	3	4	5
6. Am often down in the dumps	1	2	3	4	5
7. Would never make a high-risk investment	1	2	3	4	5
8. Can manage many things at the same time	1	2	3	4	5
9. Seek danger	1	2	3	4	5
10. Feel that I am unable to deal with things	1	2	3	4	5
11. Stick to the rules	1	2	3	4	5
12. Can tackle anything	1	2	3	4	5
13. Know how to get around rules	1	2	3	4	5
14. Am afraid of many things	1	2	3	4	5
15. Avoid dangerous situations	1	2	3	4	5
16. Think quickly	1	2	3	4	5
17. Am willing to try anything once	1	2	3	4	5
18. Need reassurance	1	2	3	4	5
19. Seek adventure	1	2	3	4	5

Scoring Key

To determine your score, combine your responses to the items above as follows:

Self-efficacy = (Item 4 + Item 8 + Item 12 + Item 16) + (30 − (Item 2 + Item 6 + Item 10 + Item 14 + Item 18))

Tolerance for risk = (Item 1 + Item 5 + Item 9 + Item 13 + Item 17 + Item 19) + (24 − (Item 3 + Item 7 + Item 11 + Item 15))

Scores for self-efficacy can range from 9 to 45. Scores of 36 or above may be considered high, while scores of 18 or below may be considered low. Scores for risk tolerance can range from 10 to 50. Scores of 40 or above may be considered high, while scores of 20 or below may be considered low.

Source: International Personality Item Pool. 2001. A Scientific Collaboration for the Development of Advanced Measures of Personality Traits and Other Individual Differences, at http://ipip.ori.org.

an organizational behavior moment
Organization Development at KBTZ

KBTZ is a large television station located in a major metropolitan area in the United States. The station is one of the largest revenue producers in its market and employs more than 180 people, considerably more than its closest competitors. It is a subsidiary of a large corporation that has diversified interests in other businesses as well as the communications field. KBTZ represents a significant portion of the corporation's profit base.

Over the past few years, substantial investments have been made in the television station by the parent corporation. These investments have not only resulted in significant tax advantages but also have established KBTZ as the local television leader in the use of sophisticated electronic equipment. The station's physical plant was remodeled at considerable expense to accommodate the new equipment and to boost its image as the leader in the market. KBTZ is a successful business and a respected member of the metropolitan community. However, in part because of the recent changes in the station and in part because of its desire to maintain its established success, the station has requested that a consultant examine important problems. You are the consultant.

In your initial meeting with Valerie Diaz, the president and general manager of KBTZ, she explained her perceptions of key problems facing the station.

> One of our biggest problems is the high stress to which our managers and associates are exposed. This is especially true with respect to time deadlines. There is no such thing as slack time in television. For example, when it is precisely six o'clock, we must be on the air with the news. All of the news material, local reporting, news interviews, and so on must be processed, edited, and ready to go at six. We can't have any half-prepared material or extended deadlines, or we lose the audience and, most likely, our sponsors. I believe this situation causes a great deal of conflict and turnover among our employees. We have a number of well-qualified and motivated employees, some of whom work here because of the glamour and excitement. But we also have a lot of problems.

Valerie concluded by saying, "I've asked you here because I believe the station needs an outside viewpoint. Our employee turnover is about 35 percent, which is too high. We are having trouble hiring qualified people who fit our culture and who can help us deal with the challenges. We must eliminate the conflicts and develop a cohesive organization to retain our profit and market-leading positions. I would like to hire you as a consultant for this job. I want you to monitor our operations and diagnose our problems."

You have now collected data within each department (there are seven departments based on function, as discussed below). All department heads have been interviewed, while other employees have responded to questionnaires concerning organizational culture and job satisfaction. The information collected during this diagnosis phase has been summarized as follows.

Interviews with Department Heads

Business Manager: "I'm very new in this job and haven't really learned the ropes yet. I previously worked in sales and in the general manager's office. This is my first managerial position, and I need help in managing my department, because I don't have any management training."

News Director: "Let me be frank with you. I've worked for the big network, and the only reason I'm here is because I wanted to come back home to live. I don't think we need you here. We don't need any new 'management programs.' My department functions smoothly, my people are creative, and I don't want you messing us up with the latest fad program."

Operations Manager: "We truly have the best department in the station. I believe in Valerie's management of the station. I also believe in working my people hard. Nobody lags in this department, or out they go. Our only problems are with the news director's people, who are confused all of the time, and the engineering group, which is lazy and uncooperative. Our effectiveness depends on these groups. I think the chief engineer is incompetent. Get rid of him, shape up the news group and the engineers, and you'll have done a great job."

Chief Engineer: "Things go pretty well most of the time, except for the unreasonableness of certain people in other departments. Some people expect us to drop whatever we're doing and immediately repair some malfunctioning equipment in their area. This is sophisticated equipment, and it can take several hours just to determine the cause of the failure. The news people just have to treat their equipment better, and the operations manager—he's up here nearly every day screaming about something. One of these days I'm going to punch his lights out!"

Program Director: "My department is okay, but the station is missing a lot of opportunities in other areas. We have a lot of people problems in some departments, especially news and sales. The chief engineer is incompetent, and the operations manager pushes his lower-level managers and associates too hard—never lets them make any decisions or take any responsibilities. The general manager, Valerie Diaz, doesn't want to face up to these problems."

Promotion Manager: "We're a small, friendly group. We have few problems—except with the news group people, who think they know more than we do. But that's just a small problem. I would like a little training in how to deal with people—motivation, communication, and that sort of stuff."

Sales Manager: "Things are just great in our department. To be sure, the sales reps complain sometimes, but I just remind them that they're the highest-paid people in the station. I think Mom [Valerie Diaz] is doing a great job as general manager of the station."

Survey of Departments

Business Office and Programming Departments. The survey showed individuals in these departments to have generally positive attitudes. Job satisfaction was somewhat mixed but still positive. These individuals did, however, have two important negative perceptions of their task environment. First, they thought that their department heads and the general manager could handle downward communication better. Second, there were several unsolicited comments about being underpaid relative to other station employees.

News Department. Managers and associates in the news department reported very high satisfaction with their jobs but extreme dissatisfaction with the department head (the news director) and very negative attitudes toward their overall work environment. Communication between managers and associates was perceived to be almost nonexistent. Associates complained of very low rewards, including pay, promotion opportunities, and managerial praise. They also complained of constant criticism, which was the only form of managerial feedback on performance. In addition, in spite of their high job satisfaction, they believed that the negative factors led them to be poorly motivated.

The severity of the problems in this department was highlighted when some associates reported that they weren't certain who their immediate manager was, because both the assignments editor and the assistant news director gave them assignments. They also reported that creativity (thought to be important in their jobs) was discouraged by the director's highly authoritarian and structured style. Many employees resented the news director, referring to him as erratic, caustic, and alcoholic.

Operations Department. Most of the operations associates were satisfied with their jobs and reported pride in their department. However, satisfaction with immediate managers was mixed. Furthermore, some associates had very positive feelings about the department head, but most held him in low regard. The associates tended to feel overworked (reporting an average 74-hour work week) and thought the department head expected too much. They also thought they were underpaid relative to their task demands, and they criticized managerial feedback on their performance. They noted that the department head never praised positive performance—he only reprimanded them for poor performance. They also reported concern over the conflict with engineering, which they believed should and could be resolved.

Engineering Department. The survey revealed that members of this department were very dissatisfied with their jobs and immediate managers. Responses also showed that department members perceived a high level of conflict between themselves and the operations and news departments, especially the operations department. They also believed the department head did not support them and that managers and associates in other departments held them in low regard. They noted that they never had department meetings and that they rarely received feedback on their performance from the chief engineer.

Promotions Department. The survey showed this department to have very positive attitudes. Job satisfaction was high, and everyone viewed their work environment positively. The few negative comments were primarily directed toward the "ineffectiveness" of the news department.

Sales Department. Very few individuals from the sales department responded to the survey. To find out why they hadn't received responses, the consultant approached several salespersons for private discussions. Nearly all of them indicated that they couldn't complete the survey honestly. As one stated, "My attitudes about this place are largely negative, and my department head is the station manager's son. I'd lose my job today if he knew what I really thought about him."

Discussion Questions

1. Identify the basic problems at KBTZ.
2. Which OD techniques would you consider using, and why?

---

team exercise
Identifying Change Pressures and Their Effects

Procedure

1. With the aid of the instructor, the class will be divided into four- or five-person groups.
2. The groups will be assigned several tasks:
   - Each group should identify several specific change pressures that are acting on their institution (e.g., college, university). The group should record these pressures as external or internal.

- Once the change pressures have been identified, the group should determine and record the effects of each change pressure on the institution.

- Each group should prepare a list of recommendations concerning what the institution should do to deal with these change pressures.

- Finally, each group should conduct an analysis of possible resistance to change. Who or what groups might resist each recommendation and why? How should the possible resistance be handled?

3. The instructor will call on each group in class, asking it to present its lists of (1) change pressures, (2) effects of change pressures, (3) recommendations, and (4) people/groups that might resist change.

4. The instructor will guide a discussion of this exercise.

Endnotes

1. Hitt, M.A., Ireland, R.D., & Hoskisson, R.E. 2009. *Strategic management: Competitiveness and globalization* (8th ed). Mason, OH: South-Western.

2. Walsh, J.P., Meyer, A.D., & Schoonhoven, C.B. 2006. A future for organization theory: Living in and living with changing organizations. *Organization Science*, 17: 657–671; Fiss, P.C., & Zajac, E.J. 2006. The symbolic management of strategic change: Sensegiving via framing and decoupling. *Academy of Management Journal*, 49: 1173–1193.

3. Huber, G.P. 2004. *The necessary nature of future firms: Attributes of survivors in a changing world.* Thousand Oaks, CA: Sage Publications.

4. Chen, W.-R., & Miller, K.D. 2007. Situational and institutional determinants of firms' R&D search intensity. *Strategic Management Journal*, 28: 368–381; Cyert, R.M., & March, J.G. 1963. *A behavioral theory of the firm.* Englewood Cliffs, NJ: Prentice Hall.

5. Berry, H. 2010. Why do firms divest? *Organization Science*, in press.

6. Rao, S.K. 2009. Re-engineering a product portfolio: Case study of a pharmaceutical merger, *Journal of Business Strategy*, 30 (6): 52–62; Wan, W.P., & Yui, D.W. 2009. From crisis to opportunity: Environmental jolt, corporate acquisitions, and firm performance. *Strategic Management Journal*, 30: 791–801.

7. Cyert & March, *A behavioral theory of the firm*; Mezias, S.F., Chen Y.-R., & Murphy, P.R. 2002. Aspiration level adaptation in an American financial services organization: A field study. *Management Science*, 48: 1285–1300.

8. Morrow, J.L., Jr., Sirmon, D.G., Hitt, M.A., & Holcomb, T.R. 2007. Creating value in the face of declining performance: Firm strategies and organizational recovery. *Strategic Management* Journal, 28: 271–283.

9. Mezias, Chen, & Murphy, Aspiration level adaptation in an American financial services organization.

10. de Figueiredo, J.M., & Kyle, M.K. 2006. Surviving the gales of creative destruction: The determinants of product turnover. *Strategic Management Journal*, 27: 241–264; Greiner, L.E. 1998. Evolution and revolution as organizations grow. *Harvard Business Review*, 76(3): 55–68; Flamholtz, E., & Hua, W. 2002. Strategic organizational development, growing pains and corporate financial performance: An empirical test. *European Management Journal*, 20: 527–536; Lynall, M.D., Goleen, B.R., & Hillman, A.J. 2003.

11. Board composition from adolescence to maturity: A multitheoretic view. *Academy of Management Review*, 28: 416–431.

11. Smith, W.S. 2009. Vitality in business: Executing a new strategy at Unilever. *Journal of Business Strategy*, 30 (4): 31–41.

12. Arthaud-Day, M.L., Certo, S.T., Dalton C.M., & Dalton, D.R. 2006. A changing of the guard: Executive and director turnover following corporate financial restatements. *Academy of Management Journal*, 49: 1119–1136.

13. Shimizu, K., & Hitt, M.A. 2005. What constrains or facilitates divestitures of formerly acquired firms? The effects of organizational inertia. *Journal of Management*, 31: 50–72.

14. Hayward, M., & Shimizu, K. 2006. De-commitment to losing strategic action: Evidence from divestiture of poorly performing acquisitions. *Strategic Management Journal*, 27: 541–557.

15. Yokota, R., & Mitsuhashi, H. 2008. Attributive change in top management teams as a driver of strategic change. *Asia Pacific Journal of Management*, 25: 297–315.

16. Boyne, G.J., & Meier, K.J. 2009. Environmental change, human resources and organizational turnaround. *Journal of Management Studies*, 46: 835–863.

17. Zhang, Y. 2008. Information asymmetry and the dismissal of newly appointed CEOs: An empirical investigation. *Strategic Management Journal*, 29: 859–872.

18. Simsek, Z., Heavey, C., & Veiga, J.F. 2010. The impact of CEO core self-evaluation on the firm's entrepreneurial orientation. *Strategic Management Journal*, 31: 110–119.

19. Huber, *The necessary nature of future firms.*

20. Bjork, B.-C., Roos, A., & Lauri, M. 2009. Scientific journal publishing: Yearly volume and open access availability. *Informationresearch*, at http://informationr.net, March.

21. Narin, F., & Olivastro, D. 1998. Linkage between patents and papers: An interim EPO/U.S. Comparison. *Scientometrics*, 41: 51–59.

22. U.S. Patent and Trademark Office. 2000. U.S. patent studies report. Washington, DC: Government Printing Office.

23. U.S. Patent and Trademark Office, U.S. patent statistics report.

24. Sinha, R., & Noble, C.H. 2008. The adoption of radical manufacturing technologies and firm survival. *Strategic Management Journal*, 29: 943–962.

25. Benner, M.J. 2010. Securities analysts and incumbent response to radical technological change: Evidence from digital photography and internet telephony. *Organization Science*, 21: 42–62; Lin, Z., Zhao, X., Ismail, K.M., & Carley, K.M. 2006. Organizational restructuring in response to crises: Lessons from computational modeling and real-world cases. *Organization Science*, 17: 598–618.

26. Taylor, A. 2010. The next generation: Technology adoption and integration through internal competition in new product development. *Organization Science*, 21; 23–41.

27. Bell, J., & Power, S. 2004. Nissan is seeking U.S. exemption on fuel efficiency. *Wall Street Journal*, March 10, p. D.12; Draper, H. 2004. "Do not call" list forces marketers to seek new ways to get attention. *Wall Street Journal*, July 7, p. 1; Latour, A., & Squeo, A.M. 2004. FCC to urge telecoms to settle on local network-access issue. *Wall Street Journal*, March 31, p. D.4.

28. Spell, C.S., & Blum, T.C. 2006. Adoption of workplace substance abuse prevention programs: Strategic choice and institutional perspectives. *Academy of Management Journal*, 49: 1125–1142.

29. Coeurderoy, R., & Murray, G. 2008. Regulatory environments and the location decision: Evidence from early foreign market entries of new-technology-based firms. *Journal of International Business Studies*, 39: 670–687; Peng, M.W., Wang, D.Y.L., & Jiang, Y. 2008. An institution-based view of international business strategy: A focus on emerging economies. *Journal of International Business Studies*, 39: 920–936.

30. Cuervo-Cazurra, A. 2008. The effectiveness of laws against bribery. *Journal of International Business Studies*, 39: 634–651.

31. Hoffmann, V.H., Trautmann, T., & Hamprecht, J. 2009. Regulatory uncertainty: A reason to postpone investments? Not necessary. *Journal of Management Studies*, 46: 1225–1253.

32. Rajagopalan, N., & Zhang, Y. 2009. Recurring failures in corporate governance: A global disease? *Business Horizons*, 52: 545–552.

33. Spell & Blum, Adoption of workplace substance abuse prevention programs.

34. Spanish Resources: Overview—Hispanics in North Carolina, 2007. CarolinasAGC, at http://www.cagc.org/spanish_res/hisp_nc.cfm, May 21; Hummel, M. 2004. Speaking the language: Booming Spanish-speaking population alters business strategies. *Greensboro News Record*, May 16, p. E.1.

35. Hitt, M.A., Ireland, R.D., & Hoskisson, R.E. 2011. *Strategic management: Competitiveness and globalization* (9th ed). Mason, OH: Cengage South-Western.

36. Hitt, M.A., Tihanyi, L., Miller T., & Connelly, B. 2006. International diversification: Antecedents, outcomes and moderators. *Journal of Management*, 32: 831–867; Meyer, K.E. 2006. Globalfocusing: From domestic conglomerates to global specialists. *Journal of Management Studies*, 43: 1109–1144.

37. Bowen, D.E., & Inkpen, A.C. 2009. Exploring the role of "global mindset" in change in international contexts, *Journal of Applied Behavioral Science*, 45: 230–260.

38. Mathews, J.A., & Zander, I. 2007. The international entrepreneurial dynamics of accelerated internationalisation. *Journal of International Business Studies*, 38: 387–403; Szulanski, G., & Jensen, R.J. 2006. Presumptive adaptation and the effectiveness of knowledge transfer. *Strategic Management Journal*, 27: 937–957.

39. Lee, S.-H. & Makhija, M. 2009. Flexibility in internationalization: Is it valuable during an economic crisis? *Strategic Management Journal*, 30: 537–555.

40. Koka, B.R., Madhavan, R., & Prescott, J.E. 2006. The evolution of interfirm networks: Environmental effects on patterns of network change. *Academy of Management Review*, 31: 721–737.

41. Latta, G. 2009. A process model of organizational change in cultural context (OC3 Model). *Journal of Leadership and Organizational Studies*, 16: 19–37.

42. See, for example, Kanter, R.M., Stein, B.A., & Jick, T.D. 1992. *The challenge of change: How companies experience it and leaders guide it.* New York: The Free Press.

43. Ford, M.W. 2006. Profiling change. *Journal of Applied Behavioral Science*, 42: 420–446; Hayes, J. 2002. *The theory and practice of change management.* New York: Palgrave; Lewin, K. 1951. Field theory in social science. New York: Harper & Row; Lewin, K. 1958. Group decisions and social change. In E.E. Maccobby, T.M. Newcomb, & E.L. Hartley (Eds.), *Readings in social psychology* (3rd ed.). Austin, TX: Holt, Rinehart & Winston.

44. Based on Goodstein, L.D., & Burke, W.W. 1993. Creating successful organizational change. *Organizational Dynamics*, 19(4): 5–18; Kanter, Stein, & Jick, *The challenge of change*; Lewin, *Field theory in social science*; Lewin, Group decisions and social change; Schein, E.H. 1987. *Process consultation (Vol. II).* Boston: Addison-Wesley; Sitkin, S. 2003. *Notes on organizational change.* Durham, NC: Fuqua School of Business.

45. Sydow, J., Schreyogg, G. & Koch, J. 2009. Organizational path dependence: Opening the black box. *Academy of Management Review*, 34: 689–709.

46. Geiger, D. 2009. Narratives and organizational dynamics. *Journal of Applied Behavioral Science*, 45: 411–436.

47. Reay, T., Golden-Biddle, K., & Germann, K. 2006. Legitimizing a new role: Small wins and microprocesses of change. *Academy of Management Journal*, 49: 977–998.

48. Based on Goodstein & Burke, Creating successful organizational change; Kanter, Stein, & Jick, *The challenge of change; Lewin, Field theory in social science*; Lewin, Group decisions and social change; Schein, *Process consultation (Vol. II)*; Sitkin, *Notes on organizational change.*

49. Filatotchev, I., & Toms, S. 2006. Corporate governance and financial constraints on strategic turnarounds. *Journal of Management Studies*, 43: 407–433.

50. Lavie, D. 2006. Capability reconfiguration: An analysis of incumbent responses to technological change. *Academy of Management Review*, 31: 153–174.

51. Furuya, N., Stevens, M.J., Bird, A., Oddou, G., Mendenhall, M. 2009. Managing the learning and transfer of global management competence: Antecedents and outcomes of Japanese repatriation effectiveness. *Journal of International Business Studies*, 40: 200–215.

52. Based on Goodstein & Burke, Creating successful organizational change; Kanter, Stein, & Jick, *The challenge of change*; Lewin, Field theory in social science; Lewin, Group decisions and social change; Schein, *Process consultation (Vol. II)*. Sitkin, Notes on organizational change.

53. See, for example, Schuster, J.R. 2004. Total rewards. *Executive Excellence*, 21 (1): 5.

54. Anand, N., Gardner, H.K., & Morris, T. 2007. Knowledge-based innovation: Emergence and embedding of new practice areas in management consulting firms. *Academy of Management Journal*, 50: 406–428.

55. See, for example, Kotter, J.P. 1996. *Leading change*. Boston: Harvard Business School Publishing.

56. Gilley, A., McMillan, H.S., & Gilley, J.W. 2009. Organizational change and characteristics of leadership effectiveness, *Journal of Leadership and Organizational Studies*, 16: 38–47.

57. See, for example, Kotter, *Leading change*

58. Ibid.

59. Ibid.

60. See Hailey, V.H., & Balogun, J. 2002. Devising context sensitive approaches to change: The example of Glaxo Wellcome. *Long Range Planning*, 35: 153–178; Kanter, Stein, & Jick, *The challenge of change*; Nohria, N., & Khurana, R. 1993. *Executing change: Seven key considerations*. Boston: Harvard Business School Publishing.

61. See Hailey & Balogun, Devising context sensitive approaches to change; Kanter, Stein, & Jick, *The challenge of change*.

62. Ibarra, H., & Sackley, N. 1995. *Charlotte Beers at Ogilvy and Mather (A)*. Boston: Harvard Business School Publishing.

63. Kanter, Stein, & Jick, *The challenge of change*.

64. Durand, R., Rao, H., & Monin, P. 2007. Code and conduct in French cuisine: Impact of code changes on external evaluations. *Strategic Management Journal*, 28: 455–472.

65. Jansen, J.J.P., George, G., Van den Bosch, F.A.J., & Volberda, H.W. 2008. Senior team attributes and organizational ambidexterity: The moderating role of transformational leadership, *Journal of Management Studies*, 45: 982–1007.

66. Marrow, A.J., Bowers, D.F., & Seashore, S.E. 1967. *Management by participation*. New York: Harper & Row.

67. Kanter, Stein, & Jick, *The challenge of change*.

68. Judson, A.S. 1991. *Changing behavior in organizations: Minimizing resistance to change*. Cambridge, MA: Basil Blackwell.

69. Abrahamson, E. 2004. Avoiding repetitive change syndrome. *Sloan Management Review*, 45 (2): 93–95.

70. Kotter, J.P., & Schlesinger, L.A. 1979. Choosing strategies for change. *Harvard Business Review*, 57 (2): 106–114.

71. Elliott, D., & Smith, D. 2006. Cultural readjustment after crisis: Regulation and learning from crisis within the UK soccer industry. *Journal of Management Studies*, 43: 290–317.

72. Kotter & Schlesinger, Choosing strategies for change.

73. David, P., Bloom, M., & Hillman, A.J. 2007. Investor activism, managerial responsiveness, and corporate social performance. *Strategic Management Journal*, 28: 91–100.

74. Kotter & Schlesinger, Choosing strategies for change.

75. See Vroom, V.H., & Yetton, P.W. 1973. *Leadership and decision making*. Pittsburgh: University of Pittsburgh Press.

76. Korsgaard, M.A., Sapienza, H.J., & Schweiger, D.M. 2002. Beaten before begun: The role of procedural justice in planning change. *Journal of Management*, 28: 497–516; Saunders, M.N.K., & Thornhill, A. 2003. Organizational justice, trust, and the management of change: An exploration. *Personnel Review*, 32: 360–375.

77. Korsgaard, Sapienza, & Schweiger, Beaten before begun.

78. Matta, E., & Beamish, P.W. 2008. The accentuated CEO career horizon problem: Evidence from international acquisitions. *Strategic Management Journal*, 29: 683–700.

79. Ryan, M.K., & Haslam, S.A. 2007. The glass cliff: Exploring the dynamics surrounding the appointment of women to precarious leadership positions. *Academy of Management Review*, 32: 549–572.

80. Duncan, A.K., & Breslin, M.A. 2009. Innovating health care delivery: The design of health services. *Journal of Business Strategy*, 30 (2.3): 13–20.

81. See Kotter & Schlesinger, Choosing strategies for change.

82. Elias, S. 2009. Employee commitment in times of change: Assessing importance of attitudes toward organizational change. *Journal of Management*, 35: 37–55.

83. Henderson, A.D., Miller, D., & Hambrick, D.C. 2006. How quickly do CEOs become obsolete? Industry dynamism, CEO tenure and company performance. *Strategic Management Journal*, 27: 447–460.

84. Kotter & Schlesinger, Choosing strategies for change.

85. Judge, T.A., Thoresen, V.P., & Welbourne, T.M. 1999. Managerial coping with organizational change: A dispositional perspective. *Journal of Applied Psychology*, 84: 107–122; Malone, J.W. 2001. Shining a new light on organizational change: Improving self-efficacy through coaching. *Organizational Dynamics*, 19(2): 27–36; Morrison, E.W., & Phelps, C.C. 1999. Taking charge at work: Extrarole efforts to initiate workplace change. *Academy of Management Journal*, 42: 403–419; Bandura, A. 1977. Self-efficacy: Toward a unifying theory of behavioral change. *Psychological Review*, 84: 191–215.

86. Cassar, G., & Friedman, H. 2009. Does self-efficacy affect entrepreneurial investment? *Strategic Entrepreneurship Journal*, 3: 241–260.

87. Judge, Thorenson, & Welbourne, Managerial coping with organizational change.

88. Ibid.

89. Laursen, K., & Salter, A. 2006. Open for innovation: The role of openness in explaining innovation performance among U.K. manufacturing firms. *Strategic Management Journal*, 27: 131–150.

90. Jick, T.D. 1991. *Donna Dubinsky and Apple Computer* (A) (B) (C): Note. Boston: Harvard Business School Publishing. For the original basis of these ideas, see Kubler-Ross, E. 1969. *On death and dying*. New York: Macmillan.

91. Ibid.

92. French, W.L., & Bell, C.H. 1999. *Organization development: Behavioral science interventions for organization improvement* (6th ed.). Upper Saddle River, NJ: Prentice Hall.

93. Worley, C.G., & Feyerherm, A.E. 2003. Reflections on the future of organization development. *Journal of Applied Behavioral Science*, 39: 97–115; Robertson, P.J., Roberts, D.R., & Porras, J.I. 1993. An evaluation of a model of planned organizational change: Evidence from a meta-analysis. In R.W. Woodman & W.A. Passmore (Eds.), *Research in organizational change and development (Vol. 7)*. Greenwich, CT: JAI Press.

94. See Egan, T.M. 2002. Organization development: An examination of definitions and dependent variables. *Organization Development Journal*, 20(2): 59–70; French & Bell, *Organization development: Behavioral science interventions for organization improvement* (6th ed.);

Schifo, R. 2004. OD in ten words or less: Adding lightness to the definitions of organizational development. *Organization Development Journal*, 22(3): 74–85; Worley & Feyerherm, Reflections on the future of organization development.

95. Paz, A.E. 2009. Transplanting management. *Journal of Applied Behavioral Science*, 45: 280–304.

96. See Beckhard, R. 1969. *Organization development: Strategies and models*. Reading, MA: Addison-Wesley.

97. See French & Bell, *Organization development*.

98. Ibid.

99. Worley & Feyerherm, Reflections on the future of organization development.

100. French & Bell, Organization development.

101. Luscher, L.S., & Lewis, M.W. 2008. Organizational change and managerial sensemaking: Working through paradox. *Academy of Management Journal*, 51: 221–240.

102. Lambrechts, F., Grieten, S., Bouwen, R., & Corthouts, F. 2009. Process consultation revisited. *Journal of Applied Behavioral Science*, 45: 39–58.

103. Guzzo, R.A., Jette, R.D., & Katzell, R.A. 1985. The effects of psychologically based intervention programs on worker productivity. *Personnel Psychology*, 38: 461–489; Neuman, G.A., Edwards, J.E., & Raju, N.S. 1989. Organization development interventions: A meta-analysis of their effects on satisfaction and other attitudes. *Personnel Psychology*, 42: 461–489.

104. See the "human processual" approaches in Friedlander, F., & Brown, D. 1974. Organization development. *Annual Review of Psychology*, 25: 313–341; Also see Porras, J.I., & Berg, P.O. 1978. The impact of organization development. *Academy of Management Review*, 3: 249–266.

105. See structural interventions in French & Bell, *Organization development*.

106. Argyris, C. 1964. T-groups for organizational effectiveness. *Harvard Business Review*, 42 (2): 60–74; French & Bell, *Organization development*.

107. Porras & Berg, The impact of organization development.

108. See team-building interventions in French & Bell, *Organization development*; also see Hackman, J.R. 2002. *Leading teams: Setting the stage for great performances*. Boston: Harvard Business School Press.

109. Morgeson, F.P., DeRue, D.S., & Karam, E.P. 2010. Leadership in teams: A functional approach to understanding leadership structures and processes. *Journal of Management*, 36: 5–39.

110. Solansky, S.T. 2008. Leadership style and team processes in self-managed teams. *Journal of Leadership and Organization Studies*, 14: 332–341.

111. Bell, C., & Rosenzweig, J. 1978. Highlights of an organization improvement program in a city government. In W.L. French, C.H. Bell, Jr., & R.A. Zawacki (Eds.), *Organization development theory, practice, and research*. Dallas: Business Publications.

112. Bowers, D.G., & Franklin, J.L. 1972. Survey-guided development: Using human resources management in organizational change. *Journal of Contemporary Business*, 1: 43–55.

113. Mabey, C. 2008. Management development and firm performance in Germany, Norway, Spain and the UK. *Journal of International Business Studies*, 39: 1327–1342.

114. Berk, A., & Kase, R. 2010. Establishing the value of flexibility created by training: Applying real options methodology to a single HR practice. *Organization Science*, in press.

115. Beck, N., Kabst, R., & Walgenbach, P. 2009. The cultural dependence of vocational training, *Journal of International Business Studies*, 40: 1374–1395.

116. Hackman, J.R., Oldham, G., Janson, R., & Purdy, K. 1975. A new strategy for job enrichment. *California Management Review*, 17(4): 57–71.

117. Kumar, K., van Fenema, P.C., & Glinow, M.A. 2009. *Journal of International Business Studies*, 40: 642–667.

118. Steps based on French, W., & Hollman, R. 1975. Management by objectives: The team approach. *California Management Review*, 17(3): 13–22.

119. Levinson, H. 2003. Management by whose objectives? *Harvard Business Review*, 81(1): 107–116.

120. Bartlett, C.A., & Wozny, M. 2004. *GE's two-decade transformation: Jack Welch's leadership*. Boston: Harvard Business School Publishing.

121. Hitt, M.A., Ireland, R.D., & Hoskisson, R.E. 2003. *Strategic management: Competitiveness and globalization* (5th ed.). Mason, OH: South-Western.

122. Song, J., & Shin, J. 2008. The paradox of technological capabilities: A study of knowledge sourcing from host countries of overseas R&D operations. *Journal of International Business Studies*, 39: 291–303; Meyer, K. 2007. Contextualizing organizational learning: Lyles and Salk in the context of their research. *Journal of International Business Studies*, 38: 27–37.

123. Gupta, A., Smith, K.G., & Shalley, C.E. 2006. The interplay between exploration and exploitation. *Academy of Management Journal*, 49: 693–706.

124. Kang, S.-C., Morris, S.S. & Snell, S.A. 2007. Relational archetypes, organizational learning and value creation: Extending the human resource architecture. *Academy of Management Review*, 32: 236–256.

125. Espedal, B. 2006. Do organizational routines change as experience changes? *Journal of Allied Behavioral Science*, 42: 469–490.

126. Bezuijen, X.M., van den Berg, P.T., van Dam, K & Thierry, H. 2009. Pygmalion and employee learning: The role of leader behaviors. *Journal of Management*, 35: 1248–1267.

127. Hirst, G., Knippenberg, D.V., & Zhou, J. 2009. A cross-level perspective on employee creativity, goal orientation, team learning behavior and individual creativity. *Academy of Management Journal*, 52: 280–293.

128. Son & Shin. The paradox of technological capabilities; Beck, Kabst, & Wallenbach. The cultural dependence of vocational training.

129. Deutschman, A. 2005. Change or die. *Fast Company*, May: 52–62.

130. Gilbert, C.G. 2006. Change in the presence of residual fit: Can competing frames coexist? *Organization Science*, 17: 150–167.

A SEA CHANGE IN STAFFING AT leapfrog innovations, inc.

Laurie L. Levesque, Suffolk University
Andrew S. Cheng, Barker Blue Digital Imaging

Court Chilton listened patiently to Dick Eaton's rundown on the potential staffing options at Leapfrog Innovations, Inc. (LFI), a small, Boston-based firm that Dick had founded ten years earlier to provide training to other companies. They had been friends since college. Dick hoped Court would provide advice on how to manage the imminent exodus of all three of LFI's full-time employees by drawing upon his MBA degree and work experiences as a consultant and a former employee of one of the largest training firms in the U.S. Dick's co-founder, Julia Douglas, had left to start her own consulting firm. The other two full-time employees had also announced their departures, one due to pregnancy and the other to attend graduate school.

Dick was unsure what role to take on partly because the three departing employees had handled oversight of the daily operations and coordination of LFI's training programs. He had absented himself from most management duties in order to focus on tasks that drew upon his creativity. Because he had worked very hard to build the firm's brand, he rejected outright the idea of selling LFI. It crossed his mind to run the company virtually and outsource all the work to facilitators and consultants. However, the most straightforward solution—or so it seemed—required him to get more involved and hire all new employees.

For months, Dick had put off deciding LFI's future and his role and now Court pushed him to address it immediately. He looked at Dick and quietly said, "If you're going to make this thing work, you're going to have to *lean in*."

Dick reflected that this phrase meant devoting his full-time effort to *running* LFI—something his co-founder had always done. He resisted, "I don't want to do that … that's not my plan."

At least, it hadn't been his plan up to that point. He had always worked off-site, limiting the scope of his role, typically visiting the office only once a week for meetings. Hiring replacement workers into the same three jobs the employees were exiting could keep his role from changing. Alternatively, he could try to take LFI to a new level of growth by taking on more management responsibilities and hiring people into newly designed jobs that complemented his own. He looked to Court as he considered the options.

THE TEAM BUILDING AND LEADERSHIP TRAINING INDUSTRY

In 2004, team building, leadership development, and training programs constituted a $13.3 billion dollar industry in the U.S.[1] Several hundred thousand firms competed in this market, ranging in size from individual contractors to companies with over ten thousand employees. The amount

of business that firms in this industry secured depended partly upon economic conditions in the industries of their client firms. For example, during the Internet boom years of 1999 and early 2000, many technology firms hired trainers to provide their employees with team-building programs geared toward the developmental needs of rapidly expanding companies. The firms used additional programs as rewards and to reinforce fun and upbeat work environments. When the economy slowed in 2000, tech firms increasingly viewed such programs as extravagances, and cut them from their budgets. The 9/11 attacks accelerated this trend, as firms cut travel to the minimum for several months. As a result, training firms experienced a slowdown in their business in 2001 and 2002, and some laid off employees. Many independent consultants struggled to get clients, and ultimately sought employment in established firms.

LEAPFROG INNOVATIONS, INC.

Dick Eaton and Julia Douglas founded Leapfrog Innovations in 1994 as a teambuilding and leadership-development firm. LFI earned a reputation for delivering high-quality programs ranging from one-time team-building experiences to coaching and consulting for improved firm performance. Julia and Dick worked closely to create a boutique training company with high-energy, high-involvement programs. The firm designed its own programs so that Dick and Julia would have complete creative control over the customization and delivery of its programs and thus its brand. Their first programs

focused largely on culture building, by creating fun learning environments that allowed participants to enhance relationships and improve communication. Julia handpicked facilitators after extensive interviews and participation in numerous LFI programs to help her deliver programs at either a client's firm or off site.

LFI's programs were distinctive because they were developed from scratch. Dick generated the concepts, by brainstorming with Julia. She then converted these into a learning experience by identifying the materials to use, the steps facilitators would follow, and how the debriefing session should unfold. In later years, all of LFI's employees and key facilitators gathered around a conference table with Dick's outline and elaborated on, debated, fleshed out, and tested new ideas until they developed a viable program. They would tweak the core program to tailor it for different clients. LFI's employees saw Dick as a creative genius who came up with complex programs that embedded experiential learning with opportunities for participants to connect with each other. Dick noted, "The programs had an electricity to them. They moved people outside their comfort zones into situations that were too big to get their arms around. It's like real work, even though it's just a metaphor."

LFI helped client firms identify their needs (e.g., desire to renew employees' energy, create more effective working relationships, increase self-awareness, etc.) and then tailored a program specifically to meet those goals. LFI offered three types of programs (see **Appendix 1**). Corporate culture programs created closer workplace relationships through fun, dynamic team bonding events. An example was The Mad, Mad, Mad, Mad Hunt™, a fast-paced urban scavenger hunt for teams. Leadership development simulations and experiential learning initiatives focused around a client firm's objectives, e.g., improving the quality of supervision. An example was Novotran™, which had teams work on complex problems (e.g., designing and building a race car out of PVC piping). The debriefing focused on the emergent strategies, teamwork, and leadership behaviors. The third type of program, Total Team Performance Solutions™ (TTPS), led to soft-skill development (e.g., communication, decision-making, meeting management). Julia worked closely with clients during the TTPS program design to develop one- or two-day workshops that combined individual assessments, team development improvement initiatives, and the teaching of models and skills. She worked with clients to roll out TTPS programs incrementally in order to create real, sustainable changes in workplace behavior. After each coaching session or workshop, clients applied the learning to actual challenges they faced. Intensive follow-up meetings insured that changes were implemented effectively over time. (See **Appendix 2** for a partial model of how LFI's service model worked.)

Successful program delivery required extensive logistical preparations prior to the actual event: sites were identified, travel reservations made, support staff hired, facilitator outlines developed, participant materials assembled, and a debriefing presentation was built around the client firm's needs. While reusable program materials were stored at LFI (e.g., markers, plungers, rubber chickens, balls, etc.), supplemental materials had to be purchased for large clients. Nearly half of LFI's programs were delivered outside of New England, which necessitated shipping these materials to arrive on-site before the facilitator. LFI hired energetic and socially adept facilitators to run its programs and debriefings. They represented LFI to the client firm's participants, as did the temporary staff that assisted on-site.

Similar to its competition, LFI experienced a decline in business in 2002, but weathered it in part because of its strong reputation in the market for original programs and superior customer relations. LFI ran a lean business, with inexpensive office space and training done at client-arranged sites. Employees received low base pay and a significant percentage of the profit-sharing. Dick shared a tip he had learned from his father: "We attended to cash flow." LFI's competition billed clients after delivery of a program and then waited for reimbursement, while LFI billed 50–75% of the fee in advance so as not to carry a balance for the purchase of materials and travel, and the hiring of facilitators and support staff. Clients accepted this arrangement because of the reputation LFI had developed for high-quality programs. Also, LFI had earned the right for the arrangement because of the time they invested developing the business relationship and demonstrating the value of the program to be delivered. At times, LFI provided deep discounts in order to stay within a client's budget.

LFI had an edge when it came to the training products they offered to clients: they custom designed programs for each client firm to meet company-specific learning goals and then "executed them nearly flawlessly," according to Dick. "I told potential clients, 'I *hate* team building. And I didn't like it when I worked at Proctor & Gamble, either. I represent the introverts at your firm. Julia represents the outgoing employees. We design programs that engage both groups." Dick and Julia drew on their own corporate experience when designing programs. They spent a lot of time talking with the clients to determine what employees needed to learn or change. Dick further explained that by starting with the learning goals, LFI worked backwards to design the correct sequence of activities and discussions that would ultimately make up the training program in order to get at "the heart of the outcomes [the executives] wanted from the training program." Leapfrog was first to market with many new program ideas. Rather than tweak programs from the public domain (e.g., ropes courses) that everyone else was using, they deconstructed why such programs were effective or fun. Taking insights about these fundamental components, Dick dreamed up never-seen-before programs, such as having employees build a miniature golf course to learn team and leadership skills, an experience that achieved the same, if not better, results as other programs. Julia noted that LFI sold clients on the idea that "you'll never have experienced this before." Two to three years after introducing a radically new type of program, LFI would hear that other training firms or local consultants had stolen and modified the concept. The changes were usually minor, because most facilitators competing with LFI weren't experienced with design. They were more experienced in running Outward Bound and/or ropes courses, both of which were originally designed for students, not workplace complexities, and usually had generic debriefings.

LEAPFROG'S REMAINING FOUNDER: DICK EATON

Dick Eaton's philosophy of management and company culture was a product of his work experiences as well as his father's influence. His father had owned a public relations firm and had shared many stories with his family. From these, Dick learned the importance of treating everyone as an equal regardless of job title. His father hosted dinners at their home for high level CEOs, explaining to Dick that he treated them no differently from anyone else: "They all look the same sitting on the can." In one of his first jobs as a Proctor & Gamble management trainee, Dick had felt "an uncomfortable fit from the start." Though he learned a lot and was promoted to a first-line manager after two years and "managed four people who were twice my age," he hated each day. With little input into his job, he did not feel enabled to help his clients: "P&G wanted to mold me into their way of thinking" and expected jobs to be done in a prescribed manner with a "salesy" style.

Dick yearned for more say in the decisions of his day-to-day work and to be more intimately involved in the development of the products he sold. He left and got his next job at an advertising agency. To his surprise, two months later when his client cancelled its marketing budget, the agency retained Dick on its payroll. This decision soon paid off as the agency landed a large account with Finast Supermarkets and needed someone to manage it. Their commitment to him as an employee made a positive impression on him. Not long after, the president of Finast left to start his own company and hired Dick as the first director of marketing for what became Staples, Inc. As the position evolved, Dick and the executive team realized that his advertising skills hadn't prepared him to do direct marketing, and he was a poor fit with the values of the executive team and the emerging corporate culture. As a result, he was asked to leave:

> Money was not my number one driver. I wasn't in a mode where I was interested in working a hundred hours a week. I had gone to search for more quality. [The executive team] had the intention of making a mark on the world, which I admired and wanted to be part of but I didn't have [that goal]. I was reducing my traditional ambition. I was going the other way in terms of fame and fortune. The traditional definition of it was not in concert with what I was feeling and seeking.

Dick then founded the Urban Outing Club and ran it out of his condo, relying on the word of mouth of his members as its only advertising. It was a membership-based adventure and social club for people seeking community and quality of life, but were too busy to plan their own fun. Dick designed and offered creative activities and interactive experiences that "broke down barriers and let members connect with one another." Though not driven by profit, Dick had a family to support and to do so adequately would have meant increasing membership exponentially beyond its four hundred members. However, he believed that commercialization would destroy the club's unique culture so he opted to turn it over to its members. Dick took his creative ideas and began planning a for-profit firm that would offer some of the same types of team building programs to corporations. He toyed with the idea of opening a few businesses, and for each, hiring people to run them.

Dick met Julia Douglas in December 1993, and they launched the initial incarnation of Leapfrog Innovations in February 1994. Early in their discussions, Dick told her:

> We are going to do this together. If we have a cash shortfall I'll be responsible for that. But anything outside of the financials, the buck stops with you. If you hire a facilitator who doesn't show up, then the call will go to you and not to me. Basically you're in charge of the day-to-day and I'll be your partner in helping to make things work but I'll only be available about half my time. So the essence of it is that if I choose to take a six-month sabbatical the business shouldn't falter.

Julia agreed to this arrangement and left IBM in Canada to move to Boston. She took a small base salary with high profit-sharing potential, and planned to work at LFI for three years while simultaneously earning a master's degree in cross-cultural consulting. After that, she planned to open her own consulting firm.

From the beginning, LFI's employees could choose from among several combinations of compensation regarding their level of base pay and how much they shared in the company's profits. To adjust for changed personal circumstances, some employees switched to a higher base pay and less profit-sharing combination. This worked well as LFI hired "really hungry, relatively young people who wanted to learn a ton and make their mark. To them, the company was more of a mission or a calling than a job," Dick observed. They loved LFI and enjoyed their colleagues.

In LFI's first ten years, there were never more than five full-time employees, even when business was at its highest level in 2000. During peak times, Julia and the other employees worked long hours to sell and deliver programs. When the economy weakened, the types of programs companies requested changed to ones where participants brought learning back into their workplaces. This shift led LFI to develop long-term client relationships and to construct customized programs to meet those clients' needs.

THE EMERGENCE OF DIFFERENTIATED ROLES AT LEAPFROG

Though a self-admitted introvert, Dick was an excellent networker. Both he and Julia could develop rapport with

anyone. Their interpersonal skills not only sold clients on the firm, it shaped their company's culture. Dick viewed LFI as a fertile ground where employees explored their skill sets, got mentored, and developed their whole selves. In this vein, he crafted a schedule for himself that included time for personal pursuits: painting, Reiki (a Japanese spiritual healing practice), community service, and his family. He went to LFI's office once a week for the staff meeting. He preferred to maintain a private office off site where he generated client leads, negotiated large client contracts, and developed new program ideas. Julia noted that "Dick had capabilities to do more than that, but he focused primarily on building client relationships and developing marketing and product ideas."

Julia noted, "I considered Leapfrog *my* baby because Dick was in the distance. While he called it a means of 'early retirement' for himself, I wanted Leapfrog to thrive, not just survive." It wasn't the pay that motivated her, because she had "one fantastic year out of ten." Instead, it was the opportunity to learn an extraordinary amount. Her future goal had always been to build her own firm when she felt ready. Julia didn't want to risk going solo until she had experience and maturity, and building and managing LFI from scratch helped her do just that. She took a lot of pride in her accomplishments at LFI. She managed day-to-day operations, sold programs to clients, handled all the logistics for getting a program prepared and delivered to the client, and usually facilitated them herself. She handled

the development work (turning the concept into a documented program) without Dick, because "figuring out how to work with him was an art." As a big picture thinker, he got mired in details, slowed the process, and made it overly complicated. Given her workload, she couldn't afford any delays in the process.

From 1995 to 1999, LFI hired various people to handle sales and program logistics (see **Appendix 3**), seeking employees who were driven by LFI's mission. Many were referrals from Dick or Julia's networks or people they met through LFI's programs. LFI hired them if there was a fit between the individual's personality and the firm's culture.

Job titles were generally avoided, particularly on the sales side of the business because Dick believed titles would suggest that LFI was a typical training firm that sold generic products. Like many start-ups, its employees willingly took on multiple responsibilities. Matt, the first employee, focused on making new sales—with the understanding that he had to make most of his income through commissions. Together, he and Julia generated more business than ever. This created capacity challenges for managing and delivering so many programs, so Steve was hired to handle program logistics. Julia managed to keep the company afloat by juggling sales, managing the operations, delivering programs, and still motivating the others. Matt was put on salary, which removed the pressure to sell every minute and allowed him to assist with program delivery. He noted, "Dick was great about giving chances and building on people's skills." When Steve left in 1997, Julia covered his responsibilities until Heidi was hired.

In late 1997, Matt left to pursue an internship for his MBA. Dick and Julia spent two to three months interviewing candidates to find someone who would represent LFI well to its clients and whose skills and personality fit with their own. In September 1998, LFI hired Dave to assist Julia with sales. Dave fielded inquiries from potential clients and worked with existing clients to sell programs to their other departments. Selling involved a needs analysis, recommending a solution, and writing a proposal. He recalled that his job wasn't that narrow: "There was a line in my job description that read, 'Lots of other stuff as necessary,'" an expectation held of all LFI employees. This included brainstorming sessions to tweak existing programs or develop new ones. "One of the best results of my experience was that I realized I had a creative side that, until then, had been untapped." He tried two ideas: marketing LFI at a trade show and offering an incentive program for hotel managers who referred business, neither of which paid off. He characterized the decision to experiment as reflective of LFI's culture—"If you had an idea and felt strongly about something then you had leeway to try it. If you made a mistake, it was not the end of the world. I didn't think I could keep making mistakes, but trying new things was the only way we were going to grow, and the only way I was going to grow professionally." He saw that as one reason why Dick was careful about hiring: "He's the kind of person who

thinks the quality and characteristics of people are just as important as the exact skill set they bring to the table."

CHANGES AND GROWTH IN STAFFING, SERVICES, AND WORK ROLES

Revenues doubled from 1999 to 2000, although LFI's infrastructure was little changed. Heidi left that year to hike the Appalachian Trail. One of the facilitators, Chris, handled logistics until Heather was hired as the logistics program manager. Business boomed and Julia worked sixty to eighty hours every week not counting travel to client sites. Her work ethic was legendary among LFI's employees and facilitators. She said, "The year 2000 itself was the most ridiculous year of my life; it was just insane." Dick suggested they hire a manager so Julia could focus on Total Team Performance Solutions™ consulting, which she now preferred over LFI's other programs. Dick did most of the interviewing that resulted in Allison's being hired, albeit more on chemistry and raw talent than experience in the industry. Dick considered her "a brilliant woman and very talented in so many ways and a great qualitative kind of person." Though she was hired to be the managing director she "had only a general idea of what that meant—nothing in writing ... it was nebulous." Allison took on responsibility for bookkeeping, client invoices, management of the physical location and staff, and the day-to-day operations of the LFI.

Allison also expected to generate revenues, but the learning curve for selling LFI's unique training

programs was steep. Dave noted that it could take a while, especially when coming from a different industry: "It required actually going to the programs and seeing them and understanding how they benefited the client organizations so you could sell them." Allison agreed, "There was so much content to learn ... early on it was a lot of watching Julia and listening and trying to really get up to speed on the programs so I could make client calls and write proposals. There really wasn't any archive of information to access that would give me all the stuff I'd need to know to say confidently to a corporate client, 'here's what we can offer, here's what it looks like, and here's what it's going to feel like.'" Given the exigencies of a busy office with few full-time workers, Allison was soon fielding client calls and trying to figure it out as she went along.

As the "logistics guru," Heather ensured that all program details were attended to in a timely manner once the account executive selected a program and facilitator. She tailored her help to meet the facilitators' individual needs and preferences. She developed forms to track information and rudimentary operational systems to improve program scheduling and delivery. She recruited, hired and trained support staff to aid these facilitators on-site. Allison and Julia mentored her, pushing Heather to gain more knowledge by aiding the facilitators on-site. "It got to the point where Allison said to me, 'Do you want to go to a client meeting too? Make calls? Try managing an account?' I could have done anything. It was up to me to say 'no, I want to try *those* things, or I'd like to do *these* things.' I could do anything as long as my original job was being done." Though the core never changed, Heather's job looked a little different with each project. In 2000, she dealt with approximately a dozen programs; in later years nearly all of LFI's programs were highly customized. Heather stated:

After the tech crash, my job became more complicated. No two programs looked the same; everything was tailored. Even our stock programs were customized. It added a ton of work for me. By 2004, my job involved so much because of customization that I definitely felt there needed to be two of me. There were two levels to my work. One was the printing and shopping and organizing. Those were my days where I could take a mental break; I could wear my jeans and sit on the floor. There was another level of coordination, dealing with the client facilities and support staff. And then there were the days I was at the programs—sometimes there were three or four programs going on in a week and I would send one off but I wouldn't get to go to it because I was going to another program. One of the things we were remiss about is that I couldn't be at every program to get all the feedback, because you learn something from each debrief.

Heather's learning came primarily from Julia and Allison; she and Dick didn't have a close relationship. He continued to work out of his other office and go in once a week for the company meeting. From Heather's view, "I didn't know Dick as well as I did Julia and Allison; he wasn't around as much as they. They were in my daily life."

Even though he wasn't on-site much, Dick felt a strong connection to LFI and its employees. He occasionally indicated to them that he "desired to capture the tacit knowledge that each person had built through their experience on the job." However, it was not "in his nature" to sit down and document his job and procedures; therefore he never pushed others to do so either. At times he would comment that LFI needed to document a procedure so that the next time they would have a checklist of what to do. "It wasn't that we didn't want to do it, but other things were always higher priority, like dealing with clients or getting a new project."

UNCERTAIN FUTURE OF LFI

In 2002, Dave decided to move west, and LFI did not replace him. By then, Julia was focused on LFI's top-level operational issues and her clients. Allison fielded incoming calls from potential clients and managed daily operations. Julia said, "Though I was sad to see Dave go, I knew that [his salary] would be better allocated elsewhere. We needed someone selling more aggressively."

The firm was doing well but needed to maintain sales. Up to that point, most employees stayed with LFI for two to five years. Turnover averaged one employee a year. Dick and Julia remained and provided stability as new people came aboard and others left (refer to **Appendix 3** for LFI's employee tenure).

Signs of major changes appeared at the end of 2003. LFI had to develop relationships with new facilitators, as its primary external facilitator was unavailable while she had her second child. In December, Allison also announced she was pregnant. A few months later, Heather found out she had been accepted into a degree program that started in the fall of 2004 so she planned to leave LFI that summer. For Julia, the year 2004 would be her tenth anniversary, and she spoke with renewed interest about leaving to start her own company and working for LFI only on a contract basis.

And around this time, Dick underwent a transformation and engaged in a lot of personal reflection as a result of his father's death. Allison observed that, "Dick did a lot of soul searching and concluded that he needed to have a drastically different role within LFI. He told us that he and the company were in a transition phase, but it was unclear what that meant." He didn't mention he had thought about increasing his involvement on-site.

Dick reflected, "I did a lot of thinking, and had a lot of conversations with people outside LFI who had very rich points of view. I reached out to seven different high level executives and consultants, some in this industry, some in related businesses, and some whose opinion I just respect." One of these individuals was Dick's longtime friend, Court, who reviewed profit and loss statements, asked questions about LFI's structure, assessed how things were run and the challenges Dick faced. After helping Dick think through all these, Court pointed out that the future of the company and who should be hired were decisions that were ultimately Dick's responsibility to make—but they all hinged on what Dick wanted the scope and focus of his own role to be and how he wanted to structure the company.

The outcomes of these conversations had not been shared with the employees. According to Allison, in early 2004 "Julia, Heather, and I were trying to create a plan that would allow us to phase out and not disrupt the company. We were definitely struggling with who we should hire and what they would be responsible for ... there was a fair amount of confusion about whether or not we were looking to recreate the model that already existed [hire new people to take on the existing roles] or we were breaking that model and starting all over again." Their conversations revolved around what the skill sets of new hires should look like and whether job descriptions reflected not just responsibilities but the LFI's culture, too.

They focused first on replacing Heather. Allison explained, "There always needs to be a program manager and it was pretty clear what the program manager needed to do. And regardless of what happened with the direction of the company, that job was pretty clear." They debated filling the "Heather of 2000" role or the "Heather of 2004" role,

the latter reflecting the more complex job that had developed around her skills and interests as well as the additional tasks she had become responsible for over the four years. Her job in 2004 was "meatier" than what it was in 2000, so it required a more experienced person, thus a higher salary. Allison and Heather interviewed candidates, many young, recent graduates with the skill level of Heather when she was initially hired. They were good with logistics and excited to shop, pack, and coordinate program materials. Some interviewees were a closer match for the "Heather of 2004" role. Heather observed that the process was interesting, "because we described the job and company, and then said, 'but nothing is going to look like this when you are here. And here we are, two people interviewing you who, by the way, won't be here when you are here.'"

By May 2004, LFI had hired no replacements. Julia had left in April and the stress was increasing. Allison's due date approached, and she was expected to leave by July. Heather would go to school in August. As Allison contemplated the situation, "I had a clear idea of what my job description was and what role needed to be filled. I created a long list of all the tasks that needed to be attended to for the general operations of LFI, ranging from client relationships, IT, marketing, finances, office management—a very long spreadsheet, incredibly

detailed—and regardless of who does it, *this stuff needs to get done.*"

Yet while Heather and Allison sought their replacements, Dick continued to work on a new company vision and his role within it. The decisions that would come out of the new vision would influence the roles that LFI needed and the responsibilities assigned to each. He even considered different business models, such as doing away with all employees and instead using a Web site to broker matches between clients and outside facilitators.

One thing was clear, though— if he kept the firm, he would do so without other investors. This self-funding limitation meant a fixed budget for salaries and benefits. If revenues remained the same, LFI could support four employees in addition to Dick. Although he always held the financial risks as an owner, his role in the firm had been limited to only those tasks that he wanted to do—mostly the creative work and handling the larger client accounts. He hadn't overseen the daily operations. "If the computers broke, somebody else dealt with it. If there was a bunch of stuff to load into a truck, I wasn't there." Dick now had a decision to make. Thinking through all this was taking time, though, and there wasn't much of that left. Julia was gone and the only other two employees would be out the door sooner rather than later. Dick realized it was time to decide the future of LFI and his job as well.

NOTE

1. "2005 Industry Report," *Training Magazine*, (December 2005), 14–28.

APPENDIX 1: OVERVIEW OF PROGRAMS OFFERED BY LEAPFROG INNOVATIONS, INC.

I. CORPORATE CULTURE BUILDING

Focus: Provide a foundation by which team members can build relationships. Create shared experiences that encourage bonding by teams.

Experience: Fun, dynamic, fast-moving.

Example: The Mad, Mad, Mad, Mad Hunt™

II. LEADERSHIP DEVELOPMENT SIMULATIONS

Focus: Experiential learning designed to meet the leadership development needs and teambuilding skills of a client firm.

Experience: Complex problems that require collaborative work, team leadership, strategic thinking.

Actual team and leader behaviors are focus of the debrief session.

Example: Novotran™

III. MULTI-PHASED, IMPROVEMENT INITIATIVES

Focus: Long-term change in soft skill development for teams and leaders (e.g., communication, decision-making, meeting management).

Experience: Intensive interaction with clients to develop program and tailor follow-up consulting. After the program ended, intensive meetings were held to ensure the changes and their implementation were successful.

Example: Total Team Performance Solutions™

APPENDIX 2: LEAPFROG'S SERVICE MODEL

Client contact is made. A Leapfrog employee meets with the client to uncover what they want their employees to learn or gain from the training program.

A Leapfrog design team tweaks existing program or creates a custom program to challenge client's employees in creative, fun ways.

For custom programs, LFI's employees discuss the concept and goals to determine how the program will be run for this specific client.

If it's a new program without support documents, the lead designer may build a facilitator manual to itemize the props and supplies needed, the steps participants will go through, and the specific questions to be asked of participants when the fun is over so they can articulate what they have learned.

A facilitator is assigned and reviews the materials. Support staff is hired as needed. Travel is arranged. Materials are bought, organized, and delivered to the training location. Payment is secured from client.

The facilitator and support staff run the program.

Participants experience the program followed by a debriefing. This is where the key learning from the program is derived. For TTPS, several meetings and follow-up coaching sessions are planned.

Source: Author illustration

APPENDIX 3: FULL-TIME EMPLOYEE TENURE AT LEAPFROG

Employee	Primary focus	1994	1995	1996	1997	1998	1999	2000	2001	2002	2003	2004	2005
Dick	sales/creative	x	x	x	x	x	x	x	x	x	x	x	x
Julia	sales/operations/ lead facilitator	x	x	x	x	x	x	x	x	x	x	**X**	
Steve	logistics		x	x	x								
Heidi	logistics					x	x						
Chris	logistics							x					
Heather	logistics								x	x	x	**X**	
Matt	sales		x	x	x	x							
Dave	sales					x	x	x	x	x			
Allison	operations/sales							x	x	x	x	**X**	

Notes:
x indicates employment at LFI
X indicates employee announcement of planned resignation from the firm during 2004

CENTURION MEDIA: doing the right thing

Carolyn Conn, St. Edward's University, Aundrea Kay Guess, St. Edward's University
Jonathan Hiatt, St. Edward's University

E ach time Richard Bennett reached across his desk for the mail and other documents his assistant had placed in his in-box, he smiled because he thought of the friendly disagreement with his wife about the "proper" way to handle this task. His approach was "top-down." Whatever was on top of the in-box was dealt with first, then down through the stack until it was all finished. His wife preferred the "priority" method, first sorting through everything to determine the urgency of each item. Bennett felt that was just a waste of time. "By the time you've gotten your stuff sorted, I've probably finished with at least one-third of the items in my in-box," he had kidded her. Bennett was thinking of his wife again that morning as he sat down at his desk. Tomorrow, July 12, 2006, was their wedding anniversary. How could forty-one years have gone by so quickly? His reminiscing was abruptly interrupted when Bennett saw the item on top of his in-box.

A special courier had delivered a package from the corporate office of Centurion Media. Inside the package was a contract signed by Joseph Fowler, the new president of his division. (Refer to **Exhibit 1** for corporate structure.) As Bennett read through the contract, he had a sick feeling. The contract required all of the cable television systems in the Centurion cable division to sell their advertising inventory at severely discounted

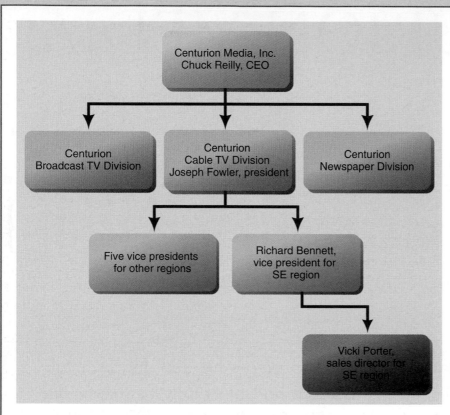

Centurion Media, Inc.
Chuck Reilly, CEO

Centurion
Broadcast TV Division

Centurion
Cable TV Division
Joseph Fowler, president

Centurion
Newspaper Division

Five vice presidents
for other regions

Richard Bennett,
vice president for
SE region

Vicki Porter,
sales director for
SE region

Exhibit 1   Centurion's Corporate Structure

rates to Northpark Media. Northpark was a national buying service that bought and resold commercial spots on cable television systems; Centurion Media owned 25 percent of Northpark's outstanding common stock. From the wording Bennett saw in the contract, Centurion Cable would lose millions of dollars in revenue both by selling commercials so cheaply to Northpark and by alienating existing customers, who would stop buying from Centurion. Because Fowler had been CEO of Northpark before coming to Centurion, Bennett immediately wondered if that relationship had played a role in the negotiation of this contract.

As a vice president in Centurion's cable division, Bennett managed cable network systems in the southeastern United States. Bennett had been a regional vice president in the cable division of Centurion Media for nearly ten years. Most of his management team had been with him from the time he began as regional vice president. They had worked hard to build relationships in the communities where they operated, and financial growth provided proof of their success. Revenues for his group's cable systems had almost doubled annually since his first year as regional vice president. His group had been recognized for their accomplishments as the "Outstanding Team" nationwide at the previous year's Centurion Media annual banquet. In Bennett's opinion, the Northpark contract would destroy everything Bennett's group had done in their region during the past ten years.

Bennett wondered if the other vice presidents had received their copies of the contract. He had to get to the bottom of this and try to avert financial calamity. He knew he had to be careful. One of Bennett's golfing buddies who was in upper management of Centurion's newspaper division had a run-in with Fowler at a corporate meeting the month after he became president of the cable division. His buddy warned Bennett not to trust Fowler. Bennett called his sales director, Vicki Porter.

Vicki, you are never going to believe what I got by special courier

Copyright © 2008 by the *Case Research Journal* and Carolyn Conn, Aundrea Kay Guess, and Jonathan Hiatt. All rights reserved to the authors and NACRA.

This case was presented to the North American Case Research Association (NACRA) at its annual meeting, October 18–20, 2007, Keystone, CO.

The authors wish to thank the individual portrayed as Richard Bennett in this case. We want to thank the editor and associate editor of the *Case Research Journal* and the anonymous reviewers for their time and valuable suggestions. This case was written to stimulate class discussion rather than to illustrate the effective or ineffective handling of a managerial situation.

This case did not occur in the cable television industry. The industry, as well as the names of all firms, their locations, and the people involved in this case have been disguised.

this morning. It's a contract signed by Joseph Fowler between Centurion Cable and Northpark Media—and we've got to sell them any of our advertising inventory they want at rates way below what we are charging this year and below many of the annual contracts we already have with advertisers for the coming year. Those customers are going to be furious if they ever hear about this—and, you know they will. Worse still is the impact this contract will have on our bottom line. We'll lose millions!

Porter said she understood Bennett's frustration, but reminded him they needed to talk to other Centurion Cable vice presidents about the Northpark contract before they did anything. Bennett said he would make a few calls, and they agreed to meet later that day to work out a strategy for dealing with the contract. Bennett had hired Vicki during his first year as vice president at Centurion Cable and had never regretted it. He respected Vicki's judgment and knew she was trustworthy and knowledgeable about the political workings of the corporate offices and boardroom of Centurion Media. He had told her numerous times she was the logical choice to be promoted into his position after he retired.

THE CABLE TELEVISION INDUSTRY

The cable television industry originated in the mountains of Pennsylvania in the late 1940s. John Walson, owner of an appliance store in rural Mahanoy City, wanted to increase sales of televisions. To improve reception and better demonstrate the televisions, he erected an antenna on top of a nearby hill and ran a cable to his store. Customers soon began asking for their houses to be connected to his antenna.

Walson charged two dollars a month for this service and by the middle of 1948 had 727 customers. He and other entrepreneurs soon began setting up similar "Community Antenna Television" (CATV) systems in rural areas where television reception was poor. By 1955, there were about 400 such systems with a total of 150,000 subscribers.[1]

Initially, CATV systems throughout the United States provided their customers with the three channels from the national broadcast networks: ABC, CBS, and NBC. Expansion of the systems and demand from customers resulted in the growth of programming to include hundreds of national cable networks (such as A&E, HBO, Showtime, ESPN, and CNN) as well as the offerings of local standard broadcast stations.

Cable television systems were established under franchise agreements within specific geographic regions. Under FCC regulations, some cable operators had been granted franchises in multiple areas of the United States. Cable operators that had multiple franchises were referred to as Multiple-System Operators (MSOs). As of 2006, the twenty-five largest MSOs served more than 61 million subscribers nationwide.[2]

Cable Television Revenues

Operators of cable television systems obtained revenue from several sources: subscriber fees for basic service, additional subscriber fees for premium programming, fees for specialty services (such as movies on-demand), and local advertising. Sales of subscriptions for basic cable service had stalled; thus, advertising revenues had become more significant to the operators of cable systems. The dramatic increase in the number of available digital cable channels resulted in ever-increasing amounts of advertising space. Nationwide, total cable revenue for 2007 was estimated at $74.7 billion, with $26.9 billion of that coming from advertising.[3]

Cable television operators sold local advertising on their systems based on a predetermined number of commercial breaks within each network program. On average there was two minutes per hour of commercial breaks. These commercials were in addition to those purchased directly by advertisers through the national cable networks. Depending upon the city and surrounding area served by a specific cable system and the demand for a given program, the local advertising rate in various markets across the United States for 2006 averaged from less than $20 per thirty-second spot to approximately $200.

TELEVISION ADVERTISING

Television advertising spots had been available for purchase from multiple sources: national broadcast (ABC, CBS, NBC); national cable networks (e.g., ESPN, MTV, CNN); local broadcast affiliates (e.g., KABC in Los Angeles, WFOR4 in Miami, and WXIA in Atlanta); and local cable (e.g., Comcast, Time-Warner, Cox). Small advertisers did not need national placement of their commercials. Instead, they targeted a local market and bought lower-priced commercials from local broadcast stations (frequently in locally-produced programs such as evening and late news) and/or from local cable operators.

Industry data for 2005 showed that audiences watched cable as much as they were watching broadcast networks, causing an increase in the demand for advertising on cable systems. For 2005, gross cable advertising revenue was estimated at $24 billion with local cable advertising at $5.6 billion. Experts predicted 10 percent annual growth for local cable advertising, 9 percent for national cable, 4 percent for national broadcast, and 1.5 percent for local broadcast.[4]

Unsold inventory of advertising in their local commercial breaks had presented challenges for the operators of cable systems. Nationally, unsold inventory on cable was equal to roughly 70 percent of the total available spots (called "avails").[5] Much of the unsold inventory was in "late night" (after "prime time") through the following "early morning" (approximately 5 A.M.).

Some internet-based companies had begun exploring ways to sell the unsold "remnant" advertising inventory in various media, including newspapers, radio, and cable television. Google had been extremely aggressive in this area. In fall 2006, Google debuted an online bidding system for selling advertising in all media. Google began this service in the newspaper and radio markets, with plans to expand

into broadcast and cable television. Most major newspaper chains and major papers, such as *The Chicago Tribune* and *The New York Times*, subscribed to Google's new bidding service. Google reported their initial ad volume sold through the system was double their projections.[6] Their public statements about the system described their plans to add spot sales on broadcast television and cable networks.[7] Some industry experts postulated that availability of online advertising order systems would force cable television programmers to partner with firms such as Google and eBay to help sell advertising on the programmers' cable and satellite networks.[8]

Some members of the radio industry had tried to keep Google at a distance, primarily because of concern their advertising would become a commodity and prices would be driven down. However, Google's position had been just the opposite, as described by Douglass Merrill, their vice president of engineering, "If you use some of the things that we understand about finding appropriate value and targeting, we might get folks who haven't advertised on radio before to advertise now.... With those advertisers comes new money; with those, rates rise."[9]

CENTURION MEDIA

Centurion Media began as a newspaper publishing business called *Centurion News* in the late-1940s. The corporate founder, Charles Reilly Sr., had the foresight in the 1950s to expand into broadcast and cable television. In order to obtain sufficient capital for his new ventures, Reilly

took the company public and named the new company Centurion Media. In 2006, Centurion Media was a diversified public corporation headquartered in Chicago, Illinois with operating divisions in several major media segments, including Centurion Broadcast Television, Centurion Cable Television, and Centurion Newspaper. A president managed each division. (Refer to **Exhibit 1** for Centurion's organization chart.)

Charles Reilly Sr. served as chief executive officer (CEO) until 1975 when he became chairman of the board. Even though it was a public corporation, Centurion Media maintained the feel of a family business. When Reilly Sr. stepped down as CEO, Charles Reilly Jr. replaced him and served in that capacity until 2001. At that time, Charles Reilly III (Chuck) was named CEO. Chuck Reilly had worked in various departments at Centurion, starting first as an errand boy during summers in high school. After graduating from college with a degree in radio, television and film, he began working full-time for one of the broadcast television stations owned by Centurion. He was well liked by his colleagues and regarded as a hard worker. They also respected him because he had started at the bottom and never used his father's and grandfather's positions as influence to get ahead in the company.

CENTURION CABLE DIVISION

As a division of Centurion Media, Centurion Cable had a president supported by six vice presidents, with operational responsibility for multiple cable television systems within specific regions of the United States. Each vice president was autonomous with primary responsibility for franchise negotiations in the cities and towns where their systems operated. Every region had its own sales department that sold advertising at the rates established by the regional vice president. The rates were based on demand for commercial placement and availability in various programming, as well as competitive market forces. The president was primarily responsible for the execution of their division's portion of the corporate strategic plan and for representing their division's interests to the upper management of Centurion Media.

In January 2006, Terrence Moore, the fourth president of Centurion in eight years, was transferred to Centurion's broadcast television division and replaced by Joseph Fowler. Moore, president for two years, had been a hands-off manager, letting the regional vice presidents run their own operations with little input or guidance from him. The management style of the new president, Fowler, was at the other end of the spectrum. A few current Centurion Cable employees had worked for Fowler at Northpark, and they described him as being dictatorial, with little patience for people who disagreed with him.

Chuck Reilly personally recruited Fowler from his position as CEO of Northpark. When Reilly introduced Fowler around Centurion's offices, Reilly noted they had been friends in college and began their media careers together at Centurion. Reilly let everyone know Fowler was a tough negotiator and had led Northpark to

impressive growth in revenues and profits. Reilly said he was expecting Fowler to have a significant impact on the cable division's bottom line in a short period of time.

NORTHPARK MEDIA

A simple concept had been the basis for Northpark Media's business. Most cable television operators could not sell all their available advertising inventory and most small businesses did not have employees dedicated to buying local airtime. Northpark negotiated with cable television operators to buy large quantities of commercial advertising at deeply discounted rates. In turn, they resold those commercial spots to small local businesses for higher prices—but at rates that were lower than what the firms could negotiate for themselves. Northpark became the intermediary between the small businesses and the local cable operators.

The company was established in 1974 and went public in 1984. Their stock traded on the New York Stock Exchange and was included as part of the Standard & Poor's 400 Mid-Cap. During fiscal year 2005 they employed nearly 13 hundred people.

Northpark Media had experienced exponential growth in sales, along with steady growth in their stock price under the leadership of CEO Joseph Fowler. In the two fiscal years ending December 2004 and 2005, revenue had grown from $358 to $553 million, with operating income rising from $61 to $104 million, and net income increased from $24 to $42 million. Northpark had minimized capital expenditures while generating increases

in earnings and cash flow. At a time when many companies in the media industry were having difficulty, Northpark was regarded as a solid investment. Bennett knew that most investment analysts who covered the publicly traded company rated it as a buy or a strong buy. Northpark had bought some commercial airtime from Centurion Media in recent years, but the amount was an insignificant portion of their total purchases. The company had formed no close trading partnerships or alliances with any particular media companies.

In late spring 2006, Centurion Media completed several purchases of Northpark stock which gave them control of approximately 25 percent of Northpark's outstanding common stock. After Centurion completed these purchases, they held two positions on Northpark's ten-member board of directors. Chuck Reilly had been persuaded by Joseph Fowler to buy the stock because Northpark was the "wave of the future" for the next few years in the media business. As Fowler reportedly described it in a meeting with Centurion Media's upper management:

> At least *until* Google and other Internet firms get the beta testing done for their technology and their internal processes ironed out, buying services such as Northpark will replace traditional sales departments. Then, in a few years Google and others will have made so many inroads into media buying that companies like Northpark won't be needed either. Centurion can get in on the action in the short-run by buying significant ownership of Northpark.

JOSEPH FOWLER

In the spring of 1999, Joseph Fowler was promoted from chief operating officer to CEO of Northpark Media. Fowler's career in media began with an internship during college in the sales department of one of Centurion Cable's systems. After graduation, he was hired as an account executive for a broadcast television station in Atlanta, Georgia. He later returned to his hometown of Boston where he worked his way up from sales to higher-level management positions at several cable systems in the area.

Fowler's reputation was that he did not take "no" for an answer. A sales assistant at Centurion Cable who had worked in a similar position at Northpark described his presidency there as "frightening," marked by indiscriminate firings of long-time employees. When he was hired as CEO of Northpark, financial news articles described Fowler's high six-figure salary, stock options, his bonuses which were based on revenue growth, and his seat on the Northpark board of directors. Only a short time after being hired as president of Centurion Cable, rumors circulated within the division that Fowler had played hard-to-get and ended up with an even higher compensation package from Centurion than what he had at Northpark. The corporate gossip was that Fowler had been allowed to keep his position on Northpark's board of directors and to retain ownership of his Northpark stock and options, although Bennett had no way of confirming this.

Chuck Reilly's memo in January 2006 announcing Fowler's hiring described his wide range of experience working in various media across the country, as well as the significant growth in Northpark's revenues and profits while he was their CEO. The memo ended with a statement about Chuck Reilly's professional respect for Fowler as a visionary in the media business and it mentioned their long-standing friendship. It also quoted Fowler as saying his personal business motto was: "Profits equal success."

THE CONTRACT REVIEW MEETING

Vicki Porter was alarmed at what Richard Bennett described over the phone. From what Bennett had read to her from the Northpark contract, their cable systems and all of those within Centurion Cable would, indeed, lose millions in advertising revenues. She could not imagine what had caused Joseph Fowler to sign a contract like that with Northpark. Was the guy that unfamiliar with Centurion's side of the industry? Or, did he just have a screw loose? She cleared her appointments for the entire afternoon in order to meet with Bennett.

When Porter arrived at Bennett's office, he was calmer than he had been on the phone that morning. But, he was dejected when he greeted her:

It's worse than I thought. I've been reading and re-reading this contract. In addition to every Centurion Cable system being *required* to sell all the advertising Northpark wants at extremely discounted rates, we have to *guarantee* that we'll run at least 90 percent of the commercials they buy. If we don't, we'll have to pay a penalty of five times the discounted ad rate. Oh yeah, and the contract wording says it *cannot* be cancelled and is *automatically renewable!*

Porter was stunned.

What do you mean? Even if I have a local advertiser who's willing to pay top dollar on the rate card—Northpark's discounted contract will take precedence over a higher rate paid by all other advertisers? Are you saying the Northpark contract also trumps annual contracts we already have in place? How's that supposed to work?

Bennett handed her the contract.

Read it for yourself. Look at section six on page four. It says the Northpark purchases of our commercials supersede all existing and future contracts with other advertisers. I don't think it can be any plainer than that.

Porter looked at section six of the contract.

That's exactly what it says. When this gets out, our sales people won't be able to sign up any new advertisers—at any price—because we won't be able to promise them their spots will actually make it on the air. There's too much chance they'll be bumped by Northpark, And, I don't even want to think about what our existing advertisers are going to say. At best, we'll lose our credibility with them. At worst, we'll get sued. Our contracts with existing advertisers contain a provision about being pre-empted only due to emergencies or other advertisers paying a *higher* rate; not a lower one!

Bennett was certain the contract meant financial disaster for Centurion. It would be one thing if Northpark bought only the unsold commercial time. But, the way he read the contract, Northpark was entitled to buy any commercial spots they wanted (prime-time and elsewhere) at deeply discounted rates. The real kicker in the contract was that all the Centurion Cable systems had to *guarantee* at least 90 percent of the spots Northpark bought would run and would not be pre-empted even if other advertisers were willing to pay more.

Bennett went on to describe telephone conversations he had earlier that day with the five other vice presidents of Centurion Cable.

After I got off the phone with you, I called every other vice president in the cable division. None of them saw this coming. Nobody can believe a contract of this magnitude could have—or would have—been kept so hush-hush. It's just not the way Centurion does things. Even though it's been like a revolving door in the president's office, everyone who's been in that position since I've been at Centurion has told the vice presidents to handle our own sales contracts. Every vice president I talked to today said this contract will make their region lose millions ... just like it will do to us.

In Bennett's southeast region in 2006, they were selling their commercial inventory at prices ranging from $80 to $180 per thirty-second spot (with an average of $100 each).

The deal that Fowler negotiated with Northpark allowed them to purchase any of Centurion's commercial advertising inventory for re-sale at prices discounted by 70 percent off the regular advertising rates. Consequently, almost overnight, Bennett's systems could be replacing revenue which averaged $100 per commercial with revenue averaging only $30 each! What had been a deeply discounted $30 spot turned into a $150 penalty if the spot purchased by Northpark did not air.

When she was hired as Sales Director, Porter began tracking the percentage of unsold inventory as well as the rates at which commercials were sold. She knew it was an important way to measure the effectiveness of her department and also to measure their progress from year to year. Before Porter joined Centurion Cable, their unsold inventory was at 80 percent, significantly higher than the industry average of 70 percent. She had steadily built her department and customer base and at the mid-point of

2006, they had achieved a level of 60 percent for unsold inventory. Porter knew that some of their success was due to a strong economy in their region. More importantly, Bennett had given her total authority to negotiate rates with customers, to build "packages" for multiple programs purchased, and to discount rates for annual contracts. As she showed two charts to Bennett (see **Exhibit 2** and **Exhibit 3**), she commented:

Look at these graphs. The first shows the dramatic decrease we have achieved in unsold inventory. Our region has gone from 80 percent when you first joined Centurion ten years ago to 60 percent for the first half of 2006. Right now we are ten percentage points below the industry average. We've achieved that while simultaneously increasing rates for the spots we sell. Our sales department worked their fannies off to achieve numbers like this. I've sacrificed a lot personally to make all this happen.

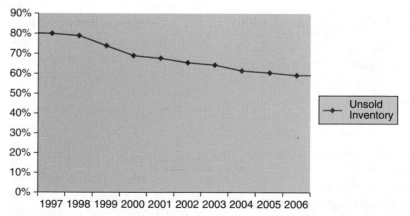

Exhibit 2   Centurion Cable—Southeast Region, Percent of Unsold Inventory, FY 1997–2006

Note: Data presented in the above chart is an average of all unsold inventory on all networks for all the systems in the southeastern region of Centurion Cable, 2006 data is for the first half of the year.

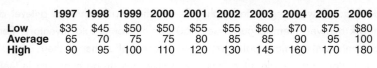

	1997	1998	1999	2000	2001	2002	2003	2004	2005	2006
Low	$35	$45	$50	$50	$55	$55	$60	$70	$75	$80
Average	65	70	75	75	80	85	85	90	95	100
High	90	95	100	110	120	130	145	160	170	180

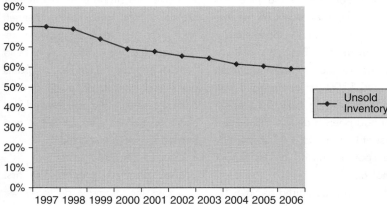

Exhibit 3   Centurion Cable—Southeast Region, Advertising Rates per :30 spot, FY 1997–2006

Note: The above rates were estimates of the average of all rates for commercials sold on all cable networks on all the systems in the southeast region of Centurion Media.

Do you think Fowler even looked at this data?

Bennett reassured Porter he knew their success in achieving the dramatic changes in advertising sales had been due to her efforts. He felt Fowler was not interested in any kind of data. There had to be something else going on. Maybe Fowler was just trying to make himself look good at the expense of everyone else.

The vice president in the Midwest region told Bennett he heard that Fowler was touting his Northpark deal as a huge revenue stream from "unsold" inventory on all the Centurion Cable systems. The word on the corporate grapevine was that Fowler had told Reilly unsold advertising inventory in every region was significantly higher than it should be and had convinced Reilly the contract would produce a large increase in revenue and profit. There was even some talk that Fowler might

centralize advertising sales for all of Centurion Cable into a single department reporting directly to his own brother, Steve. Everyone had been surprised when Fowler hired Steve as his own special assistant and gave him broad authority in areas where he had no experience or training. The thought of Steve, who had no sales experience in any industry, managing a centralized sales department for Centurion was disturbing to most of the managers and their sales staff in all of Centurion's divisions.

Prior to executing the Northpark contract, Fowler had not consulted with any of the vice presidents of Centurion Cable. Consequently, he could not have had any idea what portion of their inventory was unsold or how many annual contracts had already been signed with their customers. Bennett did not think there was any way for him to have known

how much commercial time was available to guarantee for sale to Northpark.

To get an idea of the financial impact of the Northpark contract, Bennett had prepared some very rough estimates of possible lost ad revenue for a single cable system in his own region (see **Exhibit 4**). Using a conservative figure of 5 percent for estimated inventory that Northpark might buy out from under regular advertisers, one system in the southeast region of Centurion Cable could lose an estimated $3.5 million based on regular ad rates. Northpark would be paying rates discounted by 70 percent off the regular price, causing the net decrease in revenues for Centurion to be an estimated $2.4 million. And, that figure was for only one cable system in the southeast region.

Of course, the $2.4 million figure was only an estimate for advertising revenues that might be lost from regular customers. Bennett knew that the counter argument would likely be that Northpark would sell advertising to new customers who had not previously bought on any Centurion system. But, the new sales volume would have to be more than triple any lost sales because Northpark's rates were only 30 percent of Centurion's rates to regular customers. Bennett was certain that was not possible in any market in the country.

The other vice presidents told Bennett they were outraged about the Northpark contract, but not enough to join him in going up the ladder to Chuck Reilly. They all indicated they were concerned Fowler would fire anyone who questioned him. Bennett asked Porter about a

EXHIBIT 4   Centurion Cable—Southeast Region, Bennett's Estimates of Ad Revenue Losses from Regular Advertisers for One Cable System

Average Ad Revenue per Single Cable System

4 spots per network $\times$ 24 hours per day $\times$ 365 days per year	= 35,040 avails per network
Average of 50 cable networks carried on each system	= 1,752,000 total avails
Sold inventory in 2006 was 40 percent (unsold at 60 percent)	= 700,800 estimated spots sold
Average spot rates of $100 across all networks and time slots	= $70,080,000 average revenue
$70,080,000 $\times$ potential 5 percent avails lost to Northpark	= $3,504,000
Northpark's rates discounted at 70 percent off regular rates	= $2,452,800 lost revenue *per cable system*

conference call he had earlier in the day with Centurion Media's general counsel, Tom Watson, and controller Cynthia Smith. Both had urged Bennett to "tread lightly." They said they had been involved in reviewing the contract and both thought it was a good deal that would have overall positive results from the standpoint of the entire Centurion corporation.

The comment from Tom Watson was:

After all, Centurion Media now owns 25 percent of Northpark. So, what's good for them is good for us. During our contract review meetings, Fowler briefed us on the Google and eBay plans to use their technology to auction off unsold ad inventory in newspapers, television, everything. That will be detrimental for advertising sales in all media—not just cable. Fowler's thinking ahead and looking out for us. We've needed somebody like him. Just like Chuck says—he is a visionary. Did you see what our stock price did this week? It's already increased—just on the rumors about the Northpark contract. And, Fowler's got

a seat on Northpark's board. His seat, along with our other two seats, gives us enough leverage to influence how the other seven directors vote. Fowler has close working relationships with everyone on that board. This is all good for Centurion. Do the right thing, Richard, and leave it alone.

Then Smith spoke up:

There's a lot more going on than just this one contract with Northpark, Fowler's been looking at all aspects of the cable division. He told us there are some real economies of scale and multi-million dollar savings to be gained by consolidating some administrative and, possibly, sales offices in all the regions. Those savings should offset any short-term decreases in revenues.

Apparently the corporate rumors were true. Fowler intended to eliminate all the regional sales offices. He had not shared this information with the vice presidents either. As Bennett was mentally processing what this meant for himself and other members

of his staff, Smith's next comments came as a real surprise.

You know, Richard, the media business is changing at an exponential rate. It's not like it was when you started. It won't be long until sales departments are nonexistent in all media. Advertisers will be able to go on-line and place their orders themselves and technology like Google or eBay will handle all the pricing. Fowler made a strong case to everyone at the corporate level that these changes are looming on the horizon and the Northpark contract is just a transitional step. You're only two years away from retirement. Why rock the boat at this point with a new president? Keep your head low and try to stay out of Fowler's way. He told us he'd fire anyone who did not implement the contract.

As he repeated this conversation to Porter, Bennett threw the Northpark contract down on his desk.

I've been a company man all my working life. But, if they think they can threaten me and get me to back off, they better think again. This Northpark contract stinks to high-heaven. I'm reporting this to the SEC, the FCC, Internal Audit, our external auditors, and anyone else who will listen. I've never compromised my integrity by looking the other way and I don't intend to start now.

Porter was taken aback at Smith's disclosure that Fowler might shut down all the regional sales departments. But, her more immediate concern was that any rash actions by Bennett might hasten whatever changes Fowler had planned. Porter

knew Bennett valued his ethics above all else and always put the welfare of the company and his employees and customers ahead of his own needs. However, she wanted him to consider the implications of what Smith had said:

Richard, you've got to know how much I respect you. So, don't get mad at what I'm about to say. Smith may be right. You and your wife have been looking forward to your retirement for so long. You've made plans to travel and spend more time with your kids and grandkids. If Fowler's half as

nasty as his reputation, he could really screw things up for you.

Bennett had prided himself on his ethical approach to all business decisions during his entire career. He had also been certain not to put other people at risk based on his own actions. He knew that if he was not careful, his career could end *very* soon. It was also likely that Porter would be seen as "guilty by association" and her career could also be in jeopardy. He had to be certain that whatever action he took was, in fact, doing the right thing.

NOTES

1. Eisenmann, p. 1.
2. National Cable & Telecommunications Association, "Industry Statistics" section of organization's Web site. http://www.ncta.com/ContentView.aspx?contendld=66.
3. Ibid.
4. Kara Nortman, "The Future of Television," *The Battery Charger*, June 2006. http://www.battery.com/content/news/charger/June2006/future.html.
5. Ibid.
6. Miguel Helft, "Google, Online Ad Giant, Looks at Radio and TV," *The New York Times*, March 29, 2007. http://www.nytimes.com/2007/03/29/technology/29google.html.
7. Robert Young, "Google ... the OS for Advertising," Gigaom, November 9, 2006. http://gigaom.com/2006/11/09/google-the-os-for-advertising/.
8. Linda Haugsted, "Online Ad Market Nears," *Multichannel News*, August 14, 2006, p. 2.
9. Helft.

REFERENCES

Eisenmann, Thomas R. 2000. Cable TV: From community antennas to wired cities. *Harvard Business School Working Knowledge*, July 10: 1.

Haugsted, Linda. 2006. Online ad market nears. *Multichannel News*, August 14: 2.

Helft, Miguel. 2007. Google, online ad giant, looks at radio and TV: *The New York Times*, March 29. http://www.nytimes.com/2007/03/29/technology/29google.html

National Cable & Telecommunications Association. "Industry statistics" section of organization's Web site. http://www.ncta.com/ContentView.aspx?contendld=66.

Nortman, Kara. 2006. The future of television. *The Battery Charger*, June. http://www.battery.com/content/news/charger/June2006/furure.html.

Young, Robert. 2006. Google ... the OS for advertising. Gigaom. November 9. http://gigaom.com/2006/11/09/google-the-os-for-advertising/.

glossary

achievement motivation The degree to which an individual desires to perform in terms of a standard of excellence or to succeed in competitive situations.

achievement-oriented leadership Leadership behavior characterized by setting challenging goals and seeking to improve performance.

acute stress A short-term stress reaction to an immediate threat.

affective commitment Organizational commitment due to one's strong positive attitudes toward the organization.

agreeableness The degree to which an individual is easy-going and tolerant.

ambidextrous organization An organization structure that balances formalization and standardization to help to achieve efficiency and flexibility.

anchoring bias A cognitive bias in which the first piece of information that is encountered about a situation is emphasized too much in making a decision.

approval motivation The degree to which an individual is concerned about presenting himself or herself in a socially desirable way in evaluative situations.

ascribed status Status and power that is assigned by cultural norms and depends on group membership.

aspiration–performance discrepancies Gaps between what an individual, unit, or organization wants to achieve and what it is actually achieving.

associates The workers who carry out the basic tasks.

attitude A persistent tendency to feel and behave in a favorable or unfavorable way toward a specific person, object, or idea.

attitudinal structuring Activities aimed at influencing the attitudes and relationships of the negotiating parties.

authoritarianism The degree to which an individual believes in conventional values, obedience to authority, and legitimacy of power differences in society.

brainstorming A process in which a large number of ideas are generated while evaluation of the ideas is suspended.

burnout A condition of physical or emotional exhaustion generally brought about by stress; associates and managers experiencing burnout show various symptoms, such as constant fatigue, or lack of enthusiasm for work, and increasing isolation from others.

business strategy How a firm competes for success against other organizations in a particular market.

centralization The degree to which authority for meaningful decisions is retained at the top of an organization.

centralized networks A communication network in which one or a few network members dominate communications.

changes in top management Involve the replacement of top management team members who retire or depart the company for other reasons.

charisma A leader's ability to inspire emotion and passion in his followers and to cause them to identify with the leader.

chronic stress A long-term stress reaction resulting from ongoing situations.

coalition A group whose members act together to actively pursue a common interest.

coercive power Power resulting from the ability to punish others.

cognitive biases Mental shortcuts involving simplified ways of thinking.

cognitive dissonance An uneasy feeling produced when a person behaves in a manner inconsistent with an existing attitude.

common information bias A bias in which group members overemphasize information held by a majority or the entire group while failing to be mindful of information held by one group member or a few members.

communication audit An analysis of an organization's internal and external communication to assess communication practices and capabilities and to determine needs.

communication climate Associates' perceptions regarding the quality of communication within the organization.

communication medium or communication channel The manner in which a message is conveyed.

communication The sharing of information between two or more people to achieve a common understanding about an object or situation.

competitive advantage An advantage enjoyed by an organization that can perform some aspect of its work better than competitors can or in a way that competitors cannot duplicate, such that it offers products/services that are more valuable to customers.

confirmation bias A cognitive bias in which information confirming early beliefs and ideas is sought while potentially disconfirming information is not sought.

conflict escalation The process whereby a conflict grows increasingly worse over time.

conflict A process in which one party perceives that its interests are being opposed or negatively affected by another party.

conscientiousness The degree to which an individual focuses on goals and works toward them in a disciplined way.

consideration A behavioral leadership style demonstrated by leaders who express friendship, develop mutual trust and respect, and have strong interpersonal relationships with those being led.

contingency theory of leadership effectiveness A theory of leadership that suggests that the effectiveness of a leader depends on the interaction of his style of behavior with certain characteristics of the situation.

continuance commitment Organizational commitment due to lack of better opportunities.

continuous reinforcement A reinforcement schedule in which a reward occurs after each instance of a behavior or set of behaviors.

corporate strategy The overall approach an organization uses in interacting with its environment. The emphasis is placed on growth and diversification.

cultural audit A tool for assessing and understanding the culture of an organization.

cultural fluency The ability to identify, understand, and apply cultural differences that influence communication.

cultural intelligence The ability to separate the aspects of behavior that are based in culture from those unique to the individual or all humans in general.

culture shock A stress reaction involving difficulties coping with the requirements of life in a new country.

culture Shared values and taken-for-granted assumptions that govern acceptable behavior and thought patterns in a country and give a country much of its uniqueness.

DADA syndrome A sequence of stages—denial, anger, depression, and acceptance—through which individuals can move or in which they can become trapped when faced with unwanted change.

decentralized networks A communication network in which no single network member dominates communications.

decisions Choices of actions from among multiple feasible alternatives.

decoding The process whereby a receiver perceives a sent message and interprets its meaning.

Delphi technique A highly structured decision-making process in which participants are surveyed regarding their opinions or best judgments.

demand–control model A model that suggests that experienced stress is a function of both job demands and job control. Stress is highest when demands are high but individuals have little control over the situation.

dense networks A communication network in which most or all network members communicate with many other members.

departmentalization The grouping of human and other resources into units, typically based on functional areas or markets.

destructive individual roles Roles involving self-centered behaviors that put individual needs and goals ahead of the team.

devil's advocacy A group decision-making technique that relies on a critique of a recommended action and its underlying assumptions.

dialectical inquiry A group decision-making technique that relies on debate between two subgroups that have developed different recommendations based on different assumptions.

directive leadership Leadership behavior characterized by implementing guidelines, providing information on what is expected, setting definite performance standards, and ensuring that individuals follow rules.

discrimination Behavior that results in unequal treatment of individuals based on group membership.

distributive bargaining A strategy that: (1) involves a competing, win–lose approach and (2) tends to be used when one party's goals are in direct conflict with the goals of another party.

distributive justice The degree to which people think outcomes are fair.

diversification Related to the number of different product lines or service areas in the organization.

diversity A characteristic of a group of people where differences exist on one or more relevant dimensions such as gender.

diversity-based infighting A situation in which group members engage in unproductive, negative conflict over differing views.

divisible tasks Tasks that can be separated into subcomponents.

downward communication Communication that flows from superior to subordinate.

dysfunctional conflict Conflict that is detrimental to organizational goals and objectives.

dystress Negative stress; often referred to simply as stress.

ease-of-recall bias A cognitive bias in which information that is easy to recall from memory is relied upon too much in making a decision.

effort–reward imbalance model A model that suggests that experienced stress is a function of both required effort and rewards obtained. Stress is highest when required effort is high but rewards are low.

emotional contagion Phenomenon where emotions experienced by one or a few members of a work group spread to other members.

emotional intelligence The ability to accurately appraise one's own and others' emotions, effectively regulate one's own and others' emotions, and use emotion to motivate, plan, and achieve.

emotional labor The process whereby associates must display emotions that are contrary to what they are feeling.

emotional stability The degree to which an individual easily handles stressful situations and heavy demands.

emotions Complex subjective reactions that have both a physical and mental component.

emotions States corresponding to specific feelings, such as anger, that tend to be associated with particular events, people, or other stimuli.

employee-centered leadership style A behavioral leadership style that emphasizes employees' personal needs and the development of interpersonal relationships.

encoding The process whereby a sender translates the information he or she wishes to send in a message.

environmental uncertainty The degree to which an environment is complex and changing; uncertain environments are difficult to monitor and understand.

equity theory A theory that suggests motivation is based on a person's assessment of the ratio of outcomes she receives (e.g., pay, status) for inputs on the job (e.g., effort, ability) compared to the same ratio for a comparison other.

ERG theory Alderfer's theory that suggests people are motivated by three hierarchically ordered types of needs: existence needs (E), relatedness needs (R), and growth needs (G). A person may work on all three needs at the same time, although satisfying lower-order needs often takes place before a person is strongly motivated by higher-level needs.

ethnocentrism The belief that one's culture is better than others.

eustress Positive stress that results from facing challenges and difficulties with the expectation of achievement.

expatriate An individual who leaves his or her home country to live and work in a foreign land.

expectancy theory Vroom's theory that suggests that motivation is a function of an individual's expectancy that a given amount of effort will lead to a particular level of performance, instrumentality judgments that indicate performance will lead to certain outcomes, and the valences of outcomes.

expectancy The subjective probability that a given amount of effort will lead to a particular level of performance.

expert power Power resulting from special expertise or technical knowledge

exploitative learning Learning how to more effectively use current knowledge.

exploratory learning Creating new knowledge and being innovative.

extinction A reinforcement contingency in which a behavior is followed by the absence of a previously encountered positive consequence, thereby reducing the likelihood that the behavior will be repeated in the same or similar situations.

extraversion The degree to which an individual is outgoing and derives energy from being around other people.

feedback The process whereby a receiver encodes the message received and sends it or a response to it back to the original sender.

feeling A decision style focused on subjective evaluation and the emotional reactions of others.

formal communication Communication that follows the formal structure of the organization (e.g., superior to subordinate) and entails organizationally sanctioned information.

formal groups Groups to which members are formally assigned.

formalization The degree to which rules and operating procedures are documented on paper or in company intranets.

functional conflict Conflict that is beneficial to organizational goals and objectives.

fundamental attribution error A perception problem in which an individual is too likely to attribute the behavior of others to internal rather than external causes.

glass border The unseen but strong discriminatory barrier that blocks many women from opportunities for international assignments.

global strategy A strategy by which a firm provides standard products and services to all parts of the world while maintaining a strong degree of central control in the home country.

globalization The trend toward a unified global economy where national borders mean relatively little.

goal-setting theory A theory that suggests challenging and specific goals increase human performance because they affect attention, effort, and persistence.

gossip Information that is presumed to be factual and is communicated in private or intimate settings.

group Two or more interdependent individuals who influence one another through social interaction.

groupthink A situation in which group members maintain or seek consensus at the expense of identifying and debating honest disagreements.

growth Relates to increases in sales as well as associates and managers.

halo effect A perception problem in which an individual assesses a person positively or negatively in all situations based on an existing general assessment of the person.

hardiness A personality dimension corresponding to a strong internal commitment to activities, an internal locus of control, and challenge seeking.

height The number of hierarchical levels in an organization, from the CEO to the lower-level associates.

hierarchy of needs theory Maslow's theory that suggests people are motivated by their desire to satisfy specific needs, and that needs are arranged in a hierarchy with physiological needs at the bottom and self-actualization needs at the top. People must satisfy needs at lower levels before being motivated by needs at higher levels.

hierarchy The reporting relationships depicted in an organization chart.

high-context cultures A type of culture where individuals use contextual cues to understand people and their communications and where individuals value trust and personal relationships.

high-involvement management Involves carefully selecting and training associates and giving them significant decision-making power, information, and incentive compensation.

horizontal communication Communication that takes place between and among people at the same level.

human capital imitability The extent to which the skills and talents of an organization's people can be copied by other organizations.

human capital rareness The extent to which the skills and talents of an organization's people are unique in the industry.

human capital value The extent to which individuals are capable of producing work that supports an organization's strategy for competing in the marketplace.

human capital The sum of the skills, knowledge, and general attributes of the people in an organization.

hygienes Job factors that can influence job dissatisfaction but not satisfaction.

identity groups Groups based on the social identities of members.

implicit person theories Personal theories about what personality traits and abilities occur together and how these attributes are manifested in behavior.

incivility Slightly deviant behavior with ambiguous intent to harm another person.

informal communication Communication that involves spontaneous interaction between two or more people outside the formal organization structure.

informal groups Groups formed spontaneously by people who share interests, values, or identities.

information technology An overall set of tools, based on microelectronic technology, designed to provide data, documents, and commentary as well as analysis support to individuals in an organization.

initiating structure A behavioral leadership style demonstrated by leaders who establish well-defined patterns of organization and communication, define procedures, and delineate their relationships with those being led.

instrumentality Perceived connections between performance and outcomes.

integrative bargaining A strategy that: (1) involves a collaborative, win–win approach and (2) tends to be used when the nature of the problem permits a solution that is attractive to both parties.

intelligence General mental ability used in complex information processing.

intermittent reinforcement A reinforcement schedule in which a reward does not occur after each instance of a behavior or set of behaviors.

international ethics Principles of proper conduct focused on issues such as corruption, exploitation of labor, and environmental impact.

interpersonal cohesion Team members' liking or attraction to other team members.

interpersonal communication Direct verbal or nonverbal interaction between two or more active participants.

intuition A decision style focused on developing abstractions and figurative examples for use in decision making, with an emphasis on imagination and possibilities.

job enlargement The process of making a job more motivating by adding tasks that are similar in complexity relative to the current tasks.

job enrichment The process of making a job more motivating by increasing responsibility.

job redesign Enlargement or enrichment of jobs; enrichment is the better method to enhance motivation for effective problem solving, communication, and learning.

job stress The feeling that one's capabilities, resources, or needs do not match the demands or requirements of the job.

job-centered leadership style A behavioral leadership style that emphasizes employee tasks and the methods used to accomplish them.

lateral relations Elements of structure designed to draw individuals together for interchanges related to work issues and problems.

leader–member exchange A model of leadership focused on leaders developing more positive relationships with some individuals and having more positive exchanges with these individuals.

leader–member relations The degree to which a leader is respected, is accepted as a leader, and has friendly interpersonal relations.

leadership The process of providing general direction and influencing individuals or groups to achieve goals.

learning A process through which individuals change their relatively permanent behavior based on positive or negative experiences in a situation.

legitimate power Power derived from position; also known as formal authority.

life-cycle forces Natural and predictable pressures that build as an organization grows and that must be addressed if the organization is to continue growing.

locus of control The degree to which an individual attributes control of events to self or external factors.

low-context cultures A type of culture where individuals rely on direct questioning to understand people and their communications and where individuals value efficiency and performance.

management by objectives (MBO) A management process in which individuals negotiate task objectives with their managers and then are held accountable for attainment of those objectives.

managing organizational behavior Actions focused on acquiring, developing, and applying the knowledge and skills of people.

mass customization A manufacturing technology that involves integrating sophisticated information technology and management methods to produce a flexible manufacturing system with the ability to customize products for many customers in a short time.

maximization tasks Tasks with a quantity goal.

modern racism Subtle forms of discrimination that occur despite people knowing it is wrong to be prejudiced against other racial groups and despite believing they are not racist.

monochronic time orientation A preference for focusing on one task per unit of time and completing that task in a timely fashion.

monolithic organization An organization that is homogeneous.

moods States corresponding to general positive or negative feelings disconnected from any particular event or stimulus.

motivation Forces coming from within a person that account for the willful direction, intensity, and persistence of the person's efforts toward achieving specific goals, where achievement is not due solely to ability or to environmental factors.

motivators Job factors that can influence job satisfaction but not dissatisfaction.

multicultural organization An organization in which the organizational culture values differences.

multidomestic strategy A strategy by which a firm tailors its products and services to the needs of each country or region in which it operates and gives a great deal of power to the managers and associates in those countries or regions.

need for achievement The need to perform well against a standard of excellence.

need for affiliation The need to be liked and to stay on good terms with most other people.

need for power The desire to influence people and events.

negative reinforcement A reinforcement contingency in which a behavior is followed by the withdrawal of a previously encountered negative consequence, thereby increasing the likelihood that the behavior will be repeated in the same or similar situations.

negotiation A process through which parties with different preferences and interests attempt to agree on a solution.

nominal group technique A process for group decision making in which discussion is structured and the final solution is decided by silent vote.

nonverbal communication Communication that takes place without using spoken or written language, such as communication through facial expressions and body language.

normative commitment Organizational commitment due to feelings of obligation.

norms Informal rules or standards that regulate the team's behavior.

OB Mod A formal procedure focused on improving task performance through positive reinforcement of desired behaviors and extinction of undesired behaviors.

openness to experience The degree to which an individual seeks new experiences and thinks creatively about the future.

operant conditioning theory An explanation for consequence-based learning that assumes learning results from simple conditioning and that higher mental functioning is irrelevant.

optimization tasks Tasks with a quality goal.

organization development (OD) A planned organization-wide continuous process designed to improve communication, problem solving, and learning through the application of behavioral science knowledge.

organization A collection of individuals forming a coordinated system of specialized activities for the purpose of achieving certain goals over an extended period of time.

organizational behavior The actions of individuals and groups in an organizational context.

organizational culture The values shared by associates and managers in an organization.

organizational politics Behavior that is directed toward furthering one's own self-interests without concern for the interests or well-being of others.

organizational structure Work roles and authority relationships that influence behavior in an organization.

participative leadership Leadership behavior characterized by sharing information, consulting with those who are led, and emphasizing group decision making.

path–goal leadership theory A theory of leadership based on expectancy concepts from the study of motivation, which suggests that leader effectiveness depends on the degree to which a leader enhances the performance expectancies and valences of her subordinates.

perception A process that involves sensing various aspects of a person, task, or event and forming impressions based on selected inputs.

personal conflict Conflict that arises out of personal differences between people, such as differing values, personal goals, and personalities.

personality A stable set of characteristics representing internal properties of an individual, which are reflected in behavioral tendencies across a variety of situations.

planned change A process involving deliberate efforts to move an organization or a unit from its current undesirable state to a new, more desirable state.

plural organization An organization that has a diverse workforce and takes steps to be inclusive and respectful of differences, but where diversity is tolerated rather than truly valued.

political skill The ability to effectively understand others at work and to use this knowledge to enhance one's own objectives.

polychronic time orientation A willingness to juggle multiple tasks per unit of time and to have interruptions, and an unwillingness to be driven by time.

position power The degree to which a leader can reward, punish, promote, or demote individuals in the unit or organization.

positive organizational behavior An approach to managing people that nurtures each individual's greatest strengths and helps people use them to their and the organization's advantage.

positive reinforcement A reinforcement contingency in which a behavior is followed by a positive consequence, thereby increasing the likelihood that the behavior will be repeated in the same or similar situations.

power The ability to achieve desired outcomes.

prejudice Unfair negative attitudes we hold about people who belong to social or cultural groups other than our own.

procedural conflict Conflict that arises over how work should be completed.

procedural justice The degree to which people think the procedures used to determine outcomes are fair.

process loss The difference between actual and potential team performance that is caused by diverting time and energy into maintaining the team as opposed to working on substantive tasks.

projecting A perception problem in which an individual assumes that others share his or her values and beliefs.

punctuated equilibrium model (PEM) A model of team development that suggests that teams do not go through linear stages but that team formation depends on the task at hand and the deadlines for that task.

punishment A reinforcement contingency in which a behavior is followed by a negative consequence, thereby reducing the likelihood that the behavior will be repeated in the same or similar situations.

reference point A possible level of performance used to evaluate one's current standing.

referent power Power resulting from others' desire to identify with the referent.

refreezing A phase in the change process in which leaders lock in new approaches by implementing evaluation systems that track expected behaviors, by creating reward systems that reinforce expected behaviors, and by ensuring that hiring and promotion systems support the new demands.

resistance to change Efforts to block the introduction of new approaches. Some of these efforts are passive in nature, involving tactics such as verbally supporting the change while continuing to work in the old ways; other efforts are active in nature, involving tactics such as organized protests and sabotage.

reward power Power resulting from the ability to provide others with desired outcomes.

risk-taking propensity Willingness to take chances.

risky shift A process by which group members collectively make a more risky choice than most or all of the individuals would have made working alone.

role ambiguity A situation in which goals, expectations, and/or basic job requirements are unclear.

role conflict A situation in which different roles lead to conflicting expectations.

roles Expectations shared by group members about who is to perform what types of tasks and under what conditions.

rumors Unsubstantiated information of universal interest.

satisficing decisions Satisfactory rather than optimal decisions.

self-contained tasks An integration technique whereby a department is given resources from other functional areas in order to reduce the need to coordinate with those areas.

self-efficacy An individual's belief that he or she will be able to perform a specific task in a given situation.

self-monitoring The degree to which an individual attempts to present the image he or she thinks others want to see in a given situation.

self-serving bias A perception problem in which an individual is too likely to attribute the failure of others to internal causes and the successes of others to external causes, whereas the same individual will be too likely to attribute his own failure to external causes and his own successes to internal causes.

sensing A decision style focused on gathering concrete information directly through the senses, with an emphasis on practical and realistic ideas.

servant leadership An approach to leadership focused on serving others.

simulation A representation of a real system that allows associates and managers to try various actions and receive feedback on the consequences of those actions.

slack resources An integration technique whereby a department keeps more resources on hand than absolutely required in order to reduce the need for tight communication and coordination with other departments.

social dominance orientation A general attitudinal orientation concerning whether one prefers social relationships to be equal or to reflect status differences.

social facilitation effect Improvement in individual performance when others are present.

social identity A person's knowledge that he or she belongs to certain social groups, where belonging to those groups has emotional significance.

social learning theory An explanation for consequence-based learning that acknowledges the higher mental functioning of human beings and the role such functioning can play in learning.

social loafing A phenomenon wherein people put forth less effort when they work in teams than when they work alone.

socialization model A model proposing that all leaders in a particular organization will display similar leadership styles, because all have been selected and socialized by the same organization.

socialization A process through which an organization imparts its values to newcomers.

socioemotional roles Roles that require behaviors that support the social aspects of the organization.

span of control The number of individuals a manager directly oversees.

sparse networks A communication network in which most or all network members communicate with only a few other members.

specialization The degree to which associates and managers have jobs with narrow scopes and limited variety.

standardization The degree to which rules and standard operating procedures govern behavior in an organization.

stereotype A generalized set of beliefs about the characteristics of a group of individuals.

stereotyping A perception problem in which an individual bases perceptions about members of a group on a generalized set of beliefs about the characteristics of a group of individuals.

strategic contingencies model of power A model holding that organizational units and people gain power by being able to address the major problems and issues faced by the organization.

strategic OB approach An approach that involves organizing and managing people's knowledge and skills effectively to implement the organization's strategy and gain a competitive advantage.

stress response An unconscious mobilization of energy resources that occurs when the body encounters a stressor.

stress A feeling of tension that occurs when a person perceives that a situation is about to exceed her ability to cope and consequently could endanger her well-being.

stressors Environmental conditions that cause individuals to experience stress.

structural characteristics The tangible, physical properties that determine the basic shape and appearance of an organization's hierarchy.

structural–cultural model A model holding that because women often experience lack of power, lack of respect, and certain stereotypical expectations, they develop leadership styles different from those of the men.

structuring characteristics The policies and approaches used to directly prescribe the behavior of managers and associates.

subcultures In the organizational context, groups that share values that differ from the main values of the organization.

substantive conflict Conflict that involves work content, tasks, and task goals.

sunk-cost bias A cognitive bias in which past investments of time, effort, and/or money are heavily weighted in deciding on continued investment.

supplemental organizational processes Processes in which associates and/or managers have ongoing meetings for the purpose of understanding and addressing important problems.

supportive leadership Leadership behavior characterized by friendliness and concern for individuals' well-being, welfare, and needs.

survey feedback Data obtained from questionnaires; managers receive the data for their units and are expected to hold unit meetings to discuss problems.

swift trust A phenomenon where trust develops rapidly based on positive, reciprocated task-related communications.

synergy An effect wherein the total output of a team is greater than the combined outputs of individual members working alone.

task cohesion Team members' attraction and commitment to the tasks and goals of the team.

task roles Roles that require behaviors aimed at achieving the team's performance goals and tasks.

task structure The degree to which tasks can be broken down into easily understood steps or parts.

team building A process in which members of a team work together and with a facilitator to diagnose task, process, and interpersonal problems within the team and create solutions.

team orientation The extent to which an individual works well with others, wants to contribute to team performance, and enjoys being on a team.

team Two or more people with work roles that require them to be interdependent, who operate within a larger social system (the organization), performing tasks relevant to the organization's mission, with consequences that affect others inside and outside the organization, and who have membership that is identifiable to those on the team and those not on the team.

t-group training Group exercises in which individuals focus on their actions, how others perceive their actions, and how others generally react to them; participants often learn about unintended negative consequences of certain types of behavior.

thinking A decision style focused on objective evaluation and systematic analysis.

training A process used in OD to help managers and associates to gain skills and capabilities needed to accomplish tasks in their jobs.

transactional leadership A leadership approach that is based on the exchange relationship between followers and leaders. Transactional leadership is characterized by contingent reward behavior and active management-by-exception behavior.

transformational leadership A leadership approach that involves motivating followers to do more than expected, to continuously develop and grow, to increase self-confidence, and to place the interests of the unit or organization before their own. Transformational leadership involves charisma, intellectual stimulation, and individual consideration.

transforming A phase in the change process in which leaders help to implement new approaches by providing information that supports proposed changes and by providing resources and training to bring about actual shifts in behavior.

transnational strategy A strategy by which a firm tailors its products and services to some degree to meet the needs of different countries or regions of the world but also seeks some degree of standardization in order to keep costs reasonably low.

two-factor theory Herzberg's motivation theory that suggests that job satisfaction and dissatisfaction are not opposite ends of the same continuum but are independent states and that different factors affect satisfaction and dissatisfaction.

Type A personality A personality type characterized by competitiveness, aggressiveness, and impatience.

unfreezing A phase in the change process in which leaders help managers and associates move beyond the past by providing a rationale for change, by creating guilt and/or anxiety about not changing, and by creating a sense of psychological safety concerning the change.

unitary tasks Tasks that cannot be divided and must be performed by an individual.

upward communication Communication that flows from subordinate to superior.

valence Value associated with an outcome.

values Abstract ideals that relate to proper life goals and methods for reaching those goals.

virtual electronic teams Teams that rely heavily on electronically mediated communication rather than face-to-face meetings as the means to coordinate work.

virtual teams Teams in which members work together but are separated by time, distance, or organizational structure.

organization index

name index

subject index

OB skills workbook

www.wileyplus.com

WileyPLUS is a research-based online environment for effective teaching and learning.

WileyPLUS builds students' confidence because it takes the guesswork out of studying by providing students with a clear roadmap:

- **what to do**
- **how to do it**
- **if they did it right**

It offers interactive resources along with a complete digital textbook that help students learn more. With *WileyPLUS*, students take more initiative so you'll have greater impact on their achievement in the classroom and beyond.

12th edition

ORGANIZATIONAL BEHAVIOR

John R. Schermerhorn, Jr. | Richard N. Osborn | Mary Uhl-Bien | James G. Hunt
Ohio University | Wayne State University | University of Nebraska | Texas Tech University

John Wiley & Sons, Inc.
WILEY

VICE PRESIDENT & EXECUTIVE PUBLISHER	George Hoffman
EXECUTIVE EDITOR	Lisé Johnson
DEVELOPMENTAL EDITOR	Susan McLaughlin
ASSOCIATE EDITOR	Sarah Vernon
PROJECT EDITOR	Brian Baker
ASSOCIATE DIRECTOR OF MARKETING	Amy Scholz
MARKETING MANAGER	Kelly Simmons
MARKETING ASSISTANT	Ashley Tomeck
DESIGN DIRECTOR	Harry Nolan
SENIOR CONTENT MANAGER	Dorothy Sinclair
SENIOR PRODUCTION EDITOR	Erin Bascom
SENIOR MEDIA EDITOR	Allison Morris
MEDIA SPECIALISTS	Elena Santa Maria and Thomas Caruso
PHOTO DEPARTMENT MANAGER	Hilary Newman
PHOTO RESEARCHER	Lisa Passmore
EDITORIAL ASSISTANT	Melissa Solarz
ILLUSTRATION EDITOR	Anna Melhorn
PRODUCTION MANAGEMENT SERVICES	Ingrao Associates
TEXT DESIGNER	Madelyn Lesure
COVER DESIGNER	Wendy Lai
COVER PHOTO	©ULTRA.F/Getty Images, Inc.
UMBRELLA ICON	©Monti26/Shutterstock

This book was typeset in 10/12 ITC Garamond at Aptara®, Inc. and printed and bound by Quad Graphics/Versailles. The cover was printed by Quad Graphics/Versailles.

This book is printed on acid free paper. ∞

Founded in 1807, John Wiley & Sons, Inc. has been a valued source of knowledge and understanding for more than 200 years, helping people around the world meet their needs and fulfill their aspirations. Our company is built on a foundation of principles that include responsibility to the communities we serve and where we live and work. In 2008, we launched a Corporate Citizenship Initiative, a global effort to address the environmental, social, economic, and ethical challenges we face in our business. Among the issues we are addressing are carbon impact, paper specifications and procurement, ethical conduct within our business and among our vendors, and community and charitable support. For more information, please visit our website: www.wiley.com/go/citizenship.

Evaluation copies are provided to qualified academics and professionals for review purposes only, for use in their courses during the next academic year. These copies are licensed and may not be sold or transferred to a third party. Upon completion of the review period, please return the evaluation copy to Wiley. Return instructions and a free of charge return shipping label are available at www.wiley.com/go/returnlabel. If you have chosen to adopt this textbook for use in your course, please accept this book as your complimentary desk copy. Outside of the United States, please contact your local representative.

ISBN 13 978-0-470-87820-0
          978-1-118-12931-9

Printed in the United States of America.

10 9 8 7 6 5 4 3 2 1

Dr. John R. Schermerhorn, Jr. is the Charles G. O'Bleness Professor Emeritus of Management in the College of Business at Ohio University where he teaches undergraduate and MBA courses in management, organizational behavior, and Asian business. He earned a Ph.D. in organizational behavior from Northwestern University, after receiving an M.B.A. (with distinction) in management and international business from New York University, and a B.S. in business administration from the State University of New York at Buffalo.

Dedicated to instructional excellence and serving the needs of practicing managers, Dr. Schermerhorn focuses on bridging the gap between the theory and practice of management in both the classroom and in his textbooks. He has won awards for teaching excellence at Tulane University, The University of Vermont, and Ohio University, where he was named a *University Professor*, the university's leading campus-wide award for undergraduate teaching. He also received the excellence in leadership award for his service as Chair of the Management Education and Development Division of the Academy of Management.

Dr. Schermerhorn's international experience adds a unique global dimension to his teaching and textbooks. He holds an honorary doctorate from the University of Pécs in Hungary, awarded for his international scholarly contributions to management research and education. He has also served as a Visiting Professor of Management at the Chinese University of Hong Kong, as on-site Coordinator of the Ohio University MBA and Executive MBA programs in Malaysia, and as Kohei Miura visiting professor at the Chubu University of Japan. Presently he is Adjunct Professor at the National University of Ireland at Galway, a member of the graduate faculty at Bangkok University in Thailand, and Permanent Lecturer in the PhD program at the University of Pécs in Hungary.

An enthusiastic scholar, Dr. Schermerhorn is a member of the Academy of Management, where he served as chairperson of the Management Education and Development Division. Educators and students alike know him as author of *Management 11e* (Wiley, 2011) and *Exploring Management 3e* (2012), and senior co-author of *Organizational Behavior 12/e* (Wiley, 2012). His many books are available in Chinese, Dutch, French, Indonesian, Portuguese, Russian, and Spanish language editions. Dr. Schermerhorn's published articles are found in the *Academy of Management Journal, Academy of Management Review Academy of Management Executive, Organizational Dynamics, Journal of Management Education*, and the *Journal of Management Development*.

Dr. Schermerhorn is a popular guest speaker at colleges and universities. His recent student and faculty workshop topics include innovations in business education, teaching the millennial generation, global perspectives in management education, and textbook writing and scholarly manuscript development.

Dr. John R. Schermerhorn, Jr.

Dr. James G. (Jerry) Hunt

The late Dr. James G. (Jerry) Hunt was the Paul Whitfield Horn Professor of Management, Professor of Health Organization Management, Former Director, Institute for Leadership Research, and former department Chair of Management, Texas Tech University. He received his Ph.D. and master's degrees from the University of Illinois after completing a B.S. (with honors) at Michigan Technological University. Dr. Hunt co-authored an organization theory text and *Core Concepts of Organizational Behavior* (Wiley, 2004) and authored or co-authored three leadership monographs. He founded the Leadership Symposia Series and co-edited the eight volumes based on the series. He was the former editor of the *Journal of Management* and *The Leadership Quarterly*. He presented or published some 200 articles, papers, and book chapters, and among his better-known books are *Leadership: A New Synthesis*, published by Sage, and *Out-of-the-Box Leadership*, published by JAI. The former was a finalist for the Academy of Management's 1993 Terry Distinguished Book Award. Dr. Hunt received the Distinguished Service Award from the Academy of Management, the Sustained Outstanding Service Award from the Southern Management Association, and the Barnie E. Rushing, Jr. Distinguished Researcher Award from Texas Tech University for his long-term contributions to management research and scholarship. He also lived and taught in England, Finland, and Thailand, and taught in China.

Dr. Richard N. Osborn

Dr. Richard N. Osborn is a Wayne State University Distinguished Professor, Professor of Management Emeritus, and former Board of Governors Faculty Fellow. He has received teaching awards at Southern Illinois University at Carbondale and Wayne State University, and he has also taught at Arizona State University, Monash University (Australia), Tulane University, University of Munich, and the University of Washington. He received a DBA from Kent State University after earning an MBA at Washington State University and a B.S. from Indiana University. With over 200 presentations and publications, he is a charter member of the Academy of Management Journals Hall of Fame. Dr. Osborn is a leading authority on international alliances in technology-intensive industries and is co-author of an organization theory text as well as *Basic Organizational Behavior* (John Wiley & Sons, 1995, 1998). He has served as editor of international strategy for the *Journal of World Business* and Special Issue Editor for *The Academy of Management Journal*. He serves or has served as a member of the editorial boards for *The Academy of Management Journal, The Academy of Management Review, Journal of High Technology Management, The Journal of Management, Leadership Quarterly*, and *Technology Studies*, among others. He is very active in the Academy of Management, having served as divisional program chair and president, as well as the Academy representative for the International Federation of Scholarly Associations of Management. Dr. Osborn's research has been sponsored by the Department of Defense, Ford Motor Company, National Science Foundation, Nissan, and the Nuclear Regulatory Commission, among others. In addition to teaching, Dr. Osborn spent a number of years in private industry, including a position as a senior research scientist with the Battelle Memorial Institute in Seattle, where he worked on improving the safety of commercial nuclear power.

Dr. Mary Uhl-Bien is the Howard Hawks Chair in Business Ethics and Leadership at the University of Nebraska. She earned her Ph.D. and M.B.A. in organizational behavior at the University of Cincinnati after completing an undergraduate degree in International Business and Spanish. She teaches organizational behavior, leadership, and ethics courses at the undergraduate and graduate (MBA and doctoral) levels, and has been heavily involved in executive education, teaching to business executives and physicians in the United States, China, Europe, and Saudi Arabia and to the senior executive service of the U.S. government for The Brookings Institute in Washington, D.C. She has been a visiting professor/scholar at Pablo de Olavide University in Seville, Spain, the Universidade Nova de Lisboa/Catolica Portuguesa in Lisbon, Portugal, and University Lund in Sweden.

Dr. Mary Uhl-Bien

Dr. Uhl-Bien's research interests are in leadership, followership, and ethics. In addition to her conceptual work on complexity and relational leadership, some of the empirical projects she is currently involved in include investigations of "Leadership and Adaptability in the Healthcare Industry" (a $300,000 grant from Booz Allen Hamilton), "Adaptive Leadership and Innovation: A Focus on Idea Generation and Flow" (at a major financial institution in the U.S.), and "Social Constructions of Followership and Leading Up." She has published in such journals as *The Academy of Management Journal*, the *Journal of Applied Psychology*, *The Leadership Quarterly*, the *Journal of Management*, and *Human Relations*. She won the Best Paper Award in *The Leadership Quarterly* in 2001 for her co-authored article on Complex Leadership. She has been on the editorial boards of *The Academy of Management Journal*, *The Academy of Management Review*, *The Leadership Quarterly*, *Leadership*, and *The International Journal of Complexity in Leadership and Management*, and is senior editor of the Leadership Horizons series (Information Age Publishers). Dr. Uhl-Bien has consulted with Disney, the U.S. Fish and Wildlife Service, British Petroleum, and the General Accounting Office, and served as the executive consultant for State Farm Insurance Co. from 1998–2004. She has been a Visiting Scholar in Spain, Portugal, and Sweden. Dr. Uhl-Bien has trained Russian businesspeople for the American Russian Center at the University of Alaska Anchorage from 1993–1996, worked on a USAID grant at the Magadan Pedagogical Institute in Magadan, Russia from 1995–1996, and participated in a Fulbright-Hays grant to Mexico during the summer of 2003.

Global warming, economic uncertainty, poverty, discrimination, unemployment, illiteracy . . . these are among the many issues and problems we face as citizens today. But how often do we stop and recognize our responsibilities for problem solving and positive action in this social context? What we do today will have a lasting impact on future generations. And whether we are talking about families, communities, nations, or the organizations in which we work and volunteer, the core question remains: How can we join together to best serve society?

Look again at the cover. Think about people working together and collaborating in organizations around the world. Think about how organizations and their members grow, and how individuals can expand the positive impact of society's institutions as their ideas and talents come together in supportive and nurturing work settings. And, think about the delicate balances between work and family, between individuals and teams, and between organizations and society that must be mastered in the quest for future prosperity.

Yes, our students do have a lot to consider in the complex and ever-shifting world of today. But, we believe they are up to the challenge. And, we believe that courses in organizational behavior have strong roles to play in building their capabilities to make good judgments and move organizational performance forward in positive and responsible ways.

That message is a fitting place to begin *Organizational Behavior*, 12th Edition. Everyone wants to have a useful and satisfying job and career; everyone wants all the organizations of society—small and large businesses, hospitals, schools, governments, nonprofits, and more—to perform well; everyone seeks a healthy and sustainable environment. In this context the lessons of our discipline are strong and applicable. Armed with an understanding of organizational behavior, great things are possible as people work, pursue careers, and contribute to society through positive personal and organizational accomplishments.

Organizational behavior is a discipline rich with insights for career and life skills. As educators, our job is to bring to the classroom and to students the great power of knowledge, understanding, and inquiry that characterizes our discipline and its commitment to understanding human behavior in organizations. What our students do with their talents will not only shape how organizations all contribute to society, but also fundamentally alter lives around the globe. We must do our parts as educators to help them gain the understanding and confidence to become leaders of tomorrow's organizations.

JOHN R. SCHERMERHORN, JR.
Ohio University

RICHARD N. OSBORN
Wayne State University

MARY UHL-BIEN
University of Nebraska

Organizational Behavior, 12th Edition, brings to its readers the solid and complete content core of prior editions, an enriched and exciting "OB Skills Workbook," and many revisions, updates, and enhancements that reflect today's dynamic times.

Content

All chapters are written so that they can be used in any sequence that best fits the instructor's course design. Each has also been updated to reflect new research findings and current applications and issues. For this edition, major changes were made to strengthen the research component, expand and refocus the chapters dealing with individual behavior and performance, and more fully treat the emerging directions in leadership research and thinking. A module on Research Methods in OB has been placed online to offer easy ways to further enrich the course experience.

Ethics Focus

To help students anticipate, understand, and confront the ethical challenges of work and careers today, we have continued our special feature in each chapter—*Ethics in OB*. This feature presents a situation or issue from an actual case or news report and asks a question of the student reader that requires personal reflection on the ethics and ethics implications. Examples include "Workers Concerned about Ethical Workplace, Personality Testing, Social Loafing May Be Closer than You Think, Privacy in an Age of Social Networking, and Cheat Now . . . Cheat Later."

Leadership Focus

To focus students on their roles in demonstrating leadership in organizations, we revised the leadership feature to "Finding the Leader in You." This feature helps students think about how they can develop their own leadership skills and capabilities to enhance organizational performance. Examples include Patricia Karter of Dancing Deer Baking, Jim Senegal of Costco, Karen Bryant of the Seattle Storm, and Jeff Bezos of Amazon.

Research Focus

To better communicate the timely research foundations of OB, we have continued the popular *Research Insights* found in each chapter. Each highlights an article from a respected journal such as the *Academy of Management Journal* and the *Journal of Applied Psychology*. Sample topics include interactional justice, racial bias, social loafing, demographic faultlines, and workplace identities.

Applications Focus

To help students apply the insights of OB to real situations and problems, each chapter includes *Visual Sidebars* that highlight key action points to remember—such as "Things Are Changing as the Facebook Generation Goes to Work"; *Margin Essays* that provide brief and timely examples—such as "Employee Morale Varies Around the World," and *OB and Popular Culture* that links movies and television to management insights—such as Moral Management and John Q.

Pedagogy

As always, our primary goal is to create a textbook that appeals to the student reader while still offering solid content. Through market research surveys and focus groups with students and professors, we continue to learn what features worked best from previous editions, what can be improved, and what can be added to accomplish this goal both effectively and efficiently. Our response is a pedagogical frame that combines popular elements from the last edition with new ones.

- **Chapter Opening**—a timely, real-world vignette introduces the chapter, *The Key Point* helps clarify the topic, *Chapter at a Glance* highlights major study questions, and *What's Inside* highlights the key features.
- **Inside the Chapter**—a variety of thematic embedded boxes as previously noted—*Ethics in OB, Finding the Leader in You, OB in Popular Culture,* and *Research Insight,* highlight relevant, timely, and global themes and situations that reinforce chapter content. Margin *Photo Essays* provide further short examples highlighting events and issues. To assist with chapter study and test preparation, each chapter has a running *Margin Glossary* and *Margin List Identifiers*.
- **End of Chapter**—a *Study Guide* helps students review and test their mastery of chapter content. Key components are Key Questions and Answers (keyed to opening *Chapter at a Glance* topics), *Key Terms,* and a *Self-Test* (with multiple choice, short response, and essay questions). Next Steps: Top Choices from the OB Skills Workbook highlight the Cases for Critical Thinking, Team and Experiential Exercises, and Self-Assessments found in the back of the book that complement each chapter.

The OB Skills Workbook

The end-of-text *OB Skills Workbook* has become a hallmark feature of the textbook, and it has been updated and expanded for the new edition. This edition features the Learning Style Inventory and Kouzes/Posner Student Leadership Practices Inventory. Both fit well in an OB course as opportunities for substantial student reflection and course enhancement. The five sections in the new updated workbook that offer many ways to extend the OB learning experience in creative and helpful ways are:

- Learning Style Inventory
- Student Leadership Practices Inventory
- Self-Assessment Portfolio
- Team and Experiential Exercises
- Cases for Critical Thinking

New Student and Instructor Support

Organizational Behavior, 12th Edition, is supported by a comprehensive learning package that assists the instructor in creating a motivating and enthusiastic environment.

Instructor's Resource Guide   The Instructor's Resource Guide, written by Andrea Smith-Hunter, Siena College, offers helpful teaching ideas, advice on course development, sample assignments, and chapter-by-chapter text highlights, learning objectives, lecture outlines, class exercises, lecture notes, answers to end-of-chapter material, and tips on using cases.

Test Bank   This comprehensive Test Bank, written by Amit Shah, Frostburg University, is available on the instructor portion of the Web site and consists of over 200 questions per chapter. Each chapter has true/false, multiple choice, and short answer questions. The questions are designed to vary in degree of difficulty to challenge your OB students.

   The Computerized Test Bank is for use on a PC running Windows. It contains content from the Test Bank provided within a test-generating program that allows instructors to customize their exams.

PowerPoint   This robust set of lecture/interactive PowerPoints prepared by Karen Edwards, Chemeketa Community College, is provided for each chapter to enhance your students' overall experience in the OB classroom. The PowerPoint slides can be accessed on the instructor portion of the Web site and include lecture notes to accompany each slide.

Web Quizzes   This online study guide with online quizzes varies in level of difficulty. Written by Amit Shah, Frostburg University, it is designed to help your students evaluate their individual progress through a chapter. Web quizzes are available on the student portion of the Web site. Here students will have the ability to test themselves with 15–25 questions per chapter and include true-false and multiple choice questions.

Personal Response System   The Personal Response System questions (PRS or "Clickers") for each chapter of *Organizational Behavior 12th Edition* is designed to spark discussion/debate in the OB classroom. For more information on PRS, please contact your local Wiley sales representative.

Companion Web Site The text's Web site at http://www.wiley.com/college/ schermerhorn contains myriad tools and links to aid both teaching and learning, including nearly all of the student and instructor resources.

Business Extra Select Online Courseware System http://www.wiley. com/college/bxs. Wiley has launched this program that provides an instructor with millions of content resources from an extensive database of cases, journals, periodicals, newspapers, and supplemental readings. This courseware system lends itself extremely well to the integration of real-world content and allows instructors to convey the relevance of the course content to their students.

Videos and Video Teaching Guide

Short video clips tied to the major topics in organizational behavior are available. These clips provide an excellent starting point for lectures or for general class discussion. Teaching notes for using the video clips, written by Stacy Shriver, University of Colorado, Boulder, are available on the instructor's portion of the Web site.

WileyPLUS

WileyPLUS is an innovative, research-based, online environment for effective teaching and learning.

What do students receive with *WileyPLUS*?

A Research-based Design *WileyPLUS* provides an online environment that integrates relevant resources, including the entire digital textbook, in an easy-to-navigate framework that helps students study more effectively.

- *WileyPLUS* adds structure by organizing textbook content into smaller, more manageable "chunks."
- Related media, examples, and sample practice items reinforce the learning objectives.

One-on-One Engagement With *WileyPLUS* for *Organizational Behavior, 12e,* students receive 24/7 access to resources that promote positive learning outcomes. Students engage with related examples (in various media) and sample practice items, including:

- Animated Figures
- CBS/BBC Videos

- Self-Assessments quizzes students can use to test themselves on topics such as emotional intelligence, diversity awareness, and intuitive ability.
- Management Calendar Including Daily Management Tips
- iPhone Applications for Download
- Flash Cards
- Hot Topic Modules
- Crossword Puzzles
- Self-Study Questions

Measurable Outcomes Throughout each study session, students can assess their progress and gain immediate feedback. *WileyPLUS* provides precise reporting of strengths and weaknesses, as well as individualized quizzes, so that students are confident they are spending their time on the right things. With *WileyPLUS*, students always know the exact outcome of their efforts.

What do instructors receive with *WileyPLUS*?

WileyPLUS provides reliable, customizable resources that reinforce course goals inside and outside of the classroom as well as visibility into individual student progress. Pre-created materials and activities help instructors optimize their time:

Customizable Course Plan *WileyPLUS* comes with a pre-created Course Plan designed by a subject matter expert uniquely for this course. Simple drag-and-drop tools make it easy to assign the course plan as-is or modify it to reflect your course syllabus.

Pre-created Activity Types Include:

- Questions
- Readings and Resources
- Presentation
- Print Tests
- Concept Mastery
- Project

Course Materials and Assessment Content:

- Lecture Notes PowerPoint Slides
- Classroom Response System (Clicker) Questions
- Image Gallery
- Instructor's Manual
- Gradable Reading Assignment Questions (embedded with online text)
- Question Assignments: all end-of-chapter problems
- Testbank
- Pre- and Post-Lecture Quizzes

- Web Quizzes
- Video Teaching Notes—includes questions geared towards applying text concepts to current videos

Gradebook   *WileyPLUS* provides instant access to reports on trends in class performance, student use of course materials, and progress towards learning objectives, helping inform decisions and drive classroom discussions.

WileyPLUS. Learn More. www.wileyplus.com.

Powered by proven technology and built on a foundation of cognitive research, *WileyPLUS* has enriched the education of millions of students in over 20 countries around the world.

Cases for Critical Thinking

Barry R. Armandi, *State University of New York*, David S. Chappell, *Ohio University*, Bernardo M. Ferdman, *Alliant International University*, Placido L. Gallegos, *Southwest Communications Resources, Inc.* and the *Kaleel Jamison Consulting Group. Inc.*, Carol Harvey, *Assumption College*, Ellen Ernst Kossek, *Michigan State University*, Barbara McCain, *Oklahoma City University*, Mary McGarry, *Empire State College*, Marc Osborn, *R&R Partners, Phoenix, AZ*, Franklin Ramsoomair, *Wilfrid Laurier University*, Hal Babson and John Bowen of *Columbus State Community College.*

Experiential Exercises and Self-Assessment Inventories

Barry R. Armandi, *State University of New York, Old Westbury*, Ariel Fishman, *The Wharton School, University of Pennsylvania*, Barbara K. Goza, *University of California, Santa Cruz*, D.T. Hall, *Boston University*, F.S. Hall, *University of New Hampshire*, Lady Hanson, *California State Polytechnic University, Pomona*, Conrad N. Jackson, *MPC, Inc.*, Mary Khalili, *Oklahoma City University*, Robert Ledman, *Morehouse College*, Paul Lyons, *Frostburg State University*, J. Marcus Maier, *Chapman University*, Michael R. Manning, *New Mexico State University*, Barbara McCain, *Oklahoma City University*, Annie McKee, *The Wharton School, University of Pennsylvania*, Bonnie McNeely, *Murray State University*, W. Alan Randolph, *University of Baltimore*, Joseph Raelin, *Boston College*, Paula J. Schmidt, *New Mexico State University*, Susan Schor, *Pace University*, Timothy T. Serey, *Northern Kentucky University*, Barbara Walker, *Diversity Consultant*, Paula S. Weber, *New Mexico Highlands University*, Susan Rawson Zacur, *University of Baltimore.*

acknowledgments

Organizational Behavior, 12th Edition, benefits from insights provided by a dedicated group of management educators from around the globe who carefully read and critiqued draft chapters of this edition. We are pleased to express our appreciation to the following colleagues for their contributions to this new edition.

Heidi Barclay, *Metropolitan State*
Nancy Fredericks, *San Diego State*
Cindy Geppert, *Palm Beach State College*
Jim Maddox, *Friends University*
Randy McCamey, *Tarleton State*
Wendy Smith, *U Del*
Barcley Johnson, *Western Michigan U.*
Lam Nguyen, *Palm Beach State College*

Robert Blanchard, *Salem State*
Suzanne Crampton, *Grand Valley State University*
Jody Tolan, *USC Marshall*
Gary J. Falcone, Ed.D., *LaSalle University*
Marcia Marriott, *Monroe CC*
Edward Kass, *USFCA*
Sidney Siegel, *Drexel*

We also thank those reviewers who contributed to the success of previous editions.

Merle Ace
Chi Anyansi-Archibong
Terry Armstrong
Leanne Atwater
Forrest Aven
Steve Axley
Abdul Aziz
Richard Babcock
David Baldridge
Michael Banutu-Gomez
Robert Barbato
Richard Barrett
Nancy Bartell
Anna Bavetta
Robb Bay
Hrach Bedrosian
Bonnie Betters-Reed
Gerald Biberman
Melinda Blackman
Lisa Bleich
Mauritz Blonder
Dale Blount
G. B. Bohn
William Bommer
H. Michal Boyd
Pat Buhler
Gene E. Burton
Roosevelt Butler
Ken Butterfield

Joseph F. Byrnes
Michal Cakrt
Tom Callahan
Daniel R. Cillis
Nina Cole
Paul Collins
Ann Cowden
Deborah Crown
Roger A. Dean
Robert Delprino
Emmeline De Pillis
Pam Dobies
Delf Dodge
Dennis Duchon
Michael Dumler
Ken Eastman
Norb Elbert
Theresa Feener
Janice M. Feldbauer
Claudia Ferrante
Mark Fichman
Dalmar Fisher
J. Benjamin Forbes
Dean Frear
Cynthia V. Fukami
Normandie Gaitley
Daniel Ganster
Joe Garcia
Virginia Geurin

Robert Giambatista
Manton Gibbs
Eugene Gomolka
Barbara Goodman
Stephen Gourlay
Frederick Greene
Richard Grover
Bengt Gustafsson
Peter Gustavson
Lady Alice Hanson
Don Hantula
Kristi Harrison
William Hart
Nell Hartley
Neil J. Humphreys
David Hunt
Eugene Hunt
Howard Kahn
Harriet Kandelman
Paul N. Keaton
Andrew Klein
Leslie Korb
Peter Kreiner
Eric Lamm
Donald Lantham
Jim Lessner
Les Lewchuk
Kristi M. Lewis
Robert Liden

Beverly Linnell
Kathy Lippert
Michael London
Michael Lounsbury
Carol Lucchesi
David Luther
Lorna Martin
Tom Mayes
Daniel McAllister
Douglas McCabe
James McFillen
Jeanne McNett
Charles Milton
Herff L. Moore
David Morand
David Morean
Sandra Morgan
Paula Morrow
Richard Mowday
Christopher Neck
Linda Neider
Judy C. Nixon
Regina O'Neill
Dennis Pappas
Edward B. Parks
Robert F. Pearse
Lawrence Peters
Prudence Pollard

Joseph Porac
Samuel Rabinowitz
Franklin Ramsoomair
Clint Relyea
Bobby Remington
Charles L. Roegiers
Steven Ross
Joel Rudin
Michael Rush
Robert Salitore
Terri Scandura
Mel Schnake
Holly Schroth
L. David Schuelke
Richard J. Sebastian
Anson Seers
William Sharbrough
R. Murray Sharp
Ted Shore
Allen N. Shub
Sidney Siegal
Dayle Smith
Mary Alice Smith
Walter W. Smock
Pat Sniderman
Ritch L. Sorenson
Shanthi Srinivas
Paul L. Starkey

Robert Steel
Ronni Stephens
Ron Stone
Tom Thompson
Ed Tomlinson
Sharon Tucker
Nicholas Twigg
Tony Urban
Ted Valvoda
Joyce Vincelette
David Vollrath
Andy Wagstaff
W. Fran Waller
Charles Wankel
Edward Ward
Fred A. Ware, Jr.
Andrea F. Warfield
Harry Waters, Jr.
Joseph W. Weiss
Deborah Wells
Robert Whitcomb
Donald White
Bobbie Williams
Barry L. Wisdom
Wayne Wormley
Barry Wright
Kimberly Young
Raymond Zammuto

We are grateful for all the hard work of the supplements authors who worked to develop the comprehensive ancillary package described above. We thank Andrea Smith-Hunter, Siena College, for preparing the Instructor's Resource Guide, Amit Shah, Frostburg University, for creating the Test Bank and the web quizzes, Karen Edwards, Chemeketa Community College, for developing the PowerPoint presentations, and Stacy Shriver, University of Colorado, Boulder, for writing the Video Teaching Notes. We thank Brandon Warga of Kenyon College for his chapter opening vignettes, and Robert (Lenie) Holbrook of Ohio University for both the *OB in Popular Culture* feature and the creative instructor's guide *Art Imitates Life*.

As always, the support staff at John Wiley & Sons was most helpful in the various stages of developing and producing this edition. We would especially like to thank Lisé Johnson (Acquisitions Editor), George Hoffman (Publisher), Susan McLaughlin (Developmental Editor), Sarah Vernon (Associate Editor), and Melissa Solarz (Editorial Assistant) for their extraordinary efforts in support of this project. They took OB to heart and did their very best to build a high-performance team in support of this book. We thank everyone at Wiley for maintaining the quest for quality and timeliness in all aspects of the book's content and design. Special gratitude goes to Maddy Lesure as the creative force behind the new design. We also thank Erin Bascom and Suzanne Ingrao of Ingrao Associates for their excellent production and design assistance, Allie Morris for overseeing the media development, and Amy Scholz for leading the marketing campaign. Thank you everyone!!

brief contents

contents

The Tonight Show: Things Don't Always Go as Planned

The peacock was feeling the heat.

Affiliate station owners were grumbling to NBC that *The Jay Leno Show,* the comedian's new prime-time project after passing the *Tonight Show* torch to Conan O'Brien, was bad for ratings and would turn off viewers. Even worse, Leno's show wasn't on the air yet.

High-ranking NBC exec Jeff Zucker, having earlier turned around *The Today Show,* offered a deal. Leno takes Conan's slot but is shortened to 30 minutes. Conan keeps *The Tonight Show* but moves to midnight.

The deal: It came together like an "after-school special on the *Don't*s of leadership transitions," noted HR consultant J.P. Elliot.[a] The result: A PR nightmare dubbed *The Jaypocalypse.* Public trash-talking by all parties. And the defection of a serious chunk of viewers with strong brand loyalty and purchasing power.

> *"So what does NBC do? If you are making buggy whips and no one is buying buggies anymore, do you keep making buggy whips?"*
> *—Jay Leno.*[b]

Only one day after the deal was announced, Conan released his earnest "People of Earth" statement, quickly winning fans, a visible majority of fellow comedians, and, seemingly, almost everyone on Twitter. In contrast, Leno often appeared befuddled in interviews, with only Jerry Seinfeld and Oprah supporting him in the press.

The aftermath: Eight months later, Leno was back behind the *Tonight Show* desk. Conan had a home on TBS. NBC was down viewers, sponsors, and cash, having paid $43 million to break Conan's contract.

The lesson to be learned: "The real culprit here," says consultant Elliot, "[is] NBC's lack of ability to execute their succession plan." But just whose failure was that? Perhaps that's a question best answered by Jeff Zucker as he ponders the complexities of human behavior in organizations.

Quick Summary

- After five years of waiting, Conan O'Brien takes the reins of *The Tonight Show* from Jay Leno.
- Leno, unwilling to step away, launches a prime-time talk show. Affiliates complain even before the show airs.
- To rescue Leno, NBC Universal proposes bumping Conan to 12:05 A.M., Leno to 11:35 P.M. Public acrimony ensues.
- NBC Universal spends an estimated one-third of the cost of breaking Leno's contract to fire Conan. Leno's show airs, sputters. O'Brien sells out a 30-city comedy tour before launching *Conan* on TBS.

FYI

1. Time for Conan O'Brien's Twitter followers to surpass Jay Leno's: under 60 minutes.[c]
2. Cost of breaking Leno's NBC contract: Estimated $150 million. Cost of breaking Conan's NBC contract: $45 million.[d]

1 Introducing Organizational Behavior

the key point

People in all of their rich diversity are the basic building blocks of organizations. Everyone deserves to be respected at work and to be satisfied with their jobs and accomplishments. Problems like those with the Tonight Show don't need to happen. The field of organizational behavior offers many insights into managing individuals and teams for high performance in today's new workplace.

chapter at a glance

What Is Organizational Behavior and Why Is It Important?

What Are Organizations Like as Work Settings?

What Is the Nature of Management and Leadership in Organizations?

How Do We Learn About Organizational Behavior?

ETHICS IN OB
IS MANAGEMENT A PROFESSION?

FINDING THE LEADER IN YOU
BANKER SHOWS GENEROSITY CAN TRIUMPH OVER GREED

OB IN POPULAR CULTURE
MORAL MANAGEMENT AND *JOHN Q*

RESEARCH INSIGHT
WOMEN MIGHT MAKE BETTER LEADERS

what's inside?

Introducing Organizational Behavior

LEARNING ROADMAP   Why Organizational Behavior Is Important / Scientific Foundations of Organizational Behavior / Organizational Behavior in a Changing World

Whether your career unfolds in entrepreneurship, corporate enterprise, public service, or any other occupational setting, it is always worth remembering that people are the basic building blocks of organizational success. Organizations do well when the people in them work hard to achieve high performance, as individuals and as members of teams. Creating success requires respect for everyone's needs, talents, and aspirations, as well as an understanding of the dynamics of human behavior in organizational systems.

This book is about people, everyday people like you and like us, who work and pursue careers in today's highly demanding settings. It is about people who seek fulfillment in their lives and jobs in a variety of ways and in uncertain times. It is about the challenges of leadership, ethics, globalization, technology utilization, diversity, work–life balance, and other social issues. And this book is also about how our complex environment requires people and organizations to learn and to continuously develop in the quest for high performance and promising futures.

Why Organizational Behavior Is Important

• **Organizational behavior** is the study of individuals and groups in organizations.

In this challenging era, the body of knowledge we call organizational behavior offers many insights of great value. Called OB for short, **organizational behavior** is the study of human behavior in organizations. It is an academic discipline devoted to understanding individual and group behavior, interpersonal processes, and organizational dynamics. Learning about OB can help you expand your potential for career success in the dynamic, shifting, and complex workplaces of today—and tomorrow.

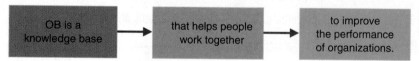

OB is a knowledge base → that helps people work together → to improve the performance of organizations.

Scientific Foundations of Organizational Behavior

As far back as a century ago, consultants and scholars were giving increased attention to the systematic study of management and organizational practices. Although the early focus was initially on physical working conditions, principles of administration, and industrial engineering, interest broadened to include the human factor. This gave impetus to research dealing with individual attitudes, group dynamics, and the relationships between managers and workers. From this historical foundation, organizational behavior emerged as a scholarly discipline devoted to scientific understanding of individuals and groups in organizations, and of the performance implications of organizational processes, systems, and structures.[1]

Interdisciplinary Body of Knowledge   Organizational behavior is an interdisciplinary body of knowledge with strong ties to the behavioral sciences—psychology, sociology, and anthropology—as well as to allied social sciences such as economics and political science. OB is unique, however, in its goals of integrating the diverse insights of these other disciplines and applying them to real-world organizational problems and opportunities. The ultimate goal of OB is to improve the performance of people, groups, and organizations, and to improve the quality of work life overall.

Use of Scientific Methods   The field of organizational behavior uses scientific methods to develop and empirically test generalizations about behavior in organizations. OB scholars often propose and test **models**—simplified views of reality that attempt to identify major factors and forces underlying real-world phenomena. These models link **independent variables**—presumed causes— with **dependent variables**—outcomes of practical value and interest. Here, for example, is a very basic model that describes one of the findings of OB research—job satisfaction (independent variable) influences absenteeism (dependent variable).

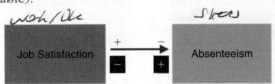

- **Models** are simplified views of reality that attempt to explain real-world phenomena.
- **Independent variables** are presumed causes that influence dependent variables.
- **Dependent variables** are outcomes of practical value and interest that are influenced by independent variables.

Notice that "+" and "−" signs in the above model indicate that as job satisfaction increases, absenteeism tends to go down, and as job satisfaction decreases, absenteeism often goes up. As you look at this model you might ask what other dependent variables are important to study in OB—perhaps things like task performance, ethical behavior, work stress, incivility, team cohesion, and leadership effectiveness. In fact, job satisfaction can also be a dependent variable in its own right. What independent variables do you believe might explain whether satisfaction will be high or low for someone doing a service job like an airline flight attendant or a managerial one like a school principal?

Figure 1.1 describes a set of research methods commonly used by OB researchers to study models and the relationships among variables. These methods are based on scientific thinking. This means (1) the process of data collection is controlled and systematic, (2) proposed explanations are carefully tested, and (3) only explanations that can be rigorously verified are accepted.

Focus on Application   As already suggested, the science of organizational behavior focuses on applications that can make a real difference in how organizations and people in them perform. Examples of the many practical research questions addressed by the discipline of OB and reviewed in this book include: How should rewards such as merit pay raises be allocated? How can jobs be designed for both job satisfaction and high performance? What are the ingredients of successful teamwork? How can a manager deal with resistance to change? Should leaders make decisions by individual, consultative, or group methods? How can "win–win" outcomes be achieved in negotiations? What causes unethical and socially irresponsible behavior by people in organizations?

Contingency Thinking   Rather than assuming that there is one "best" or universal answer to questions such as those just posed, OB recognizes that management

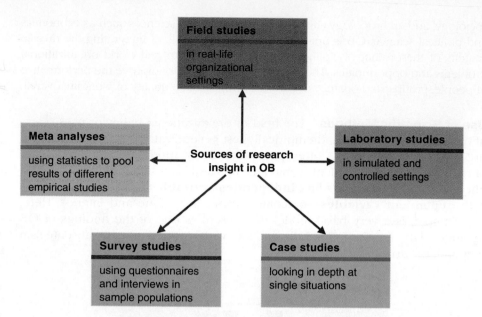

Figure 1.1 Common scientific research methods in organizational behavior.

Field studies

in real-life organizational settings

Meta analyses

using statistics to pool results of different empirical studies

Sources of research insight in OB

Laboratory studies

in simulated and controlled settings

Survey studies

using questionnaires and interviews in sample populations

Case studies

looking in depth at single situations

• **Contingency thinking** seeks ways to meet the needs of different management situations.

practices must be tailored to fit the exact nature of each situation—this is called **contingency thinking**. In fact, one of the most accepted conclusions of scientific research to date is that there is no single best way to manage people and organizations. Stated a bit differently, contingency thinking recognizes that there are no cookie-cutter solutions that can be universally applied to solve organizational problems. Responses must be crafted to best fit the circumstances and people involved. As you might expect, this is where solid scientific findings in organizational behavior become very helpful. Many examples are provided in the Research Insight feature found in each chapter.

An essential responsibility of any science is to create and test models that offer evidence-based foundations for decision making and action. A book by scholars Jeffrey Pfeffer and Robert Sutton defines **evidence-based management** as making decisions on "hard facts"—that is about what really works, rather than on "dangerous half-truths"—things that sound good but lack empirical substantiation.[2] One of the ways evidence-based thinking manifests itself in OB is through a contingency approach in which researchers identify how different situations can best be understood and handled.

• **Evidence-based management** uses hard facts and empirical evidence to make decisions.

In a time of complex globalization, for example, it's important for everyone, from managers and employees to government leaders, to understand how OB theories and concepts apply in different countries.[3] Although it is relatively easy to conclude that what works in one culture may not work as well in another, it is far harder to describe how specific cultural differences can affect such things as motivation, job satisfaction, leadership style, negotiating tendencies, and ethical behavior. Fortunately, OB is now rich with empirically based insights into cross-cultural issues.

Organizational Behavior in a Changing World

With the recent economic turmoil, financial crisis, and recession, there isn't any doubt that organizations and their members face huge challenges. Talk to friends

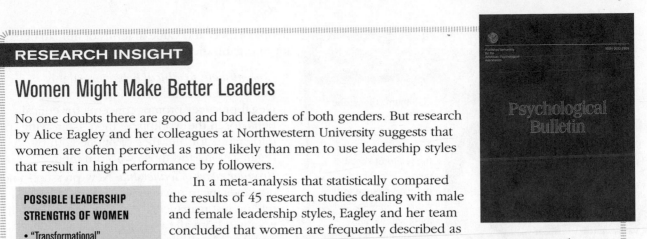

RESEARCH INSIGHT

Women Might Make Better Leaders

No one doubts there are good and bad leaders of both genders. But research by Alice Eagley and her colleagues at Northwestern University suggests that women are often perceived as more likely than men to use leadership styles that result in high performance by followers.

POSSIBLE LEADERSHIP STRENGTHS OF WOMEN

- "Transformational"
- Good at mentoring
- Very inspiring
- Encourage creativity
- Show excitement about goals
- Reward positive performance

In a meta-analysis that statistically compared the results of 45 research studies dealing with male and female leadership styles, Eagley and her team concluded that women are frequently described as leading by inspiring, exciting, mentoring, and stimulating creativity. They point out that these behaviors have "transformational" qualities that build stronger organizations through innovation and teamwork. Women also score higher on rewarding positive performance, while men score higher in punishing and correcting mistakes.

Eagley and her colleagues explain the findings in part by the fact that followers are more accepting of a transformational style when the leader is female, and that the style comes more naturally to women because of its emphasis on nurturing. They also suggest that because women may have to work harder than men to succeed, their leadership skills get tough tests and end up being better developed.

Do the Research   *What do you think: is this study on track? Conduct an interview study of people working for female and male managers. Ask the question: Do women lead differently from men? Organize the responses and prepare an analysis that answers your research question. Although not scientific, your study could prove quite insightful.*

Source: Alice H. Eagley, Mary C. Johannesen-Smith and Marloes I. van Engen, "Transformational, Transactional and Laissez-Faire Leadership: A Meta-Analysis of Women and Men," *Psychological Bulletin* 24.4 (2003), pp. 569–591.

and follow the news headlines. Jobs are still hard to come by for new college graduates; unemployment remains high; those with jobs often face the conflicting demands of work and family responsibilities. You'll notice organizations adopting new features, changing work processes and practices, and trying different strategies. At the same time, they're dealing with employees, customers, and clients whose needs, values, and tastes seem to be constantly shifting.

Things have actually been changing for quite some time in our work environments, but recent events are especially dramatic in affecting both the nature and pace of change. The comments of consultant Tom Peters seem especially relevant. He once called the changing environment of organizations a "revolution that feels something like this: scary, guilty, painful, liberating, disorienting, exhilarating, empowering, frustrating, fulfilling, confusing, and challenging. In other words, it feels very much like chaos."[4]

The environment of change in which we now live and work calls for lots of learning and continuous attention. The field of OB recognizes these trends in what

Things Are Changing as the Facebook Generation Goes to Work

Call them "Generation F," short for the Facebook Generation. They are heavily into the world of social media, and they are bringing change to the workplace. Management scholar and consultant Gary Hamel says that managers who want to work well with Gen F have to face up to a new set of expectations. Here's his view of Gen F at work.

- No one kills an idea; all ideas deserve a hearing.
- Contributions overrule credentials.
- Authority is earned, not given.
- Leaders serve; they don't command.
- People choose tasks that interest them.
- Groups are self-organizing and free formed.
- Resources flow toward good ideas and projects.
- Power comes from information sharing.
- Wisdom lies within the crowd; peer review counts.
- Community grows from shared decision making.
- Recognition and joy of accomplishment are great motivators.
- Rabble rousing is embraced, not discouraged.

people expect and value in terms of human behavior in organizations.[5]

- *Commitment to ethical behavior:* Highly publicized scandals involving unethical and illegal practices prompt concerns for ethical behavior in the workplace; there is growing intolerance for breaches of public faith by organizations and those who run them.
- *Broader views of leadership:* New pressures and demands mean organizations can no longer rely on just managers for leadership: leadership is valued from all members, found at all levels, and flows in all directions—not just top-down.
- *Emphasis on human capital and teamwork:* Success is earned through knowledge, experience, and commitments to people as valuable human assets; work is increasingly team based with a focus on peer contributions.
- *Demise of command-and-control:* Traditional hierarchical structures and practices are proving incapable of handling today's challenges; they are being replaced by shared leadership, flexible structures, and participatory work settings that fully value human capital.
- *Influence of information technology:* As new technologies—including social media—penetrate all aspects of the workplace, implications for work arrangements, organizational systems and processes, and individual behavior are continuously evolving.

- *Respect for new workforce expectations:* The new generation of workers is less tolerant of hierarchy, more high tech, and less concerned about status; organizations are paying more attention to helping members balance work and non-work responsibilities.
- *Changing concept of careers:* New economy jobs require special skill sets and a capacity for continuous skill development; more people now work as independent contractors who shift among employers rather than hold traditional full-time jobs.
- *Concern for sustainability:* Issues of sustainability are top priorities; decision making and goal setting increasingly give attention to the environment, climate justice, and preservation of resources for future generations.

Organizations as Work Settings

LEARNING ROADMAP   Organizational Behavior in Context / Organizational Environments and Stakeholders / Diversity and Multiculturalism

- **Organizations** are collections of people working together to achieve a common purpose.

In order to understand the complex field of forces that relate to human behavior in organizations, we need to begin with the nature of the "organization" itself. Simply stated, an **organization** is a collection of people working together in a division of labor to achieve a common purpose. This definition describes everything from clubs, voluntary organizations, and religious bodies to entities such as small and large businesses, schools, hospitals, and government agencies.

Organizational Behavior in Context

The behavior of people in organizations is greatly affected by context. Think about yourself. Do you act differently when you are with your friends, at school, or at work? In many cases the answer is probably "yes," and the question then becomes: "Why?" To understand behavior in any setting, we must ask ourselves how contextual factors influence it and in what ways. We also need to consider how we are affecting the context. How do our behaviors contribute to the dynamics that are happening to us and around us, and in both positive and negative ways? The bottom line is that a key aspect of understanding organizational behavior is considering the situations, or contexts, in which the behavior occurs.

One of the strongest contextual influences on OB is **organizational culture**—the shared beliefs and values that influence the behavior of organizational members. Former eBay CEO Meg Whitman calls it the "character" of the organization. She says organization culture is "the set of values and principles by which you run a company" and becomes the "moral center" that helps every member understand what is right and wrong in terms of personal behavior.[6]

Organizational cultures influence the way we feel and act in organizations. In cultures that are more authoritarian and hierarchical, people are hesitant to make decisions and take action on their own, so they tend to show little initiative and wait for approval. In other cultures, people can be extremely competitive and aggressive in the quest for performance results and rewards. Still other cultures are known for their emphasis on speed and agility in dealing with markets and environments, and in generating new ideas and innovations. How these organizational cultures affect people depends on something called "fit"—the match of organizational culture and individual characteristics. People who find a good fit tend to experience confidence and satisfaction in their work; those who find themselves in a bad fit may be more prone to withdraw, experience work stress, and even become angry and aggressive due to dissatisfaction.

Just as organizations have cultures, they also have climates. **Organizational climate** represents the shared perceptions among members regarding what the organization is like in terms of management policies, practices, events, and procedures. You have probably noticed and felt the climate in organizations that you have worked for. In some organizational climates relations among managers and employees are relaxed and informal, with lots of free-flowing communication. But in other climates, managers act distant from employees and emphasize formal work procedures and interactions, with more structured and restricted communication.

Organizational Environments and Stakeholders

Figure 1.2 shows that organizations are dynamic **open systems**. They obtain resource inputs from the environment and transform them into finished goods or services that are returned to the environment as product outputs. If everything works right, suppliers value the organization and continue to provide needed resources, employees value their work and infuse the transformation

- **Organizational culture** is a shared set of beliefs and values within an organization.

- **Organizational climate** represents shared perceptions of members regarding what the organization is like in terms of management policies and practices.

- **Open systems** transform human and material resource inputs into finished goods and services.

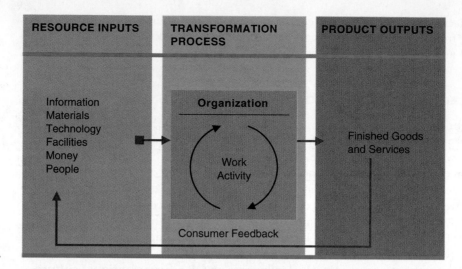

| RESOURCE INPUTS | TRANSFORMATION PROCESS | PRODUCT OUTPUTS |

Information
Materials
Technology
Facilities
Money
People

Organization

Work
Activity

Finished Goods
and Services

Consumer Feedback

Figure 1.2 Organizations are open systems that create value while interacting with their environments.

processes with their energies and intellects, and customers and clients value the organization's outputs enough to create a continuing demand for them.

We have just described a **value chain**—the sequence of activities that results in the creation of goods and services of value to customers. It begins with the acquisition of inputs, continues through their transformation into product outputs, and ends when products are distributed to customers and clients who are well served. When the value chain is well managed, the organization is able to sustain operations and, hopefully, prosper over the long run. But when the value chain breaks down due to input problems, transformation problems, or output problems, an organization's performance suffers and its livelihood may be threatened. In extreme cases the organization can be forced into bankruptcy, such as happened to General Motors and Chrysler in the recent economic downturn, or even go out of existence altogether.

A popular and useful way to describe and analyze the external environment of organizations is in terms of **stakeholders**—people, groups, and institutions that are affected by and thus have an interest or "stake" in an organization's performance. It is common in OB to recognize customers, owners, employees, suppliers, regulators, local communities, and future generations among the key stakeholders of organizations.

Although an organization should ideally operate in ways that best serve all stakeholders, the realities are that conflicting interests can create challenges for decision makers. Consider the possibilities: customers want value pricing and high-quality products, owners want profits and returns on investments, employees want secure jobs with good pay and benefits, suppliers want reliable contracts and on-time payments, regulators want compliance with laws, local communities want good organizational citizenship and community support, and future generations want environmental protection and sustainability of natural resources.

- The **value chain** is a sequence of activities that creates valued goods and services for customers.

- **Stakeholders** are people and groups with an interest or "stake" in the performance of the organization.

Diversity and Multiculturalism

Another important aspect of any organization is the makeup of the people within it. Consultant R. Roosevelt Thomas makes the point that positive organizational cultures tap the talents, ideas, and creative potential of *all* members.[7] His point focuses attention on **workforce diversity**, the presence of individual differences based on gender, race and ethnicity, age, able-bodiedness, and sexual orientation.[8] It also highlights **multiculturalism** as an attribute of organizations that emphasize pluralism, and genuine respect for diversity and individual differences.[9]

Demographic trends driving workforce diversity in American society are well recognized. There are more women working than ever before. They earn 60 percent of college degrees and fill a bit more than half of managerial jobs.[10] The proportion of African Americans, Hispanics, and Asians in the labor force is increasing. By the year 2060, people of color will constitute over 60 percent of the U.S. population; close to 30 percent of the population will be Hispanic.[11]

A key issue in any organization is **inclusion**—the degree to which the culture embraces diversity and is open to anyone who can perform a job, regardless of their diversity attributes.[12] In practice, however, valuing diversity must still be considered a work in progress. Data show, for example, that women earn only about 75 cents per dollar earned by men; female CEOs earn 85 cents per dollar earned by males. At *Fortune* 500 companies women hold only 15 CEO jobs and 6.2 percent of top-paying positions; women of color hold only 1.7 percent of corporate officer positions and 1 percent of top-paying jobs.[13] Indeed, when Ursula Burns was named CEO of Xerox, she became the first African-American woman to head a *Fortune* 500 firm.[14]

- **Workforce diversity** describes how people differ on attributes such as age, race, ethnicity, gender, physical ability, and sexual orientation.
- **Multiculturalism** refers to pluralism and respect for diversity in the workplace.

- **Inclusion** is the degree to which an organization's culture respects and values diversity.

Management and Leadership

LEARNING ROADMAP Managerial Activities and Roles / Managerial Skills / Leadership in Organizations / Ethical Management and Leadership

A **manager** is someone whose job it is to directly support the work efforts of others. Being a manager is a unique challenge with responsibilities that link closely with the field of organizational behavior. At the heart of the matter managers help other people get important things done in timely, high-quality, and personally satisfying ways. And in the workplaces of today this is accomplished more through "helping" and "supporting" than through traditional notions of "directing" and "controlling."

You'll find the word "manager" is increasingly being replaced in conversations by such terms as "coordinator," "coach," or "team leader." **Effective managers** help people achieve both high performance and job satisfaction. This definition focuses attention on two key outcomes, or dependent variables, that are important in OB. The first is **task performance**. You can think of it as the quality and quantity of the work produced or the services provided by an individual, team or work unit, or organization as a whole. The second is **job satisfaction**. It indicates how people feel about their work and the work setting.

OB is quite clear in that managers should be held accountable for both of these results. The first, performance, pretty much speaks for itself. The second, satisfaction, might give you some pause for thought. But just as a valuable machine should not be allowed to break down for lack of proper maintenance, the talents and enthusiasm of an organization's workforce should never be lost

- **Managers** are persons who support the work efforts of other people.

- An **effective manager** helps others achieve high levels of both performance and satisfaction.
- **Task performance** is the quantity and quality of work produced.
- **Job satisfaction** is a positive feeling about one's work and work setting.

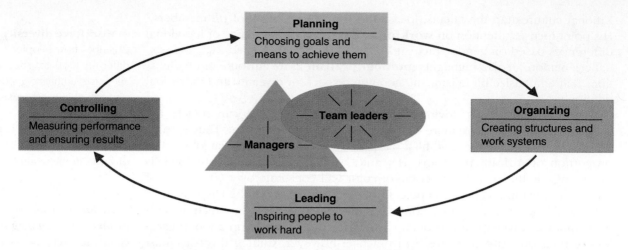

Figure 1.3 The management process of planning, organizing, leading, and controlling.

or compromised for lack of proper care. In this sense, taking care of job satisfaction today can be considered an investment in tomorrow's performance potential.

Managerial Activities and Roles

Anyone serving as a manager or team leader faces a challenging and complicated job. Among the ways that managerial work has been described and taught is through the four functions shown in Figure 1.3: planning, organizing, leading, and controlling. These functions describe what managers are supposed to do in respect to:

- **Planning**—defining goals, setting specific performance objectives, and identifying the actions needed to achieve them
- **Organizing**—creating work structures and systems, and arranging resources to accomplish goals and objectives
- **Leading**—instilling enthusiasm by communicating with others, motivating them to work hard, and maintaining good interpersonal relations
- **Controlling**—ensuring that things go well by monitoring performance and taking corrective action as necessary

In what has become a classic study, Henry Mintzberg described how managers perform these functions while fulfilling the set of 10 managerial roles shown in Figure 1.4.[15]

A manager's *interpersonal roles* involve working directly with other people, hosting and attending official ceremonies (figurehead), creating enthusiasm and serving people's needs (leader), and maintaining contacts with important people and groups (liaison). The *informational roles* involve managers exchanging information with other people, seeking relevant information (monitor), sharing it with insiders (disseminator), and sharing it with outsiders (spokesperson). A manager's *decisional roles* involve making decisions that affect other people, seeking problems to solve and opportunities to explore (entrepreneur), helping to resolve

Marginal notes:

- **Planning** sets objectives and identifies the actions needed to achieve them.
- **Organizing** divides up tasks and arranges resources to accomplish them.
- **Leading** creates enthusiasm to work hard to accomplish tasks successfully.
- **Controlling** monitors performance and takes any needed corrective action.

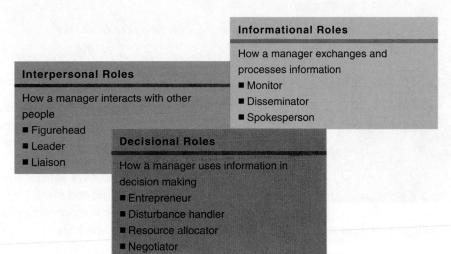

Interpersonal Roles

How a manager interacts with other people
- Figurehead
- Leader
- Liaison

Informational Roles

How a manager exchanges and processes information
- Monitor
- Disseminator
- Spokesperson

Decisional Roles

How a manager uses information in decision making
- Entrepreneur
- Disturbance handler
- Resource allocator
- Negotiator

Figure 1.4 Mintzberg's 10 roles of effective managers.

conflicts (disturbance handler), allocating resources to various uses (resource allocator), and negotiating with other parties (negotiator).

Managerial Skills

A **skill** is an ability to translate knowledge into action that results in a desired performance. Robert Katz divides the essential managerial skills into three categories—technical, human, and conceptual.[16] He further suggests that the relative importance of these skills varies across the different levels of management. Technical skills are considered more important at entry levels, where supervisors and team leaders must deal with job-specific problems. Senior executives require more conceptual skills as they face sometimes ambiguous problems and deal with complex issues of organizational mission and strategy. Human skills, which are strongly grounded in the foundations of organizational behavior, are consistently important across all managerial levels.

- A **skill** is an ability to turn knowledge into effective action.

Technical Skills A **technical skill** is an ability to perform specialized tasks using knowledge or expertise gained from education or experience. A good example is skill in using the latest communication and information technologies. In the high-tech workplaces of today, technical proficiency in database management, spreadsheet analysis, presentation software, e-mail, video chats and conferencing, and even social media is often a hiring prerequisite.

- **Technical skill** is an ability to perform specialized tasks.

Human Skills Central to all aspects of managerial work and team leadership are **human skills**, or the ability to work well with other people. They show up as a spirit of trust, enthusiasm, and genuine involvement in interpersonal relationships. A person with good human skills will have a high degree of self-awareness and a capacity for understanding or empathizing with the feelings of others. People with this skill are able to interact well with others, engage in persuasive communications, and deal successfully with disagreements and conflicts.

An important aspect of human skills is **emotional intelligence**, or EI. As defined by Daniel Goleman, EI is the ability to understand and manage emotions

- **Human skill** is the ability to work well with other people.

- **Emotional intelligence** is the ability to manage oneself and one's relationships effectively.

both personally and in relationships with others.[17] The core elements in emotional intelligence are:

- *Self-awareness*—ability to understand your own moods and emotions
- *Self-regulation*—ability to think before acting and to control bad impulses
- *Motivation*—ability to work hard and persevere
- *Empathy*—ability to understand the emotions of others
- *Social skill*—ability to gain rapport with others and build good relationships

Human skills in emotional intelligence and interpersonal relationships are essential to success in each of the managerial activities and roles previously discussed. Managers and team leaders need to develop, maintain, and work well with a wide variety of people, both inside and outside the organization.[18] These include *task networks* of specific job-related contacts, *career networks* of career guidance and opportunity resources, and *social networks* of trustworthy friends and peers.[19] It can be said in this sense that managers must develop and maintain **social capital** in the form of relationships and networks that they can call upon as needed to get work done through other people.

- **Social capital** is a capacity to get things done due to relationships with other people.

Conceptual Skills   In addition to technical and human skills, managers should be able to view the organization or situation as a whole so that problems are always solved for the benefit of everyone concerned. This capacity to think analytically and solve complex and sometimes ambiguous problems is a **conceptual skill**. It involves the ability to see and understand how systems work and how their parts are interrelated, including human dynamics. Conceptual skill is used to identify problems and opportunities, gather and interpret relevant information, and make good problem-solving decisions.

- **Conceptual skill** is the ability to analyze and solve complex problems.

Leadership in Organizations

The job of a manager has never been more demanding than it is in today's dynamic and hypercompetitive work environments. But it is also true that managers alone cannot solve all the complex problems and address all the challenging

Finding the Leader in You

BANKER SHOWS GENEROSITY CAN TRIUMPH OVER GREED

When we think of outstanding leaders we often think of heroes and celebrate their great accomplishments with national holidays such as Presidents Day (initially for Washington and Lincoln) and Martin Luther King Day. Current and former employees of City National Bank of Florida, one of the oldest and most profitable banks in the state, are considering a day that would honor their CEO, Leonard Abess.

Abess bought the bank out of bankruptcy in 1985 for $21 million, all borrowed. City National

flourished under his leadership, getting an A1 rating for financial security from TheStreet.com and joining the top 5 percent of all U.S. banks. It was sold to a Spanish bank, Caja Madrid, for almost a billion dollars. Abess didn't just take his profits and go home. He quietly took $60 million and distributed it to 471 current and former employees.

So what made Leonard Abess a hero? He didn't talk about his generosity publicly until a newspaper discovered it. Abess told the *Miami Herald* that long before the sale he had been trying to come up with a way to reward employees for their service. "I always thought some day I'm going to surprise them," Abess said. "I sure as heck don't need (the money)."

He also noted that with the recent recession, bank employees had taken quite a hit on their retirement accounts. He wanted to reach out to the staff and show his appreciation.

This wasn't the first time this heroic banker has shared his wealth. Abess is an active philanthropist who regularly contributes to local medical centers and universities.

With all the recent commentary about CEOs receiving hefty bonuses as their firms have experienced declining profitability, it is a nice reminder that some CEOs can be both excellent managers and generous leaders.

What's the Lesson Here?

Would you have made the same decision as Abess? Do you think the employees deserved the distribution, or should it go to the executives for their leadership? Would you, like Abess, have included former employees as well?

situations in organizations. In today's organizations there is more recognition that every individual contributes to his or her own performance and job satisfaction and that more people have to be engaged in the leadership process to advance new ideas and new solutions, and to challenge old ways of thinking. It is a new world of management where managers aren't the only leaders and where part of every manager's success is based on how well he or she mobilizes leadership contributions from others.

Leaders are people who use influence to create change. They have followers because other people see the value of their ideas or suggestions and choose to go along or align with them. Managers, by virtue of their positions of authority, have the opportunity to act as leaders. But they don't always do so, or do so successfully. Leaders succeed when people follow them not because they have to but because they want to. This positive influence emerges from persuasiveness, competence, and human skills. The Finding the Leader in You feature in each chapter is designed to provide role models and get you thinking about developing your leadership potential.

ETHICS IN OB

IS MANAGEMENT A PROFESSION?

The economic recession brought hardship and turmoil to lots of people and organizations. But even as firms performed poorly or failed altogether, many top executives still got high salaries, extra bonuses, and generous severance packages. This happened at the same time many workers lost their jobs, took pay cuts, or had their work hours reduced.

If that's not enough, there's the Bernard Madoff scandal. Now sentenced to 150 years in prison, he formerly lived lavishly while running an investment Ponzi scheme that bilked individuals, charitable foundations, colleges and universities, and other institutions of many billions of dollars.

Does it surprise you that a *Harvard Business Review* article pointed out that managers are now losing the public trust? To help change things for the better, the authors call for business schools to address management as a profession governed by codes of conduct that "forge an implicit social contract with society."

This is all part of a continuing debate about management ethics and corporate social responsibility. You'll hear some argue that managers should try to satisfy the interests of many different stakeholders. But others will say that managers should stick to their primary duty—acting to maximize wealth for shareholders.

Make Ethics Personal: *What is your position on the shareholder wealth versus stakeholder interest debate? Do you agree with the movement to make management a profession? Would professionalizing management really make a difference in terms of ethical accountability and everyday managerial behavior?*

Organizations are full of leaders, managers and nonmanagers alike. These are people who get listened to by their peers, by their managers, and by people below and higher up in the organization. In contrast to traditional views of leadership flowing downward, lots of leadership flows upward and side-to-side. You can be a leader among your peers by becoming the person people turn to for advice, support, or direction. You can be a leader by convincing higher management to adopt new practices suggested from your level. And, remember the notion of the manager as "coach" and "coordinator" as described earlier? Everytime you act in ways that fit these descriptions, there's no doubt you're being a leader.

Ethical Management and Leadership

Having the essential managerial and leadership skills is one thing; using them correctly to get things done in organizations is quite another. And when it comes to ethics and morality, scholar Archie B. Carroll draws a distinction between immoral managers, amoral managers, and moral managers.[20]

- An **immoral manager** chooses to behave unethically.

The **immoral manager** essentially chooses to behave unethically. She or he doesn't subscribe to any ethical principles, making decisions and acting to gain best personal advantage. Disgraced executives like Bernard Madoff and

Organization's Ethics Center of Gravity

Figure 1.5 Moral leadership, ethics mindfulness, and the virtuous shift. [*Source:* Developed from Terry Thomas, John R. Schermerhorn Jr., and John W. Dinehart, "Strategic Leadership of Ethical Behavior in Business," *Academy of Management Executive* 18 (May 2004), pp. 56–66.]

others whose unethical acts make headlines fit this billing. The **amoral manager**, by contrast, acts unethically at times but does so unintentionally. This manager fails to consider the ethics of a decision or behavior. Unintentional ethics lapses that we all must guard against include prejudice from unconscious stereotypes and attitudes, showing bias based on in-group favoritism, and claiming too much personal credit for performance accomplishments.[21] Finally, the **moral manager** incorporates ethics principles and goals into his or her personal behavior. Ethical behavior is a goal, a standard, and even a matter of routine; ethical reasoning is part of every decision, not just an occasional afterthought.

Carroll believes that the majority of managers tend to act amorally. If this is true, and because we also know there are also immoral managers around, it is very important to understand personal responsibilities for everyday ethical behavior and leadership. All organization members can and should be ethics leaders. This includes always acting as ethics role models and being willing to take stands in the face of unethical behavior by those above, below, and around them.

A review article by Terry Thomas and his colleagues describes how the "ethics center of gravity" shown in Figure 1.5 can be moved positively through moral leadership or negatively through amoral leadership.[22] In this view, a moral manager or moral leader always sets an ethics example, communicates ethics values, and champions **ethics mindfulness**—an "enriched awareness" that causes one to behave with an ethical consciousness from one decision or behavioral event to another. Moral managers and moral leaders contribute to the "virtuous shift" shown in the figure. They help create an organizational culture in which people encourage one another to act ethically as a matter of routine. One of the themes of this book, as reflected in the Ethics in OB feature in each chapter, is that ethics is the responsibility of everyone in the organization.

- An **amoral manager** fails to consider the ethics of a decision or behavior.

- A **moral manager** makes ethical behavior a personal goal.

- **Ethics mindfulness** is an enriched awareness that causes one to consistently behave with ethical consciousness.

Learning about Organizational Behavior

LEARNING ROADMAP   Learning from Experience / Learning Styles / Learning Guide to *Organizational Behavior 12/E*

Learning about OB is important because it directly benefits you. It helps you to understand how to work more effectively and be more influential in work situations. Today's knowledge-based world places a great premium on learning. Only the learners, so to speak, will be able to keep the pace and succeed in a high-tech, global, and constantly changing environment.

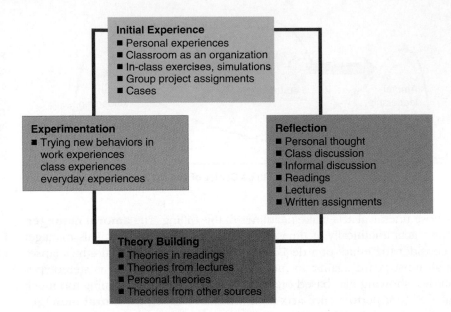

Figure 1.6 Experiential learning in an OB course.

Learning from Experience

• **Learning** is an enduring change in behavior that results from experience.

• **Lifelong learning** is continuous learning from everyday experiences.

Learning is an enduring change of behavior that results from experience. **Lifelong learning** involves learning continuously from day-to-day experiences. "Experience," in this sense, is found in work events and activities, conversations with colleagues and friends, counseling and advice provided by mentors, success models, training seminars and workshops, and other daily opportunities. Lifelong learning will in many respects be a key to your personal and career success. Now is the best time to get a serious start on the process.

Figure 1.6 shows how the content and activities of the typical OB course can fit together in an experiential learning cycle.[23] The learning sequence begins with initial experience and subsequent reflection. It grows as theory building takes place to try to explain what has happened. Theory is then tested in behavior. Textbooks, readings, class discussions, and other course assignments and activities should help you practice the phases of the learning cycle.

Notice that Figure 1.6 assigns to you a substantial responsibility for learning. Along with your instructor, we can offer examples, cases, and exercises to provide you with initial experience. We can even stimulate your reflection and theory building by presenting concepts and discussing their research and practical implications. Sooner or later, however, you must become an active participant in the process; you and only you can do the work required to take full advantage of the learning cycle.

Learning Styles

Now is also a good time to inquire further into your preferred learning style or tendencies. The end-of-book *OB Skills Workbook* includes instructions for a *Learning Styles* self-assessment.[24] If you complete it you'll get feedback on how you like to learn through receiving, processing, and recalling new information. Armed with this understanding, you can take steps to maximize your learning and

MORAL MANAGEMENT AND *JOHN Q.*

Moral managers try to act with ethical principles while immoral managers makes decisions primarily on self-interest. To be sure, many decisions in organizations are quite complicated and their ethical components may be hard to sort out.

"John Q" is the story of a desperate father's attempt to save his dying child. John Archibald (Denzel Washington) learns that his son Mike needs a heart transplant and he does not have sufficient insurance coverage. He decides to take the heart surgeon hostage in the hospital's emergency room. During a lull, the hostages and medical staff discuss how managed care insurance practices and hospital policies result in treatment decisions that are not always in the best interests of the patient. One hostage questions these practices in light of the medical profession's Hippocratic Oath. When Mike's (Daniel Smith) condition worsens, John decides to commit suicide so that a heart will be available. The heart surgeon initially balks for ethical reasons, then agrees to do the surgery. In the end, the sacrifice is not necessary. The hospital gets word that a donor heart is available and on its way.

This movie is worth watching as a study in organizational behavior. It illustrates that ethical lines can sometimes be blurry. What's "right" or "wrong" isn't always clear or agreed upon. If an insurance company refuses to pay for preventive health screening, should the doctor order it? If someone can't pay, should doctors and hospitals still provide medical care? Should a doctor adhere to hospital policies if they jeopardize the health of a patient?

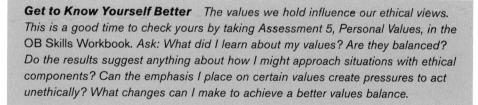

Get to Know Yourself Better   The values we hold influence our ethical views. This is a good time to check yours by taking Assessment 5, Personal Values, in the OB Skills Workbook. Ask: What did I learn about my values? Are they balanced? Do the results suggest anything about how I might approach situations with ethical components? Can the emphasis I place on certain values create pressures to act unethically? What changes can I make to achieve a better values balance.

even course success by studying in ways that best fit your learning style. So, what type of learner are you? Why not take the self-assessment and find out?

Learning Guide to *Organizational Behavior 12/E*

To facilitate your learning, the chapters in *Organizational Behavior 12/E* are presented in a logical building-block fashion. This first chapter in *Part 1* has introduced the discipline and context of OB, including its scientific foundations and link with managerial skills and leadership. *Part 2* focuses on individual behavior and performance. Key topics include diversity, values, personality, attitudes, emotions, perception, learning, and motivation. *Part 3* covers teams and teamwork, including the dynamics of decision making, conflict, and negotiation. *Part 4* examines leadership and influence processes, with an emphasis on communication and collaboration, power and politics, and important leadership theories and perspectives. *Part 5* discusses the organizational context in respect to organization cultures, structures, and designs.

At the end of the book you'll find the rich and useful *OB Skills Workbook*. It provides a variety of active learning opportunities that can help you better understand the practical applications of OB concepts, models, and theories. The Workbook contains cases for analysis, team and experiential exercises, and a portfolio of self-assessments that includes the popular Kouzes and Posner "Student Leadership Practices Inventory."

Finally, don't forget that opportunities to learn more about OB and yourself abound in everyday living. Every team project, part-time work experience, student co-curricular activity, or visit to the store, is rich in learning potential. Even our leisure pasttimes from sports to social interactions to television, movies, and on-line games offer learning insights. The OB in Popular Culture feature in each chapter is a reminder to keep your learning dialed in all the time.

1 *study guide*

Key Questions and Answers

What is organizational behavior and why is it important?

- Organizational behavior is the study of individuals and groups in organizations.

- OB is an applied discipline based on scientific methods.

- OB uses a contingency approach, recognizing that management practices must fit the situation.

- Shifting paradigms of OB reflect a commitment to ethical behavior, the importance of human capital, an emphasis on teams, the growing influence of information technology, new workforce expectations, changing notions of careers, and concern for sustainability.

What are organizations like as work settings?

- An organization is a collection of people working together in a division of labor for a common purpose.

- Organizations are open systems that interact with their environments to obtain resources and transform them into outputs returned to the environment for consumption.

- Key stakeholders in the external environments of organizations include customers, owners, suppliers, regulators, local communities, employees, and future generations.

- The organizational culture is the internal "personality" of the organization, including the beliefs and values that are shared by members.

- Positive organizational cultures place a high value on workforce diversity and multiculturalism, emphasizing respect and inclusiveness for all members.

What is the nature of management and leadership in organizations?

- Managers directly support the work efforts of others; they are increasingly expected to act more like "coaches" and "facilitators" than like "bosses" and "controllers."

- An effective manager is successful at helping others, working individually and in teams, reach high levels of both performance and job satisfaction.

- The four functions of management are planning—to set directions; organizing—to assemble resources and systems; leading—to create workforce enthusiasm; and controlling—to ensure desired results.

- Managers fulfill a variety of interpersonal, informational, and decisional roles while working with networks of people both inside and outside of the organization.

- Managerial performance is based on a combination of essential technical, human, and conceptual skills.

- Emotional intelligence is an important human skill that is an ability to recognize and manage emotions both personally and in relationships with others.

How do we learn about organizational behavior?

- Learning is an enduring change in behavior that results from experience.

- True learning about organizational behavior involves a commitment to continuous lifelong learning from one's work and everyday experiences.

- Most organizational behavior courses use multiple methods and approaches that take advantage of the experiential learning cycle.

- People vary in their learning styles; an understanding of your style can help improve learning and course success.

Terms to Know

Amoral manager (p. 17)
Conceptual skill (p. 14)
Contingency thinking (p. 6)
Controlling (p. 12)
Dependent variables (p. 5)
Effective manager (p. 11)
Emotional intelligence (p. 13)
Ethics mindfulness (p. 17)
Evidence-based management (p. 6)
Human skills (p. 13)
Immoral manager (p. 16)
Inclusion (p. 11)

Independent variables (p. 5)
Job satisfaction (p. 11)
Leading (p. 12)
Learning (p. 18)
Lifelong learning (p. 18)
Managers (p. 11)
Models (p. 5)
Moral manager (p. 17)
Multiculturalism (p. 11)
Open systems (p. 9)
Organization (p. 9)
Organizational behavior (p. 4)

Organizational climate (p. 9)
Organizational culture (p. 9)
Organizing (p. 12)
Planning (p. 12)
Skill (p. 13)
Social capital (p. 14)
Stakeholders (p. 10)
Task performance (p. 11)
Technical skill (p. 13)
Value chain (p. 10)
Workforce diversity (p. 11)

Self-Test 1

Multiple Choice

1. Which issue is most central to the field of organizational behavior? (a) ways to improve advertising for a new product (b) how to increase job satisfaction and performance among employees (c) creation of new strategy for organizational growth (d) design of a new management information system

2. What is the best description of the setting facing organizational behavior today? (a) Command-and-control is in. (b) The new generation is similar to the old. (c) Empowerment is out. (d) Work–life balance concerns are in.

3. The term "workforce diversity" refers to differences in race, age, gender, ethnicity, and _____ among people at work. (a) social status (b) personal wealth (c) able-bodiedness (d) political preference

4. Which statement about OB is most correct? (a) OB seeks "one-best-way" solutions to management problems. (b) OB is a unique science that has little relationship to other scientific disciplines. (c) OB is focused on using knowledge for practical applications. (d) OB is so modern that it has no historical roots.

5. In the open-systems view of organizations, such things as technology, information, and money are considered _____. (a) transformation elements (b) feedback (c) inputs (d) outputs

6. If the organization culture represents the character of an organization in terms of shared values, the _____ represents the shared perceptions of members about day-to-day management practices. (a) value chain (b) organization climate (c) transformation process (d) organization strategy

7. Which of the following is *not* a good match of organizational stakeholder and the interests they often hold important? (a) customers—high quality products (b) owners—returns on investments (c) future generations—value pricing (d) regulators—compliance with laws

8. Which word best describes an organizational culture that embraces multiculturalism and in which workforce diversity is highly valued? (a) inclusion (b) effectiveness (c) dynamism (d) predictability

9. The management function of _____ is concerned with creating enthusiasm for hard work among organizational members. (a) planning (b) motivating (c) controlling (d) leading

10. In the management process, _____ is concerned with measuring performance results and taking action to improve future performance. (a) disciplining (b) organizing (c) leading (d) controlling

11. Among Mintzberg's 10 managerial roles, acting as a figurehead and liaison are examples of _____ roles. (a) interpersonal (b) informational (c) decisional (d) conceptual

12. When a manager moves upward in responsibility, Katz suggests that _____ skills decrease in importance and _____ skills increase in importance. (a) human, conceptual (b) conceptual, emotional (c) technical, conceptual (d) emotional, human

13. A person with high emotional intelligence would be strong in _____, the ability to think before acting and to control disruptive impulses. (a) motivation (b) perseverance (c) self-regulation (d) empathy

14. When a person's human skills are so good that they always have relationships with other people who they can confidently ask for help and assistance at work, these skills increase the _____ of the individual. (a) analytical capacity (b) ethics mindfulness (c) social capital (d) multiculturalism

15. Class discussions, "debriefs," and individual papers based on case studies, team projects, and in-class activities are all ways an instructor tries to engage you in which part of the experiential learning cycle? (a) initial experience (b) reflection (c) theory building (d) experimentation

Short Response

16. What are the key characteristics of OB as a scientific discipline?

17. What does "valuing diversity" mean in the workplace?

18. What is an effective manager?

19. What does "self-regulation" mean when used in the context of one's emotional intelligence?

Applications Essay

20. Carla, a college junior, is participating in a special "elementary education outreach" project in her local community. Along with other students from the business school, she is going to spend the day with fourth- and fifth-grade students and introduce them to the opportunities of going to college. One of her tasks is to lead a class discussion of the question: "How is the world of work changing today?" Help Carla out by creating an outline of the major points she should discuss with the students.

Next Steps
Top Choices from
The OB Skills
Workbook

Cases for Critical Thinking	Team and Experiential Exercises	Self-Assessment Portfolio
• Trader Joe's • Management Training Dilemma	• My Best Manager • My Best Job • Graffiti Needs Assessment • Sweet Tooth	• Learning Styles • Student Leadership Practices Inventory • Managerial Assumptions • 21st Century Manager

Xerox: A Dynamic Duo

The news came as a surprise: In 1999, Xerox announced that Anne Mulcahy, a relative newcomer, had been selected as the new CEO. Dubbed the "accidental CEO" because she never aspired to the job, one of the first things she did was to recruit the best talent she could find. And one of those key players turned out to be Ursula Burns.[a]

Burns did not come to power through a traditional path. She was raised in a housing project on Manhattan's Lower East Side. Her hard-working, single mother cleaned, ironed, and provided childcare in order to give her daughter a private education and the opportunity to earn an engineering degree from Columbia University.

Together, Mulcahy and Burns have broken new ground. In 2007, when Mulcahy became CEO, Burns replaced Mulcahy as president and was appointed a seat on the board. In 2009, Mulcahy retired and Burns became CEO, marking two more firsts: the first transition of power from one woman to another at a large public company, and the first to be run by a Black woman.

> *"I think we are really tough on each other . . . in a way most people can't handle."*
> *—Anne Mulcahy referring to Ursula Burns*

Mulcahy took over when the company was in shambles. Through a strong partnership, Burns and Mulcahy saved Xerox in a major turnaround, transforming red ink to black ink within a few years. In the process, they also became a close duo, often finishing each other's sentences.

According to Burns, Mulcahy was her role model as she rose through the Xerox ranks. Burns remembers being on a panel with Mulcahy and realizing, "Wow, this woman is exactly where I am going." Mulcahy coached Burns, shooting her looks in meetings when Burns needed to listen instead of "letting my big mouth drive the discussion," said Burns with a laugh. Mulcahy pushed Burns to develop a poker face, telling her after a meeting, "Ursula, they could read your face. You have to be careful. Sometimes it's not appropriate."

Mulcahy and Burns show how individual differences can build a strong team. Their relationship is complex and sometimes contentious: "I think we are really tough on each other," says Mulcahy. "We are in a way most people can't handle. Ursula will tell me when she thinks I am so far away from the right answer." Chimes in Burns: "I try to be nice."[b]

Quick Summary
- In 1999 Xerox made a surprise announcement that Anne Mulcahy, a relative newcomer, would be their new CEO.
- Mulcahy selected Ursula Burns to partner with her in running the business. In 2009, Mulcahy retired and Burns took over as CEO, marking the first transition of power from one woman to another at a large public company, and the first to be run by a Black woman.
- Mulcahy and Burns' partnership shows how individual differences can build a strong team. They were able to save Xerox in a major turnaround by learning to share power and forging a highly successful leadership collaboration.

FYI: *Fortune* 500 companies with higher percentages of women board directors, on average, financially outperformed companies with the lowest percentages of women board directors by significant margins.

2 Individual Differences, Values, and Diversity

the key point

Organizational behavior is generated in actions of individuals interacting in context. Therefore we need to begin with an understanding of the individual. People vary in their traits, values, and personal characteristics, and as illustrated by the example of Anne Mulcahy and Ursula Burns, these individual differences can have powerful impacts in organizations.

chapter at a glance

What Are Individual Differences and Why Are They Important?

What Is Personality?

How Are Personality and Stress Related?

What Are Individual Values?

Why Is Diversity Important in the Workplace?

ETHICS IN OB
PERSONALITY TESTING

FINDING THE LEADER IN YOU
STEPHEN HAWKING SOARS DESPITE DISABILITY

OB IN POPULAR CULTURE
PERSONALITY AND *SHREK*

RESEARCH INSIGHT
TWIN STUDIES: NATURE OR NURTURE?

what's inside?

Individual Differences

LEARNING ROADMAP   Self-Awareness and Awareness of Others / Components of Self / Nature versus Nurture

People are complex. While you approach a situation one way, someone else may approach it quite differently. These differences among people can make the ability to predict and understand behavior in organizations challenging. They also contribute to what makes the study of organizational behavior so fascinating.

In OB, the term *individual differences* is used to refer to the ways in which people are similar and how they vary in their thinking, feeling, and behavior. Although no two people are completely alike, they are also not completely different. Therefore, the study of **individual differences** attempts to identify where behavioral tendencies are similar and where they are different. The idea is that if we can figure out how to categorize behavioral tendencies and identify which tendencies people have, we will be able to more accurately predict how and why people behave as they do.

Although individual differences can sometimes make working together difficult, they can also offer great benefits. The best teams often result from combining people who have different skills and approaches and who think in different ways—by putting the "whole brain" to work.[1] Capitalizing on these differences requires an understanding of what these differences are and valuing the benefits they can offer.

> • **Individual differences** are the ways in which people are similar and how they vary in their thinking, feeling, and behavior.

Self-Awareness and Awareness of Others

In this chapter we examine factors that increase awareness of individual differences—our own and others—in the workplace. Two factors that are important for this analysis are self-awareness and awareness of others. **Self-awareness** means being aware of our own behaviors, preferences, styles, biases, personalities, and so on. **Awareness of others** means being aware of these same things in others. To enhance our own awareness of these issues, we begin by understanding components of the self and how these components are developed. We then discuss what personality is, and identify the personality characteristics and values that have the most relevance for OB. As you read these concepts, think about where you fall on them. Do they sound like you? Do they sound like people you know?

> • **Self-awareness** means being aware of one's own behaviors, preferences, styles, biases, personalities, and so on.
> • **Awareness of others** is being aware of the behaviors, preferences, styles, biases, and personalities of others.

Components of Self

The ways in which an individual integrates and organizes personality and the traits they contain make up the self-concept. The **self-concept** is the view individuals have of themselves as physical, social, and spiritual or moral beings.[2] It is a way of recognizing oneself as a distinct human being.

A person's self-concept is greatly influenced by his or her culture. For example, Americans tend to disclose much more about themselves than do the English; that is, an American's self-concept is more assertive and talkative.[3]

Two related—and crucial—aspects of the self-concept are self-esteem and self-efficacy. **Self-esteem** is a belief about one's own worth based on an overall self-evaluation.[4] People high in self-esteem see themselves as capable, worthwhile,

> • **Self-concept** is the view individuals have of themselves as physical, social, spiritual, or moral beings.
> • **Self-esteem** is a belief about one's own worth based on an overall self-evaluation.

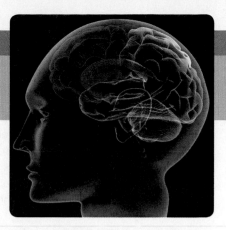

and acceptable; they tend to have few doubts about themselves. People who are low in self-esteem are full of self-doubt and are often afraid to act because of it. While OB research has shown that high self-esteem generally can boost performance and satisfaction outcomes, it can also have drawbacks. For example, when under pressure, people with high self-esteem may become boastful and act egotistically. They may also be overconfident at times and fail to obtain important information.[5]

Self-efficacy, sometimes called the "effectance motive," is a more specific version of self-esteem. It is an individual's belief about the likelihood of successfully completing a specific task. You could have high self-esteem and yet have a feeling of low self-efficacy about performing a certain task, such as public speaking.

> • **Self-efficacy** is an individual's belief about the likelihood of successfully completing a specific task.

Nature versus Nurture

What determines the development of the self? Is our personality inherited or genetically determined, or is it formed by experience? You may have heard someone say, "She acts like her mother," or, "Bobby is the way he is because of the way he was raised." These two arguments illustrate the nature/nurture controversy: Are we the way we are because of heredity—that is, genetic endowment—or because of the environments in which we have been raised and live—cultural, social, situational? As shown, these two forces actually operate in combination. Heredity consists of those factors that are determined at conception, including physical characteristics, gender, and personality factors. Environment consists of cultural, social, and situational factors.

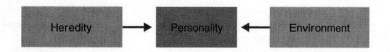

The impact of heredity on personality continues to be the source of considerable debate. Perhaps the most general conclusion we can draw is that heredity sets the limits on the extent to which our personality characteristics can be developed; environment determines development within these limits. For instance, a person could be born with a tendency toward authoritarianism, and that tendency could be reinforced in an authoritarian work environment. These limits appear to vary from one characteristic to the next, and across all characteristics there is about a 50–50 heredity–environment split.[6]

A person's development of the self is also related to the environment in which he or she was raised (i.e., "nurture"). As we show throughout this book,

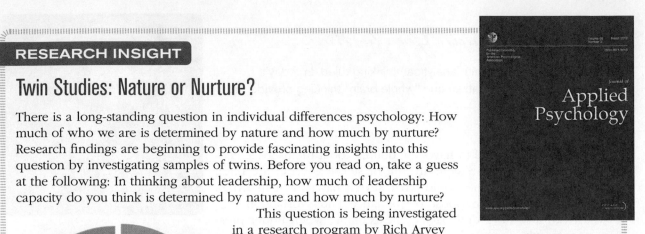

Journal of
Applied
Psychology

RESEARCH INSIGHT

Twin Studies: Nature or Nurture?

There is a long-standing question in individual differences psychology: How much of who we are is determined by nature and how much by nurture? Research findings are beginning to provide fascinating insights into this question by investigating samples of twins. Before you read on, take a guess at the following: In thinking about leadership, how much of leadership capacity do you think is determined by nature and how much by nurture?

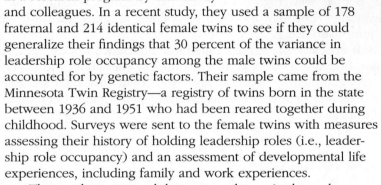

This question is being investigated in a research program by Rich Arvey and colleagues. In a recent study, they used a sample of 178 fraternal and 214 identical female twins to see if they could generalize their findings that 30 percent of the variance in leadership role occupancy among the male twins could be accounted for by genetic factors. Their sample came from the Minnesota Twin Registry—a registry of twins born in the state between 1936 and 1951 who had been reared together during childhood. Surveys were sent to the female twins with measures assessing their history of holding leadership roles (i.e., leadership role occupancy) and an assessment of developmental life experiences, including family and work experiences.

The results supported the pattern shown in the male sample—32 percent of the variance in the women's leadership role occupancy was associated with heritability. Family experience and work experience were also related to leadership role occupancy, though not surprisingly, experiences at work are more important than family experiences in shaping women's leadership development. The findings are important because they indicate that developmental experiences can help both men and women move into leadership roles.

Do the Research   How close was your guess? Do these findings correspond with what you see in your own families (e.g., with brothers and sisters or with parents and children)? How would you test the question of nature versus nurture?

Source: R. Arvey, Z. Zhang, B. Avolio, and R. Krueger (2007). "Developmental and Genetic Determinants of Leadership Role Occupancy among Women." *Journal of Applied Psychology*, 92.3 (2007), pp. 693–706.

cultural values and norms play a substantial role in the development of an individual's personality and behaviors. Contrast the individualism of U.S. culture with the collectivism of Mexican culture, for example.[7] In addition, social factors, such as family life, religion, and the many kinds of formal and informal groups in which people participate throughout their lives, can influence the nature of the self. Finally, the demands of differing *situational factors* can influence certain aspects of an individual's personality. For example, firstborns in families tend to be ambitious, enterprising, and scholarly, whereas middle children tend to be more loners, quiet, shy, and impatient.

Personality

LEARNING ROADMAP   Big Five Personality Traits / Social Traits / Personal Conception Traits / Emotional Adjustment Traits

The term **personality** encompasses the overall combination of characteristics that capture the unique nature of a person as that person reacts to and interacts with others. It combines a set of physical and mental characteristics that reflect how a person looks, thinks, acts, and feels. Think of yourself, and of your family and friends. A key part of how you interact with others depends on your own and their personalities, doesn't it? If you have a friend who has a sensitive personality, do you interact with that person differently than you do with a friend or family member who likes to joke around?

Sometimes attempts are made to measure personality with questionnaires or special tests. Frequently, personality can be inferred from behavior alone. Either way, personality is an important individual characteristic to understand. It helps us identify predictable interplays between people's individual differences and their tendencies to behave in certain ways.

> • **Personality** is the overall combination of characteristics that capture the unique nature of a person as that person reacts to and interacts with others.

Big Five Personality Traits

Numerous lists of **personality traits**—enduring characteristics describing an individual's behavior—have been developed, many of which have been used in OB research and can be looked at in different ways. A key starting point is to consider the personality dimensions that recent research has distilled from extensive lists into what is called the "Big Five":[8]

> • **Personality traits** are enduring characteristics describing an individual's behavior.

The Big Five Personality Dimensions
- *Extraversion*—outgoing, sociable, assertive
- *Agreeableness*—good-natured, trusting, cooperative
- *Conscientiousness*—responsible, dependable, persistent
- *Emotional stability*—unworried, secure, relaxed
- *Openness to experience*—imaginative, curious, broad-minded

Standardized personality tests determine how positively or negatively an individual scores on each of these dimensions. For instance, a person scoring high on openness to experience tends to ask lots of questions and to think in new and unusual ways. You can consider a person's individual personality profile across the five dimensions. In terms of job performance, research has shown that conscientiousness predicts job performance across five occupational groups of professions—engineers, police, managers, salespersons, and skilled and semiskilled employees. Predictability of the other dimensions depends on the occupational group. For instance, not surprisingly, extraversion predicts performance for sales and managerial positions.

A second approach to looking at OB personality traits is to divide them into social traits, personal conception traits, and emotional adjustment traits, and then to consider how those categories come together dynamically.

> • **Social traits** are surface-level traits that reflect the way a person appears to others when interacting in social settings.

Social Traits

Social traits are surface-level traits that reflect the way a person appears to others when interacting in various social settings. The **problem-solving style**, based

> • **Problem-solving style** reflects the way a person gathers and evaluates information when solving problems and making decisions.

PERSONALITY AND *SHREK*

Personality refers to the unique set of characteristics that determine how an individual reacts and responds to the environment. Put another way, it reflects the combination of individual traits that lead to consistent patterns of behavior. Personality is complex. One of the best frameworks for examining this concert is the Big Five Personality Traits. It consists of five dimensions, each of which has several descriptors.

When Shrek sets out on his quest to rescue Princess Fiona from the dragon for King Farquaad, he is accompanied by newfound "friend" Donkey. Donkey still does not understand the mysterious ogre and is questioning why he would set out on this quest in the first place. Shrek, growing ever impatient with the query, explains that Donkey could not possibly understand his reasoning. "Ogres are like onions," he replies. "They both have layers."

The analogy is useful when it comes to understanding anyone. In a world reduced to sound bites and stereotypes, we all want to size up other people quickly. The truth is human beings are more complicated than a single individual characteristic. You do not have to look any farther than personality to realize this.

> *Get to Know Yourself Better*   Most of the individual assessments in the OB Skills Workbook *measure some aspect of your personality. Consider this as you begin to explore your preferences and gain a better understanding of who you are. How difficult would it be for someone else to understand you? Why not spend a few minutes looking at one, Assessment 19. After you score the instrument, sit down with your roommate or a close friend and discuss the results. Is what you discovered consistent with how they see you?*

on the work of Carl Jung, a noted psychologist, is one measure representing social traits.[9] It reflects the way a person goes about gathering and evaluating information in solving problems and making decisions.

Information gathering involves getting and organizing data for use. Styles of information gathering vary from sensation to intuitive. *Sensation-type individuals* prefer routine and order and emphasize well-defined details in gathering information; they would rather work with known facts than look for possibilities. By contrast, *intuitive-type individuals* prefer the "big picture." They like solving new problems, dislike routine, and would rather look for possibilities than work with facts.

The second component of problem solving, *evaluation*, involves making judgments about how to deal with information once it has been collected. Styles of information evaluation vary from an emphasis on feeling to an emphasis on thinking. *Feeling-type individuals* are oriented toward conformity and try to accommodate themselves to other people. They try to avoid problems that may result in disagreements. *Thinking-type individuals* use reason and intellect to deal with problems and downplay emotions.

When these two dimensions (information gathering and evaluation) are combined, four basic problem-solving styles result: sensation–feeling (SF), intuitive–feeling (IF), sensation–thinking (ST), and intuitive–thinking (IT), together with summary descriptions as shown in Figure 2.1.

Research indicates that there is a fit between the styles of individuals and the kinds of decisions they prefer. For example, STs (sensation–thinkers) prefer analytical

S

Sensation–Feeling	Sensation–Thinking
Interpersonal	Technical detail oriented
Specific human detail	Logical analysis of hard data
Friendly, sympathetic	Precise, orderly
Open communication	Careful about rules and procedures
Respond to people now	Dependable, responsible
Good at:	*Good at*:
Empathizing	Observing, ordering
Cooperating	Filing, recalling
Goal: To be helpful	*Goal*: Do it correctly
Illustrated by: Anita Roddick, CEO Body Shop International (International Cosmetics Organization)	*Illustrated by*: Enita Nordeck, President Unity Forest Products (a small and growing builder's supply firm)
Intuitive–Feeling	Intuitive–Thinking
Insightful, mystical	Speculative
Idealistic, personal	Emphasize understanding
Creative, original	Synthesize, interpret
Global ideas oriented to people	Logic-oriented ideas
Human potential	Objective, impersonal, idealistic
Good at:	*Good at*:
Imagining	Discovery, inquiry
New combinations	Problem solving
Goal: To make things beautiful	*Goal*: To think things through
Illustrated by: Herb Kelleher, former CEO Southwest Airlines (a fast-growing, large, regional airline)	*Illustrated by*: Paul Allaire, former CEO, Xerox Corporation (a huge multi-national, recently innovatively reorganized)

F   T

I

Figure 2.1 Four problem-solving style summaries.

strategies—those that emphasize detail and method. IFs (intuitive–feelers) prefer intuitive strategies—those that emphasize an overall pattern and fit. Not surprisingly, mixed styles (sensation–feelers or intuitive–thinkers) select both analytical and intuitive strategies. Other findings also indicate that thinkers tend to have higher motivation than do feelers and that individuals who emphasize sensations tend to have higher job satisfaction than do intuitives. These and other findings suggest a number of basic differences among different problem-solving styles, emphasizing the importance of fitting such styles with a task's information processing and evaluation requirements.[10]

Problem-solving styles are most frequently measured by the typically 100-item *Myers-Briggs Type Indicator (MBTI)*, which asks individuals how they usually act or feel in specific situations. Firms such as Apple, AT&T, and Exxon, as well as hospitals, educational institutions, and military organizations, have used the Myers-Briggs for various aspects of management development.[11]

Personal Conception Traits

The **personal conception traits** represent the way individuals tend to think about their social and physical setting as well as their major beliefs and personal orientation concerning a range of issues.

Locus of Control   The extent to which a person feels able to control his or her own life is concerned with a person's internal–external orientation and is measured by Rotter's **locus of control** instrument.[12] People have personal conceptions about whether

- **Personal conception traits** represent individuals' major beliefs and personal orientation concerning a range of issues involving social and physical setting.
- **Locus of control** is the extent a person feels able to control his or her own life and is concerned with a person's internal–external orientation.

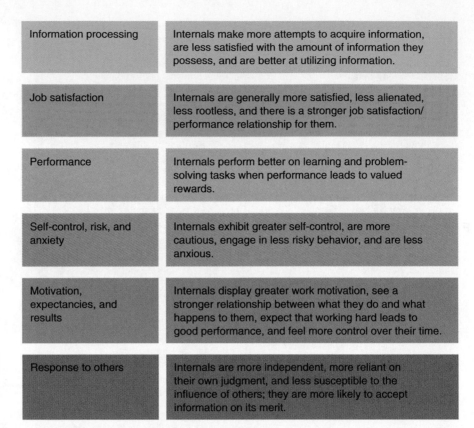

Information processing	Internals make more attempts to acquire information, are less satisfied with the amount of information they possess, and are better at utilizing information.
Job satisfaction	Internals are generally more satisfied, less alienated, less rootless, and there is a stronger job satisfaction/performance relationship for them.
Performance	Internals perform better on learning and problem-solving tasks when performance leads to valued rewards.
Self-control, risk, and anxiety	Internals exhibit greater self-control, are more cautious, engage in less risky behavior, and are less anxious.
Motivation, expectancies, and results	Internals display greater work motivation, see a stronger relationship between what they do and what happens to them, expect that working hard leads to good performance, and feel more control over their time.
Response to others	Internals are more independent, more reliant on their own judgment, and less susceptible to the influence of others; they are more likely to accept information on its merit.

Figure 2.2 Ways in which those high in internal locus of control differ from those high in external locus of control.

events are controlled primarily by themselves, which indicates an internal orientation, or by outside forces, such as their social and physical environment, which indicates an external orientation. *Internals*, or persons with an internal locus of control, believe that they control their own fate or destiny. In contrast, *externals*, or persons with an external locus of control, believe that much of what happens to them is beyond their control and is determined by environmental forces (such as fate). In general, externals are more extraverted in their interpersonal relationships and are more oriented toward the world around them. Internals tend to be more introverted and are more oriented toward their own feelings and ideas. Figure 2.2 suggests that internals tend to do better on tasks requiring complex information processing and learning as well as initiative. Many managerial and professional jobs have these kinds of requirements.

Proactive Personality   Some people in organizations are passive recipients when faced with constraints, while others take direct and intentional action to change their circumstances. The disposition that identifies whether or not individuals act to influence their environments is known as **proactive personality**. Individuals with high proactive personality identify opportunities and act on them, show initiative, take action, and persevere until meaningful change occurs. People who are low on proactivity are the opposite. They fail to identify—let alone seize—opportunities to change things. These individuals are passive and reactive, preferring to adapt to circumstances rather than change them.[13]

In the ever more demanding world of work, many companies are seeking individuals with more proactive qualities—individuals who take initiative and engage in proactive problem solving. Research supports this, showing that proactive personality is positively related to job performance, creativity, leadership, and career success.

• A **proactive personality** is the disposition that identifies whether or not individuals act to influence their environments.

Other studies have shown that proactive personality is related to team effectiveness and entrepreneurship. Moreover, when organizations try to make positive and innovative change, these changes have more positive effects for proactive individuals—they are more involved and more receptive to change. This research is showing that proactive personality is an important and desirable element in today's work environment.

Authoritarianism/Dogmatism   Both "authoritarianism" and "dogmatism" deal with the rigidity of a person's beliefs. A person high in **authoritarianism** tends to adhere rigidly to conventional values and to obey recognized authority. This person is concerned with toughness and power and opposes the use of subjective feelings. An individual high in **dogmatism** sees the world as a threatening place. This person regards legitimate authority as absolute, and accepts or rejects others according to how much they agree with accepted authority. Superiors who possess these latter traits tend to be rigid and closed. At the same time, dogmatic subordinates tend to want certainty imposed upon them.

• **Authoritarianism** is a tendency to adhere rigidly to conventional values and to obey recognized authority.

• **Dogmatism** leads a person to see the world as a threatening place and to regard authority as absolute.

From an ethical standpoint, we can expect highly authoritarian individuals to present a special problem because they are so susceptible to authority that in their eagerness to comply they may behave unethically.[14] For example, we might speculate that many of the Nazis who were involved in war crimes during World War II were high in authoritarianism or dogmatism; they believed so strongly in authority that they followed unethical orders without question.

Machiavellianism   Another personal conceptions dimension is **Machiavellianism**, which owes its origins to Niccolo Machiavelli. The very name of this sixteenth-century author evokes visions of a master of guile, deceit, and opportunism in interpersonal relations. Machiavelli earned his place in history by writing *The Prince*, a nobleman's guide to the acquisition and use of power.[15] The subject of Machiavelli's book is manipulation as the basic means of gaining and keeping control of others. From its pages emerges the personality profile of a Machiavellian—someone who views and manipulates others purely for personal gain.

• **Machiavellianism** causes someone to view and manipulate others purely for personal gain.

A person high in Machiavellian orientation approaches situations logically and thoughtfully, and is even capable of lying to achieve personal goals.[16] They are rarely swayed by loyalty, friendships, past promises, or the opinions of others, and they are skilled at influencing others. A person low in Machiavellianism tends to accept direction imposed by others in loosely structured situations and works hard to do well in highly structured situations.

Research using the Mach scales provides insight into the way high and low Machs may be expected to behave in various situations. A person with a "cool" and "detached" high-Mach personality can be expected to take control and try to exploit loosely structured environmental situations but will perform in a perfunctory, even detached, manner in highly structured situations. Where the situation permits, a high Mach might be expected to do or say whatever it takes to get his or her way. In contrast, a low Mach will tend to be much more strongly guided by ethical considerations and will be less likely to lie or cheat or to get away with lying or cheating.

Self-Monitoring   A final personal conceptions trait of special importance to managers is self-monitoring. **Self-monitoring** reflects a person's ability to adjust his or her behavior to external, situational (environmental) factors.[17] High self-monitors are sensitive to external cues and tend to behave differently in different situations. Like high Machs, high self-monitors can present a very different appearance from their true self. In contrast, low self-monitors, like their low-Mach counterparts, are not able to disguise their behaviors—"what you see is what you get."

• **Self-monitoring** is a person's ability to adjust his or her behavior to external situational (environmental) factors.

PERSONALITY TESTING

Dear [your name goes here]:

I am very pleased to invite you to a second round of screening interviews with XYZ Corporation. Your on-campus session with our representative went very well, and we would like to consider you further for a full-time position. Please contact me to arrange a visit date. We will need a full day. The schedule will include several meetings with executives and your potential team members, as well as a round of personality tests.

Thank you again for your interest in XYZ Corp. I look forward to meeting you during the next step in our recruiting process.

Sincerely,

/signed/
Human Resource Director

Getting a letter like this is great news: a nice confirmation of your hard work and performance in college. You obviously made a good first impression. But have you thought about this "personality test" thing? What do you know about them and how they are used for employment screening?

The U.S. Equal Employment Opportunity Commission says that personality tests can't have an adverse impact on members of protected groups. A report in the *Wall Street Journal* advises that lawsuits can result when employers use personality tests that weren't specifically designed for hiring decisions. Some people might even consider their use an invasion of privacy.[c]

> ***Make the Decision.*** *What are the ethical issues of personality testing? When might the use of personality tests be considered an invasion of privacy? When might their use be considered unethical? Now go back to the situation just described: Will you take the tests at XYZ? Will you ask any questions about the tests when you contact the human resource director? Is the fact that XYZ uses personality tests a positive or a negative in terms of your likely fit with the firm?*

There is also evidence that high self-monitors are closely attuned to the behavior of others and conform more readily than do low self-monitors.[18] Thus, they appear flexible and may be especially good at responding to the kinds of situational contingencies emphasized throughout this book. For example, high self-monitors should be especially good at changing their leadership behavior to fit subordinates with more or less experience, tasks with more or less structure, and so on.

Emotional Adjustment Traits

- **Emotional adjustment traits** are traits related to how much an individual experiences emotional distress or displays unacceptable acts.

Emotional adjustment traits measure how much an individual experiences emotional distress or displays unacceptable acts, such as impatience, irritability, or aggression. Inability to effectively manage stress can often affect the person's health. Although numerous such traits are cited in the literature, a frequently encountered one especially important for OB is the Type A/Type B orientation.[19]

Individuals with a **Type A orientation** are characterized by impatience, desire for achievement, and perfectionism. In contrast, those with a **Type B orientation** are characterized as more easygoing and less competitive in relation to daily events.[20] Type A people tend to work fast and to be abrupt, uncomfortable, irritable, and aggressive. Such tendencies indicate "obsessive" behavior, a fairly widespread—but not always helpful—trait among managers. Many managers are hard-driving, detail-oriented people who have high performance standards and thrive on routine. But when such work obsessions are carried to the extreme, they may lead to greater concerns for details than for results, resistance to change, overzealous control of subordinates, and various kinds of interpersonal difficulties, which may even include threats and physical violence. In contrast, Type B managers tend to be much more laid back and patient in their dealings with co-workers and subordinates.

- **Type A orientations** are characterized by impatience, desire for achievement, and a more competitive nature than Type B.
- **Type B orientations** are characterized by an easygoing and less competitive nature than Type A.

Personality and Stress

LEARNING ROADMAP   Sources of Stress / Outcomes of Stress / Managing Stress

It is but a small step from a focus on the emotional adjustment traits of Type A/Type B orientation to consideration of the relationship between personality and stress. We define **stress** as a state of tension experienced by individuals facing extraordinary demands, constraints, or opportunities. As we show, stress can be both positive and negative and is an important fact of life in our present work environment.[21]

An especially important set of stressors includes personal factors, such as individual needs, capabilities, and personality.[22] Stress can reach a destructive state more quickly, for example, when experienced by highly emotional people or by those with low self-esteem. People who perceive a good fit between job requirements and personal skills seem to have a higher tolerance for stress than do those who feel less competent as a result of a person–job mismatch.[23] This is a reason to be careful about making sure you are a good fit with your organization.

- **Stress** is tension from extraordinary demands, constraints, or opportunities.

Sources of Stress

Any look toward your career future in today's dynamic times must include an awareness that stress is something you, as well as others, are sure to encounter.[24] Stressors are the wide variety of things that cause stress for individuals. Some stressors can be traced directly to what people experience in the workplace, whereas others derive from nonwork and personal factors.

Spillover Effects Bring Work Home

American men spend four times as many hours in household and childcare responsibilities than Japanese men, and the number of hours they spend in childcare has doubled since 1965. When combined with the decreasing gap between American women and men in time spent on housework, this means that spillover effects are a concern not only for women, but also for men.

Work Stressors   Without doubt, work can be stressful, and job demands can disrupt one's work–life balance. A study of two-career couples, for example, found some 43 percent of men and 34 percent of women reporting that they worked more hours than they wanted to.[25] We know that work stressors can arise from many sources—from excessively high or low task demands, role conflicts or ambiguities, poor interpersonal relations, or career progress that is either too slow or too fast. A list of common stressors includes the following:

Possible work-related stressors

- *Task demands*—being asked to do too much or being asked to do too little
- *Role ambiguities*—not knowing what one is expected to do or how work performance is evaluated
- *Role conflicts*—feeling unable to satisfy multiple, possibly conflicting, performance expectations
- *Ethical dilemmas*—being asked to do things that violate the law or personal values
- *Interpersonal problems*—experiencing bad relationships or working with others with whom one does not get along
- *Career developments*—moving too fast and feeling stretched; moving too slowly and feeling stuck on a plateau
- *Physical setting*—being bothered by noise, lack of privacy, pollution, or other unpleasant working conditions

Life Stressors   A less obvious, though important, source of stress for people at work is the *spillover effect* that results when forces in their personal lives "spill over" to affect them at work. Such life stressors as family events (e.g., the birth of a new child), economic difficulties (e.g., loss of income by a spouse), and personal affairs (e.g., a separation or divorce) can all be extremely stressful. Since it is often difficult to completely separate work and nonwork lives, life stressors can affect the way people feel and behave on their jobs as well as in their personal lives.

Outcomes of Stress

- **Eustress** is a stress that has a positive impact on both attitudes and performance.
- **Distress** is a negative impact on both attitudes and performance.
- **Job burnout** is a loss of interest in or satisfaction with a job due to stressful working conditions.

Though stress has an important impact on our lives, it isn't always negative. Two types of stress are eustress and distress.[26] **Eustress**, or constructive stress, acts in a positive way. It occurs at moderate stress levels by prompting increased work effort, stimulating creativity, and encouraging greater diligence. You may know such stress as the tension that causes you to study hard before exams, pay attention, and complete assignments on time in a difficult class. **Distress**, or destructive stress, is dysfunctional for both the individual and the organization. An outcome of extended distress is **job burnout**, which manifests as loss of interest in and satisfaction with a job due to stressful working conditions. A person who is "burned out" feels exhausted, emotionally and physically, and is less able to deal positively with work responsibilities and opportunities. More extreme reactions sometimes appear in news reports in the form of personal attacks and crimes at work known as "desk rage" and "workplace rage."

Too much stress can overload and break down a person's physical and mental systems, resulting in absenteeism, turnover, errors, accidents, dissatisfaction, reduced performance, unethical behavior, and even illness.[27] Stanford scholar and consultant Jeffrey Pfeffer calls those organizations that create excessive stress for their members "toxic workplaces."[28]

Managers and team leaders should watch for signs of toxic workplaces by being alert to excessive distress in themselves and their co-workers. Key symptoms are deviations from normal patterns—changes from regular attendance to absenteeism, from punctuality to tardiness, from diligent work to careless work, from a positive attitude to a negative attitude, from openness to change to resistance to change, or from cooperation to hostility.

Organizations can avoid problems of toxic workplaces by building positive work environments and making significant investments in their employees. These organizations are best positioned to realize the benefits of their full talents and work potential. As Pfeffer says: "All that separates you from your competitors are the skills, knowledge, commitment, and abilities of the people who work for you. Organizations that treat people right will get high returns."[29] That, in essence, is what the study of organizational behavior is all about.

- **Coping** is a response or reaction to distress that has occurred or is threatened.
- **Problem-focused coping** mechanisms manage the problem that is causing the distress.
- **Emotion-focused coping** are mechanisms that regulate emotions or distress.

Managing Stress

Coping Mechanisms With rising awareness of stress in the workplace, interest is also growing in how to manage, or *cope*, with distress. **Coping** is a response or reaction to distress that has occurred or is threatened. It involves cognitive and behavioral efforts to master, reduce, or tolerate the demands created by the stressful situation.

Two major coping mechanisms are those that: (1) regulate emotions or distress (emotion-focused coping) and (2) manage the problem that is causing the distress (problem-focused coping). As described by Susan Folkman, **problem-focused coping** strategies include: "get the person responsible to change his or her mind," "make a plan of action and follow it," and "stand your ground and fight for what you want." **Emotion-focused coping** strategies include: "look for the silver lining, try to look on the bright side of things," "accept sympathy and understanding from someone," and "try to forget the whole thing."[30]

There are individual differences when it comes to coping mechanisms. Not surprisingly, on the Big Five, neuroticism (i.e. emotional stability) has been found to be associated with increased use of hostile reaction, escapism/fantasy, self-blame, withdrawal, wishful thinking, passivity, and indecisiveness. In contrast, people high in extraversion and optimism use rational action, positive thinking, substitution, and restraint. And individuals high in openness to experience are likely to use humor in dealing with stress. What this shows is that the more your personality allows you to approach the situation with positive affect the better off you will be.

Stress Prevention Stress prevention is the best first-line strategy in the battle against stress. It

Achievement-Striving, and Learning to Say "No"

For employees who are high in achievement-striving, it is common to be overwhelmed by good opportunities. This can lead to situations where you end up overcommitted and, perhaps, less successful in the long run. A key element of managing stress is learning to say "No."[31]

When to say no:
- Focus on what matters most—focus on your priorities
- Weigh the yes-to-stress ratio—how much added stress will this cause? Is it worth it?
- Take guilt out of the equation—guilt is inflated due to feeling of self-importance—it's ok to say no
- Sleep on it—discipline yourself to not automatically say yes; what it will cost you?

How to say no:
- Just say no—or "I'm sorry but I can't . . ."
- Be brief—state your reason and avoid elaborations or justifications . . . "I'm swamped."
- Be honest—don't fabricate reasons; the truth is always best and people do understand
- Be respectful—"I am honored to be asked but I can't do it"
- Be ready to repeat—stick to it if they ask again; just hit the replay button . . . don't give in

involves taking action to keep stress from reaching destructive levels in the first place. Work and life stressors must be recognized before one can take action to prevent their occurrence or to minimize their adverse impacts. Persons with Type A personalities, for example, may exercise self-discipline; supervisors of Type A employees may try to model a lower-key, more relaxed approach to work. Family problems may be partially relieved by a change of work schedule; simply knowing that your supervisor understands your situation may also help to reduce the anxiety caused by pressing family concerns.

Personal Wellness   To keep stress from reaching a destructive point, special techniques of stress management can be implemented. This process begins with the recognition of stress symptoms and continues with actions to maintain a positive performance edge. The term "wellness" is increasingly used these days. **Personal wellness** involves the pursuit of one's job and career goals with the support of a personal health promotion program. The concept recognizes individual responsibility to enhance and maintain wellness through a disciplined approach to physical and mental health. It requires attention to such factors as smoking, weight management, diet, alcohol use, and physical fitness. Organizations can benefit from commitments to support personal wellness. A University of Michigan study indicates that firms have saved up to $600 per year per employee by helping them to cut the risk of significant health problems.[32] Arnold Coleman, CEO of Healthy Outlook Worldwide, a health fitness consulting firm, states: "If I can save companies 5 to 20 percent a year in medical costs, they'll listen. In the end you have a well company and that's where the word 'wellness' comes from."[33]

- **Personal wellness** involves the pursuit of one's job and career goals with the support of a personal health promotion program.

Values

LEARNING ROADMAP   Sources of Values / Personal Values / Cultural Values

- **Values** are broad preferences concerning appropriate courses of action or outcomes.

Values can be defined as broad preferences concerning appropriate courses of action or outcomes. As such, values reflect a person's sense of right and wrong or what "ought" to be.[34] "Equal rights for all" and "People should be treated with respect and dignity" are representative of values. Values tend to influence attitudes and behavior. For example, if you value equal rights for all and you go to work for an organization that treats its managers much better than it does its workers, you may form the attitude that the company is an unfair place to work; consequently, you may not produce well or may perhaps leave the company. It is likely that if the company had had a more egalitarian policy, your attitude and behaviors would have been more positive.

Sources of Values

Parents, friends, teachers, siblings, education, experience, and external reference groups are all value sources that can influence individual values. Indeed, peoples' values develop as a product of the learning and experience they encounter from various sources in the cultural setting in which they live. As learning and experiences differ from one person to another, value differences result. Such differences are likely to be deep seated and difficult (though not impossible) to change; many have their roots in early childhood and the way a person has been raised.[35]

Terminal Values	Instrumental Values
A comfortable life (and prosperous)	Ambitious (hardworking)
An exciting life (stimulating)	Broad-minded (open-minded)
A sense of accomplishment (lasting contribution)	Capable (competent, effective)
A world at peace (free of war and conflict)	Cheerful (lighthearted, joyful)
A world of beauty (beauty of nature and the arts)	Clean (neat, tidy)
Equality (brotherhood, equal opportunity)	Courageous (standing up for beliefs)
Family security (taking care of loved ones)	Forgiving (willing to pardon)
Freedom (independence, free choice)	Helpful (working for others' welfare)
Happiness (contentedness)	Honest (sincere, truthful)
Inner harmony (freedom from inner conflict)	Imaginative (creative, daring)
Mature love (sexual and spiritual intimacy)	Independent (self-sufficient, self-reliant)
National security (attack protection)	Intellectual (intelligent, reflective)
Pleasure (leisurely, enjoyable life)	Logical (rational, consistent)
Salvation (saved, eternal life)	Loving (affectionate, tender)
Self-respect (self-esteem)	Obedient (dutiful, respectful)
Social recognition (admiration, respect)	Polite (courteous, well mannered)
True friendship (close companionship)	Responsible (reliable, dependable)
Wisdom (mature understanding of life)	Self-controlled (self-disciplined)

Figure 2.3 Rokeach value survey.

Personal Values

The noted psychologist Milton Rokeach has developed a well-known set of values classified into two broad categories.[36] **Terminal values** reflect a person's preferences concerning the "ends" to be achieved; they are the goals an individual would like to achieve during his or her lifetime. Rokeach divides values into 18 terminal values and 18 instrumental values as summarized in Figure 2.3. **Instrumental values** reflect the "means" for achieving desired ends. They represent *how* you might go about achieving your important end states, depending on the relative importance you attached to the instrumental values. Look at the list in Figure 2.3. What are your top five values, and what does this say about you?

Illustrative research shows, not surprisingly, that both terminal and instrumental values differ by group (for example, executives, activist workers, and union members).[37] These preference differences can encourage conflict or agreement when different groups have to deal with each other.

A more recent values schema, developed by Bruce Meglino and associates, is aimed at people in the workplace:[38]

- *Achievement*—getting things done and working hard to accomplish difficult things in life
- *Helping and concern for others*—being concerned for other people and with helping others
- *Honesty*—telling the truth and doing what you feel is right
- *Fairness*—being impartial and doing what is fair for all concerned

These four values have been shown to be especially important in the workplace; thus, the framework should be particularly relevant for studying values in OB.

Meglino and colleagues used their value schema to show the importance of value congruence between leaders and followers. **Value congruence** occurs

- **Terminal values** reflect a person's preferences concerning the "ends" to be achieved.
- **Instrumental values** reflect a person's beliefs about the means to achieve desired ends.

Meglino and associates' value categories

- **Value congruence** occurs when individuals express positive feelings upon encountering others who exhibit values similar to their own.

when individuals express positive feelings upon encountering others who exhibit values similar to their own. When values differ, or are *incongruent*, conflicts over such things as goals and the means to achieve them may result. What they found was that satisfaction with the leader by followers was greater when there was congruence in terms of achievement, helping, honesty, and fairness values.[39]

Cultural Values

• **Culture** is the learned and shared way of thinking and acting among a group of people or society.

Cultural values are also important in the increasingly global workplace. **Culture** is the learned, shared way of doing things in a particular society. It is the way, for example, in which its members eat, dress, greet and treat one another, teach their children, solve everyday problems, and so on.[40] Geert Hofstede, a Dutch scholar and consultant, refers to culture as the "software of the mind," making the analogy that the mind's "hardware" is universal among human beings.[41] But the software of culture takes many different forms. We are not born with a culture; we are born into a society that teaches us its culture. And because culture is shared among people, it helps to define the boundaries between different groups and affect how their members relate to one another.

Cultures vary in their underlying patterns of values and attitudes. The way people think about such matters as achievement, wealth and material gain, and risk and change may influence how they approach work and their relationships with organizations. A framework developed by Hofstede offers one approach for understanding how value differences across national cultures can influence human behavior at work. The five dimensions of national culture in his framework can be described as follows:[42]

Hofstede's dimensions of national cultures

• **Power distance** is a culture's acceptance of the status and power differences among its members.

1. **Power distance** is the willingness of a culture to accept status and power differences among its members. It reflects the degree to which people are likely to respect hierarchy and rank in organizations. Indonesia is considered a high-power-distance culture, whereas Sweden is considered a relatively low-power-distance culture.

• **Uncertainty avoidance** is the cultural tendency to be uncomfortable with uncertainty and risk in everyday life.

2. **Uncertainty avoidance** is a cultural tendency toward discomfort with risk and ambiguity. It reflects the degree to which people are likely to prefer structured versus unstructured organizational situations. France is considered a high uncertainty avoidance culture, whereas Hong Kong is considered a low uncertainty avoidance culture.

• **Individualism–collectivism** is the tendency of members of a culture to emphasize individual self-interests or group relationships.

3. **Individualism–collectivism** is the tendency of a culture to emphasize either individual or group interests. It reflects the degree to which people are likely to prefer working as individuals or working together in groups. The United States is a highly individualistic culture, whereas Mexico is a more collectivist one.

• **Masculinity–femininity** is the degree to which a society values assertiveness or relationships.

4. **Masculinity–femininity** is the tendency of a culture to value stereotypical masculine or feminine traits. It reflects the degree to which organizations emphasize competition and assertiveness versus interpersonal sensitivity and concerns for relationships. Japan is considered a very masculine culture, whereas Thailand is considered a more feminine culture.

• **Long-term/short-term orientation** is the degree to which a culture emphasizes long-term or short-term thinking.

5. **Long-term/short-term orientation** is the tendency of a culture to emphasize values associated with the future, such as thrift and persistence, or values that focus largely on the present. It reflects the degree to which

people and organizations adopt long-term or short-term performance horizons. South Korea is high on long-term orientation, whereas the United States is a more short-term-oriented country.

The first four dimensions in Hofstede's framework were identified in an extensive study of thousands of employees of a multinational corporation operating in more than 40 countries.[43] The fifth dimension, long-term/short-term orientation, was added from research using the Chinese Values Survey conducted by cross-cultural psychologist Michael Bond and his colleagues.[44] Their research suggested the cultural importance of Confucian dynamism, with its emphasis on persistence, the ordering of relationships, thrift, sense of shame, personal steadiness, reciprocity, protection of "face," and respect for tradition.[45]

When using the Hofstede framework, it is important to remember that the five dimensions are interrelated, not independent.[46] National cultures may best be understood in terms of cluster maps or collages that combine multiple dimensions. For example, Figure 2.4 shows a sample grouping of countries based on individualism–collectivism and power distance. Note that high power distance and collectivism are often found together, as are low power distance and individualism. Whereas high collectivism may lead us to expect a work team in Indonesia to operate by consensus, the high power distance may cause the consensus to be heavily influenced by the desires of a formal leader. A similar team operating in more individualist and low-power-distance Great Britain or America might make decisions with more open debate, including expressions of disagreement with a leader's stated preferences.

At the national level, cultural value dimensions, such as those identified by Hofstede, tend to influence the previously discussed individual sources of values. The sources, in turn, tend to share individual values, which are then reflected in the recipients' value structures. For example, in the United States the sources would tend to be influenced by Hofstede's low-power-distance dimensions (along with his others, of course), and the recipients would tend to interpret their own individual value structures through that low-power-distance lens. Similarly, people in other countries or societies would be influenced by their country's standing on such dimensions.

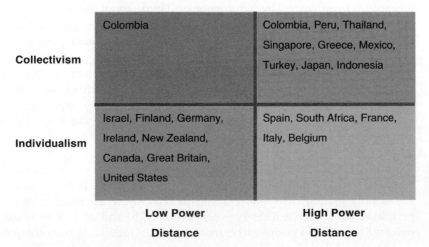

Figure 2.4 Sample country clusters on Hofstede's dimensions of individualism–collectivism and power distance.

Diversity

LEARNING ROADMAP   Importance of Diversity / Types of Diversity / Challenges in Managing Diversity

We started this chapter by saying that individual differences are important because they can offer great benefits. The discussion now comes full circle with the topic of diversity.

Importance of Diversity

Interest in workplace diversity gained prominence years ago when it became clear that the demographic makeup of the workforce was going to experience dramatic changes. At that time the workforce was primarily white male. Since then, workforce diversity has increased in both the United States and much of the rest of the world, and white males are no longer the majority in the labor force.

• **Workforce diversity** is a mix of people within a workforce who are considered to be, in some way, different from those in the prevailing constituency.

Workforce diversity refers to a mix of people within a workforce who are considered to be, in some way, different from those in the prevailing constituency. Organizations have recognized the importance of embracing policies and practices to diversify their workforces because it helps enhance competitiveness, build talent, expand organizational capabilities, and enhance access to markets (i.e., diverse customer bases).[47]

The focus on diversity is important because of the benefits diversity brings to the workplace. Current approaches focus on diversity not as something we have to manage, but as a key element of the "Global War for Talent." As described by Rob McInness in *Diversity World*:

> It is clear that the greatest benefits of workforce diversity will be experienced not by the companies that have learned to employ people *in spite of* their differences, but by the companies that have learned to employ people *because of* them.[48]

Types of Diversity

The benefits of diversity are achieved by acknowledging the strengths diversity can bring to organizations. Research shows that organizational creativity and innovation is enhanced by heterogeneity. Think about it—if you need to be creative, do you turn to people who think like you or to people who can help you think differently? Moreover, when you need to understand something you have never encountered before, such as another culture or an emerging market (e.g., the Latino market in Florida), would you turn to people who are the same as you or would you want access to co-workers familiar with those cultures? These examples show the benefits of "heterogeneous" (rather than "homogeneous") perspectives available when people bring different worldviews, cultural backgrounds, and personal experiences to the workplace.

Race and Ethnicity   Such heterogeneous perspectives can be gained from multicultural workforces with a rich mix of racial and ethnic diversity. And this diversity is only getting richer. Recent census data show an increase of 27.3 million people residing in the U.S. between 2000–2010, and of this increase, the vast majority came from people who indicated their race(s) as something other than

Racial Diversity Is Changing Attitudes

As racial diversity is increasing in the workplace, attitudes toward diversity are changing as well. The younger generation, or "Millennials" (those born between 1981 and 2000), are infusing the workplace with an appreciation for differences. Young people want to join a diverse workforce because they feel they can learn from those of different backgrounds: "Once this generation is in management positions corporate diversity will really advance," says Ron Alsop, author of *The Trophy Kids Grow Up*.

white alone, particularly those who are Hispanic or Latino.[49] More than half the growth in the total U.S. population between 2000–2010 was due to increase in the Hispanic population. While the number of whites alone grew one percent in this time period, its total proportion of the population declined from 69 percent to 64 percent. Moreover, the Asian population group grew at a faster rate than any other major race group between 2000 and 2010. Clearly, the U.S. continues to be a melting pot.

In the workplace, race and ethnicity are protected from discrimination by **Title VII of the Civil Rights Act of 1964**. This act protects individuals against employment discrimination on the basis of race and color, as well as national origin, sex, and religion. It applies to employers with 15 or more employees, including state and local governments.[50] According to Title VII, equal employment opportunity cannot be denied any person because of his/her racial group or perceived racial group, his/her race-linked characteristics (e.g., hair texture, color, facial features), or because of his/her marriage to or association with someone of a particular race or color. It also prohibits employment decisions based on stereotypes and assumptions about abilities, traits, or the performance of individuals of certain racial groups.

Title VII often brings to mind affirmative action, but movement is afoot on the affirmative action front. As Dr. Ella Bell of Dartmouth College says, it is time to redesign, rethink, and reframe what we mean by affirmative action because the issue is so much broader today. "The historical moment when affirmative action was created is not here anymore," Dr. Bell said. "We need to design an intervention that will fit this particular historical moment." According to Dr. Bell, and as the census data show, if you want to be competitive as a company, you cannot think black and white, because this is no longer a black-and-white world.[51]

Gender Women are also bringing a different set of skills and styles to the workplace. Given their unique experiences in organizations, women learn to do more with less, are resourceful, and bring an interpersonal style conducive to teamwork and innovation. This style includes listening skills, collaborative approaches to problem solving, and ability to multitask and synthesize a number of viewpoints effectively and quickly.

When women are at the top of the organization, benefits are even better. Research shows that companies with a higher percentage of female board directors and corporate officers, on average, financially outperform companies with the lowest percentages by significant margins.[52] Women leaders are beneficial

• **Title VII of the Civil Rights Act of 1964** protects individuals against employment discrimination on the basis of race and color, as well as national origin, sex, and religion.

because they encourage more women in the pipeline and act as role models and mentors for younger women. Moreover, the presence of women leaders sends important signals that an organization has a broader and deeper talent pool, is an "employer of choice," and offers an inclusive workplace.

The Leaking Pipeline   Despite these benefits to organizations, recognition that women have not penetrated the highest level, and even worse, are abandoning the corporate workforce just as they are positioned to attain these levels, has gained the attention of many organizations. The phrase **leaking pipeline** was coined to describe this phenomenon. The leaking pipeline theory gained credence with a study by Professor Lynda Gratton of the London Business School.[53] In her study she examined 61 organizations operating in 12 European countries and found that the number of women decreases the more senior the roles become.

• **Leaking pipeline** is a phrase coined to describe how women have not reached the highest levels of organizations.

• **Stereotyping** occurs when people make a generalization, usually exaggerated or oversimplified (and potentially offensive), that is used to describe or distinguish a group.

One potential reason for this is **stereotyping**. Catalyst research[54] finds that women consistently identify gender stereotypes as a significant barrier to advancement. They describe it as the "*think-leader-think-male*" mindset: the idea that men are largely seen as the leaders by default. Both men and women see women as better at stereotypically feminine "caretaking skills," such as supporting and encouraging others, and men as better at stereotypically masculine "take charge" skills, such as influencing superiors and problem solving—characteristics previously shown to be essential to leadership. These perceptions are even more salient in traditionally male-dominated fields, such as engineering and law.

This creates a *double bind* for women: If they conform to the stereotype, they are seen as weak, and if they go against the stereotype, they are going against norms of femininity. As some describe it, "damned if they do, doomed if they don't."[55] Organizations can help address these stereotypes by creating workplaces that are more meaningful and satisfying to successful women, such as cultures that are less command-and-control and status-based, and more meaning-based with less emphasis on "face-time."[56] As *Catalyst* reports, "Ultimately, it is not women's leadership styles that need to change but the structures and perceptions that must keep up with today's changing times."

Sexual Orientation   The first U.S. corporation to add sexual orientation to its nondiscrimination policy did so 30 years ago. That company was AT&T and its chairman, John DeButts, said that his company would "respect the human rights of our employees."[57] Although sexual orientation is not protected by the Equal Employment Opportunities Commission (EEOC), which addresses discrimination based on race, color, sex, religion, national origin, age, and disability,[58] many states now have executive orders protecting the rights of gay and lesbian workers. Wisconsin was the first in 1982, and as of January 2008, thirteen states prohibit workplace discrimination against gay people and seven more have extended additional protection to LGB (lesbian, gay, bisexual) people.[59]

Regardless of legislation, the workplace is beginning to improve for gay Americans. A 2010 Harris poll shows that 78 percent of heterosexual adults in the United States agree that how an employee performs at his or her job should be the standard for judging an employee, not one's sexual orientation, and 62 percent agree that all employees are entitled to equal benefits on the job, such as health insurance for partners or spouses.[60] Many businesses are paying attention because statistics show that the gay market segment is one of the fastest growing segments in the United States. The buying power of the gay/lesbian market is set

Millennials Are Shaking up the Workplace

At 83 million—the largest generation of all—Millennials are shaking up the workplace in unprecedented ways. They challenge their more senior colleagues with their techno savvy, multitasking, lower willingness to do "face time," and more casual dress and relaxed style.

to exceed $835 billion by 2011.[61] Companies wanting to tap into this market will need employees who understand and represent it.

Age It is getting harder to have discussions with managers today without the issue of age differences arising. Age, or more appropriately *generational*, diversity is affecting the workplace like never before. And with the oldest Baby Boomers turning 65, it seems that everyone has an opinion!

The controversy is being generated from Millennials, Gen Xers, and Baby Boomers mixing in the workplace—and trying to learn how to get along. The primary point of conflict: work ethic. Baby Boomers believe that Millennials are not hard working and are too "entitled." Baby Boomers value hard work, professional dress, long hours, and paying their dues—earning their stripes slowly.[62] Millennials believe Baby Boomers and Gen Xers are more concerned about the hours they work than what they produce. Millennials value flexibility, fun, the chance to do meaningful work right away, and "customized" careers that allow them the choice to go at the pace they want.

The generational mix provides an excellent example of diversity in action. For example, one thing Millennials can bring to the workplace is their appreciation for gender equality and sexual, cultural, and racial diversity—Millennials embrace these concepts more than any previous generation. Millennials also have an appreciation for community and collaboration. They can help create a more relaxed workplace that reduces some of the problems that come from too much focus on status and hierarchy.[63] Boomers and Gen Xers bring a wealth of experience, dedication, and commitment that contribute to productivity, and a sense of professionalism that is benefiting their younger counterparts. Together, Millennials and Gen Xers may be able to satisfy the Gen X desire for work–life balance through greater demand for more flexible scheduling and virtual work. Accomplishing such changes will come when all the generations learn to understand, respect—and maybe even like—one another.

Disability In recent years the "disability rights movement" has been working to bring attention and support to the needs of disabled workers.[64] The passage of the **Americans with Disabilities Act** (ADA) in 1990 has been a significant catalyst

• The **Americans with Disabilities Act** is a federal civil rights statute that protects the rights of people with disabilities.

Who's Who in Generational Differences at Work

Generation	Born between:	Percent of Today's Workforce
Matures	1922–1945	8
Baby Boomers	1946–1964	40
Generation X	1965–1980	36
Millennials	1981–2000	16

in advancing their efforts. The focus of the ADA is to eliminate employers' practices that make people with disabilities unnecessarily different. The ADA has helped to generate a more inclusive climate where organizations are reaching out more to people with disabilities. The most visible changes from the ADA have been in issues of **universal design**—the practice of designing products, buildings, public spaces, and programs to be usable by the greatest number of people. You may see this in your own college or university's actions to make their campus and classrooms more accessible.[65]

The disability rights movement is working passionately to advance a redefinition of what it means to be disabled in American society. The goal is to overcome the "stigmas" attached to disability. A **stigma** is a phenomenon whereby an individual with an attribute, which is deeply discredited by his or her society, is rejected as a result of the attribute. Because of stigmas, many are reluctant to seek coverage under the ADA because they do not want to experience discrimination in the form of stigmas.

The need to address issues of stigmas and accessibility for disabled workers is not trivial. Estimates indicate that over 50 million Americans have one or more physical or mental disabilities, and studies show these workers do their jobs as well as, or better than, nondisabled workers. Despite this, nearly three-quarters of severely disabled persons are reported to be unemployed, and almost 80 percent of those with disabilities say they want to work.[66]

- **Universal design** is the practice of designing products, buildings, public spaces, and programs to be usable by the greatest number of people.
- **Stigma** is a phenomenon whereby an individual is rejected as a result of an attribute that is deeply discredited by his or her society.

Finding the Leader in You

STEPHEN HAWKING SOARS DESPITE DISABILITY

Stephen Hawking cannot speak and does not have use of his motor skills. But he doesn't let that stop him. Renowned for his work in theoretical physics, Hawking has been an influential voice in redefining the way we see black holes and the origin of the universe. He is perhaps most recognized for his book *A Brief History of Time*, in which he works to translate Einstein's general theory of relatively and quantum theory for a general audience.

Hawking was diagnosed with ALS, or Lou Gehrig's disease, a few years after his 21st birthday. Over time, ALS has gradually crippled his body, first making him dependent on a wheelchair and private nurse, and then requiring 24-hour nursing care. He uses a voice synthesizer devised by a colleague that allows him to type rather than having to check letters off a card.

Despite his disability, Hawking has maintained an extensive program of travel, public lectures, and television appearances—even defying gravity by experiencing weightlessness on a zero-gravity flight for two hours over the Atlantic. His accomplishments and ability to live a full life, with three children and three grandchildren, have inspired people around the world. As Hawking says, "I'm sure my disability has a bearing on why I'm well known. People are fascinated by the contrast between my very limited physical powers, and the vast nature of the universe I deal with. I'm the archetype of a disabled genius, or should I say a physically challenged genius, to be politically correct. At least I'm obviously physically challenged. Whether I'm a genius is more open to doubt."[67]

What's the Lesson Here?

How do you respond to individual differences in the workplace? Are you understanding of the strengths and limitations of others? What about your own limitations and challenges? Do you work to overcome them, or do you let them bring you down?

Challenges in Managing Diversity

A Focus on Inclusion   While in the past many organizations addressed the issue of diversity from the standpoint of compliance (e.g., complying with the legal mandate by employing an Employment Equity and Affirmative Action Officer who kept track of and reported statistics), in recent years there has been a shift in focus from diversity to **inclusion**.[68] As described by Katharine Esty,[69] "This sea change has happened without fanfare and almost without notice. In most organizations, the word inclusion has been added to all the company's diversity materials with no explanation." As Esty explains, this change represents a shift from a numbers game to a focus on culture, and consideration of how organizations can create inclusive cultures for everyone.

> **Inclusion** A work environment in which all individuals are treated fairly and respectfully, have equal access to opportunities and resources, and can contribute fully to the organization's success.

The move from diversity to inclusion occurred primarily because employers began to learn that, although they were able to recruit diverse individuals, they were not able to retain them. In fact, some organizations found that after years of trying, they had *lower* representation among certain groups than they had earlier. They pieced together that this was related to the fact that the upper ranks of organizations continued to be primarily white male. In these environments, awareness and diversity training was not enough—they needed to address the issue more deeply. So, they asked different questions: Do employees in all groups and categories feel comfortable and welcomed in the organization? Do they feel included, and do they experience the environment as inclusive?[70]

Social Identity Theory   Such questions are the focus of social identity theory. **Social identity theory** was developed by social psychologists Henri Tajfel and John Turner to understand the psychological basis of discrimination.[71] According to the theory, individuals have not one, but multiple, "personal selves." Which self is activated depends on the group with which the person identifies. The mere act of identifying, or "categorizing," oneself as a member of a group will generate favoritism toward that group, and this favoritism is displayed in the form of "in-group" enhancement. This in-group favoritism occurs *at the expense of* the out-group. In terms of diversity, social identity theory suggests that simply having diversity groups makes that identity salient in peoples' minds. Individuals feel these identities and engage in **in-group** and **out-group** categorizations.

> **Social identity theory** is a theory developed to understand the psychological basis of discrimination.

The implications of this theory are pretty obvious. If organizations have strong identities around in-group and out-group based on some type of diversity group categorization, this will work against a feeling of inclusion. The important thing to remember is that simply saying we embrace you is not enough. In organizational contexts these categorizations can be subtle but powerful—and primarily noticeable to those in the "out-group" category. Organizations may not intend to create discriminatory environments, but having only a few members of a group may evoke a strong out-group identity. This may make them feel uncomfortable and less a part of the organization.

> **In-group** occurs when individuals feel part of a group and experience favorable status and a sense of belonging.
> **Out-group** occurs when one does not feel part of a group and experiences discomfort and low belongingness.

Valuing and Supporting Diversity   So how do managers and firms deal with all this? By committing to the creation of environments that welcome and embrace inclusion, and working to promote a better understanding of factors that help support inclusion in organizations. The concept of valuing diversity in organizations emphasizes appreciation of differences in creating a setting where everyone feels valued and accepted through such things as:[72]

- Strong commitment from the board and corporate officers
- Influential mentors and sponsors to provide career guidance and help navigate politics
- Opportunities for networking
- Role models from same-gender, racial, or ethnic group
- Exposure through high-visibility assignments
- An inclusive culture that values differences and does not require extensive adjustments to fit in
- Reducing subtle and subconscious stereotypes and stigmas

Valuing diversity assumes that groups will retain their own characteristics and will shape the firm as well as be shaped by it. As Dr. Santiago Rodriguez, former director of Diversity for Microsoft, says true diversity is exemplified by companies that "hire people who are different—knowing and valuing that they will change the way you do business."

2 study guide

Key Questions and Answers

What are individual differences and why are they important?

- The study of individual differences attempts to identify where behavioral tendencies are similar and where they are different to more accurately predict how and why people behave as they do.
- For people to capitalize on individual differences, they need to be aware of them. Self-awareness is being aware of our own behaviors, preferences, styles, biases, and personalities; awareness of others means being aware of these same things in others.
- Self-concept is the view individuals have of themselves as physical, social, and spiritual or moral beings. It is a way of recognizing oneself as a distinct human being.
- The nature/nurture controversy addresses whether we are the way we are because of heredity or because of the environments in which we have been raised and live.

What is personality?

- Personality captures the overall profile, or combination of characteristics, that represents the unique nature of an individual as that individual interacts with others.
- Personality is determined by both heredity and environment; across all personality characteristics, the mix of heredity and environment is about 50–50. The Big Five personality traits are extraversion, agreeableness, conscientiousness, emotional stability, and openness to experience.
- A useful personality framework consists of social traits, personal conception traits, emotional adjustment traits, and personality dynamics, where each category represents one or more personality dimensions.

How are personality and stress related?

- Stress emerges when people experience tensions caused by extraordinary demands, constraints, or opportunities in their jobs.

- Personal stressors derive from personality type, needs, and values; they can influence how stressful different situations become for different people.

- Work stressors arise from such things as excessive task demands, interpersonal problems, unclear roles, ethical dilemmas, and career disappointments.

- Nonwork stress can spill over to affect people at work; nonwork stressors may be traced to family situations, economic difficulties, and personal problems.

- Stress can be managed by prevention—such as making adjustments in work and nonwork factors; it can also be dealt with through coping mechanisms and personal wellness—taking steps to maintain a healthy body and mind capable of better withstanding stressful situations.

What are values and how do they vary across cultures?

- Values are broad preferences concerning courses of action or outcomes.

- Rokeach identifies terminal values (preferences concerning ends) and instrumental values (preferences concerning means); Meglino and his associates classify values into achievement, helping and concern for others, honesty, and fairness.

- Hofstede's five national culture values dimensions are power distance, individualism–collectivism, uncertainty avoidance, masculinity–femininity, and long-term/short-term orientation.

- Culture is the learned and shared way of doing things in a society; it represents deeply ingrained influences on the way people from different societies think, behave, and solve problems.

Why is diversity important in the workplace?

- Workforce diversity is increasing in the United States and other countries. It is important because of the benefits diverse backgrounds and perspectives can bring to the workplace.

- Rather than being something we have to "manage," diversity should be something we value.

- There are many types of diversity, but the most commonly discussed in the workplace are racial/ethnic, gender, age, disability, and sexual orientation.

- In recent years there has been a shift from a focus on diversity to a focus on inclusion. This represents a need to emphasize not only recruitment but retention.

- Social identity theory suggests that many forms of discrimination are subtle but powerful, and may occur in subconscious psychological processes that individuals of out-groups perceive in the workplace.

- Companies can value diversity by promoting cultures of inclusion that implement policies and practices to help create a more equitable and opportunity-based environment for all.

Terms to Know

Americans with Disabilities Act (p. 45)
Authoritarianism (p. 33)
Awareness of others (p. 26)
Coping (p. 37)

Culture (p. 40)
Distress (p. 36)
Dogmatism (p. 33)
Emotion-focused coping (p. 37)

Emotional adjustment traits (p. 34)
Eustress (p. 36)
Inclusion (p. 47)
Individual differences (p. 26)

Individualism–collectivism (p. 40)
In-group (p. 47)
Instrumental values (p. 39)
Job burnout (p. 36)
Leaking pipeline (p. 44)
Locus of control (p. 31)
Long-term/short-term orientation (p. 40)
Machiavellianism (p. 33)
Masculinity–femininity (p. 40)
Out-group (p. 47)
Personal conception traits (p. 31)
Personal wellness (p. 38)
Personality (p. 29)

Personality traits (p. 29)
Power distance (p. 40)
Proactive personality (p. 32)
Problem-focused coping (p. 37)
Problem-solving style (p. 29)
Self-awareness (p. 26)
Self-concept (p. 26)
Self-esteem (p. 26)
Self-efficacy (p. 27)
Self-monitoring (p. 33)
Social identity theory (p. 47)
Social traits (p. 29)
Stereotyping (p. 44)

Stigma (p. 46)
Stress (p. 35)
Terminal values (p. 39)
Title VII of the Civil Rights Act of
   1964 (p. 43)
Type A orientation (p. 35)
Type B orientation (p. 35)
Uncertainty avoidance (p. 40)
Universal design (p. 46)
Value congruence (p. 39)
Values (p. 38)
Workforce diversity (p. 42)

Self-Test 2

Multiple Choice

1. Individual differences are important because they _____. (a) mean we have to be different (b) reduce the importance of individuality (c) show that some cultural groups are superior to others (d) help us more accurately predict how and why people act as they do

2. Self-awareness is _____ awareness of others. (a) more important than (b) less important than (c) as important as (d) not at all related to

3. Self-efficacy is a form of _____. (a) self-awareness (b) self-esteem (c) nurture (d) agreeableness

4. Personality encompasses _____. (a) the overall combination of characteristics that capture the unique nature of a person (b) only the nurture components of self (c) only the nature components of self (d) how self-aware someone is

5. People who are high in internal locus of control _____. (a) believe what happens to them is determined by environmental forces such as fate (b) believe that they control their own fate or destiny (c) are highly extraverted (d) do worse on tasks requiring learning and initiative

6. Proactive personality is _____ in today's work environments. (a) punished (b) missing (c) becoming more important (d) losing importance

7. People who would follow unethical orders without question would likely be high in _____. (a) internal locus of control (b) machiavellianism (c) proactive personality and extraversion (d) authoritarianism and dogmatism

8. Managers who are hard-driving, detail-oriented, have high performance standards, and thrive on routine could be characterized as _____. (a) Type B (b) Type A (c) high self-monitors (d) low Machs

9. Eustress is _____ stress, while distress is _____ stress. (a) constructive, destructive (b) destructive, constructive (c) negative, positive (d) the most common, the most relevant

10. Coping involves both _____ and _____ elements. (a) cognitive, intellectual (b) promotion, prevention (c) problem-focused, emotion-focused (d) cultural, psychological

11. When it comes to values, _____. (a) instrumental values are more important than terminal values, (b) value congruence is what seems to be most important for satisfaction (c) it is rare that people hold similar values (d) most cultures share the same values

12. Culture is _____. (a) a person's major beliefs and personal orientation concerning a range of issues (b) the way a person gathers and evaluates information (c) the way someone appears to others when interacting in social settings (d) the learned, shared way of doing things in a particular society

13. The demographic make-up of the workforce _____. (a) has been relatively stable (b) is not related to managerial practices (c) has experienced dramatic changes in recent decades (d) is becoming less of an issue for management.

14. Companies that _____ experience the greatest benefits of workforce diversity. (a) have learned to employ people because of their differences (b) have learned to employ people in spite of their differences (c) have not worried about people's differences (d) implemented diversity programs based only on affirmative action

15. The experience in which simply having various diversity groups makes that group category salient in peoples' minds is an example of _____. (a) stigma (b) leaking pipeline (c) inclusion (d) social identity theory

Short Response

16. What are individual differences and why are they important to organizational behavior?

17. What is more influential in determining personality: nature or nurture?

18. What values were identified by Meglino and associates, and how do they relate to workplace behavior?

19. With respect to diversity and inclusion, what do we know about environments that are most conducive to valuing and supporting diversity?

Applications Essay

20. Your boss has noticed that stress levels have been increasing in your work unit, and has asked you to assess the problem and propose a plan of action for addressing it. What steps would you take to meet this request? What would be the first thing you would do, what factors would you take into consideration in conducting your assessment, and what plan of action do you think would be most promising?

Next Steps
Top Choices from
The OB Skills Workbook

These learning activities from *The OB Skills Workbook* are suggested for Chapter 2.

Cases for Critical Thinking	Team and Experiential Exercises	Self-Assessment Portfolio
• Xerox	• What Do You Value in Work? • Prejudice in Our Lives • How We View Differences • Alligator River Story	• Turbulence Tolerance Test • Your Personality Type • Time Management Profile • Personality Type

Balance through Fitness

After the birth of her first child, Lisa Druxman was eager to both get in shape and get back to work. She decided to blend her passion for fitness with motherhood and developed a series of exercises she could perform while out walking her baby. As a fitness instructor, it was only natural for her to teach the workouts to other new moms. They liked it—lots—and Stroller Strides was born.

Since then, Druxman's business has grown by leaps and bounds. In its first year, Stroller Strides expanded to coach more than 300 moms in 12 locations.[a] Today, the company boasts more than 300 franchisees teaching fitness in over 1,200 locations.[b,c]

And Druxman hasn't stopped there. She has developed Fit4Baby, BodyBack classes, videos and accessories. She also wrote *L.E.A.N. Mommy*, a book advising new moms how to maintain physical and emotional fitness.

There's another side to Stroller Strides—the "balance" side of things. Owning a franchise gives

working mothers what they want—the chance to succeed at work without losing touch with their families. "The home-based business model has great appeal, as it's both low-cost and lifestyle-friendly."

> *"My work gives me satisfaction, stimulation and inspiration. Motherhood keeps me grounded and reminds me daily of what is truly important."*
> *—Lisa Druxman, founder of Stroller Strides.*

Druxman says. "Our franchisees have the flexibility to create their business hours around the needs of their family."[d]

Her tips for success include:

1. **You create the vision** and the road map of how to get to the goal.
2. **Delegate.** Hire out everything you can so that there is progress when you are with your family.
3. **Partner up.** You may be able to get twice as much done if you have a like-minded partner.
4. **Work smart.** Make sure the time you do have is spent on the Most Important Things.
5. **Get spousal support.** Get buy-in with parenting as you grow your business.[e]

Quick Summary

- Stroller Strides encourages new moms to socialize with women like themselves while regaining their pre-pregnancy fitness.
- Market efforts and low franchising fees helped Stroller Strides expand to more than 300 franchisees in just over five years.
- Stroller Strides partnered with leading stroller manufacturer BOB to create a fitness-specific model; founder Lisa Druxman published *Lean Mommy*, a physical and emotional fitness guide for new mothers, Fit4Baby and BodyBack classes, videos and accessories.

FYI: 83% of women say that work–life balance is important to their job satisfaction.[f]

3 Emotions, Attitudes, and Job Satisfaction

the key point

The work-life balance issues faced by new moms and dads are prime examples of how emotions test us in everyday living. When we're feeling good there's hardly anything better. But when we're feeling down, it takes a toll on us and possibly others. OB scholars are very interested in how emotions, attitudes, and job satisfaction influence people's behavior. There's a lot to learn that can help you both personally and in your career.

chapter at a glance

What Are Emotions and Moods?

How Do Emotions and Moods Influence Behavior?

What Are Attitudes and How Do They Influence Behavior?

What Is Job Satisfaction and Why Is It Important?

ETHICS IN OB
WATCH OUT FOR FACEBOOK FOLLIES

FINDING THE LEADER IN YOU
DON THOMPSON SHOWS THE POWER OF LISTENING TO EMOTIONS

what's inside?

OB IN POPULAR CULTURE
MOODS AND *CRASH*

RESEARCH INSIGHT
JOB SATISFACTION SPILLOVER ONTO FAMILY LIVES

Understanding Emotions and Moods

LEARNING ROADMAP   The Nature of Emotions / Emotional Intelligence / Types of Emotions / The Nature of Moods

How do you feel when you are driving a car and are halted by a police officer? You are in class and receive a poor grade on an exam? A favorite pet passes away? You check e-mail and discover that you are being offered a job interview? A good friend walks right by without speaking? A parent or sibling or child loses his job? Or, you get this SMS from a new acquaintance: "Ur gr8☺!"?

- **Affect** is the range of feelings in the forms of emotions and moods that people experience.

These examples show how what happens to us draws out "feelings" of many forms, such as happy or sad, angry or pleased. These feelings constitute what scholars call **affect**, the range of emotions and moods that people experience in their life context.[1] Affects have important implications not only for our lives in general but also our behavior at work.[2] Lisa Druxman, featured in the opening example, might have allowed her frustration at having no time to hit the gym turn into a negative affect toward her work and personal life. Instead, she took the initiative and developed a series of exercises she could perform while walking with her baby. She then took it a step further and started Stroller Strides, a company whose franchises provide moms with a chance to succeed—with their career and their families.

The Nature of Emotions

- **Emotions** are strong positive or negative feelings directed toward someone or something.

Anger, excitement, apprehension, attraction, sadness, elation, grief . . . those are all **emotions** that appear as strong positive or negative feelings directed toward someone or something.[3] Emotions are usually intense and not long-lasting. They are always associated with a source—someone or something that makes us feel the way we do. You might feel positive emotion of elation when an instructor congratulates you on a fine class presentation; you might feel negative emotion of anger when an instructor criticizes you in front of the class. In both situations the object of your emotion is the instructor, but the impact of the instructor's behavior on your feelings is quite different in each case. And your response to the aroused emotions is likely to differ as well—perhaps breaking into a wide smile after the compliment, or making a nasty side comment or withdrawing from further participation after the criticism.

Emotional Intelligence

- **Emotional intelligence** is an ability to understand emotions and manage relationships effectively.

All of us are familiar with the notions of cognitive ability and intelligence, or IQ, which have been measured for many years. A more recent concept is **emotional intelligence**, or EI. First introduced in Chapter 1 as a component of a manager's essential human skills, it is defined by scholar Daniel Goleman as an ability to understand emotions in ourselves and others and to use that understanding to manage relationships effectively.[4] EI is demonstrated in the ways in which we deal with affect, for example, by knowing when a negative emotion is about to cause problems and being able to control that emotion so that it doesn't become disruptive.

Goleman's point about emotional intelligence is that we perform better when we are good at recognizing and dealing with emotions in ourselves and others.

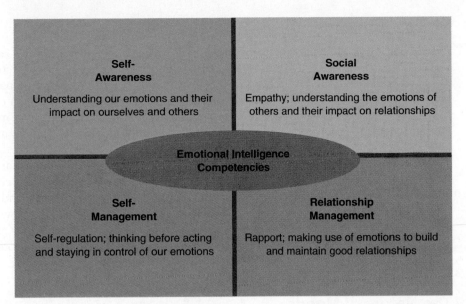

Figure 3.1 Four key emotional intelligence competencies for leadership success.

When high in EI, we are more likely to behave in ways that avoid having our emotions "get the better of us." Knowing that an instructor's criticism causes us to feel anger, for example, EI might help us control that anger, maintain a positive face, and perhaps earn the instructor's praise when we make future class contributions. If the unchecked anger caused us to act in a verbally aggressive way—creating a negative impression in the instructor's eyes—or to withdraw from all class participation—causing the instructor to believe we have no interest in the course, our course experience would likely suffer.

If you are good at knowing and managing your emotions and are good at reading others' emotions, you may perform better while interacting with other people. This applies to work and life in general, and to leadership situations.[5] Figure 3.1 identifies four essential emotional intelligence competencies that can and should be developed for leadership success and, we can say, success more generally in all types of interpersonal situations.[6] The competencies are self-awareness, social awareness, self-management, and relationship management.

Self-awareness in emotional intelligence is the ability to understand our emotions and their impact on our work and on others. You can think of this as a continuing appraisal of your emotions that results in a good understanding of them and the capacity to express them naturally. **Social awareness** is the ability to empathize, to understand the emotions of others, and to use this understanding to better relate to them. It involves continuous appraisal and recognition of others' emotions, resulting in better perception and understanding of them.

Self-management in emotional intelligence is the ability to think before acting and to be in control of otherwise disruptive impulses. It is a form of *self-regulation* in which we stay in control of our emotions and avoid letting them take over. **Relationship management** is an ability to establish rapport with others in ways that build good relationships and influence their emotions in positive ways. It shows up as the capacity to make good use of emotions by directing them toward constructive activities and improved relationships.

- **Self-awareness** is the ability to understand our emotions and their impact on us and others.
- **Social awareness** is the ability to empathize and understand the emotions of others.
- **Self-management** is the ability to think before acting and to control disruptive impulses.
- **Relationship management** is the ability to establish rapport with others to build good relationships.

Types of Emotions

Researchers have identified six major types of emotions: anger, fear, joy, love, sadness, and surprise. The key question from an emotional intelligence perspective is: Do we recognize these emotions in ourselves and others, and can we manage them well? Anger, for example, may involve disgust and envy, both of which can have very negative consequences. Fear may contain alarm and anxiety; joy may contain cheerfulness and contentment; love may contain affection, longing, and lust; sadness may contain disappointment, neglect, and shame.

• **Self-conscious emotions** arise from internal sources, and **social emotions** derive from external sources.

It is also common to differentiate between **self-conscious emotions** that arise from internal sources and **social emotions** that are stimulated by external sources.[7] Shame, guilt, embarrassment, and pride are examples of internal emotions. Understanding self-conscious emotions helps individuals regulate their relationships with others. Social emotions like pity, envy, and jealousy derive from external cues and information. An example is feeling envious or jealous upon learning that a co-worker received a promotion or job assignment that you were hoping to get.

The Nature of Moods

• **Moods** are generalized positive and negative feelings or states of mind.

Whereas emotions tend to be short-term and clearly targeted at someone or something, **moods** are more generalized positive and negative feelings or states of mind that may persist for some time. Everyone seems to have occasional

ETHICS IN OB

WATCH OUT FOR FACEBOOK FOLLIES

Facebook is fun, but if you put the wrong things on it—the wrong photo, a snide comment, and complaints about your boss—you might have to change your online status to "Just got fired!"

Bed Surfing Banker—After a Swiss bank employee called in sick with the excuse that she "needed to lie in the dark," company officials observed her surfing Facebook. She was fired and the bank's statement said it "had lost trust in the employee."

Angry Mascot—The Pittsburgh Pirates fired their mascot after he posted criticisms of team management on his Facebook page. A Twitter campaign by supporters helped him get hired back.

Short-changed Server—A former server at a pizza parlor in North Carolina used Facebook to call her customers "cheap" for not giving good tips. After finding out about the posting, her bosses fired her for breaking company policy.

Who's Right and Wrong?   You may know of other similar cases where employees ended up being penalized for things they put on their Facebook pages. But where do you draw the line? Isn't a person's Facebook page separate from one's work; shouldn't one be able to speak freely about their jobs, co-workers, and even bosses when outside the workplace? Or is there an ethical boundary that travels from work into one's public communications that needs to be respected? What are the ethics here—on the employee and the employer sides?

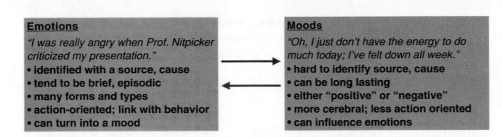

Figure 3.2 Emotions and moods are different, but can also influence one another.

moods, and we each know the full range of possibilities they represent. How often do you wake up in the morning and feel excited and refreshed and just happy, or wake up feeling grouchy and depressed and generally unhappy? And what are the consequences of these different moods for your behavior with friends and family, and at work or school?

The field of OB is especially interested in how moods affect someone's likeability and performance at work. When it comes to CEOs, for example, a *Business Week* article claims that it pays to be likable, stating that "harsh is out, caring is in."[8] Some CEOs are even hiring executive coaches to help them manage their affects to come across as more personable and friendly in relationships with others. If a CEO goes to a meeting in a good mood and gets described as "cheerful," "charming," "humorous," "friendly," and "candid," she or he may be viewed as on the upswing. But if the CEO goes into a meeting in a bad mood and is perceived as "prickly," "impatient," "remote," "tough," "acrimonious," or even "ruthless," the perception will more likely be of a CEO on the downslide.

Figure 3.2 offers a brief comparison of emotions and moods. In general, emotions are intense feelings directed at someone or something; they always have rather specific triggers; and they come in many types—anger, fear, happiness, and the like. Moods tend to be more generalized positive or negative feelings. They are less intense than emotions and most often seem to lack a clear source; it's often hard to identify how or why we end up in a particular mood.[9] But moods tend to be more long-lasting than emotions. When someone says or does something that causes a quick and intense positive or negative reaction from you, that emotion will probably quickly pass. However, a bad or good mood is likely to linger for hours or even days and influence a wide range of behaviors.

How Emotions and Moods Influence Behavior

LEARNING ROADMAP Emotion and Mood Contagion / Emotional Labor / Cultural Aspects of Emotions and Moods / Emotions and Moods as Affective Events

A while back, former CEO Mark V. Hurd of Hewlett-Packard found himself dealing with a corporate scandal. It seems that the firm had hired "consultants" to track down what were considered to be confidential leaks by members of HP's Board of Directors. When meeting the press and trying to explain the situation and resignation of board chair Patricia C. Dunn, Hurd called the actions "very disturbing" and the *Wall Street Journal* described him as speaking with "his voice shaking."[10]

We can say that Hurd was emotional and angry that the incident was causing public humiliation for him and the company. Chances are the whole episode resulted in him being in a bad mood for a while. In the short run, at least, Hurd's emotions and mood probably had spillover consequences for those working directly with him and maybe for HP's workforce as a whole. But even further, was this just a one-time reaction on his part or was it an expected pattern that he displayed whenever things went wrong?

Emotion and Mood Contagion

Although emotions and moods are influenced by different events and situations, each of us may display some relatively predictable tendencies.[11] Some people seem almost always positive and upbeat about things. For these optimists we might say the glass is nearly always half full. Others, by contrast, seem to be often negative or downbeat. They tend to be pessimists viewing the glass as half empty. Such tendencies toward optimism and pessimism not only influence the individual's behavior, they can also influence other people he or she interacts with—co-workers, friends, and family members.

- **Emotion and mood contagion** is the spillover of one's emotions and mood onto others.

Researchers are increasingly interested in **emotion and mood contagion**— the spillover effects of one's emotions and mood onto others.[12] You might think this as a bit like catching a cold from someone. Evidence shows that positive and negative emotions are "contagious" in much the same ways, even though the tendency may not be well recognized in work settings. One study found team members shared good and bad moods within two hours of being together; bad moods, interestingly, traveled person-to-person faster than good moods.[13] Other research shows that when mood contagion is positive, followers report being more attracted to their leaders and rate the leaders more highly. The mood contagion also has up and down effects on moods of co-workers and teammates, as well as family and friends.[14]

Daniel Goleman and his colleagues studying emotional intelligence believe leaders should manage emotion and mood contagion with care. "Moods that start at the top tend to move the fastest," they say, "because everyone watches the boss."[15] This was very evident as CEOs in all industries—business and nonprofit alike—struggled to deal with the impact of economic crisis on their organizations and workforces. "Moaning is not a management task," said Rupert Stadler of Audi: "We can all join in the moaning, or we can make a virtue of the plight. I am rather doing the latter."[16]

Emotional Labor

- **Emotional labor** is a situation where a person displays organizationally desired emotions in a job.

The concept of **emotional labor** relates to the need to show certain emotions in order to perform a job well.[17] Good examples come from service settings such as airline check-in personnel or flight attendants. They are supposed to appear approachable, receptive, and friendly while taking care of the things you require as a customer. Some airlines like Southwest go even further in asking service employees to be "funny" and "caring" and "cheerful" while doing their jobs.

- **Emotional dissonance** is inconsistency between emotions we feel and those we try to project.

Emotional labor isn't always easy; it can be hard to be consistently "on" in displaying the desired emotions in one's work. If you're having a bad mood day or have just experienced an emotional run-in with a neighbor, for example, being "happy" and "helpful" with a demanding customer might seem a little much to ask. Such situations can cause **emotional dissonance** where the emotions we

Two Brothers Make Being Happy a Big Business

Imagine! Yes you can! Go for it! Life is good. Well, make that really good. These dreams became realities for Bert and John Jacobs. They began selling tee shirts on Boston streets and now run an $80 million company—Life Is Good. *Inc.* magazine called it "a fine small business that only wants to make me happy." John says: "Life is good . . . don't determine that you're going to be happy when you get the new car or the big promotion or meet that special person. You can decide that you're going to be happy today."

actually feel are inconsistent with the emotions we try to project.[18] That is, we are expected to act with one emotion while we actually feel quite another.

It often requires a lot of self-regulation to display organizationally desired emotions in one's job. Imagine, for example, how often service workers struggling with personal emotions and moods experience dissonance when having to act positive toward customers.[19] Scholars call it *deep acting* when someone tries to modify their feelings to better fit the situation—such as putting yourself in the position of the air travelers whose luggage went missing and feeling the same sense of loss. *Surface acting* is hiding true feelings while displaying very different ones—such as smiling at a customer even though the words they used to express a complaint just offended you.

Cultural Aspects of Emotions and Moods

Issues of emotional intelligence, emotion and mood contagion, and emotional labor can be complicated in cross-cultural situations. General interpretations of emotions and moods appear similar across cultures, with the major emotions of happiness, joy, and love all valued positively.[20] But the frequency and intensity of emotions is known to vary somewhat. In mainland China, for example, research suggests that people report fewer positive and negative emotions as well as less intense emotions than in other cultures.[21] Norms for emotional expression also vary across cultures. In collectivist cultures that emphasize group relationships such as Japan, individual emotional displays are less likely to occur and less likely to be accepted than in individualistic cultures.[22]

Informal cultural standards called **display rules** govern the degree to which it is appropriate to display emotions. For example, British culture tends to encourage downplaying emotions, while Mexican culture is much more demonstrative in public. Overall, the lesson is that the way emotions are displayed in other cultures may not mean what they do at home. When Walmart first went to Germany, its executives found that an emphasis on friendliness embedded in its U.S. roots didn't work as well in the local culture. The more serious German shoppers did not respond well to Walmart's friendly greeters and helpful personnel. And along the same lines, Israeli shoppers seem to equate smiling cashiers with inexperience, so cashiers are encouraged to look somber while performing their jobs.[23]

• **Display rules** govern the degree to which it is appropriate to display emotions.

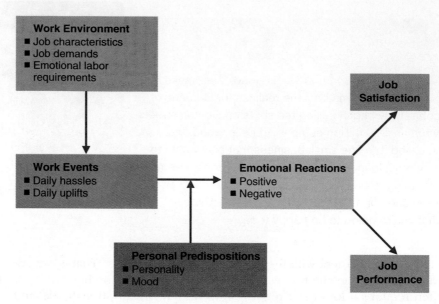

Figure 3.3 Figurative summary of Affective Events Theory.

Emotions and Moods as Affective Events

Figure 3.3 presents the Affective Events Theory as a summary for this discussion of emotions, moods, and human behavior in organizations.[24] The basic notion of the theory is that our emotions and moods are influenced by events involving other people and situations. Emotions and moods, in turn, influence the work performance and satisfaction of us and others.

The left-hand side of Figure 3.3 shows how the work environment, including the job and its emotional labor requirements, and daily work events create positive and negative emotional reactions. These influence job satisfaction and performance.[25] For example, everyone experiences hassles and uplifts on the job, sometimes many of these during a workday. Our positive and negative emotional reactions to them influence the way we work at the moment and how we feel about it.

Personal predispositions in the form of personality and moods also affect the connection between work events and emotional reactions. Someone's mood at the time can exaggerate the emotions experienced as a result of an event. If you have just been criticized by your boss, for example, you are likely to feel worse than you would otherwise when a colleague makes a joke about the length of your coffee breaks.

How Attitudes Influence Behavior

LEARNING ROADMAP   Components of Attitudes / Linking Attitudes and Behavior / Attitudes and Cognitive Consistency / Types of Job Attitudes

At one time Challis M. Lowe was one of only two African-American women among the five highest-paid executives in U.S. companies surveyed by the woman's advocacy and research organization Catalyst.[26] She became executive vice president at Ryder System after a 25-year career that included several changes of employers and lots of stressors—working-mother guilt, a failed marriage, gender

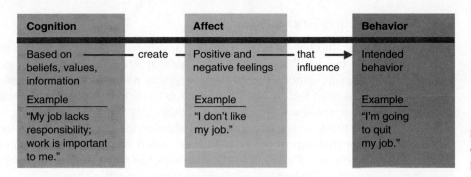

Figure 3.4 A work-related example of the three components of attitudes.

bias on the job, and an MBA degree earned part-time. Through it all she says: "I've never let being scared stop me from doing something. Just because you haven't done it before doesn't mean you shouldn't try." That, simply put, is what we would call a can-do "attitude!"

An **attitude** is a predisposition to respond in a positive or negative way to someone or something in one's environment. When you say, for example, that you "like" or "dislike" someone or something, you are expressing an attitude. But it's important to remember that an attitude, like a value, is a hypothetical construct; one never sees, touches, or actually isolates an attitude. Rather, attitudes are *inferred* from the things people say or through their behavior. Attitudes are influenced by values and are acquired from the same sources—friends, teachers, parents, role models, and culture. Attitudes, however, focus on specific people or objects. The notion that shareholders should have a voice in setting CEO pay is a value. Your positive or negative feeling about a specific company due to the presence or absence of shareholder inputs on CEO pay is an attitude.

• An **attitude** is a predisposition to respond positively or negatively to someone or something.

Components of Attitudes

The three components of an attitude are shown in Figure 3.4—cognitive, affective, and behavioral.[27] The *cognitive component* of an attitude reflects underlying beliefs, opinions, knowledge, or information a person possesses. It represents a person's ideas about someone or something and the conclusions drawn about them. The statement "My job lacks responsibility" is a belief shown in the figure. The statement "Job responsibility is important" reflects an underlying value. Together they comprise the cognitive component of an attitude toward one's work or workplace.

The *affective component* of an attitude is a specific feeling regarding the personal impact of the antecedent conditions evidenced in the cognitive component. In essence this becomes the actual attitude, such as the feeling "I don't like my job." Notice that the affect in this statement displays the negative attitude; "I don't like my job" is a very different condition than "I do like my job."

The *behavioral component* is an intention to behave in a certain way based on the affect in one's attitude. It is a predisposition to act, but one that may or may not be implemented. The example in the figure shows behavioral intent expressed as "I'm going to quit my job." Yet even with such intent, it remains to be seen whether or not the person really quits.

Linking Attitudes and Behavior

As just pointed out, the link between attitudes and behavior is tentative. An attitude expresses an intended behavior that may or may not be carried out. In general, the more specific attitudes are the stronger the relationship with eventual behavior. A person who feels "I don't like my job" may be less likely to actually quit than someone who feels "I can't stand another day with Alex harassing me at work." For an attitude to actually influence behavior, it's also necessary to have the opportunity or freedom to behave in the intended way. In today's economy there are most likely many persons who stick with their jobs while still holding negative job attitudes. The fact is they may not have any other choice.[28]

Attitudes and Cognitive Consistency

• **Cognitive dissonance** is experienced inconsistency between one's attitudes and/or between attitudes and behavior.

Leon Festinger, a noted social psychologist, uses the term **cognitive dissonance** to describe a state of inconsistency between an individual's attitudes and/or between attitudes and behavior.[29] It turns out that this is an important issue. Perhaps you have the attitude that recycling is good for the economy. You also realize you aren't always recycling everything you can. Festinger points out that such cognitive inconsistency between attitude and behavior is uncomfortable. We tend to deal with the discomfort by trying to do things to reduce or eliminate the dissonance: (1) changing the underlying attitude, (2) changing future behavior, or (3) developing new ways of explaining or rationalizing the inconsistency.

The way we respond to cognitive dissonance is influenced by the degree of control we seem to have over the situation and the rewards involved. In the case of recycling dissonance, for example, the lack of convenient recycling containers would make rationalizing easier and changing the positive attitude less likely. A reaffirmation of intention to recycle in the future might also reduce the dissonance.

Types of Job Attitudes

Even though attitudes do not always predict behavior, the link between attitudes and potential or intended behavior is an important workplace issue. Think about your daily experiences or conversations with other people about their work. It isn't uncommon to hear concerns expressed about a co-worker's "bad attitude" or another's "good attitude." Such feelings get reflected in things like job satisfaction, job involvement, organizational commitment, and employee engagement.

• **Job satisfaction** is the degree to which an individual feels positive or negative about a job.

You often hear the term "morale" used to describe how people feel about their jobs and employers. It relates to the more specific notion of **job satisfaction**, an attitude reflecting a person's positive and negative feelings toward a job, co-workers, and the work environment. Indeed, you should remember that helping others realize job satisfaction is considered one hallmark of effective managers. They create work environments in which people achieve high performance and experience high job satisfaction. This concept of job satisfaction is very important in OB and receives special attention in the following section.

• **Job involvement** is the extent to which an individual is dedicated to a job.

In addition to job satisfaction, OB scholars and researchers are interested in **job involvement**. This is the extent to which an individual feels dedicated to a job. Someone with high job involvement psychologically identifies with her or his job, and, for example, shows willingness to work beyond expectations to complete a special project. This relates to organizational citizenship behaviors as also discussed in the next section.

Employee Morale Varies around the World

A worldwide study shows that morale and what workers want varies from one country to the next. FDS International of the United Kingdom surveyed 13,832 workers in 23 countries on their job satisfaction, quality of employer-employee relations, and work-life balance. Here's how selected countries ranked. Workers with the highest morale were in the Netherlands, Ireland and Thailand (tie), and Switzerland. The United States ranked 10th in the sample and Canada ranked 11th. Japan came in 15th.

Another work attitude is **organizational commitment**, or the degree of loyalty an individual feels toward the organization. Individuals with a high organizational commitment identify strongly with the organization and take pride in considering themselves members. *Rational commitment* reflects feelings that the job serves one's financial, developmental, and professional interests. *Emotional commitment* reflects feelings that what one does is important, valuable, and of real benefit to others. Research shows that strong emotional commitments to the organization are much more powerful than rational commitments in positively influencing performance.[30]

A survey of 55,000 American workers by the Gallup Organization suggests that profits for employers rise when workers' attitudes reflect high job involvement and organizational commitment. This combination creates a high sense of **employee engagement**—something that Gallup defines as feeling "a profound connection" with the organization and "a passion" for one's job.[31] Active employee engagement shows up as a willingness to help others, to always try to do something extra to improve performance, and to speak positively about the organization. Things that counted most toward high engagement in the Gallup research were believing one has the opportunity to do one's best every day, believing one's opinions count, believing fellow workers are committed to quality, and believing a direct connection exists between one's work and the organization's mission.[32]

- **Organizational commitment** is the loyalty of an individual to the organization.

- **Employee engagement** is a strong sense of connection with the organization and passion for one's job.

Job Satisfaction and Its Importance

LEARNING ROADMAP Components of Job Satisfaction / Job Satisfaction Trends / How Job Satisfaction Influences Work Behavior / Linking Job Satisfaction and Job Performance

There is no doubt that job satisfaction is one of the most talked about of all job attitudes. It was defined earlier as an attitude reflecting a person's feelings toward his or her job or job setting at a particular point in time.[33] And when it comes to job satisfaction, several good questions can be asked. What are the major components of job satisfaction? What are the main job satisfaction findings and trends? What is the relationship between job satisfaction and job performance?

Finding the Leader in You

DON THOMPSON SHOWS THE POWER OF LISTENING TO EMOTIONS

The president's office at McDonald's world headquarters in Oak Brook, Illinois has no door; the building is configured with an open floor plan. All that fits nicely with Thompson's management style and personality. His former mentor Raymond Mines says: "He has the ability to listen, blend in, analyze and communicate. People feel at ease with him. A lot of corporate executives have little time for those below them. Don makes everyone a part of the process."

When Thompson was appointed president and chief operating officer, his boss, McDonald's vice chairman and chief executive officer, Jim Skinner said, "Don has done an outstanding job leading our U.S. business, and I am confident he will bring the same energy and innovative thinking to his new global role."

While these rosy accolades are well deserved, there was a time when Thompson had to make a bold choice. After grand success when first joining McDonald's, he ran into a period of routine accomplishment. He was getting stuck and thought it might be time to change employers. But the firm's diversity officer recommended he speak with Raymond Mines, at the time the firm's highest-ranking African-American executive. When Thompson confided that he "wanted to have an impact on

decisions," Mines told him to move out of engineering and into the operations side of the business.

Thompson listened to the advice and moved into unfamiliar territory. It got him the attention he needed to advance to ever-higher responsibilities that spanned restaurant operations, franchisee relations, and global strategic management.

Thompson now says, "I want to make sure others achieve their goals, just as I have."

What's the Lesson Here?

How attuned are you to your own emotions and to those of others? What do you do when you feel frustrated? Do you ignore it, or do you try to address it by seeking out the advice of others? Are you willing to help others by sharing your own learning with them?

Components of Job Satisfaction

Managers can infer the job satisfaction of others by careful observation and interpretation of what people say and do while going about their jobs. They can also use interviews and questionnaires to more formally assess levels of job satisfaction on a team or in an organization.[34] Two of the more popular job satisfaction questionnaires used over the years are the Minnesota Satisfaction Questionnaire (MSQ) and the Job Descriptive Index (JDI).[35] Both address components of job satisfaction with which all good managers should be concerned. The MSQ measures satisfaction with working conditions, chances for advancement, freedom to use one's own judgment, praise for doing a good job, and feelings of accomplishment, among others. The JDI measures these five job satisfaction facets.

- *The work itself*—responsibility, interest, and growth
- *Quality of supervision*—technical help and social support
- *Relationships with co-workers*—social harmony and respect
- *Promotion opportunities*—chances for further advancement
- *Pay*—adequacy of pay and perceived equity vis-à-vis others

Job Satisfaction Trends

If you watch or read the news, you'll regularly find reports on the job satisfaction of workers. You'll also find lots of job satisfaction studies in the academic literature. The results don't always agree, but they usually fall within a common range. And until recently, we generally concluded that the majority of American workers are at least somewhat satisfied with their jobs. Now, the trend has turned down.[36]

Surveys conducted by The Conference Board showed in 1987 that about 61 percent of American workers said they were satisfied; in 2009 only 45 percent were reporting job satisfaction.[37] The report states: "Fewer Americans are satisfied with all aspects of employment, and no age or income group is immune. In fact, the youngest cohort of employees (those currently under age 25) expresses the highest level of dissatisfaction ever recorded by the survey for that age group." In terms of other patterns in these data, only 51 percent of workers surveyed in 2009 said their jobs were interesting versus 70 percent in 1987. Only 51 percent said they were satisfied with their bosses versus 60 percent in 1987.

A global survey in 2011 by Accenture contacted 3,400 professionals from 29 countries around the world.[38] Results showed less than one-half were satisfied with their jobs, and that the percentage of job satisfaction was about equal between women (43%) and men (42%). But about three quarters of the respondents said they had no plans to leave their current jobs. This makes us wonder about the

OB IN POPULAR CULTURE

MOODS AND *CRASH*

None of us is immune to feelings and the influence they have on our lives. And, it really doesn't matter whether we are at work, at home, or at play. We are generally expected to be in charge of our feelings, particularly when we interact with others. This requires a good deal of self-control, and that can be difficult when **moods** take over our feelings. They are positive or negative states that persist, perhaps for quite a long time.

In *Crash,* Jean Cabot (Sandra Bullock) is talking on the telephone with her best friend, Carol. When she begins to complain about her housekeeper, Carol's response is skeptical and a bit critical. Jean starts to justify her reaction but then admits she is angry at practically everyone with whom she interacts. Her final admission is quite telling—Jean informs Carol that she wakes up angry every day. When Carol ends the conversation prematurely, Jean loses focus and ends up falling down the stairs in her house.

This scene from the movie illustrates how moods can be all consuming—affecting not only our outlook, but our relationships and even behaviors. When emotions and moods get the best of us, we may say or do things that are not in our best interests and that we may regret later. Emotional intelligence involves understanding moods, recognizing how they affect behavior, and learning to control emotions.

Get to Know Yourself Better   Take time to complete Assessment 3, The Turbulence Tolerance Test, in the OB Skills Workbook. Remember to respond as if you were the manager. What is your tolerance level for turbulence? What role might moods and emotions play in how you react to these and other situations? How can better self-awareness and emotional intelligence help you prepare to handle such things more effectively?

implications for both employees and employers when people stick with jobs that give them little satisfaction.

Both men and women in the Accenture Survey generally agreed on the least satisfying things about their jobs–being underpaid, lacking career advancement opportunities, and feeling trapped in their jobs. But gender differences were also evident. Women are less likely than men to ask for pay raises (44% vs. 48%) and for promotions (28% vs. 39%). Women are more likely to believe their careers are not "fast-tracked" (63% vs. 55%) and more likely to report that getting ahead in careers is due to hard work and long hours (68% vs. 55%). And in respect to generational differences, Gen Y workers ranked pay higher as a source of motivation (73%) than either Gen Xers (67%) or Baby Boomers (58%).

How Job Satisfaction Influences Work Behavior

Would you agree that people deserve to have satisfying work experiences? You probably do. But, is job satisfaction important in other than a "feel good" sense? How does it impact work behaviors and job performance? In commenting on the Conference Board data just summarized, for example, Lynn Franco, the director of the organization's Consumer Research Center, said: "The downward trend in job satisfaction could spell trouble for the engagement of U.S. employees and ultimately employee productivity."[39]

Withdrawal Behaviors   There is a strong relationship between job satisfaction and physical withdrawal behaviors like *absenteeism* and *turnover*. Workers who are more satisfied with their jobs are absent less often than those who are dissatisfied. Satisfied workers are also more likely to remain with their present employers, while dissatisfied workers are more likely to quit or at least be on the lookout for other jobs.[40] Withdrawal through absenteeism and turnover can be very costly in terms of lost experience, and the expenses for recruiting and training of replacements.[41]

A survey by Salary.com showed not only that employers tend to overestimate the job satisfactions of their employees, they underestimate the amount of job seeking they are doing.[42] Whereas employers estimated that 37 percent of employees were on the lookout for new jobs, 65 percent of the employees said they were job seeking by networking, Web surfing, posting resumes, or checking new job

Generations Differ in Satisfaction with Their Bosses

Would it surprise you that Millennials have somewhat different views of their bosses than their Generation X and Baby Boomer co-workers? This pattern is evident in a Kenexa survey that asked 11,000 respondents to rate their managers' performance. Results showed positive rating of boss's performance–Boomers 55%, Gen Xers 59%, Millennials 68% . . . positive rating of boss's people management–Boomers 50%, Gen Xers 53%, Millennials 62% . . . positive rating of boss's leadership–Boomers 39%, Gen Xers 43%, Millennials 51%.

possibilities. Millennials in their 20s and early 30s were most likely to engage in these "just-in-case" job searches. The report concluded that "most employers have not placed enough emphasis on important retention strategies."

There is also a relationship between job satisfaction and psychological withdrawal behaviors. They show up in such forms as daydreaming, cyber loafing by Internet surfing or personal electronic communications, excessive socializing, and even just giving the appearance of being busy when one is not. These withdrawal behaviors are indicators of work disengagement, something that Gallup researchers say as many as 71 percent of workers report feeling at times.[43]

Organizational Citizenship   Job satisfaction is also linked with **organizational citizenship behaviors**.[44] These are discretionary behaviors, sometimes called OCBs, that represent a willingness to "go beyond the call of duty" or "go the extra mile" in one's work.[45] A person who is a good organizational citizen does extra things that help others—*interpersonal OCBs*, or advance the performance of the organization as a whole—*organizational OCBs*.[46] You might observe interpersonal OCBs in a service worker who is extraordinarily courteous while taking care of an upset customer, or a team member who takes on extra tasks when a co-worker is ill or absent. Examples of organizational OCBs are co-workers who are always willing volunteers for special committee or task force assignments, and those whose voices are always positive when commenting publicly on their employer.

The flip-side of organizational citizenship shows up as **counterproductive work behaviors**.[47] Often associated with some form of job dissatisfaction, they purposely disrupt relationships, organizational culture, or performance in the workplace.[48] Counterproductive workplace behaviors cover a wide range of things from work avoidance, to physical and verbal aggression, to bad mouthing, to outright work sabotage and even theft.

> • **Organizational citizenship behaviors** are the extras people do to go the extra mile in their work.

> • **Counterproductive work behaviors** are behaviors that intentionally disrupt relationships or performance at work.

At-Home Affect   When OB scholars talk about "spillover" effects, they are often referring to how what happens to us at home can affect our work attitudes and behaviors, and how the same holds true as work experiences influence how we feel and behave at home. Research finds that people with higher daily job satisfaction show more positive affect after work.[49] In a study that measured spouse or significant other evaluations, more positive at-home affect scores were reported on days when workers experienced higher job satisfaction.[50] This issue of the job satisfaction and at-home affect link is proving especially significant as workers in today's high-tech and always-connected world struggle with work–life balance.

Linking Job Satisfaction and Job Performance

The importance of job satisfaction shows up in two decisions people make about their work— belonging and performing. The first is the *decision to belong*—that is, to join and remain a member of

Spotting Counterproductive or Deviant Workplace Behaviors

Whereas organizational citizenship behaviors help make the organization a better and more pleasant place, counterproductive or deviant behaviors do just the opposite. To varying degrees of severity, they harm the work, the people, and the organizational culture. Here are some things to look for.

- *Personal aggression*—sexual harassment, verbal abuse, physical abuse, intimidation, humiliation.
- *Production deviance*—wasting resources, avoiding work, disrupting workflow, making deliberate work errors.
- *Political deviance*—spreading harmful rumors, gossiping, using bad language, lacking civility in relationships.
- *Property deviance*—destroying or sabotaging facilities and equipment, stealing money and other resources.

an organization. This decision links job satisfaction and withdrawal behaviors, both absenteeism and turnover. The second decision, the *decision to perform*, raises quite another set of issues. We all know that not everyone who belongs to an organization, whether it's a classroom or workplace or sports team or voluntary group, performs up to expectations. So, what is the relationship between job satisfaction and performance?[51] A recent study, for example, finds that higher levels of job satisfaction are related to higher levels of customer ratings received by service workers.[52] But can it be said that high job satisfaction causes high levels of customer service performance?

Three different positions have been advanced about causality in the satisfaction–performance relationship. The first is that job satisfaction causes performance; in other words, a happy worker is a productive worker. The second is that performance causes job satisfaction. The third is that job satisfaction and performance influence one another, and are mutually affected by other factors such as the availability of rewards. Perhaps you can make a case for one or more of these positions based on your work experiences.

Satisfaction Causes Performance   If job satisfaction causes high levels of performance, the message to managers is clear. To increase employees' work performance, make them happy. But, research hasn't found a simple and direct link between individual job satisfaction at one point in time and later work performance. A sign once posted in a tavern near one of Ford's Michigan plants helps tell the story: "I spend 40 hours a week here, am I supposed to work too?" Even though some evidence exists for the satisfaction causes performance relationship among professional or higher-level employees, the best conclusion is that job satisfaction alone is not a consistent predictor of individual work performance.

Performance Causes Satisfaction   If high levels of performance cause job satisfaction, the message to managers is quite different. Instead of focusing on job satisfaction as the precursor to performance, try to create high performance as a pathway to job satisfaction. It generally makes sense that people should feel good about their jobs when they perform well. And indeed, research does find a link between individual performance measured at one time and later job satisfaction.

Figure 3.5 shows this relationship using a model from the work of Edward E. Lawler and Lyman Porter. It suggests that performance leads to rewards that, in turn, lead to

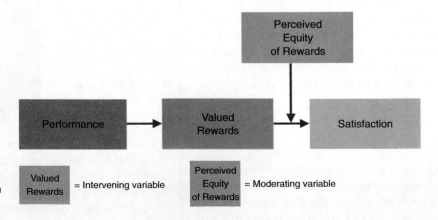

Figure 3.5 Simplified Porter-Lawler model of the performance → satisfaction relationship.

RESEARCH INSIGHT

Job Satisfaction Spillover onto Family Lives

The spillover of job satisfaction onto workers' family lives is the subject of a study published in the *Academy of Management Journal* by Remus Ilies, Kelly Schwind Wilson, and David T. Wagner. Noting that communication technologies and flexibility in work schedules have narrowed the gap between work and home, the researchers asked the question: How does daily job satisfaction spill over to affect a person's feelings and attitudes in the family role?

The research was conducted by survey and telephone interviews with 101 university employees and their spouses or significant others over a two-week period. High work–family role integration was defined as making "little distinction between their work and family roles," while low work–family role integration meant that work and family were quite segmented from one another. A key hypothesis in the research was that job satisfaction spillover from work to home on any given day would be greater for the high work–family role integration employees.

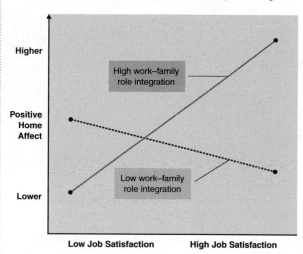

Results showed that workers displayed higher positive affect at home on days when they also reported higher job satisfaction. As shown in the figure, the expected moderating effect of work–family integration also held. Workers with high work–family role integration showed a stronger relationship between daily job satisfaction and positive affect at home versus those with low work–family role integration. In fact, among workers with low work–family integration, those who tended to segment work and family roles, positive home affect actually declined as job satisfaction increased.

Do the Research   How can the findings for the low work–family integration group be explained? What research questions does this study raise in your mind that might become the topics for further study in this area? Would you hypothesize that the job satisfaction–home spillover effects would vary by type of occupation, age of worker, family responsibilities such as number of at-home children, or other factors? Could you suggest a study that might empirically investigate these possibilities?

Source: Remus Ilies, Kelly Schwind Wilson, and David T. Wagner, "The Spillover of Daily Job Satisfaction onto Employees' Family Lives: The Facilitating Role of Work-Family Integration," *Academy of Management Journal*, Vol. 52, No. 1 (2009), pp. 87–102.

satisfaction.[53] Rewards are intervening variables in this model; when valued by the recipient, they link performance with later satisfaction. The model also includes a moderator variable—perceived equity of rewards. This indicates that performance leads to satisfaction only if rewards are perceived as fair and equitable. Although this model is a good starting point, and one that we will use again in discussing motivation and rewards in Chapter 6, we also know from experience that some people may perform well but still not like the jobs that they have to do.

Rewards Cause Both Satisfaction and Performance   The final position in the job satisfaction–performance discussion suggests that the right rewards allocated in the right ways will positively influence both performance and satisfaction. These two outcomes also influence one another. A key issue in respect to the allocation of rewards is *performance contingency*. This means that the size of the reward varies in proportion to the level of performance.

Research generally finds that rewards influence satisfaction while performance-contingent rewards influence performance.[54] The prevailing management advice is to use performance-contingent rewards well in the attempt to create both. Although giving a low performer a small reward may lead to dissatisfaction at first, the expectation is that he or she will make efforts to improve performance in order to obtain higher rewards in the future.[55]

3 *study guide*

Key Questions and Answers

What are emotions and moods?

- Affect is a generic term that covers a broad range of feelings that individuals experience as emotions and moods.

- Emotions are strong feelings directed at someone or something and that influence behavior, often with intensity and for short periods of time.

- Moods are generalized positive or negative states of mind that can be persistent influences on one's behavior.

- Emotional intelligence is the ability to detect and manage emotional cues and information. Four emotional intelligence skills or competencies are self-awareness, self-management, social awareness, and relationship management.

How do emotions and moods influence behavior in organizations?

- Emotional contagion involves the spillover effects onto others of one's emotions and moods; in other words, emotions and moods can spread from person to person.

- Emotional labor is a situation where a person displays organizationally desired emotions while performing a job.

- Emotional dissonance is a discrepancy between true feelings and organizationally desired emotions; it is linked with deep acting to try to modify true inner feelings and with surface acting to hide one's true inner feelings.

- Affective Events Theory (AET) relates characteristics of the work environment, work events, and personal predispositions to positive or negative emotional reactions and job satisfaction.

What are attitudes and how do they influence behavior in organizations?

• An attitude is a predisposition to respond in a certain way to people and things.

• Attitudes have affective, cognitive, and behavioral components.

• Although attitudes predispose individuals toward certain behaviors, they do not guarantee that such behaviors will take place.

• Individuals desire consistency between their attitudes and their behaviors, and cognitive dissonance occurs when a person's attitude and behavior are inconsistent.

• Job satisfaction is an attitude toward one's job, co-workers, and workplace.

• Job involvement is a positive attitude that shows up in the extent to which an individual is dedicated to a job.

• Organizational commitment is a positive attitude that shows up in the loyalty of an individual to the organization.

What is job satisfaction and why is it important?

• Five components of job satisfaction are the work itself, quality of supervision, relationships with co-workers, promotion opportunities, and pay.

• Job satisfaction influences physical withdrawal behaviors of absenteeism, turnover, as well as psychological withdrawal behaviors like day dreaming and cyber loafing.

• Job satisfaction is linked with organizational citizenship behaviors that are both interpersonal—such as doing extra work for a sick teammate—and organizational—such as always speaking positively about the organization.

• A lack of job satisfaction may be reflected in counterproductive work behaviors such as purposely performing with low quality, avoiding work, acting violently at work, or even engaging in workplace theft.

• Three possibilities in the job satisfaction and performance relationship are that satisfaction causes performance, performance causes satisfaction, and rewards cause both performance and satisfaction.

Terms to Know

Self-Test 3

Multiple Choice

1. A/an _____ is a rather intense but short-lived feeling about a person or a situation, while a/an _____ is a more generalized positive or negative state of mind. (a) stressor, satisfier (b) affect, attitude (c) spillover, moderator (d) emotion, mood

2. When someone is feeling anger about something a co-worker did, she is experiencing a/an _____, but when just "having a bad day overall" she is experiencing a/an _____. (a) mood, emotion (b) emotion, mood (c) affect, effect (d) dissonance, consonance

3. Emotions and moods as personal affects are known to influence _____. (a) attitudes (b) ability (c) aptitude (d) intelligence

4. If a person shows empathy and understanding of the emotions of others and uses this to better relate to them, she is displaying the emotional intelligence competency of _____. (a) self-awareness (b) emotional contagion (c) relationship management (d) social awareness

5. The _____ component of an attitude indicates a person's belief about something, while the _____ component indicates positive or negative feeling about it. (a) cognitive, affective (b) emotional, affective (c) cognitive, mood (d) behavioral, mood

6. _____ describes the discomfort someone feels when his or her behavior is inconsistent with an expressed attitude. (a) Alienation (b) Cognitive dissonance (c) Job dissatisfaction (d) Person–job imbalance

7. Affective Events Theory shows how one's emotional reactions to work events, environment, and personal predispositions can influence _____. (a) job satisfaction and performance (b) emotional labor (c) emotional intelligence (d) emotional contagion

8. The tendency of people at work to display feelings consistent with the moods of their co-workers and bosses, is known as _____. (a) emotional dissonance (b) emotional labor (c) mood contagion (d) mood stability

9. When an airline flight attendant displays organizationally desired emotions when interacting with passengers, this is an example of _____. (a) emotional labor (b) emotional contagion (c) job commitment (d) negative affect

10. A person who always volunteers for extra work or helps someone else with their work is said to be high in _____. (a) emotional labor (b) affect (c) emotional intelligence (d) organizational commitment

11. The main difference between job involvement and _____ is that the former shows a positive attitude toward the job and the latter shows a positive attitude toward the organization. (a) organizational commitment (b) employee engagement (c) job satisfaction (d) cognitive dissonance

12. Job satisfaction is known to be a good predictor of _____. (a) deep acting (b) emotional intelligence (c) cognitive dissonance (d) absenteeism

13. The best conclusion about job satisfaction in today's workforce is probably that _____. (a) it isn't an important issue (b) the only real concern is pay (c) most people are not satisfied with their jobs most of the time (d) trends show declining job satisfaction

14. Which statement about the job satisfaction–job performance relationship is most consistent with research? (a) A happy worker will be productive. (b) A productive worker will be happy. (c) A well rewarded productive worker will be happy. (d) a poorly rewarded productive worker will be happy.

15. What does "performance-contingent" refer to when rewards are discussed as possible influences on satisfaction and performance? (a) rewards are highly valued (b) rewards are frequent (c) rewards are in proportion to performance (d) rewards are based only on seniority

Short Response

16. What are the major differences between emotions and moods as personal affects?

17. Describe and give examples of the three components of an attitude.

18. List five facets of job satisfaction and briefly discuss their importance.

19. Why is cognitive dissonance an important concept for managers to understand?

Applications Essay

20. Your boss has a sign posted in her office. It says—"A satisfied worker is a high-performing worker." In a half-joking and half-serious way she points to it and says, "You are fresh out of college as a business and management major, am I right or wrong?" What is your response?

Next Steps
Top Choices from
The OB Skills Workbook

Case for Critical Thinking	Team and Experiential Exercises	Self-Assessment Portfolio
• Management Training Dilemma	• My Best Manager • My Best Job • Graffiti Needs Assessment • Sweet Tooth	• Learning Style Inventory • Student Leadership Practices Inventory • 21st Century Manager • Global Readiness Index

Just-in-time Learning Saves the Day

Right about now, you're starting to panic. Your boss has a request: The Web designer is on maternity leave. You're good with computers, so can you edit some pages on the company's Web site?

What do you do? Cross your fingers and dive in head first. That's the spirit behind Head First Labs, a series of irreverent tech tutorial books designed to help readers learn—and remember—new and complicated information by incorporating storytelling, unexpected images, and hands-on projects.

Published by O'Reilly Media, the books emphasize *just-in-time learning*, the idea of acquiring just enough knowledge to get by, where and when you need it.

Here's the core of Head First's philosophy: Sometimes you have to trick your brain. Because its primary goal is to keep you safe and out of trouble, your gray matter tends to favor the important stuff (*Danger! Fire! Angry boss!*) over what it thinks is trivial. The solution: Couple the information you need now with enough unusual images, piquant captions, and unexpected elements to kick those neurons into learning mode.

"When you learn just-in-time, you're highly motivated," says research statistician John Cook. Because you're already under the gun, "there's no need to imagine whether you might apply what you're learning."[a]

But what about those Web pages the boss asked you to edit? With the help of a Head First guide, you learn just enough to

> *"What you know is trivial. The real issue is, what do you know how to do?"*
> −Roger Schank, Director of Northwestern University's Institute for Learning Sciences[b]

make the necessary changes without crashing the site. Your grateful boss rewards you with your favorite kind of positive reinforcement: lunch on the company's dime. While you're waiting for the check, she leans in and asks, "How much do you know about databases?"

A Brain-Friendly Guide

Head First HTML with CSS & XHTML

Launch your Web career in one chapter

A learner's guide to creating standards-based Web pages

Watch out for common HTML & CSS traps and pitfalls

Learn why everyth your friends know a style is probably wr

Bend your mind around 100 puzzles & exercises

Avoid embarrassing validation mistakes

O'REILLY®

Elisabeth Freeman & Eric Freem

Quick Summary
- O'Reilly Media's Head First books provide engaging just-in-time training on dense tech topics like programming and Web design.
- The guides use unexpected pictures, real-life examples, and hands-on exercises to increase information retention.
- Companies find that just-in-time learning tools cuts training costs, minimizes employee downtime, and improves productivity.

FYI: For employees with less than 12 years of work experience, trained (on the job) workers enjoy wages that are almost 10% higher than wages of untrained workers.

4 Perception, Attribution, and Learning

the key point

In all the events and experiences of everyday living it can be a shock when people view the same thing and come to different conclusions. But this is reality—people often perceive situations in different ways. The better we understand perception and attribution and their effects on how people behave and learn, the better we can be at dealing with events, people, and relationships not only just-in-time, but also in positive ways.

chapter at a glance

What Is Perception and Why Is It Important?

What Are the Common Perceptual Distortions?

What Is the Link Between Perception, Attribution, and Social Learning?

What Is Involved in Learning by Reinforcement?

ETHICS IN OB
WORKERS REPORT VIEWS ON ETHICAL WORKPLACE CONDUCT

FINDING THE LEADER IN YOU
RICHARD BRANSON LEADS WITH PERSONALITY AND POSITIVE REINFORCEMENT

OB IN POPULAR CULTURE
POSITIVE REINFORCEMENT AND *THE BIG BANG THEORY*

RESEARCH INSIGHT
INTERACTIONAL JUSTICE PERCEPTIONS AFFECT INTENT TO LEAVE

what's inside?

The Perception Process

LEARNING ROADMAP   Factors Influencing Perception / Information Processing and the Perception Process / Perception, Impression Management, and Social Media

• **Perception** is the process through which people receive and interpret information from the environment.

Perception is the process by which people select, organize, interpret, retrieve, and respond to information from the world around them.[1] It is a way of forming impressions about ourselves, other people, and daily life experiences. It also serves as a screen or filter through which information passes before it has an effect on people. Because perceptions are influenced by many factors, different people may perceive the same situation quite differently. And since people behave according to their perceptions, the consequences of these differences can be great in terms of what happens next.

Consider the example shown in Figure 4.1. It shows substantial differences in how a performance appraisal discussion is perceived by managers and their subordinates. These managers may end up not giving much attention to things like career development, performance goals, and supervisory support since they perceive these issues were adequately addressed at performance appraisal time. But the subordinates may end up frustrated and unsatisfied because they perceive less attention was given and they want more.

Factors Influencing Perception

We can think of perception as a bubble that surrounds us and influences significantly the way we receive, interpret, and process information received from our

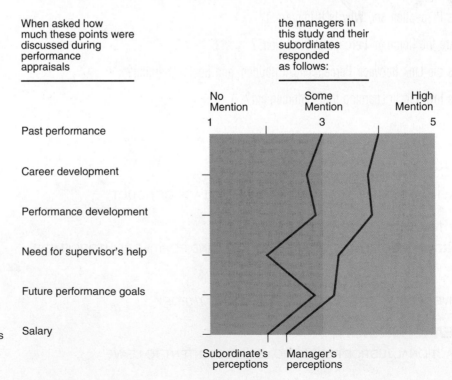

Figure 4.1 Contrasting perceptions between managers and subordinates regarding performance appraisal interviews.

environments. The many factors influencing perception include characteristics of the *perceiver*, the *setting*, and the *perceived*.

The Perceiver   A person's past experiences, needs or motives, personality, values, and attitudes may all influence the perceptual process. Someone with a strong achievement need tends to perceive a situation in terms of that need. If doing well in class is perceived as a way to help meet your achievement need, for example, you will tend to emphasize that aspect when choosing classes to take. In the same way, a person with a negative attitude toward younger workers may react antagonistically when asked to work for a young, newly hired team leader regardless of his or her competency.

The Setting   The physical, social, and organizational context can influence the perception process. When Kim Jeffrey was promoted to CEO of Nestlé Waters North America, he was perceived by subordinates as a frightening figure because he gave in to his temper and had occasional confrontations with them. Before the promotion Jeffrey's flare-ups had been tolerable, but in this new role as CEO they caused intimidation. The problem was resolved after he received feedback, learned of his subordinates' perceptions, and changed his manner and ways.[2]

The Perceived   Characteristics of the perceived person, object, or event are also important in the perception process. We talk about them in terms of contrast, intensity, figure–ground separation, size, motion, and repetition or novelty. In respect to contrast for example, one Mac computer among six HPs or one man among six women will be perceived differently than one of six Mac computers or one of six men. The latter cases have less contrast.

Intensity varies in terms of brightness, color, depth, and sound of what is being perceived. A bright red sports car stands out from a group of gray sedans; whispering or shouting stands out from ordinary conversation. This links with a concept known as figure–ground separation. Look, for example, at the illustration in Figure 4.2. What do you see, faces or a vase? It depends on which image is perceived as the background and which as the figure or object of our attention.

In the matter of size, very small or very large people tend to be perceived differently and more readily than average-sized people. In terms of motion, moving objects are perceived differently than stationary objects. And, of course, repetition or

Figure 4.2 Figure and ground illustration.

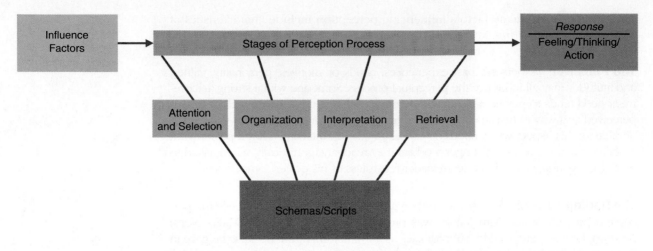

Figure 4.3 Information processing and the perception process.

frequency can also influence perceptions. Television advertisers well know that the more they put something in front of us the more likely we are to give it attention. Finally, the novelty of a situation affects its perception. A college student with streaks of hair dyed purple may be perceived quite differently by an instructor than others with a more common hair color.

Information Processing and the Perception Process

The various stages of the perception process are presented in Figure 4.3. They show that information processing during the perception process involves attention and selection, organization, interpretation, and retrieval.

Attention and Selection Our senses are constantly bombarded with so much information that if we don't screen it, we quickly become incapacitated with information overload. We tend to deal with this through **selective screening** that lets in only a tiny portion of all the information available.

• **Selective screening** allows only a portion of available information to enter our perceptions.

Some of the selective screening that we do comes from controlled processing—consciously deciding what information to pay attention to and what to ignore. Think, for example, about the last time you were at a noisy restaurant and screened out all the sounds but those of the person with whom you were talking. Some screening also takes place without conscious awareness. We often drive cars without thinking about the process; we're aware of things like traffic lights and other cars, but we don't pay conscious attention to them. This selectivity of attention and automatic information processing works well most of the time. But if a nonroutine event occurs, such as an animal darting onto the road, you may have an accident unless you quickly shift to controlled processing.

• **Schemas** are cognitive frameworks that represent organized knowledge developed through experience about people, objects, or events.

Organization Even though selective screening takes place in the attention stage, it's still necessary for us to organize information efficiently. This is done to some extent through **schemas**. These are cognitive frameworks that represent organized knowledge developed through experience about a concept or

In the World of Social Media It Pays to Take Charge of Your Script

Did you know that you already have an online brand? It's true. That's the person that you create as you profile yourself and interact with others in the world of social media. And it's a brand that endures. But does one brand do the job? Why not make sure the script fits the audience? Donna Byrd, publisher at TheRoot.com, uses LinkedIn and Twitter to voice expert opinions and publicize her company. "If you do it consistently," she says, "you can become a trusted voice in your particular area of expertise."

stimulus.[3] We commonly use script schemas, person schemas, and person-in-situation schemas.

A *script schema* is a knowledge framework that describes the appropriate sequence of events in a given situation.[4] For example, an experienced manager would use a script schema to think about the appropriate steps involved in running a meeting. A *self schema* contains information about a person's own appearance, behavior, and personality. For instance, people with decisiveness schemas tend to perceive themselves in terms of that aspect, especially in circumstances calling for leadership.

Person schemas refer to the way individuals sort others into categories, such as types or groups, in terms of similar perceived features. The terms *prototype* and *stereotype* are often used in this regard. They are abstract sets of features commonly associated with members of a category, such as a "good teammate" being intelligent, dependable, and hard-working. Once formed, they are stored in long-term memory and retrieved only when needed for a comparison of how well a person matches the schema's features. *Person-in-situation schemas* combine schemas built around persons (self and person schemas) and events (script schemas).[5]

Interpretation   Once your attention has been drawn to certain stimuli and you have grouped or organized this information, the next step is to uncover the reasons behind the actions. Even if your attention is called to the same information and you organize it in the same way your friend does, you may still interpret it differently or make different assumptions about what you have perceived. As a team leader, for example, you might interpret compliments from a team member as due to his being an eager worker; your friend might interpret the behavior as insincere flattery.

Retrieval   Each stage of the perception process becomes part of memory. This information stored in our memory must be retrieved if it is to be used. But all of us at times have trouble retrieving stored information. And memory decays, so that only some of the information may be retrieved. Schemas can make it difficult for people to remember things not included in them. If holding the prototype of a "good worker" as someone showing lots of effort, punctuality, intelligence, articulateness, and decisiveness, you may emphasize these traits and overlook others when evaluating the performance of a team member whom you generally consider good.

Perception, Impression Management, and Social Media

• **Impression management** is the systematic attempt to influence how others perceive us.

Richard Branson, CEO of the Virgin Group, is one of the richest and most famous executives in the world. He may also be the ultimate master of **impression management**, the systematic attempt to behave in ways that will create and maintain desired impressions in the eyes of others.[6] One of Branson's early business accomplishments was the successful start-up of Virgin Airlines, now a global competitor to the legacy airlines. In a memoir, the former head of British Airways, Lord King, said: "If Richard Branson had worn a shirt and tie instead of a goatee and jumper, I would not have underestimated him."[7]

Don't you wonder if creating a casual impression was part of Branson's business strategy? Whether intended or not, the chances are he's used this persona to very good advantage in other business dealings as well. It's an example of how much our impressions can count, both positive and negative, in how others perceive us. And it's not a new lesson; we've all heard it before. Who hasn't been told when heading off to a job interview—"Don't forget to make a good first impression"?

The fact is that we already practice a lot of impression management as a matter of routine in everyday life. Impression management is taking place when we dress, talk, act, and surround ourselves with things that reinforce a desirable self-image and help to convey that image to other persons. When well done, it can help us to advance in jobs and careers, form relationships with people we admire, and even create pathways to group memberships. We manage impressions by such activities as associating with the "right" people, "dressing up" and "dressing down" at the right times, making eye contact when introduced to someone, doing favors to gain approval, flattering others to impress them, taking credit for a favorable event and apologizing for a negative one, and agreeing with the opinions of others.[8]

One of the most powerful forces in impression management today might be the one least recognized—how we communicate our presence in the online world of social media. It might even be the case that this short message deserves to go viral: User beware! The brand you are building through social media may last a lifetime.

It's no secret that more and more employers are intensely scouring the Web to learn what they can about job candidates. What they are gathering are impressions, ones left in the trails of the candidates' past social media journeys. One bad photo, one bad nickname, or one bad comment sends the wrong impression and can kill a great job opportunity. When active in the online world we are creating impressions of ourselves all the time. The problem is that they may be fun in social space but harmful in professional space.

Brand Building and Impression Management in Social Networks

Don't let your social media presence get out of control. Impression management counts online as well as face-to-face, and here are some things to help you make it work for you.

• Ask: How do I want to be viewed? What are my goals in this forum?
• Ask: What am I communicating, or about to communicate, to my "public" audience?
• Ask: Before I post this item, is it something that I want my family, loved ones, or a potential employer to see?
• Do: Choose a respectable username.
• Do: Profile yourself only as you really would like to be known to others; keep everything consistent.
• Do: View your online persona as a "brand" that you are going to wear for a long time; make sure your persona and desired brand are a "fit" and not a "misfit."
• Do: Post and participate in an online forum only in ways that meet your goals for your personal brand; don't do anything that might damage it.

There's a lot to learn about impression management and social media. At a minimum it pays to keep the two social media spaces—the social and the professional—separated with a good firewall in between them. Check the sidebar for more on this topic.

Common Perceptual Distortions

LEARNING ROADMAP Stereotypes / Halo Effects / Selective Perception / Projection / Contrast Effects / Self-Fulfilling Prophecies

Given the complexity of the information streaming toward us from the environments, we use various means of simplifying and organizing our perceptions. But these simplifications can cause inaccuracies in our impressions and in the perception process more generally. Common perceptual distortions trace to the use of stereotypes and prototypes, halo effects, selective perception, projection, contrast effects, and self-fulfilling prophecies.

Stereotypes

One of the most common simplifying devices in perception is the **stereotype**. It occurs when we identify someone with a group or category, and then use the attributes perceived to be associated with the group or category to describe the individual. Although this makes things easier for us by reducing the need to deal with unique individual characteristics, it is an oversimplification. Because stereotypes obscure individual differences, we can easily end up missing the real individual. For managers this means not accurately understanding the needs, preferences, and abilities of others in the workplace.

> • A **stereotype** assigns attributes commonly associated with a group to an individual.

Some of the most common stereotypes, at work and in life in general, relate to such factors as gender, age, race, and physical ability. Why are so few top executives in industry African Americans or Hispanics? Legitimate questions can be asked about *racial and ethnic stereotypes* and about the slow progress of minority managers into America's corporate mainstream.[9] Why is it that women constitute only a small percentage of American managers sent abroad to work on international business assignments? A Catalyst study of opportunities for women in global business points to *gender stereotypes* that place women at a disadvantage compared to men for these types of opportunities. The tendency is to assume women lack the ability and/or willingness to work abroad.[10] Gender stereotypes may cause even everyday behavior to be misconstrued, for example: "He's talking with co-workers." (Interpretation: He's discussing a new deal); "She's talking with co-workers." (Interpretation: She's gossiping).[11]

Ability stereotypes and *age stereotypes* also exist in the workplace. Physically or mentally challenged candidates may be overlooked by a recruiter even though they possess skills that are perfect for the job. A talented older worker may not be promoted because a manager assumes older workers are cautious and tend to avoid risk.[12] Yet a Conference Board survey of workers 50 and older reports that 72 percent felt they could take on additional responsibilities, and two-thirds were interested in further training and development.[13] And then there's the flip side: Can a young person be a real leader, even a

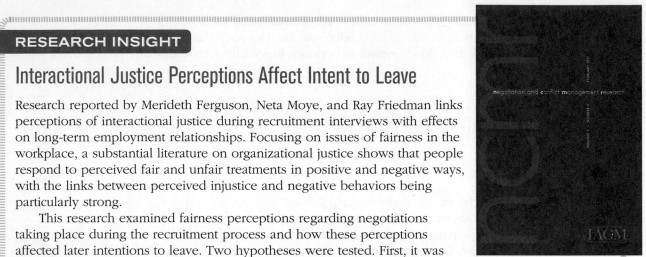

negotiation and conflict management research

IACM

RESEARCH INSIGHT

Interactional Justice Perceptions Affect Intent to Leave

Research reported by Merideth Ferguson, Neta Moye, and Ray Friedman links perceptions of interactional justice during recruitment interviews with effects on long-term employment relationships. Focusing on issues of fairness in the workplace, a substantial literature on organizational justice shows that people respond to perceived fair and unfair treatments in positive and negative ways, with the links between perceived injustice and negative behaviors being particularly strong.

This research examined fairness perceptions regarding negotiations taking place during the recruitment process and how these perceptions affected later intentions to leave. Two hypotheses were tested. First, it was hypothesized that perceived use of negotiation pressure by recruiters would have a negative impact on perceived interactional justice by job applicants. Second, it was hypothesized that perceived interactional injustice during recruiting negotiations would have a positive long-term impact on later intentions to leave by the newly hired employees.

Two studies were conducted. The first study asked a sample of 68 university alumni of a business program about their retrospective perceptions of interactional justice during job negotiations and their current intentions to leave. The second study asked a sample of recent MBA graduates to report perceptions of interactional justice during their job negotiations; they were asked six months later to report on their intentions to leave the new employer. Results from both studies offered confirmation for the two hypotheses.

In conclusion, Ferguson et al. state: "the sense of injustice one feels during a negotiation affects an employee's turnover intentions with the hiring organization . . . negotiations in the recruitment process can set the tone for the future employment relationship." They recommend future research to examine how negotiating tactics like slow responses, dishonesty, disrespect, and lack of concessions influence justice perceptions and later intent to leave. They also suggest that perceived injustice in recruiting when jobs are plentiful may lead to applicants making alternative job choices, while such injustice when jobs are scarce may result in employees accepting the jobs but harboring intent to leave when the opportunity permits.

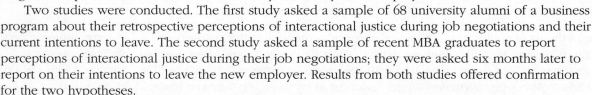

Hypothesis 1   **Hypothesis 2**

| Perceived high pressure negotiating tactics by recruiters | → | Less perceived interactional justice in job negotiation | → | More long-term intent to leave by employees |

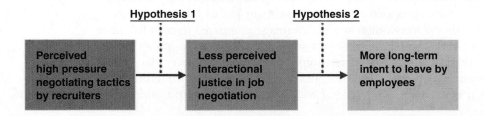

Do the Research   *What is your experience with interactional justice in the recruiting process? Can you design a study to gather the experiences of your cohorts, friends, and others on campus? How can your study pinpoint the impact of tactics such as setting a tight time limit on a job offer?*

Source: Merideth Ferguson, Neta Moye, and Ray Friedman, "The Lingering Effects of the Recruitment Experience on the Long-Term Employment Relationship," *Negotiation and Conflict Management Research*, Vol. 1 (2008), pp. 246–262.

Individual Differences Are Something to Be Celebrated

At Root Learning, a small management consulting firm in Sylvania, Ohio, and also ranked by the *Wall Street Journal* as one of America's Top Small Workplaces, the individual counts. Caricature drawings of each employee are prominently hung in the lobby with the goal of highlighting their interests and talents. CEO Jim Haudan sees this as a way of getting beyond stereotypes and making sure that everyone is viewed as a whole person. "If we pigeon-hole or just identify any of our people as a 'proofer' or an 'analyst,' it grossly limits what they're capable of," he says.

CEO? Facebook's founder and CEO Mark Zuckerberg is still in his 20s. And when current CEO Sheryl Sandberg was being recruited from Google she admits to this thought: "Wow, I'm going to work for a CEO who is quite young." "Mark is a great leader," she now says. After working for him, her perception has changed. "Mark has a real purity of vision . . . He brings people along with him."[14]

Halo Effects

A **halo effect** occurs when one attribute of a person or situation is used to develop an overall impression of that individual or situation. Like stereotypes, these distortions are more likely to occur in the organization stage of perception. Halo effects are common in our everyday lives. When meeting a new person, for example, a pleasant smile can lead to a positive first impression of an overall "warm" and "honest" person. The result of a halo effect is the same as that associated with a stereotype, however, in that individual differences are obscured.

Halo effects are particularly important in the performance appraisal process because they can influence a manager's evaluations of subordinates' work performance. For example, people with good attendance records may be viewed as intelligent and responsible while those with poor attendance records are considered poor performers. Such conclusions may or may not be valid. It is the manager's job to try to get true impressions rather than allowing halo effects to result in biased and erroneous evaluations.

• A **halo effect** uses one attribute to develop an overall impression of a person or situation.

Selective Perception

Selective perception is the tendency to single out those aspects of a situation, person, or object that are consistent with one's needs, values, or attitudes. Its strongest impact occurs in the attention stage of the perceptual process. This perceptual distortion was identified in a classic research study involving executives

• **Selective perception** is the tendency to define problems from one's own point of view.

in a manufacturing company.[15] When asked to identify the key problem in a comprehensive business policy case, each executive selected a problem consistent with his or her functional area work assignments. Most marketing executives viewed the key problem area as sales, whereas production people tended to see the problem as one of production and organization. These differing viewpoints would likely affect how each executive would approach the problem; they might also create difficulties as the executives tried to work together to improve things.

Projection

- **Projection** assigns personal attributes to other individuals.

Projection is the assignment of one's personal attributes to other individuals. It is especially likely to occur in the interpretation stage of perception. A classic error is projecting your needs, values, and views onto others. This causes their individual differences to get lost. Such projection errors can be controlled through a high degree of self-awareness and empathy—the ability to view a situation as others see it.

Suppose, for example, that you enjoy responsibility and achievement in your work. Suppose, too, that you are the newly appointed leader of a team whose jobs seem dull and routine. You may move quickly to expand these jobs so that members get increased satisfaction from more challenging tasks. Basically, you want them to experience things that you value in work. But this may not be a good decision. Instead of designing team members' jobs to best fit their needs, you have designed their jobs to best fit yours. They may be quite satisfied and productive doing jobs that seem dull and routine to you.

Contrast Effects

- A **contrast effect** occurs when the meaning of something that takes place is based on a contrast with another recent event or situation.

We mentioned earlier how a bright red sports car would stand out from a group of gray sedans. This shows a **contrast effect** in which the meaning or interpretation of something is arrived at by contrasting it with a recently occurring event or situation. This form of perceptual distortion can occur, say, when a person gives a talk following a strong speaker or is interviewed for a job following a series of mediocre applicants. A contrast effect occurs when an individual's characteristics are contrasted with those of others recently encountered who rank higher or lower on the same characteristics.

Self-Fulfilling Prophecies

A final perceptual distortion is the **self-fulfilling prophecy**—the tendency to create or find in another situation or individual that which you expected to find in the first place. A self-fulfilling prophecy is sometimes referred to as the "Pygmalion effect," named for a mythical Greek sculptor who created a statue of his ideal mate and then made her come to life.[16]

Self-fulfilling prophecies can have both positive and negative outcomes. In effect, they may create in work and personal situations that which we expect to find. Suppose you assume that team members prefer to satisfy most of their needs outside the work setting and want only minimal involvement with their jobs. Consequently, you assign simple, highly structured tasks designed to require little involvement. Can you predict what response they will have to this situation? In fact, they may show the very same lack of commitment you assumed they would

• A **self-fulfilling prophecy** is creating or finding in a situation that which you expected to find in the first place.

ETHICS IN OB

WORKERS REPORT VIEWS ON ETHICAL WORKPLACE CONDUCT

These data on ethical workplace conduct are from a survey conducted for Deloitte & Touche USA.

• 42 percent of workers say the behavior of their managers is a major influence on an ethical workplace.

• Most common unethical acts by managers and supervisors include verbal, sexual, and racial harassment, misuse of company property, and giving preferential treatment.

• Most workers consider it unacceptable to steal from an employer, cheat on expense reports, take credit for another's accomplishments, and lie on time sheets.

• Most workers consider it acceptable to ask a work colleague for a personal favor, take sick days when not ill, and use company technology for personal affairs.

• Top reasons for unethical behavior are lack of personal integrity (80%) and lack of job satisfaction (60%).

• 91 percent of workers are more likely to behave ethically when they have work–life balance; 30 percent say they suffer from poor work–life balance.

Whose Ethics Count? Shouldn't an individual be accountable for her or his own ethical reasoning and analysis? How and why is it that the ethics practices of others, including managers, influence our ethics behaviors? What can be done to strengthen people's confidence in their own ethical frameworks so that even bad management won't result in unethical practices?

have in the first place. In this case your initial expectations get confirmed as a negative self-fulfilling prophecy.

Self-fulfilling prophecies can also have a positive side. In a study of army tank crews, one set of tank commanders was told that some members of their assigned crews had exceptional abilities while others were only average. But, the crew members had been assigned randomly so that the two test groups were equal in ability. The commanders later reported that the so-called "exceptional" crew members performed better than the "average" ones. The study also revealed the commanders had given more attention and praise to the crew members for whom they had the higher expectations.[17] Don't you wonder what might happen with students and workers in general if teachers and managers adopted more uniformly positive and optimistic approaches toward them?

Perception, Attribution, and Social Learning

LEARNING ROADMAP   Importance of Attributions / Attribution Errors / Attribution and Social Learning

• **Attribution** is the process of creating explanations for events.

One of the ways in which perception exerts its influence on behavior is through **attribution**. This is the process of developing explanations or assigning perceived causes for events. It is natural for people to try to explain what they observe and the things that happen to them. What happens when you perceive that someone in a job or student group isn't performing up to expectations? How do you explain this? And, depending on the explanation, what do you do to try and correct things?

Importance of Attributions

Attribution theory helps us understand how people perceive the causes of events, assess responsibility for outcomes, and evaluate the personal qualities of the people involved.[18] It is especially concerned with whether the assumption is that an individual's behavior, such as poor performance, has been internally or externally caused. Internal causes are believed to be under an individual's control—you believe Jake's performance is poor because he is lazy. External causes are seen as coming from outside a person—you believe Kellie's performance is poor because the software she's using is out of date.

According to attribution theory, three factors influence this internal or external determination of causality: distinctiveness, consensus, and consistency. *Distinctiveness* considers how consistent a person's behavior is across different situations. If Jake's performance is typically low, regardless of the technology with which he is working, we tend to assign the poor performance to an internal attribution—there's something wrong with Jake. If the poor performance is unusual, we tend to assign an external cause to explain it—there's something happening in the work context.

Consensus takes into account how likely all those facing a similar situation are to respond in the same way. If all the people using the same technology as Jake perform poorly, we tend to assign his performance problem to an external attribution. If others do not perform poorly, we attribute Jake's poor

Cause of Poor Performance by Their Subordinates	Most Frequent Attribution	Cause of Poor Performance by Themselves
Many	Lack of *ability*	Few
Many	Lack of *effort*	Few
Few	Lack of *support*	Many

Figure 4.4 Attribution errors when explaining for poor performance.

performance to internal causation. *Consistency* concerns whether an individual responds the same way across time. If Jake performs poorly over a sustained period of time, we tend to give the poor performance an internal attribution. If his low performance is an isolated incident, we may well attribute it to an external cause.

Attribution Errors

Two perception errors are associated with the assignment of internal versus external causation—*fundamental attribution error* and *self-serving bias*.[19] Look at the data reported in Figure 4.4. When managers were asked to identify, or attribute, causes of poor performance among their subordinates, they most often blamed internal deficiencies of the individual—lack of ability and effort, rather than external deficiencies in the situation—lack of support. This demonstrates **fundamental attribution error**—the tendency to underestimate the influence of situational factors and to overestimate the influence of personal factors when evaluating someone else's behavior. When asked to identify causes of their own poor performance, however, the managers mostly cited lack of support—an external, or situational, deficiency. This indicates **self-serving bias**—the tendency to deny personal responsibility for performance problems but to accept personal responsibility for performance success.

The managerial implications of attribution theory trace back to the fact that perceptions influence behavior.[20] For example, a team leader who believes that members are not performing well and perceives the reason to be an internal lack of effort is likely to respond with attempts to "motivate" them to work harder. The possibility of changing external, situational factors that may remove job constraints and provide better organizational support may be largely ignored. This oversight could sacrifice major performance gains for the team.

- **Fundamental attribution error** overestimates internal factors and underestimates external factors as influences on someone's behavior.
- **Self-serving bias** underestimates internal factors and overestimates external factors as influences on someone's behavior.

Attribution and Social Learning

Perception and attribution are important components in **social learning theory**, which describes how learning takes place through the reciprocal interactions among people, behavior, and environment. According to the work of Albert Bandura, an individual uses modeling or vicarious learning to acquire behavior by observing and imitating others.[21] In a work situation, the model may be a higher manager or co-worker who demonstrates desired behaviors. Mentors or senior workers who befriend younger and more inexperienced protégés can also be

- **Social learning theory** describes how learning occurs through interactions among people, behavior, and environment.

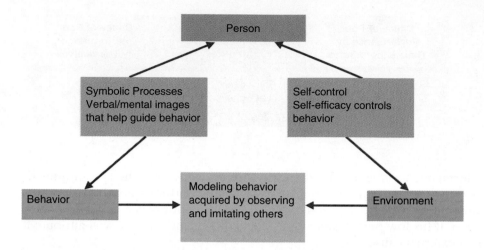

Figure 4.5 Simplified model of social learning.

• **Self-efficacy** is a person's belief that she or he is capable of performing a task.

important models. Indeed, some have argued that a shortage of mentors for women in senior management has been a major constraint to their progression up the career ladder.[22]

The symbolic processes shown in Figure 4.5 are important in social learning. Words and symbols used by managers and others in the workplace help communicate values, beliefs, and goals and thus serve as guides to an individual's behavior. For example, a "thumbs up" or other signal from the boss lets you know your behavior is appropriate. At the same time, the person's self-control is important in influencing his or her own behavior. And **self-efficacy**—the person's belief that he or she can perform adequately in a situation—is an important part of such self-control. Closely associated with the concept of self-efficacy are such terms as confidence, competence, and ability.[23]

People with high self-efficacy believe that they have the necessary abilities for a given job, that they are capable of the effort required, and that no outside events will hinder them from attaining their desired performance level.[24] In contrast, people with low self-efficacy believe that no matter how hard they try, they cannot manage their environment well enough to be successful. If you feel high self-efficacy as a student, a low grade on one test is likely to encourage you to study harder, talk to the instructor, or do other things to enable you to do well the next time. In contrast, a person low in self-efficacy would probably drop the course or give up studying. Of course, even people who are high in self-efficacy do not control their environment entirely.

Four Ways to Build or Enhance Self-Efficacy

Scholars generally recognize the following four ways of building or enhancing our self-efficacy:

1. *Enactive mastery*– gaining confidence through positive experience. The more you work at a task, so to speak, the more your experience builds and the more confident you become at doing it.

2. *Vicarious modeling*–gaining confidence by observing others. When someone else is good at a task and we are able to observe how they do it, we gain confidence in being able to do it ourselves.

3. *Verbal persuasion*–gaining confidence from someone telling us or encouraging us that we can perform the task. Hearing others praise our efforts and link those efforts with performance successes is often very motivational.

4. *Emotional arousal*–gaining confidence when we are highly stimulated or energized to perform well in a situation. A good analogy for arousal is how athletes get "psyched up" and highly motivated to perform in key competitions.

Learning by Reinforcement

When it comes to learning, the concept of reinforcement is very important in OB. It has a very specific meaning that has its origin in some classic studies in psychology.[25] **Reinforcement** is the administration of a consequence as a result of a behavior. Managing reinforcement properly can change the direction, level, and persistence of an individual's behavior. To best understand this idea, it is helpful to review concepts of conditioning and reinforcement you may have already learned in a basic psychology course.

• **Reinforcement** is the delivery of a consequence as a result of behavior.

Operant Conditioning and the Law of Effect

Classical conditioning, studied by Ivan Pavlov, is a form of learning through association that involves the manipulation of stimuli to influence behavior. The Russian psychologist "taught" dogs to salivate at the sound of a bell by ringing the bell when feeding the dogs. The sight of the food naturally caused the dogs to salivate. The dogs "learned" to associate the bell ringing with the presentation of food and to salivate at the ringing of the bell alone. Such learning through association is so common in organizations that it is often ignored until it causes considerable confusion.

The key here is to understand stimulus and conditioned stimulus. A stimulus is something that incites action and draws forth a response, such as food for the dogs. The trick is to associate one neutral stimulus—the bell ringing, with another stimulus that already affects behavior—the food. The once-neutral stimulus is called a conditioned stimulus when it affects behavior in the same way as the initial stimulus. Take a look at Figure 4.6 for a work example. Here, the boss's smiling becomes a conditioned stimulus because of its linkage to his criticisms.

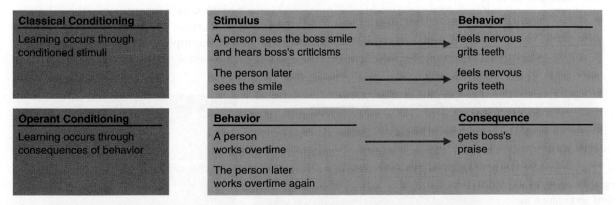

Figure 4.6 Differences between classical and operant conditioning approaches for a boss and subordinate.

An approach popularized by B. F. Skinner extends these reinforcement applications to include more than just stimulus and response behavior.[26] It involves **operant conditioning**, the process of controlling behavior by manipulating its consequences. You may think of operant conditioning as learning by reinforcement. In a work setting the goal is to use reinforcement principles to systematically reinforce desirable behavior and discourage undesirable behavior.[27]

- **Operant conditioning** is the control of behavior by manipulating its consequences.

Operant conditioning calls for examining antecedents, behavior, and consequences. The *antecedent* is the condition leading up to or "cueing" behavior. Figure 4.6 gives the example of an agreement with the boss to work overtime as needed. If the employee actually does work overtime, this is the *behavior*. The *consequence* would be the boss's praise. In operant conditioning, this consequence strengthens the behavior and makes it more likely to reoccur when the antecedent next appears.

The basis for operant conditioning rests in E. L. Thorndike's **law of effect**.[28] It is simple but powerful: Behavior that results in a pleasant outcome is likely to be repeated, whereas behavior that results in an unpleasant outcome is not likely to be repeated. The implications of this law are rather straightforward. If you want more of a behavior, you must make the consequences for the individual positive.

- The **law of effect** is that behavior followed by pleasant consequences is likely to be repeated; behavior followed by unpleasant consequences is not.

Extrinsic rewards, such as pay and praise, are positively valued work outcomes that are given to the individual by some other person. They become external reinforcers or environmental consequences that can substantially influence a person's work behaviors through the law of effect.[29] As shown in Figure 4.7, some of these are *contrived rewards* that are planned, and have direct costs and budgetary implications. Examples are pay increases and cash bonuses. Others are *natural rewards* that have no cost other than the manager's personal time and efforts. Examples are verbal praise and recognition in the workplace.

- **Extrinsic rewards** are positively valued work outcomes that are given to the individual by some other person.
- **Organizational behavior modification** is the use of extrinsic rewards to systematically reinforce desirable work behavior and discourage undesirable behavior.

The use of extrinsic rewards to systematically reinforce desirable work behavior and to discourage unwanted work behavior is known as **organizational behavior modification**, or OB Mod for short. It involves the use of four basic reinforcement strategies: positive reinforcement, negative reinforcement (or avoidance), punishment, and extinction.[30]

Positive Reinforcement

- **Positive reinforcement** strengthens a behavior by making a desirable consequence contingent on its occurrence.

B. F. Skinner and his followers advocate **positive reinforcement**—the administration of positive consequences that tend to increase the likelihood of repeating the desirable behavior in similar settings. For example, a team leader nods to a team member to express approval after she makes a useful comment during a

Contrived Extrinsic Rewards: Some Direct Cost		Natural Extrinsic Rewards: No Direct Cost	
refreshments	promotion	smiles	recognition
piped-in music	trips	greetings	feedback
nice offices	company car	compliments	asking advice
cash bonuses	paid insurance	special jobs	
merit pay increases	stock options		
profit sharing	gifts		
office parties	sport tickets		

Figure 4.7 A sample of contrived and natural extrinsic rewards that can be allocated by managers.

Finding the Leader in You

RICHARD BRANSON LEADS WITH PERSONALITY AND POSITIVE REINFORCEMENT

Sir Richard Branson, well-known founder of Virgin Group, is a believer in positive reinforcement. "For the people who work for you or with you, you must lavish praise on them at all times," he says. "If a flower is watered, it flourishes. If not it shrivels up and dies." And besides, he goes on to add: "It's much more fun looking for the best in people."

Virgin Group is a business conglomerate employing many thousands of people around the globe. It even holds a space venture—Virgin Galactic. It's all

very creative and ambitious—but that's Branson. "I love to learn things I know little about," he says.

Yet if you bump into Branson on the street you might be surprised. He's casual, he's smiling, and he's fun; he's also considered brilliant when it comes to business and leadership. His goal is to build Virgin into "the most respected brand in the world."

As the man behind the Virgin brand, Branson is described as "flamboyant," something that he doesn't deny and also considers a major business advantage that keeps him and his ventures in the public eye.

About leadership Branson says: "Having a personality of caring about people is important . . . You can't be a good leader unless you generally like people. That is how you bring out the best in them." He claims his own style was shaped by his family and childhood. At age 10 his mother put him on a 300-mile bike ride to build character and endurance. At 16 he started a student magazine. By the age of 22 he was launching Virgin record stores. And by the time he was 30 Virgin Group was running at high speed.

As for himself, Branson says he'll probably never retire. Now known as Sir Richard after being knighted, he enjoys Virgin today "as a way of life." But he also says that "In the next stage of my life I want to use our business skills to tackle social issues around the world . . . Malaria in Africa kills four million people a year. AIDS kills even more . . . I don't want to waste this fabulous situation in which I've found myself."

What's the Lesson Here?

Sir Richard obviously has confidence in himself as both a person and a leader. How much of his business and leadership success comes from management of his public impression? Is this something we might all use to advantage? And when he says "you must lavish praise all the time" on the people who work for you, is he giving us an example of the law of effect in action? Finally, Branson seems to have moved beyond the quest for personal business success; he's now talking about real social impact. Is that a natural progression for successful entrepreneurs and business executives?

sales meeting. This increases the likelihood of future useful comments from the team member, just as the leader would hope.

To begin using a strategy of positive reinforcement, we need to be aware that not all rewards end up being positive reinforcers. Recognition, for example, is both a reward and a potential positive reinforcer. But it becomes a positive reinforcer only if a person's performance later improves. Sometimes, a "reward" doesn't work as intended. For example, a team leader might praise a team member in front of others for finding errors in a report that the group had prepared. If the members then give their teammate the silent treatment, however, the worker is less likely to report such errors in the future. In this case, the "reward" fails to serve as a positive reinforcer of the desired work behavior.

- The **law of contingent reinforcement** states a reward should only be given when the desired behavior occurs.
- The **law of immediate reinforcement** states a reward should be given as soon as possible after the desired behavior occurs.

- **Shaping** is positive reinforcement of successive approximations to the desired behavior.

To have maximum reinforcement value, a reward must be delivered only if the desired behavior is exhibited. That is, the reward must be contingent on the desired behavior. This principle is known as the **law of contingent reinforcement**. For example, a supervisor's praise should be contingent on the worker's doing something identifiably well, such as giving a constructive suggestion in a meeting. Also, the reward must be given as soon as possible after the desired behavior. This is known as the **law of immediate reinforcement**.[31] If the supervisor waits for the annual performance review to praise a worker for providing constructive comments, the law of immediate reinforcement would be violated.

Shaping   The power of positive reinforcement can be mobilized through a process known as **shaping**. This is the creation of a new behavior by the positive reinforcement of successive approximations to it. For example, new machine operators in the Ford Motor casting operation in Ohio must learn a complex series of tasks in pouring molten metal into castings in order to avoid gaps, overfills, or cracks.[32] The molds are filled in a three-step process, with each step progressively more difficult than its predecessor. Astute master craftspersons first show newcomers how to pour as the first step and give praise based on what

OB IN POPULAR CULTURE

POSITIVE REINFORCEMENT AND *THE BIG BANG THEORY*

Learning is an important part of an individual's development. In the workplace, **reinforcement** can be used to help employees learn proper behavior. Through the principle of **operant conditioning**, reinforcement uses consequences to help mold the behavior of others.

In one episode of "The Big Bang Theory" Leonard, Penny, and Sheldon are watching anime on television. Penny is bored with a show she does not understand and begins to tell a story about a high school classmate named Anna Mae. Sheldon uses chocolate to get her to stop talking. Later, when Penny's cell phone rings, Sheldon again uses chocolate to get Penny to take the call in the hallway. Leonard discovers the tactic and forbids Sheldon from experimenting with Penny. Sheldon then sprays Leonard with a water bottle (punishment).

The episode is hilarious yet serious. It demonstrates how easily behavior can be influenced through the proper application of operant conditioning techniques. However, it's important to remember that what works at one point in time may not work at another. If Sheldon continues to give Penny chocolates, for example, will she eventually lose her desire for them and the reinforcement will no longer be effective?

Get to Know Yourself Better   Take a look at Experiential Exercise 12, The Downside of Punishment, in the OB Skills Workbook. The focus of the exercise is entirely on punishment. Why do you think this is the case? Have you ever experienced punishment as a student or an employee? What was your reaction? Have you ever seen a boss punish an employee in front of co-workers or customers? Is this an effective way to change behavior? If you were a teacher, how would you handle a behavior problem with a student—such as unwanted text messaging in class?

they did right. As the apprentices gain experience, they are given praise only when all of the elements of the first step are completed successfully. Once the apprentices have mastered the first step, they move to the second. Reinforcement is given only when the entire first step and an aspect of the second step are completed successfully. Over time, apprentices learn all three steps and are given contingent positive rewards immediately upon completing a casting that has no cracks or gaps. In this way behavior is shaped gradually rather than changed all at once.

Scheduling Positive Reinforcement   Positive reinforcement can be given on either continuous or intermittent schedules. **Continuous reinforcement** administers a reward each time a desired behavior occurs, whereas **intermittent reinforcement** rewards behavior only periodically. In general, continuous reinforcement draws forth a desired behavior more quickly than does intermittent reinforcement. But it is costly in the consumption of rewards, and the behavior is more easily extinguished when reinforcement is no longer present. Behavior acquired under intermittent reinforcement is more resistant to extinction and lasts longer upon the discontinuance of reinforcement. This is why shaping typically begins with a continuous reinforcement schedule and then gradually shifts to an intermittent one.

As shown in Figure 4.8, intermittent reinforcement can be given according to fixed or variable schedules. *Variable schedules* typically result in more consistent patterns of desired behavior than do fixed reinforcement schedules. *Fixed-interval schedules* provide rewards at the first appearance of a behavior after a given time has elapsed. *Fixed-ratio schedules* result in a reward each time a certain number of the behaviors have occurred. A *variable-interval schedule* rewards behavior at random times, while a *variable-ratio schedule* rewards behavior after a random number of occurrences.

> • **Continuous reinforcement** administers a reward each time a desired behavior occurs.
> • **Intermittent reinforcement** rewards behavior only periodically.

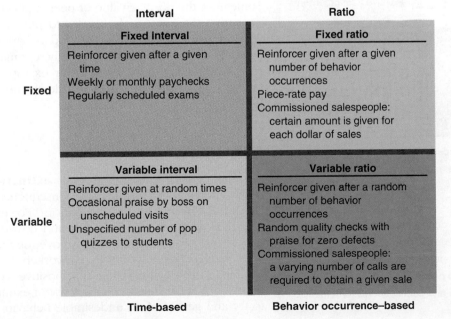

Figure 4.8 Alternative schedules of positive reinforcement.

Negative Reinforcement

- **Negative reinforcement** strengthens a behavior by making the avoidance of an undesirable consequence contingent on its occurrence.

A second reinforcement strategy used in operant conditioning is **negative reinforcement** or avoidance learning. It uses the withdrawal of negative consequences to increase the likelihood of desirable behavior being repeated. For example, the manager regularly nags a worker about being late for work and then doesn't nag when the worker next shows up on time. The term *negative reinforcement* comes from this withdrawal of the negative consequences. The strategy is also called *avoidance learning* because its intent is for the person to avoid the negative consequence by performing the desired behavior. Think of it this way. The streets may be deserted, but we still stop at a red light to avoid a traffic ticket.

Punishment

- **Punishment** discourages a behavior by making an unpleasant consequence contingent on its occurrence.
- **Extinction** discourages a behavior by making the removal of a desirable consequence contingent on its occurrence.

A third reinforcement strategy is punishment. Unlike positive reinforcement and negative reinforcement, it is intended not to encourage desired behavior but to discourage undesirable behavior. Formally defined, **punishment** is the administration of negative consequences or the withdrawal of positive consequences to reduce the likelihood of a behavior being repeated.

There is evidence that punishment administered for poor performance can lead to better performance without a significant effect on satisfaction. But punishment seen by workers as arbitrary and capricious leads to low satisfaction as well as low performance.[33] The point here is that punishment can be handled poorly, or it can be handled well as suggested in the sidebar.

It's also worth noting that punishment may be offset by positive reinforcement received from another source. Take the case of a worker being positively reinforced by peers at the same time that he is receiving punishment from the manager. Sometimes the positive value of peer support is so great that the individual chooses to put up with punishment and continues the bad behavior. As many times as a child may be verbally reprimanded by a teacher for playing jokes, for example, the "grins" offered by classmates may keep the jokes flowing in the future.

How to Make Positive Reinforcement and Punishment Work for You

Positive Reinforcement

- Clearly identify desired work behaviors.
- Maintain a diverse inventory of rewards.
- Inform everyone what must be done to get rewards.
- Recognize individual differences when allocating rewards.
- Follow the laws of immediate and contingent reinforcement.

Punishment

- Tell the person what is being done wrong.
- Tell the person what is being done right.
- Make sure the punishment matches the behavior.
- Administer the punishment in private.
- Follow the laws of immediate and contingent reinforcement.

Extinction

The final reinforcement strategy is **extinction**— the withdrawal of reinforcing consequences in order to weaken undesirable behavior. For example, Enya is often late for work and co-workers provide positive reinforcement by covering for her. The manager instructs Enya's co-workers to stop covering, thus withdrawing the positive consequences of her tardiness. This is a use of extinction to try and get rid of an undesirable behavior. But even though a successful extinction strategy decreases the frequency of or weakens behavior, the behavior is not "unlearned." It simply is not exhibited and will reappear if reinforced again.

Reinforcement Pros and Cons

The effective use of the four reinforcement strategies can help manage human behavior at work. Testimony to this effect is found in the wide application of these strategies in all sorts of work settings, and by the number of consulting firms that specialize in reinforcement techniques. But use of these approaches is not without criticism.

Some critics claim that the success of specific reinforcement programs involves isolated cases that have been analyzed without the benefit of scientific research designs. This makes it hard to conclude definitively whether the observed results were really caused by reinforcement dynamics. One critic goes so far as to argue that any improved performance may well have occurred only because of the goal setting involved—that is, because specific performance goals were clarified, and workers were individually held accountable for their accomplishment.[34] Another major criticism rests with potential value dilemmas associated with using reinforcement to influence human behavior at work. Some maintain that the systematic use of reinforcement strategies leads to a demeaning and dehumanizing view of people that stunts human growth and development.[35] Others believe managers abuse the power of their position and knowledge when they exert this external control over individual behavior.

Advocates of the reinforcement approach attack its critics head on. They agree that behavior modification involves the control of behavior, but they also argue that such control is an irrevocable part of every manager's job. The real question, they say, is how to ensure that the reinforcement strategies are done in positive and constructive ways.[36]

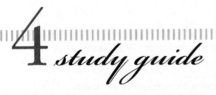

4 *study guide*

What is perception and why is it important?

- Individuals use the perception process to select, organize, interpret, and retrieve information from the world around them.

- Perception acts as a filter through which all communication passes as it travels from one person to the next.

- Because people tend to perceive things differently, the same situation may be interpreted and responded to differently by different people.

- Factors influencing perceptions include characteristics of the perceiver, the setting, and the perceived.

What are the common perceptual distortions?

- Stereotypes occur when a person is identified with a category and is assumed to display characteristics otherwise associated with members of that category.

- Halo effects occur when one attribute of a person or situation is used to develop an overall impression of the person or situation.

- Selective perception is the tendency to single out for attention those aspects of a situation or person that reinforce or emerge and are consistent with existing beliefs, values, and needs.

- Projection involves the assignment of personal attributes to other individuals.

- Contrast effects occur when an individual's characteristics are contrasted with those of others recently encountered who rank higher or lower on the same characteristics.

What is the link between perception, attribution, and social learning?

- Attribution theory addresses tendencies to view events or behaviors as primarily the results of external causes or internal causes.

- Three factors that influence the attribution of external or internal causation are distinctiveness, consensus, and consistency.

- Fundamental attribution error occurs when we blame others for performance problems while excluding possible external causes.

- Self-serving bias occurs when, in judging our own performance, we take personal credit for successes and blame failures on external factors.

- Social learning theory links perception and attribution by recognizing how learning is achieved through the reciprocal interactions among people, behavior, and environment.

What is involved in learning by reinforcement?

- Reinforcement theory recognizes that behavior is influenced by environmental consequences.

- The law of effect states that behavior followed by a pleasant consequence is likely to be repeated; behavior followed by an unpleasant consequence is unlikely to be repeated.

- Positive reinforcement is the administration of positive consequences that tend to increase the likelihood of a person's repeating a behavior in similar settings.

- Positive reinforcement should be contingent and immediate, and it can be scheduled continuously or intermittently depending on resources and desired outcomes.

- Negative reinforcement, or avoidance learning, is used to encourage desirable behavior through the withdrawal of negative consequences for previously undesirable behavior.

- Punishment is the administration of negative consequences or the withdrawal of positive consequences to reduce the likelihood of an undesirable behavior being repeated.

- Extinction is the withdrawal of reinforcing consequences to weaken or eliminate an undesirable behavior.

Terms to Know

Attribution (p. 86)
Continuous reinforcement (p. 93)
Contrast effect (p. 84)
Extinction (p. 94)
Extrinsic rewards (p. 90)
Fundamental attribution error (p. 87)
Halo effect (p. 83)
Impression management (p. 80)
Intermittent reinforcement (p. 93)
Law of contingent reinforcement (p. 92)

Law of effect (p. 90)
Law of immediate reinforcement (p. 92)
Negative reinforcement (p. 94)
Operant conditioning (p. 90)
Organizational behavior
    modification (p. 90)
Perception (p. 76)
Positive reinforcement (p. 90)
Projection (p. 84)
Punishment (p. 94)

Reinforcement (p. 89)
Schemas (p. 78)
Selective perception (p. 83)
Selective screening (p. 78)
Self-efficacy (p. 88)
Self-fulfilling prophecy (p. 85)
Self-serving bias (p. 87)
Shaping (p. 92)
Social learning theory (p. 87)
Stereotype (p. 81)

Self-Test 4

Multiple Choice

1. Perception is the process by which people _____ and interpret information.
   (a) generate (b) retrieve (c) transmit (d) verify

2. When an individual attends to only a small portion of the vast information available in the environment, this tendency in the perception process is called _____.
   (a) interpretation (b) self scripting (c) attribution (d) selective screening

3. Self-serving bias is a form of attribution error that involves _____. (a) blaming yourself for problems caused by others (b) blaming the environment for problems you caused (c) poor emotional intelligence (d) low self-efficacy

4. In fundamental attribution error, the influence of _____ as causes of a problem are _____. (a) situational factors, overestimated (b) personal factors, underestimated (c) personal factors, overestimated (d) situational factors, underestimated

5. If a new team leader changes tasks for persons on her work team mainly "because I would prefer to work the new way rather than the old," she may be committing a perceptual error known as _____. (a) halo effect (b) stereotype (c) selective perception (d) projection

6. Use of special dress, manners, gestures, and vocabulary words when meeting a prospective employer in a job interview are all examples of how people use _____. (a) projection (b) selective perception (c) impression management (d) self-serving bias

7. The perceptual tendency known as a/an _____ is associated with the "Pygmalion effect" and refers to finding or creating in a situation that which was originally expected. (a) self-efficacy (b) projection (c) self-fulfilling prophecy (d) halo effect

8. If a manager allows one characteristic of a person, say a pleasant personality, to bias performance ratings of that individual overall, the manager is falling prey to a perceptual distortion known as _____. (a) halo effect (b) stereotype (c) selective perception (d) projection

9. The underlying premise of reinforcement theory is that _____. (a) behavior is a function of environment (b) motivation comes from positive expectancy (c) higher-order needs stimulate hard work (d) rewards considered unfair are de-motivators

10. The law of _____ states that behavior followed by a positive consequence is likely to be repeated, whereas behavior followed by an undesirable consequence is not likely to be repeated. (a) reinforcement (b) contingency (c) goal setting (d) effect

11. _____ is a positive reinforcement strategy that rewards successive approximations to a desirable behavior. (a) Extinction (b) Negative reinforcement (c) Shaping (d) Merit pay

12. B. F. Skinner would argue that "getting a paycheck on Friday" reinforces a person for coming to work on Friday but would not reinforce the person for doing an extraordinary job on Tuesday. This is because the Friday paycheck fails the law of _____ reinforcement. (a) negative (b) continuous (c) immediate (d) intermittent

13. The purpose of negative reinforcement as an operant conditioning technique is to _____. (a) punish bad behavior (b) discourage bad behavior (c) encourage desirable behavior (d) offset the effects of shaping

14. Punishment _____. (a) may be offset by positive reinforcement from another source (b) generally is the most effective kind of reinforcement (c) is best given anonymously (d) should never be directly linked with its cause.

15. A defining characteristic of social learning theory is that it _____. (a) recognizes the existence of vicarious learning (b) is not concerned with extrinsic ewards (c) relies only on use of negative reinforcement (d) avoids any interest in self-efficacy

Short Response

16. Draw and briefly discuss a model showing the important stages of the perception process.

17. Select two perceptual distortions, briefly define them, and show how they can lead to poor decisions by managers.

18. Why is the law of effect useful in management?

19. Explain how the reinforcement learning and social learning approaches are similar and dissimilar to one another.

Applications Essay

20. One of your friends has just been appointed as leader of a work team. This is her first leadership assignment and she has recently heard a little about attribution theory. She has asked you to explain it to her in more detail, focusing on its possible usefulness and risks in managing the team. What will you tell her?

Case for Critical Thinking	Team and Experiential Exercises	Self-Assessment Portfolio
• Magrec, Inc.	• Decode • How We View Differences • Alligator River Story • Expatriate Assignments • Cultural Cues • Downside of Punishment	• Turbulence Tolerance Test • Global Readiness Index • Intolerance for Ambiguity

Hungry to Succeed

One in six Americans are at risk of hunger. And Feeding America wants to do something about it. With more than 200 local food banks, the nation's largest network of food banks feeds more than 37 million Americans each year by acquiring and distributing more than 3 billion pounds of food and grocery products annually.[a]

The Chicago-based charity procures donations from corporations, the food and grocery industries, individuals, government agencies, and other organizations. They distribute the food, grocery items and funds to member food banks, which distribute food to more than 61,000 agencies including food pantries, soup kitchens, and other emergency feeding centers.[b]

Founder Jon van Hengel volunteered at a Phoenix, AZ, soup kitchen in the late 1960s. During his efforts to secure donations, he was inspired by the suggestion that there should be a place where unwanted food could be stored for later use, like money in a bank. His work led to the opening of St. Mary's Food Bank Alliance, the nation's first food bank.

"Not often in your day-to-day job do you get to enjoy what you do and impact so many people."
—Jerrod Matthews, Feeding America.

In the mid-70s, St. Mary's Food Bank Alliance was given a federal grant to promote the development of food banks in other states, and America's Second Harvest was born in 1979. The charity retained this name until 2008, when it rebranded itself Feeding America to more explicitly communicate its core mission and responsibilities.

Employees and volunteers alike often cite a powerful desire to end hunger as their motivation for engaging with Feeding America, a desire sometimes influenced by first hand understanding of what it means to go without food. "In essence," the charity says on its website, "*feeding* serves a double meaning—both providing food and enriching lives."[c]

Quick Summary

- Feeding America is the nation's largest organization of food banks, with 202 participants in all 50 states and the District of Columbia.
- Centered in Chicago, it employs more than 150 people. Its board of directors includes high-ranking executives from Procter and Gamble, ConAgra, Mars Inc., and other food-centric corporations.
- After more than 30 years as America's Second Harvest, the organization rebranded itself to Feeding America to counter declining donor participation and an increasing misunderstanding about its purpose.

FYI: Last year, 14.7% of American households (17.4 million) were food insecure, the USDA's term to define a lack of daily access to food.[d]

5 Motivation Theories

the key point

Even with great talents many people fail to achieve great things. They just aren't willing to work hard enough to achieve high performance. That's obviously not a problem in Feeding America's success story. But still, many individuals underachieve, and so do the organizations they work for. The question to be answered in this chapter is: Why are some people more motivated than others in their jobs?

chapter at a glance

What Is Motivation?

What Can We Learn from the Needs Theories of Motivation?

Why Is the Equity Theory of Motivation Important?

What Are the Insights of the Expectancy Theory of Motivation?

How Does Goal Setting Influence Motivation?

ETHICS IN OB
INFORMATION GOLDMINE CREATES A DILEMMA

FINDING THE LEADER IN YOU
LORRAINE MONROE'S LEADERSHIP TURNS VISION INTO INSPIRATION

OB IN POPULAR CULTURE
EQUITY THEORY AND *ALLY BANK*

RESEARCH INSIGHT
CONSCIOUS AND SUBCONSCIOUS GOALS HAVE MOTIVATIONAL IMPACT

what's inside?

What Is Motivation?

LEARNING ROADMAP   Motivation Defined / Types of Motivation Theories

Motivation Defined

- **Motivation** refers to forces within an individual that account for the level, direction, and persistence of effort expended at work.

Motivation is defined as forces within the individual that account for the direction, level, and persistence of a person's effort expended at work. *Direction* refers to an individual's choice when presented with a number of possible alternatives (e.g., whether to pursue quality, quantity, or both in one's work). *Level* refers to the amount of effort a person puts forth (e.g., to put forth a lot or very little). *Persistence* refers to the length of time a person sticks with a given action (e.g., to keep trying or to give up when something proves difficult to attain).

Types of Motivation Theories

There are many available theories of motivation and each offers useful insights. We usually divide them into content theories and process theories.[1] While theories of both types contribute to our understanding of motivation to work, none offers a complete explanation. Our goal here is to examine the various theories, identify their key management implications, and then in the next chapter pull everything together into an integrated model of rewards, motivation, and performance.

- **Content theories** profile different needs that may motivate individual behavior.

The **content theories** of motivation focus primarily on individual needs—physiological or psychological deficiencies that we feel a compulsion to reduce or eliminate. The content theories try to explain work behaviors based on pathways to need satisfaction and on blocked needs. This chapter discusses Maslow's hierarchy of needs theory, Alderfer's ERG theory, McClelland's acquired needs theory, and Herzberg's two-factor theory.

- **Process theories** examine the thought processes that motivate individual behavior.

The **process theories** of motivation focus on how cognitive processes as thoughts and decisions within the minds of people influence their behavior. Whereas a content approach may identify job security as an important individual need, a process approach would probe further to identify why the decision to seek

Working Mother Magazine Tracks Best Employers for Women

Working Mother magazine covers issues from kids to health to personal motivation and more. Its goal is to help women "integrate their professional lives, their family lives and their inner lives." Each year it publishes a list of the "100 Best Companies for Working Mothers." In making the selections, *Working Mother* says: "All of our winning companies not only require manager training on diversity issues but also rate manager performance partly on diversity results, such as how many multicultural women advance."

job security results in certain work behaviors. Three process theories discussed in this chapter are equity theory, expectancy theory, and goal-setting theory.

Needs Theories of Motivation

LEARNING ROADMAP Hierarchy of Needs Theory / ERG Theory / Acquired Needs Theory / Two-Factor Theory

Content theories, as just noted, suggest that motivation results from our attempts to satisfy important needs. They imply that managers should be able to understand individual needs in order to create work environments that respond positively to them.

Hierarchy of Needs Theory

Abraham Maslow's **hierarchy of needs theory**, depicted in Figure 5.1, identifies five levels of individual needs. They range from self-actualization and esteem needs at the top, to social, safety, and physiological needs at the bottom.[2] The concept of a needs "hierarchy" assumes that some needs are more important than others and must be satisfied before the other needs can serve as motivators. For example, physiological needs must be satisfied before safety needs are activated; safety needs must be satisfied before social needs are activated; and so on.

Maslow's model is easy to understand and quite popular. But research evidence fails to support the existence of a precise five-step hierarchy of needs. If

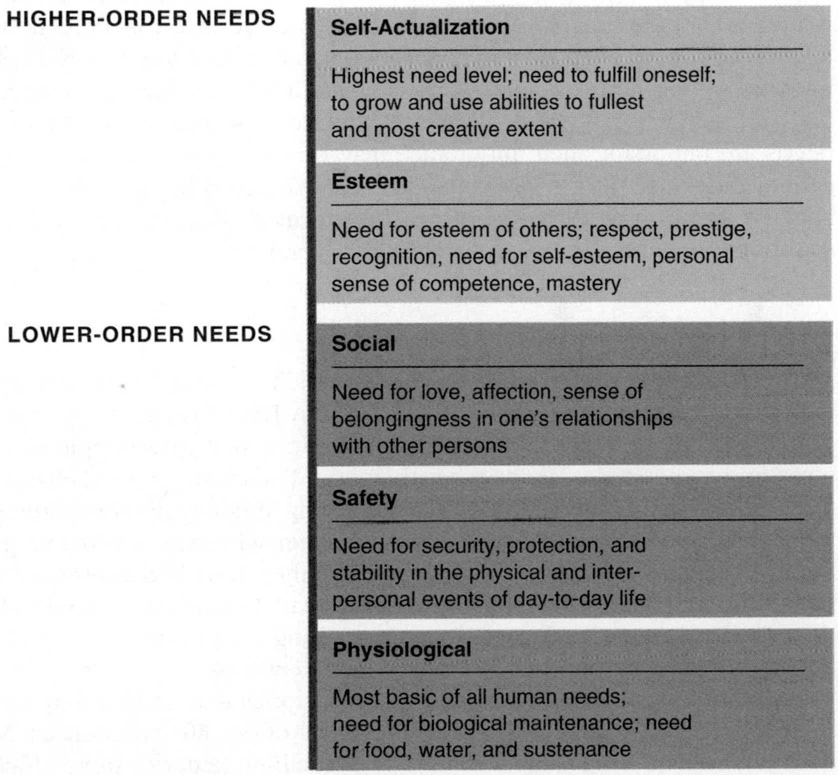

- Maslow's **hierarchy of needs theory** offers a pyramid of physiological, safety, social, esteem, and self-actualization needs.

HIGHER-ORDER NEEDS

Self-Actualization

Highest need level; need to fulfill oneself; to grow and use abilities to fullest and most creative extent

Esteem

Need for esteem of others; respect, prestige, recognition, need for self-esteem, personal sense of competence, mastery

LOWER-ORDER NEEDS

Social

Need for love, affection, sense of belongingness in one's relationships with other persons

Safety

Need for security, protection, and stability in the physical and inter-personal events of day-to-day life

Physiological

Most basic of all human needs; need for biological maintenance; need for food, water, and sustenance

Figure 5.1 Higher-order and lower-order needs in Maslow's hierarchy of needs.

anything, the needs are more likely to operate in a flexible rather than in a strict, step-by-step sequence. Some research suggests that **higher-order needs** (esteem and self-actualization) tend to become more important than **lower-order needs** (psychological, safety, and social) as individuals move up the corporate ladder.[3] Studies also report that needs vary according to a person's career stage, the size of the organization, and even geographic location.[4] There is also no consistent evidence that the satisfaction of a need at one level decreases its importance and increases the importance of the next-higher need.[5] And findings regarding the hierarchy of needs vary when this theory is examined across cultures. For instance, social needs tend to take on higher importance in more collectivist societies, such as Mexico and Pakistan, than in individualistic ones like the United States.[6]

- **Higher-order needs** in Maslow's hierarchy are esteem and self-actualization.
- **Lower-order needs** in Maslow's hierarchy are physiological, safety, and social.

ERG Theory

- Alderfer's **ERG theory** identifies existence, relatedness, and growth needs.
- **Existence needs** are desires for physiological and material well-being.
- **Relatedness needs** are desires for satisfying interpersonal relationships.
- **Growth needs** are desires for continued personal growth and development.

Clayton Alderfer's **ERG theory** is also based on needs, but it differs from Maslow's theory in three main respects.[7] First, ERG theory collapses Maslow's five needs categories into three: **existence needs**, desires for physiological and material well-being; **relatedness needs**, desires for satisfying interpersonal relationships; and **growth needs**, desires for continued personal growth and development. Second, ERG theory emphasizes a unique *frustration-regression* component. An already satisfied lower-level need can become activated when a higher-level need cannot be satisfied. If a person is continually frustrated in his or her attempts to satisfy growth needs relatedness needs can again surface as key motivators. Third, unlike Maslow's theory, ERG theory contends that more than one need may be activated at the same time.

The supporting evidence for ERG theory is encouraging, but further research would be helpful.[8] In particular, ERG theory's allowance for regression back to lower-level needs is a valuable contribution to our thinking. It may explain why in some settings, for example, worker complaints focus mainly on wages, benefits, and working conditions—things relating to existence needs. Although these needs are important, their importance may be exaggerated because the workers cannot otherwise satisfy relatedness and growth needs in their jobs. This type of analysis shows how ERG theory can offer a more flexible approach to understanding human needs than does Maslow's hierarchy.

Acquired Needs Theory

In the late 1940s psychologist David I. McClelland and his co-workers began experimenting with the Thematic Apperception Test (TAT) as a way of measuring human needs.[9] The TAT is a projective technique that asks people to view pictures and write stories about what they see. For example, McClelland showed three executives a photograph of a man looking at family photos arranged on his work desk. One executive wrote of an engineer who was daydreaming about a family outing scheduled for the next day. Another described a designer who had picked up an idea for a new gadget from remarks made by his family. The third described an engineer who was intently working on a bridge stress problem that he seemed sure to solve because of his confident look.[10]

- **Need for achievement (nAch)** is the desire to do better, solve problems, or master complex tasks.

McClelland identified themes in the TAT stories that he believed correspond to needs that are acquired over time as a result of our life experiences. **Need for achievement (nAch)** is the desire to do something better or more efficiently, to

Finding the Leader in You

LORRAINE MONROE'S LEADERSHIP TURNS VISION INTO INSPIRATION

Dr. Lorraine Monroe began her career in the New York City schools as a teacher. She went on to serve as assistant principal, principal, and vice-chancellor for Curriculum and Instruction. But her career really took off when she founded the Frederick Douglass Academy, a public school in Harlem, where she grew up.

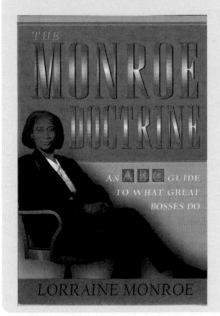

Under her leadership as principal, the school became highly respected for educational excellence. The academy's namesake was an escaped slave who later became a prominent abolitionist and civil rights leader.

Through her experiences Monroe formed a set of beliefs centered on a leader being vision-driven and follower-centered. She believes leaders must always start at the "heart of the matter" and that "the job of a good leader is to articulate a vision that others are inspired to follow." She believes in making sure all workers know they are valued, that their advice is welcome, and that workers and managers should always try to help and support one another. "I have never undertaken any project," she says, "without first imagining on paper what it would ultimately look like . . . All the doers who would be responsible for carrying out my imaginings have to be informed and let in on the dream."

About her commitment to public leadership, Monroe states: "We can reform society only if every place we live—every school, workplace, church, and family—becomes a site of reform." She now serves as a leadership consultant and runs the Lorraine Monroe Leadership Institute. Its goal is to train educational leaders in visionary leadership and help them go forth to build high-performing schools that transform children's lives.

Lorraine Monroe's many leadership ideas are summarized in what is called the "Monroe Doctrine." It begins with this advice: "The job of the leader is to uplift her people—not just as members of and contributors to the organization, but as individuals of infinite worth in their own right."

What's the Lesson Here?

How good are you at visioning? Are you able to generate visions that are persuasive and engaging to others? Do others feel inspired by your visions? If not, could it be that you need to think about how to make the vision more about them and less about you?

solve problems, or to master complex tasks. **Need for affiliation (nAff)** is the desire to establish and maintain friendly and warm relations with others. **Need for power (nPower)** is the desire to control others, to influence their behavior, or to be responsible for others.

Because each need can be linked with a set of work preferences, McClelland encouraged managers to learn how to identify the presence of nAch, nAff, and nPower in themselves and in others. Someone with a high need for achievement will prefer individual responsibilities, challenging goals, and performance feedback. Someone with a high need affiliation is drawn to interpersonal relationships and opportunities for communication. Someone with a high need for power seeks influence over others and likes attention and recognition.

Since these three needs are acquired, McClelland also believed it may be possible to teach people to develop need profiles required for success in various types of jobs. His research indicated, for example, that a moderate to high need for power that is stronger than a need for affiliation is linked with success as a

- **Need for affiliation (nAff)** is the desire for friendly and warm relations with others.
- **Need for power (nPower)** is the desire to control others and influence their behavior.

senior executive. The high nPower creates the willingness to exercise influence and control over others; the lower nAff allows the executive to make difficult decisions without undue worry over being disliked.[11]

Research lends considerable insight into the need for achievement in particular, and it includes some interesting applications in developing nations. McClelland trained businesspeople in India to think, talk, and act like high achievers by having them write stories about achievement and participate in a business game that encouraged achievement. He also had them meet with successful entrepreneurs and learn how to set challenging goals for their own businesses. Over a two-year period following these activities, he found that participants who received this training engaged in activities that created twice as many new jobs as those who did not.[12]

Two-Factor Theory

Frederick Herzberg took yet another approach in his studies of individual needs and motivation. He began by asking workers to report the times they felt exceptionally good about their jobs and the times they felt exceptionally bad about them.[13] Results showed that people talked about very different things when they reported feeling good or bad about their jobs. Herzberg explained these results using what he called the **two-factor theory**, also known as the motivator-hygiene theory. This theory identifies motivator factors as primary causes of job satisfaction and hygiene factors as primary causes of job dissatisfaction.

Hygiene factors are sources of job dissatisfaction, and they are found in the *job context* or work setting. That is, they relate more to the setting in which people work than to the nature of the work itself. The two-factor theory suggests that job dissatisfaction occurs when hygiene is poor. But it also suggests that improving the hygiene factors will not increase job satisfaction; it will only decrease job dissatisfaction. Among the hygiene factors shown on the left in Figure 5.2, perhaps the most surprising is salary. Herzberg found that a low base salary or wage makes people dissatisfied, but that paying more does not necessarily satisfy or motivate them.

Motivator factors, shown on the right in Figure 5.2, are sources of job satisfaction. These factors are found in *job content*—what people actually do in their work. They include such things as a sense of achievement, opportunities for

- Herzberg's **two-factor theory** identifies job context as the source of job dissatisfaction and job content as the source of job satisfaction.
- **Hygiene factors** in the job context are sources of job dissatisfaction.

- **Motivator factors** in the job content are sources of job satisfaction.

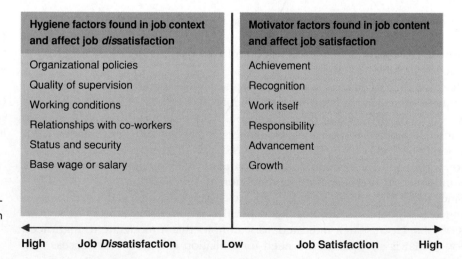

Hygiene factors found in job context and affect job *dis*satisfaction	Motivator factors found in job content and affect job satisfaction
Organizational policies	Achievement
Quality of supervision	Recognition
Working conditions	Work itself
Relationships with co-workers	Responsibility
Status and security	Advancement
Base wage or salary	Growth

High   Job *Dis*satisfaction   Low   Job Satisfaction   High

Figure 5.2 Sources of dissatisfaction and satisfaction in Herzberg's two-factor theory.

personal growth, recognition, and responsibility. According to two-factor theory, the presence or absence of satisfiers or motivators in people's jobs is the key to satisfaction, motivation, and performance. When motivator factors are minimal, low job satisfaction decreases motivation and performance. When motivator factors are substantial, high job satisfaction raises motivation and performance.

A key and controversial point to remember about two-factor theory is that job satisfaction and job dissatisfaction are separate dimensions. Taking action to improve a hygiene factor, such as by giving pay raises or creating better physical working conditions, will not make people satisfied and more motivated in their work; it will only prevent them from being less dissatisfied on these matters. To improve job satisfaction, Herzberg suggests doing **job enrichment** as a way of building more motivator factors into job content. This technique is given special attention in the next chapter as a job design alternative. For now, the implication is well summarized in this statement by Herzberg: "If you want people to do a good job, give them a good job to do."[14]

- **Job enrichment** tries to build more motivator factors into job content.

OB scholars have long debated the merits of the two-factor theory.[15] It is criticized as being method bound, or replicable only when Herzberg's original methods are used. This is a serious criticism, since the scientific approach valued in OB requires that theories be verifiable under different research methods.[16] Yet, the distinction between hygiene and motivator factors has been a useful contribution to OB. As will be apparent in the discussions of job designs and alternative work schedules in the next chapter, the notion of two factors—job content and job context—has a practical validity that adds useful discipline to management thinking.

Equity Theory of Motivation

LEARNING ROADMAP   Equity and Social Comparisons / Equity Theory Predictions and Findings / Equity and Organizational Justice

What happens when you get a grade back on a written assignment or test? How do you interpret your results, and what happens to your future motivation in the course? Such questions fall in the domain of the first process theory of motivation to be discussed here—**equity theory**. As applied to the workplace through the writing of J. Stacy Adams, equity theory argues that any perceived inequity becomes a motivating state of mind. In other words, people are motivated to behave in ways that restore or maintain equity in situations.[17]

- Adams's **equity theory** posits that people will act to eliminate any felt inequity in the rewards received for their work in comparison with others.

Equity and Social Comparisons

The basic foundation of equity theory is social comparison. Think back to the earlier questions. When you receive a grade, do you quickly try to find out what others received as well? And when you do, does the interpretation of your grade depend on how well your grade compared to those of others? Equity theory predicts that your behavior upon receiving a grade—working less or harder in the course, will be based on whether or not you perceive it as fair and equitable. Furthermore, that determination is made only after you compare your results with those received by others.

Adams argues that this logic applies equally well to the motivational consequences of rewards we receive at work. He believes that motivation is a function of how one evaluates rewards received relative to efforts made, and as compared to the rewards received by others relative to their efforts made. A key issue in this comparison is "fairness." And as you might expect, any feelings of unfairness or perceived inequity are uncomfortable; they create a state of mind we are motivated to eliminate.

Equity Theory Predictions and Findings

• **Perceived inequity** is feeling under-rewarded or over-rewarded in comparison with others.

Perceived inequity occurs when someone believes that he or she has been under-rewarded or over-rewarded for work contributions in comparison to other people. The basic equity comparison can be summarized as follows:

$$\frac{\text{Individual Outcomes}}{\text{Individual Efforts}} \begin{matrix} > \\ < \end{matrix} \frac{\text{Others' Outcomes}}{\text{Others' Efforts}}$$

OB IN POPULAR CULTURE

EQUITY THEORY AND *ALLY BANK*

Equity theory tells us that employees are motivated to eliminate perceived inequity, the feeling that stems from unfair distributions of rewards. These perceptions develop when employees receive outcomes as a result of their work effort and then make comparisons with similar others, known as referents.

Ally Bank has a number of child-themed commercials to depict unfair practices in the banking industry. The commercials resonate with viewers because we all have a fundamental understanding of what is fair and what is not. In one particular commercial, two little girls are sitting at a table with a grown man. The man turns to the first little girl and asks, "Would you like a pony?" The girl smiles and nods affirmatively and he hands her a toy pony. Then the man turns and repeats his question to the second little girl. Only this time, when the girl indicates she would like a pony, the man makes a clicking noise and a real pony emerges from behind a playhouse. The second little girl is overjoyed.

While the first girl is initially quite happy with the toy pony she received, she becomes upset when the other girl receives a real pony. This reaction illustrates equity theory and shows that we evaluate rewards within the context in which they are given. Rewards may look good on the surface. But if you find someone else getting the same reward while accomplishing less or getting a bigger reward for completing similar work, it makes your reward pale by comparison. That's not a good feeling.

Get to Know Yourself Better   *Experiential Exercise 17, Annual Pay Raises, in the* OB Skills Workbook *asks you to determine pay raises for a group of employees based on information provided about performance, co-worker assessments, and other nonperformance factors. Take a close look at employee Z. Davis. He is a good worker, but others do not see it that way. How would you handle this situation? If Davis is truly deserving and does not get a pay raise, what will he do? If you give Davis a raise, on the other hand, how will co-workers react?*

Felt negative inequity exists when an individual feels that he or she has received relatively less than others have in proportion to work inputs. *Felt positive inequity* exists when an individual feels that he or she has received relatively more than others have. When either feeling exists, the theory states that people will be motivated to act in ways that remove the discomfort and restore a sense of equity to the situation. In the case of perceived negative inequity, for example, a sense of equity might be restored by engaging in one or more of the following behaviors:

- Reduce work inputs (e.g., don't do anything extra in future).
- Change the outcomes received (e.g., ask for a bigger raise).
- Leave the situation (e.g., quit).
- Change the comparison points (e.g., compare to a different co-worker).
- Psychologically distort things (e.g., rationalize the inequity as temporary).
- Try to change the efforts of the comparison person (e.g., get a teammate to accept more work).

Research on equity theory indicates that people who feel they are over-paid (perceived positive inequity) are likely to try to increase the quantity or quality of their work, whereas those who feel they are underpaid (perceived negative inequity) are likely to try to decrease the quantity or quality of their work.[18] The research is most conclusive with respect to felt negative inequity. It appears that people are less comfortable when they are under-rewarded than when they are over-rewarded. But these findings are particularly tied to individualistic cultures in which self-interest tends to govern social compari-sons. In more collectivist cultures, the concern often runs more for equality than equity. This allows for solidarity with the group and helps to maintain harmony in social relationships.[19]

Equity theory reminds us that the motivational value of rewards is deter-mined by social comparison. It is not the reward-giver's intentions that count; it is how the recipient perceives the reward in the social context that counts. We always do well to remember the equity comparison as interven-ing between the allocation of rewards and the ultimate motivational impact for the recipient.

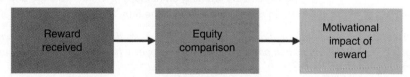

Equity and Organizational Justice

One of the basic elements of equity theory is the fairness with which people per-ceive they are being treated. This relates to an issue in organizational behavior known as **organizational justice**—how fair and equitable people view the prac-tices of their workplace. And in respect to equity theory, justice notions may enter social comparisons in four ways.[20]

Procedural justice is the degree to which the rules and procedures speci-fied by policies are properly followed in all cases to which they are applied. In

- **Organizational justice** concerns how fair and equitable people view workplace practices.
- **Procedural justice** is the degree to which rules are always properly followed to implement policies.

- **Distributive justice** is the degree to which all people are treated the same under a policy.

- **Interactional justice** is the degree to which people are treated with dignity and respect in decisions affecting them.

- **Commutative justice** is the degree to which exchanges and transactions are considered fair.

a sexual harassment case, for example, this may mean that required formal hearings are held for every case submitted for administrative review. **Distributive justice** is the degree to which all people are treated the same under a policy, regardless of race, ethnicity, gender, age, or any other demographic characteristic. In a sexual harassment case, this might mean that a complaint filed by a man against a woman would receive the same consideration as one filed by a woman against a man.

Interactional justice is the degree to which the people affected by a decision are treated with dignity and respect. Interactional justice in a sexual harassment case, for example, may mean that both the accused and accusing parties believe they have received a complete explanation of any decision made. **Commutative justice** is the degree to which exchanges and transactions among parties is considered free and fair. In the sexual harassment example again, commutative justice is present when everyone involved perceives themselves as having full access to all the available facts and information.[21]

ETHICS IN OB

INFORMATION GOLDMINE CREATES A DILEMMA

A worker opens the top of the office photocopier and finds a document someone has left behind. It's a list of performance evaluations, pay, and bonuses for 80 co-workers. She reads the document.

Lo and behold, someone considered a "nonstarter" is getting paid more than others regarded as "super workers." New hires are being brought in at substantially higher pay and bonuses than are paid to existing staff. And to make matters worse, she's in the middle of the list and not near the top, where she would have expected to be. She makes a lot less money than some others are getting.

Looking at the data, she begins to wonder why she is spending extra hours working on her laptop in the evenings and on weekends at home, trying to do a really great job for the firm. She wonders to herself:

"Should I pass this information around anonymously so that everyone knows what's going on? Or, should I quit and find another employer who fully values me for my talents and hard work?"

In the end she decided to quit, saying: "I just couldn't stand the inequity." She also decided not to distribute the information to others in the office because "it would make them depressed, like it made me depressed."

What Would You Do?   *Would you hit "print," make about 80 copies, and put them in everyone's mailboxes—or even just leave them stacked in a couple of convenient locations? That would get the information out and right into the gossip chains pretty quickly. But is this ethical? On the other hand, if you don't send out the information, is it ethical to let other workers go about their days with inaccurate assumptions about pay practices at the firm? By quitting and not sharing the information, did this worker commit an ethics miscue?*

Expectancy Theory of Motivation

Another of the process theories of motivation is Victor Vroom's **expectancy theory**.[22] It suggests that motivation is a result of a rational calculation—people will do what they can do when they want to do it.

Expectancy Terms and Concepts

In expectancy theory, and as summarized in Figure 5.3, a person is motivated to the degree that he or she believes that: (1) effort will yield acceptable performance (expectancy), (2) performance will be rewarded (instrumentality), and (3) the value of the rewards is highly positive (valence). Each of the key terms is defined as follows.

- **Expectancy** is the probability assigned by an individual that work effort will be followed by a given level of achieved task performance. Expectancy would equal zero if the person felt it were impossible to achieve the given performance level; it would equal one if a person were 100 percent certain that the performance could be achieved.

- **Instrumentality** is the probability assigned by the individual that a given level of achieved task performance will lead to various work outcomes. Instrumentality also varies from 0 to 1. Strictly speaking, Vroom's treatment of instrumentality would allow it to vary from −1 to +1. We use the probability definition here and the 0 to +1 range for pedagogical purposes; it is consistent with the instrumentality notion.

- **Valence** is the value attached by the individual to various work outcomes. Valences form a scale from −1 (very undesirable outcome) to +1 (very desirable outcome).

- Vroom's **expectancy theory** argues that work motivation is determined by individual beliefs regarding effort/ performance relationships and work outcomes.

- **Expectancy** is the probability that work effort will be followed by performance accomplishment.

- **Instrumentality** is the probability that performance will lead to various work outcomes.

- **Valence** is the value to the individual of various work outcomes.

Expectancy Theory Predictions

Vroom posits that motivation, expectancy, instrumentality, and valence are related to one another by this equation.

$$\text{Motivation} = \text{Expectancy} \times \text{Instrumentality} \times \text{Valence}$$

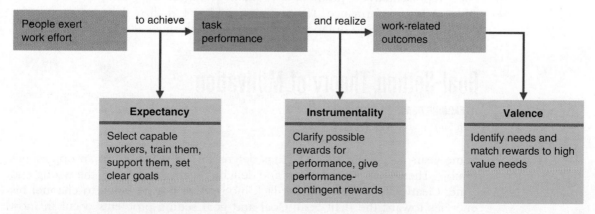

Figure 5.3 Key terms and managerial implications of Vroom's expectancy theory.

You can remember this equation simply as $M = E \times I \times V$, and the multiplier effect described by the "$\times$" signs is significant. It means that the motivational appeal of a work path is sharply reduced whenever any one or more of these factors—E, I, or V—approaches the value of zero. Conversely, for a given reward to have a high and positive motivational impact as a work outcome, the expectancy, instrumentality, and valence associated with the reward must each be high and positive.

Suppose that a manager is wondering whether or not the prospect of earning a merit pay raise will be motivational to an employee. Expectancy theory predicts that motivation to work hard to earn the merit pay will be low if *expectancy* is low—a person feels that he or she cannot achieve the necessary performance level. Motivation will also be low if *instrumentality* is low—the person is not confident a high level of task performance will result in a high merit pay raise. Motivation will also be low if *valence* is low—the person places little value on a merit pay increase. Finally, motivation will be low if any combination of these exists.

Expectancy Implications and Research

Expectancy logic argues that managers should always try to create work situations to maximize work expectancies, instrumentalities, and valences that support organizational objectives.[23] To influence expectancies, the advice is to select people with proper abilities, train them well, support them with needed resources, and identify clear performance goals. To influence instrumentality, the advice is to clarify performance–reward relationships, and then live up to them when rewards are actually given for performance accomplishments. To influence valences, the advice is to identify the needs that are important to each individual and adjust available rewards to match these needs.

A great deal of research on expectancy theory has been conducted.[24] Even though the theory has received substantial support, specific details, such as the operation of the multiplier effect, remain subject to some question. In addition, expectancy theory has proven interesting in terms of helping to explain some apparently counterintuitive findings in cross-cultural management situations. For example, a pay raise motivated one group of Mexican workers to work fewer hours. They wanted a certain amount of money in order to enjoy things other than work, rather than just getting more money in general. A Japanese sales representative's promotion to manager of a U.S. company adversely affected his performance. His superiors did not realize that the promotion embarrassed him and distanced him from his colleagues.[25]

Goal-Setting Theory of Motivation

LEARNING ROADMAP   Motivational Properties of Goals / Goal-Setting Guidelines / Goal Setting and the Management Process

Some years ago a Minnesota Vikings defensive end gathered up an opponent's fumble. Then, with obvious effort and delight, he ran the ball into the wrong end zone. Clearly, the athlete did not lack motivation. But he failed to channel his energies toward the right goal. Goal and goal setting problems occur in most work settings. Without clear goals, people may suffer from poor direction. When goals are both clear and properly set, they may be highly motivated to work towards goal accomplishment.

Motivational Properties of Goals

Goal setting is the process of developing, negotiating, and formalizing the targets or objectives that a person is responsible for accomplishing.[26] Over a number of years Edwin Locke, Gary Latham, and their associates have developed a comprehensive framework linking goals to performance. They say: "Purposeful activity is the essence of living action. If the purpose is neither clear nor challenging, very little gets accomplished."[27] Research on goal setting is extensive.[28] And, many cross-cultural studies have been conducted, including Australia, England, Germany, Japan, and the United States.[29] Although it has its critics, the basic precepts of goal-setting theory remain an important source of advice for managing human behavior in the work setting.[30]

- **Goal setting** is the process of setting performance targets.

Goal-Setting Guidelines

The implications of research on goal setting can be summarized as follows.[31]

Point—*Difficult goals are more likely to lead to higher performance than are less difficult ones.* If the goals are seen as too difficult or impossible, however, the relationship with performance no longer holds. For example, you will likely perform better as a financial services agent if you have a goal of selling 6 annuities a week than if you have a goal of selling 3. But if your goal is selling 15 annuities a week, you may consider that impossible to achieve, and your performance may well be lower than what it would be with a more realistic goal.

Point—*Specific goals are more likely to lead to higher performance than are no goals or vague or very general ones.* All too often people work with very general goals such as the encouragement to "do your best." Research indicates that more specific goals, such as selling six computers a day, are much more motivational than a simple "do your best" goal.

Point—*Task feedback, or knowledge of results, is likely to motivate people toward higher performance by encouraging the setting of higher performance goals.* Feedback lets people know where they stand and whether they are on course or off course in their efforts. For example, think about how eager you are to find out how well you did on an examination.

Point—*Goals are most likely to lead to higher performance when people have the abilities and the feelings of self-efficacy required to accomplish them.* The individual must be able to accomplish the goals

How to Make Goal Setting Work for You

- *Set challenging goals:* When viewed as realistic and attainable, more difficult goals lead to higher performance than do easy goals.
- *Set specific goals:* They lead to higher performance than do more generally stated ones, such as "do your best."
- *Provide feedback on goal accomplishment:* Make sure that people know how well they are doing with respect to goal accomplishment.

- *Build goal acceptance and commitment:* People work harder for goals they accept and believe in; they resist goals forced on them.
- *Clarify goal priorities:* Make sure that expectations are clear as to which goals should be accomplished first, and why.
- *Reward goal accomplishment:* Don't let positive accomplishments pass unnoticed; reward people for doing what they set out to do.

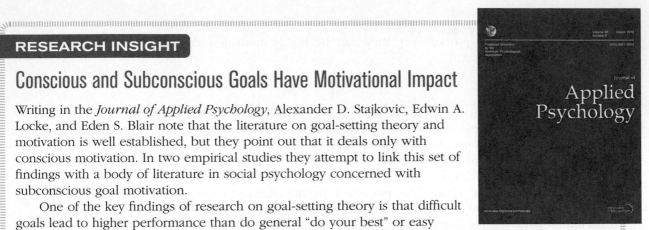

RESEARCH INSIGHT

Conscious and Subconscious Goals Have Motivational Impact

Writing in the *Journal of Applied Psychology*, Alexander D. Stajkovic, Edwin A. Locke, and Eden S. Blair note that the literature on goal-setting theory and motivation is well established, but they point out that it deals only with conscious motivation. In two empirical studies they attempt to link this set of findings with a body of literature in social psychology concerned with subconscious goal motivation.

One of the key findings of research on goal-setting theory is that difficult goals lead to higher performance than do general "do your best" or easy goals when performance feedback, goal commitment, and task knowledge are present. A research stream of social psychology literature deals with the subconscious activation of goals by primers found in environments in which goals are regularly pursued. Using this background, the researchers stated that their purpose "was to link subconscious and conscious goals by empirically examining the interaction between the two."

A pilot study and a main study were conducted with samples of undergraduate and graduate students at a university in the Midwest. Study participants were divided into two groups, with one group receiving a "priming" treatment where subjects did setup work involving identification or use of achievement-related words before they completed a performance task. In the second, or "no prime" group, only achievement-neutral words were identified or used in the setup work prior to the performance task.

In both studies the results confirmed predictions from goal-setting theory by showing that "diffi-

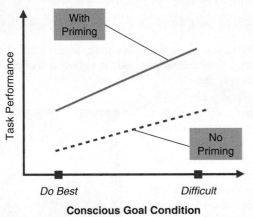

Conscious Goal Condition

cult" conscious goals increased performance relative to "easy" and "do your best" goal-setting conditions. In addition, the researchers found that subjects in primed subconscious conditions performed better than did those in unprimed subconscious conditions on both "difficult" and "do your best" goals. In other words, primed subconscious goals had positive interactions with conscious goals for both difficult and do your best goals.

The overall conclusions from these studies show that more research is needed on the links between conscious and subconscious goals with task performance. But the initial findings are favorable in suggesting that when both types of goals are used together, their motivational impact is increased.

Source: Alexander D. Stajkovic, Edwin A. Locke, and Eden S. Blair, "A First Examination of the Relationships between Primed Subconscious Goals, Assigned Conscious Goals, and Task Performance," *Journal of Applied Psychology* 91 (2006), pp. 1172–1180.

and feel confident in those abilities. To take the financial services example again, you may be able to do what is required to sell 6 annuities a week and feel confident that you can. If your goal is to sell 15, however, you may believe that your abilities are insufficient to the task, and thus you may lack the confidence to work hard enough to accomplish it.

Point—*Goals are most likely to motivate people toward higher performance when they are accepted and there is commitment to them.* Participating in the goal-setting process helps build acceptance and commitment; it creates a sense of "ownership" of the goals. But goals assigned by someone else can be equally effective when the assigners are authority figures that can have an impact, and when the subordinate can actually reach the goal. According to research, assigned goals most often lead to poor performance when they are curtly or inadequately explained.

Goal Setting and the Management Process

When we speak of goal setting and its motivational potential, the entire management process comes into play. Goals launch the process during planning, provide critical focal points for organizing and leading, and then facilitate controlling to make sure the desired outcomes are achieved. One approach that tries to integrate goals across these management functions is known as **management by objectives**. Called MBO, for short, it is essentially a process of joint goal setting between managers and those who report to them.[32] In a team setting, for example, the leader works with team members to set performance goals consistent with higher-level organizational objectives. When done throughout an organization, MBO also helps clarify the hierarchy of objectives as a series of well-defined means–ends chains.

• **Management by objectives** is a process of joint goal setting between a supervisor and a subordinate.

Figure 5.4 shows how an MBO process might utilize goal-setting principles. The joint team leader and team member discussions are designed to extend participation from the point of setting initial goals all the way to evaluating results in terms of goal attainment. As team members work to achieve their goals, the team leader's role is to actively coach them.

A fair amount of research reports some common difficulties with MBO in practice.[33] These include too much paperwork required to document goals and accomplishments, too much emphasis on goal-oriented rewards and punishments, as well as too much focus on top-down goals, goals that are easily stated and achieved, and individual instead of team goals. When these issues are resolved, managers should find that some version of this MBO approach has much to offer as an application of goal-setting theory.

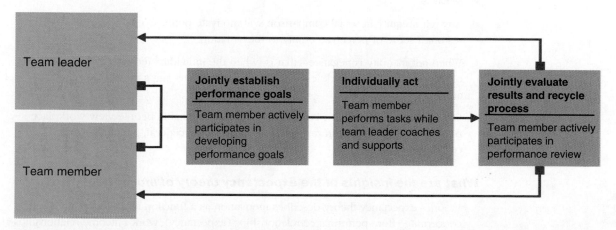

Figure 5.4 How a management by objectives process works.

5 *study guide*

Key Questions and Answers

What is motivation?

- Motivation is an internal force that accounts for the level, direction, and persistence of effort expended at work.

- Content theories—including the work of Maslow, Alderfer, McClelland, and Herzberg—focus on identifying human needs that influence behavior in the workplace.

- Process theories, such as equity theory and expectancy theory, examine the thought processes that affect decisions people make about their work efforts.

What can we learn from the needs theories of motivation?

- Maslow's hierarchy of needs theory views human needs as activated in a five-step hierarchy ranging from physiological (lowest) to safety, to social, to esteem, to self-actualization (highest).

- Alderfer's ERG theory collapses the five needs into three: existence, relatedness, and growth; it maintains that more than one need can be activated at a time.

- McClelland's acquired needs theory focuses on the needs for achievement, affiliation, and power, and it views needs as developed over time through experience and training.

- Herzberg's two-factor theory links job satisfaction to motivator factors, such as responsibility and challenge, associated with job content; it links job dissatisfaction to hygiene factors, such as pay and working conditions, associated with job context.

Why is the equity theory of motivation important?

- Equity theory points out that social comparison takes place when people receive rewards.

- Any felt inequity in social comparison will motivate people to behave in ways that restore a sense of perceived equity to the situation.

- When felt inequity is negative—that is, when the individual feels unfairly treated—he or she may decide to work less hard in the future or to quit a job for other, more attractive opportunities.

- Organizational justice is an issue of how fair and equitable people view workplace practices; it is described in respect to distributive, procedural, interactive, and commutative justice.

What are the insights of the expectancy theory of motivation?

- Vroom's expectancy theory describes motivation as a function of an individual's beliefs concerning effort–performance relationships (expectancy), work-outcome relationships (instrumentality), and the desirability of various work outcomes (valence).

- Expectancy theory states that Motivation = Expectancy × Instrumentality × Valence, and argues that managers should make each factor strong and positive in order to ensure high levels of motivation.

How does goal-setting influence motivation?

- Goal setting is the process of developing, negotiating, and formalizing performance targets or objectives.

- Goals are the most motivational when they are challenging and specific, allow for feedback on results, and create commitment and acceptance.

- Management by objectives, a process of joint goal setting between a team leader and team member, is a way of applying goal-setting theory in day-to-day management practice.

Terms to Know

Commutative justice (p. 110)
Content theories (p. 102)
Distributive justice (p. 109)
Equity theory (p. 107)
ERG theory (p. 104)
Existence needs (p. 104)
Expectancy (p. 111)
Expectancy theory (p. 111)
Goal setting (p. 113)
Growth needs (p. 104)
Hierarchy of needs theory (p. 103)

Higher-order needs (p. 104)
Hygiene factors (p. 106)
Instrumentality (p. 111)
Interactional justice (p. 110)
Job enrichment (p. 107)
Lower-order needs (p. 104)
Management by objectives, or MBO (p. 115)
Motivation (p. 102)
Motivator factors (p. 106)

Need for achievement (nAch) (p. 104)
Need for affiliation (nAff) (p. 105)
Need for power (nPower) (p. 105)
Organizational justice (p. 109)
Perceived inequity (p. 108)
Procedural justice (p. 109)
Process theories (p. 102)
Relatedness needs (p. 104)
Two-factor theory (p. 106)
Valence (p. 111)

Self-Test 5

Multiple Choice

1. Motivation is defined as the level and persistence of _____.
(a) effort (b) performance (c) need satisfaction (d) instrumentalities

2. A content theory of motivation is most likely to focus on _____.
(a) organizational justice (b) expectancy (c) equity (d) individual needs

3. A process theory of motivation is most likely to focus attention on _____.
(a) frustration–regression (b) expectancies regarding work outcomes (c) lower-order needs (d) hygiene factors

4. When a team member shows strong ego needs in Maslow's hierarchy, the team leader should find ways to link this person's work on the team task with _____.
(a) compensation tied to group performance (b) individual praise and recognition for work well done (c) lots of social interaction with other team members (d) challenging individual performance goals

5. According to McClelland, a person high in need achievement will be motivated by _____.
(a) status of being an executive (b) control and influence over other people (c) teamwork and collective responsibility (d) challenging but achievable goals

6. In Alderfer's ERG theory, the _____ needs best correspond with Maslow's higher-order needs of esteem and self-actualization.
(a) existence (b) relatedness (c) recognition (d) growth

7. Improvements in job satisfaction are most likely under Herzberg's two-factor theory when _____ are improved.
(a) working conditions (b) base salaries (c) co-worker relationships
(d) opportunities for responsibility

8. In Herzberg's two-factor theory _____ factors are found in job context.
(a) motivator (b) satisfier (c) hygiene (d) enrichment

9. Both Barry and Marissa are highly motivated college students. Knowing this I can expect them to be _____ in my class.
(a) hard working (b) high performing (c) highly satisfied (d) highly dissatisfied

10. In equity theory, the _____ is a key issue.
(a) social comparison of rewards (b) equality of rewards (c) equality of efforts
(d) absolute value of rewards

11. A manager's failure to enforce a late-to-work policy the same way for all employees is a violation of _____ justice.
(a) interactional (b) moral (c) distributive (d) procedural

12. When someone has a high and positive "expectancy" in expectancy theory of motivation, this means that the person _____.
(a) believes he or she can meet performance expectations (b) highly values the rewards being offered (c) sees a relationship between high performance and the available rewards (d) believes that rewards are equitable

13. In expectancy theory, _____ is the perceived value of a reward.
(a) expectancy (b) instrumentality (c) motivation (d) valence

14. Which goals tend to be more motivating?
(a) challenging goals (b) easy goals (c) general goals (d) no goals

15. The MBO process emphasizes _____ as a way of building worker commitment to goal accomplishment.
(a) authority (b) joint goal setting (c) infrequent feedback (d) rewards

Short Response

16. What is the frustration-regression component in Alderfer's ERG theory?

17. What does job enrichment mean in Herzberg's two-factor theory?

18. What is the difference between distributive and procedural justice?

19. What is the multiplier effect in expectancy theory?

Applications Essay

20. While attending a business luncheon, you overhear the following conversation at a nearby table. Person A: "I'll tell you this: if you satisfy your workers' needs, they'll be productive." Person B: "I'm not so sure; if I satisfy their needs, maybe they'll be real good about coming to work but not very good about working really hard while they are there." Which person do you agree with and why?

Case for Critical Thinking	Team and Experiential Exercises	Self-Assessment Portfolio
• It Isn't Fair	• What Do You Value in Work? • Teamwork and Motivation • Downsides of Punishment • Annual Pay Raises	• Managerial Assumptions • Two-Factor Profile

Los 33 Surviving on Faith Alone

Most of us know the pangs of hunger that come from missing a meal. But imagine missing breakfast, lunch, and dinner every day for two weeks. And despite having enough food to fill your belly, you intentionally limit yourself to one teaspoon of tuna each day. Could you do it?

The 33 men trapped for more than two months in a mine near Copiapó, Chile, maintained this self-discipline despite being stuck more than 3 miles underground. "As a group we had to keep faith, we had to keep hope, we had to all believe that we would survive," says Franklin Lobos, one of the miners and a former professional footballer. "We pulled together when things got rough, when there was nothing. That really bonded us."[a]

After the dust settled from the mine's collapse, the men coalesced around hard-nosed shift supervisor Luis Urzúa, a mining veteran. To keep them focused on and participating in their own survival, Urzúa divided *Los 33*, as they became known above ground, into three groups who split shifts maintaining the mine's nooks he designated as their sleeping, working, and washing areas.

> **"Life has given us a new challenge—to care more deeply, to be more present with the people we love."**
> **—Edison Pena, one of "Los 33".**[c]

Drawing on discipline learned in the Chilean military, Urzúa assigned more complex responsibilities as it became clear they would not be rescued immediately. Appropriating a pickup truck as his office, he led the men through topographically mapping their new home, regular repair of crumbling rock walls, and digging for water. To simulate night and day, he toggled the headlights of other trucks. Balancing strong leadership and democracy, Urzúa instituted a *one man, one vote* policy.

Many of the men cited a deep religious faith that divine providence would see them through. Others cited the desire to see their family and firm confidence in the rescue crew as motivating them to overcome their loneliness and worry.

Though Urzúa was the leader underground, Edison Pena has become for many the public face of the miners' personal efforts at recovery. Pena, who jogged 3 to 6 miles daily in cutoff work boots through the 1.2-mile-long halls of the mines, was invited to run the New York Marathon shortly after emerging from the depths. "I thought as I ran in the mine that I was going to beat destiny," Pena says. "I was saying to that mine, *I can outrun you. I'm going to run until you're just tired and bored of me.*"[b]

Quick Summary

- On August 26, 2010, thirty-three miners and subcontractors were trapped 3 miles underground in a collapsed mine near Copiapó, Chile.
- Shift leader Luis Urzúa quickly organized the men into three groups working 12-hour shifts to set up camp, look for escape routes, and make the best of their unforeseen accommodations.
- Psychologists credit the men's active participation in their own survival, as well as Urzúa's leadership, for keeping relative peace and solidarity during their 69 days in the mine.

FYI: 4,052,459—Number of Web page views per minute when news broke of the early start to the miners' rescue.[d]

6 Motivation and Performance

the key point

There was a lot going on with motivation and performance as Los 33 struggled together for survival in the Chilean mine. It's really the same in our busy multitasking world where work, family, and leisure are often intertwined. There's much to consider when trying to build high-performance work settings that also fit well with individual needs and goals.

chapter at a glance

What Is the Link Between Motivation, Rewards, and Performance?

What Are the Essentials of Performance Management?

How Do Job Designs Influence Motivation and Performance?

What Are the Motivational Opportunities of Alternative Work Arrangements?

ETHICS IN OB
MOTIVATION AND PERFORMANCE

FINDING THE LEADER IN YOU
SARA BLAKELY LEADS SPANX FROM IDEA TO THE BOTTOM LINE

OB IN POPULAR CULTURE
INTRINSIC/EXTRINSIC REWARDS AND NEW BALANCE

what's inside?

RESEARCH INSIGHT
RACIAL BIAS MAY EXIST IN SUPERVISOR RATINGS OF WORKERS

Motivation and Rewards

LEARNING ROADMAP   Integrated Model of Motivation / Intrinsic and Extrinsic Rewards / Pay for Performance

• **Motivation** accounts for the level and persistence of a person's effort expended at work.

Motivation was defined in Chapter 5 as forces within the individual that account for the level and persistence of an effort expended at work. In other words and as shown in the figure, motivation predicts effort. But because motivation is a property of the individual, all that managers can do is try to create work environments within which someone finds sources of motivation. As the theories in the last chapter suggest, a major key to achieving this is to build into the job and work setting a set of rewards that match well with individual needs and goals.

Integrated Model of Motivation

Figure 6.1 outlines an integrated model of motivation, one that ties together much of the previous discussion regarding the basic effort → performance → rewards relationship. Note that the figure shows job performance and satisfaction as separate but potentially interdependent work results. Performance, as first discussed in the last chapter, is influenced by *individual attributes* such as ability and experience; *organizational support* such as resources and technology; and *effort*, or the willingness of someone to work hard at what they are doing. Satisfaction results when rewards received for work accomplishments are performance contingent and perceived as equitable.

Double-check Figure 6.1 and locate where various motivation theories come into play. Reinforcement theory highlights the importance of performance contingency and immediacy in determining how rewards affect future performance. Equity theory is an issue in the perceived fairness of rewards. The content theories are useful guides to understanding individual needs that give motivational value to the possible rewards. And, expectancy theory is central to the effort → performance → reward linkage.

Intrinsic and Extrinsic Rewards

Wouldn't it be nice if we could all connect with our jobs and organizations in positive and inspirational ways? In fact, there are lots of great workplaces out there, and they become great because the managers at all levels of responsibility do things that end up turning people on to their jobs rather than off of them. This requires a good understanding of the links between motivation theories and their

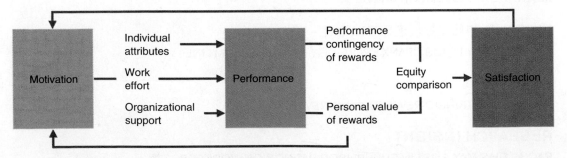

Figure 6.1 An integrated model of individual motivation to work.

Finding the Leader in You

SARA BLAKELY LEADS SPANX FROM IDEA TO THE BOTTOM LINE

"Like so many women, I bought clothes that looked amazing in a magazine or the hanger, but in reality . . . ." The words are Sara Blakely's, and her concerns led to product innovation, entrepreneurship, and ultimately, a successful big business—Spanx. With $5,000 of her own money and a new idea for "body shaping" underwear, she cut the feet out of a pair of pantyhose and never looked back.

When her first attempts to convince manufacturers to make

product samples met with resistance—with one calling it "a stupid idea"—she persisted until one agreed. She aspired to place Spanx in "high end" department stores. But again, she didn't give up, finally persuading a Neiman-Marcus buyer to sell them. Blakely kept at it, traveling extensively and energetically, some might say exhaustively. "I'm the face of the brand," she says, "and we didn't have money to advertise. I had to be out. Sitting in the office wasn't helping." She sent Oprah Winfrey samples and with her endorsement as "one of her favorite things" sales and the firm took off.

After about a year of fast-paced growth, Blakely turned operations over to a chief executive officer. This left her free to pursue creative efforts, new products, and brand development. She says

that she recognized her limits and "was eager to delegate my weaknesses." It worked. She won the national Entrepreneur of the Year Award and was voted Georgia's Woman of the Year. Her motivation to succeed extends beyond product and business goals alone. She has since started the Sara Blakely Foundation with the express purpose of "supporting and empowering women around the world."

What's the Lesson Here?

Blakely's success story obviously began with having a great product idea. But it's also tied to who she is as a person. Where would she be today without her special personality? What about her persistence in the face of adversity? What role did goal-setting play in her journey to success? Can you combine qualities like these with your ideas to build a motivational capacity for long-term career achievement?

applications. Knowing the motivation theories is part of the story. The rest involves using them to make rewards meaningful as motivational opportunities that appeal to people in all the rich diversity of their individual differences.

The typical reward systems of organizations emphasize a mix of intrinsic and extrinsic rewards. **Intrinsic rewards** are positively valued work outcomes that the individual receives directly as a result of task performance. These rewards were the foundations for Herzberg's concept of job enrichment discussed in the last chapter. He believes that people are turned on and motivated by high content jobs that are rich in intrinsic rewards. A feeling of achievement after completing a particularly challenging task with a good person–job fit is an example. You might think of it this way: Yves Chouinard, founder and CEO of Patagonia, Inc., says that "It's easy to go to work when you get paid to do what you love to do."[1]

Extrinsic rewards are positively valued work outcomes that are given to an individual or a group by some other person or source in the work setting. They might include things like sincere praise for a job well done or symbolic tokens of accomplishment such as "employee-of-the-month" awards. Importantly too, anything dealing with compensation, or the pay and benefits one receives at work,

• **Intrinsic rewards** are valued outcomes received directly through task performance.

• **Extrinsic rewards** are valued outcomes given by some other person.

INTRINSIC/EXTRINSIC REWARDS AND NEW BALANCE

Intrinsic rewards are received directly from task performance. For example, the satisfaction that comes from completing a challenging task would be an intrinsic reward. **Extrinsic rewards**, on the other hand, are derived from factors external to the job. The most common extrinsic reward is pay. While both types have positive value, extrinsic rewards typically are not as motivating because they leave the worker feeling compelled to complete a task rather than desiring to do it for sheer enjoyment.

In a popular New Balance shoe commercial, groups of high school athletes remind professional athletes about the "little things" in sports, such as floor burn, bunting, and training at dawn. The commercial ends with a statement and two questions for the professional athletes. "There are two motivations in sports. Which is yours? For love or money?"

The difference implied in this commercial is that professional athletes play sports because of the extrinsic rewards, and thus are not as motivated to do the little things, while high school athletes are motivated by intrinsic rewards. It is an important distinction for those who believe money is an effective motivator.

Get to Know Yourself Better   Take a look at Experiential Exercise 16, Motivation by Job Enrichment, in your OB Skills Workbook. Review the list of jobs. What would motivate you to do each of them? In all likelihood, your first job will not be your dream job. Now consider this. Which would you rather have—a job that is not exciting but pays really well or one that you thoroughly enjoy doing but may not provide a lavish lifestyle?

is an extrinsic reward. And like all extrinsic rewards, pay and benefits have to be well managed for positive motivational impact. How often have you heard someone say: "I'll do what I can to keep this job; the pay and benefits are unbeatable"?

Pay for Performance

Pay is not only an important extrinsic reward; it is an especially complex one. When pay functions well it can help an organization attract and retain highly capable workers. It can also help satisfy and motivate these workers to work hard to achieve high performance. But when something goes wrong with pay, the results may well be negative effects on motivation performance. Pay dissatisfaction is often reflected in bad attitudes, increased absenteeism, intentions to leave and actual turnover, poor organizational citizenship, and even adverse impacts on employees' physical and mental health.

- The essence of **performance-contingent pay** is that you earn more when you produce more and earn less when you produce less.

- **Merit pay** links an individual's salary or wage increase directly to measures of performance accomplishment.

The research of scholar and consultant Edward Lawler generally concludes that pay only serves as a motivator when high levels of job performance are viewed as the paths through which high pay can be achieved.[2] This is the essence of **performance-contingent pay** or pay for performance. It basically means that you earn more when you produce more and earn less when you produce less.

Merit Pay   It is most common to talk about pay for performance in respect to **merit pay**, a compensation system that directly ties an individual's salary or wage increase to measures of performance accomplishments during a specified time period.

Although the concept of merit pay is compelling, a survey by the Hudson Institute demonstrates that it is more easily said than done. When asked if employees who do perform better really get paid more, only 48 percent of managers and 31 percent of nonmanagers responded with agreement. And when asked if their last pay raise had been based on performance, 46 percent of managers and just 29 percent of nonmanagers said yes.[3] In fact, surveys over the past 30 or so years have found that as many as 80 percent of respondents felt that they were not rewarded for a job well done.[4]

To work well, a merit pay plan should create a belief among employees that the way to achieve high pay is to perform at high levels. This means that the merit system should be based on realistic and accurate measures of work performance. It means that the merit system should clearly discriminate between high and low performers in the amount of pay increases awarded. And it also means that any "merit" aspects of a pay increase are not confused with across-the-board "cost-of-living" adjustments.

Although well supported in theory, merit pay is also subject to criticisms. For example, merit pay plans may cause problems when they emphasize individual achievements and fail to recognize the high degree of task interdependence that is common in many organizations today. Also, if they are to be effective, merit pay systems must be consistent with overall organization strategies and environmental challenges. For example, a firm facing a tight labor market with a limited supply of highly skilled individuals might benefit more from a pay system that emphasizes employee retention rather than strict performance results.[5]

ETHICS IN OB

DRIVE TOWARD PRESENTEEISM AFFECTS BUSINESS

You wake up and you're feeling even worse than the day before. Sniffling, sneezing, coughing, you make your way to work, hoping to get through the day as best as you can. Fine, but what about everyone whom you'll come into contact with that day, and what about the impact your *presenteeism*—basically meaning that you go to work sick—can have on office productivity and your co-workers' and customers' lives in general?

Brett Gorovsky of CCH, a business information resource, says that when people come to work sick it "can take a very real hit on the bottom line." His firm reports that 56 percent of executives in one poll considered this a problem; that figure is up some 17 percent in a two-year period. Estimates are that the cost of lost productivity is as much as $180 billion annually. Just think of the costs of swine flu season.

WebMD reports a study claiming that the cost of lost productivity could be higher than what might be paid out in authorized sick days. But the fact remains: Many of us work sick because we have to if we want to be paid.

You Tell Us   What are the ethics of coming to work sick and sharing our illnesses with others? And from the management side of things, what are the ethics of not providing benefits sufficient to allow employees to stay home from work when they aren't feeling well?

- **Bonuses** are extra pay awards for special performance accomplishments.

Bonuses   Some employers award cash **bonuses** as extra pay for performance that meets certain benchmarks or is above expectations. The practice is especially common in senior executive ranks. Top managers in some industries earn annual bonuses of 50 percent or more of their base salaries. One of the motivational trends is to extend such opportunities to workers at all levels, and in both managerial and nonmanagerial jobs. Employees at Applebee's, for example, may earn "Applebucks"—small cash bonuses that are given to reward performance and increase loyalty to the firm.[6]

- **Gain sharing** rewards employees in some proportion to productivity gains.

- **Profit sharing** rewards employees in some proportion to changes in organizational profits.

Gain Sharing and Profit Sharing   Another way to link pay with performance is **gain sharing**. This gives workers the opportunity to earn more by receiving shares of any productivity gains that they help to create. Gain sharing plans are supposed to create a greater sense of personal responsibility for organizational performance improvements and increase motivation to work hard. They are also supposed to encourage cooperation and teamwork to increase productivity.[7]

Instead of rewarding employees for specific productivity gains, **profit sharing** rewards them for increased organizational profits. The more profits made, the more money that is available for distribution to employees through profit sharing.[8] Of course when profits are lower, individuals earn less due to reduced profit-sharing returns. And indeed, one criticism of the approach is that profit increases and decreases are not always a direct result of employees' efforts. Many other factors, including a bad economy, can come into play. In such cases the question is whether it is right or wrong for workers to earn less because of circumstances beyond their control.

- **Stock options** give the right to purchase shares at a fixed price in the future.

Stock Options and Employee Stock Ownership   Another way to link pay and performance is for a company to offer its employees **stock options**.[9] These options give the owner the right to buy shares of stock at a future date at a fixed or "strike" price. The expectation is that employees with stock options will be highly motivated to do their best so that the firm performs well, because they gain financially as the stock price increases. However, as the recent economic downturn reminded us, the value of the options an employee holds can decline or even zero out when the stock price falls.

- **Employee stock ownership plans** give stock to employees or allow them to purchase stock at special prices.

In **employee stock ownership plans**, or ESOPs, companies may give stock to employees or allow stock to be purchased by them at a price below market value. The incentive value of the stock awards or purchases is like the stock options. "Employee owners" should be motivated to work hard so that the organization will perform well, its stock price will rise, and as owners they will benefit from the gains. Of course, the company's stock prices can fall as well as rise.[10] During the economic crisis many people who had invested heavily in their employer's stock were hurt substantially.

- **Skill-based pay** rewards people for acquiring and developing job-relevant skills.

Skill-Based Pay   Still another alternative is to pay people according to the skills they possess, develop, and use for job performance. **Skill-based pay** rewards people for acquiring and developing job-relevant skills. Pay systems of this sort pay people for the mix and depth of skills they have, not for the particular job assignment they hold. Some advantages of skill-based pay are employee cross-training—workers learn to do one another's jobs; fewer supervisors—workers can provide more of these functions themselves; and more individual control over compensation—workers know in advance what is required to receive a pay raise. A possible disadvantage is that higher pay and training costs are not offset by greater productivity.[11]

Motivation and Performance Management

LEARNING ROADMAP Performance Management Process / Performance Measurement Methods / Performance Measurement Errors

If you want to get hired by Procter & Gamble and make it to the upper management levels, you had better be good. Not only is the company highly selective in hiring, it also carefully tracks the performance of every manager in every job they are asked to do. The firm always has at least three performance-proven replacements ready to fill any vacancy that occurs. And by linking performance to career advancement, motivation to work hard is built into the P&G management model.[12]

The effort → performance → reward relationship is evident in the P&G management approach. However, we shouldn't underestimate the challenge of managing any such performance-based reward system. As mentioned earlier, performance must be measured in ways that are accurate and respected by everyone involved. When the performance measurement fails, the motivational value of any pay or reward systems will fail as well.

Performance Management Process

The foundation for any performance management system is performance measurement as shown in Figure 6.2. And if performance measurement is to be done well, managers must have good answers to both the "Why?" and the "What?" questions.

The "Why?" question in performance management involves two purposes. Performance management serves an *evaluation purpose* when it lets people know where their actual performance stands relative to objectives and standards. Such an evaluation feeds into decisions that allocate rewards and otherwise administer

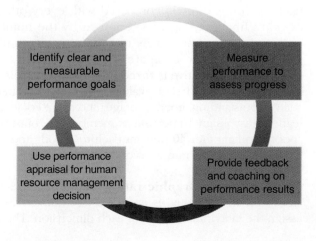

Figure 6.2 Four steps in the performance management process.

the organization's human resource management systems. Performance management serves a *developmental purpose* when it provides insights into individual strengths and weaknesses. This can be used to plan helpful training and career development activities.

The "What?" question in performance management takes us back to the old adage "what gets measured happens." It basically argues that people will do what they know is going to be measured. Given this, managers are well advised to always make sure they are measuring the right things in the right ways in the performance management process. Measurements should be based on clear job performance criteria, be accurate in assessing performance, provide a defensible basis for differentiating between high and low performance, and be useful as feedback that can help improve performance in the future.

* **Output measures** of performance assess achievements in terms of actual work results.
* **Activity measures** of performance assess inputs in terms of work efforts.

Output measures of performance assess what is accomplished in respect to concrete work results. For example, a software developer might be measured on the number of lines of code written a day or on the number of lines written that require no corrections upon testing. **Activity measures** of performance assess work inputs in respect to activities tried and efforts expended. These are often used when output measures are difficult and in cases where certain activities are known to be good predictors of eventual performance success. An example might be the use of number of customer visits made per day by a salesperson, instead of or in addition to counting the number of actual sales made.

Performance Measurement Methods

The formal procedure for measuring and documenting a person's work performance is often called *performance appraisal* or *performance assessment*. As might be expected, there are a variety of alternative performance measurement methods. They each have strengths and weaknesses that make them more appropriate for use in some situations than others.[13]

* **Ranking** in performance appraisal orders each person from best to worst.
* **Paired comparison** in performance appraisal compares each person with every other.

Comparative Methods   Comparative methods of performance measurement seek to identify one worker's standing relative to others. **Ranking** is the simplest approach and is done by rank ordering each individual from best to worst on overall performance or on specific performance dimensions. Although relatively simple to use, this method can be difficult when there are many people to consider. An alternative is the **paired comparison** in which each person is directly compared with every other person being rated. Each person's final ranking is determined by the number of pairs for which they emerged the "winner." This method also gets quite complicated when there are many people to compare.

* **Forced distribution** in performance appraisal forces a set percentage of persons into predetermined rating categories.
* **Graphic rating scales** in performance appraisal assigns scores to specific performance dimensions.

Another alternative is **forced distribution**. This method forces a set percentage of all persons being evaluated into predetermined performance categories such as outstanding, good, average, and poor. For example, it might be that a team leader must assign 10 percent of members to "outstanding," another 10 percent to "poor," and another 40 percent each to "good" and "average." This method eliminates tendencies to rate everyone about the same.

Rating Scales   **Graphic rating scales** list a variety of performance dimensions that an individual is expected to exhibit. The scales allow the manager to assign the individual scores on each dimension. The example in Figure 6.3 shows

Employee: _Jayne Burroughs_   **Supervisor:** _Dr. Cutter_
Department: _Pathology_   **Date:** _11-28_

Work Quantity		Work Quality		Cooperation	
1. Far below average	—	1. Far below average	—	1. Far below average	—
2. Below average	✓	2. Below average	—	2. Below average	✓
3. Average	—	3. Average	✓	3. Average	—
4. Above average	—	4. Above average	—	4. Above average	—
5. Far above average	—	5. Far above average	—	5. Far above average	—

Figure 6.3 Sample six-month performance reviews using graphic rating scale.

that the primary appeal of graphic rating scales is ease of use. But, because of generality they may lack real performance links to a given job.

The **behaviorally anchored rating scale** (BARS) adds more sophistication by linking ratings to specific and observable job-relevant behaviors. These include descriptions of superior and inferior performance. A sample BARS for a customer service representative is shown in Figure 6.4. Note the specificity of the behaviors and the scale values for each. Similar behaviorally anchored scales would be developed for other dimensions of the job. Even though the BARS approach is detailed and complex, and requires time to develop, it can provide specific behavioral information useful for both evaluation and development purposes.[14]

Critical Incident Diary   **Critical incident diaries** are written records that give examples of a person's work behavior that leads to either unusual performance

- The **behaviorally anchored rating scale** links performance ratings to specific and observable job-relevant behaviors.

- **Critical incident diaries** record actual examples of positive and negative work behaviors and results.

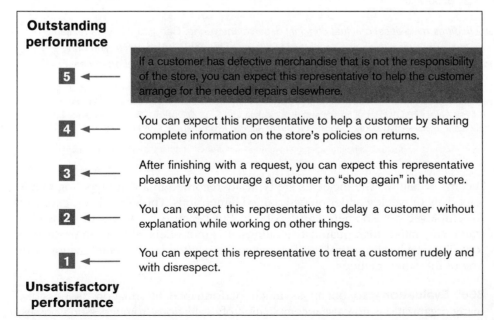

Outstanding performance

5 ← If a customer has defective merchandise that is not the responsibility of the store, you can expect this representative to help the customer arrange for the needed repairs elsewhere.

4 ← You can expect this representative to help a customer by sharing complete information on the store's policies on returns.

3 ← After finishing with a request, you can expect this representative pleasantly to encourage a customer to "shop again" in the store.

2 ← You can expect this representative to delay a customer without explanation while working on other things.

1 ← You can expect this representative to treat a customer rudely and with disrespect.

Unsatisfactory performance

Figure 6.4 Sample performance appraisal dimension from the behaviorally anchored rating scale for a customer service representative.

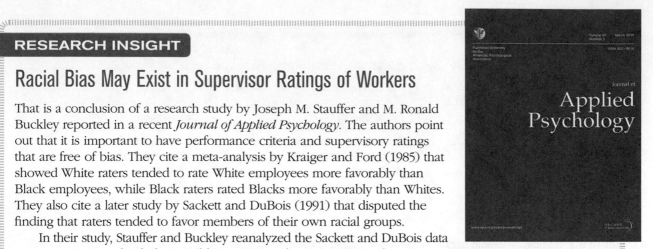

RESEARCH INSIGHT

Racial Bias May Exist in Supervisor Ratings of Workers

That is a conclusion of a research study by Joseph M. Stauffer and M. Ronald Buckley reported in a recent *Journal of Applied Psychology*. The authors point out that it is important to have performance criteria and supervisory ratings that are free of bias. They cite a meta-analysis by Kraiger and Ford (1985) that showed White raters tended to rate White employees more favorably than Black employees, while Black raters rated Blacks more favorably than Whites. They also cite a later study by Sackett and DuBois (1991) that disputed the finding that raters tended to favor members of their own racial groups.

In their study, Stauffer and Buckley reanalyzed the Sackett and DuBois data to pursue in more depth the possible interactions between rater and ratee race. The data included samples of military and civilian workers, each of whom was rated by Black and White supervisors. Their findings are that in both samples White supervisors gave significantly higher ratings to White workers than they did to Black workers, while Black supervisors also tended to favor White workers in their ratings.

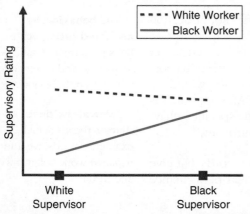

Stauffer and Buckley advise caution in interpreting these results as meaning that the rating differences are the result of racial prejudice; instead they maintain that the data aren't sufficient to address this issue. The researchers call for additional studies designed to further examine both the existence of bias in supervisory ratings and the causes of such bias. In terms of workplace implications, however, the authors are quite definitive: "If you are a White ratee then it doesn't matter if your supervisor is Black or White. If you are a Black ratee, then it is important whether your supervisor is Black or White."

Do the Research *These findings raise questions that certainly deserve answering. Can you design a research study that could discover whether or not racial bias affects instructor ratings of students? Also, when you bring this issue up with family and friends, do their experiences seem to support or deny the findings reported here?*

Source: Joseph M. Stauffer and M. Ronald Buckley, "The Existence and Nature of Racial Bias in Supervisory Ratings," *Journal of Applied Psychology* 90 (2005), pp. 586–591. Also cited: K. Kraiger and J. K. Ford, "A Meta-analysis of Ratee Race Effects in Performance Ratings," *Journal of Applied Psychology* 70 (1985), pp. 56–65; and, P. R. Sackett and C. L. Z. DuBois, "Rater-Ratee Race Effects on Performance Evaluations: Challenging Meta-Analytic Conclusions," *Journal of Applied Psychology* 76 (1991), pp. 873–877.

success or failure. The incidents are typically recorded in a diary-type log that is kept daily or weekly under predetermined dimensions. This approach is excellent for employee development and feedback. But because it consists of qualitative statements rather than quantitative ratings, it is more debatable as an evaluation tool. This is why the critical incident technique is often used in combination with one of the other methods.

360° Evaluation   To obtain as much performance information as possible, many organizations now use a combination of evaluations from a person's bosses, peers, and subordinates, as well as internal and external customers and self-ratings. Such a comprehensive approach is called a **360° evaluation**, and it is very common now in horizontal and team-oriented organization structures.[15] The 360° evaluation has also moved online with software that both collects and organizes the results of ratings from multiple sources. A typical approach asks the jobholder to do a self-rating and then discuss with the boss and perhaps a sample of the 360° participants the implications from both evaluation and counseling perspectives.

* A **360° evaluation** gathers evaluations from a jobholder's bosses, peers, and subordinates, as well as internal and external customers and self-ratings.

Performance Measurement Errors

Regardless of the method being employed, any performance measurement system should meet two criteria: **reliability**—providing consistent results each time it is used for the same person and situation, and **validity**—actually measuring dimensions with direct relevance to job performance. The following are examples of measurement errors that can reduce the reliability or validity of any performance measure.[16]

* **Reliability** means a performance measure gives consistent results.
* **Validity** means a performance measure addresses job-relevant dimensions.

* *Halo error*—results when one person rates another person on several different dimensions and gives a similar rating for each dimension.
* *Leniency error*—just as some professors are known as "easy A's," some managers tend to give relatively high ratings to virtually everyone under their supervision; the opposite is *strictness error*—giving everyone a low rating.
* *Central tendency error*—occurs when managers lump everyone together around the average, or middle, category; this gives the impression that there are no very good or very poor performers on the dimensions being rated.
* *Recency error*—occurs when a rater allows recent events to influence a performance rating over earlier events; an example is being critical of an employee who is usually on time but shows up one hour late for work the day before his or her performance rating.
* *Personal bias error*—displays expectations and prejudices that fail to give the jobholder complete respect, such as showing racial bias in ratings.

Motivation and Job Design

LEARNING ROADMAP Scientific Management / Job Enlargement and Job Rotation / Job Enrichment / Job Characteristics Model

When it comes to motivation, we might say that nothing beats a good person–job fit. This means that the job requirements fit well with individual abilities and needs. By contrast, a poor person–job fit is likely to cause performance problems and be somewhat demotivating for the worker. You might think of the goal this way:

Person + Good Job Fit = Motivation

Job design is the process through which managers plan and specify job tasks and the work arrangements that allow them to be accomplished.[17] Figure 6.5 shows three major alternative job design approaches, and also indicates how they differ in how tasks are defined and in the availability of intrinsic rewards. The

* **Job design** is the process of specifying job tasks and work arrangements.

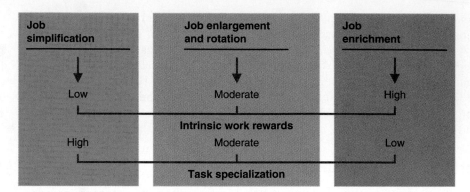

Figure 6.5 A continuum of job design strategies.

"best" job design is always one that meets organizational requirements for high performance, offers a good fit with individual skills and needs, and provides valued opportunities for job satisfaction.

Scientific Management

- Taylor's **scientific management** used systematic study of job components to develop practices to increase people's efficiency at work.

The history of scholarly interest in job design can be traced in part to Frederick Taylor's work with **scientific management** in the early 1900s.[18] Taylor and his contemporaries wanted to create management and organizational practices that would increase people's efficiency at work. Their approach was to study a job carefully, break it into its smallest components, establish exact time and motion requirements for each task to be done, and then train workers to do these tasks in the same way over and over again. Taylor's principles of scientific management can be summarized as follows:

1. Develop a "science" for each job that covers rules of motion, standard work tools, and supportive work conditions.
2. Hire workers with the right abilities for the job.
3. Train and motivate workers to do their jobs according to the science.
4. Support workers by planning and assisting their work using the job science.

These early efforts were forerunners of current industrial engineering approaches to job design that emphasize efficiency. Such approaches attempt to determine the best processes, methods, workflow layouts, output standards, and person–machine interfaces for various jobs. A good example is found at United Parcel Service (UPS), where calibrated productivity standards carefully guide workers. After analyzing delivery stops on regular van routes, supervisors generally know within a few minutes how long a driver's pickups and deliveries will take. Engineers devise precise routines for drivers, who save time by knocking on customers' doors rather than looking for doorbells. Handheld computers further enhance delivery efficiencies.

- **Job simplification** standardizes work to create clearly defined and highly specialized tasks.

Today, the term **job simplification** is used to describe a scientific management approach to job design that standardizes work procedures and employs people in routine, clearly defined, and highly specialized tasks. The machine-paced automobile assembly line is a classic example. Why is it used? The answer is increased operating efficiency gained by reducing the number of skills required to do a job, being able to hire low-cost labor, keeping the needs for job training

Burgers and Benefits Are Good at In-N-Out Burger

The work is typical fast-food routine, but the California-based hamburger chain pays employees above-average salaries, gives part-timers paid vacation, and provides full-timers with 401(K) and health insurance plans. Most managers come from the ranks, and the firm has one of the lowest turnover rates in the industry.

to a minimum, and emphasizing the accomplishment of repetitive tasks. But, the very nature of such jobs creates potential disadvantages as well—lower work quality, high rates of absenteeism and turnover, and demand for higher wages to compensate for unappealing jobs. One response to such problems is replacing people with technology. In automobile manufacturing, for example, robots now do many different kinds of work previously accomplished with human labor.

Job Enlargement and Job Rotation

Although job simplification makes the limited number of tasks easier to master, the repetitiveness can reduce motivation. This has prompted alternative job design approaches that try to make jobs more interesting by adding breadth to the variety of tasks performed.

Job enlargement increases task variety by combining into one job two or more tasks that were previously assigned to separate workers. Sometimes called *horizontal loading,* this approach increases job breadth by having the worker perform more and different tasks, but all at the same level of responsibility and challenge.

Job rotation increases task variety by periodically shifting workers among jobs involving different tasks. Also a form of horizontal-loading, the responsibility level of the tasks stays the same. The rotation can be arranged according to almost any time schedule, such as hourly, daily, or weekly schedules. An important benefit of job rotation is training. It allows workers to become more familiar with different tasks and increases the flexibility with which they can be moved from one job to another.

* **Job enlargement** increases task variety by combining into one job two or more tasks that were previously assigned to separate workers.
* **Job rotation** increases task variety by periodically shifting workers among jobs involving different tasks.

Job Enrichment

A third job design alternative traces back to Frederick Herzberg's two-factor theory of motivation described in Chapter 5. This theory suggests that jobs designed on the basis of simplification, enlargement, or rotation shouldn't be expected to deliver high levels of motivation.[19] "Why," asks Herzberg, "should a worker become motivated when one or more 'meaningless' tasks are added to previously existing ones or when work assignments are rotated among equally 'meaningless' tasks?" He recommends using **job enrichment** to build high-content jobs full of motivating factors such as responsibility, achievement, recognition, and personal growth.

* **Job enrichment** builds high-content jobs that involve planning and evaluating duties normally done by supervisors.

The content changes made possible by job enrichment involve what Herzberg calls *vertical loading* to increase job depth. This essentially means that planning and evaluating tasks normally performed by supervisors are pulled down into the job to make it bigger. Such enriched jobs, he believes, satisfy higher-order needs and increase motivation to achieve high levels of job performance.

Job Characteristics Model

OB scholars have been reluctant to recommend job enrichment as a universal solution to all job performance and satisfaction problems, particularly given the many individual differences among people at work. Their answer to the question "Is job enrichment for everyone?" is a clear "No." Present thinking focuses more on a diagnostic approach to job design developed by Richard Hackman and Greg Oldham.[20] Their job characteristics model provides a data-based approach for creating job designs with good person–job fits that maximize the potential for motivation and performance.

Core Characteristics   Figure 6.6 shows how the Hackman and Oldham model informs the process of job design. The higher a job scores on each of these five core characteristics, the higher its motivational potential and the more it is considered to be enriched.[21]

- *Skill variety*—the degree to which a job includes a variety of different activities and involves the use of a number of different skills and talents
- *Task identity*—the degree to which the job requires completion of a "whole" and identifiable piece of work, one that involves doing a job from beginning to end with a visible outcome
- *Task significance*—the degree to which the job is important and involves a meaningful contribution to the organization or society in general
- *Autonomy*—the degree to which the job gives the employee substantial freedom, independence, and discretion in scheduling the work and determining the procedures used in carrying it out
- *Job feedback*—the degree to which carrying out the work activities provides direct and clear information to the employee regarding how well the job has been done

Psychological Empowerment   A job's motivating potential can be raised by combining tasks to create larger jobs, opening feedback channels to enable workers to know how well they are doing, establishing client relationships to experience such feedback directly from customers, and employing vertical loading to create more planning and controlling responsibilities. When the core characteristics are enriched in these ways, the job creates what is often called **psychological empowerment**—a sense of personal fulfillment and purpose that arouses one's feelings of competency and commitment to the work.[22] Figure 6.6 identifies three critical psychological states that have a positive impact on individual motivation, performance, and satisfaction: (1) experienced meaningfulness of the work, (2) experienced responsibility for the outcomes of the work, and (3) knowledge of actual results of the work.

• **Psychological empowerment** is a sense of personal fulfillment and purpose that arouses one's feelings of competency and commitment to work.

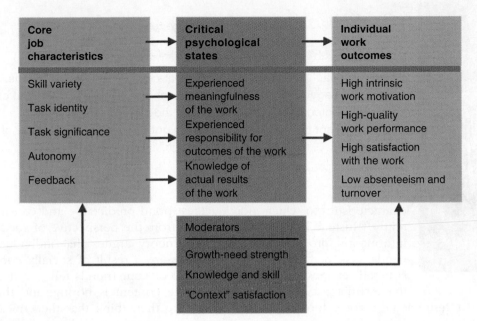

Figure 6.6 Job design considerations according to the job characteristics theory.

Moderator Variables   The five core job characteristics do not affect all people in the same way. Rather than accept Herzberg's implication that enriched jobs should be good for everyone, Hackman and Oldham suggest that enriched jobs will lead to positive outcomes only for those persons who are a good match for them, the person–job fit again. When the fit between the person and an enriched job is poor, positive outcomes are less likely and problems are more likely. "Fit" in the job characteristics model is viewed from the perspective of three moderators shown in Figure 6.6.

The first moderator variable is *growth-need strength*, or the degree to which a person desires the opportunity for self-direction, learning, and personal accomplishment at work. It is similar to Abraham Maslow's esteem and self-actualization needs and Alderfer's growth needs, as discussed in Chapter 5. The expectation here is that people high in growth-need strengths will respond positively to enriched jobs, whereas people low in growth-need strengths will find enriched jobs to be sources of anxiety.

The second moderator is *knowledge and skill*. People whose capabilities fit the demands of enriched jobs are predicted to feel good about them and perform well. Those who are inadequate or who feel inadequate in this regard are likely to experience difficulties. The third moderator is *context satisfaction*, or the extent to which an employee is satisfied with aspects of the work setting such as salary levels, quality of supervision, relationships with co-workers, and working conditions. In general, people who are satisfied with job context are more likely to do well in enriched jobs.

Research Questions and Answers   Experts generally agree that the job characteristics model and its diagnostic approach are useful, although not perfect, guides to job design.[23] One note of caution is raised by Gerald Salancik and Jeffrey Pfeffer, who question whether jobs have stable and objective

Craft Work Leads to Personal Fulfillment at Phoenix Bats

Charlie Trudeau used to make baseball bats for himself and his friends. Now major leaguers are his customers. Each bat is made by hand out of carefully selected wood and designed to the player's needs. Says Charlie, "it's got to have the right feel, it's got to have the right center of balance, and . . . there is no perfect design."

characteristics to which individuals respond predictably and consistently.[24] Instead, they view job design from the perspective of social information processing theory. This theory argues that individual needs, task perceptions, and reactions are a result of socially constructed realities. Suppose that several of your friends tell you that the instructor for a course is bad, the content is boring, and the requirements involve too much work. You may then think that the critical characteristics of the class are the instructor, the content, and the workload, and that they are all bad. All of this may substantially influence the way you perceive your instructor and the course, and the way you deal with the class— regardless of the actual characteristics.

Finally, research suggests the following answers for two common questions about job enrichment and its applications. *Should everyone's job be enriched?* The answer is clearly no. The logic of individual differences suggests that not everyone will want an enriched job. Individuals most likely to have positive reactions to job enrichment are those who need achievement, who exhibit a strong work ethic, or who are seeking higher-order growth-need satisfaction at work. Job enrichment also appears to work best when the job context is positive and when workers have the abilities needed to do the enriched job. Costs, technological constraints, and workgroup or union opposition may also make it difficult to enrich some jobs. *Can job enrichment apply to groups?* The answer is yes. The self-managing teams discussed in Chapter 7 are good examples.

Alternative Work Schedules

LEARNING ROADMAP Compressed Workweeks / Flexible Working Hours / Job Sharing / Telecommuting / Part-Time Work

New work arrangements are reshaping the traditional 40-hour week, with its 9-to-5 schedules and work done at the company or place of business. Virtually all such plans are designed to improve satisfaction by helping employees balance the demands of their work and nonwork lives.[25] They are important as concerns for "work–life balance" and more "family-friendly" employers are growing ever more apparent. If you have any doubts at all, consider these facts: 78 percent of American couples are dual wage earners; 63 percent believe they don't have enough time for spouses and partners; 74 percent believe they don't have enough time for their children; 35 percent are spending time caring for elderly relatives. Both Baby Boomers (87%) and Gen Ys (89%) rate flexible work as important; they also want opportunities to work remotely at least part of the time—Boomers (63%) and Gen Ys (69%).[26]

Compressed Workweeks

A **compressed workweek** is any scheduling of work that allows a full-time job to be completed in fewer than the standard five days. The most common form of compressed workweek is the "4/40," or 40 hours of work accomplished in four 10-hour days.

> • A **compressed workweek** allows a full-time job to be completed in fewer than the standard five days.

This arrangement has many possible benefits. For the worker, additional time off provides increased leisure time, three-day weekends, free weekdays to pursue personal business, and lower commuting costs. For the organization there may be less absenteeism and improved recruiting of new employees.[27] But there are potential disadvantages as well. Individuals can experience increased fatigue from the extended workday and have family adjustment problems. Work scheduling can be more complicated for the organization, and customers may complain because of breaks in work coverage. Union opposition to the longer workday is also a possibility, and laws requiring payment of overtime for work exceeding 8 hours of individual labor in any one day.

> • **Flexible working hours** gives individuals some amount of choice in scheduling their daily work hours.

Flexible Working Hours

Another innovative work schedule, **flexible working hours** or *flextime,* gives individuals a daily choice in the timing of their work commitments. A typical schedule requires employees to work certain hours of "core" time but leaves them free to choose their remaining hours from flexible time blocks. One person, for example, may start early and leave early, whereas another may start later and leave later.

All top 100 companies in *Working Mother* magazine's list of best employers for working moms offer flexible scheduling. Reports indicate that flexibility in dealing with nonwork obligations reduces stress and unwanted job turnover.[28] It can help reduce absenteeism, tardiness, and turnover for the organization, and can also raise organizational commitment and performance by workers. It is a way for dual-career couples to handle children's schedules as well as their own; it is a way to meet the demands of caring for elderly parents or ill family members; it is even a way to better attend to such personal affairs as medical and dental appointments, home emergencies, banking needs, and so on.

How Employers Can Beat the Mommy Drain

It's no secret that more and more employers are turning to flexibility in work schedules to better accommodate today's workers. Among them, Accenture and Booz Allen Hamilton are taking special steps to make sure they can attract and retain talented working mothers. Here is a selection of ways top employers are counteracting the "Mommy drain," and responding to Daddy's needs as well.

- Offer increased pay and extended time for maternity leave.
- Offer increased pay and extended time for parental leave.
- Allow employee pay set-asides to buy more time for maternal and parental leave.
- Create alternative and challenging jobs that require less travel.
- Make sure pay for performance plans do not discriminate against those on maternal or parental leave.
- Set up mentoring and networking systems to support working parents.
- Make sure new mothers feel they are wanted back at work.
- Keep in contact with employees on maternity and parental leaves.

Job Sharing

- In **job sharing** one full-time job is split between two or more persons who divide the work according to agreed-upon hours.

In **job sharing**, one full-time job is assigned to two or more persons who then divide the work according to agreed-upon hours. Often, each person works half a day, but job sharing can also be done on a weekly or monthly basis. Organizations benefit from job sharing when they can attract talented people who would otherwise be unable to work. An example is the qualified teacher who also is a parent. This person may be able to work only half a day. Through job sharing, two such persons can be employed to teach one class. Some job sharers report less burnout and claim that they feel recharged each time they report for work. The tricky part of this arrangement is finding two people who will work well with each other.

- **Work sharing** is when employees agree to work fewer hours to avoid layoffs.

Job sharing should not be confused with something called **work sharing**. This occurs when workers agree to cut back on the number of hours they work in order to protect against layoffs. In the recent economic crisis, for example, workers in some organizations agreed to voluntarily reduce their paid hours worked so that others would not lose their jobs. Many employers tried to manage the crisis with an involuntary form of work sharing. An example is Pella Windows which went to a four-day workweek for some 3,900 workers to avoid layoffs.[29]

Telecommuting

Technology has enabled yet another alternative work arrangement that is now highly visible in many employment sectors ranging from higher education to government, and from manufacturing to services. **Telecommuting** is work done at home or in a remote location via the use of computers and advanced telecommunications linkages with a central office or other employment locations. And it's popular; the number of workers who are telecommuting is growing daily, with corporate telecommuters now numbering at least 9 million.[30]

- **Telecommuting** is work done at home or from a remote location using computers and advanced telecommunications.

When asked what they like, telecommuters report increased productivity, fewer distractions, the freedom to be their own boss, and the benefit of having more time for themselves. Potential advantages also include more flexibility, the comforts of home, and being able to live and work in locations consistent with one's lifestyle. But there are potential negatives as well. Some telecommuters report working too much while having difficulty separating work and personal life.[31] Other complaints include not being considered as important as other workers, isolation from co-workers, decreased identification with the work team, and even the interruptions of everyday family affairs. One telecommuter says: "You have to have self-discipline and pride in what you do, but you also have to have a boss that trusts you enough to get out of the way."[32]

Part-Time Work

Part-time work has become an increasingly prominent and controversial work arrangement. In *temporary part-time work* an employee works only when needed and for less than the standard 40-hour workweek. Some choose this schedule because they like it. But others are *involuntary part-timers* who would prefer a

Telecommuter Community Forms at Jelly Columbus

A "jelly" is a co-worker community—people who meet together to do individual work in public places like libraries or coffee shops rather than at home. Jody Dzuranin of the Columbus, Ohio, Jelly says: "I call it study hall for adults . . . a nice mix of interacting in person and getting your work done silently."

full-time work schedule but do not have access to one. Someone doing *permanent part-time* work is considered a "permanent" member of the workforce, although still working fewer hours than the standard 40-hour week.

A part-time work schedule can be a benefit to people who want to supplement other jobs or who want something less than a full workweek for a variety of personal reasons. But there are downsides. When a person holds multiple part-time jobs, the work burdens can be stressful; performance may suffer on the job, and spillover effects to family and leisure time can be negative. Also, part-timers often fail to qualify for fringe benefits such as health care insurance and retirement plans. And they may be paid less than their full-time counterparts.

Many employers use part-time work to hold down labor costs and to help smooth out peaks and valleys in the business cycle. Temporary part-timers are easily released and hired as needs dictate; during difficult business times they will most likely be laid off before full-timers. The use of part-timers is growing as today's employers try to cut back labor costs. In just one year the number of involuntary part-time workers grew from 4.5 million to 9 million.[33]

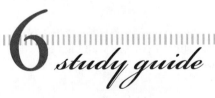

6 study guide

Key Questions and Answers

What is the link between motivation, performance, and rewards?

- The integrated model of motivation brings together insights from content, process, and learning theories around the basic effort → performance → reward linkage.

- Reward systems emphasize a mix of intrinsic rewards—such as a sense of achievement from completing a challenging task, and extrinsic rewards—such as receiving a pay increase.

- Pay for performance systems takes a variety of forms, including merit pay, gain-sharing and profit-sharing plans, stock options, and employee stock ownership.

What are the essentials of performance management?

- Performance management is the process of managing performance measurement and the variety of human resource decisions associated with such measurement.

- Performance measurement serves both an evaluative purpose for reward allocation and a development purpose for future performance improvement.

- Performance measurement can be done using output measures of performance accomplishment or activity measures of performance efforts.

- The ranking, paired comparison, and forced-distribution approaches are examples of comparative performance appraisal methods.

- The graphic rating scale and the behaviorally anchored rating scale use individual ratings on personal and performance characteristics to appraise performance.

- 360° appraisals involve the full circle of contacts a person may have in job performance—from bosses to peers to subordinates to internal and external customers.

- Common performance measurement errors include halo errors, central tendency errors, recency errors, personal bias errors, and cultural bias errors.

How do job designs influence motivation and performance?

- Job design by scientific management or job simplification standardizes work and employs people in clearly defined and specialized tasks.

- Job enlargement increases task variety by combining two or more tasks previously assigned to separate workers; job rotation increases task variety by periodically rotating workers among jobs involving different tasks; job enrichment builds bigger and more responsible jobs by adding planning and evaluating duties.

- The job characteristics model offers a diagnostic approach to job enrichment based on analysis of five core job characteristics: skill variety, task identity, task significance, autonomy, and feedback.

- The job characteristics model does not assume that everyone wants an enriched job; it indicates that job enrichment will be more successful for persons with high growth needs, requisite job skills, and context satisfaction.

What are the motivational opportunities of alternative work arrangements?

- The compressed workweek allows a full-time workweek to be completed in fewer than five days, typically offering four 10-hour days of work and three days free.

- Flexible working hours allow employees some daily choice in scheduling core and flex time.

- Job sharing occurs when two or more people divide one full-time job according to agreements among themselves and the employer.

- Telecommuting involves work at home or at a remote location while communicating with the home office as needed via computer and related technologies.

- Part-time work requires less than a 40-hour workweek and can be done on a temporary or permanent schedule.

Terms to Know

Activity measures (p. 128)

Behaviorally anchored rating scale (p. 129)

Bonuses (p. 126)

Compressed workweek (p. 137)

Critical incident diaries (p. 129)

Employee stock ownership plans (p. 126)

Extrinsic rewards (p. 123)

Flexible working hours (p. 137)

Forced distribution (p. 128)

Gain sharing (p. 126)

Graphic rating scales (p. 128)

Intrinsic rewards (p. 123)

Job design (p. 131)

Job enlargement (p. 133)

Job enrichment (p. 133)

Job rotation (p. 133)

Job sharing (p. 138)

Job simplification (p. 132)

Merit pay (p. 124)

Motivation (p. 122)

Output measures (p. 128)

Paired comparison (p. 128)

Performance-contingent pay (p. 124)

Profit sharing (p. 126)

Psychological empowerment (p. 134)

Ranking (p. 128)

Reliability (p. 131)

Scientific management (p. 132)

Skill-based pay (p. 126)

Stock options (p. 126)

Telecommuting (p. 138)

360° evaluation (p. 131)

Validity (p. 131)

Work sharing (p. 138)

Self-Test 6

Multiple Choice

1. In the integrated model of motivation, what predicts effort? (a) rewards (b) organizational support (c) ability (d) motivation

2. Pay is generally considered a/an _____ reward, while a sense of personal growth experienced from working at a task is an example of a/an _____ reward. (a) extrinsic, skill-based (b) skill-based, intrinsic (c) extrinsic, intrinsic (d) absolute, comparative

3. If someone improves productivity by developing a new work process and receives a portion of the productivity savings as a monetary reward, this is an example of a/an _____ pay plan. (a) cost-sharing (b) gain-sharing (c) ESOP (d) stock option

4. Performance measurement serves both evaluation and _____ purposes. (a) reward allocation (b) counseling (c) discipline (d) benefits calculations

5. Which form of performance assessment is an example of the comparative approach? (a) forced distribution (b) graphic rating scale (c) BARS (d) critical incident diary

6. If a performance assessment method fails to accurately measure a person's performance on actual job content, it lacks _____. (a) performance contingency (b) leniency (c) validity (d) strictness

7. A written record that describes in detail various examples of a person's positive and negative work behaviors is most likely part of which performance appraisal method? (a) forced distribution (b) critical incident diary (c) paired comparison (d) graphic rating scale

8. When a team leader evaluates the performance of all team members as "average," the possibility for _____ error in the performance appraisal is quite high. (a) personal bias (b) recency (c) halo (d) central tendency

9. Job simplification is closely associated with _____ as originally developed by Frederick Taylor. (a) vertical loading (b) horizontal loading (c) scientific management (d) self-efficacy

10. Job _____ increases job _____ by combining into one job several tasks of similar difficulty. (a) rotation, depth (b) enlargement, depth (c) rotation, breadth (d) enlargement, breadth

11. If a manager redesigns a job through vertical loading, she would most likely _____. (a) bring tasks from earlier in the workflow into the job (b) bring tasks from later in the workflow into the job (c) bring higher level or managerial responsibilities into the job (d) raise the standards for high performance

12. In the job characteristics model, a person will be most likely to find an enriched job motivating if he or she _____. (a) receives stock options (b) has ability and support (c) is unhappy with job context (d) has strong growth needs

13. In the job characteristics model, _____ indicates the degree to which an individual is able to make decisions affecting his or her work. (a) task variety (b) task identity (c) task significance (d) autonomy

14. When a job allows a person to do a complete unit of work, for example, process an insurance claim from point of receipt from the customer to the point of final resolution, it would be considered high on which core characteristic? (a) task identity (b) task significance (c) task autonomy (d) feedback

15. The "4/40" is a type of _____ work arrangement. (a) compressed workweek (b) "allow workers to change machine configurations to make different products" (c) job-sharing (d) permanent part-time

Short Response

16. Explain how a 360° evaluation works as a performance appraisal approach.

17. Explain the difference between halo errors and recency errors in performance assessment.

18. What role does growth-need strength play in the job characteristics model?

19. What are the potential advantages and disadvantages of a compressed workweek?

Applications Essay

20. Choose a student organization on your campus. Discuss in detail how the concepts and ideas in this chapter could be applied in various ways to improve motivation and performance among its members.

Next Steps

Top Choices from

The OB Skills Workbook

Cases for Critical Thinking	Team and Experiential Exercises	Self-Assessment Portfolio
• Perfect Pizzeria • Hovey and Beard	• My Fantasy Job • My Best Job • Tinkertoys • Job Design Preferences	• Personal Values • Are You Cosmopolitan? • Managerial Assumptions • Twenty-first Century Manager

Whole Foods: **Teaming Up for Success**

Only two things unite the more than 300 Whole Foods Market locations: coordinated teamwork and the inflexible rule that all food sold must be free from artificial additives, sweeteners, colorings, and preservatives.[a] The rest is up to the individual stores. This balance between dogma and freedom permits stores to make decisions based on the input from their local teams instead of solely taking orders from corporate honchos. At Whole Foods, department members work as a team. Teams within stores operate as a team. Parallel departments in regional stores team up. And all stores within each of Whole Foods' 12 regions work as a team.

While Whole Foods does have a core management team, led by founder John Mackey and co-president Walter Robb, the regions operate largely free from corporate interference. Every store becomes local, and individual departments have license to develop personalities. Each market is free to act like a neighborhood store that just happens to be part of a huge franchise.

> *"Culture is our secret weapon."*
> *—Walter Robb, co-president of Whole Foods.*[e]

John Moore, former National Marketing Director of Whole Foods, identifies a "Libertarian" theme of management running through the company. "[Whole Foods] operates under the belief stores should have the freedom to meet the needs of its unique customers and team members."[b]

Each district, headed by its own president, oversees most of the corporate functions you'd expect to be run from a company's world headquarters, like marketing, HR, and payroll. Districts procure most of their stores' products and customize new-employee training to fit their own personalities. In doing so, districts operate with the nimbleness of a regionally sized company but benefit from consumers' loyalty to a well-loved national brand.[c]

Walter Robb thinks that the glue binding the employees, stores, and regions is Whole Foods' unique corporate culture. "When people copy us," he says, "they can copy our fixtures and design, but they can't chase the culture because they're chasing a shadow."[d]

Quick Summary

- John Mackey opened the first Whole Foods Market in Austin, Texas, in 1980. The company now operates more than 300 locations in the United States and the United Kingdom.

- Instead of relying solely on top-down management, Whole Foods divides the stores into 12 districts, granting them autonomy over most purchasing and managerial decisions.

- Stores and the departments within are organized into teams. Whole Foods encourages each to develop unique local personalities and cater to their specific neighborhoods.

FYI: Whole Foods is proud of the diversity its employees represent. In one Atlanta store, employees speak over 50 languages.[f]

7 Teams in Organizations

the key point

The Whole Foods story highlights how organizations can benefit from teams and teamwork. Teams that achieve synergy bring out the best in their members in respect to performance, creativity, and enthusiasm. But we all know that teamwork isn't always easy and that teams sometimes underperform. Anyone seeking career success must be prepared to work well in a wide variety of team settings.

chapter at a glance

What Are Teams and How Are They Used in Organizations?

When Is a Team Effective?

What Are the Stages of Team Development?

How Can We Understand Teams at Work?

ETHICS IN OB
CHEAT NOW . . . CHEAT LATER

FINDING THE LEADER IN YOU
TEAMWORK TURNS NASCAR'S KEY TO THE FAST LANE

OB IN POPULAR CULTURE
SOCIAL LOAFING AND *SURVIVOR*

RESEARCH INSIGHT
MEMBERSHIP, INTERACTIONS, AND EVALUATION INFLUENCE SOCIAL LOAFING IN GROUPS

what's inside?

Teams in Organizations

The fact is that there is a lot more to teamwork than simply assigning members to the same group, calling it a "team," appointing someone as "team leader," and then expecting them all to do a great job.[1] That's part of the lesson in the opening example of Whole Foods. And it is a good introduction to the four chapters in this part of the book that are devoted to an understanding of teams and team processes. As the discussion begins, it helps to remember that the responsibilities for building high-performance teams rest not only with the manager, coach, or team leader, but also with the team members themselves. If you look now at the sidebar, you'll find a checklist of several must-have team contributions, the types of things that team members and leaders can do to help their teams achieve high performance.[2]

Head's Up—Don't Forget These "Must-Have" Contributions by Team Members

- Putting personal talents to work.
- Encouraging and motivating others.
- Accepting suggestions.
- Listening to different points of view.
- Communicating information and ideas.
- Persuading others to cooperate.
- Resolving and negotiating conflict.
- Building consensus.
- Fulfilling commitments.
- Avoiding disruptive acts and words.

Teams and Teamwork

When we think of the word "team," a variety of popular sporting teams might first come to mind, perhaps a favorite from the college ranks or from the professional leagues. For a moment, let's stick with basketball.

Scene—NBA Basketball: Scholars find that both good and bad basketball teams win more games the longer the players have been together. Why? They claim it's a "teamwork effect" that creates wins because players know each other's moves and playing tendencies.[3]

Let's not forget that teams are important in work settings as well. And whether or not a team lives up to expectations can have a major impact on how well its customers and clients are served.

Scene—Hospital Operating Room: Scholars notice that the same heart surgeons have lower death rates for similar procedures when performed in hospitals where they do more operations. Why? They claim it's because the doctors spend more time working together with members of these surgery teams. The scholars argue it's not only the surgeon's skills that count: "the skills of the team, and of the organization, matter."[4]

What is going on in these examples? Whereas a group of people milling around a coffee shop counter is just that—a "group" of people—teams like those in the examples are supposed to be something more: "groups+" if you will. That "+" factor is what distinguishes the successful NBA basketball teams from the also-rans and the best surgery teams from all the others.

In OB we define a **team** as a group of people brought together to use their complementary skills to achieve a common purpose for which they are collectively accountable.[5] Real **teamwork** occurs when team members accept and live up to their collective accountability by actively working together so that all their respective skills are best used to achieve team goals.[6]

> • A **team** is a group of people holding themselves collectively accountable for using complementary skills to achieve a common purpose.
> • **Teamwork** occurs when team members live up to their collective accountability for goal accomplishment.

What Teams Do

When we talk about teams in organizations, one of the first things to recognize is that they do many things and make many types of performance contributions. In general we can describe them as teams that recommend things, run things, and make or do things.[7]

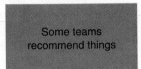

Some teams recommend things

Some teams run things

Some teams make or do things

Teams that recommend things are set up to study specific problems and recommend solutions for them. These teams typically work with a target completion date and often disband once the purpose has been fulfilled. The teams include task forces, ad hoc committees, special project teams, and the like. Members of these teams must be able to learn quickly how to pool talents, work well together, and accomplish the assigned task.

Teams that run things consist of people with the formal responsibility for leading organizations and their component parts. They may exist at all levels of responsibility, from the individual work unit composed of a team leader and team members to the top-management team composed of a CEO and other senior executives. Key issues addressed by top-management teams, for example, include identifying overall organizational purposes, goals, and values, as well as crafting strategies and persuading others to support them.[8]

Teams that make or do things are work units that perform ongoing tasks such as marketing, sales, systems analysis, or manufacturing. Members of these teams must have effective long-term working relationships with one another, the right technologies and operating systems, and the external support needed to achieve effectiveness over time. They also need energy to keep up the pace and meet the day-to-day challenges of sustained high performance.

Organizations as Networks of Teams

When it was time to reengineer its order-to-delivery process to streamline a noncompetitive and costly cycle time, Hewlett-Packard turned to a team. In just nine months, they had slashed the time, improved service, and cut costs. How did they do it? Team leader Julie Anderson said: "We took things away: no supervisors, no hierarchy, no titles, no job descriptions . . . the idea was to create a sense of personal ownership." One team member said, "No individual is going to have the best idea, that's not the way it works—the best ideas come from the collective intelligence of the team."[9] This isn't an isolated example. Organizations everywhere are using teams and teamwork to improve performance. And, the catchwords are empowerment, participation, and involvement.

• **Formal teams** are official and designated to serve a specific purpose.

The many **formal teams** found in organizations are created and officially designated to serve specific organizational purposes. Some are permanent and ongoing. They appear on organization charts as departments (e.g., market research department), divisions (e.g., consumer products division), or teams (e.g., product-assembly team). Such teams can vary in size from very small departments or teams of just a few people to large divisions employing 100 or more people. Other formal teams are temporary and short lived. They are created to solve specific problems or perform defined tasks and are then disbanded once the purpose has been accomplished. Examples include temporary committees and task forces.[10]

One way to view organizations is as interlocking networks of formal teams. On the vertical dimension the manager is a linchpin serving as a team leader at one level and a team member at the next higher level.[11] On the horizontal dimension, for example, a customer service team member may also serve on a special task force for new product development and head a committee set up to examine a sexual harassment case.

• **Informal groups** are unofficial and emerge to serve special interests.

Organizations also have vast networks of **informal groups**, ones that emerge and coexist as a shadow to the formal structure and without any assigned purpose or official endorsement. As shown in Figure 7.1, these informal groups form through personal relationships and create their own interlocking networks within the organization. *Friendship groups*, for example, consist of persons with natural affinities for one another. Their members tend to work together, sit together, take breaks together, and even do things together outside of the workplace. *Interest groups* consist of persons who share common interests. These may be job-related interests, such as an intense desire to learn more about computers, or nonwork interests, such as community service, sports, or religion.

Although informal groups can be places where people join to complain, spread rumors, and disagree with what is happening in the organization, they can also be quite helpful. Informal networks can speed up workflows as people assist each other in ways that cut across the formal structures. They can also help satisfy unmet needs, for example, by providing companionship or a sense of personal importance that is otherwise missing in someone's formal team assignments.

• **Social network analysis** identifies the informal structures and their embedded social relationships that are active in an organization.

A tool known as **social network analysis** is used to identify the informal groups and networks of relationships that are active in an organization. The analysis typically asks people to identify co-workers who most often help them, who communicate with them regularly, and who energize and deenergize them. When results are analyzed, social networks are drawn with lines running from person to person according to frequency and type of relationship maintained. This map shows how a lot of work really gets done, in contrast to the formal arrangements depicted on organization charts. Managers can use such information to better under-

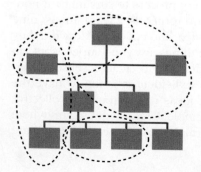

Figure 7.1 The organization as an interlocking network of informal groups.

stand organizational dynamics, and even to redesign the formal team structure for better performance.

Cross-Functional and Problem-Solving Teams

Management scholar Jay Conger calls the organization built around teams and teamwork the management system of the future and the best response to the needs for speed and adaptability in an ever-more-competitive environment.[12] He cites the example of an American jet engine manufacturer that changed from a traditional structure of functional work units to one in which people from different functions worked together in teams. The new approach cut the time required to design and produce new engines by 50 percent. Conger calls such "cross-functional" teams "speed machines."[13]

A **cross-functional team** consists of members brought together from different functional departments or work units to achieve more horizontal integration and better lateral relations. Members of cross-functional teams are expected to work together with a positive combination of functional expertise and integrative team thinking. The expected result is higher performance driven by the advantages of better information and faster decision making.

Cross-functional teams are a way of trying to beat the **functional silos problem**, also called the *functional chimneys problem*. It occurs when members of functional units stay focused on matters internal to their function and minimize their interactions with members dealing with other functions. In this sense, the functional departments or work teams create artificial boundaries, or "silos," that discourage rather than encourage interaction with other units. The result is poor integration and poor coordination with other parts of the organization. The cross-functional team is a way to break down these barriers by creating a forum in which members from different functions work together as one team with a common purpose.[14]

Organizations also use any number of **problem-solving teams**, which are created temporarily to serve a specific purpose by dealing with a specific problem or opportunity. The president of a company, for example, might convene a task force to examine the possibility of implementing flexible work hours for employees; a human resource director might bring together a committee to advise her on changes in employee benefit policies; a project team might be formed to plan and implement a new organizationwide information system.

The term **employee involvement team** applies to a wide variety of teams whose members meet regularly to collectively examine important workplace

- A **cross-functional team** has members from different functions or work units.

- The **functional silos problem** occurs when members of one functional team fail to interact with others from other functional teams.

- A **problem-solving team** is set up to deal with a specific problem or opportunity.

- An **employee involvement team** meets regularly to address workplace issues.

Teams Aren't Always Good for Productivity

A Microsoft survey of 38,000 workers worldwide raised concerns about teamwork and productivity. Results showed that the average worker believes 69% of meetings attended were ineffective. 32% of workers complained about poor communication and unclear objectives on their teams; 31% said they were unsure of priorities; 29% said that procrastination was a problem.

issues. They might discuss, for example, ways to enhance quality, better satisfy customers, raise productivity, and improve the quality of work life. Such employee involvement teams are supposed to mobilize the full extent of workers' know-how and experiences for continuous improvements. An example is what some organizations call a **quality circle**—a small team of persons who meet periodically to discuss and make propsals for ways to improve quality.[15]

• A **quality circle** team meets regularly to address quality issues.

Self-Managing Teams

In the last chapter we discussed job enrichment and its implications for individual motivation and performance. Now we can talk about a form of job enrichment for teams.

• **Self-managing** teams are empowered to make decisions to manage themselves in day-to-day work.

The **self-managing team** is a high-involvement workgroup design that is becoming increasingly well established. Sometimes called *self-directed work teams*, these teams are empowered to make the decisions needed to manage themselves on a day-to-day basis.[16] They basically replace traditional work units with teams whose members assume duties otherwise performed by a manager or first-line supervisor. Figure 7.2 shows that members of true self-managing teams make their own decisions about scheduling work, allocating tasks, training for job skills, evaluating performance, selecting new team members, and controlling the quality of work.

Most self-managing teams include between 5 and 15 members. They need to be large enough to provide a good mix of skills and resources but small enough to function efficiently. Because team members have a lot of discretion in determining

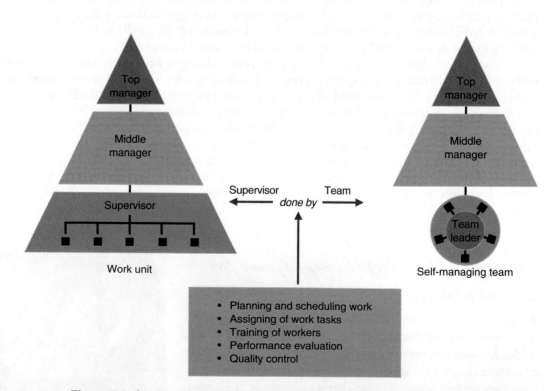

Figure 7.2 Organizational and management implications of self-managing teams.

Virtual Teams Travel the World for Texas Instruments

On any given day you can find talented engineers in Bangalore, India, laboring on complex chip designs with their counterparts in Texas. Virtual teammates are in constant contact, sending work back and forth while taking advantage of the near half-day time difference.

work pace and in distributing tasks, **multiskilling** is important. This means that team members are expected to perform many different jobs—even all of the team's jobs—as needed. Pay is ideally skill-based; the more skills someone masters, the higher the base pay.

The expected benefits of self-managing teams include productivity and quality improvements, production flexibility and faster response to technological change, reduced absenteeism and turnover, and improved work attitudes and quality of work life. But just as with all organizational changes, the shift from traditional work units to self-managing teams may have its difficulties. It may be hard for some team members to adjust to the "self-managing" responsibilities. And higher-level managers may have problems dealing with the loss of the first-line supervisor positions. Given all this, self-managing teams are probably not right for all organizations, work situations, and people. They have great potential, but they also require a proper setting and a great deal of management support. At a minimum, the essence of any self-managing team—high involvement, participation, and empowerment—must be consistent with the values and culture of the organization.

- **Multiskilling** is where team members are each capable of performing many different jobs.
- Members of **virtual teams** work together through computer mediation.

Virtual Teams

It used to be that teamwork was confined in concept and practice to those circumstances in which members could meet face to face. Information technology has changed all that. The **virtual team**, one whose members convene and work together through computer mediation rather than face-to-face, is increasingly common.[17] Working in electronic space and free from the constraints of geographical distance, members of virtual teams can do the same things as members of face-to-face groups: share information, make decisions, and complete tasks. Some steps to successful teams are summarized in the accompanying sidebar. In many ways they mirror in electronic space the essentials of good teamwork in face-to-face teams.[18]

In terms of potential advantages, virtual teams bring together people who may be located at great distances from one another.[19] Working virtually rather than face to face offers obvious cost and time efficiencies. The electronic rather than face-to-face

Don't Neglect These Steps to Successful Virtual Teams

- Select team members high in initiative and capable of self-starting.
- Select members who will join and engage the team with positive attitudes.
- Select members known for working hard to meet team goals.
- Begin with social messaging that allows members to exchange information about each other to personalize the process.
- Assign clear goals and roles so that members can focus while working alone and also know what others are doing.
- Gather regular feedback from members about how they think the team is doing and how it might do better.
- Provide regular feedback to team members about team accomplishments.

environment of the virtual team can help focus interaction and decision making on objective information rather than emotional considerations and distracting interpersonal problems. Discussions and information shared among team members can also be electronically stored for continuous access and historical record keeping.

The potential downsides to virtual teams are also real. Members of virtual teams can have difficulties establishing good working relationships. When the computer is the go-between, relationships and interactions can be different and require special attention. The lack of face-to-face interaction limits the role of emotions and nonverbal cues in the communication process, perhaps depersonalizing relations among team members.

Team Effectiveness

LEARNING ROADMAP   Criteria of an Effective Team / Synergy and Team Benefits / Social Facilitation / Social Loafing and Team Problems

There is no doubt that teams are pervasive and important in organizations; they accomplish important tasks and help members achieve satisfaction in their work. But we also know from personal experiences that teams and teamwork have their difficulties; not all teams perform well, and not all team members are always satisfied. Surely you've heard the sayings "a camel is a horse put together by a committee" and "too many cooks spoil the broth." They raise an important question: Just what are the foundations of team effectiveness?[20]

Criteria of an Effective Team

Teams in all forms and types, just like individuals, should be held accountable for their performance. And to do this we need to have some understanding of team effectiveness. In OB we define an **effective team** as one that achieves high levels of task performance, member satisfaction, and team viability.

• An **effective team** is one that achieves high levels of task performance, member satisfaction, and team viability.

| An effective team achieves high performance | → | An effective team generates high member satisfaction | → | An effective team stays viable for long-term action |

With regard to *task performance*, an effective team achieves its performance goals in the standard sense of quantity, quality, and timeliness of work results. For a formal work unit such as a manufacturing team this may mean meeting daily production targets. For a temporary team such as a new policy task force this may involve meeting a deadline for submitting a new organizational policy to the company president.

With regard to *member satisfaction*, an effective team is one whose members believe that their participation and experiences are positive and meet important personal needs. They are satisfied with their team tasks, accomplishments, and interpersonal relationships.

With regard to *team viability*, the members of an effective team are sufficiently satisfied to continue working well together on an ongoing basis. When one task is finished, they look forward to working on others in the future. Such a team has all-important long-term performance potential.

Synergy and Team Benefits

Effective teams offer the benefits of **synergy**—the creation of a whole that is greater than the sum of its parts. Synergy works within a team, and it works across teams as their collective efforts are harnessed to serve the organization as a whole. It creates the great beauty of teams: people working together and accomplishing more through teamwork than they ever could by working alone.

The performance advantages of teams over individuals are most evident in three situations.[21] First, when there is no clear "expert" for a particular task or problem, teams tend to make better judgments than does the average individual alone. Second, teams are typically more successful than individuals when problems are complex and require a division of labor and the sharing of information. Third, because they tend to make riskier decisions, teams can be more creative and innovative than individuals.

Teams are beneficial as settings where people learn from one another and share job skills and knowledge. The learning environment and the pool of experience within a team can be used to solve difficult and unique problems. This is especially helpful to newcomers, who often need help in their jobs. When team members support and help each other in acquiring and improving job competencies, they may even make up for deficiencies in organizational training systems.

Teams are also important sources of need satisfaction for their members. Opportunities for social interaction within a team can provide individuals with a sense of security through work assistance and technical advice. Team members can also provide emotional support for one another in times of special crisis or pressure. And the many contributions individuals make to teams can help members experience self-esteem and personal involvement.

> • **Synergy** is the creation of a whole greater than the sum of its parts.

Social Facilitation

This discussion moves us to another concept known as **social facilitation**—the tendency for one's behavior to be influenced by the presence of others in a group or social setting.[22] In a team context it can be a boost or a detriment to an individual member's performance contributions. Social facilitation theory suggests that working in the presence of others creates an emotional arousal or excitement that stimulates behavior and affects performance. The effect works to the positive and stimulates extra effort when one is proficient with the task at hand. An example is the team member who enthusiastically responds when asked to do something she is really good at, such as making Power Point slides for a team presentation. But the effect of social facilitation can be negative when the task is unfamiliar or a person lacks the necessary skills. A team member might withdraw or even tend toward social loafing, for example, when asked to do something he isn't very good at. An example might be having to deliver the team's final presentation in front of a class or larger audience.

> • **Social facilitation** is the tendency for one's behavior to be influenced by the presence of others in a group.

Social Loafing and Team Problems

Although teams have enormous performance potential, one of their problems is **social loafing**. Also known as the *Ringlemann effect*, it is the tendency of people to work less hard in a group than they would individually.[23] Max Ringlemann, a German psychologist, pinpointed the phenomenon by asking people to pull on a rope as hard as they could, first alone and then as part of a team.[24] Average

> • **Social loafing** occurs when people work less hard in groups than they would individually.

productivity dropped as more people joined the rope-pulling task. Ringlemann suggested that people may not work as hard in groups because their individual contributions are less noticeable in the group context and because they prefer to see others carry the workload.

You may have encountered social loafing in your work and study teams, and been perplexed in terms of how to best handle it. Perhaps you have even been surprised at your own social loafing in some performance situations. Rather than give in to the phenomenon and its potential performance losses, you can often reverse or prevent social loafing. Steps that team leaders can take include keeping group size small and redefining roles so that free-riders are more visible and peer pressures to perform are more likely, increasing accountability by making individual performance expectations clear and specific, and making rewards directly contingent on an individual's performance contributions.[25]

Other common problems of teams include personality conflicts and differences in work styles that antagonize others and disrupt relationships and accomplishments. Sometimes team members withdraw from active participation due to uncertainty over tasks or battles about goals or competing visions. Ambiguous agendas or ill-defined problems can also cause fatigue and loss of motivation when

OB IN POPULAR CULTURE

SOCIAL LOAFING AND *SURVIVOR*

While teams offer tremendous performance potential, there are also unique problems in the team context. **Social loafing** is the tendency for an individual to do less in a group than he or she would individually. Two factors increase the likelihood of loafing. The first relates to the difficulty of identifying how individuals perform. When you do not know what others are doing, they can avoid working as hard. It is tempting to say the second factor is individual laziness. However, many times individuals simply recognize that others will pick up the slack and make sure tasks are accomplished. As a result, they simply opt out.

In the ever-popular reality show *Survivor,* individual players must balance cunning and competitiveness against the need for teamwork and collaboration. In Season 10, Willard Smith finds himself a member of the successful Koror tribe. Willard's contributions are limited, so his tribe assigns him to tend the fire at night. Instead of fulfilling his obligation, Willard sleeps in the only hammock available. When morning comes, eventual winner Tom Westman complains about losing sleep because he has to "cover" for Willard. He and Gregg Carey talk about how easy it is to make a contribution to the team even if physical ability is lacking.

Westman's assessment of Willard's motives (e.g., "Why should I do it if somebody else is going to do it for me") shows that social loafing can be a difficult problem to address even when others know it is happening.

Get to Know Yourself Better *Has this been your experience when working in groups? Take the Assessment 9, Team Effectiveness, in the* OB Skills Workbook. *If the score suggests previous groups were ineffective, explore the reasons. If social loafing was a problem, how would you deal with it in the future? If there were issues with other dynamics, think about ways that you could help future group members develop greater trust, communicate more effectively, and become more committed.*

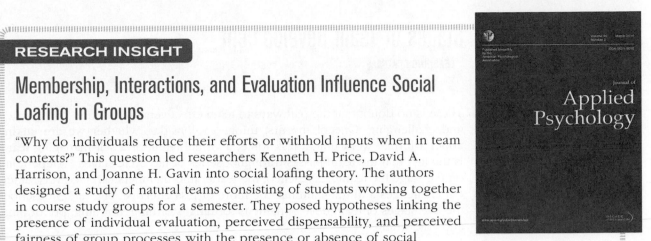

RESEARCH INSIGHT

Membership, Interactions, and Evaluation Influence Social Loafing in Groups

"Why do individuals reduce their efforts or withhold inputs when in team contexts?" This question led researchers Kenneth H. Price, David A. Harrison, and Joanne H. Gavin into social loafing theory. The authors designed a study of natural teams consisting of students working together in course study groups for a semester. They posed hypotheses linking the presence of individual evaluation, perceived dispensability, and perceived fairness of group processes with the presence or absence of social loafing.

Price and colleagues studied 144 groups with a total of 515 students in 13 undergraduate and graduate university courses. Participants completed a questionnaire before group work started and again at the end. The final questionnaire included a section asking respondents to rate the extent to which each other group member "loafed by not doing his or her share of the tasks, by leaving work for others to do, by goofing off, and by having other things to do when asked to help out."

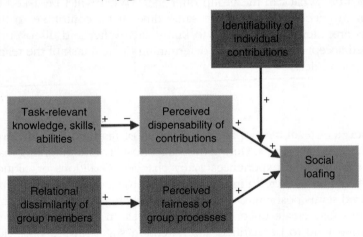

Findings showed that social loafing was negatively related to perceived fairness of group processes and positively related to perceived dispensability of one's contributions. The relationship between social loafing and perceived dispensability strengthened when individual contributions were more identifiable. Task-relevant ability was negatively associated with perceived dispensability; the presence of relational differences among members was negatively associated with perceived fairness of group processes.

Do the Research   *Build a model that explains social loafing in the teams you often work with. What are the major hypotheses? How might you test them in an actual research study?*

Source: Kenneth H. Price, David A. Harrison, and Joanne H. Gavin, "Withholding Inputs in Team Contexts: Member Composition, Interaction Processes, Evaluation Structure, and Social Loafing," *Journal of Applied Psychology* 91.6 (2006), pp. 1375–1384.

teams work too long on the wrong things with little to show for it. And finally, not everyone is always ready to do group work. This might be due to lack of motivation, but it may also stem from conflicts with other work deadlines and priorities. Low enthusiasm may also result from perceptions of poor team organization or progress, as well as from meetings that seem to lack purpose. These and other difficulties can easily turn the great potential of teams into frustration and failure.

Stages of Team Development

LEARNING ROADMAP   Forming Stage / Storming Stage / Norming Stage / Performing Stage / Adjourning Stage

There is no doubt that the pathways to team effectiveness are often complicated and challenging. One of the first things to consider, whether we are talking about a formal work unit, a task force, a virtual team, or a self-managing team, is the fact that the team passes through a series of life cycle stages.[26] Depending on the stage the team has reached, the leader and members can face very different challenges and the team may be more or less effective. Figure 7.3 describes the five stages of team development as forming, storming, norming, performing, and adjourning.[27]

Forming Stage

- The **forming stage** focuses around the initial entry of members to a team.

In the **forming stage** of team development, a primary concern is the initial entry of members to a group. During this stage, individuals ask a number of questions as they begin to identify with other group members and with the team itself. Their concerns may include "What can the group offer me?" "What will I be asked to contribute?" "Can my needs be met at the same time that I contribute to the group?" Members are interested in getting to know each other and discovering what is considered acceptable behavior, in determining the real task of the team, and in defining group rules.

Storming Stage

- The **storming stage** is one of high emotionality and tension among team members.

The **storming stage** of team development is a period of high emotionality and tension among the group members. During this stage, hostility and infighting may occur, and the team typically experiences many changes. Coalitions or cliques may form as individuals compete to impose their preferences on the group and to achieve a desired status position. Outside demands such as premature performance expectations may create uncomfortable pressures. In the process, membership expectations tend to be clarified, and attention shifts toward obstacles standing in the way of team goals. Individuals begin to understand one another's

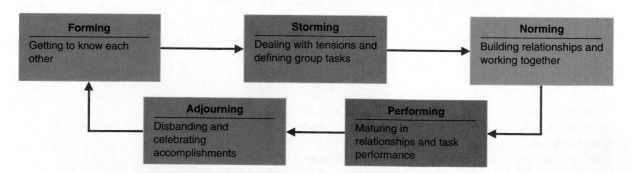

Figure 7.3 Five stages of team development.

interpersonal styles, and efforts are made to find ways to accomplish team goals while also satisfying individual needs.

Norming Stage

The **norming stage** of team development, sometimes called initial integration, is the point at which the members really start to come together as a coordinated unit. The turmoil of the storming stage gives way to a precarious balancing of forces. While enjoying a new sense of harmony team members will strive to maintain positive balance. But, holding the team together may become more important to some than successfully working on the team tasks. Minority viewpoints, deviations from team directions, and criticisms may be discouraged as members experience a preliminary sense of closeness. Some members may mistakenly perceive this stage as one of ultimate maturity. In fact, a premature sense of accomplishment at this point needs to be carefully managed in order to reach the next level of team development—performing.

> • The **norming stage** is where members start to work together as a coordinated team.

Performing Stage

The **performing stage** of team development, sometimes called total integration, marks the emergence of a mature, organized, and well-functioning team. Team members are now able to deal with complex tasks and handle internal disagreements in creative ways. The structure is stable, and members are motivated by team goals and are generally satisfied. The primary challenges are continued efforts to improve relationships and performance. Team members should be able to adapt successfully as opportunities and demands change over time. A team that has achieved the level of total integration typically scores high on the criteria of team maturity as shown in Figure 7.4.

> • The **performing stage** marks the emergence of a mature and well-functioning team.

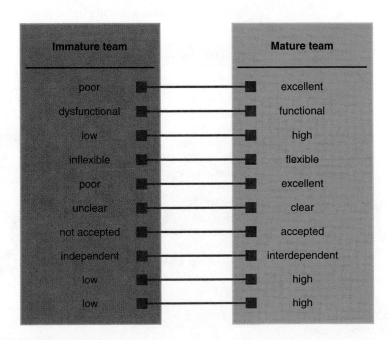

	Immature team	Mature team
1. Feedback mechanisms	poor	excellent
2. Decision-making methods	dysfunctional	functional
3. Group loyalty/cohesion	low	high
4. Operating procedures	inflexible	flexible
5. Use of member resources	poor	excellent
6. Communications	unclear	clear
7. Goals	not accepted	accepted
8. Authority relations	independent	interdependent
9. Participation in leadership	low	high
10. Acceptance of minority views	low	high

Figure 7.4 Ten criteria for measuring the maturity of a team.

Adjourning Stage

• The **adjourning stage** is where teams disband when their work is finished.

A well-integrated team is able to disband, if required, when its work is accomplished. The **adjourning stage** of team development is especially important for the many temporary teams such as task forces, committees, project teams, and the like. Their members must be able to convene quickly, do their jobs on a tight schedule, and then adjourn—often to reconvene later if needed. Their willingness to disband when the job is done and to work well together in future responsibilities, team or otherwise, is an important long-term test of team success.

Understanding Teams at Work

LEARNING ROADMAP　Open Systems Model of Teams　/　Team Resources and Setting　/　Nature of the Team Task　/　Team Size　/　Membership Composition of the Team　/　Diversity and Team Performance　/　Team Processes

Procter & Gamble's former CEO A. G. Lafley says that team effectiveness comes together when you have "the right players in the right seats on the same bus, headed in the same direction."[28] This wisdom is quite consistent with the findings of OB scholars.

Open Systems Model of Teams

The open systems model presented in Figure 7.5 shows team effectiveness being influenced by both inputs—"right players in the right seats," and by processes—"on the same bus, headed in the same direction."[29] You can remember the implications of this figure by this equation:

$$\text{Team effectiveness} = \text{Quality of inputs} \times (\text{Process gains} - \text{Process losses})$$

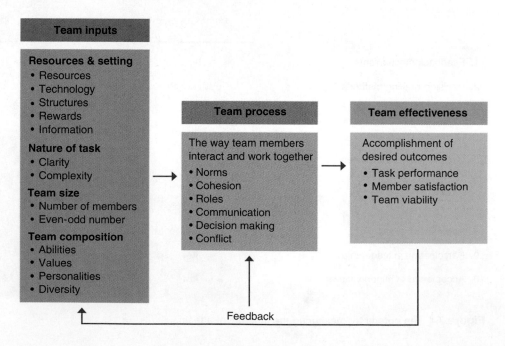

Figure 7.5 An open systems model of team effectiveness.

As we look at the prior equation on team effectiveness, the rest of this chapter focuses on the quality of inputs. The next chapter addresses the issue of process gains and losses. We start with inputs because they set the essential foundations for team performance. They set the stage for all subsequent action. And the fact is that the stronger the input foundations of a team, the better the chances for long-term effectiveness. Key team inputs include resources and setting, the nature of the task, team size, and team composition.

Team Resources and Setting

When it comes to making sure that teams have high-quality inputs, appropriate goals, well-designed reward systems, adequate resources, and appropriate technology are all essential to support the work of teams. Just as is true of an individual's performance, team performance can suffer when goals are unclear, insufficiently challenging, or arbitrarily imposed. It can also suffer if goals and rewards are focused too much on individual-level instead of group-level accomplishments. In addition, it can suffer when resources—information, budgets, work space, deadlines, rules and procedures, technologies, and the like—are insufficient to accomplish the task. By contrast, getting the right resources in place sets a strong launching pad for team success.

The importance of physical setting is evident in the attention now being given to office architecture and how well it supports teamwork. At SEI Investments, for example, employees work in a large, open space without cubicles or dividers. Each person has a private set of office furniture and fixtures, but all on

ETHICS IN OB

CHEAT NOW . . . CHEAT LATER

A study reported by Rutgers University professor Donald McCabe found that 56 percent of MBA students reported cheating by plagiarizing, downloading essays from the Web, and more. He believes the actual figure may be higher and that some respondents held back confessions for fear of losing their anonymity.

Another study, by University of Arkansas professor Tim West and colleagues, surveyed students who had cheated on an accounting test by finding answers online. When asked why, student responses ranged from being unsure that what they did was cheating, to blaming West for giving a test that had answers available on the Web, to rationalizing that "everyone cheats" and "this is how business operates."

Berkshire Hathaway chairman Warren Buffett says: "The five most dangerous words in the English language are 'Everyone else is doing it.'" Professor Alma Acevedo of the University of Puerto Rico Rio Piedras calls this the fallacy of the "assumed authority of the majority."

What's Your Position? Is this the way business operates? And just because "everyone" may be doing something, does that make it okay for us to do it as well? How often does it creep into your thinking?

wheels. Technology easily plugs and unplugs from suspended power beams that run overhead. This makes it easy for project teams to convene and disband as needed and for people to meet and converse intensely within the ebb and flow of daily work.[30]

Nature of the Team Task

Another important team input is the nature of the task. Different tasks place different demands on teams. When tasks are clear and well defined, it is easier for members to both know what they are trying to accomplish and to work together while doing it. But team effectiveness is harder to achieve with complex tasks.[31] They require lots of information exchange and intense interaction, and this all takes place under conditions of some uncertainty. To deal well with complexity, team members have to fully mobilize their talents and use the available resources well if they are to achieve desired results. Success at complex tasks, however, is a source of high satisfaction for team members.

One way to analyze the nature of the team task is in terms of its technical and social demands. The *technical demands* of a task include the degree to which it is routine or not, the level of difficulty involved, and the information requirements. The *social demands* of a task involve the degree to which issues of interpersonal relationships, egos, controversies over ends and means, and the like come into play. Tasks that are complex in technical demands require unique solutions and more information processing. Those that are complex in social demands pose difficulties for reaching agreement on goals and methods to accomplish them.

Team Size

The size of a team can have an impact on team effectiveness. As a team becomes larger, more people are available to divide up the work and accomplish needed tasks. This can boost performance and member satisfaction, but only up to a point. At some point, communication and coordination problems set in due to the sheer number of linkages that must be maintained. Satisfaction may dip, and turnover, absenteeism, and social loafing may increase. Even logistical matters, such as finding time and locations for meetings, become more difficult for larger teams.[32]

Amazon.com's founder and CEO, Jeff Bezos, is a great fan of teams. But he also has a simple rule when it comes to the size of product development teams: No team should be larger than two pizzas can feed.[33] This boils down to between five and seven members. Chances are that fewer than five may be too small to adequately share all the team responsibilities. With more than seven, individuals may find it harder to join in the discussions, contribute their talents, and offer ideas. Larger teams are also more prone to possible domination by aggressive members and have tendencies to split into coalitions or subgroups.[34]

When voting is required, odd-numbered teams are preferred to help rule out tie votes. But when careful deliberations are required and the emphasis is more on consensus, such as in jury duty or very complex problem solving, even-numbered teams may be more effective. The even number forces members to confront disagreements and deadlocks rather than simply resolve them by majority voting.[35]

Finding the Leader in You

TEAMWORK TURNS NASCAR'S KEY TO THE FAST LANE

What distinguishes a group of people from a high-performance team? For one, it's the way members work with one another to achieve common goals.

A vivid example is a NASCAR pit crew. When a driver pulls in for a pit stop, the team must jump in to perform multiple tasks flawlessly and in perfect order and unison. A second gained or lost can be crucial to a NASCAR driver's performance. Team members must be well trained and rehearsed to efficiently perform on race day. "You can't win a race with a

12-second stop, but you can lose it with an 18-second stop," says pit crew coach Trent Cherry.

Pit crew members are conditioned and trained to execute intricate maneuvers while taking care of tire changes, car adjustments, fueling, and related matters on a crowded pit lane. Each crew member is an expert at one task. But each is also fully aware of how that job fits into every other task that must be performed in a few-second pit stop interval.

The duties are carefully scripted for each individual's performance

and equally choreographed to fit together seamlessly at the team level. Every task is highly specialized and interdependent; if the jacker is late, for example, the wheel changer can't pull the wheel.

Pit crews plan and practice over and over again, getting ready for the big test of race day perfor-

mance. The crew chief makes sure that everyone is in shape, well trained, and ready to contribute to the team. "I don't want seven all-stars," Trent Cherry says, "I want seven guys who work as a team."

The NASCAR pit crews don't just get together and "wing" it on race days. The members are carefully selected for their skills and attitudes, the teams practice–practice–practice, and the pit crew leader doesn't hesitate to make changes when things aren't going well.

What's the Lesson Here?

Do you encourage teamwork, or do you do some things as a leader that might be harmful to team dynamics? Are you able to see ways to make positive changes even when things are going well? How open are you to suggestions for improvement from team members?

Membership Composition of the Team

"If you want a team to perform well, you've got to put the right members on the team to begin with." It's advice we hear a lot. There is no doubt that one of the most important input factors is the **team composition**. You can think of this as the mix of abilities, personalities, backgrounds, and experiences that the members bring to the team. The basic rule of thumb for team composition is to choose members whose talents and interests fit well with the tasks to be accomplished, and whose personal characteristics increase the likelihood of being able to work well with others.

Ability counts in team composition, and it's probably the first thing to consider in selecting members. The team is more likely to perform better when its members have skills and competencies that best fit task demands. Although talents alone cannot guarantee desired results, they do establish an important baseline of high performance potential.

Let's not forget, however, that it takes more than raw talent to generate team success. Surely you've been on teams or observed teams where there was lots of talent but very little teamwork. A likely cause is that the blend of members caused

• **Team composition** is the mix of abilities, skills, personalities, and experiences that the members bring to the team.

relationship problems over everything from needs to personality to experience to age and other background characteristics.

The **FIRO-B theory** (with FIRO standing for "fundamental interpersonal orientation") identifies differences in how people relate to one another in groups based on their needs to express and receive feelings of inclusion, control, and affection.[36] Developed by William Schultz, the theory suggests that teams whose members have compatible needs are likely to be more effective than teams whose members are more incompatible. Symptoms of incompatibilities include withdrawn members, open hostilities, struggles over control, and domination by a few members. Schultz states the management implications of the FIRO-B theory this way: "If at the outset we can choose a group of people who can work together harmoniously, we shall go far toward avoiding situations where a group's efforts are wasted in interpersonal conflicts."[37]

Another issue in team composition is *status*—a person's relative rank, prestige, or social standing. **Status congruence** occurs when a person's position within the team is equivalent in status to positions the individual holds outside of it. Any status incongruence may create problems. In high-power-distance cultures such as Malaysia, for example, the chair of a committee is expected to be the highest-ranking member of the group. When this is the case, the status congruity makes members comfortable in proceeding with their work. But if the senior member is not appointed to head the committee, perhaps because an expatriate manager from another culture selected the chair on some other criterion, members are likely to feel uncomfortable and have difficulty working together. Similar problems might occur, for example, when a young college graduate in his or her first job is appointed to chair a project team composed of senior and more experienced workers.

Diversity and Team Performance

Diversity in team composition, in the form of different values, personalities, experiences, demographics, and cultures among the members, is an important team input. And it can pose both opportunities and problems.[38]

In **homogeneous teams** where members are very similar to one another, teamwork usually isn't much of a problem. The members typically find it quite easy to work together and enjoy the team experience. But researchers warn about the risks of homogeneity. When team members are too similar in background, training, and experience, they tend to underperform even though the members may feel very comfortable with one another.[39]

In **heterogeneous teams** where members are very dissimilar, teamwork problems are more likely. The mix of diverse personalities, experiences, backgrounds,

---

- **FIRO-B theory** examines differences in how people relate to one another based on their needs to express and receive feelings of inclusion, control, and affection.

- **Status congruence** involves consistency between a person's status within and outside a group.

- In **homogeneous teams** members share many similar characteristics.

- In **heterogeneous teams** members differ in many characteristics.

Teamwork Drives Success at Cleveland Clinic

Teamwork between physicians and nonphysicians is one of the keys to success at the Cleveland Clinic. Dr. Bruce Lytle says there is no room for inflated egos. "We're not built around the notion of one superstar surrounded by supporting role players," he says.

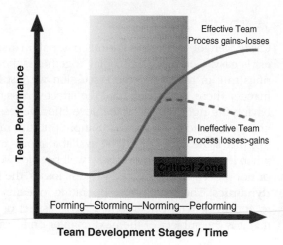

Figure 7.6 Member diversity, stages of team development, and team performance.

ages, and other personal characteristics may create difficulties as members try to define problems, share information, mobilize talents, and deal with obstacles or opportunities. Nevertheless, if—and this is a big "if"—members can work well together, the diversity can be a source of advantage and enhanced performance potential.[40]

When it comes to team process and performance difficulties due to diversity issues, the effects are especially likely in the initial stages of team development. The so-called **diversity–consensus dilemma** is the tendency for diversity to make it harder for team members to work together, even though the diversity itself expands the skills and perspectives available for problem solving.[41] These dilemmas may be most pronounced in the critical zone of the storming and norming stages of development as described in Figure 7.6. Problems may occur as interpersonal stresses and conflicts emerge from the heterogeneity. The challenge to team effectiveness is to take advantage of diversity without suffering process disadvantages.[42]

Working through the diversity–consensus dilemma can slow team development and impede relationship building, information sharing, and problem solving.[43] Some teams get stuck here and can't overcome their process problems. But if and when such difficulties are resolved, diverse teams can emerge from the critical zone shown in the figure with effectiveness and often outperform less diverse ones. Research also shows that the most creative teams include a mix of old-timers and newcomers.[44] The old-timers have the experience and connections; the newcomers bring in new talents and fresh thinking.

The diversity and performance relationship is evident in research on **collective intelligence**—the ability of a group or team to perform well across a range of tasks.[45] Researchers have found only a slight correlation between average or maximum individual member intelligence and the collective intelligence of teams. But they found strong correlations between collective intelligence and two process variables—social sensitivities within the teams and absence of conversational domination by a few members. Furthermore, collective intelligence was associated with gender diversity, specifically the proportion of females on the team. This finding was also linked to process, with researchers pointing out that females in their studies scored higher than males on social sensitivity.

• **Diversity–consensus dilemma** is the tendency for diversity in groups to create process difficulties even as it offers improved potential for problem solving.

• **Collective intelligence** is the ability of a team to perform well across a range of tasks.

Team Processes

Casey Stengel, a late and famous baseball manager, once said: "Getting good players is easy. Getting them to play together is the hard part." His comment certainly rings true in respect to the discussion we just had on diversity and team performance. There is no doubt that the effectiveness of any team depends on more than having the right inputs. To achieve effectiveness, team members must have strong and positive team processes. Simply put, the members of a team must work well together if they are to turn the available inputs into high-performance outputs. And when it comes to analyzing how well people "work together" in teams, and whether or not process gains exceed process losses, the focus is on critical **group or team dynamics**. These are forces operating in teams that affect the way members relate to and work with one another.[46] This aspect of team performance is so important that it is the subject of the next chapter on teams and teamwork.

• **Group or team dynamics** are the forces operating in teams that affect the ways members work together.

study guide

Key Questions and Answers

What are teams and how are they used in organizations?

• A team is a group of people working together to achieve a common purpose for which they hold themselves collectively accountable.

• Teams help organizations by improving task performance; teams help members experience satisfaction from their work.

• Teams in organizations serve different purposes—some teams run things, some teams recommend things, and some teams make or do things.

• Organizations consist of formal teams that are designated by the organization to serve an official purpose, as well as informal groups that emerge from special relationships but are not part of the formal structure.

• Organizations can be viewed as interlocking networks of permanent teams such as project teams and cross-functional teams, as well as temporary teams such as committees and task forces.

• Members of self-managing teams typically plan, complete, and evaluate their own work, train and evaluate one another in job tasks, and share tasks and responsibilities.

• Virtual teams, whose members meet and work together through computer mediation, are increasingly common and pose special management challenges.

When is a team effective?

• An effective team achieves high levels of task accomplishment, member satisfaction, and viability to perform successfully over the long term.

• Teams help organizations through synergy in task performance, the creation of a whole that is greater than the sum of its parts.

- Teams help satisfy important needs for their members by providing them with things like job support and social interactions.

- Team performance can suffer from social loafing when a member slacks off and lets others do the work.

- Social facilitation occurs when the behavior of individuals is influenced positively or negatively by the presence of others in a team.

What are the stages of team development?

- In the forming stage, team members come together and form initial impressions; it is a time of task orientation and interpersonal testing.

- In the storming stage, team members struggle to deal with expectations and status; it is a time when conflicts over tasks and how the team works are likely.

- In the norming or initial integration stage, team members start to come together around rules of behavior and what needs to be accomplished; it is a time of growing cooperation.

- In the performing or total integration stage, team members are well organized and well functioning; it is a time of team maturity when performance of even complex tasks becomes possible.

- In the adjourning stage, team members achieve closure on task performance and their personal relationships; it is a time of managing task completion and the process of disbanding.

How can we understand teams at work?

- Teams are open systems that interact with their environments to obtain resources that are transformed into outputs.

- The equation summarizing the open systems model for team performance is: Team Effectiveness = Quality of Inputs × (Process Gains − Process Losses).

- Input factors such as resources and setting, nature of the task, team size, and team composition, establish the core performance foundations of a team.

- Team processes include basic group or team dynamics that show up as the ways members work together to use inputs and complete tasks.

Terms to Know

Adjourning stage (p. 158)
Collective intelligence (p. 163)
Cross-functional team (p. 149)
Diversity–consensus dilemma (p. 163)
Effective team (p. 152)
Employee involvement team (p. 149)
FIRO-B theory (p. 162)
Formal teams (p. 148)
Forming stage (p. 156)
Functional silos problem (p. 149)

Group or team dynamics (p. 164)
Heterogeneous teams (p. 162)
Homogeneous teams (p. 162)
Informal groups (p. 148)
Multiskilling (p. 151)
Norming stage (p. 157)
Performing stage (p. 157)
Problem-solving team (p. 149)
Quality circle (p. 150)
Self-managing team (p. 150)

Social facilitation (p. 153)
Social loafing (p. 153)
Social network analysis (p. 148)
Status congruence (p. 162)
Storming stage (p. 156)
Synergy (p. 153)
Team (p. 147)
Team composition (p. 161)
Teamwork (p. 147)
Virtual team (p. 151)

Self-Test 7

Multiple Choice

1. The FIRO-B theory deals with _____ in teams. (a) membership compatibilities (b) social loafing (c) dominating members (d) conformity

2. It is during the _____ stage of team development that members begin to come together as a coordinated unit. (a) storming (b) norming (c) performing (d) total integration

3. An effective team is defined as one that achieves high levels of task performance, member satisfaction, and _____. (a) coordination (b) harmony (c) creativity (d) team viability

4. Task characteristics, reward systems, and team size are all _____ that can make a difference in team effectiveness. (a) processes (b) dynamics (c) inputs (d) rewards

5. The best size for a problem-solving team is usually _____ members. (a) no more than 3 or 4 (b) 5 to 7 (c) 8 to 10 (d) around 12 to 13

6. When a new team member is anxious about questions such as "Will I be able to influence what takes place?" the underlying issue is one of _____. (a) relationships (b) goals (c) processes (d) control

7. Self-managing teams _____. (a) reduce the number of different job tasks members need to master (b) largely eliminate the need for a traditional supervisor (c) rely heavily on outside training to maintain job skills (d) add another management layer to overhead costs

8. Which statement about self-managing teams is most accurate? (a) They always improve performance but not satisfaction. (b) They should have limited decision-making authority. (c) They operate with elected team leaders. (d) They should let members plan and control their own work.

9. When a team of people is able to achieve more than what its members could by working individually, this is called _____. (a) distributed leadership (b) consensus (c) team viability (d) synergy

10. Members of a team tend to become more motivated and better able to deal with conflict during the _____ stage of team development. (a) forming (b) norming (c) performing (d) adjourning

11. The Ringlemann effect describes _____. (a) the tendency of groups to make risky decisions (b) social loafing (c) social facilitation (d) the satisfaction of members' social needs

12. Members of a multinational task force in a large international business should probably be aware that _____ might initially slow the progress of the team. (a) synergy (b) groupthink (c) the diversity–consensus dilemma (d) intergroup dynamics

13. When a team member engages in social loafing, one of the recommended strategies for dealing with this situation is to _____. (a) forget about it (b) ask another member to force this person to work harder (c) give the person extra rewards and hope he or she will feel guilty (d) better define member roles to improve individual accountability

14. When a person holds a prestigious position as a vice president in a top management team, but is considered just another member of an employee involvement team that

a lower-level supervisor heads, the person might experience _____. (a) role underload (b) role overload (c) status incongruence (d) the diversity–consensus dilemma

15. The team effectiveness equation states: Team effectiveness = _____ + (Process gains − Process losses). (a) Nature of setting (b) Nature of task (c) Quality of inputs (d) Available rewards

Short Response

16. In what ways are teams good for organizations?

17. What types of formal teams are found in organizations today?

18. What are members of self-managing teams typically expected to do?

19. What is the diversity–consensus dilemma?

Applications Essay

20. One of your Facebook friends has posted this note. "Help! I have just been assigned to head a new product design team at my company. The division manager has high expectations for the team and me, but I have been a technical design engineer for four years since graduating from college. I have never 'managed' anyone, let alone led a team. The manager keeps talking about her confidence that I will be very good at creating lots of teamwork. Does anyone out there have any tips to help me master this challenge?" You smile while reading the message and start immediately to formulate your recommendations. Exactly what message will you send?

Next Steps
Top Choices from
The OB Skills Workbook

Case for Critical Thinking	Team and Experiential Exercises	Self-Assessment Portfolio
• The Forgotten Team Member	• Sweet Tooth • Interrogatories • Teamwork and Motivation • Serving on the Boundary • *Eggs*periential Exercise	• Team Effectiveness • Decision-Making Biases

Virtual Teams: Here, There, Everywhere

In an average workday, Sarah strategizes with her teammates, consults with vendors, and advises clients in several time zones. And most workdays, she's still in her pajamas.

That's one of the perks of working for a virtual team—a group whose members collaborate across time, geographic, or organizational boundaries.[a] Once favored mostly by creative agencies, call centers, and multinational businesses, a growing number of organizations trade the security of managing employees in house for managing them in virtual space. The hope is for increased performance, improved employee satisfaction, and ultimately, a wider selection of potential collaborators.

But when teamwork goes virtual, the potential risks as well as gains are real. Any deficiencies in employee performance or management oversight will be magnified through the lens of team-member separation. Given the extra effort needed for every communication, virtual team members may experience loneliness or perceive social isolation. And teams may suffer if all members don't have a high degree of trust and regard for each other.[b]

Companies wouldn't accept the risks of virtual teams if the potential payoff wasn't worth it. When teams straddle time zones, companies benefit from longer work hours, more uptime, and greater access by both fellow employees and customers. As for virtual employees, who wouldn't be happy with a flexible work schedule and a 0-minute commute?[c]

> "My deadlines now no longer affect a voice on Skype or a person writing email—they affect my friends and colleagues."
> —Angela Sasso, on meeting her virtual teammates for the first time.[d]

These days, virtual employees have an impressive suite of tools that keep them tethered to their teammates. Webcams, chat, and VoIP services like Skype are *de facto* in most remote offices. As the quote suggests, with the right technology distant strangers become real teammates and friends. Execs who insist that it feel like virtual team members are *right there* (and who have deep pockets) invest in HD-quality videoconference systems.

Quick Summary

- Facilitated by the emergence of new networking technologies and ubiquitous broadband Internet, more organizations are making frequent use of virtual teams.
- Virtual teams can reduce employee travel costs, help companies approach 24/7 uptime, and give workers more flexible work schedules.
- To succeed, virtual teams require good technology, constant communication, shared priorities and deadlines, and a high degree of trust among all members.

FYI: The virtual world of workplace learning is the subject of the bestseller, *The New Social Learning: A Guide to Transforming Organizations Through Social Media*, by Tony Bingham, Marcia Conner, and Daniel H. Pink.[e]

8 Teamwork and Team Performance

the key point

In order for any team—virtual or face-to-face—to work well and do great things, its members must get things right. This means paying attention to things like team building and team processes. Team performance can't be left to chance. Yes, teams can be hard work. But it's also worth the effort. The opportunities of teams and teamwork are simply too great to miss.

chapter at a glance

What Are High-Performance Teams and How Do We Build Them?

How Can Team Processes Be Improved?

How Can Team Communications Be Improved?

How Can Team Decisions Be Improved?

ETHICS IN OB
SOCIAL LOAFING MAY BE CLOSER THAN YOU THINK

FINDING THE LEADER IN YOU
AMAZON'S JEFF BEZOS WINS WITH TWO-PIZZA TEAMS

OB IN POPULAR CULTURE
GROUPTHINK AND MADAGASCAR

RESEARCH INSIGHT
DEMOGRAPHIC FAULTLINES POSE IMPLICATIONS FOR LEADING TEAMS

what's inside?

High-Performance Teams

LEARNING ROADMAP   Characteristics of High-Performance Teams / The Team-Building Process / Team-Building Alternatives

Are you an iPod, iPhone, iPad, MacBook, or iMac user? Have you ever wondered why Apple, Inc. keeps giving us a stream of innovative and trend-setting products?

In many ways today's Apple story started years ago with its co-founder Steve Jobs, the first Macintosh computer, and a very special team. The "Mac" was Jobs's brainchild. To create it he put together a team of high-achievers who were excited and motivated by a highly challenging task. They worked all hours and at an unrelenting pace, while housed in a separate building flying the Jolly Roger to display their independence from Apple's normal bureaucracy. The Macintosh team combined youthful enthusiasm with great expertise and commitment to an exciting goal. In the process they set a new benchmark for product innovation as well as new standards for what makes for a high-performance team.[1]

Apple remains today a hotbed of high-performing teams that harness great talents to achieve innovation. But let's not forget that there are a lot of solid contributions made by good, old-fashioned, everyday teams in all organizations—the cross-functional, problem-solving, virtual, and self-managing teams introduced in the last chapter. We also need to remember, as scholar J. Richard Hackman points out, that many teams underperform and fail to live up to their potential. They simply, as Hackman says, "don't work."[2] The question for us is: What differentiates high-performing teams from the also-rans?

Characteristics of High-Performance Teams

Teams Gain from Great Leaders and Talented Members that Do the Right Things

- Set a clear and challenging direction
- Keep goals and expectations clear
- Communicate high standards
- Create a sense of urgency
- Make sure members have the right skills

- Model positive team member behaviors
- Create early performance "successes"
- Introduce useful information
- Help members share useful information
- Give positive feedback

Some "must-have" team leadership skills are described in the sidebar. And it's appropriate that setting a clear and challenging direction is at the top of the list.[3] Again, a look back in time to the original Macintosh story sets an example. In November 1983, *Wired* magazine's correspondent Steven Levy was given a sneak look at what he had been told was the "machine that was supposed to change the world." He says: "I also met the people who created that machine. They were groggy and almost giddy from three years of creation. Their eyes blazed with Visine and fire. They told me that with Macintosh, they were going to "put a dent in the Universe." Their leader, Steven P. Jobs, told them so. They also told me how Jobs referred to this new computer: 'Insanely Great.'"[4]

Whatever the purpose or tasks, the foundation for any high-performing team is a set of members who believe in team goals and are motivated to work hard to accomplish them. Indeed, an essential criterion of a high-performance team is that the members feel "collectively accountable" for moving in what Hackman calls "a compelling direction" toward a goal. Getting to this point isn't always easy. Hackman points out that members of many teams don't agree on the goal and don't share an understanding of what the team is supposed to accomplish.[5]

Whereas a shared sense of purpose gives general direction to a team, commitment to targeted performance results makes this purpose truly meaningful. High-performance teams turn a general sense of purpose into specific performance objectives. They set standards for taking action, measuring results, and gathering performance feedback. And they provide a clear focus for solving problems and resolving conflicts.

Members of high-performance teams have the right mix of skills, including technical, problem-solving, and interpersonal skills. A high-performance team also has strong core values that help guide team members' attitudes and behaviors in consistent directions. Such values act as an internal control system keeping team members on track without outside direction and supervisory attention.

You should recall from the last chapter the notion of **collective intelligence**, or the ability of a team to do well on a wide variety of tasks. This concept really summarizes what we mean by a "high-performance" team. It is not a team that excels only once. It is a team that excels over and over again while performing different tasks over time. Researchers point out that collective intelligence is higher in teams whose processes are not dominated by one or a few members. Collective intelligence is also associated with having more female members, something researchers link to higher social sensitivity in the team process.[6]

> • **Collective intelligence** is the ability of a team to perform well across a range of tasks.

The Team-Building Process

In the sports world, coaches and managers spend a lot of time at the start of each season joining new members with old ones and forming a strong team. Yet we all know that even the most experienced teams can run into problems as a season progresses. Members slack off or become disgruntled with one another; some have performance "slumps," and others criticize them for it; some are traded gladly or unhappily to other teams.

Even world-champion teams have losing streaks. And at times even the most talented players can lose motivation, quibble among themselves, and end up contributing little to team success. When these things happen, concerned owners, managers, and players are apt to examine their problems, take corrective action to rebuild the team, and restore the teamwork needed to achieve high-performance results.[7]

Workgroups and teams face similar challenges. When newly formed, they must master many challenges as members learn how to work together while passing through the stages of team development. Even when mature, most work teams encounter problems of insufficient teamwork at different points in time. At the very least we can say that teams sometimes need help to perform well and that teamwork always needs to be nurtured.

This is why a process known as **team-building** is so important. It is a sequence of planned activities designed to gather and analyze data on the functioning of a team and to initiate changes designed to improve teamwork and increase team effectiveness.[8] When done well and at the right times, team-building can be a good way to deal with teamwork problems or to help prevent them from occurring in the first place.

> • **Team-building** is a collaborative way to gather and analyze data to improve teamwork.

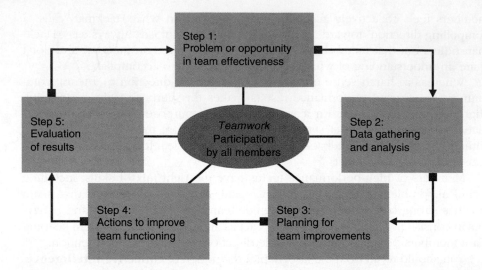

Figure 8.1 Steps in the team-building process.

The action steps for team-building are highlighted in Figure 8.1. Although it is tempting to view the process as something that consultants or outside experts are hired to do, the fact is that it can and should be part of any team leader and manager's skill set.

Team-building begins when someone notices an actual or a potential problem with team effectiveness. Data are gathered to examine the problem. This can be done by questionnaire, interview, nominal group meeting, or other creative methods. The goal is to get good answers to such questions as: "How well are we doing in terms of task accomplishment?" "How satisfied are we as individuals with the group and the way it operates?" After the answers to such questions are analyzed by team members, they then work together to plan for and accomplish improvements. This team-building process is highly collaborative and participation by all members is essential.

Team-Building Alternatives

Team-building can be accomplished in a wide variety of ways. On one fall day, for example, a team of employees from American Electric Power (AEP) went to an outdoor camp. They worked on problems such as how to get six members through a spider-web maze of bungee cords strung 2 feet above the ground. When her colleagues lifted Judy Gallo into their hands to pass her over the obstacle, she was nervous. But a trainer told the team this was just like solving a problem together at the office. The spider web was just another performance constraint, like the difficult policy issues or financial limits they might face at work. After "high-fives" for making it through the web, Judy's team jumped tree stumps together, passed hula hoops while holding hands, and more. Says one outdoor team trainer, "We throw clients into situations to try and bring out the traits of a good team."9

This was an example of the *outdoor experience approach* to team-building. It is increasingly popular and can be done on its own or in combination with other approaches. The outdoor experience places group members in a variety of

Reality Team-Building Is Catching More Attention

Some organizations are finding that borrowing ideas from "reality" TV offers novel ways to accomplish team-building and drive innovation. It sounds radical, but Best Buy sent small teams to live together for 10 weeks in Los Angeles apartments. The purpose was to demonstrate new ideas and lay the groundwork for new lines of business as well as potential independent businesses. One participant says: "Living together and knowing we only had 10 weeks sped up our team-building process."

physically challenging situations that must be mastered through teamwork. By having to work together in the face of difficult obstacles, team members are supposed to grow in self-confidence, gain more respect for each others' capabilities, and leave with a greater commitment to teamwork.

In the *formal retreat approach*, team-building takes place during an off-site "retreat." The agenda, which may cover one or more days, is designed to engage team members in the variety of assessment and planning tasks just discussed. Formal retreats are often held with the assistance of a consultant, who is either hired from the outside or made available from in-house staff. Team-building retreats are opportunities to take time away from the job to assess team accomplishments, operations, and future potential.

In a *continuous improvement approach,* the manager, team leader, or group members themselves take responsibility for regularly engaging in the team-building process. This method can be as simple as periodic meetings that implement the team-building steps; it can also include self-managed formal retreats. In all cases, the goal is to engage team members in a process that leaves them more capable and committed to continuous performance assessment and improved teamwork.

Improving Team Processes

LEARNING ROADMAP   Entry of New Members / Task and Maintenance Leadership / Roles and Role Dynamics / Team Norms / Team Cohesiveness / Inter-Team Dynamics

As more and more jobs are turned over to teams, and as more and more traditional supervisors are asked to function as team leaders, special problems and challenges of managing team processes become magnified. Team leaders and members alike must be prepared to deal positively with such issues as introducing new members, handling disagreements on goals and responsibilities, resolving delays and disputes when making decisions, reducing personality friction, and dealing with interpersonal conflicts. These are all targets for team-building. And given the complex nature of group dynamics, team-building is, in a sense, never finished. Something is always happening that creates the need for further leadership efforts to help improve team processes.

Entry of New Members

Special difficulties are likely to occur when members first get together in a new group or team, or when new members join an existing team. Problems arise as new members try to understand what is expected of them while dealing with the anxiety and discomfort of a new social setting. New members, for example, may worry about—

- *Participation*—"Will I be allowed to participate?"
- *Goals*—"Do I share the same goals as others?"
- *Control*—"Will I be able to influence what takes place?"
- *Relationships*—"How close do people get?"
- *Processes*—"Are conflicts likely to be upsetting?"

Edgar Schein points out that people may try to cope with individual entry problems in self-serving ways that may hinder team development and performance.[10] He identifies three behavior profiles that are common in such situations.

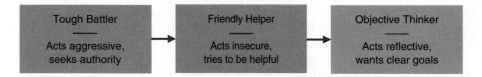

Tough Battler   The *tough battler* is frustrated by a lack of identity in the new group and may act aggressively or reject authority. This person wants answers to this question: "Who am I in this group?" The best team response may be to allow the new member to share his or her skills and interests, and then have a discussion about how these qualities can best be used to help the team.

Friendly Helper   The *friendly helper* is insecure, suffering uncertainties of intimacy and control. This person may show extraordinary support for others, behave in a dependent way, and seek alliances in subgroups or cliques. The friendly helper needs to know whether he or she will be liked. The best team response may be to offer support and encouragement while encouraging the new member to be more confident in joining team activities and discussions.

Objective Thinker   The *objective thinker* is anxious about how personal needs will be met in the group. This person may act in a passive, reflective, and even single-minded manner while struggling with the fit between individual goals and group directions. The best team response may be to engage in a discussion to clarify team goals and expectations, and to clarify member roles in meeting them.

Task and Maintenance Leadership

• **Distributed leadership** shares responsibility among members for meeting team task and maintenance needs.

Research in social psychology suggests that teams have both "task needs" and "maintenance needs," and that both must be met for teams to be successful.[11] Even though a team leader should be able to meet these needs at the appropriate times, each team member is responsible as well. This sharing of responsibilities for making task and maintenance contributions to move a group forward is called **distributed leadership**, and it is usually well evidenced in high-performance teams.

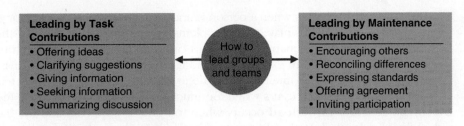

Figure 8.2 Task and maintenance leadership in team dynamics.

Figure 8.2 describes **task activities** as things team members and leaders do that directly contribute to the performance of important group tasks. They include initiating discussion, sharing information, asking information of others, clarifying something that has been said, and summarizing the status of a deliberation.[12] A team will have difficulty accomplishing its objectives when task activities are not well performed. In an effective team, by contrast, all members pitch in to contribute important task leadership as needed.

- **Task activities** directly contribute to the performance of important tasks.

The figure also shows that **maintenance activities** support the social and interpersonal relationships among team members. They help a team stay intact and healthy as an ongoing and well-functioning social system. A team member or leader can contribute maintenance leadership by encouraging the participation of others, trying to harmonize differences of opinion, praising the contributions of others, and agreeing to go along with a popular course of action. When maintenance leadership is poor, members become dissatisfied with one another, the value of their group membership diminishes, and emotional conflicts may drain energies otherwise needed for task performance. In an effective team, by contrast, maintenance activities support the relationships needed for team members to work well together over time.

- **Maintenance activities** support the emotional life of the team as an ongoing social system.

In addition to helping meet a group's task and maintenance needs, team members share additional responsibility for avoiding and eliminating any **disruptive behaviors** that harm the group process. These dysfunctional activities include bullying and being overly aggressive toward other members, showing incivility and disrespect, withdrawing and refusing to cooperate, horsing around when there is work to be done, using meetings as forums for self-confession, talking too much about irrelevant matters, and trying to compete for attention and recognition. *Incivility* or *antisocial behavior* by members can be especially disruptive of team dynamics and performance. Research shows that persons who are targets of harsh leadership, social exclusion, and harmful rumors often end up working less hard, performing less well, being late and absent more, and reducing their commitment.[13]

- **Disruptive behaviors** in teams harm the group process and limit team effectiveness.

Roles and Role Dynamics

New and old team members alike need to know what others expect of them and what they can expect from others. A **role** is a set of expectations associated with a job or position on a team. And, simply put, teams tend to perform better when their members have clear and realistic expectations regarding their tasks and responsibilities. When team members are unclear about their roles or face conflicting role demands, performance problems are likely. Although this is a common situation, it can be managed with good awareness of role dynamics and their causes.

- A **role** is a set of expectations for a team member or person in a job.

• **Role ambiguity** occurs when someone is uncertain about what is expected of him or her.

Role ambiguity occurs when a person is uncertain about his or her role or job on a team. Role ambiguities may create problems as team members find that their work efforts are wasted or unappreciated. This can even happen in mature groups if team members fail to share expectations and listen to one another's concerns.

Being asked to do too much or too little as a team member can also create problems. **Role overload** occurs when too much is expected and someone feels overwhelmed. **Role underload** occurs when too little is expected and the individual feels underused. Both role overload and role underload can cause stress, dissatisfaction, and performance problems.

• **Role overload** occurs when too much work is expected of the individual.

• **Role underload** occurs when too little work is expected of the individual.

Role conflict occurs when a person is unable to meet the expectations of others. The individual understands what needs to be done but for some reason cannot comply. The resulting tension is stressful and can reduce satisfaction. And, it can affect an individual's performance and relationships with other group members. People at work and in teams can experience four common forms of role conflict:

• **Role conflict** occurs when someone is unable to respond to role expectations that conflict with one another.

1. *Intrasender role conflict* occurs when the same person sends conflicting expectations. Example: Team leader—"You need to get the report written right away, but now I need you to help me get the Power Points ready."

2. *Intersender role conflict* occurs when different people send conflicting and mutually exclusive expectations. Example: Team leader (to you)—"Your job is to criticize our decisions so that we don't make mistakes." Team member (to you)—"You always seem so negative; can't you be more positive for a change?"

3. *Person–role conflict* occurs when a person's values and needs come into conflict with role expectations. Example: Other team members (showing agreement with each other)—"We didn't get enough questionnaires back, so let's each fill out five more and add them to the data set." You (to yourself)—"Mmm, I don't think this is right."

4. *Inter-role conflict* occurs when the expectations of two or more roles held by the same individual become incompatible, such as the conflict between work and family demands. Example: Team leader—"Don't forget the big meeting we have scheduled for Thursday evening." You (to yourself)—"But my daughter is playing in her first little-league soccer game at that same time."

• **Role negotiation** is a process for discussing and agreeing upon what team members expect of one another.

A technique known as **role negotiation** is a helpful way of managing role dynamics. It's a process where team members meet to discuss, clarify, and agree upon the role expectations each holds for the other. Such a negotiation might begin, for example, with one member writing down this request of another: "If you were to do the following, it would help me to improve my performance on the team." Her list of requests might include such things as: "respect it when I say that I can't meet some evenings because I have family obligations to fulfill"—indicating role conflict; "stop asking for so much detail when we are working hard with tight deadlines"—indicating role overload; and "try to make yourself available when I need to speak with you to clarify goals and expectations"—indicating role ambiguity.

Team Norms

• **Norms** are rules or standards for the behavior of group members.

The role dynamics we have just discussed all relate to what team members expect of one another and of themselves. This brings up the issue of team **norms**—beliefs

Beware the Sins of Deadly Meetings

The sins of deadly meetings are easy to spot, but harder to avoid: meeting scheduled in the wrong place; meeting scheduled at a bad time; people arrive late; meeting is too long; people go off topic; discussion lacks candor; right information not available; no follow-through when meeting is over.

about how members are expected to behave. They can be considered as rules or standards of team conduct.[14] Norms help members to guide their own behavior and predict what others will do. When someone violates a team norm, other members typically respond in ways that are aimed at enforcing it and bring behavior back into alignment with the norm. These responses may include subtle hints, direct criticisms, and even reprimands. At the extreme, someone violating team norms may be ostracized or even expelled.

Types of Team Norms   A key norm in any team setting is the **performance norm**. It conveys expectations about how hard team members should work and what the team should accomplish. In some teams the performance norm is high and strong. There is no doubt that all members are expected to work very hard and that high performance is the goal. If someone slacks off they get reminded to work hard or end up removed from the team. But in other teams the performance norm is low and weak. Members are left to work hard or not as they like, with little concern shown by the other members.

> • The **performance norm** sets expectations for how hard members work and what the team should accomplish.

Many other norms also influence the day-to-day functioning of teams. In order for a task force or a committee to operate effectively, for example, norms regarding attendance at meetings, punctuality, preparedness, criticism, and social behavior are needed. Teams may have norms on how members deal with supervisors, colleagues, and customers, as well as norms about honesty and ethical behavior. The following examples show norms that can have positive and negative implications for teams and organizations.[15]

- *Ethics norms*—"We try to make ethical decisions, and we expect others to do the same" (positive); "Don't worry about inflating your expense account; everyone does it here" (negative).

- *Organizational and personal pride norms*—"It's a tradition around here for people to stand up for the company when others criticize it unfairly" (positive); "In our company, they are always trying to take advantage of us" (negative).

- *High-achievement norms*—"On our team, people always want to win or be the best" (positive); "No one really cares on this team whether we win or lose" (negative).

- *Support and helpfulness norms*—"People on this committee are good listeners and actively seek out the ideas and opinions of others" (positive); "On this committee it's dog-eat-dog and save your own skin" (negative).

- *Improvement and change norms*—"In our department people are always looking for better ways of doing things" (positive); "Around here, people hang on to the old ways even after they have outlived their usefulness" (negative).

ETHICS IN OB

SOCIAL LOAFING MAY BE CLOSER THAN YOU THINK

1. *Psychology study:* A German researcher asked people to pull on a rope as hard as they could. First, they pulled alone. Second, they pulled as part of a group. Results showed that people pull harder when working alone than when working as part of a team. Such "social loafing" is the tendency to reduce effort when working in groups.

2. *Faculty office:* A student wants to speak with the instructor about his team's performance on the last group project. There were four members, but two did almost all of the work. The other two largely disappeared, showing up only at the last minute to be part of the formal presentation. His point is that the team was disadvantaged because the two "free-riders" caused reduced performance capacity for his team.

3. *Telephone call from the boss:* "John, I really need you to serve on this committee. Will you do it? Let me know tomorrow." John thinks: I'm overloaded, but I don't want to turn down the boss. I'll accept but let the committee members know about my limits. I'll be active in discussions and try to offer viewpoints and perspectives that are helpful. However, I'll tell them front that I can't be a leader or volunteer for any extra work. Some might say this is an excuse to "slack off while still doing what the boss wants." John views it as being honest.

> *You Decide*   Whether you call it "social loafing," "free-riding" or just plain old "slacking off," the issue is the same: What right do some people have to sit back in team situations and let other people do all the work? Is this ethical? Does everyone on a team have an ethical obligation to do his or her fair share of the work? And when it comes to John, does the fact that he is going to be honest with the other committee members make any difference? Isn't he still going to be a loafer, and yet earn credit with the boss for serving on the committee? Would it be more ethical for John to decline becoming a part of this committee?

How to Influence Team Norms   Team leaders and members alike can do several things to help their teams develop and operate with positive norms, ones that foster high performance as well as membership satisfaction. The first thing is to always *act as a positive role model*. In other words, be the exemplar of the norm, always living up to the norm in everyday behavior. It is helpful to hold meetings where time is set aside for members to *discuss team goals* and also *discuss team norms* that can best contribute to their achievement. Norms are too important to be left to chance. The more directly they are discussed and confronted in the early stages of team development, the better.

It's always best to try to *select members who can and will live up to the desired norms*, be sure to *provide training and support*, and then *reward and positively reinforce desired behaviors*. This is a full-cycle approach to developing positive team norms—select the right people, give them support, and then offer positive reinforcement for doing things right. Finally, teams should remember the power of team-building and *hold regular meetings to discuss team performance and plan how to improve it* in the future.

Team Cohesiveness

The **cohesiveness** of a group or team is the degree to which members are attracted to and motivated to remain part of it.[16] We might think of it as the "feel good" factor that causes people to value their membership on a team, positively identify with it, and strive to maintain positive relationships with other members. Feelings of cohesion can be a source of need satisfaction, often providing a source of loyalty, security, and esteem for team members. And because cohesive teams are such a source of personal satisfaction, their members tend to display fairly predictable behaviors that differentiate them from members of less cohesive teams—they are more energetic when working on team activities, less likely to be absent, less likely to quit the team, and more likely to be happy about performance success and sad about failures.

- **Cohesiveness** is the degree to which members are attracted to a group and motivated to remain a part of it.

Team Cohesiveness and Conformity to Norms Even though cohesive groups are good for their members, they may or may not be good for the organization. The question is: Will the cohesive team also be a high-performance team? The answer to this question depends on the match of cohesiveness with conformity to norms.

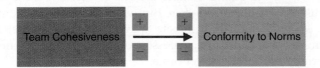

The **rule of conformity** in team dynamics states that the greater the cohesiveness of a team, the greater the conformity of members to team norms. So when the performance norms are positive in a highly cohesive work group or team, the resulting conformity to the norm should have a positive effect on both team performance and member satisfaction. This is a best-case situation for team members, the team leader, and the organization. But when the performance norms are negative in a highly cohesive group, as shown in Figure 8.3, the rule of

- The **rule of conformity** is the greater the cohesiveness, the greater the conformity of members to team norms.

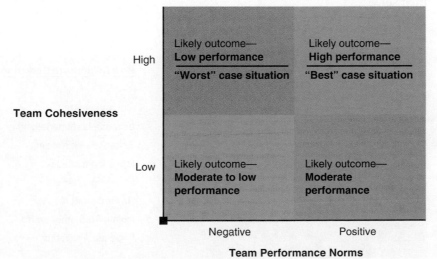

Figure 8.3 How cohesiveness and conformity to norms influence team performance.

conformity creates a worst-case situation for the team leader and the organization. Although the high cohesiveness leaves the team members feeling loyal and satisfied, they are also highly motivated to conform to the negative performance norm. In between these two extremes are two mixed-case situations for teams low in cohesion. Because there is little conformity to either the positive or negative norms, team performance will most likely fall on the moderate or low side.

How to Influence Team Cohesiveness What can be done to tackle the worst-case and mixed-case scenarios just described? The answer rests with the factors influencing team cohesiveness. Cohesiveness tends to be high when teams are more homogeneous in makeup, that is when members are similar in age, attitudes, needs, and backgrounds. Cohesiveness also tends to be high in teams of small size, where members respect one another's competencies, agree on common goals, and like to work together rather than alone on team tasks. And cohesiveness tends to increase when groups are physically isolated from others and when they experience performance success or crisis.

Figure 8.4 shows how team cohesiveness can be increased or decreased by making changes in goals, membership composition, interactions, size, rewards, competition, location, and duration. When the team norms are positive but cohesiveness is low, the goal is to take actions to increase cohesion and gain more conformity to the positive norms. But when team norms are negative and cohesiveness is high, just the opposite may have to be done. If efforts to change the norms fail, it may be necessary to reduce cohesiveness and thus reduce conformity to the negative norms.

Inter-Team Dynamics

- **Inter-team dynamics** occur as groups cooperate and compete with one another.

The presence of competition with other teams tends to increase cohesiveness within a team. This raises the issue of what happens between, not just within, teams. We call this **inter-team dynamics**. Organizations ideally operate as cooperative systems in which the various groups and teams support one another. In the real world, however, competition and inter-team problems often develop. Their consequences can be good or bad for the host organization and the teams themselves.

How to Decrease Cohesion	TARGETS	How to Increase Cohesion
Create disagreement	Goals	Get agreement
Increase heterogeneity	Membership	Increase homogeneity
Restrict within team	Interactions	Enhance within team
Make team bigger	Size	Make team smaller
Focus within team	Competition	Focus on other teams
Reward individual results	Rewards	Reward team results
Open up to other teams	Location	Isolate from other teams
Disband the team	Duration	Keep team together

Figure 8.4 Ways to increase and decrease team cohesiveness.

Demographic Faultlines Pose Implications for Leading Teams in Organizations

According to researchers Dora Lau and Keith Murnighan, strong "faultlines" occur in groups when demographic diversity results in the formation of two or more subgroups whose members are similar to and strongly identify with one another. Examples include teams with subgroups forming around age, gender, race, ethnic, occupational, or tenure differences. When strong faultlines are present, members are expected to identify more strongly with their subgroups than with the team as a whole. Lau and Murnighan predict that this will affect what happens with the team in terms of conflict, politics, and performance.

Using subjects from ten organizational behavior classes at a university, the researchers randomly assigned students to casework groups based on sex and ethnicity. After working on their cases, group members completed questionnaires about group processes and outcomes. Results showed, as predicted, that members in strong faultline groups evaluated those in their

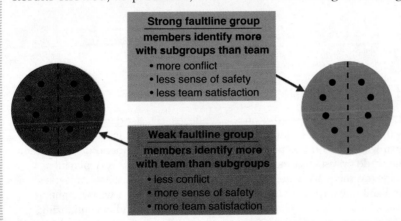

Strong faultline group
members identify more with subgroups than team
- more conflict
- less sense of safety
- less team satisfaction

Weak faultline group
members identify more with team than subgroups
- less conflict
- more sense of safety
- more team satisfaction

subgroups more favorably than did members of weak faultline groups. Members of weak faultline groups also experienced less conflict, more psychological safety, and more satisfaction than did those in strong faultline groups. More communication across faultlines had a positive effect on outcomes for weak faultline groups but not for strong faultline groups.

Do the Research *See if you can verify these findings. Be a "participant observer" in your work teams. Focus on faultlines and their effects. Keep a diary, make notes, and compare your experiences with this study in mind.*

Source: Dora C. Lau and J. Keith Murnighan, "Interactions within Groups and Subgroups: The Effects of Demographic Faultlines," *Academy of Management Journal* 48 (2005), pp. 645–659; and "Demographic Diversity and Faultlines: The Compositional Dynamics of Organizational Groups," *Academy of Management Review* 23 (1998), pp. 325–340.

On the positive side of inter-team dynamics, competition among teams can stimulate them to become more cohesive, work harder, become more focused on key tasks, develop more internal loyalty and satisfaction, or achieve a higher level of creativity in problem solving. This effect is demonstrated at virtually any intercollegiate athletic event, and it is common in work settings as well.[17] On the negative side, such as when manufacturing and sales units don't get along, inter-team dynamics may drain and divert work energies. Members may spend too much time focusing on their animosities or conflicts with another team and too little time focusing on their own team's performance.[18]

A variety of steps can be taken to avoid negative and achieve positive effects from inter-team dynamics. Teams engaged in destructive competition, for example, can be refocused on a common enemy or a common goal. Direct negotiations can be held among the teams. Members can be engaged in inter-group team-building that encourages positive interactions and helps members of different teams learn how to work more cooperatively together. Reward systems can also be refocused to emphasize team contributions to overall organizational performance and on how much teams help out one another.

Improving Team Communications

LEARNING ROADMAP   Communication Networks / Proxemics and Use of Space / Communication Technologies

Chapter 11 discusses many issues on communication and collaboration. The focus there is on such things as communication effectiveness, techniques for overcoming barriers and improving communication, and the use of collaborative

Finding the Leader in You

AMAZON'S JEFF BEZOS WINS WITH TWO-PIZZA TEAMS

Amazon.com's founder and CEO Jeff Bezos is considered one of America's top businesspersons and a technology visionary. He's also a great fan of teams. Bezos coined a simple rule when it comes to sizing the firm's product development teams: If two pizzas aren't enough to feed a team, it's too big.

The business plan for Amazon originated while Bezos was driving cross-country. He started the firm in his garage, and even when his Amazon stock grew to $500 million he was still driving a Honda and living in a small apartment in downtown Seattle. Clearly, he's a

unique personality and also one with a great business mind. His goal with Amazon was to "create the world's most customer-centric company, the place where you can find and buy anything you want online."

If you go to Amazon.com and click on the "Gold Box" at the top, you'll be tuning in to his vision. It's a place for special deals, lasting only an hour and offering everything from a power tool to a new pair of shoes. Such online innovations don't just come out of the blue. They're part and parcel of the management philosophy Bezos has instilled at the firm. The Gold Box and many of Amazon's successful innovations are products of many "two-pizza teams." Described as "small," "fast-moving," and "innovation engines," these teams typically have five to eight members and thrive on turning new ideas into business potential.

Don't expect to spot a stereotyped corporate CEO in Jeff

Bezos. His standard office attire is still blue jeans and blue collared shirt. A family friend describes him and his wife as "very playful people." Bezos views Amazon's small teams as a way of fighting bureaucracy and decentralizing, even as a company grows large and very complex. He is also a fan of what he calls fact-based decisions. He says they help to "overrule the hierarchy. The most junior person in the company can win an argument with the most senior person with fact-based decisions."

What's the Lesson Here?

Do you need to be in control as a team leader, or are you comfortable delegating? Do you consider yourself more informal or formal in your approach to leadership? How would you feel if a person junior to you had more say in a decision than you did?

communication technologies. And in teams, it is important to make sure that every member is strong and capable in basic communication and collaboration skills. In addition, however, teams must address questions like these: What communication networks are being used by the team and why? How does space affect communication among team members? Is the team making good use of the available communication technologies?

Communication Networks

Three patterns typically emerge when team members interact with one another while working on team tasks. We call them the interacting team, the co-acting team, and the counteracting team shown in Figure 8.5.

In order for a team to be effective and high-performing, the interaction pattern should fit the task at hand. Indeed, a team ideally shifts among the interaction patterns as task demands develop and change over time. One of the most common mistakes discovered during team-building is that members are not using the right interaction patterns. An example might be a student project team whose members believe every member must always be present when any work gets done on the project; in other words, no one works on his own and everything is done together.

Figure 8.5 links interaction patterns with team communication networks.[19] When task demands require intense interaction, this is best done with a **decentralized communication network**. Also called the *star network* or *all-channel network*, it operates with everyone communicating and sharing information with everyone else. Information flows back and forth constantly, with no one person serving as the center point.[20] Decentralized communication networks work well when team tasks are complex and nonroutine, perhaps tasks that involve

- In **decentralized communication networks** members communicate directly with one another.

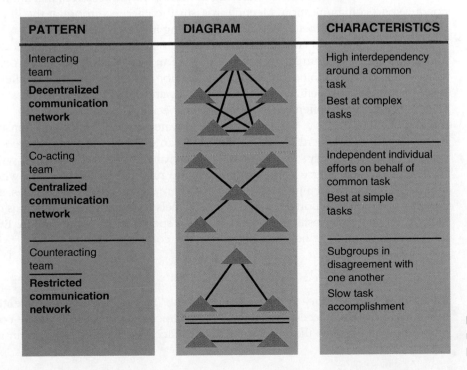

PATTERN	DIAGRAM	CHARACTERISTICS
Interacting team **Decentralized communication network**		High interdependency around a common task Best at complex tasks
Co-acting team **Centralized communication network**		Independent individual efforts on behalf of common task Best at simple tasks
Counteracting team **Restricted communication network**		Subgroups in disagreement with one another Slow task accomplishment

Figure 8.5 Communication networks and interaction patterns found in teams.

uncertainty and require creativity. Member satisfaction on such interacting teams is usually high.

• **Centralized communication networks** link group members through a central control point.

When task demands allow for more independent work by team members, a **centralized communication network** is the best option. Also called the *wheel network* or *chain network*, it operates with a central "hub" through which one member, often a formal or informal team leader, collects and distributes information. Members of such coaching teams work on assigned tasks independently while the hub keeps everyone and everything coordinated. Work is divided up among members and results are pooled to create the finished product. The centralized network works well when team tasks are routine and easily subdivided. It is usually the hub member who experiences the most satisfaction on successful coaching teams.

• **Restricted communication networks** link subgroups that disagree with one another's positions.

Counteracting teams form when subgroups emerge within a team due to issue-specific disagreements, such as a temporary debate over the best means to achieve a goal, or emotional disagreements, such as personality clashes. This creates a **restricted communication network** in which the subgroups contest each other's positions and restrict interactions with one another. The poor communication often creates problems. But there are times when it can be useful. Counteracting teams might be set up to stimulate conflict and criticism to help improve creativity or double check decisions about to be implemented.

Proxemics and Use of Space

• **Proxemics** involves the use of space as people interact.

An important but sometimes neglected part of communication in teams involves **proxemics**, or the use of space as people interact.[21] We know, for example, that office or workspace architecture is an important influence on communication behavior. It only makes sense that communication in teams might be improved by arranging physical space to best support it. This might be done by moving chairs and tables closer together, or by choosing to meet in physical spaces that are most conducive to communication. Meeting in a small conference room at the library, for example, may be a better choice than meeting in a busy coffee shop.

Some architects and consultants specialize in office design for communication and teamwork. When Sun Microsystems built its San Jose, California, facility, public spaces were designed to encourage communication among persons from different departments. Many meeting areas had no walls, and most walls were glass.[22] At Google headquarters, often called Googleplex, specially designed office "tents" are made of acrylics to allow both the sense of private personal space and transparency.[23] And at b&a advertising in Dublin, Ohio, an emphasis on open space supports the small ad agency's emphasis on creativity; after all, its Web address is www.babrain.com. Face-to-face communication is the rule at b&a to the point where internal e-mail among employees is banned. There are no offices or cubicles, and all office equipment is portable. Desks have wheels so that informal meetings can happen by people repositioning themselves for spontaneous collaboration. Even the formal meetings are held standing up in the company kitchen.[24]

Communication Technologies

It hardly seems necessary in the age of Facebook, Twitter, and Skype to mention that teams now have access to many useful technologies that can facilitate communication and reduce the need to be face to face. We live and work in an age of instant messaging, tweets and texting, wikis, online discussions, video chats, videoconferencing, and more. We are networked socially 24–7 to the extent we want, and there's no reason the members of a team can't utilize the same technologies to good advantage.

Think of technology as allowing and empowering teams to use **virtual communication networks** in which team members communicate electronically all or most of the time. Technology in virtual teamwork acts as the "hub member" in the centralized communication network and as an ever-present "electronic router" that links members in decentralized networks on an as-needed and always-ready basis. And new developments with social media keep pushing these capabilities forward. General Electric, for example, started a "Tweet Squad" to advise employees how social networking could be used to improve internal collaboration. The insurer MetLife has its own social network, connect.MetLife, which facilitates collaboration through a Facebook-like setting.[25]

Of course and as mentioned in the last chapter, certain steps need to be taken to make sure that virtual teams and communication technologies are as successful as possible. This means doing things like online team-building so that members get to know one another, learn about and identify team goals, and otherwise develop a sense of cohesiveness.[26] And we shouldn't forget protocols and everyday good manners when using technology as part of teamwork. For example, Richard Anderson, CEO of Delta Airlines, says: "I don't think it's appropriate to use Blackberrys in meetings. You might as well have a newspaper and open the newspaper up in the middle of the meeting."[27] Might we say the same for the texting now commonplace in classrooms?

* **Virtual communication networks** link team members through electronic communication.

Improving Team Decisions

LEARNING ROADMAP Ways Teams Make Decisions / Assets and Liabilities of Team Decisions / Groupthink Symptoms and Remedies / Team Decision Techniques

One of the most important activities for any team is **decision making**, the process of choosing among alternative courses of action. The quality and timeliness of decisions made and the processes through which they are arrived at can have an important impact on how teams work and what they achieve.

* **Decision making** is the process of choosing among alternative courses of action.

Ways Teams Make Decisions

Consider the many teams of which you have been and are a part. Just how do major decisions get made? Most often there's a lot more going on than meets the eye. Edgar Schein, a noted scholar and consultant, has worked extensively with teams to identify, analyze, and improve their decision processes.[28] He observes that teams may make decisions through any of six methods discussed here. Schein doesn't rule out any method, but he does point out their advantages and disadvantages.

Lack of Response In *decision by lack of response* one idea after another is suggested without any discussion taking place. When the team finally accepts an idea, all others have been bypassed and discarded by simple lack of response rather than

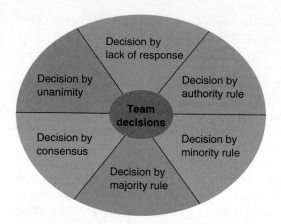

Figure 8.6 Alternative ways that teams make decisions.

by critical evaluation. This may happen early in a team's development when new members are struggling for identities and confidence. It's also common in teams with low-performance norms and when members just don't care enough to get involved in what is taking place. But whenever lack of response drives decisions, it's relatively easy for a team to move off in the wrong, or at least not the best, direction.

Authority Rule   In *decision by authority rule* the chairperson, manager, or leader makes a decision for the team. This is very time efficient and can be done with or without inputs by other members. Whether the decision is a good one or a bad one depends on if the authority figure has the necessary information and if other group members accept this approach. When an authority decision is made without expertise or member commitment, problems are likely.

Minority Rule   In *decision by minority rule* two or three people are able to dominate, or "railroad," the group into making a decision with which they agree. This is often done by providing a suggestion and then forcing quick agreement. The railroader may challenge the group with statements like: "Does anyone object? . . . No? Well, let's go ahead then." While such forcing and bullying may get the team moving in a certain direction, member commitment to making the decision successful will probably be low. "Kickback" and "resistance," especially when things get difficult, aren't unusual in these situations.

Majority Rule   One of the most common ways that groups make decisions is through *decision by majority rule*. This usually takes place as a formal vote to find the majority viewpoint. When team members get into disagreements that seem irreconcilable, for example, voting is seen to be an easy way out of the situation. But, majority rule is often used without awareness of its potential problems. The very process creates coalitions, especially when votes are taken and results are close. Those in the minority—the "losers"—may feel left out or discarded without having had a fair say. They may not be enthusiastic about implementing the decision of the "winners." Lingering resentments may hurt team effectiveness in the future if they become more concerned about winning the next vote than doing what is best for the team.

• **Consensus** is a group decision that has the expressed support of most members.

Consensus   Another of the decision alternatives in Figure 8.6 is **consensus**. It results when discussion leads to one alternative being favored by most team members and other members agree to support it. When a consensus is reached, even those who may have opposed the chosen course of action know that they have been listened to and have had a fair chance to influence the outcome. Consensus does not require unanimity. What it does require is the opportunity for any dissenting members to feel that they have been able to speak and that their voices have been heard.[29] Because of the extensive process involved in reaching a consensus decision, it may be inefficient from a time perspective. But consensus is very powerful in terms of generating commitments among members to making the final decision work best for the team.

Unanimity   A *decision by unanimity* may be the ideal state of affairs. Here, all team members whole-heartedly agree on the course of action to be taken. This "logically perfect" decision situation is extremely difficult to attain in actual practice. One reason that teams sometimes turn to authority decisions, majority voting, or even minority decisions, in fact, is the difficulty of managing the team process to achieve decisions by consensus or unanimity.

Assets and Liabilities of Team Decisions

Just as with communication networks, the best teams don't limit themselves to any one of the decision methods just described. Rather, they move back and forth using each in appropriate circumstances. In our cases, for example, we never complain when a department head makes an authority decision to have a welcome reception for new students at the start of the academic year or calls for a faculty vote on a proposed new travel policy. Yet we'd quickly disapprove if a department head made an authority decision to hire a new faculty member—something we believe should be made by faculty consensus.

The key for the department head in our example and for any team leader is to use decision methods that best fit the problems and situations at hand. This requires a good understanding of the potential assets and liabilities of team decision making.[30]

On the positive side, the more team-oriented decision methods, such as consensus and unanimity, offer the advantages of bringing more information, knowledge, and expertise to bear on a problem. Extensive discussion tends to create broader understanding of the final decision, and this increases acceptance. It also strengthens the commitments of members to follow through and support the decision.

But as we all know, team decisions can be imperfect. It usually takes a team longer to make a decision than it does an individual. Then, too, social pressures to conform might make some members unwilling to go against or criticize what appears to be the will of the majority. And in the guise of a so-called team decision, furthermore, a team leader or a few members might "railroad" or "force" other members to accept their preferred decision.

When in Doubt, Follow the Seven Steps for Consensus

It's easy to say that consensus is good. It's a lot harder to achieve consensus, especially when tough decisions are needed. Here are some tips for how members should behave in consensus-seeking teams.

1. Don't argue blindly; consider others' reactions to your points.
2. Be open and flexible, but don't change your mind just to reach quick agreement.
3. Avoid voting, coin tossing, and bargaining to avoid or reduce conflict.
4. Act in ways that encourage everyone's involvement in the decision process.
5. Allow disagreements to surface so that information and opinions can be deliberated.
6. Don't focus on winning versus losing; seek alternatives acceptable to all.
7. Discuss assumptions, listen carefully, and encourage participation by everyone.

GROUPTHINK AND *MADAGASCAR*

Cohesiveness is generally a good thing, but sometimes it can lead to problems. **Groupthink** occurs when group members fail to critically evaluate circumstances and proposed ideas. They don't actually lose the ability to criticize, they simply don't exercise it. Members go out of their way to conform, as cohesiveness actually works against the group.

In the movie *Madagascar,* four animals try to escape from the New York Central Zoo. Local residents complain about the danger, so the animals are shipped to Africa when they are captured. The animals' crates are tossed overboard during a storm and they end up in Madagascar.

Local King Julian, leader of the lemurs, hatches a plan to make friends with the mysterious animals that arrive on the island. He suggests that Alex the lion might be helpful in protecting them from other predators on the island. When Maurice, Julian's assistant, asks why predators are scared of Alex, he is quickly silenced. All the other lemurs are quick to agree with King Julian. But Alex is later discovered to be a hungry carnivore and banished from the lemur colony.

This movie segment shows how easy it is for dissension to be squelched in highly cohesive groups. King Julian, for example, demeans individuals that question his ideas or offer contrasting views. The scene also shows mind guarding. Acknowledging that Alex was a dangerous predator might force the lemurs to deal with an unpleasant reality, so they pretend it does not exist.

> *Get to Know Yourself Better*   Experiential Exercise 21, Work Team Dynamics, in the OB Skills Workbook *can be a good gauge of whether your group/team is working effectively or might be susceptible to groupthink. Take a minute and assess a group to which you currently belong. If you are the leader, what can you do to guard against groupthink? If you are not the leader, what actions would you take if your team was heading toward groupthink?*

Groupthink Symptoms and Remedies

• **Groupthink** is the tendency of cohesive group members to lose their critical evaluative capabilities.

An important potential problem that arises when teams try to make decisions is **groupthink**—the tendency of members in highly cohesive groups to lose their critical evaluative capabilities.[31] As identified by social psychologist Irving Janis, groupthink is a property of highly cohesive teams, and it occurs because team members are so concerned with harmony that they become unwilling to criticize each other's ideas and suggestions. Desires to hold the team together, feel good, and avoid unpleasantries bring about an overemphasis on agreement and an underemphasis on critical discussion. This often results in a poor decision.

By way of historical examples Janis suggests that groupthink played a role in the U.S. forces' lack of preparedness at Pearl Harbor before the United States entered World War II. It has also been linked to flawed U.S. decision making during the Vietnam War, to events leading up to the space shuttle disasters, and, most recently, to failures of American intelligence agencies regarding the status of weapons of mass destruction in Iraq. Perhaps you can think of other examples from your own experiences where otherwise well-intentioned teams end up doing the wrong things.

The following symptoms of teams displaying groupthink should be well within the sights of any team leader and member.[32]

- *Illusions of invulnerability*—Members assume that the team is too good for criticism or beyond attack.
- *Rationalizing unpleasant and disconfirming data*—Members refuse to accept contradictory data or to thoroughly consider alternatives.
- *Belief in inherent group morality*—Members act as though the group is inherently right and above reproach.
- *Stereotyping competitors as weak, evil, and stupid*—Members refuse to look realistically at other groups.
- *Applying direct pressure to deviants to conform to group wishes*—Members refuse to tolerate anyone who suggests the team may be wrong.
- *Self-censorship by members*—Members refuse to communicate personal concerns to the whole team.
- *Illusions of unanimity*—Members accept consensus prematurely, without testing its completeness.
- *Mind guarding*—Members protect the team from hearing disturbing ideas or outside viewpoints.

Groupthink Can Be Avoided When Team Leaders and Team Members Follow These Tips

- Assign the role of critical evaluator to each team member.
- Have the leader avoid seeming partial to one course of action.
- Create subgroups that each work on the same problem.
- Have team members discuss issues with outsiders and report back.
- Invite outside experts to observe and react to team processes.
- Assign someone to be a "devil's advocate" at each team meeting.
- Hold "second-chance" meetings after consensus is apparently achieved.

There is no doubt that groupthink is a serious threat to the quality of decision making in teams at all levels and in all types of organizations. But it can be managed if team leaders and members are alert to the above symptoms and quick to take action to prevent harm.[33] The accompanying sidebar identifies a number of steps to avoid groupthink or at least minimize its occurrence. For example, President Kennedy chose to absent himself from certain strategy discussions by his cabinet during the Cuban Missile Crisis. This reportedly facilitated critical discussion and avoided tendencies for members to try to figure out what the president wanted and then give it to him. As a result, the decision-making process was open and expansive, and the crisis was successfully resolved.

Team Decision Techniques

In order to take full advantage of the team as a decision-making resource, care must be exercised to avoid groupthink and otherwise manage problems in team dynamics. Team process losses often occur, for example, when meetings are poorly structured or poorly led as members try to work together. Decisions can easily get bogged down or go awry when tasks are complex, information is uncertain, creativity is needed, time is short, "strong" voices are dominant, and debates turn emotional and personal. These are times when special team decision techniques can be helpful.[34]

Brainstorming In **brainstorming**, team members actively generate as many ideas and alternatives as possible, and they do so relatively quickly and without inhibitions. IBM, for example, uses online brainstorming as part of a program

- **brainstorming** involves generating ideas through "freewheeling" and without criticism.

called Innovation Jam. It links IBM employees, customers, and consultants in an "open source" approach. Says CEO Samuel J. Palmisano: "A technology company takes its most valued secrets, opens them up to the world and says, O.K., world, you tell us what to do with them."[35]

You are probably familiar with the rules for brainstorming. First, all criticism is ruled out. No one is allowed to judge or evaluate any ideas until they are all on the table. Second, "freewheeling" is welcomed. The emphasis is on creativity and imagination; the wilder or more radical the ideas the better. Third, quantity is a goal. The assumption is that the greater the number, the more likely a superior idea will appear. Fourth, "piggy-backing" is good. Everyone is encouraged to suggest how others' ideas can be turned into new ideas or how two or more ideas can be joined into still another new idea.

Nominal Group Technique   Teams sometimes get into situations where the opinions of members differ so much that antagonistic arguments develop during discussions. At other times teams get so large that open discussion and brainstorming are awkward to manage. In such cases a structured approach called the **nominal group technique** may be helpful in face to face or virtual meetings.[36]

* The **nominal group technique** involves structured rules for generating and prioritizing ideas.

The technique begins by asking team members to respond individually and in writing to a *nominal question*, such as: "What should be done to improve the effectiveness of this work team?" Everyone is encouraged to list as many alternatives or ideas as they can. Next, participants in round-robin fashion are asked to read or post their responses to the nominal question. Each response is recorded on large newsprint or in a computer database as it is offered. No criticism is allowed. The recorder asks for any questions that may clarify specific items on the list, but no evaluation is allowed. The goal is simply to make sure that everyone fully understands each response. A structured voting procedure is then used to prioritize responses to the nominal question and identify the choice or choices having most support. This procedure allows ideas to be evaluated without risking the inhibitions, hostilities, and distortions that may occur in an open and less structured team meeting.

* The **Delphi Technique** involves generating decision-making alternatives through a series of survey questionnaires.

Delphi Technique   The Rand Corporation developed a third group-decision approach, the **Delphi Technique**, for situations when group members are unable to meet face to face. In this procedure, questionnaires are distributed online or in hard copy to a panel of decision makers. They submit initial responses to a decision coordinator. The coordinator summarizes the solutions and sends the summary back to the panel members, along with a follow-up questionnaire. Panel members again send in their responses, and the process is repeated until a consensus is reached and a clear decision emerges.

8 *study guide*

Key Questions and Answers

What are high-performance teams and how do we build them?

* Team-building is a collaborative approach to improving group process and performance.

* High-performance teams have core values, clear performance objectives, the right mix of skills, and creativity.

- Team-building is a data-based approach to analyzing group performance and taking steps to improve performance in the future.
- Team-building is participative and engages all group members in collaborative problem solving and action.

How can team processes be improved?

- Individual entry problems are common when new teams are formed and when new members join existing teams.
- Task leadership involves initiating, summarizing, and making direct contributions to the group's task agenda; maintenance leadership involves gate-keeping, encouraging, and supporting the social fabric of the group over time.
- Distributed leadership occurs when team members step in to provide helpful task and maintenance activities and discourage disruptive activities.
- Role difficulties occur when expectations for group members are unclear, overwhelming, underwhelming, or conflicting.
- Norms are the standards or rules of conduct that influence the behavior of team members; cohesiveness is the attractiveness of the team to its members.
- Members of highly cohesive groups value their membership and are very loyal to the group; they also tend to conform to group norms.
- The best situation is a team with positive performance norms and high cohesiveness; the worst is a team with negative performance norms and high cohesiveness.
- Inter-team dynamics are forces that operate between two or more groups as they cooperate and compete with one another.

How can team communications be improved?

- Effective teams vary their use of alternative communication networks and decision-making methods to best meet task and situation demands.
- Interacting groups with decentralized networks tend to perform well on complex tasks; co-acting groups with centralized networks may do well at simple tasks.
- Restricted communication networks are common in counteracting groups where subgroups form around disagreements.
- Wise choices on proxemics, or the use of space, can help teams improve communication among members.
- Information technology ranging from instant messaging, video chats, video conferencing, and more, can improve communication in teams, but it must be well used.

How can team decisions be improved?

- Teams can make decisions by lack of response, authority rule, minority rule, majority rule, consensus, and unanimity.
- Although team decisions often make more information available for problem solving and generate more understanding and commitment, their potential liabilities include social pressures to conform and greater time requirements.
- Groupthink is a tendency of members of highly cohesive teams to lose their critical evaluative capabilities and make poor decisions.
- Special techniques for team decision making include brainstorming, the nominal group technique, and the Delphi technique.

Terms to Know

Brainstorming (p. 189)
Centralized communication
    network (p. 184)
Cohesiveness (p. 179)
Collective intelligence (p. 171)
Consensus (p. 186)
Decentralized communication
    network (p. 183)
Decision making (p. 185)
Delphi Technique (p. 190)
Disruptive behavior (p. 175)

Distributed leadership (p. 174)
Groupthink (p. 188)
Inter-team dynamics (p. 180)
Maintenance activities (p. 175)
Nominal group technique (p. 190)
Norms (p. 176)
Performance norm (p. 177)
Proxemics (p. 184)
Restricted communication
    network (p. 184)
Role (p. 175)

Role ambiguity (p. 176)
Role conflict (p. 176)
Role negotiation (p. 176)
Role overload (p. 176)
Role underload (p. 176)
Rule of conformity (p. 179)
Task activities (p. 175)
Team-building (p. 171)
Virtual communication
    networks (p. 185)

Self-Test 8

Multiple Choice

1. One of the essential criteria of a true team is _____. (a) large size (b) homogeneous membership (c) isolation from outsiders (d) collective accountability

2. The team-building process can best be described as participative, data-based, and _____. (a) action-oriented (b) leader-centered (c) ineffective (d) short-term

3. A person facing an ethical dilemma involving differences between personal values and the expectations of the team is experiencing _____ conflict. (a) person-role (b) intrasender role (c) intersender role (d) interrole

4. The statement "On our team, people always try to do their best" is an example of a(n) _____ norm. (a) support and helpfulness (b) high-achievement (c) organizational pride (d) personal improvement

5. Highly cohesive teams tend to be _____. (a) bad for organizations (b) good for members (c) good for social loafing (d) bad for norm conformity

6. To increase team cohesiveness, one would _____. (a) make the group bigger (b) increase membership diversity (c) isolate the group from others (d) relax performance pressures

7. A team member who does a good job at summarizing discussion, offering new ideas, and clarifying points made by others is providing leadership by contributing _____ activities to the group process. (a) required (b) disruptive (c) task (d) maintenance

8. When someone is being aggressive, makes inappropriate jokes, or talks about irrelevant matters in a group meeting, these are all examples of _____ that can harm team performance. (a) disruptive behaviors (b) maintenance activities (c) task activities (d) role dynamics

9. If you heard from an employee of a local bank that "it's a tradition here for us to stand up and defend the bank when someone criticizes it," you could assume that the bank employees had strong _____ norms. (a) support and helpfulness (b) organizational and personal pride (c) ethical and social responsibility (d) improvement and change

10. What can be predicted when you know that a work team is highly cohesive? (a) high-performance results (b) high member satisfaction (c) positive performance norms (d) status congruity

11. When two groups are in competition with one another, _____ may be expected within each group. (a) greater cohesiveness (b) less reliance on the leader (c) poor task focus (d) more conflict

12. A co-acting group is most likely to use a(n) _____ communication network. (a) interacting (b) decentralized (c) centralized (d) restricted

13. A complex problem is best dealt with by a team using a(n) _____ communication network. (a) all-channel (b) wheel (c) chain (d) linear

14. The tendency of teams to lose their critical evaluative capabilities during decision making is a phenomenon called _____. (a) groupthink (b) the slippage effect (c) decision congruence (d) group consensus

15. When a team decision requires a high degree of commitment for its implementation, a(n) _____ decision is generally preferred. (a) authority (b) majority rule (c) consensus (d) minority rule

Short Response

16. Describe the steps in a typical team-building process.

17. How can a team leader build positive group norms?

18. How do cohesiveness and conformity to norms influence team performance?

19. How can inter-team competition be bad and good for organizations?

Applications Essay

20. Alejandro Puron recently encountered a dilemma in working with his employer's diversity task force. One of the team members claimed that a task force must always be unanimous in its recommendations. "Otherwise," she said, "we will not have a true consensus." Alejandro, the current task force leader, disagrees. He believes that unanimity is desirable but not always necessary to achieve consensus.

    Question You are a management consultant specializing in teams and teamwork. Alejandro asks for advice. What would you tell him and why?

Next Steps
Top Choices from
The OB Skills Workbook

Case for Critical Thinking	Team and Experiential Exercises	Self-Assessment Portfolio
• NASCAR's Racing Teams	• Scavenger Hunt Team-building • Work Team Dynamics • Identifying Team Norms • Work Team Culture • The Hot Seat	• Team Effectiveness • Empowering Others

Making a Big Deal Out of Nothing

For the headquarters of a leading Facebook app developer, the offices of Animoto are uncomfortably bare. On one table is a high-end Gaggia espresso machine. Scattered about are the five employees' personal computers. This spartan approach to infrastructure, as well as a killer Web service, helped Animoto grow to serve more than one million users through their Web site and two million users via their Facebook app.[a]

Animoto.com helps users build one-of-a-kind, animated slideshows from photos and music they upload. The founders, among whom are veteran TV production geeks, designed Animoto to think like a director—choreographing the images, music, and transitions for maximum emotional impact. Aside from attracting millions of consumer users, several big-name bands have used Animoto to create videos and promotional shorts.

Recognizing that bringing the tools necessary to run Animoto would sap the young startup's budget—especially if it caught on quickly—the founders brainstormed a unique approach: reworking the service to run on Amazon's self-contained Web Services platform, accepting that doing so would delay their launch by a nail-biting three months. That proved the right decision during a hectic week when their Facebook user base experienced 28-fold growth.[b]

> "We're afforded the luxury of focusing on what we're actually good at."
> —Jason Hsiao, president of Animoto.[d]

They've stayed nimble and focused on honing Animoto by outsourcing many services that conventional businesses choose to manage in-house, such as IT infrastructure (Amazon Web Services), billing and payment (PayPal/Google Checkout), e-mail (Google Apps), and sales record keeping (Salesforce.com).[c]

Animoto's Web site advertises many job openings—that's a strong sign for growth. So is the firm's success with two recent venture capital funding rounds of more than $5 million.

Quick Summary

- Animoto.com helps users create memorable slideshows by animating pictures, video clips, and music they upload. At last count their Web site had more than 2 million users, an estimated 10 percent of whom are paid subscribers.

- Recognizing the cost of hosting enough server infrastructure to accommodate rapid growth, the management team rewrote their code to run on Amazon Web Services instead of in-house servers, saving more than $2 million in processor purchases alone.

- Seeing the agility gained by focusing solely on their core talents, the company chose to outsource the management of key infrastructure services.

FYI: After tweaking their viral marketing, Animoto grew from 25,000 to 700,000 Facebook users in one week.[e]

9 Decision Making and Creativity

the key point

Not everyone has to be in an entrepreneurial environment like Animoto's to appreciate the need for good decision making and creativity. Not a day goes by that we are not involved in decisions, many of them consequential for our lives and the welfare of others. But we don't always make good decisions and sometimes we have difficulty choosing the right decision-making approaches.

chapter at a glance

What is Involved in the Decision-Making Process?

What Are the Alternative Decision-Making Models?

What Are Key Decision-Making Traps and Issues?

What Can Be Done to Stimulate Creativity in Decision Making?

ETHICS IN OB
LIFE AND DEATH AT OUTSOURCING FACTORY

FINDING THE LEADER IN YOU
ENTREPRENEUR TOM SZAKY KNOWS HOW TO MAKE SMART DECISIONS

OB IN POPULAR CULTURE
INTUITION AND U.S. AIR FLIGHT 1549

RESEARCH INSIGHT
ESCALATION OF COMMITMENT HITS BANK LOAN OFFICERS AND COLLEGE STUDENTS

what's inside?

The Decision-Making Process

LEARNING ROADMAP Steps in Decision Making / Ethical Reasoning and Decision Making / Types of Decisions / Decision Environments / Risk Management in Decision Making

It really is possible to move from dorm room to the world of entrepreneurship. Michael Dell did it—from building and selling computers in his University of Texas dorm to leading the global giant Dell Computer. Frederick Smith did it too—from writing a term paper with an interesting logistics idea at Yale University to creating Federal Express. So, you can do it too. The question is whether or not you are ready with not only good ideas, but also the ability and willingness to make good decisions. In fact, a Graduate Management Admissions Council survey reports that 25 percent of business school alumni would like more training in managing the decision-making process.[1]

In our personal lives, at work, within teams, and in management in general, a continuing stream of information, data, problems, and opportunities fuel decision making. It's a lot to sort through, and we don't always end up with the right results. In the last chapter we learned that teams make decisions in different ways, team decisions have assets and liabilities, and techniques such as brainstorming and the nominal group can help improve team decisions. Now, it's time to examine the decision-making process more thoroughly and become better prepared as leaders and members to assist teams in making high-performance decisions.

Steps in Decision Making

- **Decision making** is the process of choosing a course of action to deal with a problem or opportunity.

A common definition of **decision making** is the process of choosing a course of action for dealing with a problem or an opportunity.[2] The process is usually described in these five steps that constitute the *rational decision model*.

Define Problem	Analyze Alternatives	Make a Choice	Take Action	Evaluate Result

1. *Recognize and define the problem or opportunity*—a stage of information gathering and deliberation to specify exactly why a decision is needed and what it should accomplish. Three mistakes are common in this critical first step in decision making. First, we may define the problem too broadly or too narrowly. Second, we may focus on problem symptoms instead of causes. Third, we may choose the wrong problem to deal with.

2. *Identify and analyze alternative courses of action*—a stage where possible alternative courses of action and their anticipated consequences are evaluated for costs and benefits. Decision makers at this stage must be clear on exactly what they know and what they need to know. They should identify key stakeholders and consider the effects of each possible course of action on them.

3. *Choose a preferred course of action*—a stage where a choice is made to pursue one course of action rather than others. Criteria used in making the choice typically involve costs and benefits, timeliness of results, impact on stakeholders, and ethical soundness. Another issue is who makes the decision: team leader, team members, or some combination?

4. *Implement the preferred course of action*—a stage where actions are taken to put the preferred course of action into practice. This is a point where teams may suffer from **lack-of-participation error** because they haven't included in the decision-making process those persons whose support is necessary for its eventual implementation. Teams that use participation and involvement well gain good information and insights for better decision making, as well as team member commitments to put choices into action.

- **Lack-of-participation error** occurs when important people are excluded from the decision-making process.

5. *Evaluate results and follow up as necessary*—a stage that measures performance results against initial goals and examines both anticipated and unanticipated outcomes. This is where decision makers exercise control over their actions, being careful to ensure that the desired results are achieved and undesired side effects are avoided. It is a stage that many individuals and teams often neglect, with negative implications for their performance effectiveness.

Ethical Reasoning and Decision Making

Decision making means making choices, and these choices at each step in the decision-making process usually have a moral dimension that might easily be overlooked. Would you agree, for example, that there is a moral side to decisions such as these: Choosing to allow social loafing by a team member rather than confronting it; choosing to pursue a course of action that causes a teammate some difficulties at home; choosing to compromise on quality in order to speed up teamwork to meet deadlines; or choosing not to ask really hard questions about whether or not a team's course of action is the correct one?

Figure 9.1 links the steps in the decision-making process with corresponding issues of ethical reasoning.[3] As suggested in the figure, we are advocating that an

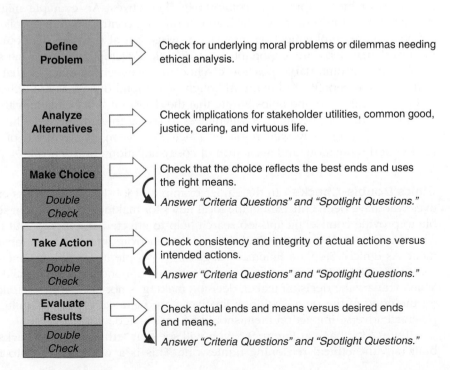

Figure 9.1 The decision-making process with embedded ethical reasoning model.

ethical reasoning approach be followed when decisions are made and that this approach be linked with steps in the decision-making process. In other words, decision making is incomplete without ethical analysis.

• **Ethics** is the philosophical study of morality.

• A **moral problem** poses major ethical consequences for the decision maker or others.

Moral Problems and Dilemmas **Ethics** is the philosophical study of morality or standards regarding good character and conduct.[4] When we apply ethical reasoning to decisions made by individuals and teams in organizations, the focus is on moral problems and dilemmas that are associated with the decision-making process. A **moral problem** is one that poses major ethical consequences for the decision maker or for others. It is possible and even easy to address a personal, management, or business problem and not properly consider any moral problems that might be associated with it. A preferred approach is to carefully examine the ethics of each alternative for all stakeholders, and make choices that minimize negative impact and maximize respect for everyone's rights.

We hear almost every day, for example, about job layoffs in a bad economy. For the manager or executive teams involved, layoffs may seem straightforward and necessary solutions to a business problem—there are insufficient sales to justify the payroll and some jobs must be cut. But this business situation also involves a moral problem. Persons losing their jobs have families, debts, and perhaps limited job options; they will be hurt even if the business benefits from lowering its costs. Although addressing the moral problem might not change the business decision, it might change how the business decision is reached and implemented. This includes addressing whether or not better alternatives to job eliminations exist and what support is offered to those who do lose jobs.

• A **moral dilemma** involves a choice between two or more ethically uncomfortable alternatives.

Sometimes problems create **moral dilemmas** in which the decision maker faces two or more ethically uncomfortable alternatives. An example might be deciding on an opportunity to make an outsourcing contract with a supplier in a country where employment discrimination exists, but also where the country is poor and new jobs are important for economic development. Such situations involve the uncomfortable position of choosing between alternatives that have both potential benefits and harm. Although such moral dilemmas are difficult to resolve, ethical reasoning helps ensure that the decisions will be made with rigor and thoughtful consideration. A willingness to pause to examine the ethics of a proposed decision may well result in a better decision, preservation of one's respect and reputation, and avoidance of costly litigation and even jail.

Ethics Double-Checks In the earlier example of job layoffs, business executives who have been criticized in the local news for making job cuts might scramble to provide counseling and job search help to affected employees. But this is after the fact, and moral conduct does not result from after-the-fact embarrassment. As ethicist Stephen Fineman suggests: "If people are unable to anticipate shame or guilt before they act in particular ways, then moral codes are invalid. . . ."[5] When you are the decision maker, decision making is not just a process followed for the good of the organization; it involves your values and your morality. And potential adverse impact on them should be anticipated.[6]

If you look back at Figure 9.1, you will see that "ethics double-checks" are built into the ethical reasoning framework. This is a way of testing to make sure our decisions meet personal moral standards. The recommended ethics double-checks ask and answer two sets of questions—criteria questions and spotlight questions. Ethicist Gerald Cavanagh and his associates identify these four **criteria questions** for assessing ethics in decision making.[7]

1. *Utility*—Does the decision satisfy all constituents or stakeholders?
2. *Rights*—Does the decision respect the rights and duties of everyone?
3. *Justice*—Is the decision consistent with the canons of justice?
4. *Caring*—Is the decision consistent with my responsibilities to care?

    The **spotlight questions** basically expose a decision to public scrutiny and forces us to consider it in the context of full transparency.[8] They are especially powerful when prospects for shame would be very upsetting.

1. "How would I feel if my family found out about this decision?"
2. "How would I feel if this decision were published in the local newspaper or posted on the Internet?"
3. "What would the person you know or know of who has the strongest character and best ethical judgment do in this situation?"

• **Criteria questions** assess a decision in terms of utility, rights, justice, and caring.

• **Spotlight questions** expose a decision to public scrutiny and full transparency.

ETHICS IN OB

LIFE AND DEATH AT OUTSOURCING FACTORY

Would you buy a product if you knew it was produced at a factory where some workers had committed suicide? Sounds extreme, doesn't it? But the fact is that a major outsourcing firm in China, Foxconn, has experienced problems with employee suicides. And guess what? It makes products for Apple, Dell, and Hewlett-Packard, among others. Over 250,000 people work in one huge complex stretching over 1 square mile in Shenzen, China. It's full of dormitories, and it has restaurants and a hospital in addition to the factory spaces. If you look closely, you'll see netting draped from the dormitories. It's designed to prevent suicides by workers jumping from the roofs.

    One Foxconn worker complains that the work is meaning-less, no conversation is allowed on the production lines, and bathroom breaks are limited. Another says: "I do the same thing every day. I have no future." A supervisor points out that the firm provides counseling services since most workers are young and this is the first time they are away from their homes. "Without their families," says the supervisor, "they're left without direction. We try to provide them with direction and help."

How Should We Act?   *People sometimes work in situations that are harmful to their health and well-being. They face abuse in the form of sexual harassment, supervisor mistreatment, co-worker incivility, unsafe conditions, overly long hours, and more. What ethical responsibilities do the firms that contract for outsourcing in foreign plants have when it comes to the conditions under which the employees work? Whose responsibility is it to make sure workers are well treated? And when it comes to consumers, should we support bad practices by continuing to buy products from firms whose outsourcing partners have been revealed to treat workers poorly?*

Types of Decisions

- **Programmed decisions** simply implement solutions that have already been determined by past experience as appropriate for the problem at hand.

- **Nonprogrammed decisions** are created to deal specifically with a problem at hand.

- A **crisis decision** occurs when an unexpected problem can lead to disaster if not resolved quickly and appropriately.

Decisions made by teams and individuals are basically attempts to deal with a specific task, resolve a performance deficiency, or take advantage of a performance opportunity. They fall into two major types—programmed decisions and nonprogrammed decisions.

Programmed decisions are made as standardized responses to recurring situations and routine problems. They deal with things a decision maker or team already has experience with. Basically, they implement alternatives that are known to be appropriate for situations that occur somewhat frequently. Examples might include decisions that deal with employee absences, compensation, or other standard human resource issues.

Nonprogrammed decisions are specifically crafted or tailored to fit a unique situation. They address novel or unexpected problems that demand a special response, one not available from a decision inventory. An example is a marketing team that has to respond to the introduction of a new product by a foreign competitor. Although past experience may help deal with this competitive threat, the immediate decision requires a creative solution based on the unique characteristics of the present market situation.

The most extreme type of nonprogrammed decision is the **crisis decision** where an unexpected problem threatens major harm and disaster if it is not resolved quickly and appropriately.[9] Acts of terrorism, workplace violence, IT failures and security breaches, ethical scandals, and environmental catastrophes are all examples. And the ability to handle crises could well be the ultimate decision-making test. Unfortunately, research indicates that we sometimes react to crises by doing exactly the wrong things.[10] Managers err in crisis situations when they isolate themselves and try to solve the problem alone or in a small, closed group. Teams do the same when they withdraw into the isolation of groupthink. In both instances the decision makers cut themselves off from access to crucial information at the very time that they need it the most.

Especially in our world of economic uncertainty, global crises, and IT security breaches, many organizations, perhaps all really strong ones, are developing formal crisis management programs. They train managers in crisis, assign people ahead of time to crisis management teams, and develop crisis management plans to deal with various contingencies. Just as fire and police departments, the Red Cross, and community groups plan ahead and train people to best handle civil and natural disasters, and airline crews train for flight emergencies, so, too, can

Crisis Is Always Tough, But These Six Rules for Crisis Management Can Help

1. *Figure out what is going on*—Take the time to understand what's happening and the conditions under which the crisis must be resolved.

2. *Remember that speed matters*—Attack the crisis as quickly as possible, trying to catch it when it is as small as possible.

3. *Remember that slow counts, too*—Know when to back off and wait for a better opportunity to make progress with the crisis.

4. *Respect the danger of the unfamiliar*—Understand the danger of all-new territory where you and others have never been before.

5. *Value the skeptic*—Don't look for and get too comfortable with agreement; appreciate skeptics and let them help you see things differently.

6. *Be ready to "fight fire with fire"*—When things are going wrong and no one seems to care, you may have to start a crisis to get their attention.

managers and work teams plan ahead and train to best deal with organizational crises.

Decision Environments

Decisions in organizations are typically made under the three conditions or environments shown in Figure 9.2—certainty, risk, and uncertainty.[11] The levels of risk and uncertainty in the decision environment tend to increase the higher one moves in management ranks. Think about this, for example, the next time you hear about Coca-Cola or Pepsi launching a new flavor or product. Is the executive team making these decisions *certain* that the results will be successful? Or, is it taking *risks* in market situations that are *uncertain* as to whether the new flavor or product will be positively received by customers?

Certain environments exist when information is sufficient to predict the results of each alternative in advance of implementation. When a person invests money in a savings account, for example, absolute certainty exists about the interest that will be earned on that money in a given period of time. Certainty is an ideal condition for problem solving and decision making. The challenge is simply to locate the alternative that offers the best or ideal solution. Unfortunately, certainty is the exception instead of the rule in most decision situations.

Risk environments exist when decision makers lack complete certainty regarding the outcomes of various courses of action, but are aware of the probabilities associated with their likely occurrence. Probabilities can be assigned through objective statistical procedures or through personal intuition. For instance, a senior production manager can make statistical estimates of quality rejects in production runs or make similar estimates based on her personal past experience. Risk is a common decision environment.

- **Certain environments** provide full information on the expected results for decision-making alternatives.

- **Risk environments** provide probabilities regarding expected results for decision-making alternatives.

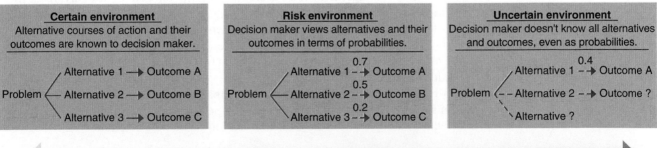

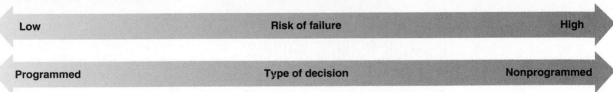

Figure 9.2   Certainty, risk, and uncertainty in organizational decision environments.
[*Source:* John R. Schermerhorn, Jr., *Management,* 10th ed. (Hoboken, NJ: Wiley, 2010). Used by permission.]

Talk about taking a risk: Ford gave Fiesta models to 100 young drivers for six months. All it asked in return was that they post their impressions on YouTube, Flickr, and Twitter. It's an interesting online campaign, but it carries a fair amount of risk since the drivers will be posting both the "goods" and the "bads." Now the firm is asking drivers to help design a new ad campaign.

• **Uncertain environments** provide no information to predict expected results for decision-making alternatives.

Uncertain environments exist when managers have so little information that they cannot even assign probabilities to various alternatives and their possible outcomes. This is the most difficult decision environment. Uncertainty forces decision makers to rely heavily on unique, novel, and often totally innovative alternatives to existing patterns of behavior. Responses to uncertainty are often heavily influenced by intuition, educated guesses, and hunches.

Risk Management in Decision Making

• **Risk management** involves anticipating risks and factoring them into decision making.

Because so many decisions are made in risk and uncertain environments, there is heightened interest in **risk management**, something often associated with insurance and finance. We use the term in general management as well, focusing on anticipating risk in situations and factoring risk alternatives into the decision-making process.[12] Risk management involves identifying critical risks and then developing strategies and assigning responsibilities for dealing with them.

KPMG, one of the world's largest consulting firms, has a large practice in enterprise risk management. It is designed to help executives identify risks to their firms and plan how to best deal with them.[13] KPMG consultants systematically ask managers to separately identify *strategic risks*—threats to overall business success; *operational risks*—threats inherent in the technologies used to reach business success; and *reputation risks*—threats to a brand or to the firm's reputation. Although they also note the importance of threats from regulatory sources, KPMG consultants pay special attention to financial threats, challenges to information systems, and new initiatives from competitors, in addition to change in the competitive setting such as economic recession or natural disasters.

Decision-Making Models

LEARNING ROADMAP Classical Decision Model / Behavioral Decision Model / Systematic and Intuitive Thinking

The field of organizational behavior has historically emphasized two alternative approaches to decision making as shown in Figure 9.3—classical and behavioral.[14] The classical decision model views people acting in a world of complete

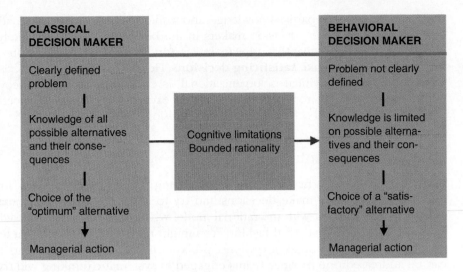

Figure 9.3 Decision making viewed from the classical and behavioral perspectives.

certainty, whereas the behavioral decision model accepts the notion of bounded rationality and suggests that people act only in terms of what they perceive about a given situation.

Classical Decision Model

The **classical decision model** views the manager or team as acting rationally and in a fully informed manner. In a certain environment, the problem is clearly defined, all possible action alternatives are known, and their consequences are clear. This allows for an **optimizing decision** that gives the absolute best solution to the problem. This model nicely fits the five-step decision-making process described earlier. It is an ideal situation of complete information where the decision maker moves through the steps one by one in a logical fashion. And it nicely lends itself to various forms of quantitative decision analysis as well as to computer-based applications.[15]

- **Classical decision model** views decision makers as acting in a world of complete certainty.
- **Optimizing decisions** give the absolute best solution to a problem.

Behavioral Decision Model

As appealing as the classical model and its rational approach may be, the reality is that many, perhaps most, decision situations faced by individuals and teams in organizations don't fit the assumptions of the model. Recognizing this, the premise of the alternative **behavioral decision model** is that people act only in terms of their perceptions, which are frequently imperfect.[16]

Behavioral scientists recognize that the human mind is a wonderful creation, capable of infinite achievements. But they also recognize that human beings have *cognitive limitations*—literally limits on what we are able to know at any point in time. These limitations restrict our information-processing capabilities. The result is that information deficiencies and overloads compromise the ability of decision makers to operate according to the classical model. Instead, they end up acting with *bounded rationality*, where things are interpreted and made sense of as perceptions and only within the context of the situation. They engage in decision making within the box of a simplified view of a more complex reality.

- **Behavioral decision model** views decision makers as acting only in terms of what they perceive about a given situation.

Armed with only partial knowledge about the available action alternatives and their consequences, decision makers in the behavioral model are likely to choose the first alternative that appears satisfactory to them. Herbert Simon calls this the tendency to make **satisficing decisions**. He states: "Most human decision making, whether individual or organizational, is concerned with the discovery and selection of satisfactory alternatives; only in exceptional cases is it concerned with the discovery and selection of optimal decisions."[17]

* **Satisficing decisions** choose the first alternative that appears to give an acceptable or satisfactory resolution of the problem.

Systematic and Intuitive Thinking

Individuals and teams may be described as using both "systematic" and "intuitive" thinking as they make decisions and try to solve problems. **Systematic thinking** is consistent with the rational model where a decision is approached in step-by-step and analytical fashion. You might recognize this style in a team member who tries to break a complex problem into smaller components that can be addressed one by one. Teams engaged in systematic thinking will try to make a plan before taking action, and to search for information and proceed with problem solving in a fact-based and logical fashion.

* **Systematic thinking** approaches problems in a rational and an analytical fashion.

We think of *intuition* as the ability to know or recognize quickly and readily the possibilities of a given situation.[18] Individuals and teams using **intuitive thinking** are more flexible and spontaneous in decision making.[19] You might observe this pattern in someone who always seems to come up with an imaginative response to a problem, often based on a quick and broad evaluation of the situation. Decision makers in this intuitive mode tend to deal with many aspects of a problem at once, search for the "big picture," jump quickly from one issue to another, and act on hunches from experience or on spontaneous ideas. This approach is common under conditions of risk and uncertainty. And because intuitive thinkers take a flexible and spontaneous approach to decision making, their presence on a team adds potential for creative problem solving and innovation.

* **Intuitive thinking** approaches problems in a flexible and spontaneous fashion.

But does this mean that we should always favor the more intuitive and less systematic approach? Most likely not—teams, like individuals, should use and combine the two approaches to solve complex problems. Amazon.com's Jeff Bezos says that when it's not possible for the firm's top managers to make systematic fact-based decisions, "you have to rely on experienced executives who've honed their instincts" and are able to make good judgments.[20] In other words, there's a place for both systematic and intuitive thinking in management decision making.

Xooglers Like Facts to Drive Decision Making

Avichal Garg started PrepMe.com with financial backing from Xooglers, ex-Google employees known for using their wealth and experience to do great things. One Xoogler describes a decision-making lesson from their time at the firm this way—"Fact-based decision-making—always rely on data. Never make an emotional decision."

Decision-Making Traps and Issues

LEARNING ROADMAP   Judgmental Heuristics / Decision Biases / Knowing When to Decide / Knowing Who to Involve / Knowing When to Quit

The pathways to good decisions can seem like a minefield of challenging issues and troublesome traps. Whether working individually or as part of a team, it is important to understand the influence of judgmental heuristics and other potential decision biases, as well as be capable in making critical choices regarding if, when, and how decisions get made.

Judgmental Heuristics

Judgment, or the use of intellect, is important in all aspects of decision making. When we question the ethics of a decision, for example, we are questioning the judgment of the person making it. Research shows that people who are prone to mistakes use biases that often interfere with the quality of decision making.[21] These biases trace back to the use of **heuristics**, which are simplifying strategies or "rules of thumb" used to make decisions. And, to be precise, such rules of thumb aren't always bad. Heuristics serve a useful purpose by making it easier to deal with uncertainty and the limited information common to problem situations. But they can also lead us toward systematic errors that affect the quality, and perhaps the ethical implications, of any decisions made.[22]

> • **Heuristics** are simplifying strategies or "rules of thumb" used to make decisions.

Availability Heuristic   The **availability heuristic** involves assessing a current event based on past occurrences that are easily available in one's memory. An example is the product development specialist who decides not to launch a new product because of her recent failure launching another one. In this case, the existence of a past product failure has negatively, and perhaps inappropriately, biased her judgment regarding how best to handle the new product.

> • The **availability heuristic** bases a decision on recent events relating to the situation at hand.

Representativeness Heuristic   The **representativeness heuristic** involves assessing the likelihood that an event will occur based on its similarity to one's stereotypes of similar occurrences. An example is the team leader who selects a new member, not because of any special qualities of the person, but only because the individual comes from a department known to have produced high performers in the past. In this case, the individual's current place of employment—not his or her job qualifications—is the basis for the selection decision.

> • The **representativeness heuristic** bases a decision on similarities between the situation at hand and stereotypes of similar occurrences.

Anchoring and Adjustment Heuristic   The **anchoring and adjustment heuristic** involves assessing an event by taking an initial value from historical precedent or an outside source and then incrementally adjusting this value to make a current assessment. An example is the executive who makes salary increase recommendations for key personnel by simply adjusting their current base salaries a percentage amount. In this case, the existing base salary becomes an "anchor" that limits subsequent salary increases. This anchor may be inappropriate, such as in the case of an individual whose market value has become substantially higher than is reflected by the base salary plus increment approach.

> • The **anchoring and adjustment heuristic** bases a decision on incremental adjustments to an initial value determined by historical precedent or some reference point.

Decision Biases

- The **confirmation error** is the tendency to seek confirmation for what is already thought to be true and not search for disconfirming information.
- The **hindsight trap** is a tendency to overestimate the degree to which an event that has already taken place could have been predicted.
- **Framing error** is solving a problem in the context perceived.

In addition to the common judgmental heuristics, decision makers are also prone to more general biases in decision making. One bias is **confirmation error**, whereby the decision maker seeks confirmation for what is already thought to be true and neglects opportunities to acknowledge or find disconfirming information. A form of selective perception, this bias involves seeking only information and cues in a situation that support a preexisting opinion.

A second bias is the **hindsight trap** where the decision maker overestimates the degree to which he or she could have predicted an event that has already taken place. One risk of hindsight is that it may foster feelings of inadequacy or insecurity in dealing with future decision situations.

A third bias is **framing error**. It occurs when managers and teams evaluate and resolve a problem in the context in which they perceive it—either positive or negative. Suppose research data show that a new product has a 40 percent market share. What does this really mean to the marketing team? A negative frame views the product as deficient because it is missing 60 percent of the market. Discussion and problem solving within this frame would likely focus on: "What are we doing wrong?" If the marketing team used a positive frame and considered a 40 percent share as a success, the conversation might have been quite different: "How can we do even better?" And by the way, we are constantly exposed to framing in the world of politics; the word used to describe it is *spin*.

Knowing When to Decide

Not only do decision makers have to be on guard against errors caused by heuristics and biases, but they also have to manage the decision-making process itself by making the right decisions in the right way at the right time.[23] One of the first issues is whether or not to actually proceed with decision making. Most people are too busy and have too many valuable things to do with their time to personally make decisions on every problem or opportunity that comes their way. A good team leader, for example, knows when to delegate decisions to others, how to set priorities, and when to abstain from acting altogether. When faced with the dilemma of whether or not to deal with a specific problem, asking and answering the following questions can sometimes help.

- *What really matters?* Small and less significant problems should not get the same time and attention as bigger ones. Even if a mistake is made, the cost of a decision error on a small problem is also small.

- *Might the problem resolve itself?* Putting problems in rank order leaves the less significant for last. Surprisingly, many of these less important problems resolve themselves or are solved by others before you get to them. This saves decision-making time and energy for better uses.

- *Is this my or our problem?* Many problems can be handled by other people. These should be delegated to people who are best prepared to deal with them; ideally, they should be delegated to people whose work they most affect.

- *Will time spent make a difference?* A really effective decision maker recognizes the difference between problems that realistically can be solved and those that are simply not solvable.

Knowing Who to Involve

You've most likely heard of this case, and the video is available on YouTube. US Airways flight 1549 hit a flock of birds on take-off from LaGuardia Airport, lost engine power, and was headed for a crash. Pilot Chesley Sullenberger III made the decision to land in the Hudson River. The landing was successful and no lives were lost. Called a "hero" for his efforts, Sullenberger described his thinking this way.[24]

> I needed to touch down with the wings exactly level. I needed to touch down with the nose slightly up. I needed to touch down at . . . a descent rate that was survivable. And I needed to touch down just above our minimum flying speed but not below it. And I needed to make all these things happen simultaneously.

Sullenberger obviously did the right thing—he made the decision himself betting on his training and experience and, literally, standing behind it with his own life on the line. But we have to be careful with the lesson from this type of case. Many new managers and team leaders make mistakes in presuming that either they must make every decision themselves or that they must turn them all over to the team itself.[25] In practice, good organizational decisions are made by

OB IN POPULAR CULTURE

INTUITION AND U.S. AIR FLIGHT 1549

Most descriptions of the decision-making process begin with the rational model. Systematic or rational thinking is often viewed as the most effective way to make decisions. By contrast, **intuition** involves being able to quickly "size up" a situation and make a decision. In some situations, it may be a better way to approach a problem.

During the afternoon of January 15, 2009, television news anchors began reporting about a plane in the Hudson River. The natural first reaction is "not another tragic plane crash." This incident was different. Captain Chesley "Sully" Sullenberger was able to successfully crash land U.S. Air Flight 1549 in the river and save the lives of all passengers and crew.

In an interview with Fox News' Greta van Susteren, Sullenberger was asked to recount what happened. The host commented, "It probably took about 20 seconds to explain; you had to make that decision like [snaps her fingers] that." Sullenberger responded, "It was sort of an instinctive moved based upon my experience and my initial read of the situation."

What Captain Sullenberger describes is an intuitive decision. Think about it. If you had been a passenger on that plane, would you want him making a systematic decision under those circumstances? The plane would have been at the bottom of the Hudson River by the time he completed Step 2. What we want is a well-trained pilot reacting on informed instinct. This is precisely why pilots spend considerable time in flight simulators—to develop the experience necessary for dealing with problems that may only occur once, if ever, in a career.

Get to Know Yourself Better   Take a look at Assessment 16, Intuitive Ability, in the OB Skills Workbook to determine the extent to which you use intuition in decision making. If your score suggests that you are uncomfortable with an intuitive decision style, you may need to work on it. Or perhaps you may simply need to rely on your experience and trust your judgment a little more.

individuals acting alone, by individuals consulting with others, and by people working together in teams. In true contingency fashion no one option is always superior to the others; who participates and how decisions are to be made should reflect the issues at hand.[26]

Three Scenarios for Successful Decision Making

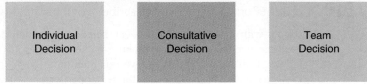

Individual Decision

Consultative Decision

Team Decision

- **Individual decisions**, or authority decisions, are made by one person on behalf of the team.
- **Consultative decisions** are made by one individual after seeking input from or consulting with members of a group.
- **Team decisions** are made by all members of the team.

When **individual decisions**, also called *authority decisions*, are made, the manager or team leader uses information that he or she possesses and decides what to do without involving others. This decision method basically assumes the decision maker is an expert on the problem at hand. In **consultative decisions**, by contrast, inputs are gathered from other persons and the decision maker uses this information to arrive at a final choice. In **team decisions**, group members work together to make the final choice, hopefully by consensus or unanimity.

Victor Vroom, Phillip Yetton, and Arthur Jago developed the framework shown in Figure 9.4 for helping managers choose the right decision-making methods for various problem situations.[27] They identify these variants of the individual, consultative, and team decision options just described.

- *AI (first variant on the authority decision):* The manager solves the problem or makes the decision alone, using information available at that time.
- *AII (second variant on the authority decision):* The manager obtains the necessary information from team members and then decides on the problem's solution. The team members provide the necessary information but do not generate or evaluate alternatives.
- *CI (first variant on the consultative decision):* The manager shares the problem with team members individually, getting their ideas and suggestions without bringing them all together. The manager then makes a decision.
- *CII (second variant on the consultative decision):* The manager shares the problem with team members, collectively obtaining their ideas and suggestions. The manager then makes a decision.
- *G (the team or consensus decision):* The manager shares the problem with team members as a total group and engages them in consensus seeking to arrive at a final decision.

Figure 9.4 is a decision tree developed from the research of Vroom and his colleagues. Though complex, it helps to illustrate how decision makers can choose among the individual, consultative, and team decision options by considering these factors: (1) required quality of the decision, (2) commitment needed from team members to implement the decision, (3) amount of information available to team leader, (4) problem structure, (5) chances team members will be committed if leader makes the decision, (6) degree to which team leader and members agree on goals, (7) conflict among team members, and (8) information available to team members.

Consultative and team decisions are recommended by this model when the leader lacks sufficient expertise and information to solve this problem alone; the problem is unclear and help is needed to clarify the situation, acceptance of the decision and commitment by others are necessary for implementation; and

Problem Attributes		Manager's Questions
QR	Quality requirement	How important is the technical quality of this decision?
CR	Commitment requirement	How important is team member commitment to the decision?
LI	Leader's information	Do you have sufficient information to make a high-quality decision?
ST	Problem structure	Is the problem well structured?
CP	Commitment probability	If you were to make the decision by yourself, is it reasonably certain that team members would be committed to the decision?
GC	Goal congruence	Do team members share the organizational goals to be attained in solving this problem?
CO	Member conflict	Is conflict among team members over preferred solutions likely?
SI	Member information	Do team members have sufficient information to make a high-quality decision?

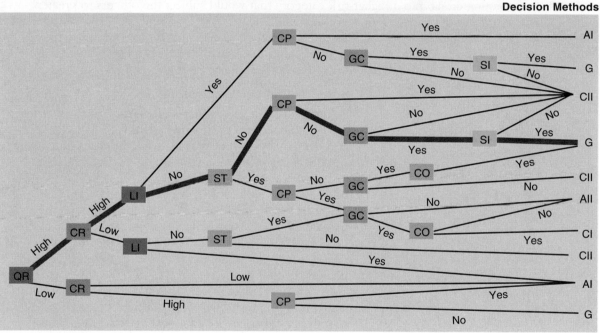

State the Problem

Figure 9.4 The Vroom-Jago model for a manager's use of alternative decision-making methods.

adequate time is available to allow for true participation. By contrast, authority decisions work best when team leaders have the expertise needed to solve the problem; they are confident and capable of acting alone; others are likely to accept and implement the decision they make; and little or no time is available for discussion. When problems must be resolved immediately, the authority decision made by the team leader may be the only option.[28]

Knowing When to Quit

After the sometimes agonizing process of making a decision is completed and implementation begins, it can be hard for decision makers to change their minds and admit a mistake even when things are clearly not going well. Instead of

RESEARCH INSIGHT

Escalation of Commitment Hits Bank Loan Officers and College Students

Study 1—Bank Loan Officers

Some individuals escalate commitment to a losing course of action when it is clear to others they should quit. McNamara, Moon, and Bromiley asked whether monitoring by more senior management would help stop escalating commitment in a group of bank loan officers.

At first glance their data seem to suggest that monitoring worked. When individual clients were put in higher-risk categories, the loan officers on these accounts were monitored more closely. Undue overcommitment to these higher-risk individuals was apparently reduced. But on closer examination the researchers found that loan officers showed "intervention avoidance" and were reluctant to place clients with deteriorating credit into a higher-risk category that would subject the officers to greater monitoring. For this group of clients, there was overcommitment by the loan officers.

McNamara et al. use their data to argue that the question of escalation is more complex than is traditionally recognized and may involve a host of organizational factors that indirectly influence the tendencies of individuals to make undesirable decision commitments.

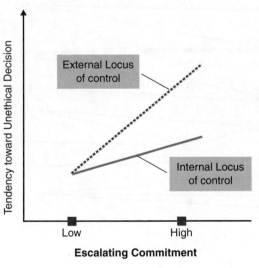

Study 2—College Students

Escalating commitments breed unethical behavior. That's the conclusion reached in an empirical study by Marc and Vera L. Street. They conducted an experiment with 155 undergraduate students working on a computerized investment task. Results showed that exposure to escalation situations increases tendencies toward unethical acts, and that the tendencies further increase with the magnitude of the escalation. Street and Street explain this link between escalation and poor ethics as driven by desires to get out of and avoid the increasing stress of painful situations.

Additional findings from the study showed that students with an external locus of control had a higher propensity to choose an unethical decision alternative than their counterparts with an internal locus of control.

Do the Research   *What role does escalating commitment play in the day-to-day performance of your work and class teams? Design a study that might identify when and why escalation is likely.*

Source: Study 1—Gerry McNamara, Henry Moon, and Philip Bromiley, "Banking on Commitment: Intended and Unintended Consequences of Organizations' Attempt to Attenuate Escalation of Commitment," *Academy of Management Journal* 45 (2002), pp. 443–452. Study 2—Marc Street and Vera L. Street, "The Effects of Escalating Commitment on Ethical Decision Making," *Journal of Business Ethics* 64 (2006), pp. 343–356.

• **Escalating commitment** is the tendency to continue a previously chosen course of action even when feedback suggests that it is failing.

backing off, the tendency is to press on to victory. This is called **escalating commitment**—continuing and renewing efforts on a previously chosen course of action, even though it is not working.[29] The tendency toward escalating commitment is reflected in the popular adage: "If at first you don't succeed, try, try, and try again."

Escalating commitments are a form of decision entrapment that leads people to do things that the facts of a situation do not justify. This is one of the most difficult aspects of decision making to convey to executives because so many of them rose to their positions by turning apparently losing courses of action into winners.[30] We should be proactive in spotting "failures" and more open to reversing decisions or dropping plans that are not working. But this is easier said than done.

The tendency to escalate commitments often outweighs the willingness to disengage from them. Decision makers may rationalize negative feedback as a temporary condition, protect their egos by not admitting that the original decision was a mistake, or characterize any negative results as a "learning experience" that can be overcome with added future effort.

Perhaps you have experienced an inability to call it quits or been on teams with similar reluctances. It's hard to admit to a mistake, especially when a lot of thought and energy went into the decision in the first place; it can be even harder when one's ego and reputation are tied up with the decision. Fortunately, researchers suggest these ideas on how to avoid getting trapped in escalating commitments.

- Set advance limits on your involvement and commitment to a particular course of action; stick with these limits.

- Make your own decisions; don't follow the lead of others because they are also prone to escalation.

- Carefully determine just why you are continuing a course of action; if there are insufficient reasons to continue, don't.

- Remind yourself of the costs of a course of action; consider saving these costs as a reason to discontinue.

Creativity in Decision Making

LEARNING ROADMAP   Stages of Creative Thinking / Personal Creativity Drivers / Team Creativity Drivers

Stages of Creative Thinking

The last chapter ended with a discussion of brainstorming and the nominal group technique as ways of improving decision making in teams. One of the things often at issue when such techniques are used is **creativity**—the generation of a novel idea or unique approach to solving performance problems or exploiting performance opportunities.[31] It often determines how well people, teams, and organizations do in response to complex challenges.[32]

Just imagine what we can accomplish with all the creative potential that exists within a team and in an organization's workforce. But how do you turn that potential into real performance? Part of the answer to this question rests with the individual team members. Part also rests with the team and organizational context in which they are asked to perform.

• **Creativity** generates unique and novel responses to problems.

Personal Creativity Drivers

Creativity is one of our greatest personal assets, even though it is sometimes untapped. One source of insight into personal creativity drivers is the three-component model of task expertise, task motivation, and creativity skills shown in Figure 9.5.[33]

Creative decisions are more likely to occur when a person has a lot of *task expertise*. Creativity typically extends in new directions a skill one is already good at. Creative decisions are also more likely when the people making them are high in *task motivation*. Creativity happens in part because people work exceptionally hard to resolve a problem or exploit an opportunity. And creative decisions are more likely when the people involved have strong *creativity skills* like the following.[34]

- Work with high energy.
- Hold ground in face of criticism.
- Accept responsibility for what happens.
- Be resourceful even in difficult situations.
- Be both systematic and intuitive.
- Be objective—step back and question assumptions.
- Use divergent thinking—think outside of the box.
- Use convergent thinking—synthesize and find correct answers.
- Use lateral thinking—look at diverse ways to solve problems.
- Transfer learning from one setting to others.

Team Creativity Drivers

If you mix creative people together on a team, will you get creative results? Not necessarily.[35] All the team creativity drivers shown in Figure 9.5 are important.

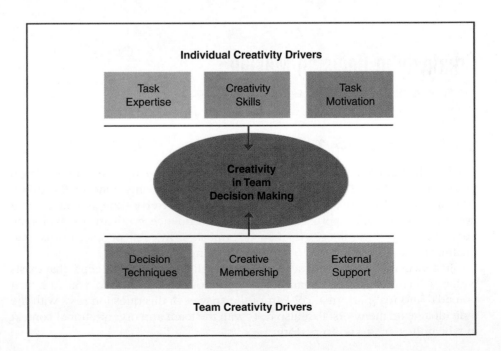

Figure 9.5 Individual and team creativity drivers.

Finding the Leader in You

ENTREPRENEUR TOM SZAKY KNOWS HOW TO MAKE SMART DECISIONS

Smart decisions led Tom Szaky from dorm-room brainstormer to Walmart supplier. And it's all based on "sustainability," "green," and "recycling." Szaky is what many call an "eco-capitalist," someone who brings environmentalism into the world of business and consumers. If you buy his book *Revolution in a Bottle* you enter the world of "upcycling"—the art, if you will, of

turning waste that isn't recyclable into reusable packaging.

While a freshman at Princeton University, Szaky was concerned about campus garbage. So he ordered a million red worms with the goal of learning how to use them to recycle the garbage and reduce landfill usage. It worked, but scaling was a problem. One thing led to another, including conversations with classmate Jon Beyer. Before long the original idea of eco-friendly waste management became a decision to sell liquid fertilizer made from worm excrement.

It was pure entrepreneurship, but Szaky points out: "The scary thing is you are always making decisions without knowing the future." While making the liquid fertilizer proved fairly easy, being able to afford the expensive plastic bottles to package it in was a lot more difficult. That's when the team expanded to three—adding entrepreneur Robin Tator. More conversations led to the idea of collecting and reusing bottles sent for recycling.

The idea worked so well that a new firm called TerraCycle quickly took shape with a mission to "find a

meaningful use for waste materials." The original liquid fertilizer became TerraCycle Plant Food. And the firm also upcycles waste products such as cookie wrappers, drink containers, and discarded juice packs into usable products from tote bags to backpacks to pencil cases. It's all about finding value in waste. Szaky says this about decision making and creativity: "Unlike most companies, which spend years in product development and testing, TerraCycle moves through these stages very quickly. First we identify a waste stream, then we figure out what we can make from that material. This is our strength—creatively solving the "what the hell do we make from it" issue. If a retailer bites, we are in full production in a matter of weeks."

What's the Lesson Here?

Are you able to make decisions quickly, or do you find yourself overanalyzing? How good are your instincts when it comes to making smart decisions? If they are not good, how can you better develop them?

Yes, the basic building block of team creativity is membership composition. If we want teams to be creative, they should be staffed with a *creative membership*. But beyond this, the use of special *decision techniques* such as brainstorming and the nominal group technique discussed in Chapter 8 can also be helpful. This is especially true when a team encounters process problems. Some of the other useful techniques when teams are trying to become more creative in decision making include:[36]

- *Associative play*—making up and telling stories, engaging in art projects, and building toy models that come to mind when dealing with a problem.
- *Cross pollination*—switching members among teams to gain insights from diverse interests, backgrounds, and experiences when working on problems.
- *Analogies and metaphors*—using analogies and metaphors to describe a problem and open pathways to creative thinking.

Even with the right members and decision techniques available, the full creative potential of a team can only be unlocked when *external support* is added to the mix. At one level this involves making creativity a strategic priority in the broader organizational context. But it also involves smaller, more everyday things that are easily missed. Team creativity is enhanced by leaders who have the patience to allow creative processes time to work themselves through a decision situation. It is also enhanced by top management that is willing to provide the resources—technology, opportunity, and space, for example, that are helpful to the creative processes.

Think creativity nurtured the next time you see a young child playing with a really neat toy. It may be from *Fisher-Price toys*, part of Mattel, Inc. In the firm's headquarters you'll find a special place called the "cave," and it's not your typical office space. Picture bean-bag chairs, soft lighting, casual seats, and couches. It's a place for brainstorming where designers, marketers, engineers, and others can meet and join in freewheeling to come up with the next great toy for preschoolers. Consultants recommend that such innovation spaces be separated from the normal workplace and be large enough for no more than 15 to 20 people.[37]

study guide

Key Questions and Answers

What is involved in the decision-making process?

- Decision making is a process of identifying problems and opportunities and choosing among alternative courses of action for dealing successfully with them.

- The steps in the decision-making process are (1) find and define the problem, (2) generate and evaluate alternatives, (3) decide on the preferred course of action, (4) implement the decision, and (5) evaluate the results.

- Ethical reasoning should be used in the decision-making process to ensure that all possible moral problems and dilemmas are dealt with properly.

- Decisions in organizations are made under conditions of certainty, risk, and uncertainty; the challenges to the decision maker are higher in risk and uncertain environments.

- Routine problems can be dealt with by programmed decisions; nonroutine or novel problems require specially crafted nonprogrammed decisions; crisis problems occur unexpectedly and can lead to disaster if not handled properly.

What are the alternative decision-making models?

- In the classical decision model, optimum decisions identifying the absolute best choice after analyzing with full information all possible alternatives and their consequences.

- In the behavioral decision model, satisficing decisions that choose the first acceptable alternative are made with limited information and bounded rationality.

- In the intuitive model, decision makers deal with many aspects of a problem at once, jump quickly from one issue to another, and act on hunches from experience or on spontaneous ideas.

What are key decision-making traps and issues?

- The use of judgmental heuristics, or simplifying rules of thumb, can lead to biased results in decision making; such heuristics include availability decisions based on recent events, representativeness decisions based on similar events, and anchoring and adjustment decisions based on historical precedents.

- Other sources of decision-making bias are confirmation error, seeking information to justify a decision already made; hindsight trap, overestimating the extent to which current events could have been predicted; and framing error, viewing a problem in a limited context.

- Individuals and teams must know when to make decisions, realizing that not every problem requires an immediate decision.

- Individuals and teams must be know who should be involved in making decisions, making use of individual, consultative, and team decisions as needed to best fit the problems and opportunities being faced.

- Individuals and teams must be able to counteract tendencies toward escalating commitment to previously chosen courses of action that are not working; they must know when to quit and abandon a course of action.

What can be done to stimulate creativity in decision making?

- Creativity is the generation of a novel idea or unique approach to solving performance problems or exploiting performance opportunities.

- Creativity in decision making can be enhanced by personal creativity drivers that include task expertise, motivation, and individual creativity skills.

- Creativity in decision making can be enhanced by team creativity drivers that include a creative membership, helpful decision techniques, and external support for creativity.

Terms to Know

Self-Test 9

Multiple Choice

1. After a preferred course of action has been implemented, the next step in the decision-making process is to _____. (a) recycle the process (b) look for additional problems or opportunities (c) evaluate results (d) document the reasons for the decision

2. In which environment does the decision maker deal with probabilities regarding possible courses of action and their consequences? (a) certain (b) risk (c) organized anarchy (d) uncertain

3. If a team approaches problems in a rational and analytical way, with members trying to solve them in step-by-step fashion, it is well described as a team using _____. (a) systematic thinking (b) intuitive thinking (c) escalating thinking (d) associative thinking

4. An individual or team that must deal with limited information and substantial risk is most likely to make decisions based on _____. (a) optimizing (b) classical decision theory (c) behavioral decision theory (d) escalation

5. A team leader who makes a decision not to launch a new product because the last new product launch failed is falling prey to the _____ heuristic. (a) anchoring (b) availability (c) adjustment (d) representativeness

6. The criteria questions for assessing ethics in decision making include the issue of _____, making sure that the decision satisfies the interests of all stakeholders. (a) utility (b) justice (c) rights (d) caring

7. In Vroom's decision-making model, the choice among individual and team decision approaches is based on criteria that include quality requirements, availability of information, and _____. (a) need for implementation commitments (b) size of the organization (c) number of people involved (d) position power of the leader

8. The saying "If at first you don't succeed, try, try again" is most associated with a decision-making tendency called _____. (a) groupthink (b) the confirmation trap (c) escalating commitment (d) associative choice

9. The _____ decision model views individuals as making optimizing decisions, whereas the _____ decision model views them as making satisficing decisions. (a) behavioral/judgmental heuristics (b) classical/behavioral (c) judgmental heuristics/ethical (d) crisis/routine

10. A common mistake by managers facing crisis situations is _____. (a) trying to get too much information before responding (b) relying too much on team decision making (c) isolating themselves to make the decision alone (d) forgetting to use their crisis management plan

11. What is a possible disadvantage of choosing to make a decision by the team rather than by the individual method? (a) people are better informed about the reason for the decision (b) it takes too long to reach a decision (c) more information is used to make the decision (d) it won't ever result in a high-quality decision

12. The _____ bases a decision on similarities between the situation at hand and stereotypes of similar occurrences. (a) representativeness heuristic (b) anchoring and adjustment heuristic (c) confirmation trap (d) hindsight trap

13. The _____ bases a decision on incremental adjustments to an initial value determined by historical precedent or some reference point. (a) representativeness heuristic (b) anchoring and adjustment heuristic (c) confirmation trap (d) hindsight trap

14. The _____ is the tendency to focus on what is already thought to be true and not to search for disconfirming information. (a) representativeness heuristic (b) anchoring and adjustment heuristic (c) confirmation trap (d) hindsight trap

15. Team creativity drivers include creative members, decision techniques, and _____. (a) task motivation (b) task expertise (c) long-term goals (d) external support

Short Response

16. What are heuristics, and how can they affect individual decision making?

17. What are the main differences among individual, consultative, and team decisions?

18. What is escalating commitment, and why is it important to recognize it in decision making?

19. What questions might a manager or team leader ask to help determine which problems to deal with and in which priority?

Applications Essay

20. As a participant in a new mentoring program between your university and a local high school, you have volunteered to give a presentation to a class of sophomores on the challenges of achieving creativity in teams. The goal is to motivate them to think creatively as individuals and to help make sure that their course teams achieve creativity as well when assignments call for it. What will you tell them?

Next Steps

Top Choices from

The OB Skills Workbook

Cases for Critical Thinking	Team and Experiential Exercises	Self-Assessment Portfolio
• Decisions, Decisions	• Decode • Lost at Sea • Entering the Unknown • Fostering the Creative Spirit	• Intuitive Ability • Decision-Making Biases

Eduardo Saverin: "You're Out."

Breaking up is hard to do. Especially with millions of dollars of venture capital at stake. Co-founder conflict is an all-too common reason entrepreneurs either dissolve startups or fundamentally alter their core management teams. Just ask Eduardo Saverin, Mark Zuckerberg's co-founder of *thefacebook*, the Harvard-based social networking site that eventually became Facebook.

From the start, notes venture capitalist and fellow Harvard alum Larry Cheng, Zuckerberg and Saverin brought fundamentally different approaches to managing their fledgling startup, which at that time was limited to Harvard students and grads. Zuckerberg, the programmer, "exuded a killer instinct" and "was not shy about sharing his aspirations of dominating the college market." Saverin, who incorporated and managed *thefacebook* from their dorm, was "jovial, likeable, and the fast follower."[a] Founders with these style differences can and do complement each other, but only when they stick together.

> *"It seemed like in all his dealings, it was a big deal to him that he be the CEO when he got the first round of financing, and that he maintain control of the company."*
> —Stephen Haggerty, former Harvard student and Facebook intern.

When they don't, there's bound to be conflict. In Facebook's case—as happens when co-founders collide—the exact details are murky, and mired in allegations. According to *Rolling Stone*, Zuckerberg sued Saverin, contending that he put the startup at risk by freezing its assets. Saverin's countersuit claimed Zuckerberg never matched his initial seed money, instead dipping into it for personal expenses.[b]

Acting alone, Zuckerberg quickly reincorporated Facebook's interests in a new version of the startup, moved to Palo Alto, California, and set about raising hundreds of millions of dollars. For years after, Facebook publicly denied Saverin's role in starting the social networking behemoth.

Though he hasn't enjoyed the celebrity attention of his co-founder, things might not be all bad for Eduardo Saverin. Though no one will confirm publicly, he's rumored to currently hold a 5 percent stake in Facebook. He has also recently been acknowledged as a co-founder on Facebook's site.

Quick Summary

- Brazilian-born Eduardo Saverin met Mark Zuckerberg during their freshman year at Harvard. One year later, Saverin incorporated and managed Zuckerberg's social networking project, *thefacebook*, from their dorm.

- Saverin invested $20,000 of his own money as seed funds to attract investors. Tensions rose when Saverin froze the company's assets after he accused Zuckerberg of spending the money on personal expenses. Zuckerberg in turn reincorporated Facebook, locked Saverin out, and moved to Palo Alto, California, where he sought venture capital by himself.

- Despite Facebook's immense success, Saverin has kept a very low profile. For years Facebook denied Saverin's role in the company's early days. But just before the release of a tell-all movie, *The Social Network*, Facebook changed its position and acknowledged Saverin as a co-founder.

FYI: According to *Forbes*, Eduardo Saverin's share in Facebook is worth $2.5 billion, and growing.[c]

10 Conflict and Negotiation

key point

The Facebook story is full of intrigue, innuendo, and unknowns. It also shows how conflict and negotiation often take center stage in organizational dynamics. Everyone has to be able to deal with them in positive ways. In teamwork and in interpersonal relationships the word "yes" can often open doors in situations prone to conflict or involving negotiations.

chapter at a glance

What Is the Nature of Conflict in Organizations?

How Can Conflict Be Managed?

What Is the Nature of Negotiation in Organizations?

What Are Alternative Strategies for Negotiation?

ETHICS IN OB
BLOGGING IS FUN, BUT BLOGGERS BEWARE

FINDING THE LEADER IN YOU
ALAN MULALLY NEGOTIATES A NEW FUTURE FOR FORD

OB IN POPULAR CULTURE
INTRAPERSONAL CONFLICT AND BECK'S

RESEARCH INSIGHT
WORDS AFFECT OUTCOMES IN ONLINE DISPUTE RESOLUTION

what's inside?

Conflict in Organizations

LEARNING ROADMAP   Types of Conflict / Levels of Conflict / Functional and Dysfunctional Conflict / Culture and Conflict

- **Conflict** occurs when parties disagree over substantive issues or when emotional antagonisms create friction between them.

The daily work of organizations revolves around people and their interpersonal relationships. We all need skills to work well with others who don't always agree with us, even in situations that are complicated and stressful.[1] **Conflict** occurs whenever disagreements exist in a social situation over issues of substance, or whenever emotional antagonisms create frictions between individuals or groups.[2] Team leaders and members can spend considerable time dealing with conflicts. Sometimes they are directly involved, and other times they act as mediators or neutral third parties to help resolve conflicts between other people.[3] Conflict dynamics are inevitable in the workplace and it's best to know how to handle them.[4]

Types of Conflict

Conflicts in teams, at work, and in our personal lives occur in at least two basic forms—substantive and emotional. Both types are common, ever present, and challenging. The question is: How well prepared are you to deal successfully with them?

- **Substantive conflict** involves fundamental disagreement over ends or goals to be pursued and the means for their accomplishment.

Substantive conflict is a fundamental disagreement over ends or goals to be pursued and the means for their accomplishment.[5] A dispute with one's boss or other team members over a plan of action to be followed, such as the marketing strategy for a new product, is an example of substantive conflict. When people work together every day, it is only normal that different viewpoints on a variety of substantive workplace issues will arise. At times people will disagree over such things as team and organizational goals, the allocation of resources, the distribution of rewards, policies and procedures, and task assignments.

- **Emotional conflict** involves interpersonal difficulties that arise over feelings of anger, mistrust, dislike, fear, resentment, and the like.

Emotional conflict involves interpersonal difficulties that arise over feelings of anger, mistrust, dislike, fear, resentment, and the like.[6] This conflict is commonly known as a "clash of personalities." How many times, for example, have you heard comments such as "I can't stand working with him" or "She always rubs me the wrong way" or "I wouldn't do what he asked if you begged me"? When emotional conflicts creep into work situations, they can drain energies and distract people from task priorities and goals. Yet, they emerge in a wide variety of settings and are common in teams, among co-workers, and in superior–subordinate relationships.

Levels of Conflict

Our first tendency may be to think of conflict as something that happens between two people, and that is certainly a valid example of what we call "interpersonal conflict." But scholars point out that conflicts in teams and organizations need to be recognized and understood in other forms as well. The full range of conflicts that we experience at work includes those emerging from the interpersonal, intrapersonal, intergroup, and interorganizational levels.

Interpersonal Conflict	Intrapersonal Conflict	Intergroup Conflict	Inter-organizational Conflict

Interpersonal conflict occurs between two or more individuals who are in opposition to one another. It may be substantive, emotional, or both. Two persons debating each other aggressively on the merits of hiring a specific job applicant is an example of a substantive interpersonal conflict. Two persons continually in disagreement over each other's choice of work attire is an example of an emotional interpersonal conflict. Interpersonal conflict often arises in the performance evaluation process. When P. J. Smoot became learning and development leader at International Paper's Memphis, Tennessee, office, for example, she recognized that the traditional concept of the boss passing judgment often fails in motivating subordinates and improving their performance. So she started a new program that began the reviews from the bottom up—with the employee's self-evaluation and a focus on the manager's job as a coach and facilitator. Her advice is to "Listen for understanding and then react honestly and constructively. Focus on the business goals, not the personality."[7]

Intrapersonal conflict is tension experienced within the individual due to actual or perceived pressures from incompatible goals or expectations. *Approach–approach conflict* occurs when a person must choose between two positive and equally attractive alternatives. An example is when someone has to choose between a valued promotion in the organization or a desirable new job with another firm. *Avoidance–avoidance conflict* occurs when a person must choose between two negative and equally unattractive alternatives. An example is being asked either to accept a job transfer to another town in an undesirable location or to have one's employment with an organization terminated. *Approach–avoidance conflict* occurs when a person must decide to do something that has both positive and negative consequences. An example is being offered a higher-paying job with responsibilities that make unwanted demands on one's personal time.

Intergroup conflict occurs between teams, perhaps ones competing for scarce resources or rewards, and perhaps ones whose members have emotional problems with one another. The classic example is conflict among functional groups or departments, such as marketing and manufacturing. Sometimes these conflicts have substantive roots, such as marketing focusing on sales revenue goals and manufacturing focusing on cost efficiency goals. Other times such conflicts have emotional roots as "egos" in the respective departments cause each to want to look better than the other in a certain situation. Intergroup conflict is quite common in organizations, and it can make the coordination and integration of task activities very difficult.[8] The growing use of cross-functional teams and task forces is one way of trying to minimize such conflicts by improving horizontal communication.

Interorganizational conflict is most commonly thought of in terms of the competition and rivalry that characterizes firms operating in the same markets. A good example is the continuing battle between U.S. businesses and their global rivals: Ford versus Hyundai, or AT&T versus Verizon, for example. But interorganizational

- **Interpersonal conflict** occurs between two or more individuals in opposition to each other.

- **Intrapersonal conflict** occurs within the individual because of actual or perceived pressures from incompatible goals or expectations.

- **Intergroup conflict** occurs among groups in an organization.

- **Interorganizational conflict** occurs between organizations.

All That Twitters Is Not Gold

Employers are finding that all that Twitters isn't gold. Problems and conflicts arise when employee "tweets" cross the line in discussing customers, new hires, and even co-workers. Two rules of thumb are finding their way into Twitter Codes of Conduct: 1–Think before you tweet. 2–Don't tweet anything you don't want your mom to read.

conflict is a much broader issue than that represented by market competition alone. Other common examples include disagreements between unions and the organizations employing their members, between government regulatory agencies and the organizations subject to their surveillance, between organizations and their suppliers, and between organizations and outside activist groups.

Functional and Dysfunctional Conflict

There is no doubt that conflict in organizations can be upsetting both to the individuals directly involved and to others affected by its occurrence. It can be quite uncomfortable, for example, to work in an environment in which two co-workers are continually hostile toward each other or two teams are always battling for top management attention. In OB, and as shown in Figure 10.1, however, we recognize that conflict can have both a functional or constructive side and a dysfunctional or destructive side.

• **Functional conflict** results in positive benefits to the group.

Functional conflict, also called *constructive conflict*, results in benefits to individuals, the team, or the organization. On the positive side, conflict can bring important problems to the surface so they can be addressed. It can cause decisions to be considered carefully and perhaps reconsidered to ensure that the right path of action is being followed. It can increase the amount of information used for decision making. And it can offer opportunities for creativity that can improve performance. Indeed, an effective manager or team leader is able to stimulate constructive conflict in situations in which satisfaction with the status quo is holding back needed change and development.

• **Dysfunctional conflict** works to the group's or organization's disadvantage.

Dysfunctional conflict, or *destructive conflict*, works to the disadvantage of an individual or team. It diverts energies, hurts group cohesion, promotes interpersonal hostilities, and overall creates a negative environment for workers. This

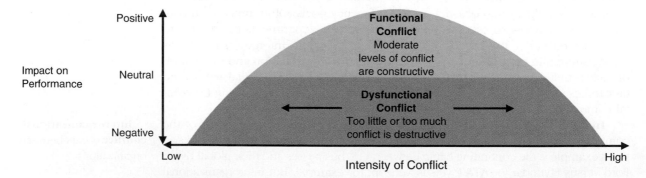

Figure 10.1 The two faces of conflict: functional conflict and dysfunctional conflict.

ETHICS IN OB

BLOGGING IS FUN, BUT BLOGGERS BEWARE

It is easy and tempting to set up your own blog, write about your experiences and impressions, and then share your thoughts with others online. So, why not do it?

Catherine Sanderson, a British citizen living and working in Paris, might have asked this question before launching her blog, *Le Petite Anglaise*. At one point it was so "successful" that she had 3,000 readers. But the Internet diary included reports on her experiences at work—and her employer, the accounting firm Dixon Wilson, wasn't at all happy when it became public knowledge.

Even though Sanderson was blogging anonymously, her photo was on the site, and the connection was eventually discovered. Noticed, too, was her running commentary about bosses, colleagues, and life at the office. One boss, she wrote, "calls secretaries 'typists.'" A Christmas party was described in detail, including an executive's "unforgivable faux pas." Under the heading "Titillation," she told how she displayed cleavage during a video conference at the office.

It's all out now. News reports said that one of the firm's partners was "incandescent with rage" after learning what Sanderson had written about him. Now Sanderson is upset. She says that she was "dooced"—a term used to describe being fired for what one writes in a blog. She wants financial damages and confirmation of her rights, on principle, to have a private blog.

Who's in the Right?   Would you agree with the observer who asks: "Say you worked for a large corporation, and in your spare time you wrote an anonymous 'insider's view' column for the *Financial Times*. Would you expect anything less than termination upon discovery?" Or would you agree with another, who asks: "Where does the influence your employer has on your day-to-day life stop?" Just what are the ethics issues here—from the blogger's and the employer's perspectives? Who has what rights when it comes to communicating in public about one's work experiences and impressions?

type of conflict occurs, for example, when two team members are unable to work together because of interpersonal differences—a destructive emotional conflict—or when the members of a work unit fail to act because they cannot agree on task goals—a destructive substantive conflict. Destructive conflicts of these types can decrease performance and job satisfaction as well as contribute to absenteeism and job turnover. Managers and team leaders should be alert to destructive conflicts and be quick to take action to prevent or eliminate them—or at least minimize any harm done.

Culture and Conflict

Society today shows many signs of cultural wear and tear in social relationships. We experience difficulties born of racial tensions, homophobia, gender gaps, and more. They arise from tensions among people who are different from one another in some way. They are also a reminder that cultural differences must be considered for their conflict potential. Consider the cultural dimension of time orientation. When persons from short-term cultures such as the United States try to work with persons from long-term cultures such as Japan, the likelihood of conflict developing is high. The same holds true when individualists work with collectivists and when persons from high-power-distance cultures work with those from low-power-distance cultures.[9]

People who are not able or willing to recognize and respect cultural differences can cause dysfunctional conflicts in multicultural teams. On the other hand, members with cultural sensitivity can help the team to unlock its performance advantages. Consider these comments from members of a joint European and American project team at Corning. "Something magical happens," says engineer John Thomas. "Europeans are very creative thinkers; they take time to really reflect on a problem to come up with the very best theoretical solution. Americans are more tactical and practical—we want to get down to developing a working solution as soon as possible." His partner at Fontainebleau in France says: "The French are more focused on ideas and concepts. If we get blocked in the execution of those ideas, we give up. Not the Americans. They pay more attention to details, processes, and time schedules. They make sure they are prepared and have involved everyone in the planning process so that they won't get blocked. But it's best if you mix the two approaches. In the end, you will achieve the best results."[10]

Conflict Management

LEARNING ROADMAP   Stages of Conflict / Hierarchical Causes of Conflict / Contextual Causes of Conflict / Indirect Conflict Management Strategies / Direct Conflict Management Strategies

• **Conflict resolution** occurs when the reasons for a conflict are eliminated.

Conflict can be addressed in many ways. But true **conflict resolution**—a situation in which the underlying reasons for dysfunctional conflict are eliminated, can be elusive. And when conflicts go unresolved, the stage is often set for future conflicts of the same or related sort. Rather than trying to deny the existence of conflict or settle on a temporary resolution, it is always best to deal with important conflicts in such ways that they are completely resolved.[11] This requires a good understanding of the stages of conflict, the potential causes of conflict, and indirect and direct approaches to conflict management.

Stages of Conflict

Most conflicts develop in stages, as shown in Figure 10.2. *Conflict antecedents* establish the conditions from which conflicts are likely to emerge. When the antecedent conditions become the basis for substantive or emotional differences between people or groups, the stage of *perceived conflict* exists. Of course, this perception may be held by only one of the conflicting parties. And there is quite a difference between perceived and *felt conflict*. When conflict is felt, it is experienced as tension that motivates the person to take action to reduce feelings of discomfort. For conflict to be resolved, all parties should perceive the conflict and feel the need to do something about it.

Manifest conflict is expressed openly in behavior. At this stage removing or correcting the antecedents results in *conflict resolution*, while failing to do so

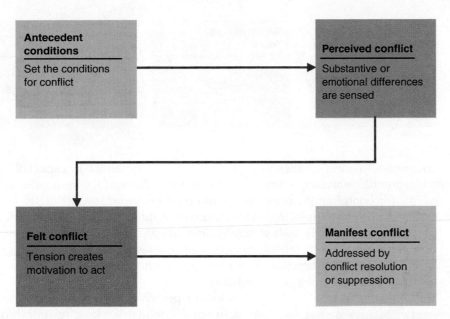

Figure 10.2 The stages of conflict.

results in *conflict suppression*. With suppression, no change in antecedent conditions occurs even though the manifest conflict behaviors may be temporarily controlled. This occurs, for example, when one or both parties choose to ignore conflict in their dealings with one another. Conflict suppression is a superficial and often temporary state that leaves the situation open to future conflicts over similar issues. Although it is perhaps useful in the short run, only true conflict resolution establishes conditions that eliminate an existing conflict and reduce the potential for it to recur in the future.

Hierarchical Causes of Conflict

The very nature of organizations as hierarchical systems provides a convenient setting for conflict to occur as individuals and teams try to work with one another. *Vertical conflict* occurs between levels and commonly involves supervisor–subordinate and team leader–team member disagreements over resources, goals, deadlines, or performance results. *Horizontal conflict* occurs between persons or groups working at the same hierarchical level. These disputes commonly involve goal incompatibilities, resource scarcities, or purely interpersonal factors. *Line–staff conflict* involves disagreements between line and staff personnel over who has authority and control over decisions on matters such as budgets, technology, and human resource practices. Also common are *role ambiguity conflicts* that occur when the communication of task expectations is unclear or upsetting in some way, such as a team member receiving different expectations from the leader and other members. Conflict is always likely when people are placed in ambiguous situations where it is hard to understand who is responsible for what, and why.

Contextual Causes of Conflict

The context of the organization as a complex network of interacting subsystems is a breeding ground for conflicts. *Task and workflow interdependencies* cause disputes and open disagreements among people and teams that are required to

Research & Development Team	Manufacturing Team	Marketing Team
Emphasizes • Product quality • Long time horizon	Emphasizes • Cost efficiency • Short time horizon	Emphasizes • Customer needs • Short time horizon

Figure 10.3 Structural differentiation as a potential source of conflict among functional teams.

cooperate to meet challenging goals.[12] Conflict potential is especially great when interdependence is high—that is, when a person or group must rely on or ask for contributions from one or more others to achieve its goals. Conflict escalates with *structural differentiation* where different teams and work units pursue different goals with different time horizons as shown in Figure 10.3. Conflict also develops out of *domain ambiguities* when individuals or teams lack adequate task direction or goals and misunderstand such things as customer jurisdiction or scope of authority.

Actual or perceived *resource scarcity* can foster destructive conflict. Working relationships are likely to suffer as individuals or teams try to position themselves to gain or retain maximum shares of a limited resource pool. They are also likely to resist having their resources redistributed to others.

Power or value asymmetries in work relationships can also create conflict. They exist when interdependent people or teams differ substantially from one another in status and influence or in values. Conflict resulting from asymmetry is likely, for example, when a low-power person needs the help of a high-power person who does not respond, when people who hold dramatically different values are forced to work together on a task, or when a high-status person is required to interact with and perhaps be dependent on someone of lower status.

Stay Alert for These Common Causes of Conflicts in Organizations

• *Unresolved prior conflicts*—When conflicts go unresolved, they remain latent and often emerge again in the future as the basis for conflicts over the same or related matters.

• *Role ambiguities*—When people aren't sure what they are supposed to do, conflict with others is likely; task uncertainties increase the odds of working at cross-purposes at least some of the time.

• *Resource scarcities*—When people have to share resources with one another and/or when they have to compete with one another for resources, the conditions are ripe for conflict.

• *Task interdependencies*—When people must depend on others doing things first before they can do their own jobs, conflicts often occur; dependency on others creates anxieties and other pressures.

• *Domain ambiguities*—When people are unclear about how their objectives or those of their teams fit with those being pursued by others, or when their objectives directly compete in win–lose fashion, conflict is likely to occur.

• *Structural differentiation*—When people work in parts of the organization where structures, goals, time horizons, and even staff compositions are very different, conflict is likely with other units.

Indirect Conflict Management Strategies

Most managers will tell you that not all conflict in teams and organizations can be resolved by getting the people involved to adopt new attitudes, behaviors, and stances toward one another. Think about it. Aren't there likely to be times when personalities and emotions prove irreconcilable? In such cases an indirect or structural approach to conflict management can often help. It uses such strategies as reduced interdependence, appeals to common goals, hierarchical referral, and alterations in the use of mythology and scripts to deal with the conflict situation.

Managed Interdependence   When workflow conflicts exist, managers can adjust the level of interdependency among teams or individuals.[13] One simple option is *decoupling*, or taking action to eliminate or reduce the required contact between conflicting parties. In some cases team tasks can be adjusted to reduce the number of required points of coordination. The conflicting parties are separated as much as possible from one another.

Buffering is another approach that can be used when the inputs of one team are the outputs of another. The classic buffering technique is to build an inventory, or buffer, between the teams so that any output slowdown or excess is absorbed by the inventory and does not directly pressure the target group. Although it reduces conflict, this technique is increasingly out of favor because it increases inventory costs.

Conflict can sometimes be reduced by assigning people to serve as liaisons between groups that are prone to conflict.[14] Persons in these *linking-pin roles* are expected to understand the operations, members, needs, and norms of their host teams. They are supposed to use this knowledge to help the team work better with others in order to accomplish mutual tasks.

Appeals to Common Goals   An *appeal to common goals* can focus the attention of conflicting individuals and teams on one mutually desirable conclusion. This elevates any dispute to the level of common ground where disagreements can be put in perspective. In a course team where members are arguing over content choices for a PowerPoint presentation, for example, it might help to remind everyone that the goal is to impress the instructor and get an "A" for the presentation and that this is only possible if everyone contributes their best.

Upward Referral   *Upward referral* uses the chain of command for conflict resolution.[15] Problems are moved up from the level of conflicting individuals or teams for more senior managers to address. Although tempting, it has limitations. If conflict is severe and recurring, the continual use of upward referral may not result in true conflict resolution. Higher managers removed from day-to-day affairs may fail to see the real causes of a conflict, and attempts at resolution may be superficial. And, busy managers may tend to blame the people involved and even act quickly to replace them.

Altering Scripts and Myths   In some situations, conflict is superficially managed by scripts, or behavioral routines, that are part of the organization's culture.[16] The scripts become rituals that allow the conflicting parties to vent their frustrations and to recognize that they are mutually dependent on one another. An example is a monthly meeting of "department heads," which is held presumably for purposes of coordination and problem solving but actually becomes just a polite forum for

INTRAPERSONAL CONFLICT AND BECK'S

Conflict can occur on any one of four levels and sometimes on multiple levels simultaneously. While we tend to think about conflicts between individuals as most serious, sometimes the agonizing choices an individual must make can be equally as difficult. **Intrapersonal conflict** arises when an individual experiences incompatible goals. Conflicts at this level are represented by having to choose between two good things, two choices each with bad outcomes (having to pick the lesser of two evils), or a single choice with pros and cons.

The Beck's commercial opens with a woman struggling to remove an article of clothing from the jaws of a dog and a room in total disarray. When the boyfriend arrives, the woman gives him an ultimatum—either the dog goes or I go—choose between man's best friend or man's better half. It is quite a dilemma. While the boyfriend acknowledges a sense of loyalty to the dog he owned for eight years, he also recognizes that the woman is the best thing that ever happened to him.

The choice in the commercial clearly illustrates an intrapersonal conflict. Whether it is approach–approach (choosing between two good things) or avoidance–avoidance (a choice involving two unequally unattractive outcomes) depends on the viewer's perspective.

Get to Know Yourself Better   Complete Assessment 18, Conflict Management Strategies, in the OB Skills Workbook. *What did you learn about your preferred style for dealing with conflict? Sometimes the styles tend to be about equal. In other cases, we may learn that we have a dominant style. What about you? If you have a dominant style, how well does it serve you?*

agreement.[17] Managers in such cases know their scripts and accept the difficulty of truly resolving any major conflicts. By sticking with the script, expressing only low-key disagreement, and then quickly acting as if everything has been taken care of, for instance, the managers can leave the meeting with everyone feeling a superficial sense of accomplishment.

Direct Conflict Management Strategies

In addition to the indirect conflict management strategies just discussed, it is also very important to understand how conflict management plays out in face-to-face fashion. Figure 10.4 shows five direct conflict management strategies that vary in their emphasis on cooperativeness and assertiveness in the interpersonal dynamics of the situation. Although true conflict resolution can occur only when a conflict is dealt with through a solution that allows all conflicting parties to "win," the reality is that direct conflict management may also pursue lose–lose and win–lose outcomes.[18]

Lose–Lose Strategies   *Lose–lose conflict* occurs when nobody really gets what he or she wants in a conflict situation. The underlying reasons for the conflict remain unaffected, and a similar conflict is likely to occur in the future. Lose–lose outcomes are likely when the conflict management strategies involve little or no assertiveness. **Avoidance** is the extreme where no one acts assertively and everyone simply pretends the conflict doesn't exist and hopes it will

• **Avoidance** involves pretending a conflict does not really exist.

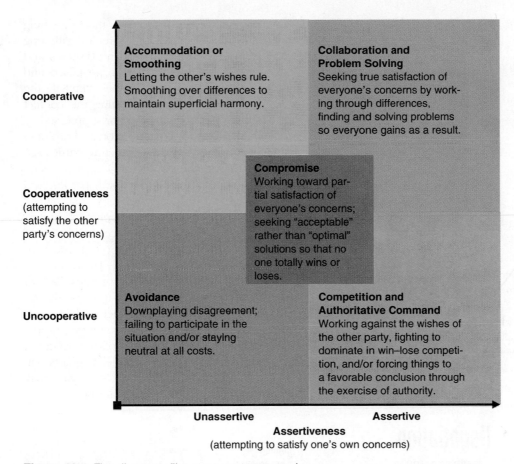

Figure 10.4 Five direct conflict management strategies.

go away. **Accommodation**, or **smoothing** as it is sometimes called, involves playing down differences among the conflicting parties and highlighting similarities and areas of agreement. This peaceful coexistence ignores the real essence of a conflict and often creates frustration and resentment. **Compromise** occurs when each party shows moderate assertiveness and cooperation, and is ultimately willing to give up something of value to the other. But because no one gets what they really wanted, the antecedent conditions for future conflicts are established.

Win–Lose Strategies   In *win–lose conflict*, one party achieves its desires at the expense and to the exclusion of the other party's desires. This is a high-assertiveness and low-cooperativeness situation. It may result from outright **competition** in which one party achieves a victory through force, superior skill, or domination. It may also occur as a result of **authoritative command**, whereby a formal authority such as manager or team leader simply dictates a solution and specifies what is gained and what is lost by whom. Win–lose strategies fail to address the root causes of the conflict and tend to suppress the desires of at least one of the conflicting parties. As a result, future conflicts over the same issues are likely to occur.

Win–Win Strategies   *Win–win conflict* is achieved by a blend of both high cooperativeness and high assertiveness.[19] **Collaboration and problem solving** involve

- **Accommodation**, or **smoothing**, involves playing down differences and finding areas of agreement.
- **Compromise** occurs when each party gives up something of value to the other.

- **Competition** seeks victory by force, superior skill, or domination.
- **Authoritative command** uses formal authority to end conflict.
- **Collaboration and problem solving** involve recognition that something is wrong and needs attention through problem solving.

- *Avoidance* may be used when an issue is trivial, when more important issues are pressing, or when people need to cool down temporarily and regain perspective.
- *Accommodation* may be used when issues are more important to others than to yourself or when you want to build "credits" for use in later disagreements.
- *Compromise* may be used to arrive at temporary settlements of complex issues or to arrive at expedient solutions when time is limited.
- *Authoritative command* may be used when quick and decisive action is vital or when unpopular actions must be taken.
- *Collaboration and problem solving* are used to gain true conflict resolution when time and cost permit.

recognition by all conflicting parties that something is wrong and needs attention. It stresses gathering and evaluating information in solving disputes and making choices. All relevant issues are raised and openly discussed. Win–win outcomes eliminate the reasons for continuing or resurrecting the conflict because nothing has been avoided or suppressed.

The ultimate test for collaboration and problem solving is whether or not the conflicting parties see that the solution to the conflict: (1) achieves each party's goals, (2) is acceptable to both parties, and (3) establishes a process whereby all parties involved see a responsibility to be open and honest about facts and feelings. When success in each of these areas is achieved, the likelihood of true conflict resolution is greatly increased. However, this process often takes time and consumes lots of energy, things to which the parties must be willing to commit. Collaboration and problem solving may not be feasible if the firm's dominant culture rewards competition too highly and fails to place a value on cooperation.[20] And, as the visual sidebar points out, each of the conflict management strategies may have advantages under certain conditions.

Negotiation

LEARNING ROADMAP   Negotiation Goals and Outcomes / Ethical Aspects of Negotiation / Organizational Settings for Negotiation

Picture yourself trying to make a decision in the following situation: You are about to order a new state-of-the-art notebook computer for a team member in your department. Then another team member submits a request for one of a different brand. Your boss says that only one brand can be ordered. Or consider this one: You have been offered a new job in another city and want to take it, but are disappointed with the salary. You've heard friends talk about how they "negotiated" better offers when taking jobs. You are concerned about the costs of relocating and would like a signing bonus as well as a guarantee of an early salary review.

The preceding examples are just two of the many situations that involve **negotiation**—the process of making joint decisions when the parties involved have different preferences.[21] Negotiation has special significance in teams and work settings, where disagreements are likely to arise over such diverse matters as wage rates, task objectives, performance evaluations, job assignments, work schedules, work locations, and more.

- **Negotiation** is the process of making joint decisions when the parties involved have different preferences.

Negotiation Goals and Outcomes

Two important goals must be considered in any negotiation: substance goals and relationship goals. *Substance goals* deal with outcomes that relate to the "content" issues under negotiation. The dollar amount of a salary offer in a recruiting situ-

Finding the Leader in You

ALAN MULALLY NEGOTIATES A NEW FUTURE FOR FORD

When Alan Mulally, a former Boeing executive, was appointed CEO of Ford Motor Company, many wondered if an "airplane guy" could run a car company. William Ford Jr. said, "Alan was the right choice and it gets more right every day."

Ford has reported record earnings, and *Fortune* magazine named Mulally executive of the year in 2010. Not too long ago, however, the picture wasn't so bright. With

the bankruptcies of both Chrysler and General Motors, Ford was fighting for its life. But Mulally was determined to transform the company for the future.

In addition to many changes to modernize plants and streamline operations, he tackled problems dealing with functional chimneys, a lack of open communication and hidden conflict among the various parts of Ford. William Ford says the firm had a culture that "loved to meet." Managers would get together to discuss the message they wanted to communicate to the top executives: all agreement and no conflict, even as all went their separate ways.

Mulally changed that with a focus on transparency, data-based decision making, and cooperation between divisions. When some of the senior executives balked and tried to complain to Ford, he refused to listen and reinforced Mulally's authority to run the firm his way.

When executives were reluctant to resolve conflicts among

themselves, Mulally remained tough: "They can either work together or they can come see me." He hasn't shied away from the United Auto Workers Union either. He negotiated new agreements that brought labor costs down to be more competitive with foreign rivals.

As one consultant noted: "The speed with which Mulally has transformed Ford into a more nimble and healthy operation has been one of the more impressive jobs I've seen. . . . without Mulally's impact Ford might well have gone out of business."

What's the Lesson Here?

How comfortable are you with conflict? Can you tolerate heated discussions around you, and can you recognize the difference between productive and nonproductive conflict? Would you be able to stand firm when others disagree with you (e.g., try to protect the status quo) or would you question your judgment?

ation is one example. *Relationship goals* deal with outcomes that relate to how well people involved in the negotiation and any constituencies they may represent are able to work with one another once the process is concluded. An example is the ability of union members and management representatives to work together effectively after a labor contract dispute has been settled.

Effective negotiation occurs when substance issues are resolved and working relationships are maintained or even improved. Three criteria for effective negotiation are:

- *Quality*—The negotiation results in a "quality" agreement that is wise and satisfactory to all sides.
- *Harmony*—The negotiation is "harmonious" and fosters rather than inhibits good interpersonal relations.
- *Efficiency*—The negotiation is "efficient" and no more time consuming or costly than absolutely necessary.

• **Effective negotiation** occurs when substance issues are resolved and working relationships are maintained or improved.

Ethical Aspects of Negotiation

Managers and others involved in negotiations should strive for high ethical standards of conduct, but this goal can get sidetracked by an overemphasis on self-interests. The motivation to behave ethically in negotiations can be put to the test by each party's desire to "get more" than the other from the negotiation and/or by a belief that there are insufficient resources to satisfy all parties.[22] After the heat of negotiations dies down, the parties may try to rationalize or explain away questionable ethics as unavoidable, harmless, or justified. Such after-the-fact rationalizations can have long-run negative consequences, such as not being able to achieve one's wishes again the next time. At the very least the unethical party may be the target of revenge tactics by those who were disadvantaged. Once some people have behaved unethically in one situation, furthermore, they may become entrapped by such behavior and more likely to display it again in the future.[23]

Organizational Settings for Negotiation

Managers and team leaders should be prepared to participate in at least four major action settings for negotiations. In *two-party negotiation* the manager negotiates directly with one other person. In a *group negotiation* the manager is part of a team or group whose members are negotiating to arrive at a common decision. In an *intergroup negotiation* the manager is part of a group that is negotiating with another group to arrive at a decision regarding a problem or situation affecting both. And in a *constituency negotiation* each party represents a broader constituency—for example, representatives of management and labor negotiating a collective bargaining agreement.

Negotiation Strategies

LEARNING ROADMAP Approaches to Distributive Negotiation / How to Gain Integrative Agreements / Common Negotiation Pitfalls / Third-Party Roles in Negotiation

When we think about negotiating for something, perhaps cars and salaries are the first things that pop into mind. But people in organizations are constantly negotiating over not only just pay and raises, but also such things as work goals or preferences and access to any variety of scarce resources—money, time, people, facilities, equipment, and so on. The general approach to, or strategy for, any negotiation can have a major influence on its outcomes.

> • **Distributive negotiation** focuses on positions staked out or declared by the parties involved, each of whom is trying to claim certain portions of the available pie.
>
> • **Integrative negotiation** focuses on the merits of the issues, and the parties involved try to enlarge the available pie rather than stake claims to certain portions of it.

In OB we generally talk about two broad negotiation strategies that differ markedly in approach and possible outcomes. **Distributive negotiation** focuses on "positions" staked out or declared by conflicting parties. Each party tries to claim certain portions of the available "pie" whose overall size is considered fixed. **Integrative negotiation**, sometimes called *principled negotiation*, focuses on the "merits" of the issues. Everyone involved tries to enlarge the available pie and find mutually agreed-upon ways of distributing it, rather than stake claims to certain portions of it.[24] Think of the conversations you overhear and are part of in team situations. The notion of "my way or the highway" is analogous to distribution negotiation; "let's find a way to make this work for both of us" is more akin to integrative negotiation.

Workers in France Negotiate by Taking Managers Hostage

Laid-off workers in Caterpillar's French plant took five managers hostage for 24 hours. The bosses were released after the company agreed to renegotiate compensation for workers losing their jobs. A poll showed some 45 percent of French people approved of such "bossnapping."

Approaches to Distributive Negotiation

Participants in distributive negotiation usually approach it as a "win–lose" episode. And, things tend to unfold in one of two directions, with neither one nor the other yielding optimal results.

"Hard" distributive negotiation takes place when each party holds out to get its own way. This leads to competition, whereby each party seeks dominance over the other and tries to maximize self-interests. The hard approach may lead to a win–lose outcome in which one party dominates and gains. Or it can lead to an impasse.

"Soft" distributive negotiation takes place when one party or both parties make concessions just to get things over with. This soft approach leads to accommodation, in which one party gives in to the other, or to compromise, in which each party gives up something of value in order to reach agreement. In either case at least some latent dissatisfaction is likely to remain.

Figure 10.5 illustrates classic two-party distributive negotiation by the example of the graduating senior negotiating a job offer with a corporate recruiter.[25] Look at the situation first from the graduate's perspective. She has told the recruiter that she would like a salary of $55,000; this is her initial offer. But she also has in mind a minimum reservation point of $50,000—the lowest salary that she will accept for this job. Thus she communicates a salary request of $55,000 but is willing to accept one as low as $50,000. The situation is somewhat the reverse from the recruiter's perspective. His initial offer to the graduate is $45,000, and his maximum reservation point is $55,000; this is the most he is prepared to pay.

The **bargaining zone** is the range between one party's minimum reservation point and the other party's maximum reservation point. In Figure 10.5, the bargaining zone is $50,000–$55,000. This is a positive bargaining zone since the reservation points of the two parties overlap. Whenever a positive bargaining zone exists, bargaining has room to unfold. Had the graduate's minimum reservation point been greater than the recruiter's maximum reservation point (for example, $57,000), no

• The **bargaining zone** is the range between one party's minimum reservation point and the other party's maximum.

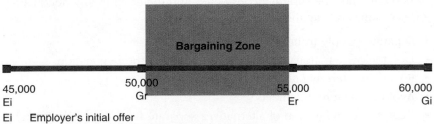

Ei   Employer's initial offer
Gr   Graduating senior's minimum reservation point
Er   Employer's maximum reservation point
Gi   Graduating senior's initial offer

Figure 10.5 The bargaining zone is classic two-party negotiation.

Sooner or Later You'll Need to Know How to Negotiate a Better Raise

We've all done it—wish we'd asked for more when negotiating a starting salary or a pay raise. Why didn't we? And, even if we did, would it have made a difference? Chances are you'll go into a salary negotiation unprepared. And you may pay a price for that. There's quite a bit of advice around for how to negotiate pay raises. A compilation of thoughts and tips follows.

• *Prepare, prepare, prepare*—do the research and find out what others make for a similar position inside and outside the organization, including everything from salary to benefits, bonuses, incentives, and job perks.

• *Document and communicate*—identify and communicate your value; put forth a set of accomplishments that show how you have saved or made money and created value for an employer, or how your skills and attributes will do so for a prospective one.

• *Advocate and ask*—be your own best advocate; in salary negotiation the rule is "Don't ask, don't get." But don't ask too soon; your boss or interviewer should be the first to bring up salary.

• *Stay focused on the goal*—the goal is to satisfy your interests to the maximum extent possible; this means everything from getting immediate satisfaction to being better positioned for future satisfaction.

• *View things from the other side*—test your requests against the employer's point of view; ask if you are being reasonable, convincing, and fair; ask how the boss could explain to higher levels and to your peers a decision to grant your request.

• *Don't overreact to bad news*—never "quit on the spot" if you don't get what you want; be willing to search for and consider alternative job offers.

room would have existed for bargaining. Classic two-party bargaining always involves the delicate tasks of first discovering the respective reservation points (one's own and the other's) and then working toward an agreement that lies somewhere within the bargaining zone and is acceptable to each party.

How to Gain Integrative Agreements

The integrative approach to negotiation is less confrontational than the distributive, and it permits a broader range of alternatives to be considered in the negotiation process. From the outset there is much more of a "win–win" orientation. Even though it may take longer, the time, energy, and effort needed to negotiate an integrated agreement can be well worth the investment. But always, the integrative or principled approach involves a willingness to negotiate based on the merits of the situation. The foundations for gaining truly integrative agreements can be described as supportive attitudes, constructive behaviors, and good information.[26]

Attitudinal Foundations   There are three attitudinal foundations of integrative agreements. First, each party must approach the negotiation with a *willingness to trust* the other party. This is a reason why ethics and maintaining relationships are so important in negotiations. Second, each party must convey a *willingness to share* information with the other party. Without shared information, effective problem solving is unlikely to occur. Third, each party must show a *willingness to ask concrete questions* of the other party. This further facilitates information sharing.

Behavioral Foundations   During a negotiation all behavior is important for both its actual impact and the impressions it leaves behind. This means the following behavioral foundations of integrative agreements must be carefully considered and included in any negotiator's repertoire of skills and capabilities:

• Separate people from the problem.
• Don't allow emotional considerations to affect the negotiation.
• Focus on interests rather than positions.
• Avoid premature judgments.
• Keep the identification of alternatives separate from their evaluation.
• Judge possible agreements by set criteria or standards.

Information Foundations   The information foundations of integrative agreements are substantial. They involve each party becoming familiar with the BATNA, or "best alternative to a negotiated agreement." That is, each party must know what he or she will do if an agreement cannot be reached. Both negotiating parties must identify and understand their personal interests in the situation. They must know what is really important to them in the case at hand. And, they must come to understand what the other party values.

Common Negotiation Pitfalls

The negotiation process is admittedly complex on ethical and many other grounds. It is subject to all the possible confusions of complex, and sometimes even volatile, interpersonal and team dynamics. And as if this isn't enough, negotiators need to guard against some common negotiation pitfalls.[27]

Fixed pie myth	Escalating commitment	Over-confidence	Too much telling	Too little listening

The first pitfall is the tendency to stake out your negotiating position based on the assumption that in order to gain your way, something must be subtracted from the gains of the other party. This *myth of the fixed pie* is a purely distributive approach to negotiation. The whole concept of integrative negotiation is based on the premise that the pie can sometimes be expanded or used to the maximum advantage of all parties, not just one.

Second, the possibility of *escalating commitment* is high when negotiations begin with parties stating extreme demands. Once demands have been stated, people become committed to them and are reluctant to back down. Concerns for protecting one's ego and saving face may lead to the irrational escalation of a conflict. Self-discipline is needed to spot tendencies toward escalation in one's own behavior as well as in the behavior of others.

Third, negotiators often develop *overconfidence* that their positions are the only correct ones. This can lead them to ignore the other party's needs. In some cases negotiators completely fail to see merits in the other party's position—merits that an outside observer would be sure to spot. Such overconfidence makes it harder to reach a positive common agreement.

Fourth, communication problems can cause difficulties during a negotiation. It has been said that "negotiation is the process of communicating back and forth for the purpose of reaching a joint decision."[28] This process can break down because of a *telling problem*—the parties don't really talk to each other, at least not in the sense of making themselves truly understood. It can also be damaged by a *hearing problem*—the parties are unable or unwilling to listen well enough to understand what the other is saying. Indeed, positive negotiation is most likely when each party engages in active listening and frequently asks questions to clarify what the other is saying. Each party occasionally needs to "stand in the other party's shoes" and to view the situation from the other's perspective.[29]

Third-Party Roles in Negotiation

Negotiation may sometimes be accomplished through the intervention of third parties, such as when stalemates occur and matters appear to be unresolvable under current circumstances. In a process called *alternative dispute resolution*, a neutral third party works with persons involved in a negotiation to help them resolve impasses and settle disputes. There are two primary forms through which it is implemented.

RESEARCH INSIGHT

Words Affect Outcomes in Online Dispute Resolution

A study of dispute resolution among eBay buyers and sellers finds that using words that give "face" were more likely than words that attack "face" to result in the settlement of online disputes. Jeanne Brett, Marla Olekans, Ray Friedman, Nathan Goates, Cameron Anderson, and Cara Cherry Lisco studied real disputes being addressed through Square Trade, an online dispute resolution service to which eBay refers unhappy customers. For purposes of the study, a "dispute" was defined as a form of conflict in which one party to a transaction made a claim that the other party rejected.

The researchers point out that most past research on dispute resolution has focused on situational and participant characteristics. In this case they adopted what they call a "language-based" approach based on the perspectives of face theory, essentially arguing that how participants use language to give and attack the face of the other party will have a major impact on results. In filing a claim, for example, an unhappy buyer might use polite words that preserve the positive self-image or face of the seller, or they might use negative words that attack this sense of face. Examples of negative words are "agitated, angry, apprehensive, despise, disgusted, frustrated, furious, and hate."

This study examined 386 eBay-generated disputes processed through Square Trade. Words in the first social interchange between parties were analyzed. Results showed that expressing negative emotions and giving commands to the other party inhibited dispute resolution, whereas providing a causal explanation, offering suggestions, and communicating firmness all made dispute resolution more likely. A hypothesis that expressing positive emotions would increase the likelihood of dispute resolution was not supported. The study also showed that the longer a dispute played out, the less likely it was to be resolved.

Dispute resolution less likely when	Dispute resolution more likely when
• Negative emotions are expressed • Commands are issued	• Causal explanation given • Suggestions are offered • Communications are firm

In terms of practical implications the researchers state: "Watch your language; avoid attacking the other's face either by showing your anger toward them, or expressing contempt; avoid signaling weakness; be firm in your claim. Provide causal accounts that take responsibility and give face." Finally, they note that these basic principles apply in other dispute resolution contexts, not just online.

Do the Research　Consider the suggestions for successful online dispute resolution. Can you design a study to test how well they apply to disputes that may occur in virtual teamwork?

Source: Jeanne Brett, Marla Olekans, Ray Friedman, Nathan Goates, Cameron Anderson, and Cara Cherry Lisco, "Sticks and Stones: Language and On-Line Dispute Resolution," *Academy of Management Journal* 50 (February 2007).

• In **arbitration** a neutral third party acts as judge with the power to issue a decision binding for all parties.

• In **mediation** a neutral third party tries to engage the parties in a negotiated solution through persuasion and rational argument.

In **arbitration**, such as the salary arbitration now common in professional sports, the neutral third party acts as a "judge" and has the power to issue a decision that is binding on all parties. This ruling takes place after the arbitrator listens to the positions advanced by the parties involved in a dispute. In **mediation**, the neutral third party tries to engage the parties in a negotiated solution through persuasion and rational argument. This is a common approach in labor–management negotiations, where trained mediators acceptable to both sides are called in to help resolve bargaining impasses. Unlike an arbitrator, the mediator is not able to dictate a solution.

10 *study guide*

What is the nature of conflict in organizations?

- Conflict appears as a disagreement over issues of substance or emotional antagonisms that create friction between individuals or teams.

- Conflict situations in organizations occur at intrapersonal, interpersonal, intergroup, and interorganizational levels.

- Moderate levels of conflict can be functional for performance, stimulating effort and creativity.

- Too little conflict is dysfunctional when it leads to complacency; too much conflict is dysfunctional when it overwhelms us.

How can conflict be managed?

- Conflict typically develops through a series of stages, beginning with antecedent conditions and progressing into manifest conflict.

- Indirect conflict management strategies include appeals to common goals, upward referral, managed interdependence, and the use of mythology and scripts.

- Direct conflict management strategies of avoidance, accommodation, compromise, competition, and collaboration show different tendencies toward cooperativeness and assertiveness.

- Lose–lose conflict results from avoidance, smoothing or accommodation, and compromise; win–lose conflict is associated with competition and authoritative command; win–win conflict is achieved through collaboration and problem solving.

What is the nature of negotiation in organizations?

- Negotiation is the process of making decisions and reaching agreement in situations where participants have different preferences.

- Managers may find themselves involved in various types of negotiation situations, including two-party, group, intergroup, and constituency negotiation.

- Effective negotiation occurs when both substance goals (dealing with outcomes) and relationship goals (dealing with processes) are achieved.

- Ethical problems in negotiation can arise when people become manipulative and dishonest in trying to satisfy their self-interests at any cost.

What are alternative strategies for negotiation?

- The distributive approach to negotiation emphasizes win–lose outcomes; the integrative or principled approach to negotiation emphasizes win–win outcomes.

- In distributive negotiation the focus of each party is on staking out positions in the attempt to claim desired portions of a "fixed pie."

- In integrative negotiation, sometimes called principled negotiation, the focus is on determining the merits of the issues and finding ways to satisfy one another's needs.

- The success of negotiations often depends on avoiding common pitfalls such as the myth of the fixed pie, escalating commitment, overconfidence, and both the telling and hearing problems.

- When negotiations are at an impasse, third-party approaches such as mediation and arbitration offer alternative and structured ways for dispute resolution.

Terms to Know

Accommodation (smoothing) (p. 229)
Arbitration (p. 236)
Authoritative command (p. 229)
Avoidance (p. 228)
Bargaining zone (p. 233)
Collaboration and problem solving (p. 229)
Competition (p. 229)

Compromise (p. 229)
Conflict (p. 220)
Conflict resolution (p. 224)
Distributive negotiation (p. 232)
Dysfunctional conflict (p. 222)
Effective negotiation (p. 231)
Emotional conflict (p. 220)
Functional conflict (p. 222)

Integrative negotiation (p. 232)
Intergroup conflict (p. 221)
Interorganizational conflict (p. 221)
Interpersonal conflict (p. 221)
Intrapersonal conflict (p. 221)
Mediation (p. 236)
Negotiation (p. 230)
Substantive conflict (p. 220)

Self-Test 10

Multiple Choice

1. A/an _____ conflict occurs in the form of a fundamental disagreement over ends or goals and the means for accomplishment. (a) relationship (b) emotional (c) substantive (d) procedural

2. The indirect conflict management approach that uses the chain of command for conflict resolution is known as _____. (a) upward referral (b) avoidance (c) smoothing (d) appeal to common goals

3. Conflict that ends up being "functional" for the people and organization involved would most likely be _____. (a) of high intensity (b) of moderate intensity (c) of low intensity (d) nonexistent

4. One of the problems with the suppression of conflicts is that it _____. (a) creates winners and losers (b) is a temporary solution that sets the stage for future conflict (c) works only with emotional conflicts (d) works only with substantive conflicts

5. When a manager asks people in conflict to remember the mission and purpose of the organization and to try to reconcile their differences in that context, she is using a conflict management approach known as _____. (a) reduced interdependence (b) buffering (c) resource expansion (d) appeal to common goals

6. An _____ conflict occurs when a person must choose between two equally attractive alternative courses of action. (a) approach–avoidance (b) avoidance–avoidance (c) approach–approach (d) avoidance–approach

7. If two units or teams in an organization are engaged in almost continual conflict and the higher manager decides it is time to deal with things through managed interdependence, which is a possible choice of conflict management approach? (a) compromise (b) buffering (c) appeal to common goals (d) upward referral

8. A lose–lose conflict is likely when the conflict management approach is one of _____. (a) collaborator (b) altering scripts (c) accommodation (d) problem solving

9. Which approach to conflict management can be best described as both highly cooperative and highly assertive? (a) competition (b) compromise (c) accommodation (d) collaboration

10. Both _____ goals should be considered in any negotiation. (a) performance and evaluation (b) task and substance (c) substance and relationship (d) task and performance

11. The three criteria for effective negotiation are _____. (a) harmony, efficiency, and quality (b) quality, efficiency, and effectiveness (c) ethical behavior, practicality, and cost-effectiveness (d) quality, practicality, and productivity

12. Which statement is true? (a) Principled negotiation leads to accommodation. (b) Hard distributive negotiation leads to collaboration. (c) Soft distributive negotiation leads to accommodation or compromise. (d) Hard distributive negotiation leads to win–win conflicts.

13. Another name for integrative negotiation is _____. (a) arbitration (b) mediation (c) principled negotiation (d) smoothing

14. When a person approaches a negotiation with the assumption that in order for him to gain his way, the other party must lose or give up something, which negotiation pitfall is being exhibited? (a) myth of the fixed pie (b) escalating commitment (c) overconfidence (d) hearing problem

15. In the process of alternative dispute resolution known as _____, a neutral third party acts as a "judge" to determine how a conflict will be resolved. (a) mediation (b) arbitration (c) conciliation (d) collaboration

Short Response

16. List and discuss three conflict situations faced by managers.

17. List and discuss the major indirect conflict management approaches.

18. Under what conditions might a manager use avoidance or accommodation?

19. Compare and contrast distributive and integrative negotiation. Which is more desirable? Why?

Applications Essay

20. Discuss the common pitfalls you would expect to encounter in negotiating your salary for your first job, and explain how you would best try to deal with them.

Next Steps

Top Choices from

The OB Skills Workbook

Case for Critical Thinking	Team and Experiential Exercises	Self-Assessment Portfolio
• The Case of the Missing Raise	• Choices • The Ugli Orange • Vacation Puzzle • Conflict Dialogues	• Conflict Management Strategies

Nordstrom: 115 Stores, 1 Inventory

Misplacing a pair of pants or favorite shirt happens to all of us from time to time. But when you're a highly successful chain of 100+ department stores, it's a bigger problem.

Seattle-based Nordstrom faced this issue recently. For nearly 100 years, the company flourished by pairing high-quality clothes with excellent customer service. But success came at a price—while the stores' fashions changed with the times, its inventory management strategy did not.

A customer who fell in love with a pair of candy red Prada pumps one day might return to her Nordstrom store 24 hours later to find they are completely out

> *"Traditional retailers have traditional ways of doing things, and sometimes those barriers are hard to break down."*
> *—Adrianne Shapira, Goldman Sachs retail analyst.*[b]

of her size. While inventory naturally fluctuates, Nordstrom associates couldn't easily locate a pair in another store or verify when they'd return to stock. And in an era of booming online sales, Nordstrom realized they were likely to lose such a customer faster than you could say, "I'll just Google that."

To catch up with competitors, Nordstrom collaborated with Accenture Consulting to unify access to inventory. After an immense overhaul of the chain's inventory management processes, customers at their laptops and associates behind sales counters see the same thing—the entire inventory of Nordstrom's 115 stores presented as one selection.

So now Nordstrom doesn't have to turn away the customer who spied that pair of candy red Pradas; she can order them online or in her local store, and they'll be shipped to her door directly from a store that has them in stock, even if it's located across the country.

Items don't stay in stock very long at Nordstrom stores these days, and that's the point. The chain is current turning inventory about twice as fast as its competitors, thanks to strong help from Web sales. And quick, continuous turnover of inventory attracts investors, even in unsure markets.[a]

Quick Summary

- 100-year-old department store Nordstrom flourished because of its sharp focus on customer service. But as competition grew fierce and sales slid, top brass conceded that the company had done so at the expense of modernizing its inventory control systems.
- Working with Accenture Consulting, Nordstrom merged the inventories of all stores into a single view accessible by both customers and retail associates.
- Nordstrom stores now keep less stock on hand, and the chain draws praise from analysts for doing so in a challenging retail environment.

FYI: Nordstrom keeps items in its inventory for an average of 62 days, compared to Macy's for 119 days and Saks for 140 days.[c]

11 Communication and Collaboration

the key point

Communication is the "lifeblood" of the organization. All organizational behavior, good and bad, stems from communication. As illustrated by Nordstrom's struggles with inventory control, effective communication creates the pathway to a more collaborative and coordinated workplace. Understanding the nature of the communication process can help us manage it more effectively in organizations.

chapter at a glance

What Is Communication?

What Are the Issues in Interpersonal Communication?

What Is the Nature of Communication in Organizations?

How Can We Build More Collaborative Work Environments?

ETHICS IN OB
PRIVACY IN THE AGE OF SOCIAL NETWORKING

FINDING THE LEADER IN YOU
IDEO SELECTS FOR COLLABORATIVE LEADERS

OB IN POPULAR CULTURE
CROSS-CULTURAL COMMUNICATION AND *THE AMAZING RACE*

RESEARCH INSIGHT
LEADERSHIP BEHAVIOR AND EMPLOYEE VOICE: IS THE DOOR REALLY OPEN?

what's inside?

The Nature of Communication

LEARNING ROADMAP   The Communication Process / Feedback and Communication / Nonverbal Communication

As workplaces become increasingly collaborative, communication is more important than ever. Social tools such as wikis and blogs are putting more communication power in the hands of employees and customers. New technologies, trends toward global real-time work, and a socially connected generation are dramatically reshaping the way work gets done. Do companies worry that this will lead to confusion and loss of control? Not at Google, IBM, and Xerox, where collaboration is becoming the new organizing principle for the workplace.

Communication is the glue that holds collaboration and organizations together. It is the way we share information, ideas, goals, directions, expectations, feelings, and emotions in the context of coordinated action. As we will see, successful organizations value and promote effective communication both at the interpersonal level and across organizational boundaries.

The Communication Process

> • **Communication** is the process of sending and receiving symbols with attached meanings.
>
> • **Noise** is anything that interferes with the effectiveness of communication.

Communication is a process of sending and receiving messages with attached meanings. The key elements in the communication process are illustrated in Figure 11.1. They include a source, which encodes an intended meaning into a message, and a receiver, which decodes the message into a perceived meaning. The receiver may or may not give feedback to the source. Although this process may appear to be elementary, it is not quite as simple as it looks. **Noise** is the term used to describe any disturbance that disrupts communication effectiveness and interferes with the transference of messages within the communication process. For example, if your stomach is growling because your class is right before lunch, or if you are worried about an exam later in the day, these can interfere with your

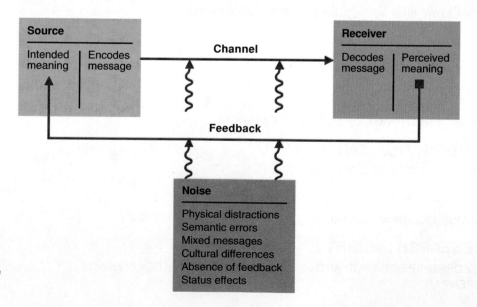

Figure 11.1 The communication process and possible sources of "noise."

ability to pay attention to what your professor and classmates are saying. In effect, they are *noise* in the communication process.

The information source, or **sender**, is a person or group trying to communicate with someone else. The source seeks to communicate, in part, to change the attitudes, knowledge, or behavior of the receiver. A team leader, for example, may want to communicate with a division manager in order to explain why the team needs more time or resources to finish an assigned project. This involves **encoding**—the process of translating an idea or thought into a message consisting of verbal, written, or nonverbal symbols (such as gestures), or some combination of them. Messages are transmitted through various **communication channels**, such as face-to-face meetings, e-mail and online discussions, written letters or memoranda, and telephone communications or voice mail, among others. The choice of channel can have an important impact on the communication process. Some people are better at using certain channels over others, and specific channels are better able to handle some types of messages. In the case of the team leader communicating with the division manager, for example, it can make quite a difference whether the message is sent face to face, in a written memo, by voice mail, or by e-mail.

The communication process is not completed even though a message is sent. The **receiver** is the individual or group of individuals to whom a message is directed. In order for meaning to be assigned to any received message, its contents must be interpreted through decoding. This process of translation is complicated by many factors, including the knowledge and experience of the receiver and his or her relationship with the sender. A message may also be interpreted with the added influence of other points of view, such as those offered by friends, co-workers, or organizational superiors. Ultimately, the decoding may result in the receiver interpreting a message in a way that is different from that originally intended by the source.

Feedback and Communication

Most receivers are well aware of the potential gap between the intended message of the source and the perceived meaning assigned to it by the recipient. As discussed in Chapter 4 on perception, learning, and attribution, this often occurs because individuals misinterpret the message by attributing motives or meanings the sender did not intend. When there are gaps in messages (and even when there aren't), receivers will often "fill in the blanks," resulting in a large potential for miscommunication in the workplace.

One way these gaps are identified and corrected is **feedback**, the process through which the receiver communicates with the sender by returning another message. Feedback represents two-way communication, going from sender to receiver and back again. Compared to one-way communication, which flows from sender to receiver only, two-way communication is more accurate and effective, although it may also be more costly and time consuming. Because of their efficiency, one-way forms of communication—memos, letters, e-mail, reports, and the like—are frequently used in work settings. One-way messages are easy for the sender but often frustrating for the receiver, who may be left unsure of just what the sender means or wants done.

In most workplaces, there is too little feedback rather than too much. This is particularly true when the feedback is negative in nature because people are

- The **sender** is a person or group trying to communicate with someone else.

- **Encoding** is the process of translating an idea or thought into a message consisting of verbal, written, or nonverbal symbols (such as gestures), or some combination of them.

- **Communication channels** are the pathways through which messages are communicated.

- The **receiver** is the individual or group of individuals to whom a message is directed.

- **Feedback** communicates how one feels about something another person has done or said.

afraid of how the feedback will be received or of raising emotions they are not prepared to handle. Words that are intended to be polite and helpful can easily end up being perceived as unpleasant and even hostile. This risk is particularly evident in the performance appraisal process. A manager or team leader must be able to do more than just complete a written appraisal to document another person's performance for the record. To serve the person's developmental needs, feedback regarding the results of the appraisal—both the praise and the criticism—must be well communicated. There is an art to giving feedback so that the receiver accepts it and uses it constructively.

Nonverbal Communication

* **Nonverbal communication** occurs through facial expressions, body motions, eye contact, and other physical gestures.

* **Presence** is the act of speaking without using words.

We all know that people communicate in ways other than the spoken or written word. Indeed, the **nonverbal communication** that takes place through facial expressions, body position, eye contact, and other physical gestures is important both to understand and to master. People who are effective communicators recognize the importance of **presence**, or the act of speaking without using words. Moreover, research on *kinesics*, the study of gestures and body postures, has shown the powerful influence that nonverbals have on how people communicate with one another.[1]

For example, the nonverbal side of communication can often hold the key to what someone is really thinking or meaning. When verbal and nonverbal do not match, research has shown that receivers will pay more attention to the nonverbal. Nonverbal can also affect the impressions we make on others. Interviewers, for example, tend to respond more favorably to job candidates whose nonverbal cues are positive, such as eye contact and erect posture, than to those displaying negative nonverbal cues, such as looking down or slouching. The art of impression management during interviews and in other situations requires careful attention to both verbal and nonverbal aspects of communication, including one's dress, timeliness, and demeanor.

Nonverbal communication can also take place through the physical arrangement of space or workspace designs, such as that found in various office layouts. *Proxemics*, the study of the way space is used, is important to communication.[2] Figure 11.2 shows three different office arrangements and the messages they may

"I am the boss!"

"I am the boss, but let's talk."

"Forget I'm the boss, let's talk."

Figure 11.2 Furniture placement and nonverbal communication in the office.

communicate to visitors. Check the diagrams against the furniture arrangement in your office or that of your instructor or a person with whom you are familiar. What are you or they saying to visitors by the choice of furniture placement?[3]

Interpersonal Communication

LEARNING ROADMAP   Communication Barriers / Active Listening / Cross-Cultural Communication

Our organizations are information rich and increasingly high tech. But even with the support provided by continuing developments in information technology, it is important to remember that people still drive organizational systems and performance. People who are willing and able to collaborate and commit their mutual talents and energies to the tasks at hand are the foundations of any high-performance organization. And to create this foundation, people must excel in interpersonal communication and not succumb to the barriers that can detract from it.

Communication Barriers

In interpersonal communication, it is important to understand the barriers that can easily create communication problems. The most common barriers in the workplace include interpersonal issues, physical distractions, and meaning, or *semantic*, barriers.

Interpersonal barriers are reflected in a quote from Ralph Waldo Emerson: "I can't hear what you say because who you are speaks so loudly."[4] Interpersonal barriers occur when individuals are not able to objectively listen to the sender due to things such as lack of trust, personality clashes, a bad reputation, or stereotypes/prejudices. In such cases, receivers and senders may distort communication by evaluating and judging a message or failing to communicate it effectively. Think of someone you don't like or a co-worker or a classmate who rubs you the wrong way. Now think about how you communicate with that person. Do you listen effectively, or do you turn him or her off? Do you share information, or do you keep your interactions short and curt, or potentially even evasive?

Such problems are indicative of selective listening and filtering. In **selective listening**, individuals block out information or only hear things that match preconceived notions. Someone who does not trust will assume the other is not telling the truth, or may "hear" things in the communication that are not accurate. An employee who believes a co-worker is incompetent may disregard important information if it comes from that person. Individuals may also **filter**, or convey only parts of the information (e.g., not tell the "whole" truth). If we don't like a co-worker, we may decide to leave out critical details or pointers that would help him or her be more successful in getting things done.

Interpersonal barriers may also occur due to ego problems or poor communication skills. Individuals with ego problems may twist what someone says to serve their own purpose, or may overly emphasize their own contributions while failing to acknowledge those of others. Poor communication skills involve failing to effectively listen, rambling on in meetings rather than presenting a concise and coherent message, or being unable to frame messages appropriate to the audience.

* **Interpersonal barriers** occur when individuals are not able to objectively listen to the sender due to things such as lack of trust, personality clashes, a bad reputation, or stereotypes/ prejudices.

* In **selective listening**, individuals block out information or only hear things that match preconceived notions.
* Senders **filter** information by conveying only certain parts that are relevant.

• Physical distractions include interruptions from noises, visitors, and the like, that interfere with communication.

Physical distractions are another barrier that can interfere with the effectiveness of a communication attempt. Some of these distractions are evident in the following conversation between an employee, George, and his manager.[5]

> Okay, George, let's hear your problem (phone rings, boss picks it up, promises to deliver the report "just as soon as I can get it done"). Uh, now, where were we—oh, you're having a problem with marketing. So, (the manager's secretary brings in some papers that need immediate signatures; he scribbles his name and the secretary leaves) . . . you say they're not cooperative? I tell you what, George why don't you (phone rings again, lunch partner drops by) . . . uh, take a stab at handling it yourself. I've got to go now.

Besides what may have been poor intentions in the first place, George's manager allowed physical distractions to create information overload. As a result, the communication with George suffered. Setting priorities and planning can eliminate this mistake. If George has something to say, his manager should set aside adequate time for the meeting. In addition, interruptions such as telephone calls, drop-in visitors, and the like should be prevented. At a minimum, George's manager could start by closing the door to the office and instructing his secretary to not disturb them.

• Semantic barriers involve a poor choice or use of words and mixed messages.

Semantic barriers involve a poor choice or use of words and mixed messages. When in doubt regarding the clarity of your written or spoken messages, the popular KISS principle of communication is always worth remembering: "Keep it short and simple." Of course, that is often easier said than done. The following illustrations of the "bafflegab" that once tried to pass as actual "executive communication" are a case in point.[6]

> A. "We solicit any recommendations that you wish to make, and you may be assured that any such recommendations will be given our careful consideration."
> B. "Consumer elements are continuing to stress the fundamental necessity of a stabilization of the price structure at a lower level than exists at the present time."

One has to wonder why these messages weren't stated more understandably: (A) "Send us your recommendations; they will be carefully considered." (B) "Consumers want lower prices."

Active Listening

"We have two ears and one mouth so we should listen twice as much as we speak."[7] This quote, a variation on that of the Greek philosopher Epictetus, indicates another common interpersonal communication pitfall: the failure to effectively listen. The ability to listen well is a distinct asset to anyone whose job success depends on communicating with other people. After all, there are always two sides to the communication process: (1) sending a message, or "telling," and (2) receiving a message, or "listening." And as the quote indicates, the emphasis should be more on the listening and less on the telling.[8]

• Active listening encourages people to say what they really mean.

Everyone in the new workplace should develop good skills in **active listening**—the ability to help the source of a message say what he or she really means. The

Finding the Leader in You

IDEO SELECTS FOR COLLABORATIVE LEADERS

IDEO has built a business based on *design thinking*—an approach that brings diverse people into heated dialogue in the hopes of generating breakthrough ideas and creative solutions. Design thinking requires a certain kind of leader, so IDEO is careful in its selection process. They seek out individuals who are smart and willing to engage in collaborative work: "We see ourselves as a mosaic of individuals, where the big picture is beautiful but each individual is different."

"We ask ourselves . . . what will this person be like at dinner, or during a brainstorm, or during a

conflict? We are eclectic, diverse and there is always room for another angle." Brainstorming is a fundamental element of design thinking, and failure is an accepted part of the culture. To succeed at IDEO, you have to be able to function with "confusion, incomplete information, paradox, irony, and fun for its own sake."

Once ideas are developed, the key becomes telling the story. Approaches such as videos, skits, immersive environments, narratives, animations, and even comic strips are used to help ideas get embraced, adopted, and elaborated faster and more efficiently. To accomplish this, IDEO promotes a "democracy of ideas." It discourages formal titles, does not have a dress code, and encourages employees to move around, especially during mental blocks. "It's

suspicious when employees are at their desk all day," according to general manager Tom Kelley, "because it makes you wonder how they pretend to work."

Stimulating interactions are encouraged by making bikes available to go from building to building and by designing lobbies to foster movement between buildings. Designers are encouraged to talk to one another in whatever forum possible, and experts commingle in offices that look like "cacophonous kindergarten classrooms." As described by Tom Peters, "Walk into the offices of IDEO design in Palo Alto, California, immediately you'll be caught up in the energy, buzz, creative disarray and sheer lunacy of it all." Lunacy or not, for IDEO, creative interaction and collaborative communication are keys to success.

What's the Lesson Here?

Would you succeed as a leader at IDEO? How would you deal with the confusion and ambiguity of the creative environment? How comfortable are you with failure?

concept comes from the work of counselors and therapists who are trained to help people express themselves and talk about things that are important to them.[9] Here are some guidelines for active listening:

1. *Listen for content*—try to hear exactly what is being said.
2. *Listen for feelings*—try to identify how the source feels about things.
3. *Respond to feelings*—let the source know feelings are recognized.
4. *Note all cues*—be sensitive to both verbal and nonverbal expressions.
5. *Reflect back*—repeat in your own words what you think you are hearing.

Take a moment to review the guidelines for active listening and then read the following conversations. How would you feel as the group leader in each case?[10]

Conversation 1

- *Group leader:* Hey, Sal, I don't get this work order. We can't handle this today. What do they think we are?
- *Branch manager:* But that's the order. So get it out as soon as you can. We're under terrific pressure this week.
- *Group leader:* Don't they know we're behind schedule already because of that software problem?
- *Branch manager:* Look, I don't decide what goes on upstairs. I just have to see that the work gets out, and that's what I'm going to do.
- *Group leader:* The team won't like this.
- *Branch manager:* That's something you'll have to work out with them, not me.

Conversation 2

- *Group leader:* Hey, Kelley, I don't get this work order. We can't handle this today. What do they think we are?
- *Branch manager:* Sounds like you're pretty upset about it.
- *Group leader:* I sure am. We're just about getting back to schedule while fighting that software breakdown. Now this comes along.
- *Branch manager:* As if you didn't have enough work to do?
- *Group leader:* Right, I don't know how to tell the team about this. They're under a real strain today. Seems like everything we do around here is rush, rush, rush.
- *Branch manager:* I guess you feel like it's unfair to load anything more on them.
- *Group leader:* Well, yes. But I know there must be plenty of pressure on everybody up the line. If that's the way it is, I'll get the word to them.
- *Branch manager:* Thanks. If you'll give it a try, I'll do my best to keep to the schedule in the future.

The second example shows active listening skills on the part of the branch manager. She responded to the group leader's communication in a way that increased the flow of information. The manager learned more about the situation, while the group leader most likely felt better after having been able to really say what she thought—after being heard. Compare these outcomes with those in the first example where the manager lacked active listening skills.

Cross-Cultural Communication

We all know that globalization is here to stay. What we might not realize is that the success of international business often rests with the quality of cross-cultural communication. And all is not well. A recent study of large firms by Accenture reports that 92 percent find that the biggest challenge in working with outsourcing providers is communication.[11] People must always exercise caution when they are involved in cross-cultural communication—whether between persons of different geographic or ethnic groupings within one country, or between persons of different national cultures.

A common problem in cross-cultural communication is **ethnocentrism,** the tendency to believe one's culture and its values are superior to those of others. It

- **Ethnocentrism** is the tendency to believe one's culture and its values are superior to those of others.

CROSS-CULTURAL COMMUNICATION AND *THE AMAZING RACE*

You hear it often enough: To be successful in today's business world you must be culturally aware. This is particularly true when it comes to communication. Being proficient in other languages is an important skill. The ability to recognize the nuances of communication in other cultures, such as body language and the use of space, is even more important. **Ethnocentrism**, the belief that the ways of our own culture are superior, must be avoided in order to communicate effectively.

In Season 6 of *The Amazing Race,* contestants travel to Dakar, Senegal, to find the final resting place of a nationally famous poet. The stress of competition combined with the difficulties of a new culture cause problems for some of the teams. Gus and Hera are clearly uncomfortable with the conditions they face. Adam and Rebecca, limited in terms of language skills, nevertheless make fun of their taxi driver's inability to communicate with them. Freddy and Kendra get into an argument with a driver over the cab fare. Kris and Jon are excited by the prospects of experiencing a new culture. At the same time, Kris is appalled by how other competitors in the race are handling the situation.

When Jonathan screams for someone to speak to him in English, he is clearly exhibiting the "ugly American behavior" that Kris abhors. It is one thing to be uncomfortable with new surroundings, but to be abusive when individuals from other cultures do not respond the way you want shows disrespect for the host country.

> ***Get to Know Yourself Better*** *Assessment 4, Global Readiness Index, in the* OB Skills Workbook *measures your global readiness. The increasingly global nature of business demands workers that understand other cultures and are comfortable interacting with individuals whose values and practices may be quite different. If you were suddenly dropped into an unfamiliar country, how would you respond?*

is often accompanied by an unwillingness to try to understand alternative points of view and to take the values they represent seriously. Another problem in cross-cultural communication arises from **parochialism**—assuming that the ways of your culture are the only ways of doing things. It is parochial for traveling American businesspeople to insist that all of their business contacts speak English, whereas it is ethnocentric for them to think that anyone who dines with a spoon rather than a knife and fork lacks proper table manners.

* **Parochialism** assumes the ways of your culture are the only ways of doing things.

The difficulties with cross-cultural communication are perhaps most obvious in respect to language differences. Advertising messages, for example, may work well in one country but encounter difficulty when translated into the language of another. Problems accompanied the introduction of Ford's European model, the "Ka," into Japan. (In Japanese, *ka* means "mosquito.") Gestures may also be used quite differently in the various cultures of the world. For example, crossed legs are quite acceptable in the United Kingdom but are rude in Saudi Arabia if the sole of the foot is directed toward someone. Pointing at someone to get his or her attention may be acceptable in Canada, but in Asia it is considered inappropriate and even offensive.[12]

The role of language in cross-cultural communication has additional and sometimes even more subtle sides. The anthropologist Edward T. Hall notes important differences in the ways different cultures use language, and he suggests that these differences often cause misunderstanding.[13] Members of **low-context cultures** are

* In **low-context cultures**, messages are expressed mainly by the spoken and written word.

ETHICS IN OB

PRIVACY IN THE AGE OF SOCIAL NETWORKING

Is there a clear line between your personal and professional life? In the age of social networking, the answer to this question is becoming less clear. Today many companies are using the Internet to evaluate employees—both current and prospective—and if you fail to maintain a "professional" demeanor, you could find yourself at a loss. There are stories of college athletes who are disciplined because of something they posted on their Web site, employees who are fired for things they say online about the company or their co-workers, or individuals who aren't hired because of a photo on their Facebook page.

To make matters more complicated, employment law in many states is still quite unclear, and in most cases, provides little protection to workers who are punished for their online postings. Take the case of Stacy Snyder, 25, a senior at Millersville University in Millersville, Pennsylvania, who was dismissed from the student teaching program at a high school and denied her teaching credential after the school staff came across a photograph on her MySpace profile showing a pirate's hat perched atop her head while she was sipping from a large plastic cup whose contents cannot be seen. The caption on the photo: "drunken pirate."

Ms. Snyder filed a lawsuit in federal court in Philadelphia contending that her rights to free expression under the First Amendment had been violated. Millersville University, in a motion asking the court to dismiss the case, countered that Ms. Snyder's student teaching had been unsatisfactory—although they acknowledged that she was dismissed based on her MySpace photograph. The university backed the school authorities' contentions that her posting was "unprofessional" and might "promote under-age drinking." It also cited a passage in the teacher's handbook that said staff members are "to be well-groomed and appropriately dressed."

> **Do the Research**   The case of Stacy Snyder and others raises interesting questions. Should what an employee does after hours, as long as no laws are broken, be any of the organization's business? Does a line need to be drawn that demarcates the boundary between an employee's work and his or her private life?

very explicit in using the spoken and written word. In these cultures, such as those of Australia, Canada, and the United States, the message is largely conveyed by the words someone uses, and not particularly by the "context" in which they are spoken. In contrast, members of **high-context cultures** use words to convey only a limited part of the message. The rest must be inferred or interpreted from the context, which includes body language, the physical setting, and past relationships—all of which add meaning to what is being said. Many Asian and Middle Eastern cultures are considered high context, according to Hall, whereas most Western cultures are low context.

> • In **high-context cultures**, words convey only part of a message, while the rest of the message must be inferred from body language and additional contextual cues.

International business experts advise that one of the best ways to gain understanding of cultural differences is to learn at least some of the language of the country that one is dealing with. Says one global manager: "Speaking and understanding the local language gives you more insight; you can avoid misunderstandings." A former American member of the board of a German multinational says:

"Language proficiency gives a [non-German] board member a better grasp of what is going on . . . not just the facts and figures but also texture and nuance."[14] Although the prospect of learning another language may sound daunting, there is little doubt that it can be well worth the effort.[15]

Organizational Communication

LEARNING ROADMAP Communication Channels / Communication Flows / Status Effects

One of the greatest changes in organizations and in everyday life in recent years has been the explosion in new communication technologies. We have moved from the world of the telephone, e-mail, photocopying, and face-to-face meetings into one of Skype, texting, twittering, blogs, wikis, video conferencing, net meetings, and more. These changes are creating more collaborative environments and are challenging traditional notions of hierarchy and structure in organizations.

Communication Channels

Organizations are designed based on bureaucratic organizing principles; that is, jobs are arranged in hierarchical fashion with specified job descriptions and formal reporting relationships. However, much information in organizations is also passed along more fluidly, through informal communication networks. These illustrate two types of information flows in organizations: formal and informal communication channels.

Formal channels follow the chain of command established by an organization's hierarchy of authority. For example, an organization chart indicates the proper routing for official messages passing from one level or part of the hierarchy to another. Because formal channels are recognized as authoritative, it is typical for communication of policies, procedures, and other official announcements to adhere to them. On the other hand, much "networking" takes place through the use of **informal channels** that do not adhere to the organization's hierarchy of authority.[16] They coexist with the formal channels but frequently diverge from them by skipping levels in the hierarchy or cutting across divisional lines. Informal channels help to create open communications in organizations and ensure that the right people are in contact with one another.[17]

A common informal communication channel is the **grapevine**, or network of friendships and acquaintances through which rumors and other unofficial information are passed from person to person. Grapevines have the advantage of being able to transmit information quickly and efficiently. They also help fulfill

- **Formal channels** follow the official chain of command.

- **Informal channels** do not follow the chain of command.

- A **grapevine** transfers information through networks of friendships and acquaintances.

Collaboration Rules the Wiki Workplace

At Google, collaborative interaction means a different kind of control over the way in which decisions are made. CEO Eric Schmidt says, "You talk about the strategy, you get people excited, you tell people what the company's priorities are, and somehow it works out."

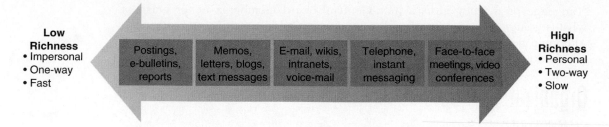

Figure 11.3 Richness of communication channels.

the needs of people involved in them. Being part of a grapevine can provide a sense of security that comes from "being in the know" when important things are going on. It also provides social satisfaction as information is exchanged interpersonally. The primary disadvantage of grapevines arises when they transmit incorrect or untimely information. Rumors can be very dysfunctional, both to people and to organizations. One of the best ways to avoid rumors is to make sure that key persons in a grapevine get the right information to begin with.

Today, the traditional communication grapevine in organizations is often technology assisted. The most common form is probably the e-mail message, but as text messaging and social networking technologies continue to evolve, so, too, do informal communication channels. In more and more organizations people are communicating officially and unofficially by blogs and wikis. As evidence of the power of technology in this regard, the U.S. military set strict regulations on blogs after becoming concerned about the messages from a proliferation of bloggers stationed in Iraq. On the other hand, reports indicate that, by 2009, wikis were used by at least 50 percent of organizations worldwide as a communications improvement tool.[18]

Channel richness indicates the capacity of a channel to convey information. And as indicated in Figure 11.3, the richest channels are face to face. Next are telephone, video conferences, and instant messaging, followed by e-mail, written memos, and letters. The leanest channels are posted notices and bulletins. When messages get more complex and open ended, richer channels are necessary to achieve effective communication. Leaner channels work well for more routine and straightforward messages, such as announcing the location of a previously scheduled meeting.

- **Channel richness** indicates the capacity of a channel to convey information.

Communication Flows

Within organizations, information flows through both the formal and informal channels just described as well as downward, upward, and laterally. **Downward communication** follows the chain of command from top to bottom. One of its major functions is to achieve influence through information. Lower-level personnel need to know what those in higher levels are doing and to be regularly reminded of key policies, strategies, objectives, and technical developments. Of special importance are feedback and information on performance results. Sharing such information helps minimize the spread of rumors and inaccuracies regarding higher-level intentions. It also helps create a sense of security and involvement among receivers who believe they know the whole story. Unfortunately, a lack of adequate downward communication is often cited as a management failure. On

- **Downward communication** follows the chain of command from top to bottom.

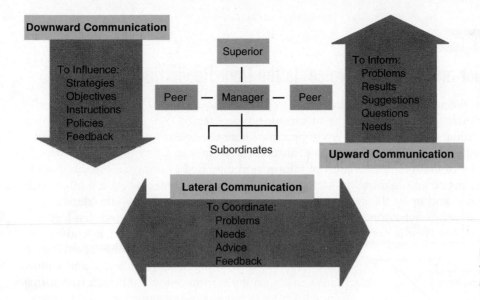

Figure 11.4 Directions for information flows in and around organizations.

the issue of corporate downsizing, for example, one sample showed that 64 percent of employees did not believe what management said, 61 percent felt uninformed about company plans, and 54 percent complained that decisions were not well explained.

The flow of messages from lower to higher organizational levels is **upward communication**. As shown in Figure 11.4, it serves several purposes. Upward communication keeps higher levels informed about what lower-level workers are doing, what their problems are, what suggestions they have for improvements, and how they feel about the organization and their jobs. Upward communication has historically been a problem in organizations due to lower-level employees filtering information that goes up, leaving many higher-level organizational managers in the dark about what is really happening in the organization.

The importance of **lateral communication** for promotion of collaborative environments in the new workplace has been a recurrent theme in this book. Today's customer-sensitive organizations need timely and accurate feedback and product information. To serve customer needs they must get the right information—and get it fast enough—into the hands of workers. Furthermore, inside the organization, people must be willing and able to communicate across departmental or functional boundaries and to listen to one another's needs as "internal customers." At IDEO, lateral communication is the basis for their core competitive advantage, *design thinking*—a collaborative approach that engages people from different disciplines in dynamic dialogue to generate breakthrough ideas and creative solutions.

Collaborative organization designs emphasize lateral communication in the form of cross-departmental committees, teams, or task forces as well as matrix structures. There is also growing attention to organizational ecology—the study of how building design may influence communication and productivity by improving lateral communications. Information technology is allowing organizations to (1) distribute information more instantaneously, (2) make more information available than ever before, (3) allow broader and more immediate access to this information, (4) encourage participation in the sharing and use of information,

• **Upward communication** is the flow of messages from lower to higher organizational levels.

• **Lateral communication** is the flow of messages at the same levels across organizations.

RESEARCH INSIGHT

Leadership Behavior and Employee Voice: Is the Door Really Open?

In today's environment, the willingness of all members to provide thoughts and ideas about critical work processes characterizes successful learning in various types of teams. Yet, despite this "learning imperative," many individuals do not work in environments where they perceive it as safe to speak up. To address these issues, James Detert and Ethan Burris engaged in a study of employee *voice*, which they define as "the discretionary provision of information intended to improve organizational functioning to someone inside an organization with the perceived authority to act, even though such information may challenge and upset the status quo of the organization and its powerholders."

In their study of leadership behaviors and employee voice, Detert and Burris found that leader positivity or personalized behavior is not enough to generate employee voice. Instead, if leaders are

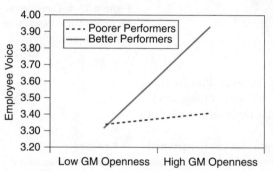

going to overcome employee restraint in speaking up, they need to indicate openness to change and willingness to act on input from below. Although transformational leader behaviors are positively related to voice, openness behaviors clearly send the stronger signal that voice is welcome. Openness behaviors are important because they provide a "safe" environment for employees to voice their opinions. The authors concluded that the signals leaders send are key inputs to employees in assessing the potential costs and benefits of speaking up.

Do the Research   *Do you think the findings are applicable to your work situation? How would you conduct a study in your workplace to find out? What other variables would you include?*

Source: J. Detert and E. Burris, "Leadership Behavior and Employee Voice: Is the Door Really Open?" *Academy of Management Journal* 50.4 (2007), pp. 869–884.

and (5) integrate systems and functions as well as use information to link with other environments in unprecedented ways.

These new forms of communication also have potential downsides. When they are largely impersonal or mostly one-way, such as e-mail, they remove non-verbal communications from the situation and thereby lose aspects that may otherwise add important context to an interaction. Studies show that recipients of e-mail are accurate less than 50 percent of the time in identifying the tone or intent of the message.[19] They may also create difficulties with understanding the emotional aspects of communication. In this respect, little smiley or frowning faces and other symbols often do not carry the message. Another problem is a failure in the electronic medium to control one's emotions, a skill considered essential in interpersonal communications.[20] Some argue, for example, that it is far easier to be blunt, overly critical, and insensitive when conveying messages electronically rather than face to face. The term **flaming** is sometimes used to describe rudeness in electronic communication. In this sense, the use of computer mediation may make people less inhibited and more impatient in what they say.

• **Flaming** is expressing rudeness when using e-mail or other forms of electronic communication.

Another very pressing reality of the new workplace is information overload and 24–7 work environments. Too much information may create stressful situations for individuals who have difficulty sorting the useful from the trivial. Even the IT giant Intel experiences e-mail problems. An employee once commented: "We're so wrapped up in sending e-mail to each other, we don't have time to be dealing with the outside."[21] The growing trend toward **presence-aware tools** that allow for real-time collaboration creates difficulties for employees trying to determine when they get to finish working. As described by Kevin Angley of SAS, there are "a lot of people who find it to be an intrusion and invasion of privacy, because they walk away from their desk for five minutes and their machine declares that they're idle, or they're reading a document on paper at their desk and all of a sudden their computer claims that they're idle." At Procter & Gamble, director of computers and communications services Laurie Heltsley says employees are told it's acceptable for people to turn their presence status to off or unavailable.[22]

- **Presence-aware tools** are software that allow a user to view others' real-time availability status and readiness to communicate.

Status Effects

Another key element of organizational communication associated with hierarchical organizing principles is status differences. **Status differences** create potential communication barriers between persons of higher and lower ranks. On the one hand, given the authority of their positions, managers may be inclined to do a lot of "telling" but not much "listening." As mentioned earlier, we know that communication is frequently biased when flowing upward in organizational hierarchies.[23] Subordinates may filter information and tell their superiors only what they think the bosses want to hear. Whether the reason is a fear of retribution for bringing bad news, an unwillingness to identify personal mistakes, or just a general desire to please, the result is the same: The higher-level decision maker may end up taking the wrong actions because of biased and inaccurate information supplied from below. This is sometimes called the **mum effect**, in reference to tendencies to sometimes keep "mum" from a desire to be polite and a reluctance to transmit bad news.[24]

- **Status differences** are differences between persons of higher and lower ranks.

- The **mum effect** occurs when people are reluctant to communicate bad news.

Collaborative Work Environments

LEARNING ROADMAP Collaboration Technologies / Interactional Transparency / Supportive Communication Principles

As we proceed deeper into the Internet age, collaborative communication is becoming less a choice and more a reality—and it is changing the face of the work environment. Collaborative environments are characterized by boundaryless information flows, more open and transparent communication, and more supportive communication dynamics.

Collaboration Technologies

In hierarchical organizing, information can often become a source of power that employees hold and use for their own advantage. With the rise of social networking tools, such as Facebook, Twitter, and YouTube, and video technologies, such as camera phones and videography, the withholding of information is becoming more and more difficult. Customers now have more information power than ever due to the power of emerging collaboration technologies.

The Changing Face of Information Power

The Internet is changing the nature of information power. In today's era of social networking and collaboration technologies, no longer can information be centralized or controlled. Wikileaks shows the challenges of keeping secrets, and Facebook shows how a youth movement can spawn a revolution in Egypt.

Instead of fighting these trends, organizations are identifying ways to capitalize on emerging technologies. At Xerox, rather than leaving the design of high-level strategy documents to a handful of people at the top of the corporate hierarchy, they set up a wiki that allows researchers in the R&D group to collaboratively generate the company's technology strategy. Chief Technology Officer Dr. Sophie VanDebroek says that with the wiki, "we'll get more content and knowledge in all of our areas of expertise . . . including everything from material science to the latest document services and solutions." At IBM, up to $100 million have been committed to sessions such as the *Innovation Jam*, where employees in more than 160 countries and their clients, business partners—and even family members—engage in online moderated discussions to glean insights that will transform industries, improve human health, and help protect the environment over the course of the coming decades.[25]

The result is a reduction of status differentials and breaking down of corporate silos. At Mars Inc., the "President's Challenge" brings together thought leaders in the company with the most senior people in Mars to explore new enabling strategies for business. As part of this exploration, team members work together to challenge and engage in "fierce debate" of proposed strategies. As a result, Mars has broken down silos and developed leaders throughout the organization. The collaborative communication has resulted in a ferment of innovation, with many new best practices being driven throughout the business.[26]

Interactional Transparency

In the financial world, "transparency" means opening the books. In the context of management, it is increasingly being used to symbolize more open and honest sharing of information. Interest in transparency concepts has been on the rise since passage of the Sarbanes-Oxley Act, which, to guard against corporate fraud, requires public organizations to disclose information concerning financial transactions.

• Interactional transparency is the open and honest sharing of information.

Interactional transparency has been conceptualized in the OB literature as the ability for both leaders and followers to be open, accountable, and honest with each other.[27] It comprises multiple components. First, transparent communication involves sharing relevant information. For example, contrary to information power games of the past, transparent communication means that individuals work together to share all pertinent information and not withhold important information from one another. Second, transparent communication involves being forthcoming regarding motives and the reasoning behind decisions. Such transparency about motives helps avoid the problem of faulty attributions that can often break down communication processes. Third, transparent communication involves proactively seeking and giving feedback. Transparent communication is two-way and collaborative, involving a free and open exchange of information.

Supportive Communication Principles

Achieving transparency requires individuals to communicate openly and honestly. However, we know that is not always the case. Avoidance continues to be a major issue in interpersonal communication. If a problem arises between employees or work groups, many individuals are much more likely to avoid than address it. Why is this?

A major reason is fear the conversation will be uncomfortable or worry that trying to talk about the problem will only make it worse. This fear often comes with a lack of understanding about how to approach difficult conversations. A set of tools known as **supportive communication principles** can help overcome this problem. These principles focus on joint problem solving with the intent of addressing communication breakdowns and changing problematic behaviors before they get to be big problems.[28]

The primary emphasis of supportive communication is to avoid defensiveness and disconfirmation. **Defensiveness** occurs when individuals feel they are being attacked and they need to protect themselves. If you are communicating with someone who begins to get angry and becomes aggressive, that person is likely feeling defensive. **Disconfirmation** occurs when an individual feels his self-worth is being questioned. A person shows a disconfirmed feeling when he or she withdraws from the conversation or starts engaging in show-off behaviors to try to look good. In either case, the communicator needs to stop the conversation and work to reduce the defensiveness and disconfirmation by refocusing the conversation and building the other person up before continuing.

This can be accomplished by using several techniques. First, focus on the problem and not the person. This helps keep the communication problem-oriented and not person-oriented. For example, instead of saying "you are bad," you would say "you are behaving badly." By focusing on behavior you are addressing something the individual can do something about—he can change his *behavior* but he can't change who he is as a person.

Second, be specific and descriptive, not global or evaluative. In the prior example, once you target the behavior, you then have to be specific about which behavior is the problem. Do not focus on too many behaviors at one time. Pick a couple of examples that illustrate the problem behavior and identify them as specifically (and as recently) as you can. Instead of saying "you never listen to me," you can say "the other day in the meeting you interrupted me three times and that made it hard for me to get my point across to the group."

Third, own the communication. As a manager, instead of saying "Corporate tells us we need to better document our work hours," you would say "I believe that better documenting our work hours will help us be more effective in running our business."

Finally, be congruent—make sure your message is consistent with your body language. If your words say "No, I'm not mad," but your body

* **Supportive communication principles** are a set of tools focused on joint problem solving.

* **Defensiveness** occurs when individuals feel they are being attacked and they need to protect themselves.
* **Disconfirmation** occurs when an individual feels his or her self-worth is being questioned.

Supportive Communication Principles

1. Focus on the problem and not the person.
   . . . Not "You are bad!" but rather "You are behaving badly."
2. Be specific and descriptive, not global or evaluative.
   . . . Avoid using never or always, as in "you never listen to me."
3. Own, rather than disown, the communication.
   . . . "I believe we need to change" rather than "Management tells us we have to change."
4. Be congruent—match the words with the body language.
   . . . Don't say "No I'm not angry!" if your body language says you are.

language conveys anger, you are being dishonest in the communication and are only provoking less open and collaborative communication.

By learning to use supportive communication principles, you can enhance your ability to communicate effectively, not only in your workplace, but also in your life.

11 *study guide*

Key Questions and Answers

What is communication?

- Collaborative communication is becoming more important as technology changes the way we work.

- Communication is the process of sending and receiving messages with attached meanings.

- The communication process involves encoding an intended meaning into a message, sending the message through a channel, and receiving and decoding the message into perceived meaning.

- Noise is anything that interferes with the communication process.

- Feedback is a return message from the original recipient back to the sender.

- To be constructive, feedback must be direct, specific, and given at an appropriate time.

- Nonverbal communication involves communication other than through the spoken word (e.g., facial expressions, body position, eye contact, and other physical gestures).

- When verbal and nonverbal do not match, research has shown that receivers will pay more attention to the nonverbal.

What are the issues in interpersonal communication?

- To create collaborative communication, people must not succumb to communication barriers.

- Interpersonal barriers detract from communication because individuals are not able to objectively listen to the sender due to personal biases; they include selective listening and filtering.

- Physical distractions are barriers due to interruptions from noises, visitors, and so on.

- Semantic barriers involve a poor choice or use of words and mixed messages.

- Active listening encourages a free and complete flow of communication from the sender to the receiver; it is nonjudgmental and encouraging.

- Parochialism and ethnocentrism contribute to the difficulties of experiencing truly effective cross-cultural communication.

What is the nature of communication in organizations?

- Organizational communication is the specific process through which information moves and is exchanged within an organization.

- Technologies continue to change the workplace, challenging traditional notions of hierarchy and structure in organizations.

- Communication in organizations uses a variety of formal and informal channels; the richness of the channel, or its capacity to convey information, must be adequate for the message.

- Information flows upward, downward, and laterally in organizations.

- Status effects in organizations may result in restricted and filtered information exchanges between subordinates and their superiors.

How can we build more collaborative work environments?

- With the rise of social networking tools, the restriction of information is becoming more and more difficult.

- Instead of fighting these trends, organizations are identifying ways to capitalize on emerging technologies that are resulting in a reduction of status differentials and breaking down of corporate silos.

- More companies are valuing transparency in communication.

- Transparency is enhanced through the use of supportive communication principles.

Terms to Know

Active listening (p. 246)
Channel richness (p. 252)
Communication (p. 242)
Communication channels (p. 243)
Defensiveness (p. 257)
Disconfirmation (p. 257)
Downward communication (p. 252)
Encoding (p. 243)
Ethnocentrism (p. 248)
Feedback (p. 243)
Filter (p. 245)
Flaming (p. 254)

Formal channels (p. 251)
Grapevine (p. 251)
High-context cultures (p. 250)
Informal channels (p. 251)
Interactional transparency (p. 256)
Interpersonal barriers (p. 245)
Lateral communication (p. 253)
Low-context cultures (p. 249)
Mum effect (p. 255)
Noise (p. 242)
Nonverbal communication (p. 244)
Parochialism (p. 249)

Physical distractions (p. 246)
Presence (p. 244)
Presence-aware tools (p. 255)
Receiver (p. 243)
Selective listening (p. 245)
Semantic barriers (p. 246)
Sender (p. 243)
Status differences (p. 255)
Supportive communication principles (p. 257)
Upward communication (p. 253)

Self-Test 11

Multiple Choice

1. In communication, _____ is anything that interferes with the transference of the message. (a) channel (b) sender (c) receiver (d) noise

2. When you give criticism to someone, the communication will be most effective when the criticism is _____. (a) general and nonspecific (b) given when the sender feels the need (c) tied to things the recipient can do something about (d) given all at once to get everything over with

3. Which communication is the best choice for sending a complex message? (a) face to face (b) written memorandum (c) e-mail (d) telephone call

4. When someone's words convey one meaning but body posture conveys something else, a(n) _____ is occurring. (a) ethnocentric message (b) lack of congruence (c) semantic problem (d) status effect

5. Personal bias is an example of _____ in the communication process. (a) an interpersonal barrier (b) a semantic barrier (c) physical distractions (d) proxemics

6. Which communication method has the most two-way characteristics? (a) e-mail (b) blog (c) voice mail (d) instant messaging

7. _____ is an example of an informal channel through which information flows in an organization. (a) The grapevine (b) Top-down communication (c) The mum effect (d) Transparency

8. New electronic communication technologies have the advantage of handling large amounts of information, but they may also make communication among organizational members _____. (a) less accessible (b) less immediate (c) more informal (d) less private

9. The study of gestures and body postures for their impact on communication is an issue of _____. (a) kinesics (b) proxemics (c) semantics (d) informal channels

10. In _____ communication the sender is likely to be most comfortable, whereas in _____ communication the receiver is likely to feel most informed. (a) one-way; two-way (b) top-down; bottom-up (c) bottom-up; top-down (d) two-way; one-way

11. A manager who spends a lot of time explaining his or her motives and engaging in frank and open dialogue could be described as using _____. (a) the KISS principle (b) transparency (c) MBO (d) the grapevine

12. _____ interfere(s) with open communication in most workplaces. (a) Status effects (b) Technology (c) Organizational ecology (d) Nonverbal communication

13. If someone is interested in proxemics as a means of improving communication with others, that person would likely pay a lot of attention to his or her _____. (a) office layout (b) status (c) active listening skills (d) 360-degree feedback

14. Among the rules for active listening is _____. (a) remain silent and communicate only nonverbally (b) confront emotions (c) don't let feelings become part of the process (d) reflect back what you think you are hearing

15. The use of supportive communication principles is helpful for _____. (a) reducing defensiveness and disconfirmation (b) the use of computer technology (c) privacy and electronic performance monitoring (d) improving the correctness of one's vocabulary

Short Response

16. Why is channel richness a useful concept for managers?

17. What place do informal communication channels have in organizations today?

18. Why is communication between lower and higher levels sometimes filtered?

19. What is the key to using active listening effectively?

Applications Essay

20. "People in this organization don't talk to one another anymore. Everything is e-mail, e-mail, e-mail. If you are mad at someone, you can just say it and then hide behind your computer." With these words, Wesley expressed his frustrations with Delta General's operations. Xiaomei echoed his concerns, responding, "I agree, but surely the managing director should be able to improve organizational communication without losing the advantages of e-mail." As a consultant overhearing this conversation, how do you suggest the managing director respond to Xiaomei's challenge?

Next Steps
Top Choices from
The OB Skills
Workbook

Case for Critical Thinking	Team and Experiential Exercises	Self-Assessment Portfolio
• The Poorly Informed Walrus	• Active Listening • Upward Appraisal • 360° Feedback	• "TT" Leadership Style • Empowering Others

Tweets Heard 'Round the World

The most powerful voice reporting from within Iran about the recent presidential election didn't belong to a single person. Rather, it was a chorus of many voices[a]:

Mohamadreza   mohamadreza **(Tehran, Iran)** It is not officially approved by any of candidates but its spreading: Tuesday national strike in Iran. #iranelection *13 June 2009 from web*

Iran Election 2009   iran09 **(Tehran, Iran)** Massive arrests are the sign of a coup! Help us to a REVOLUTION! #iranelection #newiran *13 Jun 2009 from TwitterFox*

tehranelection **(Tehran, Iran)** On my street, the crowd is pushing the police to the side. *14 Jun 2009 from web*

Yashar Khaz douzion   Yshar **(Tehran, Iran)** The rumors are spreading faster . . . Is it true that people have taken over the police station at Tajrish Sq. ?!?! #iranelection *13 June 2009 from Seesmic Desktop.*

> *"[Twitter] has emboldened the protesters, reinforced their conviction that they are not alone, and engaged populations outside Iran in an emotional, immediate way that was never possible before."*
> *−Lev Grossman, TIME Magazine*[d]

When Iran blocked text messaging and throttled Internet speeds in the days surrounding the hotly contested election, thousands of Iranians took to Twitter because of the service's worldwide visibility and low bandwidth requirements.

The early postelection tweets tended to focus on individual reactions to voting and the election's immediate aftermath. But a growing number of social media users took to tagging their tweets with *#iranelection*, which helped otherwise scattered Iranians fact-check official statements, and coordinate protests. They interconnected to build their power.

Looking back days later at the flow of *#iranelection* tweets, *Atlantic Monthly* blogger Andrew Sullivan reflected, "This is the raw data of history, as it happens."[b] U.S. intelligence services found the *#iranelection* tweets so useful that the State Department asked Twitter to delay a preplanned downtime to avoid a gap in updates.[c]

#iranelection has remained one of Twitter's most active hashtags. Today, concerned citizens and activists worldwide invoke it to call attention to human rights concerns throughout the Middle East.

Quick Summary

- In the hours after its tenth presidential election, Iran shut down text messaging and severely crippled broadband Internet speeds within the country.
- Because of its worldwide visibility and small message size, Iranian social media users turned to Twitter and the hashtag *#iranelection* to share information about the election results and pursuant protests.
- The steady stream of Iranian tweets provided more information to the outside world than CNN.

FYI: On June 16, 2009, a peak of 221,744 tweets mentioning *Iran* were sent in one hour. Around the same time, more than 23,750 tweets were tagged with *#iranelection*.[e]

12 Power and Politics

the key point

While individuals join organizations for their own reasons and goals, all members are interconnected. Power and politics are inevitable. Even though you may not be planning a protest march, you need to understand the key sources of power and how to use them to effectively manage. You also need to understand and use organizational politics to survive and thrive in today's modern organization.

chapter at a glance

What Are Power and Influence?

What Are the Key Sources of Power and Influence?

What Is Empowerment?

What Is Organizational Politics?

ETHICS IN OB
ETHICS OF INCENTIVES

FINDING THE LEADER IN YOU
NELSON MANDELA USES POWER FOR THE GREATER GOOD

OB IN POPULAR CULTURE
POLITICAL BEHAVIOR AND *SPANGLISH*

RESEARCH INSIGHT
FEMALE MEMBERS ON CORPORATE BOARDS OF DIRECTORS

what's inside?

Power and Influence

Without the power to influence, neither organizations nor individuals can accomplish much. Yet, all of us have been warned about the excesses of power. In your organizational life you will need to develop, use, and spread your ability to get things done. You will need to be powerful and exercise influence. In OB the basis for both power and politics is the degree of interconnectedness among individuals.[1] As individuals pursue their own goals within an organization, they must also deal with the interests of other individuals and their desires.[2] There are never enough resources—money, people, time, or authority—to meet everyone's needs. Choices need to be made. The analysis of choices as to who "wins" resources and rewards and how they win lies at the heart of power and politics in organizational life.

The analyses of power and politics have at least two sides. On the one hand, power and politics are important organizational tools that managers must use to get the job done. More organizational members can "win" when managers identify areas where individual and organizational interests are compatible. On the other hand, organizations are not democracies composed of individuals with equal influence. Some people have a lot more clout than others. Managers often see a "power gap" as they constantly face too many competing demands to satisfy. They must choose to favor some interests over others.[3] Yet, the astute manager also recognizes opportunities to expand power and increase accomplishment.

- **Power** is the ability to get someone else to do something you want done or the ability to make things happen or get things done the way you want.

In organizational behavior, **power** is defined as the ability to get someone to do something you want done or the ability to make things happen in the way you want them to. The essence of power is control over the behavior of others.[4] Without a direct or indirect connection it is not possible to alter the behavior of others.

- **Influence** is a behavioral response to the exercise of power.

While power is the force used to make things happen in an intended way, **influence** is what an individual has when he or she exercises power, and it is expressed by others' behavioral response to the exercise of power. In Chapters 13 and 14 we will examine leadership as a key power mechanism to make things happen. This chapter will discuss other ways that power and politics form the context for leadership influence.

Interdependence, Legitimacy, and Power

It is important to remember that the foundation for power rests in interdependence. Each member of an organization's fate is, in part, determined by the actions of all other members. All members of an organization are interdependent. It is apparent that employees are closely connected with the individuals in their workgroup, those in other departments they work with, and, of course, their supervisors. In today's modern organization the pattern of interdependence and, therefore the base for power and politics, rests on a system of authority and control.[5] In addition, organizations have societal backing to seek reasonable goals in legitimate ways.

The unstated foundation of legitimacy in most organizations is an understood and unwritten set of social mores and conventions that serve to maintain societal order. From infancy to retirement, individuals in our society are taught to obey "higher authority." In societies, "higher authority" does not always have a bureaucratic or an organizational reference but consists of those with moral authority such as tribal chiefs and religious leaders. In most organizations, "higher authority" means those close to the top of the corporate pyramid. The legitimacy of those at the top derives from their positions as representatives for various constituencies. The importance of stockholders is, in turn, a foundation for our capitalistic economic system.

Some senior executives evoke ethics and social causes in their role as authority figures because these are important foundations for the power of these institutions. For instance, consider Northwestern Mutual, the largest direct provider of individual life insurance in the United States. Here the customers actually own the firm. It's a mutual company, and none of the stock options go to the executives. Instead, dividend proceeds are given back to the customers. Former CEO Edward J. Zore, as the representative for the customers, has said, "Our mutuality is about fairness. It's about upholding strong principles." These strong principles helped Northwestern Mutual forgo the short-term profits others were posting on mortgage derivatives just before the recent financial crisis hit the insurance industry. Instead of following the crowd and seeking higher short-term gains, Northwestern Mutual charted a safer if somewhat less dramatic course to continued prosperity and growth.

Yet, just talking about the ethical and social foundations for power would not be enough to ensure that individuals comply with their supervisor's orders if they were not prone to obedience.

Obedience

The mythology of American independence and unbridled individualism is so strong we need to spend some time explaining how most of us are really quite obedient. So we turn to the seminal studies of Stanley Milgram on obedience from the early 1960s.[6]

Milgram designed experiments to determine the extent to which people would obey the commands of an authority figure, even if they believed they were endangering the life of another person. Subjects from a wide variety of occupations and ranging in age from 20 to 50 were paid a nominal fee for participation in the project. The subjects were told that the purpose of the study was to determine the effects of punishment on learning. The subjects were to be the "teachers." The "learner," a partner of Milgram's, was strapped to a chair in an adjoining room with an electrode attached to his wrist. The "experimenter," another partner of Milgram's, was dressed in a laboratory coat. Appearing impassive and somewhat stern, the "experimenter" instructed the "teacher" to read a series of word pairs to the learner and then to reread the first word along with four other terms. The learner was supposed to indicate which of the four terms was in the original pair by pressing a switch that caused a light to flash on a response panel in front of the "teacher."

The "teacher" was instructed to administer a shock to the learner each time an incorrect answer was given. This shock was to be increased one level of intensity each time the learner made a mistake. The "teacher" controlled switches that supposedly administered the electric shocks. In reality, there was no electric current in the apparatus. And the "learners" purposely made mistakes often and responded to each shock level in progressively distressing ways. If a "teacher" proved unwilling to administer a shock, the experimenter used the following sequential prods to get him or her to perform as requested. (1) "Please continue"; (2) "The experiment requires that you continue"; (3) "It is absolutely essential that you continue"; and (4) "You have no choice; you must go on." Only when the "teacher" refused to go on after the fourth prod would the experiment be stopped.

So what happened? Some 65 percent of the "teachers" actually administered an almost lethal shock to the "learners." Shocked at the results, Milgram tried a wide variety of variations (e.g., different commands to continue, a bigger gap between the teacher and the experimenter) with similar if less severe shocks. He concluded that there is a tendency for individuals to comply and be obedient—to switch off their emotions and merely do exactly what they are told to do.

The tendency to obey is powerful, and it is a major problem in the corporate boardroom where the lack of dissent due to extreme obedience to authority has been associated with the lack of rationality and questionable ethics.[7]

Acceptance of Authority and the Zone of Indifference

Obedience is not the only reason for compliance in organizations. The author of groundbreaking research in management theory and organizational studies, Chester Barnard, suggested that it also stemmed from the "consent of the governed."[8] From this notion, Barnard developed the concept of the acceptance of authority—the idea that some directives would naturally be followed while others would not. The basis of this acceptance view was the notion of an implicit contract between the individual and the firm, known as a psychological contract. These two ideas led Barnard to outline the notion of the "zone of indifference" where individuals would comply without much thought.

Acceptance of Authority In everyday organizational life Barnard argued that subordinates accepted or followed a managerial directive only if four circumstances were met.

- The subordinate can and must understand the directive.
- The subordinate must feel mentally and physically capable of carrying out the directive.
- The subordinate must believe that the directive is not inconsistent with the purpose of the organization.

- The subordinate must believe that the directive is not inconsistent with his or her personal interests.

Note the way in which the organizational purpose and personal interest requirements are stated. The subordinate does not need to understand how the proposed action will help the organization. He or she only needs to believe that the requested action is not inconsistent with the purpose of the firm. Barnard found the issue of personal interest to be more complicated, and he built his analysis on the notion of a psychological contract between the individual and the firm.

Zone of Indifference Most people seek a balance between what they put into an organization (contributions) and what they get from an organization in return (inducements). Within the boundaries of this **psychological contract**, therefore, employees will agree to do many things in and for the organization because they think they should. In exchange for the inducements, they recognize the authority of the organization and its managers to direct their behavior in certain ways. Outside of the psychological contract's boundaries, however, things become much less clear.

The notion of the psychological contract turns out to be a powerful concept, particularly in the "breach" where an individual feels the contract has been violated. When employees believe the organization has not delivered on its implicit promises, in addition to disobedience, there is less loyalty, higher turnover intentions, and less job satisfaction.[9]

Based on his acceptance view of authority, Chester Barnard calls the area in which authoritative directions are obeyed the **zone of indifference**.[10] It describes the range of requests to which a person is willing to respond without subjecting the directives to critical evaluation or judgment. Directives falling within the zone are obeyed routinely. Requests or orders falling outside the zone of indifference are not considered legitimate under terms of the psychological contract. Such "extraordinary" directives may or may not be obeyed. This link between the zone of indifference and the psychological contract is shown in Figure 12.1.

- The **psychological contract** is an unwritten set of expectations about a person's exchange of inducements and contributions with an organization.

- **Zone of indifference** is the range of authoritative requests to which a subordinate is willing to respond without subjecting the directives to critical evaluation or judgment.

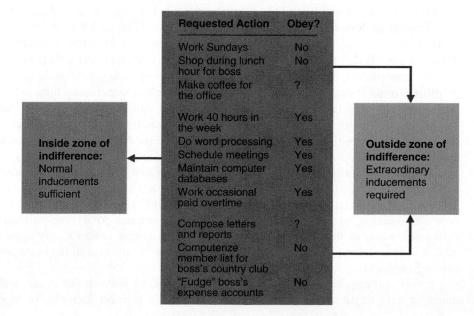

Requested Action	Obey?
Work Sundays	No
Shop during lunch hour for boss	No
Make coffee for the office	?
Work 40 hours in the week	Yes
Do word processing	Yes
Schedule meetings	Yes
Maintain computer databases	Yes
Work occasional paid overtime	Yes
Compose letters and reports	?
Computerize member list for boss's country club	No
"Fudge" boss's expense accounts	No

Inside zone of indifference: Normal inducements sufficient

Outside zone of indifference: Extraordinary inducements required

Figure 12.1 Hypothetical psychological contract for a secretary.

The zone of indifference is not fixed. There may be times when a boss would like a subordinate to do things that fall outside of the zone. In this case, the manager must enlarge the zone to accommodate additional behaviors. We have chosen to highlight a number of ethical issues that are within, or may be beyond, the typical zone of indifference. Research on ethical managerial behavior shows that supervisors can become sources of pressure for subordinates to do such things as support incorrect viewpoints, sign false documents, overlook the supervisor's wrongdoing, and conduct business with the supervisor's friends.[11] Employees might be willing to do some things for one boss but not another. In different terms, the boss has two sources of power: power position derived from his or her position in the firm, and personal power derived from the individual actions of the manager.[12]

Sources of Power and Influence

LEARNING ROADMAP   Position Power / Personal Power / Power and Influence Capacity / Relational Influence Techniques

Within each organization a manager's power is determined by his or her position and personal power, his or her individual actions, and the ability to build on combinations of these sources.

Position Power

One important source of power available to a manager stems solely from his or her position in the organization. Specifically, position power stems from the formal hierarchy or authority vested in a particular role. There are six important aspects of position power: legitimate, reward, coercive, process, information, and representative power.[13]

- **Legitimate power** or formal authority is the extent to which a manager can use the "right of command" to control other people.

Based on our discussion of obedience and the acceptance theory of authority it is easy to understand **legitimate power**, or formal hierarchical authority. It stems from the extent to which a manager can use subordinates' internalized values or beliefs that the "boss" has a "right of command" to control their behavior. For example, the boss may have the formal authority to approve or deny such employee requests as job transfers, equipment purchases, personal time off, or overtime work. Legitimate power represents the unique power a manager has because subordinates believe it is legitimate for a person occupying the managerial position to have the right to command. If this legitimacy is lost, authority will not be accepted by subordinates.

- **Reward power** is the extent to which a manager can use extrinsic and intrinsic rewards to control other people.

Reward power is the extent to which a manager can use extrinsic and intrinsic rewards to control other people. Examples of such rewards include money, promotions, compliments, or enriched jobs. Although all managers have some access to rewards, success in accessing and utilizing rewards to achieve influence varies according to the skills of the manager. While giving rewards may appear ethical, it is not always the case. The use of incentives by unscrupulous managers can be unethical.

Power can also be based on punishment instead of reward. For example, a manager may threaten to withhold a pay raise or to transfer, demote, or even

ETHICS IN OB

ETHICS OF INCENTIVES

Incentives are a major way of influencing employees. Key ethical issues in the development of incentive systems often center on voluntarism, legitimacy, and character. Voluntarism is the degree of choice the individual has over the ramifications of his or her behavior. Or in simple terms, do you choose to go after the incentive offered? For instance, telemarketers are often required to read a script that includes less than honest statements. If they read the script, they are given a bonus. If they depart from the script no bonus is given, thereby encouraging the employee to act in a way that may be considered unethical.

In addition to voluntarism, incentives are considered ethical only when their purpose is legitimate and when they do not affect the character of the individual being offered the incentive. For example, a CEO's bonus may depend on a short-term increase in the firm's stock price. Here, the incentive may be considered illegitimate if it is the only one because the firm has many goals, not just one. The larger potential bonus from the short-term stock price increase, the greater chances the CEO will manipulate it. For instance, if the potential bonus may be in the tens of millions of dollars, the CEO may be tempted to trade short-term gains (e.g., reductions in R&D) for longer-term benefits. Here, the incentive may be considered unethical because it challenges the character of the CEO.

What Would You Do?   *What would you do if you were a telemarketer given a script to read that included statements you knew weren't true? What if your boss offered you a bonus for each script you read and each sale you made based on the information in the script? Would you be tempted to read the script and close the sale in order to earn the bonus?*

---

recommend the firing of a subordinate who does not act as desired. Such **coercive power** is the extent to which a manager can deny desired rewards or administer punishments to control other people. The availability of coercive power also varies from one organization and manager to another. The presence of unions and organizational policies on employee treatment can weaken this power base considerably.

Process power is the control over methods of production and analysis. The source of this power is the placing of the individual in a position to influence how inputs are transformed into outputs for the firm, a department in the firm, or even a small group. Firms often establish process specialists who work with managers to ensure that production is accomplished efficiently and effectively. Closely related to this is control of the analytical processes used to make choices. For example, many organizations have individuals with specialties in financial analysis. They may review proposals from other parts of the firm for investments. Their power derives not from the calculation itself, but from the assignment to determine the analytical procedures used to judge the proposals.

Process power may be separated from legitimate hierarchical power simply because of the complexity of the firm's operations. A manager may have the

- **Coercive power** is the extent to which a manager can deny desired rewards or administer punishment to control other people.

- **Process power** is the control over methods of production and analysis.

formal hierarchical authority to make a decision but may be required to use the analytical schemes of others or to consult on effective implementation with process specialists. The issue of position power can get quite complex very quickly in sophisticated operations. This leads us to another related aspect of position power—the role of access to and control of information.

- **Information power** is the access to and/or the control of information.

Information power is the access information or the control of it. It is one of the most important aspects of legitimacy. The "right to know" and use information can be, and often is, conferred on a position holder. Thus, information power may complement legitimate hierarchical power. Information power may also be granted to specialists and managers who are in the middle of the information systems in the firm.

For example, the chief information officer of the firm may not only control all the computers, but may also have access to any and all information desired. Managers jealously guard the formal "right to know," because it means they are in a position to influence events, not merely react to them. Most chief executive officers believe they have the right to know about everything in "their" firm. Deeper in the organization, managers often protect information from others based on the notion that outsiders would not understand it. Engineering drawings, for example, are not typically allowed outside of the engineering department. In other instances, information is to be protected from outsiders. Marketing and advertising plans may be labeled "top secret." In most cases the nominal reason for controlling information is to protect the firm. The real reason is often to allow information holders the opportunity to increase their power.

- **Representative power** is the formal right conferred by the firm to speak for and to a potentially important group.

Representative power is the formal right conferred to an individual by the firm enabling him or her to speak as a representative for a group comprised of individuals from across departments or outside the firm. In most complex organizations there is a wide variety of constituencies that may have an important impact on the firm's operations and its success. They include such groups as investors, customers, alliance partners, and, of course, unions. In government, it is not at all unusual to find positions established to represent officials. The top job of this type is, of course, Presidential Press Secretary.

Personal Power

Personal power resides in the individual and is independent of that individual's position within an organization. Personal power is important in many well-managed firms, as managers need to supplement the power of their formal

Presidential Press Secretary

When President Barack Obama recently chose Jay Carney, the former communications chief to Vice President Joe Biden and magazine journalist, to be the next White House press secretary, he gave him more than a job—he gave him power. Carney is . . . "the face of the administration" to the press. His position of power is based on representing the President and his administration.

positions. Four bases of personal power are expertise, rational persuasion, reference, and coalitions.[14]

Expert power is the ability to control another person's behavior through the possession of knowledge, experience, or judgment that the other person does not have but needs. A subordinate follows a supervisor possessing expert power because the latter usually knows more about what is to be done or how it is to be done than does the subordinate. Expert power is relative, not absolute. So if you are the best cook in the kitchen, you have expert power until a real chef enters. Then the chef has the expert power.

Rational persuasion is the ability to control another's behavior because, through the individual's efforts, the person accepts the desirability of an offered goal and a reasonable way of achieving it. Much of what a supervisor does on a day-to-day basis involves rational persuasion up, down, and across the organization. Rational persuasion involves both explaining the desirability of expected outcomes and showing how specific actions will achieve these outcomes. Relational persuasion relies on trust.

Referent power is the ability to alter another's behavior because the person wants to identify with the power source. In this case, a subordinate obeys the manager because he or she wants to behave, perceive, or believe as the manager does. This obedience may occur, for example, because the subordinate likes the boss personally and therefore tries to do things the way the boss wants them done. In a sense, the subordinate attempts to avoid doing anything that would interfere with the boss–subordinate relationship.

A person's referent power can be enhanced when the individual taps into the morals held by another or shows a clearer long-term path to a morally desirable end. Individuals with the ability to tap into these more esoteric aspects of corporate life have "charisma" and "vision." Followership is not based on what the subordinate will get for specific actions or specific levels of performance, but on what the individual represents—a role model and a path to a morally desired future. For example, an employee can increase his or her referent power by showing subordinates how they can develop better relations with each other and how they can serve the greater good.

Coalition power is the ability to control another's behavior indirectly because the individual has an obligation to someone as part of a larger collective interest. Coalitions are often built around issues of common interest.[15] To build a coalition, individuals negotiate trade-offs in order to arrive at a common position. Individuals may also trade across issues in granting support for one another. These trade-offs and trades represent informational obligations of support. To maintain the coalition, individuals may be asked to support a position on an issue and act in accordance with the desires of the supervisor. When they do, there is a reciprocal obligation to support them on their issues. For example, members of a department should support a budget increase.

These reciprocal obligations can extend to a network of individuals as well. A network of mutual support provides a powerful collective front to protect members and to accomplish shared interests. Think about all of the required courses you must take to graduate; the list was probably developed by a coalition of professors led by their department chairs. Faculty members who support a required course from another department expect help from the supported department in getting their course on the list.

• **Expert power** is the ability to control another's behavior because of the possession of knowledge, experience, or judgment that the other person does not have but needs.

• **Rational persuasion** is the ability to control another's behavior because, through the individual's efforts, the person accepts the desirability of an offered goal and a reasonable way of achieving it.

• **Referent power** is the ability to control another's behavior because of the individual's desire to identify with the power source.

• **Coalition power** is the ability to control another's behavior indirectly because the individual owes an obligation to you or another as part of a larger collective interest.

Finding the Leader in You

NELSON MANDELA USES POWER FOR THE GREATER GOOD

It is a great film and lesson all in one. On the surface, it is a film about a rugby team in South Africa just after the transition to black rule; on a deeper level, it is about Nelson Mandela and his use of power. *Invictus* (Latin for undefeated or unconquered) is a compelling story of how Nelson Mandela used his personal power and position as president to help transform a whole society using a rugby team.

The story is simple. After being imprisoned from 1964 to 1990

Nelson Mandela becomes president in 1994. The nation is split between whites and blacks and is on the verge of an outright racial war. While the South African blacks hate the national rugby team as a symbol of white power and dominance, the Springboks are beloved by the whites. Mandela reaches across the divide the support the Springboks in their attempt to win an international title when they host the 1995 Rugby World Cup. Of course, the Springboks win, as this is a Hollywood film, but this is not the lesson.

Where does this once imprisoned leader find it within himself to not only forgive his captors, but support them? It was always there, as captured in the quote from the poem *Invictus* by William Earnest Henley, "I am the master of my fate: I am captain of my soul." Why not marginalize the white population in the same say they marginal-

ized the blacks? The blacks won the election and they are the vast majority in the nation. Why not follow the popular sentiment?

Over the objections of his advisers, Mandela provides visible support for a team that is not expected to even be in the finals. He is at the games. He meets with the team and its leader. He supports the games as evidence of a new South Africa. The nation is not black or white, it is black *and* white. This is not the old South Africa, but a new nation, and the Springboks are a new symbol of a new vision of South Africa.

What's the Lesson Here?

As a leader are you able to use your power to bring people together? Do you have it in you to forgive and move on, even when it is difficult?

Power and Influence Capacity

• **Power-oriented behavior** is action directed primarily at developing or using relationships in which other people are willing to defer to one's wishes.

A considerable portion of any manager's time is directed toward what is called **power-oriented behavior**. Power-oriented behavior is action directed primarily at developing or using relationships in which other people are willing to defer to one's wishes.[16] Figure 12.2 shows three basic dimensions of power and influence affecting a manager: downward, upward, and lateral. Also shown in the figure are the uses of personal and position power. The effective manager is one who succeeds in building and maintaining high levels of both position and personal power over time. Only then is sufficient power of the right types available when the manager needs to exercise influence on downward, lateral, and upward dimensions.

Building Position Power   Position power can be enhanced when a manager is able to demonstrate to others that their work unit is highly relevant to organizational goals, called centrality, and is able to respond to urgent organizational need, called criticality. Managers may seek to acquire a more central role in the workflow by having information filtered through them, making at least part of their job responsibilities unique, and expanding their network of communication contacts.

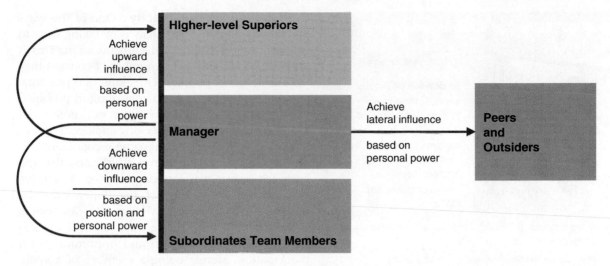

Figure 12.2 Three dimensions of managerial power and influence.

A manager may also attempt to increase task relevance to add criticality. There are many ways to do this. The manager may try to become an internal coordinator within the firm or an external representative. When the firm is in a dynamic setting of changing technology, the executive may also move to provide unique services and information to other units. A manager may shift the emphasis on his or her group's activities toward emerging issues central to the organization's top priorities. To effectively initiate new ideas and new projects may not be possible unless a manager also delegates more routine activities and expands both the task variety and task novelty for subordinates. Of course, not all attempts to build influence may be positive. Some managers are known to have defined tasks, so they are difficult to evaluate by creating an ambiguous job description or developing a unique language for their work.

Building Personal Power Personal power arises from the individual characteristics of the manager. Three personal characteristics—expertise, political savvy, and likeability—have potential for enhancing personal power in an organization. The most obvious is *building expertise*. Additional expertise may be gained by advanced training and education, participation in professional associations, and involvement in the early stages of projects.

A somewhat less obvious way to increase personal power is to learn **political savvy**—better ways to negotiate, persuade individuals, and understand the goals and means they are most willing to accept. The novice believes that most individuals are very much the same: They acknowledge the same goals and will accept similar paths toward these goals. The more astute individual recognizes important individual differences among co-workers. The most experienced managers are adept at building coalitions and developing a network of reciprocal obligations.

Finally, a manager's personal power is increased by characteristics that enhance his or her *likeability* and create personal appeal in relationships with other people. These include pleasant personality traits, agreeable behavior patterns, and attractive appearance.

• **Political savvy** is knowing how to negotiate, persuade, and deal with people regarding goals they will accept.

How the Right Skills Can Build Organizational Political Savvy

To develop political savvy, Gerald Ferris, Sherry Davidson, and Pamela Perrewé suggest cultivating your political skills. How? For starters, focus on developing four key skills:

1. Become more aware of others' concerns and improve your understanding of why they act the way they do.
2. Work on communication skills and develop friendly relationships.
3. Sharpen your ability to network by finding others inside and outside the firm who have shared interests.
4. Perfect your approach to become viewed as a person who genuinely cares for others.

Building Influence Capacity   One of the ways people build influence capacity is by taking steps to increase their visibility in the organization. This is done by (1) expanding the number of contacts they have with senior people, (2) making oral presentations of written work, (3) participating in problem-solving task forces, (4) sending out notices of accomplishments, and (5) seeking additional opportunities to increase personal name recognition.[17]

In the opening section we indicated that the basis for power was interdependence. You often can change the pattern of interdependence by developing and using coalitions. By developing coalitions and networks, executives also expand their access to information and opportunities for participation. Merely being a member of a coalition of individuals with relevant knowledge increases your expert power. With membership you have expanded sources of information and greater opportunities for participation. Remember, many important decisions are made outside formal channels and are substantially influenced by key individuals with the requisite knowledge.

Managers can also build influence capacity by controlling, or at least attempting to control, decision premises. A decision premise is a basis for defining the problem and selecting among alternatives. By defining a problem in a manner that fits your expertise, it is natural for you to be in charge of solving the problem. Thus, by controlling a decision premise the executive can subtly shift his or her position power. To effectively make this shift, it is important for goals and needs to be clear and for bargaining to be done effectively in order to show that the preferred goals and needs are best.

The astute manager does not threaten or attempt to invoke sanctions to build power. Instead, he or she combines personal power with the position of the unit to enhance total power. As the organizational context changes, different personal sources of power may become more important both alone and in combination with the individual's position power. There is an art to building power, and a key part of this art is to make effective use of a variety of influence techniques.

Relational Influence Techniques

A wide variety of techniques can be used to influence other individuals. Almost all individuals will have an opportunity to use these seven techniques:[18]

Reason: Using facts and data to support a logical argument.

Friendliness: Using flattery, goodwill, and favorable impressions.

Coalition: Using relationships with other people for support.

Bargaining: Using the exchange of benefits as a basis for negotiation.

Assertiveness: Using a direct and forceful personal approach.

Higher authority: Gaining higher-level support for one's requests.

Sanctions: Using organizationally derived rewards and punishments.

Research on these strategies suggests that reason is the most popular technique overall.[19] Friendliness, assertiveness, bargaining, and higher authority are used more frequently to influence subordinates than to influence supervisors. This pattern of attempted influence is consistent with our earlier contention that downward influence generally includes mobilization of both position and personal power sources, whereas upward influence is more likely to draw on personal power.

Truly effective managers, as suggested earlier in Figure 12.2, are able to influence their bosses as well as their subordinates. One study reports that both supervisors and subordinates view reason, or the logical presentation of ideas, as the most frequently used strategy of upward influence.[20] When queried on reasons for success and failure, however, the two groups show similarities and differences in their viewpoints. The perceived causes of success in upward influence are very similar for both supervisors and subordinates and involve the favorable content of the influence attempt, a favorable manner of its presentation, and the competence of the subordinate.[21]

The two groups do disagree, however, on the causes of failure. Subordinates attribute failure in upward influence to the closed-mindedness of the supervisor, to an unfavorable and difficult relationship with the supervisor, as well as to the content of the influence attempt. Supervisors also attribute failure to the unfavorable content of the attempt, but report additional causes of failure as the unfavorable manner in which it was presented and the subordinate's lack of competence.

Empowerment

LEARNING ROADMAP   *Keys to Empowerment / Power as an Expanding Pie / From Empowerment to Valuing People*

The concept of empowerment is part of the sweeping change taking place in today's corporations. Corporate staff is being cut back; layers of management are being eliminated; and the number of employees is being reduced as the volume of work increases. What is left is a leaner and trimmer organization staffed by fewer managers who must share more power as they go about their daily tasks. Indeed, empowerment is a key foundation of the increasingly popular self-managing work teams and other creative worker involvement groups.

Empowerment is the process by which managers help others to acquire and use the power needed to make decisions affecting themselves and their work. More than ever before, managers in progressive organizations are expected to be good at and comfortable with empowering the people with whom they work. Rather than considering power to be something to be held only at higher levels in the traditional "pyramid" of organizations, this view considers power to be something that can be shared by everyone working in flatter and more collegial structures.[22]

While empowerment has been popular and successfully implemented in the United States and Europe for over a decade, new evidence suggests it can boost performance and commitment in firms worldwide as well.[23]

• **Empowerment** is the process by which managers help others to acquire and use the power needed to make decisions affecting themselves and their work.

Keys to Empowerment

One of the bases for empowerment is a radically different view of power itself. So far, our discussion has focused on power that is exerted over other individuals.

In this traditional view, power is relational in terms of individuals. In contrast, the concept of empowerment emphasizes the ability to make things happen. Power is still relational, but in terms of problems and opportunities, not just individuals. Cutting through all of the corporate rhetoric on empowerment is quite difficult because the term has become quite fashionable in management circles. Each individual empowerment attempt needs to be examined in light of how both position power and personal power in the organization will be changed.

Changing Position Power When an organization attempts to move power down the hierarchy, it must also alter the existing pattern of position power. Changing this pattern raises some important questions. Can "empowered" individuals give rewards and sanctions based on task accomplishment? Has their new right to act been legitimized with formal authority? All too often, attempts at empowerment disrupt well-established patterns of position power and threaten middle- and lower-level managers. As one supervisor said, "All this empowerment stuff sounds great for top management. They don't have to run around trying to get the necessary clearances to implement the suggestions from my group. They never gave me the authority to make the changes, only the new job of asking for permission."

When embarking on an empowerment program, management needs to recognize the current zone of indifference and systematically move to expand it. All too often, management assumes that its directive for empowerment will be followed because management sees empowerment as a better way to manage. Management needs to show precisely how empowerment will benefit the individuals involved and provide the inducement needed to expand the zone of indifference.

Enhancing Personal Power There is also a very personal aspect to empowerment that goes far beyond the reallocation of position power to involve personal power. To be empowered individuals need to believe that their jobs are (1) meaningful to them and consistent with their values, (2) call for them to use their competence, (3) allow for discretion, and (4) have an impact. If one of these is missing, an individual may not feel empowered.[24] For instance, even in jobs the individual believes are important and consistent with their values, they need to believe they have some choice in how it is performed. Regardless of the importance, choice, or impact of a job, individuals must also believe they are competent or they will not feel empowered.

Power as an Expanding Pie

Although many firms want all employees to be empowered, it is extremely difficult to accomplish, for it often changes the dynamics among supervisors and between supervisors and subordinates. The change calls for all to understand an expanded notion of power. From a view that stresses power over others, effective empowerment emphasizes the use of power to get things done. Under the new definition of power, all employees can be more powerful and the chances of success can be enhanced. As stressed in this chapter, alterations in both position and personal power are required.

A clearer definition of roles and responsibilities may help managers to empower others. For instance, senior managers may choose to concentrate on long-term, large-scale adjustments to a variety of challenging and strategic forces in the external environment. If top management tends to concentrate on the long term and downplay quarterly mileposts, others throughout the organization must be ready and willing to make the key decisions that ensure current profitability. Further, when asked to make these decisions, lower management must believe they are not only competent to do so but can also make choices consistent with their values. By providing opportunities for creative problem solving coupled with the discretion to act, real empowerment increases the total potential power for action available in an organization.

The same basic arguments hold true in any manager–subordinate higher authority, and sanctions need to be replaced by appeals to reason. Friendliness must replace coercion, and bargaining must replace orders for compliance. Given the all too familiar history of an emphasis on coercion and compliance within firms, special support may be needed for managers so that they become comfortable in developing their own power over events and activities. For instance, one recent study found that management's efforts at increasing empowerment in order to boost performance were successful only when directly supported by individual supervision. Without leader support there is no increase in empowerment, and so there is less improvement in performance.[25]

With more and more firms adopting empowerment, the chances that you will be asked to make important decisions early in your career are much greater. Though exciting and challenging, some of the choices will present you with ethical dilemmas. You can avoid rationalizing unethical behavior by following the tips listed in the sidebar.

How to Avoid Common Rationalizations for Unethical Behavior

Choosing to be ethical involves personal sacrifice. When confronting potentially unethical actions, make sure you are not justifying your actions by suggesting that:

1. the behavior is not really illegal and so it could be morally acceptable;
2. the action appears to be in the firm's best interests even though it hurts others;
3. the action is unlikely ever to be detected; and
4. it appears that the action demonstrates loyalty to the boss, the firm, or short-term stockholder interests.

From Empowerment to Valuing People

Beyond empowering employees, a number of organizational behavior scholars argue that U.S. firms need to change how they view employees in order to sustain a competitive advantage in an increasingly global economy.[26] Although no one firm may have all of the necessary characteristics, Jeffrey Pfeffer suggests that the goals of the firm should include placing employees at the center of their strategy. To do so they need to:

- Develop employment security for a selectively recruited workforce.
- Pay high wages with incentive pay and provide potential for employee ownership.
- Encourage information sharing and participation with an emphasis on self-managed teams.
- Emphasize training and skill development by utilizing talent and cross-training.
- Pursue egalitarianism (at least symbolically) with little pay compression across units and enable extensive internal promotion.

Hard Times Mean Getting Back to the Basics

John Chambers, president and CEO of Cisco Systems, says he is "getting back to the basics in terms of focusing on the areas that a company can influence and control: cash generation, available market share gains, productivity increases, profitability and technology innovation." Chambers suggests emphasizing interactions that will favor those people who can add value and content to networks.

Of course, this also calls for taking a long-term view coupled with a systematic emphasis on measuring what works and what does not, as well as a supporting managerial philosophy. This is a long list. However, it appears consistent with the sentiments of John Chambers, CEO of Cisco, and his emphasis on people and interconnections.

Organizational Politics

LEARNING ROADMAP   Traditions of Organizational Politics / Politics of Self-Protection / Politics and Governance

Any study of power and influence inevitably leads to the subject of politics. For many, the word "politics" may conjure up thoughts of illicit deals, favors, and advantageous personal relationships. Organizational politics also seems to involve using the ends to justify the means. In this light organizational politics dates back to Machiavelli's classic fifteenth-century work, *The Prince*, which outlines how to obtain and hold power through political action. For Machiavelli, the ends did justify the means. It is important, however, to understand the importance of organizational politics and adopt a perspective that allows workplace politics to function in a much broader capacity.[27]

Traditions of Organizational Politics

There are two different traditions in the analysis of organizational politics. One tradition builds on Machiavelli's philosophy and defines *politics in terms of self-interest* and the use of nonsanctioned means. In this tradition, **organizational politics** may be formally defined as the management of influence to obtain ends not sanctioned by the organization or to obtain sanctioned ends by way of non-sanctioned influence.[28] Managers are often considered political when they seek their own goals and use means that are not currently authorized by the organization or those that push legal limits. Where there is uncertainty or ambiguity, it is often extremely difficult to tell whether or not a manager is being political in this self-serving sense.[29] For example, to earn a bonus, some mortgage brokers often neglected to verify the income of mortgage applicants. It was not illegal, but it certainly was self-serving and could be labeled political.

The second tradition treats politics as a necessary function resulting from differences in the self-interests of individuals. Here, organizational politics is viewed

• **Organizational politics** is the management of influence to obtain ends not sanctioned by the organization or to obtain sanctioned ends through nonsanctioned means and the art of creative compromise among competing interests.

OB IN POPULAR CULTURE

POLITICAL BEHAVIOR AND *SPANGLISH*

One aspect of **organizational politics** involves using legitimate means to gain nonlegitimate outcomes or using nonlegitimate means to gain any kind of outcome. Political behavior is inherently self-interested, but that does not make it bad or good. Organizations must exhibit a degree of self-interest (e.g., acting to make a profit, trying to perform better than competitors) in order to succeed.

In *Spanglish*, John Clasky (Adam Sandler) is an exceptional chef with an exclusive restaurant in California. His assistants, Pietro (Phil Rosenthal) and Gwen (Angela Goethals), are always trying to impress him. Gwen is political, agreeing with and praising the boss and always willing to do favors. Pietro is equally political, just in a more cunning fashion. He controls the actions of others and uses his own cooking skills to make himself invaluable to the boss.

What we see in both cases are employees who want to be viewed favorably by the boss. There is nothing wrong with that. Everyone has a right to "toot their own horn." However, if the actions keep one from completing legitimate job responsibilities or are designed to mask performance deficiencies, they represent bad political behaviors. Furthermore, legitimate actions that deny others the right to legitimately influence outcomes are also inappropriate political behaviors.

Get to Know Yourself Better   Take a look at Assessment 14, Machiavellianism, in the OB Skills Workbook. Machiavellian tendencies are often associated with political behavior. Take this quick test and see how you score. What does it suggest about your own preferences? Do you have a desire to control and manipulate others? Could this lead to actions that might be viewed unfavorably by co-workers? How can you make sure that you use your power appropriately and effectively?

as the art of creative compromise among competing interests. According to this view, the firm is more than just an instrument for accomplishing a task or a mere collection of individuals with a common goal. It acknowledges that the interests of individuals, stakeholders, and society must also be considered and that these interests are not always consistent with one another.

Individuals will often disagree as to whose self-interests are most valuable, whose interests should be bounded by collective interests, and how individual interests should be bounded. Politics arise because individuals need to develop compromises, avoid confrontation, and live and work together. This is especially true in organizations, where individuals join, work, and stay together because their self-interests are served. It is important to remember that both the goals of the organization and the acceptable means of achieving them are established by powerful individuals in the organization through their negotiation with others. Therefore, organizational politics is also the use of power to develop socially acceptable ends and means that balance individual and collective interests.

Political Interpretation   The two different traditions of organizational politics are reflected in the ways executives describe the effects of organizational politics on managers and their organizations. In one survey, some 53 percent of those interviewed indicated that organizational politics enhanced the achievement of organizational goals and survival. Yet some 44 percent also suggested that politics distracted individuals from organizational goals.[30]

Organizational politics is not inherently good or bad. It can serve a number of important functions, including overcoming personnel inadequacies, coping with change, and substituting for formal authority. Even in the best-managed firms, mismatches arise among managers who are learning, are burned out, lack necessary training and skills, are overqualified, or are lacking the resources needed to accomplish their assigned duties. Organizational politics provides a mechanism for circumventing these inadequacies and getting the job done. It can also facilitate adaptation to changes in the environment and technology of an organization.

Organizational politics can also help identify problems and move ambitious, problem-solving managers into action. It is quicker than restructuring, and it allows the firm to meet unanticipated problems with people and resources quickly, before small headaches become major problems. Finally, when a person's formal authority breaks down or fails to apply to a particular situation, political actions can be used to prevent a loss of influence. Managers may use political behavior to maintain operations and to achieve task continuity in circumstances where the failure of formal authority may otherwise cause problems.

Political Forecasting   Managers may gain a better understanding of political behavior in order to forecast future actions by placing themselves in the positions of other persons involved in critical decisions or events. Each action and decision can be seen as having benefits for and costs to all parties concerned. Where the costs exceed the benefits, the manager may act to protect his or her position. Figure 12.3 shows a sample payoff table for two managers, Lee and Leslie, in a problem situation involving a decision as to whether or not they should allocate resources to a special project.

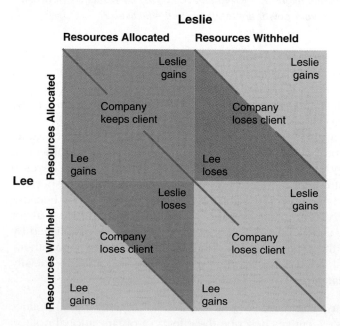

Figure 12.3 Political payoff matrix for the allocation of resources on a sample project.

If both managers authorize the resources, the project gets completed on time and their company keeps a valuable client. Unfortunately, if they do this, both Lee and Leslie spend more than they have in their budgets. Taken on its own, a budget overrun would be bad for the managers' performance records. Assume that the overruns are acceptable only if the client is kept. Thus, if both managers act, both they and the company win, as depicted in the upper-left block of the figure. Obviously, this is the most desirable outcome for all parties concerned.

Assume that Leslie acts, but Lee does not. In this case, the company loses the client, Leslie overspends the budget in a futile effort, but Lee ends up within budget. While the company and Leslie lose, Lee wins. This scenario is illustrated in the lower-left block of the figure. The upper-right block shows the reverse situation, where Lee acts but Leslie does not. In this case, Leslie wins, while the company and Lee lose. Finally, if both Lee and Leslie fail to act, each stays within budget and therefore gains, but the company loses the client.

The company clearly wants both Lee and Leslie to act. But will they? Would you take the risk of overspending the budget, knowing that your colleague may refuse to do the same? The question of trust is critical here, but building trust among co-managers and other workers can be difficult and takes time. The involvement of higher-level managers may be needed to set the stage. Yet in many organizations both Lee and Leslie would fail to act because the "climate" or "culture" too often encourages people to maximize their self-interest at minimal risk.

Subunit Power   To be effective in political action, managers should also understand the politics of subunit relations.[31] Units that directly contribute to organizational goals are typically more powerful than units that provide advice or assistance. Units toward the top of the hierarchy are often more powerful than those toward the bottom. More subtle power relationships are found among units at or near the same level in a firm. Political action links managers more formally to one another as representatives of their work units.

Five of the more typical lateral, intergroup relations a manager may engage with are workflow, service, advisory, auditing, and approval.[32] Workflow linkages involve contacts with units that precede or follow in a sequential production chain. Service ties involve contacts with units established to help with problems. For instance, an assembly-line manager may develop a service link by asking the maintenance manager to fix an important piece of equipment on a priority basis. In contrast, advisory connections involve formal staff units having special expertise, such as a manager seeking the advice of the personnel department on evaluating subordinates.

Auditing linkages involve units that have the right to evaluate the actions of others after action has been taken, whereas approval linkages involve units whose approval must be obtained before action may be taken. In general, units gain power as more of their relations with others are of the approval and auditing types. Workflow relations are more powerful than are advisory associations, and both are more powerful than service relations.

Politics of Self-Protection

Although organizational politics may be helpful to the organization as a whole, it is more commonly known and better understood in terms of self-protection.[33] Whether or not management likes it, all employees recognize that in any organization they must first watch out for themselves. In too many organizations, if the employee doesn't protect himself or herself, no one else will. Individuals can employ three common strategies to protect themselves. They can (1) avoid action and risk taking, (2) redirect accountability and responsibility, or (3) defend their turf.

Avoidance   Avoidance is quite common in controversial areas where the employee must risk being wrong or where actions may yield a sanction. Perhaps the most common reaction is to "work to the rules." That is, employees are protected when they adhere strictly to all the rules, policies, and procedures and do not allow deviations or exceptions.

Although working to the rules and playing dumb are common techniques, experienced employees often practice somewhat more subtle techniques of self-protection. These include depersonalization and stalling. Depersonalization involves treating individuals, such as customers, clients, or subordinates, as numbers, things, or objects. Senior managers don't fire long-term employees; the organization is merely "downsized" or "delayered." Routine stalling involves slowing down the pace of work to expand the task so that the individuals look as if they are working hard. With creative stalling, the employees may spend the time supporting the organization's ideology, position, or program and delaying implementation of changes they consider undesirable.

Redirecting Responsibility   Politically sensitive individuals will always protect themselves from accepting blame for the negative consequences of their actions. Again, a variety of well-worn techniques may be used for redirecting responsibility. "Passing the buck" is a common method employees and managers use. The trick here is to define the task in such a way that it becomes someone else's formal responsibility. The ingenious ways in which individuals can redefine an issue to avoid action and transfer responsibility are often amazing.

A convenient method some managers use to avoid responsibility is merely to rewrite history. If a program is successful, the manager claims to have been an early supporter. If a program fails, the manager was the one who expressed serious reservations in the first place. Whereas it is often nice to have a memo in the files in order to show one's early support or objections, some executives don't bother with such niceties. They merely start a meeting by recapping what has happened in such a way that makes them look good.

For the truly devious, there are three other techniques for redirecting responsibility. One technique is to blame the problem on someone or some group that has difficulty defending itself. Fired employees, outsiders, and opponents are often targets of such scapegoating. Closely related to scapegoating is blaming the problem on uncontrollable events.[34] The astute manager goes far beyond this natural tendency to place the blame on events that are out of his or her control. A perennial favorite is, "Given the unexpected severe decline in the overall economy, firm profitability was only somewhat below reasonable expectations." Meaning, the firm lost a bundle of money.

Should these techniques fail, there is always another possibility: Facing apparent defeat, the manager can escalate commitment to a losing cause of action. That is, when all appears lost, assert your confidence in the original action, blame the problems on not spending enough money to implement the plan fully, and embark on actions that call for increased effort. The hope is that you will be promoted, have a new job with another firm, or be retired by the time the negative consequences are recognized. It is called "skating fast over thin ice."[35]

Turf Wars at the Pentagon

The Pentagon activated Cyber Command to coordinate cyber units from all the military services. Its success depends on ending turf wars. One general is reported as saying that winning cyber battles will require "harmony of effort." But he adds "That's just not part of our DNA. . . . We are programmed to protect 'what's in it for me.' . . . It's time to start thinking about the 'what's in it for us' perspective."

Defending Turf   Defending turf is a time-honored tradition in most large organizations. As noted earlier in the chapter, managers seeking to improve their power attempt to expand the jobs their groups perform. Defending turf also results from the coalitional nature of organizations. That is, the organization may be seen as a collection of competing interests held by various departments and groups. As each group attempts to expand its influence, it starts to encroach on the activities of other groups. Turf protection is common in organizations and runs from the very lowest position to the executive suite. Note the example of the Pentagon in its attempts to end the turf wars over control of cyberspace.

Politics and Governance

From the time of the robber barons such as Jay Gould in the 1890s, Americans have been fascinated with the politics of the chief executive suite. Recent accounts of alleged and proven criminal actions emanating from the executive suites of Washington Mutual, Bear Stearns, WorldCom, Enron, Global Crossings, and Tyco have caused the media spotlight to penetrate the mysterious veil shrouding politics at the top of organizations.[36] An analytical view of executive suite dynamics may lift some of the mystery.

Agency Theory   An essential power problem in today's modern corporation arises from the separation of owners and managers. A body of work called **agency theory** suggests that public corporations can function effectively, even though their managers are self-interested and do not automatically bear the full consequences of their managerial actions. The theory argues that (1) all of society's interests are served by protecting stockholder interests, (2) stockholders have a clear interest in greater returns, and (3) managers are self-interested and unwilling to sacrifice these self-interests for others (particularly stockholders) and thus must be controlled. The term *agency theory* stems from the notion that managers are "agents" of the owners.[37] Because agency theory is very popular in economic and financial analyses of corporations, we will spend a minute discussing it.

• **agency theory** suggests that public corporations can function effectively even though their managers are self-interested and do not always automatically bear the full consequences of their managerial actions.

So what types of controls should be instituted? There are several. One type of control involves making sure that what is good for stockholders is good for management. Incentives in the pay plan for executives may be adjusted to align with the interests of management and stockholders. For example, executives may get most of their pay based on the stock price of the firm via stock options. A second type of control involves the establishment of a strong, independent board of directors, since the board is to represent the stockholders. While this may sound unusual, it is not uncommon for a CEO to pick a majority of the board members and to place many top managers on the board. For example, before General Motors went into bankruptcy the board of directors was passive. The compensation of the CEO increased even when the market share of the firm declined. Many board members were appointed at the suggestion of the old CEO, and only a few board members held large amounts of GM stock.

A third way is for stockholders with a large stake in the firm to take an active role on the board. For instance, mutual fund managers have been encouraged to become more active in monitoring management. And there is, of course, the so-called market for corporate control. For instance, poorly performing executives can be replaced by outsiders.[38]

The problem with the simple application of all of these control mechanisms is that they do not appear to work very well even for the stockholders and clearly, some suggest, not for others either. Recent studies strongly suggest that agency-based controls backfire when applied to CEOs. One study found that when options were used extensively to reward CEOs for short-term increases in the stock price, it prompted executives to make risky bets. The results were extreme with big winners and big losers. In a related investigation, the extensive use of stock options was associated with manipulation of earnings when these options were not going to give the CEOs a big bonus. These researchers concluded that "stock-based managerial incentives lead to incentive misalignment."[39]

The recent storm of controversy over CEO pay and the studies cited above illustrate questions for using a simple application of agency theory to control executives. Until the turn of the century, U.S. CEOs made about 25 to 30 times the pay of the average worker. This was similar to CEO pay scales in Europe and Japan. Today, however, many U.S. CEOs are paid 300 times the average salary of workers.[40] Why are they paid so much? It is executive compensation specialists who suggest these levels to the board of directors. The compensation specialists list the salaries of the top-paid, most successful executives as the basis for suggesting a plan for a client CEO. The board or the compensation committee of the board, selected by the current CEO and consisting mainly of other CEOs, then must decide if the firm's CEO is one of the best. If not one of the best, then why should they continue the tenure of the CEO? Of course, if the candidate CEO gets a big package, it also means that the base for subsequent comparison is increased. And round it goes.

It is little wonder that there is renewed interest in how U.S. firms are governed. Rather than proposing some quick fix based on a limited theory of the firm, it is important to come to a better understanding of different views on the politics of the executive suite. By taking a broader view, you can better understand politics in the modern corporation.

Resource Dependencies   Executive behavior can sometimes be explained in terms of resource dependencies—the firm's need for resources that are controlled by others.[41] Essentially, the resource dependence of an organization increases as (1) needed resources become more scarce, (2) outsiders have more control over needed resources, and (3) there are fewer substitutes for a particular type of resource controlled by a limited number of outsiders. Thus, one political role of the chief executive is to develop workable compromises among the competing resource dependencies facing the organization—compromises that enhance the executive's power.

To create executive-enhancing compromises, managers need to diagnose the relative power of outsiders and to craft strategies that respond differently to various external resource suppliers. For larger organizations, many strategies may center on altering the firm's degree of resource dependence. Through mergers and acquisitions, a firm may bring key resources within its control. By changing the "rules of the game," a firm may also find protection from particularly powerful outsiders. For instance, before being absorbed by another firm, Netscape sought relief from the onslaught of Microsoft by appealing to the U.S. government. Markets may also be protected by trade barriers, or labor unions may be put in check by "right to work" laws. Yet there are limits on the ability of even our largest and most powerful organizations to control all important external contingencies.

International competition has narrowed the range of options for chief executives, and they can no longer ignore the rest of the world. For instance, once U.S. firms could go it alone without the assistance of foreign corporations. Now, chief executives are increasingly leading companies in the direction of more joint ventures and strategic alliances with foreign partners from around the globe. Such "combinations" provide access to scarce resources and technologies among partners, as well as new markets and shared production costs.[42]

RESEARCH INSIGHT

Female Members on Corporate Boards of Directors

While the number of women on corporate boards of directors is increasing, there is still a lack of representation. Less than 16 percent of board members in major U.S. corporations are female. Amy Hillman, Christine Shropshire, and Albert Cannalla used a resource-dependence perspective to identify potentially important factors leading to greater participation by women on the boards of the top 1,000 U.S. firms with headquarters in the United States from 1990 to 2003. What did they find?

- Larger firms were more likely to have female board members than smaller corporations.
- Firms with more female employees were more likely to have a female board member.
- Firms with less diversification and more closely related products and services were more likely to have a female board member.
- Firms doing a lot of business with organizations that also had a female board member were more likely to have female board members.

Do the Research *What do you think the proportion of females on a board of directors is in your area? Find a list of the largest private employers in your state. Check each Web site and count the number of female directors. What do you think the proportion should be? If the board were all female, would this be a problem? If it were all male, would this be a problem?*

Source: Amy J. Hillman, Christine Shropshire, and Albert Cannalla, "Organizational Predictors of Women on Corporate Boards," *Academy of Management Journal* 5 (2007), pp. 941–968; http://www.catalyst.org/file/241/08_Census_COTE_JAN.pdf.

Organizational Governance   With some knowledge of agency theory and resource dependencies, it is much easier to understand the notion of organizational governance. **Organizational governance** refers to the pattern of authority, influence, and acceptable managerial behavior established at the top of the organization. This system establishes what is important, how issues will be defined, who should and should not be involved in key choices, and the boundaries for acceptable implementation. Students of organizational governance suggest that a "dominant coalition" comprised of powerful organizational actors is a key to understanding a firm's governance.[43]

• **Organizational governance** is the pattern of authority, influence, and acceptable managerial behavior established at the top of the organization.

Although one expects many top officers within the organization to be members of this coalition, the dominant coalition occasionally includes outsiders with access to key resources. Thus, analysis of organizational governance builds on the resource dependence perspective by highlighting the effective control of key resources by members of a dominant coalition. It also recognizes the relative power of key constituencies, such as the power of stockholders stressed in agency theory.

This dependence view of the executive suite recognizes that the daily practice of organizational governance is the development and resolution of issues. Through the governance system, the dominant coalition attempts to define reality. By accepting or rejecting proposals from subordinates, by directing questions toward the interests of powerful outsiders, and by selecting individuals who appear to espouse particular values and qualities, the pattern of governance is slowly established within the organization. Furthermore, this pattern rests, at least in part, on political foundations.

Organizational governance was an internal and a rather private matter in the past; today it is becoming more public and controversial. Some, as we noted in the discussion of agency theory, argue that senior managers don't represent shareholder interests well enough. Others are concerned that managers give too little attention to broader constituencies. We think managers should recognize the basis for their power and legitimacy and become leaders. The next two chapters are devoted to the crucial topic of leadership.

12 *study guide*

Key Questions and Answers

What are power and influence?

- Power is the ability to get someone else to do what you want him or her to do.

- Power vested in managerial positions derives from three sources: rewards, punishments, and legitimacy or formal authority.

- Influence is what you have when you exercise power.

- Position power is formal authority based on the manager's position in the hierarchy.

- Personal power is based on one's expertise and referent capabilities.

- Managers can pursue various ways of acquiring both position and personal power.

- Managers can also become skilled at using various techniques—such as reason, friendliness, and bargaining—to influence superiors, peers, and subordinates.

What are the key sources of power and influence?

- Individuals are socialized to accept power, the potential to control the behavior of others, and formal authority, the potential to exert such control through the legitimacy of a managerial position.

- The Milgram experiments illustrate that people have a tendency to obey directives that come from others who appear powerful and authoritative.

- Power and authority work only if the individual "accepts" them as legitimate.

- The zone of indifference defines the boundaries within which people in organizations let others influence their behavior.

What is empowerment?

- Empowerment is the process through which managers help others acquire and use the power needed to make decisions that affect themselves and their work.

- Clear delegation of authority, integrated planning, and the involvement of senior management are all important to implementing empowerment.

- Empowerment emphasizes power as the ability to get things done rather than the ability to get others to do what you want.

What is organizational politics?

- Politics involves the use of power to obtain ends not officially sanctioned as well as the use of power to find ways of balancing individual and collective interests in otherwise difficult circumstances.

- For the manager, politics often occurs in decision situations where the interests of another manager or individual must be reconciled with one's own.

- For managers, politics also involves subunits that jockey for power and advantageous positions vis-à-vis one another.

- The politics of self-protection involves efforts to avoid accountability, redirect responsibility, and defend one's turf.

- While some suggest that executives are agents of the owners, politics also comes into play as resource dependencies with external environmental elements that must be strategically managed.

- Organizational governance is the pattern of authority, influence, and acceptable managerial behavior established at the top of the organization.

- CEOs and managers can develop an ethical organizational governance system that is free from rationalizations.

Terms to Know

Agency theory (p. 283)
Coalition power (p. 271)
Coercive power (p. 269)
Empowerment (p. 275)

Expert power (p. 271)
Influence (p. 264)
Information power (p. 270)
Legitimate power (p. 268)

Organizational governance (p. 286)
Organizational politics (p. 278)
Political savvy (p. 273)
Power (p. 264)

Self-Test 12

Multiple Choice

1. Three bases of position power are _____. (a) reward, expertise, and coercive power (b) legitimate, experience, and judgment power (c) knowledge, experience, and judgment power (d) reward, coercive, and information power

2. _____ is the ability to control another's behavior because, through the individual's efforts, the person accepts the desirability of an offered goal and a reasonable way of achieving it. (a) Rational persuasion (b) Legitimate power (c) Coercive power (d) Charismatic power

3. A worker who behaves in a certain manner to ensure an effective boss–subordinate relationship shows _____ power. (a) expert (b) reward (c) approval (d) referent

4. One guideline for implementing a successful empowerment strategy is that _____. (a) delegation of authority should be left ambiguous and open to individual interpretation (b) planning should be separated according to the level of empowerment (c) it can be assumed that any empowering directives from management will be automatically followed (d) the authority delegated to lower levels should be clear and precise

5. The major lesson of the Milgram experiments is that _____. (a) Americans are very independent and unwilling to obey (b) individuals are willing to obey as long as it does not hurt another person (c) individuals will obey an authority figure even if it does appear to hurt someone else (d) individuals will always obey an authority figure

6. The range of authoritative requests to which a subordinate is willing to respond without subjecting the directives to critical evaluation or judgment is called the _____. (a) psychological contract (b) zone of indifference (c) Milgram experiments (d) functional level of organizational politics

7. The three basic power relationships are _____. (a) upward, downward, and lateral (b) upward, downward, and oblique (c) downward, lateral, and oblique (d) downward, lateral, and external

8. In which dimension of power and influence would a manager find the use of both position power and personal power most advantageous? (a) upward (b) lateral (c) downward (d) workflow

9. Reason, coalition, bargaining, and assertiveness are strategies for _____. (a) enhancing personal power (b) enhancing position power (c) exercising referent power (d) exercising influence

10. Negotiating the interpretation of a union contract is an example of _____. (a) organizational politics (b) lateral relations (c) an approval relationship (d) an auditing linkage

11. _____ is the ability to control another's behavior because of the possession of knowledge, experience, or judgment that the other person does not have but needs. (a) Coercive power (b) Expert power (c) Information power (d) Representative power

12. _____ is the range of authoritative requests to which a subordinate is willing to respond without subjecting the directives to critical evaluation or judgment. (a) A zone of indifference (b) Legitimate authority (c) Power (d) Politics

13. The process by which managers help others to acquire and use the power needed to make decisions affecting themselves and their work is called _____. (a) politics (b) managerial philosophy (c) authority (d) empowerment

14. The pattern of authority, influence, and acceptable managerial behavior established at the top of the organization is called _____. (a) organizational governance (b) agency linkage (c) power (d) politics

15. _____ suggests that public corporations can function effectively even though their managers are self-interested and do not automatically bear the full consequences of their managerial actions. (a) Power theory (b) Managerial philosophy (c) Virtual theory (d) Agency theory

Short Response

16. Explain how the various bases of position and personal power do or do not apply to the classroom relationship between instructor and student. What sources of power do students have over their instructors?

17. Identify and explain at least three guidelines for the acquisition of (a) position power and (b) personal power by managers.

18. Identify and explain at least four strategies of managerial influence. Give examples of how each strategy may or may not work when exercising influence (a) downward and (b) upward in organizations.

19. Define *organizational politics* and give an example of how it operates in both functional and dysfunctional ways.

Applications Essay

20. Some argue that mergers and acquisitions rarely produce positive financial gains for the shareholders. What explanations could you offer to explain why mergers and acquisitions continue?

Next Steps
Top Choices from
The OB Skills
Workbook

Case for Critical Thinking	Team and Experiential Exercises	Self-Assessment Portfolio
• Faculty Empowerment	• Interview a Leader • My Best Manager: Revisited • Power Circles	• Managerial Assumptions • Empowering Others • Machiavellianism • Personal Power Profile

Zappos Insights: Revealing Corporate Secrets

Tony Hsieh doesn't see the need to protect the secrets to Zappos's wild success. In fact, the CEO is happy to share them with anyone who comes by the office.

Hsieh has built a $635 million Internet superstore by doing two things very well: exceeding customers' expectations and driving positive word-of-mouth recommendations. Hsieh believes so strongly in the organizational culture that he's on a mission to share it with anyone who will listen.

It all comes together in a program called Zappos Insights. The core experience is a tour of Zappos's headquarters. "Company Evangelists" lead groups of 20 around the cubicles, overflowing with kitschy action figures and brightly colored balloons. Staffers

> *"We open our doors and say, 'Be part of our family and talk to anybody you want.' And you see it's the real deal."*
> *—Robert Richman, co-leader of Zappos Insights.*[d]

blow horns and ring cowbells to greet participants in the 16 weekly tours, and each department tries to offer a more outlandish welcome than the last.[a]

The tours are free, but many visitors actually come for paid one- and two-day seminars that immerse participants in the Zappos culture. The capstone of the two-day boot camp is dinner at Tony Hsieh's house, with ample time to talk customer service with the CEO himself. Seminars range from $497 to $3,997. "There are management consulting firms that charge really high rates," says Hsieh. "We wanted to come up with something that's accessible to almost any business."[b]

Those who want to learn Zappos's secrets without venturing to Las Vegas have a few options. You can subscribe to a members-only community that grants access to video interviews and chats with Zappos management or get a free copy of *Zappos Family Culture Book* about Zappos's mission and core values.

They may be giving away hard-earned knowledge, but Zappos definitely isn't losing money—profits from the seminars pay for the program, and Hsieh hopes it will some day represent 10 percent of Zappos's operating profit. "There's a huge open market," says Robert Richman, co-leader of Zappos Insights. "We were afraid that we've been talking about this for free for so long. 'Are people going to be upset we are charging for it?' Instead, the reaction is opposite."[c]

Quick Summary

- In addition to free tours of their Las Vegas headquarters, Zappos now offers one- and two-day seminars. Attendees immerse themselves in Zappos's culture, which CEO Tony Hsieh believes is inseparable from the company's success.
- Attendees have unprecedented one-on-one access to Zappos executives and managers, all of whom are happy to espouse the customer- and employee-centric policies that increase profits and retain employees year after year.
- While the project is in its infancy, Hsieh hopes to develop Zappos's management consulting business into a venture that earns 10 percent of annual profits.

FYI: Customers from over 30 countries have attended Zappos Insights seminars.[e]

13 Leadership Essentials

the key point

Not all managers are leaders and not all leaders are managers. In a managerial position, being a leader requires understanding how to adapt one's management style to the situation to generate willing and effective followership. As shown in the Zappos example, the most successful leaders are those who are able to generate strong cultures in which employees work together to get things done.

chapter at a glance

What Is Leadership?

What Are Situational Contingency Approaches to Leadership?

What Are Follower-Centered Approaches to Leadership?

What Are Inspirational and Relational Leadership Perspectives?

ETHICS IN OB
CEO PAY–IS IT EXCESSIVE?

FINDING THE LEADER IN YOU
LOOKING FOR LEADER MATCH AT GOOGLE

OB IN POPULAR CULTURE
PATH-GOAL AND *REMEMBER THE TITANS*

RESEARCH INSIGHT
PARTICIPATORY LEADERSHIP AND PEACE

what's inside?

Leadership

LEARNING ROADMAP Managers versus Leaders / Trait Leadership Perspectives / Behavioral Leadership Perspectives

Most people assume that anyone in management, particularly the CEO, is a leader. Currently, however, controversy has arisen over this assumption. We can all think of examples where managers do not perform much, if any, leadership, as well as instances where leadership is performed by people who are not in management. Researchers have even argued that failure to clearly recognize this difference is a violation of "truth in advertising" because many studies labeled "leadership" may actually be about "management."[1]

Managers versus Leaders

A key way of differentiating between managers and leaders is to argue that the role of management is to promote stability or to enable the organization to run smoothly, whereas the role of leadership is to promote adaptive or useful changes.[2] Persons in managerial positions could be involved with both management and leadership activities, or they could emphasize one activity at the expense of the other. Both management and leadership are needed, however, and if managers do not assume responsibility for both, then they should ensure that someone else handles the neglected activity. The point is that when we discuss leadership, we do not assume it is identical to management.

> • **Leadership** is the process of influencing others and the process of facilitating individual and collective efforts to accomplish shared objectives.

For our purposes, we treat **leadership** as the process of influencing others to understand and agree about what needs to be done and how to do it, and the process of facilitating individual and collective efforts to accomplish shared objectives.[3] Leadership appears in two forms: (1) formal leadership, which is exerted by persons appointed or elected to positions of formal authority in organizations, and (2) informal leadership, which is exerted by persons who become influential because they have special skills that meet the needs of others. Although both types are important in organizations, this chapter will emphasize formal leadership; informal leadership will be addressed in the next chapter.[4]

The leadership literature is vast—thousands of studies at last count—and consists of numerous approaches.[5] We have grouped these approaches into two chapters: Leadership Essentials, Chapter 13, and Leadership Challenges and Organizational Change, Chapter 14. The present chapter focuses on trait and behavioral

Change Brings Out the Leader in Us

Avon CEO Andrea Jung feels "there is a big difference between being a leader and being a manager." That difference lies in being flexible and willing to change. According to Jung, if you have difficulty with change you will have a harder time being successful as a leader.

theory perspectives, cognitive and symbolic leadership perspectives, and transformational and charismatic leadership approaches. Chapter 14 deals with such leadership challenges as how to be a moral leader, how to share leadership, how to lead across cultures, how to be a strategic leader of major units, and, of course, how to lead change. Many of the perspectives in each chapter include several models. Although each of these models may be useful to you in a given work setting, we invite you to mix and match them as necessary in your setting, just as we did earlier with the motivational models discussed in Chapter 5.

Trait Leadership Perspectives

For over a century, scholars have attempted to identify the key characteristics that separate leaders from nonleaders. Much of this work stressed traits. **Trait perspectives** assume that traits play a central role in differentiating between leaders and nonleaders in that leaders must have the "right stuff."[6] The great person-trait approach reflects the attempt to use traits to separate leaders from nonleaders. This list of possible traits identified only became longer as researchers focused on the leadership traits linked to successful leadership and organizational performance. Unfortunately, few of the same traits were identified across studies. Part of the problem involved inadequate theory, poor measurement of traits, and the confusion between managing and leading.

Fortunately, recent research has yielded promising results. A number of traits have been found that help identify important leadership strengths, as outlined in Figure 13.1. As it turns out, most of these traits also tend to predict leadership outcomes.[7]

Key traits of leaders include ambition, motivation, honesty, self-confidence, and a high need for achievement. They crave power not as an end in itself but as a means to achieve a vision or desired goals. At the same time, they must have enough emotional maturity to recognize their own strengths and weaknesses, and have to be oriented toward self-improvement. Furthermore, to be trusted, they must have authenticity; without trust, they cannot hope to maintain the loyalty of their followers. Leaders are not easily discouraged, and they stick to a chosen

> • **Trait perspectives** assume that traits play a central role in differentiating between leaders and nonleaders or in predicting leader or organizational outcomes.

Energy and adjustment or stress tolerance: Physical vitality and emotional resilience

Prosocial power motivation: A high need for power exercised primarily for the benefit of others

Achievement orientation: Need for achievement, desire to excel, drive to success, willingness to assume responsibility, concern for task objectives

Emotional maturity: Well-adjusted, does not suffer from severe psychological disorders

Self-confidence: General confidence in self and in the ability to perform the job of a leader

Integrity: Behavior consistent with espoused values; honest, ethical, trustworthy

Perseverance or tenacity: Ability to overcome obstacles; strength of will

Cognitive ability, intelligence, social intelligence: Ability to gather, integrate, and interpret information; intelligence, understanding of social setting

Task-relevant knowledge: Knowledge about the company, industry, and technical aspects

Flexibility: Ability to respond appropriately to changes in the setting

➜ **Positive Impact on Leadership Success**

Figure 13.1 Traits with positive implications for successful leadership.

course of action as they push toward goal accomplishment. At the same time, they must be able to deal with the large amount of information they receive on a regular basis. They do not need to be brilliant, but usually exhibit above-average intelligence. In addition, leaders have a good understanding of their social setting and possess extensive knowledge concerning their industry, firm, and job.

Even with these traits, however, the individual still needs to be engaged. To lead is to influence others, and so we turn to the question of how a leader should act.

Behavioral Leadership Perspectives

• The **behavioral perspective** assumes that leadership is central to performance and other outcomes.

How should managerial leaders act toward subordinates? The **behavioral perspective** assumes that leadership is central to performance and other outcomes. However, instead of underlying traits, behaviors are considered. Two classic research programs—at the University of Michigan and at the Ohio State University—provide useful insights into leadership behaviors.

Michigan Studies　In the late 1940s, researchers at the University of Michigan sought to identify the leadership pattern that results in effective performance. From interviews of high- and low-performing groups in different organizations, the researchers derived two basic forms of leader behaviors: employee-centered and production-centered. Employee-centered supervisors are those who place strong emphasis on their subordinates' welfare. In contrast, production-centered supervisors are more concerned with getting the work done. In general, employee-centered supervisors were found to have more productive workgroups than did the production-centered supervisors.[8]

These behaviors are generally viewed on a continuum, with employee-centered supervisors at one end and production-centered supervisors at the other. Sometimes, the more general terms *human-relations oriented* and *task oriented* are used to describe these alternative leader behaviors.

Ohio State Studies　At about the same time as the Michigan studies, an important leadership research program began at the Ohio State University. A questionnaire was administered in both industrial and military settings to measure subordinates' perceptions of their superiors' leadership behavior. The researchers identified two dimensions similar to those found in the Michigan studies: **consideration** and **initiating structure**.[9] A highly considerate leader was found to be one who is sensitive to people's feelings and, much like the employee-centered leader, tries to make things pleasant for his or her followers. In contrast, a leader high in initiating structure was found to be more concerned with defining task requirements and other aspects of the work agenda; he or she might be seen as similar to a production-centered supervisor. These dimensions are related to what people sometimes refer to as socioemotional and task leadership, respectively.

• A leader high in **consideration** is sensitive to people's feelings.
• A leader high in **initiating structure** is concerned with spelling out the task requirements and clarifying aspects of the work agenda.

At first, the Ohio State researchers believed that a leader high in consideration, or socioemotional warmth, would have more highly satisfied or better performing subordinates. Later results suggested, however, that many individuals in leadership positions should be high in both consideration and initiating structure. This dual emphasis is reflected in the leadership grid approach.

• **Leadership grid** is an approach that uses a grid that places concern for production on the horizontal axis and concern for people on the vertical axis.

The Leadership Grid　Robert Blake and Jane Mouton developed the leadership grid approach based on extensions of the Ohio State dimensions. **Leadership grid** results are plotted on a nine-position grid that places concern for production on the horizontal axis and concern for people on the vertical axis, where 1 is minimum concern and 9 is maximum concern. As an example, those with a 1/9 style—low concern for production and high concern for people—are termed "country club management." They do not emphasize task accomplishment but stress the attitudes, feelings, and social needs of people.[10]

Similarly, leaders with a 1/1 style—low concern for both production and people—are termed "impoverished," while a 5/5 style is labeled "middle of the road." A 9/1 leader—high concern for production and low concern for people—

RESEARCH INSIGHT

Participatory Leadership and Peace

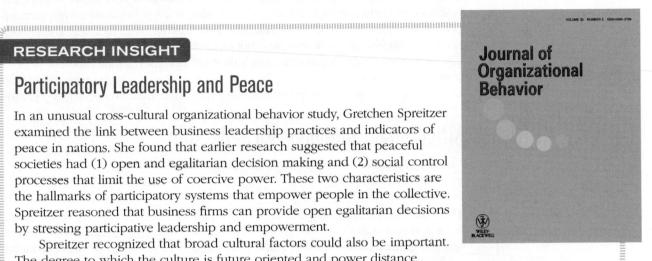

In an unusual cross-cultural organizational behavior study, Gretchen Spreitzer examined the link between business leadership practices and indicators of peace in nations. She found that earlier research suggested that peaceful societies had (1) open and egalitarian decision making and (2) social control processes that limit the use of coercive power. These two characteristics are the hallmarks of participatory systems that empower people in the collective. Spreitzer reasoned that business firms can provide open egalitarian decisions by stressing participative leadership and empowerment.

Spreitzer recognized that broad cultural factors could also be important. The degree to which the culture is future oriented and power distance appeared relevant. And she reasoned that she needed specific measures of peace. She selected two major indicators: (1) the level of corruption and (2) the level of unrest. The measure of unrest was a combined measure of political instability, armed conflict, social unrest, and international disputes. While she found a large leadership database that directly measured participative leadership, she developed the measures of empowerment from another apparently unrelated survey. Two items appeared relevant: the decision freedom individuals reported (decision freedom), and the degree to which they felt they had to comply with their boss regardless of whether they agreed with an order (compliance).

You can schematically think of this research in terms of the following model.

As one might expect with exploratory research, the findings support most of her hypotheses but not all. Participative leadership was related to less corruption and less unrest, as was the future-oriented aspect of culture. Regarding empowerment, there were mixed results; decision freedom was linked to less corruption and unrest, but the compliance measure was only linked to more unrest.

Do the Research   *Do you agree that when business used participatory leadership, it legitimated the democratically based style and increased the opportunity for individuals to express their voice? What other research could be done to determine the link between leadership and peace?*[11]

Source: Gretchen Spreitzer, "Giving Peace a Chance: Organizational Leadership, Empowerment, and Peace," *Journal of Organizational Behavior* 28 (2007), pp. 1077–1095.

has a "task management" style. Finally, a 9/9 leader, high on both dimensions, is considered to have a "team management" style; this is the ideal leader in Blake and Mouton's framework.

Cross-Cultural Implications   It is important to consider whether the findings of the Michigan, Ohio State, and grid studies transfer across national boundaries. Some research in the United States, Britain, Hong Kong, and Japan shows that the behaviors must be carried out in different ways in alternative cultures. For instance, British leaders are seen as considerate if they show subordinates how to use equipment, whereas in Japan the highly considerate leader helps subordinates with personal problems.[12] We will see this pattern again as we discuss other theories. The concept seems to transfer across boundaries, but the actual behaviors differ. Sometimes the differences are slight, but in other cases they are not. Even subtle differences in the leader's situation can make a significant difference in precisely the type of behavior needed for success. Successful leaders adjust their influence attempts to the situation.

Situational Contingency Leadership

LEARNING ROADMAP   Fiedler's Leadership Contingency View / Path-Goal View of Leadership / Hersey and Blanchard Situational Leadership Model / Substitutes for Leadership

The trait and behavioral perspectives assume that leadership, by itself, would have a strong impact on outcomes. Another development in leadership thinking has recognized, however, that leader traits and behaviors can act in conjunction with situational contingencies—other important aspects of the leadership situation—to predict outcomes. Traits are enhanced by their relevance to the leader's situational contingencies.[13] For example, achievement motivation should be most effective for challenging tasks that require initiative and the assumption of personal responsibility for success. Leader flexibility should be most predictive in unstable environments or when leaders lead different people over time.

- **Prosocial power motivation** is power oriented toward benefiting others.

   Prosocial power motivation, or power oriented toward benefiting others, is likely to be most important in situations where decision implementation requires lots of persuasion and social influence. "Strong" or "weak" situations also make a difference. An example of a strong situation is a highly formal organization with lots of rules, procedures, and policies. An example of a weak situation is one that is ambiguous and unstructured. In a strong situation traits will have less impact than in a weaker, more unstructured situation because the leader has less ability to influence the nature of the situation. In other words, leaders can't show dynamism as much when the organization restricts them.

Traits may also make themselves felt by influencing leader behaviors (e.g., a leader high in energy engages in directive, take-charge behaviors).[14] In an attempt to isolate when particular traits and specific combinations of leader behavior and situations are important, scholars have developed a number of situational contingency theories and models. Some of these theories emphasize traits, whereas others deal exclusively with leader behaviors and the setting.

Fiedler's Leadership Contingency View

Fred Fiedler's leadership contingency view argues that team effectiveness depends on an appropriate match between a leader's style, essentially a trait measure, and the demands of the situation.[15] Specifically, Fiedler considers **situational control**—the extent to which a leader can determine what his or her group is going to do—and leader style as important in determining the outcomes of the group's actions and decisions.

To measure a person's leadership style, Fiedler uses an instrument called the **least–preferred co-worker (LPC) scale**. Respondents are asked to describe the person with whom they have been able to work least well—their least preferred co-worker, or LPC—using a series of adjectives such as the following two:

Unfriendly ___ ___ ___ ___ ___ ___ ___ ___ Friendly
         1   2   3   4   5   6   7   8

Pleasant ___ ___ ___ ___ ___ ___ ___ ___ Unpleasant
       1   2   3   4   5   6   7   8

Fiedler argues that high-LPC leaders (those describing their LPC very positively) have a relationship-motivated style, whereas low-LPC leaders have a task-motivated style. Because LPC is a style and does not change across settings, the leaders' actions vary depending on the degree of situational control. Specifically, a task-motivated leader (low LPC) tends to be nondirective in high- and low-control situations, and directive in those in between. A relationship-motivated leader tends to be the opposite. Confused? Take a look at Figure 13.2 to clarify the differences between high-LPC leaders and low-LPC leaders.

Figure 13.2 shows the task-motivated leader as being more effective when the situation is high and low control, and the relationship-motivated leader as being more effective when the situation is moderate control. The figure also shows that Fiedler measures situational control with the following variables:

- Leader-member relations (good/poor)—membership support for the leader
- Task structure (high/low)—spelling out the leader's task goals, procedures, and guidelines in the group
- Position power (strong/weak)—the leader's task expertise and reward or punishment authority

- **Situational control** is the extent to which leaders can determine what their groups are going to do and what the outcomes of their actions are going to be.
- The **least-preferred co-worker (LPC) scale** is a measure of a person's leadership style based on a description of the person with whom respondents have been able to work least well.

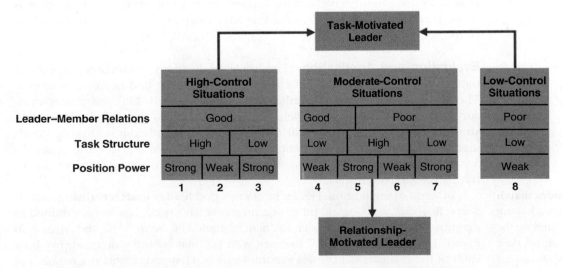

Figure 13.2 Fiedler's situational variables and their preferred leadership styles.

Consider an experienced and well-trained production supervisor of a group that is responsible for manufacturing a part for a personal computer. The leader is highly supported by his group members and can grant raises and make hiring and firing decisions. This supervisor has very high situational control and is operating in situation 1 in Figure 13.2. For such high-control situations, a task-oriented leader style is predicted as the most effective. Now consider the opposite setting. Think of the chair of a student council committee of volunteers who are unhappy about this person being the chair. They have the low-structured task of organizing a Parents' Day program to improve university–parent relations. This low-control situation also calls for a task-motivated leader who needs to behave directively to keep the group together and focus on the task; in fact, the situation demands it. Finally, consider a well-liked academic department chair who is in charge of determining the final list of students who will receive departmental honors at the end of the academic year. This is a moderate-control situation with good leader–member relations, low-task structure, and weak position power, calling for a relationship-motivated leader. The leader should emphasize nondirective and considerate relationships with the faculty.

Fiedler's Cognitive Resource Perspective   Fiedler later developed a cognitive resource perspective that built on his earlier model.[16] Cognitive resources are abilities or competencies. According to this approach, whether a leader should use directive or nondirective behavior depends on the following situational contingencies: (1) the leader's or subordinates' ability or competency, (2) stress, (3) experience, and (4) group support of the leader. Cognitive resource theory is useful because it directs us to leader or subordinate group-member ability, an aspect not typically considered in other leadership approaches.

The theory views directiveness as most helpful for performance when the leader is competent, relaxed, and supported. In this case, the group is ready, and directiveness is the clearest means of communication. When the leader feels stressed, his or her attention is diverted. In this case, experience is more important than ability. If support is low, then the group is less receptive, and the leader has less impact. Group-member ability becomes most important when the leader is nondirective and receives strong support from group members. If support is weak, then task difficulty or other factors have more impact than either the leader or the subordinates.

Evaluation and Application   The roots of Fiedler's contingency approach date back to the 1960s and have elicited both positive and negative reactions. The biggest controversy concerns exactly what Fiedler's LPC instrument measures. Some question Fiedler's behavioral interpretations that link the style measure with leader behavior in all eight conditions. Furthermore, the approach makes the most accurate predictions in situations 1 and 8 and 4 and 5; results are less consistent in the other situations.[17] Tests regarding cognitive resources have shown mixed results.[18]

In terms of application, Fiedler has developed **leader match training**, which Sears, Roebuck and Co. and other organizations have used. Leaders are trained to diagnose the situation in order to "match" their LPC score. The red arrows in Figure 13.2 suggest a "match." In cases with no "match," the training shows how each of these situational control variables can be changed to obtain a match. For instance, a leader with a low LPC and in setting 4 could change the position

• In **leader match training**, leaders are trained to diagnose the situation to match their high and low LPC scores with situational control.

Finding the Leader in You

LOOKING FOR LEADER MATCH AT GOOGLE

The news came as a surprise: Eric Schmidt was out as CEO of Google, and Larry Page was in. Schmidt had been brought in by board of directors in 2001 to provide "adult supervision" to then 27-year-old founders Larry Page and Sergey Brin. For 10 years Google's management structure was described as something of a three-ring circus, with co-founders Larry Page and Sergey Brin running the business behind the scenes, and Schmidt as the public face. Now, the three decided, it was time for Page to take the stage.

"For the last 10 years, we have all been equally involved in making decisions. This triumvirate approach has real benefits in terms

of shared wisdom, and we will continue to discuss the big decisions among the three of us. But we have also agreed to clarify our individual roles so there's clear responsibility and accountability at the top of the company," said Eric Schmidt.

The objective is to simplify the management structure and speed up decision making. "Larry will now lead product development and technology strategy, his greatest strengths . . . and he will take charge of our day-to-day operations as Google's Chief Executive Officer," according to Schmidt.

That leaves Sergey Brin, with title of co-founder, to focus on strategic projects and new products, and Schmidt to serve as executive

chairman, working externally on deals, partnerships, customers, and government outreach. As described on the official Google blog, "We are confident that this focus will serve Google and our users well in the future."

In many ways, Page is taking over at an ideal time. Google's business is doing well, with the company reporting revenues of $29.3 billion, up 24 percent from the year before and profits soaring. But the concern isn't for the present; it is for the future. As reported in *Newsweek,* "there has been a gnawing sense that Google's best days may be behind it." Google is facing tough competition from Facebook and Microsoft, and has been losing top talent to younger tech shops.

Page's job is clear: *Shake things up and knock loose some new ideas.* But it's a risky move. As reported in *Newsweek,* "Page is a computer scientist, not a business strategist. And not all founders make great leaders. Page is no Steve Jobs."

Steve Jobs or not, Page is a brilliant entrepreneur who has been heavily involved in running the business and gets along well with the engineers. The question now is whether the new leadership structure will work, and if Google has found its match between leader capabilities and company needs.

power to strong and gain a "match." Another way of getting a match is through leader selection or placement based on LPC scores.[19] For example, a low LPC leader would be selected for a position with high situational control, as in our earlier example of the manufacturing supervisor. A number of studies have been designed to test this leader match training. Although they are not uniformly supportive, more than a dozen such tests have found increases in group effectiveness following the training.[20]

We conclude that although unanswered questions concerning Fiedler's contingency theory remain, especially concerning the meaning of LPC, the perspective and the leader match program have relatively strong support.[21] The approach and training program are especially useful in encouraging situational contingency thinking.

Path-Goal View of Leadership

Another well-known approach to situational contingencies is one developed by Robert House based on the earlier work of others.[22] House's **path-goal view of managerial leadership** has its roots in the expectancy model of motivation discussed in Chapter 5. The term *path-goal* is used because of its emphasis on how a leader influences subordinates' perceptions of both work goals and personal goals, and the links, or paths, found between these two sets of goals.

The theory assumes that a leader's key function is to adjust his or her behaviors to complement situational contingencies, such as those found in the work setting. House argues that when the leader is able to compensate for things lacking in the setting, subordinates are likely to be satisfied with the leader. For example, the leader could help remove job ambiguity or show how good performance could lead to an increase in pay. Performance should improve as the paths by which (1) effort leads to performance—expectancy—and (2) performance leads to valued rewards—instrumentality—become clarified.

House's approach is summarized in Figure 13.3. The figure shows four types of leader behavior (directive, supportive, achievement-oriented, and participative) and two categories of situational contingency variables (follower attributes and work-setting attributes). The leader behaviors are adjusted to complement the situational contingency variables in order to influence subordinate satisfaction, acceptance of the leader, and motivation for task performance.

Before delving into the dynamics of the House model, it is important to understand each component. **Directive leadership** has to do with spelling out the subordinates' tasks; it is much like the initiating structure mentioned earlier. **Supportive leadership** focuses on subordinate needs and well-being and on promoting a friendly work climate; it is similar to consideration. **Achievement-oriented leadership** emphasizes setting challenging goals, stressing excellence in performance, and showing confidence in the group members' ability to achieve high standards of performance. **Participative leadership** focuses on consulting with subordinates, and seeking and taking their suggestions into account before making decisions.

Margin notes

• **Path-goal view of managerial leadership** assumes that a leader's key function is to adjust his or her behaviors to complement situational contingencies.

• **Directive leadership** spells out the what and how of subordinates' tasks.

• **Supportive leadership** focuses on subordinate needs, well-being, and promotion of a friendly work climate.

• **Achievement-oriented leadership** emphasizes setting goals, stressing excellence, and showing confidence in people's ability to achieve high standards of performance.

• **Participative leadership** focuses on consulting with subordinates and seeking and taking their suggestions into account before making decisions.

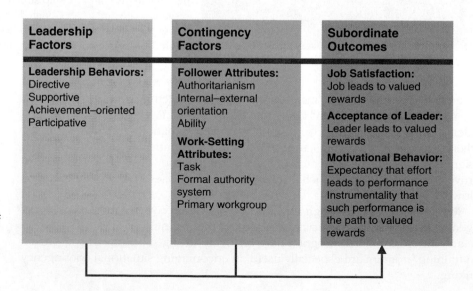

Figure 13.3 Summary of major path-goal relationships in House's leadership approach.

Important subordinate characteristics are *authoritarianism* (close-mindedness, rigidity), *internal-external orientation* (i.e., locus of control), and *ability*. The key work-setting factors are the nature of the subordinates' tasks (task structure), the *formal authority system*, and the *primary workgroup*.

Predictions from Path-Goal Theory   Directive leadership is predicted to have a positive impact on subordinates when the task is ambiguous; it is predicted to have just the opposite effect for clear tasks. In addition, the theory predicts that when ambiguous tasks are being performed by highly authoritarian and closed-minded subordinates, even more directive leadership is called for.

Supportive leadership is predicted to increase the satisfaction of subordinates who work on highly repetitive tasks or on tasks considered to be unpleasant, stressful, or frustrating. In this situation the leader's supportive behavior helps compensate for adverse conditions. For example, many would consider traditional assembly-line jobs to be highly repetitive, perhaps even unpleasant or frustrating. A supportive supervisor could help make these jobs more enjoyable. Achievement-oriented leadership is predicted to encourage subordinates to strive for higher performance standards and to have more confidence in their ability to meet challenging goals. For subordinates in ambiguous, nonrepetitive jobs, achievement-oriented leadership should increase their expectations that effort leads to desired performance.

Participative leadership is predicted to promote satisfaction on nonrepetitive tasks that allow for the ego involvement of subordinates. For example, on a challenging research project, participation allows employees to feel good about dealing independently with the demands of the project. On repetitive tasks, open-minded or nonauthoritarian subordinates will also be satisfied with a participative leader. On a task where employees screw nuts on bolts hour after hour, for example, those who are nonauthoritarian will appreciate having a leader who allows them to get involved in ways that may help break up the monotony.

Evaluation and Application   House's path-goal approach has been with us for more than 30 years. Early work provided some support for the theory in general and for the particular predictions discussed earlier.[23] However, current assessments by well-known scholars have pointed out that many aspects have not been tested adequately, and there is very little current research concerning the theory.[24] House recently revised and extended path-goal theory into the theory of work-unit leadership. It's beyond our scope to discuss the details of this new theory, but as a base the new theory expands the list of leader behaviors beyond those in path-goal theory, including aspects of both leadership theory and emerging challenges of leadership.[25] It remains to be seen how much research it will generate.

In terms of application there is enough support for the original path-goal theory to suggest two possibilities. First, training could be used to change leadership behavior to fit the situational contingencies. Second, the leader could be taught to diagnose the situation and learn how to try to change the contingencies, as in leader match.

Hersey and Blanchard Situational Leadership Model

Like other situational contingency approaches, the **situational leadership model** developed by Paul Hersey and Kenneth Blanchard indicates that there is

• The **situational leadership model** focuses on the situational contingency of maturity or "readiness" of followers.

OB IN POPULAR CULTURE

PATH-GOAL AND *REMEMBER THE TITANS*

A leader following the **Path-Goal View** will adjust her or his style in response to a number of situations that may exist. If followers lack ability, a directive style might be used. If the work is unpleasant, a supportive approach is needed. Achievement-oriented and participative styles can be used to increase follower motivation. A leader must be aware of the conditions that exist and help clear the paths that lead followers to achieve goals (both individual and organizational).

In *Remember the Titans,* legendary Coach Herman Boone (Denzel Washington) has a daunting task. In assuming the position of head football coach at the newly integrated T.C. Williams High School, he demonstrates Path-Goal leadership. Boone knows that many of the players will not respect a "colored" coach. When it comes to practice, he uses a very directive leadership style—my way or else, get the plays right or expect to run. At the same time, he respects the difficulties his players face. When Louie Lastik (Ethan Suplee) says he does not have the grades to go to college, Boone whispers that they will work on his grades together because he does not want that to keep Lastik from going to college. "Let's just keep that between you and me," he adds at the end.

Herman Boone clearly knew when to be tough and when to use a softer, more understanding approach. He was clearly the leader, making tough decisions even in situations involving assistant coaches and star players. Still, he recognized the impact his leadership would have on the lives of the young men who played for him.

> *Get to Know Yourself Better*   Coach Boone was an effective coach because he knew what it took to get a team in shape and meet the individual needs of his players. What about you? Complete Assessment 11, Leadership Style, in the OB Skills Workbook to see if your concern for task is balanced in terms of your concern for people. Too much emphasis on one aspect over the other could lead to problems. Can you show enough concern for individuals and still keep them focused on getting the job done?

no single best way to lead.[26] Hersey and Blanchard focus on the situational contingency of maturity, or "readiness," of followers, in particular. Readiness is the extent to which people have the ability and willingness to accomplish a specific task. Hersey and Blanchard argue that "situational" leadership requires adjusting the leader's emphasis on task behaviors—for instance, giving guidance and direction—and relationship behaviors—for example, providing socioemotional support—according to the readiness of followers to perform their tasks. Figure 13.4 identifies four leadership styles: delegating, participating, selling, and telling. Each emphasizes a different combination of task and relationship behaviors by the leader. The figure also suggests the following situational matches as the best choice of leadership style for followers at each of four readiness levels.

A "telling" style (S1) is best for low follower readiness (R1). The direction provided by this style defines roles for people who are unable and unwilling to take responsibility themselves; it eliminates any insecurity about the task that must be done.

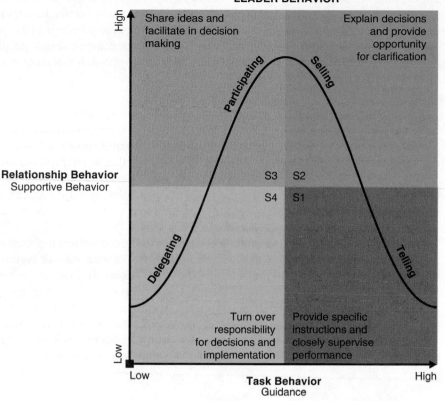

LEADER BEHAVIOR

High

Share ideas and facilitate in decision making

Explain decisions and provide opportunity for clarification

Participating

Selling

Relationship Behavior
Supportive Behavior

S3   S2

S4   S1

Delegating

Telling

Low

Turn over responsibility for decisions and implementation

Provide specific instructions and closely supervise performance

Low   **Task Behavior**   High
Guidance

Follower Readiness

R4	R3	R2	R1
Able and Willing or Confident	Able but Unwilling or Insecure	Unable but Willing or Confident	Unable or Unwilling or Insecure

Figure 13.4 Hersey and Blanchard model of situational leadership.

A "selling" style (S2) is best for low-to-moderate follower readiness (R2). This style offers both task direction and support for people who are unable but willing to take task responsibility; it involves combining a directive approach with explanation and reinforcement in order to maintain enthusiasm.

A "participating" style (S3) is best for moderate-to-high follower readiness (R3). Able but unwilling followers require supportive behavior in order to increase their motivation; by allowing followers to share in decision making, this style helps enhance the desire to perform a task.

A "delegating" style (S4) is best for high readiness (R4). This style provides little in terms of direction and support for the task at hand; it allows able and willing followers to take responsibility for what needs to be done.

This situational leadership approach requires that the leader develop the capability to diagnose the demands of situations and then choose and implement the appropriate leadership response. The model gives specific attention to followers and their feelings about the task at hand and suggests that effective leaders focus on emerging changes in the level of readiness of the people involved in the work.

In spite of its considerable history and incorporation into training programs by a large number of firms, this situational leadership approach has received very little systematic research attention.[27]

Substitutes for Leadership

A final situational contingency approach is leadership substitutes.[28] Scholars using this approach have developed a perspective indicating that sometimes managerial leadership makes essentially no difference. These researchers contend that certain individuals, jobs, and organization variables can serve as substitutes for leadership or neutralize a managerial leader's impact on subordinates. Some examples of these variables are shown in Figure 13.5.

Substitutes for leadership make a leader's influence either unnecessary or redundant in that they replace the leader's influence. For example, in Figure 13.5 it will be unnecessary and perhaps impossible for a leader to provide the kind of task-oriented direction already available from an experienced, talented, and well-trained subordinate. In contrast, neutralizers can prevent a leader from behaving in a certain way or nullify the effects of a leader's actions. If a leader has little formal authority or is physically separated, for example, his or her leadership may be neutralized even though task supportiveness may still be needed.

> • **Substitutes for leadership** make a leader's influence either unnecessary or redundant in that they replace a leader's influence.

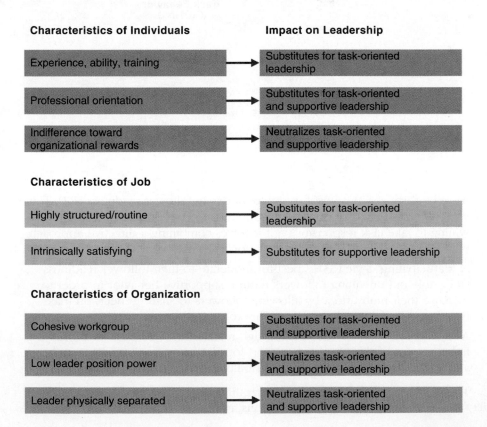

Figure 13.5 Some examples of leadership substitutes and neutralizers.

Research suggests some support for the general notion of substitutes for leadership.[29] First, studies involving Mexican, U.S., and Japanese workers suggests both similarities and differences between various substitutes in the countries examined. Again, there were subtle but important differences across the national samples. Second, a systematic review of 17 studies found mixed results for the substitutes theory. The review suggested a need to broaden the list of substitutes and leader behaviors. It was also apparent that the approach is especially important in examining self-directed work teams. In such teams, for example, in place of a hierarchical leader specifying standards and ways of achieving goals (task-oriented behaviors), the team might set its own standards and substitute them for those of the leader's.

Central to the substitutes for leadership perspective is the question of whether leadership makes a difference at all levels of the organization. At least one researcher has suggested that at the very top of today's complex firms, the leadership of the CEO makes little difference compared to environmental and industry forces.[30] These leaders are typically accountable to so many groups of people for the resources they use that their leadership impact is greatly constrained, so the argument goes. Instead of a dramatic and an important effect, much of the impact a top leader has is little more than symbolic. Further, much of what is described as CEO leadership is actually part of explanations to legitimize their actions.

Such symbolic treatment of leadership occurs particularly when performance is either extremely high or extremely low or when the situation is such that many people could have been responsible for the performance. The late James Meindl and his colleagues call this phenomenon the **romance of leadership**, whereby people attribute romantic, almost magical, qualities to leadership.[31] Consider the firing of a baseball manager or football coach whose team does not perform well. Neither the owner nor anyone else is really sure why the poor showing occurred. But the owner can't fire all the players, so a new team manager is brought in to symbolize "a change in leadership" that is "sure to turn the team around."

• **Romance of leadership** involves people attributing romantic, almost magical, qualities to leadership.

Follower-Centered Approaches

LEARNING ROADMAP   Implicit Leadership Theories / Implicit Followership Theories

So far we have dealt with leader traits, leader behavior, and the situations facing the leader and his or her subordinates. But what about followers and their part in the leadership process? Interestingly, until very recently, issues of followership have been largely ignored in leadership research. It seems that our fascination with leaders has caused us to overlook the importance of followers. As discussed in this section, this issue is addressed in cognitive approaches to leadership, but is also becoming its own field of study in newly emerging work on followership.

Implicit Leadership Theories (ILTs)

In the mid-1970s, Dov Eden and Uri Leviatan[32] wrote an article in which they concluded that "leadership factors are in the mind of the respondent." This radical idea sparked what is known as the *cognitive revolution* in leadership, in which researchers recognized that if leadership resides in the minds of followers, then it is imperative to discover what followers are thinking.[33]

Scholars began using cognitive categorization theory to learn more about how followers process information regarding leaders.[34] Recall from Chapter 4 on perception and attribution that cognitive categorization is a type of mental shortcut that helps us simplify our cognitive understanding of the world by attaching labels when we are faced with a stimulus target. For example, think about your first day of class. Did you look around the room and find yourself making assessments of the teacher, and even your classmates? Were your assessments accurate? This is the process of cognitive categorization, and it occurs automatically and spontaneously when individuals categorize others on the basis of visually salient cues (e.g., age, race, gender, and appearance) and social roles (e.g., leader and follower). We do it because it helps us process and act on information quickly and easily.

Leadership Categorization Theory In leadership research, these ideas developed into leadership categorization theory. According to this theory, individuals naturally classify people as leaders or nonleaders using implicit theories. **Implicit leadership theories** are preconceived notions about the attributes (e.g., traits and behaviors) associated with leaders.[35] They reflect the structure and content of "cognitive categories" used to distinguish leaders from nonleaders.

These attributes, or leadership **prototypes**, are mental images of the characteristics that make a "good" leader, or that a "real" leader would possess. Individuals engage in a two-stage categorization process.[36] First, relevant prototypes, such as those shown in Table 13.1, are activated and the target person is compared with the prototype. Second, the target person is categorized as a leader or nonleader depending on the fit with the prototype.

For example, think of someone you consider to be a great leader. Make a list of attributes you associate with that person as a leader. These images that come to mind represent your implicit theory of leadership. The words you listed represent your "prototypes" for effective leadership. Now look at Table 13.1. Are the attributes you listed in the table? Chances are they are in the list, which is a measure of the implicit leadership theories developed in research by Lynn Offermann and colleagues.[38]

* **Implicit leadership theories** are preconceived notions about the attributes associated with leaders that reflect the structure and content of "cognitive categories" used to distinguish leaders from nonleaders.
* **Prototypes** are a mental image of the characteristics that comprise an implicit theory.

Table 13.1 Implicit Leadership Theories Prototypes

Prototype	Description
Sensitivity	Sympathetic, sensitive, compassionate, understanding
Dedication	Dedicated, disciplined, prepared, hard-working
Tyranny	Domineering, power-hungry, pushy, manipulative
Charisma	Charismatic, inspiring, involved, dynamic
Attractiveness	Attractive, classy, well-dressed, tall
Masculinity	Male, masculine
Intelligence	Intelligent, clever, knowledgeable, wise
Strength	Strong, forceful, bold, powerful

Source: Offermann, L. R., Kennedy, John K., Jr., & Wirtz, P. W. (1994). Implicit leadership theories: Content, structure, and generalizability. *Leadership Quarterly, 5,* 43–58.

Through sampling individuals about their implicit theories, research has identified eight predominant factors, both positive and negative, in peoples' images of leaders: sensitivity, dedication, tyranny, charisma, attractiveness, masculinity, intelligence, and strength. The prototypes show that people view leaders in a positive fashion and hold them to high standards. However, the negative prototypes also reveal that people recognize the possibility for leaders, who are in positions of power, to use that power negatively, such as to dominate, control, and manipulate others.

Since these factors were developed from an American sample, we should expect differences in prototypes by country and by national culture. For example, a typical business leader prototype in Japan is described as responsible, educated, trustworthy, intelligent, and disciplined, whereas the counterpart in the United States is portrayed as determined, goal-oriented, verbally skilled, industrious, and persistent.[39] More in-depth insights on such prototypes, as related to culture, are provided by the broadscale Project GLOBE discussed in the next chapter.

Implicit Followership Theories

Although research on implicit theories has been around since the early 1980s, it wasn't until 2010 that these ideas were applied to followers. This work is now rapidly developing as the study of followership. **Followership** is defined as the behaviors of individuals acting in relation to leaders.[40] To understand these behaviors, researchers are investigating whether an association exists between followers' implicit theories and the nature of their interactions with leaders.

Followership Categorization Theory Paralleling the approach described earlier in leadership categorization theory, Dr. Thomas Sy developed a measure of **implicit followership theory** (IFT) that we can refer to as followership categorization theory.[41] Again using the concept of implicit theories, this research gathered the prototypical behavior of followers as described by leaders.

Using a sample of managers, the investigator asked leaders to identify characteristics associated with effective followers, ineffective followers, and subordinates. He then analyzed the responses to see whether categories of prototypes emerged. The result, as shown in Table 13.2, is an 18-item implicit followership

• **Followership** is defined as the behaviors of individuals acting in relation to leaders.

• **Implicit followership theories** are preconceived notions about prototypical and antiprototypical followership behaviors and characteristics.

Table 13.2 Implicit Followership Theories Prototypes and Antiprototypes

Prototypical/ Antiprototypical	Category	Description
Prototypical	Industry	Hardworking, Productive, Goes above and beyond
Prototypical	Enthusiasm	Excited, Outgoing, Happy
Prototypical	Good Citizen	Loyal, Reliable, Team player
Antiprototypical	Conformity	Easily influenced, Follows trends, Soft spoken
Antiprototypical	Insubordination	Arrogant, Rude, Bad Tempered
Antiprototypical	Incompetence	Uneducated, Slow, Inexperienced

Source: Sy, T. (2010). What do you think of followers? Examining the content, structure, and consequences of implicit followership theories. *Organizational Behavior and Human Decision Processes, 113*(2), 73–84.

theory (IFT) scale that contains two main factors: followership prototype and followership antiprototype. Followership prototype consists of factors associated with good followers, including being "industrious," having enthusiasm, and being a good organizational citizen. Followership antiprototype consists of behaviors associated with ineffective followership, including conformity, insubordination, and incompetence.

Although this work is very new, it has important practical implications. For example, if we think about leaders and recognize they have implicit theories of followers represented by follower prototypes, these prototypes may play a key role in shaping leaders' judgments of and reactions to followers. Remember that categorization processes are spontaneous and automatic. This suggests that leaders make assessments of followers very quickly and very early on in the relationship. Followers who fulfill leaders' prototypes will be judged more positively than those who match the follower antiprototype. It could also be that leaders' implicit followership theories (IFTs) may predispose them to certain socioemotional experiences. For example, leaders who endorse more prototypic perceptions of followers may be more likely to generate more positive affective tones in their workgroups, whereas leaders who endorse more antiprototypic perceptions of followers may generate more negative emotion with the group.

The Social Construction of Followership

- **Social construction** approaches describe individual behavior as "constructed" in context, as people act and interact in situations.

Using a somewhat different approach, Melissa Carsten and colleagues are exploring followership through a lens of "social construction."[42] According to **social construction** approaches, individual behavior is "constructed" in context, as people act and interact in situations. Social constructions are influenced by two things: the individuals' implicit theories about how they *should* act, and the nature of the situation in which they find themselves. For example, have you ever been in situations where you think you should do one thing but find yourself doing another? This is because your implicit belief is interacting with the situation to influence your behavior.

- **Passive followership beliefs** are beliefs that followers should be passive, deferent, and obedient to authority.
- **Proactive followership beliefs** are beliefs that followers should express opinions, take initiative, and constructively question and challenge leaders.

Using a social construction approach, Carsten and colleagues found that followers tend to act in different ways according to their beliefs and the context. Some followers hold **passive beliefs**, viewing their roles in the classic sense of following—as passive, deferential, and obedient to authority (i.e., a passive belief). Others hold **proactive beliefs**, viewing their role as expressing opinions, taking initiative, and constructively questioning and challenging leaders (i.e., a proactive belief). These proactive followership beliefs more closely resemble leading (e.g., followers acting as leaders) than following. Not surprisingly, proactive beliefs were found to be strong among "high potentials"—people who have been identified by their organizations as demonstrating the skills and capabilities to be promoted to higher-level leadership positions in their organization. This makes sense. It suggests that one key to advancement in organizations is being able to demonstrate the ability to lead not only downward, but upward.

Because social construction is dependent on context, findings also show that not everyone is able to act according to their followership beliefs. This occurs when the work environment does not support the belief. Individuals holding proactive beliefs reported they could not be proactive when they were operating in authoritarian or bureaucratic work climates because these environments suppressed their ability to take the initiative and speak up. In this environment they were frustrated—they felt stifled and were not able to work to their potential.

Alternatively, individuals with passive beliefs reported cases where an empowering climate encouraged them to offer ideas and opinions, but these situations were uncomfortable because their natural inclinations as followers were to follow rather than be empowered. They were stressed by leaders' demands that they be more proactive, and weren't comfortable engaging in those behaviors. These cases of mismatch created dissonance for these individuals, leading to varying levels of stress and discontent.

Although this work is still developing, similar to discussions of the importance of person–job fit, when the mismatch between one's followership beliefs and the work context is ongoing and pervasive it is likely to create strong feelings of dissonance. These feelings can be detrimental to workplace functioning, such as making one dissatisfied or highly stressed in their job, and potentially leading to high levels of burnout.

Inspirational and Relational Leadership Perspectives

LEARNING ROADMAP   Charismatic Leadership / Transactional and Transformational Leadership / Leader–Member Exchange Theory

The role of the follower is also considered in inspirational and relational perspectives to leadership. Like follower-centered approaches, these perspectives consider how followers view and interact with leaders.

Charismatic Leadership

One of the reasons leadership is considered so important is simply because most of us think of leaders as highly inspirational individuals—heroes and heroines. We think of prominent individuals who appear to have made a significant difference by inspiring followers to work toward great accomplishments. In the study of leadership, this inspirational aspect has been studied extensively under the notions of charismatic leadership.

Studies of charismatic leadership have provided an extensive body of evidence indicating that **charismatic leaders**, by force of their personal abilities, are capable of having a profound and extraordinary effect on followers.[43] Findings show that charismatic leaders are high in need for power and have high feelings of self-efficacy and conviction in the moral rightness of their beliefs. Their need for power motivates them to want to be leaders, and this need is then reinforced by their conviction of the moral rightness of their beliefs. The feeling of self-efficacy, in turn, makes these individuals believe they are capable of being leaders. These traits also influence such charismatic behaviors as role modeling, image building, articulating simple and dramatic goals, emphasizing high expectations, showing confidence, and arousing follower motives.

Some of the more interesting and important work based on aspects of charismatic theory involves a study of U.S. presidents.[44] The research showed that behavioral charisma was substantially related to presidential performance and that the kind of personality traits described in the theory, along with response to crisis among other things, predicted behavioral charisma for the sample of presidents.[45]

The charisma trait also has a potential negative side as seen in infamous leaders such as Adolf Hitler and Josef Stalin, who had been considered charismatic.

• **Charismatic leaders** are those leaders who are capable of having a profound and extraordinary effect on followers.

Negative, or "dark-side," charismatic leaders emphasize personalized power and focus on themselves—whereas positive, or "bright-side," charismatic leaders emphasize socialized power that tends to positively empower their followers.[46] This helps explain the differences between a dark-side leader such as David Koresh, leader of the Branch Davidian sect, and a bright-side leader such as Martin Luther King Jr.[47]

Jay Conger and Rabindra Kanungo have developed a three-stage charismatic leadership model.[48] In the initial stage the leader critically evaluates the status quo. Deficiencies in the status quo lead to formulations of future goals. Before developing these goals, the leader assesses available resources and constraints that stand in the way of the goals. The leader also assesses follower abilities, needs, and satisfaction levels. In the second stage, the leader formulates and articulates the goals along with an idealized future vision. Here, the leader emphasizes articulation and impression-management skills. Then, in the third stage, the leader shows how these goals and the vision can be achieved. The leader emphasizes innovative and unusual means to achieve the vision.

Martin Luther King Jr. illustrated these three stages in his nonviolent civil rights approach, thereby changing race relations in this country. Conger and Kanungo have argued that if leaders use behaviors such as vision articulation, environmental sensitivity, and unconventional behavior, rather than maintaining the status quo, followers will tend to attribute charismatic leadership to them. Such leaders are also seen as behaving quite differently from those labeled "noncharismatic."[49]

Transactional and Transformational Leadership

Building on notions originated by James MacGregor Burns, as well as on ideas from charismatic leadership theory, Bernard Bass has developed an approach that focuses on both transactional and transformational leadership.[50]

• **Transactional leadership** involves leader–follower exchanges necessary for achieving routine performance agreed upon between leaders and followers.

Transactional Leadership   Transactional leadership involves leader–follower exchanges necessary for achieving routine performance agreed upon between leaders and followers. Transactional leadership is similar to most of the leadership approaches mentioned earlier. These exchanges involve four dimensions:

1. *Contingent rewards*—various kinds of rewards in exchange for mutually agreed-upon goal accomplishment.
2. *Active management by exception*—watching for deviations from rules and standards and taking corrective action.
3. *Passive management by exception*—intervening only if standards not met.
4. *Laissez-faire*—abdicating responsibilities and avoiding decisions.

Transformational leadership goes beyond this routine accomplishment, however. For Bass, transformational leadership occurs when leaders broaden and elevate their followers' interests, when they generate awareness and acceptance of the group's purposes and mission, and when they stir their followers to look beyond their own self-interests to the good of others.

• **Transformational leadership** occurs when leaders broaden and elevate followers' interests and stir followers to look beyond their own interests to the good of others.

Transformational Leadership   Transformational leadership has four dimensions: charisma, inspiration, intellectual stimulation, and individualized consideration.

Charisma provides vision and a sense of mission, and it instills pride along with follower respect and trust. For example, Steve Jobs, who founded Apple Computer, showed charisma by emphasizing the importance of creating the Macintosh as a radical new computer and has since followed up with products such as the iPod, iPhone, and iPad.

Inspiration communicates high expectations, uses symbols to focus efforts, and expresses important purposes in simple ways. As an example, in the movie *Patton*, George C. Scott stood on a stage in front of his troops with a wall-sized American flag in the background and ivory-handled revolvers in holsters at his side. Soldiers were told not to die for their country but make the enemy die for theirs. **Intellectual stimulation** promotes intelligence, rationality, and careful problem solving. For instance, your boss encourages you to look at a very difficult problem in a new way. **Individualized consideration** provides personal attention, treats each employee individually, and coaches and advises. This occurs, for example, when your boss drops by and makes remarks reinforcing your worth as a person.

Bass concludes that transformational leadership is likely to be strongest at the top-management level, where there is the greatest opportunity for proposing and communicating a vision. However, for Bass, it is not restricted to the top level; it is found throughout the organization. Furthermore, transformational leadership operates in combination with transactional leadership. Leaders need both transformational and transactional leadership in order to be successful, just as they need to display both leadership and management abilities.[51]

Reviews have summarized a large number of studies using Bass's transformational approach. These reviews report significant favorable relationships between Bass's leadership dimensions and various aspects of performance and satisfaction, as well as extra effort, burnout and stress, and predispositions to act as innovation champions on the part of followers. The strongest relationships tend to be associated with charisma or inspirational leadership, although in most cases the other dimensions are also important. These findings are consistent with those reported elsewhere.[52] They broaden leadership outcomes beyond those cited in many leadership studies.

Issues in Charismatic and Transformational Leadership In respect to leaders and leadership development, it is reasonable to ask: Can people be trained in charismatic/transformational leadership? According to research in this area, the answer is yes. Bass and his colleagues have put a lot of work into developing such training efforts. For example, they have created a workshop where leaders are given initial feedback on their scores on Bass's measures. The leaders then devise improvement programs to strengthen their weaknesses and work with the trainers to develop their leadership skills. Bass and Avolio report findings that demonstrate the beneficial effects of this training. They also report the effectiveness of team training and programs tailored to individual firms' needs.[53] Similarly, Conger and Kanungo propose training to develop the kinds of behaviors summarized in their model.

Approaches with special emphasis on vision often emphasize training. Kouzes and Posner report results of a week-long training program at AT&T. The program involved training leaders on five dimensions oriented around developing, communicating, and reinforcing a shared vision. According to Kouzes and

- **Charisma** provides vision and a sense of mission, and it instills pride along with follower respect and trust.
- **Inspiration** communicates high expectations, uses symbols to focus efforts, and expresses important purposes in simple ways.
- **Intellectual stimulation** promotes intelligence, rationality and careful problem solving, by for example, encouraging looking at a very difficult problem in a new way.
- **Individualized consideration** provides personal attention, treats each employee individually, and coaches and advises.

ETHICS IN OB

CEO PAY—IS IT EXCESSIVE?

In corporate America today, there seems to be a perception that CEOs have a tremendous influence on company success, whereas workers are more or less interchangeable. In fact, CEO compensation is typically over 260 times greater than the compensation provided to the median full-time employee. A typical CEO will earn more in one workday than the average worker will earn all year.

While the pay gap between top executives and the average American worker has traditionally been relatively large, it has grown tremendously over the past few decades. For the decade 1995–2005, CEO compensation rose nearly 300 percent while the average employee salary rose less than 5 percent—both occurring during a timeframe in which average corporate profits rose by a little over 100 percent.

In support of rising CEO salaries, the argument has been made that companies have to pay a lot to attract the best executive talent and need to pay for performance. However, pay levels are now such that many CEOs are assured of getting rich no matter how the company performs. In fact, over 80 percent of executives receive bonuses even during down years for the stock market.

In the midst of the recent economic downturn, one might expect this gap to be significantly reduced. Surprisingly, though, that has not occurred, and the pay gap remains very high by historical standards. Many people continue to be shocked by the exorbitant salaries and bonuses received by top executives, especially at a time when many companies are laying off employees and freezing salaries among lower-level workers.

An underlying question seems to be whether it is ethical for a company to eliminate hundreds or thousands of jobs while its CEO remains very highly compensated.

What Do You Think? Is it ethical for executives to reap such high rewards when employees are being laid off and shareholders are seeing little to no return on their investment? Should CEO pay be capped at some multiple of the average worker's pay? Should CEOs be forced to take a pay cut during this difficult financial period? What are the consequences (both positive and negative) of unrestricted CEO salaries? If you were the CEO of a company that was struggling financially and was in the process of laying off thousands of employees, would you voluntarily give up some of your compensation?

Posner, leaders showed an average 15 percent increase in these visionary behaviors 10 months after participating in the program.[54] Similarly, Sashkin and Sashkin have developed a leadership approach that emphasizes various aspects of vision and organizational culture change. They discuss a number of ways to train leaders to be more visionary and to enhance cultural change.[55] All of these leadership training programs involve a heavy hands-on workshop emphasis so that leaders do more than just read about vision.

A second issue in leadership and leadership development involves this question: Is charismatic/transformational leadership always good? As pointed out earlier, dark-side charismatics, such as Adolf Hitler, can have a negative effect on followers. Similarly, charismatic/transformational leadership is not always helpful. Sometimes emphasis on a vision diverts energy from more important day-to-day activities. It is also important to note that such leadership by itself is not sufficient. That leadership needs to be used in conjunction with all of the leadership theories discussed in this chapter. Finally, charismatic and transformational leadership is important not only at the top of an organization. A number of experts argue that for an organization to be successful, it must apply at all levels of organizational leadership.

Leader–Member Exchange Theory

While charismatic and inspirational theories emphasize leader behavior, relational leadership theories adopt a different perspective: They view leadership as produced in the *relationship* between leaders and followers. The most prominent of these theories is **leader–member exchange (LMX) theory**.

LMX theory shows that leaders develop differentiated relationships with subordinates in their work groups.[56] Some relationships are high-quality (high LMX) "partnerships," characterized by mutual influence, trust, respect, and loyalty. These relationships are associated with more challenging job assignments, increased leader attention and support, and more open and honest communication. Other relationships are low quality (low LMX), more in line with traditional supervisory relationships. Low-quality relationships are characterized by formal status and strict adherence to rules of the employment contract. They have low levels of interaction, trust, and support.

According to LMX theory, leadership is generated when leaders and followers are able to develop "incremental influence" with one another that produces behavior above and beyond what is required by the work contract. Returning to our discussion of managers and leaders at the beginning of the chapter, we can state that LMX approaches assume that managers are leaders when, through development of high-quality relationships, they are able to generate "willing followership" with subordinates in their work unit.

These differentiated relationships are important for subordinates because they have strong associations with work outcomes.[57] Research shows that high-quality LMX is associated with increased follower satisfaction and productivity, decreased turnover, increased salaries, and faster promotion rates. Low-quality relationships are associated with negative work outcomes, including low job satisfaction and commitment, greater feelings of unfairness, lower performance, and higher stress. Recent discussions of LMX suggest that to generate strong leadership, managers should try to develop high-quality relationships with all subordinates.

The LMX approach continues to receive increasing emphasis in organizational behavior research literature worldwide. The evidence for the benefits of high-quality relationships is robust, and the implications for both managers and employees are quite clear. Relationships matter, and working to develop them— whether you are a leader or a follower—is critical in terms of both organizational and personal career outcomes.

• **Leader–member exchange (LMX) theory** emphasizes the quality of the working relationship between leaders and followers.

13 *study guide*

Key Questions and Answers

What is leadership?

- Leadership is the process of influencing others to understand and agree about what needs to be done and how to do it, and the process of facilitating individual and collective efforts to accomplish shared objectives.

- Leadership and management differ in that management is designed to promote stability or to make the organization run smoothly, whereas the role of leadership is to promote adaptive change.

- Trait or great-person approaches argue that leader traits have a major impact on differentiating between leaders and nonleaders or predicting leadership outcomes.

- Traits are considered relatively innate and hard to change.

- Similar to trait approaches, behavioral theories argue that leader behaviors have a major impact on outcomes.

- The Michigan and Ohio State approaches are important leader behavior theories.

- Leader behavior theories are especially suitable for leadership training.

What is situational contingency leadership?

- Leader situational contingency approaches argue that leadership, in combination with various situational contingency variables, can have a major impact on outcomes.

- The effects of traits are enhanced to the extent of their relevance to the situational contingencies faced by the leader.

- Strong or weak situational contingencies influence the impact of leadership traits.

- Fiedler's contingency theory, House's path-goal theory, Hersey and Blanchard's situational leadership theory, and substitutes for leadership theory are particularly important specific situational contingency approaches.

- Sometimes, as in the case of the substitutes for leadership approach, the role of situational contingencies replaces that of leadership, so that leadership has little or no impact in itself.

What are follower-centered approaches to leadership?

- Follower-centered approaches focus on how followers view leaders and how they view themselves. The former are called implicit leadership theories (ILTs), and the latter are called implicit followership theories (IFTs).

- Implicit leadership theories (ILTs) are part of leadership categorization theory. They describe the cognitive categorization processes individuals use to identify characteristics, or prototypes, of traits and behaviors they associate with leaders (and nonleaders).

- Typical prototypes of leaders are sensitivity, dedication, tyranny, charisma, attractiveness, masculinity, intelligence, and strength. They reflect both the positive and negative elements of leaders.

- Followership is defined as the behaviors of individuals acting in relation to leaders. Followership categorization theory is the study of implicit followership theories that leaders hold of followers.

- Prototypical follower behaviors have been identified as industriousness (e.g., hard-working), having enthusiasm, and being a good citizen. Follower antiprototypes include conformity, insubordination, and incompetence.

- Implicit followership theories have also been studied relative to social constructions of follower roles. Social construction approaches consider individuals' beliefs regarding how they should act and the contexts in which they act.

- Social construction perspectives of followership have identified passive and proactive followership beliefs. Passive beliefs are consistent with classic definitions of followers as obedient, passive, and deferential, while proactive beliefs reflect include expressing opinions, taking the initiative, and constructively challenging leaders.

What are inspirational and relational leadership perspectives?

- Inspirational and relational leadership perspectives focus on how leaders motivate and build relationships with followers to achieve performance beyond expectations.

- Particularly important among inspirational approaches are Bass's transformational/transactional theory and House's and Conger and Kanungo's charismatic perspectives.

- Transformational behaviors include charisma, inspiration, intellectual stimulation, and individualized consideration. Transactional behaviors include contingent reward, management-by-exception, and laissez-faire leadership.

- Charismatic/transformational leadership is not always good, as shown by the example of Adolf Hitler.

- The most prominent relational leadership theory is leader–member exchange (LMX).

- LMX describes how leaders develop relationships with some subordinates that are high quality and some that are low quality. Subordinates in high-quality relationships receive much better benefits and outcomes than those in low-quality LMX.

- The most effective leaders should develop high-quality relationships with all subordinates.

Terms to Know

Achievement-oriented leadership (p. 300)
Behavioral perspective (p. 294)
Charisma (p. 311)
Charismatic leaders (p. 309)
Consideration (p. 294)
Directive leadership (p. 300)
Followership (p. 307)

Implicit followership theories (IFTs) (p. 307)
Implicit leadership theories (ILTs) (p. 306)
Individualized consideration (p. 311)
Initiating structure (p. 294)
Inspiration (p. 311)
Intellectual stimulation (p. 311)

Leader match training (p. 298)
Leader–member exchange (LMX) theory (p. 313)
Leadership (p. 292)
Leadership grid (p. 294)
Least-preferred co-worker (LPC) scale (p. 297)
Participative leadership (p. 300)

Self-Test 13

Multiple Choice

1. Leadership is _____. (a) equivalent to management (b) being in charge (c) the process of influencing others to get things done (d) holding a formal position

2. In comparing leadership and management, _____. (a) leadership promotes stability and management promotes change (b) leadership promotes change and management promotes stability (c) leaders are born but managers are developed (d) the two are pretty much the same

3. The earliest theory of leadership stated that individuals become leaders because of _____. (a) the behavior of those they lead (b) the traits they possess (c) the particular situation in which they find themselves (d) being very tall

4. The behavioral approaches to leadership show that the most common types of leadership behaviors relate to _____. (a) empowering and motivating (b) directing and controlling (c) guiding and visioning (d) relationships and tasks

5. Leadership grid research suggests that the most effective managers are (a) high, high (b) high, low (c) low, high (d) middle of the road

6. Leader traits will have less of an impact in a(n) _____ situation than in a(n) _____ situation. (a) prototypical, antiprototypical (b) implicit, explicit (c) weak, strong (d) favorable, unfavorable

7. A key finding in Fiedler's contingency theory is the importance of _____. (a) leader match (b) implicit theories (c) prosocial power motivation (d) task-oriented leadership behavior

8. Path-goal has its roots in the _____ theory of motivation. (a) hierarchy (b) equity (c) manifest need (d) expectancy

9. Substitutes for leadership research suggests that in certain situations leadership _____. (a) has no substitutes (b) is contingent upon traits (c) makes no difference (d) substitutes for management

10. When followers attribute superior qualities to leaders, it is referred to as _____. (a) substitutes for leadership (b) romance of leadership (c) implicit leadership theories (d) follower-centered approaches to leadership

11. The idea that leadership resides in the minds of followers represents the _____ in leadership. (a) cognitive revolution (b) contingency approach (c) behavioral approach (d) substitutes neutralizer

12. _____ is defined as the behaviors of individuals acting in relation to leaders. (a) Subordination (b) Prototyped (c) Implicit theory (d) Followership

13. Conformity, insubordination, and incompetence represent followership _____. (a) prototypes (b) antiprototypes (c) social construction (d) dissonance

14. Findings regarding charismatic leadership indicate that _____. (a) anyone can be a charismatic leader (b) charisma is the most desirable leadership style (c) there is a potential negative side to charismatic leadership (d) charismatics are found to have the best interests of followers in mind

15. Research showing that leaders develop differentiated relationship with followers is known as _____. (a) leader-member exchange theory (b) transformational leadership theory (c) transactional leadership theory (d) follower-centered theory

Short Response

16. Define "leadership" and contrast it with "management."

17. How do situational contingency theories relate to behavioral approaches to leadership theory?

18. Describe the difference between transactional and transformational theories of leadership.

19. What are the characteristics of low and high LMX relationships?

Applications Essay

20. Your manager at work just called you into the office to inform you that you are being promoted to supervisor. You are excited and nervous at the same time: You want to do a good job in this position but you are not sure how. Your friend is taking an OB course, so you decided to ask him for advice. What does he tell you?

Next Steps

Top Choices from

The OB Skills Workbook

Cases for Critical Thinking	Team and Experiential Exercises	Self-Assessment Portfolio
• The New Vice President	• Interview a Leader • Leadership Skills Inventories • Leadership and Participation in Decision Making	• Student Leadership Practices Inventory • Least-Preferred Co-worker Scale • Leadership Style • "TT" Leadership Style

Ready About: Don't Lose Your Bearings

Mark Berns has a flair for navigating treacherous waters.

A passionate sailor, Berns also heads Ready About, a consulting firm that guides companies through potentially disruptive changes, such as strategic realignments, mergers, and acquisitions.

Plans for organizational change often look lucrative on paper and meet resounding approval at the highest levels of management. But

> *"If culture is a company's DNA, acquisitions are a bit like gene splicing. You want to combine the best of both worlds so you don't end up with Frankenstein, Inc."*
> *—Mark Berns.*[b]

they can go awry when they fail to account for a company's intangible—but often most valuable—assets. These can include group or corporate culture, operational strategy, and trusted avenues of internal communication. It doesn't help matters if key employees resist the coming change because they resent the strategy or don't have enough information about what's going to happen.

Enter Ready About, named after the command a captain issues to make sure his crew is ready to chart a new course. Berns and his team help organizations thrive before and after big changes. They specialize in organizational strategy, team effectiveness, and mergers and acquisitions.

Whether brought into a company to manage change or keeping in close contact as a consulting partner, Ready About makes sure companies stay watchful of the "soft" assets that bring them value.

Berns himself has been involved in more than 100 acquisitions, and he's quick to emphasize the importance of culture in defining an organization. "I see culture as the story we tell about ourselves," he says. "It's mission, vision, and our relationships with each other and the broader world. It's the all-out company effort to support a food pantry. It's even that we always dress casually and have muffins on Friday."[a]

Quick Summary

- Ready About helps clients manage and survive large organizational changes such as mergers, acquisitions, and strategy realignments.
- Immersed in day-to-day operations, many companies lack the perspective to understand how organizational change will affect their soft assets, such as company culture and successful internal communication.
- Ready About's consulting emphasizes helping companies understand and monitor the health of these resources while managing operational or material change.

FYI: 83% of mergers fail to increase shareholder value.[c]

14 Leadership Challenges and Organizational Change

the key point

Some challenges of leadership and organizational change are quite new; others have been recognized for decades. In leadership, these issues are addressed relative to moral persuasion, cultural differences, and strategy. Moreover, one of the key challenges to leaders, as illustrated in the Ready About chapter opener, is managing change.

chapter at a glance

What Is Moral Leadership?

What Is Shared Leadership?

How Do You Lead Across Cultures?

How Do You Lead Organizational Change?

ETHICS IN OB
COLLEGE ATHLETES MAKE ETHICAL CHOICES

FINDING THE LEADER IN YOU
PATRICIA KARTER USES CORE VALUES AS HER GUIDE

OB IN POPULAR CULTURE
AUTHENTIC LEADERSHIP AND *BRAVEHEART*

RESEARCH INSIGHT
CEO VALUES MAKE A DIFFERENCE

what's inside?

Moral Leadership

LEARNING ROADMAP Authentic Leadership / Spiritual Leadership / Servant Leadership / Ethical Leadership

All of us are aware of recent concerns about moral leadership issues. American International Group (AIG), for example, joined the growing list of firms such as Enron and Merrill Lynch, which at one time had highly questionable leadership. It appears that leaders of various government, religious, and educational entities made decisions based on short-term individual gain rather than long-term collective benefit.

As these problems have gained attention and scrutiny, there has been a stronger emphasis in research on topics including authentic leadership, servant leadership, spiritual leadership, and ethical leadership. These are the topics we will cover in our treatment of moral leadership. Essentially the moral leader is attempting to use transcendent values to stimulate action that is considered beneficial. The challenge of moral leadership starts with who you are and what you think the job of a leader should be.

Authentic Leadership

Authentic leadership essentially argues "know thyself."[1] It involves both owning one's personal experiences (values, thoughts, emotions, and beliefs) and acting in accordance with one's true self (expressing what you really think and believe, and acting accordingly). Although no one is perfectly authentic, authenticity is something to strive for. It reflects the unobstructed operation of one's true or core self. It also underlies virtually all other aspects of leadership, regardless of the particular theory or model involved.

Those high in authenticity are thought to have optimal self-esteem, or genuine, true, stable, and congruent self-esteem, as opposed to fragile self-esteem based on outside responses. Leaders who desire authentic leadership should have genuine relationships with followers and associates and display transparency, openness, and trust.[2] All of these points draw on psychological well-being emphasized in positive psychology literature.[3] For instance, Nelson Mandela is considered an authentic leader.

• **Self-efficacy** is a person's belief that he or she can perform adequately in a situation.

• **Optimism** is the expectation of positive outcomes.

• **Hope** is the tendency to look for alternative pathways to reach a desired goal.

• **Resilience** is the ability to bounce back from failure and keep forging ahead.

In positive psychology we find emphasis on **self-efficacy**, which is an individual's belief about the likelihood of successfully completing a specific task; **optimism**, the expectation of positive outcomes; **hope**, the tendency to look for alternative pathways to reach a desired goal; and **resilience**, the ability to bounce back from failure and keep forging ahead. An increase in any one of these traits is seen as increasing the others. These are important traits for a leader to demonstrate and are believed to positively influence his or her followers.

Perhaps the most important aspect of authentic leadership is the notion that being a leader begins with you and your perspective on leading others. But being authentic is just one aspect of moral leadership. A second feature is your view of the leader's task.

Spiritual Leadership

In contrast to authentic leadership, spiritual leadership can be seen as a field of inquiry within the broader setting of workplace spirituality.[4] Western religious

OB IN POPULAR CULTURE

AUTHENTIC LEADERSHIP AND *BRAVEHEART*

Contemporary leadership styles are based heavily on the values of leaders. **Authentic leadership** exists when a leader knows her or his values and leads in accordance with them. An authentic leader will develop genuine relationships with others. Characteristics associated with this style of leadership include self-efficacy, optimism, hope, and resilience.

Braveheart is an account loosely based on the life of William Wallace, the Guardian of Scotland, who helped liberate Scotland from England. In the movie, nobleman Robert the Bruce (Angus Macfayden), the seventeenth Earl of Scotland, finds out that Wallace (Mel Gibson) has started a rebellion. He reports to his father, who advises him to embrace the movement while he opposes it. Frustrated, the younger Bruce describes Wallace as a commoner who fights with passion and inspires others. When the father suggests a meeting with the nobles, the younger Bruce complains that they are all talk (with no action).

William Wallace brings about change because he fights not for himself, but for the rights of all Scotsmen. He exhibits self-efficacy in his belief that he can defeat the English when others have been unsuccessful. He is optimistic that he can obtain freedom for Scotland—even to the point of death. There is a hope that this freedom will allow fellow Scotsmen to live a life he dreams about. Finally, he is resilient, fighting against incredible odds, including betrayal by the Scottish nobles.

> *Get to Know Yourself Better*   At its core, authentic leadership is about knowing yourself. This requires not only understanding your strengths and weaknesses, but also knowing your core values and acting in line with them. The OB Skills Workbook provides self-assessments that paint a picture of you as a leader. Is your leadership style in accordance with your core values? What factors work against your ability to be authentic as a leader, and how do you deal with these?

theology and practice coupled with leadership ethics and values provide much of the base for the actions of a spiritual leader. As one might expect with a view based on religion, there is considerable disagreement. One key point of contention is whether spirituality and religion are the same. To some, spirituality stems from their religion. For others, it does not. Researchers note that organized religions provide rituals, routines, and ceremonies, thereby providing a vehicle for achieving spirituality. Of course, one could be considered religious by following religious rituals but could lack spirituality, or one could reflect a strong spirituality without being religious.

Even though spiritual leadership does not yet have a strong research base in organizational behavior, there has been some research resulting in the term *Spiritual Leadership Theory*, or *SLT*. It is a causal leadership approach for organizational transformation designed to create an intrinsically motivated, learning organization. Spiritual leadership includes values, attitudes, and behaviors required to intrinsically motivate the leader and others to have a sense of spiritual survival through calling and membership. In other words, the leader and followers experience meaning in their lives, believe they make a difference, and feel understood and appreciated. Such a sense of leader and follower survival tends to create

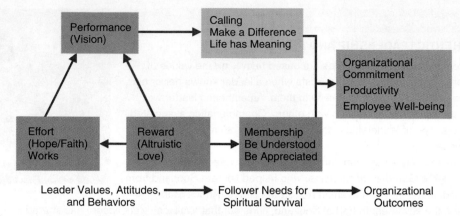

Figure 14.1 Causal model of spiritual leadership theory.
Source: Lewis W. Fry, Steve Vitucci, and Marie Cedillo, "Spiritual Leadership and Army Transformation: Theory, Measurement, and Establishing a Baseline," *The Leadership Quarterly* 16.5 (2005), p. 838.

value congruence across the strategic, empowered team and at the individual level; it ultimately encourages higher levels of organizational commitment, productivity, and employee well-being.

Figure 14.1 summarizes a causal model of spiritual leadership. It shows three core qualities of a spiritual leader: *Vision*—defining the destination and journey, reflecting high ideals, encouraging hope/faith; *Altruistic love*—trust/loyalty as well as forgiveness/acceptance/honesty, courage, and humility; *Hope/Faith*—endurance, perseverance, do what it takes, have stretch goals.

Servant Leadership

Servant leadership, developed by Robert K. Greenleaf, is based on the notion that the primary purpose of business should be to create a positive impact on the organization's employees as well as the community. In an essay he wrote about servant leadership in 1970, Greenleaf said: "The servant-leader *is* servant first. . . . It begins with the natural feeling that one wants to serve, to serve *first*. Then conscious choice brings one to aspire to lead."[5]

The servant leader is attuned to basic spiritual values and, in serving these, assists others including colleagues, the organization, and society. Viewed in this way servant leadership is not a unique example of leadership but rather a special kind of service. The servant leader helps others discover their inner spirit, earns and keeps the trust of their followers, exhibits effective listening skills, and places the importance of assisting others over self-interest. It is best demonstrated by those with a vision and a desire to serve others first rather than by those seeking leadership roles. Servant leadership is usually seen as a philosophical movement, with the support of the Greenleaf Center for Servant Development, an international nonprofit organization founded by Robert K. Greenleaf in 1964 and headquartered in Indiana. The Center promotes the understanding and practice of servant leadership, holds conferences, publishes books and materials, and sponsors speakers and seminars throughout the world.

While servant leadership is not rooted in OB research, its guiding philosophy is consistent with that of the other aspects of moral leadership discussed here. In this case, the power of modeling service is the basis for influencing others. You lead to serve and ask others to follow; their followership then becomes a special form of service.

Ethical Leadership

There is no simple definition of ethical leadership. However, many believe that ethical leadership is characterized by caring, honest, principled, fair, and balanced choices by individuals who act ethically, set clear ethical standards, communicate about ethics with followers, and reward as well as punish others based on ethical or unethical conduct.[6] Figure 14.2 summarizes the similarities and differences among ethical, authentic, spiritual, and transformational leadership. A key similarity cutting across all these dimensions is role modeling. Altruism, or concern for others, and integrity are also important similarities. Leaders influence others by appealing to transcendent values. In terms of differences, authentic leaders stress authenticity and self-awareness and tend to be more transactional than do the other leaders. Ethical leaders emphasize moral concerns, while spiritual leaders stress visioning, hope, and faith, as well as work as a vocation.

Transformational leaders emphasize values, vision, and intellectual stimulation. Taken as a whole, it is clear that any of these related approaches are important and ready for systematic empirical and conceptual development. Even servant leadership would lend itself to further developments.[7] Despite the lack of research, ethical leadership can and should be a driving force for improving today and tomorrow's leaders. Take a look at Ethics in OB for one example.[8]

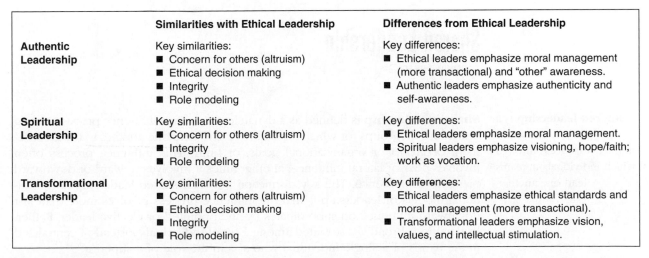

	Similarities with Ethical Leadership	Differences from Ethical Leadership
Authentic Leadership	Key similarities: ■ Concern for others (altruism) ■ Ethical decision making ■ Integrity ■ Role modeling	Key differences: ■ Ethical leaders emphasize moral management (more transactional) and "other" awareness. ■ Authentic leaders emphasize authenticity and self-awareness.
Spiritual Leadership	Key similarities: ■ Concern for others (altruism) ■ Integrity ■ Role modeling	Key differences: ■ Ethical leaders emphasize moral management. ■ Spiritual leaders emphasize visioning, hope/faith; work as vocation.
Transformational Leadership	Key similarities: ■ Concern for others (altruism) ■ Ethical decision making ■ Integrity ■ Role modeling	Key differences: ■ Ethical leaders emphasize ethical standards and moral management (more transactional). ■ Transformational leaders emphasize vision, values, and intellectual stimulation.

Figure 14.2 Similarities and differences between ethical, spiritual, authentic, and transformational theories of leadership.
Source: Michael E. Brown and Linda K. Trevino, "Ethical Leadership: A Review and Future Directions," *The Leadership Quarterly* 17.6 (December 2006), p. 598.

COLLEGE ATHLETES MAKE ETHICAL CHOICES

During a volleyball game, player A hits the ball over the net. The ball barely grazes off player B's fingers and lands out of bounds. However, the referee does not see player B touch the ball. Because the referee is responsible for calling rule violations, player B is not obligated to report the violation and lose the point. Do you "strongly agree," "agree," are "neutral" about, "disagree," or "strongly disagree" that player B should be silent? At an increasing rate, athletes are answering "strongly agree." In other words, winning is more important than fair play.

The above is one example of work conducted by Sharon Stoll, a University of Idaho faculty member and administrator, to see if athletes are as morally developed as the normal population. A 20-year study of some 80,000 high school, college, and professional athletes, showed that the athletes' responses on moral reasoning are less ethical than those of nonathletes. From the time male athletes enter big-time sports, their moral reasoning does not improve and it sometimes declines. The same has also recently become true of female athletes.

As part of a leadership role in this problem, Stoll has developed an educational program as a component of "Winning with Character." The universities of Georgia and Maryland, among other athletic programs, hold weekly group discussions with athletes about ethical problem areas.

> ***Make Ethics Personal***   *Would you expect the ethical response differences between athletes and nonathletes? What kinds of details might you suggest be included in the weekly group discussions?*

Shared Leadership

LEARNING ROADMAP   Shared Leadership in Work Teams / Shared Leadership and Self-Leadership

• **Shared leadership** is a dynamic, interactive influence process through which individuals in teams lead one another.

Shared leadership is defined as a dynamic, interactive influence process among individuals in groups for which the objective is to lead one another to the achievement of group or organizational goals, or both. This influence process often involves peer or lateral influence; at other times it involves upward or downward hierarchical influence. The key distinction between shared leadership and traditional models of leadership is that the influence process involves more than just downward influence on subordinates by an appointed or elective leader. Rather, leadership is broadly distributed among a set of individuals instead of centralized in the hands of a single individual who acts in the role of a superior.[9]

Shared Leadership in Work Teams

So far our treatment of leadership has tended to treat it as vertical influence. The notion of vertical leadership is best depicted by the old Westerns of Hollywood fame. A single rider wearing a white hat and riding a white horse—the bad guys wear black hats and ride black horses—arrives in town. The townsfolk are passive and docile while they stand by and watch as the hero cleans up the town, eliminates the bad guys, and declares, "My work here is done." You should recognize that leadership is not restricted to the vertical influence of the lone figure in a white hat but extends to other people as well. Shared and vertical leadership can be more specifically illustrated in terms of self-directing work teams.

Locations of Shared Leadership Leadership can come from outside or inside the team. Within a team, leadership can be assigned to one person, rotate across team members, or even be shared simultaneously as different needs arise across time.[10] Outside the team, leaders can be traditional, formally designated, first-level supervisors, or outside vertical (top down) leaders of a self-managing team whose duties tend to be quite different from those of a traditional supervisor. Often these nontraditional leaders are called coordinators or facilitators. A key part of their job is to provide resources to their unit and serve as a liaison with other units, all without the authority trappings of traditional supervisors. Here, team members tend to carry out traditional managerial/leadership functions internal to the team along with direct performance activities.

The activities or functions vary and could involve a designated team role or even be defined more generally as a process to facilitate shared team performance. In the latter case, you are likely to see job rotation activities, along with skill-based pay, where workers are paid for the mix and depth of skills they possess as opposed to the skills of a given job assignment they might hold.

Desired Shared Conditions The key element to successful team performance is to create and maintain conditions for that performance. Although a wide variety of characteristics may be important for the success of a specific effort, five important characteristics have been identified across projects: (1) efficient, goal-directed effort; (2) adequate resources; (3) competent, motivated performance; (4) a productive, supportive climate; and (5) a commitment to continuous improvement.

Efficient, Goal-Directed Effort The key here is to coordinate the effort both inside and outside the team. Team leaders can play a crucial role and need to coordinate individual efforts with those of the team, as well as team efforts with those of the organization or major subunit. Among other things, such coordination calls for shared visions and goals.

Leaders Unlock Talent Through Diversity

Max DePree is a noted author and former CEO of the innovative furniture maker Herman Miller, Inc. He says "It is fundamental that leaders endorse the concept of persons" and that "this begins with an understanding of the diversity of people's gifts, talents, and skills."

Adequate Resources   Teams rely on their leaders to obtain enough equipment, supplies, and so on to carry out the team's goals. These are often handled by the outside facilitator and almost always involve internal and external negotiations enabling the facilitator to do his or her negotiating outside the team.

Competent, Motivated Performance   Team members need the appropriate knowledge, skills, abilities, and motivation to perform collective tasks well. Leaders may be able to influence team composition so as to enhance shared efficacy and performance. We often see this demonstrated with short-term teams such as task forces.

A Productive, Supportive Climate   Here, we are talking about high levels of cohesiveness, mutual trust, and cooperation among team members. Sometimes these aspects are part of a team's "interpersonal climate." Team leaders contribute to this climate by role-modeling and supporting relationships that build the high levels of cohesion, trust, and collaboration. Team leaders can also work to enhance shared beliefs about team efficacy and collective capability.

Commitment to Continuous Improvement and Adaptation   A successful team should be able to adapt to changing conditions. Again, both internal and external team leaders may play a role. The focus on continuous improvement may be through formal mechanisms. Often, however, teams recognize that a failure to strive for improvement actually results in a deterioration of performance.

Shared Leadership and Self-Leadership

These shared and vertical self-directing team activities tend to encourage self-leadership activities. Self-leadership can help both the individual and the team. All members, at one point or another, are expected to be leaders. Self-leadership represents a portfolio of self-influence strategies that positively influence individual behavior, thought processes, and related activities. Self-leadership activities are divided into three broad categories: behavior-focused, natural-reward, and constructive-thought-pattern strategies.[11]

Behavior-Focused Strategies   Behavior-focused strategies tend to increase self-awareness, leading to the handling of behaviors involving necessary but not always pleasant tasks. These strategies include personal observation, goal setting, reward, self-correcting feedback, and practice. Self-observation involves examining your own behavior in order to increase awareness of when and why you engage in certain behaviors. Such examination identifies behaviors that should be changed, enhanced, or eliminated. Poor performance could lead to informal self-notes documenting the occurrence of unproductive behaviors. Such heightened awareness is a first step toward behavior change.

Self-Rewards   It helps if you, as a team member, set high but reachable goals and provide yourself with rewards when they are reached. Self-rewards can be quite useful in moving behaviors toward goal attainment. Self-rewards can be real (e.g., a steak dinner or a new outfit) or imaginary (imagining a steak dinner or a new outfit). Also, such things as the rehearsal of desired behaviors you know will lead to self-established goals before the actual performance can prove quite

Innocent Protects Its Identity

Coco-Cola invested $44 million in Innocent, the highly regarded British maker of healthy smoothies. Innocent uses recycled bottles, gives 10 percent of profits to charity, and follows ethical marketing practices, all while selling a product consumers love. By not allowing Coke to have a majority stake for its millions, Innocent plans to keep its identity and integrity while gaining the advantages of Coke's global reach.

useful. Rehearsals allow you to perfect skills that will be needed when the actual performance is required.

Constructive Thought Patterns   Constructive thought patterns focus on the creation or alteration of cognitive thought processes. Self-analysis and improvement of belief systems, mental imagery of successful performance outcomes, and positive self-talk can help. Developing a mental image of the necessary actions allows you to think about what needs to be accomplished and how it will be accomplished before the stress of performance takes hold.

These activities can influence and control the team members' thoughts through the use of cognitive strategies designed to facilitate ways of thinking that can positively affect performance. Where these activities occur, they tend to serve as partial substitutes for hierarchical leadership even though they may be encouraged in a shared situation in contrast to a vertical leadership setting.

A final thought is in order before we move on. Leadership should not be restricted to the traditional style of vertical leadership, nor should the focus be primarily on shared leadership. Shared leadership appears in many forms and is often used successfully in combination with vertical leadership. As with a number of the leadership approaches discussed in this book, various contingencies operate that influence the emphasis that should be devoted to each of the leadership perspectives.

Leadership across Cultures

LEARNING ROADMAP   The GLOBE Perspective / Leadership Aspects and Culture / Culturally Endorsed Leadership Matches / Universally Endorsed Aspects of Leadership

At some point in your career you will confront the challenge of cross-cultural leadership. This may come in the form of leading team members from different cultures, or it may come when you are offered your first international assignment. Or it might happen when you are asked to join in a cooperative venture with a foreign-based supplier or distributor. There are a wide variety of approaches to meeting the challenge of cross-cultural leadership. A major research project conducted by an international team of researchers provides an excellent overview of the factors you need to consider. Called Project GLOBE, it outlines the common dimensions of leadership that are important, as well as the significant differences in how effective managers lead in different cultures.

The GLOBE Perspective

Project GLOBE (Global Leadership and Organizational Behavior Effectiveness Research Program) is an ambitious program involving over 17,000 managers from 951 organizations functioning in 62 nations throughout the world. The project, which is led by Robert House, has involved over 140 country co-investigators, as well as a coordinating team and a number of research associates.[12]

The GLOBE approach argues that leadership variables and cultural variables can be meaningfully applied at societal and organizational levels. Congruence between cultural expectations and leadership is expected to yield superior performance. The central assumption behind the model, shown in Figure 14.3, is that the attributes and entities that differentiate a specified culture predict organizational practices, leader attributes, and behaviors that are most often carried out and are most effective in that culture.

A variety of leadership assumptions are evident in the Globe theoretical model as summarized in Figure 14.3. For example, societal cultural norms, values, and practices affect leaders' attributes and behaviors, as do organizational forms, cultures, and practices. Founders and organization members are immersed in their own societal cultures as well as in the prevailing practices in their industries. Societal cultural norms, values, and practices also affect organizational culture and practices. Both societal culture and organizational culture, in turn, influence the culturally endorsed leadership prototype. And leader attributes and behaviors affect organizational forms, cultures, and practices.

Figure 14.3 also shows that acceptance of leaders by followers facilitates leadership effectiveness. Leaders who are not accepted by organization members will find it more difficult and arduous to influence these members than leaders who

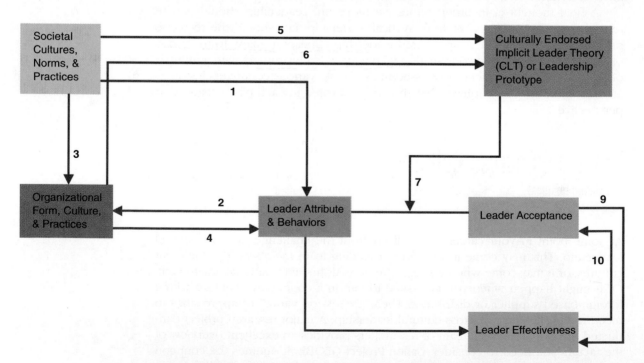

Figure 14.3 A simplified version of the original GLOBE theoretical model.
Source: See Robert J. House, Paul J. Hanges, Mansour Javidan, Peter W. Dorfman, and Vipin Gupta (eds.), *Culture, Leadership, and Organizations* (Thousand Oaks, CA: Sage, 2004).

are accepted. Furthermore, leader effectiveness over time increases leader acceptance. Demonstrated leader effectiveness causes some members to adjust their behaviors toward the leader in positive ways. Those followers who do not accept the leader are likely to leave the organization either voluntarily or involuntarily.

Leadership Aspects and Culture

So far the GLOBE researchers have identified and studied six broad-based dimensions that can be more or less effective in different cultures. These leadership dimensions are as follows.

- *Charismatic/value-based*—the extent to which the leader inspires, motivates, and expects high-performance outcomes
- *Team-oriented*—the degree to which the leader stresses team building and implementation of a common goal among team members
- *Participative*—the degree to which subordinates are involved in making an implementation
- *Humane-oriented*—the degree to which the leader stresses support, consideration, compassion, and generosity
- *Autonomous*—the degree to which the leader stresses independent and individualistic leadership
- *Self-protective*—the degree to which the leader stresses ensuring the safety and security of the individual, self-centered, and face saving

In addition to these leadership dimensions, the GLOBE researchers also identified and studied variations in national cultures. They chose to emphasize cultural aspects known to have some relationship to effective leadership. The presumption was that leaders in different cultures would be required to adjust their approaches to best fit these cultural differences. In other words, effective leadership is based on a good fit of leadership approach and culture. The nine dimensions of societal/cultural used in the GLOBE studies are:

1. *Assertiveness:* assertive, confrontational, and aggressive approaches in relationships versus nonconfrontational approaches
2. *Future orientation:* future-oriented behaviors such as delaying gratification and investing in the future versus a stress on immediate gratification
3. *Gender egalitarianism:* belief that the collective minimizes gender inequality versus asserting major differences by gender
4. *Uncertainty avoidance:* reliance on social norms, rules, and the like to alleviate future unpredictability versus adaptation to rapid change
5. *Power distance:* expectation that power is equally distributed versus large differences in the power of positions and individuals
6. *Institutional collectivism:* organization/society rewards and collective resources/action versus individual rewards
7. *In-group collectivism:* individual's expression of pride, loyalty, and similar attitudes in organizations/families versus individualism
8. *Performance orientation:* the collective's encouragement/reward of group for performance improvement versus rewards for membership
9. *Humane orientation:* the collective encouragement/reward of individuals for being fair, generous, and kind.

Sample Country	Societal Cluster	Leadership Dimensions					
		Charismatic/ Value-Based	Team-Oriented	Partici-pative	Humane-Oriented	Autono-mous	Self-Protective
Russia	Eastern Europe	M	M	L	M	H	H
Argentina	Latin America	H	H	M	M	L	H
France	Latin Europe	H	M	M	L	L	M
China	Confucian Asia	M	H	L	H	M	H
Sweden	Nordic Europe	H	M	H	L	M	L
United States	Anglo	H	M	H	H	M	L
Nigeria	Sub-Saharan Africa	M	M	M	H	L	L
India	Southern Asia	H	H	L	H	M	H
Germany	Germanic Europe	H	L	H	M	H	L
Egypt	Middle East	L	L	L	M	M	H

Figure 14.4 Summary of GLOBE comparisons for culturally endorsed leadership dimensions. *Source:* Mansour Javidan, Peter W. Dorfman, Mary Sully de Luque, and Robert J. House, "In the Eye of the Beholder: Cross Cultural Lessons in Leadership from Project GLOBE," *Academy of Management Perspectives* 20.7 (2006), pp. 67–90.
Note: H = high rank; M = medium rank; L = low rank as a culturally endorsed leadership dimension.

Although each culture has its own unique pattern across these nine dimensions, nations do have enough similarities to be grouped in societal clusters. These clusters often form around geographic areas where there is a common language and an extensive pattern of interaction. For example, Argentina is a member of the Latin American societal cluster, whereas India is a member of the Southern Asian societal cluster. Figure 14.4 shows some of the major societal clusters identified in Project GLOBE and highlights a representative country for each cluster.

Culturally Endorsed Leadership Matches

So far GLOBE researchers have matched cultural and leadership dimensions for over 62 countries and have collapsed them to form 10 geographic clusters. For the six broad-based leadership dimensions, Figure 14.4 shows the degree to which a particular aspect of leadership is endorsed with an H for highly endorsed, an M for moderately endorsed, and an L for not endorsed. Where an emphasis on a specific leadership dimension is matched with an H on a cultural dimension, it is labeled a **culturally endorsed leadership dimension**. This aspect of leadership is characteristic of what individuals in the culture expect from an effective leader.

Perhaps the best way to grasp this complicated perspective is to examine the patterns across the leadership dimensions by cluster in Figure 14.4. For example, in the United States the charismatic dimension is highly endorsed, whereas the protective dimension is not. For team orientation, endorsement is medium. In Russia, the self-protective dimension is culturally endorsed. Note the differences in the degree to which specific dimensions of leadership are endorsed or refuted. For instance, there is a very sharp contrast between the Anglo cluster (of which the United States is a part) and the Middle East.

• A **culturally endorsed leadership dimension** is one that members of a culture expect from effective leaders.

Journal of Organizational Behavior

RESEARCH INSIGHT

CEO Values Make a Difference

Although there has been a lot of discussion about how the values of the CEO impact performance, comparatively few comprehensive studies have been done. Recently, Y. Berson, S. Oreg, and T. Dvir started to remedy this gap with a study of CEO values, organizational culture, and performance. They suggested that individuals are drawn to and stay with organizations that have value priorities similar to their own. That includes the CEO. Furthermore, the CEO reinforces some values over others, and this has a measurable impact on the organizational culture. The organizational culture, then, emphasizes some aspects of performance over others.

The researchers hypothesized and found the following in a study of some 22 CEOs and their firms in Israel: CEOs tend to place a high priority on self-direction or security or benevolence. This priority tends to emphasize a particular type of organizational culture. Specifically, when a CEO values self-direction, there is more cultural emphasis on innovation; when a CEO values security, there is more cultural emphasis on bureaucracy; and when a CEO values benevolence, the culture is more supportive of its members. Then they linked aspects of organizational culture with specific elements of performance (organizational outcomes). More innovation was associated with higher sales growth. A bureaucratic culture was linked to efficiency, while a supportive culture was associated with greater employee satisfaction. In sum, CEO values are linked to organizational culture, which, in turn, is associated with organizational outcomes. Schematically, it looks like this:

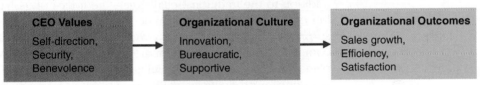

CEO Values	Organizational Culture	Organizational Outcomes
Self-direction, Security, Benevolence	Innovation, Bureaucratic, Supportive	Sales growth, Efficiency, Satisfaction

What Do You Think?   *Do you think this study would transfer to firms located in North America? Is it possible that firms with an established innovative culture select a CEO that values self-direction?*

Source: Yair Berson, Shaul Oreg, and Taly Dvir, "CEO Values, Organizational Culture and Firm Outcomes." *Journal of Organizational Behavior* 29 (2008), pp. 615–633.

Universally Endorsed Aspects of Leadership

Finally, GLOBE seeks to understand which attributes of leadership are universally endorsed. To date, across the sampled countries, some aspects of leadership are associated with effective leadership while others portray ineffective leadership. Leadership described in terms of integrity, charismatic-visionary, charismatic-inspirational, and team-oriented are almost universally endorsed as indications of outstanding leadership. Leadership described in terms of irritability, egocentricity, noncooperativeness, malevolence, as well as being a loner, dictatorial, and ruthless, are identified as indicators of ineffective leadership. Some aspects of leadership were seen as effective in only some national samples and involved characterizing leaders as individualistic, status conscious, risk taking, or self-sacrificing.

The important point to remember is that there are dramatically different expectations for leaders in different cultures. Leading across cultures is far from simple, as this overview of the GLOBE project suggests. Throughout the book we have stressed integrity, and the discussion of shared leadership emphasizes a team orientation. These aspects of leadership appear to be important in most cultures. In many respects the GLOBE perspective on leadership highlights the difficulty in prescribing exactly what a leader should do in our increasingly global economy. As your career progresses and you become more engaged in cross-cultural leadership, it will be important for you to go beyond a universalist view to study cultural expectations. Each culture is unique, and the pattern of cultural expectations for leaders is also unique.

Leading Organizational Change

LEARNING ROADMAP   Contexts for Leadership Action / Leaders as Change Agents / Planned Change Strategies / Resistance to Change

Leaders can also change the situation facing them and their followers. Change leadership deals with the idea that an organization needs to master the challenges of change while creating a satisfying, healthy, and effective workplace for its employees. For over a decade firms have dealt with a "new economy [that] has ushered in great business opportunities—and great turmoil."[13] The terms *turmoil* and *turbulence* are particularly salient in the current economic environment. In addition to the traditional challenges, the forces of globalization provide a number of problems and opportunities, and the new economy is constantly springing surprises on even the most experienced organizational executives. Flexibility, competence, and commitment are the rules of the day. People in the new workplace must be comfortable dealing with adaptation and continuous change, along with greater productivity, willingness to learn from the successes of others, total quality, and continuous improvement.

To deal with all of these concerns and more, we will examine leaders as change agents, phases of planned change, change strategies, and resistance to change.

Contexts for Leadership Action

During the recent recession, it became quite clear that leaders are facing new and unique challenges. Not only have North American-based firms fully entered the information age, they have recognized the need to innovate or die. The old titans of the industrial age, the Fords, the GMs, the U.S. Steels, today look like remnants of a bygone era. Now we send tweets instead of handwritten letters; we check e-mails on our Blackberry or iPad anytime and anywhere; and we even display our photos electronically on our blogs or social networking sites, instead of in frames or photo albums. Increasingly, leaders in every level of the organization are confronting the necessity and challenges of continual innovation and the uncertainty of the age. Simply put, leaders need to be acutely aware of the setting in which they lead.[14] And the leadership needed in a routine setting is not the same leadership that is needed in other contexts.[15]

Contextual leadership perspectives detail the conditions facing the leader and then suggest the type of leadership that is needed for success. In organizational behavior, the term **context** is used to describe the collection of opportunities and constraints that affect the occurrence and meaning of behavior as well as the relationships among variables.[16] The different contexts may be described in terms of the stability and uncertainty facing the leader and his or her other unit.

For most managers there are three major sources of instability. The first is market and environmental instability. During a recession, for example, the market is extremely unstable. Second is technological instability, where what is produced and how it is produced are changing. For example, competitors may be innovating rapidly but in ways your firm cannot easily predict. Finally, there is firm instability with an emphasis on process and procedure or internal administration instability. An example is an internal production and delivery system that needs changing, but the instability is so great that the design changes cannot keep up with system demands. In other words, managers cannot clear the swamp because the alligators keep eating the workers.

Four Leadership Contexts These sources of instability can be combined to depict the overall character of the opportunities and constraints facing the leader. For simplicity consider the four contexts in Figure 14.5.[17] In context 1 (Stability), stable conditions exist, and the focus is on adjusting and creating internal operations to enhance system goals. This is often the context for earlier leadership perspectives. Note that to measure success, the leader should judge progress on the basis of goals assigned to his or her unit.

In context 2 (Crisis), there are identifiable and dramatic departures from prior practice and sudden threats to high-priority goals, providing little or no response time. For many managers the current recession is such a crisis and calls for dramatic action and active leadership where charismatic and transformational leadership can be particularly important. Although the situation appears dire, leaders are aware of factors contributing to the crisis and can develop action plans to try and weather the storm. For example, in a recession, downsizing is a way to preserve

> • **Context** is the collection of opportunities and constraints that affect the occurrence and meaning of behavior and the relationships among variables.

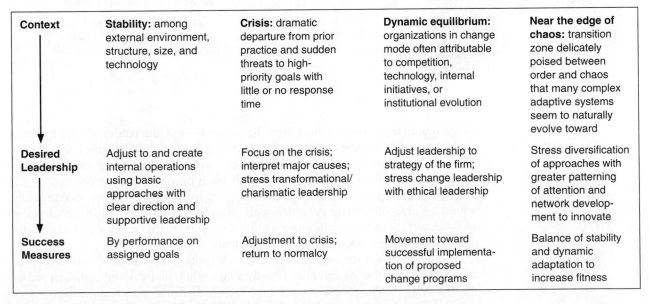

Context	Stability: among external environment, structure, size, and technology	Crisis: dramatic departure from prior practice and sudden threats to high-priority goals with little or no response time	Dynamic equilibrium: organizations in change mode often attributable to competition, technology, internal initiatives, or institutional evolution	Near the edge of chaos: transition zone delicately poised between order and chaos that many complex adaptive systems seem to naturally evolve toward
Desired Leadership	Adjust to and create internal operations using basic approaches with clear direction and supportive leadership	Focus on the crisis; interpret major causes; stress transformational/ charismatic leadership	Adjust leadership to strategy of the firm; stress change leadership with ethical leadership	Stress diversification of approaches with greater patterning of attention and network development to innovate
Success Measures	By performance on assigned goals	Adjustment to crisis; return to normalcy	Movement toward successful implementation of proposed change programs	Balance of stability and dynamic adaptation to increase fitness

Figure 14.5 Four situational contexts, the desired leadership, and how to measure success.
Source: Based on Osborn, Hunt, and Jauch (2002).

Finding the Leader in You

PATRICIA KARTER USES CORE VALUES AS HER GUIDE

Sweet is what one gets when digging into one of Dancing Deer Baking's Cherry Almond Ginger Chew cookies. Co-founded by Trish Karter, Dancing Deer sells over $10 million of cookies, cakes, and brownies a year. Each product is made with all-natural ingredients, packaged in recycled materials, and comes from inner-city Boston.

This story began for Karter in 1994 when she and her husband made a $20,000 Angel investment in a talented baker and set her up in a former pizza shop. Karter hadn't planned on working in the company, but growth came quickly and for the company to prosper, their baker partner, Suzanne Lombardi, needed more support and Karter jumped in. Customer demand led to product development and expansion; many positive press call outs and industry awards, such as being recognized on national TV as having the "best cake in the nation" and winning (the first of 11) Sophie awards, the food industry's equivalent of the Oscars, fueled growth further.

It isn't always easy for a leader to stay on course and in control while changing structures, adding people, and dealing with competition. But for Karter the anchor point has always been clear—let core values be the guide. Dancing Deer's employees get stock options and a package of benefits well above the industry standard; 35 percent of the sales price from the firm's Sweet Home line of cake and cookie gifts are donated to fund scholarships for homeless and at-risk mothers. When offered a chance to make a large cookie sale to Williams-Sonoma, Karter declined. Why? Because to fulfill the order would have required the use of preservatives, and that violated the company's values.

Williams-Sonoma was so impressed that it contracted to develop bakery mixes and eventually, many more products and a substantial relationship. Instead of losing an opportunity, by sticking with her values, Karter's firm gained more sales.

"There's more to life than selling cookies," says the Dancing Deer's Web site, "but it's not a bad way to make a living." And Karter hopes growth will soon make Dancing Deer "big enough to make an impact, to be a social economic force." As she says on www.dancingdeer.com: "It has been an interesting journey. Our successes are due to luck, a tremendous amount of dedication and hard work, and a commitment to having fun while being true to our principles. We have had failures as well—and survived them with a sense of humor."

What's the Lesson Here?

Do you know your core values? Do those core values guide your leadership decisions? Have you ever had your core values tested, and how did you respond?

the firm until the economy improves. To judge success, the leader should monitor the degree to which the unit is coping with the crisis and make sure it is on track to return to normal operations. While those in the middle can face a crisis, in cases of a dramatic downturn the firm may even bring in a new CEO.

In context 3 (Dynamic Equilibrium), organizational stability occurs only within a range of shifting priorities with programmed change efforts. This is the well-known dynamic equilibrium setting found in many analyses of corporate strategy, strategic leadership, and change leadership.

Context 4 (Near the Edge of Chaos) is a transition zone poised between order and chaos. Here, the system must rapidly adjust while maintaining sufficient stability to learn.[18] While globally operating high-tech firms are classic examples of those at the edge of chaos,[19] more conventional analyses of today's corporations have suggested that many firms are moving toward the edge of chaos. Why? By moving forward with a balance of exploration and exploitation, they find superior performance. Poised near the edge of chaos, firms stress innovation, responsiveness, and adaptability over routine efficiency.

Near the edge of chaos, context 4 leaders operate in uncertainty where no one person can actually describe the challenges and opportunities facing the firm. The context is just too complex. With this level of complexity some of the traditional aspects of leadership are expected to yield very poor performance. For example, transformational leadership often fails simply because no single leader is capable of charting the necessary goals and paths to keep the system viable.[20] More transactional leadership appears to provide stability but often reinforces sticking to a failed approach. The challenge is to stimulate innovation while keeping the learning environment stable.

Patterning of Attention and Network Development   Recent research suggests that in order to meet context challengers, leaders need to emphasize two often neglected aspects of leadership, patterning of attention and network development.[21] **Patterning of attention** involves isolating and communicating important information from a potentially endless stream of events, actions, and outcome. The term *patterning* is used to stress the establishment of a norm where the leader is expected to ask questions, raise issues, and help gather information for unit members. The leader is not telling others what the goal is or how to reach it. Nor is the leader stressing an ideology or a moral position. The leader is merely stimulating discussion among others in the setting. This discussion, in turn, produces new knowledge and information as individuals develop coping strategies.

In combination, greater patterning of attention and network development increases the size, interconnectedness, and diversity of the unit to provide a variety of world views. By increasing the depth and breadth of talent in combination with increased interaction, the chances are much greater that the unit will isolate reachable goals and develop a sustaining way of accomplishing them. Too much patterning of attention and/or network development, however, can decrease the chances of effective adaptation. This becomes the case when there is too much talk and not enough action. Managers must realize that patterning of attention and network development is a delicate balancing act. Finally, network leadership can be an important aspect of influence in many contexts. An example of how it is used to establish a philanthropic entity can be found in the accompanying sidebar.[22]

Leaders as Change Agents

While change is the watchword for most firms, it is important to separate transformational from incremental change. Some of this change may be described as radical change, or frame-breaking change.[23] This is **transformational change**,

Networking Leadership for the Greater Good

Managers can emphasize leadership by encouraging the formation of giving circles that bring people together for a charitable purpose.

A number of charities may arise informally or as part of a formal voluntary organization. Here are some tips for establishing the circles.

- Find out who is interested in participating in a giving circle comprised of employees who will contribute a fixed amount of money and/or time toward a charitable cause.

- Once the circle is established, provide a schedule of meeting times and locations.

- Assign an appropriate number of people, depending on the size of the group, to bring forward a cause for support.

- Educate members in a variety of activities and organizations in order to get more people involved.

- Decide on the scope of the charitable cause, whether broad, narrow, or variable.

- Keep in touch with other volunteer organizations and giving circles.

- **Patterning of attention** involves isolating and communicating what information is important and what is given attention from a potentially endless stream of events, actions, and outcome.

- **Transformational change** radically shifts the fundamental character of an organization.

How to Increase Your Chances of Success with Transformational Change

- Develop a sense of urgency.
- Have a powerful guiding coalition.
- Have a compelling vision.
- Communicate the vision.
- Empower others to act.
- Celebrate short-term wins.
- Build on accomplishments.
- Institutionalize results.

- **Incremental change** builds on the existing ways of operating to enhance or extend them in new directions.

- **Unplanned change** occurs spontaneously or randomly.

- **Planned change** is a response to someone's perception of a performance gap—a discrepancy between the desired and actual state of affairs.

- **Performance gap** is a discrepancy between the desired and the actual conditions.

which results in a major overhaul of the organization or its component systems. Organizations experiencing transformational change undergo significant shifts in basic characteristics, including the overall purpose/mission, underlying values and beliefs, and supporting strategies and structures.[24] In today's business environments, transformational changes are often initiated by a critical event, such as a new CEO, a new ownership brought about by merger or takeover, or a dramatic failure in operating results. When it occurs in the life cycle of an organization, such radical change is intense and all encompassing.[25]

The most common form of change is **incremental change**, or frame-bending change. This type of change, being part of an organization's natural evolution, is frequent and less traumatic than other types of change. Typical incremental changes include the introduction of new products, technologies, systems, and processes. Although the nature of the organization remains relatively the same, incremental change builds on the existing ways of operating to enhance or extend them in new directions. The capability of improving continuously through incremental change is an important asset in today's demanding business environment.

The success of both radical and incremental change in organizations depends in part on change agents who lead and support the change processes. These are individuals and groups who take responsibility for changing the existing behavior patterns of another person or even the entire social system. Although change agents are sometimes consultants hired from outside the organization, most managers in today's dynamic times are expected to act in the capacity of change agents. Indeed, this responsibility is essential to the leadership role. Simply put, being an effective change agent means being effective at "change leadership."

Planned and Unplanned Change   Not all change in organizations is the result of a change agent's direction. **Unplanned changes** can occur spontaneously or randomly. They may be disruptive, such as a wildcat strike that ends in a plant closure, or beneficial, such as an interpersonal conflict that results in a new procedure designed to improve the flow of work between two departments. When the forces of unplanned change appear, the goal is to act quickly in order to minimize negative consequences and maximize possible benefits. In many cases, an unplanned change can be turned into an advantage.

In contrast, **planned change** is the result of specific efforts led by a change agent. It is a direct response to someone's perception of a performance gap—a discrepancy between the desired and actual state of affairs. **Performance gaps** may represent problems to be solved or opportunities to be explored. Most planned changes are efforts intended to deal with performance gaps in ways that benefit an organization and its members. The processes of continuous improvement require constant vigilance to spot performance gaps and to take action to resolve them.

Change Is Shorthand for Opportunity

For Fred Smith, founder and CEO of FedEx, "change is shorthand for opportunity." He claims, "You'll get extinguished if you think you will not have to change." Organizational change calls for a high degree of trust and outstanding communication capability.

Forces and Targets for Change   The driving forces for change are ever present in and around today's dynamic work settings. They are found in the organization–environment relationship, with mergers, strategic alliances, and divestitures among the examples of organizational attempts to redefine their relationships in challenging social and political environments. They are found in the organizational life cycle, with changes in culture and structure among the examples of how organizations must adapt as they evolve from birth through growth and toward maturity. They are found in the political nature of organizations, with changes in internal control structures, including benefits and reward systems that attempt to deal with shifting political currents.

Planned change based on any of these forces can be internally directed toward a wide variety of organizational components, most of which have already been discussed in this book. As shown in Figure 14.6, these targets include organizational

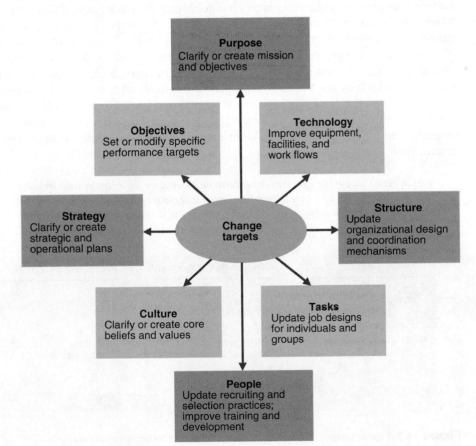

Figure 14.6 Organizational targets for planned change.

purpose, strategy, structure, and people, as well as objectives, culture, tasks, and technology. When considering these targets, it must be recognized that they are highly intertwined in the workplace. Changes in any one are likely to require or involve changes in others. For example, a change in the basic tasks—what people do—is inevitably accompanied by a change in technology—the way in which tasks are accomplished. Changes in tasks and technology usually require alterations in structures, including changes in the patterns of authority and communication as well as in the roles of workers. These technological and structural changes can, in turn, necessitate changes in the knowledge, skills, and behaviors of the members of the organization.[26] In all cases, tendencies to accept easy-to-implement, but questionable, "quick fixes" to problems should be avoided.

Planned Change Strategies

There are a variety of *power change strategies* utilized to mobilize power, exert influence over others, and get people to support planned change efforts. Three pure strategies—force–coercion, rational persuasion, and shared power—are described in Figure 14.7. Each of these strategies builds from the various bases of social power. Note in particular that each power source has somewhat different implications for the planned change process.[27]

• **Force–coercion strategy** uses authority, rewards, and punishments to create change.

Force–Coercion   A **force–coercion strategy** uses authority, rewards, or punishments as primary inducements to change. Here, the leader acts unilaterally to "command" change through the formal authority of his or her position, to induce change via an offer of special rewards, or to bring about change through threats of punishment. People respond to this strategy mainly out of the fear of being punished if they do not comply with a change directive or out of the desire to gain a reward if they do. Coercion compliance is usually temporary and continues only as long as the leader is present. With reliance on legitimate authority and rewards, compliance remains as long as supervision is visible and rewards keep coming. The actions as a change agent using the force–coercion strategy might match the following profile:

> *You believe that people who run things are motivated by self-interest and by what the situation offers in terms of potential personal gain or loss. Since you feel that people change only in response to such motives, you try to find out where their*

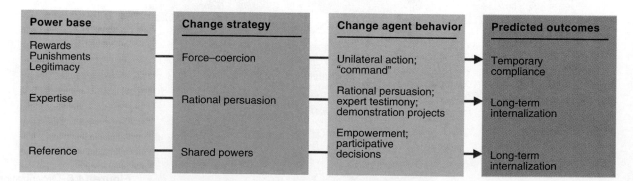

Figure 14.7 Power bases, change strategies, and predicted change outcomes.

vested interests lie and then put the pressure on. If you have formal authority, you use it. If not, you resort to whatever possible rewards and punishments you have access to and do not hesitate to threaten others with these weapons. Once you find a weakness, you exploit it and are always wise to work "politically" by building supporting alliances wherever possible.[28]

Rational Persuasion   Change agents using a **rational persuasion strategy** attempt to bring about change through the use of special knowledge, empirical support, or rational arguments. This strategy assumes that rational people will be guided by reason and self-interest in deciding whether or not to support a change. Expert power is mobilized to convince others that the change will leave them better off than before. It is sometimes referred to as an empirical-rational strategy of planned change. When successful, this strategy results in a longer-lasting, more naturalized change than does force–coercion. A change agent taking the rational persuasion approach to a change situation might behave as follows:

> *You believe that people are inherently rational and are guided by reason in their actions and decision making. Once a specific course of action is demonstrated to be in a person's self-interest, you assume that reason and rationality will cause the person to adopt it. Thus, you approach change with the objective of communicating—through information and facts—the essential "desirability" of change from the perspective of the person whose behavior you seek to influence. If this logic is effectively communicated, you are sure of the person who is adopting the proposed change.*[29]

> • **Rational persuasion strategy** uses facts, special knowledge, and rational argument to create change.

Shared Power   A **shared-power strategy** actively involves the people who will be affected by a change in planning and making key decisions relating to this change. Sometimes called a normative-reeducative approach, this strategy tries to develop directions and support for change through involvement and empowerment. It builds essential foundations, such as personal values, group norms, and shared goals, so that support for a proposed change emerges naturally. Managers using normative-reeducative approaches draw on the power of personal reference and share power by allowing others to participate in planning and implementing the change. Given this high level of involvement, the strategy is likely to result in a longer-lasting and internalized change. A change agent who shares power and adopts a normative-reeducative approach to change is likely to fit this profile:

> • **Shared-power strategy** uses participatory methods and emphasizes common values to create change.

> *You believe that people have complex motivations and behave as they do as a result of sociocultural norms and commitments to these norms. You also recognize that changes in these orientations involve changes in attitudes, values, skills, and significant relationships, not just changes in knowledge, information, or intellectual rationales for action and practice. Thus, when seeking to change others, you are sensitive to the supporting or inhibiting effects of group pressures and norms. In working with people, you try to find out their side of things and identify their feelings and expectations.*[30]

Resistance to Change

In organizations, **resistance to change** is any attitude or behavior that indicates unwillingness to make or support a desired alteration. Leaders often view any resistance as something that must be "overcome" in order for change to be successful. This is not always the case, however. It is helpful to view resistance to

> • **Resistance to change** is any attitude or behavior that indicates unwillingness to make or support a desired change.

change as feedback that the leader can use to facilitate gaining change objectives.[31] The essence of this constructive approach to resistance is to recognize that when people resist change, they are defending something that is important to them that appears to be threatened.

Why People Resist Change People have many reasons to resist change—fear of the unknown, insecurity, lack of a felt need to change, threat to vested interests, contrasting interpretations, and lack of resources, among other possibilities. A work team's members, for example, may resist the introduction of an advanced workstation of computers because they have never used the operating system and are apprehensive. They may wonder whether the new computers will eventually be used as justification for "getting rid" of certain members of their department, or they may believe that they have been doing their jobs just fine and do not need the new computers. These and other viewpoints often create resistance to even the best and most well-intended planned changes.

Resistance to the Change Itself Sometimes a leader experiences resistance to the change itself. People may reject a change because they believe it is not worth their time, effort, or attention. They may believe that the proposed change asks them to do more for less. To minimize resistance in such cases, the leader should make sure that everyone who may be affected by a change knows how it satisfies the following criteria.[32]

>*Benefit*—The change should have a clear advantage for the people being asked to change; it should be perceived as "a better way."
>
>*Compatibility*—The change should be as compatible as possible with the existing values and experiences of the people being asked to change.
>
>*Complexity*—The change should be no more complex than necessary; it must be as easy as possible for people to understand and use.
>
>*Triability*—The change should be something that people can try on a step-by-step basis and make adjustments as things progress.

Resistance to the Change Strategy Leaders must also be prepared to deal with resistance to the change strategy. Someone who attempts to bring about change via force–coercion, for example, may create resistance among individuals who resent management of leadership by "command" or the use of threatened punishment. People may resist a rational persuasion strategy in which the data are suspect or the expertise of advocates is not clear. They may resist a shared-power strategy that even appears manipulative and insincere.

Resistance to the Change Agent Resistance to a leader implementing the change often involves personality differences and a poor history of relationships. Leaders who are isolated and aloof from other persons in the change situation, who appear self-serving, or who have a high emotional involvement in the changes are especially prone to such problems. Research indicates that leaders who differ from other persons on such dimensions as age, education, and socio-economic status may encounter greater resistance to change.[33]

How to Deal with Resistance An informed leader has many options available for dealing positively with resistance to change. Figure 14.8 summarizes insights

Method ⟶	Use when ⟶	Advantages ⟶	Disadvantages
Education & communication	People lack information or have inaccurate information	Creates willingness to help with the change	Can be very time consuming
Participation & involvement	Other people have important information and/or power to resist	Adds information to change planning; builds commitment to the change	Can be very time consuming
Facilitation & support	Resistance traces to resource or adjustment problems	Satisfies directly specific resource or adjustment needs	Can be time consuming; can be expensive
Negotiation & agreement	A person or group will "lose" something because of the change	Helps avoid major resistance	Can be expensive; can cause others to seek similar "deals"
Manipulation & cooptation	Other methods don't work or are too expensive	Can be quick and inexpensive	Can create future problems if people sense manipulation
Explicit & implicit coercion	Speed is important and change agent has power	Quick; overpowers resistance	Risky if people get "mad"

Figure 14.8 Methods for dealing with resistance to change.

into how and when each of these methods may be used to deal with resistance to change. Regardless of the chosen strategy, it is always best to remember that the presence of resistance typically suggests that something can be done to achieve a better fit among the change, the situation, and the people affected. A good leader deals with resistance to change by listening to feedback and acting accordingly.[34]

The first approach in dealing with resistance to change is through *education and communication*. The objective is to teach people about a change before it is implemented and to help them understand the logic of the change. Education and communication seem to work best when resistance is based on inaccurate or incomplete information. A second way is the use of participation and involvement. With the goal of allowing others to help design and implement the changes, this approach asks people to contribute ideas and advice or to work on task forces or committees that may be leading the change. This is useful when the leader does not have all the information needed to successfully handle a problem situation. Here, for instance, the increased use of patterning of attention and network development by the leader may help resolve tensions.

Facilitation and support help to deal with resistance by providing help—both emotional and material—for people experiencing the hardships of change. Here a leader increases consideration by actively listening to problems and complaints. This is matched with a greater initiating structure whereby the leader provides training in the new ways and helps others to overcome performance pressures. Facilitation and support are highly recommended when people are frustrated by work constraints and difficulties encountered in the change process.

A *negotiation and agreement approach* offers incentives to actual or potential change resistors. Trade-offs are arranged to provide special benefits in exchange for assurances that the change will not be blocked. It is most useful when dealing with a person or group that will lose something of value as a result of the planned change.

Frustrated managers may attempt to use *manipulation and co-optation* in covert attempts to influence others, selectively providing information and consciously structuring events so that the desired change occurs. Although manipulation and co-optation are common when other tactics do not work, only the more astute and experienced executives find they can gain temporary reductions in resistance.

In a crisis, some leaders find that in order to overcome resistance to change they must resort to *explicit or implicit coercion*. Often, resistors are threatened with a variety of undesirable consequences if they do not go along with the plan. In a crisis, the temporary compliance to the change may be all that is necessary to weather the storm. Unfortunately, crises are much rarer than the use of this approach. When the crisis is past, even the temporary use of coercion means that leaders will need to embark on a new change program that stresses facilitation and support.

Finally, it is important to recognize the history, change, and culture of the firm as it undergoes planned change. Often a planned change will yield unanticipated alterations in the culture of the organization. We will spend the next chapter delving into the concept of organizational culture and the necessity to promote innovation, a unique kind of planned change.

14 *study guide*

Key Questions and Answers

What is moral leadership?

- Moral leadership includes authentic leadership, servant leadership, and spiritual and ethical leadership.

- Authentic leadership emphasizes owning one's personal experiences and acting in accordance with one's true or core self which underlies virtually all other aspects of leadership.

- Servant leadership is where the leader is attuned to basic spiritual values and, in serving these, serves others, including colleagues, the organization, and society.

- Spiritual leadership is a field of inquiry within the broader setting of workplace spirituality; it includes values, attitudes, and behaviors required to intrinsically motivate self and others to have a sense of spiritual survival through calling and membership.

- Ethical leadership emphasizes moral concerns.

What is shared leadership?

- Shared leadership is a dynamic, interactive influence process among individuals in groups for which the objective is to lead one another to the achievement of group or organizational goals or both.

- The influence process often involves peer or lateral influence and at other times involves upward or downward hierarchical influence within a team.

- Though broader than traditional vertical leadership, shared leadership may be used in combination with it.

- Self-leadership techniques can be used to improve the effectiveness of shared leadership.

How do you lead across cultures?

- Cross-cultural leadership emphasizes Project GLOBE (Global Leadership and Organizational Behavior Effectiveness Research Program), which involves 62 societies, 951 organizations, and about 140 country co-investigators.

- It assumes that the attributes and entities that differentiate a specified culture predict organizational practices and leader attributes and behaviors that are most often carried out and most effective in that culture.

- It identifies a number of potentially important aspects of culture that form the basis for culturally based leader prototypes.

- It matches key aspects of leadership to the important aspects of culture to identify endorsed elements of leadership.

- It suggests both universally endorsed elements of leadership and those unique to a particular culture and group of nations.

How do you lead organizational change?

- Change leadership helps deal with the idea of an organization that masters the challenges of both radical and incremental change while still creating a satisfying, healthy, and effective employee workplace.

- Change leadership deals with leaders as change agents, phases of planned change, change strategies, and resistance to change.

- Radical or transformational change results in a major overhaul of the organization or its component systems.

- Incremental or frame-bending change as part of an organization's natural evolution is frequent and less traumatic than radical change.

- Change agents are individuals and groups who take responsibility for changing the existing behavior pattern or social system; being a change agent is an integral part of a manager's leadership role.

- Planned change strategies consist of force–coercion, rational persuasion, and shared power.

- Dealing with resistance to change involves education and communication, participation and involvement, facilitation and support, negotiation and agreement, manipulation and co-optation, and explicit or implicit agreement.

Terms to Know

Self-Test 14

Multiple Choice

1. Authentic leadership _____. (a) is easily attainable (b) is the most common type of leadership (c) involves acting in accordance with one's true or core self (d) focuses on awareness of others

2. Research on project GLOBE found that _____. (a) some dimensions of leadership are universally endorsed (b) there are no commonalities in leadership across cultures (c) expectations for leaders are pretty similar across cultures (d) risk-taking and self-sacrificing are the most important aspects of leadership

3. The _____ leader helps others discover their inner spirit, earns and keeps the trust of their followers, exhibits effective listening skills, and places the importance of assisting others over self-interest. (a) ethical (b) shared (c) servant (d) spiritual

4. _____ is a causal leadership approach for organizational transformation designed to create an intrinsically motivated, learning organization. (a) Servant leadership (b) Spiritual leadership (c) Shared leadership (d) Ethical leadership

5. Shared leadership _____. (a) emphasizes managerial relationships (b) is an extension of participative leadership (c) replaces vertical leadership (d) is a dynamic, interactive influence process

6. Characteristics that are important for successful team performance include all but which of the following? (a) a strong vertical leader (b) efficient, goal directed effort (c) commitment to continuous improvement (d) competent, motivated performance

7. Which of the following is not one of the three broad categories of self-leadership? (a) constructive-thought-pattern strategies (b) natural-reward (c) behavior-focused (d) achievement-focus

8. In shared leadership teams, non-traditional leaders are often called _____. (a) task leaders (b) project managers (c) facilitators (d) mentors

9. Contexts are usually described in terms of _____ and _____. (a) high, low (b) stability, uncertainty (c) shared, vertical (d) individualism, collectivism

10. In edge of chaos contexts, transformational leadership _____. (a) is highly successful (b) is better than transactional (c) is the same as patterning of attention (d) often fails

11. Two often neglected aspects of leadership are _____ and _____. (a) transformational, transactional (b) shared, vertical (c) patterning of attention, network development (d) strategic, contextual

12. Which type of change radically shifts the fundamental character of an organization? (a) transformational (b) incremental (c) transactional (d) hierarchical

13. The most common form of change is _____. (a) transformational (b) incremental (c) transactional (d) hierarchical

14. In a _____ strategy, leaders use authority, rewards or punishments as primary inducements to change. (a) rational persuasion (b) shared power (c) benefit-compatibility (d) force-coercion

15. _____ is a change approach in which managers offer incentives to actual or potential change resistors. (a) Manipulation and co-optation (b) Explicit or implicit coercion (c) Negotiation and agreement (d) Education and communication

Short Response

16. Explain three ways in which shared leadership can be used in a self-directed work team.

17. What are the three core qualities of a spiritual leader?

18. What should a manager do when forces for unplanned change appear?

19. What internal and external forces push for change in organizations?

Applications Essay

20. When Jorge Maldanado became general manager of the local civic recreation center, he realized that many changes would be necessary to make the facility a true community resource. Having the benefit of a new bond issue, the center had the funds for new equipment and expanded programming. All he needed to do now was get the staff committed to new initiatives. Unfortunately, his first efforts have been met with considerable resistance to change. A typical staff comment is, "Why do all these extras? Everything is fine as it is." How can Jorge use the strategies for dealing with resistance to change, as discussed in the chapter, to move the change process along?

Next Steps

Top Choices from *The OB Skills Workbook*

Case for Critical Thinking	Team and Experiential Exercises	Self-Assessment Portfolio
• Novo Nordisk	• Cultural Cues	• A Twenty-First Century Manager • Global Readiness Index

Social Media and Corporations: Don't Cross the Line When You Go Online

When you think of "shameless self-promotion on Twitter", what industry do you think of first? Whatever your choice, there's a good chance it's not Wall Street.

But it's not for lack of wanting. Though investment banking has been slower than most industries to dive headfirst into self-promotion via Twitter and Facebook, many young professionals are eager to reach out to existing and potential customers using social media tools. But firms are cautious about how bankers represent themselves to a public wary of corporate hijinks and poor decision-making. Add to this a very complex regulatory environment surrounding how businesses in banking industry must monitor and store official communications, and you start to understand why Wall Street has been more tentative than most industries to get with the times.

> *"It would be nice to say, 'OK, we have a social media strategy and here it is.' But that's not the way this story is being played out."*
> *—Todd Estabrook, chief marketing officer for Common-wealth Financial.*[c]

"Who could blame any firm operating in a regulated industry for taking a cautious approach in the face of all that?" asks social media expert Kip Gregory, principal of The Gregory Group. "Especially in financial services, which is at its core an industry built around the management of risk. The question is: How do you, as a competitor in this business, choose to respond to a clearly shifting landscape?"[a]

Some firms ban all social media use by employees. Others are taking a predictably cautious approach to exploring social media. For example, Morgan Stanley's position—"There are substantial restrictions on its use right now, but we are continuing to review the issue."—is itself shorter than a single tweet. But many investment professionals are eager to learn how they can make positive use of social media's persuasive powers.

"We're trying to rally the troops and recognize that you just can't have a policy in place that prohibits this," says John N. Travagline, vice president of compliance for the trade group Insurance Marketplace Standards Association. "People realize this is something that's here to stay. We've just got to figure out leading solutions—the right way to do this."[b] How can executives manage this emerging aspect of the corporate culture?

Quick Summary

- Communications by Wall Street firms and employees are restricted by intensely detailed regulatory guidelines, which present a challenge for individual employees who wish to promote themselves using social media tools.
- Especially cautious about maintaining a positive image, some firms forbid employees from using social media to promote themselves or their firms.

FYI: According to a 2010 study by asset management advisory company kasina, 48% of financial advisors visit LinkedIn; 43% visit Facebook.[d]

15 Organizational Culture and Innovation

the key point

Since people spend much of their adult lives in and around organizations, they are often absorbed into the organization culture. While the organizational culture provides meaning and stability, most organizations also contain a number of subcultures and countercultures. To operate as an effective manager you will need to understand the various layers of culture and the important role of stories, rites, and rituals. While culture provides stability, organizations also need innovation to survive. Balancing the need for innovation and stability can be a managerial challenge of the first order as illustrated in the case of Wall Street firms and social media.

chapter at a glance

What Is Organizational Culture?

How Do You Understand an Organizational Culture?

What Is Innovation and Why Is It Important?

How Can We Manage Organizational Culture and Innovation?

ETHICS IN OB

AGE BECOMES AN ISSUE IN JOB LAYOFFS

FINDING THE LEADER IN YOU

CHRISTINE SPECHT PUTS A NEW FACE ON COUSINS SUBS

OB IN POPULAR CULTURE

CORPORATE CULTURE AND *THE FIRM*

RESEARCH INSIGHT

TEAM FACTORS AND INNOVATION

what's inside?

Can you imagine eliminating all of your Facebook friends or passing up the opportunity to Twitter the most recent news? It is also like getting disconnected from the world. Although Wall Street executives want to control the use of social media, they also clearly recognize that being interconnected is a part of the larger U.S. culture and rapidly becoming a global standard. This is just one of the newer issues executives are confronting as they attempt to manage organizational culture.

Organizational Culture

LEARNING ROADMAP   Functions of Organizational Culture / Subcultures and Countercultures / National Culture and Corporate Culture

• **Organizational or corporate culture** is the system of shared actions, values, and beliefs that develops within an organization and guides the behavior of its members.

Organizational or corporate culture is the system of shared actions, values, and beliefs that develops within an organization and guides the behavior of its members.[1] In the business setting, this system is often referred to as the corporate culture. Each organization has its own unique culture. Just as no two individual personalities are the same, no two organizational cultures are identical. Yet, there are some common cultural elements that yield stability and meaning for organizations. Management scholars and consultants believe that some cultural elements can have a major impact on the performance of organizations and the quality of work life experienced by their members.[2] In this chapter we will examine the functions of organizational culture and various levels of cultural analysis to understand the powerful force of organizational culture.

Functions of Organizational Culture

Through their collective experience, members of an organization can solve two extremely important survival issues.[3] The first issue is one of external adaptation: What precisely needs to be accomplished, and how can it be done? The second is known as internal integration: How do members resolve the daily problems associated with living and working together?

• **External adaptation** deals with reaching goals, the tasks to be accomplished, the methods used to achieve the goals, and the methods of coping with success and failure.

External Adaptation   Issues of **external adaptation** deal with ways of reaching goals, tasks to be accomplished, methods used to achieve the goals, and methods of coping with success and failure. Through their shared experiences, members may develop common views that help guide their day-to-day activities. Organizational members need to know the real mission of the organization, not just the pronouncements to key constituencies, such as stockholders. By talking to one another, members will naturally develop an understanding of how they contribute to the mission. This view may emphasize the importance of human resources. On the other hand, employees may see themselves as cogs in a machine, or a cost to be reduced.

Each group of individuals in an organization tends to (1) separate more important from less important external forces, (2) develop ways to measure their accomplishments, and (3) create explanations for why goals are not always met. At Dell, the retailer of computers and consumer electronics, managers, for example, have moved away from judging their progress against specific targets to estimating the degree to which they are moving a development process forward. They work on improving participation and commitment. They don't blame a poor

Winning Culture at Sherwin-Williams

Christopher Connor, chairman and CEO of Sherwin-Williams, describes his firm's "winning culture" in terms of providing "a place where individuals get promoted based on performance to build wealth—real wealth." Sherwin-Williams managers believe in providing training and developmental experiences for all its employees.

economy or upper-level managers for the firm's failure to reach a profit target. In difficult times they stress the progress all have made in their collective effort.[4]

The final issues in external adaptation deal with two important, but often neglected, aspects of coping with external reality. First, individuals need to develop acceptable ways of telling outsiders just how good they really are. At 3M, for example, employees talk about the quality of their products and the many new, useful products they have brought to the market. Second, individuals must collectively know when and how to admit defeat. At 3M, the answer is easy for new projects: At the beginning of the development process, members establish "drop" points at which to quit the development effort and redirect it. When they quit, project managers are careful not to suggest that the group has failed but stress that what they have learned increases the chances that the next project will succeed to market.[5]

In sum, external adaptation involves answering important instrumental or goal-related questions concerning coping with reality: What is the real mission? How do we contribute? What are our goals? How do we reach our goals? What external forces are important? How do we measure results? What do we do if we do not meet specific targets? How do we tell others how good we are? When do we quit? Chris Connor of Sherwin-Williams expressed his firm's approach to external adaptation in terms of winning.[6]

The process of **internal integration** often begins with the establishment of a unique identity. Through dialogue and interaction, members begin to characterize their world. They may see it as malleable or fixed, filled with opportunities or threats. Real progress toward innovation can only begin when group members believe that they can change important parts of the world around them and that what appears to be a threat is actually an opportunity for change.

Three important aspects of working together are (1) deciding who is a member of the group and who is not, (2) developing an informal understanding of acceptable and unacceptable behavior, and (3) separating friends from enemies. These are important issues for managers as well. A key to effective total quality management, for instance, is that subgroups in the organization need to view their immediate supervisors as members of the group. The immediate supervisor is expected to represent the group to friendly higher managers. Of course, should management not be seen as friendly, the process of improving quality could quickly break down.[7] For example, Aetna, one of the nation's leading diversified health care benefits companies, describes its corporate culture as one where employees "work together openly, share information freely and build on each other's ideas to continually create the next better way. Nothing is impossible to our Aetna team. We are eager, ambitious learners and continuous innovators. And we are succeeding. Every day."[8]

• **Internal Integration** deals with the creation of a collective identify and with ways of working and living together.

To work together effectively, individuals need to decide collectively how to allocate power, status, and authority. They need to establish a shared understanding of who will get rewards and sanctions for specific types of actions. Too often, managers fail to recognize these important aspects of internal integration. A manager may fail to explain the basis for a promotion and to show why this reward, the status associated with it, and the power given to the newly promoted individual are consistent with commonly shared beliefs.

Collections of individuals also need to work out acceptable ways to communicate and develop guidelines for friendships. Although these aspects of internal integration may appear esoteric, they are vital. For example, to function effectively as a team, all must recognize that some members will be closer than others; friendships are inevitable.[9]

Resolving the issues of internal integration helps individuals develop a shared identity and a collective commitment. It may well lead to longer-term stability and provide a lens for members to make sense of their part of the world. In sum, internal integration involves answers to important questions associated with living together. What is our unique identity? How do we view the world? Who is a member? How do we allocate power, status, and authority? How do we communicate? What is the basis for friendship? Answering these questions is important to organizational members because the organization is more than just a place to work.

Subcultures and Countercultures

Whereas smaller firms often have a single dominant culture with a universal set of shared actions, values, and beliefs, most larger organizations contain several subcultures as well as one or more countercultures.[10]

• **Subcultures** are groups who exhibit unique patterns of values and philosophies not consistent with the dominant culture of the larger organization or system.

Subcultures   **Subcultures** are groups of individuals who exhibit a unique pattern of values and a philosophy that is consistent with the organization's dominant values and philosophy.[11] While subcultures are unique, their members' values do not clash with those of the larger organization. Interestingly, strong subcultures are often found in task forces, teams, and special project groups in organizations. The subculture emerges to bind individuals working intensely together to accomplish a specific task. For example, there are strong subcultures of stress engineers and liaison engineers in the Boeing Renton plant. These highly specialized groups must solve knotty technical issues to ensure that Boeing planes are safe. Though distinct, these groups of engineers also share in the dominant values of Boeing.

• **Countercultures** are groups where the patterns of values and philosophies outwardly reject those of the organization or social system.

Countercultures   In contrast, **countercultures** are groups whose patterns of values and philosophies outwardly reject those of the larger organization or social system.[12] When Stephen Jobs reentered Apple Computer as its CEO, he quickly formed a counterculture within Apple. Over the next 18 months, numerous clashes occurred as the followers of the former CEO Gil Amelio fought to maintain their place and the old culture. Jobs won and so did Apple. His counterculture became dominant and the company thrived.[13]

Every large organization imports potentially important subcultural groupings when it hires employees from the larger society. In North America, for instance, subcultures and countercultures may naturally form based on ethnic, racial, gender, generational, or locational similarities. In Japanese organizations, subcultures often form based on the date of graduation from a university, gender, or geographic location. In European firms, ethnicity and language play an important part in developing subcultures, as does gender. In many less developed nations, language, education, religion, or family social status are often grounds for forming popular subcultures and countercultures.

Within an organization, mergers and acquisitions may produce adjustment problems. Employers and managers of an acquired firm may hold values and assumptions that are inconsistent with those of the acquiring firm. This is known as the "clash of corporate cultures."[14] One example is the difficulty Bank of America faced when it gave huge bonuses to traders after acquiring Merrill Lynch.[15]

National Culture and Corporate Culture

Most organizations originate in one national culture and incorporate many features from this host national culture even when they expand internationally. The difference between Sony's corporate emphasis on group achievements and Zenith's emphasis on individual engineering excellence, for example, can be traced to the Japanese emphasis on collective action versus the U.S. emphasis on individualism. National cultural values may also become embedded in the expectations of important organizational constituencies and in generally accepted solutions to problems.

When moving across national cultures, managers need to be sensitive to national cultural differences so that their actions do not violate common assumptions in the underlying national culture. To improve morale at General Electric's French subsidiary, Chi. Generale de Radiologie, American managers invited all of the European managers to a "get-acquainted" meeting near Paris. The Americans gave out colorful t-shirts with the GE slogan, "Go for One," a typical maneuver in many American training programs. The French resented the t-shirts. One outspoken individual said, "It was like Hitler was back, forcing us to wear uniforms. It was humiliating." Firms often face problems in developing strong ethical standards, particularly when they import societal subgroups.

Importing Societal Subgroups   Beyond becoming culturally sensitive, difficulties often arise with importing groupings from the larger society. Some of these groupings are relevant to the organization whereas others may be quite destructive. At the one extreme, senior managers can merely accept societal divisions and work within the confines of the larger culture. This approach presents three primary difficulties. First, subordinated groups, such as members of a specific religion or ethnic group, are likely to form into a counterculture and to work more diligently to change their status than to better the firm. Second, the firm may find it extremely difficult to cope with broader cultural changes. For instance, in the United States the expected treatment of women, ethnic minorities, and the disabled has changed dramatically over the last 20 years. Firms that merely accept old customs and prejudices have experienced a greater loss of key personnel and increased communication difficulties, as well as greater interpersonal conflict, than have their more progressive counterparts. Third, firms that accept and build on natural divisions from the larger culture may find it extremely difficult to develop sound international operations. For example, many Japanese firms have experienced substantial difficulties adjusting to the equal treatment of women in their U.S. operations.[16]

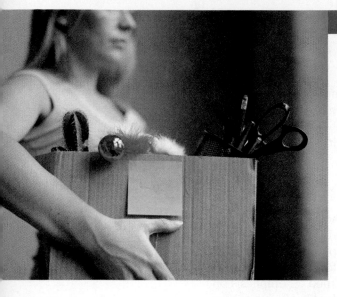

ETHICS IN OB

AGE BECOMES AN ISSUE IN JOB LAYOFFS

Job cuts need to be made in a bad economy. Who gets laid off? Sarah is young, single, and years out of college; she is hard working, topped the performance ratings this year, and always steps forward when volunteers are needed for evening work or travel. Mary is in her mid-40s, has two children, and her husband is a pediatrician; her performance is good, always at or above average during performance reviews, but she has limited time available for evening work and out-of-town travel.

Who gets picked for the layoff, Sarah or Mary? Chances are it's going to be Sarah. The *Wall Street Journal* reports that younger workers are at greater risk of layoffs because many employers use a "last in/first out" rule when cutting back staff. This is true even though the younger workers tend to earn less than their older counterparts and may even be outperforming them. One reason is conflict avoidance; who wants to face an age discrimination lawsuit? Another is the emotional toll that making layoff decisions places on managers; it just seems easier to let go the younger person who probably has fewer complicating personal and family situations.

David Schauer, a school superintendent in Phoenix, says he sent layoff notices to 68 teachers all in their first year of employment. He says, "My worst fear is that really good people will leave teaching." Nicole Ryan, a teacher in New York, received just such a notice. She says: "I knew it was coming because, based on seniority, I was lower on the totem pole." But, she adds: "It didn't make it any easier."

What's Right?   *Are managers doing the right things when they lay off younger workers first, even when they are high performers? Is it correct to take "personal and family" factors into account when making decisions on who gets to keep their jobs and who doesn't? Is it fair that younger workers have more to fear about keeping their jobs because some managers are unwilling to face possible age discrimination claims from older workers?*

Building on National Cultural Diversity   At the other extreme, managers can work to eradicate all naturally occurring national subcultures and countercultures. Firms are struggling to develop what Taylor Cox calls the multicultural organization. The **multicultural organization** is a firm that values diversity but systematically works to block the transfer of societally based subcultures into the fabric of the organization.[17] Because Cox focuses on some problems unique to the United States, his prescription for change may not apply to organizations located in other countries with much more homogeneous populations.

Cox suggests a five-step program for developing the multicultural organization. First, the organization should develop pluralism with the objective of multibased socialization. To accomplish this objective, members of different naturally occurring groups need to school one another to increase knowledge and information and to eliminate stereotyping. Second, the firm should fully integrate its structure so that there is no direct relationship between a naturally occurring group and any particular job—for instance, there are no distinct male or female

• **Multicultural organization** is a firm that values diversity but systematically works to block the transfer of societally based subcultures into the fabric of the organization.

jobs. Third, the firm must integrate the informal networks by eliminating barriers and increasing participation. That is, it must break down existing societally based informal groups. Fourth, the organization should break the linkage between naturally occurring group identity and the identity of the firm. Fifth, the organization must actively work to eliminate interpersonal conflict based on either the group identity or the natural backlash of the largest societally based grouping.

Understanding Organizational Cultures

LEARNING ROADMAP   Layers of Cultural Analysis / Stories, Rites, Rituals, and Symbols / Cultural Rules and Roles / Shared Values, Meanings, and Organizational Myths

Some aspects of organizational culture are easy to see. Yet, not all aspects of organizational culture are readily apparent because they are buried deep in the shared experience of organizational members. It may take years to understand some deeper aspects of the culture. This complexity has led some to examine different layers of analysis ranging from easily observable to deeply hidden aspects of corporate culture.

Layers of Cultural Analysis

Figure 15.1 illustrates the observable aspects of culture, shared values, and underlying assumptions as three layers.[18] The deeper one digs, the more difficult it is to discover the culture but the more important an aspect becomes.

The first layer concerns **observable culture**, or "the way we do things around here." Important parts of an organization's culture emerge from the collective experience of its members. These emergent aspects of the culture help make it unique and may well provide a competitive advantage for the organization. Some of these aspects may be observed directly in day-to-day practices. Others may have to be discovered—for example, by asking members to tell stories of important incidents in the history of the organization. We often learn about the unique aspects of the organizational culture through descriptions of specific events.[19] By observing employee actions, listening to stories, and asking members to interpret what is going on, one can begin to understand the organization's culture. The observable culture includes the unique stories, ceremonies, and corporate rituals that make up the history of the firm or a group within the firm.

The second layer recognizes that shared values can play a critical part in linking people together and can provide a powerful motivational mechanism for members of the culture. Many consultants suggest that organizations should develop a "dominant and coherent set of shared values."[20] The term *shared* in cultural analysis

• **Observable culture** is the way things are done in an organization

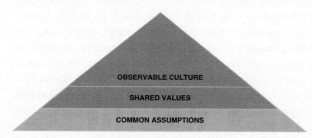

Figure 15.1 Three levels of analysis in studying organizational culture.

OBSERVABLE CULTURE

SHARED VALUES

COMMON ASSUMPTIONS

implies that the group is a whole. Not every member may agree with the shared values, but they have all been exposed to them and have often been told they are important. At Microsoft a shared culture value is a passion for technology.

At the deepest layer of cultural analysis are common cultural assumptions; these are the taken-for-granted truths that collections of corporate members share as a result of their joint experience. It is often extremely difficult to isolate these patterns, but doing so helps explain why culture invades every aspect of organizational life.

Stories, Rites, Rituals, and Symbols

To begin understanding a corporate culture, it is often easiest to start with stories. Organizations are rich with stories of winners and losers, successes and failures. Perhaps one of the most important stories concerns the founding of the organization. The founding story often contains the lessons learned from the heroic efforts of an embattled entrepreneur, whose vision may still guide the firm. The story of the founding may be so embellished that it becomes a **saga**—a heroic account of accomplishments.[21] Sagas are important because they are used to tell new members the real mission of the organization, how the organization operates, and how individuals can fit into the company. Rarely is the founding story totally accurate, and it often glosses over some of the more negative aspects of the founders. Such is the case with Monterey Pasta.[22]

> • **Saga** is an embellished heroic account of accomplishments.

On its Web site, the organization says of its history, "The Monterey Pasta Company was launched from a 400-square-foot storefront on Lighthouse Avenue in Monterey, California in 1989. . . . The founders started their small fresh pasta company in response to the public's growing interest in healthy gourmet foods. Customers were increasingly excited about fresh pasta given its superior quality and nutritional value, as well as ease of preparation. . . . The company soon accepted its first major grocery account. . . . In 1993, the company completed its first public offering." The Web site fails to mention another interesting aspect of the firm. An unsuccessful venture into the restaurant business in the mid-1990s provided a significant distraction, and substantial losses were incurred before the company refocused on its successful retail business. But why ruin a good founding story?

If you have job experience, you may well have heard stories concerning the following questions: How will the boss react to a mistake? Can someone move from the bottom to the top of the company? What will get me fired? These are common story topics in many organizations.[23] Often, the stories provide valuable but hidden information about who is more equal than others, whether jobs are secure, and how things are really controlled. In essence, the stories begin to suggest how organizational members view the world and live together.

Some of the most obvious aspects of organizational culture are rites and rituals.[24] **Rites** are standardized and recurring activities that are used at special times to influence the behaviors and understanding of organizational members; **rituals** are systems of rites. It is common, for example, for Japanese workers and managers to start their workdays together with group exercises and singing of the "company song." Separately, the exercises and song are rites. Together, they form part of a ritual. In other settings, such as Mary Kay Cosmetics, scheduled ceremonies reminiscent of the Miss America pageant (a ritual) are used regularly to spotlight positive work achievements and reinforce high-performance expectations with awards, including gold and diamond pins and fur stoles.

- **Rites** are standardized and recurring activities used at special times to influence the behaviors and understanding of organizational members.
- **Rituals** are systems of rites.

Rituals and rites may be unique to particular groups within the organization. Subcultures often arise from the type of technology deployed by the unit, the specific function being performed, and the specific collection of specialists in the unit. A unique language may well maintain the boundaries of the subculture. Often, the language of a subculture, and its rituals and rites, emerge from the group as a form of jargon. In some cases, the special language starts to move outside the firm and begins to enter the larger society. For instance, look at Microsoft Word's specialized language, with such words as hyperlink, frames, and quick parts. It's a good thing they also provide a Help button defining each.

Another observable aspect of corporate culture centers on the symbols found in organizations. A **cultural symbol** is any object, act, or event that serves to transmit cultural meaning. Good examples are the corporate uniforms worn by UPS and Federal Express delivery personnel.

- A **cultural symbol** is any object, act, or event that serves to transmit cultural meaning.

Cultural Rules and Roles

Organizational culture often specifies when various types of actions are appropriate and where individual members stand in the social system. These cultural rules and roles are part of the normative controls of the organization and emerge from its daily routines.[25] For instance, the timing, presentation, and methods of communicating authoritative directives are often quite specific to each organization. In one firm, meetings may follow a set rigid agenda. The manager could go into meetings to tell subordinates what to do and how to accomplish tasks. Private conversations prior to the meeting might be the place for any new ideas or critical examination. In other firms, meetings might be forums for dialogue and discussion, where managers set agendas and then let others offer new ideas, critically examine alternatives, and fully participate. Take a look at how R&R Partners uses what it calls a SWARM.[26]

The Swarm at R&R Partners

R&R Partners is a midsized advertising and lobbying firm headquartered in Las Vegas. It has a creative culture where everyone is expected to constantly be providing new ideas. When creativity is needed, all members are invited into the "war room" to brainstorm. These brainstorming sessions are called a SWARM.

Finding the Leader in You

CHRISTINE SPECHT PUTS A NEW FACE ON COUSINS SUBS

As the second generation to head Cousins Subs, Christine Specht stresses the importance of culture. She makes it perfectly clear that her focus is on the key attributes of the organization founded by her father and his cousin.

Specht notes, "Our food is better; our sandwiches are bigger. More importantly, they are made by people who really care about serving the guests . . . we have a great organizational culture of people who really care about the company and the guest."

For Christine Specht, it is imperative to continue the cultural traditions of Cousins while at the same time making sure the firm is new, vital, and viable. When Specht unveiled a new logo and restaurant design for Cousins Subs, she explained that it was a great time to evolve their look with a logo that while fresh and modern, incorporated the "pride of our family heritage" and shared the story of Cousins Subs with their loyal patrons.

While Specht emphasizes tradition at Cousins, she also looks to the future. When she first became president of the organization she visited all of the franchise operations. Based on this experience, she reorganized the central office operations. The visits helped build trust, and as the economy entered the recession the new central office operations were instrumental in reducing costs for all the

franchise holders. These changes also led to a revamped training program for those who own, and want to own, a Cousins' franchise.

Since becoming president, Specht continues to focus on the cornerstone of the brand—"*Better Bread. Better Subs.*" And it is as true today as it was 30 years ago when cousins Bill Specht and Jim Sheppard started the company. The cousins worked with a local baker to create a unique recipe for their bread that is still baked fresh several times a day in every Cousins store.

What's the Lesson Here?

How comfortable are you with managing change? How can you use stories, rituals, and symbols to reinforce aspects of the culture you want to keep? How much innovation would you introduce and how quickly?

Shared Values, Meanings, and Organizational Myths

To describe an organization's culture more fully, it is necessary to go deeper than the observable aspects. To many researchers and managers, shared common values lie at the very heart of organizational culture.

Shared Values   Shared values help turn routine activities into valuable and important actions, tie the corporation to the important values of society, and possibly provide a very distinctive source of competitive advantage. In organizations, what works for one person is often taught to new members as the correct way to think and feel. Important values are then attributed to these solutions to everyday problems. By linking values and actions, the organization taps into some of the strongest and deepest realms of the individual. The tasks a person performs are given not only meaning but also value: What one does is not only workable but correct, right, and important.

Some successful organizations share some common cultural characteristics.[27] Organizations with "strong cultures" possess a broadly and deeply shared value system. Unique, shared values can provide a strong corporate identity, enhance collective commitment, provide a stable social system, and reduce the need for formal and bureaucratic controls. For firms in a very stable domestic environment, several consultants suggest that firms develop a "strong culture."[28] By this, they basically mean:

- A widely shared real understanding of what the firm stands for, often embodied in slogans
- A concern for individuals over rules, policies, procedures, and adherence to job duties
- A recognition of heroes whose actions illustrate the company's shared philosophy and concerns
- A belief in ritual and ceremony as important to members and to building a common identity
- A well-understood sense of the informal rules and expectations so that employees and managers understand what is expected of them
- A belief that what employees and managers do is important and that it is important to share information and ideas

When it is established over a long period of time, a strong culture can be a double-edged sword. A strong culture and value system can reinforce a singular and sometimes outdated view of the organization and its environment. If dramatic changes are needed, it may be very difficult to change the organization. For years General Motors had a "strong" culture. But as the global auto industry changed, GM could not. It took bankruptcy to shake it to its foundations and provide the impetus for radical change.

Shared Meanings   When you are observing the actions within a firm, it is important to keep in mind the three levels of analysis we mentioned earlier. What you see as an outside observer may not be what organizational members experience because members may link actions to values and unstated assumptions. For instance, in the aftermath of 9/11 many casual observers saw crane operators moving wreckage from an 18-acre pile of rubble that was once the Twin Towers at the World Trade Center complex into waiting trucks.

If you probe the values and assumptions about what these individuals are doing, however, you get an entirely different picture from those actually doing the work. They were not just hauling away the remnants of the Twin Towers at the World Trade Center complex. They were rebuilding America. These workers had infused a larger shared meaning—or sense of broader purpose—into their tasks. Through interaction with one another, and as reinforced by the rest of their organizations and the larger society, their work had deeper meaning. In this deeper sense, organizational culture is a "shared" set of meanings and perceptions.

In most corporations, these shared meanings and perceptions may not be as dramatic as those shared at Ground Zero, yet in most firms employees create and learn a deeper aspect of their culture.[29] Often one finds a series of common assumptions known to most everyone in the corporation: "We are different." "We are better at. . . ." "We have unrecognized talents." Cisco Systems provides an excellent example. Senior managers often share common assumptions, such as "We are good stewards" and "We are competent managers" and "We are practical innovators." Like values, such assumptions become reflected in the organizational culture.

How the Mighty Fall

In his new book, *How the Mighty Fall*, consultant and author Jim Collins asks what can be learned from the failures of previously great companies. He likens corporate decline to a "disease"—the firm looks good on the outside but is sick on the inside. The first stage of decline is "hubris born of success," a point at which arrogance in leadership leads to strategic neglect.

As with a "strong culture," shared meanings and perceptions can be a double-edged sword. While a deeper shared perception can provide managers with a common base for decision making to develop an effective organization, Jim Collins notes in his book *How Do the Mighty Fall*, that firms may begin to decline if managers share an unrealistic positive perception of their firm.[30]

Organizational Myths   In many firms, a key aspect of the shared common assumptions involves organizational myths. **Organizational myths** are unproven and frequently unstated beliefs that are accepted uncritically. Often corporate mythology focuses on cause–effect relationships and assertions by senior management that cannot be empirically supported.[31] Although some may scoff at organizational myths and want to see rational, hard-nosed analysis replace mythology, each firm needs a series of managerial myths.[32] Myths allow executives to redefine impossible problems into more manageable components. Myths can facilitate experimentation and creativity, and they allow managers to govern. Of course, there is also a potential downside to the power of myths.

Three common myths may combine to present major risk problems.[33] The first common myth is the presumption that at least senior management has *no risk bias*. This myth is often expressed as, "Although others may be biased, I am able to define problems and develop solutions objectively." We are all subject to bias in varying degrees and in varying ways. As an issue becomes more complex, it is much more likely there are several biased viable interpretations.

A second common myth is *the presumption of administrative competence*. Managers at all levels are subject to believing that their part of the firm is okay and just needs minor improvements in implementation. As we have documented throughout this book, such is rarely the case. In almost all firms, there is often considerable room for improvement. One particularly damaging manifestation of this myth is that new process and product innovations can be managed in the same way as older ones.

A third common myth is *the denial of trade-offs;* their group, unit, or firm can avoid making undesirable trade-offs and simultaneously please nearly every constituency. Whereas the denial of trade-offs is common, it can be a dangerous myth in some firms. An emphasis on a single goal often means that other goals are neglected. For example, throughout this book we have emphasized ethics to remind the reader that ethics does not stem from the search for higher efficiency. It is a worthy goal among several.

• **Organizational myth** is a commonly held cause-effect relationship or assertion that cannot be supported empirically.

OB IN POPULAR CULTURE

CORPORATE CULTURE AND *THE FIRM*

All organizations have cultures, some stronger than others, and these are reinforced in a variety of ways. **Corporate culture** is reflected in the shared values and beliefs and the actions of employees that reflect them. Culture is important and can be a competitive advantage. Consider the cultures of the United States Marine Corps or most fraternities and sororities. Membership in any one of those organizations creates an identify that defines a person for life.

In *The Firm*, hotshot lawyer Mitch McDeere (Tom Cruise) accepts a position at the Memphis law firm of Bendini, Lambert, & Locke. After graduating first in his Harvard Law School class, he knows what it means to work hard. He shows up early on the first day and finds himself alone in the firm's law library. Sometime later, Lamar Quin (Terry Kinney) arrives to show him around. When Mitch says he "thought he would jump start the bar exam," Lamar quickly responds, "Good because no associate of the firm ever failed the bar exam." Throughout the day, McDeere is greeted by a series of lawyers bringing binders and offering help. Each leaves the office with the same admonishment—"No associate of the firm has ever failed the bar exam."

Corporate culture is reinforced through stories, rites, rituals, and symbols. Rites are special activities that hold important meaning throughout the organization. Like rites of passage, these activities may represent tests that employees are expected to pass. At Bendini, Lambert, & Locke, the bar exam was the measure of success. If you wanted to stay with the firm, you had better pass.

Get to Know Yourself Better Do you think much about organizational culture? Take a look at Assessment 22, Which Culture Fits You? in the OB Skills Workbook. What does it reveal about your preference? While person–organization fit is important, you may not have the luxury of choosing the "right" organization upon graduating. Could you work in an organization that had any one of the other three cultures? What challenges might this present for you?

As illustrated in Figure 15.2, these myths may combine to yield purposeful unintended consequences.

Purposeful unintended consequences arise from the collective application of these three myths. Purposeful unintended consequences are dramatic, unanticipated benefits or costs arising from the implementation of a way of doing business. Often these unintended consequences are dire. They are purposeful because they stem from unexamined myths—myths managers think apply to others and not themselves.

The recent financial meltdown in mortgage-backed securities is an example.[34] Over the last decade, banks and financial institutions bought and sold mortgage-backed derivatives (complex financial instruments) under the myths that they could (1) accurately judge the risk themselves and value them accurately (they were not risk biased), (2) administer these complex instruments in a manner similar to traditional mortgages (the presumption of administrative competence), and (3) gain great short-term returns without risking long-term profitability (denial of trade-offs). These combined myths allowed the managers to dismiss collectively the potential of a systematic meltdown of the entire financial system (the

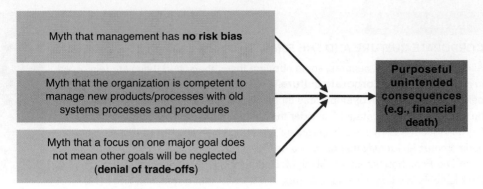

Figure 15.2 Purposeful unintended consequences arising from organizational myths.

dire unintended consequence). Yet, by the end of 2008 and the beginning of 2009 the global financial system almost collapsed from these and related problems. Was the unintended consequence pursued on purpose? Yes and no. No one manager sought a meltdown. Yet, collectively, millions of mortgages were granted to individuals with questionable credit and used to develop new types of financial instruments. It took unprecedented actions by many central banks and governments to avert a collapse.

And yet, mortgage-backed securities and derivatives were one of the financial system's major innovations toward the turn of the century. They were an important way to broaden the financial support for housing. Initially they appeared quite successful and provided financial institutions with a way to grow and prosper. So, we turn to the topic of innovation to delve more deeply into this important factor for growth and prosperity.

Innovation in Organizations

LEARNING ROADMAP   The Process of Innovation / Product and Process Innovations / Balancing Exploration and Exploitation

When analysis stresses commonly shared actions, values, and common assumptions across the entire organization, it can appear that firms are static, unchanging entities. It is quite clear that much of the organization's culture and its structure emphasize stability and control. Yet, we all know that the world is changing and that firms must change with it. The best organizations don't stagnate; they consistently innovate to the extent that innovation becomes a part of everyday operations.

• **Innovation** is the process of creating new ideas and putting them into practice.

Innovation is the process of creating new ideas and putting them into practice.[35] It is the means by which creative ideas find their way into everyday practices—ideally practices that contribute to improved customer service or organizational productivity. There are a variety of ways to look at innovation. Here, we will examine it as a process, separate product from process innovation, and note the tensions between the early development of ideas and the task of implementation.

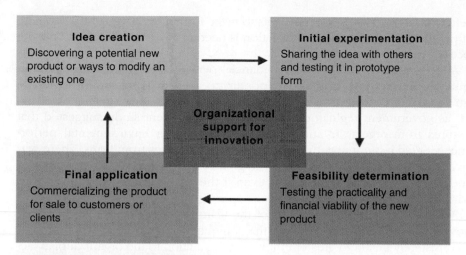

Figure 15.3 The innovation process: a case of new product development.

The Process of Innovation

One easy way to look at the complex process of innovation is to break it down into four steps (see Figure 15.3).

1. *Idea creation*—to create an idea through spontaneous creativity, ingenuity, and information processing
2. *Initial experimentation*—to establish the idea's potential value and application
3. *Feasibility determination*—to identify anticipated costs and benefits
4. *Final application*—to produce and market a new product or service, or to implement a new approach to operations

It takes many creative ideas to establish a base for initial experimentation. Moreover, many successful initial experiments are just not feasible. Even among the few feasible ideas, only the rare idea actually makes it into application. Finally, innovative entities benefit from and require top-management support. Senior managers can and must provide good examples for others, eliminate obstacles to innovation, and try to get things done that make innovation easier.

By emphasizing the innovation process, innovative entities often adapt a different culture from the ones typically found where more routine operations are paramount. Innovative entities look to the future, are willing to cannibalize existing products in their development of new ones, have a high tolerance for risk, have a high tolerance for mistakes, respect well-intentioned ideas that just do not work, prize creativity, and reward and give special attention to idea generators, information keepers, product champions, and project leaders. They also prize empowerment and emphasize communication up, down, and across all individuals in the unit.[36]

Although it is convenient to depict the process as a sequential four-step affair, you should be aware that in practice the process of innovation is often quite messy. Take a look at Figure 15.3. With initial experimentation, for instance, the very act of sharing ideas with others can, and often does, yield a completely new set of ideas. Even in final application, the process does not stop, as astute innovators carefully listen to customers and clients to make further improvements. Also note that organizational support for innovation is needed in each step in this ongoing process.

Although the desire to improve financial performance is often important in stimulating innovation, it is also important to note that innovation can arise from the firm's desire to be more legitimate in the eyes of key stakeholders, such as government regulators. For example, one recent study suggested that pressures from regulators and a prior record of poor environmental performance yielded more innovative environmental responses from firms. There was an exception, however, in that firms with greater slack resources did not respond as positively to regulatory pressures even if they had a record of poorer prior environmental performance.[37]

Research also shows the results of the team factors associated with greater innovation. It is clear from this work that a number of important team processes are consistently linked to greater innovation in addition to the organizational factors noted above.

Product and Process Innovations

Product innovations result in the introduction of new or improved goods or services to better meet customer needs. A number of studies suggest that the key difficulty associated with product development is the integration across all of the units needed to move from the idea stage to final implementation.[38] Culturally, new product development often challenges existing practice, existing value structures, and common understandings. For instance, by its very definition, product innovation means that the definition of the business will change. Many firms find it difficult to cannibalize their existing product lineup in the hope that new products will be even more successful. Yet, this is what often needs to be done.[39]

Product innovation is so important that a number of government-based initiatives have been launched to help spur the development of new products. Individuals proposing initiatives point to the revolution resulting from development of the Internet, the hope for new green technologies, and the promise of medical breakthroughs to change the human condition. One important new study suggests that corporate culture, rather than national policy, makes the biggest difference with radical product innovation.[40]

A number of interrelated firms may share the product innovation process.[41] Generally speaking, large complex products are often combinations of individual components from a variety of corporations. At the extreme, there is open innovation where each firm knows what the others are doing. Control is exercised by a common design, often under the direction of a single integrator who maintains the dominant design. This is often the model in computer software, for instance. It is important to note that the development and control of the dominant design can be linked to extremely high profitability.[42] Furthermore, the dominant design is often not the best technical solution—it is the solution most often adopted by a large number of users.

Where the product innovation process is less open, firms often find that coordination with lead users can help provide design insights.[43] Yet, firms typically confront waning commitment to product innovation. Although no solution is perfect, several studies suggest that the development of multidisciplinary teams

• **Product innovations** introduce new goods or services to better meet customer needs.

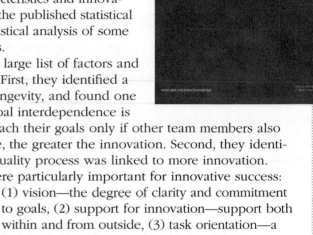

RESEARCH INSIGHT

Team Factors and Innovation

What characteristics of innovation teams are linked to success? Because so much innovation depends on teams of individuals, a large volume of work has been done on the linkage between team characteristics and innovation. Here, the authors systematically reviewed all the published statistical studies over the last 30 years and conducted a statistical analysis of some 100 studies with a technique called a meta-analysis.

As you might expect, they started with a very large list of factors and found that a handful were particularly important. First, they identified a series of input variables, such as team size and longevity, and found one major factor they called goal interdependence. Goal interdependence is essentially the degree to which individuals can reach their goals only if other team members also reach theirs. The higher the goal interdependence, the greater the innovation. Second, they identified a host of team processes in which a higher quality process was linked to more innovation.

The authors found that six team processes were particularly important for innovative success:

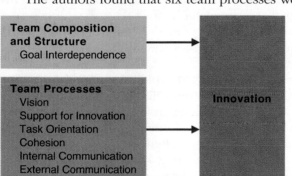

(1) vision—the degree of clarity and commitment to goals, (2) support for innovation—support both within and from outside, (3) task orientation—a climate for excellence, (4) cohesion—a commitment to the team and maintenance of group membership, (5) internal communications—quality interactions within the group, and (6) external communications—quality interactions with outsiders. For instance, if there was greater support for innovation, there was greater success. These six factors are in the schematic.

> **Do the Research**   Were you surprised that some composition factors such as size were not consistently important? Of the six important team factors, which ones do you think would be most important for idea generation? Which factors might be particularly critical for successful implementation?

Source: U. Hulsher, N. Anderson, and J. Salgado, "Team-Level Predictors of Innovation at Work: A Comprehensive Meta-Analysis Spanning Three Decades of Research, *Journal of Applied Psychology* 94.5 (2009), pp. 1128–1145.

can help maintain broader commitment. Of course, just the inclusion of individuals with diverse skills, interests, and perspectives calls for astute management. As we said earlier, the innovation process is far from easy.

Process innovations result in the introduction of new and better work methods and operations. Perhaps one of the most interesting and difficult types of process improvement is that of management innovation.[44] Obviously, much management innovation comes from the vast industry known as management consulting, Unfortunately, many of the new management practices emanating from these outside units are more fashions and fads than workable

• **Process innovations** introduce into operations new and better ways of doing things.

solutions to the problems faced by individual firms. The key to successful managerial innovation often involves extensive interaction with peers, subordinates, and superiors. As astute managers try new practices, they compare initial implementation with the reactions of peers and subordinates to refine and modify the practice. Often this process of trial and error takes several iterations before the practice becomes accepted well enough to provide the intended benefits.

Balancing Exploration and Exploitation

As suggested by Figure 15.3, the innovation continuum runs from exploration to exploitation.[45] In the early stages of innovation, time, energy, and effort to explore potentials are necessary. These early phases are the result of the research and development units found in so many companies. Yet, too much emphasis on exploration will yield a whole list of potential ideas for new products and processes to new clients and customers in new markets, but little pay-off. It is also important to stress *exploitation* to capture the economic value stemming from exploration.[46] **Exploitation** often focuses on refinement and reuse of existing products and processes. Refining an existing product to make it more saleable in a new market is an example of exploitation. Of course, too much emphasis on exploitation and the firm loses its competitive edge because its products become obsolete and its processes less effective and efficient than those of competitors.

The admonition to balance exploration and exploitation sounds very simple, but it comes with a major problem. **Exploration** calls for the organization and its managers to stress freedom and radical thinking and therefore opens the firm to big changes—or what some call radical innovations.[47] Although some radical departures are built on existing competencies, often the adoption of a radically new product or process means that the existing knowledge within a firm is invalidated.[48] Conversely, an emphasis on exploitation stresses control and evolutionary development. Such exploitation can be planned with tight budgets, careful forecasts, and steady implementation. It is often much easier to stress exploitation because most organizations have a structure and culture that emphasize stability and control.[49]

Managers may attempt to solve this tension between exploration and exploitation in a variety of ways. One partial solution is to have separate units for the two types of activities. For example, some firms rely heavily on cooperative R&D arrangements with other firms for exploration and keep a tight rein on exploitation within the firm.[50] Others rely on middle managers to reconcile the tensions stemming from attempts to link explorative and exploitative groups. However, the desired mix of explorative and exploitative may well depend on the industry setting.

Recent research suggests a more culturally oriented solution based on the notion of an ambidextrous organization. There appear to be four critical factors in building an ambidextrous organization:

1. Managers must recognize the tension between exploration and exploitation.
2. Managers should realize that one form of thinking based on a single perspective is inappropriate.

• **Exploitation** focuses on refinement and reuse of existing products and processes.

• **Exploration** calls for the organization and its managers to stress freedom and radical thinking and therefore opens the firm to big changes–or what some call radical innovations.

3. Managers need to discuss with their subordinates the paradoxes arising from simultaneously thinking about big ideas and sound incremental improvements.

4. Managers must encourage subordinates to embrace these paradoxes and use them as motivations to provide creative solutions.[51]

Managing Organizational Culture and Innovation

LEARNING ROADMAP   Management Philosophy and Strategy / Building, Reinforcing, and Changing Culture / Tensions Between Cultural Stability and Innovation

Good managers are able to reinforce and support an existing strong culture. They are also able to help build resilient cultures in situations where they are absent. The best managers also recognize that effectively managing an organization culture involves incorporation of the innovation process as well.

Management Philosophy and Strategy

The process of managing organizational culture calls for a clear understanding of the organizational subculture at the top and a firm recognition of what can and cannot be changed. The first step in managing an organizational culture is for management to recognize its own subculture. Key aspects of the top-management subculture are often referred to in the OB literature by the term *management philosophy*. A **management philosophy** links important goals with key collaboration issues and comes up with a series of general ways by which the firm will manage its affairs.[52] Specifically, it (1) establishes generally understood boundaries for all members of the firm, (2) provides a consistent way of approaching new and novel situations, and (3) helps hold individuals together by assuring them of a known path toward success. In other words, it is the way in which top management addresses the questions of external adaptation.

When the management philosophy stresses security and stability, management reinforces such values as benevolence. Such firms tend to be less innovative than when the management philosophy is more self-directive and reinforces risk taking. When the management philosophy stresses reaching out to others, embracing novel situations, and collectively developing a new path toward new visions of success, there is greater innovation.[53]

> • A **management philosophy** links key goal-related issues with key collaboration issues to come up with general ways by which the firm will manage its affairs.

How to Become a Better Culture Manager

To develop a strong management culture, managers need to:

- Emphasize a shared understanding of what the unit stands for.
- Stress a concern for members over rules and procedures.
- Talk about heroes of the past and their contributions.
- Develop rituals and ceremonies for the members.
- Reinforce informal rules and expectations consistent with shared values.
- Promote the sharing of ideas and information.
- Provide employees with emotional support.
- Make a commitment to understand all members.
- Support progressive thinking by all members.

For instance, the management philosophy at Cisco Systems links the strategic concerns of growth, profitability, and customer service with observable aspects of culture and desired underlying values. While elements of a management philosophy may be formally documented in a corporate plan or statement of business philosophy, it is the understood fundamentals these documents signify that form the heart of a successfully developed management philosophy.[53A]

Building, Reinforcing, and Changing Culture

Managers can modify the visible aspects of culture, such as the language, stories, rites, rituals, and sagas. They can change the lessons drawn from common stories and even encourage individuals to see the reality they see. Because of their positions, senior managers can interpret situations in new ways and can adjust the meanings attached to important corporate events. They can create new rites and rituals. Executives can back these initiatives with both their words and their actions. This takes time and an enormous amount of energy, but the long-run benefits can be great. This is the approach found at Cisco Systems.[54]

One of the key ways management influences the organizational culture is through the reward systems it establishes. In many larger U.S.-based firms, the reward system matches the overall strategy of the firm and reinforces the culture emerging from day-to-day activities. Two patterns of reward systems, strategies, and corporate cultures are common. The first is a steady-state strategy matched with hierarchical rewards and consistent with what can be labeled a clan culture. Specifically, rewards emphasize and reinforce a culture characterized by long-term commitment, fraternal relationships, mutual interests, and collegiality with heavy pressures to conform from peers and with superiors acting as mentors. Firms with this pattern were in such industries as power generation, chemicals, mining, and pharmaceuticals.

In contrast was a second pattern in which the strategy stressed evolution and change. Here the rewards emphasized and reinforced a more market culture. That is, rewards emphasized a contractual link between employee and employer, focused on short-term performance, and stressed individual initiative with very little pressure from peers to conform and with supervisors acting as resource allocators. Firms with this pattern were often in such industries as restaurants, consumer products, and industrial services.[55]

Beyond reward systems, top managers can set the tone for a culture and for cultural change. Managers at Aetna Life and Casualty Insurance built on its humanistic traditions to provide basic skills to highly motivated but underqualified individuals. Even in the highly cost-competitive steel industry, Nucor executives built on basic entrepreneurial values in U.S. society to reduce the number of management levels by half.

Each of these examples illustrates how managers can help foster a culture that provides answers to important questions concerning external adaptation and internal integration. Recent work on the linkages between corporate culture and financial performance reaffirms the importance of an emphasis on helping employees adjust to the environment. It also suggests that this emphasis alone is not sufficient. Neither is an emphasis solely on stockholders or customers associated with long-term economic performance. Instead, managers must work to emphasize all three issues simultaneously.

The need to provide a balanced emphasis can be seen when executives violate ethical and legal standards as in the case of misleading earning statements. One key study found that while the fines levied for "cooking the books" may appear small, other costs were far more substantial. The real costs to these firms came from a loss of their reputation in the business community. Customers lost confidence, suppliers demanded greater assurances, and, of course, the entire financial community undervalued the firm so that loan costs were higher, stock prices were lower, and scrutiny was more extensive. How big is big? The fines averaged about $23 million a firm. The estimated financial cost from the loss of reputation was estimated at 7.5 times the average fine. That yielded a loss of some $196 million.[56]

Early research on culture and cultural change often emphasized direct attempts by senior management to alter the values and assumptions of individuals by resocializing them—that is, trying to change their hearts so that their minds and actions would follow.[57] The goal was to establish a clear, consistent organization-wide consensus. More recent work suggests that this unified approach of working through values may not be either possible or desirable.[58]

Trying to change people's values from the top down without also changing how the organization operates and recognizes the importance of individuals does not work very well. Look again at the example of Cisco Systems. Here managers realized that maintaining a dynamic, change-oriented culture is a mix of managerial actions, decisions about technology, and initiatives from all employees. The values are not set and imposed from someone on high. The shared values emerge, and they are not identical across all of Cisco's operating sites. For instance, subtle but important differences emerge across their operations in Silicon Valley, the North Carolina operation, and the Australian setting.

Tensions Between Cultural Stability and Innovation

Although organizational cultures help individuals cope with external adaptation and internal integration, the enduring pattern of observable actions, shared values, and common assumptions often does not evolve as quickly as required by innovations. **Organizational cultural lag** is a condition in which dominant cultural patterns are inconsistent with new emerging innovations.[59] As we suggested earlier, observable aspects of organizational culture such as rites, rituals, and cultural symbols often have powerful underlying meaning for organizational members. In a way they are symbols of prior successful ways to cope with external adaptation and internal integration. Individuals are often wary of abandoning the successful for an unproven new approach. One scholar notes that there can be a major "cultural drag on innovation from cultural legacies."[60] These legacy effects come from an overreliance on rule following and reinforcement of old existing patterns of action.

Thus, one of the key challenges to management in promoting innovation where there are widely held and strong attached-to shared values and common assumptions is to show how they apply to the new innovations. When managers see an opportunity to develop new visions, create new strategies, and move the organization in new directions, they need to balance rule changing and rule

* **Organizational cultural lag** is a condition where dominant cultural patterns are inconsistent with new emerging innovations.

following.[61] If left uncontrolled, rule changing can yield runaway industry change that can quickly lead to chaos. While rule following can lead to a more stable industry structure and/or controlled industry change, there is also a danger of reinforcing cultural lag.

15 *study guide*

Key Questions and Answers

What is organizational culture?

- Organizational or corporate culture is the system of shared actions, values, and beliefs that develops within an organization and guides the behavior of its members.

- The functions of the corporate culture include responding to both external adaptation and internal integration issues.

- Most organizations contain a variety of subcultures, and a few have countercultures that can sometimes become the source of potentially harmful conflicts.

- The corporate culture also reflects the values and implicit assumptions of the larger national culture.

How do you understand an organizational culture?

- Organizational cultures may be analyzed in terms of observable actions, shared values, and common assumptions (the taken-for-granted truths).

- Observable aspects of culture include the stories, rites, rituals, and symbols that are shared by organization members.

- Cultural rules and roles specify when various types of actions are appropriate and where individual members stand in the social system.

- Shared meanings and understandings help everyone know how to act and expect others to act in various circumstances.

- Common assumptions are the taken-for-granted truths that are shared by collections of corporate members.

What is innovation and why is it important?

- Innovation is the process of creating new ideas and then implementing them in practical applications.

- Steps in the innovation process normally include idea generation, initial experimentation, feasibility determination, and final application.

- Common features of highly innovative organizations include supportive strategies, cultures, structures, staffing, and senior leadership.

- Product innovations result in improved goods or services; process innovations result in improved work methods and operations.

- Process innovations introduce into operations new and better ways of doing things.

- While it is necessary to balance exploration and exploitation, it is difficult to accomplish.

How can we manage organizational culture and innovation?

- Executives may manage many aspects of the observable culture directly.

- Nurturing shared values among the membership is a major challenge for executives.

- Adjusting actions to common understandings limits the decision scope of even the CEO.

- There are tensions between the tendency for cultural stability in most firms and the need to innovate.

Terms to Know

Countercultures (p. 350)
Cultural symbol (p. 355)
Exploitation (p. 364)
Exploration (p. 364)
External adaptation (p. 348)
Innovation (p. 360)
Internal integration (p. 349)

Management philosophy (p. 365)
Multicultural organization (p. 352)
Observable culture (p. 353)
Organizational cultural lag (p. 367)
Organizational or corporate
   culture (p. 348)
Organizational myth (p. 358)

Process innovations (p. 363)
Product innovations (p. 362)
Rites (p. 355)
Rituals (p. 355)
Saga (p. 354)
Subcultures (p. 350)

Self-Test 15

Multiple Choice

1. Culture concerns all of the following except _____. (a) the collective concepts shared by members of a firm (b) acquired capabilities (c) the personality of the leader (d) the beliefs of members

2. The three levels of cultural analysis highlighted in the text concern _____. (a) observable culture, shared values, and common assumptions (b) stories, rites, and rituals (c) symbols, myths, and stories (d) manifest culture, latent culture, and observable artifacts

3. External adaptation concerns _____. (a) the unproven beliefs of senior executives (b) the process of coping with outside forces (c) the vision of the founder (d) the processes working together

4. Internal integration concerns _____. (a) the process of deciding the collective identity and how members will live together (b) the totality of the daily life of members as they see and describe it (c) expressed unproven beliefs that are accepted uncritically and used to justify current actions (d) groups of individuals with a pattern of values that rejects those of the larger society

5. When Japanese workers start each day with the company song, this is an example of a(n) _____. (a) symbol (b) myth (c) underlying assumption (d) ritual

6. _____ is a sense of broader purpose that workers infuse into their tasks as a result of interaction with one another. (a) A rite (b) A cultural symbol (c) A foundation myth (d) A shared meaning

7. The story of a corporate turnaround attributed to the efforts of a visionary manager is an example of _____. (a) a saga (b) a foundation myth (c) internal integration (d) a latent cultural artifact

8. The process of creating new ideas and putting them into practice is _____. (a) innovation (b) creative destruction (c) product innovation (d) process innovation

9. Any object, act, or event that serves to transmit cultural meaning is called _____. (a) a saga (b) a cultural symbol (c) a cultural lag (d) a cultural myth

10. Groups where the patterns of values outwardly reject those of the larger organization are _____. (a) external adaptation rejectionist (b) cultural lag (c) countercultures (d) organizational myths

11. Groups with unique patterns of values and philosophies that are consistent with the dominant organizational culture are called _____. (a) countercultures (b) subcultures (c) sagas (d) rituals

12. A _____ links key goal-related issues with key collaboration issues to come up with general ways by which the firm will manage its affairs. (a) managerial philosophy (b) cultural symbol (c) ritual (d) saga

13. Commonly held cause–effect relationships that cannot be empirically supported are referred to as _____. (a) cultural lags (b) rituals (c) management philosophy (d) organizational myths

14. The patterns of values and philosophies that outwardly reject those of the larger organization or social system are called _____. (a) sagas (b) organizational development (c) rituals (d) countercultures

15. _____ is a condition in which dominant cultural patterns are inconsistent with new emerging innovations. (a) Organizational cultural lag (b) Management philosophy (c) Internal integration (d) External adaptation

Short Response

16. Describe the five steps Taylor Cox suggests need to be developed to help generate a multicultural organization or pluralistic company culture.

17. List the three aspects that help individuals and groups work together effectively and illustrate them through practical examples.

18. Give an example of how cultural rules and roles affect the atmosphere in a college classroom. Provide specific examples from your own perspective.

19. What are the major elements of a strong corporate culture?

Applications Essay

20. Discuss why managers should balance exploration and exploitation when seeking greater innovation.

Next Steps

Top Choices from *The OB Skills Workbook*

Case for Critical Thinking	Team and Experiential Exercises	Self-Assessment Portfolio
• Never on a Sunday	• How We View Differences • Workgroup Culture • Fast-Food Technology • Alien Invasion	• Are You Cosmopolitan? • Team Effectiveness • Which Culture Fits You?

Employee Autonomy: **A Little Freedom Goes a Long Way**

Turn them loose. Get the management layers off their backs, the bureaucratic shackles off their feet, and the functional barriers out of their way.[a]

Jack Welch Jr., the former CEO and chairman of General Electric, knew how to get the most out of his employees; he was an ardent believer in giving them clear goals and the freedom to excel according to their own rules.

He's not alone. There's a growing consensus that organizations benefit when they give employees more autonomy in their jobs. Consider these methods:

> *"So long as it fits in with managing the workload, flexibility is okay. It's not that old-school thought of, 'You have to be at your work (place) to be at work.'"*
> *—Edweana Wenkart, Tsuki Communications, on telecommuting.*[e]

- *Side projects:* Google understands that employees are more productive and engaged when projects stir their passions, so Googlers can spend some of their time on projects of their own invention. The results include Gmail, Google News, and dozens of Labs features.[b]

- *Hackfests:* Pizza + beer + programmers = inspired coding. From startups to Facebook, companies find that sponsoring all-night programming sessions is a cheap way to develop new products (and camaraderie) in a flash.

- *Flex time and telecommuting:* Employees who can come in late, leave early, or work from home are more likely to stay with a company that helps them balance their work and home lives.

- *Predictability:* Ironically, freedom even comes from structure. When job roles are clearly defined, employees can succeed without concern for overstepping boundaries. For example, at American Express, it's company practice that junior managers bear individual leadership, middle managers execute policy, and vice presidents lead strategic initiatives.[c]

"If leaders create the right environment and engage in the right behaviors, employees will give their best to the organization," says author David Witt. "This leads to a greater sense of excitement and passion at work that leads to better customer service."[d] Clear goals need to be matched to a structure that facilitates goal attainment.

Quick Summary
- Companies are increasingly exploring alternatives to rigid rules and bureaucratic structures in order to keep valued employees and increase their productivity.
- These measures often align with harnessing employees' passions, giving them flexible work schedules, or more clearly defining their roles.

FYI: Google employees are expected to spend up to 20% of their time on self-led projects that combine their skills and passions.

16 Organizational Goals and Structures

the key point

Organizations are collections of people working together to achieve common goals. While employees value autonomy, executives need to make the organization's goals clear and structure the organization to reach those goals. To effectively manage you will need to know how to organize a hierarchy and control it. You will also need to know how to organize the work to be done and effectively coordinate with others.

chapter at a glance

What Are the Different Types of Organizational Goals?

What Are the Hierarchical Aspects of Organizations?

How Is Work Organized and Coordinated?

What Are Bureaucracies and What Are the Common Forms?

ETHICS IN OB
FLATTENED INTO EXHAUSTION

FINDING THE LEADER IN YOU
KAREN BRYANT WINS BY STAYING FOCUSED ON GOALS

OB IN POPULAR CULTURE
HIERARCHY AND *RATATOUILLE*

RESEARCH INSIGHT
COORDINATION IN TEMPORARY ORGANIZATIONS

what's inside?

Ever think about working for a large firm and all of that bureaucracy? Rigid rules, elaborate procedures, multiple layers, and narrow jobs were once the hallmarks of large firms. Google and GE are but two examples of large firms that have stressed new ways of organizing to boost autonomy and give all employees much more say in both what goals to pursue and how to reach these goals. Although it is a challenge to develop goals that serve both employees and the organization and to match these goals to effective structures, this challenge must be met to be successful.

Organizational Goals

LEARNING ROADMAP Societal Goals / Output Goals / Systems Goals

The notion that organizations have goals is very familiar simply because our world is one comprised of organizations.[1] Most of us are born, go to school, work, and retire in organizations. Without organizations and their limited, goal-directed behavior, modern societies would simply cease to exist. We would need to revert to older forms of social organization based on royalty, clans, and tribes. Organizational goals are so pervasive we rarely give them more than passing notice.

No firm can be all things to all people. By selecting goals, firms also define who they are and what they will try to become. The choice of goals involves the type of contribution the firm makes to the larger society and the types of outputs it seeks.[2] Managers decide how to link conditions considered desirable for enhanced survival prospects with its societal and output desires.[3] From these basic choices, executives can work with subordinates to develop ways of accomplishing the chosen targets. The goals of the firm should be consistent and compatible with the way in which it is organized.

Societal Goals

• **Societal goals** reflect the intended contributions of an organization to the broader society.

Organizations do not operate in a social vacuum, but rather they reflect the needs and desires of the societies in which they operate. **Societal goals** reflect an organization's intended contributions to the broader society.[4] Organizations normally serve a specific societal function or an enduring need of the society. Astute top-level managers build on the professed societal contribution of the organization by relating specific organizational tasks and activities to higher purposes. By contributing to the larger society, organizations gain legitimacy, a social right to operate, and more discretion for their nonsocietal goals and operating practices. By claiming to provide specific types of societal contributions, an organization can also make legitimate claims over resources, individuals, markets, and products.

• **Mission statements** are written statements of organizational purpose.

Often, the social contribution of the firm is part of its mission statement. **Mission statements** are written statements of organizational purpose. Weaving a mission statement together with an emphasis on implementation to provide direction and motivation is an executive order of the first magnitude. A good mission statement states whom the firm will serve and how it will go about accomplishing its societal purpose.[5] Hope Labs is a good example of a firm building on a clearly stated social purpose.

We would expect to see the mission statement of a political party linked to generating and allocating power for the betterment of citizens. Mission statements for universities often profess to both develop and disseminate knowledge. Courts are expected to integrate the interests and activities of citizens. Finally, business firms are expected to provide economic sustenance and material well-being.[6]

Video Games Bring Hope and Health

Pam Omidyar, an immunology researcher and gaming enthusiast, founded the nonprofit Hope Labs to "improve the health and quality of life of young people with chronic illness." It produced the video game Re-Mission where players move the nanorobot Roxxi through the body of a cancer patient to destroy cancer cells. The game helps young patients stick to their medication schedules.

Organizations that can more effectively translate the positive character of their societal contribution into a favorable image have an advantage over firms that neglect this sense of purpose. Executives who link their firm to a desirable mission can lay claim to important motivational tools that are based on a shared sense of noble purpose. Some executives and consultants talk of a "strategic vision" that links highly desirable and socially appealing goals to the contributions a firm intends to make. The first step is a clear and compelling mission statement.

When it introduced its new all electric zero-turning riding lawnmower, the Hustler Zeon, Paul Mullet, president of Hustler Turf Equipment, restated his firm's mission "to provide innovative and durable outdoor power equipment, maximizing customer noble purpose."[7] The mission statement of Hustler Turf Equipment is a good example.

Output Goals

Organizations need to refine their societal contributions in order to target their efforts toward a particular group.[8] In the United States, for example, it is generally expected that the primary beneficiary of business firms is the stockholder. Interestingly, in Japan employees are much more important, and stockholders are considered as important as banks and other financial institutions. Although each organization may have a primary beneficiary, its mission statement may also recognize the interests of many other parties. Thus, business mission statements often include service to customers, the organization's obligations to employees, and its intention to support the community.

As managers consider how they will accomplish their firm's mission, many begin with a very clear statement of which business they are in.[9] This statement can form the basis for long-term planning and may help prevent huge organizations from diverting too many resources to peripheral areas. For some corporations, answering the question of which business they are in may yield a more detailed statement concerning their products and services. These product and service goals provide an important basis for judging the firm. **Output goals** define the type of business an organization is in and provide some substance to the more general aspects of mission statements.

* **Output goals** are the goals that define the type of business an organization is in.

Systems Goals

Historically, fewer than 10 percent of the privately owned businesses founded in a typical year can be expected to survive to their twentieth birthday.[10] The survival rate for public organizations is not much better. Even in organizations for which survival is not an immediate problem, managers seek specific types of conditions within their firms that minimize the risk of demise and promote survival. These conditions are positively stated as systems goals.

• **Systems goals** are concerned with the conditions within the organization that are expected to increase its survival potential.

Systems goals are concerned with the conditions within the organization that are expected to increase the organization's survival potential. The list of systems goals is almost endless, since each manager and researcher links today's conditions to tomorrow's existence in a different way. For many organizations, however, the list includes growth, productivity, stability, harmony, flexibility, prestige, and human-resource maintenance. In some businesses, analysts consider market share and current profitability important systems goals, while many suggest that innovation and quality are also considered important.[11]

In a very practical sense, systems goals represent short-term organizational characteristics that higher-level managers wish to promote. Systems goals often must be balanced against one another. For instance, a productivity and efficiency drive, if taken too far, may reduce the flexibility of an organization even in a downturn. For example, PepsiCo's CEO Indra Nooyi, eliminated plants and over 3,000 jobs, yet she also knows she must expand PepsiCo's operations in China.[12]

Often different parts of the organization are asked to pursue different types of systems goals. For example, higher-level managers may expect to see their production operations strive for efficiency while pressing for innovation from their R&D lab and promoting stability in their financial affairs. The relative importance of different systems goals can vary substantially across various types of organizations. Although we may expect the University of British Columbia or the University of New South Wales to emphasize prestige and innovation (in the form of research), few expect such businesses as Pepsi or Coke to subordinate growth and profitability to prestige. We expect to see some societal expectations and output desires used to justify the incorporation of some systems goals.

Systems goals are important to firms because they provide a roadmap that helps them link together various units of their organization to assure survival. Well-defined systems goals are practical and easy to understand; they focus the manager's attention on what needs to be done. Accurately stated systems goals also offer managers flexibility in devising ways to meet important targets. They can be used to balance the demands, constraints, and opportunities facing the firm. Recent research suggests incorporating integrity and ethics into the desired system goals characteristics.

The choices managers make regarding systems goals should naturally form a basis for dividing the work of the firm—a basis for developing a formal structure. In other words, to ensure success, management needs to match decisions regarding what to accomplish with choices concerning an appropriate way to organize in reaching these goals. Since the formal structure is so important, we will detail the types of choices managers can make in organizing, controlling, and coordinating the tasks needed to reach goals.

Hierarchy and Control

The formal structure of an organization outlines the jobs to be done, the persons who are to perform specific activities, and the ways the total tasks of the organization are to be accomplished. In other words, the formal structure is the skeleton of the firm.[13] The formal structure shows the planned pattern of positions, job duties, and the lines of authority among different parts of the enterprise. The pattern selected provides the organization with specific strengths to reach toward some goals more than others. Traditionally, the formal structure of the firm has also been called the division of labor. Some still use this terminology to isolate decisions concerning formal structure from choices regarding the division of markets and/or technology. We will deal with environmental and technology issues after we discuss the structure as a foundation for managerial action.

Organizations as Hierarchies

In larger organizations, there is a clear separation of authority and duties by rank. How authority is specialized is known as vertical specialization. **Vertical specialization** is an organization's hierarchical division of labor that distributes formal authority and establishes where and how critical decisions are to be made. This division creates a hierarchy of authority—an arrangement of work positions in order of increasing authority.[14]

• **Vertical specialization** is a hierarchical division of labor that distributes formal authority.

The Organization Chart Diagrams that depict the formal structures of organizations are known as **organizational charts**. A typical chart shows the various positions, the position holders, and the lines of authority that link them to one another. Figure 16.1 presents a partial organization chart for a large university. The total chart allows university employees to locate their positions in the structure

• **Organizational charts** are diagrams that depict the formal structures of organizations.

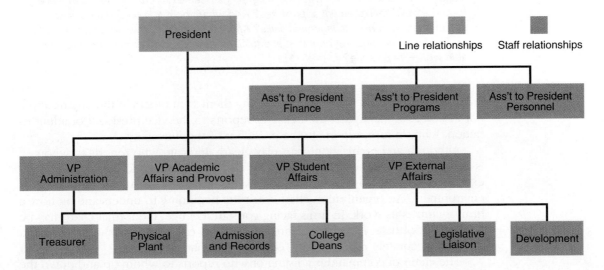

Figure 16.1 A partial organization chart for a state university.

FLATTENED INTO EXHAUSTION

Dear Stress Doctor:

My boss has come up with this great idea of cutting some supervisor positions, assigning more workers to those of us who remain, and calling us "coaches" instead of supervisors. She says this is all part of a new management approach to operate with a flatter structure and more empowerment.

For me this means a lot more work coordinating the activities of 17 operators instead of the 6 that I previously supervised. I can't get everything cleaned up on my desk most days, and I end up taking a lot of paperwork home.

As my organization "restructures" and cuts back staff, it puts a greater burden on those of us that remain. We get exhausted, and our families get short-changed and even angry. I even feel guilty now taking time to watch my daughter play soccer on Saturday mornings. Sure, there's some decent pay involved, but that doesn't make up for the heavy price I'm paying in terms of lost family times.

But you know what? My boss doesn't get it. I never hear her ask: "Henry, are you working too much; don't you think it's time to get back on a reasonable schedule?" No! What I often hear instead is "Look at Andy; he handles our new management model really well, and he's a real go-getter. I don't think he's been out of here one night this week before 8 PM."

What am I to do, just keep it up until everything falls apart one day? Is a flatter structure with fewer managers always best? Am I missing something in regard to this "new management?"

Sincerely,
Overworked in Cincinnati

Get the Ethics Straight   Is it ethical to restructure, cut management levels, and expect the remaining managers to do more work? Or is it simply the case that managers used to the "old" ways of doing things need extra training and care while learning "new" management approaches? And what about this person's boss—is she on track with her management skills? Aren't managers supposed to help people understand their jobs, set priorities, and fulfill them, while still maintaining a reasonable work–life balance?

and to identify the lines of authority linking them with others in the organization. For instance, in this figure, the treasurer reports to the vice president of administration, who, in turn, reports to the president of the university.

Although an organization chart may clearly indicate who reports to whom, it is also important to recognize that it does not show how work is completed, who exercises the most power over specific issues, or how the firm will respond to its environment. An organization chart is just the beginning to understanding how a firm organizes its work. In firms facing constant change, the formal chart may be quickly out of date. However, organization charts can be important to the extent that they accurately represent the "chain of command."

The chain of command is a listing of who reports to whom up and down the firm and shows how executives, managers, and supervisors are hierarchically connected. Traditional management theory suggests that each individual should have one boss and each unit one leader. Under these circumstances, there is a "unity of command." Unity of command is considered necessary to avoid confusion, to assign accountability to specific individuals, and to provide clear channels of communication up and down the organization.

Span of Control   The number of individuals reporting to a supervisor is called the **span of control**. Narrower spans of control are expected when tasks are complex, when subordinates are inexperienced or poorly trained, or when tasks call for team effort. Unfortunately, narrow spans of control yield many organizational levels. The excessive number of levels is not only expensive, but it also makes the organization unresponsive to necessary change. Communications in such firms often become less effective because they are successively screened and modified so that subtle but important changes are ignored. Furthermore, with many levels, managers are removed from the action and become isolated.

- **Span of control** refers to the number of individuals reporting to a supervisor.

New information technologies now allow organizations to broaden the span of control, flatten their formal structures, and still maintain control of complex operations. At Nucor, for instance, senior managers pioneered the development of "minimills" for making steel and developed what they call "lean" management. At the same time, management has expanded the span of control with extensive employee education and training backed by sophisticated information systems. The result: Nucor has only four levels of management from the bottom to the top.[15]

Line and Staff Units   A very useful way to examine the vertical division of labor is to separate line and staff units. **Line units** and personnel conduct the major business of the organization. The production and marketing functions are two examples. In contrast, **staff units** and personnel assist the line units by providing specialized expertise and services, such as accounting and public relations. For example, the vice president of administration in a university as depicted in Figure 16.1 heads a staff unit, as does the vice president of student affairs.

- **Line units** are workgroups that conduct the major business of the organization.
- **Staff units** assist the line units by performing specialized services to the organization.

Firms often make two additional useful distinctions regarding line and staff. One distinction is the nature of the relationship of a unit in the chain of command. A staff department, such as the office of the VP for External Affairs shown in Figure 16.1, may be divided into subordinate units, such as Legislative Liaison and Development. Although all units reporting to a higher-level staff unit are considered staff from an organizational perspective, some subordinate staff units are charged with conducting the major business of the higher unit—they have a line relationship up the chain of command. In Figure 16.1 both Legislative Liaison and Development are staff units with a line relationship to the unit immediately above them in the chain of command—the VP for External Affairs. Why the apparent confusion? It is a matter of history, with the notion of line and staff originally coming from the military with its emphasis on command. In a military sense, the VP for External Affairs is the commander of this staff effort—the individual responsible for this activity and the one held accountable.

A second useful distinction for both line and staff units concerns the amount and types of contacts each maintains with outsiders to the organization. Some units are mainly internal in orientation; others are more external in focus. In general, internal line units (e.g., production) focus on transforming raw materials and information into products and services, whereas external line units (e.g., marketing) focus on maintaining linkages to suppliers, distributors, and customers.

Internal staff units (e.g., accounting) assist the line units in performing their function. Normally, they specialize in specific technical or financial areas. External staff units (e.g., public relations) also assist the line units, but the focus of their actions is on linking the firm to its environment and buffering internal operations. To recap: the Legislative Liaison unit is external staff with a line relationship to the office of the VP for External Affairs.

Staff units can be assigned predominantly to senior-, middle-, or lower-level managers. When staff is assigned predominantly to senior management, the capability of senior management to develop alternatives and make decisions is expanded. When staff is at the top, senior executives can directly develop information and alternatives and check on the implementation of their decisions. Here, the degree of vertical specialization in the firm is comparatively lower because senior managers plan, decide, and control via their centralized staff. With new information technologies, fewer firms are placing most staff at the top. They are replacing internal staff with information systems and placing talented individuals farther down the hierarchy. For instance, executives at giant international glass bottle maker O-I have shifted staff from top management to middle management. When staff are moved to the middle of the organization, middle managers now have the specialized help necessary to expand their role.

Many firms are also beginning to ask whether certain staff should be a permanent part of the organization at all, and some are outsourcing many of their staff functions while others are using new technologies to replace staff.[16] Outsourcing by large firms has been a boon for smaller corporations as they perform staff functions for larger corporations. For some time, firms have used information technology to streamline operations and reduce staff to lower costs and raise productivity.[17] One way to facilitate these actions is to provide line managers and employees with information and managerial techniques designed to expand on their analytical and decision-making capabilities—that is, to replace internal staff.[18]

Controls Are a Basic Feature

• **Control** is the set of mechanisms used to keep actions and outputs within predetermined limits.

Distributing formal authority calls for control. **Control** is the set of mechanisms used to keep action or outputs within predetermined limits. Control deals with setting standards, measuring results versus standards, and instituting corrective action. We should stress that effective control occurs before action actually begins. For instance, in setting standards, managers must decide what will be measured and how accomplishment will be determined. While there are a wide variety of organizational controls, they are roughly divided into output, process, and social controls.

Output Controls   Earlier in this chapter, we suggested that systems goals are a roadmap that ties together the various units of the organization to achieve a practical objective. Developing targets or standards, measuring results against these targets, and taking corrective action are all steps involved in developing output controls.[19] **Output controls** focus on desired targets and allow managers to use their own methods to reach defined targets. Most modern organizations use output controls as part of an overall method of managing by exception.

• **Output controls** are controls that focus on desired targets and allow managers to use their own methods for reaching defined targets.

Output controls are popular because they promote flexibility and creativity and they facilitate dialogue concerning corrective actions. Reliance on outcome controls separates what is to be accomplished from how it is to be accomplished.

Finding the Leader in You

KAREN BRYANT WINS BY STAYING FOCUSED ON GOALS

In March 2008 when the new owners of the WNBA's Seattle Storm announced Karen Bryant as the new Storm CEO, success was far from clear. Known as KB, Bryant was a local high school basketball superstar with a modest record as a collegian. As a high school coach she had a three-year record of only 24 and 44 before leaving. Even her initial stint as a basketball executive looked like a failure when the local professional team and league folded. But Bryant did not quit, and she rebounded with a top position with the Seattle Storm team.

As the new CEO of the Storm in 2008 the prospects looked dire. The matched men's team, the Seattle Supersonics, had been sold and moved to Oklahoma. Even rabid basketball fans were furious over the "loss of professional basketball" in Seattle. The Storm remained only because four local businesswomen and community leaders bought the women's team. Yet, KB saw opportunity. "Sometimes there were other priorities. Now, there's no lack of clarity. There's no confusion about what our resources are, nor are there any surprises." Bryant set clear compatible goals: (1) world-class basketball, (2) fan accessibility and affordability, (3) a sense of community, and (4) a successful business model.

She delivered. In 2009, even without the deep pockets so typical of professional sports teams, the Storm fielded a competitive team, set ticket prices that allowed the whole family to attend a game, and stressed extensive community involvement. In 2010 the Storm organization reached the goals initially set by KB—the WNBA championship! The championship is not the end of the story but a milestone. Now the challenge is to maintain success. For a once marginal collegiate player and failed coach, this most recent success must be vindication for her hard work, executive skills, and dedication.

What's the Lesson Here?

How well do you deal with failure? Are you able to persist in the face of difficult challenges? Can you keep a focus and drive toward results when times get tough or situations feel overwhelming?

Thus, the discussion of goals is separated from the dialogue concerning methods. This separation can facilitate the movement of power down the organization, as senior managers are reassured that individuals at all levels will be working toward the goals senior management believes are important, even as lower-level managers innovate and introduce new ways to accomplish these goals.

Process Controls   Few organizations run on outcome controls alone. Once a solution to a problem is found and successfully implemented, managers do not want the problem to recur, so they institute process controls. **Process controls** attempt to specify the manner in which tasks are accomplished. There are many types of process controls, but three groups have received considerable attention: (1) policies, procedures, and rules; (2) formalization and standardization; and (3) total quality management controls.

> • **Process controls** are controls that attempt to specify the manner in which tasks are to be accomplished.

Policies, Procedures, and Rules   Most organizations implement a variety of policies, procedures, and rules to help specify how goals are to be accomplished.

Usually, we think of a *policy* as a guideline for action that outlines important objectives and broadly indicates how an activity is to be performed. A policy allows for individual discretion and minor adjustments without direct clearance by a higher-level manager. *Procedures* indicate the best method for performing a task, show which aspects of a task are the most important, or outline how an individual is to be rewarded.

Many firms link *rules* and *procedures*. Rules are more specific, rigid, and impersonal than policies. They typically describe in detail how a task or a series of tasks is to be performed, or they indicate what cannot be done. They are designed to apply to all individuals, under specified conditions. For example, most car dealers have detailed instruction manuals for repairing a new car under warranty, and they must follow very strict procedures to obtain reimbursement from the manufacturer for warranty work.

Rules, procedures, and policies are often employed as substitutes for direct managerial supervision. Under the guidance of written rules and procedures, the organization can specifically direct the activities of many individuals. It can ensure virtually identical treatment across even distant work locations. For example, a McDonald's hamburger and fries taste much the same whether they are purchased in Chicago, Indianapolis, Los Angeles, or Toronto simply because the ingredients and the cooking methods follow written rules and procedures.

• **Formalization** is written documentation of work rules, policies, and procedures.

Formalization and Standardization   **Formalization** refers to the written documentation of rules, policies, and procedures to guide behavior and decision making. Beyond substituting for direct management supervision, formalization is often used to simplify jobs. Written instructions allow individuals with less training to perform comparatively sophisticated tasks. Written procedures may also be available to ensure that a proper sequence of tasks is executed, even if this sequence is performed only occasionally.

• **Standardization** is the degree to which the range of actions in a job or series of jobs is limited.

Most organizations have developed additional methods for dealing with recurring problems or situations. **Standardization** is the degree to which the range of allowable actions in a job or series of jobs is limited so that actions are performed in a uniform manner. It involves the creation of guidelines so that similar work activities are repeatedly performed in a similar fashion. Such standardized methods may come from years of experience in dealing with typical situations, or they may come from outside training. For instance, if you are late in paying your credit card, the bank will automatically send you a notification and start an internal process of monitoring your account.

Total Quality Management   The process controls discussed so far—policies, procedures, rules, formalization, and standardization—represent the lessons of experience within an organization. That is, managers institute these process controls based on experience typically one at a time. Often there is no overall philosophy for using control to improve the general operations of the company. Another way to institute process controls is to establish a total quality management process within the firm.

W. Edwards Deming is the modern-day founder of the total quality management movement.[20] When Deming's ideas were not generally accepted in the United States, he found an audience in Japan. Thus, to some managers, Deming's ideas appear in the form of the best Japanese business practices.

1. Create a consistency of purpose in the company to (a) innovate, (b) put resources into research and education, and (c) put resources into maintaining equipment and new production aids.

2. Learn a new philosophy of quality to improve every system.

3. Require statistical evidence of process control and eliminate financial controls on production.

4. Require statistical evidence of control in purchasing parts; this will mean dealing with fewer suppliers.

5. Use statistical methods to isolate the sources of trouble.

6. Institute modern on-the-job training.

7. Improve supervision to develop inspired leaders.

8. Drive out fear and instill learning.

9. Break down barriers between departments.

10. Eliminate numerical goals and slogans.

11. Constantly revamp work methods.

12. Institute massive training programs for employees in statistical methods.

13. Retrain people in new skills.

14. Create a structure that will push, every day, on the above 13 points.

Figure 16.2 Deming's 14 Points of Quality Management

The heart of Deming's approach was to institute a process approach to continual improvement based on statistical analyses of the firm's operations. Around this core idea, Deming built a series of 14 points for managers to implement. As shown in Figure 16.2, the points emphasize everyone working together using statistical controls to improve continually. All levels of management are to be involved in the quality program. Managers are to improve supervision, train employees, retrain employees in new skills, and create a structure that supports the quality program. Where the properties of the firm's outcomes are well defined, as in most manufacturing operations, Deming's system and emphasis on quality work well. This is especially true when implemented in conjunction with empowerment and participative management.

The Illusion of Control   One of the myths in management is the illusion of control. There are many variations of this myth, but one centers on the formal controls themselves. Many managers want to believe they can specify all of the relevant goals for subordinates as well as how they are to be accomplished. With too many output and process goals, subordinates appear to have very little flexibility. However, as the number of output and process controls escalates, so do the conflicts between the output and process controls. The result is that subordinates begin to pick and choose which controls they follow and managers only have the illusion that subordinates are reaching toward the specified goals.[21]

Centralization and Decentralization

Different firms use very different mixes of vertical specialization, output controls, process controls, and managerial techniques to allocate the authority or discretion to act.[22] The farther up the hierarchy of authority the discretion to spend money, to hire people, and to make similar decisions is moved, the greater the degree of **centralization**. The more such decisions are delegated, or moved down the hierarchy of authority, the greater the degree of **decentralization**. Greater centralization is often adopted when the firm faces a single major threat to its survival.

• **Centralization** is the degree to which the authority to make decisions is restricted to higher levels of management.

• **Decentralization** is the degree to which the authority to make decisions is given to lower levels in an organization's hierarchy.

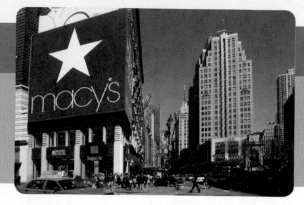

Thus, it is little wonder that armies tend to be centralized and that firms facing bankruptcy increase centralization. Recent research even suggests that governmental agencies may improve their performance through centralization when in a defensive mode.[23]

Greater decentralization generally provides higher subordinate satisfaction and a quicker response to a diverse series of unrelated problems. Decentralization also assists in the on-the-job training of subordinates for higher-level positions. Decentralization is now a popular approach in many industries. For instance, Union Carbide is pushing responsibility down the chain of command, as are SYSCO and Hewlett-Packard. In each case, the senior managers hope to improve both performance quality and organizational responsiveness. Closely related to decentralization is the notion of participation. Many people want to be involved in making decisions that affect their work. Participation results when a manager delegates some authority for such decision making to subordinates in order to include them in the choice process. Employees may want a say both in what the unit objectives should be and in how they may be achieved.[24]

Governmental agencies find that increasing decentralization helps them effectively explore innovations.[25] For instance, Macy's has successfully experimented with moving decisions down the chain of command and increasing participation.

Organizing and Coordinating Work

LEARNING ROADMAP　Traditional Types of Departments / Coordination

• **Horizontal specialization** is a division of labor through the formation of work units or groups within an organization.
• **Coordination** is the set of mechanisms used in an organization to link the actions of its subunits into a consistent pattern.

Managers must divide the total task into separate duties and group similar people and resources together.[26] Organizing work is formally known as **horizontal specialization**, a division of labor that establishes specific work units or groups within an organization. This aspect of the organization is also called departmentation. Whatever is divided up horizontally in two or more departments must also be integrated.[27] **Coordination** is the set of mechanisms that an organization uses to link the actions of their units into a consistent pattern. This linkage includes mechanisms to link managers and staff units, operating units with each other, and divisions with each other. Managers use a mix of personal and impersonal methods of coordination to tie the efforts of departments together.

HIERARCHY AND *RATATOUILLE*

Unfortunately, bureaucracy tends to a get a "bad rap" most of the time. Yet organizations must have rules and structure to operate effectively. Large companies organize into departments and distribute responsibilities and authority in hierarchical fashion. This is known as **vertical specialization**, the division of labor that shows authority relationships, decision making, and the chain of command. This is usually spelled out in an organization chart.

Pixar's *Ratatouille* is the story about a rat named Remy that aspires to be a great cook like his hero, Chef Auguste Gusteau. Following an accident that separates Remy from the rest of his family, he finds himself in Paris. In a short time, he is peering down through a skylight into the restaurant made famous by the now departed Gusteau. He observes the cooking activity taking place in the kitchen and can name all the roles and relationships that exist between the staff. Guided by an apparition of Gusteau himself, he learns that all positions in the kitchen are critical—even that of the garbage boy.

What we learn from *Ratatouille* is that hierarchy and authority are necessary to keep the work flowing smoothly. While some positions have more power and responsibility than others, each individual has a contribution to make and must be willing to do so if the organization is to be successful.

Get to Know Yourself Better   By now, you are probably quite used to participating in organizations with a lot of structure. Take a look at Assessment 21, Organizational Design Preference, *in the* OB Skills Workbook *to determine your comfort level with this environment. If you score high, you will probably function effectively in an organization with a high degree of vertical specialization. On the other hand, if your score is low, you may like working for a smaller, newer company where the structure is a little more flexible.*

Traditional Types of Departments

Since the pattern of departmentation is so visible and important in a firm, managers often refer to their pattern as the departmental structure. While most firms use a mix of various types of departments, it is important to look at the traditional types and what they do and do not provide the firm.[28]

Functional Departments   Grouping individuals by skill, knowledge, and action yields a pattern of **functional departmentation**. Recall that Figure 16.1 shows the partial organization chart for a large university in which each department has a technical specialty. Marketing, finance, production, and personnel are important functions in business. In many small firms, this functional pattern dominates. Even large firms use this pattern in technically demanding areas. Figure 16.3 summarizes the advantages and disadvantages of the functional pattern. With all of these advantages, it is not surprising that the functional form is extremely popular. It is used in most organizations, particularly toward the bottom of the hierarchy. The extensive use of functional departments also has some disadvantages. Organizations that rely heavily on functional specialization may expect the following tendencies to emerge over time: an emphasis on quality from a technical standpoint, rigidity to change, and difficulty in coordinating the actions of different functional areas.

• **Functional departmentation** is grouping individuals by skill, knowledge, and action.

Major Advantages and Disadvantages of Functional Specialization	
Advantages	**Disadvantages**
1. Yields very clear task assignments, consistent with an individual's training.	1. May reinforce the narrow training of individuals.
2. Individuals within a department can easily build on one another's knowledge, training, and experience.	2. May yield narrow, boring, and routine jobs.
3. Provides an excellent training ground for new managers.	3. Communication across technical area is complex and difficult.
4. It is easy to explain.	4. "Top-management overload" with too much attention to cross-functional problems.
5. Takes advantage of employee technical quality.	5. Individuals may look up the organizational hierarchy for direction and reinforcement rather than focus attention on products, services, or clients.

Figure 16.3 Major advantages and disadvantages of functional specialization.

• **Divisional departmentation** groups individuals and resources by products, territories, services, clients, or legal entities.

Divisional Departments   In **divisional departments** individuals and resources are grouped by products, territories, services, clients, or legal entities. For example, Land O' Lakes organizes around divisions for its various types of products.

A divisional pattern is often used to meet diverse external threats and opportunities. As shown in Figure 16.4, the major advantages of the divisional pattern are its flexibility in meeting external demands, spotting external changes, integrating specialized individuals deep within the organization, and focusing on the delivery of specific products to specific customers. Among its disadvantages are duplication of effort by function, the tendency for divisional goals to be placed above corporate interests, and conflict among divisions. It is also not the most desirable structure for training individuals in technical areas; firms that rely on this pattern may fall behind technically to competitors with a functional pattern.

Many larger, geographically dispersed organizations that sell to national and international markets may rely on departmentation by geography. The savings in time, effort, and travel can be substantial, and each territory can adjust to regional differences. Organizations that rely on a few major customers may organize their people and resources by client. Here, the idea is to focus attention on the needs of the individual customer. To the extent that customer needs are unique, departmentation by customer can also reduce confusion and increase synergy.

Organizations expanding internationally may also form divisions to meet the demands of complex host-country ownership requirements. For example, NEC, Sony, Nissan, and many other Japanese corporations have developed U.S. divisional subsidiaries to service their customers in the U.S. market. Some huge European-based corporations such as Philips and Nestlé have also adopted a divisional structure in their expansion to the United States. Similarly, most of the internationalized U.S.-based firms, such as IBM, GE, and DuPont, have incorporated the divisional structure as part of their internalization programs.

Cooperative Land O' Lakes

Land O' Lakes is more than just a brand of butter; it is a cooperative that sells dairy products and helps farmer members buy supplies. The cooperative is organized into divisions for (1) dairy operations, (2) feed, (3) seed, and (4) crop nutrients and crop protection products.

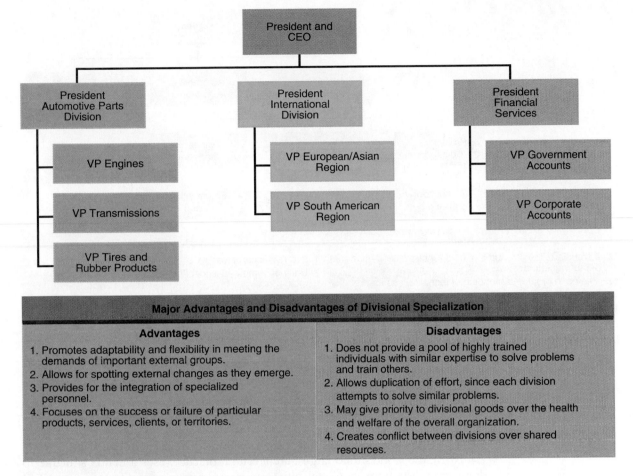

Major Advantages and Disadvantages of Divisional Specialization	
Advantages	**Disadvantages**
1. Promotes adaptability and flexibility in meeting the demands of important external groups. 2. Allows for spotting external changes as they emerge. 3. Provides for the integration of specialized personnel. 4. Focuses on the success or failure of particular products, services, clients, or territories.	1. Does not provide a pool of highly trained individuals with similar expertise to solve problems and train others. 2. Allows duplication of effort, since each division attempts to solve similar problems. 3. May give priority to divisional goods over the health and welfare of the overall organization. 4. Creates conflict between divisions over shared resources.

Figure 16.4 A divisional pattern of departmentation.

Matrix Structures   Originally from the aerospace industry, a third unique form of departmentation called the matrix structure was developed and is now becoming more popular.[29] In aerospace efforts, projects are technically very complex, involving hundreds of subcontractors located throughout the world. Precise integration and control are needed across many sophisticated functional specialties and corporations. This is often more than a functional or divisional structure can provide, for many firms do not want to trade the responsiveness of the divisional form for the technical emphasis provided by the functional form. Thus, **matrix departmentation** uses both the functional and divisional forms simultaneously. Figure 16.5 shows the basic matrix arrangement for an aerospace program. Note the functional departments on one side and the project efforts on the other. Workers and supervisors in the middle of the matrix have two bosses—one functional and one project.

Figure 16.5 summarizes the major advantages and disadvantages of the matrix form of departmentation. The key disadvantage of the matrix method is the loss of unity of command. Individuals can be unsure as to what their jobs are, whom they report to for specific activities, and how various managers are to administer the effort. It can also be a very expensive method because it relies on individual managers to coordinate efforts deep within the firm. Despite these limitations, the

• **Matrix departmentation** is a combination of functional and divisional patterns wherein an individual is assigned to more than one type of unit.

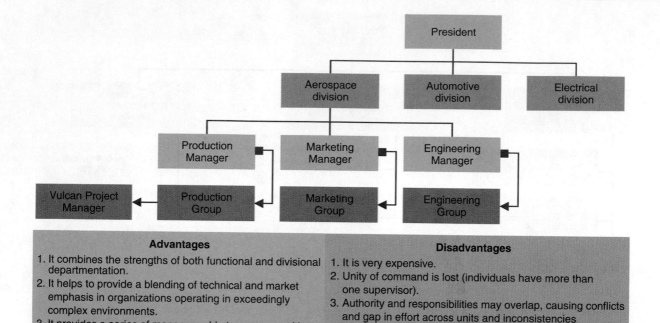

Figure 16.5 A matrix pattern of departmentation in an aerospace division.

matrix structure provides a balance between functional and divisional concerns. Many problems can be resolved at the working level, where the balance among technical, cost, customer, and organizational concerns can be dealt with.

NBBJ, the world's third largest architectural practice, uses a matrix structure to draw specialists from its global offices to complete major design projects. NBBJ executives use senior contact staff in a local design studio to identify and focus on a client's specific needs. They coordinate across the global locations to supplement a local studio's staff.[30] Many organizations also use elements of the matrix structure without officially using the term *matrix*. For example, special project teams, coordinating committees, and task forces can be the beginnings of a matrix. These temporary structures can be used within a predominantly functional or divisional form and without upsetting the unity of command or hiring additional managers.

Which form of departmentation should be used? As the matrix concept suggests, it is possible to departmentalize by two different methods at the same time. Actually, organizations often use a mixture of departmentation forms. It is often desirable to divide the effort (group people and resources) by two methods at the same time in order to balance the advantages and disadvantages of each. These mixed forms help firms use their division of labor to capitalize on environmental opportunities, capture the benefits of larger size, and realize the potential of new technologies in pursuit of its strategy.

Coordination

As noted earlier, whatever is divided up horizontally in two departments must also be integrated.[31] Coordination is the set of mechanisms that an organization uses to

The Challenge of Decentralization

CEO William Weldon of Johnson and Johnson (the pharmaceutical, medical device, and consumer packaged goods manufacturer) noted, "I think that the downside to decentralization . . . is actually the coordination. It is trying to get people together . . . sometimes there is enough to do in their own group and now we are asking them to cross boundaries and work together . . . , that is the challenge—the coordination."

link the actions of their units into a consistent pattern. Coordination is needed at all levels of management, not just across a few scattered units. Much of the coordination within a unit is handled by its manager. Smaller organizations may rely on their management hierarchy to provide the necessary consistency and integration. As the organization grows, however, managers become overloaded. For example, when Johnson and Johnson moved to become more decentralized, CEO William Weldon immediately noted the difficulties of coordination.

Personal Methods of Coordination   Personal methods of coordination produce synergy by promoting dialogue and discussion, innovation, creativity, and learning, both within and across organizational units. Personal methods allow the organization to address the particular needs of distinct units and individuals simultaneously. There is a wide variety of personal methods of coordination.[32] Perhaps the most popular is direct contact between and among organizational members. As new information technologies have moved into practice, the potential for developing and maintaining effective contact networks has expanded. For example, many executives use e-mail and text messaging to supplement direct personal communication. Direct personal contact is also associated with the ever-present "grapevine." Although the grapevine is notoriously inaccurate in its role as the corporate rumor mill, it is often both accurate enough and quick enough that managers cannot ignore it. Instead, managers need to work with and supplement the rumor mill with accurate information.

Managers are often assigned to numerous committees to improve coordination across departments. Even though committees are generally expensive and have a very poor reputation as time wasters, they can become an effective personal mechanism for mutual adjustment across unit heads. Committees can be effective in communicating complex qualitative information and in helping managers whose units must work together to adjust schedules, workloads, and work assignments to increase productivity. As more organizations develop flatter structures with greater delegation, they are finding that task forces can be quite useful. Whereas committees tend to be long lasting, task forces are typically formed with a more limited agenda. Individuals from different parts of the organization are assembled into a task force to identify and solve problems that cut across different departments.

The appropriate mix of personal coordination methods and tailoring them to the individual skills, abilities, and experience of subordinates also vary with the type of task. As the Research Insights feature suggests, a variety of methods can be tailored to match different individuals and the settings in which they operate. Personal methods are only one important part of coordination. The manager may also establish a series of impersonal mechanisms.

Organization Science

RESEARCH INSIGHT

Coordination in Temporary Organizations

Many individuals have jobs that take them to a number of temporary settings such as a corporate task force, an alliance, or a special project. Coordinating the actions of the members in these temporary arrangements is often a challenge. However, research by Beth Bechky offers some insight. She studied the workers on a movie set—not the actors or producer—but the crew who set up and ran the equipment, shot the movie, and made sure the sound was perfect. These individuals are generally "independent" contractors whose work must mesh quickly even though they have only been together a few hours.

How do they do it in the short-lived organization of a movie set? According to Bechky, they negotiate their roles with each other. Each has his or her own specialization and assignment, but they must be coordinated with all others. While all recognize each other's career progression (some have more experience and they are looked to for guidance), they recognize that the current assignment is one of many they may want to work on in the future. All are on their best behavior so that they will be hired for the next movie.

To successfully coordinate, Bechky found that the more experienced crew members may provide enthusiastic thanks and may politely admonish the other less-experienced crew members. To enforce an emerging order and maintain coordination, they use humor, polite ribbing, sarcastic comments, and teasing. Public display of anger is rare and frowned upon. With these mechanisms in place, it only takes a few hours for the crew to emerge as an integrated unit.

To transfer the findings to a student group, try and build a simplified model of the factors mentioned in the description. It might look somewhat like this:

Pick a student group to perform a team case study with majors in different areas (such as accounting, finance, management). See if the members self-assign to specialized areas based on their major. Look for variations in experience and check if there is a

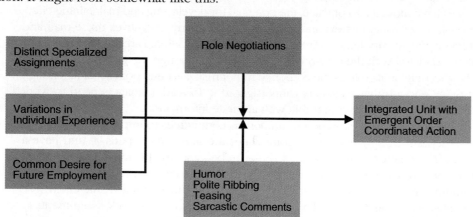

common desire for high performance. As the group starts to work on the project, observe whether they negotiate distinct roles. Do they use humor, teasing, or sarcastic comments to coalesce? Do they form an integrated group with an identified order and coordinated action, or do just a few actually run the show?

Do the Research   *Would you expect a student group to form-up much the way the professionals do? If the student group does not use humor or teasing, what do they use to gain coordinated action?*

Source: Beth A. Bechky, "Gaffers, Gofers, and Grips: Role-based Coordination in Temporary Organizations" *Organization Science* 17.1 (2006), pp. 3–23.

Shiseido Consolidation Increases Sales and Profits

With all the talk of decentralizing, sometimes consolidation makes sense. At Shiseido, Japan's largest cosmetic company with a global reach, President and CEO Shinzo Maeda announced the results of a three-year effort to reorganize North American operations by consolidating three large separate divisions into one integrated unit. The goal was to increase coordination. The results were a dramatic increase in sales and profits as the once separate divisions were able to focus as one unit.

Impersonal Methods of Coordination   Impersonal methods of coordination produce synergy by stressing consistency and standardization so that individual pieces fit together. Impersonal coordination methods are often refinements and extensions of process controls with an emphasis on formalization and standardization. Larger organizations often have written policies and procedures, such as schedules, budgets, and plans that are designed to mesh the operations of several units into a whole by providing predictability and consistency.

Historically, firms used specialized departments to coordinate across units. However, this method is very expensive and often results in considerable rigidity. The most highly developed form of impersonal coordination comes with the adoption of a matrix structure. As noted earlier, this form of departmentation is designed to coordinate the efforts of diverse functional units. Many firms are using cross-functional task forces instead of maintaining specialized departments or implementing a matrix.

The final example of impersonal coordination mechanisms is undergoing radical change in many modern organizations. Originally, management information systems were developed and designed so that senior managers could coordinate and control the operations of diverse subordinate units. These systems were intended to be computerized substitutes for schedules, budgets, and the like. In the hands of astute managers, however, the management information system becomes an electronic network, linking individuals throughout the organization. Using decentralized communication systems that connect all members allows once centralized systems to evolve into a supplement to personal coordination.

In the United States there is an aversion to controls, as the culture prizes individuality, democracy, and individual free will. Managers often institute controls under the title of coordination. Since some of the techniques are used for both, many managers suggest that all efforts at control are for coordination. It is extremely important to separate these two functions simply because the reactions to controls and coordination are quite different. The underlying logic of control involves setting targets, measuring performance, and taking corrective action to meet goals normally assigned by higher management. Thus, many employees see an increase in controls as a threat based on a presumption that they have been doing something wrong. The logic of coordination is to get unit actions and interactions meshed together into a unified whole. While control involves the vertical exercise of formal authority involving targets, measures, and corrective action, coordination stresses cooperative problem solving. Experienced employees recognize the difference between controls and coordination regardless of what the boss calls it.[33] Increasing controls rarely solves problems of coordination, and emphasizing coordination to solve control issues rarely works.

Bureaucracy and Beyond

LEARNING ROADMAP   Mechanistic Structures and the Machine Bureaucracy / Organic Structures and the Professional Bureaucracy / Hybrid Structures

In the developed world, most firms are bureaucracies. In OB this term has a very special meaning, beyond its negative connotation. The famous German sociologist Max Weber suggested that organizations would thrive if they became bureaucracies by emphasizing legal authority, logic, and order.[34] Ideally, **bureaucracies** rely on a division of labor, hierarchical control, promotion by merit with career opportunities for employees, and administration by rule.

Weber argued that the rational and logical idea of bureaucracy was superior to building the firm based on charisma or cultural tradition. The "charismatic" ideal-type organization was overly reliant on the talents of one individual and could fail when the leader leaves. Too much reliance on cultural traditions blocked innovation, stifled efficiency, and was often unfair. Since the bureaucracy prizes efficiency, order, and logic, Weber hoped that it could also be fair to employees and provide more freedom for individual expression than is allowed when tradition dominates or dictators rule. Many interpreted Weber as suggesting that bureaucracy or some variation of this ideal form, though far from perfect, would dominate modern society.[35] For large organizations the bureaucratic form is predominant. Yet, the bureaucracy poses an interesting series of challenges for managers as illustrated in the sidebar.

Just as interpretations of Weber have evolved over time, so has the notion of a bureaucracy.[36] We will discuss two popular basic types of bureaucracies: the mechanistic structure and machine bureaucracy and the organic structure and professional bureaucracy as well as some hybrid approaches. Each type is a different mix of the basic elements discussed in this chapter, and each mix yields firms with a slightly different blend of capabilities and natural tendencies. That is, each type of bureaucracy allows the firm to pursue some goals more easily than others. Although charismatic leadership and cultural traditions are still important in each of these, it is the rational, legal, and efficiency aspects of the firm that characterize modern corporations.

- **Bureaucracy** is an ideal form of organizations, the characteristics of which were defined by the German sociologist Max Weber.

- **Mechanistic type or machine bureaucracy** emphasizes vertical specialization with impersonal coordination and a heavy reliance on standardization, formalization, rules, policies, and procedures.

Managerial Challenges in a Bureaucracy

- Overspecialization with conflicts between highly specialized units
- Overreliance on the chain of command rather than bottom-up problem solving
- Objectification of senior executives as rulers rather than problem solvers for others
- Overemphasis on conformity
- Rules as ends in and of themselves

Mechanistic Structures and the Machine Bureaucracy

The **mechanistic type of bureaucracy** emphasizes vertical specialization and control.[37] Organizations of this type stress rules, policies, and procedures; specify techniques for decision making; and emphasize developing well-documented control systems backed by a strong middle management and supported by a centralized staff. There is often extensive use of the functional pattern of departmentation throughout the firm. Henry Mintzberg uses the term *machine bureaucracy* to describe an organization structured in this manner.[38]

The mechanistic design results in a management emphasis on routine for efficiency. Firms often used this design in pursuing a strategy of becoming a low-cost leader. Until the implementation of new information systems, most large-scale firms in basic industries were machine bureaucracies. Included in this long list were all of the auto firms, banks, insurance companies, steel mills, large retail establishments, and government offices. Efficiency was achieved through extensive vertical and horizontal specialization tied together with elaborate controls and impersonal coordination mechanisms.

There are, however, limits to the benefits of specialization backed by rigid controls. Employees do not like rigid designs, so motivation becomes a problem. Unions further solidify narrow job descriptions by demanding fixed work rules and regulations to protect employees from the extensive vertical controls. Key employees may leave. In short, using a machine bureaucracy can hinder an organization's capacity to adjust to subtle external changes or new technologies.

Organic Structures and the Professional Bureaucracy

The **organic type or professional bureaucracy** is much less vertically oriented than its mechanistic counterpart is; it emphasizes horizontal specialization. Procedures are minimal, and those that do exist are not as formalized. The organization relies on the judgments of experts and personal means of coordination. When controls are used, they tend to back up professional socialization, training, and individual reinforcement. Staff units are placed toward the middle of the organization. Because this is a popular design in professional firms, Mintzberg calls it a professional bureaucracy.[39]

- **Organic type or professional bureaucracy** emphasizes horizontal specialization, extensive use of personal coordination, and loose rules, policies, and procedures.

Your university is probably a professional bureaucracy that looks like a broad, flat pyramid with a large bulge in the center for the professional staff. Power in this ideal type rests with knowledge. Other examples of organic types of bureaucracy include most hospitals and social service agencies.

Compared to the machine bureaucracy, the professional bureaucracy is usually better for problem solving and for serving individual customer needs. Since lateral relations and coordination are emphasized, centralized direction by senior management is less intense. Thus, this type is good at detecting external changes and adjusting to new technologies, but at the sacrifice of responding to central management direction.[40] Firms using this pattern found it easier to pursue product quality, to quickly respond to customers, and to use innovation as strategies.

Hybrid Structures

Many very large firms found that neither the mechanistic nor the organic approach was suitable for all of their operations. Adopting a machine bureaucracy would overload senior management and yield too many levels of management. Yet, adopting an organic type would mean losing control and becoming too inefficient. Senior managers may instead opt for one of a number of hybrid types of bureaucracies.

We have briefly introduced two of the more common hybrid types earlier in the chapter. One is an extension of the divisional pattern of departmentation and sometimes called a divisional firm. Here, the firm is composed of quasi-independent divisions so that different divisions can be more or less organic or mechanistic. Although the divisions may be treated as separate businesses, they often share a similar mission and systems goals.[41] When adopting this hybrid type, each division can pursue a different strategy.

• **Conglomerates** are firms that own several different unrelated business.

A second hybrid is the true conglomerate. A **conglomerate** is a single corporation that contains a number of unrelated businesses. On the surface these firms look like divisionalized firms, but when the various businesses of the divisions are unrelated, the term *conglomerate* is applied.[42] For instance, General Electric is a conglomerate that has divisions in unrelated businesses and industries, ranging from producing light bulbs to designing and servicing nuclear reactors to building jet engines. Most state and federal entities are also, by necessity, conglomerates. For instance, a state governor is the chief executive officer of those units concerned with higher education, welfare, prisons, highway construction and maintenance, police, and the like.

The conglomerate type also simultaneously illustrates three important points: (1) All structures are combinations of the basic elements; (2) there is no one best structure—it all depends on a number of factors such as the size of the firm, its environment, its technology, and, of course, its strategy; and (3) the firm does not stand alone but is part of a larger network of firms that competes against other networks.

16 *study guide*

Key Questions and Answers

What are the different types of organizational goals?

• Societal goals: Organizations make specific contributions to society and gain legitimacy from these contributions.

• A societal contribution focused on a primary beneficiary may be represented in the firm's mission statement.

• Output goals: As managers consider how they will accomplish their firm's mission, many begin with a very clear statement of which business they are in.

• Firms often specify output goals by detailing the types of specific products and services they offer.

• Systems goals: Corporations have systems goals to show the conditions managers believe will yield survival and success.

• Growth, productivity, stability, harmony, flexibility, prestige, and human-resource maintenance are examples of systems goals.

What are the hierarchical aspects of organizations?

• The formal structure is also known as the firm's division of labor.

• The formal structure defines the intended configuration of positions, job duties, and lines of authority among different parts of the enterprise.

• Vertical specialization is used to allocate formal authority within the organization and may be seen on an organization chart.

• Vertical specialization is the hierarchical division of labor that specifies where formal authority is located.

- Typically, a chain of command exists to link lower-level workers with senior managers.

- The distinction between line and staff units also indicates how authority is distributed, with line units conducting the major business of the firm and staff providing support.

- Managerial techniques, such as decision support and expert computer systems, are used to expand the analytical reach and decision-making capacity of managers to minimize staff.

- Control is the set of mechanisms the organization uses to keep action or outputs within predetermined levels.

- Output controls focus on desired targets and allow managers to use their own methods for reaching these targets.

- Process controls specify the manner in which tasks are to be accomplished through (1) policies, rules, and procedures; (2) formalization and standardization; and (3) total quality management processes.

- Firms are learning that decentralization often provides substantial benefits.

How is work organized and coordinated?

- Horizontal specialization is the division of labor that results in various work units and departments in the organization.

- Three main types or patterns of departmentation are observed: functional, divisional, and matrix. Each pattern has a mix of advantages and disadvantages.

- Organizations may successfully use any type, or a mixture, as long as the strengths of the structure match the needs of the organization.

- Coordination is the set of mechanisms an organization uses to link the actions of separate units into a consistent pattern.

- Personal methods of coordination produce synergy by promoting dialogue, discussion, innovation, creativity, and learning.

- Impersonal methods of control produce synergy by stressing consistency and standardization so that individual pieces fit together.

What are bureaucracies and what are the common forms?

- The bureaucracy is an ideal form based on legal authority, logic, and order that provides superior efficiency and effectiveness.

- Mechanistic, organic, and hybrid are common types of bureaucracies.

- Hybrid types include the divisionalized firm and the conglomerate. No one type is always superior to the others.

Terms to Know

Self-Test 16

Multiple Choice

1. The major types of goals for most organizations are _____. (a) societal, personal, and output (b) societal, output, and systems (c) personal and impersonal (d) profits, corporate responsibility, and personal (e) none of the above

2. The formal structures of organizations may be shown in a(n) _____. (a) environmental diagram (b) organization chart (c) horizontal diagram (d) matrix depiction (e) labor assignment chart

3. A major distinction between line and staff units concerns _____. (a) the amount of resources each is allowed to utilize (b) linkage of their jobs to the goals of the firm (c) the amount of education or training they possess (d) their use of computer information systems (e) their linkage to the outside world

4. The division of labor by grouping people and material resources into regional groups deals with _____. (a) specialization (b) coordination (c) divisionalization (d) vertical specialization (e) goal setting

5. Control involves all but _____. (a) measuring results (b) establishing goals (c) taking corrective action (d) comparing results with goals (e) selecting manpower

6. Grouping individuals and resources in the organization around products, services, clients, territories, or legal entities is an example of _____ specialization. (a) divisional (b) functional (c) matrix (d) mixed form (e) hybrid

7. Grouping resources into departments by skill, knowledge, and action is the _____ pattern. (a) functional (b) divisional (c) vertical (d) means–end chains (e) matrix

8. A matrix structure _____. (a) reinforces unity of command (b) is inexpensive (c) is easy to explain to employees (d) gives some employees two bosses (e) yields a minimum of organizational politics

9. _____ is the concern for proper communication enabling the units to understand one another's activities. (a) Control (b) Coordination (c) Specialization (d) Departmentation (e) Division of Labor

10. Compared to the machine bureaucracy (mechanistic type), the professional bureaucracy (organic type) _____. (a) is more efficient for routine operations (b) has more vertical specialization and control (c) is larger (d) has more horizontal specialization and coordination mechanism (e) is smaller

11. Written statements of organizational purpose are called _____. (a) mission statements (b) formalization (c) mean–ends chains (d) formal organization charts

12. _____ is grouping individuals by skill, knowledge, and action yields. (a) Divisional departmentation (b) Functional departmentation (c) Hybrid structuration (d) Matrix departmentation

13. The division of labor through the formation of work units or groups within an organization is called _____. (a) control (b) vertical specialization (c) horizontal specialization (d) coordination

14. _____ is the set of mechanisms used in an organization to link the actions of its subunits into a consistent pattern. (a) Departmentation (b) Coordination (c) Control (d) Formal authority

15. The set of mechanisms used to keep actions and outputs within predetermined limits is called _____. (a) coordination (b) vertical specialization (c) control (d) formalization

16. _____ describes how formal authority is distributed and establishes where and how critical decisions are to be made. (a) Vertical/horizontal specialization (b) Centralization/decentralization (c) Control/coordination (d) Bureaucratic/charismatic

17. Grouping people together by skill, knowledge, and action yields a _____ pattern of departmentation. (a) functional (b) divisional (c) matrix (d) dispersed

18. _____ in an organization provide specialized expertise and services. (a) Staff units and personnel (b) Line units and personnel (c) Cross-functional teams (d) Auditing units

19. One of the advantages of a _____ is that it helps provide a blending of technical and market emphases in organizations operating in exceedingly complex environments. (a) functional structure (b) matrix structure (c) divisional structure (d) conglomerate structure

20. _____ goals are the goals that define the type of business an organization is in. (a) Divisional (b) Systems (c) Societal (d) Output

Short Response

21. Compare and contrast output goals with systems goals.

22. Describe the types of controls used in organizations.

23. What are the major advantages and disadvantages of functional departmentation?

24. What are the major advantages and disadvantages of matrix departmentation?

Applications Essay

25. Describe some of the side effects of organizational controls in a large mechanistically structured organization such as the United States Postal Service.

Next Steps
Top Choices from
The OB Skills Workbook

Cases for Critical Thinking	Team and Experiential Exercises	Self-Assessment Portfolio
• First Community Financial	• Tinker Toys • Organizations Alive • Fast-Food Technology • Alien Invasion	• Twenty-First-Century Manager • Organizational Design Preference

American Airlines and Citibank: Leading the Charge for Frequent Flyer Miles

"I'm not one to recommend taking on any new credit card lightly," says Joe Brancatelli, publisher of business travel Web site www.joesentme.com, "but once in a while, an offer comes along that's irresistible."[a]

That's exactly the reaction American Airlines and Citibank®, paired by a mutual interest in protecting profits during an economic slump, hope consumers have to their co-branded Citi®/AAdvantage® credit card. The card, launched in 1987, provides casual customers and frequent travelers alike the opportunity to earn American Airlines AAdvantage® miles with a simple promise: Earn miles for everyday purchases.

> "As long as [the airlines] don't mess with the consumer perception of the value in their programs, they're a perpetual money-making machine."
> –Gary Leff, Inside Flyer.[c]

Cardholders earn one mile per dollar spent on purchases with the card, with multipliers or accelerators invoked for promotional special offers—for example, 2 miles per dollar spent on all grocery purchases for a limited time. But the biggest draw for American customers is often the signing incentive, which is typically a compelling offer of American Airlines AAdvantage bonus miles, awarded for achieving a pre-determined (but reasonable) spending threshold within the first several months of having the card (e.g., 30,000 bonus miles after spending $750 within 4 months of becoming a cardmember).

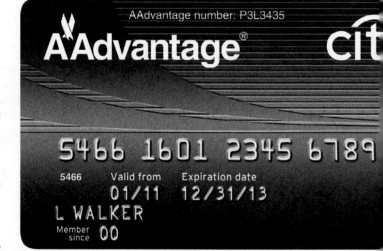

Beyond the miles, monthly mailings, and marketing hype, it's a strong example of a cross-industry alliance that provides mutual benefit to partners in volatile and highly competitive markets. Both partners know that the allure of destinations unknown can powerfully motivate consumers. Citi realizes thousands of new customers (or in some cases, existing customers adding a second card to their wallet), many funneling much more of their monthly spending through a Citi credit card than they'd ever planned.

American benefits from a much-welcomed influx of cash—Citi purchases AAdvantage miles in bulk at an undisclosed price that generally favors American.[b] And the promise of "miles for every purchase" keeps customers actively engaged in a relationship with American: cardholders are suddenly taking a second look at flying when they might ordinarily drive, or choosing American over a better-priced competitor.

Given the competition in both the airline and financial industries, do you think this alliance has what it takes to go the distance? If not, which partner would be at a greater disadvantage if the relationship dissolved?

Quick Summary
- American Airlines and Citibank, a partnership initiated in 1987, release a co-branded Citi®/AAdvantage® credit card.
- Along with an initial signing bonus, cardholders earn AAdvantage miles for nearly every purchase they make with the card.
- The partnership is mutually beneficial: Citibank purchases miles in bulk from American Airlines, which in turn provides Citi with new customers through a compelling incentive for members—the promise of travel.

FYI: 52% of frequent flyers polled believe that credit card spending should not qualify customers for elite status.[d]

17 Strategy, Technology, and Organizational Design

the key point

Organizations use strategy, technology, and design options to respond to opportunities and challenges in their competitive landscapes. The American Airlines and Citibank alliance is but one example. You need to understand the basic linkages among strategy, technology, and design. And it is important to understand how to lead under different environmental circumstances.

chapter at a glance

Why Are Strategy and Organizational Learning Important?

What Is Organizational Design, and How Is It Linked to Strategy?

How Does Technology Influence Organizational Design?

How Does the Environment Influence Organizational Design?

How Should the Whole Organization Be Led Strategically?

ETHICS IN OB
SOCIAL ENTREPRENEUR TACKLES ILLITERACY, TURNS DREAM INTO PROGRESS

FINDING THE LEADER IN YOU
JIM SINEGAL'S STRATEGY AT COSTCO IS TO NOT FOLLOW THE CROWD

OB IN POPULAR CULTURE
ADHOCRACY AND *THE EX*

RESEARCH INSIGHT
CEO VALUES MAKE A DIFFERENCE

what's inside?

As the example of the American Airlines-Citibank alliance suggests, executives of leading firms are taking a very sophisticated view of what their firms can do, how they can compete, and who they need as partners to insure success. Today, executives think about choices. What contributions to society should their firms make? How should the firm be positioned in the environment? Can the firm alter the environment in its favor either alone or with others? And how should the whole firm be lead? The key to success is to integrate such choices into an overall pattern—a strategy for success.

Strategy and Organizational Learning

LEARNING ROADMAP   Strategy / Organizational Learning / Linking Strategy and Organizational Learning

Strategy

• **Strategy** positions the organization in the competitive environment and implements actions to compete successfully.

Strategy is the process of positioning the organization in the competitive environment and implementing actions to compete successfully. It is a pattern in a stream of decisions.[1] Choosing the types of contributions the firm intends to make to the larger society, precisely whom it will serve, and exactly what it will provide to others are conventional ways in which the firm begins the pattern of decisions and corresponding implementations that define its strategy.

The Strategy Process   The strategy process is ongoing. It should involve individuals at all levels of the firm to ensure that there is a recognizable, consistent pattern—yielding a superior capability over rivals—up and down the firm and across all of its activities. This recognizable pattern involves many facets to develop a sustainable and unique set of dynamic capabilities.

Obviously, a successful strategy does not evolve in a vacuum but is driven by the goals emphasized, the size of the enterprise, the nature of the technology used by the firm, and its setting as well as the structure used to implement the strategy. In this chapter, we will emphasize the development of dynamic capabilities via organizational learning as an enduring feature of a successful strategy.

Strategy and Co-Evolution   With astute senior management, the firm can co-evolve. That is, the firm can adjust to both internal and external changes even as it shapes some of the challenges facing it. Co-evolution is a process,[2] and one aspect of this process is repositioning the firm in its setting as the setting changes. A shift in the environment may call for adjusting the firm's scale of operations. Senior management can also guide the process of positioning and repositioning in the environment.

Co-evolution may call for changes in technology. For instance, a firm can introduce new products into new markets. It can change parts of its environment by joining with others to compete. However, senior management must also have the necessary internal capabilities if it is to shape its environment. It cannot introduce new products without extensive product development capabilities or rush into a new market it does not understand. Shaping capabilities via the organization's design is a dynamic aspect of co-evolution. Corning is an example of a firm that effectively innovates and uses partners to commercialize its innovations across the globe.

Corning's Strategy Has a Global Reach

Although Corning is an innovation-driven firm engaged in a variety of advanced materials and technologies, it does not commercialize its new products alone. For instance, it is exploring the development of more effective wafered silicon photovoltaic (PV) cells with Hemlock Semiconductor.

Strategy as a Pattern of Decisions   The second aspect of strategy is a pattern in the stream of decisions. In a recent poll of some 750 CEOs, Samuel Palmisano, CEO of IBM, reported that two-thirds of the respondents reported being inundated with change and new competitors. Most saw their primary focus as that of adjusting their firm's processes, management, and culture to the new learning challenges. Most called for collaboration with other firms and suggested that they would emphasize learning to innovate.[3]

As the environment, strategy, and technology shift, we expect to see changes in the pattern of decisions selected within an organization. For example, IBM was once known as *big blue*, a button-down, white-shirt, blue-tie-and-black-shoe, second-to-market imitator with the bulk of its business centered on mainframe computers. The company is now a major hub in e-commerce and is on the cutting edge as an integrator across systems, equipment, and service.

Organizational Learning

Organizational learning is the process of acquiring knowledge and using information to adapt successfully to changing circumstances. For organizations to learn, they must engage in knowledge acquisition, information distribution, information interpretation, and organizational retention in adapting successfully to changing circumstances.[4] In simpler terms, organizational learning involves the adjustment of actions based on the organization's experience and that of others. The challenge is doing to learn and learning to do.

> • **Organizational learning** is the process of knowledge acquisition, information distribution, information interpretation, and organizational retention.

How Organizations Acquire Knowledge   Firms obtain information in a variety of ways and at different rates during their histories. Perhaps the most important information is obtained from sources outside the firm at the time of its founding. During the firm's initial years, its managers copy, or mimic, what they believe are the successful practices of others.[5] As they mature, however, firms can also acquire knowledge through experience and systematic search.

Mimicry is the copying of the successful practices of others. Mimicry is particularly important to the new firm because (1) it provides workable, if not ideal, solutions to many problems; (2) it reduces the number of decisions that need to be analyzed separately, allowing managers to concentrate on more critical issues; and (3) it establishes legitimacy or acceptance by employees, suppliers, and customers and narrows the choices calling for detailed explanation.

> • **Mimicry** is the copying of the successful practices of others.

A primary way to acquire knowledge is through experience. All organizations and managers can learn in this manner. Besides learning by doing, managers can also systematically embark on structured programs to capture the lessons to be learned from failure and success.[6] For instance, a well-designed research and

development program allows managers to learn as much through failure as through success.[7]

Vicarious learning involves capturing the lessons of others' experiences. Typically, successful vicarious learning involves both scanning and grafting.[8]

Scanning involves looking outside the firm and bringing back useful solutions. At times, these solutions are applied to recognized problems. More often, these solutions float around management until they are needed to solve a problem.[9] Astute managers can contribute to organizational learning by scanning external sources, such as competitors, suppliers, industry consultants, customers, and leading firms.

Grafting is the process of acquiring individuals, units, or firms to bring in useful knowledge. Almost all firms seek to hire experienced individuals from other firms simply because experienced individuals may bring with them a completely new series of solutions. Contracting out or outsourcing is the reverse of grafting and involves asking outsiders to perform a particular function. Whereas virtually all organizations contract out and outsource, the key question for managers is often what to keep.

- **Vicarious learning** involves capturing the lessons of others' experiences.
- **Scanning** involves looking outside the firm and bringing back useful solutions.
- **Grafting** is the process of acquiring individuals, units, or firms to bring in useful knowledge.

Information Distribution and Interpretation   Once information is obtained, managers must establish mechanisms to distribute relevant information to the individuals who may need it. A primary challenge in larger firms is to locate quickly who has the appropriate information and who needs specific types of information.

Although data collection is helpful, it is not enough. Data are not information; the information must be interpreted. Information within organizations is a collective understanding of the firm's goals and of how the data relate to one of the firm's stated or unstated objectives within the current setting. Unfortunately, a number of common problems often thwart the process of developing multiple interpretations.[10] Chief among the problems of interpretation are self-serving interpretations. Among managers, the ability to interpret events, conditions, and history to their own advantage is almost universal. Managers and employees alike often see what they have seen in the past or see what they want to see.

Retention   Organizations contain a variety of mechanisms that can be used to retain useful information.[11] In addition to individual employees, documents, the internal information systems, and external archives and individuals, organizations can also retain information through their formal structures and ecology.

The organization's formal structure and the positions in an organization are mechanisms for storing information. Landing on the deck of a U.S. Navy aircraft carrier, for example, is dangerous. There have historically been several accidents. After each accident an investigation is conducted to prevent a similar occurrence. Based on this investigation individuals are trained in specific remedial actions and assigned to specific positions during landings. Over time as each individual trains

SOCIAL ENTREPRENEUR TACKLES ILLITERACY, TURNS DREAM INTO PROGRESS

There was a time when John Wood was just another, albeit up-and-coming, Microsoft executive. Now he's a social entrepreneur fighting the scourge of illiteracy through a nonprofit called Room to Read. What began as a dream of making a contribution to the fight against illiteracy has become a reality, one that grows stronger each day.

During a successful career as a Microsoft executive, his life changed on a vacation to the Himalayas of Nepal. Wood was shocked at the lack of schools. He discovered a passion that determines what he calls the "second chapter" in his life: to provide the lifelong benefits of education to poor children. He quit his Microsoft job and started Room to Read. So far, the organization has built over 100 schools and 1,000 libraries in Cambodia, India, Nepal, Vietnam, and Laos.

Noting that one-seventh of the global population can't read or write, Wood says: "I don't see how we are going to solve the world's problems without literacy." The Room to Read model is so efficient that it can build schools for as little as $6,000. *Time* magazine has honored Wood and his team as "Asian Heroes," and *Fast Company* magazine tapped his organization for a Social Capitalist Award.

> ***Could You Do It?***   *What social problems do you see in your community, and which of them seems most pressing in terms of negative consequences? Who seems to be stepping forward in the attempt to solve the problems in innovative ways? Where and how might you engage in social entrepreneurship and make a very personal contribution to what is taking place? What, if anything, is holding you back?*

the next generation of position holders, the Navy retains the lessons learned from prior accidents through these positions.

The *physical structures* (or *ecology*, in the language of learning theorists) are potentially important mechanisms used to store information. For example, a traditional way of ordering parts is known as the "two-bin" system. One bin is always kept in reserve. Once an individual opens the reserve bin, he or she automatically orders replacements. In this way, the plant never runs out of parts.

Linking Strategy and Organizational Learning

As this quick overview of strategy and learning suggests, there are many strategies and many ways to learn. Historically, these two concepts have been discussed separately. Often strategy is linked to economic perspectives of the firm, whereas learning is discussed with organizational change. Today, however, many OB scholars recognize that to compete successfully in the twenty-first century global economy, individuals, units, and firms will need to learn continually. A firm based in a developed nation cannot successfully compete with firms based in developing countries just by being more efficient, any more than an individual in western Europe or North America can afford to work for the same wages as laborers from developing countries.

Production technology now spreads globally; transportation of goods is cheap, and the delivery of many services cuts across national boundaries. However, this does not mean that firms in developed nations are doomed. Firms can know more about their local markets; they can carefully select what they produce, what services they provide, what they buy, and how to build capability. They must learn and use their strategy to provide the necessary balance between exploration and exploitation of new ideas.[12] They must be capable of sustained learning at the organizational level to capture the lessons from exploring new technologies and exploiting existing markets.[13]

It is important to emphasize that sustaining a competitive strategy with consistent learning involves more than just a commitment by individuals; it calls for a systematic adjustment of the organization's structure and processes to alterations in the size and scope of operations, the technology selected, and the environmental setting. The process involved in making these dynamic adjustments is known as organizational design. As illustrated in Finding the Leader in You, old strategies based, for example, on low costs, also call for valuing employees as a basis for learning.

Strategy and Organizational Design

LEARNING ROADMAP Organizational Design and Strategic Decisions / Organizational Design, Age, and Growth / Smaller Size and the Simple Design

- **Organizational design** is the process of choosing and implementing a structural configuration for an organization.

Organizational design is the process of choosing and implementing a structural configuration.[14] It goes beyond just indicating who reports to whom and what types of jobs are contained in each department. The design process takes the basic structural elements and molds them to the firm's desires, demands, constraints, and choices. The choice of an appropriate organizational design is contingent upon several factors, including the size of the firm, its operations and information technology, its environment, and, of course, the strategy it selects for growth and survival.

For example, IBM's senior management has selected a form of organization for each component of IBM that matches that component's contribution to the whole. The overall organizational design matches the technical challenges facing IBM, allows it to adjust to new developments, and helps it shape its competitive landscape. Above all, the design promotes the development of individual skills and abilities, but different designs stress different skills and abilities. See, for instance, the activities IBM supports for Naoki Abe in its Yorktown Research Center. As we discuss each major contingency factor, we will highlight the design option the firm's managers need to consider and link these options to aspects of innovation and learning.[15]

Organizational Design and Strategic Decisions

To show the intricate intertwining of strategy and organizational design, it is important to reiterate and extend the dualistic notion of strategy.[16] Recall that strategy is a positioning of the firm in its environment to provide it with the

capability to succeed. Strategy is also a pattern in the stream of decisions. Here we will emphasize that what the firm intends to do must be backed up by capabilities for implementation in a setting that facilitates success.

Historically, executives were told that firms had available a limited number of economically determined generic strategies that were built upon the foundations of such factors as efficiency and innovation.[17] If the firm wanted efficiency, it should adopt the machine bureaucracy (many levels of management backed with extensive controls replete with written procedures). If it wanted innovation, it should adopt a more organic form (fewer levels of management with an emphasis on coordination). Today the world of corporations is much more complex, and executives have found much more sophisticated ways of competing.

Now many senior executives emphasize the skills and abilities that their firms need to compete and to remain agile and dynamic in a rapidly changing world.[18] The structural configuration or organizational design of the firm should not only facilitate the types of accomplishment desired by senior management, but also allow individuals to experiment, grow, and develop competencies so that the firm can learn and can evolve its strategy.[19] Over time, the firm may develop specific administrative and technical skills as middle- and lower-level managers institute minor adjustments to solve specific problems. As they learn, so can their firms if the individual learning of employees can be transferred across and up the organization's hierarchy.

Organizational Design, Age, and Growth

Most organizations want to grow and grow old. Growing old also means that the firm has a record of success, has been able to develop an effective strategy, and has been able to learn. However, aging also exposes the firm to a number of adjustment problems.

As organizations grow, the design of the firm needs to be adjusted.[20] Large organizations cannot simply be bigger versions of their smaller counterparts. With growth the direct interpersonal contact among all members in an organization must be managed. For instance, when the number of individuals in a firm is increased arithmetically, the number of possible interconnections between these individuals increases geometrically.

The Perils of Growth and Age   As organizations age and begin to grow beyond their simple structure, they become more rigid, inflexible, and resistant to change.[21] Both managers and employees begin to believe their prior success will continue into the future without an emphasis on innovation or learning. The organization or department becomes subject to routine scripts.

• A **managerial script** is a series of well-known routines for problem identification and alternative generation and analysis common to managers within a firm.

A **managerial script** is a series of well-known routines for problem identification and alternative generation and analysis common to managers within a firm.[22] Different organizations have different scripts, often based on what has worked in the past. In a way, the script is a ritual that reflects the "memory banks" held by the corporation. However, managers become bound by what they have seen. They may not be open to what is actually occurring. They may be unable to unlearn. Few managers question a successful script. Consequently, they start solving today's problems with yesterday's solutions. Managers often initiate small, incremental improvements based on existing solutions instead of creating new approaches to identify underlying problems.

Overcoming Inertia   For large organizations a key challenge in overcoming inertia is eliminating the vertical, horizontal, external, and geographic barriers that block desired action, innovation, and learning.[23] These barriers include overemphasizing vertical relations that can block communication up and down the firm; overemphasizing functions, product lines, or organizational units that block effective coordination; maintaining rigid lines of demarcation between the firm and its partners that isolate it from others; and reinforcing natural cultural, national, and geographical borders that can limit globally coordinated action. In breaking down such barriers, the goal is not necessarily to eliminate them altogether, but to make them more permeable.[24]

There are several major factors associated with the inability to dynamically co-evolve and develop a cycle with positive benefits.[25] Beyond inertia is hubris. Too few senior executives are willing to challenge their own actions or those of their firms because they see a history of success. An issue related to inertia and hubris is excessive detachment. Executives often believe they can manage far-flung, diverse operations just through analysis of reports and financial records. They lose touch and fail to make the needed unique and special adaptations required of all firms.

Although inertia, hubris, and detachment are common maladies, they are not the automatic fate of all corporations. Firms can successfully co-evolve. As we have repeatedly demonstrated, managers are constantly trying to reinvent their firms. They hope to initiate a benefit cycle—a pattern of successful adjustment followed by further improvements.[26] General Mills, IBM, Cisco, and Microsoft are examples of firms experiencing a benefit cycle. In this cycle, the same problems do not keep recurring as the firm develops adequate mechanisms for learning. The firm has few major difficulties with the learning process, and managers continually attempt to improve knowledge acquisition, information distribution, information interpretation, and organizational memory.

Smaller Size and the Simple Design

Larger organizations are more complex than smaller firms. The design of small firms is directly influenced by its core operations technology whereas larger firms have many core operations technologies in a wide variety of much more specialized

Finding the Leader in You

JIM SINEGAL'S STRATEGY AT COSTCO IS TO NOT FOLLOW THE CROWD

According to CEO Jim Sinegal, "Costco is able to offer lower prices . . . by eliminating virtually all the frills and costs historically associated with conventional wholesalers. . . . We run a tight operation with extremely low overhead."

On the surface it sounds much like most large-box discount retailers who pursue a low-cost strategy in order to effectively compete. So what is the difference? For one, Costco invests in its employees. They pay nearly all

full-time employees full benefits, including health care and retirement. Base wages are among the highest in the industry, and the company also promotes from within. It is not at all unusual to find a store manager who started her career with Costco. The emphasis on employees is rare in the discount retail sector. For many competitors, a low-cost strategy means low wages and restricted benefits. And, of course, devaluing employees means not learning much from employees.

How does Costco do it? Costco stores have a comparatively limited range of items, which cuts carrying costs. Most Costco stores have, at any given time, 5,000 items compared to about 100,000 for Walmart. Costco also tends to carry a greater number of higher-end products with very low margins to

stimulate store excitement. As a result, Costco is the fifth largest retailer in the United States, with over 53 million cardholders and 250,000 employees. With global sales approaching $75 billion, Costco currently ranks 29th on the *Fortune* global 500 list.

In the short term Costco could probably make more money with lower wages and benefits. But that would be inconsistent with Sinegal's vision of building a long-term business. To him, treating employees well is consistent with nurturing and developing customer loyalty.

What's the Lesson Here?

In developing a strategy for your group, will you always follow the crowd? As a leader, what type of learning do you promote, and how would you design it into your operations?

units. While all larger firms are bureaucracies, smaller firms need not be. In larger firms, additional complexity calls for a more sophisticated organizational design. Such is not the case for the small firm. For smaller firms the simple design is most appropriate.

The **simple design** is a configuration involving one or two ways of specializing individuals and units. Vertical specialization and control typically emphasize levels of supervision without elaborate formal mechanisms (for example, rulebooks and policy manuals), and the majority of the control resides in the manager. Thus, the simple design tends to minimize bureaucracy and to rest more heavily on the leadership of the manager.

The simple design pattern is appropriate for many small firms, such as family businesses, retail stores, and small manufacturing firms.[27] The strengths of the simple design are simplicity, flexibility, and responsiveness to the desires of a central manager—in many cases, the owner. Because a simple design relies heavily on the manager's personal leadership, however, this configuration is only as effective as is the senior manager.

One example is B&A Travel, a small travel agency owned by Helen Druse. Reporting to Helen is a part-time staff member, Jane Bloom, for accounting and

• **Simple design** is a configuration involving one or two ways of specializing individuals and units.

finance. Jane also keeps the dedicated computer system operating. Joan Wiland heads the operations arm and supervises eight travel agents. Although each of the travel agents specializes in a geographical area, all take client requests for different types of trips. Coordination is achieved through their dedicated intranet and Internet connections. Joan uses weekly meetings and a lot of personal contact by Helen and Joan to coordinate everyone. Control is enhanced by the computerized reservation system they all use. Helen makes sure each agent has a monthly sales target and she routinely chats with important clients about their level of service. Helen realizes that developing participation from even the newest associate is an important tool in maintaining a "fun" atmosphere.

Technology and Organizational Design

LEARNING ROADMAP   Operations Technology and Organizational Design / Adhocracy as a Design Option for Innovation and Learning / Information Technology and Organizational Design

Although the design for an organization should reflect its size, it must also be adjusted to fit technological opportunities and requirements.[28] Successful organizations are said to arrange their internal structures to meet the dictates of their dominant "operations technologies" or workflows and, more recently, information technology opportunities.[29] **Operations technology** is the combination of resources, knowledge, and techniques that creates a product or service output for an organization.[30] **Information technology** is the combination of machines, artifacts, procedures, and systems used to gather, store, analyze, and disseminate information for translating it into knowledge.[31]

> • **Operations technology** is the combination of resources, knowledge, and techniques that creates a product or service output for an organization.
> • **Information technology** is the combination of machines, artifacts, procedures, and systems used to gather, store, analyze, and disseminate information for translating it into knowledge.

Operations Technology and Organizational Design

As researchers in OB have charted the links between operations technology and organizational design, two common classifications for operations technology have received considerable attention: Thompson's and Woodward's classifications.

Thompson's View of Technology   James D. Thompson classified technologies based on the degree to which the technology could be specified and the degree of interdependence among the work activities with categories called intensive, mediating, and long-linked.[32] Under *intensive technology*, there is uncertainty as to how to produce desired outcomes. A group of specialists must be brought together interactively to use a variety of techniques to solve problems. Examples are found in a hospital emergency room or a research and development laboratory. Coordination and knowledge exchange are of critical importance with this kind of technology.

Mediating technology links parties that want to become interdependent. For example, banks link creditors and depositors and store money and information to facilitate such exchanges. Whereas all depositors and creditors are indirectly interdependent, the reliance is pooled through the bank. The degree of coordination among the individual tasks with pooled technology is substantially reduced, and information management becomes more important than coordinated knowledge application.

Under *long-linked technology*, also called mass production or industrial technology, the way to produce the desired outcomes is known. The task is broken down into a number of sequential steps. A classic example is the automobile assembly line. Control is critical, and coordination is restricted to making the sequential linkages work in harmony.

Three Types of Operations Technologies

| Intensive | Mediating | Long linked |

Woodward's View of Technology   Joan Woodward also divides technology into three categories: small-batch, mass production, and continuous-process manu-facturing.[33] In units of *small-batch production*, a variety of custom products are tai-lor-made to fit customer specifications, such as tailor-made suits. The machinery and equipment used are generally not very elaborate, but considerable craftsmanship is often needed. In *mass production*, the organization produces one or a few products through an assembly-line system. The work of one group is highly dependent on that of another, the equipment is typically sophisticated, and the workers are given very detailed instructions. Automobiles and refrigerators are produced in this way.

Organizations using *continuous-process technology* produce a few products using considerable automation. Classic examples are automated chemical plants and oil refineries.

From her studies, Woodward concluded that the combination of structure and technology was critical to the success of the organizations. When technology and organizational design were matched properly, a firm was more successful. Specifi-cally, successful small-batch and continuous-process plants had flexible structures with small workgroups at the bottom; more rigidly structured plants were less suc-cessful. In contrast, successful mass-production operations were rigidly structured and had large workgroups at the bottom. Since Woodward's studies, various other investigations have supported this technological imperative. Today we recognize that operations technology is just one factor involved in the success of an organization.[34]

Adhocracy as a Design Option for Innovation and Learning

The influence of operations technology is clearly seen in small organizations and in specific departments within large firms. In some instances, managers and employees simply do not know the appropriate way to service a client or to pro-duce a particular product. This is an extreme example of Thompson's intensive type of technology, and it may be found in some small-batch processes where a team of individuals must develop a unique product for a particular client.

Mintzberg suggests that at these technological extremes, the "adhocracy" may be an appropriate design.[35] An **adhocracy** is characterized by

- Few rules, policies, and procedures
- Substantial decentralization

• **Adhocracy** emphasizes shared, decentralized decision making; extreme horizontal specialization; few levels of management; the virtual absence of formal controls; and few rules, policies, and procedures.

- Shared decision making among members
- Extreme horizontal specialization (as each member of the unit may be a distinct specialist)
- Few levels of management
- Virtually no formal controls

This design emphasizes innovation and learning. The adhocracy is particularly useful when an aspect of the firm's operations technology presents two sticky problems:

1. The tasks facing the firm vary considerably and provide many exceptions, as in a management consulting firm. Or

2. Problems are difficult to define and resolve.[36]

The adhocracy places a premium on professionalism and coordination in problem solving.[37] Large firms may use temporary task forces, form special committees, and even contract with consulting firms to provide the creative problem identification and problem solving that the adhocracy promotes. For instance, Microsoft creates autonomous departments to encourage talented employees to

OB IN POPULAR CULTURE

ADHOCRACY AND *THE EX*

Organizational design is often dictated by a company's business. When the business environment is fluid because of rapid changes in the marketplace, organizational designs have to be equally flexible. One extreme form is the **adhocracy**, where strict centralized hierarchical structure is replaced by one that relies more on groups made up of highly specialized individuals.

Out of work, Tom Reilly (Zach Braff) lands a job at Sunburst with the help of his father-in-law. Tom is in for a bit of a rude awakening. Sunburst is unlike anything from his previous professional experience. He arrives his first day to find an open-air office with employees singing, riding motorized skateboard scooters, and casually dressed. New co-workers arrive with the imaginary "yes" ball, which is designed to encourage cooperation and positive thinking. Later in the afternoon, everyone in the workgroup meets to discuss ideas and welcome Tom. When Tom unintentionally offends a co-worker, he learns about the practice of "mushiwaki," where employees accept responsibility for their actions without having to publicly apologize.

Although the scene is meant to be comical, it does reflect a trend in newer businesses toward more open designs that give employees incredible freedom and control. Decisions are usually made in groups, so there is a high degree of interaction across functions. Professionalism and personal responsibility take the place of rules and procedures.

Get to Know Yourself Better   Perhaps your instructor had you complete Exercise 34, Entering the Unknown, in the OB Skills Workbook. If not, take a moment to examine it. The exercise is designed to explore how individuals interact when they are new to a group, but it can be just as applicable to joining new organizations. You will soon be transitioning from a very structured world (i.e., school) to one that may be much looser. Expectations in this new environment may be even higher than before. How will you adjust and perform, particularly if you are not accustomed to the freedom?

develop new software programs. Allied Chemical and 3M set up quasi-autonomous groups to work through new ideas.

We should note, however, that the adhocracy is notoriously inefficient. Many managers are reluctant to adopt this form because they appear to lose control of day-to-day operations. The implicit strategy consistent with the adhocracy is a stress on quality and individual service as opposed to efficiency. With more advanced information technology, firms are beginning to combine an adhocracy with bureaucratic elements based on advanced information systems.

Information Technology and Organizational Design

Recall that we defined information technology as the combination of machines, artifacts, procedures, and systems used to gather, store, analyze, and disseminate information.[38] Information technology (IT), the Web, and the computer are virtually inseparable, and they have fundamentally changed the organization design of firms to capture new competencies.[39] While some suggest that IT refers only to computer-based systems used in the management of the enterprise, we take a broader view. With substantial collateral advances in telecommunication options, advances in the computer as a machine are much less profound than those information technology changes affecting how firms manage all of their parts.

From an organizational standpoint, IT can be used, among other things, as a partial substitute for some operations as well as some process controls and impersonal methods of coordination. IT has a strategic capability as well as a capability for transforming information into knowledge. For instance, most financial firms could not exist without IT because it is now the base for the industry. Financial institutions created completely new aspects of their industry based on IT, such as exotic derivatives; it is now painfully obvious that these new aspects of the industry have outpaced the ability of management to control them. Information technology, just as operations technology, can yield great good or great harm.

IT as a Substitute   Old bureaucracies prospered and dominated other firms in part because they provided efficient production through specialization and through the way they managed their information. Old bureaucracies programmed jobs through rules, policies, and procedures, as well as other process controls.[40] In many organizations, the initial implementation of IT displaced the most routine, highly specified, and repetitive jobs where they were highly programmed.[41] A second wave of substitution replaced process controls and informal coordination mechanisms. For instance, if you apply for a credit card, a computer program, not a person, will check your credit history and other financial information. If your application passes several preset tests, you are issued a credit card.

IT to Add Capability   IT has also long been recognized for its potential to add capability.[42] Married to machines, IT became advanced manufacturing technology when computer-aided design (CAD) was combined with computer-aided manufacturing (CAM) to yield the automated manufacturing cell. More complex decision-support systems have provided middle and lower-level managers with programs to aid in analyzing complex problems rather than merely ratifying routine choices. IT systems can also empower individuals, expanding their jobs and making them both interesting and challenging. The emphasis on narrowly defined jobs replete with process controls imposed by middle management can be transformed to

Amazon's Expansion Means More Than Just Books

Amazon.com was founded by Jeff Bezos in 1995 with the intention of selling books directly to customers via the Internet. It has rapidly expanded into a virtual general store. With sales over $24 billion and over 24,000 employees, Amazon.com has one of the best-recognized Web site addresses and is the hub of a virtual network of organizations.

broadly envisioned, interesting jobs based on IT-embedded processes with output controls. The IT system can handle the routine operations while individuals deep within the organization deal with the exceptions.

The Virtual Organization and IT Opportunities   Shortly before the turn of the last century, e-business exploded upon the scene.[43] Today e-business is integrated into the virtual organization, just as on-site project teams morphed into virtual project teams.

Whether it is business to business (B2B) or business to consumers (B2C), a whole new set of firms have evolved with information technology at the core of their operations. One of the more flamboyant early entrants to the B2C world is Amazon.com.

It is interesting to examine the transformation in the design of this firm to illustrate the notion of co-evolution and the ability to learn with advanced IT. Initially when Amazon just sold books, it was organized as a simple structure. As it grew, it became more complex by adding divisions devoted to each of its separate product areas. To remain flexible and promote growth in both the volume of operations and the capabilities of employees, it did not develop an extensive bureaucracy. There are still very few levels of management. It built separate organizational components based on product categories (divisional structure) with minimal rules, policies, and procedures. In other words, the organizational design it adopted appeared to be relatively conventional.[44]

What was not conventional was the use of IT for learning about customers and for coordinating and tracking operations and the development of extensive partnerships via IT. In comparison to Amazon.com, many other new dot-com firms adopted a variation of the adhocracy as their design pattern. The thinking was that e-business was fundamentally different from the old bricks-and-mortar operations. The managers of these firms forgot two important liabilities of the adhocracy as they grew. First, there are limits on the size of an effective adhocracy. Second, the actual delivery of their products and services did not require continual product innovation but rested more firmly on responsiveness to clients and maintaining efficiency.

The Virtual Organization   As IT has become widespread, firms are finding that it can be the basis for a new way to compete. Some executives have started to develop "virtual organizations."[45] A **virtual organization** is an ever-shifting constellation of firms, with a lead corporation, that pools skills, resources, and experiences to thrive jointly. This ever-changing collection most likely has a relatively stable group of actors (usually independent firms) that normally includes customers, research centers, suppliers, and distributors all connected to each other. The lead firm possesses a critical competence that all need and therefore

• A **virtual organization** is an ever-shifting constellation of firms, with a lead corporation, that pools skills, resources, and experiences to thrive jointly.

directs the constellation. While this critical competence may be a key operations technology or access to customers, it always includes IT as a base for connecting the firms.

The virtual organization works if it operates by some unique rules and is led in a most untypical way. First, the production system that yields the products and services needs to be a partner network among independent firms where they are bound together by mutual trust and collective survival. As customers desire change, the proportion of work done by any member firm might also change and the membership itself may change. In a similar fashion, the introduction of a new operations technology could shift the proportion of work among members or call for the introduction of new members. Second, this partner network needs to develop and maintain (1) an advanced information technology (rather than just face-to-face interaction), (2) trust and cross-owning of problems and solutions, and (3) a common shared culture.

The virtual organization can be highly resilient, extremely competent, innovative, and reasonably efficient—characteristics that are usually trade-offs. Executives in the lead firm need to have the vision to see how the network of participants will both effectively compete with consistent enough patterns to be recognizable and still rapidly adjust to technological and environmental changes.[46]

What to Do When You Are Managing a "Virtual" Project.

1. Establish a set of mutually reinforcing motives for participation, including a share in success.
2. Stress self-governance and make sure there are a manageable number of high-quality contributors.
3. Outline a set of rules that members can adapt to their individual needs.
4. Encourage joint monitoring and sanctions of member behavior.
5. Stress shared values, norms, and behavior.
6. Develop effective work structures and processes via project management software.
7. Emphasize the use of technology for communication and norms about how to use it.

Virtual Projects   More than likely, someday you will be involved with a "virtual" network of task forces and temporary teams to both define and solve problems. Here the members will only connect electronically. Recent work on participants of the virtual teams suggests you will need to rethink what it means to "manage." Instead of telling others what to do, you will need to treat your colleagues as unpaid volunteers who expect to participate in governing the meetings and who are tied to the effort only by a commitment to identify and solve problems.[47]

Environment and Organizational Design

LEARNING ROADMAP   Environmental Complexity / Using Networks and Alliances

An effective organizational design also reflects powerful external forces as well as size and technological factors. Organizations, as open systems, need to receive input from the environment and in turn to sell output to their environment. Therefore, understanding the environment is important.[48]

The **general environment** is the set of cultural, economic, legal-political, and educational conditions found in the areas in which the organization operates.

• The **general environment** is the set of cultural, economic, legal-political, and educational conditions found in the areas in which the organization operates.

Firms expanding globally encounter multiple general environments. At one time, firms could separate foreign and domestic operations into almost distinct operating entities, but this is rarely the case now.

• The **specific environment** is the set of owners, suppliers, distributors, government agencies, and competitors with which an organization must interact to grow and survive.

The owners, suppliers, distributors, government agencies, and competitors with which an organization must interact to grow and survive constitute its **specific environment**. A firm typically has much more choice in the composition of its specific environment than its general environment. Although it is often convenient to separate the general and specific environmental influences on the firm, managers need to recognize the combined impact of both

Environmental Complexity

A basic concern to address when analyzing the environment of the organization is its complexity. A more complex environment provides an organization with more opportunities and more problems. **Environmental complexity** refers to the magnitude of the problems and opportunities in the organization's environment, as evidenced by three main factors: the degree of richness, the degree of interdependence, and the degree of uncertainty stemming from both the general and the specific environment.

• **Environmental complexity** is the magnitude of the problems and opportunities in the organization's environment as evidenced by the degree of richness, interdependence, and uncertainty.

Environmental Richness   Overall, the environment is richer when the economy is growing, when individuals are improving their education, and when everyone that the organization relies upon is prospering. For businesses, a richer environment means that economic conditions are improving, customers are spending more money, and suppliers (especially banks) are willing to invest in the organization's future. In a rich environment, more organizations survive, even if they have poorly functioning organizational designs. A richer environment is also filled with more opportunities and dynamism—the potential for change. The organizational design must allow the company to recognize these opportunities and capitalize on them. The opposite of richness is decline. For business firms, the current general recession is a good example of a leaner environment.

Environmental Interdependence   The link between external interdependence and organizational design is often subtle and indirect. The organization may co-opt powerful outsiders by including them. For instance, many large corporations have financial representatives from banks and insurance companies on their boards of directors. One example is Fab India, a premium brand of hand-woven products that encourages its 20,000 plus artisan workers to become stockholders.

Fab India Artists Are Its Most Important Shareholders

A premium retail brand in India, Fab India sells hand-woven products produced by artisan workers. It also invites them to become shareholders and sets up centers to specialize in each region's special crafts. CEO William Bissell says: "We're somewhere between the 17th century, with our artisan suppliers, and the 21st century with our consumers."

The organization may also adjust its overall design strategy to absorb or buffer the demands of a more powerful external element. Perhaps the most common adjustment is the development of a centralized staff department to handle an important external group. Few large U.S. corporations lack some type of centralized governmental relations group, for example. Where service to a few large customers is critical, the organization's departmentation is likely to switch from a functional to a divisionalized form.[49]

Uncertainty and Volatility   Environmental uncertainty and volatility can be particularly damaging to large bureaucracies. In times of change, investments quickly become outmoded, and internal operations no longer work as expected. The obvious organizational design response to uncertainty and volatility is to opt for a more flexible organic form. At the extremes, movement toward an adhocracy may be important. However, these pressures may run counter to those that come from large size and operations technology. In these cases, it may be too hard or too time consuming for some organizations to make the design adjustments. Thus, the organization may continue to struggle while adjusting its design just a little bit at a time. Some firms can deal with the conflicting demands from environmental change and need for internal stability by developing alliances.

Using Networks and Alliances

In today's complex global economy, organizational design must go beyond the traditional boundaries of the firm.[50] Firms must learn to co-evolve by altering their environment. Two ways are becoming more popular: (1) the management of networks and (2) the development of alliances. Many North American firms are learning from their European and Japanese counterparts to develop networks of linkages to the key firms they rely on. In Europe, for example, one finds *informal combines* or *cartels*. Here, competitors work cooperatively to share the market in order to decrease uncertainty and improve favorability for all. Except in rare cases, these arrangements are often illegal in the United States.

In Japan, the network of relationships among well-established firms in many industries is called a *keiretsu*. There are two common forms. The first is a bank-centered *keiretsu* in which firms link to one another directly through cross-ownership and historical ties to one bank. The Mitsubishi group is a good example of a company that grew through cross-ownership. In the second type, a *vertical keiretsu*, a key manufacturer is at the hub of a network of supplier firms or distributor firms. The manufacturer typically has both long-term supply contracts with members and cross-ownership ties. These arrangements help isolate Japanese firms from stockholders and provide a mechanism for sharing and developing technology. Toyota is an example of a firm at the center of a *vertical keiretsu*.

A specialized form of network organization is evolving in U.S.-based firms as well. Here, the central firm specializes in core activities, such as design, assembly, and marketing, and works with a small number of participating suppliers on a long-term basis for both component development and manufacturing efficiency. The central firm is the hub of a network where others need it more than it needs any other member. Although Nike was a leader in the development of these relationships, now it is difficult to find a large U.S. firm that does not outsource extensively.

• **Interfirm alliances** are announced cooperative agreements or joint ventures between two independent firms.

Another option is to develop **interfirm alliances**, which are cooperative agreements or joint ventures between two independent firms.[51] Often, these agreements involve corporations that are headquartered in different nations. In high-tech areas, such as robotics, semiconductors, advanced materials (ceramics and carbon fibers), and advanced information systems, a single company often does not have all of the knowledge necessary to bring new products to the market. Alliances are quite common in such high-technology industries. Through their international alliances, high-tech firms seek to develop technology and to ensure that their solutions standardize across regions of the world.

Developing and effectively managing an alliance is a managerial challenge of the first order. Firms are asked to cooperate rather than compete. The alliance's sponsors normally have different and unique strategies, cultures, and desires for the alliance itself. Both the alliance managers and sponsoring executives must be patient, flexible, and creative in pursuing the goals of the alliance and each sponsor. It is little wonder that some alliances are terminated prematurely.[52]

Of course, alliances are but one way of altering the environment. The firm can also invest in the projects of other firms through corporate venture capital. It may acquire other companies to bring their expertise directly into the firm. All of these can be beneficial.[53] However, these initiatives need to be related to the strategy of the firm and its technology. And all of these alert us to the fact that in addition to organizational design, strategy and learning call for leadership of the whole organization.

Strategic Leadership of the Whole Organization

LEARNING ROADMAP Strategic Leadership and the Challenges at Multiple Levels /
Developing a Top-Management Team / Using Top-Management Leadership Skills

• **Strategic leadership** is leadership of a quasi-independent unit, department, or organization.

Even with an organizational design perfectly matched to the size, technology, and environment of the firm, it must still be led. Leading the whole effort is often called strategic leadership.[54] When the focus is on **strategic leadership**, it is the study of leading a quasi-independent unit, department, or organization. Although many focus on the individual at the top of the pyramid, such as the chief executive officer or the president of the United States, research suggests that strategic leadership is not rooted in just the top-management team or the CEO.[55] The top-management team as a group is also important. For example, if there is greater diversity in the challenges and opportunities facing the firm, the top-management team should be more diverse.[56] So leading the whole organization calls for understanding the unique challenges facing both the individual at the top and the top-management team. Whereas the head of the organization needs to understand the challenges of the job, the top-management team needs to develop an effective group process that will cope with the struggles and opportunities facing the firm.

Strategic Leadership and the Challenges at Multiple Levels

Starting from the bottom, organizations can be separated into three major zones: (1) the production zone, (2) the administrative zone, and (3) the systems zone. As the names imply, the challenge to the leader across the zones vary. That is, leadership requirements at different levels or echelons of management differ.[57] Each echelon gets more complex than the one beneath it in terms of its leadership and managerial requirements. Leaders at top levels have special responsibilities since their influence cascades throughout the organization.

One way of expressing the increasing complexity of the levels is in terms of how long it takes to see the results of the key decisions required at any given level. The timeframe can range from 3 months or so at the lowest level, which emphasizes hands-on work performance and practical judgment to solve ongoing problems, to 20 years or more at the top.

Because problems become increasingly complex from the lower levels to the upper levels of the organization, you can expect that managers at each level must demonstrate increasing cognitive and behavioral complexity in order to deal with an increase in organizational complexity. **Cognitive complexity** deals with the degree to which individuals perceive nuances and subtle differences, whereas **behavioral complexity** centers on the possession of a repertoire of roles and the ability to selectively apply them. In other terms cognitively complex individuals see more subtle variations, and those who are behaviorally complex can act in a wider variety of roles than those who are less complex.

One way of measuring a manager's cognitive complexity is in terms of how far into the future he or she can develop a vision. Accompanying such a vision should be an increasing range and sophistication of leadership behaviors.

When there is a focus on complexity at the top, researchers often stress how strategic leadership cascades deep within the organization. One example of such cascading, indirect leadership is the leadership-at-a-distance. Even individuals several levels above a unit can influence the style and tone of what occurs in a unit. The systems zone leadership at the top of an organization is normally responsible for producing complex systems, organizing acquisition of major resources, creating vision, developing strategy and policy, and identifying organizational design. These functions call for a much broader conception of leadership. In many respects leadership of this zone combines leadership and management as choices made at the top cascade down the organization. One subtle example of cascading leadership is known as "intent of the commander" where middle-level leaders try to mimic what they think the top-level leader would do in their situation.[58] Researchers have linked CEO values to culture and then to organizational outcomes as the values of the CEO cascaded down.[59]

Leadership of the organization also involves a face-to-face influence as well. Regardless of the level, leaders must engage in direct supervision and must be effective followers. The saying is that "everyone has a boss." And even most CEOs would argue that those near the top must act as a team and the notion of shared leadership at the top of the organization is clearly relevant.[60] The top-management team is particularly important.

- **Cognitive complexity** is the degree to which individuals perceive nuances and subtle differences.
- **Behavioral complexity** is the possession of a repertoire of roles and the ability to selectively apply them.

Developing a Top-Management Team

Top-management teams (TMTs) refer to the relatively small group of executives at the very top of the organization or the leaders of the firm. Often the top-management team is composed of 3 to 10 executives.[61] The composition of the top-management team is important because the collective nature, temperament, outlook, and interactions among these individuals alter the choices made in the leadership of the organization.

Journal of
Organizational
Behavior

VOLUME 32 NUMBER 7 ISSN 0934–3796

WILEY-
BLACKWELL

RESEARCH INSIGHT

CEO Values Make a Difference

Although there has been a lot of discussion about how the values of the CEO impact performance, comparatively few comprehensive studies have been done. Recently, Y. Berson, S. Oreg, and T. Dvir started to remedy this gap with a study of CEO values, organizational culture, and performance. They suggested that individuals are drawn to and stay with organizations that have value priorities similar to their own. That includes the CEO. Furthermore, the CEO reinforces some values over others, and this has a measurable impact on the organizational culture. The organizational culture, then, emphasizes some aspects of performance over others.

The researchers hypothesized and found the following in a study of some 22 CEOs and their firms in Israel: CEOs tend to place a high priority on self-direction or security or benevolence. This priority tends to emphasize a particular type of organizational culture. Specifically, when a CEO values self-direction, there is more cultural emphasis on innovation; when a CEO values security, there is more cultural emphasis on bureaucracy; and when a CEO values benevolence, the culture is more supportive of its members. Then they linked aspects of organizational culture with specific elements of performance (organizational outcomes). More innovation was associated with higher sales growth. A bureaucratic culture was linked to efficiency, while a supportive culture was associated with greater employee satisfaction. In sum, CEO values are linked to organizational culture, which, in turn, is associated with organizational outcomes. Schematically, it looks like this:

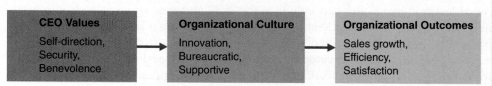

Do the Research Do you think this study would transfer to firms located in North America? Is it possible that firms with an established innovative culture select a CEO that values self-direction?

Source: Yair Berson, Shaul Oreg, and Taly Dvir, "CEO Values, Organizational Culture and Firm Outcomes," *Journal of Organizational Behavior* 29 (2008), pp. 615–633.

The composition of a top-management team can have a major influence on how an organization operates in terms of the shared culture, decision-making, and management styles, and even on the ethical foundation of day-to-day workplace behaviors.

Much of the research on top-management teams uses demographic characteristics as proxies for harder-to-obtain psychological variables. Such variables as age, tenure, education, and functional background are used in this perspective. Researchers typically attempt to link such variables to various kinds of organizational outcomes, including sales growth, innovation, and executive turnover.[62]

Because of conflicting findings, researchers have been working to enrich this approach. One important review argues that a given TMT is likely to face a variety of different situations over time. Demographic composition may be relatively stable, but the tasks are dynamic and variable. Sometimes team members have

Top-Management Team Composition Influences Organization

The composition of a top-management team can have a major influence on how an organization operates in terms of a shared culture, decision making, and even the ethical foundation of day-to-day workplace behaviors.

similar information (symmetric) and interests, and sometimes not (asymmetric). With asymmetric information and symmetric interests, there is an opportunity for the top-management team to develop new innovative solutions. For example, when considering a merger, some executives may have information on the potential partner's finances, on its management style and strategy, or on the partner's connections with others. The team may initially move to buy the new partner but sell off selected portions of the new business.

In today's dynamic environment it is desirable for top-management teams to have a variety of skills, experiences, and emergent theories that are basically explanations of what might happen and why. Diversity of the skills and abilities of the team can promote debate and discussion, which can lead to more comprehensive, balanced, and effective initiatives for improvement.[63] Homogeneous top-management groups are less likely to identify and respond to subtle but important variations. This can result in stale strategies, unresponsiveness, and dulling consistency. Of course, there are practical limits to the degree of diversity and the range of emergent theories that top-management can effectively discuss. Too much variation can yield excessive discussion and paralysis by analysis.[64]

The TMT researchers argue that group process must be handled differently and effectively for dynamic versus less dynamic settings. Not only should the composition of the top management team be adjusted to the degree of change facing the firm, but there should also be adjustments in group process. With change facing the firm, there needs to be more emphasis on processing information, a representation of broader interests, a strong recognition of existing power asymmetries, and additional emphasis on developing new emergent theories of action.[65]

Using Top-Management Leadership Skills

So far we have suggested that the challenges at the top are unique, that leaders need to be cognitively complex with a far-reaching vision and possess behavioral complexity. We also noted the importance of the cascading effects of leadership at the top and the critical role of the top-management team. Now it is time to put all of this together in a model developed by Boal and Hooijberg. Their model focuses on the tensions and complexity faced by strategic leaders and is shown in Figure 17.1.[66]

In their model, Boal and Hooijberg express the challenges at the top in terms of tensions among desirable conditions. They describe these tensions as stemming from Emergent Theories and the Competing Values Framework (CVF).[67] Specifically, tensions exist between (1) flexibility versus control and (2) internal focus versus external focus. The flexibility versus control dimension contrasts actions focused on goal clarity and efficiency and those emphasizing adaptation to people and the external environment. The internal versus external focus dimension distinguishes between social actions emphasizing such internal effectiveness measures as employee satisfaction versus a focus on external effectiveness measures such as market share and profitability.

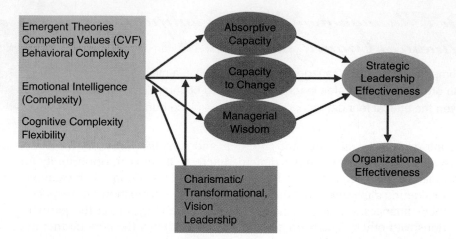

Figure 17.1 Boal and Hooijberg Perspective on Strategic Leadership. [*Source:* Kimberly B. Boal and Robert Hooijberg, "Strategic Leadership Research: Moving On." *The Leadership Quarterly* 11 (2009).]

Combinations of these tensions yield a variety of potential roles that can be used in addressing these tensions. In the terms used by Boal and Hooijberg, a leadership role is a set of influence attempts crafted to meet a specific combination of challenges.[68] For instance, the leader may be asked to deal with the combination of (1) the need for high flexibility coupled with high-control requirements in addition to (2) a call for high emphasis on external performance but a low requirement for internal effectiveness. This need would suggest that the leader perform one role. A different combination would ask the leader to perform a slightly different role. Although it is possible to detail the leadership roles for each possible combination, the point of our discussion is to stress the wide variety of roles the leader may need to perform. Also note that the leader needs to see the tensions in combination (the need for cognitive complexity) as well as be able to act accordingly (behavioral complexity).

Overall, executives who can display a large repertoire of leadership roles and know when to apply these roles are more likely to be effective than leaders who have a small role repertoire and who indiscriminately apply these roles. Since the challenges often shift, executives need cognitive and behavioral complexity as well as flexibility. Of course, they may understand and see the differences between their subordinates and superiors but not be able to behaviorally differentiate so as to satisfy the demands of each group. It is not always possible to successfully influence others.

Figure 17.1 shows that CVF, behavioral complexity, emotional complexity, and cognitive complexity are directly associated with absorptive capacity, capacity to change, and managerial wisdom as well as with charismatic/transformational leadership and vision. In other words, the block to the left shows the challenges and opportunities facing those at and near the top. The leadership of these individuals, both alone and in combination, alters the degree to which the firm can adjust day-to-day management. As the complexity of the challenges and opportunities increases, there is more stress on the organization. How it is led then becomes more important.

Organizational Competencies and Strategic Leadership Finally, consistent with the research of Boal and Hooijberg, it is important to recognize key organizational competencies and link them with strategic leadership effectiveness and ultimately with organizational effectiveness.[69] The first key competency is absorptive capacity. **Absorptive capacity** is the ability to learn. It involves the capacity to recognize new information, assimilate it, and apply it to new ends. It utilizes processes necessary to improve the organization–environment fit. Absorptive capacity of strategic leaders in the top-management team is of particular importance because those in such a position have a unique ability to change or reinforce organizational action patterns.

> • **Absorptive capacity** is the ability to learn.

The second key competency is adaptive capacity. **Adaptive capacity** refers to the ability to change. Boal and Hooijberg argue that in the new, fast-changing competitive landscape, organizational success calls for strategic flexibility—that is, the ability to respond quickly to competitive conditions. The third key competency is **managerial wisdom**, which involves the ability to perceive variation in the environment and understand the social actors and their relationships. Thus, emotional intelligence is called for, and the leader must be able to take the right action at the right moment.

> • **Adaptive capacity** refers to the ability to change.

> • **Managerial wisdom** is the ability to perceive variations in the environment and understand the social actors and their relationships.

An Example of the Model   Let's look at an integrative example of an engineering company that, at one time, had 100 percent of its contracts with the Department of Defense. Alice Smith left the meeting with the top-management team with a clear mandate—a company reorientation was necessary given a pending decline in the U.S. defense budget. The company had to reconceptualize its organizational system to ensure future profitability and continued employment for all. Contract bidding procedures changed; the company no longer needed to comply with numerous government regulations in terms of its contracts, and executive leaders had to acquire new customers. All of this called for a capacity to change, the adsorption of new skills, and the wisdom to choose a viable new path. These leaders formulated future visions and emphasized organizational transformation. They hired others to help retrain themselves and their workforce. They even appeared charismatic, if not visionary, as they pushed the pace of change. As strategic leaders high in behavioral complexity and emotional intelligence, they spotted new consumer trends for variations of existing products and moved quickly to capture new markets even as they phased out their old contracts.[70] Some two years after their fateful meeting, the firm was in the middle of a fundamental transition. The future looked bright, and before long it would be time to plan for another change.

17 *study guide*

Key Questions and Answers

Why are strategy and organizational learning important?

- Strategy is the process of positioning the organization in the competitive environment and implementing actions to compete successfully. It is a pattern in a stream of decisions.

- Organizational learning is the process of acquiring knowledge and using information to adapt successfully to changing circumstances.

- For organizations to learn, they must engage in knowledge acquisition, information distribution, information interpretation, and organizational retention in adapting successfully to changing circumstances.

- Firms use mimicry, experience, vicarious learning, scanning, and grafting to acquire information.

- Firms establish mechanisms to convert information into knowledge. Chief among the problems of interpretation are self-serving interpretations.

- Firms retain information through individuals, transformation mechanisms, formal structure, physical structure, external archives, and their IT system.

- To compete successfully, individuals, units, and firms will need to constantly learn because of changes in the scope of operations, technology, and the environment.

What is organizational design, and how is it linked to strategy?

- Organizational design is the process of choosing and implementing a structural configuration for an organization.

- Organizational design is a way to implement the positioning of the firm in its environment.

- Organizational design provides a basis for a consistent stream of decisions.

- Strategy and organizational design are interrelated and must evolve with changes in size, technology, and the environment.

- The design of a large organization is far more complex than that of a small firm.

- With aging, firms become subject to routine managerial scripts. Large organizations will need to systematically break down boundaries limiting learning.

- Smaller firms often adopt a simple structure because it works, is cheap, and stresses the influence of the leader.

How does technology influence organizational design?

- Operations technology and organizational design should be interrelated to ensure the firm produces the desired goods and/or services.

- Adhocracy is an organizational design used in technology-intense settings.

- Information technology is the combination of machines, artifacts, procedures, and systems used to gather, store, analyze, and disseminate information for translating it into knowledge.

- IT provides an opportunity to change the design by substitution, for learning, and to capture strategic advantages.

- IT forms the basis for the virtual organization.

How does the environment influence organizational design?

- Organizations, as open systems, need to receive inputs from the environment and, in turn, to sell outputs to their environment.

- The environment is more complex when it is richer and more interdependent with higher volatility and greater uncertainty.

- The more complex the environment, the greater the demands on the organization, and firms should respond with more complex designs.

- Firms need not stand alone but can develop network relationships and alliances to cope with greater environmental complexity.

- By honing the knowledge gained in this text you can develop the skills to compete successfully in the twenty-first century and become a leader.

How should the whole organization be led strategically?

- When the focus is on strategic leadership, this is leadership of a quasi-independent unit, department, or organization.

- The expectations for leaders, the timeframe for their actions, and the complexity of the assignments increase as one moves up the organizational hierarchy.

- Strategic leadership, as used here, includes the leadership of both the CEO and the top-management team.

- Boal and Hooijberg's view of strategic leadership uses emergent theories: cognitive complexity, emotional intelligence (complexity), and behavioral complexity as well as charismatic, transformational, and visionary leadership to influence absorptive capacity, capacity to change, and managerial wisdom, which in turn influence effectiveness.

Terms to Know

Absorptive capacity (p. 421)
Adaptive capacity (p. 421)
Adhocracy (p. 409)
Behavioral complexity (p. 417)
Cognitive complexity (p. 417)
Environmental complexity (p. 414)
General environment (p. 413)
Grafting (p. 402)

Information technology (p. 408)
Interfirm alliances (p. 416)
Managerial wisdom (p. 421)
Managerial script (p. 406)
Mimicry (p. 401)
Operations technology (p. 408)
Organizational design (p. 404)
Organizational learning (p. 401)

Scanning (p. 402)
Simple design (p. 407)
Specific environment (p. 414)
Strategic leadership (p. 416)
Strategy (p. 400)
Vicarious learning (p. 402)
Virtual organization (p. 412)

Self-Test 17

Multiple Choice

1. The design of the organization needs to be adjusted to all but _____. (a) the environment of the firm (b) the strategy of the firm (c) the size of the firm (d) the operations and information technology of the firm (e) the personnel to be hired by the firm

2. _____ is the combination of resources, knowledge, and techniques that creates a product or service output for an organization. (a) Information technology (b) Strategy (c) Organizational learning (c) Operations technology (d) The general environment (e) The benefit cycle

3. _____ is the combination of machines, artifacts, procedures, and systems used to gather, store, analyze, and disseminate information for translating it into

knowledge. (a) The specific environment (b) Strategy (c) Operations technology (d) Information technology (e) Organizational decline

4. Which of the following is an accurate statement about an adhocracy? (a) The design facilitates information exchange and learning. (b) There are many rules and policies. (c) Use of IT is always minimal. (d) IT handles routine problems efficiently. (e) IT is quite common in older industries.

5. The set of cultural, economic, legal-political, and educational conditions in the areas in which a firm operates is called the _____. (a) task environment (b) specific environment (c) industry of the firm (d) environmental complexity (e) general environment

6. The segment of the environment that refers to the other organizations with which an organization must interact in order to obtain inputs and dispose of outputs is called _____. (a) the general environment (b) the strategic environment (c) the learning environment (d) the technological setting (e) the specific environment

7. _____ are announced cooperative agreements or joint ventures between two independent firms. (a) Mergers (b) Acquisitions (c) Interfirm alliances (d) Adhocracies (e) Strategic configurations

8. The process of knowledge acquisition, organizational retention, and information distribution and interpretation is called _____. (a) vicarious learning (b) experience (c) organizational learning (d) an organizational myth (e) a self-serving interpretation

9. Three methods of vicarious learning are _____. (a) scanning, grafting, and contracting out (b) grafting, contracting out, and mimicry (c) maladaptive specialization, scanning, and grafting (d) scanning, grafting, and mimicry (e) experience, mimicry, and scanning

10. The process of acquiring individuals, unit, and/or firms to bring in useful knowledge to the organization is called _____. (a) grafting (b) strategy (c) scanning (d) mimicry

11. Regarding the organizational design for a small firm compared to a large firm, _____. (a) they are almost the same (b) they are fundamentally different (c) a large firm is just a larger version of a small one (d) the small firm has more opportunity to use information technology

12. Organizations with well-defined and stable operations technologies _____. (a) have more opportunity to substitute decision-support systems (DSS) for managerial judgment than do firms relying on more variable operations technologies (b) have less opportunity to substitute decision-support systems for managerial judgment than do firms relying on more variable operations technologies (c) are less able to develop international alliances (d) are more able to develop international alliances

13. Adhocracies tend to favor _____. (a) vertical specialization and control (b) horizontal specialization and coordination (c) extensive centralization (d) a rigid strategy

14. With extensive use of IT, _____. (a) more staff are typically added (b) firms can develop a virtual organization (c) firms can move internationally (d) firms can reduce redundancy

15. Environmental complexity _____. (a) refers to the set of alliances formed by senior management (b) refers to the overall level of problems and opportunities stemming from munificence, interdependence, and volatility (c) is restricted to the

general environment of organizations (d) is restricted to other organizations with which an organization must interact in order to obtain inputs and dispose of outputs

16. The strategy of a firm _____. (a) is the process of positioning the organization in the competitive environment and implementing actions to compete successfully. It is a pattern in a stream of decisions (b) is only a process of positioning the organization to compete (c) is only a pattern in a stream of decisions (d) is a process of acquiring knowledge, organizational retention, and distributing and interpreting information

17. An interfirm alliance is _____. (a) an extreme example of an adhocracy (b) an announced cooperative agreement or joint venture between two independent firms (c) always short-lived (d) a sign of organizational weakness

18. Copying of the successful practices of others is called _____. (a) mimicry (b) scanning (c) grafting (d) strategy

19. _____ is the process of choosing and implementing a structural configuration for an organization. (a) Strategy (b) Organizational design (c) Grafting (d) Scanning

20. Boal and Hooijberg _____. (a) argue against the notion of strategic leadership theory (b) have a theory with lots of research support (c) have a theory emphasizing leadership tensions and complexity (d) have a theory that is largely obsolete

Short Response

21. Explain why a large firm could not use a simple structure.

22. Explain the deployment of IT and its uses in organizations.

23. Describe the effect of operations technology on an organization from both Thompson's and Woodward's points of view.

24. What are the three primary determinants of environmental complexity?

Applications Essay

25. Why would Ford Motors want to shift to a matrix design organization for the design and development of cars and trucks but not do so in its manufacturing and assembly operations?

Next Steps

Top Choices from

The OB Skills Workbook

Case for Critical Thinking	Team and Experiential Exercises	Self-Assessment Portfolio
• Mission Management and Trust • Novo Nordisk	• Tinker Toys • Organizations Alive • Alien Invasion • Interview a Leader • Force-Field Analysis	• A Twenty-first-Century Manager • Group Effectiveness • Organizational Design Preferences • "TT" Leadership

THE OB SKILLS WORKBOOK

Featuring
The Jossey-Bass/Pfeiffer
Classroom Collection

Pfeiffer
An Imprint of WILEY

JOSSEY-BASS
An Imprint of WILEY
Now you know.

SUGGESTED USES AND APPLICATIONS OF WORKBOOK MATERIALS

1. Learning Styles

Activity	Suggested Part	Overview
1. *Learning Styles Inventory— Online at: www.wiley.com/ college/schermerhorn*	1	This online inventory provides insight into a person's relative strengths on seven alternative approaches to learning, described as: visual learner, print learner, auditory learner, interactive learner, haptic learner, kinesthetic learner, and olfactory learner.
2. *Study Tips for Different Learning Styles*	1	This reading included in the workbook provides study tips for learners with different tendencies and strengths.

2. Student Leadership Practices Inventory by Kouzes and Posner

Activity	Suggested Part	Overview
1. *Student Leadership Practices Inventory— Student Workbook*	All	This workbook includes a worksheet to help interpret feedback and plan improvement in each leadership practice assessed, sections on how to compare scores with the normative sample and how to share feedback with constituents, and more than 140 actual steps students can take to get results.
2. *Student Leadership Practices Inventory— Self*	All	This 30-item inventory will help students evaluate their performance and effectiveness as a leader. Results from the simple scoring process help students prepare plans for personal leadership development.
3. *Student Leadership Practices Inventory— Observer*	All	This version of the LPI is used by others to assess the individual's leadership tendencies, thus allowing for comparison with self-perceptions.

3. Self-Assessment Portfolio

See companion Web site for online versions of many assessments: www.wiley.com/college/schermerhorn

Assessment	Suggested Chapter	Cross-References and Integration
1. *Managerial Assumptions*	1 Organizational Behavior Today	leadership
2. *A Twenty-First-Century Manager*	1 Organizational Behavior Today 14 Leadership Challenges and Organizational Change 16 Organizational Goals and Structures 17 Strategy, Technology, and Organizational Design	leadership; decision making; globalization

Assessment	Suggested Chapter	Cross-References and Integration
3. Turbulence Tolerance Test	1 Organizational Behavior Today 2 Individual Differences, Values, and Diversity	perception; individual differences; organizational change and stress
4. Global Readiness Index	3 Emotions, Attitudes, and Job Satisfaction 14 Leadership Challenges and Organizational Change	diversity; culture; leading; perception; management skills; career readiness
5. Personal Values	3 Emotions, Attitudes, and Job Satisfaction 6 Motivation and Performance	perception; diversity and individual differences; leadership
6. Intolerance for Ambiguity	4 Perception, Attribution, and Learning	perception; leadership
7. Two-Factor Profile	5 Motivation Theories 6 Motivation and Performance	job design; perception; culture; human resource management
8. Are You Cosmopolitan?	6 Motivation and Performance 15 Organizational Culture and Innovation	diversity and individual differences; organizational culture
9. Group Effectiveness	7 Teams in Organizations 8 Teamwork and Team Performance 15 Organizational Culture and Innovation 17 Strategy, Technology, and Organizational Design	organizational designs and cultures; leadership
10. Least Preferred Co-worker Scale	13 Foundations for Leadership	diversity and individual differences; perception; group dynamics and teamwork
11. Leadership Style	13 Foundations for Leadership	diversity and individual differences; perception; group dynamics and teamwork
12. "TT" Leadership Style	11 Communication and Collaboration 13 Foundations for Leadership	diversity and individual differences; perception; group dynamics and teamwork
13. Empowering Others	8 Teamwork and Team Performance 11 Communication and Collaboration 12 Power and Politics	leadership; perception and attribution
14. Machiavellianism	12 Power and Politics	leadership; diversity and individual differences
15. Personal Power Profile	12 Power and Politics	leadership; diversity and individual differences
16. Your Intuitive Ability	9 Creativity and Decision Making	diversity and individual differences

Assessment	Suggested Chapter	Cross-References and Integration
17. *Decision-Making Biases*	7 Teams in Organizations 9 Creativity and Decision Making	teams and teamwork; communication; perception
18. *Conflict Management Strategies*	10 Conflict and Negotiation	diversity and individual differences; communication
19. *Your Personality Type*	2 Individual Differences, Values, and Diversity	diversity and individual differences; job design
20. *Time Management Profile*	2 Individual Differences, Values, and Diversity	diversity and individual differences
21. *Organizational Design Preference*	16 Organizational Goals and Structures 17 Strategy, Technology, and Organizational Design	job design; diversity and individual differences
22. *Which Culture Fits You?*	15 Organizational Culture and Innovation	perception; diversity and individual differences

4. Team and Experiential Exercises

Selections from *The Pfeiffer Annual Training*

Activity	Suggested Part	Overview
A. *Sweet Tooth: Bonding Strangers into a Team*	Parts 1, 3, 4	Perception, teamwork, decision making, communication
B. *Interrogatories: Identifying Issues and Needs*	Parts 1, 3, 4	Current issues, group dynamics, communication
C. *Decode: Working with Different Instructions*	Parts 3, 4	Decision making, leadership, conflict, teamwork
D. *Choices: Learning Effective Conflict Management Strategies*	Parts 1, 2, 3, 4, 5	Conflict, negotiation, communication, decision making
E. *Internal/External Motivators: Encouraging Creativity*	Parts 2, 4, 5	Creativity, motivation, job design, decision making
F. *Quick Hitter: Fostering the Creative Spirit*	Parts 4, 5	Creativity, decision making, communication

Additional Team and Experiential Exercises

Exercise	Suggested Chapter	Cross-References and Integration
1. *My Best Manager*	1 Introducing Organizational Behavior 3 Emotions, Attitudes, and Job Satisfaction	leadership

Exercise	Suggested Chapter	Cross-References and Integration
2. Graffiti Needs Assessment	1 Introducing Organizational Behavior	human resource management; communication
3. My Best Job	1 Introducing Organizational Behavior 6 Motivation and Performance	motivation; job design; organizational cultures
4. What Do You Value in Work?	5 Motivation Theories	diversity and individual differences; performance management and rewards; motivation; job design; decision making
5. My Asset Base	3 Emotions, Attitudes, and Job Satisfaction 4 Perception, Attribution, and Learning	perception and attribution; diversity and individual differences; groups and teamwork; decision making
6. Expatriate Assignments	4 Perception, Attribution, and Learning 15 Organizational Culture and Innovation	perception and attribution; diversity and individual differences; decision making
7. Cultural Cues	14 Leadership Challenges and Organizational Change	perception and attribution; diversity and individual differences; decision making; communication; conflict; groups and teamwork
8. Prejudice in Our Lives	3 Emotions, Attitudes, and Job Satisfaction	perception and attribution; decision making; conflict; groups and teamwork
9. How We View Differences	3 Emotions, Attitudes, and Job Satisfaction 4 Perception, Attribution, and Learning 15 Organizational Culture and Innovation	culture; international; diversity and individual differences; decision making; communication; conflict; groups and teamwork
10. Alligator River Story	4 Perception, Attribution, and Learning	diversity and individual differences; decision making; communication; conflict; groups and teamwork
11. Teamwork and Motivation	5 Motivation Theories	performance management and rewards; groups and teamwork
12. The Downside of Punishment	5 Motivation Theories	motivation; perception and attribution; performance management and rewards
13. Tinkertoys	6 Motivation and Performance 16 Organizational Goals and Structures 17 Strategy, Technology, and Organizational Design	organizational structure; design and culture; groups and teamwork
14. Job Design Preferences	6 Motivation and Performance	motivation; job design; organizational design; change
15. My Fantasy Job	6 Motivation and Performance	motivation; individual differences; organizational design; change
16. Motivation by Job Enrichment	6 Motivation and Performance	motivation; job design; perception; diversity and individual differences; change

Exercise	Suggested Chapter	Cross-References and Integration
17. *Annual Pay Raises*	5 Motivation Theories 6 Motivation and Performance	motivation; learning and reinforcement; perception and attribution; decision making; groups and teamwork
18. *Serving on the Boundary*	7 Teams in Organizations	intergroup dynamics; group dynamics; roles; communication; conflict; stress
19. *Eggsperiential Exercise*	7 Teams in Organizations	group dynamics and teamwork; diversity and individual differences; communication
20. *Scavenger Hunt—Team Building*	8 Teamwork and Team Performance	groups; leadership; diversity and individual differences; communication; leadership
21. *Work Team Dynamics*	8 Teamwork and Team Performance	groups; motivation; decision making; conflict; communication
22. *Identifying Team Norms*	8 Teamwork and Team Performance	groups; communication; perception and attribution
23. *Workgroup Culture*	8 Teamwork and Team Performance 15 Organizational Culture and Innovation	groups; communication; perception and attribution; job design; organizational culture
24. *The Hot Seat*	8 Teamwork and Team Performance	groups; communication; conflict and negotiation; power and politics
25. *Interview a Leader*	12 Power and Politics 13 Foundations for Leadership	performance management and rewards; groups and teamwork; new workplace; organizational change and stress
26. *Leadership Skills Inventories*	13 Foundations for Leadership	individual differences; perception and attribution; decision making
27. *Leadership and Participation in Decision Making*	13 Foundations for Leadership	decision making; communication; motivation; groups; teamwork
28. *My Best Manager: Revisited*	12 Power and Politics	diversity and individual differences; perception and attribution
29. *Active Listening*	11 Communication and Collaboration	group dynamics and teamwork; perception and attribution
30. *Upward Appraisal*	6 Motivation and Performance 11 Communication and Collaboration	perception and attribution; performance management and rewards
31. *360° Feedback*	6 Motivation and Performance 11 Communication and Collaboration	communication; perception and attribution; performance management and rewards
32. *Role Analysis Negotiation*	9 Creativity and Decision Making	communication; group dynamics and teamwork; perception and attribution; communication; decision making
33. *Lost at Sea*	9 Creativity and Decision Making	communication; group dynamics and teamwork; conflict and negotiation
34. *Entering the Unknown*	9 Creativity and Decision Making 10 Conflict and Negotiation	communication; group dynamics and teamwork; perception and attribution

Exercise	Suggested Chapter	Cross-References and Integration
35. *Vacation Puzzle*	10 Conflict and Negotiation	conflict and negotiation; communication; power; leadership
36. *The Ugli Orange*	9 Creativity and Decision Making 10 Conflict and Negotiation	communication; decision making
37. *Conflict Dialogues*	10 Conflict and Negotiation	conflict; communication; feedback; perception; stress
38. *Force-Field Analysis*	9 Creativity and Decision Making	decision making; organization structures, designs, cultures
39. *Organizations Alive!*	16 Organizational Goals and Structures 17 Strategy, Technology, and Organizational Design	organizational design and culture; performance management and rewards
40. *Fast-Food Technology*	15 Organizational Culture and Innovation 16 Organizational Goals and Structures	organizational design; organizational culture; job design
41. *Alien Invasion*	15 Organizational Culture and Innovation 16 Organizational Goals and Structures 17 Strategy, Technology, and Organizational Design	organizational structure and design; international; diversity and individual differences; perception and attribution
42. *Power Circles Exercise*	12 Power and Politics	influence; power; leadership; change management

5. Cases for Critical Thinking

Case	Suggested Chapter	Cross-References and Integration
1a. *Trader Joe's*	1 Introducing Organizational Behavior	human resource management; organizational cultures; innovation; information technology; leadership
1b. *Management Training Dilemma*	1 Introducing Organizational Behavior	ethics and decision making; communication; conflict and negotiation
2. *Ursula Burns, Xerox*	2 Individual Differences, Values, and Diversity	diversity and individual differences; perception and attribution; performance management; job design; communication; conflict; decision making
3. *Lois Quam, Tysvar, LLC*	3 Emotions, Attitudes, and Job Satisfaction	organizational cultures; globalization; innovation; motivation
4. *MagRec, Inc.*	4 Perception, Attribution, and Learning	ethics and diversity; organizational structure, design, and culture; decision making; organizational change

Case	Suggested Chapter	Cross-References and Integration
5. It Isn't Fair	5 Motivation Theories	perception and attribution; performance management and rewards; communication; ethics and decision making
6a. Perfect Pizzeria	6 Motivation and Performance	organizational design; motivation; performance management and rewards
6b. Hovey and Beard	6 Motivation and Performance	organizational cultures; globalization; communication; decision making
7. The Forgotten Group Member	7 Teams in Organizations	teamwork; motivation; diversity and individual differences; perception and attribution; performance management and rewards; communication; conflict; leadership
8. NASCAR's Racing Teams	8 Teamwork and Team Performance	organizational cultures; leadership; motivation and reinforcement; communication
9. Decisions, Decisions	9 Creativity and Decision Making	organizational structure; organizational cultures; change and innovation; group dynamics and teamwork; diversity and individual differences
10. The Missing Raise	10 Conflict and Negotiation	change; innovation and stress; job designs; communication; power and politics
11. The Poorly Informed Walrus	11 Communication and Collaboration	diversity and individual differences; perception and attribution
12. Faculty Empowerment	12 Power and Politics	change; innovation and stress; job designs; communication; power and politics
13a. The New Vice President	13 Foundations for Leadership	leadership; performance management and rewards; diversity and individual differences; communication; conflict and negotiation; power and influence
13b. Southwest Airlines	14 Leadership Challenges and Organizational Change	leadership; performance management and rewards; diversity and individual differences; communication; conflict and negotiation; power and influence
14. Novo Nordisk	14 Leadership Challenges and Organizational Change	leadership; performance management and rewards; diversity and individual differences; communication; conflict and negotiation; power and influence
15. Never on a Sunday	15 Organizational Culture and Innovation	ethics and diversity; organizational structure, design, and culture; decision making; organizational change
16. First Community Financial	16 Organizational Goals and Structures	organizational structure, designs, and culture; performance management and rewards
17. Mission Management and Trust	17 Strategy, Technology, and Organizational Design	organizational structure, designs, and culture; performance management and rewards

LEARNING STYLE INVENTORY

This is a Wiley resource—www.wiley.com/college/schermerhorn

Step 1.

Take the Learning Style Instrument at www.wiley.com/college/schermerhorn

Step 2.

The instrument will give you scores on seven learning styles:

1. Visual learner—focus on visual depictions such as pictures and graphs
2. Print learner—focus on seeing written words
3. Auditory learner—focus on listening and hearing
4. Interactive learner—focus on conversation and verbalization
5. Haptic learner—focus on sense of touch or grasp
6. Kinesthetic learner—focus on physical involvement
7. Olfactory learner—focus on smell and taste

Step 3.

Consider your top four rankings among the learning styles. They suggest your most preferred methods of learning.

Step 4.

Read the following study tips for the learning styles. Think about how you can take best advantage of your preferred learning styles.

WHAT ARE LEARNING STYLES?

Have you ever repeated something to yourself over and over to help remember it? Or does your best friend ask you to draw a map to someplace where the two of you are planning to meet, rather than just tell her the directions? If so, then you already have an intuitive sense that people learn in different ways. Researchers in learning theory have developed various categories of learning styles. Some people, for example, learn best by reading or writing. Others learn best by using various senses—seeing, hearing, feeling, tasting, or even smelling. When you understand how you learn best, you can make use of learning strategies that will optimize the time you spend studying. To find out what your particular learning style is, go to www.wiley.com/college/boone and take the learning styles quiz you find there. The quiz will help you determine your primary learning style:

Visual Learner   Auditory Learner   Haptic Learner   Olfactory Learner
Print Learner   Interactive Learner   Kinesthetic Learner

Then, consult the information below and on the following pages for study tips for each learning style. This information will help you better understand your learning style and how to apply it to the study of business.

Study Tips for Visual Learners

If you are a Visual Learner, you prefer to work with images and diagrams. It is important that you see information.

Visual Learning
- Draw charts/diagrams during lecture.
- Examine textbook figures and graphs.
- Look at images and videos on WileyPLUS and other Web sites.

- Pay close attention to charts, drawings, and handouts your instructor uses.
- Underline; use different colors.
- Use symbols, flowcharts, graphs, different arrangements on the page, white spaces.

Visual Reinforcement
- Make flashcards by drawing tables/ charts on one side and definition or description on the other side.
- Use art-based worksheets; cover labels on images in text and then rewrite the labels.

Study Tips for Visual Learners (Continued)

- Use colored pencils/markers and colored paper to organize information into types.
- Convert your lecture notes into "page pictures." To do this:
  - Use the visual learning strategies outlined above.

  - Reconstruct images in different ways.
  - Redraw pages from memory.
  - Replace words with symbols and initials.
  - Draw diagrams where appropriate.

  - Practice turning your visuals back into words.

If visual learning is your weakness: If you are not a Visual Learner but want to improve your visual learning, try re-keying tables/charts from the textbook.

Study Tips for Print Learners

If you are a Print Learner, reading will be important but writing will be much more important.

Print Learning

- Write text lecture notes during lecture.
- Read relevant topics in textbook, especially textbook tables.
- Look at text descriptions in animations and Web sites.
- Use lists and headings.
- Use dictionaries, glossaries, and definitions.
- Read handouts, textbooks, and supplementary library readings.
- Use lecture notes.

Print Reinforcement

- Rewrite your notes from class, and copy classroom handouts in your own handwriting.

- Make your own flashcards.
- Write out essays summarizing lecture notes or text book topics.
- Develop mnemonics.
- Identify word relationships.
- Create tables with information extracted from textbook or lecture notes.
- Use text-based worksheets or crossword puzzles.
- Write out words again and again.
- Reread notes silently.
- Rewrite ideas and principles into other words.
- Turn charts, diagrams, and other illustrations into statements.

- Practice writing exam answers.
- Practice with multiple choice questions.
- Write paragraphs, especially beginnings and endings.
- Write your lists in outline form.
- Arrange your words into hierarchies and points.

If print learning is your weakness: If you are not a Print Learner but want to improve your print learning, try covering labels of figures from the textbook and writing in the labels.

Study Tips for Auditory Learners

If you are an Auditory Learner, then you prefer listening as a way to learn information. Hearing will be very important, and sound helps you focus.

Auditory Learning

- Make audio recordings during lecture. Do not skip class; hearing the lecture is essential to understanding.
- Play audio files provided by instructor and textbook.
- Listen to narration of animations.
- Attend lecture and tutorials.
- Discuss topics with students and instructors.
- Explain new ideas to other people.
- Leave spaces in your lecture notes for later recall.
- Describe overheads, pictures, and visuals to somebody who was not in class.

Auditory Reinforcement

- Record yourself reading the notes and listen to the recording.
- Write out transcripts of the audio files.
- Summarize information that you have read, speaking out loud.
- Use a recorder to create self-tests.
- Compose "songs" about information.
- Play music during studying to help focus.
- Expand your notes by talking with others and with information from your textbook.

- Read summarized notes out loud.
- Explain your notes to another auditory learner.
- Talk with the instructor.
- Spend time in quiet places recalling the ideas.
- Say your answers out loud.

If auditory learning is your weakness: If you are not an Auditory Learner but want to improve your auditory learning, try writing out the scripts from pre-recorded lectures.

Study Tips for Interactive Learners

If you are an Interactive Learner, you will want to share your information. A study group will be important.

Interactive Learning
- Ask a lot of questions during lecture or TA review sessions.
- Contact other students, via e-mail or discussion forums, and ask them to explain what they learned.

Interactive Reinforcement
- "Teach" the content to a group of other students.

- Talking to an empty room may seem odd, but it will be effective for you.
- Discuss information with others, making sure that you both ask and answer questions.
- Work in small group discussions, making a verbal and written discussion of what others say.

If interactive learning is your weakness: If you are not an Interactive Learner but want to improve your interactive learning, try asking your study partner questions and then repeating them to the instructor.

Study Tips for Haptic Learners

If you are a Haptic Learner, you prefer to work with your hands. It is important to physically manipulate material.

Haptic Learning
- Take blank paper to lecture to draw charts/tables/diagrams.
- Using the textbook, run your fingers along the figures and graphs to get a "feel" for shapes and relationships.

Haptic Reinforcement
- Trace words and pictures on flashcards.

- Perform electronic exercises that involve drag-and-drop activities.
- Alternate between speaking and writing information.
- Observe someone performing a task that you would like to learn.
- Make sure you have freedom of movement while studying.

If haptic learning is your weakness: If you are not a Haptic Learner but want to improve your haptic learning, try spending more time in class working with graphs and tables while speaking or writing down information.

Study Tips for Kinesthetic Learners

If you are a Kinesthetic Learner, it will be important that you involve your body during studying.

Kinesthetic Learning
- Ask permission to get up and move during lecture.
- Participate in role-playing activities in the classroom.
- Use all your senses.
- Go to labs; take field trips.
- Listen to real-life examples.
- Pay attention to applications.
- Use trial-and-error methods.
- Use hands-on approaches.

Kinesthetic Reinforcement
- Make flashcards; place them on the floor, and move your body around them.
- Move while you are teaching the material to others.
- Put examples in your summaries.
- Use case studies and applications to help with principles and abstract concepts.
- Talk about your notes with another kinesthetic person.

- Use pictures and photographs that illustrate an idea.
- Write practice answers.
- Role-play the exam situation.

If kinesthetic learning is your weakness: If you are not a Kinesthetic Learner but want to improve your kinesthetic learning, try moving flashcards to reconstruct graphs and tables, etc.

Study Tips for Olfactory Learners

If you are an Olfactory Learner, you will prefer to use the senses of smell and taste to reinforce learning. This is a rare learning modality.

Olfactory Learning
- During lecture, use different scented markers to identify different types of information.

Olfactory Reinforcement
- Rewrite notes with scented markers.
- If possible, go back to the computer lab to do your studying.

- Burn aromatic candles while studying.
- Try to associate the material that you're studying with a pleasant taste or smell.

If olfactory learning is your weakness:
If you are not an Olfactory Learner but want to improve your olfactory learning, try burning an aromatic candle or incense while you study, or eating cookies during study sessions.

STUDENT LEADERSHIP PRACTICES INVENTORY

STUDENT WORKBOOK

James M. Kouzes

Barry Z. Posner, Ph.D.

Jossey-Bass Publishers • San Francisco

Jossey-Bass/Pfeiffer Classroom Collection

ISBN: 0-7879-4425-4

Jossey-Bass is a registered trademark of Jossey-Bass Inc., a Wiley Company.

Printed in the United States of America.

Jossey-Bass books and products are available through most bookstores. To contact Jossey-Bass directly, call (888) 378-2537, fax to (800) 605-2665, or visit our Web site at www.josseybass.com.

Substantial discounts on bulk quantities of Jossey-Bass books are available to corporations, professional associations, and other organizations. For details and discount information, contact the special sales department at Jossey-Bass.

Printing 10 9 8 7 6 5 4 3 2

This book is printed on acid-free, recycled stock that meets or exceeds the minimum GPO and EPA requirements for recycled paper.

CONTENTS

People WHO BECOME
leaders
DON'T *always* **seek**
THE **challenges**
THEY **face.**
CHALLENGES
also SEEK **leaders.**

1
Leadership: What People Do When They're Leading

"*Leadership is everyone's business.*" That's the conclusion we have come to after nearly two decades of research into the behaviors and actions of people who are making a difference in their organizations, clubs, teams, classes, schools, campuses, communities, and even their families. We found that leadership is an observable, learnable set of practices. Contrary to some myths, it is not a mystical and ethereal process that cannot be understood by ordinary people. Given the opportunity for feedback and practice, those with the desire and persistence to lead—to make a difference—can substantially improve their ability to do so.

The *Leadership Practices Inventory* (LPI) is part of an extensive research project into the everyday actions and behaviors of people, at all levels and across a variety of settings, as they are leading. Through our research we identified five practices that are common to all leadership experiences. In collaboration with others, we extended our findings to student leaders and to school and college environments and created the student version of the LPI.[1] The LPI is a tool, not a test, designed to assess your current leadership skills. It will identify your areas of strength as well as areas of leadership that need to be further developed.

The *Student LPI* helps you discover the extent to which you (in your role as a leader of a student group or organization) engage in the following five leadership practices:

Challenging the Process. Leaders are pioneers—people who seek out new opportunities and are willing to change the status quo. They innovate, experiment, and explore ways to improve the organization. They treat mistakes as learning experiences. Leaders also stay prepared to meet whatever challenges may confront them. *Challenging the Process* involves

- Searching for opportunities
- Experimenting and taking risks

As an example of Challenging the Process, one student related how innovative thinking helped him win a student class election: "I challenged the process in more than one way. First, I wanted people to understand that elections are not necessarily popularity contests, so I campaigned on the issues and did not promise things that could not possibly be done. Second, I challenged the incumbent positions. They thought they would win easily because they were incumbents, but I showed them that no one has an inherent right to a position."

---

[1]For more information on our original work, see *The Leadership Challenge: How to Keep Getting Extraordinary Things Done in Organizations* (Jossey-Bass Publishers).

Challenging the Process for a student serving as treasurer of her sorority meant examining and abandoning some of her leadership beliefs: "I used to believe, 'If you want to do something right, do it yourself.' I found out the hard way that this is impossible to do. . . . One day I was ready to just give up the position because I could no longer handle all of the work. My adviser noticed that I was overwhelmed, and she turned to me and said three magic words: 'Use your committee.' The best piece of advice I would pass along about being an effective leader is that it is okay to experiment with letting others do the work."

Inspiring a Shared Vision.

Leaders look toward and beyond the horizon. They envision the future with a positive and hopeful outlook. Leaders are expressive and attract other people to their organization and teams through their genuineness. They communicate and show others how their interests can be met through commitment to a common purpose. *Inspiring a Shared Vision* involves

- Envisioning an uplifting future
- Enlisting others in a common vision

Describing his experience as president of his high school class, one student wrote: "It was our vision to get the class united and to be able to win the spirit trophy. . . . I told my officers that we could do anything we set our minds on. Believe in yourself and believe in your ability to accomplish things."

Enabling Others to Act.

Leaders infuse people with energy and confidence, developing relationships based on mutual trust. They stress collaborative goals. They actively involve others in planning, giving them discretion to make their own decisions. Leaders ensure that people feel strong and capable. *Enabling Others to Act* involves

- Fostering collaboration
- Strengthening people

It is not necessary to be in a traditional leadership position to put these principles into practice. Here is an example from a student who led his team as a team member, not from a traditional position of power: "I helped my team members feel strong and capable by encouraging everyone to practice with the same amount of intensity that they played games with. Our practices improved throughout the year, and by the end of the year had reached the point I was striving for: complete involvement among all players, helping each other to perform at our very best during practice times."

Modeling the Way.

Leaders are clear about their personal values and beliefs. They keep people and projects on course by behaving consistently with these values and modeling how they expect others to act. Leaders also plan projects and break them down into achievable steps, creating opportunities for small wins. By focusing on key priorities, they make it easier for others to achieve goals. *Modeling the Way* involves

- Setting the example
- Achieving small wins

Working in a business environment taught one student the importance of Modeling the Way. She writes: "I proved I was serious because I was the first one on the job and the last one to leave. I came prepared to work and make the tools available to my crew. I worked alongside them and in no way portrayed an attitude of superiority. Instead, we were in this together."

Encouraging the Heart.

Leaders encourage people to persist in their efforts by linking recognition with accomplishments and visibly recognizing contributions to the common vision. They express pride in the achievements of the group or organization, letting others know that their efforts are appreciated. Leaders also find ways to celebrate milestones. They nurture a team spirit, which enables people to sustain continued efforts. *Encouraging the Heart* involves

- Recognizing individual contributions
- Celebrating team accomplishments

While organizing and running a day camp, one student recognized volunteers and celebrated accomplishments through her actions. She explains: "We had a pizza party with the children on the last day of the day camp. Later, the volunteers were sent thank you notes and 'valuable volunteer awards' personally signed by the day campers. The pizza party, thank you notes, and awards served to encourage the hearts of the volunteers in the hopes that they might return for next year's day camp."

Somewhere,
sometime,
THE *leader within*
EACH OF US
MAY get
THE CALL
to STEP forward.

2
Questions Frequently Asked About the *Student LPI*

Question 1: What are the right answers?

Answer: There are no universal right answers when it comes to leadership. Research indicates that the more frequently you are perceived as engaging in the behavior and actions identified in the *Student LPI,* the more likely it is that you will be perceived as an effective leader. The higher your scores on the Student LPI-Observer, the more others perceive you as (1) having personal credibility, (2) being effective in running meetings, (3) successfully representing your organization or group to nonmembers, (4) generating a sense of enthusiasm and cooperation, and (5) having a high-performing team. In addition, findings show a strong and positive relationship between the extent to which people report their leaders engaging in this set of five leadership practices and how motivated, committed, and productive they feel.

Question 2: How reliable and valid is the Student LPI?

Answer: The question of reliability can be answered in two ways. First, the *Student LPI* has shown sound psychometric properties. The scale for each leadership practice is internally reliable, meaning that the statements within each practice are highly correlated with one another. Second, results of multivariate analyses indicate that the statements within each leadership practice are more highly correlated (or associated) with one another than they are between the five leadership practices.

In terms of validity (or "So what difference do the scores make?"), the *Student LPI* has good face validity and predictive validity. This means, first, that the results make sense to people. Second, scores on the *Student LPI* significantly differentiate high-performing leaders from their less successful counterparts. Whether measured by the leader, his or her peers, or student personnel administrators, those student leaders who engage more frequently, rather than less frequently, in the five leadership practices are more effective.

Question 3: Should my perceptions of my leadership practices be consistent with the ratings other people give me?

Answer: Research indicates that trust in the leader is essential if other people (for example, fellow members of a group, team, or organization) are going to follow that person over time. People must experience the leader as believable, credible, and trustworthy. Trust—whether in a leader or any other person—is developed through consistency in behavior. Trust is further established when words and deeds are congruent.

This does not mean, however, that you will always be perceived in exactly the same way by every person in every situation. Some people may not see you as often as others do, and therefore they may rate you differently on the same behavior. Some people simply may not know you as well as others do. Also you may appropriately behave differently in different situations, such as in a crisis versus during more stable times. Others may have different expectations of you, and still others may perceive the rating descriptions (such as "once in a while" or "fairly often") differently.

Therefore, the key issue is not whether your self-ratings and the ratings from others are exactly the same, but whether people perceive consistency between what you say you do and what you actually do. The only way you can know the answer to this question is to solicit feedback. The Student LPI-Observer has been designed for this purpose.

Research indicates that people tend to see themselves more positively than others do. The Student LPI-Self norms are consistent with this general trend; scores on the Student LPI-Self tend to be somewhat higher than scores on the Student LPI-Observer. *Student LPI* scores also tend to be higher than LPI scores of experienced managers and executives in the private and public sector.

Question 4: Can I change my leadership practices?

Answer: It is certainly possible—even for experienced people—to learn new skills. You will increase your chances of changing your behavior if you receive feedback on what level you have achieved with a particular skill, observe a positive model of that skill, set some improvement goals for yourself, practice the skill, ask for updated feedback on your performance, and then set new goals. The practices that are assessed with the *Student LPI* fall into the category of learnable skills.

But some things can be changed only if there is a strong and genuine inner desire to make a difference. For example, enthusiasm for a cause is unlikely to be developed through education or job assignments; it must come from within.

Use the information from the *Student LPI* to better understand how you currently behave as a leader, both from your own perspective and from the perspective of others. Note where there are consistencies and inconsistencies. Understand which leadership behaviors and practices you feel comfortable engaging in and which you feel uncomfortable with. Determine which leadership behaviors and practices you can improve on, and take steps to improve your leadership skills and gain confidence in leading other people and groups. The following sections will help you to become more effective in leadership.

> Perhaps NONE OF
> us knows
> OUR *true strength*
> UNTIL **challenged**
> TO **bring**
> *it* **forth.**

3
Recording Your Scores

On pages W-18 through W-21 are grids for recording your *Student LPI* scores. The first grid (Challenging the Process) is for recording scores for items 1, 6, 11, 16, 21, and 26 from the Student LPI-Self and Student LPI-Observer. These are the items that relate to behaviors involved in Challenging the Process, such as searching for opportunities, experimenting, and taking risks. An abbreviated form of each item is printed beside the grid as a handy reference.

In the first column, which is headed "Self-Rating," write the scores that you gave yourself. If others were asked to complete the Student LPI-Observer and if the forms were returned to you, enter their scores in the columns (A, B, C, D, E, and so on) under the heading "Observers' Ratings." Simply transfer the numbers from page W-18 of each Student LPI-Observer to your scoring grids, using one column for each observer. For example, enter the first observer's scores in column A, the second observer's scores in column B, and so on. The grids provide space for the scores of as many as ten observers.

After all scores have been entered for Challenging the Process, total each column in the row marked "Totals." Then add all of the totals for observers; do not include the "self" total. Write this grand total in the space marked "Total of All Observers' Scores." To obtain the average, divide the grand total by the number of people who completed the Student LPI-Observer. Write this average in the blank provided. The sample grid shows how the grid would look with scores for self and five observers entered.

	SELF-RATING	OBSERVERS' RATINGS										TOTAL OF ALL OBSERVERS' SCORES
		A	B	C	D	E	F	G	H	I	J	
1. Seeks challenge	5	4	2	4	4	2						
6. Keeps current	4	4	3	4	4	3						
11. Initiates experiment	3	3	2	2	2	1						
16. Looks for ways to improve	4	3	2	3	5	3						
21. Asks "What can we learn?"	2	3	2	3	3	2						
26. Lets others take risks	5	3	3	2	3	2						
TOTALS	23	20	14	18	21	13						86

TOTAL SELF-RATING: _____23_____   AVERAGE OF ALL OBSERVERS: ___17.2___

The other four grids should be completed in the same manner.

The second grid (Inspiring a Shared Vision) is for recording scores to the items that pertain to envisioning the future and enlisting the support of others. These include items 2, 7, 12, 17, 22, and 27.

The third grid (Enabling Others to Act) pertains to items 3, 8, 13, 18, 23, and 28, which involve fostering collaboration and strengthening others.

The fourth grid (Modeling the Way) pertains to items about setting an example and planning small wins.

These include items 4, 9, 14, 19, 24, and 29.

The fifth grid (Encouraging the Heart) pertains to items about recognizing contributions and celebrating accomplishments. These are items 5, 10, 15, 20, 25, and 30.

Grids for Recording *Student LPI* Scores

Scores should be recorded on the following grids in accordance with the instructions on page W-17. As you look at individual scores, remember the rating system that was used:

- "1" means that you *rarely or seldom* engage in the behavior.
- "2" means that you engage in the behavior *once in a while*.
- "3" means that you *sometimes* engage in the behavior.
- "4" means that you engage in the behavior *fairly often*.
- "5" means that you engage in the behavior *very frequently*.

After you have recorded all of your scores and calculated the totals and averages, turn to page W-21 and read the section on interpreting scores.

Challenging the Process

	SELF-RATING	OBSERVERS' RATINGS									
		A	B	C	D	E	F	G	H	I	J
1. Seeks challenge											
6. Keeps current											
11. Initiates experiment											
16. Looks for ways to improve											
21. Asks "What can we learn?"											
26. Lets others take risks											
TOTALS											

TOTAL OF ALL OBSERVERS' SCORES

TOTAL SELF-RATING: _____   AVERAGE OF ALL OBSERVERS: _____

Inspiring a Shared Vision

	SELF-RATING	OBSERVERS' RATINGS									
		A	B	C	D	E	F	G	H	I	J
2. Describes ideal capabilities											
7. Looks ahead and communicates future											
12. Upbeat and positive communicator											
17. Finds common ground											
22. Communicates purpose and meaning											
27. Enthusiastic about possibilities											
TOTALS											

TOTAL OF ALL OBSERVERS' SCORES

TOTAL SELF-RATING: _____   AVERAGE OF ALL OBSERVERS: _____

Enabling Others to Act

	SELF-RATING	OBSERVERS' RATINGS									
		A	B	C	D	E	F	G	H	I	J
3. Includes others in planning											
8. Treats others with respect											
13. Supports decisions of others											
18. Fosters cooperative relationships											
23. Provides freedom and choice											
28. Lets others lead											
TOTALS											

TOTAL OF ALL OBSERVERS' SCORES

TOTAL SELF-RATING: _____   AVERAGE OF ALL OBSERVERS: _____

Modeling the Way

	SELF-RATING	OBSERVERS' RATINGS									
		A	B	C	D	E	F	G	H	I	J
4. Shares beliefs about leading											
9. Breaks projects into steps											
14. Sets personal example											
19. Talks about guiding values											
24. Follows through on promises											
29. Sets clear goals and plans											
TOTALS											

TOTAL OF ALL OBSERVERS' SCORES

TOTAL SELF-RATING: _____   AVERAGE OF ALL OBSERVERS: _____

Encouraging the Heart

	SELF-RATING	OBSERVERS' RATINGS									
		A	B	C	D	E	F	G	H	I	J
5. Encourages other people											
10. Recognizes people's contributions											
15. Praises people for job well done											
20. Gives support and appreciation											
25. Finds ways to publicly celebrate											
30. Tells others about group's good work											
TOTALS											

TOTAL OF ALL OBSERVERS' SCORES

TOTAL SELF-RATING: _____   AVERAGE OF ALL OBSERVERS: _____

> THE unique ROLE
> OF leaders
> IS TO *take us*
> TO places
> WE'VE never
> *been* before.

4
Interpreting Your Scores

This section will help you to interpret your scores by looking at them in several ways and by making notes to yourself about what you can do to become a more effective leader.

Ranking Your Ratings

Refer to the previous chapter, "Recording Your Scores." On each grid, look at your scores in the blanks marked "Total Self-Rating." Each of these totals represents your responses to six statements about one of the five leadership practices. Each of your totals can range from a low of 6 to a high of 30.

In the blanks that follow, write "1" to the left of the leadership prac- tice with the highest total self-rating, "2" by the next-highest total self- rating, and so on. This ranking represents the leadership practices with which you feel most comfort- able, second-most comfortable, and so on. The practice you identify with a "5" is the practice with which you feel least comfortable.

Again refer to the previous chapter, but this time look at your scores in the blanks marked "Average of All Observers." The number in each blank is the average score given to you by the people you asked to complete the Student LPI-Observer. Like each of your total self-ratings, this number can range from 6 to 30.

In the blanks that follow, write "1" to the right of the leadership practice with the highest score, "2" by the next-highest score, and so on. This ranking represents the leader- ship practices that others feel you use most often, second-most often, and so on.

Self	Observers
_____ Challenging the Process	_____
_____ Inspiring a Shared Vision	_____
_____ Enabling Others to Act	_____
_____ Modeling the Way	_____
_____ Encouraging the Heart	_____

Comparing Your Self-Ratings to Observers' Ratings

To compare your Student LPI-Self and Student LPI-Observer assessments, refer to the "Chart for Graphing Your Scores" on the next page. On the chart, designate your scores on the five leadership practices (Challenging, Inspiring, Enabling, Modeling, and Encouraging) by marking each of these points with a capital "S" (for "Self"). Connect the five resulting "S scores" with a *solid line* and label the end of this line "Self" (see sample chart below).

If other people provided input through the Student LPI-Observer, designate the average observer scores (see the blanks labeled "Average of All Observers" on the scoring grids) by marking each of the points with a capital "O" (for "Observer"). Then connect the five resulting "O scores" with a *dashed line* and label the end of this line "Observer" (see sample chart). Completing this process will provide you with a graphic representation (one solid and one dashed line) illustrating the relationship between your self-perception and the observations of other people.

Chart for Graphing Your Scores

Percentile	Challenging the Process	Inspiring a Shared Vision	Enabling Others to Act	Modeling the Way	Encouraging the Heart
100%	30 29 28 27	30 29 28	30	30 29 28 27	30
					29
90%	26	27	29		
	25	26	28	26	28
80%		O 25			27
	24		S	25	
70%		S	26		26
	23			24	
60%	22	23	O	O 23	Self
50%		22	25		Observer 24
40%	S	21	24	S	23
30%	20	20		21	22
		19	23	20	21
20%	19 O	18	22	19	20
	18	17	21	18	19
10%	17 16 15	16 15 14	20 19 18	17 16	18 17 16

Chart for Graphing Your Scores

Percentile	Challenging the Process	Inspiring a Shared Vision	Enabling Others to Act	Modeling the Way	Encouraging the Heart
100%	30 29 28	30 29	30	30 29 28	30
	27	28	29	27	29
90%	26	27			28
	25	26	28	26	27
80%					
	24	25	27	25	
70%					26
	23	24	26	24	
60%		23			25
	22			23	
50%		22	25		24
	21			22	
40%		21	24		23
	20	20			22
30%	20			21	
		19	23	20	21
20%	19	18	22	19	20
	18	17	21	18	19
10%	17	16 15	20		18
	16 15	14	19 18	17 16	17 16

Percentile Scores

Look again at the "Chart for Graphing Your Scores." The column to the far left represents the Student LPI-Self percentile rankings for more than 1,200 student leaders. A percentile ranking is determined by the percentage of people who score at or below a given number. For example, if your total self-rating for "Challenging" is at the 60th percentile line on the "Chart for Graphing Your Scores," this means that you assessed yourself higher than 60 percent of all people who have completed the *Student LPI;* you would be in the top 40 percent in this leadership practice. Studies indicate that a "high" score is one at or above the 70th percentile, a "low" score is one at or below the 30th percentile, and a score that falls between those ranges is considered "moderate."

Using these criteria, circle the "H" (for "High"), the "M" (for "Moderate"), or the "L" (for "Low") for each leadership practice on the "Range of Scores" table below. Compared to other student leaders around the country, where do your leadership practices tend to fall? (Given a "normal distribution," it is expected that most people's scores will fall within the moderate range.)

Range of Scores

In my perception				In others' perception			
Practice	**Rating**			**Practice**	**Rating**		
Challenging the Process	H	M	L	Challenging the Process	H	M	L
Inspiring a Shared Vision	H	M	L	Inspiring a Shared Vision	H	M	L
Enabling Others to Act	H	M	L	Enabling Others to Act	H	M	L
Modeling the Way	H	M	L	Modeling the Way	H	M	L
Encouraging the Heart	H	M	L	Encouraging the Heart	H	M	L

Exploring Specific Leadership Behaviors

Looking at your scoring grids, review each of the thirty items on the *Student LPI* by practice. One or two of the six behaviors within each leadership practice may be higher or lower than the rest. If so, on which specific items is there variation? What do these differences suggest? On which specific items is there agreement? Please write your thoughts in the following space.

Challenging the Process

_____

_____

_____

Inspiring a Shared Vision

_____

_____

_____

_____

_____

_____

Enabling Others to Act

_____

_____

_____

_____

_____

_____

Modeling the Way

_____

_____

_____

Encouraging the Heart

_____

_____

_____

_____

_____

**Comparing Observers'
Responses to One Another**

Study the Student LPI-Observer
scores for each of the five leadership
practices. Do some respondents'
scores differ significantly from others? If so, are the differences local-
ized in the scores of one or two people? On which leadership practices
do the respondents agree? On which
practices do they disagree? If you
try to behave basically the same
with all the people who assessed
you, how do you explain the difference in ratings? Please write your
thoughts in the following space.

_____

_____

_____

_____

_____

_____

_____

_____

_____

_____

_____

_____

_____

Wanting TO LEAD AND
believing THAT
YOU *can lead* ARE THE
departure POINTS
ON THE PATH TO **leadership.**
LEADERSHIP IS AN ART—
A *performing* art—
AND THE **instrument**
IS THE **self.**

5
Summary and Action-Planning Worksheets
....

Take a few moments to summarize your *Student LPI* feedback by completing the following Strengths and Opportunities Summary Worksheet. Refer
to the "Chart for Graphing Your Scores," the "Range of Scores" table, and
any notes you have made.

After the summary worksheet you
will find some suggestions for getting started on meeting the leadership challenge. With these suggestions in mind, review your *Student
LPI* feedback and decide on the actions you will take to become an
even more effective leader. Then
complete the Action-Planning
Worksheet to spell out the steps you
will take. (One Action-Planning
Worksheet is included in this workbook, but you may want to develop
action plans for several practices or
behaviors. You can make copies of
the blank form before you fill it in or
just use a separate sheet of paper for
each leadership practice you plan to
improve.)

**Strengths and Opportunities
Summary Worksheet**

Strengths

Which of the leadership practices
and behaviors are you most comfortable with? Why? Can you do more?

_____

_____

_____

_____

_____

_____

_____

Areas for Improvement

What can you do to use a practice more frequently? What will it take to feel more comfortable?

_____

_____

_____

_____

_____

_____

_____

The following are ten suggestions for getting started on meeting the leadership challenge.

Prescriptions for Meeting the Leadership Challenge

Challenge the Process
- Fix something
- Adopt the "great ideas" of others

Inspire a Shared Vision
- Let others know how you feel
- Recount your "personal best"

Enable Others to Act
- Always say "we"
- Make heroes of other people

Model the Way
- Lead by example
- Create opportunities for small wins

Encourage the Heart
- Write "thank you" notes
- Celebrate, and link your celebrations to your organization's values

Action-Planning Worksheet

1. What would you like to be better able to do?

_____

_____

_____

_____

_____

_____

_____

_____

_____

_____

2. What specific actions will you take?

_____

_____

_____

_____

_____

_____

_____

_____

3. What is the first action you will take? Who will be involved? When will you begin?

Action _____

_____

_____

People Involved _____

_____

_____

_____

Target Date _____

4. Complete this sentence: "I will know I have improved in this leadership skill when . . ."

_____

_____

_____

_____

5. When will you review your progress? _____

About the Authors

James M. Kouzes is chairman of TPG/Learning Systems, which makes leadership work through practical, performance-oriented learning programs. In 1993 *The Wall Street Journal* cited Jim as one of the twelve most requested "nonuniversity executive-education providers" to U.S. companies. His list of past and present clients includes AT&T, Boeing, Boy Scouts of America, Charles Schwab, Ciba-Geigy, Dell Computer, First Bank System, Honeywell, Johnson & Johnson, Levi Strauss & Co., Motorola, Pacific Bell, Stanford University, Xerox Corporation, and the YMCA.

Barry Z. Posner, PhD, is dean of the Leavey School of Business, Santa Clara University, and professor of organizational behavior. He has received several outstanding teaching and leadership awards, has published more than eighty research and practitioner-oriented articles, and currently is on the editorial review boards for *The Journal of Management Education, The Journal of Management Inquiry,* and *The Journal of Business Ethics.* Barry also serves on the board of directors for Public Allies and for The Center for Excellence in Non-Profits. His clients have ranged from retailers to firms in health care, high technology, financial services, manufacturing, and community service agencies.

Kouzes and Posner are coauthors of several best-selling and award-winning leadership books. *The Leadership Challenge: How to Keep Getting Extraordinary Things Done in Organizations* (2nd ed., 1995), with over 800,000 copies in print, has been reprinted in fifteen languages, has been featured in three video programs, and received a Critic's Choice award from the nation's newspaper book review editors. *Credibility: How Leaders Gain and Lose It, Why People Demand It* (1993) was chosen by *Industry Week* as one of the five best management books of the year. Their latest book is *Encouraging the Heart: A Leader's Guide to Rewarding and Recognizing Others* (1998).

STUDENT LEADERSHIP PRACTICES INVENTORY—SELF

Your Name: _____

Instructions

On the next two pages are thirty statements describing various leadership behaviors. Please read each statement carefully. Then rate *yourself* in terms of *how frequently* you engage in the behavior described. *This is not a test* (there are no right or wrong answers).

Consider each statement in the context of the student organization (for example, club, team, chapter, group, unit, hall, program, project) with which you are most involved. The rating scale provides five choices:

(1) If you RARELY or SELDOM do what is described in the statement, circle the number one (1).
(2) If you do what is described ONCE IN A WHILE, circle the number two (2).
(3) If you SOMETIMES do what is described, circle the number three (3).
(4) If you do what is described FAIRLY OFTEN, circle the number four (4).
(5) If you do what is described VERY FREQUENTLY or ALMOST ALWAYS, circle the number five (5).

Please respond to every statement.

In selecting the response, be realistic about the extent to which you *actually* engage in the behavior. Do *not* answer in terms of how you would like to see yourself or in terms of what you should be doing. Answer in terms of how you *typically behave*. The usefulness of the feedback from this inventory will depend on how honest you are with yourself about how frequently you actually engage in each of these behaviors.

For example, the first statement is "I look for opportunities that challenge my skills and abilities." If you believe you do this "once in a while," circle the number 2. If you believe you look for challenging opportunities "fairly often," circle the number 4.

When you have responded to all thirty statements, please turn to the response sheet on the back page and transfer your responses as instructed. Thank you.

STUDENT LEADERSHIP PRACTICES INVENTORY-SELF

How frequently do you typically engage in the following behaviors and actions? *Circle* the number that applies to each statement.

1 SELDOM OR RARELY	2 ONCE IN A WHILE	3 SOMETIMES	4 FAIRLY OFTEN	5 VERY FREQUENTLY

1. I look for opportunities that challenge my skills and abilities.	1	2	3	4	5
2. I describe to others in our organization what we should be capable of accomplishing.	1	2	3	4	5
3. I include others in planning the activities and programs of our organization.	1	2	3	4	5
4. I share my beliefs about how things can be run most effectively within our organization.	1	2	3	4	5
5. I encourage others as they work on activities and programs in our organization.	1	2	3	4	5
6. I keep current on events and activities that might affect our organization.	1	2	3	4	5
7. I look ahead and communicate about what I believe will affect us in the future.	1	2	3	4	5
8. I treat others with dignity and respect.	1	2	3	4	5
9. I break our organization's projects down into manageable steps.	1	2	3	4	5
10. I make sure that people in our organization are recognized for their contributions.	1	2	3	4	5
11. I take initiative in experimenting with the way we do things in our organization.	1	2	3	4	5
12. I am upbeat and positive when talking about what our organization is doing.	1	2	3	4	5
13. I support the decisions that other people in our organization make on their own.	1	2	3	4	5
14. I set a personal example of what I expect from other people.	1	2	3	4	5
15. I praise people for a job well done.	1	2	3	4	5
16. I look for ways to improve whatever project or task I am involved in.	1	2	3	4	5
17. I talk with others about how their own interests can be met by working toward a common goal.	1	2	3	4	5
18. I foster cooperative rather than competitive relationships among people I work with.	1	2	3	4	5
19. I talk about the values and principles that guide my actions.	1	2	3	4	5
20. I give people in our organization support and express appreciation for their contributions.	1	2	3	4	5
21. I ask, "What can we learn from this experience?" when things do not go as we expected.	1	2	3	4	5
22. I speak with conviction about the higher purpose and meaning of what we are doing.	1	2	3	4	5
23. I give others a great deal of freedom and choice in deciding how to do their work.	1	2	3	4	5
24. I follow through on the promises and commitments I make in this organization.	1	2	3	4	5
25. I find ways for us to celebrate our accomplishments publicly.	1	2	3	4	5
26. I let others experiment and take risks even when outcomes are uncertain.	1	2	3	4	5
27. I show my enthusiasm and excitement about what our organization is doing.	1	2	3	4	5
28. I provide opportunities for others to take on leadership responsibilities.	1	2	3	4	5
29. I make sure that we set goals and make specific plans for the projects we undertake.	1	2	3	4	5
30. I make it a point to tell others about the good work done by our organization.	1	2	3	4	5

Transferring the Scores

After you have responded to the thirty statements on the previous two pages, please transfer your responses to the blanks below. This will make it easier to record and score your responses. Notice that the numbers of the statements are listed *horizontally*. Make sure that the number you assigned to each statement is transferred to the appropriate blank. Fill in a response for every item.

1. _____	2. _____	3. _____	4. _____	5. _____
6. _____	7. _____	8. _____	9. _____	10. _____
11. _____	12. _____	13. _____	14. _____	15. _____
16. _____	17. _____	18. _____	19. _____	20. _____
21. _____	22. _____	23. _____	24. _____	25. _____
26. _____	27. _____	28. _____	29. _____	30. _____

Further Instructions

Please write your name here: _____

Please bring this form with you to the workshop (seminar or class) or return this form to:

_____

_____

_____

_____

If you are interested in feedback from other people, ask them to complete the Student LPI-Observer, which provides you with perspectives on your leadership behaviors as perceived by others.

Printed in the United States of America.

Jossey-Bass Publishers
350 Sansome Street
San Francisco, California 94104
(888) 378-2537
Fax (800) 605-2665

www.josseybass.com

Printing 10 9 8 7 6 5 4 3

This instrument is printed on acid-free, recycled stock that meets or exceeds the minimum GPO and EPA requirements for recycled paper.

ISBN: 0-7879-4426-2

STUDENT LEADERSHIP PRACTICES INVENTORY—OBSERVER

Name of Leader: _____

Instructions

On the next two pages are thirty descriptive statements about various leadership behaviors. Please read each statement carefully. Then rate *the person who asked you to complete this form* in terms of *how frequently* he or she typically engages in the described behavior. *This is not a test* (there are no right or wrong answers).

Consider each statement in the context of the student organization (for example, club, team, chapter, group, unit, hall, program, project) with which that person is most involved or with which you have had the greatest opportunity to observe him or her. The rating scale provides five choices:

(1) If this person RARELY or SELDOM does what is described in the statement, circle the number one (1).
(2) If this person does what is described ONCE IN A WHILE, circle the number two (2).
(3) If this person SOMETIMES does what is described, circle the number three (3).
(4) If this person does what is described FAIRLY OFTEN, circle the number four (4).
(5) If this person does what is described VERY FREQUENTLY or ALMOST ALWAYS, circle the number five (5).

Please respond to every statement.

In selecting the response, be realistic about the extent to which this person *actually* engages in the behavior. Do *not* answer in terms of how you would like to see this person behaving or in terms of what this person should be doing. Answer in terms of how he or she *typically behaves*. The usefulness of the feedback from this inventory will depend on how honest you are about how frequently you observe this person actually engaging in each of these behaviors.

For example, the first statement is, "He or she looks for opportunities that challenge his or her skills and abilities." If you believe this person does this "once in a while," circle the number 2. If you believe he or she looks for challenging opportunities "fairly often," circle the number 4.

When you have responded to all thirty statements, please turn to the response sheet on the back page and transfer your responses as instructed. Thank you.

STUDENT LEADERSHIP PRACTICES INVENTORY—OBSERVER

How frequently does this person typically engage in the following behaviors and actions? *Circle* the number that applies to each statement:

1 SELDOM OR RARELY	2 ONCE IN A WHILE	3 SOMETIMES	4 FAIRLY OFTEN	5 VERY FREQUENTLY

He or she:

1. looks for opportunities that challenge his or her skills and abilities.	1	2	3	4	5
2. describes to others in our organization what we should be capable of accomplishing.	1	2	3	4	5
3. includes others in planning the activities and programs of our organization.	1	2	3	4	5
4. shares his or her beliefs about how things can be run most effectively within our organization.	1	2	3	4	5
5. encourages others as they work on activities and programs in our organization.	1	2	3	4	5
6. keeps current on events and activities that might affect our organization.	1	2	3	4	5
7. looks ahead and communicates about what he or she believes will affect us in the future.	1	2	3	4	5
8. treats others with dignity and respect.	1	2	3	4	5
9. breaks our organization's projects down into manageable steps.	1	2	3	4	5
10. makes sure that people in our organization are recognized for their contributions.	1	2	3	4	5
11. takes initiative in experimenting with the way we do things in our organization.	1	2	3	4	5
12. is upbeat and positive when talking about what our organization is doing.	1	2	3	4	5
13. supports the decisions that other people in our organization make on their own.	1	2	3	4	5
14. sets a personal example of what he or she expects from other people.	1	2	3	4	5
15. praises people for a job well done.	1	2	3	4	5
16. looks for ways to improve whatever project or task he or she is involved in.	1	2	3	4	5
17. talks with others about how their own interests can be met by working toward a common goal.	1	2	3	4	5
18. fosters cooperative rather than competitive relationships among people he or she works with.	1	2	3	4	5
19. talks about the values and principles that guide his or her actions.	1	2	3	4	5
20. gives people in our organization support and expresses appreciation for their contributions.	1	2	3	4	5
21. asks "What can we learn from this experience?" when things do not go as we expected.	1	2	3	4	5
22. speaks with conviction about the higher purpose and meaning of what we are doing.	1	2	3	4	5
23. gives others a great deal of freedom and choice in deciding how to do their work.	1	2	3	4	5
24. follows through on the promises and commitments he or she makes in this organization.	1	2	3	4	5
25. finds ways for us to celebrate our accomplishments publicly.	1	2	3	4	5
26. lets others experiment and take risks even when outcomes are uncertain.	1	2	3	4	5
27. shows his or her enthusiasm and excitement about what our organization is doing.	1	2	3	4	5
28. provides opportunities for others to take on leadership responsibilities.	1	2	3	4	5
29. makes sure that we set goals and make specific plans for the projects we undertake.	1	2	3	4	5
30. makes it a point to tell others about the good work done by our organization.	1	2	3	4	5

Transferring the Scores

After you have responded to the thirty statements on the previous two pages, please transfer your responses to the blanks below. This will make it easier to record and score your responses. Notice that the numbers of the statements are listed *horizontally*. Make sure that the number you assigned to each statement is transferred to the appropriate blank. Fill in a response for every item.

1. ____	2. ____	3. ____	4. ____	5. ____
6. ____	7. ____	8. ____	9. ____	10. ____
11. ____	12. ____	13. ____	14. ____	15. ____
16. ____	17. ____	18. ____	19. ____	20. ____
21. ____	22. ____	23. ____	24. ____	25. ____
26. ____	27. ____	28. ____	29. ____	30. ____

Further Instructions

The above scores are for (name of person): _____

Please bring this form with you to the workshop (seminar or class) or return this form to:

_____

_____

_____

_____

ISBN: 0-7879-4427-0

Printed in the United States of America.

Jossey-Bass Publishers
350 Sansome Street
San Francisco, California 94104
(888) 378-2537
Fax (800) 605-2665

www.josseybass.com

Printing 10 9 8 7 6 5 4 3 2 1

This instrument is printed on acid-free, recycled stock that meets or exceeds the minimum GPO and EPA requirements for recycled paper.

SELF-ASSESSMENT PORTFOLIO

Find online versions of many assessments at www.wiley.com/college/schermerhorn

Managerial Assumptions

Instructions
Read the following statements. Write "Yes" if you agree with the statement, or "No" if you disagree with it. Force yourself to take a "yes" or "no" position for every statement.

1. Are good pay and a secure job enough to satisfy most workers?

2. Should a manager help and coach subordinates in their work?
3. Do most people like real responsibility in their jobs?
4. Are most people afraid to learn new things in their jobs?
5. Should managers let subordinates control the quality of their work?
6. Do most people dislike work?
7. Are most people creative?
8. Should a manager closely supervise and direct work of subordinates?

Source: Schermerhorn, John R., Jr., *Management,* 5th ed. (New York, John Wiley & Sons, Inc., 1996), p. 51. By permission.

9. Do most people tend to resist change?
10. Do most people work only as hard as they have to?
11. Should workers be allowed to set their own job goals?
12. Are most people happiest off the job?
13. Do most workers really care about the organization they work for?
14. Should a manager help subordinates advance and grow in their jobs?

Scoring

Count the number of "yes" responses to items 1, 4, 6, 8, 9, 10, 12; write that number here as [X = ____]. Count the number of "yes" responses to items 2, 3, 5, 7, 11, 13, 14; write that score here [Y = ____].

Interpretation

This assessment gives insight into your orientation toward Douglas McGregor's Theory X (your "X" score) and Theory Y (your "Y" score) assumptions. You should review the discussion of McGregor's thinking in Chapter 1.1 and consider further the ways in which you are likely to behave toward other people at work. Think, in particular, about the types of "self-fulfilling prophecies" you are likely to create.

ASSESSMENT 2

A Twenty-First-Century Manager

Instructions

Rate yourself on the following personal characteristics. Use this scale.

S =	Strong, I am very confident with this one.
G =	Good, but I still have room to grow.
W =	Weak, I really need work on this one.
? =	Unsure, I just don't know.

1. *Resistance to stress:* The ability to get work done even under stressful conditions.
2. *Tolerance for uncertainty:* The ability to get work done even under ambiguous and uncertain conditions.
3. *Social objectivity:* The ability to act free of racial, ethnic, gender, and other prejudices or biases.
4. *Inner work standards:* The ability to personally set and work to high-performance standards.
5. *Stamina:* The ability to sustain long work hours.
6. *Adaptability:* The ability to be flexible and adapt to changes.
7. *Self-confidence:* The ability to be consistently decisive and display one's personal presence.
8. *Self-objectivity:* The ability to evaluate personal strengths and weaknesses and to understand one's motives and skills relative to a job.
9. *Introspection:* The ability to learn from experience, awareness, and self-study.

Source: See *Outcome Management Project,* Phase I and Phase II Reports (St. Louis: American Assembly of Collegiate Schools of Business, 1986 & 1987).

10. *Entrepreneurism:* The ability to address problems and take advantage of opportunities for constructive change.

Scoring

Give yourself 1 point for each S, and 1/2 point for each G. Do not give yourself points for W and ? responses. Total your points and enter the result here [PMF = ____].

Interpretation

This assessment offers a self-described *profile of your management foundations* (*PMF*). Are you a perfect 10, or is your PMF score something less than that? There shouldn't be too many 10s around. Ask someone who knows you to assess you on this instrument. You may be surprised at the differences between your PMF score as self-described and your PMF score as described by someone else. Most of us, realistically speaking, must work hard to grow and develop continually in these and related management foundations. This list is a good starting point as you consider where and how to further pursue the development of your managerial skills and competencies. The items on the list are recommended by the American Assembly of Collegiate Schools of Business (AACSB) as skills and personal characteristics that should be nurtured in college and university students of business administration. Their success—and yours—as twenty-first-century managers may well rest on (1) an initial awareness of the importance of these basic management foundations and (2) a willingness to strive continually to strengthen them throughout your work career.

Turbulence Tolerance Test

Instructions

The following statements were made by a 37-year-old manager in a large, successful corporation. How would you like to have a job with these characteristics? Using the following scale, write your response to the left of each statement.

> 4 = I would enjoy this very much; it's completely acceptable.
>
> 3 = This would be enjoyable and acceptable most of the time.
>
> 2 = I'd have no reaction to this feature one way or another, or it would be about equally enjoyable and unpleasant.
>
> 1 = This feature would be somewhat unpleasant for me.
>
> 0 = This feature would be very unpleasant for me.

_____ 1. I regularly spend 30 to 40 percent of my time in meetings.

_____ 2. Eighteen months ago my job did not exist, and I have been essentially inventing it as I go along.

_____ 3. The responsibilities I either assume or am assigned consistently exceed the authority I have for discharging them.

_____ 4. At any given moment in my job, I have on average about a dozen phone calls to be returned.

_____ 5. There seems to be very little relation between the quality of my job performance and my actual pay and fringe benefits.

_____ 6. About 2 weeks a year of formal management training is needed in my job just to stay current.

_____ 7. Because we have very effective equal employment opportunity (EEO) in my company and because it is thoroughly multinational, my job consistently brings me into close working contact at a professional level with people of many races, ethnic groups and nationalities, and of both sexes.

_____ 8. There is no objective way to measure my effectiveness.

_____ 9. I report to three different bosses for different aspects of my job, and each has an equal say in my performance appraisal.

_____ 10. On average, about a third of my time is spent dealing with unexpected emergencies that force all scheduled work to be postponed.

_____ 11. When I have to have a meeting of the people who report to me, it takes my secretary most of a day to find a time when we are all available, and even then I have yet to have a meeting where everyone is present for the entire meeting.

_____ 12. The college degree I earned in preparation for this type of work is now obsolete, and I probably should go back for another degree.

_____ 13. My job requires that I absorb 100–200 pages of technical materials per week.

_____ 14. I am out of town overnight at least one night per week.

_____ 15. My department is so interdependent with several other departments in the company that all distinctions about which departments are responsible for which tasks are quite arbitrary.

Source: Peter B. Vail, _Managing as a Performance Art: New Ideas for a World of Chaotic Change_ (San Francisco: Jossey-Bass, 1989), pp. 8–9. Used by permission.

_____ 16. In about a year I will probably get a promotion to a job in another division that has most of these same characteristics.

_____ 17. During the period of my employment here, either the entire company or the division I worked in has been reorganized every year or so.

_____ 18. While there are several possible promotions I can see ahead of me, I have no real career path in an objective sense.

_____ 19. While there are several possible promotions I can see ahead of me, I think I have no realistic chance of getting to the top levels of the company.

_____ 20. While I have many ideas about how to make things work better, I have no direct influence on either the business policies or the personnel policies that govern my division.

_____ 21. My company has recently put in an "assessment center" where I and all other managers will be required to go through an extensive battery of psychological tests to assess our potential.

_____ 22. My company is a defendant in an antitrust suit, and if the case comes to trial, I will probably have to testify about some decisions that were made a few years ago.

_____ 23. Advanced computer and other electronic office technology is continually being introduced into my division, necessitating constant learning on my part.

_____ 24. The computer terminal and screen I have in my office can be monitored in my bosses' offices without my knowledge.

Scoring

Total your responses and divide the sum by 24; enter the score here [TTT = _____].

Interpretation

This instrument gives an impression of your tolerance for managing in turbulent times—something likely to characterize the world of work well into the future. In general, the higher your TTT score, the more comfortable you seem to be with turbulence and change—a positive sign. For comparison purposes, the average scores for some 500 MBA students and young managers was 1.5–1.6. The test's author suggests the TTT scores may be interpreted much like a grade point average in which 4.0 is a perfect A. On this basis, a 1.5 is below a C! How did you do?

● ● ASSESSMENT 4 ●

Global Readiness Index

Instructions

Use the scale to rate yourself on each of the following items to establish a baseline measurement of your readiness to participate in the global work environment.

Rating Scale

> 1 = Very Poor
> 2 = Poor
> 3 = Acceptable
> 4 = Good
> 5 = Very Good

Source: Developed from "Is Your Company Really Global,"
Business Week (December 1, 1997).

_____ 1. I understand my own culture in terms of its expectations, values, and influence on communication and relationships.

_____ 2. When someone presents me with a different point of view, I try to understand it rather than attack it.

_____ 3. I am comfortable dealing with situations where the available information is incomplete and the outcomes unpredictable.

_____ 4. I am open to new situations and am always looking for new information and learning opportunities.

_____ 5. I have a good understanding of the attitudes and perceptions toward my culture as they are held by people from other cultures.

_____ 6. I am always gathering information about other countries and cultures and trying to learn from them.

_____ 7. I am well informed regarding the major differences in government, political systems, and economic policies around the world.

_____ 8. I work hard to increase my understanding of people from other cultures.

_____ 9. I am able to adjust my communication style to work effectively with people from different cultures.

_____ 10. I can recognize when cultural differences are influencing working relationships and adjust my attitudes and behavior accordingly.

Interpretation

To be successful in the twenty-first-century work environment, you must be comfortable with the global economy and the cultural diversity that it holds. This requires a *global mind-set* that is receptive to and respectful of cultural differences, *global knowledge* that includes the continuing quest to know and learn more about other nations and cultures, and *global work skills* that allow you to work effectively across cultures.

Scoring

The goal is to score as close to a perfect "5" as possible on each of the three dimensions of global readiness. Develop your scores as follows.

Items (1 + 2 + 3 + 4)/4
= _____ Global Mind-Set Score

Items (5 + 6 + 7)/3
= _____ Global Knowledge Score

Items (8 + 9 + 10)/3
= _____ Global Work Skills Score

ASSESSMENT 5

Personal Values

Instructions

Below are 16 items. Rate how important each one is to you on a scale of 0 (not important) to 100 (very important). Write the numbers 0–100 on the line to the left of each item.

Not important				Somewhat important				Very important		
0	10	20	30	40	50	60	70	80	90	100

_____ 1. An enjoyable, satisfying job.

_____ 2. A high-paying job.

_____ 3. A good marriage.

_____ 4. Meeting new people; social events.

_____ 5. Involvement in community activities.

_____ 6. My religion.

_____ 7. Exercising, playing sports.

_____ 8. Intellectual development.

_____ 9. A career with challenging opportunities.

_____ 10. Nice cars, clothes, home, etc.

_____ 11. Spending time with family.

_____ 12. Having several close friends.

_____ 13. Volunteer work for not-for-profit organizations, such as the cancer society.

Source: Robert N. Lussier, *Human Relations in Organizations,* 2nd ed. (Homewood, IL: Richard D. Irwin, 1993). By permission.

_____ 14. Meditation, quiet time to think, pray, etc.

_____ 15. A healthy, balanced diet.

_____ 16. Educational reading, TV, self-improvement programs, etc.

Scoring

Transfer the numbers for each of the 16 items to the appropriate column below, then add the two numbers in each column.

	Professional	Financial	Family	Social
	1. _____	2. _____	3. _____	4. _____
	9. _____	10. _____	11. _____	12. _____
Totals	_____	_____	_____	_____

	Community	Spiritual	Physical	Intellectual
	5. _____	6. _____	7. _____	8. _____
	13. _____	14. _____	15. _____	16. _____
Totals	_____	_____	_____	_____

Interpretation

The higher the total in any area, the higher the value you place on that particular area. The closer the numbers are in all eight areas, the more well-rounded you are. Think about the time and effort you put forth in your top three values. Is it sufficient to allow you to achieve the level of success you want in each area? If not, what can you do to change? Is there any area in which you feel you should have a higher value total? If yes, which, and what can you do to change?

ASSESSMENT 6

Intolerance for Ambiguity

Instructions

To determine your level of tolerance (intolerance) for ambiguity, respond to the following items. PLEASE RATE EVERY ITEM; DO NOT LEAVE ANY ITEM BLANK. Rate each item on the following seven-point scale:

1	2	3	4	5	6	7
strongly disagree	moderately disagree	slightly disagree		slightly agree	moderately agree	strongly agree

Rating

_____ 1. An expert who doesn't come up with a definite answer probably doesn't know too much.

_____ 2. There is really no such thing as a problem that can't be solved.

_____ 3. I would like to live in a foreign country for a while.

_____ 4. People who fit their lives to a schedule probably miss the joy of living.

_____ 5. A good job is one where what is to be done and how it is to be done are always clear.

Source: Based on Budner, S., "Intolerance of Ambiguity as a Personality Variable," _Journal of Personality,_ Vol. 30, No. 1 (1962), pp. 29–50.

_____ 6. In the long run it is possible to get more done by tackling small, simple problems rather than large, complicated ones.

_____ 7. It is more fun to tackle a complicated problem than it is to solve a simple one.

_____ 8. Often the most interesting and stimulating people are those who don't mind being different and original.

_____ 9. What we are used to is always preferable to what is unfamiliar.

_____ 10. A person who leads an even, regular life in which few surprises or unexpected happenings arise really has a lot to be grateful for.

_____ 11. People who insist upon a yes or no answer just don't know how complicated things really are.

_____ 12. Many of our most important decisions are based on insufficient information.

_____ 13. I like parties where I know most of the people more than ones where most of the people are complete strangers.

_____ 14. The sooner we all acquire ideals, the better.

_____ 15. Teachers or supervisors who hand out vague assignments give a chance for one to show initiative and originality.

_____ 16. A good teacher is one who makes you wonder about your way of looking at things.

_____ Total

Scoring

The scale was developed by S. Budner. Budner reports test–retest correlations of .85 with a variety of samples (mostly students and health care workers). Data, however, are more than 30 years old, so mean shifts may have occurred. Maximum ranges are 16–112, and score ranges were from 25 to 79, with a grand mean of approximately 49.

The test was designed to measure several different components of possible reactions to perceived threat in situations which are new, complex, or insoluble. Half of the items have been reversed.

To obtain a score, first *reverse* the scale score for the eight "reverse" items, 3, 4, 7, 8, 11, 12, 15, and 16 (i.e., a rating of 1 = 7, 2 = 6, 3 = 5, etc.), then add up the rating scores for all 16 items.

Interpretation

Empirically, low tolerance for ambiguity (high intolerance) has been positively correlated with:

- Conventionality of religious beliefs
- High attendance at religious services
- More intense religious beliefs
- More positive views of censorship
- Higher authoritarianism
- Lower Machiavellianism

The application of this concept to management in the 1990s is clear and relatively self-evident. The world of work and many organizations are full of ambiguity and change. Individuals with a *higher* tolerance for ambiguity are far more likely to be able to function effectively in organizations and contexts in which there is a high turbulence, a high rate of change, and less certainty about expectations, performance standards, what needs to be done, and so on. In contrast, individuals with a lower tolerance for ambiguity are far more likely to be unable to adapt or adjust quickly in turbulence, uncertainty, and change. These individuals are likely to become rigid, angry, stressed, and frustrated when there is a high level of uncertainty and ambiguity in the environment. High levels of tolerance for ambiguity, therefore, are associated with an ability to "roll with the punches" as organizations, environmental conditions, and demands change rapidly.

Two-Factor Profile

Instructions

On each of the following dimensions, distribute a total of 10 points between the two options. For example:

Summer weather   (_7_) ....(_3_) Winter weather

1. Very responsible job   (____) ....(____) Job security

2. Recognition for   (____) ....(____) Good relations
   work accomplishments   with co-workers

3. Advancement   (____) ....(____) A boss who knows
   opportunities at work   his/her job well

4. Opportunities to grow   (____) ....(____) Good working
   and learn on the job   conditions

5. A job that I can   (____) ....(____) Supportive rules,
   do well   policies of employer

6. A prestigious or   (____) ....(____) A high base wage
   high-status job   or salary

Scoring

Summarize your total scores for all items in the *left-hand column* and write it here:
MF = ____.
Summarize your total scores for all items in the *right-hand column* and write it here:
HF = ____.

Interpretation

The "MF" score indicates the relative importance that you place on motivating or satisfier factors in Herzberg's two-factor theory. This shows how important job content is to you.
The "HF" score indicates the relative importance that you place on hygiene or dissatisfier factors in Herzberg's two-factor theory. This shows how important job context is to you.

Are You Cosmopolitan?

Instructions

Answer the questions using a scale of 1 to 5: 1 representing "strongly disagree"; 2, "somewhat disagree"; 3, "neutral"; 4, "somewhat agree"; and 5, "strongly agree."

____ 1. You believe it is the right of the professional to make his or her own decisions about what is to be done on the job.

_____

Source: Developed from Joseph A. Raelin, *The Clash of Cultures, Managers and Professionals* (Harvard Business School Press, 1986).

_____ 2. You believe a professional should stay in an individual staff role regardless of the income sacrifice.

_____ 3. You have no interest in moving up to a top administrative post.

_____ 4. You believe that professionals are better evaluated by professional colleagues than by management.

_____ 5. Your friends tend to be members of your profession.

_____ 6. You would rather be known or get credit for your work outside rather than inside the company.

_____ 7. You would feel better making a contribution to society than to your organization.

_____ 8. Managers have no right to place time and cost schedules on professional contributors.

Scoring and Interpretation

A "cosmopolitan" identifies with the career profession, and a "local" identifies with the employing organization. Total your scores. A score of 30–40 suggests a cosmopolitan work orientation, 10–20 a "local" orientation, and 20–30 a mixed orientation.

ASSESSMENT 9

Group Effectiveness

Instructions

For this assessment, select a specific group you work with or have worked with; it can be a college or work group. For each of the eight statements below, select how often each statement describes the group's behavior. Place the number 1, 2, 3, or 4 on the line next to each of the 8 numbers.

Usually	Frequently	Occasionally	Seldom
1	2	3	4

_____ 1. The members are loyal to one another and to the group leader.

_____ 2. The members and leader have a high degree of confidence and trust in each other.

_____ 3. Group values and goals express relevant values and needs of members.

_____ 4. Activities of the group occur in a supportive atmosphere.

_____ 5. The group is eager to help members develop to their full potential.

_____ 6. The group knows the value of constructive conformity and knows when to use it and for what purpose.

_____ 7. The members communicate all information relevant to the group's activity fully and frankly.

_____ 8. The members feel secure in making decisions that seem appropriate to them.

Scoring

_____ Total. Add up the eight numbers and place an X on the continuum below that represents the score.

Effective group   8 . . . 16 . . . 24 . . . 32   Ineffective group

Interpretation

The lower the score, the more effective the group. What can you do to help the group become more effective? What can the group do to become more effective?

Least Preferred Co-worker Scale

Instructions

Think of all the different people with whom you have ever worked—in jobs, in social clubs, in student projects, or whatever. Next, think of the *one person* with whom you could work *least* well—that is, the person with whom you had the most difficulty getting a job done. This is the one person—a peer, boss, or subordinate—with whom you would least want to work. Describe this person by circling numbers at the appropriate points on each of the following pairs of bipolar adjectives. Work rapidly. There are no right or wrong answers.

Pleasant	8 7 6 5 4 3 2 1	Unpleasant
Friendly	8 7 6 5 4 3 2 1	Unfriendly
Rejecting	1 2 3 4 5 6 7 8	Accepting
Tense	1 2 3 4 5 6 7 8	Relaxed
Distant	1 2 3 4 5 6 7 8	Close
Cold	1 2 3 4 5 6 7 8	Warm
Supportive	8 7 6 5 4 3 2 1	Hostile
Boring	1 2 3 4 5 6 7 8	Interesting
Quarrelsome	1 2 3 4 5 6 7 8	Harmonious
Gloomy	1 2 3 4 5 6 7 8	Cheerful
Open	8 7 6 5 4 3 2 1	Guarded
Backbiting	1 2 3 4 5 6 7 8	Loyal
Untrustworthy	1 2 3 4 5 6 7 8	Trustworthy
Considerate	8 7 6 5 4 3 2 1	Inconsiderate
Nasty	1 2 3 4 5 6 7 8	Nice
Agreeable	8 7 6 5 4 3 2 1	Disagreeable
Insincere	1 2 3 4 5 6 7 8	Sincere
Kind	8 7 6 5 4 3 2 1	Unkind

Scoring

This is called the "least preferred co-worker scale" (LPC). Compute your LPC score by totaling all the numbers you circled; enter that score here [LPC = ____].

Interpretation

The LPC scale is used by Fred Fiedler to identify a person's dominant leadership style. Fiedler believes that this style is a relatively fixed part of one's personality and is therefore difficult to change. This leads Fiedler to his contingency views, which suggest that the key to leadership success is finding (or creating) good "matches" between style and situation. If your score is 73 or above, Fiedler considers you a "relationship-motivated" leader; if your score is 64 and below, he considers you a "task-motivated" leader. If your score is between 65 and 72, Fiedler leaves it up to you to determine which leadership style is most like yours.

Source: Fred E. Fiedler and Martin M. Chemers, *Improving Leadership Effectiveness: The Leader Match Concept,* 2nd ed. (New York: John Wiley & Sons, Inc., 1984). Used by permission.

Leadership Style

Instructions

The following statements describe leadership acts. Indicate the way you would most likely act if you were leader of a workgroup, by circling whether you would most likely behave in this way:

> always (A); frequently (F); occasionally (O); seldom (S); or never (N)

A F O S N   1. Act as group spokesperson.
A F O S N   2. Encourage overtime work.
A F O S N   3. Allow members complete freedom in their work.
A F O S N   4. Encourage the use of uniform procedures.
A F O S N   5. Permit members to solve their own problems.
A F O S N   6. Stress being ahead of competing groups.
A F O S N   7. Speak as a representative of the group.
A F O S N   8. Push members for greater effort.
A F O S N   9. Try out ideas in the group.
A F O S N   10. Let the members work the way they think best.
A F O S N   11. Work hard for a personal promotion.
A F O S N   12. Tolerate postponement and uncertainty.
A F O S N   13. Speak for the group when visitors are present.
A F O S N   14. Keep the work moving at a rapid pace.
A F O S N   15. Turn members loose on a job.
A F O S N   16. Settle conflicts in the group.
A F O S N   17. Focus on work details.
A F O S N   18. Represent the group at outside meetings.
A F O S N   19. Avoid giving the members too much freedom.
A F O S N   20. Decide what should be done and how it should be done.
A F O S N   21. Push for increased production.
A F O S N   22. Give some members authority to act.
A F O S N   23. Expect things to turn out as predicted.
A F O S N   24. Allow the group to take initiative.
A F O S N   25. Assign group members to particular tasks.
A F O S N   26. Be willing to make changes.
A F O S N   27. Ask members to work harder.
A F O S N   28. Trust members to exercise good judgment.
A F O S N   29. Schedule the work to be done.
A F O S N   30. Refuse to explain my actions.
A F O S N   31. Persuade others that my ideas are best.
A F O S N   32. Permit the group to set its own pace.
A F O S N   33. Urge the group to beat its previous record.
A F O S N   34. Act without consulting the group.
A F O S N   35. Ask members to follow standard rules.
            T ____   P ____

Scoring

1. Circle items 8, 12, 17, 18, 19, 30, 34, and 35.
2. Write the number 1 in front of a *circled item number* if you responded S (seldom) or N (never) to that item.

3. Write a number 1 in front of *item numbers not circled* if you responded A (always) or F (frequently).
4. Circle the number 1's which you have written in front of items 3, 5, 8, 10, 15, 18, 19, 22, 24, 26, 28, 30, 32, 34, and 35.
5. *Count the circled number 1's.* This is your score for leadership *concern for people.* Record the score in the blank following the letter P at the end of the questionnaire.
6. *Count the uncircled number 1's.* This is your score for leadership *concern for task.* Record this number in the blank following the letter T.

"TT" Leadership Style

Instructions

For each of the following 10 pairs of statements, divide 5 points between the two according to your beliefs, perceptions of yourself, or according to which of the two statements characterizes you better. The 5 points may be divided between the a and b statements in any one of the following ways: 5 for a, 0 for b; 4 for a, 1 for b; 3 for a, 2 for b; 1 for a, 4 for b; 0 for a, 5 for b, but not equally (2 1/2) between the two. Weigh your choices between the two according to the one that characterizes you or your beliefs better.

1. (a) As leader I have a primary mission of maintaining stability.
   (b) As leader I have a primary mission of change.
2. (a) As leader I must cause events.
   (b) As leader I must facilitate events.
3. (a) I am concerned that my followers are rewarded equitably for their work.
   (b) I am concerned about what my followers want in life.
4. (a) My preference is to think long range: what might be.
   (b) My preference is to think short range: what is realistic.
5. (a) As a leader I spend considerable energy in managing separate but related goals.
   (b) As a leader I spend considerable energy in arousing hopes, expectations, and aspirations among my followers.

6. (a) Although not in a formal classroom sense, I believe that a significant part of my leadership is that of teacher.
   (b) I believe that a significant part of my leadership is that of facilitator.
7. (a) As leader I must engage with followers at an equal level of morality.
   (b) As leader I must represent a higher morality.
8. (a) I enjoy stimulating followers to want to do more.
   (b) I enjoy rewarding followers for a job well done.
9. (a) Leadership should be practical.
   (b) Leadership should be inspirational.
10. (a) What power I have to influence others comes primarily from my ability to get people to identify with me and my ideas.
    (b) What power I have to influence others comes primarily from my status and position.

Scoring

Circle your points for items 1b, 2a, 3b, 4a, 5b, 6a, 7b, 8a, 9b, 10a and add up the total points you allocated to these items; enter the score here [**T** = ____]. Next, add up the total points given to the uncircled items 1a, 2b, 3a, 4b, 5a, 6b, 7a, 8b, 9a, 10b; enter the score here [**T** = ____].

Interpretation

This instrument gives an impression of your tendencies toward "transformational" leadership (your **T** score) and "transactional" leadership (your **T** score). You may want to refer to the discussion of these concepts in Chapter 4. Today, a lot of attention is being given to the transformational aspects of leadership—those personal qualities that inspire a sense of vision and desire for extraordinary accomplishment in followers. The most successful leaders of the future will most likely be strong in both "T"s.

Source: Questionnaire by W. Warner Burke, Ph.D. Used by permission.

Empowering Others

Instructions

Think of times when you have been in charge of a group—this could be a full-time or part-time work situation, a student workgroup, or whatever. Complete the following questionnaire by recording how you feel about each statement according to this scale.

> 1 = Strongly disagree
> 2 = Disagree
> 3 = Neutral
> 4 = Agree
> 5 = Strongly agree

When in charge of a group I find:

____ 1. Most of the time other people are too inexperienced to do things, so I prefer to do them myself.

____ 2. It often takes more time to explain things to others than just to do them myself.

____ 3. Mistakes made by others are costly, so I don't assign much work to them.

Source: Questionnaire adapted from L. Steinmetz and R. Todd, *First Line Management,* 4th ed. (Homewood, IL: BPI/Irwin, 1986), pp. 64–67. Used by permission.

____ 4. Some things simply should not be delegated to others.

____ 5. I often get quicker action by doing a job myself.

____ 6. Many people are good only at very specific tasks, and thus can't be assigned additional responsibilities.

____ 7. Many people are too busy to take on additional work.

____ 8. Most people just aren't ready to handle additional responsibilities.

____ 9. In my position, I should be entitled to make my own decisions.

Scoring

Total your responses; enter the score here [____].

Interpretation

This instrument gives an impression of your *willingness to delegate*. Possible scores range from 9 to 45. The higher your score, the more willing you appear to be to delegate to others. Willingness to delegate is an important managerial characteristic. It is essential if you—as a manager—are to "empower" others and give them opportunities to assume responsibility and exercise self-control in their work. With the growing importance of empowerment in the new workplace, your willingness to delegate is well worth thinking about seriously.

Machiavellianism

Instructions

For each of the following statements, circle the number that most closely resembles your attitude.

Statement	Disagree			Agree	
	A Lot	A Little	Neutral	A Little	A Lot
1. The best way to handle people is to tell them what they want to hear.	1	2	3	4	5
2. When you ask someone to do something for you, it is best to give the real reason for wanting it rather than reasons that might carry more weight.	1	2	3	4	5
3. Anyone who completely trusts someone else is asking for trouble.	1	2	3	4	5
4. It is hard to get ahead without cutting corners here and there.	1	2	3	4	5
5. It is safest to assume that all people have a vicious streak, and it will come out when they are given a chance.	1	2	3	4	5
6. One should take action only when it is morally right.	1	2	3	4	5
7. Most people are basically good and kind.	1	2	3	4	5
8. There is no excuse for lying to someone else.	1	2	3	4	5
9. Most people forget more easily the death of their father than the loss of their property.	1	2	3	4	5
10. Generally speaking, people won't work hard unless forced to do so.	1	2	3	4	5

Scoring and Interpretation

This assessment is designed to compute your Machiavellianism (Mach) score. Mach is a personality characteristic that taps people's power orientation. The high-Mach personality is pragmatic, maintains emotional distance from others, and believes that ends can justify means. To obtain your Mach score, add up the numbers you checked for questions 1, 3, 4, 5, 9, and 10. For the other four questions, reverse the numbers you have checked, so that 5 becomes 1; 4 is 2; and 1 is 5. Then total both sets of numbers to find your score. A random sample of adults found the national average to be 25. Students in business and management typically score higher.

The results of research using the Mach test have found: (1) men are generally more Machiavellian than women; (2) older adults tend to have lower Mach scores than younger adults; (3) there is no significant difference between high Machs and low Machs on measures of intelligence or ability; (4) Machiavellianism is not significantly related to demographic characteristics such as educational level or marital status; and (5) high Machs tend to be in professions that emphasize the control and manipulation of people—for example, managers, lawyers, psychiatrists, and behavioral scientists.

Source: From R. Christie and F. L. Geis, *Studies in Machiavellianism* (New York: Academic Press, 1970). By permission.

Personal Power Profile

Contributed by Marcus Maier, Chapman University

Instructions

Below is a list of statements that may be used in describing behaviors that supervisors (leaders) in work organizations can direct toward their subordinates (followers). First, carefully read each descriptive statement, thinking in terms of *how you prefer to influence others*. Mark the number that most closely represents how you feel. Use the following numbers for your answers.

> 5 = Strongly agree
> 4 = Agree
> 3 = Neither agree nor disagree
> 2 = Disagree
> 1 = Strongly disagree

To influence others, I would prefer to:	Strongly Disagree	Disagree	Neither Agree nor Disagree	Agree	Strongly Agree
1. Increase their pay level	1	2	3	4	5
2. Make them feel valued	1	2	3	4	5
3. Give undesirable job assignments	1	2	3	4	5
4. Make them feel like I approve of them	1	2	3	4	5
5. Make them feel that they have commitments to meet	1	2	3	4	5
6. Make them feel personally accepted	1	2	3	4	5
7. Make them feel important	1	2	3	4	5
8. Give them good technical suggestions	1	2	3	4	5
9. Make the work difficult for them	1	2	3	4	5
10. Share my experience and/or training	1	2	3	4	5
11. Make things unpleasant here	1	2	3	4	5
12. Make being at work distasteful	1	2	3	4	5
13. Influence their getting a pay increase	1	2	3	4	5
14. Make them feel like they should satisfy their job requirements	1	2	3	4	5
15. Provide them with sound job-related advice	1	2	3	4	5
16. Provide them with special benefits	1	2	3	4	5
17. Influence their getting a promotion	1	2	3	4	5
18. Give them the feeling that they have responsibilities to fulfill	1	2	3	4	5
19. Provide them with needed technical knowledge	1	2	3	4	5
20. Make them recognize that they have tasks to accomplish	1	2	3	4	5

Source: Modified version of T. R. Hinken and C. A. Schriesheim, "Development and Application of New Scales to Measure the French and Raven (1959) Bases of Social Power," *Journal of Applied Psychology,* Vol. 74 (1989), pp. 561–567.

Scoring

Using the grid below, insert your scores from the 20 questions and proceed as follows: *Reward power*—sum your response to items 1, 13, 16, and 17 and divide by 4. *Coercive power*—sum your response to items 3, 9, 11, and 12 and divide by 4. *Legitimate power*—sum your response to questions 5, 14, 18, and 20 and divide by 4. *Referent power*—sum your response to questions 2, 4, 6, and 7 and divide by 4. *Expert power*—sum your response to questions 8, 10, 15, and 19 and divide by 4.

Reward		Coercive		Legitimate		Referent		Expert	
1	____	3	____	5	____	2	____	8	____
13	____	9	____	14	____	4	____	10	____
16	____	11	____	18	____	6	____	15	____
17	____	12	____	20	____	7	____	19	____
Total	____		____		____		____		____
Divide by 4	____		____		____		____		____

Interpretation

A high score (4 and greater) on any of the five dimensions of power implies that you prefer to influence others by employing that particular form of power. A low score (2 or less) implies that you prefer not to employ this particular form of power to influence others. This represents your power profile. Your overall power position is not reflected by the simple sum of the power derived from each of the five sources. Instead, some combinations of power are synergistic in nature—they are greater than the simple sum of their parts. For example, referent power tends to magnify the impact of other power sources because these other influence attempts are coming from a "respected" person. Reward power often increases the impact of referent power, because people generally tend to like those who give them things that they desire. Some power combinations tend to produce the opposite of synergistic effects, such that the total is less than the sum of the parts. Power dilution frequently accompanies the use of (or threatened use of) coercive power.

ASSESSMENT 16

Intuitive Ability

Instructions

Complete this survey as quickly as you can. Be honest with yourself. For each question, select the response that most appeals to you.

1. When working on a project, do you prefer to:
   (a) Be told what the problem is but be left free to decide how to solve it?
   (b) Get very clear instructions about how to go about solving the problem before you start?
2. When working on a project, do you prefer to work with colleagues who are:
   (a) Realistic?
   (b) Imaginative?

3. Do you most admire people who are:
   (a) Creative?
   (b) Careful?
4. Do the friends you choose tend to be:
   (a) Serious and hard working?
   (b) Exciting and often emotional?
5. When you ask a colleague for advice on a problem you have, do you:
   (a) Seldom or never get upset if he or she questions your basic assumptions?
   (b) Often get upset if he or she questions your basic assumptions?
6. When you start your day, do you:
   (a) Seldom make or follow a specific plan?
   (b) Usually first make a plan to follow?

Source: AIM Survey (El Paso, TX: ENFP Enterprises, 1989). Copyright © 1989 by Weston H. Agor. Used by permission.

7. When working with numbers do you find that you:
   (a) Seldom or never make factual errors?
   (b) Often make factual errors?
8. Do you find that you:
   (a) Seldom daydream during the day and really don't enjoy doing so when you do it?
   (b) Frequently daydream during the day and enjoy doing so?
9. When working on a problem, do you:
   (a) Prefer to follow the instructions or rules when they are given to you?
   (b) Often enjoy circumventing the instructions or rules when they are given to you?
10. When you are trying to put something together, do you prefer to have:
    (a) Step-by-step written instructions on how to assemble the item?
    (b) A picture of how the item is supposed to look once assembled?
11. Do you find that the person who irritates you *the most* is the one who appears to be:
    (a) Disorganized?
    (b) Organized?
12. When an expected crisis comes up that you have to deal with, do you:
    (a) Feel anxious about the situation?
    (b) Feel excited by the challenge of the situation?

Scoring

Total the number of "a" responses circled for questions 1, 3, 5, 6, 11; enter the score here [A = ____]. Total the number of "b" responses for questions 2, 4, 7, 8, 9, 10, 12; enter the score here [B = ____]. Add your "a" and "b" scores and enter the sum here [A + B = ____]. This is your *intuitive score*. The highest possible intuitive score is 12; the lowest is 0.

Interpretation

In his book *Intuition in Organizations* (Newbury Park, CA: Sage, 1989), pp. 10–11, Weston H. Agor states: "Traditional analytical techniques . . . are not as useful as they once were for guiding major decisions. . . . If you hope to be better prepared for tomorrow, then it only seems logical to pay some attention to the use and development of intuitive skills for decision making." Agor developed the prior survey to help people assess their tendencies to use intuition in decision making. Your score offers a general impression of your strength in this area. It may also suggest a need to further develop your skill and comfort with more intuitive decision approaches.

ASSESSMENT 17

Decision-Making Biases

Instructions

How good are you at avoiding potential decision-making biases? Test yourself by answering the following questions:

1. Which is riskier:
   (a) driving a car on a 400-mile trip?
   (b) flying on a 400-mile commercial airline flight?
2. Are there more words in the English language:
   (a) that begin with "r"?
   (b) that have "r" as the third letter?
3. Mark is finishing his MBA at a prestigious university. He is very interested in the arts and at one time considered a career as a musician. Is Mark more likely to take a job:
   (a) in the management of the arts?
   (b) with a management consulting firm?

Source: Incidents from Max H. Bazerman, *Judgment in Managerial Decision Making,* 3rd ed. (New York: John Wiley & Sons, Inc., 1994), pp. 13–14. Used by permission.

4. You are about to hire a new central-region sales director for the fifth time this year. You predict that the next director should work out reasonably well since the last four were "lemons" and the odds favor hiring at least one good sales director in five tries. Is this thinking
   (a) correct?
   (b) incorrect?
5. A newly hired engineer for a computer firm in the Boston metropolitan area has 4 years' experience and good all-around qualifications. When asked to estimate the starting salary for this employee, a chemist with very little knowledge about the profession or industry guessed an annual salary of $35,000. What is your estimate?
   $____ per year

Scoring

Your instructor will provide answers and explanations for the assessment questions.

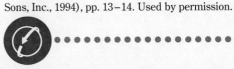

Interpretation

Each of the preceding questions examines your tendency to use a different judgmental heuristic. In his book *Judgment in Managerial Decision Making,* 3rd ed. (New York: John Wiley & Sons, 1994), pp. 6–7, Max Bazerman calls these heuristics "simplifying strategies, or rules of thumb" used in making decisions. He states, "In general, heuristics are helpful, but their use can sometimes lead to severe errors. . . . If we can make managers aware of the potential adverse impacts of using heuristics, they can then decide when and where to use them." This assessment offers an initial insight into your use of such heuristics. An informed decision maker understands the heuristics, is able to recognize when they appear, and eliminates any that may inappropriately bias decision making.

Test yourself further. Before hearing from your instructor, go back and write next to each item the name of the judgmental heuristic (see Chapter 2 text discussion) that you think applies.

Then write down a situation that you have experienced and in which some decision-making bias may have occurred. Be prepared to share and discuss this incident with the class.

ASSESSMENT 18

Conflict Management Strategies

Instructions

Think of how you behave in conflict situations in which your wishes differ from those of others. In the space to the left, rate each of the following statements on a scale of "1" "not at all" to "5" "very much."

When I have a conflict at work, school, or in my personal life, I do the following:

____ **1.** I give in to the wishes of the other party.
____ **2.** I try to realize a middle-of-the-road solution.
____ **3.** I push my own point of view.
____ **4.** I examine issues until I find a solution that really satisfies me and the other party.
____ **5.** I avoid a confrontation about our differences.
____ **6.** I concur with the other party.
____ **7.** I emphasize that we have to find a compromise solution.
____ **8.** I search for gains.
____ **9.** I stand for my own and the other's goals.
____ **10.** I avoid differences of opinion as much as possible.
____ **11.** I try to accommodate the other party.
____ **12.** I insist we both give in a little.
____ **13.** I fight for a good outcome for myself.
____ **14.** I examine ideas from both sides to find a mutually optimal solution.
____ **15.** I try to make differences seem less severe.
____ **16.** I adapt to the other party's goals and interests.
____ **17.** I strive whenever possible towards a fifty-fifty compromise.
____ **18.** I do everything to win.
____ **19.** I work out a solution that serves my own as well as other's interests as much as possible.
____ **20.** I try to avoid a confrontation with the other person.

Scoring

Total your scores for items as follows.
Yielding tendency: 1+6+11+16 = ____ .

_____

Source: This instrument is described in Carsten K. W. De Drew, Arne Evers, Bianca Beersma, Esther S. Kluwer, and Aukje Nauta, "A Theory-Based Measure of Conflict Management Strategies in the Workplace," *Journal of Organizational Behavior,* vol. 22 (2001), pp. 645–668. Used by permission.

Compromising tendency: 2+7+12+17 = ____.
Forcing tendency: 3+8+13+18 = ____.
Problem-solving tendency: 4+9+14+19 = ____.
Avoiding tendency: 5+10+15+20 = ____.

Interpretation

Each of the scores above approximates one of the conflict management styles discussed in the chapter. Look back to Figure 15.4 and make the match ups. Although each style is part of management, only collaboration or problem solving leads to true conflict resolution. You should consider any patterns that may be evident in your scores and think about how to best handle the conflict situations in which you become involved.

ASSESSMENT 19

Your Personality Type

Instructions
How true is each statement for you?

	Not True at All		Not True or Untrue		Very True
1. I hate giving up before I'm absolutely sure that I'm licked.	1	2	3	4	5
2. Sometimes I feel that I should not be working so hard, but something drives me on.	1	2	3	4	5
3. I thrive on challenging situations. The more challenges I have, the better.	1	2	3	4	5
4. In comparison to most people I know, I'm very involved in my work.	1	2	3	4	5
5. It seems as if I need 30 hours a day to finish all the things I'm faced with.	1	2	3	4	5
6. In general, I approach my work more seriously than most people I know.	1	2	3	4	5
7. I guess there are some people who can be nonchalant about their work, but I'm not one of them.	1	2	3	4	5
8. My achievements are considered to be significantly higher than those of most people I know.	1	2	3	4	5
9. I've often been asked to be an officer of some group or groups.	1	2	3	4	5

Scoring
Add all your scores to create a total score = ____.

Interpretation
Type A personalities (hurried and competitive) tend to score 36 and above. Type B personalities (relaxed) tend to score 22 and below. Scores of 23–35 indicate a balance or mix of Type A and Type B.

Source: From *Job Demands and Worker Health* (HEW Publication No. [NIOSH] 75–160) (Washington, DC: US Department of Health, Education and Welfare, 1975), pp. 253–254.

Time Management Profile

Instructions

Complete the following questionnaire by indicating "Y" (yes) or "N" (no) for each item. Be frank and allow your responses to create an accurate picture of how you tend to respond to these kinds of situations.

___ 1. When confronted with several items of similar urgency and importance, I tend to do the easiest one first.

___ 2. I do the most important things during that part of the day when I know I perform best.

___ 3. Most of the time I don't do things someone else can do; I delegate this type of work to others.

___ 4. Even though meetings without a clear and useful purpose upset me, I put up with them.

___ 5. I skim documents before reading them and don't complete any that offer a low return on my time investment.

___ 6. I don't worry much if I don't accomplish at least one significant task each day.

___ 7. I save the most trivial tasks for that time of day when my creative energy is lowest.

___ 8. My workspace is neat and organized.

Source: Suggested by a discussion in Robert E. Quinn, Sue R. Faerman, Michael P. Thompson, and Michael R. McGrath, *Becoming a Master Manager: A Contemporary Framework* (New York: John Wiley & Sons, Inc., 1990), pp. 75–76.

___ 9. My office door is always "open"; I never work in complete privacy.

___ 10. I schedule my time completely from start to finish every workday.

___ 11. I don't like "to do" lists, preferring to respond to daily events as they occur.

___ 12. I "block" a certain amount of time each day or week that is dedicated to high-priority activities.

Scoring

Count the number of "Y" responses to items 2, 3, 5, 7, 8, 12. [Enter that score here ___.] Count the number of "N" responses to items 1, 4, 6, 9, 10, 11. [Enter that score here ___.] Add together the two scores.

Interpretation

The higher the total score, the closer your behavior matches recommended time management guidelines. Reread those items where your response did not match the desired one. Why don't they match? Do you have reasons why your behavior in this instance should be different from the recommended time management guideline? Think about what you can do (and how easily it can be done) to adjust your behavior to be more consistent with these guidelines. For further reading, see Alan Lakein, *How to Control Your Time and Your Life* (New York: David McKay), and William Oncken, *Managing Management Time* (Englewood Cliffs, NJ: Prentice Hall, 1984).

Organizational Design Preference

Instructions

To the left of each item, write the number from the following scale that shows the extent to which the statement accurately describes your views.

> 5 = strongly agree
>
> 4 = agree somewhat
>
> 3 = undecided
>
> 2 = disagree somewhat
>
> 1 = strongly disagree

I prefer to work in an organization where:

1. Goals are defined by those in higher levels.
2. Work methods and procedures are specified.
3. Top management makes important decisions.
4. My loyalty counts as much as my ability to do the job.

Source: John F. Veiga and John N. Yanouzas, *The Dynamics of Organization Theory: Gaining a Macro Perspective* (St. Paul, MN: West, 1979), pp. 158–160. Used by permission.

5. Clear lines of authority and responsibility are established.
6. Top management is decisive and firm.
7. My career is pretty well planned out for me.
8. I can specialize.
9. My length of service is almost as important as my level of performance.
10. Management is able to provide the information I need to do my job well.
11. A chain of command is well established.
12. Rules and procedures are adhered to equally by everyone.
13. People accept authority of a leader's position.
14. People are loyal to their boss.
15. People do as they have been instructed.
16. People clear things with their boss before going over his or her head.

Scoring

Total your scores for all questions. Enter the score here [_____].

Interpretation

This assessment measures your preference for working in an organization designed along "organic" or "mechanistic" lines. The higher your score (above 64), the more comfortable you are with a mechanistic design; the lower your score (below 48), the more comfortable you are with an organic design. Scores between 48 and 64 can go either way. This organizational design preference represents an important issue in the new workplace. Indications are that today's organizations are taking on more and more organic characteristics. Presumably, those of us who work in them will need to be comfortable with such designs.

Which Culture Fits You?

Instructions

Check one of the following organization "cultures" in which you feel most comfortable working.

1. A culture that values talent, entrepreneurial activity, and performance over commitment; one that offers large financial rewards and individual recognition.
2. A culture that stresses loyalty, working for the good of the group, and getting to know the right people; one that believes in "generalists" and step-by-step career progress.
3. A culture that offers little job security; one that operates with a survival mentality, stresses that every individual can make a difference, and focuses attention on "turnaround" opportunities.
4. A culture that values long-term relationships; one that emphasizes systematic career development, regular

Source: Developed from Carol Hymowitz, "Which Corporate Culture Fits You?" *Wall Street Journal* (July 17, 1989), p. B1.

training, and advancement based on gaining of functional expertise.

Scoring

These labels identify the four different cultures: 1 = "the baseball team," 2 = "the club," 3 = "the fortress," and 4 = "the academy."

Interpretation

To some extent, your future career success may depend on working for an organization in which there is a good fit between you and the prevailing corporate culture. This assessment can help you learn how to recognize various cultures, evaluate how well they can serve your needs, and recognize how they may change with time. A risk taker, for example, may be out of place in a "club" but fit right in with a "baseball team." Someone who wants to seek opportunities wherever they may occur may be out of place in an "academy" but fit right in with a "fortress."

TEAM AND EXPERIENTIAL EXERCISES

Selections from The Pfeiffer Training Annuals

A. SWEET TOOTH:
BONDING STRANGERS INTO A TEAM

Procedure:

The general idea is just to relax, have fun, and get to know one another while completing a task. Form groups of five. All groups in the room will be competing to see which one can first complete the following items with the name of a candy bar or sweet treat. The team that completes the most items correctly first will win a prize.

Source: Robert Allan Black, *The 2002 Annual Volume 1, Training/© 2002 John Wiley & Sons, Inc.*

1. Pee Wee . . . , baseball player.
2. Dried up cows.
3. Kids' game minus toes.
4. Not bad and more than some.
5. Explosion in the sky.
6. Polka . . . .
7. Rhymes with Bert's, dirts, hurts.
8. Happy place to drink.
9. Drowning prevention device.
10. Belongs to a mechanic from Mayberry's cousin.

11. They're not "lesses"; they're . . . .
12. Two names for a purring pet.
13. Takes 114 licks to get to the center of these.
14. Sounds like asteroids.
15. A military weapon.
16. A young flavoring.
17. Top of mountains in winter.
18. To catch fish you need to . . . .
19. Sounds like riddles and fiddles.

Questions for discussion:
- What lessons about effective teamwork can be learned from this activity?
- What caused each subgroup to be successful?
- What might be learned about effective teamwork from what happened during this activity?
- What might be done next time to increase the chances of success?

Variation
- Have the individual subgroups create their own lists of clues for the names of candies/candy bars/sweets. Collect the lists and make a grand list using one or two from each group's contribution. Then hold a competition among the total group.

B. INTERROGATORIES: IDENTIFYING ISSUES AND NEEDS

Procedure:

This activity is an opportunity to discover what issues and questions people have brought to the class. The instructor will select from the topic list below. Once a topic is raised, participants should ask any questions they have related to that topic. No one is to *answer* a question at this time. The goal is to come up with as many questions as possible in the time allowed. Feel free to build on a question already asked, or to share a completely different question.

Interrogatories Starter Topic List

- Class requirements
- Coaching
- Communication
- Customers
- Instant messaging
- Job demands
- Leadership
- Management
- Meetings
- Mission
- Performance appraisal
- Personality
- Priorities
- Project priorities
- Quality
- Rules
- Service
- Social activities
- Success
- Task uncertainty
- Teamwork
- Time
- Training
- Values
- Work styles

Questions for discussion:
- How did you feel about this process?
- What common themes did you hear?
- What questions would you most like to have answered?

Source: Cher Holton, *The 2002 Annual: Volume 1, Training/© 2002 John Wiley & Sons, Inc.*

C. DECODE: WORKING WITH DIFFERENT INSTRUCTIONS

Procedure:

1. You are probably familiar with codes and cryptograms from your childhood days. In a cryptogram, each letter in the message is replaced by another letter of the alphabet. For example, LET THE GAMES BEGIN! may become this cryptogram:

YZF FOZ JUKZH CZJVQ!

In the cryptogram Y replaces L, Z replaces E, F replaces T, and so on. Notice that the same letter substitutions are used throughout this cryptogram: Every E in the sentence is replaced by a Z, and every T is replaced by an F.

Here's some information to help you solve cryptograms:

Letter Frequency

The most commonly used letters of the English language are *e, t, a, i, o, n, s, h,* and *r*.

The letters that are most commonly found at the beginning of words are *t, a, o, d,* and *w*.

The letters that are most commonly found at the end of words are *e, s, d,* and *t*.

Word Frequency

One-letter words are either *a* or *I*.

The most common two-letter words are *to, of, in, it, is, as, at, be,* we, he, so, on, an, or, do, if, up, by, and *my*.

The most common three-letter words are *the, and, are, for, not, but, had, has, was, all, any, one, man, out, you, his, her,* and *can*.

The most common four-letter words are *that, with, have, this, will, your, from, they, want, been, good, much, some,* and *very*.

2. The goal of the activity is to learn to work together more effectively in teams. Form into groups of four to seven members each. Have members briefly share their knowledge of solving cryptogram puzzles.

3. In this exercise all groups will be asked to solve the same cryptogram. If a team correctly and completely solves the cryptogram within two minutes, it will earn two hundred points. If it takes more than two minutes but fewer than three minutes, the team will earn fifty points.

4. Before working on the cryptogram, each participant will receive an Instruction Sheet with hints on how to solve cryptograms. Participants can study this sheet for two minutes only. They may not mark up the Instruction Sheet but they may take notes on an index card or a blank piece of paper. The Instruction Sheets will be taken back after two minutes.

5. At any time a group can send one of its members to ask for help from the instructor. The instructor will decode any *one* of the words in the cryptogram selected by the group member.

6. After the points are tallied, the instructor will lead class discussion.

DECODE CRYPTOGRAM

ISV'B JZZXYH BPJB BPH SVQE

_____

UJE BS UCV CZ BS FSYTHBH

_____

ZSYHBCYHZ BPH AHZB UJE BS

_____

UCV CZ BS FSSTHWJBH UCBP

_____

SBPHWZ—Z. BPCJMJWJOJV

_____

Source: Sivasailam "Thiagi" Thiagarajan, *The 2003 Annual: Volume 1, Training/© 2003 John Wiley & Sons, Inc.*

D. CHOICES: LEARNING EFFECTIVE CONFLICT MANAGEMENT STRATEGIES

Procedure: Form teams of three.

Assume you are a group of top managers who are responsible for an organization of seven departments. Working as a team, choose an appropriate strategy to intervene in the situations below when the conflict must be managed in some way. Your choices are *withdrawal, suppression, integration, compromise,* and *authority.* Refer to the list below for some characteristics of each strategy. Write your team's choice following each situation number. Engage in discussion led by the instructor.

CHOICES: STRATEGIES AND CONTINGENCIES

Withdrawal Strategy

Use When (Advantages)
- Choosing sides is to be avoided
- Critical information is missing
- The issue is outside the group
- Others are competent and delegation is appropriate
- You are powerless

Be Aware (Disadvantages)
- Legitimate action ceases
- Direct information stops
- Failure can be perceived
- Cannot be used in a crisis

Suppression (and Diffusion) Strategy

Use When (Advantages)
- A cooling down period is needed
- The issue is unimportant
- A relationship is important

Be Aware (Disadvantages)
- The issue may intensify
- You may appear weak and ineffective

Integration Strategy

Use When (Advantages)
- Group problem solving is needed
- New alternatives are helpful
- Group commitment is required
- Promoting openness and trust

Be Aware (Disadvantages)
- Group goals must be put first
- More time is required for dialogue
- It doesn't work with rigid, dull people

Compromise Strategy

Use When (Advantages)
- Power is equal
- Resources are limited
- A win-win settlement is desired

Be Aware (Disadvantages)
- Action (a third choice) can be weakened
- Inflation is encouraged
- A third party may be needed for negotiation

Authority Strategy

Use When (Advantages)
- A deadlock persists
- Others are incompetent
- Time is limited (crisis)
- An unpopular decision must be made
- Survival of the organization is critical

Be Aware (Disadvantages)
- Emotions intensify quickly
- Dependency is promoted
- Winners and losers are created

Source: Chuck Kormanski, Sr., and Chuck Kormanski, Jr., *The 2003 Annual: Volume 1, Training/© 2003 John Wiley & Sons, Inc.*

Situation #1

Two employees of the support staff have requested the same two-week vacation period. They are the only two trained to carry out an essential task using a complex computer software program that cannot be mastered quickly. You have encouraged others to learn this process so there is more backup for the position, but heavy workloads have prevented this from occurring.

Situation #2

A sales manager has requested a raise because there are now two salespeople on commission earning higher salaries. The work performance of this individual currently does not merit a raise of the amount requested, mostly due to the person turning in critical reports late and missing a number of days of work. The person's sales group is one of the highest rated in the organization, but this may be the result of having superior individuals assigned to the team, rather than to the effectiveness of the manager.

Situation #3

It has become obvious that the copy machine located in a customer service area is being used for a variety of personal purposes, including reproducing obscene jokes. A few copies have sometimes been found lying on or near the machine at the close of the business day. You have mentioned the matter briefly in the organization's employee newsletter, but recently you have noticed an increase in the activity. Most of the office staff seems to be involved.

Situation #4

Three complaints have filtered upward to you from long-term employees concerning a newly hired individual. This person has a pierced nose and a visible tattoo. The work performance of the individual is adequate and the person does not have to see customers; however, the employees who have complained allege that the professional appearance of the office area has been compromised.

Situation #5

The organization has a flex-time schedule format that requires all employees to work the core hours of 10 A.M. to 3 P.M., Monday through Friday. Two department managers have complained that another department does not always maintain that policy. The manager of the department in question has responded by citing recent layoffs and additional work responsibilities as reasons for making exceptions to policy.

Situation #6

As a result of a recent downsizing, an office in a coveted location is now available. Three individuals have made a request to the department manager for the office. The manager has recommended that the office be given to one of the three. This individual has the highest performance rating, but was aided in obtaining employment with the company by the department manager, who is a good friend of the person's family. Colleagues prefer not to work with this individual, as there is seldom any evidence of teamwork.

Situation #7

Two department managers have requested a budget increase in the areas of travel and computer equipment. Each asks that your group support this request. The CEO, not your group, will make the final decision. You are aware that increasing funds for one department will result in a decrease for others, as the total budget figures for all of these categories are set.

Situation #8

Few of the management staff attended the Fourth of July picnic held at a department manager's country home last year. This particular manager, who has been a loyal team player for the past twenty-one years, has indicated that he/she plans to host the event again this year. Many of you have personally found the event to be boring, with little to do but talk and eat. Already a few of the other managers have suggested that the event be held at a different location with a new format or else be cancelled.

Situation #9

It has come to your attention that a manager and a subordinate in the same department are having a romantic affair openly in the building. Both are married to other people. They have been taking extended lunch periods, yet both remain beyond quitting time to complete their work. Colleagues have begun to complain that neither is readily available mid-day and that they do not return messages in a timely manner.

Situation #10

Two loyal department managers are concerned that a newly hired manager who is wheelchair-bound has been given too much in the way of accommodations beyond what is required by the Americans with Disabilities Act. They have requested similar changes to make their own work lives easier. Specifically, they cite office size and location on the building's main floor as points of contention.

E. INTERNAL/EXTERNAL MOTIVATORS: ENCOURAGING CREATIVITY

Procedure:

1. This interactive, experience-based activity is designed to increase participants' awareness of creativity and creative processes. Begin by thinking of a job that you now hold or have held. Then complete Questions 1 and 2 from the Internal/External Motivators Questionnaire (see below).
2. Form into groups. Share your questionnaire results and make a list of responses to Question 1.
3. Discuss and compare rankings of major work activities listed for Question 2. Make a list with at least two responses from each participant.
4. Individually record your answers to Questions 3 and 4 below. Then share your answers and again list member responses within your group.
5. Individually, compare your responses to Questions 1 and 2 with your responses to Questions 3 and 4. Then answer Question 5. Again, share with the group and make a group list of answers to Question 5 for the recorder, who is to record these answers on the flip chart. (Ten minutes.)

Questions for Discussion:

- What was the most important part of this activity for you?
- What have you learned about motivation?
- What impact will having done this activity have for you back in the workplace?
- How will what you have learned change your leadership style or future participation in a group?
- What will you do differently based on what you have learned?

INTRINSIC/EXTRINSIC MOTIVATORS QUESTIONNAIRE

1. How could you do your job in a more creative manner? List some ways in the space below:

2. List four or five major work activities or jobs you perform on a regular basis in the left-hand boxes on the following chart. Use a seven-point scale that ranges from 1 (low) to 7 (high) to rate each work activity on three separate dimensions: (a) level of difficulty, (b) potential to motivate you, and (c) opportunity to add value to the organization.

Source: Elizabeth A. Smith, *The 2003 Annual: Volume 1, Training/© 2003 John Wiley & Sons, Inc.*

Major Work Activity	Level of Difficulty	Potential to Motivate	Opportunity to Add Value
1.			
2.			
3.			
4.			
5.			

3. List five motivators or types of rewards that would encourage you to do your job in a more creative manner.

4. List three motivators or types of rewards from Question 3 above that you believe would *definitely increase your creativity*. Indicate whether these motivators are realistic or unrealistic in terms of your job or work setting. Indicate whether each is intrinsic or extrinsic.

Motivators	Realistic/ Unrealistic	Intrinsic	Extrinsic
1.			
2.			
3.			

5. List three types of work activities you like to perform and the motivators or rewards that would stimulate and reinforce your creativity.

Work Activity	Rewards That Reinforce Creativity
1.	
2.	
3.	

F. QUICK HITTER: FOSTERING THE CREATIVE SPIRIT

Part A Procedure:

1. Write the Roman numeral nine (IX) on a sheet of paper.
2. Add one line to make six. After you have one response, try for others.

Questions for discussion:

- What does solving this puzzle show us about seeing things differently?
- Why don't some people consider alternatives easily?
- What skills or behaviors would be useful for us to develop our ability to see different points of view?

Part B Procedure:

1. Rent the video or DVD of "Patch Adams." In this video Patch (Robin Williams) is studying to become a doctor, but he does not look, act, or think like a traditional doctor. For Patch, humor is the best medicine. He is always willing to do unusual things to make his patients laugh. Scenes from this video can be revealing to an OB class.

2. Show the first Patch Adams scene (five minutes)—this is in the psychiatric hospital where Patch has admitted himself after a failed suicide attempt. He meets Arthur in the hospital. Arthur is obsessed with showing people four fingers of his hand and asking them: "How many fingers can you see?" Everybody says four. The scene shows Patch visiting Arthur to find out the solution. Arthur's answer is: "If you only focus on the problem, you will never see the solution. Look further. You have to see what other people do not see."

3. Engage the class in discussion of these questions and more:
   - How does this film clip relate to Part A of this exercise?
   - What restricts our abilities to look beyond what we see?
   - How can we achieve the goal of seeing what others do not see?

4. Show the second Patch Adams scene (five minutes)—this is when Patch has left the hospital and is studying medicine. Patch and his new friend Truman are having breakfast. Truman is reflecting on the human mind and on the changing of behavioral patterns (the adoption of programmed answers) as a person grows older. Patch proposes to carry out the Hello Experiment. The objective of the experiment is "to change the programmed answer by changing the usual parameters."

5. Engage the class in discussion of these questions and more:
   - What is a programmed answer?
   - What is the link between our programmed answers and our abilities to exhibit creativity?
   - How can we "deprogram" ourselves?

6. Summarize the session with a wrap-up discussion of creativity, including barriers and ways to encourage it.

Source: Mila Gascó Hernández and Teresa Torres Coronas, *The 2003 Annual: Volume 1, Training/© 2003 John Wiley & Sons, Inc.*

Additional Team and Experiential Exercises

EXERCISE 1

My Best Manager

Procedure

1. Make a list of the attributes that describe the best manager you ever worked for. If you have trouble identifying an actual manager, make a list of attributes you would like the manager in your next job to have.
2. Form a group of four or five persons and share your lists.
3. Create one list that combines all the unique attributes of the "best" managers represented in your group. Make sure that you have all attributes listed, but list each only once. Place a check mark next to those that were reported by two or more members. Have one of your members prepared to present the list in general class discussion.
4. After all groups have finished Step 3, spokespersons should report to the whole class. The instructor will make a running list of the "best" manager attributes as viewed by the class.
5. Feel free to ask questions and discuss the results.

EXERCISE 2

Graffiti Needs Assessment: Involving Students in the First Class Session

Contributed by Barbara K. Goza, Visiting Associate Professor, University of California at Santa Cruz, and Associate Professor, California State Polytechnic University, Pomona. From *Journal of Management Education*, 1993.

Procedure

1. Complete the following sentences with as many endings as possible.
   1. When I first came to this class, I thought . . .
   2. My greatest concern this term is . . .
   3. In 3 years I will be . . .
   4. The greatest challenge facing the world today is . . .
   5. Organizational behavior specialists do . . .
   6. Human resources are . . .
   7. Organizational research is . . .
   8. The most useful question I've been asked is . . .
   9. The most important phenomenon in organizations is . . .
   10. I learn the most when . . .
2. Your instructor will guide you in a class discussion about your responses. Pay careful attention to similarities and differences among various students' answers.

EXERCISE 3

My Best Job

Procedure

1. Make a list of the top five things you expect from your first (or next) full-time job.
2. Exchange lists with a nearby partner. Assign probabilities (or odds) to each goal on your partner's list to indicate how likely you feel it is that the goal can be

accomplished. (*Note:* Your instructor may ask that everyone use the same probabilities format.)

3. Discuss your evaluations with your partner. Try to delete superficial goals or modify them to become more substantial. Try to restate any unrealistic goals to make them more realistic. Help your partner do the same.

4. Form a group of four to six persons. Within the group, have everyone share what they now consider to be the most "realistic" goals on their lists. Elect a spokesperson to share a sample of these items with the entire class.

5. Discuss what group members have individually learned from the exercise. Await further class discussion led by your instructor.

EXERCISE 4

What Do You Value in Work?

Procedure

1. The following nine items are from a survey conducted by Nicholas J. Beutell and O. C. Brenner ("Sex Differences in Work Values," *Journal of Vocational Behavior,* Vol. 28, pp. 29–41, 1986). Rank the nine items in terms of how important (9 = most important) they would be to you in a job.

   How important is it to you to have a job that:
   ____ Is respected by other people?
   ____ Encourages continued development of knowledge and skills?
   ____ Provides job security?
   ____ Provides a feeling of accomplishment?
   ____ Provides the opportunity to earn a high income?
   ____ Is intellectually stimulating?
   ____ Rewards good performance with recognition?
   ____ Provides comfortable working conditions?
   ____ Permits advancement to high administrative responsibility?

2. Form into groups as designated by your instructor. Within each group, the *men in the group* will meet to develop a consensus ranking of the items as they think the *women* in the Beutell and Brenner survey ranked them. The reasons for the rankings should be shared and discussed so they are clear to everyone. The *women in the group* should not participate in this ranking task. They should listen to the discussion and be prepared to comment later in class discussion. A spokesperson for the men in the group should share the group's rankings with the class.

3. (*Optional*) Form into groups as designated by your instructor, but with each group consisting entirely of men or women. Each group should meet and decide which of the work values members of the *opposite* sex ranked first in the Beutell and Brenner survey. Do this again for the work value ranked last. The reasons should be discussed, along with reasons that each of the other values probably was not ranked first . . . or last. A spokesperson for each group should share group results with the rest of the class.

Source: Adapted from Roy J. Lewicki, Donald D. Bowen, Douglas T. Hall, and Francine S. Hall, *Experiences in Management and Organizational Behavior,* 3rd ed. (New York: John Wiley & Sons, Inc., 1988), pp. 23–26. Used by permission.

My Asset Base

A business has an asset base or set of resources that it uses to produce a good or service of value to others. For a business, these are the assets or resources it uses to achieve results, including capital, land, patented products or processes, buildings and equipment, raw materials, and the human resources or employees, among others.

Each of us has an asset base that supports our ability to accomplish the things we set out to do. We refer to our personal assets as *talents, strengths,* or *abilities.* We probably inherit our talents from our parents, but we acquire many of our abilities and strengths through learning. One thing is certain: we feel very proud of the talents and abilities we have.

Procedure

1. Printed here is a T chart that you are to fill out. On the right-hand side of the T, list four or five of your accomplishments—*things you have done of which you are most proud.* Your accomplishments should only include those things for which you can take credit, those *things for which you are primarily responsible.* If you are proud of the sorority to which you belong, you may be justifiably proud, but don't list it unless you can argue that the sorority's excellence is due primarily to your efforts. However, if you feel that having been invited to join the sorority is a major accomplishment for you, then you may include it.

   When you have completed the right-hand side of the chart, fill in the left-hand side by listing *talents, strengths,* and *abilities,* that you have that have enabled you to accomplish the outcomes listed on the right-hand side.

My Asset Base

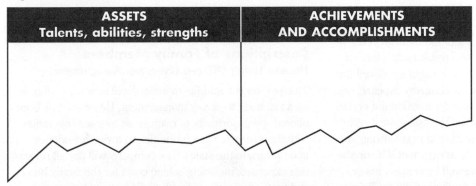

ASSETS Talents, abilities, strengths	ACHIEVEMENTS AND ACCOMPLISHMENTS

2. Share your lists with other team members. As each member shares his or her list, pay close attention to your own perceptions and feelings. Notice the effect this has on your attitudes toward the other team members.
3. Discuss these questions in your group:
   1. How did your attitudes and feelings toward other members of the team change as you pursued the activity? What does this tell you about the process whereby we come to get to know and care about people?
   2. How did you feel about the instructions the instructor provided? What did you expect to happen? Were your expectations accurate?

Source: Adapted from Donald D. Bowen et al., *Experiences in Management and Organizational Behavior,* 4th ed. (New York: John Wiley & Sons, Inc., 1997).

Expatriate Assignments

Contributed by Robert E. Ledman, Morehouse College

This exercise focuses on issues related to workers facing international assignments. It illustrates that those workers face a multitude of issues. It further demonstrates that managers who want employees to realize the maximum benefits of international assignments should be aware of, and prepared to deal with, those issues. Some of the topics that are easily addressed with this exercise include the need for culture and language training for the employees and their families and the impact that international assignments may have on an employee's family and how that may affect an employee's willingness to seek such assignments.

Procedure

1. Form into "families" of four or five. Since many students today have only one parent at home, it is helpful if some groups do not have students to fill both parental roles in the exercise. Each student is assigned to play a family member and given a description of that person.

2. Enter into a 20-minute discussion to explore how a proposed overseas assignment will affect the family members. Your goal is to try to reach a decision about whether the assignment should be taken. You must also decide whether the entire family or only the family member being offered the assignment will relocate. The assignment is for a minimum of two years, with possible annual extensions resulting in a total of four years, and your family, or the member offered the assignment, will be provided, at company expense, one trip back to the states each year for a maximum period of 15 days. The member offered the assignment will not receive any additional housing or cost-of-living supplements described in the role assignment if he or she chooses to go overseas alone and can expect his or her living expenses to exceed substantially the living allowance being provided by the company. In your discussion, address the following questions:

   1. What are the most important concerns your family has about relocating to a foreign country?
   2. What information should you seek about the proposed host country to be able to make a more informed decision?

Source: Robert E. Ledman, Gannon University. Presented in the Experiential Exercise Track of the 1996 ABSEL Conference and published in the *Proceedings* of that conference.

3. What can the member offered the assignment do to make the transition easier if he or she goes overseas alone? If the whole family relocates?
4. What should the member offered the assignment do to ensure that this proposed assignment will not create unnecessary stress for him or her and the rest of the family?
5. What lessons for managers of expatriate assignees are presented by the situation in this exercise?

Try to reach some "family" consensus. If a consensus is not possible, however, resolve any differences in the manner you think the family in the role descriptions would ultimately resolve any differences.

3. Share your answers with the rest of the class. Explain the rationale for your answers and answer questions from the remainder of the class.
4. (*Optional*) After each group has reported on a given question, the instructor may query the class about how their answers are consistent, or inconsistent, with common practices of managers as described in the available literature.

Descriptions of Family Members
Person Being Offered Overseas Assignment

This person is a middle- to upper-level executive who is on a fast track to senior management. He or she has been offered the opportunity to manage an overseas operation, with the assurance of a promotion to a vice presidency upon return to the states. The company will pay all relocation expenses, including selling costs for the family home and the costs associated with finding a new home upon return. The employer will also provide language training for the employee and cultural awareness training for the entire family. The employee will receive a living allowance equal to 20 percent of his or her salary. This should be adequate to provide the family a comparable standard of living to that which is possible on the employee's current salary.

Spouse of the Person Offered an Overseas Assignment (Optional)

This person is also a professional with highly transferable skills and experience for the domestic market. It is unknown how easily he or she may be able to find employment in the foreign country. This person's income, though less than his or her spouse's, is necessary if the couple is to continue paying for their child's college tuition and to prepare for the next child to enter college in two years. This person has spent 15 years developing a career, including completing a degree at night.

Oldest Child

This child is a second-semester junior in college and is on track to graduate in 16 months. Transferring at this time would probably mean adding at least one semester to complete the degree. He or she has been dating the same person for over a year; they have talked about getting married immediately after graduation, although they are not yet formally engaged.

Middle Child

This child is a junior in high school. He or she has already begun visiting college campuses in preparation for applying in the fall. This child is involved in a number of school activities; he or she is a photographer for the yearbook and plays a varsity sport. This child has a learning disability for which services are being provided by the school system.

Youngest Child

This child is a middle school student, age 13. He or she is actively involved in Scouting and takes piano lessons. This child has a history of medical conditions that have required regular visits to the family physician and specialists. This child has several very close friends who have attended the same school for several years.

EXERCISE 7

Cultural Cues

Contributed by Susan Rawson Zacur and W. Alan Randolph, University of Baltimore

Introduction

In the business context, culture involves shared beliefs and expectations that govern the behavior of people. In this exercise, *foreign culture* refers to a set of beliefs and expectations different from those of the participant's home culture (which has been invented by the participants).

Procedure

1. (10–15 minutes) Divide into two groups, each with color-coded badges. For example, the blue group could receive blue Post-it notes and the yellow group could receive yellow Post-it notes. Print your first name in bold letters on the badge and wear it throughout the exercise.

   Work with your group members to invent your own cultural cues. Think about the kinds of behaviors and words that will signify to all members that they belong together in one culture. For each category provided below, identify and record at least one important attribute for your culture.

Cultural Cues:	Your Culture:
Facial expression:	_____
Eye contact (note: you must have some eye contact in order to observe others):	_____
Handshake:	_____
Body language (note: must be evident while standing):	_____
Key words or phrases:	_____

Source: Adapted by Susan Rawson Zacur and W. Alan Randolph from *Journal of Management Education,* Vol. 17, No. 4 (November 1993), pp. 510–516.

Once you have identified desirable cultural aspects for your group, practice them. It is best to stand with your group and to engage one another in conversations involving two or three people at a time. Your aim in talking with one another is to learn as much as possible about each other—hobbies, interests, where you live, what your family is like, what courses you are taking, and so on, all the while practicing the behaviors and words on the previous page. It is not necessary for participants to answer questions of a personal nature truthfully. Invention is permissible because the conversation is only a means to the end of cultural observation. Your aim at this point is to become comfortable with the indicators of your particular culture. Practice until the indicators are second nature to you.

2. Now assume that you work for a business that has decided to explore the potential for doing business with companies in a different culture. You are to learn as much as possible about another culture. To do so, you will send from one to three representatives from your group on a "business trip" to the other culture. These representatives must, insofar as possible, behave in a manner that is consistent with your culture. At the same time, each representative must endeavor to learn as much as possible about the people in the other culture, while keeping eyes and ears open to cultural attributes that will be useful in future negotiations with foreign businesses. (*Note:* At no time will it be considered ethical behavior for the representative to ask direct questions about the foreign culture's attributes. These must be gleaned from firsthand experience.)

  While your representatives are away, you will receive one or more exchange visitors from the other culture, who will engage in conversation as they attempt to learn more about your organizational culture. You must strictly adhere to the cultural aspects of your own culture while you converse with the visitors.

3. (5–10 minutes) All travelers return to your home cultures. As a group, discuss and record what you have learned about the foreign culture based on the exchange of visitors. This information will serve as the basis for orienting the next representatives who will make a business trip.

4. (5–10 minutes) Select one to three different group members to make another trip to the other culture to check out the assumptions your group has made about the other culture. This "checking out" process will consist of actually practicing the other culture's cues to see whether they work.

5. (5–10 minutes) Once the traveler(s) have returned and reported on findings, as a group prepare to report to the class what you have learned about the other culture.

EXERCISE 8

Prejudice in Our Lives

Contributed by Susan Schor of Pace University and Annie McKee of The Wharton School, University of Pennsylvania, with the assistance of Ariel Fishman of The Wharton School

Procedure

1. As a large class group, generate a list of groups that tend to be targets of prejudice and stereotypes in our culture—such groups can be based on gender, race, ethnicity, sexual orientation, region, religion, and so on. After generating a list, either as a class or in small groups, identify a few common positive and negative stereotypes associated with each group. Also consider relationships or patterns that exist between some of the lists. Discuss the implications for groups that have stereotypes that are valued in organizations versus groups whose stereotypes are viewed negatively in organizations.

2. As an individual, think about the lists you have now generated, and list those groups with which you identify. Write about an experience in which you

were stereotyped as a member of a group. Ask yourself the following questions and write down your thoughts:

1. What group do I identify with?
2. What was the stereotype?
3. What happened? When and where did the incident occur? Who said what to whom?
4. What were my reactions? How did I feel? What did I think? What did I do?
5. What were the consequences? How did the incident affect myself and others?

3. Now, in small groups, discuss your experiences. Briefly describe the incident and focus on how the incident made you feel. Select one incident from the ones shared in your group to role-play for the class. Then, as a class, discuss your reactions to each role play. Identify the prejudice or stereotype portrayed, the feelings the situation evoked, and the consequences that might result from such a situation.

4. Think about the prejudices and stereotypes you hold about other people. Ask yourself, "What groups do I feel prejudice toward? What stereotypes do I hold about members of each of these groups?" How may such a prejudice have developed—did a family member or close friend or television influence you to stereotype a particular group in a certain way?

5. Now try to identify implications of prejudice in the workplace. How do prejudice and stereotypes affect workers, managers, relationships between people, and the organization as a whole? Consider how you might want to change erroneous beliefs as well as how you would encourage other people to change their own erroneous beliefs.

How We View Differences

Contributed by Barbara Walker

Introduction

Clearly, the workplace of the future will be much more diverse than it is today: more women, more people of color, more international representation, more diverse lifestyles and ability profiles, and the like. Managing a diverse workforce and working across a range of differences is quickly becoming a "core competency" for effective managers.

Furthermore, it is also becoming clear that diversity in a work team can significantly enhance the creativity and quality of the team's output. In today's turbulent business environment, utilizing employee diversity will give the manager and the organization a competitive edge in tapping all of the available human resources more effectively. This exercise is an initial step in the examination of how we work with people whom we see as different from us. It is fairly simple, straightforward, and safe, but its implications are profound.

Source: Exercise developed by Barbara Walker, a pioneer on work on valuing differences. Adapted for this volume by Douglas T. Hall. Used by permission of Barbara Walker.

Procedure

1. Read the following:

Imagine that you are traveling in a rental car in a city you have never visited before. You have a one-hour drive on an uncrowded highway before you reach your destination. You decide that you would like to spend the time listening to some of your favorite kind of music on the car radio.

The rental car has four selection buttons available, each with a preset station that plays a different type of music. One plays *country music,* one plays *rock,* one plays *classical,* and one plays *jazz.* Which type of music would you choose to listen to for the next hour as you drive along? (Assume you want to relax and just stick with one station; you don't want to bother switching around between stations.)

2. Form into groups based on the type of music that you have chosen. All who have chosen country will meet in an area designated by the instructor. Those who chose rock will meet in another area, and so on. In your groups, answer the following question. Appoint one member to be the spokesperson to report your answers back to the total group.

Question

For each of the other groups, what words would you use to describe people who like to listen to that type of music?

3. Have each spokesperson report the responses of her or his group to the question in Step 2. Follow with class discussion of these additional questions:
   1. What do you think is the purpose or value of this exercise?
   2. What did you notice about the words used to describe the other groups? Were there any *surprises* in this exercise for you?
   3. Upon what sorts of data do you think these images were based?

4. What term do we normally use to describe these generalized perceptions of another group?
5. What could some of the consequences be?
6. How do the perceptual processes here relate to other kinds of intergroup differences, such as race, gender, culture, ability, ethnicity, health, age, nationality, and so on?
7. What does this exercise suggest about the ease with which intergroup stereotypes form?
8. What might be ways an organization might facilitate the valuing and utilizing of differences between people?

EXERCISE 10

Alligator River Story

The Alligator River Story

There lived a woman named Abigail who was in love with a man named Gregory. Gregory lived on the shore of a river. Abigail lived on the opposite shore of the same river. The river that separated the two lovers was teeming with dangerous alligators. Abigail wanted to cross the river to be with Gregory. Unfortunately, the bridge had been washed out by a heavy flood the previous week. So she went to ask Sinbad, a riverboat captain, to take her across. He said he would be glad to if she would consent to go to bed with him prior to the voyage. She promptly refused and went to a friend named Ivan to explain her plight. Ivan did not want to get involved at all in the situation. Abigail felt her only alternative was to accept Sinbad's terms. Sinbad fulfilled his promise to Abigail and delivered her into the arms of Gregory. When Abigail told Gregory about her amorous escapade in order to cross the river, Gregory cast her aside with disdain. Heartsick and rejected, Abigail turned to Slug with her tail of woe. Slug, feeling compassion for Abigail, sought out Gregory and beat him brutally. Abigail was overjoyed at the sight of Gregory getting his due. As the sun set on the horizon, people heard Abigail laughing at Gregory.

Procedure

1. Read "The Alligator River Story."
2. After reading the story, rank the five characters in the story beginning with the one whom you consider the most offensive and end with the one whom you consider the least objectionable. That is, the character who seems to be the most reprehensible to you should be entered first in the list following the story, then the second most reprehensible, and so on, with the least reprehensible or objectionable being entered fifth. Of course, you will have your own reasons as to why you rank them in the order that you do. Very briefly note these too.
3. Form groups as assigned by your instructor (at least four persons per group with gender mixed).
4. Each group should:
   1. Elect a spokesperson for the group
   2. Compare how the group members have ranked the characters
   3. Examine the reasons used by each of the members for their rankings
   4. Seek consensus on a final group ranking
5. Following your group discussions, you will be asked to share your outcomes and reasons for agreement or nonagreement. A general class discussion will then be held.

Source: From Sidney B. Simon, Howard Kirschenbaum, and Leland Howe, *Values Clarification, The Handbook,* rev. ed., © 1991, Values Press, P.O. Box 450, Sunderland, MA. 01375.

Teamwork and Motivation

Contributed by Dr. Barbara McCain, Oklahoma City University

Procedure

1. Read this situation.

You are the *owner* of a small manufacturing corporation. Your company manufactures widgets—a commodity. Your widget is a clone of nationally known widgets. Your widget, "WooWoo," is less expensive and more readily available than the nationally known brand. Presently, the sales are high. However, there are many rejects, which increases your cost and delays the delivery. You have 50 employees in the following departments: sales, assembly, technology, and administration.

2. In groups, discuss methods to motivate all of the employees in the organization—rank them in terms of preference.

3. Design an organization motivation plan that encourages high job satisfaction, low turnover, high productivity, and high-quality work.

4. Is there anything special you can do about the minimum-wage service worker? How do you motivate this individual? On what motivation theory do you base your decision?

5. Report to the class your motivation plan. Record your ideas on the board and allow all groups to build on the first plan. Discuss additions and corrections as the discussion proceeds.

Worksheet

Individual Worker	Team Member
Talks	
Me oriented	
Department focused	
Competitive	
Logical	
Written messages	
Image	
Secrecy	
Short-term sighted	
Immediate results	
Critical	
Tenure	

Directions: Fill in the right-hand column with descriptive terms. These terms should suggest a change in behavior from individual work to teamwork.

The Downside of Punishment

Contributed by Dr. Barbara McCain, Oklahoma City University

Procedure

There are numerous problems associated with using punishment or discipline to change behavior. Punishment creates negative effects in the workplace. To better understand this, work in your group to give an example of each of the following situations:

1. Punishment may not be applied to the person whose behavior you want to change.

2. Punishment applied over time may suppress the occurrence of socially desirable behaviors.

3. Punishment creates a dislike of the person who is implementing the punishment.

4. Punishment results in undesirable emotions such as anxiety and aggressiveness.

5. Punishment increases the desire to avoid punishment.

6. Punishing one behavior does not guarantee that the desired behavior will occur.

7. Punishment follow-up requires allocation of additional resources.

8. Punishment may create a communication barrier and inhibit the flow of information.

Source: Adapted from class notes: Dr. Larry Michaelson, Oklahoma University.

Tinker Toys

Contributed by Bonnie McNeely, Murray State University

Materials Needed
Tinker Toy sets.

Source: Adapted from Bonnie McNeely, "Using the Tinker Toy Exercise to Teach the Four Functions of Management," *Journal of Management Education,* Vol. 18, No. 4 (November 1994), pp. 468–472.

Procedure
1. Form groups as assigned by the instructor. The mission of each group or temporary organization is to build the tallest possible Tinker Toy tower. Each group should determine worker roles: at least four students will be builders, some will be consultants who offer suggestions, and the remaining students

will be observers who remain silent and complete the observation sheet provided below.

2. Rules for the exercise:
   1. Fifteen minutes allowed to plan the tower, but *only 60 seconds* to build.
   2. No more than two Tinker Toy pieces can be put together during the planning.
   3. All pieces must be put back in the box before the competition begins.
   4. Completed tower must stand alone.

Observation Sheet

1. What planning activities were observed?

   Did the group members adhere to the rules?

2. What organizing activities were observed?

   Was the task divided into subtasks? Division of labor?

3. Was the group motivated to succeed? Why or why not?

4. Were any control techniques observed?

   Was a timekeeper assigned?

   Were backup plans discussed?

5. Did a clear leader emerge from the group?

   What behaviors indicated that this person was the leader?

   How did the leader establish credibility with the group?

6. Did any conflicts within the group appear?

   Was there a power struggle for the leadership position?

EXERCISE 14

Job Design Preferences

Procedure

1. Use the left column to rank the following job characteristics in the order most important *to you* (1—highest to 10—lowest). Then use the right column to rank them in the order you think they are most important *to others*.

   ____ Variety of tasks ____
   ____ Performance feedback ____
   ____ Autonomy/freedom in work ____
   ____ Working on a team ____
   ____ Having responsibility ____
   ____ Making friends on the job ____

_____ Doing all of a job, not part _____
_____ Importance of job to others _____
_____ Having resources to do well _____
_____ Flexible work schedule _____

2. Form workgroups as assigned by your instructor. Share your rankings with other group members. Discuss where you have different individual preferences and where your impressions differ from the preferences of others. Are there any major patterns in your group—for either the "personal" or the "other" rankings? Develop group consensus rankings for each column. Designate a spokesperson to share the group rankings and results of any discussion with the rest of the class.

·· EXERCISE 15 ·

My Fantasy Job

Contributed by Lady Hanson, California State Polytechnic University, Pomona

Procedure

1. Think about a possible job that represents what you consider to be your ideal or "fantasy" job. For discussion purposes, try to envision it as a job you would hold within a year of finishing your current studies. Write down a brief description of that job in the space below. Start the description with the following words—*My fantasy job would be* . . .

2. Review the description of the Hackman/Oldham model of Job Characteristics Theory offered in the textbook. Note in particular the descriptions of the core characteristics. Consider how each of them could be maximized in your fantasy job. Indicate in the spaces that follow how specific parts of your fantasy job will fit into or relate to each of the core characteristics.

   1. Skill variety: _____

   2. Task identity: _____

   3. Task significance: _____

   4. Autonomy: _____

   5. Job feedback: _____

3. Form into groups as assigned by your instructor. In the group have each person share his or her fantasy job and the descriptions of its core characteristics. Select one person from your group to tell the class as a whole about her or his fantasy job. Be prepared to participate in a general discussion regarding the core characteristics and how they may or may not relate to job performance and job satisfaction. Consider also the likelihood that the fantasy jobs of class members are really attainable—in other words: Can "fantasy" become fact?

Motivation by Job Enrichment

Contributed by Diana Page, University of West Florida

Procedure

1. Form groups of five to seven members. Each group is assigned one of the following categories:
   1. Bank teller
   2. Retail sales clerk
   3. Manager, fast-food service (e.g., McDonald's)
   4. Wait person
   5. Receptionist
   6. Restaurant manager
   7. Clerical worker (or bookkeeper)
   8. Janitor
2. As a group, develop a short description of job duties for the job your group has been assigned. The list should contain approximately four to six items.
3. Next, using job characteristics theory, enrich the job using the specific elements described in the theory. Develop a new list of job duties that incorporate any or all of the core job characteristics suggested by Richard Hackman and Greg Oldham, such as skill variety, task identity, and so on. Indicate for each of the new job duties which job characteristic(s) was/were used.
4. One member of each group should act as the spokesperson and will present the group's ideas to the class. Specifically describe one or two of the old job tasks. Describe the modified job tasks. Finally, relate the new job tasks the group has developed to specific job core characteristics such as skill variety, skill identity, and so on.
5. The group should also be prepared to discuss these and other follow-up questions:
   1. How would a manager go about enlarging but not enriching this job?
   2. Why was this job easy or hard?
   3. What are the possible constraints on actually accomplishing this enrichment in the workplace?
   4. What possible reasons are there that a worker would *not* like to have this newly enriched job?

Annual Pay Raises

Procedure

1. Read the following job descriptions and decide on a percentage pay increase for each of the eight employees.
2. Make salary increase recommendations for each of the eight managers that you supervise. There are no formal company restrictions on the size of raises you give, but the total for everyone should not exceed the $10,900 (a 4 percent increase in the salary pool) that has been budgeted for this purpose. You have a variety of information on which to base the decisions, including a "productivity index" (PI), which

Industrial Engineering computes as a quantitative measure of operating efficiency for each manager's work unit. This index ranges from a high of 10 to a low of 1. Indicate the percentage increase *you* would give each manager in the blank space next to each manager's name. Be prepared to explain why.

_____ *A. Alvarez*   Alvarez is new this year and has a tough workgroup whose task is dirty and difficult. This is a hard position to fill, but you don't feel Alvarez is particularly good. The word around is that the other managers agree with you. PI = 3. Salary = $33,000.

_____ *B. J. Cook*   Cook is single and a "swinger" who enjoys leisure time. Everyone laughs at the problems B.J. has getting the work out, and you feel it certainly is lacking. Cook has been in the job two years. PI = 3. Salary = $34,500.

_____ *Z. Davis*   In the position three years, Davis is one of your best people, even though some of the other managers don't agree. With a spouse who is independently wealthy, Davis doesn't need money but likes to work. PI = 7. Salary = $36,600.

_____ *M. Frame*   Frame has personal problems and is hurting financially. Others gossip about Frame's performance, but you are quite satisfied with this second-year employee. PI = 7. Salary = $34,700.

_____ *C. M. Liu*   Liu is just finishing a fine first year in a tough job. Highly respected by the others, Liu has a job offer in another company at a 15 percent increase in salary. You are impressed, and the word is that the money is important. PI = 9. Salary = $34,000.

_____ *B. Ratin*   Ratin is a first-year manager whom you and the others think is doing a good job. This is a bit surprising since Ratin turned out to be a "free spirit" who doesn't seem to care much about money or status. PI = 9. Salary = $33,800.

_____ *H. Smith*   Smith is a first-year manager recently divorced and with two children to support as a single parent. The others like Smith a lot, but your evaluation is not very high. Smith could certainly use extra money. PI = 5. Salary = $33,000.

_____ *G. White*   White is a big spender who always has the latest clothes and a new car. In the first year on what you would call an easy job, White doesn't seem to be doing very well. For some reason, though, the others talk about White as the "cream of the new crop." PI = 5. Salary = $33,000.

3. Convene in a group of four to seven persons and share your raise decisions.
4. As a group, decide on a new set of raises and be prepared to report them to the rest of the class. Make sure that the group spokesperson can provide the rationale for each person's raise.
5. The instructor will call on each group to report its raise decisions. After discussion, an "expert's" decision will be given.

•• EXERCISE 18 ••

Serving on the Boundary

Contributed by Joseph A. Raelin, Boston College

Procedure

The objective of this exercise is to experience what it is like being on the boundary of your team or organization and to experience the boundary person's divided loyalties.

1. As a full class, decide on a stake you are willing to wager on this exercise. Perhaps it will be 5¢ or 10¢ per person or even more.

2. Form into teams. Select or elect one member from your team to be an expert. The expert will be the person most competent in the field of international geography.
3. The experts will then form into a team of their own.
4. The teams, including the expert team, are going to be given a straightforward question to work on. Whichever team comes closest to deriving the correct answer will win the pool from the stakes already collected. The question is any one of the following as assigned by the instructor: (a) What is the airline distance between Beijing and Moscow (in miles)? (b) What is the highest point in Texas (in feet)? (c) What was the number of American battle deaths in the Revolutionary War?
5. Each team should now work on the question, including the expert team. However, after all the teams come up with a verdict, the experts will be allowed to return to their "home" team to inform the team of the expert team's deliberations.
6. The expert team members are now asked to reconvene as an expert team. They should determine their final answer to the question. Then, they are to face a decision. The instructor will announce that for a period of up to two minutes, any expert may either return to their home team (to sink or swim with the answer of the home team) or remain with the expert team. As long as two members remain in the expert team, it will be considered a group and may vie for the pool. Home teams, during the two-minute decision period, can do whatever they would like to do—within bounds of normal decorum—to try to persuade their expert member to return.
7. After the two minutes are up, teams will hand in their verdicts to the question, and the team with the closest answer (up or down) will be awarded the pool.
8. Class members should be prepared to discuss the following questions:
   1. What did it feel like to be a boundary person (the expert)?
   2. What could the teams have done to corral any of the boundary persons who chose not to return home?

EXERCISE 19

Eggsperiential Exercise

Contributed by Dr. Barbara McCain, Oklahoma City University

Materials Needed

1 raw egg per group

6 plastic straws per group

1 yard of plastic tape

1 large plastic jar

Procedure

1. Form into equal groups of five to seven people.
2. The task is to drop an egg from the chair onto the plastic without breaking the egg. Groups can evaluate the materials and plan their task for 10 minutes. During this period the materials may not be handled.
3. Groups have 10 minutes for construction.
4. One group member will drop the egg while standing on top of a chair in front of the class. One by one a representative from each group will drop their eggs.
5. Optional: Each group will name the egg.

6. Each group discusses their individual/group behaviors during this activity. Optional: This analysis may be summarized in written form. The following questions may be utilized in the analysis:
   1. What kind of group is it? Explain.
   2. Was the group cohesive? Explain.
   3. How did the cohesiveness relate to performance? Explain.
   4. Was there evidence of groupthink? Explain.
   5. Were group norms established? Explain.
   6. Was there evidence of conflict? Explain.
   7. Was there any evidence of social loafing? Explain.

Scavenger Hunt—Team Building

Contributed by Michael R. Manning and Paula J. Schmidt, New Mexico State University

Introduction

Think about what it means to be a part of a team—a successful team. What makes one team more successful than another? What does each team member need to do in order for their team to be successful? What are the characteristics of an effective team?

Procedure

1. Form teams as assigned by your instructor. Locate the items on the list below while following these important rules:
   1. Your team *must stay together at all times*—that is, you cannot go in separate directions.
   2. Your team must return to the classroom in the time allotted by the instructor.

   The team with the most items on the list will be declared the most successful team.

2. Next, reflect on your team's experience. What did each team member do? What was your team's strategy? What made your team effective? Make a list of the most important things your team did to be successful. Nominate a spokesperson to summarize your team's discussion for the class. What items were similar between teams? That is, what helped each team to be effective?

Source: Adapted from Michael R. Manning and Paula J. Schmidt, *Journal of Management Education,* "Building Effective Work Teams: A Quick Exercise Based on a Scavenger Hunt" (Thousand Oaks, CA: Sage Publications, 1995), pp. 392–398. Used by permission. Reference for list of items for scavenger hunt from C. E. Larson and F. M. Lafas, *Team Work: What Must Go Right/What Can Go Wrong* (Newbury Park, CA: Sage Publications, 1989).

Items for Scavenger Hunt

Each item is to be identified and brought back to the classroom.

1. A book with the word "team" in the title.
2. A joke about teams that you share with the class.
3. A blade of grass from the university football field.
4. A souvenir from the state.
5. A picture of a team or group.
6. A newspaper article about a team.
7. A team song to be composed and performed for the class.
8. A leaf from an oak tree.
9. Stationery from the dean's office.
10. A cup of sand.
11. A pine cone.
12. A live reptile. (*Note:* Sometimes a team member has one for a pet or the students are ingenious enough to visit a local pet store.)
13. A definition of group "cohesion" that you share with the class.
14. A set of chopsticks.
15. Three cans of vegetables.
16. A branch of an elm tree.
17. Three unusual items.
18. A ball of cotton.
19. The ear from a prickly pear cactus.
20. A group name.

(*Note:* Items may be substituted as appropriate for your locale.)

Work Team Dynamics

Introduction

Think about your course work team, a work team you are involved in for another course, or any other team suggested by the instructor. Indicate how often each of the following statements accurately reflects your experience in the team. Use this scale:

Source: Adapted from William Dyer, *Team Building,* 2nd ed. (Reading, MA: Addison-Wesley, 1987), pp. 123–125.

___ 1. My ideas get a fair hearing.

___ 2. I am encouraged for innovative ideas and risk taking.

___ 3. Diverse opinions within the team are encouraged.

___ 4. I have all the responsibility I want.

___ 5. There is a lot of favoritism shown in the team.

___ 6. Members trust one another to do their assigned work.

___ 7. The team sets high standards of performance excellence.

___ 8. People share and change jobs a lot in the team.

___ 9. You can make mistakes and learn from them on this team.

___ 10. This team has good operating rules.

Procedure

Form groups as assigned by your instructor. Ideally, this will be the team you have just rated. Have all team members share their ratings, and make one master rating for the team as a whole. Circle the items on which there are the biggest differences of opinion. Discuss those items and try to find out why they exist. In general, the better a team scores on this instrument, the higher its creative potential. If everyone has rated the same team, make a list of the five most important things members can do to improve its operations in the future. Nominate a spokesperson to summarize the team discussion for the class as a whole.

EXERCISE 22

Identifying Team Norms

Procedure

1. Choose an organization you know quite a bit about.
2. Complete the questionnaire below, indicating your responses using one of the following:

> 1. Strongly agree or encourage it.
> 2. Agree with it or encourage it.
> 3. Consider it unimportant.
> 4. Disagree with or discourage it.
> 5. Strongly disagree with or discourage it.

If an employee in this organization were to . . . *Most other employees would:*

1. Show genuine concern for the problems that face the organization and make suggestions about solving them . . .   ___
2. Set very high personal standards of performance . . .   ___
3. Try to make the workgroup operate more like a team when dealing with issues or problems . . .   ___
4. Think of going to a supervisor with a problem . . .   ___
5. Evaluate expenditures in terms of the benefits they will provide for the organization . . .   ___

6. Express concern for the well-being of other members of the organization . . . ____
7. Keep a customer or client waiting while looking after matters of personal convenience . . . ____
8. Criticize a fellow employee who is trying to improve things in the work situation . . . ____
9. Actively look for ways to expand his or her knowledge to be able to do a better job . . . ____
10. Be perfectly honest in answering this questionnaire . . . ____

Scoring

A = +2, B = +1, C = 0, D = –1, E = –2

1. Organizational/Personal Pride
   Score ____
2. Performance/Excellence
   Score ____
3. Teamwork/Communication
   Score ____
4. Leadership/Supervision
   Score ____
5. Profitability/Cost-Effectiveness
   Score ____
6. Colleague/Associate Relations
   Score ____
7. Customer/Client Relations
   Score ____
8. Innovativeness/Creativity
   Score ____
9. Training/Development
   Score ____
10. Candor/Openness
   Score ____

EXERCISE 23 ·

Workgroup Culture

Contributed by Conrad N. Jackson, MPC Inc.

Procedure

The bipolar scales on this instrument can be used to evaluate a group's process in a number of useful ways. Use it to measure where you see the group to be at present. To do this, *circle* the number that best represents *how you see the culture of the group*. You can also indicate how you think the group *should* function by using a different symbol, such as a square (**) or a caret (^), to indicate how you saw the group at some time in the past.

1. If you are assessing your own group, have everyone fill in the instrument, summarize the scores, then discuss their bases (what members say and do that has led to these interpretations) and implications. This is often an extremely productive intervention to improve group or team functioning.

2. If you are assessing another group, use the scores as the basis for your feedback. Be sure to provide specific feedback on behavior *you have observed* in addition to the subjective interpretations of your ratings on the scales in this instrument.

3. The instrument can also be used to compare a group's self-assessment with the assessment provided by another group.

1. Trusting	1 : 2 : 3 : 4 : 5	Suspicious
2. Helping	1 : 2 : 3 : 4 : 5	Ignoring, blocking
3. Expressing feelings	1 : 2 : 3 : 4 : 5	Suppressing feelings
4. Risk taking	1 : 2 : 3 : 4 : 5	Cautious
5. Authenticity	1 : 2 : 3 : 4 : 5	Game playing
6. Confronting	1 : 2 : 3 : 4 : 5	Avoiding
7. Open	1 : 2 : 3 : 4 : 5	Hidden, diplomatic

Source: Adapted from Donald D. Bowen et al., *Experiences in Management and Organizational Behavior,* 4th ed. (New York: John Wiley & Sons, Inc., 1997.)

The Hot Seat

Contributed by Barry R. Armandi, SUNY–Old Westbury

Procedure
1. Form into groups as assigned by your instructor.
2. Read the following situation.

A number of years ago, Professor Stevens was asked to attend a departmental meeting at a university. He had been on leave from the department, but a junior faculty member discreetly requested that he attend to protect the rights of the junior faculty. The Chair, or head of the department, was a typical Machiavellian, whose only concerns were self-serving. Professor Stevens had had a number of previous disagreements with the Chair. The heart of the disagreements centered around the Chair's abrupt and domineering style and his poor relations with the junior faculty, many of whom felt mistreated and scared.

The department was a conglomeration of different professorial types. Included in the mix were behavioralists, generalists, computer scientists, and quantitative analysts. The department was embedded in the school of business, which had three other departments. There was much confusion and concern among the faculty, since this was a new organizational design. Many of the faculty were at odds with each other over the direction the school was now taking.

At the meeting, a number of proposals were to be presented that would seriously affect the performance and future of certain junior faculty, particularly those who were behavioral scientists. The Chair, a computer scientist, disliked the behaviorists, who he felt were "always analyzing the motives of people." Professor Stevens, who was a tenured full professor and a behaviorist, had an objective to protect the interests of the junior faculty and to counter the efforts of the Chair.

Including Professor Stevens, there were nine faculty present. The accompanying diagram below shows the seating

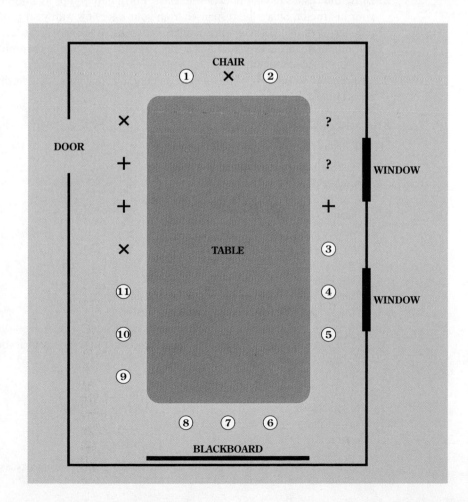

arrangement and the layout of the room. The ×s signify those faculty who were allies of the Chair. The +s are those opposed to the Chair and supportive of Professor Stevens, and the ?s were undecided and could be swayed either way. The circled numbers represent empty seats. Both ?s were behavioralists, and the + next to them was a quantitative analyst. Near the door, the first × was a generalist, the two +s were behavioralists, and the second × was a quantitative analyst. The diagram shows the seating of everyone but Professor Stevens, who was the last one to enter the room. Standing at the door, Professor Stevens

surveyed the room and within 10 seconds knew which seat was the most effective to achieve his objective.

3. Answer the following questions in your group.
   1. Which seat did Professor Stevens select and why?
   2. What is the likely pattern of communication and interaction in this group?
   3. What can be done to get this group to work harmoniously?

EXERCISE 25

Interview a Leader

Contributed by Bonnie McNeely, Murray State University

Procedure

1. Make an appointment to interview a leader. It can be a leader working in a business or nonprofit organization, such as a government agency, school, and so on. Base the interview on the form provided here, but feel free to add your own questions.
2. Bring the results of your interview to class. Form into groups as assigned by your instructor. Share the responses from your interview with your group and compare answers. What issues were similar? Different? Were the stress levels of leaders working in nonprofit organizations as high as those working in for-profit firms? Were you surprised at the number of hours per week worked by leaders?
3. Be prepared to summarize the interviews done by your group as a formal written report if asked to do so by the instructor.

Interview Questionnaire

Student's Name _____ Date _____

1. Position in the organization (title):
2. Number of years in current position:
   Number of years of managerial experience:
3. Number of people directly supervised:
4. Average number of hours worked a week:
5. How did you get into leadership?
6. What is the most rewarding part of being a leader?
7. What is the most difficult part of your job?
8. What would you say are the *keys to success* for leaders?
9. What advice do you have for an aspiring leader?
10. What type of ethical issues have you faced as a leader?
11. If you were to enroll in a leadership seminar, what topics or issues would you want to learn more about?
12. (Student question)

Gender: M _____ F _____ Years of formal education _____
Level of job stress: Very high _____ High _____ Average _____ Low _____
Profit organization _____ Nonprofit organization _____
Additional information/Comments:
_____

Source: Adapted from Bonnie McNeely, "Make Your Principles of Management Class Come Alive," *Journal of Management Education,* Vol. 18, No. 2 (May 1994), pp. 246–249.

Leadership Skills Inventories

Procedure

1. Look over the skills listed below and ask your instructor to clarify those you do not understand.
2. Complete each category by checking either the "Strong" or "Needs Development" category in relation to your own level with each skill.
3. After completing each category, briefly describe a situation in which each of the listed skills has been utilized.
4. Meet in your groups to share and discuss inventories. Prepare a report summarizing major development needs in your group.

Instrument

	Strong	Needs Development	Situation
Communication			
Conflict management			
Delegation			
Ethical behavior			
Listening			
Motivation			
Negotiation			
Performance appraisal and feedback			
Planning and goal setting			
Power and influence			
Presentation and persuasion			
Problem solving and decision making			
Stress management			
Team building			
Time management			

Leadership and Participation in Decision Making

Procedure

1. For the 10 situations described here, decide which of the three styles you would use for that unique situation. Place the letter A, P, or L on the line before each situation's number.

   A—authority; make the decision alone without additional inputs.
   P—consultative; make the decision based on group inputs.
   L—group; allow the group to which you belong to make the decision.

Decision Situations

_____ 1. You have developed a new work procedure that will increase productivity. Your boss likes the idea and wants you to try it within a few weeks. You view your employees as fairly capable and believe that they will be receptive to the change.

_____ 2. The industry of your product has new competition. Your organization's revenues have been dropping. You have been told to lay off three of your ten employees in two weeks. You have been the supervisor for over one year. Normally, your employees are very capable.

_____ 3. Your department has been facing a problem for several months. Many solutions have been tried and have failed. You finally thought of a solution, but you are not sure of the possible consequences of the change required or its acceptance by the highly capable employees.

_____ 4. Flextime has become popular in your organization. Some departments let each employee start and end work whenever they choose. However, because of the cooperative effort of your employees, they must all work the same eight hours. You are not sure of the level of interest in changing the hours. Your employees are a very capable group and like to make decisions.

_____ 5. The technology in your industry is changing faster than the members of your organization can keep up. Top management hired a consultant who has given the recommended decision. You have two weeks to make your decision. Your employees are capable, and they enjoy participating in the decision-making process.

_____ 6. Your boss called you on the telephone to tell you that someone has requested an order for your department's product with a very short delivery date. She asked that you call her back with the decision about taking the order in 15 minutes. Looking over the work schedule, you realize that it will be very difficult to deliver the order on time. Your employees will have to push hard to make it. They are cooperative, capable, and enjoy being involved in decision making.

_____ 7. A change has been handed down from top management. How you implement it is your decision. The change takes effect in one month. It will personally affect everyone in your department. The acceptance of the department members is critical to the success of the change. Your employees are usually not too interested in being involved in making decisions.

_____ 8. You believe that productivity in your department could be increased. You have thought of some ways that may work, but you're not sure of them. Your employees are very experienced; almost all of them have been in the department longer than you have.

_____ 9. Top management has decided to make a change that will affect all of your employees. You know that they will be upset because it will cause them hardship. One or two may even quit. The change goes into effect in 30 days. Your employees are very capable.

_____ 10. A customer has offered you a contract for your product with a quick delivery date. The offer is open for two days. Meeting the contract deadline would require employees to work nights and weekends for six weeks. You cannot require them to work overtime. Filling this profitable contract could help get you the raise you want and feel you deserve. However, if you take the contract and don't deliver on time, it will hurt your chances of getting a big raise. Your employees are very capable.

2. Form groups as assigned by your instructor. Share and compare your choices for each decision situation. Reconcile any differences and be prepared to defend your decision preferences in general class discussion.

My Best Manager: Revisited

Contributed by J. Marcus Maier, Chapman University

Procedure

1. Refer to the list of qualities—or profiles—the class generated earlier in the course for the "Best Manager."
2. Looking first at your Typical Managers profile, suppose you took this list to 100 average people on the street (or at the local mall) and asked them whether ____ (Trait X, quality Y) was "more typical of men or of women in our culture." What do you think *most* of them would say? That ____ (X, Y etc.) is more typical of *women?* or of *men?* or of neither/both?[1] Do this for every trait on your list(s). (5 minutes)
3. Now do the same for the qualities we generated in our Best Manager profile. (5 min.)
4. A straw vote is taken, one quality at a time, to determine the class's overall gender identification of each trait, focusing on the Typical Managers profile (10–15 min.). Then this is repeated for the Best Manager profile (10–15 min.).[2]
5. Discussion. What do you see in the data this group has generated? How might you interpret these results? (15–20 min.)

Source: Based on Maier's 1993 article, "The Gender Prism," *Journal of Management Education,* 17(3), 285–314. 1994 Fritz Roethlisberger Award Recipient for Best Paper (Updated, 1996).

[1] This gets the participants to move outside of their *own* conceptions to their awareness of *societal* definitions of masculinity and femininity.

[2] This is done by a rapid show of hands, looking for a clear majority vote. An "f" (for "feminine") is placed next to those qualities that a clear majority indicate are more typical of women, an "m" (for "masculine") next to those qualities a clear majority indicate would be more typical of men. (This procedure parallels the median-split method used in determining Bem Sex Role Inventory classifications.) If no clear majority emerges (i.e., if the vote is close), the trait or quality is classified as "both" (f/m). The designations "masculine" or "feminine" are used (rather than "men" or "women") to underscore the socially constructed nature of each dimension.

Active Listening

Contributed by Robert Ledman, Morehouse College

Procedure

1. Review active listening skills and behaviors as described in the textbook and in class.
2. Form into groups of three. Each group will have a listener, a talker, and an observer (if the number of students is not evenly divisible by three, two observers are used for one or two groups).
3. The "talkers" should talk about any subject they wish, but only *if* they are being actively listened to. Talkers should stop speaking as soon as they sense active listening has stopped.
4. The "listeners" should use a list of active listening skills and behaviors as their guide, and practice as many of them as possible to be sure the talker is kept

---

Source: Adapted from the presentation entitled "An Experiential Exercise to Teach Active Listening," presented at the Organizational Behavior Teaching Conference, Macomb, IL, 1995.

talking. Listeners should contribute nothing more than "active listening" to the communication.

5. The "observer" should note the behaviors and skills used by the listener and the effects they seemed to have on the communication process.

6. These roles are rotated until each student has played every role.

7. The instructor will lead a discussion of what the observers saw and what happened with the talkers and listeners. The discussion focuses on what behaviors from the posted list have been present, which have been absent, and how the communication has been affected by the listener's actions.

•• EXERCISE 30 ••

Upward Appraisal

Procedure

1. Form workgroups as assigned by your instructor.
2. The instructor will leave the room.
3. Convene in your assigned workgroups for a period of 10 minutes. Create a list of comments, problems, issues, and concerns you would like to have communicated to the instructor in regard to the course experience to date. *Remember,* your interest in the exercise is twofold: (a) to communicate your feelings to the instructor and (b) to learn more about the process of giving and receiving feedback.
4. Select one person from the group to act as spokesperson in communicating the group's feelings to the instructor.
5. The spokespersons should briefly convene to decide on what physical arrangement of chairs, tables, and so forth is most appropriate to conduct the feedback session. The classroom should then be rearranged to fit the desired specifications.
6. While the spokespersons convene, persons in the remaining groups should discuss how they expect the forthcoming communications event to develop. Will it be a good experience for all parties concerned? Be prepared to critically observe the actual communication process.
7. The instructor should be invited to return, and the feedback session will begin. Observers should make notes so that they may make constructive comments at the conclusion of the exercise.
8. Once the feedback session is complete, the instructor will call on the observers for comments, ask the spokespersons for reactions, and open the session to discussion.

•• EXERCISE 31 ••

360° Feedback

Contributed by Timothy J. Serey, Northern Kentucky University

Introduction

The time of performance reviews is often a time of genuine anxiety for many organizational members. On the one hand, it is an important organizational ritual and a key part of the Human Resource function. Organizations usually codify the process and provide a mechanism to appraise performance. On the other hand, it is rare for managers to feel comfortable with this process. Often, they feel discomfort over "playing God." One possible reason for this is that managers rarely receive formal training about how to provide feedback. From the manager's point of view, if done properly, giving feedback is at the very heart of his or her job as "coach" and "teacher." It is an investment in the professional development of another person, rather than the punitive element we so often associate with hearing from "the boss." From the subordinate's perspective, most people want to know where they stand, but this is usually tempered by a fear of "getting it in the neck." In many organizations, it is rare to receive straight, non-sugar-coated feedback about where you stand.

Procedure

1. Review the section of the book dealing with feedback before you come to class. It is also helpful if individuals make notes about their perceptions and feelings about the course *before* they come to class.
2. Groups of students should discuss their experiences, both positive and negative, in this class. Each group should determine the dimensions of evaluating the class itself *and* the instructor. For example, students might select criteria that include the practicality of the course, the way the material is structured and presented (e.g., lecture or exercises), and the instructor's style (e.g., enthusiasm, fairness).
3. Groups select a member to represent them in a subgroup that next provides feedback to the instructor before the entire class.
4. The student audience then provides the subgroup with feedback about their effectiveness in this exercise. That is, the larger class provides feedback to the subgroup about the extent to which students actually put the principles of effective feedback into practice (e.g., descriptive, not evaluative; specific, not general).

Source: Adapted from Timothy J. Serey, *Journal of Management Education,* Vol. 17, No. 2 (May 1993). © 1993 by Sage Publications, Inc. Reprinted by permission of Sage Publications.

EXERCISE 32

Role Analysis Negotiation

Contributed by Paul Lyons, Frostburg State University

Introduction

A role is the set of various behaviors people expect from a person (or group) in a particular position. These role expectations occur in all types of organizations, such as one's place of work, school, family, clubs, and the like. Role ambiguity takes place when a person is confused about the expectations of the role. And sometimes, a role will have expectations that are contradictory—for example, being loyal to the company when the company is breaking the law.

The Role Analysis Technique, or RAT, is a method for improving the effectiveness of a team or group. RAT helps to clarify role expectations, and all organization members have responsibilities that translate to expectations. Determination of role requirements, by consensus—involving all concerned—will ultimately result in more effective and mutually satisfactory behavior. Participation and collaboration in the definition and

Source: Adapted from Paul Lyons, "Developing Expectations with the Role Analysis Technique," *Journal of Management Education.* Vol. 17, No. 3 (August 1993), pp. 386–389. © Sage Publications.

analysis of roles by group members should result in clarification regarding who is to do what as well as increase the level of commitment to the decisions made.

Procedure

Working alone, carefully read the course syllabus that your instructor has given you. Make a note of any questions you have about anything for which you need clarification or understanding. Pay particular attention to the performance requirements of the course. Make a list of any questions you have regarding what, specifically, is expected of you in order for you to be successful in the course. You will be sharing this information with others in small groups.

EXERCISE 33

Lost at Sea

Introduction

Consider this situation. You are adrift on a private yacht in the South Pacific when a fire of unknown origin destroys the yacht and most of its contents. You and a small group of survivors are now in a large raft with oars. Your location is unclear, but you estimate being about 1,000 miles south–southwest of the nearest land. One person has just found in her pockets five $1 bills and a packet of matches. Everyone else's pockets are empty. The following items are available to you on the raft.

	A	B	C
Sextant	___	___	
Shaving mirror	___	___	
5 gallons of water	___	___	
Mosquito netting	___	___	
1 survival meal	___	___	
Maps of Pacific Ocean	___	___	
Floatable seat cushion	___	___	
2 gallons oil-gas mix	___	___	
Small transistor radio	___	___	
Shark repellent	___	___	
20 square feet black plastic	___	___	
1 quart of 20-proof rum	___	___	
15 feet of nylon rope	___	___	
24 chocolate bars	___	___	
Fishing kit	___	___	

Source: Adapted from "Lost at Sea: A Consensus-Seeking Task," in *The 1975 Handbook for Group Facilitators.* Used with permission of University Associates, Inc.

Procedure

1. *Working alone,* rank in Column A the 15 items in order of their importance to your survival ("1" is most important and "15" is least important).
2. *Working in an assigned group,* arrive at a "team" ranking of the 15 items and record this ranking in Column B. Appoint one person as group spokesperson to report your group rankings to the class.
3. *Do not write in Column C* until further instructions are provided by your instructor.

●●●●●●● **EXERCISE 34** ●●

Entering the Unknown

Contributed by Michael R. Manning, New Mexico State University; Conrad N. Jackson, MPC Inc., Huntsville, Alabama; and Paula S. Weber, New Mexico Highlands University

Procedure

1. Form into groups of four or five members. In each group spend a few minutes reflecting on members' typical entry behaviors in new situations and their behaviors when they are in comfortable settings.
2. According to the instructor's directions, students count off to form new groups of four or five members each.
3. The new groups spend the next 15–20 minutes getting to know each other. There is no right or wrong way to proceed, but all members should become more aware of their entry behaviors. They should act in ways that can help them realize a goal of achieving comfortable behaviors with their group.
4. Students review what has occurred in the new groups, giving specific attention to the following questions:
   1. What topics did your group discuss (content)? Did these topics involve the "here and now" or were they focused on "there and then"?
   2. What approach did you and your group members take to the task (process)? Did you try to initiate or follow? How? Did you ask questions? Listen? Respond to others? Did you bring up topics?
   3. Were you more concerned with how you came across or with how others came across to you? Did you play it safe? Were you open? Did you share things even though it seemed uncomfortable or risky? How was humor used in your group? Did it add or detract?
   4. How do you feel about the approach you took or the behaviors you exhibited? Was this hard or easy? Did others respond the way you had anticipated? Is there some behavior you would like to do more of, do better, or do less of?
   5. Were your behaviors the ones you had intended (goals)?
5. Responses to these questions are next discussed by the class as a whole. (*Note:* Responses will tend to be mixed within a group, but between groups there should be more similarity.) This discussion helps individuals become aware of and understand their entry behaviors.
6. Optional individuals have identified their entry behaviors; each group can then spend 5–10 minutes discussing members' perceptions of each other:
   1. What behaviors did they like or find particularly useful? What did they dislike?

2. What were your reactions to others? What ways did they intend to come across? Did you see others in the way they had intended to come across?
(Alternatively, if there is concern about the personal nature of this discussion, ask the groups to discuss what they liked/didn't like without referring to specific individuals.)

EXERCISE 35

Vacation Puzzle

Contributed by Barbara G. McCain and Mary Khalili, Oklahoma City University

Procedure

Can you solve this puzzle? Give it a try and then compare your answers with those of classmates. Remember your communicative skills!

Puzzle

Khalili, McCain, Middleton, Porter, and Quintaro teach at Oklahoma City University. Each gets two weeks of vacation a year. Last year, each took his or her first week in the first five months of the year and his or her second week in the last five months. If each professor took each of his or her weeks in a different month from the other professors, in which months did each professor take his or her first and second week?

Here are the facts:

1. McCain took her first week before Khalili, who took *hers* before Porter; for their second week, the order was reversed.
2. The professor who vacationed in March also vacationed in September.
3. Quintaro did not take her first week in March or April.
4. Neither Quintaro nor the professor who took his or her first week in January took his or her second week in August or December.
5. Middleton took her second week before McCain but after Quintaro.

Month	Professor
January	
February	
March	
April	
May	
June	
July	
August	
September	
October	
November	
December	

Source: Adapted to classroom activity by Dr. Mary Khalili.

The Ugli Orange

Introduction

In most work settings, people need other people to do their job, benefit the organization, and forward their career. Getting things done in organizations requires us to work together in cooperation, even though the ultimate objectives of those other people may be different from our own. Your task in the present exercise is learning how to achieve this cooperation more effectively.

Procedure

1. The class will be divided into pairs. One student in each pair will read and prepare the role of Dr. Roland, and one will play the role of Dr. Jones (role descriptions to be distributed by instructor). Students should read their respective role descriptions and prepare to meet with their counterpart (see Steps 2 and 3).
2. At this point the group leader will read a statement. The instructor will indicate that he or she is playing

the role of Mr. Cardoza, who owns the commodity in question. The instructor will tell you
1. How long you have to meet with the other
2. What information the instructor will require at the end of your meeting
After the instructor has given you this information, you may meet with the other firm's representative and determine whether you have issues you can agree to.
3. Following the meetings (negotiations), the spokesperson for each pair will report any agreements reached to the entire class. The observer for any pair will report on negotiation dynamics and the process by which agreement was reached.
4. Questions to consider:
1. Did you reach a solution? If so, what was critical to reaching that agreement?
2. Did you and the other negotiator trust one another? Why or why not?
3. Was there full disclosure by both sides in each group? How much information was shared?
4. How creative and/or complex were the solutions? If solutions were very complex, why do you think this occurred?
5. What was the impact of having an "audience" on your behavior? Did it make the problem harder or easier to solve?

Source: Adapted from Hall et al., *Experiences in Management and Organizational Behavior,* 3rd ed. (New York: John Wiley and Sons, Inc.), 1988. Originally developed by Robert J. House. Adapted by D. T. Hall and R. J. Lewicki, with suggested modifications by H. Kolodny and T. Ruble.

Conflict Dialogues

Contributed by Edward G. Wertheim, Northeastern University

Procedure

1. Think of a conflict situation at work or at school and try to re-create a segment of the dialogue that gets to the heart of the conflict.
2. Write notes on the conflict dialogue using the following format

Introduction

- Background
- My goals and objectives

- My strategy
- Assumptions I am making

Dialogue (re-create part of the dialogue below and try to put what you were really thinking in parentheses).

- *Me:*
- *Other:*
- *Me:*
- *Other, etc.*

3. Share your situation with members of your group. Read the dialogue to them, perhaps asking someone to play the role of "other."
4. Discuss with the group:
   1. The style of conflict resolution you used (confrontation, collaboration, avoidance, etc.)
   2. The triggers to the conflict, that is, what really set you off and why
   3. Whether or not you were effective
   4. Possible ways of handling this differently
5. Choose one dialogue from within the group to share with the class. Be prepared to discuss your analysis and also possible alternative approaches and resolutions for the situation described.

EXERCISE 38

Force-Field Analysis

Procedure

1. Choose a situation in which you have high personal stakes (for example, how to get a better grade in course X; how to get a promotion; how to obtain a position).
2. Using a version of the Sample Force-Field Analysis Form on the next page, apply the technique to your situation.
   1. Describe the situation as it now exists.
   2. Describe the situation as you would like it to be.
   3. Identify those "driving forces"—the factors that are presently helping to move things in the desired direction.
   4. Identify those "restraining forces"—the factors that are presently holding things back from moving in the desired direction.
3. Try to be as specific as possible in terms of the above in relation to your situation. You should attempt to be exhaustive in your listing of these forces. List them all!
4. Now go back and classify the strength of each force as weak, medium, or strong. Do this for both the driving and the restraining forces.
5. At this point you should rank the forces regarding their ability to influence or control the situation.
6. In small groups share your analyses. Discuss the usefulness and drawbacks to using this method for personal situations and its application to organizations.
7. Be prepared to share the results of your group's discussion with the rest of the class.

Sample Force-Field Analysis Form

Current Situation:	Situation as You Would Like It to Be:
Driving Forces:	**Restraining Forces:**

Organizations Alive!

Contributed by Bonnie L. McNeely, Murray State University

Procedure

1. Find a copy of the following items from actual organizations. These items can be obtained from the company where you now work, a parent's workplace, or the university. Universities have mission statements, codes of conduct for students and faculty, organizational charts, job descriptions, performance appraisal forms, and control devices. Some student organizations also have these documents. All the items do not have to come from the same organization. *Bring these items to class.*

   1. Mission statement
   2. Code of ethics
   3. Organizational chart
   4. Job description
   5. Performance appraisal form
   6. Control device

2. Form groups in class as assigned by your instructor. Share your items with the group, as well as what you learned while collecting these items. For example, did you find that some firms have a mission, but it is not written down? Did you find that job descriptions existed, but they were not really used or had not been updated in years?

Source: Adapted from Bonnie L. McNeely, "Make Your Principles of Management Class Come Alive," *Journal of Management Education,* Vol. 18, No. 2 (May 1994), pp. 246–249.

EXERCISE 40

Fast-Food Technology

Contributed by D. T. Hall, Boston University, and F. S. Hall, University of New Hampshire

Introduction

A critical first step in improving or changing any organization is *diagnosing* or analyzing its present functioning.

Many change and organization development efforts fall short of their objectives because this important step was not taken or was conducted superficially. To illustrate this, imagine how you would feel if you went to your doctor complaining of stomach pains and he recommended surgery without conducting any tests, without obtaining any further information, and without a careful physical examination. You would probably switch doctors! Yet managers often attempt major changes with correspondingly little diagnostic work in advance. (It could be said that they undertake vast projects with half-vast ideas.)

In this exercise, you will be asked to conduct a group diagnosis of two different organizations in the fast-food business. The exercise will provide an opportunity to integrate much of the knowledge you have gained in other exercises and in studying other topics. Your task will be to describe the organizations as carefully as you can in terms of several key organizational concepts. Although the organizations are probably very familiar to you, try to step back and look at them as though you were seeing them for the first time.

Procedure

1. In groups of four or six people, your assignment is described below.

One experience most people in this country have shared is that of dining in the hamburger establishment known as McDonald's. In fact, someone has claimed that twenty-fifth-century archeologists may dig into the ruins of our present civilization and conclude that twentieth-century religion was devoted to the worship of golden arches.

Your group, Fastalk Consultants, is known as the shrewdest, most insightful, and most overpaid management consulting firm in the country. You have been hired by the president of McDonald's to make recommendations for improving the motivation and performance of personnel in their franchise operations. Let us assume that the key job activities in franchise operations are food preparation, order-taking and dealing with customers, and routine cleanup operations.

Recently the president of McDonald's has come to suspect that his company's competitors—such as Burger King, Wendy's, Jack-in-the-Box, Dunkin' Donuts, various pizza establishments, and others—are making heavy inroads into McDonald's market. He has also hired a market research firm to investigate and compare the relative merits of the sandwiches, french fries, and drinks served in McDonald's and the competitors, and has asked the market research firm to assess the advertising campaigns of the two organizations. Hence, you will not need to be concerned with marketing issues, except as they may have an impact on employee behavior. The president wants *you* to look into the *organization* of the franchises to determine the strengths and weaknesses of each. Select a competitor that gives McDonald's a good "run for its money" in your area.

The president has established an unusual contract with you. *He wants you to make your recommendations based upon your observations as a customer.* He does not want you to do a complete diagnosis with interviews, surveys, or behind-the-scenes observations. He wants your report in two parts. Remember, the president wants concrete, specific, and practical recommendations. Avoid vague generalizations such as "improve communications" or "increase trust." Say very clearly *how* management can improve organizational performance. Substantiate your recommendations by reference to one or more theories of motivation, leadership, small groups, or job design.

Part I

Given his organization's goals of profitability, sales volume, fast and courteous service, and cleanliness, the president of McDonald's wants an analysis that will *compare and contrast McDonald's and the competitor* in terms of the following concepts:
- Organizational goals
- Organizational structure
- Technology
- Environment
- Employee motivation
- Communication
- Leadership style
- Policies/procedures/rules/standards
- Job design
- Organizational climate

Part II

Given the corporate goals listed under Part I, what specific actions might McDonald's management and franchise owners take in the following areas to achieve these goals (profitability, sales volume, fast and courteous service, and cleanliness)?
- Job design and workflow
- Organizational structure (at the individual restaurant level)
- Employee incentives
- Leadership
- Employee selection

How do McDonald's and the competition differ in these aspects? Which company has the best approach?

2. Complete the assignment by going as a group to one McDonald's and one competitor's restaurant. If possible, have a meal in each place. To get a more valid comparison, visit a McDonald's and a competitor located in the same area. After observing each restaurant, meet with your group and prepare your 10-minute report to the executive committee.
3. In class, each group will present its report to the rest of the class, who will act as the executive committee. The group leader will appoint a timekeeper to be sure

that each group sticks to its 10-minute time limit. Possible discussion questions include:

1. What similarities are there between the two organizations?
2. What differences are there between the organizations?
3. Do you have any "hunches" about the reasons for the particular organizational characteristics you found? For example, can you try to explain why one organization might have a particular type of structure? Incentive system? Climate?
4. Can you try to explain one set of characteristics in terms of some other characteristics you found? For example, do the goals account for structure? Does the environment explain the structure?

EXERCISE 41

Alien Invasion

Procedure

This is an exercise in organizational culture. You will be assigned to a team (if you are not already in one) and instructed to visit an organization by your instructor.

1. Visit the assigned site as a team working under conditions set forth in the "situation" below.
2. Take detailed notes on the cultural forms that you observe.
3. Prepare a presentation for the class that describes these forms and draw any inferences you can about the nature of the culture of the organization—its ideologies, values, and norms of behavior.
4. Be sure to explain the basis of your inferences in terms of the cultural forms observed.

You will have 20 minutes to report your findings, so plan your presentation carefully. Use visual aids to help your audience understand what you have found.

Situation

You are Martians who have just arrived on Earth in the first spaceship from your planet. Your superiors have ordered you to learn as much about Earthlings and the way they behave as you can without doing anything to make them aware that you are Martians. It is vital for the future plans of your superiors that you do nothing to disturb the Earthlings. Unfortunately, Martians communicate by emitting electromagnetic waves and are incapable of speech, so you cannot talk to the natives. Even if you did, it is reported by the usually reliable Bureau of Interplanetary Intelligence that Earthlings may become cannibalistic if annoyed. However, the crash course in Earth languages taught by the bureau has enabled you to read the language.

Remember, these instructions limit your data collection to observation and request that you *not* talk to the "natives." There are two reasons for this instruction. First, your objective is to learn what the organization does when it is simply going about its normal business and not responding to a group of students asking questions. Second, you are likely to be surprised at how much you can learn by simply observing if you put your mind to it. Many skilled managers employ this ability in sensing what is going on as they walk through their plant or office area.

Since you cannot talk to people, some of the cultural forms (legends, sagas, etc.) will be difficult to spot unless you are able to pick up copies of the organization's promotional literature (brochures, company reports, advertisements) during your visit. Do not be discouraged, because the visible forms such as artifacts, setting, symbols, and (sometimes) rituals can convey a great deal about the culture. Just keep your eyes, ears, and antennae open!

Source: Adapted from Donald D. Bowen et al., *Experiences in Management and Organizational Behavior,* 4th ed. (New York: John Wiley & Sons, Inc., 1997).

Power Circles

Contributed by Marian C. Schultz, University of West Florida

This exercise is designed to examine power and influence in the classroom setting. Specifically, it allows you to identify the combination of power bases used by your instructor in accomplishing his or her objectives for the course.

Procedure

1. Recall that the instructor's power includes the following major bases: (a) the authority that comes from the instructor's position (position power), (b) the knowledge, skill, and expertise of the instructor in the subject area (expert power), and (c) the regard in which you personally hold the instructor (referent power).

2. Indicate the configuration of power that is most evident in the way the instructor behaves in the course overall and according to the following "power circle." This circle can be filled in to represent the relative emphasis on the three power bases (e.g., 60 percent position, 30 percent expert, and 10 percent referent). Use the grid at the right to draw/fill in the circle to show the profile of instructor's power. The instructor will also complete a self-perceived power circle profile.

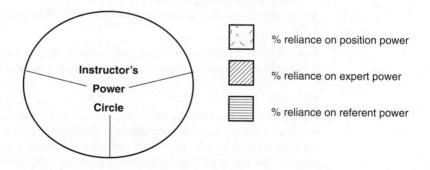

3. Consider also some possible special situations in which the instructor would have to use his or her power in the classroom context. Draw one power circle for each of the following situations, showing for each the power profile most likely to be used by the instructor to accomplish his or her goal.
   ○ Instructor wants to change the format of the final examination.
   ○ Instructor wants to add an additional group assignment to course requirements.
   ○ Instructor wants to have students attend a special two-hour guest lecture on a Saturday morning.
   ○ Instructor wants students to come to class better prepared for discussions of assigned material.
   ○ The instructor will also complete a self-perceived power circle profile for each situation.

4. Share your power circles with those developed by members of your assigned group. Discuss the profiles and the reasons behind them in the group. Appoint one group member as spokesperson to share results in general class discussion. Discuss with the group the best way to communicate this feedback effectively to the instructor in the presence of all class members, and help prepare the spokesperson for the feedback session.

5. Have the instructor share his or her power profiles with the class. Ask the instructor to comment on any differences between the self-perceptions and the views of the class. Comment as a class on the potential significance to leaders and managers of differences in the way they perceive themselves and the ways they are perceived by others.

6. Discuss with the instructor and class how people may tend to favor one or more of the power bases (i.e., to develop a somewhat predictable power circle profile). Discuss as well how effective leaders and managers need to use power contingently, and modify their use of different power bases and power circle profiles to best fit the needs of specific influence situations.

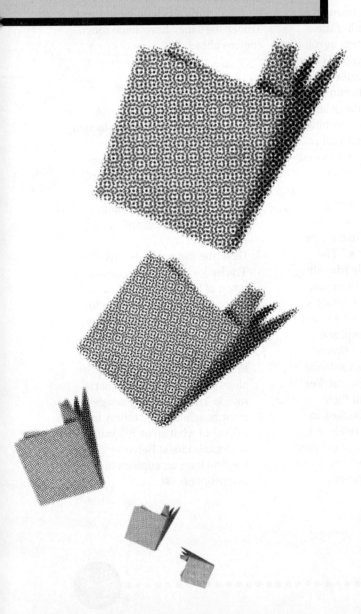

CASES FOR CRITICAL THINKING

While vacationing in the Caribbean, founder "Trader" Joe Coulombe discovered a way to differentiate his 7-Eleven–style corner stores from those of his competitors. Joe observed that consumers are more likely to try new things while on vacation. With a nautical theme and cheerful guides sporting Hawaiian shirts, Joe transformed his stores into oases of value by replacing humdrum sundries with exotic, one-of-a-kind foods priced persuasively below any reasonable competitor.[1]

For over fifty years, Trader Joe's has competed with such giants as Whole Foods and Dean & DeLuca. So what is its recipe for success? The company applies its pursuit of value to every facet of its operations. Buyers travel all over the world in search of great tasting foods and beverages. By focusing on natural ingredients, inspiring flavors, and buying direct from the producer whenever possible, Trader Joe's is able to keep costs down. The chain prides itself on its thriftiness and cost-saving measures, proclaiming, "We run a pretty lean ship," "Every penny we save is a penny you save," and "Our CEO doesn't even have a secretary."[2]

"When you look at food retailers," says Richard George, professor of food marketing at St. Joseph's University, "there is the low end, the big middle, and then there is the cool edge—that's Trader Joe's."[3] But how does Trader Joe's compare with other stores with an edge, such as Whole Foods? Both obtain products locally and from all over the world. Each values employees and strives to offer the highest quality. However, there's no mistaking that Trader Joe's is cozy and intimate, whereas Whole Foods' spacious stores offer an abundance of choices. By limiting its stock and selling quality products at low prices, Trader Joe's sells twice as much per square foot than other supermarkets.[4] Most retail mega-markets, such as Whole Foods, carry between 25,000 and 45,000 products; Trader Joe's stores only carry around 4,000.[5] But this scarcity benefits both Trader Joe's and its customers. According to Swarthmore professor Barry Schwartz, author of The Paradox of Choice: Why Less Is More, "Giving people too much choice can result in paralysis. . . . [R]esearch shows that the more options you offer, the less likely people are to choose any."[6]

Despite the lighthearted tone suggested by marketing materials and in-store ads, Trader Joe's aggressively courts friendly, customer-oriented employees by writing job descriptions highlighting desired soft skills ("ambitious and adventurous, enjoy smiling and have a strong sense of values") as much as actual retail experience.[7]

Trader Joe's connects with its customers because of the culture of product knowledge and customer involvement that its management cultivates among store employees. Trader Joe's considers its responsible, knowledgeable, and friendly "crew" to be critical to its success. Therefore they nurture their employees with a promote-from-within philosophy.

Each employee is encouraged to taste and learn about the products and to engage customers to share what they've experienced. Most shoppers recall instances when helpful crew members took the time to locate or recommend particular items. Says one employee,

"Our customers don't just come here to buy a loaf of bread. They can do that anywhere. They come to try new things. They come to see a friendly face. They come because they know our names and we know theirs. But most of all, they come because we can tell them why not all Alaskan salmon has to come from Alaska or the difference between a Shiraz and a Syrah. The flow of ideas and information at the store level is always invigorating."[8]

When it comes to showing its appreciation for its employees, Trader Joe's puts its money where its mouth is. Those who work for Trader Joe's earn considerably more than their counterparts at other chain grocers. Starting benefits include medical, dental, and vision insurance, company-paid retirement, paid vacation, and a 10% employee discount.[9] Being a privately owned company and a little media shy, Trader Joe's has been keeping some of its financial information confidential these days, but outside estimates suggest that managers make at least $120K per year.[10]

Outlet managers are highly compensated, substantially more than at other retailers, partly because they know the Trader Joe's system inside and out (managers are hired only from within the company). Future leaders enroll in training programs such as Trader Joe's University that foster in them the loyalty necessary to run stores according to both company and customer expectations, teaching managers to imbue their part-timers with the customer-focused attitude shoppers have come to expect.[11]

So it came as a horrifying surprise to many of those shoppers that Trader Joe's had a new nickname: "Traitor Joe's." The usually environmentally friendly company fared the worst of the national chains on Greenpeace's recently released seafood sustainability scorecard. Greenpeace's study, *Carting Away the Oceans: How Grocery Stores are Emptying the Seas,* ranked 20 supermarket companies by assessing their seafood policies and checked to see whether they sold red-listed seafood—those that are overfished and need to be conserved to ensure their survival.[12] Greenpeace surveys found Trader Joe's selling 15 of the 22 red-list seafoods.[12] In response to strong feedback from its customers—and, no doubt, to a Greenpeace-built lookalike *Traitor Joe's* Web site—Trader Joe's was quick to respond. The company promised to only offer sustainable seafood by the end of 2012, remove red-listed seafood from its shelves, and improve its product labeling to provide consumers with more accurate information about seafood products.[13]

Will Trader Joe's keep its promises to consumers, and will it pass the cost of doing so on to them? As buyers are increasingly mindful of how and where each dollar is spent, Trader Joe's may have some tough choices ahead.

Discussion Questions

1. How does Trader Joe's design jobs for increased job satisfaction and higher performance?
2. In what ways does Trader Joe's demonstrate the importance of each responsibility in the management process—planning, organizing, leading, and controlling?
3. Describe the methods that show Trader Joe's knows the importance of human capital.
4. Does Trader Joe's response to the *Traitor Joe's* campaign demonstrate contingency thinking? Why or why not?
5. Research Question: What do the blogs and current news reports say? Is Trader Joe's a management benchmark for others to follow? In what areas relevant to Organizational Behavior does the firm have an edge on the competition? ■

CASE 1B
Management Training Dilemma

Developed by John R. Schermerhorn, Jr., Ohio University

Shane Alexander is the personnel director of the Central State Medical Center. One of her responsibilities is to oversee the hospital's supervisory training programs. Recently Shane attended a professional conference where a special "packaged" training program was advertised for sale. The package includes a set of videotaped lectures by a distinguished management consultant plus a workbook containing readings, exercises, cases, tests, and other instructional aids. The subjects covered in the program include motivation, group dynamics, communication skills, leadership effectiveness, performance appraisal, and the management of planned change.

In the past Shane felt that the hospital had not lived up to its supervisory training goals. One of the reasons for this was the high cost of hiring external consultants to do the actual instruction. This packaged program was designed, presumably, so that persons from within the hospital could act as session coordinators. The structure of the program provided through the videotapes and workbook agenda was supposed to substitute for a consultant's expertise. Because of this, Shane felt that use of the packaged program could substantially improve supervisory training in the hospital.

The cost of the program was $3,500 for an initial purchase of the videotapes plus 50 workbooks. Additional workbooks were then available at $8 per copy. Before purchasing the program, Shane needed the approval of the senior administrative staff.

At the next staff meeting Shane proposed purchasing the training program. She was surprised at the response. The hospital president was noncommittal; the vice-president was openly hostile; and the three associate administrators were varied in their enthusiasm. It was the vice-president's opinion that dominated the discussion. He argued that to invest in such a program on the assumption that it would lead to improved supervisory practices was unwise. "This is especially true in respect to the proposed program," he said. "How could such a package possibly substitute for the training skills of an expert consultant?"

Shane argued her case and was left with the following challenge. The administrators would allow $1,000 to be spent to rent the program with 30 workbooks. It would be up to Shane to demonstrate through a trial program that an eventual purchase would be worthwhile.

There were 160 supervisors in the hospital. The program was designed to be delivered in eight $2\frac{1}{2}$ hour sessions. It was preferred to schedule one session per week, with no more than 15 participants per session.

Shane knew that she would have to present very strong evidence to gain administrative support for the continued use of the program. Given the opportunity, she decided to implement a trial program in such a way that conclusive evidence on the value of the packaged training would be forthcoming.

Review Questions

1. If you were Shane, what type of research design would you use to test this program? Why?
2. How would the design actually be implemented in this hospital setting?
3. What would be your research hypothesis? What variables would you need to measure to provide data that could test this hypothesis? How would you gather these data?
4. Do you think the administrator's request for "proof before purchase" was reasonable? Why or why not? ■

CASE 2
Xerox

At Xerox, Diversity equals Success. The equation certainly has worked for them! According to *Fortune* magazine's annual reputation survey, Xerox is the world's most admired company in the computer industry. According to Anne Mulcahy, Xerox Chairman and former CEO, "Diversity is about more than race and gender. It's about more than numbers. It's about inclusion. Diversity means creating an environment where all employees can grow to their fullest potential." Xerox knows that employees with different ways of thinking, and different ways of perceiving the world, are employees who create innovative solutions. In a business like Xerox, whose lifeblood is fresh ideas, this variety of perspectives is a priceless resource—and a key to achieving critical business results.[1]

Innovation keeps Xerox at the forefront of their industry. In fact, nearly 5% of revenue is dedicated to Research & Development and Engineering. Says Mulcahy, "Investing in innovation was indeed the best decision I've ever made. Despite the economic slowdown in technology spending, Xerox is still the prominent player in our industry, with a No. 1 revenue share. And at a time when we had a bunker-like mentality to save our company, we also empowered a small but entrepreneurial team to create our services business. Good thing we did. The offerings from Xerox Global Services have never been more relevant for our customers, who are knocking on our door looking for any way to save money . . . We're able to move quickly on these opportunities right now because we decided to fund innovation back then." With recent annual revenue of $21.6 billion, Xerox is the world's largest technology-and-services company specializing in document management.[2]

Xerox provides the document industry's broadest portfolio of offerings. Digital systems include color and black-and-white printing and publishing systems, digital presses and "book factories," advanced and basic multifunction systems, laser and solid ink network printers, copiers, and fax machines. No competitor can match Xerox's services expertise, which includes: helping businesses develop online document archives, analyzing how employees can most efficiently share documents and knowledge in the office, operating in-house print shops or mailrooms, and building Web-based processes for personalizing direct mail, invoices, brochures and more. Xerox also offers associated software, support, and even supplies such as toner, paper, and ink.[3]

By recognizing and respecting diversity and empowering individuality, Xerox creates productive people and an innovative company. Theirs is a corporate culture of inclusion whose commitment to diversity can be traced back to its very first chairman, Joseph C. Wilson. Chairman Wilson took proactive steps to create a more diverse workforce in response to race riots in the 1960s. With then Xerox President C. Peter McCullough, Wilson called for increased hiring of African Americans in an effort to achieve equality among its workforce. Throughout the 1970s Xerox established an internal affirmative action office and began to hire a significant number of minority employees.[4]

Xerox placed emphasis on the advancement of minorities and females in the 1980s. It was during this time that Barry Rand, an African American, was named the first minority president of a division. Xerox's Balanced Workforce Strategy (BWF) aimed to achieve unbiased representation for women and minorities throughout the organization at all times, including throughout times of restructuring. During the influx of women in its workforce Xerox recognized their struggle balancing work and family commitments. In response, Xerox Human Resources (HR) initiated "flex time" and other HR policies to maintain a high level of productivity and satisfaction among its workforce.[5]

In the 1990s sexual orientation was included in the company's Equal Opportunity/Affirmative Action and On-discrimination policy, GALAXe Pride at Work (a caucus group for gay, lesbian, bisexual, and transgender employees) was established, and Xerox began to provide domestic partner benefits for gay, lesbian, bisexual, and transgender employees. Annual diversity employee round-

tables with senior managers were initiated, providing employees the opportunity to engage in unfiltered communication with management about best practices, strengths, and weaknesses of Xerox's diversity initiatives.[6]

Xerox's view on a diverse workforce is most eloquently expressed by Xerox Chairman Anne M. Mulcahy:

I'm convinced diversity is a key to success. Experience tells us that the most diverse companies—companies ruled by a hierarchy of imagination and filled with people of all ages, races, and backgrounds—are the most successful over time. Somehow, diversity breeds creativity. Maybe it's because people with different backgrounds challenge each other's underlying assumptions, freeing everybody from convention and orthodoxy. We provide a shining proof point that diversity in all its wonderful manifestations is good for business . . . good for our country . . . and good for people.[7]

Xerox is proud to say that women and minorities make up more than 50% of its workforce. About 48.2% of Xerox senior executives are women, people of color, or both. The employee roster is made up of roughly 30% African-Americans, Latinos, Asians, and Native Americans. In fact, Xerox has been rated as one of the Top 10 companies in hiring minorities, women, disabled, and gay and lesbian employees by *Fortune, Forbes, Working Mother, Latino Style,* and *Enable* magazines. It is among *Working Mother*'s top 100 family friendly companies for women—and has been for the past 15 years.[8]

In 2007 Ursula Burns was named the first African-American female president of Xerox Corporation. In July 2009 she succeeded Anne M. Mulcahy as CEO. It was the first female-to-female hand-off in Fortune

500 history. Burns' philosophy echoes Mulcahy's:

"The power of our people development model is that it recognizes the value of diversity from entry-level positions to the top seats. When you've been at it as long as we have, the bench gets pretty strong of next generation leaders who represent the real world: black, white, male, female, Hispanic, Asian from different religions and with different beliefs. What they all have in common is strong skills, a solid work ethic, commitment and a will to win."[9]

With Ursula Burns at the helm, and a 100 percent rating on the Human Rights Campaign Foundation's Corporate Equality Index *and* its Best Places to Work survey, there's no doubt about it—

Xerox's commitment to diversity is still going strong.[10]

Review Questions

1. How would Xerox define diversity? How has its definition changed over the years?
2. What are the seven reasons why Xerox should be motivated to diversify their workforce? Illustrate how Xerox shows it values workplace diversity.
3. Does Xerox embody or defy the "leaking pipeline" phenomenon? Why?
4. Research question: Compare Xerox to other Fortune 500 companies. How are women and minorities represented at the highest levels of each organization? How can these statistics be improved upon? ∎

CASE 3
Lois Quam
. . . .
Founder, Tysvar, LLC

A fter accompanying Will Steger on a trip to Norway and the Arctic Circle, Lois Quam's interest in global climate change was sparked. There she witnessed firsthand the astonishing changes in the polar ice masses and the resulting impact on wildlife. Inspired by Steger's call for action to reduce global climate change, in 2009 Lois Quam left Piper Jaffray, a leading international investment bank, to become the founder and CEO of Tysvar, LLC, a privately held, Minnesota-based New Green Economy and health care reform incubator.[1] In 2010, Quam was selected by President Barack Obama to head the Global Health Initiative. This case is a retrospective of her executive experience at Tysvar.

"I'm focused on ways to finding solutions to really significant problems and taking those ideas to full potential," Quam said. "I want to bring the green economy to reality in a way that is much broader than financing. I want to focus on areas where I can make the most difference bringing the green economy to scale."[2]

Tysvar works with investors who can create the change they wish to see in the world rather than simply reacting to events as they unfold. The company is a strategic advisor and incubator of ideas, organizations, and people working to facilitate and build the New Green Economy (NGE) to scale. Tysvar's goal is to contribute to a viable, profitable, and socially responsible industry of sustainability, clean technology, and renewable energy sources.[3]

Conscientiously working to play their part to create a more sustainable world for the next generation, Tysvar's efforts include new creation of NGE industries, jobs, and investment opportunities, contributing to building NGE public policy frameworks, trade for import/export of clean technologies, and renewable energy sources around the world.[4]

"We stand on the brink of a very exciting time in the world," according to Quam. The interest in developing renewable energy sources to replace dwindling fossil fuel supplies and reduce carbon dioxide emissions is worldwide. "It is a very difficult time in the financial markets right now to do this, but that will change. Good companies will find ways to get things done."[5]

"I am an optimist about our future," said Quam, "Which is why I started Tysvar. The challenges we face from climate change are immense, but so are our capabilities, and the rewards and benefits to humanity are even greater in the New Green Economy."[6]

Lois Quam named her company after the hometown of her grandfather, Nels Quam. Tysvar is a majestically beautiful area in western Norway which is becoming a clean technology hub as part of Norway's growing NGE leadership and will soon be the site of the world's largest off-shore wind farm.[7]

Lois Quam has continually worked for a better tomorrow. In 2005, Quam was named Norwegian American of the Year. She believes there is much to learn from Norway: From balancing work and life, allowing parents to fully participate in the economy while still being active parents, to how successfully Norway is immersing itself in new energy technologies such as wind and biomass. As an arctic oil producing nation with a carbon tax since 1993, Norway has reinvested its oil wealth to become a world leader in renewable energy.[8, 9]

Internationally recognized as a visionary and leader on universal health-care reform and the emerging NGE, Lois Quam embodies the skill sets needed to succeed in this new economy. Named in 2006 by *Fortune* magazine as one of America's "50 Most Powerful Women," Quam has worked as head of Strategic Investments, Green Economy & Health at Piper Jaffray, a leading international investment bank; served as president and CEO of the Public and Senior Markets segment at UnitedHealth Group, a $30 billion division she helped create and run; chaired the Minnesota Health Care Access Commission, which led to legislation that brought health insurance to tens of thousands of Minnesotans; and served as a senior advisor to Hillary Clinton's task force on health-care reform. She graduated magna cum laude from Macalester College in St. Paul and went on to attend the University of Oxford as a Rhodes Scholar, earning a master's degree in philosophy, politics, and economics.[10]

Lois Quam believes the New Green Economy will produce high quality jobs, improve our national security via less dependence on foreign fuels, and prevent the most damaging consequence of all: irreversible and diminishing climate change. She and Tysvar are committed to establishing universal health-care reform in America. They believe universal health care is the answer for dependable, affordable health care for all Americans and that it is necessary to help rebuild the American economy and restore American competitiveness worldwide.[11]

Recognizing this, President Obama recently appointed Quam executive director of the State Department's Global Health Initiative. This $63 billion project will help developing countries improve their health care systems, with a special emphasis on women, children, and newborns.[12] In accepting this position, Quam decided to step down as CEO of the company she founded and hand leadership to Norwegian Terje Mikalsen, co-founder and former chairman of Norsk Data.

"Although we are sad to see Lois leave the firm, Tysvar will continue to follow through on her vision to help bring the new green economy to scale and make quality health care affordable and accessible to everyone," Mikalsen said on Tysvar's Web site. "We wish Lois all the best as she assumes her new position at the State Department. Her vision and leadership will help improve health care delivery and access for millions of people around the world."[13]

On Earth Day Lois Quam gave a speech at the University of St. Thomas on the emerging opportunities in the NGE after which she said, "I enjoyed sharing . . . how we can all use these key capabilities as a platform for doing something you love. Imagine: helping to build the NGE with a purposeful passion. It doesn't get much better than that!"[14]

In another speech she illustrated her philosophy:

The change required to combat climate change and conserve biodiversity will create a change in business and society similar to the Industrial Revolution. The new energy realities require nothing short of an energy revolution, a thorough retooling of our energy economy in ways that match up with the realities of the 21st century. It will affect every aspect of daily life and business, creating an immense set of opportunities for investors, businesses and individuals.

For investors, there are highly diverse and immense opportunities to create and scale new sources of energy, adapt our current methods of production and improve daily life in ways that drive down global warming emissions.

It will also create unprecedented depth and breadth of opportunities for businesses and investors. . . . clean energy will always be in strong demand . . . the world will always have massive energy needs, and they will always have to be balanced against the needs of the environment . . . the clean energy industry is fueled by the laws of nature—and there is no force as powerful or promising.

Think about what we can achieve working together at this conference and as a region . . . and think about the time sometime in the future when our work is reaching critical mass, when our environment is safer and our energy is cleaner, when we too will have our eureka moments, our moments of life-changing and world-changing discovery.[15]

As individuals, organizations, and countries answer the call for action, we look forward to achieving Lois Quam's vision of the future.

Review Questions

1. How does Lois Quam use emotions and moods in her speeches to convey her viewpoint? Cite examples to support your statements.

2. Based on what you have learned about Lois Quam, create hypotheses about the attitudes of her colleagues at Tysvar while using the three basic components of attitudes in your theories.

3. Take a moment to research the Global Health Initiative. Why do you believe Lois Quam was chosen to lead this program?

4. Research question: Search news reports, Web sites, and blogs to find out more information on Tysvar. How is the company faring in its quest to make the world cleaner and safer for future generations? What implications might that have on Tysvar's employees, their attitudes, and job satisfaction? ■

CASE 4
MAGREC, Inc.

Developed by Mary McGarry, Empire State College and Barry R. Armandi, SUNY-Old Westbury

Background

MagRec, Incorporated was started by Mr. Leed, a brilliant engineer (he has several engineering patents) who was a group manager at Fairchild Republic. The company's product was magnetic recording heads, a crucial device used for reading, writing, and erasing data on tapes and disks.

Like any other startup, MagRec had a humble beginning. It struggled during the early years, facing cash-flow and technical problems. After a slow start, it grew rapidly and gained 35 percent of the tape head market, making it the second-largest supplier in North America. Financially, the company suffered heavily because of price erosions caused by Far East competition. Unlike all its competitors, the company resisted moving its manufacturing operations off-shore. But the company accumulated losses to a point of bankruptcy. Finally MagRec entered a major international joint venture and received many new sales orders. Things looked good again. But . . .

Pat's Dilemma

When Fred Marsh promoted me to Sales Manager, I was in seventh heaven. Now, six months later, I feel I am in hell. This is the first time in my life that I am really on my own. I have been working with other people all my life. I tried my best and what I could not solve, I took upstairs. Now it's different because I am the boss (or am I?). Fred has taught me a lot. He was my mentor and gave me this job when he became vice president. I have always respected him and listened to his judgment. Now thinking back I wonder whether I should have listened to him at all on this problem.

It started one late Friday evening. I had planned to call my West Coast customer, Partco, to discuss certain contract clauses. I wanted to nail this one fast (Partco had just been acquired by Volks, Inc.). Partco was an old customer. In fact, through good and bad it had always stayed with us. It was also a *major* customer. I was about to call Partco when Dinah Coates walked in clutching a file. I had worked with Dinah for three years. She was good. I knew that my call to Partco would have to wait. Dinah had been cleaning out old files and came across a report about design and manufacturing defects in Partco heads. The report had been written nine years ago. The cover memo read as follows:

To: Ken Smith, Director of Marketing
From: Rich Grillo, V.P. Operations
Sub: Partco Head Schedule

This is to inform you that due to pole-depth problems in design, the Partco heads (all 514 in test) have failed. They can't reliably meet the reading requirements. The problem is basically a design error in calculations. It can be corrected. However, the fix will take at least six months.

Meanwhile, Ron Scott in production informs me that the entire 5,000 heads (the year's production) have already been pole-slotted, thus they face the same problem.

Ken, I don't have to tell you how serious this is, but how can we OK and ship them to Partco knowing that they'll cause read error problems in the field? My engineering and manufacturing people realize this is the number one priority. By pushing the Systems Tech job back we will be back on track in less than six months. In the interim I can modify Global Widgets heads. This will enable us to at least continue shipping some product to Partco. As a possible alternate I would like to get six Partco drives. Michaels and his team feel that with quick and easy changes in the drives tape path they can get the head to work. If this is true we should be back on track within six to eight weeks.

A separate section of the report reads as follows:

Confidential
(Notes from meeting with Don Updyke and Rich Grillo)

Solution to Partco heads problem
All Partco heads can be reworked (.8 hrs. ea.—cost insignificant) to solve Partco's read problems by grinding an extra three-thousandths of an inch off the top of the head. This will reduce the overall pole depth to a point where no read errors occur. The heads will fully meet specifications in all respects except one, namely life. Don estimates that due to the reduced chrome layer (used for wear) the heads' useful life will be 2500 hours instead of 6000 hours of actual usage.

Our experience is that no customer keeps accurate records to tell actual usage and life. Moreover, the cost is removed since Partco sells drives to MegaComputer, who sells systems to end-users. The user at the site hardly knows or rarely complains about extra costs such as the replacement of a head 12 to 18 months down the line instead of the normal 2 years. Besides, the service technicians always innovatively believe in and offer plausible explanations—such as the temperature must be higher than average—or they really must be using the computer a lot.

I have directed that the heads be reworked and shipped to Partco. I also instructed John to tell Partco that due to inclement weather this week's shipment will be combined with next week's shipment.

Dinah was flabbergasted. The company planned to sell products deliberately that it knew would not meet life requirements, she said, "risking our reputation as a quality supplier. Partco and others buy our heads thinking they are the best. Didn't we commit fraud through outright misrepresentation?"

Dinah insisted I had to do something. I told her I would look into the matter and get back to her by the end of next week.

Over the weekend I kept thinking about the Partco issue. We had no customer complaints. Partco had always been extremely pleased with our products and technical support. In fact, we were their sole suppliers. MegaComputer had us placed on the preferred, approved ship to stock, vendors list. It was a fact that other vendors were judged against our standards. MegaComputer's Quality Control never saw our product or checked it.

Monday morning I showed the report to Fred. He immediately recollected it and began to explain the situation to me.

MagRec had been under tremendous pressure and was growing rapidly at the time. "That year we had moved into a new 50,000 sq. ft. building and went from 50 or 60 employees to over 300. Our sales were increasing

dramatically." Fred was heading Purchasing at the time and every week the requirements for raw materials would change. "We'd started using B.O.A.s (Broad Order Agreements, used as annual purchasing contracts) guaranteeing us the right to increase our numbers by 100 percent each quarter. The goal was to maintain the numbers. If we had lost Partco then, it could have had a domino effect and we could have ended up having no customers left to worry about."

Fred went on to explain that it had only been a short-term problem that was corrected within the year and no one ever knew it existed. He told me to forget it and to move the file into the back storage room. I conceded. I thought of all the possible hassles. The thing was ancient history anyway. Why should I be concerned about it? I wasn't even here when it happened.

The next Friday Dinah asked me what I had found out. I told her Fred's feelings on the matter and that I felt he had some pretty good arguments regarding the matter. Dinah became angry. She said I had changed since my promotion and that I was just as guilty as the crooks who'd cheated the customers by selling low-life heads as long-life heads. I told her to calm down. The decision was made years ago. No one got hurt and the heads weren't defective. They weren't causing any errors.

I felt bad but figured there wasn't much to do. The matter was closed as far as I was concerned, so I returned to my afternoon chores. Little was I to know the matter was not really closed.

That night Fred called me at 10:00. He wanted me to come over to the office right away. I quickly changed, wondering what the emergency was. I walked into Fred's office. The coffee was going. Charlie (Personnel Manager) was there.

Rich Grillo (V.P. Operations) was sitting on the far side of Fred's conference table. I instinctively headed there for that was the designated smoking corner.

Ken (Director of Marketing) arrived 15 minutes later. We settled in. Fred began the meeting by thanking everyone for coming. He then told them about the discovery of the Partco file and filled them in on the background. The problem now was that Dinah had called Partco and gotten through to their new vice president, Tim Rand. Rand had called Fred at 8 P.M. at home and said he was personally taking the Red Eye to find out what this was all about. He would be here in the morning.

We spent a grueling night followed by an extremely tense few weeks. Partco had a team of people going through our tests, quality control, and manufacturing records. Our production slipped, and overall morale was affected.

Mr. Leed personally spent a week in California assuring Partco that this would never happen again. Though we weathered the storm, we had certain losses. We were never to be Partco's sole source again. We still retained 60 percent of their business but had to agree to lower prices. The price reduction had a severe impact. Although Partco never disclosed to anyone what the issues were (since both companies had blanket nondisclosure agreements), word got around that Partco was paying a lower price. We were unable to explain to our other customers why Partco was paying this amount. Actually I felt the price word got out through Joe Byrne (an engineer who came to Partco from Systems Tech and told his colleagues back at Systems Tech that Partco really knew how to negotiate prices down). He was unaware, however, of the real issues. Faced with customers who perceived they were being treated inequitably, we experienced problems. Lowering prices meant incurring losses; not lowering them meant losing customers. The next two financial quarters saw sales dollars decline by 40 percent. As the sales manager, I felt pretty rotten presenting my figures to Fred.

With regard to Dinah, I now faced a monumental problem. The internal feeling was she should be avoided at all costs. Because of price erosions, we faced cutbacks. Employees blamed her for production layoffs. The internal friction kept mounting. Dinah's ability to interface effectively with her colleagues and other departments plummeted to a point where normal functioning was impossible.

Fred called me into his office two months after the Partco episode and suggested that I fire Dinah. He told me that he was worried about results. Although he had nothing personally against her, he felt that she must go because she was seriously affecting my department's overall performance. I defended Dinah by stating that the Partco matter would blow over and given time I could smooth things out. I pointed out Dinah's accomplishments and stated I really wanted her to stay. Fred dropped the issue, but my problem persisted.

Things went from bad to worse. Finally, I decided to try to solve the problem myself. I had known Dinah well for many years and had a good relationship with her before the incident. I took her to lunch to address the issue. Over lunch, I acknowledged the stress the Partco situation had put on her and suggested that she move away for a while to the West Coast, where she could handle that area independently.

Dinah was hurt and asked why I didn't just fire her already. I responded by accusing her of causing the problem in the first place by going to Partco.

Dinah came back at me, calling me a lackey for having taken her story to Fred and having brought his management message back. She said I hadn't even attempted a solution and that I didn't have the guts to stand up for what was right. I was only interested in protecting my backside and keeping Fred happy. As her manager, I should have protected her and taken some of the heat off her back. Dinah refused to transfer or to quit. She told me to go ahead and fire her, and she walked out.

I sat in a daze as I watched Dinah leave the restaurant. What the heck went wrong? Had Dinah done the morally right thing? Was I right in defending MagRec's position? Should I have taken a stand with Fred? Should I have gone over Fred's head to Mr. Leed? Am I doing the right thing? Should I listen to Fred and fire Dinah? If not, how do I get my department back on track? What am I saying? If Dinah is right, shouldn't I be defending her rather than MagRec?

Review Questions

1. Place yourself in the role of the manager. What should you do now? After considering what happened, would you change any of your behaviors?
2. Do you think Dinah was right? Why or why not? If you were she and you had it to do all over again, would you do anything differently? If so, what and why?
3. Using cognitive dissonance theory, explain the actions of Pat, Dinah, and Fred. ∎

CASE 5
It Isn't Fair
. . . .

Developed by Barry R. Armandi, SUNY–Old Westbury

Mary Jones was in her senior year at Central University and interviewing for jobs. Mary was in the top 1 percent of her class, active in numerous extracurricular activities, and highly respected by her professors. After the interviews, Mary was offered positions with every company with which she interviewed. After much thought, she decided to take the offer from Universal Products, a multinational company. She felt that the salary was superb ($40,000), there were excellent benefits, and there was good potential for promotion.

Mary started work a few weeks after graduation and learned her job assignments and responsibilities thoroughly and quickly. Mary was asked on many occasions to work late because report deadlines were often moved forward. Without hesitation she said "Of course!" even though as an exempt employee she would receive no overtime.

Frequently she would take work home with her and use her personal computer to do further analyses. At other times she would come into the office on weekends to monitor the progress of her projects or just to catch up on the ever-growing mountain of correspondence.

On one occasion her manager asked her to take on a difficult assignment. It seemed that the company's Costa Rican manufacturing facility was having production problems. The quality of one of the products was highly questionable, and the reports on the matter were confusing. Mary was asked to be part of a team to investigate the quality and reporting problems. The team stayed in poor accommodations for the entire three weeks they were there. This was because of the plant's location near its resources, which happened to be in the heart of the jungle. Within the three-week period the team had located the source of the quality problem, corrected it, and altered the reporting documents and processes. The head of the team, a quality engineer, wrote a note to Mary's manager stating the following: "Just wanted to inform you of the superb job Mary Jones did down in Costa Rica. Her suggestions and insights into the reporting system were invaluable. Without her help we would have been down there for another three weeks, and I was getting tired of the mosquitoes. Thanks for sending her."

Universal Products, like most companies, has a yearly performance review system. Since Mary had been with the company for a little over one year, it was time for her review. Mary entered her manager's office nervous, since this was her first review ever and she didn't know what to expect. After closing the door and exchanging the usual pleasantries, her manager, Tom, got right to the point.

Tom: Well, Mary, as I told you last week this meeting would be for your annual review. As you are aware, your performance and compensation are tied together. Since the philosophy of the company is to reward those who perform, we take these reviews very sincerely. I have spent a great deal of time thinking about your performance over the

past year, but before I begin I would like to know your impressions of the company, your assignments, and me as a manager.

Mary: Honestly, Tom, I have no complaints. The company and my job are everything I was led to believe. I enjoy working here. The staff are all very helpful. I like the team atmosphere, and my job is very challenging. I really feel appreciated and that I'm making a contribution. You have been very helpful and patient with me. You got me involved right from the start and listened to my opinions. You taught me a lot and I'm very grateful. All in all I'm happy being here.

Tom: Great, Mary, I was hoping that's the way you felt because from my vantage point, most of the people you worked with feel the same. But before I give you the qualitative side of the review, allow me to go through the quantitative appraisal first. As you know, the rankings go from 1 (lowest) to 5 (highest). Let's go down each category and I'll explain my reasoning for each.

Tom starts with category one (Quantity of Work) and ends with category ten (Teamwork). In each of the categories, Tom has either given Mary a 5 or a 4. Indeed, only two categories have a 4 and Tom explains these are normal areas for improvement for most employees.

Tom: As you can see, Mary, I was very happy with your performance. You have received the highest rating I have ever given any of my subordinates. Your attitude, desire, and help are truly appreciated. The other people on the Costa Rican team gave you glowing reports, and speaking with the plant manager, she felt that you helped her understand the reporting system better than anyone else. Since your performance has

been stellar, I'm delighted to give you a 10 percent increase effective immediately!

Mary: (mouth agape, and eyes wide) Tom, frankly I'm flabbergasted! I don't know what to say, but thank you very much. I hope I can continue to do as fine a job as I have this last year. Thanks once again.

After exchanging some parting remarks and some more thank-you's, Mary left Tom's office with a smile from ear to ear. She was floating on air! Not only did she feel the performance review process was uplifting, but her review was outstanding and so was her raise. She knew from other employees that the company was only giving out a 5 percent average increase. She figured that if she got that, or perhaps 6 or 7, she would be happy. But to get 10 percent . . . wow!! Imagine . . .

Sue: Hi, Mary! Lost in thought? My, you look great. Looks like you got some great news. What's up?

Susan Stevens was a recent hire, working for Tom. She had graduated from Central University also, but a year after Mary. Sue had excelled while at Central, graduating in the top 1 percent of her class. She had laudatory letters of recommendation from her professors and was into many after-school clubs and activities.

Mary: Oh, hi, Sue! Sorry, but I was just thinking about Universal and the opportunities here.

Sue: Yes, it truly is . . .

Mary: Sue, I just came from my performance review and let me tell you, the process isn't that bad. As a matter of fact I found it quite rewarding, if you get my drift. I got a wonderful review, and can't wait till next year's. What a great company!

Sue: You can say that again! I couldn't believe them hiring me right out of college at such a good salary. Between you and me, Mary, they started me at $45,000. Imagine that? Wow, was I impressed. I just couldn't believe that they would . . . Where are you going, Mary? Mary? What's that you say, "It isn't fair"? What do you mean? Mary? Mary . . .

Review Questions

1. Indicate Mary's attitudes before and after meeting Sue. If there was a change, why?
2. What do you think Mary will do now? Later?
3. What motivation theory applies best to this scenario? Explain. ■

CASE 6A
Perfect Pizzeria
. . . .

Perfect Pizzeria in Southville, in deep southern Illinois, is the second-largest franchise of the chain in the United States. The headquarters is located in Phoenix, Arizona. Although the business is prospering, employee and managerial problems exist.

Each operation has one manager, an assistant manager, and from two to five night managers. The managers of each pizzeria work under an area supervisor. There are no systematic criteria for being a manager or becoming a manager trainee. The franchise has no formalized training period for the manager. No college education is required. The managers for whom the case observer worked during a four-year period were relatively young (ages 24 to 27) and only one had completed college. They came from the ranks of night managers or assistant managers, or both. The night managers were chosen for their ability to perform the duties of the regular employees. The assistant managers worked a two-hour shift during the luncheon period five days a week to gain knowledge about bookkeeping and management. Those becoming managers remained at that level unless they expressed interest in investing in the business.

The employees were mostly college students, with a few high school students performing the less challenging jobs. Since Perfect Pizzeria was located in an area with few job opportunities, it had a relatively easy task of filling its employee quotas. All the employees, with the exception of the manager, were employed part time and were paid the minimum wage.

The Perfect Pizzeria system is devised so that food and beverage costs and profits are computed according to a percentage. If the percentage of food unsold or damaged in any way is very low, the manager gets a bonus. If the percentage is high, the manager does not receive a bonus; rather, he or she receives only his or her normal salary.

There are many ways in which the percentage can fluctuate. Since the manager cannot be in the store 24 hours a day, some employees make up for their paychecks by helping themselves to the food. When a friend comes in to order a pizza, extra ingredients are put on the friend's pizza. Occasional nibbles by 18 to 20 employees throughout the day at the meal table also raise the percentage figure. An occasional bucket of sauce may be spilled or a pizza accidentally burned.

In the event of an employee mistake, the expense is supposed to come from the individual. Because of peer pressure, the night manager seldom writes up a bill for the erring employee. Instead, the establishment takes the loss and the error goes unnoticed until the end of the month when the inventory is taken. That's when the manager finds out that the percentage is high and that there will be no bonus.

In the present instance, the manager took retaliatory measures. Previously, each employee was entitled to a free pizza, salad, and all the soft drinks he or she could drink for every 6 hours of work. The manager raised this figure from 6 to 12 hours of work. However, the employees had received these 6-hour benefits for a long time. Therefore, they simply took advantage of the situation whenever the manager or the assistant was not in the building. Although the night manager theoretically had complete control of the operation in the evenings, he did not command the respect that the manager or assistant manager did. This was because he received the same pay as the regular employees, he could not reprimand other employees, and he was basically the same age or sometimes even younger than the other employees.

Thus, apathy grew within the pizzeria. There seemed to be a further separation between the manager and his workers, who started out as a closely knit group. The manager made no attempt to alleviate the problem, because he felt it would iron itself out. Either the employees that were dissatisfied would quit or they would be content to put up with the new regulations. As it turned out, there was a rash of employee dismissals. The manager had no problem filling the vacancies with new workers, but the loss of key personnel was costly to the business.

With the large turnover, the manager found that he had to spend more time in the building, supervising and sometimes taking the place of inexperienced workers. This was in direct violation of the franchise regulation, which stated that a manager would act as a supervisor and at no time take part in the actual food preparation. Employees were not placed under strict supervision with the manager working alongside them. The operation no longer worked smoothly because of differences between the remaining experienced workers and the manager concerning the way in which a particular function should be performed.

After a two-month period, the manager was again free to go back to his office and leave his subordinates in charge of the entire operation. During this two-month period, the percentage had returned to the previous low level, and the manager received a bonus each month. The manager felt that his problems had been resolved and that conditions would remain the same, since the new personnel had been properly trained.

It didn't take long for the new employees to become influenced by the other employees. Immediately after the manager had returned to his supervisory role, the percentage began to rise. This time the manager took a bolder step. He cut out any benefits that the employees had—no free pizzas, salads, or drinks. With the job market at an even lower ebb than usual, most employees were forced to stay. The appointment of a new area supervisor made it impossible for the manager to "work behind the counter," since the super-

visor was centrally located in Southville.

The manager tried still another approach to alleviate the rising percentage problem and maintain his bonus. He placed a notice on the bulletin board stating that if the percentage remained at a high level, a lie detector test would be given to all employees. All those found guilty of taking or purposefully wasting food or drinks would be immediately terminated. This did not have the desired effect on the employees, because they knew if they were all subjected to the test, all would be found guilty and the manager would have to dismiss all of them. This would leave him in a worse situation than ever.

Even before the following month's percentage was calculated, the manager knew it would be high. He had evidently received information from one of the night managers about the employees' feelings toward the notice. What he did not expect was that the percent-

age would reach an all-time high. That is the state of affairs at the present time.

Review Questions

1. Consider the situation where the manager changed the time period required to receive free food and drink from 6 to 12 hours of work. Try to apply each of the motivational approaches to explain what happened. Which of the approaches offers the most appropriate explanation? Why?
2. Repeat Question 1 for the situation where the manager worked beside the employees for a time and then later returned to his office.
3. Repeat Question 1 for the situation as it exists at the end of the case.
4. Establish and justify a motivational program based on one or a combination of motivation theories to deal with the situation as it exists at the end of the case. ■

CASE 6B
Hovey and Beard Company

Source: Abridged and adapted from George Strauss and Alex Bavelas, "Group Dynamics and Intergroup Relations" (under the title "The Hovey and Beard Case"), in *Money and Motivation*, ed. William F. Whyte (New York: Harper & Row, 1955).

The Hovey and Beard Company manufactures a variety of wooden toys, including animals, pull toys, and the like.[1] The toys were manufactured by a transformation process that began in the wood room. There, toys were cut, sanded, and partially assembled. Then the toys were dipped into shellac and sent to the painting room.

In years past, the painting had been done by hand, with each employee working with a given toy until its painting was completed. The toys were predominantly two-colored, although a few required more colors. Now in response to increased demand for the toys, the painting operation was changed so that the painters sat in a line by an endless chain of hooks. These hooks moved continuously in front of the painters and passed into a long horizontal oven. Each painter sat in a booth designed to carry away fumes and to backstop excess paint. The painters would take a toy from a nearby tray, position it in a jig inside the painting cubicle, spray on the color according to a pattern, and then hang the toy on a passing hook. The rate at which the hooks moved was calculated by the engineers so that each painter, when fully trained, could hang a painted toy on each hook before it passed beyond reach.

The painters were paid on a group bonus plan. Since the operation was new to them, they received a learning bonus that decreased by regular amounts each month. The learning bonus was scheduled to vanish in six months, by which time it was expected that they would be on their own—that is, able to meet the production standard and earn a group bonus when they exceeded it.

By the second month of the training period, trouble developed. The painters learned more slowly than had been anticipated and it began to look as though their production would stabilize far below what was planned. Many of the hooks were going by empty. The painters complained that the hooks moved too fast and that the engineer had set the rates wrong. A few painters quit and had to be replaced with new ones. This further aggravated the learning problem. The team spirit that the management had expected to develop through the group bonus was not in evidence except as an expression of what the engineers called "resistance." One painter, whom the group regarded as its leader (and the management regarded as the ring-leader), was outspoken in taking the complaints of the group to the supervisor. These complaints were that the job

was messy, the hooks moved too fast, the incentive pay was not correctly calculated, and it was too hot working so close to the drying oven.

A consultant was hired to work with the supervisor. She recommended that the painters be brought together for a general discussion of the working conditions. Although hesitant, the supervisor agreed to this plan.

The first meeting was held immediately after the shift was over at 4 P.M. It was attended by all eight painters. They voiced the same complaints again: the hooks went by too fast, the job was too dirty, and the room was hot and poorly ventilated. For some reason, it was this last item that seemed to bother them most. The supervisor promised to discuss the problems of ventilation and temperature with the engineers, and a second meeting was scheduled. In the next few days the supervisor had several talks with the engineers. They, along with the plant superintendent, felt that this was really a trumped-up complaint and that the expense of corrective measures would be prohibitively high.

The supervisor came to the second meeting with some apprehensions. The painters, however, did not seem to be much put out. Rather, they had a proposal of their own to make. They felt that if several large fans were set up to circulate the air around their feet, they would be much more comfortable. After some discussion, the supervisor agreed to pursue the idea. The supervisor and the consultant discussed the idea of fans with the superintendent. Three large propeller-type fans were purchased and installed.

The painters were jubilant. For several days the fans were moved about in various positions until they were placed to the satisfaction of the group. The painters seemed com-

pletely satisfied with the results, and the relations between them and the supervisor improved visibly.

The supervisor, after this encouraging episode, decided that further meetings might also prove profitable. The painters were asked if they would like to meet and discuss other aspects of the work situation. They were eager to do this. Another meeting was held and the discussion quickly centered on the speed of the hooks. The painters maintained that the engineer had set them at an unreasonably fast speed and that they would never be able to fill enough of them to make a bonus.

The discussion reached a turning point when the group's leader explained that it wasn't that the painters couldn't work fast enough to keep up with the hooks but that they couldn't work at that pace all day long. The supervisor explored the point. The painters were unanimous in their opinion that they could keep up with the belt for short periods if they wanted to. But they didn't want to because if they showed they could do this for short periods then they would be expected to do it all day long. The meeting ended with an unprecedented request by the painters: "Let us adjust the speed of the belt faster or slower depending on how we feel." The supervisor agreed to discuss this with the superintendent and the engineers.

The engineers reacted negatively to the suggestion. However, after several meetings it was granted that there was some latitude within which variations in the speed of the hooks would not affect the finished product. After considerable argument with the engineers, it was agreed to try out the painters' idea.

With misgivings, the supervisor had a control with a dial marked "low, medium, fast" installed at the booth of the group leader. The speed of the belt could now be adjusted anywhere between the lower and upper limits that the engineers had set.

The painters were delighted and spent many lunch hours deciding how the speed of the belt should be varied from hour to hour throughout the day. Within a week the pattern had settled down to one in which the first half hour of the shift was run on a medium speed (a dial setting slightly above the point marked "medium"). The next two and a half hours were run at high speed, and the half hour before lunch and the half hour after lunch were run at low speed. The rest of the afternoon was run at high speed with the exception of the last 45 minutes of the shift, which was run at medium.

The constant speed at which the engineers had originally set the belt was actually slightly below the "medium" mark on the control dial; the average speed at which the painters were running the belt was on the high side of the dial. Few, if any, empty hooks entered the oven, and inspection showed no increase of rejects from the paint room.

Production increased, and within three weeks (some two months before the scheduled ending of the learning bonus) the painters were operating at 30 to 50 percent above the level that had been expected under the original arrangement. Naturally, their earnings were correspondingly higher than anticipated. They were collecting their base pay, earning a considerable piece-rate bonus, and still benefiting from the learning bonus. They were earning more now than many skilled workers in other parts of the plant.

Management was besieged by demands that the inequity between the earnings of the painters and those of other workers in the plant be taken care of. With growing irritation between the superintendent and the supervisor, the engineers and supervisor, and the superintendent and engineers, the situation came to a head when the superintendent revoked the learning bonus and returned the painting operation to its original status: the hooks moved again at their constant, time-studied, designated speed. Production dropped again and within a month all but two of the eight painters had quit. The supervisor stayed on for several months, but, feeling aggrieved, left for another job.

Review Questions

1. How does the painters' job score on the core job characteristics before and after the changes were made? How can the positive impact of the job redesign be explained?

2. Was the learning bonus handled properly in this case? How can its motivational impact be explained? What alternative approaches could have been taken with similar motivational results?

3. How do you explain the situation described in the last paragraph of the case? How could this outcome have been avoided by appropriate managerial actions? ■

CASE 7
The Forgotten Group Member

Developed by Franklin Ramsoomair, Wilfred Laurier University

The Organizational Behavior course for the semester appeared to promise the opportunity to learn, enjoy, and practice some of the theories and principles in the textbook and class discussions. Christine Spencer was a devoted, hard-working student who had been maintaining an A–average to date. Although the skills and knowledge she had acquired through her courses were important, she was also very concerned about her grades. She felt that grades were paramount in giving her a competitive edge when looking for a job and, as a third-year student, she realized that she'd soon be doing just that.

Sunday afternoon. Two o'clock. Christine was working on an accounting assignment but didn't seem to be able to concentrate. Her courses were working out very well this semester, all but the OB. Much of the mark in that course was to be based on the quality of groupwork, and so she felt somewhat out of control. She recollected the events of the past five weeks. Professor Sandra Thiel had divided the class into groups of five people and had given them a major group assignment worth 30 percent of the final grade. The task was to analyze a seven-page case and to come up with a written analysis. In addition, Sandra had asked the groups to present the case in class, with the idea that the rest of the class members would be "members of the board of directors of the company" who would be listening to how the manager and her team dealt with the problem at hand.

Christine was elected "Team Coordinator" at the first group meeting. The other members of the group were Diane, Janet, Steve, and Mike. Diane was quiet and never volunteered suggestions, but when directly asked, she would come up with high-quality ideas. Mike was the clown. Christine remembered that she had suggested that the group should get together before every class to discuss the day's case. Mike had balked, saying "No way!! This is an 8:30 class, and I barely make it on time anyway! Besides, I'll miss my *Happy Harry* show on television!" The group couldn't help but laugh at his indignation. Steve was the businesslike individual, always wanting to ensure that group meetings were guided by an agenda and noting the tangible results achieved or not achieved at the end of every meeting. Janet was the reliable one who would always have more for the group than was expected of her. Christine saw herself as meticulous and organized and as a person who tried to give her best in whatever she did.

It was now week 5 into the semester, and Christine was deep in thought about the OB assignment. She had called everyone to arrange a meeting for a time that would suit them all, but she seemed to be running into a roadblock. Mike couldn't make it, saying that he was working that night as a member of the campus security force. In fact, he seemed to miss most meetings and would send in brief notes to Christine, which she was supposed to discuss for him at the group meetings. She wondered how to deal with this. She also remembered the incident last week. Just before class started, Diane, Janet, Steve, and she were joking with one another before class. They were laughing and enjoying themselves before Sandra came in. No one noticed that Mike had

slipped in very quietly and had unobtrusively taken his seat.

She recalled the cafeteria incident. Two weeks ago, she had gone to the cafeteria to grab something to eat. She had rushed to her accounting class and had skipped breakfast. When she got her club sandwich and headed to the tables, she saw her OB group and joined them. The discussion was light and enjoyable as it always was when they met informally. Mike had come in. He'd approached their table. "You guys didn't say you were having a group meeting," he blurted. Christine was taken aback.

We just happened to run into each other. Why not join us?"

"Mike looked at them, with a noncommittal glance. "Yeah . . . right," he muttered, and walked away.

Sandra Thiel had frequently told them that if there were problems in the group, the members should make an effort to deal with them first. If the problems could not be resolved, she had said that they should come to her. Mike seemed so distant, despite the apparent camaraderie of the first meeting.

An hour had passed, bringing the time to 3 P.M., and Christine found herself biting the tip of her pencil. The written case analysis was due next week. All the others had

done their designated sections, but Mike had just handed in some rough handwritten notes. He had called Christine the week before, telling her that in addition to his course and his job, he was having problems with his girlfriend. Christine empathized with him. Yet, this was a group project! Besides, the final mark would be peer evaluated. This meant that whatever mark Sandra gave them could be lowered or raised, depending on the group's opinion about the value of the contribution of each member. She was definitely worried. She knew that Mike had creative ideas that could help to raise the overall mark. She was also concerned for him. As she listened to the music in the background, she wondered what she should do.

Review Questions

1. How could an understanding of the stages of group development assist Christine in leadership situations such as this one?
2. What should Christine understand about individual membership in groups in order to build group processes that are supportive of her work group's performance?
3. Is Christine an effective group leader in this case? Why or why not? ■

CASE 8
NASCAR'S Racing Teams

Developed by David S. Chappell, Ohio University, modified by Hal Babson, Columbus State Community College and John R. Schermerhorn, Jr., Ohio University

The most popular team sport, based on total spectator audience, is not basketball, baseball, football, or even soccer: it is stock car racing. The largest stock car racing group in the world is the National Association for Stock Car Auto Racing (NASCAR), which recently celebrated its 60th year. The NASCAR Sprint Cup Series (formerly known as the Winston Cup or Nextel Cup) kicks off in February and runs through November. Along the way it serves as a marketing powerhouse.

Not only are over 3.5 million fans attracted to NASCAR's Sprint Cup races, but another 218 million watched them on television last year.[1,2] Drivers are involved in cable network shows as well as syndicated radio shows each week. NASCAR's official Web site, at www.nascar.com, consistently ranks among the top league sites on the Internet and generates well over 1 billion page views year-after-year.[3] Companies such as the Coca-Cola Co. and Nationwide Insurance take advantage of NASCAR's popularity with merchandise, collectibles, apparel, accessories, toys, and other marketing tie-ins. The race cars themselves have been described by some as "200 mile-per-hour billboards."

Jeff Gordon is one of NASCAR's most successful and well-known drivers; he's been a sensation ever since he started racing go-carts and quarter-midget cars at the age of 5. But as the driver of a successful race car he represents just the most visible part of an incredibly complex racing organization—a high-performance system whose ultimate contribution takes place on race day. For several years a team known as the Rainbow Warriors handled Gordon's car. Their leader was crew chief Ray Evernham, recognized by many as one of the very best in the business. Posted on the wall of his workshop was this sign:

Success is a ruthless competitor, for it flatters and nourishes our weaknesses and lulls us into complacency.

While Gordon represented the star attraction, many believed that it was Evernham who pulled the whole act together. He was responsible for a group of over 120 technicians and mechanics with an annual budget estimated between $10 and $12 million! And he had strong opinions as to what it takes to consistently

finish first: painstaking preparation, egoless teamwork, and thoroughly original strategizing—principles that apply to any high-performance organization.

Evernham believed that teams needed to experiment with new methods and processes. When he assembled his Rainbow Warriors pit crew, none of them had Nextel/Winston Cup experience and none worked on the car in any other capacity. With the use of a pit crew coach, the Rainbow Warriors provide Gordon with an approximately one-second advantage with each pit stop, which, at a speed of 200 miles per hour, equates to 300 feet of race track. "When you coach and support a superstar like Jeff Gordon, you give him the best equipment possible, you give him the information he needs, and then you get out of the way. But racing is a team sport. Everyone who races pretty much has the same car and the same equipment. What sets us apart is our people. I like to talk about our 'team IQ'—because none of us is as smart as all of us."

Said Evernham, "I think a lot about people, management, and psychology: Specifically, how can I motivate my guys and make them gel as a team? I surround them with ideas about teamwork. I read every leadership book I can get my hands on. One thing that I took from my reading is the idea of a 'circle of strength.' When the Rainbow Warriors meet, we always put our chairs in a circle. That's a way of saying that we're stronger as a team than we are on our own."

Evernham backed up this belief in team by emphasizing team performance over individual performance. When the car won a race, everyone shared in the prize money. In addition, when Evernham earned money through personal-service activities such as

speaking tours and autograph signings, he shared what he earned with the team. "I wouldn't be in a position to earn that income if it weren't for the team. Everyone should feel as if his signature is on the finished product."

Steve Letarte had some pretty big shoes to fill when he became Jeff Gordon's crew chief. After a series of successful title runs, Letarte was recently transferred to Gordon teammate Dale Earnhardt's team with the intention of bringing about "a more professional and ultimately more successful Earnhardt."[4]

But don't cry for Jeff Gordon. Under new pit boss Alan Gustafson, the #24 crew is performing as strongly as ever: In the current season, Gordon has spent 50% more miles at the front of the pack than the number two racer.[5]

It's not only the fans who have noticed what goes on in the NASCAR pit crews and racing teams. The next time you fly on United Airlines, check out the ground crews. You might notice some similarities with the teams handling pit stops for NASCAR racers. In fact, there's a good chance the members of the ramp crews have been through what has been called "Pit Crew U."[6] United is among many organizations that are sending employees to Pit Instruction and Training in Mooresville, North Carolina. At the same facility where real racing crews train, United's ramp workers learn to work under pressure while meeting the goals of teamwork, safety, and job preparedness. The objective is to replace work practices that may sometimes result in aircraft delays and service inadequacies—things that a NASCAR team must avoid in order to stay competitive in races. "It's stuff you can carry back like cleaning up your work area, being set up for that airplane to arrive like the pit crews are ready for that car to get here," said Marc Abbatacola of Chicago's O'Hare International Airport.[7]

Joe Konkel agreed: "The PIT training supports all the major principles of Georgia-Pacific . . . the need for everyone to have the necessary skill, commitment, ownership, and teamwork to advance the vision. Safety, compliance, and efficiency work together and become a result of this focus. This fosters pride, ownership, and a clear understanding of each person's individual advantage as part of the team."

High-performance teams may be inherited, but must be maintained. They do not happen by chance; rather, they are the result of good recruiting and meticulous attention to learning every detail of the job.

Review Questions

1. In what ways do Evernham's leadership tactics prove consistent with the characteristics and ideas on high performance teams and teamwork advanced in the text?
2. If you were hired as Jeff Gordon's new pit crew chief, what team norms would you expect to be in place?
3. What can someone who takes over a highly successful team from a leader like Evernham do to maintain and even improve team success in the future?
4. Research question: Pit crews are often in the news. See what you can find out about pit crew performance. Ask: What distinguishes the "high performance" pit crews from the "also rans?" ∎

CASE 9
Decisions, Decisions
....

Developed by John R. Schermerhorn, Jr.

The Case of the Wedding Ring

Setting—A woman is preparing for a job interview.

Dilemma—She wants the job desperately and is worried that her marital status might adversely affect the interview.

Decision—Should she or should she not wear her diamond engagement ring?

Considerations—When queried for a column in *The Wall Street Journal*, some women claimed that they would try to hide their marital status during a job interview.[1] One says: "Although I will never remove my wedding band, I don't want anyone to look at my engagement ring and think, she doesn't need this job, what is she doing working?" Even the writer remembers that she considered removing her engagement ring some years back when applying for a job. "I had no idea about the office culture," she said. "I didn't want anyone making assumptions, however unreasonable, about my commitment to work."

Wellness or Invasive Coercion?

Setting—Scotts Miracle-Gro Company, Marysville, Ohio.

Dilemma—Corporate executives are concerned about rising health-care costs. CEO Jim Hagedorn backs an aggressive wellness program and anti-smoking campaign to improve health of employees and reduce health-care costs for the firm. Scott employees are asked to take extensive health-risk assessments; failure to do so increases their health insurance premiums by $40 a month. Employees found to have "moderate to high" health risks are assigned health coaches and given action plans; failure to comply adds another $67 per month. In states where the practice is legal, the firm will not hire a smoker and tests new employees for nicotine use. In response to complaints that the policy is intrusive, Hagedorn says: "If people understand the facts and still choose to smoke, it's suicidal. And we can't encourage suicidal behavior."

Decision—Is Hagedorn doing the right thing by leading Scotts's human resource policies in this direction?

Considerations—Joe Pellegrini's life was probably saved by his employer. After urging from a Scotts's health coach he saw his doctor about weight and cholesterol concerns. This led to a visit with a heart specialist who inserted two stents, correcting a 95% blockage. Scott Rodrigues' life was changed by his employer; he is suing Scotts's for wrongful dismissal. A smoker, he claims that he was fired after failing a drug test for nicotine even though he wasn't informed about the test and had been told the company would help him stop smoking. CEO Hagedorn says: "This is an area where CEOs are afraid to go. A lot of people are watching to see how badly we get sued."[2]

Super Sales Woman Won't Ask for Raise

Setting—A woman is described as a "productive star" and "super-successful" member of an 18 person sales force.[3]

Dilemma—She finds out that both she and the other woman

salesperson are being paid 20% less than the men. Her sister wants her to talk with her boss and ask for more pay. She says: "No, I'm satisfied with my present pay and I don't want to 'rock the boat'." The sister can't understand how and why she puts up with this situation, allowing herself to be paid less than a man for at least equal and quite possibly better performance.

Considerations—In the past ten years women have lost ground relative to men when it comes to pay; whereas they previously earned 75.7 cents for each dollar earned by a man, a decade later they are earning 74.7 cents. Some claim that one explanation for the wage gap and its growing size is that women tolerate the situation and allow it to continue, rather than confronting the gap in their personal circumstances and trying to change it.

Wal-Mart Goes Public with Annual Bonuses

Setting—Wal-Mart executives released to the public information on the annual bonuses paid to store employees.[4]

Dilemma—Wal-Mart's founder, Sam Walton, started the bonus program in 1986 as a way of linking employees with the firm's financial success. Historically Wal-Mart did not divulge the annual bonuses. Recently the firm has received considerable negative publicity regarding the wages paid to employees and the benefits they are eligible to receive. But a spokesperson indicated that going public with the bonuses was not a response to such criticism. A former human resource executive at the firm says: "This is just an example of how they really treat their people well and they're putting it out there to let the facts speak for themselves."

Considerations—Some 813,759 employees shared a bonus pool of $529.8 million. A current employee said she received "substantially over $1,000," and that this was higher than the prior year's bonus. Wal-Mart is planning to give the bonuses on a quarterly basis to link them more frequently with performance. One of the firm's critics, WakeUpWalMart.com, was critical, charging: "Wal-Mart values are so misplaced that it gives executives hundreds of millions in bonuses and the mere crumbs to associates."

Review Questions

1. Use the decision-making model presented in the chapter to map the decisions being made in these situations. Identify how, where, and why different decisions might be made.
2. What are the issues involved in these situations? How are they best addressed by the decision makers?
3. Find other decision-making examples that raise similar issues and quandaries. Share them with classmates and analyze the possible decisions. ∎

CASE 10
The Case of the Missing Raise

Prepared by John R. Schermerhorn, Jr., Ohio University

It was late February, and Marsha Lloyd had just completed an important long-distance telephone call with Professor Fred Massie, head of the Department of Management at Central University. During the conversation Marsha accepted an offer to move from her present position at Private University, located in the East, to Central in the Midwest as an Assistant Professor. Marsha and her husband John then shared the following thoughts.

Marsha: "Well, it's final."
John: "It's been a difficult decision, but I know it will work out for the best."
Marsha: "Yes, however, we are leaving many things we like here."
John: "I know, but remember, Professor Massie is someone you respect a great deal and he is offering you a challenge to come and introduce new courses at Central. Besides, he will surely be a pleasure to work for."
Marsha: "John we're young, eager and a little adventurous. There's no reason we shouldn't go."
John: "We're going dear."

Marsha Lloyd began the fall semester eagerly. The points discussed in her earlier conversations with Fred were now real challenges, and she was teaching new undergraduate and graduate courses in Central's curriculum. Overall, the transition to Central had been pleasant. The nine faculty members were warm in welcoming her, and Marsha felt it would be good working with them. She also felt comfortable with the performance standards that appeared to exist in the department. Although it was certainly not a "publish or perish" situation, Fred had indicated during the recruiting process that research and publications would be given increasing weight along with teaching and service in future departmental decisions. This was consistent with Marsha's personal belief that a professor should live up to each of these responsibilities. Although there was some conflict in evidence among the faculty over what weighting and standards should apply to these performance areas, she sensed some consensus that the multiple responsibilities should be respected.

It was April, and spring vacation time. Marsha was sitting at home reflecting upon her experiences to date at Central. She was pleased. Both she and John had adjusted very well to Midwestern life. Although there were things they both missed from their prior location, she was in an interesting new job and they found the rural environment of Central very satisfying. Marsha had also received positive student feedback on her fall semester courses, had presented two papers at a recent professional meeting, and had just been informed that two of her papers would be published by a journal. This was a good record and she felt satisfied. She had been working hard and it was paying off.

The spring semester had ended and Marsha was preoccupied. It was time, she thought, for an end-of-the-year performance review by Fred Massie. This anticipation had been stimulated, in part, by a recent meeting of the College faculty in which the Dean indicated that a 7% pay raise pool was now available for the coming year. He was encouraging department chairpersons to distribute this money differentially based on performance merit. Marsha had listened closely to the Dean and liked what she heard. She felt this meant that Central was really trying to establish a performance-oriented reward system. Such a system was consistent with her personal philosophy and, indeed, she taught such reasoning in her courses.

Throughout May, Marsha kept expecting to have a conversation with Fred Massie on these topics. One day, the following memo appeared in her faculty mailbox.

MEMORANDUM
TO: Fellow Faculty
FROM: Fred
RE: Raises for Next Year

The Dean has been most open about the finances of the College as evidenced by his detail and candor regarding the budget at the last faculty meeting. Consistent with that philosophy I want to provide a perspective on raises and clarify a point or two.

The actual dollars available to our department exclusive of the chairman total 7.03%. In allocating those funds I have attempted to reward people on the basis of their contribution to the life of the Department and the University, as well as professional growth and development. In addition, it was essential this year to adjust a couple of inequities which had developed over a period of time. The distribution of increments was the following:

| 5% or less | 3 | 7+%–9% | 3 |
| 5+%–7% | 2 | More than 9% | 2 |

Marsha read the memo with mixed emotions. Initially, she was upset that Fred had obviously made the pay raise decisions without having spoken first with her about her performance. Still, she felt good because she was sure to be one of those receiving a 9+% increase. "Now," she mused to herself, "it will be good to sit down with Fred and discuss not only this past year's efforts, but my plans for next year's as well."

Marsha was disappointed when Fred did not contact her for such a discussion. Furthermore, she found herself frequently involved in informal conversations with other faculty members who were speculating over who received the various pay increments.

One day Carla Block, a faculty colleague, came into Marsha's office and said she had asked Fred about her raise. She received a 7+% increase, and also learned that the two 9+% increases had been given to senior faculty members. Marsha was incredulous. "It can't be," she thought, "I was a top performer this past year. My teaching and publications records are strong, and I feel I've been a positive force in the department." She felt Carla could be mistaken and waited to talk the matter out with Fred.

A few days later another colleague reported to Marsha the results of a similar conversation with Fred. This time Marsha exploded internally. She felt she deserved just reward.

The next day Marsha received a computerized notice on her pay increment from the Accounting Office. Her raise was 7.2%. That night, after airing her feelings with John, Marsha telephoned Fred at home and arranged to meet with him the next day.

Fred Massie knocked on the door to Marsha's office and entered. The greetings were cordial. Marsha began the conversation. "Fred, we've always been frank with one another and now I'm concerned about my raise," she said. "I thought I had a good year, but I understand that I've received just an average raise." Fred Massie was a person who talked openly, and Marsha could trust him. He responded to Marsha in this way.

Yes, Marsha, you are a top performer. I feel you have made great contributions to the Department. The two 9+% raises went to correct "inequities" that had built up over a period of time for two senior people. I felt that since the money was available this year that I had a responsibility to make the adjustments. If we don't consider them, you received one of the three top raises, and I consider any percentage differences between these three very superficial. I suppose I could have been more discriminating at the lower end of the distribution, but I can't give zero increments. I know you had a good year. It's what I expected when I hired you. You haven't let me down. From your perspective I know you feel you earned an "A," and I agree. I gave you a "B+". I hope you understand why.

Marsha sympathized with Fred's logic and felt good having spoken with him. Although she wasn't happy, she understood Fred's position. Her final comment to Fred was this. "You know, it's not the absolute dollar value of the raise that hurts. It's the sense of letdown. Recently, for example, I turned down an extensive consulting job that would have paid far more than the missing raise. I did so because I felt it would require too many days away from the office. I'm not sure my colleagues would make that choice."

In the course of a casual summer conversation, Carla mentioned to Marsha that she heard two of the faculty who had received 4+% raises had complained to Fred and the Dean. After lodging the complaints they had received additional salary increments. "Oh great," Marsha responded to herself, "I thought I had put this thing to rest."

About three weeks later, Marsha, Fred, Carla, and another colleague were in a meeting with the Dean. Although the meeting was on a separate matter, something was said which implied that Carla had also received an additional pay increment. Marsha confronted the Dean and learned that this was the case. Carla had protested to Fred and the

Dean, and they raised her pay on the justification that an historical salary inequity had been overlooked. Fred was visibly uncomfortable as a discussion ensued on how salary increments should be awarded and what had transpired in the department in this respect.

Fred eventually excused himself to attend another meeting. Marsha and the others continued to discuss the matter with the Dean and the conversation became increasingly heated. Finally, they each rose to terminate the meeting and Marsha felt compelled to say one more thing. "It's not that I'm not making enough money," she said to the Dean, "but I just don't feel I received my fair share, especially in terms of your own stated policy of rewarding faculty on the basis of performance merit."

With that remark, Marsha left the meeting. As she walked down the hall to her office, she said to herself, "Next year there will be no turning down consulting jobs because of a misguided sense of departmental responsibility."

Review Questions

1. What is Marsha's conflict management style and how has it influenced events in this case? What were Marsha's goals and what conflict management style would have worked best in helping her achieve them?
2. What is Fred's conflict management style and how has it influenced events in this case?
3. Once Marsha found out what her raise was to be, how could she have used the notion and elements of distributive negotiation to create a situation where Fred would make a raise adjustment that was favorable and motivating for her? ■

CASE 11
The Poorly Informed Walrus

Developed by Barbara McCain, Oklahoma City University

"How's it going down there?" barked the big walrus from his perch on the highest rock near the shore. He waited for the good word.

Down below the smaller walruses conferred hastily among themselves. Things weren't going well at all, but none of them wanted to break the news to the Old Man. He was the biggest and wisest walrus in the herd, and he knew his business, but he had such a terrible temper that every walrus in the herd was terrified of his ferocious bark.

"What will we tell him?" whispered Basil, the second-ranking walrus. He well remembers how the

Old Man had raved and ranted at him the last time the herd had caught less than its quota of herring, and he had no desire to go through that experience again. Nevertheless, the walrus noticed for several weeks that the water level in the nearby Arctic bay had been falling constantly, and it had become necessary to travel much farther to catch the dwindling supply of herring. Someone should tell the Old Man; he would probably know what to do. But who? and how?

Finally Basil spoke up: "Things are going pretty well, Chief," he said. The thought of the receding water line made his heart grow heavy, but he went on: "As a matter of fact, the beach seems to be getting larger."

The Old Man grunted. "Fine, fine," he said. "That will give us a bit more elbow room." He closed his eyes and continued basking in the sun.

The next day brought more trouble. A new herd of walruses moved in down the beach and, with the supply of herring dwindling, this invasion could be dangerous. No one wanted to tell the Old Man, though only he could take the steps necessary to meet this new competition.

Reluctantly, Basil approached the big walrus, who was still sunning himself on the large rock. After some smalltalk, he said, "Oh, by the way, Chief, a new herd of walruses seems to have moved into our territory." The Old Man's eyes snapped open, and he filled his great lungs in preparation for a mighty bellow. But Basil added quickly, "Of course, we don't anticipate any trouble. They don't look like herring eaters to me. More likely interested in minnows. And as you know, we don't bother with minnows ourselves."

The Old Man let out the air with a long sigh. "Good, good," he said. "No point in our getting excited over nothing then, is there?"

Things didn't get any better in the weeks that followed. One day, peering down from the large rock, the Old Man noticed that part of the herd seemed to be missing. Summoning Basil, he grunted peevishly. "What's going on, Basil? Where is everyone?" Poor Basil didn't have the courage to tell the Old Man that many of the younger walruses were leaving every day to join the new herd. Clearing his throat nervously, he said, "Well

Chief, we've been tightening up things a bit. You know, getting rid of some of the dead wood. After all, a herd is only as good as the walruses in it."

"Run a tight ship, I always say," the Old Man grunted. "Glad to hear that all is going so well."

Before long, everyone but Basil had left to join the new herd, and Basil realized that the time had come to tell the Old Man the facts. Terrified but determined, he flopped up to the large rock. "Chief," he said, "I have bad news. The rest of the herd has left you." The old walrus was so astonished that he couldn't even work up a good bellow. "Left

me?" he cried. "All of them? But why? How could this happen?"

Basil didn't have the heart to tell him, so he merely shrugged helplessly.

"I can't understand it," the old walrus said. "And just when everything was going so well."

Review Questions

1. What barriers to communication are evident in this fable?
2. What communication "lessons" does this fable offer to those who are serious about careers in the new workplace? ■

CASE 12
Faculty Empowerment and the Changing University Environment

Source: Developed by John Bowen, Columbus State Community College

In a typical university, the instructor enjoys a very high level of empowerment and opportunity for creativity in achieving course objectives. Within general limitations of the course description, instructors tend to have a good deal of flexibility in selecting course content, designing instructional activities, and selecting assignments. This allows them to tailor courses in varying ways to do what may seem to work best in a given situation. For example, an instructor teaching a course four times a year may design one section to cover course content in a somewhat different manner or with a slightly different focus due to the unique background and interests of the students. Since not all students learn or can be effectively evaluated in exactly the same way, an instructor normally is able to respond to varying situations by the way in which the text is used, the specific activities assigned, and choice of tests and other means of measuring student performance.

One of the settings in which instructor empowerment has been especially functional is the presence of adult learners (those working full-time and attending school part-time, or returning to school after substantial work experience).

Often adult learners have quite different needs than the more traditional student. Course variations that include unique learning opportunities that tap their work experiences and that accommodate the nature of their work schedules are often necessary. Flexibility and responsiveness by the instructor is also important. A major news event may create intense student interest in a course-related topic, but it might not occur at the specific point in the course in which the topic was scheduled to be covered, and the level of interest might require more time being allocated to the discussion than was originally planned. Assignment schedules and requirements are also a challenge when dealing with adult learners. Not all have work schedules such that they have the same amount of work week after week, but instead they may have variations in workloads that may include substantial travel commitments.

Where instructors have a good deal of empowerment, quality of education is maintained through instructor selection and development and through oversight by department heads. The supervision often includes reviews of any changes in course plans, learning activities, exams, assignments, and syllabus. This is facilitated by reviews of student feedback and through personal observation of the instructor conducting a class.

Regardless of the extent to which such quality control measures may or may not work, competition among colleges and universities is beginning to have an impact on faculty empowerment. In the past, schools tended to focus on a given geographic area, certain fields of study, or a particular class of students. Thus, competitive pressures were often relatively minimal. Today competition in the education market is not just local or even national, but is becoming increasingly global. Accelerating the trend is the use of online classes that can enable students in distant locations to take classes over the Internet.

The need to compete for revenues and to contain costs has also produced pressure for universities to operate more like businesses. This has, in some cases, resulted in more standardization of courses and instructional methods, consequently reducing the traditional empowerment of instructors. As an example of what is being done, consider two universities: Upstate University and Downstate University. Upstate and Downstate share two commonalities: (1) each sees their primary target student market as the working adult and (2) each is increasing the use of standardization in instructional methods.

Upstate University focuses on the working adult: 82 percent of its 8,200 students are employed and the average age is 32. It still holds traditional face-to-face classes on its main campus and in nearby communities, but its programs now include standardized online courses (including a program for military personnel) in both masters and undergraduate degree programs. It has developed a "Balanced Learning Format" approach involving standardized quality, content, and delivery for its courses—both online and traditional courses.

Downstate University was started to provide a means through which poor but qualified students could work and pay for their education. The school offers both undergraduate and masters degree programs. Enrollment at the main campus is now approximately 2,000 students but it has over 19,000 other students attending around the nation and around the world. Those students attend classes online and at 37 other campuses in 20 states—most of those students are working adults.

Upstate has standardized its courses so that certain specific activities and points are to be covered in each class session. The instructor does not set the assignments (problems, text questions, etc.). Rather, the

student taking the course can go online and see what is required for both the instructor and student. The amount of time to be devoted to particular discussion or activities must follow a given script for each class session or at least be within guidelines in which some flexibility may exist. As a result, all instructors covering a given class session will be following the same script—often saying and doing much the same thing. This approach largely limits creativity to the person or persons involved in developing and modifying the course. Any ideas to change the course would normally have to be approved by that developer. Changes are infrequent, however, perhaps because some instructors might be unwilling to contact the course developer and take the time to argue the need for a change.

Downstate is modifying its courses in ways that are similar to the approach taken at Upstate, although not identical. Standardized test banks are being used. Objective test questions are to be randomly selected from within the test banks and scored by computer, thus reducing subjective evaluation (and any possible favoritism) by individual instructors.

At both Upstate and Downstate, online instruction is playing an increasingly important role. The goal is to assure that all online interaction between students and instructors is proper and consistent with school policies. Online classes are conducted so that any communication must be either at the class Web site or through use of the school's own e-mail system. Thus the institution can monitor not only what goes on in the "electronic classroom" (the Web site for the course) but also in what might be comparable to the private chats which traditional students in the past had in the instructor's office. Furthermore, to the extent that a course is online and that all activity is completed using either the course Web site or the school's e-mail system, protection is provided to both students and instructors. There is always proof available that an assignment was or was not received on time; student complaints or grade challenges are much more verifiable.

From the perspective of administration at both universities, the approach to more standardization ensures uniformity of quality in instructional delivery across settings, students, and instructors. It also provides a benefit in regards to the recruitment of adjunct (part-time) instructors that are increasingly used. Since not all such instructors have the same level of creativity and experience, having a standardized course and common script for all to follow is presumed to help maintain quality of instruction across instructors and course sections. Many instructors—especially those who have taught in the past under empowered conditions, find the new developments at both Upstate and Downstate frustrating. They believe that their prerogatives and talents as professionals are not being fully respected.

Review Questions

1. Would you rather be a student in a class that has been standardized or one in which the instructor has a high degree of empowerment? Why?
2. What issues involving power and politics are involved in moving from a setting that encouraged faculty empowerment to one that required much more standardization of instruction? How would you deal with those issues if you were involved in university administration?
3. In the specific case of adult learners and use of multiple instructors, is it possible to reach a compromise between standardization and empowerment so that the benefits of standardization can be obtained while still allowing for the flexibility that comes with empowerment? How can this apply to courses taught online versus face-to-face? ■

CASE 13
The New Vice President
....

[*Note:* Please read only those parts identified by your instructor. Do not read ahead.]

Part A

When the new president at Mid-West U took over, it was only a short time before the incumbent vice president announced his resignation. Unfortunately, there was no one waiting in the wings, and a hiring freeze prevented a national search from commencing.

Many faculty leaders and former administrators suggested that the president appoint Jennifer Treeholm, the Associate Vice President for Academic Affairs, as interim. She was an extremely popular person on campus and had 10 years of experience in the role of associate vice president. She knew everyone and everything about the campus. Jennifer, they assured him, was the natural choice. Besides, Jennifer *deserved* the job. Her devotion to the school was unparalleled, and her energy knew no bounds. The new president, acting on advice from many campus leaders, appointed Jennifer interim vice president for a term of up to three years. He also agreed that she could be a candidate for the permanent position when the hiring freeze was lifted.

Jennifer and her friends were ecstatic. It was high time more women moved into important positions on campus. They went out for dinner to their every-Friday-night watering hole to celebrate and reflect on Jennifer's career.

Except for a brief stint outside of academe, Jennifer's entire career had been at Mid-West U. She started out teaching Introductory History, then, realizing she wanted to get on the tenure track, went back to school and earned her Ph.D. at Metropolitan U while continuing to teach at Mid-West. Upon completion of her degree, she was appointed as an assistant professor and eventually earned the rank of associate based on her popularity and excellent teaching.

Not only was Jennifer well liked, but she devoted her entire life, it seemed, to Mid-West, helping to form the first union, getting grants, writing skits for the faculty club's annual follies, and going out of her way to befriend everyone who needed support.

Eventually, Jennifer was elected president of the Faculty Senate. After serving for two years, she was offered the position of associate vice president. During her 10 years as associate vice president, she handled most of the academic complaints, oversaw several committees, wrote almost all of the letters and reports

Source: Adapted from Donald D. Bowen et al., *Experiences in Management and Organizational Behavior.* 4th ed. (New York: Wiley, 1997).

for the vice president, and was even known to run personal errands for the president. People just knew they could count on Jennifer.

Review Questions

1. At this point, what are your predictions about Jennifer as the interim vice president?
2. What do you predict will be her management/leadership style?
3. What are her strengths? Her weaknesses? What is the basis for your assessment?

After you have discussed Part A, please read Part B.

Part B

Jennifer's appointment as interim vice president was met with great enthusiasm. Finally the school was getting someone who was "one of their own," a person who understood the culture, knew the faculty, and could get things done.

It was not long before the campus realized that things were not moving and that Jennifer, despite her long-standing popularity, had difficulty making tough decisions. Her desire to please people and to try to take care of everyone made it difficult for her to choose opposing alternatives. (To make matters worse, she had trouble planning, organizing, and managing her time.)

What was really a problem was that she did not understand her role as the number-two person at the top of the organization. The president expected her to support him and his decisions without question. Over time the president also expected her to implement some of his decisions—to do his dirty work. This became particularly problematic when it involved firing people or saying "no" to old faculty cronies. Jennifer also found herself uncomfortable with the other members of the president's senior staff.

Although she was not the only woman (the general counsel, a very bright, analytical woman was part of the group), Jennifer found the behavior and decision-making style to be different from what she was used to.

Most of the men took their lead from the president and discussed very little in the meetings. Instead, they would try to influence decisions privately. Often a decision arrived in a meeting as a "fait accompli." Jennifer felt excluded and wondered why, as vice president, she felt so powerless.

In time, she and the president spent less and less time together talking and discussing how to move the campus along. Although her relations with the men on the senior staff were cordial, she talked mostly to her female friends.

Jennifer's friends, especially her close-knit group of longtime female colleagues, all assured her that it was because she was "interim." "Just stay out of trouble," they told her. Of course this just added to her hesitancy when it came to making tough choices.

As the president's own image on campus shifted after his "honeymoon year," Jennifer decided to listen to her friends rather than follow the president's lead. After all, her reputation on campus was at stake.

Review Questions

1. What is the major problem facing Jennifer?
2. What would you do if you were in her position?
3. Would a man have the same experience as Jennifer?
4. Are any of your predictions about her management style holding up?

Part C

When the hiring freeze was lifted and Jennifer's position was able to be filled, the president insisted on a

national search. Jennifer and her friends felt this was silly, given that she was going into her third year in the job. Nonetheless, she entered the search process.

After a year-long search, the Search Committee met with the president. The external candidates were not acceptable to the campus. Jennifer, they recommended, should only be appointed on a permanent basis if she agreed to change her management style.

The president mulled over his dilemma, then decided to give Jennifer the benefit of the doubt and the opportunity. He appointed her permanent provost, while making the following private agreement with her.

1. She would organize her office and staff and begin delegating more work to others.
2. She would "play" her number-two position, backing the president and echoing his position on the university's vision statement.
3. She would provide greater direction for the Deans who report to her.

Jennifer agreed to take the position. She was now the university's first female vice president and presided over a council of 11 deans, three of whom were her best female friends. Once again, they sought out their every-Friday-night watering hole for an evening of dinner and celebration.

Review Questions

1. If you were Jennifer, would you have accepted the job?
2. What would you do as the new, permanent, vice president?
3. Will Jennifer change her management style? If so, in what ways?
4. What are your predictions for the future?

Part D

Although people had predicted that things would be better once Jennifer was permanently in the job, things in fact became more problematic. People now expected Jennifer to be able to take decisive action. She did not feel she could.

Every time an issue came up, she would spend weeks, sometimes months, trying to get a sense of the campus. Nothing moved once it hit her office. After a while, people began referring to the vice president's office as "the black hole" where things just went in and disappeared.

Her immediate staff were concerned and frustrated. Not only did she not delegate effectively, but her desire to make things better led her to try to do more and more herself.

The vice president's job also carried social obligations and requests. Here again, she tried to please everyone and often ran from one evening obligation to another, trying to show her support and concern for every constituency on campus. She was exhausted, overwhelmed, and knowing the mandate under which she was appointed, anxious about the president's evaluation of her behavior.

The greatest deterioration occurred within her Dean's Council. Several of the male Deans, weary of waiting for direction from Jennifer regarding where she was taking some of the academic proposals of the president, had started making decisions without Jennifer's approval.

"Loose cannons," was how she described a couple of them. "They don't listen. They just march out there on their own."

One of the big problems with two of the deans was that they just didn't take "no" for an answer when it came from Jennifer. Privately, each conceded that her "no" sounded like a "maybe." She always left room open to renegotiate.

Whatever the problem, and there were several by now, Jennifer's ability to lead was being questioned. Although her popularity was as high as ever, more and more people on campus were expressing their frustrations with what sometimes appeared as mixed signals from her and the president and sometimes was seen as virtually no direction. People wanted priorities. Instead, crisis management reigned.

Review Questions

1. If you were president, what would you do?
2. If you were Jennifer, what would you do?

Conclusion

Jennifer had a few "retreats" with her senior staff. Each time, she committed herself to delegate more, prioritize, and work on time management issues, but within 10 days or so, everything was back to business as usual.

The president decided to hire a person with extensive corporate experience to fill the vacant position of Vice President of Finance and Administration. The new man was an experienced team player who had survived mergers, been fired and bounced back, and had spent years in the number-two position in several companies. Within a few months he had earned the respect of the campus as well as the president and was in fact emerging as the person who really ran the place. Meanwhile, the president concentrated on external affairs and fundraising.

Jennifer felt relieved. Her role felt clearer. She could devote herself to academic and faculty issues and she was out from under the pressure to play "hatchet man."

As she neared the magic age for early retirement, she began to talk more and more about what she wanted to do next. ■

CASE 14
Novo Nordisk
●●●●●●●●●●●●●●●●●●●●●●●●●

D uring the last decade, it seemed no matter where we looked we found evidence of the erosion of business ethics and the basic concepts of right and wrong. Respected corporations and individuals who spent years building their reputations of integrity seemingly lost theirs overnight— perhaps forever. But some companies hold themselves to a higher set of standards and recognize that their business practices have lasting and worldwide effects. Let's look at one example.

Headquartered in Denmark, Novo Nordisk is a company whose concerns run beyond the financial bottom line. Novo Nordisk not only manufactures and markets pharma-ceutical products and services, it realizes that responsible business is good business.

One of the world's leading producers of insulin, Novo Nordisk also makes insulin analogs (genetically engineered forms of insulin), injection devices, and diabetes education materials. Its products include analogs Levemir and NovoRapid and the revolutionary FlexPen, a pre-filled insulin injection tool. In addition to its diabetes portfolio, the firm has products in the areas of blood clotting management, human growth hormone, and hormone replacement therapy.[1]

Today, diabetes is recognized as a pandemic; and only half of all people with type 2 diabetes are diagnosed. Novo Nordisk works with policy makers and social influencers to improve the quality of life for those with diabetes, to find a cure for type 1 diabetes, and to help prevent the onset of type 2 diabetes. The company has framed a strategy for inclusive access to diabetes care. The ambition to ultimately defeat diabetes is at the core of Novo Nordisk's vision. This vision puts the company's objectives in perspective and inspires employees in their work. It is a beacon that keeps everyone's focus on creating long-term shareholder value and leveraging the company's unique qualities to gain competitive advantage.

In making decisions and managing their business, Novo Nordisk's Triple Bottom Line business principle balances three considerations: Is it economically viable? Is it socially responsible? And is it environmentally sound? This ensures that decision-making balances financial growth with corporate responsibility, short-term gains with long-term profitability, and shareholder return with other stakeholder interests. The Triple Bottom Line is built into their corporate governance structures, management tools, individual performance assessments, and rewards.

Novo Nordisk strives to manage its business in a way that ensures corporate profitability and growth, while it seeks to leave a positive economic footprint in the community. Its environmentally sound decisions acknowledge the company's concern for its impact on the world as well as the bioethical implications of its activities. As part of Novo Nordisk's ambitious non-financial targets, it aims to achieve a 10% reduction in the company's CO_2 emissions by 2014, compared with its 2004 emission levels. In 2009, the company announced that it had already reduced CO_2 emissions by 9% and water consumption by 17%, even as production and sales increased![2]

Novo Nordisk adopted the Balanced Scorecard as the company-wide management tool for measuring its progress. As part of their payment package, individuals are rewarded for performance that meets or exceeds the financial and non-financial targets in the Balanced Scorecard. Financial performance is guided by a set of four long-term targets focusing on growth, profitability, financial return, and cash generation. Non-financial performance targets include job creation, the ability to manage environmental impacts and optimize resource efficiency, and social impacts related to employees, patients, and communities.[3] Novo Nordisk deeply considers the people who rely on the company's products and its employees, as well as the impact of their business on society.

Corporate sustainability—the ability to sustain and develop business in the long-term perspective, in harmony with society—is an ethos clearly practiced by Novo Nordisk, and the company believes that it drives their success in business. Surveys indicate that ethical behavior in business today is the number one driver of reputation for pharmaceutical companies. Any company that is not perceived by the public as behaving in an ethical manner is likely to lose business, and it takes a long time to regain trust.

For Novo Nordisk, a business with integrity and innovation, its commitment to corporate sustainability has always been based on values. In this case, it's clear that doing the right thing makes a direct return on their bottom line.

Review Questions

1. What leadership style dominates at Novo Nordisk? Cite examples to support your opinion.
2. How does Novo Nordisk's leadership influence its organizational design and shape its competitive strategy?
3. Describe Novo Nordisk's philosophy in relation to transformational change, planned and unplanned change, and the strategies it has used to create change.
4. In what ways do you think Novo Nordisk employees might be asked to utilize self-leadership techniques to improve the effectiveness of the culture of shared leadership?
5. Research Question: Check up on the strides Novo Nordisk has made for diabetes recently. Have they made any progress and garnered the attention of influential people or organizations? How might cultural expectations and leadership enhance or limit their success? ∎

CASE 15
Never on a Sunday

Developed by Anne C. Cowden, California State University, Sacramento and John R. Schermerhorn, Jr., Ohio University

McCoy's Building Supply Centers of San Marcos, Texas, have been in continuous successful operation for over 70 years in an increasingly competitive retail business. McCoy's is one of the nation's largest family-owned and -managed building-supply companies, serving 10 million customers a year in a regional area currently covering New Mexico, Texas, Oklahoma, Arkansas, Mississippi, and Louisiana. McCoy's strategy has been to occupy a niche in the market of small and medium-sized cities.

McCoy's grounding principle is acquiring and selling the finest-quality products that can be found and providing quality service to customers. As an operations-oriented company. McCoy's has always managed without many layers of management. Managers are asked to concentrate on service-related issues in their stores: get the merchandise on the floor, price it, sell it, and help the customer carry it out. The majority of the administrative workload is handled through headquarters so that store employees can concentrate on customer service. The top management team (Emmett McCoy and his two sons, Brian and Mike, who serve as co-presidents) has established 11 teams of managers drawn from the different regions McCoy's stores cover. The teams meet regularly to discuss new products, better ways for product delivery, and a host of items integral to maintaining customer satisfaction. Team leadership is rotated among the managers.

McCoy's has a workforce of 70 percent full-time and 30 percent part-time employees. McCoy's philosophy values loyal, adaptable, skilled employees as the most essential element of its overall success. To operationalize this philosophy, the company offers extensive on-the-job training. The path to management involves starting at the store level and learning all facets of operations before advancing into a management program. All management trainees are required to relocate to a number of stores. Most promotions come from within. Managers are rarely recruited from the outside. This may begin to change as the business implements more technology requiring greater reliance on college-educated personnel.

Permeating all that McCoy's does is a strong religious belief, including a strong commitment to community. The firm has a long-standing reputation of fair dealing that is a source of pride for all employees.

Many McCoy family members are Evangelical Christians who believe in their faith through letting their "feet do it"—that is, showing their commitment to God through action, not just talk. Although their beliefs and values permeate the company's culture in countless ways, one very concrete way is reflected in the title of this case: Never on a Sunday. Even though it's a busy business day for retailers, all 103 McCoy's stores are closed on Sunday.

Atlanta, Georgia

Courteous service fuels growth at Chick-fil-A. But don't plan on stopping in for a chicken sandwich on a Sunday; all of the chain's 1,250 stores are closed. It is a tradition started by 85-year-old founder Truett Cathy, who believes that employees deserve a day of rest. Known as someone who believes in placing "people before profits," Truett has built a successful and fast growing fast-food franchise.

Headquartered in Atlanta, where its first restaurant was opened, Chick-fil-A is wholly owned by Truett's family and is now headed by his son. It has a reputation as a great employer, processing about 10,000 inquiries each year for 100 open restaurant operator jobs. Chick-fil-A's turnover among restaurant operators is only 3%, compared to an industry average as high as 50%. It is also a relatively inexpensive franchise, costing $5,000, compared to the $50,000 that is typical of its competitors.

The president of the National Restaurant Association Educational Foundation says: "I don't think there's any chain that creates such a wonderful culture around the way they treat their people and the respect they have for their employees."

Truett asks his employees to always say "my pleasure" when thanked by a customer. He says: "It's important to keep people happy." The results seem to speak for themselves. Chick-fil-A is the twenty-fifth largest restaurant chain in the United States, and reached over $2 billion in sales in 2006.[1]

Review Questions

1. How have the personal beliefs of the McCoy and Cathy families influenced the organizational cultures of their firms?
2. What lessons for developing high-performance organizational cultures can these two cases provide for other firms that aren't family run?
3. What would be the challenges for a new leader who is interested in moving her organization in the direction of the McCoy or Chick-fil-A cultures? ■

CASE 16
First Community Financial

Developed by Marcus Osborn, RSR Partners

First Community Financial is a small business lender that specializes in asset-based lending and factoring for a primarily small-business clientele. First Community's business is generated by high-growth companies in diverse industries, whose capital needs will not be met by traditional banking institutions. First Community Financial will lend in amounts up to $1 million, so its focus is on small business. Since many of the loans that it administers are viewed by many banks as high-risk loans, it is important that the sales staff and loan processors have a solid working relationship. Since the loans and factoring deals that First Community finances are risky, the interest that it charges is at prime plus 6 percent or sometimes higher.

First Community is a credible player in the market because of its history and the human resource policies of the company. The company invests in its employees and works to assure that turnover is low. The goal of this strategy is to develop a consistent, professional team that has more expertise than its competitors.

Whereas Jim Adamany, president and CEO, has a strong history in the industry and is a recognized expert in asset-based lending and factoring, First Community has one of the youngest staff and management teams in the finance industry. In the banking industry, promotions are slow in coming, because many banks employ conservative personnel programs. First Community, however, has recruited young, ambi-

tious people who are specifically looking to grow with the company. As the company grows, so will the responsibility and rewards for these young executives. In his early thirties, for example, Matt Vincent is a vice president; at only 28, Brian Zcray is director of marketing.

Since First Community has a diverse product line, it must compete in distinct markets. Its factoring products compete with small specialized factoring companies. Factoring is a way for businesses to improve their cash flow by selling their invoices at a discount. Factoring clients are traditionally the smallest clients finance companies must serve. Education about the nature of the product is crucial if the company is to be successful, since this is often

a new approach to financing for many companies. First Community's sales staff is well trained in understanding its product lines and acts as the client's representative as they work through the approval process.

To assure the loans or factoring deals fit within the risk profile of the company, First Community must ask many complex financial questions. Many small businesses are intimidated by credit officers, so First Community handles all of these inquiries through the business development officers. The business development officers, in turn, must understand the needs of their credit officers, who are attempting to minimize risk to the company while maintaining a friendly rapport with the client. By centralizing the client contract through educated sales representatives, First Community is able to ask the hard financial questions and still keep the clients interested in the process. A potential customer can be easily discouraged by a credit administrator's strong questioning about financial background. Utilizing the business development officers as an intermediary reduces the fear of many applicants about the credit approval process. Thus, a sales focus is maintained throughout the recruitment and loan application process.

Internally at First Community Financial there is a continual pressure between the business development staff and the credit committee. The business development staff is focused on bringing in new clients. Their compensation is in large part dependent on how many deals they can execute for the company. Like sales staff in any industry, they are aggressive and always look for new markets for business. The sales staff sells products from both the finance department and the factoring department, so they must interact with credit officers from each division. In each of these groups are credit administrators specifically responsible for ensuring that potential deals meet the lending criteria of the organization. While the business development officer's orientation is to bring in more and more deals, the credit administrator's primary goal is to limit bad loans.

The pressure develops when business development officers bring in potential loans that are rejected by the credit administrators. Since the business development officers have some experience understanding the credit risks of their clients, they often understand the policy reasoning for denying or approving a loan. The business development officers have additional concerns that their loans that have potential to be financed are approved because many of the referral sources of the sales staff will only refer deals to companies that are lending. If First Community fails to help many of a bank's referral clients, that source of business may dry up, as bankers refer deals to other lending institutions.

These structural differences are handled by focused attempts at improving communication. As noted before, the First Community staff experiences an extremely low turnover rate. This allows for the development of a cohesive team. With a cohesive staff, the opportunity to maintain frank and open communication helps bridge the different orientations of the sales staff and the administration divisions. A simple philosophy that the opinions of all staff are to be respected is continually implemented.

Since approving a loan is often a policy decision, the sales staff and the loan administrators can have an open forum to discuss whether a loan will be approved. CEO Jim Adamany approves all loans, but since he values the opinions of all of his staff, he provides them all an opportunity to communicate. Issues such as the

loan history for an applicant's industry, current bank loan policies, and other factors can be openly discussed from multiple perspectives.

Review Questions

1. What coordinative mechanisms does First Community use to manage the potential conflict between its sales and finance/auditing functions?
2. What qualities should First Community emphasize in hiring new staff to ensure that its functional organizational structure will not yield too many problems?
3. What are the key types of information transfer that First Community needs to emphasize, and how is this transmitted throughout the firm?
4. Why might a small finance company have such a simple structure while a larger firm might find this structure inappropriate? ∎

CASE 17
Mission Management and Trust
••

Developed by Marcus Osborn, RSR Partners

With more than 500 business and political leaders in attendance from across the state of Arizona, CEO Carmen Bermúdez of Mission Management and Trust accepted the prestigious ATHENA Award. The ATHENA, which is presented by the Arizona Chamber of Commerce, is annually awarded to companies that have a demonstrated track record in promoting women's issues within their company and the community. The 50-pound bronze statue that was presented to Mission Management and Trust was particularly special for the company's leadership because it was a tangible demonstration of their commitment to the community and to women's issues.

Mission Management and Trust is a small, newly formed company of just eight employees that has already made great headway in an industry that is dominated by giant corporations. When it began, Mission was the first minority- and women-owned trust company in the nation.

The trust management industry provides services to individuals, organizations, and companies who want their assets managed and protected by specialized outside firms. Mission Management provides personal service to its customers at a level of sophistication that is unusual for a firm of its small size.

Understanding that the trust management business is highly competitive, Mission developed a unique strategy that highlighted socially conscious policies combined with good business relations.

When the company was formed, it was created with more than the goal of just making a profit. Founder Carmen Bermúdez started Mission with three principal goals in mind. "1. To run a top-quality trust company; 2. To promote within the company and, by example, increase opportunities for women and minorities; and 3. To donate a portion of all revenue to charitable projects supported by clients and staff." As these statements demonstrate, Mission Management and Trust was created with a specific purpose that was focused not just on the business of trust management but on the responsibility of being a good corporate citizen.

Even with these lofty goals, Mission faced the problem of finding clients who not only wanted quality services but were not hindered by some of the potential sacrifices a socially conscious investment company might make. Many investors want a high rate of return for their trusts, and social policy is of a much lesser concern. This was not the market Mission wanted to address, so it had to be selective in developing a client base.

Mission needed to find clients that fit its social philosophy about investing and corporate responsibility. The ideal customers would be individuals and organizations that were committed to socially conscious policies and wanted an investment strategy that reflected this commitment. Mission found a perfect niche in the market with religious institutions. Churches and other civic organizations across the nation have trusts that they use to fund special projects and maintain operating expenses. They need effective service, but in many cases these organizations must be mindful of investing in companies and other projects that do not reflect their ideals. For example, a trust company that invests in companies in the highly profitable liquor and cigarette industries would not be consistent with the philosophy of many religious organizations. Mission services this niche by developing an organization that is structurally designed to make socially conscious decisions.

Mission has already begun to meet one of its principal goals, which is to donate a portion of its profits to charities. It donated $4,500

to causes ranging from Catholic Community Services to the Jewish Community Center scholarship program. These donations not only fulfill a goal of the organization but assist in the socially conscious client recruitment. Mission's target client base will find Mission a much more attractive trust company because of its charity programs. A religious organization can be comforted with the reality that some of the dollars it spends on trust management will be recycled into causes it promotes itself. The Mission policy makes good social policy, but it also makes good marketing sense. Understanding your clients is crucial to developing a small business, and Mission has mastered this principle.

Mission makes the most of its commitment to charitable causes by keeping its clients informed about the trust's activities and, more importantly, its community activities. *The Mission Bell,* a regular publication of Mission Management and Trust, details news and issues about the trust industry, company activities, and, most importantly, how Mission's social responsibility philosophy is being implemented. The name *Mission Bell* is more consistent with a religious publication than a corporate investing sheet, but it is consistent with its clients' needs. The name of the publication and its content clarifies Mission's role and purpose. For example, the *Mission Bell* summer issue presented articles on new hires, breaking investment news, and an article about how Mission is working with other groups to support socially responsible corporate investing. Thus, the Mission philosophy is clearly defined in its marketing and communication strategies.

To be consistent with the goals of the organizations, Carmen Bermúdez collected a small staff of highly experienced individuals whose backgrounds and principles

fit Mission's ideals. She frequently comments that the best business decision she ever made was "giving preference to intelligent, talented, compatible people whose main attribute was extensive experience." Mission employees are not just experts in the field of finance but leaders in their communities. These dual qualifications fulfill three important requirements that are crucial for the company's success. First, community involvement creates an appreciation of the investment sensitivities that are required by the organizations that Mission services. Second, individuals who are involved in the community have well-developed contacts that can be useful in business recruitment. Finally, socially active employees are committed to the purpose of the organization and help unify the corporate culture within Mission.

The Mission case is a clear example of how matching a philosophy with a market can bear solid results. Mission's commitment to its ideals is evident and reflected in all of its business practices. When human resources, investing, marketing, and strategic planning decisions are made with unified goals in mind, the chances are good that a strong, successful corporate culture will develop.

Review Questions

1. How do the mission elements of Mission Management differ from most firms?
2. Does donating to charity before the firm is fully established mean that Mission is not demonstrating financial prudence?
3. Could Mission's unique mission contribute to effective coordination as well as adjustment to the market?
4. Would Mission's unique mission still yield success with more traditional investors? ■

Notes

Case 1 References

[1] Deborah Orr, "The Cheap Gourmet," *Forbes* (April 10, 2006).

[2] www.traderjoes.com/how_we_do_biz.html accessed July 10, 2009.

[3] Deborah Orr, "The Cheap Gourmet," *Forbes* (April 10, 2006).

[4] Business Week Online. February 21, 2008.

[5] Beth Kowitt. "Inside the Secret World of Trader Joe's." *Fortune.* Posted 8/23/10. http://money.cnn.com/2010/08/20/news/companies/inside_trader_joes_full_version.fortune/index.htm. Accessed 2/6/11.

[6] Marianne Wilson, "When Less Is More," *Chain Store Age* (November 2006).

[7] Irwin Speizer, "The Grocery Chain That Shouldn't Be," *Fast Company* (February 2004).

[8] http://www.traderjoes.com/meet_our_crew.html accessed July 10, 2009.

[9] www.traderjoes.com/benefits.html accessed July 10, 2009.

[10] "Trader Joe's Store Manager Salary." *GlassDoor.com.* http://www.glassdoor.com/Salary/Trader-Joe-s-Store-Manager-Salaries-E5631_D_KO13,26.htm. Accessed 2/6/11.

[11] http://www.huffingtonpost.com/2009/07/13/the-greenpeace-vs-trader_n_230891.html (accessed July 22, 2009)

[12] http://go.greenpeaceusa.org/seafood/scorecards/trader-joes.pdf (accessed July 22, 2009)

[13] "Traitor Who?" *Traitor Joe's.* http://www.traitorjoe.com/who.htm#update. Accessed 3/1/11.

Case 2 References

[1] How Xerox Diversity Breeds Business Success. (Accessed August 3, 2009 at http://a1851.g.akamaitech.net/f/1851/2996/24h/cacheB.xerox.com/downloads/usa/en/d/Diversity_Brochure_2006.pdf)

[2] "Xerox Reports Fourth-Quarter 2010 Earnings." *Wall Street Journal.* Posted 1/26/11. http://online.wsj.com/article/PR-CO-20110126-903779.html. Accessed 3/1/11.

[3] http://www.xerox.com/go/xrx/template/019d.jsp?view=Factbook&id=Overview&Xcntry=USA&Xlang=en_US&Xseg=xnet (accessed July 7, 2009)

[4] http://www.xerox.com/downloads/usa/en/n/nr_Xerox_Diversity_Timeline_2008.pdf (accessed July 7, 2009)

[5] Ibid.

[6] Ibid.

[7] http://www.xeroxcareers.com/working-xerox/diversity.aspx (accessed July 7, 2009)

[8] "Diversity, Inclusion and Opportunity." *Xerox 2010 Report on Global Citizenship.* http://www.xerox.com/corporate-citizenship-2010/employee-engagement/diversity.html. Accessed 3/1/11.

[9] How Xerox Diversity Breeds Business Success.

[10] http://www.hrc.org/documents/HRC_Corporate_Equality_Index_2009.pdf (accessed July 8, 2009)

Case 3 References

[1] http://www.linkedin.com/in/loisquam (accessed July 18, 2009)

[2] http://www.startribune.com/business/42640682.html (accessed July 5, 2009)

[3] http://tysvar.com

[4] http://tysvar.com/our-vision/ (accessed July 5, 2009)

[5] www.morrissuntribune.com/articles/index.cfm?id=16258&se (accessed July 18, 2009)

[6] http://tysvar.com/our-work/ (accessed July 5, 2009)

[7] http///tysvar.com; http://tysvar.com/green-blog/ (accessed July 5, 2009)

[8] http://tcbmag.blogs.com/debatable/2008/02/qa-with-lois-qu.htmlQ (accessed July 5, 2009)

[9] http://www.linkedin.com/in/loisquam (accessed July 18, 2009)

[10] http://tysvar.com/lois-quam.com (accessed July 5, 2009)

[11] Rachel Keranen. "Health Care Exec Lois Quam to Lead Global Health Project." *Minneapolis St. Paul Business Journal.* Posted 1/26/11. http://www.bizjournals.com/twincities/news/2011/01/26/health-industry-vet-lois-quam-named-to.html. Accessed 3/1/11.

[12] Ibid.

[13] "Statement of Terje Mikalsen, CEO of Tysvar, Regarding the Appointment of Lois Quam to Head Global Health at the State Department." *Tysvar.* Posted 1/26/11. http://tysvar.com/news/. Accessed 3/1/11.

[14] http://tysvar.com/our-work (accessed July 5, 2009)

[15] http://www.piperjaffray.com/pdf/lois_quam_speech.pdf (accessed July 18, 2009)

Case 8 References

[1] "NASCAR Sprint Cup Race Track Seating Capacity and Attendance Chart." *Jayski.com.* http://jayski.com/pages/tracks-seating.htm. Accessed 3/5/11.

[2] "2010 NASCAR Sprint Cup TV Ratings." *Jayski.com.* http://jayski.com/pages/tvratings2010.htm. Accessed 3/5/11.

[3] http://www.nascar.com/guides/about/nascar/ accessed July 13, 2009.

[4] David Caraviello. "For Earnhardt, Letarte brings 'needed' change'." *NASCAR.* Posted 12/2/10. http://www.nascar.com/news/101202/dearnhardtjr-sletarte-champions-week-cw/index.html?eref=/drivers/dps/dearnhardtjr. Accessed 3/5/11.

[5] "Statistics." *NASCAR.* http://www.nascar.com/kyn/nbtn/. Accessed 3/5/11.

[6] http://www.visitpit.com/about-us/testimonials/ accessed July 13, 2009.

[7] Ibid.

Case 9 References

[1] Information from Sara Schaefer Munoz, "Is Hiding Your Wedding Band Necessary at a Job Interview?" *The Wall Street Journal* (March 15, 2007), p. D3.

[2] Information and quotes from "Get Healthy—Or Else," *Business Week* (February 26, 2007), cover story; and, "Wellness—or Orwellness?" *Business Week* (March 19, 2007), cover story.

[3] Information from "Anne Fisher, "Why Women Get Paid Less," *Fortune* (March 20, 2007), retrieved from www.fortune.com.

[4] Information from Marcus Kabel, "Wal-Mart Goes Public with Annual Bonuses," *The Columbus Dispatch* (March 23, 2007), pp. H1, H2.

Case 14 References

[1] www.hoovers.com (accessed July 22, 2009).

[2] http://www.environmentalleader.com/2009/02/05/novo-nordisk-cuts-co2-emissions-9/ accessed July 12, 2009.

[3] Ibid.

Case 15 Reference

[1] Information from "Daniel Yee, "Chick-Fil-A Recipe Winning Customers," *The Columbus Dispatch* (September 9, 2006), p. D1.

360° evaluation gathers evaluations from a jobholder's bosses, peers, and subordinates, as well as internal and external customers and self-ratings.

Absorptive capacity is the ability to learn.

Accommodation, or **smoothing** involves playing down differences and finding areas of agreement.

Achievement-oriented leadership emphasizes setting goals, stressing excellence, and showing confidence in people's ability to achieve high standards of performance.

Active listening encourages people to say what they really mean.

Activity measures of performance assess inputs in terms of work efforts.

Adaptive capacity refers to the ability to change.

Adhocracy emphasizes shared, decentralized decision making; extreme horizontal specialization; few levels of management; the virtual absence of formal controls; and few rules, policies, and procedures.

Adjourning stage is where teams disband when their work is finished.

Affect is the range of feelings in the forms of emotions and moods that people experience.

Agency theory suggests that public corporations can function effectively even though their managers are self-interested and do not always automatically bear the full consequences of their managerial actions.

Americans with Disabilities Act is a federal civil rights statute that protects the rights of people with disabilities.

Anchoring and adjustment heuristic bases a decision on incremental adjustments to an initial value determined by historical precedent or some reference point.

Attitude is a predisposition to respond positively or negatively to someone or something.

Attribution is the process of creating explanations for events.

Authoritarianism is a tendency to adhere rigidly to conventional values and to obey recognized authority.

Authoritative command uses formal authority to end conflict.

Availability heuristic bases a decision on recent events relating to the situation at hand.

Avoidance involves pretending a conflict does not really exist.

Awareness of others is being aware of the behaviors, preferences, styles, biases, and personalities of others.

Bargaining zone is the range between one party's minimum reservation point and the other party's maximum.

Behavioral complexity is the possession of a repertoire of roles and the ability to selectively apply them.

Behavioral decision model views decision makers as acting only in terms of what they perceive about a given situation.

Behavioral perspective assumes that leadership is central to performance and other outcomes.

Behaviorally anchored rating scale links performance ratings to specific and observable job-relevant behaviors.

Bonuses are extra pay awards for special performance accomplishments.

Brainstorming involves generating ideas through "freewheeling" and without criticism.

Bureaucracy is an ideal form of organizations, the characteristics of which were defined by the German sociologist Max Weber.

Centralization is the degree to which the authority to make decisions is restricted to higher levels of management.

Centralized communication networks link group members through a central control point.

Certain environments provide full information on the expected results for decision-making alternatives.

Channel richness indicates the capacity of a channel to convey information.

Charisma provides vision and a sense of mission, and it instills pride along with follower respect and trust.

Charismatic leaders are those leaders who are capable of having a profound and extraordinary effect on followers.

Classical decision model views decision makers as acting in a world of complete certainty.

Coalition power is the ability to control another's behavior indirectly because the individual owes an obligation to you or another as part of a larger collective interest.

Coercive power is the extent to which a manager can deny desired rewards or administer punishment to control other people.

Cognitive complexity is the degree to which individuals perceive nuances and subtle differences.

Cognitive dissonance is experienced inconsistency between one's attitudes and/or between attitudes and behavior.

Cohesiveness is the degree to which members are attracted to a group and motivated to remain a part of it.

Collaboration and problem solving involves recognition that something is wrong and needs attention through problem solving.

Collective intelligence is the ability of a team to perform well across a range of tasks.

Communication is the process of sending and receiving symbols with attached meanings.

Communication channels are the pathways through which messages are communicated.

Commutative justice is the degree to which exchanges and transactions are considered fair.

Competition seeks victory by force, superior skill, or domination.

Compressed workweek allows a full-time job to be completed in fewer than the standard five days.

Compromise occurs when each party gives up something of value to the other.

Conceptual skill is the ability to analyze and solve complex problems.

Confirmation error is the tendency to seek confirmation for what is already thought to be true and not search for disconfirming information.

Conflict occurs when parties disagree over substantive issues or when emotional antagonisms create friction between them.

Conflict resolution occurs when the reasons for a conflict are eliminated.

Conglomerates are firms that own several different unrelated businesses.

Consensus is a group decision that has the expressed support of most members.

Consideration is sensitive to people's feelings.

Consultative decisions are made by one individual after seeking input from or consulting with members of a group.

Content theories profile different needs that may motivate individual behavior.

Context is the collection of opportunities and constraints that affect the occurrence and meaning of behavior and the relationships among variables.

Continuous reinforcement administers a reward each time a desired behavior occurs.

Contrast effect occurs when the meaning of something that takes place is based on a contrast with another recent event or situation.

Control is the set of mechanisms used to keep actions and outputs within predetermined limits.

Controlling monitors performance and takes any needed corrective action.

Coordination is the set of mechanisms used in an organization to link the actions of its subunits into a consistent pattern.

Coping is a response or reaction to distress that has occurred or is threatened.

Countercultures are groups where the patterns of values and philosophies outwardly reject those of the organization or social system.

Counterproductive work behaviors are behaviors that intentionally disrupt relationships or performance at work.

Creativity generates unique and novel responses to problems.

Crisis decision occurs when an unexpected problem can lead to disaster if not resolved quickly and appropriately.

Criteria questions assess a decision in terms of utility, rights, justice, and caring.

Critical incident diaries record actual examples of positive and negative work behaviors and results.

Cross-functional team has members from different functions or work units.

Cultural symbol is any object, act, or event that serves to transmit cultural meaning.

Culturally endorsed leadership dimension is one that members of a culture expect from effective leaders.

Culture is the learned and shared way of thinking and acting among a group of people or society.

Decentralization is the degree to which the authority to make decisions is given to lower levels in an organization's hierarchy.

Decentralized communication networks members communicate directly with one another.

Decision making is the process of choosing among alternative courses of action.

Defensiveness occurs when individuals feel they are being attacked and they need to protect themselves.

Delphi Technique involves generating decision-making alternatives through a series of survey questionnaires.

Dependent variables are outcomes of practical value and interest that are influenced by independent variables.

Directive leadership spells out the what and how of subordinates' tasks.

Disconfirmation occurs when an individual feels his or her self-worth is being questioned.

Display rules govern the degree to which it is appropriate to display emotions.

Disruptive behaviors in teams harm the group process and limit team effectiveness.

Distress is a negative impact on both attitudes and performance.

Distributed leadership shares responsibility among members for meeting team task and maintenance needs.

Distributive justice is the degree to which all people are treated the same under a policy.

Distributive negotiation focuses on positions staked out or declared by the parties involved, each of whom is trying to claim certain portions of the available pie.

Diversity–consensus dilemma is the tendency for diversity in groups to create process difficulties even as it offers improved potential for problem solving.

Divisional departmentation groups individuals and resources by products, territories, services, clients, or legal entities.

Dogmatism leads a person to see the world as a threatening place and to regard authority as absolute.

Downward communication follows the chain of command from top to bottom.

Dysfunctional conflict works to the group's or organization's disadvantage.

Effective manager helps others achieve high levels of both performance and satisfaction.

Effective negotiation occurs when substance issues are resolved and working relationships are maintained or improved.

Effective team is one that achieves high levels of task performance, member satisfaction, and team viability.

Emotion and mood contagion is the spillover of one's emotions and mood onto others.

Emotion-focused coping are mechanisms that regulate emotions or distress.

Emotional conflict involves interpersonal difficulties that arise over feelings of anger, mistrust, dislike, fear, resentment, and the like.

Emotional dissonance is inconsistency between emotions we feel and those we try to project.

Emotional intelligence is an ability to understand emotions and manage relationships effectively.

Emotional labor is a situation where a person displays organizationally desired emotions in a job.

Emotions are strong positive or negative feelings directed toward someone or something.

Employee engagement is a strong sense of connection with the organization and passion for one's job.

Employee involvement team meets regularly to address workplace issues.

Employee stock ownership plans give stock to employees or allow them to purchase stock at special prices.

Empowerment is the process by which managers help others to acquire and use the power needed to make decisions affecting themselves and their work.

Encoding is the process of translating an idea or thought into a message consisting of verbal, written, or nonverbal symbols (such as gestures), or some combination of them.

Environmental complexity is the magnitude of the problems and opportunities in the organization's environment as evidenced by the degree of richness, interdependence, and uncertainty.

Equity theory posits that people will act to eliminate any felt inequity in the rewards received for their work in comparison with others.

ERG theory identifies existence, relatedness, and growth needs.

Ethics is the philosophical study of morality.

Ethics mindfulness is an enriched awareness that causes one to consistently behave with ethical consciousness.

Ethnocentrism is the tendency to believe one's culture and its values are superior to those of others.

Eustress is a stress that has a positive impact on both attitudes and performance.

Evidence-based management uses hard facts and empirical evidence to make decisions.

Existence needs are desires for physiological and material well-being.

Expectancy is the probability that work effort will be followed by performance accomplishment.

Expectancy theory argues that work motivation is determined by individual beliefs regarding effort/ performance relationships and work outcomes.

Expert power is the ability to control another's behavior because of the possession of knowledge, experience, or judgment that the other person does not have but needs.

Exploitation focuses on refinement and reuse of existing products and processes.

Exploration calls for the organization and its managers to stress freedom and radical thinking and therefore opens the firm to big changes—or what some call radical innovations.

External adaptation deals with reaching goals, the tasks to be accomplished, the methods used to achieve the goals, and the methods of coping with success and failure.

Extinction discourages a behavior by making the removal of a desirable consequence contingent on its occurrence.

Extrinsic rewards are valued outcomes given by some other person.

Feedback communicates how one feels about something another person has done or said.

Filter information by conveying only certain parts that are relevant.

FIRO-B theory examines differences in how people relate to one another based on their needs to express and receive feelings of inclusion, control, and affection.

Flaming is expressing rudeness when using e-mail or other forms of electronic communication.

Flexible working hours gives individuals some amount of choice in scheduling their daily work hours.

Followership is defined as the behaviors of individuals acting in relation to leaders.

Force–coercion strategy uses authority, rewards, and punishments to create change.

Forced distribution in performance appraisal forces a set percentage of persons into predetermined rating categories.

Formal channels follow the official chain of command.

Formal teams are official and designated to serve a specific purpose.

Formalization is written documentation of work rules, policies, and procedures.

Forming stage focuses around the initial entry of members to a team.

Framing error is solving a problem in the context perceived.

Functional conflict results in positive benefits to the group.

Functional departmentation is grouping individuals by skill, knowledge, and action.

Functional silos problem occurs when members of one functional team fail to interact with others from other functional teams.

Fundamental attribution error overestimates internal factors and underestimates external factors as influences on someone's behavior.

Gain sharing rewards employees in some proportion to productivity gains.

General environment is the set of cultural, economic, legal-political, and educational conditions found in the areas in which the organization operates.

Goal setting is the process of setting performance targets.

Grafting is the process of acquiring individuals, units, or firms to bring in useful knowledge.

Grapevine transfers information through networks of friendships and acquaintances.

Graphic rating scales in performance appraisal assigns scores to specific performance dimensions.

Group or team dynamics are the forces operating in teams that affect the ways members work together.

Groupthink is the tendency of cohesive group members to lose their critical evaluative capabilities.

Growth needs are desires for continued personal growth and development.

Halo effect uses one attribute to develop an overall impression of a person or situation.

Heterogeneous team members differ in many characteristics.

Heuristics are simplifying strategies or "rules of thumb" used to make decisions.

Hierarchy of needs theory offers a pyramid of physiological, safety, social, esteem, and self-actualization needs.

High-context cultures words convey only part of a message, while the rest of the message must be inferred from body language and additional contextual cues.

Higher-order needs in Maslow's hierarchy are esteem and self-actualization.

Hindsight trap is a tendency to overestimate the degree to which an event that has already taken place could have been predicted.

Homogeneous team members share many similar characteristics.

Hope is the tendency to look for alternative pathways to reach a desired goal.

Horizontal specialization is a division of labor through the formation of work units or groups within an organization.

Human skill is the ability to work well with other people.

Hygiene factors in the job context are sources of job dissatisfaction.

Immoral manager chooses to behave unethically. An amoral manager fails to consider the ethics of a decision or behavior.

Implicit followership theories are preconceived notions about prototypical and antiprototypical followership behaviors and characteristics.

Implicit leadership theories are preconceived notions about the attributes associated with leaders that reflect the structure and content of "cognitive categories" used to distinguish leaders from nonleaders.

Impression management is the systematic attempt to influence how others perceive us.

In-group occurs when individuals feel part of a group and experience favorable status and a sense of belonging.

Inclusion is the degree to which an organization's culture respects and values diversity.

Incremental change builds on the existing ways of operating to enhance or extend them in new directions.

Independent variables are presumed causes that influence dependent variables.

Individual decisions or authority decisions, are made by one person on behalf of the team.

Individual differences are the ways in which people are similar and how they vary in their thinking, feeling, and behavior.

Individualism–collectivism is the tendency of members of a culture to emphasize individual self-interests or group relationships.

Individualized consideration   provides personal attention, treats each employee individually, and coaches and advises.

Influence   is a behavioral response to the exercise of power.

Informal channels   do not follow the chain of command.

Informal groups   are unofficial and emerge to serve special interests.

Information power   is the access to and/or the control of information.

Information technology   is the combination of machines, artifacts, procedures, and systems used to gather, store, analyze, and disseminate information for translating it into knowledge.

Initiating structure   is concerned with spelling out the task requirements and clarifying aspects of the work agenda.

Innovation   is the process of creating new ideas and putting them into practice.

Inspiration   communicates high expectations, uses symbols to focus efforts, and expresses important purposes in simple ways.

Instrumental values   reflect a person's beliefs about the means to achieve desired ends.

Instrumentality   is the probability that performance will lead to various work outcomes.

Integrative negotiation   focuses on the merits of the issues, and the parties involved try to enlarge the available pie rather than stake claims to certain portions of it.

Intellectual stimulation   promotes intelligence, rationality, and careful problem solving by, for example, encouraging looking at a very difficult problem in a new way.

Inter-team dynamics   occur as groups cooperate and compete with one another.

Interactional justice   is the degree to which people are treated with dignity and respect in decisions affecting them.

Interactional transparency   is the open and honest sharing of information.

Interfirm alliances   are announced cooperative agreements or joint ventures between two independent firms.

Intergroup conflict   occurs among groups in an organization.

Intermittent reinforcement   rewards behavior only periodically.

Internal integration   deals with the creation of a collective identity and with ways of working and living together.

Interorganizational conflict   occurs between organizations.

Interpersonal barriers   occur when individuals are not able to objectively listen to the sender due to things such as lack of trust, personality clashes, a bad reputation, or stereotypes/prejudices.

Interpersonal conflict   occurs between two or more individuals in opposition to each other.

Intrapersonal conflict   occurs within the individual because of actual or perceived pressures from incompatible goals or expectations.

Intrinsic rewards   are valued outcomes received directly through task performance.

Intuitive thinking   approaches problems in a flexible and spontaneous fashion.

Job burnout   is a loss of interest in or satisfaction with a job due to stressful working conditions.

Job design   is the process of specifying job tasks and work arrangements.

Job enlargement   increases task variety by combining into one job two or more tasks that were previously assigned to separate workers.

Job enrichment   builds high-content jobs that involve planning and evaluating duties normally done by supervisors.

Job involvement   is the extent to which an individual is dedicated to a job.

Job rotation   increases task variety by periodically shifting workers among jobs involving different tasks.

Job satisfaction   is the degree to which an individual feels positive or negative about a job.

Job sharing   is where one full-time job is split between two or more persons who divide the work according to agreed-upon hours.

Job simplification   standardizes work to create clearly defined and highly specialized tasks.

Lack-of-participation error   occurs when important people are excluded from the decision-making process.

Lateral communication   is the flow of messages at the same levels across organizations.

Law of contingent reinforcement   states a reward should only be given when the desired behavior occurs.

Law of effect   states that behavior followed by pleasant consequences is likely to be repeated; behavior followed by unpleasant consequences is not.

Law of immediate reinforcement   states a reward should be given as soon as possible after the desired behavior occurs.

Leader match training is when leaders are trained to diagnose the situation to match their high and low LPC scores with situational control.

Leader–member exchange (LMX) theory emphasizes the quality of the working relationship between leaders and followers.

Leadership is the process of influencing others and the process of facilitating individual and collective efforts to accomplish shared objectives.

Leadership grid is an approach that uses a grid that places concern for production on the horizontal axis and concern for people on the vertical axis.

Leading creates enthusiasm to work hard to accomplish tasks successfully.

Leaking pipeline is a phrase coined to describe how women have not reached the highest levels of organizations.

Learning is an enduring change in behavior that results from experience.

Least-preferred co-worker (LPC) scale is a measure of a person's leadership style based on a description of the person with whom respondents have been able to work least well.

Legitimate power or formal authority is the extent to which a manager can use the "right of command" to control other people.

Lifelong learning is continuous learning from everyday experiences.

Line units are workgroups that conduct the major business of the organization.

Locus of control is the extent a person feels able to control his or her own life and is concerned with a person's internal–external orientation.

Long-term/short-term orientation is the degree to which a culture emphasizes long-term or short-term thinking.

Low-context cultures messages are expressed mainly by the spoken and written word.

Lower-order needs in Maslow's hierarchy are physiological, safety, and social.

Machiavellianism causes someone to view and manipulate others purely for personal gain.

Maintenance activities support the emotional life of the team as an ongoing social system.

Management by objectives is a process of joint goal setting between a supervisor and a subordinate.

Management philosophy links key goal-related issues with key collaboration issues to come up with general ways by which the firm will manage its affairs.

Managerial script is a series of well-known routines for problem identification and alternative generation and analysis common to managers within a firm.

Managerial wisdom is the ability to perceive variations in the environment and understand the social actors and their relationships.

Managers are persons who support the work efforts of other people.

Masculinity–femininity is the degree to which a society values assertiveness or relationships.

Matrix departmentation is a combination of functional and divisional patterns wherein an individual is assigned to more than one type of unit.

Mechanistic type or machine bureaucracy emphasizes vertical specialization with impersonal coordination and a heavy reliance on standardization, formalization, rules, policies, and procedures.

Merit pay links an individual's salary or wage increase directly to measures of performance accomplishment.

Mimicry is the copying of the successful practices of others.

Mission statements are written statements of organizational purpose.

Models are simplified views of reality that attempt to explain real-world phenomena.

Moods are generalized positive and negative feelings or states of mind.

Moral dilemma involves a choice between two or more ethically uncomfortable alternatives.

Moral manager makes ethical behavior a personal goal.

Moral problem poses major ethical consequences for the decision maker or others.

Motivation refers to forces within an individual that account for the level, direction, and persistence of effort expended at work.

Motivator factors in the job content are sources of job satisfaction.

Multicultural organization is a firm that values diversity but systematically works to block the transfer of societally based subcultures into the fabric of the organization.

Multiculturalism refers to pluralism and respect for diversity in the workplace.

Multiskilling is where team members are each capable of performing many different jobs.

Mum effect occurs when people are reluctant to communicate bad news.

Need for achievement (nAch) is the desire to do better, solve problems, or master complex tasks.

Need for affiliation (nAff) is the desire for friendly and warm relations with others.

Need for power (nPower) is the desire to control others and influence their behavior.

Negative reinforcement strengthens a behavior by making the avoidance of an undesirable consequence contingent on its occurrence.

Negotiation is the process of making joint decisions when the parties involved have different preferences.

Noise is anything that interferes with the effectiveness of communication.

Nominal group technique involves structured rules for generating and prioritizing ideas.

Nonprogrammed decisions are created to deal specifically with a problem at hand.

Nonverbal communication occurs through facial expressions, body motions, eye contact, and other physical gestures.

Norming stage is where members start to work together as a coordinated team.

Norms are rules or standards for the behavior of group members.

Observable culture is the way things are done in an organization.

Open systems transform human and material resource inputs into finished goods and services.

Operant conditioning is the control of behavior by manipulating its consequences.

Operations technology is the combination of resources, knowledge, and techniques that creates a product or service output for an organization.

Optimism is the expectation of positive outcomes.

Optimizing decisions give the absolute best solution to a problem.

Organic type or professional bureaucracy emphasizes horizontal specialization, extensive use of personal coordination, and loose rules, policies, and procedures.

Organizational behavior is the study of individuals and groups in organizations.

Organizational behavior modification is the use of extrinsic rewards to systematically reinforce desirable work behavior and discourage undesirable behavior.

Organizational charts are diagrams that depict the formal structures of organizations.

Organizational citizenship behaviors are the extras people do to go the extra mile in their work.

Organizational climate represents shared perceptions of members regarding what the organization is like in terms of management policies and practices.

Organizational commitment is the loyalty of an individual to the organization.

Organizational cultural lag is a condition where dominant cultural patterns are inconsistent with new emerging innovations.

Organizational culture is a shared set of beliefs and values within an organization.

Organizational design is the process of choosing and implementing a structural configuration for an organization.

Organizational governance is the pattern of authority, influence, and acceptable managerial behavior established at the top of the organization.

Organizational justice concerns how fair and equitable people view workplace practices.

Organizational learning is the process of knowledge acquisition, information distribution, information interpretation, and organizational retention.

Organizational myth is a commonly held cause-effect relationship or assertion that cannot be supported empirically.

Organizational or corporate culture is the system of shared actions, values, and beliefs that develops within an organization and guides the behavior of its members.

Organizational politics is the management of influence to obtain ends not sanctioned by the organization or to obtain sanctioned ends through nonsanctioned means and the art of creative compromise among competing interests.

Organizations are collections of people working together to achieve a common purpose.

Organizing divides up tasks and arranges resources to accomplish them.

Out-group occurs when one does not feel part of a group and experiences discomfort and low belongingness.

Output controls are controls that focus on desired targets and allow managers to use their own methods for reaching defined targets.

Output goals are the goals that define the type of business an organization is in.

Output measures of performance assess achievements in terms of actual work results.

Paired comparison in performance appraisal compares each person with every other.

Parochialism assumes the ways of your culture are the only ways of doing things.

Participative leadership focuses on consulting with subordinates and seeking and taking their suggestions into account before making decisions.

Passive followership beliefs are beliefs that followers should be passive, deferent, and obedient to authority.

Path-goal view of managerial leadership assumes that a leader's key function is to adjust his or her behaviors to complement situational contingencies.

Patterning of attention involves isolating and communicating what information is important and what is given attention from a potentially endless stream of events, actions, and outcome.

Perceived inequity is feeling under-rewarded or over-rewarded in comparison with others.

Perception   is the process through which people receive and interpret information from the environment.

Performance gap   is a discrepancy between the desired and the actual conditions.

Performance norm   sets expectations for how hard members work and what the team should accomplish.

Performance-contingent pay   is that you earn more when you produce more and earn less when you produce less.

Performing stage   marks the emergence of a mature and well-functioning team.

Personal conception traits   represent individuals' major beliefs and personal orientation concerning a range of issues involving social and physical setting.

Personal wellness   involves the pursuit of one's job and career goals with the support of a personal health promotion program.

Personality   is the overall combination of characteristics that capture the unique nature of a person as that person reacts to and interacts with others.

Personality traits   are enduring characteristics describing an individual's behavior.

Physical distractions   include interruptions from noises, visitors, and the like, that interfere with communication.

Planned change   is a response to someone's perception of a performance gap—a discrepancy between the desired and actual state of affairs.

Planning   sets objectives and identifies the actions needed to achieve them.

Political savvy   is knowing how to negotiate, persuade, and deal with people regarding goals they will accept.

Positive reinforcement   strengthens a behavior by making a desirable consequence contingent on its occurrence.

Power   is the ability to get someone else to do something you want done or the ability to make things happen or get things done the way you want.

Power distance   is a culture's acceptance of the status and power differences among its members.

Power-oriented behavior   is action directed primarily at developing or using relationships in which other people are willing to defer to one's wishes.

Presence   is the act of speaking without using words.

Presence-aware tools   are software that allow a user to view others' real-time availability status and readiness to communicate.

Proactive followership beliefs   are beliefs that followers should express opinions, take initiative, and constructively question and challenge leaders.

Proactive personality   is the disposition that identifies whether or not individuals act to influence their environments.

Problem-focused coping   mechanisms manage the problem that is causing the distress.

Problem-solving style   reflects the way a person gathers and evaluates information when solving problems and making decisions.

Problem-solving team   is set up to deal with a specific problem or opportunity.

Procedural justice   is the degree to which rules are always properly followed to implement policies.

Process controls   are controls that attempt to specify the manner in which tasks are to be accomplished.

Process innovations   introduce into operations new and better ways of doing things.

Process power   is the control over methods of production and analysis.

Process theories   examine the thought processes that motivate individual behavior.

Product innovations   introduce new goods or services to better meet customer needs.

Profit sharing   rewards employees in some proportion to changes in organizational profits.

Programmed decisions   simply implement solutions that have already been determined by past experience as appropriate for the problem at hand.

Projection   assigns personal attributes to other individuals.

Prosocial power motivation   is power oriented toward benefiting others.

Prototypes   are a mental image of the characteristics that comprise an implicit theory.

Proxemics   involves the use of space as people interact.

Psychological contract   is an unwritten set of expectations about a person's exchange of inducements and contributions with an organization.

Psychological empowerment   is a sense of personal fulfillment and purpose that arouses one's feelings of competency and commitment to work.

Punishment   discourages a behavior by making an unpleasant consequence contingent on its occurrence.

Quality circle   is a team that meets regularly to address quality issues.

Ranking   in performance appraisal orders each person from best to worst.

Rational persuasion   is the ability to control another's behavior because, through the individual's efforts, the person accepts the desirability of an offered goal and a reasonable way of achieving it.

Rational persuasion strategy   uses facts, special knowledge, and rational argument to create change.

Receiver   is the individual or group of individuals to whom a message is directed.

Referent power   is the ability to control another's behavior because of the individual's desire to identify with the power source.

Reinforcement   is the delivery of a consequence as a result of behavior.

Relatedness needs   are desires for satisfying interpersonal relationships.

Relationship management   is the ability to establish rapport with others to build good relationships.

Reliability   means a performance measure gives consistent results.

Representative power   is the formal right conferred by the firm to speak for and to a potentially important group.

Representativeness heuristic   bases a decision on similarities between the situation at hand and stereotypes of similar occurrences.

Resilience   is the ability to bounce back from failure and keep forging ahead.

Resistance to change   is any attitude or behavior that indicates unwillingness to make or support a desired change.

Restricted communication networks   link subgroups that disagree with one another's positions.

Reward power   is the extent to which a manager can use extrinsic and intrinsic rewards to control other people.

Risk environments   provide probabilities regarding expected results for decision-making alternatives.

Risk management   involves anticipating risks and factoring them into decision making.

Rites   are standardized and recurring activities used at special times to influence the behaviors and understanding of organizational members.

Rituals   are systems of rites.

Role   is a set of expectations for a team member or person in a job.

Role ambiguity   occurs when someone is uncertain about what is expected of him or her.

Role conflict   occurs when someone is unable to respond to role expectations that conflict with one another.

Role negotiation   is a process for discussing and agreeing upon what team members expect of one another.

Role overload   occurs when too much work is expected of the individual.

Role underload   occurs when too little work is expected of the individual.

Romance of leadership   involves people attributing romantic, almost magical, qualities to leadership.

Rule of conformity   states that the greater the cohesiveness, the greater the conformity of members to team norms.

Saga   is an embellished heroic account of accomplishments.

Satisficing decisions   choose the first alternative that appears to give an acceptable or satisfactory resolution of the problem.

Scanning   involves looking outside the firm and bringing back useful solutions.

Schemas   are cognitive frameworks that represent organized knowledge developed through experience about people, objects, or events.

Scientific management   uses systematic study of job components to develop practices to increase people's efficiency at work.

Selective listening   is when individuals block out information or only hear things that match preconceived notions.

Selective perception   is the tendency to define problems from one's own point of view.

Selective screening   allows only a portion of available information to enter our perceptions.

Self-awareness   is the ability to understand our emotions and their impact on us and others.

Self-concept   is the view individuals have of themselves as physical, social, spiritual, or moral beings.

Self-conscious emotions   arise from internal sources, and **social emotions** derive from external sources.

Self-efficacy   is a person's belief that he or she can perform adequately in a situation.

Self-esteem   is a belief about one's own worth based on an overall self-evaluation.

Self-fulfilling prophecy   is creating or finding in a situation that which you expected to find in the first place.

Self-management   is the ability to think before acting and control disruptive impulses.

Self-managing   teams are empowered to make decisions to manage themselves in day-to-day work.

Self-monitoring   is a person's ability to adjust his or her behavior to external situational (environmental) factors.

Self-serving bias   underestimates internal factors and overestimates external factors as influences on someone's behavior.

Semantic barriers   involve a poor choice or use of words and mixed messages.

Sender   is a person or group trying to communicate with someone else.

Shaping   is positive reinforcement of successive approximations to the desired behavior.

Shared leadership   is a dynamic, interactive influence process through which individuals in teams lead one another.

Shared-power strategy   uses participatory methods and emphasizes common values to create change.

Simple design is a configuration involving one or two ways of specializing individuals and units.

Situational control is the extent to which leaders can determine what their groups are going to do and what the outcomes of their actions are going to be.

Situational leadership model focuses on the situational contingency of maturity or "readiness" of followers.

Skill is an ability to turn knowledge into effective action.

Skill-based pay rewards people for acquiring and developing job-relevant skills.

Social awareness is the ability to empathize and understand the emotions of others.

Social capital is a capacity to get things done due to relationships with other people.

Social construction approaches describe individual behavior as "constructed" in context, as people act and interact in situations.

Social facilitation is the tendency for one's behavior to be influenced by the presence of others in a group.

Social identity theory is a theory developed to understand the psychological basis of discrimination.

Social learning theory describes how learning occurs through interactions among people, behavior, and environment.

Social loafing occurs when people work less hard in groups than they would individually.

Social network analysis identifies the informal structures and their embedded social relationships that are active in an organization.

Social traits are surface-level traits that reflect the way a person appears to others when interacting in social settings.

Societal goals reflect the intended contributions of an organization to the broader society.

Span of control refers to the number of individuals reporting to a supervisor.

Specific environment is the set of owners, suppliers, distributors, government agencies, and competitors with which an organization must interact to grow and survive.

Spotlight questions expose a decision to public scrutiny and full transparency.

Staff units assist the line units by performing specialized services to the organization.

Stakeholders are people and groups with an interest or "stake" in the performance of the organization.

Standardization is the degree to which the range of actions in a job or series of jobs is limited.

Status congruence involves consistency between a person's status within and outside a group.

Status differences are differences between persons of higher and lower ranks.

Stereotype assigns attributes commonly associated with a group to an individual.

Stereotyping occurs when people make a generalization, usually exaggerated or oversimplified (and potentially offensive), that is used to describe or distinguish a group.

Stigma is a phenomenon whereby an individual is rejected as a result of an attribute that is deeply discredited by his or her society.

Stock options give the right to purchase shares at a fixed price in the future.

Storming stage is one of high emotionality and tension among team members.

Strategic leadership is leadership of a quasi-independent unit, department, or organization.

Strategy positions the organization in the competitive environment and implements actions to compete successfully.

Stress is tension from extraordinary demands, constraints, or opportunities.

Subcultures are groups who exhibit unique patterns of values and philosophies not consistent with the dominant culture of the larger organization or system.

Substantive conflict involves fundamental disagreement over ends or goals to be pursued and the means for their accomplishment.

Substitutes for leadership make a leader's influence either unnecessary or redundant in that they replace a leader's influence.

Supportive communication principles are a set of tools focused on joint problem solving.

Supportive leadership focuses on subordinate needs, well-being, and promotion of a friendly work climate.

Synergy is the creation of a whole greater than the sum of its parts.

Systematic thinking approaches problems in a rational and an analytical fashion.

Systems goals are concerned with the conditions within the organization that are expected to increase its survival potential.

Task activities directly contribute to the performance of important tasks.

Task performance is the quantity and quality of work produced.

Team is a group of people holding themselves collectively accountable for using complementary skills to achieve a common purpose.

Team-building is a collaborative way to gather and analyze data to improve teamwork.

Team composition is the mix of abilities, skills, personalities, and experiences that the members bring to the team.

Team decisions are made by all members of the team.

Teamwork occurs when team members live up to their collective accountability for goal accomplishment.

Technical skill is an ability to perform specialized tasks.

Telecommuting is work done at home or from a remote location using computers and advanced telecommunications.

Terminal values reflect a person's preferences concerning the "ends" to be achieved.

Title VII of the Civil Rights Act of 1964 protects individuals against employment discrimination on the basis of race and color, as well as national origin, sex, and religion.

Trait perspectives assume that traits play a central role in differentiating between leaders and nonleaders or in predicting leader or organizational outcomes.

Transactional leadership involves leader–follower exchanges necessary for achieving routine performance agreed upon between leaders and followers.

Transformational change radically shifts the fundamental character of an organization.

Transformational leadership occurs when leaders broaden and elevate followers' interests and stir followers to look beyond their own interests to the good of others.

Two-factor theory identifies job context as the source of job dissatisfaction and job content as the source of job satisfaction.

Type A orientations are characterized by impatience, desire for achievement, and a more competitive nature than Type B.

Type B orientations are characterized by an easy-going and less competitive nature than Type A.

Uncertain environments provide no information to predict expected results for decision-making alternatives.

Uncertainty avoidance is the cultural tendency to be uncomfortable with uncertainty and risk in everyday life.

Universal design is the practice of designing products, buildings, public spaces, and programs to be usable by the greatest number of people.

Unplanned change occurs spontaneously or randomly.

Upward communication is the flow of messages from lower to higher organizational levels.

Valence is the value to the individual of various work outcomes.

Validity means a performance measure addresses job-relevant dimensions.

Value chain is a sequence of activities that creates valued goods and services for customers.

Value congruence occurs when individuals express positive feelings upon encountering others who exhibit values similar to their own.

Values are broad preferences concerning appropriate courses of action or outcomes.

Vertical specialization is a hierarchical division of labor that distributes formal authority.

Vicarious learning involves capturing the lessons of others' experiences.

Virtual communication networks link team members through electronic communication.

Virtual organization is an ever-shifting constellation of firms, with a lead corporation, that pools skills, resources, and experiences to thrive jointly.

Virtual teams work together through computer mediation.

Work sharing is when employees agree to work fewer hours to avoid layoffs.

Workforce diversity is a mix of people within a workforce who are considered to be, in some way, different from those in the prevailing constituency.

Zone of indifference is the range of authoritative requests to which a subordinate is willing to respond without subjecting the directives to critical evaluation or judgment.

Self-Test 1

Multiple Choice
1. b **2.** d **3.** c **4.** c **5.** c **6.** b **7.** c **8.** a **9.** d
10. d **11.** a **12.** c **13.** c **14.** c **15.** a

Short Response
16. OB as a scientific discipline has the following characteristics: a) It is an interdisciplinary body of knowledge, drawing upon insights from such allied social sciences as sociology and psychology. b) OB researchers use scientific methods to develop and test models and theories about human behavior in organizations. c) OB focuses on application, trying to develop from science practical insights that can improve organizations. d) OB uses contingency thinking, trying to fit explanations to situations rather than trying to find "one best" answer that fits all situations.

17. The term "valuing diversity" is used to describe behavior that respects individual differences. In the workplace this means respecting the talents and potential contributions of people from different races and of different genders, ethnicities, and ages, for example.

18. An effective manager is one who is able to work with and support other people so that long-term high performance is achieved. This manager is able to maintain an environment for sustainable high performance by creating conditions for job satisfaction as well as high task performance.

19. Emotional intelligence is an ability to understand and manage emotions well, both personally and in interactions with others. Self-regulation is an important emotional intelligence competency. It is the capacity to think before taking action, and thus make sure that actions are functional rather than dysfunctional. It is the capacity to quickly spot tendencies to behave in disruptive or unhelpful ways due to an emotional reaction to a person or situation, and then control those tendencies to avoid bad behavior.

Applications Essay
20. Carla is about to lead an important discussion since the world of work will certainly be different by the time these sixth graders are ready to enter the workforce. As they look ahead, she should encourage them to consider the following points:

- Commitment to ethical behavior
- Importance of knowledge and experience in the form of "human capital"
- Less emphasis on boss-centered "command and control"
- Emphasis on teamwork
- Emphasis on use of computers and information technology
- Respect for people and their work expectations
- More people working for themselves and more job/employer shifting by people; fewer people working a lifetime for one organization

Of course, one of Carla's greatest challenges will be to express these concepts in words and examples that sixth graders will understand. Your answer should reflect that use of language and examples.

Self-Test 2

Multiple Choice
1. d **2.** c **3.** b **4.** a **5.** b **6.** c **7.** d **8.** b **9.** a
10. c **11.** b **12.** d **13.** c **14.** a **15.** d

Short Response
16. Individual differences reflect the ways in which people are similar and how they vary in their thinking, feeling, and behavior. They are important in organizational behavior because by categorizing behavioral tendencies of different types of people, and then identifying groups to which individuals (including ourselves) belong, we can more accurately predict why and how people behave as they do.

17. Both nature and nurture are important, and research isn't conclusive as to whether one is more influential than the other. Some studies show there is a 50-50 split, while the twin studies show that about 32% of variance in leadership is related to nurture. What is clear is that who we are is affected by *both* the genes we inherit and the environments in which we are raised.

18. Meglino and colleagues found that the most common values held by people in the workplace are those related to achievement, helping and concern for others, honesty, and fairness. When individuals in organizations share values with those around them, they experience greater satisfaction; when their values differ from those around them, they may experience conflict over such things as goals and how to achieve them.

19. Environments that are most conducive to diversity are those that appreciate differences, create a setting where everyone feels valued and accepted, and recognize the benefits diversity brings to workplace and organizational functioning. Such environments offer commitment to inclusion from the highest levels, opportunities for networking and mentoring, and role models and exposure to high visibility assignments for diverse groups.

Applications Essay

20. The first step would be to identify the source of the stress. It is important at this stage to gather data from multiple perspectives (e.g., employees, managers, HR) and to create a safe environment for people to provide input to ensure accurate information. Factors you should consider are: Is the stress due to personal issues of employees, or workplace issues? Are some employees more stressed than others, and if so why? How do individual differences come into play, if at all? What workplace or organizational factors are causing the stress? How much agreement is there about the causes of the stress? What are the effects of the stress, and who is most affected? Once you have gathered enough information that you are satisfied you have a complete picture of the situation, develop an action plan. This plan should (a) make sure to address the appropriate source, (b) be realistic and impactful, and (c) be one that will not cause more stress. Typically many stress issues can be resolved with good communication and support, and by working with individuals to find ways they can manage the factors causing their stress. Managers need to be careful to avoid environments that are highly stressful and lead to burnout, such as fear climates, environments that are too individually competitive (pitting employees against one another), not dealing with poor performers, overly stressful change situations, and bad communication. The most promising plan of action would be one that helps both employees and managers understand specific steps and techniques for reducing stress.

Self-Test 3

Multiple Choice

1. d **2.** b **3.** a **4.** d **5.** a **6.** b **7.** a **8.** c **9.** a
10. d **11.** a **12.** d **13.** d **14.** c **15.** c

Short Response

16. Emotions and moods are both part of what is called affect, or the range of feelings that people experience in their life context. An emotion is a strong positive or negative feeling directed toward someone or something. It is usually intense, not long-lasting, and always associated with a source—someone or something that makes you feel the way you do. An example is the positive emotion of elation a student feels when congratulated by an instructor. A mood is a more generalized positive and negative feeling or state of mind that may persist for some time. An example is someone who wakes up and just fells "grouchy" that day. See Figure 3.2 for additional material to fit this answer.

17. The three components of an attitude are cognition, affect, and behavior. Cognition might occur as the belief that "I think being a management major is important to my future career." Affect might occur as "I feel really good about taking this organizational behavior course." Behavior might occur as the intention of "I am going to study hard and earn an 'A' in the course." The cognition influences affect which influences intended behavior. But the behavior is only that—an intention. As we well know, there are lots of things that happen during a semester that might lead an otherwise well-intentioned management major who likes his or her OB course to not study hard enough to earn an A grade.

18. Here are five aspects of job satisfaction that are commonly measured. (1) Work itself: responsibility, interest, and growth; (2) Quality of supervision: technical and social support; (3) Relationships with co-workers: social harmony and respect; (4) Promotion opportunities: chances for further advancement; (5) Pay: adequacy and perceived equity vis-à-vis others. Although it depends on the individual and the context, in general each of these can be considered equally important.

19. Cognitive dissonance describes a state of inconsistency between an individual's attitudes and his or her behavior. Such inconsistency can result in changing attitudes, changing future behavior, or developing new ways to explain the inconsistency. The amount of control an individual has over the situation and the magnitude of the reward tend to influence which of these actions will be chosen.

Applications Essay

20. The heart of the issue rests with the satisfaction—performance relationship as discussed in this chapter. Does satisfaction cause performance? It appears that satisfaction alone is no guarantee of high-level job performance. Although a satisfied worker is likely not to quit and to have good attendance, his or her performance still remains uncertain. In the integrated model of motivation, performance is a function not only of motivation and effort, but also of individual attributes and organizational support. Thus I would be cautious in focusing only on creating satisfied workers and high-performing ones. I would try to make sure that the rewards for performance create satisfaction. I would also try to make sure that the satisfied worker has the right abilities, training, and other support needed to perform a job really well. Assuming that satisfaction alone will always lead to high performance seems risky at best; it leaves too many other important considerations left untouched, an example of which is described in the study of satisfaction in groups across time.

Self-Test 4

Multiple Choice

1. b **2.** d **3.** b **4.** c **5.** d **6.** c **7.** c **8.** a **9.** a
10. d **11.** c **12.** c **13.** c **14.** a **15.** a

Short Response

16. A model similar to that in Figure 4.2 should be drawn to include a brief discussion of the perception process as discussed in the chapter.

17. There are six perceptual distortions listed and discussed in the chapter—stereotype, halo effect, selective perception, projection, contrast, and self-fulfilling prophecies. You may select any two and briefly note how they distort the perceptual process.

18. The law of effect states that a behavior followed by a pleasant consequence is likely to be repeated and a behavior followed by an unpleasant consequence is unlikely to be repeated. Managers and people at work deal regularly with others who exhibit desirable and undesirable behaviors. By understanding the law of effect, they should be able to strengthen the desired behaviors and weaken the undesired ones by manipulating consequences.

19. Reinforcement learning focuses on behavior as a function of its consequences, while social learning theory emphasizes observational learning and the importance of perception and attribution. Thus, people respond to how their perceptions and attributions help define consequences, and not to the objective consequences as emphasized in reinforcement learning.

Applications Essay

20. A good example to illustrate attribution is the fundamental attribution error as opposed to the self-serving bias. You should explain the fundamental attribution error as the tendency to underestimate the influence of situational factors and to overestimate the influence of personal factors in evaluating someone else's behaviors. In contrast, the self-serving bias is the tendency to deny personal responsibility for performance problems but accept personal responsibility for performance success. Then follow up with an example of each and implications for managing the department.

Self-Test 5

Multiple Choice

1. a **2.** d **3.** b **4.** b **5.** d **6.** d **7.** d **8.** c **9.** a **10.** a **11.** c **12.** a **13.** d **14.** a **15.** b

Short Response

16. Basically, the frustration-regression principle in Alderfer's ERG theory states that when one level of need is unsatisfied (or frustrated) the individual can revert back (or regress) to seek further satisfaction of a lower level need. For example, if a need for psychological growth in one's job is frustrated, the person may regress back to place more emphasis on satisfying relatedness needs.

17. According to Herzberg the job content or satisfier factors are what really motivate people to work hard. They include such things as feelings of responsibility, opportunities for advancement and growth, and job challenges. In order to build these things into jobs and make them more motivational, Herzberg recommends job enrichment—that is adding job content factors by moving into a job things traditionally done by higher levels such as planning and controlling responsibilities.

18. Distributive justice is when everyone is treated by the same rules with no one getting special favors or exceptions; procedural justice is when all rules and procedures are properly followed.

19. Expectancy theory states that Motivation = Expectancy × Instrumentality × Valence. The presence of multiplication signs creates the "multiplier effect." This means that a "0" in expectancy or instrumentality or valence creates a "0" for motivation. In other words, the multiplier effect is that all three factors—expectancy, instrumentality, valence—must be positive in order for motivation to be positive.

Applications Essay

20. The issue in this case boils down to motivation to work hard. A job might provide lots of satisfaction for someone—relationships, good pay, etc., and they may not work hard because there is no link between receiving the need satisfaction and doing a really good job every day. To apply the needs theories of motivation, managers need to link opportunities for need satisfaction with tasks and activities that are important to getting the job done well. In other words, hard work on things important to the organization are viewed as pathways toward individual need satisfaction. In this case, as perhaps Person B would be suggesting, individuals will work hard because they are satisfying important needs by doing important job-relevant things.

Self-Test 6

Multiple Choice

1. d **2.** c **3.** b **4.** b **5.** a **6.** c **7.** b **8.** d **9.** c **10.** d **11.** c **12.** d **13.** d **14.** a **15.** a

Short Response

16. In a traditional evaluation the employee's performance is evaluated by the supervisor. In the 360° evaluation the employee's performance is evaluated by those with whom he or she works, including supervisor, peers, subordinates, and perhaps even customers. The 360° evaluation also typically includes a self-evaluation. When the results of all evaluations are analyzed and compared, the employee has a good sense of his or her accomplishments and areas for improvement. This evaluation can then be discussed with the supervisor.

17. A halo error in performance appraisal occurs when one attribute or behavior inappropriately influences the overall appraisal. For example, an individual may have a unique style of dress but be a very high performer. If the evaluator lets his or her distaste for the dress style negatively bias the overall performance evaluation, a halo error has occurred. A recency error occurs when a performance appraisal is biased due to the influence of recent events. In other words, the performance appraisal is based on most recent performance and may not be an accurate reflection of performance for a full evaluation period. For example, I might have a very bad week just prior to an evaluation due to family problems. If my supervisor uses that week's performance to negatively bias the evaluation even though for the prior six months I had been a very strong performer, recency error would have occurred.

18. Growth-need strength is a moderator variable in the job characteristics model. In other words, it sets the condition under which an individual will or will not respond positively to the job characteristics. When an individual is high in growth-need strength, the prediction is that he or she will respond positively to a job high in the core characteristics and therefore largely enriched. However, when the individual has low-growth-need strength, the prediction is that he or she will not respond positively to high core characteristics and may be dissatisfied and less productive in such enriched job conditions.

19. The compressed workweek, or 4–40 schedule, offers employees the advantage of a three-day weekend. However, it can cause problems for the employer in terms of ensuring that operations are covered adequately during the normal five-day workweek. Also, the compressed workweek will entail more complicated work scheduling. In addition, some employees find that the schedule is tiring and can cause family adjustment problems.

Applications Essay

20. There are many things that can be done to use rewards and performance management well in the context of student organizations. On the reward side the most appropriate thing is to make sure that those who get the benefits from the organization are the ones who do the work. For example, if there is a fund-raiser to support a student trip, only those who actively raise the money should get financial support for the trip. And possibly, the financial support should be proportionate to the amount of time and effort each person contributed to raising the funds. Also it is probably quite common that little or no evaluation is done of how people perform in offices and special assignments in the student organizations. Many possible ways of creating and using more formal evaluation systems could be established. For example, officers could be rated on a BARS scale developed by the membership to reflect the

desirable officer behaviors. These ratings could take place every month or two, and individuals who perform poorly can be counseled or removed, while those who perform well can be praised and continued.

Self-Test 7

Multiple Choice

1. a **2.** b **3.** d **4.** c **5.** b **6.** d **7.** b **8.** d **9.** d **10.** c **11.** b **12.** c **13.** d **14.** c **15.** c

Short Response

16. Teams are potentially good for organizations for several reasons. They are good for people, they can improve creativity, they sometimes make the best decisions, they gain commitment to decisions, they help control the behavior of their members, and they can help to counterbalance the effects of large organization size.

17. Permanent formal groups appear on organization charts and serve an ongoing purpose. These groups may include departments, divisions, teams, and the like. Temporary groups are created to solve a specific problem or perform a defined task and are then disbanded. Examples are committees, cross-functional task forces, and project teams.

18. Self-managing teams take different forms. A common pattern, however, involves empowering team members to make decisions about the division of labor and scheduling, to develop and maintain the skills needed to perform several different jobs for the team, to help train one another to learn those jobs, and to help select new team members.

19. The diversity-consensus dilemma occurs when a team with high membership diversity gets caught between diversity advantages and disadvantages. On the one hand the team has the potential advantages of many viewpoints, perspectives, and enriched information. On the other hand it suffers the potential pitfalls of members having a hard time learning how to work well with one another; this can make it hard to reach consensus.

Applications Essay

20. Saw your message and wanted to respond. Don't worry. There is no reason at all that a great design engineer can't run a high-performance project team. Go into the job with confidence, but try to follow some basic guidelines as you build and work with the team. First off, remember that a "team" isn't just a "group." You have to make sure that the members identify highly with the goals and will hold themselves collectively accountable for results—and that includes you. I suggest that you communicate high-performance standards right from the beginning. Set the tone in the first team meeting and even create a sense of urgency to get things going. Be sure that the members have the right skills, and find ways to create some early "successes" for them. Don't let them drift apart; make sure they spend a lot of time together. Give lots of positive feedback as the project develops and, perhaps most importantly, model the expected behaviors yourself. Go for it!

Self-Test 8

Multiple Choice

1. d **2.** a **3.** a **4.** b **5.** b **6.** c **7.** c **8.** a **9.** b
10. b **11.** a **12.** d **13.** a **14.** a **15.** c

Short Response

16. Team building usually begins when someone notices that a problem exists or may develop in the group. Members then work collaboratively to gather data, analyze the situation, plan for improvements, and implement the plan. Everyone is expected to participate in each step, and the group as a whole is expected to benefit from continuous improvement.

17. To help build positive norms, a team leader must first act as a positive role model. She or he should carefully select members for the team and be sure to reinforce and reward members for performing as desired. She or he should also hold meetings to review performance, provide feedback, and discuss and agree on goals.

18. A basic rule of team dynamics is that members of highly cohesive groups tend to conform to group norms. Thus, when group norms are positive for performance, the conformity is likely to create high-performance outcomes. When the norms are negative, however, the conformity is likely to create low-performance outcomes.

19. Inter-team competition can create problems in the way groups work with one another. Ideally, an organization is a cooperative system in which groups are well integrated and help one another out as needed. When groups get competitive, however, there is a potential dysfunctional side. Instead of communicating with one another, they decrease communication. Instead of viewing one another positively, they develop negative stereotypes of one another. Instead of viewing each other as mutual partners in the organization, they become hostile and view one another more as enemies. Although inter-team competition can be good by adding creative tension and encouraging more focused efforts, this potential negative side should not be forgotten.

Applications Essay

20. I would tell Alejandro that consensus and unanimity are two different, but related, things. Consensus results from extensive discussion and lots of "give and take" in which group members share ideas and listen carefully to one another. Eventually, one alternative emerges that is preferred

by most. Those who disagree, however, know that they have been listened to and have had a fair chance to influence the decision outcome. Consensus, therefore, does not require unanimity. What it does require is the opportunity for any dissenting members to feel they have been able to speak and be sincerely listened to. A decision by unanimity that generates 100 percent agreement on an issue may be the ideal state of affairs, but it is not always possible to achieve. Thus, Alejandro should always try to help members work intensively together, communicate well with one another, and sincerely share ideas and listen. However, he should not be concerned for complete unanimity on every issue. Rather, consensus should be the agreed-upon goal in most cases.

Self-Test 9

Multiple Choice

1. c **2.** b **3.** a **4.** c **5.** b **6.** a **7.** a **8.** c **9.** a
10. c **11.** b **12.** a **13.** b **14.** c **15.** d

Short Response

16. Heuristics are simplifying strategies, or "rules of thumb," that people use to make decisions. They make it easier for individuals to deal with uncertainty and limited information, but they can also lead to biased results. Common heuristics include availability-making decisions based on recent events; representativeness-making decisions based on similar events; and anchoring and adjustment-making decisions based on historical precedents.

17. Individual, or authority, decisions are made by the manager or team leader acting alone based on information that he or she possesses. Consultative decisions are made by the manager or team leader after soliciting input from other persons. Group decisions are made when the manager or team leader asks others to participate in problem solving. The ideal form of the group decision is true consensus.

18. Escalating commitment is the tendency to continue with a previously chosen course of action even though feedback indicates that it is not working. This can lead to a waste of time, money, and other resources, in addition to the sacrificing of the opportunity to pursue a course of action offering more valuable results. Escalating commitment is encouraged by the popular adage, "If at first you don't succeed try, try, again." Another way to look at it is "throwing good money after bad."

19. Most people are too busy to respond personally to every problem that comes their way. The effective manager and team leader knows when to delegate decisions to others, how to set priorities, and when to abstain from acting altogether. Questions to ask include: Is the problem easy to deal with? Might the problem resolve itself? Is this my decision to make? Is this a solvable problem within the context of the organization?

Applications Essay

20. This is what I would say in the mentoring situation. First, teams can be great for creativity but they have to be set up and then led so that their creative potential is fully realized. To start with, the team needs to have at least some highly creative members. They bring to the team context valuable insights, new ideas, and enthusiasm for finding new ways of doing things. These are people who already have strong creativity skills such as high energy, resourcefulness, intuition, and lateral thinking. With people like this as part of the team it will have a strong baseline of team creativity skills in place. Then it is important to give this team management and organizational support to harness this creativity potential. The team leader has to believe in and want team creativity, he or she has to be patient and allow time for creative processes to work, and he or she also needs to make sure the team has all the resources it needs to do creative work. An organizational culture in which creativity is valued is also an asset since it provides a broader context of support for what the team is trying to accomplish. When people throughout the organization value creativity, it tends to pull others along and also support their creative efforts. When creativity is expected and even evaluated as part of performance appraisals, it is also further encouraged by the surrounding organizational context.

Self-Test 10

Multiple Choice

1. c **2.** a **3.** b **4.** b **5.** d **6.** c **7.** b **8.** c **9.** d
10. c **11.** a **12.** c **13.** c **14.** a **15.** b

Short Response

16. Managers can be faced with the following conflict situations: vertical conflict—conflict that occurs between hierarchical levels; horizontal conflict—conflict that occurs between those at the same hierarchical level; line-staff conflict—conflict that occurs between line and staff representatives; role conflict—conflict that occurs when the communication of task expectations is inadequate or upsetting.

17. The major indirect conflict management approaches include the following: appeals to common goals—involves focusing the attention of potentially conflicting parties on one mutually desirable conclusion; hierarchical referral—using the chain of command for conflict resolution; organizational redesign—including decoupling, buffering, linking pins, and liaison groups; use of myths and scripts—managing superficially through behavioral routines (scripts) or to hide conflict by denying the necessity to make a tradeoff in conflict resolution.

18. You should acknowledge that different styles may be appropriate under different conditions. Avoidance is the extreme form of nonattention and is most commonly used when the issue is trivial, when more important issues are pressing, or when individuals need to cool off. An accommodation strategy is used when an issue is more important to the other party than it is to you, or to build social credits.

19. Distributive negotiation focuses on staking out positions and claiming portions of the available "pie." It usually takes the form of hard negotiation—the parties maximize their self-interests and hold out to get their own way—or soft negotiation—one party is willing to make concessions in order to reach an agreement. Distributive negotiation can lead to competition, compromise, or accommodation, but it tends to be win-lose oriented in all cases. Integrative negotiation focuses on the merits of an issue and attempts to enlarge the available "pie." It may lead to avoidance, compromise, or collaboration. It tends to be more win-win oriented and seeks to satisfy the needs and interests of all parties.

Applications Essay

20. When negotiating the salary for your first job, you should attempt to avoid the common pitfalls of negotiation. These include falling prey to the myth of the "fixed pie"; nonrational escalation of conflict, such as trying to compare the proposed salary to the highest offer you have heard; overconfidence; and ignoring other's needs (the personnel officer probably has a fixed limit). While the initial salary may be very important to you, you should also recognize that it may not be as significant as what type of job you will have and whether you will have an opportunity to move up in the firm.

Self-Test 11

Multiple Choice

1. d **2.** c **3.** a **4.** b **5.** a **6.** d **7.** a **8.** d **9.** a
10. a **11.** b **12.** a **13.** a **14.** d **15.** a

Short Response

16. Channel richness is a useful concept for managers because it describes the capacity of a communication channel to convey and move information. For example, if a manager wants to convey basic and routine information to a lot of people, a lean channel such as the electronic bulletin or written memorandum may be sufficient. However, if the manager needs to convey a complicated message and one that may involve some uncertainty, a richer channel such as the face-to-face meeting may be necessary. Simply put, the choice of channel may have a lot of impact on the effectiveness of a communication attempt.

17. Informal communication channels are very important in today's organizations. Modern work environments place great emphasis on cross-functional relationships and communication. Employee involvement and participation in decision making are very important. This requires that people know and talk with one another, often across departmental lines. Progressive organizations make it easy for people to interact and meet outside of formal work assignments and relationships. When people know one another, they can more easily and frequently communicate with one another.

18. Status effects can interfere with the effectiveness of communication between lower and higher levels in an organization. Lower-level members are concerned about how the higher-level members will respond, especially if the information being communicated is negative or unfavorable. In such cases, a tendency exists to filter or modify the information to make it as attractive as possible to the recipient. The result is that high-level decision makers in organizations sometimes act on inaccurate or incomplete information. Although their intentions are good, they just aren't getting good information from their subordinates.

19. Active listening works by increasing the flow of information to help the communicator analyze the issue being processed. In active listening, the focus should be on the communicator, not the listener. At the beginning of the conversation the listener helps increase information flow to open up communication by listening for content and feelings. The listener also uses reinforcing statements to support those feelings and create a safe environment. Once the information has been processed, the listener helps the communicator identify a course of action by turning to reflecting and advising statements that help represent what the communicator expressed.

Applications Essay

20. Organizations depend on communication flowing upward, downward, and laterally. Rapid developments in technology have led to a heavy reliance on computers to assist in the movement of this information. E-mail is one part of an electronic organizational communication system. Research suggests that people may fall prey to the "impersonality" of computer-based operations and that the personal or face-to-face side of communication may suffer. Rather than eliminate e-mail and other forms of computer-mediated communication, however, the managing director should work hard to establish proper e-mail protocols and provide many other avenues for communication. The managing director can serve as a role model in his or her use of e-mail, in being regularly available for face-to-face interactions, by holding regular meetings, and by "wandering around" frequently to meet and talk with people from all levels. In addition, the director can make sure that facility designs and office arrangements support interaction and make it less easy for people to disappear behind computer screens. Finally, the director must

actively encourage communication of all types and not allow himself or herself to get trapped into serving as a classic example of the "e-mail boss."

Self-Test 12

Multiple Choice

1. d **2.** a **3.** d **4.** d **5.** c **6.** b **7.** a **8.** c **9.** d
10. a **11.** b **12.** a **13.** d **14.** a **15.** d

Short Response

16. For the first part of the question, you should consider the notions of reward, coercive, legitimate, expert, and referent power. The response should recognize the difference between position sources and personal sources. The second part of the question concerns the power of lower level participants in organizational settings. Link the sources of power with Bernard's acceptance theory of authority.

17. The text introduces five basic guidelines for increasing position power. They are (1) increase your centrality and criticality in the organization; (2) increase the personal discretion and flexibility of your job; (3) build into your job tasks that are difficult to evaluate; (4) increase the visibility of your job performance; (5) increase the relevance of your tasks to the organization. The text also identifies three basic guidelines for acquiring personal power. They are: (1) increase your knowledge and information as it relates to the job; (2) increase your personal attractiveness; (3) increase your effort in relation to key organizational tasks.

18. The text identifies seven basic strategies of managerial influence: reason, friendliness, coalition, bargaining, assertiveness, higher authority, and sanctions. You should be able to express them in everyday language along with an example. Each of these strategies is available to the manager in the downward influence attempt; however, the choices in upward attempts may be more limited. In the exercise of upward influence, influence attempts can be expected frequently to include assertiveness, friendliness, and reason.

19. Organizational politics is formally defined as "the management of influence to obtain ends not sanctioned by the organization or to obtain sanctioned ends through nonsanctioned means." Yet it can also be viewed as the art of creative compromise among competing interests. You should be able to express these apparently conflicting views in everyday language that communicates a sense of understanding. It is important that politics not be viewed as an entirely dysfunctional phenomenon that can result in people becoming dissatisfied and feeling emotionally distraught or estranged from the organizational situation. In particular, the functional aspects of organizational politics include helping managers to overcome personal inadequacies, cope with change, channel personal contacts, and substitute for formal authority.

Applications Essay

20. While the financial implications to stockholders from merger and acquisition seems to vary considerably, one lesson is quite clear—the senior executive of the acquiring firm gains power and influence. Further, a chief reason for senior executives involuntarily leaving firms is being taken over by another corporation. Thus, some executives believe that it is merge or be merged so they would rather be on the acquiring end.

Self-Test 13

Multiple Choice

1. c **2.** b **3.** b **4.** d **5.** a **6.** c **7.** a **8.** d **9.** c
10. b **11.** a **12.** d **13.** b **14.** c **15.** a

Short Response

16. Leadership is the process of influencing others and facilitating effort in order to accomplish shared objectives. Leadership tends to emphasize adaptive or useful change, whereas management is designed to promote stability or to enable the organization to run smoothly.

17. Behavioral approaches to leadership indicate that leader behaviors, such as task-oriented and relationship-oriented behavior, are related to leadership effectiveness. Situational theories also acknowledge the importance of behaviors, but add that the effectiveness of these behaviors will depend on (i.e., is contingent upon) the situation. In some situations, such as highly structured situations where employees know what to do, relationship-oriented behavior will be more effective. In other situations, where individuals do not know what to do, task-oriented behavior will be more effective.

18. Transactional and transformational leadership theories are both part of the full range leadership theory developed by Bass and colleagues, but differ in an important way. Transactional leadership is focused on leader-follower exchanges necessary for achieving routine performance, while transformational leadership is focused on motivating performance beyond expectations. Transactional leadership behaviors include contingent rewards, management by exception, and laissez-faire, whereas transformational leadership behaviors include charisma, inspiration, intellectual stimulation, and individualized consideration. Although early theorizing on this model believed that transformational leadership would be the preferred style, later research showed that both transactional and transformational leadership are important and necessary to managerial leadership.

19. Leader-member exchange theory says that rather than having an "average" leadership style, managers develop differentiated relationships with their subordinates. With some subordinates these relationships are high quality (high LMX), involving high levels of trust, respect, consideration, loyalty, etc. With others (low LMX), these relationships are characterized by low trust (or distrust), lack of respect and loyalty, and reduced work effort. High quality LMX relationships generate very positive outcomes for organizations, whereas low quality relationships are associated with a range of negative outcomes for the individuals involved and the organization.

Applications Essay

20. Your friend tells you that there is no easy answer but there are some basics to keep in mind. Effective leadership involves using various types of behaviors appropriate to a situation. These behaviors generally include things associated with relationships (e.g., consideration) and task (e.g., initiating structure). Effective leadership is also associated with certain kinds of traits, such as integrity, self-confidence, trustworthiness, and intelligence. Leaders need to know their strengths and weaknesses, and if they are not able to use a range of effective behaviors they should try to match situations to their style. If you are charismatic that will help you to motivate employees, but you have to be careful because it can have negative effects. Moreover, both transactional and transformational behaviors are beneficial (and he gives you a list of those behaviors). Finally, you need to recognize the importance of followers and of the relationships you develop. The bottom line is that the best leaders are those who are high in self-awareness and awareness of others, who work to generate effective work (not friendship) relationships with all employees and motivate strong task performance as well as positive job attitudes.

Self-Test 14

Multiple Choice

1. c **2.** a **3.** c **4.** b **5.** d **6.** a **7.** d **8.** c **9.** b
10. d **11.** c **12.** a **13.** b **14.** d **15.** c

Short Response

16. Three ways in which shared leadership can be used in self-directed work teams are (1) behavior-focused strategies that tend to increase self-awareness, leading to the behaviors involving necessary but not always pleasant tasks; (2) self rewards in conjunction with behavior-focused strategies; and (3) constructive thought patterns that focus on the creation or alteration of cognitive thought processes. The student should then elaborate on each of these along the lines of the discussion in the chapter.

17. The three core qualities of a spiritual leader are vision, altruistic love, and hope/faith. Vision defines the destination and journey, reflects high ideals, and encourages hope/faith. Altruistic love develops trust and loyalty, as well as forgiveness, acceptance, honesty, courage, and humility. Hope/faith addresses endurance, perseverance, and motivates others to do what it takes by using stretch goals.

18. Not all change in organizations is planned. Unplanned change—that which occurs spontaneously or by surprise—can be useful. The appropriate goal in managing unplanned change is to act immediately once the change is recognized to minimize any negative consequences and maximize any possible benefits. The goal is to take best advantage of the change situation by learning from the experience.

19. External forces for change are found in the relationship between an organization and its environment. Examples are the pressures of mergers, strategic alliances, and divestitures. Internal forces for change include those found in different lifecycle demands as the organization passes from birth through growth and toward maturity. Internal forces also include the political nature of organizations as reflected in authority and reward systems.

Applications Essay

20. Jorge may begin his attempts to deal with resistance to change by using education and communication. Through one-on-one discussions, group presentations, and even visits to other centers he can better inform his staff about the nature and logic of the changes. He should also utilize participation and involvement by allowing others (for example, in a series of task forces) to help choose the new equipment and design the new programs. In all this he should offer enough facilitation and support to help everyone deal with any hardships the changes may cause. He should be especially alert to listen to any problems and complaints that may arise. On certain matters, Jorge might use negotiation and agreement to exchange benefits for staff support. In the extreme case, manipulation and cooperation through covert attempts to influence others might be used to achieve needed support, although this is not advisable. Similarly, explicit or implicit coercion would use force to get people to accept change at any cost. Our advice would be to stick with the first four strategies as much as possible and avoid the latter two.

Self-Test 15

Multiple Choice

1. c **2.** a **3.** b **4.** a **5.** d **6.** d **7.** a **8.** a **9.** b
10. c **11.** b **12.** a **13.** d **14.** d **15.** a

Short Response

16. Cox's theory is designed for organizations that are located in the United States. His ideas may not be easily expanded to multinational corporations headquartered in other cultures. Cox believes that it is important for culturally divergent groups within an organization to communicate and educate one another. This helps subgroups become more tolerant and interactive with other portions of the organization. Second, the organization needs to make sure that one type of cultural group is not segregated into one type of position. When cultural subgroups are spread throughout the organization, the levels of interaction increase as the stereotyping decreases. The company also needs to help restructure many of its informal lines of communication. By encouraging the integration of the informal communication, subgroups become more involved with one another. The organization must also ensure that no one group is associated with the company's outside image. A company that is perceived to be uniform in its culture attracts individuals who are from a similar culture. Finally, Cox states that interpersonal conflict that is based on group identity needs to be controlled.

17. Groups first need to define who is in the group and who is not. Criteria for both formal and informal groups need to be established to provide a framework for membership. Second, the group needs to set standards of behavior. These standards should consist of a series of informal rules that describe proper behavior and activities for the members. Finally, group members need to identify the friends and adversaries of the group. The identification process helps the group build alliances throughout the organization when they attempt to get projects and ideas completed.

18. If you have not had full-time employment, think seriously about this question because it is designed to help you appreciate the importance of organizational rules and roles. Formal rules should be covered to show that they help dictate procedures individuals use. Informal interaction should be discussed as well. Such questions as, "How are subgroups treated?" "Do different instructors have different rules?" and "Are Seniors treated differently from Sophomores in this system?" could all be potential subtopics.

19. The first element is the need for a widely shared philosophy. Although this first element seems vague, an effective company philosophy is anything but abstract. An organization member needs to be exposed to what the firm stands for. The firm's mission needs to be articulated often and throughout the organization. Organizations should put people ahead of rules and general policy mandates. When staffers feel included and important in a system they feel more loyal and accepting of the culture. Every company has heroes or individuals who have succeeded beyond expectations. Companies with strong company cultures allow the stories of these individuals to become well known throughout the organization. Through these stories, workers need to make sure that they understand the rituals and ceremonies that are important to the company's identity. Maintaining and enhancing these rituals helps many organizations keep a strong corporate culture. Informal rules and expectations must be evident so that workers understand what is expected of them and the organization. Finally, employees need to realize that their work is important; their work and knowledge should be networked throughout the company. The better the communication system in the company, the better the company's culture.

Applications Essay

20. An overemphasis on exploration is likely to yield a great number of new ideas, programs, and initiatives, but comparatively little effective commercialization. In contrast, an overemphasis on exploitation often results in small incremental changes to existing products in existing markets and does not yield the changes often dictated by environmental and technological change. Thus, most OB researchers stress the need for some type of balance. There are a variety of ways to do this. The most ambitious is to develop an ambidextrous organization that stresses both. Often, however, senior managers ask some parts to stress exploration and others exploitation. Here they recognize the tension and are prepared to reconcile opposing views.

Self-Test 16

Multiple Choice

1. b **2.** b **3.** b **4.** c **5.** e **6.** a **7.** a **8.** d **9.** b
10. d **11.** a **12.** b **13.** c **14.** b **15.** c **16.** b **17.** a
18. a **19.** b **20.** d

Short Response

21. Output goals are designed to help an organization define its overall mission and to help define the kind of business it is in. Output goals can often help define the types of products and the relationships that the company has with its consumers. Output goals often help demonstrate how a company fits into society. The second kind of organizational goal is the systems goal. A systems goal helps the company realize what behaviors it needs to maintain for its survival. The systems goal provides the means for the ends. It is important to recognize the importance of systems goals for day-to-day operations.

22. Control is the set of mechanisms used to keep action and/or outputs within predetermined limits. Two types of controls are often found in organizations. Output controls focus on desired targets to allow managers discretion in using different methods for reaching these targets. Process controls attempt to specify the manner in which tasks are accomplished. Policies, procedures, and rules as well as formalization and standardization can be seen as types of process controls. Total Quality Management can be seen

as a systemic way of managing processes within the firm and thus be viewed as a control mechanism.

23. The first advantage is that functional specialization can yield clear task assignments that replicate an individual's training and experience. Functional specialization also provides the ability for departmental colleagues to build upon one another's knowledge and experience. The functional approach also provides an excellent training ground for new managers. Finally, this system is easy to explain because members can understand the role of each group even though they do not understand a particular individual's functions. There are some major disadvantages to the system as well. The system may reinforce overspecialization. Many jobs within the system may become boring and too routine. The lines of communication within the organization may become overly complex. Top management is often overloaded with too many problems that should be addressed at a lower level. Many top managers spend too much time dealing with cross-functional issues. Finally, many individuals look up in the hierarchy for reinforcement instead of focusing their attention on products, services, and clients.

24. A matrix combines the strengths of both the functional and divisional departmentation. For instance, divisional specialization provides the organization with adaptability and flexibility to meet important demands of key external groups. With the matrix, this emphasis is blended with a stress on technical affairs found under functional departmentation. Unfortunately, there is a cost for this blending. Unity of command is lost. The authority and responsibilities of managers may overlap, causing conflict. And this form may be expensive.

Applications Essay

25. The notion that the Postal Service is a mechanistic bureaucracy is important because it suggests that there are already many controls built into the system by the division of labor. You should recognize several primary side effects that are exhibited when control mechanisms are placed on an individual in an organization such as the Postal Service. There is often a difficulty in balancing organizational controls. As one control is emphasized, others may be neglected. Controls often force managers to emphasize the "quick fix" instead of long-term planning. Often, controls lead to solutions that are not customized to specific problems (i.e., "across the board cuts"). Planning and documentation can become burdensome and limit the amount of action that actually occurs. Managers often become more concerned with internal paperwork than with problem solving or customers. And there are far too many supervisors and managers. Controls that are vaguely designed are often ineffective and unrealistic. As a result, the manager may interpret the control as he or she wants. The "do the best you can" goal that is commonly given to managers in the Postal Service is an example of this concept. Controls that are inserted drastically and harshly often cause panic among managers and administrators. A swift change in the territories of postal delivery clerks is an example. Finally, many goals and controls are inserted without the appropriate resources. This practice can make the attainment of goals difficult, if not impossible.

Self-Test 17

Multiple Choice
1. e **2.** c **3.** d **4.** a **5.** e **6.** e **7.** c **8.** c **9.** a
10. a **11.** b **12.** a **13.** b **14.** b **15.** b **16.** a **17.** b
18. a **19.** b **20.** c

Short Response
21. There are a number of ways to answer this question. Actually, a very large firm could use a simple structure but its chances of reaching its goals and surviving would be small. As the firm grows so does the complexity inside and individuals become overwhelmed if the firm does not evolve into a bureaucracy. Recall that a bureaucracy involved labor that is divided so that each worker was specialized. Every worker would have well-defined responsibilities and authorities. To complement this specialization, the organization should be arranged hierarchically. Authority should be arranged from the bottom up. A worker should be promoted only on the basis of merit and technical competence. Most importantly, employees are to work under rules and guidelines that were impersonal and applied to all staffers equally.

22. Information technology is the combination of machines, artifacts, procedures, and systems used to gather, store, analyze, and disseminate information for translating it into knowledge. It can be used as (a) a partial substitute for some operations as well as some process controls and impersonal methods of coordination, (b) a capability for transforming information to knowledge for learning, and (c) a strategic capability.

23. James Thompson believed that technology could be divided into three categories—intensive, mediating, or long linked. An intensive technology occurs when uncertainty exists as to how to produce the desired outcomes. Teams of specialists are brought together to pool knowledge and resources to solve the problem. An interdependence among specialists develops because all parties need one another to fulfill the project successfully. This technology often occurs in the research and development portion of organizations. A mediating technology allows various parties to become interdependent. For example, the ATM network that most banks utilize allows customers to bank at other institutions and still be tied to their home bank, automatically. Without this technology, the banking industry would not be so well

linked. The technology helps determine the nature of the banks' relationships with one another. Finally, Thompson believed that long-linked technologies had a unique effect on organizations as well. Long-linked technology is more commonly known as industrial technology. This type of knowledge allows organizations to produce goods in mass quantities. The assembly line designed by Henry Ford is one of the early examples of long-linked technology. Thompson uses these distinctions to highlight the various impacts that technology has on organizations. His approach differs greatly from Joan Woodward's approach, which focuses more on the mode of production. Woodward divides technology into three areas: small-batch manufacturing, mass production, and continuous process custom goods. Crafts persons are often characterized as small producers who must alter production to fit the needs of each client. Mass production technology deals with production of uniform goods for a mass market. The production design is altered to maximize speed while limiting product styles. The last type of technology deals with continuous-process technology. Oil refineries and chemical plants are classic examples of this type of technology. These industries are intensely automated and produce the same products without variation.

24. We define environmental complexity as an estimate of the magnitude of the problems and opportunities in an organization's environment as influenced by three main factors: degree of richness, degree of interdependence, and degree of uncertainty. Environmental richness is shown by an environment that is improving around the company. The economy is growing, and people are investing and spending money. Internally, the company may be growing, and its employees may be prospering as well. In a rich environment, organizations can succeed despite their poor organizational structure. An environment that is not rich allows only well-organized companies to survive in the long run. The second major factor in environmental complexity is the level of interdependence. This factor focuses on the relationships an organization needs to develop to compete in a certain setting. How free is that organization to conduct business? Uncertainty and volatility are the final factors that make up complexity. Organizations must decide how to deal with markets and environments that are continually changing and where the rate of change is changing.

Applications Essay
25. In the design and development of cars and trucks, Ford must recognize both the voice of the customer and a whole series of extremely complex technical requirements. If the company violates either the customer requirements or the technical requirements, it will not be able to develop a profitable vehicle. In the product and assembly plants these conflict forces are not as prominent, and the firm may opt for a simpler structure.

CHAPTER 1

ENDNOTES

[1] For a general overview see Jay W. Lorsch (ed.), *Handbook of Organizational Behavior* (Englewood Cliffs, NJ: Prentice Hall, 1987); and Julian Barling, Cary Li Cooper, and Stewart Clegg (eds.), *The Sage Handbook of Organizational Behavior*, Volumes 1 and 2 (San Francisco: Sage, 2009).

[2] Jeffrey Pfeffer and Robert I. Sutton, *Hard Facts, Dangerous Half-Truths, and Total Nonsense: Profiting from Evidence-Based Management* (Boston: Harvard Business School Press, 2006). See also Jeffrey Pfeffer and Robert I. Sutton, "Management Half-Truths and Nonsense," *California Management Review* 48.3 (2006), pp. 77–100; and Jeffrey Pfeffer and Robert I. Sutton, "Evidence-Based Management," *Harvard Business Review* (January 2006), R0601E.

[3] Geert Hofstede, "Cultural Constraints in Management Theories," *Academy of Management Executive* 7 (1993), pp. 81–94.

[4] John Huey, "Managing in the Midst of Chaos," *Fortune* (April 5, 1993), pp. 38–48. See also Tom Peters, *Thriving on Chaos* (New York: Knopf, 1991); Jay R. Galbraith, Edward E. Lawler III, and Associates, *Organizing for the Future: The New Logic for Managing Organizations* (San Francisco: Jossey-Bass, 1993); William H. Davidow and Michael S. Malone, *The Virtual Corporation Structuring and Revitalizing the Corporation of the 21st Century* (New York: HarperBusiness, 1993); Charles Handy, *The Age of Unreason* (Boston: Harvard Business School Press, 1994); Peter Drucker, *Managing in a Time of Great Change* (New York: Truman Talley, 1995); Peter Drucker, *Management Challenges for the 21st Century* (New York: Harper, 1999); Jeffrey Pfeffer, "Building Sustainable Organizations: The Human Factor," *Academy of Management Perspectives* (February, 2010), pp. 34–45.

[5] For historical foundations see Jay A. Conger, *Winning 'Em Over: A New Model for Managing in the Age of Persuasion* (New York: Simon & Schuster, 1998), pp. 180–181; Stewart D. Friedman, Perry Christensen, and Jessica DeGroot, "Work and Life: The End of the Zero-Sum Game," *Harvard Business Review* (November/December 1998), pp. 119–129; C. Argyris, "Empowerment: The Emperor's New Clothes," *Harvard Business Review* (May/June 1998), pp. 98–105.

[6] Rajiv Dutta, "eBay's Meg Whitman on Building a Company's Culture," *Business Week* (March 27, 2009): businessweek.com.

[7] R. Roosevelt Thomas Jr., *Beyond Race and Gender* (New York: AMACOM, 1992), p. 10; see also R. Roosevelt

Thomas Jr., "From 'Affirmative Action' to 'Affirming Diversity,'" *Harvard Business Review* (November/December 1990), pp. 107–117; R. Roosevelt Thomas Jr., with Marjorie I. Woodruff, *Building a House for Diversity* (New York: AMACOM, 1999).

[8] A baseline report on diversity in the American workplace is *Workforce 2000: Work and Workers in the 21st Century* (Indianapolis, IN: Hudson Institute, 1987). For comprehensive discussions see Martin M. Chemers, Stuart Oskamp, and Mark A. Costanzo, *Diversity in Organization: New Perspectives for a Changing Workplace* (Beverly Hills, CA: Sage, 1995); Robert T. Golembiewski, *Managing Diversity in Organizations* (Tuscaloosa: University of Alabama Press, 1995).

[9] See Taylor Cox Jr., "The Multicultural Organization," *Academy of Management Executive* 5 (1991), pp. 34–47; *Cultural Diversity in Organizations: Theory, Research and Practice* (San Francisco: Berrett-Koehler, 1993).

[10] "In CEO Pay, Another Gender Gap." *BusinessWeek* (November 24, 2008), p. 22; "The View from the Kitchen Table," *Newsweek* (January 26, 2009), p. 29; and Del Jones, "Women Slowly Gain on Men," *USA Today* (January 2, 2009), p. 6B; Catalyst research reports at www.catalyst.org; "Nicking the Glass Ceiling," *BusinessWeek* (June 9, 2009), p. 18.

[11] We're Getting Old," *The Wall Street Journal* (March 26, 2009), p. D2; and Les Christie, "Hispanic Population Boom Fuels Rising U.S. Diversity," *CnnMoney:* www.cnn.com; and Betsy Towner, "The New Face of 50+ America," *AARP Bulletin* (June 2009), p. 31. "Los U.S.A.: Latino Population Grows Faster, Spreads Wider," *The Wall Street Journal* (March 25, 2011), p. A1. See also U.S. Census Bureau reports at www.factfinder.census.gov.

[12] Thomas and Woodruff (1998).

[13] Conor Dougherty, "Strides by Women, Still a Wage Gap," *The Wall Street Journal* (March 1, 2011), p. A3; "In CEO Pay, Another Gender Gap," op. cit.; Jones, op. cit.; Catalyst, op. cit.; Women in Top Jobs; Information from Del Jones, "Women Slowly Gain on Corporate America," *USA Today* (January 2, 2009), p. 6B; "Catalyst 2008 Census of the Fortune 500 Reveals Women Gained Little Ground Advancing to Business Leadership Positions," *Catalyst Press Release* (December 8, 2008); www.catalyst.org/press_release.

[14] William M. Bulkeley, "Xerox Names Burns Chief as Mulcahy Retires Early," *The Wall Street Journal* (May 22, 2009), pp. B1, B2.

[15] Mintzberg (1973). See also Henry Mintzberg, *Mintzberg on Management* (New York: Free Press, 1989); "Rounding Out the Manager's Job," *Sloan Management Review* (Fall 1994), pp. 11–26.

[16] Robert L. Katz, "Skills of an Effective Administrator, *Harvard Business Review* 52 (September/October 1974), p. 94. See also Richard E. Royatzis, *The Competent Manager: A Model for Effective Performance* (New York: Wiley, 1982).

[17] Daniel Goleman, *Emotional Intelligence* (New York: Bantam, 1995); Daniel Goleman, *Working with Emotional Intelligence* (New York: Bantam, 1998). See also Daniel Goleman, "What Makes a Leader," *Harvard Business Review* (November/December 1998), pp. 93–102; and "Leadership That Makes a Difference," *Harvard Business Review* (March/April 2000), pp. 79–90, quote from p. 80.

[18] Kotter (1982); "What Effective General Managers Really Do," *Harvard Business Review* 60 (November/December 1982), p. 161. See Kaplan (1986).

[19] Herminia Ibarra, "Managerial Networks," Teaching Note: 9-495-039, Harvard Business School Publishing, Boston.

[20] Archie B. Carroll, "In Search of the Moral Manager," *Business Horizons* (March/April 2001), pp. 7–15.

[21] See Mahzarin R. Banagji, Max H. Bazerman, and Dolly Chugh, "How (Un)ethical Are You?" *Harvard Business Review* (December 2003), pp. 56–64.

[22] Terry Thomas, John R. Schermerhorn Jr., and John W. Dinehart, "Strategic Leadership of Ethical Behavior in Business," *Academy of Management Executive* (2004), pp. 56–66.

[23] For a discussion of experiential learning, see D. Christopher Kayes, "Experiential Learning and Its Critics: Preserving the Role of Experience in Management Learning and Education," *Academy of Management Learning and Education* 1.2 (2002), pp. 137–149.

[24] See Institute for Learning Styles, *Perceptual Modality Preferences Survey*: www.learningstyles.org.

FEATURES AND MARGIN PHOTOS

Opener: [a] "Jay Leno vs. Conan O'Brien: When Succession Planning Goes Very, Very Wrong." *Managing the Curve.* Posted 1/14/10, http://www.managingthecurve.com/jay-leno-vs-conan-obrien-when-succession-planning-goes-very-very-wrong. Accessed 12/30/10. [b] "Jay Leno Talks Back: An Exclusive Interview with *B&C.*" *Broadcasting & Cable.* Posted 11/2/09, 2:00 AM. http://www.broadcastingcable.com/article/366971-Jay Leno Talks Back: An Exclusive Interview with B C.php. Accessed 12/30/10. [c] "Conan O'Brien Joins Twitter: New Account EXPLODES with Followers." *The Huffington Post.* Posted 2/24/10, 6:16 PM. http://www.huffingtonpost.com/2010/02/24/conan-obrien-joins-twitte n 475722.html. Retrieved 12/29/10. [d] "Conan's $32m leap for joy," *New York Post.* Posted 1/20/10, 4:09 AM. http://www.nypost.com/p/news/national/conan leap for joy Xem23v4HiRT w0PWPs3HKiL#ixzz0dA8QSiFl. Retrieved 12/29/10.

Ethics in OB: Rakesh Khuran and Nitin Noria, "It's Time to Make Management a True Profession," *Harvard Business Review* (October 2008), pp. 70–77.

Finding the Leader in You: M. Brannigan, "Miami banker gives $60 million of his own to employees," www.MiamiHerald.com (February 14, 2009); www.thestreet.com; A. James Memmott, "Leonard Abbess—a banker who gave away millions," Muckety News (February 26, 2009).

Facebook Generation—Gary Hamel, "The Facebook Generation vs. the Fortune 500," opensource.com (September 22, 2010). *Skills and Managerial Work*—Information and quotes from Sandy Shore, "Could You Fill the Leader's Shoes?" *The Columbus Dispatch* (May 30, 2010), p. D3.

CHAPTER 2

ENDNOTES

[1] See Dorothy Leonard and Susan Strauss, "Putting Your Company's Whole Brain to Work," *Harvard Business Review* 75.4 Jul–Aug 1997, pp. 110–121. Also, Daniel Pink's *A Whole New Mind: Why Right-Brainers Will Rule the Future* (New York: Riverhead Books, 2005).

[2] Viktor Gecas, "The Self-Concept," in *Annual Review of Sociology* 8, ed. Ralph H. Turner and James F. Short Jr. (Palo Alto, CA: Annual Review, 1982), p.3. Also see Arthur P. Brief and Ramon J. Aldag, "The Self in Work Organizations: A Conceptual Review," *Academy of Management Review* (January 1981), pp. 75–88; Jerry J. Sullivan, "Self Theories and Employee Motivation," *Journal of Management* (June 1989), pp. 345–363.

[3] Compare Philip Cushman, "Why the Self Is Empty," *American Psychologist* (May 1990), pp. 599–611.

[4] Based in part on a definition in Gecas, 1982, p. 3.

[5] Suggested by J. Brockner, *Self-Esteem at Work* (Lexington, MA: Lexington Books, 1988), p. 144; John A. Wagner III and John R. Hollenbeck, *Management of Organizational Behavior* (Englewood Cliffs, NJ: Prentice-Hall, 1992), pp. 100–101.

[6] See N. Brody, *Personality: In Search of Individuality* (San Diego, CA: Academic Press, 1988), pp. 68–101; C. Holden, "The Genetics of Personality," *Science* (August 7, 1987), pp. 598–601.

[7] See Geert Hofstede, 1984.

[8] M. R. Barrick and M. K. Mount, "The Big Five Personality Dimensions and Job Performance: A Meta Analysis," *Personnel Psychology* 44 (1991), pp. 1–26; M. R. Barrick and M. K. Mount, "Autonomy as a Moderator of the Relationships between the Big Five Personality Dimensions and Job Performance," *Journal of Applied Psychology* (February 1993), pp. 111–118.

[9] See David A. Whetten and Kim S. Cameron, *Developing Management Skills*, 3rd ed. (New York: HarperCollins, 1995), p. 72.

[10] Raymond G. Hunt, Frank J. Kryzstofiak, James R. Meindl, and Abdalla M. Yousry, "Cognitive Style and

Decision Making," *Organizational Behavior and Human Decision Processes* 44.3 (1989), pp. 436–453. For additional work on problem-solving styles, see Ferdinand A. Gul, "The Joint and Moderating Role of Personality and Cognitive Style on Decision Making," *Accounting Review* (April 1984), pp. 264–277; Brian H. Kleiner, "The Interrelationship of Jungian Modes of Mental Functioning with Organizational Factors: Implications for Management Development," *Human Relations* (November 1983), pp. 997–1012; James L. McKenney and Peter G. W. Keen, "How Managers' Minds Work," *Harvard Business Review* (May–June 1974), pp. 79–90.

[11] Some examples of firms using the Myers-Briggs Type Indicators are given in J. M. Kunimerow and L. W. McAllister, "Team Building with the Myers-Briggs Type Indicator: Case Studies," *Journal of Psychological Type* 15 (1988), pp. 26–32; G. H. Rice Jr. and D. P. Lindecamps, "Personality Types and Business Success of Small Retailers," *Journal of Occupational Psychology* 62 (1989), pp. 177–182; B. Roach, *Strategy Styles and Management Types: A Resource Book for Organizational Management Consultants* (Stanford, CA: Balestrand, 1989).

[12] J. B. Rotter, "Generalized Expectancies for Internal versus External Control of Reinforcement," *Psychological Monographs* 80 (1966), pp. 1–28.

[13] See J. Michael Crant, "Proactive Behavior in Organizations," *Journal of Management* 26 (2000), pp. 435–462. See also T. S. Bateman, and J. M. Crant, "The proactive component of organizational behavior," *Journal of Organizational Behavior* 14 (1993), pp. 103–118.

[14] Don Hellriegel, John W. Slocum Jr., and Richard W. Woodman, *Organizational Behavior*, 5th ed. (St. Paul, MN: West, 1989), p. 46; Wagner and Hollenbeck (1992), chapter 4.

[15] Niccolo Machiavelli, *The Prince*, trans. George Bull (Middlesex, UK: Penguin, 1961).

[16] Richard Christie and Florence L. Geis, *Studies in Machiavellianism* (New York: Academic Press, 1970).

[17] See M. Snyder, *Public Appearances/Private Realities: The Psychology of Self-Monitoring* (New York: Freeman, 1987).

[18] Snyder, 1987.

[19] Adapted from R. W. Bonner, "A Short Scale: A Potential Measure of Pattern A Behavior," *Journal of Chronic Diseases* 22 (1969). Used by permission.

[20] See Meyer Friedman and Ray Roseman, *Type A Behavior and Your Heart* (New York: Knopf, 1974). For another view, see Walter Kiechel III, "Attack of the Obsessive Managers," *Fortune* (February 16, 1987), pp. 127–128.

[21] Arthur P. Brief, Randall S. Schuler, and Mary Van Sell, *Managing Job Stress* (Boston: Little, Brown, 1981).

[22] See Orlando Behling and Arthur L. Darrow, *Managing Work-Related Stress* (Chicago: Science Research Associates, 1984).

[23] Behling and Darrow, 1984.

[24] A review of research is available in Steve M. Jex, *Stress and Job Performance* (Thousand Oaks, CA: Sage, 1998).

[25] "Couples Dismayed at Long Workdays, New Study Finds," *Columbus Dispatch* (January 23, 1999), p. 5A.

[26] See H. Selye, *The Stress of Life*, rev. ed. (New York: McGraw-Hill, 1976).

[27] See John D. Adams, "Health, Stress and the Manager's Life Style," *Group and Organization Studies* 6 (1981), pp. 291–301.

[28] Jeffrey Pfeffer, *The Human Equation: Building Profits by Putting People First* (Boston: Harvard Business School Press, 1998). Quotations are from Alan M. Webber, "Danger: Toxic Company," *Fast Company* (November 1998), p. 152.

[29] Pfeffer, 1998.

[30] See Susan Folkman "Personal Control and Stress and Coping Processes: A Theoretical Analysis," *Journal of Personality and Social Psychology*, 1984, Vol. 46, No. 4, p. 844.

[31] See "Stress relief: When and how to say no" by Mayo Clinic Staff (www.mayoclinic.com/health/stress-relief/SR00039).

[32] Information from Mike Pramik, "Wellness Programs Give Businesses Healthy Bottom Line," *Columbus Dispatch* (January 18, 1999), pp. 10–11.

[33] Pramik, 1999.

[34] See P. E. Jacob, J. J. Flink, and H. L. Schuchman, "Values and Their Function in Decision Making," *American Behavioral Scientist* 5, suppl. 9 (1962), pp. 6–38.

[35] See M. Rokeach and S. J. Ball Rokeach, "Stability and Change in American Value Priorities, 1968–1981," *American Psychologist* (May 1989), pp. 775–784.

[36] Milton Rokeach, *The Nature of Human Values* (New York: Free Press, 1973).

[37] See W. C. Frederick and J. Weber, "The Values of Corporate Managers and Their Critics: An Empirical Description and Normative Implications," *Business Ethics Research Issues and Empirical Studies*, ed. W. C. Frederick and L. E. Preston (Greenwich, CT: JAI Press, 1990), pp. 123–144.

[38] Bruce M. Meglino and Elizabeth C. Ravlin, "Individual Values in Organizations: Concepts, Controversies and Research," *Journal of Management* 24 (1998), pp. 351–389.

[39] Meglino and Ravlin, 1998.

[40] Geert Hofstede, *Culture's Consequences: International Differences in Work-Related Values*, 2nd ed. (Beverly Hills, CA: Sage, 2001); Fons Trompenaars and Charles Hampden-Turner, *Riding the Waves of Culture: Understanding Cultural Diversity in Global Business*, 2nd ed. (New York: McGraw-Hill, 1998). For an excellent discussion of culture, see also "Culture: The Neglected Concept," in *Social Psychology Across Cultures*, 2nd ed., Peter B. Smith and Michael Harris Bond (Boston: Allyn &

Bacon, 1998). See also Michael H. Hoppe, "An Interview with Geert Hofstede," *Academy of Management Executive* 18 (2004), pp. 75–79; Harry C. Triandis, "The Many Dimensions of Culture," *Academy of Management Executive* 18 (2004), pp. 88–93.

[41] Geert Hofstede, *Culture and Organizations: Software of the Mind* (London: McGraw-Hill, 1991).

[42] Hofstede, 2001; Geert Hofstede and Michael H. Bond, "The Confucius Connection: From Culture Roots to Economic Growth," *Organizational Dynamics* 16 (1988), pp. 4–21.

[43] Hofstede, 2001.

[44] Chinese Culture Connection, "Chinese Values and the Search for Culture-Free Dimensions of Culture," *Journal of Cross-Cultural Psychology* 18 (1987), pp. 143–164.

[45] Hofstede and Bond, 1988; Geert Hofstede, "Cultural Constraints in Management Theories," *Academy of Management Executive* 7 (1993), pp. 81–94. For a further discussion of Asian and Confucian values, see also Jim Rohwer, Asia Rising: *Why America Will Prosper as Asia's Economies Boom* (New York: Simon & Schuster, 1995).

[46] For an example, see John R. Schermerhorn Jr. and Michael H. Bond, "Cross-Cultural Leadership Dynamics in Collectivism 1 High Power Distance Settings," *Leadership and Organization Development Journal* 18 (1997), pp. 187–193.

[47] Adapted from Rob McInnes, Diversity World, www.diversityworld.com.

[48] Rob McInnes, "Workforce Diversity: Changing the Way You Do Business," accessed May 3, 2009 from http://www.diversityworld.com/Diversity/workforce_diversity.htm.

[49] See Karen R. Humes, Nicholas A. Jones, and Roberto R. Ramirez, "Overview of Race and Hispanic Origin: 2010," 2010 Census Briefs (C2010BR-02), United States Census Bureau, U.S. Department of Commerce, Economic and Statistics Administration.

[50] Accessed May 5, 2009 from http://www.eeoc.gov/types/race.html.

[51] See Sam Ali, "Ward Connerly's Comments at the March 2011 DiversityInc Conference," Mar 31, 2011, DiversityInc.com (http://www.diversityinc.com/article/8350/Ward-Connerlys-Comments-at-the-March-2011-Diversity-Inc-Conference/).

[52] See Lois Joy, "Advancing Women Leaders: The Connection between Women Corporate Board Directors and Women Corporate Officers." Catalyst, 2008. email: info@catalyst.org; www.catalyst.org.

[53] See Lynda Gratton "Inspiring Women: Corporate Best Practice in Europe," The Lehman Brothers Centre for Women in Business, 2007.

[54] See Catalyst report "The Double-Bind Dilemma for Women in Leadership: *Damned if You Do, Doomed if You Don't,*" 2007. email: info@catalyst.org; www.catalyst.org.

[55] See Catalyst report "The Double-Bind Dilemma for Women in Leadership: *Damned if You Do, Doomed if You Don't,*" 2007. email: info@catalyst.org; www.catalyst.org.

[56] See Catalyst report "The Double-Bind Dilemma for Women in Leadership: *Damned if You Do, Doomed if You Don't,*" 2007. email: info@catalyst.org; www.catalyst.org; "The Leaking Pipeline: Where are our Female Leaders?" Pricewaterhouse Coopers report, March 2008. PwC Gender Advisory Council, www.pwc.com/women.

[57] See "The Workplace Improves for Gay Americans," Dec 17, 2007 GFN News. Accessed May 5, 2009 from http://www.gfn.com/recordDetails.php?page_id=19&section_id=22&pcontent_id=18.

[58] http://www.eeoc.gov/facts/fs-orientation_parent_marital_political.html.

[59] See "The Workplace Improves for Gay Americans," Dec. 17, 2007 GFN News. Accessed May 5, 2009 from http://www.gfn.com/recordDetails.php?page_id=19&section_id=22&pcontent_id=18.

[60] http://www.pollingreport.com/civil.htm.

[61] See Lauren Prince, "Marketers: Buying Power of Gays to Exceed $835 Billion." Dec. 8, 2007. Accessed May 4, 2009 from http://www.gfn.com/recordDetails.php?page_id=19&section_id=18&pcontent_id=2.

[62] See Carol Mithers, "Workplace Wars," in *Ladies' Home Journal,* May 2009, pp. 104–109.

[63] Mithers, 2009.

[64] http://www.accessiblesociety.org/topics/ada/index.htm.

[65] http://www.accessiblesociety.org/topics/ada/index.htm.

[66] Fernandez (1991); Patrick Digh, "Finding New Talent in a Tight Market," *Mosaics* 4.3 (March–April, 1998), pp. 1, 4–6.

[67] http://www.hawking.org.uk/index.php/about-stephen/questionsandanswers.

[68] www.shrm.org/.../Diversity_CLA_Definitions_of_Diversity_Inclusion.ppt

[69] http://www.accessiblesociety.org/topics/ada/index.htm.

[70] See Katharine Esty, "From Diversity to Inclusion," April 30, 2007, http://www.boston.com/jobs/nehra/043007.shtml, downloaded May 3, 2009.

[71] See Henri Tajfel and John Turner, (1979), "An Integrative Theory of Intergroup Conflict," in Austin, G. William; Worchel, Stephen. *The Social Psychology of Intergroup Relations.* Monterey, CA: Brooks-Cole. pp. 94–109.

[72] http://www.catalystwomen.org/press_room/factsheets/factwoc3.htm. Accessed May 4, 2009.

FEATURES AND MARGIN PHOTOS

Opener: [a] Betsy Morris, "Xerox's Dynamic Duo," *Fortune* (Nov. 19, 2007), accessed online at http://money.cnn.com/magazines/fortune/fortune_archive/2007/10/15/100536857/index.htm. [b] Heidi Brown, "Burns Succeeds Mulcahy at Xerox in First Big Woman-to-Woman

CEO Transition," Forbes.com (May 21, 2009), accessed online at http://www.forbes.com/2009/05/21/xerox-ceo-mulcahy-burns-forbes-woman-leadership-tech.html. ᶜ *Source:* Catalyst, *The Bottom Line: Corporate Performance and Women's Representation on Boards* (2007).

Ethics in OB: Information from Victoria Knight, "Personality Tests as Hiring Tools," *The Wall Street Journal* (March 15, 2006), p. B3C.

Finding the Leader in You: http://www.hawking.org.uk/index.php/about-stephen/questionsandanswers.

Whole Brain—See Dorothy Leonard and Susan Strauss, "Putting Your Company's Whole Brain to Work," *Harvard Business Review* 75.4 Jul–Aug 1997, pp. 110–121. Also, Daniel Pink's *A Whole New Mind: Why Right-Brainers Will Rule the Future* (New York: Riverhead Books, 2005). *Spillover Effect:* Jibu, Renge. How American men's participation in housework and childcare affects wives' careers. Working paper, July 2007, Center for the Education of Women, University of Michigan, www.cew.umich.edu.

CHAPTER 3

ENDNOTES

[1] These concept definitions and discussions are based on J. M. George, "Trait and State Affect," p. 45 in *Individual Differences in Behavior in Organizations,* ed. K. R. Murphy (San Francisco: Jossey-Bass, 1996); N. H. Frijda, "Moods, Emotion Episodes and Emotions," pp. 381–403 in *Handbook of Emotions,* ed. M. Lewis and J. M. Haviland (New York: Guilford Press, 1993); H. M. Weiss and R. Cropanzano, "Affective Events Theory: A Theoretical Discussion of the Structure, Causes, and Consequences of Affective Experiences at Work," pp. 17–19 in *Research in Organizational Behavior,* 18, eds. B. M. Staw and L. L. Cummings (Greenwich, CT: JAI Press, 1996); P. Ekman and R. J. Davidson (eds.), *The Nature of Emotions: Fundamental Questions* (Oxford, UK: Oxford University Press, 1994; Frijda, 1993, p. 381.

[2] For an example see Mary Ann Hazen, "Grief and the Workplace," *Academy of Management Perspective* 22 (August 2008), pp. 78–86.

[3] J. A. Fuller, J. M. Stanton, G. G. Fisher, C. Spitzmuller, S. S. Russell, and P. C. Smith, "A Lengthy Look at the Daily Grind: Time Series Analysis of Events, Mood, Stress, and Satisfaction," *Journal of Applied Psychology* 88 (2003), pp. 1019–1033; C. J. Thoreson, S. A. Kaplan, A. P. Barsky, C. R. Warren, and K. de Chermont, "The Affective Underpinnings of Job Perceptions and Attitudes; A Meta-Analytic Review and Integration," *Psychological Bulletin* 129 (2003), pp. 914–925.

[4] Daniel Goleman, "Leadership That Gets Results," *Harvard Business Review* (March–April 2000), pp. 78–90. See also his books *Emotional Intelligence* (New York: Bantam Books, 1995) and *Working with Emotional Intelligence* (New York: Bantam Books, 1998).

[5] See Davies L. Stankow and R. D. Roberts, "Emotion and Intelligence: In Search of an Elusive Construct," *Journal of Personality and Social Psychology* 75 (1998), pp. 989–1015; I. Greenstein, *The Presidential Difference: Leadership Style from FDR to Clinton* (Princeton, NJ: Princeton University Press, 2001); Goleman, op. cit. (2000).

[6] Goleman, op. cit. (1998).

[7] J. P. Tangney and K. W. Fischer (eds.), *"Self-conscious Emotions: The Psychology of Shame, Guilt, Embarrassment and Price* (New York: Guilford Press, 1995); J. L. Tracy and R. W. Robbins, "Putting the Self into Self-Conscious Emotions: A Theoretical Model," *Psychological Inquiry* 15 (2004), pp. 103–125; D. Keltner and C. Anderson, "Saving Face for Darwin: The Functions and Uses of Embarrassment," *Current Directions in Psychological Science* 9 (2000), pp. 187–192; J. S. Beer, E. A. Heery, D. Keltner, D. Scabini, and R. T. Knight, "The Regulatory Function of Self-Conscious Emotion: Insights from Patients with Orbitofrontal Damage," *Journal of Personality and Social Psychology* 85 (2003), pp. 594–604; R. P. Vecchio, "Explorations of Employee Envy: Feeling Envious and Feeling Envied," *Cognition and Emotion* 19 (2005), pp. 69–81; C. F. Poulson II, "Shame and Work," pp. 490–541 in *Emotions in the Workplace: Research, Theory, and Practice,* eds. N. M. Ashkanasy, W. Zerby, and C. E. J. Hartel (Westport, CT: Quorum Books).

[8] Diane Brady, "Charm Offensive," *BusinessWeek* (June 26, 2006), pp. 76–80.

[9] Lewis and Haviland, op. cit.

[10] Damon Darlin and Matt Richtel, "Chairwoman Leaves Hewlett in Spying Furor," *The Wall Street Journal* (September 23, 2006), pp. Al, A9.

[11] R. E. Lucas, A. E. Clark, Y. Georgellis, and E. Deiner, "Unemployment Alters the Set Points for Life Satisfaction," *Psychological Science* 15 (2004), pp. 8–13; C. Graham, A. Eggers, and S. Sukhtaner, "Does Happiness Pay?: An Exploration Based on Panel Data from Russia," *Journal of Economic Behaviour and Organization* 55 (November 2004), pp. 319–342; G. L. Clore, N. Schwartz, and M. Conway, "Affective Causes and Consequences of Social Information Processing," pp. 323–417 in *Handbook of Social Cognition,* Vol. 1, eds. R. S. Wyer Jr. and T. K. Srull (Hillsdale, NJ: Erlbaum, 1994); K. D. Vohs, R. F. Baumeister, and G. Lowenstein, *Do Emotions Help or Hurt Decision Making?* (New York: Russell Sage Foundation Press, 2007; H. M. Weiss, J. P. Nicholas, and C. S. Daus, "An Examination of the Joint Effects of Affective Experiences and Job Beliefs on Job Satisfaction and Variations in Affective Experiences over Time," *Organizational Behavior and Human Decision Processes* 78 (1999), pp. 1–24;

N. M. Ashkanasy, "Emotion and Performance," *Human Performance* 17 (2004), pp. 137–144.

[12] See Robert G. Lord, Richard J. Klimoski, and Ruth Knafer (eds.), *Emotions in the Workplace: Understanding the Structure and Role of Emotions in Organizational Behavior* (San Francisco: Jossey-Bass, 2002); Roy L. Payne and Cary L. Cooper (eds.), *Emotions at Work: Theory Research and Applications for Management* (Chichester, UK: John Wiley & Sons, 2004): Daniel Goleman and Richard Boyatzis, "Social Intelligence and the Biology of Leadership," *Harvard Business Review* (September 2008), Reprint R0809E.

[13] Caroline Bartel and Richard Saavedra, "The Collective Construction of Work Group Moods," *Administrative Science Quarterly* 45 (June 2000), pp. 197–231.

[14] Joyce K. Bono and Remus Ilies, "Charisma, Positive Emotions and Mood Contagion," *Leadership Quarterly* 17 (2006), pp. 317–334, Goleman and Boyatzis, op. cit.

[15] Daniel Goleman, Richard Boyatzis, and Annie McKie, *Primal Leadership: Realizing the Power of Emotional Intelligence* (Boston: Harvard Business School Publishing, 2002); quote from "Managing the Mood Is Crucial When Times Are Tough," *Financial Times* (March 24, 2009).

[16] Quote from ibid.

[17] S. M. Kruml and D. Geddes, "Catching Fire without Burning Out: Is There an Ideal Way to Perform Emotional Labor?" pp. 177–188 in *Emotions in the Workplace,* ed. N. M. Ashkanasy, C. E. J. Hartel, and W. J. Zerby (New York: Quorum, 2000).

[18] A. Grandey, "Emotional Regulation in the Workplace: A New Way to Conceptualize Emotional Labor, "*Journal of Occupational Health Psychology* 5.1 (2000), pp. 95–110; R. Cropanzano, D. E. Rupp, and Z. S. Byrne, "The Relationship of Emotional Exhaustion to Work Attitudes, Job Performance and Organizational Citizenship Behavior," *Journal of Applied Psychology* (2003), pp. 160–169.

[19] W. Tasi and Y. Huang, "Mechanisms Linking Employee Affective Delivery and Customer Behavioral Intentions," *Journal of Applied Psychology* 87 (2002), pp. 1001–1008.

[20] M. Eid and E. Diener, "Norms for Experiencing Emotions in Different Cultures: Inter- and Intranational Differences," *Journal of Personality and Social Psychology* 81.5 (2001), pp. 869–885.

[21] Ibid. (2001).

[22] B. Mesquita, "Emotions in Collectivist and Individualist Contexts," *Journal of Personality and Social Psychology* 80.1 (2001), pp. 68–74.

[23] D. Rubin, "Grumpy German Shoppers Distrust the Wal-Mart Style," *Seattle Times* (December 30, 2001), p. a15; A. Rafaeli, "When Cashiers Meet Customers: An Analysis of Supermarket Cashiers," *Academy of Management Journal* (1989), pp. 245–273.

[24] H. M. Weiss and R. Cropanzano, "An Affective Events Approach to Job Satisfaction," pp. 1–74 in *Research in Organizational Behavior,* Vol. 18, ed. B. M. Staw and L. L. Cummings

(Greenwich, CT: JAI Press, 1996); N. M. Ashkanasy and C. S. Daus, "Emotion in the Workplace: New Challenges for Managers," *Academy of Management Executive* 16 (2002), pp. 76–86.

[25] A. G. Miner and C. L. Hulin, *Affective Experience at Work: A Test of Affective Events Theory.* Poster presented at the 15th annual conference of the Society for Industrial and Organizational Psychology (2000).

[26] Information and quote from Joann S. Lublin, "How One Black Woman Lands Her Top Jobs: Risks and Networking," *The Wall Street Journal* (March 4, 2003), p. B1.

[27] Compare Martin Fishbein and Icek Ajzen, *Belief, Attitude, Intention and Behavior: An Introduction to Theory and Research* (Reading, MA: Addison-Wesley, 1973).

[28] See A. W. Wicker, "Attitude Versus Action: The Relationship of Verbal and Overt Behavioral Responses to Attitude Objects," *Journal of Social Issues* (Autumn 1969), pp. 41–78.

[29] L. Festinger, *A Theory of Cognitive Dissonance* (Palo Alto, CA: Stanford University Press, 1957).

[30] See "The Things They Do for Love," *Harvard Business Review* (December 2004), pp. 19–20.

[31] Tony DiRomualdo, "The High Cost of Employee Disengagement" (July 7, 2004), www.wistechnology.com.

[32] Information from Sue Shellenbarger, "Employers Are Finding It Doesn't Cost Much to Make a Staff Happy." *The Wall Street Journal* (November 19, 1977), p. B1; see also "Job Satisfaction on the Decline." *The Conference Board* (July 2002).

[33] See, for example, Remus Ilies, Kelly Schwind Wilson, and David T. Wagner, "The Spillover of Daily Job Satisfaction onto Employees' Family Lives: The Facilitating Role of Work-Family Integration," *Academy of Management Journal* 52 (February 2009), pp. 87–102.

[34] See W. E. Wymer and J. M. Carsten, "Alternative Ways to Gather Opinions," *HR Magazine* 37.4 (April 1992), pp. 71–78.

[35] The Job Descriptive Index (JDI) is available from Dr. Patricia C. Smith, Department of Psychology, Bowling Green State University; the Minnesota Satisfaction Questionnaire (MSQ) is available from the Industrial Relations Center and Vocational Psychology Research Center, University of Minnesota.

[36] See ibid.; Timothy A. Judge, "Promote Job Satisfaction through Mental Challenge," Chapter 6 in Edwin A. Locke (ed.), *The Blackwell Handbook of Principles of Organizational Behavior* (Malden, MA: Blackwell, 2004): "U.S. Employees More Dissatisfied with Their Jobs," *Associated Press* (February 28, 2005), www.msnbc.com; "U.S. Job Satisfaction Keeps Falling, The Conference Board Reports Today," *The Conference Board* (February 28, 2005), www.conference-board.org; Salary.com, op. cit. (2009).

[37] Data reported in Jeannine Aversa, "Happy Workers Harder to Find," *The Columbus Dispatch* (January 5, 2010), pp. A1, A4. Data from "U.S. Job Satisfaction the Lowest in Two Decades," press release, *The Conference Board* (January 5, 2010), retrieved January 6, 2010 from: http://www.conference-board.org.

[38] Despite Low Job Satisfaction, Employees Unlikely to Seek New Jobs, Accenture Research Reports, Prefer to Focus on Creating Opportunities with Current Employers" (March 4, 2011): newsroom.accenture.com/article_display.cfm?article_id=5163.

[39] The Conference Board, op. cit.

[40] For historical research see B. M. Staw, "The Consequences of Turnover," *Journal of Occupational Behavior* 1 (1980), pp. 253–273; J. P. Wanous, *Organizational Entry* (Reading, MA: Addison-Wesley, 1980).

[41] C. N. Greene, "The Satisfaction-Performance Controversy," *Business Horizons* 15 (1972), pp. 31–41; M. T. Iaffaldano and P. M. Muchinsky, "Job Satisfaction and Job Performance: A Meta-Analysis," *Psychological Bulletin* 97 (1985), pp. 251–273; D. Organ, "A Reappraisal and Reinterpretation of the Satisfaction-Causes-Performance Hypothesis," *Academy of Management Review* 2 (1977), pp. 46–53; P. Lorenzi, "A Comment on Organ's Reappraisal of the Satisfaction-Causes-Performance Hypothesis," *Academy of Management Review* 3 (1978), pp. 380–382.

[42] Salary.com, "Survey Shows Impact of Downturn on Job Satisfaction," *OH&S: Occupational Health and Safety* (February 7, 2009), www.ohsonline.com.

[43] Tony DiRomualdo, "The High Cost of Employee Disengagement" (July 7, 2004), www.wistechnology.com.

[44] Dennis W. Organ, *Organizational Citizenship Behavior: The Good Soldier Syndrome* (Lexington, MA: Lexington Books, 1988); Dennis W. Organ, "Organizational Citizenship Behavior: It's Constructive Cleanup Time," *Human Performance* 10 (1997), pp. 85–97.

[45] See Mark C. Bolino and William H. Turnley, "Going the Extra Mile: Cultivating and Managing Employee Citizenship Behavior," *Academy of Management Executive* 17 (August 2003), pp. 60–67.

[46] See Venetta I. Coleman and Walter C. Borman, "Investigating the Underlying Structure of the Citizenship Performance Domain," *Human Resource Management Review* 10 (2000), pp. 115–126.

[47] Sandra L. Robinson and Rebecca J. Bennett, "A Typology of Deviant Workplace Behaviors: A Multidimensional Scaling Study," *Academy of Management Journal* 38 (1995), pp. 555–572.

[48] Reeshad S. Dalal, "A Meta-Analysis of the Relationship Among Organizational Citizenship Behavior and Counterproductive Work Behavior," *Journal of Applied Psychology* 90 (2005), pp. 1241–1255.

[49] Timothy A. Judge and Remus Ilies, "Affect and Job Satisfaction: A Study of Their Relationship at Work and at Home," *Journal of Applied Psychology* 89 (2004), pp. 661–673.

[50] Ilies et al., op. cit. (2009).

[51] See Benjamin Schneider, Paul J. Hanges, D. Brent Smith, and Amy Salvaggio, "Which Comes First: Employee Attitudes or Organizational, Financial, and Market Performance?" *Journal of Applied Psychology* 88.5 (2003), pp. 836–851.

[52] See Satoris S. Culbertson, "Do Satisfied Employees Mean Satisfied Customers?" *The Academy of Management Perspectives* 23 (February 2009), pp. 76–77.

[53] L. W. Porter and E. E. Lawler III, *Managerial Attitudes and Work Performance* (Homewood, IL: Irwin, 1968).

[54] Schneider, Hanges, Smith, and Salvaggio, op. cit.

[55] Ibid.

FEATURES AND MARGIN PHOTOS

Opener: [a] "Welcome Potential Franchisees!" *Stroller Strides.* http://strollerstrides.com/franchisee.php. Accessed 1/6/11. [b] "Stroller Strides," *International Franchise Organization.* www.franchise.org/Stroller_Strides_franchise.aspx. Accessed 1/7/11. [c] "Stroller Strides Hosts National Conference." MarketWire. Posted 10/28/10. 2:33 PM. http://www.marketwire.com/press-release/Stroller-Strides-Hosts-National-Conference-1343349.htm. Accessed 1/6/11. [d] "Stroller Strides Home-Based Business Model May Be the Future of Franchising." *Stroller Strides.* Posted 12/9/09. http://strollerstrides.com/blog/?p=967. Accessed 1/5/11. [e] www.entrepreneur.com/startingabusiness/mompreneur/mompreneurcolumnistlisadruxman/article203980.html [f] "Different Factors Create Job Satisfaction for Men and Women in IT." *TechRepublic.* Posted 3/11/10. http://blogs.techrepublic.com.com/career/?p=1855. Accessed 1/7/11.

Ethics in OB: Information from Joe O'Shea, "How a Facebook Update Can Cost You Your Job," *Irish Independent* (September 1, 2010), p. 34.

Finding the Leader in You: Don Thompson: Information from Julie Bennett, "McGolden Opportunity," *Franchise Times* (February, 2008), www.franchisetimes.com; www.mcdonalds.com.

Life Is Good—Information from Leigh Buchanan, "Life Lessons, *Inc.* (June 6, 2006), www.inc.com/magazine/; "A Fortune Coined from Cheerfulness Entrepreneurship," *Financial Times* (May 20, 2009); www.lifeisgood.com/about/. *Employee morale*—Information from *What Workers Want: A Worldwide Study of Attitudes to Work and Work-Life Balance* (London: FDS International Limited, 2007). *Generations Differ*—Information and quotes from "Generation Gap: On Their Bosses, Millennials Happier Than Boomers," *The Wall Street Journal* (November 15, 2010), p. B6.

CHAPTER 4

ENDNOTES

[1] H. R. Schiffmann, *Sensation and Perception: An Integrated Approach*, 3rd ed. (New York: Wiley, 1990).

[2] Example from John A. Wagner III and John R. Hollenbeck, *Organizational Behavior*, 3rd ed. (Upper Saddle River, NJ: Prentice-Hall, 1998), p. 59.

³ See Georgia T. Chao and Steve W. J. Kozlowski, "Employee Perceptions on the Implementation of Robotic Manufacturing Technology," *Journal of Applied Psychology* 71 (1986), pp. 70–76; Steven F. Cronshaw and Robert G. Lord, "Effects of Categorization, Attribution, and Encoding Processes in Leadership Perceptions," *Journal of Applied Psychology* 72 (1987), pp. 97–106.

⁴ See Robert G. Lord, "An Information Processing Approach to Social Perceptions, Leadership, and Behavioral Measurement in Organizations," pp. 87–128 in *Research in Organizational Behavior* 7, ed. B. M. Staw and L. L. Cummings (Greenwich, CT: JAI Press, 1985); T. K. Srull and R. S. Wyer, *Advances in Social Cognition* (Hillsdale, NJ: Erlbaum, 1988); U. Neisser, *Cognitive and Reality* (San Francisco: Freeman, 1976), p. 112.

⁵ See J. G. Hunt, *Leadership: A New Synthesis* (Newbury Park, CA: Sage, 1991), ch. 7; R. G. Lord and R. J. Foti, "Schema Theories, Information Processing, and Organizational Behavior," pp. 20–48 in *Thinking Organization*, ed. H. P. Simms Jr. and D. A. Gioia (San Francisco: Jossey-Bass, 1986); S. T. Fiske and S. E. Taylor, *Social Cognition* (Reading, MA: Addison-Wesley, 1984).

⁶ See William L. Gardner and Mark J. Martinko, "Impression Management in Organizations," *Journal of Management* (June 1988), p. 332.

⁷ Quotation from Sheila O'Flanagan, "Underestimate Casual Dressers at Your Peril," *Irish Times* (July 22, 2005).

⁸ See B. R. Schlenker, *Impression Management: The Self-Concept, Social Identity, and Interpersonal Relations* (Monterey, CA: Brooks/Cole, 1980); W. L. Gardner and M. J. Martinko, "Impression Management in Organizations," *Journal of Management* (June 1988), p. 332; R. B. Cialdini, "Indirect Tactics of Image Management: Beyond Banking," pp. 232–252 in *Impression Management in the Organization*, ed. R. A. Giacolini and P. Rosenfeld (Hillsdale, NJ: Erlbaum, 1989), pp. 45–71; and Sandy Wayne and Robert Liden, "Effects of Impression Management on Performance Ratings," *Academy of Management Journal* (February 2005), pp. 232–252.

⁹ See, for example, Stephan Thernstrom and Abigail Thernstrom, *America in Black and White* (New York: Simon & Schuster, 1997); David A. Thomas and Suzy Wetlaufer, "A Question of Color: A Debate on Race in the U. S. Workspace, "*Harvard Business Review* 2 (September–October 1997), pp. 118–132.

¹⁰ Information from "Misconceptions about Women in the Global Arena Keep Their Number Low," www.catalystwomen.org/home.html.

¹¹ These examples are from Natasha Josefowitz, *Paths to Power* (Reading, MA: Addison-Wesley, 1980), p. 60. For more on gender issues, see Gray N. Powell (ed.), *Handbook of Gender and Work* (Thousand Oaks, CA: Sage, 1999).

¹² For a recent report on age discrimination, see Joseph C. Santora and William J. Seaton, "Age Discrimination:

Alive and Well in the Workplace?" *The Academy of Management Perspectives* 22 (May 2008), pp. 103–104.

¹³ Survey reported in Kelly Greene, "Age Is Still More Than a Number," *The Wall Street Journal* (April 10, 2003), p. D2.

¹⁴ "Facebook Gets Down to Business," *BusinessWeek* (April 20, 2009), p. 30.

¹⁵ Dewitt C. Dearborn and Herbert A. Simon, "Selective Perception: A Note on the Departmental Identification of Executives," *Sociometry* 21 (1958), pp. 140–144.

¹⁶ J. Sterling Livingston, "Pygmalion in Management," *Harvard Business Review* (July–August 1969), pp. 81–89.

¹⁷ D. Eden and A. B. Shani, "Pygmalion Goes to Boot Camp," *Journal of Applied Psychology* 67 (1982), pp. 194–199.

¹⁸ See H. H. Kelley, "Attribution in Social Interaction," in E. Jones et al. (eds.), *Attribution: Perceiving the Causes of Behavior* (Morristown, NJ: General Learning Press, 1972).

¹⁹ See Terence R. Mitchell, S. G. Green, and R. E. Wood, "An Attribution Model of Leadership and the Poor Performing Subordinate," pp. 197–234, in *Research in Organizational Behavior*, ed. Barry Staw and Larry L. Cummings (New York: JAI Press, 1981); John H. Harvey and Gifford Weary, "Current Issues in Attribution Theory and Research," *Annual Review of Psychology* 35 (1984), pp. 427–459.

²⁰ See F. Fosterling, "Attributional Retraining: A Review," *Psychological Bulletin* (November 1985), pp. 496–512.

²¹ Albert Bandura, *Social Learning Theory* (Englewood Cliffs, NJ: Prentice-Hall, 1977); and Albert Bandura, *Self-Efficacy: The Exercise of Control* (New York: W. H. Freeman, 1997).

²² See, for example, A. M. Morrison, R. P. White, and E. Van Velsor, *Breaking the Glass Ceiling* (Reading, MA: Addison-Wesley, 1987); J. D. Zalesny and J. K. Ford, "Extending the Social Information Processing Perspective: New Links to Attitudes, Behaviors and Perceptions," *Organizational Behavior and Human Decision Processes* 47 (1990), pp. 205–246; M. E. Gist, C. Schwoerer, and B. Rosen, "Effects of Alternative Training Methods of Self-Efficacy and Performance in Computer Software Training," *Journal of Applied Psychology* 74 (1989), pp. 884–891; D. D. Sutton and R. W. Woodman, "Pygmalion Goes to Work: The Effects of Supervisor Expectations in a Retail Setting," *Journal of Applied Psychology* 74 (1989), pp. 943–950; M. E. Gist, "The Influence of Training Method on Self-Efficacy and Idea Generation among Managers," *Personnel Psychology* 42 (1989), pp. 787–805.

²³ Bandura, op. cit., 1977 and 1997.

²⁴ See M. E. Gist, "Self Efficacy: Implications in Organizational Behavior and Human Resource Management," *Academy of Management Review* 12 (1987), pp. 472–485; A. Bandura, "Self-Efficacy Mechanisms in Human Agency," *American Psychologist* 37 (1987), pp. 122–147.

²⁵ For good overviews of reinforcement-based views, see W. E. Scott Jr. and P. M. Podsakoff, *Behavioral Prin-*

ciples in the Practice of Management (New York: Wiley, 1985); Fred Luthans and Robert Kreitner, *Organizational Behavior Modification and Beyond* (Glenview, IL: Scott Foresman, 1985).

[26] For some of B. F. Skinner's work, see *Walden Two* (New York: Macmillan, 1948); *Science and Human Behavior* (New York: Macmillan, 1953); *Contingencies of Reinforcement* (New York: Appleton-Century-Crofts, 1969).

[27] Fred Luthans and Robert Kreitner, *Organizational Behavior Modification* (Glenview, IL: Scott Foresman, 1975); Fred Luthans and Robert Kreitner, *Organizational Behavior Modification and Beyond* (Glenview, IL: Scott Foresman, 1985); and Fred Luthans and Alexander D. Stajkovic, "Reinforce for Performance: The Need to Go Beyond Pay and Even Rewards," *Academy of Management Executive* 13 (1999), pp. 49–57.

[28] E. L. Thorndike, *Animal Intelligence* (New York: Macmillan, 1911), p. 244.

[29] Example adapted from Luthans and Kreitner (1985), op. cit., 1985.

[30] Luthans and Kreitner, op. cit., 1985.

[31] Both laws are stated in Keith L. Miller, *Principles of Everyday Behavior Analysis* (Monterey, CA: Brooks/Cole, 1975), p. 122.

[32] This example is based on a study by Barbara Price and Richard Osborn, "Shaping the Training of Skilled Workers," working paper (Detroit: Department of Management, Wayne State University, 1999).

[33] A. R. Korukonda and James G. Hunt, "Pat on the Back Versus Kick in the Pants: An Application of Cognitive Inference to the Study of Leader Reward and Punishment Behavior," *Group and Organization Studies* 14 (1989), pp. 199–234.

[34] Edwin A. Locke, "The Myths of Behavior Mod in Organizations," *Academy of Management Review* 2 (October 1977), pp. 543–553. For a counterpoint, see Jerry L. Gray, "The Myths of the Myths about Behavior Mod in Organizations: A Reply to Locke's Criticisms of Behavior Modification," *Academy of Management Review* 4 (January 1979), pp. 121–129.

[35] Robert Kreitner, "Controversy in OBM: History, Misconceptions, and Ethics," in Lee Frederiksen (ed.), *Handbook of Organizational Behavior Management* (New York: Wiley, 1982), pp. 71–91.

[36] W. E. Scott Jr. and P. M. Podsakoff, *Behavioral Principles in the Practice of Management* (New York: Wiley, 1985); also see W. Clay Hamner, "Reinforcement Theory and Contingency Management in Organizational Settings," pp. 139–165 in *Motivation and Work Behavior* (4th ed.), ed. Richard M. Steers and Lyman W. Porters (New York: McGraw-Hill, 1987); Luthans and Kreitner, op. cit. (1985); Charles C. Manz and Henry P. Sims Jr., *Superleadership* (New York: Berkeley, 1990).

FEATURES AND MARGIN PHOTOS

Opener: [a] "Just-in-case versus just-in-time," *The Endeavour.* Posted 3/3/10. http://www.johndcook.com/blog/2010/03/03/just-in-case-versus-just-in-time/. Accessed 1/6/11. [b] "Best Technology: Just-in-Time Learning," *Fast Company.* Posted 10/31/96. http://www.fastcompany.com/magazine/05/corpu3.html. Accessed 1/6/11.

Ethics in OB: Information from Deloitte LLP, "Leadership Counts: 2007 Deloitte & Touché USA Ethics & Workplace Survey Results," *Kiplinger Business Resource Center* (June 2007), www.kiplinger.com.

Finding the Leader in You: Information and quotes from the corporate Web sites and from The Entrepreneur's Hall of Fame, www.1tbn.com/halloffame.html; *Knowledge@Wharton*, "The Importance of Being Richard Branson," Wharton School Publishing (June 3, 2005), www.whartonsp.com.

Donna Byrd—Information from Temple Hemphill, "Bull Market: Now is the Time to Take Advantage of Web 2.0," *BlackMBA* (Winter 2008/2009), pp. 63–66. See also Brian Solis, *Engage: The Complete Guide for Brands and Businesses* (Hoboken, NJ: John Wiley & Sons, 2010). *Elsewhere class*—Information from Dalton Conley, "Welcome to Elsewhere," *Newsweek* (January 26, 2009), pp. 25–26.

CHAPTER 5

ENDNOTES

[1] See John P. Campbell, Marvin D. Dunnette, Edward E. Lawler III, and Karl E. Weick Jr., *Managerial Behavior Performance and Effectiveness* (New York: McGraw-Hill, 1970), ch. 15.

[2] Abraham Maslow, *Eupsychian Management* (Homewood, IL: Irwin, 1965); Abraham Maslow, *Motivation and Personality*, 2nd ed. (New York: Harper & Row, 1970).

[3] Lyman W. Porter, "Job Attitudes in Management: Perceived Importance of Needs as a Function of Job Level," *Journal of Applied Psychology* 47 (April 1963), pp. 141–148.

[4] Douglas T. Hall and Khalil E. Nougaim, "An Examination of Maslow's Need Hierarchy in an Organizational Setting," *Organizational Behavior and Human Performance* 3 (1968), pp. 12–35; John M. Ivancevich, "Perceived Need Satisfactions of Domestic versus Overseas Managers," *Journal of Applied Psychology* 54 (August 1969), pp. 274–278.

[5] Mahmoud A. Wahba and Lawrence G. Bridwell, "Maslow Reconsidered: A Review of Research on the Need Hierarchy Theory," *Academy of Management Proceedings* (1974), pp. 514–520; Edward E. Lawler III and J. Lloyd Shuttle, "A Causal Correlation Test of the Need Hierarchy Concept," *Organizational Behavior and Human Performance* 7 (1973), pp. 265–287.

[6] Nancy J. Adler, *International Dimensions of Organizational Behavior*, 2nd ed. (Boston: PWS-Kent, 1991), p. 153; Richard M. Hodgetts and Fred Luthans, *International Management* (New York: McGraw-Hill, 1991), ch. 11.

[7] Clayton P. Alderfer, "An Empirical Test of a New Theory of Human Needs," *Organizational Behavior and Human Performance* 4 (1969), pp. 142–175; Clayton P. Alderfer, *Existence, Relatedness, and Growth* (New York: Free Press, 1972); Benjamin Schneider and Clayton P. Alderfer, "Three Studies of Need Satisfaction in Organizations," *Administrative Science Quarterly* 18 (1973), pp. 489–505.

[8] Lane Tracy, "A Dynamic Living Systems Model of Work Motivation," *Systems Research* 1 (1984), pp. 191–203; John Rauschenberger, Neal Schmidt, and John E. Hunter, "A Test of the Need Hierarchy Concept by a Markov Model of Change in Need Strength," *Administrative Science Quarterly* 25 (1980), pp. 654–670.

[9] Sources pertinent to this discussion are David C. McClelland, *The Achieving Society* (New York: Van Nostrand, 1961); David C. McClelland, "Business, Drive and National Achievement," *Harvard Business Review* 40 (July/August 1962), pp. 99–112; David C. McClelland, "That Urge to Achieve," *Think* (November/December 1966), pp. 19–32; G. H. Litwin and R. A. Stringer, *Motivation and Organizational Climate* (Boston: Division of Research, Harvard Business School, 1966), pp. 18–25.

[10] George Harris, "To Know Why Men Do What They Do: A Conversation with David C. McClelland," *Psychology Today* 4 (January 1971), pp. 35–39.

[11] David C. McClelland and David H. Burnham, "Power Is the Great Motivator," *Harvard Business Review* 54 (March/April 1976), pp. 100–110; David C. McClelland and Richard E. Boyatzis, "Leadership Motive Pattern and Long-Term Success in Management," *Journal of Applied Psychology* 67 (1982), pp. 737–743.

[12] P. Miron and D. C. McClelland, "The Impact of Achievement Motivation Training in Small Businesses," *California Management Review* (Summer 1979), pp. 13–28.

[13] The complete two-factor theory is well explained by Herzberg and his associates in Frederick Herzberg, Bernard Mausner, and Barbara Bloch Synderman, *The Motivation to Work*, 2nd ed. (New York: Wiley, 1967); Frederick Herzberg, "One More Time: How Do You Motivate Employees?" *Harvard Business Review* 46 (January/February 1968), pp. 53–62.

[14] From Herzberg (1968), op. cit.

[15] See Robert J. House and Lawrence A. Wigdor, "Herzberg's Dual-Factor Theory of Job Satisfaction and Motivation: A Review of the Evidence and a Criticism," *Personnel Psychology* 20 (Winter 1967), pp. 369–389.

[16] Adler, op. cit.; Nancy J. Adler and J. T. Graham, "Cross Cultural Interaction: The International Comparison Fallacy," *Journal of International Business Studies* (Fall 1989), pp. 515–537; Frederick Herzberg, "Workers' Needs: The Same Around the World," *Industry Week* (September 27, 1987), pp. 29–32.

[17] See, for example, J. Stacy Adams, "Toward an Understanding of Inequality," *Journal of Abnormal and Social Psychology* 67 (1963), pp. 422–436; J. Stacy Adams, "Inequity in Social Exchange," in L. Berkowitz (ed.), *Advances in Experimental Social Psychology* 2 (New York: Academic Press, 1965), pp. 267–300.

[18] Adams, op. cit. (1965).

[19] These issues are discussed in C. Kagitcibasi and J. W. Berry, "Cross-Cultural Psychology: Current Research and Trends," *Annual Review of Psychology* 40 (1989), pp. 493–531.

[20] See Blair Sheppard, Roy J. Lewicki, and John Minton, *Organizational Justice: The Search for Fairness in the Workplace* (New York: Lexington Books, 1992); Jerald Greenberg, *The Quest for Justice on the Job: Essays and Experiments* (Thousand Oaks, CA: Sage, 1995); Robert Folger and Russell Cropanzano, *Organizational Justice and Human Resource Management* (Thousand Oaks, CA: Sage, 1998); and Mary A. Konovsky, "Understanding Procedural Justice and Its Impact on Business Organizations," *Journal of Management* 26 (2000), pp. 489–511.

[21] Interactional justice is described by Robert J. Bies, "The Predicament of Injustice: The Management of Moral Outrage," in L. L. Cummings and B. M. Staw (eds.), *Research in Organizational Behavior* 9 (Greenwich, CT: JAI Press, 1987), pp. 289–319. The example is from Carol T. Kulik and Robert L. Holbrook, "Demographics in Service Encounters: Effects of Racial and Gender Congruence on Perceived Fairness," *Social Justice Research* 13 (2000), pp. 375–402. On commutative justice see Marion Fortin and Martin Fellenz, "Hypocrisies of Fairness: Towards a More Reflexive Ethical Base in Organizational Justice Research and Practice," *Journal of Business Ethics*, vol. 78 (2008), pp. 415–433.

[22] Victor H. Vroom, *Work and Motivation* (New York: Wiley, 1964).

[23] Ibid.

[24] See Terence R. Mitchell, "Expectancy Models of Job Satisfaction, Occupational Preference and Effort: A Theoretical, Methodological, and Empirical Appraisal," *Psychological Bulletin* 81 (1974), pp. 1053–1077; Mahmoud A. Wahba and Robert J. House, "Expectancy Theory in Work and Motivation: Some Logical and Methodological Issues," *Human Relations* 27 (January 1974), pp. 121–147; Terry Connolly, "Some Conceptual and Methodological Issues in Expectancy Models of Work Performance Motivation," *Academy of Management Review* 1 (October 1976), pp. 37–47; and Terrence Mitchell, "Expectancy-Value Models in Organizational Psychology," in N. Feather (ed.), *Expectancy, Incentive and Action* (New York: Erlbaum & Associates, 1980).

[25] See Adler, op. cit.

[26] Edwin A. Locke, Karyll N. Shaw, Lise M. Saari, and Gary P. Lathan, "Goal Setting and Task Performance: 1969–1980," *Psychological Bulletin* 90 (July/November 1981), pp. 125–152; Edwin A. Locke and Gary P. Latham,

"Work Motivation and Satisfaction: Light at the End of the Tunnel," *Psychological Science* 1.4 (July 1990), pp. 240–246; Edwin A. Locke and Gary Latham, *A Theory of Goal-Setting and Task Performance* (Englewood Cliffs, NJ: Prentice Hall, 1990).

27 Edwin A. Locke and Gary P. Latham, "Has Goal Setting Gone Wild, or Have Its Attackers Abandoned Good Scholarship?" *The Academy of Management Perspective* 23 (February 2009), pp. 17–23.

28 Gary P. Latham and Edwin A. Locke, "Goal Setting— A Motivational Technique That Works," *Organizational Dynamics* 8 (Autumn 1979), pp. 68–80; Gary P. Latham and Timothy P. Steele, "The Motivational Effects of Participation versus Goal-Setting on Performance," *Academy of Management Journal* 26 (1983), pp. 406–417; Miriam Erez and Frederick H. Kanfer, "The Role of Goal Acceptance in Goal Setting and Task Performance," *Academy of Management Review* 8 (1983), pp. 454–463; R. E. Wood and E. A. Locke, "Goal Setting and Strategy Effects on Complex Tasks," in B. Staw and L. L. Cummings (eds.), *Research in Organizational Behavior* (Greenwich, CT: JAI Press, 1990).

29 See E. A. Locke and G. P. Latham, "Work Motivation and Satisfaction," *Psychological Science* 1.4 (July 1990), p. 241.

30 For recent debate on goal setting, see Lisa D. Ordóñez, Maurice E. Schwitzer, Adam D. Galinsky, and Max H. Bazerman, "Goals Gone Wild: The Systematic Side Effects of Overprescribing Goal Setting," *The Academy of Management Perspective* 23 (February 2009), pp. 6–16; Locke and Latham, op. cit. (2009).

31 Ibid.

32 For a good review of MBO, see Anthony P. Raia, *Managing by Objectives* (Glenview, IL: Scott Foresman, 1974).

33 Ibid. Steven Kerr summarizes the criticisms well in "Overcoming the Dysfunctions of MBO," *Management by Objectives* 5.1 (1976).

FEATURES AND MARGIN PHOTOS

Opener: [a] "How We Work." *Feeding America.* http://feedingamerica.org/our-network/how-we-work.aspx. Accessed 1/6/11. [b] "Feeding America Employment Video." *Feeding America.* http://feedingamerica.org/Home/careers.aspx. Accessed 1/6/11. [c] "Our Brand." *Feeding America.* http://feedingamerica.org/about-us/our-brand.aspx. Accessed 1/6/11. [d] "Hunger and Poverty Statistics." *Feeding America.* http://feedingamerica.org/faces-of-hunger/hunger-101/hunger-and-poverty-statistics.aspx. Accessed 1/7/11. Quote from (http://feedingamerica.org/careers.aspx). Photo from http://blog.feedingamerica.org/2010/03/shepard-faireys-feeding-america-poster/.

Ethics in OB: Information on this situation from Jared Sandberg, "Why You May Regret Looking at Papers Left on the Office Copier," *Wall Street Journal* (June 20, 2006), p. B1.

Finding the Leader in You: Information and quotes from Lorraine Monroe, "Leadership Is About Making Vision Happen—What I Call 'Vision Acts,'" *Fast Company* (March 2001), p. 98; Lorraine Monroe Leadership Institute Web site: www.lorrainemonroe.com. See also Lorraine Monroe, *Nothing's Impossible: Leadership Lessons from Inside and Outside The Classroom* (New York: PublicAffairs Books, 1999), and *The Monroe Doctrine: An ABC Guide to What Great Bosses Do* (New York: PublicAffairs Books, 2003).

Working Mother Media—Quote from Information from workingmother.com (retrieved September 29, 2006 and August 1, 2008).

CHAPTER 6

ENDNOTES

1 Steve Hamm, "A Passion for the Plan," *BusinessWeek* (August 21, 2B 2006), pp. 92–94. See also Yvon Chouinard, *Let My People Go Surfing: The Education of a Reluctant Businessman* (New York: Penguin, 2006).

2 For complete reviews of theory, research, and practice see Edward E. Lawler III, *Pay and Organizational Effectiveness* (New York: McGraw-Hill, 1971); Edward E. Lawler III, *Pay and Organizational Development* (Reading, MA: Addison-Wesley, 1981); Edward E. Lawler III, "The Design of Effective Reward Systems," in Jay W. Lorsch (ed.), *Handbook of Organizational Behavior* (Englewood Cliffs, NJ: Prentice-Hall, 1987), pp. 255–271.

3 "Reasons for Pay Raises," *BusinessWeek* (May 29, 2006), p. 11.

4 As an example, see D. B. Balkin and L. R. Gómez-Mejia (eds.), *New Perspectives on Compensation* (Englewood Cliffs, NJ: Prentice-Hall, 1987).

5 Jone L. Pearce, "Why Merit Pay Doesn't Work: Implications from Organization Theory," in Balkin and Gómez-Mejia op. cit., pp. 169–178; Jerry M. Newman, "Selecting Incentive Plans to Complement Organizational Strategy," in Balkin and Gómez-Mejia op. cit., pp. 214–224; Edward E. Lawler III, "Pay for Performance: Making It Work," *Compensation and Benefits Review* 21 (1989), pp. 55–60.

6 Erin White, "How to Reduce Turnover," *The Wall Street Journal* (November 21, 2005), p. B5.

7 See Brian Graham-Moore, "Review of the Literature," in Brian Graham-Moore and Timothy L. Ross (eds.), *Gainsharing* (Washington, DC: Bureau of National Affairs, 1990), p. 20.

8 S. E. Markham, K. D. Scott, and B. L. Little, "National Gainsharing Study: The Importance of Industry Differences," *Compensation and Benefits Review* (January/February 1992), pp. 34–45.

9 Jeffrey Pfeffer and John F. Veiga, "Putting People First for Organizational Success," *Academy of Management Executive* 13 (May 1999), pp. 37–48.

[10] L. R. Gómez-Mejia, D. B. Balkin, and R. L. Cardy, *Managing Human Resources* (Englewood Cliffs, NJ: Prentice-Hall, 1995), pp. 410–411.

[11] N. Gupta, G. E. Ledford, G. D. Jenkins, and D. H. Doty, "Survey Based Prescriptions for Skill-Based Pay," *American Compensation Association Journal* 1.1 (1992), pp. 48–59; L. W. Ledford, "The Effectiveness of Skill-Based Pay," *Perspectives in Total Compensation* 1.1 (1991), pp. 1–4.

[12] Mina Kines, "P&G's Leadership Machine," *Fortune* (April 14, 2009).

[13] For more details, see G. P. Latham and K. N. Wexley, *Increasing Productivity through Performance Appraisal* (2nd ed.); Stephen J. Carroll and Craig E. Schneier, *Performance Appraisal and Review Systems* (Glenview, IL: Scott Foresman, 1982).

[14] See George T. Milkovich and John W. Boudreau, *Personnel/Human Resource Management: A Diagnostic Approach*, 5th ed. (Plano, TX: Business Publications, 1988).

[15] Mark R. Edwards and Ann J. Ewen, *360-Degree Feedback: The Powerful New Tool for Employee Feedback and Performance Improvement* (New York: Amacom, 1996).

[16] For discussion of many of these errors, see David L. Devries, Ann M. Morrison, Sandra L. Shullman, and Michael P. Gerlach, *Performance Appraisal on the Line* (Greensboro, NC: Center for Creative Leadership, 1986), Ch. 3.

[17] For an overall discussion see Greg R. Oldham and J. Richard Hackman, "Not What It Was and Not What It Will Be: The Future of Job Design Research," *Journal of Organizational Behavior* 31 (2010), pp. 463–479.

[18] Frederick W. Taylor, *The Principles of Scientific Management* (New York: Norton, 1967).

[19] Frederick Herzberg, "One More Time: How Do You Motivate Employees?" *Harvard Business Review* 46 (January/February 1968), pp. 53–62.

[20] For a complete description, see J. Richard Hackman and Greg R. Oldham, *Work Redesign* (Reading, MA: Addison-Wesley, 1980).

[21] See J. Richard Hackman and Greg Oldham, "Development of the Job Diagnostic Survey," *Journal of Applied Psychology* 60 (1975), pp. 159–170.

[22] See, for example, Kenneth D. Thomas and Betty A. Velthouse, "Cognitive Elements of Empowerment: An 'Interpretive' Model of Intrinsic Task Motivation," *Academy of Management Review*, 15.4 (1990), pp. 666–681.

[23] For forerunner research, see Charles L. Hulin and Milton R. Blood, "Job Enlargement, Individual Differences, and Worker Responses," *Psychological Bulletin* 69 (1968), pp. 41–55; Milton R. Blood and Charles L. Hulin, "Alienation, Environmental Characteristics and Worker Responses," *Journal of Applied Psychology* 51 (1967), pp. 284–290.

[24] Gerald Salancik and Jeffrey Pfeffer, "An Examination of Need-Satisfaction Models of Job Attitudes," *Administrative Science Quarterly* 22 (1977), pp. 427–456; Gerald Salancik and Jeffrey Pfeffer, "A Social Information Processing Approach to Job Attitude and Task Design," *Administrative Science Quarterly* 23 (1978), pp. 224–253.

[25] For overviews, see Allan R. Cohen and Herman Gadon, *Alternative Work Schedules: Integrating Individual and Organizational Needs* (Reading, MA: Addison-Wesley, 1978); and Jon L. Pearce, John W. Newstrom, Randall B. Dunham, and Alison E. Barber, *Alternative Work Schedules* (Boston: Allyn & Bacon, 1989). See also Sharon Parker and Toby Wall, *Job and Work Design* (Thousand Oaks, CA: Sage, 1998).

[26] Data reported in "A Saner Workplace," *BusinessWeek* (June 1, 2009), pp. 66–69, and based on excerpt from Claire Shipman and Katty Kay, *Womenomics: Write Your Own Rules for Success* (New York: Harper Business, 2009); and "A to Z of Generation Y Attitudes," *Financial Times* (June 18, 2009).

[27] See Sue Shellenbarger, "What Makes a Company a Great Place to Work," *The Wall Street Journal* (October 4, 2007), p. D1.

[28] Olga Kharif, "Chopping Hours, Not Heads," *BusinessWeek* (January 5, 2009), p. 85.

[29] Sue Shellenbarger, "Does Avoiding a 9-to-5 Grind Make You a Target for Layoffs?" *The Wall Street Journal* (April 22, 2009), p. D1.

[30] See Wayne F. Cascio, "Managing a Virtual Workplace," *Academy of Management Executive*, Vol. 14 (2000), pp. 81–90.

[31] Quote from Phil Porter, "Telecommuting Mom Is Part of a National Trend," *Columbus Dispatch* (November 29, 2000), pp. H1, H2.

[32] "Hurting, But Often Uncounted," *BusinessWeek* (April 20, 2009), p. 20.

FEATURES AND MARGIN PHOTOS

Opener: [a] "Chile miners came to blows, but swore to keep details secret," *The Telegraph*. Posted 10/15/10, 8:00 PM. http://www.telegraph.co.uk/news/worldnews/south-america/chile/8067501/Chile-miners-came-to-blows-but-swore-to-keep-details-secret.html. Accessed 1/11/11. [b] "Chilean Miner Edison Pena Prepares for NY Marathon," *PIX 11*. Posted 11/6/10, 10:13 PM. http://www.wpix.com/news/wpix-new-york-marathon,0,7054964.story. Accessed 1/11/11. [c] *MSNBC.com*. [d] "How Massive Was the Chilean Miners' Rescue Online?" *Mashable*. Posted 10/18/10. http://mashable.com/2010/10/18/chilean-miners-rescue-news-numbers/. Accessed 1/11/11.

Ethics in OB: Information from Reuters, "Coming to Work Sick Affects Biz," *Economic Times Bangalore* (January 28, 2007), p. 14; www.webmd.com.

Finding the Leader in You: Information from Andrew Ward, "Spanx Queen Firms up the Bottom Line," *Financial Times* (November 30, 2006), p. 7; and Simona Covel, "A Dated Industry Gets a Modern Makeover," *The Wall Street Journal* (August 7, 2008), p. B9.

In-N-Out Burger—Stacy Perman, "In-N-Out Burger: Professionalizing Fast Food," *BusinessWeek* (April 9, 2009); Stacy Perman, "Fast Food, Family Feuds," *The Wall Street Journal* (April 15, 2009), p. A.13. *Jelly Columbus*—Information from Mararet Harding, "Uncommon Co-Workers," *The Columbus Dispatch* (March 22, 2009), p. D1. *Phoenix Bats*—Information from Scott Priestle, "Hitting It Off," *The Columbus Dispatch* (March 31, 2009).

CHAPTER 7

ENDNOTES

[1] See, for example, Jon R. Katzenbach and Douglas K. Smith, "The Discipline of Teams," *Harvard Business Review* (March/April 1993a), pp. 111–120; Jon R. Katzenbach and Douglas K. Smith, *The Wisdom of Teams: Creating the High-Performance Organization* (Boston: Harvard Business School Press, 1993b).

[2] Katzenbach and Smith (1993a), op. cit., p. 112.

[3] Information from Scott Thurm, "Teamwork Raises Everyone's Game," *The Wall Street Journal* (November 7, 2005), p. B7.

[4] Ibid.

[5] Katzenbach and Smith (1993a, 1993b), op. cit.

[6] For a good overview, see Greg L. Stewart, Charles C. Manz, and Henry P. Sims, *Team Work and Group Dynamics* (New York: Wiley, 1999).

[7] Katzenbach and Smith (1993a, 1993b), op. cit.

[8] See Jon R. Katzenbach, "The Myth of the Top Management Team," *Harvard Business Review* 75 (November/December 1997), pp. 83–91.

[9] Information from Stratford Shermin, "Secrets of HP's 'Muddled' Team," *Fortune* (March 18, 1996), pp. 116–120.

[10] See Stewart, Manz, and Sims, pp. 43–44.

[11] Rensis Likert, *New Patterns of Management* (New York: McGraw-Hill, 1961).

[12] Jay A. Conger, *Winning 'Em Over: A New Model for Managing in the Age of Persuasion* (New York: Simon & Schuster, 1998).

[13] Ibid., p. 191.

[14] See Jay R. Galbraith, *Designing Organizations* (San Francisco: Jossey-Bass, 1998).

[15] Robert P. Steel, Anthony J. Mento, Benjamin L. Dilla, Nestor Ovalle, and Russell F. Lloyd, "Factors Influencing the Success and Failure of Two Quality Circles Programs," *Journal of Management* 11.1 (1985), pp. 99–119; Edward E. Lawler III and Susan A. Mohrman, "Quality Circles: After the Honeymoon," *Organizational Dynamics* 15.4 (1987), pp. 42–54.

[16] See, for example, Paul S. Goodman, Rukmini Devadas, and Terri L. Griffith Hughson, "Groups and Productivity: Analyzing the Effectiveness of Self-Managing Teams," Chapter 11 in John R. Campbell and Richard J. Campbell, *Productivity in Organizations* (San Francisco: Jossey-Bass, 1988); Jack Orsbrun, Linda Moran, Ed Musslewhite, and John H. Zenger, with Craig Perrin, *Self-Directed Work Teams: The New American Challenge* (Homewood, IL: Business One Irwin, 1990); Dale E. Yeatts and Cloyd Hyten, *High Performing Self-Managed Work Teams* (Thousand Oaks, CA: Sage, 1997).

[17] See D. Duarte and N. Snyder, *Mastering Virtual Teams: Strategies, Tools, and Techniques That Succeed* (San Francisco: Jossey-Bass, 1999); Jessica Lipnack and Jeffrey Stamps, *Virtual Teams: Reaching across Space, Time, and Organizations with Technology* (New York: Wiley, 1997).

[18] For reviews see Wayne F. Cascio, "Managing a Virtual Workplace," *Academy of Management Executive* 14 (2000), pp. 81–90; Sheila Simsarian Webber, "Virtual Teams: A Meta-Analysis," www.shrm.org/foundation/findings.asp.

[19] Stacie A. Furst, Martha Reeves, Benson Rosen, and Richard S. Blackburn, "Managing the Life Cycle of Virtual Teams," *Academy of Management Executive* 18.2 (2004), pp. 6–11; ibid.; Duarte and Schneider, op. cit.; Lipnack and Stamps, op. cit.; and J. Richard Hackman by Diane Coutu, "Why Teams Don't Work," *Harvard Business Review* (May 2009), pp. 99–105.

[20] See, for example, J. Richard Hackman and Nancy Katz, "Group Behavior and Performance," Chapter 32, pp. 1208–1251, in Susan T. Fiske, Daniel T. Gilbert, and Gardner Lindzey (eds.), *Handbook of Social Psychology,* Fifth Edition (Hoboken, NJ: Wiley, 2010).

[21] Marvin E. Shaw, *Group Dynamics: The Psychology of Small Group Behavior,* 2nd ed. (New York: McGraw-Hill, 1976).

[22] Bib Latané, Kipling Williams, and Stephen Harkins, "Many Hands Make Light the Work: The Causes and Consequences of Social Loafing," *Journal of Personality and Social Psychology* 37 (1978), pp. 822–832; E. Weklon and G. M. Gargano, "Cognitive Effort in Additive Task Groups: The Effects of Shared Responsibility on the Quality of Multi-Attribute Judgments," *Organizational Behavior and Human Decision Processes* 36 (1985), pp. 348–361; John M. George, "Extrinsic and Intrinsic Origins of Perceived Social Loafing in Organizations," *Academy of Management Journal* (March 1992), pp. 191–202; W. Jack Duncan, "Why Some People Loaf in Groups While Others Loaf Alone," *Academy of Management Executive* 8 (1994), pp. 79–80.

[23] D. A. Kravitz and B. Martin, "Ringelmann Rediscovered," *Journal of Personality and Social Psychology* 50 (1986), pp. 936–941.

[24] John M. George, "Extrinsic and Intrinsic Origins of Perceived Social Loafing in Organizations," *Academy of Management Journal* (March 1992), pp. 191–202; and W. Jack Duncan, "Why Some People Loaf in Groups While Others Loaf Alone," *Academy of Management Executive* 8 (1994), pp. 79–80.

[25] A classic article by Richard B. Zajonc, "Social Facilitation," *Science* 149 (1965), pp. 269–274.

26 See, for example, Leland P. Bradford, *Group Development*, 2nd ed. (San Francisco: Jossey-Bass, 1997).

27 J. Steven Heinen and Eugene Jacobson, "A Model of Task Group Development in Complex Organization and a Strategy of Implementation," *Academy of Management Review* 1 (October 1976), pp. 98–111; Bruce W. Tuckman, "Developmental Sequence in Small Groups," *Psychological Bulletin* 63 (1965), pp. 384–399; Bruce W. Tuckman and Mary Ann C. Jensen, "Stages of Small Group Development Revisited," *Group & Organization Studies* 2 (1977), pp. 419–427.

28 Quote from Alex Markels, "Money & Business," *U.S. News online* (October 22, 2006).

29 Ibid.

30 Example from "Designed for Interaction," *Fortune* (January 8, 2001), p. 150.

31 David M. Herold, "The Effectiveness of Work Groups," in Steven Kerr (ed.), *Organizational Behavior* (New York: Wiley, 1979), p. 95; see also the discussion of group tasks in Stewart, Manz, and Sims, op. cit., pp. 142–143.

32 F. J. Thomas and C. F. Fink, "Effects of Group Size," in Larry L. Cummings and William E. Scott (eds.), *Readings in Organizational and Human Performance* (Homewood, IL: Irwin, 1969), pp. 394–408.

33 Robert D. Hof, "Amazon's Risky Bet," *BusinessWeek* (November 13, 2006), p. 52.

34 Thomas and Fink, op. cit.

35 Shaw, op. cit.

36 William C. Schultz, *FIRO: A Three-Dimensional Theory of Interpersonal Behavior* (New York: Rinehart, 1958).

37 William C. Schultz, "The Interpersonal Underworld," *Harvard Business Review* 36 (July/August 1958), p. 130.

38 See Daniel, R. Ilgen, Jeffrey A. LePiner, and John R. Hollenbeck, "Effective Decision Making in Multinational Teams," in P. Christopher Earley and Miriam Erez (eds.), *New Perspectives on International Industrial/Organizational Psychology* (San Francisco: New Lexington Press, 1997), pp. 377–409.

39 Matt Golosinski, "Teamwork Takes Center Stage," *Northwestern* (Winter 2005), p. 39.

40 Daniel R. Ilgen, Jeffrey A. LePine, and John R. Hollenbeck, "Effective Decision Making in Multinational Teams," in P. Christopher Earley and Miriam Erez (eds.), *New Perspectives on International Industrial/Organizational Psychology* (San Francisco: New Lexington Press, 1997); Warren Watson, "Cultural Diversity's Impact on Interaction Process and Performance," *Academy of Management Journal* 16 (1993).

41 L. Argote and J. E. McGrath, "Group Processes in Organizations: Continuity and Change," in C. L. Cooper and I. T. Robertson (eds.), *International Review of Industrial and Organizational Psychology* (New York: Wiley, 1993), pp. 333–389.

42 See Ilgen, LePiner, and Hollenbeck, op. cit.

43 Golosinski, op. cit., p. 39.

44 "Dream Teams," *Northwestern* (Winter 2005), p. 10; and Matt Golosinski, "Teamwork Takes Center Stage," *Northwestern* (Winter 2005), p. 39.

45 Anita Williams Woolley, Christopher F. Chabris, Alex Pentland, Nada Hasmi, and Thomas W. Malone, "Evidence for a Collective Intelligence Factor in the Performance of Human Groups," *Science* 330 (October 29, 2010), pp. 686–688.

45a Woolley et al., op. cit.

46 George C. Homans, *The Human Group* (New York: Harcourt Brace, 1950).

FEATURES AND MARGIN PHOTOS

Opener: [a] "About Whole Foods Market." *Whole Foods Market.* http://www.wholefoodsmarket.com/company/. Accessed 1/12/11. [b] "The Winning Ways of Whole Foods Market." *Brand Autopsy.* Posted 10/16/2005. http://brandautopsy.typepad.com/brandautopsy/2005/10/the_winning_way.html. Accessed 1/12/11. [c] "Whole Foods/Wild Oats Merger Implications." *Brand Autopsy.* Posted 2/24/07. http://brandautopsy.typepad.com/brandautopsy/2007/02/implications_of.html. Accessed 1/12/11. "Whole Foods cultivates its philosophy amid rapid change." *Statesman.com.* Posted 2/28/2005. http://www.statesman.com/business/content/business/stories/archive/022005_wholefoods.html. Accessed 1/12/11. [d] Ibid.

Ethics in OB: Information from "MBAs 'Cheat Most,'" *Financial Times* (September 21, 2006), p. 1; "The Devil Made Me Do It," *BusinessWeek* (July 24, 2006), p. 10; Karen Richardson, "Buffett Advises on Scandals: Avoid Temptations," *The Wall Street Journal* (October 10, 2006), p. A9; Alma Acevedo, "Of Fallacies and Curricula: A Case of Business Ethics," *Teaching Business Ethics* 5 (2001), pp. 157–170.

Finding the Leader in You: Information and quotes from Allen St. John, "Racing's Fastest Pit Crew," *The Wall Street Journal* (May 9, 2008), p. W4; see also "High-Octane Business Training," *BizEd* (July/August 2008), p. 72.

Microsoft—Information from "Two Wasted Days at Work," *CNNMoney.com* (March 16, 2005), www.cnnmoney.com. *Cleveland Clinic*—Information from "Getting to No. 1," *Continental.com Magazine* (March 2009), pp. 48–49.

CHAPTER 8

ENDNOTES

1 See Owen Linzmeyer and Owen W. Linzmeyer, *Apple Confidential 2.0: The Definitive History of the World's Most Colorful Company* (San Francisco: No Starch Press, 2004); and Jeffrey L. Cruikshank, *The Apple Way* (New York: McGraw-Hill, 2005).

2 Diane Coutu, "Why Teams Don't Work," *Harvard Business Review* (May 2009), pp. 99–105.

[3] Ibid.

[4] Steven Levy, "Insanely Great," *Wired* (February 1994), www.wired.com.

[5] Ibid.

[6] Anita Williams Woolley, Christopher F. Chabris, Alex Pentland, Nada Hasmi, and Thomas W. Malone," "Evidence for a Collective Intelligence Factor in the Performance of Human Groups," *Science* 330 (October) 29, 2010), pp. 686–688.

[7] For an interesting discussion of sports teams, see Ellen Fagenson-Eland, "The National Football League's Bill Parcells on Winning, Leading, and Turning around Teams," *Academy of Management Executive* 15 (August 2001), pp. 48–57; and Nancy Katz, "Sport Teams as a Model for Workplace Teams: Lessons and Liabilities," *Academy of Management Executive* 15 (August 2002), pp. 56–69.

[8] See William D. Dyer, *Team Building*, 3rd ed. (Reading, MA: Addison-Wesley, 1995).

[9] Dennis Berman, "Zap! Pow! Splat!" *BusinessWeek*, Enterprise Issue (February 9, 1998), p. ENT22.

[10] Developed from a discussion by Edgar H. Schein, *Process Consultation* (Reading, MA: Addison-Wesley, 1969), pp. 32–37; Edgar H. Schein, *Process Consultation*, Vol. 1 (Reading, MA: Addison-Wesley, 1988), pp. 40–49.

[11] The classic work is Robert F. Bales, "Task Roles and Social Roles in Problem-Solving Groups," in Eleanor E. Maccoby, Theodore M. Newcomb, and E. L. Hartley (eds.), *Readings in Social Psychology* (New York: Holt, Rinehart & Winston, 1958).

[12] For a good description of task and maintenance functions, see John J. Gabarro and Anne Harlan, "Note on Process Observation," Note 9-477-029 (Harvard Business School, 1976).

[13] Christine Porath and Christine Pearson, "How Toxic Colleagues Corrode Performance," *Harvard Business Review* (April 2009), p. 24.

[14] See Daniel C. Feldman, "The Development and Enforcement of Group Norms," *Academy of Management Review* 9 (1984), pp. 47–53.

[15] See Robert F. Allen and Saul Pilnick, "Confronting the Shadow Organization: How to Select and Defeat Negative Norms," *Organizational Dynamics* (Spring 1973), pp. 13–17; and Alvin Zander, *Making Groups Effective* (San Francisco: Jossey-Bass, 1982), Ch. 4; Feldman, op.cit.

[16] For a summary of research on group cohesiveness, see Marvin E. Shaw, *Group Dynamics* (New York: McGraw-Hill, 1971), pp. 110–112, 192.

[17] See Jay R. Galbraith, *Designing Organizations* (San Francisco: Jossey-Bass, 1998).

[18] Jerry Yoram Wind and Jeremy Main, *Driving Change: How the Best Companies Are Preparing for the 21st Century* (New York: Free Press, 1998), p. 135.

[19] The concept of interacting, coacting, and counteracting groups is presented in Fred E. Fiedler, *A Theory of Leadership Productivity* (New York: McGraw-Hill, 1967).

[20] Research on communication networks is found in Alex Bavelas, "Communication Patterns in Task-Oriented Groups," *Journal of the Acoustical Society of America* 22 (1950), pp. 725–730. See also "Research on Communication Networks," as summarized in Shaw (1976), pp. 137–153.

[21] A classic work on proxemics is Edward T. Hall's book, *The Hidden Dimension* (Garden City, NY: Doubleday, 1986).

[22] Mirand Wewll, "Alternative Spaces Spawning Desk-Free Zones," *The Columbus Dispatch* (May 18, 1998), pp. 10–11.

[23] "Tread: Rethinking the Workplace," *BusinessWeek* (September 25, 2006), p. IN.

[24] Amy Saunders, "A Creative Approach to Work," *The Columbus Dispatch* (May 2, 2008), pp. C1, C9.

[25] Michelle Conlin and Douglas MacMillan, "Managing the Tweets," *BusinessWeek* (June 1, 2009), pp. 20–21.

[26] See Wayne F. Cascio, "Managing a Virtual Workplace," *Academy of Management Executive* 14 (2000), pp. 81–90; Sheila Simsarian Webber, "Virtual Teams: A Meta-Analysis," http://www.shrm.org/foundation/findings.asp; and Stacie A. Furst, Martha Reeves, Benson Rosen, and Richard S. Blackburn, "Managing the Life Cycle of Virtual Teams," *Academy of Management Executive* 18 (2004), pp. 6–20.

[27] Adam Bryant, "He Wants Subjects, Verbs and Objects," *The New York Times* (April 26, 2009), www.nytimes.com.

[28] The discussion is developed from Schein (1988), op. cit., pp. 69–75.

[29] Developed from guidelines presented in the classic article by Jay Hall, "Decisions, Decisions, Decisions," *Psychology Today* (November 1971), pp. 55–56.

[30] Norman R. F. Maier, "Assets and Liabilities in Group Problem Solving," *Psychological Review* 74 (1967), pp. 239–249.

[31] Irving L. Janis, "Groupthink," *Psychology Today* (November 1971), pp. 33–36; Irving L. Janis. *Groupthink*, 2nd ed. (Boston: Houghton Mifflin, 1982). See also J. Longley and D. G. Pruitt, "Groupthink: A Critique of Janis' Theory," in L. Wheeler (ed.), *Review of Personality and Social Psychology* (Beverly Hills, CA: Sage, 1980); Carrie R. Leana, "A Partial Test of Janis's Groupthink Model: The Effects of Group Cohesiveness and Leader Behavior on Decision Processes," *Journal of Management* 1.1 (1985), pp. 5–18. See also Jerry Harvey, "Managing Agreement in Organizations: The Abilene Paradox," *Organizational Dynamics* (Summer 1974), pp. 63–80.

[32] See Janis, op. cit. (1971, 1982).

[33] Gayle W. Hill, "Group Versus Individual Performance: Are Two Leads Better Than One?" *Psychological Bulletin* 91 (1982), pp. 517–539.

[34] These techniques are well described in George P. Huber, *Managerial Decision Making* (Glenview, IL: Scott, Foresman, 1980); Andre L. Delbecq, Andrew L. Van de Ven, and David H. Gustafson, *Group Techniques for Program Planning: A Guide to Nominal Groups and Delphi*

Techniques (Glenview, IL: Scott, Foresman. 1975); William M. Fox, "Anonymity and Other Keys to a Successful Problem-Solving Meeting," *National Productivity Review* 8 (Spring 1989), pp. 145–156.

[35] Information from Jessi Hempel, "Big Blue Brainstorm," *BusinessWeek* (August 7, 2006), p. 70.

[36] Delbecq et al., op. cit.

FEATURES AND MARGIN PHOTOS

Opener: [a] Anne Powell, Gabriele Piccoli, and Blake Ives. "Virtual teams: a review of current literature and directions for future research." *The DATA BASE for Advances in Information Systems.* Vol. 35, issue 31, 2004. [b] *Time-Management-Guide.com.* [c] "Virtual Team Benefits." *Exforsys Inc.* http://www.exforsys.com/career-center/virtual-team/virtual-team-benefits.html. Accessed 1/13/11. [d] www.leadingvirtually.com/?p-59). [e] Published by ASTD & Berrett-Koehler (2010).

Ethics in OB: Information from Ken Gordon, "Tressel's Way Transforms OSU into 'Model Program,'" *Columbus Dispatch* (January 5, 2007), pp. A1, A4.

Finding the Leader in You: Information and quotes from Robert D. Hof, "Amazon's Risky Bet," *Business Week* (November 13, 2006), p. 52; Jon Neale, "Jeff Bezos," *Business-Wings* (February 16, 2007): www.businesswings.com.uk; Alan Deutschman, "Inside the Mind of Jeff Bezos," *Fast Company* (December 19, 2007); www.fastcompany.com/magazine/85; and http://en.wikipedia.org/wiki/Jeff_Bezos.

Deadly Meetings—Developed from Eric Matson, "The Seven Sins of Deadly Meetings," *Fast Company* (April/May 1996), p. 122. *Reality Team Building*—Information from Reena Jana, "Real Life Imitates *Real World*," *BusinessWeek* (March 23 & 30, 2009), p. 42.

CHAPTER 9

ENDNOTES

[1] "Skills Stakeholders Want," *Biz-Ed* (May/June 2009), p. 11.

[2] For concise overviews, see Susan J. Miller, David J. Hickson, and David C. Wilson, "Decision-Making in Organizations" in Steward R. Clegg, Cynthia Hardy, and Walter Nord (eds.), *Handbook of Organizational Studies* (London: Sage, 1996); George P. Huber, *Managerial Decision Making* (Glenview, IL: Scott Foresman, 1980), pp. 293–312.

[3] This figure and the related discussion are developed from conversations with Dr. Alma Acevedo of the University of Puerto Rico at Rio Piedras and from her articles "Of Fallacies and Curricula: A Case of Business Ethics," *Teaching Business Ethics* 5 (2001), pp. 157–170; and "Business Ethics: An Introduction," Working Paper (2009).

[4] Acevedo, op cit. (2009).

[5] Stephen Fineman, "Emotion and Organizing," in Clegg, Hardy, and Nord (eds.) (1996), pp. 542–580.

[6] For discussion of ethical frameworks for decision making, see Joseph R. Desjardins, *Business, Ethics and the Environment* (Upper Saddle River, NJ: Pearson Education, 2007); Linda A. Trevino and Katherine A. Nelson, *Managing Business Ethics* (New York: Wiley, 1995); Saul W. Gellerman, "Why 'Good' Managers Make Bad Ethical Choices," *Harvard Business Review* 64 (July/August 1986), pp. 85–90; and Barbara Ley Toffler, *Tough Choices: Managers Talk Ethics* (New York: Wiley, 1986).

[7] Based on Gerald F. Cavanagh, *American Business Values*, 4th ed. (Upper Saddle River, NJ: Prentice-Hall, 1998).

[8] www.josephsoninstitute.org.

[9] For scholarly reviews, see Dean Tjosvold, "Effects of Crisis Orientation on Managers' Approach to Controversy in Decision Making," *Academy of Management Journal* 27 (1984), pp. 130–138; and Ian I. Mitroff, Paul Shrivastava, and Firdaus E. Udwadia, "Effective Crisis Management," *Academy of Management Executive* 1 (1987), pp. 283–292.

[10] Ibid.

[11] This section stems from the classic work on decision making found in Michael D. Cohen, James G. March, and Johan P. Olsen, "The Garbage Can Model of Organizational Choice," *Administrative Science Quarterly* 17 (1972), pp. 1–25; and James G. March and Herbert A. Simon, *Organizations* (New York: Wiley, 1958), pp. 137–142.

[12] See, for example, Jonathan Rosenoer and William Scherlis, "Risk Gone Wild," *Harvard Business Review* (May 2009), p. 26.

[13] See KPMG, Enterprise Risk Management Services, www.kpmg.com.

[14] This traditional distinction is often attributed to Herbert Simon, *Administrative Behavior* (New York: Free Press, 1945); see also Herbert Simon, *The New Science of Management Decision* (New York: Harper and Row, 1960).

[15] For a historical review, see Leight Buchanan and Andrew O'Connell, "Thinking Machines," *Harvard Business Review* 84.1 (2006), pp. 38–49. For recent applications, see Jiju Antony, Raj Anand, Maneesh Kumar, and M. K. Tiwari, "Multiple Response Optimization Using Taguchi Methodology and Nero-Fuzzy Based Model," *Journal of Manufacturing Technology Management* 17.7 (2006), pp. 908–112; and Craig Boutilier, "The Influence of Influence Diagrams on Artificial Intelligence," *Decision Analysis* 2.4 (2005), pp. 229–232.

[16] Also see Mary Zey (ed.), *Decision Making: Alternatives to Rational Choice Models* (Thousand Oaks, CA: Sage, 1992).

[17] March and Simon, *Organizations* op. cit., (1958).

[18] For a good discussion, see Watson H. Agor, *Intuition in Organizations: Leading and Managing Productively* (Newbury Park, CA: Sage, 1989); Herbert A. Simon, "Making Management Decisions: The Role of Intuition and Emotion," *Academy of Management Executive* 1 (1987),

pp. 57–64; Orlando Behling and Norman L. Eckel, "Making Sense Out of Intuition," *Academy of Management Executive* 1 (1987), pp. 57–64; Orlando Behling and Norman L. Eckel, "Making Sense Out of Intuition," *Academy of Management Executive* 5 (1991), pp. 46–54.

[19] Agor, op cit. (1989).

[20] Alan Deutschman, "Inside the Mind of Jeff Bezos," *Fast Company* 85 (August 2004), www.fastcompany.com.

[21] The classic work in this area is found in a series of articles by D. Kahneman and A. Tversky, "Subjective Probability: A Judgment of Representativeness," *Cognitive Psychology* 3 (1972), pp. 430–454; "On the Psychology of Prediction," *Psychological Review* 80 (1973), pp. 237–251; "Prospect Theory: An Analysis of Decision under Risk," *Econometrica* 47 (1979), pp. 263–291; "Psychology of Preferences," *Scientific American* (1982), pp. 161–173; and "Choices, Values, Frames," *American Psychologist* 39 (1984), pp. 341–350.

[22] See Max H. Bazerman, *Judgment in Managerial Decision Making*, 6th ed. (New York: Wiley, 2005).

[23] See discussion by James A. F. Stoner, *Management*, 2nd ed. (Englewood Cliffs, NJ: Prentice Hall, 1982), pp. 167–168.

[24] Quote from Susan Carey, "Pilot 'in Shock' as He landed Jet in River," *The Wall Street Journal* (February 9, 2009), p. A6.

[25] They may also try and include too many others as shown by Phillip G. Clampitt and M. Lee Williams, "Decision Downsizing," *MIT Sloan Management Review* 48.2 (2007), pp. 77–89.

[26] Victor H. Vroom and Arthur G. Jago, *The New Leadership: Managing Participation in Organizations* (Englewood Cliffs, NJ: Prentice-Hall, 1988). This is based on earlier work by Victor H. Vroom, "A New Look in Managerial Decision-Making," *Organizational Dynamics* (Spring 1973), pp. 66–80; and Victor H. Vroom and Phillip Yetton, *Leadership and Decision-Making* (Pittsburgh: University of Pittsburgh Press, 1973).

[27] Vroom and Yetton, op. cit. (1973); and Vroom and Jago, op. cit. (1988).

[28] See the discussion by Victor H. Vroom, "Leadership and the Decision Making Process," *Organizational Dynamics* 28 (2000), pp. 82–94.

[29] Barry M. Staw, "The Escalation of Commitment to a Course of Action," *Academy of Management Review* 6 (1981), pp. 577–587; Barry M. Staw and Jerry Ross, "Knowing When to Pull the Plug," *Harvard Business Review* 65 (March/April 1987), pp. 68–74. See also Glen Whyte, "Escalating Commitment to a Course of Action: A Reinterpretation," *Academy of Management Review* 11 (1986), pp. 311–321.

[30] Joel Brockner, "The Escalation of Commitment to a Failing Course of Action: Toward Theoretical Progress," *Academy of Management Review* 17 (1992), pp. 39–61; and J. Ross and B. M. Staw, "Organizational Escalation and Exit: Lessons from the Shoreham Nuclear Power Plant," *Academy of Management Journal* 36 (1993), pp. 701–732.

[31] See, for example, Roger von Oech's books, *A Whack on the Side of the Head* (New York: Warner Books, 1983); and *A Kick in the Seat of the Pants* (New York: Harper & Row, 1986).

[32] See Cameron M. Ford and Dennis A. Gioia, *Creative Action in Organizations* (Thousand Oaks, CA: Sage, 1995).

[33] Teresa M. Amabile, "Motivating Creativity in Organizations," *California Management Review* 40 (Fall 1997), pp. 39–58.

[34] Developed from discussions by Edward DeBono, *Lateral Thinking: Creativity Step-by-Step* (New York: HarperCollins, 1970); John S. Dacey and Kathleen H. Lennon, *Understanding Creativity* (San Francisco: Jossey-Bass, 1998); and Bettina von Stamm, *Managing Innovation, Design and Creativity* (Chichester, England: Wiley, 2003).

[35] R. Drazen, M. Glenn, and R. Kazanijan, "Multilevel Theorizing about Creativity in Organizations: A Sensemaking Perspective," *Academy of Management Review* 21 (1999), pp. 286–307.

[36] Developed from discussions by DeBono (1970); Dacey and Lennon (1998); and Von Stamm, (2003).

[37] See "Mosh Pits for Creativity," *BusinessWeek* (November 7, 2005), pp. 98–99.

FEATURES AND MARGIN PHOTOS

Opener: [a] "Animoto makes video edits a snap," *USA Today.* Posted 8/26/09, 12:36 PM. http://www.usatoday.com/tech/news/2009-08-25-online-edit-video_N.html. Accessed 1/12/11. [b] "Animoto: The No-Infrastructure Startup," *Fast Company.* Posted 9/3/08. http://www.fastcompany.com/articles/2008/09/interview-animoto.html?page. Accessed 1/12/11. [c] Ibid. [d] Ibid. [e] Ibid.

Ethics in OB: Information and quotes from "Life and Death at the iPad Factory," *Bloomberg BusinessWeek* (June 7–13, 2010), pp. 35–36.

OB in Popular Culture: Quote from Chesley Sullenberger III from Robert I. Sutton, "In Praise of Simple Competence," *BusinessWeek* (April 13, 2009), p. 67.

Ford—Information from Matthew Dolan, "Ford Takes Online Gamble with New Fiesta," *The Wall Sreet Journal* (April 8, 2009), p. B8. *Google*—Quotes from Dan Fost, "Keeping It All in the Family," *The New York Times* (November 13, 2008), p. 6.

CHAPTER 10

ENDNOTES

[1] See, for example, Henry Mintzberg, *The Nature of Managerial Work* (New York: Harper & Row, 1973); and John R. P. Kotter, *The General Managers* (New York: Free Press, 1982).

[2] One of the classic discussions is by Richard E. Walton, *Interpersonal Peacemaking: Confrontations and*

Third-Party Consultation (Reading, MA: Addison-Wesley, 1969).

[3] Kenneth W. Thomas and Warren H. Schmidt, "A Survey of Managerial Interests with Respect to Conflict," *Academy of Management Journal* 19 (1976), pp. 315–318.

[4] For a good overview, see Richard E. Walton, *Managing Conflict: Interpersonal Dialogue and Third Party Roles*, 2nd ed. (Reading, MA: Addison-Wesley, 1987); and Dean Tjosvold, *The Conflict-Positive Organization: Stimulate Diversity and Create Unity* (Reading, MA: Addison-Wesley, 1991).

[5] Walton (1969).

[6] Ibid.

[7] Information from Hal Lancaster, "Performance Reviews: Some Bosses Try a Fresh Approach," *The Wall Street Journal* (December 1, 1998), p. B1.

[8] Richard E. Walton and John M. Dutton, "The Management of Interdepartmental Conflict: A Model and Review," *Administrative Science Quarterly* 14 (1969), pp. 73–84.

[9] Geert Hofstede, *Culture's Consequences: International Differences in Work-Related Values* (Beverly Hills, CA: Sage, 1980); and Geert Hofstede, "Cultural Constraints in Management Theories," *Academy of Management Executive* 7 (1993), pp. 81–94.

[10] Information from "Capitalizing on Diversity: Navigating the Seas of the Multicultural Workforce and Workplace," *BusinessWeek*, Special Advertising Section (December 4, 1998).

[11] These stages are consistent with the conflict models described by Alan C. Filley, *Interpersonal Conflict Resolution* (Glenview, IL: Scott Foresman, 1975); and Louis R. Pondy, "Organizational Conflict: Concepts and Models," *Administrative Science Quarterly* (September 1967), pp. 269–320.

[12] Information from Ken Brown and Gee L. Lee. "Lucent Fires Top China Executives," *The Wall Street Journal* (April 7, 2004), p. A8.

[13] Walton and Dutton (1969).

[14] Rensis Likert and Jane B. Likert, *New Ways of Managing Conflict* (New York: McGraw-Hill, 1976).

[15] See Jay Galbraith, *Designing Complex Organizations* (Reading, MA: Addison-Wesley, 1973); and David Nadler and Michael Tushman, *Strategic Organizational Design* (Glenview, IL: Scott Foresman, 1988).

[16] E. M. Eisenberg and M. G. Witten, "Reconsidering Openness in Organizational Communication," *Academy of Management Review* 12 (1987), pp. 418–426.

[17] R. G. Lord and M. C. Kernan, "Scripts as Determinants of Purposeful Behavior in Organizations," *Academy of Management Review* 12 (1987), pp. 265–277.

[18] See Filley (1975); and L. David Brown, *Managing Conflict at Organizational Interfaces* (Reading, MA: Addison-Wesley, 1983).

[19] Ibid., pp. 27, 29.

[20] For discussions, see Robert R. Blake and Jane Strygley Mouton, "The Fifth Achievement," *Journal of Applied Behavioral Science* 6 (1970), pp. 413–427; Kenneth Thomas, "Conflict and Conflict Management," in M. D. Dunnett (ed.), *Handbook of Industrial and Organizational Behavior* (Chicago: Rand McNally, 1976), pp. 889–935; and Kenneth W. Thomas, "Toward Multi-Dimensional Values in Teaching: The Examples of Conflict Behaviors," *Academy of Management Review* 2 (1977), pp. 484–490.

[21] See Roger Fisher and William Ury, *Getting to Yes: Negotiating Agreement Without Giving In* (New York: Penguin, 1983). See also James A. Wall Jr., *Negotiation: Theory and Practice* (Glenview, IL: Scott Foresman, 1985).

[22] Roy J. Lewicki and Joseph A. Litterer, *Negotiation* (Homewood, IL: Irwin, 1985), pp. 315–319.

[23] Ibid., pp. 328–329.

[24] The following discussion is based on Fisher and Ury (1983); and Lewicki and Litterer (1985).

[25] This example is developed from Max H. Bazerman, *Judgment in Managerial Decision Making*, 2nd ed. (New York: Wiley, 1991), pp. 106–108.

[26] For a detailed discussion, see Fisher and Ury (1983); and Lewicki and Litterer (1985).

[27] Developed from Bazerman (1991), pp. 127–141.

[28] Fisher and Ury (1983), p. 33.

[29] Lewicki and Litterer (1985), pp. 177–181.

FEATURES AND MARGIN PHOTOS

Opener: [a] "Where in the World is Eduardo Saverin?" *Thinking about Thinking.* Posted June 15, 2009. http://larrycheng.com/2009/06/15/where-in-the-world-is-eduardo-saverin/. Accessed 1/18/2011. [b] "The Battle For Facebook." *Rolling Stone.* Posted 10/15/10, 12:45 PM. http://www.rollingstone.com/culture/news/the-battle-for-facebook-20100915. Accessed 1/18/11. [c] "Eduardo Saverin." *Forbes.* http://www.forbes.com/profile/eduardo-saverin. Accessed 1/18/11.

Ethics in OB: Information from Bridget Jones, Blogger-Fire Fury, CNN.com (July 19, 2006).

Finding the Leader in You: Information and quotes from David Kiley, "Ford's Savior?" *BusinessWeek* (March 16, 2009), pp. 31–34; and, Alex Taylor III, "Fixing up Ford," *Fortune* (May 14, 2009).

Workplace Bullying Institute—Mickey Meece, "Backlash: Women Bullying Women at Work," *The New York Times* (May 10, 2009), www.nytimes.com. *Caterpillar in France*—David Gauthier-Villars and Leila Abboud, "In France, CEOs Can Become Hostages," *The Wall Street Journal* (April 3, 2009), pp. B1, B4; "Bossnapping of Executives Wins 45% Backing in Poll," *The Wall Street Journal* (April 8, 2009), p. A8.

CHAPTER 11

ENDNOTES

[1] See Richard L. Birdwhistell, *Kinesics and Context* (Philadelphia: University of Pennsylvania Press, 1970).

[2] Edward T. Hall, *The Hidden Dimension* (Garden City, NY: Doubleday, 1966).

[3] See D. E. Campbell, "Interior Office Design and Visitor Response," *Journal of Applied Psychology* 64 (1979), pp. 648–653; P. C. Morrow and J. C. McElroy, "Interior Office Design and Visitor Response: A Constructive Replication," *Journal of Applied Psychology* 66 (1981), pp. 646–650.

[4] Variation on quote by Ralph Waldo Emerson, http://www.quotationspage.com/quotes/Ralph_Waldo_Emerson/. Feb 15, 2009.

[5] Information from "Chapter 2.2," *Kellogg* (Winter 2004), p. 6; "Room to Read," *Northwestern* (Spring 2007), pp. 32–33.

[6] The statements are from *BusinessWeek* (July 6, 1981), p. 107.

[7] Epictetus quote found at http://thinkexist.com/quotation/we_have_two_ears_and_one_mouth_so_that_we_can/7650.html. Feb 15, 2009.

[8] M. P. Rowe and M. Baker, "Are You Hearing Enough Employee Concerns?" *Harvard Business Review* 62 (May/June 1984), pp. 127–135.

[9] This discussion is based on Carl R. Rogers and Richard E. Farson, "Active Listening" (Chicago: Relations Center of the University of Chicago).

[10] Modified from an example in ibid.

[11] N. Shivapriya, "Accenture All Set to Venture into Corporate Training," *Economic Times* (February 17, 2007), p. 5.

[12] See C. Bamum and N. Woliansky, "Taking Cues from Body Language," *Management Review* (78) 1989, p. 59; S. Bochner (ed.), *Cultures in Contact: Studies in Cross-Cultural Interaction* (London: Pergamon, 1982); A. Furnham and S. Bochner, *Culture shock: Psychological Reactions to Unfamiliar Environments* (London: Methuen, 1986); "How Not to Do International Business," *BusinessWeek* (April 12, 1999); Yon Kagegama, "Tokyo Auto Show Highlights," *Associated Press* (October 24, 2001).

[13] Edward T. Hall, *Beyond Culture* (New York: Doubleday, 1976).

[14] Quotes from "Lost in Translation," *The Wall Street Journal* (May 18, 2004), pp. B1, B6.

[15] See Gary P. Ferraro. "The Need for Linguistic Proficiency in Global Business," *Business Horizons* 39 (May/June 1966), pp. 39–46.

[16] Networking is considered an essential managerial activity by Kotter (1982).

[17] Thomas J. Peters and Robert H. Waterman Jr., *In Search of Excellence* (New York: Harper & Row, 1983).

[18] Patricia Kitchen, "Businesses Beginning to See Benefits of Employee Wikis," *The Columbus Dispatch* (March 26, 2007), pp. C1, C2.

[19] Diane Brady, "*#!@the E-Mail. Can We Talk?" *BusinessWeek* (December 4, 2006), pp. 109–110.

[20] See Daniel Goleman, *Social Intelligence: The New Science of Human Relationships* (New York: Bantam Books, 2006).

[21] Katherine Reynolds Lewis, "Digital Debris," *Columbus Dispatch* (February 26, 2007), p. B1.

[22] "Four presence potholes to avoid," *Network World* 24 (1) (January 8, 2007), p. 28.

[23] This research is reviewed by John C. Athanassiades, "The Distortion of Upward Communication in Hierarchical Organizations," *Academy of Management Journal* 16 (June 1973), pp. 207–226.

[24] F. Lee, "Being Polite and Keeping Mum. How Bad News Is Communicated in Organizational Hierarchies," *Journal of Applied Social Psychology* 23 (1983), pp. 1124–1149.

[25] *The Wiki Workplace,* by Don Tapscott and Anthony D. Williams, BusinessWeek Online, 00077135, accessed March 26, 2007.

[26] Andre Martin, *The President's Challenge: Creating the Space for Transformation,* internal company document, copyright Mars Inc., 2008.

[27] C. Crossley and G. Vogelsang, "Measuring interactional transparency and testing its impact on trust and psychological capital," working paper, University of Nebraska, 2009.

[28] D. A. Whetten and K. S. Cameron, *Developing Management Skills* (New York: Prentice Hall, 2006).

FEATURES AND MARGIN PHOTOS

Opener: [a] "Nordstrom Beats Macy's and Saks by Moving Inventories." *Bloomberg.* Posted 4/8/09, 4:19 PM. http://www.bloomberg.com/apps/news?pid=newsarchive&sid=a54WN3jQ6TEs. Accessed 1/18/11. [b] "Nordstrom Uses Web to Locate Items and Increase Sales." *The New York Times.* Posted 8/23/2010. http://www.nytimes.com/2010/08/24/business/24shop.html. Accessed 1/18/21. [c] Bloomberg.com.

Ethics in OB: "Request Puts Employees in a Tough Spot," *Columbus Dispatch* (May 28, 2006). p. B3.

Finding the Leader in You: Description of design thinking found on IDEO Web page at www.ideo.com. Feb 22, 2009. Information taken from Web site at http://www.ideo.com/culture/careers/. Feb 22, 2009. Quotes can be found in Harvard Business School case 9-600-143 titled "IDEO Product Development," April 26, 2007, written by Stefan Thomke and Ashok Nimgade, pp. 5–6. See also T. Peters, "The Peters Principles," *Forbes ASAP,* September 13, 1993, p. 180.

Randall Stross, "How to Lose Your Job on Your Own Time," *The New York Times,* December 30, 2007 (late ed., sec. 3, col. 0, Money and Business/Financial Desk; Digital Domain, p. 3).

The Wiki Workplace—Don Tapscott and Anthony D. Williams, BusinessWeek Online, 00077135, accessed March 26, 2007.

CHAPTER 12

ENDNOTES

[1] Several scholars emphasize interdependence, such as W. Richard Scott and Gereal F. Davis, *Organizations and Organizing: Rational, Natural and Open Systems Perspectives* (Upper Saddle River, NJ: Pearson-Prentice Hall, 2007).

[2] The most extensive early work was done by Jeffrey Pfeffer, *Organizations and Organization Theory* (Boston: Pitman, 1983); Jeffrey Pfeffer and Gerald R. Salancik, *The External Control of Organizations* (Englewood Cliffs, NJ: Prentice Hall, 1978).

[3] Rosabeth Moss Kanter, "Power Failure in Management Circuit," *Harvard Business Review* (July–August 1979), pp. 65–75.

[4] John R. P. French and Bertram Raven, "The Bases of Social Power," in Dorwin Cartwright (ed.) *Group Dynamics: Research and Theory* (Evanston, IL: Row, Peterson, 1962), pp. 607–623.

[5] Pfeffer (1983); Pfeffer and Salancik (1978).

[6] Stanley Milgram, "Behavioral Study of Obedience," in Dennis W. Organ (ed.), *The Applied Psychology of Work Behavior* (Dallas, TX: Business Publications, 1978), pp. 384–398. Also see Stanley Milgram, "Behavioral Study of Obedience," *Journal of Abnormal and Social Psychology* 67 (1963), pp. 371–378; Stanley Milgram, "Group Pressure and Action Against a Person," *Journal of Abnormal and Social Psychology* 69 (1964), pp. 137–143; "Some Conditions of Obedience and Disobedience to Authority," *Human Relations* 1 (1965), pp. 57–76; *Obedience to Authority* (New York: Harper and Row, 1974).

[7] Randal Morck, "Behavioral Finance in Corporate Governance: Economics and the Ethics of the Devil's Advocate," *Journal of Management and Governance* 12.2 (2008), pp. 179–191; N. Craig Smith, Sally S. Simpson, and Chun-Yao Huang, "Why Managers Fail to Do the Right Thing: An Empirical Study of Ethical and Illegal Conduct," *Business Ethics Quarterly* 17.4 (2007), pp. 633–649.

[8] Chester Barnard, *The Functions of the Executive* (Cambridge, MA: Harvard University Press, 1938).

[9] For recent studies, see Karin A. Orvis, Nicole M. Dudley, and Jose M Corlina, "Conscientiousness and Reactions to Psychological Contract Breach: A Longitudinal Field Study," *Journal of Applied Psychology* 93.5 (2008), pp. 1183–1195; Prashant Bordia, Simion Lyod D. Restubog, and Robert L. Tang, "When Employees Strike Back: Investigating Mediating Mechanisms between Psychological Contract Breach and Work Place Deviance, *Journal of Applied Psychology* 93.5 (2008), pp. 1004–1010. For a review, see Neil Conway and Rob B. Briner, *Understanding Psychological Contracts at Work: Critical Evaluation of Theory and Research* (Oxford, UK: Oxford University Press, 2005).

[10] Barnard (1938).

[11] See Joseph R. DesJardins, *Business Ethics and the Environment: Imagining a Sustainable Future* (Upper Saddle River, NJ: Pearson-Prentice Hall, 2007); Steven N. Brenner and Earl A. Mollander, "Is the Ethics of Business Changing?" *Harvard Business Review* 55 (February 1977), pp. 57–71; Barry Z. Posner and Warren H. Schmidt, "Values and the American Manager: An Update," *California Management Review* 26 (Spring 1984), pp. 202–216.

[12] French and Raven (1962).

[13] We have added process, information, and representative power to the French and Raven list.

[14] We have added coalition power to the French and Raven list.

[15] See Jean-Jacques Herings, Gerald Van Der Lean, and Doif Tallman, "Social Structured Games," *Theory and Decision* 62.1 (2007), pp. 1–30; and William Matthew Bowler, "Organizational Goals Versus the Dominant Coalition: A Critical View of the Value of Organizational Citizenship Behavior," *Journal of Behavior and Applied Management* 7.3 (2006), pp. 258–277.

[16] For an interesting but different take on power, networks, and visibility, see Calvin Morrill, Mayer N. Zold, and H. Roa, "Covert Political Conflict in Organizations: Challenges from Below," *American Sociological Review* 29 (2003), pp. 391–416.

[17] David Kipinis, Stuart M. Schmidt, Chris Swaffin-Smith, and Ian Wilkinson, "Patterns of Managerial Influence: Shotgun Managers, Tacticians, and Bystanders," *Organizational Dynamics* 12 (1984), pp. 60–69.

[18] Ibid. David Kipinis, Stuart M. Schmidt, and Ian Wilkinson, "Intraorganizational Influence Tactics: Explorations in Getting One's Way," *Journal of Applied Psychology* 65 (1980), pp. 440–452.

[19] See Conway and Briner (2005).

[20] Warren Schilit and Edwin A. Locke, "A Study of Upward Influence in Organizations," *Administrative Science Quarterly* 27 (1982), pp. 301–316.

[21] Ibid; also see Amil Somech and Anat Drach-Zahavy, "Relative Power and Influence Strategy: The Effect of Agent-target Organizational Power on Superiors' Choices of Influence Strategies," *Journal of Organizational Behavior* 23.2 (2002), pp. 167–194.

[22] For discussion of empowerment, see Scott E. Seibert, Seth R. Silver, and W. Allan Randolph, "Taking Empowerment to the Next Level: A Multiple-level Model of Empowerment, Performance and Satisfaction," *Academy of Management Journal* 47.3 (2004), pp. 37–53; John E. Mathieu, Lucky L. Gibson, and Thomas M. Ruddy, "Empowerment and Team Effectiveness: An Empirical Test of an Integrated Model," *Journal of Applied Psychology* 91.1 (2006), pp. 1–10; Jean M Bartunek and Gretchen M. Spreitzer, "The Interdisciplinary Career of a Popular Construct Used in Management: Empowerment in the Late 20th Century," *Journal of Management Inquiry* 15.3 (2006), pp. 255–274.

[23] M. Anita, M. Liu, W. M. Chiu, and R. Fellows, "Enhancing Commitment Through Work Empowerment," *Engineering, Construction and Architectural Management* 14.6 (2007), pp. 568–574.

[24] G. Spreitzer, "Taking Stock: A Review of More Than Twenty Years of Research on Empowerment at Work." In C. Cooper and J. Barling (eds.), *The Handbook of Organizational Behavior* (Thousand Oaks, CA: Sage, 2007), pp. 314–339; J. M Bartunek and G. Spreitzer, "The Interdisciplinary Career of a Popular Construct Used in Management: Empowerment in the Late 20th Century," *Journal of Management Inquiry* 15:3 (2006), 255–273; G. M Spreitzer, "Empowerment," in S. Rogelberg (ed.), *Encyclopedia of Industrial and Organizational Psychology* (Thousand Oaks, CA: Sage, 2006), pp 202–206.

[25] M. S. Logan and D. Ganster, "The Effects of Empowerment on Attitudes and Performance: The Role of Social Support and Empowerment Beliefs," *Journal of Management Studies* 44 (2007), pp. 1523–1531.

[26] J. Pfeffer, "Producing Sustainable Competitive Advantage through the Effective Management of People," *Academy of Management Executive* 19.4 (2005), pp. 85–115.

[27] Useful reviews include a chapter in Robert H. Miles, *Macro Organizational Behavior* (Santa Monica, CA: Goodyear, 1980); Bronston T. Mayes and Robert W. Allen, "Toward a Definition of Organizational Politics," *Academy of Management Review* 2 (1977), pp. 672–677; Dan Farrell and James C. Petersen, "Patterns of Political Behavior in Organizations," *Academy of Management Review* 7 (1982), pp. 403–412; D. L. Madison, R. W. Allen, L. W. Porter, and B. T. Mayes, "Organizational Politics: An Exploration of Managers' Perceptions," *Human Relations* 33 (1980), pp. 92–107.

[28] Pfeffer (1981).

[29] For a discussion, see Christopher Gresov and Carroll Stephen, "Context of Interunit Influence Attempts," *Administrative Science Quarterly* 38.2 (1993), pp. 252–304.

[30] Warren K. Schilit and Edwin A. Locke, "A Study of Upward Influence in Organizations," *Administrative Science Quarterly* 27 (1982), pp. 304–316.

[31] Mayes and Allen (1977), p. 675; James L. Hall and Joel L. Leldecker, "A Review of Vertical and Lateral Relations: A New Perspective for Managers," pp. 138–146 in Patrick Connor, (ed.), *Dimensions in Modern Management*, 3rd ed. (Boston: Houghton Mifflin, 1982); John P. Kotter, "Power, Success, and Organizational Effectiveness," *Organizational Dynamics* 6 (1978), pp. 27–43.

[32] See Susan William and Rick Wilson, "Group Support Systems, Power, and Influence in an Organization: A Field Study," *Decision Sciences* 28.4 (1997), pp. 911–938.

[33] B. Ashforth and R. T. Lee, "Defensive Behavior in Organizations: A Preliminary Model," *Human Relations* (July 1990), pp. 621–648; personal communication with Blake Ashforth, March 2006; Pfeffer (1983).

[34] For discussion of attribution theory, see Simon Tagger and Michell Neubert, "The Impact of Poor Performers on Team Outcomes: An Empirical Examination of Attribution Theory," *Personnel Psychology* 57.4 (2004), pp. 935–979; Robert G. Lord and Karen Maher, "Alternative Information-Processing Models and Their Implications," *Academy of Management Review* 15.1 (1990), pp. 9–29.

[35] For more extensive discussions, see Richard Ritte and Steven Levy, *The Ropes to Skip and the Ropes to Know: Studies in Organizational Behavior*, 7th ed. (Hoboken, NJ: Wiley, 2006); Gerry Griffin and Ciaran Parker, *Games Companies Play: An Insider's Guide to Surviving Politics* (Hoboken, NJ: Wiley, 2004).

[36] See J. M. Ivancevich, T. N. Deuning, J. A. Gilbert, and R. Konopaske, "Deterring White-Collar Crime," *Academy of Management Executive* 17.2 (2003), pp. 114–128.

[37] See J. P. O'Connor Jr., R. Priem, and K. M. Gilly, "Do CEO Stock Options Prevent or Promote Fraudulent Financial Reporting," *Academy of Management Journal* 49.3 (2006), pp. 483–500; D. Dalton, C. Daily, A. E. Ellstrand, and J. L. Johnson, "Meta-Analysis of Financial Performance and Quality: Fusion or Confusion," *Academy of Management Journal* 46.1 (1998), pp. 13–26.

[38] Ibid.

[39] Gerard Sanders and Donald Hambrick, "Swinging for the Fences: The Effects of CEO Stock Options on Company Risk Taking and Performance," *Academy of Management Journal* 50.5 (2007), pp. 1055–1078; Xiaomeng Zhang, Kathryn Bartol, Ken Smith, Michael Pfarrer, and Dmitry Khanin, "CEOS on the Edge: Earnings Manipulation and Stock-Based Incentive Misalignment," *Academy of Management Journal* 51.2 (2008), pp. 241–258.

[40] See David Henry, "Worker vs. CEO Pay: Room to Run," *BusinessWeek* (October 30, 2006), pp. 13–14; Takao Kato and Katsuyuii Kubo, "CEO Compensation and Firm Performance in Japan, Evidence from New Panel Data on Individual CEO Pay," *Journal of the Japanese and International Economics* 20.1 (2006), pp. 1–31; Jeffery Moriarty, "Do CEOs Get Paid Too Much," *Business Ethics Quarterly* 15.15 (2005), pp. 257–266; O'Connor, Priem, and Gilly (2006); C. Daily, D. Dalton, and A. A. Cannella, Jr., "Corporate Governance: Decades of Dialog and

Data," *Academy of Management Review* 28 (2003), pp. 114–128.

[41] See Pfeffer (1983).

[42] Richard N. Osborn, "Strategic Leadership and Alliances in a Global Economy," Working Paper, Department of Business, Wayne State University (2007).

[43] The notion of a dominant coalition was a key concept in James D. Thompson, *Organizations in Action* (New York: McGraw-Hill, 1967). Also see Rony Simons and Randall S. Peterson, "When to Let Them Duke It Out," *Harvard Business Review* 84.6 (2006), pp. 23–49; M. Firth, P. M. Y. Fund, and O. M. Rui, "Firm Performance, Governance Structure, and Top Management Turnover in a Transition Economy," *Journal of Management Studies* 43.6 (2006), pp. 1289–1299; John A. Pearce, "A Structural Analysis of Dominant Coalitions in Small Banks," *Journal of Management* 21.6 (1995), pp. 1075–1096.

FEATURES AND MARGIN PHOTOS

Opener: [a] Tweets compiled from http://www.breakingtweets.com/2009/06/13/violence-escalates-in-iran-first-deaths-reported-communication-cut-off/. Accessed 1/25/11. [b] "The Tweeters In Iran." *The Atlantic.* Posted 6/18/09, 8:07 AM. http://andrewsullivan.theatlantic.com/the_daily_dish/2009/06/the-tweeters-in-iran.html. Accessed 1/25/11. [c] "U.S. Government Asks Twitter to Stay Up for #IranElection Crisis." *Mashable.* 6/16/09. http://mashable.com/2009/06/16/twitter-iran/. Accessed 1/25/11. [d] "Iran Protests: Twitter, the Medium of the Movement." *TIME.* Posted 6/17/09. http://www.time.com/time/world/article/0,8599,1905125,00.html. Accessed 1/25/11. [e] "Mind-blowing #IranElection Stats: 221,744 Tweets Per Hour at Peak." *Mashable.* Posted 6/17/09. http://mashable.com/2009/06/17/iranelection-crisis-numbers/. Accessed 1/25/11.

Ethics in OB: Based on Ruth W. Grant, "Ethics and Incentives: A Political Approach," *The American Political Science Review* 100:1 (2006), pp. 29–40.

Finding the Leader in You: Roger Ebert (December 9, 2009). "Invictus." *Chicago Sun-Times.* (http://rogerebert.suntimes.com/apps/pbcs.dll/article?AID=/20091209/REVIEWS/912099994). http://invictusmovie.warnerbros.com.

Turf Wars at the Pentagon—"Before the Pentagon Can Defeat Cyberattackers, It Must End Internal Turf Wars," *NDIA Business and Technology Magazine,* July 13, 2010, pp. 13–16. *Corporate Citizenship at Citi Bank*—Dan Keeler, "Companies at the cutting edge of corporate responsibility are weaving their citizenship efforts into the strategic heart of the business," *Global Finance* (June 10, 2010 pp. 1–4.); http://community.nasdaq.com/News/2010-06/corporate-social-responsibility.aspx?storyid=23968#ixzz1D2OYTVgL. *Presidential Press Secretary*—www.csmonitor.com/USA/Politics/2011/0127/Jay-Carney-tapped-for-White-House-press-secretary (Jan 27, 2011). *Cisco Systems—Getting Back to Basics* www.cisco.com.

How the Right Skills Can Build Organizational Political Savvy adpted from—Gerald Ferris, Sherry Davidson and Pamela Perrewe, *Political Skill at Work* (Mountain View, CA: Davis-Black Publishing, 2005. How to Avoid Common Rationalizations for Ethic Behavior Adapt from Saul W. Gellerman, "Why Good Managers Made Bad Ethical Decisions," *Harvard Business Review* 64 (July/August 1986) pp. 85–90.

CHAPTER 13

ENDNOTES

[1] Arthur G. Bedeian and James G. Hunt, "Academic Amnesia and Vestigial Assumptions of Our Forefathers," *The Leadership Quarterly* 17 (2006), pp. 190–205.

[2] See J. P. Kotter, *A Force for Change: How Leadership Differs from Management* (New York: Free Press, 1990).

[3] Gary Yukl, *Leadership in Organizations*, 6th ed. (Upper Saddle River, NJ: Prentice Hall, 2006), p. 8.

[4] Ibid.

[5] See Bernard M. Bass, *Bass and Stogdill's Handbook of Leadership*, 3rd ed. (New York: Free Press, 1990).

[6] See Alan Bryman, *Charisma and Leadership in Organizations* (London: Sage, 1992), ch. 5; Ralph M. Stogdill, *Handbook of Leadership* (New York: Free Press, 1974).

[7] Based on information from Robert J. House and Ram Aditya, "The Social Scientific Study of Leadership: QuoVadis?" *Journal of Management* 23 (1997), pp. 409–474; Shelley A. Kirkpatrick and Edwin A. Locke, "Leadership: Do Traits Matter?" *The Executive* 5.2 (1991), pp. 48–60; Gary Yukl, *Leadership in Organizations*, 3rd ed. (Upper Saddle River, NJ: Prentice-Hall, 1998), ch. 10.

[8] Rensis Likert, *New Patterns of Management* (New York: McGraw-Hill, 1961).

[9] Bass (1990), ch. 24.

[10] Robert R. Blake and Jane S. Mouton, *The Managerial Grid* (Houston: Gulf Publishing Co., 1991), p. 29.

[11] Gretchen Spreitzer, "Giving Peace a Chance: Organizational Leadership, Empowerment, and Peace," *Journal of Organizational Behavior* 28 (2007), pp. 1077–1095.

[12] See M. F. Peterson, "PM Theory in Japan and China: What's in It for the United States?" *Organizational Dynamic,* 16 (Spring 1988), pp. 22–39; J. Misumi and M. F. Peterson, "The Performance-Maintenance Theory of Leadership: Review of a Japanese Research Program," *Administrative Science Quarterly* 30 (1985), pp. 198–223; P. B. Smith, J. Misumi, M. Tayeb, M. F. Peterson, and M. Bond, "On the Generality of Leadership Style Measures Across Cultures," paper presented at the International Congress of Applied Psychology, Jerusalem, July 1986.

[13] House and Aditya (1997).

[14] Kirkpatrick and Locke (1991); Yukl (1998), ch. 10; J. G. Hunt and G. E. Dodge, "Management in Organiza-

tions," *Handbook of Psychology* (Washington, DC: American Psychological Association, 2000).

[15] This section is based on Fred E. Fiedler and Martin M. Chemers, *Leadership* (Glenview, IL: Scott, Foresman, 1974).

[16] This discussion of cognitive resource theory is based on Fred E. Fiedler and Joseph E. Garcia, *New Approaches in Effective Leadership* (New York: Wiley, 1987).

[17] See L. H. Peters, D. D. Harke, and J. T. Pohlmann, "Fiedler's Contingency Theory of Leadership: An Application of the Meta-Analysis Procedures of Schmidt and Hunter," *Psychological Bulletin* 97 (1985), pp. 274–285.

[18] Yukl (2006).

[19] F. E. Fiedler, Martin Chemers, and Linda Mahar, *Improving Leadership Effectiveness: The Leader Match Concept*, 2nd ed. (New York: Wiley, 1985).

[20] For documentation, see Fred E. Fiedler and Linda Mahar, "The Effectiveness of Contingency Model Training: A Review of the Validation of Leader Match," *Personnel Psychology* 32 (Spring 1979), 45–62; Fred E. Garcia, Cecil H. Bell, Martin M. Chemers, and Dennis Patrick, "Increasing Mine Productivity and Safety Through Management Training and Organization Development: A Comparative Study," *Basic and Applied Social Psychology* 5.1 (March 1984), pp. 1–18; Arthur G. Jago and James W. Ragan, "The Trouble with Leader Match Is That It Doesn't Match Fiedler's Contingency Model," *Journal of Applied Psychology* 71 (November 1986), pp. 555–559; Yukl (1998); R. Ayman, M. M. Chemers, and F. E. Fiedler, "The Contingency Model of Leadership Effectiveness: Its Levels of Analysis," *The Leadership Quarterly* 6.2 (Summer 1995), pp. 147–168.

[21] See Yukl (1998); R. Ayman, M. M. Chemers, and F. E. Fiedler, "The Contingency Model of Leadership Effectiveness: Its Levels of Analysis," *The Leadership Quarterly* 6.2 (Summer 1995), pp. 141–188.

[22] This section is based on Robert J. House and Terence R. Mitchell, "Path-Goal Theory of Leadership," *Journal of Contemporary Business* 3 (Autumn 1977), pp. 81–97.

[23] House and Mitchell (1977).

[24] C. A. Schriesheim and L. L. Neider, "Path-Goal Theory: The Long and Winding Road," *The Leadership Quarterly* 7 (1996), pp. 317–321; M. G. Evans, "Commentary on R. J. House's Path-Goal Theory of Leadership Effectiveness," *The Leadership Quarterly* 7 (1996), pp. 305–309.

[25] R. J. House, "Path-Goal Theory of Leadership: Lessons, Legacy, and a Reformulated Theory," *The Leadership Quarterly* 7 (1996), pp. 323–352.

[26] See the discussion of this approach in Paul Hersey and Kenneth H. Blanchard, *Management of Organizational Behavior* (Englewood Cliffs, NJ: Prentice Hall, 1988); Paul Hersey, Kenneth Blanchard, and Dewey E. Johnson, *Management of Organizational Behavior*, 8th ed. (Upper Saddle River, NJ: Prentice Hall, 2001).

[27] R. P. Vecchio and C. Fernandez, "Situational Leadership Theory Revisited," in M. Schnake (ed.), *1995 Southern Management Association Proceedings* (Valdosta, GA: Georgia Southern University, 1995), pp. 137–139; Claude L. Graeff, "Evolution of Situational Leadership Theory: A Critical Review," *The Leadership Quarterly* 8 (1997), pp. 153–170.

[28] The discussion in this section is based on Steven Kerr and John Jermier, "Substitutes for Leadership: Their Meaning and Measurement," *Organizational Behavior and Human Performance* 22 (1978), pp. 375–403; Jon P. Howell, David E. Bowen, Peter W. Dorfman, Steven Kerr, and Phillip M. Podsakoff, "Substitutes for Leadership: Effective Alternatives to Ineffective Leadership," *Organizational Dynamics* 19.1 (Summer 1990), pp. 21–38.

[29] Phillip M. Podsakoff, Peter W. Dorfman, Jon P. Howell, and William D. Todor, "Leader Reward and Punishment Behaviors: A Preliminary Test of a Culture-Free Style of Leadership Effectiveness," *Advances in Comparative Management* 2 (1989), pp. 95–138; T. K. Peng, "Substitutes for Leadership in an International Setting," unpublished manuscript, College of Business Administration, Texas Tech University (1990); P. M. Podsakoff and S. B. MacKenzie, "Kerr and Jermier's Substitutes for Leadership Model: Background, Empirical Assessment, and Suggestions for Future Research," *The Leadership Quarterly* 8.2 (1997), pp. 117–132.

[30] See J. Pfeffer, "Management as Symbolic Action: The Creation and Maintenance of Organizational Paradigms," in Cummings and Staw, *Research in Organizational Behavior*, vol. 3 (Greenwich, CT: JAI Press, 1981), pp. 1–52.

[31] James R. Meindl, "On Leadership: An Alternative to the Conventional Wisdom," in Staw and Cummings, *Research Organizational Behavior*, vol. 3 (Greenwich, CT: JAI Press, 1981), pp. 159–203; compare with Bryman (1992); also see James G. Hunt and Jay A. Conger (eds.), *The Leadership Quarterly* 10.2 (1999), special issue.

[32] D. Eden and U. Leviatan. "Implicit Leadership Theory as a Determinant of the Factor Structure Underlying Supervisory Behavior Scales," *Journal of Applied Psychology* 60 (1975), pp. 736–741.

[33] Lord, R. & Emrich, C. (2001). Thinking outside the box by looking inside the box: Extending the cognitive revolution in leadership research. *The Leadership Quarterly, 11*(4), 551–579.

[34] See T. R. Mitchell, S. G. Green, and R. E. Wood, "An Attribution Model of Leadership and the Poor Performing Subordinate: Development and Validation," in L. L. Cummings and B. M. Staw (eds.), *Research in Organizational Behavior*, vol. 3 (Greenwich, CT: JAI Press, 1981), pp. 197–234

[35] Robert Lord and Karen Maher, *Leadership and Information Processing* (Boston: Unwin Hyman).

[36] Thomas Sy et al. (2010). "Leadership Perceptions as a Function of Race-Occupation Fit: The Case of Asian Americans." *Journal of Applied Psychology.*

[37] Lynn R. Offermann, John K. Kennedy, Jr., & Philip Wirtz, (1994). Implicit leadership theories: Content, structure, and generalizability. *Leadership Quarterly, 5*, 43–58.

[38] Ibid.

[39] C. R. Gerstner and D. B. Day, "Cross-Cultural Comparison of Leadership Prototypes," *The Leadership Quarterly* 5 (1994), pp. 122–134.

[40] Carsten, M., Uhl-Bien, M., West, B., Patera, J., & McGregor, R. (2010). Exploring social constructions of followership. *The Leadership Quarterly, 21*(3), 543–562.

[41] Sy, T. (2010). What do you think of followers? Examining the content, structure, and consequences of implicit followership theories. *Organizational Behavior and Human Decision Processes, 113*(2), 73–84.

[42] Carsten et al. (2010).

[43] See R. J. House, "A 1976 Theory of Charismatic Leadership," in J. G. Hunt and L. L. Larson (eds.), *Leadership: The Cutting Edge* (Carbondale: Southern Illinois University Press, 1977), pp. 189–207.

[44] R. J. House, W. D. Spangler, and J. Woycke, "Personality and Charisma in the U.S. Presidency," *Administrative Science Quarterly* 36 (1991), pp. 364–396.

[45] Pillai and E. A. Williams, "Does Leadership Matter in the Political Arena? Voter Perceptions of Candidates' Transformational and Charismatic Leadership and the 1996 U.S. Presidential Vote," *The Leadership Quarterly* 9 (1998), pp. 397–416.

[46] Adapted from Jeffery S. Mio, Ronald E. Riggio, Shana Levin, and Renford Reese, "Presidential Leadership Charisma: The Effects of Metaphor," *The Leadership Quarterly* 16 (2005), pp. 287–294.

[47] See Jane M. Howell and Bruce J. Avolio, "The Ethics of Charismatic Leadership: Submission or Liberation," *Academy of Management Executive* 6 (May 1992), pp. 43–54.

[48] Jay Conger and Rabindra N. Kanungo, *Charismatic Leadership in Organizations* (San Francisco: Jossey-Bass, 1998).

[49] Conger and Kanungo (1998).

[50] See B. M. Bass, *Leadership and Performance Beyond Expectations* (New York: Free Press, 1985); Bryman (1992), pp. 98–99.

[51] B. M. Bass, *A New Paradigm of Leadership* (Alexandria, VA: U.S. Army Research Institute for the Behavioral and Social Sciences, 1996).

[52] Bryman (1992), ch. 6; B. M. Bass and B. J. Avolio, "Transformational Leadership: A Response to Critics," in M. M. Chemers and R. Ayman (eds.), *Leadership Theory and Practice: Perspectives and Directions* (San Diego, CA: Academic Press, 1993), pp. 49–80; Kevin B. Lowe, K. Galen Kroeck, and Nagaraj Sivasubramanium, "Effectiveness Correlates of Transformational and Transactional Leadership: A Meta-Analytic Review of the MLQ Literature," *Leadership Quarterly* 7 (1996), pp. 385–426.

[53] Bass (1996); Bass and Avolio (1993).

[54] See J. R. Kouzes and B. F. Posner, *The Leadership Challenge: How to Get Extraordinary Things Done in Organizations* (San Francisco: Jossey-Bass, 1991).

[55] Marshall Sashkin and Molly G. Sashkin, *Leadership That Matters* (San Francisco: Berrett-Koehler, 2003), ch. 10.

[56] G. B. Graen and M. Uhl-Bien, "Relationship-Based Approach to Leadership: Development of Leader-Member Exchange (LMX) Theory of Leadership over 25 Years: Applying a Multi-Level Multi-Domain Perspective," *The Leadership Quarterly* 6 (1995), pp. 219–247.

[57] Gerstner, C.R., & Day, D.V. (1997). Meta-analytic review of leader-member exchange theory: correlates and construct ideas. *Journal of Applied Psychology, 82*, 827–844.

FEATURES AND MARGIN PHOTOS

Opener: [a] "Zappos Retails Its Culture." *Business Week.* Posted 12/30/09, 5:00 PM. http://www.businessweek.com/magazine/content/10_02/b4162057120453.htm. Accessed 1/18/11. [b] "Zappos Launches Insights Service." *AdWeek.* Posted 12/15/08. http://www.adweek.com/aw/content_display/news/digital/e3i1ccc5c91366de3d9c9a65c32df3b5cdc. Accessed 1/18/11. [c] "Zappos's grand mission doesn't involve selling shoes." *MarketWatch.* Posted 9/13/10, 7:04 PM. http://www.marketwatch.com/story/zaposs-grand-mission-goes-beyond-selling-shoes-2010-09-13. Accessed 1/18/11. [d] Ibid. [e] Ibid.

Ethics in OB: This situation was reported in the *Columbus Dispatch* (March 8, 2006), p. D2.

Finding the Leader in You: James Temple, "Google's Larry Page must prove he has CEO skills," SFGate.com, Sun Jan 23, 2011. "Meet the New Boss: Google Cofounder Larry Page is ready to show the world he's all grown up," *Newsweek*.com, Jan 23, 2011.

Official Google Blog: http://googleblog.blogspot.com/2011/01/update-from-chairman.html.

Avon CEO Andrea Jung—www.avon.com.

CHAPTER 14

ENDNOTES

[1] Based on Bruce J. Avolio and William L. Gardner, "Authentic Leadership Development: Getting to the Root of Positive Forms of Leadership," *The Leadership Quarterly* 16 (2005), pp. 315–338; William L. Gardner, Bruce J. Avolio, Fred Luthans, Douglas R. May, and Fred O. Walumba, "'Can You See the Real Me?' A Self-Based Model of Authentic Leader and Follower Development," *The Leadership Quarterly* 16 (2005), pp. 343–372;

[2] Bill George, Peter Sims, Andrew N. McLean, and Diana Mayer, "Discovering Your Authentic Leadership," *Harvard Business Review* (February, 2007), pp. 1–9.

[3] For a more extended discussion based on positive psychology, see Avolio and Gardner, 2005.

[4] James K. Dittmar, "An Interview with Larry Spears," *Journal of Leadership & Organizational Studies* 13 (2006), pp. 108–118.

[5] Based on Lewis W. Fry, "Toward a Paradigm of Spiritual Leadership," *The Leadership Quarterly* 16 (2005), pp. 619–622; Lewis W. Fry, Steve Vitucci, and Marie Cedillo, "Spiritual Leadership and Army Transformation: Theory, Measurement, and Establishing a Baseline," *The Leadership Quarterly* 16.5 (2005), pp. 835–862.

[6] For a discussion, see Michael E. Brown and Linda K. Trevino, "Ethical Leadership: A Review and Future Directions," *The Leadership Quarterly* 17, 6 (2006), pp. 579–609.

[7] Michael E. Brown and Linda K. Trevino, "Ethical Leadership: A Review and Future Directions," *The Leadership Quarterly* 17 (2006), pp. 595–616.

[8] L. Jon Wertheim, "Do College Athletics Corrupt?" *Sports Illustrated* (March 5, 2007), p. 67.

[9] This discussion relies heavily on that of Katrina A. Zalatan and Gary Yukl, "Team Leadership," in George R. Goethals, Georgia J. Sorenson, and James McGregor Burns, *Encyclopedia of Leadership*, vol. A (Great Barrington, MA, Berkshire/Sage, 2004), pp. 1529–1552.

[10] See Mary Uhl-Bien, Russ Marion, and Bill McKelvey, "Complexity Leadership Theory: Shifting Leadership from the Industrial Age to the Knowledge Era," *The Leadership Quarterly* 18(4) (2007), pp. 298–318.

[11] For specific aspects of self leadership, see Jeffery D. Houghton, Christopher P. Neck, and Charles C. Manz, "Self Leadership and Super Leadership," in Craig L. Pearce and Jay A. Conger (eds.), *Shared Leadership* (Thousand Oaks, CA: Sage Publications, 2003), pp. 123–140.

[12] This discussion is built primarily upon Robert J. House, Paul J. Hanges, Mansour Javidan, Peter W. Dorfman, and Vipin Gupta (eds.), *Culture, Leadership, and Organizations* (Thousand Oaks, CA: Sage Publications, 2004); Mansour Javidan, Peter W. Dorfman, Mary Sully de Luque, and Robert J. House, "In the Eye of the Beholder: Cross Cultural Lessons in Leadership from Project GLOBE," *Academy of Management Perspectives* 20.1 (2006), pp. 67–90.

[13] Michael Beer and Nitin Mitra, "Cracking the Code of Change," *Harvard Business Review* (May–June 2000), p. 133.

[14] L. W. Porter and G. B. McLaughlin, "Leadership and the Organizational Context: Like the Weather," *The Leadership Quarterly* 17 (2006), pp. 559–573.

[15] Osborn, Hunt, and Jauch, 2002.

[16] Gary Johns, "The Essential Impact of Context on Organizations Behavior," *Academy of Management Review* 31.2 (2006), pp. 386–408.

[17] Based on Osborn, Hunt, and Jauch (2002).

[18] R. Marion, *The Edge of Organization: Chaos and Complexity Theories of Formal Social Systems* (Thousand Oaks, CA: Sage, 1999).

[19] Osborn, Hunt, and Jauch (2002).

[20] R. N. Osborn and R. Marion, "Contextual Leadership, Transformational Leadership and the Performance of Innovation Seeking Alliances." *The Leadership Quarterly* (in press).

[21] Osborn, Hunt, and Jauch (2002).

[22] Adopted from Karlene Grabner, "Giving Circles Bring People Together for the Sake of Charity." *Lubbock Avalarche Journal* (November 12, 2006), p. 6.

[23] See David Nadler and Michael Tushman, *Strategic Organizational Design* (Glenview, IL: Scott, Foresman, 1988); Noel M. Tichy, "Revolutionize Your Company," *Fortune* (December 13, 1993), pp. 114–118.

[24] Jerry I. Porras and Robert C. Silvers, "Organization Development and Transformation," *Annual Review of Psychology* 42 (1991), pp. 51–78.

[25] Ibid.

[26] The classic description of organizations on these terms is by Harold J. Leavitt, "Applied Organizational Change in Industry: Structural, Technological and Humanistic Approaches," in James G. March (ed.), *Handbook of Organizations* (Chicago: Rand McNally, 1965). This application is developed from Robert A. Cooke, "Managing Change in Organizations," in Gerald Zaltman (ed.), *Management Principles for Nonprofit Organizations* (New York: American Management Association, 1979). See also David A. Nadler, "The Effective Management of Organizational Change," pp. 358–369, in Jay W. Lorsch (ed.), *Handbook of Organizational Behavior* (Englewood Cliffs, NJ: Prentice-Hall, 1987).

[27] The change strategies are described in Robert Chin and Kenneth D. Benne, "General Strategies for Effecting Changes in Human Systems," pp. 22–45, in Warren G. Bennis, Kenneth D. Benne, Robert Chin, and Kenneth E. Corey *The Planning of Change,* 3rd ed. (New York: Holt, Rinehart & Winston, 1969).

[28] Example developed from an exercise reported in J. William Pfeffer and John E. Jones, *A Handbook of Structural Experiences for Human Relations Training*, vol. II (La Jolla, CA: University Associates, 1973).

[29] Judith A. Ross, "Making Every Leadership Moment Matter," *Harvard Management Update* (September, 2006), pp. 3–5.

[30] Pfeffer and Jones, 1973.

[31] Donald Klein, "Some Notes on the Dynamics of Resistance to Change: The Defender Role," in Bennis et al., 1969, pp. 117–124.

[32] See Everett M. Roberts, *Communication of Innovations*, 3rd ed. (New York: Free Press, 1993).

[33] Everett M. Roberts, 1993.

[34] John P. Kotter and Leonard A. Schlesinger, "Choosing Strategies for Change," *Harvard Business Review* 57 (March–April 1979), pp. 109–112.

FEATURES AND MARGIN PHOTOS

Opener: "A Culture in Acquisitions." *Lyons Solutions,* LLC. http://lyonssolutions.com/culture-in-acquisitions.html. Accessed 1/25/11.

Ethics in OB: L. Jon Wertheim, "Do College Athletics Corrupt?" *Sports Illustrated* (March 5, 2007), p.67.

Finding the Leader in You: Information and quotes from Stacy Perman, "Scones and Social Responsibility," *BusinessWeek* (August 21/28, 2006), p. 38; and www.dancingdeer.com.

Leaders Understanding Diversity—Max DePree's books include *Leadership Jazz* (New York: Dell, 1993) and *Leadership Is an Art* (New York: Broadway Business, 2004), and *Leading Without Power: Finding Hope in Serving Community* (San Francisco: Jossey-Bass, 2003). *Change Is Opportunity*—Fred Smith of FedEx on Change—Ellen Florian, "I Have a Cast-Iron Stomach," *Fortune* (August 1, 2006).

CHAPTER 15

ENDNOTES

[1] This treatment and many analyses of corporate culture are based on Edgar Schein, "Organizational Culture," *American Psychologist* 45 (1990), pp. 109–119; and E. Schein, *Organizational Culture and Leadership* (San Francisco: Jossey-Bass, 1985).

[2] For a recent treatment, see Ali Danisman, C. R. Hinnings, and Trevor Slack, "Integration and Differentiation in Institutional Values: An Empirical Investigation in the Field of Canadian National Sport Organizations," *Canadian Journal of Administrative Sciences* 23.4 (2006), pp. 301–315.

[3] Schein (1990).

[4] See www.dellapp.us.dell.com.

[5] This example was reported in an interview with Edgar Schein, "Corporate Culture Is the Real Key to Creativity," *Business Month* (May 1989), pp. 73–74.

[6] www.Sherwinwilliams.com.

[7] Schein (1990).

[8] www.aetna.com.

[9] Schein (1990).

[10] For an extended discussion, see J. M. Beyer and H. M. Trice, "How an Organization's Rites Reveal Its Culture," *Organizational Dynamics* (Spring 1987), pp. 27–41.

[11] A. Cooke and D. M. Rousseau, "Behavioral Norms and Expectations: A Quantitative Approach to the Assessment of Organizational Culture," *Group and Organizational Studies* 13 (1988), pp. 245–273.

[12] Mary Trefry, "A Double-edged Sword: Organizational Culture in Multicultural Organizations," *International Journal of Management* 23 (2006), pp. 563–576; J. Martin and C. Siehl, "Organization Culture and Counterculture," *Organizational Dynamics* 12 (1983), pp. 52–64.

[13] www.apple-history.com.

[14] For a recent discussion of the clash of corporate cultures, see George Lodorfos and Agyenim Boateng, "The Role of Culture in the Merger and Acquisition Process: Evidence from the European Chemical Industry," *Management Decision* 44 (2006), pp. 1405–1410.

[15] See R. N. Osborn, "The Culture Clash at BofA," Working Paper, Department of Management, Wayne State University, 2008.

[16] Osborn (2008).

[17] Taylor Cox Jr., "The Multicultural Organization," *Academy of Management Executive* 2.2 (May 1991), pp. 34–47.

[18] See Schein (1985), pp. 52–57, and Schein (1990).

[19] For a discussion from a different perspective, see Anat Rafaeli and Michael G. Pratt (eds.), *Artifacts and Organizations: Beyond Mere Symbols* (Mahwah, NJ: Erlbaum, 2006).

[20] For early work, see T. Deal and A. Kennedy, *Corporate Culture* (Reading, MA: Addison-Wesley, 1982); and T. Peters and R. Waterman, *In Search of Excellence* (New York: Harper & Row, 1982), while more recent studies are summarized in Joanne Martin and Peter Frost, "The Organizational Culture War Games: The Struggle for Intellectual Dominance," in Stewart R. Clegg, Cynthia Hardy, and Walter R. Nord (eds.), *Handbook of Organization Studies* (London: Sage, 1996), pp. 599–621.

[21] Schein (1990).

[22] www.montereypasta.com.

[23] H. Gertz, *The Interpretation of Culture* (New York: Basic Books, 1973).

[24] See Rafaeli and Pratt (2006) and Beyer and Trice (1987).

[25] H. M. Trice and J. M. Beyer, "Studying Organizational Cultures through Rites and Ceremonials," *Academy of Management Review* 3 (1984), pp. 633–669.

[26] This description was provided by Marcus B. Osborn.

[27] J. Martin, M. S. Feldman, M. J. Hatch, and S. B. Sitkin, "The Uniqueness Paradox in Organizational Stories," *Administrative Science Quarterly* 28 (1983), pp. 438–453; *BusinessWeek* (November 23, 1992), p. 117.

[28] For a recent study, see John Barnes, Donald W. Jackson, Michael D. Hutt, and Ajith Kumar, "The Role of Culture Strength in Shaping Sales Force Outcomes," *Journal of Personal Setting and Sales Management* 26.3 (2006), pp. 255–269. This tradition of strong cultures goes back to work by Deal and Kennedy (1982) and Peters and Waterman (1982).

[29] Trice and Beyer (1984).

[30] J. Collins, *How Do the Mighty Fall* (New York, HarperCollins, 2009).

[31] R. N. Osborn and D. Jackson, "Leaders, River Boat Gamblers or Purposeful Unintended Consequences," *Academy of Management Journal* 31 (1988), pp. 924–947.

[32] For an interesting twist, see John Connolly, "High Performance Cultures," *Business Strategy Review* 17 (2006), pp. 19–32; a more conventional treatment may be found in Martin, Feldman, Hatch, and Sitkin (1983).

[33] Osborn and Jackson (1988).

[34] R. N. Osborn, "Purposeful Unintended Consequences and Systemic Financial Risk," Working Paper, Department of Management, Wayne State University (2009).

[35] For the classic popular work, see Peter F. Drucker, *Innovation and Entrepreneurship* (New York: Harper, 1985); Edward B. Roberts, "Managing Invention and Innovation," *Research Technology Management* (January/February 1989), pp. 1–19 provides a practitioner perspective, whereas an interesting extended case study is provided by John Clark, *Managing Innovation and Change* (Thousand Oaks, CA: Sage, 1995).

[36] Miller (2008).

[37] P. Berrone, L. Gelabert, A. Fosfuri, and L. Gomez-Mejia, "Can Institutional Forces Create Competitive Advantage? An Empirical Examination of Environmental Innovation," *2008 Academy of Management Proceedings* (2008).

[38] D. Dougherty, "Organizing for Innovation," in Clegg, Hardy, and Nord (eds.), *Handbook of Organization Studies* (1996), pp. 424–439.

[39] For a discussion of product cannibalization, see S. Netessie and T. Taylor, "Product Line Design and Production Technology," *Marketing Science* 26.1 (2007), pp. 101–118.

[40] Gerard J. Tellis, Jaideep C. Prabhu, and Rajesh K. Chandy, "Radical Innovation Across Nations: The Preeminence of Corporate Culture," *Journal of Marketing* 73.1 (2009), pp. 3–23.

[41] N. Clymer and S. Asaba, " A New Approach for Understanding Dominant Design: The Case of the Ink-jet Printer," *Journal of Engineering and Technology Management* 25.3 (2008), pp. 137–152.

[42] V. Acha, "Open by Design: The Role of Design in Open Innovation," *2008 Academy of Management Proceedings* (2008), pp. 1–6.

[43] One of the first to emphasize the role of lead uses was E. von Hipple, *The Sources of Innovation* (New York: Oxford University Press, 1988).

[44] See J. Birkinshaw, G. Hamel, and M. Mol, "Management Innovation," *Academy of Management Review* 33 (2008), pp. 825–845.

[45] The terms exploration and exploitation were popularized by James G. March. See James G. March, "Exploration and Exploitation in Organizational Learning," *Organization Science* 2.1 (1991), pp. 71–87.

[46] For a recent review, see Sung-Choon Kang, Shad S. Morris, and Scot A. Shell, "Relational Archetypes, Organizational Learning, and Value Creation: Extending the Human Resource Architecture," *Academy of Management Review* 32 (2007), pp. 236–256.

[47] Tellis, Prabhu, and Chandy (2009). For an extended discussion of radical innovation, see R. N. Osborn and C. C. Baughn, *An Assessment of the State of the Field of Organizational Design* (Alexandria, VA: U.S. Army Research Institute, 1994).

[48] See M. Tushman and P. Anderson, "Technological Discontinuities and Organizational Environments," *Administrative Science Quarterly* 31 (1986), pp. 439–465.

[49] M. Tushman and C. O. Reilly, "Ambidextrous Organizations: Managing Evolutionary and Revolutionary Change," *California Management Review* 38.4 (1996), pp. 8–30.

[50] M. Tokman, R. G. Richey, L. Marino, and K. M. Weaver, "Exploration, Exploitation and Satisfaction in Supply Chain Portfolio Strategy," *Journal of Business Logistics* 28 (2007), pp. 25–48.

[51] See C. Mirow, K. Hoelzle, and H. Gemueden, "The Ambidextrous Organization in Practice: Barriers to Innovation within Research and Development," *2008 Academy of Management Proceedings* (2008), pp. 1–6.

[52] This section was originally based on Osborn and Baughn (1994).

[53] Y. Berson, S. Oreg, and T. Dvir, "CEO Values, Organizational Culture and Firm Outcomes," *Journal of Organizational Behavior* 29 (2008), pp. 615–633.

[54] www.cisco.com.

[55] J. Kerr and J. Slocum, "Managing Corporate Culture through Reward Systems," *Academy of Management Executive* 19.4 (2005), pp. 130–138.

[56] J. Karpoff, D. S. Lee, and Gerald Martin, "A Company's Reputation Is What Gets Fried When Its Books Are Cooked," uwnews.org (2007).

[57] Martin and Frost (1996).

[58] For example, see Tellis, Prabhu, and Chandy (2009).

[59] For an excellent review, see C. Miller, *Formalization and Innovation: An Ethnographic Study of Process Formalization* (Ann Arbor, MI: Proquest, 2008).

[60] Ibid., p. 391.

[61] See K. Boal and P. Schultz, "Storytelling, Time and Evolution: The Role of Strategic Leadership in Complex Adaptive Systems," *The Leadership Quarterly* 18 (2007), pp. 411–428; and A. Grove, *Only the Paranoid Survive* (New York: Doubleday, 1996).

FEATURES AND MARGIN PHOTOS

Opener: [a] Ellen Uzelac. "Social Networking: Going Online Without Crossing the Line." *AdvisorOne.* Posted 3/1/210. http://www.advisorone.com/article/social-networking-going-online-without-crossing-line. Accessed 3/5/11. [b] *Ibid.* [c] *Ibid.* [d] *Ibid.*

Ethics in OB: Information and quotes from Dana Mattioli. "With Jobs Scarce, Age Becomes an Issue." *The Wall Street Journal* (May 19, 2009), p. D4.

Finding the Leader in You: www.Cousinssubs.com; "Having words with Christine Sprecht," *Nations Restaurant News* 42:49 (2008), p. 78.; www.associatedcontent.com/article/972566/christine_specht_continues_family_legacy.html. www.franchisedirect.com/news/sandwichbagelfranchises/cousins-subs.

Winning Culture at Sherwin-Williams—www.sherwin-williams.com. *Shared Passions at Microsoft*—www.microsoft.com. *The Swarm at R&R Partners*—rrpartners.com. *How the Mighty Fall*—Jim Collins, *How the Mighty Fall*—Harper Business 2009.

CHAPTER 16

ENDNOTES

[1] The bulk of this chapter was originally based on Richard N. Osborn, James G. Hunt, and Lawrence R. Jauch, *Organization Theory: Integrated Text and Cases* (Melbourne, FL: Krieger, 1985). For a more recent but consistent view, see Lex Donaldson, "The Normal Science of Structural Contingency Theory," in Stewart R. Clegg, Cynthia Hardy, and Walter R. Nord (eds.), *Handbook of Organizational Studies* (London: Sage, 1996), pp. 57–76. For a more advanced treatment, see W. Richard Scott and Gerald F. Davis, *Organizations and Organizing: Rational and Open Systems* (Englewood Cliffs, NJ: Prentice-Hall, 2007).

[2] Osborn et al. (1985), Scott and Davis (2007).

[3] Osborn, Hunt, and Jauch (1985).

[4] H. Talcott Parsons, *Structure and Processes in Modern Societies* (New York: Free Press, 1960).

[5] See B. Bartkus, M. Glassman, and B. McAfee, "Mission Statement Quality and Financial Performance," *European Management Journal* 24.1 (2006), pp. 66–79; J. Peyrefitte and F. R. David, "A Content Analysis of the Mission Statements of United States Firms in Four Industries," *International Journal of Management* 23.2 (2006), pp. 296–305; Terri Lammers, "The Effective and Indispensable Mission Statement," *Inc.* 7.1 (August 1992), p. 23; and I. C. MacMillan and A. Meshulack, "Replacement versus Expansion: Dilemma for Mature U.S. Businesses," *Academy of Management Journal* 26 (1983), pp. 708–726.

[6] Osborn, Hunt, and Jauch (1985).

[7] Anonymous, "Making Vision Statements Meaningful," *The British Journal of Administrative Management* (April/May 2006), p. 17; and L. Larwood, C. M. Falbe, M. Kriger, and P. M. Miesing, "Structure and Meaning of Organizational Vision," *Academy of Management Journal* 38 (1995), pp. 740–770.

[8] See Scott and Davis (2007); Stewart R. Clegg and Cynthia Hardy, "Organizations, Organization and Organizing," in Clegg, Hardy, and Nord (eds.), *Handbook of Organizational Studies* (1996), pp. 1–28; and William H.

Starbuck and Paul C. Nystrom, "Designing and Understanding Organizations," in P. C. Nystrom and W. H. Starbuck (eds.), *Handbook of Organizational Design: Adapting Organizations to Their Environments* (New York: Oxford University Press, 1981).

[9] See Jeffery Pfeffer, "Barriers to the Advance of Organization Science," *Academy of Management Review* 18.4 (1994), pp. 599–620; Richard M. Cyert and James G. March, *A Behavioral Theory of the Firm* (Englewood Cliffs, NJ: Prentice-Hall, 1963). A historical view of organizational goals is also found in Charles Perrow, *Organizational Analysis: A Sociological View* (Belmont, CA: Wadsworth, 1970) and in Richard H. Hall, "Organizational Behavior: A Sociological Perspective," in Jay W. Lorsch (ed.), *Handbook of Organizational Behavior* (Englewood Cliffs, NJ: Prentice-Hall, 1987), pp. 84–95.

[10] See Osborn, Hunt, and Jauch (1985) for the historical rates, and for differences in survival rates by time of formation in the development of a technology, see R. Agarwal, M. Sarkar, and R. Echambadi, "The Conditioning Effect of Time on Firm Survival: An Industry Life Cycle Approach," *Academy of Management Journal* 25 (2002), pp. 971–985.

[11] J. Beyer, D. P. Ashmos, and R. N. Osborn, "Contrasts in Enacting TQM: Mechanistic vs. Organic Ideology and Implementation," *Journal of Quality Management* 1 (1997), pp. 13–29; and for an early treatment, see Paul R. Lawrence and Jay W. Lorsch, *Organization and Environment* (Homewood, IL: Irwin, 1969).

[12] Kate Klonick, "Pepsi's CEO a Refreshing Change" (August 15, 2006): www.abcnews.go.com; Diane Brady, "Indra Nooyi: Keeping Cool in Hot Water," *BusinessWeek* (June 11, 2007), special report; Indra Nooyi, "The Best Advice I Ever Got," *CNNMoney* (April 30, 2008), www.cnnmony.com; and, "Indra Nooyi," *The Wall Street Journal* (November 10, 2008), p. R3.

[13] Osborn, Hunt, and Jauch (1985).

[14] For reviews, see Scott and Davis (2007); Osborn, Hunt, and Jauch (1985); Clegg, Hardy, and Nord (1996).

[15] See www.nucor.com.

[16] For instance, J. Gao, R. Kishore, K. Nam, H. R. Rao, and H. Song, "An Investigation of the Factors that Influence the Duration of IT Outsourcing Relationships," *Decision Support Systems* 42.4 (2007), pp. 21–37; J. E. M. McGee, M. J. Dowling, and W. L. Megginson, "Cooperative Strategy and New Venture Performance: The Role of Business Strategy and Management Experience," *Strategic Management Journal* 16 (1995), pp. 565–580; and James B. Quinn, *Intelligent Enterprise: A Knowledge and Service Based Paradigm for Industry* (New York: Free Press, 1992).

[17] F. T. Rothaemel, M. A. Hitt, and L. A. Jobe, "Balancing Vertical Integration and Strategic Outsourcing: Effects on Product Portfolio, Product Success, and Firm Performance," *Strategic Management Journal* 27.11 (2006), pp. 1033–1049. Also see L. F. Cranor and S. Greensteing (eds.),

Communications Policy and Information Technology: Promises, Problems and Prospects (Cambridge, MA: MIT Press, 2002); P. Candace Deans, Global Information Systems and Technology: Focus on the Organization and Its Functional Areas (Harrisburg, PA: Ideal Group Publishing, 1994); and Osborn, Hunt, and Jauch (1985).

[18] Haim Levy and Deborah Gunthorpe, Introduction to Investments, 2nd ed. (Cincinnati, OH: South-Western, 1999); and L. F. Cranor and S. Greensteing (eds.), Communications Policy and Information Technology: Promises, Problems and Prospects (Cambridge, MA: MIT Press, 2002).

[19] William G. Ouchi and M. A. McGuire, "Organization Control: Two Functions," Administrative Science Quarterly 20 (1977), pp. 559–569.

[20] This discussion is adapted from W. Edwards Deming, "Improvement of Quality and Productivity through Action by Management," Productivity Review (Winter 1982): pp. 12–22; Edwards Deming, Quality, Productivity and Competitive Position (Cambridge, MA: MIT Center for Advanced Engineering, 1982).

[21] R. Durand, "Predicting a Firm's Forecasting Ability: The Roles of Organizational Illusion of Control and Organizational Attention." Strategic Management Journal, 24 (September 2003), pp. 821–838.

[22] For related reviews, see Scott and Davis (2007); Osborn, Hunt, and Jauch (1985); Clegg, Hardy, and Nord (1996).

[23] Rhys Andrews, George A. Boyne, Jennifer Law, and Richard M Walker, "Centralization, Organization Strategy, and Public Service Performance," Journal of Public Administration Research and Theory 19.1 (2009), pp. 57–81.

[24] See C. Bradley, "Succeeding by Organizational Design Decisions," Irelands Business Review 11.1 (2006), pp. 24–29; Osborn, Hunt, and Jauch (1985), pp. 273–303, for a discussion of centralization/decentralization.

[25] Rhys et al. (2009).

[26] For reviews of structural tendencies and their influence on outcomes, also see Scott and Davis (2007); Clegg, Hardy, and Nord (1996).

[27] See P. R. Lawrence and J. W. Lorsch, Organization and Environment: Managing Differentiation and Integration (Homewood, IL: Richard D. Irwin, 1967).

[28] Osborn, Hunt, and Jauch (1985).

[29] For a good discussion of the early use of matrix structures, see Stanley Davis, Paul Lawrence, Harvey Kolodny, and Michael Beer, Matrix (Reading, MA: Addison-Wesley, 1977).

[30] www.NBBJ.com.

[31] Lawrence and Lorsch (1967).

[32] See Osborn, Hunt, and Jauch (1985); Scott and Davis (2007).

[33] Chris P. Long, Corinee Bendersky, and Calvin Morrill, "Fair Control: Complementarities between Types of Managerial Controls and Employees' Fairness Evalua-

tions," 2008 Academy of Management Proceedings (2008), pp. 362–368.

[34] Max Weber, The Theory of Social and Economic Organization, translated by A. M. Henderson and H. T. Parsons (New York: Free Press, 1947).

[35] Stephen Cummings and Todd Bridgman, "The Strawman: The Reconfiguration of Max Weber in Management Textbooks and Why It Matters," 2008 Academy of Management Proceedings (2008), pp. 243–249.

[36] Ibid.

[37] These relationships were initially outlined by Tom Burns and G. M. Stalker, The Management of Innovation (London: Tavistock, 1961).

[38] See Henry Mintzberg, Structure in Fives: Designing Effective Organizations (Englewood Cliffs, NJ: Prentice-Hall, 1983).

[39] Ibid.

[40] Ibid.

[41] See Osborn, Hunt, and Jauch (1984) for an extended discussion.

[42] See Peter Clark and Ken Starkey, Organization Transitions and Innovation—Design (London: Pinter Publications, 1988).

FEATURES AND MARGIN PHOTOS

Opener: [a] "During Jack Welch's tenure, GE increased its market capitalization by over $400 billion." Opportunist Magazine. Posted 12/1/10. http://opportunistmagazine.com/during-jack-welch%E2%80%99s-tenure-ge-increased-its-market-capitalization-by-over-400-billion-name/. Accessed 1/25/11. [b] "The Google Way: Give Engineers Room." The New York Times. Posted 10/21/07.http://www.nytimes.com/2007/10/21/jobs/21pre.html. Accessed 1/25/11. [c] "Freedom & Welfare: Amex's All Inclusive Mantra." The Economic Times. http://www.ideas.economictimes.com/Freedom-welfare.aspx. Accessed 1/25/11. [d] "The Leadership-Profit Chain–How Leadership Impacts Employee Passion and Customer Devotion." Blanchard LeaderChat. Posted 4/28/10. http://leaderchat.org/2010/04/28/the-leadership-profit-chain-how-leadership-impacts-employee-passion-and-customer-devotion/. Accessed 1/25/11. [e] "Harnessing Gen Y's Passion at Work." Vodafone. Posted 7/3/07. http://www.vodafone.com.au/business/businessense/cultureandleadership/genyspassion/index.htm. Accessed 1/25/11.

Finding the Leader in You: www.wnba/storm. Allison Espiritu, "Seattle Storm Ownership Awarded Business of the Year," Ballard Tribune (2009), March 26, p. B1.

Video Games Bring Hope and Health—"Hope Lab Video Games for Health," Fast Company (December 2008/January 2009), p. 116 and www.hopelab.org. Hustler Turf Equipment Maximize Profitability, Satisfaction and Value—www.hustlerturf.com. My Macy's Successfully Personalizes Local Stores—Robert Klara, "For the New Macy's, All Marketing Is Local," Mediaweek (June 7, 2010), pp. 20, 23. *Cooperative Land O'Lakes*—www.landolakes. com. *The Challenge of Decentralization*—"Johnson & Johnson CEO William Weldon: Leadership in a Decentralized Company," www.knowledge.wharton.upenn.edu/article. (June 25, 2008). *Shiseido Consolidation Increases Sales and Profits*—www.shiseido.com/2008 annual report.

CHAPTER 17

ENDNOTES

[1] This view of strategy was drawn from several sources, including David Simon, Michael Hitt, and Duane Ireland, "Managing Firm Resources in Dynamic Environments to Create Value: Looking Inside the Black Box," *Academy of Management Review* 32 (2007), pp. 273–292; Alfred D. Chandler, *The Visible Hand: The Managerial Revolution in America* (Cambridge, MA: Belknap, 1977); Michael E. Porter, *Competitive Strategy* (New York: Free Press, 1980); L. R. Jauch and R. N. Osborn, "Toward an Integrated Theory of Strategy," *Academy of Management Review* 6 (1981), pp. 491–498; B. Wernefelt, "A Resource-based View of the Firm," *Strategic Management Journal* 5 (1984), pp. 171–180; J. B. Barney, "Firm Resources and Sustained Competitive Advantage," *Journal of Management* 17 (1991), pp. 99–120; Michael A. Hitt, R. Duane Ireland, and Robert E. Hoskisson, *Strategic Management: Competition and Globalization* (Cincinnati, OH: Southwestern, 2001).

[2] Russ Marion, *The Edge of Organization: Chaos and Complexity Theories of Formal Social Systems* (London: Sage, 1999); Arie Lewin, Chris Long, and Timothy Caroll, "The Coevolution of New Organizational Forms," *Organization Science* 10 (1999), pp. 535–550.

[3] Samuel J. Palmisano, "The New CIO: Setting the Innovation Agenda," speech for the first IBM CIO Leadership Forum, Monte Carlo, www.IBM.com.

[4] G. Huber, "Organizational Learning: The Contributing Process and the Literature," *Organization Science* 2.1 (1991), pp. 88–115.

[5] J. W. Myer and B. Rowan, "Institutionalized Organizations: Formal Structure as Myth and Ceremony," *American Journal of Sociology* 83 (1977), pp. 340–363.

[6] See Bjame Espedal, "Do Organization Routines Change as Experience Changes," *The Journal of Applied Behavior Science* 42.4 (2006), pp. 468–491.

[7] M. Mumford, "The Leadership Quarterly Special Issue on Leading Innovation," *Leadership Quarterly* 14 (2003), pp. 385–387; and M. Mumford, G. Scott, B. Gaddis, B. Strange, and J. Strange, "Leading Creative People: Orchestrating Expertise and Relationships," *Leadership Quarterly* 13 (2002), pp. 705–750.

[8] See Raji Srinivasan, Pamela Haunschild, and Rajdeep Grewal, "Vicarious Learning in Product Development Introductions in the Early Years of a Converging Market," *Management Science* 53.1 (2007), pp. 16–29.

[9] James G. March, *Decisions and Organizations* (Oxford: Basil Blackwell, 1988).

[10] For an illustration with dire consequences, see R. N. Osborn and D. H. Jackson, "Leaders, Riverboat Gamblers, or Purposeful Unintended Consequences in the Management of Complex Technologies," *Academy of Management Journal* 31 (1988), pp. 924–947.

[11] O. P. Walsch and G. R. Ungson, "Organization Memory," *Academy of Management Review* 16.1 (1991), pp. 57–91.

[12] Jansen, Van Bosh, and Volberda (2006).

[13] Simon, Hitt, and Ireland (2007).

[14] This discussion of organizational design was initially based on R. N. Osborn, J. G. Hunt, and L. Jauch, *Organization Theory Integrated Text and Cases* (Melbourne, FL: Krieger, 1984), pp. 123–215. For a more advanced treatment, see W. Richard Scott and Gerald F. Davis, *Organizations and Organizing: Rational and Open Systems* (Englewood Cliffs, NJ: Prentice-Hall, 2007).

[15] http://domino.research.ibm.com/comm/research_people and Naoki, Abe "Optimizing Debt Collections Using Constrained Reinforcement Learning," Paper presented at the 16th Annual Association for Computing Machinery International Conference, Washington, D.C. (July 2010) nsf/pages/nabe.index.html.

[16] Simon, Hitt, and Ireland (2007); Marion (1999); Jauch and Osborn (1981).

[17] Porter (1980).

[18] For example, Simon, Hitt, and Ireland (2007).

[19] Jeffery Pfeffer, "Producing Sustainable Competitive Advantage through the Effective Management of People," *Academy of Management Executive* 19.4 (2005), pp. 85–115.

[20] Osborn, Hunt, and Jauch (1985).

[21] This inertia may be due to both fixed routines and resources; see Gilbert Clark, "Unbundling the Structure of Inertia: Resource Versus Routine Rigidity," *Academy of Management Journal* 48.6 (2005), pp. 741–763.

[22] See R. Lord and M. Kernan, "Scripts as Determinants of Purposeful Behavior in Organizations," *Academy of Management Review* 12 (1987), pp. 265–278; A. L. Stinchcombe, *Economic Sociology* (New York: Academic Press, 1983).

[23] This treatment of the boundaryless organization is based on R. Ashkenas, D. Ulrich, T. Jick, and S. Kerr, *The Boundaryless Organization: Breaking the Chains of Organizational Structure* (San Francisco, CA: Jossey-Bass, 1995). For earlier discussion, also see R. Golembiewski, *Men, Management and Morality* (New Brunswick, NJ: Transaction, 1989). For a critical review, see R. Golembiewski, "The Boundaryless Organization: Breaking the Chains of Organizational Structure, A Review," *International Journal of Organizational Analysis* 6 (1998), pp. 267–270.

24 S. Kerr and D. Ulrich, "Creating the Boundaryless Organization: The Radical Reconstruction of Organization Capabilities," *Planning Review* 23 (1995), pp. 41–44.

25 See Scott and Davis (2007); David A. Nadler and Michael L. Tushman, *Competing by Design: The Power of Organizational Architecture* (New York: Oxford University Press, 1997); Jack Veiga and Kathleen Dechant, "Wired World Woes: www.help," *Academy of Management Executive* 11.3 (1997), pp. 73–79.

26 A. A. Marcus, *Business and Society: Ethics Government and the World of Economy* (Homewood, IL: Richard D. Irwin, 1993).

27 See Henry Mintzberg, *Structure in Fives: Designing Effective Organizations* (Englewood Cliffs, NJ: Prentice-Hall, 1983), pp. 76–83.

28 See Scott and Davis (2007); Osborn, Hunt, and Jauch (1984).

29 Ibid.

30 See Peter M. Blau and Richard A. Schoenner, *The Structure of Organizations* (New York: Basic Books, 1971); Joan Woodward, *Industrial Organization: Theory and Practice* (London: Oxford University Press, 1965).

31 Gerardine DeSanctis, "Information Technology," in Nigel Nicholson (ed.), *Blackwell Encyclopedic Dictionary of Organizational Behavior* (Cambridge, MA: Blackwell, 1995), pp. 232–233.

32 James D. Thompson, *Organization in Action* (New York: McGraw-Hill, 1967).

33 Woodward (1965).

34 For an updated review, see Scott and Davis (2007). This discussion also incorporates Osborn, Hunt, and Jauch (1984); and Louis Fry, "Technology-Structure Research: Three Critical Issues," *Academy of Management Journal* 25 (1982), pp. 532–552.

35 Mintzberg (1983).

36 See Henry Mintzberg and Alexandra McHugh, "Strategy Formulation in an Adhocracy," *Administrative Science Quarterly* 30.2 (1985), pp. 160–193.

37 Halit Keskis, Ali E. Akgun, Ayse Gunsel, and Salih Imamoglu, "The Relationship between Adhocracy and Clan Cultures and Tacit Oriented KM Strategy," *Journal of Transnational Management* 10.3 (2005), pp. 39–51.

58 DeSanctis (1995).

39 Prashant C. Palvia, Shailendra C. Palvia, and Edward M. Roche, *Global Information Technology and Systems Management: Key Issues and Trends* (Nashua, NH: Ivy League Publishing, 1996).

40 Osborn, Hunt, and Jauch (1984).

41 Jaana Woiceshyn, "The Role of Management in the Adoption of Technology: A Longitudinal Investigation," *Technology Studies* 4.1 (1997), pp. 62–99; Melissa A. Schilling, "Technological Lockout: An Integrative Model of the Economic and Strategic Factors Driving Technological Success and Failure," *Academy of Management Review* 23.2 (1998), pp. 267–284.

42 David Lei, Michael Hitt, and Richard A. Bettis, "Dynamic Capabilities and Strategic Management," *Journal of Management* 22 (1996), pp. 547–567.

43 Michael A. Hitt, R. Duane Ireland, and Robert E. Hoskisson, *Strategic Management: Competitiveness and Globalization* (Cincinnati, OH: South-Western College Publishing, 2007).

44 www.amazon.com.

45 While this form is known under a variety of names, we emphasize the information technology base that makes it possible. See Peter Senge, Benjamin B. Lichtenstein, Katrin Kaeufer, Hilary Bradbury, and John S. Carol, "Collaborating for Systematic Change," *MIT Sloan Management Review* 48.2 (2007), pp. 44–59; Josh Hyatt, "The Soul of a New Team," *Fortune* 153.11 (2006), pp. 134–145; M. L. Markus, B. Manville, and C. E. Agres, "What Makes a Virtual Organization Work," *MIT Sloan Management Review* 42 (2002), pp. 13–27; B. Hedberg, G. Hahlgren, J. Hansson, and N. Olve, *Virtual Organizations and Beyond* (New York: Wiley, 2001); and Janice Beyer, Danti P. Ashmos, and R. N. Osborn, "Contrasts in Enacting TQM: Mechanistic vs Organic Ideology and Implementation," *Journal of Quality Management* 1 (1997), pp. 13–29.

46 M. L. Markus, B. Manville, and C. E. Agres, "What Makes a Virtual Organization Work," *MIT Sloan Management Review* 42 (2002), pp. 13–27.

47 Ibid.

48 This section is based on R. N. Osborn, "The Evolution of Strategic Alliances in High Technology," Working Paper, Detroit: Department of Business, Wayne State University (2007); R. N. Osborn and J. G. Hunt, "The Environment and Organization Effectiveness," *Administrative Science Quarterly* 19 (1974), pp. 231–246; and Osborn, Hunt, and Jauch (1984). For a more extended discussion, see P. Kenis and D. Knoke, "How Organizational Field Networks Shape Interorganizational Information Rates," *Academy of Management Journal* 27 (2002), pp. 275–294.

49 See R. N. Osborn and C. C. Baughn, "New Patterns in the Formation of U.S. Japanese Cooperative Ventures," *Columbia Journal of World Business* 22 (1988), pp. 57–65.

50 This section is based on R. N. Osborn, "International Alliances: Going Beyond the Hype," *Mt Eliza Business Review* 6 (2003), pp. 37–44; S. Reddy, J. F. Hennart, and R. Osborn, "The Prevalence of Equity and Non-equity Cross-boarder Linkages: Japanese Investments in the U.S.," *Organization Studies* 23 (2002), pp. 759–780; Wepin Tsai, "Knowledge Transfer in Interorganizational Networks: Effects of Network Position and Absorptive Capacity on Business Unit Innovation and Performance," *Academy of Management Journal* 44.5 (2001), pp. 996–1004.

51 Osborn (2007).

[52] Osborn (2002).

[53] Osborn (2003).

[54] R. N. Osborn, J. G. Hunt, and L. R. Jauch, "Toward a Contextual Theory of Leadership. *The Leadership Quarterly* 13 (2002), pp. 797–837.

[55] For a discussion of top-management teams, see Amy C. Edmonson, Michael A. Roberto, and Michael D. Watkins, "A Dynamic Model of Top Management Team Effectiveness: Matching Unstructured Task Streams," *The Leadership Quarterly* 14 (2003), pp. 297–325.

[56] See Michael D. Mumford, Alison Lantes, Jay J. Caughron, and Tamara L Friedrich, "Charismatic, Ideological and Pragmatic Leadership: Multi-level Influences on Emergence and Performance," *The Leadership Quarterly* 19.2 (2008), pp. 144–160.

[57] This discussion of the multiple-level perspective is based primarily on James G. Hunt, *Leadership: A New Synthesis* (Thousand Oaks, CA: Sage, 1991); and Ken Shepard, Jerry L. Gray, James G. (Jerry) Hunt, and Sarah McArthur (eds.), *Organization Design, Levels of Work and Human Capability* (Ontario, Canada: Global Organization Design Society, 2007), p. 534.

[58] Gerry Larsson, Thorvald Haerem, Misa Sjöberg, Aida Alvinius, and Björn Bakken, "Indirect Leadership under Severe Stress: A Qualitative Inquiry into the 2004 Kosovo Riots," *International Journal of Organizational Analysis* 15.1 (2007), pp. 23–35.

[59] Yair Berson, Shaul Oreg, and Taly Dvir, "CEO Values, Organizational Culture and Firm Outcomes." *Journal of Organizational Behavior* 29 (2008), pp. 615–633.

[60] See R. Marion and M. Uhl-Bien, "Leadership in Complex Organizations," *The Leadership Quarterly* 12.4 (2001), pp. 389–418.

[61] D. C. Hambrick, "Top Management Teams," in Nigel Nicholson (ed.), *Blackwell Encyclopedic Dictionary of Organizational Behavior* (Oxford, England: Blackwell, 1995), pp. 567–568.

[62] This discussion of top-management teams draws heavily on A. C. Edmonson, Michael A. Roberto, and Michael D. Watkins, "A Dynamic Model of Top Management Team Effectiveness: Matching Unstructured Task Streams," *The Leadership Quarterly* 14 (2003), pp. 297–325.

[63] For a discussion of top-management teams, see D. C. Hambrick, T. S. Cho, and M. J. Chen, "The Influence of Top Management Team Heterogeneity on Firm's Competitive Moves," *Administrative Science Quarterly* 41 (1996), pp. 659–684; T. Simons, L. H. Pelled, and K. A. Smith, "Making Use of Difference, Diversity, Debate and Decision Comprehensiveness in Top Management Teams," *Academy of Management Journal* 42 (1999), pp. 662–673.

[64] Osborn, Hunt, and Jauch, (2002).

[65] Kimberly B. Boal and Robert Hooijberg, "Strategic Leadership Research: Moving On," *The Leadership Quarterly* 1 (2000), pp. 515–550.

[66] This discussion of strategic leadership perspective is based primarily on ibid.

[67] Robert E. Quinn, Sue R. Faerman, Michael P. Thompson, and Michael R. McGrath, *Becoming a Master Manager,* 4th ed. (Hoboken, NJ: Wiley, 2006).

[68] Boal and Hooijberg (2000).

[69] Ibid.

[70] Ibid.

FEATURES AND MARGIN PHOTOS

Opener: [a] "It's About the Money, Not the Frequent Flier." *The New York Times.* Posted 8/2/10. http://www.nytimes.com/2010/08/03/business/03road.html. Accessed 1/31/11. [b] "Buying Your Way to the Top." *InsideFlyer.* Posted 5/10/10. http://www.insideflyer.com/articles/article.php?key=5983. Accessed 1/31/11. [c] Ibid. [d] Ibid. American Airlines customers multiply their frequent flyer miles with purchases from specific retailers. (http://www.aa.com/i18n/AAdvantage/partners/retailGifts/main.jsp?from=Nav)

Finding the Leader in You: www.costco.com

Corning's Global Reach—www.corning.com. *Building Research Skills at IBM*—www.IBM.com. *Amazon's Expansion Means More Than Just Books*—www.amazon.com. *Fab India Artists Are Its Most Important Shareholders*—"Weaving a New Kind of Company," *BusinessWeek* (March 23 & 30, 2009), pp. 64–65.

CHAPTER 1

Page 2: Kevin Winter/Getty Images, Inc. *Page 7:* The Psychological Bulletin is copyrighted by the American Psychological Association. Front cover reproduced with permission. *Page 8:* Aluma Images/Radius Images/Masterfile. *Page 14:* David Zalubowski/AP/Wide World Photos. *Page 15:* Charles Trainor, Jr./MCT/Landov LLC. *Page 16:* Jin Lee/Bloomberg/Getty Images, Inc. *Page 19:* New Line Cinema/Photofest.

CHAPTER 2

Page 24: Courtesy Xerox Corporation. *Page 27:* Vasilly Yakobchuk/iStockphoto. *Page 28:* The Journal of Applied Psychology is copyrighted by the American Psychological Association. Front cover reproduced with permission. *Page 30:* Dreamworks/Photofest. *Page 34:* Tek Image/ Photo Researchers, Inc. *Page 35:* digital skillet/iStockphoto. *Page 37:* Fuse/Getty Images, Inc. *Page 43:* Dean Mitchell/ iStockphoto. *Page 45:* Gregory Kramer/Getty Images, Inc. *Page 46:* NewsCom.

CHAPTER 3

Page 52: Zuma Press/NewsCom. *Page 56:* Loic Venance/ AFP/Getty Images, Inc. *Page 59:* Michael Dwyer/AP/Wide World Photos. *Page 63:* Dario Pignatelli/Bloomberg/Getty Images, Inc. *Page 64:* Yves Logghe/AP/Wide World Photos. *Page 65:* Bull's Eye Entertainment/Lions Gate Films/ Photofest. *Page 66:* Ricky John Molloy/Getty Images, Inc. *Page 69:* Claus Christensen/Getty Images, Inc.

CHAPTER 4

Page 74: Used with permission by O'Reilly Media. *Page 79:* Courtesy Washington Post Digital. *Page 80:* Chris Jackson/Getty Images, Inc. *Page 82:* Reprinted with permission of John Wiley & Sons, Inc. *Page 83:* Reprinted with permission of Root Learning, Inc. ©Root Learning, Inc., 2011. All rights reserved. *Page 84:* Jupiterimages/ Getty Images, Inc. *Page 85:* Izvorinka Jankovic/iStockphoto. *Page 88:* Nicole Waring/Getty Images, Inc. *Page 91:* Rosie Greenway/Getty Images, Inc. *Page 92:* CBS/Cliff Lipson/ Landov LLC. *Page 94:* Fuse/Getty Images, Inc.

CHAPTER 5

Page 100: Artwork by Shepard Fairey. Reproduced with permission. *Page 102:* Scott Hortop/Getty Images, Inc. *Page 105:* Copyright ©2003 by Lorraine Monroe. Reprinted by permission of PUBLICAFFAIRS, a member of Perseus Books Group. All rights reserved. *Page 108:* Emmerich-Webb/Getty Images, Inc. *Page 110:* DAJ/Getty Images, Inc. *Page 113:* Joshua Hodge/Getty Images, Inc.

Page 114: The Journal of Applied Psychology is copyrighted by the American Psychological Association. Front cover reproduced with permission.

CHAPTER 6

Page 120: Timothy A. Clary/AFP/Getty Images, Inc. *Page 123:* Michael Schwarz/NewsCom. *Page 124:* Laurent Grandguillot/ REA/Redux Pictures. *Page 125:* Rubberball/iStockphoto. *Page 130:* The Journal of Applied Psychology is copyrighted by the American Psychological Association. Front cover reproduced with permission. *Page 133:* Zuma Press/NewsCom. *Page 136:* Eric Albright/Dispatch Photo. *Page 137:* Mango Productions/Corbis. *Page 139:* Jupiter Images/Getty Images, Inc.

CHAPTER 7

Page 144: Elise Amendola/AP/Wide World Photos. *Page 146:* Monalyn Gracia/Corbis Images. *Page 149:* endopack/ iStockphoto. *Page 151 (top):* Masterfile. *Page 151 (bottom):* Peter Wynn Thompson/The New York Times/Redux Pictures. *Page 153:* iStockphoto. *Page 154:* CBS/Landov LLC. *Page 155:* The Journal of Applied Psychology is copyrighted by the American Psychological Association. Front cover reproduced with permission. *Page 159:* Commercial Eye/Getty Images, Inc. *Page 161:* George Tiedemann/GT Images/©Corbis. *Page 162:* Scott Shaw/The Plain Dealer/ Landov LLC.

CHAPTER 8

Page 168: Steve Chenn/©Corbis. *Page 170:* Helen King/ ©Corbis Images. *Page 173:* Ruth Fremson/The New York Times/Redux Pictures. *Page 177:* Tadej Zupancic/iStockphoto. *Page 178:* Tetra Images/Getty Images, Inc. *Page 182:* John Angelillo/©Corbis. *Page 187:* Digital Vision/Getty Images, Inc. *Page 188:* Dreamworks/Photofest. *Page 189:* Ryan McVay/Stone/Getty Images, Inc.

CHAPTER 9

Page 194: ©Animoto. Reproduced with permission. *Page 199:* REUTERS/Jason Lee/Landov LLC. *Page 200:* Gary S. Chapman/Getty Images, Inc. *Page 202:* Mark Elias/ Bloomberg/Getty Images, Inc. *Page 204:* Peter DaSilva/ The New York Times/Redux Pictures. *Page 207:* Steven Day/©AP/Wide World Photos. *Page 213:* Photo by Dara Seabridge, Courtesy TerraCycle, Inc.

CHAPTER 10

Page 218: Jason Kempin/Getty Images, Inc. *Page 222:* Comstock Images/Getty Images, Inc. *Page 223:* Magali Delporte/eyevine/Redux Pictures. *Page 226:* Steve Prezant/

Corbis Images. *Page 227:* diego cervo/iStockphoto. *Page 228:* Chris Collins/Corbis Images, Inc. *Page 230:* image 100/ ©Corbis. *Page 231:* STAN HONDA/AFP/Getty Images, Inc. *Page 233:* Francois Henry/REA/Redux Pictures. *Page 234:* Josef Lindau/Corbis Images.

CHAPTER 11

Page 240: David Zalubowski/©AP/Wide World Photos. *Page 247:* Courtesy of IDEO. *Page 249:* CBS/Nancy Daniels/ Landov LLC. *Page 250:* CJG-Technology/Alamy. *Page 251:* NewsCom. *Page 256:* Manoocher Deghati/©AP/Wide World Photos. *Page 257:* Getty Images, Inc.

CHAPTER 12

Page 262: Atta Kenare/AFP/Getty Images, Inc. *Page 265:* Stan Honda/AFP/Getty Images, Inc. *Page 269:* Images Bazaar/Getty Images, Inc. *Page 270:* Charles Dharapak/ ©AP/Wide World Photos. *Page 272:* Kim Ludbrook/ epa/©Corbis. *Page 274:* Jose Luis Pelaez/Getty Images, Inc. *Page 277:* Steve Hix/Somos Images/Fuse/Getty Images, Inc. *Page 278:* Jacob Kepler/Bloomberg/Getty Images, Inc. *Page 279:* Columbia Pictures/Marshak, Bob/NewsCom. *Page 283:* Age fototstock/Photolibrary.

CHAPTER 13

Page 290: Brad Swonetz/Redux Pictures. *Page 292:* Marty Lederhandler/©AP/Wide World Photos. *Page 295:* Reprinted with permission of John Wiley & Sons, Inc. *Page 299:* David Strick/Redux Pictures. *Page 302:* Tracy Bennett/ Disney Enterprises/ZUMA Press/NewsCom. *Page 312:* Photodisc/Getty Images, Inc.

CHAPTER 14

Page 318: Photo by Joel Cipes. Provided courtesy of Mark Berns. *Page 321:* 20th Century Fox/Photofest. *Page 324:* DreamPictures/VStock/Getty Images, Inc. *Page 325:* Michael L. Abramson/Time Life Pictures/Getty Images, Inc. *Page 327:* Edmond Terakopian/©AP/Wide World Photos. *Page 331:* Reprinted with permission of John Wiley & Sons, Inc. *Page 334:* Courtesy Dancing Deer Baking Company, Inc. *Page 335:* John Lund/Marc Romanelli/Getty Images, Inc. *Page 336:* Tim KItchen/ Getty Images, Inc. *Page 337:* Rogelio Solis/©AP/Wide World Photos.

CHAPTER 15

Page 346: Scott Dunlap/Getty Images, Inc. *Page 349:* Alex Wong/Getty Images, Inc. *Page 352:* Image Source/ Getty Images, Inc. *Page 354:* Dan Levine/AFP/Getty Images, Inc. *Page 355:* Thomas Barwick/Getty Images, Inc. *Page 356:* Courtesy of Cousins Submarines, Inc. *Page 358:* Carrie Devorah/WENN/NewsCom. *Page 359:* Paramount Pictures/Photofest. *Page 363:* The Journal of Applied Psychology is copyrighted by the American Psychological Association. Front cover reproduced with permission. *Page 365:* Southern Stock/Blend/Getty Images, Inc.

CHAPTER 16

Page 372: Tim Brakemeier/dpa/picture-alliance/NewsCom. *Page 375:* HopeLab/©AP/Wide World Photos. *Page 376:* Courtesy Hustler Turf Equipment, Hustler Zeon: All electric zero-turn-mower. *Page 378:* Tetra Images/Getty Images, Inc. *Page 381:* Photo by Jesse D. Garrabrant/ NBAE/Getty Images, Inc. *Page 384:* Mike Booth/Alamy. *Page 386:* NewsCom. *Page 389:* Keith Meyers/The New York Times/Redux Pictures. *Page 390:* Reprinted by permission. Cover of Organizational Science, Volume 22, Number 2, March–April 2011. Copyright 2011, the Institute for Operations Research and the Management Sciences (INFORMS), 7240 Parkway Drive, Suite 300, Hanover, MD 21076 USA. *Page 391:* TORU YAMANAKA/AFP/Getty Images, Inc. *Page 392:* Robert Daly/Getty Images, Inc.

CHAPTER 17

Page 393: Jesse D. Garrabrant/NBAE/Getty Images, Inc. *Page 397:* Buena Vista/Photofest. *Page 398:* Courtesy of the American Airlines AAdvantage Program. *Page 401:* Courtesy Corning, Inc. *Page 402:* Tom and Dee Ann McCarthy/©Corbis. *Page 403:* Scripps Howard Photo Service/ NewsCom. *Page 405:* Courtesy Naoki Abe. *Page 407:* Peter Yates/The New York Times/Redux Pictures. *Page 409 (left):* Stefano Lunardi/Age Fotostock America, Inc. *Page 409 (center):* Keith Brofsky/Getty Images, Inc. *Page 409 (right):* ©vario images GmbH & Co. KG/Alamy Limited. *Page 410:* The Kobal Collection, Ltd. *Page 412:* Mueller H./laif/Redux Pictures. *Page 413:* Flying Colours, Ltd/ Getty Images, Inc. *Page 414:* India Today Group/Getty Images, Inc. *Page 418:* Reprinted with permission of John Wiley & Sons, Inc. *Page 419:* Thinkstock/Getty Images, Inc.